Hotel facilities

In general the hotels we recommend have full bathroom and toilet facilities in each room. However, this may not be the case for certain rooms in categories , , *and* .

- **30 rm** — *Number of rooms*
- *Lift (elevator)*
- *Air conditioning*
- *Television in room*
- *Establishment either partly or wholly reserved for non-smokers*
- *Telephone in room: outside calls connected by the operator*
- *Telephone in room: direct dialling for outside calls*
- *Rooms accessible to disabled people*
- *Meals served in garden or on terrace*
- *Outdoor or indoor swimming pool*
- *Exercise room – Sauna*
- *Garden*
- *Hotel tennis court – Golf course and number of holes*
- *Fishing available to hotel guests. A charge may be made*
- 150 — *Equipped conference hall: maximum capacity*
- *Hotel garage (additional charge in most cases)*
- *Car park for customers only*
- *Dogs are not allowed in all or part of the hotel*
- Fax — *Telephone document transmission*
- *May-October* — *Dates when open, as indicated by the hotelier*
- *season* — *Probably open for the season – precise dates not available*

Where no date or season is shown, establishments are open all year round

- LL35 OSB — *Postal code*
- (Forte) — *Hotel Group (See list at end of the Guide)*

Animals

It is forbidden to bring domestic animals (dogs, cats...) into Great Britain and Ireland.

Dear Reader

This 23rd edition of the Michelin Guide to Great Britain and Ireland offers the latest selection of hotels and restaurants.

Independently compiled by our inspectors, the Guide provides travellers with a wide choice of establishments at all levels of comfort and price.

We are committed to providing readers with the most up to date information and this edition has been produced with the greatest care.

That is why only this year's guide merits your complete confidence.

Thank you for your comments, which are always appreciated.

Bon voyage ———

Contents

Choosing a hotel or restaurant

This guide offers a selection of hotels and restaurants to help the motorist on his travels. In each category establishments are listed in order of preference according to the degree of comfort they offer.

Categories

Hotel	Restaurant	
	XXXXX	*Luxury in the traditional style*
	XXXX	*Top class comfort*
	XXX	*Very comfortable*
	XX	*Comfortable*
	X	*Quite comfortable*
		Simple comfort
		Other recommended accommodation, at moderate prices
without rest.		*The hotel has no restaurant*
	with rm	*The restaurant also offers accommodation*

Peaceful atmosphere and setting

Certain establishments are distinguished in the guide by the red symbols shown below.
Your stay in such hotels will be particularly pleasant or restful, owing to the character of the building, its decor, the setting, the welcome and services offered, or simply the peace and quiet to be enjoyed there.

to	*Pleasant hotels*
XXXXX to X	*Pleasant restaurants*
« Park »	*Particularly attractive feature*
	Very quiet or quiet, secluded hotel
	Quiet hotel
≤ sea	*Exceptional view*
≤	*Interesting or extensive view*

The maps located at the beginning of each regional section in the guide indicate places with such peaceful, pleasant hotels and restaurants.

By consulting them before setting out and sending us your comments on your return you can help us with our enquiries.

Cuisine

Stars

Certain establishments deserve to be brought to your attention for the particularly fine quality of their cooking. ***Michelin stars*** *are awarded for the standard of meals served. For each of these restaurants we indicate three culinary specialities typical of their style of cooking to assist you in your choice.*

❀❀❀ **Exceptional cuisine, worth a special journey**

One always eats here extremely well, sometimes superbly. Fine wines, faultless service, elegant surroundings. One will pay accordingly !

❀❀ **Excellent cooking, worth a detour**

Specialities and wines of first class quality. This will be reflected in the price.

❀ **A very good restaurant in its category**

The star indicates a good place to stop on your journey. But beware of comparing the star given to an expensive « de luxe » establishment to that of a simple restaurant where you can appreciate fine cooking at a reasonable price.

The red Meals

Whilst appreciating the quality of the cooking in restaurants with a star, you may, however, wish to find some serving a perhaps less elaborate but nonetheless always carefully prepared meal.

Certain restaurants seem to us to answer this requirement.
We bring them to your attention by marking them with a red **Meals** *in the text of the Guide.*

Please refer to the map of stars and **Meals** *rated restaurants located at the beginning of each regional section in the guide.*

Prices

Prices quoted are valid for autumn 1995. Changes may arise if goods and service costs are revised. Your recommendation is self-evident if you always walk into a hotel guide in hand.
Hotels and restaurants in bold type have supplied details of all their rates and have assumed responsibility for maintaining them for all travellers in possession of this guide.
Prices are given in £ sterling, except for the Republic of Ireland where Irish pounds (punt) are quoted. Where no mention **s., t.,** *or* **st.** *is shown, prices may be subject to the addition of service charge, V.A.T., or both (V.A.T. does not apply in the Channel Islands).*

Meals

Meals 13.00/24.00	**Set meals** *Lunch* 13.00, *dinner* 24.00 – *including cover charge, where applicable*
Meals 15.00/25.00	*See page 7*
s.	*Service only included*
t.	*V.A.T. only included*
st.	*Service and V.A.T. included*
🍷 6.00	*Price of 1/2 bottle or carafe of house wine*
Meals a la carte 20.00/25.00	**A la carte meals** *The prices represent the range of charges from a simple to an elaborate 3 course meal and include a cover charge where applicable*
☕ 8.50	*Charge for full cooked breakfast (i.e. not included in the room rate)* *Continental breakfast may be available at a lower rate*

⌂ : Dinner in this category of establishment will generally be offered from a fixed price menu of limited choice, served at a set time to residents only. Lunch is rarely offered. Many will not be licensed to sell alcohol.

Rooms

rm 50.00/80.00 — *Lowest price* 50.00 *per room for a comfortable single and highest price* 80.00 *per room for the best double*

rm ☕ 55.00/75.00 — *Full cooked breakfast (whether taken or not) is included in the price of the room*

Short breaks (SB.)

Many hotels offer a special rate for a stay of two or more nights which comprises dinner, room and breakfast usually for a minimum of two people. Please enquire at hotel for rates.

Alcoholic beverages-conditions of sale

The sale of alcoholic drinks is governed in Great Britain and Ireland by licensing laws which vary greatly from country to country.

Allowing for local variations, restaurants may stay open and serve alcohol with a bona fide meal during the afternoon. Hotel bars and public houses are generally open between 11am and 11pm at the discretion of the licensee. Hotel residents, however, may buy drinks outside the permitted hours at the discretion of the hotelier.

Children under the age of 14 are not allowed in bars.

Deposits

Some hotels will require a deposit, which confirms the commitment of customer and hotelier alike. Make sure the terms of the agreement are clear.

Credit cards

AE VISA JCB — *Credit cards accepted by the establishment: Access (MasterCard, Eurocard) – American Express – Diners Club – Visa – Japan Credit Bureau*

Towns

✉ York	*Postal address*
☎ 01225 Bath	*STD dialling code (name of exchange indicated only when different from name of the town). Omit 0 when dialling from abroad*
401 M 27, ⑩	*Michelin map and co-ordinates or fold*
West Country G.	*See the Michelin Green Guide England : The West Country*
pop. 1057	*Population. (Crown copyright 1991. Published by permission of the Controller of Her Majesty's Stationery Office.)*
BX **A**	*Letters giving the location of a place on the town plan*
18	*Golf course and number of holes (handicap usually required, telephone reservation strongly advised)*
✻, ⇐	*Panoramic view, viewpoint*
✈	*Airport*
☎ 261 1234	*Place with a motorail connection; further information from telephone number listed*
⛴	*Shipping line*
⛴	*Passenger transport only*
ℹ	*Tourist Information Centre*

Standard Time

In winter standard time throughout the British Isles is Greenwich Mean Time (G.M.T.). In summer British clocks are advanced by one hour to give British Summer Time (B.S.T.). The actual dates are announced annually but always occur over weekends in March and October.

Sights

Star-rating

★★★	*Worth a journey*
★★	*Worth a detour*
★	*Interesting*
AC	*Admission charge*

Location

See	*Sights in town*
Envir.	*On the outskirts*
Exc.	*In the surrounding area*
N, S, E, W	*The sight lies north, south, east or west of the town*
A 22	*Take road A 22, indicated by the same symbol on the Guide map*
2 m.	*Mileage*

Car, tyres

The wearing of seat belts in Great Britain is obligatory for drivers, front seat passengers and rear seat passengers where seat belts are fitted. It is illegal for front seat passengers to carry children on their lap.

In the Republic of Ireland seat belts are compulsory, if fitted, for drivers and front seat passengers. Children under 12 are not allowed in front seats unless in a suitable safety restraint.

Michelin tyre suppliers

ATS Tyre dealers

The location of the nearest ATS tyre dealer can be obtained by contacting the address below between 9am and 5pm.

ATS HOUSE
180-188 Northolt Rd.
Harrow,
Middlesex HA2 OED
(0181) 423 2000

Motoring organisations

The major motoring organisations in Great Britain and Ireland are the Automobile Association and the Royal Automobile Club. Each provides services in varying degrees for non-resident members of affiliated clubs.

AUTOMOBILE ASSOCIATION
Fanum House
BASINGSTOKE, Hants.,
RG21 2EA
℘ (01256) 20123

ROYAL AUTOMOBILE CLUB
RAC House, Lansdowne Rd.
CROYDON, Surrey CR9 2JA
℘ (0181) 686 2525

AUTOMOBILE ASSOCIATION
108-110 Great-Victoria St.
BELFAST, BT2 7AT
℘ (01232) 328924

ROYAL AUTOMOBILE CLUB
RAC House, 79 Chichester St.
BELFAST, BT1 4JR
℘ (01232) 240261

AUTOMOBILE ASSOCIATION
23 Rock Hill
BLACKROCK
Co-Dublin
℘ (01) 283-3555

ROYAL AUTOMOBILE CLUB
RAC IRELAND
New Mount House
22-24 Lower Mount St.
DUBLIN 2
℘ (01) 760113

Town plans

Hotels – Restaurants

Sights

Place of interest and its main entrance
Interesting place of worship

Roads

Motorway
Junctions : complete, limited
Dual carriageway with motorway characteristics
Main traffic artery
A 2 Primary route
- (network currently being reclassified)
One-way street – Unsuitable for traffic, street subject to restrictions
Pedestrian street
Piccadilly Shopping street – Car park
Gateway – Street passing under arch – Tunnel
Low headroom (16'6" max.) on major through routes
Station and railway
Funicular – Cable-car
Lever bridge – Car ferry

Various signs

Tourist Information Centre
Mosque – Synagogue
Communications tower or mast – Ruins
Garden, park, wood – Cemetery
Stadium – Racecourse – Golf course
Golf course (with restrictions for visitors)
View – Panorama
Monument – Fountain – Hospital
Pleasure boat harbour – Lighthouse
Airport – Underground station
Ferry services :
- passengers and cars
Main post office with poste restante, telephone
Public buildings located by letter :
C H - County Council Offices – Town Hall
M T U - Museum – Theatre – University, College
POL. - Police (in large towns police headquarters)

London

BRENT SOHO Borough – Area
Borough boundary – Area boundary

Ami lecteur

Cette 23e édition du Guide Michelin Great Britain and Ireland propose une sélection actualisée d'hôtels et de restaurants.

Réalisée en toute indépendance, par nos inspecteurs, elle offre au voyageur de passage un large choix d'adresses à tous les niveaux de confort et de prix.

Toujours soucieux d'apporter à nos lecteurs l'information la plus récente, nous avons mis à jour cette édition avec le plus grand soin.

C'est pourquoi, seul le Guide de l'année en cours mérite votre confiance.

Merci de vos commentaires toujours appréciés.

Michelin vous souhaite « Bon voyage ! »

Sommaire

Le choix d'un hôtel, d'un restaurant

Ce guide vous propose une sélection d'hôtels et restaurants établie à l'usage de l'automobiliste de passage. Les établissements, classés selon leur confort, sont cités par ordre de préférence dans chaque catégorie.

Catégories

	XXXXX	*Grand luxe et tradition*
	XXXX	*Grand confort*
	XXX	*Très confortable*
	XX	*De bon confort*
	X	*Assez confortable*
		Simple mais convenable
		Autre ressource hôtelière conseillée, à prix modérés
without rest.		*L'hôtel n'a pas de restaurant*
	with rm	*Le restaurant possède des chambres*

Agrément et tranquillité

Certains établissements se distinguent dans le guide par les symboles rouges indiqués ci-après.
Le séjour dans ces hôtels se révèle particulièrement agréable ou reposant.
Cela peut tenir d'une part au caractère de l'édifice, au décor original, au site, à l'accueil et aux services qui sont proposés, d'autre part à la tranquillité des lieux.

à	*Hôtels agréables*
XXXXX à X	*Restaurants agréables*
« Park »	*Élément particulièrement agréable*
	Hôtel très tranquille ou isolé et tranquille
	Hôtel tranquille
< sea	*Vue exceptionnelle*
<	*Vue intéressante ou étendue.*

Les localités possédant des établissements agréables ou tranquilles sont repérées sur les cartes placées au début de chacune des régions traitées dans ce guide.

Consultez-les pour la préparation de vos voyages et donnez-nous vos appréciations à votre retour, vous faciliterez ainsi nos enquêtes.

L'installation

Les chambres des hôtels que nous recommandons possèdent, en général, des installations sanitaires complètes. Il est toutefois possible que dans les catégories , , et , certaines chambres en soient dépourvues.

30 rm *Nombre de chambres*
Ascenseur
Air conditionné
Télévision dans la chambre
Établissement entièrement ou en partie réservé aux non-fumeurs
Téléphone dans la chambre relié par standard
Téléphone dans la chambre, direct avec l'extérieur
Chambres accessibles aux handicapés physiques
Repas servis au jardin ou en terrasse
Piscine : de plein air ou couverte
Salle de remise en forme – Sauna
Jardin de repos
9 *Tennis à l'hôtel – Golf et nombre de trous*
Pêche ouverte aux clients de l'hôtel (éventuellement payant)
150 *Salles de conférences : capacité maximum*
Garage dans l'hôtel (généralement payant)
P *Parking réservé à la clientèle*
Accès interdit aux chiens (dans tout ou partie de l'établissement)
Fax *Transmission de documents par télécopie*
May-October *Période d'ouverture, communiquée par l'hôtelier*
season *Ouverture probable en saison mais dates non précisées. En l'absence de mention, l'établissement est ouvert toute l'année.*
LL35 OSB *Code postal de l'établissement*
(Forte) *Chaîne hôtelière (voir liste en fin de guide)*

Animaux

L'introduction d'animaux domestiques (chiens, chats...) est interdite en Grande-Bretagne et en Irlande.

La table

Les étoiles

Certains établissements méritent d'être signalés à votre attention pour la qualité de leur cuisine. Nous les distinguons par **les étoiles de bonne table**. *Nous indiquons, pour ces établissements, trois spécialités culinaires qui pourront orienter votre choix.*

✿✿✿ **Une des meilleures tables, vaut le voyage**

On y mange toujours très bien, parfois merveilleusement, grands vins, service impeccable, cadre élégant... Prix en conséquence.

✿✿ **Table excellente, mérite un détour**

Spécialités et vins de choix... Attendez-vous à une dépense en rapport.

✿ **Une très bonne table dans sa catégorie**

L'étoile marque une bonne étape sur votre itinéraire. Mais ne comparez pas l'étoile d'un établissement de luxe à prix élevés avec celle d'une petite maison où à prix raisonnables, on sert également une cuisine de qualité.

Meals

Tout en appréciant les tables à « étoiles », on peut souhaiter trouver sur sa route un repas plus simple mais toujours de préparation soignée. Certaines maisons nous ont paru répondre à cette préoccupation.

Le mot **Meals** *rouge les signale à votre attention dans le texte de ce guide.*

Consultez les cartes des localités (étoiles de bonne table et **Meals***) placées au début de chacune des régions traitées dans ce guide.*

Les prix

Les prix que nous indiquons dans ce guide ont été établis en automne 1995. Ils sont susceptibles de modifications, notamment en cas de variations des prix des biens et services.

Entrez à l'hôtel le guide à la main, vous montrerez ainsi qu'il vous conduit là en confiance.

Les prix sont indiqués en livres sterling (1 £ = 100 pence), sauf en République d'Irlande où ils sont donnés en « Punts ».

Lorsque les mentions **s., t.,** *ou* **st.** *ne figurent pas, les prix indiqués peuvent être majorés d'un pourcentage pour le service, la T.V.A., ou les deux. (La T.V.A. n'est pas appliquée dans les Channel Islands.)*

Les hôtels et restaurants figurent en gros caractères lorsque les hôteliers nous ont donné tous leurs prix et se sont engagés, sous leur propre responsabilité, à les appliquer aux touristes de passage porteurs de notre guide.

Repas

Meals 13.00/24.00 — **Repas à prix fixe**
Déjeuner 13.00, *dîner* 24.00. *Ces prix s'entendent couvert compris*

Meals 15.00/25.00 — *Voir page 19*

s. — *Service compris*

t. — *T.V.A. comprise*

st. — *Service et T.V.A. compris (prix nets)*

🍷 6.00 — *Prix de la 1/2 bouteille ou carafe de vin ordinaire*

Meals à la carte 20.00/25.00 — **Repas à la carte**
Le 1er prix correspond à un repas simple mais soigné, comprenant : petite entrée, plat du jour garni, dessert. Le 2e prix concerne un repas plus complet, comprenant : hors-d'œuvre, plat principal, fromage ou dessert. Ces prix s'entendent couvert compris

☕ 8.50 — *Prix du petit déjeuner à l'anglaise, s'il n'est pas compris dans celui de la chambre. Un petit déjeuner continental peut être obtenu à moindre prix*

⌂: *Dans les établissements de cette catégorie, le dîner est servi à heure fixe exclusivement aux personnes ayant une chambre. Le menu, à prix unique, offre un choix limité de plats. Le déjeuner est rarement proposé. Beaucoup de ces établissements ne sont pas autorisés à vendre des boissons alcoolisées.*

Chambres

rm 50.00/80.00 *Prix minimum* 50.00 *d'une chambre pour une personne et prix maximum* 80.00 *de la plus belle chambre occupée par deux personnes*

rm ☕ 55.00/75.00 *Le prix du petit déjeuner à l'anglaise est inclus dans le prix de la chambre, même s'il n'est pas consommé*

« Short breaks » (SB.)

Certains hôtels proposent des conditions avantageuses ou « Short Break » pour un séjour minimum de 2 nuits. Ce forfait calculé par personne, pour 2 personnes au minimum, comprend la chambre, le diner et le petit déjeuner. Se renseigner auprès de l'hôtelier.

La vente de boissons alcoolisées

En Grande-Bretagne et en Irlande, la vente de boissons alcoolisées est soumise à des lois pouvant varier d'une région à l'autre.
D'une façon générale, les hôtels, les restaurants et les pubs peuvent demeurer ouverts l'après-midi et servir des boissons alcoolisées dans la mesure où elles accompagnent un repas suffisamment consistant. Les bars ferment après 23 heures.
Néanmoins, l'hôtelier a toujours la possibilité de servir, à sa clientèle, des boissons alcoolisées en dehors des heures légales.
Les enfants au-dessous de 14 ans n'ont pas accès aux bars.

Les arrhes

Certains hôteliers demandent le versement d'arrhes. Il s'agit d'un dépôt-garantie qui engage l'hôtelier comme le client. Bien faire préciser les dispositions de cette garantie.

Cartes de crédit

Cartes de crédit acceptées par l'établissement : Access (Eurocard) – American Express – Diners Club – Visa – Japan Credit Bureau

Les villes

✉ York	*Bureau de poste desservant la localité*
☏ 01225 Bath	*Indicatif téléphonique interurbain suivi, si nécessaire, de la localité de rattachement (de l'étranger, ne pas composer le 0)*
401 M 27, ⑩	*Numéro des cartes Michelin et carroyage ou numéro du pli*
West Country G.	*Voir le guide vert Michelin England : The West Country*
pop. 1057	*Population*
BX **A**	*Lettres repérant un emplacement sur le plan*
18	*Golf et nombre de trous (Handicap généralement demandé, réservation par téléphone vivement recommandée)*
✻, <	*Panorama, point de vue*
✈	*Aéroport*
☏ 261 1234	*Localité desservie par train-auto. Renseignements au numéro de téléphone indiqué*
⛴	*Transports maritimes*
⛴	*Transports maritimes (pour passagers seulement)*
ℹ	*Information touristique*

Heure légale

Les visiteurs devront tenir compte de l'heure officielle en Grande Bretagne : une heure de retard sur l'heure française.

Les curiosités

Intérêt

★★★	*Vaut le voyage*
★★	*Mérite un détour*
★	*Intéressant*
AC	*Entrée payante*

Situation

See	*Dans la ville*
Envir.	*Aux environs de la ville*
Exc.	*Excursions dans la région*
N, S, E, W	*La curiosité est située : au Nord, au Sud, à l'Est, à l'Ouest*
A 22	*On s'y rend par la route A 22, repérée par le même signe sur le plan du Guide*
2 m.	*Distance en miles*

La voiture, les pneus

En Grande-Bretagne, le port de la ceinture de sécurité est obligatoire pour le conducteur et le passager avant ainsi qu'à l'arrière, si le véhicule en est équipé. La loi interdit au passager avant de prendre un enfant sur ses genoux. En République d'Irlande, le port de la ceinture de sécurité est obligatoire pour le conducteur et le passager avant, si le véhicule en est équipé. Les enfants de moins de 12 ans ne sont pas autorisés à s'asseoir à l'avant, sauf si le véhicule est muni d'un système d'attache approprié.

Fournisseurs de pneus michelin

ATS Spécialistes du pneu

Des renseignements sur le plus proche point de vente de pneus ATS pourront être obtenus en s'informant entre 9 h et 17 h à l'adresse indiquée ci-dessous.

ATS HOUSE
180-188 Northolt Rd.
Harrow,
Middlesex HA2 OED
(0181) 423 2000

Automobile clubs

Les principales organisations de secours automobile dans le pays sont l'Automobile Association et le Royal Automobile Club, toutes deux offrant certains de leurs services aux membres de clubs affilés.

AUTOMOBILE ASSOCIATION
Fanum House
BASINGSTOKE, Hants.,
RG21 2EA
☎ (01256) 20123

AUTOMOBILE ASSOCIATION
108-110 Great-Victoria St.
BELFAST, BT2 7AT
☎ (01232) 328924

AUTOMOBILE ASSOCIATION
23 Rock Hill
BLACKROCK
Co-Dublin
☎ (01) 283-3555

ROYAL AUTOMOBILE CLUB
RAC House, Lansdowne Rd,
CROYDON, Surrey CR9 2JA
☎ (0181) 686 2525

ROYAL AUTOMOBILE CLUB
RAC House, 79 Chichester St.
BELFAST, BT1 4JR
☎ (01232) 240261

ROYAL AUTOMOBILE CLUB
RAC IRELAND New Mount House
22-24 Lower Mount St.
DUBLIN 2
☎ (01) 760113

Les plans

ⓐ ●a *Hôtels – Restaurants*

Curiosités

Bâtiment intéressant et entrée principale

Édifice religieux intéressant

Voirie

M 1 *Autoroute*

- échangeurs : complet, partiel

Route à chaussées séparées de type autoroutier

Grand axe de circulation

A 2 *Itinéraire principal (Primary route)*

- réseau en cours de révision

Sens unique – Rue impraticable, réglementée

Rue piétonne

Piccadilly P *Rue commerçante – Parc de stationnement*

Porte – Passage sous voûte – Tunnel

15'5 *Passage bas (inférieur à 16'6") sur les grandes voies de circulation*

Gare et voie ferrée

Funiculaire – Téléphérique, télécabine

B *Pont mobile – Bac pour autos*

Signes divers

Information touristique

Mosquée – Synagogue

Tour ou pylône de télécommunication – Ruines

Jardin, parc, bois – Cimetière

Stade – Hippodrome – Golf

Golf (réservé)

Vue – Panorama

Monument – Fontaine – Hôpital

Port de plaisance – Phare

Aéroport – Station de métro

Transport par bateau :

- passagers et voitures

Bureau principal de poste restante, téléphone

Bâtiment public repéré par une lettre :

C H *- Bureau de l'Administration du Comté – Hôtel de ville*

M T U *- Musée – Théâtre – Université, grande école*

POL. *- Police (commissariat central)*

Londres

BRENT SOHO *Nom d'arrondissement (borough) – de quartier (area)*

Limite de « borough » – d'« area »

Amico Lettore

Questa 23esima edizione della Guida Michelin Great Britain and Ireland propone una selezione aggiornata di alberghi e ristoranti.

Realizzata dai nostri ispettori in piena autonomia offre al viaggiatore di passaggio un'ampia scelta a tutti i livelli di confort e prezzo.

Con l'intento di fornire ai nostri lettori l'informazione più recente, abbiamo aggiornato questa edizione con la massima cura. Per questo solo la Guida dell'anno in corso merita pienamente la vostra fiducia.

Grazie delle vostre segnalazioni sempre gradite.

Michelin vi augura « Buon Viaggio ! »

Sommario

La scelta di un albergo, di un ristorante

Questa guida vi propone una selezione di alberghi e ristoranti stabilita ad uso dell'automobilista di passaggio. Gli esercizi, classificati in base al confort che offrono, vengono citati in ordine di preferenza per ogni categoria.

Categorie

	XXXXX	*Gran lusso e tradizione*
	XXXX	*Gran confort*
	XXX	*Molto confortevole*
	XX	*Di buon confort*
	X	*Abbastanza confortevole*
		Semplice, ma conveniente
		Altra risorsa, consigliata per prezzi contenuti
without rest.		*L'albergo non ha ristorante*
	with rm	*Il ristorante dispone di camere*

Amenità e tranquillità

Alcuni esercizi sono evidenziati nella guida dai simboli rossi indicati qui di seguito. Il soggiorno in questi alberghi dovrebbe rivelarsi particolarmente ameno o riposante.
Ciò può dipendere sia dalle caratteristiche dell'edificio, dalle decorazioni non comuni, dalla sua posizione e dal servizio offerto, sia dalla tranquillità dei luoghi.

a	*Alberghi ameni*
XXXXX a X	*Ristoranti ameni*
« Park »	*Un particolare piacevole*
	Albergo molto tranquillo o isolato e tranquillo
	Albergo tranquillo
sea	*Vista eccezionale*
	Vista interessante o estesa

Le località che possiedono degli esercizi ameni o tranquilli sono riportate sulle carte che precedono ciascuna delle regioni trattate nella guida.

Consultatele per la preparazione dei vostri viaggi e, al ritorno, inviateci i vostri pareri ; in tal modo agevolerete le nostre inchieste.

Installazioni

Le camere degli alberghi che raccomandiamo possiedono, generalmente, delle installazioni sanitarie complete. È possibile tuttavia che nelle categorie ⌂⌂, ⌂, *e* ⌂ *alcune camere ne siano sprovviste.*

30 rm	*Numero di camere*
	Ascensore
	Aria condizionata
TV	*Televisione in camera*
	Esercizio riservato completamente o in parte ai non fumatori
	Telefono in camera collegato con il centralino
	Telefono in camera comunicante direttamente con l'esterno
	Camere di agevole accesso per portatori di handicap
	Pasti serviti in giardino o in terrazza
	Piscina : all'aperto, coperta
	Palestra – Sauna
	Giardino da riposo
9	*Tennis appartenente all'albergo – Golf e numero di buche*
	Pesca aperta ai clienti dell'albergo (eventualmente a pagamento)
150	*Sale per conferenze : capienza massima*
	Garage nell'albergo (generalmente a pagamento)
P	*Parcheggio riservato alla clientela*
	Accesso vietato ai cani (in tutto o in parte dell'esercizio)
Fax	*Trasmissione telefonica di documenti*
May-October	*Periodo di apertura, comunicato dall'albergatore*
season	*Probabile apertura in stagione, ma periodo non precisato. Gli esercizi senza tali menzioni sono aperti tutto l'anno.*
LL35 OSB	*Codice postale dell'esercizio*
(Forte)	*Catena alberghiera (Vedere la lista alla fine della Guida)*

Animali

L'introduzione di animali domestici (cani, gatti...), in Gran Bretagna e in Irlanda, è vietata.

La tavola

Le stelle

*Alcuni esercizi meritano di essere segnalati alla vostra attenzione per la qualità tutta particolare della loro cucina. Noi li evidenziamo con le « **stelle di ottima tavola** ». Per questi ristoranti indichiamo tre specialità culinarie e alcuni vini locali che potranno aiutarvi nella scelta.*

✿✿✿ **Una delle migliori tavole, vale il viaggio**
Vi si mangia sempre molto bene, a volte meravigliosamente, grandi vini, servizio impeccabile, ambientazione accurata... Prezzi conformi.

✿✿ **Tavola eccellente, merita una deviazione**
Specialità e vini scelti...
Aspettatevi una spesa in proporzione.

✿ **Un'ottima tavola nella sua categoria**
La stella indica una tappa gastronomica sul vostro itinerario.
Non mettete però a confronto la stella di un esercizio di lusso, dai prezzi elevati, con quella di un piccolo esercizio dove, a prezzi ragionevoli, viene offerta una cucina di qualità.

Meals

Pur apprezzando le tavole a « stella », si desidera alle volte consumare un pasto più semplice ma sempre accuratamente preparato.

Alcuni esercizi ci son parsi rispondenti a tale esigenza e sono contraddistinti nella guida con **Meals** *in rosso.*

Consultate le carte delle località con stelle e con **Meals** *che precedono ciascuna delle regioni trattate nella guida.*

I prezzi

I prezzi che indichiamo in questa guida sono stati stabiliti nell'autunno 1995. Potranno pertanto subire delle variazioni in relazione ai cambiamenti dei prezzi di beni e servizi.

Entrate nell'albergo o nel ristorante con la guida alla mano, dimostrando in tal modo la fiducia in chi vi ha indirizzato.

Gli alberghi e i ristoranti vengono menzionati in carattere grassetto quando gli albergatori ci hanno comunicato tutti i loro prezzi e si sono impegnati, sotto la propria responsabilità, ad applicarli ai turisti di passaggio, in possesso della nostra guida.

I prezzi sono indicati in lire sterline (1 £ = 100 pence) ad eccezione per la Repubblica d'Irlanda dove sono indicati in « punts ».

Quando non figurano le lettere **s., t.,** *o* **st.** *i prezzi indicati possono essere maggiorati per il servizio o per l'I.V.A. o per entrambi. (L'I.V.A. non viene applicata nelle Channel Islands).*

Pasti

Meals 13.00/24.00	**Prezzo fisso**
	Pranzo 13.00, *cena* 24.00. *Questi prezzi comprendono il coperto*
Meals 15.00/25.00	*Vedere p. 31*
s.	*Servizio compreso*
t.	*I.V.A. compresa*
st.	*Servizio ed I.V.A. compresi (prezzi netti)*
6.00	*Prezzo della mezza bottiglia o di una caraffa di vino*
Meals a la carte 20.00/25.00	**Alla carta**
	Il 1° prezzo corrisponde ad un pasto semplice comprendente : primo piatto, piatto del giorno con contorno, dessert. Il 2° prezzo corrisponde ad un pasto più completo comprendente : antipasto, piatto principale, formaggio e dessert
	Questi prezzi comprendono il coperto
8.50	*Prezzo della prima colazione inglese se non è compreso nel prezzo della camera. Una prima colazione continentale può essere ottenuta a minor prezzo*

⌂ : *Negli alberghi di questa categoria, la cena viene servita, ad un'ora stabilita, esclusivamente a chi vi allogia. Il menu, a prezzo fisso, offre una scelta limitata di piatti. Raramente viene servito anche il pranzo. Molti di questi esercizi non hanno l'autorizzazione a vendere alcolici.*

Camere

rm 50.00/80.00 *Prezzo minimo* 50.00 *per una camera singola e prezzo massimo* 80.00 *per la camera più bella per due persone*

rm ☕ 55.00/75.00 *Il prezzo della prima colazione inglese è compreso nel prezzo della camera anche se non viene consumata*

« Short breaks » (SB.)

Alcuni alberghi propongono delle condizioni particolarmente vantaggiose o short break per un soggiorno minimo di due notti.
Questo prezzo, calcolato per persona e per un minimo di due persone, comprende : camera, cena e prima colazione. Informarsi presso l'albergatore.

La vendita di bevande alcoliche

In Gran Bretagna e Irlanda la vendita di bevande alcoliche è soggetta a leggi che possono variare da una regione all'altra.

In generale gli alberghi, i ristoranti e i pub possono restare aperti il pomeriggio e servire bevande alcoliche nella misura in cui queste accompagnano un pasto abbastanza consistente.
I bar chiudono dopo le ore 23.00.

L'albergatore ha tuttavia la possibilità di servire alla clientela bevande alcoliche anche oltre le ore legali.

Ai ragazzi inferiori ai 14 anni è vietato l'accesso ai bar.

La caparra

Alcuni albergatori chiedono il versamento di una caparra. Si tratta di un deposito-garanzia che impegna tanto l'albergatore che il cliente.
Vi raccomandiamo di farvi precisare le norme riguardanti la reciproca garanzia di tale caparra.

Carte di credito

AE VISA JCB *Carte di credito accettate dall'esercizio*
Access (Eurocard) – American Express – Diners Club – Visa – Japan Credit Bureau

Le città

✉ York	*Sede dell'ufficio postale*
☎ 01225 Bath	*Prefisso telefonico interurbano (nome del centralino indicato solo quando differisce dal nome della località). Dall'estero non formare lo 0*
401 M 27, ⑩	*Numero della carta Michelin e del riquadro o numero della piega*
West Country G.	*Vedere la Guida Verde Michelin England : The West Country*
pop. 1057	*Popolazione*
BX **A**	*Lettere indicanti l'ubicazione sulla pianta*
18	*Golf e numero di buche (handicap generalmente richiesto, prenotazione telefonica vivamente consigliata)*
※, ←	*Panorama, vista*
✈	*Aeroporto*
✆ 261 1234	*Località con servizio auto su treno. Informarsi al numero di telefono indicato*
⛴	*Trasporti marittimi*
⛴	*Trasporti marittimi (solo passeggeri)*
ℹ	*Ufficio informazioni turistiche*

Ora legale

I visitatori dovranno tenere in considerazione l'ora ufficiale in Gran Bretagna : un'ora di ritardo sull'ora italiana.

Le curiosità

Grado di interesse

★★★	*Vale il viaggio*
★★	*Merita una deviazione*
★	*Interessante*
AC	*Entrata a pagamento*

Ubicazione

See	*Nella città*
Envir.	*Nei dintorni della città*
Exc.	*Nella regione*
N, S, E, W	*La curiosità è situata : a Nord, a Sud, a Est, a Ovest*
A 22	*Ci si va per la strada A 22 indicata con lo stesso segno sulla pianta*
2 m.	*Distanza in miglia*

L'automobile, I pneumatici

In Gran Bretagna, l'uso delle cinture di sicurezza è obbligatorio per il conducente e il passeggero del sedile anteriore, nonchè per i sedili posteriori, se ne sono equipaggiati. La legge non consente al passaggero davanti di tenere un bambino sulle ginocchia.

Nella Repubblica d'Irlanda, l'uso delle cinture di sicurezza è obbligatorio per il conducente e il passeggero davanti, se il veicolo ne è equipaggiato. I bambini di meno di 12 anni non sono autorizzati a viaggiare sul sedile anteriore, a meno che questo non sia fornito di un sistema di sicurezza espressamente concepito per loro.

Rivenditori di pneumatici Michelin ATS Specialista in pneumatici

Potrete avere delle informazioni sul più vicino punto vendita di pneumatici ATS, rivolgendovi, tra le 9 e le 17, all'indirizzo indicato qui di seguito :

ATS HOUSE
180-188 Northolt Rd.
Harrow,
Middlesex HA2 OED
(0181) 423 2000

Automobile clubs

Le principali organizzazioni di soccorso automobilistico sono l'Automobile Association ed il Royal Automobile Club : entrambe offrono alcuni loro servizi ai membri dei club affiliati.

AUTOMOBILE ASSOCIATION
Fanum House
BASINGSTOKE, Hants.,
RG21 2EA
☎ (01256) 20123

ROYAL AUTOMOBILE CLUB
RAC House, Lansdowne Rd,
CROYDON, Surrey CR9 2JA
☎ (0181) 686 2525

AUTOMOBILE ASSOCIATION
108-110 Great-Victoria St.
BELFAST, BT2 7AT
☎ (01232) 328924

ROYAL AUTOMOBILE CLUB
RAC House, 79 Chichester St.
BELFAST, BT1 4JR
☎ (01232) 240261

AUTOMOBILE ASSOCIATION
23 Rock Hill
BLACKROCK
Co-Dublin
☎ (01) 283-3555

ROYAL AUTOMOBILE CLUB
RAC IRELAND
New Mount House
22-24 Lower Mount St.
DUBLIN 2
☎ (01) 760113

Le piante

Alberghi – Ristoranti

Curiosità

Edificio interessante ed entrata principale
Costruzione religiosa interessante

Viabilità

Autostrada
- svincoli : completo, parziale,
Strada a carreggiate separate di tipo autostradale
Asse principale di circolazione
Itinerario principale
- (« Primary route », rete stradale in corso di revisione)
Senso unico – Via impraticabile, a circolazione regolamentata
Via pedonale
Piccadilly *Via commerciale – Parcheggio*
Porta – Sottopassaggio – Galleria
Sottopassaggio (altezza inferiore a 16'6") sulle grandi vie di circolazione
Stazione e ferrovia
Funicolare – Funivia, Cabinovia
Ponte mobile – Battello per auto

Simboli vari

Ufficio informazioni turistiche
Moschea – Sinagoga
Torre o pilone per telecomunicazioni – Ruderi
Giardino, parco, bosco – Cimitero
Stadio – Ippodromo – Golf
Golf riservato
Vista – Panorama
Monumento – Fontana – Ospedale
Porto per imbarcazioni da diporto – Faro
Aeroporto – Stazione della Metropolitana
Trasporto con traghetto :
- passeggeri ed autovetture
Ufficio centrale di fermo posta, telefono
Edificio pubblico indicato con lettera :
C H *- Sede dell'Amministrazione di Contea – Municipio*
M T U *- Museo – Teatro – Università, grande scuola*
POL. *- Polizia (Questura, nelle grandi città)*

Londra

BRENT SOHO *Nome del distretto amministrativo (borough) – del quartiere (area)*
Limite del « borough » – di « area »

Lieber Leser

Die 23. Ausgabe des Michelin-Hotelführers Great Britain and Ireland bietet Ihnen eine aktualisierte Auswahl an Hotels und Restaurants.

Von unseren unabhängigen Hotelinspektoren ausgearbeitet, bietet der Hotel führer dem Reisenden eine große Auswahl an Hotels und Restaurants in jeder Kategorie sowohl was den Preis als auch den Komfort anbelangt.

Stets bemüht, unseren Lesern die neueste Information anzubieten, wurde diese Ausgabe mit größter Sorgfalt erstellt.

Deshalb sollten Sie immer nur dem aktuellen Hotelführer Ihr Vertrauen schenken.

Ihre Kommentare sind uns immer willkommen.

Michelin wünscht Ihnen "Gute Reise !"

Inhaltsverzeichnis

Wahl eines Hotels, eines Restaurants

Die Auswahl der in diesem Führer aufgeführten Hotels und Restaurants ist für Durchreisende gedacht. In jeder Kategorie drückt die Reihenfolge der Betriebe (sie sind nach ihrem Komfort klassifiziert) eine weitere Rangordnung aus.

Kategorien

	XXXXX	*Großer Luxus und Tradition*
	XXXX	*Großer Komfort*
	XXX	*Sehr komfortabel*
	XX	*Mit gutem Komfort*
	X	*Mit Standard Komfort*
		Bürgerlich
		Preiswerte, empfehlenswerte Gasthäuser und Pensionen
without rest.		*Hotel ohne Restaurant*
	with rm	*Restaurant vermietet auch Zimmer*

Annehmlichkeiten

Manche Häuser sind im Führer durch rote Symbole gekennzeichnet (s. unten). Der Aufenthalt in diesen ist wegen der schönen, ruhigen Lage, der nicht alltäglichen Einrichtung und Atmosphäre sowie dem gebotenen Service besonders angenehm und erholsam.

bis	*Angenehme Hotels*
XXXXX bis X	*Angenehme Restaurants*
« Park »	*Besondere Annehmlichkeit*
	Sehr ruhiges, oder abgelegenes und ruhiges Hotel
	Ruhiges Hotel
sea	*Reizvolle Aussicht*
	Interessante oder weite Sicht

Die den einzelnen Regionen vorangestellten Übersichtskarten, auf denen die Orte mit besonders angenehmen oder ruhigen Häusern eingezeichnet sind, helfen Ihnen bei der Reisevorbereitung. Teilen Sie uns bitte nach der Reise Ihre Erfahrungen und Meinungen mit. Sie helfen uns damit, den Führer weiter zu verbessern.

Einrichtung

Die meisten der empfohlenen Hotels verfügen über Zimmer, die alle oder doch zum größten Teil mit einer Naßzelle ausgestattet sind. In den Häusern der Kategorien , , und kann diese jedoch in einigen Zimmern fehlen.

30 rm	*Anzahl der Zimmer*
	Fahrstuhl
	Klimaanlage
	Fernsehen im Zimmer
	Hotel ganz oder teilweise reserviert für Nichtraucher
	Zimmertelefon mit Außenverbindung über Telefonzentrale
	Zimmertelefon mit direkter Außenverbindung
	Für Körperbehinderte leicht zugängliche Zimmer
	Garten-, Terrassenrestaurant
	Freibad, Hallenbad
	Fitneßraum – Sauna
	Liegewiese, Garten
	Hoteleigener Tennisplatz – Golfplatz und Lochzahl
	Angelmöglichkeit für Hotelgäste, evtl. gegen Gebühr
150	*Konferenzräume : Höchstkapazität*
	Hotelgarage (wird gewöhnlich berechnet)
	Parkplatz reserviert für Gäste
	Hunde sind unerwünscht (im ganzen Haus bzw. in den Zimmern oder im Restaurant)
Fax	*Telefonische Dokumentenübermittlung*
May-October	*Öffnungszeit, vom Hotelier mitgeteilt*
season	*Unbestimmte Öffnungszeit eines Saisonhotels. Die Häuser, für die wir keine Schließungszeiten angeben, sind im allgemeinen ganzjährig geöffnet*
LL35 OSB	*Angabe des Postbezirks (hinter der Hoteladresse)*
(Forte)	*Hotelkette (Liste am Ende des Führers)*

Tiere

Das Mitführen von Haustieren (Hunde, Katzen u. dgl.) bei der Einreise in Großbritannien und Irland ist untersagt.

Küche

Die Sterne

Einige Häuser verdienen wegen ihrer überdurchschnittlich guten Küche Ihre besondere Beachtung. Auf diese Häuser weisen die Sterne hin.

*Bei den mit « **Stern** » ausgezeichneten Betrieben nennen wir drei kulinarische Spezialitäten, die Sie probieren sollten.*

✿✿✿ **Eine der besten Küchen : eine Reise wert**
Man ißt hier immer sehr gut, öfters auch hervorragend, edle Weine, tadelloser Service, gepflegte Atmosphäre ... entsprechende Preise.

✿✿ **Eine hervorragende Küche : verdient einen Umweg**
Ausgesuchte Menus und Weine ... angemessene Preise.

✿ **Eine sehr gute Küche : verdient Ihre besondere Beachtung**
Der Stern bedeutet eine angenehme Unterbrechung Ihrer Reise.
Vergleichen Sie aber bitte nicht den Stern eines sehr teuren Luxusrestaurants mit dem Stern eines kleineren oder mittleren Hauses, wo man Ihnen zu einem annehmbaren Preis eine ebenfalls vorzügliche Mahlzeit reicht.

Meals

Wir glauben, daß Sie neben den Häusern mit « Stern » auch solche Adressen interessieren werden, die einfache, aber sorgfältig zubereitete Mahlzeiten anbieten.

Meals *im Text weist auf solche Häuser hin.*

Siehe Karten der Orte mit « Stern » und **Meals***, die den einzelnen im Führer behandelten Regionen vorangestellt sind.*

Preise

Die in diesem Führer genannten Preise wurden uns im Herbst 1995 angegeben. Sie können sich mit den Preisen von Waren und Dienstleistungen ändern.

Halten Sie beim Betreten des Hotels den Führer in der Hand. Sie zeigen damit, daß Sie aufgrund dieser Empfehlung gekommen sind.

Die Preise sind in Pfund Sterling angegeben (1 £ = 100 pence) mit Ausnahme der Republik Irland wo sie in Punts angegeben sind.

Wenn die Buchstaben **s., t.,** *oder* **st.** *nicht hinter den angegebenen Preisen aufgeführt sind, können sich diese um den Zuschlag für Bedienung und/oder MWSt erhöhen (keine MWSt auf den Channel Islands).*

Die Namen der Hotels und Restaurants, die ihre Preise genannt haben, sind fett gedruckt. Gleichzeitig haben sich diese Häuser verpflichtet, die von den Hoteliers selbst angegebenen Preise den Benutzern des Michelin-Führers zu berechnen.

Mahlzeiten

Meals 13.00/24.00	**Feste Menupreise** *Mittagessen* 13.00, *Abendessen* 24.00 *(inkl. Couvert)*
Meals 15.00/25.00	*Siehe Seite 43*
s.	*Bedienung inkl.*
t.	*MWSt inkl.*
st.	*Bedienung und MWSt inkl.*
6.00	*Preis für 1/2 Flasche oder eine Karaffe Tafelwein*

Meals a la carte 20.00/25.00	**Mahlzeiten « à la carte »** *Der erste Preis entspricht einer einfachen aber sorgfältig zubereiteten Mahlzeit, bestehend aus kleiner Vorspeise, Tagesgericht mit Beilage und Nachtisch. Der zweite Preis entspricht einer reichlicheren Mahlzeit mit Vorspeise, Hauptgericht, Käse oder Nachtisch (inkl. Couvert)*
8.50	*Preis des englischen Frühstücks, wenn dieser nicht im Übernachtungspreis enthalten ist. Einfaches, billigeres Frühstück (Continental breakfast) erhältlich*

: In dieser Hotelkategorie wird ein Abendessen normalerweise nur zu bestimmten Zeiten für Hotelgäste angeboten. Es besteht aus einem Menu mit begrenzter Auswahl zu festgesetztem Preis. Mittagessen wird selten angeboten. Viele dieser Hotels sind nicht berechtigt, alkoholische Getränke auszuschenken.

Zimmer

rm 50.00/80.00 *Mindestpreis* 50.00 *für ein Einzelzimmer und Höchstpreis* 80.00 *für das schönste Doppelzimmer*

rm ☕ 55.00/75.00 *Übernachtung mit englischem Frühstück, selbst wenn dieses nicht eingenommen wird*

« Short breaks » (SB.)

Einige Hotels bieten Vorzugskonditionen für einen Mindestaufenthalt von zwei Nächten oder mehr (Short Break). Der Preis ist pro Person kalkuliert, bei einer Mindestbeteiligung von zwei Personen und schließt das Zimmer, das Abendessen und das Frühstück ein.

Ausschank alkoholischer Getränke

In Großbritannien und Irland unterliegt der Ausschank alkoholischer Getränke gesetzlichen Bestimmungen, die in den einzelnen Gegenden verschieden sind.

Generell können Hotels, Restaurants und Pubs nachmittags geöffnet sein und alkoholische Getränke ausschenken, wenn diese zu einer entsprechend gehaltvollen Mahlzeit genossen werden. Die Bars schließen nach 23 Uhr. Hotelgästen können alkoholische Getränke jedoch auch außerhalb der Ausschankzeiten serviert werden.

Kindern unter 14 Jahren ist der Zutritt zu den Bars untersagt.

Anzahlung

Einige Hoteliers verlangen eine Anzahlung. Diese ist als Garantie sowohl für den Hotelier als auch für den Gast anzusehen.

Kreditkarten

AE VISA JCB *Vom Haus akzeptierte Kreditkarten :*
Access (Eurocard) – American Express – Diners Club – Visa (Carte Bleue) – Japan Credit Bureau

Städte

✉ York	*Zuständiges Postamt*
☏ 01225 Bath	*Vorwahlnummer und evtl. zuständiges Fernsprechamt (bei Gesprächen vom Ausland aus wird die erste Null weggelassen)*
401 M 27, ⑩	*Nummer der Michelin-Karte und Koordinaten des Planfeldes oder Faltseite*
West Country G.	*Siehe auch den grünen Michelinführer « England : The West Country »*
pop. 1057	*Einwohnerzahl*
BX **A**	*Markierung auf dem Stadtplan*
18	*Öffentlicher Golfplatz und Lochzahl (Handicap erforderlich, telefonische Reservierung empfehlenswert)*
☼, <	*Rundblick, Aussichtspunkt*
✈	*Flughafen*
☏ 261 1234	*Ladestelle für Autoreisezüge – Nähere Auskünfte unter der angegebenen Telefonnummer*
⛴	*Autofähre*
⛴	*Personenfähre*
ℹ	*Informationsstelle*

Uhrzeit

In Großbritannien ist eine Zeitverschiebung zu beachten und die Uhr gegenüber der deutschen Zeit um 1 Stunde zurückzustellen.

Sehenswürdigkeiten

Bewertung

★★★	*Eine Reise wert*
★★	*Verdient einen Umweg*
★	*Sehenswert*
AC	*Eintritt (gegen Gebühr)*

Lage

See	*In der Stadt*
Envir.	*In der Umgebung der Stadt*
Exc.	*Ausflugsziele*
N, S, E, W	*Im Norden (N), Süden (S), Osten (E), Westen (W) der Stadt*
A 22	*Zu erreichen über die Straße A 22*
2 m.	*Entfernung in Meilen*

Das Auto, die Reifen

In Großbritannien herrscht Anschnallpflicht für Fahrer, Beifahrer und auf dem Rücksitz, wenn Gurte vorhanden sind. Es ist verboten, Kinder auf den Vordersitzen auf dem Schoß zu befördern. In Irland besteht für den Fahrer und den Beifahrer Anschnallpflicht, wenn Gurte vorhanden sind. Kinder unter 12 Jahren dürfen allerdings nicht auf den Vordersitzen befördert werden, es sei denn es existiert ein entsprechender Kindersitz.

Lieferanten von Michelin-Reifen

ATS Reifenhändler

Die Anschrift der nächstgelegenen ATS-Verkaufsstelle erhalten Sie auf Anfrage (9-17 Uhr) bei

ATS HOUSE
180-188 Northolt Rd.
Harrow, Middlesex HA2
OED (0181) 423 2000

Automobilclubs

Die wichtigsten Automobilclubs des Landes sind die Automobile Association und der Royal Automobile Club, die den Mitgliedern der der FIA angeschlossenen Automobilclubs Pannenhilfe leisten und einige ihrer Dienstleistungen anbieten.

AUTOMOBILE ASSOCIATION
Fanum House
BASINGSTOKE, Hants.,
RG21 2EA
✆ (01256) 20123

ROYAL AUTOMOBILE CLUB
RAC House, Lansdowne Rd.
CROYDON, Surrey CR9 2JA
✆ (0181) 686 2525

AUTOMOBILE ASSOCIATION
108-110 Great-Victoria St.
BELFAST, BT2 7AT
✆ (01232) 328924

ROYAL AUTOMOBILE CLUB
RAC House, 79 Chichester St.
BELFAST, BT1 4JR
✆ (01232) 240261

AUTOMOBILE ASSOCIATION
23 Rock Hill
BLACKROCK
Co-Dublin
✆ (01) 283-3555

ROYAL AUTOMOBILE CLUB
RAC IRELAND
New Mount House
22-24 Lower Mount St.
DUBLIN 2
✆ (01) 760113

Stadtpläne

@ ●a *Hotels – Restaurants*

Sehenswürdigkeiten

Sehenswertes Gebäude mit Haupteingang
Sehenswerter Sakralbau

Straßen

Autobahn
- Anschlußstellen : Autobahneinfahrt und/oder-ausfahrt,
Schnellstraße mit getrennten Fahrbahnen
Hauptverkehrsstraße
A 2 *Fernverkehrsstraße (Primary route)*
- Netz wird z.z. neu eingestuft
Einbahnstraße – Gesperrte Straße, mit Verkehrsbeschränkungen
Fußgängerzone
Piccadilly P *Einkaufsstraße – Parkplatz*
Tor – Passage – Tunnel
Unterführung (Höhe angegeben bis 16'6") auf Hauptverkehrsstraßen
Bahnhof und Bahnlinie
Standseilbahn – Seilschwebebahn
B *Bewegliche Brücke – Autofähre*

Sonstige Zeichen

Informationsstelle
Moschee – Synagoge
Funk-, Fernsehturm – Ruine
Garten, Park, Wäldchen – Friedhof
Stadion – Pferderennbahn – Golfplatz
Golfplatz (Zutritt bedingt erlaubt)
Aussicht – Rundblick
Denkmal – Brunnen – Krankenhaus
Jachthafen – Leuchtturm
Flughafen – U-Bahnstation
Schiffsverbindungen : Autofähre
Hauptpostamt (postlagernde Sendungen), Telefon
Öffentliches Gebäude, durch einen Buchstaben gekennzeichnet :
C H *- Sitz der Grafschaftsverwaltung – Rathaus*
M T U *- Museum – Theater – Universität, Hochschule*
POL. *- Polizei (in größeren Städten Polizeipräsidium)*

London

BRENT SOHO *Name des Verwaltungsbezirks (borough) – des Stadtteils (area)*
Grenze des « borough » – des « area »

County abbreviations
Abréviations des comtés
Abbreviazioni delle contee
Abkürzungen der Grafschaften

England

Avon	*Avon*	**Kent**	*Kent*
Bedfordshire	*Beds.*	**Lancashire**	*Lancs.*
Berkshire	*Berks.*	**Leicestershire**	*Leics.*
Buckinghamshire	*Bucks.*	**Lincolnshire**	*Lincs.*
Cambridgeshire	*Cambs.*	**Merseyside**	*Mersey.*
Cheshire	*Ches.*	**Norfolk**	*Norfolk*
Cleveland	*Cleveland*	**Northamptonshire**	*Northants.*
Cornwall	*Cornwall*	**Northumberland**	*Northd*
Cumbria	*Cumbria*	**North Yorkshire**	*N. Yorks.*
Derbyshire	*Derbs.*	**Nottinghamshire**	*Notts.*
Devon	*Devon*	**Oxfordshire**	*Oxon.*
Dorset	*Dorset*	**Shropshire**	*Shrops.*
Durham	*Durham*	**Somerset**	*Somerset*
East Sussex	*E. Sussex*	**South Yorkshire**	*S. Yorks.*
Essex	*Essex*	**Staffordshire**	*Staffs.*
Gloucestershire	*Glos.*	**Suffolk**	*Suffolk*
Greater Manchester	*Gtr. Manchester*	**Surrey**	*Surrey*
Hampshire	*Hants.*	**Tyne and Wear**	*Tyne and Wear*
Hereford and Worcester	*Heref. & Worcs.*	**Warwickshire**	*Warks.*
Hertfordshire	*Herts.*	**West Midlands**	*W. Mids.*
Humberside	*Humbs.*	**West Sussex**	*W. Sussex*
Isle of Wight	*I.O.W.*	**West Yorkshire**	*W. Yorks.*
		Wiltshire	*Wilts.*

Wales

Clwyd	*Clwyd*	**Mid Glamorgan**	*M. Glam.*
Dyfed	*Dyfed*	**Powys**	*Powys*
Gwent	*Gwent*	**South Glamorgan**	*S. Glam.*
Gwynedd	*Gwynedd*	**West Glamorgan**	*W. Glam*

Local government in England, Scotland and Wales is being reorganised with effect from April 1996. The names and boundaries of local authorities, as listed in this guide, may be subject to change.

Starred establishments
Les établissements à étoiles
Gli esercizi con stelle
Die Stern-Restaurants

England

Bray-on-Thames *Waterside Inn*
London *Chez Nico at Ninety Park Lane (at Grosvenor House H.)*
– *The Restaurant, Marco Pierre White (at Hyde Park H.)*
– *La Tante Claire*

England

Bristol *Lettonie*
London *Le Gavroche*
– *Pied à Terre*
Longridge *Paul Heathcote's*
Oxford *Le Manoir aux Quat' Saisons*
Reading *L'Ortolan*

Scotland

Ullapool *Altnaharrie Inn*

Republic of Ireland

Dublin *Patrick Guilbaud*

England

Baslow *Fischer's at Baslow Hall*
Bath *Lucknam Park*
Blackburn *Northcote Manor*
Bourton-on-the-Water *Lords of the Manor*
Bradford *Restaurant Nineteen*
Bristol *Harvey's*
– *Hunstrete House*
Broadway *Buckland Manor*
Brockenhurst *Le Poussin*
Bury *Normandie*
Chagford *Gidleigh Park*
Cheltenham *Le Champignon Sauvage*
– *Epicurean*
Chester *Arkle (at Chester Grosvenor H.)*
Earl Stonham *Mr. Underhill's*
Faversham *Read's*
Grantham *Harry's Place*
Great Malvern *Croque-en-Bouche*
Haslemere *Fleur de Sel*
Ilkley *Box Tree*
Leeds *Pool Court at 42*
London *Aubergine*
– *The Canteen*
– *Capital*
– *Connaught*
– *L'Escargot*
– *Four Seasons (at Four Seasons H.)*
– *Fulham Road*
– *Greenhouse*
– *Grill Room at the Café Royal*
– *Halkin*
– *Interlude de Chavot*
– *Leith's*
– *Oriental (at Dorchester H.)*
– *Les Saveurs*
– *The Square*
Ludlow *Merchant House*
Minster Lovell *Lovells at Windrush Farm*
Newcastle upon Tyne *21 Queen St.*
New Milton *Chewton Glen*
Norwich *Adlard's*
Oakham *Hambleton Hall*
Plymouth *Chez Nous*

Storrington *Manley's*
Taplow *Waldo's (at Cliveden)*
Taunton *Castle*
Truro *Pennypots*
Ullswater *Sharrow Bay Country House*
Waterhouses *Old Beams*
Winteringham *Winteringham Fields*

Wales

Llyswen *Llangoed Hall*
Pwllheli *Plas Bodegroes*

Scotland

Aberfoyle *Braeval*
Balloch *Georgian Room (at Cameron House H.)*
Fort William *Inverlochy Castle*
Glasgow *One Devonshire Gardens*
Gullane *La Potinière*
Port Appin *Airds*
Portpatrick *Knockinaam Lodge*

Northern Ireland

Bangor *Shanks*
Belfast *Roscoff*

Channel Islands

St. Aubin (Jersey) *Broome's*
St. Saviour (Jersey) *Longueville Manor*

Republic of Ireland

Ahakista *Shiro*
Dublin *The Commons*
- *Thornton's*
Kenmare *Park*
- *Sheen Falls Lodge*

Further establishments which merit your attention

Autres tables qui méritent votre attention

Altre tavole particolarmente interessanti

Weitere empfehlenswerte Häuser

Meals

England

Bath	*Hole in the Wall*
Blakeney	*Morston Hall*
Bridgnorth	*Old Vicarage*
Brimfield	*Poppies*
Calstock	*Danescombe Valley*
Cambridge	*22 Chesterton Road*
Cheltenham	*Epicurean Bistro*
Dorking	*Partners West Street*
Drewsteignton	*Hunts Tor*
Eastbourne	*Hungry Monk*
Fordingbridge	*Three Lions*
Fowey	*Food for Thought*
Frampton-on-Severn	*Savery's*
Goring	*Leatherne Bottel*
Halifax	*Design House*
Hastings	*Röser's*
Kenilworth	*Simpson's*
Keswick	*Swinside Lodge*
King's Lynn	*Congham Hall*
-	*Rococo*
Leeds	*Leodis Brasserie*
-	*Rascasse*
London	*Alastair Little*
-	*Al Bustan*
-	*Atelier*
-	*Bibendum*
-	*Bistrot Bruno*
-	*Blue Print Café*
-	*Le Caprice*
-	*Chutney Mary*
-	*Clarke's*
-	*Fifth Floor (at Harvey Nichols)*
-	*Hilaire*
-	*Ivy*
-	*Kensington Place*
-	*Malabar*
-	*Nico Central*
-	*Percy's*
-	*Le Pont de la Tour*
-	*River Café*
-	*Simply Nico*
-	*Zafferano*
Maiden Newton	*Le Petit Canard*
Midhurst	*Cowdray Room (at Angel H.)*
Milford-on-Sea	*Rocher's*
Moulsford	*Beetle & Wedge*
Newcastle upon Tyne	*Café 21*
-	*Forsters*
-	*Horton Grange*
Old Burghclere	*Dew Pond*
Padstow	*Seafood*
Pateley Bridge	*Dusty Miller*
Portsmouth	*Bistro Montparnasse*
Preston	*Heathcotes Brasserie*
Royal Tunbridge Wells	*Cheevers*
Rushlake Green	*Stone House*
St Ives	*Pig "n" Fish*
St Keverne	*Volnay*
Shepton Mallet	*Bowlish House*
Southend-on-Sea	*Paris*
Storrington	*Old Forge*
Tadworth	*Gemini*
Totnes	*Floyd's Inn (sometimes)*
Towcester	*Vine House*
Wiveliscombe	*Langley House*

Wales

Llanrwst	*Chandler's Brasserie*
Llansanffraid Glan Conwy	*Old Rectory*

Scotland

Achiltibuie	*Summer Isles*
Dalry	*Braidwoods*
Edinburgh	*Atrium*

Glasgow	*Ubiquitous Chip*
Gullane	*Greywalls*
Kingussie	*The Cross*
Linlithgow	*Champany Inn*
Muir of Ord	*Dower House*
Skye (Isle of)	*Harlosh House*

Northern Ireland

Portrush	*Ramore*

Channel Islands

Gorey (Jersey)	*Jersey Pottery (Garden Rest.)*
–	*Village Bistro*

Republic of Ireland

Bunratty	*MacCloskey's*
Caherdaniel	*Loaves and Fishes*
Cashel	*Chez Hans*
Castlebaldwin	*Cromleach Lodge*
Cork	*Cliffords*
Dingle	*Doyle's Seafood Bar*
Dublin	*Chapter One*
–	*L'Ecrivain*
–	*Ernie's*
–	*Roly's Bistro*
Glandore	*Rectory*
Gorey	*Marlfield House*
Kenmare	*d'Arcy's Old Bank House*
–	*Lime Tree*

Particularly pleasant Hotels
Hôtels agréables
Alberghi ameni
Angenehme Hotels

England

London	*Claridge's*	**New Milton**	*Chewton Glen*
–	*Dorchester*	**Taplow**	*Cliveden*
–	*Savoy*		

Republic of Ireland

Straffan *Kildare H & Country Club*

England

Aylesbury	*Hartwell House*
Bath	*Lucknam Park*
Ipswich	*Hintlesham Hall*
London	*Connaught*
Melton Mowbray	*Stapleford Park*
Oxford	*Le Manoir aux Quat' Saisons*
Ston Easton	*Ston Easton Park*

Wales

Llyswen *Llangoed Hall*

Scotland

Dunkeld	*Kinnaird*
Fort William	*Inverlochy Castle*
Glasgow	*One Devonshire Gardens*

Republic of Ireland

Kenmare	*Park*
–	*Sheen Falls Lodge*

England

Bath	*Homewood Park*
Bolton Abbey	*Devonshire Arms Country House*
Bourton-on-the-water	*– Lords of the Manor*
–	*Lower Slaughter Manor*
Bristol	*Hunstrete House*
Broadway	*Buckland Manor*
Castle Combe	*Manor House*
Chagford	*Gidleigh Park*
Cheltenham	*On the Park*
Chipping Campden	*Charingworth Manor*
East Grinstead	*Gravetye Manor*
Evershot	*Summer Lodge*
Gillingham	*Stock Hill Country House*
Grasmere	*Michael's Nook Country House*
Kidderminster	*Brockencote Hall*
Leeds	*42 The Calls*
London	*Blakes*
–	*Durley House*
–	*Goring*
–	*Halkin*
–	*Pelham*
–	*22 Jermyn Street*
Newbury	*Hollington House*

Oakham *Hambleton Hall*
Royal Leamington Spa *Mallory Court*
Sandiway *Nunsmere Hall*
Sutton Coldfield *New Hall*
Tetbury *Close*
Ullswater *Sharrow Bay Country House*
York *Middlethorpe Hall*

Wales

Llandudno *Bodysgallen Hall*

Scotland

Arisaig *Arisaig House*
Dunblane *Cromlix House*
Eriska (Isle of) *Isle of Eriska*
Inverness *Culloden House*
Port Appin *Airds*

Channel Islands

St Saviour (Jersey) *Longueville Manor*

Republic of Ireland

Gorey *Marlfield House*
Mallow *Longueville House*
Wicklow *Tinakilly House*

England

Bradford-on-Avon *Woolley Grange*
Brampton *Farlam Hall*
Cuckfield *Ockenden Manor*
King's Lynn *Congham Hall*
Lewdown *Lewtrenchard Manor*
Liskeard *Well House*
Littlehampton *Bailiffscourt*
London *Sloane*
– *Sydney House*
Oxford *Old Parsonage*
Prestbury *White House Manor*
Purton *Pear Tree at Purton*
South Molton *Whitechapel Manor*
Tetbury *Calcot Manor*
Ullswater *Old Church*
Wareham *Priory*
Windermere *Holbeck Ghyll*
Woodstock *Feathers*

Wales

Llandrillo *Tyddyn Llan Country House*
Machynlleth *Ynyshir Hall*
Talsarnau *Maes-y-Neuadd*

Scotland

Aberfeldy *Farleyer House*
Achiltibuie *Summer Isles*
Alloa *Gean House*
Ballater *Tullich Lodge*
Gullane *Greywalls*
Kentallen *Ardsheal House*
Lewis & Harris (Isle of) *Ardvourlie Castle*
Portpatrick *Knockinaam Lodge*
Skye (Isle of) *Kinloch Lodge*
Ullapool *Altnaharrie Inn*
Whitebridge *Knockie Lodge*

Northern Ireland

Annalong *Glassdrumman Lodge*

Republic of Ireland

Ballingarry *Mustard Seed at Echo Lodge*
Cashel Bay *Cashel House*
Castlebaldwin *Cromleach Lodge*
Donegal *St Ernan's House*
Kanturk *Assolas Country House*
Shanagarry *Ballymaloe House*
Skibbereen *Liss Ard Lake Lodge*

England

Ashwater *Blagdon Manor Country*
Blakeney *Morston Hall*
Branscombe *The Look Out*
Bary St Edmunds *Twelve Angel Hill* (without rest)
Buttermere *Pickett Howe*
Calne *Chilvester Hill House*
Calstock *Danescombe Valley*
Canterbury *Thruxted Oast* (without rest)
Chipping Campden *Malt House*
Cranbrook *Old Cloth Hall*
Dulverton *Ashwick House*
Holmes Chapel *Brereton House*
Horley *Langshott Manor*
Keswick *Swuiside Lodge*
Leominster *The Marsh*
Marlborough *Old Vicarage* (without rest)
Melksham *Sandridge Park*

Porlock *Oaks*
Rushlake Green *Stone House*
Staverton *Kingston House*
Swaffham *Strattons*
Teignmouth *Thomas Luny House*
Tintagel *Trebrea Lodge*
Tonbridge *Goldhill Mill* (without rest)
Veryan *Crugsillick Manor*
Wiveliscombe *Langley House*
York *4 South Parade* (without rest)

Wales

Betws-y-Coed *Tan-y-Foel*
Llansanffraid Glan Conwy *Old Rectory*

Scotland

Arran (Isle of) *Kilmichael Country House*
Auchencairn *Collin House*
Banff *Eden House*
Lewis & Harris (Isle of) *Scarista House*
Lochinver *Albannach*
Maybole *Ladyburn*
Muir of Ord *Dower House*
Nairn *Lochloy House*
Oban *Glenfeochan House*

Northern Ireland

Holywood *Rayanne House*

Republic of Ireland

Bagenalstown *Kilgraney Country House*
Kenmare *Sallyport House* (without rest)
Kilkenny *Blanchville House*
Leenane *Delphi Lodge*
Wicklow *Old Rectory*

England

Askrigg *Helm Country House*
Benenden *Crit Hall*
Bethersden *Little Hodgeham*
Billingshurst *Old Wharf* (without rest)
Boroughbridge *Brafferton Hall*
Chipping Campden *Holly Mount* (without rest)
Cirencester *Shawswell Country House*
Cockermouth *Low Hall*
– *New House Farm*
Coniston *Appletree Holme*
Crackington Haven *Manor Farm*
East Retford *Old Plough*
Faversham *Frith Farm House*
Grindon *Porch Farmhouse*
Hayling Island *Cockle Warren Cottage*
Honiton *Cokesputt House*
Hutton-Le-Hole *Burnley House*
Iron Bridge *Severn Lodge* (without rest)
Lewes *Millers* (without rest)
Lizard *Landewedrack House*
Norwich *Old Rectory* (without rest)
Otley *Bowerfield House*
St Blazey *Nanscawen House* (without rest)
Seaford *Old Parsonage* (without rest)
Stow-on-the-Wold *College House*
Tetbury *Tavern House* (without rest)
Thame *Upper Green Farm* (without rest)
Thoralby *Littleburn*
Wiveliscombe *Jews Farm House*
Worcester *Upton House*
Wroxham *Garden Cottage* (without rest)

Wales

Bala *Fron Feuno Hall*
Betws-y-Coed *Penmachno Hall*
Cowbridge *Stembridge Farmhouse* (without rest)

Scotland

Edinburgh *Drummond House* (without rest)
– *17 Abercromby Place* (without rest)
– *Sibbet House* (without rest)
– *27 Heriot Row*
Fort William *Grange* (without rest)
Mull (Isle of) *Ardfenaig*

Northern Ireland

Belfast *Cottage* (without rest)
Coleraine *Greenhill House*

Republic of Ireland

Inistioge *Berryhill*

Particularly pleasant Restaurants
Restaurants agréables
Ristoranti ameni
Angenehme Restaurants

XXXX

England

Bray-on-Thames *Waterside Inn (with rm)*
London *Grill Room at the Café Royal*
– *Oriental (at Dorchester H.)*
Taplow *Waldo's (at Cliveden)*
Winteringham *Winteringham Fields (with rm)*

XXX

England

Baslow *Fischer's at Baslow Hall (with rm)*
Cheltenham *Epicurean*
Emsworth *36 on the Quay*
Henley-on-Thames *Stonor Arms (with rm)*
Leeds *Pool Court at 42*
London *Le Pont de la Tour*
– *Quaglino's*
Lymington *Gordleton Mill (with rm)*
Moreton-in-Marsh *Marsh Goose*
Moulsford *Beetle & Wedge (with rm)*
Reading *L'Ortolan*
Romsey *Old Manor House*
Sheffield *Old Vicarage*
Winchcombe *Wesley House (with rm)*

Scotland

Kingussie *The Cross (with rm)*
Peat Inn *Peat Inn (with rm)*

Republic of Ireland

Glandore *Rectory*

XX

England

Cheltenham *Epicurean Bistro*
Earl Stonham *Mr Underhill's*
Eastbourne *Hungry Monk*
Fowey *Food for Thought*
Goring *Leatherne Bottel*
Grantham *Harry's Place*
Newcastle upon Tyne *Horton Grange (with rm)*
Padstow *Seafood (with rm)*
Salisbury *Howard's House (with rm)*
Waterhouses *Old Beams (with rm)*

Wales

Brechfa *Ty Mawr Country House (with rm)*
Llanrwst *Cae'r Berllan (with rm)*

Republic of Ireland

Ahakista *Shiro*

X

England

Thirsk *Crab & Lobster*

Channel Islands

Jersey (Gorey) *Jersey Pottery (Garden Rest.)*

Republic of Ireland

Kenmare *Lime Tree*

England

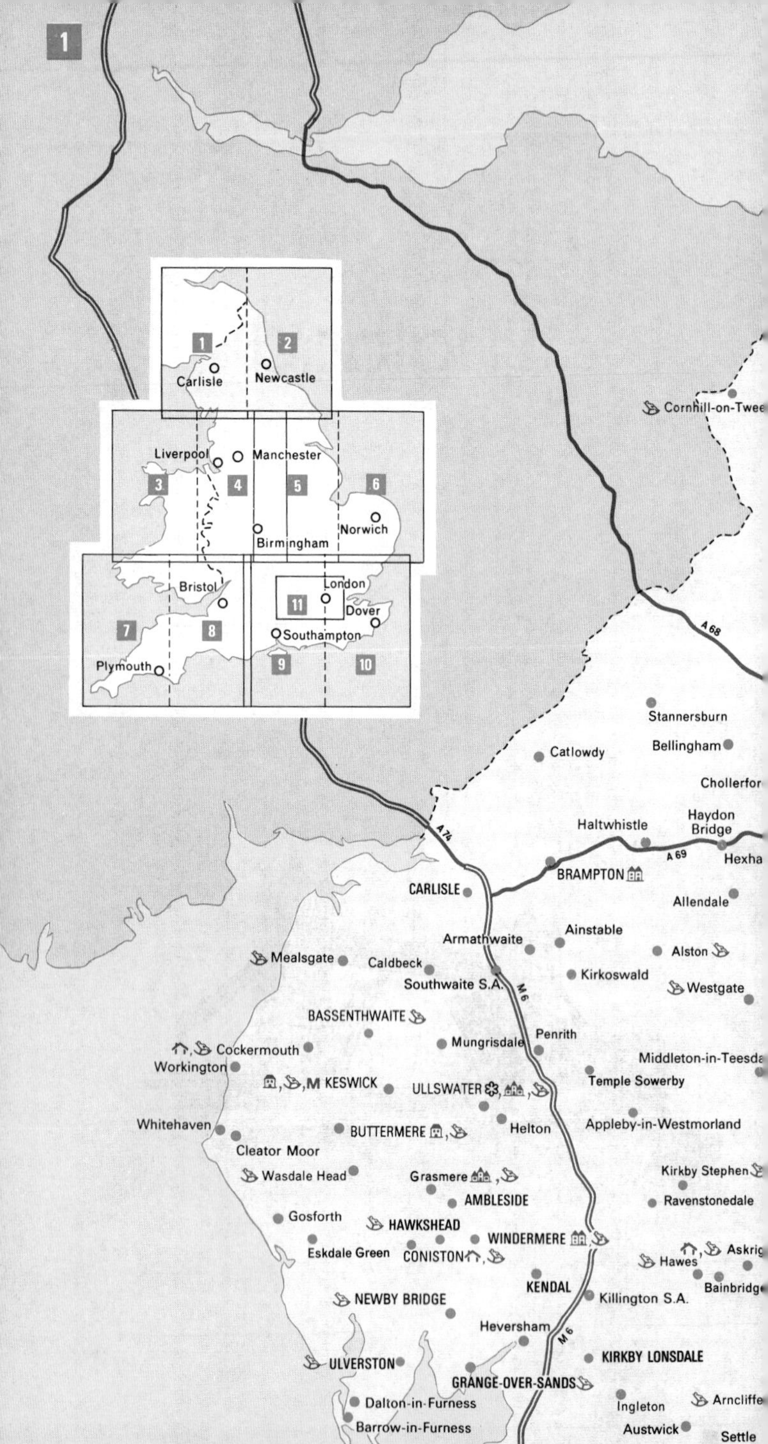
1
1
2
Carlisle
Newcastle
Liverpool
Manchester
3
4
5
6
Norwich
Birmingham
Bristol
London
11
Dover
7
8
Southampton
Plymouth
9
10
Cornhill-on-Twee
A 68
Stannersburn
Bellingham
Catlowdy
Chollerfor
Haltwhistle
Haydon Bridge
A 74
A 69
Hexha
BRAMPTON
CARLISLE
Allendale
Armathwaite
Ainstable
Alston
Mealsgate
Caldbeck
Southwaite S.A.
Kirkoswald
Westgate
M6
BASSENTHWAITE
Penrith
Cockermouth
Mungrisdale
Middleton-in-Teesda
Workington
M KESWICK
ULLSWATER
Temple Sowerby
Whitehaven
BUTTERMERE
Helton
Appleby-in-Westmorland
Cleator Moor
Wasdale Head
Grasmere
Kirkby Stephen
AMBLESIDE
Ravenstonedale
Gosforth
HAWKSHEAD
WINDERMERE
Askrig
Eskdale Green
CONISTON
Hawes
Bainbridge
KENDAL
Killington S.A.
NEWBY BRIDGE
Heversham
M6
KIRKBY LONSDALE
ULVERSTON
GRANGE-OVER-SANDS
Dalton-in-Furness
Ingleton
Arncliffe
Barrow-in-Furness
Austwick
Settle

Place with at least
a hotel or restaurant ● Ripon
a pleasant hotel or restaurant
a quiet, secluded hotel
a restaurant with Meals (M)
See this town for establishments located in its vicinity LEICESTER
Localité offrant au moins
une ressource hôtelière ● Ripon
un hôtel ou restaurant agréable
un hôtel très tranquille, isolé
une bonne table à Meals (M)
Localité groupant dans le texte les ressources de ses environs LEICESTER
La località possiede come minimo
una risorsa alberghiera ● Ripon
Albergo o ristorante ameno
un albergo molto tranquillo, isolato
un'ottima tavola con Meals (M)
La località raggruppa nel suo testo le risorse dei dintorni LEICESTER
Ort mit mindestens
einem Hotel oder Restaurant ● Ripon
ein angenehmes Hotel oder Restaurant
einem sehr ruhigen und abgelegenen Hotel
einem Restaurant mit Meals (M)
Ort mit Angaben über Hotels und Restaurants in der Umgebung LEICESTER
Berwick-upon-Tweed
BAMBURGH
Belford
Seahouses
Wooler
Powburn
ALNWICK
Alnmouth
Rothbury
Kirkwhelpington
Ashington
Morpeth
A 696
Whitley Bay
Tynemouth
orbridge
Wylam
NEWCASTLE UPON TYNE
M, with rm.
GATESHEAD
South Shields
Ebchester
Sunderland
Washington
Carterway Heads
Washington S.A.
Blanchland
Chester-le-Street
DURHAM
Crook
Bowburn
A1
Hamsterley
HARTLEPOOL
Bishop Auckland
Redcar
ARNARD CASTLE
STOCKTON-ON-TEES
Staithes
Thornaby-on-Tees
Middlesbrough
Loftus
Greta Bridge
DARLINGTON
Yarm
Great Ayton
WHITBY
Stokesley
Scotch Corner
eeth
Moulton
GREAT BROUGHTON
RICHMOND
Goathland
Rosedale Abbey
Patrick Brompton
NORTHALLERTON
Hutton-le-Hole
oralby
W. Witton
Bedale
Leeming Bar
Lastingham
Kirkbymoorside
SCARBOROUGH
MIDDLEHAM
E. Witton
Pickhill
Appleton le Moors
PICKERING
THIRSK
HELMSLEY
Masham
ETTLEWELL
Hovingham
Ripon
EASINGWOLD
MALTON
PATELEY BRIDGE
Bridlington
Sheriff Hutton
BOROUGHBRIDGE
sington

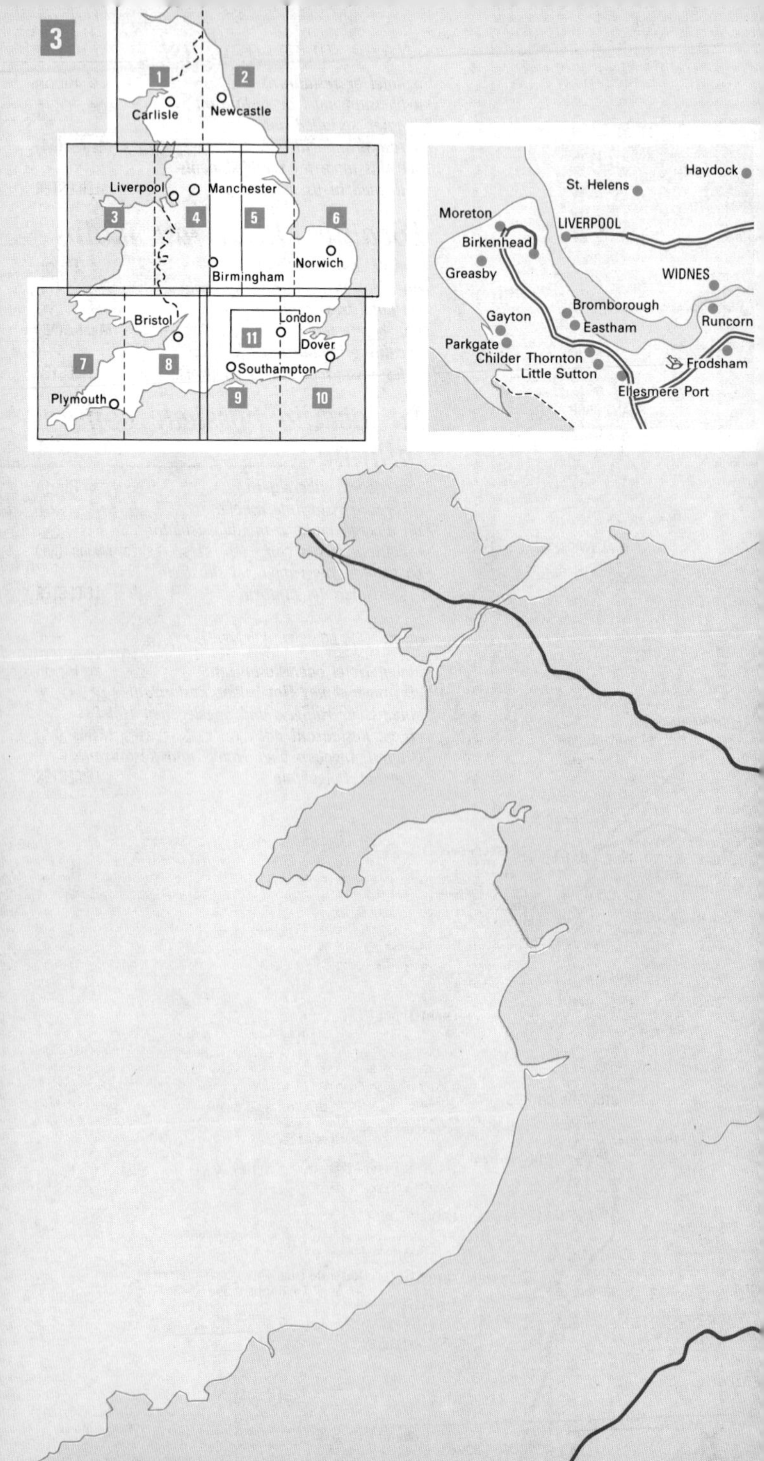
3
1
2
Carlisle
Newcastle
Liverpool
Manchester
3
4
5
6
Birmingham
Norwich
Bristol
London
11
Dover
7
8
Southampton
Plymouth
9
10
Haydock
St. Helens
Moreton
LIVERPOOL
Birkenhead
Greasby
WIDNES
Bromborough
Gayton
Eastham
Runcorn
Parkgate
Childer Thornton
Frodsham
Little Sutton
Ellesmere Port

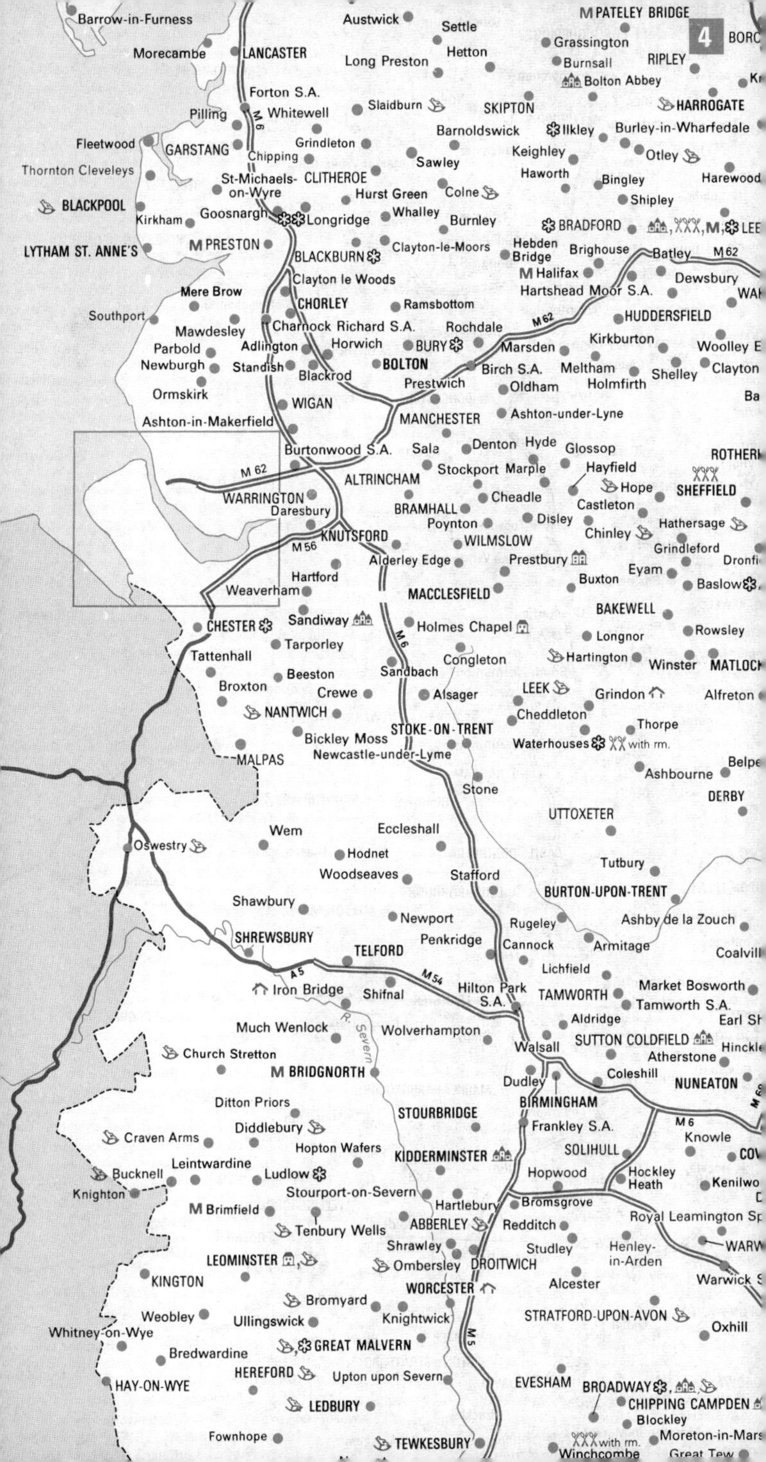
4
Barrow-in-Furness
Morecambe
LANCASTER
Austwick
Settle
Long Preston
Hetton
PATELEY BRIDGE
Grassington
Burnsall
Bolton Abbey
RIPLEY
Forton S.A.
Pilling
Whitewell
Slaidburn
SKIPTON
HARROGATE
Fleetwood
GARSTANG
Grindleton
Chipping
Barnoldswick
Ilkley
Burley-in-Wharfedale
Sawley
Keighley
Otley
Thornton Cleveleys
St-Michaels-on-Wyre
CLITHEROE
Haworth
Harewood
Bingley
BLACKPOOL
Hurst Green
Colne
Shipley
Kirkham
Goosnargh
Longridge
Whalley
Burnley
BRADFORD
LYTHAM ST. ANNE'S
PRESTON
BLACKBURN
Clayton-le-Moors
Hebden Bridge
Brighouse
Batley
M 62
Halifax
Dewsbury
Clayton le Woods
Hartshead Moor S.A.
Mere Brow
CHORLEY
Ramsbottom
HUDDERSFIELD
Southport
Charnock Richard S.A.
Rochdale
Mawdesley
M 62
Kirkburton
Parbold
Adlington
Horwich
BURY
Marsden
Woolley
Newburgh
Standish
BOLTON
Birch S.A.
Meltham
Shelley
Clayton
Blackrod
Prestwich
Oldham
Holmfirth
Ormskirk
WIGAN
Ashton-under-Lyne
Ashton-in-Makerfield
MANCHESTER
Denton
Hyde
Glossop
Burtonwood S.A.
Sala
ROTHER
M 62
Stockport
Marple
Hayfield
ALTRINCHAM
Hope
SHEFFIELD
WARRINGTON
Cheadle
BRAMHALL
Castleton
Daresbury
Poynton
Disley
Hathersage
KNUTSFORD
WILMSLOW
Chinley
M 56
Grindleford
Alderley Edge
Prestbury
Hartford
Eyam
Buxton
Baslow
Weaverham
MACCLESFIELD
BAKEWELL
Sandiway
CHESTER
Holmes Chapel
Longnor
Rowsley
Tarporley
M 6
Tattenhall
Congleton
Hartington
Winster
MATLOC
Sandbach
Beeston
Broxton
Crewe
Alsager
LEEK
Grindon
Alfreton
NANTWICH
Cheddleton
STOKE-ON-TRENT
Thorpe
Bickley Moss
Waterhouses
with rm.
Newcastle-under-Lyme
MALPAS
Ashbourne
Stone
DERBY
UTTOXETER
Wem
Eccleshall
Oswestry
Hodnet
Tutbury
Woodseaves
Stafford
BURTON-UPON-TRENT
Shawbury
Newport
Ashby de la Zouch
Rugeley
SHREWSBURY
Penkridge
TELFORD
Cannock
Armitage
Coalvill
Lichfield
A 5
M 54
Iron Bridge
Shifnal
Hilton Park S.A.
TAMWORTH
Market Bosworth
Tamworth S.A.
Aldridge
Much Wenlock
R. Severn
Wolverhampton
Walsall
SUTTON COLDFIELD
Church Stretton
Atherstone
BRIDGNORTH
Dudley
Coleshill
NUNEATON
BIRMINGHAM
Ditton Priors
STOURBRIDGE
M 6
Frankley S.A.
Diddlebury
Craven Arms
Hopton Wafers
SOLIHULL
Knowle
KIDDERMINSTER
Leintwardine
Bucknell
Ludlow
Hopwood
Hockley Heath
Kenilwo
Knighton
Stourport-on-Severn
Hartlebury
Bromsgrove
Brimfield
Royal Leamington Sp
Tenbury Wells
ABBERLEY
Redditch
Shrawley
Studley
Henley-in-Arden
LEOMINSTER
Ombersley
DROITWICH
KINGTON
Alcester
Warwick
WORCESTER
Bromyard
Weobley
Ullingswick
Knightwick
STRATFORD-UPON-AVON
Oxhill
Whitney-on-Wye
M 5
Bredwardine
GREAT MALVERN
HEREFORD
Upton upon Severn
EVESHAM
BROADWAY
HAY-ON-WYE
CHIPPING CAMPDEN
LEDBURY
Blockley
Fownhope
with rm.
Moreton-in-Mars
TEWKESBURY
Winchcombe
Great Tew

5
PATELEY BRIDGE
BOROUGHBRIDGE
RIPLEY
Knaresborough
HARROGATE
Burley-in-Wharfedale
Wetherby
Otley
Bingley
Harewood
Shipley
LEEDS
Batley
M 62
Dewsbury
HUDDERSFIELD
WAKEFIELD
Wentbridge
Woolley Edge S.A.
Clayton West
Shelley
Barnsley
A1
Sheriff Hutton
YORK
Tadcaster
Selby
Monk Fryston
Ferrybridge S.A.
Barnsdale Bar
DONCASTER
Bridlington
GREAT DRIFFIELD
Pocklington
Market Weighton
Brandesburton
BEVERLEY
South Cave
Little Weighton
Wressle
M 62
A 63
KINGSTON-UPON-HULL
Winteringham with rm
SCUNTHORPE
Epworth
Great Grimsby
Cleethorp
Binbrook
Conisholm
Louth
Market Rasen
Gringley
Bawtry
ROTHERHAM
SHEFFIELD
M 18
Blyth
East Retford
Todwick
Hope
Hathersage
Grindleford
Dronfield
Eyam
Baslow with rm.
Clowne
Worksop
A1
Markham Moor
R. Trent
BAKEWELL
Chesterfield
Longnor
Rowsley
Winster
MATLOCK
South Normanton
Grindon
Alfreton
M 1
LINCOLN
Horncastle
Woodhall Spa
Beckingham
Southwell
NEWARK-ON-TRENT
Thorpe
with rm.
Ashbourne
Belper
Gunthorpe
NOTTINGHAM
DERBY
Bingham
GRANTHAM
A 17
Sleaford
Boston
Tutbury
CASTLE DONINGTON
Colsterworth
LOUGHBOROUGH
Spalding
Whaplode
Bourne
Ashby de la Zouch
MELTON MOWBRAY
Armitage
Coalville
Markfield
Market Deeping
Market Bosworth
Tamworth S.A.
LEICESTER
OAKHAM
STAMFORD
PETERBOROUGH
Earl Shilton
UPPINGHAM
Blaby
Hinckley
Atherstone
King's Cliffe
Coleshill
NUNEATON
Corby
Stilton
M 69
MARKET HARBOROUGH
OUNDLE
Chatteris
M 6
Lutterworth
Desborough
Knowle
Aldwincle
COVENTRY
Kettering
Keyston
Hockley Heath
RUGBY
Old
Thrapston S.A.
Huntingdon
ST. IVES
Kenilworth
Dunchurch
WELLINGBOROUGH
Royal Leamington Spa
DAVENTRY
Holdenby
Buckden
Henley-in-Arden
WARWICK
NORTHAMPTON
Rushden
ST. NEOTS
Weedon Bec
Castle Ashby
A 45
Warwick S.A.
A1
Caxton
Horton
M 40
A 428
Oxhill
Roade
Sandy
TOWCESTER
Stoke Bruerne
BEDFORD
Biggleswade
Culworth
Newport Pagnell
STONY STRATFORD
MILTON KEYNES
Melbourn
BANBURY
CHIPPING CAMPDEN
Flitwick
Aspley Guise
Blockley
Brackley
Woburn
Letchworth
Moreton-in-Marsh
Deddington
Buckingham
Toddington S.A.
Baldock
Great Tew
Chipping Norton
HITCHIN

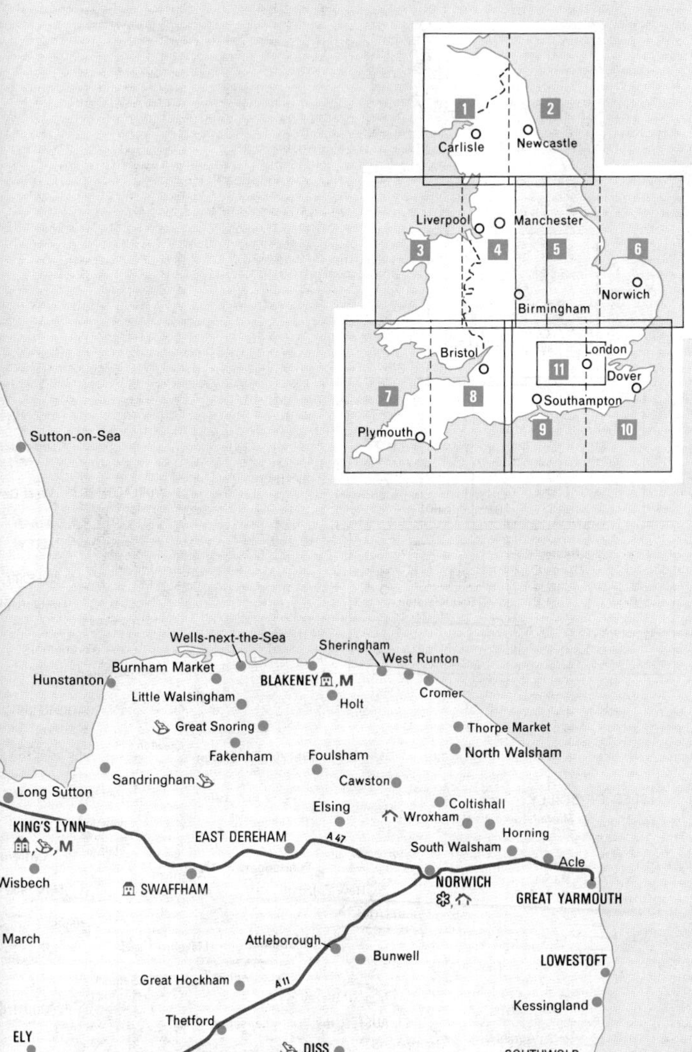
1
2
Carlisle
Newcastle
Liverpool
Manchester
3
4
5
6
Norwich
Birmingham
Bristol
London
11
Dover
7
8
Southampton
Plymouth
9
10
Sutton-on-Sea
Wells-next-the-Sea
Sheringham
West Runton
Burnham Market
Hunstanton
BLAKENEY, M
Cromer
Little Walsingham
Holt
Great Snoring
Thorpe Market
Fakenham
Foulsham
North Walsham
Sandringham
Cawston
Long Sutton
Coltishall
Elsing
Wroxham
KING'S LYNN
M
Horning
EAST DEREHAM
A 47
South Walsham
Acle
Wisbech
SWAFFHAM
NORWICH
GREAT YARMOUTH
March
Attleborough
Bunwell
LOWESTOFT
Great Hockham
A 11
Kessingland
Thetford
ELY
DISS
SOUTHWOLD
Eye
Walberswick
Gislingham
Barton Mills
Westleton
BURY ST. EDMUNDS
FRAMLINGHAM
NEWMARKET
Leiston
A 45
STOWMARKET
Earl Stonham
AMBRIDGE M
Aldeburg
Needham Market
Otley
A 11
Claydon
Lavenham
Chelsworth
WOODBRIDGE
Long Melford
Haverhill
Clare
SUDBURY
Hadleigh
IPSWICH
SAFFRON WALDEN
Stoke-by-Nayland
ewport
Great Yeldham
Nayland
Dedham
Higham
Felixstowe
Thaxted
Wethersfield
Bures
Harwich and

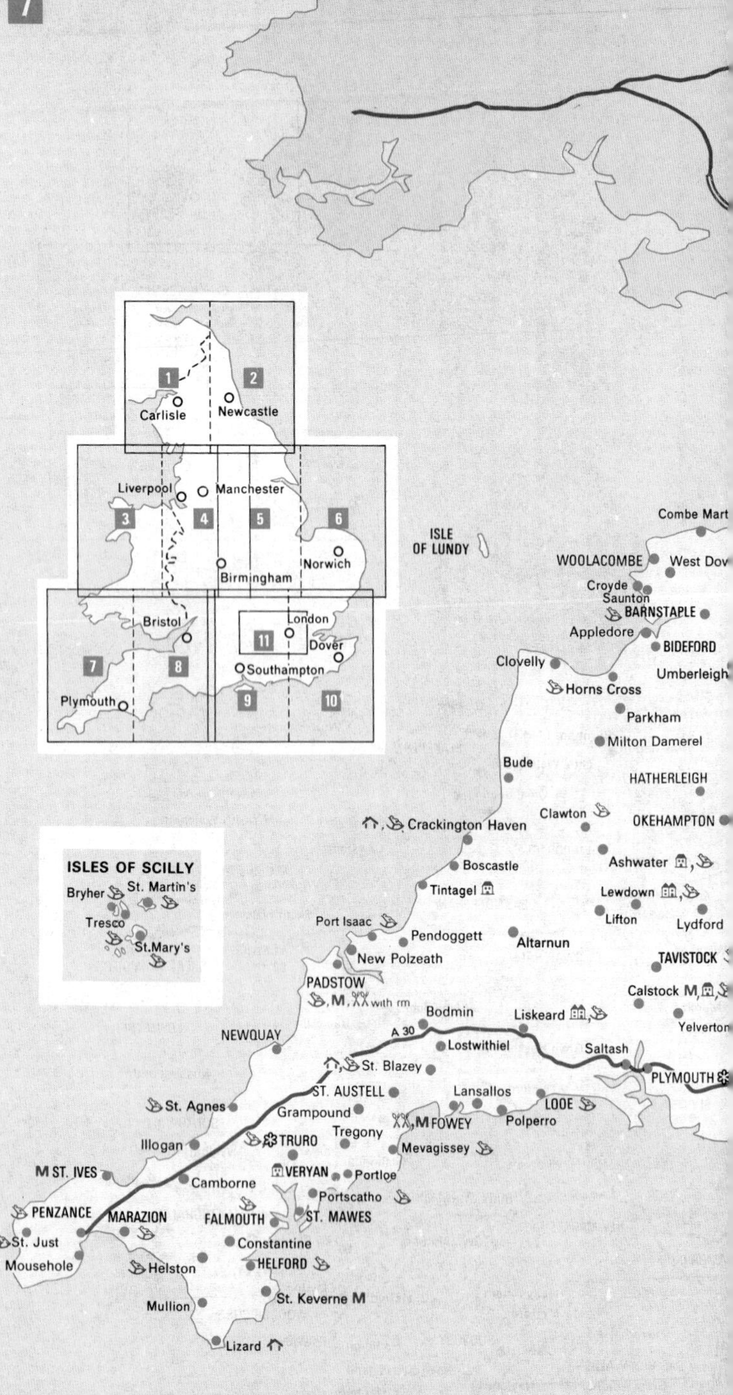

1
2
Carlisle
Newcastle
Liverpool
Manchester
3
4
5
6
Birmingham
Norwich
Bristol
London
11
Dover
7
8
Southampton
Plymouth
9
10
ISLE OF LUNDY
ISLES OF SCILLY
Bryher
St. Martin's
Tresco
St.Mary's
Combe Mart
WOOLACOMBE
West Dov
Croyde
Saunton
BARNSTAPLE
Appledore
BIDEFORD
Clovelly
Umberleigh
Horns Cross
Parkham
Milton Damerel
Bude
HATHERLEIGH
Clawton
OKEHAMPTON
Crackington Haven
Ashwater
Boscastle
Tintagel
Lewdown
Lifton
Lydford
Port Isaac
Pendoggett
Altarnun
New Polzeath
TAVISTOCK
PADSTOW
M, with rm
Calstock M
Bodmin
Liskeard
Yelverton
NEWQUAY
A 30
Lostwithiel
Saltash
St. Blazey
PLYMOUTH
ST. AUSTELL
Lansallos
St. Agnes
Grampound
LOOE
M FOWEY
Polperro
Tregony
Illogan
TRURO
Mevagissey
M ST. IVES
VERYAN
Portloe
Camborne
Portscatho
PENZANCE
MARAZION
FALMOUTH
ST. MAWES
St. Just
Constantine
Mousehole
Helston
HELFORD
St. Keverne M
Mullion
Lizard

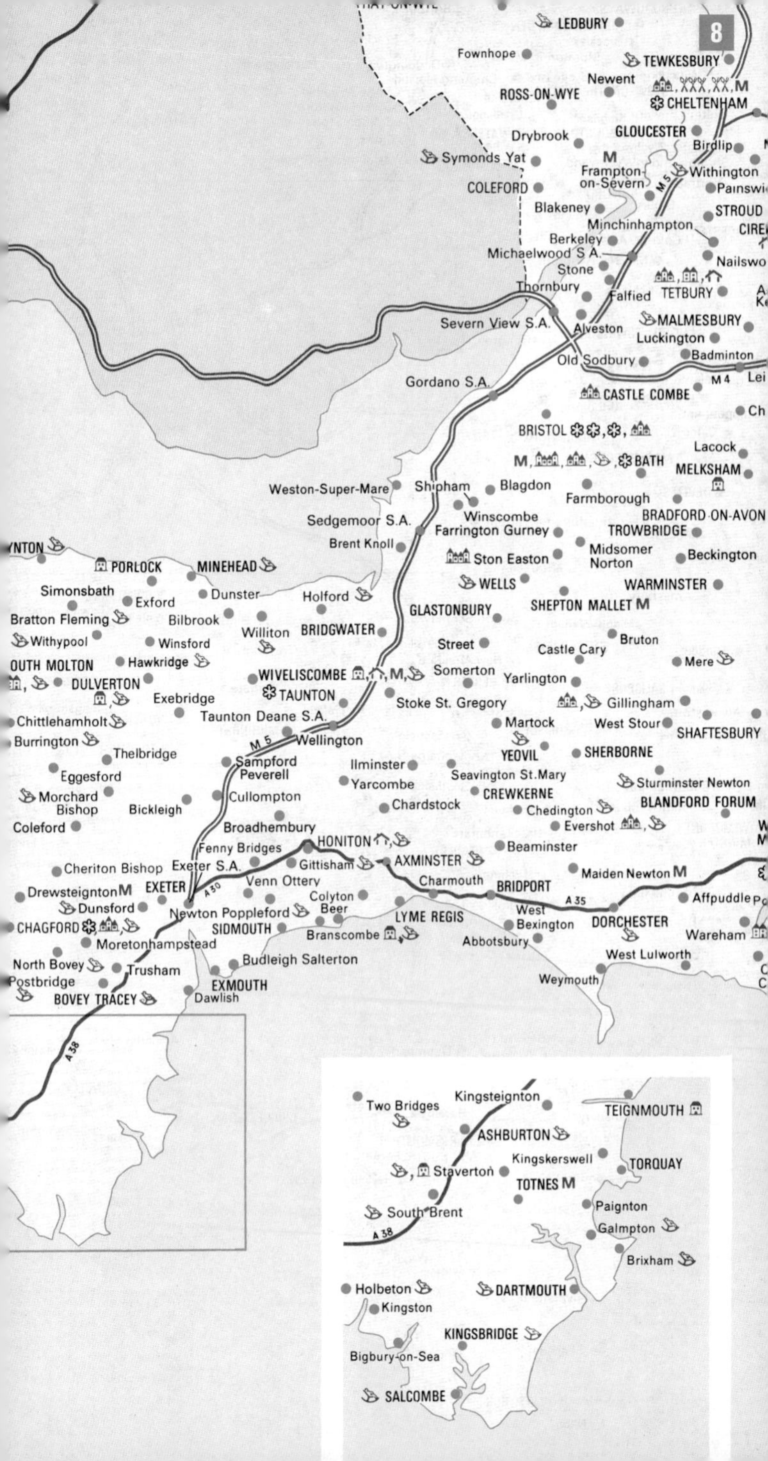

8
LEDBURY
Fownhope
TEWKESBURY
Newent
ROSS-ON-WYE
CHELTENHAM
GLOUCESTER
Drybrook
Birdlip
Symonds Yat
Frampton-on-Severn
Withington
COLEFORD
Painswick
Blakeney
STROUD
Minchinhampton
Berkeley
Michaelwood S.A.
Nailsworth
Stone
Thornbury
Falfied
TETBURY
Severn View S.A.
Alveston
MALMESBURY
Luckington
Old Sodbury
Badminton
M 4
Gordano S.A.
CASTLE COMBE
BRISTOL
Lacock
BATH
MELKSHAM
Weston-Super-Mare
Shipham
Blagdon
Farmborough
Winscombe
BRADFORD-ON-AVON
Sedgemoor S.A.
Farrington Gurney
TROWBRIDGE
Brent Knoll
Ston Easton
Midsomer Norton
Beckington
LYNTON
PORLOCK
MINEHEAD
WELLS
WARMINSTER
Simonsbath
Exford
Dunster
Holford
GLASTONBURY
SHEPTON MALLET
Bratton Fleming
Bilbrook
Withypool
Winsford
Williton
BRIDGWATER
Bruton
Street
Castle Cary
SOUTH MOLTON
Hawkridge
Mere
DULVERTON
WIVELISCOMBE
Somerton
Yarlington
TAUNTON
Exebridge
Stoke St. Gregory
Gillingham
Taunton Deane S.A.
Chittlehamholt
Martock
West Stour
Burrington
Wellington
SHAFTESBURY
YEOVIL
SHERBORNE
Thelbridge
M 5
Sampford Peverell
Ilminster
Eggesford
Seavington St.Mary
Yarcombe
Sturminster Newton
Morchard Bishop
Cullompton
CREWKERNE
Bickleigh
Chardstock
Chedington
BLANDFORD FORUM
Coleford
Broadhembury
Evershot
HONITON
Fenny Bridges
Beaminster
Exeter S.A.
Gittisham
AXMINSTER
Cheriton Bishop
Maiden Newton
Venn Ottery
Charmouth
Drewsteignton
EXETER
A 30
BRIDPORT
Colyton
A 35
Affpuddle
Dunsford
Beer
Newton Poppleford
LYME REGIS
West Bexington
DORCHESTER
CHAGFORD
SIDMOUTH
Branscombe
Wareham
Moretonhampstead
Abbotsbury
West Lulworth
North Bovey
Trusham
Budleigh Salterton
Postbridge
EXMOUTH
Weymouth
BOVEY TRACEY
Dawlish
A 38
Two Bridges
Kingsteignton
TEIGNMOUTH
ASHBURTON
Kingskerswell
TORQUAY
Staverton
TOTNES
South Brent
Paignton
A 38
Galmpton
Brixham
Holbeton
DARTMOUTH
Kingston
KINGSBRIDGE
Bigbury-on-Sea
SALCOMBE

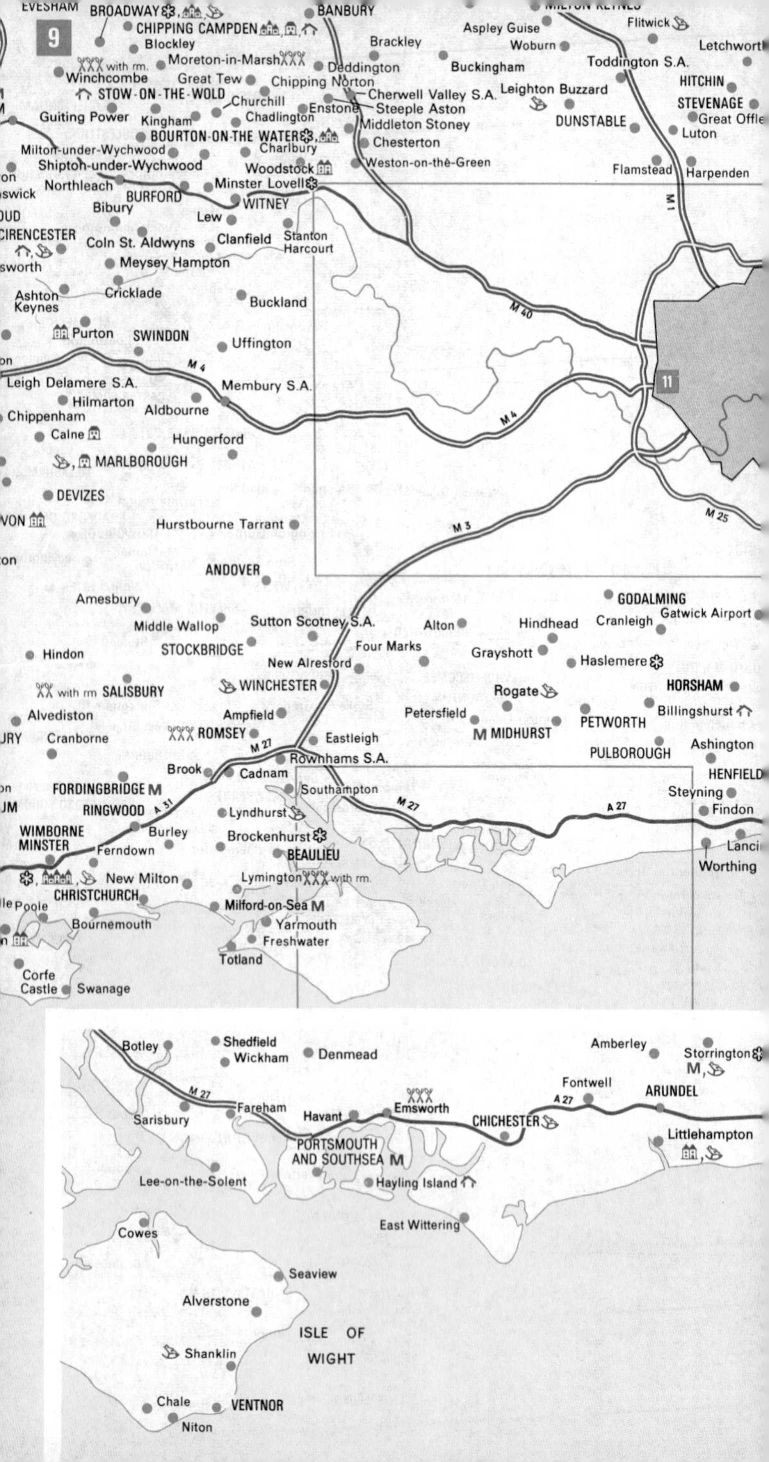
9
EVESHAM
BROADWAY
CHIPPING CAMPDEN
Blockley
with rm.
Moreton-in-Marsh
Winchcombe
Great Tew
STOW-ON-THE-WOLD
Churchill
Guiting Power
Kingham
Chadlington
BOURTON-ON-THE WATER
Milton-under-Wychwood
Charlbury
Shipton-under-Wychwood
Woodstock
Northleach
Minster Lovell
BURFORD
WITNEY
Bibury
Lew
CIRENCESTER
Coln St. Aldwyns
Clanfield
Stanton Harcourt
Meysey Hampton
Ashton Keynes
Cricklade
Buckland
Purton
SWINDON
Uffington
M 4
Leigh Delamere S.A.
Membury S.A.
Hilmarton
Aldbourne
Chippenham
Calne
Hungerford
MARLBOROUGH
DEVIZES
Hurstbourne Tarrant
ANDOVER
Amesbury
Middle Wallop
Sutton Scotney S.A.
STOCKBRIDGE
Hindon
with rm SALISBURY
WINCHESTER
Alvediston
Ampfield
ROMSEY
Cranborne
M 27
Eastleigh
Rownhams S.A.
Brook
Cadnam
FORDINGBRIDGE
Southampton
RINGWOOD
A 31
Lyndhurst
WIMBORNE MINSTER
Burley
Brockenhurst
Ferndown
BEAULIEU
New Milton
Lymington
with rm.
CHRISTCHURCH
Poole
Milford-on-Sea
Bournemouth
Yarmouth
Freshwater
Totland
Corfe Castle
Swanage
BANBURY
Brackley
Deddington
Chipping Norton
Enstone
Cherwell Valley S.A.
Steeple Aston
Middleton Stoney
Chesterton
Weston-on-the-Green
Aspley Guise
Woburn
Buckingham
Leighton Buzzard
Flitwick
Toddington S.A.
Letchworth
HITCHIN
STEVENAGE
Great Offley
DUNSTABLE
Luton
Flamstead
Harpenden
M 1
M 40
11
M 4
M 3
M 25
GODALMING
Alton
Hindhead
Cranleigh
Gatwick Airport
Four Marks
Grayshott
New Alresford
Haslemere
Rogate
HORSHAM
Petersfield
Billingshurst
MIDHURST
PETWORTH
Ashington
PULBOROUGH
HENFIELD
M 27
Steyning
A 27
Findon
Worthing
Botley
Shedfield
Wickham
Denmead
Amberley
Storrington
Fontwell
ARUNDEL
M 27
Sarisbury
Fareham
Havant
Emsworth
A 27
CHICHESTER
Littlehampton
PORTSMOUTH AND SOUTHSEA
Lee-on-the-Solent
Hayling Island
East Wittering
Cowes
Seaview
Alverstone
ISLE OF WIGHT
Shanklin
Chale
VENTNOR
Niton

10
Clare
Melbourn
SAFFRON WALDEN
Newport
Great Yeldham
Nayland
Stoke-by-Nayland
Higham
Dedham
Felixstowe
Baldock
Clavering
Thaxted
Wethersfield
Bures
Earls Colne
Manningtree
Harwich and Dovercourt
Wix
STANSTED AIRPORT
Coggeshall
COLCHESTER
Braintree
Great Dunmow
Felsted
Brightlingsea
ISHOP'S STORTFORD
WARE
Hertford
Witham
Clacton-on-Sea
West Mersea
M 11
CHELMSFORD
Maldon
M 25
Battlesbridge
Burnham-on-Crouch
Wickford
Rochford
Basildon
Southend-on-Sea M
LONDON
North Stifford
Gravesend
Rochester
Birchington
Whitstable
Herne Bay
Broadstairs
Medway S.A.
Newington
M 20
Cobham
RAMSGATE
West Malling
FAVERSHAM
Selling
Sandwich
Warren Street
CANTERBURY
M 25
MAIDSTONE
Lenham
DEAL
M 23
Pluckley
M 20
Wye
Edenbridge
Brenchley
Horley
Penshurst
Frittenden
ASHFORD
Turners Hill
M ROYAL TUNBRIDGE WELLS
Bethersden
DOVER
EAST GRINSTEAD
Goudhurst
Biddenden
RAWLEY
Hartfield
CRANBROOK
Folkestone
FOREST ROW
Wadhurst
Tenterden
Hythe
Ardingly
Crowborough
Hawkhurst
Benenden
A 259
Cuckfield
MAYFIELD
Ticehurst
Wittersham
New Romney
Heathfield
Sedlescombe
aywards Heath
Uckfield
Rushlake Green
RYE
Hickstead
Halland
Battle
Winchelsea
Lewes
Herstmonceux
A 27
Bexhill
RIGHTON AND HOVE
HAILSHAM
Hastings and St. Leonards M
Alfriston
Pevensey
ottingdean
EASTBOURNE
SEAFORD
1
2
Carlisle
Newcastle
Liverpool
Manchester
3
4
5
6
Norwich
Birmingham
Bristol
London
11
Dover
7
8
Southampton
Plymouth
9
10

11
LONDON ✿✿✿, ✿✿, ✿, M, XXXXX, XXXX, XXX
Waddesdon
Horton-cum-Studley
Aylesbury
Aston Clinton
Tring
Long Crendon
OXFORD
THAME
Welwyn
St.Albans
Hatfield
Hertingfordbury
Stanstead Abbots
Sawbridgeworth
Harlow
Brookmans Park
HEMEL HEMPSTEAD
Kings Langley
Cheshunt
Epping
South Mimms S.A.
Waltham Abbey
Great Missenden
Chipperfield
Ingatestone
Chislehampton
Chinnor
Little Chalfont
Chenies
Borehamwood
ABINGDON
Amersham
Watford
Elstree
Brentwood
Dorchester
Speen
High Wycombe
Ibstone
Buckhurst Hill
WALLINGFORD
BEACONSFIELD
Chalfont St. Peter
Harwell
East Horndon
Nettlebed
Gerrards Cross
Marlow
Cookham
Moulsford XXX with rm., M
Hurley-on-Thames
Taplow ✿, XXXX
XXX with rm.
MAIDENHEAD
HENLEY-ON-THAMES
Burnham
Streatley
Goring M, XX
Knowl Hill
Slough
Thurrock S.A.
Purfleet
XXXX with rm. ✿✿✿ Bray-on-Thames
Thames
Dartford
Sonning-on-Thames
Windsor
Yattendon
Bradfield
READING ✿✿ XXX
Staines
Bracknell
Egham
Reading S.A.
Wokingham
ASCOT
Shepperton
Thatcham
NEWBURY
Chertsey
Walton-on-Thames
Farningham
Padworth
Crowthorne
Bagshot
Weybridge
ESHER
Silchester
BRANDS HATCH
Old Burghclere M
Chobham
Stratfield Turgis
Yateley
Camberley
COBHAM
Epsom
Wrotham Heath
Frimley
Tadworth M
Fleet S.A.
Ripley
HOOK
Fleet
Ockham
SEVENOAKS
Westerham
Farnborough
BASINGSTOKE
Crondall
Redhill
Godstone
TONBRIDGE
North Waltham
Odiham
FARNHAM
GUILDFORD
M Dorking
Reigate
A 40
M 40
M 1
M 11
A 11
A 41
A 40
M 25
M 4
A 4
A 316
A 23
A 20
M 20
M 3

ABBERLEY Heref. and Worcs. 403 404 M 27 – pop. 654 – ✉ Worcester – ☎ 01299.
♦London 137 – ♦Birmingham 27 – Worcester 13.

The Elms ⛰, WR6 6AT, W : 2 m. on A 443 ☎ 896666, Fax 896804, ←, « Queen Anne mansion », park – TV ☎ P – 40. AE VISA.
Meals (bar lunch Monday to Saturday)/dinner 24.00 **st.** and a la carte 7.15 – 9.95 – **24 rm** 105.00/148.00 **st.**, 1 suite – SB.

Manor Arms ⛰, Abberley Village, WR6 6BN, ☎ 896507, Fax 896723, – TV ☎ P. AE VISA
Meals (bar lunch)/dinner a la carte 9.50/18.00 **st.** 4.00 **10 rm** 30.00/40.00 **st.**

at Little Witley SE : 4 m. by A 443 – ✉ Worcester – ☎ 01886 :

Ribston House ⛰, Bank Rd, WR6 6LS, ☎ 888750, Fax 888925, – P.
booking essential – **Meals** (communal dining) – **3 rm** (dinner included) 35.00/70.00 **st.** – SB.

ABBOTSBURY Dorset 403 404 M 32 **The West Country G.** – pop. 422 – ☎ 01305.
See : Town★★ - Chesil Beach★★ - Swannery★ *AC* – Sub-Tropical Gardens★ *AC*.
Envir. : St. Catherine's Chapel★, ½ m. uphill (30 mn rtn on foot).
Exc. : Maiden Castle★★ (←★) NE : 7½ m.
♦London 146 – Exeter 50 – Bournemouth 44 – Weymouth 10.

Ilchester Arms, 9 Market St., DT3 4JR, ☎ 871243, Fax 871225 – rest TV ☎ P. VISA.
accommodation closed 24 and 25 December – **Meals** a la carte 9.50/16.25 **t.** – 4.45 – **10 rm** 39.50 **st.** – SB.

ABBOT'S SALFORD Warks. 403 404 O 27 – see Evesham (Heref. and Worcs.).

ABINGDON Oxon. 403 404 Q 28 **Great Britain G.** – pop. 30 771 – ☎ 01235.
See : Town★ – County Hall★.
18 Drayton Park, Steventon Rd, Drayton, ☎ 550607.
25 Bridge St., OX14 3HN ☎ 522711.
♦London 64 – ♦Oxford 6 – Reading 25.

Upper Reaches (Forte Heritage), Thames St., OX14 3JA, ☎ 522311, Fax 555182 – TV ☎ P – 70. AE VISA JCB
Meals 11.95/19.95 **st.** 6.00 – 8.75 – **25 rm** 85.00/95.00 **st.** – SB.

Abingdon Lodge, Marcham Rd, OX14 1TZ, W : 1 m. on A 415 ☎ 553456, Fax 554117 – rm TV ☎ P – 140. AE VISA.
Meals 8.50/12.35 **st.** and a la carte – 6.50 – **63 rm** 69.00/84.00 **st.** – SB.

at Frilford W : 3¾ m. on A 415 – ✉ Abingdon – ☎ 01865 :

Dog House, Frilford Heath, OX13 6QJ, NE : 1 ¼ m. by A 338 on Cothill rd ☎ 390830, Fax 390860, – rm TV ☎ P
19 rm.

at Kingston Bagpuize W : 7 m. by A 415 – ✉ Abingdon – ☎ 01865 :

Fallowfields ⛰, Faringdon Rd, OX13 5BH, ☎ 820416, Fax 821275, heated, – TV ☎ P
Meals (lunch by arrangement)/dinner 21.50 **s.** 4.95 – **3 rm** 65.00/74.00 **s.**

ACLE Norfolk 404 Y 26 **Great Britain G.** – pop. 2 208 – ☎ 01493.
Envir. : The Broads★.
♦London 118 – Great Yarmouth 8 – ♦Norwich 11.

Forte Travelodge, Acle by pass, NR1 3BE, on A 47 at junction with B 1140 ☎ 751970, Reservations (Freephone) 0800 850950 – TV P. AE VISA.
Meals (grill rest.) – **40 rm** 34.50 **t.**

ADDERBURY Oxon. 403 404 Q 27 – see Banbury.

ADLINGTON Ches. – see Macclesfield.

ADLINGTON Lancs. 402 404 M 23 – pop. 5 653 – ☎ 01257.
♦London 217 – ♦Liverpool 35 – ♦Manchester 21 – Preston 16.

Gladmar, Railway Rd, PR6 9RG, ☎ 480398, Fax 482681, – TV ☎ P. AE VISA.
Meals (residents only) (dinner only) 11.50 **st.** 3.50 – **20 rm** 37.00/58.00 **st.**

AFFPUDDLE Dorset 403 404 N 31 **The West Country G.** – pop. 447 – ✉ Dorchester – ☎ 01305.
Envir. : Moreton Church★★, S : 2½ m. by B 3390.
Exc. : Bere Regis (St. John the Baptist Church★★) NE : 3½ m. by B 3390 and A 35.
♦London 121 – Bournemouth 19 – Exeter 60 – ♦Southampton 47 – Weymouth 14.

Old Vicarage ⛰ without rest., DT2 7HH, ☎ 848315, « Tastefully furnished Georgian house », – TV P.
closed Christmas - New Year – **3 rm** 22.50/40.00.

AINSTABLE Cumbria 401 402 L 19 pop. 523 – ✉ Carlisle – ☎ 01768.
♦London 304 – ♦Carlisle 19 – Kendal 45 – Lancaster 62.

- **New Crown Inn,** CA4 9QQ, ☎ 896273 – TV P. VISA
  Meals (in bar) a la carte 8.80/15.15 **t.** 4.10 – **3 rm** 27.50/45.00 **t.** – SB.

ALBERBURY Shrops. 402 403 L 25 – see Shrewsbury.

ALBRIGHTON Shrops. 402 403 L 25 – see Shrewsbury.

ALBURY Surrey – see Guildford.

ALCESTER Warks. 403 404 O 27 pop. 5 697 – ☎ 01789.
♦London 104 – ♦Birmingham 20 – Cheltenham 27 – Stratford-upon-Avon 8.

- **Kings Court,** Kings Coughton, B49 5QQ, N : 1½ m. on A 435 ☎ 763111, Fax 400242, – TV ☎ & P – 100. AE VISA
  accommodation closed 24 to 30 December – **Meals** 14.00 **t.** and a la carte 5.95 – **42 rm** 49.00/70.00 **t.**
- **Throckmorton Arms,** Coughton, B49 5HX, N : 2¼ m. on A 435 ☎ 762879, Fax 762654 – TV ☎ P. AE VISA.
  closed 25 and 26 December – **Meals** (closed Sunday dinner) 10.95/15.95 **st.** and a la carte – **10 rm** 45.00/60.00 **st.**

ALDBOURNE Wilts. 403 404 P 29 – pop. 2 194 – ☎ 01672.
♦London 77 – ♦Oxford 36 – ♦Southampton 53 – Swindon 9.

- XX **Raffles,** 1 The Green, SN8 2BW, ☎ 540700, Fax 540038 – AE VISA
  closed lunch Monday and Saturday, Sunday dinner, 2 weeks August-September, 25 to 30 December and Bank Holidays – **Meals** (light lunch Tuesday to Friday)/dinner a la carte 11.05/20.15 **t.** 4.80.

We suggest:

For a successful tour, that you prepare it in advance.

Michelin maps and guides will give you a great deal of useful information on route planning, places of interest, accommodation, prices etc.

ALDEBURGH Suffolk 404 Y 27 – pop. 2 654 – ☎ 01728.
Thorpeness Golf Hotel, Thorpeness ☎ 452176.
The Cinema, High St., IP15 5AU ☎ 453637 (summer only).
♦London 97 – ♦Ipswich 24 – ♦Norwich 41.

- **Wentworth,** Wentworth Rd, IP15 5BD, ☎ 452312, Fax 454343, ← – rm TV ☎ P. AE VISA
  closed 27 December-8 January – **Meals** 13.50/17.50 **t.** – **38 rm** 55.00/110.00 **t.** – SB.
- **White Lion,** Market Cross Pl., IP15 5BJ, ☎ 452720, Fax 452986, ← – TV ☎ P – 100. AE VISA
  Meals (bar lunch Monday to Saturday)/dinner 16.95 **st.** and a la carte 5.25 – **38 rm** 59.50/80.00 **st.** – SB.
- **Brudenell** (Forte), The Parade, IP15 5BU, ☎ 452071, Fax 454082, ← – TV ☎ P – 45. AE VISA JCB
  Meals (bar lunch in winter) 9.95/16.95 **t.** and a la carte 5.55 – 8.50 – **47 rm** 60.00/90.00 **t.** – SB.
- **Uplands,** Victoria Rd, IP15 5DX, ☎ 452420, Fax 454872, – TV ☎ P. AE VISA.
  closed 23 December-3 January – **Meals** (dinner only) 14.50 **t.** and a la carte 4.00 – **20 rm** 47.00/65.00 **t.** – SB.
- X New Regatta, 171-173 High St., IP15 5AN, ☎ 452011, Fax 452011.
- X **Lighthouse,** 77 High St., IP15 5AU, ☎ 453377, Fax 453377. VISA
  closed 15-31 January – **Meals** 15.75 **t.** (dinner) and lunch a la carte 11.20/19.60 4.00.

ALDERHOLT Hants. – see Fordingbridge.

ALDERLEY EDGE Ches. 402 403 404 N 24 – pop. 4 482 – ☎ 01625.
Wilmslow, Great Warford, Mobberley ☎ (01565) 872148 – Brook Lane ☎ 585583.
♦London 187 – Chester 34 – ♦Manchester 14 – ♦Stoke-on-Trent 25.

- **Alderley Edge,** Macclesfield Rd, SK9 7BJ, ☎ 583033, Fax 586343, – TV ☎ P – 120. AE VISA.
  Meals - (see below) – 8.50 – **32 rm** 87.00/125.00 **t.** – SB.
- **De Trafford Arms** (Premier), London Rd, SK9 7AA, ☎ 583881, Fax 586625 – rm TV ☎ P – 40. AE VISA.
  Meals (grill rest.) a la carte 9.50/18.90 **st.** 6.95 – 4.45 – **37 rm** 39.50 **st.** – SB.
- XXX **Alderley Edge** (at Alderley Edge H.), Macclesfield Rd, SK9 7BJ, ☎ 583033, Fax 586343, – P. AE VISA
  Meals 9.50/21.95 **t.** and a la carte 7.50.

ALDRIDGE W. Mids. 402 403 404 O 26 – pop. 26 458 (inc. Walsall Wood) – ✉ Walsall – ☎ 01922.

◆London 130 – ◆Birmingham 12 – Derby 32 – ◆Leicester 40 – ◆Stoke-on-Trent 38.

Plan : see Birmingham p.3

Fairlawns, 178 Little Aston Rd, WS9 0NU, E : 1 m. on A 454 ☎ 55122, Fax 743210 – rest TV ☎ P – 80. AE VISA JCB CT **n**
Meals *(closed Saturday lunch and Sunday dinner to non-residents)* 12.75/22.50 **t.** and a la carte 5.50 – **31 rm** ☕ 45.00/80.00 **t.**, 4 suites.

ATS 106 Leighswood Rd, Walsall ☎ 51968/53970

ALDWINCLE Northants. 402 404 S 26 – pop. 310 – ✉ Kettering – ☎ 01832.

◆London 84 – ◆Cambridge 40 – ◆Leicester 40 – Northampton 26 – Peterborough 18.

The Maltings without rest., Main St., NN14 3EP, ☎ 720233, Fax 720326, – TV P. VISA.
closed Christmas – **3 rm** ☕ 32.00/44.00 **st.**

ALFRETON Derbs 402 403 404 P 24 – pop. 8 276 – ☎ 01773.

18 Shirland, Lower Delves ☎ 834935 – 18 Ormonde Fields, Nottingham Rd, Codnor, Ripley ☎ 742987.

◆London 134 – Derby 13 – ◆Nottingham 19 – ◆Sheffield 27.

Forte Travelodge, Old Swanwick Colliery Rd, DE55 1HJ, S : ¾ m. by A 61 at junction with A 38 ☎ 520040, Fax 521087, Reservations (Freephone) 0800 850950 – rm rest TV ☎ P – 50. AE VISA.
Meals (grill rest.) – **61 rm** 34.50 **t.**

ALFRISTON E. Sussex 404 U 31 – pop. 1 721 – ✉ Polegate – ☎ 01323.

◆London 66 – Eastbourne 9 – Lewes 10 – Newhaven 8.

Star Inn (Forte Heritage), High St., BN26 5TA, ☎ 870495, Fax 870922 – TV ☎ P – 30. AE VISA JCB
Meals 12.25/18.95 **st.** 6.95 – ☕ 9.25 – **34 rm** 75.00/87.50 **st.** – SB.

XX **Moonrakers,** High St., BN26 5TD, ☎ 870472 – AE VISA
Meals (dinner only) 12.95 **t.** and a la carte 4.50.

ALLENDALE Northd. 401 402 N 19 – pop. 2 123 – ✉ Hexham – ☎ 01434.

9 High Studdon, Allenheads Rd ☎ (0191) 267 5875.

◆London 314 – ◆Carlisle 39 – ◆Newcastle upon Tyne 33.

Thornley House, NE47 9NH, W : ¾ m. on Whitfield rd ☎ 683255, – P
Meals (communal dining) 9.50 – **3 rm** ☕ 26.50/35.00.

ALLESLEY W. Mids. 403 404 P 26 – see Coventry.

ALNE N. Yorks. – see Easingwold.

ALNMOUTH Northd. 401 402 P 17 **Great Britain G.** – pop. 586 – ☎ 01665.

Envir. : Warkworth Castle★ *AC*, S : 4 m. by B 1338 and A 1068.

9 Alnmouth Village, Marine Rd. ☎ 830370.

◆London 314 – ◆Edinburgh 90 – ◆Newcastle upon Tyne 37.

Marine House, 1 Marine Rd, NE66 2RW, ☎ 830349, ←, – TV P. VISA
Meals 15.95 **st.** 5.50 – **10 rm** ☕ (dinner included) 82.00 **st.** – SB.

High Buston Hall, High Buston, NE66 3QH, SW: 2 ¼ m. by B 1338 off A 1068 ☎ 830341, Fax 830341, « Georgian house » – TV P.
closed December and January – **Meals** (by arrangement)(communal dining) 25.00 **s.** – **3 rm** ☕ 35.00/60.00 **s.** – SB.

The Grange without rest., Northumberland St., NE66 2RJ, ☎ 830401, ←, – TV P.
April-October – **5 rm** ☕ 21.00/46.00 **t.**

ALNWICK Northd. 401 402 O 17 **Great Britain G.** – pop. 7 419 – ☎ 01665.

See : Town ★ – Castle★★ *AC*.

Exc. : Dunstanburgh Castle★ *AC*, NE : 8 m. by B 1340 and Dunstan rd (last 2½ m. on foot).

18 Swansfield Park ☎ 602632.

The Shambles, NE66 1TN ☎ 510665.

◆London 320 – ◆Edinburgh 86 – ◆Newcastle upon Tyne 34.

White Swan, Bondgate Within, NE66 1TD, ☎ 602109, Fax 510400 – rest TV ☎ P – 150. AE VISA
Meals (bar lunch Monday to Saturday)/dinner 16.95 **st.** 4.95 – **55 rm** ☕ 59.00/64.00 **st.** – SB.

Oaks, South Rd, NE66 2PN, SE : ½ m. ☎ 510014, Fax 603219 – TV ☎ P. AE VISA
Meals 18.50 **t.** (dinner) and a la carte 13.40/21.95 **t.** – **13 rm** ☕ 45.00/65.00 **t.** – SB.

Bondgate House, 20 Bondgate Without, NE66 1PN, ☎ 602025, Fax 602554 – TV P. VISA.
Meals (by arrangement) 12.00 4.50 – **8 rm** ☕ 23.00/40.00 **st.** – SB.

at Eglingham NW : 7 m. on B 6346 – ✉ Alnwick – ☎ 01665 :

Ogle House, NE66 2TZ, ☎ 578264, – ⅀ TV P
closed January and December – **Meals** 10.95 **s.** 3.95 – **3 rm** 30.00/50.00 **t.** – SB.

ALPORT Derbs. – see Bakewell.

ALSAGER Ches. 402 403 404 N 24 **Great Britain G.** – pop. 11 912 – ✉ Stoke-on-Trent (Staffs.) – ☎ 01270.

Envir. : Little Moreton Hall★★ *AC*, NE : 4 m. by A 50 and A 34.

♦London 180 – Chester 36 – ♦ Liverpool 49 – ♦ Manchester 32 – ♦ Stoke-on-Trent 11.

Manor House, Audley Rd, ST7 2QQ, SE : ¾ m. ☎ 884000, Fax 882483, – rm TV ☎ ♿ P – 200. AE VISA.
Meals *(closed Saturday lunch)* 10.95/17.50 **st.** and a la carte 5.45 – **56 rm** 64.00/94.00 **st.** – SB.

Sappho Cottage, 118 Crewe Rd, ST7 2JA, ☎ 882033, – rm TV P.
Meals (by arrangement) (communal dining) 12.00 **s.** – **3 rm** 27.50/42.00 **s.**

ALSTON Cumbria 401 402 M 19 – pop. 2 065 – ☎ 01434.

Alston Moor, The Hermitage ☎ 381675.

The Railway Station, CA9 3JB ☎ 381696 (summer only).

♦London 309 – ♦Carlisle 28 – ♦Newcastle upon Tyne 45.

Lovelady Shield Country House, Nenthead Rd, CA9 3LF, E : 2½ m. on A 689 ☎ 381203, Fax 381515, ←, , – rest TV ☎ P. AE VISA.
closed 4 January-4 February – **Meals** (bar lunch)/dinner 25.50 **t.** 6.95 – **12 rm** (dinner included) 73.00/154.00 **t.** – SB.

Nent Hall Country House, CA9 3LQ, E : 2½ m. on A 689 ☎ 381584, Fax 382668, – TV ☎ ♿ P. AE VISA
Meals 23.00 (dinner) and a la carte 10.85/23.00 – **18 rm** 50.00/85.00 **st.** – SB.

Le Guide change, changez de **guide Michelin** *tous les ans.*

ALTARNUN Cornwall 403 G 32 pop. 2 405 – ✉ Launceston – ☎ 01566.

♦London 279 – Exeter 56 – ♦Plymouth 36 – Truro 39.

Penhallow Manor Country House, PL15 7SJ, ☎ 86206, Fax 86179, – rest TV ☎ P. AE VISA.
closed 8 January-14 February – **Meals** (bar lunch)/dinner 17.50 **t.** 4.50 – **7 rm** 30.00/70.00 **st.** – SB.

ALTON Hants. 404 R 30 – pop. 16 356 – ☎ 01420.

Old Odiham Rd ☎ 84774.

7 Cross and Pillory Lane, GU34 1HL ☎ 88448.

♦London 53 – Reading 24 – ♦Southampton 29 – Winchester 18.

Swan (Forte), High St., GU34 1AT, ☎ 83777, Fax 87975 – TV ☎ P – 50. AE VISA
Meals (bar lunch Monday to Saturday)/dinner 16.95 **t.** and a la carte **6.95** – 8.50 – **36 rm** 60.00/75.00 **st.** – SB.

Grange, London Rd, GU34 4EG, NE : 1 m. on A 339 ☎ 86565, Fax 541346, – TV ☎ P – 80. AE VISA JCB
closed 24 to 31 December – **Meals** *(closed Saturday lunch)* a la carte 12.65/22.65 **t.** 4.50 – **30 rm** 49.50/75.00 **t.** – SB.

Alton House, Normandy St., GU34 1DW, ☎ 80033, Fax 89222, heated, , – TV ☎ P – 120. AE VISA
Meals 10.95/11.95 **t.** and a la carte 4.00 – 6.50 – **39 rm** 45.00/65.00 **t.**

ALTRINCHAM Gtr. Manchester 402 403 404 N 23 – pop. 10 356 – ☎ 0161.

Altrincham Municipal, Stockport Rd, Timperley ☎ 928 0761 – Ringway, Hale Mount, Hale Barns ☎ 904 9609.

Stamford New Road, WA14 1EJ ☎ 941 7337.

♦London 191 – Chester 30 – ♦Liverpool 30 – ♦Manchester 8.

Cresta Court, Church St., WA14 4DP, on A 56 ☎ 927 7272, Fax 926 9194 – rm rest TV ☎ P – 250. AE VISA
Meals 7.75/9.60 **st.** and a la carte – **138 rm** 59.95/88.00 **t.** – SB.

Woodland Park, Wellington Rd, WA15 7RG, off A 560 ☎ 928 8631, Fax 941 2821 – rest TV ☎ P – 200. AE VISA.
Meals *(closed lunch Saturday and Sunday)* 15.50 **t.** (dinner) and a la carte 15.40/24.95 **t.** – **45 rm** 69.50/95.00 **t.**

Pelican Lodge (Premier), Manchester Rd, West Timperley, WA14 5NH, N : 2 m. on A 56 ☎ 962 7414, Fax 962 3456 – rm TV ☎ P. AE VISA.
Meals *(closed Saturday lunch)* a la carte 10.20/14.70 **st.** 3.95 – 4.45 – **48 rm** 39.50 **st.** – SB.

at Hale SE : 1 m. on B 5163 – ✉ Altrincham – ☎ 0161 :

X **Est, Est, Est!,** 183 Ashley Rd, WA15 9SD, ☎ 928 1811 – AE VISA
closed 25 December – **Meals** - Italian - 9.95/12.95 **t.** and a la carte 4.95.

at Halebarns SE : 3 m. on A 538 – ✉ Altrincham – ☎ 0161 :

Four Seasons, Manchester Airport, Hale Rd, WA15 8XW, ☎ 904 0301, Fax 980 1787, – rm rest TV – 120. AE VISA
Meals (bar lunch Saturday) 13.75/17.95 **st.** and a la carte – 10.50 – **90 rm** 97.50/118.50 **st.**, 4 suites – SB.

at Bowdon SW : 1 m. – ✉ Altrincham – ☎ 0161 :

Bowdon, Langham Rd, WA14 2HT, ☎ 928 7121, Fax 927 7560 – TV – 130. AE VISA.
Meals 10.95/14.95 **st.** and a la carte – 7.95 – **82 rm** 58.00/79.00 **st.** – SB.

ATS 74 Oakfield Rd ☎ 929 5803

ALVEDISTON Wilts. 404 N 30 pop. 85 – ✉ Salisbury – ☎ 01722.
♦London 107 – Bournemouth 23 – ♦Bristol 55 – Dorchester 37 – Salisbury 12 – Shaftesbury 8.

X **Crown Inn** with rm, SP5 5JY, ☎ 780335, « Part 17C inn », – TV. AE VISA
Meals a la carte 15.55/20.30 **t.** – **3 rm** 25.00/40.00 **t.**

ALVELEY Shrops. – see Bridgnorth.

ALVERSTONE I.O.W. 403 404 Q 32 – see Wight (Isle of).

ALVESTON Avon 403 404 M 29 – pop. 3 620 – ✉ Bristol – ☎ 01454.
♦London 127 – ♦Bristol 11 – Gloucester 23 – Swindon 42.

Alveston House, BS12 2LJ, on A 38 ☎ 415050, Fax 415425, – TV – 85. AE VISA
Meals 10.75/17.00 **st.** and a la carte 5.75 – **30 rm** 65.50/79.50 **st.** – SB.

Forte Posthouse, Thornbury Rd, BS12 2LL, on A 38 ☎ 412521, Fax 413920, heated, – rm TV – 100. AE VISA.
Meals a la carte 14.40/22.85 **t.** 6.95 – 7.95 – **74 rm** 59.00 **st.** – SB.

ALWALTON Cambs. 402 404 T 26 – see Peterborough.

AMBERLEY Glos. 403 404 N 28 – see Stroud.

AMBERLEY W. Sussex 404 S 31 Great Britain G. – pop. 525 – ✉ Arundel – ☎ 01798.
Envir. : Bignor Roman Villa (mosaics★) *AC*, NW : 3½m. by B 2139 via Bury.
♦London 56 – ♦Brighton 24 – ♦Portsmouth 31.

Amberley Castle, BN18 9ND, SW : ½ m. on B 2139 ☎ 831992, Fax 831998, « 14C castle, 12C origins », , park – rest TV – 40. AE VISA.
Queen's Room : Meals 19.50/45.00 **t.** and dinner a la carte 8.95 – 5.00 – **15 rm** 130.00/275.00 **t.** – SB.

AMBLESIDE Cumbria 402 L 20 Great Britain G. – pop. 2 905 – ☎ 0153 94.
Envir. : Lake Windermere★★ – Dove Cottage, Grasmere★ *AC* AY **A** – Brockhole National Park Centre★ *AC*, SE : 3 m. by A 591 AZ.
Exc. : Wrynose Pass★★, W : 7½m. by A 593 AY – Hard Knott Pass★★, W : 10 m. by A 593 AY.
Old Courthouse, Church St., LA22 0BT ☎ 32582 (summer only) AZ – Main Car Park, Waterhead, LA22 0EN ☎ 32729 (summer only) BY.
♦London 278 – ♦Carlisle 47 – Kendal 14.

Plan on next page

Rothay Manor, Rothay Bridge, LA22 0EH, S : ½ m. on A 593 ☎ 33605, Fax 33607, ←, – rest TV. AE VISA. BY **r**
closed 2 January-9 February – **Meals** (buffet lunch Monday to Saturday)/dinner 23.00 **t.** 5.00 – **15 rm** 78.00/128.00 **t.**, 3 suites – SB.

Ambleside Salutation, Lake Rd, LA22 9BX, ☎ 32244, Fax 34157 – rest TV. AE VISA JCB AZ **r**
Meals (bar lunch)/dinner 18.50 **st.** and a la carte 5.15 – **29 rm** 51.50/83.00 **st.** – SB.

Kirkstone Foot Country House, Kirkstone Pass Rd, LA22 9EH, NE : ¼ m. ☎ 32232, Fax 32232, – rest TV. AE VISA JCB AZ **c**
closed 3 January-10 February and 10 to 23 December – **Meals** (dinner only) 19.95 **t.** – **13 rm** (dinner included) 55.00/115.00 **t.** – SB.

Borrans Park, Borrans Rd, LA22 0EN, ☎ 33454, – TV. VISA. BY **a**
closed 18 to 28 December – **Meals** (dinner only) 16.00 **st.** 4.95 – **12 rm** 39.00/78.00 **st.** – SB.

Elder Grove, Lake Rd, LA22 0DB, ☎ 32504 – rest TV. AE VISA JCB AZ **a**
mid February-mid November – **Meals** (bar lunch)/dinner 16.00 **t.** and a la carte 4.50 – **12 rm** (dinner included) 42.00/84.00 **t.** – SB.

AMBLESIDE GRASMERE

Lake Rd . . . . AZ

Borrans Rd. . . . . BY 2
Broadgate . . . . BZ 3
Cheapside . . . . AZ 4
Church St. . . . . AZ 6
Compston St . . . . AZ 8
Easedale Rd. . . . . BZ 10
Kelswick Rd. . . . . AZ 12
King St . . . . AZ 13
Market Pl . . . . AZ 14
North Rd . . . . AZ 17
Old Lake Rd. . . . . AZ 20
St. Mary's Lane . . . . AZ 22
Smithy Brow . . . . AZ 23
Swan Hill . . . . AY 24

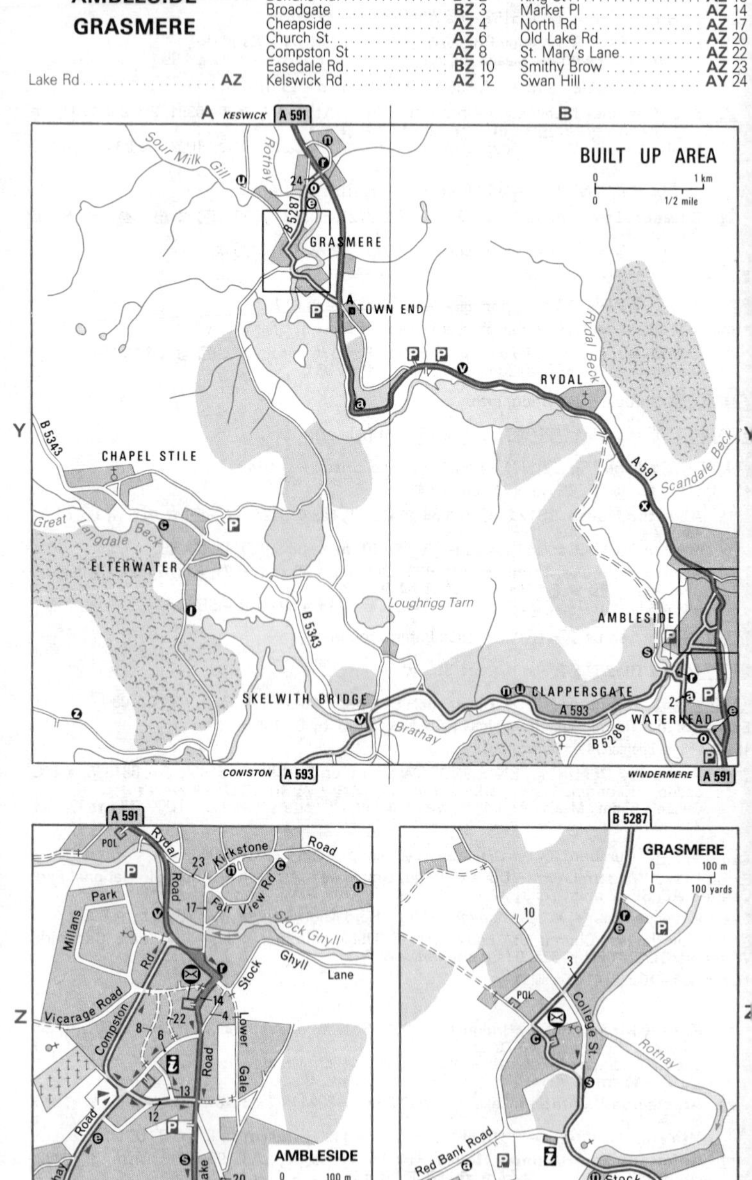

Town plans: *roads most used by traffic and those on which guide listed hotels and restaurants stand are fully drawn; the beginning only of lesser roads is indicated.*

Rothay Garth, Rothay Rd, LA22 0EE, ℘ 32217, Fax 34400, – TV ☎ P. AE VISA JCB. AZ e
Meals 18.50 **t.** (dinner) and lunch a la carte 14.50/22.50 **t.** 5.20 – **15 rm** (dinner included) 63.00/126.00 **t.**, 1 suite – SB.

Laurel Villa, Lake Rd, LA22 0DB, ℘ 33240 – TV P. AE VISA. AZ s
closed mid December-mid January – **Meals** (booking essential) (dinner only) 25.00 **st.** – **8 rm** 50.00/80.00 **st.**

Riverside, Under Loughrigg, LA22 9LJ, ℘ 32395, Fax 32395, – rest TV ☎ P. VISA. BY s
March-November – **Meals** (bar lunch)/dinner 18.00 **t.** and a la carte 5.20 – **9 rm** (dinner included) 56.00/100.00 **t.** – SB.

Crow How, Rydal Rd, LA22 9PN, NW : ½ m. on A 591 ℘ 32193, ←, – rest TV P. AE VISA BY x
closed December and January – **Meals** (dinner only) 12.75 **st.** 4.75 – **9 rm** 24.00/65.00 **st.** – SB.

Drunken Duck Inn, Barngates, LA22 0NG, SW : 3 m. by A 593 off B 5286 ℘ 36347, Fax 36781, ←, « Part 16C inn » – TV ☎ P. AE VISA BY
closed 25 December – **Meals** (in bar) a la carte 11.15/15.40 **t.** – **9 rm** 50.00/79.00 **t.**

Rowanfield Country House, Kirkstone Rd, LA22 9ET, NE : ¾ m. ℘ 33686, ← Lake Windermere and Coniston Old Man, – TV P. VISA JCB. AZ u
mid March-mid November and Christmas-New Year – **Meals** (by arrangement) 16.00 **st.** – **7 rm** 41.00/56.00 **st.** – SB.

Chapel House, Kirkstone Rd, LA22 9DZ, ℘ 33143 – . AZ n
closed January-February (restricted service November and December) – **Meals** 15.00 **st.** 4.25 – **10 rm** (dinner included) 38.50/82.50 – SB.

Glass House, Rydal Rd, LA22 9AN, ℘ 32137, Fax 31139, « Converted mill » – . VISA
Meals (light lunch)/dinner a la carte approx. 17.65 **st.** AZ v

at Waterhead S : 1 m. on A 591 – BY – ✉ Ambleside – ☎ 015394 :

Wateredge, Borrans Rd, LA22 0EP, ℘ 32332, Fax 31878, ←, « Part 17C fishermen's cottages, lakeside setting », – rest TV ☎ P. AE VISA JCB. BY o
closed mid December-early February – **Meals** (light lunch)/dinner 26.90 **t.** 7.00 – **23 rm** (dinner included) 73.00/166.00 **t.** – SB.

Regent, Borrans Rd, LA22 0ES, ℘ 32254, Fax 31474, – rest TV ☎ P. VISA BY e
Meals (bar lunch)/dinner 19.95 **t.** and a la carte 5.00 – **22 rm** 50.00/95.00 **t.** – SB.

at Clappersgate W : 1 m. on A 593 – BY – ✉ Ambleside – ☎ 015394 :

Nanny Brow Country House, LA22 9NF, ℘ 32036, Fax 32450, ←, « Landscaped gardens », – TV ☎ P. AE VISA JCB BY u
Meals (dinner only) 27.50 **t.** 6.00 – **15 rm** (dinner included) 65.00/150.00 **t.**, 3 suites – SB.

Grey Friar Lodge, LA22 9NE, ℘ 33158, Fax 33158, ←, – TV P. BY n
March-October – **Meals** (residents only) (dinner only) 15.50 **st.** 3.75 – **8 rm** 29.00/60.00 **st.**

at Skelwith Bridge W : 2½ m. on A 593 – AY – ✉ Ambleside – ☎ 0153 94 :

Skelwith Bridge, LA22 9NJ, ℘ 32115, Fax 34254 – rest TV ☎ P. VISA JCB
closed 10 to 26 December – **Meals** (bar lunch Monday to Saturday)/dinner 17.45 **st.** 5.00 – **29 rm** 40.50/85.00 **st.** – SB. AY v

at Little Langdale W : 4½ m. by A 593 – ✉ Langdale – ☎ 0153 94 :

Three Shires Inn, LA22 9NZ, ℘ 37215, ←, – P. AY z
closed Christmas and January except New Year – **Meals** (bar lunch)/dinner 17.50 **st.** and a la carte 4.50 – **10 rm** 35.00/70.00 **st.** – SB.

at Elterwater W : 4½ m. by A 593 off B 5343 – AY – ✉ Ambleside – ☎ 0153 94 :

Langdale H. & Country Club, Great Langdale, LA22 9JD, NW : 1 ¼ m. on B 5343 ℘ 37302, Fax 37694, , , , , park, , squash – rest TV ☎ P – 90. AE VISA. AY c
Meals (dinner only) a la carte 16.45/28.40 **st.** 6.65 – **65 rm** 103.00/196.00 **st.** – SB.

Eltermere Country House, LA22 9HY, ℘ 37207, ←, – rest TV P.
Meals *(closed Monday to Thursday December and January)* (dinner only) 17.50 **t.** 5.50 – **18 rm** 27.00/75.00 **st.** – SB. AY i

at Great Langdale W : 6 m. by A 593 on B 5343 – AY – ✉ Ambleside – ☎ 0153 94 :

Long House, LA22 9JS, ℘ 37222, ← Langdale valley, – P. VISA.
Meals (by arrangement) 10.50 – **3 rm** 26.00/48.00 **st.**

For the quickest route use the Michelin Main Road Maps*:*
970 Europe, 976 Czech Republic-Slovak Republic, 980 Greece, 984 Germany,
985 Scandinavia-Finland, 986 Great Britain and Ireland, 987 Germany-Austria-Benelux,
988 Italy, 989 France, 990 Spain-Portugal and 991 Yugoslavia.

AMERSHAM (Old Town) Bucks. 404 S 28 – pop. 17 629 – ☎ 01494.

♦London 29 – Aylesbury 16 – ♦Oxford 33.

Crown (Forte Heritage), 16 High St., HP7 0DH, ☎ 721541, Fax 431283, « Former coaching inn », – ⇔ TV ☎ P – 30. AE VISA JCB.
Meals 10.25/21.00 **t.** and dinner a la carte 5.70 – ☐ 8.50 – **22 rm** 85.00/95.00 **st.**, 1 suite – SB.

King's Arms, High St., HP7 0DJ, ☎ 726333, Fax 433480 – P. AE VISA JCB
closed Sunday dinner, Monday and 26 to 30 December – **Meals** 11.50/25.00 **t.** and a la carte 4.25.

Romna, 20-22 The Broadway, HP7 0HP, ☎ 433732 – . AE VISA
closed 25 and 26 December – **Meals** - Indian - (buffet lunch Sunday) 5.95/10.50 **t.** and a la carte.

AMESBURY Wilts. 403 404 O 30 The West Country G. – pop. 6 656 – ☎ 01980.

Envir. : Stonehenge★★★ *AC*, W : 2 m. by A 303 – Exc. : Wilton (Wilton House★★★ *AC*, Royal Wilton Carpet Factory★ *AC*) SW : 13 m. by A 303, B 3083 and A 36.

Redworth House, Flower Lane, SP4 7HE ☎ 622833.

♦London 87 – ♦Bristol 52 – Taunton 66.

Forte Travelodge, SP4 7AS, N : ¼ m. at junction of A 303 with A 345 ☎ 624966, Reservations (Freephone) 0800 850950 TV P. AE VISA.
Meals (grill rest.) – **32 rm** 34.50 **t.**

Mandalay without rest., 15 Stonehenge Rd, SP4 7BA, ☎ 623733, – ⇔ TV P. VISA.
closed 15 to 30 January – **3 rm** ☐ 25.00/36.00 **st.**

AMPFIELD Hants. 403 404 P 30 – pop. 1 523 – ✉ Romsey – ☎ 01794.

18 Ampfield (Par Three), Winchester Rd ☎ 368480.

♦London 79 – Bournemouth 31 – Salisbury 19 – ♦Southampton 11 – Winchester 7.

Potters Heron (Country Club), Winchester Rd, SO51 9ZF, on A 31 ☎ (01703) 266611, Fax 251359, – ⇔ TV ☎ P – 150. AE VISA
Meals *(closed Saturday lunch)* 9.75/17.95 **st.** and a la carte 4.75 – ☐ 7.50 – **54 rm** 65.00 **st.** – SB.

Keats, Winchester Rd, SO51 9BQ, on A 31 ☎ 368252 – P. AE VISA JCB
closed Sunday, Monday and Bank Holidays – **Meals** - Italian - 8.00 **t.** (lunch) and a la carte 16.60/26.40 **t.** 5.40.

AMPNEY CRUCIS Glos. 403 404 O 28 – see Cirencester.

ANDOVER Hants. 403 404 P 30 – pop. 34 647 – ☎ 01264.

9 51 Winchester Rd ☎ 323980 – Town Mill House, Bridge St., SP10 1BL ☎ 324320.

♦London 74 – Bath 53 – Salisbury 17 – Winchester 11.

Ashley Court, Micheldever Rd, SP11 6LA, by London Street and Wolversdene Rd ☎ 357344, Fax 356755, , – ⇔ rm TV ☎ P – 120. AE VISA.
Meals 11.50/13.90 **st.** and dinner a la carte 5.55 – **35 rm** ☐ 49.50/85.00 **st.** – SB.

White Hart, Bridge St., SP10 1BH, ☎ 352266, Fax 323767 – ⇔ rm TV ☎ P – 65. AE VISA
closed 24 to 27 December – **Meals** 14.95 **t.** and a la carte 4.95 – ☐ 7.95 – **20 rm** 55.00/85.00 **t.** – SB.

at Barton Stacey SE : 5½ m. by A 303 – ✉ Andover – ☎ 01264 :

Forte Travelodge, SO21 3NP, on A 303 ☎ 720260, Reservations (Freephone) 0800 850950 – TV P. AE VISA.
Meals (grill rest.) – **20 rm** 34.50 **t.**

ATS 51a New St. ☎ 323606/7

ANSTY Warks. – see Coventry (West Midlands).

APPLEBY-IN-WESTMORLAND Cumbria 402 M 20 – pop. 2 570 (inc. Bongate) – ☎ 01768 3.

18 Appleby, Brackenber Moor ☎ 51432 – Moot Hall, Boroughgate, CA16 6XD ☎ 51177.

♦London 285 – ♦Carlisle 33 – Kendal 24 – ♦Middlesbrough 58.

Appleby Manor , Roman Rd, CA16 6JB, E : 1 m. by B 6542 and Station Rd ☎ 51571, Fax 52888, <, , – TV ☎ P – 40. AE VISA JCB
Meals 18.95/25.95 **st.** 5.95 – **30 rm** ☐ 64.00/98.00 **st.** – SB.

Tufton Arms, Market Sq., CA16 6XA, ☎ 51593, Fax 52761, – TV ☎ P – 100. AE VISA
Meals 18.50 **t.** (dinner) and a la carte 12.00/26.75 **t.** 3.75 – **19 rm** ☐ 42.50/120.00 **t.**, 2 suites – SB.

Royal Oak Inn, Bongate, CA16 6UN, SE : ½ m. on B 6542 ☎ 51463, Fax 52300, « Part 16C and 17C inn » – ⇔ rest TV ☎ P. AE VISA JCB
closed 25 December – **Meals** a la carte 9.95/16.50 **t.** 5.00 – **9 rm** ☐ 28.00/75.00 **t.** – SB.

APPLEDORE Devon 403 H 30 – ☎ 01237.
London 228 – Barnstaple 12 – Exeter 46 – Plymouth 61 – Taunton 63.

West Farm, Irsha St., EX39 1RY, W : ¼ m. ☎ 425269, « 17C house », – rm.
Meals (by arrangement) (communal dining) 20.00 **s.** – **3 rm** 37.50/50.00 **s.** – SB.

APPLETON LE MOORS N. Yorks 402 R 21 pop. 178 – ☎ 01751.
London 242 – Middlesbrough 37 – Scarborough 26 – York 37.

Appleton Hall Country House, YO6 6TF, ☎ 417227, Fax 417540, – rest. AE VISA
Meals (dinner only and Sunday lunch)/dinner 18.95 **t.** – **8 rm** (dinner included) 60.00/120.00 **t.**, 2 suites – SB.

ARDINGLY W. Sussex 404 T 30 pop. 1 594 – ☎ 01444.
London 37 – Brighton 20 – Crawley 11.

Ardingly Inn, Street Lane, RH17 6UA, ☎ 892214, Fax 892942, – AE VISA.
Meals a la carte 10.70/17.85 **t.** 4.50 – **6 rm** 30.00/45.00 **t.**

ARMATHWAITE Cumbria 401 402 L 19 – ✉ Carlisle – ☎ 01697 4.
London 302 – Carlisle 17 – Kendal 46 – Lancaster 60.

Dukes Head, Front St., CA4 9PB, ☎ 72226, – VISA
closed 25 December – **Meals** a la carte 11.50/15.75 **t.** 4.10 – **6 rm** 22.50/45.00 **t.** – SB.

ARMITAGE Staffs. 402 403 404 O 25 – pop. 4 426 (inc. Handscare) – ✉ Rugeley – ☎ 01543.
London 135 – Birmingham 25 – Derby 26 – Stoke-on-Trent 25.

Old Farmhouse, Rugeley Rd, WS15 4AT, on A 513 ☎ 490353, Fax 491932 – AE VISA
closed Saturday lunch, Sunday dinner, Monday, last 2 weeks August and first 2 weeks January – **Meals** 8.95/9.95 **t.** and a la carte 4.95.

ARNCLIFFE N. Yorks. 402 N 21 – pop. 79 – ✉ Skipton – ☎ 01756.
London 232 – Kendal 41 – Leeds 41 – Preston 50 – York 52.

Amerdale House, BD23 5QE, ☎ 770250, Fax 770250, ←, – rest. VISA.
mid March-mid November – **Meals** (dinner only) 24.00 **t.** – **11 rm** (dinner included) 64.50/115.00 **st.** – SB.

ARUNDEL W. Sussex 404 S 31 Great Britain G. – pop. 3 033 – ☎ 01903.
See : Castle★ *AC.*
61 High St., BN18 9AJ ☎ 882268.
London 58 – Brighton 21 – Southampton 41 – Worthing 9.

Norfolk Arms, 22 High St., BN18 9AD, ☎ 882101, Fax 884275 – – 100. AE VISA
Meals 9.95/19.95 **st.** – **34 rm** 44.95/79.90 **st.** – SB.

Arundel, 16-18 Chichester Rd, BN18 0AD, W : 1 m. on A 27 ☎ 882677, Fax 884154 – rm – 140. AE VISA
Meals a la carte 11.05/21.00 **t.** 4.40 – **27 rm** 65.00/85.00 **t.** – SB.

Howards, Crossbush, BN18 9PQ, E : 1 m. on A 27 ☎ 882655, Fax 883384 –
Meals (carving rest.) – **9 rm.**

Arundel Park Inn, Station Rd, BN18 9JL, E : ½ m. on A 27 ☎ 882588, Fax 883808 – AE VISA.
Meals a la carte 10.70/18.20 **t.** 5.25 – **12 rm** 38.00/48.00 **t.**

Portreeves Acre without rest., The Causeway, BN18 9JL, ☎ 883277, –
closed 1 week Christmas – **3 rm** 26.00/40.00 **st.**

at **Burpham** NE : 3 m. by A 27 – ✉ Arundel – ☎ 01903 :

Burpham Country, Old Down, BN18 9RJ, ☎ 882160, Fax 882160, ←, – rest. VISA.
Meals (dinner only) 16.50 **t.** 4.75 – **10 rm** 31.50/70.00 **t.** – SB.

George and Dragon, BN18 9RR, ☎ 883131 – AE VISA JCB
closed Sunday dinner – **Meals** (dinner only and Sunday lunch)/dinner 15.95 **t.** 5.50.

at **Walberton** W : 3 m. by A 27 off B 2132 – ✉ Arundel – ☎ 01243 :

Stakis Arundel, Avisford Park, Yapton Lane, BN18 0LS, on B 2132 ☎ 551215, Fax 552481, ←, heated, , park, , squash – rest – 300. AE VISA
Meals (buffet lunch) 16.50/25.00 **st.** and dinner a la carte 6.50 – 9.50 – **121 rm** 80.00/121.00 **st.**, 5 suites – SB.

ASCOT Berks. 404 R 29 – pop. 150244 (inc Sunningdale) – ☎ 01344.

Mill Ride, North Ascot ✆ 886777.

◆London 36 – Reading 15.

Royal Berkshire (Hilton) 🔇, London Rd, Sunninghill, SL5 OPP, E : 2 m. on A 329 ✆ 23322, Fax 27100, « Queen Anne mansion », fitness, sauna, indoor pool, garden, park, tennis, squash – TV ☎ P – 70. Cards: AE, Diners, VISA, JCB
Meals - (see ***Stateroom*** below) – 14.00 – **60 rm** 120.00/165.00 **st.**, 3 suites – SB.

Berystede (Forte Heritage), Bagshot Rd, Sunninghill, SL5 9JH, S : 1 ½ m. on A 330 ✆ 23311, Fax 872301, heated pool, garden, park – lift, non-smoking rm TV ☎ P – 120. Cards: AE, Diners, VISA, JCB
Meals 15.50/21.00 **st.** and a la carte 8.50 – 9.50 – **90 rm** 95.00/130.00 **st.**, 1 suite – SB.

Royal Foresters, London Rd, SL5 8DR, W : 1½ m. on A 329 ✆ 884747, Fax 884115 – TV ☎ P
Meals (grill rest.) – **33 rm.**

Stateroom (at Royal Berkshire H.), London Rd, Sunninghill, SL5 0PP, E : 2 m. on A 329 ✆ 23322, Fax 27100, garden – P. Cards: AE, Diners, VISA, JCB
Meals *(closed Saturday lunch)* (booking essential) 16.00/35.00 **st.** and a la carte 10.00.

Ciao Ninety, 6 Hermitage Par., High St., SL5 7TE, ✆ 22285 – air conditioning. Cards: AE, Diners, VISA
closed Saturday lunch – **Meals** - Italian - 12.00 **t.** (lunch) and a la carte 14.70/26.00 **t.** 4.00.

at Sunninghill S : 1½ m. by A 329 on B 3020 – ✉ Ascot – ☎ 01344 :

Highclere, Kings Rd, SL5 9AD, ✆ 25220, Fax 872528 – TV ☎ P. Cards: AE, VISA. no dogs
Meals *(closed Sunday dinner)* a la carte 12.00/25.50 **t.** – **11 rm** 60.00/90.00 **t.**

Jade Fountain, 38 High St., SL5 9NE, ✆ 27070 – air conditioning. Cards: AE, Diners, VISA
closed 24 to 27 December – **Meals** - Chinese (Canton, Peking) - 12.50/25.00 **t.** and a la carte.

ASENBY N. Yorks. – see Thirsk.

ASHBOURNE Derbs. 402 403 404 O 24 **Great Britain G.** – pop. 6 300 – ☎ 01335.

Envir. : Dovedale★★ (Ilam Rock★) NW : 6 m. by A 515.

13 Market Pl., DE6 1EU ✆ 343666.

◆London 146 – Derby 14 – ◆Manchester 48 – ◆Nottingham 33 – ◆Sheffield 44.

Callow Hall 🔇, Mappleton Rd, DE6 2AA, W : ¾ m. by Union St. ✆ 343403, Fax 343624, fishing, garden, park – non-smoking rest TV ☎ & P. Cards: AE, Diners, VISA. no dogs
closed 25 and 26 December – **Meals** *(closed Sunday dinner to non-residents)* (lunch by arrangement)/dinner 14.75/29.50 **t.** and dinner a la carte 4.75 – **16 rm** 65.00/140.00 **t.** – SB.

Ashbourne Lodge, Derby Rd, DE6 1XH, SE : 1 m. on A 52 ✆ 346666, Fax 346549 – lift non-smoking rm air conditioning rest TV ☎ & P – 200. Cards: AE, Diners, VISA. no dogs
Meals (bar lunch)/dinner 14.95 **st.** and a la carte 5.80 – **48 rm** 65.00/80.00 **st.**, 2 suites – SB.

ATS Airfield Ind. Est., Blenheim Rd ✆ 344644

ASHBURTON Devon 403 I 32 **The West Country G.** – pop. 3 660 – ☎ 01364.

Envir. : Dartmoor National Park★★ (Brent Tor ≤★★, Haytor Rocks ≤★).

◆London 220 – Exeter 20 – ◆Plymouth 23.

Holne Chase 🔇, TQ13 7NS, W : 3 m. on Two Bridges rd ✆ 631471, Fax 631453, ≤, fishing, garden, park – non-smoking rest TV ☎ P – 25. Cards: AE, Diners, VISA
Meals 14.50/21.00 **st.** and a la carte 5.60 – **14 rm** 50.00/115.00 **st.** – SB.

Dartmoor Lodge, Peartree Cross, TQ13 7JW, ✆ 652232, Fax 653990 – lift non-smoking rm TV ☎ & P – 40. Cards: AE, VISA, JCB
Meals (bar lunch)/dinner a la carte 9.05/17.20 **t.** 4.65 – 5.95 – **30 rm** 33.00/44.00 **t.** – SB.

Gages Mill, Buckfastleigh Rd, TQ13 7JW, SW : 1 m. ✆ 652391, garden – non-smoking rest TV P. no dogs
closed February and December – **Meals** (by arrangement) 10.00 **t.** 3.50 – **8 rm** 23.00/46.00 **t.**

at Holne W : 4½ m. by Two Bridges rd – ✉ Ashburton – ☎ 01364 :

Wellpritton Farm 🔇, TQ13 7RX, E : 1 m. ✆ 631273, park – P. no dogs
Meals 9.00 **st.** – **4 rm** 17.50/35.00 – SB.

at Poundsgate W : 5 m. on Princetown rd – ✉ Newton Abbot – ☎ 01364 :

Leusdon Lodge 🔇, Lower Town, TQ13 7PE, NE : 1 m. by Princetown rd, off Leusdon rd ✆ 631304, Fax 631599, ≤, garden – non-smoking TV ☎ P. Cards: VISA
closed January and February – **Meals** (lunch by arrangement) 15.00/22.50 **t.** – **7 rm** 40.00/100.00 **t.** – SB.

Bitte beachten Sie die Geschwindigkeitsbeschränkungen in Großbritannien
- 60 mph (= 96 km/h) außerhalb geschlossener Ortschaften
- 70 mph (= 112 km/h) auf Straßen mit getrennten Fahrbahnen und Autobahnen.

ASHBY DE LA ZOUCH Leics. 402 403 404 P 25 – pop. 10 595 – ☎ 01530.

Willesley Park, Measham Rd ✆ 411532.

North St., LE65 1HU ✆ 411767.

◆London 119 – ◆Birmingham 29 – ◆Leicester 18 – ◆Nottingham 22.

- **Fallen Knight,** Kilwardby St., LE65 2FQ, ✆ 412230, Fax 417596 – ▮ TV ☎ P – 70. AE VISA.
  Meals 9.95/17.50 **t.** and a la carte 4.95 – **24 rm** 64.00/112.00 **t.** – SB.
- **Rajni,** 48 Tamworth Rd, LE65 2PR, S : ½ m. on B 5006 ✆ 560349 – P. AE VISA
  closed Friday lunch and 25 December – **Meals** - Indian - a la carte 7.15/14.85 **t.**

ATS Kilwardby St. ✆ 412791

ASHFORD Kent 404 W 30 – pop. 52 002 – ☎ 01233.

18 The Churchyard, TN23 1QG ✆ 629165.

◆London 56 – Canterbury 14 – ◆Dover 24 – Hastings 30 – Maidstone 19.

- **Eastwell Manor** (Q.M.H.), Eastwell Park, Boughton Lees, TN25 4HR, N : 3 m. by A 28 on A 251 ✆ 219955, Fax 635530, ≤, « Reconstructed period mansion in formal gardens », park, – ▮ rest TV ☎ P – 80. AE VISA
  Meals 19.50/28.50 **t.** and a la carte 11.00 – **20 rm** 107.50/165.00 **t.**, 3 suites – SB.
- **Ashford International** (Q.M.H.), Simone Weil Av., TN24 8UX, ✆ 219988, Group Telex 96498, Fax 627708, , , – ▮ rm TV ☎ P – 400. AE VISA
  Meals (carving lunch) 13.90/17.90 **st.** 6.25 – 9.50 – **198 rm** 82.50 **st.**, 2 suites – SB.
- **Forte Posthouse,** Canterbury Rd, TN24 8QQ, ✆ 625790, Fax 643176, – rm TV ☎ P – 100. AE VISA JCB
  Meals a la carte 11.85/22.85 **st.** – 7.95 – **60 rm** 56.00 **st.** – SB.
- **Master Spearpoint,** Canterbury Rd, Kennington, TN24 9QR, NE : 2 m. on A 28 ✆ 636863, Fax 610119, – TV ☎ P – 60. AE VISA
  Meals (carving lunch) 4.95/13.50 **t.** and dinner a la carte 4.60 – **34 rm** 57.70/65.00 **t.** – SB.

at Hothfield NW : 3½ m. by A 20 – ✉ Ashford – ☎ 01233 :

- **Holiday Inn Garden Court,** Maidstone Rd, TN26 1AR, N : 1 m. on A 20 ✆ 713333, Fax 712082, , – ▮ rm rest TV ☎ P – 25. AE VISA
  Meals (bar lunch)/dinner a la carte 10.00/18.95 **st.** 4.50 – 6.95 – **104 rm** 57.50 **st.**
- **Travel Inn,** Maidstone Rd, Hothfield Common, TN26 1AP, on A 20 ✆ 712571, Fax 713945 – rm TV P. AE VISA.
  Meals (grill rest.) – 4.95 – **40 rm** 34.50 **t.**

ATS Henwood Ind. Est., Hythe Rd, Henwood ✆ 622450/624891

ASHFORD-IN-THE-WATER Derbs. 402 403 404 O 24 – see Bakewell.

ASHINGTON Northd. 401 402 P 18 – pop. 27 962 – ☎ 01670.

◆London 303 – ◆Edinburgh 102 – ◆Newcastle upon Tyne 17.

- Lakeside, Queen Elizabeth II Country Park, Woodhorn, NE63 9AT, N : 2½ m. by A 197 on A 189 ✆ 862001, Fax 860986, , – TV ☎ P – 130
  20 rm.

ASHINGTON W. Sussex 404 S 31 – pop. 2 852 – ✉ Pulborough – ☎ 01903.

◆London 50 – ◆Brighton 20 – Worthing 9.

- **Mill House** , Mill Lane, RH20 3BZ, ✆ 892426, Fax 892855, – TV ☎ P – 40. AE VISA JCB
  Meals 12.95/16.95 **st.** 4.25 – **12 rm** 47.00/97.00 **st.** – SB.
- **Willows,** London Rd, RH20 3JR, on A 24 ✆ 892575 – P. AE VISA
  closed Monday – **Meals** (dinner only and Sunday lunch)/dinner 19.15 **t.** 4.95.

ATS Lintonville Terr. ✆ 817013/817038

ASHPRINGTON Devon 403 I 32 – see Totnes.

ASHTON-IN-MAKERFIELD Gtr. Manchester 402 M 23 – ✉ Wigan – ☎ 01942.

◆London 199 – ◆Liverpool 21 – ◆Manchester 20.

- **Bay Horse** (Premier), 53 Warrington Rd, WN4 9PJ, S : ½ m. on A 49 ✆ 725032, Fax 719302 – rm TV ☎ P. AE VISA.
  Meals (grill rest.) a la carte 7.10/11.00 **st.** 3.95 – 4.45 – **28 rm** 39.50 **st.** – SB.

ASHTON KEYNES Wilts. 403 404 O 29 – pop. 1 682 – ☎ 01285.

◆London 98 – ◆Bristol 40 – Gloucester 27 – ◆Oxford 42 – Swindon 14.

- **Two Cove House,** SN6 6NS, off Park Place ✆ 861221, – rest P.
  closed Christmas – **Meals** (by arrangement) (communal dining) 16.50 **s.** – **3 rm** 27.00/50.00 **s.**

ASHTON-UNDER-LYNE Gtr. Manchester 402 403 404 N 23 – pop. 43 906 – 0161.

London 209 – Leeds 40 – Manchester 7 – Sheffield 34.

York House, York Pl., off Richmond St., OL6 7TT, 330 5899, Fax 343 1613, – TV ☎ P – 40. AE VISA JCB.
Meals *(closed Saturday lunch and Sunday)* 8.75/15.00 **st.** and a la carte – **34 rm** 46.00/66.00 **st.** – SB.

Woodlands with rm, 33 Shepley Rd, Audenshaw, M34 5DL, S : 2 m. by A 635, Audenshaw Rd and Guide Lane (A 6017) on B 6169 336 4241 – TV ☎ P. VISA.
closed Saturday lunch, Sunday, Monday, 1 week Easter, 2 weeks August and 1 week Christmas-New Year – **Meals** 15.95 **t.** and a la carte – **3 rm** 40.00/60.00 **t.**

ASHWATER Devon 403 H 31 pop. 623 – Beaworthy – 01409.

London 238 – Bideford 26 – Exeter 43 – Launceston 7 – Plymouth 34.

Blagdon Manor Country, EX21 5DF, NW : 2 m. by Holsworthy rd on Blagdon rd 211224, Fax 211634, ≤, « Part 17C Manor », – TV P. AE VISA.
Meals (residents only) (communal dining) (dinner only) 17.00 **st.** 4.50 – **7 rm** 45.00/90.00 **st.** – SB.

ASKRIGG N. Yorks. 402 N 21 – pop. 1 002 – Leyburn – 01969.

London 251 – Kendal 32 – Leeds 70 – York 63.

King's Arms, Market Sq., DL8 3HQ, 650258, Fax 650635, « Part 18C, part 19C coaching inn » – rest TV ☎ P. AE VISA JCB
Clubroom : Meals (dinner only and Sunday lunch)/dinner 25.00 **t.** – **Silks Grill : Meals** a la carte 14.25/18.90 **t.** – **10 rm** 50.00/85.00 **t.** – SB.

Winville, Main St., DL8 3HG, 650515, Fax 650594, – TV ☎ P. VISA
Meals 17.95 **st.** and dinner a la carte 9.95/15.65 **st.** 5.50 – **10 rm** 42.00/64.00 **st.** – SB.

Helm Country House, Helm, DL8 3JF, W: 1 ¼m, turning right at No Through Rd sign 650443, Fax 650443, ≤, « Part 17C stone cottage » – TV ☎ P.
closed November-2 January – **Meals** 16.00 5.00 – **3 rm** 40.00/58.00 **s.** – SB.

ASPLEY GUISE Beds. 404 S 27 – pop. 2 236 – 01908.

Woburn Sands, West Hill 582264 – Millbrook, Ampthill (01525) 840252.

London 52 – Bedford 13 – Luton 16 – Northampton 22.

Moore Place, The Square, MK17 8DW, 282000, Fax 281888, – TV ☎ P – 50. AE VISA
closed 26 to 30 December – **Meals** 14.50/17.00 **st.** and a la carte 6.95 – **53 rm** 65.00/100.00 **st.**, 1 suite.

When looking for a quiet hotel
use the maps found in the introductory pages
or look for establishments with the sign or .

ASTON CLINTON Bucks. 404 R 28 – pop. 3 980 – Aylesbury – 01296.

London 42 – Aylesbury 4 – Oxford 26.

Bell Inn, London Rd, HP22 5HP, 630252, Fax 631250, « Courtyard and gardens » – rest TV ☎ P – 150. AE VISA
Meals 10.00/30.00 **t.** and a la carte 8.25 – 7.95 – **15 rm** 50.00/70.00 **st.**, 6 suites – SB.

ATHERSTONE Warks. 403 404 P 26 – pop. 8 047 – 01827.

London 120 – Birmingham 22 – Coventry 15 – Leicester 30.

Chapel House with rm, Friar's Gate, CV9 1EY, 718949, Fax 717702, « Part Georgian former dower house », – TV ☎. AE VISA JCB.
closed 25-26 December and 1 January – **Meals** *(closed Sunday)* (lunch by arrangement) 24.00 **t.** 6.50 – **11 rm** 42.00/65.00 **t.**

ATTLEBOROUGH Norfolk 404 X 26 – pop. 7 604 – 01953.

London 94 – Cambridge 47 – Norwich 15.

Sherbourne Country House, Norwich Rd, NR17 2JX, NE :½ m. 454363, Fax 453509, – TV ☎ P. VISA
closed 25 and 26 December – **Meals** (bar lunch)/dinner a la carte 13.15/19.40 **st.** – **7 rm** 29.00/65.00 **st.** – SB.

ATS London Rd 453883

AUSTWICK N. Yorks. 402 M 21 pop. 467 – Lancaster (Lancs.) – 0152 42.

London 259 – Kendal 28 – Lancaster 20 – Leeds 46.

The Traddock, LA2 8BY, 51224, Fax 51224, – TV ☎ P. VISA.
Meals 19.50 **st.** (dinner) and lunch a la carte 13.00/17.00 **st.** 3.75 – **11 rm** 34.00/65.00.

Wood View without rest., The Green, LA2 8BB, 51268, – TV P
March-October – **5 rm** 26.00/40.00 **st.**

AVON Hants. – see Ringwood.

AXMINSTER Devon 403 L 31 The West Country G. – pop. 5 181 – ☎ 01297.

Envir. : Lyme Regis★ - The Cobb★, SE : 5½m. by A 35 and A 3070.

The Old Courthouse, Church St., EX13 5AQ ☎ 34386 (summer only).

London 156 – Exeter 27 – Lyme Regis 5.5 – Taunton 22 – Yeovil 24.

Fairwater Head Country House, Hawkchurch, EX13 5TX, NE : 3 ¾ m. by A 35 off B 3165 ☎ 678349, Fax 678459, ← Axe Vale, – rest. AE VISA
March-November and Christmas – **Meals** (bar lunch Monday to Saturday)/dinner 20.50 **st.** and a la carte 4.20 – **21 rm** (dinner included) 78.50/138.00 **st.** – SB.

at Membury N : 4½ m. by A 35 and Stockland rd – ✉ Axminster – ☎ 01404 :

Lea Hill, EX13 7AQ, ☎ 881881, ←, « Part 14C Devon longhouse », AE VISA
closed January – **Meals** (bar lunch)/dinner 14.95 **t.** and a la carte 4.95 – **9 rm** 45.00/88.00 **st.** – SB.

AYLESBURY Bucks. 404 R 28 Great Britain G. – pop. 145 931 (Vale of Aylesbury) – ☎ 01296.

Envir. : Waddesdon Manor (Collection★★) NW : 5½m. by A 41.

18 Weston Turville, New Rd ☎ 24084 – 9 Hulcott Lane, Bierton ☎ 393644.

8 Bourbon St., HP20 2RR ☎ 330559.

London 46 – Birmingham 72 – Northampton 37 – Oxford 22.

Hartwell House, Oxford Rd, HP17 8NL, SW : 2 m. on A 418 ☎ 747444, Fax 747450, ←, « Part Jacobean, part Georgian house, former residence of Louis XVIII », park, – 80. AE VISA
Meals 18.25/39.50 **st.** and a la carte 9.50 – 12.95 – **34 rm** 98.00/235.00 **st.**, 13 suites – SB.

Forte Posthouse, Aston Clinton Rd, HP22 5AA, SE : 2 m. on A 41 ☎ 393388, Telex 838820, Fax 392211, rm rest – 100. AE VISA
Meals (bar lunch Saturday) a la carte 11.95/20.45 **st.** 4.95 – 7.95 – **92 rm** 59.00 **st.**, 2 suites – SB.

Holiday Inn Garden Court without rest., Buckingham Rd, HP19 3FY, N : 1 m. on A 413 ☎ 398839, Fax 394108 – 30. AE VISA JCB.
7.50 – **40 rm** 53.50 **st.**

ATS Gatehouse Way ☎ 433177

BABBACOMBE Devon 403 J 32 – see Torquay.

BADBY Northants. – see Daventry.

BADINGHAM Suffolk 404 Y 27 – see Framlingham.

BADMINTON Avon 403 404 N 29 – pop. 2 167 – ☎ 01454.

London 114 – Bristol 19 – Gloucester 26 – Swindon 33.

Petty France, Dunkirk, GL9 1AF, NW : 3 m. on A 46 ☎ 238361, Fax 238768, rest – 25. AE VISA
Meals a la carte 16.75/26.50 **st.** 5.95 – **20 rm** 49.00/110.00 **st.** – SB.

Bodkin House, Dunkirk, GL9 1AF, NW : 3 m. on A 46 ☎ 238310, Fax 238422 – AE VISA JCB
Meals *(closed Sunday dinner)* 8.95/14.50 and a la carte 4.50 – **8 rm** 49.00/65.00 **t.** – SB.

BAGINTON Warks. 403 404 P 26 – see Coventry.

BAGSHOT Surrey 404 R 29 – pop. 5 190 – ☎ 01276.

London 37 – Reading 17 – Southampton 49.

Pennyhill Park, London Rd, GU19 5ET, SW : 1 m. on A 30 ☎ 471774, Fax 473217, ←, heated, 9, park, rm – 50. AE VISA JCB.
Meals 20.50/29.50 **t.** and a la carte 9.75 – 13.00 – **70 rm** 125.00/140.00, 6 suites – SB.

Cricketers, London Rd, GU19 5HR, N : ½ m. on A 30 ☎ 473196, Fax 451357, AE VISA.
Meals (grill rest.) a la carte 8.70/17.90 **t.** 4.90 – 4.95 – **27 rm** 39.50 **st.**

BAINBRIDGE N. Yorks. 402 N 21 – pop. 474 – ✉ Wensleydale – ☎ 01969.

London 249 – Kendal 31 – Leeds 68 – York 61.

Rose and Crown, DL8 3EE, ☎ 650225, Fax 650735 – VISA
Meals (bar lunch Monday to Saturday)/dinner 16.00 **t.** and a la carte – **12 rm** 26.50/43.00 **t.** – SB.

BAKEWELL Derbs. 402 403 404 O 24 Great Britain G. – pop. 3 818 – ☎ 01629.

Envir. : Chatsworth★★★ (Park and Garden★★★) *AC*, NE : 2½m. by A 619 – Haddon Hall★★ *AC*, SE : 2 m. by A 6.

Old Market Hall, Bridge St., DE4 5DS ☎ 813227.

London 160 – Derby 26 – Manchester 37 – Nottingham 33 – Sheffield 17.

Rutland Arms, The Square, DE45 1BT, ☎ 812812, Fax 812309 – rest – 80. AE VISA
Meals 8.75/17.50 **t.** and a la carte – **36 rm** 45.00/85.00 **t.** – SB.

Milford House, Mill St., DE45 1DA, ☎ 812130, – TV P. VISA.
April-October – **Meals** (by arrangement) 15.90 **t.** 5.00 – **12 rm** 36.00/72.00 **t.** – SB.

Renaissance, Bath St., DE45 1BX, ☎ 812687 – . VISA
closed Sunday dinner, Monday and 6 to 20 May – **Meals** 15.95 **t.** 4.90.

at Hassop N : 3½ m. by A 619 on B 6001 – ✉ Bakewell – ☎ 01629 :

Hassop Hall, DE45 1NS, ☎ 640488, Fax 640577, ≤, « Part 16C hall », , park, – TV P. AE VISA JCB.
accommodation closed 3 days at Christmas – **Meals** *(closed Monday lunch and Sunday dinner)* 14.00/28.00 **t.** 5.75 – 8.95 – **13 rm** 70.00/125.00 **t.**

at Great Longstone N : 4 m. by A 619 off B 6001 – ✉ Bakewell – ☎ 01629 :

Croft, DE45 1TF, ☎ 640278, – rest TV P. VISA.
closed 3 January-2 February – **Meals** (dinner only) 21.50 **t.** 4.25 – **9 rm** 60.00/95.00 **t.** – SB.

at Alport S : 4 m. by A 6 off B 5056 – ✉ Bakewell – ☎ 01629 :

Rock House without rest., DE45 1LG, ☎ 636736, – P.
3 rm 20.00/40.00.

at Ashford-in-the-Water NW : 1¾ m. by A 6 and A 6020 on B 6465 – ✉ Bakewell – ☎ 01629 :

Riverside Country House, Fennel St., DE45 1QF, ☎ 814275, Fax 812873, – TV P. AE VISA.
Meals 11.50/29.00 **t.** and a la carte 6.00 – 5.00 – **15 rm** 75.00/99.00 **t.** – SB.

BALDERSTONE Lancs. – see Blackburn.

BALDOCK Herts. 404 T 28 – pop. 9 232 – ☎ 01462.
♦London 42 – Bedford 20 – ♦Cambridge 21 – Luton 15.

Forte Travelodge, A 1 Great North Road, Hinxworth (southbound carriageway), SG7 5EX, NW : 3 m. by A 507 on A 1 ☎ 835329, Reservations (Freephone) 0800 850950 – TV P. AE VISA.
Meals (grill rest.) – **40 rm** 34.50 **t.**

BALSALL COMMON W. Mids. – see Coventry.

BAMBER BRIDGE Lancs. 402 M 22 – see Preston.

BAMBURGH Northd. 401 402 O 17 Great Britain G. – pop. 582 – ☎ 01668.
See : Castle★ *AC.*
♦London 337 – ♦Edinburgh 77 – ♦Newcastle upon Tyne 51.

Lord Crewe Arms, Front St., NE69 7BL, ☎ 214243, Fax 214273 – TV P. VISA
Easter-October – **Meals** (bar lunch)/dinner 17.95 **t.** – **23 rm** 27.50/68.00 **t.** – SB.

at Waren Mill W : 2¾ m. on B 1342 – ✉ Belford – ☎ 01668 :

Waren House, NE70 7EE, ☎ 214581, Fax 214484, ≤, – TV P. AE VISA JCB.
Meals (dinner only) 22.50 **st.** 6.50 – **5 rm** 74.00/124.00 **st.**, 2 suites – SB.

BANBURY Oxon. 403 404 P 27 Great Britain G. – pop. 39 906 – ☎ 01295.
Exc. : Upton House★ *AC*, NW : 7 m. by A 422.
18 Cherwell Edge, Chacombe ☎ 711591.
Banbury Museum, 8 Horsefair, OX16 0AA ☎ 259855.
♦London 76 – ♦Birmingham 40 – ♦Coventry 25 – ♦Oxford 23.

Whately Hall (Forte Heritage), Horsefair, by Banbury Cross, OX16 0AN, ☎ 263451, Fax 271736, « Part 17C hall », – TV P – 80. AE VISA JCB.
Meals *(closed Saturday lunch)* 12.00/20.00 **st.** and a la carte 7.25 – 9.00 – **72 rm** 70.00/85.00 **st.**, 2 suites – SB.

Banbury House, 27-29 Oxford Rd, OX16 9AH, ☎ 259361, Fax 270954 – TV P – 70. AE VISA
closed 25 to 30 December – **Meals** (bar lunch Monday to Saturday)/dinner 15.75 **st.** and a la carte 4.50 – 8.25 – **48 rm** 69.00/99.00 **t.** – SB.

Easington House, 50 Oxford Rd, OX16 9AN, ☎ 270181, Fax 269527, – TV P. AE VISA
closed 24 December-2 January – **Meals** *(closed Sunday and Bank Holidays)* (dinner only) a la carte approx. 13.75 **st.** 4.75 – **12 rm** 47.50/75.00 **st.** – SB.

Prospect House without rest., 70 Oxford Rd, OX16 9AN, ☎ 268749, – TV P. AE VISA.
9 rm 28.00/45.00 **st.**

at Adderbury S : 3 m. on A 4260 – ✉ Banbury – ☎ 01295 :

Red Lion, The Green, OX17 3LU, ☎ 810269, Fax 811906, « Part 16C inn » – ☎ P. AE VISA JCB.
Meals a la carte 13.20/17.20 **st.** – **14 rm** 45.00/55.00 **st.** – SB.

at North Newington W : 2 ¼ m. by B 4035 – ✉ Banbury – ☎ 01295 :

La Madonette Country Guest House without rest., OX15 6AA, ☎ 730212, Fax 730363, – ☎ P. VISA JCB.
5 rm 32.00/58.00 **t.**

at Wroxton NW : 3 m. by B 4100 on A 422 – ✉ Banbury – ☎ 01295 :

Wroxton House, Silver St., OX15 6QB, ☎ 730777, Fax 730800 – ☎ P – 50. AE VISA
Meals *(closed Saturday lunch)* 15.50/22.50 **t.** and a la carte – **31 rm** 65.00/95.00 **t.**, 1 suite – SB.

at Shenington NW : 6 m. by A 41 off A 422 – ✉ Banbury – ☎ 01295 :

Sugarswell Farm, OX15 6HW, NW : 2 ¼ m. on Edge Hill rd ☎ 680512, Fax 680512, – P.
Meals (by arrangement) 20.00 **st.** – **3 rm** 38.00/55.00 **st.**

ATS Beaumont Ind. Est., Beaumont Close ☎ 253525

BANTHAM Devon – see Kingsbridge.

BARDWELL Suffolk 404 W 27 – see Bury St. Edmunds.

BARFORD Warks. 403 404 P 27 – see Warwick.

BAR HILL Cambs. 404 U 27 – see Cambridge.

BARNARD CASTLE Durham 402 O 20 **Great Britain G.** – pop. 4 783 – ☎ 01833.

See : Bowes Museum★ *AC*.

Exc. : Raby Castle★ *AC*, NE : 6½m. by A 688.

Harmire Rd ☎ 38355.

43 Galgate, DL12 8EL ☎ 690909.

London 258 – Carlisle 63 – Leeds 68 – Middlesbrough 31 – Newcastle upon Tyne 39.

Jersey Farm, Darlington Rd, DL12 8TA, E : 1 ½ m. on A 67 ☎ 638223, Fax 631988, park – ☎ P – 150. VISA
Meals (carving rest.) (bar lunch Monday to Friday)/dinner 15.00 **t.** 5.00 – **16 rm** 50.00/80.00 **t.**, 4 suites – SB.

at Romaldkirk NW : 6 m. by A 67 on B 6277 – ✉ Barnard Castle – ☎ 01833 :

Rose and Crown, DL12 9EB, ☎ 650213, Fax 650828, « Part 18C coaching inn » – rest ☎ P. VISA
closed 25 and 26 December – **Meals** *(closed Sunday dinner)* (bar lunch Monday to Saturday)/dinner 24.95 **st.** 5.90 – **10 rm** 55.00/75.00 **st.**, 2 suites – SB.

BARNARD GATE Oxon. 403 404 P 28 – see Witney.

BARNOLDSWICK Lancs. 402 N 22 pop. 10 038 – ☎ 01282.

London 239 – Manchester 33 – Preston 30.

Monks House, 5 Manchester Rd, BB8 5NZ, ☎ 814423.
Meals (by arrangement) (communal dining) 7.00 – **4 rm** 16.00/32.00.

BARNSDALE BAR W. Yorks. 402 404 Q 23 – ✉ Pontefract – ☎ 01977.

London 181 – Leeds 22 – Nottingham 53 – Sheffield 26.

Forte Travelodge, WF8 3JB, on A 1 ☎ 620711, Reservations (Freephone) 0800 850950 – P. AE VISA.
Meals (grill rest.) – **56 rm** 34.50 **t.**

BARNSLEY Glos. 403 404 O28 – see Cirencester.

BARNSLEY S. Yorks. 402 404 P 23 – pop. 220 937 – ☎ 01226.

18 Wakefield Rd, Staincross ☎ 382856 – 18 Silkstone, Field Head, Elmhirst Lane ☎ 790328 – 9 Wombwell Hillies, Wentworth View, Wombwell ☎ 754433.

56 Eldon St., S70 2JL ☎ 206757.

London 177 – Leeds 21 – Manchester 36 – Sheffield 15.

Ardsley House (Q.M.H.), Doncaster Rd, Ardsley, S71 5EH, E: 2 ¾ m. on A 635 ☎ 309955, Fax 205374, – rest ☎ P – 250. AE VISA
Meals *(closed lunch Saturday and Bank Holidays)* 10.75/17.35 **st.** and a la carte 5.60 – 8.75 – **73 rm** 60.00/75.00 **st.** – SB.

Forte Travelodge, Doncaster Rd, S70 3PE, E: 2½ m. on A 635 ☎ 298799, Reservations (Freephone) 0800 850950 – TV & P. VISA.
Meals (grill rest.) – **32 rm** 34.50 **t.**

Periquito, Regent St., S70 2HQ, ☎ 731010, Fax 248719, – rm TV ☎ P – 150. VISA JCB
Meals (lunch by arrangement)/dinner 14.00 **t.** and a la carte 6.95 – 6.50 – **49 rm** 44.00 **st.**

ATS Huddersfield Rd ☎ 281888/287406 ATS Wombwell Lane, Aldham Bridge, Wombwell ☎ 753511

BARNSTAPLE Devon 403 H 30 **The West Country G.** – pop. 20 740 – 01271.

See : Town★ - Long Bridge★.

Envir. : Arlington Court★★ (Carriage Collection★) *AC*, NE : 6 m. by A 39.

18, 9 Chulmleigh, Leigh Rd ☎ (01769) 580519.

to the Isle of Lundy (Lundy Co.) (2 h 15 mn).

North Devon Library, Tuly St., EX31 1TY ☎ 388583/388584.

◆London 222 – Exeter 40 – Taunton 51.

Barnstaple, Braunton Rd, EX31 1LE, W : 1½ m. on A 361 ☎ 76221, Fax 24101, , , – rest TV ☎ P – 250. VISA
Meals 8.50/14.50 **t.** and a la carte – 5.00 – **57 rm** 47.00/59.00 **t.** – SB.

XX **Lynwood House** with rm, Bishops Tawton Rd, EX32 9EF, S : 1½ m. by A 361 and Newport rd ☎ 43695, Fax 79340 – rest TV ☎ P. VISA
Meals *(closed Sunday)* 13.95 **t.** (lunch) and a la carte 19.00/36.00 **t.** 5.05 – **5 rm** 40.50/60.50 **t.** – SB.

at Bishop's Tawton S : 2¾ m. by A 39 on A 377 – ✉ Barnstaple – 01271 :

Downrew House , EX32 0DY, SE : 1½ m. on Chittlehampton rd ☎ 42497, Fax 23947, <, heated, , park, – rest TV ☎ P – 40. VISA
closed January – **Meals** 8.95/17.50 **t.** and dinner a la carte 4.80 – **12 rm** (dinner included) 56.00/120.00 **t.** – SB.

Halmpstone Manor , EX32 0EA, SE : 3 m. by Chittlehampton rd ☎ 830321, Fax 830826, <, , park – rest TV ☎ P. VISA
closed January and November – **Meals** (lunch by arrangement)/dinner 30.00 **st.** 5.40 – **5 rm** 65.00/100.00 **t.**

ATS Pottington Ind. Est., Braunton Rd ☎ 42294/5

BARROW-IN-FURNESS Cumbria 402 K 21 – pop. 73 125 – 01229.

18 Rakesmoore Lane, Hawcoat ☎ 825444 – 18 Furness, Walney Island ☎ 471232.

Forum 28, Duke St., LA14 1HU ☎ 870156.

◆London 295 – Kendal 34 – Lancaster 47.

Abbey House, Abbey Rd, LA13 0PA, NE : 2 m. ☎ 838282, Fax 820403, « Lutyens house », , park – TV ☎ P – 100. VISA
Meals *(closed Saturday lunch)* 5.95/22.50 **t.** and dinner a la carte 4.50 – **30 rm** 59.95/79.95 **t.** – SB.

Arlington House, 200/202 Abbey Rd, LA14 5LD, N : 1 m. ☎ 831976, heated – TV ☎ P. VISA.
Meals *(closed Sunday)* (dinner only) a la carte 12.50/21.00 **t.** 4.50 – **8 rm** 52.00/70.00 **t**

ATS 149-151 Ainslie St. ☎ 828513/828663

BARTON MILLS Suffolk. 404 V 26 – pop. 832 – 01638.

◆London 72 – Cambridge 21 – ◆Ipswich 37 – ◆Norwich 40.

Forte Travelodge, Fiveways Roundabout, IP28 6AE, on A 11 ☎ 717675, Reservations (Freephone) 0800 850950 – TV & P. VISA.
Meals (grill rest.) – **32 rm** 34.50 **t.**

BARTON STACEY Hants. 403 404 P 30 – see Andover.

BARTON UNDER NEEDWOOD Staffs. – see Burton-upon-Trent.

BARWICK Somerset 403 404 M 31 – see Yeovil.

BASFORD Staffs. – see Stoke-on-Trent.

BASILDON Essex 404 V 29 – pop. 161 124 – 01268.

18 Clayhill Lane, Sparrow's Hearne, Kingswood ☎ 533297 – 18, 9 Langdon Hills, Lower Dunton Rd, Bulphan ☎ 548444.

◆London 30 – Chelmsford 17 – Southend-on-Sea 13.

Forte Posthouse, Cranes Farm Rd, SS14 3DG, NW : 2¼ m. by A 176 on A 1235 ☎ 533955, Fax 530119, , , 18, , squash – rm TV ☎ P – 250. VISA JCB.
Meals a la carte 14.35/24.20 **t.** 6.95 – 7.95 – **110 rm** 59.00 **st.** – SB.

🏨 **Travel Inn,** Felmores, East Mayne, SS13 1BW, N : 1½ m. on A 132 ☎ 522227, Fax 530092 – ⛔ rm 📺 ♿ 🅟. 💳 AE ⓓ VISA. ⛔
closed Christmas – **Meals** (grill rest.) – ☕ 4.95 – **32 rm** 34.50 **t.**

🏨 **Campanile,** A 127 Southend Arterial Rd, Pipp's Hill, SS14 3AE, NW : 1 m. by A 176 at junction with A 127 ☎ 530810, Fax 286710 – ⛔ rm 📺 ☎ ♿ 🅟 – 🎤 30. 💳 AE ⓓ VISA
Meals 10.35 **st.** 🍷 4.95 – ☕ 4.50 – **97 rm** 35.75 **t.** – SB.

ATS Archers Field ☎ 525177

BASINGSTOKE Hants. 403 404 Q 30 – pop. 77 837 – ☎ 01256.

⛳ Test Valley, Micheldever Rd, Overton ☎ 771737 – ⛳ Weybrook Park, Sherborne, St Johns ☎ 20347.

ℹ Willis Museum, Old Town Hall, Market Pl., RG21 1QD ☎ 817618.

♦London 55 – Reading 17 – ♦Southampton 31 – Winchester 18.

BASINGSTOKE

London Street . . . . Y 19
Upper Church Street . . . . Y 24
Winchester Street . . . . Y 27

Aldermaston Road . . . . Z 2
Beaconsfield Road . . . . Y 3
Buckland Avenue . . . . Z 5
Chequers Road . . . . Y 6
Church Street . . . . Y 7
Churchill Way . . . . Z 9
Churchill Way East . . . . Z 10
Council Road . . . . Y 12
Cross Street . . . . Y 13
Fairfields Road . . . . Y 14
Houndmills Road . . . . Z 17
New Road . . . . Y 20
Reading Road . . . . Z 22
Southern Ringway . . . . Z 23
Victoria Street . . . . Y 25
Wote Street . . . . Y 28

North is at the top on all town plans.

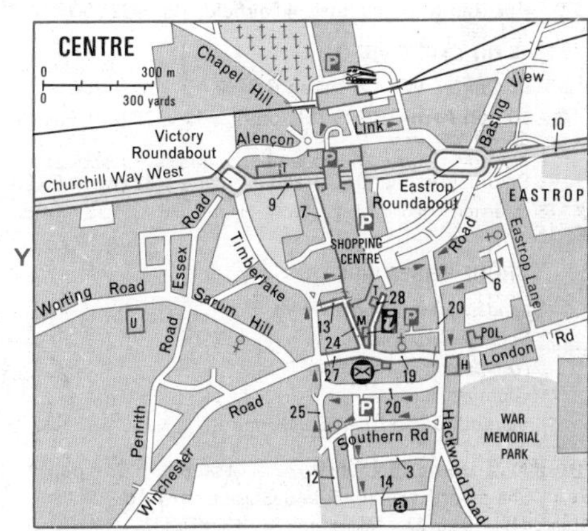

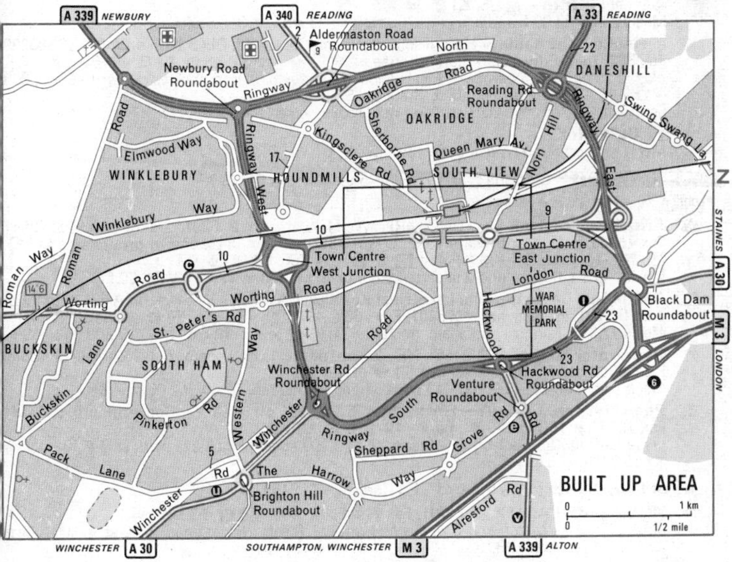

Audleys Wood (Thistle), Alton Rd, RG25 2JT, S : 1 ½ m. on A 339 ✆ 817555, Fax 817500, « Gothic Renaissance mansion », park – rm – 50. AE VISA JCB. Z v
Meals *(closed lunch Saturday and Bank Holidays)* 14.95/28.50 **st.** and a la carte 7.20 – 9.25 – **69 rm** 88.00/108.00 **st.**, 2 suites – SB.

Hilton National, Old Common Rd, Black Dam, RG21 3PR, ✆ 460460, Fax 840441, – rm rest – 150 Z i
Meals (carving rest.) – **141 rm.**

Forte Posthouse, Grove Rd, RG21 3EE, S : 1 m. at junction of A 339 with A 30 ✆ 468181, Fax 840081 – rm – 150. AE VISA JCB Z e
Meals a la carte 14.95/21.70 **st.** – 7.95 – **84 rm** 69.00 **st.** – SB.

Travel Inn, Worting Rd, RG22 6PG, ✆ 811477, Fax 819329 – rm. AE VISA. Z c
Meals (grill rest.) – 4.95 – **49 rm** 34.50 **t.**

Forte Travelodge, Stag & Hounds, Winchester Road, RG22 6HN, ✆ 843566, Reservations (Freephone) 0800 850950 – . AE VISA. Z u
Meals (grill rest.) – **32 rm** 34.50 **t.**

Fernbank without rest., 4 Fairfields Rd, RG21 3DR, ✆ 21191, Fax 21191 – . VISA. Y a
16 rm 40.00/52.00 **st.**

at Oakley W : 4 ¾ m. on B 3400 – Z – 01256 :

Beach Arms, RG23 7EP, on B 3400 ✆ 780210, Fax 780557, – – 25. AE VISA JCB
closed 25 and 26 December – **Meals** *(closed Sunday dinner)* (bar lunch Monday to Saturday)/dinner 9.95 **t.** and a la carte – **32 rm** 55.00/75.00 **t.**

ATS Moniton Trading Est., West Ham Lane ✆ 51431/2 ATS Armstrong Rd, Daneshill East ✆ 462448

BASLOW Derbs. 402 403 404 P 24 **Great Britain G.** – pop. 1 757 – Bakewell – 01246.
See : Chatsworth★★★ (Park and Garden★★★) *AC.*
♦London 161 – Derby 27 – ♦Manchester 35 – ♦Sheffield 13.

Cavendish, DE45 1SP, on A 619 ✆ 582311, Fax 582312, ≤ Chatsworth Park, – rest – 25. AE VISA.
Meals 23.75/32.00 **t.** and a la carte – 9.20 – **23 rm** 79.00/125.00 **t.** – SB.

XXX ✿ **Fischer's at Baslow Hall** (Fischer) with rm, Calver Rd, DE45 1RR, on A 623 ✆ 583259, Fax 583818, « Edwardian manor house », – rest . AE VISA.
closed 25 and 26 December – **Meals** *(closed Sunday dinner to non-residents)* 19.50/38.00 **t.** – 7.25 – **5 rm** 75.00/120.00 **t.**, 1 suite – SB
Spec. Turbot on black ink risotto, Roast calves liver, Chocolate fondant tartlet with cherries.

XX **Cafe Max**
Meals *(closed Sunday)* a la carte 15.80/24.10 **t.**

BASSENTHWAITE Cumbria 401 402 K 19 – pop. 433 – 01768 7.
♦London 300 – ♦Carlisle 24 – Keswick 7.

Armathwaite Hall, CA12 4RE, W : 1 ½ m. on B 5291, Keswick ✆ 76551, Fax 76220, ≤ Bassenthwaite Lake, « Part 18C mansion in extensive grounds », , , park, – rest – 100. AE VISA
Meals 14.95 **t.** (lunch) and a la carte 29.85/44.40 **t.** – **43 rm** 50.00/190.00 **t.** – SB.

Castle Inn, Bassenthwaite Lake, Near Keswick, CA12 4RG, W : 1 m. on A 591 at junction with B 5291, Keswick ✆ 76401, Fax 76604, , , – . AE VISA
Meals 17.95 **t.** (dinner) and a la carte 19.90/24.70 **t.** 7.95 – **49 rm** 56.00/108.00 **t.** – SB.

Overwater Hall, CA5 1HH, NE : 2 ¼ m. by A 591 on Uldale rd, Carlisle ✆ 76566, Fax 76566, ≤, , park – rest . VISA
Meals (dinner only) 19.95 **st.** – **13 rm** (dinner included) 51.00/102.00 **st.** – SB.

Pheasant Inn, CA13 9YE, SW : 3 ¼ m. by B 5291 off A 66, Cockermouth ✆ 76234, Fax 76002, « 16C inn », , park – rest . VISA.
closed 24 and 25 December – **Meals** 12.00/20.00 **st.** and lunch a la carte **st.** 4.40 – **20 rm** 56.00/104.00 **st.** – SB.

at Ireby N : 4½ m. on Ireby rd – Carlisle – 01697 3 :

Woodlands, CA5 1EX, ✆ 71791, Fax 71482, – . VISA JCB
closed 2 weeks March and 2 weeks November – **Meals** *(dinner only)* 15.00 **st.** 4.00 – **8 rm** 20.00/50.00 **st.** – SB.

BATH Avon 403 404 M 29 The West Country G. – pop. 78 689 – ☎ 01225.

See : City★★★ – Royal Crescent★★★ AV (No 1 Royal Crescent★★ *AC* AV **D**) – The Circus★★★ AV – Museum of Costume★★★ *AC* AV **M2** – Royal Photographic Society National Centre of Photography★★ *AC* BV **M4** – Roman Baths★★ *AC* BX **B** – Holburne Museum and Crafts Study Centre★★ *AC* Y **M1** – Pump Room★ BX **A** - Assembly Rooms★ AV – Bath Abbey★ BX – Pulteney Bridge★ BV – Bath Industrial Heritage Centre★ *AC* AV **M3**.

Envir. : Lansdown Crescent★★ (Somerset Place★) Y – Claverton (American Museum★★ *AC*, Claverton Pumping Station★ *AC*) E : 3 m. by A 36 Y – Camden Crescent★ Y – Beckford Tower and Museum *AC* (prospect★) Y **M6**.

Exc. : Corsham Court★★ *AC*, NE : 8½m. by A 4 – Dyrham Park★ *AC*, N : 6½m. by A 4 and A 46 – Norton St. Philip (George Inn★) S : 7¼m. by A 367 – Z - and B 3110.

18, 9 Tracy Park, Bath Rd, Wick ☎ 0117 937 2251 – 18 Lansdown ☎ 425007 – 18 Sham Castle, North Rd ☎ 425182 – 9 Entry Hill ☎ 834248.

The Colonnades, 11-13 Bath St., BA1 1SW ☎ 462831.

London 119 – ◆Bristol 13 – ◆Southampton 63 – Taunton 49.

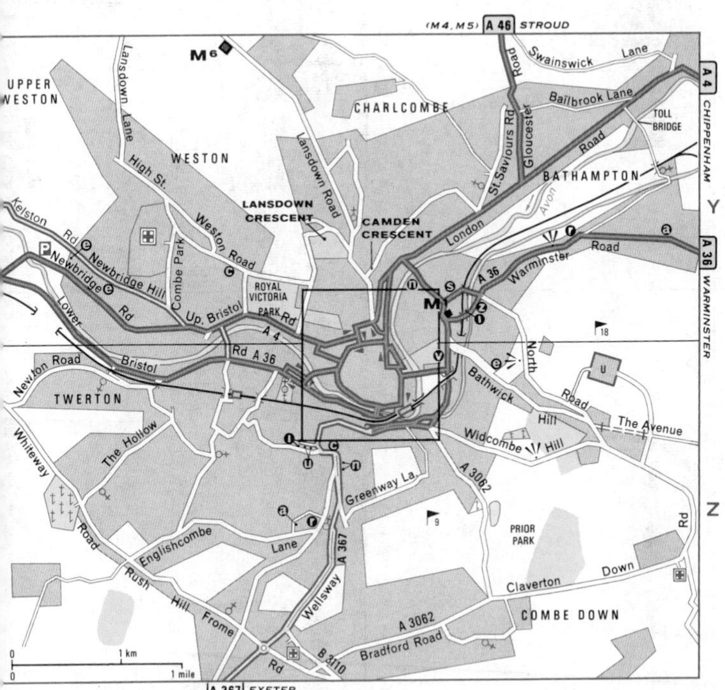

Bath Spa (Forte), Sydney Rd, BA2 6JF, ☎ 444424, Fax 444006, « Part 19C mansion in landscaped gardens », – rm – 120. AE VISA JCB
Alfresco Colonnade : Meals a la carte 13.30/30.95 **t.** – (see also ***Vellore*** below) – 13.50 – **91 rm** 119.00/189.00 **t.**, 7 suites – SB. Y **z**

Royal Crescent (Q.M.H.), 16 Royal Cres., BA1 2LS, ☎ 739955, Fax 339401, ‹, « Tastefully restored Georgian town houses », – – 60. AE VISA JCB AV **a**
Meals 14.50/45.00 **st.** and a la carte – 12.50 – **38 rm** 98.00/240.00 **st.**, 4 suites – SB.

The Priory, Weston Rd, BA1 2XT, ☎ 331922, Fax 448276, ‹, heated, – rest . AE VISA Y **c**
Meals 12.00/38.50 **st.** and a la carte 6.50 – 5.00 – **21 rm** 85.00/225.00 **st.** – SB.

Queensberry, Russell St., BA1 2QF, ☎ 447928, Fax 446065, « Georgian town houses » – . AE VISA. AV **x**
closed 24 to 30 December – **Meals** - (see ***Olive Tree*** below) – 7.50 – **22 rm** 89.00/164.00 **st.** – SB.

Hilton National, Walcot St., BA1 5BJ, ☎ 463411, Fax 464393, – – 240. AE VISA JCB. BV **i**
Meals 11.50/17.50 **st.** and a la carte – 10.25 – **148 rm** 85.00/105.00 **st.**, 2 suites – SB.

BATH

Gay Street	AV	
Green Street	BV	21
Milsom Street	BV	
New Bond Street	BV	31
Ambury	BX	2
Argyle Street	BV	3
Bennett Street	AV	4
Bridge Street	BVX	6
Broad Quay	BX	7
Chapel Row	AVX	9
Charles Street	AX	10
Charlotte Street	AV	12
Cheap Street	BX	13
Churchill Bridge	BX	14
Circus Place	AV	16
Grand Parade	BX	17
Great Stanhope Street	AV	18
Guinea Lane	BV	23
Henry Street	BX	24
Lower Borough Walls	BX	26
Monmouth Place	AVX	28
Monmouth Street	AX	30
New Orchard Street	BX	32
Nile Street	AV	34
Northgate Street	BVX	35
Old Bond Street	BX	36
Orange Grove	BX	3
Pierrepont Street	BX	3
Quiet Street	BV	4
Russell Street	AV	4
Southgate Street	BX	4
Stanley Road	BX	4
Terrace Walk	BX	4
Upper Borough Walls	BX	4
Westgate Buildings	AX	4
Westgate Street	ABX	5
Wood Street	AV	5
York Street	BX	5

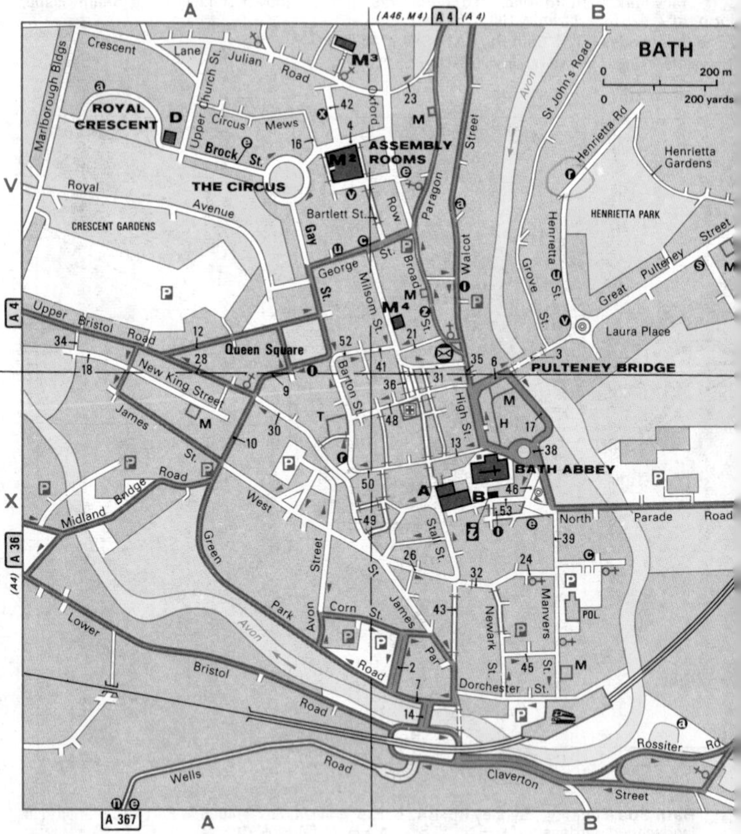

Fountain House without rest., 9-11 Fountain Buildings, Lansdown Rd, BA1 5DV ☎ 338622, Fax 445855 – 🛗 TV ☎. AE ⓓ VISA — BV
13 suites 92.00/168.00 **st.**.

Francis (Forte Heritage), Queen Sq., BA1 2HH, ☎ 424257, Fax 319715 – 🛗 TV ☎ Ⓟ – 80. AE ⓓ VISA JCB. — AV
Meals (bar lunch Saturday) 10.25/18.95 **st.** and a la carte – ☕ 9.25 – **92 rm** 78.00/98.00 **st**
1 suite – SB.

Pratt's, South Par., BA2 4AB, ☎ 460441, Fax 448807 – 🛗 TV ☎ – 50. AE ⓓ VISA — BX
Meals (bar lunch Monday to Saturday)/dinner 14.75 **t.** and a la carte 🍷 6.00 – **46 rm** ☕ 49.95/89.90 **t.** – SB.

Stakis Bath, Widcombe Basin, BA2 4JP, ☎ 338855, Fax 428941 – 🛗 TV ☎ Ⓟ – 75. AE ⓓ VISA — BX
Meals 13.50/16.95 **st.** and dinner a la carte – ☕ 9.75 – **96 rm** 65.00/105.00 **t.** – SB.

Compass Abbey, North Par., BA1 1LG, ☎ 461603, Fax 447758 – 🛗 📺 ☎ – 🏛 40. AE VISA BX **e**
Meals 6.50/14.95 **st.** and dinner a la carte 4.20 – **54 rm** 55.00/85.00 **st.** – SB.

Brompton House without rest., St. John's Rd, Bathwick, BA2 6PT, ☎ 420972, Fax 420505, – 📺 ☎ P. AE VISA JCB. Y **n**
closed 4 days at Christmas and New Year – **16 rm** 32.00/68.00 **st.**

Dukes, Great Pulteney St., BA2 4DN, ☎ 463512, Fax 483733 – rest 📺 ☎. AE VISA BV **s**
closed 5 days at Christmas – **Meals** (dinner only) 15.50 **st.** 6.00 – **22 rm** 50.00/90.00 **st.** – SB.

Sydney Gardens without rest., Sydney Rd, BA2 6NT, ☎ 464818, ←, – 📺 ☎ P. AE VISA JCB Y **i**
closed Christmas and early January – **6 rm** 49.00/75.00 **st.**

Siena, 25 Pulteney Rd, BA2 4EZ, ☎ 425495, Fax 469029, – rest 📺 ☎ P – 🏛 25. AE VISA JCB Z **v**
Meals (bar lunch)/dinner 16.95 **t.** and a la carte 4.95 – **14 rm** 42.50/77.50 **t.** – SB.

Bloomfield House without rest., 146 Bloomfield Rd, BA2 2AS, ☎ 420105, Fax 481958, ←, – 📺 ☎ P. VISA. Z **r**
6 rm 35.00/95.00 **st.**

Paradise House without rest., 86-88 Holloway, BA2 4PX, ☎ 317723, Fax 482005, ←, – 📺 ☎. AE VISA. Z **c**
closed Christmas – **9 rm** 42.00/68.00 **t.**

Holly Lodge without rest., 8 Upper Oldfield Park, BA2 3JZ, ☎ 424042, Fax 481138, ←, – 📺 ☎ P. AE VISA. Z **i**
6 rm 48.00/85.00 **st.**

Cranleigh without rest., 159 Newbridge Hill, BA1 3PX, ☎ 310197, Fax 423143 – 📺 P. VISA. Y **e**
closed Christmas – **5 rm** 38.00/60.00 **st.**

Haydon House without rest., 9 Bloomfield Park, off Bloomfield Rd, BA2 2BY, ☎ 444919, Fax 444919, – 📺 ☎. AE VISA JCB. Z **a**
5 rm 40.00/70.00 **st.**

Leighton House without rest., 139 Wells Rd, BA2 3AL, ☎ 314769, – 📺 ☎ P. VISA. AX **e**
8 rm 42.00/68.00 **st.**

Somerset House, 35 Bathwick Hill, BA2 6LD, ☎ 466451, Fax 317188, ←, – ☎ P. AE VISA Z **e**
Meals (dinner only Monday to Saturday and Sunday lunch November-May)/dinner 18.30 **st.** 4.25 – **10 rm** (dinner included) 47.75/95.50 **st.** – SB.

Villa Magdala without rest., Henrietta Rd, BA2 6LX, ☎ 466329, Fax 483207, – 📺 ☎ P. AE VISA JCB. BV **r**
17 rm 45.00/75.00 **t.**

Bath Tasburgh without rest., Warminster Rd, Bathampton, BA2 6SH, ☎ 425096, Fax 463842, ←, – 📺 ☎ P. AE VISA. Y **r**
13 rm 38.00/72.00 **t.**

Laura Place without rest., 3 Laura Pl., Great Pulteney St., BA2 4BH, ☎ 463815, Fax 310222 – 📺 ☎ P. AE VISA. BV **v**
closed 21 December-1 March – **8 rm** 52.00/85.00 **st.**

Dorian House without rest., 1 Upper Oldfield Park, BA2 3JX, ☎ 426336, Fax 444699, – 📺 ☎ P. AE VISA. Z **u**
8 rm 42.00/70.00 **st.**

Orchard Lodge without rest., Warminster Rd, Bathampton, BA2 6XG, ☎ 466115, Fax 446050, – 📺 ☎ P. VISA Y **a**
14 rm 35.00/55.00 **st.**

Cheriton House without rest., 9 Upper Oldfield Park, BA2 3JX, ☎ 429862, Fax 428403, – 📺 P. VISA. Z **u**
closed Christmas and New Year – **9 rm** 35.00/60.00 **st.**

Blairgowrie House without rest., 55 Wellsway, BA2 4RT, ☎ 332266 – 📺. Z **n**
3 rm 32.00/50.00 **st.**

Rosemary House, 63 Wellsway, BA2 4RT, ☎ 425667 – 📺. Z **n**
closed 23 to 31 December – **Meals** (by arrangement) 12.50 **t.** – **3 rm** 30.00/52.00 **st.**

Greenways without rest., 1 Forester Rd, Bathwick, BA2 6QF, ☎ 310132, Fax 310132 – 📺 Y **s**
closed Christmas – **3 rm** 35.00/54.00 **s.**

Kennard without rest., 11 Henrietta St., BA2 6LL, ☎ 310472, Fax 460054 – 📺 ☎. AE VISA. BV **u**
13 rm 35.00/64.00 **t.**

01225

Oakleigh without rest., 19 Upper Oldfield Park, BA2 3JX, 315698, Fax 448223 – TV P. VISA. Z i
4 rm 35.00/60.00 **st.**

Brocks without rest., 32 Brock St., BA1 2LN, 338374, Fax 334245 – TV. VISA. AV e
closed 2 weeks January – **6 rm** 40.00/56.00 **t.**

Oldfields without rest., 102 Wells Rd, BA2 3AL, 317984, Fax 444471, – TV P. VISA. AX n
14 rm 30.00/65.00 **t.**

XXXX **Vellore** (at Bath Spa H.), Sydney Rd, BA2 6JF, 444424, Fax 444006, – P. AE VISA JCB Y z
Meals (dinner only and Sunday lunch) 16.50/35.00 **t.** and a la carte 9.50.

XX **Clos du Roy,** 1 Seven Dials, Saw Close, BA1 1EN, 444450, Fax 460218 – AE VISA JCB AX r
closed 25 December and 1 January – **Meals** 8.95/18.50 **st.** and a la carte 4.50.

XX **Hole in the Wall,** 16 George St., BA1 2EH, 425242, Fax 425242 – AE VISA AV u
closed Sunday – **Meals** 7.00/14.50 **t.** and a la carte approx. 19.50 **t.**

XX **Garlands,** 7 Edgar Buildings, George St., BA1 2EE, 442283 – AE VISA AV c
closed Monday, 25-26 December and first week January – **Meals** 13.95 **t.** (lunch) and dinner a la carte 18.95/22.30 **t.**

XX **Olive Tree** (at Queensberry H.), Russell St., BA1 2QF, 447928, Fax 446065 – . AE VISA AV x
closed lunch Sunday and Bank Holiday Mondays and 24 to 30 December – **Meals** 9.50/18.00 **t.** and a la carte.

XX **Sukhothai,** 90a Walcot St., BA1 5BG, 462463, Fax 462463 – . AE VISA BV a
closed Sunday – **Meals** - Thai - 6.00/22.00 **t.** and a la carte 3.50.

X **New Moon,** Seven Dials, Saw Close, BA1 1EN, 444407 – AE VISA JCB AX r
Meals 8.25/18.50 **st.** and a la carte **t.** 6.60.

X **Tilleys Bistro,** 3 North Parade Passage, BA1 1NX, 484200 – . VISA BX i
closed Sunday lunch and 24 to 28 December – **Meals** 6.60 **t.** (lunch) and dinner a la carte 12.50/17.40 **t.**

X **Woods,** 9-13 Alfred St., BA1 2QX, 314812, Fax 443146 – VISA AV v
closed Sunday dinner and 24 to 26 December – **Meals** 12.00 **t.** (dinner) and a la carte 11.00/19.95 **t.** 4.50.

X **Moon and Sixpence,** 6a Broad St., BA1 5LJ, 460962 BV z
Meals 5.50/18.95 **t.** and dinner a la carte.

at Box NE : 5½ m. on A 4 - Y – Corsham (Wilts.) – 01225 :

Hermitage without rest., Bath Rd, SN13 8DT, 744187, Fax 744187, heated, – TV P.
5 rm 35.00/48.00 **s.**

Manor Farm without rest., Wadswick, SN13 9JB, SE : 2 m. by A 365 off B 3109 810700, Fax 810307, « Working Farm », , park – TV P. VISA JCB.
April-October – **3 rm** 25.00/42.00.

at Colerne (Wilts.) NE : 6½ m. by A 4 – Y – and Bannerdown rd – Bath – 01225

Lucknam Park, SN14 8AZ, N : ½ m. on Marshfield rd 742777, Fax 743536, « Early 18C country house in park », , , , – rest TV P – 25. AE VISA JCB.
Meals 22.50/42.50 **t.** – 5.50 – **38 rm** 110.00/200.00 **t.**, 4 suites – SB
Spec. Ceviche of South Coast monkfish, rocket and herb salad, Roast Suffolk lamb on a potato cage, red wine and mint olive oil sauce, Chocolate tear drops filled with iced coffee parfait, praline and caramel.

at Bathford E : 3½ m. by A 4 – Y – off A 363 – Bath – 01225 :

Old School House, Church St., BA1 7RR, 859593, Fax 859590, – TV P. VISA.
Meals (by arrangement) 21.50 **st.** 7.65 – **4 rm** 48.00/70.00 **st.**

at Monkton Combe SE : 4½ m. by A 36 – Bath – 01225 :

Monks Hill without rest., BA2 7HL, 833028, Fax 833028, Limpley Stoke Valley, – TV P. VISA.
3 rm 35.00/65.00 **st.**

at Limpley Stoke (Lower) SE : 5½ m. by A 36 - Y - off B 3108 – Bath – 01225 :

Cliffe, Cliffe Drive, Crowe Hill, BA3 6HY, 723226, Fax 723871, , heated, – rest TV P. AE VISA JCB
Meals 15.00/23.00 **t.** and a la carte 4.00 – **11 rm** 68.00/105.00 **t.** – SB.

at Winsley (Wilts) SE : 6 ½ m. by A 36 – Y – on B 3108 – ✉ Bradford-on-Avon – ☎ 01225 :

Burghope Manor ⛰ without rest., BA15 2LA, off B 3108 ℘ 723557, Fax 723113, « 13C manor house », ⛬ – ⊭ TV **P**. AE VISA JCB. ✻
closed Christmas and New Year – **5 rm** 55.00/70.00 **st.**

at Hinton Charterhouse S : 5 ¾ m. by A 367 – Z – on B 3110 – ✉ Bath – ☎ 01225 :

Homewood Park ⛰, BA3 6BB, E : 1 ¼ m. off A 36 (North) ℘ 723731, Fax 723820, ⩽, « Part Georgian country house », ⛬, park, ✂ – ⊭ rest TV ☎ **P**. AE ⓓ VISA JCB. ✻
Meals 13.50/28.50 **st.** and a la carte 28.50/37.50 **st.** – **15 rm** 90.00/150.00 **st.** – SB.

Green Lane House without rest., Green Lane, BA3 6BL, ℘ 723631 – AE VISA. ✻
4 rm 24.00/49.00.

at Norton St. Philip (Somerset) S : 7 ¼ m. by A 367 – Z – on B 3110 – ✉ Bath (Avon) – ☎ 01373 :

Monmouth Lodge without rest., BA3 6LH, ℘ 834367, ⛬ – ⊭ TV **P**. ✻
closed 20 to 31 December – **3 rm** 40.00/55.00.

The Plaine without rest., BA3 6LE, ℘ 834723, Fax 834101, « 16C cottages » – ⊭ TV **P**. AE ⓓ VISA. ✻
3 rm 35.00/50.00.

at Bitton NW : 5 ¾ m. by A 4 - Y - on A 431 – ✉ Bristol – ☎ 0117 :

Gaites House ⛰, Swineford, BS15 6LR, SE : ¾ m. on A 431 ℘ 932 9800, Fax 932 8882, ⩽, ⛬ – ⊭ rm TV ☎ **P**. AE ⓓ VISA
Meals (by arrangement) (residents only) (communal dining) (dinner only) 20.00 **s.** – **3 rm** 45.00/80.00 **s.**

ATS London Rd ℘ 338899/338924

La guida cambia, cambiate la guida ogni anno.

BATHFORD Avon 403 404 M 29 – see Bath.

BATLEY W. Yorks. 402 O 22 – ☎ 01924.
♦London 205 – ♦Leeds 9 – ♦Manchester 40 – ♦Middlesbrough 76 – ♦Sheffield 31.

Alder House, Towngate Rd, Healey Lane, WF17 7HR, ℘ 444777, Fax 442644, ⛬ – TV ☎ **P** – 🏛 80. AE VISA
Meals (bar lunch Monday to Saturday and Sunday dinner) 13.95 **st.** and a la carte 🍷 4.95 – **21 rm** 46.00/70.00 **st.**

BATTLE E. Sussex 404 V 31 **Great Britain G.** – pop. 5 732 – ☎ 01424.
See : Town★ – Abbey and Site of the Battle of Hastings★ *AC.*
ℹ 88 High St., TN33 0AQ ℘ 773721.
♦London 55 – ♦Brighton 34 – Folkestone 43 – Maidstone 30.

Netherfield Place ⛰, TN33 9PP, NW : 2 m. by A 2100 on Netherfield rd ℘ 774455, Fax 774024, ⩽, « Georgian style country house », ⛬, park, ✂ – TV ☎ **P** – 🏛 50. AE ⓓ VISA. ✻
closed last 2 weeks December – **Meals** 16.00/24.50 **t.** and a la carte 🍷 5.50 – **14 rm** 60.00/145.00 **t.** – SB.

Powdermills ⛰, Powdermill Lane, TN33 0SP, S : 1½ m. by A 2100 on B 2095 ℘ 775511, Fax 774540, ⩽, « Part Georgian gunpowdermill, antiques », 🏊, 🎣, ⛬, park – TV ☎ **P** – 🏛 250. AE ⓓ VISA JCB
Meals - (see *Orangery* below) – **23 rm** 49.00/120.00 **t.** – SB.

Burnt Wood House, Powdermill Rd, TN33 0SU, S : 2 m. on B 2095 ℘ 775151, Fax 775151, ⩽, 🏊 heated, ⛬, park, ✂ – TV ☎ **P**. AE ⓓ VISA
Meals a la carte 10.65/17.50 **t.** 🍷 6.95 – **10 rm** 45.00/55.00 **t.** – SB.

George, 23 High St., TN33 0EA, ℘ 774466, Fax 774853 – TV ☎ **P** – 🏛 50
22 rm.

Little Hemingfold ⛰, Hastings Rd, TN33 0TT, SE : 1 ¾ m. on A 2100 ℘ 774338, Fax 775351, ⩽, « Lakeside setting », 🎣, ⛬, park, ✂ – ⊭ rest TV ☎ **P**. AE ⓓ VISA. ✻
Meals (dinner only) 19.50 **t.** 🍷 5.50 – **12 rm** 35.00/68.00 **t.** – SB.

XX **Orangery** (at Powdermills H.), Powdermill Lane, TN33 0SP, S : 1 ½ m. by A 2100 on B 2095 ℘ 775511, Fax 774540, ⛬ – **P**. AE ⓓ VISA JCB
Meals *(closed Sunday dinner January-February)* 13.50/21.50 **t.** 🍷 6.50.

BATTLESBRIDGE Essex 404 V 29 – ✉ Wickford – ☎ 01245.
♦London 31 – Chelmsford 11 – Southend-on-Sea 9.

Lodge Country Inn, Hayes Chase, Burnham Rd, SS11 7QT, NE : 1 ¾ m. on A 132 ℘ 320060, Fax 320007, ⛬ – TV ☎ **P**. AE VISA. ✻
Meals 10.95 **st.** and a la carte 🍷 4.50 – **6 rm** 39.95/44.45 **st.**

BAWTRY S. Yorks 402 403 404 Q 23 pop. 2 696 – ✉ Doncaster – ☎ 01302.

Austerfield Park, Cross Lane ☎ 710841.

♦London 157 – ♦Leeds 37 – Lincoln 30 – ♦Nottingham 36 – ♦Sheffield 20.

Crown (Forte), High St., DN10 6JW, ☎ 710341, Fax 711798 – rm TV ☎ P – 150. AE VISA
Meals (bar lunch Monday to Saturday)/dinner a la carte 14.90/20.20 **s.** 5.55 – 8.50 – **57 rm** 40.00/50.00 **t.** – SB.

BEACONSFIELD Bucks. 404 S 29 – pop. 10 543 – ☎ 01494.

♦London 26 – Aylesbury 19 – ♦Oxford 32.

De Vere Bellhouse, Oxford Rd, HP9 2XE, E : 1 ¾ m. on A 40 ☎ (01753) 887211, Fax 888231, squash – rm TV ☎ P – 450. AE VISA
Meals 16.50/18.50 **st.** and a la carte 4.95 – **133 rm** 110.00/120.00 **st.**, 3 suites – SB.

Leigh House, 53 Wycombe End, HP9 1LX, ☎ 676348, Fax 676348 – AE VISA
Meals - Chinese (Peking) - 12.00/17.50 **t.** and a la carte.

La Lanterna, 57 Wycombe End, HP9 1LX, ☎ 675210 –
Meals - Italian rest..

China Diner, 7 The Highway, Station Rd, Beaconsfield New Town, HP9 1QD, ☎ 673345 – AE VISA
closed 25 to 27 December – **Meals** - Chinese - 14.50/20.00 **t.** and a la carte 4.25.

at Wooburn Common SW : 3½ m. by A 40 – ✉ Beaconsfield – ☎ 01628 :

Chequers Inn, Kiln Lane, HP10 0JQ, SW : 1 m. on Bourne End rd ☎ 529575, Fax 850124 – TV ☎ P – 45. AE VISA.
Meals 14.95/17.95 **t.** and a la carte – **17 rm** 72.50/90.00 **t.** – SB.

Si vous cherchez un hôtel tranquille,
consultez d'abord les cartes de l'introduction
ou repérez dans le texte les établissements indiqués avec le signe ou .

BEAMINSTER Dorset 403 L 31 – ☎ 01308.

♦London 154 – Exeter 45 – Taunton 30 – Weymouth 29.

Bridge House, DT8 3AY, ☎ 862200, Fax 863700, – rest TV ☎ P. AE VISA JCB
Meals (light lunch)/dinner 17.45 **t.** 4.50 – **14 rm** 50.50/94.75 **t.** – SB.

The Lodge, DT8 3BL, on A 3066 ☎ 863468, « Georgian country house », – TV P. VISA JCB
Meals (dinner only) 16.00 **st.** 4.00 – **3 rm** 30.00/80.00 **st.** – SB.

BEARSTED Kent 404 V 30 – see Maidstone.

BEAULIEU Hants. 403 404 P 31 **Great Britain G.** – pop. 726 – ✉ Brockenhurst – ☎ 01590.

See : Town★★ - National Motor Museum★★ *AC*.

Envir. : Buckler's Hard★ (Maritime Museum★ *AC*) SE : 2 m..

♦London 102 – Bournemouth 24 – ♦Southampton 13 – Winchester 23.

Montagu Arms, Palace Lane, SO42 7ZL, ☎ 612324, Fax 612188, « Part 18C inn, gardens » – rest TV ☎ P – 30. AE VISA
Meals 14.95/19.90 **t.** and dinner a la carte 10.00 – **22 rm** 69.90/149.90 **t.**, 2 suites – SB.

at Bucklers Hard S : 2½ m. – ✉ Brockenhurst – ☎ 01590 :

Master Builder's House, SO42 7XB, ☎ 616253, Fax 616297, ←, – rm TV ☎ P – 40. AE VISA
Meals 12.50/15.50 **t.** and a la carte – **23 rm** 70.00/140.00 **st.** – SB.

BECKINGHAM Lincs. 402 404 R 24 – pop. 263 – ✉ Fenton Claypole – ☎ 01636.

♦London 124 – Leicester 43 – Lincoln 20 – ♦Nottingham 28 – ♦Sheffield 46.

Black Swan, Hillside, LN5 0RF, ☎ 626474, – P. VISA
closed Sunday dinner, Monday, 2 weeks August and 25 to 30 December – **Meals** (booking essential) (lunch by arrangement)/dinner a la carte 16.20/24.75 **t.** 4.30.

BECKINGTON Somerset 403 404 N 30 pop. 903 – ✉ Bath (Avon) – ☎ 01373.

♦London 110 – ♦Bristol 27 – ♦Southampton 54 – Swindon 37.

Forte Travelodge without rest., BA3 6SF, on A 36 ☎ 830251, Reservations (Freephone) 0800 850950 – TV P. AE VISA.
40 rm 34.50 **t.**

Woolpack Inn with rm, Warminster Rd, BA3 6SP, ☎ 831244, Fax 831223, « Part 16C inn », – TV ☎ P. VISA JCB.
Meals a la carte 19.70/26.60 **t.** – **10 rm** 49.50/84.50 **t.** – SB.

BECKWITHSHAW N. Yorks. 402 P 22 – see Harrogate.

BEDALE N. Yorks. 402 P 21 – pop. 3 319 – ✉ Darlington – ☎ 01677.

Leyburn Rd ☎ 422568 – Bedale Hall, DL8 1AA ☎ 424604 (summer only).

♦London 225 – ♦Leeds 45 – ♦Newcastle Upon Tyne 30 – York 38.

Hyperion House without rest., 88 South End, DL8 2DS, ☎ 422334, – rm. *closed Christmas and New Year* – **3 rm** 20.00/36.00.

Plummer's, 7-10 North End, DL8 1AF, ☎ 423432, Fax 423432 – AE VISA
Meals 9.45 **st.** (lunch) and a la carte 12.70/21.70 **st.**

BEDFORD Beds. 404 S 27 – pop. 73 917 – ☎ 01234.

Bedfordshire, Bromham Rd, Biddenham ☎ 353241 – Mowsbury, Kimbolton Rd ☎ 216374/771041 – 10 St. Paul's Sq., MK40 1SL ☎ 215226.

♦London 59 – ♦Cambridge 31 – Colchester 70 – ♦Leicester 51 – Lincoln 95 – Luton 20 – ♦Oxford 52 – Southend-on-Sea 85.

Barns (Country Club), Cardington Rd, MK44 3SA, E : 2 m. on A 603 ☎ 270044, Fax 273102, – rm – 120. AE VISA
Meals (bar lunch Saturday) 11.00/25.00 **t.** and a la carte 5.75 – 7.50 – **48 rm** 67.00 **t.** – SB.

Bedford Swan, The Embankment, MK40 1RW, ☎ 346565, Fax 212009, – – 300. AE VISA
Meals 13.25/15.00 **st.** and a la carte 5.60 – **110 rm** 72.00/82.00 **st.**, 1 suite – SB.

Shakespeare, Shakespeare Rd, MK40 2DX, ☎ 213147, Fax 214524 – rest. AE VISA JCB.
Meals *(closed Sunday)* (dinner only) 11.00 **st.** 3.25 – **19 rm** 42.50/60.00 **st.**

Wayfarer, 403 Goldington Rd, Goldington, MK41 0DS, E : 2 m. on A 428 ☎ 272707, Fax 272707, – AE VISA.
Meals (grill rest.) a la carte 9.50/17.45 **st.** – **29 rm** 55.00/65.00 **st.** – SB.

at Elstow S : 2 m. by A 6 off A 5134 – ✉ Bedford – ☎ 01234 :

St. Helena, High St., MK42 9XP, ☎ 344848, « Part 16C house », – AE VISA
closed Saturday lunch, Sunday and Monday – **Meals** 17.75/28.50 **t.** 7.95.

at Houghton Conquest S : 6½ m. by A 6 – ✉ Bedford – ☎ 01234 :

Knife and Cleaver with rm, The Grove, MK45 3LA, ☎ 740387, Fax 740900, – AE VISA
closed 27 to 30 December – **Meals** *(closed Sunday dinner)* (bar lunch Saturday) 11.95/17.50 **t.** and a la carte 6.00 – **9 rm** 45.00/69.00 **t.**

at Marston Moretaine SW : 6¼ m. by A 6 off A 421 – ✉ Bedford – ☎ 01234 :

Forte Travelodge, Beancroft Rd junction, MK43 0PZ, on A 421 ☎ 766755, Reservations (Freephone) 0800 850950 – AE VISA.
Meals (grill rest.) – **32 rm** 34.50 **t.**

Moreteyne Manor, Woburn Rd, MK43 0NG, ☎ 767003, « 16C moated manor house », – VISA
closed Sunday dinner and Monday except December – **Meals** 10.00/17.95 **st.** and a la carte.

ATS 3 London Rd ☎ 358838

BEER Devon 403 K 31 The West Country G. – pop. 1 415 – ✉ Seaton – ☎ 01297.

Envir. : Seaton (≤★★) N ¾m..

Axe Cliff, Squires Lane, Axmouth, Seaton ☎ 24371.

♦London 170 – Exeter 22 – Taunton 28.

Anchor Inn, Fore St., EX12 3ET, ☎ 20386, ≤ – VISA.
closed 3 days at Christmas – **Meals** a la carte 12.40/25.75 **t.** 5.50 – **8 rm** 34.50/59.00 **t.**

BEESTON Ches. 402 403 404 L 24 – pop. 196 – ✉ Tarporley – ☎ 01829.

♦London 186 – Chester 15 – ♦Liverpool 40 – Shrewsbury 32.

Wild Boar, Whitchurch Rd, Bunbury, CW6 9NW, on A 49 ☎ 260309, Fax 261081, « Part 17C timbered house » – rm rest – 50. AE VISA
Meals 14.50/20.50 **t.** and a la carte 6.50 – **37 rm** 71.50/88.00 **t.** – SB.

BEESTON Notts. 402 403 404 Q 25 – see Nottingham.

BELCHAMP WALTER Essex 404 W 27 – see Sudbury.

BELFORD Northd. 401 402 O 17 – pop. 1 177 – ☎ 01668.

♦London 335 – ♦Edinburgh 71 – ♦Newcastle upon Tyne 49.

Blue Bell, Market Pl., NE70 7NE, ☎ 213543, Fax 213787, – rest. AE VISA
Meals (bar lunch)/dinner 21.00 **t.** and a la carte 4.75 – **17 rm** 44.00/92.00 **t.** – SB.

Purdy Lodge, Adderstone Services, NE70 7JU, on A 1 at junction with B 1341 ☎ 213000, Fax 213111 – AE VISA
Meals (bar lunch)/dinner a la carte 9.00/24.20 **st.** – 4.95 – **20 rm** 37.50 **st.**

BELLINGHAM Northd. 401 402 N 18 pop. 1 164 – ✉ Hexham – ☎ 01434.

Boggle Hole ☎ 220530.

Main St., NE48 2BQ ☎ 220616.

♦London 315 – Carlisle 48 – Newcastle upon Tyne 33.

Riverdale Hall ⓢ, NE48 2JT, E : ½ m. ☎ 220254, Fax 220457, ≤, ⓢ, ⓢ, ⓢ – TV ☎ P. AE VISA JCB
Meals 18.00 (dinner) and a la carte 10.15/19.65 **st.** 4.95 – **19 rm** ⊐ 40.00/76.00 **st.** – SB.

Westfield House, NE48 2DP, ☎ 220340, Fax 220340, – ⓢ P. VISA.
Meals (communal dining) (by arrangement) 13.50 **st.** – **5 rm** ⊐ 25.00/50.00.

BELPER Derbs. 402 403 404 P 24 – pop. 16 960 – ☎ 01332.

♦London 141 – Derby 8 – ♦Manchester 55 – ♦Nottingham 17.

Makeney Hall Country House ⓢ, Makeney, Milford, DE56 0RU, S : 2 m. by A 6 ☎ 842999, Fax 842777, – ⓢ rm TV ☎ ⓢ P – 180. AE VISA
Meals *(closed Saturday lunch)* 10.50/22.50 **t.** and a la carte – ⊐ 8.50 – **44 rm** 65.00/90.00 **t.**, 1 suite – SB.

BENENDEN Kent 404 V 30 pop. 1 727 – ✉ Cranbrook – ☎ 01580.

♦London 50 – Hastings 20 – Maidstone 20.

Crit Hall, Cranbrook Rd, TN17 4EU, W : 1 m. on B 2086 ☎ 240609, Fax 241743, – ⓢ TV P. VISA.
closed 15 December-10 January – **Meals** (by arrangement) (communal dining) 17.50 **st.** 3.50 – **3 rm** ⊐ 30.00/50.00 **st.** – SB.

During the season, particularly in resorts, it is wise to book in advance.

BEPTON W. Sussex – see Midhurst.

BERKELEY Glos. 403 404 M 28 **Great Britain G.** – pop. 1 550 – ☎ 01453.

See : Berkeley Castle** *AC*.

Exc. : Wildfowl and Wetlands Trust, Slimbridge* *AC*, NE : 6½ m. by B 4066 and A 38.

♦London 129 – ♦Bristol 20 – ♦Cardiff 50 – Gloucester 18.

Prince of Wales, Berkeley Rd, GL13 9HD, NE : 2 ½ m. by B 4066 on A 38 ☎ 810474, Fax 511370, – TV ☎ P – 200. AE VISA JCB
Meals 15.00/20.00 **st.** and a la carte 4.95 – ⊐ 5.95 – **41 rm** 39.00/55.00 **st.** – SB.

Old School House, 34 Canonbury St., GL11 9BG, ☎ 811711, Fax 511761 – TV ☎ P. VISA
Meals 9.95/13.95 **t.** and a la carte 4.50 – **7 rm** ⊐ 38.00/48.50 **t.** – SB.

BERKSWELL W. Mids. 403 404 P 26 – see Coventry.

BERWICK-UPON-TWEED Northd. 401 402 O 16 **Great Britain and Scotland G.** – pop. 26 731 – ☎ 01289.

See : Town* - Walls*.

Envir. : Foulden*, NW : 5 m. – Paxton House (Chippendale furniture*) *AC*, W : 5 m. by A 6105, A 1 and B 6461.

Exc. : SW : Tweed Valley** – Eyemouth Museum* *AC*, N : 7½ m. by A 1 and A 1107 – Holy Island* (Priory ruins* *AC*, Lindisfarne Castle* *AC*) SE : 9 m. by A 1167 and A 1.

Goswick Beal ☎ 387256 – Magdalene Fields ☎ 306384.

Castlegate Car Park, TD15 1JS ☎ 330733.

♦London 349 – ♦Edinburgh 57 – ♦Newcastle upon Tyne 63.

Marshall Meadows Country House ⓢ, TD15 1UT, N : 2 ¾ m. by A 1167 and A 1 ☎ 331133, Fax 331438, , park, – TV ☎ P. VISA
Meals 18.00 **t.** (dinner) and a la carte 12.00/29.00 **t.** 5.00 – **17 rm** ⊐ 55.00/75.00 **t.**, 1 suite – SB.

Harberton, 181 Main St., Spittal, TD15 1RP, SE : 2¼ m. by A 1167 ☎ 308813, ≤, – ⓢ TV P.
closed Christmas and New Year – **Meals** 10.00 **s.** – **5 rm** ⊐ 17.50/44.00 **s.**

ATS 78-80 Church St. ☎ 308222

BETHERSDEN Kent 404 W 30 – pop. 1 341 – ✉ Ashford – ☎ 01233.

♦London 63 – Folkestone 20 – Maidstone 27.

Little Hodgeham ⓢ, Smarden Rd, TN26 3HE, W : 2 m. ☎ 850323, « 15C cottage, antique furniture », ⓢ, – ⓢ rest P.
mid March-October – **Meals** (by arrangement) (communal dining) 17.50 **s.** 6.50 – **3 rm** ⊐ (dinner included) 59.00/69.00 **s.**

BEVERLEY Humbs. 402 S 22 Great Britain G. – pop. 12 914 – ✉ Kingston-upon-Hull – ☎ 01482.

See : Town★ - Minster★★ – St. Mary's Church★.

18 The Westwood ✆ 867190.

The Guildhall, Register Sq., HU17 9AU ✆ 867430/883898.

London 188 – Kingston-upon-Hull 8 – Leeds 52 – York 29.

Beverley Arms (Forte), North Bar Within, HU17 8DD, ✆ 869241, Fax 870907 – 60.
Meals *(closed Bank Holidays)* 10.50/17.95 **st.** and a la carte 5.25 – 8.95 – **57 rm** 60.00/90.00 **st.** – SB.

Kings Head, 38 Market Pl., HU17 9AH, ✆ 868103, Fax 871201 –
accommodation closed 25 December – **Meals** 6.95 **t.** and a la carte 4.50 – **12 rm** 39.50/49.50 **st.** – SB.

Lairgate, 30 Lairgate, HU17 8EP, ✆ 882141, Fax 861067 –
Meals 8.95/15.00 **t.** and dinner a la carte 5.00 – **22 rm** 40.00/65.00 **st.** – SB.

Cerutti 2, Beverley Station, Station Sq., HU17 0AS, ✆ 866700 –
closed Sunday and Bank Holidays – **Meals** a la carte 13.50/20.75 **t.**

at Tickton NE : 3½ m. by A 1035 – ✉ Kingston-upon-Hull – ☎ 01964 :

Tickton Grange, HU17 9SH, on A 1035 ✆ 543666, Fax 542556, – 60.
Meals 12.95/19.95 **t.** 5.25 – 7.50 – **18 rm** 49.50/59.50 **st.**

at Walkington SW : 3½ m. by A 164 – ✉ Beverley – ☎ 01482 :

Manor House with rm, Northlands, Newbald Rd, HU17 8RT, NE : 1 m. by Northgate ✆ 881645, Fax 866501, « Late 19C house, conservatory », –
Meals (dinner only) 15.00 **t.** and a la carte 4.00 – 8.50 – **7 rm** 70.00/100.00 **st.** – SB.

ATS 379 Grovehill Rd ✆ 386855/3882644

BEXHILL E. Sussex 404 V 31 – pop. 38 905 – ☎ 01424.

18 Cooden Beach ✆ 842040 – 18 Highwoods, Ellerslie Lane ✆ 212625.

De La Warr Pavilion, Marina, TN40 1DP ✆ 212023.

London 66 – Brighton 32 – Folkestone 42.

Jarvis Cooden Beach, Cooden Sea Rd, Cooden Beach, TN39 4TT, W : 2 m. on B 2182 ✆ 842281, Fax 846142, heated, – 140.
Meals 9.95/15.00 **st.** and a la carte 4.50 – **41 rm** 70.00/113.00 **st.** – SB.

Lychgates, 5a Church St., Old Town, TN40 2HE, ✆ 212193 –
closed Sunday to Tuesday, 2 weeks in summer and Bank Holiday Mondays – **Meals** (booking essential) (lunch by arrangement) 10.00/21.95 5.50.

BIBURY Glos. 403 404 O 28 Great Britain G. – pop. 570 – ✉ Cirencester – ☎ 01285.

See : Village★.

London 86 – Gloucester 26 – Oxford 30.

Swan, GL7 5NW, ✆ 740695, Fax 740473, « Attractively furnished inn with gardens and trout stream », – rest
Meals (dinner only and Sunday lunch)/dinner 21.50 **st.** and a la carte 26.45/39.30 **st.** 6.50 – **Jankowski's Brasserie : Meals** a la carte 13.70/18.00 **st.** 6.50 – **18 rm** 89.00/210.00 **st.** – SB.

Cotteswold House without rest., Arlington, GL7 5ND, on B 4425 ✆ 740609 –
3 rm 25.00/38.00.

BICKLEIGH Devon 403 J 31 The West Country G. – pop. 3 595 – ✉ Tiverton – ☎ 01884.

See : Village★★ - Bickleigh Mill Craft Centre and Farms★★ *AC* – Bickleigh Castle★ *AC*.

Envir. : Tiverton : Museum★ *AC*, N : 2½m. by A 396 – Knightshayes Court★ *AC*, N : 4 m. by A 396.

Exc. : Uffculme (Coldharbour Mill★★ *AC*) NE : 7½m..

18 Post Hill Tiverton ✆ 252114.

London 195 – Exeter 9 – Taunton 31.

Fisherman's Cot, EX16 8RW, on A 396 ✆ 855289, Fax 855241, « Riverside setting », – rm
Meals (carving lunch)/dinner a la carte 8.40/13.20 **t.** 6.50 – **23 rm** 46.00/66.00 **t.**

Bickleigh Cottage, Bickleigh Bridge, EX16 8RJ, on A 396 ✆ 855230, « Part 17C thatched cottage, riverside setting », –
April-October – **Meals** (residents only) (dinner only) 11.50 – **9 rm** 22.50/47.50.

BICKLEY MOSS Ches. 402 404 L 24 – ✉ Malpas – ☎ 01829.

London 180 – Birmingham 63 – Chester 16 – Shrewsbury 27 – Stoke-on-Trent 25.

Cholmondeley Arms, Cholmondeley, SY14 8BT, N : 1 ½ m. on A 49 ✆ 720300, Fax 720123, –
closed 25 December – **Meals** a la carte 11.70/15.85 **t.** 5.55 – **4 rm** 36.00/49.00 **st.** – SB.

BIDDENDEN Kent 404 V 30 Great Britain G. – pop. 2 205 – ✉ Ashford – ☎ 01580.
Envir. : Sissinghurst Castle★ *AC*, W : 3 m. by A 262.
♦London 51 – Folkestone 29 – Hastings 23 – Maidstone 14.

XX **West House,** 28 High St., TN27 8AH, ☎ 291341 – P. AE VISA
closed Sunday dinner, Monday, 1 week April and 1 week October – **Meals** - Italian - 5.45/16.50 **st.** and a la carte 4.95.

BIDEFORD Devon 403 H 30 The West Country G. – pop. 13 066 – ☎ 01237.
See : Bridge★★ – Burton Art Gallery★ *AC*.
Envir. : Appledore★, N : 2 m.
Exc. : Clovelly★★, W : 11 m. by A 39 and B 3237 – Lundy Island★★, NW : by ferry – Great Torrington (Dartington Crystal★ *AC*) SE : 7½m. by A 386.
18 Royal North Devon, Golf Links Rd, Westward Ho ☎ 473824 – 9 Torrington, Weare Trees ☎ (01805) 622229.
to the Isle of Lundy (Lundy Co.) (2 h 15 mn).
Victoria Park, The Quay, EX39 2QQ ☎ 477676/421853.
♦London 231 – Exeter 43 – ♦Plymouth 58 – Taunton 60.

Durrant House, Heywood Rd, Northam, EX39 3QB, N : 1 ¼ m. by B 3235 on A 386 ☎ 472361, Fax 421709, – TV ☎ P – 400. AE VISA
closed 2 weeks January – **Meals** (bar lunch)/dinner 17.50 **t.** and a la carte 5.50 – **123 rm** 40.00/81.00 **t.**, 2 suites – SB.

Newbridge, Heywood Rd, Northam, EX39 3QA, N : 1 ¼ m. by B 3235 on A 386 ☎ 474989, Fax 474989 – rest TV ☎ P. VISA.
Meals *(closed Sunday dinner to non-residents)* (dinner only and Sunday lunch)/dinner 16.00 **t.** 4.50 – **10 rm** 35.00/70.00 **t.** – SB.

at Instow N : 3 m. by A 386 on B 3233 – ✉ Bideford – ☎ 01271 :

Commodore, Marine Par., EX39 4JN, ☎ 860347, Fax 861233, ← Taw and Torridge estuaries, – TV ☎ P – 200
20 rm.

at Eastleigh NE : 2½ m. by A 386 (via Old Barnstaple Rd) – ✉ Bideford – ☎ 01271 :

Pines, EX39 4PA, ☎ 860561, Fax 860561, ←, – TV ☎ P. VISA
Meals (by arrangement) 14.00 **st.** – **5 rm** 28.00/50.00 **st.** – SB.

ATS New Rd ☎ 472451

BIGBURY-ON-SEA Devon 403 I 33 – pop. 600 – ✉ Kingsbridge – ☎ 01548.
♦London 196 – Exeter 42 – ♦Plymouth 17.

Henley, Folly Hill, TQ7 4AR, ☎ 810240, Fax 810020, ← Bigbury Bay and Bolt Tail, – TV ☎ P. AE VISA
April-October – 3.75 – **7 rm** (dinner included) 42.00/90.00 **st.** – SB.

BIGGLESWADE Beds. 404 T 27 – ☎ 01767.
♦London 44 – Bedford 11 – ♦Cambridge 23 – Peterborough 37.

Stratton House, London Rd, SG18 8ED, ☎ 312442, Fax 600416 – TV ☎ P – 30. AE VISA.
Meals 6.95/10.95 **st.** and a la carte 3.70 – 4.95 – **31 rm** 30.00/38.00 **st.**

BILBROOK Somerset 403 J 30 – ✉ Minehead – ☎ 01984.
Envir. : Washford – Cleeve Abbey★★ *AC*, E : 1 m. by A 39 – Dunster★★ – Castle★★ *AC* (upper rooms ←★) Water Mill★ *AC*, St. George's Church★, Dovecote★, NW : 3 m. by A 39.
♦London 179 – ♦Bristol 56 – Minehead 7 – Taunton 17.

Dragon House, TA24 6HQ, on A 39 ☎ 40215, Fax 41340, « Part 18C », – TV ☎ P
9 rm.

BILBROUGH N. Yorks. 402 Q 22 – see York.

BILLESLEY Warks. – see Stratford-upon-Avon.

BILLINGSHURST W. Sussex 404 S 30 – pop. 5 770 – ☎ 01403.
♦London 44 – ♦Brighton 24 – Guildford 25 – ♦Portsmouth 40.

Forte Travelodge, Five Oaks, Stane St., RH14 9AE, N : 1 m. on A 29 ☎ 78271 Reservations (Freephone) 0800 850950 – TV P. AE VISA.
Meals (grill rest.) – **26 rm** 34.50 **t.**

Old Wharf without rest., Wharf Farm, Newbridge, RH14 0JG, W : 1 ¾ m. on A 27 ☎ 784096, Fax 784096, ←, « Restored canalside warehouse », , park – TV ☎ P. AE VISA.
closed 2 weeks Christmas-New Year – 5.50 – **4 rm** 40.00/50.00 **t.**

XX **Gables,** Pulborough Rd, Parbrook, RH14 9EU, S : ½ m. on A 29 ☎ 782571, Fax 784094 P. AE VISA
closed Saturday lunch, Sunday dinner, Monday, 2 weeks April-May and Bank Holidays 15.25/20.75 **t.** 5.50.

BILSBURROW Lancs. – see Garstang.

BINBROOK Lincs. 402 404 T 23 pop. 1 605 – 01472.

London 162 – Great Grimsby 10 – Lincoln 26 – Scunthorpe 32.

Hoe Hill, Swinhope, LN3 6HX, NE : 1 m. on B 1203 ℘ 398206, – rm. *closed January* – **Meals** (by arrangement) (communal dining) 12.00 – **4 rm** 15.00/50.00 **s.**

BINGHAM Notts. 402 404 R 25 pop. 7 057 – 01949.

London 125 – Lincoln 28 – Nottingham 11 – Sheffield 35.

Bingham Court, Ming House, Market St., NG13 8AB, ℘ 831831, Fax 838833 – . *closed 25 and 26 December* – **Meals** - (see ***Yeung Sing*** below) – **15 rm** 39.00/50.00 **t.**

Yeung Sing (at Bingham Court H.), Ming House, Market St., NG13 8AB, ℘ 831222, Fax 838833 – . *closed 25 and 26 December* – **Meals** - Chinese (Canton) - (dinner only and Sunday lunch)/dinner 18.00 **t.** and a la carte.

ATS 1 Moorbridge Rd ℘ 837717

BINGLEY W. Yorks. 402 O 22 – pop. 28 196 – Bradford – 01274.

St. Ives Est. ℘ 562436.

London 204 – Bradford 6 – Skipton 13.

Jarvis Bankfield, Bradford Rd, BD16 1TU, SE : 1 ½ m. on A 650 ℘ 567123, Fax 551331, – rm rest – 200. **Meals** (carving rest.) (bar lunch Saturday) 7.95/15.00 **t.** and dinner a la carte – 8.50 – **103 rm** 69.00/89.00 **st.** – SB.

Five Rise Locks, Beck Lane, BD16 4DD, ℘ 565296, Fax 568828 – rest. *closed Christmas and New Year* – **Meals** 14.00 **st.** 4.00 – **9 rm** 45.00/55.00 **st.**

Holroyd House, Beck Rd, Micklethwaite, BD16 3JN, N : 1 ¾ m. by A 650 and Micklethwaite Lane ℘ 562464, – . **Meals** (by arrangement) 11.00 **s.** – **3 rm** 18.00/36.00.

Christophers', 7-9 Chapel Lane, BD16 2NG, ℘ 510742 – *closed Sunday and first 2 weeks January* – **Meals** 9.25/14.95 **t.** and a la carte.

BINLEY W. Mids. – see Coventry.

BIRCHINGTON Kent 404 X 29 pop. 9 859 – 01843.

London 71 – Dover 20 – Maidstone 40 – Margate 5.

Crown Inn (Cherry Brandy House), Ramsgate Rd, Sarre, CT7 OLF, SW : 4 m. on A 28 ℘ 847808, Fax 847914 – rm. **Meals** (bar lunch and Sunday dinner)/dinner a la carte 15.10/22.10 **t.** – **12 rm** 43.50/66.75 **t.** – SB.

BIRCH SERVICE AREA Gtr. Manchester 402 ㉒ 403 ③ 404 ⑩ – Heywood (Lancs.) – 0161.

Granada Lodge without rest., OL10 2QH, on M 62, between junctions 18 and 19 ℘ 655 3403, Fax 655 3358, Reservations (Freephone) 0800 555300 – – **39 rm** 39.95 **st.**

BIRDLIP Glos. 403 404 N 28 **Great Britain G.** – Gloucester – 01452.

Envir. : Crickley Hill Country Park (<*) N : 1½m. by B 4070 and A 417.

London 107 – Bristol 51 – Gloucester 9 – Oxford 44 – Swindon 24.

Royal George, GL4 8JH, ℘ 862506, Fax 862277, – rm – 100. **Meals** a la carte 12.15/21.95 **st.** – **34 rm** 55.00/65.00 **t.** – SB.

Kingshead House, GL4 8JH, ℘ 862299 – *closed Saturday lunch, Sunday dinner, Monday, 12 days summer and 1 and 2 January* – **Meals** 24.00 **t.** (dinner) and lunch a la carte 16.75/21.75 **t.** 6.00.

BIRKENHEAD Mersey. 402 403 K 23 – pop. 14 900 – 0151.

Arrowe Park, Woodchurch ℘ 677 1527 – Prenton, Golf Links Rd, Prenton ℘ 608 1461.

to Liverpool and Wallasey (Mersey Ferries).

Woodside Visitors Centre, Woodside Ferry Terminal, L41 6DU ℘ 647 6780.

London 222 – Liverpool 2.

Plan : see Liverpool p. 3

Bowler Hat, 2 Talbot Rd, Oxton, L43 2HH, ℘ 652 4931, Fax 653 8127, – 200. AX **Meals** 9.95/19.55 **t.** and a la carte 4.75 – **32 rm** 62.50/88.00 **t.** – SB.

Beadles, 15 Rosemount, Oxton, L43 5SG, ℘ 653 9010 – AX *closed Sunday, Monday, 2 weeks February and 2 weeks August-September* – **Meals** (dinner only) a la carte approx. 19.75 **t.**

ATS 40 Mill Lane, Wallasey, Wirral ℘ 638 1949/8606

BIRMINGHAM W. Mids. 403 404 O 26 **Great Britain G.** – pop. 961 041 – ☎ 0121.

See : City★ – Museum and Art Gallery★★ JZ **M2** – Barber Institute of Fine Arts★★ (at Birmingham University) EX – Museum of Science and Industry★ JY **M3** – Cathedral of St. Philip (stained glass portrayals★) KYZ.

Envir. : Aston Hall★★ FV **M.**

Exc. : Black Country Museum★, Dudley, NW : 10 m. by A 456 and A 4123 AU.

Edgbaston, Church Rd ✆ 454 1736, FX – Hilltop, Park Lane, Handsworth ✆ 554 4463, CU – Hatchford Brook, Coventry Rd, Sheldon ✆ 743 9821, HX – Brand Hall, Heron Rd, Oldbury, Warley ✆ 552 2195, BU – Harborne Church Farm, Vicarage Rd, Harborne ✆ 427 1204, EX.

Birmingham Airport : ✆ 767 5511, E : 6½m. by A 45 DU.

Convention & Visitor Bureau, 2 City Arcade, B2 4TX ✆ 643 2514 – Convention & Visitor Bureau, National Exhibition Centre, B40 1NT ✆ 780 4321 – Birmingham Airport, Information Desk, B26 3QJ ✆ 767 7145/7146.

♦London 122 – ♦Bristol 91 – ♦Liverpool 103 – ♦Manchester 86 – ♦Nottingham 50.

Town plans : Birmingham pp. 2-7
Except where otherwise stated see pp. 6 and 7

Hyatt Regency, 2 Bridge St., B1 2JZ, ✆ 643 1234, Telex 335097, Fax 616 2323, ≤, – rm TV ☎ – 250. AE VISA. JZ **a**
Meals - (see ***Number 282*** below) – 12.00 – **315 rm** 99.00 **st.**, 4 suites – SB.

Swallow, 12 Hagley Rd, B16 8SJ, ✆ 452 1144, Fax 456 3442, – rm TV ☎ – 25. AE VISA p. 4 FX **c**
Langtrys : Meals *(closed Sunday) a la carte* 19.35/32.20 **st.** 8.00 – (see also ***Sir Edward Elgar's*** below) – **94 rm** 130.00/150.00 **st.**, 4 suites – SB.

Holiday Inn Crowne Plaza, Central Sq., Holliday St., B1 1HH, ✆ 631 2000, Fax 643 9018, – rm TV ☎ – 150. AE VISA JZ **z**
Meals 13.95/17.95 **st.** and a la carte 8.50 – 10.95 – **281 rm** 108.00/118.00 **st.**, 3 suites – SB.

Copthorne, Paradise Circus, B3 3HJ, ✆ 200 2727, Telex 339026, Fax 200 1197, – rm rest TV ☎ – 180. AE VISA JCB. JZ **e**
Meals a la carte 15.30/28.70 **st.** 6.00 – 10.60 – **209 rm** 110.00/135.00, 3 suites.

Jonathan's, 16-24 Wolverhampton Rd, Oldbury, B68 0LH, W : 4 m. by A 456 ✆ 429 3757, Fax 434 3107, « Authentic Victorian furnishings and memorabilia » – rest TV ☎. AE VISA p. 2 BU **e**
Meals - English - *(closed Sunday dinner)* 12.90/24.50 **t.** and a la carte 6.00 – **19 rm** 69.00/118.00 **st.**, 11 suites – SB.

Grand (Q.M.H.), Colmore Row, B3 2DA, ✆ 607 9955, Fax 233 1465 – rm rest TV ☎ – 500. AE VISA JKY **c**
Meals 12.95/18.50 **st.** and a la carte. 7.00 – 9.95 – **171 rm** 87.50/102.50 **st.**, 2 suites – SB.

Plough and Harrow (Forte), 135 Hagley Rd, Edgbaston, B16 8LS, ✆ 454 4111, Fax 454 1868, – TV ☎ – 70. AE VISA JCB p. 4 EX **a**
Meals *(closed Saturday lunch)* 11.25/16.95 **t.** and a la carte 6.05 – 7.95 – **42 rm** 75.00 **st.**, 2 suites – SB.

Forte Crest, Smallbrook Queensway, B5 4EW, ✆ 643 8171, Fax 631 2528, squash – rm TV ☎ – 630. AE VISA JCB KZ **o**
Meals 12.95/14.95 **st.** and a la carte – 10.85 – **252 rm** 89.00/119.00 **st.**, 1 suite – SB.

Strathallan Thistle, 225 Hagley Rd, Edgbaston, B16 9RY, ✆ 455 9777, Telex 336680, Fax 454 9432 – rm rest TV ☎ – 170. AE VISA JCB p. 4 EX **i**
Meals *(closed Saturday lunch)* 12.25/17.25 **st.** and a la carte 5.25 – 9.25 – **163 rm** 79.00/89.00 **st.**, 4 suites.

Novotel, 70 Broad St., B1 2HT, ✆ 643 2000, Telex 335556, Fax 643 9796, – rm rest TV ☎ – 250. AE VISA p. 4 FV **a**
Meals 13.95/17.95 **st.** and a la carte 5.50 – 8.00 – **148 rm** 71.00/81.00 **st.**

Chamberlain, Alcester St., B12 0PJ, ✆ 606 9000, Fax 606 9001 – rest rest TV ☎ – 400. AE VISA. FX **r**
Meals *(closed Saturday lunch)* (carving rest.) 6.00/9.00 **t.** – **250 rm** 35.00/40.00 **t.**

Royal Angus Thistle, St. Chad's, Queensway, B4 6HY, ✆ 236 4211, Fax 233 2195 – rm TV ☎ – 140. AE VISA JCB KY **s**
Meals *(closed Saturday lunch)* 12.50/16.50 6.35 – 9.25 – **131 rm** 79.00/99.00 **st.** 2 suites – SB.

Apollo (Mount Charlotte), 243 Hagley Rd, Edgbaston, B16 9RA, ✆ 455 0271, Telex 336759, Fax 456 2394 – rm rest TV ☎ – 150. AE VISA JCB p. 4 EX **o**
Meals *(closed Saturday lunch and Bank Holidays)* (carving lunch) 9.95/12.80 **st** and a la carte 5.30 – 8.75 – **124 rm** 58.00/68.00 **st.**, 2 suites – SB.

Asquith House, 19 Portland Rd, off Hagley Rd, Edgbaston, B16 9HN, ☎ 454 5282, Fax 456 4668, « Attractive furnishings », – TV ☎. AE VISA. p. 4 EX **c**
closed Christmas – **Meals** (by arrangement Sunday dinner and Bank Holidays) 17.00/35.95 **t.** and a la carte 4.95 – **10 rm** 51.10/67.00 **t.**

Westbourne Lodge, 27-29 Fountain Rd, Edgbaston, B17 8NJ, ☎ 429 1003, Fax 429 7436, – TV ☎ P. AE VISA. p. 4 EV **x**
Meals 9.95/14.95 **t.** 5.00 – **18 rm** 42.00/52.00 **t.**

Copperfield House, 60 Upland Rd, Selly Park, B29 7JS, ☎ 472 8344, Fax 415 5655, – rest TV ☎ P. AE VISA p. 4 FX **a**
Meals (bar lunch)/dinner 17.75 **st.** – **17 rm** 47.50/67.50 **t.** – SB.

Bearwood Court, 360-366 Bearwood Rd, Bearwood, B66 4ET, ☎ 429 9731, Fax 429 6175 – TV ☎ P. VISA. EV **e**
Meals *(closed lunch Sunday and Bank Holidays)* 5.50/18.00 **st.** and dinner a la carte 4.50 – **24 rm** 25.00/46.00 **st.**

Travel Inn, 20-22 Bridge St., B1 2JH, ☎ 633 4820, Fax 633 4779 – rm TV P – 40. AE VISA. JZ **c**
Meals (grill rest.) – 4.95 – **54 rm** 34.50 **t.**

Quality Cobden (Friendly), 166-174 Hagley Rd, Edgbaston, B16 9NZ, ☎ 454 6621, Fax 456 2935, , – rm TV ☎ P – 100. AE VISA JCB. p. 4 EX **e**
Meals 8.95/13.50 **st.** and a la carte 4.75 – 7.75 – **230 rm** 54.50/70.00 **st.** – SB.

Hagley Court, 229 Hagley Rd, Edgbaston, B16 9RP, ☎ 454 6514, Fax 456 2722 – TV ☎ P. AE VISA JCB. p. 4 EX **s**
closed 24 December-2 January – **Meals** *(closed Friday to Sunday)* (dinner only) 13.95 **st.** and a la carte 4.95 – **27 rm** 45.00/69.00 **st.** – SB.

Campanile, 55 Irving St., B1 1DH, ☎ 622 4925, Fax 622 4195 – TV ☎ P – 25. AE VISA p. 4 FX **e**
Meals (grill rest.) 10.35 **t.** and a la carte 4.65 – 4.50 – **47 rm** 35.75 **t.**

XXXX **Sir Edward Elgar's** (at Swallow H.), 12 Hagley Rd, B16 8SJ, ☎ 452 1144, Fax 456 3442 – P. AE VISA p. 4 FX **c**
closed Saturday lunch – **Meals** 17.50/30.00 **st.** and a la carte 8.00.

XX **Number 282** (at Hyatt Regency H.), 2 Bridge St., B1 2JZ, ☎ 643 1234, Fax 616 2323 – . AE VISA JZ **a**
Meals 12.75/35.00 **t.** and a la carte 7.00.

XX **Henry's,** 27 St. Paul's Sq., B3 1RB, ☎ 200 1136, Fax 200 1190 – . AE VISA JY **a**
closed Sunday and Bank Holidays – **Meals** - Chinese (Canton) - 13.00/20.00 **t.** and a la carte.

XX **Dynasty,** 93-103 Hurst St., B5 4TE, ☎ 622 1410 – AE VISA JCB KZ **e**
Meals - Chinese - (lunch by arrangement) 11.50 **st.** (dinner) and a la carte approx. 12.00/19.30 **st.**

XX Henry Wong, 283 High St., Harborne, B17 9QH, ☎ 427 9799 – p. 4 EX **n**
Meals - Chinese (Canton) rest..

XX **Maharaja,** 23-25 Hurst St., B5 4AS, ☎ 622 2641 – . AE VISA KZ **i**
closed Sunday, last week July and first week August – **Meals** - North Indian - a la carte 8.35/16.20 **t.**

XX **Franzl's,** 151 Milcote Rd, Bearwood, Smethwick, B67 5BN, ☎ 429 7920, Fax 429 1615 – AE VISA p. 4 EV **a**
closed Sunday, Monday and first 3 weeks August – **Meals** - Austrian - (dinner only) 13.45/19.45 **st.** 4.50.

at Hall Green SE : 5 ¾ m. by A 41 on A 34 – ✉ Birmingham – ☎ 0121 :

Robin Hood (Toby), Stratford Rd, B28 9ES, ☎ 745 9900, Fax 733 1075 – TV ☎ P. AE VISA GX **a**
Meals (grill rest.) 9.25 **st.** and a la carte 5.00 – **30 rm** 59.95/69.95 **st.** – SB.

at Birmingham Airport SE : 9 m. by A 45 - DU – ✉ Birmingham – ☎ 0121 :

Novotel, Passenger Terminal, B26 3QL, ☎ 782 7000, Telex 338158, Fax 782 0445 – rm rest TV ☎ – 35. AE VISA
closed 24-25 December – **Meals** *(closed lunch Saturday, Sunday and Bank Holidays)* 12.00/18.00 **st.** and a la carte 6.50 – 7.50 – **195 rm** 72.50/119.00 **st.**

Forte Posthouse, Coventry Rd, B26 3QW, on A 45 ☎ 782 8141, Fax 782 2476 – rm TV ☎ P – 130. AE VISA JCB
Meals a la carte 10.70/22.15 **st.** 5.75 – 7.95 – **136 rm** 56.00 **st.** – SB.

at National Exhibition Centre SE : 9½ m. on A 45 – DU – ✉ Birmingham – ☎ 0121 :

Birmingham Metropole, Bickenhill, B40 1PP, ☎ 780 4242, Telex 336129, Fax 780 3923, , , – rm TV ☎ P – 2000. AE VISA
closed Christmas and New Year – **Meals** (carving rest.) 23.50 **st.** – **Primavera : Meals** - Italian - a la carte 28.45/35.50 **st.** – **787 rm** 145.00/220.00, 15 suites – SB.

Arden, Coventry Rd, B92 0EH, ☎ (01675) 443221, Fax 443221, , , – TV ☎ P – 170. AE VISA JCB
Meals (bar lunch Saturday) 12.10 **t.** and a la carte 4.85 – 8.00 – **146 rm** 69.00/79.00 **st.**

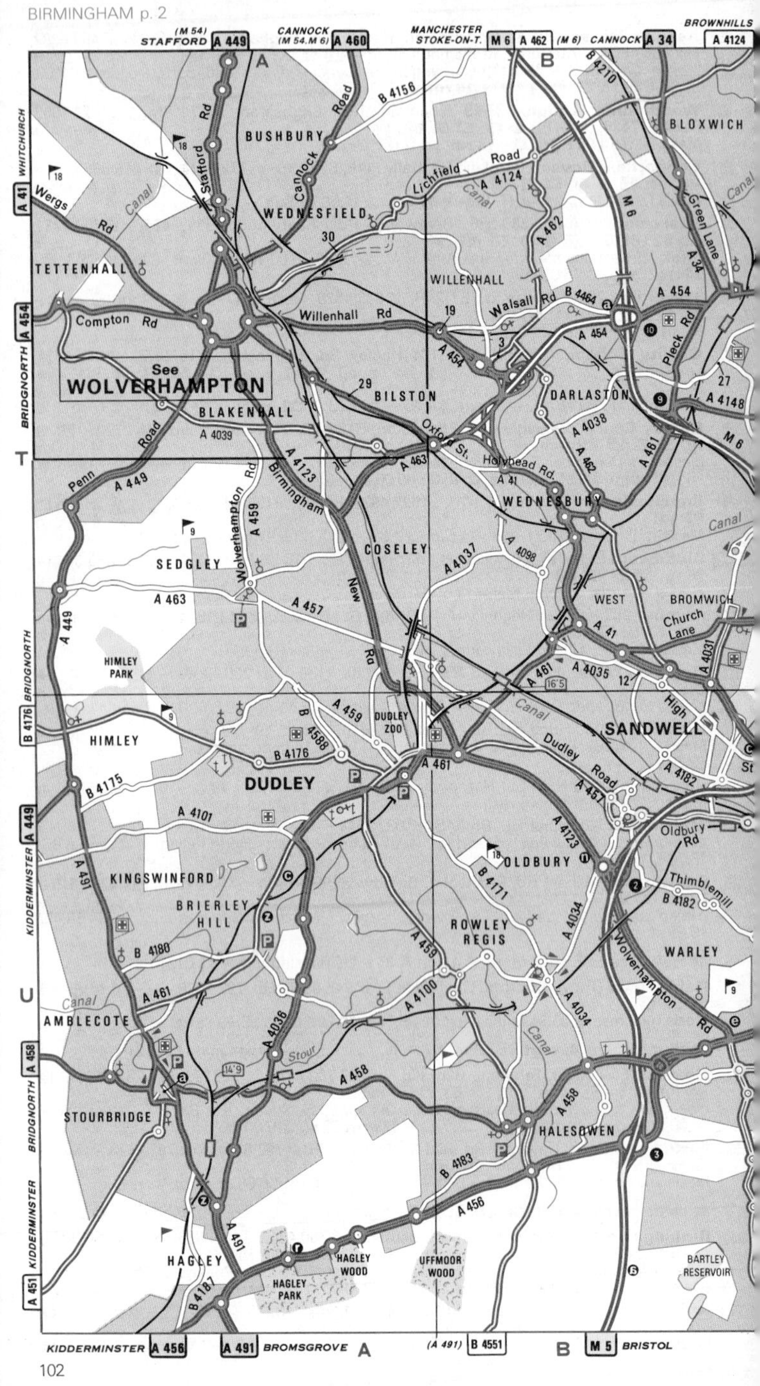
(M 54) STAFFORD A 449
CANNOCK (M 54.M 6) A 460
MANCHESTER STOKE-ON-T. M 6
A 462 (M 6) CANNOCK A 34
BROWNHILLS A 4124
WHITCHURCH A 41
BRIDGNORTH A 454
BRIDGNORTH B 4176
KIDDERMINSTER A 449
BRIDGNORTH A 458
KIDDERMINSTER A 451
KIDDERMINSTER A 456
A 491 BROMSGROVE
(A 491) B 4551
M 5 BRISTOL
BUSHBURY
WEDNESFIELD
BLOXWICH
TETTENHALL
WILLENHALL
See WOLVERHAMPTON
BILSTON
BLAKENHALL
DARLASTON
WEDNESBURY
SEDGLEY
COSELEY
WEST BROMWICH
HIMLEY PARK
HIMLEY
DUDLEY
DUDLEY ZOO
SANDWELL
KINGSWINFORD
BRIERLEY HILL
OLDBURY
ROWLEY REGIS
WARLEY
AMBLECOTE
STOURBRIDGE
HALESOWEN
HAGLEY
HAGLEY PARK
HAGLEY WOOD
UFFMOOR WOOD
BARTLEY RESERVOIR
Wergs Rd
Compton Rd
Stafford Rd
Cannock Road
Lichfield Road
Willenhall Rd
Walsall Rd
Green Lane
Pleck Rd
Penn Road
Wolverhampton Rd
Birmingham
New Rd
Oxford St.
Holyhead Rd.
Church Lane
High
Dudley Road
Oldbury Rd
Thimblemill
Wolverhampton Rd
Canal
Stour
A
B
T
U

BIRMINGHAM AND WOLVERHAMPTON
ENLARGED AREA

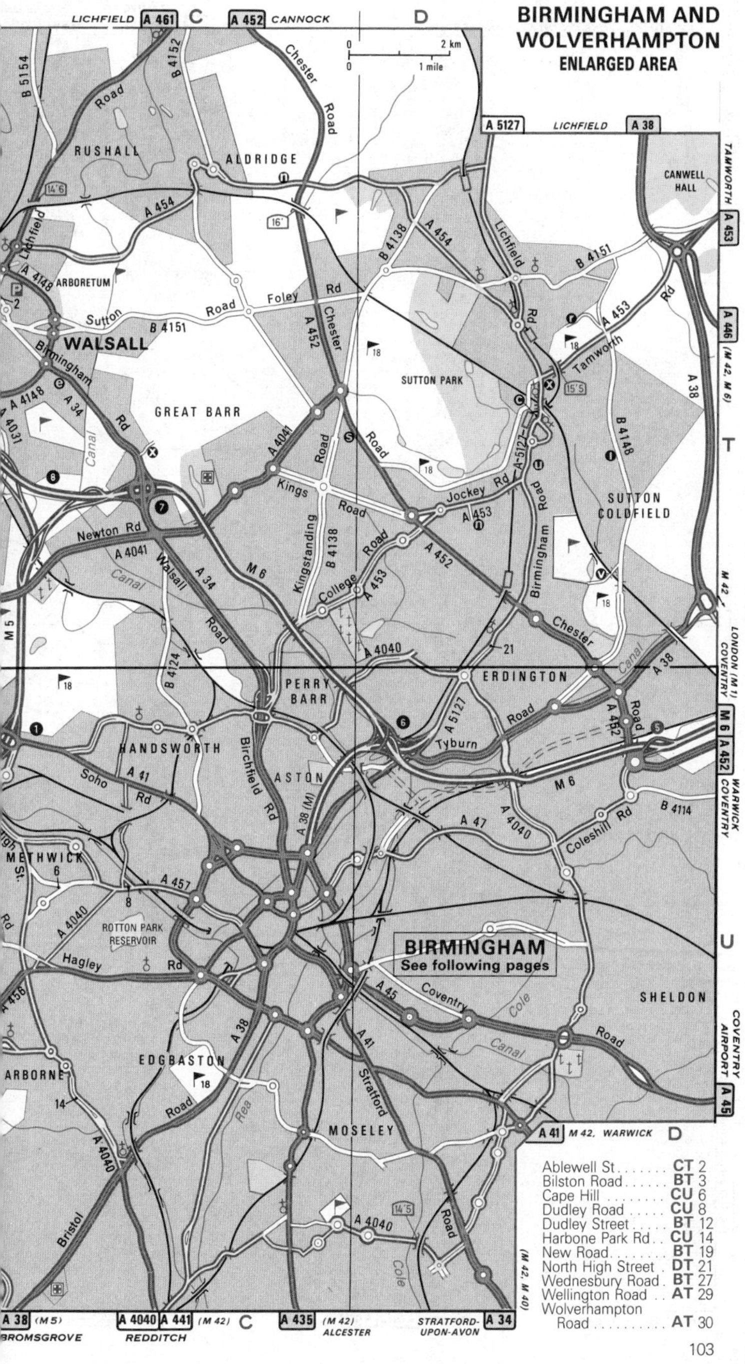

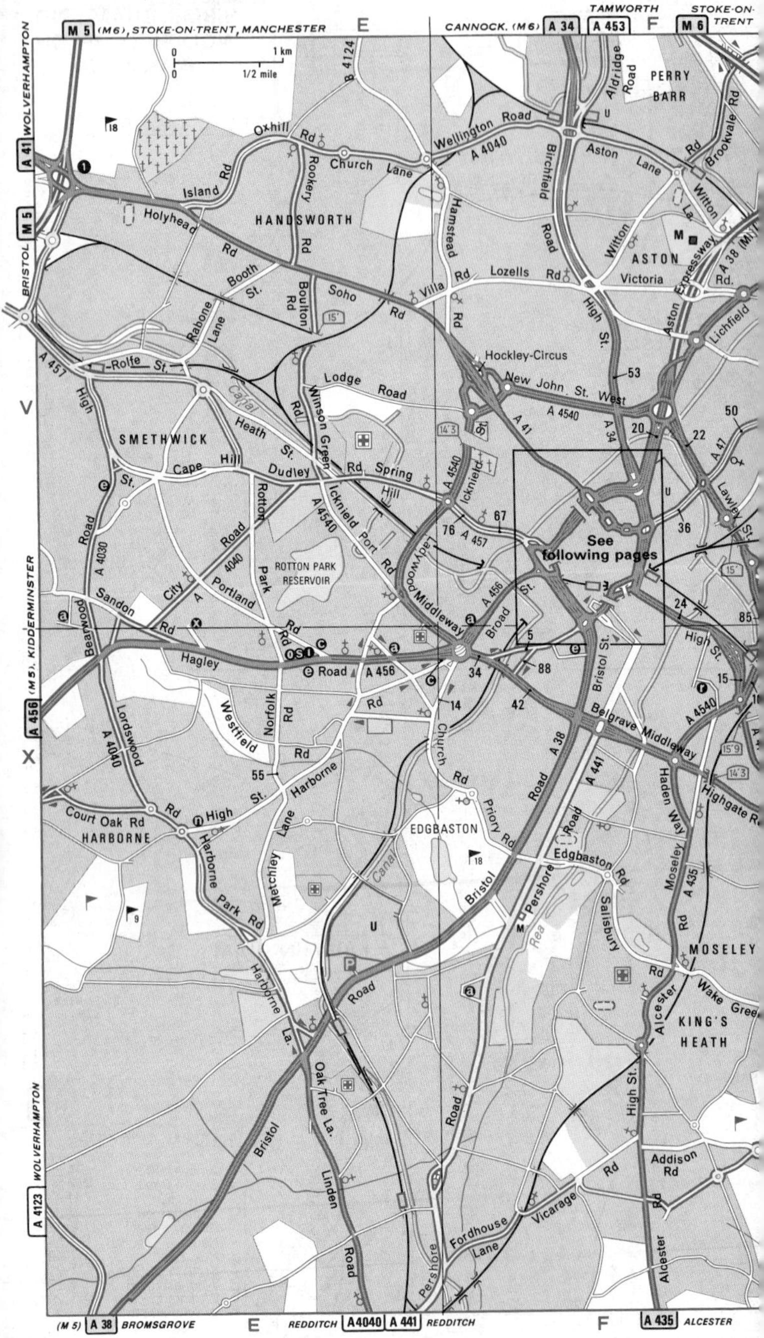

M 5 (M6), STOKE-ON-TRENT, MANCHESTER
E
CANNOCK. (M6) A 34
TAMWORTH A 453
F
M 6 STOKE-ON-TRENT
0 1 km
0 1/2 mile
A 41 WOLVERHAMPTON
M 5 BRISTOL
A 456 (M5), KIDDERMINSTER
A 4123 WOLVERHAMPTON
V
X
PERRY BARR
HANDSWORTH
ASTON
SMETHWICK
ROTTON PARK RESERVOIR
EDGBASTON
HARBORNE
MOSELEY
KING'S HEATH
Hockley-Circus
See following pages
Holyhead Rd
Island Rd
Oxhill Rd
Church Lane
Rookery Rd
Wellington Road
A 4040
Aldridge Road
Birchfield Road
Aston Lane
Brookvale Rd
Witton La.
Witton
Aston Expressway
A 38 (M)
Victoria Rd.
Hamstead Rd
Villa Rd
Lozells Rd
High St.
Soho Rd
Booth St.
Boulton Rd
Rabone Lane
Rolfe St.
A 457
High St.
Lodge Road
New John St. West
A 4540
A 41
A 34
Lichfield
A 47
Lawley St.
Winson Green Rd
Heath St.
Canal
Cape Hill
Dudley Rd
Spring Hill
Icknield St.
Icknield Port Rd
Rotton Park
Portland Rd
City Road A 4040
Sandon Rd
Bearwood Road
A 4030
Ladywood Middleway
A 456
Broad St.
Hagley Road A 456
Norfolk Rd
Westfield Rd
Lordswood A 4040
Harborne Rd
Church Rd
Bristol St.
Belgrave Middleway
A 38 Road
A 441
Haden Way
Highgate Rd
A 4540
High St.
Court Oak Rd
High St.
Harborne Park Rd
Metchley Lane
Harborne Lane
Priory Rd
Pershore Road
Edgbaston Rd
Salisbury Rd
Moseley Rd A 435
Alcester Rd
Wake Green
Rea
Bristol Road
Harborne La.
Oak Tree La.
Linden Road
Pershore Road
Fordhouse Lane
Vicarage Rd
Addison Rd
Alcester Rd
B 4124
53 20 22 50 67 76 36 24 85 15 5 34 88 42 14 55
(M 5) A 38 BROMSGROVE
E
REDDITCH A4040 A 441 REDDITCH
F
A 435 ALCESTER

BUILT UP AREA

Bath Row	FX 5
Bordesley Middleway	FX 10
Calthorpe Rd	FX 14
Camp Hill	FX 15
Corporation St.	FV 20
Darmouth Middleway	FV 22
Digbeth	FV 24
Dudley Park Rd	GX 25
High St.	GV 31
Islington Row Middleway	FX 34
Jennen's Rd	FV 36
Lee Bank Middleway	FX 42
Nechell's Parkway	FV 50
New Town Row	FV 53
Nursery Rd	EX 55
Saltley Rd	GV 66
Sand Pits Parade	FV 67
Solihull Lane	GX 74
Summer Hill Rd	FV 76
Watery Lane	FV 85
Westley Rd	GX 87
Wheeley's Lane	FX 88

For Street Index see Birmingham p. 7

CENTRE

Albert St. . . . . **KZ** 2
Bull St. . . . . **KY** 13
Dale End . . . . **KZ** 21
Hall St. . . . . **JY** 29
Holloway Circus . . . . **JZ** 32
James Watt Queensway . . **KY** 35
Jennen's Rd . . . . **KY** 36
Lancaster Circus . . . . **KY** 39
Lancaster St. . . . . **KY** 41
Masshouse Circus . . . . **KY** 43
Moor St. Queensway . . . . . **KZ** 46
Navigation St. . . . . **JZ** 49
Newton St. . . . . **KY** 52
Paradise Circus . . . . **JZ** 56
Priory Queensway . . . . **KY** 57
St Chads Circus . . . . **JKY** 62
St Chads Ringway . . . . **KY** 63
St Martin's Circus . . . . **KZ** 64
Shadwell St. . . . . **KY** 70
Smallbrook Queensway . . . **KZ** 71
Snow Hill Queensway . . . . **KY** 73
Summer Row . . . . **JY** 77
Temple Row . . . . **KZ** 80
Waterloo St. . . . . **JZ** 84

For Street Index
see Birmingham p. 7

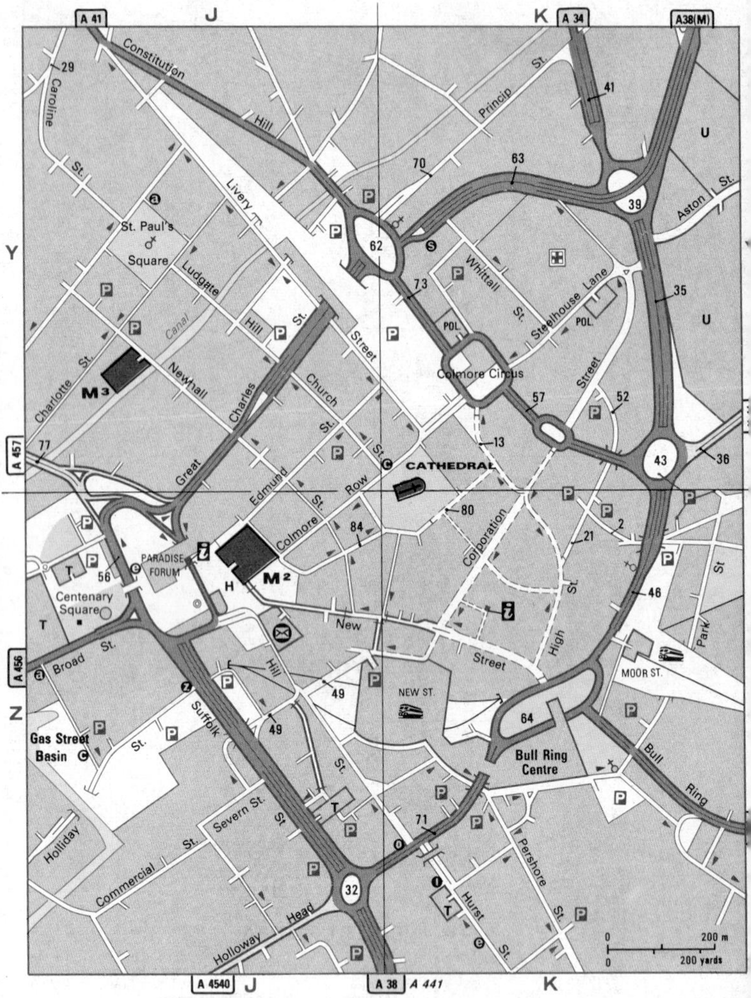

« Short Breaks »

Many hotels now offer a special rate for a stay of 2 nights which includes dinner, bed and breakfast.

STREET INDEX TO BIRMINGHAM TOWN PLANS

« Short Breaks » (SB)

De nombreux hôtels proposent des conditions avantageuses pour un séjour de deux nuits comprenant la chambre, le dîner et le petit déjeuner.

at Northfield SW : 6 m. by A 38 – CU – ✉ Birmingham – ☎ 0121 :

Norwood, 87-89 Bunbury Rd, B31 2ET, via Church rd ☎ 411 2202, Fax 411 2202, – TV ☎ P. VISA JCB
Meals *(closed Saturday and Sunday)* (dinner only) 15.00 6.50 – **15 rm** 40.00/75.00 **st.**

at Oldbury W : 7 ¾ m. by A 456 on A 4123 – ✉ Birmingham – ☎ 0121 :

Forte Travelodge, Wolverhampton Rd, B69 2BH, on A 4123 ☎ 552 2967, Reservations (Freephone) 0800 850950 – TV P. AE VISA. BU **n**
Meals (grill rest.) – **33 rm** 34.50 **t.**

at Great Barr NW : 6 m. on A 34 – ✉ Birmingham – ☎ 0121 :

Forte Posthouse, Chapel Lane, B43 7BG, ☎ 357 7444, Fax 357 7503, – rm TV ☎ P – 120. AE VISA JCB. CT **x**
Meals a la carte 15.20/23.60 **t.** – 7.95 – **192 rm** 56.00 **st.** – SB.

at West Bromwich NW : 6 m. on A 41 – ✉ Birmingham – ☎ 0121 :

Moat House Birmingham (Q.M.H.), Birmingham Rd, B70 6RS, ☎ 609 9988, Fax 525 7403 – rm rest TV ☎ P – 180. AE VISA JCB BU **c**
Meals 6.50/14.95 **st.** and a la carte 5.95 – 8.50 – **171 rm** 65.00/90.00 **st.** – SB.

ATS 1558 Pershore Rd., Stirchley ☎ 458 2951
ATS 158 Slade Rd, Erdington ☎ 327 2783
ATS 1189 Chester Rd, Erdington ☎ 373 6104/382 7533
ATS 94 Aldrige Rd, Perry Barr ☎ 356 5925/6632
ATS 314 Bearwood Rd, Bearwood ☎ 420 2000
ATS 427 Bordesley Green, Bordesley Green ☎ 772 6514
ATS 43 Whitmore Rd, Small Heath ☎ 772 2571
ATS 341 Dudley Rd, Winson Green ☎ 454 2588/2536
ATS Dudley Rd, Halesowen ☎ 550 2464
ATS 947 Bristol Rd South, Northfield ☎ 475 1244
ATS 87 Old Meeting St., West Bromwich ☎ 553 3495

For the quickest route use the ***Michelin Main Road Maps*** *:*
970 Europe, 976 Czech Republic-Slovak Republic, 980 Greece, 984 Germany, 985 Scandinavia-Finland, 986 Great Britain and Ireland, 987 Germany-Austria-Benelux, 988 Italy, 989 France, 990 Spain-Portugal and 991 Yugoslavia.

BIRTLE Gtr. Manchester – see Bury.

BISHOP AUCKLAND Durham 401 402 P 20 – pop. 23 154 – ☎ 01388.

High Plains, Durham Rd ☎ 602198 – Oakleaf, School Aycliffe Lane, Newton Aycliffe ☎ (01325) 310820 – Woodham G. & C.C., Burnhill Way, Newton Aycliffe ☎ (01325) 318346.

London 253 – Carlisle 73 – Middlesbrough 24 – Newcastle upon Tyne 28 – Sunderland 25.

Park Head, Park View Terrace, New Coundon, DL14 8QB, NE : 1 ¾ m. by A 689 on A 688 ☎ 661727, Fax 661727 – TV ☎ P
31 rm.

ATS Cockton Hill ☎ 603681

BISHOPS FROME Heref. and Worcs. – see Ledbury.

BISHOP'S HULL Somerset – see Taunton.

BISHOP'S STORTFORD Herts. 404 U 28 – pop. 27 874 – ☎ 01279.

Stansted Airport : ☎ 680500, NE : 3½ m.

The Old Monastery, Windhill, CM23 2ND ☎ 652274.

London 34 – Cambridge 27 – Chelmsford 19 – Colchester 33.

The Cottage , 71 Birchanger Lane, CM23 5QA, NE : 2¼ m. by B 1383 on Birchanger rd ☎ 812349, Fax 812349, « Part 17C and 18C cottages », – TV ☎ P. VISA JCB.
closed 24 to 27 December – **Meals** (by arrangement) 11.00 **st.** – **14 rm** 30.00/47.00 **st.**

at Hatfield Heath SE : 6 m. on A 1060 – ✉ Bishop's Stortford – ☎ 01279 :

Down Hall Country House, CM22 7AS, S : 1 ½ m. ☎ 731441, Fax 730416, ←, « 19C Italianate mansion », , park, – TV ☎ P – 200. AE VISA JCB
Meals 16.50/19.95 **t.** and a la carte – 9.25 – **103 rm** 86.00/145.00 **st.** – SB.

ATS 14 Burnt Mill, Harlow ☎ 421965

BISHOP'S TAWTON Devon 403 H 30 – see Barnstaple.

BITTON Avon 403 404 M 29 – see Bath.

BLABY Leics. 402 403 404 Q 26 – pop. 6 538 – ☎ 01162.

London 100 – Coventry 10 – Leicester 4 – Northampton 38.

Time Out (Regal), 15 Enderby Rd, LE8 4GD, ☎ 2787898, Fax 2781974, – TV ☎ P – 40. AE VISA.
Meals 15.00/20.00 **st.** 5.25 – **25 rm** 49.50/79.00 **t.** – SB.

BLACKBURN Lancs. 402 M 22 – pop. 136 612 – ☎ 01254.

Pleasington ✆ 202177 – Wilpshire, 72 Whalley Rd ✆ 248260/249691 – Great Harwood, Harwood Bar ✆ 884391 – King George's Hall, Northgate, BB2 1AA ✆ 53277.

London 228 – Leeds 47 – Liverpool 39 – Manchester 24 – Preston 11.

Millstone, Church Lane, Mellor, BB2 7JR, NW : 4 m. by A 677 ✆ 813333, Fax 812628 – rm – 25. AE VISA
Meals 11.50/20.00 **st.** and a la carte 6.95 – **17 rm** 69.00/88.00 **st.**, 1 suite – SB.

at Langho N : 4½ m. on A 666 – ✉ Whalley – ☎ 01254 :

XXX ✿ **Northcote Manor** (Haworth) with rm, Northcote Rd, BB6 8BE, N : ½ m. on A 59 at junction with A 666 ✆ 240555, Fax 246568, – . AE VISA.
Meals 17.80/40.00 **t.** and a la carte 23.00/34.50 **t.** – **14 rm** 85.00/110.00 **t.** – SB
Spec. Bury black pudding and pink trout with mustard and watercress sauce, Breast of Goosnargh chicken 'Hindle Wakes', Damson souffle with prune and Armagnac ice cream.

at Balderstone NW : 6½ m. by A 677 off A 59 – ✉ Blackburn – ☎ 01254 :

Boddington Arms, Myerscough Rd, BB2 7LE, on A 59 ✆ 813900, Fax 814079 – . AE VISA.
Meals (grill rest.) 7.00/12.00 **st.** and a la carte 5.10 – 4.95 – **20 rm** 45.00 **t.** – SB.

ATS Pendle St., Copy Nook ✆ 55963/59272/665115

BLACKPOOL Lancs. 402 K 22 **Great Britain G.** – pop. 146 069 – ☎ 01253.

See : Tower★ AC AY A – Blackpool Park, North Park Drive ✆ 393960, BY – Poulton-le-Fylde, Myrtle Farm, Breck Rd ✆ 892444.

Blackpool Airport : ✆ 343434, S : 3 m. by A 584.

1 Clifton St., FY1 1LY ✆ 321623 – Pleasure Beach, 11 Ocean Boulevard, South Promenade, FY4 1PL ✆ 403223 (summer only).

London 246 – Leeds 88 – Liverpool 56 – Manchester 51 – Middlesbrough 123.

Plan on next page

Imperial (Forte), North Promenade, FY1 2HB, ✆ 23971, Fax 751784, ≤, – rm – 400. AE VISA JCB — AY c
Meals 16.75 **st.** (dinner) and a la carte 20.20/31.15 **st.** – 9.95 – **173 rm** 104.00/139.00 **st.**, 7 suites – SB.

Pembroke, North Promenade, FY1 2JQ, ✆ 23434, Fax 27864, ≤, – rm rest – 900. AE VISA JCB — AY x
The Promenade : Meals (buffet rest.) 11.25/16.95 **st.** 7.75 – **The Crystal Room : Meals** (dinner only) 23.00 **st.** and a la carte **st.** 7.75 – **268 rm** 112.00/139.00 **st.**, 6 suites – SB.

Village H. & Leisure Club, East Park Drive, FY3 8LL, ✆ 838866, Fax 798800, , squash – rm – 600. AE VISA. — BZ a
Meals *(closed Saturday lunch)* (grill rest.) 15.50 **st.** (dinner) and a la carte 14.00/18.00 **st.** – **166 rm** 85.00/95.00 **st.** – SB.

Savoy, Queens Promenade, FY2 9SJ, ✆ 352561, Fax 500735 – – 300. AE VISA. — AY a
Meals (bar lunch Monday to Saturday)/dinner 13.50 **t.** and a la carte – **125 rm** 30.00/110.00 **t.**, 6 suites – SB.

Libertys on the Square without rest., Cocker Square, North Promenade, FY1 1RX, ✆ 291155, ≤ – . VISA. — AY n
2.95 – **24 rm** 35.00 **st.**

Warwick, 603-609 New South Promenade, FY4 1NG, ✆ 342192, Fax 405776, – – 50. AE VISA JCB — BZ u
Meals (bar lunch)/dinner 12.95 **st.** – **50 rm** 40.00/88.00 **st.** – SB.

Berwyn, 1-2 Finchley Rd, Gynn Sq., FY1 2LP, ✆ 352896, Fax 594391 – . VISA. — AY e
Meals (dinner only) 15.00 **t.** 4.00 – **20 rm** (dinner included) 30.00/70.00 **t.** – SB.

Shellard, 18-20 Dean St., South Shore, FY4 1AU, ✆ 342679 – rest . VISA. — AZ a
Meals (dinner only) 18.50 **st.** 3.90 – **20 rm** 27.00/66.00 **t.**

Sunray, 42 Knowle Av., off Queens Promenade, FY2 9TQ, ✆ 351937, Fax 593307 – . AE VISA — BY c
closed 15 December-5 January – **Meals** (by arrangement) 12.00 **st.** – **9 rm** 25.00/56.00 **st.** – SB.

Burlees, 40 Knowle Av., off Queen's Promenade, FY2 9TQ, ✆ 354535 – . VISA. — BY c
closed December and January – **Meals** 7.50 **st.** 4.50 – **9 rm** 21.00/46.00 **st.** – SB.

Bambi without rest., 27 Bright St., South Shore, FY4 1BS, ✆ 343756 – . AE VISA. — AZ c
closed December and January – **5 rm** 16.00/32.00.

X **September Brasserie,** 15-17 Queen St., FY1 1PU, ✆ 23282 – AE VISA JCB. — AY r
closed Sunday, Monday, 2 weeks winter and 2 weeks summer – **Meals** 15.95 **t.** (dinner) and a la carte 16.50/23.50 **t.** 5.00.

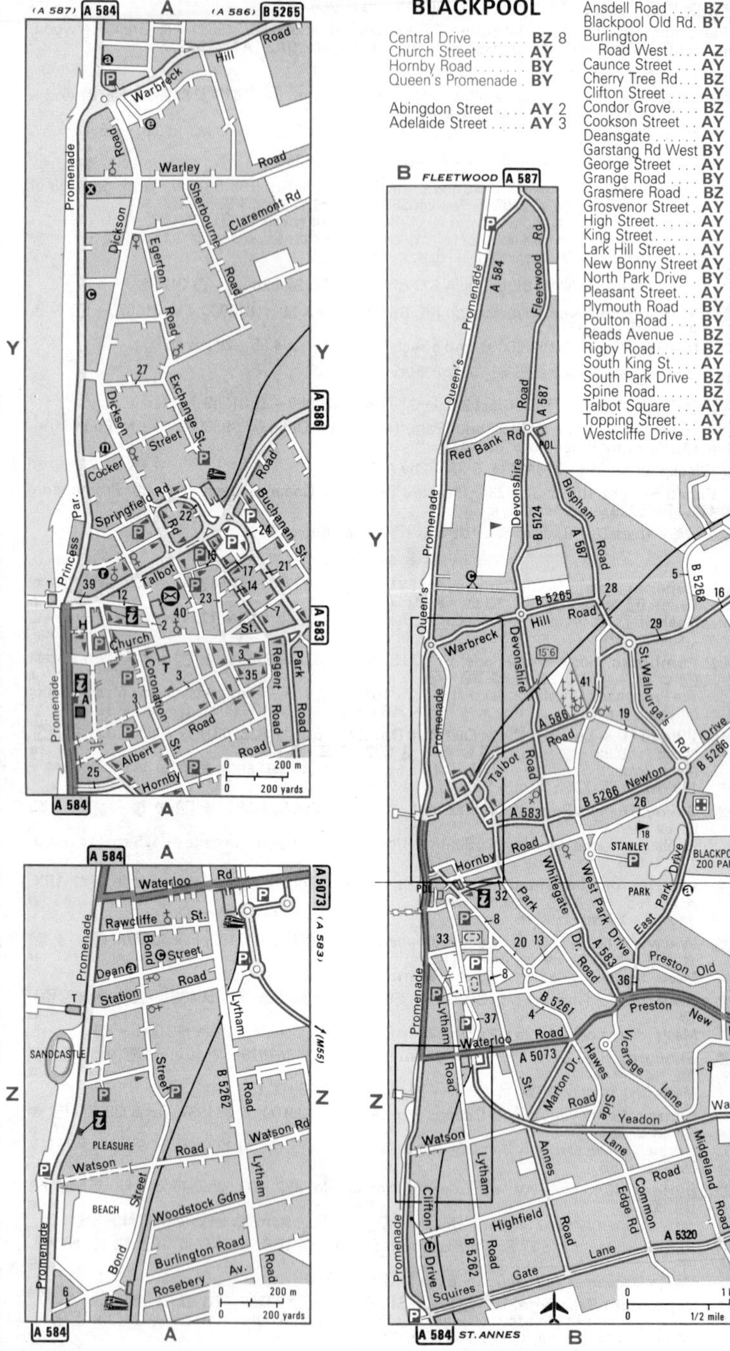
BLACKPOOL
Central Drive BZ 8
Church Street AY
Hornby Road BY
Queen's Promenade BY
Abingdon Street AY 2
Adelaide Street AY 3
Ansdell Road BZ 4
Blackpool Old Rd. BY 5
Burlington Road West AZ 6
Caunce Street AY 7
Cherry Tree Rd. BZ 9
Clifton Street AY 12
Condor Grove BZ 13
Cookson Street AY 14
Deansgate AY 15
Garstang Rd West BY 16
George Street AY 17
Grange Road BY 19
Grasmere Road BZ 20
Grosvenor Street AY 21
High Street AY 22
King Street AY 23
Lark Hill Street AY 24
New Bonny Street AY 25
North Park Drive BY 26
Pleasant Street AY 27
Plymouth Road BY 28
Poulton Road BY 29
Reads Avenue BZ 32
Rigby Road BZ 33
South King St. AY 35
South Park Drive BZ 36
Spine Road BZ 37
Talbot Square AY 39
Topping Street AY 40
Westcliffe Drive BY 41
(A 587) A 584
(A 586) B 5265
Warbreck Hill Road
Warley Road
Dickson Road
Promenade
Sherbourne Road
Claremont Rd
Egerton Road
Exchange St.
Cocker Street
Springfield Rd
Buchanan St.
Princess Par.
Talbot Rd
Church St.
Coronation St.
Regent Road
Park Road
Albert Road
Hornby Road
0 200 m
0 200 yards
A 586
A 583
A 584
Waterloo Rd
Rawcliffe St.
Bond Street
Deansgate
Station Road
Lytham Road
SANDCASTLE
PLEASURE BEACH
Watson Road
Watson Rd
Woodstock Gdns
Burlington Road
Rosebery Av.
B 5262
A 5073
(A 583)
(M55)
FLEETWOOD A 587
Queen's Promenade
Fleetwood Rd
Red Bank Rd
Devonshire Road
Bispham Road
B 5124
B 5265 Hill Road
B 5268
St. Walburga's Rd
B 5266 Newton Drive
Whitegate Dr.
West Park Drive
East Park Drive
STANLEY PARK
BLACKPOOL ZOO PARK
Preston Old Rd
Preston New Rd
Vicarage Lane
Hawes Side Lane
Yeadon Way
Marton Dr.
Midgeland Road
Common Edge Rd
Highfield Road
Annes St.
Squires Gate Lane
Clifton Drive
A 5320
0 1 km
0 1/2 mile
A 584 ST. ANNES

at Little Thornton NE : 5 m. by A 586 – BY – off A 588 – ✉ Blackpool – ☎ 01253 :

River House with rm, Skippool Creek, Wyre Rd, FY5 5LF, ☎ 883497, Fax 892083, ←, – TV ☎ P. VISA
Meals *(closed Sunday)* (booking essential) 18.50 **t.** and a la carte 7.50 – **5 rm** 65.00/ 80.00 **t.** – SB.

at Little Singleton NE : 6 m. by A 586 – BY – on A 585 – ✉ Blackpool – ☎ 01253 :

Mains Hall, 86 Mains Lane, FY6 7LE, ☎ 885130, Fax 894132, – rm TV ☎ P. AE VISA
Meals (lunch by arrangement)/dinner a la carte 20.00/30.00 **st.** 5.50 – **10 rm** 58.00/ 130.00 **st.**

at Singleton NE : 7 m. by A 586 – BY – on B 5260 – ✉ Blackpool – ☎ 01253 :

Singleton Lodge, Lodge Lane, FY6 8LT, N : ¼ m. on B 5260 ☎ 883854, Fax 894432, – TV ☎ P. AE VISA
closed 25-26 December and 1 January – **Meals** *(closed Sunday dinner and Bank Holidays)* (dinner only and Sunday lunch)/dinner 14.50 **t.** 5.00 – **12 rm** 52.00/70.00 **t.** – SB.

ATS Clifton Rd, Marton ☎ 695033/4

BLACKROD Lancs. 402 404 M 23 – ☎ 01942.
London 220 – Burnley 25 – Liverpool 31 – Manchester 16 – Preston 18.

Georgian House, Manchester Rd, BL6 5RU, SE : 1 ½ m. by B 5408 on A 6 ☎ 814598, Fax 813427, – rm TV ☎ P – 200. AE VISA
Meals 10.70/19.50 **st.** and a la carte 4.95 – **100 rm** 80.00/114.25 **st.** – SB.

Prices For full details of the prices quoted in the guide, consult the introduction.

BLACKWATER Cornwall 403 E 33 – see Truro.

BLAGDON Avon 403 L 30 pop. 1 900 – ✉ Bristol.
London 140 – Bristol 18 – Taunton 24.

Butcombe Farm without rest., Aldwick Lane, BS18 6UW, N : 1 ½ m. by Station Rd ☎ (01761) 462380, Fax 462300, ←, « Farmhouse of 15C origin », heated, park – TV ☎ P. VISA JCB.
5 rm 39.00/49.00 **t.**

Aldwick Court Farm without rest., Aldwick Lane, BS18 7RF, N : 2 ¼ m. by Station Rd ☎ (01934) 862305, Fax 863308, park, – TV P.
closed December and January – **3 rm** 28.00/45.00 **s.**

BLAKENEY Glos. 403 404 M 28 – ☎ 01594.
London 134 – Bristol 31 – Gloucester 16 – Newport 31.

Viney Hill Country, Viney Hill, GL15 4LT, S : ¾ m. by A 48 ☎ 516000, Fax 516018, – TV P. VISA.
Meals (by arrangement) 18.00 **st.** 4.20 – **6 rm** 32.00/42.00 **st.** – SB.

BLAKENEY Norfolk 404 X 25 – pop. 1 628 – ✉ Holt – ☎ 01263.
London 127 – King's Lynn 37 – Norwich 28.

Blakeney, The Quay, NR25 7NE, ☎ 740797, Fax 740795, ←, – rest TV ☎ P – 200. AE VISA JCB
Meals (light lunch)/dinner 16.00 **t.** and a la carte 4.30 – **59 rm** 59.00/118.00 **t.** – SB.

Manor, The Quay, NR25 7ND, ☎ 740376, Fax 741116, – rest TV ☎ P
closed 4 to 26 January – **Meals** (bar lunch Monday to Saturday)/dinner 15.50 **st.** and a la carte 4.75 – **37 rm** 25.00/80.00 **st.** – SB.

White Horse, 4 High St., NR25 7AL, ☎ 740574 – TV P. AE VISA.
Meals *(closed Sunday and Monday)* (bar lunch Tuesday to Saturday)/dinner a la carte 13.00/20.00 **t.** 4.00 – **9 rm** 30.00/70.00 **t.**

at Cley next the Sea E : 1½ m. on A 149 – ✉ Holt – ☎ 01263 :

George & Dragon, High St., NR25 7RN, ☎ 740652, Fax 741275, – TV P
Meals a la carte 9.65/16.75 **t.** – **8 rm** 30.00/65.00 **t.**

Cley Mill, NR25 7NN, ☎ 740209, Fax 740209, ←, « 18C redbrick windmill on saltmarshes », – P.
closed 10 January-29 February – **Meals** (by arrangement) 15.50 **st.** – **6 rm** 31.00/ 63.00 **st.**

at Morston W : 1½ m. on A 149 – ✉ Holt – ☎ 01263 :

Morston Hall, NR25 7AA, ☎ 741041, Fax 741041, – TV ☎ P. AE VISA
closed January and February – **Meals** (dinner only and Sunday lunch)/dinner 25.00 **st.** 5.00 – **6 rm** (dinner included) 80.00/150.00 **st.** – SB.

BLANCHLAND Northd. 401 402 N 19 – pop. 135 – ✉ Consett (Durham) – ☎ 01434.

♦London 298 – ♦Carlisle 47 – ♦Newcastle upon Tyne 24.

Lord Crewe Arms 🔇, DH8 9SP, ☎ 675251, Fax 675337, « Part 13C abbey », – TV ☎ – 25. AE VISA
Meals (bar lunch Monday to Saturday)/dinner 25.00 **st.** 7.00 – **18 rm** 70.00/98.00 **st.** – SB.

BLANDFORD FORUM Dorset 403 404 N 31 The West Country G. – pop. 7 957 – ☎ 01258.

See : Town★.

Envir. : Kingston Lacy★★ *AC*, SE : 5½m. by B 3082 – Royal Signals Museum★, NE : 2 m. by B 3082.

Exc. : Milton Abbas★, SW : 8 m. by A 354.

18 Ashley Wood, Tarrant Rawston ☎ 452253 – 18 The Mid Dorset, Belchalwell ☎ 861386.

Marsh & Ham Car Park, West St., DT11 7AW ☎ 454770.

♦London 124 – Bournemouth 17 – Dorchester 17 – Salisbury 24.

Crown, West St., DT11 7AJ, ☎ 456626, Fax 451084, – rm TV ☎ P – 100. AE VISA
closed 25 to 29 December – **Meals** *(closed Saturday lunch and Bank Holiday Mondays)* 12.75 **t.** and a la carte 4.75 – **32 rm** 58.00/68.00 **t.** – SB.

at Pimperne NE : 2½ m. on A 354 – ✉ Blandford Forum – ☎ 01258 :

Anvil, Salisbury Rd, DT11 8UQ, ☎ 453431, Fax 480182 – TV ☎ P. AE VISA
Meals a la carte 12.80/21.00 **st.** 5.00 – **9 rm** 47.50/75.00 **st.**

Fairfield House, Church Rd, DT11 8UB, ☎ 456756, Fax 452123, – TV P. AE VISA.
Meals *(closed Sunday)* (dinner only) a la carte 15.20/22.15 **st.** – **5 rm** 44.00/75.00 **st.** – SB.

at Tarrant Monkton NE : 5½ m. by A 354 – ✉ Blandford Forum – ☎ 01258 :

Langton Arms, DT11 8RX, ☎ 830225, Fax 830053, – TV ☎ P. VISA
Meals (bar lunch Monday to Saturday) (in bar Sunday dinner and Monday)/dinner a la carte 9.85/16.75 **st.** 3.50 – **6 rm** 39.00/54.00 **st.** – SB.

at Farnham NE : 7½ m. by A 354 – ✉ Blandford Forum – ☎ 01725 :

Museum, DT11 8DE, ☎ 516261, – TV ☎ P. VISA.
closed 25 December – **Meals** (booking essential) 7.50/18.00 **t.** and a la carte 4.95 – **4 rm** 35.00/65.00 **t.**

BLAWITH Cumbria 402 K 21 – see Coniston.

BLEDINGTON Glos. 403 404 P 28 – see Stow-on-the-Wold.

BLOCKLEY Glos. 403 404 O 27 – pop. 1 668 – ✉ Moreton-in-Marsh – ☎ 01386.

♦London 89 – ♦Birmingham 40 – Gloucester 29 – ♦Oxford 33.

Crown Inn, High St., GL56 9EX, ☎ 700245, Fax 700247, « Converted 15C coach house and cottages », – TV ☎ P. AE VISA
Meals a la carte 18.15/30.85 **t.** 7.95 – **21 rm** 53.00/78.00 **t.** – SB.

BLUNSDON Wilts. 403 404 O 29 – see Swindon.

BLYTH Notts. 402 403 404 Q 23 – pop. 1 867 – ✉ Worksop – ☎ 01909.

♦London 166 – Doncaster 13 – Lincoln 30 – ♦Nottingham 32 – ♦Sheffield 20.

Granada Lodge without rest., Hilltop roundabout, S81 8HG, N : ¾ m. by B 6045 at junction of A 1 (M) with A 614 ☎ 591841, Fax 591831, Reservations (Freephone) 0800 555300 – TV ☎ P. AE VISA.
39 rm 39.95 **st.**

Forte Travelodge, A 1 southbound, S81 8EL, SE : 1 m. by A 634 on A 1 ☎ 591775, Reservations (Freephone) 0800 850950 – TV P. AE VISA.
Meals (grill rest.) – **32 rm** 34.50 **t.**

BODENHAM Heref. and Worcs. 403 L 29 – see Leominster.

BODINNICK-BY-FOWEY Cornwall – see Fowey.

BODMIN Cornwall 403 F 32 – ☎ 01208.

Shire House, Mount Folly Sq., PL31 2DQ ☎ 76616.

♦London 270 – Newquay 18 – ♦Plymouth 32 – Truro 23.

Treffry Farmhouse without rest., Lanhydrock, PL30 5AF, S : 2¼ m. by B 3268 on Lanivet rd ☎ 74405, Fax 74405, « Working farm », , park – TV P.
closed Christmas and New Year – **3 rm** 25.00/40.00 **s.**

ATS Church Sq. ☎ 74353/73757

BODYMOOR HEATH Staffs. 402 403 404 O 26 – see Tamworth.

BOLDON Tyne and Wear 401 402 O 19 – see Newcastle upon Tyne.

BOLLINGTON Ches. 402 403 404 N 24 – see Macclesfield.

BOLTON Gtr. Manchester 402 404 M 23 – pop. 258 584 – ☎ 01204.

Regent Park, Links Rd, Chorley New Road ☎ 844170 – Lostock Park ☎ 843278 – Bolton, Old Links, Chorley Old Rd, Montserrat ☎ 840050.

Town Hall, Victoria Sq, BL1 1RU ☎ 364333.

London 214 – Burnley 19 – Liverpool 32 – Manchester 11 – Preston 23.

Bolton Moat House (Q.M.H.), 1 Higher Bridge St., BL1 2EW, ☎ 879988, Fax 380777, « Cloisters restaurant in 19C church », – rm rest – 300. AE VISA JCB.
Meals *(closed Saturday lunch)* (carving lunch) 10.95/22.00 **st.** and a la carte 6.20 – 9.75 – **126 rm** 83.00/99.00 **st.**, 2 suites – SB.

Beaumont (Forte), Beaumont Rd, BL3 4TA, SW : 2½ m. on A 58 ☎ 651511, Fax 61064 – rm – 120. AE VISA
Meals 13.80 **t.** and a la carte 4.65 – 7.95 – **95 rm** 55.00/80.00 **t.** – SB.

Pack Horse, Nelson Sq., Bradshawgate, BL1 1DP, ☎ 527261, Fax 364352 – – 250. AE VISA.
Meals (buffet lunch) (dancing Friday evening)/dinner 10.95 **st.** and a la carte 4.90 – **72 rm** 45.00/100.00 **st.** – SB.

Broomfield, 33-35 Wigan Rd, Deane, BL3 5PX, SW : 1 ½ m. on A 676 ☎ 61570, Fax 650932 – rest . AE VISA
Meals *(closed Friday to Sunday)* (residents only)(dinner only) 12.00 **t.** and a la carte 3.75 – **15 rm** 26.50/42.00 **st.**

at Egerton N : 3½ m. on A 666 – ✉ Bolton – ☎ 01204 :

Egerton House, Blackburn Rd, BL7 9PL, ☎ 307171, Fax 593030, squash – rm – 150. AE VISA.
Meals *(closed Saturday lunch)* 12.00/16.50 **t.** and a la carte 5.50 – 7.95 – **32 rm** 75.00/87.50 **t.** – SB.

at Bromley Cross N : 4 m. by A 666 on B 6472 – ✉ Bolton – ☎ 01204 :

Last Drop Village, Hospital Rd, BL7 9PZ, ☎ 591131, Fax 304122, « Village created from restored farm buildings », squash – rm – 200. AE VISA JCB
Meals *(closed Saturday lunch)* 15.50/20.50 **t.** and a la carte – 8.50 – **80 rm** 80.00/93.00 **t.**, 3 suites – SB.

ATS Foundry St. ☎ 522144/527841/388681
ATS Moss Bank Way, Astley Bridge, Bolton (ASDA car park) ☎ 300057
ATS Chorley Rd, Fourgates, Westhoughton ☎ 813024

BOLTON ABBEY N. Yorks. 402 O 22 **Great Britain G.** – pop. 117 – ✉ Skipton – ☎ 01756.

See : Bolton Priory★ *AC.*

London 216 – Harrogate 18 – Leeds 23 – Skipton 6.

Devonshire Arms Country House, BD23 6AJ, ☎ 710441, Fax 710564, <, « Part 17C restored coaching inn », park, – – 150. AE VISA JCB
Burlington : **Meals** 17.95/40.00 **st.** and a la carte – **39 rm** 105.00/165.00 **st.**, 2 suites – SB.

BONCHURCH I.O.W. 403 404 Q 32 – see Wight (Isle of).

BOREHAMWOOD Herts. 404 T 29 – pop. 29 837 – ☎ 0181.

London 10 – Luton 20.

Plan : see Greater London (North West)

Elstree Moat House (Q.M.H.), Barnet by pass, WD6 5PU, at junction of A 5135 with A 1 ☎ 214 9988, Fax 207 3194, – rm rest – 400. AE VISA. CT s
Meals (bar lunch Saturday and Bank Holidays) 12.95/16.70 **t.** and a la carte 6.75 – 9.95 – **118 rm** 95.00/135.00 **st.** – SB.

Oaklands Toby, Studio Way, WD6 5JY, off Elstree Way (A 5135) ☎ 905 1455, Fax 905 1370 – rm – 35. AE VISA. CT i
Meals (grill rest.) 6.95 **t.** and a la carte 4.95 – **38 rm** 67.00/77.00 **t.**

Per spostarvi più rapidamente utilizzate le **carte Michelin** *"Grandi Strade" :*
n° 970 Europa, *n°* 976 Rep. Ceca/Slovacchia, *n°* 980 Grecia, *n°* 984 Germania,
n° 985 Scandinavia-Finlandia, *n°* 986 Gran Bretagna-Irlanda, *n°* 987 Germania-Austria-Benelux,
n° 988 Italia, *n°* 989 Francia, *n°* 990 Spagna-Portogallo, *n°* 991 Jugoslavia.

BOROUGHBRIDGE N.Yorks 402 P 21 pop. 2 910 – ☎ 01423.

◆London 215 – ◆Leeds 19 – ◆Middlesbrough 36 – York 16.

Rose Manor, Horsefair, YO5 9LL, ☎ 322245, Fax 324920, – rm – 200. AE VISA.
Meals (bar lunch Monday to Saturday)/dinner 17.50 **t.** and a la carte 4.25 – 8.50 – **17 rm** 62.00/75.00 **t.** – SB.

at Brafferton Helperby NE : 5 m. by B 6265 and Easingwold rd on Helperby rd – ✉ York – ☎ 01423 :

Brafferton Hall, , YO6 2NZ, ☎ 360352, Fax 360352, – . AE VISA
Meals (by arrangement) (communal dining) 20.00 **s.** – **4 rm** 30.00/60.00 **s.**

Laurel Farm , YO6 2NZ, ☎ 360436, Fax 360436, , , park, –
Meals (by arrangement) (communal dining) 15.00 **st.** 2.00 – **3 rm** 19.00/38.00 **st.**

BORROWDALE Cumbria 402 K 20 – see Keswick.

BOSCASTLE Cornwall 403 F 31 **The West Country G.** – ☎ 01840.

See : Village★.

Envir. : Tintagel Church★ – Old Post Office★.

Exc. : Boscastle★, NE : 3 m. off B 3263 – Delabole Quarry★, SE : 4 m. by B 3263 and by-roads.

◆London 260 – Bude 14 – Exeter 59 – ◆Plymouth 43.

Bottreaux House, PL35 0BG, S : ¾ m. by B 3263 on B 3266 ☎ 250231 – rest . AE VISA
Meals *(closed Sunday)* (dinner only) a la carte 9.00/15.50 **s.** – **7 rm** 25.00/40.00.

St. Christopher's, High St., PL35 0BD, S : ¾ m. by B 3263 off B 3266 ☎ 250412 – rest . VISA JCB
March-October – **Meals** (by arrangement) 9.00 **s.** 2.80 – **9 rm** 18.00/38.00 **s.** – SB.

Old Coach House without rest., Tintagel Rd, PL35 0AS, S : ¾ m. on B 3263 ☎ 250398, Fax 250346 – . AE VISA.
March-October – **6 rm** 24.00/48.00 – SB.

BOSHAM W. Sussex 404 R 31 – see Chichester.

BOSTON Lincs. 402 404 T 25 **Great Britain G.** – pop. 53 226 – ☎ 01205.

See : St. Botolph's Church★.

Exc. : Tattershal Castle★, NW : 15 m. by A 1121, B 1192 and A 153.

18 Cowbridge, Horncastle Rd ☎ 362306.

Blackfriars Arts Centre, Spain Lane, PE21 6HP ☎ 356656.

◆London 122 – Lincoln 35 – ◆Nottingham 55.

Friendly Stop Inn, Bicker Bar Roundabout, PE20 3AN, SW : 8 m. at junction of A 17 with A 52 ☎ 820118, Fax 820228, – rm rest – 60. AE VISA JCB.
Meals 9.75 **st.** and dinner a la carte 4.75 – 5.75 – **55 rm** 36.50/52.00 **t.** – SB.

ATS London Rd ☎ 362854

BOTLEY Hants. 403 404 Q 31 – pop. 2 436 – ✉ Southampton – ☎ 01489.

18 Botley Park H. & C.C., Winchester Rd, Boorley Green ☎ 780888 ext : 444.

◆London 83 – ◆Portsmouth 17 – ◆Southampton 6 – Winchester 11.

Botley Park, Winchester Rd, Boorley Green, SO32 2UA, NW : 1 ½ m. on B 3354 ☎ 780888, Fax 789242, , , , 18, park, , squash – rest – 200. AE VISA
Meals 13.25/21.95 and a la carte – 8.95 – **100 rm** 90.00/122.00 **t.** – SB.

BOUGHTON Kent – see Faversham.

BOUGHTON MONCHELSEA Kent – see Maidstone.

BOURNE Lincs. 402 404 S 25 – pop. 9 988 – ☎ 01778.

◆London 101 – ◆Leicester 42 – Lincoln 35 – ◆Nottingham 42.

Bourne Eau House, 30 South St., PE10 9LY, on A 15 ☎ 423621, « Part Elizabethan and Georgian house », – .
closed Christmas and Easter – **Meals** *(closed Sunday)* (residents only) (communal dining) (dinner only) 18.00 **s.** – **3 rm** 35.00/60.00 **st.**

Toft House, Main Rd, Toft, PE10 0JT, SW : 3 m. by A 151 on A 6121 ☎ 590614, Fax 590264, 18, – – 70. VISA.
Meals *(closed Sunday dinner)* 14.50 **t.** 3.80 – **22 rm** 40.00/60.00 **t.**

ATS 18 Abbey Rd ☎ 422811

BOURNE END Herts. 404 S 28 – see Hemel Hempstead.

BOURNEMOUTH Dorset 403 404 O 31 The West Country G. – pop. 151 302 – ☎ 01202.

See : Compton Acres★★ (English Garden ≤★★★) *AC* AX – Bournemouth Museums★ (Russell-Cotes Art Gallery and Museum *AC* DZ - Shelley Rooms *AC* EX).

Queens Park, Queens Park West Drive ☎ 396198/302611, DV – Meyrick Park, Central Drive ☎ 290307 CY.

Bournemouth (Hurn) Airport : ☎ 593939, N : 5 m. by Hurn - DV.

Westover Rd, BH1 2BU ☎ 789789.

♦London 114 – ♦Bristol 76 – ♦Southampton 34.

Plans on following pages

Carlton, Meyrick Rd, East Overcliff, BH1 3DN, ☎ 552011, Fax 299573, ≤, heated, – rest – 140. AE VISA EZ **a**
Meals 12.50/25.00 **t.** and a la carte 8.50 – **65 rm** 95.00/125.00 **t.**, 5 suites – SB.

Royal Bath (De Vere), Bath Rd, BH1 2EW, ☎ 555555, Fax 554158, ≤, – – 400. AE VISA. DZ **a**
Meals (dinner only and Sunday lunch)/dinner 23.00 **t.** and a la carte – **Oscars : Meals** *(closed Sunday)* (dinner only) 15.50/28.50 **t.** and a la carte – **124 rm** 115.00/140.00 **st.**, 7 suites – SB.

Swallow Highcliff, 105 St. Michael's Rd, West Cliff, BH2 5DU, ☎ 557702, Fax 292734, ≤, heated, – – 450. AE VISA JCB CZ **z**
Meals 9.75/17.95 **st.** and a la carte – **154 rm** 82.00/125.00 **st.**, 3 suites – SB.

Norfolk Royale, Richmond Hill, BH2 6EN, ☎ 551521, Fax 299729, – rm rest – 90. AE VISA. CY **u**
Meals (bar lunch)/dinner 18.00 **t.** and a la carte 5.00 – **90 rm** 90.00/120.00 **st.**, 5 suites – SB.

Stakis Bournemouth, Westover Rd, BH1 2BZ, ☎ 557681, Fax 554918, ≤, – – 100. AE VISA. DZ **n**
Meals *(closed Saturday lunch)* 12.50/18.50 **st.** and dinner a la carte – **104 rm** 95.00/150.00, 6 suites – SB.

East Cliff Court, East Overcliff Drive, BH1 3AN, ☎ 554545, Fax 557456, ≤, heated – rest – 100. AE VISA EZ **v**
Meals 6.25/14.25 3.50 – **70 rm** 30.00/60.00 – SB.

Marsham Court, Russell-Cotes Rd, East Cliff, BH1 3AB, ☎ 552111, Fax 294744, ≤, heated – – 200. AE VISA. DZ **e**
Meals (bar lunch)/dinner 16.00 **st.** 4.95 – **85 rm** 51.00/107.00 **st.**, 1 suite – SB.

Miramar, 19 Grove Rd, East Overcliff, BH1 3AU, ☎ 556581, Fax 291242, ≤, – rest – 80. AE VISA DZ **u**
Meals 10.25/16.25 **t.** 5.95 – **39 rm** 55.00/114.00 **st.** – SB.

New Durley Dean, 28 Westcliff Rd, BH2 5HE, ☎ 557711, Fax 292815, – rest – 80. AE VISA JCB. CZ **a**
Meals (bar lunch Monday to Saturday)/dinner 10.95 **st.** – **112 rm** 49.00/118.00 **st.** – SB.

Round House (Forte), Meyrick Rd, The Lansdowne, BH1 2PR, ☎ 553262, Fax 557698 – rm – 100. AE VISA JCB. DY **a**
Meals 8.95/22.85 **st.** and a la carte 5.80 – 7.95 – **98 rm** 55.00 **st.** – SB.

Chesterwood, East Overcliff Drive, BH1 3AR, ☎ 558057, Fax 556285, ≤, heated – rest . AE VISA EZ **i**
Meals (bar lunch)/dinner a la carte 7.50/13.00 **t.** 4.50 – **51 rm** 45.00/110.00 **st.** – SB.

Connaught, West Hill Rd, West Cliff, BH2 5PH, ☎ 298020, Fax 298028, – – 40. AE VISA CZ **s**
Meals (bar lunch Monday to Saturday)/dinner 14.50 **st.** and a la carte – **59 rm** 58.00/116.00 **st.**, 1 suite – SB.

Durley Hall, Durley Chine Rd, BH2 5JS, ☎ 751000, Fax 757585, – – 120. AE VISA. CZ **e**
Meals (buffet lunch Monday to Saturday)/dinner 16.50 **st.** and a la carte 4.70 – **81 rm** 50.00/100.00 **st.** – SB.

Queens, Meyrick Rd, East Cliff, BH1 3DL, ☎ 554415, Fax 294810, – rest – 200. AE VISA EYZ **r**
Meals 8.50/18.95 **t.** and dinner a la carte 4.75 – **110 rm** 47.50/95.00 **t.** – SB.

Courtlands, 16 Boscombe Spa Rd, East Cliff, BH5 1BB, ☎ 302442, Fax 309880, heated – rest – 45. AE VISA DX **o**
Meals (bar lunch Monday to Saturday)/dinner 15.00 and a la carte – **58 rm** 42.90/78.00 **t.** – SB.

Bournemouth Heathlands, 12 Grove Rd, East Cliff, BH1 3AY, ☎ 553336, Fax 555937, heated – – 250. AE VISA EZ **c**
Meals (bar lunch Monday to Saturday)/dinner 16.50 **st.** – **113 rm** (dinner included) 35.00/70.00 **st.**, 2 suites – SB.

Hinton Firs, 9 Manor Rd, East Cliff, BH1 3HB, ☎ 555409, Fax 299607, heated – rest . VISA. EY **n**
Meals (dinner only and Sunday lunch October-May)/dinner 13.25 **st.** and a la carte 3.80 – **52 rm** (dinner included) 35.50/110.00 **st.** – SB.

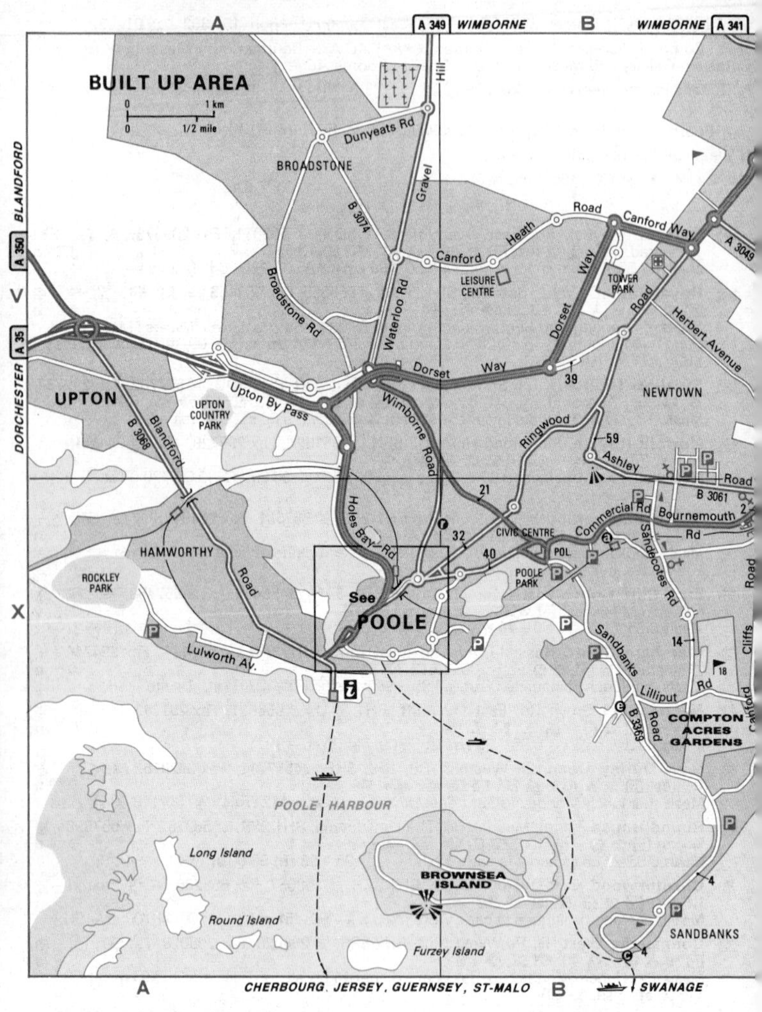

BOURNEMOUTH AND POOLE

Old Christchurch Road .... **DY**
Square (The) .... **CY** 63
Westover Road .... **DZ** 75

Archway Road .... **BX** 2
Banks Road .... **BX** 4
Boscombe Overcliff Road .... **EX** 6
Boscombe Spa Road ..... **DX** 7
Branksome Wood Road ... **CY** 9
Chessel Avenue .... **EX** 10
Clarendon Road .... **CX** 12
Commercial Road .... **CY** 13
Compton Avenue .... **BX** 14
Cranleigh Road .... **EV** 16
Durley Road .... **CZ** 17
Ensbury Park Road .... **CV** 19
Exeter Road .... **CDZ** 20
Fernside Road .... **ABX** 21
Fir Vale Road .... **DY** 23
Gervis Place .... **DY** 24
Gloucester Road .... **EV** 26
Hinton Road .... **DZ** 27
Lansdowne (The) .... **DY** 28
Lansdowne Road .... **DY** 30
Leven Avenue .... **CX** 31
Longfleet Road .... **BX** 32
Madeira Road .... **DY** 34
Manor Road .... **EY** 35
Meyrick Road .... **EYZ** 36
Old Wareham Road ...... **BV** 39
Parkstone Road .... **BX** 40
Pinecliff Road .... **CX** 42
Post Office Road .... **CY** 43
Priory Road .... **CZ** 45
Queen's Road .... **CX** 46
Richmond Hill .... **CY** 47
Richmond Park Road ..... **DV** 48
Russell Cotes Road .... **DZ** 49
St. Michael's Road .... **CZ** 51
St. Paul's Road .... **EY** 52
St. Peter's Road .... **DY** 53
St. Stephen's Road .... **CY** 55
St. Swithuns Road South .. **EY** 56
Seabourne Road .... **EV** 57
Seamoor Road .... **CX** 58
Sea View Road .... **BV** 59
Southbourne Grove .... **EX** 61
Southbourne Overcliff Drive .... **EX** 62
Suffolk Road .... **CY** 64
Surrey Road .... **CX** 66
Triangle (The) .... **CY** 67
Upper Hinton Road ...... **DZ** 68
Wessex Way .... **CX** 70
West Cliff Promenade ..... **CZ** 71
Western Road .... **CX** 73

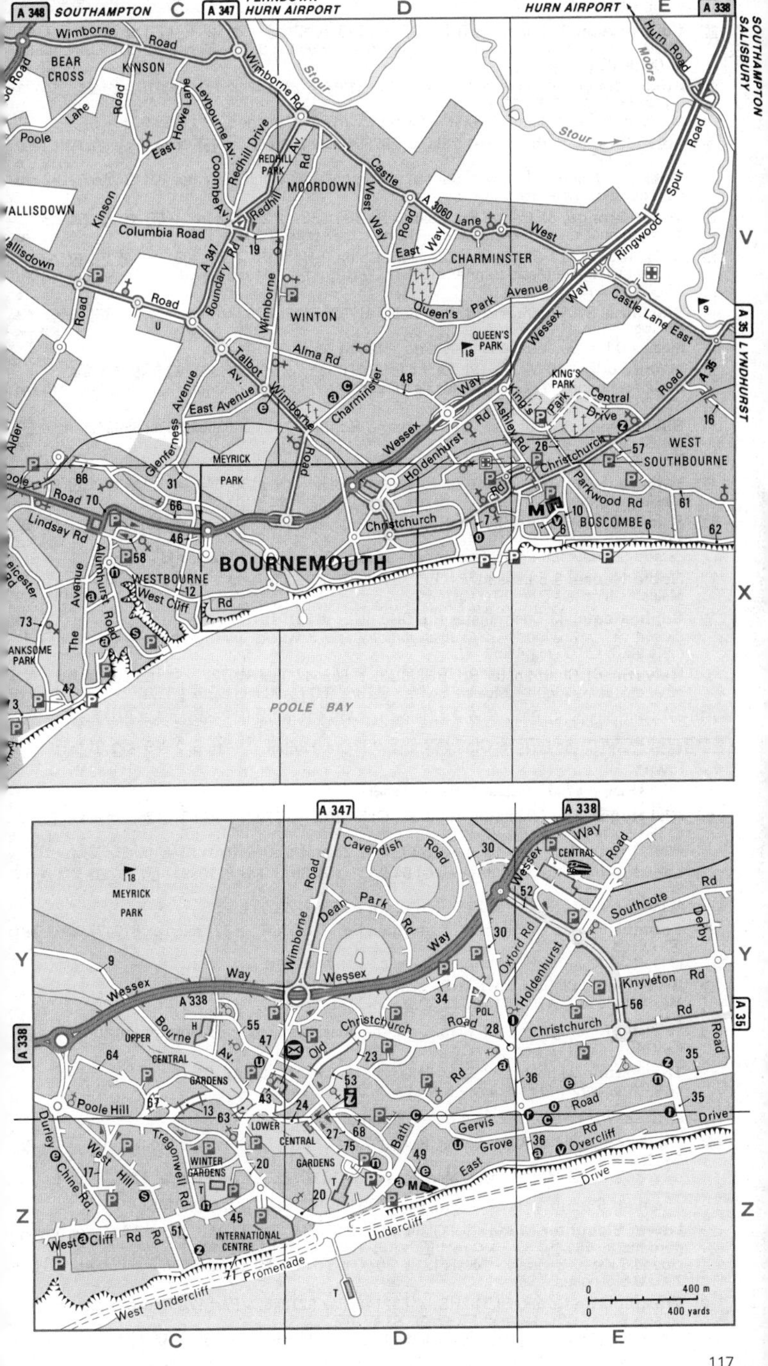

A 348 SOUTHAMPTON
A 347 FERNDOWN HURN AIRPORT
HURN AIRPORT
A 338
SOUTHAMPTON SALISBURY
C
D
E
V
X
Y
Z
A 35 LYNDHURST
BEAR CROSS
KINSON
Wimborne Road
Stour
Moors
Hurn Road
Spur Road
Poole Lane
Leybourne Av.
East Howe Lane
Redhill Drive
Coombe Av.
REDHILL PARK
MOORDOWN
Castle Lane
A 3060
West Way
East Way
CHARMINSTER
WALLISDOWN
Kinson
Columbia Road
Wallisdown Road
A 347
Boundary Rd
Redhill Av.
Wimborne
WINTON
Queen's Park Avenue
QUEEN'S PARK
Wessex Way
Ringwood
Castle Lane East
Talbot Av.
Alma Rd
Charminster
East Avenue
Glenferness Avenue
KING'S PARK
King's Park
Central Drive
Ashley Rd
Holdenhurst Rd
Christchurch
WEST SOUTHBOURNE
MEYRICK PARK
Poole Road
Lindsay Rd
Alumhurst Road
The Avenue
WESTBOURNE
West Cliff Rd
BOURNEMOUTH
Parkwood Rd
BOSCOMBE
BRANKSOME PARK
POOLE BAY
A 347
A 338
Cavendish Road
Dean Park Rd
Wimborne Road
CENTRAL
Southcote Rd
Derby
Knyveton Rd
Oxford Rd
Holdenhurst
MEYRICK PARK
Wessex Way
A 338
Bourne Av.
UPPER CENTRAL GARDENS
Old Christchurch Rd
Christchurch Road
POL.
Christchurch Rd
A 35
Road
Poole Hill
LOWER CENTRAL GARDENS
Bath
Gervis Road
Grove
East Overcliff Drive
Durley Chine Rd.
West Hill
Tregonwell Rd
WINTER GARDENS
INTERNATIONAL CENTRE
West Cliff Rd
Promenade
Undercliff
West Undercliff
0 400 m
0 400 yards

Collingwood, 11 Priory Rd, BH2 5DF, ☎ 557575, – rest. VISA. **Meals** (bar lunch Monday to Saturday)/dinner 15.95 **t.** 3.75 – **53 rm** (dinner included) 47.00/94.00 **t.** – SB. CZ **n**

Anglo-Swiss, 16 Gervis Rd, East Cliff, BH1 3EQ, ☎ 554794, Fax 299615, – – 80. AE VISA. EY **e**
Meals (bar lunch)/dinner 10.00 **t.** – **64 rm** (dinner included) 49.00/98.00 **t.** – SB.

Belvedere, 14 Bath Rd, BH1 2EU, ☎ 297556, Fax 294699 – – 80. AE VISA JCB. DYZ **c**
Meals (bar lunch Monday to Saturday)/dinner 10.00 **t.** and a la carte 10.85/16.50 – **62 rm** 32.00/85.00 **t.** – SB.

Tudor Grange, 31 Gervis Rd, East Cliff, BH1 3EE, ☎ 291472, – . VISA
Meals (dinner only) 9.00 **st.** 4.25 – **12 rm** 23.00/60.00 **st.** – SB. EY **o**

Cliff House, 113 Alumhurst Rd, Alum Chine, BH4 8HS, ☎ 763003, – .
Easter-October – **Meals** (dinner only) 12.00 **st.** 3.50 – **11 rm** (dinner included) 27.00/78.00 **st.** – SB. CX **s**

Sinclair's, 31 Alumhurst Rd, BH4 8EN, ☎ 752777, Fax 752778, – . CX **n**
Meals 7.00/18.00 and dinner a la carte – **20 rm** 14.00/34.00 **st.**

Wood Lodge, 10 Manor Rd, East Cliff, BH1 3EY, ☎ 290891, – . VISA
closed January and February – **Meals** (dinner only and Sunday lunch) 10.95 **t.** 4.40 – **15 rm** 25.00/58.00 **t.** – SB. EY **z**

Silver Trees without rest., 57 Wimborne Rd, BH3 7AL, ☎ 556040, Fax 556040, – . AE VISA. CV **e**
5 rm 25.00/41.00.

Valberg, 1A Wollstonecraft Rd, Boscombe, BH5 1JQ, ☎ 394644, – rest .
Meals (by arrangement) 7.00 – **10 rm** 25.00/40.00 **st.** – SB. EX **v**

Salathai, 1066 Christchurch Rd, Boscombe East, BH7 6DS, ☎ 420772 – . AE VISA EV **z**
closed Sunday and 25-26 December – **Meals** - Thai - 7.95/17.00 **t.** and a la carte.

Noble House, 3-5 Lansdowne Rd, BH1 1RZ, ☎ 291277 – . AE VISA JCB
Meals - Chinese - 5.80/19.00 **st.** and a la carte. DEY **i**

Sophisticats, 43 Charminster Rd, BH8 8UE, ☎ 291019 CV **a**
closed Sunday, Monday, 2 weeks January and 2 weeks July – **Meals** (dinner only) a la carte 18.65/23.00 **t.** 4.25.

Helvetia, 61 Charminster Rd, BH8 8UE, ☎ 555447, Fax 319722 – . AE VISA
closed Sunday lunch – **Meals** - Swiss - 5.20/18.50 **t.** and a la carte 4.50. DV **c**

ATS 892 Christchurch Rd, Boscombe ☎ 424457 ATS 1 Fernside Rd, Poole ☎ 733301/733326

BOURTON-ON-THE-WATER Glos. 403 404 O 28 Great Britain G. – pop. 2 999 – 01451.

See : Town★.

London 91 – Birmingham 47 – Gloucester 24 – Oxford 36.

Dial House, The Chestnuts, High St., GL54 2AN, ☎ 822244, Fax 810126, – . AE VISA.
Meals (light lunch)/dinner a la carte 13.20/22.25 **st.** 6.50 – **10 rm** 41.50/96.00 **st.** – SB.

Lansdowne Villa, Lansdowne, GL54 2AT, ☎ 820673, Fax 822099 – . VISA JCB.
Meals (residents only) 14.00 3.75 – **12 rm** 26.00/43.00 **t.** – SB.

Coombe House without rest., Rissington Rd, GL54 2DT, ☎ 821966, Fax 810477, – . AE VISA.
closed 24, 25 and 31 December – **7 rm** 38.00/64.00 **st.**

Broadlands, Clapton Row, GL54 2DN, ☎ 822002 – rest .
Meals 10.50 **st.** 3.75 – **11 rm** 30.00/58.00 **st.**

at Little Rissington E : 1 ¾ m. on Little Rissington rd – ✉ Bourton-on-the-Water – 01451 :

Touchstone without rest., GL54 2ND, ☎ 822481, – .
closed January and February – **3 rm** 25.00/38.00 **st.**

at Great Rissington SE : 3¼ m. – ✉ Cheltenham – 01451 :

Lamb Inn, GL54 2LP, ☎ 820388, Fax 820724, « Part 17C Cotswold stone inn », – . AE VISA
closed 25 and 26 December – **Meals** a la carte 10.50/15.00 **t.** – **12 rm** 32.00/75.00 **t.**

at Lower Slaughter NW : 1 ¾ m. by A 429 – ✉ Cheltenham – 01451 :

Lower Slaughter Manor, GL54 2HP, ☎ 820456, Fax 822150, , « 17C manor house, gardens », , , – rest – 25. AE VISA.
closed 3 weeks January – **Meals** 12.95/36.50 **t.** 8.50 – **12 rm** (dinner included) 145.00/290.00 **t.**, 2 suites – SB.

Washbourne Court, GL54 2HS, ☎ 822143, Fax 821045, « Part 17C house in picturesque village », , – rest . AE VISA.
Meals (light lunch)/dinner 25.95 **t.** and a la carte – **13 rm** 78.00/130.00 **t.**, 6 suites – SB.

at Upper Slaughter NW : 2 ¾ m. by A 429 – ✉ Cheltenham – ☎ 01451 :

✿ **Lords of the Manor** ⛰, GL54 2JD, ✆ 820243, Fax 820696, ≤, « Part 17C manor house », park – rest TV ☎ P – 30. AE VISA JCB.
closed 2 to 11 January – **Meals** 14.95/29.50 **st.** and dinner a la carte approx. 34.50 **t.** 6.50 – **27 rm** 80.00/190.00 **st.** – SB
Spec. Foie gras, scallop and bacon salad with a Sauternes dressing, Trelough duckling, spiced pearl barley risotto, pear and apricot chutney, Fine apple tart on caramel sauce with sultana and Calvados ice cream.

BOVEY TRACEY Devon 403 I 32 **The West Country G.** – pop. 4 884 – ✉ Newton Abbot – ☎ 01626.
See : St. Peter, St. Paul and St. Thomas of Canterbury Church★.
Envir. : Dartmoor National Park★★ (Brent Tor ≤★★, Haytor Rocks ≤★).
18 Newton Abbot ✆ 52460.
♦London 214 – Exeter 14 – ♦Plymouth 32.

Edgemoor, Haytor Rd, TQ13 9LE, W : 1 m. on B 3387 ✆ 832466, Fax 834760, – rest TV ☎ P – 50. AE VISA
Meals (booking essential) 10.75/21.90 **t.** 4.15 – **12 rm** 46.95/99.95 **t.** – SB.

Coombe Cross, Coombe Cross, TQ13 9EY, E : ½ m. on B 3344 ✆ 832476, Fax 835298, ≤, – rest TV ☎ P. AE VISA JCB
closed 21 November-31 December – **Meals** (bar lunch)/dinner 18.95 **st.** 6.00 – **24 rm** 40.00/64.00 – SB.

Front House Lodge, East St., TQ13 9EL, ✆ 832202, Fax 832202, – TV P. AE VISA JCB.
Meals (by arrangement) 15.00 **st.** – **6 rm** 25.00/44.00 **st.**

at Haytor W : 2½ m. on B 3387 – ✉ Bovey Tracey – ☎ 01364 :

Bel Alp House ⛰, TQ13 9XX, on B 3387 ✆ 661217, Fax 661292, ≤ countryside, « Country house atmosphere », – rest TV ☎ ♿ P. VISA
March-November – **Meals** (booking essential) (light lunch)/dinner 30.00 5.00 – **9 rm** 78.00/156.00 **t.** – SB.

at Haytor Vale W : 3½ m. by B 3387 – ✉ Newton Abbot – ☎ 01364 :

Rock Inn, TQ13 9XP, ✆ 661305, Fax 661242, « 18C inn », – TV ☎ P. AE VISA JCB.
Meals (bar lunch)/dinner 20.95 **t.** and a la carte 6.25 – **10 rm** 29.50/51.00 **t.** – SB.

BOWBURN Durham 401 402 P 19 – pop. 5 141 – ☎ 0191.
♦London 265 – Durham 3 – ♦Middlesbrough 20.

Road Chef Lodge without rest., Tursdale, DH6 5NP, at junction of A 1(M) with A 177 ✆ 377 3666, Fax 377 1448, Reservations (Freephone) 0800 834719 – TV ☎ ♿ P.
closed Christmas – **38 rm** 37.50 **st.**

BOWDON Gtr. Manchester 402 403 404 M 23 – see Altrincham.

BOWLAND BRIDGE Cumbria – see Newby Bridge.

BOWNESS-ON-WINDERMERE Cumbria 402 L 20 - see Windermere.

BOX Avon 403 404 M 29 – see Bath.

BRACKENTHWAITE Cumbria – see Buttermere.

BRACKLEY Northants. 403 404 Q 27 – pop. 9 113 – ☎ 01280.
2 Bridge St., NN13 5EP ✆ 700111.
♦London 67 – ♦Birmingham 53 – Northampton 21 – ♦Oxford 21.

Crown, 20 Market Pl., NN13 7DP, ✆ 702210, Fax 701840 – TV ☎ – 60. AE VISA.
Meals 9.50 **st.** (dinner) and a la carte 7.40/14.35 **st.** 6.95 – **18 rm** 50.00/65.00 **t.** – SB.

ATS Station Building, Northampton Rd ✆ 702000/703188

BRACKNELL Berks. 404 R 29 – pop. 50 325 – 01344.

Downshire, Easthampstead Park, Wokingham 302030.

The Look Out, Nine Mile Ride, RG12 7QW 868196.

London 35 – Reading 11.

Coppid Beech, John Nike Way, RG12 8TF, NW : 3 m. by A 329 on B 3408 303333, Fax 301200, – rm rest – 350. AE VISA. **Rowans : Meals** *(closed Saturday lunch)* 17.50/39.50 **t.** and a la carte 8.25 – **205 rm** 105.00/195.00 **t.** – SB.

Hilton National, Bagshot Rd, RG12 3QJ, S : 2 m. on A 322 424801, Fax 487454, – rm rest – 200. AE VISA JCB **Meals** *(closed Saturday lunch)* 12.95/14.95 **st.** and a la carte 5.60 – 10.75 – **167 rm** 95.00/130.00 **t.** – SB.

BRADFIELD Berks. 403 404 Q 29 – pop. 1 570 – Reading – 01734.

London 56 – Oxford 28 – Reading 7.

Boot Farm without rest., Southend Rd., Southend, RG7 6ES, SW : 2 m. 744298, – . **4 rm** 25.00/38.00 **t.**

BRADFIELD COMBUST Suffolk – see Bury St. Edmunds.

BRADFORD W. Yorks. 402 O 22 **Great Britain G.** – pop. 457 344 – 01274.

See : City★.

West Bowling, Newall Hall, Rooley Lane 724449 BY – Woodhall Hills, Woodhall Rd, Calverley, Pudsley (0113) 256 4771/225 4594 – Bradford Moor, Scarr Hall, Pollard Lane 638313 BX – East Bierley, South View Rd 681023 BX – Queensbury, Brighouses Road 882155, AY.

Leeds and Bradford Airport : (0113) 250 9696, NE : 6 m. by A 658 BX.

National Museum of Photography, Film & TV, Pictureville, BD1 1NQ 753678.

London 212 – Leeds 9 – Manchester 39 – Middlesbrough 75 – Sheffield 45.

Plan of Enlarged Area : see Leeds

Stakis Bradford, Hall Ings, BD1 5SH, 734734, Fax 306146 – rm rest – 700. AE VISA BZ **e** **Meals** 6.50/17.95 **st.** and a la carte – 8.95 – **116 rm** 69.00/84.00 **st.**, 4 suites – SB.

Victoria, Bridge St., BD1 1JX, 728706, Fax 736358, – – 150. AE VISA JCB BZ **a** **Meals** *(closed Saturday lunch and Sunday)* 7.95/9.95 **st.** and a la carte – 10.00 – **57 rm** 49.00/79.00 **st.**, 3 suites.

Tong Village, The Pastures, Tong Lane, BD4 0RP, SE : 4 ¾ m. by A 650 and B 6135 on Tong Lane 2854646, Fax 2853661, , – rm – 250. AE VISA **Meals** a la carte 10.65/19.60 **st.** – 7.50 – **58 rm** 65.00/96.00 **st.**, 1 suite – SB. BY

Guide Post, Common Rd, Low Moor, BD12 OST, S : 3 m. by A 641 off A 638 607866, Fax 671085 – – 100. AE VISA. on plan of Leeds AX **c** **Meals** *(closed Saturday lunch)* 8.95/14.95 **t.** and dinner a la carte 3.65 – **43 rm** 50.00/85.00 **t.**

Novotel Bradford, Euroway Trading Estate, Merrydale Rd, BD4 6SA, S : 3 ½ m. by A 641 and A 6117 off M 606 683683, Fax 651342, heated – rm – 300. AE VISA on plan of Leeds AX **a** **Meals** 12.50 and a la carte 4.95 – 7.50 – **125 rm** 42.50 **st.**

Park Drive, 12 Park Drive, Heaton, BD9 4DR, 480194, Fax 484869, – . AE VISA. AX **e** **Meals** (bar lunch)/dinner 12.00 **st.** and a la carte – **11 rm** 46.00/56.00 **st.** – SB.

Brow Top Farm without rest., Baldwin Lane, Clayton, BD14 6PS, SW : 4½ m. by A 647 off Baldwin Lane 882178, « Working farm », – . AY *closed Christmas* – **3 rm** 20.00/30.00.

XXX **Restaurant Nineteen** (Smith) with rm, 19 North Park Rd, Heaton, BD9 4NT, 492559 – . AE VISA. AX **n** *closed Sunday, Monday, 1 week May-June, 2 weeks August-September and 1 week Christmas-New Year* – **Meals** (dinner only) 25.00 **t.** 6.50 – **4 rm** 65.00/75.00 **t.** – SB Spec. Red mullet sausage with pesto noodles, Roasted cornfed chicken with Parma ham, goats cheese and plum tomatoes, Orange tart with lemon sorbet.

XXX **Bombay Brasserie**, Simes St., Westgate, BD1 3RB, 737564, Fax 370515, « Former Baptist church » – . VISA AZ **a** **Meals** - Indian - 8.95/17.50 **t.** and a la carte 4.00.

at Gomersal SE : 7 m. by A 650 on A 651 – BY – Bradford – 01274 :

Gomersal Park, Moor Lane, BD19 4LJ, NW : 1 ½ m. by A 651 off A 652 869386, Fax 861042, , – – 200. AE VISA **Meals** *(closed Saturday lunch)* 7.95/16.50 **st.** and a la carte 5.95 – 7.25 – **49 rm** 70.00/80.00 **st.**, 1 suite – SB.

ATS 8 Cranmer Rd 632233/632106
ATS 177 Thornton Rd 731141/723015
ATS Tong Street (ASDA) 680155

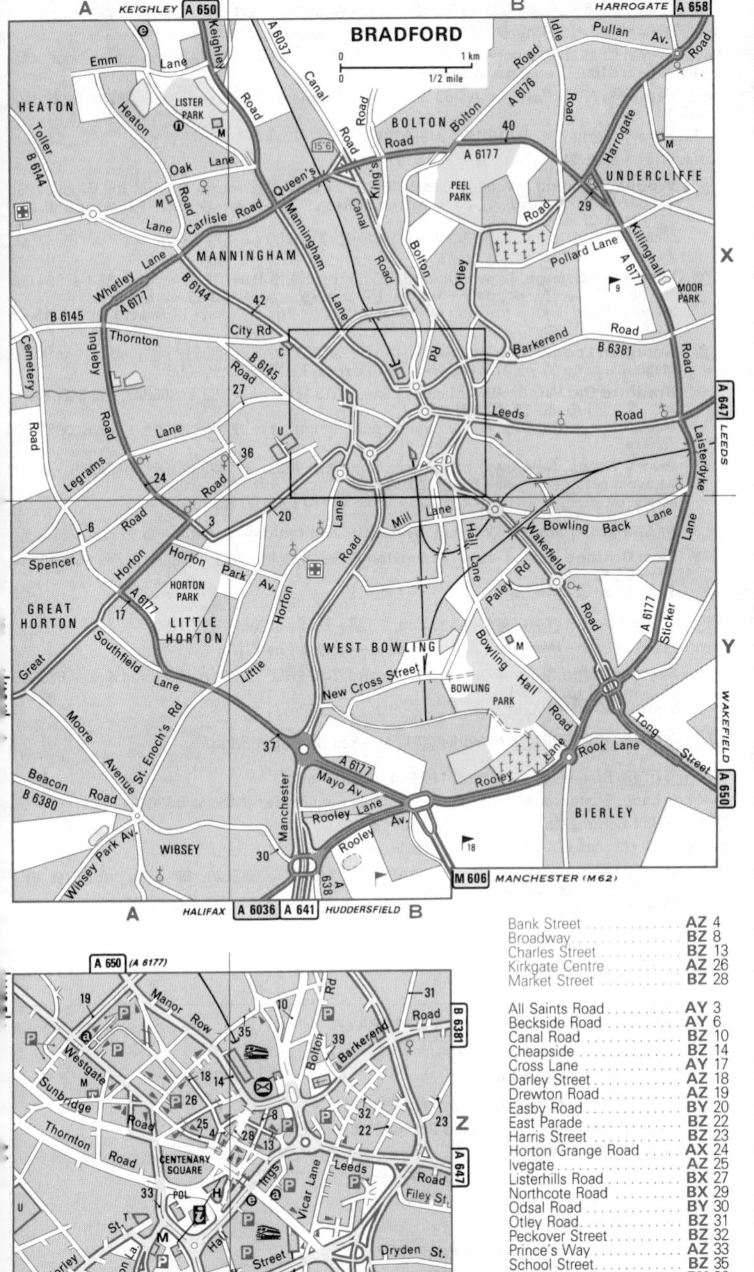

Street	Grid	No.
Bank Street	AZ	4
Broadway	BZ	8
Charles Street	BZ	13
Kirkgate Centre	AZ	26
Market Street	BZ	28

Street	Grid	No.
All Saints Road	AY	3
Beckside Road	AY	6
Canal Road	BZ	10
Cheapside	BZ	14
Cross Lane	AY	17
Darley Street	AZ	18
Drewton Road	AZ	19
Easby Road	BY	20
East Parade	BZ	22
Harris Street	BZ	23
Horton Grange Road	AX	24
Ivegate	AZ	25
Listerhills Road	BX	27
Northcote Road	BX	29
Odsal Road	BY	30
Otley Road	BZ	31
Peckover Street	BZ	32
Prince's Way	AZ	33
School Street	BZ	35
Shearbridge Road	BX	36
Smiddles Lane	BY	37
Stott Hill	BZ	39
Valley View Grove	BX	40
White Abbey Road	BX	42

BRADFORD-ON-AVON Wilts. 403 404 N 29 The West Country G. – pop. 8 815 – ☎ 01225.

See : Town★★ - Saxon Church of St. Lawrence★★ – Bridge★.

Envir. : Great Chalfield Manor★ (All Saints★) *AC*, NE : 3 m. by B 3109 – Westwood Manor★ *AC*, S : 1½m. by B 3109 – Top Rank Tory (≤★).

Exc. : Bath★★★, NW : 7½m. by A 363 and A 4 – Corsham Court★★ *AC*, NE : 6½m. by B 3109 and A 4.

ℹ The Library, Bridge St., BA15 1BY ℘ 865797.

◆London 118 – ◆ Bristol 24 – Salisbury 35 – Swindon 33.

Woolley Grange, Woolley Green, BA15 1TX, NE : ¾ m. by B 3107 on Woolley St. ℘ 864705, Fax 864059, ≤, « 17C manor house », heated, park, – rest TV ☎ P – 40. AE VISA
Meals 28.00 **st.** (dinner) and lunch a la carte 10.00/25.00 5.40 – **18 rm** 80.00/165.00 **st.**, 2 suites – SB.

Widbrook Grange, Trowbridge Rd, Widbrook, BA15 1UH, SE : 1 m. on A 363 ℘ 864750, Fax 862890, , , , park – rest TV ☎ & P – 25. AE VISA JCB.
Meals *(closed Friday to Sunday)* (residents only) (dinner only) 19.50 **st.** 6.50 – **18 rm** 32.50/85.00 **st.**

Georgian Lodge, 25 Bridge St., BA15 1BY, ℘ 862268, Fax 862218 – TV.
Meals a la carte 11.70/21.00 **st.** 4.50 – **10 rm** 30.00/55.00 **st.** – SB.

Bradford Old Windmill, 4 Masons Lane, BA15 1QN, on A 363 ℘ 866842, Fax 866648, ≤, – TV P. AE VISA.
Meals - Ethnic Vegetarian - (by arrangement) (communal dining) 18.00 **s.** – **4 rm** 39.00/75.00 **s.**

Priory Steps, Newtown, off Market St., BA15 1NQ, ℘ 862230, Fax 866248, ≤, « 17C weavers cottages », – TV P. VISA.
Meals (by arrangement) 16.00 3.90 – **5 rm** 44.00/58.00 **st.** – SB.

at Monkton Farleigh NW : 4 m. by A 363 – ✉ Bradford-on-Avon – ☎ 01225 :

Fern Cottage without rest., 74 Monkton Farleigh, BA15 2QJ, ℘ 859412, Fax 859018, – TV P.
3 rm 30.00/50.00 **st.**

BRADWELL Derbs. 402 403 404 O 24 pop. 1 728 – ✉ Sheffield – ☎ 01433.

◆London 181 – Derby 51 – ◆Manchester 32 – ◆Sheffield 16 – ◆Stoke-on-Trent 41.

Stoney Ridge without rest., Granby Rd, S30 2HU, W : ¾ m. by Gore Lane ℘ 620538, , – TV P. VISA
3 rm 26.00/48.00 **st.**

BRAFFERTON HELPERBY N. Yorks 402 P 21 – see Boroughbridge.

BRAINTREE Essex 404 V 28 – pop. 118 883 – ☎ 01376.

18 Kings Lane, Stisted ℘ 346079 – 9 Towerlands, Panfield Rd ℘ 552487/326802.

ℹ Town Hall Centre, Market Sq., CM7 6YG ℘ 550066.

◆London 45 – ◆Cambridge 38 – Chelmsford 12 – Colchester 15.

White Hart, Bocking End, CM7 9AB, ℘ 321401, Fax 552628, – rm TV ☎ P – 40. AE VISA.
Meals (grill rest.) a la carte 12.85/17.80 **st.** 5.25 – **31 rm** 59.50/71.00 **st.** – SB.

ATS 271-275 Rayne Rd ℘ 323306

BRAITHWAITE Cumbria 401 402 K 20 – see Keswick.

BRAMHALL Ches. 402 403 404 N 23 – ✉ Stockport – ☎ 0161.

♦London 190 – Chesterfield 35 – ♦Manchester 11.

Bramhall Moat House (Q.M.H.), Bramhall Lane South, SK7 2EB, on A 5102 ☏ 439 8116, Fax 440 8071, – rm – 110.
closed 25 to 30 December – **Meals** (bar lunch)/dinner 14.50 **st.** and a la carte 6.85 – **65 rm** 79.00/89.00 **st.**

at Woodford S : 2 m. on A 5102 – ✉ Bramhall – ☎ 0161 :

Olivers, 547 Chester Rd, SK7 1PR, on A 5102 ☏ 440 8715 – .
closed Sunday dinner and Monday – **Meals** a la carte 17.20/23.40 **t.** 4.95.

BRAMHOPE W. Yorks. 402 P 22 – see Leeds.

BRAMLEY Surrey 404 S 30 – see Guildford.

BRAMLEY S. Yorks. 402 403 404 Q 23 – see Rotherham.

BRAMPTON Cumbria 401 402 L 19 Great Britain G. – pop. 3 957 – ☎ 0169 77.

Envir. : Hadrian's Wall★★, NW : by A 6077.

18 Talkin Tarn ☏ 2255.

Moot Hall, Market Pl., CA8 IRA ☏ 3433 (summer only).

♦London 317 – ♦Carlisle 9 – ♦Newcastle upon Tyne 49.

Farlam Hall , CA8 2NG, SE : 2 ¾ m. on A 689 ☏ 46234, Fax 46683, ≤, « Gardens » – .
closed 25 to 30 December – **Meals** (dinner only) 28.50 **t.** 6.75 – **12 rm** (dinner included) 95.00/210.00 **t.** – SB.

Kirby Moor Country House, Longtown Rd, CA8 2AB, N : ½ m. on A 6071 ☏ 3893, Fax 41847, – .
closed 25 and 26 December – **Meals** (light lunch)/dinner 12.95 **t.** and a la carte 4.95 – **6 rm** 38.50/48.00 **t.** – SB.

at Kirkcambeck N : 7 ¾ m. by A 6071 and Walton rd – ✉ Brampton – ☎ 0169 77 :

Cracrop Farm , CA8 2BW, W : 1 m. by B 6318 on Stapleton rd ☏ 48245, Fax 48333, ≤, « Working farm », , – .
Meals (by arrangement) (communal dining) 14.00 **st.** – **4 rm** 20.00/44.00 **st.**

at Lanercost NE : 2 m. by A 689 – ✉ Brampton – ☎ 0169 77 :

Abbey Bridge Inn, CA8 2HG, ☏ 2224, Fax 2224 – rm .
closed 25 December – **Meals** a la carte 15.00/17.25 **t.** – **7 rm** 20.00/50.00 **t.** – SB.

at Talkin S : 2 ¾ m. by B 6413 – ✉ Brampton – ☎ 0169 77 :

Hullerbank , CA8 1LB, NE : ½ m. by Hallbankgate rd ☏ 46668, – .
Meals (by arrangement) 11.00 **st.** – **3 rm** 25.00/40.00 **st.** – SB.

BRANDESBURTON Humbs. 402 T 22 pop. 1 835 – ✉ Great Driffield – ☎ 01964.

♦London 197 – ♦Kingston-upon-Hull 16 – York 37.

Burton Lodge, YO25 8RU, S : ½ m. on A 165 ☏ 542847, Fax 542847, 18, , – rest
Meals (residents only)(dinner only) 12.00 **st.** 4.50 – **9 rm** 35.00/45.00 **st.** – SB.

BRANDON Warks. 403 404 P 26 – see Coventry (W. Mids.).

BRANDS HATCH Kent – ✉ Dartford – ☎ 01474.

9 Corinthian, Gay Dawn Farm, Fawkham, Dartford ☏ 707559.

♦London 22 – Maidstone 18.

Brands Hatch Thistle (Mt. Charlotte), DA3 8PE, on A 20 ☏ 854900, Fax 853220 – rm rest – 270.
Meals *(closed lunch Saturday and Bank Holidays)* 14.95/19.95 **t.** and a la carte 7.25 – 9.50 – **135 rm** 70.00/80.00 **st.**, 2 suites – SB.

at Fawkham Green E : 1 ½ m. by A 20 – ✉ Ash Green – ☎ 01474 :

Brands Hatch Place, DA3 8NQ, ☏ 872239, Fax 879652, , , , , park, , squash – rest – 120.
Meals *(closed Saturday lunch)* 13.25/19.95 **st.** and a la carte 6.75 – **41 rm** 80.00/120.00 **st.** – SB.

BRANSCOMBE Devon 403 K 32 The West Country G. – pop. 501 – ✉ Seaton – ☎ 01297.

See : Village★.

Envir. : Seaton (≤★★) NW : 3 m.

♦London 167 – Exeter 20 – Lyme Regis 11.

- **The Look Out** ⛺, EX12 3DP, S : ¾ m. by Beach rd ☎ 680262, Fax 680272, ≤ cliffs and Beer Head, « Tastefully converted coastguards cottages », 🌳 – TV ☎ P
  closed 4 days Christmas – **Meals** *(closed Monday)* (dinner only) 17.50/22.50 **t.** 5.25 – **5 rm** ☕ 55.00/86.00 **t.** – SB.
- **Masons Arms,** EX12 3DJ, ☎ 680300, Fax 680500, « 14C inn » – TV ☎ P – 🏛 60. VISA
  Meals (bar lunch Monday to Saturday)/dinner a la carte 14.00/18.50 **t.** – **21 rm** ☕ 22.00/74.00 **st.** – SB.

BRANSTON Lincs. 402 404 S 24 – see Lincoln.

BRANSTON Staffs. – see Burton-upon-Trent.

BRATTON FLEMING Devon 403 I 30 pop. 1 813 – ✉ Barnstaple – ☎ 01598.

♦London 228 – Barnstaple 6 – Exeter 46 – Taunton 36.

- **Bracken House** ⛺, EX31 4TG, ☎ 710320, ≤, 🌳 – TV ♿ P. VISA
  mid March-mid November – **Meals** (dinner only) 15.00 **t.** – **8 rm** ☕ (dinner included) 46.00/94.00 **t.** – SB.

BRAUNSTONE Leics. 402 403 404 Q 26 – see Leicester.

BRAY-ON-THAMES Berks. 404 R 29 – pop. 8 121 – ✉ Maidenhead – ☎ 01628.

♦London 34 – Reading 13.

Plan : see Maidenhead

- **Monkey Island,** SL6 2EE, SE : ¾ m. by Upper Bray Rd and Old Mill Lane ☎ 23400, Fax 784732, ≤, « Island on River Thames », 🎣, 🌳 – TV ☎ P – 🏛 150. AE ⓞ VISA. ✻
  closed 26 December-7 January – **Meals** *(closed Saturday lunch)* 14.00/25.00 **st.** and a la carte 7.50 – ☕ 10.00 – **23 rm** 85.00/100.00 **st.**, 2 suites – SB.
- XXXX ✻✻✻ **Waterside Inn** (Roux) with rm, Ferry Rd, SL6 2AT, ☎ 20691, Fax 784710, « ≤ Thames-side setting », 🌳 – ▤ rest TV ☎ P. ⓞ VISA JCB. ✻ X s
  closed 26 December-26 January – **Meals** - French - *(closed Tuesday lunch, Sunday dinner from 3rd weekend October-2nd weekend April, Monday and Bank Holidays)* 29.00/65.50 **st.** and a la carte 56.10/86.00 **st.** 11.50 – **6 rm** 130.00/160.00 **st.**, 1 suite
  Spec. Tronçonnettes de homard poêlées minute au Porto blanc, Filets de lapereau grillés aux marrons glacés, Soufflé chaud aux framboises.

BREADSALL Derbs. – see Derby.

BREDONS NORTON 403 404 N 28 – see Tewkesbury.

BREDWARDINE Heref. and Worcs. 403 L 27 – ✉ Hereford – ☎ 01981.

♦London 150 – Hereford 12 – Newport 51.

- **Bredwardine Hall** ⛺, HR3 6DB, ☎ 500596, 🌳 – ⊬ TV P. ✻
  March-October – **Meals** (by arrangement) 12.00 4.50 – **4 rm** ☕ 33.00/50.00 **st.** – SB.

BRENCHLEY Kent 404 V 30 – pop. 2 756 – ✉ Tonbridge – ☎ 01892.

⛳18 Moatlands, Watermans Lane ☎ 724400.

♦London 44 – ♦Brighton 41 – Hastings 28 – Maidstone 15.

- **Bull Inn,** High St., TN12 7NQ, ☎ 722701, Fax 723248 – ⊬ rm TV P. ✻
  Meals 12.00/17.00 **t.** 3.50 – **4 rm** ☕ 24.00/45.00 **t.** – SB.

BRENT KNOLL Somerset 403 L 30 – pop. 1 142 – ✉ Highbridge – ☎ 01278.

⛳18 Brean, Coast Rd, Burnham-on-Sea ☎ 751595.

♦London 151 – ♦Bristol 33 – Taunton 21.

- **Battleborough Grange,** Bristol Rd, TA9 4HJ, E : 2 m. on A 38 ☎ 760208, Fax 760208, 🌳 – TV ☎ P – 🏛 90. AE ⓞ VISA. ✻
  Meals 17.00 **st.** and a la carte 4.50 – **16 rm** ☕ 42.50/65.00 **st.** – SB.

Les prix Pour toutes précisions sur les prix indiqués dans ce guide, reportez-vous à l'introduction.

BRENTWOOD Essex 404 V 29 – pop. 70 597 – ☎ 01277 – 18 Bentley, Ongar Road ℘ 373179.
9, 18, Warley Park, Magpie Lane, Little Warley ℘ 224891.
14 Ongar Rd, CM15 9AX ℘ 200300.
♦London 22 – Chelmsford 11 – Southend-on-Sea 21.

Marygreen Manor, London Rd, CM14 4NR, SW : 1 ¼ m. on A 1023 ℘ 225252, Telex 995182, Fax 262809, – rm – 50. AE VISA.
Meals 12.00/25.00 **t.** and a la carte 5.50 – 9.00 – **32 rm** 88.00/155.00 **st.**, 1 suite.

Forte Posthouse, Brook St., CM14 5NF, SW : 1½ m. on A 1023 ℘ 260260, Fax 264264, – rest – 100. AE VISA.
Meals a la carte 15.00/22.40 **st.** 5.95 – 7.95 – **113 rm** 69.00 **st.** – SB.

ATS Fairfield Rd ℘ 211079
ATS Unit 30, Wash Rd, Hutton Ind. Est., Hutton ℘ 262877

BRETFORTON Heref. and Worcs. 403 404 O 27 – see Evesham.

BRIDGNORTH Shrops. 402 403 404 M 26 **Great Britain G.** – pop. 50 511 – ☎ 01746.
Exc. : Ironbridge Gorge Museum★★ *AC* (The Iron Bridge★★ - Coalport China Museum★★ - Blists Hill Open Air Museum★★ - Museum of the River and Visitor Centre★) NW : 8 m. by B 4373.
18 Stanley Lane ℘ 763315.
The Library, Listley St., WV16 4AW ℘ 763358.
♦London 146 – ♦Birmingham 26 – Shrewsbury 20 – Worcester 29.

Cross Lane House, Astley Abbotts, WV16 4SJ, N : 1 ¾ m. on B 4373 ℘ 764887, Fax 768667, – VISA.
Meals (residents only) (dinner only) 18.50 **st.** 5.50 – **9 rm** 37.50/75.00 **st.** – SB.

Croft, 11 St. Mary's St., WV16 4DW, ℘ 762416 – rest AE VISA
Meals (by arrangement) 12.95 **st.** 5.25 – **12 rm** 30.50/48.00 **st.** – SB.

at Worfield NE : 4 m. by A 454 – ✉ Bridgnorth – ☎ 01746 :

Old Vicarage , WV15 5JZ, ℘ 716497, Fax 716552, – AE VISA
closed 22 December-15 January – **Meals** (residents only Sunday dinner) (dinner only and Sunday lunch)/dinner 24.00/35.00 **t.** 9.00 – **12 rm** 65.00/120.00 **t.**, 2 suites – SB.

at Hampton Loade SE : 6¼ m. by A 442 – ✉ Bridgnorth – ☎ 01746 :

Haywain, WV15 6HD, ℘ 780404, Fax 780533, – AE VISA
Meals *(closed Sunday dinner and Monday)* (dinner only and Sunday lunch)/dinner 19.25/23.95 **t.** 3.95.

at Alveley SE : 7 m. by A 442 – ✉ Bridgnorth – ☎ 01746 :

Mill, Birdsgreen, WV15 6HL, NE : ¾ m. ℘ 780437, Fax 780850, , park – – 150. AE VISA JCB.
Meals 8.70/18.50 **t.** and a la carte 5.00 – **21 rm** 47.50/110.00 **t.** – SB.

BRIDGWATER Somerset 403 L 30 **The West Country G.** – pop. 34 610 – ☎ 01278.
See : Town★ – Castle Street★ – St. Mary's★ – Admiral Blake Museum★ *AC*.
Envir. : Westonzoyland (St. Mary's Church★★) SE : 4 m. by A 372 – North Petherton (Church Tower★★) S : 3½m. by A 38.
Exc. : Stogursey Priory Church★★, NW : 14 m. by A 39.
18 Enmore Park,Enmore ℘ 671244.
50 High St., TA6 3BL ℘ 427652 (summer only).
♦London 160 – ♦Bristol 39 – Taunton 11.

Watergate, 10-11 West Quay, TA6 3DB, ℘ 423847, Fax 423847 –
8 rm.

Friarn Court, 37 St. Mary St., TA6 3LX, ℘ 452859, Fax 452988 – AE VISA.
Meals *(closed Sunday)* (dinner only) 20.00 **st.** and a la carte 4.50 – 2.00 – **16 rm** 39.90/59.90 **st.** – SB.

at North Petherton S : 3 m. on A 38 – ✉ Bridgwater – ☎ 01278 :

Walnut Tree Inn, TA6 6QA, ℘ 662255, Telex 46529 WT, Fax 663946 – rest – 90. AE VISA JCB.
Meals a la carte 13.90/19.00 **t.** 4.30 – **27 rm** 54.00/66.00 **t.**, 1 suite – SB.

ATS Friarn St. ℘ 455891/455795

BRIDLINGTON Humbs. 402 T 21 **Great Britain G.** – pop. 32 163 – 01262.

Envir. : Flamborough Head★, NE : 5½m. by B 1255 and B 1259 – Burton Agnes Hall★ *AC* SW : 6 m. by A 166.

Belvedere Rd 672092/606367 – Flamborough Head, Lighthouse Rd, Flamborough 850333.

25 Prince St., YO15 2NP 673474/606383.

London 236 – Kingston-upon-Hull 29 – York 41.

Expanse, North Marine Drive, YO15 2LS, 675347, Fax 604928, ← – P. VISA.
Meals 8.25/13.75 **st.** and dinner a la carte 5.20 – **48 rm** 27.50/65.00 **st.** – SB.

ATS Springfield Av. 675571

BRIDPORT Dorset 403 L 31 **The West Country G.** – pop. 7 2785 – 01308.

Exc. : Parnham House★★ *AC*, N : 6 m. by A 3066 – Lyme Regis★ - The Cobb★, W : 11 m. by A 35 and A 3052.

Bridport and West Dorset, East Cliff, West Bay 422597.

32 South St., DT6 3NQ 424901.

London 150 – Exeter 38 – Taunton 33 – Weymouth 19.

Roundham House, Roundham Gdns, West Bay Rd, DT6 4BD, S : 1 m. by B 3157 422753, ←, – rest P. VISA.
closed January, February and November – **Meals** (dinner only and Sunday lunch)/dinner 14.50 **st.** 5.00 – **8 rm** 50.00/90.00 **st.** – SB.

Britmead House, 154 West Bay Rd, DT6 4EG, S : 1 m. on B 3157 422941, – rest P. AE VISA JCB
Meals 12.00 **st.** 3.75 – **7 rm** 31.00/54.00 **st.** – SB.

Riverside, West Bay, DT6 4EZ, 422011 – VISA JCB
Meals - Seafood - *closed Sunday dinner, Monday and early December-early March* (booking essential) a la carte 13.50/26.00 **t.** 5.95.

at Powerstock NE : 4 m. by A 3066 – Bridport – 01308 :

Three Horseshoes Inn, DT6 3TF, 485328 – P. AE VISA JCB
Meals 10.50/16.50 **t.** and a la carte 4.50 – **4 rm** 24.00/50.00 **t.** – SB.

at Shipton Gorge SE : 3 m. by A 35 – Bridport – 01308 :

Innsacre Farmhouse without rest., Shipton Lane, DT6 4LJ, N : 1 m. 456137, Fax 456137, – P. VISA
closed 2 weeks November and Christmas – **6 rm** 45.00/58.00 **st.**

ATS Victoria Grove 423661/2

BRIGHOUSE W. Yorks. 402 O 22 – pop. 9 806 – 01484.

London 213 – Bradford 12 – Burnley 28 – Manchester 35 – Sheffield 39.

Forte Crest, Clifton Village, HD6 4HW, SE : 1 m. on A 644 400400, Telex 518204, Fax 400068, , – P – 200. AE VISA JCB
Meals *(closed Saturday lunch)* 12.00/20.00 **st.** and a la carte 6.50 – 10.85 – **92 rm** 95.00 **st.**, 2 suites – SB.

Brook's, 6 Bradford Rd, HD6 1RW, 715284, Fax 712641 – . VISA
closed Sunday and 2 weeks January – **Meals** (dinner only) 18.95 **t.** 3.95.

BRIGHTLINGSEA Essex 404 X 28 – 01206.

London 71 – Cambridge 61 – Colchester 11 – Ipswich 28 – Southend-on-Sea 52.

Birch House without rest., Church Rd, CO7 0QT, 302877, – P.
3 rm 22.50/38.50 **st.**

BRIGHTON AND HOVE E. Sussex 404 T 31 **Great Britain G.** – pop. 228 946 (inc. Hove) – 01273.

See : Town★★ - Royal Pavilion★★★ *AC* CZ – Seafront★★ – The Lanes★ BCZ – St. Bartholomew's★ *AC* CX **B** – Art Gallery and Museum (20C decorative arts★) CY **M.**

Envir. : Devil's Dyke (←★) NW : 5 m. by Dyke Rd (B 2121) BY.

East Brighton, Roedean Rd 604838 CV – The Dyke, Dyke Rd 857296, BV – Hollingbury Park, Ditchling Rd 552010, CV – Waterhall, Devils Dyke Rd 508658, AV.

Shoreham Airport : 452304, W : 8 m. by A 27 AV.

10 Bartholomew Sq., BN1 1JS 323755.

London 53 – Portsmouth 48 – Southampton 61.

Grand (De Vere), Kings Rd, BN1 2FW, ✆ 321188, Fax 202694, ≤, 800. VISA — BZ **v**
Meals 16.00/28.00 **t.** and a la carte – **195 rm** 130.00/165.00 **st.**, 5 suites – SB.

Brighton Thistle, Kings Rd, BN1 2GS, ✆ 206700, Fax 820692, ≤, rm – 300. VISA JCB — CZ **n**
Meals 14.50 **st.** and dinner a la carte 6.00 – (see also ***La Noblesse*** below) – 9.75 – **200 rm** 120.00/165.00 **st.**, 4 suites – SB.

Brighton Metropole, Kings Rd, BN1 2FU, ✆ 775432, Telex 877245, Fax 207764, ≤, rm rest – 1200. VISA — BZ **s**
Meals 17.50/17.95 **t.** and a la carte – **312 rm** 132.00/173.00 **st.**, 16 suites – SB.

Bedford, Kings Rd, BN1 2JF, ✆ 329744, Fax 775877, ≤, rest – 450. VISA — BZ **c**
Meals (carving rest.) 13.95/35.00 **st.** and a la carte – **125 rm** 102.00/144.00 **st.**, 4 suites – SB.

Old Ship, Kings Rd, BN1 1NR, ✆ 329001, Fax 820718 – – 300. VISA. — CZ **c**
Meals (dancing Saturday evening) 14.00/20.00 **st.** and a la carte – **151 rm** 65.00/125.00 **st.**, 1 suite – SB.

Topps, 17 Regency Sq., BN1 2FG, ✆ 729334, Fax 203679 – VISA JCB. — BZ **a**
Meals *(closed Sunday and Monday)* (dinner only) 18.95 and a la carte 3.95 – **15 rm** 45.00/79.00 **st.** – SB.

Brighton Oak, West St., BN1 2RQ, ✆ 220033, Fax 778000 – rm rest – 200. VISA — BZ **i**
Meals (bar lunch Monday to Saturday)/dinner 12.75 **st.** and a la carte 5.95 – 6.95 – **136 rm** 46.00/105.00 **st.**, 2 suites – SB.

Adelaide, 51 Regency Sq., BN1 2FF, ✆ 205286, Fax 220904 – rest. VISA. — BZ **z**
Meals *(closed Sunday and Wednesday)* (residents only) (dinner only) 14.50 **st.** 4.00 – **12 rm** 34.00/75.00 **st.** – SB.

Twenty One, 21 Charlotte St., BN2 1AG, ✆ 686450 – VISA JCB. — CV **i**
Meals *(closed Sunday and Monday)* (by arrangement) (dinner only) 15.95 **t.** 4.50 – **6 rm** 35.00/68.00 **t.**

Harvey's without rest., 1 Broad St., BN2 1TJ, ✆ 699227 – . — CZ **e**
closed Christmas – **8 rm** 20.00/50.00 **st.**

Allendale, 3 New Steine, BN2 1PB, ✆ 675436, Fax 602603 – rest. VISA. — CZ **u**
closed 23 to 29 December – **Meals** (by arrangement) 12.50/15.00 **st.** – **12 rm** 30.00/70.00 **st.**

Prince Regent without rest., 29 Regency Sq., BN1 2FH, ✆ 329962, Fax 748162 – . VISA JCB. — BZ **u**
closed Christmas – **20 rm** 35.00/55.00 **t.**

Kempton House, 33-34 Marine Par., BN2 1TR, ✆ 570248, Fax 570248, ≤ – . VISA — CZ **a**
Meals (by arrangement) – **12 rm** 32.00/52.00 **st.**

New Steine without rest., 12a New Steine, BN2 1PB, ✆ 681546 – . — CZ **v**
closed January and February – **11 rm** 18.00/45.00 **st.**

La Noblesse (at Brighton Thistle H.), Kings Rd, BN1 2GS, ✆ 206700, Fax 820692 – — CZ **n**
Meals *(closed Saturday lunch, Sunday and Monday)* 16.50/23.00 **st.** 6.00.

One Paston Place, 1 Paston Pl., Kemp Town, BN2 1HA, ✆ 606933, Fax 675685 – . VISA — CV **a**
closed Sunday, Monday, 1 to 15 January and 1 to 15 August – **Meals** 14.50 **t.** (lunch) and a la carte 23.00/27.50 **t.**

Whytes, 33 Western St., BN1 2PG, ✆ 776618 – VISA — BZ **o**
closed Sunday – **Meals** (dinner only) 15.50/18.95 **t.**

Black Chapati, 12 Circus Par., off New England Rd, BN1 4GW, ✆ 699011 – VISA
closed Sunday, Monday, 1 week June and 1 week Christmas – **Meals** - Indian Specialities - (dinner only) a la carte 15.50/20.50 **t.** — CX **a**

Foggs, 5 Little Western St., BN1 2PU, ✆ 735907 – VISA JCB — BY **e**
closed 25 December-31 January – **Meals** (dinner only) a la carte 18.60/22.50 **t.** 3.60.

at Hove – ✆ 01273 :

Imperial, First Av., BN3 2GU, ✆ 777320, Fax 777310 – – 100. VISA
Meals 13.95 **st.** and a la carte 8.95 – **75 rm** 45.00/70.00 **st.** – SB. — AZ **e**

Whitehaven, 34 Wilbury Rd, BN3 3JP, ✆ 778355, Fax 731177, – . VISA — AX **c**
Meals *(closed Saturday lunch and Sunday)* 7.95/19.95 **t.** 5.25 – **17 rm** 40.00/60.00 **st.** – SB.

BRIGHTON AND HOVE

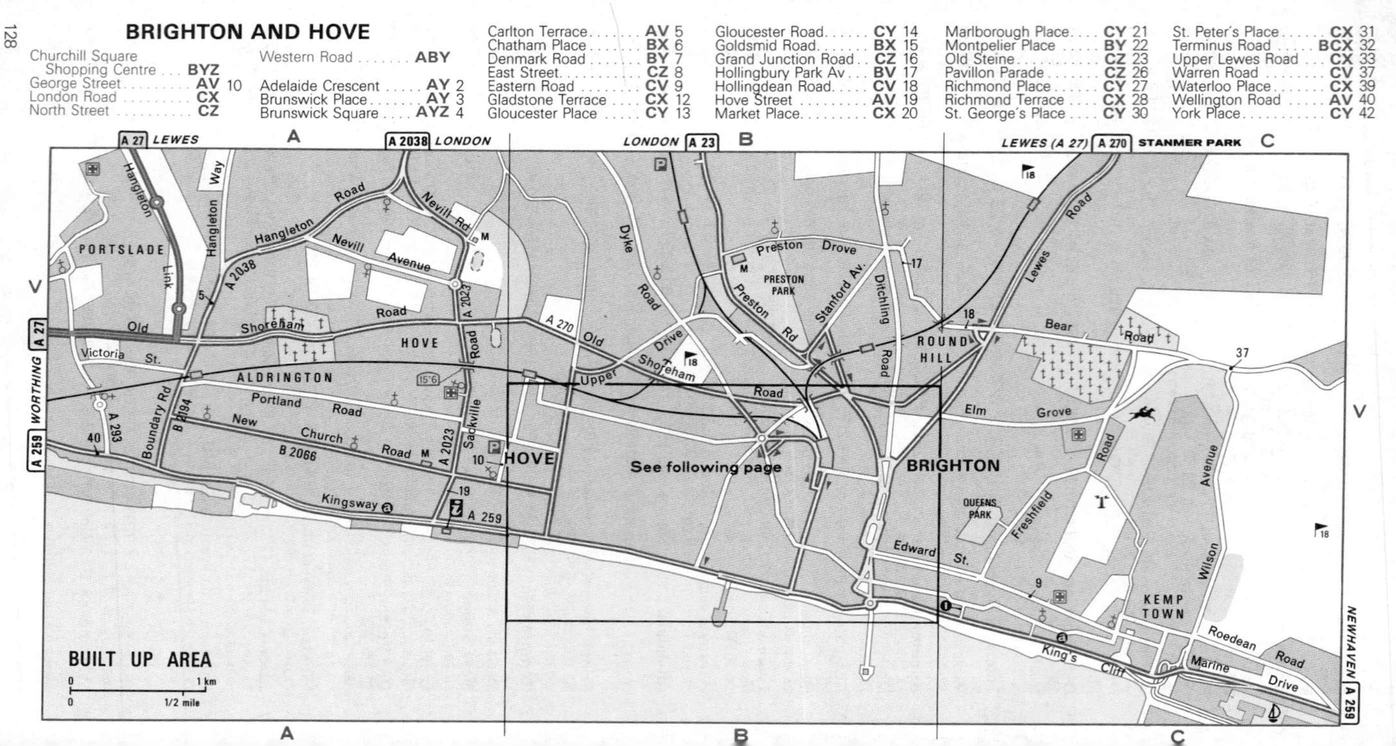

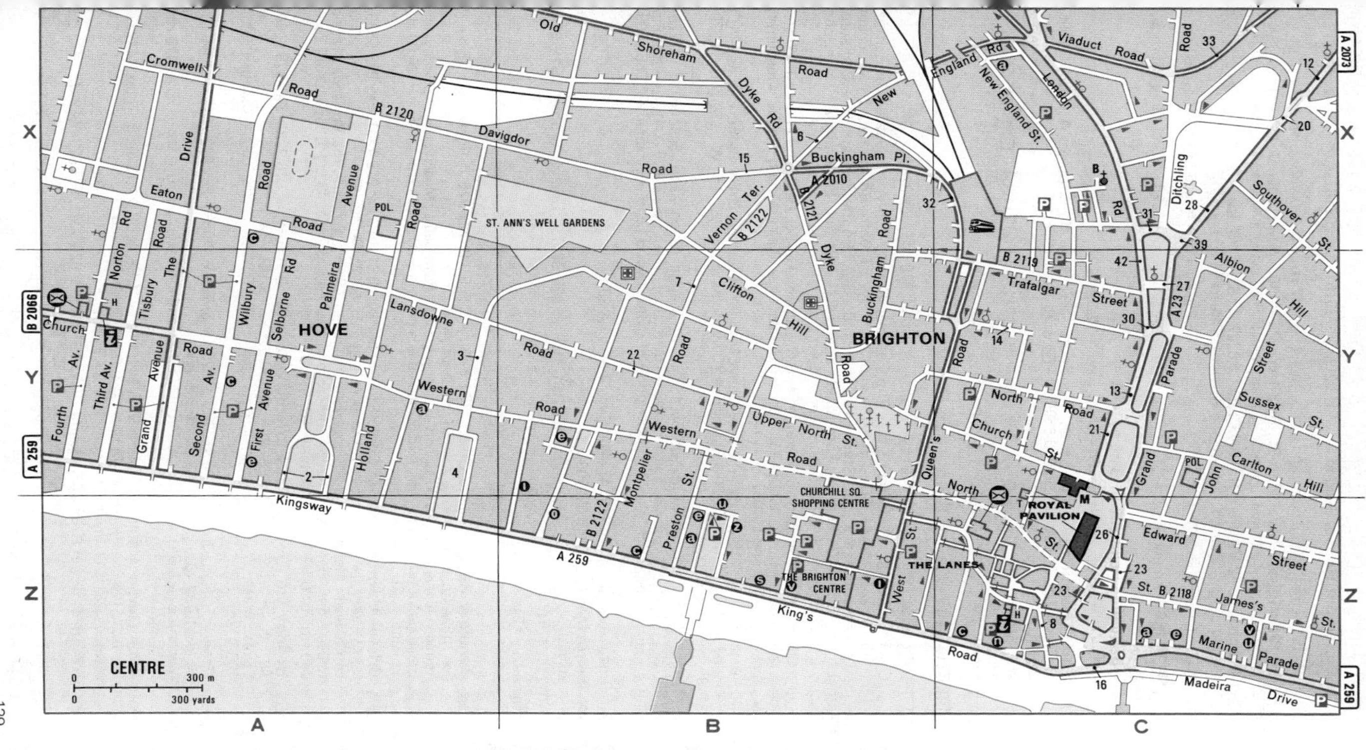

A 2073
A 259
B 2066
A 259
X
Y
Z
A
B
C
BRIGHTON
HOVE
ROYAL PAVILION
THE LANES
CHURCHILL SQ. SHOPPING CENTRE
THE BRIGHTON CENTRE
ST. ANN'S WELL GARDENS
Kingsway
King's Road
Madeira Drive
Marine Parade
Queen's Road
North Road
Church St.
North St.
West St.
Western Road
Upper North St.
Dyke Road
Dyke Rd
Clifton Hill
Montpelier Road
Preston St.
Buckingham Road
Buckingham Pl.
Trafalgar Street
Grand Parade
Edward Street
St. James's St.
Carlton Hill
John St.
Sussex St.
Albion Hill
Southover St.
Ditchling Road
Viaduct Road
London Rd
New England St.
New England Rd
New England Road
Shoreham Road
Old Shoreham Road
Vernon Ter.
Davigdor Road
Lansdowne Road
Holland Road
Palmeira Avenue
Selborne Rd
Wilbury Road
First Avenue
Second Av.
Grand Avenue
The Drive
Eaton Road
Cromwell Road
Tisbury Road
Norton Rd
Third Av.
Fourth Av.
Church Road
A 23
A 2010
B 2118
B 2119
B 2120
B 2121
B 2122
POL
CENTRE
0
300 m
300 yards

Claremont House, Second Av., BN3 2LL, ☎ 735161, Fax 735161, – TV ☎. AE VISA JCB — AY c
Meals (dinner only) 9.50 **st.** and a la carte 4.00 – **12 rm** 45.00/68.00 **st.** – SB.

Le Classique, 37 Waterloo St., BN3 1AY, ☎ 734140 – . AE VISA — BY i
closed Sunday – **Meals** - French - (dinner only) 15.25 **t.** and a la carte 4.25.

Quentin's, 42 Western Rd, BN3 1JD, ☎ 822734. AE VISA — AZ a
closed Saturday lunch, Sunday and Monday – **Meals** 14.95 **t.** 4.25.

ATS 40 Bristol Gdns ☎ 680150/686344 — ATS Franklin Rd, Portslade ☎ 415327/414488

BRIMFIELD Heref. and Worcs. 403 404 L 27 **Great Britain G.** – pop. 626 – ✉ Ludlow (Shrops.) – ☎ 01584.

Envir. : Berrington Hall★ *AC*, S : 3 m. by A 49.

♦London 149 – ♦Birmingham 41 – Hereford 21 – Shrewsbury 32 – Worcester 33.

Forte Travelodge without rest., Woofferton, SY8 4AL, N : ½ m. on A 49 ☎ 711695, Reservations (Freephone) 0800 850950 – TV P. AE VISA.
32 rm 34.50 **t.**

Poppies (at The Roebuck) with rm, SY8 4NE, ☎ 711230, Fax 711654 – TV ☎ P. VISA
closed 25 and 26 December – **Meals** *(closed Sunday and Monday)* 20.00 **t.** (lunch) and dinner a la carte 27.00/36.00 **t.** 7.50 – **3 rm** 45.00/60.00 **t.**

BRIMSCOMBE Glos. 403 404 N 28 – see Stroud.

BRISTOL Avon 403 404 M 29 **The West Country G.** – pop. 376 146 – ☎ 0117.

See : City★★ – St. Mary Redcliffe★★ DZ – The Georgian House★★ AX **A** - Industrial Museum★★ CZ **M2** - SS Great Britain★★ *AC* AX **B** – The Old City★ CYZ : Theatre Royal★★ CZ **T** - Merchant Seamen's Almshouses★ **K** – St. Stephen's City★ CY **D** - St. John the Baptist★ CY – Cathedral District★ CYZ (Bristol Cathedral★, Lord Mayor's Chapel★) – Bristol "Exploratory"★ DZ - John Wesley's New Room★ DY **E** – City Museum and Art Gallery★ AX **M**.

Envir. : Clifton★★ AX (Suspension Bridge★★★, R.C. Cathedral of SS. Peter and Paul★★ **F**, Bristol Zoological Gardens★★ *AC*, Village★) – Blaise Hamlet★★ - Blaise Castle House Museum★, NW : 5 m. by A 4018 and B 4057 AV.

Exc. : Bath★★★, SE : 13 m. by A 4 BX – Chew Magna★ (Stanton Drew Stone Circles★ *AC*) S : 8 m. by A 37 - BX - and B 3130 – Clevedon★ (Clevedon Court★ *AC*, ≤★) W : 11½m. by A 370, B 3128 – AX – and B 3130.

Mangotsfield, Carsons Rd ☎ 956 5501, BV – Beggar Bush Lane, Failand ☎ (01275) 393117/393474, AX – Knowle, Fairway, West Town Lane, Brislington ☎ 977 6341, BX – Long Ashton ☎ (01275) 392229, AX – Stockwood Vale, Stockwood Lane, Keynsham ☎ 986 6505, BX.

Bristol Airport : ☎ (01275) 474444, SW : 7 m. by A 38 AX.

Temple Meads ☎ 0345 090700.

St. Nicholas Church, St. Nicholas St., BS1 1UE ☎ 926 0767 – Bristol Airport, BS19 3DY ☎ (01275) 474444.

♦London 121 – ♦Birmingham 91.

Plans on following pages

Swallow Royal, College Green, BS1 5TA, ☎ 925 5100, Fax 925 1515, – rm TV ☎ P – 250. AE VISA JCB — CZ a
Terrace : Meals 12.50/20.00 **st.** and a la carte 7.00 – **Palm Court : Meals** *(closed Sunday and Bank Holidays)* (dinner only) 23.50 **st.** and a la carte 7.00 – **230 rm** 95.00/126.00 **st.**, 12 suites – SB.

Bristol Marriott, 2 Lower Castle St., Old Market, BS1 3AD, ☎ 929 4281, Fax 922 5838, ≤, – rm TV ☎ P – 600. AE VISA. — DY s
Le Chateau : Meals *(closed Sunday)* (dinner only) 19.95 **t.** 7.25 – **The Brasserie : Meals** *(closed Saturday lunch)* 14.25 **t.** (dinner) and a la carte 16.25/26.45 **t.** 7.25 – 10.25 – **280 rm** 75.00/89.00 **st.**, 9 suites – SB.

Holiday Inn Crowne Plaza Bristol, Victoria St., BS1 6HY, ☎ 976 9988, Fax 925 5040, – rm rest TV ☎ P – 180. AE VISA JCB — DZ a
Spires : Meals 17.00 **st.** (dinner) and a la carte 11.95/28.20 **st.** – 10.00 – **128 rm** 95.00/190.00 **st.** – SB.

Grand (Thistle), Broad St., BS1 2EL, ☎ 929 1645, Telex 449889, Fax 922 7619 – rm rest TV ☎ P – 600. AE VISA JCB — CY a
Meals *(closed Saturday lunch)* 14.50/17.50 **st.** and a la carte 5.20 – 8.75 – **178 rm** 85.00/95.00 **st.**, 4 suites – SB.

Avon Gorge (Mount Charlotte), Sion Hill, Clifton, BS8 4LD, ☎ 973 8955, Telex 444237, Fax 923 8125, ≤ – rm TV ☎ – 100. AE VISA JCB — AX x
Meals 11.25/15.00 **st.** and a la carte 5.10 – **74 rm** 75.00/100.00 **st.**, 2 suites – SB.

Hilton National Bristol, Redcliffe Way, BS1 6NJ, ☎ 926 0041, Fax 923 0089, – rm rest TV ☎ P – 300. AE VISA JCB — DZ n
Meals *(closed Saturday lunch)* 16.50/36.00 **st.** and a la carte – 10.75 – **201 rm** 95.00/105.00 **st.**

Berkeley Square, 15 Berkeley Sq., BS8 1HB, ℘ 925 4000, Fax 925 2970 – |♦| TV ☎ . AE VISA AX i
Meals *(closed Saturday lunch and Sunday)* (bar lunch)/dinner a la carte 14.55/24.80 **t.** 5.25 – **42 rm** 79.00/105.00 **st.**, 1 suite – SB.

St. Vincent Rocks (Forte), Sion Hill, Clifton, BS8 4BB, ℘ 973 9251, Fax 923 8139, ← – TV ☎ – 50. AE VISA AX c
Meals (dinner only and Sunday lunch)/dinner 15.95 **t.** and a la carte 6.05 – 8.50 – **46 rm** 67.50/90.00 **st.** – SB.

Westbury Park without rest., 37 Westbury Rd, BS9 3AU, ℘ 962 0465, Fax 962 8607 – TV ☎. AE VISA AV u
8 rm 29.50/48.00 **s.**

Forte Travelodge, Cribbs Causeway, BS10 8TL, junction 17, M5 ℘ 501530 – TV . AE VISA. AV e
Meals (grill rest.) – **40 rm** 34.50 **t.**

Downlands without rest., 33 Henleaze Gdns, BS9 4HH, ℘ 962 1639, Fax 962 1639 – TV. VISA AV s
9 rm 25.00/48.00 **s.**

XXX ✿ **Harveys,** 12 Denmark St., BS1 5DQ, ℘ 927 5034, Fax 927 5003, « Medieval cellars and wine museum » – . AE VISA CY c
closed Saturday lunch, Sunday and Bank Holidays – **Meals** 16.00/38.00 **st.** and a la carte 29.50/39.50 **st.**
Spec. Sautéed fresh langoustines with hazelnut and truffle, Seared scallop and leek salad with warm potatoes, sweet lime vinaigrette, Warm chocolate tart with white chocolate and pecan ice cream.

XX ✿✿ **Lettonie** (Blunos), 9 Druid Hill, Stoke Bishop, BS9 1EW, ℘ 968 6456, Fax 968 6943 (probably moving during 1996) – AE VISA AV a
closed Sunday, Monday, 2 weeks August and 2 weeks Christmas – **Meals** - French - (booking essential) 17.95/34.50 **t.** 7.85
Spec. Seared scallops on a parsnip purée with reduced chicken juices, Roast skirt of beef with a rich truffle sauce, Mascarpone and peach vinegar ice cream with raspberries.

XX **Markwicks,** 43 Corn St., BS1 1HT, ℘ 926 2658, Fax 926 2658 – AE VISA CY i
closed Saturday lunch, Sunday, Easter, last 2 weeks August, Christmas-New Year and Bank Holidays – **Meals** 16.00/19.50 **t.** and a la carte 5.50.

XX **Hunt's,** 26 Broad St., BS1 2HG, ℘ 926 5580, Fax 926 5580 – AE VISA CY r
closed Saturday lunch, Sunday, Monday, 1 week Easter, 1 week late August and 10 days Christmas – **Meals** 12.95 **t.** (lunch) and a la carte 18.95/27.95 **t.**

XX **Redcliffs,** Redcliff Quay, 125 Redcliff St., BS1 6HQ, ℘ 987 2270, Fax 930 4255, ← – AE VISA DZ e
closed Sunday dinner and 25 December – **Meals** 10.50/15.50 **t.** and a la carte.

XX **China Palace,** 18a Baldwin St., BS1 1SE, ℘ 926 2719, Fax 925 6168 – . AE VISA JCB
Meals - Chinese - a la carte 21.45/35.75 **st.** 4.50. CY x

XX **Glass Boat,** Welsh Back, nr Bristol Bridge, BS1 4SB, ℘ 929 0704, Fax 929 7338 – AE VISA DY a
closed Saturday lunch, Sunday and 24 to 27 December – **Meals** 9.50/16.50 **t.** and a la carte.

XX **Michaels,** 129 Hotwell Rd, BS8 4RU, ℘ 927 6190, Fax 925 3629 – . AE VISA
closed Sunday dinner, 28 August-1 September, 26 December and 1 January – **Meals** (dinner only and Sunday lunch)/dinner 15.00 **t.** 4.25. AX z

XX **Du Gourmet,** 43 Whiteladies Rd, BS8 2LS, ℘ 973 6230, Fax 923 7394 – . AE VISA JCB AX v
closed Saturday lunch, Sunday, 24 December-2 January and Bank Holidays – **Meals** a la carte 14.25/20.90 **t.** 4.50.

XX **Jameson's,** 30-32 Upper Maudlin St., BS2 8DJ, ℘ 927 6565 – AE VISA CY e
closed Saturday lunch, Sunday dinner and Bank Holidays – **Meals** a la carte 12.85/20.80 **t.**

X **Bistro Twenty One,** 21 Cotham Road South, Kingsdown, BS6 5TZ, ℘ 942 1744 – AE VISA JCB AX s
closed Saturday lunch and Sunday – **Meals** 12.95 **st.** and a la carte.

X **Howards,** 1a/2a Avon Crescent, Hotwells, BS1 6XQ, ℘ 926 2921 – AE VISA
closed Saturday lunch, Sunday, 25-26 December and Bank Holidays – **Meals** 13.00/15.00 **st.** and a la carte. AX a

at Patchway N : 6½ m. on A 38 – BV – ✉ Bristol – 01454 :

Aztec, Aztec West Business Park, BS12 4TS, N : 1 m. by A 38 ℘ 201090, Fax 201593, , , , squash – |♦| rm rest TV ☎ – 200. AE VISA
Meals 13.50/20.00 **st.** and a la carte 6.95 – **109 rm** 86.00/116.00 **st.**, 2 suites – SB.

Stakis Bristol, Woodlands Lane, Bradley Stoke, BS12 4JF, N : 1 m. by A 38 ℘ 201144, Fax 612022, , , – rm rest TV ☎ – 80. AE VISA.
Meals *(closed Saturday lunch)* (carving rest.) 10.00/16.50 **t.** and dinner a la carte – 9.75 – **108 rm** 92.00/102.00 **st.** – SB.

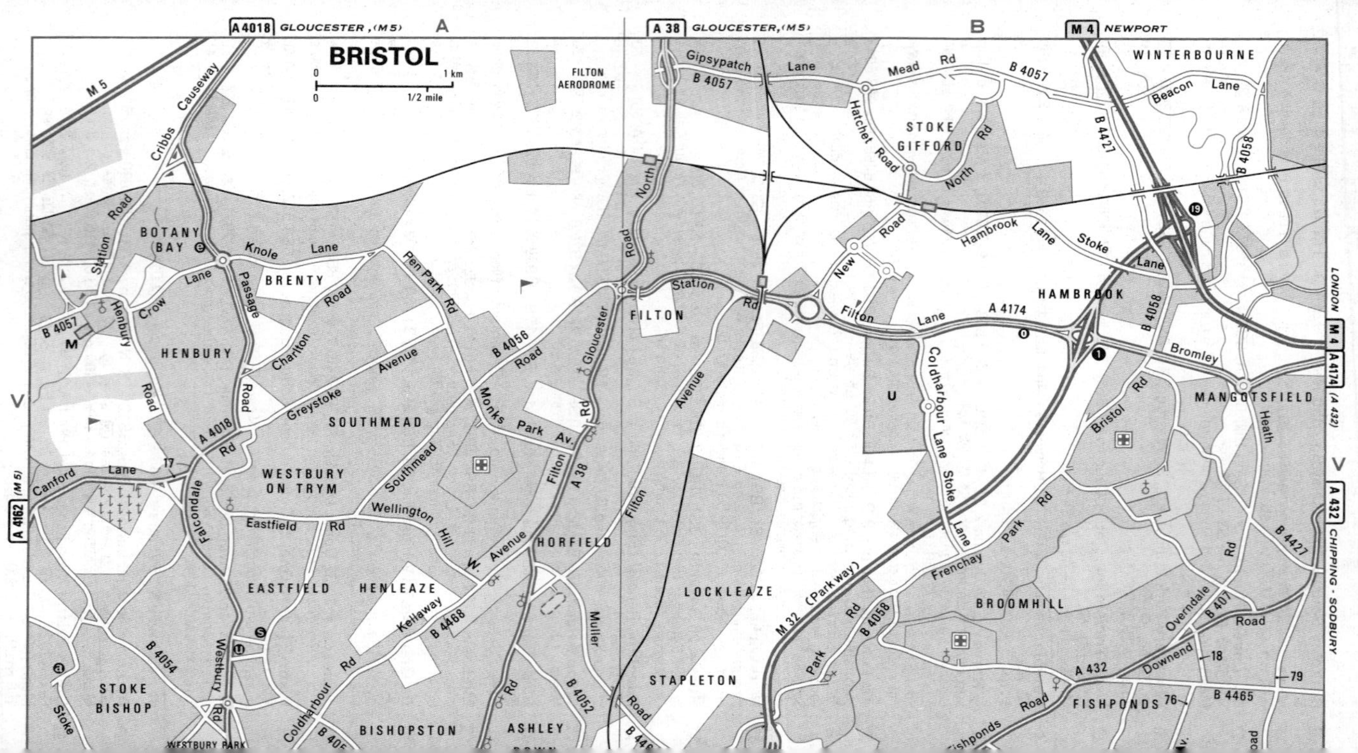
A 4018 GLOUCESTER, (M5)
A
A 38 GLOUCESTER, (M5)
B
M 4 NEWPORT
BRISTOL
0 1 km
0 1/2 mile
FILTON AERODROME
M 5
Cribbs Causeway
Station Road
BOTANY BAY
Knole Lane
Lane
Passage Road
BRENTY
Crow
Henbury
B 4057
M
HENBURY
Road
Charlton Road
Greystoke Avenue
Pen Park Rd
SOUTHMEAD
A 4018
Rd
Canford Lane
17
A 4162 (M 5)
Falcondale
WESTBURY ON TRYM
Southmead
Wellington Hill
Eastfield Rd
W. Avenue
EASTFIELD
HENLEAZE
Kellaway
B 4468
Westbury Rd
STOKE BISHOP
B 4054
Stoke
WESTBURY PARK
Coldharbour Rd
B 405
BISHOPSTON
ASHLEY
B 4052
Muller
HORFIELD
B 4056
Road
Monks Park Av.
Gloucester Rd
Filton A 38
North Road
Gipsypatch Lane
B 4057
FILTON
Station Rd
Filton Avenue
LOCKLEAZE
STAPLETON
Road
B 446
Hatchet Road
Mead Rd
B 4057
STOKE GIFFORD
North Rd
B 4427
WINTERBOURNE
Beacon Lane
B 4058
New Road
Hambrook Lane
Stoke Lane
HAMBROOK
Filton Lane
A 4174
U
Coldharbour Lane
Stoke Lane
Bromley
B 4058
MANGOTSFIELD
Heath
Bristol Rd
LONDON M 4 A 4174 (A 432)
A 432 CHIPPING - SODBURY
Frenchay Park Rd
M 32 (Park way)
Park Rd
B 4058
BROOMHILL
Rd
B 4427
Overndale
B 407
Road
Downend
18
A 432
79
FISHPONDS
76
B 4465
Road
Fishponds

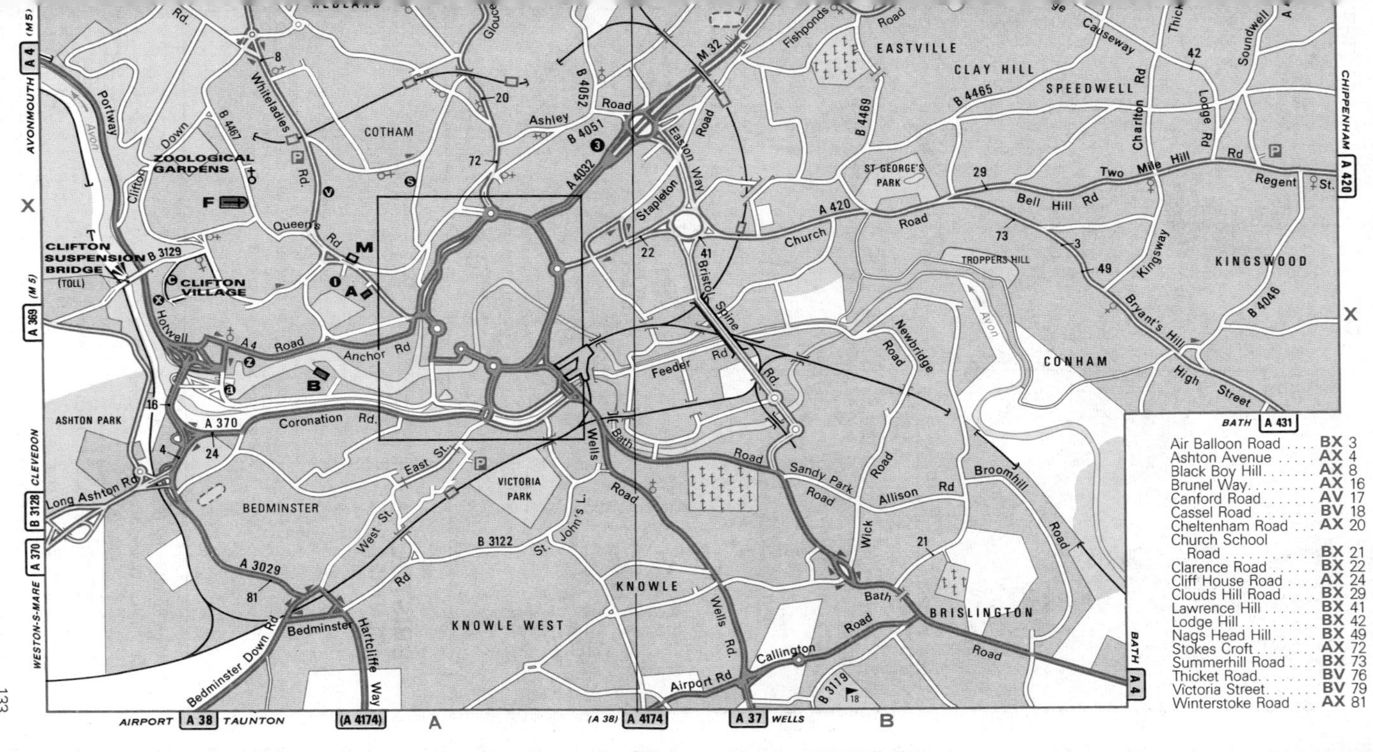
CHIPPENHAM A 420
BATH A 431
BATH A 4
AVONMOUTH A 4 (M5)
A 369 (M 5)
CLEVEDON B 3128
WESTON-S-MARE A 370
AIRPORT A 38 TAUNTON
(A 4174)
(A 38) A 4174
A 37 WELLS
A
B
Air Balloon Road . . . . BX 3
Ashton Avenue . . . . . AX 4
Black Boy Hill. . . . . . . AX 8
Brunel Way. . . . . AX 16
Canford Road . . . . AV 17
Cassel Road . . . . BV 18
Cheltenham Road . . . AX 20
Church School
Road . . . . BX 21
Clarence Road . . . . . . BX 22
Cliff House Road . . . . AX 24
Clouds Hill Road . . . . BX 29
Lawrence Hill . . . . BX 41
Lodge Hill . . . . BX 42
Nags Head Hill . . . . . . BX 49
Stokes Croft . . . . AX 72
Summerhill Road . . . . BX 73
Thicket Road. . . . . BV 76
Victoria Street. . . . . . . BV 79
Winterstoke Road . . . AX 81
EASTVILLE
CLAY HILL
SPEEDWELL
KINGSWOOD
CONHAM
BRISLINGTON
KNOWLE
KNOWLE WEST
BEDMINSTER
COTHAM
TROPPERS HILL
ST GEORGE'S PARK
VICTORIA PARK
ASHTON PARK
ZOOLOGICAL GARDENS
CLIFTON SUSPENSION BRIDGE (TOLL)
CLIFTON VILLAGE
Portway
Avon
Whiteladies Rd.
Queen's Rd
Hotwell Road
Anchor Rd
Coronation Rd.
Long Ashton Rd
Bedminster Down Rd
Hartcliffe Way
Wells Road
Bath Road
Sandy Park Road
Wick Road
Allison Rd
Broomhill Road
Newbridge Road
Feeder Rd
Bristol Spine Rd.
Easton Way
Stapleton Road
Church Road
Bell Hill Rd
Two Mile Hill Rd
Regent St.
Bryant's Hill
High Street
Kingsway
Charlton Rd
Lodge Rd
Causeway
Fishponds Road
Ashley Road
Callington Road
Airport Rd
East St.
West St.
St. John's L.
M 32
A 4032
A 420
A 370
A 3029
A 4
B 4052
B 4051
B 4469
B 4465
B 4046
B 4467
B 3129
B 3122
B 3119

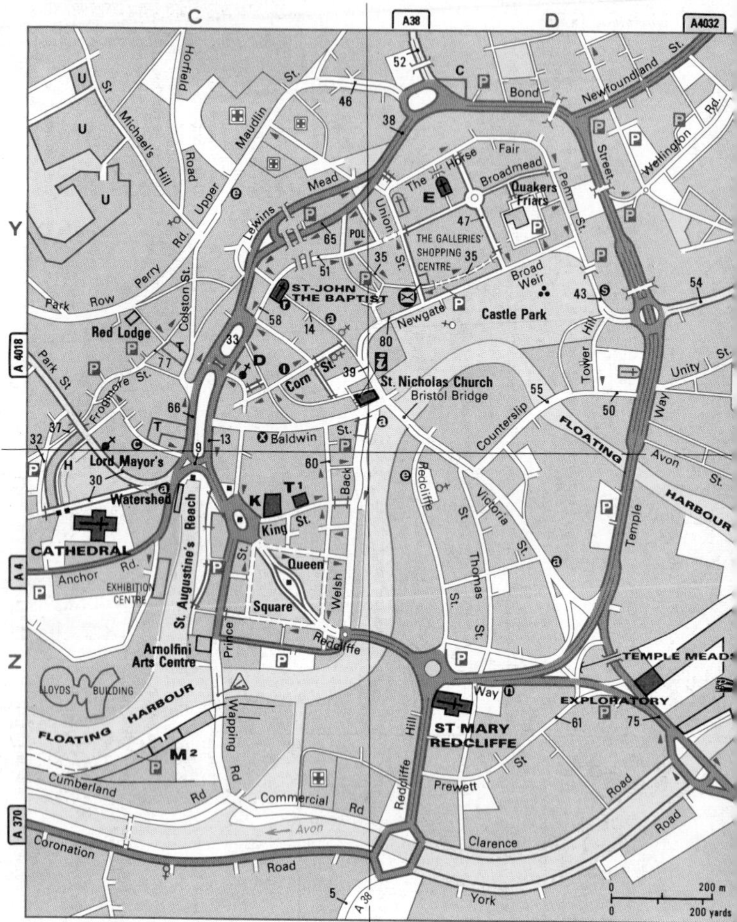

BRISTOL
CENTRE

Broadmead . . . . DY
Fairfax Street . . . . CDY 35
Galleries' (The)
  Shopping Centre . . . . . . DY
Horse Fair (The) . . . . DY
Merchant Street . . . . DY 47
Nelson Street . . . . CY 51
Park Street . . . . CY

Bedminster Parade . . . . CZ 5
Bridgehead . . . . CZ 9
Broad Quay . . . . CYZ 13
Broad Street . . . . CY 14
College Green . . . . CZ 30
College Street . . . . CYZ 32
Colston Avenue . . . . CY 33
Frog Lane . . . . CY 37
Haymarket . . . . DY 38
High Street . . . . CDY 39
Lower Castle St. . . . . DY 43
Marlborough St. . . . . CDY 46

Narrow Plain . . . . DY 5
North Street . . . . DY 5
Old Market St. . . . . DY 5
Passage Street . . . . DY 5
Quay Street . . . . CY 5
Queen Charlotte St. . . . . . . CZ 6
Redcliffe Mead Lane . . . . . DZ 6
Rupert Street . . . . CY 6
St. Augustine's Parade . . . . CY 6
Temple Gate . . . . DZ 7
Trenchard Street . . . . CY 7
Wine Street . . . . DY 8

at Hambrook NE : 5½ m. by M 32 on A 4174 – ✉ Bristol – ☎ 0117 :

🏨 **Forte Crest,** Filton Rd, BS16 1QX, ☎ 956 4242, Fax 956 9735, ⛹, ≘s, 🏊, 🌳, park – 🛗 ⛔ rm ▤ rest 📺 ☎ 🅿 – 🏛 500. AE ⓘ VISA JCB. ✂ BV o
Meals 12.50/18.00 **st.** and a la carte 6.00 – ☕ 10.85 – **193 rm** 91.00/101.00 **st.**, 4 suites – SB.

at Winterbourne NE : 7½ m. by M 32 and A 4174 on B 4058 – BV – ✉ Bristol – ☎ 01454 :

🏨 **Jarvis Grange H. & Country Club,** Northwoods, BS17 1RP, NW : 2 m. by B 4057 on B 4427 ☎ 777333, Fax 777447, ≘s, 🏊 – ⛔ rm 📺 ☎ 🅿 – 🏛 150. AE ⓘ VISA. ✂
Meals *(closed Saturday lunch)* 14.95/17.95 **st.** and a la carte – ☕ 9.50 – **52 rm** 89.00/99.00 **st.** – SB.

at Saltford SE : 7½ m. on A 4 – BX – ✉ Bristol – ☎ 01225 :

⌂ **Brunel's Tunnel House,** High St., BS18 3BQ, off Beech Rd ☎ 873873, Fax 874875, 🌳 – ⛔ rest 📺 ☎ 🅿. AE VISA. ✂
closed 24 to 26 December – **Meals** (by arrangement) 14.00 **st.** 4.00 – **7 rm** ☕ 49.00/57.00 **st.**

at Chelwood SE : 8½ m. by A 37 – BX – on A 368 – ✉ Bristol – ☎ 01761 :

🏨 **Chelwood House,** BS18 4NH, SW : ¾ m. on A 37 ☎ 490730, Fax 490730, ≤, 🌳 – ⛔ rest 📺 ☎ 🅿. AE ⓘ VISA JCB. ✂
closed first 2 weeks January – **Meals** *(closed Sunday dinner to non-residents)* (dinner only) a la carte 17.00/23.40 **st.** 5.00 – **10 rm** ☕ 49.00/85.00 **st.** – SB.

at Hunstrete SE : 10 m. by A 4 and A 37 – BX – off A 368 – ✉ Bristol – ☎ 01761 :

🏨 ✿ **Hunstrete House** 🐦, BS18 4NS, ☎ 490490, Fax 490732, ≤, 🏛, « 18C country house, gardens and deer park », 🏊 heated, 🎾 – ⛔ rest 📺 ☎ 🅿. AE ⓘ VISA. ✂
Meals 15.00/40.00 **t.** and a la carte 7.50 – **22 rm** ☕ 115.00/165.00 **t.**, 1 suite – SB
Spec. Roast risotto of langoustine and salmon with saffron sauce, Fillet of beef with green pepper and port sauce, Raspberry and vanilla parfait.

at Stanton Wick S : 9 m. by A 37 and A 368 on Stanton Wick rd – BX – ✉ Bristol – ☎ 01761 :

🏨 **Carpenters Arms,** BS18 4BX, ☎ 490202, Fax 490763 – ⛔ rm 📺 ☎ 🅿. AE ⓘ VISA. ✂ – **Meals** a la carte 12.00/25.00 **t.** 4.00 – **12 rm** ☕ 45.50/59.50 **t.** – SB.

ATS 68-72 Avon St. ☎ 971 1269
TS 551 Gloucester Rd, Horfield ☎ 951 4525
TS 58-60 Broad St., Staple Hill ☎ 956 4741/56 5396/956 4594/ 957 1483
ATS 34-38 St. Johns Lane, Bedminster ☎ 977 6418/977 0674

BRIXHAM Devon 403 J 32 **The West Country G.** – pop. 15 865 – ☎ 01803.

nvir. : Berry Head★ (≤★★★) NE : 1½ m.

The Old Market House, The Quay, TQ5 8TB ☎ 852861.

London 230 – Exeter 30 – ♦Plymouth 32 – Torquay 8.

🏨 **Berry Head** 🐦, Berry Head Rd, TQ5 9AL, ☎ 853225, Fax 882084, ≤ Torbay, 🌳 – 📺 ☎ 🅿. AE VISA. ✂
Meals 15.00 **st.** (dinner) and a la carte 13.75/24.00 **st.** 5.10 – **16 rm** ☕ 45.00/110.00 **st.** – SB.

BROAD CAMPDEN Glos. – see Chipping Campden.

BROAD CHALKE Wilts. 403 404 O 30 – see Salisbury.

BROADHEMBURY Devon 403 K 31 pop. 617 – ✉ Honiton – ☎ 01404.

London 191 – Exeter 17 – Honiton 5 – Taunton 23.

✕ **Drewe Arms,** EX14 0NF, ☎ 841267, « Part 13C thatched inn », 🌳 – 🅿
closed Sunday dinner – **Meals** - Seafood - 17.95 **t.** and a la carte.

BROADSTAIRS Kent 404 Y 29 – pop. 23 691 (inc. St. Peter's) – ☎ 01843.

North Foreland, Kingsgate, Broadstairs ☎ 862140.

6b High St., CT10 1IH ☎ 862242.

London 78 – ♦Dover 21 – Maidstone 47.

🏨 **Castlemere,** 15 Western Esplanade, CT10 1TD, ☎ 861566, Fax 866379, ≤, 🌳 – 📺 ☎ 🅿. VISA
Meals (light lunch)/dinner 14.95 **t.** 4.65 – **36 rm** ☕ 35.00/76.00 **t.** – SB.

✕✕ **Marchesi,** 18 Albion St., CT10 1LU, ☎ 862481, Fax 861509, ≤ – 🅿. AE VISA
closed Sunday dinner and 26 to 30 December – **Meals** 8.95/14.50 **st.** and a la carte 5.10.

BROADWATER Herts. – see Stevenage.

BROADWAY Heref. and Worcs. 403 404 O 27 Great Britain G. – pop. 2 775 – ☎ 01386.

See : Town★.

Envir. : Country Park (Broadway Tower ✻★★), SE : 2 m. by A 44 – Snowshill Manor★ (Terrac Garden★) *AC*, S : 2½ m.

ℹ 1 Cotswold Court, WR12 7AA ✆ 852937 (summer only).

♦London 93 – ♦Birmingham 36 – Cheltenham 15 – Worcester 22.

Lygon Arms, High St., WR12 7DU, ✆ 852255, Fax 858611, « Part 16C inn », ... – ... 80. AE VISA JCB
Meals 21.00/33.00 **t.** and a la carte – 8.25 – **60 rm** 95.00/155.00, 5 suites – SB.

Broadway, The Green, WR12 7AA, ✆ 852401, Fax 853879, ... – TV ☎ P. AE VISA
Meals (bar lunch Monday to Saturday)/dinner 16.50 **st.** and a la carte 4.75 – **19 rm** 45.00/74.00 **st.** – SB.

Collin House ⛰, Collin Lane, WR12 7PB, NW : 1 ¼ m. by A 44 ✆ 858354, ... – P VISA.
closed 24 to 29 December – **Meals** 15.00/24.00 **st.** 4.95 – **7 rm** 45.00/97.00 **st.** – SB.

Windrush House, Station Rd, WR12 7DE, ✆ 853577, ... – TV P
closed Christmas – **Meals** (by arrangement) – **5 rm** 25.00/44.00 **t.** – SB.

Olive Branch without rest., 78 High St., WR12 7AJ, ✆ 853440, Fax 853440, ... – TV P AE.
7 rm 19.50/45.00 **st.**

Small Talk Lodge, Keil Close, 32 High St., WR12 7DP, ✆ 858953 – rest TV P. VISA.
Meals (by arrangement) 15.00 **st.** 4.80 – **8 rm** 30.00/50.00 **st.** – SB.

Whiteacres without rest., Station Rd, WR12 7DE, ✆ 852320, ... – TV P.
March-October – **6 rm** 42.00 **st.**

at Willersey (Glos.) N : 2 m. on B 4632 – ✉ Broadway – ☎ 01386 :

Old Rectory ⛰ without rest., Church St., WR12 7PN, ✆ 853729, Fax 858061, ... – TV ☎ P. VISA.
closed 1 week Christmas – **8 rm** 40.00/95.00 **st.**

at Willersey Hill (Glos.) E : 2 m. by A 44 – ✉ Broadway – ☎ 01386 :

Dormy House, WR12 7LF, ✆ 852711, Fax 858636, ... – rest TV ☎ P – 200. AE VISA
closed 25 and 26 December – **Meals** (bar lunch Saturday) 15.00/26.50 **t.** and a la cart 5.00 – **46 rm** 60.00/120.00 **t.**, 3 suites – SB.

at Buckland (Glos.) SW : 2¼ m. by B 4632 – ✉ Broadway – ☎ 01386 :

✿ **Buckland Manor** ⛰, WR12 7LY, ✆ 852626, Fax 853557, ←, « Part 13C manor i extensive gardens », heated, ... – rest TV ☎ P. AE VISA.
Meals 22.70 **t.** (lunch) and a la carte 30.65/40.35 **t.** 7.90 – **13 rm** 150.00/325.00 **t.** – SB
Spec. Pithivier of Cornish scallops with caviar and chives, Garlic and herb coated rack of lamb with a rosemary ju Glazed summer berries with a basket of homemade cinnamon ice cream.

at Wormington (Glos.) SW : 4 ¼ m. by B 4632 on Wormington rd – ✉ Broadway ☎ 01386 :

Leasow House ⛰ without rest., Laverton Meadow, WR12 7NA, E : 1 ¼ m. ✆ 584526 Fax 584596, ←, ... – TV ☎ ♿ P. AE VISA
7 rm 38.00/60.00.

BROADWELL Glos. 403 404 O 28 – see Stow-on-the-Wold.

BROCKENHURST Hants. 403 404 P 31 **Great Britain G.** – pop. 7 680 – ☎ 01590.

Envir. : New Forest** (Rhinefield Ornamental Drive**, Bolderwood Ornamental Drive**).

Brockenhurst Manor, Sway Rd ☎ 623332.

London 99 – Bournemouth 17 – ◆Southampton 14 – Winchester 27.

Rhinefield House ⚘, Rhinefield Rd, SO42 7QB, NW : 3 m. ☎ 622922, Fax 622800, « Victorian country mansion, formal gardens », Ꮀ6, ≘s, ⛱ heated, park, ✂ – ⇔ rm ▣ ☎ 🅟 – 🏔 80. ▣ AE ⓘ VISA. ✂
Meals *(closed Saturday lunch)* 6.95/21.50 **t.** and a la carte 🕯 5.00 – **34 rm** ☐ 85.00/155.00 **t.** – SB.

Careys Manor, Lyndhurst Rd, SO42 7RH, on A 337 ☎ 623551, Fax 622799, Ꮀ6, ≘s, ⛱, ⛲ – ⇔ ▣ ☎ 🅟 – 🏔 100. ▣ AE ⓘ VISA JCB
Meals (dancing Saturday evening) 13.95/21.95 **t.** and a la carte – (see also ***Le Blaireau*** below) – **79 rm** ☐ 69.00/159.00 **t.** – SB.

Balmer Lawn, Lyndhurst Rd, SO42 7ZB, on A 337 ☎ 623116, Fax 623864, ≤, Ꮀ6, ≘s, ⛱ heated, ⛱, ⛲, ✂, squash – |♦| ⇔ ▣ ☎ ♿ 🅟 – 🏔 100. ▣ AE ⓘ VISA JCB
Meals (bar lunch Monday to Saturday)/dinner 15.50 **st.** and a la carte 🕯 6.75 – **55 rm** ☐ 57.50/94.00 **st.** – SB.

Whitley Ridge ⚘, Beaulieu Rd, SO42 7QL, E : 1 m. on B 3055 ☎ 622354, Fax 622856, ⛲, ✂ – ▣ ☎ 🅟. ▣ AE ⓘ VISA
Meals (bar lunch)/dinner 19.00/20.00 **t.** and a la carte – **13 rm** ☐ 52.00/94.00 **t.** – SB.

Cottage without rest., Sway Rd, SO42 7SH, ☎ 622296, Fax 623014, ⛲ – ⇔ ▣ 🅟. ▣ VISA
closed December and January – **7 rm** ☐ 28.50/74.00 **t.**

XXX ✿ **Le Poussin** (Aitken), The Courtyard, rear of 49-51 Brookley Rd, SO42 7RB, ☎ 623063, Fax 622912, ⛱ – ⇔. ▣ VISA
closed Sunday dinner, Monday, Tuesday and 2 weeks January – **Meals** (booking essential) 10.00/25.00 **t.** 🕯 6.00
Spec. Tagliatelle with wild New Forest mushrooms, rosemary and a cream sauce, New Forest game, Rich chocolate truffle cake with white chocolate ice cream.

X **Le Blaireau** (at Carey's Manor H.), SO42 7RH, ☎ 623032 – 🅟. ▣ AE ⓘ VISA JCB
Meals - French - 9.95/12.95 **t.** and a la carte.

BROMBOROUGH Mersey. 402 403 L 24 – pop. 14 518 – ✉ Wirral – ☎ 0151.

Raby Hall Rd ☎ 334 2155.

London 210 – Chester 14 – ◆Liverpool 6.5 – ◆Manchester 46.

The Village H. & Leisure Club, Pool Lane, L62 4UE, on A 41 ☎ 643 1616, Fax 643 1420, Ꮀ6, ≘s, ⛱, ✂, squash – |♦| ▤ rest ▣ ☎ ♿ 🅟 – 🏔 200. ▣ AE VISA
Meals (bar lunch Monday to Saturday)/dinner 11.95 and a la carte 🕯 5.75 – **89 rm** ☐ 77.00/87.00 **t.**

Travel Inn, High St., L62 7HZ, ☎ 334 2917, Telex 628225, Fax 334 0443 – ⇔ rm ▣ 🅟 – 🏔 80. ▣ AE ⓘ VISA. ✂
Meals (grill rest.) – ☐ 4.95 – **32 rm** 34.50 **t.**

BROME Suffolk 404 X 26 – see Diss (Norfolk).

BROMLEY CROSS Gtr. Manchester 402 404 M 23 – see Bolton.

BROMSGROVE Heref. and Worcs. 403 404 N 26 – pop. 91 544 – ☎ 01527.

Bromsgrove Museum, 26 Birmingham Rd, B61 0DD ☎ 831809.

London 117 – ◆Birmingham 14 – ◆Bristol 71 – Worcester 13.

Stakis Bromsgrove, Birmingham Rd, B61 0JB, N : 2½ m. on A 38 ☎ (0121) 447 7888, Fax 447 7273, Ꮀ6, ≘s, ⛱, ⛲ – ⇔ rm ▤ rest ▣ ☎ ♿ 🅟 – 🏔 80. ▣ AE ⓘ VISA
Meals *(closed Saturday lunch)* 12.50/17.95 **st.** and dinner a la carte 🕯 7.50 – ☐ 8.95 – **130 rm** 94.00/115.00 **st.**, 10 suites – SB.

Pine Lodge, 85 Kidderminster Rd, B61 9AB, W : 1 m. on A 448 ☎ 576600, Fax 878981, Ꮀ6, ≘s, ⛱ – |♦| ⇔ rm ▤ rest ▣ ☎ ♿ 🅟 – 🏔 200. ▣ AE ⓘ VISA
Meals (light lunch Saturday) 9.95/18.00 **st.** and a la carte – **112 rm** ☐ 89.00/100.00 **st.**, 2 suites – SB.

Perry Hall (Jarvis), 13 Kidderminster Rd, B61 7JN, ☎ 579976, Fax 575998, ⛲ – ⇔ rm ▣ ☎ 🅟 – 🏔 70. ▣ AE ⓘ VISA JCB
Meals 11.95/15.95 **st.** and a la carte 🕯 4.95 – ☐ 8.50 – **58 rm** 75.00/85.00 **st.** – SB.

Bromsgrove Country, 249 Worcester Rd, Stoke Heath, B61 7JA, SW : 2 m. ☎ 835522, Fax 871257, ⛲ – ⇔ rm ▣ 🅟. ▣ VISA. ✂
closed Christmas-New Year – **Meals** (residents only) (dinner only) 12.00 **st.** 🕯 4.50 – ☐ 5.00 – **10 rm** 40.00/49.00 **st.**

XXX **Grafton Manor** with rm, Grafton Lane, B61 7HA, SW : 1 ¾ m. by Worcester Rd ☎ 579007, Fax 575221, « 16C and 18C manor », ⛲, park – ▣ ☎ 🅟. ▣ AE ⓘ VISA. ✂
Meals *(closed Saturday lunch)* 18.50/31.50 **st.** 🕯 6.75 – **7 rm** ☐ 85.00/125.00 **st.**, 2 suites – SB.

BROMYARD Heref. and Worcs. 403 404 M 27 – pop. 3 401 – ✆ 01885.

T.I.C. & Heritage Centre, 1 Rowberry St., HR7 4DX ✆ 482038.

London 138 – Hereford 15 – Leominster 13 – Worcester 14.

- **Falcon,** Broad St., HR7 4BT, ✆ 483034, Fax 488818 – TV ☎ P. VISA
  Meals (carving rest.) 4.50/12.50 **st.** and a la carte 3.50 – **8 rm** 39.50/49.50 **st.** – SB.
- **Granary**, Church House Farm, HR7 4NA, N : 4 ¼ m. by B 4214, Edvin Loach rd an Ripplewood rd ✆ 410345, « Working farm » – TV P
  Meals (by arrangement) a la carte approx. 14.00 **t.** 3.50 – **5 rm** 19.00/38.00 **t.**

BROOK Hants. 403 404 P 31 – ✉ Lyndhurst – ✆ 01703.

London 92 – Bournemouth 24 – Southampton 14.

- **Bell Inn,** SO43 7HE, ✆ 812214, Fax 813958, 18 – TV ☎ P. AE VISA
  Meals (bar lunch Monday to Saturday)/dinner 23.50 **st.** and a la carte 5.00 – **25 rr** 45.00/90.00 **st.** – SB.

BROOKMANS PARK Herts. 404 T 28 – pop. 5 238 (inc. Little Heath) – ✆ 01707.

London 21 – Luton 21.

- **Villa Rosa,** 3 Great North Rd, AL9 6LB, SE : 1 ¾ m. on A 1000 ✆ 651444, Fax 654970 – AE VISA JCB
  closed Saturday lunch, Sunday and Bank Holidays – **Meals** - Italian - a la carte 12.80/26.40 4.55.

BROUGHTON Lancs. 402 L 22 – see Preston.

BROUGHTON S. Humbs. 402 S 23 – see Scunthorpe.

BROXTED Essex 404 U 28 – see Stansted Airport.

BROXTON Ches. 402 403 L 24 – pop. 417 – ✆ 01829.

London 197 – Birmingham 68 – Chester 12 – Manchester 44 – Stoke-on-Trent 29.

- **Broxton Hall Country House,** Whitchurch Rd, CH3 9JS, on A 41 at junction with A 53 ✆ 782321, Fax 782330, « Part 17C timbered house », – TV ☎ P. AE VISA
  closed 25 December – **Meals** 9.50/23.90 **t.** and lunch a la carte 5.50 – **11 rm** 65.00 80.00 **st.** – SB.
- **Egerton Arms,** Whitchurch Rd, CH3 9JW, on A 41 at junction with A 534 ✆ 78224 Fax 782352 – TV P. AE VISA
  Meals a la carte 10.95 **t.** 4.95 – 5.25 – **7 rm** 30.00 **t.**

BRUSHFORD Somerset 403 J 30 – see Dulverton.

BRUTON Somerset 403 404 M 30 **The West Country G.** – pop. 2 111 – ✆ 01749.

Exc. : Stourhead★★★ *AC*, W : 8 m. by B 3081.

London 118 – Bristol 27 – Bournemouth 44 – Salisbury 35 – Taunton 36.

- **Truffles,** 95 High St., BA10 0AR, ✆ 812255 – VISA
  closed Sunday dinner and Monday – **Meals** (booking essential lunch Tuesday t Friday) 13.50/20.95 **st.** 4.25.

BRYHER Cornwall 403 ㉚ – see Scilly (Isles of).

BUCKDEN Cambs. 404 T 27 – pop. 2 534 – ✉ Huntingdon – ✆ 01480.

London 65 – Bedford 15 – Cambridge 20 – Northampton 31.

- **George,** Great North Rd, PE18 9XA, ✆ 810307, Fax 811274 – TV ☎ P. AE VISA.
  Meals 9.50/14.50 **st.** and a la carte 5.00 – **16 rm** 53.00/70.00 **st.** – SB.
- **Lion,** High St., PE18 9XA, ✆ 810313, Fax 811070, « Part 15C inn » – TV ☎ P. AE VISA JCB
  Meals 8.50/17.00 **t.** and a la carte 3.75 – **15 rm** 57.50/82.00 **t.** – SB.

BUCKHURST HILL Essex 404 ㊸ – pop. 11 243 – ✆ 0181.

London 13 – Chelmsford 25.

Plan : see Greater London (North-East)

- **Roebuck** (Forte), North End, IG9 5QY, ✆ 505 4636, Fax 504 7826 – TV ☎ P – 150 AE VISA HT
  Meals 10.25/16.95 **st.** and a la carte 6.05 – 8.50 – **29 rm** 60.00/70.00 **st.** – SB.

BUCKINGHAM Bucks. 403 404 Q 27 **Great Britain G.** – pop. 10 774 – ✆ 01280.

Exc. : Claydon House★ *AC*, S : 8 m. by A 413.

18 Silverstone, Silverstone Rd, Stowe ✆ 850005.

London 64 – Birmingham 61 – Northampton 20 – Oxford 25.

- **Villiers,** 3 Castle St., MK18 1BS, ✆ 822444, Fax 822113 – rest TV ☎ P – 250. AE VISA.
  Meals (bar lunch Monday to Saturday)/dinner 13.95 **st.** and a la carte 4.50 – **34 rn** 65.00/79.00 **st.**, 1 suite – SB.

Buckingham Lodge, Buckingham Ring Rd, MK18 1RY, W : 1 ¼ m. by A 413 on A 421 ☏ 822622, Fax 823074, Ⓛ, ≘s, ⛆ – ⇔ rm ▤ rest ▣ ☎ ♿ ℗ – 🏛 160. ⓢ AE VISA
Meals (carving lunch Sunday) 7.75/11.50 **st.** and a la carte 🍷 5.95 – ☐ 6.25 – **70 rm** 65.00/84.00 **t.** – SB.

BUCKLAND Glos. 403 404 O 27 – see Broadway (Heref. and Worc.).

BUCKLAND Oxon. 403 404 P 28 – ✉ Faringdon – ☎ 01367 87.
London 78 – ◆Oxford 16 – Swindon 15.

Lamb Inn with rm, Lamb Lane, SN7 8QN, ☏ 0484 – ▣ ☎ ℗. ⓢ VISA JCB
Meals (restricted menu Monday) (bar lunch)/dinner a la carte 10.65/22.40 **t.** – **4 rm** ☐ 35.00/70.00 **t.**

BUCKLERS HARD Hants. 403 404 P 31 – see Beaulieu.

BUCKNELL Shrops. 403 L 26 – pop. 898 – ☎ 01547.
London 158 – ◆Birmingham 55 – Hereford 29 – Shrewsbury 31.

Bucknell House 🌿 without rest., SY7 0AD, on B 4367 ☏ 530248, 🎣, 🌳, park, 🎾 – ▣ ℗
closed December and January – **3 rm** ☐ 22.00/36.00 **s.**

BUDE Cornwall 403 G 31 The West Country G. – pop. 6 512 (inc. Poughill) – ☎ 01288.
See : The Breakwater★★ – Compass Point (<★).
Envir. : Poughill★★ (Church★★) N : 2½ m. - E : Tamar River★★ – Kilkhampton (Church★) NE : ½ m. by A 39 – Stratton (Church★) E : 1 ½ m. – Launcells (Church★) E : 3 m. by A 3072 – Marhamchurch (St. Morwenne's Church★) SE : 2½ m. by A 39 – Poundstock★ (<★★, church★, guildhouse★) S : 4½ m. by A 39.
Exc. : Jacobstow (Church★) S : 7 m. by A 39.
⛳ Burn View ☏ 352006.
ℹ Bude Vistor Centre, The Crescent, EX23 8LE ☏ 354240.
London 252 – Exeter 51 – ◆Plymouth 44 – Truro 53.

Hartland, EX23 8JY, ☏ 355661, Fax 355664, <, ⛆ heated – |‡| ▣ ☎ ℗
Easter-October and Christmas – **Meals** 13.25/20.00 **st.** – **29 rm** ☐ 37.00/70.00 **t.** – SB.

Camelot, Downs View, EX23 8RE, ☏ 352361, Fax 355470, 🌳 – ⇔ rest ▣ ☎ ℗. ⓢ VISA. 🐕
March-October – **Meals** (dinner only) 14.00 **st.** and a la carte 🍷 4.50 – **21 rm** ☐ 26.00/52.00 **st.** – SB.

Bude Haven, Flexbury Av., EX23 8NS, ☏ 352305 – ⇔ rest ▣ ℗. ⓢ AE VISA
Meals 5.00/9.00 **st.** 🍷 3.50 – **11 rm** ☐ 22.00/38.00 **st.**

Meva Gwin, Upton, EX23 0LY, S : 1¼ m. on coast rd ☏ 352347, Fax 352347, < – ⇔ rest ▣ ℗. ⓢ VISA. 🐕
10 April-4 October – **Meals** 8.50 🍷 3.30 – **13 rm** ☐ 22.00/44.00 **t.**

BUDLEIGH SALTERTON Devon 403 K 32 The West Country G. – pop. 4 710 – ☎ 01395.
Envir. : East Budleigh (Church★) N : 2½ m. by A 376 – Bicton★ (garden★) *AC*, N : 3 m. by A 376.
⛳ East Devon, North View Rd ☏ 443370.
ℹ Fore St., EX9 6NG ☏ 445275.
London 215 – Exeter 16 – ◆Plymouth 55.

Long Range, Vales Rd, EX9 6HS, by Raleigh Rd ☏ 443321, 🌳 – ⇔ ▣. 🐕
Meals 12.50 **st.** 🍷 3.75 – **6 rm** ☐ 22.50/43.00 **st.** – SB.

BUDOCK WATER Cornwall – see Falmouth.

BUNWELL Norfolk 404 X 26 – pop. 795 – ☎ 01953.
London 102 – ◆Cambridge 51 – ◆Norwich 16.

Bunwell Manor 🌿, Bunwell St., NR16 1QU, NW : 1 m. ☏ 788304, 🌳 – ▣ ☎ ℗. ⓢ AE VISA
Meals 12.95/19.45 **t.** and a la carte 🍷 3.90 – **10 rm** ☐ 40.00/65.00 **t.** – SB.

BURBAGE Wilts. 403 404 O 29 – see Marlborough.

BURES Suffolk 404 W 28 – ☎ 01787.
London 54 – ◆Cambridge 53 – Colchester 8 – ◆Ipswich 25.

Butlers 🌿, Colne Rd, Bures Hamlet, CO8 5DN, SW : 1 ½ m. via Station Hill ☏ 227243, <, « 17C farmhouse », 🌳, park – ⇔ ℗. 🐕
Meals (by arrangement) (communal dining) 15.00 **st.** – **3 rm** ☐ 19.00/55.00 **st.**

BURFORD Oxon. 403 404 P 28 – pop. 1 807 – ☎ 01993.

18 ℰ 822149.

The Brewery, Sheep St., OX18 4LP ℰ 823558/823590.

♦London 76 – ♦Birmingham 55 – Gloucester 32 – ♦Oxford 20.

Bay Tree, 12-14 Sheep St., OX18 4LW, ℰ 822791, Fax 823008, « 16C house, antique furnishings », – rest. AE VISA JCB
Meals 11.50/22.50 **t.** and a la carte – **20 rm** 65.00/110.00 **t.**, 2 suites – SB.

Golden Pheasant, 91 High St., OX18 4QA, ℰ 823223, Fax 822621 – rest. AE VISA.
Meals 16.95 **t.** and a la carte **t.** 9.95 – **12 rm** 42.00/92.00 **t.** – SB.

Lamb Inn, Sheep St., OX18 4LR, ℰ 823155, Fax 822228, « Part 14C inn, antique furnishings », – rest. VISA.
closed 25 and 26 December – **Meals** (bar lunch Monday to Friday)/dinner 24.00 **t.** and a la carte – **16 rm** 37.50/95.00 **t.** – SB.

Andrews without rest., 99 High St., OX18 4QA, ℰ 823151, Fax 823240, – . VISA JCB.
closed 23 to 26 December – **8 rm** 50.00/85.00 **st.**

Inn For All Seasons, The Barringtons, OX18 4TN, W : 3¼ m. on A 40 ℰ (01451) 844324 Fax 844375, – . AE VISA.
Meals (bar lunch)/dinner 15.75 **st.** and a la carte 4.75 – **10 rm** 41.50/75.00 **st.** – SB.

Forte Travelodge, Berry Barn, OX7 5TB, on A 40 (Burford roundabout) ℰ 822699 Reservations (Freephone) 0800 850950 – . AE VISA
Meals (grill rest.) – **40 rm** 34.50 **t.**

at Fulbrook NE : ¾ m. on A 361 – ✉ Burford – ☎ 01993 :

Elm House, Meadow Lane, OX18 4BW, ℰ 823611, Fax 823937, – . VISA JCB
Meals 17.00 and a la carte 4.50 – **7 rm** 33.00/60.00 – SB.

En saison, *surtout dans les stations fréquentées, il est prudent de retenir à l'avance. Cependant, si vous ne pouvez pas occuper la chambre que vous avez retenue, prévenez immédiatement l'hôtelier.*

Si vous écrivez à un hôtel à l'étranger, joignez à votre lettre un coupon-réponse international (disponible dans les bureaux de poste).

BURLAND Ches. – see Nantwich.

BURLEY Hants. 403 404 O 31 **Great Britain G.** – pop. 1 438 – ✉ Ringwood – ☎ 01425.

Envir. : New Forest★★ (Rhinefield Ornamental Drive★★, Bolderwood Ornamental Drive★★).

9 Burley, Ringwood ℰ 402431.

♦London 102 – Bournemouth 17 – ♦Southampton 17 – Winchester 30.

Toad Hall, The Cross, BH24 4AB, ℰ 403448, Fax 402505 – . AE VISA.
Meals a la carte 16.40/25.40 **st.** – **8 rm** 45.00/60.00 **t.** – SB.

BURLEY IN WHARFEDALE W. Yorks. 402 O 22 – ☎ 01943.

♦London 218 – Bradford 14 – Harrogate 15 – ♦Leeds 14 – Preston 52.

XX **David Woolley's,** 78 Main St., LS29 7BT, ℰ 864602 – . VISA
closed Sunday and Monday – **Meals** (dinner only) 13.95 **t.** and a la carte 4.50.

BURNHAM Bucks. 404 S 29 – pop. 11 169 – ☎ 01628.

♦London 33 – ♦Oxford 37 – Reading 17.

Burnham Beeches (Q.M.H.), Grove Rd, SL1 8DP, NW : 1 m. by Britwell Rd ℰ 429955, Fax 603994, , , , , park, – rm – 180. AE VISA
Grays : Meals *(closed Saturday lunch)* 22.50 **t.** 10.25 – 10.00 – **73 rm** 93.00/120.00 **t.** 2 suites – SB.

BURNHAM MARKET Norfolk 404 W 25 **Great Britain G.** – pop. 898 – ☎ 01328.

Envir. : Holkham Hall★★ *AC*, E : 3 m. by B 1155.

♦London 128 – ♦Cambridge 71 – ♦Norwich 36.

Hoste Arms, The Green, PE31 8HD, ℰ 738257, Fax 730103, « 17C inn », – rest. VISA
Meals (bar lunch)/dinner 15.75 **t.** – **15 rm** 56.00/100.00 **t.**

BURNHAM-ON-CROUCH Essex 404 W 29 – pop. 7 067 – ☎ 01621.

♦London 52 – Chelmsford 19 – Colchester 32 – Southend-on-Sea 25.

XXX **Contented Sole,** 80 High St., CM0 8AA, ℰ 782139. VISA
closed Sunday dinner, Monday, 2 weeks August-September and 23 December-22 January – **Meals** 11.95/17.95 **t.** and a la carte 6.00.

BURNLEY Lancs. 402 N 22 – pop. 91 130 – ☎ 01282.

9, 18 Towneley, Towneley Park, Todmorden Rd ☎ 451636 – 18 Glen View ☎ 421045.

Burnley Mechanics, Manchester Rd, BB11 1JA ☎ 455485.

London 236 – Bradford 32 – Leeds 37 – Liverpool 55 – Manchester 25 – Middlesbrough 104 – Preston 22 – Sheffield 68.

Oaks, Colne Rd, Reedley, BB10 2LF, NE : 2½ m. on A 56 ☎ 414141, Fax 33401, – rm – 150.
Quills : Meals 18.00 **st.** and a la carte 6.95 – **56 rm** 72.00/108.00 **st.** – SB.

Rosehill House, Rosehill Av., Manchester Rd, BB11 2PW, ☎ 453931, Fax 455628, –
Meals (lunch by arrangement)/dinner 12.50 **st.** and a la carte 6.50 – **20 rm** 40.00/62.00 **st.**

Forte Travelodge, Cavalry Barracks, Barracks Rd, BB11 4AS, W : ½ m. at junction of A 671 with A 679 ☎ 416039, Reservations (Freephone) 0800 850950 –
Meals (grill rest.) – **32 rm** 34.50 **t.**

ATS Healey Wood Rd ☎ 22409/38423/51624

BURNSALL N. Yorks. 402 O 21 – pop. 108 – ✉ Skipton – ☎ 01756.

London 223 – Bradford 26 – Leeds 29.

Red Lion, BD23 6BU, ☎ 720204, Fax 720292 – rest
Meals (bar lunch Monday to Saturday)/dinner 10.95/19.95 **t.** 6.00 – **11 rm** 44.50/74.00 **t.** – SB.

BURNT YATES N. Yorks. – see Ripley.

BURPHAM W. Sussex 404 S 30 – see Arundel.

BURRINGTON Devon 403 I 31 – pop. 533 – ☎ 01769.

London 260 – Barnstaple 14 – Exeter 28 – Taunton 50.

Northcote Manor , EX37 9LZ, NW : 1½ m. by Barnstaple rd ☎ 560501, Fax 560770, , park, – rest
Meals (booking essential) (lunch residents only)/dinner 10.00/22.50 **t.** 5.50 – **11 rm** 79.00/129.00 **st.**, 1 suite – SB.

BURSTALL Suffolk – see Ipswich.

BURTON-UPON-TRENT Staffs. 402 403 404 O 25 – pop. 60 525 – ☎ 01283.

18 Branston G – 18, Craythorne Road, Stretton ☎ 564329.

Unit 40, Octagon Centre, New St., DE14 3TN ☎ 516609/508589.

London 128 – Birmingham 29 – Leicester 27 – Nottingham 27 – Stafford 27.

Queens, 1 Bridge St., DE14 1SY, ☎ 564993, Fax 517556 – – 100.
Meals *(closed Saturday lunch)* 7.95/12.50 **t.** and a la carte 4.75 – **24 rm** 59.50/69.50 **t.**, 3 suites.

Stanhope Arms, Ashby Rd East, DE15 0PU, SE : 2½ m. on A 50 ☎ 217954, Fax 226199 – – 150.
Meals 20.00 **t.** and a la carte 3.95 – 5.95 – **23 rm** 45.50 **t.**

at Stretton N : 3½ m. by A 50 off A 5121 – ✉ Burton-upon-Trent – ☎ 01283 :

Dovecliff Hall with rm, Dovecliff Rd, DE13 0DJ, ☎ 531818, Fax 516546, , « Carefully restored Georgian house, gardens », , , park –
closed 1 week December and 2 weeks summer – **Meals** *(closed lunch Monday and Saturday, Sunday dinner and Bank Holidays)* 9.50/18.50 **t.** and dinner a la carte 8.00 – **7 rm** 55.00/105.00 **t.** – SB.

at Rolleston-on-Dove N : 3 ¾ m. by A 50 on Rolleston Rd – ✉ Burton-upon-Trent – ☎ 01283 :

Brookhouse Inn, Brookside, DE13 9AA, ☎ 814188, Fax 813644, « Part 17C house, antiques », –
Meals *(closed Saturday lunch and Sunday dinner)* 13.25 **t.** (lunch) and a la carte 16.95/29.65 **t.** 4.95 – **19 rm** 65.00/85.00 **t.** – SB.

at Newton Solney NE : 3 m. by A 50 on B 5008 – ✉ Burton-upon-Trent – ☎ 01283 :

Newton Park (Jarvis), Newton Rd, DE15 0SS, ☎ 703568, Fax 703214, – rm – 100.
Meals 9.95/15.95 **st.** and dinner a la carte – 8.00 – **50 rm** 85.00/95.00 **st.** – SB.

at Branston SW : 1½ m. on A 5121 – ✉ Burton-upon-Trent – ☎ 01283 :

Riverside , Riverside Drive, off Warren Lane, DE14 3EP, ☎ 511234, Fax 511441, , – – 150.
Meals *(closed Saturday lunch)* 10.95/16.50 **t.** and a la carte – **22 rm** 59.00/69.00 **t.**

Old Vicarage, 2 Main St., DE14 3EX, ☎ 533222, Fax 540258 –
closed Saturday lunch, Sunday dinner, Monday, and first 2 weeks August – **Meals** 9.95/22.95 **st.** 5.00.

at Barton-under-Needwood SW : 5 m. by A 5121 on A 38 – ✉ Burton-upon-Trent – ☎ 01283 :

Forte Travelodge, Lichfield Rd, DE13 8EG, on A 38 (northbound carriageway) ☎ 716343, Reservations (Freephone) 0800 850950 – TV ♿ P. AE VISA. 🐕
Meals (grill rest.) – **20 rm** 34.50 **t.**

Forte Travelodge, DE13 8EG, on A 38 (southbound carriageway) ☎ 716784 Reservations (Freephone) 0800 850950 – TV ♿ P. AE VISA. 🐕
Meals (grill rest.) – **40 rm** 34.50 **t.**

ATS All Saints Rd ☎ 565994/563170

BURTONWOOD SERVICE AREA Ches. 402 M 23 – ✉ Warrington – ☎ 01925.

Forte Travelodge, WA5 3AY, M 62 (westbound carriageway) ☎ 710376, Reservations (Freephone) 0800 850950 – TV ♿ P. AE VISA. 🐕
Meals (grill rest.) – **40 rm** 34.50 **t.**

BURY Gtr. Manchester 402 N 23 403 ② 404 N 23 – pop. 176 760 – ☎ 0161 – 9 Hill Top, Lowes Rd, Walmersley ☎ 764 1231.

The Mets Art Centre, Market St., BL9 0BN ☎ 705 5111.

♦London 211 – ♦Leeds 45 – ♦Liverpool 35 – ♦Manchester 9.

Est, Est, Est!, 703 Manchester Rd, BL9 9SS, on A 56 ☎ 766 4869 – ▤ P. AE VISA
closed 25 December and lunch 26 December – **Meals** - Italian - 9.95/12.95 **t.** and a la carte 4.95.

at Walmersley N : 1 ¾ m. on A 56 – ✉ Bury – ☎ 01706 :

Red Hall, Manchester Rd, BL9 5NA, N : 1 ¼ m. on A 56 ☎ 822476, Fax 828086 – rest TV ☎ P – 35. AE VISA. 🐕
closed 24 December-4 January – **Meals** *(closed lunch Monday and Saturday)* 9.95/19.50 **t.** and a la carte 5.00 – **20 rm** 50.00/62.00 **t.**

at Birtle NE : 3 m. by B 6222 – ✉ Bury – ☎ 0161 :

✿ **Normandie,** Elbut Lane, BL9 6UT, ☎ 764 1170, Fax 764 4866, ← – TV ☎ P. AE VISA JCB. 🐕
closed 3 to 9 April, 26 December-6 January and Bank Holidays except 25 December – **Meals** French - *(closed Sunday and lunch Monday and Saturday)* (booking essential) 12.50/18.95 **t.** and a la carte 21.25/35.00 **t.** 6.00 – 6.95 – **23 rm** 49.00/79.00 **t.**
Spec. Steamed sea bass with olive oil and couscous, Breast of Goosnargh chicken with pea ravioli, smoked bacon and lettuce, Hot banana soufflé with toffee ice cream.

ATS John St. ☎ 764 2830/6860

BURY ST. EDMUNDS Suffolk 404 W 27 **Great Britain G.** – pop. 31 327 – ☎ 01284.

See : Town★ – Abbey and Cathedral★.

Envir. : Ickworth House★ *AC*, SW : 3 m. by A 143.

18 Fornham Park G.

6 Angel Hill, IP33 1UZ ☎ 764667.

♦London 79 – ♦Cambridge 27 – ♦Ipswich 26 – ♦Norwich 41.

Angel, 3 Angel Hill, IP33 1LT, ☎ 753926, Fax 750092 – rest TV ☎ P – 140. AE VISA
Meals 13.95/19.75 **st.** and a la carte – **41 rm** 65.00/95.00 **st.**, 1 suite – SB.

Priory, Tollgate, IP32 6EH, N : 1 ¾ m. by A 1101 on B 1106 ☎ 766181, Fax 767604, rest TV ☎ P – 60. AE VISA. 🐕
closed 26 to 28 December – **Meals** *(closed Sunday lunch)* 17.50/24.00 **t.** and a la carte 4.25 – **27 rm** 65.00/89.00 **t.** – SB.

Butterfly, Symonds Rd, IP32 7BW, SE : 1 ½ m. by A 1302 and A 134 at junction with A 1 ☎ 760884, Fax 755476 – rm TV ☎ ♿ P – 40. AE VISA
Meals 12.25 **t.** and a la carte 4.50 – 6.95 – **66 rm** 52.00 **t.** – SB.

Twelve Angel Hill without rest., 12 Angel Hill, IP33 1UZ, ☎ 704088, Fax 725549, TV ☎ P. AE VISA. 🐕
closed January – **6 rm** 45.00/75.00 **st.**

Ounce House, 13 Northgate St., IP33 1HP, ☎ 761779, Fax 768315, – TV ☎ P. VISA. 🐕
Meals (by arrangement) (communal dining) 18.00 **t.** 3.50 – **3 rm** 40.00/75.00 **st.**

Abbey without rest., 35 Southgate St., IP33 2AZ, ☎ 762020, Fax 724770 – TV ☎ P AE VISA. 🐕
12 rm 39.50/59.50 **st.**

Mortimer's, 31 Churchgate St., IP33 1RG, ☎ 760623, Fax 761611 . AE VISA JCB
closed Saturday lunch, Sunday, 2 weeks August-September, 24 December-5 January and Bank Holidays – **Meals** - Seafood - a la carte 11.85/21.20 **t.**

at Pakenham NE : 5½ m. by A 143 – ✉ Bury St. Edmunds – ☎ 01359 :

Hamling House ♨, Bull Rd, IP31 2LW, ✆ 230934, Fax 232298, ⛲ – ⇔ rest TV ☎ P. AE ⓓ VISA
Meals *(closed Sunday dinner)* 11.50/16.50 **st.** 3.00 – **7 rm** ⊡ 48.00/64.00 **t.** – SB.

at Ixworth NE : 7 m. by A 143 – ✉ Bury St. Edmunds – ☎ 01359 :

XX **Theobalds,** 68 High St., IP31 2HJ, ✆ 231707 – VISA JCB
closed Saturday lunch, Sunday dinner, Monday, 1 week August and Bank Holidays – **Meals** 12.00 **t.** and a la carte 25.50/28.50 **t.** 7.00.

at Bardwell NE : 9¾ m. by A 143 and A 1088 on Bardwell rd – ✉ Bury St. Edmunds – ☎ 01359 :

Six Bells Country Inn, The Green, IP31 1AW, ✆ 250820, ⛲ – TV ☎ P. VISA.
closed 25 and 26 December – **Meals** a la carte 12.15/20.40 **st.** – **8 rm** ⊡ 40.00/55.00 **st.** – SB.

at Rougham Green SE : 4 m. by A 1302 and A 134 off A 14 – ✉ Bury St. Edmunds – ☎ 01359 :

Ravenwood Hall, IP30 9JA, ✆ 270345, Fax 270788, heated, ⛲, park, – ⇔ rm TV ☎ P – 150. AE ⓓ VISA
Meals 16.95/18.90 **t.** and a la carte 5.50 – **14 rm** ⊡ 59.00/97.00 **st.** – SB.

at Bradfield Combust SE : 4½ m. on A 134 – ✉ Bury St. Edmunds – ☎ 01284 :

Bradfield House, Sudbury Rd, IP30 0LR, ✆ 386301, ⛲ – ⇔ rest TV ☎ P. VISA JCB.
closed 1 week January and last week August – **Meals** *(closed Sunday dinner and Monday to non-residents)* 15.50/19.50 **t.** and a la carte 5.95 – **4 rm** ⊡ 45.00/80.00 **t.** – SB.

ATS Units 1 and 3, Ailwin Rd, Moreton Hall Ind. Est. ✆ 705610

BUTTERMERE Cumbria 402 K 20 – pop. 139 – ✉ Cockermouth – ☎ 0176 87.

London 306 – Carlisle 35 – Kendal 43.

Bridge, CA13 9UZ, ✆ 70252, Fax 70252, ← – ⇔ rest ☎ P. VISA
Meals (booking essential) 12.00/19.00 **t.** 4.95 – **22 rm** ⊡ (dinner included) 53.00/106.00 **t.** – SB.

at Brackenthwaite NW : 4 m. on B 5289 – ✉ Cockermouth – ☎ 01900 :

Pickett Howe ♨, CA13 9UY, ✆ 85444, Fax 85209, ←, « Part 17C longhouse », ⛲ – ⇔ TV ☎ P. VISA.
mid March-mid November – **Meals** (residents only) (communal dining) (dinner only) 21.00 **st.** 3.90 – **4 rm** ⊡ 70.00/72.00 **st.**

BUTTERTON Staffs. – see Leek.

BUXTON Derbs. 402 403 404 O 24 – pop. 19 854 – ☎ 01298.

Buxton and High Peak, Townend ✆ 23453.

The Cresent, SK17 6BQ ✆ 25106.

London 172 – Derby 38 – Manchester 25 – Stoke-on-Trent 24.

Lee Wood, 13 Manchester Rd, SK17 6TQ, on A 5004 ✆ 23002, Fax 23228, ⛲ – ⇔ rm TV ☎ P – 100. AE ⓓ VISA
Meals 11.95/19.95 **t.** and a la carte 5.00 – **38 rm** ⊡ 62.00/88.00 **t.** – SB.

Brookfield Hall ♨, Long Hill, SK17 6SU, NW : 1¾ m. on A 5004 ✆ 24151, Fax 24151, ←, « Victorian country house », ⛲ – TV ☎ P
7 rm.

Coningsby, 6 Macclesfield Rd, SK17 9AH, ✆ 26735, Fax 26735, ⛲ – ⇔ TV P.
closed December – **Meals** (by arrangement) (communal dining) 13.50 4.00 – **3 rm** ⊡ 50.00 **s.**

Lakenham, 11 Burlington Rd, SK17 9AL, ✆ 79209 – TV P
Meals (by arrangement) 10.00 – **6 rm** ⊡ 30.00/44.00.

ATS Staden Lane, off Ashbourne Rd ✆ 25608/25655

BYFORD Heref. and Worcs. 403 L 27 – see Hereford.

CADNAM Hants. 403 404 P 31 – pop. 1 866 – ☎ 01703.

London 91 – Salisbury 16 – Southampton 8 – Winchester 19.

Walnut Cottage without rest., Old Romsey Rd, SO40 2NP, off A 31 ✆ 812275, ⛲ – TV P.
closed 23 to 27 December – **3 rm** ⊡ 28.00/43.00.

CALCOT Glos. – see Tetbury.

CALDBECK Cumbria 401 402 K 19 – pop. 688 – ✉ Wigton – ☎ 01697 4.

♦London 308 – ♦Carlisle 13 – Keswick 16 – Workington 23.

Parkend , Park End, CA7 8HH, SW : 1½ m. on B 5299 ☎ 78494, « Converted 17 farmhouse », – rest TV P. AE VISA
closed 8 to 31 January – **Meals** (by arrangement) approx. 10.40 **t.** 4.25 – **3 rm** 32.00 48.00 **t.**

CALNE Wilts. 403 404 O 29 **The West Country G.** – pop. 13 894 – ☎ 01249.

Envir. : Bowood House★ *AC*, (Library ≤★) SW : 2 m. by A 4 – Avebury★★ (The Stones★ Church★) E : 6 m. by A 4.

Bowood G. & C.C., Derry Hill ☎ 822228.

♦London 91 – ♦Bristol 33 – Swindon 17.

Chilvester Hill House, SN11 OLP, W : ¾ m. by A 4 on Bremhill rd ☎ 813981 Fax 814217, heated, – rest TV P. AE VISA.
closed 1 week low season – **Meals** (booking essential) (residents only) (communal dining (dinner only) 22.00 **st.** 4.35 – **3 rm** 40.00/75.00 **st.**

ATS Unit 4, Maundrell Rd., Portemarsh Ind. Est. ☎ 821622

CALSTOCK Cornwall 403 H 32 **The West Country G.** – pop. 5 964 – ✉ Tavistock – ☎ 01822.

Envir. : Tamar River★★ – Cotehele★ *AC*, SW : 1 m. - Morwellham★ *AC*, NE : 1½ m.

♦London 246 – Exeter 48 – ♦Plymouth 22.

Danescombe Valley , Lower Kelly, PL18 9RY, W : ½ m. ☎ 832414, Fax 832414, Viaduct and Tamar Valley, « Country house atmosphere » – rest P. AE VISA.
closed Wednesday, Thursday, 1 January-28 March and 28 October-23 December – **Meal** (dinner only) 30.00 **st.** 4.00 – **5 rm** 75.00/125.00 **st.**

Les prix — Pour toutes précisions sur les prix indiqués dans ce guide, reportez-vous à l'introduction.

CAMBERLEY Surrey 404 R 29 – pop. 46 120 – ☎ 01276.

♦London 40 – Reading 13 – ♦Southampton 48.

Frimley Hall (Forte Heritage) , Lime Av. via Conifer Drive, GU15 2SB, E : ¾ m. o Portsmouth Rd (A 325) ☎ 28321, Fax 691253, – TV ☎ P – 60. AE VIS JCB
Meals 14.75/21.95 **st.** and a la carte – 8.75 – **66 rm** 98.00/108.00 **st.** – SB.

CAMBORNE Cornwall 403 E 33 – ☎ 01209.

♦London 299 – Falmouth 14 – Penzance 16 – Truro 14.

Tyack's, 27 Commercial St., TR14 8LD, ☎ 612424, Fax 612435 – rm TV ☎ P. VISA JCB.
Meals 10.50/11.50 **t.** and a la carte 5.00 – **15 rm** 45.00/90.00 **st.** – SB.

CAMBRIDGE Cambs. 404 U 27 **Great Britain G.** – pop. 91 933 – ☎ 01223.

See : Town★★★ – St. John's College★★★ *AC* Y – King's College★★ (King's Colleg Chapel★★★) Z The Backs★★ YZ – Fitzwilliam Museum★★ Z **M1** – Trinity College★★ Y – Cla College★ Z **B** – Kettle's Yard★ Y **M2** – Queen's College★ *AC* Z.

Cambridgeshire Moat House Hotel, Bar Hill ☎ (01954) 780555 X.

Cambridge Airport : ☎ 61133, E : 2 m. on A 1303 X.

Wheeler St., CB2 3QB ☎ 322640.

♦London 55 – ♦Coventry 88 – ♦Kingston-upon-Hull 137 – ♦Ipswich 54 – ♦Leicester 74 – ♦Norwich 61 – ♦Nottingham 8 – ♦Oxford 100.

Plan opposite

Garden House (Q.M.H.), Granta Pl., off Mill Lane, CB2 1RT, ☎ 259988, Fax 316605, – rm TV ☎ P – 250. AE VISA. Z
Le Jardin : Meals 9.95/23.00 **t.** and a la carte – 11.95 – **118 rm** 95.00/140.00 **t.** – SB.

University Arms (De Vere), Regent St., CB2 1AD, ☎ 351241, Fax 315256 – rm ☎ P – 300. AE VISA Z
Meals 11.50/18.00 **st.** and a la carte 6.50 – **114 rm** 50.00/100.00, 1 suite – SB.

Holiday Inn, Downing St., CB2 3DT, ☎ 464466, Fax 464440, – rm TV ☎ – 150. AE VISA JCB Z
Meals (bar lunch Monday to Saturday)/dinner 17.50 **t.** and a la carte – **197 rm** 89.00 104.00 **st.**, 2 suites – SB.

Gonville, Gonville Pl., CB1 1LY, ☎ 366611, Fax 315470 – rest TV ☎ P – 20 AE VISA. Z
Meals 12.50/15.00 **st.** and a la carte 6.50 – **63 rm** 71.00/89.00 **st.** – SB.

Arundel House, 53 Chesterton Rd, CB4 3AN, ☎ 367701, Fax 367721 – rest TV P – 50. AE VISA. Y
closed 25 and 26 December – **Meals** 8.75/14.95 **t.** and a la carte 4.65 – 2.25 – **105 r** 28.00/77.00 **t.** – SB.

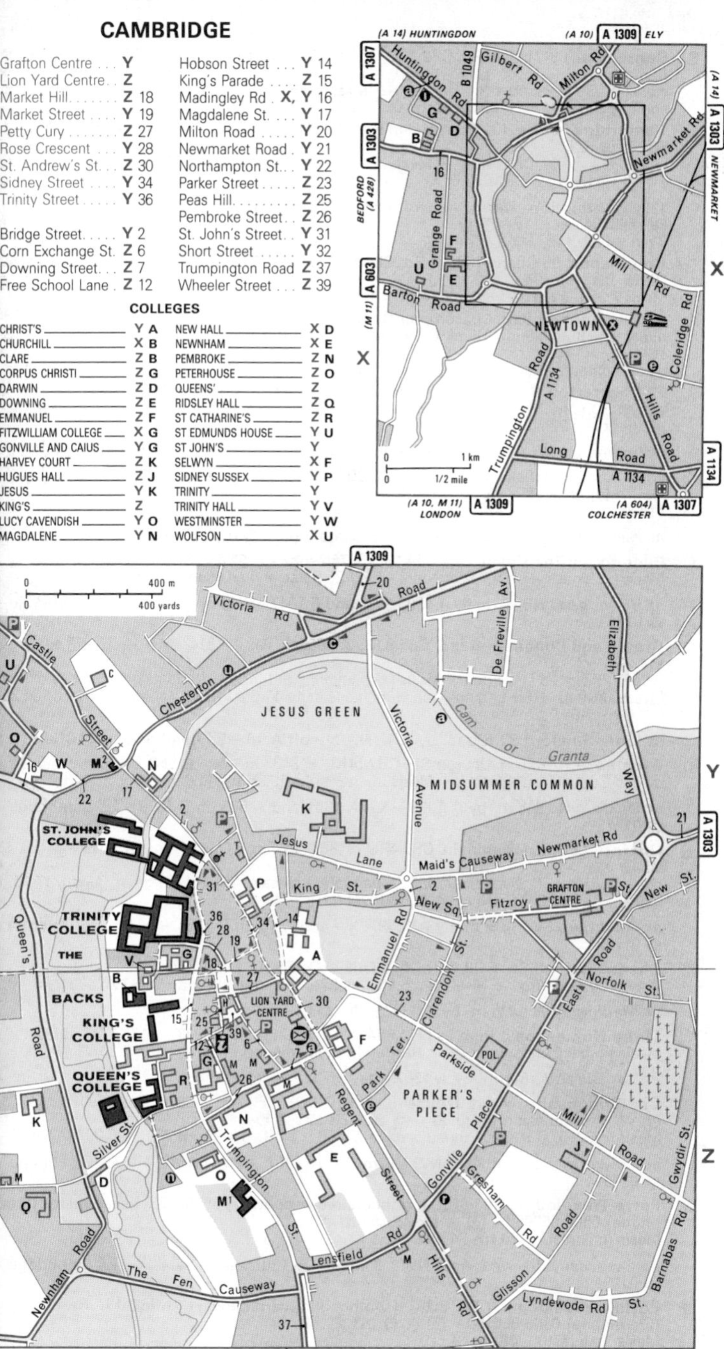
CAMBRIDGE
Grafton Centre . . . Y
Lion Yard Centre . . Z
Market Hill . . . . Z 18
Market Street . . . . Y 19
Petty Cury . . . . Z 27
Rose Crescent . . . Y 28
St. Andrew's St. . . Z 30
Sidney Street . . . . Y 34
Trinity Street . . . . . Y 36
Bridge Street . . . . . Y 2
Corn Exchange St. Z 6
Downing Street . . . Z 7
Free School Lane . Z 12
Hobson Street . . . Y 14
King's Parade . . . . Z 15
Madingley Rd . X, Y 16
Magdalene St. . . . Y 17
Milton Road . . . . . Y 20
Newmarket Road . Y 21
Northampton St. . . Y 22
Parker Street . . . . . Z 23
Peas Hill . . . . Z 25
Pembroke Street . . Z 26
St. John's Street . . Y 31
Short Street . . . . . Y 32
Trumpington Road Z 37
Wheeler Street . . . Z 39
COLLEGES
CHRIST'S Y A
CHURCHILL X B
CLARE Z B
CORPUS CHRISTI Z G
DARWIN Z D
DOWNING Z E
EMMANUEL Z F
FITZWILLIAM COLLEGE X G
GONVILLE AND CAIUS Y G
HARVEY COURT Z K
HUGUES HALL Z J
JESUS Y K
KING'S Z
LUCY CAVENDISH Y O
MAGDALENE Y N
NEW HALL X D
NEWNHAM X E
PEMBROKE Z N
PETERHOUSE Z O
QUEENS' Z
RIDSLEY HALL Z Q
ST CATHARINE'S Z R
ST EDMUNDS HOUSE Y U
ST JOHN'S Y
SELWYN X F
SIDNEY SUSSEX Y P
TRINITY Y
TRINITY HALL Y V
WESTMINSTER Y W
WOLFSON X U
(A 14) HUNTINGDON
(A 10) A 1309 ELY
(A 14) A 1303 NEWMARKET
BEDFORD (A 428) A 1303
(M 11) A 603
(A 10, M 11) LONDON A 1309
(A 604) COLCHESTER A 1307
A 1307
A 1134
Huntingdon Rd
Gilbert Rd
Milton Rd
B 1049
Newmarket Rd
Grange Road
Barton Road
Mill Rd
Coleridge Rd
NEWTOWN
Trumpington Road
Hills Road
Long Road
A 1134
0 1 km
0 1/2 mile
X
Y
Z
A 1309
0 400 m
0 400 yards
Victoria Rd
Road
De Freville Av.
Elizabeth Way
Castle Street
Chesterton
JESUS GREEN
Victoria Avenue
Cam or Granta
MIDSUMMER COMMON
ST. JOHN'S COLLEGE
TRINITY COLLEGE
THE BACKS
KING'S COLLEGE
QUEEN'S COLLEGE
Queen's Road
Jesus Lane
King St.
Maid's Causeway
Newmarket Rd
New Sq.
Fitzroy
GRAFTON CENTRE
New St.
East Road
Norfolk St.
Emmanuel Rd
Clarendon St.
LION YARD CENTRE
Park Ter.
Parkside
PARKER'S PIECE
Regent Street
Trumpington St.
Silver St.
Mill Road
Gwydir St.
Gonville Place
Gresham Rd
Road
Barnabas Rd
Lensfield Rd
Hills Rd
Glisson
Lyndewode Rd
St.
Newnham Road
The Fen Causeway
POL
A 1303
A 1309
A 1307

Centennial, 63-71 Hills Rd, CB2 1PG, ℘ 314652, Fax 315443 – rm. VISA. X x
closed 23 December-2 January – **Meals** (lunch by arrangement)/dinner 15.00 t. and a la carte 4.00 – **39 rm** 55.00/75.00 **t.** – SB.

Cambridge Lodge, 139 Huntingdon Rd, CB3 0DQ, ℘ 352833, Fax 355166, – . VISA X
closed 27 to 30 December – **Meals** *(closed Saturday lunch)* 9.95/19.95 **t.** and a la carte 4.50 – **11 rm** 55.00/72.50 **t.** Y a

136 Huntingdon Road without rest., 136 Huntingdon Rd, CB3 0HL, ℘ 365285, Fax 568304, – X a
3 rm 32.00/52.00.

Brooklands, 95 Cherry Hinton Rd, CB1 4BS, ℘ 242035, Fax 242035, – . VISA. X e
Meals 7.95 – **5 rm** 28.00/45.00 **st.**

Midsummer House, Midsummer Common, CB4 1HA, ℘ 69299, Fax 302672, « Attractively situated beside River Cam, overlooking Midsummer Common », – VISA Y a
closed Saturday lunch, Sunday dinner and Monday – **Meals** 17.00/35.00 **st.** and a la carte.

22 Chesterton Road, 22 Chesterton Rd, CB4 3AX, ℘ 351880 – VISA Y c
closed Sunday, Monday and 1 week Christmas to New Year – **Meals** (booking essential) (dinner only) 22.50 **t.**

at Impington N : 2 m. on B 1049 at junction with A 14 – X – ✉ Cambridge – 01223 :

Forte Posthouse, Lakeview, Bridge Rd, CB4 4PH, ℘ 237000, Fax 233426, – rm – 60
118 rm.

at Histon N : 3 m. on B 1049 – X – ✉ Cambridge – 01223 :

Phoenix, 20 The Green, CB4 4JA, ℘ 233766 – . VISA
Meals - Chinese (Peking, Szechuan) - 6.50/25.50 **st.** and a la carte 4.00.

at Horningsea NE : 4 m. by A 1303 – X – and B 1047 on Horningsea rd – ✉ Cambridge – 01223 :

Crown and Punchbowl Inn, CB5 9JG, ℘ 860643, Fax 441814, – rm . VISA.
closed 25 and 26 December – **Meals** *(closed lunch Saturday)* (residents only Sunday dinner (meals in bar) 15.95 **t.** (dinner) and lunch a la carte 11.35/15.95 **t.** 4.00 – **5 rm** 36.25, 63.00 **t.** – SB.

at Little Shelford S : 5½ m. by A 1309 – X – off A 10 – ✉ Cambridge – 01223 :

Sycamore House, 1 Church St., CB2 5HG, ℘ 843396 – . VISA
closed Sunday and Monday – **Meals** (dinner only) 19.95 **t.** 4.50.

at Duxford S : 9½ m. by A 1309 – X – A 1301 and A 505 on B 1379 – ✉ Cambridge – 01223 :

Duxford Lodge, Ickleton Rd, CB2 4RU, ℘ 836444, Fax 832271, – – 30. VISA
closed 26 to 30 December and 1 January – **Meals** *(closed Saturday lunch)* 17.75 **t.** and a la carte 5.00 – **15 rm** 68.00/89.50 **t.**

at Fowlmere SW : 8¾ m. by A 1309 – X – and A 10 on B 1368 – ✉ Royston (Herts.) – 01763 :

Chequers, High St., SG8 7SR, ℘ 208369 – . VISA
closed 25 December – **Meals** 14.25 **st.** (lunch) and dinner a la carte 15.60/26.40 **st.** 4.40.

at Madingley W : 4½ m. by A 1303 – X – 01954 :

Three Horseshoes, High St., CB3 8AB, ℘ 210221, Fax 212043 – . VISA
Meals (in bar Sunday and Bank Holiday Monday dinner) a la carte 15.50/26.00 4.00.

at Bar Hill NW : 5½ m. by A 1307 – X – off A 14 – 01954 :

Cambridgeshire Moat House (Q.M.H.), CB3 8EU, ℘ 249988, Fax 780010, , , , squash – – 200. VISA
Meals 5.75/15.00 **t.** and dinner a la carte 5.50 – 9.95 – **99 rm** 75.00/95.00 **t.** – SB.

at Lolworth Service Area NW : 6 m. by A 1307 – X – on A 14 – ✉ Cambridge – 01954 :

Forte Travelodge, CB3 8DR, (northbound carriageway) ℘ 781335, Reservations (Freephone) 0800 850950 – . VISA.
Meals (grill rest.) – **20 rm** 34.50 **t.**

at Swavesey Service Area NW : 8 m. by A 1307 on A 14 – X – ✉ Cambridge – 01954 :

Forte Travelodge, CB4 5QR, (southbound carriageway) ℘ 789113, Reservation (Freephone) 0800 850950 – . VISA.
Meals (grill rest.) – **36 rm** 34.50 **t.**

ATS 143 Histon Rd ℘ 351431

CANNOCK Staffs. 402 403 404 N 25 **Great Britain G.** – pop. 88 833 – ☎ 01543.

Exc. : Weston Park★★ *AC*, W : 11 m. by A 5.

Cannock Park, Stafford Rd ☎ 578850.

◆London 135 – ◆Birmingham 20 – Derby 36 – ◆Leicester 51 – Shrewsbury 32 – ◆Stoke-on-Trent 28.

Roman Way (Regal), Watling St., Hatherton, WS11 1SH, SW : 1 ¼ m. by A 4601 on A 5 ☎ 572121, Fax 502742 – rm – 120. VISA
Meals 14.50 and a la carte 6.00 – **56 rm** 61.00/64.00 **st.** – SB.

Travel Inn, Watling St., WS11 1SJ, SW : 1 m. at junction of A 4601 with A 5 ☎ 572721, Fax 466130 – rm – 100. VISA.
Meals (grill rest.) – 4.95 – **38 rm** 34.50 **t.**

ATS Cannock Rd, Chadsmoor ☎ 574580/504985 ATS Cannock Rd, Heath Hayes ☎ 274200

CANON PYON Heref. and Worcs. 403 L 27 – see Hereford.

CANTERBURY Kent 404 X 30 **Great Britain G.** – pop. 123 947 – ☎ 01227.

See : City★★★ - Cathedral★★★ Y - St. Augustine's Abbey★★ *AC* YZ **K** – King's School★ Y **B** – Mercery Lane★ Y **12** - Christ Church Gate★ Y **A** – Weavers★ Y **D** – Hospital of St. Thomas the Martyr, Eastbridge★ Y **E** – Poor Priests Hospital★ *AC* Y **M1** – St. Martin's Church★ Y **N** – West Gate★ *AC* Y **R**.

34 St. Margaret's St., CT1 2TG ☎ 766567.

◆London 59 – ◆Brighton 76 – ◆Dover 15 – Maidstone 28 – Margate 17.

Plan on next page

County, High St., CT1 2RX, ☎ 766266, Fax 451512 – – 180. VISA JCB. Y **n**
Meals – (see ***Sullys*** below) – 8.50 – **72 rm** 71.00/95.00 **t.**, 1 suite.

Chaucer (Forte Heritage), Ivy Lane, CT1 1TU, ☎ 464427, Fax 450397 – – 100. VISA JCB Z **c**
Meals 11.95/18.95 **t.** and a la carte 7.05 – 8.75 – **42 rm** 70.00/85.00 **st.** – SB.

Falstaff (Country Club), 8-12 St. Dunstan's St., CT2 8AF, ☎ 462138, Fax 463525 – rm – 50. VISA Y **a**
Meals a la carte 12.50/19.50 **st.** 4.95 – 7.50 – **24 rm** 68.00/85.00 **st.** – SB.

Thanington without rest., 140 Wincheap, CT1 3RY, ☎ 453227, Fax 453225, – . VISA JCB. Z **s**
10 rm 46.00/65.00 **st.**

Victoria, 59 London Rd, CT2 8JY, ☎ 459333, Fax 781552 – Y **i**
Meals (grill rest.) – **33 rm.**

Pilgrims, 15 The Friars, CT1 2AS, ☎ 464531, Fax 762514 – . VISA. Y **c**
Meals (dinner only) a la carte 11.95/17.50 **st.** – **14 rm** 45.00/55.00 **st.** – SB.

Ebury, 65-67 New Dover Rd, CT1 3DX, ☎ 768433, Fax 459187, , – rest . VISA Z **r**
closed mid December-mid January – **Meals** (dinner only) (light dinner Sunday) a la carte 10.10/14.50 **t.** 4.50 – **15 rm** 41.00/65.00 **t.** – SB.

Pointers, 1 London Rd, CT2 8LR, ☎ 456846, Fax 831131 – . VISA JCB
closed 23 December to 14 January – **Meals** (dinner only) 13.50 **t.** 4.50 – **13 rm** 38.00/55.00 **t.** – SB. Y **e**

Ann's House without rest., 63 London Rd, CT2 8JZ, ☎ 768767, Fax 768172, – . VISA. Y **r**
18 rm 18.00/46.00 **st.**

Magnolia House, 36 St. Dunstan's Terr., CT2 8AX, ☎ 765121, Fax 765121, – . VISA. Y **s**
Meals (November-February) (by arrangement) 20.00 **st.** – **7 rm** 36.00/80.00 **t.** – SB.

Alexandra House without rest., 1 Roper Rd, CT2 7EH, ☎ 767011, Fax 786617, – . Y **u**
7 rm 22.00/50.00.

Highfield without rest., Summer Hill, Harbledown, CT2 8NH, W : by Rheims way, ☎ 462772, Fax 462772, – . VISA JCB.
closed Christmas-3 January – **8 rm** 27.00/50.00 **st.**

Clare Ellen without rest., 9 Victoria Rd, CT1 3SG, ☎ 760205, Fax 784482, – . VISA. Z **u**
6 rm 22.00/45.00 **s.**

Zan Stel Lodge without rest., 140 Old Dover Rd, CT1 3NX, ☎ 453654, – .
4 rm 26.00/46.00.

XXX **Sullys** (at County H.), High St., CT1 2RX, ☎ 766266, Fax 451512 – . VISA JCB
Meals 13.50/19.50 **t.** and a la carte. Y **n**

XX **Tuo e Mio,** 16 The Borough, CT1 2DR, ☎ 761471 – VISA Y **o**
closed Tuesday lunch, Monday, last 2 weeks February and last 2 weeks August – **Meals** - Italian - 13.50 **st.** (lunch) and a la carte 13.50/22.50 **st.** 3.75.

CANTERBURY

Burgate	Y
Butchery Lane	Y 5
Guildhall Street	Y 6
High Street	Y 8
Mercery Lane	Y 12
Palace Street	Y
St. George's Street	Z 17
St. Margaret's Street	YZ 18
St. Peter's Street	Y 20
Beercart Lane	YZ 2
Borough (The)	Y 4
Lower Bridge Street	Z 9
Lower Chantry Lane	Z 1
Rhodaus Town	Z 1
Rosemary Lane	Z 1
St. George's Place	Z 1
St. Mary's Street	Z 1
St. Radigund's Street	Y 2
Upper Bridge Street	Z 2
Watling Street	Z 2

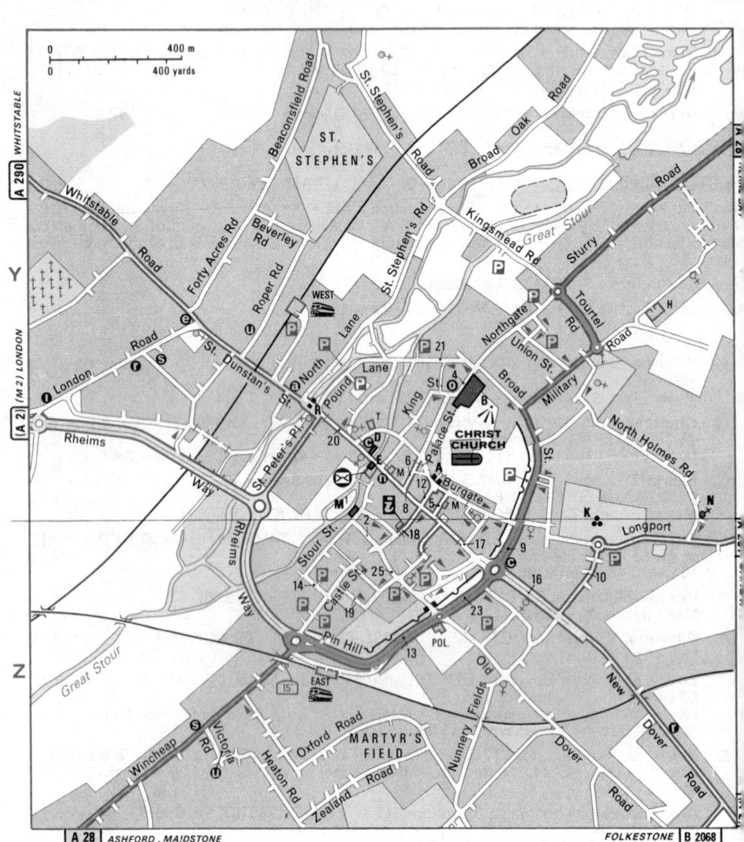

at Littlebourne E : 3 ¾ m. on A 257 – Z – ✉ Canterbury – ☎ 01227 :

Bow Window Inn, 50 High St., CT3 1ST, ☎ 721264, Fax 721250 – TV P. AE VISA
Meals *(closed Sunday dinner)* a la carte 13.75/20.20 **t.** 4.75 – **8 rm** 35.00/58.00 **t.** – SB

at Chartham SW : 3 ¼ m. by A 28 – Z – ✉ Canterbury – ☎ 01227 :

Thruxted Oast without rest., Mystole, CT4 7BX, SW : 1 ¼ m. by Rattington St. and Cockering Rd on Mystole Lane ☎ 730080, ←, – TV ☎ P. AE VISA.
closed Christmas – **3 rm** 65.00/75.00 **s.**

at Chartham Hatch W : 3 ¼ m. by A 28 – Z – ✉ Canterbury – ☎ 01227 :

Howfield Manor, Howfield Lane, CT4 7HQ, SE : 1 m. ☎ 738294, Fax 731535, – TV
P – 80. AE VISA JCB.
Meals – (see ***Old Well*** below) – **13 rm** 62.50/95.00 **st.** – SB.

Old Well (at Howfield Manor H.), Howfield Lane, CT4 7HQ, SE : 1 m. ☎ 73829
Fax 731535, – P. AE VISA JCB
Meals 13.95/18.95 **st.** and a la carte 4.85.

ATS 29 Sturry Rd ☎ 464867/765021

CARBIS BAY Cornwall 403 D 33 – see St. Ives.

CARCROFT S. Yorks. 402 403 404 Q 23 – see Doncaster.

CARLISLE Cumbria 401 402 L 19 **Great Britain G.** – pop. 100 562 – ☎ 01228.

See : Town★ - Cathedral★ (Painted Ceiling★) AY **E** – Tithe Barn★ BY **A**.

Envir. : Hadrian's Wall★★, N : by A 7 AY.

18 Aglionby ℘ 513303 BY – 18 Stoneyholme, St. Aidan's Rd ℘ 34856, BY – 9 Dalston Hall, Dalston ℘ 710165, AZ.

✈ Carlisle Airport ℘ 573641, NW : 5½m. by A 7 BY and B 6264 – **Terminal** : Bus Station, Lowther Street.

℘ 0345 090700.

ℹ Carlisle Visitor Centre, Old Town Hall, Green Market, CA3 8JH ℘ 512444.

♦London 317 – ♦Blackpool 95 – ♦Edinburgh 101 – ♦Glasgow 100 – ♦Leeds 124 – ♦Liverpool 127 – ♦Manchester 122 – ♦Newcastle upon Tyne 59.

CARLISLE

Botchergate .... **BZ**
Castle Street .... **BY** 6
English Street .... **BY** 13
Scotch Street .... **BY** 19
The Lanes Shopping Centre .... **BY**

Annetwell Street .... **AY** 2
Bridge Street .... **AY** 3
Brunswick Street .... **BZ** 4
Cecil Street .... **BZ** 5
Charlotte Street .... **AZ** 7
Chiswick Street .... **BY** 8
Church Street .... **AY** 10
Eden Bridge .... **BY** 12
Lonsdale Street .... **BY** 14

Lowther Street .... **BY** 15
Port Road .... **AY** 16
St. Marys Gate .... **BY** 17
Spencer Street .... **BY** 20
Tait Street .... **BZ** 21
Victoria Viaduct .... **ABZ** 24
West Tower Street .... **BY** 26
West Walls .... **ABY** 27
Wigton Road .... **AZ** 29

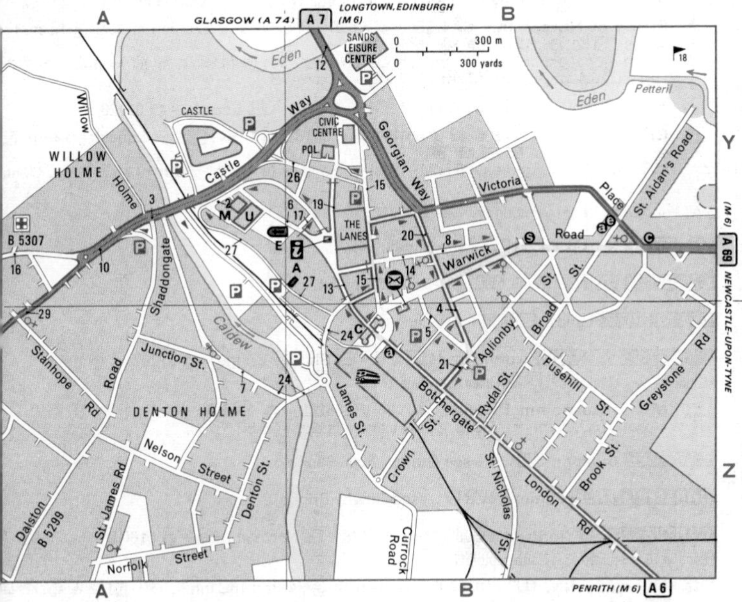

Cumbrian (Regal), Court Sq., CA1 1QY, ℘ 31951, Fax 47799 – |‡| ⇔ rm TV ☎ & ⇔ P – 300. AE VISA. ✻ BZ **a**
Meals 9.50/15.50 **st.** – **70 rm** ⊐ 70.00/95.00 **st.** – SB.

Cumbria Park, 32 Scotland Rd, CA3 9DG, N : 1 m. on A 7 ℘ 22887, Fax 514796 – |‡| ⇔ rm TV ☎ P – 100. AE VISA JCB. ✻
closed 25 and 26 December – **Meals** (bar lunch Sunday) 16.50 **t.** (dinner) and a la carte 15.85/24.35 **t.** – **49 rm** ⊐ 65.00/82.50 **t.** – SB.

Gosling Bridge (Premier), Kingstown Rd, CA3 0AT, N : 1 ¾ m. on A 7 ℘ 515294, Fax 515220 – ⇔ rm TV ☎ & P
Meals (grill rest.) – **30 rm.**

Beeches, Wood St., CA1 2SF, E : 1 ½ m. by A 69 off Victoria Rd ☎ 511962, –
Meals (by arrangement in winter) 10.95 **st.** – **3 rm** 30.00/35.00 **st.** – SB.

Courtfield House, 169 Warwick Rd, CA1 1LP, ☎ 22767 – BY
Meals (by arrangement) 7.00 – **4 rm** 20.00/35.00.

Fern Lee, 9 St. Aidan's Rd, CA1 1LT, ☎ 511930 – BY
Meals (by arrangement) 8.00 **st.** – **5 rm** 22.00/40.00 **st.** – SB.

Langleigh House without rest., 6 Howard Pl., CA1 1HR, ☎ 30440 – BY
3 rm 25.00/36.00.

Avondale, 3 St. Aidan's Rd, CA1 1LT, ☎ 23012 – BY
Meals (by arrangement) (communal dining) 8.00 – **3 rm** 22.00/38.00.

XX **No. 10,** 10 Eden Mount, Stanwix, CA3 9LY, N : ¾ m. on A 7. ☎ 24183 – VISA
closed Sunday, first week November and February – **Meals** (dinner only) a la carte 13.45 20.00 **t.** 3.80.

at Kingstown N : 3 m. by A 7 – BY – at junction 44 of M 6 – ✉ Carlisle – ☎ 01228 :

Forte Posthouse, Park House Rd, Kingstown, CA3 0HR, on A 7 ☎ 31201, Fax 43178, – rm VISA JCB
Meals a la carte 14.45/22.85 **st.** 10.25 – 7.95 – **93 rm** 59.00 **st.** – SB.

at High Crosby NE : 5 m. by A 7 and B 6264 – BY – off A 689 – ✉ Carlisle – ☎ 01228

Crosby Lodge Country House, CA6 4QZ, ☎ 573618, Fax 573428, ‹, « 18C countr mansion », – rest VISA JCB.
closed 24 December to 21 January – **Meals** *(closed Sunday dinner to non-residents)* 15.50 30.50 **t.** and a la carte 7.50 – **11 rm** 68.00/95.00 **t.** – SB.

at Faugh E : 8 ¼ m. by A 69 – BY – and Heads Nook rd – ✉ Carlisle – ☎ 01228 :

String of Horses Inn, CA4 9EG, ☎ 70297, Fax 70675, « 17C inn », heated rest VISA.
accommodation closed 24 and 25 December – **Meals** 14.95 **t.** (lunch) and a la cart approx. 16.40 **t.** 4.25 – **12 rm** 58.00/98.00 **t.** – SB.

at Wetheral E : 6 ¼ m. by A 69 – BZ – on B 6263 – ✉ Carlisle – ☎ 01228 :

Crown, CA4 8ES, on B 6263 ☎ 561888, Fax 561637, squash – rm – 175. VISA
Meals (bar lunch Saturday) 9.50/18.00 **st.** and a la carte 6.95 – **50 rm** 72.00/118.00 **st** 1 suite – SB.

ATS Rosehill Ind. Est., Montgomery Way ☎ 25277

CARLTON N. Yorks. 402 O 21 – see Middleham.

CARLYON BAY Cornwall 403 F 33 – see St. Austell.

CARNFORTH Lancs. 402 L 21 – see Lancaster.

CARTERWAY HEADS Northd 401 402 O 19 – ✉ Shotley Bridge – ☎ 01207.
London 272 – Carlisle 59 – Newcastle upon Tyne 21.

XX **Manor House Inn,** DH8 9LX, on A 68 ☎ 255268 – VISA
closed 25 December – **Meals** 16.50 **st.** and a la carte 3.50.

CARTMEL Cumbria 402 L 21 – see Grange-over-Sands.

CARTMELL FELL Cumbria 402 L 21 – see Newby Bridge.

CASTLE ASHBY Northants. 404 R 27 – pop. 138 – ✉ Northampton – ☎ 01604.
London 76 – Bedford 15 – Northampton 11.

Falcon, NN7 1LF, ☎ 696200, Fax 696673, « Part 16C inn », – VISA JCB
Meals 19.50 **t.** and a la carte 4.50 – **16 rm** 62.50/75.00 **t.** – SB.

CASTLE CARY Somerset 403 404 M 30 – pop. 1 904 – ☎ 01963.
London 125 – Bristol 28 – Taunton 31 – Yeovil 13.

George, Market Pl., BA7 7AH, ☎ 350761, Fax 350035 – VISA
Meals *(closed Sunday dinner)* (bar lunch Monday to Saturday)/dinner 9.40 20.50 a la carte **t.** 3.75 – **15 rm** 55.00/70.00 **t.** – SB.

XX **Bond's** with rm, Ansford Hill, Ansford, BA7 7JP, N : ¾ m. by Ansford Rd on A 37 ☎ 350464, Fax 350464, – VISA.
closed 1 week Christmas – **Meals** (light lunch)/dinner 12.50/19.75 **t.** 4.25 – **7 rm** 38.00 80.00 **t.** – SB.

CASTLE COMBE Wilts. 403 404 N 29 The West Country G. – pop. 347 – ✉ Chippenham – ☎ 01249 – See : Village★★.

♦London 110 – ♦Bristol 23 – Chippenham 6.

- **Manor House** ⑤, SN14 7HR, ☏ 782206, Fax 782159, « Part 14C manor house in park », heated, 18, park, % – ⊁ rest TV ☎ P. AE VISA.
  Meals 16.95/32.00 **t.** and a la carte – ⊡ 11.00 – **40 rm** 95.00/295.00 **t.**, 2 suites – SB.
- **Castle Inn,** SN14 7HN, ☏ 783030, Fax 782315, « Part 12C » – ⊁ rest TV ☎. AE VISA JCB.
  Meals 12.50/27.00 **st.** 6.50 – **7 rm** ⊡ 65.00/95.00 **st.** – SB.

at Ford S : 1 ¾ m. on A 420 – ✉ Chippenham – ☎ 01249 :

- **White Hart Inn,** SN14 8RP, ☏ 782213, Fax 783075 – TV ☎ P. AE VISA
  Meals 12.75/14.00 **t.** and a la carte 4.00 – **11 rm** ⊡ 43.00/59.00 **t.** – SB.

at Nettleton Shrub W : 2 m. by B 4039 on Nettleton rd (Fosse Way) – ✉ Chippenham – ☎ 01249 :

- **Fosse Farmhouse,** SN14 7NJ, ☏ 782286, Fax 783066, park – ⊁ rest TV P. AE VISA JCB.
  Meals 15.00/25.00 **t.** and lunch a la carte 6.00 – **6 rm** ⊡ 40.00/110.00 **t.** – SB.

CASTLE DONINGTON Leics. 402 403 404 P 25 – pop. 6 313 – ✉ Derby – ☎ 01332.

✈ East Midlands Airport : ☏ 852852, S : by B 6540 and A 453.

♦London 123 – ♦Birmingham 38 – ♦Leicester 23 – ♦Nottingham 13.

- **Hilton National,** East Midlands Airport, Derby Rd, Lockington, DE74 2YW, E : 3 ¼ m. by B 6540 on A 453 at junction with A 6 and M 1 ☏ (01509) 674000, Telex 341031, Fax 672412, Ls, ≘s, – ⊁ rm TV ☎ & P – 350. AE VISA JCB
  closed 26 to 30 December – **Meals** (bar lunch Saturday) 11.75/17.50 **st.** and dinner a la carte 5.65 – **Zen : Meals** - Japanese (Teppan Yaki) - *(closed Sunday and Bank Holidays)* 24.00/30.00 **st.** 5.65 – ⊡ 10.50 – **151 rm** 95.00/140.00 **st.**, 1 suite – SB.
- **Donington Thistle,** East Midlands Airport, DE74 2SH, SE : 3 ¼ m. by B 6540 on A 453 ☏ 850700, Fax 850823, Ls, ≘s, – ⊁ rm rest TV ☎ & P – 220. AE VISA JCB
  Meals (bar lunch Saturday and Bank Holidays) 14.00/19.95 **st.** and a la carte 6.50 – ⊡ 8.95 – **108 rm** 85.00/140.00 **st.**, 2 suites – SB.
- Priest House ⑤, Kings Mills, DE74 2RR, W : 1 ¾ m. by Park Lane ☏ 810649, Fax 811141, ←, « Riverside setting », park – TV ☎ P – 130 – **43 rm**, 2 suites.
- **Donington Manor,** High St., DE74 2PP, ☏ 810253, Fax 850330 – TV ☎ P – 80. AE VISA.
  closed 26 to 30 December – **Meals** 8.90/10.75 **st.** and a la carte 4.40 – **34 rm** ⊡ 54.00/72.50 **st.**

at Isley Walton SW : 1 ¾ m. by B 6540 on A 453 – ✉ Derby – ☎ 01332 :

- **Park Farmhouse,** Melbourne Rd, DE74 2RN, W : ¾ m. ☏ 862409, Fax 862364, ← – TV ☎ P. AE VISA JCB
  closed Christmas – **Meals** (residents only) (dinner only) a la carte 14.15/17.45 4.25 – **9 rm** ⊡ 41.00/66.00 **t.** – SB.

CASTLETON Derbs. 402 403 404 O 23 Great Britain G. – pop. 689 – ✉ Sheffield (South Yorks.) – ☎ 01433 – Envir. : Blue John Caverns★ *AC*, W : 1 m.

♦London 181 – Derby 49 – ♦Manchester 30 – ♦Sheffield 16 – ♦Stoke-on-Trent 39.

- **Ye Olde Nags Head,** S30 2WH, ☏ 620248, Fax 620614 – TV ☎ P. AE VISA.
  Meals 13.95/19.95 **t.** and a la carte 4.50 – **8 rm** ⊡ 42.50/90.00 **t.**

CATLOWDY Cumbria 401 402 L 18 – ✉ Carlisle – ☎ 01228.

♦London 333 – ♦Carlisle 16 – ♦Dumfries 36 – Hawick 31 – ♦Newcastle upon Tyne 65.

- **Bessiestown Farm** ⑤, CA6 5QP, ☏ 577219, Fax 577219, park – ⊁ TV P. AE VISA.
  Meals (by arrangement) 10.00 **s.** – **4 rm** ⊡ 26.50/45.00 **s.**

CAWSTON Norfolk 404 X 25 Great Britain G. – pop. 2 265 – ✉ Norwich – ☎ 01603.

Envir. : Blicking Hall★★ *AC*, NE : 5 m. by B 1145 and B 1354.

♦London 122 – Cromer 15 – King's Lynn 42 – ♦Norwich 13.

- **Grey Gables** ⑤, Norwich Rd, NR10 4EY, S : 1 m. ☏ 871259, %, – ⊁ rest TV ☎ P. VISA
  closed 24 to 26 December – **Meals** (lunch by arrangement)/dinner 12.50/21.50 **st.** 5.75 – **8 rm** ⊡ 28.00/60.00 **t.** – SB.

CAXTON Cambs. – ☎ 01954.

♦London 67 – Bedford 18 – ♦Cambridge 12 – Huntingdon 7.

- **Church Farm** ⑤, Gransden Rd, CB3 8PL, ☏ 719543, Fax 718999, « Part 17C farm-house », %, – ⊁ P.
  Meals (by arrangement) (communal dining) 17.50 **st.** – **3 rm** ⊡ 27.50/55.00 **st.**

CHADDESLEY CORBETT Heref. and Worcs. 403 404 N 26 – see Kidderminster.

CHADLINGTON Oxon. 403 404 P 28 – pop. 1 310 – ☎ 01608.
♦London 74 – Cheltenham 32 – ♦Oxford 18 – Stratford-upon-Avon 25.

Manor ⛓, OX7 3LX, ✆ 676711, Fax 676674, ←, 🌳, park – ⛔ rest TV ☎ P. VISA JCB.
Meals (dinner only) 25.50 **st.** 4.50 – **7 rm** 60.00/119.00 **st.** – SB.

Chadlington House, OX7 3LZ, ✆ 676437, Fax 676503, 🌳 – ⛔ rest TV ☎ P. AE VISA.
closed January and February – **Meals** (residents only) (dinner only) 15.00 **t.** 4.00 – **10 rm** 30.00/60.00 **t.** – SB.

CHAGFORD Devon 403 I 31 **The West Country G.** – pop. 1 417 – ☎ 01647.
Envir. : Dartmoor National Park★★ (Brent Tor ←★★, Haytor Rocks ←★).
♦London 218 – Exeter 17 – ♦Plymouth 28.

✿ **Gidleigh Park** ⛓, TQ13 8HH, NW : 2 m. by Gidleigh Rd ✆ 432367, Fax 432574, ← Teign Valley, woodland and Meldon Hill, « Timbered country house, water garden », park, – ⛔ rest TV ☎ P. AE VISA
Meals (booking essential) 26.00/57.50 **st.** 9.00 – **13 rm** (dinner included) 205.00/375.00 **st.**, 2 suites – SB
Spec. Terrine of duck confit, foie gras and shallots, Lobster fricassee with vegetables and herbs, Stuffed leg of rabbit with wild mushrooms.

Thornworthy House ⛓, Thornworthy, TQ13 8EY, SW : 3 m. by Fernworthy rd on Thornworthy rd ✆ 433297, Fax 433297, ←, « Country house atmosphere », 🌳, park, – ⛔ TV P.
closed 7 to 31 January – **Meals** (by arrangement) (dinner only) 22.50 **st.** 4.50 – 5.00 – **3 rm** 18.00/53.00 **st.**

Glendarah House without rest., Lower St., TQ13 8BZ, ✆ 433270, Fax 433483, ←, 🌳 – ⛔ TV P. VISA.
closed 2 weeks December – **6 rm** 25.00/54.00 **st.**

at Sandy Park NE : 2¼ m. on A 382 – ✉ Chagford – ☎ 01647 :

Mill End, TQ13 8JN, on A 382 ✆ 432282, Fax 433106, « Country house with water mill », 🌳 – TV ☎ P. AE VISA JCB
closed 8 to 19 January and 9 to 19 December – **Meals** 9.95 **t.** (lunch) and dinner a la carte 23.50 **t.** 5.75 – **16 rm** 35.00/85.00 **t.** – SB.

Great Tree ⛓, TQ13 8JS, on A 382 ✆ 432491, Fax 432562, ←, « Country house atmosphere », 🌳, park – ⛔ rest TV ☎ P. AE VISA.
Meals (lunch by arrangement)/dinner 12.50/19.95 **t.** 4.50 – **10 rm** 50.00/98.00 **t.** – SB.

at Easton NE : 1½ m. on A 382 – ✉ Chagford – ☎ 01647 :

Easton Court, TQ13 8JL, ✆ 433469, Fax 433469, « Part 15C thatched house », 🌳 – ⛔ rest TV ☎. AE VISA
closed January – **Meals** (dinner only) 25.00 **t.** 4.00 – **7 rm** (dinner included) 64.00/116.00 **st.** – SB.

CHALE I.O.W. – see Wight (Isle of).

CHALFONT ST. PETER Bucks. 404 S 29 – pop. 12 664 – ✉ Chalfont St. Giles – ☎ 01494.
18 Harewood Downs, Cokes Lane, Chalfont St. Giles ✆ 762308.
♦London 24 – ♦Oxford 43.

XXX **Water Hall,** Amersham Rd, SL9 OPA, N : ½ m. on A 413 ✆ 873430 – P. AE VISA
closed dinner 25 December and 26 December – **Meals** - French - 14.50/19.50 **st.** and a la carte 5.00.

CHAPELTOWN N. Yorks. 402 403 404 P 23 – see Sheffield.

CHARDSTOCK Devon 403 L 31 **The West Country G.** – pop. 725 – ✉ Axminster – ☎ 01460.
Envir. : Chard (Museum★) *AC*, N : 3 m. by A 358.
♦London 160 – Exeter 31 – Lyme Regis 9.5 – Taunton 20 – Yeovil 21.

Tytherleigh Cot, EX13 7BN, ✆ 221170, Fax 221291, heated, 🌳 – ⛔ rest TV ☎ P. AE VISA
Meals (dinner only) 24.35 **st.** – **19 rm** 55.00/123.00 **st.** – SB.

CHARINGWORTH Glos. – see Chipping Campden.

CHARLBURY Oxon. 403 404 P 28 – pop. 2 694 – ☎ 01608.
♦London 72 – ♦Birmingham 50 – ♦Oxford 15.

Bell, Church St., OX7 3PP, ✆ 810278, Fax 811447 – TV ☎ P – 50. AE VISA
Meals 15.00/20.00 **st.** and a la carte 4.60 – **14 rm** 50.00/75.00 **st.** – SB.

CHARLECOTE Warks. 403 404 P 27 – see Stratford-upon-Avon.

CHARLESTOWN Cornwall 403 F 32 – see St. Austell.

CHARLTON W. Sussex 404 R 31 – see Chichester.

CHARMOUTH Dorset 403 L 31 – pop. 1 497 – ✉ Bridport – ☎ 01297.

♦London 157 – Dorchester 22 – Exeter 31 – Taunton 27.

- **White House,** 2 Hillside, The Street, DT6 6PJ, ☎ 560411, Fax 560702 – TV ☎ P. AE VISA
  closed December and January – **Meals** (dinner only) 18.50 **st.** and a la carte **st.** 5.75 – **11 rm** 36.00/112.00 **st.** – SB.
- **Thatch Lodge,** The Street, DT6 6PQ, ☎ 560407, Fax 560407, « Part 14C thatched cottage », – TV P. VISA JCB
  Meals (dinner only) 13.50/17.00 **st.** 5.50 – **8 rm** 35.00/64.00 **st.** – SB.
- **Hensleigh,** Lower Sea Lane, DT6 6LW, ☎ 560830 – rest TV P. AE VISA
  March-October – **Meals** (by arrangement) 11.50 **st.** 4.80 – **11 rm** 26.00/52.00 **st.** – SB.
- **Newlands House,** Stonebarrow Lane, DT6 6RA, ☎ 560212, – TV P.
  March-October – **Meals** (by arrangement) 13.50 **st.** 3.50 – **12 rm** 25.75/51.50 **t.** – SB.

CHARNOCK RICHARD SERVICE AREA Lancs. 402 L 23 – ✉ Chorley – ☎ 01257.

♦London 212 – ♦Liverpool 27 – ♦Manchester 31 – Preston 10.

- **Forte Travelodge,** Mill Lane, PR7 5LR, M6 between junctions 27 and 28 (northbound carriageway) ☎ 791746, Reservations (Freephone) 0800 850950 – TV P – 50. AE VISA
  Meals (grill rest.) – **100 rm** 34.50 **t.**

CHARTHAM Kent 404 X 30 – see Canterbury.

CHARTHAM HATCH Kent 404 X 30 – see Canterbury.

Europe

If the name of the hotel
is not in bold type,
on arrival ask the hotelier his prices.

CHATTERIS Cambs. 402 404 U 26 – pop. 7 261 – ☎ 01345.

♦London 85 – ♦Cambridge 26 – ♦Norwich 71.

- **Cross Keys,** 16 Market Hill, PE16 6BA, ☎ 693036, Fax 693036 – TV ☎ P. AE VISA JCB
  Meals a la carte 8.95/15.25 **st.** and a la carte 5.00 – **7 rm** 21.00/45.00 **st.** – SB.

CHEADLE Ches. 402 403 N 23 – ☎ 0161.

♦London 200 – ♦Manchester 7 – ♦Stoke-on-Trent 33.

- **Village H. & Leisure Club,** Cheadle Rd, SK8 1HW, S : ¾ m. by A 5149 ☎ 428 0404, Fax 428 1191, squash – TV ☎ P – 200. AE VISA
  Meals (grill rest.) (bar lunch)/dinner 15.00 **st.** and a la carte – **73 rm** 77.50/95.00 **st.** – SB.
- **Spring Cottage** without rest., 60 Hulme Hall Rd, Cheadle Hulme, SK8 6JZ, S : 2¼ m. by A 5149 on B 5095 ☎ 485 1037 – TV P. VISA
  6 rm 20.00/39.00 **s.**

CHEDDLETON Staffs. 402 403 404 N 24 – pop. 4 088 – ✉ Leek – ☎ 01538.

♦London 125 – ♦Birmingham 48 – Derby 33 – ♦Manchester 42 – ♦Stoke-on-Trent 11.

- **Choir Cottage,** Ostlers Lane, via Hollows Lane, ST13 7HS, ☎ 360561 – rest TV P.
  closed Christmas – **Meals** (by arrangement) 15.00 **st.** – **3 rm** 35.00/53.00 **st.**

CHEDINGTON Dorset 403 L 31 – pop. 100 – ✉ Beaminster – ☎ 01935.

18 Halstock, Common Lane ☎ 891689 – 9 Chedington Court, South Perrott, Beaminster ☎ 891413.

♦ London 148 – Dorchester 17 – Taunton 25.

- **Chedington Court**, DT8 3HY, ☎ 891265, Fax 891442, countryside, « Country house in landscaped gardens », 9, park – TV ☎ P. AE VISA
  closed January – **Meals** (dinner only) 27.50 **st.** 5.00 – **10 rm** 85.00/190.00 **st.** – SB.
- **Hazel Barton** without rest., DT8 3HY, ☎ 891613, Fax 891370, – TV ☎ P. VISA
  closed Christmas – **4 rm** 75.00/95.00 **st.**

CHELMSFORD Essex 404 V 28 – pop. 91 109 – ☎ 01245.

E Block, County Hall, Market Rd, CM1 1GG ☎ 283400.

♦London 33 – ♦Cambridge 46 – ♦Ipswich 40 – Southend-on-Sea 19.

- **County,** 29 Rainsford Rd, CM1 2QA, ☎ 491911, Fax 492762 – TV ☎ P – 200. AE VISA
  closed 27 to 30 December – **Meals** a la carte 20.40/27.85 **st.** 5.95 – **35 rm** 64.00/94.00 **st.** – SB.
- **Travel Inn,** Chelmsford Service Area, Colchester Rd, Springfield, CM2 5PY, NE : at junction of A 12 with A 138 and A 130 ☎ 464008, Fax 464010 – rm TV P – 35. AE VISA
  Meals (grill rest.) – 4.95 – **60 rm** 34.50 **t.**

at Great Baddow SE : 3 m. by A 414 – ✉ Chelmsford – ☎ 01245 :

Pontlands Park, West Hanningfield Rd, CM2 8HR, ☎ 476444, Fax 478393, <, heated, – – 40. AE VISA
closed first week January – **Meals** *(closed Monday and Saturday lunch and Sunday dinner to non-residents)* 14.00/18.00 **t.** and a la carte 8.00 – 9.00 – **16 rm** 75.00/110.00 **t.**, 1 suite.

ATS 375 Springfield Rd ☎ 257795
ATS Chelmer Village Centre, Springfield (ASDA car park) ☎ 465676
ATS Town Centre, Inchbonnie Rd, South Woodham Ferrers (ASDA car park) ☎ 324999

CHELSWORTH Suffolk 404 W 27 – pop. 141 – ✉ Ipswich – ☎ 01449.

♦London 68 – Colchester 21 – ♦Ipswich 16.

Peacock Inn, The Street, IP7 7HU, ☎ 740758, « 14C inn », – rm . VISA
Meals *(closed dinner Sunday and Monday)* a la carte 12.00/21.00 **t.** – **4 rm** 25.00/45.00 **t.**

CHELTENHAM Glos. 403 404 N 28 Great Britain G. – pop. 103 115 – ☎ 01242.

See : Town★ – Pittville Pump Room★ *AC* A **A.**

Exc. : Sudeley Castle★ (Paintings★) *AC*, NE : 7 m. by B 4632 A.

18 Cleeve Hill ☎ (0124 267) 2025 A – 18 Cotswold Hills, Ullenwood ☎ 522421, A.

77 Promenade, GL50 1PP ☎ 522878.

♦London 99 – ♦Birmingham 48 – ♦Bristol 40 – Gloucester 9 – ♦Oxford 43.

Plan opposite

Queen's (Forte Heritage), Promenade, GL50 1NN, ☎ 514724, Fax 224145, – rm – 200. AE VISA JCB B n
Regency : Meals 15.00/42.50 **st.** and a la carte 6.95 – 9.75 – **74 rm** 65.00/130.00 **st.** – SB.

Cheltenham Park, Cirencester Rd, Charlton Kings, GL53 8EA, ☎ 222021, Fax 226935, park – rm rest – 350. AE VISA A e
Meals (dinner only) 19.50 **st.** and a la carte 5.75 – **153 rm** 80.00/100.00 **st.**, 1 suite – SB.

On the Park, 38 Evesham Rd, GL52 2AH, ☎ 518898, Fax 511526 – . AE VISA C r
closed 1 week January – **Meals** 14.50/21.50 **t.** and a la carte 5.95 – 8.00 – **12 rm** 70.00/145.00 **st.** – SB.

Golden Valley Thistle, Gloucester Rd, GL51 0TS, W : 2 m. on A 40 ☎ 232691, Fax 221846, – rm rest – 220. AE VISA JCB.
Burford Room : Meals 14.50/35.00 **st.** 5.95 – 8.75 – **120 rm** 84.00/104.00 **st.**, 4 suites – SB.

Prestbury House, The Burgage, GL52 3DN, NE : 1½ m. by Prestbury Rd (B 4632) off New Barn Lane ☎ 529533, Fax 227076, – – 30. AE VISA A r
Meals *(closed Sunday dinner)* 21.50/28.50 **t.** and a la carte 4.75 – **17 rm** 68.00/80.00 **st.** – SB.

Charlton Kings, London Rd, Charlton Kings, GL52 6UU, ☎ 231061, Fax 241900, – . AE VISA JCB A c
Meals 15.95/21.00 **st.** and a la carte 5.40 – **14 rm** 49.00/88.00 **st.** – SB.

Lypiatt House, Lypiatt Rd, GL50 2QW, ☎ 224994, Fax 224996 – . AE VISA. B c
Meals (by arrangement) (dinner only) 21.50 **st.** 4.80 – **10 rm** 48.00/68.00 **st.**

Milton House, 12 Royal Parade, Bayshill Rd, GL50 3AY, ☎ 582601, Fax 222326 – . AE VISA. B e
Meals (by arrangement) (dinner only) 16.00/25.00 **st.** – **8 rm** 38.50/68.00 **st.**

Regency House, 50 Clarence Sq., GL50 4JR, ☎ 582718, Fax 262697, – . AE VISA. C c
closed 24 December-2 January – **Meals** (by arrangement) 10.00/15.95 **st.** 4.00 – **8 rm** 32.50/48.00 **st.** – SB.

Wyastone, Parabola Rd, GL50 3BG, ☎ 245549, Fax 522659 – . AE VISA. B i
closed 21 December-2 January – **Meals** (dinner only) a la carte 13.50/17.50 **st.** 5.50 – **12 rm** 46.25/65.25 **st.**

Stretton Lodge, Western Rd, GL50 3RN, ☎ 570771, Fax 528724, – . AE VISA. B v
Meals (by arrangement) (dinner only) 15.00 **st.** – **5 rm** 38.00/62.00 **s.**

Travel Inn, Tewkesbury Rd, Uckington, GL51 9SL, NW : 1¾ m. on A 4019 at junction with B 4634 ☎ 233847, Fax 244887 – rm . AE VISA. A a
Meals (grill rest.) – 4.95 – **40 rm** 34.50 **t.**

Hannaford's, 20 Evesham Rd, GL52 2AB, ☎ 515181, Fax 515181 – . AE VISA.
closed 23 December-2 January – **Meals** (by arrangement) 13.50 – **8 rm** 31.00/55.00 – SB. C u

Beaumont House, 56 Shurdington Rd, GL53 0JE, ☎ 245986, Fax 520044, – rest . AE VISA. A u
closed 24 to 27 December – **Meals** (by arrangement) 15.95 **t.** – **17 rm** 38.00/60.00 **t.** – SB.

CHELTENHAM

Street	Grid	No.
High Street	BC	
Pittville Street	C	26
Portland Street	C	27
Promenade (The)	BC	28
Regent Arcade Shopping Centre	C	
Winchcombe Street	C	38
Berkeley Street	C	4
Clarence Street	C	6
Crescent Terrace	B	7
Deep Street	A	9
Dunalley Street	C	10
Henrietta Street	C	13
High Street (PRESTBURY)	A	14
Keynsham Road	C	15
Knapp Road	B	16
Montpellier Avenue	B	17
Montpellier Walk	B	18
North Street	C	20
Norwood Road	B	21
Oriel Road	C	22
Regent Street	C	29
Rodney Road	C	30
Royal Well Road	BC	32
St. James Street	C	33
St. Margaret's Road	C	35
Sandford Mill Road	C	36
Sandford Terrace	C	37

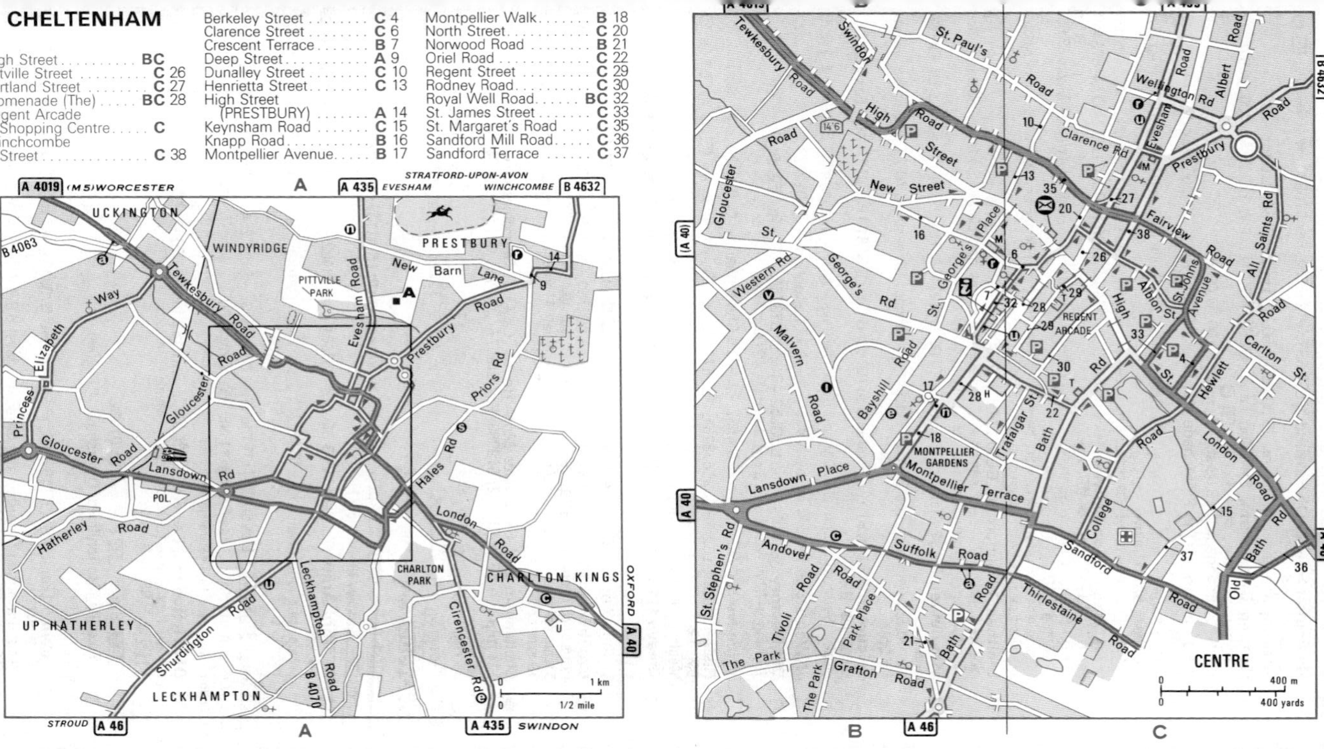

Hollington House, 115 Hales Rd, GL52 6ST, ✆ 256652, Fax 570280, – rest. VISA. A s
Meals (by arrangement) approx. 15.00 **st.** 4.50 – **9 rm** 37.50/60.00 **st.** – SB.

Hunting Butts Farm, Swindon Lane, GL50 4NZ, N : 1 ½ m. by A 435 ✆ 524982, « Working farm », – rest A n
Meals (by arrangement) 9.00 **st.** – **7 rm** 21.00/37.00 **st.**

XXX ✿ **Epicurean,** 81 The Promenade (1st Floor), GL51 1PJ, ✆ 222466, Fax 222474 – AE VISA B u
closed Saturday lunch, Sunday and Bank Holidays – **Meals** 15.00/50.00 **t.** 9.00 - (see also ***Epicurean Bistro*** below)
Spec. Braised beef with foie gras and garlic mash, Parsley soup with oysters and caviar Chantilly, Hot pear soufflé.

XX ✿ **Le Champignon Sauvage** (Everitt-Matthias), 24-26 Suffolk Rd, GL50 2AQ, ✆ 573449, Fax 573449 – AE VISA JCB B a
closed Saturday lunch, Sunday, 24 December-3 January and Bank Holidays – **Meals** 17.50/29.50 **t.** 4.50
Spec. Salmon poached in duck fat with a black pudding jus, Chump of Cinderford lamb with sweet spiced couscous and a cardamon jus, Warm pistachio tart with orange and liquorice sorbet.

XX **Staithes,** 12 Suffolk Rd, GL50 2AQ, ✆ 260666 – . AE VISA B a
closed Sunday, 2 weeks summer, 2 weeks Christmas and Bank Holidays – **Meals** (lunch by arrangement)/dinner a la carte 13.85/24.40 **t.**

XX **Mayflower,** 32-34 Clarence St., GL50 3NX, ✆ 522426, Fax 251667 – . AE VISA JCB B r
closed Sunday lunch and 25 to 28 December – **Meals** - Chinese - 6.70/25.50 **t.** and a la carte 6.95.

XX **Epicurean Bistro,** 81 The Promenade (Ground floor), GL51 1PJ, ✆ 222466, Fax 222474 – AE VISA B u
closed Saturday lunch, Sunday and Bank Holidays – **Meals** a la carte 11.50/18.00 **t.** 6.25.

at Woolstone N : 6 ¼ m. by A 435 – A – ✉ Cheltenham – 01242 :

Old Rectory without rest., GL52 4RG, ✆ 673766, – .
13 March-19 November – **3 rm** 28.00/40.00 **st.**

at Cleeve Hill NE : 4 m. on B 4632 – A – ✉ Cheltenham – 01242 :

Rising Sun, GL52 3PX, ✆ 676281, Fax 673069, ≤, – rm . AE VISA.
Meals 13.95/19.95 **st.** and a la carte 4.95 – **24 rm** 55.00/65.00 – SB.

Cleeve Hill without rest., GL52 3PR, ✆ 672052, ≤, – . AE VISA.
9 rm 45.00/75.00 **st.**

at Shurdington SW : 3 ¾ m. on A 46 – A – ✉ Cheltenham – 01242 :

Greenway, GL51 5UG, ✆ 862352, Fax 862780, ≤, « Part 16C Cotswold country house, gardens » – – 30. AE VISA.
Meals *(closed lunch Saturday and Bank Holiday Mondays)* 17.50/30.00 **t.** and a la carte – **19 rm** 87.50/180.00 **t.** – SB.

Cheltenham and Gloucester Moat House (Q.M.H.), Shurdington Rd, GL3 4PB, SW : 1 ¼ m. on A 46 ✆ (01452) 519988, Fax 519977, – rm – 345
98 rm, 2 suites.

ATS Chosen View Rd ✆ 521288 ATS 99-101 London Rd ✆ 519814

CHELWOOD Avon – see Bristol.

CHENIES Bucks. 404 S 28 – pop. 258 – ✉ Rickmansworth (Herts.) – 01923.
♦London 30 – Aylesbury 18 – Watford 7.

Bedford Arms (Thistle), WD3 6EQ, ✆ 283301, Fax 284825, – rm . AE VISA JCB.
Meals (bar lunch Saturday) 15.00/21.00 **t.** and a la carte 7.50 – 8.75 – **10 rm** 95.00/145.00 **t.**

CHERITON BISHOP Devon 403 I 31 The West Country G. – pop. 754 – ✉ Exeter – 01647.
Exc. : Crediton (Holy Cross Church★) NE : 6½m. by A 30.
♦London 211 – Exeter 10 – ♦Plymouth 51.

Old Thatch Inn, EX6 6HJ, ✆ 24204, « Part 16C inn » – . VISA.
closed first 2 weeks November – **Meals** a la carte 7.65/12.50 **st.** 3.95 – **3 rm** 33.00/45.00 **st.** – SB.

CHERTSEY Surrey 404 S 29 ㊷ – 01932.
18, 18, 9 Foxhills, Stonehill Rd, Ottershaw ✆ 872050.
♦London 28.

Crown, 7 London St., KT16 8AP, ✆ 564657, Fax 570839 – rm – 100. AE VISA
Meals (bar lunch Saturday and Bank Holidays) 6.95 **st.** (lunch) and dinner a la carte 14.15/19.50 **st.** – **30 rm** 84.00/125.00 **st.**

CHERWELL VALLEY SERVICE AREA Oxon. – ✉ Bicester – ☎ 01869.

Granada Lodge without rest., Northampton Rd, Ardley, OX6 9RD, M 40, junction 10 ☎ 346060, Fax 345030, Reservations (Freephone) 0800 555300 – ⇔ TV ☎ ♿ P. AE VISA. ✻
64 rms 39.95 **st.**

CHESHUNT Herts. 404 T 28 – pop. 57 998 – ✉ Broxbourne – ☎ 01992.

18 Cheshunt Park, Park Lane ☎ 629777.

♦London 22 – ♦Cambridge 40 – ♦Ipswich 70 – Luton 34 – Southend-on-Sea 39.

Cheshunt Marriott, Halfhide Lane, Turnford, EN10 6NG, NW : 1 ¼ m. on B 176 ☎ 451245, Fax 440120, Ls, ▢, ⛱ – ▮ ⇔ rm ▤ TV ☎ ♿ P – ♕ 120. AE ⓞ VISA JCB
Meals (bar lunch Saturday) 11.00/23.00 **t.** and a la carte 🍷 5.25 – ☕ 7.95 – **133 rm** 82.00/130.00 **s.**, 12 suites – SB.

CHESTER Ches. 402 403 L 24 **Great Britain G.** – pop. 115 971 – ☎ 01244.

See : City★★ - The Rows★★ – Cathedral★ – City Walls★.

Envir. : Chester Zoo★ *AC*, N : 3 m. by A 5116.

18 Upton-by-Chester, Upton Lane ☎ 381183 – 18 Curzon Park ☎ 675130.

i Town Hall, Northgate St., CH1 2HJ ☎ 317962 – Chester Visitor Centre, Vicars Lane, CH1 1QX ☎ 351609/318916.

♦London 207 – Birkenhead 7 – ♦Birmingham 91 – ♦Liverpool 19 – ♦Manchester 40 – Preston 52 – ♦Sheffield 76 – ♦Stoke-on-Trent 38.

CHESTER

Bridge Street 3
Eastgate Street 5
Northgate Street 18
Watergate Street

Boughton 2
Frodsham Street 6
Grosvenor Park Road 7
Grosvenor Street 8
Handbridge 10
Little St. John Street 12
Liverpool Road 13

Lower Bridge Street 15
Nicholas Street 17
Parkgate Road 20
Pepper Street 21
St. John Street 23
St. Martins Way 24
Vicar's Lane 25

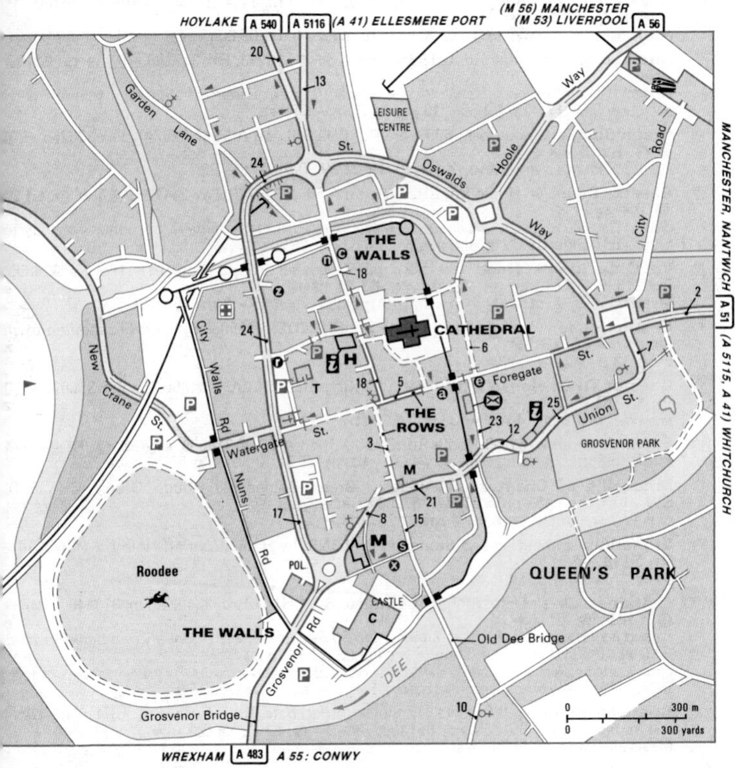

Chester Grosvenor, Eastgate St., CH1 1LT, ✆ 324024, Fax 313246, Fitness, ≘ – |♦| ▤ TV ☎ ♿ P – ⚓ 250. AE ◐ VISA JCB. ✂ **a**
closed 25 and 26 December – **Brasserie : Meals** a la carte 20.70/28.65 **t.** 🍷 5.50 – (see also *Arkle* below) – ☕ 9.95 – **83 rm** 115.00/190.00, 3 suites.

Crabwall Manor ⛬, Parkgate Rd, Mollington, CH1 6NE, NW : 2 ¼ m. on A 540 ✆ 851666, Fax 851400, « Part 16C manor », garden – ▤ rest TV ☎ P – ⚓ 80. AE ◐ VISA JCB. ✂
Meals - (see *Crabwall Manor* below) – ☕ 8.50 – **42 rm** 98.50/130.00 **st.**, 6 suites – SB.

Moat House Chester (Q.M.H.), Trinity St., CH1 2BD, ✆ 899988, Fax 316118, Fitness, ≘ – |♦| ✗ rm ▤ rest TV ☎ ♿ P – ⚓ 500. AE ◐ VISA **r**
Meals 13.00/27.50 **st.** and a la carte 🍷 6.95 – ☕ 9.00 – **146 rm** 95.00/145.00 **st.**, 6 suites – SB.

Mollington Banastre, Parkgate Rd, Mollington, CH1 6NN, NW : 2 ¼ m. on A 540 ✆ 851471, Fax 851165, Fitness, ≘, pool, garden, squash – |♦| ✗ rm TV ☎ P – ⚓ 250. AE ◐ VISA
Meals *(closed Saturday lunch)* 12.00/23.00 **st.** and a la carte 🍷 8.50 – **63 rm** ☕ 80.00/135.00 **st.** – SB.

Hoole Hall (Regal), Warrington Rd, Hoole, CH2 3PD, NE : 2 m. on A 56 ✆ 350011, Fax 320251 – |♦| ✗ rm ▤ rest TV ☎ ♿ P – ⚓ 150
99 rm.

Redland without rest., 64 Hough Green, CH4 8JY, SW : 1 m. by A 483 on A 5104 ✆ 671024, Fax 681309, « Victorian town house », ≘ – TV ☎ P. ✂
12 rm ☕ 40.00/70.00 **t.**

Blossoms (Forte Heritage), St. John St., CH1 1HL, ✆ 323186, Fax 346433 – |♦| ✗ TV ☎ – ⚓ 30
64 rm. **e**

Forte Posthouse, Wrexham Rd, CH4 9DL, S : 2 m. on A 483 ✆ 680111, Fax 674100, Fitness, ≘, pool, garden – ✗ rm ▤ rest TV ☎ P – ⚓ 100. AE ◐ VISA
Meals a la carte approx. 15.00 **t.** 🍷 5.50 – **105 rm** 56.00/69.50 **st.**

Cavendish, 42-44 Hough Green, CH4 8JQ, SW : 1 m. by A 483 on A 5104 ✆ 675100, garden – TV ☎ P. AE VISA. ✂
Meals (residents only) 15.00/20.00 **st.** – **18 rm** ☕ 40.00/65.00 **t.** – SB.

Alton Lodge, 78 Hoole Rd, CH2 3NT, on A 56 ✆ 310213, Fax 319206 – TV ☎ P. VISA JCB. ✂
closed Christmas and New Year – **Meals** *(closed Friday to Sunday)* (dinner only) a la carte 9.85/17.90 **t.** 🍷 4.50 – **16 rm** ☕ 35.00/43.50 **st.**

Green Bough without rest., 60 Hoole Rd, CH2 3NL, on A 56 ✆ 326241, Fax 326265 – TV ☎ P. AE VISA JCB
closed Christmas and New Year – **20 rm** ☕ 39.00/58.00 **t.** – SB.

Chester Court, 48 Hoole Rd, CH2 3NL, on A 56 ✆ 320779, Fax 344795 – TV ☎ P. AE ◐ VISA JCB. ✂
closed 24 December to 2 January – **Meals** *(closed Sunday dinner)* (bar lunch Monday to Saturday)/dinner 18.60 **st.** and a la carte 🍷 6.50 – **20 rm** ☕ 38.00/52.00 **st.** – SB.

Ye Olde King's Head (Premier), 48/50 Lower Bridge St., CH1 1RS, ✆ 324855, Fax 315693, « 16C inn » – TV ☎ 🚗. AE ◐ VISA. ✂ **s**
Meals 6.50/25.00 **st.** and lunch a la carte 🍷 5.95 – ☕ 4.45 – **8 rm** 39.50 **st.**

Castle House without rest., 23 Castle St., CH1 2DS, ✆ 350354, « Part Elizabethan town house » – TV. VISA **x**
5 rm ☕ 22.00/44.00 **s.**

Chester Town House without rest., 23 King St., CH1 2AH, ✆ 350021, Fax 350021 – TV P. VISA **z**
closed Christmas – **4 rm** ☕ 35.00/48.00 **st.**

Edwards House, 61-63 Hoole Rd, CH2 3NJ, on A 56 ✆ 318055 – TV ☎ P. VISA. ✂
Meals (by arrangement) 9.45 **st.** 🍷 4.00 – **10 rm** ☕ 21.00/40.00 **st.**

Mitchell's of Chester without rest., Green Gables, 28 Hough Green, CH4 8JQ, SW : 1 m. by A 483 on A 5104 ✆ 679004, garden – TV P. ✂
closed 20 to 28 December – **4 rm** ☕ 25.00/40.00.

Stone Villa without rest., 3 Stone Pl., CH2 3NR, by Hoole Way off Hole Rd ✆ 345014 – ✗ TV P. ✂
6 rm ☕ 23.00/40.00 **s.**

XXXX ✿ **Arkle** (at Chester Grosvenor H.), Eastgate St., CH1 1LT, ✆ 324024, Fax 313246 – ✗ ▤ P. AE ◐ VISA JCB **a**
closed Monday lunch, Sunday dinner, 24 to 30 December, 1 to 8 January and Bank Holidays – **Meals** 18.50/37.00 **t.** and dinner a la carte 33.50/44.75 **t.** 🍷 5.50
Spec. Roasted scallops with a tomato brandade, sweet garlic and cherry tomatoes, Pot roasted Bresse pigeon with scented cabbage and pigeon mousse, Ice cream of Bailey's liqueur with caramel wafers.

XXX **Crabwall Manor** (at Crabwall Manor H.), Parkgate Rd, Mollington, CH1 6NE, NW : 2¼ m. on A 540 ✆ 851666, Fax 851400, garden – ▤ P. AE ◐ VISA JCB
Meals a la carte 25.50/34.25 **st.**

CHOLLERFORD Northd. 401 402 N 18 Great Britain G. – ✉ Hexham – 01434.
Envir. : Hadrian's Wall★★ – Chesters★ (Bath House★) *AC*, W : ½ m. by B 6318.
◆London 303 – ◆Carlisle 36 – ◆Newcastle upon Tyne 21.

George (Swallow), NE46 4EW, ℘ 681611, Fax 681727, ≤, « Riverside gardens », – rm – 65.
Meals 13.50/19.50 **st.** and a la carte – **48 rm** 85.00/125.00 **st.** – SB.

CHORLEY Lancs. 402 404 M 23 – pop. 34 618 – 01257.
Duxbury Park, Duxbury Hall Rd ℘ 265380 – Shaw Hill Hotel G.
◆London 222 – ◆Blackpool 30 – ◆Liverpool 32 – ◆Manchester 26.

Yarrow Bridge (Premier), Bolton Rd, PR7 4AB, S : 1 m. on A 6 ℘ 265989, Fax 230821 – rm
Meals (grill rest.) a la carte approx. 8.90 **st.** 3.95 – 4.45 – **29 rm** 39.50 **t.** – SB.

at Whittle-le-Woods N : 2 m. on A 6 – ✉ Chorley – 01257 :

Shaw Hill H. Golf & Country Club, Preston Rd, PR6 7PP, ℘ 269221, Fax 261223, – – 200.
closed 26 December – **Vardon : Meals** *(closed Saturday lunch and Bank Holidays)* 17.95 **st.** and a la carte – **30 rm** 53.00/85.00 **st.** – SB.

Parkville Country House, 174 Preston Rd, PR6 7HE, ℘ 261881, Fax 273171, –
Meals *(closed Sunday)* (dinner only) 25.00 **st.** and a la carte 14.50/25.00 **st.** – **13 rm** 55.00/70.00 **st.** – SB.

ATS 18 Westminster Rd ℘ 262000/265472

CHORLTON CUM HARDY Gtr. Manchester 402 403 404 N 23 – see Manchester.

CHRISTCHURCH Dorset 403 404 O 31 The West Country G. – pop. 40 865 – 01202.
See : Town★ – Priory★.
Envir. : Hengistbury Head★ (≤★★) SW : 4½ m. by A 35 and B 3059.
Highcliffe Castle, 107 Lymington Rd, Highcliffe-on-Sea ℘ (01425) 272953 – Barrack Rd, Iford ℘ 473817.
23 High St., BH23 1AB ℘ 471780.
◆London 111 – Bournemouth 6 – Salisbury 26 – ◆Southampton 24 – Winchester 39.

Travel Inn, Somerford Rd, BH23 3QG, E : 2 m. by A 35 on B 3059 ℘ 485376, Fax 474939 – rm
Meals (grill rest.) – 4.95 – **38 rm** 34.50 **t.**

Splinters, 12 Church St., BH23 1BW, ℘ 483454, Fax 483454 –
closed 2 weeks January – **Meals** 11.50/24.00 **t.** 5.50.

at Mudeford SE : 2 m. – ✉ Christchurch – 01202 :

Avonmouth (Forte Heritage), 95 Mudeford, BH23 3NT, ℘ 483434, Fax 479004, ≤, heated, – – 60.
Meals (bar lunch Monday to Saturday)/dinner 15.95 **st.** 6.75 – 8.50 – **41 rm** 65.00/90.00 **st.** – SB.

Waterford Lodge, 87 Bure Lane, Friars Cliff, BH23 4DN, ℘ (01425) 272940, Fax 279130, – – 80.
Meals 13.95/32.00 **t.** and a la carte 5.50 – **17 rm** 73.00/100.00 **t.** – SB.

CHURCHILL Oxon. 403 404 P 28 – pop. 502 – ✉ Chipping Norton – 01608.
◆London 79 – ◆Birmingham 46 – Cheltenham 29 – ◆Oxford 23 – Swindon 31.

Forge House without rest., OX7 6NJ, ℘ 658173 –
4 rm 35.00/46.00 **st.**

CHURCH STRETTON Shrops. 402 403 L 26 Great Britain G. – pop. 4 161 – 01694.
Envir. : Wenlock Edge★, E : by B 4371.
Trevor Hill ℘ 722281.
◆London 166 – ◆Birmingham 46 – Hereford 39 – Shrewsbury 14.

Mynd House, Ludlow Rd, Little Stretton, SY6 6RB, SW : 1 m. on B 4370 ℘ 722212, Fax 724180, –
closed January and 2 weeks summer – **Meals** (booking essential) (bar lunch)/dinner a la carte 18.95/25.00 **st.** 5.50 – **7 rm** 38.00/60.00 **st.**, 1 suite – SB.

Rectory Farm without rest., Woolstaston, SY6 6NN, NW : 5½ m. by A 49 ℘ 751306, ≤, « 17C timbered house », –
closed mid December and January – **3 rm** 27.00/40.00 **st.**

Belvedere, Burway Rd, SY6 6DP, ℘ 722232, Fax 722232, –
closed 17 to 30 December – **Meals** (by arrangement) 9.00 **st.** 3.75 – **12 rm** 21.00/46.00 **st.**

ATS Crossways ℘ 722526/722112

CHURT Surrey 404 R 30 – see Farnham.

CIRENCESTER Glos. 403 404 O 28 Great Britain G. – pop. 17 085 – ☎ 01285.

See : Town★ – Church of St. John the Baptist★ – Corinium Museum★ (Mosaic pavements★) AC.

Envir. : Fairford : Church of St. Mary★ (stained glass windows★★) E : 7 m. by A 417.

Cheltenham Rd ✆ 653939.

Corn Hall, Market Pl., GL7 2NW ✆ 654180.

◆London 97 – ◆Bristol 37 – Gloucester 19 – ◆Oxford 37.

Jarvis Fleece, Market Pl., GL7 2NZ, ✆ 658507, Fax 651017 – TV ☎ P – 25. AE VISA
Meals (bar lunch Monday to Saturday)/dinner 13.95 **t.** and a la carte 6.95 – 8.50 – **30 rm** 69.00/89.00 **t.** – SB.

Wimborne House, 91 Victoria Rd, GL7 1ES, ✆ 653890, – TV P.
closed Christmas – **Meals** (by arrangement) 5.50 **st.** – **5 rm** 20.00/35.00 **st.**

Ivy House without rest., 2 Victoria Rd, GL7 1EN, ✆ 656626 – TV.
closed Christmas – **4 rm** 27.00/40.00 **st.**

Harry Hare's, 3 Gosditch St., GL7 2AG, ✆ 652375, Fax 641691, – AE VISA.
Meals a la carte 13.95/23.45 **t.** 4.25.

at Rendcomb N : 6¼ m. by A 417 off A 435 – ✉ Cirencester – ☎ 01285 :

Shawswell Country House without rest., GL7 7HD, N : 1½ m. on No Through Rd ✆ 831779, ←, « Part 17C and 18C house », , park – TV P.
closed December and January – **5 rm** 30.00/55.00 **st.**

at Barnsley NE : 4 m. by A 429 on B 4425 – ✉ Cirencester – ☎ 01285 :

Village Pub, GL7 5EF, ✆ 740421 – TV ☎ P. AE VISA JCB
closed 25 December – **Meals** a la carte 9.15/14.65 **t.** 4.50 – **5 rm** 29.00/44.00 **t.**

at Ampney Crucis E : 2¾ m. by A 417 – ✉ Cirencester – ☎ 01285 :

Crown of Crucis, GL7 5RS, on A 417 ✆ 851806, Fax 851735, – TV ☎ P – 80. AE VISA
closed 24 to 30 December – **Meals** (bar lunch)/dinner 18.00 **t.** and a la carte 4.95 – **25 rm** 49.00/68.00 **t.** – SB.

Waterton Garden Cottage, GL7 5RY, S : ½ m. by Driffield rd turning right into unmarked driveway ✆ 851303, « Converted Victorian stables, walled garden », heated – rm P.
closed Christmas (booking essential) – **Meals** (by arrangement) (communal dining) 20.00 – **3 rm** 25.00/45.00 **st.**

at Ewen SW : 3¼ m. by A 429 – ✉ Cirencester – ☎ 01285 :

Wild Duck Inn, Drake's Island, GL7 6BY, ✆ 770310, Fax 770310, « Part 16C former farm buildings », – TV ☎ P. AE VISA.
Meals a la carte 12.00/20.45 **t.** – 5.00 – **10 rm** 48.00/75.00 **t.**

at Kemble SW : 4 m. by A 433 on A 429 – ✉ Cirencester – ☎ 01285 :

Smerrill Barns without rest., GL7 6BW, N : 1¼ m. on A 429 ✆ 770907, Fax 770706 – TV P. VISA.
7 rm 30.00/45.00 **s.**

at Stratton NW : 1¼ m. on A 417 – ✉ Cirencester – ☎ 01285 :

Stratton House, Gloucester Rd, GL7 2LE, ✆ 651761, Fax 640024, – TV ☎ P – 150. AE VISA
Meals (bar lunch Monday to Saturday)/dinner 15.75 **st.** and a la carte – **41 rm** 59.95/89.95 – SB.

ATS 1 Mercian Close, Watermoor End ✆ 657761

CLACTON-ON-SEA Essex 404 X 28 – ☎ 01255.

West Rd ✆ 424331.

23 Pier Av, CO15 1QD ✆ 423400.

◆London 76 – Chelmsford 37 – Colchester 14 – ◆Ipswich 28.

Chudleigh, 13 Agate Rd, Marine Parade West, CO15 1RA, ✆ 425407, Fax 425407 – rest TV P. AE VISA JCB
Meals *(closed Saturday and Sunday lunch November-February)* (bar lunch) 11.50 **t.** 3.75 – **10 rm** 29.50/48.00 **st.**

ATS 46 High St. ✆ 420659

CLANFIELD Oxon. 403 404 P 28 – pop. 1 709 (inc. Shilton) – ☎ 01367 81.

◆London 76 – ◆Oxford 20 – Swindon 17.

XXX **Plough at Clanfield** with rm, Bourton Rd, OX18 2RB, on A 4095 ✆ 810222, Fax 810596, « Small Elizabethan manor house », – rest TV ☎ P. AE VISA JCB.
Meals 14.95/30.00 **t.** 5.75 – **6 rm** 65.00/115.00 **t.** – SB.

CLAPPERSGATE Cumbria – see Ambleside.

CLARE Suffolk 404 V 27 – ✉ Sudbury – ☎ 01787.

♦London 67 – ♦Cambridge 27 – Colchester 24 – ♦Ipswich 32 – Bury St.Edmunds 16.

Bell, Market Hill, CO10 8NN, ☎ 277741, Fax 278474, « Part 16C coaching inn » – rest – 70
23 rm.

CLAVERING Essex 404 U 28 – pop. 1 663 – ✉ Saffron Walden – ☎ 01799.

♦London 44 – ♦Cambridge 25 – Colchester 44 – Luton 29.

Cricketers with rm, CB11 4QT, ☎ 550442, Fax 550882, – . VISA.
Meals (bar lunch Monday to Saturday)/dinner 15.00/20.00 **st.** 4.20 – 5.00 – **6 rm** 50.00/60.00 **st.**

CLAWTON Devon 403 H 31 The West Country G. – pop. 292 – ✉ Holsworthy – ☎ 01409.

Envir. : W : Tamar River★★.

♦London 240 – Exeter 39 – ♦Plymouth 36.

Court Barn Country House, EX22 6PS, W : ½ m. ☎ 271219, Fax 271309, – rm . VISA JCB
Meals (booking essential) 10.50/20.00 **t.** 3.95 – **8 rm** 30.00/70.00 **t.** – SB.

CLAYDON Suffolk 404 X 27 – ☎ 01473.

♦London 80 – Bury St.Edmunds 22 – ♦Cambridge 51 – Colchester 20 – ♦Ipswich 3.

Claydon Country House, 16-18 Ipswich Rd, IP6 0AR, ☎ 830382, Fax 832476, – . VISA.
Meals a la carte 10.65/22.75 **t.** – **14 rm** 42.50/69.50 **t.** – SB.

CLAYGATE Surrey 404 ㊷ – see Esher.

CLAYTON-LE-MOORS Lancs 402 M 22 – pop. 6 146 – ✉ Accrington – ☎ 01254.

♦London 232 – Blackburn 3.5 – Lancaster 37 – ♦Leeds 44 – Preston 14.

Dunkenhalgh, Blackburn Rd, BB5 5JP, SW : 1½ m. on A 678 ☎ 398021, Fax 872230, , , – rm – 400. VISA
Meals (bar lunch Saturday) 10.95/28.00 **st.** and a la carte – 7.95 – **79 rm** 76.50/102.50 **t.**, 1 suite – SB.

Sparth House, Whalley Rd, BB5 5RP, ☎ 872263, Fax 872263, – rest – 100. VISA.
Meals *(closed Sunday dinner)* 13.25/15.75 **st.** and a la carte – **16 rm** 48.25/78.50 **st.** – SB.

CLAYTON-LE-WOODS Lancs. – pop. 14 173 – ✉ Chorley – ☎ 01772.

♦London 220 – ♦Liverpool 31 – ♦Manchester 26 – Preston 5.5.

Pines, Preston Rd, PR6 7ED, on A 6 at junction with B 5256 ☎ 38551, Fax 629002, – rm – 200. VISA.
closed 25 and 26 December – **Meals** 9.50/17.50 **t.** and a la carte – **37 rm** 50.00/85.00 **t.**, 2 suites – SB.

CLAYTON WEST W. Yorks 402 404 P 23 – ✉ Huddersfield – ☎ 01484.

♦London 190 – ♦Leeds 19 – ♦Manchester 35 – ♦Sheffield 24.

Bagden Hall, Wakefield Rd, Scissett, HD8 9LE, SW : 1 m. on A 636 ☎ 865330, Fax 861001, , , park – – 90. VISA.
Meals *(closed Sunday dinner)* 8.95/15.95 **t.** and a la carte 5.25 – **17 rm** 60.00/100.00 **t.** – SB.

CLEARWELL Glos. – see Coleford.

CLEATOR MOOR Cumbria 402 J 20 – ☎ 01946.

♦London 317 – ♦Carlisle 31 – Keswick 25 – Whitehaven 7.

Ennerdale Country House, Cleator, CA23 3DT, S : 1½ m. by B 5295 on A 5086 ☎ 813907, Fax 815260, – – 75. VISA.
Meals 10.00/20.00 **st.** and dinner a la carte 6.00 – **20 rm** 79.00/99.00 **st.** – SB.

CLEETHORPES Humbs. 402 404 U 23 – pop. 32 719 – ☎ 01472.

ℹ 42-43 Alexandra Rd, DN35 8LE ☎ 200220.

♦London 171 – Boston 49 – Lincoln 38 – ♦Sheffield 77.

Plan : see Great Grimsby

Kingsway, Kingsway, DN35 0AE, ☎ 601122, Fax 601381, ← – . VISA. BZ **a**
closed 25 and 26 December – **Meals** 9.50/15.95 **t.** and a la carte 5.20 – **50 rm** 55.00/77.00 **t.** – SB.

CLEEVE HILL Glos. 403 404 N 28 – see Cheltenham.

CLEY NEXT THE SEA Norfolk 404 X 25 – see Blakeney.

CLIMPING W. Sussex 404 S 31 – see Littlehampton.

CLITHEROE Lancs 402 M 22 – pop. 13 548 – ☎ 01200.
Whalley Rd ☎ 22618.
12-14 Market Pl., BB7 2DA ☎ 25566.
London 64 – Blackpool 35 – Manchester 31.

Brooklyn, 32 Pimlico Rd, BB7 2AH, ☎ 28268 – TV. AE VISA.
closed 24 December to 2 January – **Meals** (by arrangement) 10.50 **s.** – **4 rm** 26.00/40.00 **s.** – SB.

Auctioneer, New Market St., BB7 2JW, ☎ 27153 – AE VISA
closed Monday and Tuesday – **Meals** 6.25/16.75 **t.** and lunch a la carte 5.00.

at Waddington N : 1 ¾ m. on B 6478 – ✉ Clitheroe – ☎ 01200 :

Peter Barn without rest., Rabbit Lane, via Cross Lane, BB7 3JH, NW : 1 ½ m. by B 6478 ☎ 28585, – P.
closed Christmas and New Year – **3 rm** 25.00/39.00 **st.**

ATS Salthill Rd ☎ 23011

CLOVELLY Devon 403 G 31 **The West Country G.** pop. 439 – ✉ Bideford – ☎ 01237.
See : Village★★.
Envir. : SW : Tamar River★★.
Exc. : Hartland : Hartland Church★ – Hartland Quay★ (viewpoint★★) – Hartland Point ≤★★★, W : 6½m. by B 3237 and B 3248 – Morwenstow (Church★, cliffs★★), SW : 11 ½ m. by A 39.
London 241 – Barnstaple 18 – Exeter 52 – Penzance 92.

Red Lion, The Quay, EX39 5TF, ☎ 431237, Fax 431044, ≤ – TV ☎ P. VISA.
Meals (bar lunch October-March) 20.95 **t.** (dinner) and lunch a la carte 3.65 – **11 rm** 39.00/63.00 **t.** – SB.

Le Guide change, changez de **guide Michelin** *tous les ans.*

CLOWNE Derbs. 402 403 404 Q 24 **Great Britain G.** – pop. 7 234 – ☎ 01246.
Exc. : Bolsover Castle★ *AC*, S : 6 m. by B 6417 and A 632.
London 156 – Derby 40 – Lincoln 35 – Nottingham 30 – Sheffield 12.

Van Dyk, Worksop Rd, S43 4TD, N : ¾ m. by A 618 on A 619 ☎ 810219, Fax 819566 – TV ☎ P – 120. AE VISA
Meals *(closed Sunday dinner)* 18.75 **st.** and a la carte 5.25 – **16 rm** 40.00/50.00 **st.**

COALVILLE Leics. 402 403 404 P 25 – pop. 3 846 – ☎ 01530.
Snibston Discovery Park, Ashby Rd, LE67 3LN ☎ 813608.
London 115 – Birmingham 32 – Leicester 15 – Nottingham 25.

Hermitage Park, Whitwick Rd, LE67 3FA, off High St. ☎ 814814, Fax 814202, – rest TV ☎ P – 30. AE VISA.
Meals 7.95/10.95 **t.** and a la carte 5.95 – **24 rm** 65.00/69.50 **st.**, 1 suite.

COATHAM MUNDEVILLE Durham 402 P 20 – see Darlington.

COBHAM Kent 404 V 29 – pop. 15 254 (inc. Oxshott) – ✉ Gravesend – ☎ 01474.
London 27 – Maidstone 13 – Rochester 6.

Ye Olde Leather Bottle, The Street, DA12 3BZ, ☎ 814327, Fax 812086, « 17C inn », – TV ☎ P
7 rm.

COBHAM Surrey 404 S 30 – pop. 10 252 – ☎ 01932.
London 24 – Guildford 10.

Plan : see Greater London (South-West)

Hilton National, Seven Hills Rd South, KT11 1EW, W : 1 ½ m. by A 245 ☎ 864471, Fax 868017, , , , , park, , squash – rm TV ☎ P – 300. AE VISA JCB. by A 3 AZ
Meals (bar lunch Saturday) (dancing Friday and Saturday evenings) 16.50/26.00 **t.** and a la carte 5.00 – 10.75 – **146 rm** 120.00/135.00 **st.**, 3 suites.

Cedar House, Mill Rd, KT11 3AN, ☎ 863424, Fax 862023, – TV ☎ P. AE VISA. by A 307 AZ
closed 25 December to 1 January – **Meals** *(closed Sunday and Monday)* (dinner only) 19.95 **t.** and a la carte 5.50 – **6 rm** 40.00/80.00 **t.**

at Stoke D'Abernon SE : 1½ m. on A 245 – AZ – ✉ Cobham – ☎ 01372 :

Woodlands Park, Woodlands Lane, KT11 3QB, on A 245 ☎ 843933, Fax 842704, , park, – TV ☎ P – 300. AE VISA.
Meals *(closed Saturday lunch and Sunday dinner)* 12.50/15.00 **st.** and a la carte 5.00 – 9.25 – **57 rm** 110.00/140.00 **st.**, 1 suite.

COCKERMOUTH Cumbria 401 402 J 20 – pop. 7 702 – 01900.

Embleton (0176 87) 76223.

Town Hall, Market St., CA13 9NP 822634.

London 306 – Carlisle 25 – Keswick 13.

Trout, Crown St., CA13 0EJ, 823591, Fax 827514, – rest – 50.
Meals 8.95/16.45 **t.** and a la carte 5.15 – **23 rm** 57.95/84.95 **t.** – SB.

Low Hall, Brandlingill, CA13 0RE, S : 3¼ m. by A 5086 on Lorton rd 826654, – .
March-October – **Meals** 17.00 **st.** – **5 rm** (dinner included) 36.00/100.00 **st.**

New House Farm, Lorton, CA13 9UU, SE : 5¼ m. by B 5292 on B 5289 85404, « Part 17C and 19C farmhouse », park – .
Meals 20.00 **st.** 4.75 – **3 rm** 45.00/60.00 **s.**

COGGESHALL Essex 404 W 28 – pop. 5 220 – Colchester – 01376.

London 49 – Braintree 6 – Chelmsford 16 – Colchester 9.

White Hart, Market End, CO6 1NH, 561654, Fax 561789, « Part 15C guildhall », – .
Meals - Italian (in bar Sunday dinner) 14.95 **t.** and a la carte 5.95 – **18 rm** 61.50/97.00 **t.**

Baumann's Brasserie, 4-6 Stoneham St., CO6 1TT, 561453, Fax 563762 –
closed Saturday lunch, Sunday dinner, Monday and first 2 weeks January – **Meals** 9.95 **t.** (lunch) and a la carte 17.20/24.70 **t.**

COLCHESTER Essex 404 W 28 Great Britain G. – pop. 142 515 – 01206.

See : Castle and Museum★ *AC.*

Birch Grove, Layer Rd 734276 – , Earls Colne (01787) 224466.

1 Queen St., CO1 2PJ 282920.

London 52 – Cambridge 48 – Ipswich 18 – Luton 76 – Southend-on-Sea 41.

George, 116 High St., CO1 1TD, 578494, Fax 761732 – – 80.
Meals 5.25/20.00 **t.** and a la carte – 7.50 – **46 rm** 59.50/110.00 **t.** – SB.

Rose and Crown, East St., Eastgates, CO1 2TZ, 866677, Fax 866616, « Part 15C inn » – rm – 100.
Meals 15.95 **t.** and a la carte – **28 rm** 58.00/99.00 **t.** – SB.

Red Lion, 43 High St., CO1 1DJ, 577986, Fax 578207, « Part 15C inn » – – 40.
Meals 13.95 **st.** and a la carte 8.95 – **24 rm** 50.00/80.00 **st.**

Butterfly, Old Ipswich Rd, CO7 7QY, NE : 4¼ m. by A 1232 at junction of A 12 with A 120 (via sliproad to A 120) 230900, Fax 231095 – rm – 80.
Meals 12.25 **t.** and a la carte – 6.95 – **50 rm** 52.00/80.00 **t.** – SB.

Four Sevens, 28 Inglis Rd, CO3 3HU, off Maldon Rd (B 1022) 46093, Fax 46093, – .
Meals (by arrangement) 10.00 – **6 rm** 25.00/40.00.

North Hill Exchange Brasserie, 19-20 North Hill, CO1 1DZ, 769988, Fax 766898 –
closed Sunday – **Meals** 7.50/21.50 **st.** and a la carte 4.50.

Warehouse Brasserie, 12a Chapel St. North, CO2 7AT, 765656, Fax 765656 – .
closed Sunday dinner, 25-26 December and Bank Holiday Mondays – **Meals** 10.25 **t.** (lunch) and a la carte 12.75/17.70 **t.** 3.95.

at Eight Ash Green W : 4 m. by A 604 – Colchester – 01206 :

Forte Posthouse, Abbotts Lane, CO6 3QL, at junction of A 604 with A 12 767740, Fax 766577, – rm – 110.
Meals a la carte approx. 12.00/24.15 **st.** 6.25 – 7.95 – **110 rm** 56.00 **st.** – SB.

at Marks Tey W : 5 m. by A 12 at junction with A 120 – Colchester – 01206 :

Marks Tey, London Rd, CO6 1DU, on B 1408 210001, Fax 212167, – rm rest – 250.
closed 25 to 30 December – **Meals** 10.95/13.50 **st.** and a la carte 4.95 – 6.00 – **109 rm** 56.00/57.50 **st.**, 1 suite – SB.

ATS East Hill 866484/867471
ATS 451 Ipswich Rd 841404
ATS Telford Way, Severalls Park Ind. Est. 845641

COLEFORD Devon 403 I 31 – Crediton – 01363.

London 214 – Barnstaple 29 – Exeter 14 – Taunton 42.

New Inn, EX17 5BZ, 84242, Fax 85044, « Part 13C thatched inn » – rm .
closed 25 and 26 December – **Meals** (in bar) a la carte 10.10/15.00 **st.** 4.50 – **3 rm** 33.00/52.00 **st.** – SB.

COLEFORD Glos. 403 404 M 28 **Great Britain G.** – pop. 9 567 – ☎ 01594.

Envir. : W : Wye Valley★.

18 Forest of Dean, Lords Hills ☎ 832583 – 18 Forest Hills, Mile End Rd ☎ 810620.

27 Market Place, GL16 8AE ☎ 836307.

London 143 – Bristol 28 – Gloucester 19 – Newport 29.

Speech House (Forte Heritage), Forest of Dean, GL16 7EL, NE : 3 m. by B 4028 on B 4226 ☎ 822607, Fax 823658, – – TV ☎ P – 40. AE VISA JCB
Meals (bar lunch Monday to Saturday)/dinner 17.95 **t.** 7.30 – 9.25 – **14 rm** 60.00/115.00 **t.** – SB.

at Clearwell S : 2 m. by B 4228 – ✉ Coleford – ☎ 01594 :

Wyndham Arms, GL16 8JT, ☎ 833666, Fax 836450 – TV ☎ P – 40. AE VISA JCB
Meals 7.75/16.25 **t.** and a la carte 5.50 – **17 rm** 46.50/61.00 **t.** – SB.

Tudor Farmhouse, High St., GL16 8JS, ☎ 833046, Fax 837093, – rm TV ☎ P. AE VISA JCB.
closed 24 to 29 December – **Meals** *(closed Sunday)* (dinner only) 15.95 **t.** and a la carte – **8 rm** 45.00/62.00 **t.**, 1 suite – SB.

COLERNE Wilts. 403 404 M 29 – see Bath (Avon).

COLESHILL Warks. 403 404 O 26 – pop. 6 324 – ✉ Birmingham (W. Mids.) – ☎ 01675.

London 113 – Birmingham 8 – Coventry 11.

Swan, High St., B46 3BL, ☎ 464107, Fax 467493 – TV ☎ P – 60. AE VISA.
Meals *(closed Saturday lunch)* 12.25 **st.** and a la carte 3.75 – 5.00 – **32 rm** 49.00 **st.**

Coleshill, 152 High St., B46 3BG, ☎ 465527, Fax 464013 – TV ☎ P – 150. AE VISA.
Meals a la carte 13.00/20.00 **st.** 4.25 – **23 rm** 65.00/85.00 **st.** – SB.

COLNE Lancs. 402 N 22 – pop. 18 776 – ☎ 01282.

9 Law Farm, Skipton Old Rd ☎ 863391 – 9 Ghyll Brow, Barnoldswick ☎ 842466.

London 234 – Manchester 29 – Preston 26.

Higher Slipper Hill Farm , Foulridge, BB8 7LY, NW : 3¾ m. by A 56 and B 6251 on Barrowford rd ☎ 863602, ←, – TV P. AE VISA.
closed 1 week Christmas-New Year – **Meals** *(closed Saturday and Sunday)* (residents only) (dinner only) 6.95 **st.** and a la carte 6.95 – **9 rm** 38.80/50.50 **st.**

ATS North Valley Road ☎ 870645

COLN ST. ALDWYNS Glos. – ✉ Cirencester – ☎ 01285.

London 101 – Bristol 53 – Gloucester 20 – Swindon 15.

New Inn, GL7 5AN, ☎ 750651, Fax 750657, « 16C inn » – TV ☎ P. AE VISA JCB.
Meals (bar lunch Monday to Saturday)/dinner 21.00 **t.** 4.50 – 3.00 – **14 rm** 50.00/90.00 **t.** – SB.

COLSTERWORTH Lincs. 402 404 S 25 – pop. 1 452 – ☎ 01476.

London 105 – Grantham 8 – Leicester 29 – Nottingham 32 – Peterborough 14.

Granada Lodge without rest., Granada Service Area, NG33 5JR, at A 151/A 1 (southbound carriageway) ☎ 860686, Fax 861078, Reservations (Freephone) 0800 555300 – TV ☎ P – 30. AE VISA.
36 rm 39.95 **st.**

Forte Travelodge, NG33 5JJ, E : ½ m. by B 6403 on A 1 (southbound carriageway) ☎ 861181, Reservations (Freephone) 0800 850950 – TV P. AE VISA
Meals (grill rest.) – **32 rm** 34.50 **t.**

Forte Travelodge, New Fox, South Witham, LE15 8AU, S : 3 m. by B 6403 on A 1 (northbound carriageway) ☎ (01572) 767586, Reservations (Freephone) 0800 850950 – TV P. AE VISA
Meals (grill rest.) – **32 rm** 34.50 **t.**

COLTISHALL Norfolk 404 Y 25 **Great Britain G.** – pop. 2 315 – ✉ Norwich – ☎ 01603.

Envir. : The Broads★.

London 133 – Norwich 8.

Norfolk Mead , Church St., NR12 7DN, ☎ 737531, Fax 737521, heated, , , park – rest TV ☎ P. AE VISA.
closed 2 weeks January-February – **Meals** *(closed Sunday dinner and Bank Holidays)* (dinner only) 24.75 **t.** and a la carte – **10 rm** 55.00/89.00 **t.** – SB.

COLYTON Devon 403 K 31 **The West Country G.** – pop. 2 782 – ☎ 01297.

See : Town★ - Church★.

Envir. : Axmouth (←★) SE : 3 m. by B 3161, A 3052 and B 3172.

London 160 – Exeter 23 – Lyme Regis 7.

Old Bakehouse, Lower Church St., EX13 6ND, ℘ 552518 – TV P. VISA
Meals a la carte 8.50/20.00 **st.** and a la carte – **6 rm** 21.50/43.00 **st.** – SB.

Swallows Eaves, Colyford, EX13 6QJ, SE : 1 ¼ m. on A 3052 ℘ 553184, – TV P.
closed December and January – **Meals** (dinner only) 18.00 **st.** 5.10 – **8 rm** 30.50/70.00 **st.** – SB.

COMBE MARTIN Devon 403 H 30 – pop. 3 165 – ✉ Ilfracombe – ☎ 01271.
See : Ilfracombe : Hillsborough (≤★★) *AC*, Capstone Hill★ (≤★), St. Nicholas' Chapel (≤★) *AC*.
Cross St., EX34 0DH ℘ 883319 (summer only).
♦London 218 – Exeter 56 – Taunton 58.

XX **Just Johnsons,** King St., EX34 0BS, ℘ 883568 – VISA
closed Monday, Tuesday and Bank Holidays in winter and Sunday – **Meals** (dinner only) a la carte 15.30/19.80 3.80.

COMPTON ABBAS Dorset – see Shaftesbury.

CONGLETON Ches. 402 403 404 N 24 **Great Britain G.** – pop. 21 539 – ☎ 01260.
Envir. : Little Moreton Hall★★ *AC*, SW : 3 m. by A 34.
Biddulph Rd ℘ 273540.
Town Hall, High St., CW12 1BN ℘ 271095.
♦London 183 – ♦Liverpool 50 – ♦Manchester 25 – ♦Sheffield 46 – ♦Stoke-on-Trent 13.

Sandhole Farm without rest., Hulme Walfield, CW12 2JH, N : 2 ¼ m. on A 34 ℘ 224419, Fax 224766, , park – TV ☎ P. VISA
13 rm 33.00/43.00 **t.**

ATS Brookside ℘ 273720

CONISHOLME Lincs. – ☎ 01507.
♦London 164 – Boston 44 – Great Grimsby 15.

Wickham House without rest., Church Lane, LN11 7LX, off A 1031 ℘ 358465, – TV P.
closed Christmas and New Year – **3 rm** 37.00 **st.**

CONISTON Cumbria 402 K 20 **Great Britain G.** – pop. 1 304 – ☎ 0153 94.
Envir. : Coniston Water★ – Brantwood★ *AC*, SE : 2 m. on east side of Coniston Water.
Ruskin Av., LA21 8EH ℘ 41533 (summer only).
♦London 285 – ♦Carlisle 55 – Kendal 22 – Lancaster 42.

Coniston Lodge, Station Rd, LA21 8HH, ℘ 41201 – TV ☎ P. VISA.
Meals *(closed Sunday and Monday)* (dinner only) 17.50 **t.** 6.95 – **6 rm** 39.00/68.00 **t.** – SB.

Sun, LA21 8HQ, ℘ 41248, ≤, – rest TV ☎ P. VISA
closed 24 to 26 December and restricted opening during winter – **Meals** (bar lunch)/dinner 15.00 **t.** and a la carte 5.50 – **11 rm** 27.50/66.00 **t.** – SB.

at Torver SW : 2 ¼ m. on A 593 – ✉ Coniston – ☎ 0153 94 :

Wheelgate Country House, Little Arrow, LA21 8AU, NE : ¾ m. on A 593 ℘ 41418, « Part 17C farmhouse », – TV P. VISA JCB.
March-November – **Meals** (dinner only) 18.50 **t.** 5.25 – **8 rm** 33.00/66.00 **t.** – SB.

Old Rectory , LA21 8AX, NE : ¼ m. by A 593 ℘ 41353, Fax 41156, ≤, – TV P. VISA
Meals (residents only) (dinner only) 15.50 **t.** 4.75 – **8 rm** (dinner included) 40.00/94.00 **t.** – SB.

Arrowfield Country without rest., Little Arrow, LA21 8AU, NE : ¾ m. on A 593 ℘ 41741, ≤, – TV P.
closed December and January – **5 rm** 21.00/46.00 **st.**

at Water Yeat S : 6 ½ m. by A 593 on A 5084 – ✉ Ulverston – ☎ 01229 :

Water Yeat, LA12 8DJ, ℘ 885306, – rm P.
closed January-mid February and 1 week June-July – **Meals** (by arrangement) 17.50 **st.** 5.00 – **7 rm** 21.00/55.00 **st.** – SB.

at Blawith S : 7 ¼ m. by A 593 on A 5084 – ✉ Ulverston – ☎ 01229 :

Appletree Holme , LA12 8EL, W : 1 m. taking unmarked road opposite church and then right hand fork ℘ 885618, ≤, – TV ☎ P. VISA.
Meals 22.50 **st.** 4.25 – **4 rm** (dinner included) 60.00/126.00 **st.** – SB.

CONSTANTINE Cornwall 403 E 33 – ✉ Plymouth – ☎ 01326.
♦London 303 – Falmouth 15 – Penzance 25 – Truro 24.

Trengilly Wartha, Nancenoy, TR11 5RP, S : 1 ½ m. by Fore St. off Port Navas rd ℘ 340332, Fax 340332, – TV ☎ P. VISA JCB
Meals (bar lunch)/dinner 19.00 **st.** 4.80 – **6 rm** 39.00/59.00 **st.** – SB.

CONSTANTINE BAY Cornwall 403 E 32 – see Padstow.

COOKHAM Berks. 404 R 29 Great Britain G. – pop. 5 752 – ✉ Maidenhead – ☎ 01628.
See : Stanley Spencer Gallery★ *AC.*
♦London 32 – High Wycombe 7 – Reading 16.

XX **Alfonso's,** 19 Station Hill Par., SL6 9BR, ☎ 525775 – AE VISA JCB
closed Saturday lunch, Sunday, 2 weeks August and Bank Holidays – **Meals** 16.50 **t.** (lunch) and a la carte 16.50/25.00 **t.** 4.50.

XX Peking Inn, 49 High St., SL6 9SL, ☎ 520900 –
Meals - Chinese (Peking), Thai rest..

COPDOCK Suffolk 404 X 27 – see Ipswich.

COPTHORNE W. Sussex 404 T 30 – see Crawley.

CORBRIDGE Northd. 401 402 N 19 Great Britain G. – pop. 3 533 – ☎ 01434.
Envir. : Hadrian's Wall★★, N : 3 m. by A 68 – Corstopitum★ *AC*, NW : ½ m.
Hill St., NE45 5AA ☎ 632815 (summer only).
♦London 300 – Hexham 3 – ♦Newcastle upon Tyne 18.

Lion of Corbridge, Bridge End, NE45 5AX, ☎ 632504, Fax 632571 – TV ☎ & P. AE VISA JCB.
Meals (bar lunch)/dinner 13.95/18.00 **t.** and a la carte 4.50 – **14 rm** 46.00/53.50 **t.** – SB.

Riverside without rest., Main St., NE45 5LE, ☎ 632942, Fax 633883 – TV P. VISA JCB
closed mid December-mid January – **10 rm** 25.00/48.00 **t.**

Wheatsheaf, St. Helens St., NE45 5HE, ☎ 632020, Fax 632801 – TV ☎ P
6 rm.

XXX **Ramblers Country House,** Farnley, NE45 5RN, S : 1 m. on Riding Mill Rd ☎ 632424, Fax 633656 – P. AE VISA
closed Sunday dinner and Monday – **Meals** - German - (dinner only and Sunday lunch) 17.95 **t.** and a la carte.

XX **Valley,** The Old Station House, Station Rd, NE45 5AY, S : ½ m. by Riding Mill rd ☎ 633434, Fax 633923 – AE VISA
Meals - Indian – (dinner only) 22.50 **t.** and a la carte 12.00/21.50 **st.**

CORBY Northants. 404 R 26 Great Britain G. – pop. 53 044 – ☎ 01536.
Envir. : Boughton House★★ *AC*, S : 5½ m. by A 6116 and A 43.
18 Stamford Rd, Weldon ☎ 260756.
Civic Centre, George St., NN17 1QB ☎ 407507.
♦London 100 – ♦Leicester 26 – Northampton 22 – Peterborough 24.

Stakis Carlton Manor, Geddington Rd, NN18 8ET, SE : 1 ¾ m. on A 6116 ☎ 401020, Fax 400767, – rest TV ☎ & P – 190. AE VISA JCB.
Meals *(closed Saturday lunch and Sunday dinner to non-residents)* (lunch booking essential) 12.75/14.75 **t.** and a la carte – 8.50 – **102 rm** 75.00/112.00 **st.**, 2 suites – SB.

Rockingham Forest (Forte), Rockingham Rd, NN17 1AE, ☎ 401348, Fax 266383 – TV ☎ P – 400. AE VISA
Meals (bar lunch Monday to Saturday)/dinner 14.95 **st.** and a la carte 5.80 – **69 rm** 55.00/75.00 **st.** – SB.

ATS St. James's Rd ☎ 269519

CORFE CASTLE Dorset 403 404 N 32 The West Country G. – pop. 1 335 – ✉ Wareham – ☎ 01929.
See : Castle★ (≤★★) *AC.*
♦London 129 – Bournemouth 18 – Weymouth 23.

Mortons House, 45 East St., BH20 5EE, ☎ 480988, Fax 480820, ≤, « Elizabethan manor », – TV ☎ P. AE VISA
Meals 15.00/22.50 **t.** – **16 rm** 60.00/80.00 **t.**, 1 suite – SB.

CORNHILL-ON-TWEED Northd. 401 402 N 17 – pop. 317 – ☎ 01890.
♦London 345 – ♦Edinburgh 49 – ♦Newcastle upon Tyne 59.

Tillmouth Park , TD12 4UU, NE : 2½ m. on A 698 ☎ 882255, Fax 882540, ≤, « 19C country house », , , park – TV ☎ P. AE VISA
Meals 23.50 **t.** and lunch a la carte 6.25 – **14 rm** 70.00/125.00 **t.**

Coach House, Crookham, TD12 4TD, E : 4 m. on A 697 ☎ 820293, – rest & P. VISA
Easter-mid November – **Meals** 15.50 **t.** – **9 rm** 21.00/68.00 **t.**

CORSE LAWN Heref. and Worcs. – see Tewkesbury (Glos.).

COSGROVE Northants. 404 R 27 – see Stony Stratford.

COSHAM Hants. 403 404 Q 31 – see Portsmouth and Southsea.

COVENEY Cambs. – see Ely.

COVENTRY W. Mids. 403 404 P 26 **Great Britain G.** – pop. 294 387 – 01203.

See : City★ - Cathedral★★★ *AC* AV – Old Cathedral★ AV **A** – Museum of British Road Transport★ *AC* AV **M1**.

Finham Park 411123 BZ – Windmill Village, Birmingham Rd, Allesley 407241, – Sphinx, Sphinx Drive 451361.

Bayley Lane, CV1 5RN 832303/832304,.

London 100 – Birmingham 18 – Bristol 96 – Nottingham 52.

Plans on following pages

De Vere, Cathedral Sq., CV1 5RP, 633733, Fax 225299 – rm rest – 400. AE VISA AV **n**
Meals (bar lunch Saturday) 12.00/22.50 **t.** and a la carte – **180 rm** 85.00/95.00 **st.**, 10 suites – SB.

Brooklands Grange, Holyhead Rd, CV5 8HX, 601601, Fax 601277, – . AE VISA. AY **e**
closed 26 to 29 December – **Meals** *(closed lunch Saturday and Bank Holidays)* 16.95 **t.** and a la carte – **30 rm** 80.00/100.00 **t.**

Leofric (Regal), Broadgate, CV1 1LZ, 221371, Fax 551352 – rm rest – 600. AE VISA JCB. AV **r**
Meals 5.95/15.00 **st.** and a la carte 3.95 – 7.50 – **89 rm** 79.50/94.50 **t.**, 5 suites – SB.

Travel Inn, Rugby Rd, Binley Woods, CV3 2TA, at junction of A 46 with A 428 636585, Fax 431178 – rm – 32. AE VISA. BZ **n**
Meals (grill rest.) – 4.95 – **50 rm** 34.50 **t.**

Ashbourne without rest., 33 St. Patricks Rd, CV1 2LP, 229518 – . AV **a**
5 rm 25.00/35.00 **st.**

Crest without rest., 39 Friars Rd, CV1 2LJ, 227822, Fax 227244 – . AV **e**
closed 25 and 26 December – **4 rm** 20.00/40.00.

at Longford N : 4 m. on B 4113 – Coventry – 01203 :

Novotel, Wilsons Lane, CV6 6HL, 365000, Fax 362422, heated, – rm rest – 200. AE VISA BV **v**
Meals (bar lunch)/dinner 11.50 **t.** and a la carte 4.95 – 7.50 – **98 rm** 42.50 **st.**

at Walsgrave NE : 3 m. on A 4600 – Coventry – 01203 :

Hilton National, Paradise Way, The Triangle, CV2 2ST, NE : 1 m. by A 4600 603000, Fax 603011, , , – rm – 600. AE VISA JCB
Meals (bar lunch Saturday) 12.75/16.95 **st.** and a la carte 8.00 – 10.95 – **169 rm** 95.00 **st.**, 3 suites – SB. BX **c**

Forte Posthouse, Hinckley Rd, CV2 2HP, NE : ½ m. on A 4600 613261, Fax 621736, , , – rm rest – 425. AE VISA BX **e**
Meals a la carte 13.35/23.90 **st.** 6.25 – 7.95 – **147 rm** 56.00 **st.** – SB.

at Ansty (Warks.) NE : 5¾ m. by A 4600 – BY – on B 4065 – Coventry – 01203 :

Ansty Hall, CV7 9HZ, 612222, Fax 602155, « Part 17C mansion », , park – rm – 80. AE VISA.
Meals (bar lunch)/dinner 25.95 **t.** 5.20 – **30 rm** 70.00/90.00 **t.** – SB.

at Binley E : 3½ m. on A 428 – Coventry – 01203 :

Coombe Abbey , Brinklow Rd, CV3 2AB, E : 2 m. on B 4027 450450, Fax 635101, , « Former Cistercian abbey of 12C origins with formal gardens by Capability Brown », , park – rm – 120. AE VISA.
Meals 12.50/22.50 **st.** and a la carte – 10.50 – **61 rm** 95.00/295.00 **st.**, 2 suites – SB.

at Brandon (Warks.) E : 6 m. on A 428 – BZ – Coventry – 01203 :

Brandon Hall (Forte Heritage) , Main St., CV8 3FW, 542571, Fax 544909, , park, squash – – 90. AE VISA JCB
Meals 16.95/19.95 **st.** and a la carte 8.00 – 10.00 – **60 rm** 80.00/110.00 **st.** – SB.

at Ryton on Dunsmore SE : 4¾ m. by A 45 – Coventry – 01203 :

Coventry Knight (Country Club), London Rd, CV8 3DY, on A 45 (northbound carriageway) 301585, Fax 301610 – rm rest – 250. AE VISA.
Meals *(closed Saturday lunch)* 9.95/25.00 **t.** and a la carte – 7.50 – **47 rm** 65.00 **t.**, 2 suites – SB. BZ **u**

at Baginton (Warks.) S : 3 m. by A 4114 and A 444 off A 45 (off westbound carriageway and Howes Lane turning) – Coventry – 01203 :

Old Mill, Mill Hill, CV8 2BS, 302241, Fax 307070, « Converted corn mill », – . AE VISA. BZ **e**
Meals (grill rest.) a la carte 7.15/18.40 **t.** – 5.50 – **20 rm** 54.00 **t.** – SB.

COVENTRY

Broadgate . . . . AV 6
Corporation Street . . . . AV
Shopping Precincts . . . . AV

Bayley Lane . . . . AV 3
Bishop Street . . . . AV 5
Burges . . . . AV 7
Earl Street . . . . AV 10
Fairfax Street . . . . AV 12
Far Gosford Street . . . . AV 13
Gosford Street . . . . AV 15
Greyfriars Lane . . . . AV 16
Hales Street . . . . AV 17
Hearsall Lane . . . . AY 21
High Street . . . . AV 22
Ironmonger Row . . . . . . AV 23
Jordan Well . . . . AV 26
Leicester Row . . . . AV 29
Light Lane . . . . AV 30
Little Park Street . . . . . AV 31
Primrose Hill Street . . . . AV 34
Queen Victoria Road . . . AV 35
St. Johns (Ringway) . . . . AV 38
St. Nicholas (Ringway) . . AV 39
Swanswell (Ringway) . . . AV 40
Trinity Street . . . . AV 41
Upper Well Street . . . . . AV 43
Vecqueray Street . . . . . . AV 45
Victoria Street . . . . AV 46
Warwick Row . . . . AV 49
White Street . . . . AV 51
Windsor Street . . . . AV 52
White Friars (Ringway) . . AV 54

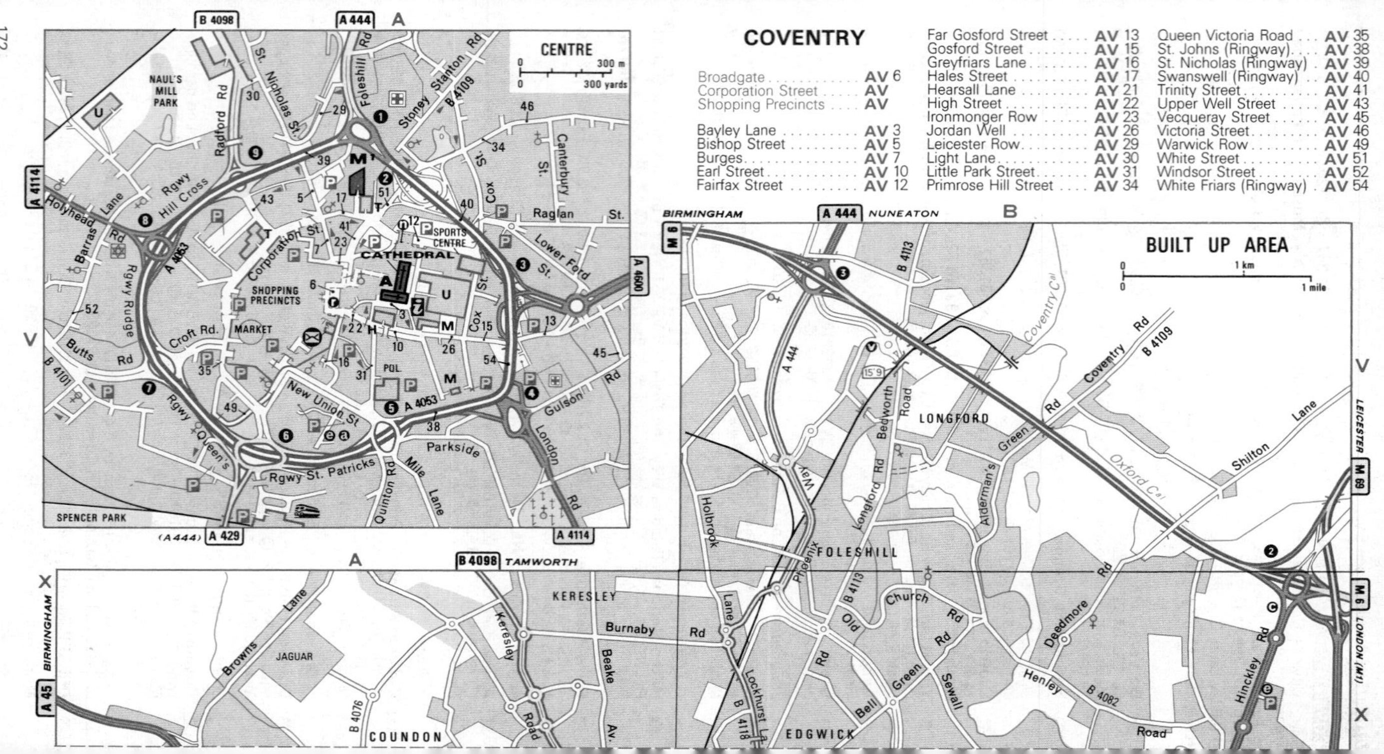

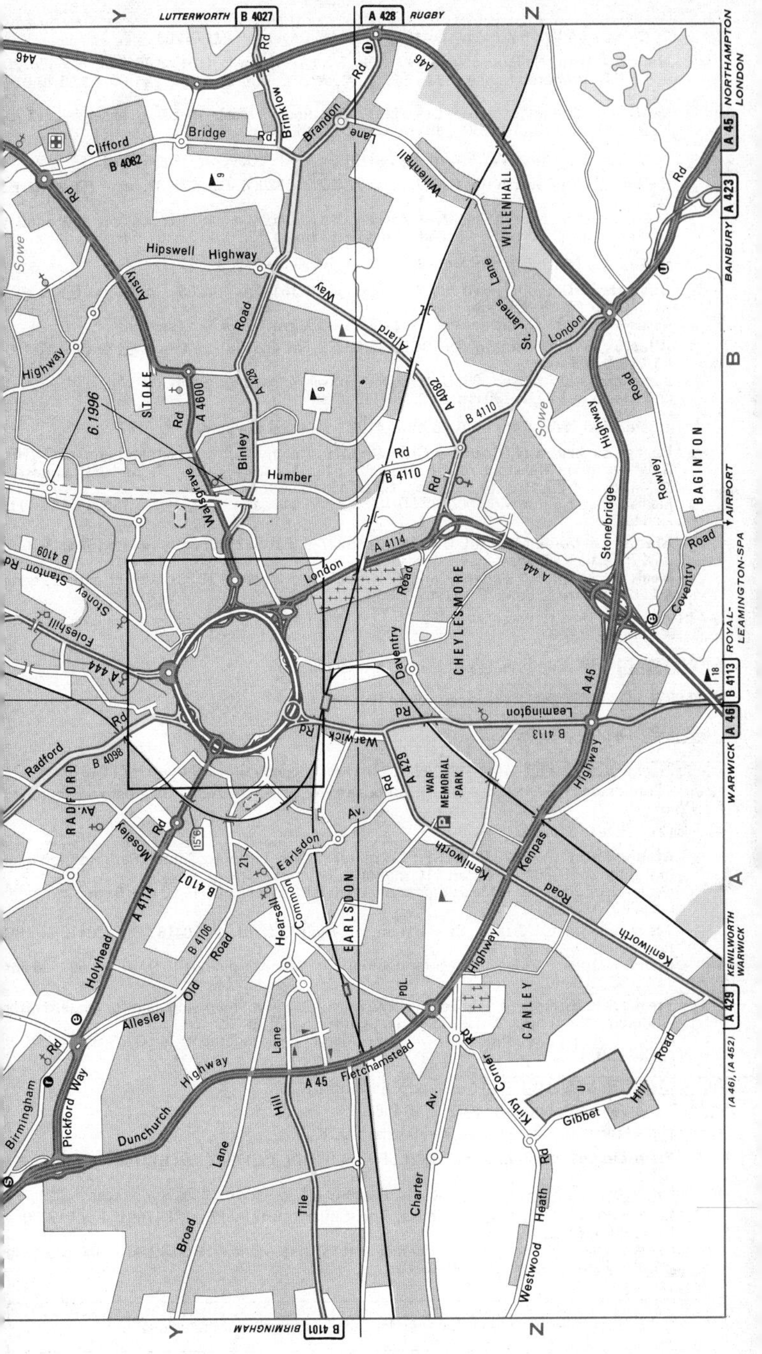
LUTTERWORTH B 4027
A 428 RUGBY
NORTHAMPTON LONDON
A 45
A 423
BANBURY
AIRPORT
ROYAL-LEAMINGTON-SPA
B 4113
A 46
WARWICK
KENILWORTH WARWICK
A 429
(A 46), (A 452)
B 4101 BIRMINGHAM
Y
Z
A
B
A46
Clifford
Bridge
Rd.
B 4082
Brinklow
Brandon
Rd
Lane
Willenhall
WILLENHALL
Hipswell
Highway
Sowe
Ansty
Rd
Way
Allard
A 4082
STOKE
A 4600
A 428
Binley
Road
Humber
B 4110
St. James
Lane
London
Stonebridge
Highway
Road
Rowley
BAGINTON
Coventry
Road
A 444
CHEYLESMORE
Daventry
Road
London
A 4114
Walsgrave
6.1996
Stoney Stanton Rd
B 4109
Foleshill
A 444
Radford
B 4098
RADFORD
Av.
Moseley
Rd
A 4114
B 4107
Holyhead
B 4106
Road
Old
Allesley
Highway
Dunchurch
Pickford Way
Birmingham
Rd
Warwick Rd
A 429
WAR MEMORIAL PARK
Kenilworth
Road
Kenpas
Highway
Leamington
B 4113
Rd
A 45
Earlsdon
Av.
EARLSDON
Common
Hearsall
Lane
Hill
Tile
A 45
Fletchamstead
POL
CANLEY
Highway
Charter
Av.
Corner
Kirby
Rd
Gibbet
Hill
Road
Westwood
Heath
Rd
Broad
Lane
Kenilworth

at Berkswell W : 6½ m. by B 4101 – AY – ✉ Coventry – ☎ 01203 :

Nailcote Hall, Nailcote Lane, CV7 7DE, S : 1½ m. on B 4101 ✆ 466174, Fax 470720, « Part 17C timbered house », ₣₲, ≘s, ▣, ⛳9, 🐴, 🎾 – 📺 ☎ ♿ 🅟 – 🏛 100. 🅰 AE ⓓ VISA. ✂
Meals a la carte approx. 15.00 **t.** 🍷 6.50 – **Oak Room : Meals** (booking essential) 17.75/26.50 **t.** and a la carte 🍷 6.50 – **38 rm** ▭ 120.00/150.00 **st.** – SB.

at Balsall Common W : 6¾ m. by B 4101 – AY – ✉ Coventry – ☎ 01676 :

Haigs, 273 Kenilworth Rd, CV7 7EL, on A 452 ✆ 533004, Fax 535132, 🐴 – 📺 ☎ 🅟. 🅰 VISA. ✂
closed 26 December-4 January – **Meals** *(closed Sunday dinner)* (dinner only and Sunday lunch)/dinner 17.00 **t.** and a la carte 🍷 4.80 – **13 rm** ▭ 52.50/68.50 **st.** – SB.

at Allesley NW : 3 m. on A 4114 – ✉ Coventry – ☎ 01203 :

Coventry Hill (Forte), Rye Hill, CV5 9PH, ✆ 402151, Fax 402235 – 🛗 ⚞ rm 📺 ☎ 🅟 – 🏛 110. 🅰 AE ⓓ VISA JCB AXY **s**
Meals 9.95/14.95 **st.** and a la carte – ▭ 7.95 – **180 rm** 49.00/75.00 **st.** – SB.

Allesley, Birmingham Rd, CV5 9GP, ✆ 403272, Fax 405190 – 🛗 ▤ rest 📺 ☎ 🅟 – 🏛 400. 🅰 AE ⓓ VISA JCB AY **r**
accommodation closed 25 December – **Meals** *(closed Saturday lunch)* 12.50/14.00 **t.** and a la carte 🍷 4.50 – **90 rm** ▭ 95.00/115.00 **st.**

at Meriden NW : 6 m. by A 45 on B 4102 – AX – ✉ Coventry – ☎ 01676 :

Forest of Arden H. Country Club Resort (Country Club), Maxstoke Lane, CV7 7HR, NW : 2¾ m. by Maxstoke rd ✆ 522335, Fax 523711, ₣₲, ≘s, ▣, ⛳18, 🎣, park, 🎾, squash – 🛗 ⚞ ▤ rest 📺 ☎ ♿ 🅟 – 🏛 150. 🅰 AE ⓓ VISA. ✂
Meals *(closed Saturday lunch)* 16.50/19.50 **t.** and a la carte – ▭ 9.00 – **150 rm** 115.00 **t.**, 2 suites.

Manor (De Vere), Main Rd, CV7 7NH, ✆ 522735, Fax 522186, 🐴 – ⚞ rm 📺 ☎ ♿ 🅟 – 🏛 275. 🅰 AE ⓓ VISA
Meals *(closed lunch Saturday and Bank Holiday Mondays)* 13.95/16.95 **st.** and a la carte 🍷 4.25 – **74 rm** ▭ 85.00/95.00 **st.** – SB.

ATS Ashmore Lake Way, Willenhall ✆ (01902) 602555/605098

ATS Kingswood Close, off Holbrook Lane, Holbrooks ✆ 638554

COWAN BRIDGE Cumbria 402 M 21 – see Kirkby Lonsdale.

COWES I.O.W. 403 404 PQ 31 – see Wight (Isle of).

COWLEY Oxon. – see Oxford.

CRACKINGTON HAVEN Cornwall 403 G 31 **The West Country G.** – ✉ Bude – ☎ 01840.

Envir. : Poundstock* (≤**, church*, guildhouse*) NE : 5½m. by A 39 – Jacobstow (Church*) E : 3½ m.

◆London 262 – Bude 11 – Truro 42.

Manor Farm 🐦, EX23 0JW, SE : 1¼ m. taking first left onto Church Park Rd then take first right ✆ 230304, ≤, « Part 11C manor », 🐴, park – ⚞ 🅟. ✂
closed 25 December – **Meals** (communal dining) (dinner only) 15.00 **s.** – **5 rm** ▭ (dinner included) 42.00/84.00 **s.**

Trevigue 🐦, EX23 0LQ, SE : 1¼ m. on High Cliff rd ✆ 230418, Fax 230418, « 16C farmhouse » – ⚞ 🅟. ✂
March-October – **Meals** (by arrangement) (communal dining) 15.00 **s.** 🍷 3.50 – **6 rm** ▭ 50.00/60.00 **s.**

Treworgie Barton 🐦, St. Gennys, EX23 0NL, E : 2¼ m. following sign for Dizzard after white church on right ✆ 230233, ≤, 🐴, park – ⚞ 📺 🅟. ✂
closed October, December and January – **Meals** (by arrangement) 14.00 – **3 rm** ▭ 20.00/46.00 – SB.

CRANBORNE Dorset 403 404 O 31 – pop. 667 – ☎ 01725.

⛳18, ⛳9 Crane Valley, Verwood ✆ (01202) 814088.

◆London 107 – Bournemouth 21 – Salisbury 18 – ◆Southampton 30.

Fleur De Lys, Wimborne St., BH21 5PP, on B 3078 ✆ 517282, Fax 517765 – 📺 ☎ 🅟. 🅰 VISA
Meals (bar lunch)/dinner 11.95 **st.** and a la carte 🍷 4.95 – **8 rm** ▭ 26.30/45.00 **st.** – SB.

XX **La Fosse** with rm, London House, The Square, BH21 5PR, ✆ 517604, Fax 517778 – ⚞ rest 📺. 🅰 AE VISA. ✂
Meals *(closed Saturday lunch, Sunday dinner and Monday)* 9.00/12.00 **t.** and a la carte 🍷 4.50 – **3 rm** ▭ 32.50/55.00 **t.** – SB.

CRANBROOK Kent 404 V 30 **Great Britain G.** – pop. 4 670 – ☎ 01580.

Envir. : Sissinghurst Castle★ *AC*, NE : 2½ m. by A 229 and A 262.

ℹ Vestry Hall, Stone St., TN17 3HA ☎ 712538 (summer only).

♦London 53 – Hastings 19 – Maidstone 15.

- **Kennel Holt** 🐦, Goudhurst Rd, TN17 2PT, NW : 2 ¼ m. by A 229 on A 262 ☎ 712032, Fax 715495, « Gardens » – 🚭 rest TV ☎ P. AE VISA JCB. 🐕
  Meals *(closed Sunday dinner to non-residents and Monday)* (lunch by arrangement)/ dinner 20.00/25.00 **t.** 5.00 – **9 rm** 105.00/125.00 **st.**
- **Old Cloth Hall** 🐦, TN17 3NR, E : 1 m. by Tenterden Rd ☎ 712220, Fax 712220, ←, « Tudor manor house, gardens », 🏊, park, 🎾 – TV P. 🐕
  closed Christmas – **Meals** (lunch by arrangement) (residents only) (unlicensed)/ dinner 25.00 **s.** – **3 rm** 45.00/95.00 **s.**
- **Hartley Mount,** TN17 3QX, S : ½ m. on A 229 ☎ 712230, Fax 715733, 🌳, 🎾 – 🚭 TV ☎ 🚗 P. AE VISA JCB. 🐕
  Meals 12.50/15.50 **st.** and a la carte 5.50 – **5 rm** 55.00/75.00 **st.** – SB.
- **Hancocks Farmhouse** 🐦, Tilsden Lane, TN17 3PH, E : ¾ m. by Tenterden Rd off Benenden rd ☎ 714645, ←, « 16C half timbered farmhouse » – 🚭 TV P. 🐕
  Meals (by arrangement) 19.00 **s.** – **3 rm** 35.00/60.00 **s.**

at Sissinghurst NE : 1 ¾ m. by B 2189 on A 262 – ✉ Cranbrook – ☎ 01580 :

- **Rankins,** The Street, TN17 2JH, ☎ 713964 – VISA
  closed Sunday dinner, Monday, Tuesday, 1 week August and Bank Holidays – **Meals** (dinner only and Sunday lunch)/dinner 25.95/23.50 **t.** 3.90.

Die Preise Einzelheiten über die in diesem Führer angegebenen Preise finden Sie in der Einleitung.

CRANLEIGH Surrey 404 S 30 – pop. 11 479 – ☎ 01483.

⛳ Fernfell G. & C.C., Barhatch Lane ☎ 268855.

♦London 42 – ♦Brighton 36 – Reading 36 – ♦Southampton 58.

- **La Barbe Encore,** High St., GU6 8AE, ☎ 273889 – AE VISA
  closed Saturday lunch, Sunday dinner, Monday and 25-26 December – **Meals** - French - 15.95/24.40 **st.** 4.70.

CRANTOCK Cornwall 403 E 32 – see Newquay.

CRAVEN ARMS Shrops. 402 403 L 26 **Great Britain G.** pop. 1 892 – ☎ 01588.

Envir. : Wenlock Edge★, NE : by B 4368.

♦London 170 – ♦Birmingham 47 – Hereford 32 – Shrewsbury 21.

- **Old Rectory** 🐦, Hopesay, SY7 8HD, W : 3 ¾ m. by B 4368 ☎ 660245, ←, « Part 17C », 🌳 – 🚭 TV P. 🐕
  closed Christmas – **Meals** (by arrangement) (communal dining) 18.00 6.00 – **3 rm** 30.00/60.00.

CRAWLEY W. Sussex 404 T 30 – pop. 87 644 – ☎ 01293.

⛳ (2x) Cottesmore, Buchan Hill ☎ 528256 – ⛳, ⛳ Tilgate Forest, Titmus Drive, Tilgate ☎ 530103 – ⛳ Gatwick Manor, London Rd, Lowfield Heath ☎ 538587 – ⛳ Horsham Rd, Pease Pottage ☎ 521706.

♦London 33 – ♦Brighton 21 – Lewes 23 – Royal Tunbridge Wells 23.

Plan of enlarged area : see Gatwick

- **Holiday Inn London Gatwick,** Langley Drive, Tushmore Roundabout, RH11 7SX, ☎ 529991, Telex 877311, Fax 515913, Fø, ≘s, 🏊 – 🛗 🚭 rm ▤ rest TV ☎ ♿ P – 🏛 250. AE ⓓ VISA JCB BY **n**
  Meals 12.50/25.00 **st.** and dinner a la carte – 10.95 – **215 rm** 79.00 **st.**, 2 suites.
- **George** (Forte), High St., RH10 1BS, ☎ 524215, Fax 548565 – 🚭 TV ☎ P – 🏛 50. AE ⓓ VISA JCB. 🐕 BY **o**
  Meals *(closed dinner 24 to 26 December)* (bar lunch Monday to Saturday)/dinner 16.95 **t.** and a la carte – 8.50 – **81 rm** 58.00/78.00 **t.** – SB.
- **Goffs Park,** 45 Goffs Park Rd, Southgate, RH11 8AX, ☎ 535447, Fax 542050, 🌳 – TV ☎ P – 🏛 80. AE ⓓ VISA. 🐕 AZ **s**
  Meals (dancing Friday and Saturday evenings) (bar lunch)/dinner 13.90 **st.** and a la carte – 7.75 – **64 rm** 49.00 **st.**

at Copthorne NE : 4½ m. on A 264 – BY – ☎ 01342 :

- **Copthorne London Gatwick,** Copthorne Way, RH10 3PG, ☎ 714971, Fax 717375, Fø, ≘s, 🌳, park, squash – 🚭 rm ▤ rest TV ☎ P – 🏛 110. AE ⓓ VISA JCB
  Lion D'Or : Meals *(closed Saturday lunch and Sunday) 8.50/25.00* **st.** and a la carte – **Brasserie : Meals** 17.00 **st.** and a la carte – 10.50 – **222 rm** 98.00/118.00 **st.**, 5 suites – SB.
- **Copthorne Effingham Park,** West Park Rd, RH10 3EU, on B 2028 ☎ 714994, Fax 716039, ←, Fø, ≘s, 🏊, ⛳, 🌳, park – 🛗 🚭 rm ▤ rest TV ☎ ♿ P – 🏛 600. AE ⓓ VISA. 🐕
  Meals 15.50 **t.** (lunch) and dinner a la carte 21.85/35.35 **t.** – 9.95 – **119 rm** 98.00 **st.**, 3 suites.

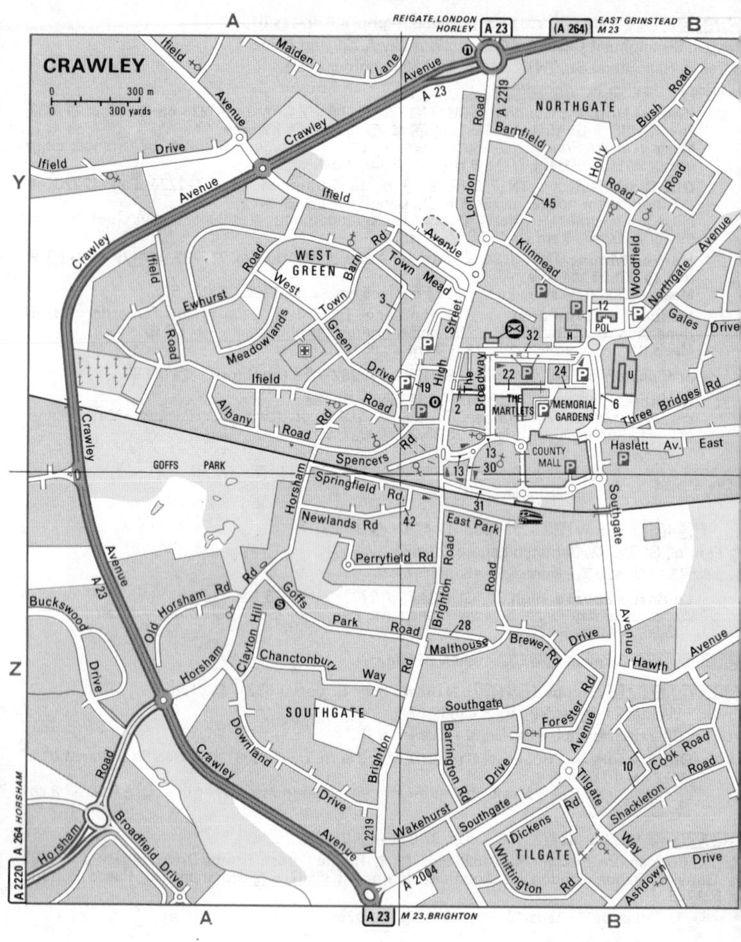

Broad Walk	BY 2	Buckmans Road	AY 3	Southgate Road	BZ 28
County Mall Shopping Centre	BZ	College Road	BY 6	Station Road	BY 30
High Street	BY	Drake Road	BZ 10	Station Way	BZ 31
Queens Square	BY 22	Exchange Road	BY 12	The Boulevard	BY 32
The Broadway	BY	Haslett Av. West	BY 13	Titmus Drive	BZ 34
The Martlets	BY	Orchard Street	BY 19	West Street	ABZ 42
		Queensway	BY 24	Woolborough Road	BY 45

at Three Bridges E : 1 m. on Haslett Avenue East – BY – ✉ Crawley – ☎ 01293 :

Scandic Crown, Tinsley Lane South, RH11 1NP, N : ½ m. by Hazelwick Av. ☎ 561186, Telex 87485, Fax 561169, – rm – 210. AE VISA. plan of Gatwick Y **n**
closed 24 December-2 January – **Meals** 16.00 **t.** and a la carte – 9.95 – **151 rm** 80.00/95.00 **t.**

at Maidenbower E : 2½ m. by Haslett Av. and Worth Rd on B 2036 – BY – ✉ Crawley – ☎ 01293 :

Europa Gatwick, Balcombe Rd, RH10 7ZR, on B 2036 ☎ 886666, Fax 886781, – rm – 150. AE VISA. plan of Gatwick Z **a**
– **Mediterranee : Meals** 13.50 **st.** – 9.95 – **207 rm** 66.00/77.00 **st.**, 4 suites.

ATS Reynolds Rd, West Green ☎ 533151/2

Richiedete nelle librerie il catalogo delle pubblicazioni Michelin

CREWE Ches. 402 403 404 M 24 – pop. 63 351 – ☎ 01270.

Queen's Park Drive ☎ 666724.

London 174 – Chester 24 – ◆Liverpool 49 – ◆Manchester 36 – ◆Stoke-on-Trent 15.

Forte Travelodge, Alsager Rd, Barthomley, CW2 5PT, SE : 5½ m. by A 5020 on A 500 at junction with M 6 ☎ 883157, Reservations (Freephone) 0800 850950 – TV & P. AE VISA.
Meals (grill rest.) – **42 rm** 34.50 **t.**

ATS Gresty Rd ☎ 256285

CREWKERNE Somerset 403 L 31 **The West Country G.** – pop. 6 437 – ☎ 01460.

Envir. : Forde Abbey★ *AC*, SW : 8 m. by B 3165 and B 3162 – Clapton Court Gardens★ *AC*, S : 3½ m. by B 3165.

Exc. : Montacute House★★ *AC*, NE : 7 m. by A 30 – Parnham House★★ *AC*, SE : 7½ m. by A 356 and A 3066.

Windwhistle G. & C.C., Cricket St. Thomas, Chard ☎ 30231.

London 145 – Exeter 38 – ◆Southampton 81 – Taunton 20.

Broadview, 43 East St., TA18 7AG, ☎ 73424, – TV P. VISA.
Meals (by arrangement) 12.00 **s.** – **3 rm** 35.00/50.00.

at Haselbury Plucknett NE : 2¾ m. by A 30 on A 3066 – ✉ Crewkerne – ☎ 01460 :

Oak House, North St., TA18 7RB, ☎ 73625, « 16C thatched cottage », – rest P
Easter-October – **Meals** (by arrangement) 10.50 **st.** – **7 rm** 21.00/48.00 **st.** – SB.

at North Perrot E : 3½ m. by A 30 on A 3066 – ✉ Crewkerne – ☎ 01460 :

Manor Arms, TA18 7SG, ☎ 72901, « 16C inn » – TV P. VISA JCB.
Meals (in bar Sunday dinner and Monday) a la carte 7.85/13.75 **t.** 3.75 – **5 rm** 32.00/48.00 **t.** – SB.

at Misterton SE : 1½ m. on A 356 – ✉ Crewkerne – ☎ 01460 :

Yew Trees, Silver St., TA18 8NB, ☎ 77192, – P.
closed Christmas – **Meals** (by arrangement) 7.00 – **3 rm** 19.00/38.00 **s.**

CRICK Northants. 403 404 Q 26 – see Rugby.

CRICKLADE Wilts 403 404 O 29 – pop. 4 680 – ☎ 01793.

Cricklade Hotel, Common Hill ☎ 750751.

◆London 90 – ◆Bristol 45 – Gloucester 27 – ◆Oxford 34 – Swindon 6.

Cricklade H. & Country Club, Common Hill, SN6 6HA, SW : 1 m. on B 4040 ☎ 750751, Fax 751767, ≤, , , , park, – TV ☎ P – 120. AE VISA JCB.
Meals 13.00/21.00 **t.** and a la carte 5.75 – **46 rm** 74.00/108.00 **t.** – SB.

CROCKERTON Wilts. – see Warminster.

CROFT-ON-TEES Durham 402 P 20 – see Darlington.

CROMER Norfolk 404 X 25 – pop. 5 022 – ☎ 01263.

Royal Cromer, Overstrand Rd ☎ 512884.

Bus Station, Prince of Wales Rd, NR27 9HS ☎ 512497.

◆London 132 – ◆Norwich 23.

Morden House, 20 Cliff Av., NR27 0AN, ☎ 513396, – TV P.
Meals 12.00 – **6 rm** 21.00/42.00 – SB.

Birch House, 34 Cabbell Rd, NR27 9HX, ☎ 512521 – TV. VISA.
Meals 7.00 – **8 rm** 16.00/38.00 **s.** – SB.

CRONDALL Hants. 404 R 30 – pop. 6 113 – ☎ 01252.

◆London 56 – Reading 21 – Winchester 30.

Chesa, Bowling Alley, GU10 5RJ, N : 1 m. ☎ 850328, Fax 850328 – P. AE VISA
closed Sunday to Tuesday, first 2 weeks January and last 2 weeks August – **Meals** (booking essential) (light lunch by arrangement)/dinner 10.00/30.00 **t.** 5.90.

CRONTON Ches. 402 403 404 L 23 – see Widnes.

CROOK Durham 401 402 O 19 – pop. 6 390 – ✉ Bishop Auckland – ☎ 01388.

Low Job's Hill ☎ 762429.

◆London 261 – ◆Carlisle 65 – ◆Middlesbrough 34 – ◆Newcastle upon Tyne 27.

Greenhead without rest., Fir Tree, DL15 8BL, SW : 3½ m. by A 689 off A 68 ☎ 763143, – TV P. VISA.
7 rm 35.00/50.00 **s.**

CROSBY Mersey. 402 403 K 23 – see Liverpool.

CROSTHWAITE Cumbria 402 L 21 – see Kendal.

CROWBOROUGH E. Sussex 404 U 30 – pop. 5 685 – ☎ 01892.

♦London 45 – ♦Brighton 25 – Maidstone 26.

Winston Manor, Beacon Rd, TN6 1AD, on A 26 ☎ 652772, Fax 665537, [gym], [sauna], [pool] – [TV] ☎ [P] – 250. [credit cards]
Meals (light lunch Monday to Saturday)/dinner 16.95/16.75 **t.** and a la carte 4.75 – **48 rm** 50.00/90.00 **t.** – SB.

ATS Church Rd ☎ 662100

CROWTHORNE Berks. 404 R 29 – pop. 19 166 – ☎ 01344.

♦London 42 – Reading 15.

Waterloo (Forte), Dukes Ride, RG45 7NW, on B 3348 ☎ 777711, Fax 778913 – [TV] [P] – 50. [credit cards]
Meals (bar lunch Monday to Saturday)/dinner 16.95 **st.** and a la carte 5.80 – 8.50 **58 rm** 70.00/115.00 **st.** – SB.

Beijing, 103 Old Wokingham Rd, RG11 6LH, NE : ¾ m. by A 3095 ☎ 778802 – [P]. [credit cards]
closed Sunday lunch – **Meals** - Chinese - 15.50/18.50 **t.** and a la carte.

CROXDALE Durham – see Durham.

CROYDE Devon 403 H 30 **The West Country G.** – ✉ Braunton – ☎ 01271.

♦London 232 – Barnstaple 10 – Exeter 50 – Taunton 61.

Kittiwell House, St. Mary's Rd, EX33 1PG, ☎ 890247, Fax 890469, « 16C thatche Devon longhouse » – rm [TV] ☎ [P]. [credit cards]
closed mid January-mid February – **Meals** (dinner only and Sunday lunch)/dinner 16.90 and a la carte – **12 rm** (dinner included) 54.00/108.00 **t.** – SB.

Croyde Bay House [quiet], Moor Lane, Croyde Bay, EX33 1PA, NW : 1 m. by Baggy Poin rd ☎ 890270, ≤ Croyde Bay, [garden] – rest [TV] [P]. [credit cards]
March-mid November – **Meals** (dinner only) 17.90 **t.** – **7 rm** (dinner included) 59.00 98.00 **t.**

Whiteleaf without rest., Hobbs Hill, EX33 1PN, ☎ 890266, [garden] – [TV] ☎ [P]. [credit cards]
closed 2 weeks April-May, 2 weeks July, 2 weeks October and January-February – **Meal** *(closed Monday to Wednesday in winter)* a la carte 15.25/19.00 4.00 – **3 rm** 35.00 54.00 **s.** – SB.

CRUDWELL Wilts. 403 404 N 29 – see Malmesbury.

CUCKFIELD W. Sussex 404 T 30 – pop. 4 057 (inc. Cuckfield Rural) – ☎ 01444.

♦London 40 – ♦Brighton 15.

Ockenden Manor [quiet], Ockenden Lane, RH17 5LD, ☎ 416111, Fax 415549, « Part 16C manor », [garden] – rest [TV] ☎ [P] – 50. [credit cards].
Meals 17.00/35.00 **t.** and a la carte 27.85/41.20 **t.** 6.50 – 5.00 – **20 rm** 85.00/175.00 **t.** 2 suites – SB.

CULLOMPTON Devon 403 J 31 **The West Country G.** – pop. 7 159 – ☎ 01884.

See : Town★ – St. Andrew's Church★.

Envir. : Uffculme (Coldharbour Mill★★ *AC*) NE : 5½m. by B 3181 and B 3391.

Exc. : Killerton★★, SW : 6½m. by B 3181 and B 3185.

Padbrook Park ☎ 38286.

♦London 197 – Exeter 15 – Taunton 29.

Manor, 2-4 Fore St., EX15 1JL, ☎ 32281, Fax 38344 – [TV] ☎ [P]. [credit cards]
Meals (bar lunch)/dinner a la carte 13.85/20.15 **t.** 3.50 – **10 rm** 41.50/53.50 **t.** – SB.

Lower Beers [quiet], Brithem Bottom, EX15 1NB, NW : 2 ¾ m. by B 3181 ☎ 32257 Fax 32257, « 16C farmhouse », [garden] – [P].
closed mid December-mid January – **Meals** (by arrangement) (communal dining) 25.00 **st** 5.00 – **4 rm** 30.00/60.00 **st.**

CULWORTH Northants. 404 Q 27 – ✉ Banbury (Oxon.) – ☎ 01295.

♦London 84 – ♦Birmingham 48 – ♦Coventry 23 – ♦Oxford 31.

Fulford House [quiet] without rest., The Green, OX17 2BB, ☎ 760355, Fax 768304, « 17C house », [garden] – rm [TV] [P].
closed mid December-February – **3 rm** 34.00/56.00 **s.**

CUMNOR Oxon. 403 404 P 28 – see Oxford.

CURDWORTH W. Mids. – see Sutton Coldfield.

DALTON-IN-FURNESS Cumbria 402 K 21 – pop. 7 550 – ☎ 01229.

The Dunnerholme, Duddon Rd, Askham-in-Furness ☎ 262675.

♦London 283 – Barrow-in-Furness 3.5 – Kendal 30 – Lancaster 41.

Clarence House Country, Skelgate, LA15 8BQ, N : ¼ m. ☎ 462508, Fax 467177, [garden] – [TV] ☎ [P] – 40. [credit cards]
closed 25 and 26 December – **Meals** 8.95/25.00 **st.** and a la carte 8.40 – **17 rm** 60.00 75.00 **st.** – SB.

DARESBURY Ches. 402 403 404 M 23 – pop. 1 579 – ✉ Warrington – ☎ 01925.

London 197 – Chester 16 – Liverpool 22 – Manchester 25.

Lord Daresbury (De Vere), Chester Rd, WA4 4BB, on A 56 ☎ 267331, Fax 265615, squash – rm – 300.
Meals *(closed Saturday lunch)* 14.00/20.00 **st.** and a la carte 6.00 – **140 rm** 95.00/115.00 **st.** – SB.

DARLEY ABBEY Derbs. 402 403 404 P 25 – see Derby.

DARLINGTON Durham 402 P 20 – pop. 98 906 – ☎ 01325.

Blackwell Grange, Briar Close ☎ 464464 – Stressholme, Snipe Lane ☎ 461002.

Teesside Airport : ☎ 332811, E : 6 m. by A 67.

4 West Row, DL1 5PL ☎ 382698.

London 251 – Leeds 61 – Middlesbrough 14 – Newcastle upon Tyne 35.

Blackwell Grange Moat House (Q.M.H.), Blackwell Grange, DL3 8QH, SW : 1 m. on A 167 ☎ 380888, Fax 380899 – 300.
Meals 9.25/17.95 **st.** and a la carte 5.95 – 9.50 – **99 rm** 85.00/150.00 **st.** – SB.

Swallow King's Head, Priestgate, DL1 1NW, ☎ 380222, Fax 382006 – rm – 200.
Meals 8.50/15.25 **st.** and a la carte – **85 rm** 78.00/95.00 **st.** – SB.

Woodland House without rest., 63 Woodland Rd, DL3 7BQ, ☎ 461908
8 rm 20.00/40.00 **s.**

Sardis, 196 Northgate, DL1 1QU, ☎ 461222
closed Sunday, Monday, 1 to 9 January, 1 week spring, 2 weeks August and Bank Holidays – **Meals** 16.50 **t.** (dinner) and a la carte 15.50/21.00 **t.**

at Coatham Mundeville N : 4 m. on A 167 – ✉ Darlington – ☎ 01325 :

Hall Garth Golf & Country Club (Regal), DL1 3LU, E : ¼ m. on Brafferton rd ☎ 300400, Fax 310083 – rm – 300.
closed 24 to 26 December – **Meals** *(closed Saturday lunch and Sunday dinner)* 10.95/19.95 **t.** and a la carte 4.95 – **39 rm** 75.00/95.00 **st.**, 1 suite – SB.

at Teesside Airport E : 5½ m. by A 67 – ✉ Darlington – ☎ 01325 :

St. George (Mount Charlotte), DL2 1RH, ☎ 332631, Fax 333851, squash – rm – 150.
Meals *(closed lunch Monday and Saturday and Sunday dinner* 8.50/15.50 **st.** and a la carte 4.85 – **58 rm** 70.00/80.00 **st.**, 1 suite – SB.

at Croft-on-Tees S : 3½ m. on A 167 – ✉ Darlington – ☎ 01325 :

Clow Beck House without rest., Monk End Farm, DL2 2SW, W : ½ m. by South Parade ☎ 721075, Fax 720419, « Working farm », park
5 rm 30.00/47.00.

at Headlam NW : 6 m. by A 67 – ✉ Gainford – ☎ 01325 :

Headlam Hall, DL2 3HA, ☎ 730238, Fax 730790, « Part Jacobean and part Georgian manor house », park – rest – 150.
closed 25 December – **Meals** 11.00 **t.** (lunch) and a la carte 19.00/23.50 **t.** 3.50 – **24 rm** 55.00/75.00 **t.**, 2 suites – SB.

at Heighington NW : 6 m. by A 68 off A 6072 – ✉ Darlington – ☎ 01325 :

Eldon House without rest., East Green, DL5 6PP, ☎ 312270
3 rm 27.00/45.00 **s.**

at Redworth NW : 7 m. by A 68 on A 6072 – ✉ Bishop Auckland – ☎ 01388 :

Redworth Hall H. & Country Club, DL5 6NL, on A 6072 ☎ 772442, Fax 775112, « Part 18C and 19C manor house of Elizabethan origins », park, squash – rm rest – 300.
Crozier Conservatory : Meals 9.50/17.95 **t.** and a la carte 7.25 - (see also ***Blue Room*** below) – **96 rm** 98.00/150.00 **st.**, 4 suites – SB.

Blue Room (at Redworth Hall H. & Country Club), DL5 6NL, on A 6072 ☎ 772442, Fax 775112, « Part 18C and 19C manor house of Elizabethan origins », park
closed Sunday – **Meals** (dinner only) a la carte 23.25/31.45 **t.** 7.25.

ATS Albert St., off Neasham Rd ☎ 469271/469693

Jährlich eine neue Ausgabe
Aktuellste Informationen, jährlich für Sie!

DARTFORD Kent 404 U 29 pop. 79 439 – ☎ 01322.

The Clocktower, Suffolk Rd, DA1 1EJ ℘ 343243.

London 20 – Hastings 51 – Maidstone 22.

Stakis Dartford Bridge, Masthead Close, Crossways Business Park, DA2 6QF, NE 2½ m. by A 226, Cotton Lane and Crossways Boulevard ℘ 284444, Fax 288225, ... – ... rm ... – 240. AE VISA
Meals *(closed lunch Saturday and Bank Holidays)* 9.50/18.50 **t.** and a la carte – 9.50 – **171 rm** 77.00/102.00 **st.**, 4 suites – SB.

Campanile, Dartford Bridge, Clipper Boulevard West, Edison's Park, Crossways, DA 6QN, NE : 3 m. by A 226, Cotton Lane and Galleon Boulevard ℘ 278925, Fax 278948 ... rm ... – 30. AE VISA
Meals 15.00 **st.** and a la carte 4.50 – 4.50 – **80 rm** 36.50 **st.** – SB.

DARTINGTON Devon 403 I 32 – see Totnes.

DARTMOUTH Devon 403 J 32 The West Country G. – pop. 5 712 – ☎ 01803.

See : Town★★ - Dartmouth Castle (≤★★★) *AC*.

Exc. : Start Point (≤★) S : 13 m. (including 1 m. on foot).

The Engine House, Mayor's Av., TQ6 9YY ℘ 834224.

London 236 – Exeter 36 – Plymouth 35.

Royal Castle, 11 The Quay, TQ6 9PS, ℘ 833033, Fax 835445, ≤ – ... rest ... VISA
Meals (bar lunch Monday to Saturday)/dinner 20.25 **t.** 5.55 – **25 rm** (dinner included) 50.00/135.00 **t.** – SB.

Dart Marina (Forte Heritage), Sandquay, TQ6 9PH, ℘ 832580, Fax 835040, ≤ – ... AE VISA JCB
Meals 25.00 **st.** (dinner) and a la carte 14.95/21.15 **st.** – **35 rm** 50.00/100.00 **st.** – SB.

Ford House, 44 Victoria Rd, TQ6 9DX, ℘ 834047, Fax 834047, ... – ... AE VISA
mid March-November – **Meals** (residents only) (communal dining) (dinner only) (unlicensed) 25.00 **st.** – **3 rm** 50.00/65.00 **st.** – SB.

Wavenden House without rest., Compass Cove, TQ6 0JN, S : 1¼ m. via Warfleet by Newcomen Rd, off Castle Rd ℘ 833979, ≤ River Dart and sea, ... – ...
closed Christmas-New Year – **3 rm** 25.00/38.00 **st.**

Wadstray House without rest., Blackawton, TQ9 7DE, W : 4 ½ m. on A 3122 ℘ 712539, ... – ...
3 rm 30.00/50.00 **st.**

Carved Angel, 2 South Embankment, TQ6 9BH, ℘ 832465, Fax 835141, ≤ Dart Estuary – ...
closed Sunday dinner, Monday, 2 January-15 February, 24 to 26 and 28 December – **Meals** 15.00/47.50 **st.** and lunch a la carte 7.50.

Exchange, 5 Higher St., TQ6 9RB, ℘ 832022, Fax 832022 – VISA
closed Tuesday – **Meals** (light lunch)/dinner 13.00 and a la carte 4.85.

Billy Budd's, 7 Foss St., TQ6 9DW, ℘ 834842 – VISA
closed Sunday, Monday, 4 weeks February-March and 1 week November – **Meals** (booking essential) (light lunch)/dinner a la carte approx. 19.90 **t.**

at Stoke Fleming SW : 3 m. on A 379 – ✉ Dartmouth – ☎ 01803 :

Stoke Lodge, Cinders Lane, TQ6 0RA, ℘ 770523, Fax 770851, ≤, ..., heated, ... – ... AE VISA
Meals 9.75/16.95 **t.** and a la carte 5.95 – **24 rm** 42.50/85.00 **t.** – SB.

New Endsleigh, New Rd, TQ6 0NR, ℘ 770381 – ... VISA.
closed January – **Meals** (bar lunch)/dinner 9.95 **t.** and a la carte 4.50 – **12 rm** 27.00/49.00 **t.** – SB.

DAVENTRY Northants 404 Q 27 – pop. 26 886 – ☎ 01327.

9 Norton Rd ℘ 702829 – 18 Hellidon Lakes Hotel & C.C., Hellidon, Daventry ℘ 62550 – 18 Staverton Park, Staverton ℘ 705911.

Moot Hall, Market Sq., NN11 4BH ℘ 300277.

London 79 – Coventry 23 – Northampton 13 – Oxford 46.

Daventry, Ashby Rd, NN11 5SG, N : 2 m. on A 361 ℘ 301777, Fax 706313, ... – ... rest ... – 600. AE VISA
Meals (bar lunch Monday to Saturday)/dinner 20.00 **st.** 5.75 – 8.25 – **136 rm** 80.00/90.00 **st.**, 2 suites – SB.

Britannia, London Rd, NN11 4EN, SE : ¾ m. on A 45 ℘ 77333, Fax 300420 – ... – 350. AE VISA
Meals (carving rest.) (bar lunch Saturday) 9.95/15.95 **st.** and dinner a la carte 4.75 – **144 rm** 67.50/85.00 **st.**, 4 suites – SB.

at Badby S : 3½ m. by A 45 on A 361 – ✉ Daventry – 01327 :

Windmill Inn, Main St., NN11 6AN, ☎ 702363, Fax 311521 – TV ☎ P. VISA
Meals a la carte 9.50/17.50 **t.** 5.25 – **8 rm** 42.50/55.00 **t.** – SB.

at Hellidon SW : 9½ m. by A 45 and A 361 on Hellidon rd – ✉ Daventry – 01327 :

Hellidon Lakes H. & Country Club, NN11 6LN, SW : ¼ m. ☎ 262550, Fax 262559, ←, park, – TV ☎ P – 200. VISA JCB.
Meals 19.50/22.50 **t.** and a la carte – **43 rm** 90.00/115.00 **t.**, 2 suites – SB.

DAWLISH Devon 403 J 32 – pop. 11 929 – 01626.
Warren ☎ 862255.
The Lawn, EX7 9PW ☎ 863589.
London 215 – Exeter 13 – ♦Plymouth 40 – Torquay 11.

Langstone Cliff, Dawlish Warren, EX7 0NA, N : 2 m. by A 379 ☎ 865155, Fax 867166, heated, – TV ☎ P – 400. VISA
Meals (lunch by arrangement Monday to Saturday) 10.50/14.50 **st.** 4.00 – **68 rm** 40.00/70.00 **st.** – SB.

DEAL Kent 404 Y 30 – pop. 28 504 – 01304.
Walmer & Kingsdown, The Leas, Kingsdown ☎ 373256.
Town Hall, High St., CT14 6BB ☎ 369576.
London 78 – Canterbury 19 – Dover 8.5 – Margate 16.

Sutherland House, 186 London Rd, CT14 9PT, ☎ 362853, Fax 361268 – rm TV P. VISA JCB.
Meals (by arrangement) 18.50 3.50 – **5 rm** 35.00/48.00 **st.** – SB.

at Kingsdown S : 2¾ m. by A 258 on B 2057 – ✉ Deal – 01304 :

Blencathra Country without rest., Kingsdown Hill, CT14 8EA, off Upper St. ☎ 373725, – TV P.
5 rm 17.00/38.00 **st.**

at Finglesham NW : 3½ m. by A 258 and Burgess Green on The Street – ✉ Deal – 01304 :

Finglesham Grange without rest., CT14 0NQ, NW : ¾ m. on Eastry rd ☎ 611314, – P.
April-October – **3 rm** 25.00/45.00 **s.**

ATS 40 Gilford Rd ☎ 361543

DEDDINGTON Oxon. 403 404 Q 28 – pop. 2 319 – 01869.
London 72 – ♦Birmingham 46 – ♦Coventry 33 – ♦Oxford 18.

Holcombe, High St., OX15 0SL, ☎ 338274, Fax 337167, – TV ☎ P. VISA
closed 2 to 14 January – **Meals** 12.95/28.50 **t.** and a la carte 7.50 – **17 rm** 58.00/110.00 **t.** – SB.

Dexter's, 37 Market Pl., OX15 0SE, ☎ 338813 – VISA JCB
closed Tuesday lunch, Sunday dinner, Monday and January – **Meals** a la carte 14.50/22.50 **t.** 5.00.

DEDHAM Essex 404 W 28 **Great Britain G.** – pop. 1 847 – ✉ Colchester – 01206.
Envir. : Stour Valley★ – Flatford Mill★, E : 6 m. by B 1029, A 12 and B 1070.
London 63 – Chelmsford 30 – Colchester 8 – ♦Ipswich 12.

Maison Talbooth, Stratford Rd, CO7 6HN, W : ½ m. ☎ 322367, Fax 322752, ←, – TV ☎ P. VISA.
Meals - (see ***Le Talbooth*** below) – 7.50 – **9 rm** 85.00/140.00 **st.**, 1 suite – SB.

XXX **Le Talbooth,** Gun Hill, CO7 6HP, W : 1 m. ☎ 323150, Fax 322309, « Part Tudor house in attractive riverside setting », – P. VISA
Meals 13.50/20.95 and a la carte 10.00.

XX **Fountain House & Dedham Hall** with rm, Brook St., CO7 6AD, ☎ 323027, – rest TV P. VISA.
Meals *(closed Sunday dinner and Monday)* (dinner only and Sunday lunch)/dinner 18.50 **t.** 7.50 – **6 rm** 38.00/57.00 **st.**

DENMEAD Hants. 403 Q 31 – 01705.
♦London 70 – ♦Portsmouth 11 – ♦Southampton 27.

XX **Barnard's,** Hambledon Rd, PO7 6NU, ☎ 257788, – VISA
closed lunch Tuesday and Saturday, Sunday, Monday, 2 weeks August and 1 week Christmas-New Year – **Meals** 13.50/15.50 **t.** and a la carte.

DENTON Gtr. Manchester 402 404 N 23 – pop. 35 813 – ☎ 0161.

Denton, Manchester Rd ☎ 336 3218.

♦London 196 – Chesterfield 41 – ♦Manchester 6.

Old Rectory, Meadow Lane, Haughton Green, M34 1GD, S : 2 m. by A 6017, Two Tre Lane and Haughton Green Rd ☎ 336 7516, Fax 320 3212, – rest rest – 80. AE VISA
Meals 11.95/15.95 **st.** and a la carte – **36 rm** 63.00/85.00 **st.** – SB.

DERBY Derbs. 402 403 404 P 25 **Great Britain G.** – pop. 218 802 – ☎ 01332.

See : City★ – Museum and Art Gallery★ (Collection of Derby Porcelain★) YZ **M1** – Royal Crow Derby Museum★ *AC* Z **M2**.

Envir. : Kedleston Hall★★ *AC*, NW : 4½ m. by Kedleston Rd X.

Wilmore Rd, Sinfin ☎ 766323 – Mickleover, Uttoxeter Rd ☎ 513339 – Kedleston Pa ☎ 840035 – , Breadsall Priory Hotel G – Allestree Park, Allestree Hall ☎ 550616.

East Midlands Airport, Castle Donington : ☎ 852852, SE : 12 m. by A 6 X.

Assembly Rooms, Market Pl., DE1 3AH ☎ 255802.

♦London 132 – ♦Birmingham 40 – ♦Coventry 49 – ♦Leicester 29 – ♦Manchester 62 – ♦Nottingham 16 – ♦Sheffield 47 ♦Stoke-on-Trent 35.

Plan opposite

Midland, Midland Rd, DE1 2SQ, ☎ 345894, Fax 293522, – rm – 150. AE VISA Z
closed Christmas-New Year – **Meals** *(closed lunch Saturday and Bank Holidays)* 11.2 16.00 **t.** – 7.50 – **99 rm** 69.50/117.50 **t.** – SB.

La Gondola, 220 Osmaston Rd, DE23 8JX, ☎ 332895, Fax 384512 – – 70. AE VISA. X
Meals - Italian - *(closed Sunday)* (dancing Saturday) 7.50/16.50 **t.** and a la carte 5.75 – 4.50 – **19 rm** 45.00/56.00 **st.**, 1 suite – SB.

Periquito, 119 London Rd, DE1 2QR, ☎ 340633, Fax 293502 – rm – 15 AE VISA JCB Z
Meals 8.50/14.00 **st.** and a la carte 4.75 – 6.50 – **101 rm** 46.00 **st.** – SB.

Oast House (Premier), Foresters Leisure Park, 220 Osmaston Park Rd, DE3 8A ☎ 270027, Fax 270528 – rm – 40. AE VISA. X
Meals (grill rest.) a la carte 10.15/13.15 **st.** – 4.45 – **26 rm** 39.50 **st.** – SB.

European Inn without rest., Midland Rd, DE1 2SL, ☎ 292000, Fax 293940 – – 100. AE VISA Z
5.75 – **88 rm** 39.00 **st.**

New Water Margin, 72-74 Burton Rd, DE1 1TG, ☎ 364754, Fax 290482 – . VISA JCB Z
Meals - Chinese (Canton) - 11.00/17.00 **t.** and a la carte 3.40.

G.C's, 22 Iron Gate, DE1 3GP, ☎ 368732 – . AE VISA JCB Y
closed Monday lunch, Sunday, 25-28 December and Bank Holiday Mondays – **Meals** 7.5 13.50 **t.** and a la carte 5.00.

at Darley Abbey N : 1¾ m. on A 6 (Duffield Rd) – X – ✉ Derby – ☎ 01332 :

Darleys on the River, Darley Abbey Mills, DE22 1DZ, E : ½ m. by Mileash Lane and Ol Lane ☎ 364987, Fax 364987, – . AE VISA
closed Sunday dinner and Bank Holidays – **Meals** 11.95 **t.** (lunch) and a la carte 21.40 26.80 **st.**

at Breadsall NE : 4 m. by A 52 off A 61 – X – ✉ Derby – ☎ 01332 :

Breadsall Priory H. Country Club Resort (Country Club), Moor Rd, Morley, DE7 6DL NE : 1¼ m. by Rectory Lane ☎ 832235, Fax 833509, , , , , , , squash – rest – 90. AE VISA.
Meals *(closed Saturday lunch)* 10.25/25.00 **st.** and dinner a la carte 7.50 – 10.00 **91 rm** 95.00/108.00 **st.** – SB.

at Littleover SW : 2½ m. on A 5250 – ✉ Derby – ☎ 01332 :

La Villa, 222 Rykneld Rd, DE3 7AP, SW : 1¾ m. on A 5250 ☎ 510161, Fax 514010, –
Meals - Italian rest. – **16 rm.**

Forte Posthouse, Pastures Hill, DE23 7BA, ☎ 514933, Fax 518668, – rm – 60. AE VISA JCB X
Meals a la carte 11.85/19.85 **st.** – 7.95 – **60 rm** 56.00 **st.**, 2 suites – SB.

at Mickleover SW : 3 m. by A 38 and A 516 – ✉ Derby – ☎ 01332 :

Mickleover Court, Etwall Rd, DE3 5XX, ☎ 521234, Fax 521238, , , – rm – 200. AE VISA
Avesbury : Meals 14.50/21.00 **st.** and a la carte 6.00 – **Stelline : Meals** - Italian - a la cart 11.35/22.70 **st.** 6.00 – **71 rm** 89.50/99.50 **st.** – SB.

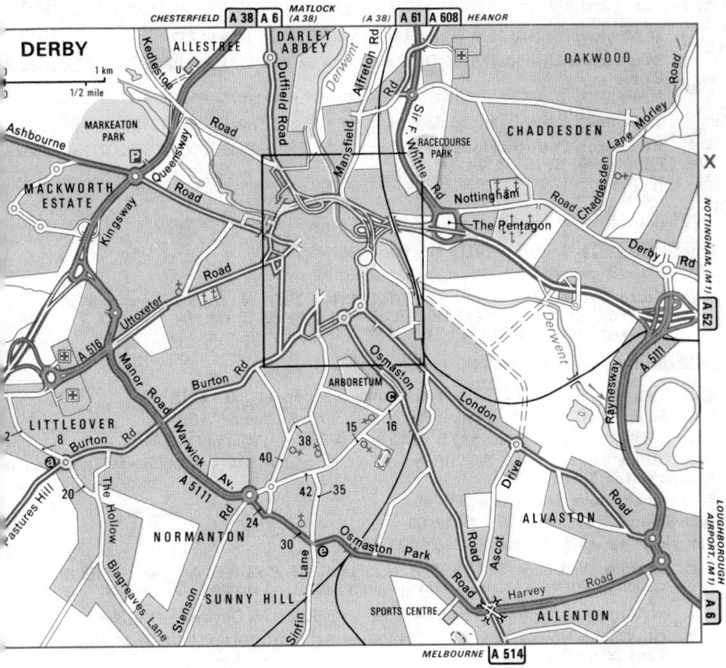

CHESTERFIELD A 38 A 6 MATLOCK (A 38)
(A 38) A 61 A 608 HEANOR
DERBY
1 km
1/2 mile
ALLESTREE
DARLEY ABBEY
Kedleston
Duffield Road
Derwent
Alfreton Rd
Rd
OAKWOOD
Road
Ashbourne
MARKEATON PARK
Queensway
Road
Mansfield
Sir F. Whittle Rd
RACECOURSE PARK
CHADDESDEN
Lane Morley
Chaddesden
X
MACKWORTH ESTATE
Road
Kingsway
Nottingham
Road
The Pentagon
NOTTINGHAM (M 1)
Derby Rd
Road
Uttoxeter
A 516
A 52
Derwent
Raynesway
A 5111
Manor Road
Burton Rd
ARBORETUM
Osmaston
London
LITTLEOVER
Burton Rd
Warwick Av.
A 5111
Rd
The Hollow
Pastures Hill
NORMANTON
Drive
Road
ALVASTON
LOUGHBOROUGH AIRPORT, (M 1)
Osmaston Park
Road
Ascot
Road
Harvey
Road
Blagreaves Lane
Stenson
SUNNY HILL
Lane
Sinfin
SPORTS CENTRE
ALLENTON
A 6
MELBOURNE A 514

A 6
A 61
CENTRE
200 m
200 yards
Mansfield Road
Sir F. Whittle Road
Derwent
Garden St.
Lodge La.
Alkmund's
Saint
Fox Street
Stores Road
Way
Nottingham
Road
Y
Eastgate
A 52
POL.
Friar Gate
Ford St.
Derwent St.
M1
Morledge
The Cock Pitt
A 516
Curzon St.
Macklin St.
MARKET
EAGLE
CENTRE
Station App.
Siddals Rd
Park St.
Traffic St.
Z
Street
Street
Green
Osmaston
Railway Ter.
Canal St.
Abbey
Gerard
Road
London
Road
MIDLAND
Burton
Lane
Litchurch St.
Road
A 5250 (A 38)
Mill Hill
M2
A 514
A 6

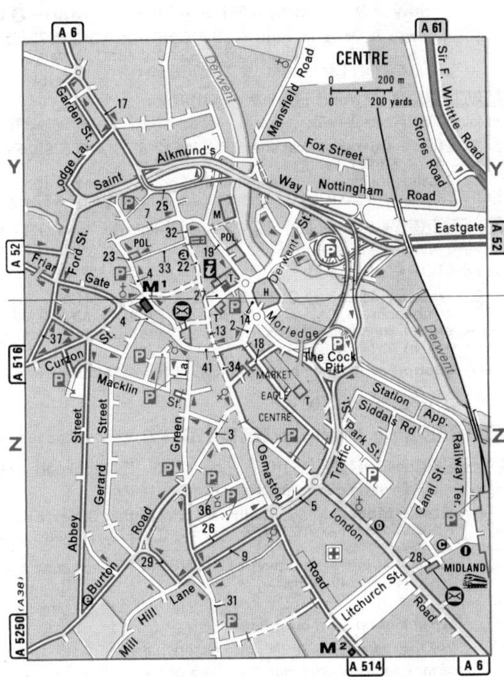

at Mackworth NW : 2 3⁄4 m. by A 52 – X – ✉ Derby – ☎ 01332 :

Mackworth, Ashbourne Rd, DE22 4LY, on A 52 ☎ 824324, Fax 824692, – TV ☎ P. AE VISA
Meals (carving rest.) 8.95 **t.** (lunch) and a la carte – **14 rm** 44.50/59.00 **t.**

at Kedleston NW : 4 m. by Kedleston Rd – X – ✉ Derby – ☎ 01332 :

Kedleston Country House, Kedleston Rd, DE22 5JD, E : 2 m. ☎ 559202, Fax 558822 TV ☎ ♿ P. AE VISA.
Meals *(closed Sunday dinner)* 8.95/16.95 **st.** and a la carte 6.25 – **14 rm** 39.50/56.00 **st.** – SB.

ATS Gosforth Rd, off Ascot Drive ☎ 340854 ATS 67 Bridge St. ☎ 347327

DESBOROUGH Northants. 404 R 26 – pop. 7 351 – ☎ 01536.
London 83 – Birmingham 52 – Leicester 20 – Northampton 20.

Forte Travelodge, Harborough Rd, NN14 2UG, N : 1 ½ m. on A 6 ☎ 76203 Reservations (Freephone) 0800 850950 – TV ♿ P. AE VISA.
Meals (grill rest.) – **32 rm** 34.50 **t.**

DETHICK Derbs. – see Matlock.

DEVIZES Wilts. 403 404 O 29 **The West Country G.** – pop. 11 250 – ☎ 01380.
See : St. John's Church★★ – Market Place★ – Devizes Museum★ *AC.*
Envir. : Potterne (Porch House★★) S : 2½ m. by A 360 – E : Vale of Pewsey★.
Exc. : Stonehenge★★★ *AC,* SE : 16 m. by A 360 and A 344 – Avebury★★ (The Stones★, Church★) NE : 7 m. by A 361.
Erlestoke Sands, Erlestoke ☎ 831069.
39 St. John's St., SN10 1BN ☎ 729408.
London 98 – Bristol 38 – Salisbury 25 – Swindon 19.

Rathlin, Wick Lane, SN10 5DP, S : ¾ m. by A 360 ☎ 721999, – rest TV P.
closed Christmas – **Meals** (by arrangement) 8.50 **st.** – **3 rm** 25.00/40.00 **st.**

at Market Lavington S : 6 m. by A 360 on B 3098 – ✉ Devizes – ☎ 01380 :

Old Coach House without rest., 21 Church St., SN10 4DU, ☎ 812879, – TV P.
4 rm 22.00/40.00 **st.**

at Rowde NW : 2 m. by A 361 on A 342 – ✉ Devizes – ☎ 01380 :

George & Dragon, High St., SN10 2PN, on A 342 ☎ 723053, Fax 724738, – P. VISA
closed Sunday, Monday, 25 December and 1 January – **Meals** (booking essential) 10.00 **t.** (lunch) and a la carte 12.50/29.50 **t.**

DEWSBURY W. Yorks. 402 P 22 – ☎ 01924.
London 205 – Leeds 9 – Manchester 40 – Middlesbrough 76 – Sheffield 31.

Heath Cottage, Wakefield Rd, WF12 8ET, ☎ 465399, Fax 459405 – rm TV ☎ P 70. VISA.
Meals (meals by arrangement Sunday dinner) (booking essential Bank Holiday Mondays) 10.00/19.00 **t.** and dinner a la carte 4.50 – **27 rm** 45.00/60.00 **t.** – SB.

DIDDLEBURY Shrops. 402 403 L 26 **Great Britain G.** – pop. 911 – ✉ Craven Arms – ☎ 01584.
Envir. : NW : Wenlock Edge★.
London 169 – Birmingham 46.

Delbury Hall , SY7 9DH, on B 4368 ☎ 841267, Fax 841441, ←, « Country house atmosphere », , , park, – TV ☎ P. VISA.
closed Christmas – **Meals** (by arrangement) (communal dining) (dinner only) 25.00 **s.** 5.00 – **3 rm** 50.00/80.00 **s.**

Glebe Farm without rest., SY7 9DH, ☎ 841221, « Part Elizabethan house », – TV P.
3 rm 28.00/52.00 **st.**

DIDSBURY Gtr. Manchester 402 403 404 N 23 – see Manchester.

DISLEY Ches. 402 403 404 N 23 – pop. 4 590 – ✉ Stockport – ☎ 01663.
London 187 – Chesterfield 35 – Manchester 12.

Stakis Moorside , Mudhurst Lane, Higher Disley, SK12 2AP, SE : 2 m. by Buxton Old Rd ☎ 764151, Fax 762794, ←, , , , 9, , squash – rm TV ☎ P – 50. AE VISA
Meals (bar lunch Saturday) 12.50/20.00 **st.** and a la carte 4.50 – 8.50 – **94 rm** 80.00/100.00 **st.**, 1 suite – SB.

When looking for a quiet hotel
use the maps found in the introductory pages
or look for establishments with the sign or .

DISS Norfolk 404 X 26 – pop. 6 301 – ☎ 01379.

Meres Mouth, Mere St., IP22 3AG ☎ 650523.

London 98 – ♦Ipswich 25 – ♦Norwich 21 – Thetford 17.

Malt House, Palgrave, IP22 1AE, SW : 1 m. by Denmark St. ☎ 642107, Fax 640315, « Gardens », – – rm TV P. VISA.
closed 20 December-5 January – **Meals** (by arrangement) (communal dining) 17.00 **s.** – **3 rm** 30.00/60.00 **s.** – SB.

Weavers, Market Hill, IP22 3JZ, ☎ 642411 – VISA JCB
closed Saturday lunch, Sunday, Monday, 2 weeks late August and 1 week Christmas – **Meals** 9.95/12.00 **st.** and dinner a la carte.

at Gissing NE : 5 m. by Burston rd – ✉ Diss – ☎ 01379 :

Old Rectory , Rectory Rd, IP22 3XB, ☎ 677575, Fax 674427, ←, , – TV P. VISA.
closed 3 days at Christmas – **Meals** *(closed Monday and Thursday)* (by arrangement) (communal dining) (dinner only) (unlicensed) 20.00 **st.** – **3 rm** 36.00/58.00 **s.**

at Scole E : 2½ m. by A 1066 on A 143 – ✉ Diss – ☎ 01379 :

Scole Inn, Norwich Rd, IP21 4DR, ☎ 740481, Fax 740762, « 17C inn » – rest TV ☎ P – 40. AE VISA.
Meals *(closed Saturday lunch)* 9.95/14.95 **st.** and a la carte – **23 rm** (dinner included) 60.00/89.00 **st.** – SB.

at Brome (Suffolk) SE : 2¾ m. by A 143 on B 1077 – ✉ Eye – ☎ 01379 :

Oaksmere , IP23 8AJ, ☎ 870326, Fax 870051, « Part 16C house, topiary gardens », park – TV ☎ P – 40
11 rm.

at South Lopham W : 5½ m. on A 1066 – ✉ Diss – ☎ 01379 :

Malting Farm without rest., Blo Norton Rd, IP22 2HT, ☎ 687201, ←, « Working farm » – P. .
closed Christmas and New Year – **3 rm** 25.00/38.00.

at Fersfield NW : 7 m. by A 1066 – ✉ Diss – ☎ 01379 :

The Strenneth , Airfield Rd, IP22 2BP, ☎ 688182, Fax 688260, – TV P. VISA
Meals (by arrangement) 13.00 – **7 rm** 25.00/44.00 – SB.

ATS Shelfanger Rd ☎ 642861

DITTON PRIORS Shrops. 403 404 M 26 – pop. 680 – ✉ Bridgnorth – ☎ 01746.

London 154 – ♦Birmingham 34 – Ludlow 13 – Shrewsbury 21.

Middleton Lodge without rest., Middleton Priors, WV16 6UR, N : 1 m. ☎ 712228, « Part 17C hunting lodge », – TV P.
closed Christmas – **3 rm** 25.00/55.00.

Howard Arms, WV16 6SQ, ☎ 712200, – P. VISA
closed Sunday dinner, Monday and 2 weeks September – **Meals** (dinner only and Sunday lunch)/dinner 24.00 **t.** 4.85.

DODDISCOMBSLEIGH Devon – see Exeter.

DONCASTER S. Yorks. 402 403 404 Q 23 – pop. 288 854 – ☎ 01302.

Doncaster Town Moor, Bawtry Rd, Bellevue ☎ 533778 – Crookhill Park, Conisborough ☎ (01709) 862979 – Wheatley, Amthorpe Rd ☎ 831655 – Owston Park, Owston Hall, Owston ☎ 330821.

Central Library, Waterdale, DN1 3JE ☎ 734309.

London 173 – ♦Kingston-upon-Hull 46 – ♦Leeds 30 – ♦Nottingham 46 – ♦Sheffield 19.

Doncaster Moat House (Q.M.H.), Warmsworth, DN4 9UX, SW : 2¾ m. on A 630 ☎ 799988, Fax 310197, , , – rm TV ☎ P – 350. AE VISA JCB
Meals *(closed lunch Saturday and Bank Holidays)* 9.95/18.75 **t.** and a la carte 5.20 – 8.50 – **98 rm** 83.50/105.00 **t.**, 2 suites – SB.

Danum Swallow, High St., DN1 1DN, ☎ 342261, Fax 329034 – rm TV ☎ P – 350. AE VISA
Meals *(closed Saturday lunch)* 7.95/15.95 **st.** and a la carte 5.50 – **64 rm** 78.00/90.00 **st.**, 2 suites – SB.

Grand St. Leger, Racecourse Roundabout, Bennetthorpe, DN2 6AX, SE : 1½ m. on A 638 ☎ 364111, Fax 329865 – TV ☎ P – 60. AE VISA.
Meals 11.95/16.95 **t.** and a la carte 4.80 – **20 rm** 66.00/90.00 **t.**

Punch's (Toby), Bawtry Rd, Bessacarr, DN4 7BS, SE : 3 m. on A 638 ☎ 370037, Fax 532281 – rm TV ☎ P – 40. AE VISA JCB
Meals (grill rest.) 7.90/18.00 and a la carte 5.00 – **24 rm** 52.00/62.00 **st.** – SB.

Campanile, Doncaster Leisure Park, Bawtry Rd, DN4 7PD, SE : 2 m. on A 638 ☎ 370770, Fax 370813 – rm TV ☎ P – 30. AE VISA
Meals 10.35 **t.** and a la carte 4.95 – 4.50 – **50 rm** 35.75 **st.**

at Rossington SE : 6 m. on A 638 – ✉ Doncaster – ☎ 01302 :

Mount Pleasant, Great North Rd, DN11 0HP, on A 638 ☎ 868219, Fax 865130, – 60. AE VISA JCB.
Meals 8.50/16.00 **t.** and a la carte 4.00 – **30 rm** 48.00/73.00 **t.**, 1 suite – SB.

at Carcroft NW : 6½ m. on A 1 – ✉ Doncaster – ☎ 01302 :

Forte Travelodge, Great North Rd, (northbound carriageway) ☎ 330841, Reservatio (Freephone) 0800 850950 – . AE VISA.
Meals (grill rest.) – **40 rm** 34.50 **t.**

ATS Heavnens Walk ☎ 367337/367338/360249/340797

DORCHESTER Dorset 403 404 M 31 The West Country G. – pop. 15 037 – ☎ 01305.

See : Town★ - Dorset County Museum★ *AC.*

Envir. : Maiden Castle★★ (≤★) SW : 2½m. – Puddletown Church★, NE : 5½m. by A 35.

Exc. : Moreton Church★★, E : 7½ m. – Bere Regis (St. John the Baptist Church★★) NE : 11 r by A 35 – Athelhampton★ *AC*, NE : 6½ m. by A 35 - Cerne Abbas★, N : 7 m. by A 352.

18 Came Down ☎ 812531.

Unit 11, Antelope Walk, Dorchester, DT1 1BE ☎ 267992.

London 135 – Bournemouth 27 – Exeter 53 – Southampton 53.

King's Arms, 30 High East St., DT1 1HF, ☎ 265353, Fax 260269 – rm – 80. AE VISA.
Meals 8.95/19.50 **t.** and a la carte – 4.45 – **31 rm** 39.50/99.00 **t.** – SB.

Wessex Royale, 32 High West St., DT1 1UP, ☎ 262660, Fax 251941 – – 100. AE VISA JCB
Meals 12.00 **t.** and dinner a la carte 6.95 – **23 rm** 39.95/49.95 **st.** – SB.

Casterbridge without rest., 49 High East St., DT1 1HU, ☎ 264043, Fax 26088 « Georgian town house » – . AE VISA.
closed 25 and 26 December – **14 rm** 32.00/65.00 **st.**

Yalbury Cottage, Lower Bockhampton, DT2 8PZ, E : 2 ¼ m. by B 3150 an Bockhampton rd ☎ 262382, Fax 266412, – . VISA JCB.
closed 2 weeks January – **Meals** (dinner only and Sunday lunch) 17.50 **st.** 4.50 – **8 r** (dinner included) 60.00/100.00 **st.** – SB.

Westwood House without rest., 29 High West St., DT1 1UP, ☎ 268018, Fax 250282 – . AE VISA
7 rm 29.50/59.50 **st.**

Junction, 42 Great Western Rd, DT1 1UF, ☎ 268826 – – 60. VISA.
closed 25 December – **Meals** *(closed dinner Friday to Sunday)* (in bar) a la cart approx. 7.95 **t.** 3.95 – 4.50 – **6 rm** 32.00/41.00 **st.**

Mock Turtle, 34 High West St., DT1 1UP, ☎ 264011 – VISA
closed 1-2 January and 26-27 December – **Meals** *(closed lunch Monday and Saturday ar Sunday)* 13.75 **t.** (lunch) and dinner a la carte 15.75/20.50 **t.** 5.75.

Shapla Tandoori, 14 High East St., DT1 1HH, ☎ 269202 –
Meals - Indian rest.

at Frampton NW : 6 m. by B 3147 and A 37 on A 356 – ✉ Dorchester – ☎ 01300 :

Hyde Farm House, DT2 9NG, NW :½ m. on A 356 ☎ 320272, ≤, « Part 18C and 19 house », – rm .
Meals (dinner only) (unlicensed) 12.50 **st.** – **3 rm** 25.00/50.00 **st.**

ATS Unit 4, Great Western Ind. Centre ☎ 264756

DORCHESTER Oxon. 403 404 Q 29 Great Britain G. – pop. 1 5037 – ☎ 01865.

See : Town★.

Exc. : Ridgeway Path★★.

London 51 – Abingdon 6 – Oxford 8 – Reading 17.

George, 23 High St., OX10 7HH, ☎ 340404, Fax 341620, « Part 14C coaching inn », – 40. AE VISA.
closed 27 to 30 December – **Meals** a la carte 18.75/28.75 **t.** – **17 rm** 55.00/70.00 **t.** – SB.

White Hart, 26 High St., OX10 7HN, ☎ 340074, Fax 341082, « 17C coaching inn » – – 35. AE VISA JCB
Meals a la carte 13.20/19.25 **t.** 4.50 – **14 rm** 55.00/85.00 **t.**, 4 suites – SB.

Dieser Führer ist kein vollständiges Hotel- und Restaurantverzeichnis.
Um den Ansprüchen aller Touristen gerecht zu werden,
haben wir uns auf eine Auswahl in jeder Kategorie beschränkt.

DORKING Surrey 404 T 30 – pop. 10 604 – ☎ 01306.

London 26 – ♦Brighton 39 – Guildford 12 – Worthing 33.

Burford Bridge (Forte Heritage), Box Hill, RH5 6BX, N : 1 ½ m. on A 24 ☎ 884561, Fax 880386, heated, – – 150. AE VISA
Meals a la carte 18.45/34.20 **t.** 6.95 – 10.95 – **48 rm** 85.00 **st.**

White Horse (Forte), High St., RH4 1BE, ☎ 881138, Fax 887241 – – 50. AE VISA
Meals 12.25/17.95 **t.** 6.55 – 8.50 – **68 rm** 75.00/85.00 **st.** – SB.

Forte Travelodge, Reigate Rd, RH4 1QB, E : ½ m. on A 25 ☎ 740361, Reservations (Freephone) 0800 850950 – . AE VISA.
Meals (grill rest.) – **29 rm** 34.50 **t.**

Partners West Street, 2-4 West St., RH4 1BL, ☎ 882826 – . AE VISA
closed Saturday lunch, and Sunday dinner – **Meals** 11.95/15.00 **t.** and a la carte 22.65/33.85 **t.** 5.50.

DORMINGTON Heref. and Worcs. – see Hereford.

DORRINGTON Shrops. 402 403 L 26 – see Shrewsbury.

DOULTING 403 404 M 30 – see Shepton Mallet.

LES GUIDES VERTS MICHELIN

Paysages, monuments
Routes touristiques
Géographie
Histoire, Art
Itinéraires de visite
Plans de villes et de monuments

DOVER Kent 404 Y 30 **Great Britain G.** – pop. 103 216 – ☎ 01304.

See : Castle★★ *AC* Y.

to France (Calais) (P & O European Ferries Ltd) (1 h 15), (Calais) (Hoverspeed Ltd) frequent services (35 mn) – to France (Calais) (Stena Line) frequent services (1 h 30 mn).

Townwall St., CT16 1JR ☎ 205108.

♦London 76 – ♦Brighton 84.

Plan on next page

Forte Posthouse, Singledge Lane, Whitfield, CT16 3LF, NW : 3 ½ m. by A 256 on A 2 ☎ 821222, Fax 825576 – rm – 40. AE VISA JCB Z **o**
Meals a la carte 13.00/22.85 **st.** 6.95 – 7.95 – **67 rm** 56.00 **st.** – SB.

County (Q.M.H.), Townwall St., CT16 1SZ, ☎ 509955, Telex 96458, Fax 213230, – rm – 80. AE VISA Y **z**
Meals 16.95/17.95 **st.** and a la carte 5.55 – 8.95 – **79 rm** 65.00/96.00 **st.** – SB.

Travel Inn, Folkestone Rd, CT15 7AB, SW : 2 ½ m. on B 2011 ☎ 213339, Fax 214504 – rm . AE VISA.
closed 24 and 25 December – **Meals** (grill rest.) – 4.95 – **30 rm** 34.50 **t.**

East Lee without rest., 108 Maison Dieu Rd, CT16 1RT, ☎ 210176, Fax 210176 – . VISA. Y **o**
4 rm 30.00/40.00 **st.**

Penny Farthing without rest., 109 Maison Dieu Rd, CT16 1RT, ☎ 205563 – . Y **i**
6 rm 21.00/40.00.

Number One without rest., 1 Castle St., CT16 1QH, ☎ 202007, – . Y **u**
closed 4 days Christmas – **5 rm** 25.00/40.00.

St. Martins and Ardmore without rest., 17-18 Castle Hill Rd, CT16 1QW, ☎ 205938, Fax 208229 – . VISA. Y **r**
10 rm 25.00/45.00 **st.**

at St. Margaret's at Cliffe NE : 4 m. by A 258 – Z – on B 2058 – ✉ Dover – ☎ 01304 :

Wallett's Court with rm, West Cliffe, CT15 6EW, NW : ¾ m. on B 2058 ☎ 852424, Fax 853430, « Part 17C manor house », , – rest . VISA.
closed 24 to 27 December – **Meals** *(closed Sunday)* (dinner only) 27.00 **st.** 8.00 – **10 rm** 50.00/80.00 **st.** – SB.

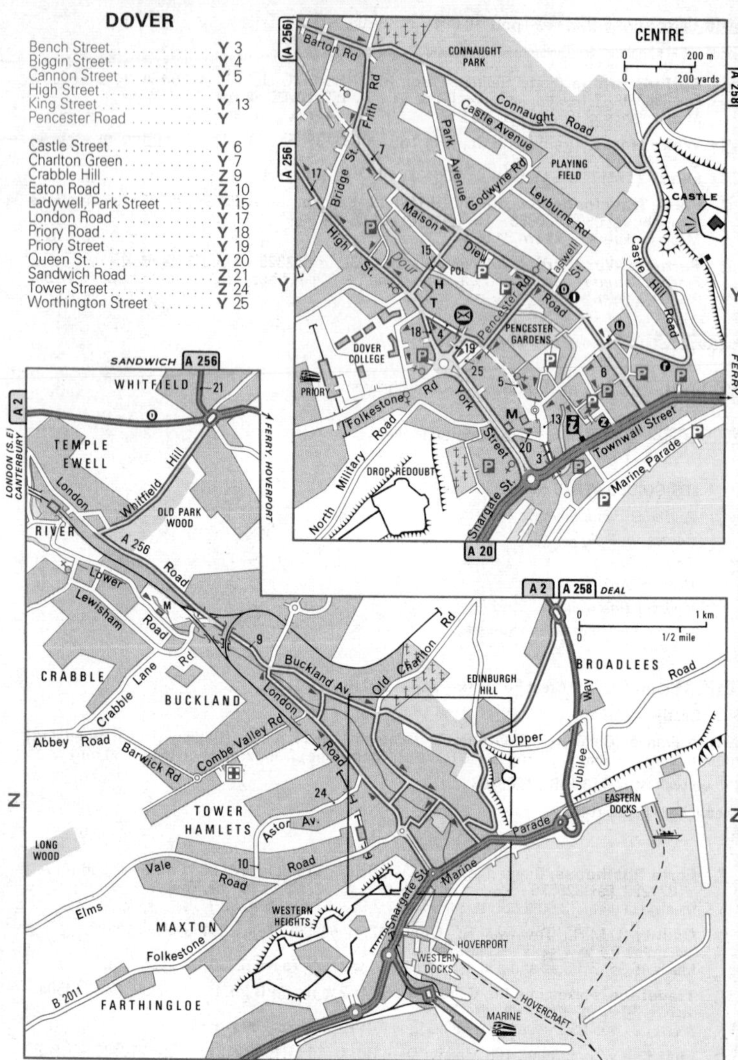

DOVERIDGE Derbs. 402 403 404 O 25 – see Uttoxeter.

DOWN HATHERLEY Glos. – see Gloucester.

DOWNTON Wilts. 403 404 O 31 – see Salisbury.

DREWSTEIGNTON Devon 403 I 31 **The West Country G.** – pop. 668 – ☎ 01647.
Envir. : Dartmoor National Park★★ (Brent Tor ⋞★★, Haytor Rocks ⋞★).
◆London 216 – Exeter 15 – ◆Plymouth 46

⌂ **Hunts Tor,** EX6 6QW, ✆ 281228 – ⇸ rest TV
March-October – **Meals** (booking essential) 17.00 **st.** – **4 rm** ⊐ 30.00/65.00 **st.**

DRIFFIELD Humbs. 402 S 21 – see Great Driffield.

DRIFT Cornwall – see Penzance.

DROITWICH Heref. and Worcs. 403 404 N 27 – pop. 20 966 – ☎ 01905.

Ombersley, Bishopswood Rd ✆ 620747.

St. Richard's House, Victoria Sq., WR9 8DS ✆ 774312.

London 129 – ♦Birmingham 20 – ♦Bristol 66 – Worcester 6.

Forte Travelodge, Rashwood Hill, WR9 8DA, NE : 1 ½ m. on A 38 ✆ (01527) 861545, Reservations (Freephone) 0800 850950 – TV & P. AE VISA.
Meals (grill rest.) – **32 rm** 34.50 **t.**

Rossini, 6 Worcester Rd, WR9 8AB, ✆ 794799 – P. AE VISA
closed Sunday and 25-26 December – **Meals** - Italian - 11.50/19.90 **t.** and a la carte 4.90.

at Feckenham E : 7 ¼ m. on B 4090 – ✉ Redditch – ☎ 01527 :

Steps, 6 High St., B96 6HS, ✆ 892678 – rm
Meals (by arrangement) 12.00 – **3 rm** 20.00/38.00 **s.**

at Smite S : 3 ¾ m. by B 4090, A 38 off A 4538 – ✉ Worcester – ☎ 01905 :

Pear Tree, WR3 8SY, ✆ 756565, Fax 756777 – TV & P – 30. AE VISA JCB.
Meals a la carte 10.50/16.00 **st.** 4.95 – **22 rm** 55.00/68.50 **st.**, 2 suites.

at Hadley Heath SW : 4 m. by Ombersley Way, A 4133 and Ladywood rd – ✉ Droitwich – ☎ 01905 :

Hadley Bowling Green Inn, WR9 0AR, ✆ 620294, Fax 620771 – rest TV P
14 rm.

DRONFIELD Derbs. 402 403 404 P 24 – pop. 13 335 – ✉ Sheffield (S. Yorks.) – ☎ 01246.

London 158 – Derby 30 – ♦ Nottingham 31 – ♦ Sheffield 6.

Manor House, 10-15 High St., S18 6PY, ✆ 413971, Fax 412104 – TV P – 25. AE VISA
Meals *(closed Monday lunch and Sunday dinner)* (residents only Monday dinner) 14.00 **t.** and a la carte 6.95 – **10 rm** 45.00/75.00 **t.** – SB.

Chantry, Church St., S18 6QB, ✆ 413014, Fax 413014, – TV P. AE VISA.
Meals *(closed Sunday)* (residents only) (dinner only) 12.00 **t.** 5.20 – **8 rm** 40.00/50.00 **st.**

Horsleygate Hall without rest., Horsleygate Lane, Holmesfield, S18 5WD, W : 3 ½ m. by B 5056 off B 6054 ✆ (0114) 2890333, « Part Victorian, part Georgian house », – P. – **3 rm** 21.00/40.00 **st.**

DRYBROOK Glos. 403 404 M 28 – ☎ 01594.

London 149 – ♦Bristol 34 – Gloucester 12 – Newport 35.

Cider Press, The Cross, GL17 9EB, ✆ 544472 – . VISA
closed Monday lunch, Tuesday and first 2 weeks January – **Meals** (lunch by arrangement) (dinner by arrangement Sunday and Monday) 15.35/20.35 **t.**

DUDDENHOE END Essex 404 U 27 – see Saffron Walden.

DUDLEY W. Mids. 402 403 404 N 26 **Great Britain G.** – pop. 304 615 – ☎ 01384.

See : Black Country Museum★.

Swindon, Bridgnorth Rd ✆ (01902) 897031 – Sedgley, Sandyfields Rd ✆ (01902) 880503.

39 Churchill Shopping Centre, DY2 7BL, ✆ 457494.

London 132 – ♦Birmingham 10 – Wolverhampton 6.

Plan : see Birmingham p. 2

Copthorne Merry Hill, The Waterfront, Level St., Brierley Hill, DY5 1UR, SW : 2 ¼ m. by A 461 ✆ 482882, Fax 482773, – rm rest TV & P – 250. AE VISA JCB AU **z**
Meals 17.75 **st.** and a la carte 7.15 – 10.25 – **129 rm** 94.00/119.00 **s.**, 9 suites – SB.

Ward Arms (Regal), Birmingham Rd, DY1 4RN, NE : ¾ m. on A 461 ✆ 458070, Fax 457502 – rm TV & P – 100. AE VISA
Meals *(closed Saturday lunch)* 9.00/9.95 **t.** and a la carte 5.25 – **72 rm** 64.00/68.00 **st.**

Forte Travelodge without rest., Dudley Rd, Brierley Hill, DY5 1LQ, SW : 2 m. on A 461 ✆ 481579, Reservations (Freephone) 0800 850950 – TV & P. AE VISA. AU **c**
32 rm 34.50 **t.**

ATS Oakeywell St. ✆ 238047

DULVERTON Somerset 403 J 30 **The West Country G.** – pop. 1 870 (inc. Brushford) – ☎ 01398.

See : Village★ – **Envir.** : Tarr Steps★★, NW : 6 m. by B 3223.

London 198 – Barnstaple 27 – Exeter 26 – Minehead 18 – Taunton 27.

Ashwick House, TA22 9QD, NW : 4 ¼ m. by B 3223 ✆ 323868, Fax 323868, <, « Country house atmosphere », – rest TV P.
Meals (dinner only and Sunday lunch)/dinner 22.75 **t.** 5.95 – **6 rm** (dinner included) 70.00/138.00 **t.** – SB.

at Brushford SW : 1 ¾ m. on B 3223 – ✉ Dulverton – ☎ 01398 :

Carnarvon Arms, TA22 9AE, ℘ 323302, Fax 324022, heated, ⚲, ⚘, park, ✂ – TV – P – 100. AE VISA
Meals 10.50/22.50 **t.** and lunch a la carte – **24 rm** ⊐ 35.00/80.00 **t.**, 1 suite – SB.

DUNCHURCH Warks. 403 404 Q 26 – pop. 2 904 (inc. Thurlaston) – ✉ Rugby – ☎ 01788.
♦London 90 – ♦Coventry 12 – ♦Leicester 24 – Northampton 26.

Forte Travelodge, London Rd, Thurlaston, CV23 9LG, NW : 2½ m. on A 45 ℘ 52153
Reservations (Freephone) 0800 850950 – TV & P. AE VISA. ✻
Meals (grill rest.) – **40 rm** 34.50 **t.**

DUNSFORD Devon 403 I 31 – pop. 1212 – ☎ 01647.
♦London 206 – Exeter 6 – ♦Plymouth 35.

Rock House ⚲, EX6 7EP, SE : 1½ m. by B 3212 off Christow rd ℘ 252514, ≤, ⚘, park
P. ✻
Meals 22.50 **st.** 3.00 – **3 rm** ⊐ 55.00 **st.**

DUNSLEY N. Yorks. – see Whitby.

DUNSTABLE Beds. 404 S 28 – pop. 32 845 – ☎ 01582.
18 Tilsworth, Dunstable Rd ℘ (01525) 210721/210722.
ℹ The Library, Vernon Pl., LU5 4HA ℘ 471012.
♦London 40 – Bedford 24 – Luton 4.5 – Northampton 35.

Old Palace Lodge, Church St., LU5 4RT, ℘ 662201, Fax 696422 – ⇕ ✻ rm ▤ rest TV
P – 35. AE ⓓ VISA JCB
Meals *(closed Saturday lunch)* 14.50/17.50 **st.** and a la carte – ⊐ 8.75 – **49 rm** 73.5
83.50 **st.**

Highwayman, London Rd, LU6 3DX, SE : 1 m. on A 5 ℘ 601122, Fax 603812 – TV ☎
P – 40. AE ⓓ VISA. ✻
Meals (lunch by arrangement Monday to Saturday) a la carte 8.45/12.90 **st.** – **51 r**
⊐ 47.00/56.00 **st.** – SB.

at Hockliffe NW : 3¼ m. on A 5 – ✉ Dunstable – ☎ 01525 :

Forte Travelodge, LU7 9LZ, ℘ 211177, Reservations (Freephone) 0800 850950 – TV
P. AE VISA. ✻
Meals (grill rest.) – **28 rm** 34.50 **t.**

DUNSTER Somerset 403 J 30 **The West Country G.** – pop. 848 – ✉ Minehead – ☎ 01643.
See : Town★★ - Castle★★ *AC* (Upper rooms ≤★) – Dunster Water Mill★ *AC* – St. Georg
Church★ – Dovecote★.
Envir. : Exmoor National Park★★ (Dunkery Beacon★★★, Watersmeet★, Valley of the Rocks
Vantage Point★) – Cleeve Abbey★★ *AC*, SE : 5 m. by A 39 – Timberscombe (Church★) SW
3½ m. by A 396.
♦London 184 – ♦Bristol 61 – Exeter 40 – Taunton 22.

Luttrell Arms (Forte Heritage), 36 High St., TA24 6SG, ℘ 821555, Fax 821567, « Part 15
inn », ⚘ – ✻ TV ☎. AE ⓓ VISA JCB
Meals (bar lunch Monday to Saturday)/dinner 19.95 **st.** and a la carte – ⊐ 8.50 – **27 r**
75.00/95.00 **st.** – SB.

Exmoor House, 12 West St., TA24 6SN, ℘ 821268, ⚘ – ✻ TV. AE ⓓ VISA JCB
closed December and January – **Meals** (dinner only) 15.50 **st.** 4.90 – **7 rm** ⊐ 34.5
59.00 **st.** – SB.

DURHAM Durham 401 402 P 19 **Great Britain G.** – pop. 36 937 – ☎ 0191.
See : City★★★ - Cathedral★★★ (Nave★★★, Chapel of the Nine Altars★★★, Sanctuary Knocker
B – Oriental Museum★★ *AC* (at Durham University by A 167) B – City and Riverside (Prebenc
Bridge ≤★★★ A , Framwellgate Bridge ≤★★ B) – Monastic Buildings (Cathedral Treasury
Central Tower ≤★) B – Castle★ (Norman chapel★) *AC* B.
18 Mount Oswald, South Rd ℘ 386 7527.
ℹ Market Pl., DH1 3NJ ℘ 384 3720.
♦London 267 – ♦Leeds 77 – ♦Middlesbrough 23 – Sunderland 12.

Plan opposite

Royal County (Swallow), Old Elvet, DH1 3JN, ℘ 386 6821, Fax 386 0704, ⚲, ≘s, ⊠ –
✻ rm ▤ rest TV ☎ & P – 120. AE ⓓ VISA B
County : **Meals** 13.00/21.00 **st.** and a la carte 6.75 – **Bowes Brasserie** : **Meals** 6.5
10.50 **st.** and a la carte 6.75 – **149 rm** ⊐ 85.00/130.00 **st.**, 1 suite – SB.

Three Tuns Swallow, New Elvet, DH1 3AQ, ℘ 386 4326, Fax 386 1406 – ✻ rm TV
P – 250. AE ⓓ VISA JCB B
Meals *(closed Saturday lunch)* 10.00/17.00 **st.** and a la carte 6.95 – **46 rm** ⊐ 89.0
109.00 **st.**, 1 suite – SB.

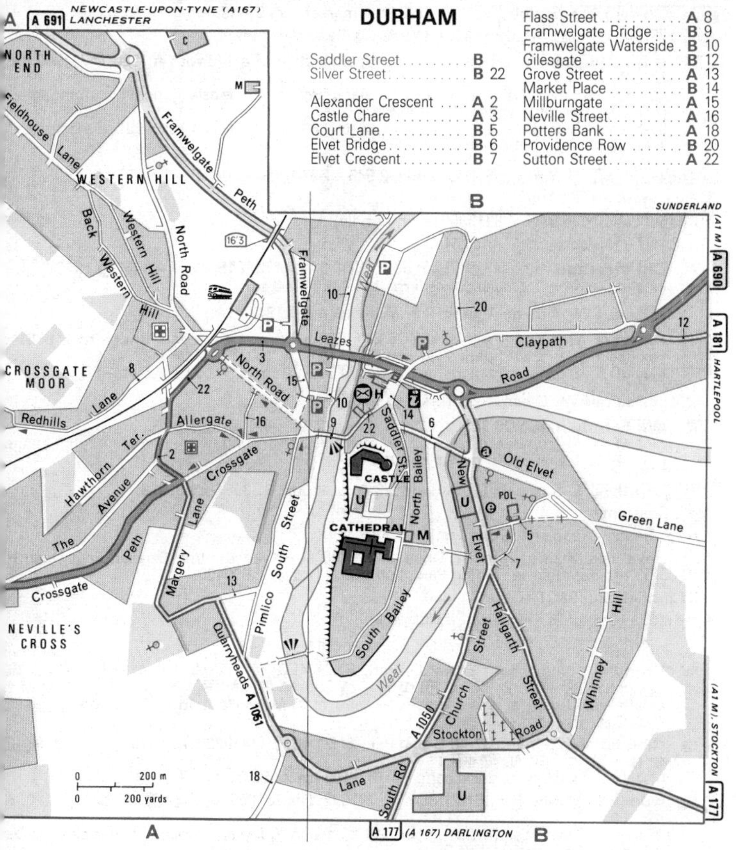

at Croxdale S : 3 m. by A 1050 on A 167 – B – ✉ Durham – ☎ 0191 :

Bridge Toby, DH1 3SP, ☎ 378 0524, Fax 378 9981 – ⇔ rm TV ☎ P – 🎤 50. AE ① VISA

Meals (grill rest.) 8.75 **t.** and a la carte – **46 rm** ☐ 52.00/62.00 **st.** – SB.

ATS Finchale Rd, Newton Hall ☎ 384 1810 ATS Mill Rd, Langley Moor ☎ 378 0262

DUXFORD Cambs. 404 U 27 – see Cambridge.

EAGLESCLIFFE Cleveland 402 P 20 – see Stockton-on-Tees.

EARL'S COLNE Essex 404 W 28 pop. 3 769 – ✉ Colchester – ☎ 01787.

London 55 – Cambridge 33 – Chelmsford 22 – Colchester 10.

Elm House, 14 Upper Holt St., CO6 2PG, on A 604 ☎ 222197, ⚘ – ⇔ rm
closed Christmas and New Year – **Meals** (by arrangement) (communal dining) 15.00 **s.** – **3 rm** ☐ 19.00/50.00 **s.**

EARL SHILTON Leics. 403 404 Q 26 – pop. 9 101 – ✉ Leicester – ☎ 01455.

London 107 – Birmingham 35 – Coventry 16 – Leicester 9 – Nottingham 35.

Mill on the Soar, Coventry Rd, Sutton in the Elms, LE9 6JU, SE : 4½ m. by B 581 on B 4114 ☎ 282419, Fax 285937, ⚘ – TV ☎ P – 🎤 40. AE ① VISA. ⚘
Meals (in bar) a la carte 9.00/13.85 **t.** 🍷 4.10 – ☐ 4.95 – **20 rm** 39.50 **t.**

EARL SOHAM Suffolk 404 X 27 – see Framlingham.

The Guide is updated annually so renew your Guide every year.

EARL STONHAM Suffolk 404 X 27 – ✉ Stowmarket – ☎ 01449.

♦London 81 – ♦Cambridge 47 – ♦Ipswich 10 – ♦Norwich 33.

XX ✿ **Mr. Underhill's** (Bradley), IP14 5DW, at junction of A 140 with A 1120 ✆ 711206 – Ⓟ VISA
closed Sunday dinner, Monday and Bank Holidays – **Meals** (lunch by arrangement) (booking essential)/dinner 21.00/34.25 **t.** 5.75
Spec. Roast smoked haddock on a bed of spinach and sorrel, Fillet of beef with white truffle and local wild mushrooms, Italian style bread and butter pudding.

EASINGWOLD N. Yorks. 402 Q 21 – pop. 3 545 – ✉ York – ☎ 01347.

Stillington Rd ✆ 821486.

Chapel Lane, YO6 3AE ✆ 821530 (summer only).

♦London 217 – ♦Middlesbrough 37 – York 14.

Old Vicarage without rest., Market Pl., YO6 3AL, ✆ 821015, – TV Ⓟ.
closed December and January – **5 rm** 24.00/42.00 **st.**

at Alne SW : 4 m. on Alne Rd – ✉ Aldwark – ☎ 01347 :

Aldwark Manor, Aldwark, YO6 2NF, SW : 3½ m. by Aldwark Bridge rd ✆ 838146 Fax 838867, ←, 18, , park – rest TV ☎ Ⓟ – 100. AE VISA
Meals 9.50/24.00 **st.** and dinner a la carte 4.50 – **20 rm** 50.00/80.00 **st.** – SB.

at Raskelf W : 2¾ m. – ✉ York – ☎ 01347 :

Old Farmhouse, YO6 3LF, ✆ 821971, Fax 822392 – rest TV ☎ Ⓟ
closed 22 December-31 January – **Meals** *(closed Sunday to non-residents)* (dinner only) 17.00 **t.** 4.00 – **10 rm** 29.00/50.00 **t.** – SB.

EASTBOURNE E. Sussex 404 U 31 **Great Britain G.** – pop. 81 395 – ☎ 01323.

See : Seafront★.

Envir. : Beachy Head★★★, SW : 3 m. by B 2103 Z.

18, 9 Royal Eastbourne, Paradise Drive ✆ 729738 Z – 18 Eastbourne Downs, East Dean R ✆ 720827, – 9 Eastbourne Golfing Park, Lottbridge Drove ✆ 520400.

3 Cornfield Rd, BN21 4QL ✆ 411400.

♦London 68 – ♦Brighton 25 – ♦Dover 61 – Maidstone 49.

Plan opposite

Grand (De Vere), King Edward's Par., BN21 4EQ, ✆ 412345, Fax 412233, ←, , heated, , – rm TV ☎ Ⓟ – 350. AE VISA Z
Meals 19.00/25.00 **st.** and a la carte – (see also ***Mirabelle*** below) – **149 rm** 95.00/160.00 **st.**, 15 suites – SB.

Cavendish (De Vere), 37-40 Grand Par., BN21 4DH, ✆ 410222, Fax 410941, ← – ☎ Ⓟ – 200. AE VISA X
Meals 6.95/17.50 **st.** and a la carte 4.75 – **108 rm** 80.00/145.00 **st.**, 4 suites – SB.

Queen's, Marine Par., BN21 3DY, ✆ 722822, Fax 731056, ← – TV ☎ Ⓟ – 120. VISA. Y
closed 18 November-18 December and 2 January-6 March – **Meals** (dinner only) 9.00 **st.** 3.95 – **106 rm** 39.00/64.00 **st.**

Lansdowne, King Edward's Par., BN21 4EE, ✆ 725174, Fax 739721, ← – TV ☎ 130. AE VISA JCB Z
closed 1 to 13 January – **Meals** 15.00 **t.** (dinner) and a la carte 7.50/9.50 **t.** 5.00 – **122 rm** 49.00/94.00 **st.** – SB.

Langham, Royal Par., BN22 7AH, ✆ 731451, Fax 646623, ← – TV ☎. AE VISA JCB
Meals 6.95/9.95 **t.** and dinner a la carte 5.00 – **87 rm** (dinner included) 34.95/69.90 **t.** – SB. Z

Wish Tower, King Edward's Par., BN21 4EB, ✆ 722676, Fax 721474, ← – TV ☎ 40. AE VISA Z
Meals (bar lunch Monday to Saturday)/dinner 18.95 **t.** 5.00 – **65 rm** 58.00/116.00 **t.** – SB.

Brownings, 28 Upperton Rd, BN21 1JS, ✆ 724358, Fax 731288, heated – TV ☎ Ⓟ 40. AE VISA. Z
Meals *(closed Sunday dinner)* (dinner only and Sunday lunch)/dinner 12.95 **t.** – **10 rm** 38.00/60.00 **t.**

Oban, King Edward's Par., BN21 4DS, ✆ 731581, Fax 731581 – TV ☎. AE VISA X
closed January and February – **Meals** (bar lunch)/dinner 15.50 and a la carte – **31 rm** 30.00/70.00 **st.** – SB.

Camelot Lodge, 35 Lewes Rd, BN21 2BU, ✆ 725207 – rest TV Ⓟ. VISA. V
April-October – **Meals** (by arrangement) 8.00 **st.** – **9 rm** 24.50/43.00 **st.**

Far End, 139 Royal Par., BN22 7LH, ✆ 725666 – rest TV Ⓟ Y
Meals (by arrangement) – **10 rm** 18.00/44.00 **s.**

Cherry Tree, 15 Silverdale Rd, BN20 7AJ, ✆ 722406 – rest TV ☎. AE VISA.
Meals (by arrangement) 16.50 **t.** 3.50 – **10 rm** 22.00/54.00 **t.** – SB. Z

Southcroft, 15 South Cliff Av., BN20 7AH, ✆ 729071 – . Z
Meals (by arrangement) 7.00 **st.** 2.50 – **6 rm** 21.00/42.00 **st.** – SB.

EASTBOURNE

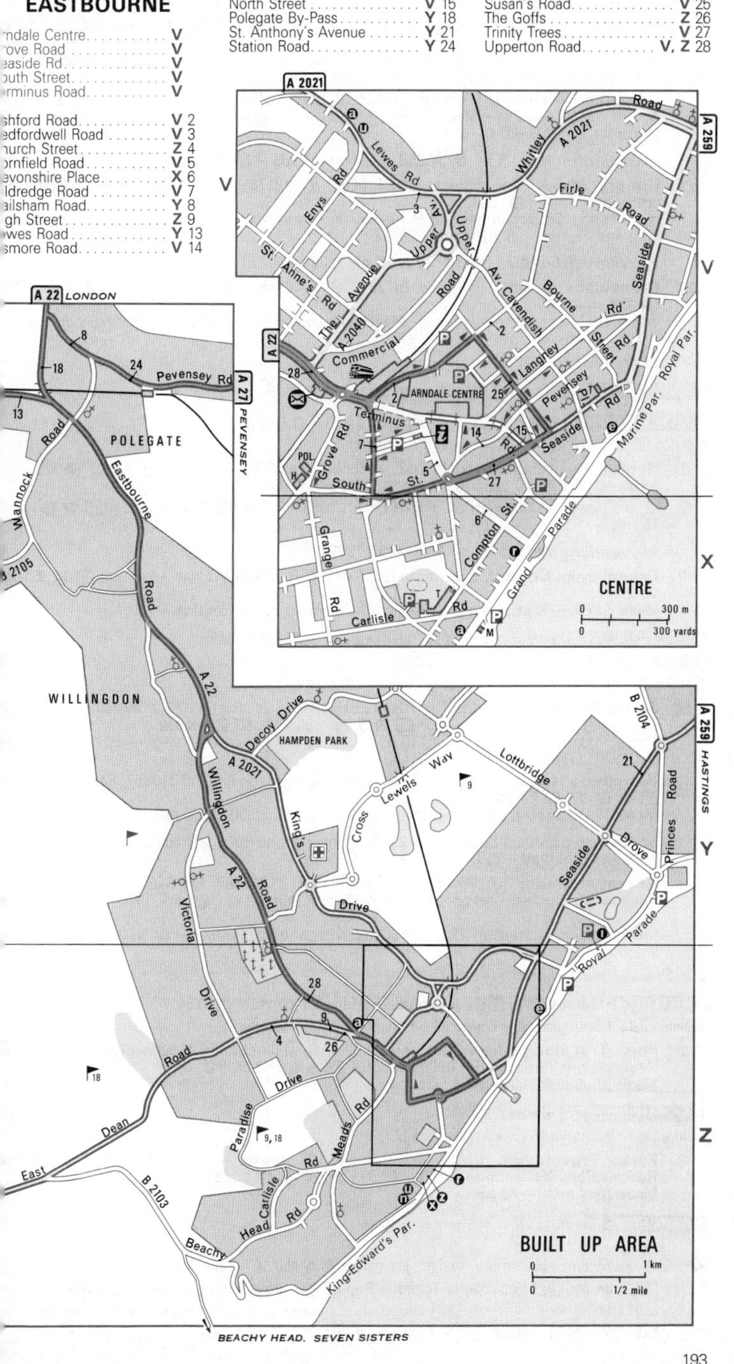

A 2021
Lewes Rd
Whitley Road
A 2021
A 259
Firle Road
Enys Rd
Upper Av.
Upper
St. Anne's Rd
The Avenue
A 2040
Road
Cavendish Av.
Bourne
Seaside
Rd
Royal Par.
Commercial
A 22
ARNDALE CENTRE
Langney
Street
Rd
Pevensey Rd
Terminus
Grove Rd
POL.
South St.
Seaside
Marine Par.
Compton St.
Grange Rd
Parade
Grand
Carlisle Rd
CENTRE
300 m
300 yards
V
X
A 22 LONDON
Pevensey Rd
A 27 PEVENSEY
POLEGATE
Wannock Road
Eastbourne
Road
B 2105
WILLINGDON
A 22
Decoy Drive
HAMPDEN PARK
A 2021
Lewels Way
Lottbridge
Cross
King's
Willingdon
Road
Drive
B 2104
A 259 HASTINGS
Road
Princes
Drove
Seaside
Victoria
Drive
Royal Parade
Road
Dean
East
Drive
Paradise
Rd
Meads
B 2103
Head Carlisle Rd
Beachy
King Edward's Par.
BUILT UP AREA
1 km
1/2 mile
Y
Z
BEACHY HEAD. SEVEN SISTERS

XXXX **Mirabelle** (at Grand H.), King Edward's Par., BN21 4EQ, ✆ 410771, Fax 412233 – ▤ AE VISA Z
closed Sunday, Monday, first 2 weeks January and first 2 weeks August – **Meals** *(closed Sunday and Monday)* 15.50/29.00 **st.** and a la carte.

XX **Downland** with rm, 37 Lewes Rd, BN21 2BU, ✆ 732689 – TV ☎ P. AE VISA JCB. V
closed 1 to 25 January – **Meals** *(closed Monday)* (dinner only) 17.50 **t.** and a la carte 4.50 – **14 rm** 27.50/65.00 **t.** – SB.

at Jevington NW : 6 m. by A 259 – Z – on B 2105 – ✉ Polegate – ☎ 01323 :

XX **Hungry Monk,** The Street, BN26 5QF, ✆ 482178, Fax 483989, « Part Elizabethan cottages », – P. AE
closed 24 to 26 December and Bank Holiday Mondays – **Meals** (booking essential) (dinner only and Sunday lunch)/dinner 22.90 **t.**

at Wilmington NW : 6½ m. by A 22 on A 27 – Y – ✉ Eastbourne – ☎ 01323 :

XX **Crossways** with rm, Lewes Rd, BN26 5SG, ✆ 482455, Fax 487811, – TV ☎ P. VISA JCB.
closed 23 December-23 January – **Meals** *(closed Sunday and Monday)* (dinner only) 24.95 5.95 – **7 rm** 42.00/70.00 **st.** – SB.

ATS Langney Rise ✆ 761971

EAST BUCKLAND Devon 403 I 30 – see South Molton.

EAST DEREHAM Norfolk 404 W 25 – pop. 13 333 – ☎ 01362.
♦London 109 – ♦Cambridge 57 – King's Lynn 27 – ♦Norwich 16.

George, Swaffham Rd, NR19 2AZ, ✆ 696801, Fax 695711 – TV ☎ P. AE VISA
Meals 10.00 **t.** and a la carte – **7 rm** 40.00/48.00 **t.**, 1 suite.

King's Head, 42 Norwich St., NR19 1AD, ✆ 693842, Fax 693776, – TV ☎ P
15 rm.

at Wendling W : 5½ m. by A 47 – ☎ 01362 :

Greenbanks County, Swaffham Rd, NR19 2AR, ✆ 687742, – rest TV P. VISA
Meals 6.00/26.00 **st.** and a la carte 5.00 – **5 rm** 32.00/52.00 **st.** – SB.

EAST GRINSTEAD W. Sussex 404 T 30 – pop. 24 383 – ☎ 01342.
Copthorne, Borers Arm Rd ✆ 712508.
♦London 32 – ♦Brighton 29 – Eastbourne 33 – Lewes 21 – Maidstone 32.

Jarvis Felbridge, London Rd, RH19 2BH, NW : 1 ½ m. on A 22 ✆ 326992, Fax 41077, heated, – TV ☎ P – 350. AE VISA
Meals *(closed Saturday lunch)* 10.50/15.50 **st.** and a la carte 4.95 – 5.00 – **90** 65.00/75.00 **st.** – SB.

Woodbury House, Lewes Rd, RH19 3UD, SE : ½ m. on A 22 ✆ 313657, Fax 314801, TV ☎ P. AE VISA JCB.
Meals 12.00/20.50 **t.** and a la carte 5.00 – **14 rm** 70.00/85.00 **st.**

at Gravetye SW : 4 ½ m. by B 2110 taking second turn left towards West Hoathly – ✉ East Grinstead – ☎ 01342 :

Gravetye Manor, Vowels Lane, RH19 4LJ, ✆ 810567, Fax 810080, ≤, « 16C manor house with gardens and grounds by William Robinson », park – rest TV ☎ P. VISA.
Meals (booking essential) 22.00/28.00 and a la carte 35.00/49.00 – 10.00 – **18 rm** 100.00/205.00 **s.**

ATS London Rd, North End ✆ 410740

EASTHAM Mersey. 402 403 L 24 – pop. 15 011 – ✉ Wirral – ☎ 0151.
♦London 209 – ♦Birmingham 45 – Chester 13 – ♦Liverpool 7.5 – ♦Manchester 45.

Forte Travelodge, New Chester Rd, L62 9AQ, at junction of M 53 with A 41 ✆ 327 248 Reservations (Freephone) 0800 850950 – TV P. AE VISA.
Meals (grill rest.) – **31 rm** 34.50 **t.**

EAST HORNDON Essex – ☎ 01277.
♦London 21 – Chelmsford 13 – Southend-on-Sea 17.

Forte Travelodge, CM13 3LL, on A 127 (eastbound carriageway) ✆ 8108 Reservations (Freephone) 0800 850950 – TV P. AE VISA.
Meals (grill rest.) – **22 rm** 34.50 **t.**

EASTLEIGH Devon 403 H 30 – see Bideford.

Pour voyager rapidement, utilisez les **cartes Michelin "Grandes Routes"** :
970 Europe, 976 République Tchèque-République Slovaque, 980 Grèce, 984 Allemagne, 985 Scandinavie-Finlande, 986 Grande-Bretagne-Irlande, 987 Allemagne-Autriche-Benelux, 988 Italie, 989 France, 990 Espagne-Portugal, 991 Yougoslavie.

EASTLEIGH Hants. 403 P 31 – pop. 105 999 – ✆ 01703.

Fleming Park, Magpie Lane ✆ 612797.

Southampton (Eastleigh) Airport : ✆ 620021.

Town Hall Centre, Leigh Rd, SO50 4DE ✆ 641261.

London 74 – Winchester 8 – Southampton 4.

Forte Posthouse, Leigh Rd, SO50 9PG, ✆ 619700, Fax 643945, rm rest 200. VISA JCB.
Meals 9.75/25.00 **t.** and a la carte 6.95 – 7.95 – **113 rm** 59.00 **t.**, 3 suites – SB.

Forte Travelodge, Twyford Rd, SO5 4LF, N : 1m. on A 335 ✆ 616813, Reservations (Freephone) 0800 850950 – VISA.
Meals (grill rest.) – **32 rm** 34.50 **t.**

ATS Dutton Lane, Bishopstoke Rd ✆ 613027/613393

EASTLING Kent 404 W 30 – see Faversham.

EASTON Devon 403 I 31 – see Chagford.

EAST RETFORD Notts. 402 404 R 24 – pop. 20 6793 – ✆ 01777.

London 148 – Lincoln 23 – Nottingham 31 – Sheffield 27.

Old Plough, Top Street, North Wheatley, DN22 9DB, NE : 5 m. by A 620 ✆ (01427) 880916, ←, – .
Meals (by arrangement) (communal dining) 14.50 **st.** 3.25 – **3 rm** 27.50/55.00 **st.**

ATS Babworth Rd ✆ 706501

Great Britain and *Ireland* is now covered
by an *Atlas* at a scale of 1 inch to 4.75 miles.

Three easy to use versions: Paperback, Spiralbound and Hardback.

EAST WITTERING W. Sussex 404 R 31 – pop. 3 431 – ✉ Chichester – ✆ 01243.

London 74 – Brighton 37 – Portsmouth 25.

Clifford's Cottage, Bracklesham Lane, Bracklesham Bay, PO20 8JA, E : 1 m. by B 2179 on B 2198 ✆ 670250 – VISA JCB
closed Sunday dinner, Monday, last week February and first 2 weeks November – **Meals** (dinner only and Sunday lunch)/dinner 17.50 **t.** and a la carte 4.50.

EAST WITTON N. Yorks. 402 O 21 pop. 153 – ✉ Leyburn – ✆ 01969.

London 238 – Leeds 45 – Middlesbrough 30 – York 39.

Blue Lion with rm, DL8 4SN, ✆ 624273, Fax 624189, « 19C inn », – VISA
Meals (in bar Tuesday to Saturday lunch, Sunday dinner and Monday) dinner a la carte 16.95/26.15 **t.** 6.95 – **9 rm** 39.50/70.00 **t.** – SB.

EBCHESTER Durham 401 402 O 19 – ✉ Consett – ✆ 01207.

Consett and District, Elmfield Rd, Consett ✆ 502186.

London 275 – Carlisle 64 – Newcastle upon Tyne 16.

Raven, Broomhill, DH8 6RY, SE : ¾ m. on B 6309 ✆ 560367, Fax 560262, ← – VISA.
Meals *(closed Sunday dinner)* (bar lunch Monday to Saturday)/dinner 17.95 **st.** and a la carte 4.95 – **28 rm** 52.00/69.00 **st.** – SB.

ECCLES Gtr. Manchester 402 403 404 M 23 – see Manchester.

ECCLESHALL Staffs. 402 403 404 N 25 – pop. 4 606 – ✆ 01785.

London 149 – Birmingham 33 – Derby 40 – Shrewsbury 26 – Stoke-on-Trent 12.

George, Castle St., ST21 6DF, ✆ 850300, Fax 851452 – VISA
Meals 12.95 **t.** (lunch) and a la carte 13.25/20.40 **t.** 4.25 – **10 rm** 45.00/60.00 **st.** – SB.

Badger Inn, Green Lane, ST21 6BA, S : ¼ m. by A 519 ✆ 850564 – rest VISA.
Meals 8.85/9.50 **st.** and a la carte 3.75 **4 rm** 20.00/40.00 **st.** – SB.

EDENBRIDGE Kent 404 U 30 Great Britain G. – pop. 7 581 – ✆ 01732.

Envir. : Hever Castle★ *AC*, E : 2½m. – Chartwell★ *AC*, N : 3 m. by B 2026.

Crouch House Rd ✆ 867381.

London 35 – Brighton 36 – Maidstone 29.

Honours Mill, 87 High St., TN8 5AU, ✆ 866757, « Carefully renovated 18C mill » – VISA
closed Saturday lunch, Sunday dinner, Monday and 2 weeks Christmas-New Year – **Meals** 15.50/32.75 **st.**

EGERTON Gtr. Manchester 402 ㉑ 403 ② 404 ⑨ – see Bolton.

EGGESFORD Devon 403 I 31 – ☎ 01769.

♦London 215 – Barnstaple 18 – Exeter 22 – Taunton 48.

Fox and Hounds, EX18 7JZ, ℘ 580345, Fax 580262, park – rest – 80. VISA.
Meals 9.50/17.50 **t.** and a la carte 3.50 – **18 rm** 35.50/65.00 **t.** – SB.

EGHAM Surrey 404 S 29 – pop. 6 370 – ☎ 01784.

♦London 29 – Reading 21.

Runnymede, Windsor Rd, TW20 0AG, on A 308 ℘ 436171, Fax 436340, – rm – 350. AE VISA.
Meals (bar lunch Saturday) (dancing Saturday evening) 16.95/35.00 **t.** – 11.95 – **171 rm** 113.00/152.00 **st.** – SB.

Great Fosters, Stroude Rd, TW20 9UR, S : 1 ¼ m. by B 388 ℘ 433822, Fax 472455 « Elizabethan mansion, gardens », heated, park, – – 65. AE VISA.
Meals 9.95/22.50 **t.** and a la carte 5.00 – **42 rm** 85.00/178.50 **t.**, 2 suites.

EGLINGHAM Northd. 401 402 O 17 – see Alnwick.

EIGHT ASH GREEN Essex 404 W 28 – see Colchester.

ELLESMERE PORT Mersey. 403 L 24 – ☎ 0151.

♦London 211 – Birkenhead 9 – Chester 9 – ♦Liverpool 11 – ♦Manchester 44.

Holiday Inn, Centre Island, Waterways, Lower Mersey St., L65 2AL, NE : 1 ½ m. by A 5032 (junction 9 M 53) ℘ 356 8111, Fax 356 8444, – rm rest – 120. AE VISA JCB.
Meals 8.00/25.00 **t.** and a la carte – 7.50 – **83 rm** 65.00/75.00 – SB.

ELMDON Essex 404 U 27 – see Saffron Walden.

ELSING Norfolk 404 X 25 pop. 261 – ✉ East Dereham – ☎ 01362.

♦London 118 – ♦Cambridge 66 – King's Lynn 33 – ♦Norwich 15.

Bartles Lodge, Church St., NR20 3EA, ℘ 637177, – . VISA
Meals (dinner only) 8.50 **st.** 3.50 – **7 rm** 27.00/55.00 **st.**

ELSLACK N. Yorks. 402 N 22 – see Skipton.

ELSTOW Beds. 404 S 27 – see Bedford.

ELSTREE Herts. 404 T 29 – ☎ 0181.

Watling St. ℘ 953 6115.

♦London 10 – Luton 22.

Plan : see Greater London (North West)

Edgwarebury (Country Club), Barnet Lane, WD6 3RE, ℘ 953 8227, Fax 207 3668, park, – – 60. AE VISA CT
Meals 17.95/24.50 **t.** and dinner a la carte – 7.50 – **47 rm** 80.00/125.00 **t.** – SB.

ELTERWATER Cumbria – see Ambleside.

ELY Cambs. 404 U 26 **Great Britain G.** – pop. 11 345 – ☎ 01353.

See : Cathedral★★ *AC.*

Exc. : Wicken Fen★, SE : 9 m. by A 10 and A 1123.

Cambridge Rd ℘ 662751.

Oliver Cromwells House, 29 St. Mary's St., CB7 4HF ℘ 662062.

♦London 74 – ♦Cambridge 16 – ♦Norwich 60.

Lamb, 2 Lynn Rd, CB7 4EJ, ℘ 663574, Fax 666350 – – 25. AE VISA.
Meals 8.00/14.75 **t.** and a la carte 4.95 – **32 rm** 55.00/90.00 **t.** – SB.

Forte Travelodge, Witchford Rd, CB6 3NN, W : 1 m. on A 10/A 142 roundabout, E by pass ℘ 668499, Reservations (Freephone) 0800 850950 – . AE VISA.
Meals (grill rest.) – **39 rm** 34.50 **t.**

Old Fire Engine House, 25 St. Mary's St., CB7 4ER, ℘ 662582, – . VISA
closed Sunday dinner, 2 weeks Christmas-New Year and Bank Holidays – **Meals** - English (booking essential) a la carte 17.30/22.55 **t.**

at Littleport N : 5 ¾ m. on A 10 – ✉ Ely – ☎ 01353 :

Fen House, 2 Lynn Rd, CB6 1QG, ℘ 860645 – . VISA
closed Sunday and Monday – **Meals** (dinner only) 24.50 **t.** 5.50.

at Coveney NW : 6½ m. by A 142 – ✉ Ely – ☎ 01353 :

Hill House Farm without rest., 9 Main St., CB6 2DJ, ℘ 778369, – .
3 rm 25.00/38.00.

ATS 11 Broad St. ℘ 662758/662801

EMPINGHAM Leics. 402 404 S 26 – see Stamford (Lincs.).

EMSWORTH Hants. 404 R 31 – pop. 9 692 – ☎ 01243.

♦London 75 – ♦Brighton 37 – ♦Portsmouth 10.

Brookfield, 93-95 Havant Rd, PO10 7LF, ✆ 373363, Fax 376342, – rest TV ☎ P – 50. AE VISA.
closed 24 December-2 January – **Meals** 13.95 **t.** and a la carte 4.95 – **40 rm** 49.00/73.50 **t.** – SB.

Forte Travelodge without rest., PO10 7RB, E : ½ m. on A 27 (eastbound carriageway) ✆ 370877, Reservations (Freephone) 0800 850950 – TV P. AE VISA
40 rm 34.50 **t.**

36 on the Quay, 47 South St., The Quay, PO10 7EG, ✆ 375592, Fax 374429 – AE VISA
closed Sunday April-September, Sunday dinner and Tuesday October-March and 2 weeks September-October – **Meals** 19.95/29.95 **t.** 6.50.

Spencer's, 36 North St., PO10 7DG, ✆ 372744 – . AE VISA
closed Sunday, Monday and 25-26 December – **Meals** 18.50 **t.** (dinner) and lunch a la carte 13.40/19.45 **t.** 5.70.

ENSTONE Oxon. 403 404 P 28 – pop. 1 523 – ✉ Chipping Norton – ☎ 01608.

♦London 73 – ♦Birmingham 48 – Gloucester 32 – ♦Oxford 18.

Swan Lodge, OX7 4NE, on A 44 ✆ 678736, – TV P.
Meals (by arrangement) 10.00 **st.** – **5 rm** 30.00/45.00 – SB.

EPPING Essex 404 U 28 – ☎ 01992.

♦London 18 – ♦Cambridge 40 – Chelmsford 21 – Southend-on-Sea 37.

Neil's, 142 High St., CM16 4AG, ✆ 576767 – VISA
closed Sunday, Monday, 2 to 4 January and 2 to 16 April – **Meals** a la carte 24.00/27.50 **t.** 4.75.

EPSOM Surrey 404 ㉚ – pop. 67 007 (inc. Ewell) – ☎ 01372.

18 Longdown Lane South, Epsom Downs ✆ 721666 – 18 Horton Park C.C., Hook Rd ✆ (0181) 393 8400.

♦London 17 – Guildford 16.

Plan : see Greater London (South-West)

Le Raj, 211 Fir Tree Rd, Epsom Downs, KT19 3LB, SE : 2¼ m. by B 289 and B 284 on B 291 ✆ (01737) 371371, Fax 371067 – . AE VISA CZ
closed 25 and 26 December – **Meals** - Indian - a la carte 14.85/27.40 **t.**

EPWORTH Humbs. 402 404 R 23 – ✉ Doncaster – ☎ 01427.

♦London 170 – ♦Leeds 48 – Lincoln 31 – ♦Sheffield 39.

Epworth Tap, 9-11 Market Pl., DN9 1EU, ✆ 873333, Fax 875020 – AE VISA
closed Sunday to Tuesday, first 2 weeks January and first week September – **Meals** (booking essential) (dinner only) 17.50 **t.** and a la carte 4.00.

ESCRICK N. Yorks. 402 Q 22 – see York.

ESHER Surrey 404 S 29 – pop. 5 849 – ☎ 01372.

9 Thames Ditton & Esher, Portsmouth Rd ✆ (0181) 398 1551 BZ – 9 Moore Place, Portsmouth Rd ✆ 463533 BZ – 9, 9 Sandown Park, More Lane ✆ 463340 BZ.

♦London 20 – ♦Portsmouth 58.

Plan : see Greater London (South-West)

Good Earth, 14-18 High St., KT10 9RT, ✆ 462489 – . AE VISA BZ e
closed 24 to 27 December – **Meals** - Chinese - 11.75/26.00 **t.** and a la carte 4.25.

La Orient, 63 High St., KT10 9RQ, ✆ 466628 – . AE VISA BZ a
Meals - South East Asian - a la carte 12.00/20.00 **t.** 3.75.

at Claygate SE : 1 m. by A 244 – ✉ Esher – ☎ 01372 :

Les Alouettes, 7 High St., KT10 0JW, ✆ 464882, Fax 465337 – . AE VISA BZ n
closed Saturday lunch, Sunday dinner, Monday, 26 to 30 December and Bank Holidays – **Meals** - French - 15.50/22.50 **t.** and a la carte 5.50.

Le Petit Pierrot, 4 The Parade, KT10 0NU, ✆ 465105, Fax 467642 – AE VISA BZ r
closed Saturday lunch, Sunday and Bank Holidays – **Meals** - French - 9.95/18.95 **t.** 4.85.

ESKDALE GREEN Cumbria 402 K 20 **Great Britain G.** – pop. 316 – ✉ Holmrook – ☎ 0194 67.

Exc. : Hard Knott Pass★★, E : 6 m. – Wrynose Pass★★, E : 8 m.

♦London 312 – ♦Carlisle 59 – Kendal 60.

Bower House Inn , CA19 1TD, W : ¾ m. ✆ 23244, Fax 23308, – TV ☎ P – 40. AE VISA.
Meals (bar lunch)/dinner 18.50 **st.** and a la carte 3.70 – **24 rm** 46.00/60.00 – SB.

EVERCREECH Somerset 403 404 M 30 – see Shepton Mallet.

EVERSHOT Dorset 403 404 M 31 – pop. 225 – ✉ Dorchester – ☎ 01935.

♦London 149 – Bournemouth 39 – Dorchester 12 – Salisbury 53 – Taunton 30 – Yeovil 10.

Summer Lodge ⛰, Summer Lane, DT2 0JR, ☎ 83424, Fax 83005, « Part Georgian dower house », heated, ☐, ☐ – ☐ rest ☐ ☎ Ⓟ. ☐ AE ☐ VISA
Meals 23.50/32.50 **t.** 6.50 – **17 rm** 100.00/185.00 **st.** – SB.

Rectory House, Fore St., DT2 0JW, ☎ 83273, Fax 83273, ☐ – ☐ rest ☐ Ⓟ. ☐ VISA. ☐
closed December – **Meals** (by arrangement) 17.00 **t.** 3.50 – **6 rm** 30.50/75.00 **t.** – SB.

Great Britain and Ireland is now covered by an Atlas at a scale of 1 inch to 4.75 miles.

Three easy to use versions: Paperback, Spiralbound and Hardback.

EVESHAM Heref. and Worcs. 403 404 O 27 – pop. 17 823 – ☎ 01386.

The Almonry, Abbey Gate, WR11 4BG ☎ 446944.

♦London 99 – ♦Birmingham 30 – Cheltenham 16 – ♦Coventry 32.

Evesham, Coopers Lane, WR11 6DA, off Waterside ☎ 765566, Fax 765443, Reservations (Freephone)0800 716969, ☐, ☐ – ☐ ☎ Ⓟ. ☐ AE ☐ VISA
closed 25 and 26 December – **Meals** a la carte 16.25/24.50 **st.** 6.50 – **40 rm** 60.00/90.00 **st.** – SB.

Waterside, 56-59 Waterside, WR11 6JZ, ☎ 442420, ☐, ☐ – ☐ ☎ Ⓟ. ☐ AE VISA
Meals 5.00/15.00 **t.** and a la carte – **15 rm** 38.60/71.60 **t.** – SB.

Riverside ⛰, The Parks, Offenham Rd, WR11 5JP, NW : 2 m. by Waterside and B 4035 off B 4510 ☎ 446200, Fax 40021, ≤, ☐, ☐ – ☐ rest ☐ ☎ Ⓟ. ☐ VISA. ☐
Meals *(closed Sunday dinner and Monday)* 16.95/21.95 **st.** and lunch a la carte 6.95 – **7 rm** 60.00/80.00 **st.** – SB.

at Harvington N : 3¾ m. by A 4184 and A 435 off B 439 – ✉ Evesham – ☎ 01386 :

Mill at Harvington ⛰, Anchor Lane, WR11 5NR, SE : 1½ m. by B 439 ☎ 870688 Fax 870688, ≤, « 18C mill with riverside garden », heated, ☐, ☐ – ☐ ☎ Ⓟ. ☐ AE ☐ VISA. ☐
closed 24 to 28 December – **Meals** 12.25/23.50 **st.** 4.50 – **15 rm** 54.00/85.00 **st.** – SB.

at Abbot's Salford (Warks.) N : 4¾ m. by A 4184 and A 435 on B 439 – ✉ Evesham – ☎ 01386 :

Salford Hall, WR11 5UT, ☎ 871300, Fax 871301, « Tudor mansion with early 17C extension and gatehouse », ☐, ☐, ☐ – ☐ rest ☐ ☎ Ⓟ – ☐ 50. ☐ AE ☐ VISA JCB. ☐
closed 22 to 30 December – **Meals** 14.95/27.50 **t.** 6.50 – **33 rm** 75.00/130.00 **t.** – SB.

at Bretforton E : 3½ m. on B 4035 – ✉ Evesham – ☎ 01386 :

Bretforton Manor ⛰ without rest., WR11 5JH, ☎ 833111, Fax 833111, ☐ – ☐ ☐ Ⓟ ☐ AE VISA. ☐
closed Christmas – **3 rm** 50.00/85.00 **st.**

ATS Worcester Road ☎ 765313

EWEN Glos. 403 404 O 28 – see Cirencester.

EXEBRIDGE Somerset 403 J 30 – ✉ Dulverton – ☎ 01398.

♦London 194 – Exeter 23 – Minehead 19 – Taunton 23.

Anchor Inn, TA22 9AZ, NW : ¼ m. on B 3222 ☎ 323433, « Riverside setting », ☐, ☐ – ☐ ☎ Ⓟ. ☐ VISA
Meals (bar lunch Monday to Saturday)/dinner 25.00 **t.** and a la carte 4.95 – **6 rm** 35.00/70.00 – SB.

EXETER Devon 403 J 31 The West Country G. – pop. 98 125 – ☎ 01392.

See : City★★ - Cathedral★★ Z – Maritime Museum★★ *AC* Z – Royal Albert Memorial Museum★ Y.

Envir. : Holy Cross Church★.

Exc. : Killerton★★ *AC*, NE : 7 m. by B 3181 V – Ottery St. Mary★ (St. Mary's★★) E : 12 m. by B 3183 – Y - A 30 and B 3174.

18 Downes Crediton, Hookway ☎ (01363) 773991.

Exeter Airport : ☎ 367433, E : 5 m. by A 30 V – **Terminal** : St. David's and Central Stations.

Civic Centre, Paris St., EX1 IRP ☎ 265700 – Exeter Services, Sandygate (M 5), EX2 7N ☎ 437581/79088.

♦London 201 – Bournemouth 83 – ♦Bristol 83 – ♦Plymouth 46 – ♦Southampton 110.

EXETER

BUILT UP AREA

lackboy Road . . . . V 8
uddle Lane . . . . X 9
utts Road . . . . X 12
ast Wonford Hill . . . . X 17
eavitree Road . . . . VX 20
Hill Lane . . . . V 21
Marsh Barton Road . . . . X 25
Mount Pleasant Road . . . . . . V 29
North Street
HEAVITREE . . . . X 32
Old Tiverton Road . . . . V 35
Polsloe Road . . . . V 39
Prince Charles Road . . . . V 41
Prince of Wales Road . . . . . . V 42
St. Andrew's Road . . . . V 48
Summer Lane . . . . V 51
Sweetbriar Lane . . . . VX 52
Trusham Road . . . . X 53
Union Road . . . . V 54
Whipton Lane . . . . X 55
Wonford Road . . . . X 57
Wonford Street . . . . X 58
Woodwater Lane . . . . X 60

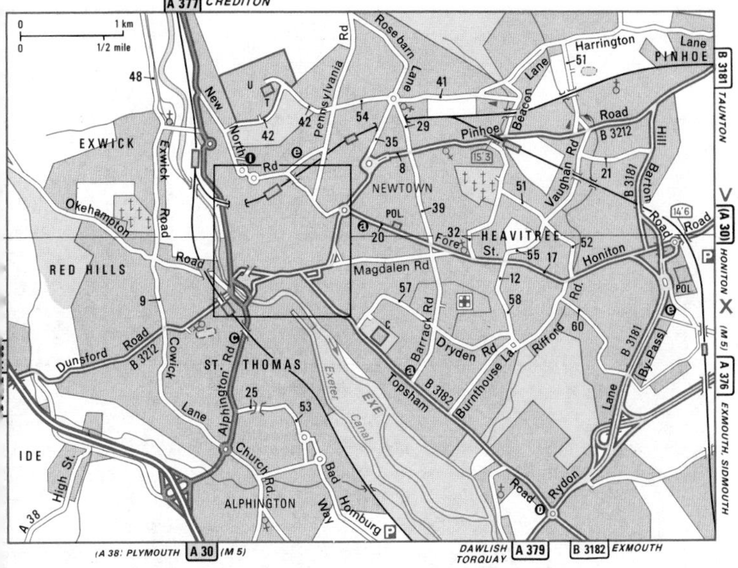

Forte Crest, Southernhay East, EX1 1QF, 412812, Fax 413549, – rm rest – 150. Z **a**
Meals 12.75/18.95 **st.** and a la carte 6.50 – 10.50 – **109 rm** 90.00 **st.**, 1 suite – SB.

Rougemont Thistle, Queen St., EX4 3SP, 54982, Fax 420928 – rm rest – 300. Y **x**
Meals 9.95/16.95 **st.** and a la carte – **88 rm** 73.00/83.00, 2 suites – SB.

Royal Clarence (Q.M.H.), Cathedral Yard, EX1 1HB, 319955, Fax 439423 – rest – 120. Y **z**
Meals 11.35/16.00 **t.** and lunch a la carte 8.50 – 8.95 – **55 rm** 90.00/99.00 **t.**, 1 suite – SB.

Buckerell Lodge, Topsham Rd, EX2 4SQ, 52451, Fax 412114, – rm – 60. X **a**
Meals 14.95/23.95 5.95 – 8.95 – **52 rm** 39.00/85.00 **t.** – SB.

St. Olaves Court, Mary Arches St., EX4 3AZ, 217736, Fax 413054, – . Z **e**
Meals - (see ***Golsworthy's*** below) – 6.00 – **17 rm** 65.00/95.00 **t.** – SB.

Exeter Arms Toby, Rydon Lane, Middlemoor, EX2 7HL, E : 3 m. on B 3181 435353, Fax 420826 – – 80. X **e**
Meals (grill rest.) a la carte 8.25/18.00 – **37 rm** 48.00/58.00 **t.** – SB.

Devon, Matford, EX2 8XU, S : 3 m. by A 377 on A 379 59268, Fax 413142 – – 100.
Meals (carving lunch)/dinner 15.50 **st.** and a la carte 5.25 – **41 rm** 52.00/69.00 **st.**

St. Andrews, 28 Alphington Rd, EX2 8HN, 76784, Fax 50249 – . X **c**
closed Christmas-New Year – **Meals** (bar lunch)/dinner a la carte 12.90/18.00 **t.** 4.35 – **16 rm** 38.00/53.00 **t.**

Edwardian without rest., 30-32 Heavitree Rd, EX1 2LQ, 76102, Fax 76102 – . V **a**
closed Christmas – **13 rm** 23.00/46.00 **st.**

Travel Inn, 398 Topsham Rd, EX2 6HE, 875441, Fax 876174 – rm . X **o**
Meals (grill rest.) – 4.95 – **45 rm** 34.50 **t.**

EXETER
CENTRE

Bedford St. . . . . Y 6
Fore St. . . . . Z
Guildhall
  Shopping Centre . . . . Y
High St. . . . . Y

Alphington Rd. . . . . Z 2
Barnfield Rd . . . . Z 3
Bartholomew Rd. . . . . Z 5
Castle St. . . . . Y 13
Cowick St. . . . . Z 15
Edmund St. . . . . Z 18
King St. . . . . Z 22
Mary Arches St. . . . . Z 26
Mint (The) . . . . Z 28

New Bridge St. . . . . Z 31
Palace Gate. . . . . Z 36
Paul St. . . . . Y 37
Preston St. . . . . Z 40
Princesshay . . . . Y 44
Quay Hill. . . . . Z 45
Queen's Terrace. . . . . Y 46
St. Martin's Lane . . . . Y 49
Summerland. . . . . Y 50

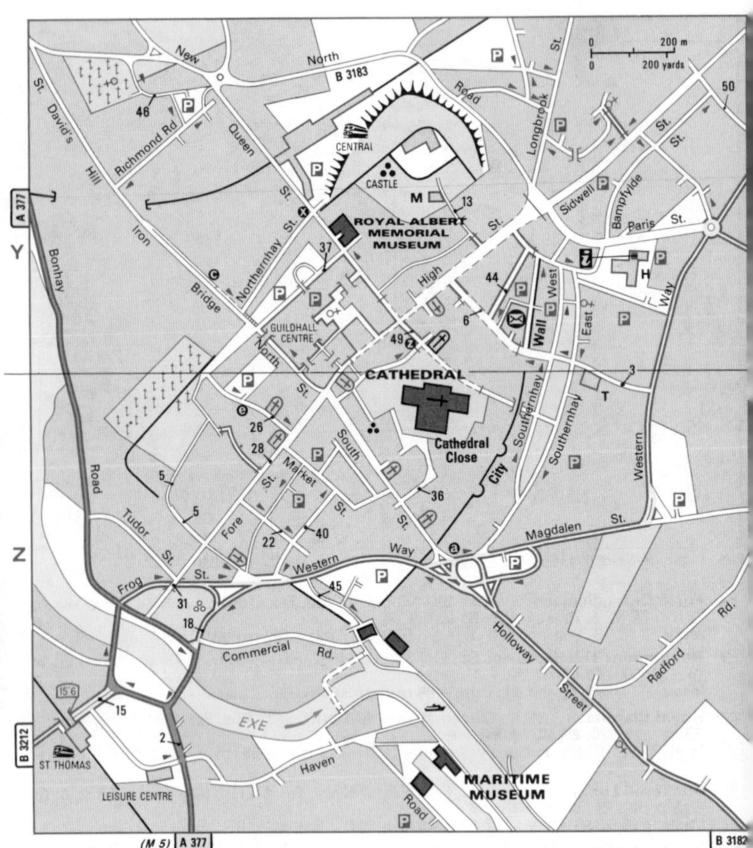

The Grange without rest., Stoke Hill, EX4 7JH, N : 1 ¾ m. by Old Tiverton Rd
59723, heated, – . – **3 rm** 20.00/35.00.

Raffles, 11 Blackall Rd, EX4 4HD, 70200 – . AE VISA V
Meals 12.00 **st.** 3.50 – **7 rm** 28.00/40.00 **st.** – SB.

Park View without rest., 8 Howell Rd, EX4 4LG, 71772, Fax 53047 – . AE
VISA. – **15 rm** 20.00/43.00 **t.** V

Golsworthy's (at St. Olaves Court H.), Mary Arches St., EX4 3AZ, 217736, Fax 413054
– . AE VISA Z
closed lunch Saturday and Sunday – **Meals** 13.50 **t.** and a la carte 4.75.

Lamb's, 15 Lower North St., EX4 3ET, 54269, Fax 431145 – . VISA Y
Meals *(closed Saturday lunch, Sunday and Monday)* 10.00/17.00 **t.** and a la carte 4.50.

at Pinhoe NE : 2 m. by A 30 – V – Exeter – 01392 :

Gipsy Hill, Gipsy Hill Lane, via Pinn Lane, EX1 3RN, 465252, Fax 464302,
rm – 120. AE VISA
closed 26 to 30 December – **Meals** 6.50/15.00 **st.** and a la carte 4.50 – **38 rm** 60.00
80.00 **st.** – SB.

at Huxham N : 5 m. by A 377 off A 396 – V – ✉ Exeter – ☎ 01392 :

XX **Barton Cross** with rm, Stoke Canon, EX5 4EJ, ✆ 841245, Fax 841942, « Part 17C thatched cottages », – rest TV ☎ P. AE VISA
Meals 14.50/22.50 **t.** and a la carte 6.00 – **7 rm** 63.50/85.00 **st.** – SB.

at Whimple NE : 9 m. by A 30 – V – ✉ Exeter – ☎ 01404 :

Woodhayes, EX5 2TD, ✆ 822237, Fax 822337, « Georgian country house », – rest TV ☎ P. AE VISA.
Meals (booking essential) (lunch residents only) 15.00/25.00 **st.** – **6 rm** (dinner included) 85.00/130.00 **st.**

at Kennford S : 5 m. on A 38 – X – ✉ Exeter – ☎ 01392 :

Fairwinds, EX6 7UD, ✆ 832911, Fax 832911 – TV ☎ P. VISA.
closed 5 to 31 December – **Meals** *(closed Sunday November-February)* (bar lunch)/dinner 13.50 3.95 – **8 rm** 22.00/46.00 – SB.

Gissons Arms, EX6 7UD, ✆ 832444 – TV ☎ P. VISA
Meals a la carte 8.45/19.50 **st.** 4.25 – **6 rm** 30.00/45.00 **st.** – SB.

at Doddiscombsleigh SW : 10 m. by B 3212 off B 3193 – X – ✉ Exeter – ☎ 01647 :

Nobody Inn, EX6 7PS, ✆ 252394, Fax 252978, ←, « Part 16C inn », – ☎ P. AE VISA.
closed 25 December – **Meals** *(closed Sunday and Monday)* (bar lunch)/dinner a la carte 12.60/17.50 **t.** 3.50 – **7 rm** 23.00/59.00 **st.**

at Ide SW : 3 m. by A 377 – X – ✉ Exeter – ☎ 01392 :

XX **Old Mill**, 20 High St., EX2 9RN, ✆ 59480 – P. AE VISA
closed Saturday lunch, Sunday and 25 to 29 December – **Meals** (lunch by arrangement)/dinner 14.00 **t.** and a la carte.

ATS 276/280 Pinhoe Road, Polsloe Bridge ✆ 55465

EXETER SERVICE AREA Devon 403 J 31 – ✉ Exeter – ☎ 01392.

Sandygate, EX2 7NJ ✆ 43581/79088.

Granada, Moor Lane, Sandygate, EX2 4AR, M 5 Junction 30 ✆ 74044, Fax 410406 – rm TV ☎ P – 70.
Meals (grill rest.) – **76 rm.**

EXFORD Somerset 403 J 30 – ☎ 01643.

London 193 – Exeter 41 – Minehead 14 – Taunton 33.

Crown, TA24 7PP, ✆ 831554, Fax 831665, – TV ☎ P. AE VISA JCB
Meals (bar lunch Monday to Saturday)/dinner 22.00 **t.** and a la carte 5.90 – **17 rm** 38.00/76.00 **t.** – SB.

EXMOUTH Devon 403 J 32 The West Country G. – pop. 30 386 – ☎ 01395.

Envir. : A la Ronde★ *AC*, N : 2 m. by B 3180.

Alexandra Terr., EX8 1NZ ✆ 263744.

London 210 – Exeter 11.

Imperial (Forte), The Esplanade, EX8 2SW, ✆ 274761, Fax 265161, ←, heated, – TV ☎ P – AE VISA JCB
Meals (bar lunch Monday to Saturday)/dinner 16.95 **t.** 8.50 – **57 rm** 60.00/85.00 **t.** – SB.

Barn, Foxholes Hill, EX8 2DF, E : 1 m. ✆ 224411, Fax 224411, ←, – rest TV ☎ P – 50. VISA.
closed Christmas and New Year – **Meals** (bar lunch Monday to Saturday)/dinner 13.00 **st.** 5.25 – **11 rm** 32.00/64.00 **st.** – SB.

at Lympstone N : 3 m. by A 376 – ✉ Exmouth – ☎ 01395 :

XX **River House** with rm, The Strand, EX8 5EY, ✆ 265147, ← Exe Estuary – rest TV ☎. AE VISA.
Meals *(closed Sunday and Monday)* 25.95/29.50 **t.** and lunch a la carte – 6.50 – **2 rm** 55.00/74.00 **t.** – SB.

EYAM Derbs. 402 403 404 O 24 pop. 1 018 – ✉ Sheffield – ☎ 01433.

London 163 – Derby 29 – Manchester 32 – Sheffield 12.

Miners Arms, Water Lane, S30 1RG, ✆ 630853 – TV P. VISA
closed first 2 weeks January – **Meals** *(closed Sunday dinner and Monday)* (bar lunch Tuesday to Saturday)/dinner a la carte 15.70/17.15 **t.** 4.50 – **6 rm** 25.00/45.00 **t.**

EYE Suffolk 404 X 27 – pop. 1 741 – ☎ 01379.

London 94 – Ipswich 19 – Thetford 23.

Four Horseshoes, Thornham Magna, IP23 7HD, SW : 5 m. by B 1117 off A 140 ✆ 678777, Fax 678134, – TV ☎ P. AE VISA
Meals a la carte 13.90/21.70 **st.** – **8 rm** 35.00/50.00 **st.**

EYTON Heref. and Worcs. – see Leominster.

FAKENHAM Norfolk 404 W 25 pop. 6 471 – 01328.

◆London 111 – ◆Cambridge 64 – ◆Norwich 27.

Sculthorpe Mill, Lynn Rd, Sculthorpe, NR21 9QG, W : 2 ½ m. on A 148 856161, Fax 856651, – .
Meals (bar lunch Monday to Saturday)/dinner 14.95 **t.** and a la carte 4.95 – **6 rm** 35.00/65.00 **t.** – SB.

FALFIELD Avon 403 404 M 29 – 01454.

◆London 132 – ◆Bristol 16 – Gloucester 22.

Gables, Bristol Rd, GL12 8DL, on A 38 260502, Fax 261821, , – rm – 150.
Meals (bar lunch Monday to Saturday)/dinner 14.50 **st.** and a la carte 4.50 – 4.50 – **32 rm** 45.00/60.00 **st.** – SB.

FALMOUTH Cornwall 403 E 33 **The West Country G.** – pop. 19 217 – 01326.

See : Town★ – Pendennis Castle★ (≤★★) *AC* B.

Envir. : Glendurgan Garden★★ *AC*, SW : 4½ m. by Swanpool Rd A – Mawnan Parish Church★ (≤★★) S : 4 m. by Swanpool Rd A – Cruise to Truro★ – Cruise along Helford River★.

Exc. : Trelissick Garden★★ (≤★★) NW : 13 m. by A 39 and B 3289 A – Carn Brea (≤★★) NW : 10 m. by A 393 A – Gweek (Setting★, Seal Sanctuary★) SW : 8 m. by A 39 and Treverva rd – Wendron (Poldark Mine★) *AC*, SW : 12½ m. by A 39 – A and A 394.

18 Swanpool Rd 314296 A – 9 Budock Vean Hotel 250288.

28 Killigrew St., TR11 3PN 312300.

◆London 308 – Penzance 26 – ◆Plymouth 65 – Truro 11.

Plan opposite

Greenbank, Harbourside, TR11 2SR, 312440, Fax 211362, ≤ harbour, , – rm – 40. A a
closed 24 December-14 January – **Nightingales : Meals** 23.95/35.00 **t.** and a la carte – **61 rm** 65.45/159.50 **t.** – SB.

Royal Duchy, Cliff Rd, TR11 4NX, 313042, Fax 319420, ≤, , , – . B a
Meals (dancing Saturday evening) 8.95/17.50 **t.** and a la carte 4.50 – **40 rm** (dinner included) 60.00/173.00 **t.**, 2 suites – SB.

St. Michael's of Falmouth (Regal), Gyllyngvase Beach, Seafront, TR11 4NB, 312707, Fax 211772, ≤, , , , – – 60. . A z
Meals (bar lunch Monday to Saturday)/dinner 16.00 **st.** and a la carte 5.50 – **65 rm** 59.00/118.00 **t.** – SB.

Penmere Manor , Mongleath Rd, TR11 4PN, 211411, Fax 317588, , , heated, , – rm – 60. A e
closed 24 to 27 December – **Meals** (bar lunch)/dinner 19.00 **st.** and a la carte – **38 rm** 57.00/105.00 **st.** – SB.

Carthion, Cliff Rd, TR11 4AP, 313669, Fax 212828, ≤, – . B v
Meals (bar lunch)/dinner 10.00 **st.** and a la carte 4.95 – **18 rm** 44.00/96.00 **t.**

Broadmead, 66-68 Kimberley Park Rd, TR11 2DD, 315704, Fax 311048 – rest . A u
closed Christmas-New Year – **Meals** (bar lunch)/dinner 11.75 **t.** 4.50 – **12 rm** 26.00/52.00 **t.** – SB.

Prospect House, 1 Church Rd, Penryn, TR10 8DA, NW : 2 m. by A 39 on B 3292 373198, Fax 373198, – rest .
Meals (by arrangement) (communal dining) 18.00 **s.** 5.00 – **3 rm** 30.00/55.00 **s.**

Gyllyngvase House, Gyllyngvase Rd, TR11 4DJ, 312956, – rest B s
April-October – **Meals** 9.00 **st.** 4.80 – **15 rm** 19.00/42.00 **st.** – SB.

Trevaylor, 8 Pennance Rd, TR11 4EA, 313041, ≤ – rest . A r
May-September – **Meals** 6.00 **st.** 3.00 – **7 rm** (dinner included) 25.00/44.50 **st.**

Rosemullion, Gyllyngvase Hill, TR11 4DF, 314690 – B c
13 rm.

Melvill House, 52 Melvill Rd, TR11 4DQ, 316645, Fax 211608 – . B o
closed Christmas and New Year – **Meals** (by arrangement) 8.00 – **7 rm** 22.50/38.00 – SB

Tresillian House, 3 Stracey Rd, TR11 4DW, 312425 – rest . A n
April-October – **Meals** 12.50 **st.** 4.00 – **12 rm** (dinner included) 29.10/58.20 **st.** – SB.

Esmond, 5 Emslie Rd, TR11 4BG, 313214 – . B e
closed Christmas – **Meals** (by arrangement) 8.00 **st.** 3.25 – **7 rm** 16.00/32.00 **st.**

FALMOUTH

Church Street . . . . B
High Street . . . . A
Market Street . . . . A 33

Arwenack Street . . . . B 2
Avenue Road . . . . B 3
Beacon Road . . . . A 4
Belmont Road . . . . A 7
Berkeley Vale . . . . A 8
Boscawen Road . . . . A 9
Budock Terrace . . . . A 13
Conway Road . . . . A 14
De Pass Road . . . . B 15
Emslie Road . . . . B 18
Fenwick Road . . . . A 19
Glasney Road . . . . A 20
Grovehill Crescent . . . . . B 23
Gyllyngvase Hill . . . . B 24
Gyllyngvase Road . . . . . . B 25
Kimberley Place . . . . A 28
Langton Road . . . . A 29
Madeira Walk . . . . A 30
Marlborough Crescent . . . . A 34
Park Terrace . . . . A 35
Pendennis Road . . . . B 38
Swanpool Road . . . . A 39
Symons Hill . . . . A 40
Tredova Crescent . . . . . . A 43
Trescobeas Road . . . . . . A 44
Wellington Terrace . . . . . A 45
Windsor Terrace . . . . A 48
Wodehouse Terrace . . . . . A 49

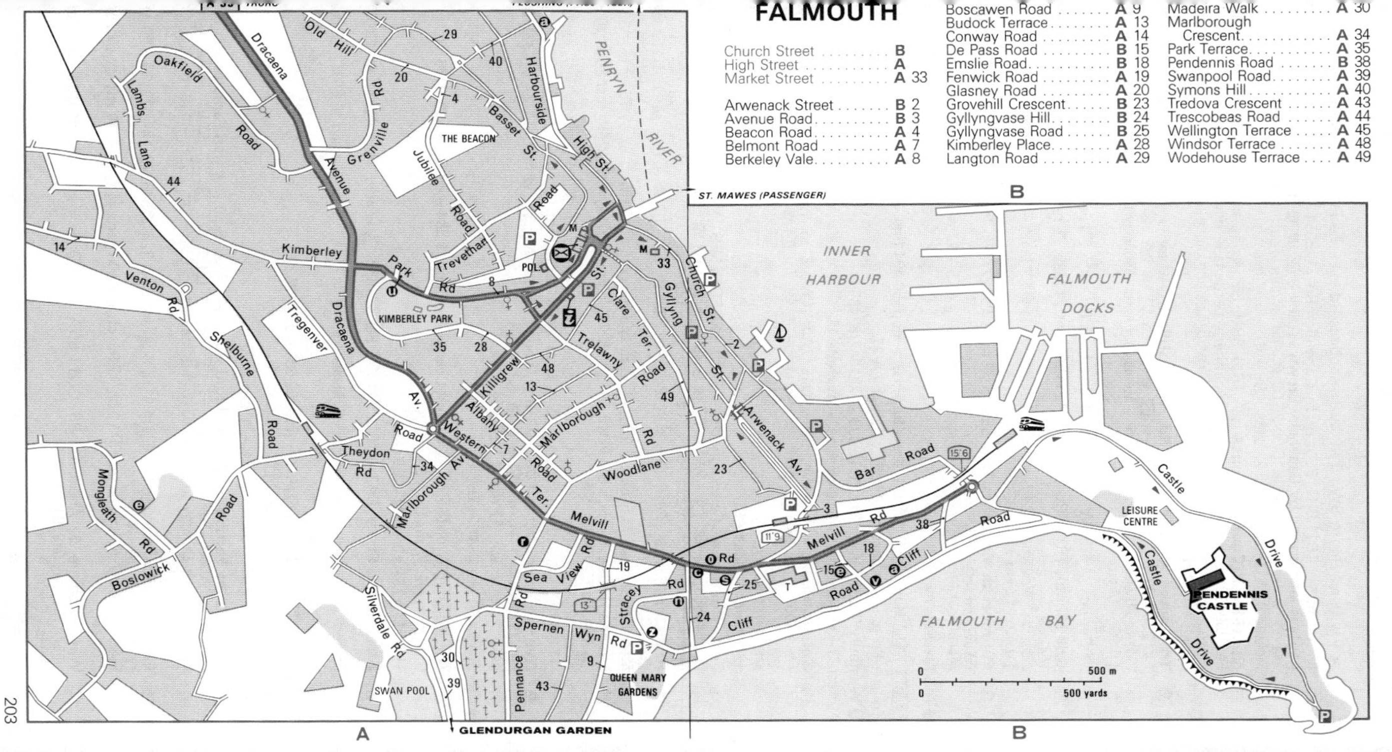

at Mawnan Smith SW : 5 m. by Trescobeas Rd – A – ✉ Falmouth – ☎ 01326 :

Meudon ⑤, TR11 5HT, E : ½ m. by Carwinion Rd ☎ 250541, Fax 250543, « ≤ Terraced gardens landscaped by Capability Brown », park – TV ☎ P. VISA AE VISA
March-November – **Meals** 15.00/25.00 **st.** and lunch a la carte 6.00 – **28 rm** (dinner included) 75.00/170.00 **st.**, 2 suites – SB.

Nansidwell Country House ⑤, TR11 5HU, SE : ¼ m. by Carwinion Rd ☎ 250340, Fax 250440, ≤, « Country house atmosphere, gardens », park, ✂ – TV ☎ P. VISA
closed 2 January-1 February – **Meals** 15.75/25.00 **t.** and dinner a la carte – 4.00 – **12 rm** 85.00/154.00 **st.**

Trelawne ⑤, Maenporth Rd, TR11 5HS, E : ¾ m. by Carwinion Rd ☎ 250226, Fax 250909, ≤, ▣, – rest TV ☎ P. AE ⓓ VISA.
closed 28 December-12 February – **Meals** (bar lunch Monday to Saturday)/dinner 23.50 **st.** 4.90 – **14 rm** 35.00/80.00 **st.** – SB.

at Budock Water W : 2 ¼ m. by Trescobeas Rd – A – ✉ Falmouth – ☎ 01326 :

Crill Manor, TR11 5BL, S : ¾ m. ☎ 211880, Fax 211229, heated, – TV ☎ P. VISA.
closed 1 November-23 December and 1 January-1 March – **Meals** (dinner only) 13.95 **t.** 4.40 – **12 rm** 49.00/98.00 **t.** – SB.

Penmorvah Manor ⑤, TR11 5ED, S : ¾ m. ☎ 250277, Fax 250509, – rm TV ☎ P. AE VISA JCB.
Meals (bar lunch)/dinner 13.95 **st.** and a la carte 4.75 – **27 rm** 35.00/80.00 **st.** – SB.

ATS Dracaena Av. ☎ 319233

FAREHAM Hants. 403 404 Q 31 **Great Britain G.** – pop. 50 434 (inc. Portchester) – ☎ 01329.
Envir. : Portchester castle★ *AC*, SE : 2½m. by A 27.
Westbury Manor, West St., PO16 0JJ ☎ 221342/824896.
London 77 – Portsmouth 9 – Southampton 13 – Winchester 19.

Solent, Rookery Av., Whiteley, PO15 7AJ, NW : 5 m. by A 27 ☎ (01489) 880000, Fax 880007, ▣, park, ✂, squash – rm TV ☎ P – 250. AE ⓓ VISA
Meals *(closed Saturday lunch)* 13.50/20.00 **st.** and a la carte 6.95 – **81 rm** 85.00/120.00 **st.**, 7 suites – SB.

Forte Posthouse, Cartwright Drive, Titchfield, PO15 5RS, W : 2¾ m. on A 27 ☎ 844644, Fax 844666, ▣ – rm TV ☎ P – 140. AE ⓓ VISA JCB
Meals a la carte 13.75/20.30 **st.** 6.95 – 7.95 – **126 rm** 59.00/68.00 **t.** – SB.

Red Lion, East St., P016 0BP, ☎ 822640, Fax 823579, – TV ☎ P – 80. AE ⓓ VISA.
Meals *(closed Saturday lunch)* 9.50/24.00 **st.** and a la carte – **42 rm** 55.00/75.00 **st.** – SB.

Lysses House, 51 High St., PO16 7BQ, ☎ 822622, Fax 822762, – rest TV ☎ P – 100. AE ⓓ VISA.
closed 24 December-2 January – **Meals** *(closed Saturday lunch, Sunday and Bank Holidays)* 11.95/18.50 **st.** and a la carte 4.70 – **21 rm** 53.00/69.00 **st.**

Avenue House without rest., 22 The Avenue, PO14 1NS, W : ½ m. on A 27 ☎ 232175, Fax 232196, – rm TV ☎ P. AE VISA
closed Christmas – **17 rm** 39.50/54.00 **st.**

ATS Queens Rd ☎ 234941/280032

FARMBOROUGH Avon 403 M 29 **The West Country G.** – pop. 1 084 – ✉ Bath – ☎ 01761.
Exc. : Bath★★★, NE : 7½m. by A 39 and A 4.
London 137 – Bath 7.5 – Bristol 12 – Wells 13.

Streets, The Street, BA3 1AR, ☎ 471452, Fax 471452, heated, – TV ☎ P. AE VISA.
closed 20 December-1 January – **Meals** (residents only) (dinner only) 14.80 **t.** – **8 rm** 42.00/60.00 **st.**

FARNBOROUGH Hants. 404 R 30 – pop. 52 535 – ☎ 01252.
18 Southwood, Ively Rd ☎ 548700.
London 41 – Reading 17 – Southampton 44 – Winchester 33.

Forte Crest Farnborough, Lynchford Rd, GU14 6AZ, S : 1 ½ m. on Farnborough Rd (A 325) ☎ 545051, Fax 377210, ▣ – rm TV ☎ P – 120. AE ⓓ VISA JCB
Meals (closed Sunday lunch) 17.95 **t.** and a la carte 6.50 – 10.95 – **110 rm** 109.00/140.00 **st.** – SB.

Falcon, 68 Farnborough Rd, GU14 6TH, S : ¾ m. on A 325 ☎ 545378, Fax 522539 – TV ☎ P. AE ⓓ VISA.
Meals *(closed Saturday lunch)* 12.95/17.95 **st.** and a la carte 5.75 – **30 rm** 67.75/79.00 **st.**

Wings Cottage, 32 Alexandra Rd, GU14 6DA, S : 1 ¼ m. by A 325 off Boundary Rd ☎ 544141, Fax 549361 –
Meals - Chinese rest.

ARNHAM Dorset 403 404 N 31 – see Blandford Forum.

ARNHAM Surrey 404 R 30 – pop. 30 428 – ☏ 01252.

Farnham Park,(Par Three) ☏ 715216.

Vernon House, 28 West St., GU9 7DR ☏ 715109.

London 45 – Reading 22 – ♦Southampton 39 – Winchester 28.

Bush (Forte Heritage), The Borough, GU9 7NN, ☏ 715237, Fax 733530, – – 60. AE VISA JCB
Meals a la carte 11.95/28.70 **st.** 7.55 – 9.00 – **66 rm** 75.00/95.00 **st.**

Bishop's Table, 27 West St., GU9 7DR, ☏ 710222, Fax 733494, – AE VISA.
closed 24 December-4 January – **Meals** *(closed Saturday lunch, 26 to 30 December and 2 to 4 January)* 16.50/27.50 **t.** 6.10 – **16 rm** 70.00/85.00 **t.** – SB.

Banaras, 40 Downing St., GU9 7PH, ☏ 734081 – AE VISA
Meals - Indian - (buffet lunch Sunday) 8.95/15.95 **st.** and a la carte 3.95.

at Churt S : 5¾ m. on A 287 – ☏ 01428 :

Pride of the Valley, Tilford Rd, GU10 2LE, E : 1½ m. by Hale House Lane ☏ 605799, Fax 605875, – . AE VISA JCB
Meals - Italian - a la carte 16.45/23.80 **t.** 4.65 – **11 rm** 50.00/70.00 **t.**

ARNINGHAM Kent 404 U 29 – ✉ Dartford – ☏ 01322.

London 18 – Hastings 46 – Maidstone 20.

Lion, High St., DA4 0DP, ☏ 866035, Fax 864357, –
Meals (grill rest.) – **7 rm.**

ARRINGTON GURNEY Avon 403 404 M 30 The West Country G. – pop. 780 – ✉ Bristol – ☏ 01761.

nvir. : Downside Abbey★ (Abbey Church★) SE : 5 m. by A 37 and B 3139.

xc. : Wells★★ - Cathedral★★★, Vicars' Close★, Bishop's Palace★ *AC* (≤★★) SW : 8 m. by A 39 Chew Magna★ (Stanton Drew Stone Circles★ *AC*) NW : 9½m. by A 37 and B 3130.

London 132 – Bath 13 – ♦Bristol 12 – Wells 8.

Country Ways, Marsh Lane, BS18 5TT, ☏ 452449, Fax 453360, – rest .
VISA.
closed 1 week Christmas – **Meals** (lunch by arrangement) (residents only Sunday dinner) a la carte 18.80/22.80 **t.** – **6 rm** 55.00/75.00 **t.** – SB.

AR SAWREY Cumbria 402 L 20 – see Hawkshead.

AUGH Cumbria – see Carlisle.

AVERSHAM Kent 404 W 30 – pop. 17 070 – ☏ 01795.

Fleur de Lys Heritage Centre, 13 Preston St., ME13 8NS ☏ 534542.

London 52 – ♦Dover 26 – Maidstone 21 – Margate 25.

✿ **Read's** (Pitchford), Painter's Forstal, ME13 0EE, SW : 2¼ m. by A 2 ☏ 535344, Fax 591200, , – AE VISA JCB
closed Sunday, Monday, last 2 weeks August and 26 December – **Meals** 16.50/25.00 **t.** and a la carte 25.00/32.00 **t.** 6.50
Spec. Scallops with a warm potato salad, white truffle oil and chives, Best end of Romney Marsh lamb, garlicky potatoes and miniature ratatouille, Chocoholics anonymous.

at Boughton SE : 3 m. by A 2 – ✉ Faversham – ☏ 01227 :

White Horse Inn, The Street, ME13 9AX, ☏ 751343, Fax 751090 –
13 rm.

at Eastling SW : 5 m. by A 2 – ✉ Faversham – ☏ 01795 :

Frith Farm House , Otterden, ME13 0DD, NW : 2 m. ☏ 890701, Fax 890009, –
. VISA.
Meals (by arrangement) (communal dining) 17.50 **st.** – **3 rm** 30.00/54.00 **st.**

ATS 20 North Lane ☏ 534039

AWKHAM GREEN Kent – see Brands Hatch.

ECKENHAM Heref. and Worcs. 403 404 O 27 – see Droitwich.

FELIXSTOWE Suffolk 404 Y 28 – pop. 23 189 – ECD : Wednesday – 01394.
Felixstowe Ferry, Ferry Rd ☎ 286834.
to Harwich (Orwell & Harwich Navigation Co. Ltd) 5 daily (14 mn).
Leisure Centre, Undercliff Road West, IP11 8AB ☎ 276770.
London 84 – Ipswich 11.

Orwell (Q.M.H.), Hamilton Rd, IP11 7DX, ☎ 309955, Fax 670687, – 200. AE VISA
Meals 13.50/17.50 **st.** and a la carte 6.50 – 9.00 – **57 rm** 63.50/77.50 **st.**, 1 suite – SB.

Waverley, Wolsey Gdns, IP11 7DF, ☎ 282811, Fax 670185, – 70. VISA
Meals 7.30/15.70 **t.** and a la carte 4.50 – 7.95 – **19 rm** 49.95/85.00 **t.** – SB.

Garfield Lodge, 12 Garfield Rd, IP11 7PU, ☎ 274843, –
Meals 10.00 **st.** – **5 rm** 18.00/36.00 **st.** – SB.

ATS 4-8 Sunderland Rd, Carr Rd Ind. Est. ☎ 675604 — ATS Crescent Rd ☎ 277596/277888

FELSTED Essex 404 V 28 – pop. 2 512 – ✉ Great Dunmow – 01371.
London 39 – Cambridge 31 – Chelmsford 9 – Colchester 24.

Rumbles Cottage, Braintree Rd, CM6 3DJ, ☎ 820996 – VISA
closed Saturday lunch, Sunday dinner and Monday – **Meals** (lunch by arrangement dinner 12.50 **t.** and a la carte 4.00.

FENNY BRIDGES Devon 403 K 31 – ✉ Honiton – 01404.
London 166 – Exeter 12.

Greyhound Inn, EX14 0BJ, on A 30 ☎ 850380, Fax 850812, « 17C thatched inn », AE VISA
Meals a la carte approx. 14.00 4.25 – **10 rm** (dinner included) 39.00/44.00 **t.** – SB.

FERNDOWN Dorset 403 404 O 31 – pop. 25 177 – 01202.
London 108 – Bournemouth 6 – Dorchester 27 – Salisbury 23.

Dormy (De Vere), New Rd, BH22 8ES, on A 347 ☎ 872121, Fax 895388, , squash – rm – 250. AE VISA
Meals *(closed Saturday lunch)* 12.50/22.00 **st.** and a la carte – **123 rm** 95.00/120.00 **st** 5 suites – SB.

Travel Inn, Ringwood Rd, Tricketts Cross, BH22 9BB, NE : 1 m. on A 348 ☎ 874210 rm AE VISA
Meals (grill rest.) – 4.95 – **32 rm** 34.50 **t.**

FERRYBRIDGE SERVICE AREA W. Yorks. – ✉ Leeds – 01977.
London 178 – Leeds 14 – Doncaster 14 – Rotherham 28 – York 28.

Granada Lodge without rest., WF11 0AF, at junction 33 of M 62 with A 1 ☎ 67048[illegible] Reservations (Freephone) 0800 555300 – AE VISA
35 rm 39.95 **st.**

FERSFIELD Norfolk – see Diss.

FINDON W. Sussex 404 S 31 – ✉ Worthing – 01903.
London 49 – Brighton 13 – Southampton 50 – Worthing 4.

Findon Manor, High St., BN14 0TA, off A 24 ☎ 872733, Fax 877473, « Part 16C ston[e] and flint house », – 40. AE VISA
Meals 12.95/19.95 **t.** and a la carte 5.95 – **11 rm** 45.00/80.00 **t.** – SB.

FINEDON Northants. 404 S 26 – see Wellingborough.

FINGLESHAM Kent – see Deal.

FIVE ASHES E. Sussex. – see Mayfield.

FLAMSTEAD Herts. 404 S 28 – pop. 1 399 – ✉ St. Albans – 01582.
London 32 – Luton 5.

Hertfordshire Moat House (Q.M.H.), London Rd, AL3 8HH, on A 5 ☎ 449988 Fax 842282, – rm rest – 300. AE VISA
Meals (bar lunch Saturday) 10.95/16.95 **st.** and dinner a la carte 6.20 – 9.50 – **89 rm** 70.00/75.00 **st.** – SB.

Si vous cherchez un hôtel tranquille,
consultez d'abord les cartes de l'introduction
ou repérez dans le texte les établissements indiqués avec le signe ou .

LEET Hants. 404 R 30 – ☎ 01252.

ondon 40 – Basingstoke 11 – Reading 17.

Lismoyne, Church Rd, GU13 8NA, ☎ 628555, Fax 811761, – rest – 100. AE VISA
Meals 12.40/14.95 **st.** and a la carte 5.25 – **44 rm** 60.00/82.00 **st.** – SB.

LEET SERVICE AREA Hants. – ✉ Basingstoke – ☎ 01252.

Forte Travelodge, Hartley Witney, RG27 8BN, M3 between junctions 4a and 5 (southbound carriageway) ☎ 815587, Reservations (Freephone) 0800 850950 – . AE VISA.
Meals (grill rest.) – **40 rm** 34.50 **t.**

LEETWOOD Lancs. 402 K 22 – pop. 27 227 – ☎ 01253.

Fleetwood, Golf House, Princes Way ☎ 873114.

to the Isle of Man (Douglas) (Isle of Man Steam Packet Co. Ltd) (summer only) h 20 mn).

Ferry Office, Ferry Dock, The Esplanade, FY7 6DL ☎ 773953.

ondon 245 – ♦Blackpool 10 – Lancaster 28 – ♦Manchester 53.

North Euston, The Esplanade, FY7 6BN, ☎ 876525, Fax 777842, – – 120. AE VISA.
Meals (bar lunch Saturday) 10.50/16.75 **t.** and a la carte 5.00 – **54 rm** 47.50/68.00 **t.** – SB.

ATS 238 Dock St. ☎ 771211

LITWICK Beds. 404 S 27 – pop. 11 283 – ☎ 01525.

ondon 45 – Bedford 13 – Luton 12 – Northampton 28.

Flitwick Manor, Church Rd, MK45 1AE, off Dunstable Rd ☎ 712242, Fax 718753, , « 18C manor house », , park, – rest . AE VISA.
Meals 19.45/39.00 **t.** 6.45 – **15 rm** 90.00/190.00 **t.** – SB.

OLKESTONE Kent 404 X 30 **Great Britain G.** – pop. 45 280 – ☎ 01303.

ee : The Leas★ (★) Z.

to France (Boulogne) (Hoverspeed Ltd) 4-5 daily (55 mn).

Harbour St., CT20 1QN ☎ 258594.

ondon 76 – ♦Brighton 76 – ♦Dover 8 – Maidstone 33.

Plan on next page

Clifton, The Leas, CT20 2EB, ☎ 851231, Fax 851231, , – – 80. AE VISA JCB Z **r**
Meals 9.95/17.00 **t.** and a la carte 7.95 – **80 rm** 55.00/149.00 **t.** – SB.

Wards, 39 Earls Av., CT20 2HB, ☎ 245166, Fax 254480 – – 50. AE VISA JCB. X **c**
Meals *(closed Sunday dinner and Bank Holidays)* a la carte 11.70/21.00 **t.** 3.75 – **10 rm** 50.00/90.00 **t.** – SB.

Banque without rest., 4 Castle Hill Av., CT20 2QT, ☎ 253797, Fax 253797, – . AE VISA. Z **z**
12 rm 25.00/50.00 **st.**

Travel Inn, Cherry Garden Lane, CT19 4AP, NW : 1 ¼ m. by A 259 at junction 13 M 20 ☎ 273620, Fax 273641 – . AE VISA X **b**
Meals (grill rest.) – 4.95 – **40 rm** 34.50 **t.**

Harbourside without rest., 14 Wear Bay Rd, CT19 6AT, ☎ 256528, Fax 241299, , , – . AE VISA. X **e**
6 rm 30.00/60.00 **st.**

La Tavernetta, Leaside Court, Clifton Gdns, CT20 2ED, ☎ 254955 – AE VISA Z **n**
closed Sunday and Bank Holidays – **Meals** - Italian - 9.50/13.50 **t.** and a la carte 4.15.

Paul's, 2a Bouverie Rd West, CT20 2RX, ☎ 259697, Fax 226647 – VISA Z **e**
closed 3 days Christmas – **Meals** 15.85/16.55 **t.** and a la carte 4.25.

ATS 318/324 Cheriton Rd ☎ 275198/275121

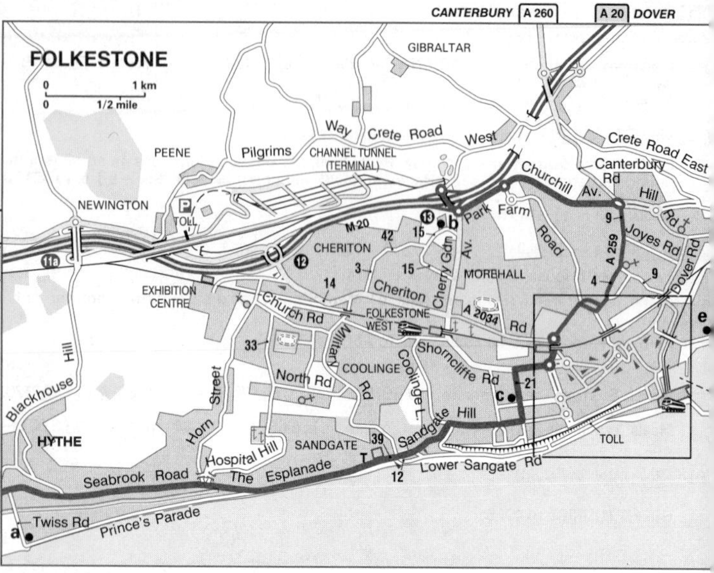

FOLKESTONE

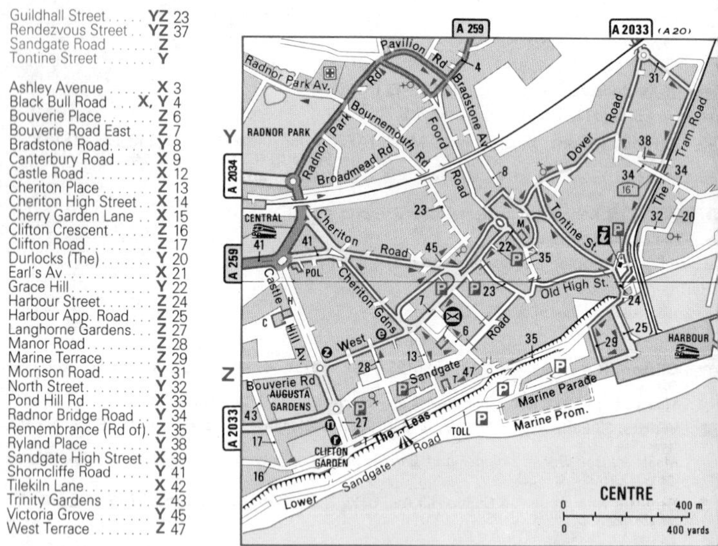

FONTWELL W. Sussex – ✉ Arundel – ☎ 01243.

🅸 Little Chef Complex, BN18 0SD ℘ 543269.

♦London 60 – Chichester 6 – Worthing 15.

🏨 **Forte Travelodge,** BN18 0SB, at A 27/A 29 roundabout ℘ 543973, Reservation (Freephone) 0800 850950 – TV ♿ 🅿. AE VISA. ✈
Meals (grill rest.) – **32 rm** 34.50 **t.**

FORD Wilts. – see Castle Combe.

FORDINGBRIDGE Hants. 403 404 O 31 – pop. 5 893 – ☎ 01425.

Salisbury St., SP6 1AB ☎ 654560 (summer only).

London 101 – Bournemouth 17 – Salisbury 11 – Winchester 30.

XX **Hour Glass,** Salisbury Rd, Burgate, SP6 1LX, N : 1 m. on A 338 ☎ 652348, « 14C thatched cottage », – P. VISA
closed Sunday dinner, Monday and 2 weeks November – **Meals** 8.95/17.95 **st.** 4.50.

at Woodgreen NE : 4 m. by B 3078 – ✉ Fordingbridge – ☎ 01725 :

Cottage Crest without rest., Castle Hill, SP6 2AX, ☎ 512009, ←, – TV P.
3 rm 25.00/38.00 **st.**

at Stuckton SE : 1 m. by B 3078 – ✉ Fordingbridge – ☎ 01425 :

X **Three Lions,** Stuckton Rd, SP6 2HF, ☎ 652489, Fax 656144 – P. VISA
closed Sunday dinner, Monday except Bank Holidays and 22 January-12 February – **Meals** a la carte 17.35/25.00 **t.** 7.50.

at Alderholt SW : 2 m. – ✉ Fordingbridge – ☎ 01425 :

XX **Moonacre,** SP6 3BB, ☎ 653142 – P. VISA
closed Sunday dinner, Monday and 2 weeks March – **Meals** (dinner only and Sunday lunch)/dinner 11.00 **t.** and a la carte 3.75.

When visiting Great Britain,
use the Michelin Green Guide **"Great Britain".**
- *Detailed descriptions of places of interest*
- *Touring programmes*
- *Maps and street plans*
- *The history of the country*
- *Photographs and drawings of monuments, beauty spots, houses...*

FOREST ROW E. Sussex 404 U 30 – pop. 4 762 – ☎ 01342.

18 Royal Ashdown Forest, Chapel Lane, Forest Row ☎ 822018.

London 35 – Brighton 26 – Eastbourne 30 – Maidstone 32.

Brambletye, The Square, RH18 5EZ, ☎ 824144, Fax 824833 – TV ☎ P. AE VISA.
Meals (carving lunch)/dinner 14.95 **st.** and a la carte 3.95 – **22 rm** 54.00/69.50 **st.** – SB.

Chequers Inn, The Square, RH18 5ES, ☎ 823333, Fax 825454 – TV ☎ P. AE VISA JCB.
Meals 10.95/25.00 **t.** and a la carte 6.95 – **21 rm** 38.50/60.00 **st.** – SB.

at Wych Cross S : 2½ m. on A 22 – ✉ Forest Row – ☎ 01342 :

Ashdown Park, RH18 5JR, E : ¾ m. on Hartfield rd ☎ 824988, Fax 826206, ←, « Part 19C manor house in extensive gardens », , , , 9, park, , squash – TV ☎ – 150. AE VISA.
Anderida : Meals 17.00/27.00 **st.** and a la carte – **89 rm** 99.00/124.00 **st.**, 6 suites – SB.

Roebuck (Jarvis), RH18 5JL, ☎ 823811, Fax 824790, – rm TV ☎ P – 110
30 rm.

FORTON SERVICE AREA Lancs. – ✉ Forton – ☎ 01524.

(M 6) Forton, Bay Horse, LA2 9DU ☎ 792181.

Pavilion Lodge without rest., LA2 9DU, on M 6 ☎ 792227, Fax 791703 – TV P
41 rm 39.95 **t.**

FOTHERINGHAY Northants. 404 S 26 – see Oundle.

FOULSHAM Norfolk – pop. 1 379 – ✉ East Dereham – ☎ 01362.

London 121 – Cambridge 69 – King's Lynn 31 – Norwich 18.

X **The Gamp,** Claypit Lane, NR20 5RW, ☎ 684114 – P. VISA
closed Tuesday lunch, Sunday dinner, Monday and first 2 weeks January – **Meals** 10.95 **st.** and a la carte 4.50.

FOUR MARKS Hants. 403 404 Q 30 – pop. 2 814 – ✉ Alton – ☎ 01420.

London 58 – Guildford 24 – Reading 29 – Southampton 24.

Forte Travelodge, 156 Winchester Rd, GU34 5HZ, on A 31 ☎ 562659, Reservations (Freephone) 0800 850950 – TV P. AE VISA.
Meals (grill rest.) – **31 rm** 34.50 **t.**

FOWEY Cornwall 403 G 32 **The West Country G.** – pop. 2 123 – ☎ 01726.

See : Town★★.

Envir. : Gribbin Head★★ (≤★★) 6 m. rtn on foot – Bodinnick (≤★★) - Lanteglos Church★ E : 5 m. by ferry – Polruan (≤★★) SE : 6 m. by ferry – Polkerris★, W : 2 m. by A 3082.

ℹ The Post Office, 4 Custom House Hill, PL23 1AA ℘ 833616.

◆London 277 – Newquay 24 – ◆Plymouth 34 – Truro 22.

Marina, 17 The Esplanade, PL23 1HY, ℘ 833315, Fax 832779, ≤ Fowey river and harbour – rest TV ☎. AE VISA JCB
closed January and February – **Meals** (dinner only) 12.00 **t.** and a la carte 4.95 – **11 rm** 51.00/68.00 **t.** – SB.

Carnethic House , Lambs Barn, PL23 1HQ, NW : ¾ m. on A 3082 ℘ 833336 Fax 833336, heated, – rest TV P. AE VISA.
closed December and January – **Meals** (bar lunch)/dinner 14.00 **st.** 3.50 – **8 rm** 40.00/60.00 **st.** – SB.

Ocean View without rest., 24 Tower Park, PL23 1JB, ℘ 832283, ≤, – .
April-September – **4 rm** 20.00/40.00 **st.**

Food for Thought, 4 Town Quay, PL23 1AT, ℘ 832221, Fax 832060, « Converted coastguard's cottage on quayside » – VISA
closed Sunday, January and February – **Meals** (dinner only) 15.95 **t.** and a la carte 18.40/27.40 **t.**

at Bodinnick-by-Fowey E : ¼ m. via car ferry – ✉ Fowey – ☎ 01726 :

Old Ferry Inn, PL23 1LX, ℘ 870237, Fax 870116, ≤ Fowey Estuary and town, « Part 16C inn » – TV P. VISA JCB
Meals (bar lunch)/dinner a la carte 17.00/23.00 **t.** 4.50 – **12 rm** 35.00/70.00 **t.**

FOWLMERE Cambs. 404 U 27 – see Cambridge.

FOWNHOPE Heref. and Worcs. 403 404 M 27 – pop. 900 – ✉ Hereford – ☎ 01432.

◆London 132 – ◆Cardiff 46 – Hereford 6 – Gloucester 27.

Green Man Inn, HR1 4PE, ℘ 860243, Fax 860207, – rest TV ☎ P. AE VISA
Meals (bar lunch Monday to Saturday)/dinner a la carte approx. 14.20 **t.** 4.95 – **19 rm** 32.00/51.00 **t.** – SB.

Bowens Country House, HR1 4PS, on B 4224 ℘ 860430, Fax 860430, – rest TV P. VISA.
Meals (by arrangement) 11.50 **t.** 3.15 – **12 rm** 20.00/52.00 **t.** – SB.

FRAMLINGHAM Suffolk 404 Y 27 – pop. 2 697 – ✉ Woodbridge – ☎ 01728.

◆London 92 – ◆Ipswich 19 – ◆Norwich 42.

Crown (Forte), Market Hill, IP13 9AN, ℘ 723521, Fax 724274, « 16C inn » – TV ☎ P. AE VISA JCB
Meals 8.95/17.95 **t.** and dinner a la carte 5.95 – 8.50 – **14 rm** 60.00/120.00 **t.** – SB.

at Badingham NE : 3¼ m. by B 1120 on A 1120 – ✉ Woodbridge – ☎ 01728 :

Colston Hall without rest., IP13 8LB, E : ¾ m. by A 1120 on Bruisyard rd ℘ 638375, , park – P.
3 rm 25.00/40.00 **st.**

at Earl Soham W : 3½ m. by B 1119 on A 1120 – ✉ Woodbridge – ☎ 01728 :

Abbey House without rest., Monk Soham, IP13 7EN, NW : 2 ½ m. by Kenton rd ℘ 685225, – P.
April-October – **3 rm** 22.00/44.00 **st.**

FRAMPTON Dorset 403 404 M 31 – see Dorchester (Dorset).

FRAMPTON-ON-SEVERN Glos. 403 404 M 28 – pop. 1 383 – ☎ 01452.

◆London 121 – ◆Bristol 48 – Gloucester 14.

Savery's, The Green, GL2 7EA, ℘ 740077 – AE VISA
closed Sunday, Monday and 25 December – **Meals** (dinner only) 25.95 **t.**

Dans ce guide

un même symbole, un même mot,
imprimé en noir ou en rouge, en maigre ou en **gras**,
n'ont pas tout à fait la même signification.
Lisez attentivement les pages explicatives.

FRANKLEY SERVICE AREA W. Mids. 403 404 ⑲ – ✉ Birmingham – ☎ 0121.

Plan : see Birmingham p. 2

Granada Lodge without rest., B32 4AR, M5, between junctions 3 and 4 (southbound carriageway) ☎ 550 3261, Fax 501 2880, Reservations (Freephone) 0800 555300 – ⇔ TV ☎ ♿ P. AE VISA.
60 rm 39.95 **st.** BU **a**

FRANT Kent 404 U 30 – see Royal Tunbridge Wells.

FRESHWATER BAY I.O.W. 403 404 P 31 – see Wight (Isle of).

FRIETH Bucks. – see Henley-on-Thames (Oxon.).

FRILFORD Oxon. 403 404 P 28-29 – see Abingdon.

FRIMLEY Surrey 404 R 30 – pop. 5 661 – ✉ Camberley – ☎ 01276.
London 39 – Reading 17 – ♦Southampton 47.

One Oak Toby, 114 Portsmouth Rd, GU15 1HS, NE : 1 m. on A 325 ☎ 691939, Fax 676088 – ⇔ rm TV ☎ P – 30. AE VISA.
Meals (grill rest.) 7.90 **t.** (lunch) and a la carte 9.30/18.00 **t.** – **40 rm** 69.95/82.00 **t.**

FRITTENDEN Kent 404 V 30 – pop. 2 055 (inc. Sissinghurst) – ☎ 01580 80.
London 50 – Folkestone 34 – Hastings 23 – Maidstone 13.

Maplehurst, Mill Lane, TN17 2DT, NW : 1 m. ☎ 852203, Fax 852203, « Converted water mill », heated, – ⇔ TV P. VISA.
Meals 18.00 **s.** 4.00 – **3 rm** 38.00/56.00 **s.**

FRODSHAM Ches. 402 403 404 L 24 – pop. 8 903 – ✉ Warrington – ☎ 01928.
London 203 – Chester 11 – ♦Liverpool 21 – ♦Manchester 29 – ♦Stoke-on-Trent 42.

Forest Hills, Overton Hill, WA6 6HH, S : 1 ¾ m. by B 5152 ☎ 735255, Fax 735517, ≤, , , , squash – ⇔ rm TV ☎ P – 200. AE VISA
Meals *(closed Saturday lunch)* (carving lunch Sunday) 10.95 **st.** and lunch a la carte 13.20/23.95 **st.** – 8.25 – **57 rm** 75.00 **st.** – SB.

Heathercliffe Country House, Manley Rd, WA6 6HB, S : 1 ½ m. by B 5152 ☎ 733722, Fax 735667, ≤, , park – ⇔ rest TV ☎ P. AE VISA
Meals *(closed to non-residents Saturday lunch, Sunday dinner and Bank Holiday Mondays)* 10.95/12.45 **st.** and a la carte 5.95 – **9 rm** 64.00/95.00 **st.** – SB.

Old Hall, Main St., WA6 7AB, ☎ 732052, Fax 739046, – TV ☎ P – 30. AE VISA JCB
Meals 7.75/13.50 **t.** and a la carte 4.95 – **20 rm** 55.75/69.00 **st.**, 1 suite.

ATS Brooklyn Garage, Chester Rd ☎ 733555

FULBROOK Oxon. 403 404 P 28 – see Burford.

GALMPTON Devon 403 J 32 – ✉ Brixham – ☎ 01803.
♦London 229 – ♦Plymouth 32 – Torquay 6.

Maypool Park, Maypool, TQ5 0ET, SW : 1 m. by Greenway Rd ☎ 842442, Fax 845782, ≤, – ⇔ TV ☎ P – 30. AE VISA.
A Taste of Taylors : Meals (lunch by arrangement)/dinner 20.00 **t.** 6.00 – **10 rm** 40.00/85.00 **t.** – SB.

GARFORTH W. Yorks. 402 P 22 – see Leeds.

GARSTANG Lancs. 402 L 22 – pop. 3 948 – ☎ 01995.
Discovery Centre, Council Offices, High St., PR3 1FU ☎ 602125.
♦London 233 – ♦Blackpool 13 – Manchester 41.

Crofters, Cabus, PR3 1PH, W : ¾ m. on A 6 ☎ 604128, Fax 601646 – TV ☎ P – 200. AE VISA
Meals (dancing Saturday evening) (bar lunch Monday to Saturday)/dinner 9.50/17.50 **t.** and a la carte 4.75 – 5.00 – **19 rm** 30.00/65.00 **t.** – SB.

Pickerings, Garstang Rd, Catterall, PR3 0HD, S : 1 ½ m. on B 6430 ☎ 602133, Fax 602100, – TV ☎ P – 25. AE VISA
Meals *(closed Saturday lunch and Bank Holidays)* 10.50/28.50 **st.** 5.25 – **16 rm** 37.50/69.00 **st.** – SB.

at Bilsborrow S : 3 ¾ m. by B 6430 on A 6 – ✉ Preston – ☎ 01995 :

Guy's Thatched Hamlet, Canalside, St. Michaels Rd, PR3 0RS, off A 6 ☎ 640010, Fax 640141 – TV ☎ P. AE VISA JCB
Meals *(closed Sunday)* 6.50 **st.** (lunch) and a la carte 12.00/21.50 **st.** 4.25 – 5.00 – **53 rm** 33.00 **st.** – SB.

Olde Duncombe House without rest., Garstang Rd, PR3 0RE, ☎ 640336 – TV ☎ P. AE VISA
10 rm 32.50/45.00 **st.**

GATESHEAD Tyne and Wear 401 402 P 19 **Great Britain G.** – pop. 199 588 – ☎ 0191.

Exc. : Beamish : North of England Open Air Museum★★ *AC*, SW : 6 m. by A 692 and A 6076 BX

Ravensworth, Moss Heaps, Wrekenton ☎ 487 6014/487 2843 – Heworth, Gingling Gate ☎ 469 2137 BX.

Central Library, Prince Consort Rd, NE8 4LN ☎ 477 3478 BX – Metrocentre, Portcullis, 7 The Arcade, NE11 9YL ☎ 460 6345 AX.

London 282 – Durham 16 – Middlesbrough 38 – Newcastle upon Tyne 1 – Sunderland 11.

Plan : see Newcastle upon Tyne

Newcastle/Gateshead Marriott, Metro Centre, NE11 9XF, ☎ 493 2233, Fax 493 2030, – rm ☎ – 400. AE VISA JCB. AX
Meals (bar lunch Monday to Saturday)/dinner 16.50 **st.** and a la carte – 10.25 – **150 rm** 98.00/150.00 **st.** – SB.

Swallow, High West St., NE8 1PE, ☎ 477 1105, Fax 478 7214, – rm ☎ – 350. AE VISA. BX
Meals (carving lunch) (bar lunch Saturday) 6.95/20.00 **st.** and dinner a la carte 4.60 – **99 rm** 70.00/95.00 **st.**, 4 suites – SB.

Gibside Arms, Front St., Whickham, NE16 4JG, ☎ 488 9292, Fax 488 8000 – rest ☎. AE VISA
closed 23 December-1 January – **Meals** 13.75 **st.** (dinner) and a la carte 15.15/21.55 **st.** – **45 rm** 59.00/78.00 **st.** – SB.

at Low Fell S : 2 m. by A 167and Belle Vue Bank – **BX** – ✉ Gateshead – ☎ 0191 :

Eslington Villa, 8 Station Rd, NE9 6DR, ☎ 487 6017, Fax 420 0667, – rest ☎. AE VISA
closed 1 week Christmas and Bank Holidays – **Meals** *(closed Saturday lunch, Sunday dinner and Bank Holidays)* 10.95/19.95 **t.** and a la carte 4.75 – **12 rm** 44.50/74.50 **t.**

ATS Earlsway/First Av., Team Valley Trading Est. ☎ 4910081

GATWICK AIRPORT W. Sussex 404 T 30 – ✉ Crawley – ☎ 01293.

Gatwick Airport : ☎ 535353.

International Arrivals, South Terminal, RH6 0NP ☎ 560108.

London 29 – Brighton 28.

Plan opposite

London Gatwick Airport Hilton, South Terminal, RH6 0LL, ☎ 518080, Telex 877021 Fax 528980, – rm ☎ – 500. AE VISA JCB Y
Meals 12.95/23.50 **st.** and a la carte 8.75 – 11.95 – **547 rm** 130.00/165.00 **st.**, 3 suites.

Ramada H. Gatwick, Povey Cross Rd, RH6 0BE, ☎ 820169, Telex 87440, Fax 820259, squash – rm ☎ – 180. AE VISA Y
Meals *(closed Saturday lunch)* 15.50/16.50 **st.** and a la carte – 10.50 – **250 rm** 80.00/90.00 **st.**, 5 suites.

Forte Crest, Gatwick Airport (North Terminal), RH6 0PH, ☎ 567070, Telex 87202 Fax 567739, – rm ☎ – 350. AE VISA JCB Y
Meals 12.95/15.95 **st.** and dinner a la carte 6.95 – 9.95 – **450 rm** 99.00/110.00 **st.** 6 suites – SB.

Forte Posthouse, Povey Cross Rd, RH6 0BA, ☎ 771621, Fax 771054, heated – rm rest ☎ – 120. AE VISA Y
Meals a la carte 13.00/22.85 **t.** 6.95 – 7.95 – **210 rm** 56.00 **t.** – SB.

Travel Inn, Longbridge Way, Gatwick Airport (North Terminal), RH6 0NX, ☎ 568158 – rm rest – 35. AE VISA. Y
Meals (grill rest.) – 4.95 – **121 rm** 34.50 **t.**

Forte Travelodge without rest., Church Rd, Lowfield Heath, RH11 0PQ, ☎ (01693) 533441, Fax 535369, Reservations (Freephone) 0800 850950 – ☎. AE VISA Y
126 rm 34.50 **t.**

ATS Building 238B, Perimeter Rd South ☎ 568333/568555

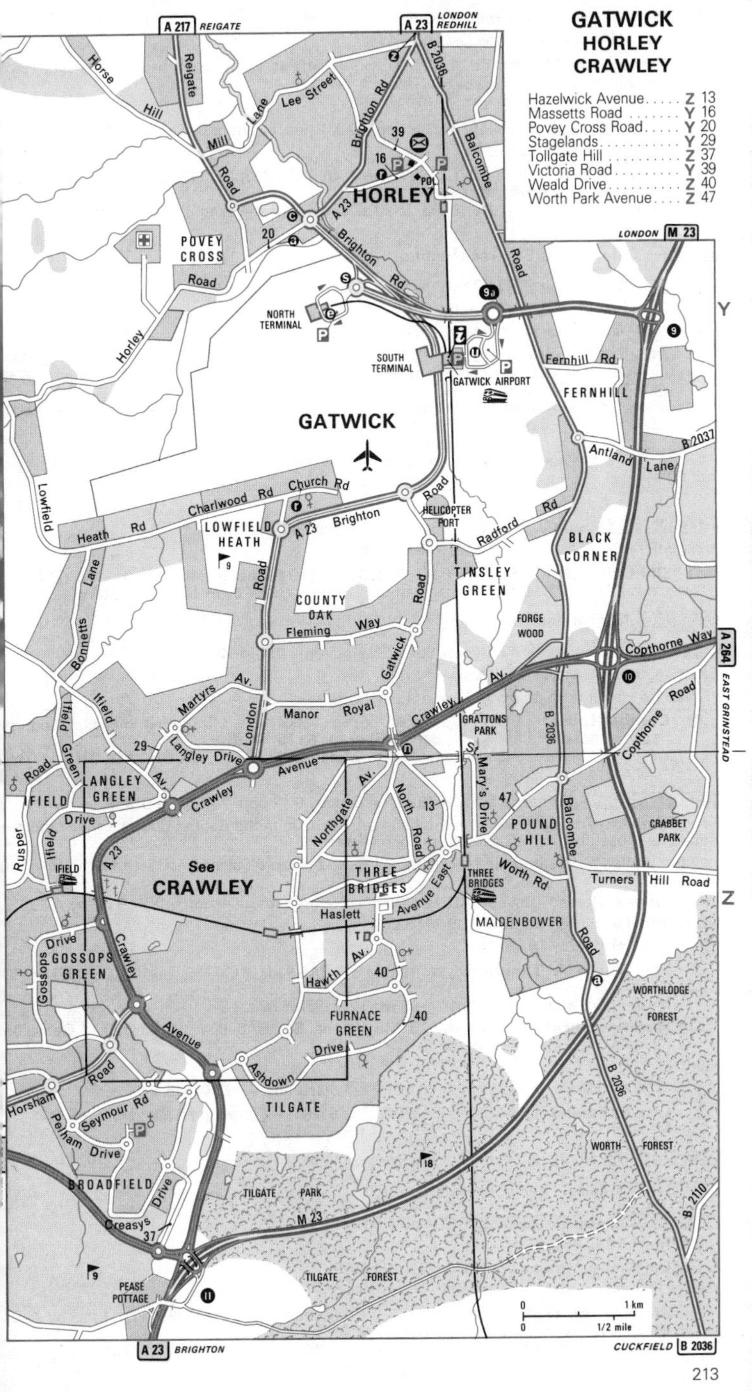
GATWICK
HORLEY
CRAWLEY
Hazelwick Avenue Z 13
Massetts Road Y 16
Povey Cross Road Y 20
Stagelands Y 29
Tollgate Hill Z 37
Victoria Road Y 39
Weald Drive Z 40
Worth Park Avenue Z 47
A 217 REIGATE
A 23 LONDON REDHILL
LONDON M 23
A 264 EAST GRINSTEAD
A 23 BRIGHTON
CUCKFIELD B 2036
Y
Z
Horse Hill
Reigate Road
Mill Lane
Lee Street
Brighton Rd
Balcombe Road
HORLEY
POVEY CROSS
Road
Horley
NORTH TERMINAL
SOUTH TERMINAL
GATWICK AIRPORT
GATWICK
Fernhill Rd
FERNHILL
Antland Lane
B 2037
Lowfield
Charlwood Rd
Church Rd
Heath Rd
LOWFIELD HEATH
Brighton
HELICOPTER PORT
Radford Rd
BLACK CORNER
TINSLEY GREEN
COUNTY OAK
Fleming Way
Gatwick Road
FORGE WOOD
Copthorne Way
Bonnetts Lane
Ifield Av.
Martyrs Av.
Manor Royal
Crawley Av.
GRATTONS PARK
B 2036
Copthorne Road
Langley Drive
London Road
Ifield Green
LANGLEY GREEN
IFIELD
Crawley Avenue
Northgate Av.
North Road
St Mary's Drive
POUND HILL
Balcombe Road
CRABBET PARK
Rusper
Ifield Drive
IFIELD
See CRAWLEY
THREE BRIDGES
Worth Rd
Turners Hill Road
Haslett Avenue East
MAIDENBOWER
Gossops Drive
GOSSOPS GREEN
Crawley Avenue
Hawth Av.
FURNACE GREEN
WORTHLODGE FOREST
Ashdown Drive
TILGATE
Horsham Road
Seymour Rd
Pelham Drive
BROADFIELD
Drive
TILGATE PARK
WORTH FOREST
B 2110
Creasys
M 23
PEASE POTTAGE
TILGATE FOREST
1 km
1/2 mile

GAYTON Mersey. – ✉ Wirral – ☎ 0151.
◆London 206 – Birkenhead 12 – Chester 13 – ◆Liverpool 10.

Travel Inn, Chester Rd, L60 3FD, on A 540 at junction with A 551 ℘ 342 1982, Fax 342 8983 – ⇔ rm TV & P. AE VISA. ✻
Meals (grill rest.) – ☐ 4.95 – **37 rm** 34.50 **t.**

GERRARDS CROSS Bucks. 404 S 29 – pop. 20 001 (inc. Chalfont St.Peter) – ☎ 01753.
◆London 22 – Aylesbury 22 – ◆Oxford 36.

De Vere Bull, Oxford Rd, SL9 7PA, on A 40 ℘ 885995, Fax 885504, – |♦| TV ☎ P – 200. AE VISA. ✻
Meals (bar lunch Saturday) 11.95/27.90 **st.** and dinner a la carte 8.50 – **93 rm** ☐ 110.00/160.00 **st.**, 2 suites – SB.

GILLAN Cornwall 403 E 33 – see Helford.

GILLINGHAM Dorset 403 404 N 30 The West Country G. – pop. 6 934 – ☎ 01747 :
Exc. : Stourhead★★★ *AC*, N : 9 m. by B 3092, B 3095 and B 3092.
◆London 116 – Bournemouth 34 – ◆Bristol 46 – ◆Southampton 52.

Stock Hill Country House ⑤, Wyke, SP8 5NR, W : 1 ½ m. on B 3081 ℘ 823626, Fax 825628, « Victorian country house, antiques », ≦s, , , park, ✂ – ⇔ rest TV ☎ P. AE VISA. ✻
Meals *(closed Monday lunch)* (booking essential) (lunch by arrangement)/dinner 19.00/32.00 **t.** 7.20 – **8 rm** ☐ (dinner included) 100.00/235.00 **t.**, 1 suite – SB.

I prezzi Per ogni chiarimento sui prezzi qui riportati, consultate le spiegazioni alle pagine dell'introduzione.

GISLINGHAM Suffolk 404 X 27 – pop. 822 – ✉ Eye – ☎ 01379.
◆London 93 – ◆Cambridge 45 – ◆Ipswich 20 – ◆Norwich 30.

Old Guildhall, Mill St., IP23 8JT, ℘ 783361, « 15C former guildhall », – ⇔ TV P
closed January – **Meals** (by arrangement) 12.50 **s.** 6.00 – **3 rm** ☐ 35.00/50.00 **s.** – SB.

GISSING Norfolk – see Diss.

GITTISHAM Devon 403 K 31 – pop. 602 – ✉ Honiton – ☎ 01404.
Envir. : Ottery St. Mary★ – St. Mary's★.
◆London 164 – Exeter 14 – Sidmouth 9 – Taunton 21.

Combe House ⑤, EX14 0AD, ℘ 42756, Fax 46004, ≤, « Elizabethan mansion, country house atmosphere », , , park – TV ☎ P. AE VISA
closed third week January-early March – **Meals** 9.50/22.00 **st.** – **14 rm** ☐ 65.00/131.00 **st.**, 1 suite.

GLASTONBURY Somerset 403 L 30 The West Country G. – pop. 7 747 – ☎ 01458.
See : Town★★ - Abbey★★ (Abbots Kitchen★) *AC* – St. John the Baptist Church★★ – Somerset Rural Life Museum★ *AC* – Glastonbury Tor★ (≤★★★).
Envir. : Wells★★ - Cathedral★★★, Vicars' Close★, Bishop's Palace★ *AC* (≤★★) NE : 5 ½ m. by A 39.
Exc. : Wookey Hole★★ (Caves★ *AC*, Papermill★, Fairground Collection★) NE : 8 m. by A 39.
ℹ The Tribunal, 9 High St., BA6 9DP ℘ 832954.
◆London 136 – ◆Bristol 26 – Taunton 22.

The Who'd 'A' Thought It, Northload St., BA6 9JJ, ℘ 834460, Fax 831039 – TV ☎. AE VISA. ✻
Meals 7.95 **t.** and a la carte 4.25 – **6 rm** ☐ 35.95/55.00 **t.** – SB.

Number Three without rest., 3 Magdalene St., BA6 9EW, ℘ 832129, « Georgian house », – ⇔ TV ☎ P. VISA. ✻
closed January – ☐ 5.50 – **5 rm** 50.00/65.00.

at West Pennard E : 3½ m. on A 361 – ✉ Glastonbury – ☎ 01458 :

Lion at Pennard, BA6 8NH, ℘ 832941, Fax 832941 – TV ☎ P. AE VISA JCB. ✻
Meals (in bar) a la carte 10.25/16.75 **t.** – **7 rm** ☐ 30.00/50.00 **t.**

GLEWSTONE Heref. and Worcs. – see Ross-on-Wye.

GLOOSTON Leics. – see Market Harborough.

GLOSSOP Derbs. 402 403 404 O 23 – pop. 30 771 – ☎ 01457.
⛳ Sheffield Rd ℘ 865247.
ℹ The Gatehouse, Victoria St., SK13 8HT ℘ 855920.
◆London 194 – ◆Manchester 18 – ◆Sheffield 25.

Wind in the Willows ⑤, Hurst Rd, Derbyshire Level, SK13 9PT, E : 1 m. by A 57 ℘ 868001, Fax 853354, – TV ☎ P – 30. AE VISA. ✻
Meals (residents only) (dinner only) 17.50 **st.** 5.50 – **12 rm** ☐ 58.00/90.00 **st.**

GLOUCESTER

Street	Grid	No.
Eastgate Shopping Centre	Y	
Eastgate Street	Y	10
Northgate Street	Y	16
Southgate Street	Y	
Barnwood By-Pass	Z	3
Black Dog Way	Y	5
Commercial Road	Y	6
Cotteswold Road	Z	8
Derby Road	Z	9
Great Western Road	Y	12
Heathville Road	Y	13
King Edward's Avenue	Z	14
Lower Westgate Street	Y	15
Parkend Road	Z	17
Parliament Street	Y	18
Pitt Street	Y	19
Quay Street	Y	20
Royal Oak Road	Y	21
St. Aldate Street	Y	22
St. Johns Lane	Y	23
Southern Avenue	Z	24
Spa Road	Y	26
Stroud Road	Z	28
Tredworth Road	Z	30
Worcester Street	Y	31

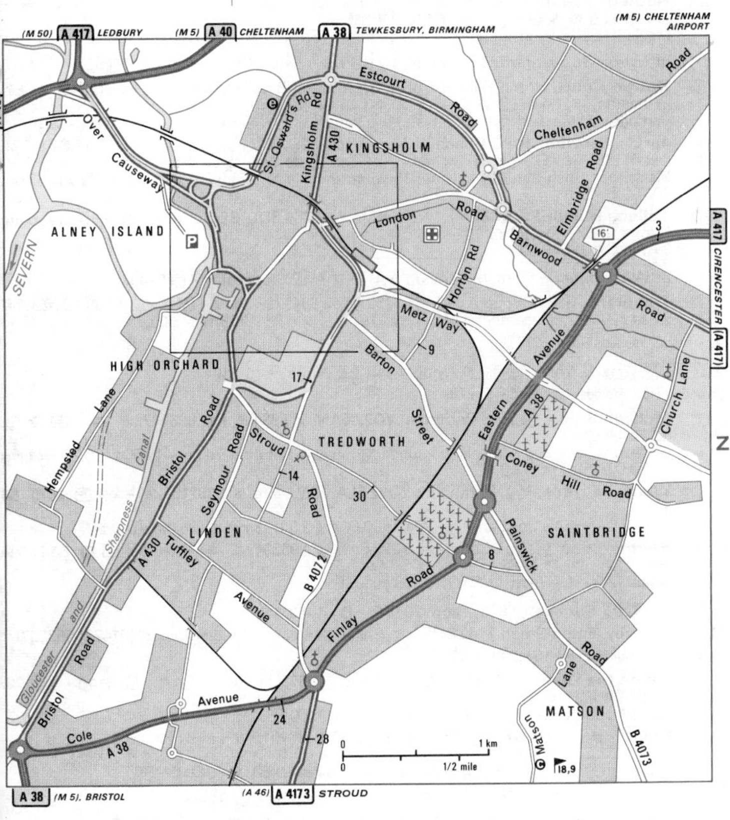

Benutzen Sie auf Ihren Reisen in Europa
die **Michelin-Länderkarten** 1 : 1 000 000.

GLOUCESTER Glos. 403 404 N 28 **Great Britain G.** – pop. 101 608 – 01452.

See : City★ - Cathedral★★ Y – The Docks★ Y – Bishop Hooper's Lodging★ *AC* Y **M.**

18, 9 Gloucester Hotel, Matson Lane 525653.

St Michael's Tower, The Cross, GL1 1PD 421188.

♦London 106 – ♦Birmingham 52 – ♦Bristol 38 – ♦Cardiff 66 – ♦Coventry 57 – Northampton 83 – ♦Oxford 48 – ♦Southampton 98 – ♦Swansea 92 – Swindon 35.

Plans on preceding page

Forte Posthouse, Crest Way, Barnwood, GL4 7RX, E : 3 m. by A 417 613311, Fax 371036, – rm – 100. AE VISA
Meals a la carte 12.95/22.15 **t.** – **122 rm** 59.00 **t.**, 1 suite.

Jarvis Gloucester H. & Country Club, Robinswood Hill, GL4 9EA, SE : 3 m. by B 4073 525653, Fax 307212, , 18, 9, , squash – rm – 180. AE VISA Z **c**
closed 25 and 26 December – **Meals** *(closed Saturday lunch)* 12.80/14.50 **st.** and a la carte – 8.50 – **102 rm** 89.00/109.00 **st.**, 5 suites – SB.

Travel Inn, Tewkesbury Rd, Longford, GL2 9BE, N : 1 ¾ m. on A 38 523519, Fax 300924 – rm . AE VISA.
Meals (grill rest.) – 4.95 – **40 rm** 34.50 **t.**

Yeungs, St. Oswald's Rd, Cattle Market, GL1 2SR, 309957 – . AE VISA Z **e**
closed Monday lunch and Sunday – **Meals** - Chinese - 12.00/22.50 **t.** and a la carte 5.00.

at Down Hatherley NE : 3¼ m. by A 38 – Z – Gloucester – 01452 :

Hatherley Manor, Down Hatherley Lane, GL2 9QA, 730217, Fax 731032, – rest – 250. AE VISA
Meals 10.50/17.25 **st.** and dinner a la carte 4.75 – 7.95 – **56 rm** 65.00/78.00 **st.** – SB.

at Upton St. Leonards SE : 3½ m. by B 4073 – Z – Gloucester – 01452 :

Hatton Court, Upton Hill, GL4 8DE, S : ¾ m. on B 4073 617412, Fax 612945, , , heated, – – 60. AE VISA JCB.
Carringtons : Meals 10.00/19.95 **t.** and a la carte 5.75 – **45 rm** 85.00/125.00 **t.** – SB.

Jarvis Bowden Hall, Bondend Lane, GL4 8ED, E : 1 m. by Bondend rd 614121, Fax 611885, , , , , , park – rm – 85. AE VISA
Meals (bar lunch Saturday)/dinner 15.95 **st.** and a la carte 5.25 – 7.50 – **72 rm** 85.00/102.00 **t.** – SB.

Bullens Manor Farm without rest., High St., GL4 8DL, SE : ½ m. 616463, « Working farm », park – .
3 rm 23.00/40.00.

at Witcombe SE : 7 m. by A 40 on A 417 – Z – Gloucester – 01452 :

Travel Inn, GL3 4SS, on A 417 862521, Fax 864926 – rm . AE VISA.
closed 24 to 27 December – **Meals** (grill rest.) – 4.95 – **39 rm** 34.50 **t.**

ATS St. Oswalds Rd 527329

GOATHLAND N. Yorks. 402 R 20 – pop. 444 – Whitby – 01947.

♦London 248 – ♦Middlesbrough 36 – York 38.

Mallyan Spout , The Common, YO22 5AN, 896486, Fax 896327, , – . AE VISA
closed 25 December – **Meals** (bar lunch Monday to Saturday)/dinner 18.50 **t.** 6.25 – **24 rm** 50.00/150.00 **t.** – SB.

Whitfield House , Darnholm, YO22 5LA, NW : ¾ m. 896215, – . VISA
closed December and January – **Meals** 10.00 **t.** 3.50 – **8 rm** 25.00/50.00 **t.**

Heatherdene , The Common, Y022 5AN, 896334, , – rest . AE VISA
Meals 12.95 **st.** – **7 rm** 30.00/65.00 **st.** – SB.

GODALMING Surrey 404 S 30 – pop. 20 086 – 01483.

18 West Surrey, Enton Green 421275 – 9 Shillinglee Park, Chiddingfold (01428) 653237.

♦London 38 – Guildford 5 – ♦Southampton 51.

Inn on the Lake, Ockford Rd, GU7 1RH, 415575, Fax 860445, – – 120. AE VISA JCB
Meals 10.00/16.50 **t.** and a la carte – **17 rm** 75.00/85.00 **t.** – SB.

Kings Arms and Royal, High St., GU7 1EB, 421545, Fax 415403, – – 40. AE VISA.
Meals (grill rest.) a la carte approx. 12.00 **t.** – **16 rm** 50.00/60.00 **t.** – SB.

at Hascombe SE : 3½ m. on B 2130 – Godalming – 01483 :

White Horse, The Street, GU8 4JA, 208258, Fax 208200, – AE VISA
closed 25 December – **Meals** (in bar Sunday dinner) 22.00 **t.** and a la carte 2.50.

ATS Meadrow 421845/422219

En haute saison, et surtout dans les stations, il est prudent de retenir à l'avance.

GODSTONE Surrey 404 T 30 – pop. 5 515 – ☎ 01342.

London 22 – Brighton 36 – Maidstone 28.

XXX **La Bonne Auberge,** Tilburstow Hill, South Godstone, RH9 8JY, S : 2 ¼ m. ℘ 892318, Fax 893435, – P. AE VISA
closed Sunday dinner, Monday and 26 to 30 December – **Meals** - French - 15.50/25.00 **st.** and a la carte 5.50.

GOLCAR W. Yorks. – see Huddersfield.

GOLDEN GREEN Kent 404 U 30 – see Tonbridge.

GOMERSAL W. Yorks. 402 O 22 – see Bradford.

GOODWOOD W. Sussex 404 R 31 – see Chichester.

GOOSNARGH Lancs. 402 L 22 pop. 1 087 – ✉ Preston – ☎ 01772.

London 238 – Blackpool 18 – Preston 6.

XX **Solo,** Goosnargh Lane, PR3 2BP, ℘ 865206, Fax 865206 – P. AE VISA JCB
Meals (dinner only and Sunday lunch)/dinner 21.00 **t.** 4.90.

GORDANO SERVICE AREA Avon – ✉ Bristol – ☎ 01275.

Forte Travelodge, BS20 9XG, M 5 : junction 19 ℘ 373709, Reservations (Freephone) 0800 850950 – TV ♿ P. AE VISA
Meals (grill rest.) – **40 rm** 34.50 **t.**

We suggest:

For a successful tour, that you prepare it in advance.
***Michelin maps** and **guides** will give you a great deal of useful information on route planning, places of interest, accommodation, prices etc.*

GORING Berks 403 404 Q 29 The West Country G. – pop. 4 193 (inc. Streatley) – ☎ 01491.

Exc. : Ridgeway Path★★.

London 56 – Oxford 16 – Reading 12.

XX **Leatherne Bottel,** RG8 0HS, N : 1 ½ m. by B 4009 ℘ 872667, ≤, « Thames-side setting » – P. AE VISA
closed 25 December – **Meals** (booking essential) a la carte 20.95/30.95 **t.**

GORLESTON-ON-SEA Norfolk 404 Z 26 – see Great Yarmouth.

GOSFORTH Cumbria 402 J 20 – pop. 1 568 – ✉ Seascale – ☎ 0194 67.

18 Seascale, The Banks ℘ 28202/28800.

London 317 – Kendal 55 – Workington 21.

Westlakes, Gosforth Rd, CA20 1HP, on A 595 ℘ 25221, Fax 25099, – TV ☎ P. AE VISA.
Meals *(closed Sunday lunch)* a la carte 13.00/20.25 **st.** 4.50 – **9 rm** 45.00/55.00 **st.**

GOSFORTH Tyne and Wear 401 402 P 18 – see Newcastle upon Tyne.

GOUDHURST Kent 404 V 30 Great Britain G. – pop. 2 498 – ✉ Cranbrook – ☎ 01580.

Envir. : Sissinghurst Castle★ *AC*, E : 5½ m. by A 262.

London 45 – Hastings 22 – Maidstone 13.

Star and Eagle, High St., TN17 1AL, ℘ 211512, Fax 211416, « 14C inn » – TV ☎ P. AE VISA.
Meals a la carte 9.40/19.65 **t.** 4.65 – **11 rm** 35.00/48.00 **t.**

GOVETON Devon 403 I 33 – see Kingsbridge.

GRAMPOUND Cornwall 403 F 33 The West Country G. – ✉ Truro – ☎ 01726.

Envir. : Trewithen★★★ *AC*, W : 2 m. by A 390 – Probus★ (tower★, Country Demonstration Garden★ *AC*) W : 2½ m. by A 390.

London 287 – Newquay 16 – Plymouth 44 – Truro 8.

XX **Eastern Promise,** 1 Moor View, TR2 4RT, ℘ 883033 – P. AE VISA JCB
closed Wednesday – **Meals** - Chinese - (booking essential) (dinner only) 17.90 **st.** and a la carte 3.75.

GRANGE-IN-BORROWDALE Cumbria 402 K 20 – see Keswick.

GRANGE-OVER-SANDS Cumbria 402 L 21 **Great Britain G.** – pop. 3 867 – ☎ 0153 95.

Envir. : Cartmel Priory★, NW : 3 m.

18 Meathop Rd ✆ 33180 – 9 Grange Fell, Fell Rd ✆ 32536.

☐ Victoria Hall, Main St., LA11 6PT ✆ 34026 (summer only).

◆London 268 – Kendal 13 – Lancaster 24.

Netherwood, Lindale Rd, LA11 6ET, ✆ 32552, Fax 34121, ≤ Morecambe Bay, ☐, park – ☐ ☐ rest ☐ ☎ ☐ – 150. ☐ VISA
Meals 12.00/23.00 **t.** and lunch a la carte 4.75 – **29 rm** ☐ 45.00/110.00 **t.** – SB.

Graythwaite Manor ☐, Fernhill Rd, LA11 7JE, ✆ 32001, Fax 35549, ≤ gardens and Morecambe Bay, « Extensive flowered gardens », park, ☐ – ☐ ☎ ☐ ☐. ☐ AE VISA JCB. ☐
closed 3 to 24 January – **Meals** 9.50/22.00 **t.** and a la carte 4.15 – **22 rm** ☐ (dinner included) 57.00/120.00 **t.** – SB.

at Lindale NE : 2 m. on B 5277 – ☒ Grange-over-Sands – ☎ 0153 95 :

Greenacres, LA11 6LP, ✆ 34578, Fax 34578 – ☐ ☐ ☐. ☐ VISA. ☐
closed December – **Meals** (by arrangement) 13.50 **st.** – **5 rm** ☐ 32.00/56.00 **st.** – SB.

at Witherslack NE : 5 m. by B 5277 off A 590 – ☎ 0153 95 :

Old Vicarage ☐, Church Rd, LA11 6RS, ✆ 52381, Fax 52373, « Part Georgian country house », ☐, ☐ – ☐ rest ☐ ☎ ☐. ☐ AE ☐ VISA JCB
Meals (booking essential) (dinner only and Sunday lunch)/dinner 26.50 **t.** 11.00 – **14 rm** ☐ 59.00/138.00 **t.** – SB.

at Cartmel NW : 3 m. – ☎ 0153 95 :

Aynsome Manor ☐, LA11 6HH, N : ¾ m. by Newby Bridge rd and Wood Broughton rd ✆ 36653, Fax 36016, ☐ – ☐ rest ☐ ☎ ☐. ☐ AE VISA
closed 2 to 27 January – **Meals** *(closed Sunday dinner to non-residents)* (dinner only and Sunday lunch)/dinner 18.50 **t.** 5.00 – **12 rm** ☐ (dinner included) 58.00/104.00 **t.** – SB.

Uplands ☐ with rm, Haggs Lane, LA11 6HD, E : 1 m. ✆ 36248, Fax 36248, ≤, ☐ – ☐ rest ☐ ☎ ☐. ☐ AE VISA
closed 1 January-7 March – **Meals** *(closed Monday)* (booking essential) 14.50/26.00 **t.** – **5 rm** ☐ (dinner included) 75.00/138.00 **t.** – SB.

GRANTHAM Lincs. 402 404 S 25 **Great Britain G.** – pop. 33 243 – ☎ 01476.

See : St. Wulfram's Church★.

Envir. : Belton House★ *AC*, N : 2½ m. by A 607.

Exc. : Belvoir Castle★★ *AC*, W : 6 m. by A 607.

18, 9 Belton Park, Belton Lane, Londonthorpe Rd ✆ 67399 – 18 (2x), 9 Belton Woods Hotel ✆ 593200.

☐ The Guildhall Centre, St. Peter's Hill, NG31 6PZ ✆ 66444.

◆London 113 – ◆Leicester 31 – Lincoln 29 – ◆Nottingham 24.

De Vere Belton Woods, Belton, NG32 2LN, N : 2 m. on A 607 ✆ 593200, Fax 74547, ☐, ☐, ☐, 18, 9, ☐, park, ☐, squash – ☐ ☐ rm ☐ ☎ ☐ ☐ – 275. ☐ AE ☐ VISA. ☐
Manor : **Meals** (lunch by arrangement)/dinner 21.00 **st.** and a la carte – **Plus Fours** : **Meals** 12.50/15.50 **st.** and a la carte – **132 rm** ☐ 105.00/115.00 **t.**, 4 suites – SB.

Swallow, Swingbridge Rd, NG31 7XT, S : 1 ¼ m. at junction of A 607 with A 1 southbound sliproad ✆ 593000, Fax 592592, ☐, ☐, ☐ – ☐ ☐ ☎ ☐ ☐ – 200. ☐ AE ☐ VISA JCB
Meals 9.50/17.75 **st.** and a la carte 4.00 – **88 rm** ☐ 91.00/101.00 **st.**, 1 suite – SB.

Angel and Royal (Forte), High St., NG31 6PN, ✆ 65816, Fax 67149, « Part 13C » – ☐ ☐ ☎ ☐ – 30. ☐ AE ☐ VISA JCB. ☐
Meals (bar lunch Monday to Saturday)/dinner 16.95 **st.** and a la carte 5.55 – ☐ 8.95 – **29 rm** 45.00/65.00 **st.** – SB.

at Hough-on-the-Hill N : 6¾ m. by A 607 on Hough Rd – ☒ Grantham – ☎ 01400 :

Brownlow Arms, NG32 2AZ, ✆ 250234, Fax 250772, « Part 17C inn », ☐ – ☐ ☎ ☐. ☐ AE VISA. ☐
Meals *(closed Monday lunch and Sunday dinner)* (in bar) a la carte 12.70/23.05 **st.** 3.65 – **5 rm** ☐ 30.00/47.00 **st.**

at Great Gonerby NW : 2 m. on B 1174 – ☒ Grantham – ☎ 01476 :

☐ **Harry's Place** (Hallam), 17 High St., NG31 8JS, ✆ 61780 – ☐. ☐ VISA
closed Sunday, Monday and 25-26 December – **Meals** (booking essential) a la carte 29.00/42.00 **t.** 10.00
Spec. Poached Filey lobster with a lobster coral hollandaise and herb fettuccine, Lincolnshire salt marsh teal roasted with red wine, Madeira and thyme, Strawberry and butterscotch tart.

at Grantham Service Area NW : 3 m on B 1174 at junction with A 1 – ☒ Grantham – ☎ 01476 :

Forte Travelodge, NG32 2AB, ✆ 77500, Reservations (Freephone) 0800 850950 – ☐ ☐ ☐. ☐ AE VISA. ☐
Meals (grill rest.) – **40 rm** 34.50 **t.**

ATS East St. ✆ 590222 ATS Elmer St. South ✆ 590444

GRASMERE Cumbria 402 K 20 Great Britain G. – ✉ Ambleside – ☎ 0153 94.

See : Dove Cottage★ *AC* AY **A**.

Envir. : Lake Windermere★★, SE : by A 591 AZ.

ℹ Redbank Rd, LA22 9SW ✆ 35245 (summer only) – BZ.

♦London 282 – ♦Carlisle 43 – Kendal 18.

Plans : see Ambleside

Michaels Nook Country House ⛰, LA22 9RP, NE : ½ m. off A 591, turning by Swan H. ✆ 35496, Fax 35645, ≤ mountains and countryside, « Antiques and gardens », park – ⇔ rest TV ☎ P. AE VISA. ⛔ AY **n**
Meals (booking essential) 27.50/46.00 **t.** 7.05 – **12 rm** ⊇ (dinner included) 120.00/270.00 **st.**, 2 suites – SB.

Wordsworth, Stock Lane, LA22 9SW, ✆ 35592, Fax 35765, ≘s, ▣, ⛲ – |‡| ⇔ rest ▤ rest TV ☎ P – 🏛 130. AE VISA. ⛔ BZ **s**
Prelude : Meals 17.50/29.50 **t.** and a la carte 7.50 – **35 rm** ⊇ 62.00/150.00 **t.**, 2 suites – SB.

Swan (Forte Heritage), LA22 9RF, on A 591 ✆ 35551, Fax 35741, ≤, ⛲ – ⇔ TV ☎ P. AE VISA JCB AY **r**
Meals 11.25/21.00 **t.** and a la carte – ⊇ 8.95 – **36 rm** 70.00/90.00 **t.** – SB.

Gold Rill, Red Bank Rd, LA22 9PU, ✆ 35486, Fax 35486, ≤ heated, ⛲ – ⇔ rest TV ☎ P. VISA. ⛔ BZ **a**
closed 7 to 25 January – **Meals** (bar lunch)/dinner 18.50 **st.** 5.40 – **24 rm** ⊇ (dinner included) 54.00/128.00 **st.** – SB.

White Moss House, Rydal Water, LA22 9SE, S : 1½ m. on A 591 ✆ 35295, Fax 35516, ⛲ – ⇔ rest TV ☎ P. VISA. ⛔ BY **v**
mid March-early December – **Meals** *(closed Sunday)* (booking essential) (dinner only) 27.50 **t.** 5.95 – **5 rm** ⊇ (dinner included) 87.00/174.00 **t.**, 1 suite – SB.

Red Lion, Red Lion Sq., LA22 9SS, ✆ 35456, Fax 35579, ⛹, ≘s, ⛲ – |‡| ⇔ rest TV ☎ P – 🏛 60. AE VISA JCB BZ **c**
closed 15 to 19 December – **Meals** (bar lunch)/dinner 16.50 **st.** and a la carte 4.85 – **34 rm** ⊇ (dinner included) 53.00/114.00 **t.** – SB.

Rothay Garden, Broadgate, LA22 9RJ, ✆ 35334, Fax 35723, ⛲ – ⇔ rest TV ☎ P. VISA AY **e**
Meals 7.95/17.50 **t.** and lunch a la carte – **25 rm** ⊇ (dinner included) 49.50/99.00 **t.** – SB.

Oak Bank, Broadgate, LA22 9TA, ✆ 35217, Fax 35685, ⛲ – ⇔ rest TV ☎ P. VISA JCB
closed January and 3 days Christmas – **Meals** (bar lunch)/dinner 17.50 **t.** – **15 rm** ⊇ 40.00/120.00 **st.** – SB. BZ **e**

Grasmere, Broadgate, LA22 9TA, ✆ 35277, Fax 35277, ⛲ – ⇔ rest TV ☎ P. VISA JCB BZ **r**
closed January – **Meals** (dinner only) 15.00 **st.** 5.50 – **12 rm** ⊇ (dinner included) 45.00/104.00 **st.** – SB.

Lancrigg Vegetarian Country House ⛰, Easedale Rd, LA22 9QN, W : ½ m. on Easedale Rd ✆ 35317, Fax 35058, ≤ Easedale Valley, ⛲, park – ⇔ rest TV P. VISA. ⛔ AY **u**
Meals (dinner only) 19.50 **st.** – **13 rm** ⊇ (dinner included) 39.00/140.00 **st.** – SB.

Bridge House, Stock Lane, LA22 9SN, ✆ 35425, Fax 35523, ⛲ – ⇔ rest TV ☎ P. VISA JCB. ⛔ BZ **n**
closed 4 to 23 December and 2 January-14 February – **Meals** (dinner only and Sunday lunch)/dinner 14.00 **t.** and a la carte – **12 rm** ⊇ (dinner included) ⊇ 35.00/90.00 **t.** – SB.

Rothay Lodge ⛰ without rest., White Bridge, LA22 9RH, ✆ 35341, ⛲ – ⇔ TV P. ⛔
March-October – **6 rm** ⊇ 25.00/45.00. AY **o**

Banerigg without rest., Lake Rd, LA22 9PW, S : ¾ m. on A 591 ✆ 35204, ≤, ⛲ – ⇔ P. ⛔ AY **a**
closed 24 to 26 December – **7 rm** ⊇ 24.00/48.00 **t.** – SB.

GRASSENDALE Mersey 402 403 L 23 – see Liverpool.

GRASSINGTON N. Yorks. 402 O 21 – pop. 1 102 – ✉ Skipton – ☎ 01756.

ℹ National Park Centre, Hebden Rd, BD23 5LB ✆ 752774 (summer only).

♦London 240 – Bradford 30 – Burnley 28 – ♦Leeds 37.

Ashfield House, BD23 5AE, ✆ 752584, ⛲ – ⇔ TV P. VISA. ⛔
closed early November-mid February and 1 week May-June – **Meals** (by arrangement) 14.50 4.00 – **7 rm** ⊇ (dinner included) 53.00/86.00 **st.** – SB.

GRAVESEND Kent 404 V 29 – pop. 51 435 – ☎ 01474.

to Tilbury (White Horse Ferries Ltd) frequent services daily (5 mn).

10 Parrock St., DA12 1ET ☎ 337600 – London 25 – Dover 54 – Maidstone 16 – Margate 53.

Quality Manor, Hever Court Rd, Singlewell, DA12 5UQ, SE : 2½ m. by A 227 off A 2 ☎ 353100, Fax 354978, – rm rest – 200. AE VISA.
Meals *(closed Saturday, Sunday and Bank Holidays)* (bar lunch)/dinner 27.65 **t.** and a la carte 8.25 – 7.95 – **38 rm** 65.00 **st.**

Overcliffe, 15-16 Overcliffe, DA11 0EF, ☎ 322131, Fax 536737 – AE VISA
Meals (dinner only) a la carte 15.40/20.45 **t.** – **29 rm** 50.00/80.00 **t.** – SB.

GRAVETYE E. Sussex – see East Grinstead.

GRAYSHOTT Hants. 404 R 30 pop. 2 113 – ✉ Hindhead (Surrey) – ☎ 01428.

London 46 – Portsmouth 31.

Woods Place, Headley Rd, GU26 6LB, ☎ 605555, Fax 605555.

GREASBY Mersey. 402 ㉜ 403 ⑫ – pop. 56 077 – ✉ Wirral – ☎ 0151.

London 220 – Liverpool 9.

Twelfth Man Lodge, Greasby Rd, L49 2PP, on B 5139 ☎ 677 5445, Fax 678 5085 – rm AE VISA.
Meals a la carte 9.15/16.75 **t.** – 4.95 – **30 rm** 39.00 **t.**

GREAT AYTON N. Yorks. 402 Q 20 **Great Britain G.** – pop. 4 759 – ✉ Middlesbrough (Cleveland) – ☎ 01642 – **See** : Captain Cook Birthplace Museum★ *AC.*

High Green Car Park, TS9 6BJ ☎ 722835 (summer only).

London 245 – Leeds 63 – Middlesbrough 7 – York 48.

Ayton Hall, Low Green, TS9 6PS, ☎ 723595, Fax 722149, – AE VISA.
Meals 12.95/23.00 **t.** and dinner a la carte – **9 rm** 55.00/125.00 **t.**

at Ingleby Greenhow S : 3 ¾ m. by Easby rd on Ingleby rd – ✉ Middlesbrough (Cleveland) – ☎ 01642 :

Manor House Farm, TS9 6RB, S : 1 m. via lane to manor, next to church ☎ 722384,
closed 15 to 29 December – **Meals** (by arrangement) 15.50 **st.** 5.00 – **3 rm** (dinner included) 52.50/85.00 **st.** – SB.

GREAT BADDOW Essex 404 V 28 – see Chelmsford.

GREAT BARR W. Mids. 403 404 O 26 – see Birmingham.

GREAT BROUGHTON N. Yorks. 402 Q 20 – pop. 937 (inc. Little Broughton) – ✉ Middlesbrough (Cleveland) – ☎ 01642 – London 241 – Leeds 61 – Middlesbrough 10 – York 54.

Wainstones, 31 High St., TS9 7EW, ☎ 712268, Fax 711560 – AE VISA.
Meals a la carte 12.85/19.10 **st.** 3.95 – **23 rm** 49.95/63.50 **st.** – SB.

GREAT DRIFFIELD Humbs. 402 S 21 **Great Britain G.** – pop. 9 463 – ✉ York – ☎ 01377.

Exc. : Burton Agnes Hall★ *AC*, NE : 6 m. by A 166 – Sledmere House★ *AC*, NW : 8 m. by A 166 and B 1252 – Driffield, Sunderlandwick ☎ 253116 – Hainsworth Park, Brandesburton ☎ (01964) 542362 – London 201 – Kingston-upon-Hull 21 – Scarborough 22 – York 29.

Star Inn, Warter Rd, North Dalton, YO25 9UX, SW : 7 m. by A 164 and A 163 on B 1246 ☎ 217688 – VISA.
Meals (bar lunch)/dinner a la carte 7.95/17.85 **t.** 3.95 – **7 rm** 29.50/39.50 **t.** – SB.

at Lockington S : 9¾ m. by A 164 – ✉ Great Driffield – ☎ 01430 :

Rockingham Arms, 52 Front St., YO25 9SH, ☎ 810607 – VISA
closed Sunday, Monday, 25 to 26 December and Bank Holidays – **Meals** (dinner only) 21.95 **st.** 4.95.

ATS 14 Westgate ☎ 252386/253628

GREAT DUNMOW Essex 404 V 28 – pop. 5 621 – ☎ 01371.

London 42 – Cambridge 27 – Chelmsford 13 – Colchester 24.

Saracen's Head (Forte), High St., CM6 1AG, ☎ 873901, Fax 875743 – – 60. AE VISA JCB
Meals (bar lunch Monday to Saturday)/dinner 16.95 **t.** – 8.50 – **24 rm** 70.00/95.00 **t.** – SB.

Starr with rm, Market Pl., CM6 1AX, ☎ 874321, Fax 876337 – – 35. AE VISA
closed first week January – **Meals** *(closed Saturday lunch and Sunday dinner)* 11.50/37.50 **t.** and lunch a la carte 5.50 – **8 rm** 55.00/100.00 **st.**

GREAT GONERBY Lincs. 402 404 S 25 – see Grantham.

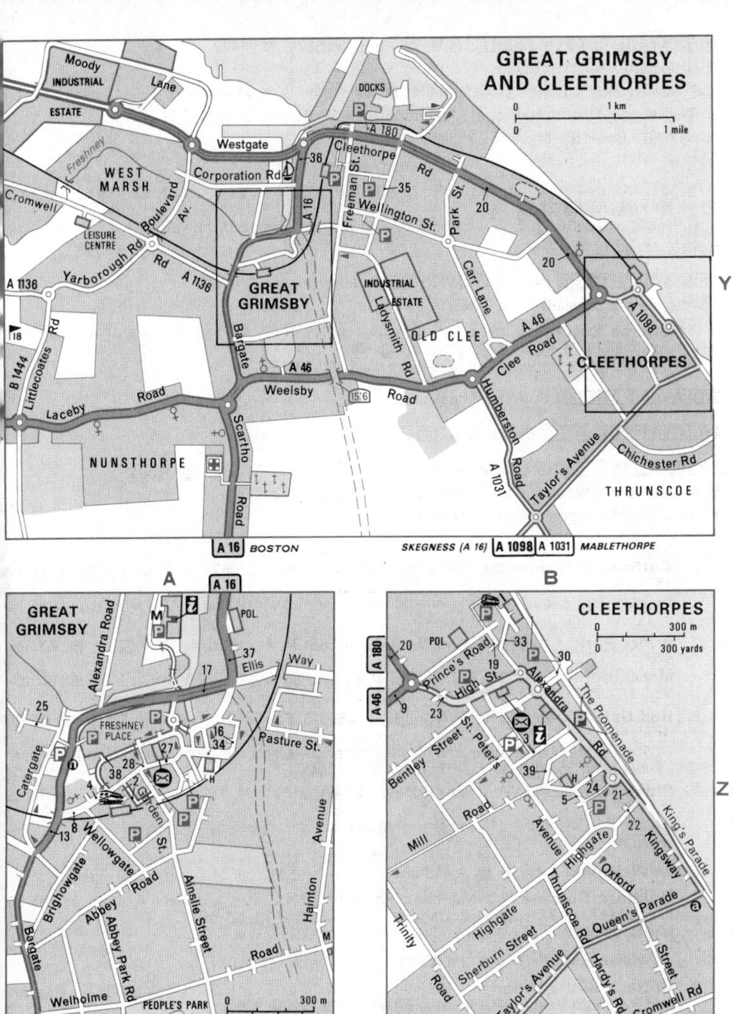

Abbeygate . . . . **AZ** 2
Freeman Street . . . . **Y**
Freshney Place
Shopping Centre . . . . **AZ**
St. Peter's Avenue . . . . **BZ**

Albert Road . . . . **BZ** 3
Bethlehem Street . . . . **AZ** 4
Cambridge Street . . . . **BZ** 5
Church Lane . . . . **AZ** 8
Clee Road . . . . **BZ** 9

Deansgate . . . . **AZ** 13
East Street . . . . **AZ** 16
Frederick Ward
Way . . . . **AZ** 17
Grant Street . . . . **BZ** 19
Grimsby Road . . . . **Y, BZ** 20
High Cliff Road . . . . **BZ** 21
Humber Street . . . . **BZ** 22
Isaac's Hill . . . . **BZ** 23
Knoll Street . . . . **BZ** 24
Lord Street . . . . **AZ** 25

Osborne Street . . . . **AZ** 27
Sea Road . . . . **BZ** 30
South St Mary's
Gate . . . . **AZ** 31
Station Road . . . . **BZ** 33
Town Hall Square . . . . **AZ** 34
Victor Street . . . . **Y** 35
Victoria Street North . . . . **Y** 36
Victoria Street South . . . . . **AZ** 37
Victoria Street West . . . . . . **AZ** 38
Yarra Road . . . . **BZ** 39

We suggest:

For a successful tour, that you prepare it in advance.
Michelin maps *and* **guides** *will give you a great deal of useful information on route planning, places of interest, accommodation, prices etc.*

GREAT GRIMSBY Humbs. 402 404 T 23 – pop. 90 517 – ☎ 01472.

Littlecoates Rd ☎ 342823 Y.

Humberside Airport : ☎ (01652) 680256, W : 13 m. by A 46 and A 18 Y.

The National Fishing Heritage, Alexandra Dock, DN31 1UF ☎ 342422 BZ.

London 172 – Boston 50 – Lincoln 36 – Sheffield 75.

Plan on preceding page

St. James (Forte), St. James Sq., DN31 1EP, ☎ 359771, Fax 241427, – rm – 70. AE VISA AZ **n**
Meals a la carte 11.25/20.45 **st.** 4.25 – 8.95 – **125 rm** 55.00 **t.** – SB.

ATS 2 Abbey Rd ☎ 358151

GREAT HOCKHAM Norfolk 404 W 26 – ✉ Attleborough – ☎ 01953.

London 86 – Cambridge 41 – Norwich 23.

Church Cottage without rest., Breckles, NR17 1EW, N : 1 ½ m. by A 1075 ☎ 498286, Fax 498320, heated, – .
closed 20 December-5 January – **3 rm** 17.00/34.00 **s.**

GREAT LANGDALE Cumbria – see Ambleside.

GREAT LONGSTONE Derbs. 402 403 404 O 24 – see Bakewell.

GREAT MALVERN Heref. and Worcs. 403 404 N 27 – pop. 31 537 – ☎ 01684.

Winter Gdns Complex, Grange Rd, WR14 3HB ☎ 892289 B.

London 127 – Birmingham 34 – Cardiff 66 – Gloucester 24.

Plan opposite

Cotford, 51 Graham Rd, WR14 2HU, ☎ 574680, Fax 572952, – rest . VISA B **o**
closed 22 December-8 January – **Meals** (dinner only) 16.00 **st.** 4.50 – **16 rm** 36.00/60.00 **st.**

Priory Park, 4 Avenue Rd, WR14 3AG, ☎ 565194, Fax 892646, – . VISA. B **x**
Meals (booking essential) 10.00/20.00 **st.** and a la carte 6.00 – **6 rm** 38.00/68.00 **st.** – SB.

Red Gate, 32 Avenue Rd, WR14 3BJ, ☎ 565013, Fax 565013, – . AE VISA JCB. B **r**
closed 24 to 26 December and 2 weeks spring – **Meals** *(closed Sunday)* (residents only) (dinner only) 15.00 **st.** 4.00 – **7 rm** 30.00/54.00 **t.**

Sidney House, 40 Worcester Rd, WR14 4AA, ☎ 574994, ←, – rest . AE VISA. B **s**
closed 24 December-25 January – **Meals** (by arrangement) 20.00 **st.** – **8 rm** 20.00/59.00 **st.**

at Welland SE : 4½ m. by A 449 on A 4104 – A – ✉ Great Malvern – ☎ 01684 :

Holdfast Cottage , Marlbank Rd, WR13 6NA, W : ¾ m. on A 4104 ☎ 310288, Fax 311117, « 17C country cottage », – . VISA
Meals (dinner only) 17.00 **st.** 5.50 – **8 rm** 44.00/80.00 **st.** – SB.

at Malvern Wells S : 2 m. on A 449 – ✉ Malvern – ☎ 01684 :

Cottage in the Wood , Holywell Rd, WR14 4LG, ☎ 575859, Fax 560662, ← Severn and Evesham Vales, – rest . AE VISA. A **z**
Meals 9.95 **st.** (lunch) and a la carte 18.75/23.00 **st.** 7.50 – **20 rm** 68.00/135.00 **st.** – SB.

Essington , Holywell Rd, WR14 4LQ, ☎ 561177, Fax 561177, ←, – . AE VISA A **e**
Meals (booking essential) (dinner only) 15.00 **t.** 5.50 – **8 rm** 35.00/64.00 **t.** – SB.

Old Vicarage, Hanley Rd, WR14 4PH, ☎ 572585, ←, – A **c**
Meals (by arrangement) 13.50 **st.** 4.50 – **6 rm** 30.00/45.00 **st.** – SB.

✪ **Croque-en-Bouche** (Marion Jones), 221 Wells Rd, WR14 4HF, ☎ 565612, Fax 565612 – . VISA A **u**
closed Sunday to Tuesday, Wednesday October-May, 1 week May, 2 weeks September and Christmas-New Year – **Meals** (booking essential) (dinner only) 21.00/33.50 **st.** 5.40
Spec. Japanese style selections, Roast leg of Welsh lamb with couscous, preserved lemon and pimiento, Salads and herbs from the garden.

Planters, 191-193 Wells Rd, WR14 9HB, ☎ 575065 – VISA A **a**
closed Sunday and Monday except Bank Holidays – **Meals** - Oriental - (booking essential) (dinner only) 19.95 **t.** and a la carte.

at Wynds Point S : 4 m. on A 449 – ✉ Malvern – ☎ 01684 :

Malvern Hills, British Camp, WR13 6DW, ☎ 540237, Fax 540327, – . VISA. A **s**
Meals 8.00/20.00 **st.** and a la carte 6.10 – **16 rm** 30.00/50.00 **st.** – SB.

GREAT MALVERN

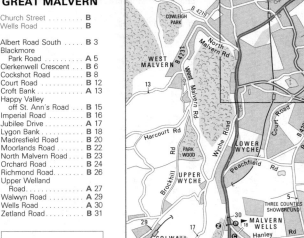

Church Street . . . . B
Wells Road . . . . B

Albert Road South . . . . . B 3
Blackmore
Park Road . . . . A 5
Clerkenwell Crescent . . . B 6
Cockshot Road . . . . B 8
Court Road . . . . B 12
Croft Bank . . . . A 13
Happy Valley
off St. Ann's Road . . . B 15
Imperial Road . . . . B 16
Jubilee Drive . . . . A 17
Lygon Bank . . . . B 18
Madresfield Road . . . . . . B 20
Moorlands Road . . . . B 22
North Malvern Road . . . . B 23
Orchard Road . . . . B 24
Richmond Road . . . . B 26
Upper Welland
Road . . . . A 27
Walwyn Road . . . . A 29
Wells Road . . . . A 30
Zetland Road . . . . B 31

Town plans
roads most used
by traffic and those
on which guide listed
hotels and restaurants
stand are fully drawn;
the beginning only
of lesser roads
is indicated.

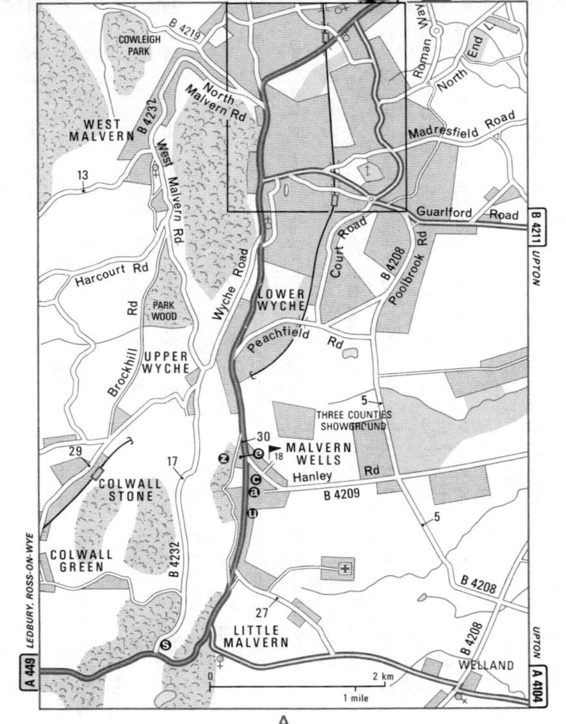

GREAT MILTON Oxon. 403 404 Q 28 – see Oxford.

GREAT MISSENDEN Bucks. 404 R 28 – pop. 7 980 (inc. Prestwood) – ☎ 01494.
♦London 34 – Aylesbury 10 – Maidenhead 19 – ♦Oxford 35.

XX **La Petite Auberge,** 107 High St., HP16 0BB, ℘ 865370 – VISA
closed Sunday, 3 weeks Christmas-New Year and Bank Holidays – **Meals** - French - (dinne only) a la carte 22.90/29.30 **t.**

GREAT OFFLEY Herts. 404 S 28 – ✉ Hitchin – ☎ 01462.
♦London 40 – Bedford 14 – ♦Cambridge 29 – Luton 6.

Red Lion, Kings Walden Rd, SG5 3DZ, ℘ 768281, Fax 768792, – TV ☎ P. AE VISA
Meals *(closed Sunday dinner)* 10.00/12.00 **t.** and a la carte 4.00 – 5.00 – **5 rm** 45.00, 55.00 **st.**

GREAT RISSINGTON Glos. – see Bourton-on-the-Water.

GREAT SNORING Norfolk 404 W 25 – pop. 191 – ✉ Fakenham – ☎ 01328.
♦London 115 – ♦Cambridge 68 – ♦Norwich 28.

Old Rectory , Barsham Rd, NR21 0HP, ℘ 820597, Fax 820048, « Country house atmosphere », – rest TV ☎ P. AE VISA JCB.
closed 24 to 27 December – **Meals** (booking essential) (dinner only) 22.50 **t.** 5.15 – **6 rm** 68.00/89.00 **t.** – SB.

GREAT TEW Oxon. 403 404 P 28 – pop. 145 – ☎ 01608.
♦London 75 – ♦Birmingham 50 – Gloucester 42 – ♦Oxford 21.

Falkland Arms, OX7 4DB, ℘ 683653, Fax 683656, « 17C inn in picturesque village », – TV.
closed 25 December – **Meals** *(closed Sunday and Monday except Bank Holidays)* (in bar) (lunch only) a la carte approx. 9.50 **st.** – **4 rm** 30.00/50.00 **st.**

GREAT YARMOUTH Norfolk 404 Z 26 **Great Britain G.** – pop. 87 724 – ☎ 01493.
Envir. : The Broads★.
18 Gorleston, Warren Rd ℘ 661911 – 18 Beach House, Caister-on-Sea ℘ 720421.
Marine Parade, NR30 2EJ ℘ 842195/846345 (summer only).
♦London 126 – ♦Cambridge 81 – ♦Ipswich 53 – ♦Norwich 20.

Carlton, 1-5 Kimberley Terr., Marine Par., NR30 3JE, ℘ 855234, Fax 852220 – rm TV ☎ – 150. AE VISA
Meals (bar lunch Monday to Saturday)/dinner 14.95 **st.** and a la carte – **88 rm** 57.00, 79.00 **st.**, 2 suites – SB.

Regency Dolphin, 14-15 Albert Sq., NR30 3JH, ℘ 855070, Fax 853798, , , heated, – TV ☎ P – 120. AE VISA
Meals 8.95/13.50 **st.** and a la carte 4.50 – **48 rm** 55.00/85.00 **st.**, 1 suite – SB.

Imperial, North Drive, NR30 1EQ, ℘ 851113, Fax 852229 – rest TV ☎ P – 140 AE VISA
Rambouillet : Meals *(closed lunch Saturday and Bank Holidays)* 11.50/18.50 **st.** and a la carte 6.25 – **39 rm** 60.00/80.00 **st.** – SB.

Two Bears, Southtown Rd, NR31 0HU, on A 12 ℘ 603198, – TV ☎ P. AE VISA
Meals 8.50/13.95 **t.** and a la carte 4.25 – 6.50 – **11 rm** 40.00/50.00 **st.** – SB.

at Gorleston-on-Sea S : 3 m. on A 12 – ✉ Great Yarmouth – ☎ 01493 :

Cliff, Cliff Hill, NR31 6DH, ℘ 662179, Fax 653617, – rm TV ☎ P – 170. AE VISA.
Meals 15.50 **t.** and a la carte 6.50 – **38 rm** 62.00/88.00 **t.**, 1 suite – SB.

ATS Suffling Rd ℘ 858211

GREAT YELDHAM Essex 404 V 27 – ✉ Colchester – ☎ 01787.
♦London 58 – ♦Cambridge 29 – Chelmsford 24 – Colchester 21 – ♦Ipswich 37.

XX **White Hart,** Poole St., CO9 4HJ, ℘ 237250, Fax 238044, « 16C inn », – P. AE VISA
Meals a la carte 11.70/24.40 **t.** 7.50.

GRENOSIDE S. Yorks. 402 403 404 P 23 – see Sheffield.

GRETA BRIDGE Durham 402 O 20 – ☎ 01833.
♦London 253 – ♦Carlisle 63 – ♦Leeds 63 – ♦Middlesbrough 32.

Morritt Arms, DL12 9SE, ℘ 627232, Fax 627392, , – rest TV ☎ P – 150. AE VISA
Meals 10.00/15.00 **t.** and dinner a la carte 4.00 – **17 rm** 50.00/95.00 **t.** – SB.

GRIMSBY Humbs. 402 404 T 23 – see Great Grimsby.

GRIMSTON Norfolk – see King's Lynn.

GRINDLEFORD Derbs. 402 403 404 P 24 – ✉ Sheffield (S. Yorks.) – ☎ 01433.

London 165 – Derby 31 – ◆Manchester 34 – ◆Sheffield 10.

Maynard Arms, Main Rd, S30 1HP, ℘ 630321, Fax 630445, ←, 🌳 – ⇔ rest TV ☎ P – 🏛 120. VISA. ✻
Meals 10.95/18.00 **t.** and a la carte 5.95 – **11 rm** ☐ 49.00/85.00 **t.** – SB.

GRINDLETON Lancs. 402 M 22 – pop. 1 446 (inc. West Bradford) – ✉ Bolton-by-Bowland – ☎ 01200.

London 241 – ◆Blackpool 38 – Lancaster 25 – ◆Leeds 45 – ◆Manchester 33.

Harrop Fold Country Farmhouse ⛰, Harrop Fold, BB7 4PJ, N : 2 3/4 m. by Slaidburn Rd ℘ 447600, ←, « 17C longhouse », 🌳, park – ⇔ rest TV ☎ P. VISA. ✻
Meals *(closed Monday and Tuesday lunch)* (lunch by arrangement)/dinner 18.50 **st.** and a la carte 3.50 – **8 rm** ☐ 39.50/65.00 **st.** – SB.

GRINDON Staffs. pop. 242 – ✉ Leek – ☎ 01538.

London 118 – ◆Birmingham 70 – Derby 26 – ◆Manchester 42 – ◆Stoke-on-Trent 20.

Porch Farmhouse ⛰, ST13 7TP, ℘ 304545, « Part 17C », 🌳 – ⇔ TV P
Meals (by arrangement) (communal dining) 18.00 **s.** – **3 rm** ☐ (dinner included) 40.00/80.00 **s.**

GRINGLEY Notts. 402 S 23 – ✉ Doncaster – ☎ 01777.

London 163 – ◆Leeds 43 – Lincoln 24 – ◆Nottingham 42 – ◆Sheffield 26.

Old Vicarage, DN10 4RF, on High St. ℘ 817248, Fax 817248, ←, 🌳, ✂ – ⇔ P. VISA. ✻
closed 24 December-2 January – **Meals** (by arrangement) (communal dining) 17.00 **s.** 3.50 – **3 rm** ☐ 30.00/50.00 **s.** – SB.

When visiting Great Britain,
use the Michelin Green Guide **"Great Britain".**

- *Detailed descriptions of places of interest*
- *Touring programmes*
- *Maps and street plans*
- *The history of the country*
- *Photographs and drawings of monuments, beauty spots, houses...*

GRIZEDALE Cumbria 402 K 20 – see Hawkshead.

GUILDFORD Surrey 404 S 30 – pop. 122 378 – ☎ 01483.

ℹ 14 Tunsgate, GU1 3QT ℘ 444007 Y.

◆London 33 – ◆Brighton 43 – Reading 27 – ◆Southampton 49.

Plan on next page

Angel Posting House and Livery, High St., GU1 3DP, ℘ 64555, Fax 33770, « 16C coaching inn with 13C vaulted cellar » – TV ☎ – 🏛 70. AE ⓓ VISA. ✻ — Y e
Meals 10.00/18.50 **t.** and dinner a la carte – ☐ 8.50 – **18 rm** 105.00 **st.**, 3 suites – SB.

Forte Crest, Egerton Rd, GU2 5XZ, ℘ 574444, Fax 302960, ₺, ≘s, 🏊, 🌳 – ⇔ rm TV ☎ ♿ P – 🏛 120. AE ⓓ VISA JCB — Z v
Meals 13.95/18.95 **t.** and a la carte 6.75 – ☐ 10.85 – **109 rm** 109.00 **st.**, 2 suites – SB.

Travel Inn, Stoke Rd, GU1 1UP, N : 1 1/2 m. by A 320 on A 25 ℘ 304932, Fax 304935 – ⇔ rm TV ♿ P. AE ⓓ VISA — Z a
Meals (grill rest.) – ☐ 4.95 – **60 rm** 34.50 **t.**

Rumwong, 16-18 London Rd, GU1 2AF, ℘ 36092 – ▤ — Y a
Meals - Thai rest.

Café de Paris, 35 Castle St., GU1 3UQ, ℘ 34896 – AE ⓓ VISA — Y u
closed Saturday lunch, Sunday, last week July, first week August and Bank Holidays – **Meals** - French - 12.50 **t.** and a la carte.

at Shere E : 6 3/4 m. by A 246 off A 25 – Z – ✉ Guildford – ☎ 01483 :

Kinghams, Gomshall Lane, GU5 9HB, ℘ 202168 – P. AE VISA JCB
closed Sunday dinner, Monday, 25 and 26 December – **Meals** 10.00/15.00 **t.** and a la carte 4.50.

at Albury E : 6 3/4 m. by A 25 – Z – on A 248 – ✉ Guildford – ☎ 01483 :

Drummond Arms, GU5 9AG, ℘ 202039, Fax 202039 – TV P. VISA. ✻
Meals (in bar Sunday dinner and Monday) 9.95/14.95 **t.** 5.15 – ☐ 6.00 – **7 rm** 38.00/50.00 **st.** – SB.

at Bramley S : 3 m. on A 281 – Z – ✉ Guildford – ☎ 01483 :

Bramley Grange, Horsham Rd, GU5 0BL, on A 281 ℘ 893434, Fax 893835, 🌳, ✂ – ⇔ rm ▤ rest TV ☎ P – 🏛 70. AE VISA
Meals *(closed Saturday lunch)* 14.75 **t.** and a la carte 6.00 – **45 rm** ☐ 80.00/90.00 **t.** – SB.

GUILDFORD

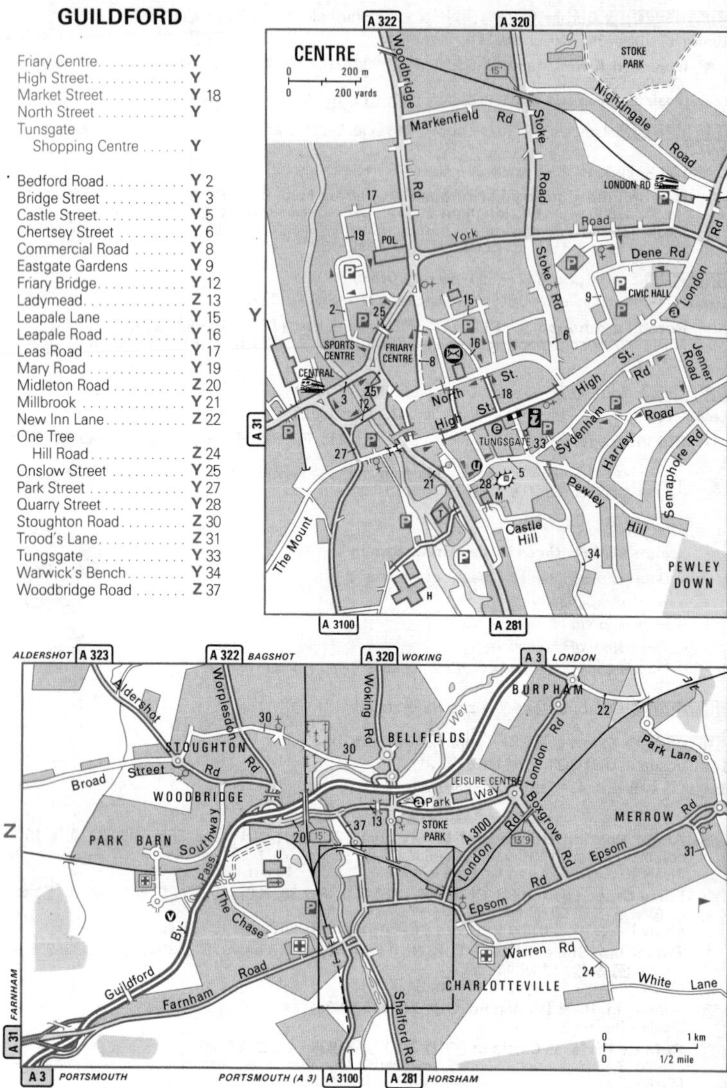

GUITING POWER Glos. 403 404 O 28 – ✉ Cheltenham – ☎ 01451.
♦London 95 – ♦Birmingham 47 – Gloucester 30 – ♦Oxford 39.

↑ **Guiting Guest House,** Post Office Lane, GL54 5TZ, ℘ 850470, Fax 850034, « 16C farmhouse » – ⅀ rm 📺 Ⓟ
closed Christmas – **Meals** (by arrangement) 15.00 **st.** – **3 rm** ⊐ 28.00/45.00 **st.**

GULWORTHY Devon 403 H 32 – see Tavistock.

GUNTHORPE Notts. pop. 646 – ☎ 0115.

London 132 – Lincoln 32 – ◆Nottingham 12 – ◆Sheffield 40.

Unicorn, Gunthorpe Bridge, NG14 7FB, SE : 1 ½ m. by A 6097 and Gunthorpe (riverside) rd ✆ 966 3612, Fax 966 4801, – rest TV ☎ P. AE VISA.
Meals (grill rest.) 10.75 **t.** (lunch) and dinner a la carte 10.60/16.40 **t.** 4.25 – **16 rm** 49.50/69.50 **st.**

HACKNESS N. Yorks. 402 S 21 – see Scarborough.

HADLEIGH Suffolk 404 W 27 – pop. 6 595 – ☎ 01473.

Toppesfield Hall, IP7 5DN ✆ 823824.

London 72 – ◆Cambridge 49 – Colchester 17 – ◆Ipswich 10.

Edgehill, 2 High St., IP7 5AP, ✆ 822458, – TV P.
closed Christmas to New Year – **Meals** (by arrangement) (dinner only) 14.50 **st.** and a la carte – **9 rm** 35.00/65.00 **st.** – SB.

HADLEY HEATH Heref. and Worcs. – see Droitwich.

HAGLEY W. Mids. 403 404 N 26 – see Stourbridge.

HAILEY Oxon. 403 404 P 28 – see Witney.

HAILSHAM E. Sussex 404 U 31 – pop. 14 906 – ☎ 01323.

Wellshurst G. & C.C., North St., Hellingly ✆ (01435) 813636.

The Library, Western Rd, BN27 3DN ✆ 844426.

◆London 57 – ◆Brighton 23 – Eastbourne 7 – Hastings 20.

Boship Farm, Lower Dicker, BN27 4AT, NW : 3 m. by A 295 on A 22 ✆ 844826, Fax 843945, heated, – rm TV ☎ P – 120. AE VISA
Meals *(closed Saturday lunch)* 7.45/16.45 **t.** and a la carte 5.45 – **44 rm** 49.95/89.90 **t.**, 2 suites – SB.

Forte Travelodge, Boship Roundabout, Lower Dicker, BN27 4DT, NW : 3 m. by A 295 on A 22 ✆ 844556, Reservations (Freephone) 0800 850950 – TV P. AE VISA.
Meals (grill rest.) – **40 rm** 34.50 **t.**

at Magham Down NE : 2 m. by A 295 on A 271 – ✉ Hailsham – ☎ 01323 :

Olde Forge, BN27 1PN, ✆ 842893, Fax 842893 – TV ☎ P. AE VISA
closed 25 December-2 January – **Meals** (dinner only) 12.95 **t.** and a la carte 3.95 – **7 rm** 37.50/60.00 **st.** – SB.

HALE Gtr. Manchester 402 403 404 M 23 – see Altrincham.

HALEBARNS Gtr. Manchester – see Altrincham.

HALIFAX W. Yorks. 402 O 22 – pop. 91 069 – ☎ 01422.

18 Halifax Bradley Hall, Holywell Green ✆ 374108 – 18 Halifax West End, Paddock Lane, Highroad Well ✆ 353608, 18 Union Lane, Ogden ✆ 244171 – 9 Ryburn, Norland, Sowerby Bridge ✆ 831355 – 9 Elland, Hammerstones Leach Lane, Hullen Edge ✆ 372505 – 9 Lightcliffe, Knowle Top Rd ✆ 202459.

Piece Hall, HX1 1RE ✆ 368725.

◆London 205 – Bradford 8 – Burnley 21 – ◆Leeds 15 – ◆Manchester 28.

Holdsworth House, Holdsworth Rd, Holmfield, HX2 9TG, N : 3 m. by A 629 and Shay Lane ✆ 240024, Fax 245174, « Part 17C house », – TV ☎ P – 80. AE VISA
Meals *(closed Saturday lunch)* 12.50/21.50 **st.** and a la carte 4.25 – 6.50 – **36 rm** 72.50/90.00 **st.**, 4 suites – SB.

Hilton National Huddersfield, Ainley Top, HD3 3RH, S : 5 ¾ m. at junction of A 629 with A 643 ✆ 375431, Fax 310067, – rm rest TV ☎ P – 400. AE VISA JCB
Meals *(closed Saturday lunch)* (carving lunch) 12.75/16.95 **st.** and dinner a la carte 5.50 – 10.25 – **113 rm** 78.00 **st.**, 1 suite – SB.

Imperial Crown, 42-46 Horton St., HX1 1BR, ✆ 342342, Fax 349866 – rm TV ☎ P – 150. AE VISA.
Meals (bar lunch)/dinner 14.50 **t.** and a la carte – **39 rm** 63.50/74.50 **st.**, 2 suites – SB.

Imperial Crown Lodge without rest., 31 Square Rd, HX1 1QG, ✆ 320000, Fax 349866 – TV P. AE VISA.
6.95 – **15 rm** 42.50 **st.**

Design House (Restaurant), Dean Clough (Gate 5), HX3 5AX, ✆ 383242, Fax 322732 – P. AE VISA
closed Saturday lunch, Sunday, 25 and 26 December – **Meals** 12.95 **t.** (lunch) and a la carte 13.95/24.40 **t.** 5.25.

ATS Hope St. ✆ 365892/360819

Prices For full details of the prices quoted in the guide, consult the introduction.

HALLAND E. Sussex 404 U 31 – ✉ Lewes – ☎ 01825.
♦London 48 – ♦Brighton 16 – Eastbourne 16 – Royal Tunbridge Wells 19.

Halland Forge, BN8 6PW, on A 22 ☎ 840456, Fax 840773, park – TV ☎ P. AE VISA JCB.
Meals 10.00/21.50 **t.** and a la carte 5.80 – 8.00 – **20 rm** 46.00/58.00 **t.** – SB.

HALL GREEN W. Mids. 402 403 404 O 26 – see Birmingham.

HALNAKER W. Sussex – see Chichester.

HALTWHISTLE Northd 401 402 M 19 **Great Britain G.** – pop. 3 773 – ☎ 01434.
Envir. : Hadrian's Wall★★, N : 4½ m. by A 6079 – Housesteads★★ *AC*, NE : 6 m. by B 6318 – Roman Army Museum★ *AC*, NW : 5 m. by A 69 and B 6318 – Vindolanda (Museum★) *AC*, NE 5 m. by A 69 – Steel Rig (≤★) NE : 5½ m. by B 6318.
9 Banktop, Greenhead ☎ (016977) 47367.
Church Hall, Main St., NE49 0BE ☎ 322002.
♦London 335 – ♦Carlisle 22 – ♦Newcastle upon Tyne 37.

Bellister Castle, NE49 0HZ, S : 1 m. by A 69 on Alston rd ☎ 320391, Fax 320391 « Castellated manor house of 17C origins », – rm P.
Meals (by arrangement) (communal dining) 22.50 **st.** – **3 rm** 33.00/65.00 **st.**

Ashcroft without rest., Lantys Lonnen, NE49 0DA, ☎ 320213, « Gardens » – P.
closed 22 December-5 January – **8 rm** 16.00/36.00.

HAMBLETON Leics. – see Oakham.

HAMBROOK Avon 403 404 M 29 – see Bristol.

HAMPTON LOADE Shrops. 402 403 404 M 26 – see Bridgnorth.

HAMSTEAD MARSHALL Berks. 403 404 P29 – see Newbury.

HAMSTERLEY Durham 401 402 O 19 – pop. 397 – ✉ Bishop Auckland – ☎ 01388.
♦London 260 – ♦Carlisle 75 – ♦Middlesbrough 30 – ♦Newcastle upon Tyne 22.

Grove House, Hamsterley Forest, DL13 3NL, W : 3¾ m. via Bedburn ☎ 488203, – P.
closed Christmas and New Year – **Meals** (by arrangement) 12.50 **s.** – **3 rm** 25.00/50.00.

HANDFORTH Ches. 402 403 404 N 23 – see Wilmslow.

HANSLOPE Bucks. 404 R 27 – see Milton Keynes.

HANWOOD Shrops. 402 403 L 25 – see Shrewsbury.

HAREWOOD W. Yorks. 402 P 22 – pop. 3 222 – ✉ Leeds – ☎ 0113.
♦London 214 – Harrogate 9 – ♦Leeds 10 – York 20.

Harewood Arms, Harrogate Rd, LS17 9LH, on A 61 ☎ 288 6566, Fax 288 6064, – TV ☎ P. AE VISA.
Meals 8.50/15.95 **t.** and dinner a la carte 4.95 – **24 rm** 65.00/78.00 **t.**

HARLOW Essex 404 U 28 – pop. 74 629 – ☎ 01279.
18 Nazeing, Middle St. ☎ (01992) 893798/893915.
♦London 22 – ♦Cambridge 37 – ♦Ipswich 60.

Churchgate Manor, Churchgate St., Old Harlow, CM17 0JT, E : 3¼ m. by A 414 and B 183 ☎ 420246, Fax 437720, – rest TV ☎ P – 170. AE VISA JCB
Meals (bar lunch Saturday) 14.95/17.95 **t.** and a la carte 5.50 – 8.95 – **82 rm** 69.00/82.00 **t.**, 3 suites – SB.

Harlow Moat House (Q.M.H.), Southern Way, CM18 7BA, SE : 2¼ m. by A 1025 on A 414 ☎ 829988, Fax 635094 – rm TV ☎ P – 150. AE VISA.
Meals (carving rest.) (bar lunch Saturday and Bank Holidays) 10.50/16.50 **st.** 5.70 – 9.50 – **118 rm** 65.00 **st.** – SB.

Travel Inn, Cambridge Rd, Old Harlow, CM20 2EP, NE : 3¼ m. by A 414 on A 1184 ☎ 442545, Fax 452169 – rm TV P. AE VISA.
Meals (grill rest.) – 4.95 – **38 rm** 34.50 **t.**

ATS 14 Burnt Mill ☎ 421965

HARNHAM Wilts. 403 404 O 30 – see Salisbury.

HAROME N. Yorks. – see Helmsley.

We suggest:

For a successful tour, that you prepare it in advance.
Michelin maps and guides will give you a great deal of useful information on route planning, places of interest, accommodation, prices etc.

HARPENDEN Herts. 404 S 28 – pop. 27 294 – ☎ 01582.

London 32 – Luton 6.

Harpenden House (Q.M.H.), 18 Southdown Rd, AL5 1PE, ☎ 449955, Fax 769858, – rm ☎ – 150. AE VISA.
Meals *(closed Saturday lunch)* 14.95/22.85 **st.** and a la carte 7.00 – 10.00 – **52 rm** 85.00/102.00 **st.**, 1 suite – SB.

Glen Eagle, 1 Luton Rd, AL5 2PX, ☎ 760271, Fax 460819, – rest ☎ – 80. AE VISA.
closed 26 to 30 December – **Meals** (light meal Saturday lunch, Sunday dinner and Bank Holidays) 12.50/14.50 **st.** and a la carte 6.00 – 8.75 – **51 rm** 73.50/83.50 **st.** – SB.

Chef Peking, 5-6 Church Green, AL5 2TP, ☎ 769358 – . AE VISA JCB
Meals - Chinese (Peking, Szechuan) - 10.00 **t.** and a la carte 4.00.

GRÜNE REISEFÜHRER

Landschaften, Baudenkmäler
Sehenswürdigkeiten
Fremdenverkehrsstraßen
Tourenvorschläge
Stadtpläne und Übersichtskarten

HARROGATE N. Yorks. 402 P 22 **Great Britain G.** – pop. 143 526 – ☎ 01423.

See : Town★.

Exc. : Fountains Abbey★★★ *AC* :- Studley Royal★★ *AC* (<★ from Anne Boleyn's Seat) Fountains Hall (Façade★), N : 13 m. by A 61 and B 6265 AY – Harewood House★★ (The Gallery★) *AC*, S : 7½ m. by A 61 BZ.

Forest Lane Head ☎ 863158 – Follifoot Rd, Pannal ☎ 871641 – Oakdale ☎ 567162 – Crimple Valley, Hookstone Wood Rd ☎ 883485.

Royal Baths Assembly Rooms, Crescent Rd, HG1 2RR ☎ 525666.

London 211 – Bradford 18 – ◆Leeds 15 – ◆Newcastle Upon Tyne 76 – York 22.

Plan on next page

Nidd Hall, Nidd, HG3 3BN, N : 4¼ m. by A 61 on B 6165 ☎ 771598, Fax 770931, <, « 19C manor house », park, squash – ☎ – 250. AE VISA JCB.
Meals (light lunch Saturday) 21.50/26.50 **st.** – **56 rm** 95.00/150.00 **st.**, 3 suites – SB.

Majestic (Forte), Ripon Rd, HG1 2HU, ☎ 568972, Fax 502283, squash – rm ☎ – 300. AE VISA JCB — AY **c**
Meals (bar lunch)/dinner 19.95 **t.** and a la carte – 11.95 – **152 rm** 84.00/110.00 **st.**, 4 suites – SB.

Old Swan, Swan Rd, HG1 2SR, ☎ 500055, Fax 501154, – ☎ – 350. AE VISA — AY **e**
Meals (bar lunch Monday to Saturday)/dinner 19.00 **t.** and a la carte – 10.25 – **126 rm** 89.50/114.00 **st.**, 10 suites – SB.

Harrogate Moat House (Q.M.H.), Kings Rd, HG1 1XX, ☎ 849988, Telex 57575, Fax 524435, < – rm rest ☎ – 350. AE VISA. — BY **x**
Abbey : Meals (carving rest.) (dinner only) 11.50 **st.** 6.50 – **Boulevard : Meals** *(closed Saturday lunch, Sunday dinner and Monday)* 17.00 **st.** (dinner) and a la carte 15.75/28.00 **st.** 6.50 – 9.00 – **205 rm** 99.00/128.00 **st.**, 9 suites – SB.

St. George (Swallow), 1 Ripon Rd, HG1 2SY, ☎ 561431, Fax 530037, – rm ☎ – 150. AE VISA — AY **o**
Meals (buffet lunch) 11.75/16.95 **st.** and dinner a la carte 5.50 – **91 rm** 85.00/105.00 **st.**, 1 suite – SB.

Crown (Forte), Crown Pl., HG1 2RZ, ☎ 567755, Fax 502284 – ☎ – 300. AE VISA JCB — AZ **i**
Meals (bar lunch Monday to Saturday)/dinner 17.95 **t.** and a la carte 6.95 – 8.95 – **116 rm** 75.00/83.00 **st.**, 5 suites – SB.

Balmoral, Franklin Mount, HG1 5EJ, ☎ 508208, Fax 530652, « Antique furnishings » – rest ☎. AE VISA — BY **v**
Meals 12.50/18.50 **t.** and a la carte 6.50 – 8.50 – **19 rm** 69.00/99.00 **st.**, 1 suite – SB.

Grants, Swan Rd, HG1 2SS, ☎ 560666, Fax 502550 – rest ☎ – 70. AE VISA JCB. — AY **s**
Meals 10.95/16.95 **t.** 5.95 – **41 rm** 90.00/125.00 **t.**, 1 suite – SB.

Studley, 28 Swan Rd, HG1 2SE, ☎ 560425, Fax 530967 – ☎. AE VISA
Meals 20.75 **t.** (dinner) and a la carte 17.75/22.00 **t.** 5.10 – **34 rm** 68.00/110.00 **st.**, 2 suites – SB. — AZ **x**

Hospitality Inn (Mount Charlotte), Prospect Pl., West Park, HG1 1LB, ☎ 564601, Telex 57530, Fax 507508 – ☎ – 150. AE VISA JCB. — BZ **v**
Meals (bar lunch Monday to Saturday)/dinner 15.50 **st.** and a la carte – 8.50 – **66 rm** 68.00/89.00 **st.**, 5 suites – SB.

HARROGATE

Cambridge Street	BZ	3
James Street	BZ	15
Montpelier Parade	AZ	18
Parliament Street	AZ	22
Albert Street	BZ	2
Cheltenham Cres.	BYZ	4
Cheltenham Parade	BYZ	7
Commercial Street	BY	8
Crescent Road	AZ	10
Hampsthwaite Road	AY	13
Knapping Hill	AY	16
North Park Road	BCZ	19
Oxford Street	BZ	20
Springfield Avenue	ABY	23
Swan Road	AYZ	24
Westmorland Street	BY	26
Wheatlands Rd East	CZ	27

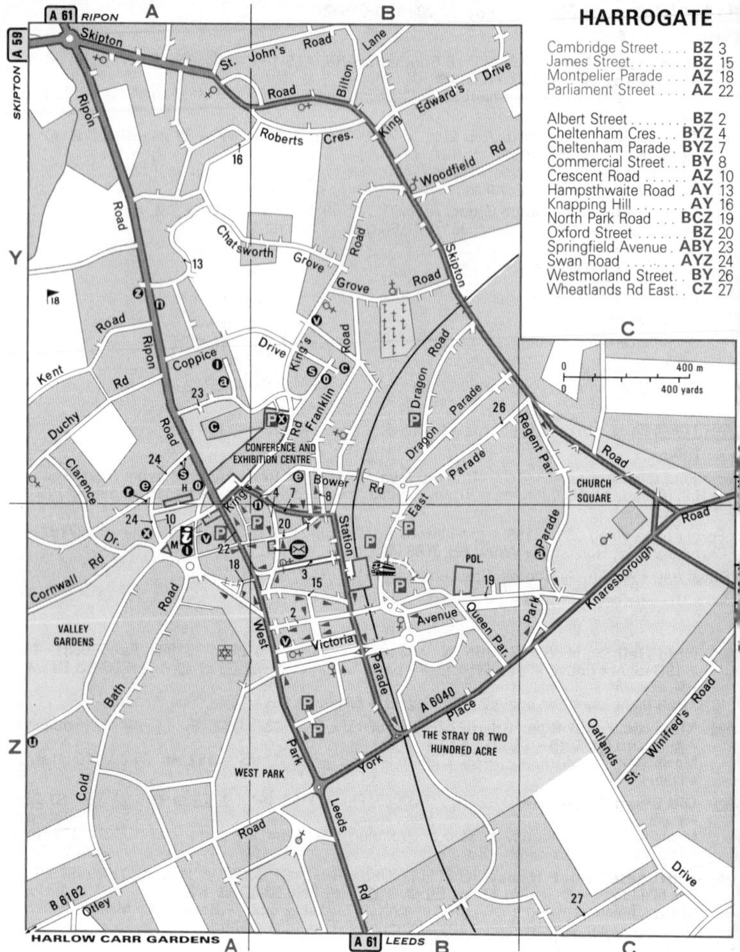

Ruskin, 1 Swan Rd, HG1 2SS, ℘ 502045, Fax 506131, – TV P. VISA AY
Meals *(closed Sunday)* (dinner only) 17.95 **st.** and a la carte **st.** 4.95 – **7 rm** 45.00/78.00 **st.** – SB.

White House, 10 Park Par., HG1 5AH, ℘ 501388, Fax 527973, – rest TV P. AE VISA. CZ
Meals *(closed Sunday)* (booking essential) (lunch by arrangement) 14.50 **t.** (lunch and a la carte 16.25/21.70 **t.** 4.95 – **10 rm** 82.50/125.00 **t.**, 1 suite – SB.

Britannia Lodge, 16 Swan Rd, HG1 2SA, ℘ 508482, Fax 526840 – rest TV P. AE VISA JCB. AYZ
Meals 7.50/12.50 **t.** 5.00 – **12 rm** 47.50/70.00 **t.** – SB.

Alexa House, 26 Ripon Rd, HG1 2JJ, ℘ 501988, Fax 504086 – TV P. VISA AY
Meals (lunch by arrangement)/dinner 7.00/11.50 **st.** 4.50 – **13 rm** 35.00/58.00 **st.** – SB

Abbey Lodge, 29-31 Ripon Rd, HG1 2JL, ℘ 569712, Fax 530570 – TV P. VISA AY
Meals (dinner only) 17.50 **t.** 4.95 – **17 rm** 28.00/59.00 **t.** – SB.

Brookfield House without rest., 5 Alexandra Rd, HG1 5JS, ☎ 506646, Fax 523151 – ⇔ TV ☎ P. VISA. ✻ BY s
6 rm ☐ 38.00/55.00 **st.**

Alexandra Court without rest., 8 Alexandra Rd, HG1 5JS, ☎ 502764, Fax 523151 – ⇔ TV ☎ P. VISA. ✻ BY o
14 rm ☐ 40.00/60.00 **t.**

Garden House, 14 Harlow Moor Drive, HG2 0JX, ☎ 503059 – ⇔ rest TV. AE VISA. ✻ AZ u
closed 24 December-2 January – **Meals** (by arrangement) 11.00 **t.** 3.00 – **7 rm** ☐ 22.00/45.00 **t.** – SB.

Arden House, 69-71 Franklin Rd, HG1 5EH, ☎ 509224, Fax 561170 – ⇔ rest TV ☎ P. AE VISA BY c
closed Christmas and New Year – **Meals** 15.00 **st.** 3.50 – **14 rm** ☐ 27.00/55.00 **st.** – SB.

Knabbs Ash ⛰ without rest., Felliscliffe, HG3 2LT, W : 5 ½ m. on A 59 ☎ 771040, Fax 771515, ≤, – ⇔ TV P. ✻
3 rm ☐ 25.00/40.00 **st.**

Stoney Lea without rest., 13 Spring Grove, HG1 2HS, ☎ 501524 – TV. ✻ AY i
closed Christmas-New Year – **7 rm** ☐ 26.00/40.00 **st.**

Ashwood House without rest., 7 Spring Grove, HG1 2HS, ☎ 560081, Fax 527928 – ⇔ TV. ✻ AY a
closed 24 December-2 January – **8 rm** ☐ 27.00/49.00.

Knox Mill House ⛰ without rest., Knox Mill Lane, HG3 2AE, N : 1 ½ m. by A 61 ☎ 560650, ≤ – P. ✻
3 rm ☐ 34.00/38.00 **s.**

XX **The Bistro,** 1 Montpellier Mews, HG1 2TG, ☎ 530708, – AE VISA AZ v
closed Sunday, Monday and 1 week Christmas – **Meals** a la carte 9.50/20.50 **t.**

XX **Grundy's,** 21 Cheltenham Cres., HG1 1DH, ☎ 502610 – AE VISA BYZ n
closed Sunday, 2 weeks January-February, 2 weeks July-August and Bank Holidays – **Meals** (dinner only) 13.95 **t.** and a la carte.

XX **La Bergerie,** 11-13 Mount Par., HG1 1BX, ☎ 500089, Fax 560837 – VISA AY e
closed Sunday and Bank Holidays – **Meals** - French - (dinner only) 16.50 **t.** and a la carte 6.80.

X **Drum and Monkey,** 5 Montpellier Gdns, HG1 2TF, ☎ 502650 – VISA AZ v
closed Sunday and 24 December-2 January – **Meals** - Seafood - (booking essential) a la carte 10.05/24.10 **t.** 3.45.

at Beckwithshaw SW : 2 ¾ m. on B 6162 AZ – ✉ Harrogate – ☎ 01423 :

Sandringham, Otley Rd, HG3 1QL, ☎ 500722, Fax 530509, « Antiques and memorabilia » – ⇔ rest TV ☎ P. AE VISA. ✻
Meals *(closed Sunday dinner and Monday)* (by arrangement to non-residents) 16.00/35.00 **st.** – **6 rm** ☐ 55.00/95.00 **st.**, 1 suite – SB.

at Markington NW : 8 ¾ m. by A 61 – AY – ✉ Harrogate – ☎ 01423 :

Hob Green ⛰, HG3 3PJ, SW : ½ m. ☎ 770031, Fax 771589, ≤, « Country house in extensive parkland », – TV ☎ P. AE VISA JCB. ✻
Meals (bar lunch Monday to Saturday)/dinner a la carte 16.70/23.15 **st.** 4.95 – **11 rm** ☐ 70.00/95.00 **st.**, 1 suite – SB.

ATS Leeds Rd, Pannal ☎ 879194

HARTFIELD E. Sussex 404 U 30 – pop. 2 026 – ☎ 01892.

London 47 – ♦Brighton 28 – Maidstone 25.

Bolebroke Mill ⛰ without rest., Edenbridge Rd, TN7 4JP, N : 1 ¼ m. by B 2026 on unmarked rd ☎ 770425, Fax 770425, « Part early 17C cornmill, original features », – ⇔ TV P. AE VISA. ✻
March-November – **5 rm** ☐ 48.00/70.00.

HARTFORD Ches. 402 403 404 M 24 – pop. 4 605 – ☎ 01606.

London 188 – Chester 15 – ♦Liverpool 31 – ♦Manchester 25.

Hartford Hall, 81 School Lane, CW8 1PW, ☎ 75711, Fax 782285, – TV ☎ P – 35
19 rm, 1 suite.

HARTINGTON Derbs. 402 403 404 O 24 – pop. 1 604 (inc. Dovedale) – ✉ Buxton – ☎ 01298.

London 168 – Derby 36 – ♦Manchester 40 – ♦Sheffield 34 – Stoke-on-Trent 22.

Biggin Hall ⛰, Biggin, SK17 0DH, SE : 2 m. by B 5054 ☎ 84451, Fax 84681, ≤, « 17C hall », – ⇔ rest TV P. VISA JCB. ✻
Meals (by arrangement) 14.50 **st.** 4.50 – ☐ 3.50 – **17 rm** 30.00/80.00 **st.** – SB.

HARTLEBURY Heref. and Worcs. 403 N 26 – pop. 2 253 – ☎ 01299.

London 135 – ♦Birmingham 20 – Worcester 11.

Forte Travelodge, Crossway Green, DX11 6DR, S : 2 ½ m. by B 4193 on A 449 (southbound carriageway) ☎ 250553, Reservations (Freephone) 0800 850950 – TV ♿ P. AE VISA. ✻
Meals (grill rest.) – **32 rm** 34.50 **t.**

HARTLEPOOL Cleveland 402 Q 19 – pop. 90 409 – ☎ 01429.

Seaton Carew, Tees Rd ☎ 266249/261040 – Castle Eden and Peterlee ☎ 836220 – Ha Warren ☎ 274398.

Teesside Airport : ☎ (01325) 332811, SW : 20 m. by A 689, A 1027, A 135 and A 67.

Civic Centre, Victoria Rd, TS24 8AY ☎ 266522 ext : 2408/2407.

London 263 – Durham 19 – Middlesbrough 9 – Sunderland 21.

Grand, Swainson St., TS24 8AA, ☎ 266345, Fax 265217 – 150. AE VISA.
Meals (carving rest.) (bar lunch Monday to Saturday)/dinner 11.50 **st.** and a la carte – **50 r** 45.00/70.00 **st.** – SB.

York, 185-187 York Rd, TS26 9EE, ☎ 867373, Fax 867220 – TV. AE VISA.
Meals *(closed Monday dinner and Sunday)* 8.95/10.95 **st.** and a la carte 4.95 – **13 r** 25.00/48.00 **st.** – SB.

at Seaton Carew SE : 2 m. on A 178 – ☎ 01429 :

Marine, 5-7 The Front, TS25 1BS, ☎ 266244, Fax 864144, – TV. AE VISA.
Meals (carving rest.) (bar lunch Saturday) 6.95/8.95 **st.** and a la carte – **25 rm** 45.0 65.00 **st.**

Krimo's, 8 The Front, TS25 1BS, ☎ 266120 – VISA
closed Saturday lunch, Sunday, Monday, 1 January, last 2 weeks September and 24 26 December – **Meals** 6.00/14.95 **st.** and a la carte 3.90.

ATS York Rd ☎ 275552

HARTSHEAD MOOR SERVICE AREA W. Yorks. 402 O 22 – ✉ Brighouse – ☎ 01274.

London 213 – Bradford 8 – Burnley 31 – Manchester 35 – Sheffield 39.

Forte Travelodge, Clifton, HD6 4RJ, M 62 between junctions 25 and 26 (eastboun carriageway) ☎ 851706, Reservations (Freephone) 0800 850950 – TV. AE VIS
Meals (grill rest.) – **40 rm** 34.50 **t.**

HARVINGTON Heref. and Worcs. 403 404 027 – see Evesham.

HARWELL Oxon. 403 404 Q 29 pop. 2 404 – ☎ 01235.

London 64 – Oxford 16 – Reading 18 – Swindon 22.

Kingswell, Reading Rd, OX11 0LZ, S : ¾ m. on A 417 ☎ 833043, Telex 83173, Fax 8331 – TV – 30. AE VISA.
Meals 12.50/17.50 **t.** and a la carte 5.25 – **19 rm** 68.00/90.00 **t.** – SB.

HARWICH and DOVERCOURT Essex 404 X 28 – pop. 15 374 (Harwich) – ☎ 01255.

Station Rd, Parkeston ☎ 503616.

to Germany (Hamburg) (Scandinavian Seaways) 1 daily (19 h 30 mn) – to Denma (Esbjerg) (Scandinavian Seaways) (18 h 30 mn) – to The Netherlands (Hook of Holland) (Ster Line) 2 daily (6 h 30 mn) day, (9 h 30 mn) night – to Sweden (Gothenburg) (Scandinavia Seaways) (24 h).

to Felixstowe (Orwell & Harwich Navigation Co. Ltd) 5 daily (14 mn).

Essex County Council, Parkeston Quay, CO12 4SP ☎ 506139.

London 78 – Chelmsford 41 – Colchester 20 – Ipswich 23.

Pier at Harwich with rm, The Quay, CO12 3HH, ☎ 241212, Fax 551922, – TV. AE VISA.
closed 25 and 26 December – **Meals** - Seafood - 12.50/16.50 **t.** and a la carte 5.95 4.00 – **6 rm** 45.00/72.50 **st.** – SB.

ATS 723 Main Rd, Dovercourt ☎ 508314

HASCOMBE Surrey – see Godalming.

HASELBURY PLUCKNETT Somerset 403 L 31 – see Crewkerne.

HASLEMERE Surrey 404 R 30 – pop. 7 326 – ☎ 01428.

London 47 – Brighton 46 – Southampton 44.

Lythe Hill, Petworth Rd, GU27 3BQ, E : 1½ m. on B 2131 ☎ 651251, Fax 644131, , park, – TV – 60. AE VISA JCB
Meals *(closed Saturday dinner and Sunday lunch)* 17.50/19.50 **st.** and a la carte 7.2
Auberge de France : Meals - French - *(closed Monday)* (dinner only and Sunday lunch dinner 22.50 **st.** and a la carte 7.25 – 8.00 – **28 rm** 74.00/95.00 **st.**, 12 suites – SB.

Georgian, High St., GU27 2JY, ☎ 651555, Fax 661304, , squash – TV. AE VISA
Meals 12.50/15.95 **t.** and a la carte 5.00 – 6.95 – **24 rm** 67.00/85.00 **st.**, 1 suite – SB.

Fleur de Sel (Perraud), 23-27 Lower St., GU27 2NY, ☎ 651462, Fax 661568 – AE VIS JCB
closed Saturday lunch, Sunday dinner, Monday, 1 week February and 2 weeks Augus September – **Meals** - French - 12.50/26.00 **t.** 6.60
Spec. Cornish crab cake with mango sauce, Roast Scottish salmon, sauce vierge, Crème brûlée flavoured with vanill

ASTINGS and ST. LEONARDS E. Sussex 404 V 31 – pop. 80 820 – ⊛ 01424.

[golf] Beauport Park, Battle Rd, St. Leonards, ℘ 852977.

4 Robertson Terr., TN34 1EZ ℘ 781111 – Fishmarket, The Stade, TN34 1EZ ℘ 781111 ummer only).

ondon 65 – ♦Brighton 37 – Folkestone 37 – Maidstone 34.

HASTINGS AND ST. LEONARDS

ing's Road AZ 22
ondon Road AZ
orman Road AZ
ueen's Road BZ
obertson Street BZ 27
Vellington Place BZ 35

Bourne (The) BY 4
Cambridge Gardens BZ 5
Castle Street BZ 7
Castle Hill Road BZ 8
Cornwallis Gardens BZ 9
Cornwallis Terrace BZ 10
Denmark Place BZ 13
Dorset Place BZ 15
Gensing Road AZ 16
George Street BY 18

Grosvenor Crescent AY 19
Harold Place BZ 20
Marine Court AZ 23
Rock-a-Nore Road BY 30
St. Helen's Park Road BY 31
Sedlescombe Road South AY 32
Silchester Road AZ 33
Warrior Square AZ 34
Wellington Square BZ 36
White Rock Road BZ 38

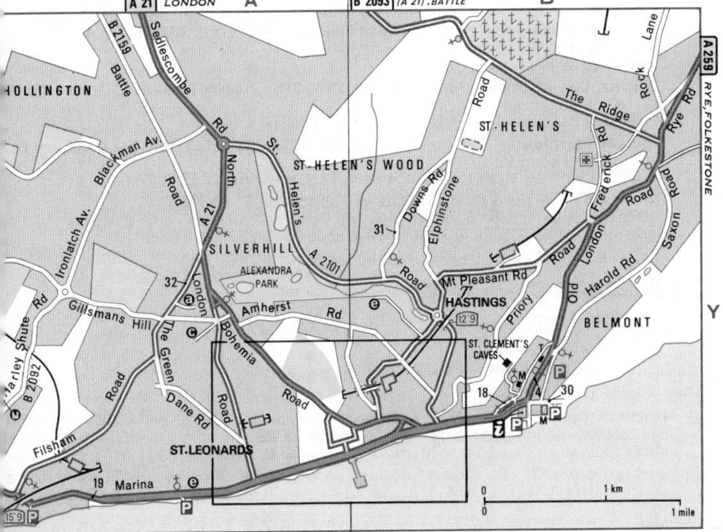

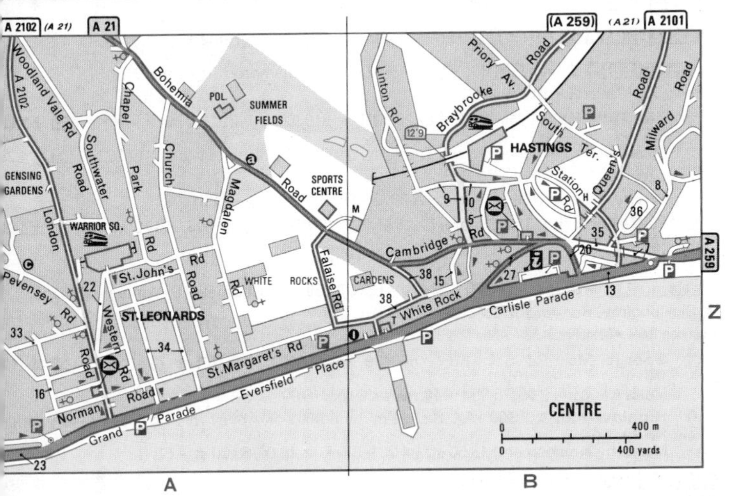

Royal Victoria, Marina, TN38 0BD, ℘ 445544, Fax 721995, ≤ – |♦| TV ☎ – 🅰 70. 🅰 🅴 **AY**
⊕ VISA. ✻
Meals (bar lunch Monday to Saturday)/dinner 13.00/17.00 **st.** and a la carte 4.50 – **50 rm** 65.00/90.00 **t.** – SB.

Beauport Park ⊛, Battle Rd, TN38 8EA, NW : 3½ m. at junction of A 2100 with B 215 ℘ 851222, Fax 852465, ≤, « Formal garden », heated, 18, park, ✻ – ▤ rest TV ☎ P 60. AE ⊕ VISA JCB
Meals 15.00/18.00 **t.** and a la carte 5.00 – 8.50 – **23 rm** 65.00/95.00 **t.** – SB.

Cinque Ports, Summerfields, Bohemia Rd, TN34 1ET, ℘ 439222, Fax 437277 – TV ☎ – 250. AE ⊕ VISA JCB **AZ**
Meals 6.00/14.00 **st.** and a la carte – 6.50 – **40 rm** 49.00 **st.** – SB.

Tower House, 26-28 Tower Rd West, TN38 0RG, ℘ 427217, – TV. AE ⊕ VISA ✻ **AY**
Meals (dinner only) 11.50 **st.** 4.00 – **10 rm** 25.00/50.00 **st.**

Eagle House, 12 Pevensey Rd, TN38 0JZ, ℘ 430535, Fax 437771 – TV ☎ P. AE VISA. ✻ **AZ**
Meals *(closed Sunday lunch)* (dinner only) 18.95 **st.** 3.60 – **19 rm** 31.60/49.00 **st.**

Parkside House without rest., 59 Lower Park Rd, TN34 2LD, ℘ 433096, Fax 421431, TV. VISA. ✻ **BY**
5 rm 25.00/52.00 **s.**

Chimes, 1 St. Matthews Gdns, Silverhill, TN38 0TS, ℘ 434041, Fax 434041, – TV. VISA. ✻ **AY**
Meals (by arrangement) 10.00 **s.** – **9 rm** 19.00/42.00 **s.**

Filsham Farmhouse, 111 Harley Shute Rd, TN38 8BY, ℘ 433109, Fax 461061, « Pa 17C », – rm TV P **AY**
closed Christmas – **Meals** (by arrangement) 12.50 **s.** – **3 rm** 25.00/50.00.

XX **Röser's,** 64 Eversfield Pl., TN37 6DB, ℘ 712218 – AE ⊕ VISA **BZ**
closed Saturday lunch, Sunday, Monday, first week January and 2 weeks August September – **Meals** 15.95/18.95 **st.** and a la carte 23.45/39.35 **st.** 5.95.

ATS Menzies Rd, Pondswood Ind. Est., St. Leonards-on-Sea ℘ 427780/424567

HATCH BEAUCHAMP Somerset 403 K 30 – see Taunton.

HATFIELD Herts. 404 T 28 **Great Britain G.** – pop. 24 238 – ☎ 01707.

See : Hatfield House★★ *AC*.

18 Hatfield London C.C., Bedwell Park, Essendon ℘ 642624.

♦London 27 – Bedford 38 – ♦Cambridge 39.

Hatfield Oak, Roehyde Way, AL10 9AF, S : 2 m. by B 6426 on A 1001 ℘ 275701 Fax 266033 – rm TV ☎ & P – 120. AE ⊕ VISA
Meals 16.25 **st.** and a la carte – **76 rm** 65.00/87.50 **st.** – SB.

Jarvis Comet, 301 St. Albans Rd West, AL10 9RH, W : 1 m. by B 6426 on A 1057 a junction with A 1001 ℘ 265411, Fax 264019 – rm TV ☎ P – 150. AE ⊕ VISA ✻
Meals *(closed Saturday lunch)* (carving rest.) 9.50/18.95 **st.** 6.25 – 8.00 – **55 rm** 79.00 89.00 **st.** – SB.

HATFIELD HEATH Essex. 404 U 28 – see Bishop's Stortford (Herts.).

HATHERLEIGH Devon 403 H 31 – pop. 1 542 – ✉ Okehampton – ☎ 01837.

♦London 230 – Exeter 29 – ♦Plymouth 38.

The Tally Ho, 14 Market St., EX20 3JN, ℘ 810306, « Part 16C inn » – rm TV. VISA. ✻
Meals *(closed Wednesday and Thursday)* (bar lunch)/dinner a la carte 12.55/33.70 **t.** 4.2 – 2.75 – **3 rm** 30.00/50.00 **t.**

at Sheepwash NW : 5½ m. by A 3072 – ✉ Beaworthy – ☎ 01409 :

Half Moon Inn, The Square, EX21 5NE, ℘ 231376, Fax 231673, « 17C inn », – TV ☎ P. VISA
Meals (bar lunch)/dinner 18.25 **t.** 5.00 – **15 rm** 34.00/75.00 **t.**

HATHERSAGE Derbs. 402 403 404 P 24 – pop. 2 858 – ✉ Sheffield (S. Yorks.) – ☎ 01433.

18 Sickleholme, Bamford ℘ 651306.

♦London 165 – ♦Manchester 33 – ♦Sheffield 10.

George, Main Rd, S30 1BB, ℘ 650436, Fax 650099 – TV ☎ P – 30. AE ⊕ VISA
Meals a la carte 9.05/20.95 **t.** – **18 rm** 59.50/75.00 **t.** – SB.

Highlow Hall ⊛, S30 1AX, S : 1½ m. by B 6001 on Abney rd ℘ 650393, ≤, , park P. ✻
Meals (by arrangement) 13.50 **st.** 4.95 – **6 rm** 18.00/60.00 **st.** – SB.

HATTON Warks. – see Warwick.

AVANT Hants. 404 R 31 – pop. 46 510 – ☎ 01705.

1 Park Rd South, PO9 1HA ☎ 480024.

London 70 – ♦Brighton 39 – ♦Portsmouth 9 – ♦Southampton 22.

Bear, 15 East St., PO9 1AA, ☎ 486501, Fax 470551 – rm – 100. VISA.
Meals a la carte 12.85/21.70 **t.** – **42 rm** 49.50/69.50 **st.** – SB.

ATS 60-62 Bedhampton Rd ☎ 483018/451570

HAVERHILL Suffolk 404 V 27 – ☎ 01440.

London 59 – ♦Cambridge 19 – Chelmsford 32 – Colchester 30 – ♦Ipswich 44.

XX **Mill House,** 11 Mill Rd, CB9 8BD, ☎ 712123 – VISA
closed Saturday lunch, Sunday dinner and Monday – **Meals** 14.95 **t.** and a la carte 10.35/19.85 **t.**

HAWES N. Yorks. 402 N 21 – pop. 1 117 – ☎ 01969.

Dales Countryside Museum, Station Yard, DL8 3NT ☎ 667450 (summer only).

London 253 – Kendal 27 – ♦Leeds 72 – ♦York 65.

Simonstone Hall, Simonstone, DL8 3LY, N : 1 ½ m. on Muker rd ☎ 667255, Fax 667741, ≤, « Part 18C country house », – VISA JCB
Meals 9.00/23.00 **t.** 6.25 – **10 rm** 36.00/114.00 **t.** – SB.

Stone House, Sedbusk, DL8 3PT, N : 1 m. by Muker rd on Askrigg rd ☎ 667571, Fax 667720, ≤, « Collections of ornaments and curios », – rest VISA JCB
closed January and restricted bookings December – **Meals** (dinner only) 15.95 **t.** 4.20 – **18 rm** 31.50/76.00 **t.** – SB.

Rookhurst Georgian Country House, Gayle, DL8 3RT, S : ½ m. by Gayle rd ☎ 667454, Fax 667454, – VISA JCB.
closed 25 and 26 December and 8 to 31 January – **Meals** (booking essential) (residents only) (dinner only) 20.00 **t.** 7.50 – **5 rm** (dinner included) 60.00/112.00 **t.** – SB.

Cockett's, Market Pl., DL8 3RD, ☎ 667312, Fax 667162, – VISA JCB.
closed 4 January-10 February and 14 to 28 December – **Meals** 15.95 **st.** (dinner) and a la carte 8.00/23.45 **t.** 4.95 – **8 rm** 35.00/64.00 **st.**

Herriot's, Main St., DL8 3QU, ☎ 667536 – VISA
April-October – **Meals** a la carte 8.65/15.00 **t.** 3.95 – **7 rm** 23.00/46.00 **t.**

Brandymires, Muker Rd, DL8 3PR, ☎ 667482 –
February-mid October – **Meals** (by arrangement) 11.00 3.50 – **4 rm** 26.00/36.00 **st.**

X **Bulls Head** with rm, Market Pl., DL8 3RD, ☎ 667437, Fax 667048 – rm VISA JCB.
Meals *(closed Sunday)* (light meals Tuesday to Saturday lunch and Monday) a la carte 15.50/27.50 **t.** 3.50 – **3 rm** 25.00/43.00 **st.** – SB.

HAWKHURST Kent 404 V 30 Great Britain G. – pop. 4 217 – ☎ 01580.

Envir. : Bodiam Castle★★ *AC*, SE : 3½ m. by B 2244.

London 47 – Folkestone 34 – Hastings 14 – Maidstone 19.

Tudor Court, Rye Rd, TN18 5DA, E : ¾ m. on A 268 ☎ 752312, Fax 753966, ≤, « Gardens », – rest – 60. VISA JCB
Meals 10.50/14.95 **t.** and dinner a la carte 4.50 – **18 rm** 49.00/83.00 **t.** – SB.

HAWKRIDGE Somerset 403 J 30 The West Country G. – ✉ Dulverton – ☎ 0164 385.

Envir. : Tarr Steps★★, NE : 2½ m.

Exc. : Exmoor National Park★★.

London 203 – Exeter 32 – Minehead 17 – Taunton 32.

Tarr Steps, TA22 9PY, NE : 1½ m. ☎ 851293, Fax 851218, ≤, park – VISA
closed February-mid March – **Meals** (dinner only and Sunday lunch)/dinner 21.50 **t.** 4.00 – **11 rm** 38.00/76.00 **t.** – SB.

HAWKSHEAD Cumbria 402 L 20 Great Britain G. – pop. 570 – ✉ Ambleside – ☎ 0153 94.

See : Village★.

Envir. : Lake Windermere★★ – Coniston Water★ (Brantwood★, on east side), SW : by B 5285.

Main Car Park, LA22 0NT ☎ 36525 (summer only).

London 283 – ♦Carlisle 52 – Kendal 19.

Highfield House, Hawkshead Hill, LA22 0PN, W : ½ m. on B 5285 (Coniston rd) ☎ 36344, Fax 36793, ≤ Kirkstone Pass and Fells, – rest VISA
closed 2 to 26 January and 22 to 26 December – **Meals** (bar lunch)/dinner 16.50 **st.** – **11 rm** 35.00/73.00 **st.** – SB.

Rough Close Country House ⛰, LA22 0QF, S : 1½ m. on Newby Bridge rd ✆ 3637(– ⇌ Ⓟ. VISA
April-October (restricted bookings March) – **Meals** 12.00 **t.** 5.00 – **5 rm** (dinner in cluded) 43.50/77.00 **t.**

Ivy House, Main St., LA22 ONS, ✆ 36204 – ⇌ rest Ⓟ
March-October – **Meals** 10.50 **t.** 3.40 – **11 rm** 38.50/77.00 **t.** – SB.

Bracken Fell ⛰ without rest., Barngates Rd, Outgate, LA22 0NH, N : 1 m. by B 5286 o Barngate rd ✆ 36289, – ⇌ Ⓟ.
closed January and December – **7 rm** 30.00/41.00 **s.**

at Near Sawrey SE : 2 m. on B 5285 – ✉ Ambleside – ☎ 0153 94 :

Ees Wyke Country House ⛰, LA22 0JZ, ✆ 36393, Fax 36393, ≤ Esthwaite Water an Grizedale Forest, – ⇌ rest TV Ⓟ. AE
closed January and February – **Meals** (booking essential) (dinner only) 18.00 **st.** 5.00 **8 rm** (dinner included) 50.00/100.00 **st.**

Sawrey Country House ⛰, LA22 0LF, ✆ 36387, Fax 36010, ≤, – ⇌ TV Ⓟ. VIS JCB
March-mid November – **Meals** 16.50/21.50 **st.** 4.00 – **10 rm** 46.50/123.00 **st.** – SB.

at Far Sawrey SE : 2½ m. on B 5285 – ✉ Ambleside – ☎ 0153 94 :

West Vale, LA22 0LQ, ✆ 42817, ≤ – ⇌ rest Ⓟ.
March-October – **Meals** 10.00 – **8 rm** 22.00/44.00 **t.**

at Grizedale SW : 2¾ m. – ✉ Ambleside – ☎ 0153 94 :

Grizedale Lodge ⛰, LA22 0QL, ✆ 36532, Fax 36572 – ⇌ TV Ⓟ. VISA
closed 2 January-17 February – **Meals** (bar lunch)/dinner 21.50 **t.** – **9 rm** (dinne included) 62.50/107.00 **t.** – SB.

HAWNBY N. Yorks 402 Q 21 – see Helmsley.

HAWORTH W. Yorks. 402 O 22 **Great Britain G.** – pop. 4 956 – ✉ Keighley – ☎ 01535.
See : Haworth Parsonage and the Brontës★ *AC* – 2-4 West Lane, BD22 8EF ✆ 642329.
London 213 – Burnley 22 – Leeds 22 – Manchester 34.

Old White Lion, 6 West Lane, BD22 8DU, ✆ 642313, Fax 646222 – TV ☎ Ⓟ – 70. AE VISA – **Meals** (bar lunch Monday to Saturday)/dinner 16.50 **t.** and a la carte 4.2 – **14 rm** 38.00/60.00 **t.** – SB.

Ferncliffe, Hebden Rd, BD22 8RS, on A 6033 ✆ 643405, ≤ – TV Ⓟ. VISA
closed 26 to 30 December – **Meals** (by arrangement) 11.95 **t.** and a la carte 4.95 – **6 rn** 19.50/50.00 **t.** – SB.

Weaver's with rm, 15 West Lane, BD22 8DU, ✆ 643822, « Converted weaver cottages » – ⇌ rest TV ☎. AE VISA.
closed first 2 weeks January and last 2 weeks July – **Meals** *(closed Sunday and Monday)* (dinner only) 11.95 **t.** and a la carte 4.25 – **4 rm** 49.50/69.50 **t.**

HAYDOCK Mersey. 402 403 404 M 23 – pop. 10 965 – ✉ St Helens – ☎ 01942.
London 198 – Liverpool 17 – Manchester 18.

Haydock Thistle, Penny Lane, WA11 9SG, NE : ½ m. on A 599 ✆ 272000, Fax 711092 – ⇌ rm rest TV ☎ Ⓟ – 300. AE VISA JCB
Meals 14.00/19.50 **st.** and a la carte 5.95 – 8.75 – **135 rm** 79.00/89.00 **st.**, 4 suites – SB

Forte Posthouse, Lodge Lane, Newton-le-Willows, WA12 0JG, NE : 1 m. on A 4 ✆ 717878, Fax 718419, – ⇌ rm rest TV ☎ Ⓟ – 180. AE VISA JCB. – **Meals** a la carte 14.20/25.00 **st.** 4.95 – 7.95 – **136 rm** 59.00 **st.** – SB.

Forte Travelodge, Piele Rd, WA11 9TL, on A 580 ✆ 272055, Reservations (Freephone 0800 850950 – TV Ⓟ. AE VISA
Meals (grill rest.) – **40 rm** 34.50 **t.**

HAYDON BRIDGE Northd. 401 402 N 19 – ✉ Hexham – ☎ 01434.
London 344 – Carlisle 31 – Newcastle upon Tyne 27.

Geeswood House, Whittis Rd, NE47 6AQ, ✆ 684220, – ⇌.
closed 25 and 26 December – **Meals** (communal dining) 10.00 **st.** – **3 rm** 20.00/34.00 **st** – SB.

HAYFIELD Derbs. 402 403 404 O 23 pop. 2 567 – ✉ Stockport (Ches.) – ☎ 01663.
London 191 – Manchester 22 – Sheffield 29.

Waltzing Weasel, New Mills Rd, Birch Vale, SK12 5BT, W : ½ m. on A 6015 ✆ 743402 Fax 743402, ≤, – TV ☎ Ⓟ. AE VISA.
Meals (carving lunch) 12.50/23.50 **st.** 4.50 – **8 rm** 45.00/95.00 **st.**

Old Bank House without rest., SK12 5EP, off Church St. ✆ 747354 – TV
3 rm 20.00/38.00 – SB.

Bridge End, 7 Church St., SK12 5JE, ✆ 747321, Fax 742121 – Ⓟ. AE VISA
Meals *(closed Sunday dinner and Monday)* (dinner only and Sunday lunch)/dinner a la carte 15.00/25.00 **t.** and a la carte 5.50.

HAYLING ISLAND Hants. 404 R 31 – pop. 14 054 – ✆ 01705.

Links Lane ✆ 463712/463777.

Beachlands Seafront, PO11 0AG ✆ 467111 (summer only).

London 77 – ♦Brighton 45 – ♦Southampton 28.

- **Cockle Warren Cottage,** 36 Seafront, PO11 9HL, ✆ 464961, Fax 464838, heated, – rm TV ☎ P. AE VISA.
Meals (by arrangement) 26.50 **st.** 4.75 – 6.50 – **5 rm** 45.00/84.00 **st.**

HAYTOR Devon – see Bovey Tracey.

HAYTOR VALE Devon – see Bovey Tracey.

HAYWARDS HEATH W. Sussex 404 T 31 pop. 22 624 – ✆ 01444.

Paxhill Park, East Mascalls Lane, Lindfield ✆ 484467.

London 41 – ♦Brighton 16.

- **Birch,** Lewes Rd, RH17 7SF, E : ¾ m. on A 272 ✆ 451565, Fax 440109 – rm TV ☎ ♿ P – 60. AE VISA JCB
Meals 10.95/15.95 and a la carte 5.50 – **53 rm** 65.00/90.00 **st.** – SB.

ATS Gower Rd ✆ 412640/454189

HEADLAM Durham – see Darlington.

HEATHFIELD E. Sussex 404 U 31 – pop. 6 280 – ✆ 01435.

London 51 – ♦Brighton 23 – Eastbourne 16.

- **Risingholme** without rest., 38 High St., TN21 8LS, ✆ 864645, – TV P.
4 rm 25.00/40.00 **s.**

HEATHROW AIRPORT Middx. – see Hillingdon (Greater London).

HEBDEN BRIDGE W. Yorks. 402 N 22 – pop. 3 681 – ✉ Halifax – ✆ 01422

Wadsworth ✆ 842896.

1 Bridge Gate, HX7 8EX ✆ 843831.

London 223 – Burnley 13 – ♦Leeds 24 – ♦Manchester 25.

- **Carlton,** Albert St., HX7 8ES, ✆ 844400, Fax 843117 – TV ☎ – 100. AE VISA
Meals 7.50/18.50 **t.** and a la carte – **18 rm** 59.00/79.00 **t.** – SB.
- **Redacre Mill,** Mytholmroyd, HX7 5DQ, SE : 1 ½ m. by A646 off Westfield Terr. ✆ 885563, « Converted canalside warehouse », – TV P. VISA.
Meals (bar lunch)/dinner 12.50 **s.** – **5 rm** 35.00/50.00 **s.** – SB.
- **Kitties,** 52 Market St., HX7 6AA, ✆ 842956 – AE VISA
closed Sunday dinner, Monday and 25 December-31 January – **Meals** (dinner only and Sunday lunch)/dinner 15.50/23.70 **t.** 5.50.

HEDON Humbs. 402 T 22 – see Kingston-upon-Hull.

HEIGHINGTON Durham 402 P20 – see Darlington.

HELFORD Cornwall 403 E 33 **The West Country G.** – ✉ Helston – ✆ 01326.

Envir. : Lizard Peninsula★.

Exc. : Helston (Flora Day Furry Dance★★) (May) W : 11 m.

London 324 – Falmouth 15 – Penzance 22 – Truro 27.

- **Riverside** with rm, TR12 6JU, ✆ 231443, Fax 231103, ←, « Converted cottages in picturesque setting », – TV P.
March-October – **Meals** (dinner only) 32.00 **st.** 5.00 – 6.00 – **5 rm** 65.00/95.00 **st.**, 1 suite.

at Gillan SE : 3 m. – ✉ Helston – ✆ 01326 :

- **Tregildry**, TR12 6HG, ✆ 231378, Fax 231561, ← Gillan Creek, sea, – TV P. VISA.
March-October – **Meals** (bar lunch)/dinner 17.50 **t.** 4.50 – **10 rm** 36.00/70.00 **t.** – SB.

HELLIDON Northants. 404 Q 27 – see Daventry.

HELMSLEY N. Yorks. 402 Q 21 **Great Britain G.** – pop. 1 833 – ✆ 01439.

Envir. : Rievaulx Abbey★★ *AC*, NW : 2½ m. by B 1257.

Ampleforth College, 56 High St. ✆ 770678.

Town Hall, Market Pl., YO6 5BL ✆ 770173 (summer only).

London 234 – ♦Middlesbrough 29 – York 24.

- **Black Swan** (Forte Heritage), Market Pl., YO6 5BJ, ✆ 770466, Fax 770174, « Part 16C inn », – TV ☎ P. AE VISA JCB
Meals 15.00/26.00 **st.** and a la carte 7.00 – 9.50 – **44 rm** 85.00/170.00 **st.** – SB.

Feathers, Market Pl., YO6 5BH, ℘ 770275, Fax 771101, – TV P. VISA
closed 23 December-3 January – **Meals** (bar lunch)/dinner a la carte 19.75 **t.** – **17 rm** 30.00/60.00 **t.**

Laskill Farm, YO6 5BN, NW : 6 ¼ m. by B 1257 ℘ 798268, « Working farm », rest TV P
Meals (by arrangement) (communal dining) 13.00 **st.** – **7 rm** 18.50/45.00 **st.**

at Harome E : 2 ¾ m. by A 170 – ✉ York – ☎ 01439 :

Pheasant, YO6 5JG, ℘ 771241, , – rest TV ☎ ♿ P.
March-November – **Meals** (bar lunch available all year)/dinner 18.50 **t.** 3.50 – **12 rm** (dinner included) 58.50/117.00 **t.**, 2 suites – SB.

at Nawton E : 3 ¼ m. on A 170 – ✉ York – ☎ 01439 :

Plumpton Court, High St., YO6 5TT, ℘ 771223, – P.
mid March-October – **Meals** (by arrangement) 11.00 **st.** 4.90 – **8 rm** 32.00/50.00 **st.**

at Nunnington SE : 6 ¼ m. by A 170 off B 1257 – ✉ York – ☎ 01439 :

Ryedale Lodge with rm, Station Rd, YO6 5XB, W : 1 m. ℘ 748246, Fax 694633, « Converted railway station », , – rest TV ☎ P. VISA.
Meals (dinner only) 26.75 **t.** 5.00 – **7 rm** 47.50/81.00 **t.** – SB.

at Old Byland NW : 5 m. by B 1257 – ☎ 01439 :

Valley View Farm , YO6 5LG, ℘ 798221, « Working farm », , park – TV P. VISA
Meals 12.00 **s.** 3.50 – **4 rm** 25.00/50.00 **s.** – SB.

at Hawnby NW : 6 ¼ m. by B 1257 – ✉ Helmsley – ☎ 01439 :

Hawnby , YO6 5QS, ℘ 798202, Fax 798417, , – TV ☎ P. VISA.
closed Christmas, January and February – **Meals** (bar lunch)/dinner 15.00 **t.** 4.25 – **6 rm** (dinner included) 64.00/98.00 **t.** – SB.

HELSTON Cornwall 403 E 33 – ☎ 01326.

♦London 306 – Falmouth 13 – Penzance 14 – Truro 17.

Nansloe Manor , Meneage Rd, TR13 0SB, ℘ 574691, Fax 564680, – rest TV P. VISA.
closed 25 December-5 January – **Meals** 11.50 **st.** (lunch) and a la carte 18.00/24.00 **st.** 5.50 – **7 rm** 45.00/110.00 **st.** – SB.

ATS Clodgey Lane ℘ 562656

HELTON Cumbria 401 402 L 20 – ✉ Penrith – ☎ 01931.

♦London 287 – ♦Carlisle 26 – Kendal 24 – Workington 43.

Beckfoot Country House , CA10 2QB, S : 1 ¼ m. ℘ 713241, Fax 713391, ≤, rest TV P.
March-November – **Meals** (dinner only) 15.00 – **6 rm** 29.00/58.00 – SB.

HEMEL HEMPSTEAD Herts. 404 S 28 – pop. 79 235 – ☎ 01442.

Little Hay Golf Complex, Box Lane, Bovington ℘ 833798 – Boxmoor, 18 Box Lane ℘ 242434 – Dacorum Information Centre, HP1 1HA ℘ 234222.

♦London 30 – Aylesbury 16 – Luton 10 – Northampton 46.

Forte Posthouse, Breakspear Way, HP2 4UA, E : 2 ½ m. on A 414 ℘ 25112 Fax 211812, , , – rm TV ☎ ♿ P – 60. VISA.
Meals a la carte 14.00/21.00 **st.** – 7.95 – **146 rm** 69.00 **st.** – SB.

Boxmoor Lodge, London Rd, HP1 2RA, W : 1 m. on A 4251 ℘ 230770, Fax 252230 – ☎ ♿ P. VISA JCB.
Meals *(closed lunch Monday and Saturday and Sunday)* 13.95/16.95 **t.** and a la carte 5. – **18 rm** 48.00/70.00 **t.** – SB.

at Bourne End W : 2 ¼ m. on A 4251 – ✉ Hemel Hempstead – ☎ 01442 :

Travel Inn, Stoney Lane, HP1 2SB, W : 1 ¼ m. by A 4251 off A 41 ℘ 879149, Fax 8791 – rm TV ♿ P – 35. VISA.
Meals (grill rest.) – 4.95 – **60 rm** 34.50 **t.**

HENFIELD W. Sussex 404 T 31 pop. 4 796 – ☎ 01903.

♦London 47 – ♦Brighton 10 – Worthing 11.

Tottington Manor, Edburton, BN5 9LJ, SE : 3 ½ m. by A 2037 on Fulking rd ℘ 81575 Fax 879331, ≤, – TV ☎ P. VISA JCB.
closed 26 to 30 December – **Meals** *(closed Sunday dinner)* 19.00 **t.** (dinner) and a la carte 20.90/25.35 **t.** 5.00 – **6 rm** 37.50/70.00 **t.** – SB.

at Wineham NE : 3 ½ m. by A 281, B 2116 and Wineham Lane – ✉ Henfield – ☎ 0140

Frylands without rest., BN5 9BP, W : ¼ m. taking left turn at telephone box ℘ 71021 Fax 711449, ≤, « Part Elizabethan farmhouse », heated, , , park – TV P.
closed 21 December-1 January – **3 rm** 20.00/36.00 **s.**

HENLEY-IN-ARDEN Warks. 403 404 O 27 – pop. 1 814 – ☎ 01564.

London 104 – ♦Birmingham 15 – Stratford-upon-Avon 8 – Warwick 8.5.

Ashleigh House without rest., Whitley Hill, B95 5DL, E : 1 ¾ m. on Warwick Rd ℘ 792315, Fax 794133, – TV ☎ P. VISA
10 rm 35.00/45.00 **st.**

HENLEY-ON-THAMES Oxon. 404 R 29 – pop. 10 558 – ☎ 01491.

Huntercombe, Nuffield ℘ 641207.

Town Hall, Market Place, RG9 2AQ ℘ 578034.

London 40 – ♦Oxford 23 – Reading 9.

Shepherds without rest., Rotherfield Greys, RG9 4QL, W : 3½ m. by Peppard rd on Shepherds Green rd ℘ 628413, – TV P.
closed Christmas and New Year – **4 rm** 22.00/48.00 **s.**

Villa Marina, 18 Thameside, RG9 1BH, ℘ 575262 – AE VISA
Meals - Italian - 5.50 **t.** (lunch) and a la carte 15.80/20.90 **t.** 4.50.

at Stonor N : 4 m. by A 4130 on B 480 – ✉ Henley-on-Thames – ☎ 01491 :

Stonor Arms with rm, RG9 6HE, ℘ 638345, Fax 638863, – TV ☎ P. AE VISA.
Stonor : Meals *(closed Sunday)* (dinner only) 29.50/35.25 **t.** – **8 rm** 85.00/95.00 **t.**, 1 suite – SB.

Blades : Meals a la carte 18.00/23.40 **t.**

at Frieth (Bucks.) NE : 7½ m. by A 4155 – ✉ Henley-on-Thames – ☎ 01494 :

Yew Tree, RG9 6RJ, ℘ 882330, Fax 882927 – P. AE VISA
Meals 13.95/18.95 **t.** and a la carte 7.25.

When looking for a quiet hotel
use the maps found in the introductory pages
or look for establishments with the sign or .

HEREFORD Heref. and Worcs. 403 L 27 **Great Britain G.** – pop. 50 234 – ☎ 01432.

See : City★ - Cathedral★★ (Mappa Mundi★) A **A** – Old House★ A **B.**

Exc. : Kilpeck (Church of SS. Mary and David★★) SW : 8 m. by A 465 B.

Raven's Causeway, Wormsley ℘ 830219 – Belmont Lodge, Belmont ℘ 352666 – , Hereford Municipal, Holmer Rd ℘ 278178 B.

1 King Street, HR4 9BW ℘ 268430.

London 133 – ♦Birmingham 51 – ♦Cardiff 56.

Plan on next page

Green Dragon (Forte Heritage), Broad St., HR4 9BG, ℘ 272506, Fax 352139 – TV ☎ – 200. AE VISA JCB A **e**
Meals 8.00/28.00 **t.** and a la carte 7.05 – 9.00 – **80 rm** 65.00/75.00 **t.**, 3 suites – SB.

County H. Hereford (Q.M.H.), Belmont Rd, HR2 7BP, SW : 1½ m. on A 465 ℘ 299955, Fax 275114 – TV ☎ P – 300. AE VISA JCB B **c**
Meals (carving lunch)/dinner 7.95/16.95 **st.** and a la carte 5.95 – 9.00 – **60 rm** 59.50/69.50 **st.** – SB.

Castle Pool, Castle St., HR1 2NR, ℘ 356321, Fax 356321, – TV ☎ P. AE VISA
Meals 8.50/16.50 **st.** and a la carte 3.90 – **26 rm** 50.00/82.00 **st.** – SB. A **a**

Travel Inn, Holmer Rd, Holmer, HR4 9RS, N : 1 ¾ m. on A 49 ℘ 274853, Fax 343003 – rm TV P. AE VISA.
Meals (grill rest.) – 4.95 – **39 rm** 34.50 **t.**

Merton, 28 Commercial Rd, HR1 2BD, ℘ 265925, Fax 354983, – TV ☎. AE VISA. A **n**
Meals (bar lunch)/dinner a la carte 14.50/21.00 **t.** 5.00 – **17 rm** 50.00/75.00 **t.** – SB.

Somerville, 12 Bodenham Rd, HR1 2TS, ℘ 273991, – TV ☎ P. AE VISA B **i**
closed Christmas and New Year – **Meals** (by arrangement) 11.50 **st.** 4.00 – **10 rm** 20.00/51.00 **st.** – SB.

Ferncroft, 144 Ledbury Rd, HR1 2TB, ℘ 265538, – TV P. VISA. B **a**
closed second week December-first week January – **Meals** (by arrangement) 25.00 **t.** 3.75 – **11 rm** 21.00/45.00 **t.**

Ramblers Court, Whitestone, HR1 3SD, NE : 4 m. by A 465 on A 4103 ℘ 850128, – rest TV P
Meals (by arrangement) 10.95 **st.** 3.95 – 5.00 – **4 rm** 25.00/40.00 **st.**

HEREFORD

Broad Street . . . . A 7
Commercial Street . . . A 13
High Street . . . . A 19
High Town. . . . . A 20
Maylord Orchards
Shopping Centre. . . A

Aubrey St. . . . . A 3
Berrington St. . . . . A 5

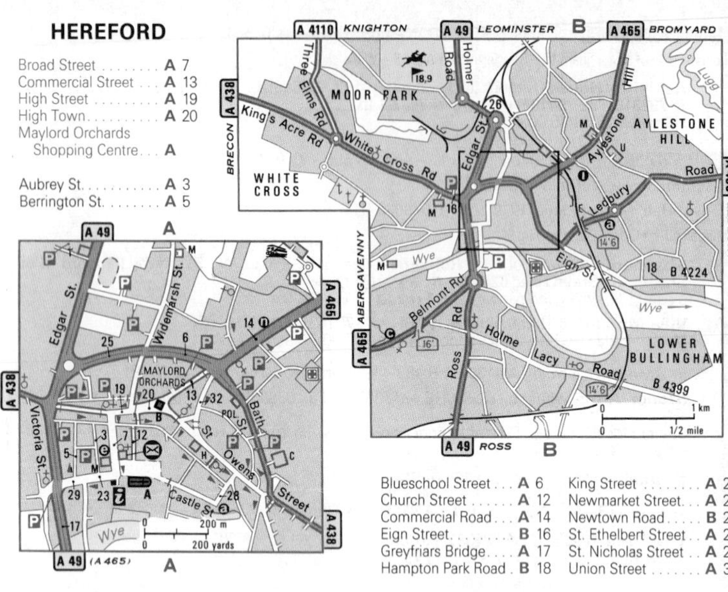

Blueschool Street . . . A 6
Church Street . . . . . . A 12
Commercial Road . . . A 14
Eign Street. . . . . B 16
Greyfriars Bridge. . . . A 17
Hampton Park Road . B 18

King Street . . . . A 2
Newmarket Street. . . A 2
Newtown Road . . . . . B 2
St. Ethelbert Street . . A 2
St. Nicholas Street . . A 2
Union Street . . . . A 3

at Marden N : 5¾ m. by A 49 – B – ✉ Hereford – ☎ 01568 :

The Vauld Farm ⛺, HR1 3HA, NE : 1½ m. by Urdimarsh rd ℘ 797898, « 16C timbere farmhouse », 🌳 – Ⓟ. ✻
Meals (by arrangement) (communal dining) 15.00 **s.** – **4 rm** ⊏ 20.00/50.00 **st.**, 1 suite.

at Canon Pyon N : 7 m. on A 4110 – B – ✉ Hereford – ☎ 01432 :

Hermitage Manor ⛺ without rest., HR4 8NR, S : 1 m. on A 4110 ℘ 760317, ≤ Vale c Hereford, 🌳 – ⇆ TV Ⓟ. ✻
March-October – **3 rm** ⊏ 30.00/50.00.

at Dormington E : 5¼ m. on A 438 – B – ✉ Hereford – ☎ 01432 :

Dormington Court without rest., HR1 4DA, ℘ 850370, Fax 850370, 🌳 – TV Ⓟ. ⊡ VIS JCB
8 rm ⊏ 29.00/50.00 **st.**

at Much Birch S : 5½ m. on A 49 – B – ✉ Hereford – ☎ 01981 :

Pilgrim, Ross Rd, HR2 8HJ, ℘ 540742, Fax 540620, ≤, 🌳 – ⇆ TV ☎ Ⓟ – 🏛 45. ⊡ ⊡ ⓓ VISA. ✻
Meals (bar lunch)/dinner 19.50 **st.** and a la carte 🍷 5.45 – **20 rm** ⊏ 49.50/69.50 **st.** – SB.

at Ruckhall W : 5 m. by A 49 off A 465 – B – ✉ Eaton Bishop – ☎ 01981 :

Ancient Camp Inn ⛺, HR2 9QX, ℘ 250449, Fax 251581, ≤ River Wye and countrysid – TV ☎ Ⓟ. ⊡ VISA JCB. ✻
Meals *(closed Sunday dinner and Monday to non-residents)* (bar lunch)/dinner 15.00 and a la carte 🍷 5.00 – **5 rm** ⊏ 35.00/58.00 **t.**

at Byford W : 7½ m. by A 438 – B – ✉ Hereford – ☎ 01981 :

Old Rectory, HR4 7LD, on A 438 ℘ 590218, Fax 590499, 🌳 – ⇆ TV Ⓟ. ✻
March-November – **Meals** (by arrangement) 12.50 **s.** – **3 rm** ⊏ 23.00/40.00 **s.**

ATS 6 Kyrle St. ℘ 265491

HERMITAGE Dorset - see Sherborne.

HERNE BAY Kent 404 X 29 – pop. 31 861 – ☎ 01227.

Herne Bay, Eddington ℘ 374097.

12 William Street, CT6 5EJ ℘ 361911.

♦London 63 – ♦Dover 24 – Maidstone 32 – Margate 13.

Northdown without rest., 14 Cecil Park, CT6 6DL, ℘ 372051, Fax 372051, 🌳 – TV ☎ ⊡ AE VISA. ✻
5 rm ⊏ 19.00/42.00 **st.**

HERSTMONCEUX E. Sussex 404 U 31 – pop. 3 898 – ☎ 01323.
♦London 63 – Eastbourne 12 – Hastings 14 – Lewes 16.

XX **Sundial,** Gardner St., BN27 4LA, ☎ 832217, « Converted 16C cottage », – P. AE VISA
closed Sunday dinner, Monday, 7 August-first week September and Christmas-20 January – **Meals** - French - 15.50/24.50 **t.** and a la carte 5.50.

HERTFORD Herts. 404 T 28 – pop. 22 176 – ☎ 01992.
The Castle, SG14 1HR ☎ 584322.
♦London 24 – ♦Cambridge 35 – Luton 26.

Hall House, Broad Oak End, SG14 2JA, NW : 1 ¾ m. by A 119 and Bramfield Rd ☎ 582807, Fax 582807, – TV P. VISA.
closed Christmas-New Year – **Meals** (by arrangement) 20.00 **s.** – **3 rm** 48.00/65.00 **s.**

HERTINGFORDBURY Herts. 404 T 28 – pop. 633 – ✉ Hertford – ☎ 01992.
♦London 26 – Luton 18.

White Horse (Forte Heritage), Hertingfordbury Rd, SG14 2LB, ☎ 586791, Fax 550809, – TV ☎ P – 50. AE VISA
Meals *(closed Saturday lunch)* 10.95/18.95 **t.** and a la carte 7.30 – 8.75 – **42 rm** 70.00/90.00 **st.** – SB.

HETHERSETT Norfolk 404 X 26 – see Norwich.

HETTON N. Yorks. 402 N 21 – pop. 151 – ✉ Skipton – ☎ 01756.
♦London 237 – Burnley 25 – ♦Leeds 33.

XXX **Angel Inn,** BD23 6LT, ☎ 730263, Fax 730363, « Attractive 18C inn » – P. AE VISA
closed Sunday dinner and 1 week January – **Meals** (bar lunch Monday to Saturday)/dinner 22.95 **t.** 5.90.

HEVERSHAM Cumbria 402 L 21 pop. 639 – ✉ Milnthorpe – ☎ 0153 95.
♦London 270 – Kendal 7 – Lancaster 18 – ♦Leeds 72.

Blue Bell, Princes Way, LA7 7EE, on A 6 ☎ 62018, Fax 62455, – rest TV ☎ P – 80. AE VISA
Meals 11.95/17.50 **t.** and a la carte 5.95 – **21 rm** 34.50/68.00 **t.** – SB.

HEXHAM Northd. 401 402 N 19 **Great Britain G.** – pop. 11 342 – ☎ 01434.
See : Abbey★ (Saxon Crypt★★, Leschman chantry★).
Envir. : Hadrian's Wall★★, N : 4½ m. by A 6079.
Exc. : Housesteads★★, NW : 12½ m. by A 6079 and B 6318.
18 Spital Park ☎ 602057 – 18 Slaley Hall G & C.C., Slaley ☎ 673350 – 9 Tynedale, Tyne Green ☎ 608154.
The Manor Office, Hallgate, NE46 1XD ☎ 605225.
♦London 304 – ♦Carlisle 37 – ♦Newcastle upon Tyne 21.

Slaley Hall, Slaley, NE47 0BY, SE : 7 ½ m. by B 6306 on Riding Mill rd ☎ 673350, Fax 673962, ≤, , , , 18, , park, – rm TV ☎ P – 450. AE VISA JCB
Imperial : Meals *(closed Saturday lunch)* 14.50/32.50 **st.** and a la carte 7.50 – **Fairways : Meals** a la carte 18.00/25.25 **st.** 7.50 – **125 rm** 107.00/125.00 **st.**, 17 suites – SB.

Beaumont, Beaumont St., NE46 3LT, ☎ 602331, Fax 602331 – TV ☎ – 80. AE VISA JCB.
closed 25 and 26 December – **Meals** 15.75 **t.** (dinner) and a la carte 11.00/26.50 **t.** 4.00 – 6.50 – **23 rm** 47.00/75.00 **t.** – SB.

County, Priestpopple, NE46 1PS, ☎ 602030 – TV ☎. AE VISA
Meals a la carte 7.50/21.00 **t.** 4.50 – **9 rm** 45.00/58.00 **t.** – SB.

Middlemarch without rest., Hencotes, NE46 2EB, ☎ 605003 – TV P.
3 rm 26.00/50.00.

West Close House without rest., Hextol Terr., NE46 2AD, by Allendale Rd ☎ 603307, – P.
4 rm 19.00/46.00 **st.**

XX **Black House,** Dipton Mill Rd, NE46 1RZ, S : 1 ¼ m. by B 6306 and Whitley Chapel rd ☎ 604744 – P. VISA
closed Sunday, Monday and 25 to 30 December – **Meals** (dinner only) a la carte 15.50/27.50 **t.**

ATS Haugh Lane ☎ 602394

HEYTESBURY Wilts. 403 404 N 30 – see Warminster.

HICKSTEAD W. Sussex – ☎ 01444.
♦London 40 – ♦Brighton 8.

Forte Travelodge, Jobs Lane, RH17 5N7, off A 23 ☎ 881377, Reservations (Freephone) 0800 850950 – TV P. AE VISA.
Meals (grill rest.) **40 rm** 34.50 **t.**

HIGHAM Suffolk 404 W 28 – pop. 119 – ✉ Colchester – ☎ 01206.

◆London 55 – Colchester 10 – ◆Ipswich 11.

- **Old Vicarage** without rest., CO7 6JY, ☎ 337248, ≤, « 16C former vicarage », heated, , park, – TV P
3 rm 32.00/56.00 **st.**

HIGH CROSBY Cumbria 401 402 L 19 – see Carlisle.

HIGH WYCOMBE Bucks. 404 R 29 – pop. 71 718 – ☎ 01494.

18 Hazlemere G & C.C., Penn Rd, Hazlemere ☎ 714722 – 18, 18 Wycombe Heights, Rayners Av., Loudwater ☎ 816686.

6 Cornmarket, HP11 2BW ☎ 421892.

◆London 34 – Aylesbury 17 – ◆Oxford 26 – Reading 18.

- **Forte Posthouse,** Handy Cross, HP11 1TL, SW : 1½ m. by A 404 ☎ 442100, Fax 439071 – rm rest TV ☎ P – 100. AE VISA JCB.
Meals a la carte 14.35/24.20 **st.** 6.25 – 7.95 – **106 rm** 69.00 – SB.
- **Alexandra,** Queen Alexandra Rd, HP11 2JX, ☎ 463494, Fax 463560 – TV ☎ P. AE VISA.
closed 21 December-3 January – **Meals** *(closed Bank Holidays and weekends)* (dinner only) a la carte 9.45/18.40 **t.** 4.25 – 7.90 – **29 rm** 59.00 **st.**, 1 suite.

ATS Copyground Lane ☎ 525101/438019

HILLSFORD BRIDGE Devon – see Lynton.

HILMARTON Wilts. 403 404 O 29 pop. 1 781 – ✉ Calne – ☎ 01249.

◆London 94 – ◆Bristol 36 – Salisbury 39 – Swindon 14.

- **Burfoots,** 1 The Close, SN11 8TH, ☎ 760492, Fax 760609, heated, – TV.
Meals (by arrangement) 11.50 – **3 rm** 17.50/45.00 **st.**

Prices For full details of the prices quoted in the guide, consult the introduction.

HILTON PARK SERVICE AREA W. Mids. – ✉ Wolverhampton – ☎ 01922.

- **Pavilion Lodge** without rest., WV11 2DR, M 6 between junctions 10 A and 11 ☎ 414100 Fax 418762 – TV P
64 rm 39.95 **t.**

HINCKLEY Leics. 402 403 404 P 26 – pop. 40 608 – ☎ 01455.

Hinckley Library, Lancaster Rd, LE10 0AT ☎ 635106.

◆London 103 – ◆Birmingham 31 – ◆Coventry 12 – ◆Leicester 14.

- **Sketchley Grange,** Sketchley Lane, LE10 3HU, S : 1½ m. by B 4109 (Rugby Rd) ☎ 251133, Fax 631384, – rm rest TV ☎ P – 280. AE VISA
Meals *(closed Sunday dinner)* 10.95/19.50 **st.** and a la carte 4.95 – **38 rm** 59.50/94.50 **st.** – SB.

ATS 5 Leicester Rd ☎ 632022/635835

HINDHEAD Surrey 404 R 30 – ☎ 01428.

◆London 47 – ◆Portsmouth 33.

- **Undershaw** with rm, 1 Portsmouth Rd, GU26 6AH, ☎ 604039, Fax 604205, – TV ☎ P AE VISA.
closed 7 days Easter, last 2 weeks August, 23 December-2 January and Bank Holidays – **Meals** (closed Sunday dinner and Monday lunch) 12.50 **t.** and a la carte approx. 38.50 4.90 – 8.00 – **5 rm** 60.00/120.00 **t.**

HINDON Wilts. 403 404 N 30 – pop. 489 – ✉ Salisbury – ☎ 01747.

◆London 107 – Bath 28 – Bournemouth 40 – Salisbury 15.

- **Lamb at Hindon,** SP3 6DP, ☎ 820573, Fax 820605 – rest TV ☎ P. AE VISA JCB.
Meals 10.00/25.00 **t.** and lunch a la carte 5.00 – **13 rm** 30.00/70.00 **t.** – SB.

HINTLESHAM Suffolk 404 X 27 – see Ipswich.

HINTON CHARTERHOUSE Avon – see Bath.

HISTON Cambs. 404 U 27 – see Cambridge.

HITCHIN Herts. 404 T 28 – pop. 32 221 – ☎ 01462.

◆London 40 – Bedford 14 – ◆Cambridge 26 – Luton 9.

- **Lord Lister,** Park St., SG4 9AH, ☎ 432712, Fax 438506 – rm TV ☎ P. AE VISA
Meals *(closed Saturday and Sunday)* (residents only) (dinner only) 10.00 **t.** and a la carte 5.90 – **21 rm** 46.00/60.00 **st.**

at Little Wymondley SE : 2½ m. by A 602 – ✉ Hitchin – ☎ 01438 :

Blakemore Thistle, Blakemore End Rd, SG4 7JJ, ℘ 355821, Telex 825479, Fax 742114, heated, – rm – 200. AE VISA
Meals 10.50/17.50 **st.** and a la carte 5.25 – 8.75 – **80 rm** 70.00/80.00 **st.**, 2 suites.

Redcoats Farmhouse with rm, Redcoats Green, SG4 7JR, S : ½ m. ℘ 729500, Fax 723322, « Part 15C farmhouse », – . AE VISA.
closed 1 week Christmas and Bank Holiday Mondays – **Meals** *(closed Sunday dinner)* 14.00/18.00 **t.** and a la carte 4.75 – **13 rm** 53.00/93.00 **st.** – SB.

HOCKLEY HEATH W. Mids. 403 404 O 26 – pop. 14 538 – ✉ Solihull – ☎ 01564.

London 117 – Birmingham 11 – Coventry 17.

Nuthurst Grange Country House, Nuthurst Grange Lane, B94 5NL, S : ¾ m. by A 3400 ℘ 783972, Fax 783919, – – 40. AE VISA.
Meals - (see below) – 9.90 – **15 rm** 95.00/145.00 **t.** – SB.

Travel Inn, Stratford Rd, B94 6NX, on A 3400 ℘ 782144, Fax 783197 – rm – 40. AE VISA
Meals (grill rest.) – 4.95 – **40 rm** 34.50 **t.**

Nuthurst Grange, Nuthurst Grange Lane, B94 5NL, S : ¾ m. by A 3400 ℘ 783972, Fax 783919, – . AE VISA
Meals *(closed Saturday lunch)* 16.90/42.50 **t.** 6.90.

HOCKLIFFE Beds. 404 S 28 – see Dunstable.

HOO GREEN Ches. – see Knutsford.

HODNET Shrops. 402 403 404 M 25 – pop. 1 405 – ☎ 01630.

London 166 – Birmingham 50 – Chester 32 – Stoke-on-Trent 22 – Shrewsbury 14.

Bear, Shrewsbury St., TF9 3NH, ℘ 685214, Fax 685787 – . VISA.
Meals a la carte 9.00/19.50 **t.** 4.00 – **6 rm** 30.00/55.00 **t.** – SB.

at Stoke-on-Tern E : 2 ¼ m. by A 442 on Stoke-on-Tern rd – ✉ Market Drayton – ☎ 01630 :

Stoke Manor without rest., TF9 2DU, E : ½ m. on Wistanswick rd ℘ 685222, Fax 685666, « Working farm with vintage tractor collection », – .
closed December – **3 rm** 25.00/50.00 **t.**

HOLBETON Devon 403 I 32 – pop. 541 – ☎ 01752.

London 236 – Exeter 40 – Plymouth 10 – Torquay 26.

Alston Hall Country House , Alston, PL8 1HN, SW : 2½ m. ℘ 830555, Fax 830494, , , , , , , – – 70. AE VISA
Meals 15.00/24.00 **t.** 6.00 – **20 rm** 67.50/120.00 **t.** – SB.

HOLDENBY Northants. pop. 88 – ✉ Northampton – ☎ 01604.

London 77 – Birmingham 58 – Leicester 26 – Northampton 6.

Lynton House with rm, NN6 8DJ, SE : ¼ m. ℘ 770777, Fax 770777, – . AE VISA.
Meals - Italian - *(closed Monday lunch, Sunday and Bank Holidays)* 13.75/24.75 **t.** 6.95 – 7.50 – **5 rm** 56.00/69.00 **t.**

HOLFORD Somerset 403 K 30 **Great Britain G.** – pop. 307 – ✉ Bridgwater – ☎ 01278.

Envir. : Stogursey Priory Church★★, W : 4½ m.

London 171 – Bristol 48 – Minehead 15 – Taunton 22.

Combe House , Holford Combe, TA5 1RZ, S : 1 m. ℘ 741382, « Country house atmosphere », , , , – rest . AE VISA.
mid March-October – **Meals** (bar lunch)/dinner 17.00 **st.** 4.60 – **19 rm** 36.00/88.00 **st.** – SB.

HOLMES CHAPEL Ches. 402 403 404 M 24 – pop. 5 369 – ☎ 01477.

London 181 – Chester 25 – Liverpool 41 – Manchester 24 – Stoke-on-Trent 20.

Old Vicarage, Knutsford Rd, Cranage, CW4 8EF, NW : ½ m. on A 50 ℘ 532041, Fax 535728 – – 30. AE VISA.
Church's Brasserie : Meals a la carte 14.25/19.50 **st.** 5.50 – **25 rm** 65.00/77.00 **st.** – SB.

Holly Lodge, 70 London Rd, CW4 7AS, on A 50 ℘ 537033, Fax 535823 – rm – 140 – **33 rm.**

Cottage Rest. and Lodge, London Rd, Allostock, WA16 9LU, N : 3 m. on A 50 ℘ (01565) 722470, Fax 722749 – rm . AE VISA.
Meals *(closed Sunday dinner to non-residents)* 10.95/18.00 **t.** and a la carte 4.50 – **12 rm** 56.00/66.00 **t.** – SB.

Brereton House , Mill Lane, Brereton, CW4 8AU, SE : 1 m. by A 54 ℘ 534511, Fax 534511, – . VISA JCB.
closed 23 December-3 January – **Meals** (residents only) (dinner only) (unlicensed) 17.50 **st.** – **6 rm** 45.00/65.00 **st.**

HOLMFIRTH W. Yorks. 402 404 O 23 – pop. 21 979 – ✉ Huddersfield – ☎ 01484.
ℹ 49-51 Huddersfield Rd, HD7 1JP ☎ 687603.
♦London 195 – ♦Leeds 23 – ♦Manchester 25 – ♦Sheffield 22.

Holme Castle, Holme, HD7 1QG, ☎ 686764, Fax 687775, ≤ – ⇔ TV P. AE VISA.
Meals (by arrangement) 19.00 **st.** 5.60 – **8 rm** ☐ 30.00/65.00 **st.**

HOLNE Devon 403 I 32 – see Ashburton.

HOLT Norfolk 404 X 25 – pop. 2 972 – ☎ 01263.
♦London 124 – King's Lynn 34 – ♦Norwich 22.

Yetman's, 37 Norwich Rd, NR25 6SA, ☎ 713320 – ⇔. AE VISA
closed Monday, Tuesday, 1 week June and 3 weeks October – **Meals** (dinner only and lunch Saturday and Sunday) 23.50/30.00 **t.** 6.25.

ATS Hempstead Rd Ind. Est. ☎ 712015

HOLYWELL Cambs. 404 T 27 – see St. Ives (Cambs.).

HONILEY Warks. – see Warwick

HONITON Devon 403 K 31 The West Country G. – pop. 9 008 – ☎ 01404.
See : All Hallows Museum★ *AC.*
Envir. : Ottery St. Mary★ (St. Mary's★) SW : 5 m. by A 30 and B 3177.
Exc. : Faraway Countryside Park (≤★) *AC,* SE : 6½m. by A 375 and B 3174.
ℹ Lace Walk Car Park, EX14 8LT ☎ 43716.
♦London 186 – Exeter 17 – ♦Southampton 93 – Taunton 18.

Deer Park ⚘, Buckerell Village, Weston, EX14 0PG, W : 2 ½ m. by A 30 ☎ 41266 Fax 46598, ≤, ≘, heated, ⚘, park, ⚘, squash – TV ☎ P – 60. AE VISA
Meals 14.00/23.00 **st.** and a la carte 6.00 – **25 rm** ☐ 40.00/130.00 **s.** – SB.

at Wilmington E : 3 m. on A 35 – ✉ Honiton – ☎ 01404 :

Home Farm, EX14 9JR, on A 35 ☎ 831278, Fax 831411, « Part 16C thatched farm », – ⇔ rest TV ☎ P. AE VISA
Meals 12.00 **t.** and a la carte 5.95 – **13 rm** ☐ 30.00/56.00 **t.** – SB.

at Payhembury NW : 7½ m. by A 30 – ✉ Honiton – ☎ 01404 :

Cokesputt House ⚘, EX14 0HD, ☎ 841289, ≤, « Part 17C and 18C house », – ⇔ P. AE VISA.
Meals (booking essential) (communal dining) 17.00 **st.** – **3 rm** ☐ 29.00/58.00 **st.**

HONLEY W. Yorks. 402 404 O 23 – see Huddersfield.

HOOK Hants. 404 R 30 – pop. 6 003 – ✉ Basingstoke – ☎ 01256.
♦London 47 – Reading 13 – ♦Southampton 35.

Basingstoke Country, Scures Hill, Nately Scures, RG27 9JS, W : 1 m. on A 3 ☎ 764161, Fax 768341, ≘, – rest TV ☎ P – 170. AE VISA JCB
Meals 12.25/19.50 **st.** and a la carte 6.00 – ☐ 8.75 – **70 rm** 82.50/130.00 **st.** – SB.

Raven, Station Rd, RG27 9HS, ☎ 762541, Fax 768677, ≘ – ⇔ rm TV ☎ P – 90. AE VISA.
Meals 15.50 **t.** and a la carte 4.95 – **38 rm** ☐ 60.00/70.00 **t.**

White Hart, London Rd, RG27 9DZ, on A 30 ☎ 762462, Fax 768351, – TV ☎ P. VISA
Meals a la carte 11.00/22.00 **st.** – **22 rm** ☐ 57.00/64.00 **st.**

Hook House, London Rd, RG27 9EQ, W : ½ m. on A 30 ☎ 762630, Fax 760232, « Pa Georgian house », – ⇔ TV ☎ P. AE VISA.
closed Christmas – **Meals** (dinner only) a la carte approx. 13.10 **t.** 7.00 – **6 rm** ☐ 45.00 st

at Rotherwick N : 2 m. by A 30 and B 3349 on Rotherwick rd – ✉ Basingstoke ☎ 01256 :

Tylney Hall ⚘, RG27 9AJ, S : 1 ½ m. by Newnham rd on Ridge Lane ☎ 76488 Fax 768141, « 19C mansion in extensive gardens by Gertrude Jekyll », ≘, heate, park, – TV ☎ P – 100. AE VISA JCB.
Meals 19.50/28.00 **st.** and a la carte 8.05 – **83 rm** ☐ 104.00/164.00 **st.**, 8 suites – SB.

HOOK Wilts. – see Swindon.

HOPE Derbs. 402 403 404 O 23 – ✉ Sheffield – ☎ 01433.
♦London 180 – Derby 50 – ♦Manchester 31 – ♦Sheffield 15 – ♦Stoke-on-Trent 40.

Underleigh ⚘, S30 2RF, N : 1 m. by Edale rd ☎ 621372, Fax 621372, ≤, – ⇔ rest P. VISA.
Meals (communal dining) 24.00 **s.** 4.25 – **6 rm** ☐ 35.00/56.00 **s.** – SB.

HOPE COVE Devon 403 I 33 – see Salcombe.

HOPTON WAFERS Shrops. 403 404 M 26 – pop. 609 – ✉ Kidderminster – ☎ 01299.
London 150 – ◆Birmingham 32 – Shrewsbury 38.

- **Crown Inn,** DY14 0NB, on A 4117 ☎ 270372, Fax 271127 – TV ☎ P. VISA. ✻
  Meals *(closed 25 December)* a la carte 14.75/21.75 **st.** 5.50 – **8 rm** 42.50/70.00 **st.** – SB.

HOPWOOD W. Mids. – ✉ Birmingham – ☎ 0121.
London 131 – ◆Birmingham 8.

- **Westmead** (Country Club), Redditch Rd, B48 7AL, on A 441 ☎ 445 1202, Fax 445 6163, – rm rest TV ☎ P – 250. AE VISA. ✻
  Meals a la carte 11.20/20.20 **st.** – 7.50 – **58 rm** 69.00/85.00 **st.** – SB.

HORLEY Surrey 404 T 30 – pop. 19 267 – ☎ 01293.
London 27 – ◆Brighton 26 – Royal Tunbridge Wells 22.

Plan : see Gatwick

- **Chequers Thistle,** Brighton Rd, RH6 8PH, on A 23 ☎ 786992, Fax 820625, – rm TV ☎ P – 60. AE VISA JCB. ✻ Y z
  Meals *(closed Saturday lunch)* 11.75/18.00 **t.** and a la carte 8.95 – 8.75 – **78 rm** 80.00/90.00 **t.** – SB.
- **Langshott Manor,** Langshott, RH6 9LN, N : by A 23 turning right at Chequers Thistle onto Ladbroke Rd ☎ 786680, Fax 783905, « Part Elizabethan manor house », – rm TV ☎ P. AE VISA. ✻
  closed 24 to 30 December – **Meals** (booking essential) (lunch by arrangement) 24.00/26.50 **st.** 6.50 – **7 rm** 91.00/124.00 **st.** – SB.
- **Lawn** without rest., 30 Massetts Rd, RH6 7DE, ☎ 775751, Fax 821803, – TV P. AE VISA JCB Y r
  7 rm 31.00/42.00 **st.**

Les prix Pour toutes précisions sur les prix indiqués dans ce guide, reportez-vous à l'introduction.

HORNCASTLE Lincs. 402 404 T 24 pop. 4 994 – ☎ 01507.
London 140 – Boston 19 – Great Grimsby 31 – Lincoln 21.

- **Admiral Rodney,** North St., LN9 5DX, ☎ 523131, Fax 523104 – rm TV ☎ P – 120. AE VISA. ✻
  Meals *(closed Sunday dinner)* (carving lunch) 8.25 **t.** and dinner a la carte 10.00/15.65 **t.** 4.95 – **31 rm** 42.50/70.00 **t.** – SB.

HORNING Norfolk 404 Y 25 **Great Britain G.** – pop. 1 070 – ✉ Norwich – ☎ 01692.
Envir. : The Broads★ – ◆London 122 – Great Yarmouth 17 – ◆Norwich 11.

- **Petersfield House** , Lower St., NR12 8PF, ☎ 630741, Fax 630745, – TV ☎ P. AE VISA
  Meals (dancing Saturday evening) 13.50/18.50 **t.** and a la carte 4.75 – **18 rm** 60.00/75.00 **t.** – SB.

HORNINGSEA Cambs. 404 U 27 – see Cambridge.

HORNINGSHAM Wilts. 403 404 N 30 – see Warminster.

HORNS CROSS Devon 403 H 31 **The West Country G.** – ✉ Bideford – ☎ 01237.
Exc. : Clovelly★★, NW : 7 m. by A 39 and B 3237.
London 237 – Barnstaple 15 – Exeter 48.

- **Foxdown Manor** , Foxdown, EX39 5PJ, S : 1 m. ☎ 451325, Fax 451525, ←, , heated, , park, – TV ☎ P. VISA. ✻
  Meals *(closed Sunday lunch)* 13.95/30.00 **t.** 4.30 – **7 rm** (dinner included) 76.00/142.00 **t.**, 1 suite – SB.
- **Lower Waytown** without rest., EX39 5DN, NE : 1 ¼ m. on A 39 ☎ 451787, – TV P. ✻
  April-October – **3 rm** 32.00/47.50 **s.**

HORSFORTH W. Yorks. 402 P 22 – see Leeds.

HORSHAM W. Sussex 404 T 30 – pop. 42 552 – ☎ 01403.
Mannings Heath, Goldings Lane ☎ 210168.
9 Causeway, RH12 1HE ☎ 211661.
London 39 – ◆Brighton 23 – Guildford 20 – Lewes 25 – Worthing 20.

- **South Lodge** , Brighton Rd, Lower Beeding, RH13 6PS, SE : 5 m. on A 281 ☎ 891711, Fax 891766, ←, « Victorian mansion, gardens », 18, , park, – rest TV ☎ P – 80. AE VISA JCB. ✻
  Meals 16.00/25.00 **t.** and dinner a la carte 9.00 – 10.00 – **37 rm** 110.00/175.00 **t.**, 2 suites – SB.

Cisswood House, Sandygate Lane, Lower Beeding, RH13 6NF, SE : 3 ¾ m. on A 281 ✆ 891216, Fax 891621, ☐, ☐ – ☐ ☎ ☐ – ☐ 150. ☐ ☐ VISA. ☐
closed Easter and Christmas-New Year – **Meals** *(closed Sunday and last 2 weeks August)* 18.50/23.50 **t.** ☐ 5.00 – ☐ 5.00 – **30 rm** 70.00/110.00 **st.**, 2 suites – SB.

Travel Inn, The Station, 57 North St., RH12 1RB, ✆ 250141, Fax 270797 – ☐ rm ☐ ☐ ☐. ☐ ☐ ☐ VISA
Meals (grill rest.) ☐ 4.95 – ☐ 4.95 – **40 rm** 34.50 **t.**

Jeremy's (at the Crabtree), Brighton Rd, Lower Beeding, RH13 6PT, SE : 5¼ m. on A 281 ✆ 891257, Fax 891606 – ☐ ☐. ☐ VISA
closed dinner Sunday – **Meals** 21.50 **t.** (dinner) and lunch a la carte 11.95/17.70 **t.**

at Slinfold W : 4 m. by A 281 off A 264 – ☒ Horsham – ☐ 01403 :

Random Hall, Stane St., RH13 7QX, W : ½ m. on A 29 ✆ 790558, Fax 791046, « Part 16C farmhouse » – ☐ ☎ ☐. ☐ ☐ VISA. ☐
Meals 9.95/19.35 **st.** ☐ 4.50 – ☐ 8.00 – **15 rm** 55.00 **st.** – SB.

ATS Nightingale Road ✆ 267491/251736

HORSHAM ST. FAITH Norfolk 404 X 25 – see Norwich.

HORTON Dorset 403 404 O 31 – see Wimborne Minster.

When visiting Ireland,
use the **Michelin Green Guide "Ireland".**
- *Detailed descriptions of places of interest*
- *Touring programmes*
- *Maps and street plans*
- *The history of the country*
- *Photographs and drawings of monuments, beauty spots, houses...*

HORTON Northants. 404 R 27 – pop. 574 – ☒ Northampton – ☐ 01604.
♦London 66 – Bedford 18 – Northampton 6.

French Partridge, Newport Pagnell Rd, NN7 2AP, ✆ 870033, Fax 870032 – ☐
closed Sunday, Monday, 2 weeks Easter, 3 weeks August and 2 weeks Christmas – **Meal** (booking essential) (dinner only) 24.00 **st.** ☐ 6.00.

HORTON-CUM-STUDLEY Oxon. 403 404 Q 28 – pop. 453 – ☒ Oxford – ☐ 01865.
♦London 57 – Aylesbury 23 – ♦Oxford 7.

Studley Priory ☐, OX33 1AZ, ✆ 351203, Fax 351613, ≤, « Elizabethan manor house i park », ☐, ☐ – ☐ ☎ ☐ – ☐ 25. ☐ ☐ ☐ VISA JCB. ☐
Meals 22.50/30.00 **t.** ☐ 8.00 – **18 rm** ☐ 95.00/150.00 **st.**, 1 suite – SB.

HORWICH Lancs. 402 404 M 23 – pop. 18 017 – ☒ Bolton – ☐ 01204.
♦London 214 – Liverpool 32 – ♦Manchester 18 – Preston 19.

Swallowfield, Chorley New Rd, BL6 6HN, SE : ¾ m. on A 673 ✆ 697914, Fax 468900 ☐ ☎ ☐ – ☐ 25. ☐ ☐ ☐ VISA JCB
closed 2 weeks Christmas – **Meals** (bar lunch Monday to Saturday)/dinner 13.50 **st.** ☐ 3.75 **32 rm** ☐ 45.00/60.00 **st.** – SB.

ATS 101 Chorley New Rd ✆ 68077/68806

HOTHFIELD Kent 404 W 30 – see Ashford.

HOUGH-ON-THE-HILL Lincs. – see Grantham.

HOUGHTON CONQUEST Beds. 404 S 27 – see Bedford.

HOVE E. Sussex 404 T 31 – see Brighton and Hove.

HOVINGHAM N. Yorks. 402 R 21 – pop. 322 – ☒ York – ☐ 01653.
♦London 235 – ♦Middlesbrough 36 – York 25.

Worsley Arms, YO6 4LA, ✆ 628234, Fax 628130, « Part 19C coaching inn », ☐ – ☐ ☐ ☐ – ☐ 25. ☐ ☐ VISA
Meals (bar lunch Monday to Saturday) 15.00/24.00 **st.** – **22 rm** ☐ 70.00/98.00 **st.** – SB.

HOWTOWN Cumbria – see Ullswater.

HUDDERSFIELD W. Yorks. 402 404 O 23 – pop. 147 726 – ☐ 01484.
18, 9 Bradley Park, Bradley Rd ✆ 539988 – 18 Woodsome Hall, Fenay Bridge ✆ 602971 18 Outlane, Slack Lane ✆ (01422) 374762 – 18 Meltham, Thick Hollins Hall ✆ 850227 18 Fixby Hall, Lightridge Rd ✆ 420110, - 18 Crosland Heath ✆ 653216.
High Street Building, 3-5 Albion St., HD1 2NW ✆ 430808.
♦London 191 – Bradford 11 – ♦Leeds 15 – ♦Manchester 25 – ♦Sheffield 26.

George, St. George's Sq., HD1 1JA, ✆ 515444, Fax 435056 – rm – 150.
Meals *(closed Saturday lunch)* 9.95/17.95 **st.** and a la carte 6.00 – **59 rm** 79.00/99.00 **st.**, 1 suite – SB.

Lodge, 48 Birkby Lodge Rd, Birkby, HD2 2BG, N : 1 ½ m. by A 629 and Blacker Rd ✆ 431001, Fax 421590, – – 30.
closed Bank Holidays – **Meals** *(closed Saturday lunch and Sunday dinner)* 11.25/24.70 **t.** – **11 rm** 55.00/75.00 **t.**

Briar Court, Halifax Rd, Birchencliffe, HD3 3NT, NW : 2 m. on A 629 ✆ 519902, Fax 431812 – rm – 90.
closed Bank Holidays – **Meals** 14.95 **t.** (dinner) and a la carte 10.45/22.35 **t.** 5.75 – **44 rm** 63.00/73.00 **t.**, 3 suites.

Wellfield House, 33 New Hey Rd, Marsh, HD3 4AL, W : 1 ½ m. on A 640 ✆ 425776, Fax 532122, « Victorian house », – rest.
closed 24 December-2 January – **Meals** *(closed Sunday dinner)* (residents only) 12.50/15.50 **st.** 3.95 – **5 rm** 40.00/55.00 **st.**

Huddersfield, 37-47 Kirkgate, HD1 1QT, ✆ 512111, Fax 435262, – .
Meals 9.50/14.50 **st.** and a la carte 4.95 – **46 rm** 47.50/80.00 **st.** – SB.

Elm Crest, 2 Queens Rd, HD2 2AG, off Edgerton Rd (A 629) ✆ 530990, Fax 516227 – .
Meals (by arrangement) 16.00 **st.** 5.00 – **8 rm** 32.00/57.00 **st.** – SB.

The Mallows without rest., 55 Spring St., Springwood, HD1 4AZ, ✆ 544684 – .
closed 21 December-4 January – **6 rm** 17.50/40.00 **st.**

at Honley S : 4 m. by A 616 – ✉ Huddersfield – 01484 :

Mustards and Punch, 6 Westgate, HD7 2AA, ✆ 662066.
closed lunch Monday and Saturday, Sunday, 25 December and 1 January – **Meals** 10.00 **t.** (lunch) and a la carte 20.00/30.00 **t.** 7.95.

at Golcar W : 3 ½ m. by A 62 on B 6111 – ✉ Huddersfield – 01484 :

Weaver's Shed, Knowl Rd, via Scar Lane, HD7 4AN, ✆ 654284, Fax 654284, « Converted 18C woollen mill » – .
closed Saturday lunch, Sunday, Monday, first 2 weeks January and 2 weeks July-August – **Meals** 10.95 **t.** (lunch) and a la carte 17.25/27.85 **t.**

at Outlane NW : 4 m. on A 640 – ✉ Huddersfield – 01422 :.

Old Golf House (Country Club), New Hey Rd, HD3 3YP, ✆ 379311, Fax 372694 – rm rest – 100.
Meals 9.95 **t.** (lunch) and a la carte 14.85/19.15 **t.** 5.80 – 7.50 – **48 rm** 62.00/69.00 **st.** – SB.

ATS Leeds Rd ✆ 534441

HULL Humbs. 402 S 22 – see Kingston-upon-Hull.

HUNGERFORD Berks. 403 404 P 29 The West Country G. – pop. 6 174 – 01488.

Envir. : Littlecote★★ (arms and armour★, Roman mosaic floor★) *AC*, NW : 2 m. by A 4 and B 4192.

Exc. : Savernake Forest★★ (Grand Avenue★★★) W : 7 m. by A 4.

London 74 – ♦Bristol 57 – ♦Oxford 28 – Reading 26 – ♦Southampton 46.

Bear at Hungerford, 17 Charnham St., RG17 0EL, on A 4 ✆ 682512, Fax 684357 – rm – 75.
Meals 11.45/24.00 **st.** and a la carte 5.50 – 8.75 – **41 rm** 69.00/115.00 **st.** – SB.

Three Swans, 117 High St., RG17 0DL, ✆ 682721, Fax 681708 – rm – 70.
Meals 11.95 **st.** and a la carte 4.45 – **15 rm** 55.00/70.00 **st.** – SB.

Marshgate Cottage, Marsh Lane, RG17 0QX, W : ¾ m. by Church St. ✆ 682307, Fax 685475, ←, – rm.
closed Christmas-New Year – **Meals** (by arrangement) 12.50 **st.** – **9 rm** 35.50/48.50 **st.**

Just William's, 50 Church St., RG17 0JH, ✆ 681199 –
closed Sunday, 25 December, 1 January and Bank Holidays – **Meals** 16.50/20.00 **t.** and a la carte 3.95.

HUNSTANTON Norfolk 402 404 V 25 – pop. 4 736 – 01485.

Golf Course Road ✆ 532811 – The Green, PE36 5BQ ✆ 532610.

London 120 – ♦Cambridge 60 – ♦Norwich 45.

Le Strange Arms, Golf Course Rd, PE36 6JJ, N : 1 m. by A 149 ✆ 534411, Fax 534724, ←, – – 120.
Meals (dinner only and Sunday lunch)/dinner 25.00 **t.** and a la carte – **36 rm** 48.00/80.00 **t.**

Claremont without rest., 35 Greevegate, PE36 6AF, ℘ 533171 – ⇆ TV
7 rm ⊐ 22.00/44.00 **st.**

Fieldsend without rest., 26 Homefields Rd, PE36 5HL, ℘ 532593 – TV P. ✗
3 rm ⊐ 25.00/42.00 **t.**

Pinewood without rest., 26 Northgate, PE36 6AP, ℘ 533068 – ⇆ TV P. AE VISA
8 rm ⊐ 25.00/50.00 **st.**

HUNSTRETE Avon 403 404 M 29 – see Bristol.

HUNTINGDON Cambs. 404 T 26 – pop. 15 424 – ☎ 01480.

18 Brampton Park, Buckden Rd ℘ 434700 – 9 Hemingford Abbots, New Farm Lodge, Cambridge Rd ℘ 495000.

The Library, Princes St., PE18 6PH ℘ 388588.

♦London 69 – Bedford 21 – ♦Cambridge 16.

Old Bridge, 1 High St., PE18 6TQ, ℘ 452681, Fax 411017, – ⇆ rest TV ☎ P – 50. AE VISA JCB
Meals *(closed dinner 25 December to non-residents)* a la carte 15.75/28.70 **st.** 5.65 –
26 rm ⊐ 69.50/120.00 **st.**

George (Forte), George St., PE18 6AB, ℘ 432444, Fax 453130 – ⇆ TV ☎ P – 150. AE VISA JCB
Meals (bar lunch Monday to Saturday)/dinner 20.00 **st.** and a la carte 6.95 – ⊐ 8.75 –
24 rm 60.00/75.00 **st.** – SB.

Forte Travelodge, PE18 9JF, SE : 5 ½ m. on A 14 (eastbound carriageway) ℘ (01954) 230919, Reservations (Freephone) 0800 850950 – TV ♿ P. AE VISA ✗
Meals (grill rest.) – **40 rm** 34.50 **t.**

ATS Nursery Rd ℘ 451031/451515

"Short Breaks" (SB)

De nombreux hôtels proposent des conditions avantageuses
pour un séjour de deux nuits
comprenant la chambre, le dîner et le petit déjeuner.

HURLEY-ON-THAMES Berks. 404 R 29 – pop. 1 712 – ✉ Maidenhead – ☎ 01628.

♦London 38 – ♦Oxford 26 – Reading 12.

Ye Olde Bell (Jarvis), High St., SL6 5LX, ℘ 825881, Fax 825939, « Part 12C inn », TV ☎ P – 130. AE VISA. ✗
Meals 14.95/18.95 **st.** and a la carte 7.85 – ⊐ 9.50 – **35 rm** 85.50/105.00 **t.**, 1 suite – SB.

HURSTBOURNE TARRANT Hants. 403 404 P 30 – pop. 700 – ✉ Andover – ☎ 01264.

♦London 77 – ♦Bristol 77 – ♦Oxford 38 – ♦Southampton 33.

Esseborne Manor , SP11 0ER, NE : 1½ m. on A 343 ℘ 736444, Fax 736725, , TV ☎ P. AE VISA. ✗
Meals 15.50 **st.** (lunch) and a la carte 6.00 – **10 rm** ⊐ 84.00/112.00 **st.** – SB.

HURST GREEN Lancs. 402 M 22 – ✉ Clitheroe – ☎ 01254.

♦London 236 – Blackburn 12 – Burnley 13 – Preston 12.

Shireburn Arms, Whalley Rd, BB7 9QJ, on B 6243 ℘ 826518, Fax 826208, – TV ☎ P. AE VISA
Meals 7.80/20.00 **t.** and dinner a la carte 5.50 – **14 rm** ⊐ 39.00/54.00 **t.** – SB.

HUTTON-LE-HOLE N. Yorks. 402 R 21 pop. 162 – ☎ 01751.

♦London 244 – Scarborough 27 – York 33.

Burnley House without rest., YO6 6UA, ℘ 417548, Fax 417174, « Georgian farmhouse », – ⇆ TV P. ✗
March-November – **3 rm** ⊐ 45.00/60.00 **st.**

Hammer and Hand, YO6 6UA, ℘ 417300 – ⇆ TV P
Meals (by arrangement) 11.50 **st.** 3.25 – **3 rm** ⊐ 35.00/45.00 **st.** – SB.

HUXHAM Devon – see Exeter.

HUYTON Mersey. 402 403 L 23 – see Liverpool.

HYDE Gtr. Manchester 402 403 404 N 23 – ☎ 0161.

♦London 202 – ♦Manchester 10.

Village Leisure, Captain Clarke Rd, Dunkinfield, SK14 4QG, NW : 1 ¼ m. by A 6... ℘ 368 1456, Fax 367 8343, , , squash – TV ☎ P – 150. AE VISA
Meals (grill rest.) (bar lunch Monday to Saturday)/dinner 12.00 **t.** and a la carte 5.50
89 rm ⊐ 57.50/68.00 **st.**

HYTHE Kent 404 X 30 – pop. 13 751 – ☎ 01303.
Sene Valley, Sene, Folkestone ☎ 268513.
Prospect Rd Car Park, CT21 5NH ☎ 267799 (summer only).
♦London 68 – Folkestone 6 – Hastings 33 – Maidstone 31.

Plan : see Folkestone

Hythe Imperial, Prince's Par., CT21 6AE, ☎ 267441, Fax 264610, ≤, squash – rest – 200. AE VISA X a
Meals 15.00/20.00 **st.** and a la carte 6.00 – **98 rm** 88.00/110.00 **st.**, 2 suites – SB.

Stade Court, West Par., CT21 6DT, ☎ 268263, Fax 261803, ≤ – rm – 35. AE VISA JCB
Meals 9.95/16.50 **t.** and a la carte 6.00 – **42 rm** 61.50/85.00 **t.** – SB.

IBSTONE Bucks 404 R 29 – pop. 254 – ✉ High Wycombe – ☎ 01491.
♦London 39 – ♦Oxford 20 – Reading 19.

Fox of Ibstone Country, HP14 3GG, ☎ 638722, Fax 638873, –
9 rm.

IDE Devon 403 J 31 – see Exeter.

IFFLEY Oxon – see Oxford.

ILKLEY W. Yorks. 402 O 22 – pop. 13 530 – ☎ 01943.
Myddleton ☎ 607277.
Station Rd, LS29 8HA ☎ 602319.
♦London 210 – Bradford 13 – Harrogate 17 – ♦Leeds 16 – Preston 46.

Rombalds, 11 West View, Wells Rd, LS29 9JG, ☎ 603201, Fax 816586 – – 50. AE VISA JCB
closed 27 to 30 December – **Meals** *(closed Sunday lunch)* 9.95/14.95 **t.** and a la carte 4.65 – **13 rm** 74.00/100.00 **st.**, 2 suites – SB.

Grove, 66 The Grove, LS29 9PA, ☎ 600298, Fax 600298 – rest . AE VISA JCB
closed Christmas – **Meals** (bar lunch)/dinner 13.00 **st.** 3.60 – **6 rm** 38.00/54.00 **st.**

XXX ✿ **Box Tree,** 37 Church St., LS29 9DR, ☎ 608484, Fax 607186 – AE VISA
closed Sunday dinner, Monday, and last 2 weeks January – **Meals** 22.50/29.50 **st.** and lunch a la carte 4.95
Spec. Confit of quail with broad beans and a tarragon sauce, Steamed breast of guinea fowl, braised leg and foie gras sauce, Warm chocolate fondant with a coffee bean sauce.

ILLOGAN Cornwall 403 E 33 **The West Country G.** – pop. 13 095 – ✉ Redruth – ☎ 01209.
Envir. : Portreath★, NW : 2 m. by B 3300 – Hell's Mouth★, SW : 5 m. by B 3301.
♦London 305 – Falmouth 14 – Penzance 17 – Truro 11.

Aviary Court ⛰, Mary's Well, TR16 4QZ, NW : ¾ m. by Alexandra Rd ☎ 842256, Fax 843744, – . AE VISA
Meals *(closed Sunday dinner)* (dinner only and Sunday lunch)/dinner 12.50 **t.** and a la carte 5.50 – **6 rm** 40.00/58.00 **t.**

ILMINSTER Somerset 403 L 31 **The West Country G.** – pop. 4 162 – ☎ 01460.
See : Town★ - St. Mary's★★.
Envir. : Barrington Court Gardens★ *AC*, NE : 3½ m. by B 3168.
♦London 145 – Taunton 12 – Yeovil 17.

Forte Travelodge, Southfield Roundabout, Horton Cross, TA19 9PT, NW : 1 ½ m. at junction of A 303 with A 358 ☎ 53748, Reservations (Freephone) 0800 850950 – . AE VISA
Meals (grill rest.) – **32 rm** 34.50 **t.**

IMPINGTON Cambs. – see Cambridge.

INGATESTONE Essex 404 V 28 – pop. 4 815 (inc. Fryering) – ✉ Chelmsford – ☎ 01277.
♦London 27 – Chelmsford 6.

Ivy Hill, Writtle Rd, Margaretting, CM4 0EW, NE : 2¼ m. by A 12 ☎ 353040, Fax 355038, heated, – – 80. AE VISA
Meals *(closed Saturday lunch and Sunday dinner)* 16.95 **st.** 5.50 – 6.95 – **34 rm** 70.00/85.00 **st.**

This Guide is not a comprehensive list of all hotels and restaurants, nor even of all good hotels and restaurants in Great Britain and Ireland.

Since our aim is to be of service to all motorists, we must show establishments in all categories and so we have made a selection of some in each.

INGLEBY GREENHOW N. Yorks. 402 Q 20 – see Great Ayton.

INGLETON N. Yorks. 402 M 21 – pop. 1 979 – ✉ Carnforth (Lancs.) – ☎ 0152 42.

ℹ Community Centre Car Park, LA6 3HJ ☎ 41049 (summer only).

♦London 266 – Kendal 21 – Lancaster 18 – ♦Leeds 53.

- **Pines Country House,** Kendall Rd, LA6 3HN, NW : ¼ m. on A 65 ☎ 41252, Fax 41252, – TV P. VISA
  Meals (by arrangement) 11.50 **t.** 3.75 – **5 rm** 28.00/40.00 **st.** – SB.
- **Ferncliffe Country,** 55 Main St., LA6 3HJ, ☎ 42405 – rest TV P
  February-October – **Meals** 12.50 **st.** – **5 rm** 26.00/40.00 **st.** – SB.
- **Riverside Lodge,** 24 Main St., LA6 3HJ, ☎ 41359, ←, – rest TV P
  closed Christmas and January – **Meals** (by arrangement) 12.50 **st.** – **6 rm** 26.00/38.00 – SB.

INSTOW Devon 403 H 30 – see Bideford.

IPSWICH Suffolk 404 X 27 **Great Britain G.** – pop. 130 157 – ☎ 01473.

See : Christchurch Mansion (collection of paintings★) X **B**.

18 Rushmere Heath ☎ 727109 – 18, 9 Purdis Heath, Bucklesham Rd ☎ 727474 – 18 Fynn Valley, Witnesham ☎ 785463.

ℹ St Stephens Church, St Stephens Lane, IP1 1DP ☎ 258070.

♦London 76 – ♦Norwich 43.

Plan opposite

- **Belstead Brook,** Belstead Rd, IP2 9HB, SW : 2½ m. ☎ 684241, Fax 681249, – TV ☎ & P – 60. AE VISA Z **u**
  Meals *(closed Saturday lunch)* 12.50/18.50 **st.** and a la carte 5.70 – 7.95 – **74 rm** 68.00/78.00 **st.**, 2 suites – SB.
- **Suffolk Grange** (Country Club), The Havens, Ransomes Europark, IP3 9SJ, SE : 3½ m. by A 1156 and Nacton Rd at junction with A 14 ☎ 272244, Fax 272484, – rm rest TV ☎ & P – 180. AE VISA
  Meals (bar lunch Saturday) a la carte 10.20/22.90 **st.** – 7.50 – **60 rm** 65.00/79.00 **st.** – SB.
- **Marlborough,** Henley Rd, IP1 3SP, ☎ 257677, Fax 226927, – rest TV ☎ P – 50. AE VISA JCB Y **e**
  Meals (bar lunch Saturday) 8.50/17.15 **t.** and a la carte – **21 rm** 61.50/71.50 **t.**, 1 suite – SB.
- **Novotel,** Greyfriars Rd, IP1 1UP, ☎ 232400, Fax 232414 – rm TV ☎ & P – 180. AE VISA JCB X **c**
  Meals 12.00/16.00 **st.** and a la carte – 7.50 – **100 rm** 55.00 **st.**
- **Highview House,** 56 Belstead Rd, IP2 8BE, ☎ 688659, – TV ☎ P. VISA JCB. Z **c**
  Meals *(closed Friday to Sunday)* (dinner only) 12.95 **st.** and a la carte **11 rm** 38.50/48.50 **st.**
- **Bombay,** 6 Orwell Pl., IP4 1BB, ☎ 251397 – AE VISA X **a**
  Meals - Indian - 6.95/14.95 **t.** and a la carte 3.95.
- **Kwoks Rendezvous,** 23 St. Nicholas St., IP1 1TW, ☎ 256833, Fax 256833. AE VISA
  closed Saturday lunch, Sunday, 2 weeks early Spring and Bank Holidays – **Meals** - Chinese (Peking) - 14.95/19.95 **t.** and a la carte 5.95. X **o**
- **St. Peter's,** 35-37 St. Peter's St., IP1 1XP, ☎ 210810, Fax 210810 – P. AE VISA
  closed Sunday and Monday – **Meals** a la carte 13.95/20.85 **t.** 5.00. X **r**
- **Galley,** 25 St. Nicholas St., IP1 1TW, ☎ 281131, Fax 281131 – . AE VISA JCB X **s**
  closed Sunday and Bank Holidays – **Meals** 5.50/22.00 **st.** and a la carte 5.25.
- **Mortimer's on the Quay,** Wherry Quay, IP4 1AS, ☎ 230225, Fax 761611 – AE VISA JCB X **n**
  closed Saturday lunch, Sunday, 2 weeks August-September, 24 December-5 January and Bank Holidays – **Meals** - Seafood - a la carte 11.85/21.20 **t.**

at Copdock SW : 4 m. by A 1214 off A 1071 – Z – ✉ Ipswich – ☎ 01473 :

- **Ipswich Moat House** (Q.M.H.), Old London Rd, IP8 3JD, ☎ 730444, Fax 730801, – rm TV ☎ & P – 500. AE VISA
  Meals (carving rest.) 7.95/19.50 **st.** 5.25 – 8.50 – **74 rm** 59.00/95.00 **st.** – SB.

at Burstall W : 4½ m. by A 1214 off A 1071 – Y – ✉ Ipswich – ☎ 01473 :

- **Mulberry Hall**, IP8 3DP, ☎ 652348, « 16C farmhouse », – P.
  closed Christmas – **Meals** (by arrangement) (communal dining) 14.00 **s.** – **3 rm** 17.00/34.00 **s.**

at Hintlesham W : 5 m. by A 1214 on A 1071 – Y – ✉ Ipswich – ☎ 01473 :

- **Hintlesham Hall**, IP8 3NS, ☎ 652334, Fax 652463, ←, « Georgian country house of 16C origins », heated, 18, park, – rest TV ☎ P – 30. AE VISA
  Meals (residents only Saturday lunch) 18.50/24.00 **st.** and a la carte 27.75/42.50 **st.** – 6.50 – **29 rm** 85.00/200.00 **st.**, 4 suites – SB.

ATS White Elm St. ☎ 217157

IPSWICH

Buttermarket Centre .... X 9
Carr Street .... X 10
Corn Hill .... X 16
Tavern Street X
Tower Ramparts Centre . X 47
Westgate Street .... X 52

Argyle Street .... X 2
Back Hamlet .... Z 3
Birkfield Drive .... Z 5
Bond Street .... X 6
Bridgwater Road .... Z 7
Chevallier Street .... Y 13
College Street .... X 15
Dogs Head Street .... X 18
Ellenbrook Road .... Z 19
Falcon Street .... X 21
Fore Hamlet .... Z 22
Franciscan Way .... X 24
Friars Street .... X 25
Grey Friars Road .... X 26
Grove Lane .... YZ 28
Handford Road .... X, Y 30
Lloyds Avenue .... X 31
Lower Orwell Street .... X 32
Northgate Street .... X 33
Orwell Place .... X 34
Queen Street .... X 37
St. Helen's Street .... X, Y 39
St. Margarets Street .... X 40
St. Nicholas Street ..... X 41
St. Peter's Street .... X 42
Salthouse Street .... X 43
Silent Street .... X 46
Upper Orwell Street .... X 49
Waterworks Street ...... X 51
Yarmouth Road .... Y 54

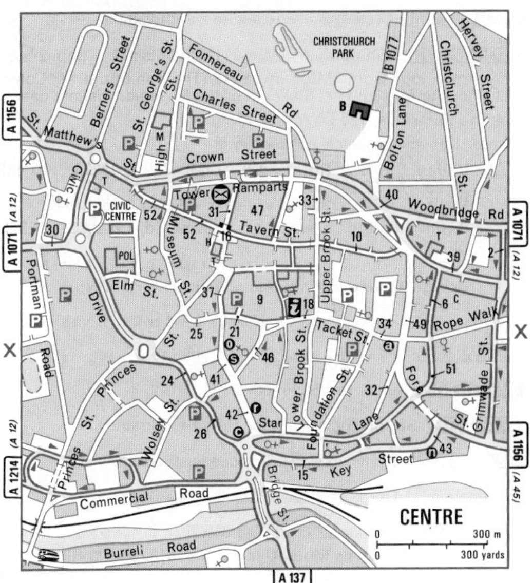

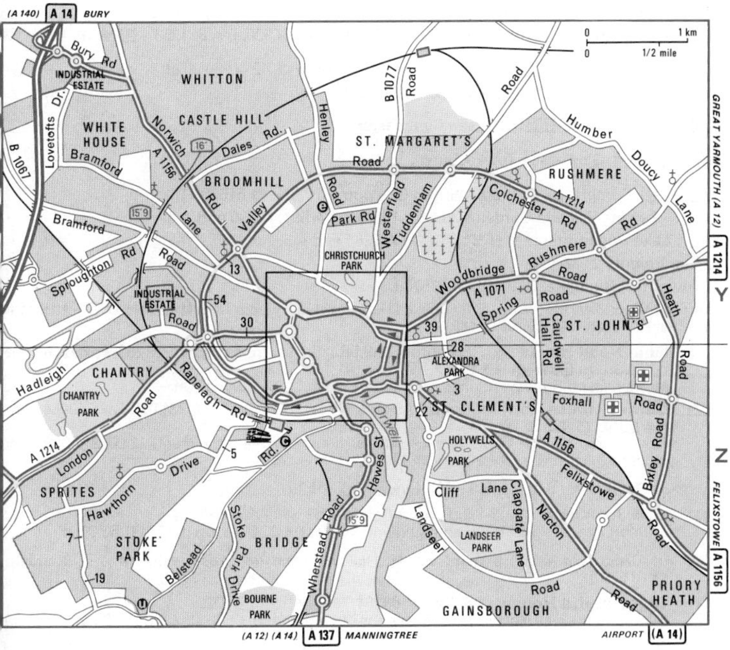

(A 140) A 14 BURY

BURY Rd
INDUSTRIAL ESTATE
WHITTON
Lovetofts Dr.
B 1067
WHITE HOUSE
Bramford
CASTLE HILL
Norwich A 1156
Dales Rd.
Henley Road
B 1077 Road
Road
ST. MARGARET'S
Road
Humber Doucy Lane
BROOMHILL
Valley Rd
Lane
Park Rd
Westerfield Tuddenham
Colchester A 1214 Rd
RUSHMERE
Rd
Bramford Road
Sproughton Rd
INDUSTRIAL ESTATE
Road
CHRISTCHURCH PARK
Woodbridge
A 1071
Rushmere Road
Spring Road
Cauldwell Hall Rd
ST. JOHN'S
Heath Road
Hadleigh
CHANTRY
CHANTRY PARK
Road
Ranelagh Rd
ALEXANDRA PARK
ST. CLEMENT'S
Foxhall Road
A 1214
London Road
Drive
Rd.
Hawes St.
Orwell
HOLYWELLS PARK
A 1156
Felixstowe Road
Bixley Road
SPRITES
Hawthorn
STOKE PARK
Belstead
Stoke Park Drive
BRIDGE
Wherstead Road
BOURNE PARK
Landseer
Cliff Lane
Clapgate Lane
LANDSEER PARK
Nacton Road
PRIORY HEATH
GAINSBOROUGH
GREAT YARMOUTH (A 12) A 1214
FELIXSTOWE A 1156
Y
Z
0 1 km
0 1/2 mile
(A 12) (A 14) A 137 MANNINGTREE
AIRPORT A 14

Europe

If the name of the hotel
is not in bold type,
on arrival ask the hotelier his prices.

IREBY Cumbria 401 402 K 19 – see Bassenthwaite.

IRON BRIDGE Shrops. 403 404 M 26 **Great Britain G.** – pop. 2 583 – ☎ 01952.

See : Ironbridge Gorge Museum★★ *AC* (The Iron Bridge★★, Coalport China Museum★★, Blists Hill Open Air Museum★★, Museum of the River and visitors centre★).

ℹ 4 The Wharfage, TF8 7AW ✆ 432166.

♦London 135 – ♦Birmingham 36 – Shrewsbury 18.

- **Valley,** Buildwas Rd, TF7 8DW, on B 4380 ✆ 432247, Fax 432308, – rest – 250. VISA.
  Meals 16.50/17.50 **st.** and a la carte – **34 rm** 62.00/72.00 **st.** – SB.
- **Severn Lodge** without rest., New Rd, TF8 7AS, ✆ 432148, Fax 432148, –
  closed Christmas and New Year – **3 rm** 36.00/48.00 **s.**
- **Bridge House** without rest., Buildwas, TF8 7BN, W : 2 m. on B 4380 ✆ 432105, « 17C cottage », –
  closed 3 weeks Christmas-New Year – **4 rm** 28.00/50.00.

ISLEY WALTON Leics. – see Castle Donington.

IVY HATCH Kent – see Sevenoaks.

IXWORTH Suffolk 404 W 27 – see Bury St. Edmunds.

JEVINGTON E. Sussex 404 U 31 – see Eastbourne.

KEDLESTON Derbs. 402 403 404 P 25 – see Derby.

KEIGHLEY W. Yorks. 402 O 22 – ☎ 01535.

Branshaw, Branshaw Moor, Oakworth ✆ 643235 – Riddlesden, Howden Rough ✆ 602148.

♦London 200 – Bradford 10 – Burnley 20.

- **Beeches** (Toby), Bradford Rd, BD21 4BB, ✆ 610611, Fax 610037 – rm – 30. VISA.
  Meals (grill rest.) 7.90 **t.** (lunch) and a la carte – **43 rm** 60.00/70.00 **t.** – SB.
- **Dalesgate,** 406 Skipton Rd, Utley, BD20 6HP, ✆ 664930, Fax 611253 – VISA
  Meals (dinner only) 10.50 **st.** and a la carte – **21 rm** 42.00/55.00 **st.**

ATS 69-73 Bradford Rd, Riddlesden ✆ 607533/607933

KEMBLE Glos. 403 404 N 28 – see Cirencester.

KEMERTON Glos. – see Tewkesbury.

KENDAL Cumbria 402 L 21 **Great Britain G.** – pop. 24 785 – ☎ 01539.

Envir. : Levens Hall and Garden★ *AC*, S : 4½ m. by A 591, A 590 and A 6.

Exc. : Lake Windermere★★, NW : 8 m. by A 5284 and A 591.

The Heights ✆ 724079.

ℹ Town Hall, Highgate, LA9 4DL ✆ 725758.

♦London 270 – Bradford 64 – Burnley 63 – ♦Carlisle 49 – Lancaster 22 – ♦Leeds 72 – ♦Middlesbrough 77 – ♦Newcastle upon Tyne 104 – Preston 44 – Sunderland 88.

- **Lane Head House** , Helsington, LA9 5RJ, S : 1¾ m. on A 6 ✆ 731283, Fax 721023, – rm VISA JCB.
  Meals *(closed Sunday)* (dinner only) 16.00 – **7 rm** 35.00/75.00 **st.** – SB.
- **Garden House,** Fowl-Ing Lane, LA9 6PH, NE : ½ m. by A 685 ✆ 731131, Fax 740064, – VISA
  closed 26 to 30 December – **Meals** (lunch by arrangement) 12.00/21.00 **t.** and dinner a la carte 6.00 – **10 rm** 47.50/78.00 **t.** – SB.

at Selside N : 6 m. on A 6 – ✉ Kendal – ☎ 01539 :

- **Low Jock Scar** , LA8 9LE, off A 6 ✆ 823259, –
  March-October – **Meals** (by arrangement) 14.00 **st.** 3.50 – **5 rm** 27.00/50.00 **st.**

at Crosthwaite W : 5 ¼ m. via All Hallows Lane on Crosthwaite rd – ✉ Kendal – ☎ 01539 5 :

- **Crosthwaite House,** LA8 8BP, ✆ 68264, – rest
  mid January-mid November – **Meals** (by arrangement) 12.00 **st.** 5.00 – **6 rm** 20.00/40.00 **st.**
- **Punch Bowl Inn** with rm, LA8 8HR, ✆ 68237, Fax 68875, « Part 16C coaching inn » – VISA
  closed Christmas Day – **Meals** (booking essential) 9.50 **t.** (dinner) and a la carte 11.50/16.00 **t.** 5.00 – **3 rm** 25.00/40.00 **t.**

ATS Mintsfeet Est. ✆ 721559/723802

ENILWORTH Warks. 403 404 P 26 Great Britain G. – pop. 21 966 – ☎ 01926.

e : Castle★ *AC.*

The Library, 11 Smalley Pl., CV8 1QG ☎ 52595/50708.

ondon 102 – ♦Birmingham 19 – ♦Coventry 5 – Warwick 5.

De Montfort, The Square, CV8 1ED, ☎ 55944, Fax 57830 – lift, ⇔ rm TV ☎ P – 300. AE VISA
Meals *(closed Saturday lunch)* 8.50/17.50 **st.** – **96 rm** ☐ 80.00/90.00 **st.** – SB.

Chesford Grange, Chesford Bridge, CV8 2LD, SE : 1 ¾ m. on A 452 ☎ 59331, Fax 59075, park – lift ⇔ rm TV ☎ P – 800. AE VISA.
Meals *(closed Saturday lunch)* 15.50 **st.** and a la carte 7.75 – **129 rm** ☐ 75.00/85.00 **st.**, 1 suite – SB.

Victoria Lodge without rest., 180 Warwick Rd, CV8 1HU, ☎ 512020, Fax 58703, – ⇔ TV ☎ P. AE VISA JCB.
7 rm ☐ 34.00/49.00 **st.**

Castle Laurels, 22 Castle Rd, CV8 1NG, ☎ 56179, Fax 54954 – ⇔ TV ☎ P. VISA.
closed 23 December-2 January – **Meals** *(closed Friday to Sunday)* (residents only) (dinner only) a la carte approx. 12.00 **t.** 7.95 – **12 rm** ☐ 30.00/54.00 **st.**

Abbey without rest., 41 Station Rd, CV8 1JD, ☎ 512707, Fax 859148 – TV.
7 rm ☐ 19.00/40.00.

XX **Simpson's,** 101-103 Warwick Rd, CV8 1HL, ☎ 864567 – P. AE VISA JCB
closed Saturday lunch and Sunday – **Meals** 13.95/19.95 **t.** 5.75.

XX **Bosquet,** 97a Warwick Rd, CV8 1HP, ☎ 852463 – AE VISA
closed Sunday, Monday, 3 weeks August and 1 week Christmas – **Meals** - French - (lunch by arrangement) 21.00 **t.** and a la carte 5.50.

Your recommendation is self-evident if you always walk into a hotel Guide in hand.

ENNFORD Devon 403 J 32 – see Exeter.

ERNE BRIDGE Heref. and Worcs. – see Ross-on-Wye.

ESSINGLAND Suffolk 404 Z 26 – ☎ 01502.

ondon 112 – ♦Ipswich 39 – ♦Norwich 32.

Old Rectory without rest., 157 Church Rd, NR33 7SQ, ☎ 740020, – TV P
May-September – **3 rm** ☐ 24.00/44.00 **t.**

ESWICK Cumbria 402 K 20 Great Britain G. – pop. 4 836 – ☎ 0176 87.

nvir. : Derwentwater★ X – Thirlmere (Castlerigg Stone Circle★), E : 1½m. X **A.**

Threlkeld Hall ☎ 79324.

Moot Hall, Market Sq., CA12 5JR ☎ 72645 – at Seatoller, Seatoller Barn, Borrowdale, eswick, CA12 5XN ☎ 77294 (summer only).

London 294 – ♦Carlisle 31 – Kendal 30.

Plan on next page

Underscar Manor, Applethwaite, CA12 4PH, N : 1 ¾ m. by A 591 on Underscar rd ☎ 75000, Fax 74904, ≤ Derwent Water and Fells, « Italianate Victorian country house », park – TV ☎ P. AE VISA.
Meals - (see below) – **11 rm** ☐ (dinner included) 75.00/250.00 **t.** – SB.

Brundholme Country House, Brundholme Rd, CA12 4NL, ☎ 74495, Fax 73536, ≤, – ⇔ rest TV ☎ P. AE VISA X e
closed December and January – **Meals** (dinner only) a la carte 17.25/20.50 **t.** 4.50 – **11 rm** ☐ 40.00/110.00 **t.** – SB.

Lyzzick Hall, Underskiddaw, CA12 4PY, NW : 2½ m. on A 591 ☎ 72277, Fax 72278, ≤, heated, – ⇔ rest TV ☎ P. AE VISA.
closed 3 days at Christmas and February – **Meals** 10.00/21.50 **t.** and a la carte 4.75 – **25 rm** ☐ 36.00/72.00 **t.**

Dale Head Hall, Thirlmere, CA12 4TN, SE : 5 ¾ m. on A 591 ☎ 72478, Fax 71070, ≤ Lake Thirlmere, « Lakeside setting », – ⇔ ☎ P. AE VISA JCB.
Meals (dinner only) 24.50 **st.** – **9 rm** ☐ (dinner included) 87.00/124.00 **st.** – SB.

Grange Country House, Manor Brow, Ambleside Rd, CA12 4BA, ☎ 72500, ≤, – ⇔ TV ☎ P. VISA. Y u
10 March-5 November – **Meals** (light lunch)/dinner 16.50 **st.** 4.40 – **10 rm** ☐ (dinner included) 100.00 **st.** – SB.

Applethwaite Country House, Underskiddaw, CA12 4PL, NW : 1 ¾ m. by A 591 on Ormathwaite rd ☎ 72413, ≤, – ⇔ rest TV P. VISA.
closed Christmas and New Year – **Meals** (dinner only) 15.50 **st.** – **12 rm** ☐ (dinner included) 44.50/89.00 **st.** – SB.

KESWICK

North is at the top on all town plans.

Les plans de villes sont disposés le Nord en haut.

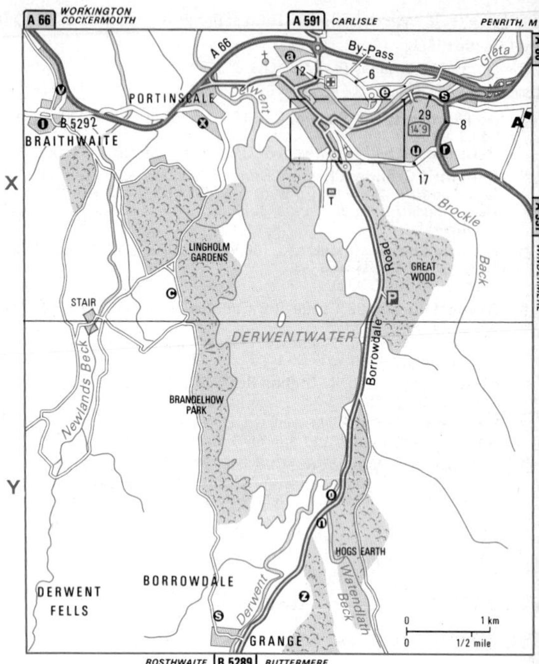

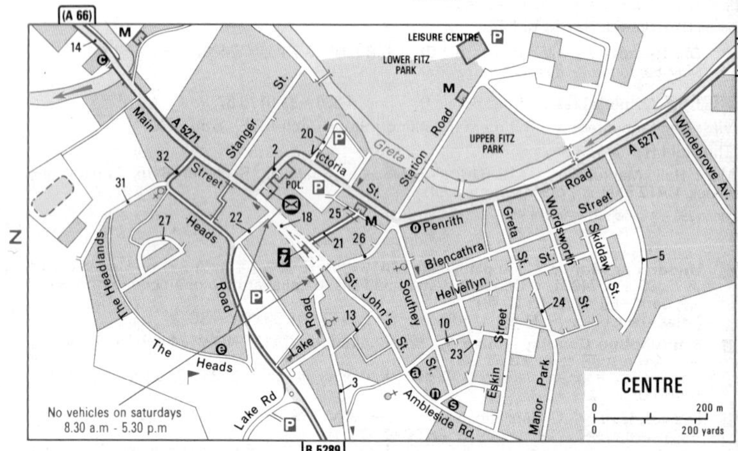

Chaucer House, Ambleside Rd, CA12 4DR, ℘ 72318, Fax 75551 – rest. Z a
AE VISA JCB.
closed December and January – **Meals** (lunch by arrangement)/dinner 15.75 **t.** and a la carte 4.80 – **35 rm** 35.00/70.00 **t.** – SB.

Lairbeck, Vicarage Hill, CA12 5QB, ℘ 73373, – VISA. X
closed January and February – **Meals** (dinner only) 14.00 **st.** 4.00 – **14 rm** (dinner included) 31.00/90.00 **st.** – SB.

Crow Park, The Heads, CA12 5ER, ℘ 72208, Fax 74776, – Z
VISA
closed last 3 weeks January – **Meals** (dinner only) 14.00 **st.** – **28 rm** 27.50/57.00 **st.** – SB

Acorn House without rest., Ambleside Rd, CA12 4DL, ☎ 72553, Fax 75322 – ⇔ TV P. VISA. Z s
mid February-mid November – **10 rm** ☐ 27.50/60.00 **st.**

Brackenrigg Country House, Thirlmere, CA12 4TF, SE : 3 m. on A 591 ☎ 72258, – TV P.
April-October – **Meals** (by arrangement) 15.00 – **6 rm** ☐ 22.50/48.00 – SB.

Claremont House, Chestnut Hill, CA12 4LT, ☎ 72089, ←, – ⇔ P. X r
closed 3 days Christmas – **Meals** (by arrangement) 16.75 **s.** 5.50 – **5 rm** ☐ 35.00/48.00 **s.**

Greystones, Ambleside Rd, CA12 4DP, ☎ 73108 – ⇔ TV P. VISA. Z n
March-mid November – **Meals** (by arrangement) 13.00 **st.** 4.00 – **8 rm** ☐ 22.50/45.00 **st.**

Craglands, Penrith Rd, CA12 4LJ, ☎ 74406, ← – ⇔ TV P. X s
closed Christmas and restricted bookings January-March – **Meals** (by arrangement) 15.00 **s.** – **4 rm** ☐ 24.00/44.00 **s.** – SB.

Linnett Hill, 4 Penrith Rd, CA12 4HF, ☎ 73109 – ⇔ TV P. VISA JCB. Z o
Meals 12.50 **t.** 4.50 – **10 rm** ☐ 24.00/45.00 **t.** – SB.

XX **Underscar Manor** (at Underscar Manor H.), Applethwaite, CA12 4PH, N : 1 ¾ m. by A 591 on Underscar rd ☎ 75000, Fax 74904, ← Derwent Water and Fells, « Italianate Victorian country house », park – ⇔ P. AE VISA
Meals 18.50/35.00 **t.** and a la carte 7.00.

X **La Primavera,** Greta Bridge, High Hill, CA12 5NX, ☎ 74621 – P. VISA Z c
closed 16 January-4 March – **Meals** - Italian - (closed Monday except Bank Holidays) 10.95/18.95 **t.** and a la carte 5.50.

at Threlkeld E : 4 m. by A 591 off A 66 – X – ✉ Keswick – ☎ 0176 87 :

Scales Farm, CA12 4SY, NE : 1 ¾ m. on A 66 ☎ 79660, – ⇔ rest TV P
closed Christmas – **Meals** (by arrangement) 15.00 – **5 rm** ☐ 28.00/46.00 **s.** – SB.

at Borrowdale S : on B 5289 – ✉ Keswick – ☎ 0176 87 :

Stakis Keswick Lodore, CA12 5UX, ☎ 77285, Fax 77343, ←, heated, , park, squash – ⇔ rest TV ☎ P – 70. AE VISA JCB. Y n
Meals (bar lunch Monday to Saturday)/dinner 20.50 **st.** and a la carte – **69 rm** ☐ (dinner included) 69.50/139.00 **st.**, 1 suite – SB.

Mary Mount, CA12 5UU, ☎ 77223, ←, – TV P. VISA Y o
closed January – **Meals** a la carte 11.75/15.55 **t.** 4.40 – **14 rm** ☐ 25.00/53.00 **t.**

Greenbank , CA12 5UY, ☎ 77215, ←, – ⇔ P. Y z
closed December and January – **Meals** (dinner only) 12.00 **st.** 3.00 – **10 rm** ☐ (dinner included) 38.00/76.00 **st.** – SB.

at Grange-in-Borrowdale S : 4 ¾ m. by B 5289 – Y – ✉ Keswick – ☎ 0176 87 :

Borrowdale Gates Country House , CA12 5UQ, ☎ 77204, Fax 77254, ← Borrowdale Valley, – ⇔ rest TV ☎ P. AE VISA. Y s
closed 2 to 31 January and 2 to 19 December – **Meals** (bar lunch Monday to Saturday)/dinner 21.50 **t.** 5.25 – **22 rm** ☐ (dinner included) 63.50/133.00 – SB.

at Rosthwaite S : 6 m. on B 5289 – Y – ✉ Keswick – ☎ 0176 87 :

Hazel Bank , CA12 5XB, ☎ 77248, ←, – ⇔ TV P. VISA JCB
6 April-25 October – **Meals** (dinner only) – **6 rm** ☐ (dinner included) 43.00/86.00 **st.**

at Seatoller S : 8 m. on B 5289 – Y – ✉ Keswick – ☎ 0176 87 :

Seatoller House, CA12 5XN, ☎ 77218, ← Borrowdale, – ⇔ P
April-October – **Meals** (by arrangement) (communal dining) 5.50 – **9 rm** ☐ (dinner included) 34.50/66.00 **t.**

at Portinscale W : 1 ½ m. by A 66 – ✉ Keswick – ☎ 0176 87 :

Swinside Lodge , Newlands, CA12 5UE, S : 1 ½ m. on Grange Rd ☎ 72948, Fax 72948, ← Catbells and Causey Pike, – ⇔ TV P. X c
closed mid December-mid February – **Meals** (unlicensed) (dinner only) 27.50 **t.** – **7 rm** ☐ (dinner included) 60.00/135.00 **t.** – SB.

Derwent Cottage , CA12 5RF, ☎ 74838, – ⇔ TV P. VISA JCB. X x
March-October – **Meals** (residents only) (dinner only) 15.00 **st.** 3.50 – **5 rm** ☐ 54.00/64.00 **st.** – SB.

at Braithwaite W : 2 m. by A 66 on B 5292 – ✉ Keswick – ☎ 0176 87 :

Ivy House, CA12 5SY, ☎ 78338, Fax 78113 – ⇔ rest TV ☎ P. AE VISA. X i
closed January – **Meals** (dinner only) 18.95 **t.** 3.95 – **12 rm** ☐ (dinner included) 46.95/99.90 **t.** – SB.

Middle Ruddings, CA12 5RY, on A 66 ☎ 78436, Fax 78438, – ⇔ rest TV ☎ P. VISA JCB X v
closed 25 and 26 December – **Meals** (closed Monday) (bar lunch)/dinner a la carte 15.00 **t.** – **11 rm** ☐ 38.00/66.00 **t.** – SB.

Cottage in The Wood , Whinlatter Pass, CA12 5TW, NW : 1 ¾ m. on B 5292 ☎ 78409, ←, – ⇔ P. VISA JCB
mid March-mid November – **Meals** (dinner only) 18.00 **st.** 4.30 – **7 rm** ☐ (dinner included) 53.00/84.00 **st.** – SB.

at Thornthwaite W : 3½ m. by A 66 – X – ✉ Keswick – ☎ 0176 87 :

Thwaite Howe 🔇, CA12 5SA, ☎ 78281, Fax 78529, ≤ Skiddaw and Derwent Valley, ⚘ – ⇔ 📺 ☎ 🅿
March-October – **Meals** (dinner only) 15.00 **st.** 🍷 4.00 – **8 rm** ☕ (dinner included) 58.50/87.00 **st.** – SB.

KETTERING Northants. 404 R 26 pop. 76 150 – ☎ 01536.

ℹ The Coach House, Sheep St., NN16 0AN ☎ 410266/410333.

◆London 88 – ◆Birmingham 54 – ◆Leicester 16 – Northampton 24.

Kettering Park, Kettering Parkway, NN15 6XT, S : 2¼ m. by A 509 (Wellingborough rd) at junction with A 14 ☎ 416666, Fax 416171, Lб, ≘s, 🏊, ⚘, squash – |$| ⇔ rm 📺 ☎ 🅿 🚶 200. 🔲 AE ⓪ VISA
Meals (bar lunch Saturday) 13.50/22.00 **st.** and a la carte 🍷 6.95 – **82 rm** ☕ 81.00/110.00 **st.** 3 suites – SB.

Periquito, Market Pl., NN16 0AJ, ☎ 520732, Fax 411036 – ⇔ rm 📺 ☎ 🅿 – 🚶 150. 🔲 AE ⓪ VISA JCB
Meals (bar lunch Monday to Saturday)/dinner 14.00 **st.** and a la carte – ☕ 6.50 – **40 rm** 46.00, 1 suite – SB.

Travel Inn, Rothwell Rd, NN16 8XF, NW : 1¼ m. at junction of A 14 with A 43 ☎ 310082, Fax 310104 – ⇔ rm 📺 ♿ 🅿. 🔲 AE ⓪ VISA
Meals (grill rest.) – ☕ 4.95 – **39 rm** 34.50 **t.**

ATS Northfield Av. ☎ 512832

I prezzi — Per ogni chiarimento sui prezzi qui riportati, consultate le spiegazioni alle pagine dell'introduzione.

KETTLEWELL N. Yorks. 402 N 21 – pop. 297 (inc. Starbotton) – ✉ Skipton – ☎ 01756.

◆London 237 – Bradford 33 – ◆Leeds 40.

Cam Lodge 🔇, BD23 5QU, ☎ 760276, ⚘ – ⇔ 🅿. ✻
April-September – **Meals** 12.00 **s.** – **3 rm** ☕ 20.00/40.00 **s.**

at Starbotton NW : 1¾ m. on B 6160 – ✉ Skipton – ☎ 01756 :

Hilltop Country 🔇, BD23 5HY, ☎ 760321, ≤, « 17C stone built house », ⚘, park – ⇔ 📺 🅿. ✻
April-October – **Meals** (by arrangement) 15.00 **st.** 🍷 4.60 – **5 rm** ☕ 36.00/50.00 **st.**

KEXBY N. Yorks. – see York.

KEYSTON Cambs. 404 S 26 – pop. 257 (inc. Bythorn) – ✉ Huntingdon – ☎ 01832.

◆London 75 – ◆Cambridge 29 – Northampton 24.

XX **Pheasant Inn,** Village Loop Rd, PE18 0RE, ☎ 710241, Fax 710340 – ⇔ 🅿. 🔲 AE ⓪ VISA
Meals a la carte 19.00/27.00 **t.**

KIDDERMINSTER Heref. and Worcs. 403 404 N 26 – pop. 105 644 – ☎ 01562.

ℹ Severn Valley Railway Station, Comberton Hill, DY10 1QX ☎ 829400 (summer only).

◆London 139 – ◆Birmingham 17 – Shrewsbury 34 – Worcester 15.

Stone Manor, Stone, DY10 4PJ, SE : 2½ m. on A 448 ☎ 777555, Fax 777834, ≤, 🏊, ⚘, park, 🎾 – ⇔ rm 📺 ☎ 🅿 – 🚶 150. 🔲 AE ⓪ VISA. ✻
Meals 11.50/16.95 **t.** and a la carte 🍷 6.95 – ☕ 7.25 – **51 rm** 45.00/72.00 **t.**, 1 suite – SB.

Gainsborough House, Bewdley Hill, DY11 6BS, ☎ 820041, Fax 66179 – ⇔ 📺 ☎ 🅿 🚶 240. 🔲 AE ⓪ VISA
Meals (bar lunch Saturday) 12.50 **t.** (dinner) and a la carte 17.10/23.80 **t.** 🍷 6.50 – **42 rm** ☕ 60.00/75.00 **t.** – SB.

Collingdale, 197 Comberton Rd, DY10 1VE, ☎ 515460 – 📺 🅿
Meals (by arrangement) 7.50 **st.** 🍷 3.50 – **9 rm** ☕ 17.50/38.00 **st.**

at Chaddesley Corbett SE : 4½ m. by A 448 – ✉ Kidderminster – ☎ 01562 :

Brockencote Hall 🔇, DY10 4PY, on A 448 ☎ 777876, Fax 777872, ≤, « Part 19C mansion in park », ⚘ – ⇔ rest 📺 ☎ ♿ 🅿 – 🚶 30. 🔲 AE ⓪ VISA. ✻
Meals *(closed Saturday lunch)* a la carte 17.50/37.50 **st.** 🍷 5.90 – **17 rm** ☕ 80.00/135.00 **st.** – SB.

ATS Park St. ☎ 744668/744843

KIDLINGTON Oxon. 403 404 Q 28 – see Oxford.

KILLINGTON LAKE SERVICE AREA Cumbria 402 M 21 – ✉ Kendal – ☎ 01539.

Road Chef Lodge without rest., LA8 0NW, M 6 between junctions 36 and 37 (southbound carriageway) ☎ 621666, Fax 621660 – ⇔ 📺 ☎ ♿ 🅿. ✻
closed Christmas and New Year – **36 rm** 37.50 **st.**

KILSBY Northants. 403 404 Q 26 – see Rugby (Warks.).

KINGHAM Oxon. 403 404 P 28 – pop. 1 434 – ☎ 01608.

♦London 81 – Gloucester 32 – ♦Oxford 25.

Mill House ⛰, OX7 6UH, ☏ 658188, Fax 658492, – TV ☎ P – 70. AE VISA.
Meals 12.95/27.00 **t.** and a la carte 5.35 – **23 rm** 55.00/100.00 **t.** – SB.

KINGSBRIDGE Devon 403 I 33 **The West Country G.** – pop. 5 081 – ☎ 01548.

See : Town★ – Boat Trip to Salcombe★★ *AC*.

Exc. : Prawle Point (≤★★★) SE : 10 m. around coast by A 379.

Thurlestone ☏ 560405.

The Quay, TQ7 1HS ☏ 853195.

♦London 236 – Exeter 36 – ♦Plymouth 20 – Torquay 21.

Kings Arms, Fore St., TQ7 1AB, ☏ 852071, Fax 852977, – TV ☎ P – 40. VISA JCB
Meals 4.50/10.00 **t.** and a la carte 3.50 – **11 rm** 30.00/60.00 **t.** – SB.

at Goveton NE : 2½ m. by A 381 – ✉ Kingsbridge – ☎ 01548 :

Buckland-Tout-Saints ⛰, TQ7 2DS, ☏ 853055, Fax 856261, ≤, « Queen Anne mansion », park – rest TV ☎ P. AE VISA JCB
Meals (booking essential) 14.50/25.00 – **13 rm** 75.00/150.00 **t.** – SB.

at Chillington E : 5 m. on A 379 – ✉ Kingsbridge – ☎ 01548 :

White House, TQ7 2JX, ☏ 580580, Fax 581124, – TV ☎ P. AE VISA
Easter-December – **Meals** *(closed Monday)* (dinner only) 14.00 **st.** 4.50 – **7 rm** 44.00/70.00 **st.** – SB.

at Torcross E : 7 m. on A 379 – ✉ Kingsbridge – ☎ 01548 :

The Venture without rest., TQ7 2TQ, ☏ 580314, ≤ – TV
February-October – **3 rm** 18.00/36.00 **s.**

at Thurlestone W : 4 m. by A 381 – ✉ Kingsbridge – ☎ 01548 :

Thurlestone ⛰, TQ7 3NN, ☏ 560382, Fax 561069, ≤, heated, 9, squash – rest rest TV ☎ P – 100. VISA.
Meals 9.50/35.00 **st.** and lunch a la carte 5.50 – **68 rm** 55.00/110.00 **st.** – SB.

at Bantham W : 5 m. by A 379 – ✉ Kingsbridge – ☎ 01548 :

Sloop Inn, TQ7 3AJ, ☏ 560489, Fax 561940 – TV P
closed 25 and 26 December – **Meals** a la carte 10.20/16.05 **t.** – **5 rm** 28.00/56.00 **t.** – SB.

ATS Union Rd ☏ 853247/852699

KING'S CLIFFE Northants. 404 S 26 – ✉ Peterborough – ☎ 01780.

♦London 93 – ♦Leicester 21 – Northampton 19 – Peterborough 7.

King's Cliffe House, 31 West St., PE8 6XB, ☏ 470172, – P
closed Sunday to Tuesday, 25-26 December and 1 January – **Meals** (dinner only) a la carte 15.25/22.25 **st.** 5.00.

KINGSDOWN Kent 404 Y 30 – see Deal.

KINGSKERSWELL Devon 403 J 32 – pop. 4 210 – ✉ Torquay – ☎ 01803.

♦London 219 – Exeter 21 – ♦Plymouth 33 – Torquay 4.

Pitt House, 2 Church End Rd, TQ12 5DS, ☏ 873374, « 15C thatched dower house », – P. VISA
closed Sunday dinner, Monday, 2 weeks January and 2 weeks summer – **Meals** (light lunch)/dinner 20.00 **t.** and a la carte.

KINGS LANGLEY Herts 404 S 28 – ☎ 01923.

♦London 26 – Luton 14.

Langleys, Hempstead Rd, WD4 8BR, ☏ 263150, Fax 264061 – rm TV P. AE VISA.
Meals (grill rest.) a la carte 9.35/12.45 **t.** 3.75 – 4.95 – **40 rm** 34.00 **t.**

KING'S LYNN Norfolk 402 404 V 25 **Great Britain G.** – pop. 41 281 – ☎ 01553.

Exc. : Houghton Hall★★ *AC*, NE : 14 ½ m. by A 148 – Four Fenland Churches★ (Terrington St. Clement, Walpole St. Peter, West Walton, Walsoken) SW : by A 47.

Eagles, School Rd, Tilney All Saints ☏ 827147.

The Old Gaol House, Saturday Market Pl., PE30 5DQ ☏ 763044.

♦London 103 – ♦Cambridge 45 – ♦Leicester 75 – ♦Norwich 44.

Knights Hill, Knights Hill Village, South Wootton, PE30 3HQ, NE : 4 ½ m. on A 148 at junction with A 149 ☏ 675566, Fax 675568, – TV ☎ P – 300. AE VISA JCB.
Meals (bar lunch Monday to Saturday)/dinner 15.50 **st.** and a la carte – 7.00 – **52 rm** 70.00/100.00 **t.** – SB.

Duke's Head (Forte), Tuesday Market Pl., PE30 1JS, ℘ 774996, Fax 763556 – 200.
Meals *(closed Saturday lunch)* 10.95/18.95 **st.** and a la carte 5.55 – 8.50 – **71 rm** 60.00/70.00 **st.** – SB.

Butterfly, Beveridge Way, PE30 4NB, S : 2¼ m. by Hardwick Rd at junction of A 10 with A 47 ℘ 771707, Fax 768027 – rm – 40.
Meals 12.25 **t.** and a la carte 4.50 – 6.95 – **50 rm** 52.00 **t.** – SB.

Russet House, 53 Goodwins Rd, PE30 5PE, ℘ 773098, Fax 773098, – rest.
closed 22 to 27 December – **Meals** *(closed Sunday)* (booking essential) (dinner only) 13.50 **t.** 4.20 – **12 rm** 30.00/51.75 **t.**

Fairlight Lodge without rest., 79 Goodwins Rd, PE30 5PE, ℘ 762234, Fax 770280, –
closed 24 to 27 December – **7 rm** 25.00/38.00 **s.**

Rococo, 11 Saturday Market Pl., PE30 5DQ, ℘ 771483 –
closed Monday lunch, Sunday and 25 to 30 December – **Meals** (booking essential) 9.00/25.50 **t.**

at Grimston NE : 6¼ m. by A 148 – ✉ King's Lynn – 01485 :

Congham Hall , Lynn Rd, PE32 1AH, ℘ 600250, Fax 601191, ≤, « Part Georgian manor house, herb garden », heated, , park, – rest – 25.
Meals – **Orangery** (booking essential Saturday lunch) 15.00/32.00 **t.** and lunch a la carte 6.50 – **12 rm** 65.00/130.00 **t.**, 2 suites – SB.

at Tottenhill S : 5¼ m. on A 10 – ✉ King's Lynn – 01553 :

Oakwood House, PE33 0RH, N : ½ m. on A 10 ℘ 810256, –
Meals (dinner only) a la carte 9.15/16.00 **st.** 4.15 – **10 rm** 30.00/40.00 **st.** – SB.

ATS 4 Oldmedow Rd, Hardwick Rd Trading Est. ℘ 774035

Prices For full details of the prices quoted in the guide, consult the introduction.

KINGSTEIGNTON Devon 403 J 32 – pop. 8 913 – ✉ Newton Abbot – 01626.

♦London 223 – Exeter 17 – ♦Plymouth 33 – Torquay 7.

Passage House, Hackney Lane, TQ12 3QH, S : ½ m. ℘ 55515, Fax 63336, ≤, – – 150
38 rm, 1 suite.

KINGSTON Devon 403 I 33 – pop. 364 – ✉ Kingsbridge – 01548.

♦London 237 – Exeter 41 – ♦Plymouth 11.

Trebles Cottage , TQ7 4PT, ℘ 810268, Fax 810268, –
Meals 14.00 **st.** 6.50 – **5 rm** 32.00/60.00 **st.** – SB.

KINGSTON BAGPUIZE Oxon. 403 404 P 28 – see Abingdon.

KINGSTON-UPON-HULL Humbs. 402 S 22 Great Britain G. – pop. 310 636 – 01482.

Exc. : Burton Constable★ *AC*, NE : 9 m. by A 165 and B 1238 – Z.

Springhead Park, Willerby Rd ℘ 656309 – Sutton Park, Salthouse Rd ℘ 374242.

Humberside Airport : ℘ (01652) 688456, S : 19 m. by A 63 – **Terminal** : Coach Service.

to The Netherlands (Rotterdam) (North Sea Ferries) (13 h 30 mn) – to The Netherlands (Zeebrugge) (North Sea Ferries) (13 h 45 mn).

Central Library, Albion St., HU1 3TF ℘ 223344 – King George Dock, Hedon Rd, HU9 5PR ℘ 702118 – 75-76 Carr Lane, HU1 3RQ ℘ 223559.

♦London 183 – ♦Leeds 61 – ♦Nottingham 94 – ♦Sheffield 68.

Plan opposite

Forte Crest, Castle St., HU1 2BX, ℘ 225221, Fax 213299, – rm – 120. Y n
Meals 8.50/30.00 **st.** and a la carte 6.75 – 10.85 – **99 rm** 70.00/120.00 **st.** – SB.

Quality Royal (Friendly), Ferensway, HU1 3UF, ℘ 325087, Fax 323172, – rm rest – 450. Y a
Meals 9.00/13.50 **st.** and a la carte 4.75 – 7.75 – **155 rm** 57.50/94.00 **st.** – SB.

Travel Inn, Ferriby Rd, Hessle, HU13 0JA, W : 7 m. by A 63 off A 164 ℘ 645285, Fax 645299 – rm
Meals (grill rest.) – 4.95 – **40 rm** 34.50 **t.**

Campanile, Beverley Rd, Freetown Way, HU2 9AN, ℘ 325530, Fax 587538 – rm – 30. X a
Meals 10.35 **t.** 4.65 – 4.50 – **47 rm** 36.50 **t.**

KINGSTON-UPON-HULL

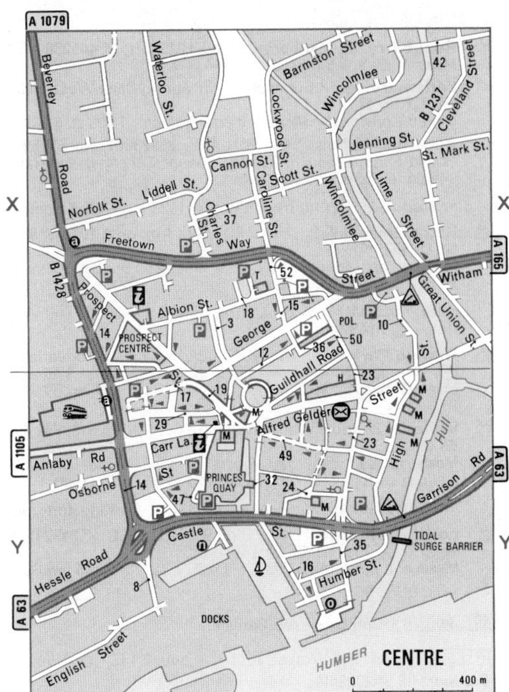

BEVERLEY, YORK A 1079

SUTTON-ON-HULL
18
BRIDLINGTON HORNSEA
Greenwood Av.
Sutton Road
Endike Lane
INDUSTRIAL ESTATE
Hull
Hall Road
Beverley
Road B 1237
Saltshouse Road
Sutton Road
Leads
SUTTON INGS
A 165
Cottingham Rd
U
STONEFERRY
Ings Rd
Road
B 1233
Clough Road
Reckitt Avenue
13
Chanterlands
Road
Stoneferry
EAST PARK
Z
Bricknell Avenue
SCULCOATES
James
SUMMERGANGS
25
9
33
15
43
Preston Rd
Lane
31
Beverley Road
Rd
Holderness
44
44
Avenue
Marfleet
WITHERNSEA HEDON
Hull
Spring Bank
West Spring Bank
A 1033
Walton St.
WEST PARK
Hedon Road
Anlaby Road
ALEXANDRA DOCK
KING GEORGE DOCK
Rd. A 63
Boulevard
Road
Garrisson
ZEEBRUGGE ROTTERDAM
HUMBER
Hessle A 1105
BUILT UP AREA
0
2 km
0
1 mile
HUMBER BRIDGE LEEDS A 63

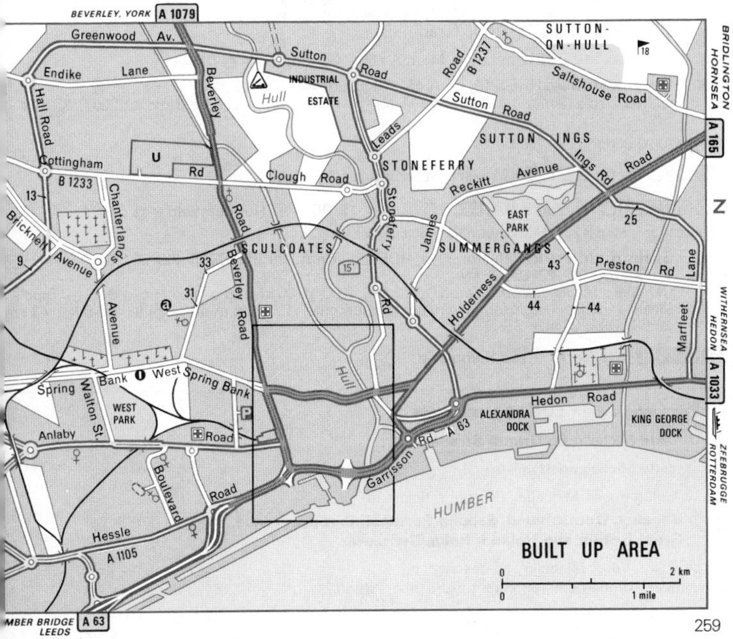

Roseberry, 86 Marlborough Av., HU5 3JT, ☎ 445256 – TV. VISA. Z
Meals 10.00 **s.** – **5 rm** 17.00/44.00 **s.**

Earlsmere, 76-78 Sunnybank, off Spring Bank West, HU3 1LQ, ☎ 341977, Fax 473714 – TV. VISA Z
closed Christmas – **Meals** (by arrangement) 12.00 **st.** 3.00 – **15 rm** 18.80/41.10 **st.**

Cerutti's, 10 Nelson St., HU1 1XE, ☎ 328501, Fax 587597 – P. VISA Y
closed Saturday lunch, Sunday, 1 week Christmas and Bank Holidays – **Meals** - Seafood a la carte 15.75/28.00 **t.** 6.25.

at Hedon E : 6½ m. by A 63 on A 1033 – Z – ✉ Kingston-upon-Hull – ☎ 01482 :

Kingstown, Hull Rd, HU12 8DJ, W : 1 m. on A 1033 ☎ 890461, Fax 890713 – TV ☎ & P AE VISA.
Meals (in bar Monday to Saturday lunch and Sunday)/dinner 15.95 **st.** and a la carte 4.45 – **34 rm** 62.00/85.00 **st.** – SB.

at Willerby W : 5 m. by A 1079, Spring Bank – Z – and Willerby Rd – ✉ Kingston-upon-Hull – ☎ 01482 :

Grange Park, Main St., HU10 6EA, N : 1 m. by Beverley Rd ☎ 656488, Fax 655848, – rm rest TV ☎ & P – 350. AE VISA
Meals 8.95/16.50 **st.** and a la carte – 8.50 – **97 rm** 59.50/69.50 **st.**, 4 suites – SB.

Willerby Manor, Well Lane, HU10 6ER, ☎ 652616, Fax 653901, – TV ☎ P – 500. AE VISA.
Meals *(closed Saturday lunch, Sunday dinner and Bank Holidays)* 12.00/14.00 **st** and a la carte 4.90 – 7.25 – **32 rm** 59.00/82.00 **st.**

at North Ferriby W : 7 m. on A 63 – Z – ✉ Kingston-upon-Hull – ☎ 01482 :

Forte Posthouse, Ferriby High Rd, HU14 3LG, ☎ 645212, Fax 643332 – rm rest TV ☎ P – 100. AE VISA JCB
Meals a la carte 14.75/22.85 **t.** 6.25 – 7.95 – **95 rm** 60.00 **st.** – SB.

ATS Great Union St. ☎ 29044 ATS Scott St. ☎ 29370/225502

KINGSTOWN Cumbria – see Carlisle.

KINGTON Heref. and Worcs. 403 K 27 – pop. 2 197 – ☎ 01544 :

Bradnor Hill ☎ 230340.

London 152 – Birmingham 61 – Hereford 19 – Shrewsbury 54.

Penrhos Court, HR5 3LH, E : 1½ m. on A 44 ☎ 230720, Fax 230754, « Part 15C and 16C house with medieval cruck hall », – TV ☎ P – 25. AE VISA JCB.
closed 1 to 14 February – **Meals** (dinner only) (booking essential) 28.00 **st.** and a la carte 6.00 – **11 rm** 60.00/140.00 **st.** – SB.

at Lyonshall E : 2½ m . by A 44 on A 480 – ✉ Kington – ☎ 01544 :

Church House, HR5 3HR, on A 44 ☎ 340350, – P.
closed 24 December-1 January – **Meals** (by arrangement) 9.00 – **3 rm** 20.00/36.00 **s.** – SB.

ATS 20-22 Bridge St. ☎ 230350

KINVER Staffs. 403 404 N 26 – see Stourbridge (W. Mids).

KIRKBURTON W. Yorks. 402 404 O 23 ⑳ pop. 15 187 – ✉ Huddersfield – ☎ 01484.

London 195 – Leeds 20 – Manchester 32 – Sheffield 22.

Springfield Park, Penistone Rd, HD8 0PE, on A 629 ☎ 607788, Fax 607961 – rm TV ☎ P – 140. AE VISA
Old Mill : Meals *(closed Saturday lunch)* 8.00/15.00 **st.** and a la carte **t.** 6.85 – **Topo's : Meals** - Italian - *(closed Monday)* (dinner only) 15.00 **st.** and a la carte 6.85 – **43 rm** 63.50/85.00 **st.** – SB.

KIRBY HILL N. Yorks. – see Richmond.

KIRKBY LONSDALE Cumbria 402 M 21 – pop. 2 076 – ✉ Carnforth (Lancs.) – ☎ 0152 42.

18 Scaleber Lane, Barbon ℘ 36365 – 9 Casterton, Sedbergh Rd ℘ 71592.

24 Main St., LA6 2AE ℘ 71437.

London 259 – Carlisle 62 – Kendal 13 – Lancaster 17 – Leeds 58.

Whoop Hall Inn, Burrow with Burrow, LA6 2HP, SE : 1 m. on A 65 ℘ 71284, Fax 72154, – rm TV ☎ P. AE VISA JCB
Meals (bar lunch)/dinner 15.00 **t.** and a la carte 4.95 – **22 rm** 45.00/65.00 **t.** – SB.

Pheasant Inn, Casterton, LA6 2RX, NE : 1 ¼ m. on A 683 ℘ 71230, Fax 71230, – rest TV ☎ P. VISA
Meals *(closed Monday)* (bar lunch)/dinner a la carte 14.20/21.45 **t.** 5.50 – **10 rm** 37.50/64.00 **t.**

at Cowan Bridge (Lancs.) SE : 2 m. on A 65 – ✉ Carnforth (Lancs.) – ☎ 0152 42 :

Hipping Hall, LA6 2JJ, SE : ½ m. on A 65 ℘ 71187, Fax 72452, – TV ☎ P. AE VISA
March-November – **Meals** (residents only) (communal dining) (dinner only) 21.00 **st.** 3.75 – **5 rm** 63.00/89.00 **st.**, 2 suites – SB.

Snooty Fox, 33 Main St., LA6 2AH, ℘ 71308, Fax 72642, « Jacobean inn » – rm TV P. AE VISA
Meals a la carte 11.45/23.95 **st.** 4.75 – **9 rm** 26.00/49.50 **st.**

KIRKBYMOORSIDE N. Yorks. 402 R 21 – pop. 3 825 – ☎ 01751.

18 Manor Vale ℘ 431525.

London 244 – Scarborough 26 – York 33.

George and Dragon, 17 Market Pl., YO6 6AA, ℘ 433334, Fax 433334, « Part 17C coaching inn », – rest TV ☎ P. VISA.
Meals (bar lunch Monday to Saturday)/dinner a la carte 13.40/17.60 **t.** 5.00 – **19 rm** 45.00/72.00 **t.** – SB.

KIRKBY STEPHEN Cumbria 402 M 20 – pop. 2 209 – ☎ 0176 83.

Market St., CA17 4QN ℘ 71199 (summer only).

London 285 – Carlisle 48 – Kendal 24.

Ing Hill Lodge, Mallerstang Dale, CA17 4JT, S : 4 ½ m. on B 6259 ℘ 71153, Fax 71153, ≤ Mallerstang Dale, – TV P
Meals (by arrangement) 12.50 **st.** 3.50 – **3 rm** 25.00/50.00 **st.** – SB.

KIRKCAMBECK Cumbria 401 402 L 18 – see Brampton.

KIRKHAM Lancs. 402 L 22 – pop. 6 311 – ✉ Preston – ☎ 01772.

London 240 – Blackpool 9 – Preston 7.

Cromwellian, 16 Poulton St., PR4 2AB, ℘ 685680, Fax 685680 – AE VISA
closed Sunday, Monday, 1 week February and 1 week October – **Meals** (dinner only) a la carte 16.50/23.50 **st.** 5.95.

KIRKOSWALD Cumbria 401 402 L 19 – pop. 1 281 – ✉ Penrith – ☎ 01768.

London 300 – Carlisle 23 – Kendal 41 – Lancaster 58.

Prospect Hill, CA10 1ER, N : ¾ m. on Armathwaite rd ℘ 898500, Fax 898088, ≤, « Converted 18C farm buildings », – P. AE VISA.
closed 24 to 27 December – **Meals** (dinner only) a la carte 12.50/19.00 **t.** 5.00 – **11 rm** 21.00/75.00 **t.** – SB.

KIRKWHELPINGTON Northd. 401 402 N/O 18 Great Britain G. – pop. 353 – ✉ Morpeth – ☎ 01830.

Envir. : Wallington House★ *AC*, E : 3½m. by A 696 and B 6342.

London 305 – Carlisle 46 – Newcastle upon Tyne 20.

Shieldhall, Wallington, NE61 4AQ, SE : 2 ½ m. by A 696 on B 6342 ℘ 540387, Fax 540387, – P.
February-October – **Meals** (by arrangement) 13.95 – **4 rm** 25.00/46.00.

KNARESBOROUGH N. Yorks. 402 P 21 – pop. 13 848 – ☎ 01423.

18 Boroughbridge Rd ℘ 863219.

35 Market Place, HG5 8AL ℘ 866886 (summer only).

London 217 – Bradford 21 – Harrogate 3 – Leeds 18 – York 18.

Dower House, Bond End, HG5 9AL, ℘ 863302, Fax 867665, , , , – rm TV ☎ P – 65. AE VISA.
Meals (bar lunch Monday to Saturday)/dinner 18.50 **t.** and a la carte – **31 rm** 55.00/90.00 **t.**, 1 suite – SB.

KNIGHTWICK Heref. and Worcs. 403 404 M 27 – pop. 87 – ✉ Worcester – ☎ 01886.

London 132 – Hereford 20 – Leominster 18 – Worcester 8.

Talbot, WR6 5PH, on B 4197 ℘ 821235, Fax 821060, , , squash – TV ☎ P. VISA
Meals a la carte 15.50/22.40 **t.** 4.50 – **10 rm** 31.00/56.50 **t.** – SB.

KNOWLE W. Mids. 403 404 O 26 – pop. 11 203 – ✉ Solihull – ☎ 01564.

♦London 108 – ♦Birmingham 9 – Coventry 10 – Warwick 11.

Bridgewater, 2110 Warwick Rd, B93 0EE, S : 1½ m. on A 4141 ℘ 771177, Fax 770141, – rest TV ☎ P. AE VISA
Meals 12.30/18.00 **t.** and a la carte – **20 rm** 57.50/70.00 **t.** – SB.

Greswolde Arms, 1657 High St., B93 0LL, ℘ 772711, Fax 770354 – rm TV ☎ & P – 150. AE VISA.
Meals 8.95/12.75 **st.** and a la carte 6.10 – 5.00 – **36 rm** 49.00 **t.**

KNOWL HILL Berks. 404 R 29 – ✉ Twyford – ☎ 01628.

Hennerton, Crazies Hill Rd, Wargrave ℘ (01734) 401000/404778.

♦London 38 – Maidenhead 5 – Reading 8.

Bird in Hand, Bath Rd, RG10 9UP, ℘ 826622, Fax 826748, – TV ☎ & P. AE VISA JCB.
closed 24 to 30 December – **Meals** 9.95/15.00 **st.** and a la carte 5.75 – **15 rm** 67.50/90.00 **st.** – SB.

KNUTSFORD Ches. 402 403 404 M 24 – pop. 13 352 – ☎ 01565.

Council Offices, Toft Rd, WA16 6TA ℘ 632611/632210.

♦London 187 – Chester 25 – ♦Liverpool 33 – ♦Manchester 18 – ♦Stoke-on-Trent 30.

Cottons, Manchester Rd, WA16 0SU, NW : 1½ m. on A 50 ℘ 650333, Fax 755351, , , – rm TV ☎ & P – 200. AE VISA
Magnolia : Meals 13.50/20.00 **st.** and a la carte 6.95 – **73 rm** 84.00/124.00 **st.**, 9 suites – SB.

Longview, 55 Manchester Rd, WA16 0LX, ℘ 632119, Fax 652402 – TV ☎ P. AE VISA
closed 24 December-1 January – **Meals** *(closed Sunday and Bank Holidays)* (lunch by arrangement)/dinner a la carte 15.75/22.40 **st.** 5.00 – **23 rm** 53.00/100.00 – SB.

Forte Travelodge, Chester Rd, Tabley, WA16 0PP, NW : 2¾ m. by A 5033 on A 556 ℘ 652187, Reservations (Freephone) 0800 850950 – TV & P. AE VISA.
Meals (grill rest.) – **32 rm** 34.50 **t.**

Belle Epoque Brasserie with rm, 60 King St., WA16 6DT, ℘ 633060, Fax 634150, « Art Nouveau », – TV – 60. AE VISA.
closed Bank Holidays – **Meals** *(closed Saturday lunch and Sunday)* 10.50 **st.** (lunch) and a la carte 12.50/27.50 **st.** – 5.50 – **7 rm** 40.00/50.00 **st.**

Treasure Village, 84 King St., WA16 6EG, ℘ 651537 – . AE VISA
closed Saturday lunch – **Meals** - Chinese - 4.80/22.00 **t.** and a la carte 6.20.

Est, Est, Est !, 81 King St., WA16 6DX, ℘ 755487, Fax 651151 – . AE VISA
closed 25 December – **Meals** - Italian - 9.95/12.95 **t.** and a la carte 4.95.

at Mobberley NE : 2½ m. by A 537 on B 5085 – ✉ Knutsford – ☎ 01565 :

Laburnum Cottage without rest., Knutsford Rd, WA16 7PU, W : ¾ m. on B 5085 ℘ 872464, Fax 872464, « Gardens » – TV P.
5 rm 38.00/48.00 **st.**

Hinton, Town Lane, WA16 7HH, on B 5085 ℘ 873484, Fax 873484, – TV ☎ P. AE VISA.
Meals (by arrangement) 9.50 – **6 rm** 30.00/48.00.

at Over Peover SE : 5 m. by A 50 and Stocks Lane – ✉ Knutsford – ☎ 01625 :

The Dog, Wellbank Lane, Peover Heath, WA16 8UP, ℘ 861421, Fax 861421 – TV P. VISA.
Meals (in bar) a la carte 12.30/15.30 **t.** – **3 rm** 39.50/59.50 **t.**

at Hoo Green NW : 3½ m. on A 50 – ✉ Knutsford – ☎ 01565 :

Kilton Inn (Premier), Warrington Rd, WA16 0PZ, ℘ 830420, Fax 830411 – rm TV ☎ & P. AE VISA.
Meals (grill rest.) 12.00 3.95 – 4.45 – **28 rm** 32.50/39.50 **st.** – SB.

ATS Malt St. ℘ 652224

LACOCK Wilts. 403 404 N 29 **The West Country G.** – pop. 1 068 – ✉ Chippenham – ☎ 01249.

See : Village★ - Lacock Abbey★ *AC* – High St.★, St. Cyriac★, Fox Talbot Museum of Photography★ *AC*.

♦London 109 – Bath 16 – ♦Bristol 30 – Chippenham 3.

Sign of the Angel, 6 Church St., SN15 2LA, ℘ 730230, Fax 730527, « Part 14C and 15C former wool merchant's house in National Trust village », – TV ☎. AE VISA
closed 22 to 31 December – **Meals** - English - *(closed Monday lunch)* a la carte 10.25/26.50 **t.** 5.00 – **9 rm** 50.00/93.00 **t.** – SB.

LANCASTER Lancs. 402 L 21 **Great Britain G.** – pop. 123 856 – ☎ 01524.

See : Castle★ *AC*.

18 Ashton Hall, Ashton-with-Stodday ✆ 752090 – 9 Lansil, Caton Rd ✆ 39269.

29 Castle Hill, LA1 1YN ✆ 32878.

♦London 252 – ♦Blackpool 26 – Bradford 62 – Burnley 44 – ♦Leeds 71 – ♦Middlesbrough 97 – Preston 26.

Lancaster House, Green Lane, LA1 4GJ, S : 3 ¼ m. by A 6 ✆ 844822, Fax 844766, ₺, ≘s, ☒ – ⇔ rm ☑ ☎ ♿ ℗ – ♔ 120. ☒ AE ⦿ VISA JCB
Gressingham : Meals 9.95/18.50 **st.** and a la carte – **80 rm** ☐ 82.00/117.00 **st.** – SB.

Forte Posthouse, Waterside Park, Caton Rd, LA1 3RA, NE : 1 ½ m. on A 683 ✆ 65999, Fax 841265, ₺, ≘s, ☒, ☞ – |♦| ⇔ rm ☑ ☎ ♿ ℗ – ♔ 120. ☒ AE ⦿ VISA JCB. ✻
Meals a la carte approx. 15.95 **t.** – ☐ 7.95 – **115 rm** 59.00 **st.**

Edenbreck House without rest., Sunnyside Lane, off Ashfield Av., LA1 5ED, by Westbourne Rd, near the station ✆ 32464, ☞ – ☑ ℗
5 rm ☐ 25.00/50.00.

at Carnforth N : 6 ¼ m. on A 6 – ☎ 01524 :

New Capernwray Farm ⑤, Capernwray, LA6 1AD, NE : 3 m. by B 6254 ✆ 734284, Fax 734284, ≤, « 17C former farmhouse », ☞ – ⇔ ☑ ℗. ☒ VISA JCB
Meals (communal dining) 18.50 **s.** – **3 rm** ☐ 36.00/62.00 **s.**

LANCING W. Sussex 404 S 31 – ☎ 01273.

♦London 59 – ♦Brighton 4 – ♦Southampton 53.

Sussex Pad, Old Shoreham Rd, BN15 0RH, E : 1 m. off A 27 ✆ 454647, Fax 453010 – ☑ ☎ ℗. ☒ AE ⦿ VISA JCB
Meals 14.00/16.50 **t.** and a la carte ₰ 5.50 – **19 rm** ☐ 56.00/72.00 **t.**

LANERCOST Cumbria 401 402 L 19 – see Brampton.

LANGHO Lancs. 402 M 22 - see Blackburn.

LANSALLOS Cornwall 403 G 32 – pop. 1 625 – ✉ Fowey – ☎ 01726.

♦London 273 – ♦Plymouth 30.

Carneggan House ⑤, Lanteglos-by-Fowey, PL23 1NW, NW : 2 m. on Polruan rd ✆ 870327, Fax 870327, ≤, ☞ – ☑ ℗. ☒ AE VISA
closed 22 to 28 December – **Meals** (by arrangement) 17.00/25.00 **st.** ₰ 3.00 – **3 rm** ☐ 25.00/54.00 **st.**

LARKFIELD Kent 404 V 30 – see Maidstone.

LASTINGHAM N. Yorks. 402 R 21 – pop. 87 – ✉ York – ☎ 01751.

♦London 244 – Scarborough 26 – York 32.

Lastingham Grange ⑤, YO6 6TH, ✆ 417345, ≤, « Country house atmosphere », ☞, park – ⇔ rest ☑ ☎ ℗. ✻
March-November – **Meals** (light lunch)/dinner 23.50 **t.** ₰ 4.50 – **12 rm** ☐ 67.75/125.75 **t.** – SB.

LAVENHAM Suffolk 404 W 27 **Great Britain G.** – pop. 1 693 – ✉ Sudbury – ☎ 01787.

See : Town★★ – Churchof SS. Peter and Paul★.

Lady St., CO10 9RA ✆ 248207 (summer only).

♦London 66 – ♦Cambridge 39 – Colchester 22 – ♦Ipswich 19.

Swan (Forte Heritage), High St., CO10 9QA, ✆ 247477, Fax 248286, « Part 14C timbered inn », ☞ ⇔ ☑ ☎ ℗ – ♔ 45. ☒ AE ⦿ VISA JCB
Meals 13.95/29.50 **t.** – ☐ 9.95 – **45 rm** 70.00/120.00 **t.**, 2 suites – SB.

Angel, Market Pl., CO10 9QZ, ✆ 247388, Fax 248344, « 15C inn », ☞ – ☑ ☎ ℗. ☒ AE VISA. ✻
closed 25 and 26 December – **Meals** a la carte 11.40/16.15 **t.** ₰ 3.95 – **8 rm** ☐ 37.50/50.00 **t.** – SB.

XX **Great House** with rm, Market Pl., CO10 9QZ, ✆ 247431, Fax 248007, « Part 14C timbered house » – ☑ ☎. ☒ AE VISA
closed 3 weeks January – **Meals** - French - *(closed Sunday dinner and Monday except Bank Holidays)* 16.95 **t.** (dinner) and a la carte 14.15/24.25 **t.** ₰ 6.90 – **1 rm** ☐ 50.00/68.00 **t.**, **3 suites** 60.00/80.00 **t.** – SB.

LEA Lancs. – see Preston.

LEAMINGTON SPA Warks. 403 404 P 27 – see Royal Leamington Spa.

LEDBURY Heref. and Worcs. 403 404 M 27 – pop. 5 119 – 01531.

1 Church Lane, HR8 1DH 636147.

London 119 – Hereford 14 – Newport 46 – Worcester 16.

Feathers, High St., HR8 1DS, 635266, Fax 632001, « Timbered 16C inn », squash – 120. AE VISA
Meals a la carte 14.40/28.40 **t.** – **11 rm** 59.50/95.00 **t.** – SB.

Wall Hills, Hereford Rd, HR8 2PR, 632833, – VISA
closed Christmas and New Year – **Meals** 16.75 **st.** 4.50 – **3 rm** 37.00/57.00 **st.** – SB.

Barn House, New St., HR8 2DX, 632825, « Part 17C House », – 30.
Meals (by arrangement) – **3 rm** 38.00/54.00 **st.** – SB.

at Wellington Heath N : 2 m. by B 4214 – Ledbury – 01531 :

Hope End, Hope End, HR8 1JQ, N : ¾ m. 633613, Fax 636366, « 18C house, restored Georgian gardens », park – rest VISA JCB.
closed mid December-first week February – **Meals** (booking essential) (dinner only) 30.00 **t.** 4.50 – **9 rm** 85.00/140.00 **t.** – SB.

at Bishops Frome NW : 8 m. on B 4214 – Worcester – 01531 :

Five Bridges, WR6 5BX, SW : 1¼ m.on A 4103 640340 – VISA JCB
Meals 10.50/15.00 **t.** and a la carte 15.70/24.65 **t.**

LEEDS W. Yorks. 402 P 22 **Great Britain G.** – pop. 680 722 – 0113.

See : City★ - City Art Gallery★ *AC* DZ **M.**

Envir. : Kirkstall Abbey★ *AC*, NW : 3 m. by A 65 BV – Templenewsam★ (decorative arts★) *AC*, E : 5 m. by A 64 and A 63 CX **D.**

Exc. : Harewood House★★ (The Gallery★) *AC*, N : 8 m. by A 61 CV.

18, 18 Temple Newsam, Temple Newsam Rd, Halton 264 5624 CV – 18 Gotts Park, Armley Ridge Rd, 234 2019 BV – 18 Middleton Park, Ring Rd, Beeston Park, Middleton 270 9506 CX – 18, 9 Moor Allerton, Coal Rd, Wike 266 1154 – 18 Howley Hall, Scotchman Lane, Morley (01924) 472432 – 9 Roundhay, Park Lane 266 2695, CV.

Leeds - Bradford Airport : 250 9696, NW : 8 m. by A 65 and A 658 BV.

The Arcade, City Station, LS1 1PL 247 8301/247 8302.

London 204 – Liverpool 75 – Manchester 43 – Newcastle upon Tyne 95 – Nottingham 74.

Plans on following pages

Oulton Hall (De Vere), Rothwell Lane, Oulton, LS26 8HN, SE : 5½ m. by A 61 and A 639 282 1000, Fax 282 8066, 18, squash – rest – 330. AE VISA CX **a**
Bronte : Meals *(closed Saturday lunch)* 12.95/23.45 **st.** and a la carte – **150 rm** 115.00/125.00 **st.**, 2 suites – SB.

Leeds Marriott, 4 Trevelyan Sq., Boar Lane, LS1 6ET, 236 6366, Fax 236 6367, – rm – 350. AE VISA DZ **x**
Dyson's : Meals 15.95 **st.** (lunch) and a la carte 15.00/18.50 **st.** – 11.25 – **241 rm** 89.00 **st.**, 3 suites – SB.

42 The Calls, 42 The Calls, LS2 7EW, 244 0099, Fax 234 4100, « Converted riverside grain mill » – rm – 55. AE VISA DZ **z**
closed 5 days at Christmas – **Meals** - (see ***Pool Court at 42*** below) (see also ***Brasserie Forty Four*** below) – 10.00 – **38 rm** 95.00/140.00 **st.**, 3 suites – SB.

Holiday Inn Crown Plaza, Wellington St., LS1 4DL, 244 2200, Fax 244 0460, – rm – 200. AE VISA JCB CZ **c**
Meals *(closed Saturday lunch)* 9.95/17.50 **st.** and a la carte 6.00 – 11.50 – **120 rm** 115.00 **st.**, 5 suites – SB.

Hilton National Leeds, Neville St., LS1 4BX, 244 2000, Telex 557143, Fax 243 3577, – rm – 300. AE VISA JCB DZ **r**
Meals 9.50/17.95 **st.** and a la carte 4.25 – 10.50 – **186 rm** 93.00 **st.**, 20 suites – SB.

Queen's (Forte), City Sq., LS1 1PL, 243 1323, Fax 242 5154 – rm – 600. AE VISA JCB DZ **a**
Meals 10.50/19.50 **st.** and a la carte – 11.50 – **182 rm** 75.00/100.00 **t.**, 6 suites – SB.

Weetwood Hall, Otley Rd, LS16 5PS, NW : 4 m. on A 660 230 6000, Fax 230 6095, – rest – 150 BV **c**
108 rm.

Haley's, Shire Oak Rd, Headingley, LS6 2DE, NW : 2 m. off Otley Rd (A 660) 278 4446, Fax 275 3342 – – 25. AE VISA CV **s**
closed 26 to 30 December – **Meals** *(closed Sunday dinner to non-residents)* (dinner only) (Sunday lunch September-May) a la carte 18.45/23.90 **st.** 5.10 – **22 rm** 95.00/112.00 **st.** – SB.

Metropole, King St., LS1 2HQ, 245 0841, Fax 242 5156 – rm – 200. AE VISA CZ **e**
Meals *(closed Saturday lunch)* 12.95/16.95 **t.** and dinner a la carte 6.50 – 8.50 – **81 rm** 78.00/120.00 **st.** – SB.

Merrion Thistle, Merrion Centre, 17 Wade Lane, LS2 8NH, ✆ 243 9191, Fax 242 3527 – rest – 80. DZ **e**
Meals 14.75 **t.** and a la carte 8.75 – 8.75 – **108 rm** 79.00/89.00 **t.**, 1 suite – SB.

Golden Lion (Mount Charlotte), 2 Lower Briggate, LS1 4AE, ✆ 243 6454, Fax 242 9327 – rm – 120. DZ **v**
Meals *(closed lunch Sunday and Bank Holidays)* 8.95/13.95 **st.** and dinner a la carte 4.60 – **89 rm** 85.00/95.00 **st.** – SB.

Aragon, 250 Stainbeck Lane, LS7 2PS, ✆ 275 9306, Fax 275 7166, – . CV **c**
closed 24 December-2 January – **Meals** 10.50 **st.** and a la carte – **13 rm** 39.75/47.50 **st.**

Pinewood, 78 Potternewton Lane, LS7 3LW, ✆ 262 2561, Fax 262 2561, – rest . . AY **a**
Meals (by arrangement) 9.50 **t.** – **10 rm** 35.00/42.00 **t.** – SB.

Ash Mount without rest., 22 Wetherby Rd, Oakwood, LS8 2QD, ✆ 265 8164, Fax 265 8164, – . CV **u**
11 rm 21.00/44.00 **st.**

Pool Court at 42 (at 42 The Calls H.), 42-44 The Calls, LS2 8AQ, ✆ 244 4242, Fax 234 3332, , « Riverside setting » – DZ **z**
closed Saturday lunch, Sunday and Bank Holidays – **Meals** 22.00/26.50 **t.** 7.80
Spec. Whitby crab ravioli scented with basil, sauce vierge, Loin of venison with deep fried polenta, asparagus and balsamic dressing, Orange and ginger bavarois with passion fruit sorbet.

Leodis Brasserie, Victoria Mill, Sovereign St., LS1 4BJ, ✆ 242 1010, Fax 243 0432 – . AZ **e**
closed Saturday lunch, Sunday, 25 to 26 December and 1 January – **Meals** 11.95 **t.** and a la carte 14.55/25.55 **t.** 5.50.

Rascasse, Canal Wharf, Water Lane , LS11 5BB, ✆ 244 6611, Fax 244 0736, ← – . Z **e**
closed Saturday lunch – **Meals** 13.00 **t.** (lunch) and a la carte 17.50/25.75 **t.** 6.00.

Brasserie Forty Four (at 42 The Calls H.), 42-44 The Calls, LS2 8AQ, ✆ 234 3232, Fax 234 3332 – . DZ **z**
closed Saturday lunch, Sunday, 5 days at Christmas and Bank Holidays – **Meals** 11.95 **t.** (lunch) and a la carte 14.15/23.15 **t.** 7.90.

Maxi's, 6 Bingley St., LS3 1LX, off Kirkstall Rd ✆ 244 0552, Fax 234 3902, « Pagoda, ornate decor » – . AZ **a**
Meals - Chinese (Canton, Peking) - 16.00 **t.**

Lucky Dragon, Templar Lane, LS2 7LP, ✆ 245 0520, Fax 245 0520 – . DZ **u**
closed 25 and 26 December – **Meals** - Chinese (Cantonese) - 14.00/15.00 **st.** and a la carte 4.50.

Hereford Beefstouw, Calls Landing, 38 The Calls, LS2 7EW, ✆ 245 3870, Fax 243 9035, « Converted riverside warehouse » – . DZ **c**
Meals (grill rest.) a la carte 12.90/28.00 **st.** 5.75.

Sous le nez en ville, Quebec House, Quebec St., LS1 2HA, ✆ 244 0108, Fax 245 0240 – CZ **a**
closed Saturday lunch, Sunday and Bank Holidays – **Meals** 13.95 **st.** (dinner) and a la carte 13.05/23.85 **st.**

La Grillade, 31-33 East Par., LS1 5PS, ✆ 245 9707, Fax 242 6112 – . CZ **n**
closed Sunday – **Meals** - French Brasserie - 9.25 **t.** and a la carte 3.95.

at Seacroft NE : 5½ m. at junction of A 64 with A 6120 – ✉ Leeds – 0113 :

Stakis Leeds, Ring Rd, LS14 5QF, ✆ 273 2323, Fax 232 3018 – rm rest – 250. CV **a**
Meals *(closed lunch Saturday and Bank Holidays)* 9.50/15.25 **st.** and dinner a la carte 4.50 – 8.50 – **100 rm** 75.00/85.00 **st.** – SB.

at Garforth E : 6 m. by A 63 – CV – at junction with A 642 – ✉ Leeds – 0113 :

Hilton National, Wakefield Rd, LS25 1LH, ✆ 286 6556, Fax 286 8326, , , – rm rest – 350.
Meals *(closed Saturday lunch)* (carving lunch) 10.50/17.00 **st.** and a la carte 5.35 – 10.25 – **144 rm** 82.50/105.00 **st.** – SB.

Aagrah, Aberford Rd, LS25 1BA, on A 642 ✆ 287 6606 – .
closed 25 December – **Meals** - Indian - (dinner only) a la carte 10.60/17.50 **t.** 4.00.

at Pudsey W : 5¾ m. by A 647 – ✉ Leeds – 01274 :

Aagrah, 483 Bradford Rd, LS28 8ED, on A 647 ✆ 668818, Fax 668818 – . BV **e**
closed 25 December – **Meals** - Indian - (dinner only and Sunday lunch)/dinner a la carte 10.60/17.50 **t.** 4.00.

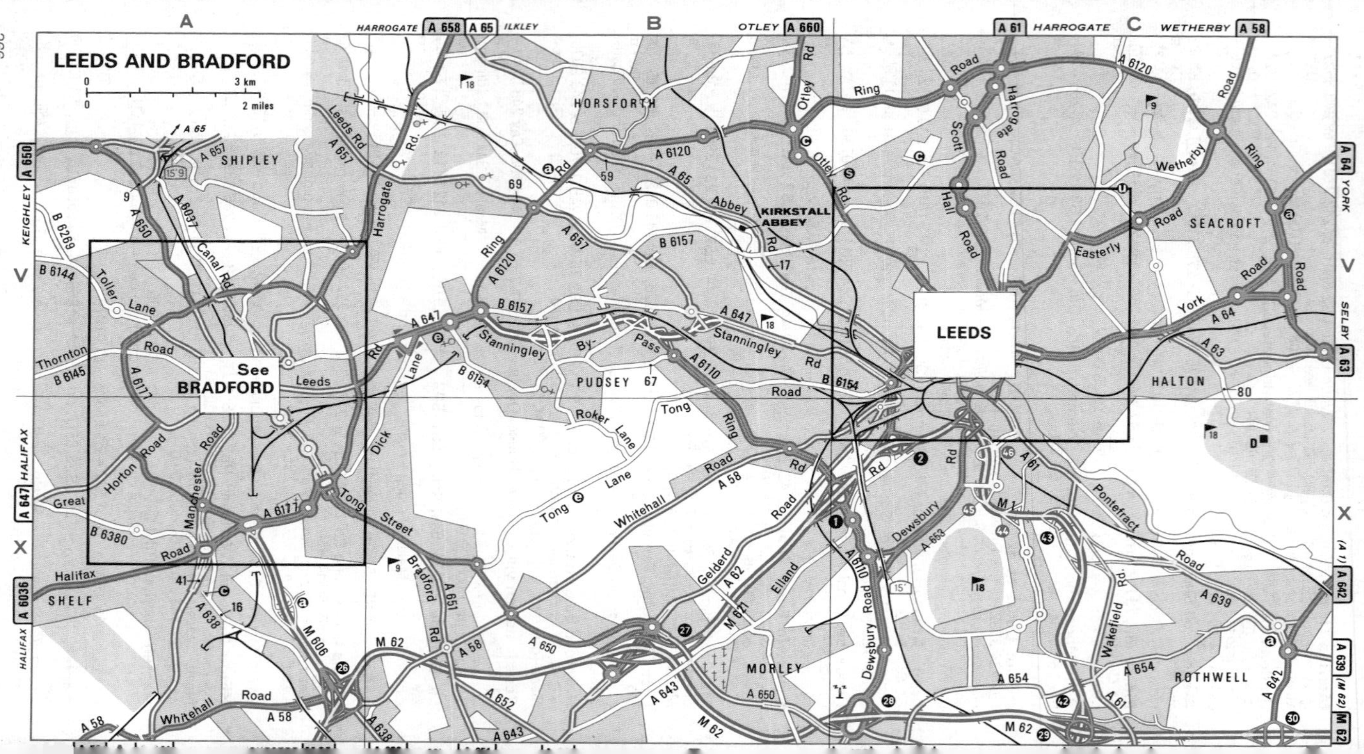
LEEDS AND BRADFORD
0 3 km
0 2 miles
A
B
C
V
X
HARROGATE A 658
A 65 ILKLEY
OTLEY A 660
A 61 HARROGATE
WETHERBY A 58
A 64 YORK
SELBY A 63
(A 1) A 642
A 639 (M 62)
M 62
KEIGHLEY A 650
HALIFAX A 647
HALIFAX A 6036
SHIPLEY
HORSFORTH
KIRKSTALL ABBEY
SEACROFT
HALTON
PUDSEY
MORLEY
ROTHWELL
SHELF
LEEDS
See BRADFORD

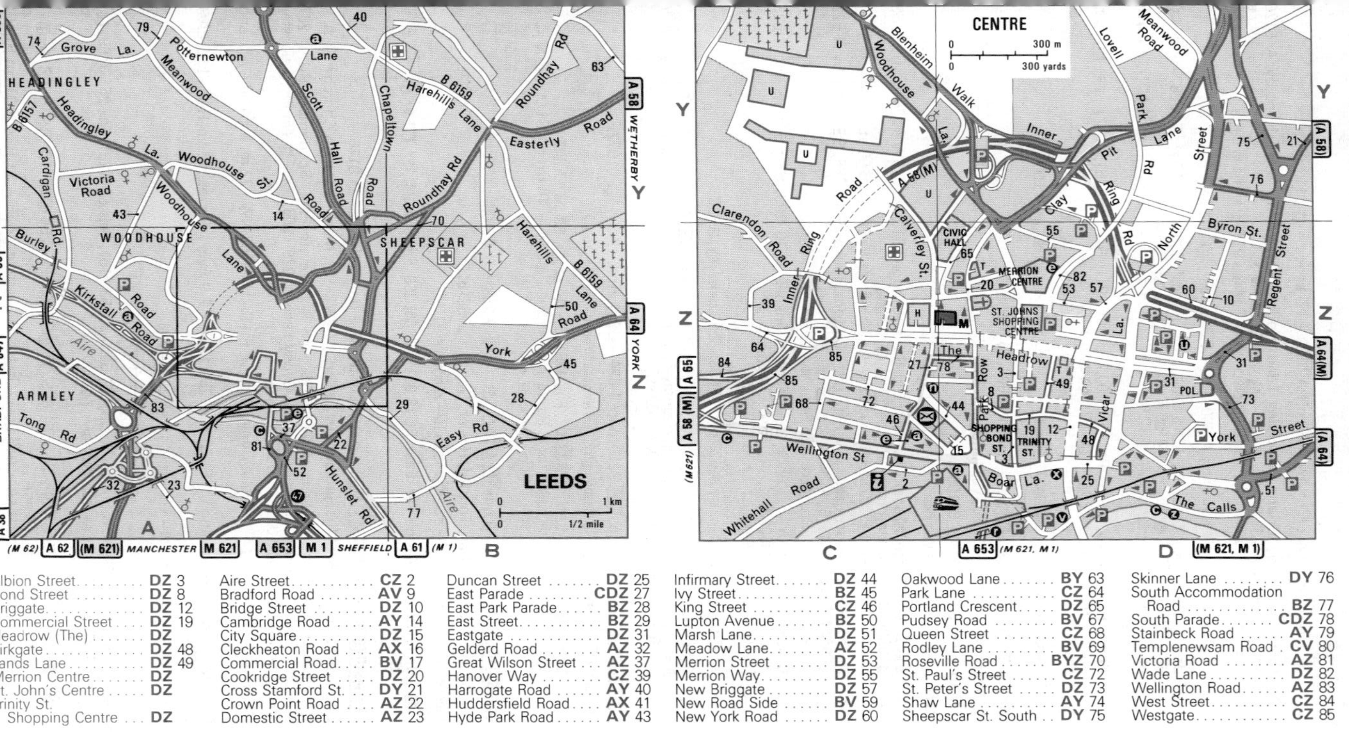
LEEDS
CENTRE
0 300 m
0 300 yards
0 1 km
0 1/2 mile
HEADINGLEY
WOODHOUSE
SHEEPSCAR
ARMLEY
A 660 SKIPTON
A 65 ILKLEY
A 647 BRADFORD
A 38
(M 62) A 62 (M 621) MANCHESTER M 621 A 653 M 1 SHEFFIELD A 61 (M 1)
A 58 WETHERBY
A 64 YORK
A 64 (M)
(M 621, M 1)
CIVIC HALL
MERRION CENTRE
ST. JOHNS SHOPPING CENTRE
SHOPPING BOND ST.
TRINITY ST.
POL
Headingley La.
Woodhouse La.
Woodhouse St.
Potternewton Lane
Scott Hall Road
Chapeltown Road
Harehills Lane
Roundhay Rd
Easterly Road
Kirkstall Road
York Road
Hunslet Rd
Easy Rd
Tong Rd
Wellington St
Whitehall Road
Clarendon Road
Inner Ring Road
Calverley St.
The Headrow
Park Row
Vicar La.
Boar La.
The Calls
York Street
Regent Street
North Street
Byron St.
Blenheim Walk
Aire

at Horsforth NW : 5 m. by A 65 off A 6120 – ✉ Leeds – ☎ 0113 :

✗ **Paris,** Calverley Bridge, Calverley Lane, Rodley, LS13 1NP, SW : 1 m. by A 6120 ☎ 258 1885, Fax 239 0651 – ▤ 🅟 – 🏛 40. ⚀ AE ⓓ VISA BV **a**
closed Saturday lunch and 26 to 28 December – **Meals** 9.95 **t.** and a la carte.

at Bramhope NW : 8 m. on A 660 – BV – ✉ Leeds – ☎ 0113 :

Jarvis Parkway, Otley Rd, LS16 8AG, S : 2 m. on A 660 ☎ 267 2551, Fax 267 4410, ⚲, ≘s, ⛶, ⌘, ✂ – ⎇ ⇆ rm ▣ ☎ ♿ 🅟 – 🏛 250. ⚀ AE ⓓ VISA
Meals *(closed Saturday lunch)* 12.95/14.95 **st.** and dinner a la carte – ☐ 8.50 – **105 rm** 95.00 **st.** – SB.

Forte Posthouse, Leeds Rd, LS16 9JJ, ☎ 284 2911, Fax 284 3451, ←, ⚲, ≘s, ⛶, ⌘, park – ⎇ ⇆ rm ▣ ☎ 🅟 – 🏛 160. ⚀ AE ⓓ VISA JCB
Meals 7.95 **st.** and a la carte 🍷 6.95 – ☐ 7.95 – **123 rm** 69.00 **t.**, 1 suite – SB.

ATS Cross Green Lane ☎ 245 9423 — ATS 2 Regent St. ☎ 243 0652

LEEK Staffs. 402 403 404 N 24 – pop. 19 850 – ☎ 01538.

⛳18 Westwood, Newcastle Rd, Wallbridge ☎ 398385.

ℹ Market Pl., ST13 5HH ☎ 381000.

♦London 122 – Derby 30 – ♦Manchester 39 – ♦Stoke-on-Trent 12.

Bank End Farm Motel ⛰, Leek Old Rd, Longsdon, ST9 9QJ, SW : 2 ½ m. by A 53 ☎ 383638, « Working farm », ⛶ – ▣ ☎ 🅟. ⚀ VISA
Meals (dinner only) 17.50 **st.** and a la carte 🍷 4.95 – **9 rm** ☐ 28.00/46.00 **st.**

Pethills Bank Cottage ⛰ without rest., Bottom House, ST13 7PF, SE : 6 m. by A 523 ☎ 304277, Fax 304575, ←, ⌘ – ⇆ ▣ 🅟. ✻
closed Christmas and January-28 February – **3 rm** ☐ 31.00/42.00.

Country Cottage ⛰, Back Lane Farm, Winkhill, ST13 7PJ, SE : 5 ½ m. by A 523 ☎ 308273, Fax 308098, ←, ⌘, park – ⇆ ▣ 🅟. ✻
Meals 11.50 **st.** – **4 rm** ☐ 19.50/37.00 **st.**

at Butterton E : 8 m. by A 523 off B 5053 – ✉ Leek – ☎ 01538 :

Black Lion Inn, ST13 7ST, ☎ 304232, « 18C inn », ⌘ – ▣ 🅟. ⚀ AE VISA. ✻
Meals (in bar except Friday and Saturday dinner and Sunday lunch)/dinner a la carte 11.00/20.15 **st.** 🍷 4.95 – **3 rm** ☐ 30.00/47.00 **st.**

LEEMING BAR N. Yorks. 402 P 21 – pop. 1 824 – ✉ Northallerton – ☎ 01677.

♦London 235 – ♦Leeds 44 – ♦Middlesbrough 30 – ♦Newcastle upon Tyne 52 – York 37.

White Rose, DL7 9AY, ☎ 422707, Fax 425123 – ▣ ☎ 🅟. ⚀ AE ⓓ VISA
Meals (bar lunch)/dinner 7.75/11.95 **st.** and a la carte 🍷 3.90 – **18 rm** ☐ 31.00/45.00 **st.** – SB.

LEE-ON-THE-SOLENT Hants. 403 404 Q 31 – pop. 7 259 – ☎ 01705.

⛳9 Gosport & Stokes Bay, Fort Rd, Haslar, Gosport ☎ 581625.

♦London 81 – ♦Portsmouth 13 – ♦Southampton 15 – Winchester 23.

Belle Vue, 39 Marine Par. East, PO13 9BW, ☎ 550258, Fax 552624, ← – ▣ ☎ 🅟
27 rm.

LEICESTER Leics. 402 403 404 Q 26 Great Britain G. – pop. 318 518 – ☎ 0116.

See : Guildhall★ BY **B** – Museum and Art Gallery★ CY **M2** – St. Mary de Castro Church★ BY **A**.

⛳18 Leicestershire, Evington Lane ☎ 273 6035, AY – ⛳18 Western Park, Scudamore Rd ☎ 287 6158/287 2339 – ⛳18 Humberstone Heights, Gypsy Lane ☎ 276 1905, AX – ⛳18 Oadby, Leicester Road Racecourse ☎ 270 0215/270 9052, AY.

✈ East Midlands Airport, Castle Donington : ☎ (01332) 852852 NW : 22 m. by A 50 – AX - and M1.

ℹ St. Margaret's Bus Station, LE1 3TY ☎ 251 1301 – 7-9 Every Street, Town Hall , LE1 6AG ☎ 265 0555.

♦London 107 – ♦Birmingham 43 – ♦Coventry 24 – ♦Nottingham 26.

Plans on following pages

Holiday Inn, 129 St. Nicholas Circle, LE1 5LX, ☎ 253 1161, Telex 341281, Fax 251 3169, ⚲, ≘s, ⛶ – ⎇ ⇆ rm ▤ ▣ ☎ ♿ 🅟 – 🏛 250 BY **c**
187 rm, 1 suite.

Grand (Jarvis), 73 Granby St., LE1 6ES, ☎ 255 5599, Fax 254 4736 – ⎇ ⇆ rm ▣ ☎ 🅟 – 🏛 450. ⚀ AE ⓓ VISA JCB CY **o**
Meals *(closed Saturday lunch)* 9.95/14.95 **t.** and a la carte 🍷 6.95 – ☐ 8.50 – **91 rm** 81.50/96.50 **t.**, 1 suite – SB.

Belmont House, De Montfort St., LE1 7GR, ✆ 254 4773, Fax 247 0804 – 🛗 ⇔ rm 📺 ☎ 🅟 – 🏛 100. 🅢 AE ⓓ VISA JCB. ✂ CY **c**
closed 25 to 28 December – **Meals** *(closed lunch Saturday)* 11.50/18.50 **t.** and a la carte 🍷 5.75 – ☕ 8.50 – **65 rm** 65.00/83.00 **st.** – SB.

Spindle Lodge, 2 West Walk, LE1 7NA, ✆ 233 8801, Fax 233 8804 – ⇔ rest 📺 ☎ 🅟. 🅢 VISA JCB CY **r**
closed 21 December-1 January – **Meals** (by arrangement) 12.00 **st.** – **13 rm** ☕ 26.50/59.50 **st.**

Scotia, 10 Westcotes Drive, LE3 0QR, ✆ 254 9200, Fax 254 9200 – 📺 AY **c**
Meals (by arrangement) 8.45 **st.** 🍷 4.25 – **11 rm** ☕ 27.00/42.00 **st.**

Welford Place, 9 Welford Place, LE1 6ZH, ✆ 247 0758, Fax 247 1843 – 🅢 AE ⓓ VISA CY **s**
Meals 10.50/15.00 **st.** and a la carte 🍷 8.05.

Man Ho, 14-16 King St., LE1 6RJ, ✆ 255 7700, Fax 254 5629 – 🅢 AE VISA CY **u**
Meals - Chinese – 6.50/18.00 **t.** and a la carte.

Curry Pot, 78-80 Belgrave Rd, LE4 5AS, ✆ 253 8256, Fax 262 5125 – 🅢 AE ⓓ VISA AX **e**
closed Sunday – **Meals** - Indian - a la carte 13.95/23.60 **t.** 🍷 5.35.

Curry House, 64 London Rd, LE2 0QD, ✆ 255 0688. 🅢 AE ⓓ VISA CY **e**
closed Sunday – **Meals** - Indian - 10.00/30.00 **t.** and a la carte 🍷 3.65.

LEICESTER

BUILT UP AREA

Asquith Way .... **AY** 2
Belgrave Road .... **AX** 4
Braunstone Avenue .... **AY** 10
Braunstone Lane East .... **AY** 13
Braunstone Way .... **AY** 14
Checketts Road .... **AX** 17
Fosse Road North .... **AX** 22
Fullhurst Avenue .... **AY** 23
Glenfrith Way .... **AX** 24
Henley Road .... **AX** 29
Humberstone Road .... **AX** 34
King Richards Road .... **AY** 37
Knighton Road .... **AY** 38
Loughborough Road .... **AX** 40
Marfitt Street .... **AX** 41
Middleton Street .... **AY** 44
Stoughton Road .... **AY** 66
Upperton Road .... **AY** 68
Walnut Street .... **AY** 69
Wigston Lane .... **AY** 75
Woodville Road .... **AY** 76
Wyngate Drive .... **AY** 78

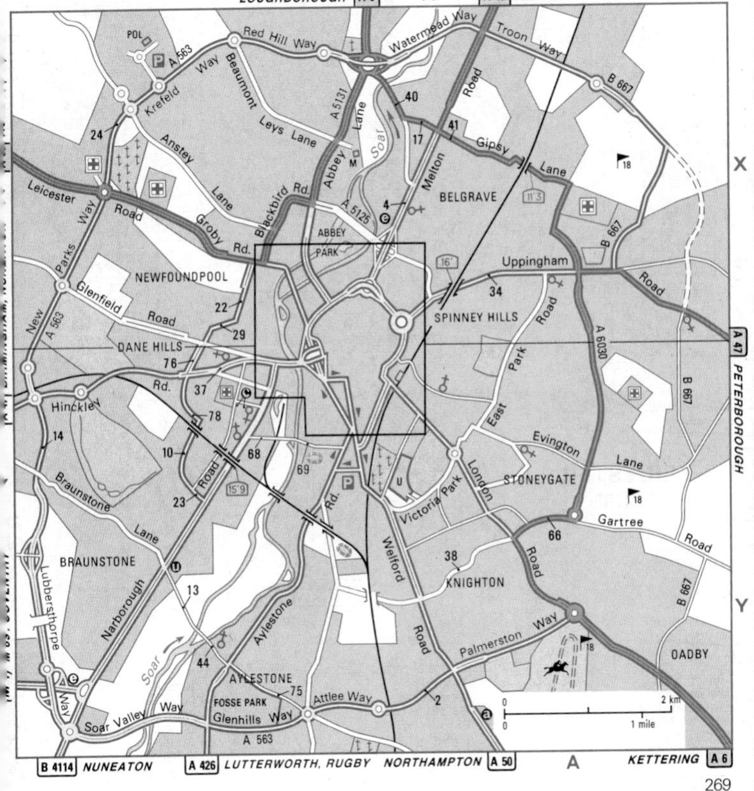

at Rothley N : 5 m. by A 6 – AX – on B 5328 – ✉ Leicester – ☎ 0116 :

Rothley Court (Forte Heritage) ⛵, Westfield Lane, LE7 7LG, W : ½ m. on B 5328 ☎ 237 4141, Fax 237 4483, ≤, « Part 13C house and 11C chapel », 🌳 – 🚭 TV ☎ P – 🏛 100. AE ⓓ VISA
Meals *(closed Saturday lunch)* 15.95/25.00 **st.** and a la carte 🍷 7.55 – ☕ 8.75 – **34 rm** 75.00/85.00, 1 suite – SB.

Limes, 35 Mountsorrel Lane, LE7 7PS, ☎ 230 2531 – 🚭 rest ▤ TV ☎ P. AE VISA JCB. ✻
closed 23 December-2 January – **Meals** (residents only) (dinner only) 7.00/15.00 **st.** and a la carte 🍷 4.95 – **11 rm** ☕ 39.50/55.00 **st.**

at Thrussington NE : 10 m. by A 46 – AX – ✉ Leicester – ☎ 01664 :

Forte Travelodge, Green Acres Filling Station, LE7 8TF, on A 46 (southbound carriageway) ☎ 424525, Reservations (Freephone) 0800 850950 – TV ♿ P. AE VISA. ✻
Meals (grill rest.) – **32 rm** 34.50 **t.**

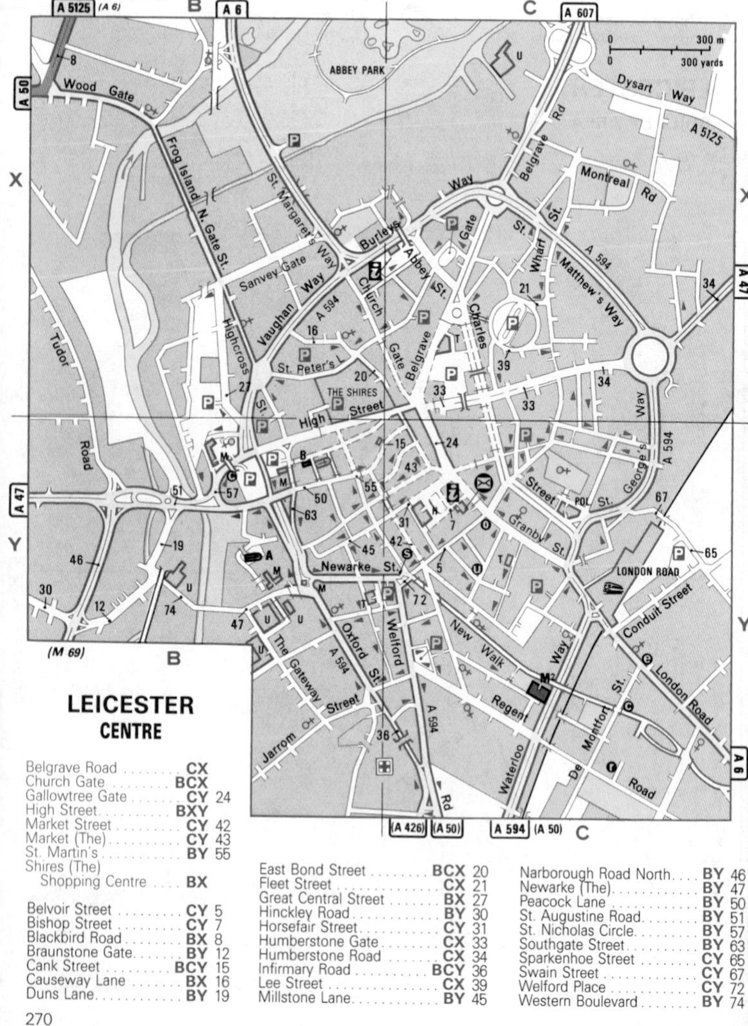

Belgrave Road CX
Church Gate . . . . . BCX
Gallowtree Gate . . . . . CY 24
High Street . . . . . BXY
Market Street . . . . . CY 42
Market (The) . . . . . CY 43
St. Martin's . . . . . BY 55
Shires (The) Shopping Centre . . . . BX

Belvoir Street . . . . . CY 5
Bishop Street . . . . . CY 7
Blackbird Road . . . . . BX 8
Braunstone Gate . . . . . BY 12
Cank Street . . . . . BCY 15
Causeway Lane . . . . . BX 16
Duns Lane . . . . . BY 19
East Bond Street . . . . . BCX 20
Fleet Street . . . . . CX 21
Great Central Street . . . . . BX 27
Hinckley Road . . . . . BY 30
Horsefair Street . . . . . CY 31
Humberstone Gate . . . . . CX 33
Humberstone Road . . . . . CX 34
Infirmary Road . . . . . BCY 36
Lee Street . . . . . CX 39
Millstone Lane . . . . . BY 45
Narborough Road North . . . . BY 46
Newarke (The) . . . . . BY 47
Peacock Lane . . . . . BY 50
St. Augustine Road . . . . . BY 51
St. Nicholas Circle . . . . . BY 57
Southgate Street . . . . . BY 63
Sparkenhoe Street . . . . . CY 65
Swain Street . . . . . CY 67
Welford Place . . . . . CY 72
Western Boulevard . . . . . BY 74

at Wigston Fields SE : 3 ¼ m. on A 50 – ✉ Leicester – ☎ 0116 :

Stage, 299 Leicester Rd, LE18 1JW, ℰ 288 6161, Fax 281 1874, Ⅰ₆, ≘s, ▢ – ⇹ rm ▤ rest ▢ ☎ ♿ ℗ – 🏟 250. ▢ AE ◑ VISA JCB. ✻ AY a
Meals 8.95/13.95 **st.** and a la carte 🍾 6.95 – **71 rm** ☐ 67.00/85.00 **st.** – SB.

at Braunstone SW : 2 m. on A 46 – ✉ Leicester – ☎ 0116 :

Stakis Leicester, LE3 2WQ, SW : 1 ¾ m. by A 46 ℰ 263 0066, Fax 263 0627, Ⅰ₆, ≘s, ▢, ⛲ – ⇹ rm ▤ rest ▢ ☎ ♿ ℗ – 🏟 200. ▢ AE ◑ VISA AY e
Meals (bar lunch Saturday) 12.95/17.95 **st.** and a la carte 🍾 8.00 – ☐ 8.95 – **130 rm** 92.00/102.00 **t.**, 10 suites – SB.

Forte Posthouse, Braunstone Lane East, LE3 2FW, ℰ 263 0500, Fax 282 3623 – 🛗 ⇹ rm ▤ rest ▢ ☎ ℗ – 🏟 80. ▢ AE ◑ VISA JCB AY u
Meals a la carte 13.35/24.20 **st.** – ☐ 7.95 – **165 rm** 59.00 **st.** – SB.

at Leicester Forest East W : 3 m. on A 47 – AY – ✉ Leicester – ☎ 0116 :

Red Cow, Hinckley Rd, LE3 3PG, ℰ 238 7878, Fax 238 6539 – ⇹ rm ▢ ☎ ♿ ℗. ▢ AE ◑ VISA. ✻
Meals (grill rest.) 7.25 **st.** (lunch) and a la carte 8.50/13.45 🍾 4.10 – ☐ 4.95 – **31 rm** 39.50 **st.**

Travel Inn, Hinckley Rd, LE3 3GD, ℰ 239 4677, Fax 239 3429 – ⇹ rm ▢ ♿ ℗. ▢ AE ◑ VISA
Meals (grill rest.) – ☐ 4.95 – **40 rm** 34.50 **t.**

ATS 16 Wanlip St. ℰ 262 4281 — ATS 31 Woodgate ℰ 262 5611

LEIGH DELAMERE SERVICE AREA Wilts. – ✉ Chippenham – ☎ 01666.

Granada Lodge without rest., SN14 6LB, M 4 between junctions 18 and 17 (eastbound carriageway) ℰ 837691, Fax 837112, Reservations (Freephone) 0800 555300 – ⇹ ▢ ☎ ♿ ℗. ▢ AE VISA. ✻
– **51 rm** 39.95 **st.**

LEIGHTON BUZZARD Beds. 404 S 28 – pop. 32 610 – ☎ 01525.

⛳ Plantation Rd ℰ 373811/373812 – ⛳ Aylesbury Vale, Wing ℰ 240196.

♦London 47 – Bedford 20 – Luton 12 – Northampton 30.

Grove farm ⛰, Grove, LU7 0QU, S : 3 ½ m. by A 4146, A 505 and B 488 on Grove Church rd ℰ 372225, Fax 854565, ⩽, ≘s, ▢, ⛲, park – ⇹ ▢ ℗. ▢ AE VISA. ✻
Meals (communal dining) (dinner only) 15.00/20.00 **st.** – **3 rm** ☐ 35.00/70.00 **st.**

ATS Grovebury Road ℰ 376158

LEINTWARDINE Shrops. 403 L 26 – ✉ Craven Arms – ☎ 01547.

♦London 156 – ♦Birmingham 55 – Hereford 24 – Worcester 40.

Upper Buckton Farm ⛰, Buckton, SY7 0JU, W : 2 m. by A 4113 and Buckton rd ℰ 540634, ⩽, « Working farm », ⛲ – ⇹ ℗. ✻
Meals (by arrangement) 16.00 **st.** – **3 rm** ☐ 20.00/40.00 – SB.

LEISTON Suffolk 404 Y 27 – ☎ 01728.

♦London 110 – ♦Cambridge 78 – ♦Ipswich 31 – ♦Norwich 38.

Theberton Grange Country House ⛰, Theberton, IP16 4RR, N : 2½ m. by B 1122 off Kelsale rd ℰ 830625, ⛲ – ⇹ ▢ ℗. ▢ AE ◑ VISA. ✻
Meals (residents only) (dinner only) 15.00 **st.** 🍾 4.00 – **6 rm** ☐ 30.00/70.00 **st.**

LENHAM Kent 404 W 30 pop. 3 103 – ✉ Maidstone – ☎ 01622.

♦London 45 – Folkestone 28 – Maidstone 9.

Lime Tree with rm, 8-10 The Limes, The Square, ME17 2PQ, ℰ 859509, Fax 850096 – ▢ ☎. ▢ AE ◑ VISA. ✻
Meals *(closed Sunday dinner and Monday lunch except Bank Holidays)* 10.95/19.95 **t.** and a la carte 🍾 8.50 – **7 rm** ☐ 37.50/47.50 **st.**

LEOMINSTER Heref. and Worcs. 403 L 27 **Great Britain G.** – pop. 10 037 – ☎ 01568.

Envir. : Berrington Hall★ *AC*, N : 3 m. by A 49.

⛳ Ford Bridge ℰ 612863.

ℹ 1 Corn Square, HR6 8LR ℰ 616460 (summer only).

♦London 141 – ♦Birmingham 47 – Hereford 13 – Worcester 26.

Talbot, West St., HR6 8EP, ℰ 616347, Fax 614880 – ▢ ☎ ℗ – 🏟 100. ▢ AE ◑ VISA JCB
Meals 10.00/15.50 **t.** and a la carte 🍾 6.10 – **20 rm** ☐ 45.00/64.00 **t.** – SB.

Heath House ⛰, Humber, Stoke Prior, HR6 0NF, SE : 3 ¾ m. by A 44 on Risbury rd ℰ 760385 – ℗. ✻
March-November – **Meals** (by arrangement) (communal dining) 12.00/17.00 **st.** 🍾 3.00 – **3 rm** ☐ 17.00/44.00 **st.**

at Bodenham E : 1 ¼ m. on A 417 – ✉ Hereford – ☎ 0156 884 :

Maund Court, HR1 3JA, E : 1 ¼ m. on A 417 ☎ 797282, heated, – TV P
March-October – **Meals** (by arrangement) 12.00/14.00 **st.** – **4 rm** 18.00/36.00 **st.**

at Eyton NW : 2 m. by B 4361 – ✉ Leominster – ☎ 01568 :

The Marsh, HR6 0AG, ☎ 613952, « Part 14C timbered house », – TV ☎ P. AE VISA.
closed January – **Meals** (dinner only and Sunday lunch)/dinner 19.95 **st.** 9.50 – **4 rm** 80.00/110.00 **st.** – SB.

ATS Market Mill, Dishley St. ☎ 612679/614114

LETCHWORTH Herts. 404 T28 – pop. 20 626 – ☎ 01462.

◆London 40 – Bedford 22 – ◆Cambridge 22 – Luton 14.

Broadway Toby, The Broadway, SG6 3NZ, ☎ 480111, Fax 481563 – rm TV ☎ P – 180. AE VISA.
Meals (grill rest.) 7.90 **t.** and a la carte – **35 rm** 51.95/61.95 **st.** – SB.

ATS Unit 21, Jubilee Trade Centre, Works Rd ☎ 670517

LEW Oxon. 403 404 P 28 pop. 59 – ✉ Oxford – ☎ 01993.

◆London 68 – Gloucester 36 – ◆Oxford 14.

Farmhouse, University Farm, OX18 2AU, ☎ 850297, Fax 850965, – TV ☎ P. VISA.
closed Christmas and New Year – **Meals** *(closed Sunday)* (residents only Monday to Thursday) (dinner only) 19.00 – **6 rm** 35.00/60.00 **s.** – SB.

LEWDOWN Devon 403 H 32 The West Country G. – ☎ 01566.

Envir. : Lydford★★ (Lydford Gorge★★) E : 4 m..

Exc. : Launceston★ - Castle★ (≤★) St. Mary Magdalene★, South Gate★, W : 8 m. by A 30 and A 388.

◆London 238 – Exeter 37 – ◆Plymouth 22.

Lewtrenchard Manor, EX20 4PN, S : ¾ m. by Lewtrenchard rd ☎ 783256, Fax 783332, « 17C manor house and gardens », park – rest TV ☎ P – 50. AE VISA
Meals (lunch by arrangement Monday to Saturday)/dinner 16.00/32.00 **t.** 5.00 – **8 rm** 75.00/140.00 **t.** – SB.

LEWES E. Sussex 404 U 31 Great Britain G. – pop. 15 376 – ☎ 01273.

See : Town★ (High Street★, Keere Street★) – Castle (≤★) *AC.*

Exc. : Sheffield Park Garden★ *AC,* N : 9½m. by A 275.

18 Chapel Hill ☎ 473245.

187 High St., BN7 2DE ☎ 483448.

◆London 53 – Brighton 8 – Hastings 29 – Maidstone 43.

Millers without rest., 134 High St., BN7 1XS, ☎ 475631, – TV.
closed 5 November and 20 December-5 January – **3 rm** 43.00/48.00 **s.**

Hillside without rest., Rotten Row, BN7 1TN, ☎ 473120, – .
3 rm 20.00/40.00 **s.**

Pailin, 20 Station St., BN7 2DB, ☎ 473906 – AE VISA JCB
closed Sunday and 25 to 26 December – **Meals** - Thai - a la carte 9.45/17.95 **t.**

ATS 18 North St. ☎ 477972/3

LICHFIELD Staffs. 402 403 404 O 25 Great Britain G. – pop. 28 666 – ☎ 01543.

See : City★ - Cathedral★★ *AC.*

18, 9 Seedy Mill, Elmhurst ☎ 417333.

Donegal House, Bore St., WS13 6NE ☎ 252109.

◆London 128 – ◆Birmingham 16 – Derby 23 – ◆Stoke-on-Trent 30.

Little Barrow, Beacon St., WS13 7AR, ☎ 414500, Fax 415734 – TV ☎ P – 100. AE VISA.
Meals 9.00/12.50 **st.** and a la carte 4.25 – **24 rm** 45.00/60.00 **st.** – SB.

Thrales, 40-44 Tamworth St., WS13 6JJ, (corner of Backcester Lane) ☎ 255091.

ATS Eastern Av. ☎ 414200

En saison, *surtout dans les stations fréquentées, il est prudent de retenir à l'avance. Cependant, si vous ne pouvez pas occuper la chambre que vous avez retenue, prévenez immédiatement l'hôtelier.*

Si vous écrivez à un hôtel à l'étranger, joignez à votre lettre un coupon-réponse international (disponible dans les bureaux de poste).

LIFTON Devon 403 H 32 **The West Country G.** – pop. 964 – ☎ 01566.

Envir. : Launceston★ - Castle★ (<★) St. Mary Magdalene★, South Gate★, W : 4½m. by A 30 and A 388.

London 238 – Bude 24 – Exeter 37 – Launceston 4 – ◆Plymouth 32.

- **Lifton Hall,** PL16 0DR, ☎ 784863, Fax 784770 – rest. – **Meals** (bar lunch) – (see ***Herbs*** below) – **11 rm** 56.00/100.00 **st.** – SB.
- **Arundell Arms,** Fore St., PL16 0AA, ☎ 784666, Fax 784494, – rest – 100. *closed 3 days Christmas* – **Meals** 16.50/30.75 **t.** 5.50 – **29 rm** 61.00/97.00 **st.** – SB.
- **Thatched Cottage**, Sprytown, PL16 0AY, E : 1 ¼ m. by old A 30 ☎ 784224, Fax 784334, – rest. **Meals** 19.50/21.50 **st.** (dinner) and lunch a la carte 9.70/15.00 **t.** 5.70 – **5 rm** 35.00/90.00 **t.** – SB.
- XX **Herbs** (at Lifton Hall H.), PL16 0DR, ☎ 784863, Fax 784770 *closed Sunday and Monday* – **Meals** (dinner only) 21.00 **st.** and a la carte 5.50.

LIMPLEY STOKE Avon – see Bath.

LINCOLN Lincs. 402 404 S 24 **Great Britain G.** – pop. 80 218 – ☎ 01522.

See : City★★ - Cathedral and Precincts★★★ *AC* Y – High Bridge★★ Z **9** – Usher Gallery★★ *AC* YZ **11** – Jew's House★ Y – Castle★ *AC* Y.

Envir. : Doddington Hall★ *AC*, W : 6 m. by B 1003 – Z – and B 1190.

Exc. : Gainsborough Old Hall★ *AC*, NW : 19 m. by A 57 – Z – and A 156.

Carholme, Carholme Rd ☎ 523725.

Humberside Airport : ☎ (01652) 688456, N : 32 m. by A 15 – Y – M 180 and A 18.

9 Castle Hill, LN1 3AA ☎ 529828.

London 140 – Bradford 81 – ◆Cambridge 94 – ◆Kingston-upon-Hull 44 – ◆Leeds 73 – ◆Leicester 53 – ◆Norwich 104 – Nottingham 38 – ◆Sheffield 48 – York 82.

Plan on next page

- **White Hart** (Forte Heritage), Bailgate, LN1 3AR, ☎ 526222, Fax 531798, « Antique furniture » – – 70. Y **c** **Meals** 9.95/22.95 **st.** and a la carte 6.25 – 9.95 – **35 rm** 85.00/105.00 **st.**, 13 suites – SB.
- **Courtyard by Marriott,** Brayford Side North, LN1 1YW, ☎ 544244, Fax 560805, – rm – 30. Z **a** **Meals** 9.95/11.95 **t.** and a la carte 6.00 – **95 rm** 55.00 **t.** – SB.
- **Forte Posthouse,** Eastgate, LN2 1PN, ☎ 520341, Fax 510780 – rm – 90. Y **z** **Meals** a la carte 14.75/22.85 **t.** – 7.95 – **70 rm** 59.00 **st.** – SB.
- **D'Isney Place** without rest., Eastgate, LN2 4AA, ☎ 538881, Fax 511321, – . Y **e** **17 rm** 51.00/84.00 **st.**
- **Damons Motel,** 997 Doddington Rd, LN6 3SE, SW : 4 ¼ m. by A 15 on B 1190 at junction with A 46 ☎ 500422, Fax 689719, – rm. **Meals** *(closed 25 December)* (grill rest.) (booking essential) a la carte 8.75/23.50 **st.** 4.75 – 3.50 – **47 rm** 34.00/36.50 **st.**
- **Minster Lodge** without rest., 3 Church Lane, LN2 1QJ, ☎ 513220, Fax 513220 – . Y **a** **6 rm** 39.00/50.00 **t.**
- **Hillcrest,** 15 Lindum Terr., LN2 5RT, ☎ 510182, Fax 510182, <, – . Y **o** *closed 23 December-3 January* – **Meals** *(closed Sunday lunch and Bank Holidays)* (bar lunch) dinner a la carte 12.30/15.20 **t.** 4.00 – **17 rm** 45.00/62.50 **t.** – SB.
- **Carline** without rest., 3 Carline Rd, LN1 1HL, ☎ 530422 – . Y **i** *closed Christmas and New Year* – **10 rm** 20.00/40.00 **t.**
- **Travel Inn,** Lincoln Rd, Canwick Hill, LN4 2RF, SE : 1 ¾ m. on B 1188 ☎ 525216, Fax 542521 – rm **Meals** (grill rest.) – 4.95 – **40 rm** 34.50 **t.**
- **Tennyson,** 7 South Park Av., LN5 8EN, ☎ 521624, Fax 521624 – rest. **Meals** 12.00 **s.** 4.50 – **8 rm** 26.00/38.00 **s.** – SB.
- **ABC Charisma** without rest., 126 Yarborough Rd, LN1 1HP, ☎ 543560, < – . Y **v** **11 rm** 21.00/40.00 **st.**
- **Rowan Lodge** without rest., 58 Pennell St., LN5 7TA, ☎ 529589 – . Z **v** **3 rm** 16.00/28.00 **s.**
- XX **Jew's House,** Jew's House, 15 The Strait, LN2 1JD, ☎ 524851, « 12C town house » – . YZ **x** *closed Monday lunch, Sunday and Bank Holiday Mondays* – **Meals** 10.95/25.00 **t.** and a la carte.

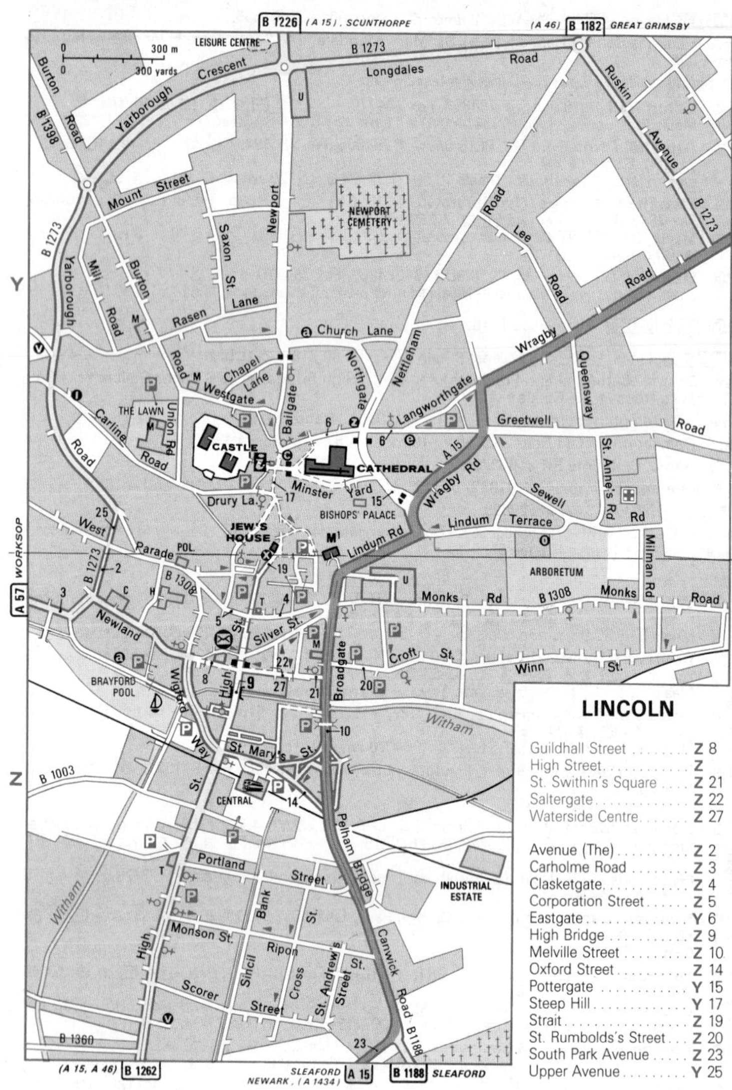

at Washingborough E : 3 m. by B 1188 – Z – on B 1190 – ✉ Lincoln – ☎ 01522 :

Washingborough Hall 🏠, Church Hill, LN4 1BE, ☎ 790340, Fax 792936, heated, rm TV ☎ P – 45. AE VISA
closed Christmas – **Meals** (lunch by arrangement)/dinner 10.50/22.50 **t.** and a la carte
12 rm 52.00/84.00 **st.** – SB.

at Branston SE : 3 m. on B 1188 – Z – ☎ 01522 :

Moor Lodge, Sleaford Rd, LN4 1HU, ☎ 791366, Fax 794389 – TV ☎ P – 150. VISA
Meals a la carte 11.05/20.25 **st.** 4.75 – **25 rm** 55.00/75.00 **st.** – SB.

ATS Crofton Rd, Allenby Rd Trading Est. ☎ 527225

LINDALE Cumbria 402 L 21 – see Grange-over-Sands.

LISKEARD Cornwall 403 G 32 The West Country G. – pop. 7 657 – ☎ 01579.

See : Church★.

Exc. : Lanhydrock★★, W : 1½m. by A 38 and A 390 – NW : Bodmin Moor★★ - St. Endellion Church★★ - Altarnun Church★ - St. Breward Church★ - Blisland★ (church★) - Camelford★ – Cardinham Church★ - Michaelstow Church★ - St. Kew★ (church★) - St. Mabyn Church★ – St. Neot★ (Parish Church★★) - St. Sidwell's, Laneast★ - St. Teath Church★ - St. Tudy★ – Launceston★ – Castle★ (≤★) St. Mary Magdalene★, South Gate★, NE : 19 m. by A 390 and A 388.

London 261 – Exeter 59 – ♦Plymouth 18 – Truro 37.

Well House ⑤, St. Keyne, PL14 4RN, S : 3 ½ m. on St. Keyne Well rd ✆ 342001, Fax 343891, ≤, heated, ⛲, ✂ – TV ☎ P. VISA
Meals (booking essential) 29.70 4.25 – ☐ 7.50 – **7 rm** 60.00/105.00 **t.**

Old Rectory ⑤, Duloe Rd, St. Keyne, PL14 4RL, S : 3 ¼ m. on B 3254 ✆ 342617, ⛲ – ⅹ rest TV ☎ P. AE VISA. ✻
closed Christmas – **Meals** (booking essential) (dinner only) a la carte 13.50/16.00 **st.** 7.90 – **8 rm** ☐ 30.00/60.00 **st.** – SB.

ATS 10 Dean St. ✆ 345489/345247

LITTLEBOURNE Kent 404 X30 – see Canterbury.

LITTLEBURY GREEN Essex 404 O 27 – see Saffron Walden.

LITTLE CHALFONT Bucks. 404 S 29 – pop. 3 991 – ☎ 01494.

Lodge Lane, Amersham ✆ 764877.

London 31 – Luton 20 – ♦Oxford 37.

Chalfont Dynasty, 9 Nightingales Corner, HP7 9PZ, ✆ 764038 – AE ⓓ VISA
Meals - Chinese (Peking) - 6.95/10.00 **t.** and a la carte 5.75.

LITTLEHAMPTON W. Sussex 404 S 31 – ☎ 01903.

London 64 – ♦Brighton 18 – ♦Portsmouth 31.

Bailiffscourt ⑤, Climping St., Climping, BN17 5RW, W : 2 ¾ m. by A 259 ✆ 723511, Fax 723107, « Reconstructed "medieval" house », ⛲, ⛲, park, ✂ – ⅹ rest TV ☎ P – 35. AE ⓓ VISA
Meals 17.50/32.50 **t.** and a la carte 39.40/50.95 **t.** 7.00 – **27 rm** ☐ 85.00/125.00 **t.** – SB.

Amberley Court without rest., Crookthorn Lane, Climping, BN17 5QU, W : 1 ¾ m. by B 2187 off A 259 ✆ 725131, Fax 734555, ⛲ – ⅹ TV P. ✻
3 rm ☐ 25.00/48.00 **st.**

ATS Church St. ✆ 713085/716919

LITTLE LANGDALE Cumbria 402 K 20 – see Ambleside.

LITTLE LANGFORD Wilts. - see Salisbury.

LITTLEOVER Derbs. 402 403 404 P 25 – see Derby.

LITTLE PETHERICK Cornwall 403 F 32 – see Padstow.

LITTLEPORT Cambs 404 U 26 – see Ely.

LITTLE RISSINGTON Glos. 403 404 O 28 – see Bourton-on-the-Water.

LITTLE SHELFORD Cambs. 404 U 27 – see Cambridge.

LITTLE SINGLETON Lancs. – see Blackpool.

LITTLE SUTTON Ches. – ✉ South Wirral – ☎ 0151.

♦London 208 – Chester 12 – ♦Liverpool 9 – ♦Manchester 48.

Woodhey, Berwick Rd, L66 4PS, at junction with A 550 ✆ 339 5121, Fax 339 3214, ⛲, – ▤ rest TV ☎ ♿ P – 200. AE ⓓ VISA
Meals *(closed Saturday lunch)* 12.95 **t.** (dinner) and a la carte 16.00/21.00 **t.** 6.95 – ☐ 7.95 – **53 rm** 65.00/80.00 **t.** – SB.

LITTLE THORNTON Lancs. 402 L 22 – see Blackpool.

LITTLE WALSINGHAM Norfolk 404 W 25 – – ✉ Walsingham – ☎ 01328.

♦London 117 – ♦Cambridge 67 – Cromer 21 – ♦Norwich 32.

White Horse Inn, Fakenham Rd, East Barsham, NR21 0LH, S : 2 ¼ m. on B 11
820645, Fax 820645 – TV P. AE VISA
Meals 4.95/5.95 **t.** and a la carte 3.50 – **3 rm** 30.00/52.00 **t.**

Old Bakehouse with rm, 33-35 High St., NR22 6BZ, 820454 – TV. VISA.
closed 2 weeks January-February, 1 week June and 2 weeks November – **Meals** *(close Sunday, Monday and Tuesday November-Easter)* (dinner only) 13.00 **t.** and a la carte 4.90 – **3 rm** 25.00/42.00 **st.**

LITTLE WEIGHTON Humbs. 402 S 22 – ✉ Cottingham – ☎ 01482.

♦London 184 – ♦Kingston-upon-Hull 8 – ♦Leeds 45 – York 31.

Rowley Manor, HU20 3XR, SW : ½ m. by Rowley Rd 848248, Fax 849900, « Georgian manor house », – TV ☎ P – 80. AE VISA
Meals 18.95/21.90 **t.** and a la carte 5.25 – **16 rm** 60.00/70.00 **t.** – SB.

LITTLEWICK GREEN Berks. 404 R 29 – see Maidenhead.

LITTLE WITLEY Heref. and Worcs. 403 404 M 27 – see Abberley.

LITTLE WYMONDLEY Herts. 404 T 28 – see Hitchin.

VERPOOL Mersey. 402 403 L 23 **Great Britain G.** – pop. 452 450 – 0151.

e : City★ – Walker Art Gallery★★ DY **M2** – Liverpool Cathedral★★ (Lady Chapel★) EZ – etropolitan Cathedral of Christ the King★★ EY – Albert Dock★ CZ (Merseyside Maritime useum★ *AC* **M1** - Tate Gallery Liverpool★).

c. : Speke Hall★ *AC*, SE : 8 m. by A 561 BX.

Allerton Municipal, Allerton Rd ✆ 428 1046 – Liverpool Municipal, Ingoe Lane, Kirkby 546 5435, BV – Bowring, Bowring Park, Roby Rd, Huyton ✆ 489 1901.

Liverpool Airport : ✆ 486 8877, SE : 6 m. by A 561 BX – **Terminal** : Pier Head.

to Isle of Man (Douglas) (Isle of Man Steam Packet Co. Ltd) (4 h) – to Northern Ireland elfast) (Norse Irish Ferries Ltd) (11 h).

to Birkenhead (Mersey Ferries) (10 mn) – to Wallasey (Mersey Ferries) (20 mn).

Merseyside Welcome Centre, Clayton Square Shopping Centre, L1 1QR ✆ 709 3631 – lantic Pavilion, Albert Dock, L3 4AA ✆ 708 8854.

ondon 219 – ◆Birmingham 103 – ◆Leeds 75 – ◆Manchester 35.

Town plans : Liverpool pp. 2-5

Liverpool Moat House (Q.M.H.), Paradise St., L1 8JD, ✆ 471 9988, Fax 709 2706, – – rm – 400. DZ **n**
Meals 10.95/16.25 **t.** and dinner a la carte – 9.50 – **244 rm** 97.50 **t.**, 7 suites – SB.

Atlantic Tower Thistle (Mt. Charlotte), 30 Chapel St., L3 9RE, ✆ 227 4444, Fax 236 3973, ← – rm – 100. CY **r**
Meals *(closed Saturday lunch)* 7.95/19.25 and a la carte 4.95 – 8.95 – **223 rm** 78.00/98.00 **st.**, 3 suites – SB.

Campanile, Wapping and Chaloner St., L3 4AJ, ✆ 709 8104, Fax 709 8725 – rm – 30. CZ **a**
Meals 10.35 **st.** and a la carte 4.95 – 4.50 – **80 rm** 35.75.

Travel Inn, Queens Dr., West Derby, L13 0DL, E : 4 m. on A 5058 (Ringroad) ✆ 228 4724, Fax 220 7610 – rm BV **a**
Meals (grill rest.) – 4.95 – **40 rm** 34.50 **t.**

Dolby, 36-42 Chaloner St., Queens Dock, L3 4DE, ✆ 708 7272, Fax 708 7266, ← – rm . DZ **c**
Meals (dinner only) 8.50 **t.** and a la carte 4.50 – 3.50 – **64 rm** 29.50 **st.**

Ristorante Del Secolo, 36-40 Stanley St., L1 6AL, ✆ 236 4004 – DY **e**
closed Saturday lunch and Sunday – **Meals** - Italian - a la carte 16.85/25.15 5.95.

Est, Est, Est !, Unit 5-6, Edward Pavilion, Albert Dock, L3 4AA, ✆ 708 6969, Fax 709 4912 – CZ **e**
closed 25 December – **Meals** - Italian - 9.95/12.95 **t.** and a la carte 4.75.

at Crosby N : 5½ m. on A 565 – AV – 0151 :

Blundellsands, The Serpentine, Blundellsands, L23 6YB, W : 1 ¼ m. via College Rd, Mersey Rd and Agnes Rd ✆ 924 6515, Fax 931 5364 – rm – 250. .
Meals *(closed Saturday lunch)* 7.50/13.50 **t.** and a la carte – **41 rm** 59.50/78.00 **t.** – SB.

at Netherton N : 6 m. by A 5038 off A 5036 – AV – ✉ Liverpool – 0151 :

Park (Premier), Dunningsbridge Rd, L30 3SU, on A 5036 ✆ 525 7555, Fax 525 2481 – rm – 100. .
Meals *(closed Saturday lunch)* a la carte 7.90/17.75 **st.** 4.25 – 4.45 – **62 rm** 32.50 **st.** – SB.

at Huyton E : 8¼ m. by A 5047 and A 5080 – BX – on B 5199 – ✉ Liverpool – 0151 :

Logwood Mill, Fallows Way, L35 1RZ, SE : 3 ¼ m. by A 5080 off Windy Arbor Rd ✆ 449 2341, Fax 449 3832, – rm – 200. .
Meals *(closed Saturday lunch)* 10.95/25.00 **st.** and a la carte 3.45 – **62 rm** 69.50/99.50 **st.** – SB.

Derby Lodge, Roby Rd, L36 4HD, SW : 1 m. on A 5080 ✆ 480 4440, Fax 480 8132, – – 150. .
Meals *(closed Saturday lunch)* 15.50 **st.** (dinner) and a la carte 17.90/35.75 **st.** 4.10 – **19 rm** 55.00/75.00 **st.** – SB.

Travel Inn, Wilson Rd, Tarbock, L36 6AD, SE : 2 ¼ m. on A 5080 ✆ 480 9614, Fax 480 9361 – rm . .
Meals (grill rest.) – 4.95 – **40 rm** 34.50 **t.**

at Grassendale SE : 4½ m. on A 561 – BX – ✉ Liverpool – 0151 :

Gulshan, 544-546 Aigburth Rd, L19 3QG, on A 561 ✆ 427 2273 – .
closed 25 December – **Meals** - Indian - (dinner only) a la carte 12.35/20.15 **t.** 5.95.

at Woolton SE : 6 m. by A 562 – BX – A 5058 and Woolton Rd – ✉ Liverpool – 0151 :

Woolton Redbourne, Acrefield Rd, L25 5JN, ✆ 428 2152, Fax 421 1501, « Victorian house, antiques », – .
Meals (residents only) (dinner only) 22.95 **st.** 5.95 – **18 rm** 58.00/120.00 **st.** – SB.

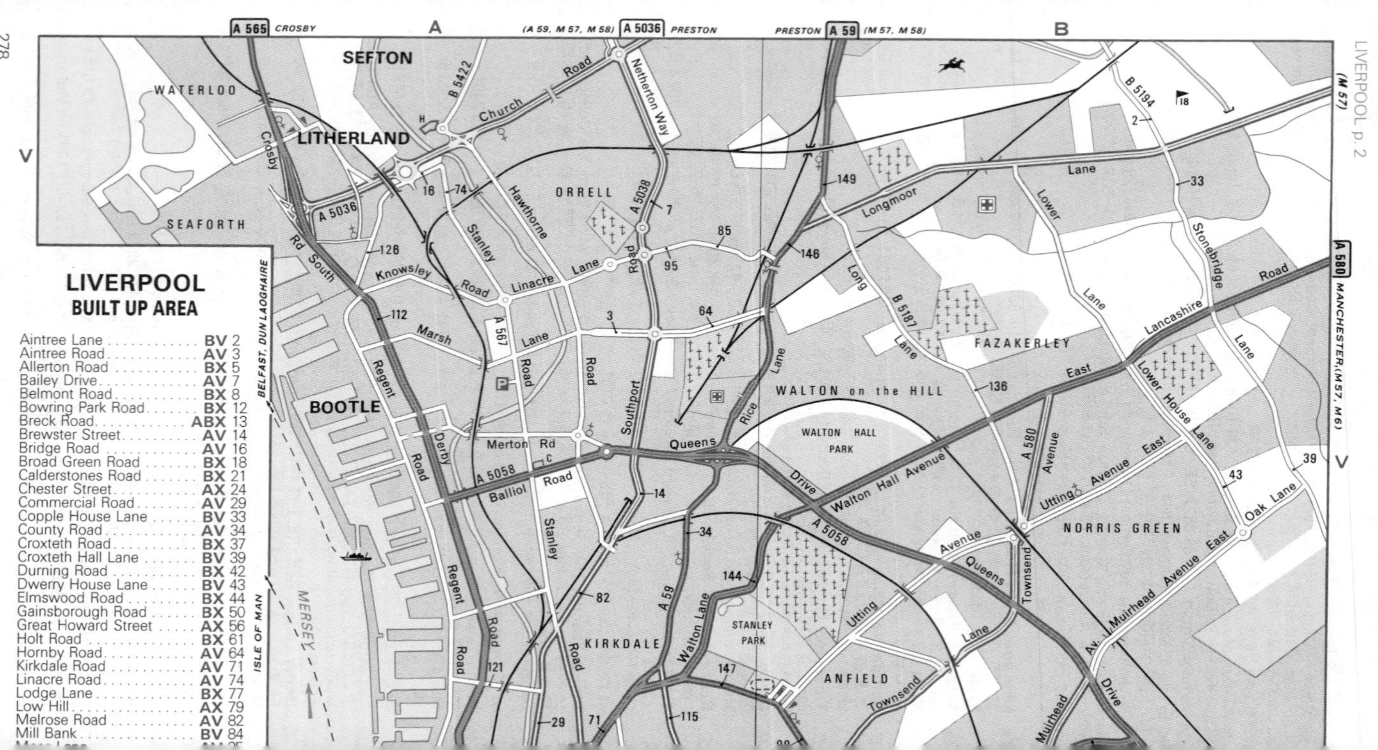

LIVERPOOL
BUILT UP AREA

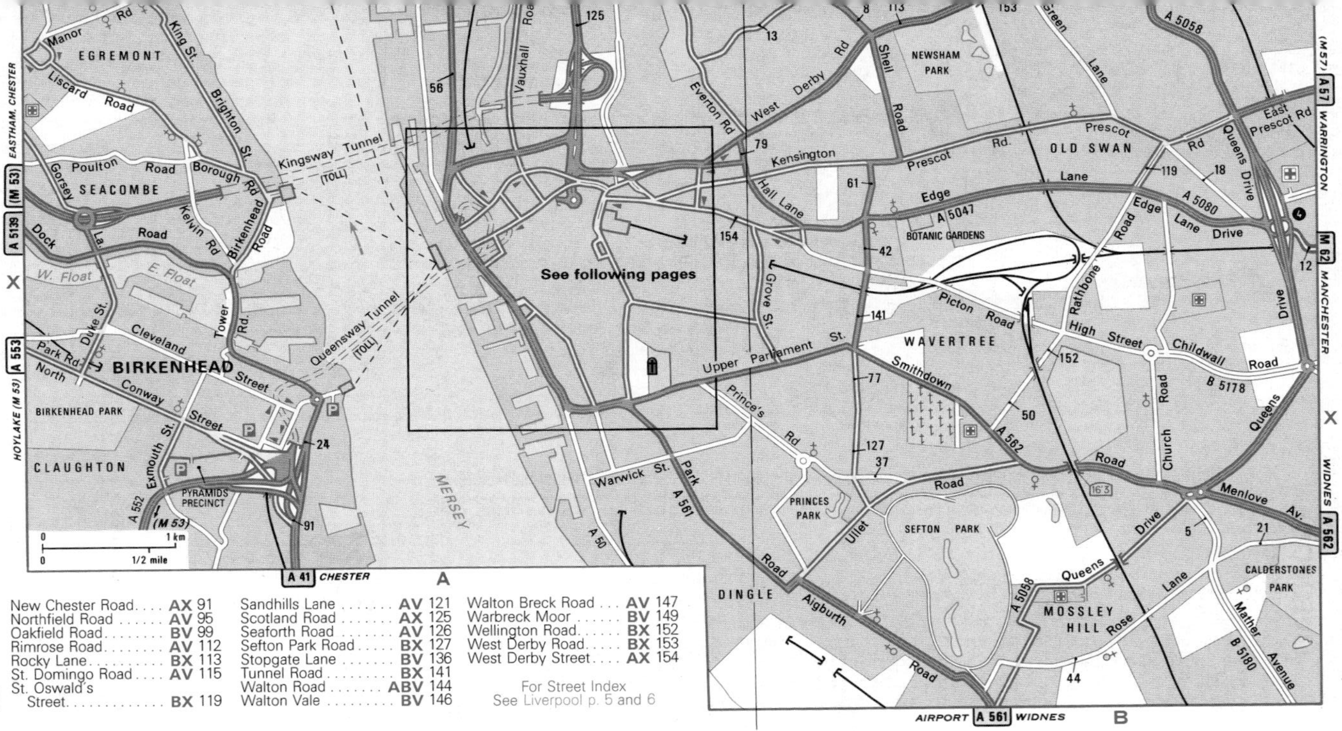

For Street Index
See Liverpool p. 5 and 6

LIVERPOOL
CENTRE

Street	Grid	No.
Argyle St.	DZ	6
Blackburne Pl.	EZ	11
Brunswick Rd.	EY	19
Canning Pl.	CZ	23
Churchill Way	DY	25
Clarence St.	EYZ	26
College Lane	DZ	28
Commutation Row	DY	30
Cook St.	CY	32
Crosshall St.	DY	36
Daulby St.	EY	40
Erskine St.	EY	45
Fontenoy St.	DY	48
Forrest St.	DZ	49
George's Dock Gate	CY	51
Grafton St.	DZ	53
Great Charlotte St.	DY	54
Great Howard St.	CY	56
Hatton Garden	DY	57
Haymarket	DY	58
Hood St.	DY	62
Houghton St.	DY	65
Huskisson St.	EZ	66
James St.	CY	68
King Edward St.	CY	69
Knight St.	EZ	72
Leece St.	EZ	73
Liver St.	CZ	76
Mansfield St.	DEY	80
Mathew St.	CDY	81
Moss St.	EY	86
Mount St.	EZ	88
Myrtle St.	EZ	89
Newington	DZ	92
New Quay	CY	93
North John St.	CY	96
Norton St.	DY	97
Parker St.	DY	103
Prescot St.	EY	105
Prince's Rd	EZ	107
Ranelagh St.	DY	108
Richmond St.	DY	109
Roe St.	DY	114
St. James Pl.	EZ	117
St. John's Lane	DY	118
School Lane	DYZ	122
Scotland Pl.	DY	123
Sefton St.	DZ	129
Seymour St.	EY	130
Skelhorne St.	DY	133
Stanley St.	CDY	135
Suffolk St.	DZ	137
Tarleton St.	DY	139
Victoria St.	DY	143
Water St.	CY	150
William Brown St.	DY	156
York St.	DZ	157

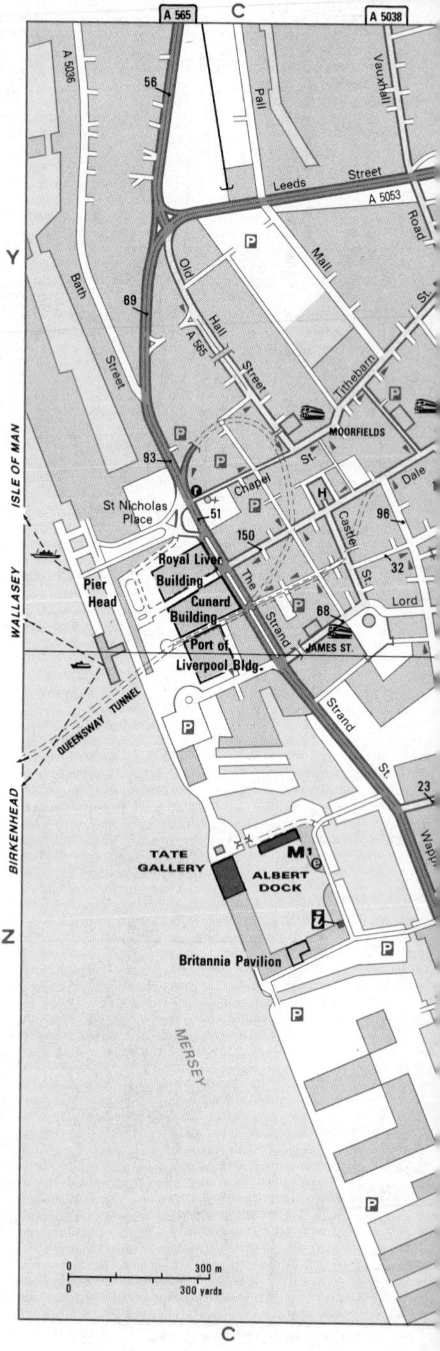

GREEN TOURIST GUIDES

Picturesque scenery, buildings
Attractive routes
Touring programmes
Plans of towns and buildings.

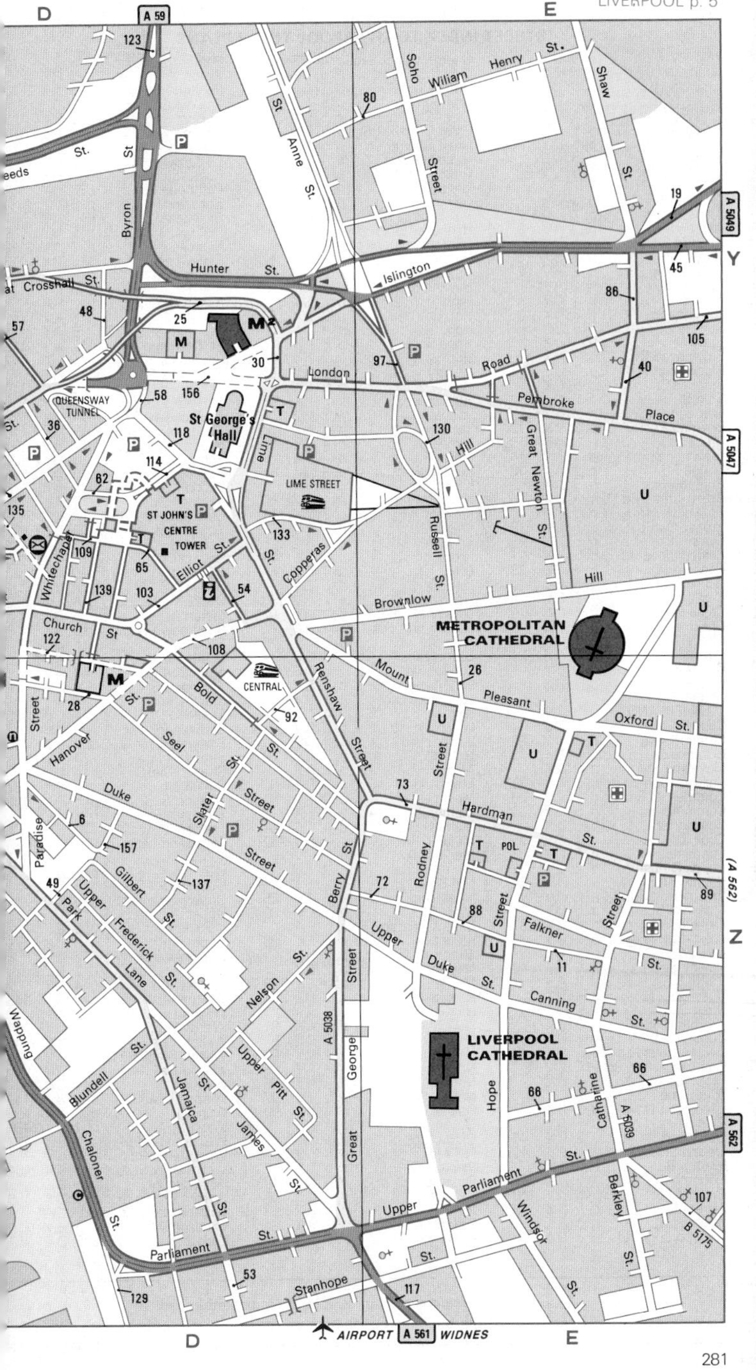

D
E
A 59
A 5049
A 5047
(A 562)
A 562
Y
Z
William
Henry
St.
Soho
Shaw
Anne
St.
Street
Leeds
Byron
Hunter
Crosshall
Islington
London
Road
Pembroke
Place
QUEENSWAY TUNNEL
St George's Hall
LIME STREET
ST JOHN'S CENTRE TOWER
Lime
Elliot
Copperas
Hill
Great
Newton
Russell
Brownlow
METROPOLITAN CATHEDRAL
Whitechapel
Church
CENTRAL
Bold
Renshaw
Mount
Pleasant
Oxford
Hanover
Seel
Slater
Duke
Paradise
Hardman
Rodney
POL
Falkner
Gilbert
Upper
Frederick
Park
Lane
Berry
Nelson
Canning
Catharine
LIVERPOOL CATHEDRAL
Hope
Wapping
Blundell
Jamaica
Pitt
James
George
Great
A 5038
A 5039
Chaloner
Parliament
Windsor
Berkley
B 5175
Stanhope
AIRPORT
A 561
WIDNES

STREET INDEX TO LIVERPOOL TOWN PLANS

Street	Page	Grid	No.
Bold St.	p. 5	DZ	
Church St.	p. 5	DY	
Lime St.	p. 5	DY	
London Rd	p. 5	DEY	
Lord St.	p. 4	CDY	
Parker St.	p. 5	DY	103
Ranelagh St.	p. 5	DY	108
Renshaw St.	p. 5	DEZ	
St. Johns Centre	p. 5	DY	
Aigburth Rd	p. 3	BX	
Aintree Lane	p. 2	BV	2
Aintree Rd	p. 2	AV	3
Allerton Rd	p. 3	BX	5
Argyle St.	p. 5	DZ	6
Bailey Drive	p. 2	AV	7
Balliol Rd	p. 2	AV	
Bath St.	p. 4	CY	
Belmont Rd	p. 3	BX	8
Berkley St.	p. 5	EZ	
Berry St.	p. 5	DZ	
Birkenhead Rd	p. 3	AX	
Blackburne Pl.	p. 5	EZ	11
Blundell St.	p. 5	DZ	
Bold St.	p. 5	DZ	
Borough Rd	p. 3	AX	
Bowring Park Rd	p. 3	BX	12
Breck Rd	p. 3	ABX	13
Brewster St.	p. 2	AV	14
Bridge Rd	p. 2	AV	16
Brighton St.	p. 3	AX	
Broad Green Rd	p. 3	BX	18
Brownlow Hill	p. 5	DEY	
Brunswick Rd	p. 5	EY	19
Byron St.	p. 5	DY	
Calderstones Rd	p. 3	BX	21
Canning Pl.	p. 4	CZ	23
Canning St.	p. 5	EZ	
Castle St.	p. 4	CY	
Catharine St.	p. 5	EZ	
Chaloner St.	p. 5	DZ	
Chapel St.	p. 4	CY	
Chester St.	p. 3	AX	24
Childwall Rd	p. 3	BX	
Church Rd	p. 3	BX	
Church Rd LITHERLAND	p. 2	AV	
Church St.	p. 5	DY	
Churchill Way	p. 5	DY	25
Clarence St.	p. 5	EYZ	26
Cleveland St.	p. 3	AX	
College Lane	p. 5	DZ	28
Commercial Rd	p. 2	AV	29
Commutation Row	p. 5	DY	30
Conway St.	p. 3	AX	
Cook St.	p. 4	CY	32
Copperas Hill	p. 5	DE	
Copple House La.	p. 2	BV	33
County Rd	p. 2	AV	34
Crosby Rd South	p. 2	AV	
Crosshall St.	p. 5	DY	36
Croxteth Rd	p. 3	BX	37
Croxteth Hall Lane	p. 2	BV	39
Dale St.	p. 4	CDY	
Daulby St.	p. 5	EY	40
Derby Rd	p. 2	AV	
Duke St.	p. 5	DZ	
Duke St. BIRKENHEAD	p. 3	AX	
Durning Rd	p. 3	BX	42
Dwerry House Lane	p. 2	BV	43
East Lancashire Rd	p. 2	BV	
East Prescot Rd	p. 3	BX	
Edge Lane	p. 3	BX	
Edge Lane Drive	p. 3	BX	
Elliot St.	p. 5	DY	
Elmswood Rd	p. 3	BX	44
Erskine St.	p. 5	EY	45
Everton Rd	p. 3	AX	
Exmouth St.	p. 3	AX	
Fontenoy St.	p. 5	DY	48
Forrest St.	p. 5	DZ	49
Freeman St.	p. 3	AX	
Gainsborough Rd	p. 3	BX	50

Street	Page	Grid	No.
George's Dock Lane	p. 4	CY	51
Gilbert St.	p. 5	DZ	
Gorsey Lane	p. 3	AX	
Grafton St.	p. 5	DZ	53
Great Charlotte St.	p. 5	DY	54
Great Crosshall St.	p. 5	DY	
Great George St.	p. 5	DY	
Great Howard St.	p. 4	CY	56
Great Newton St.	p. 5	EY	
Green Lane	p. 3	BX	
Grove St.	p. 3	BX	
Hall Lane	p. 3	BX	
Hannover St.	p. 5	DZ	
Hardman St.	p. 5	EZ	
Hatton Garden	p. 5	DY	57
Haymarket	p. 5	DY	58
Hawthorne Rd	p. 2	AV	
High St.	p. 3	BX	
Holt Rd	p. 3	BX	61
Hood St.	p. 5	DY	62
Hope St.	p. 5	EZ	
Hornby Rd	p. 2	AV	64
Houghton St.	p. 5	DY	65
Hunter St.	p. 5	DY	
Huskisson St.	p. 5	EZ	66
Islington	p. 5	EY	
Jamaica St.	p. 5	DZ	
James St.	p. 4	CY	68
Kelvin Rd	p. 3	AX	
Kensington	p. 3	BX	
King St.	p. 3	AX	
King Edward St.	p. 4	CY	69
Kirkdale Rd	p. 2	AV	71
Knight St.	p. 5	EZ	72
Knowsley Rd	p. 2	AV	
Leece St.	p. 5	EZ	73
Leeds St.	p. 4	CY	
Lime St.	p. 5	DY	
Linacre Rd	p. 2	AV	74
Linacre Lane	p. 2	AV	
Liscard Rd	p. 3	AX	
Liver St.	p. 5	CZ	76
Lodge Lane	p. 3	BX	77
London Rd	p. 5	DEY	
Long Lane	p. 2	BV	
Longmoor Lane	p. 2	BV	
Lord St.	p. 4	CDY	
Lower House Lane	p. 2	BV	
Lower Lane	p. 2	BV	
Low Hill	p. 3	ABX	79
Manor Rd	p. 2	AX	
Mansfield St.	p. 5	DEY	80
Marsh Lane	p. 2	AV	
Mather Av.	p. 3	BX	
Mathew St.	p. 4	CDY	81
Melrose Rd	p. 2	AV	82
Menlove Av.	p. 3	BV	
Merton Rd	p. 2	AV	
Mill Bank	p. 2	BV	84
Moss Lane	p. 2	AV	85
Moss St.	p. 5	EY	86
Mount Pleasant	p. 5	EZ	
Mount St.	p. 5	EZ	88
Muirhead Av.	p. 2	BV	
Muirhead Av. East	p. 2	BV	
Myrtle St.	p. 5	EZ	89
Nelson St.	p. 5	DZ	
Netherton Way	p. 2	AV	
New Chester Rd	p. 3	AX	91
Newington	p. 5	DZ	92
New Quay	p. 4	CY	93
Northfield Rd	p. 2	AV	95
North John St.	p. 4	CY	96
Norton St.	p. 5	EY	97
Oakfield Rd	p. 2	BV	99
Old Hall St.	p. 4	CY	
Oxford St.	p. 5	EZ	
Pall Mall	p. 4	CY	
Paradise St.	p. 5	DZ	
Parker St.	p. 5	DY	103
Park Lane	p. 5	DZ	
Park Rd	p. 3	AX	
Park Rd North	p. 3	AX	
Parliament St.	p. 5	DZ	

Street	Page	Grid	No.
Pembroke Pl.	p. 5	EY	
Picton Rd	p. 3	BX	
Poulton Rd	p. 3	AX	
Prescot Rd	p. 3	BX	
Prescot St.	p. 5	EY	105
Prince's Rd	p. 5	EZ	107
Queens Drive	p. 3	BX	
Queensway	p. 3	AX	
Ranelagh St.	p. 5	DY	108
Rathbone Rd	p. 3	BX	
Renshaw Rd	p. 5	DZ	
Rice Lane	p. 2	AV	
Richmond St.	p. 5	DY	109
Rimrose Rd	p. 2	AV	112
Rocky Lane	p. 3	BX	113
Rodney St.	p. 5	EZ	
Roe St.	p. 5	DY	114
Rose Lane	p. 3	BX	
Russel St.	p. 5	EY	
St. Anne St.	p. 5	DY	
St. Domingo Rd	p. 2	AV	115
St. James Pl.	p. 5	EZ	117
St. James St.	p. 5	DZ	
St. John's Lane	p. 5	DY	118
St. Johns Centre	p. 5	DY	
St. Nicholas Pl.	p. 4	CY	
St. Oswald's St.	p. 3	BX	119
Sandhills Lane	p. 2	AV	121
School Lane	p. 5	DYZ	122
Scotland Pl.	p. 5	DY	123
Scotland Rd	p. 3	AX	125
Seaforth Rd	p. 2	AV	126
Seel St.	p. 5	DZ	
Sefton Park Rd	p. 3	BX	127
Sefton St.	p. 3	DZ	129
Seymour St.	p. 5	EY	130
Shaw St.	p. 5	EY	
Sheil Rd	p. 3	BX	
Skelhorne St.	p. 5	EY	133
Slater St.	p. 5	DZ	
Smithdown Rd	p. 3	BX	
Soho St.	p. 5	EY	
South John St.	p. 4	CYZ	
Southport Rd	p. 2	AV	
Stanhope St.	p. 5	DZ	
Stanley Rd	p. 2	AV	
Stanley St.	p. 4	CDY	135
Stonebridge Lane	p. 2	BV	
Stopgate Lane	p. 2	BV	136
Strand St.	p. 4	CZ	
Strand (The)	p. 4	CY	
Suffolk St.	p. 5	DZ	137
Tarleton St.	p. 5	DY	139
Tithebarn St.	p. 4	CY	
Townsend Av.	p. 2	BV	
Townsend Lane	p. 2	BV	
Tunnel Rd	p. 3	BX	141
Ullet Rd	p. 3	BX	
Upper Duke St.	p. 5	EZ	
Upper Frederick St.	p. 5	DZ	
Upper Parliament St.	p. 5	EZ	
Upper Pitt	p. 5	DZ	
Utting Av.	p. 2	AV	
Utting Av. East	p. 2	BV	
Vauxhall Rd	p. 4	CY	
Victoria St.	p. 5	DY	143
Walton Lane	p. 2	AV	
Walton Rd	p. 2	ABV	144
Walton Vale	p. 2	BV	146
Walton Breck Rd	p. 2	AV	147
Walton Hall Av.	p. 2	BV	
Wapping	p. 4	CDZ	
Warbreck Moor	p. 2	BV	149
Warwick	p. 3	AX	
Water St.	p. 4	CY	150
Wellington Rd	p. 3	BX	152
West Derby Rd	p. 3	BX	153
West Derby St.	p. 3	AX	154
Whitechapel	p. 5	DY	
William Brown St.	p. 5	DY	156
William Henry St.	p. 5	EY	
Windsor St.	p. 5	EZ	
York St.	p. 5	DZ	157

The names of main shopping streets are indicated in red at the beginning of the list of streets.

ATS 15/37 Caryl St. ✆ 709 8032
TS Wilson Road, Huyton ✆ 489 8386/7
TS 190-194 St. Mary's Rd, Garston ✆ 427 3665
TS 73-77 Durning Rd, Wavertree ✆ 263 7604
ATS Musker St., Crosby ✆ 931 3166
ATS Unit E, Liver Ind. Est., Long Lane, Aintree ✆ 524 1000

IZARD Cornwall 403 E 34 **The West Country G.** – 01326.

nvir. : Lizard Peninsula★ - Mullion Cove★★ (Church★) - Kynance Cove★★ - Cadgwith★ - overack★ – Cury★ (Church★) - Gunwalloe Fishing Cove★ - St. Keverne (Church★) - Landewednack★ (Church★) – Mawgan-in-Meneage (Church★) - Ruan Minor (Church★) - St. Anthoy-in-Meneage★.

London 326 – Penzance 24 – Truro 29.

- **Landewednack House**, Church Cove, TR12 7PQ, ✆ 290909, Fax 290192, ≤, « Part 17C rectory », – TV P. VISA.
  Meals (booking essential) (residents only) (dinner only) 12.50 – **3 rm** 28.00/72.00 **t.**
- **Penmenner House,** Penmenner Rd, TR12 7NR, ✆ 290370, ≤, – TV P. AE VISA.
  closed Christmas and New Year – **Meals** (by arrangement) 12.50 **st.** – **8 rm** 25.00/46.00 **st.**
- **Parc Brawse House,** Penmenner Rd, TR12 7NR, ✆ 290466, Fax 290466, ≤, rest TV P. VISA
  Meals (by arrangement) 9.50 **st.** – **7 rm** 14.00/37.00 **st.** – SB.

OCKINGTON Humbs – see Great Driffield.

LOFTUS Cleveland 402 R 20 – pop. 7 315 – ✉ Saltburn-by-the-Sea – 01287.

London 264 – ♦Leeds 73 – ♦Middlesbrough 17 – Scarborough 36.

- **Grinkle Park**, Easington, TS13 4UB, SE : 3½ m. by A 174 ✆ 640515, Fax 641278, ≤, park, – TV P. AE VISA.
  Meals 9.50/15.95 **t.** and dinner a la carte – **20 rm** 65.00/85.00 **t.** – SB.

LOLWORTH SERVICE AREA Cambs. – see Cambridge.

London

04 folds ㊷ to ㊹ – London G. – pop. 6 679 699 – ☎ 0171 or 0181: see heading of each area

✈ Heathrow, ℘ (0181) 759 4321, p. 8 AX – **Terminal :** Airbus (A1) from Victoria, Airbus (A2) om Paddington – Underground (Piccadilly line) frequent service daily.

✈ Gatwick, ℘ (01293) 535353 and ℘ (0181) 763 2020, p. 9 : by A 23 EZ and M 23 – **Terminal :** oach service from Victoria Coach Station (Flightline 777, hourly service) – Railink (Gatwick xpress) from Victoria (24 h service).

✈ London City Airport ℘ (0171) 474 5555, p. 7 : HV.

✈ Stansted, at Bishop's Stortford, ℘ (01279) 680500, Fax 662066, NE : 34 m. p. 7 : by M 11 JT nd A 120.

ritish Airways, Victoria Air Terminal : 115 Buckingham Palace Rd, SW1, ℘ (0171) 834 9411, ax 828 7142, p. 32 BX.

Euston ℘ (0345) 090700.

British Travel Centre, 12 Regent St., Piccadilly Circus, SW1Y 4PQ ℘ (0171) 971 0026.
elfridges, basement Services, Arcade, Selfridges Store, Oxford St. WI ℘ (0171) 730 3488.
ictoria Station Forecourt SWI ℘ (0171) 730 3488.

Sights
Curiosités – Le curiosità
Sehenswürdigkeiten

HISTORIC BUILDINGS AND MONUMENTS

Palace of Westminster★★★ : House of Lords★★, Westminster Hall★★ (hammerbeam roof★★★ Robing Room★, Central Lobby★, House of Commons★, Big Ben★, Victoria Tower★ p. 26 LY Tower of London★★★ (Crown Jewels★★★, White Tower or Keep★★★, St. John's Chapel★★ Beauchamp Tower★ Tower Hill Pageant★) p. 27 PVX.

Banqueting House★★ p. 26 LX – Buckingham Palace★★ (Changing of the Guard★★, Roy Mews★★) p. 32 BVX – Kensington Palace★★ p. 24 FX – Lincoln's Inn★★ p. 33 EV – Londo Bridge★ p. 27 PVX – Royal Hospital Chelsea★★ p. 31 FU – St. James's Palace★★ p. 29 EP – Sout Bank Arts Centre ★★ (Royal Festival Hall★, National Theatre★, County Hall★) p. 26 MX – Th Temple★★ (Middle Temple Hall★) p. 22 MV – Tower Bridge★★ p. 27 PX.

Albert Memorial★ p. 30 CQ – Apsley House★ p. 28 BP – Burlington House★ p. 29 EM – Charte house★ p. 23 NOU – Commonwealth Institute★ p. 24 EY – Design Centre★ p. 29 FM – Georg Inn★, Southwark p. 27 PX – Gray's Inn★ p. 22 MU – Guildhall★ (Lord Mayor's Show★★) p. 23 O – Imperial College of Science and Technology★ p. 30 CR – Dr Johnson's House★ p. 23 NUV **A** Lancaster House★ p. 29 EP – Leighton House★ p. 24 EY – Linley Sambourne House★ p. 24 EY Lloyds Building★★ p. 23 PV – Mansion House★ (plate and insignia★★) p. 23 PV **P** – Th Monument★ (✲★) p. 23 PV **G** – Old Admiralty★ p. 26 KLX – Royal Exchange★ p. 23 PV **V** – Roy Opera Arcade★ (New Zealand House) p. 29 FGN – Royal Opera House★ (Covent Garden) p. 3 DX – Somerset House★ p. 33 EXY – Spencer House★★ p. 29 DP – Staple Inn★ p. 22 MU **Y** Theatre Royal★ (Haymarket) p. 29 GM – Westminster Bridge★ p. 26 LY.

CHURCHES

The City Churches

St. Paul's Cathedral★★★ (Dome ⋞★★★) p. 23 NOV.

St. Bartholomew the Great★★ (choir★) p. 23 OU **K** – St. Dunstan-in-the-East★★ p. 23 PV **F** St. Mary-at-Hill★★ (woodwork★★, plan★) p. 23 PV **B** – Temple Church★★ p. 22 MV.

All Hallows-by-the-Tower (font cover★★ brasses★) p. 23 PV **Y** – Christ Church★ p. 23 OU **E** St. Andrew Undershaft (monuments★) p. 23 PV **A** – St. Bride★ (steeple★★) p. 23 NV **J** St. Clement Eastcheap (panelled interior★★) p. 23 PV **E** – St. Edmund the King and Mart (tower and spire★) p. 23 PV **D** – St-Giles Cripplegate★ p. 23 OU **N** – St. Helen Bishopsgate (monuments★★) p. 23 PUV **R** – St. James Garlickhythe (tower and spire★, sword rests★) p. 2 OV **R** – St. Magnus the Martyr (tower★, sword rest★) p. 23 PV **K** – St. Margaret Lothbury (tower and spire★, woodwork★, screen★, font★) p. 23 PU **S** – St. Margaret Pattens (spire★ woodwork★) p. 23 PV **N** – St. Martin-within-Ludgate (tower and spire★, door cases★) p. 2 NOV **B** – St. Mary Abchurch★ (reredos★★, tower and spire★, dome★) p. 23 PV **X** – S Mary-le-Bow (tower and steeple★★) p. 23 OV **G** – St. Michael Paternoster Royal (tower an spire★) p. 23 OV **D** – St. Nicholas Cole Abbey (tower and spire★) p. 23 OV **F** – St. Olave★ p. 2 PV **S** – St. Peter upon Cornhill (screen★) p. 23 PV **L** – St. Stephen Walbrook★ (tower an steeple★, dome★), p. 23 PV **Z** – St. Vedast (tower and spire★, ceiling★), p. 23 OU **E**.

Other Churches

Westminster Abbey★★★ (Henry VII Chapel★★★, Chapel of Edward the Confessor★★, Chapt House★★, Poets' Corner★) p. 26 LY.

Southwark Cathedral★★ p. 27 PX.

Queen's Chapel★ p. 29 EP – St. Clement Danes★ p. 33 EX – St. James's★ p. 29 EM St. Margaret's★ p. 26 LY **A** – St. Martin-in-the-Fields★ p. 33 DY – St. Paul's★ (Covent Garde p. 33 DX – Westminster Roman Catholic Cathedral★ p. 26 KY **B**.

PARKS

Regent's Park★★★ p. 21 HI (terraces★★), Zoo★★★.

Hyde Park – Kensington Gardens★★ (Orangery★) pp. 24 and 25 – St. James's Park★★ p. 26 KX

TREETS AND SQUARES

ne City★★★ p. 23 NV.

edford Square★★ p. 22 KLU – Belgrave Square★★ p. 32 AVX – Burlington Arcade★★ p. 29 DM – ne Mall★★ p. 29 FP – Piccadilly★ p. 29 EM – The Thames★★ pp. 25-27 – Trafalgar Square★★ 33 DY – Whitehall★★ (Horse Guards★) p. 26 LX.

arbican★ p. 23 OU – Bond Street★ pp. 28-29 CK-DM – Canonbury Square★ p. 23 NS – Carlton ouse Terrace★ p. 29 GN – Cheyne Walk★ p. 25 GHZ – Covent Garden★ p. 33 DX – Fitzroy quare★ p. 22 KU – Jermyn Street★ p. 29 EN – Merrick Square★ p. 27 OY – Montpelier Square★ 31 EQ – The Piazza★(Covent Garden) p. 33 DX – Piccadilly Arcade★ p. 29 DEN – Portman quare★ p. 28 AJ – Queen Anne's Gate★ p. 26 KY – Regent Street★ p. 29 EM – Piccadilly Circus★ 29 FM – St. James's Square★ p. 29 FN – St. James's Street★ p. 29 EN – Shepherd Market★ 28 CN – Soho★ p. 29 – Trinity Church Square★ p. 27 OY – Victoria Embankment gardens★ 33 DEXY – Waterloo Place★ p. 29 FN.

IUSEUMS

ritish Museum★★★ p. 22 LU – National Gallery★★★ p. 29 GM – Science Museum★★★ p. 30 CR – ate Gallery★★★ p. 26 LZ – Victoria and Albert Museum★★★ p. 31 DR.

ourtauld Institute Galleries★★ (Somerset House) p. 33 EXY – Museum of London★★ p. 23 U **M** – National Portrait Gallery★★ p. 29 GM – Natural History Museum★★ p. 30 CS – ueen's Gallery★★ p. 32 BV – Wallace Collection★★ p. 28 AH.

ock Museum★ (Guildhall) p. 22 OU – Imperial War Museum★ p. 27 NY – London Transport useum★ p. 33 DX – Madame Tussaud's★ p. 21 IU **M** – Museum of Mankind★ p. 29 DM – ational Army Museum★ p. 31 FU – Percival David Foundation of Chinese Art★ p. 22 KLT **M** – r John Soane's Museum★ p. 22 MU **M** – Wellington Museum★ p. 28 BP.

UTER LONDON

lackheath p. 11 HX terraces and houses★, Eltham Palace★ **A** – **Brentford** p. 8 BX Syon ark★★, gardens★ – **Bromley** p. 10 GY The Crystal Palace Park★ – **Chiswick** p. 9 CV Chiswick all★★, Chiswick House★ **D**, Hogarth's House★ **E** – **Dulwich** p. 10 Picture Gallery★ FX **X** – **reenwich** pp. 10 and 11 : Cutty Sark★★ GV **F**, Footway Tunnel(⩽ ★★) – National Maritime useum★★ (Queen's House★★) GV **M**, Royal Naval College★★ (Painted Hall★, the Chapel★) GV , The Park and Old Royal Observatory★ (Meridian Building : collection★★) HV **K**, Ranger's ouse★ GX **N** – **Hampstead** Kenwood House★★ (Adam Library★★, paintings★★) p. 5 EU **P**, enton House★, The Benton Fletcher Collection★ p. 20 ES – **Hampton Court** p. 8 BY (The alace★★★, gardens★★★, Fountain Court★, The Great Vine★)– **Kew** p. 9 CX Royal Botanic ardens★★★ : Palm House★★, Temperate House★, Kew Palace or Dutch House★★, Orangery★, agoda★, Japanese Gateway★ – **Hendon**★ p. 5, Royal Air Force Museum★★ CT **M** – **Houn-ow** p. 8 BV Osterley Park★★ – **Lewisham** p. 10 GX Horniman Museum★ **M** – **Richmond** pp. 8 nd 9 : Richmond Park★★, ✲★★★ CX, Richmond Hill✲★★ CX, Richmond Bridge★★ BX **R**, chmond Green★★ BX **S** (Maids of Honour Row★★, Trumpeter's House★), Asgill House★ BX , Ham House★★ BX **V** – **Shoreditch** p. 6 FU Geffrye Museum★ **M** – **Tower Hamlets** p. 6 GV anary Wharf★ St. Katharine Dock★ **Y** – **Twickenham** p. 8 BX Marble Hill House★ **Z**, Straw-erry Hill★ **A** .

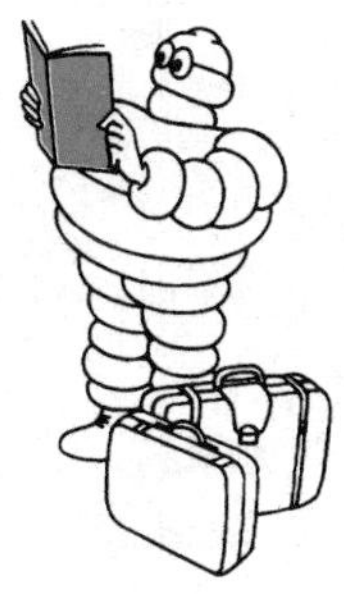

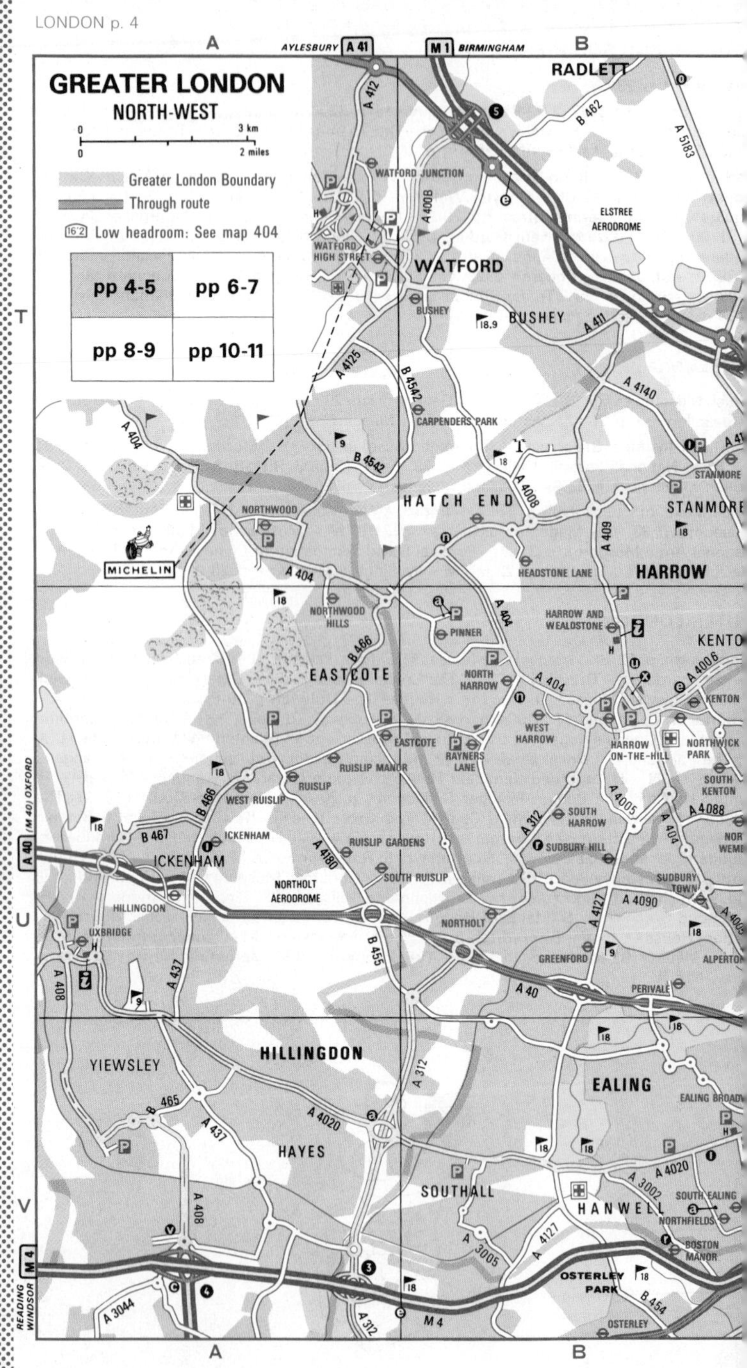
GREATER LONDON
NORTH-WEST
0 3 km
0 2 miles
Greater London Boundary
Through route
Low headroom: See map 404
pp 4-5
pp 6-7
pp 8-9
pp 10-11
A
B
T
U
V
AYLESBURY A 41
M 1 BIRMINGHAM
RADLETT
WATFORD JUNCTION
WATFORD HIGH STREET
WATFORD
ELSTREE AERODROME
BUSHEY
HATCH END
STANMORE
HARROW
NORTHWOOD
NORTHWOOD HILLS
PINNER
CARPENDERS PARK
HEADSTONE LANE
HARROW AND WEALDSTONE
KENTON
NORTH HARROW
EASTCOTE
WEST HARROW
HARROW ON-THE-HILL
NORTHWICK PARK
RAYNERS LANE
RUISLIP MANOR
RUISLIP
WEST RUISLIP
ICKENHAM
SOUTH HARROW
SOUTH KENTON
SUDBURY HILL
SUDBURY TOWN
RUISLIP GARDENS
SOUTH RUISLIP
NORTHOLT AERODROME
NORTHOLT
HILLINGDON
UXBRIDGE
GREENFORD
ALPERTON
PERIVALE
YIEWSLEY
HAYES
EALING
EALING BROADW
SOUTHALL
HANWELL
SOUTH EALING
NORTHFIELDS
BOSTON MANOR
OSTERLEY PARK
OSTERLEY
MICHELIN
A 40 (M 40) OXFORD
M 4 READING WINDSOR
A 412
B 462
A 5183
A 4008
A 411
A 4125
B 4542
A 4140
A 404
A 4008
A 409
A 404
B 466
A 4006
A 4005
A 4088
A 312
A 4180
B 467
A 4127
A 4090
B 455
A 437
A 408
A 40
B 465
A 4020
A 3002
A 3005
A 3044
A 312
M 4
B 454

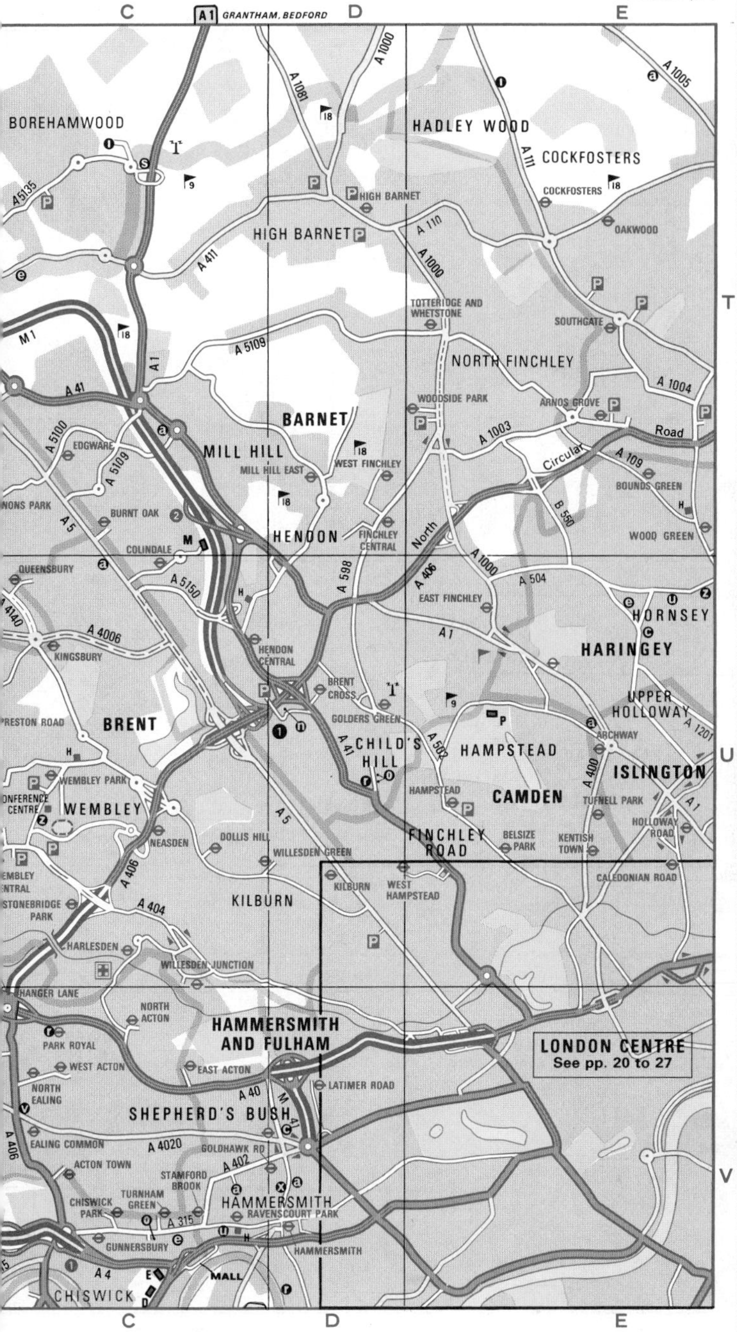
GRANTHAM, BEDFORD
BOREHAMWOOD
HADLEY WOOD
COCKFOSTERS
HIGH BARNET
OAKWOOD
TOTTERIDGE AND WHETSTONE
SOUTHGATE
NORTH FINCHLEY
WOODSIDE PARK
ARNOS GROVE
BARNET
MILL HILL
EDGWARE
MILL HILL EAST
WEST FINCHLEY
Circular
Road
North
BOUNDS GREEN
BURNT OAK
HENDON
FINCHLEY CENTRAL
WOOD GREEN
COLINDALE
QUEENSBURY
EAST FINCHLEY
HORNSEY
KINGSBURY
HENDON CENTRAL
HARINGEY
BRENT CROSS
GOLDERS GREEN
UPPER HOLLOWAY
PRESTON ROAD
BRENT
CHILD'S HILL
HAMPSTEAD
ARCHWAY
ISLINGTON
WEMBLEY PARK
WEMBLEY
CAMDEN
TUFNELL PARK
HOLLOWAY ROAD
NEASDEN
DOLLIS HILL
FINCHLEY ROAD
BELSIZE PARK
KENTISH TOWN
WILLESDEN GREEN
STONEBRIDGE PARK
KILBURN
WEST HAMPSTEAD
CALEDONIAN ROAD
HARLESDEN
WILLESDEN JUNCTION
HANGER LANE
NORTH ACTON
HAMMERSMITH AND FULHAM
PARK ROYAL
WEST ACTON
EAST ACTON
LATIMER ROAD
LONDON CENTRE
See pp. 20 to 27
NORTH EALING
SHEPHERD'S BUSH
EALING COMMON
GOLDHAWK RD
ACTON TOWN
STAMFORD BROOK
TURNHAM GREEN
CHISWICK PARK
HAMMERSMITH
RAVENSCOURT PARK
GUNNERSBURY
MALL
CHISWICK

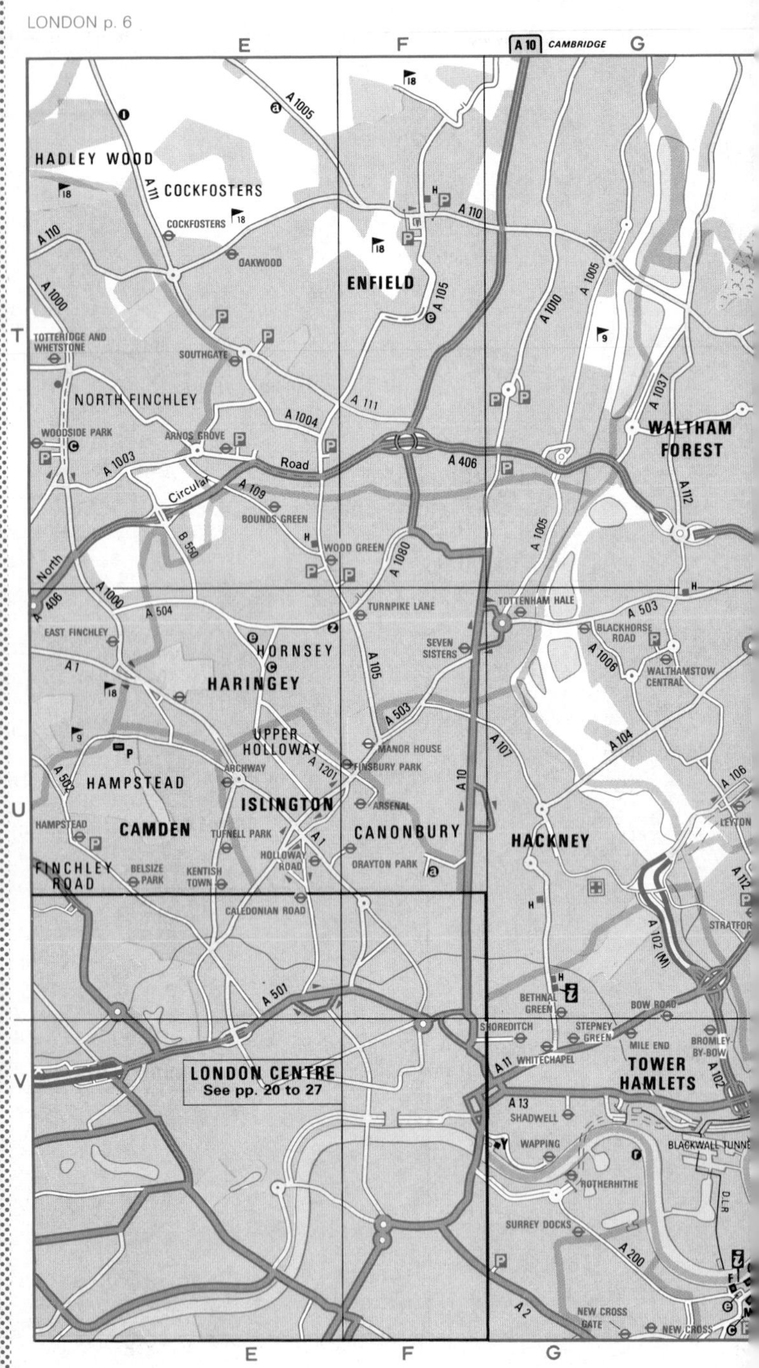
E
F
A 10 CAMBRIDGE
G
HADLEY WOOD
COCKFOSTERS
COCKFOSTERS
OAKWOOD
ENFIELD
TOTTERIDGE AND WHETSTONE
SOUTHGATE
NORTH FINCHLEY
WOODSIDE PARK
ARNOS GROVE
BOUNDS GREEN
WOOD GREEN
WALTHAM FOREST
North Circular Road
EAST FINCHLEY
HORNSEY
HARINGEY
TURNPIKE LANE
SEVEN SISTERS
TOTTENHAM HALE
BLACKHORSE ROAD
WALTHAMSTOW CENTRAL
UPPER HOLLOWAY
MANOR HOUSE
FINSBURY PARK
ARCHWAY
HAMPSTEAD
ISLINGTON
ARSENAL
CAMDEN
TUFNELL PARK
CANONBURY
HACKNEY
LEYTON
HOLLOWAY ROAD
DRAYTON PARK
FINCHLEY ROAD
BELSIZE PARK
KENTISH TOWN
CALEDONIAN ROAD
STRATFORD
BETHNAL GREEN
BOW ROAD
SHOREDITCH
STEPNEY GREEN
MILE END
BROMLEY-BY-BOW
WHITECHAPEL
TOWER HAMLETS
LONDON CENTRE
See pp. 20 to 27
SHADWELL
WAPPING
BLACKWALL TUNNEL
ROTHERHITHE
SURREY DOCKS
NEW CROSS GATE
NEW CROSS
DLR
T
U
V

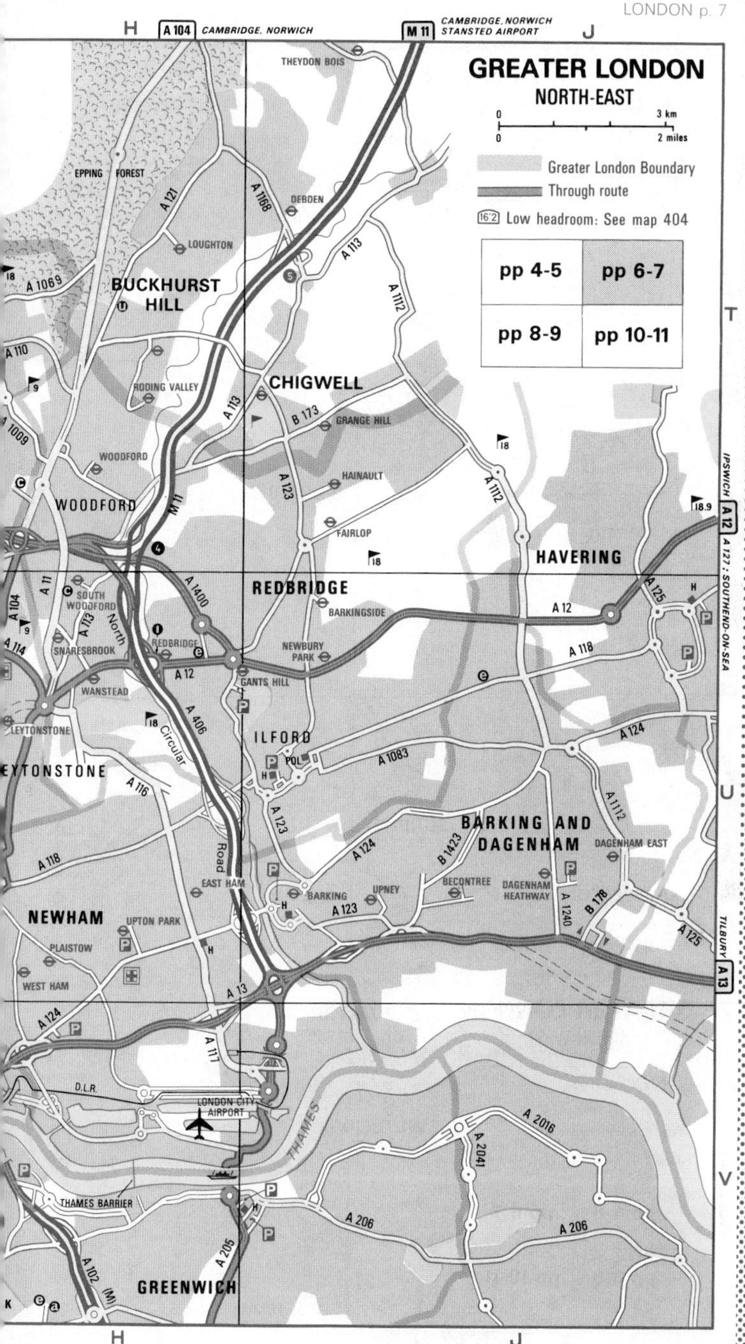
GREATER LONDON
NORTH-EAST
0 3 km
0 2 miles
Greater London Boundary
Through route
Low headroom: See map 404
pp 4-5
pp 6-7
pp 8-9
pp 10-11
A 104 CAMBRIDGE, NORWICH
M 11 CAMBRIDGE, NORWICH STANSTED AIRPORT
THEYDON BOIS
EPPING FOREST
DEBDEN
LOUGHTON
BUCKHURST HILL
CHIGWELL
RODING VALLEY
GRANGE HILL
WOODFORD
HAINAULT
FAIRLOP
HAVERING
REDBRIDGE
SOUTH WOODFORD
BARKINGSIDE
NEWBURY PARK
SNARESBROOK
GANTS HILL
WANSTEAD
LEYTONSTONE
ILFORD
North Circular Road
BARKING AND DAGENHAM
DAGENHAM EAST
BECONTREE
DAGENHAM HEATHWAY
EAST HAM
BARKING
UPNEY
NEWHAM
UPTON PARK
PLAISTOW
WEST HAM
D.L.R.
LONDON CITY AIRPORT
THAMES
THAMES BARRIER
GREENWICH
IPSWICH A 12
A 127 : SOUTHEND-ON-SEA
TILBURY A 13
A 121
A 1168
A 113
A 1112
A 1069
A 110
A 1009
B 173
A 123
M11
A 1400
A 11
A 104
A 114
A 12
A 118
A 406
A 116
A 1083
A 124
A 125
B 1423
A 1240
B 178
A 13
A 117
A 2016
A 2041
A 206
A 205
A 102 (M)
H
J
T
U
V

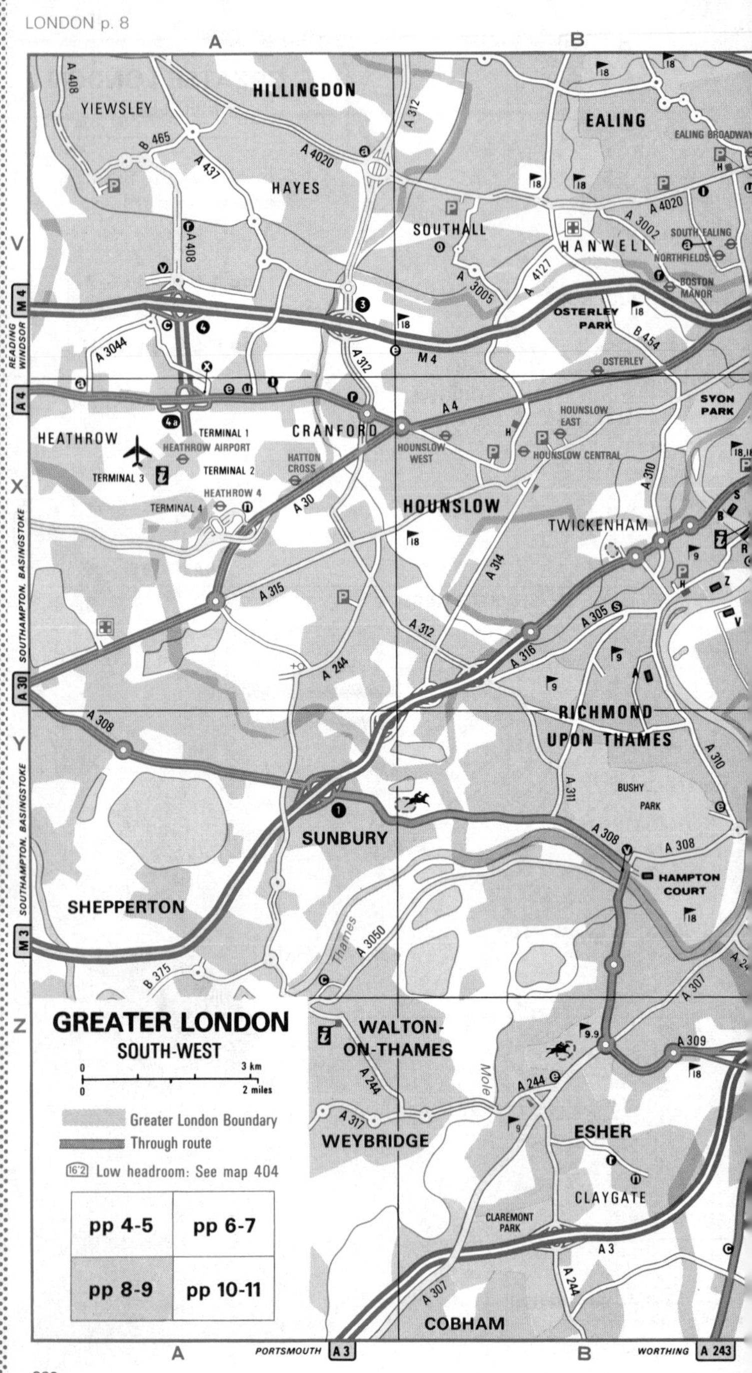
A
B
V
X
Y
Z
HILLINGDON
YIEWSLEY
HAYES
SOUTHALL
EALING
EALING BROADWAY
HANWELL
SOUTH EALING
NORTHFIELDS
BOSTON MANOR
OSTERLEY PARK
OSTERLEY
SYON PARK
HEATHROW
TERMINAL 1
HEATHROW AIRPORT
TERMINAL 2
TERMINAL 3
HEATHROW 4
TERMINAL 4
CRANFORD
HATTON CROSS
HOUNSLOW WEST
HOUNSLOW EAST
HOUNSLOW CENTRAL
HOUNSLOW
TWICKENHAM
RICHMOND UPON THAMES
BUSHY PARK
HAMPTON COURT
SUNBURY
SHEPPERTON
Thames
WALTON-ON-THAMES
Mole
WEYBRIDGE
ESHER
CLAYGATE
CLAREMONT PARK
COBHAM
M 4
READING WINDSOR
A 4
SOUTHAMPTON, BASINGSTOKE
A 30
M 3
PORTSMOUTH
A 3
WORTHING
A 243
A 408
B 465
A 437
A 4020
A 312
A 3002
A 3005
A 4127
B 454
A 3044
A 315
A 244
A 314
A 310
A 305
A 316
A 308
A 311
A 3050
B 375
A 307
A 309
A 317
GREATER LONDON
SOUTH-WEST
0
3 km
0
2 miles
Greater London Boundary
Through route
16'2 Low headroom: See map 404
pp 4-5
pp 6-7
pp 8-9
pp 10-11

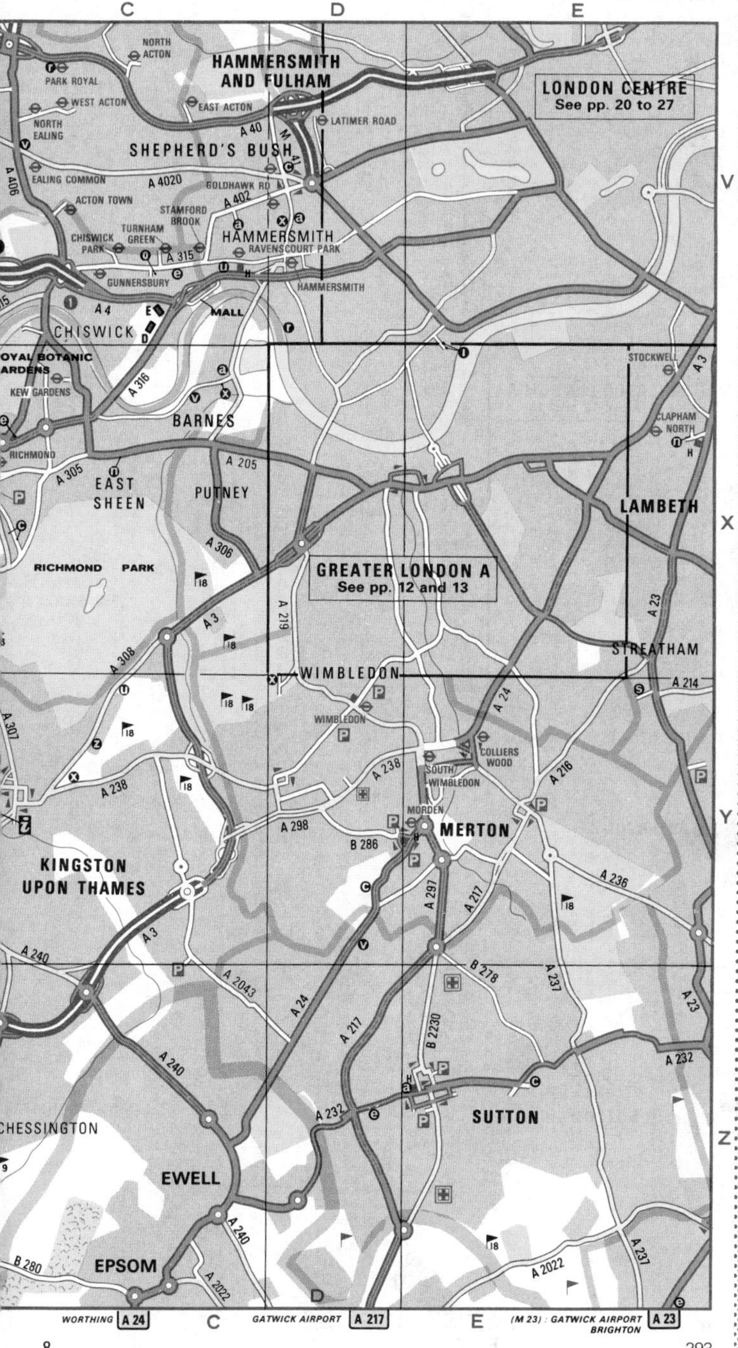
C
D
E
HAMMERSMITH AND FULHAM
LONDON CENTRE
See pp. 20 to 27
NORTH ACTON
PARK ROYAL
WEST ACTON
EAST ACTON
LATIMER ROAD
NORTH EALING
SHEPHERD'S BUSH
EALING COMMON
GOLDHAWK RD
ACTON TOWN
STAMFORD BROOK
CHISWICK PARK
TURNHAM GREEN
HAMMERSMITH
RAVENSCOURT PARK
GUNNERSBURY
MALL
CHISWICK
ROYAL BOTANIC GARDENS
KEW GARDENS
BARNES
RICHMOND
EAST SHEEN
PUTNEY
STOCKWELL
CLAPHAM NORTH
LAMBETH
RICHMOND PARK
GREATER LONDON A
See pp. 12 and 13
STREATHAM
WIMBLEDON
COLLIERS WOOD
SOUTH WIMBLEDON
MORDEN
MERTON
KINGSTON UPON THAMES
SUTTON
CHESSINGTON
EWELL
EPSOM
V
X
Y
Z
WORTHING A 24
GATWICK AIRPORT A 217
(M 23) : GATWICK AIRPORT BRIGHTON A 23

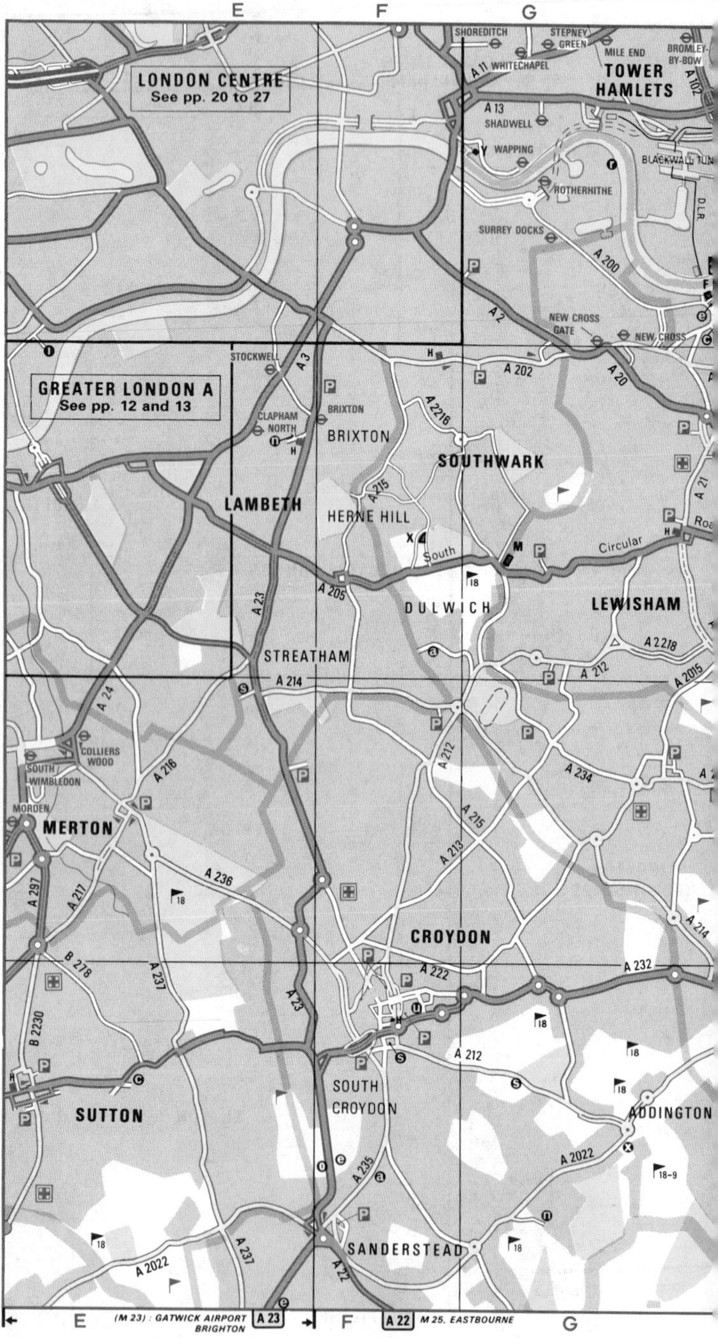

E
F
G
LONDON CENTRE
See pp. 20 to 27
GREATER LONDON A
See pp. 12 and 13
SHOREDITCH
STEPNEY GREEN
MILE END
BROMLEY-BY-BOW
WHITECHAPEL
TOWER HAMLETS
SHADWELL
WAPPING
ROTHERHITHE
BLACKWALL TUN
SURREY DOCKS
NEW CROSS GATE
NEW CROSS
STOCKWELL
CLAPHAM NORTH
BRIXTON
SOUTHWARK
LAMBETH
HERNE HILL
South Circular
DULWICH
LEWISHAM
STREATHAM
COLLIERS WOOD
SOUTH WIMBLEDON
MORDEN
MERTON
CROYDON
SOUTH CROYDON
ADDINGTON
SUTTON
SANDERSTEAD
V
X
Y
Z
A 11
A 13
A 102
A 200
A 2
A 20
A 202
A 3
A 2216
A 215
A 205
A 23
A 214
A 2218
A 212
A 2015
A 24
A 216
A 234
A 236
A 213
A 297
A 217
A 237
B 278
A 222
A 232
B 2230
A 2022
A 235
A 22
A 21
DLR
E
(M 23) : GATWICK AIRPORT BRIGHTON
A 23
F
A 22
M 25, EASTBOURNE
G

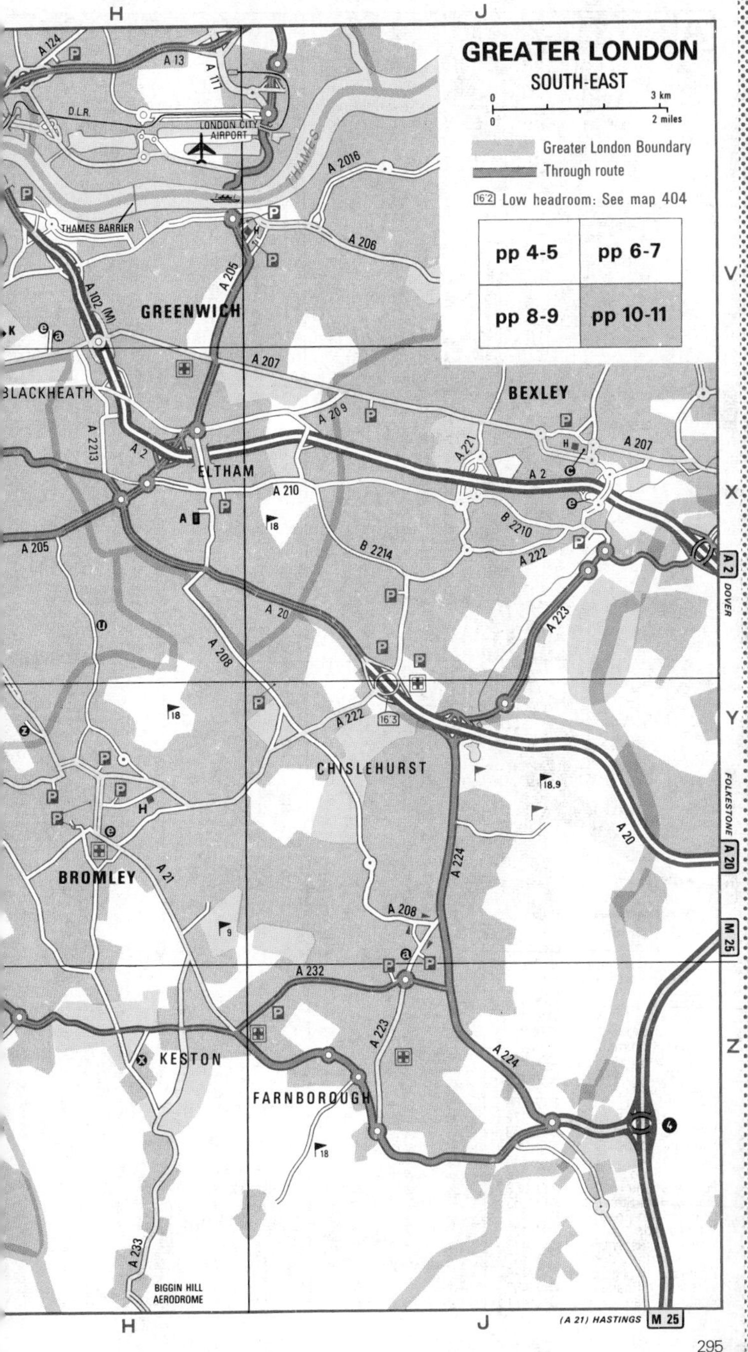
GREATER LONDON
SOUTH-EAST
0 3 km
0 2 miles
Greater London Boundary
Through route
16'2 Low headroom: See map 404
pp 4-5
pp 6-7
pp 8-9
pp 10-11
H
J
V
X
Y
Z
LONDON CITY AIRPORT
D.L.R.
THAMES
THAMES BARRIER
GREENWICH
BLACKHEATH
ELTHAM
BEXLEY
CHISLEHURST
BROMLEY
KESTON
FARNBOROUGH
BIGGIN HILL AERODROME
A 124
A 13
A 111
A 2016
A 206
A 205
A 102 (M)
A 207
A 209
A 2213
A 2
A 221
A 210
B 2210
B 2214
A 222
A 20
A 223
A 208
A 224
A 21
A 232
A 233
A 2 DOVER
FOLKESTONE A 20
M 25
(A 21) HASTINGS M 25

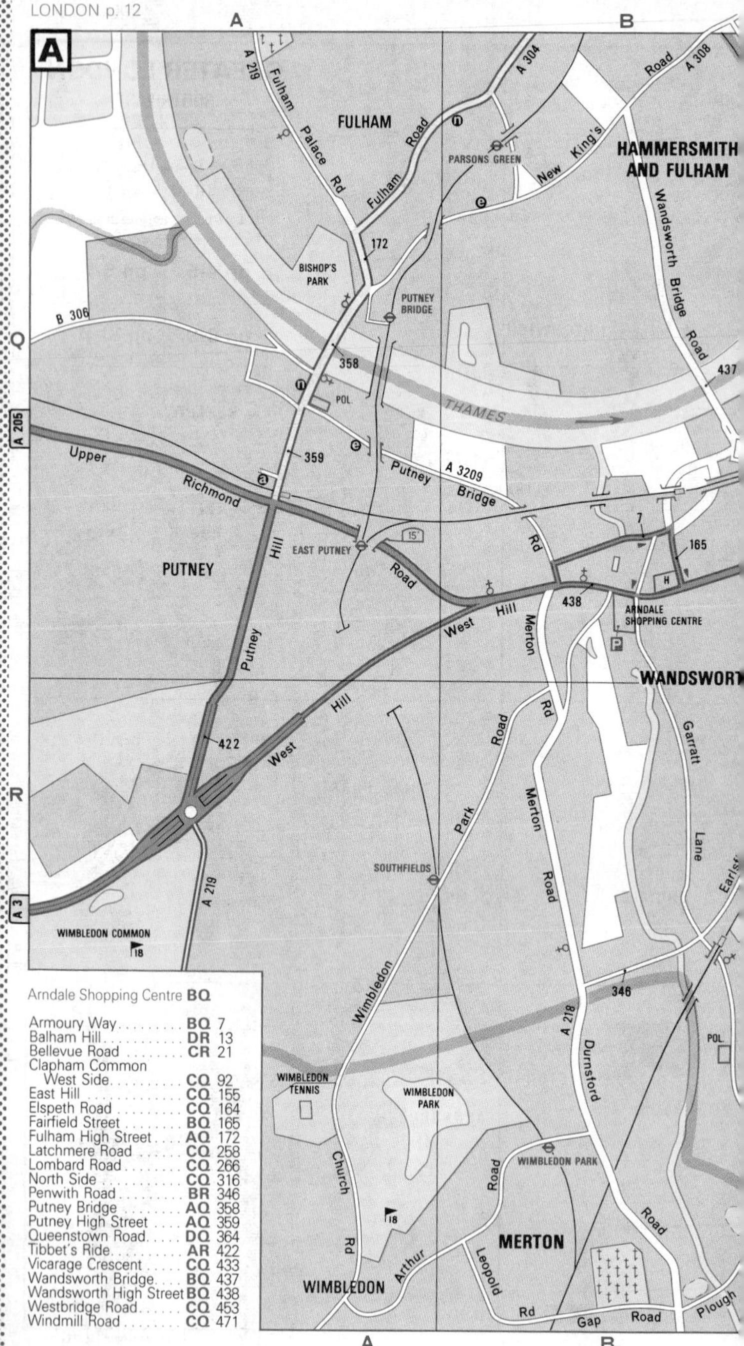

Arndale Shopping Centre **BQ**

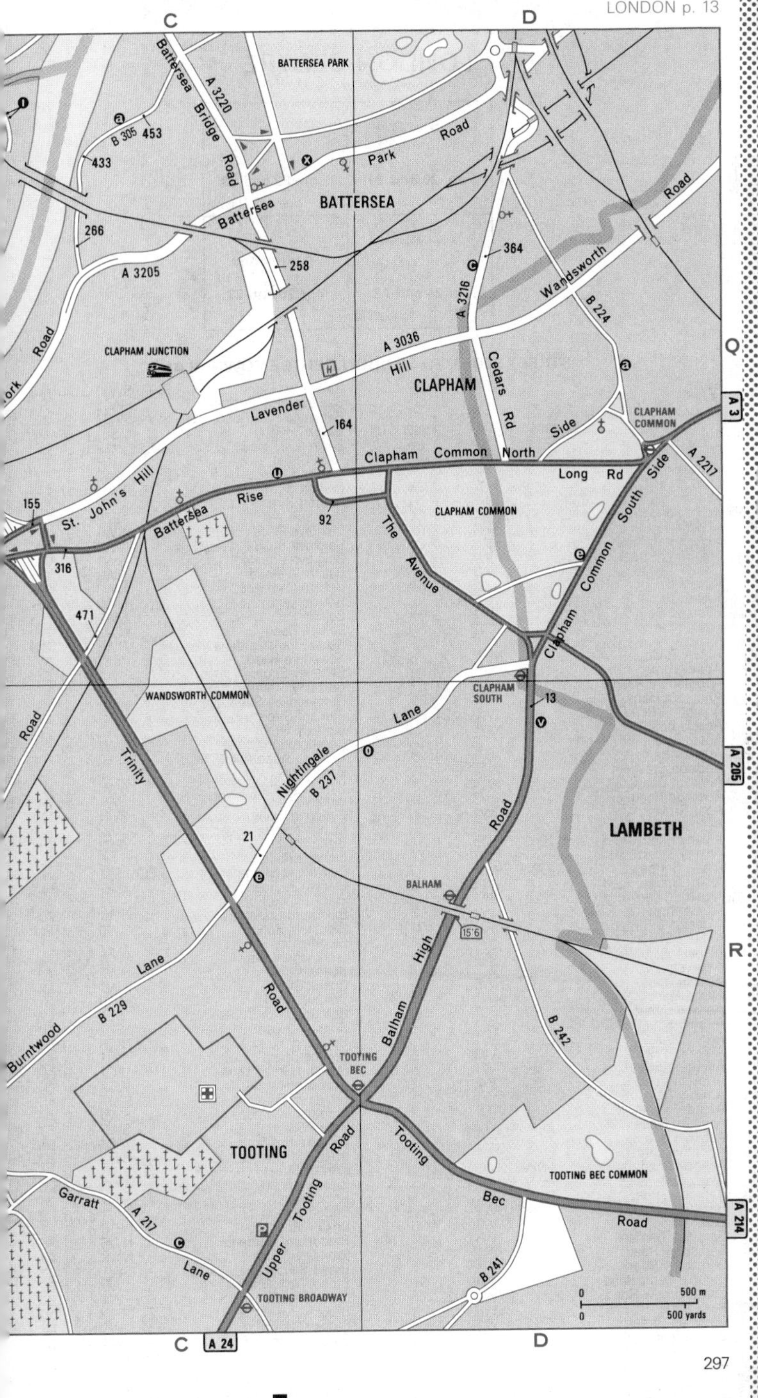
C
D
BATTERSEA PARK
Battersea Bridge Road
A 3220
B 305
453
433
Park Road
BATTERSEA
Battersea
266
A 3205
258
364
A 3216
Wandsworth Road
B 224
CLAPHAM JUNCTION
A 3036
Hill
Lavender
CLAPHAM
Cedars Rd
Q
A 3
CLAPHAM COMMON
Side
164
Clapham Common North
Long Rd
A 2217
St. John's Hill
Battersea
Rise
155
316
92
The Avenue
CLAPHAM COMMON
South Side
Clapham Common
471
WANDSWORTH COMMON
CLAPHAM SOUTH
13
Lane
Nightingale
B 237
Road
Trinity
Road
A 205
LAMBETH
21
BALHAM
15'6
High
R
Lane
B 229
Burntwood
Road
Balham
B 242
TOOTING BEC
TOOTING
Road
Tooting
Bec
Road
TOOTING BEC COMMON
A 214
Garratt
A 217
Lane
Upper Tooting
B 241
TOOTING BROADWAY
0
500 m
500 yards
C
A 24
D

LONDON CENTRE

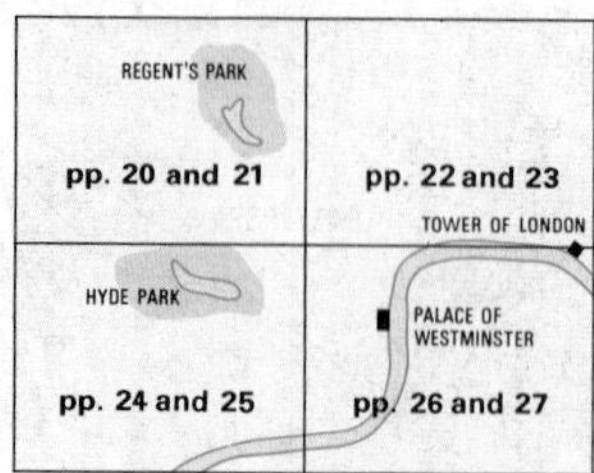

STREET INDEX TO LONDON CENTRE TOWN PLANS

Street	District	Page	Grid	No.
Brushfield Street	E1	p. 23	PU	
Bruton Street	W1	p. 28	CM	
Bryanston Square	W1	p. 21	HU	
Bryanston Street	W1	p. 28	AK	
Buckingham Gate	SW1	p. 32	CV	56
Buckingham Palace Road	SW1	p. 32	AY	
Bunhill Row	EC1	p. 23	PU	
Bury Street	SW1	p. 29	EN	
Bute Street	SW7	p. 30	CS	59
Byward Street	EC3	p. 23	PV	62
Cadogan Gardens	SW3	p. 31	FS	
Cadogan Place	SW1	p. 31	FR	
Cadogan Square	SW1	p. 31	FS	
Cadogan Street	SW3	p. 31	ET	
Caledonian Road	N1, N7	p. 22	MS	
Cale Street	SW3	p. 31	DT	
Calshot Street	N1	p. 22	MT	
Calthorpe Street	WC1	p. 22	MT	65
Camberwell New Road	SE5	p. 27	NZ	
Camberwell Road	SE5	p. 27	OZ	
Cambridge Circus	WC2	p. 29	GK	
Cambridge Square	W2	p. 33	EZ	67
Camden High Street	NW1	p. 22	JS	
Camden Road	E11	p. 22	KS	
Camden Street	NW1	p. 22	KS	
Camomile Street	EC3	p. 23	PU	71
Campden Hill Road	W8	p. 24	EX	
Cannon Street	EC4	p. 23	OV	
Canonbury Road	N1	p. 23	NS	
Canonbury Square	N1	p. 23	NS	
Carey Street	WC2	p. 33	EV	
Carlisle Place	SW1	p. 32	BX	
Carlos Place	W1	p. 28	BM	
Carlton Gardens	SW1	p. 29	FP	74
Carlton Hill	NW8	p. 20	FS	
Carlton House Terrace	SW1	p. 29	FN	
Carlton Vale	NW6	p. 20	ET	
Carriage Drive East	SW11	p. 25	IZ	
Carriage Drive North	SW11	p. 25	IZ	75
Carriage Road (the)	SW7, SW11	p. 31	EQ	
Castle Lane	SW1	p. 32	CX	
Cavendish Square	W1	p. 28	CJ	
Central Street	EC1	p. 23	OT	
Chalk Farm Road	NW1	p. 21	IS	
Chancery Lane	WC2	p. 33	EV	
Chandos Place	WC2	p. 33	DY	
Chandos Street	W1	p. 28	CH	
Chapel Market	N1	p. 23	NS	78
Chapel Street	SW1	p. 32	AV	
Chapter Road	SE17	p. 27	OZ	
Charlbert Street	NW8	p. 21	HT	79
Charles II Street	SW1	p. 29	FN	
Charles Street	W1	p. 28	CN	
Charing Cross	SW1	p. 33	DY	
Charing Cross Road	WC2	p. 29	GJ	
Charterhouse Square	EC1	p. 23	OU	81
Charterhouse Street	EC1	p. 23	NU	83
Cheapside	EC2	p. 23	OV	
Chelsea Bridge	SW1, SW8	p. 25	IZ	
Chelsea Bridge Road	SW1	p. 25	IZ	
Chelsea Embankment	SW3	p. 25	HZ	
Chelsea Manor Street	SW3	p. 31	EU	
Chelsea Square	SW3	p. 31	DU	
Cheltenham Terrace	SW3	p. 31	FT	
Chepstow Crescent	W11	p. 32	AZ	84
Chepstow Place	W2	p. 32	AZ	
Chepstow Road	W2	p. 32	AZ	
Chesham Place	SW2	p. 31	FR	
Chesham Street	SW1	p. 31	FS	
Chester Road	NW1	p. 21	IT	
Chester Row	SW1	p. 32	AY	
Chester Square	SW1	p. 32	AX	88
Chester Street	SW1	p. 32	AV	
Cheval Place	SW7	p. 31	ER	
Cheyne Walk	SW3, SW10	p. 25	GZ	
Chilworth Street	W2	p. 32	CZ	90
Chippenham Road	W9	p. 20	EU	
Chiswell Street	EC1	p. 23	OU	
Church Row	NW3	p. 20	ES	
Church Street	NW8, NW2	p. 21	GU	
Circus Road	NW8	p. 21	GT	
City Road	EC1	p. 23	NT	
Clapham Road	SW9	p. 26	MZ	
Clarendon Place	W2	p. 33	EZ	93
Clarendon Road	W11	p. 24	EX	
Claverton Street	SW1	p. 26	KZ	
Clayton Street	SE11	p. 26	MZ	
Clerkenwell Road	EC1	p. 23	NU	
Cleveland Gardens	W2	p. 32	CZ	94
Cleveland Square	W2	p. 32	CZ	
Cleveland Street	W1	p. 22	KU	
Cleveland Terrace	W2	p. 32	CZ	
Clifford Street	W1	p. 29	DM	
Cliveden Place	SW1	p. 31	FS	
Cockspur Street	SW1	p. 29	GN	
Collingham Gardens	SW5	p. 30	AT	99
Collingham Road	SW5	p. 30	AT	101
Commercial Street	E1	p. 23	PU	
Conduit Street	W1	p. 29	DL	
Connaught Square	W2	p. 33	EZ	103
Connaught Street	W2	p. 33	EZ	
Constantine Road	NW3	p. 20	ES	106
Constitution Hill	SW1	p. 32	AV	
Copenhagen Street	N1	p. 22	LS	
Cork Street	W1	p. 29	DM	
Cornwall Crescent	W11	p. 20	EV	107
Cornwall Gardens	SW7	p. 30	AR	
Cornwall Road	SE1	p. 26	MX	108
Corporation Row	EC1	p. 23	NT	110
Courtfield Gardens	SW5	p. 30	AT	
Courtfield Road	SW7	p. 30	BS	
Coventry Street	W1	p. 29	FM	
Cowcross Street	EC1	p. 23	NU	113
Cranbourn Street	WC2	p. 33	DX	115
Cranley Gardens	SW7	p. 30	CT	
Craven Hill	W2	p. 32	CZ	
Craven Road	W2	p. 33	DZ	
Craven Street	WC2	p. 33	DY	
Craven Terrace	W2	p. 33	DZ	
Crawford Place	W1	p. 21	HU	116
Crawford Street	W1	p. 21	HU	
Cromwell Crescent	SW5	p. 24	EZ	119
Cromwell Place	SW7	p. 30	CS	120
Cromwell Road	SW7, SW5	p. 30	CS	
Crowndale Road	NW1	p. 22	KS	
Crucifix Lane	SE1	p. 27	PX	125
Culross Street	W1	p. 28	AM	
Curtain Road	EC2	p. 23	PT	126
Curzon Street	W1	p. 28	BN	
Cut (The)	SE1	p. 27	NX	
Dante Road	SE11	p. 27	NZ	129
D'Arblay Street	W1	p. 29	EK	
Davies Street	W1	p. 28	BK	
Dawes Road	SW6	p. 24	EZ	
Dawson Place	W2	p. 32	AZ	
Deanery Street	W1	p. 28	BN	132
Dean Street	W1	p. 29	FJ	
De Beauvoir Road	N1	p. 23	PS	
Delancey Street	NW1	p. 21	JS	
Delaware Road	W9	p. 20	FT	
Denbigh Street	SW1	p. 26	KZ	
Denman Street	W1	p. 29	FM	133
Denmark Street	WC2	p. 29	GJ	134
De Vere Gardens	W8	p. 30	BQ	
Devonshire Street	W1	p. 21	IU	
Devonshire Terrace	W2	p. 32	CZ	136
Dorset Road	SW8	p. 26	LZ	
Dorset Street	W1	p. 28	AH	
Dovehouse Street	SW3	p. 31	DU	
Dover Street	W1	p. 29	DM	
Downham Road	N1	p. 23	PS	
Downing Street	SW1	p. 26	LX	138
Downshire Hill	NW3	p. 20	ES	139
Draycott Avenue	SW3	p. 31	ET	
Draycott Place	SW3	p. 31	ET	
Drayton Gardens	SW10	p. 30	BT	
Druid Street	SE1	p. 27	PY	
Drury Lane	WC2	p. 33	DV	
Dufferin Street	EC1	p. 23	OT	141
Duke of Wellington Place	SW1	p. 32	AV	142
Duke of York Street	SW1	p. 29	EN	143
Duke's Place	EC3	p. 23	PV	145
Duke Street	W1	p. 28	BK	
Duke Street ST. JAMES	SW1	p. 29	EN	146
Duncannon Street	WC2	p. 33	DY	147
Dunraven Street	W1	p. 28	AL	149
Dunton Road	SE1	p. 27	PZ	
Durham Street	SE11	p. 26	MZ	150
Eagle Wharf Road	N1	p. 23	OS	
Eardley Crescent	SW5	p. 24	EZ	151
Earlham Street	WC2	p. 33	DV	153
Earl's Court Road	W8, SW5	p. 24	EY	
Eastbourne Terrace	W2	p. 33	DZ	
Eastcastle Street	W1	p. 29	EJ	
Eastcheap	EC3	p. 23	PV	154
East Heath Road	NW3	p. 20	ES	
East Road	N1	p. 23	PT	
East Street	SE17	p. 27	PZ	
Eaton Place	SW1	p. 32	AX	
Eaton Square	SW1	p. 32	AX	
Ebury Bridge	SW1	p. 25	IZ	156
Ebury Street	SW1	p. 32	AY	
Ebury Bridge Road	SW1	p. 25	IZ	
Eccleston Bridge	SW1	p. 32	BY	157
Eccleston Square	SW1	p. 32	BY	
Eccleston Street	SW1	p. 32	AY	

Street	District	Page	Grid	No.
Edgware Road	W2	p. 21	**GU**	
Edith Grove	SW10	p. 24	**FZ**	
Edith Road	W14	p. 24	**EZ**	
Edwardes Square	W8	p. 24	**EY**	158
Egerton Gardens	SW3	p. 31	**DS**	160
Egerton Terrace	SW3	p. 31	**DR**	161
Egerton Gardens Mews	SW3	p. 31	**ER**	162
Elephant and Castle	SE11	p. 27	**OY**	
Elephant Road	SE17	p. 27	**OZ**	163
Elgin Avenue	W9	p. 20	**FT**	
Elizabeth Street	SW1	p. 32	**AY**	
Elm Park Gardens	SW10	p. 30	**CU**	
Elm Park Road	SW3	p. 30	**CU**	
Elsworthy Road	NW3	p. 21	**GS**	
Elvaston Place	SW7	p. 30	**BR**	
Elystan Place	SW3	p. 31	**ET**	
Elystan Street	SW3	p. 31	**DT**	
Endell Street	WC2	p. 33	**DV**	
England's Lane	NW3	p. 21	**HS**	
Englefield Road	N1	p. 23	**PS**	
Ennismore Gardens	SW7	p. 31	**DQ**	
Essex Road	N1	p. 23	**OS**	
Essex Street	WC2	p. 33	**EX**	
Estcourt Road	SW6	p. 24	**EZ**	
Eton Avenue	NW3	p. 21	**GS**	
Euston Road	NW1	p. 22	**LT**	
Evelyn Gardens	SW7	p. 30	**CU**	
Eversholt Street	NW1	p. 22	**KT**	
Exeter Street	WC2	p. 33	**DX**	
Exhibition Road	SW7	p. 30	**CQ**	
Fairfax Road	NW6	p. 20	**FS**	
Fairhazel Gardens	NW6	p. 20	**FS**	
Falmouth Road	SE1	p. 27	**OY**	
Farm Street MAYFAIR	W1	p. 28	**BM**	
Fann Street	W1	p. 23	**OU**	166
Farringdon Road	EC1	p. 23	**NU**	
Farringdon Street	EC4	p. 23	**NU**	168
Fenchurch Street	EC3	p. 23	**PV**	
Fentiman Road	SW8	p. 26	**LZ**	
Fernhead Road	W9	p. 20	**ET**	
Fetter Lane	EC4	p. 23	**NU**	169
Fifth Avenue	W10	p. 20	**ET**	
Filmer Road	SW6	p. 24	**EZ**	
Finborough Road	SW10	p. 30	**AU**	
Finchley Road	NW8, NW3 NW2, NW11	p. 21	**GS**	
Fitzalan Street	SE11	p. 26	**MZ**	
Fitzjohn's Avenue	NW3	p. 21	**GS**	
Fitzroy Square	W1	p. 22	**KU**	
Fleet Road	NW3	p. 20	**ES**	
Fleet Street	EC4	p. 22	**MV**	
Flint Street	SE17	p. 27	**PZ**	
Flood Street	SW3	p. 31	**EU**	
Floral Street	WC2	p. 33	**DX**	
Foulis Terrace	SW7	p. 30	**CT**	170
Foxley Road	SW9	p. 27	**NZ**	
Frampton Street	NW8	p. 21	**GT**	
Francis Street	SW1	p. 32	**CY**	
Franklin's Row	SW3	p. 31	**FU**	
Frith Street	W1	p. 29	**FK**	
Frognal	NW3	p. 20	**ES**	
Frognal Rise	NW3	p. 20	**ES**	171
Fulham Road	SW3, SW10, SW6	p. 24	**EZ**	
Garden Row	SE1	p. 27	**NY**	173
Garrick Street	WC2	p. 33	**DX**	
Garway Road	W2	p. 32	**BZ**	
Gayton Road	NW3	p. 20	**ES**	
George Street	W1	p. 28	**AJ**	
Gerrard Street	W1	p. 29	**GL**	174
Gilbert Street	W1	p. 28	**BL**	175
Gillingham Street	SW1	p. 32	**BY**	
Gilston Road	SW10	p. 30	**BU**	
Giltspur Street	EC1	p. 23	**OU**	178
Glasshouse Street	W1	p. 29	**EM**	179
Glendower Place	SW7	p. 30	**CS**	180
Gliddon Road	W14	p. 24	**EZ**	182
Gloucester Avenue	NW1	p. 21	**IS**	
Gloucester Place	W1, NW1	p. 21	**HU**	
Gloucester Road	SW7	p. 30	**BR**	
Gloucester Square	W2	p. 33	**EZ**	
Gloucester Street	SW1	p. 27	**JZ**	
Gloucester Terrace	W2	p. 32	**CZ**	
Golborne Road	W10	p. 20	**EU**	
Golden Square	W1	p. 29	**EL**	
Goodge Street	W1	p. 22	**KU**	184
Goswell Road	EC1	p. 23	**OT**	
Gower Street	WC1	p. 22	**KU**	
Gracechurch Street	EC3	p. 23	**PV**	187
Grafton Street	W1	p. 29	**DM**	
Grange Road	SE1	p. 27	**PY**	
Granville Place	W1	p. 28	**AK**	188
Gray's Inn Road	WC1	p. 22	**LT**	
Gt. Castle Street	W1	p. 29	**DJ**	189
Gt. Cumberland Place	W1	p. 33	**EZ**	191
Gt. Dover Street	SE1	p. 27	**PY**	
Gt. Eastern Street	EC2	p. 23	**PT**	192
Gt. George Street	SW1	p. 26	**LY**	193
Gt. Marlborough Street	W1	p. 29	**EK**	
Gt. Peter Street	SW1	p. 26	**LY**	
Gt. Queen Street	WC2	p. 33	**DV**	
Gt. Russell Street	WC1	p. 22	**LU**	
Gt. Smith Street	SW1	p. 26	**LY**	196
Gt. Suffolk Street	SE1	p. 27	**OX**	
Gt. Tower Street	EC3	p. 23	**PV**	197
Gt. Western Road	W9, W11	p. 20	**EU**	
Gt. Windmill Street	W1	p. 29	**FM**	
Greek Street	W1	p. 29	**GK**	198
Greencroft Gardens	NW6	p. 20	**FS**	
Green Street	W1	p. 28	**AL**	
Grenville Place	SW7	p. 30	**BS**	
Gresham Street	EC2	p. 23	**OU**	
Greville Place	NW6	p. 20	**FS**	
Greycoat Place	SW1	p. 26	**KY**	200
Greyhound Road	W6, W14	p. 24	**EZ**	
Grosvenor Crescent	SW1	p. 32	**AV**	
Grosvenor Gardens	SW1	p. 32	**BX**	
Grosvenor Place	SW1	p. 32	**AV**	
Grosvenor Road	SW1	p. 26	**JZ**	
Grosvenor Square	W1	p. 28	**BL**	
Grosvenor Street	W1	p. 28	**BL**	
Grove End Road	NW8	p. 21	**GT**	
Guildhouse Street	SW1	p. 32	**BY**	201
Guilford Street	WC1	p. 22	**LU**	
Gunter Grove	SW10	p. 24	**FZ**	202
Gunterstone Road	W14	p. 24	**EZ**	203
Hackney Road	E2	p. 23	**PT**	
Half Moon Street	W1	p. 28	**CN**	
Halford Road	SW6	p. 24	**EZ**	
Halkin Street	SW1	p. 32	**AV**	
Halliford Street	N1	p. 23	**OS**	
Hall Road	NW8	p. 20	**FT**	
Hamilton Place	W1	p. 28	**BP**	205
Hamilton Terrace	NW8	p. 20	**FT**	
Hammersmith Road	W14, W6	p. 24	**EZ**	207
Hampstead Grove	NW3	p. 20	**ES**	208
Hampstead High Street	NW3	p. 20	**ES**	209
Hampstead Road	NW1	p. 22	**KT**	
Hanover Square	W1	p. 28	**CK**	210
Hanover Street	W1	p. 29	**DK**	
Hans Crescent	SW1	p. 31	**ER**	
Hans Place	SW1	p. 31	**ER**	
Hans Road	SW3	p. 31	**ER**	
Harcourt Terrace	SW10	p. 30	**AU**	
Harley Street WESTMINSTER	W1	p. 28	**CH**	
Harleyford Road	SE11	p. 26	**LZ**	
Harleyford Street	SE11	p. 26	**MZ**	211
Harper Road	SE1	p. 27	**OY**	
Harriet Street	SW1	p. 31	**FQ**	214
Harrington Gardens	SW7	p. 30	**BT**	
Harrington Road	SW7	p. 30	**CS**	215
Harrow Road	W2, W9 W10, NW10	p. 20	**FU**	
Harwood Road	SW6	p. 24	**FZ**	
Hasker Street	SW3	p. 31	**ES**	
Haverstock Hill	NW3	p. 21	**HS**	
Haymarket	SW1	p. 29	**FM**	
Hay's Mews	W1	p. 28	**BN**	
Heath Street	NW3	p. 20	**ES**	
Hemingford Road	N1	p. 22	**MS**	
Henrietta Place	W1	p. 28	**BJ**	
Henrietta Street	WC2	p. 33	**DX**	217
Herbrand Street	WC1	p. 22	**LT**	218
Hercules Road	SE1	p. 26	**MY**	219
Hereford Road	W2	p. 32	**AZ**	
Hertford Street	W1	p. 28	**BP**	220
Heygate Street	SE17	p. 27	**OZ**	
High Holborn	WC1	p. 22	**LU**	
Hill Street	W1	p. 28	**BN**	
Hobart Place	SW1	p. 32	**AX**	
Holbein Place	SW1	p. 31	**FT**	
Holbein Mews	SW1	p. 31	**FT**	223
Holborn	EC1	p. 22	**MU**	
Holborn Viaduct	EC1	p. 23	**NU**	
Holland Park	W11	p. 24	**EX**	
Holland Park Avenue	W11	p. 24	**EX**	
Holland Park Gardens	W11	p. 24	**EX**	224
Holland Road	W14	p. 24	**EY**	
Holland Street	W8	p. 24	**EY**	
Holland Walk	W8	p. 24	**EY**	225
Holland Villas Road	W14	p. 24	**EY**	
Holles Street	W1	p. 28	**CJ**	
Hollybush Hill	E11	p. 20	**ES**	227
Hollywood Road	SW10	p. 30	**BU**	
Horseferry Road	SW1	p. 26	**KY**	
Horseguards Avenue	SW1	p. 26	**LX**	228

Street	District	Page	Grid	No.
Norfolk Crescent	W2	p. 33	**EZ**	310
Norfolk Square	W2	p. 33	**DZ**	313
North Audley Street	W1	p. 28	**AK**	314
North Carriage Drive	W2	p. 33	**EZ**	
North End Road	W14, SW6	p. 24	**EZ**	
North Row	W1	p. 28	**AL**	
Northumberland Avenue	WC2	p. 26	**LX**	317
Notting Hill Gate	W11	p. 32	**AZ**	
Nutley Terrace	NW3	p. 20	**ES**	
Nuttall Street	N1	p. 23	**PS**	
Oakley Street	SW3	p. 31	**DU**	
Offord Road	N1	p. 22	**MS**	
Old Bailey	EC4	p. 23	**NV**	318
Old Broad Street	EC2	p. 23	**PU**	319
Old Brompton Road	SW7, SW5	p. 30	**BT**	
Old Burlington Street	W1	p. 29	**DM**	322
Old Church Street	SW3	p. 30	**CU**	
Old Compton Street	W1	p. 29	**GK**	323
Old Kent Road	SE1, SE15	p. 27	**PZ**	
Old Marylebone Road	NW1	p. 21	**HU**	324
Old Park Lane	W1	p. 28	**BP**	
Old Street	EC1	p. 23	**OT**	
Olympia Way	W14	p. 24	**EY**	326
Onslow Gardens	SW7	p. 30	**CT**	
Onslow Square	SW7	p. 30	**CT**	
Orange Street	WC2	p. 29	**GM**	
Orchard Street	W1	p. 28	**AK**	
Ordnance Hill	NW8	p. 21	**GS**	
Orme Court	W2	p. 32	**BZ**	328
Ormonde Gate	SW3	p. 31	**FU**	329
Ornan Road	NW3	p. 20	**ES**	331
Ossulton Street	NW1	p. 22	**LT**	
Outer Circle	NW1	p. 21	**HT**	
Oxford Circus	W1	p. 29	**DJ**	
Oxford Square	W2	p. 33	**EZ**	332
Paddington Street	W1	p. 21	**IU**	333
Page Street	SW1	p. 26	**LZ**	
Page's Walk	SE1	p. 27	**PY**	
Palace Court	W2	p. 32	**BZ**	
Palace Gardens Terrace	W8	p. 32	**AZ**	335
Palace Gate	W8	p. 30	**BQ**	
Palace Street	SW1	p. 32	**BX**	
Pall Mall	SW1	p. 29	**FN**	
Palmer Street	SW1	p. 32	**CV**	
Pancras Road	NW1	p. 22	**KS**	
Panton Street	SW1	p. 29	**FM**	336
Parade (The)	SW11	p. 25	**HZ**	
Park Crescent	W1	p. 21	**IU**	337
Parker Street	WC2	p. 33	**DV**	
Parkgate Road	SW11	p. 25	**HZ**	
Park Lane	W1	p. 28	**AM**	
Park Road	NW1, NW8	p. 21	**HT**	
Park Street	W1	p. 28	**AL**	
Park Village East	NW1	p. 21	**JS**	
Park Walk	SW10	p. 30	**CU**	
Parkway	NW1	p. 21	**JS**	
Parliament Hill	NW3	p. 20	**ES**	
Parliament Street	SW1	p. 26	**LY**	340
Parry Street	SW8	p. 26	**LZ**	341
Paul Street	EC2	p. 23	**PT**	
Pelham Street	SW7	p. 31	**DS**	
Pembridge Gardens	W2	p. 32	**AZ**	
Pembridge Road	W11	p. 32	**AZ**	
Pembridge Square	W2	p. 32	**AZ**	
Pembridge Villas	W11	p. 32	**AZ**	
Pembrocke Gardens	W8	p. 24	**EY**	342
Pembrocke Road	W8	p. 24	**EZ**	
Penn Street	N1	p. 23	**PS**	343
Penton Place	WC1	p. 27	**OS**	
Penton Rise	WC1	p. 22	**MT**	344
Penton Street	N1	p. 22	**MT**	345
Pentonville Road	N1	p. 22	**LT**	
Penywern Road	SW5	p. 24	**FZ**	347
Percival Street	EC1	p. 23	**NT**	
Petty France	SW1	p. 32	**CV**	
Philbeach Gardens	SW5	p. 24	**EZ**	348
Piccadilly Circus	W1	p. 29	**FM**	
Pilgrimage Street	SE1	p. 27	**PY**	349
Pimlico Road	SW1	p. 25	**IZ**	
Pitfield Street	N1	p. 23	**PT**	
Poland Street	W1	p. 29	**EJ**	
Pond Street	NW3	p. 20	**ES**	
Pont Street	SW1	p. 31	**ER**	
Poole Street	N1	p. 23	**PS**	350
Porchester Gardens	W2	p. 32	**BZ**	
Porchester Road	W2	p. 20	**FU**	351
Porchester Terrace	W2	p. 32	**CZ**	
Portland Place	W1	p. 21	**JU**	
Portland Street	SE17	p. 27	**PZ**	
Portman Square	W1	p. 28	**AJ**	
Potman Street	W1	p. 28	**AK**	
Portugal Street	WC2	p. 33	**EV**	
Poultry	EC2	p. 23	**OV**	352
Praed Street	W2	p. 21	**GV**	
Pratt Street	NW1	p. 22	**KS**	
Primrose Hill Road	NW3	p. 21	**HS**	
Prince Albert Road	NW1, NW8	p. 21	**HS**	
Prince Consort Road	SW7	p. 30	**CR**	
Prince's Gardens	SW7	p. 30	**CR**	
Prince's Street	W1	p. 29	**DK**	
Princes Street	EC2	p. 23	**PV**	
Queen Anne's Gate	SW1	p. 26	**KY**	
Queen Anne Street	W1	p. 28	**BH**	
Queensberry Place	SW7	p. 30	**CS**	
Queensborough Terrace	W2	p. 32	**CZ**	
Queen's Circus	SW8	p. 25	**IZ**	
Queen's Gardens	W2	p. 32	**CZ**	
Queen's Gate	SW7	p. 30	**BQ**	
Queen's Gate Gardens	SW7	p. 30	**BR**	
Queen's Gate Place	SW7	p. 30	**BR**	
Queen's Gate Terrace	SW7	p. 30	**BR**	
Queen's Grove	NW8	p. 21	**GS**	
Queen Street	EC4	p. 23	**OV**	
Queen's Walk	SW1	p. 29	**DN**	
Queensway	W2	p. 32	**BZ**	
Queen Victoria Street	EC4	p. 23	**OV**	
Radnor Place	W2	p. 33	**DZ**	
Radnor Walk	SW3	p. 31	**EU**	
Randolph Avenue	W9	p. 20	**FT**	
Randoplh Street	NW1	p. 22	**KS**	
Rawlings Street	SW3	p. 31	**ES**	
Redcliffe Gardens	SW10	p. 30	**AU**	
Redcliffe Square	SW10	p. 30	**AU**	
Redesdale Street	SW3	p. 31	**EU**	3
Red Lion Street	WC1	p. 22	**MU**	
Reeves Mews	W1	p. 28	**AM**	
Regency Street	SW1	p. 26	**KZ**	
Regent's Park Road	NW1	p. 21	**HS**	
Richmond Avenue	N1	p. 22	**MS**	
Robert Street	NW1	p. 22	**JT**	
Rochester Row	SW1	p. 32	**CY**	
Rodney Road	N1	p. 27	**OZ**	
Roland Gardens	SW7	p. 30	**BT**	
Roman Way	N7	p. 22	**MS**	
Romilly Street	W1	p. 29	**GL**	3
Rosebery Avenue	EC1	p. 22	**MT**	
Rosslyn Hill	NW3	p. 20	**ES**	
Rossmore Road	NW1	p. 21	**HT**	3
Royal College Street	NW1	p. 22	**KS**	
Royal Crescent	W11	p. 24	**EX**	3
Royal Hospital Road	SW3	p. 31	**FU**	
Rupert Street	W1	p. 29	**FL**	
Russell Square	WC1	p. 22	**LU**	
Russell Street	WC2	p. 33	**DX**	
Rutland Gate	SW7	p. 31	**DQ**	
Rylston Road	SW6	p. 24	**EZ**	
Sackville Street	W1	p. 29	**EM**	
St. Albans Grove	W8	p. 28	**AR**	
St. Andrews Street	EC4	p. 23	**NU**	3
St. Bride Street	EC4	p. 23	**NV**	3
St. George's Drive	SW1	p. 26	**KZ**	
St. George's Road	SE1	p. 27	**NY**	
St. George's Square	SW1	p. 26	**KZ**	
St. George Street	W1	p. 29	**DL**	
St. Giles Circus	W1, WC1, WC2	p. 29	**GJ**	
St. Giles High Street	WC2	p. 33	**DV**	3
St. James's Place	SW1	p. 29	**EN**	
St. James's Square	SW1	p. 29	**FN**	
St. James's Street	SW1	p. 29	**EN**	
St. James Street	E17	p. 33	**DX**	
St. John Street	EC1	p. 23	**NT**	
St. John's Wood High Street	NW8	p. 21	**GT**	3
St. John's Wood Park	NW8	p. 21	**GS**	3
St. John's Wood Road	NW8	p. 21	**GT**	
St. Leonard's Terrace	SW3	p. 31	**FU**	
St. Martin's Lane	WC2	p. 33	**DY**	
St. Martin's-le-Grand	EC1	p. 23	**OU**	3
St. Pancras Way	NW1	p. 22	**KS**	
St. Paul's Road	N1	p. 23	**OS**	
St. Petersburgh Place	W2	p. 32	**BZ**	
St. Peter's Street	N1	p. 23	**OS**	
St. Thomas Street	SE1	p. 27	**PX**	
Sardinia Street	WC2	p. 33	**EV**	3
Savile Row	W1	p. 29	**DM**	
Savoy Place	WC2	p. 33	**DY**	
Savoy Street	WC2	p. 33	**EX**	
Scarsdale Villas	W8	p. 24	**EY**	
Seagrave Road	SW6	p. 24	**EZ**	
Serle Street	WC2	p. 33	**EV**	
Serpentine Road	W2	p. 28	**AP**	
Seymour Street	W1, W2	p. 28	**AK**	
Shaftesbury Avenue	W1, WC2	p. 29	**FL**	
Sheffield Terrace	W8	p. 24	**EX**	
Shelton Street	WC2	p. 33	**DX**	
Shepherdess Walk	N1	p. 23	**OT**	
Shepherd Market	W1	p. 28	**CN**	

hepherd Street W1 p. 28 **BP**
hirland Road W9 p. 20 **ET**
horeditch High Street E1 p. 23 **PT** 384
horts Gardens WC2 p. 33 **DV**
dmouth Street WC1 p. 22 **LT** 385
nclair Road W14 p. 24 **EY**
loane Avenue SW3 p. 31 **ET**
loane Square SW1 p. 31 **FT**
mith Street SW3 p. 31 **EU**
nows Fields SE1 p. 27 **PX** 386
oho Square W1 p. 29 **FJ**
outhampton Row WC1 p. 22 **LU** 387
outhampton Street WC2 p. 33 **DX** 388
outh Audley Street W1 p. 28 **BM**
outh Eaton Place SW1 p. 32 **AY** 389
outh End Road NW3 p. 20 **ES**
outh Hill NW3 p. 20 **ES** 390
outh Lambeth Road SW8 p. 26 **LZ**
outh Molton Street W1 p. 28 **BK**
outh Parade SW3 p. 30 **CU**
outh Place EC2 p. 23 **PU** 391
outh Street W1 p. 28 **BN**
outh Terrace SW7 p. 31 **DS**
outhwark Bridge SE1, EC4 p. 27 **OV** 395
outhwark Bridge Road SE1 p. 27 **OY**
outhwark Street SE1 p. 27 **OX**
outhwick Street W2 p. 33 **EZ**
pa road SE16 p. 27 **PY**
pencer Street EC1 p. 23 **NT** 398
pital Square E1 p. 23 **PU** 399
pring Street W2 p. 33 **DZ**
tamford Street SE1 p. 26 **MX**
tanhope Gardens SW7 p. 30 **BS**
tanhope Place W2 p. 33 **EZ** 400
tanhope Terrace W2 p. 33 **DZ**
tar Road W14 p. 24 **EZ**
toreys Gate SW1 p. 26 **LY** 402
trand WC2 p. 33 **DY**
tratton Street W1 p. 29 **DN**
umner Place SW7 p. 30 **CT**
umner Street SE1 p. 27 **OX**
un Street EC2 p. 23 **PU**
urrey Street WC2 p. 33 **EX**
ussex Gardens W2 p. 33 **DZ**
ussex Place W2 p. 33 **DZ**
ussex Square W2 p. 33 **DZ** 404
utherland Avenue W9 p. 20 **FU**
utherland Street SW1 p. 25 **JZ**
winton Street WC1 p. 22 **LT**
ydney Place SW7 p. 31 **DT** 405
ydney Street SW3 p. 31 **DT**
ymons Street SW3 p. 31 **FT** 407
abard Street SE1 p. 27 **OY** 408
achbrook Street SW1 p. 26 **KZ**
algarth Road W14, W6 p. 24 **EZ**
avistock Place WC1 p. 22 **LT**
avistock Square WC1 p. 22 **LT** 409
avistock Street WC2 p. 33 **DX**
edworth Square SW3 p. 31 **EU**
emple Place WC2 p. 33 **EX**
empleton Place SW5 p. 24 **EZ** 410
erminus Place SW1 p. 32 **BX** 412
hayer Street W1 p. 28 **BJ** 413
heobald's Road WC1 p. 22 **LU**
hirleby Road SW1 p. 32 **CX** 416
hornhill Road N1 p. 22 **MS**
hreadneedle Street EC2 p. 23 **PV** 417
hrogmorton Street EC2 p. 23 **PU** 418
hurloe Place SW7 p. 30 **CS** 420
hurloe Square SW7 p. 31 **DS**
hurlow Street SE17 p. 27 **PZ**
ilney Street W1 p. 28 **BN** 421
ite Street SW3 p. 31 **EU**
ooley Street SE1 p. 27 **BX**
othill Street SW1 p. 26 **KY**
ottenham Court Road W1 p. 22 **KU**
ower Bridge E1 p. 27 **PX**
ower Bridge Road SE1 p. 27 **PY**
ower Hill EC3 p. 23 **PV** 425
rafalgar Avenue SE15 p. 27 **PZ**
rafalgar Square WC2, SW1 p. 33 **DY**
rebovir Road SW5 p. 24 **FZ** 426
regunter Road SW10 p. 30 **BU**
revor Place SW7 p. 31 **EQ**
revor Square SW7 p. 31 **ER**
rinity Church Square SE1 p. 27 **OY**
rinity Street SE1 p. 27 **OY**
yers Street SE11 p. 26 **MZ**
Jnion Street SE1 p. 27 **NX**
Jpper Belgrave Street SW1 p. 32 **AX**
Jpper Berkeley Street W1 p. 33 **EZ**
Jpper Brook Street W1 p. 28 **AM**
Jpper Grosvenor Street W1 p. 28 **AM**

Upper Ground SE1 p. 27 **NX** 428
Upper St. Martin's Lane WC2 p. 33 **DX** 430
Upper Street N1 p. 23 **NS**
Upper Thames Street EC4 p. 23 **OV** 431
Upper Woburn Place WC1 p. 22 **LT** 432
Vale (The) SW3 p. 30 **CU**
Vanston Place SW6 p. 24 **EZ**
Vassal Road SW9 p. 27 **NZ**
Vauxhall Bridge SW1, SE1 p. 26 **LZ**
Vauxhall Bridge Road SW1 p. 32 **BY**
Vauxhall Street SE11 p. 26 **MZ**
Vauxhall Walk SE11 p. 26 **LZ**
Vere Street W1 p. 28 **BJ**
Victoria Embankment SW1 WC2, EC4 p. 33 **DY**
Victoria Grove W8 p. 30 **BR**
Victoria Road KENSINGTON W8 p. 30 **BQ**
Victoria Street SW1 p. 32 **BX**
Vigo Street W1 p. 29 **EM**
Villiers Street WC2 p. 33 **DY**
Vincent Square SW1 p. 26 **KZ**
Vincent Street SW1 p. 26 **LZ** 436
Virginia Road E2 p. 23 **PT**
Walterton Road W9 p. 20 **ET**
Walton Street SW3 p. 31 **ES**
Walworth Road SE17 p. 27 **OZ**
Wandsworth Road SW8 p. 26 **LZ**
Wardour Street W1 p. 29 **FJ**
Warrington Crescent W9 p. 20 **FT**
Warwick Avenue W2, W9 p. 20 **FU** 441
Warwick Road SW5, W14 p. 24 **EZ**
Warwick Street W1 p. 29 **EM** 444
Warwick Way SW1 p. 25 **JZ**
Waterloo Bridge WC2, SE1 p. 33 **EY**
Waterloo Place SW1 p. 29 **FN**
Waterloo Road SE1 p. 27 **NY**
Waverton Street W1 p. 28 **BN**
Webber Street SE1 p. 27 **NY**
Weighhouse Street W1 p. 28 **BK**
Welbeck Street W1 p. 28 **BH**
Wellington Road NW8 p. 21 **GT**
Wellington Street WC2 p. 33 **DX**
Wells Street W1 p. 29 **EJ**
Wells Way SE5 p. 27 **PZ**
Well Walk NW3 p. 20 **ES**
Westbourne Crescent W2 p. 33 **DZ** 448
Westbourne Grove W2, W11 p. 32 **AZ**
Westbourne Park Road W2, W11 p. 20 **EU**
Westbourne Park Villas W2 p. 20 **FU** 449
Westbourne Street W2 p. 33 **DZ** 450
Westbourne Terrace W2 p. 33 **DZ**
Westbourne Road N7 p. 22 **MS**
Westbourne Terrace Road W2 p. 20 **FU** 452
West Cromwell Road SW5, W14 p. 24 **EZ**
West Halkin Street SW1 p. 31 **FR**
Westminster Bridge SW1, SE1 p. 26 **LY**
Westminster Bridge Road SE1 p. 26 **MY**
Weston Street SE1 p. 27 **PY**
West Smithfield EC1 p. 23 **NU** 454
Westway N18 p. 20 **EU**
Wetherby Gardens SW5 p. 30 **BT**
Wharfdale Road N1 p. 22 **LS** 455
Wharf Road N1 p. 23 **OT**
Whiston Road E2 p. 23 **PS**
Whitcomb Street WC2 p. 29 **GM**
Whitechapel High Street E1 p. 23 **PU** 456
Whitecross Street EC1, EC2 p. 23 **OT**
Whitehall SW1 p. 26 **LX**
Whitehall Court SW1 p. 26 **LX** 460
Whitehall Place SW1 p. 26 **LX** 462
Whitehead's Grove SW3 p. 31 **ET** 463
Whitmore Road N1 p. 23 **PS** 464
Wigmore Street W1 p. 28 **BJ**
Wild Street WC2 p. 33 **DV**
William IV Street WC2 p. 33 **DY** 467
William Street SW1 p. 31 **FQ** 468
Willoughby Road NW3 p. 20 **ES** 470
Willow Road NW3 p. 20 **ES**
Willow Walk SE1 p. 27 **PY**
Wilson Street EC2 p. 23 **PU**
Wilton Place SW1 p. 31 **FQ**
Wilton Road SW1 p. 32 **BY**
Wilton Street SW1 p. 32 **AX**
Wimpole Street W1 p. 28 **BH**
Woburn Place WC1 p. 22 **LT**
Woods Mews W1 p. 28 **AL**
Wormwood Street EC2 p. 23 **PU** 472
Worship Street EC2 p. 23 **PU**
Wyndham Road SE5 p. 27 **OZ**
York Road SE1 p. 27 **MY**
York Way N1, N7 p. 22 **LS**
Young Street W8 p. 30 **AQ**

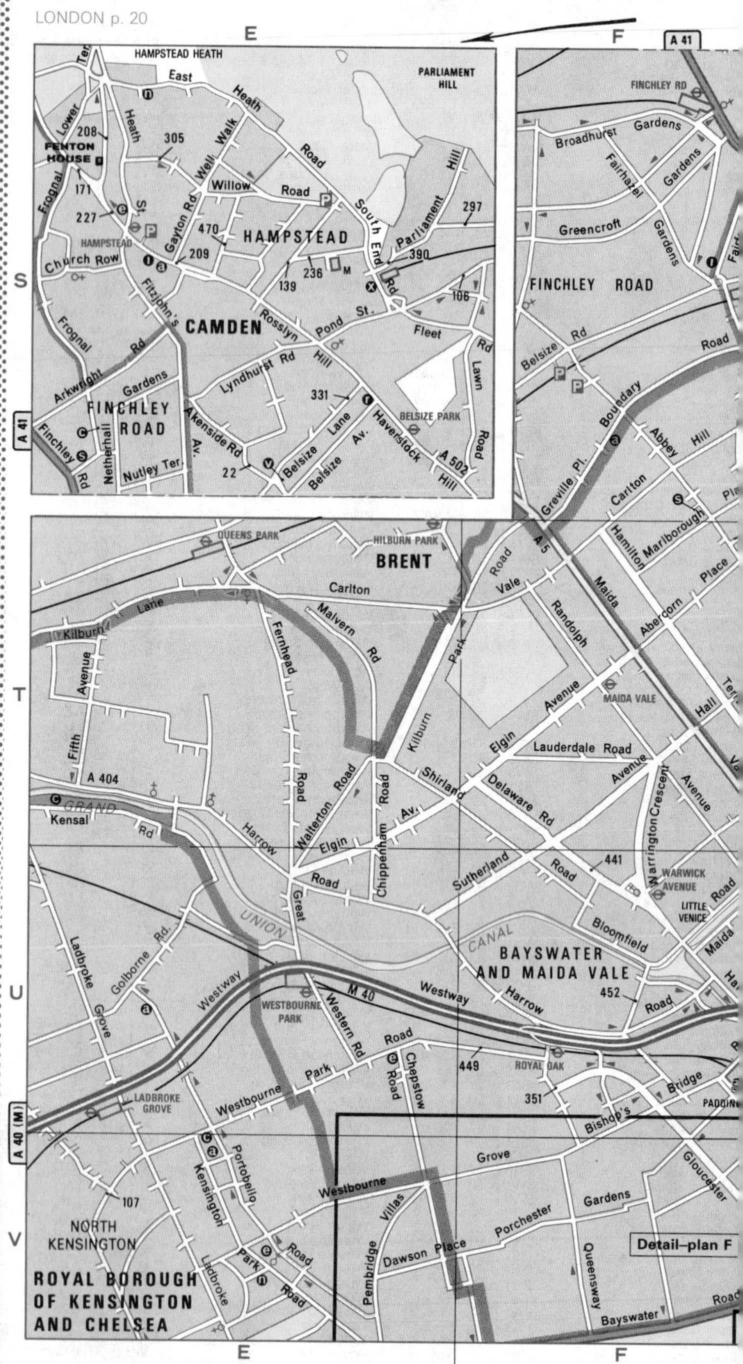
HAMPSTEAD HEATH
PARLIAMENT HILL
FENTON HOUSE
HAMPSTEAD
CAMDEN
FINCHLEY ROAD
BELSIZE PARK
FINCHLEY RD
QUEENS PARK
KILBURN PARK
BRENT
MAIDA VALE
WARWICK AVENUE
LITTLE VENICE
BAYSWATER AND MAIDA VALE
WESTBOURNE PARK
ROYAL OAK
LADBROKE GROVE
NORTH KENSINGTON
ROYAL BOROUGH OF KENSINGTON AND CHELSEA
Detail-plan F
Westway
Harrow Road
Kilburn Lane
Carlton Vale
Maida Vale
Elgin Avenue
Shirland Road
Sutherland Avenue
Westbourne Park Road
Westbourne Grove
Bayswater Road
Ladbroke Grove
Portobello Road
Kensington Park Road
Pembridge Villas
Dawson Place
Porchester Gardens
Queensway
Haverstock Hill
Fitzjohn's Av.
Rosslyn Hill
Finchley Rd
Boundary Road
Abbey Road
Belsize Rd
Greville Pl.
A 41
A 5
A 404
A 502
A 40 (M)
M 40

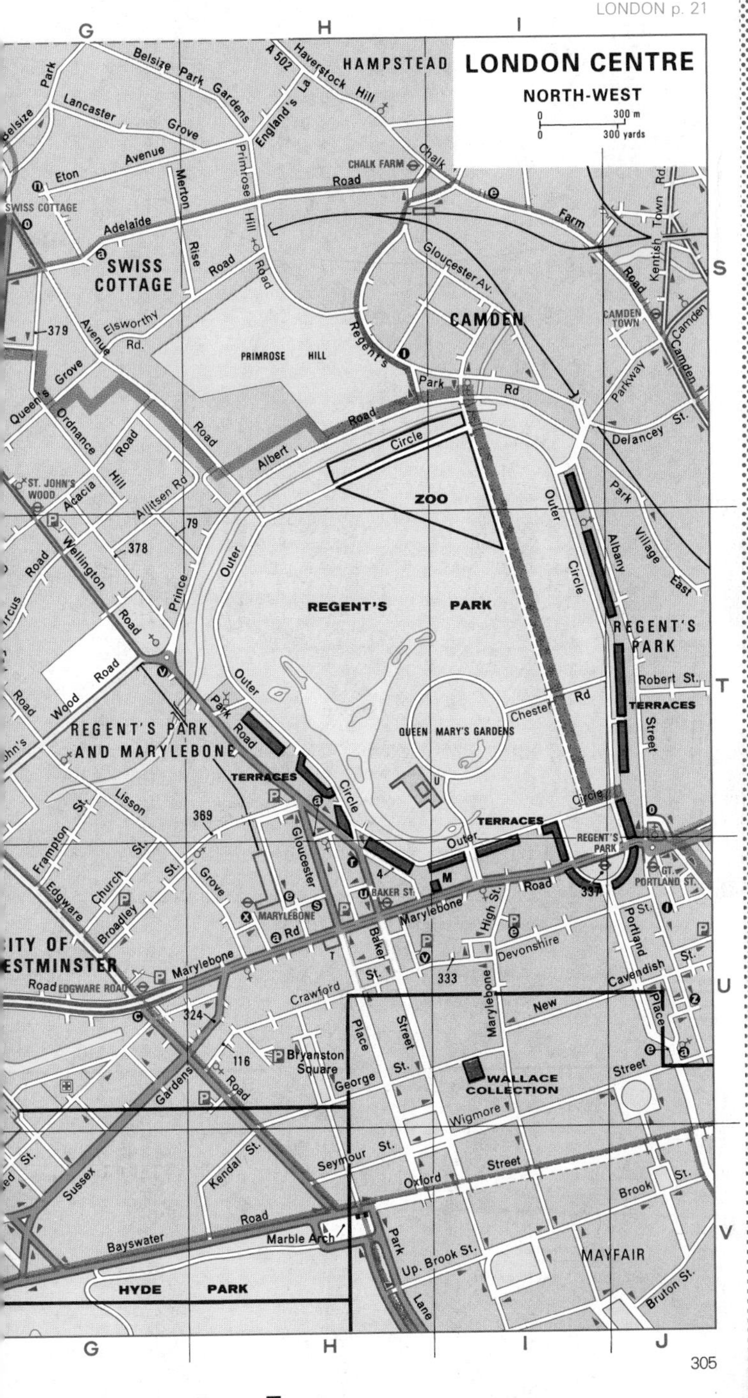
LONDON CENTRE
NORTH-WEST
300 m
300 yards
HAMPSTEAD
SWISS COTTAGE
CAMDEN
PRIMROSE HILL
ZOO
REGENT'S PARK
QUEEN MARY'S GARDENS
REGENT'S PARK AND MARYLEBONE
TERRACES
CITY OF WESTMINSTER
WALLACE COLLECTION
HYDE PARK
MAYFAIR
CHALK FARM
CAMDEN TOWN
ST. JOHN'S WOOD
BAKER ST.
MARYLEBONE
EDGWARE ROAD
GT. PORTLAND ST.
Marble Arch
Bryanston Square
Oxford Street
Bayswater Road
Marylebone Road
Park Lane
G
H
I
J
S
T
U
V

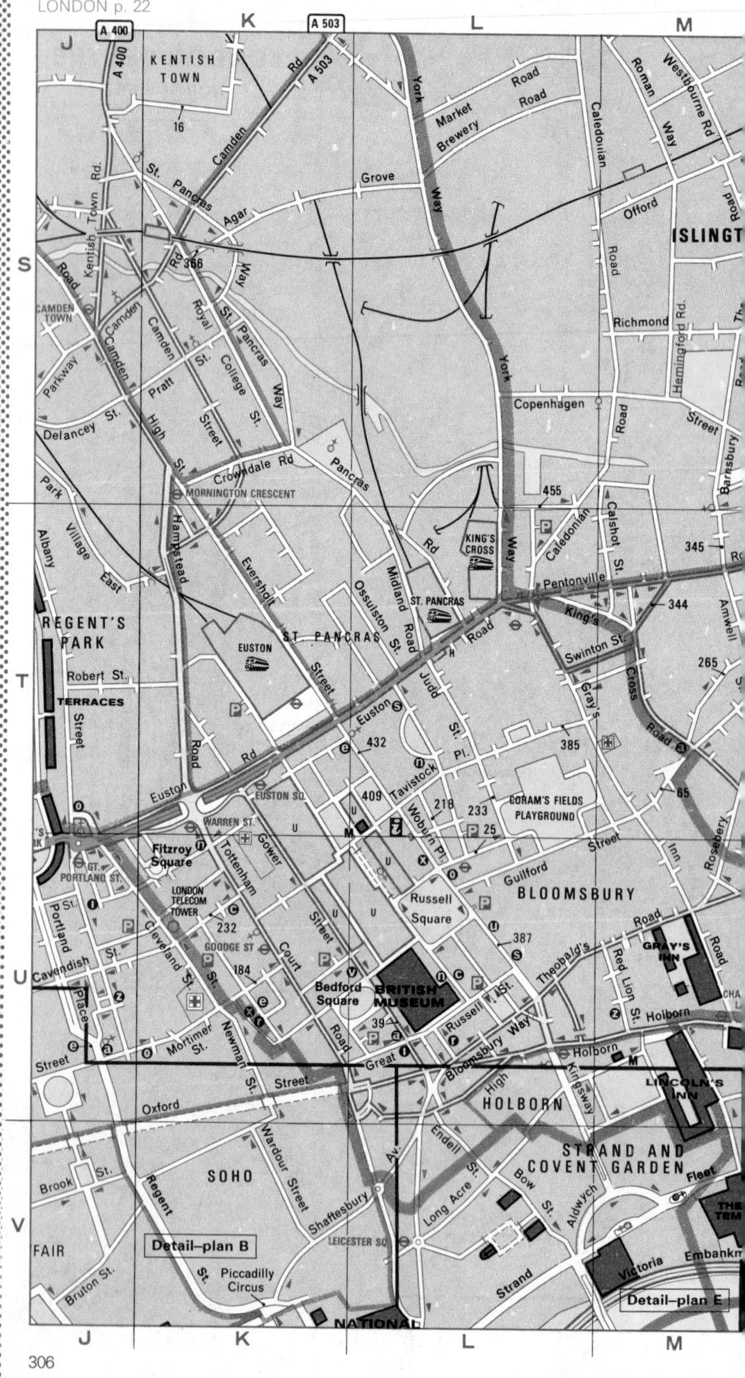
KENTISH TOWN
CAMDEN TOWN
REGENT'S PARK
TERRACES
ST. PANCRAS
EUSTON
KING'S CROSS
ST. PANCRAS
MORNINGTON CRESCENT
EUSTON SQ.
WARREN ST.
GOODGE ST
LONDON TELECOM TOWER
Fitzroy Square
GT. PORTLAND ST.
CORAM'S FIELDS PLAYGROUND
BLOOMSBURY
Russell Square
Bedford Square
BRITISH MUSEUM
GRAY'S INN
LINCOLN'S INN
HOLBORN
STRAND AND COVENT GARDEN
SOHO
LEICESTER SQ
Piccadilly Circus
NATIONAL
ISLINGT
Detail-plan B
Detail-plan E
FAIR

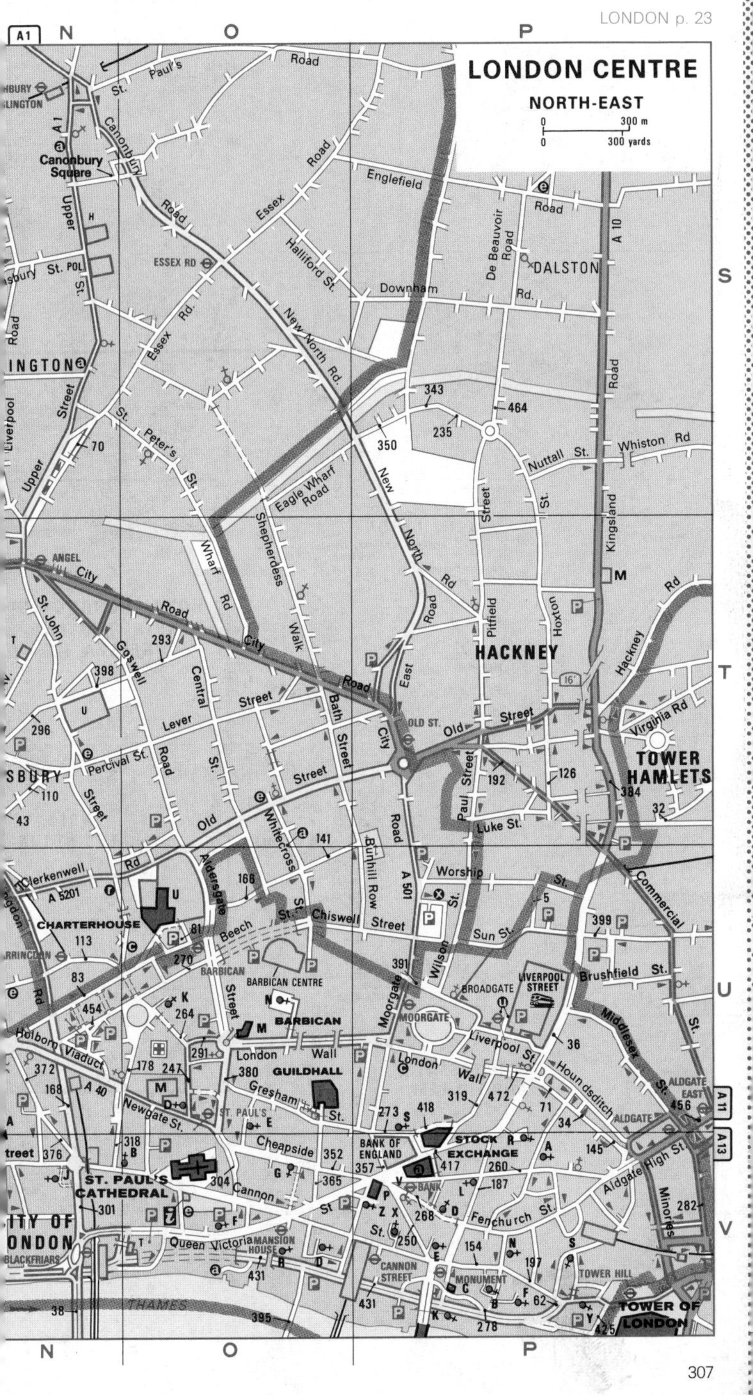
LONDON CENTRE
NORTH-EAST
0 300 m
0 300 yards
N
O
P
S
T
U
V
Canonbury Square
DALSTON
HACKNEY
TOWER HAMLETS
CHARTERHOUSE
BARBICAN CENTRE
BARBICAN
GUILDHALL
BANK OF ENGLAND
STOCK EXCHANGE
ST. PAUL'S CATHEDRAL
MANSION HOUSE
CANNON STREET
MONUMENT
TOWER HILL
TOWER OF LONDON
LIVERPOOL STREET
BROADGATE
MOORGATE
ALDGATE
ALDGATE EAST
ANGEL
ESSEX RD
OLD ST.
BLACKFRIARS
THAMES

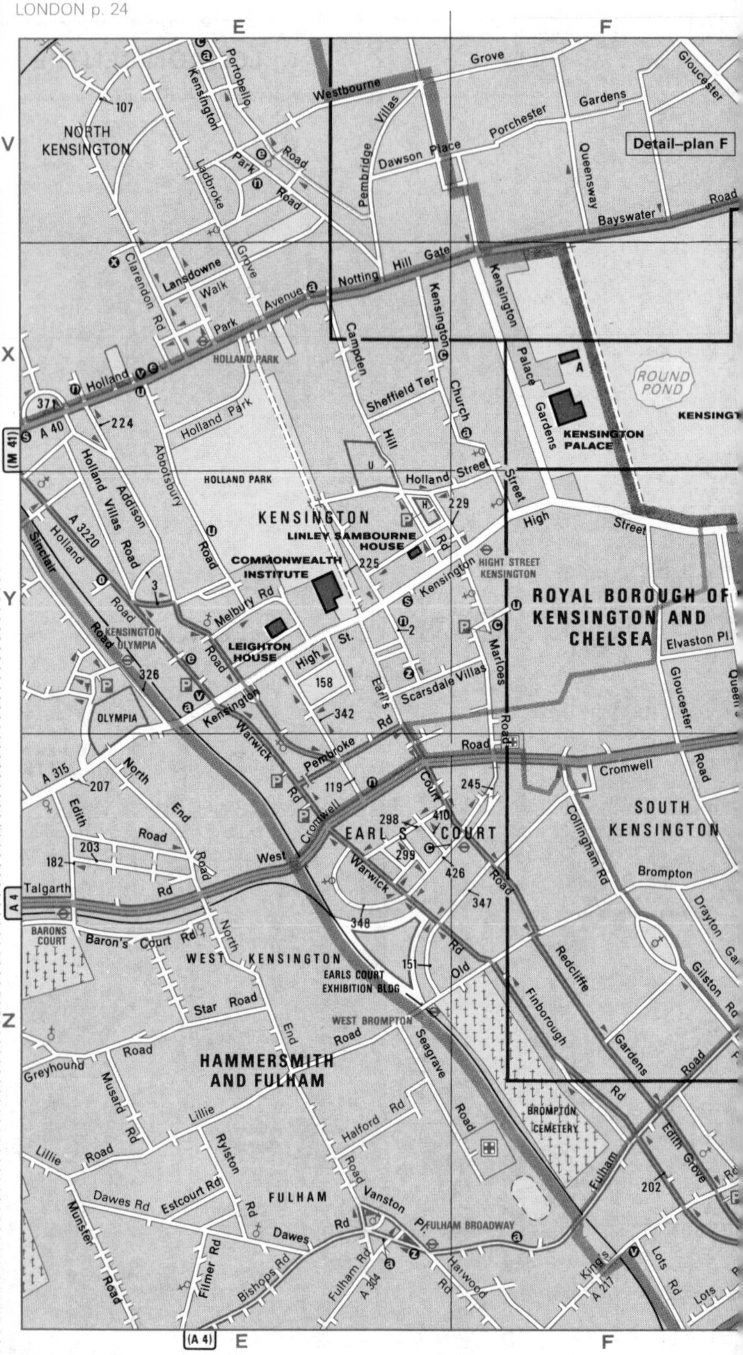

E
F
V
X
Y
Z
Detail–plan F
NORTH KENSINGTON
KENSINGTON
ROYAL BOROUGH OF KENSINGTON AND CHELSEA
SOUTH KENSINGTON
EARL'S COURT
WEST KENSINGTON
HAMMERSMITH AND FULHAM
FULHAM
HOLLAND PARK
KENSINGTON PALACE
ROUND POND
LINLEY SAMBOURNE HOUSE
COMMONWEALTH INSTITUTE
LEIGHTON HOUSE
KENSINGTON OLYMPIA
OLYMPIA
HIGH STREET KENSINGTON
EARLS COURT EXHIBITION BLDG
WEST BROMPTON
BROMPTON CEMETERY
BARONS COURT
FULHAM BROADWAY
Westbourne Grove
Bayswater Road
Notting Hill Gate
Holland Park Avenue
Kensington High Street
Cromwell Road
Talgarth Rd
Kensington Church Street
Kensington Palace Gardens
Earl's Court Road
Warwick Road
North End Road
Lillie Road
Fulham Road
Kings Road
A 40
A 3220
A 315
A 4
(M 41)
(A 4)
A 304
A 217

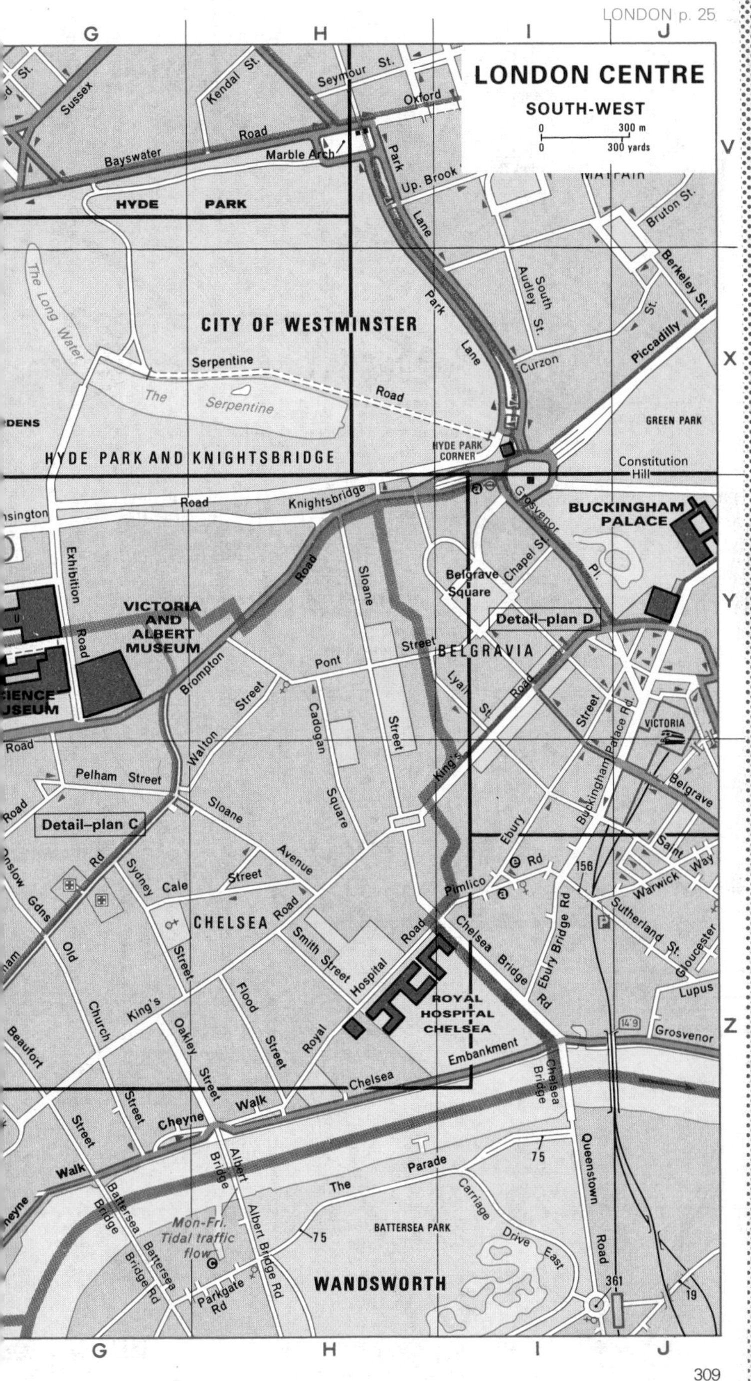
LONDON CENTRE
SOUTH-WEST
0 300 m
0 300 yards
G
H
I
J
V
X
Y
Z
Seymour St.
Kendal St.
Sussex
Oxford
Road
Bayswater
Marble Arch
Park
Up. Brook
Lane
HYDE
PARK
Bruton St.
Berkeley St.
South Audley St.
St.
The Long Water
CITY OF WESTMINSTER
Park
Lane
Piccadilly
Curzon
Serpentine
The
Serpentine
Road
GREEN PARK
DENS
HYDE PARK CORNER
HYDE PARK AND KNIGHTSBRIDGE
Constitution Hill
Road
Knightsbridge
Grosvenor
BUCKINGHAM PALACE
nsington
Exhibition
Road
Road
Sloane
Chapel St.
Belgrave Square
Pl.
VICTORIA AND ALBERT MUSEUM
Detail-plan D
Street
BELGRAVIA
Pont
Brompton
Lyall
St.
Road
Street
Street
Street
CIENCE
USEUM
Cadogan
Palace Rd.
VICTORIA
Road
Walton
Buckingham
Pelham Street
King's
Belgrave
Sloane
Square
Road
Detail-plan C
Ebury
Saint
Rd
Avenue
Way
Rd
156
Warwick
Sydney
Cale
Street
Pimlico
nslow Gdns
Sutherland St.
Gloucester
CHELSEA
Road
Road
Smith Street
Chelsea Bridge
Ebury Bridge Rd
Old
Street
Hospital
Lupus
ROYAL HOSPITAL CHELSEA
Flood
Church
King's
Beaufort
Oakley
Street
Royal
Grosvenor
Embankment
Chelsea Bridge
Street
Chelsea
Street
Street
Walk
Cheyne
Queenstown
Walk
Albert Bridge
75
Parade
The
neyne
Battersea Bridge
Carriage
Drive
East
Mon-Fri. Tidal traffic flow
Albert Bridge Rd
75
BATTERSEA PARK
Road
Battersea Bridge Rd
Parkgate Rd
WANDSWORTH
361
19

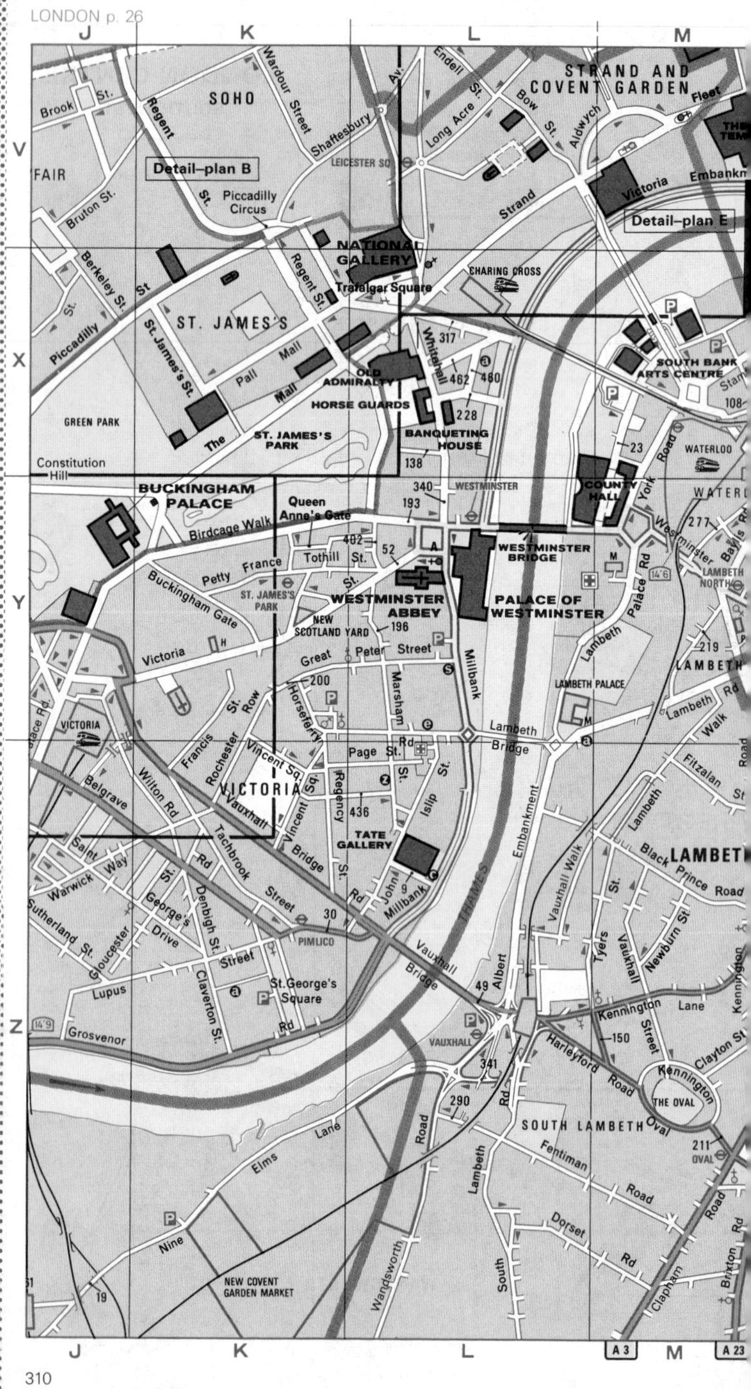
SOHO
STRAND AND COVENT GARDEN
Detail-plan B
Detail-plan E
NATIONAL GALLERY
Trafalgar Square
CHARING CROSS
ST. JAMES'S
SOUTH BANK ARTS CENTRE
OLD ADMIRALTY
HORSE GUARDS
BANQUETING HOUSE
GREEN PARK
ST. JAMES'S PARK
Constitution Hill
BUCKINGHAM PALACE
WATERLOO
COUNTY HALL
WESTMINSTER
Queen Anne's Gate
WESTMINSTER BRIDGE
WESTMINSTER ABBEY
PALACE OF WESTMINSTER
NEW SCOTLAND YARD
LAMBETH PALACE
LAMBETH
VICTORIA
TATE GALLERY
PIMLICO
St. George's Square
VAUXHALL
THE OVAL
SOUTH LAMBETH
OVAL
NEW COVENT GARDEN MARKET
THAMES

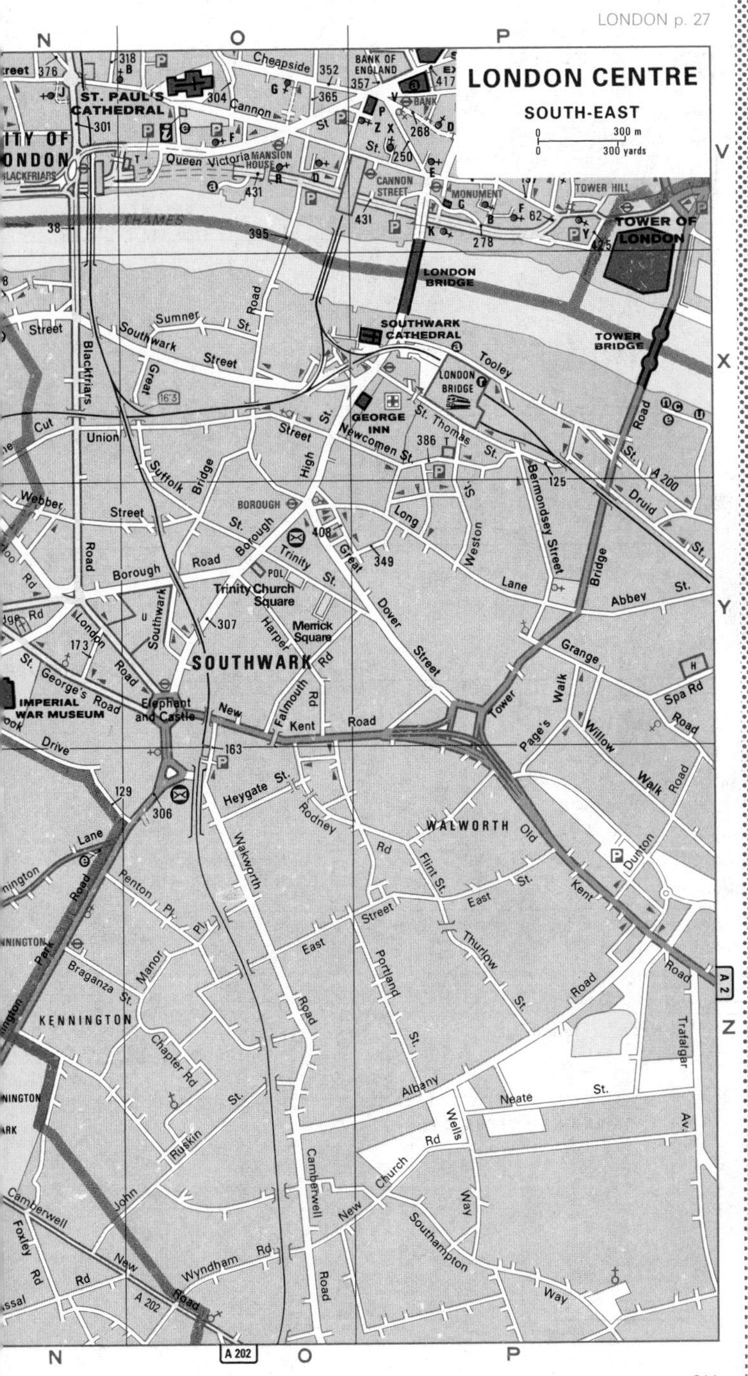
LONDON CENTRE
SOUTH-EAST
300 m
300 yards
ST. PAUL'S CATHEDRAL
TOWER OF LONDON
LONDON BRIDGE
SOUTHWARK CATHEDRAL
TOWER BRIDGE
GEORGE INN
SOUTHWARK
IMPERIAL WAR MUSEUM
Elephant and Castle
WALWORTH
KENNINGTON
Trinity Church Square
Merrick Square
BANK OF ENGLAND
MANSION HOUSE
CANNON STREET
MONUMENT
TOWER HILL
BOROUGH
THAMES
A 200
A 2
A 202

B
WALLACE COLLECTION
Portman Square
Grosvenor Square
Berkeley Square
Cavendish Sq.
REGENT'S PARK AND MARYLEBONE
CITY OF WESTMINSTER
MAYFAIR
HYDE PARK
HYDE PARK AND KNIGHTSBRIDGE
MARBLE ARCH
BOND ST.
GREEN PARK
Shepherd Market
APSLEY HOUSE WELLINGTON MUSEUM
Oxford Street
Piccadilly
Park Lane
Serpentine Road
0 200 m
0 200 yards

Street	Grid	No.
Arlington Street	DN	6
Avery Row	CL	12
Bateman Street	FK	18
Berwick Street	FK	26
Binney Street	BL	35
Carlton Gardens	FP	74
Deanery Street	BN	132
Denman Street	FM	133
Denmark Street	GJ	134
Duke of York Street	EN	143
Duke Street ST. JAMES	EN	146
Dunraven Street	AL	149
Gerrard Street	GL	174
Gilbert Street	BL	175
Glasshouse Street	EM	179
Granville Place	AK	188
Great Castle Street	DJ	189
Greek Street	GK	198
Hamilton Place	BP	205
Hanover Square	CK	210
Hertford Street	BP	220
Leicester Square	GM	261
Manchester Square	AJ	281
Market Place	DJ	286
Marylebone Lane	BJ	287
North Audley Street	AK	314
Old Burlington Street	DM	322
Old Compton Street	GK	323
Panton Street	FM	336
Romilly Street	GL	368
Thayer Street	BJ	413
Tilney Street	BN	421
Warwick Street	EM	444

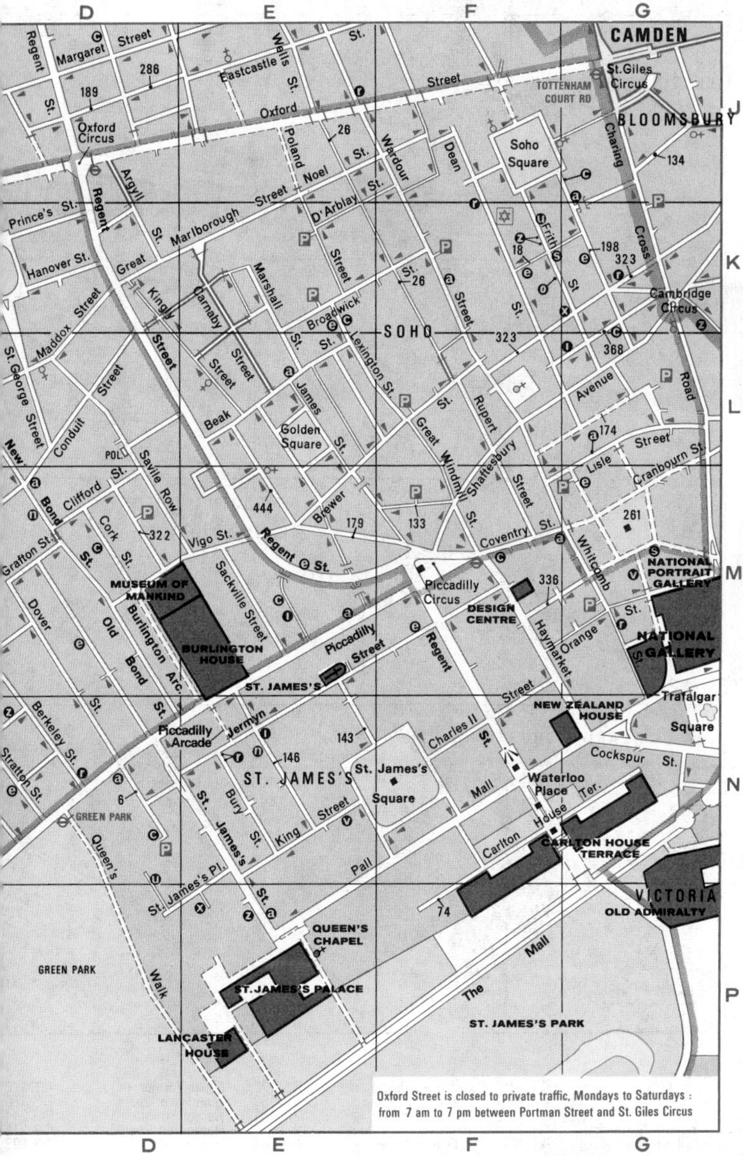

Oxford Street is closed to private traffic, Mondays to Saturdays : from 7 am to 7 pm between Portman Street and St. Giles Circus

HYDE PARK AND KNIGHTSBRIDGE
KENSINGTON GARDENS
ALBERT MEMORIAL
ROYAL ALBERT HALL
ROYAL COLLEGE OF MUSIC
IMPERIAL COLLEGE OF SCIENCE AND TECHNOLOGY
ROYAL COLLEGE OF ART
SCIENCE MUSEUM
GEOLOGICAL MUSEUM
NATURAL HISTORY MUSEUM
KENSINGTON
SOUTH KENSINGTON
EARL'S COURT
BROMPTON CEMETERY
GLOUCESTER RD
SOUTH KENSINGTON
The Boltons

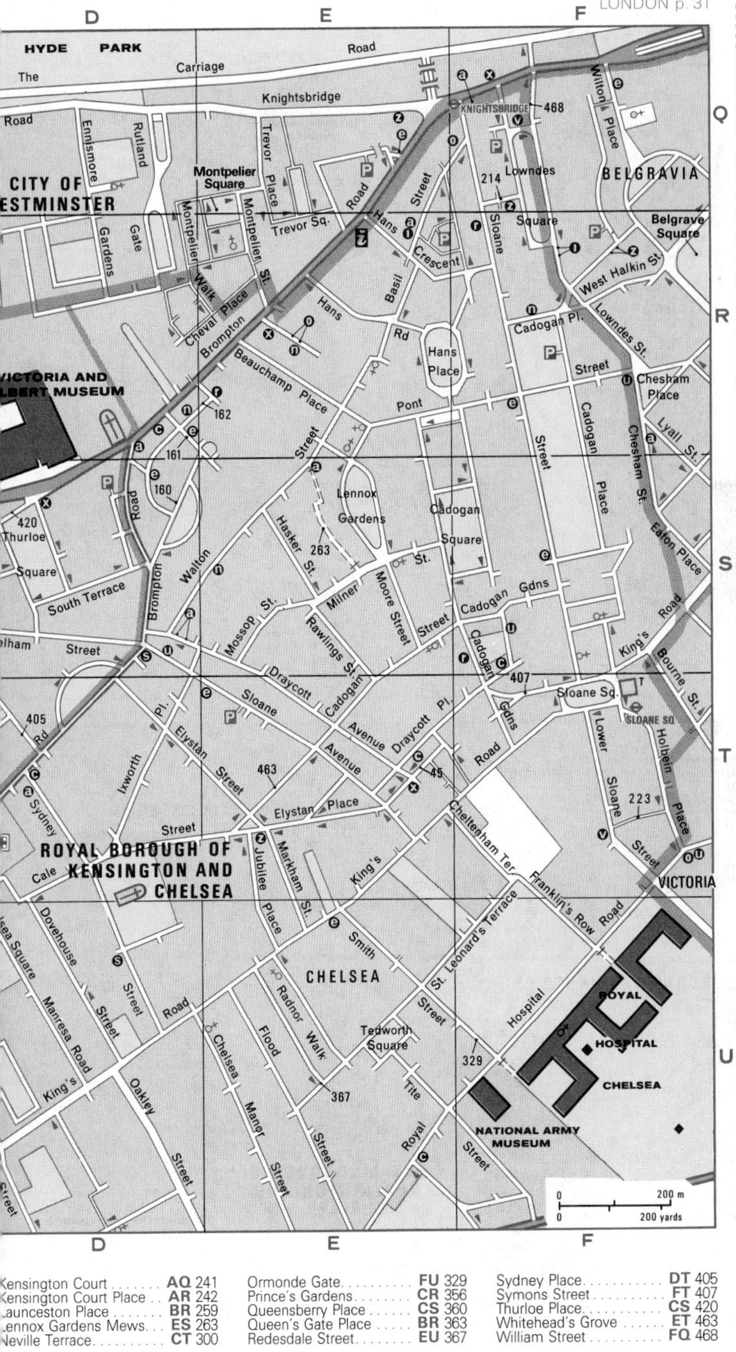
D
E
F
Q
R
S
T
U
HYDE PARK
The Carriage Road
Knightsbridge
KNIGHTSBRIDGE
468
CITY OF WESTMINSTER
BELGRAVIA
Montpelier Square
Ennismore Gardens
Rutland Gate
Trevor Place
Trevor Sq.
Montpelier Walk
Montpelier St.
Lowndes Square
214
Sloane Street
Hans Crescent
Belgrave Square
West Halkin St.
Cheval Place
Brompton Road
Hans Rd
Basil Street
Cadogan Pl.
Lowndes St.
Hans Place
Beauchamp Place
VICTORIA AND ALBERT MUSEUM
162
161
160
Pont Street
Chesham Place
Lyall St.
Cadogan Place
Chesham St.
Lennox Gardens
Cadogan Square
420
Thurloe Square
Hasker St.
263
Eaton Place
Milner St.
Moore Street
Walton Street
South Terrace
Mossop St.
Rawlings St.
Cadogan Gdns
King's Road
Bourne St.
Pelham Street
Draycott Avenue
Cadogan Street
407
Sloane Sq.
SLOANE SQ.
Sloane Avenue
405
Sydney Rd
Draycott Pl.
Lower Sloane Street
Holbein Place
Elystan Street
Ixworth Pl.
463
45
Elystan Place
223
Cheltenham Ter.
Franklin's Row
Street
ROYAL BOROUGH OF KENSINGTON AND CHELSEA
Cale Street
Jubilee Place
Markham St.
King's Road
VICTORIA
St. Leonard's Terrace
Royal Hospital Road
Dovehouse Street
Chelsea Square
Smith Street
CHELSEA
Radnor Walk
ROYAL HOSPITAL CHELSEA
Manresa Road
Chelsea Manor Street
Flood Street
Tedworth Square
329
367
Tite Street
Oakley Street
NATIONAL ARMY MUSEUM
Royal Street
0 200 m
0 200 yards

A B C

D

WELLINGTON ARCH
142
GREEN PARK
Constitution Hill
QUEEN VICTORIA MEMORIAL
The Mall
St. James's Park Lake
ST. JAMES'S
ST. JAMES'S PARK
BUCKINGHAM PALACE GARDENS
BUCKINGHAM PALACE
QUEEN'S GALLERY
Birdcage Walk
T
Grosvenor Cres.
Halkin
St.
Chapel St.
Grosvenor Place
Chester St.
Belgrave Square
Upper Belgrave St.
Wilton St.
56
CITY OF WESTMINSTER
Petty France
Palmer St.
ROYAL MEWS
BELGRAVIA
Palace St.
Castle La.
56
St.
274
48
Grosvenor Gdns
Rd
Pl.
Hobart Pl.
Belgrave Place
Place Square
Lower Belgrave St.
Victoria St.
Street
H
Victoria St.
Howick Pl.
8
Eaton
Eaton
Road
Square
88
412
Ashley Pl.
416
Street
Row
King's
Eccleston
Street
Carlisle Place
WESTMINSTER CATHEDRAL
Eaton
88
Elizabeth
Palace
VICTORIA
Vauxhall
Wilton
Francis
VICTORIA
Rochester
Vincent Square
St.
Hudson's Pl.
St.
Bridge
389
Chester Row
389
Ebury
Street
Buckingham
157
Gillingham
Tachbrook
Road
Hugh Street
Belgrave Rd
201
Eccleston Square
Warwick Way
St.
Road
0 200 m
0 200 yards

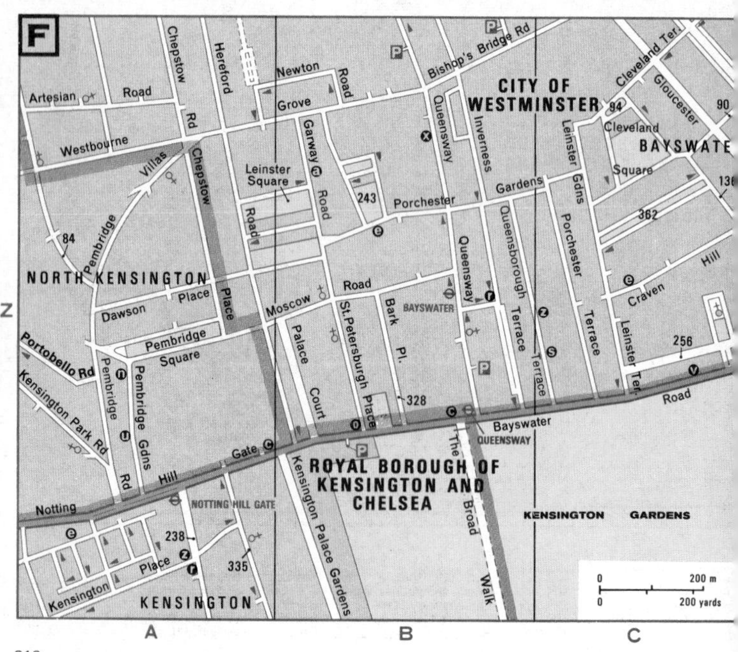

A B C

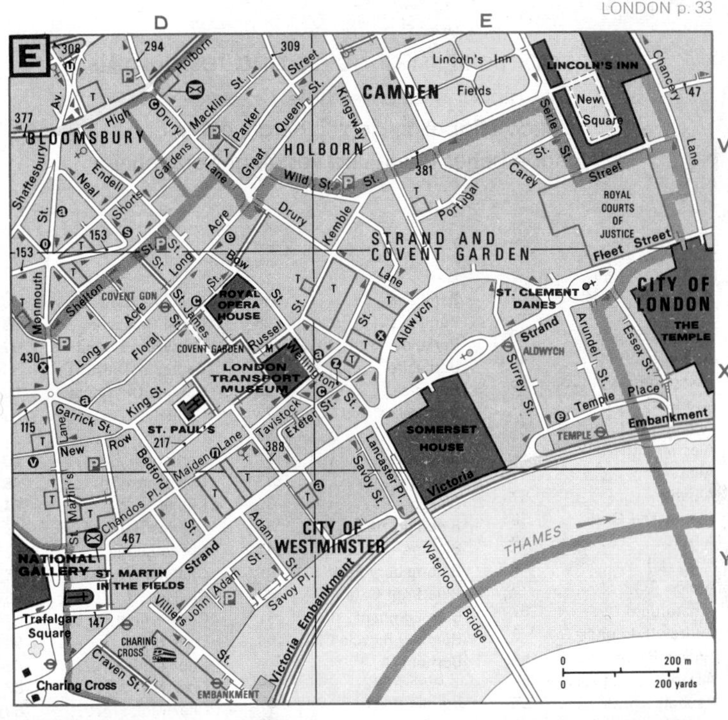

D E

PADDINGTON
REGENT'S PARK AND MARYLEBONE
ND MAIDA VALE
Edgware Road
Marble Arch
Bayswater Road
LANCASTER GATE
FOUNTAIN GARDEN
North Carriage Drive
HYDE PARK
HYDE PARK AND KNIGHTSBRIDGE
Z

D E

Artillery Row **CVX** 8	Eccleston Bridge **BY** 157	Orme Court **BZ** 328
Bream's Buildings **EV** 47	Great Cumberland Place **EZ** 191	Oxford Square **EZ** 332
Bressenden Place **BX** 48	Guildhouse Street **BY** 201	Palace Gardens Terrace **AZ** 335
Buckingham Gate **CV** 56	Henrietta Street **DX** 217	Queen's Gardens **CZ** 362
Cambridge Square **EZ** 67	Hyde Park Square **EZ** 234	St. Giles High Street **DV** 377
Chepstow Crescent **AZ** 84	Kensington Church Street **AZ** 238	Sardinia Street **EV** 381
Chester Square **AX** 88	Kensington Gardens Square **BZ** 243	Southampton Street **DX** 388
Chilworth Street **CZ** 90	Lancaster Gate **CDZ** 256	South Eaton Place **AY** 389
Clarendon Place **EZ** 93	Lancaster Terrace **DZ** 257	Stanhope Place **EZ** 400
Cleveland Gardens **CZ** 94	Lower Grosvenor Place **BX** 274	Sussex Square **DZ** 404
Connaught Square **EZ** 103	Museum Street **DV** 294	Terminus Place **BX** 412
Cranbourn Street **DX** 115	New Oxford Street **DV** 308	Thirleby Road **CX** 416
Devonshire Terrace **CZ** 136	Newton Street **DV** 309	Upper St. Martin's Lane **DX** 430
Duke of Wellington Place **AV** 142	Norfolk Crescent **EZ** 310	Westbourne Crescent **DZ** 448
Duncannon Street **DY** 147	Norfolk Square **DZ** 313	Westbourne Street **DZ** 450
Earlham Street **DV** 153		William IV Street **DY** 467

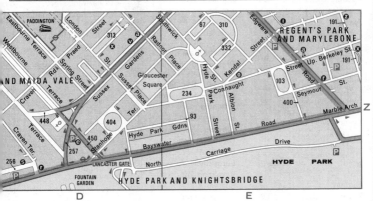

Alphabetical list of hotels and restaurants
Liste alphabétique des hôtels et restaurants
Elenco alfabetico degli alberghi e ristoranti
Alphabetisches Hotel- und Restaurantverzeichnis

G

H

I

J

K

S

T

U - V - W

X - Y - Z

Don't confuse:

Comfort of hotels : 🏨 ... 🏨, 🏨, 🏠
Comfort of restaurants : XXXXX X
Quality of the cuisine : ✿✿✿, ✿✿, ✿, **Meals**

Alphabetical list of areas included
Liste alphabétique des quartiers cités
Elenco alfabetico dei quartieri citati
Liste der erwähnten Bezirke

Starred establishments in London
Les établissements à étoiles de Londres
Gli esercizi con stelle a Londra
Die Stern-Restaurants Londons

✿✿✿

		Area	Page
XXXX	**Chez Nico at Ninety Park Lane** (at Grosvenor House H.)	Mayfair	68
XXXX	**La Tante Claire**	Chelsea	56
XXXX	**The Restaurant, Marco Pierre White** (at Hyde Park H.)	Hyde Park & Knightsbridge	66

✿✿

		Area	Page
XXXX	**Le Gavroche**	Mayfair	68
XX	**Pied à Terre**	Bloomsbury	48

✿

		Area	Page
🏨	**Connaught**	Mayfair	67
🏨	**Capital**	Chelsea	55
🏨	**Halkin**	Belgravia	66
XXXX	**Four Seasons** (at Four Seasons H.)	Mayfair	68
XXXX	**Grill Room** at the Café Royal	Soho	72
XXXX	**Oriental** (at Dorchester H.)	Mayfair	68
XXXX	**Les Saveurs**	Mayfair	68
XXX	**Aubergine**	Chelsea	56
XXX	**The Canteen**	Chelsea	56
XXX	**L'Escargot**	Soho	72
XXX	**Interlude de Chavot**	Regents Park and Marylebone	70
XXX	**Leith's**	North Kensington	59
XXX	**The Square**	St. James's	71
XX	**Fulham Road**	Chelsea	56
XX	**Greenhouse**	Mayfair	68

Further establishments which merit your attention
Autres tables qui méritent votre attention
Altre tavole particolarmente interessanti
Weitere empfehlenswerte Häuser

Meals

		Area	Page
XXX	**Bibendum**	Chelsea	56
XXX	**Chutney Mary**	Chelsea	56
XXX	**Fifth Floor** (at Harvey Nichols)	Chelsea	56
XXX	**Ivy**	Strand and Covent Garden	73
XXX	**Le Pont de la Tour**	Bermondsey	63
XX	**Al Bustan**	Belgravia	66
XX	**Atelier**	Soho	72
XX	**Le Caprice**	St. James's	71
XX	**Clarke's**	Kensington	58
XX	**Hilaire**	South Kensington	60
XX	**Nico Central**	Regent's Park and Marylebone	70
XX	**Percy's**	North Harrow	52
XX	**River Café**	Hammersmith	51
XX	**Simply Nico**	Victoria	74
XX	**Zafferano**	Belgravia	66
X	**Alastair Little**	Soho	72
X	**Bistrot Bruno**	Soho	73
X	**Blue Print Café**	Bermondsey	63
X	**Kensington Place**	Kensington	58
X	**Malabar**	Kensington	58

Particularly pleasant hotels and restaurants

Hôtels et restaurants agréables

Alberghi e ristoranti ameni

Angenehme Hotels und Restaurants

Restaurants classified according to type

Restaurants classés suivant leur genre

Ristoranti classificati secondo il loro genere

Restaurants nach Art und Einrichtung geordnet

Bistro

Seafood

Argentinian

XX **Gaucho Grill** (City of Westminster - *Mayfair*) 68

Chinese

XXX ✿ **Oriental** (City of Westminster - *Mayfair*) 68

XX **Inn of Happiness** (City of Westminster - *Victoria*) 74

XX **Pearl** (City of Westminster - *Hyde Park and Knightsbridge*) 66

XX **Princess Garden** (City of Westminster - *Mayfair*) 68

XX **West ZENders** (City of Westminster - *Strand and Covent Garden*). 73

XX **Zen Central** (City of Westminster - *Mayfair*) 68

XX **Four Regions** (Richmond-Upon-Thames - *Richmond*) 63

XX **Good Earth** (Barnet - *Mill Hill*) 46

XX **Good Earth** (Royal Borough of Kensington & Chelsea - *Chelsea*). 57

XX **Ho-Ho** (Redbridge - *South Woodford*) 62

XX **Hunan** (City of Westminster - *Victoria*) 75

XX **Imperial City** (City of London) 49

XX **Ken Lo's Memories of China** (City of Westminster - *Victoria*) 75

XX **Mao Tai** (Hammersmith & Fulham - *Fulham*) 51

XX **Maxim** (Ealing - *Ealing*) 50

XX **Ming** (City of Westminster - *Soho*) 72

XX **Mr Tang's Mandarin** (Harrow - *Stanmore*) 52

XX **Park Inn** (Royal Borough of Kensington & Chelsea - *North Kensington*) 59

XX **Peking Diner** (Bromley - *Bromley*). 47

XX **Poons** (City of Westminster - *Bayswater and Maida Vale*) 65

XX **Poons of Russel Square** (Camden - *Bloomsbury*) 48

XX **Red** (Royal Borough of Kensington & Chelsea - *Chelsea*) 57

XX **Royal China** (Wandsworth - *Putney*) 64

XX **Sampan's** (City of Westminster - *Regent's Park & Marylebone*) 70

XX **Shanghai** (Royal Borough of Kensington & Chelsea - *Kensington*) . 58

XX **Swan** (Harrow - *Hatch End*) 52

XX **Taste of China** (Harrow - *Central Harrow*) 52

XX **Treasure of China** (Greenwich - *Greenwich*) 51

XX **Willow** (Croydon - *Addington*) 50

XX **Xian** (Bromley - *Orpington*) 47

XX **ZeNW3** (Camden - *Hampstead*) 48

X **Fung Shing** (City of Westminster - *Soho*) 73

X **Jasmin** (Wandsworth - *Clapham*) . 64

X **Mandarin** (Royal Borough of Kensington & Chelsea - *Kensington*) . 58

X **Poons** (City of Westminster - *Soho*) 73

English

XXX **Shepherds** (City of Westminster - *Victoria*) 74

XX **English Garden** (Royal Borough of Kensington & Chelsea - *Chelsea*). 56

XX **Green's** (City of Westminster - *St. James's*) 71

XX **Hudson's** (City of Westminster - *Regent's Park & Marylebone*) 70

XX **Rules** (City of Westminster - *Strand & Covent Garden*) 73

X **Tate Gallery** (City of Westminster - *Victoria*) 75

X **Alfred** (Camden - *Bloomsbury*) 48

French

XXXX ✿✿✿ **Chez Nico at Ninety Park Lane** (City of Westminster - *Mayfair*) 68

XXXX **Oak Room** (City of Westminster - *Mayfair*) 68

XXXX ✿✿ **Gavroche (Le)** (City of Westminster - *Mayfair*) 68

XXXX ✿ **Saveurs (Les)** (City of Westminster - *Mayfair*) 68

XXXX ✿✿✿ **Tante Claire (La)** (Royal Borough of Kensington & Chelsea - *Chelsea*) 56

XXX **Auberge de Provence** (City of Westminster - *Victoria*) 74

XXX **Interlude de Chavot** (City of Westminster - *Regent's Park & Marylebone*) 70

XXX **Jardin des Gourmets (Au)** (City of Westminster - *Soho*) 72

French

- XX **Associés (Les)** (Haringey - *Crouch End*) 52
- XX **Brasserie St. Quentin** (Royal Borough of Kensington & Chelsea - *Chelsea*) 56
- XX **Chez Moi** (Royal Borough of Kensington & Chelsea - *North Kensington*) 59
- XX **Dordogne (La)** (Hounslow - *Chiswick*) 54
- XX **Escargot Doré (L')** (Kensington - *Kensington*) 58
- XX **Grafton (The)** (Lambeth - *Clapham Common*) 61
- XX **Gravier's** (Kingston-upon-Thames - *Kingston*) 61
- XX **Mon Plaisir** (Camden - *Bloomsbury*) 48
- XX **Poissonnerie de l'Avenue** (Royal Borough of Kensington & Chelsea - *Chelsea*) 56
- XX **Pomme d'Amour (La)** (Royal Borough of Kensington & Chelsea - *Kensington*) 5
- XX **Quai (Le)** (City of London) 4
- XX **Truffe Noire (La)** (Southwark - *Southwark*) 6
- X **Aventure (L')** (City of Westminster - *Regent's Park & Marylebone*) 7
- X **Balzac** (Hammersmith & Fulham - *Shepherd's Bush*)) 5
- X **Grignote (La)** (Camden - *Hampstead*) 4
- X **Lobster Pot** (Lambeth - *Kennington*) 6
- X **Magno's Brasserie** (City of Westminster - *Strand & Covent Garden*) 7
- X **Muscadet (Le)** (City of Westminster - *Regent's Park & Marylebone*) 7
- X **Poule au Pot (La)** (City of Westminster - *Victoria*) 7
- X **Rouxl Britannia** (Islington - *Finsbury*) 54
- X **Soulard** (Hackney - *Dalston*) 51

Hungarian

- XX **Gay Hussar** (City of Westminster - *Soho*) 72

Indian & Pakistani

- XXX **Bengal Clipper** (Southwark - *Bermondsey*) 63
- XXX **Bombay Brasserie** (Royal Borough of Kensington & Chelsea - *South Kensington*) 60
- XXX **Chutney Mary (Anglo-Indian)** (Royal Borough of Kensington & Chelsea - *Chelsea*) 56
- XX **Café Lazeez** (Royal Borough of Kensington & Chelsea - *South Kensington*) 60
- XX **Delhi Brasserie** (Royal Borough of Kensington & Chelsea - *South Kensington*) 60
- XX **Gaylord** (City of Westminster - *Regent's Park & Marylebone*) 70
- XX **Gopal's** (City of Westminster - *Soho*) 72
- XX **Khan's of Kensington** (Royal Borough of Kensington & Chelsea - *South Kensington*) 60
- XX **Laguna Tandoori** (Ealing - *Ealing*) 50
- XX **Memories of India** (Royal Borough of Kensington & Chelsea - *South Kensington*) 60
- XX **Red Fort** (City of Westminster - *Soho*) 72
- XX **Tabaq** (Wandsworth - *Wandsworth*) 64
- XX **Tamarind** (City of Westminster - *Mayfair*) 68
- XX **Tandoori Nights** (Hammersmith & Fulham - *Hammersmith*) 51
- X **Bombay Bicycle Club** (Wandsworth - *Wandsworth*) 64
- X **Jaflong** (Harrow - *South Harrow*) 52
- X **Jashan** (Haringey - *Hornsey*) 52
- X **Malabar** (Royal Borough of Kensington & Chelsea - *Kensington*) 58

Irish

- XX **Mulligans** (City of Westminster - *Mayfair*) 69

Italian

Halkin (City of Westminster - *Belgravia*) 66
L'Incontro (City of Westminster - *Victoria*) 74
Santini (City of Westminster - *Victoria*) 74
Amico (L') (City of Westminster - *Victoria*) 75
Caldesi (City of Westminster - *Regent's Park & Marylebone*) 70
Daphne's (Royal Borough of Kensington & Chelsea - *Chelsea*) 56
Del Buongustaio (Wandsworth - *Putney*) 64
Fenice (La) (Royal Borough of Kensington & Chelsea - *Kensington*) 58
Finezza (La) (Royal Borough of Kensington & Chelsea - *Chelsea*) 56
Giannino's (Bromley - *Keston*) 47
Gran Paradiso (City of Westminster - *Victoria*) 75
Luigi's (Southwark - *Dulwich*) 63
Mezzaluna (Barnet - *Child's Hill*) 46
Orchard (Camden - *Hampstead*) 48
Orsino (Royal Borough of Kensington & Chelsea - *North Kensington*) 59
Orso (City of Westminster - *Strand & Covent Garden*) 73
Portico (City of London) 49
River Café (Hammersmith and Fulham - *Hammersmith*) 51
San Vincenzo (Al) (City of Westminster - *Bayswater & Maida Vale*) 65
Scala (La) (Barking and Dagenham - *Chadwell Heath*) 46
Toto's (Royal Borough of Kensington & Chelsea - *Chelsea*) 56
Trattoria Sorrentina (Harrow - *Central Harrow*) 52
Veranda (La) (Sutton - *Carshalton*) 63
Zafferano (City of Westminster - *Belgravia*) 66
Accento (L') (City of Westminster - *Bayswater and Maida Vale*) 65
Alba (Islington - *Finsbury*) 54
Altro (L') (Royal Borough of Kensington & Chelsea - *North Kensington*) 59
Bertorelli's (City of Westminster - *Strand & Covent Garden*) 73
Cantina Del Ponte (Southwark - *Bermondsey*) 63
Castelletto (Il) (Camden - *Bloomsbury*) 48
Cibo (Royal Borough of Kensington & Chelsea - *Kensington*) 58
Enoteca (Wandsworth - *Putney*) 72
Florians (Haringey - *Crouch End*) 52
Fontana (La) (City of Westminster - *Victoria*) 75
Mario (Croydon - *Croydon*) 50
Olivo (City of Westminster - *Victoria*) 75
Paolo's (Ealing - *Ealing*) 50
Riva (Richmond-Upon-Thames - *Barnes*) 62
Roberto's (Hillingdon - *Ickenham*) 53
Villa Medici (City of Westminster - *Victoria*) 75

Japanese

Benihana (Royal Borough of Kensington & Chelsea - *Chelsea*) 56
Suntory (City of Westminster - *St. James's*) 71
Tatsuso (City of London) 49
Asuka (City of Westminster - *Regent's Park & Marylebone*) 70
Benihana (Camden - *Hampstead*) 48
Matsuri (City of Westminster - *St. James's*) 72
Miyama (City of London) 49
Shogun (City of Westminster - *Mayfair*) 69
Abeno (Brent - *Colindale*) 46
Imari (Camden - *Holborn*) 49
Imari (City of London) 49
Nakamura (City of Westminster - *Regent's Park & Marylebone*) 70

Lebanese

Polish

Spanish

Swedish

Thai

Vietnamese

Boroughs and areas

Greater London is divided, for administrative purposes, into 32 boroughs plus the City : the sub-divide naturally into minor areas, usually grouped around former villages or quarte which often maintain a distinctive character.

BARKING and DAGENHAM p. 7.

Chadwell Heath – ✉ Essex – ☎ 0181.

XX **La Scala** (first floor), 19a High Rd, RM6 6PU, ✆ 983 8818 – |‡| P. AE ⓓ VISA JU
closed Saturday lunch, Sunday and Bank Holidays – **Meals** - Italian - 11.90/23.90 and a la carte 4.50.

BARNET pp. 4 and 5.

Brent Cross – ✉ NW2 – ☎ 0181.

Holiday Inn Garden Court, Tilling Rd, NW2 1LP, ✆ 201 8686, Fax 455 4660 – |‡| r TV ☎ & P – 50. AE ⓓ VISA JCB. DU
Meals (bar lunch Monday to Saturday)/dinner 11.95 **st.** and a la carte – 9.95 – **152 r** 85.00 **st.**

Child's Hill – ✉ NW2 – ☎ 0171.

XX **Mezzaluna,** 424 Finchley Rd, NW2 2HY, ✆ 794 0452 – AE VISA DU
closed Saturday lunch and Monday – **Meals** - Italian - a la carte 19.50/27.50 **t.** 5.00.

X **Quincy's,** 675 Finchley Rd, NW2 2JP, ✆ 794 8499 – . AE VISA DU
closed Sunday, Monday and 1 week Christmas – **Meals** (booking essential) (dinn only) 25.00 **t.** 4.50.

X **Laurent,** 428 Finchley Rd, NW2 2HY, ✆ 794 3603 – AE VISA DU
closed Sunday, first 3 weeks August and Bank Holidays – **Meals** - Couscous - a la car approx. 12.90 **t.**

Mill Hill – ✉ NW7 – ☎ 0181.

18 100 Barnet Way, Mill Hill ✆ 959 2282 CT.

XX **Good Earth,** 143 The Broadway, NW7 4RN, ✆ 959 7011, Fax 959 1464 – . AE VISA
closed 24 to 27 December – **Meals** - Chinese - 10.00 **t.** and a la carte 8.00. CT

BEXLEY pp. 10 and 11.

Bexley – ✉ Kent – ☎ 01322.

Forte Posthouse, Black Prince Interchange, Southwold Rd, DA5 1ND, on A 2 ✆ 52690 Fax 526113 – |‡| rm TV ☎ & P – 70. AE ⓓ VISA JX
Meals a la carte 17.05/24.20 **t.** 7.95 – 7.95 – **100 rm** 59.00/69.00 **st.**, 2 suites.

Bexleyheath – ✉ Kent – ☎ 0181.

Swallow, 1 Broadway, DA6 7JZ, ✆ 298 1000, Fax 298 1234, – |‡| rm TV & P – 200. AE ⓓ VISA JX
Galleria : Meals *(closed Sunday)* 14.50/26.00 **st.** and a la carte 6.00 – **Copper : Meals** 13.5 19.50 **st.** 6.00 – **142 rm** 90.00/130.00 **st.** – SB.

BRENT pp. 4 and 5.

Colindale – ✉ Middx. – ☎ 0181.

X **Abeno,** Yaohan Plaza, 399 Edgware Rd, NW9 0JJ, ✆ 205 1131, Fax 201 3022 – VISA JCB CU
Meals - Japanese (Okonomi-Yaki) - 7.80/18.80 **t.** and a la carte.

Wembley – ✉ Middx – ☎ 0181.

Hilton National Wembley, Empire Way, HA9 8DS, ✆ 902 8839, Fax 900 2201, – |‡| rm rest TV ☎ P – 300. AE ⓓ VISA. CU
Celebrities : Meals (carving rest.) 16.25/19.75 **st.** – **Terracotta : Meals** - Italian - (dinner only) la carte 16.40/26.70 **st.** 8.00 – 10.95 – **306 rm** 119.00/196.00 **st.**

BROMLEY pp. 10 and 11.

, Cray Valley, Sandy Lane, St. Paul's Cray, Orpington ☏ (01689) 831927, JY.

Bromley – ✉ Kent – ☎ 0181 – Magpie Hall Lane ☏ 462 7014 HY.

Bromley Court, Bromley Hill, BR1 4JD, ☏ 464 5011, Fax 460 0899, – – 150. AE VISA HY z
Meals *(closed Saturday lunch)* 16.95 **st.** and a la carte 4.85 – **116 rm** 82.00/91.00 **st.** – SB.

Peking Diner, 71 Burnt Ash Lane, BR1 5AA, ☏ 464 7911 – . AE VISA HX u
closed Sunday dinner and 25-26 December – **Meals** - Chinese (Peking) - 12.50/23.00 **t.** and a la carte 4.75.

Keston – ✉ Kent – ☎ 01689.

Giannino's, 6 Commonside, BR2 6BP, ☏ 856410 – AE VISA HZ x
closed Sunday, Monday and first 2 weeks August – **Meals** - Italian - 14.75/16.75 **t.** and a la carte 4.75.

Orpington – ✉ Kent – ☎ 01689.

High Elms, High Elms Rd, Downe, Orpington ☏ 858175.

Xian, 324 High St., BR6 0NG, ☏ 871881 – . AE VISA JCB JY a
closed Sunday lunch and 1 week August – **Meals** - Chinese (Peking, Szechuan) - 6.50/13.00 **t.** and a la carte 5.20.

CAMDEN Except where otherwise stated see pp. 20-23.

Bloomsbury – ✉ NW1/W1/WC1 – ☎ 0171.

34-37 Woburn Pl., WC1H 0JR ☏ 580 4599.

Holiday Inn Kings Cross, 1 Kings Cross Rd, WC1X 9HX, ☏ 833 3900, Fax 917 6163, <, , , , squash – rm – 220. AE VISA JCB. MT a
Meals 17.95 **t.** (dinner) and a la carte 15.80/30.15 **t.** 6.00 – 9.75 – **397 rm** 99.00 **st.** 8 suites.

Russell (Forte), Russell Sq., WC1B 5BE, ☏ 837 6470, Telex 24615, Fax 837 2857 – rm rest – 400. AE VISA JCB. LU o
Meals 13.50/16.50 **t.** – 10.50 – **326 rm** 120.00/160.00 **st.**, 2 suites – SB.

Grafton (Radisson Edwardian), 130 Tottenham Court Rd, W1P 9HP, ☏ 388 4131, Telex 297234, Fax 387 7394 – rm – 100. AE VISA JCB. KU n
Meals *(closed Saturday lunch)* 18.50/35.00 **st.** and a la carte – 10.00 – **317 rm** 120.00/150.00 **st.**, 7 suites – SB.

Marlborough (Radisson Edwardian), 9-14 Bloomsbury St., WC1B 3QD, ☏ 636 5601, Telex 298274, Fax 636 0532 – rest – 200. AE VISA JCB. LU i
Meals 16.95/35.00 **st.** and a la carte – 10.95 – **167 rm** 135.00/180.00 **st.**, 2 suites – SB.

Mountbatten (Radisson Edwardian), 20 Monmouth St., WC2H 9HD, ☏ 836 4300, Telex 298087, Fax 240 3540 – rm rest – 75. AE VISA JCB.
Meals *(closed lunch Saturday and Sunday)* 18.00/35.00 **st.** and a la carte – 13.50 – **121 rm** 160.00/210.00 **st.**, 6 suites – SB. p.33 DV o

Kenilworth (Radisson Edwardian), 97 Great Russell St., WC1B 3LB, ☏ 637 3477, Telex 25842, Fax 631 3133 – rm rest – 100. AE VISA JCB. LU a
Meals (carving rest.) 16.95/35.00 **st.** and a la carte – 10.00 – **187 rm** 120.00/150.00 **st.**

Montague, 12-20 Montague St., WC1B 5BJ, ☏ 637 1001, Telex 23307, Fax 637 2506 – rm rest – 120. AE VISA JCB. LU c
closed 24 to 26 December – **Meals** 12.50 **t.** and dinner a la carte 6.00 – **107 rm** 99.00/170.00 **st.**, 2 suites.

Blooms, 7 Montague St., WC1B 5BP, ☏ 323 1717, Fax 636 6498 – . AE VISA JCB. LU n
Meals (in bar) a la carte 14.00/23.50 **st.** 6.00 – **27 rm** 100.00/160.00 **st.** – SB.

Bloomsbury Park (Mount Charlotte), 126 Southampton Row, WC1B 5AD, ☏ 430 0434, Telex 25757, Fax 242 0665 – rm – 25. AE VISA JCB. LU u
Meals *(closed Friday to Sunday and Bank Holidays)* (dinner only) 13.95 **st.** and a la carte 4.70 – 8.50 – **95 rm** 84.00/140.00 **st.** – SB.

Bonnington, 92 Southampton Row, WC1B 4BH, ☏ 242 2828, Telex 261591, Fax 831 9170 – rm rest – 250. AE VISA JCB LU s
Meals *(closed lunch Saturday and Sunday)* 10.00/17.75 **st.** and a la carte 7.60 – **215 rm** 85.00/105.00 **st.**

Academy, 17-21 Gower St., WC1E 6HG, ☏ 631 4115, Fax 636 3442, – rest . AE VISA JCB. KLU v
GHQ : Meals *(closed lunch Saturday and Sunday)* (residents and members only for dinner) 12.95/16.95 **t.** 5.50 – 10.10 – **33 rm** 86.95/170.40 **st.**

Harlingford without rest., 61-63 Cartwright Gdns, WC1H 9EL, ✆ 387 1551, Fax 387 4616 – ⊠ – TV ☎. AE VISA LT
44 rm ☐ 55.00/69.00 **st.**

Mabledon Court without rest., 10-11 Mabledon Pl., WC1H 9BA, ✆ 388 3866, Fax 387 5686 – TV ☎. AE VISA JCB. ✻ LT
closed 24 December-1 January – **31 rm** ☐ 52.00/62.00 **st.**

✻✻ **Pied à Terre** (Neat), 34 Charlotte St., W1P 1HJ, ✆ 636 1178, Fax 916 1171 – ▤. AE ⓓ VISA JCB KU
closed Saturday lunch, Sunday, last 2 weeks August, last week December and first week January – **Meals** 19.50/39.50 **st.** 7.00
Spec. Skate wing with poached egg, parsley sauce and potato salad, Duck breast baked in rösti potatoes with a leg and gizzard confit, Rice pudding with mango, lime purée and pineapple sorbet.

Neal Street, 26 Neal St., WC2H 9PS, ✆ 836 8368, Fax 497 1361 – AE ⓓ VISA p. 33 DV
closed Sunday and Bank Holidays – **Meals** a la carte 15.00/40.00 **t.** 6.50.

Mon Plaisir, 21 Monmouth St., WC2H 9DD, ✆ 836 7243, Fax 379 0121 – AE ⓓ VISA JCB p. 33 DV
closed Saturday lunch, Sunday, 1 week Christmas-New Year and Bank Holidays – **Meals** - French - 13.95 **st.** and a la carte 5.80.

Poons of Russell Square, 50 Woburn Pl., WC1H 0JZ, ✆ 580 1188 – ▤. AE ⓓ VISA JCB LU
closed 24 to 27 December – **Meals** - Chinese - 9.50/20.00 **t.** and a la carte.

Bleeding Heart, Bleeding Heart Yard, EC1N 8SJ, off Greville St., Hatton Garden ✆ 242 2056, Fax 831 1402, – AE ⓓ VISA NU
closed Saturday, Sunday and 24 December-4 January – **Meals** a la carte 16.85/23.70 **t.** 3.95.

Il Castelletto, 17 Bury Pl., WC1A 2IB, ✆ 405 2232 – ▤. AE ⓓ VISA LU
closed Saturday lunch, Sunday and Bank Holidays – **Meals** - Italian - 14.00 **t.** and a la carte 4.75.

Alfred, 245 Shaftesbury Av., WC2H 8EH, ✆ 240 2566, Fax 497 0672 – ▤. AE ⓓ VISA p. 33 DV
closed Sunday, Christmas-New Year and Bank Holidays – **Meals** - English - 15.90 **t.** and a la carte 15.85/22.40 **t.** 5.00.

Euston – ✉ WC1 – ☎ 0171.

Euston Plaza, 17/18 Upper Woburn Pl., WC1H 0HT, ✆ 383 4105, Fax 383 4106, – rm ▤ TV ☎ ♿ – 130. AE ⓓ VISA JCB. ✻ KLT
Meals 15.00 **t.** (dinner) and a la carte 12.25/26.40 **st.** – ☐ 9.50 – **150 rm** 112.00/129.00 **st.** – SB.

Hampstead – ✉ NW3 – ☎ 0171.

Winnington Rd, Hampstead ✆ 455 0203.

Swiss Cottage without rest., 4 Adamson Rd, NW3 3HP, ✆ 722 2281, Fax 483 4588, « Antique furniture » – TV ☎ – 50. AE ⓓ VISA. ✻ GS
55 rm ☐ 75.00/140.00 **st.**, 5 suites.

Forte Posthouse, 215 Haverstock Hill, NW3 4RB, ✆ 794 8121, Fax 435 5586 – rm TV ☎ Ⓟ – 30. AE ⓓ VISA JCB ES
Meals a la carte 15.40/23.85 **st.** 5.25 – ☐ 7.95 – **140 rm** 69.00 **st.** – SB.

Sandringham without rest., 3 Holford Rd, Hampstead Village, NW3 1AD, ✆ 435 1569, Fax 431 5932, – TV ☎. AE VISA. ✻ ES
17 rm ☐ 60.00/105.00 **st.**

Langorf without rest., 20 Frognal, NW3 6AG, ✆ 794 4483, Fax 435 9055 – TV ☎. AE ⓓ VISA. ✻ ES
☐ 2.50 – **31 rm** 55.00/90.00 **st.**, 5 suites.

Charles Bernard, 5-7 Frognal, NW3 6AL, ✆ 794 0101, Fax 794 0100 – TV ☎ Ⓟ. AE ⓓ VISA. ✻ ES
Meals (bar lunch)/dinner 15.00 **st.** and a la carte – **57 rm** ☐ 57.50/66.00 **st.**

Benihana, 100 Avenue Rd, NW3 3HF, ✆ 586 9508, Fax 586 6740 – ▤. AE ⓓ VISA JCB GS
closed Monday lunch and 25 December – **Meals** - Japanese (Teppan-Yaki) - 8.45/13.95 **t.** and a la carte.

ZeNW3, 83-84 Hampstead High St., NW3 1RE, ✆ 794 7863, Fax 794 6956 – ▤. AE ⓓ VISA ES
closed Christmas – **Meals** - Chinese - 12.00/24.50 **t.** and a la carte.

Orchard, 12a Belsize Terr., NW3 4AX, ✆ 794 4288 – ▤. VISA ES
closed Monday lunch, Sunday dinner and Bank Holidays – **Meals** - Italian - a la carte 18.90/26.50 **t.** 5.50.

X **Café des Arts,** 82 Hampstead High St., NW3 1RE, ✆ 435 3608 – AE VISA ES **i**
closed 25 and 26 December – **Meals** a la carte 13.95/22.55 **t.** 6.50.

X **Cucina,** 45a South End Rd, NW3 2QB, ✆ 435 7814, Fax 435 7815 – AE VISA JCB
closed Sunday dinner – **Meals** 13.95 **t.** (dinner) and a la carte 17.20/19.95 **t.** 5.95. ES **x**

X **La Grignote,** 77 Heath St., NW3 6UG, ✆ 433 3455 – VISA ES **e**
closed lunch Monday to Friday, 24-28 December and last 2 weeks August – **Meals** - French – 14.50/16.75 **t.** 5.75.

Holborn – ✉ WC2 – 0171.

Drury Lane Moat House (Q.M.H.), 10 Drury Lane, High Holborn, WC2B 5RE, ✆ 208 9988, Telex 8811395, Fax 831 1548 – rm – 60. AE VISA JCB p. 33 DV **c**
Meals *(closed lunch Saturday, Sunday and Bank Holidays)* a la carte 14.00/20.95 **t.** 7.15 – 10.75 – **151 rm** 125.00/149.00 **st.**, 2 suites – SB.

X **Imari,** 71 Red Lion St., WC1R 4NA, ✆ 405 0486, Fax 431 8071 – AE VISA JCB
closed Saturday, Sunday and Bank Holidays – **Meals** - Japanese - 8.00/25.00 **t.** and a la carte 4.00. MU **z**

Regent's Park – ✉ NW1 – 0171.

White House, Albany St., NW1 3UP, ✆ 387 1200, Telex 24111, Fax 388 0091, – rm rest – 110. AE VISA JCB. JT **o**
Meals 19.50/23.50 **t.** and a la carte 6.50 – 10.75 – **584 rm** 125.00/145.00 **st.**, 2 suites.

XX **Odette's,** 130 Regent's Park Rd, NW1 8XL, ✆ 586 5486 – AE VISA HS **i**
closed Saturday lunch, Sunday, 2 weeks Christmas and Bank Holidays – **Meals** 10.00 **t.** (lunch) and a la carte 15.50/28.50 **t.** 5.95.

X **Belgo Noord,** 72 Chalk Farm Rd, NW1 8AN, ✆ 267 0718, Fax 267 7508 – AE VISA
Meals 10.00/12.50 **t.** and a la carte. IS **e**

Swiss Cottage – ✉ NW3 – 0171.

Regents Park Marriott, 128 King Henry's Rd, NW3 3ST, ✆ 722 7711, Fax 586 5822, – rm – 400. AE VISA JCB. GS **a**
Meals 18.95/15.95 **t.** and a la carte – 11.85 – **298 rm** 145.00/150.00 **s.**, 5 suites – SB.

XX **Peter's Chateaubriand,** 65 Fairfax Rd, NW6 4EE, ✆ 624 5804 – AE VISA JCB
closed Saturday lunch, 1-2 January and 26-27 December – **Meals** 10.95/12.95 **t.** and a la carte. FS **i**

X **Thai Pepper,** 115 Finchley Rd, NW3 6HY, ✆ 722 0026 – AE VISA GS **v**
closed lunch Saturday and Sunday and Bank Holidays – **Meals** - Thai - 10.00/17.00 **t.** and a la carte 3.90.

ITY OF LONDON – 0171 Except where otherwise stated see p. 23.

XXX **Tatsuso,** 32 Broadgate Circle, EC2M 2QS, ✆ 638 5863, Fax 638 5864 – AE VISA JCB PU **u**
closed Saturday, Sunday, and Bank Holidays – **Meals** - Japanese - (booking essential) 21.00/70.00 **t.** and a la carte.

XX **Brasserie Rocque** (Restaurant), 37 Broadgate Circle, EC2M 2QS, ✆ 638 7919, Fax 628 5899, – AE VISA PU **u**
closed Saturday, Sunday and Bank Holidays – **Meals** (lunch only) 23.75 **t.** and a la carte 5.00.

XX **Le Quai,** Riverside Walkway, 1 Broken Wharf, EC4V 3QQ, off High Timber St. ✆ 236 6480, Fax 236 6479 – AE VISA JCB OV **a**
closed Saturday, Sunday and 21 December-5 January – **Meals** - French - (dinner booking essential) 25.50/32.50 **t.**

XX **Miyama,** 17 Godliman St., EC4V 5BD, ✆ 489 1937, Fax 236 0325 – AE VISA JCB
closed Saturday dinner, Sunday and Bank Holidays – **Meals** - Japanese - 15.00/60.00 **t.** and a la carte 6.00. OV **e**

XX **Imperial City,** Royal Exchange, Cornhill, EC3V 3LL, ✆ 626 3437, Fax 338 0125 – AE VISA PV **a**
closed Saturday, Sunday and Bank Holidays – **Meals** - Chinese - 14.90/24.90 **t.** and a la carte.

XX **Portico,** 5 Philpot Lane, EC3M 8AQ, ✆ 929 2229, Fax 929 0924 – AE VISA JCB
closed Saturday, Sunday, 25-26 December and Bank Holidays – **Meals** - Italian - (lunch only) 10.95 **t.** and a la carte 21.50/24.35 **t.** 5.50. PV **c**

X **Imari,** 20 Copthall Av., EC2R 7DN, ✆ 628 3611, Fax 628 8958 – AE VISA JCB
closed Saturday, Sunday and Bank Holidays – **Meals** - Japanese - 8.50/45.00 **t.** and a la carte 4.00. PU **c**

CROYDON pp. 10 and 11.

Addington – ✉ Surrey – ☎ 0181 – 18, 18, 9 Addington Court, Featherbed Lane ✆ 6 0281/2/3, GZ – 18 The Addington, Shirley Church Rd ✆ 777 1055 GZ.

XX **Willow,** 88 Selsdon Park Rd, CR2 8JT, ✆ 657 4656 – ▤ P. AE VISA GZ
closed 25 to 27 December – **Meals** - Chinese (Peking, Szechuan) - 13.50/16.50 and a la carte 4.50.

Coulsdon – ✉ Surrey – ☎ 0181.

Coulsdon Manor ⛰, Coulsdon Court Rd, via Stoats Nest Rd, CR5 2LL, ✆ 668 041 Fax 668 3118, 18, squash – ▤ rest TV ☎ P – 180. AE VISA EZ
Manor House : Meals 14.95/19.95 **t.** and a la carte 6.60 – **35 rm** ☐ 85.00/115.00 **st.** – SB

Croydon – ✉ Surrey – ☎ 0181.

Katherine St., CR9 1ET ✆ 253 1009.

Hilton National, Waddon Way, Purley Way, CR9 4HH, ✆ 680 3000, Fax 681 6171, – rm ▤ TV ☎ & P – 400. AE VISA JCB. FZ
Meals 19.00 **st.** 7.00 – ☐ 10.95 – **168 rm** 89.00 **st.** – SB.

Croydon Park, 7 Altyre Rd, CR9 5AA, ✆ 680 9200, Fax 760 0426, squash – rm ▤ TV ☎ P – 300. AE VISA JCB FZ
Oscars : Meals 13.95/14.95 **t.** and a la carte 4.95 – **211 rm** ☐ 95.00 **st.**, 1 suite – SB.

Forte Posthouse, Purley Way, CR9 4LT, ✆ 688 5185, Fax 681 6438, – rm TV ☎ – 170. AE VISA. FZ
Meals a la carte 16.00/20.95 **st.** – ☐ 7.95 – **83 rm** 59.00 **st.** – SB.

Windsor Castle Toby, 415 Brighton Rd, South Croydon, CR2 6EJ, ✆ 680 45 Fax 680 5121, – rm TV ☎ P. AE VISA. FZ
Meals (grill rest.) 7.90 **t.** and a la carte – **29 rm** ☐ 62.00/95.00 **t.** – SB.

Travel Inn, Coombe Rd, CR0 5RB, on A 212 ✆ 686 2030, Fax 686 6435, – rm TV P. AE VISA. GZ
Meals (grill rest.) – ☐ 4.95 – **39 rm** 34.50 **t.**

X **Mario,** 299 High St., CR0 1QL, ✆ 686 5624 – AE VISA FZ
closed Saturday lunch, Monday dinner, Sunday and last 2 weeks August – **Meals** - Ital - 12.50 **t.** and a la carte.

Sanderstead – ✉ Surrey – ☎ 0181.

18 Selsdon Park Hotel, Addington Rd, Sanderstead ✆ 657 8811 GZ.

Selsdon Park, Addington Rd, CR2 8YA, ✆ 657 8811, Fax 651 6171, heat 18, park, squash – rm TV ☎ P – 150. AE VISA JCB GZ
Meals (dancing Saturday) 15.50/27.50 **t.** and a la carte – ☐ 10.50 – **163 rm** 95.00/150.00 7 suites – SB.

EALING pp. 4 and 5.

Ealing – ✉ W5 – ☎ 0181.

18 West Middlesex, Greenford Rd ✆ 574 3450 BV – 9 Horsenden Hill, Woodland R ✆ 902 4555 BU.

Carnarvon, Ealing Common, W5 3HN, ✆ 992 5399, Fax 992 7082 – rm TV ☎ 200. AE VISA JCB. CV
Meals 14.50 **t.** (dinner) and a la carte 16.95/22.40 **t.** 5.50 – ☐ 9.95 – **145 rm** 89.0 110.00 **st.**

XX **Maxim,** 153-155 Northfield Av., W13 9QT, ✆ 567 1719 – ▤. AE VISA BV
closed Sunday lunch and 25 to 29 December – **Meals** - Chinese (Peking) - 11.90/26.0 and a la carte.

XX **Laguna Tandoori,** 1-4 Culmington Par., Uxbridge Rd, W13 9BD, ✆ 579 9992 – ▤. VISA JCB BV
closed 25 December – **Meals** - Indian - 7.00/20.00 **t.** and a la carte 3.35.

X **Noughts 'n' Crosses,** 77 The Grove, W5 5LL, ✆ 840 7568, Fax 840 1905 – AE JCB BV
closed Sunday dinner, Monday, August and 26 December-4 January – **Meals** (dinner o and Sunday lunch)/dinner 19.90 **t.** 4.90.

X **Paolo's,** 7 Hanger Green, W5 3EL, ✆ 997 8560 – AE VISA CV
closed Saturday lunch, Sunday, Easter, Christmas and Bank Holidays – **Meals** - Ital - 15.00/25.00 **t.** and a la carte 4.50.

Hanwell – ✉ W7 – ☎ 0181 – 18 Brent Valley, Church Rd, ✆ 567 1287 BV.

Wellmeadow Lodge, 24 Wellmeadow Rd, W7 2AL, ✆ 567 7294, Fax 566 3468, – TV ☎. AE VISA JCB. BV
Meals (by arrangement) 15.00 **t.** – **8 rm** ☐ 60.00/107.00 **t.**

ENFIELD pp. 6 and 7.

Lee Valley, Picketts Lock Lane, Edmonton ℘ 803 3611 GT.

Enfield – ✉ Middx – ☎ 0181.

Whitewebbs, Beggars Hollow, Clay Hill ℘ 363 4454, N : 1 m. FT.

Royal Chace, The Ridgeway, EN2 8AR, ℘ 366 6500, Fax 367 7191, heated, – 270. ET **a**
closed 25 to 28 December – **Meals** *(closed Saturday lunch, Sunday dinner and Bank Holidays)* 14.50/17.95 **st.** and a la carte 4.65 – **92 rm** 71.50/87.50 **t.**

Oak Lodge, 80 Village Rd, Bush Hill Park, EN1 2EU, ℘ 360 7082, – . FT **e**
Meals (by arrangement) a la carte 17.50 **st.** 5.50 **5 rm** 59.50/79.50 **st.** – SB.

Hadley Wood – ✉ Herts – ☎ 0181.

West Lodge Park, off Cockfosters Rd, EN4 0PY, ℘ 440 8311, Fax 449 3698, park – – 80. ET **i**
Meals 19.50/24.50 **st.** 6.25 – 9.50 – **45 rm** 67.00/176.50 **st.** – SB.

GREENWICH pp. 10 and 11.

Blackheath – ✉ SE3 – ☎ 0181.

Bardon Lodge, 15 Stratheden Rd, SE3 7TH, ℘ 853 4051, Fax 858 7387, – – 40. HV **a**
Lamplight : Meals *(closed Sunday dinner)* (bar lunch Monday to Saturday)/dinner 13.95 **t.** and a la carte – 4.95 – **30 rm** 53.50/80.00 **t.**

Vanbrugh, 21 St. John's Park, SE3 7TD, ℘ 853 5505 (Reservations : 853 4051), Fax 858 7387, – .
Meals - (see ***Bardon Lodge*** above) – 4.95 – **30 rm** 53.50/80.00 **t.**

Greenwich – ✉ SE10 – ☎ 0181.

46 Greenwich Church St., SE10 9BL ℘ 858 6376.

Treasure of China, 10-11 Nelson Rd, SE10 9JB, ℘ 858 9884, Fax 293 5327 – . GV **e**
Meals - Chinese (Peking, Szechuan) - 25.00 **t.** and a la carte 3.40.

Spread Eagle, 1-2 Stockwell St., SE10 9JN, ℘ 853 2333 – . GV **c**
closed Sunday dinner, 25 to 30 December and Bank Holiday Mondays – **Meals** 15.00 **t.** and dinner a la carte 4.50.

HACKNEY – p.23.

Dalston – ✉ N 1 – ☎ 0171.

Soulard, 113 Mortimer Rd, N1 4JY, ℘ 254 1314 – PS **e**
closed Sunday, Monday, 15 August for 3 weeks and 1 week Christmas – **Meals** - French - (dinner only) a la carte 15.45/19.70 **t.** 8.50.

HAMMERSMITH and FULHAM Except where otherwise stated see pp. 24-25.

Fulham – ✉ SW6 – ☎ 0171.

La Reserve, 422-428 Fulham Rd, SW6 1DU, ℘ 385 8561, Fax 385 7662, « Contemporary decor » – rm FZ **a**
37 rm.

Blue Elephant, 4-6 Fulham Broadway, SW6 1AA, ℘ 385 6595, Fax 386 7665 – . EZ **z**
closed Saturday lunch and 24 to 27 December – **Meals** - Thai - (booking essential) 29.00/34.00 **t.** and a la carte 6.25.

Mao Tai, 58 New Kings Rd., Parsons Green, SW6 4LS, ℘ 731 2520 – .
closed Saturday lunch and 25 to 27 December – **Meals** - Chinese (Szechuan) - 18.50 **t.** and a la carte. p. 12 BQ **e**

Fleurie, 755 Fulham Rd, SW6 5UU, ℘ 371 0695 – BQ **n**
Meals (lunch by arrangement Monday to Saturday) 14.95/16.50 **t.** and dinner a la carte.

Le Midi, 488 Fulham Rd, SW6 5NH, ℘ 386 0657 – EZ **a**
closed 4 days Christmas – **Meals** a la carte 12.25/17.45 **t.**

Hammersmith – ✉ W6/W12/W14 – ☎ 0181.

River Café, Thames Wharf, Rainville Rd, W6 9HA, ℘ 381 8824, Fax 381 6217 –
closed Sunday dinner, 25 December-1 January and Bank Holidays – **Meals** - Italian - a la carte 27.00/35.50 **t.** 7.50. DV **r**

Tandoori Nights, 319-321 King St., W6 9NH, ℘ 741 4328 – . p. 9 CV **u**
closed 25 and 26 December – **Meals** - Indian - 9.95/15.00 **st.** and a la carte 5.95.

Snows on the Green, 166 Shepherd's Bush Rd, Brook Green, W6 7P
(0171) 603 2142, Fax 602 7553 – VISA p. 9 CV
closed Saturday lunch, Sunday dinner, 10 days Christmas-New Year and Bank Holidays – **Meals** 12.50 **t.** (lunch) and a la carte 17.00/24.85 **t.** 5.00.

Brackenbury, 129-131 Brackenbury Rd, W6 0BQ, 748 0107, Fax 741 0905 – AE VISA p. 9 CV
closed lunch Monday and Saturday, Sunday dinner, 10 days Christmas-New Year and Bank Holidays – **Meals** a la carte 14.50/18.25 **t.**

Shepherd's Bush – W12/W14 – 0171.

Wilsons, 236 Blythe Rd, W14 0HJ, 603 7267 – AE VISA p.9 DV
closed Sunday dinner and 24 to 31 December – **Meals** (dinner only and Sunday lunch) a la carte 16.00/18.75 **t.** 4.50.

Balzac, 4 Wood Lane, W12 7DT, 743 5370 – AE VISA DV
closed Saturday lunch, Sunday, first week January and Bank Holidays – **Meals** - French Bistro a la carte 16.50/21.20 **t.**

HARINGEY pp. 6 and 7.

Crouch End – N 8 – 0181.

Les Associés, 172 Park Rd, N8 8JY, 348 8944 – VISA EU
closed lunch Tuesday and Saturday, Sunday, Monday, 10 days Easter and 10 days August – **Meals** - French - 15.95/25.00 **t.** and dinner a la carte.

Florians, 4 Topsfield Par., Middle Lane, N8 8RP, 348 8348 – VISA EU
closed 24 to 26 December and 1 January – **Meals** - Italian - a la carte 15.20/22.95 **t.** 5.60

Hornsey – N8 – 0181.

Jashan, 19a Turnpike Lane, N8 0EP, 340 9880, Fax 347 8770 – EU
Meals - Indian rest..

HARROW pp. 4 and 5.

Central Harrow – Middx – 0181.

Civic Centre, Station Rd, HA1 2XF 424 1103/424 1100 BU.

Cumberland, 1 St. John's Rd, HA1 2EF, 863 4111, Fax 861 5668, – rm – 130. AE VISA. BU
Meals 11.50/17.50 **st.** and a la carte – **81 rm** 65.00/90.00 **t.** – SB.

Trattoria Sorrentina, 6 Manor Par., Sheepcote Rd, HA1 2JN, 427 9411, Fax 427 94 – . AE VISA BU
closed Saturday lunch and Sunday – **Meals** - Italian - 12.95 **t.** (lunch) and a la carte 22.2 27.50 **t.**

Taste of China, 174 Station Rd, HA1 2RH, 863 2080 – . AE VISA BU
Meals - Chinese - a la carte 14.00/20.00 **t.**

Hatch End – Middx – 0181.

Swan, 322-326 Uxbridge Rd, HA5 4HR, 428 8821 – . AE VISA JCB BT
Meals - Chinese (Peking) - 20.00/26.00 **st.** and a la carte 4.20.

Kenton – Middx. – 0181.

Travel Inn, Kenton Rd, HA3 8AT, 907 1671, Fax 909 1604 – rm . AE VISA. BU
Meals (grill rest.) – 4.95 – **44 rm** 34.50 **t.**

North Harrow – Middx. – 0181.

Percy's, 66-68 Station Rd, HA2 7SJ, 427 2021, Fax 427 8134 – . AE VISA
closed Sunday and 27 December-3 January – **Meals** (booking essential) a la carte 21.0 27.00 **t.** 4.90. BU

Pinner – Middx. – 0181.

Friends, 11 High St., HA5 5PJ, 866 0286 – . AE VISA BU
closed Sunday dinner, 25 and 26 December and Bank Holidays – **Meals** 13.95/18.50 and a la carte.

Olde Village Bakery, 33 High St., HA5 5PS, 868 4704 – AE VISA BU
Meals 10.00 **st.** and a la carte 4.50.

South Harrow – Middx. – 0181.

Jaflong, 299 Northolt Rd, HA2 8JA, 864 7345 – . AE VISA BU
Meals - Indian - 4.50 **t.** (lunch) and a la carte 11.90/16.70 **t.**

Stanmore – Middx – 0181.

Mr Tang's Mandarin, 28 The Broadway, HA7 4DW, 954 0339 – . AE VISA BT
Meals - Chinese (Peking) - 15.00/25.00 **t.** and a la carte.

HAVERING pp. 6 and 7.

Hornchurch by A 12 – JT – on A 127 – ✉ Essex – ☎ 01708.

Palms (Hilton), Southend Arterial Rd (A 127), RM11 3UJ, ☎ 346789, Fax 341719, – rm – 270 – **137 rm.**

Romford by A 118 – JU – ✉ Essex – ☎ 01708.

18, 9 Havering, Risebridge, Risebridge Chase, Lower Bedfords Rd ☎ 741429 JT.

Coach House, 48 Main Rd, RM1 3DB, on A 118 ☎ 751901, Fax 730290, – . VISA.
Meals *(closed Friday to Sunday)* (in bar) 4.95 – **32 rm** 29.50/49.50 **t.**

HILLINGDON pp. 4 and 8 – 18 Haste Hill, The Drive ☎ (01927) 422877 AU – 18 Harefield Pl., The Drive ☎ (01895) 231169, by B 467 AU.

Hayes – ✉ Middx. – ☎ 0181.

Travel Inn, 362 Uxbridge Rd, UB4 0HF, ☎ 573 7479, Fax 569 1204 – rm . AE VISA. AV **a**
Meals (grill rest.) – 4.95 – **40 rm** 34.50 **t.**

Heathrow Airport – ✉ Middx – ☎ 0181 – Heathrow Terminals 1,2,3, Underground Station Concourse, TW6 2JA ☎ (0171) 824 8844.

Radisson Edwardian, 140 Bath Rd, Hayes, UB3 5AW, ☎ 759 6311, Telex 23935, Fax 759 4559, , , – rm – 500. AE VISA JCB. AX **e**
Henleys : Meals *(closed lunch Saturday and Sunday)* 19.90/28.00 **st.** and a la carte 6.50 – **Brasserie : Meals** 11.95 **st.** and a la carte – 13.00 – **442 rm** 153.00/215.00 **st.**, 17 suites.

Holiday Inn Crowne Plaza Heathrow London, Stockley Rd, West Drayton, UB7 9NA, ☎ (01895) 445555, Telex 934518, Fax 445122, , , , 9 – rm – 200. AE VISA JCB AV **v**
Marlowe : Meals *(closed Sunday)* (dinner only) 23.95 **t.** and a la carte – **Cafe Galleria : Meals** 15.95/17.50 **t.** and a la carte – 11.50 – **372 rm** 110.00/125.00 **st.**, 2 suites.

Sheraton Skyline, Bath Rd, Hayes, UB3 5BP, ☎ 759 2535, Telex 934 254, Fax 750 9150, , – rm – 500. AE VISA JCB AX **u**
Colony Room : Meals (dinner only) 32.00 **t.** and a la carte – **Cafe Jardin : Meals** a la carte 16.50/29.00 **t.** 7.00 – 12.00 – **344 rm** 180.00/190.00 **st.**, 5 suites.

London Heathrow Hilton, Terminal 4, TW6 3AF, ☎ 759 7755, Telex 925094, Fax 759 7579, , , – rm – 240. AE VISA JCB AX **n**
Brasserie : Meals 17.95/29.00 **st.** and a la carte 7.95 – **Zen Oriental : Meals** 25.00/30.00 **st.** and a la carte – 11.95 – **392 rm** 145.00/159.00 **st.**, 4 suites – SB.

Forte Crest, Sipson Rd, West Drayton, UB7 0JU, ☎ 759 2323, Telex 934280, Fax 897 8659 – rm – 100. AE VISA JCB. AV **c**
Sampans : Meals - Chinese - (dinner only) 15.50/21.95 **t.** and a la carte 7.50 – **Tutto : Meals** (carving rest.) 16.95 **st.** and a la carte 7.50 – 10.75 – **570 rm** 99.00/110.00, 2 suites – SB.

Excelsior Heathrow (Forte), Bath Rd, West Drayton, UB7 0DU, ☎ 759 6611, Telex 24525, Fax 759 3421, , , – rm – 700. AE VISA JCB. AX **x**
Meals (carving rest.) 15.50/16.95 **st.** 7.25 – **Wheeler's : Meals** *(closed lunch Saturday and Sunday)* a la carte 24.95/32.95 **st.** 7.25 – 11.45 – **817 rm** 99.00/110.00 **st.**, 10 suites – SB.

Sheraton Heathrow, Colnbrook bypass, West Drayton, UB7 0HJ, ☎ 759 2424, Telex 851 934331, Fax 759 2091 – rm – 50. AE VISA JCB.
Meals 18.50 **t.** and a la carte – 12.50 – **426 rm** 160.00/170.00 **t.**, 4 suites. AVX **a**

Forte Posthouse, Bath Rd, Hayes, UB3 5AJ, ☎ 759 2552, Fax 564 9265 – rm rest – 40. AE VISA JCB AX **i**
Meals a la carte approx. 15.00 **t.** 5.50 – **186 rm** 59.50/69.50 **st.**

Heathrow Park (Thistle), Bath Rd, Longford, West Drayton, UB7 0EQ, W : off A4, ☎ 759 2400, Telex 934093, Fax 759 5278 – rm – 700. AE VISA JCB
Meals (carving lunch) 12.75/15.75 **st.** and a la carte 5.50 – 8.75 – **306 rm** 75.00/160.00 **st.** – SB.

Ickenham – ✉ Middx. – ☎ 01895.

Roberto's, 15 Long Lane, UB10 8QU, ☎ 632519 – . AE VISA JCB AU **i**
closed Saturday lunch and Sunday – **Meals** - Italian - a la carte 12.30/27.75 **t.** 6.50.

Yiewsley – ✉ Middx. – ☎ 0181.

Waterfront Brasserie, The Arena, Stockley Park, UB11 1AA, ☎ 899 1733, Fax 899 1711 – . AE VISA AV **r**
closed Saturday lunch, dinner Monday to Wednesday, Sunday and 1 to 7 January – **Meals** (dancing Friday) 17.50 **t.** and a la carte.

HOUNSLOW pp. 8 and 9.

Wyke Green, Syon Lane, Isleworth (0181) 560 8777 BV – Airlinks, Southall Lane 56 1418 ABV – Hounslow Heath, Staines Rd 570 5271 BX.

24 The Treaty Centre, Hounslow High St., TW3 1ES 572 8279.

Chiswick – W4 – 0181.

La Dordogne, 5 Devonshire Rd, W4 2EU, 747 1836, Fax 994 9144 – AE VISA JCB *closed lunch Saturday and Sunday and Bank Holidays* – **Meals** - French - a la carte 18.20/30.30 **t.** 4.90. CV

The Chiswick, 131 Chiswick High Rd, W4 2ED, 994 6887, Fax 747 8708 – AE VISA *closed Saturday lunch, Sunday dinner, 1 week Christmas-New Year and Bank Holidays Mondays* – **Meals** 8.50 **t.** and a la carte 4.50. CV

Cranford – Middx. – 0181.

Jarvis International Heathrow, Bath Rd, TW5 9QE, 897 2121, Fax 897 7014, – rm – 100. AE VISA JCB. AX
Meals *(closed lunch Saturday and Sunday)* 10.00/22.00 **t.** and a la carte 7.00 – 10.50 – **72 rm** 89.00/99.00 **st.**, 1 suite – SB.

Heston Service Area – Middx. – 0181.

Granada Lodge without rest., TW5 9NA, on M 4 (between junctions 2 and 3 westbound carriageway) 574 7271, Fax (0177) 352 1087, Reservations (Freephone) 0800 555300 – . AE VISA ABV
71 rm 39.95 **st.**

ISLINGTON Except where otherwise stated see pp. 20-23.

Canonbury – N1 – 0171.

Anna's Place, 90 Mildmay Park, N1 4PR, 249 9379 p. 6 FU
closed Sunday, Monday, 2 weeks Easter, 4 weeks August and 2 weeks Christmas – **Meals** Swedish - (booking essential) 14.95 **t.** (lunch) and a la carte 17.65/22.35 **t.**

Finsbury – WC1/EC1/EC2 – 0171.

Stephen Bull's Bistro, 71 St. John St., EC1M 4AN, 490 1750, Fax 490 3128 – . AE VISA NU
closed Saturday lunch, Sunday, 1 week Christmas and Bank Holidays – **Meals** a la carte 17.20/25.45 **t.** 5.00.

Le Mesurier, 113 Old St., EC1V 9JR, 251 8117, Fax 608 3504 – AE VISA JCB *closed Saturday, Sunday, 3 weeks August, 2 weeks Christmas-New Year and Bank Holidays* – **Meals** (booking essential) (lunch only) a la carte 17.50/23.00 **t.** 4.50. OT

Rouxl Britannia, Triton Court, 14 Finsbury Sq., EC2A 1RP, 256 6997 – VISA *closed Saturday, Sunday, 25 December-1 January and Bank Holidays* – **Le Restaurant : Meals** - French - (lunch only) 21.75 **st.** 5.75 – **Le Café : Meals** - French - (lunch only) a la carte 12.75/17.05 **st.** 5.50. PU

Quality Chop House, 94 Farringdon Rd, EC1R 3EA, 837 5093 MT
closed Saturday lunch and 24 December-2 January – **Meals** a la carte 16.25/23.50 **t.**

Alba, 107 Whitecross St., EC1Y 8JH, 588 1798 – . AE VISA OT
closed Saturday, Sunday, Christmas-New Year and Bank Holidays – **Meals** - Italian - a la carte 13.60/21.00 **t.**

St. John, 26 St. John St., EC1M 4AY, 251 0848, Fax 251 4090 – AE VISA JCB *closed Sunday dinner, Easter and 24 December-2 January* – **Meals** a la carte 12.50/23.00 7.00. OU

Peasant, 240 St. John St., EC1V 4PH, 336 7726 – AE VISA NT
closed Saturday lunch, Sunday, 23 December-4 January and Bank Holidays – **Meals** a la carte 15.50/17.50 **t.**

Islington – N1 – 0171.

Granita, 127 Upper St., N1 1PQ, 226 3222 – . VISA NS
closed Tuesday lunch, Monday, 1 week Easter, last 2 weeks August and 10 days Christmas – **Meals** 13.95 **t.** (lunch) and dinner a la carte 19.40/22.40 **t.**

Euphorium, 203 Upper St., N1 1RQ, 704 6909. VISA NS
closed Monday and Saturday lunch, Sunday, 25 December-3 January and Good Friday – **Meals** a la carte 18.00/21.00 **t.**

KENSINGTON and CHELSEA (Royal Borough of).

Chelsea – SW1/SW3/SW10 – 0171 – Except where otherwise stated see pp. and 31.

Hyatt Carlton Tower, 2 Cadogan Pl., SW1X 9PY, 235 1234, Telex 2194 Fax 245 6570, <, , , , – rm – 150. AE VISA JCB FR
Chelsea Room : Meals 18.50/29.50 **t.** and a la carte – **Rib Room** (824 7053) : **Meals** 23.50/29.50 **t.** and a la carte – 15.50 – **194 rm** 225.00/270.00, 30 suites.

Sheraton Park Tower, 101 Knightsbridge, SW1X 7RN, ✆ 235 8050, Telex 917222, Fax 235 8231, ≤ – |‡| ⇔ rm ▤ TV ☎ ♿ P – 🔑 60. AE ① VISA JCB. ✗ FQ **v**
Meals 22.50/35.00 **st.** and a la carte 7.50 – **267 rm** ▭ 220.00/285.00 **s.**, 22 suites.

Conrad London, Chelsea Harbour, SW10 0XG, ✆ 823 3000, Fax 351 6525, ≤, Lδ, ≘s, ▭ – |‡| ⇔ rm ▤ TV ☎ ♿ ⇔ – 🔑 200. AE ① VISA JCB. ✗ p. 13 CQ **i**
Meals 16.00/24.00 **t.** and a la carte 8.00 – ▭ 17.00, **159 suites** 150.00/280.00 – SB.

Durley House, 115 Sloane St., SW1X 9PJ, ✆ 235 5537, Fax 259 6977, « Tastefully furnished Georgian town house », ⛲, ✂ – |‡| TV ☎. AE VISA. ✗ FS **e**
Meals (room service only) a la carte approx. 22.50 – ▭ 12.50 –, **11 suites** 195.00/300.00 **s.**

✿ **Capital,** 22-24 Basil St., SW3 1AT, ✆ 589 5171, Fax 225 0011 – |‡| ▤ TV ☎ ⇔ – 🔑 25. AE ① VISA. ✗ ER **a**
Meals 25.00/40.00 **st.** and a la carte 41.00/47.50 **st.** 7.95 – ▭ 14.00 – **48 rm** 167.00/290.00 **s.**
Spec. Grilled langoustines with ginger, lemon and cucumber, Roasted Scotch beef fillet with garlic, shallots and thyme, Assiette of vanilla.

Draycott, 24-26 Cadogan Gdns, SW3 2RP, ✆ 730 6466, Fax 730 0236, ⛲ – |‡| TV ☎. AE ① VISA JCB. ✗ FS **c**
Meals (room service only) – ▭ 12.95 – **25 rm** 100.00/250.00 **t.**

Cadogan, 75 Sloane St., SW1X 9SG, ✆ 235 7141, Fax 245 0994, ⛲, ✂ – |‡| ⇔ rm ▤ rest TV ☎ – 🔑 40. AE ① VISA. ✗ FR **e**
Meals *(closed Saturday lunch)* 12.90/21.90 **t.** and a la carte 6.25 – ▭ 13.50 – **60 rm** 125.00/180.00 **st.**, 5 suites – SB.

Franklin, 28 Egerton Gdns., SW3 2DB, ✆ 584 5533, Fax 584 5449, « Tastefully furnished town house », ⛲ – |‡| ⇔ ▤ TV ☎ P. AE ① VISA. ✗ DS **e**
Meals (room service only) a la carte 20.00/35.00 **st.** 7.00 – ▭ 12.50 – **35 rm** 120.00/210.00 **s.**, 1 suite.

Basil Street, 8 Basil St., SW3 1AH, ✆ 581 3311, Fax 581 3693 – |‡| TV ☎ – 🔑 55. AE ① VISA JCB. ✗ FQ **o**
Meals (carving lunch Saturday) 14.95/23.00 **t.** 6.00 – ▭ 12.50 – **92 rm** 125.00/185.00 **t.**, 1 suite.

Chelsea, 17-25 Sloane St., SW1X 9NU, ✆ 235 4377, Fax 235 3705 – |‡| ⇔ rm ▤ TV ☎ – 🔑 100. AE ① VISA JCB. ✗ FR **r**
Meals 14.95/19.50 **t.** and a la carte 7.00 – ▭ 12.50 – **219 rm** 145.00/155.00 **s.**, 5 suites.

Sydney House, 9-11 Sydney St., SW3 6PU, ✆ 376 7711, Fax 376 4233, « Tastefully furnished Victorian town house » – |‡| TV ☎. AE ① VISA DT **a**
Meals (room service only) – ▭ 12.00 – **21 rm** 120.00/180.00 **s.**

Egerton House, 17-19 Egerton Terr., SW3 2BX, ✆ 589 2412, Fax 584 6540, « Tastefully furnished Victorian town house », ⛲ – |‡| ▤ TV ☎. AE ① VISA. ✗ DR **e**
Meals (room service only) – ▭ 12.50 – **27 rm** 120.00/180.00, 1 suite.

Sloane, 29 Draycott Pl., SW3 2SH, ✆ 581 5757, Fax 584 1348, « Victorian town house, antiques » – |‡| ▤ TV ☎. AE ① VISA. ✗ ET **c**
Meals (room service only) a la carte 14.00/17.50 7.50 – ▭ 8.00 – **12 rm** 120.00/190.00.

Fenja without rest., 69 Cadogan Gdns, SW3 2RB, ✆ 589 7333, Fax 581 4958, ⛲ – |‡| ⇔ TV ☎. AE ① VISA. ✗ FS **r**
▭ 11.75 – **12 rm** 130.00/195.00 **t.**

Beaufort without rest., 33 Beaufort Gdns, SW3 1PP, ✆ 584 5252, Telex 929200, Fax 589 2834, « English floral watercolour collection » – |‡| ▤ TV ☎. AE ① VISA JCB. ✗ ER **n**
28 rm 110.00/215.00 **s.**

Eleven Cadogan Gardens, 11 Cadogan Gdns, SW3 2RJ, ✆ 730 3426, Fax 730 5217, Lδ – |‡| TV ☎ FS **u**
55 rm, 5 suites.

Parkes without rest., 41 Beaufort Gdns., SW3 1PW, ✆ 581 9944, Fax 581 1999 – |‡| TV ☎. AE ① VISA. ✗ ER **x**
17 rm ▭ 98.00 **s.**, 16 suites 135.00/215.00 **s.**

Knightsbridge, 12 Beaufort Gdns., SW3 1PT, ✆ 589 9271, Fax 823 9692 – |‡| TV ☎. AE ① VISA JCB. ✗ ER **o**
Meals (room service only) – **44 rm** ▭ 80.00/120.00 **st.**, 6 suites.

Claverley without rest., 13-14 Beaufort Gdns, SW3 1PS, ✆ 589 8541, Fax 584 3410 – |‡| ⇔ TV ☎. AE ① VISA. ✗ ER **o**
32 rm ▭ 65.00/180.00 **t.**

L'Hotel, 28 Basil St., SW3 1AT, ✆ 589 6286, Fax 225 0011 – |‡| TV ☎. AE ① VISA. ✗ ER **i**
Le Metro : Meals *(closed Sunday and Bank Holidays)* a la carte 12.45/18.00 **t.** – ▭ 6.50 – **12 rm** 145.00/160.00 **st.**

XXXX ✿✿✿ **La Tante Claire** (Koffmann), 68-69 Royal Hospital Rd, SW3 4HP, ✆ 352 6045, Fax 352 3257 – ▤. EN AE ◑ VISA EU c
closed Saturday, Sunday, 1 week Easter, last 3 weeks August and 1 week Christmas – **Meals** - French - (booking essential) 26.00/60.00 **st.** and a la carte 53.00/68.00 **st.**
Spec. Coquilles St.Jacques à la planche, sauce encre, Pied de cochon aux morilles, Croustade de pommes caramelisée.

XXX **Waltons,** 121 Walton St., SW3 2HP, ✆ 584 0204, Fax 581 2848 – ▤. EN AE ◑ VISA JCB DS a
closed 25 December dinner and 26 December – **Meals** 14.75/21.00 **t.** and a la carte 🍷 5.00.

XXX **Bibendum,** Michelin House, 81 Fulham Rd, SW3 6RD, ✆ 581 5817, Fax 823 7925 – ▤. EN AE VISA DS s
closed 24 to 28 December – **Meals** 27.00 **t.** (lunch) and dinner a la carte 25.00/44.00 **t.** 🍷 5.95.

XXX ✿ **The Canteen,** Harbour Yard, Chelsea Harbour, SW10 0XD, ✆ 351 7330, Fax 351 6189 – ▤. EN VISA p. 13 CQ
Meals a la carte approx. 24.85 **t.**
Spec. Risotto of sea scallops Provençal, Pavé of halibut with fennel, watercress and a warm aioli dressing, Tarte Tatin of pears.

XXX **Fifth Floor** (at Harvey Nichols), Knightsbridge, SW1X 7RJ, ✆ 235 5250, Fax 823 2207 – ▤. EN AE ◑ VISA JCB FQ a
closed Sunday dinner and 25 and 26 December – **Meals** 21.50 **t.** and dinner a la carte 19.00/35.75 **t.** 🍷 10.00.

XXX ✿ **Aubergine** (Ramsay), 11 Park Walk, SW10 0AJ, ✆ 352 3449, Fax 351 1770 – ▤. EN AE ◑ VISA CU
closed Saturday lunch, Sunday, first 2 weeks August, 2 weeks Christmas and Bank Holidays – **Meals** (booking essential) 19.50/34.00 **t.** 🍷 9.00
Spec. Sautéed sea scallops with creamed fennel and a light ginger cream, Pot au feu of Bresse pigeon with stuffed cabbage, Three crèmes brûlées.

XXX **Turner's,** 87-89 Walton St., SW3 2HP, ✆ 584 6711, Fax 584 4441 – ▤. EN AE ◑ VISA ES
closed Saturday lunch, 25 to 30 December and Bank Holidays – **Meals** 13.50/38.75 **st.** and a la carte 🍷 6.75.

XXX **Chutney Mary,** 535 King's Rd, SW10 0SZ, ✆ 351 3113, Fax 351 7694 – ▤. EN AE ◑ VISA JCB p. 24 FZ
closed 25 December dinner and 26 December – **Meals** - Anglo-Indian - a la carte 21.45/30.05 **t.**

XXX **Albero & Grana,** Chelsea Cloisters, 89 Sloane Av., SW3 3DX, ✆ 225 1048, Fax 581 3259 – ▤. EN AE ◑ VISA ET
closed Sunday – **Meals** - Spanish - (dinner only) a la carte 25.50/40.00 **t.** 🍷 6.00.

XXX Benihana, 77 King's Rd, SW3 4NX, ✆ 376 7799, Fax 376 7377 – ▤ EU
Meals - Japanese (Teppan-Yaki) rest..

XX ✿ **Fulham Road,** 257-259 Fulham Rd, SW3 6HY, ✆ 351 7823, Fax 376 4971 – EN AE VISA CU
closed Saturday lunch, Sunday, 1 week Christmas and Bank Holidays – **Meals** 19.00 (lunch) and a la carte 29.00/42.00 **t.** 🍷 7.00
Spec. Celeriac remoulade with pancetta, Assiette of duck with braised chicory, Papillotte of fruit with cinnamon ice cream.

XX **English Garden,** 10 Lincoln St., SW3 2TS, ✆ 584 7272 – ▤. EN AE ◑ VISA JCB ET
closed 25 and 26 December – **Meals** - English - 14.75 **t.** (lunch) and a la carte 23.25/30.00 🍷 5.00.

XX **Brasserie St. Quentin,** 243 Brompton Rd, SW3 2EP, ✆ 589 8005, Fax 584 6064 – ▤. EN AE ◑ VISA JCB DR
Meals - French - a la carte 14.70/29.10 **t.** 🍷 4.90.

XX **Poissonnerie de l'Avenue,** 82 Sloane Av., SW3 3DZ, ✆ 589 2457, Fax 581 3360 – ▤ EN AE ◑ VISA JCB DS
closed Sunday, Easter, 24 December-3 January and Bank Holidays – **Meals** - French Seafood - 16.50/26.00 **st.** and a la carte 🍷 5.50.

XX **Daphne's,** 112 Draycott Av., SW3 3AE, ✆ 589 4257, Fax 581 2232 – ▤. EN AE ◑ VISA DS
closed Christmas-New Year – **Meals** - Italian - a la carte 20.25/33.75 **t.**

XX **La Finezza,** 62-64 Lower Sloane St., SW1N 8BP, ✆ 730 8639 – ▤. EN AE ◑ VISA FT
closed Sunday and Bank Holidays – **Meals** - Italian - a la carte 22.50/43.00 **t.** 🍷 7.50.

XX **Grill St. Quentin,** 3 Yeoman's Row, SW3 2AL, ✆ 581 8377, Fax 584 6064 – ▤. EN AE ◑ VISA JCB ER
Meals a la carte 14.30/29.80 **t.** 🍷 4.90.

XX **Busabong Too,** 1a Langton St., SW10 0JL, ✆ 352 7414 – ▤. EN AE ◑ VISA JCB p. 24 FZ
Meals - Thai - (dinner only) 24.95 **t.** and a la carte.

XX **Toto's,** Walton House, Walton St., SW3 2JH, ✆ 589 0075 – EN AE ◑ VISA JCB ES
closed 25 and 26 December – **Meals** - Italian - 19.50 **st.** (lunch) and a la carte approx. 35.00 **st.**

XX **Red,** 8 Egerton Garden Mews, SW3 2EH, ☎ 584 7007, Fax 589 3152 – AE VISA JCB DR **n**
Meals - Chinese - 5.00/35.00 **t.** and a la carte 4.00.

XX **Good Earth,** 233 Brompton Rd, SW3 2EP, ☎ 584 3658, Fax 823 8769 – ▤. AE VISA JCB DR **c**
Meals - Chinese - 8.00/30.00 **t.** and a la carte 4.00.

XX **Dan's,** 119 Sydney St., SW3 6NR, ☎ 352 2718, Fax 352 3265 – AE VISA DU **s**
closed Saturday lunch, Sunday and 1 week Christmas-New Year – **Meals** a la carte 15.50/26.00 **t.** 5.00.

X **Thierry's,** 342 King's Rd, SW3 5UR, ☎ 352 3365, Fax 352 3365 – ▤. AE VISA JCB CU **c**
closed Christmas – **Meals** a la carte 18.65/30.20 **t.** 5.50.

X **R Bar,** 4 Sydney St., SW3 6PP, ☎ 352 3433, Fax 376 4972 – ▤. AE VISA DT **c**
closed Bank Holidays – **Meals** a la carte 16.15/25.70 **t.**

X **Kartouche,** 329-331 Fulham Rd, SW10 9QL, ☎ 823 3515, Fax 823 3991 – ▤. AE VISA BU **c**
Meals a la carte 15.50/24.00 **t.** 5.00.

X **Monkey's,** 1 Cale St., Chelsea Green, SW3 3QT, ☎ 352 4711 – ▤. VISA ET **z**
closed Saturday, Sunday, 2 weeks Easter and last 3 weeks August – **Meals** 15.00/22.50 **t.** and a la carte 5.50.

X **Beit Eddine,** 8 Harriet St., SW1X 9JW, ☎ 235 3969 – AE VISA FQ **z**
Meals - Lebanese - a la carte 20.00/24.00 **t.** 6.50.

Earl's Court – ✉ SW5/SW10 – ☎ 0171 – Except where otherwise stated see pp. 30 and 31.

Periquito, 34-44 Barkston Gdns., SW5 0EW, ☎ 373 7851, Fax 370 6570 – rm TV ☎ – 120. AE VISA JCB AT **e**
Meals 7.50/9.50 **st.** and a la carte 6.50 – 8.50 – **75 rm** 69.00/77.00 **st.** – SB.

Albany, 4-12 Barkston Gdns., SW5 0EN, ☎ 370 6116, Fax 244 8024 – ▤ rest TV ☎ – 30. AE VISA. AT **a**
Meals a la carte 10.50/13.20 **st.** – **Dynasty : Meals** - Chinese - (dinner only) a la carte 10.50/15.50 **st.** – 7.50 – **79 rm** 86.00/106.00 – SB.

Comfort Inn, 22-32 West Cromwell Rd, SW5 9QJ, ☎ 373 3300, Fax 835 2040 – rm ▤ TV ☎ – 80. AE VISA JCB. p. 24 EZ **n**
Meals 13.50 **st.** and a la carte 6.00 – 7.75 – **125 rm** 72.00/90.00 **st.** – SB.

Henley House, 30 Barkston Gdns., SW5 0EN, ☎ 370 4111, Fax 370 0026, – rest TV ☎. AE VISA JCB. AT **e**
Meals (by arrangement) (dinner only) (unlicensed) 14.50 **st.** – 3.40 – **20 rm** 55.00/84.00 **st.**

Rushmore without rest., 11 Trebovir Rd, SW5 9LS, ☎ 370 3839, Fax 370 0274 – TV ☎. AE VISA JCB. p. 24 EZ **c**
5.00 – **22 rm** 59.00/95.00 **st.**

Amsterdam without rest., 7 Trebovir Rd, SW5 9LS, ☎ 370 2814, Fax 244 7608, – TV ☎. AE VISA JCB. p. 24 EZ **c**
2.75 – **20 rm** 49.00/65.00 **st.**

X **Chez Max,** 168 Ifield Rd, SW10 9AF, ☎ 835 0874 – VISA AU **c**
closed Bank Holidays – **Meals** 10.00/25.50 **t.** 7.00.

Kensington – ✉ SW7/W8/W11/W14 – ☎ 0171 – Except where otherwise stated see pp. 24-27.

The Milestone without rest., 1-2 Kensington Court, W8 5DL, ☎ 917 1000, Fax 917 1010, – rm ▤ TV ☎. AE VISA. p. 30 AQ **u**
15.00 – **50 rm** 200.00/245.00 **st.**, 6 suites.

Halcyon, 81 Holland Park, W11 3RZ, ☎ 727 7288, Fax 229 8516 – ▤ TV ☎. AE VISA JCB. EX **u**
The Room : Meals *(closed Saturday lunch)* 21.00/32.00 **t.** – 13.80 – **40 rm** 165.00/250.00 **st.**, 3 suites.

Copthorne Tara, Scarsdale Pl., W8 5SR, ☎ 937 7211, Telex 918834, Fax 937 7100 – rm ▤ TV ☎ – 500. AE VISA JCB. FY **u**
Brasserie : Meals 17.50 **st.** and a la carte 6.90 – **Jerome K. Jerome : Meals** *(closed Sunday and Bank Holidays)* (dinner only) a la carte 25.30/43.00 **t.** 6.90 – 11.50 – **815 rm** 115.00/150.00 **st.**, 10 suites.

Kensington Park (Thistle), 16-32 De Vere Gdns, W8 5AG, ☎ 937 8080, Telex 929643, Fax 937 7616 – rm ▤ rest TV ☎ – 120. AE VISA.
Moniques Brasserie : Meals 14.75 **t.** and a la carte – **Cairngorm Grill : Meals** *(closed Sunday and Monday)* (dinner only) 19.95 **t.** and a la carte 7.00 – 10.75 – **326 rm** 125.00/155.00 **t.**, 6 suites. p. 30 BQ **e**

London Kensington Hilton, 179-199 Holland Park Av., W11 4UL, ☎ 603 3355, Fax 602 9397 – rm ▤ TV ☎ – 300. AE VISA JCB EX **s**
Meals 5.00/35.00 **t.** and a la carte 7.60 **Hiroko : Meals** - Japanese - *(closed Monday)* 15.00/32.00 **t.** and a la carte 7.00 – 13.00 – **602 rm** 130.00/150.00 **st.**, 1 suite.

Hilton National London Olympia, 380 Kensington High St., W14 8NL, 603 333, Telex 22229, Fax 603 4846, – rm rest – 400. EY
Meals (bar lunch Saturday) 12.95/30.00 **t.** and a la carte 8.95 – 11.75 – **395 rm** 115.00/125.00 **st.**, 10 suites – SB.

Kensington Close (Forte), Wrights Lane, W8 5SP, 937 8170, Telex 2391, Fax 937 8289, squash – rm rest – 180. FY
Meals 15.95 **st.** and a la carte – 10.00 – **530 rm** 105.00 – SB.

Holland Court without rest., 31 Holland Rd, W14 8HJ, 371 1133, Fax 602 9114, – EY
22 rm 65.00/90.00 **st.**

Russell Court without rest., 9 Russell Rd, W14 8JA, 603 1222, Fax 603 1222 – EY
18 rm 55.00/65.00 **st.**

Clarke's, 124 Kensington Church St., W8 4BH, 221 9225, Fax 229 4564 – EX
closed Saturday, Sunday, 2 weeks August, 10 days Christmas and Bank Holidays – **Meals** 26.00/37.00 **st.** 6.00.

La Pomme d'Amour, 128 Holland Park Av., W11 4UE, 229 8532, Fax 221 4096 – EX
closed Saturday lunch and Sunday – **Meals** - French - 17.50/22.00 **t.** and a la carte.

L'Escargot Doré, 2-4 Thackeray St., W8 5ET, 937 8508, Fax 937 8508 – p. 30 AQR
closed Saturday lunch, Sunday, 25-26 December and Bank Holidays – **Meals** - French - 15.50 **t.** and a la carte 5.80.

Belvedere in Holland Park, Holland House, off Abbotsbury Rd, W8 6LU, 602 123, « 19C orangery in park » – EY
closed Sunday dinner, 25 December and 1 January – **Meals** a la carte 17.50/26.00 **t.**

La Fenice, 148 Holland Park Av., W11 4UE, 221 6090, Fax 221 4096 – EX
closed Saturday lunch and Monday – **Meals** - Italian - 9.50/17.00 **t.** and a la carte 4.00.

Launceston Place, 1a Launceston Pl., W8 5RL, 937 6912, Fax 938 2412 – p. 30 BR
closed Saturday lunch, Sunday dinner and Bank Holidays – **Meals** 13.50/16.50 and a la carte.

Arcadia, Kensington Court, 35 Kensington High St., W8 5BA, 937 4294, Fax 937 439 – p. 30 AQ
closed lunch Saturday and Sunday, 25-26 December and 1 January – **Meals** 13.95 (lunch) and a la carte 24.00/25.00 **t.** 5.90.

Boyd's, 135 Kensington Church St., W8 7LP, 727 5452, Fax 221 0615 – p. 32 AZ
closed Sunday, first 2 weeks January and 4 days Easter – **Meals** 15.00 (lunch) and a la carte 22.00/34.00 **t.** 6.50.

Phoenicia, 11-13 Abingdon Rd, W8 6AH, 937 0120, Fax 937 7668 – EY
closed 24 and 25 December – **Meals** - Lebanese - (buffet lunch) a la carte 14.60/17.75 5.00.

Shanghai, 38c-d Kensington Church St., W8 4BX, 938 2501 – FX
Meals - Chinese rest.

Kensington Place, 201 Kensington Church St., W8 7LX, 727 3184, Fax 229 2025 – p. 32 AZ
closed 3 days Christmas – **Meals** 13.50 **t.** (lunch) and a la carte 17.00/29.00 **t.** 4.75.

Cibo, 3 Russell Gdns, W14 8EZ, 371 6271, Fax 602 1371 – EY
closed lunch Saturday and Bank Holidays, Sunday dinner and 1 to 7 January – **Meals** Italian - a la carte 20.00/30.00 **t.** 5.90.

Abingdon, 54 Abingdon Rd, W8 6AP, 937 3339, Fax 795 6388 – EY
closed Sunday dinner, 25 and 26 December – **Meals** 8.95 **t.** (lunch) and a la carte 14.50/20.70 **t.**

Avenue West Eleven, 157 Notting Hill Gate, W11 3LF, 221 8144 – EX
closed Saturday lunch and Bank Holidays – **Meals** 15.50 **t.** and a la carte 19.45/24.00 4.75.

Malabar, 27 Uxbridge St., W8 7TQ, 727 8800 – p. 32 AZ
closed last week August and 4 days at Christmas – **Meals** - Indian - (booking essential) (buffet lunch Sunday) a la carte 14.15/26.80 **st.** 4.60.

Wódka, 12 St. Albans Grove, W8 5PN, 937 6513, Fax 937 8621 – p. 30 AR
closed lunch Saturday and Sunday and Bank Holidays – **Meals** - Polish - 12.00 (lunch) and a la carte 17.30/22.30 **t.** 4.20.

Mandarin, 197c Kensington High St., W8 6BA, 937 1551 – EY
closed 24 to 26 December – **Meals** - Chinese - 12.50/16.00 **t.** and a la carte 4.80.

North Kensington – ✉ W2/W10/W11 – ☎ 0171 – Except where otherwise stated see pp. 20-23.

Pembridge Court, 34 Pembridge Gdns, W2 4DX, ☎ 229 9977, Fax 727 4982, « Collection of antique clothing » – rest. p. 32 AZ **n**
Meals (residents only) (restricted menu) (dinner only) a la carte 12.95/19.40 **t.** 5.25 – **20 rm** 100.00/160.00 **t.**

Abbey Court without rest., 20 Pembridge Gdns, W2 4DU, ☎ 221 7518, Fax 792 0858, « Tastefully furnished Victorian town house ». p. 32 AZ **u**
22 rm 80.00/160.00 **t.**

Portobello, 22 Stanley Gdns, W11 2NG, ☎ 727 2777, Fax 792 9641, « Attractive town house in Victorian terrace » – EV **n**
25 rm.

Leith's, 92 Kensington Park Rd, W11 2PN, ☎ 229 4481 –.
closed lunch Saturday to Monday, Sunday dinner, 18 August-1 September and 24 December-7 January – **Meals** 19.50 **t.** (lunch) and dinner a la carte 29.50/39.50 **t.** 7.75
Spec. Pan fried salmon fillet with cèpes, boulangère potatoes and oxtail broth, Pithivier of veal sweetbreads, crisp vegetables and hazelnut vinaigrette, Leith's traditional roast duckling with a light orange jus. EV **e**

Chez Moi, 1 Addison Av., Holland Park, W11 4QS, ☎ 603 8267, Fax 603 3898 –. p. 24 EX **n**
closed Saturday lunch, Sunday dinner and Bank Holidays – **Meals** - French - 15.00 **t.** (lunch) and a la carte 18.75/31.00 **t.** 4.80.

Orsino, 119 Portland Rd, W11 4LN, ☎ 221 3299, Fax 229 9414 – EX **x**
closed 24 and 25 December – **Meals** - Italian - 13.50 **t.** (lunch) and a la carte 21.80/26.50 **t.** 5.50.

Park Inn, 6 Wellington Terr., Bayswater Rd, W2 4LW, ☎ 229 3553, Fax 229 3553 –. AZ **c**
Meals - Chinese Seafood (Peking) - 4.80/12.00 **t.** and a la carte 4.90.

L'Altro, 210 Kensington Park Rd, W11 1NR, ☎ 792 1066, Fax 792 1077 –. EUV **c**
closed Sunday dinner, Easter, 4 days Christmas and Bank Holidays – **Meals** - Italian - a la carte 20.25/34.50 **t.** 6.25.

192, 192 Kensington Park Rd, W11 2ES, ☎ 229 0482 – EV **a**
closed 25 to 26 December and Bank Holidays – **Meals** a la carte 16.75/25.75 **t.**

Canal Brasserie, Canalot Studios, 222 Kensal Rd, W10 5BN, ☎ (0181) 960 2732 – ET **c**
closed lunch Saturday and Sunday and dinner Monday and Tuesday – **Meals** a la carte 11.75/17.50 **t.**

Brasserie du Marché aux Puces, 349 Portobello Rd, W10 5SA, ☎ (0181) 968 5828 – EU **a**
closed Sunday, Monday and 5 days at Christmas – **Meals** 10.95 **t.** and a la carte 17.75/20.50 **t.** 5.50.

Surinder's, 109 Westbourne Park Rd, W2 5QL, ☎ 229 8968 – EU **e**
closed Sunday, Monday, Easter, approx. 2 weeks August and Christmas – **Meals** (dinner only) 14.95 **t.**

South Kensington – ✉ SW5/SW7/W8 – ☎ 0171 – Except where otherwise stated see pp. 30 and 31.

Gloucester, 4-18 Harrington Gdns, SW7 4LH, ☎ 373 6030, Fax 373 0409 – rm – 400. BS **r**
Meals a la carte 19.45/27.90 **st.** – 14.50 – **542 rm** 176.25/193.90 **st.**, 6 suites.

Harrington Hall, 5-25 Harrington Gdns, SW7 4JW, ☎ 396 9696, Group Telex 290603, Fax 396 9090, – rm – 250. BT **n**
Wetherby's : Meals 16.00/18.50 **st.** and a la carte 7.00 – 11.00 – **200 rm** 120.00/165.00 **st.**

Pelham, 15 Cromwell Pl., SW7 2LA, ☎ 589 8288, Fax 584 8444, « Tastefully furnished Victorian town house » –. CS **z**
Kemps : Meals *(closed Sunday lunch and Saturday)* 12.50 **t.** (lunch) and a la carte 16.50/26.00 **t.** 6.50 – 11.50 – **34 rm** 120.00/170.00 **t.**, 3 suites.

Blakes, 33 Roland Gdns, SW7 3PF, ☎ 370 6701, Telex 8813500, Fax 373 0442, « Antique oriental furnishings » – rest. BU **n**
Meals a la carte 40.00/62.00 **st.** 9.00 – 17.50 – **45 rm** 135.00/495.00 **st.**, 6 suites.

Rembrandt, 11 Thurloe Pl., SW7 2RS, ☎ 589 8100, Telex 295828, Fax 225 3363, – rm rest – 250. DS **x**
Meals 15.95 **st.** and a la carte 5.00 – 9.75 – **195 rm** 115.00/155.00 **st.** – SB.

Swallow International, Cromwell Rd, SW5 0TH, ☎ 973 1000, Telex 27260, Fax 244 8194, – rm rest – 200. AS **c**
Meals 13.75/17.00 **st.** and a la carte 5.50 – 10.75 – **414 rm** 110.00/125.00 **st.**, 2 suites – SB.

Regency, 100 Queen's Gate, SW7 5AG, ☎ 370 4595, Telex 267594, Fax 370 5555, – rm rest – 100. CT **e**
Meals *(closed lunch Saturday and Sunday)* 16.50/18.50 **st.** and a la carte 6.00 – 12.00 – **192 rm** 115.00 **s.**, 6 suites – SB.

Vanderbilt (Radisson Edwardian), 68-86 Cromwell Rd, SW7 5BT, 589 2424, Telex 946944, Fax 225 2293 – rest – 120. AE VISA JCB. BS v
Meals 13.50/35.00 **st.** and a la carte – 9.50 – **223 rm** 97.00/125.00 **st.** – SB.

Jury's Kensington, 109-113 Queen's Gate, SW7 5LR, 589 6300, Telex 262180, Fax 581 1492 – rest – 80. AE VISA. CT i
Meals (bar lunch)/dinner 17.95 **st.** and a la carte 5.25 – 10.50 – **171 rm** 110.00/225.00 **st.** – SB.

Forum (Inter-Con), 97 Cromwell Rd, SW7 4DN, 370 5757, Group Telex 919663, Fax 373 1448, <, – rm rest – 400. AE VISA JCB. BS x
Meals 11.50/13.50 **st.** and a la carte 8.50 – 11.00 – **906 rm** 140.00/160.00 **st.**, 4 suites.

Gore, 189 Queen's Gate, SW7 5EX, 584 6601, Fax 589 8127, « Attractive decor » – rm AE VISA JCB BR n
closed 25 and 26 December – **Bistrot 190 : Meals** (only members and residents may book) a la carte 14.00/23.00 **t.** 6.00 – (see also ***Downstairs at One Ninety*** below) – 9.50 – **54 rm** 112.00/218.00 **st.**

Number Sixteen without rest., 16 Sumner Pl., SW7 3EG, 589 5232, Fax 584 8615, « Attractively furnished Victorian town houses », – AE VISA. CT c
8.00 – **36 rm** 68.00/155.00 **st.**

Cranley without rest., 10-12 Bina Gardens, SW5 0LA, 373 0123, Fax 373 9497, « Tasteful decor, antiques » – AE VISA. BT c
12.00 – **32 rm** 120.00/140.00 **st.**, 4 suites.

John Howard, 4 Queen's Gate, SW7 5EH, 581 3011, Telex 8813397, Fax 589 8403 – AE VISA JCB. BQ i
Meals *(closed Sunday)(dinner only)* 12.50 **t.** and a la carte – 9.50 – **43 rm** 79.00/99.00 **st.** 9 suites.

Kensington Plaza, 61 Gloucester Rd, SW7 4PE, 584 8100, Telex 8950993, Fax 823 9175 – rest – 40. AE VISA. BS e
Mongolian Brasserie : Meals (dinner only) 18.00 **t.** 9.50 – 5.25 – **88 rm** 75.00/90.00 **st.**

Cranley Gardens without rest., 8 Cranley Gdns, SW7 3DB, 373 3232, Telex 894489 Fax 373 7944 – AE VISA JCB BT e
5.50 – **85 rm** 65.00/95.00 **t.**

Five Sumner Place without rest., 5 Sumner Pl., SW7 3EE, 584 7586, Fax 823 9962 – AE VISA JCB. DR a
13 rm 69.00/99.00 **s.**

Aster House without rest., 3 Sumner Pl., SW7 3EE, 581 5888, Fax 584 4925, – VISA. CT u
12 rm 65.00/113.00 **st.**

Hotel 167 without rest., 167 Old Brompton Rd, SW5 0AN, 373 3221, Fax 373 3360 – AE VISA JCB. BT
6.50 – **19 rm** 60.00/82.00 **st.**

XXX **Bombay Brasserie,** Courtfield Close, 140 Gloucester Rd, SW7 4UH, 370 4040 Fax 835 1669, « Raj-style decor, conservatory garden » – VISA BS a
closed 25 and 26 December – **Meals** - Indian - (buffet lunch) 14.95 **t.** and dinne a la carte 19.50/24.00 **t.** 6.50.

XX **Hilaire,** 68 Old Brompton Rd, SW7 3LQ, 584 8993, Fax 581 2949 – AE VISA CT r
closed Saturday lunch, Sunday and Bank Holidays – **Meals** (booking essential) 20.50/28.50 **t.** and dinner a la carte 25.50/33.50 **t.** 8.00.

XX **Shaw's,** 119 Old Brompton Rd, SW7 3RN, 373 7774, Fax 370 5102 – AE VISA BT v
closed Saturday lunch, Sunday dinner, 1 week Easter, last 2 weeks August, 1 weel Christmas-New Year and Bank Holidays – **Meals** 17.50/29.75 **t.** 9.50.

XX **Downstairs at One Ninety,** 190 Queen's Gate, SW7 5EU, 581 5666, Fax 581 8172 – AE VISA JCB BR
closed Sunday – **Meals** - Seafood - (booking essential) (dinner only) a la carte 17.75/28.50

XX **Khan's of Kensington,** 3 Harrington Rd, SW7 3ES, 581 2900, Fax 581 2900 – AE VISA CS
closed 25 and 26 December – **Meals** - Indian - 7.50/30.00 **t.** and a la carte 3.95.

XX **Tui,** 19 Exhibition Rd, SW7 2HE, 584 8359 – AE VISA JCB CS
closed 5 days at Christmas and Bank Holiday Mondays – **Meals** - Thai - 10.00 st (lunch) and a la carte 13.50/20.20 4.10.

XX **Delhi Brasserie,** 134 Cromwell Rd, SW7 4HA, 370 7617, Fax 244 8639 – AE VISA AS
closed 25 and 26 December – **Meals** - Indian - 15.95 **t.** and a la carte 8.95.

XX **Café Lazeez,** 93-95 Old Brompton Rd, SW7 3LD, 581 9993, Fax 581 8200 – VISA JCB CT
Restaurant : Meals - North Indian - (dinner only) a la carte 11.65/22.75 **t.** 4.40.
X **Café : Meals** a la carte 11.65/22.75 **t.**

XX **Memories of India,** 18 Gloucester Rd, SW7 4RB, 589 6450 – AE VISA JCB BR
closed 25 and 26 December – **Meals** - Indian - 14.50/20.00 **t.** and a la carte.

X **The Establishment,** 1 Gloucester Rd, SW7 4PP, ☏ 589 7969, Fax 581 9996 – ▤. AE VISA BR **c**
closed Monday lunch, 25 and 26 December and Easter – **Meals** a la carte 19.00/25.00 **t.** 9.00.

X **Bangkok,** 9 Bute St., SW7 3EY, ☏ 584 8529, Fax 823 7883 – ▤. VISA CS **v**
closed Sunday, Christmas-New Year and Bank Holidays – **Meals** - Thai Bistro - a la carte 15.60/24.40 **t.**

KINGSTON UPON THAMES pp. 8 and 9.

18 Home Park, Hampton Wick ☏ (0181) 977 6645, BY.

Chessington – ✉ Surrey – ☎ 01372.

Travel Inn, Leatherhead Rd, KT9 2NE, on A 243 ☏ 744060, Fax 720889 – rm TV. AE VISA. BZ **c**
Meals (grill rest.) – 4.95 – **42 rm** 34.50 **t.**

Kingston – ✉ Surrey – ☎ 0181.

Kingston Lodge (Forte Heritage), Kingston Hill, KT2 7NP, ☏ 541 4481, Fax 547 1013 – ▤ rest TV ☎ – 60. AE VISA JCB CY **u**
Meals 14.95/19.95 **t.** and a la carte 7.05 – 8.75 – **62 rm** 99.00/130.00 **st.**

XX **Gravier's,** 9 Station Rd, Norbiton, KT2 7AA, ☏ 549 5557 – AE VISA JCB CY **x**
closed Saturday lunch, Sunday, 1 week Easter, 1 week August, 1 week Christmas and Bank Holidays – **Meals** - French Seafood - a la carte 19.00/27.80 **t.** 4.75.

X **Ayudhya,** 14 Kingston Hill, KT2 7NH, ☏ 549 5984 – AE VISA CY **z**
closed Monday lunch, Easter Sunday, 25-26 December and 1 January – **Meals** - Thai - a la carte 13.70/19.90 **st.**

LAMBETH Except where otherwise stated see pp.10 and 11.

Brixton – ✉ SW9 – ☎ 0171.

X **Twenty Trinity Gardens,** 20 Trinity Gdns, SW9 8DP, ☏ 733 8838 – VISA EX **n**
closed Sunday, last 2 weeks August and 26 to 30 December – **Meals** (dinner only) 17.50 **t.** 7.75.

Clapham Common – ✉ SW4 – ☎ 0171.

Windmill on the Common, Clapham Common South Side, SW4 9DE, ☏ (0181) 673 4578, Fax 675 1486, – rm ▤ rest TV ☎. AE VISA.
Meals *(closed Sunday dinner)* (bar lunch Monday to Saturday)/dinner a la carte 13.75/17.75 **t.** – **29 rm** 75.00/85.00 **st.** DQ **e**

XX **The Grafton,** 45 Old Town, SW4 0JL, ☏ 627 1048 – AE VISA p. 13 DQ **a**
closed Saturday lunch, Sunday, last 3 weeks August and 1 week Christmas – **Meals** - French - 12.95/18.50 **t.** and a la carte 5.00.

Kennington – ✉ SE11 – ☎ 0171.

X **Lobster Pot,** 3 Kennington Lane, SE11 4RG, ☏ 582 5556, Fax 582 9751 – AE VISA JCB NZ **e**
closed Sunday, Monday and 25 December-2 January – **Meals** - French Seafood 14.50/29.50 **st.** and a la carte.

Lambeth – ✉ SE1 – ☎ 0171.

Novotel Waterloo, 113 Lambeth Rd, SE1 7LS, ☏ 793 1010, Fax 793 0202, – rm ▤ TV ☎ – 40. AE VISA. LY **a**
Meals (bar lunch)/dinner a la carte 10.85/23.15 **st.** 5.50 – 8.50 – **185 rm** 99.00/115.00 **st.**, 2 suites.

Streatham – ✉ SW16 – ☎ 0181.

Barrow House without rest., 45 Barrow Rd, SW16 5PE, ☏ 677 1925, Fax 677 1925, « Victoriana », – . EY **s**
closed 23 to 27 December – **5 rm** 25.00/45.00 **st.**

Waterloo – ✉ SE1 – ☎ 0171.

XX **RSJ,** 13a Coin St., SE1 8YQ, ☏ 928 4554 – ▤. AE VISA p. 27 NX **e**
closed Saturday lunch, Sunday, 25 December and 1 January – **Meals** 15.95 **t.** and a la carte 5.95.

LONDON HEATHROW AIRPORT – see Hillingdon, London p. 56.

MERTON pp. 8 and 9.

Morden – ✉ Morden – ☎ 0181.

Forte Travelodge, Epsom Rd, SM4 5PH, SW : on A 24 ☏ 640 8227, Reservations (Freephone) 0800 850950 – TV. AE VISA. DY **c**
Meals (grill rest.) – **32 rm** 34.50 **t.**

Wimbledon – ✉ SW19 – ☎ 0181.

Cannizaro House (Thistle) 🐿, West Side, Wimbledon Common, SW19 4UF, ☎ 879 1464, Fax 879 7338, ≤, « 18C country house overlooking Cannizaro Park », – lift – ⇆ rm TV ☎ P – 🏢 45. AE VISA JCB. DXY **x**
Meals 21.55/25.75 **t.** and a la carte – ☕ 9.75 – **44 rm** 115.00/175.00 **t.**, 2 suites – SB.

REDBRIDGE pp. 6 and 7.

ℹ Town Hall, High Rd, IG1 1DD ☎ (0181) 478 3020 ext 2126.

Ilford – ✉ Essex – ☎ 0181.

⛳ Wanstead Park Rd ☎ 554 5174, HU – ⛳ Fairlop Waters, Forest Rd, Barkingside ☎ 500 9911 JT.

Travel Inn, Redbridge Lane East, IG4 5BG, ☎ 550 6451 – ⇆ rm TV ♿ P. AE VISA. HU **i**
Meals (grill rest.) – ☕ 4.95 – **40 rm** 34.50 **t.**

Forte Travelodge, Beehive Lane, RG4 5DR, ☎ 550 4248, Reservations (Freephone) 0800 850950 – TV ♿ P. AE VISA. HU **e**
Meals (grill rest.) – **32 rm** 34.50 **t.**

South Woodford – ✉ Essex – ☎ 0181.

Ho-Ho, 20 High Rd, E18 2QL, ☎ 989 1041 – ▤. AE VISA HU **c**
closed Saturday lunch – **Meals** - Chinese (Peking, Szechuan) - a la carte 14.70/21.50 **st.**

Woodford – ✉ Essex – ☎ 0181.

Woodford Moat House (Q.M.H.), 30 Oak Hill, Woodford Green, IG8 9NY, ☎ 787 9988, Fax 506 0941, – lift TV ☎ P – 🏢 150. AE VISA. HT **c**
Meals (bar lunch Saturday and Bank Holidays) 15.00 **st.** (lunch) and a la carte 16.00/23.50 **st.** 🍷 7.50 – ☕ 9.50 – **99 rm** 70.00/80.00 **st.** – SB.

RICHMOND-UPON-THAMES pp. 8 and 9.

Barnes – ✉ SW13 – ☎ 0181.

Sonny's, 94 Church Rd, SW13 0DQ, ☎ 748 0393, Fax 748 2698 – ▤. AE VISA CX **x**
closed Sunday dinner – **Meals** 13.50 **t.** (lunch) and a la carte 🍷 8.75.

Riva, 169 Church Rd, SW13 9HR, ☎ 748 0434 – AE VISA CX **a**
closed Saturday lunch, last 2 weeks August, Christmas-New Year and Bank Holidays – **Meals** - Italian - a la carte 17.00/28.00 **t.** 🍷 6.75.

River Brasserie, 15 High St., SW13 9LW, ☎ 876 1471 – VISA CX **v**
Meals a la carte 12.50/21.45 **t.**

East Sheen – ✉ SW14 – ☎ 0181.

Crowther's, 481 Upper Richmond Rd West, SW14 7PU, ☎ 876 6372 – ▤. VISA
closed Saturday lunch, Sunday, Monday, 2 weeks August and 1 week Christmas – **Meals** (booking essential) 16.50/22.00 **t.** 🍷 4.50. CX **n**

Hampton Court – ✉ Surrey – ☎ 0181.

Mitre, Hampton Court Rd, KT8 9BN, ☎ 979 9988, Fax 979 9777, ≤, « Riverside setting » – lift ⇆ rm TV ☎ P – 🏢 25. AE VISA. BY **v**
Meals (bar lunch Saturday)/a la carte 19.00/23.95 **t.** – ☕ 8.50 – **35 rm** 99.00/145.00 **t.**, 1 suite.

Hampton Wick – ✉ Surrey – ☎ 0181.

Chase Lodge, 10 Park Rd, KT1 4AS, ☎ 943 1862, Fax 943 9363 – TV ☎ P. AE VISA JCB BY **e**
Meals (lunch by arrangement Monday to Saturday)/dinner a la carte 11.95/15.50 **t.** 🍷 3.95 – **9 rm** ☕ 48.00/107.00 **t.** – SB.

Richmond – ✉ Surrey – ☎ 0181.

⛳, ⛳ Richmond Park, Roehampton Gate ☎ 876 3205/1795 CX – ⛳ Sudbrook Park ☎ 940 1463 CX.

ℹ Old Town Hall, Whittaker Av., TW9 1TP ☎ 940 9125.

Petersham 🐿, Nightingale Lane, Richmond Hill, TW10 6UZ, ☎ 940 7471, Telex 928556, Fax 940 9998, ≤, – lift TV ☎ P – 🏢 50. AE VISA. CX **c**
Meals - (see ***Nightingales*** below) – **54 rm** ☕ 97.00/160.00 **st.** – SB.

Richmond Gate, 158 Richmond Hill, TW10 6RP, ☎ 940 0061, Fax 332 0354, Lδ, ≘s, ▢, squash – ⇆ rm TV ☎ P – 🏢 45. AE VISA JCB. CX **c**
Gates Restaurant : Meals *(closed Saturday lunch)* 15.50/25.95 **t.** and dinner a la carte 🍷 7.50 – **Gates Bistro : Meals** *(closed Saturday, Sunday and 24 December-3 January)* (dinner only) 15.50 **t.** and a la carte 🍷 7.50 – ☕ 10.00 – **64 rm** 95.00/155.00 **t.** – SB.

Bingham, 61-63 Petersham Rd, TW10 6UT, ☎ 940 0902, Fax 948 8737, – TV ☎ – 30. AE VISA. CX z
Meals *(closed Sunday and Bank Holidays)* (dinner only) 11.75 **t.** and a la carte 4.25 – **23 rm** 67.50/95.00 **t.**

XXX **Nightingales** (at Petersham H.), Nightingale Lane, Richmond Hill, TW10 6UZ, ☎ 940 7471, Telex 928556, Fax 940 9998, ←, – P. AE VISA CX c
Meals 17.50/25.00 **t.** and a la carte 8.50.

XX **Four Regions,** 102-104 Kew Rd, TW9 2PQ, ☎ 940 9044, Fax 332 6130 – . AE VISA CX e
Meals - Chinese - 10.00/30.00 **t.** and a la carte 5.00.

X **Burnt Chair,** 5 Duke St., TW9 1HP, ☎ 940 9488 – VISA BX e
closed Sunday, 2 weeks August and 1 week December – **Meals** (dinner only) 15.00 **t.** and a la carte 4.15.

X **Chez Lindsay,** 11 Hill Rise, TW10 6UQ, ☎ 948 7473 – VISA BX c
closed Sunday, Monday and 25 to 27 December – **Meals** - French Bistro - 9.95 **t.** (lunch) and a la carte 18.75/24.75 **t.** 5.75.

Twickenham – ✉ Middx. – ☎ 0181.

Twickenham Park, Staines Rd ☎ 783 1698, BX.

44 York St., TW1 3BZ ☎ 891 1411.

XX **McClements,** 2 Whitton Rd, TW1 1BJ, ☎ 744 9598, Fax 890 1372 – . VISA BX s
closed Sunday and Monday – **Meals** 15.00/25.00 **t.** and a la carte 6.00.

SOUTHWARK Except where otherwise stated see pp. 10 and 11.

Bermondsey – ✉ SE1 – ☎ 0171.

XXX **Le Pont de la Tour,** 36d Shad Thames, Butlers Wharf, SE1 2YE, ☎ 403 8403, Fax 403 0267, ←, , « Riverside setting » – . AE VISA p. 27 PX c
closed Good Friday and 4 days Christmas – **Meals** (in bar Saturday lunch) 26.50 **t.** (lunch) and dinner a la carte 27.00/37.25 **t.** 6.20.

XXX **Bengal Clipper,** Cardamom Building, Shad Thames, Butlers Wharf, SE1 2YE, ☎ 357 9001, Fax 357 9002 – . AE VISA JCB PX e
Meals - Indian - 30.00 **t.** and a la carte.

X **Blue Print Café,** Design Museum, Shad Thames, Butlers Wharf, SE1 2YD, ☎ 378 7031, Fax 378 6540, ←, « Riverside setting », – AE VISA p. 27 PX u
closed Sunday dinner, 4 days at Christmas and 1 January – **Meals** a la carte 16.75/25.25 **t.**

X **Cantina Del Ponte,** 36c Shad Thames, Butlers Wharf, SE1 2YE, ☎ 403 5403, Fax 403 0267, ←, « Riverside setting » – AE VISA p. 27 PX c
closed Sunday dinner, Good Friday and 5 days at Christmas – **Meals** - Italian-Mediterranean - a la carte 19.40/25.25 **t.**

X **Butlers Wharf Chop House,** 36e Shad Thames, Butlers Wharf, SE1 2YE, ☎ 403 3403, Fax 403 3414, « Riverside setting, ←Tower Bridge » – AE VISA PX n
closed Saturday lunch, Sunday dinner, Good Friday and 1 January – **Meals** 22.75 **t.** (lunch) and dinner a la carte 17.45/27.75 **t.**

Dulwich – ✉ SE19 – ☎ 0181.

XX **Luigi's,** 129 Gipsy Hill, SE19 1QS, ☎ 670 1843 – . AE VISA JCB FX a
Meals - Italian - a la carte 16.20/25.00 4.50.

Rotherhithe – ✉ SE16 – ☎ 0171.

Scandic Crown, 265 Rotherhithe St., Nelson Dock, SE16 1EJ, ☎ 231 1001, Telex 290295, Fax 231 0599, ←, , , , – rm rest TV ☎ P – 350. AE VISA JCB. GV r
closed 24 to 28 December – **Meals** 18.95 **st.** and dinner a la carte 6.50 – 9.50 – **384 rm** 95.00/115.00 **st.**, 2 suites.

Southwark – ✉ SE1 – ☎ 0171.

XX **La Truffe Noire,** 29 Tooley St., SE1 2QF, ☎ 378 0621, Fax 403 0689 – . AE VISA JCB p. 27 PX a
closed Sunday, 23 December-3 January and Bank Holidays – **Meals** - French - 18.00/22.00 **t.** and a la carte 5.00.

X **Café dell'Ugo,** 56-58 Tooley St., SE1 2SZ, ☎ 407 6001, Fax 357 8806 – . AE VISA PX r
closed Sunday and Bank Holidays – **Meals** a la carte 16.15/26.85 **t.** 4.00.

SUTTON pp. 8 and 9.

Carshalton – ✉ Surrey – ☎ 0181.

XX **La Veranda,** 18-19 Beynon Rd, SM5 3RL, ☎ 647 4370 – . AE VISA EZ c
closed Sunday and Bank Holidays – **Meals** a la carte 25.00/35.00 **t.**

Sutton – ✉ Surrey – ☎ 0181.

18, 9 Oak Sports Centre, Woodmansterne Rd, Carshalton ☎ 643 8363.

Holiday Inn, Gibson Rd, SM1 2RF, ☎ 770 1311, Fax 770 1539, – rest – 220. AE VISA JCB EZ
Meals *(closed lunch August)* a la carte 17.00/27.00 **st.** – 10.50 – **115 rm** 110.00/120.00 **st.**, 1 suite – SB.

Thatched House, 135-141 Cheam Rd, SM1 2BN, ☎ 642 3131, Fax 770 0684, – – 50. VISA JCB. DZ
Meals 14.50 **t.** (dinner) and lunch a la carte 8.70/17.45 **t.** 4.95 – **26 rm** 42.50/62.50 **st.** – SB.

XX **Partners Brasserie,** 23 Stonecot Hill, SM3 9HB, ☎ 644 7743 – . AE VISA DY
closed Saturday lunch, Sunday, Monday and 1 week Christmas – **Meals** a la carte 12.85/16.20 4.00.

WANDSWORTH Except where otherwise stated see pp. 12 and 13.

Battersea – ✉ SW8/SW11 – ☎ 0171.

XX **Ransome's Dock,** 35-37 Parkgate Rd, SW11 4NP, ☎ 223 1611, Fax 924 2614 – AE VISA p. 25 HZ
closed Sunday dinner, 1 week August and Christmas – **Meals** 11.50 **t.** (lunch) and a la carte 17.50/24.75 **t.** 5.50.

XX **Chada,** 208-210 Battersea Park Rd, SW11 4ND, ☎ 622 2209, Fax 924 2178 – . AE VISA JCB CQ
closed Saturday lunch and Bank Holidays – **Meals** - Thai - a la carte 17.25/25.90 **st.**

X **The Stepping Stone,** 123 Queenstown Rd, SW8 3RH, ☎ 622 0555, Fax 622 4230 – AE VISA DQ
closed Saturday lunch, Sunday dinner, 24 to 30 December and Bank Holiday Mondays – **Meals** 10.00 **t.** (lunch) and a la carte 15.00/24.25 **t.**

X **B Square,** 8 Battersea Sq., SW11 3RA, ☎ 924 2288, Fax 924 6450 – AE VISA CQ
closed 1 week Christmas – **Meals** 15.00 **t.** 6.95.

Clapham – ✉ SW11 – ☎ 0171.

X **Jasmin,** 50/52 Battersea Rise, SW11 1EG, ☎ 228 0336 – AE VISA CQ
Meals - Chinese (Canton, Peking) - 5.50/8.80 **t.** and a la carte 4.25.

Putney – ✉ SW15 – ☎ 0181.

XX Royal China, 3 Chelverton Rd, SW15 1RN, ☎ 788 0907, Fax 785 2305 – AQ
Meals - Chinese rest..

XX **Del Buongustaio,** 283 Putney Bridge Rd, SW15 2PT, ☎ 780 9361, Fax 789 9659 – . AE VISA AQ
closed Saturday lunch, Sunday June-mid September and 10 days Christmas-New Year – **Meals** - Italian - 9.50 **t.** (lunch) and a la carte 17.65/19.80 **t.** 5.80.

X **Enoteca,** 28 Putney High St., SW15 1SQ, ☎ 785 4449 – AE VISA AQ
closed lunch Saturday and Bank Holidays, Sunday and 25 to 30 December – **Meals** - Italian - 9.50 **t.** (lunch) and a la carte 14.65/20.25 **t.** 4.50.

Tooting – ✉ SW17 – ☎ 0181.

X **Oh Boy,** 843 Garratt Lane, SW17 0PG, ☎ 947 9760, Fax 879 7867 – . AE VISA JCB CR
Meals - Thai - (dinner only) 15.50 **st.** and a la carte 3.90.

Wandsworth – ✉ SW12/SW17/SW18 – ☎ 0181.

XX **Tabaq,** 47 Balham Hill, SW12 9DR, ☎ 673 7820, Fax 673 2701 – . AE VISA JCB DR
closed Sunday – **Meals** - Indian - 9.25 **t.** (lunch) and a la carte 11.70/27.50 **t.** 4.25.

XX **Chez Bruce,** 2 Bellevue Rd, SW17 7EG, ☎ 672 0114 – . AE VISA CR
closed lunch Monday and Saturday, Sunday dinner, 1 week Christmas and Bank Holidays – **Meals** 15.00/22.00 **t.**

X **Bombay Bicycle Club,** 95 Nightingale Lane, SW12 8NX, ☎ 673 6217 – AE VISA DR
Meals - Indian - (dinner only) 15.00 **t.** and a la carte 5.75.

WESTMINSTER (City of).

Bayswater and Maida Vale – ✉ W2/W9 – ☎ 0171 – Except where otherwise stated see pp. 32 and 33.

Royal Lancaster, Lancaster Terr., W2 2TY, ☎ 262 6737, Telex 24822, Fax 724 3191, ≤ – rm – 1400. AE VISA JCB. DZ
La Rosette : Meals 22.50/27.50 **t.** and a la carte 8.00 – **Pavement Cafe : Meals** a la carte 15.10/26.85 **t.** 8.00 – 14.50 – **398 rm** 154.00/170.00 **st.**, 20 suites – SB.

London Metropole, Edgware Rd, W2 1JU, ☎ 402 4141, Telex 23711, Fax 724 8866, ≤, – rm – 1200. AE VISA JCB. p. 21 GU
Meals (buffet rest.) - (see also ***Aspects*** below) – 14.95 – **719 rm** 145.00/210.00 **st.**, 26 suites.

Whites (Thistle), Bayswater Rd, 90-92 Lancaster Gate, W2 3NR, ℘ 262 2711, Telex 24771, Fax 262 2147 – rm. AE VISA JCB. CZ v
Meals *(closed Saturday lunch)* 16.00/21.50 **t.** and a la carte 7.15 – 11.25 – **52 rm** 155.00/235.00 **t.**, 2 suites – SB.

London Embassy (Jarvis), 150 Bayswater Rd, W2 4RT, ℘ 229 1212, Fax 229 2623 – rm rest – 60. AE VISA BZ o
Meals (carving rest.) 15.95 **st.** and a la carte – 9.50 – **192 rm** 99.00/119.00 **st.**, 1 suite.

Plaza on Hyde Park (Hilton), 1-7 Lancaster Gate, W2 3LG, ℘ 262 5022, Telex 8954372, Fax 724 8666 – rm – 30. AE VISA JCB. DZ r
Meals 12.75 **st.** and a la carte 6.70 – **402 rm** 90.00/103.00 **st.** – SB.

Stakis London Coburg, 129 Bayswater Rd, W2 4RJ, ℘ 221 2217, Group Telex 268235, Fax 229 0557 – rm rest – 100. AE VISA JCB. BZ c
Meals (dinner only) 15.00 **t.** and a la carte 4.75 – 8.50 – **131 rm** 88.00/99.00 **st.**, 1 suite – SB.

Hyde Park Towers, 41-51 Inverness Terr., W2 3JN, ℘ 221 8484, Fax 792 3201 – rest – 45. AE VISA BZ r
Meals 11.00/15.00 **st.** and a la carte – 7.50 – **115 rm** 86.00/120.00 **st.**

Queen's Park, 48 Queensborough Terr., W2 3SS, ℘ 229 8080, Fax 792 1330 – rest – 80. AE VISA JCB. CZ s
Meals (dinner only) 15.00 **st.** and a la carte 6.00 – 7.50 – **86 rm** 90.00/110.00 **st.**

Mornington without rest., 12 Lancaster Gate, W2 3LG, ℘ 262 7361, Fax 706 1028 – rm. AE VISA DZ s
68 rm 85.00/115.00 **st.**

Phoenix without rest., 1 Kensington Garden Sq., W2 4BH, ℘ 229 2494, Telex 298854, Fax 727 1419 –. AE VISA JCB. BZ e
5.50 – **125 rm** 69.00/89.00 **st.**

Byron without rest., 36-38 Queensborough Terr., W2 3SH, ℘ 243 0987, Telex 263431, Fax 792 1957 –. AE VISA. CZ z
41 rm 75.50/89.00 **t.**, 1 suite.

Delmere, 130 Sussex Gdns, W2 1UB, ℘ 706 3344, Fax 262 1863 –. AE VISA JCB. DZ v
Meals *(closed Sunday and Christmas-New Year)* (dinner only) 16.00 **st.** and a la carte 6.25 – 6.00 – **38 rm** 73.00/91.00 **st.**

Gresham without rest., 116 Sussex Gdns, W2 1UA, ℘ 402 2920, Fax 402 3137 –. AE VISA JCB. DZ a
5.00 – **38 rm** 60.00/75.00 **st.**

Norfolk Plaza without rest., 29-33 Norfolk Sq., W2 1RX, ℘ 723 0792, Fax 224 8770 –. AE VISA JCB. DZ x
6.00 – **81 rm** 75.00/98.00 **st.**, 6 suites.

Comfort Inn, 18-19 Craven Hill Gdns, W2 3EE, ℘ 262 6644, Fax 262 0673 – rm. AE VISA. CZ e
Meals 12.00/15.00 **t.** and a la carte 5.00 – 3.50 – **60 rm** 69.00/91.00 **st.**

XX **Aspects** (at London Metropole H.), Edgware Rd, W2 1JU, ℘ 402 4141, Telex 23711, Fax 724 8866, ≤ London –. AE VISA JCB p. 21 GU c
closed Saturday lunch, Sunday and Bank Holidays – **Meals** 19.95/29.95 **t.** and a la carte 8.75.

XX **Poons,** Unit 205, Whiteleys, Queensway, W2 4YN, ℘ 792 2884 –. AE VISA BZ x
closed 24 to 27 December – **Meals** - Chinese - 10.00/15.00 **t.** and a la carte.

XX **Al San Vincenzo,** 30 Connaught St., W2 2AE, ℘ 262 9623 – VISA EZ o
closed Saturday lunch and Sunday – **Meals** - Italian - (booking essential) a la carte 25.00/32.50 **t.** 7.50.

X **L'Accento,** 16 Garway Rd, W2 4NH, ℘ 243 2201, Fax 243 2201 – VISA JCB BZ a
Meals - Italian - 14.00 **t.** and a la carte 16.00/23.50 **t.** 6.50.

Belgravia – ✉ SW1 – 0171 – Except where otherwise stated see pp. 30 and 31.

Lanesborough, 1 Lanesborough Pl., SW1X 7TA, ℘ 259 5599, Telex 911866, Fax 259 5606, – rm – 90. AE VISA JCB.
The Conservatory : Meals 23.00/29.50 **st.** and a la carte – 17.00 – **86 rm** 185.00/350.00 **s.**, 9 suites. p. 25 IY a

Berkeley, Wilton Pl., SW1X 7RL, ℘ 235 6000, Telex 919252, Fax 235 4330, – – 220. AE VISA JCB. FQ e
Restaurant : Meals *(closed Saturday)* 23.00/25.50 **st.** and a la carte 8.00 – 17.00 – **132 rm** 192.00/304.00 **s.**, 27 suites.

Halkin, 5 Halkin St., SW1X 7DJ, 333 1000, Fax 333 1100, « Contemporary inte design » – rm – 25. AE VISA JCB. p. 32 AV
Meals - Italian - *(closed lunch Saturday and Sunday and 25-26 December)* 36.50/45.00 and a la carte 34.00/45.00 **st.** 9.50 – 13.50 – **36 rm** 200.00/250.00 **s.**, 5 suites – SB
Spec. Pan fried foie gras with Castelluccio lentils, Ravioli with scallops and parsley purée, Roasted sea bass with tomato soup, sour cream and caviar.

Sheraton Belgravia, 20 Chesham Pl., SW1X 8HQ, 235 6040, Telex 9190 Fax 259 6243 – rm – 40. AE VISA JCB. FR
Meals *(closed Saturday lunch)* 21.95 **st.** (lunch) and a la carte 22.00/32.00 **st.** 5.50 – 11.50 – **82 rm** 170.00/215.00 **s.**, 7 suites – SB.

Lowndes (Hyatt), 21 Lowndes St., SW1X 9ES, 823 1234, Telex 919065, Fax 235 11 – rm – 25. AE VISA JCB. FR
Brasserie 21 : Meals a la carte approx. 16.45 **t.** 8.25 – 12.25 – **77 rm** 190.00 **s.**, 1 sui

Diplomat without rest., 2 Chesham St., SW1X 8DT, 235 1544, Fax 259 6153 – AE VISA JCB. FR
26 rm 70.00/120.00 **t.**

Zafferano, 15 Lowndes St., SW1X 9ES, 235 5800, Fax 235 1971 – AE VISA
closed Saturday lunch, Sunday and 2 weeks August – **Meals** - Italian - 13.50/21.50 **t.** 8.

Al Bustan, 27 Motcomb St., SW1X 8JU, 235 8277, Fax 235 1668 – AE VISA FR
closed 25 December and 1 January – **Meals** - Lebanese - 15.00/35.00 **t.** and a la carte 18.5 21.00 **t.** 6.00.

Motcombs, 26 Motcomb St., SW1X 8JU, 235 6382, Fax 245 6351 – AE
closed Saturday lunch, Sunday, Easter and Bank Holidays – **Meals** 14.75 **t.** (lunc and a la carte. FR

Hyde Park and Knightsbridge – SW1/SW7 – 0171 – pp. 30 and 31.

Hyde Park (Forte), 66 Knightsbridge, SWIX 7LA, 235 2000, Fax 235 4552, – rm – 250. AE VISA JCB. FQ
Park Room : Meals - Italian - 26.00/38.00 **t.** and a la carte 10.00 – (see also ***The Restaura Marco Pierre White*** below) – 15.00 – **166 rm** 205.00/255.00 **s.**, 19 suites – SB.

Knightsbridge Green without rest., 159 Knightsbridge, SW1X 7PD, 584 62 Fax 225 1635 – AE VISA. EQ
closed 4 days at Christmas – 9.50 – **12 rm** 80.00/110.00 **st.**, 12 suites 125.00 **st.**.

The Restaurant, Marco Pierre White, (at Hyde Park H.), 66 Knightsbrid SW1X 7LA, 259 5380, Fax 235 4552 – AE VISA FQ
closed Saturday lunch, Sunday, 2 weeks August, 2 weeks Christmas and Bank Holiday
Meals (booking essential) 29.50/70.00 **t.** 16.00
Spec. Ballotine of salmon with crayfish, herbs, fromage blanc and caviar, Panaché of sea scallops, sauce Nero, Sou of bitter chocolate with a bitter chocolate sauce.

Pearl, 22 Brompton Rd, SW1X 7QN, 225 3888, Fax 225 0252 – AE JCB
closed 24 to 26 December – **Meals** - Chinese - 20.00 **t.** and a la carte 5.00. EQ

Mayfair – W1 – 0171 – pp. 28 and 29.

Dorchester, Park Lane, W1A 2HJ, 629 8888, Telex 887704, Fax 409 0114, – rm – 500. AE VISA JCB. BN
Grill Room : Meals – English – 24.50/32.00 **st.** and a la carte 27.50/44.00 **st.** 12.00 – (s also ***Oriental*** below) – 16.00 – **195 rm** 210.00/265.00 **s.**, 49 suites – SB.

Claridge's, Brook St., W1A 2JQ, 629 8860, Telex 21872, Fax 499 2210 – rm – 200. AE VISA JCB. BL
Restaurant : Meals 29.00/45.00 **st.** and a la carte 10.00 – **Causerie : Meals** *(closed Saturd Sunday and Bank Holidays)* 19.50 **st.** (dinner) and a la carte 28.50/37.50 **st.** 10.00 – 16.50 – **142 rm** 220.00/295.00 **s.**, 63 suites – SB.

Four Seasons, Hamilton Pl., Park Lane, W1A 1AZ, 499 0888, Telex 2277 Fax 493 1895, – rm – 500. AE VISA JCB. BP
Lanes : Meals 22.75/25.00 **st.** and dinner a la carte 22.50/57.50 **st.** 7.50 – (see also ***Fo Seasons*** below) – 15.50 – **201 rm** 210.00/275.00 **s.**, 26 suites.

Le Meridien Piccadilly (Forte), 21 Piccadilly, W1V 0BH, 734 8000, Telex 2579 Fax 437 3574, squash – rm – 250. AE VISA JCB. EM
Terrace Garden : Meals 16.50/19.50 **t.** and a la carte 8.00 – (see also ***Oak Room*** below) – 14.75 – **248 rm** 215.00/255.00, 18 suites.

Grosvenor House (Forte), Park Lane, W1A 3AA, 499 6363, Telex 24871, Fax 493 334 – rm – 1500. AE VISA JCB. AM
Café Nico : Meals 21.00/26.00 **st.** and a la carte – **Pasta Vino : Meals** *(closed Saturday lun and Sunday)* a la carte 21.50/33.00 **t.** 8.00 – (see also ***Chez Nico at Ninety Park Lane*** belo – 15.50 – **383 rm** 195.00/295.00, 71 suites.

London Hilton on Park Lane, 22 Park Lane, W1Y 4BE, 493 8000, Telex 248 Fax 493 4957, Panoramic view of London, – rm – 1000. VISA JCB. BP
Trader Vics (208 4113) : **Meals** *(closed Saturday lunch and Sunday dinne* 12.00 **t.** (lunch) and a la carte 24.00/33.00 **t.** – **Park Brasserie : Meals** a la carte 23.70/31.45 – (see also ***Windows*** below) – 14.95 – **395 rm** 195.00/300.00 **st.**, 52 suites.

Connaught, Carlos Pl., W1Y 6AL, ☎ 499 7070, Fax 495 3262 – rest. BM **e**
The Restaurant : Meals (booking essential) 25.00/35.00 **t.** and a la carte 24.60/72.30 **t.** 11.00 – **Grill Room : Meals** *(closed lunch Saturday and Sunday)* (booking essential) 25.00/35.00 **t.** and a la carte 24.60/72.30 **t.** 11.00 – **66 rm** 198.00/265.00 **s.**, 24 suites
Spec. Sole "Jubilee", Prelude gourmande Connaught, Sherry trifle "Wally Ladd".

47 Park Street, 47 Park St., W1Y 4EB, ☎ 491 7282, Fax 491 7281 – AM **c**
Meals (room service)(see also ***Le Gavroche*** below) – 17.00 –, **52 suites** 245.00/550.00 **s.**.

Brown's (Forte), 29-34 Albemarle St., W1X 4BP, ☎ 493 6020, Fax 493 9381 – rm – 70. DM **e**
Meals (bar lunch Saturday) 23.65/32.00 **t.** and a la carte 9.50 – 15.00 – **110 rm** 195.00/225.00, 6 suites.

Park Lane, Piccadilly, W1Y 8BX, ☎ 499 6321, Telex 21533, Fax 499 1965, – rm – 300. CP **x**
Brasserie on the Park : Meals a la carte 15.75/31.50 **st.** – (see also ***Bracewells*** below) – 14.25 – **278 rm** 152.75/246.75 **st.**, 30 suites.

Britannia (Inter-Con), Grosvenor Sq., W1A 3AN, ☎ 629 9400, Telex 23941, Fax 629 7736, – rm – 100. BM **x**
Adams : Meals 17.50/19.50 **t.** and a la carte 6.50 – **Best of Both Worlds : Meals** 17.95 **t.** and a la carte 6.50 – (see also ***Shogun*** below) – 13.95 – **305 rm** 145.00/230.00, 12 suites.

Westbury (Forte), Conduit St., W1A 4UH, ☎ 629 7755, Telex 24378, Fax 495 1163 – rm – 120. DM **a**
La Mediterranée 22.50 **t.** and a la carte 8.00 – 14.50 – **231 rm** 145.00/185.00 **st.**, 13 suites – SB.

May Fair Inter-Continental, Stratton St., W1A 2AN, ☎ 629 7777, Telex 262526, Fax 629 1459, – rm – 290. DN **z**
Meals (see ***The Chateau*** below) – 14.50 – **262 rm** 185.00/320.00, 25 suites.

Inter-Continental, 1 Hamilton Pl., Hyde Park Corner, W1V 0QY, ☎ 409 3131, Telex 25853, Fax 409 7460, – rm – 1000. BP **o**
Meals 13.00 **s.** (dinner) and a la carte 20.00/50.00 **s.** 8.75 – (see also ***Le Soufflé*** below) – 15.00 – **426 rm** 240.00 **s.**, 34 suites – SB.

Athenaeum, 116 Piccadilly, W1V 0BJ, ☎ 499 3464, Fax 493 1860, – rm – 55. CP **s**
Bulloch's at 116 : Meals *(closed lunch Saturday and Sunday)* 29.00/42.00 **t.** and a la carte 9.00 – 14.50 – **111 rm** 175.00/185.00, 33 suites.

Marriott, Duke St., Grosvenor Sq., W1A 4AW, ☎ 493 1232, Telex 268101, Fax 491 3201, – rm – 600. BL **a**
Diplomat : Meals *(closed Saturday lunch)* 19.50 **t.** (lunch) and a la carte 14.25/26.50 **t.** 8.25 – 12.25 – **212 rm** 200.00 **s.**, 11 suites – SB.

Chesterfield, 35 Charles St., W1X 8LX, ☎ 491 2622, Fax 491 4793 – rm rest – 110. CN **c**
Butlers : Meals *(closed Saturday lunch)* 10.00/23.50 **t.** and a la carte 7.95 – 10.95 – **106 rm** 130.00/199.00 **s.**, 4 suites.

Holiday Inn, 3 Berkeley St., W1X 6NE, ☎ 493 8282, Telex 24561, Fax 629 2827 – rm – 60. DN **r**
Meals 15.75/19.50 **st.** and a la carte 9.50 – 10.95 – **183 rm** 150.00/165.00 **st.**, 2 suites.

Washington, 5-7 Curzon St., W1Y 8DT, ☎ 499 7000, Telex 24540, Fax 495 6172 – rm – 80. CN **s**
Meals *(closed lunch Saturday and Sunday)* 19.95 **st.** (dinner) and a la carte 7.95 – 10.95 – **169 rm** 175.00/195.00 **st.**, 4 suites.

Flemings, 7-12 Half Moon St., W1Y 7RA, ☎ 499 2964, Fax 629 4063 – rest – 45. CN **z**
Meals 9.00/25.00 **st.** and a la carte 8.75 – 10.50 – **120 rm** 120.00/185.00 **st.**, 10 suites.

Green Park, Half Moon St., W1Y 8BP, ☎ 629 7522, Telex 28856, Fax 491 8971 – rm – 70. CN **a**
Meals *(closed lunch Saturday and Sunday)* 12.95/14.50 **st.** and a la carte 7.00 – 10.25 – **160 rm** 120.00/174.00 **st.**, 1 suite.

London Mews Hilton, 2 Stanhope Row, W1Y 7HE, ☎ 493 7222, Fax 629 9423 – rm – 50. BP **u**
Meals (restricted menu) a la carte 14.20/24.75 **st.** – 11.75 – **71 rm** 155.00/195.00 **t.**, 1 suite.

XXXXX **Oak Room** (at Le Meridien Piccadilly H.), 21 Piccadilly, W1V OBH, ☎ 465 1640, Telex 25795, Fax 437 3574 – ▤. AE VISA JCB EM a
closed Saturday lunch, Sunday, 3 weeks August, 26 to 30 December and Bank Holidays – **Meals** - French - 25.00/46.00 **t.** and a la carte 40.50/48.50 **t.**

XXXXX ✿✿✿ **Chez Nico at Ninety Park Lane** (Ladenis) (at Grosvenor House H.), Park Lane, W1A 3AA, ☎ 409 1290, Fax 355 4877 – ▤. AE VISA AM e
closed Saturday lunch, Sunday, 4 days at Easter, 10 days at Christmas and Bank Holiday Mondays – **Meals** - French - (booking essential) 29.00/65.00 **st.**
Spec. Rosette of scallops, Sea bass with olive crust, Assiette gourmande.

XXXX ✿✿ **Le Gavroche** (Roux), 43 Upper Brook St., W1Y 1PF, ☎ 408 0881, Fax 409 0939 – ▤ AE VISA AM c
closed Saturday, Sunday, 23 December-2 January and Bank Holidays – **Meals** - French - (booking essential) 37.00/75.00 **st.** and a la carte 50.60/87.50 **st.** 🍾 10.00
Spec. Ragoût de langoustines et pied de cochon à la graine de moutarde, Pigeonneau en vessie aux deux céleris, Parfait au chocolat blanc et framboises.

XXXX ✿ **Oriental** (at Dorchester H.), Park Lane, W1A 2HJ, ☎ 629 8888, Telex 887704 Fax 409 0114 – ▤. AE VISA JCB BN a
closed Saturday lunch, Sunday and August – **Meals** - Chinese (Canton) - 22.50/32.00 **st** and a la carte 26.80/62.50 **st.** 🍾 12.00
Spec. Shredded chicken and cucumber served cold with sesame mustard sauce, Deep fried sole with chilli bean sauce and asparagus tips "Oriental style", Stir fried beef with lemon grass and black pepper.

XXXX ✿ **Four Seasons** (at Four Seasons H.), Hamilton Pl., Park Lane, W1A 1AZ, ☎ 499 0888 Telex 22771, Fax 493 1895 – ▤. AE VISA JCB BP a
Meals 19.50/45.00 **st.** and a la carte 39.25/52.25 **st.** 🍾 7.50
Spec. Cassoulet terrine with a flageolet bean vinaigrette, Cannelloni of salmon, aubergine and basil with a tomato butter sauce, Raspberry crunch with an almond and pistachio cream.

XXXX **Windows** (at London Hilton on Park Lane), 22 Park Lane, W1Y 4BE, ☎ 493 8000, ≤ London – ▤. AE VISA JCB BP e
closed Sunday dinner – **Meals** (buffet lunch Sunday) 35.95/44.00 **t.** and dinner a la carte

XXXX ✿ **Les Saveurs,** 37a Curzon St., W1Y 7AF, ☎ 491 8919, Fax 491 3658 – ▤. AE VISA
closed Saturday, Sunday, 2 weeks August, 24 December-9 January and Bank Holidays – **Meals** - French - 17.00/42.00 **t.** 🍾 9.00 BN
Spec. Terrine of duck foie gras with marinated aubergine, Scallops smoked 'a la minute' with horseradish cream and potatoes, Warm chocolate and pistachio fondant.

XXXX **Le Soufflé** (at Inter-Continental H.), 1 Hamilton Pl., Hyde Park Corner, W1V 0QY ☎ 409 3131, Telex 25853, Fax 409 7460 – ▤. AE VISA JCB BP
closed Saturday lunch, Sunday dinner, Monday and 2 weeks Christmas-New Year – **Meals** 27.50/43.00 **t.** and a la carte 🍾 10.00.

XXX **Princess Garden,** 8-10 North Audley St., W1Y 1WF, ☎ 493 3223, Fax 629 3130 – ▤. AE VISA JCB AL
closed 1 week Christmas – **Meals** - Chinese (Peking, Szechuan) - 35.00/55.00 **t** and a la carte 🍾 8.00.

XXX **Bracewells** (at Park Lane H.), Piccadilly, W1Y 8BX, ☎ 753 6725, Fax 499 1965 – Ⓟ. AE VISA JCB CP
closed Saturday lunch, Sunday and August – **Meals** 19.50 **st.** (lunch) and a la carte 24.75/32.75 **st.** 🍾 7.50.

XXX **The Chateau** (at May Fair Inter-Continental H.), Stratton St., W1A 2AN, ☎ 915 2842 Fax 629 1459 – ▤. AE VISA JCB DN
Meals 22.00/29.50 **st.** and a la carte 🍾 8.00.

XXX **Scotts,** 20 Mount St., W1Y 6HE, ☎ 629 5248, Fax 499 8246 – ▤. AE VISA JCB
closed Saturday lunch, Sunday and Bank Holidays – **Meals** - Seafood - 15.50 **t** and a la carte 🍾 4.75. BM

XXX **Zen Central,** 20 Queen St., W1X 7PJ, ☎ 629 8089, Fax 493 6181 – ▤. AE VISA
closed 4 days at Christmas – **Meals** - Chinese - 28.00/42.00 **t.** and a la carte. CN

XX **Tamarind,** 20 Queen St., W1X 7PJ, ☎ 629 3561, Fax 499 5034 – AE VISA JCB
closed Saturday lunch and 25 to 29 December – **Meals** - Indian - 13.50 **t** (lunch) and a la carte 22.75/27.75 **t.** 🍾 8.00. CN

XX ✿ **Greenhouse,** 27a Hay's Mews, W1X 7RJ, ☎ 499 3331 – ▤. AE VISA BN
closed Saturday lunch, Christmas and Bank Holidays – **Meals** a la carte 23.65/34.35 **t.** 🍾 7.50
Spec. Smoked haddock with Welsh rarebit, Salmon fish cakes, Apricot sponge pudding.

XX **Bentley's,** 11-15 Swallow St., W1R 7HD, ☎ 734 4756, Fax 287 2972 – ▤. AE VISA JCB EM
closed Sunday, 24 December-4 January and Bank Holidays – **Meals** - Seafood - 19.50 **t** and a la carte 🍾 7.50.

XX **Nicole's,** 158 New Bond St., W1V 9PA, ☎ 499 8408, Fax 499 7522 – ▤. AE VISA
closed Saturday dinner and Sunday – **Meals** a la carte 23.00/27.50 **t.** DM

XX **Langan's Brasserie,** Stratton St., W1X 5FD, ☎ 491 8822 – ▤. AE VISA
closed Saturday lunch, Sunday, 1 January, Easter, 25 December and Bank Holidays – **Meals** (booking essential) a la carte 19.30/28.15 **t.** 🍾 6.50. DN

XX **Gaucho Grill,** 19 Swallow St., W1R 7HD, ☎ 734 4040, Fax 287 1427 – ▤. AE VISA
Meals - Argentinian - a la carte 12.85/21.85 **t.** 🍾 6.00. EM

XX **Mulligans,** 13-14 Cork St., W1X 1PF, ☎ 409 1370, Fax 409 2732 – ▤. AE ⓓ VISA JCB
closed Saturday lunch and Sunday – **Meals** - Irish - a la carte 18.75/25.85 **t.** DM **c**

XX **Shogun** (at Britannia H.), Adams Row, W1Y 5DE, ☎ 493 1255 – ▤. AE ⓓ VISA JCB
closed Monday – **Meals** - Japanese - (dinner only) 32.00 **t.** and a la carte. BM **x**

X **O'Keefe's,** 19 Dering St., W1R 9AA, ☎ 495 0878 – VISA CK **e**
closed Saturday dinner, Sunday, 25-26 December and Bank Holidays – **Meals** 10.00/20.00 **t.** and a la carte 5.75.

Regent's Park and Marylebone – ✉ NW1/NW6/NW8/W1 – ☎ 0171 – Except where otherwise stated see pp. 28 and 29.

Basement Services Arcade, Selfridges Store, Oxford St., W1 ☎ 824 8844.

Landmark London, 222 Marylebone Rd, NW1 6JQ, ☎ 631 8000, Fax 631 8092, « Victorian Gothic architecture, atrium and winter garden », – rm ▤ – 350. AE ⓓ VISA JCB. p. 21 HU **a**
The Dining Room : Meals 18.00/45.00 **t.** and a la carte 10.50 – 15.50 – **307 rm** 160.00/255.00 **s.**, 2 suites – SB.

Churchill Inter-Continental, 30 Portman Sq., W1A 4ZX, ☎ 486 5800, Telex 264831, Fax 486 1255, – rm ▤ – 200. AE ⓓ VISA JCB. AJ **x**
Meals *(closed Saturday lunch)* 21.50 **t.** and a la carte 6.00 – 16.00 – **406 rm** 195.00/235.00 **s.**, 37 suites.

Langham Hilton, 1 Portland Pl., W1N 4JA, ☎ 636 1000, Fax 323 2340, – rm ▤ – 250. AE ⓓ VISA JCB. p. 21 JU **e**
Memories of the Empire : Meals 23.00/29.95 **st.** and a la carte 8.60 – 15.20 – **360 rm** 195.00/280.00 **s.**, 20 suites.

Selfridge (Thistle), Orchard St., W1H 0JS, ☎ 408 2080, Group Telex 22361, Fax 629 8849 – rm ▤ – 220. AE ⓓ VISA JCB. AK **e**
Fletchers : Meals *(closed Saturday lunch and Sunday)* 16.95/24.00 **st.** and a la carte – **Orchard : Meals** 12.95 **st.** 5.20 – 10.75 – **293 rm** 155.00/185.00 **st.**, 2 suites – SB.

Radisson SAS Portman, 22 Portman Sq., W1H 9FL, ☎ 208 6000, Telex 261526, Fax 208 6001, – rm ▤ – 350. AE ⓓ VISA JCB. AJ **o**
Meals 9.50 **t.** (lunch) and a la carte 15.00/31.00 **t.** 9.00 – 12.50 – **272 rm** 158.60/199.75 **st.**, 7 suites.

Berkshire (Radisson Edwardian), 350 Oxford St., W1N 0BY, ☎ 629 7474, Telex 22270, Fax 629 8156 – rm ▤ – 40. AE ⓓ VISA JCB. BK **n**
Meals *(closed Saturday, Sunday and Bank Holiday lunch)* 23.40 **st.** and a la carte – 13.50 – **145 rm** 160.00/210.00 **st.**, 2 suites – SB.

London Regent's Park Hilton, 18 Lodge Rd, NW8 7JT, ☎ 722 7722, Telex 23101, Fax 483 2408 – rm ▤ – 150. AE ⓓ VISA JCB. p. 21 GT **v**
Minsky's : Meals 15.95/19.95 **t.** and a la carte 9.75 – **Kashinoki : Meals** - Japanese - *(closed Monday, 25-26 December and 1 January)* 9.00/30.00 **t.** 8.00 – 12.50 – **374 rm** 126.00/142.00 **st.**, 3 suites.

Clifton Ford, 47 Welbeck St., W1M 8DN, ☎ 486 6600, Telex 22569, Fax 486 7492 – ▤ – 150. AE ⓓ VISA. BH **a**
Meals 16.00/18.00 **st.** and a la carte 4.65 – 13.50 – **191 rm** 140.00/155.00 **s.**, 2 suites.

Montcalm, Great Cumberland Pl., W1A 2LF, ☎ 402 4288, Telex 28710, Fax 724 9180 – rm ▤ – 80. AE ⓓ VISA JCB. p. 33 EZ **x**
Crescent : Meals *(closed Saturday lunch and Sunday)* 19.50/43.00 **t.** and dinner a la carte 6.50 – 14.25 – **102 rm** 165.00/185.00, 14 suites.

Marble Arch Marriott, 134 George St., W1H 6DN, ☎ 723 1277, Telex 27983, Fax 402 0666, – rm ▤ rest – 150. AE ⓓ VISA JCB. p. 33 EZ **i**
Meals 8.00/25.00 **st.** and a la carte 7.50 – 11.85 – **239 rm** 150.00/190.00 – SB.

Berners, 10 Berners St., W1A 3BE, ☎ 636 1629, Telex 25759, Fax 580 3972 – rm ▤ rest – 150. AE ⓓ VISA JCB. EJ **r**
Meals 17.20/22.15 **t.** and a la carte – 11.75 – **226 rm** 132.00/185.00 **st.**, 3 suites.

Forte Crest Regent's Park, Carburton St., W1P 8EE, ☎ 388 2300, Telex 22453, Fax 387 2806 – rm ▤ rest – 220. AE ⓓ VISA JCB. p. 21 JU **i**
Meals 15.95/25.00 **st.** and a la carte 6.60 – 11.95 – **315 rm** 125.00/140.00 **st.**, 2 suites – SB.

St. George's (Forte), Langham Pl., W1N 8QS, ☎ 580 0111, Fax 436 7997, ← – rm AE ⓓ VISA JCB. p. 21 JU **a**
Meals - (see *The Heights* below) – 13.95 – **83 rm** 140.00/150.00 **st.**, 3 suites.

Rathbone without rest., Rathbone St., W1P 2LB, ☎ 636 2001, Telex 28728, Fax 636 3882 – rm ▤ AE ⓓ VISA JCB. p. 22 KU **x**
10.00 – **72 rm** 125.00/150.00 **st.**

Dorset Square, 39-40 Dorset Sq., NW1 6QN, ☎ 723 7874, Fax 724 3328, « Attractively furnished Regency town houses », – ▤ AE VISA. p. 21 HU **s**
Meals *(closed Sunday lunch and Saturday)* 11.95 **t.** (lunch) and a la carte 22.00/27.00 **t.** – 10.00 – **37 rm** 85.00/160.00 **s.** – SB.

25 Dorset Square without rest., 25 Dorset Sq., NW1 6QN, ☎ 724 6031, Fax 723 0194, « Regency town houses » – AE ⓓ VISA. HU **e**
, **12 suites** 100.00/157.00 **st.**

Durrants, 26-32 George St., W1H 6BJ, ☎ 935 8131, Fax 487 3510, « Converted Georgia houses with Regency façade » – lift TV ☎ – 60. VISA. AH
Meals 17.00 **t.** and a la carte 5.35 – 8.95 – **90 rm** 86.00/106.00 **st.**, 3 suites.

Savoy Court, Granville Pl., W1H 0EH, ☎ 408 0130, Telex 8955515, Fax 493 2070 – rest TV ☎. AE VISA JCB. AK
Meals 13.50/35.00 and a la carte – 9.00 – **95 rm** 90.00/130.00 **st.** – SB.

Langham Court, 31-35 Langham St., W1N 5RE, ☎ 436 6622, Fax 436 6622 – lift TV ☎ 80. AE VISA JCB. p. 21 JU
Meals *(closed lunch Saturday and Sunday)* 16.95/18.95 **t.** and a la carte 7.95 – 9.50
56 rm 85.00/99.00 **st.**

Stakis London Harewood, Harewood Row, NW1 6SE, ☎ 262 2707, Telex 29722 Fax 262 2975 – lift rm rest TV ☎. AE VISA. p. 21 HU
Meals (dinner only) 16.00 **st.** and a la carte – 9.00 – **92 rm** 78.00/98.00 **st.**

Hart House without rest., 51 Gloucester Pl., W1H 3PE, ☎ 935 2288, Fax 935 8516 – TV ☎ AE VISA JCB. AH
16 rm 50.00/80.00 **st.**

Lincoln House without rest., 33 Gloucester Pl., W1H 3PD, ☎ 486 7630, Fax 486 0166 TV ☎. AE VISA JCB. AJ
22 rm 57.00/79.00 **st.**

Bryanston Court without rest., 56-60 Great Cumberland Pl., W1H 7DD, ☎ 262 314 Fax 262 7248 – lift TV ☎. AE VISA JCB. p. 33 EZ
54 rm 70.00/85.00 **t.**

Regents Park without rest., 156 Gloucester Pl., NW1 6DT, ☎ 258 1911, Fax 258 0288 TV ☎. AE VISA JCB. HT
29 rm 50.00/70.00 **st.**

XXX ✻ **Interlude de Chavot** (Chavot), 5 Charlotte St., W1P 1HD, ☎ 637 0222, Fax 637 0224 AE VISA JCB p. 22 KU
closed Saturday lunch, Sunday and Bank Holidays – **Meals** - French - 26.50 **t.**
Spec. Pithivier of quail, Roast poulet noir, fondant potatoes, Chocolate tart.

XX **The Heights** (at St. George's H.), Langham Pl., W1N 8QS, ☎ 636 1939, Fax 753 0259 London – lift. AE VISA JCB JU
closed Saturday lunch, Sunday, last 2 weeks August and Bank Holidays – **Meals** 19.50 (lunch) and dinner a la carte 23.20/30.40 **t.** 9.00.

XX **Hudson's,** 221b Baker St., NW1 4XE, ☎ 935 3130, Fax 224 3005 – AE VISA JCB HU
closed 25 December – **Meals** - English - 14.00/16.50 **t.** and a la carte 9.25.

XX **Nico Central,** 35 Great Portland St., W1N 5DD, ☎ 436 8846, Fax 355 4877 – AE VISA DJ
closed Saturday lunch, Sunday, 4 days Easter, 10 days Christmas and Bank Holida Mondays – **Meals** 23.50/26.00 **st.** 9.00.

XX **Caldesi,** 15-17 Marylebone Lane, W1M 5FE, ☎ 935 9226, Fax 929 0924 – AE VIS JCB BJ
closed Saturday lunch, Sunday and Bank Holidays – **Meals** - Italian - a la carte 15.00/26.00 4.50.

XX **Gaylord,** 79-81 Mortimer St., W1N 7TB, ☎ 580 3615, Fax 631 5077 – AE VISA JCB p. 22 KU
Meals - Indian - 11.95/12.95 **t.** and a la carte 4.50.

XX **Maroush III,** 62 Seymour St., W1H 5AF, ☎ 724 5024, Fax 706 3493 – AE VISA EZ
Meals - Lebanese - 8.00/30.00 **t.** and a la carte 8.50.

XX **Stephen Bull,** 5-7 Blandford St., W1H 3AA, ☎ 486 9696, Fax 490 3128 – AE VISA BH
closed Saturday lunch, Sunday, 1 week Christmas and Bank Holidays – **Meals** 13.00 (lunch) and a la carte 21.75/30.00 **t.** 6.00.

XX **Baboon,** Jason Court, 76 Wigmore St., W1H 9DQ, ☎ 224 2992, Fax 224 2992 – AE VISA JCB BJ
closed Saturday lunch, Sunday, 1 week Christmas and Bank Holidays – **Meals** 12.50/17.00 and a la carte 5.25.

XX Sampan's (at Cumberland H.), Marble Arch, W1A 4RF, ☎ 262 1234 AK
Meals - Chinese (Canton) rest..

XX **Asuka,** Berkeley Arcade, 209a Baker St., NW1 6AB, ☎ 486 5026, Fax 224 1741 – AE VISA JCB p. 21 HU
closed Saturday lunch, Sunday and Bank Holidays – **Meals** - Japanese - 13.50/37.00 and a la carte.

X **Le Muscadet,** 25 Paddington St., W1M 3RF, ☎ 935 2883 – VISA HU
closed Saturday lunch, Sunday, last 3 weeks August and 2 weeks Christmas-New Year – **Meals** - French - a la carte 20.50/24.05 **t.** 8.20.

X L'Aventure, 3 Blenheim Terr., NW8 0EH, ☎ 624 6232, Fax 625 5548
Meals - French rest. p. 20 FS

X **Nakamura,** 31 Marylebone Lane, W1M 5FH, ☎ 935 2931, Fax 935 2931 – AE VISA JCB BJ
closed lunch Sunday and Bank Holidays, Saturday, 1 week late August and 24 to 2 December – **Meals** - Japanese - 12.00/29.90 **t.** and a la carte.

Langan's Bistro, 26 Devonshire St., W1N 1RJ, ℘ 935 4531 – ▤. AE VISA p. 21 IU **e**
closed Saturday lunch, Sunday, Easter, Christmas and Bank Holidays – **Meals** 17.95 **t.**

Zoe, 3-5 Barrett St., St. Christopher's Pl., W1M 5HH, ℘ 224 1122, Fax 935 5444 – ▤. AE VISA BJ **a**
closed Sunday and Bank Holidays – **Meals** a la carte 14.30/23.85 **t.**

Union Café, 96 Marylebone Lane, W1M 5FP, ℘ 486 4860 – VISA BH **c**
closed Saturday, Sunday, last 2 weeks August, first 2 weeks January and Bank Holidays – **Meals** a la carte 15.50/21.50 **t.**

St. James's – ✉ W1/SW1/WC2 – 0171 – pp. 28 and 29.

Ritz, Piccadilly, W1V 9DG, ℘ 493 8181, Fax 493 2687, « Elegant restaurant in Louis XVI style » – rm ▤ TV ☎ – 50. AE VISA JCB. DN **a**
Louis XVI : Meals (dancing Friday and Saturday evenings) 28.00/49.00 **st.** and a la carte – **Italian Garden : Meals** (summer only) (lunch only) 28.00 **st.** – 16.50 – **116 rm** 200.00/275.00, 14 suites – SB.

Dukes, 35 St. James's Pl., SW1A 1NY, ℘ 491 4840, Fax 493 1264 – ▤ TV ☎ – 50. AE VISA JCB. EP **x**
Meals (residents only) a la carte 35.00/60.00 **st.** 7.50 – 12.50 – **53 rm** 125.00/160.00 **s.**, 11 suites 210.00/400.00 **s.**

22 Jermyn Street, 22 Jermyn St., SW1Y 6HL, ℘ 734 2353, Fax 734 0750 – TV ☎. AE VISA JCB. FM **e**
Meals (restricted room service only) a la carte 16.50/27.50 **t.** 8.00 – 14.00 – **5 rm** 170.00 **s.**, **13 suites** 225.00/250.00 **s.**.

Stafford, 16-18 St. James's Pl., SW1A 1NJ, ℘ 493 0111, Fax 493 7121 – ▤ rest TV ☎ – 35. AE VISA JCB. DN **u**
closed 3 January-22 April – **Meals** *(closed Saturday lunch)* 19.50/25.00 **st.** and a la carte 7.50 – 14.00 – **69 rm** 170.00/225.00 **s.**, 4 suites.

Forte Crest Cavendish, 81 Jermyn St., SW1Y 6JF, ℘ 930 2111, Fax 839 2125 – rm ▤ rest TV ☎ – 80. AE VISA JCB. EN **i**
Meals 16.50/19.50 **t.** and a la carte 7.95 – 13.50 – **252 rm** 140.00/160.00 **st.**, 3 suites – SB.

Royal Trafalgar Thistle, Whitcomb St., WC2H 7HG, ℘ 930 4477, Fax 925 2149 – rm TV ☎. AE VISA JCB. GM **r**
Meals 14.75 **t.** and a la carte 6.40 – 10.25 – **108 rm** 109.00/135.00 **st.** – SB.

Hospitality Inn Piccadilly (Mount Charlotte) without rest., 39 Coventry St., W1V 8EL, ℘ 930 4033, Telex 8950058, Fax 925 2586 – ▤ rest TV ☎. AE VISA JCB. – 9.75 – **92 rm** 115.00/130.00 **st.** FGM **a**

Pastoria, 3-6 St. Martin's St., off Leicester Sq., WC2H 7HL, ℘ 930 8641, Telex 25538, Fax 925 0551 – ▤ rest TV ☎ – 60. AE VISA JCB. GM **v**
Meals *(closed Saturday lunch and Sunday)* 15.00/35.00 **st.** and a la carte – 9.25 – **58 rm** 125.00/165.00 **st.** – SB.

Quaglino's, 16 Bury St., SW1Y 6AL, ℘ 930 6767, Fax 839 2866 – ▤. AE VISA
closed 2 days at Christmas – **Meals** (booking essential) 13.50 **t.** (lunch) and a la carte 21.65/30.95 **t.** 6.25. EN **r**

Suntory, 72-73 St. James's St., SW1A 1PH, ℘ 409 0201, Fax 499 0208 – ▤. AE VISA JCB – *closed Sunday and Bank Holidays* – **Meals** - Japanese - 15.00/90.00 **st.** and a la carte 31.70/86.00 **st.** 12.00. EP **z**

Overton's, 5 St. James's St., SW1A 1EF, ℘ 839 3774, Fax 839 4330 – ▤. AE VISA JCB EP **a**
closed Saturday and Sunday, 10 days Christmas-New Year and Bank Holidays – **Meals** - Seafood - 21.00/27.50 **t.** 5.75.

✿ **The Square,** 32 King St., SW1Y 6RJ (expected move during 1996 to 10 Bruton St., Mayfair, W1), ℘ 839 8787, Fax 321 2124 – ▤. AE VISA EN **v**
closed lunch Saturday and Sunday – **Meals** a la carte 28.00/33.00 **t.**
Spec. Seared tuna with tartare of vegetables and soy wilted greens, Peppered fillet of beef, Parmesan, meat juices and truffle oil, Warm salad of duck, deep fried vegetables and balsamic vinegar.

Le Caprice, Arlington House, Arlington St., SW1A 1RT, ℘ 629 2239, Fax 493 9040 – ▤. AE VISA DN **c**
closed 24 December-2 January – **Meals** a la carte 22.25/35.50 **t.**

Green's, 36 Duke St., SW1Y 6DF, ℘ 930 4566, Fax 491 7463 – ▤. AE VISA EN **n**
closed Sunday dinner, 25, 26 and 31 December and 1 January – **Meals** - English - a la carte 19.00/31.00 **t.** 5.00.

Criterion Brasserie Marco Pierre White, 224 Piccadilly, WIV 9LB, ℘ 930 0488, Fax 930 8190, « 19C Neo-Byzantine decor » – AE VISA FM **c**
closed 25-26 December and 1 January – **Meals** a la carte 19.40/22.70 **t.** 10.00.

Matsuri, 15 Bury St., SW1Y 6AL, ℘ 839 1101, Fax 930 7010 – ▤. AE VISA JCB
closed Sunday and Bank Holidays – **Meals** - Japanese (Teppan-Yaki, Sushi) - 10.50/53.50 **t.** and a la carte. EN **r**

Soho – ✉ W1/WC2 – ☎ 0171 – pp. 28 and 29.

Hampshire (Radisson Edwardian), Leicester Sq., WC2H 7LH, ☎ 839 9399, Telex 91484 Fax 930 8122 – rm – 80. AE VISA JCB. GM
Meals 19.50/15.00 **st.** and a la carte – 13.50 – **120 rm** 195.00/230.00 **st.**, 4 suites SB.

Hazlitt's without rest., 6 Frith St., W1V 5TZ, ☎ 434 1771, Fax 439 1524 – . AE VISA JCB FK
closed 4 days at Christmas – **22 rm** 102.00/130.00 **s.**, 1 suite.

XXXX ✿ **Grill Room at the Café Royal** (Forte), 68 Regent St., W1R 6EL, ☎ 437 909 Fax 439 7672, « Rococo decoration » – . AE VISA JCB EM
closed Saturday lunch, Sunday and Bank Holidays – **Meals** 24.00/39.0 **st.** and a la carte 35.00/51.50 **st.** 9.00
Spec. Escalopes of fresh foie gras with a ragoût of celeriac and truffle sauce, Seared fillet of sea bass with fenr sundried tomatoes and saffron, Lemon meringue with Sauternes, raspberries and pistachio sauce.

XXX **Au Jardin des Gourmets**, 5 Greek St., W1V 6NA, ☎ 437 1816, Fax 437 0043 – . VISA GJ
closed lunch Saturday and Bank Holidays, Sunday, Christmas and Easter. – **Restaurar Meals** - French - 17.50 **t.** and a la carte.
XX **Brasserie**, *closed lunch Saturday and Bank Holidays and Sunday* – **Meals** 10.95 and a la carte 6.25.

XXX **Lindsay House**, 21 Romilly St., W1V 5TG, ☎ 439 0450, Fax 581 2848 – . AE JCB GL
closed 25 and 26 December – **Meals** 10.00 **t.** (lunch) and a la carte 23.50/29.25 5.00.

XXX ✿ **L'Escargot**, 48 Greek St., W1V 5LQ, ☎ 437 2679, Fax 437 0790 – . AE VISA GK
Brasserie : **Meals** *(closed Saturday lunch and Sunday)* 21.50/23.50 **t.** – **Dining Room : Mea** *(closed Saturday lunch, Sunday, Monday and August)* 25.00/30.00 **t.**
Spec. Escabèche of salmon, Roast duck with parsley jus, Raspberry soufflé.

XX **Red Fort**, 77 Dean St., W1V 5HA, ☎ 437 2115, Fax 434 0721 – . AE VISA FJK
Meals -Indian - (buffet lunch) 12.50 **t.** (lunch) and a la carte 21.85/25.85 **t.**

XX **Mezzo**, Lower ground floor, 100 Wardour St., W1V 3LE, ☎ 314 4000, Fax 314 4040 – AE VISA FK
closed 24 to 26 December – **Meals** 19.50 **t.** (lunch) and a la carte 17.50/25.50 **t.**

XX **Soho Soho** (first floor), 11-13 Frith St., W1V 5TS, ☎ 494 3491, Fax 437 3091 – . VISA JCB FK
closed Saturday lunch, Sunday and Bank Holidays – **Meals** 15.95 **t.** (dinne and a la carte approx. 22.00 **t.**

XX **Brasserie at the Café Royal** (Forte), 68 Regent St., W1R 6EL, ☎ 437 9090 Fax 439 7672 – . AE VISA JCB EM
closed Sunday dinner – **Meals** 13.50/16.50 **st.** and a la carte 7.25.

XX **Ming**, 35-36 Greek St., W1V 5LN, ☎ 734 2721, Fax 435 0812 – . AE VIS JCB GK
closed Sunday, Bank Holiday lunch and 25 and 26 December – **Meals** - Chinese - 10.00 20.00 **t.** and a la carte 6.50.

XX **Lexington**, 45 Lexington St., W1R 3LG, ☎ 434 3401, Fax 287 2997 – . AE VISA EK
closed Saturday lunch, Sunday, 1 week Christmas-New Year and Bank Holidays **Meals** 10.00 **t.** (dinner) and a la carte 16.25/23.75 **t.**

XX **Gopal's**, 12 Bateman St., W1V 5TD, ☎ 434 0840 – . AE VISA FK
closed 25 and 26 December – **Meals** - Indian - a la carte 12.15/14.90 **t.**

XX **Gay Hussar**, 2 Greek St., W1V 6NB, ☎ 437 0973 – . AE VISA GJ
closed Sunday and Bank Holidays – **Meals** - Hungarian - 16.00 (lunch) and a la carte 18.10/26.60 **t.** 7.50.

XX **Atelier**, 41 Beak St., W1R 3LE, ☎ 287 2057 – AE VISA EL
closed Saturday lunch, Sunday, 2 weeks August, 2 weeks Christmas-New Year and Ban Holidays – **Meals** 17.00 **t.** and a la carte 22.75/28/75 **t.** 7.95.

X **dell 'Ugo**, 56 Frith St., W1V 5TA, ☎ 734 8300, Fax 734 8784 – AE VISA FK
closed Sunday and Bank Holidays – **Meals** a la carte 15.95/26.15 **t.**

X **Sri Siam**, 16 Old Compton St., W1V 5PE, ☎ 434 3544 – . AE VISA GK
closed Sunday lunch – **Meals** - Thai - 9.95 **t.** and a la carte 4.60.

X **Alastair Little**, 49 Frith St., W1V 5TE, ☎ 734 5183 – AE VISA JCB FK
closed Saturday lunch, Sunday and Bank Holidays – **Meals** (booking essential) 25.00 (lunch) and a la carte 28.00/40.00 6.00.

X **Bistrot Bruno,** 63 Frith St., W1V 5TA, ℘ 734 4545, Fax 287 1027 – ▤. AE ◑ VISA
closed Saturday lunch, Sunday and Christmas – **Meals** 25.00/35.00 **t.** FK **z**

X **Poons,** 4 Leicester St., Leicester Sq., WC2 7BL, ℘ 437 1528 – ▤. AE VISA GM **e**
closed 24 to 27 December – **Meals** - Chinese - a la carte 7.50/15.00 **t.** 6.50.

X **Andrew Edmunds,** 46 Lexington St., W1R 3LH, ℘ 437 5708 – AE VISA EK **c**
closed Easter, August Bank Holiday and 23 December-2 January – **Meals** a la carte 12.00/17.00 **t.** 4.25.

X **Fung Shing,** 15 Lisle St., WC2H 7BE, ℘ 734 0284 – ▤. AE ◑ VISA GL **a**
Meals - Chinese (Canton) - 12.50/20.00 **t.** and a la carte 4.75.

X **Saigon,** 45 Frith St., W1V 5TE, ℘ 437 7109, Fax 734 1668 – ▤. AE ◑ VISA FGK **x**
closed Sunday and Bank Holidays – **Meals** - Vietnamese - 15.80/19.50 **t.** 8.50.

Strand and Covent Garden – ✉ WC2 – 0171 – Except where otherwise stated see p. 33.

Savoy, Strand, WC2R 0EU, ℘ 836 4343, Telex 24234, Fax 240 6040, – rm ▤ TV ☎ – 500. AE ◑ VISA JCB. DEY **a**
Grill : Meals *(closed Saturday lunch, Sunday, August and Bank Holidays)* 31.00 **st.** (dinner) and a la carte 27.40/44.25 **st.** 8.60 – **River : Meals** 28.00/40.00 **st.** and a la carte 45.00/61.00 **st.** 8.60 – 16.25 – **154 rm** 200.00/325.00 **s.**, 48 suites – SB.

Waldorf (Forte), Aldwych, WC2B 4DD, ℘ 836 2400, Telex 24574, Fax 836 7244 – rm ▤ rm TV ☎ – 450. AE ◑ VISA JCB EX **x**
Meals (in bar Sunday lunch) 23.00/35.00 **t.** and a la carte 6.75 – 13.50 – **286 rm** 165.00/190.00 **s.**, 6 suites – SB.

Howard, Temple Pl., WC2R 2PR, ℘ 836 3555, Telex 268047, Fax 379 4547 – rm ▤ TV ☎ – 100. AE ◑ VISA JCB. EX **e**
Meals 25.00 **st.** and a la carte 4.75 – 15.50 – **133 rm** 200.00/236.00 **st.**, 2 suites.

XXX **Ivy,** 1 West St., WC2H 9NE, ℘ 836 4751, Fax 497 3644 – ▤. AE ◑ VISA p. 29 GK **z**
closed dinner 24 to 28 December and lunch Bank Holidays – **Meals** a la carte 22.25/35.50 **t.**

XXX **WestZENders,** 4a Upper St. Martin's Lane, WC2H 9EA, ℘ 497 0376, Fax 497 0378 – ▤. AE ◑ VISA DX **x**
closed 25 December – **Meals** - Chinese - a la carte 16.50/21.50 **t.**

XX **Rules,** 35 Maiden Lane, WC2E 7LB, ℘ 836 5314, Fax 497 1081, « London's oldest restaurant with collection of antique cartoons, drawings and paintings » – AE ◑ VISA DX **n**
closed 23 to 26 December – **Meals** - English - 12.95 **t.** (lunch) and a la carte 20.95/23.15 **t.** 4.60.

XX **Christopher's,** 18 Wellington St., WC2E 7DD, ℘ 240 4222, Fax 240 3357 – AE ◑ VISA EX **z**
closed Saturday lunch, Sunday, 25-26 December and Bank Holidays – **Meals** a la carte 22.50/45.00 6.00.

XX **Orso,** 27 Wellington St., WC2E 7DA, ℘ 240 5269, Fax 497 2148 – ▤ EX **z**
closed 24 and 25 December – **Meals** - Italian - (booking essential) a la carte 15.50/25.50 **t.** 5.50.

XX **L'Estaminet,** 14 Garrick St., off Floral St., WC2 9BJ, ℘ 379 1432 – AE VISA DX **a**
closed Sunday and Bank Holidays – **Meals** - French - a la carte 20.50/24.00 **t.**

XX **Sheekey's,** 28-32 St. Martin's Court, WC2N 4AL, ℘ 240 2565, Fax 240 0545 – ▤. AE ◑ VISA DX **v**
Meals - Seafood - 15.95/18.75 **t.** and a la carte.

XX **Bertorelli's,** 44a Floral St., WC2E 9DA, ℘ 836 3969, Fax 836 1868 – ▤. AE ◑ VISA JCB DX **c**
closed Sunday and 25-26 December – **Meals** - Italian - a la carte 15.30/27.15 **t.**

X **Le Café du Jardin,** 28 Wellington St., WC2E 7BD, ℘ 836 8769, Fax 836 4123 – ▤. AE ◑ VISA EX **a**
Meals 13.50 **t.** (lunch) and a la carte 16.95/26.95 **t.** 4.50.

X **Magno's Brasserie,** 65a Long Acre, WC2E 9JH, ℘ 836 6077, Fax 379 6184 – ▤. AE ◑ VISA JCB DV **e**
closed Saturday lunch, Sunday, Christmas and Bank Holidays – **Meals** - French - 13.50/16.50 **t.** and a la carte.

X **Joe Allen,** 13 Exeter St., WC2E 7DT, ℘ 836 0651, Fax 497 2148 – ▤ EX **c**
closed 24 and 25 December – **Meals** a la carte 16.50/22.00 **t.**

Victoria – ✉ SW1 – ☎ 0171 – Exceptwhere otherwise stated see p. 32.
ℹ Victoria Station Forecourt, SW1V 1JU ☎ 824 8844.

St. James Court, Buckingham Gate, SW1E 6AF, ☎ 834 6655, Telex 938075 Fax 630 7587, – rm – 180. CX
Café Mediterranée : Meals 12.50/25.00 **st.** and a la carte – (see also ***Auberge de Provence*** and ***Inn of Happiness*** below) – 14.00 – **375 rm** 140.00/175.00, 18 suites.

Royal Horseguards Thistle, 2 Whitehall Court, SW1A 2EJ, ☎ 839 3400, Telex 917096 Fax 925 2263 – rest – 60. p. 26 LX
Meals (light meals Saturday and Sunday) 12.95 **t.** and a la carte – 10.25 – **373 rm** 118.00/200.00 **st.**, 3 suites.

Stakis London St. Ermin's, Caxton St., SW1H 0QW, ☎ 222 7888, Fax 222 6914 – rm rest – 250. CX
Meals *(closed Saturday and Sunday lunch)* (carving rest.) 12.75/16.50 **t.** and a la carte
Caxton Grill : Meals *(closed Saturday and Sunday)* a la carte 18.75/40.90 **t.** – 9.75 **283 rm** 119.00/139.00 **st.**, 7 suites – SB.

Goring, 15 Beeston Pl., Grosvenor Gdns, SW1W 0JW, ☎ 396 9000, Telex 919166 Fax 834 4393 – – 50. BX
Meals 18.00/35.00 **t.** 8.00 – 12.50 – **72 rm** 130.00/165.00 **s.**, 5 suites – SB.

Royal Westminster Thistle, 49 Buckingham Palace Rd, SW1W 0QT, ☎ 834 1821 Telex 916821, Fax 931 7542 – rm – 160.
Meals *(closed Sunday)* (bar lunch)/dinner 21.95 **st.** and a la carte – 10.25 – **134 rm** 122.00/145.00 **st.** – SB. BX

Grosvenor Thistle, 101 Buckingham Palace Rd, SW1W 0SJ, ☎ 834 9494, Telex 916006 Fax 630 1978 – rm – 200. BX
Meals (carving rest.) 14.50/16.35 **st.** and a la carte 6.00 – 8.95 – **360 rm** 99.00/145.00 **st.**, 6 suites.

Dolphin Square, Dolphin Sq., SW1V 3LX, ☎ 834 3800, Fax 798 8735, , squash – rest – 50. KZ
Meals 11.95/17.95 **st.** and dinner a la carte – 11.95 – **14 rm** 99.00/125.00 **st.**, **137 suites** 130.00/148.00 **st.**

Rubens, 39-41 Buckingham Palace Rd, SW1W 0PS, ☎ 834 6600, Telex 916577 Fax 828 5401 – rm rest – 75. BX
Meals *(closed Saturday and Sunday lunch)* (carving rest.) 14.95 **st.** and a la carte 8.00 – 9.95 – **179 rm** 110.00/150.00 **st.**, 1 suite.

Scandic Crown, 2 Bridge Pl., SW1V 1QA, ☎ 834 8123, Telex 914973, Fax 828 1099, – rm – 180. BY
Meals 16.95/25.00 **st.** and a la carte 5.00 – 10.95 – **205 rm** 120.00/160.00 **st.**, 5 suites – SB.

Rochester, 69 Vincent Sq., SW1P 2PA, ☎ 828 6611, Fax 233 6724 – rest – 60. CY
Meals 17.95 **st.** and a la carte 6.95 – 7.50 – **70 rm** 109.00/129.00 **st.**

Winchester without rest., 17 Belgrave Rd, SW1V 1RB, ☎ 828 2972, Fax 828 5191 – – **18 rm** 60.00/70.00 **st.** BY

Windermere, 142-144 Warwick Way, SW1V 4JE, ☎ 834 5163, Fax 630 8831 – rest . BY
Meals (residents only) (dinner only) 9.00 **t.** and a la carte – **23 rm** 46.00/82.00 **t.**

Collin House without rest., 104 Ebury St., SW1W 9QD, ☎ 730 8031, Fax 730 8031 – *closed 2 weeks Christmas* – **13 rm** 36.00/60.00 **t.** AY

XXX **Auberge de Provence** (at St. James Court H.), Buckingham Gate, SW1E 6AF ☎ 821 1899, Fax 630 7587 – . CX
closed Saturday lunch, Sunday, 1 week January, 2 weeks August and Bank Holidays – **Meals** - French - 24.50/40.00 **t.**

XXX **Inn of Happiness** (at St. James Court H.), Buckingham Gate, SW1E 6AF, ☎ 821 1931 Fax 630 7587 – . CX
closed Saturday lunch – **Meals** - Chinese - (buffet lunch Sunday) 17.50/30.00 **st.** and a la carte.

XXX **L'Incontro,** 87 Pimlico Rd, SW1W 8PH, ☎ 730 6327, Fax 730 5062 – . p. 31 FT
closed lunch Saturday and Sunday, 25-26 December and Bank Holidays – **Meals** - Italian - 18.50 **t.** (lunch) and a la carte 28.00/45.50 **t.**

XXX **Santini,** 29 Ebury St., SW1W 0NZ, ☎ 730 4094, Fax 730 0544 – . ABX
closed lunch Saturday and Sunday and 25-26 December – **Meals** - Italian - 18.30 **t.** (lunch) and a la carte 24.00/43.00 **t.**

XXX **Shepherd's,** Marsham Court, Marsham St., SW1P 4LA, ☎ 834 9552, Fax 233 6047 – p. 26 LZ
closed Saturday, Sunday, Christmas and Bank Holidays – **Meals** - English - (booking essential) 20.95 **t.**

XX **Simply Nico,** 48a Rochester Row, SW1P 1JU, ☎ 630 8061 – . CY
closed Saturday lunch, Sunday, 4 days at Easter, 10 days Christmas-New Year and Bank Holidays – **Meals** (booking essential) 24.00/26.00 **st.** 9.00.

XX **Atrium,** 4 Millbank, SW1P 3JA, ☎ 233 0032, Fax 233 0010 – . LY
closed Saturday lunch, Sunday, Christmas and Bank Holidays – 15.95/18.95 **t.**

XX **Mijanou,** 143 Ebury St., SW1W 9QN, ☎ 730 4099, Fax 823 6402 – ⊁ ▤. AE ⓓ VISA AY **n**
closed Saturday, Sunday, 1 week Easter, 3 weeks August and 2 weeks Christmas – **Meals** 12.00/38.50 **t.** and a la carte.

XX **Ken Lo's Memories of China,** 67-69 Ebury St., SW1W 0NZ, ☎ 730 7734, Fax 730 2992 – ▤. AE ⓓ VISA JCB AY **u**
closed Sunday lunch and Bank Holidays – **Meals** - Chinese - 15.25/29.80 **t.** and a la carte.

XX **L'Amico,** 44 Horseferry Rd, SW1P 2AF, ☎ 222 4680 – AE ⓓ VISA
closed Saturday, Sunday and Bank Holidays – **Meals** - Italian - (booking essential) 16.50/28.00 **t.** and a la carte. p. 26 LY **e**

XX **Hunan,** 51 Pimlico Rd, SW1W 8NE, ☎ 730 5712 – AE VISA p. 25 IZ **a**
closed Sunday lunch and 24 and 25 December – **Meals** - Chinese (Hunan) - a la carte 13.80/18.80 **t.** 🍷 4.50.

XX **Tate Gallery,** Tate Gallery, Millbank, SW1P 4RG, ☎ 887 8877, Fax 887 8007, « Rex Whistler murals » – ▤. VISA p. 26 LZ **c**
closed Sunday, 24 to 26 December and Bank Holidays – **Meals** (booking essential) (lunch only) 12.00/25.00 **t.**

XX **Gran Paradiso,** 52 Wilton Rd, SW1V 1DE, ☎ 828 5818, Fax 828 3608 – AE ⓓ VISA JCB BY **a**
closed Saturday lunch, Sunday, last 2 weeks August and Bank Holidays – **Meals** - Italian - a la carte 16.50/21.60 **t.** 🍷 4.50.

X **Olivo,** 21 Eccleston St., SW1W 9LX, ☎ 730 2505 – ▤. AE VISA AY **z**
closed Saturday lunch, Sunday, 1 week Christmas and Bank Holidays – **Meals** - Italian - 15.50 **t.** (lunch) and dinner a la carte 18.05/25.30 **t.**

X **La Poule au Pot,** 231 Ebury St., SW1W 8UT, ☎ 730 7763 – ▤. AE ⓓ VISA
Meals - French - 12.95 **t.** (lunch) and dinner a la carte 25.85/34.85 **t.** 🍷 5.00. p. 25 IZ **e**

X **Villa Medici,** 35 Belgrave Rd, SW1 5AX, ☎ 828 3613, Fax 402 5358 – AE ⓓ VISA JCB BY **c**
closed Saturday lunch and Sunday – **Meals** - Italian - a la carte approx. 17.90 **t.** 🍷 8.00.

X **La Fontana,** 101 Pimlico Rd, SW1W 8PH, ☎ 730 6630, Fax 730 5577 – AE ⓓ VISA JCB
closed Bank Holidays – **Meals** - Italian - a la carte 21.00/28.00 **t.** 🍷 6.00. p. 31 FT **o**

LONGBRIDGE Warks. – see Warwick.

LONG CRENDON Bucks. 403 404 R 28 pop. 505 – ✉ Aylesbury – ☎ 01844.

♦London 50 – Aylesbury 11 – ♦Oxford 15.

- ✗ **Angel Inn,** Bicester Rd, HP18 9EE, ☎ 208268, « Part 16C inn » – P. AE VISA
  closed Sunday dinner – **Meals** a la carte 14.00/22.95 **t.** 4.75.

LONG EATON Derbs. 402 403 404 Q 25 – see Nottingham (Notts.).

LONGFORD W. Mids. 403 404 P 26 – see Coventry.

LONG MARSTON N. Yorks. 402 Q 22 – see York.

LONG MARSTON Warks. – see Stratford-upon-Avon.

LONG MELFORD Suffolk 404 W 27 **Great Britain G.** – pop. 3 519 – ☎ 01787.

See : Melford Hall★ *AC*.

♦ London 62 – ♦Cambridge 34 – Colchester 18 – ♦Ipswich 24.

- **Bull** (Forte Heritage), Hall St., CO10 9JG, ☎ 378494, Fax 880307, « Part 15C coaching inn » – TV ☎ P – 60. AE VISA JCB
  Meals 11.95/23.95 **t.** and a la carte 6.80 – 8.50 – **25 rm** 60.00/100.00 **t.** – SB.
- **Black Lion,** The Green, CO10 9DN, ☎ 312356, Fax 374557 – TV ☎ P. AE VISA JCB
  Countrymen : Meals *(closed Sunday dinner and Monday lunch)* 13.75/18.75 **t.** and a la carte 4.25 – **8 rm** 45.00/85.00 **t.**, 1 suite – SB.
- **George and Dragon,** Hall St., CO10 9JB, ☎ 371285, Fax 312428, – TV ☎ P – 30. VISA
  Meals a la carte 10.75/15.95 **st.** 3.50 – **6 rm** 30.00/50.00 **st.**
- ✗✗✗ **Chimneys,** Hall St., CO10 9JR, ☎ 379806, Fax 312294, « Part 16C cottage », – AE VISA
  closed Sunday dinner – **Meals** 17.50/25.50 **t.** and a la carte.
- ✗ **Scutchers Bistro,** Westgate St., CO10 9DP, on A 1092 ☎ 310200, Fax 310620, – AE VISA
  closed Sunday, first 2 weeks March and Bank Holiday Mondays – **Meals** a la carte 12.70/18.70 **t.**

LONGNOR Staffs. 402 403 404 O 24 – pop. 1 580 – ✉ Buxton – ☎ 01298.

♦London 161 – Derby 29 – ♦Manchester 31 – ♦Stoke-on-Trent 22.

- Ye Olde Cheshire Cheese, High St., SK17 0NS, ☎ 83218 – TV P
  3 rm.

LONG PRESTON N. Yorks. 402 N 21 – ✉ Skipton – ☎ 01729.

♦London 232 – Bradford 28 – Kendal 36 – ♦Leeds 47.

- **Country House,** BD23 4NJ, ☎ 840246, , – TV P.
  closed mid December-February – **Meals** (residents only) (dinner only) (unlicensed) 12.50 **t.** – **7 rm** 25.00/50.00 **t.**

LONGRIDGE Lancs. 402 M 22 – pop. 7 349 – ☎ 01772.

♦London 241 – Blackburn 12 – Burnley 18.

- ✗✗✗ ✿✿ **Paul Heathcote's** (Heathcote), 104-106 Higher Rd, PR3 3SY, NE : ½ m. by B 5269 following signs for Jeffrey Hill ☎ 784969, Fax 785713 – . AE VISA
  closed lunch Tuesday to Thursday, Saturday lunch and Monday – **Meals** 22.50/35.00 **st.** and a la carte 30.00/38.50 **t.** 8.00
  Spec. Roasted lobster with dried citrus fruit, celery and lobster juice, Breast of Goosnargh duckling with caramelised apples and cider potatoes, Bread and butter pudding with apricot coulis and clotted cream.

LONGSTOCK Hants. 403 404 P 30 – see Stockbridge.

LONG SUTTON Lincs. 404 U 25 – pop. 4 938 – ☎ 01406.

♦London 100 – Lincoln 51 – ♦Leicester 67 – ♦Norwich 54.

- **Forte Travelodge,** Wisbech Rd, PE12 9AG, SE : 1 m. at junction of A 17 with A 1101 ☎ 362230, Reservations (Freephone) 0800 850950 – TV ♿ P. AE VISA.
  Meals (grill rest.) – **40 rm** 34.50 **t.**

> This Guide is not a comprehensive list of all hotels and restaurants, nor even of all good hotels and restaurants in Great Britain and Ireland.
>
> Since our aim is to be of service to all motorists, we must show establishments in all categories and so we have made a selection of some in each.

LOOE Cornwall 403 G 32 The West Country G. – pop. 5 265 – 01503.

See : Town★ – Monkey Sanctuary★ AC.

Bin Down (0150) 34 239 – Whitsand Bay Hotel, Portwrinkle, Torpoint 30276.

The Guildhall, Fore St., PL13 1AA 262072 (summer only).

London 264 – Plymouth 21 – Truro 39.

Klymiarven, Barbican Hill, East Looe, PL13 1BH, E : 2 m. by A 387 off B 3253 or access from town on foot 262333, ≤ Looe and harbour, heated, – . VISA
closed January – **Meals** (bar lunch)/dinner 15.00 **st.** and a la carte 3.75 – **14 rm** 39.00/78.00 **t.** – SB.

Harescombe Lodge, Watergate, PL13 2NE, NW : 2 ¾ m. by A 387 turning right opposite Waylands Farm onto single track road 263158, – .
Meals (by arrangement) 10.00 – **3 rm** 40.00 **s.**

at Sandplace N : 2¼ m. on A 387 – Polperro – 01503 :

Polraen Country House, PL13 1PJ, 263956, Fax 263956, – rest . VISA
Meals 7.95/15.00 **t.** and a la carte 4.95 – **5 rm** 35.00/55.00 **t.** – SB.

at Widegates NE : 3½ m. on B 3253 – Looe – 01503 :

Coombe Farm, PL13 1QN, on B 3253 240223, ≤ countryside, heated, , park –
March-October – **Meals** 12.00 **st.** – **10 rm** 20.00/52.00 **st.** – SB.

at Talland Bay SW : 4 m. by A 387 – Looe – 01503 :

Talland Bay, PL13 2JB, 272667, Fax 272940, ≤, « Country house atmosphere », , heated, – rest . AE VISA.
closed January – **Meals** (bar lunch Monday to Saturday)/dinner 20.00 **t.** and a la carte 4.85 – **17 rm** (dinner included) 65.00/170.00 **t.**, 2 suites – SB.

Allhays Country House, PL13 2JB, 272434, Fax 272929, ≤, – rest . AE VISA JCB
closed Christmas and New Year – **Meals** (dinner only) 14.00 **st.** 4.80 – **7 rm** 28.00/72.00 **st.** – SB.

LOSTWITHIEL Cornwall 403 G 32 The West Country G. – pop. 2 452 – 01208.

Envir. : Lanhydrock★★, N : 4 m. by B 3268 – Restormel Castle★ AC (✻★) N : 1 m. – Bodmin (St. Petroc Church★) NW : 6 m. by B 3268.

Lostwithiel G & C.C., Lower Polscoe 873550 – Lanhydrock, Lostwithiel Road, Bodmin 73600.

Lostwithiel Community Centre, Liddicoat Rd, PL22 0HE 872207.

London 273 – Plymouth 30 – Truro 23.

Restormel Lodge, 17 Castle Hill, PL22 0DD, on A 390 872223, Fax 873568, heated, – . AE VISA
Meals (bar lunch)/dinner 15.00 **t.** and a la carte 4.25 – **32 rm** 45.00/62.00 **t.** – SB.

LOUGHBOROUGH Leics. 402 403 404 Q 25 – pop. 46 867 – 01509.

Lingdale, Joe Moore's Lane, Woodhouse Eaves 890703.

John Storer House, Wards End, LE11 3HA 218113.

London 117 – Birmingham 41 – Leicester 11 – Nottingham 15.

Quality Friendly, New Ashby Rd, LE11 0EX, W : 2 m. on A 512 211800, Fax 211868, , , , – rm – 225. AE VISA
Meals 9.50/13.50 **st.** and dinner a la carte – 7.75 – **94 rm** 57.50/82.00 **st.**

Cedars, Cedar Rd, LE11 2AB, SE : 1 m. by Leicester Rd 214459, Fax 233573, , heated, – . AE VISA.
Meals *(closed Sunday dinner)* (bar lunch Monday to Saturday)/dinner 11.95 **t.** 4.80 – **36 rm** 43.00/53.00 **t.**

Garendon Lodge, 136 Leicester Rd, LE11 2AQ, S : ¾ m. on A 6 211120 – . AE VISA.
Meals 6.00 **s.** – **4 rm** 25.00/38.00 **s.** – SB.

Garendon Park, 92 Leicester Rd, LE11 2AQ, S : ½ m. on A 6 236557, Fax 265559 – rest . AE VISA JCB
Meals a la carte approx. 11.60 **st.** – **9 rm** 20.00/45.00 **st.** – SB.

at Quorndon SE : 3 m. by A 6 – Loughborough – 01509 :

Quorn Country, 66 Leicester Rd, LE12 8BB, 415050, Fax 415557, – rm rm – 50. AE VISA
Meals *(closed Saturday lunch)* 10.95/18.95 **t.** and a la carte – 8.95 – **17 rm** 79.50/92.00 **t.**, 2 suites – SB.

Quorn Grange, 88 Wood Lane, LE12 8DB, 412167, Fax 415621, – – 100. AE VISA JCB
Meals *(closed Saturday lunch)* 9.85/25.30 **st.** and a la carte – 6.85 – **16 rm** 72.00/88.00 **st.**, 1 suite.

ATS Bridge St. 218447/218472

LOUTH Lincs. 402 404 U 23 pop. 14 248 – ☎ 01507.

♦London 156 – Boston 34 – Great Grimsby 17 – Lincoln 26.

Kenwick Park ⛱, LN11 8NR, SE : 2 ¼ m. by B 1520 on A 157 ☎ 608806, Fax 60802?, ≘s, 18, park, squash – ⚓ rest TV ☎ P – 30. AE VISA
Meals a la carte 18.95/29.95 **st.** 4.50 – **19 rm** 79.50/120.00 **st.** – SB.

Beaumont, 66 Victoria Rd, LN11 0BX, ☎ 605005, Fax 607768 – TV ☎ P – 100. AE VISA.
Meals 13.95 **t.** and a la carte 5.50 – **16 rm** 40.00/70.00 **t.** – SB.

Brackenborough Arms, Cordeaux Corner, Brackenborough, LN11 0SZ, N : 2 m. by A 16 ☎ 609169, Fax 609413 – TV ☎ P – 30. AE VISA JCB.
closed 25 and 26 December – **Meals** (bar dinner Sunday) a la carte 14.25/22.45 **t.** 5.00 – **18 rm** 52.50/54.50 **t.** – SB.

ATS 179 Newmarket ☎ 601975

LOWER SLAUGHTER Glos. 403 404 O 28 – see Bourton-on-the-Water.

LOWESTOFT Suffolk 404 Z 26 **Great Britain G.** – pop. 62 907 – ☎ 01502.

Envir. : The Broads★.

18, 9 Rookery Park, Carlton Colville ☎ 560380.

East Point Pavillion, Royal Plain, NR33 0AP ☎ 523000.

♦London 116 – ♦Ipswich 43 – ♦Norwich 30.

Hatfield, Esplanade, NR33 0QP, ☎ 565337, Fax 511885 – TV ☎ P – 55. AE VISA.
Meals 11.00/15.00 **t.** and a la carte 4.95 – **33 rm** 45.00/98.00 **t.** – SB.

Rockville House, 6 Pakefield Rd, NR33 0HS, ☎ 581011, Fax 581011 – ⚓ rest TV. VISA.
closed Christmas-New Year – **Meals** 10.75 **st.** 2.75 – **7 rm** 21.00/43.00 **st.** – SB.

at Oulton NW : 2 m. by B 1074 – ✉ Lowestoft – ☎ 01502 :

Parkhill, Parkhill, NR32 5DQ, N : ½ m. on A 1117 ☎ 730322, Fax 731695, – ⚓ TV ☎ P – 150. AE VISA
Meals *(closed Sunday dinner)* 12.00/25.00 **st.** and a la carte 5.00 – **16 rm** 48.00/60.00 **st.**, 2 suites – SB.

ATS 263 Whapload Rd ☎ 561581

LOW FELL Tyne and Wear – see Gateshead.

LOWICK BRIDGE Cumbria 402 K 21 – see Ulverston.

LOW LAITHE N. Yorks. – see Pateley Bridge.

LUCKINGTON Wilts. 403 404 N 29 pop. 508 – ✉ Chippenham – ☎ 01666.

♦London 116 – ♦Bristol 20 – Gloucester 32 – Swindon 27.

Manor Farm without rest., Alderton, SN14 6NL, SE : 1¼ m. by Alderton rd ☎ 840271, – ⚓ TV P.
3 rm 28.00/50.00 **s.**

LUDLOW Shrops. 403 L 26 **Great Britain G.** – pop. 9 395 – ☎ 01584.

See : Town★ – Castle★ *AC* – Feathers Hotel★ – St. Laurence's Parish Church★ (Misericords★).

Exc. : Stokesay Castle★ *AC*, NW : 6½m. by A 49.

Castle St., SY8 1AS ☎ 875053.

♦London 162 – ♦Birmingham 39 – Hereford 24 – Shrewsbury 29.

Feathers, Bull Ring, SY8 1AA, ☎ 875261, Fax 876030, « Part Elizabethan house » – ⚓ rest TV ☎ P – 60. AE VISA
Meals 11.00/19.50 **st.** and a la carte 5.00 – **40 rm** 72.00/140.00 **st.** – SB.

Overton Grange, Hereford Rd, SY8 4AD, S : 1 ¾ m. on B 4361 ☎ 873500, Fax 873524 – TV ☎ P – 160. AE VISA.
Meals 11.50/19.50 **t.** and a la carte 4.95 – **16 rm** 35.00/92.00 **t.** – SB.

Dinham Hall, Dinham, SY8 1EJ, ☎ 876464, Fax 876019, ≘s, – TV ☎ P. AE VISA JCB
Meals 19.50 **st.** (dinner) and lunch a la carte 10.70/17.25 **st.** 5.90 – **11 rm** 62.00/105.00 **st.** – SB.

Cliffe ⛱, Dinham, SY8 2JE, W : ½ m. via Dinham Bridge ☎ 872063, – TV ☎ P. VISA
Meals *(closed Sunday dinner)* (bar lunch Monday to Saturday)/dinner 11.95 **st.** – **9 rm** 27.50/54.00 **t.** – SB.

⌂ **Number Twenty Eight,** 28 Lower Broad St., SY8 1PQ, ☎ 876996, Fax 876996 – ⊭ rest TV. AE VISA
Meals 16.00 **st.** 5.75 – **4 rm** 40.00/60.00 **st.** – SB.

⌂ **Dinham Weir,** Dinham Bridge, SY8 1EH, ☎ 874431, ≤, – ⊭ rm TV ☎ P. AE VISA JCB.
Meals 12.50 **st.** and a la carte – **8 rm** 50.00/65.00 **st.** – SB.

⌂ **Cecil,** Sheet Rd, SY8 1LR, ☎ 872442, Fax 872442, – ⊭ TV P. VISA
Meals (by arrangement) 11.00 **st.** 3.50 – **10 rm** 18.00/42.00 **st.** – SB.

XX ✿ **Merchant House** (Hill), Lower Corve St., SY8 1DU, ☎ 875438, Fax 875438 – ⊭. AE VISA JCB
closed Sunday, Monday and 1 week June – **Meals** (dinner only and lunch Friday and Saturday) 27.50 **st.**
Spec. Grilled red mullet with ginger, garlic and tomato, Roast rack of lamb with Jabron potato, Rhubarb and frangipane tart.

XX **Oaks,** 17 Corve St., SY8 1DA, ☎ 872325 – ⊭. VISA
closed Monday, 2 weeks January and 1 week November – **Meals** (lunch booking essential) 15.70/22.70 **t.** 7.75.

ATS Weeping Cross Lane ☎ 872401

LUTON Beds. 404 S 28 **Great Britain G.** – pop. 171 671 – ☎ 01582.
See : Luton Hoo★ (Wernher Collection★★) *AC* X.
Stockwood Park, London Rd ☎ 413704, X – 18, 9 South Beds, Warden Hill Rd, ☎ 575201.
Luton International Airport : ☎ 405100, E : 1½m. X – **Terminal** : Luton Bus Station.
65-67 Bute St., LU1 2EY ☎ 401579.
London 35 – ◆Cambridge 36 – ◆Ipswich 93 – ◆Oxford 45 – Southend-on-Sea 63.

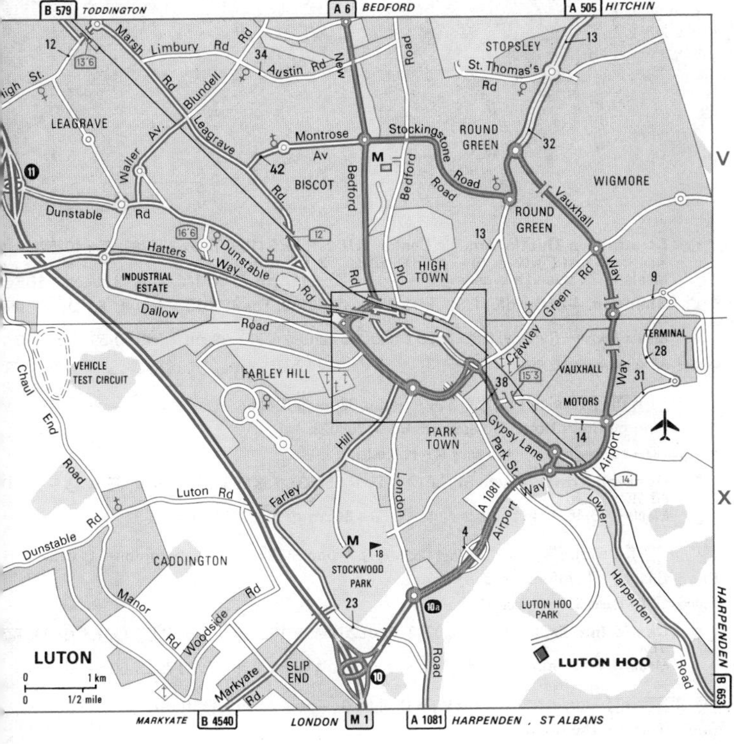

Capability Green	X 4	Kimpton Road	X 14	Stopsley Way	X 32
Eaton Green Road	V 9	Newlands Road	X 23	Trinity Road	V 34
Grange Avenue	V 12	Percival Way	X 28	Windmill Road	X 38
Hitchin Road	V 13	Spittlesey Road	X 31	Woodland Avenue	V 42

LUTON

Arndale Centre . . . . YZ
George St . . . . Z

Bute Street . . . . Y 3
Church Street . . . . Y 5
Dallow Road . . . . Y 7
Dunstable Road . . . . Y 8
King Street . . . . Z 16
Liverpool Road . . . . Y 17
Manchester Street . . . . Y 19
Market Hill . . . . Z 20
Mill Street . . . . Y 2
Old Bedford Road . . . . Y 2
Park Square . . . . Z 2
Park Street West . . . . Z 2
Silver Street . . . . Y 3
Upper George Street . . . . Z 3
Windmill Road . . . . Z 3

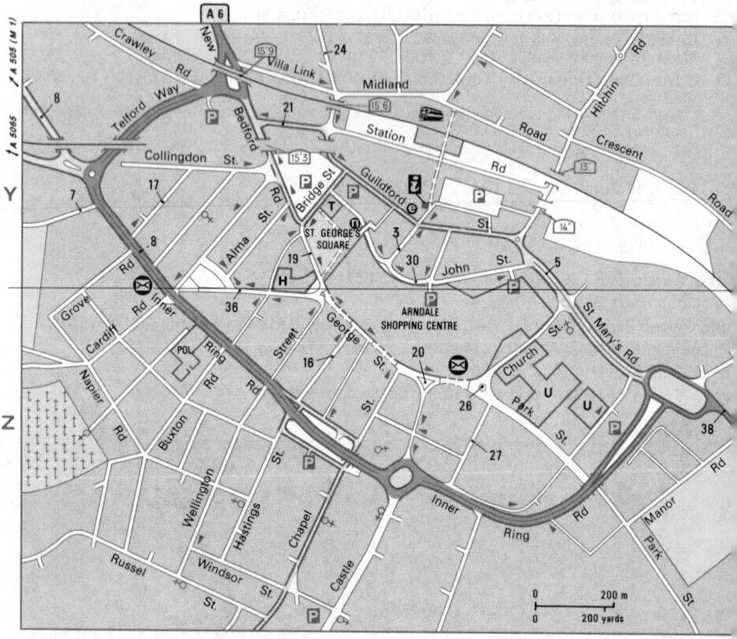

Strathmore Thistle, Arndale Centre, LU1 2TR, ✆ 34199, Telex 825763, Fax 402528 – rm rest – 300. AE VISA JCB. Y
Meals 17.25 **st.** and a la carte 5.50 – 8.75 – **147 rm** 78.00/110.00 **st.**, 3 suites – SB.

Shannon, 40a Guildford St., LU1 2PA, ✆ 482119, Fax 482818 – TV. AE VISA Y
Meals *(closed Sunday)* 6.95/12.95 **t.** and a la carte 4.00 – **28 rm** 49.50/59.50 **t.** – SB.

ATS 67 Kingsway ✆ 597519 ATS High St., Oakley Rd, Leagrave ✆ 507020/59238

LUTTERWORTH Leics. 403 404 Q 26 – pop. 7 380 – 01455.

Ullesthorpe Court Hotel, Frolesworth Rd ✆ 209023.

London 93 – Birmingham 34 – Coventry 14 – Leicester 16.

Denbigh Arms, 24 High St., LE17 4AD, ✆ 553537, Fax 556627 – rm TV – 50. AE VISA
Meals 6.95/16.95 **st.** and a la carte 5.50 – **34 rm** 55.00/80.00 **st.** – SB.

LYDFORD Devon 403 H 32 **The West Country G.** – pop. 1 734 – ✉ Okehampton – 01822.

See : Village★★ (Lydford Gorge★★).

London 234 – Exeter 33 – Plymouth 24.

Castle Inn, EX20 4BH, ✆ 820242, Fax 820454, « 16C inn », – TV. AE VISA JCB
Meals (bar lunch)/dinner 14.95 **t.** and a la carte 4.65 – **8 rm** 28.75/57.50 **t.** – SB.

LYME REGIS Dorset 403 L 31 **The West Country G.** – pop. 3 566 – 01297.

See : Town★ – The Cobb★.

Timber Hill ✆ 442963/442043.

Guildhall Cottage, Church St., DT7 3BS ✆ 442138.

London 160 – Dorchester 25 – Exeter 31 – Taunton 27.

Alexandra, Pound St., DT7 3HZ, ℘ 442010, Fax 443229, ≤, – TV ☎ P. VISA.
closed mid December-late January – **Meals** 12.50/18.00 **t.** and a la carte 4.55 – **26 rm** 45.00/105.00 **t.** – SB.

Kersbrook, Pound Rd, DT7 3HX, ℘ 442596, – TV P. VISA.
closed 5 January-12 February – **Meals** (restricted menu Sunday dinner residents only) (dinner only) 9.50 **t.** and a la carte 4.50 – **10 rm** 45.50/70.00 **t.** – SB.

Red House without rest., Sidmouth Rd, DT7 3ES, W : ¾ m. on A 3052 ℘ 442055, Fax 442055, – TV P.
March-November – **3 rm** 30.00/48.00 **s.**

White House without rest., 47 Silver St., DT7 3HR, ℘ 443420, ≤ – TV P
Easter-October – **7 rm** 18.00/40.00 **st.**

at Uplyme (Devon) NW : 1 ¼ m. on A 3070 – ✉ Lyme Regis – 01297 :

Amherst Lodge Farm without rest., DT7 3XH, NW : 1 m. by A 3070, taking left turn in Yawl to Cathole ℘ 442773, – TV P.
March-October – **3 rm** 30.00/57.50 **s.**

LYMINGTON Hants. 403 404 P 31 – pop. 7 838 – 01590.

to the Isle of Wight (Yarmouth) (Wightlink Ltd) frequent services daily (30 mn).

St. Barb Museum & Visitor Information Centre, New St. ℘ 672422 (summer only).

London 104 – Bournemouth 18 – Southampton 19 – Winchester 32.

Stanwell House, 15 High St., SO41 9AA, ℘ 677123, Fax 677756, – TV ☎ – 25. VISA
Meals 12.95/14.95 **t.** and a la carte – **33 rm** 55.00/85.00 **t.** – SB.

Passford House, Mount Pleasant Lane, Mount Pleasant, SO41 8LS, NW : 2 m. by A 337 and Sway rd ℘ 682398, Fax 683494, ≤, heated, park, – TV ☎ P – 80. VISA JCB
Meals 11.95/22.50 **t.** and a la carte 6.75 – **54 rm** 75.00/135.00 **t.**, 1 suite – SB.

Albany House, 3 Highfield, SO41 9GB, ℘ 671900, – rest TV P.
closed Christmas – **Meals** (by arrangement) 14.50 **st.** – **3 rm** 26.00/56.00 **st.** – SB.

Efford Cottage, Everton, SO41 0JD, W : 2 m. on A 337 ℘ 642315, Fax 642315, – TV P
Meals (by arrangement) 15.00 **st.** – **3 rm** 34.00/40.00 **s.** – SB.

Gordleton Mill with rm, Silver St., Hordle, SO41 6DJ, NW : 3½ m. by A 337 and Sway Rd ℘ 682219, Fax 683073, « Part 17C mill, riverside setting », – rest TV ☎ P. VISA JCB.
closed 2 to 17 January – **Provence : Meals** - French - *(closed Monday)* (booking essential) 20.00/40.00 **t.** and a la carte 43.00/48.00 **t.** – **7 rm** 97.00/129.00 **t.** – SB.

Limpets, 9 Gosport St., SO41 9BG, ℘ 675595 – VISA
closed November and 25-26 December – **Meals** *(closed Sunday and Monday)* 17.00/22.00 **t.** and a la carte.

ATS Marsh Lane ℘ 675938/9

LYMPSTONE Devon 403 J 32 – see Exmouth.

LYNDHURST Hants. 403 404 P 31 **Great Britain G.** – pop. 3 141 – 01703.

Envir. : New Forest★★ (Bolderwood Ornamental Drive★★, Rhinefield Ornamental Drive★★).

18, 9 Dibden, Main Rd ℘ 845596 – 18 New Forest, Southampton Rd ℘ 282752.

New Forest Museum & Visitor Centre, Main Car Park, SO43 7NY ℘ 282269.

London 95 – Bournemouth 20 – Southampton 10 – Winchester 23.

Parkhill, Beaulieu Rd, SO43 7FZ, SE : 1 ¼ m. on B 3056 ℘ 282944, Fax 283268, ≤, « Tastefully furnished country house », heated, park – rest TV ☎ P – 45. VISA JCB.
Meals 15.00/35.00 **t.** and a la carte 7.95 – **17 rm** 53.00/126.00 **t.**, 3 suites – SB.

Crown, 9 High St., SO43 7NF, ℘ 282922, Fax 282751, – TV ☎ P – 35. VISA JCB
Meals (bar lunch Monday to Saturday)/dinner 17.00 **st.** and a la carte 6.00 – **38 rm** 68.00/120.00 **st.**, 1 suite – SB.

Beaulieu, Beaulieu Rd, SO42 7YQ, SE : 3½ m. on B 3056 ℘ 293344, Fax 292729, – rest TV ☎ P – 30. VISA
Meals (dinner only and Sunday lunch)/dinner 25.00 **st.** and a la carte 5.40 – **17 rm** 45.00/85.00 **st.**, 1 suite – SB.

Ormonde House, Southampton Rd, SO43 7BT, ℘ 282806, Fax 282004, – rest TV ☎ P. VISA
closed 18 to 28 December – **Meals** *(closed Sunday)* (dinner only) (by arrangement) 14.00 **st.** 6.00 – **14 rm** 30.00/70.00 **st.** – SB.

Whitemoor House, Southampton Rd, SO43 7BU, ℘ 282186 – TV P. VISA.
Meals (by arrangement) 15.00 – **6 rm** 25.00/60.00 **st.** – SB.

LYNMOUTH Devon 403 I 30 – see Lynton.

LYNTON Devon 403 I 30 The West Country G. – pop. 1 870 (inc. Lynmouth) – ☎ 01598.

See : Town★ (≤★★).

Envir. : Valley of the Rocks★, W : 1 m. – Watersmeet★, E : 1½m. by A 39.

Exc. : Exmoor National Park★★ – Doone Valley★, SE : 7 ½ m. by A 39 (access from Oare on foot).

Town Hall, Lee Rd, EX35 6BT ☎ 752225.

London 206 – Exeter 59 – Taunton 44.

Lynton Cottage, North Walk Hill, EX35 6ED, ☎ 752342, Fax 752597, ≤ bay and Countisbury Hill, – TV ☎ P. AE VISA JCB
closed January – **Meals** (lunch by arrangement)/dinner 28.50 **st.** and a la carte 15.00/25.50 **st.** 6.00 – **16 rm** (dinner included) 60.00/143.00 **st.** – SB.

Hewitt's at the Hoe, North Walk, EX35 6HJ, ☎ 752293, Fax 752489, ≤ bay and Countisbury Hill, « Victorian house in wooded cliffside setting », park – TV ☎ P. VISA JCB
closed December and January – **Meals** (dinner only) 16.00 **st.** 5.00 – **9 rm** 29.00/70.00 **st.**

Highcliffe House, Sinai Hill, EX35 6AR, ☎ 752235, Fax 752235, ≤ bay and Countisbury Hill, « Antiques », – TV P. VISA.
Meals (residents only) (dinner only) 16.50 **st.** 5.25 – **6 rm** 45.00/70.00 **st.** – SB.

Seawood, North Walk, EX35 6HJ, ☎ 752272, ≤ bay and headland – rest TV P
April-October – **Meals** (dinner only) 12.00 **t.** – **12 rm** (dinner included) 37.00/74.00 **t.** – SB.

Castle Hill House, Castle Hill, EX35 6JA, ☎ 752291, Fax 752291 – rest TV. VISA JCB
Meals (dinner only) a la carte 10.95/15.00 **st.** 4.50 – **9 rm** 25.00/40.00 **st.** – SB.

Chough's Nest, North Walk, EX35 6HJ, ☎ 753315, ≤ bay and Countisbury Hill – TV P. AE VISA.
April-October – **Meals** 13.50 **st.** 3.60 – **12 rm** 29.00/58.00 **st.**

Victoria Lodge, 30-31 Lee Rd, EX35 6BS, ☎ 753203, Fax 753203, – TV P. VISA
closed December and January – **Meals** 14.00 4.00 – **10 rm** 30.00/60.00 **st.** – SB.

Rockvale, Lee Rd, EX35 6HW, off Lee Rd ☎ 752279, ≤ – TV ☎ P. VISA.
March-October – **Meals** (by arrangement) 12.00 **st.** 3.50 – **8 rm** 18.00/44.00 **st.** – SB.

Longmead House, 9 Longmead, EX35 6DQ, ☎ 752523, – P
April-October – **Meals** 11.00 **st.** 4.00 – **8 rm** 16.00/42.00 **st.** – SB.

at Lynmouth – ☎ 01598 :

Tors, EX35 6NA, ☎ 753236, Fax 752544, ≤ Lynmouth and bay, heated, – TV ☎ P. AE VISA JCB
closed 3 January-1 March – **Meals** 19.00 **st.** (dinner) and a la carte 17.50/25.50 **st.** 5.75 – **35 rm** 37.00/94.00 **st.** – SB.

Rising Sun, Harbourside, EX35 6EQ, ☎ 753223, Fax 753480, ≤, « Part 14C inn », – TV ☎. AE VISA.
Meals (lunch by arrangement) a la carte 21.50/31.00 **st.** 6.50 – **15 rm** 44.50/95.00 **st.**, 1 suite – SB.

Countisbury Lodge, Tors Park, EX35 6NB, off Countisbury Hill ☎ 752388, ≤ – P. VISA
March-mid November and Christmas – **Meals** 13.00 **st.** 4.00 – **6 rm** 49.00/54.00 **st.** – SB.

Heatherville, Tors Park, EX35 6NB, by Tors Rd ☎ 752327, ≤ – rest TV P
Easter-October – **Meals** 13.00 **s.** – **8 rm** 22.50/45.00 **s.** – SB.

Seaview Villa, 6 Summerhouse Path, EX35 6ES, off Watersmeet Rd ☎ 753460 – TV
Meals (communal dining) 11.50 **s.** 3.50 – **6 rm** 16.50/40.00 **s.** – SB.

at Hillsford Bridges SE : 4½ m. by A 39 – ✉ Lynton – ☎ 01598 :

Combe Park, EX35 6LE, ☎ 752356, – rest P
April-October – (dinner only) 18.00 **t.** 8.50 – **9 rm** (dinner included) 63.00/95.00 **t.** – SB.

at Woody Bay W : 3¼ m. on Coast road – ✉ Parracombe – ☎ 01598 :

Woody Bay, EX31 4QX, ☎ 763264, Fax 763264, ≤ Woody Bay – rest TV P. VISA
restricted opening November-March – **Meals** (bar lunch)/dinner 17.50 **st.** and a la carte 4.75 – **12 rm** (dinner included) 48.00/96.00 **st.** – SB.

at Martinhoe W : 4¼ m. via Coast road – ✉ Barnstaple – ☎ 01598 :

Old Rectory, EX31 4QT, ☎ 763368, Fax 763567, – TV P.
Easter-October – **Meals** (dinner only) 25.00 **t.** 6.00 – **8 rm** (dinner included) 65.00/120.00 **t.** – SB.

LYONSHALL Heref. and Worcs. 403 L 27 – see Kington.

LYTHAM Lancs. 402 L 22 – see Lytham St. Anne's.

The Guide is updated annually so renew your Guide every year.

LYTHAM ST. ANNE'S Lancs. 402 L 22 – pop. 40 866 – ☎ 01253.

Fairhaven, Lytham Hall Park, Ansdell ☎ 736741 – St. Annes Old Links, Highbury Rd ☎ 723597.

290 Clifton Drive South, FY8 1LH ☎ 725610.

London 237 – Blackpool 7 – Liverpool 44 – Preston 13.

Dalmeny, 19-33 South Promenade, FY8 1LX, ☎ 712236, Fax 724447, ≤, squash – rest – 200. VISA.
closed 24 to 26 December – **C'est la vie : Meals** *(closed Sunday and Monday)* a la carte 14.85/23.85 **t.** – **Carvery : Meals** 10.00/12.50 **t.** and a la carte – 6.00 – **130 rm** 40.00/89.00 **st.** – SB.

Bedford, 307-311 Clifton Drive South, FY8 1HN, ☎ 724636, Fax 729244, – rest – 100. VISA JCB
Meals 7.50/15.00 **st.** and a la carte 4.25 – **36 rm** 37.50/59.00 **st.** – SB.

at Lytham SE : 3 m. by A 584 – ☎ 01253 :

Clifton Arms, West Beach, FY8 5QJ, ☎ 739898, Fax 730657, ≤, – – 150. VISA.
Meals 13.50/20.00 **st.** and a la carte 7.50 – **40 rm** 79.00/99.00 **st.**, 3 suites – SB.

MACCLESFIELD Ches. 402 403 404 N 24 – pop. 49 024 – ☎ 01625.

The Tytherington ☎ 434562 – Shrigley Hall, Shrigley Park, Pott Shrigley ☎ 575755.

Council Offices, Town Hall, SK10 1DX ☎ 504114.

London 186 – Chester 38 – Manchester 18 – Stoke-on-Trent 21.

Sutton Hall, Bullocks Lane, Sutton, SK11 0HE, SE : 2 m. by A 523 ☎ (01260) 253211, Fax 252538, park – . VISA.
Meals 10.95/19.95 **st.** 5.65 – **10 rm** 68.95/85.00 **st.**

Chadwick House, 55 Beech Lane, SK10 2DS, N : ¼ m. on A 538 ☎ 615558, Fax 615558, – . VISA.
Meals *(closed Friday to Sunday)* (residents only) (dinner only) 8.95 **st.** 3.00 – **13 rm** 38.00/60.00 **st.**

at Bollington N : 3½ m. by A 523 on B 5090 – ✉ Macclesfield – ☎ 01625 :

Mauro's, 88 Palmerston St., SK10 5PW, ☎ 573898 – VISA
closed Saturday lunch and Sunday – **Meals** - Italian - (lunch first Sunday each month) a la carte 13.65/26.75 **t.**

at Adlington N : 5 m. on A 523 – ✉ Macclesfield – ☎ 01625 :

Shrigley Hall, Shrigley Park, Pott Shrigley, SK10 5SB, E : 2 m. on Pott Shrigley rd ☎ 575757, Fax 573323, « Early 19C country house in park », squash – rm – 250. VISA
Oakridge : Meals *(closed Saturday lunch)* (dancing Saturday evening) 16.50/19.50 **st.** and a la carte 4.50 – **156 rm** 60.00/150.00 **st.** – SB.

Forte Travelodge, London Rd South, SK12 4NA, on A 523 ☎ 875292, Reservations (Freephone) 0800 850950 – . VISA
Meals (grill rest.) – **32 rm** 34.50 **t.**

ATS 115 Hurdsfield Rd ☎ 425481/425233/424237

MACKWORTH Derbs. 402 403 404 P 25 – see Derby.

MADINGLEY Cambs. 404 U 27 – see Cambridge.

MAGHAM DOWN E. Sussex – see Hailsham.

MAIDENBOWER W. Sussex – see Crawley.

MAIDENCOMBE Devon 403 J 32 – see Torquay.

MAIDENHEAD Berks. 404 R 29 – pop. 59 605 – ☎ 01628.

Bird Hill, Drift Rd, Hawthorn Hill ☎ 771030/75588/26035 – Shoppenhangers Rd ☎ 24693 X.

The Library, St. Ives Rd, SL6 1QU ☎ 781110.

London 33 – Oxford 32 – Reading 13.

Plan on next page

Holiday Inn Maidenhead, Manor Lane, SL6 2RA, ☎ 23444, Fax 770035, squash – rm rest – 400. VISA JCB. X n
Promenade : Meals *(closed lunch Saturday and Bank Holidays)* 15.95/19.50 **st.** and a la carte 9.95 – 11.50 – **187 rm** 120.00/135.00 **st.**, 2 suites.

Fredrick's, Shoppenhangers Rd, SL6 2PZ, ☎ 35934, Fax 771054, – – 150. VISA. X c
closed 24 to 30 December – **Meals** - (see below) – **36 rm** 138.00/185.00 **t.**, 1 suite.

MAIDENHEAD

High Street . . . . **Y**
Nicholson's Walk
 Shopping Centre . . . . . **YZ**

Bad Godesberg Way . . . . . **Y** 2
Belmont Park Avenue . . . . **V** 3
Blackamoor Lane . . . . **V** 5
Boyn Hill Avenue . . . . **Z** 6
Braywick Road . . . . **Z** 7
Bridge Street . . . . **Y** 9
College Road . . . . **V** 13
Cookham Road . . . . **Y** 14
Crescent (The) . . . . **Y** 15
Ferry Road . . . . **X** 17
Frascati Way . . . . **YZ** 18
Furze Platt Road . . . . **V** 20
Grenfell Place . . . . **Z** 21
Gringer Hill . . . . **V** 22
Harrow Lane . . . . **V** 24
High Street
 BRAY-ON-THAMES . . . **X** 25
King's Grove . . . . **Z** 27
Linden Avenue . . . . **V** 28
Lower Cookham Road . . . **V** 29
Manor Lane . . . . **X** 31
Market Street . . . . **Y** 32
Norreys Drive . . . . **X** 35
Oldfield Road . . . . **V** 36
Ray Street . . . . **V** 38
Ray Mill Rd West . . . . **V** 39
St. Ives Road . . . . **Y** 41
St. Mark's Road . . . . **V** 42
Stafferton Way . . . . **Z** 43
Upper Bray Road . . . . **X** 45

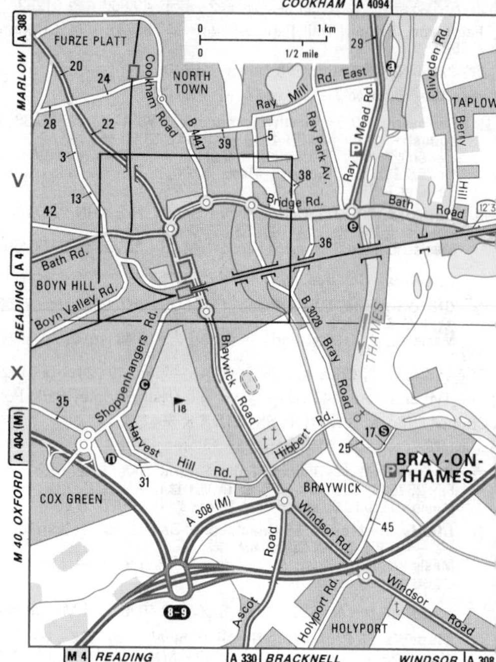

For business or tourist interest :
MICHELIN Red Guide
Main Cities EUROPE.

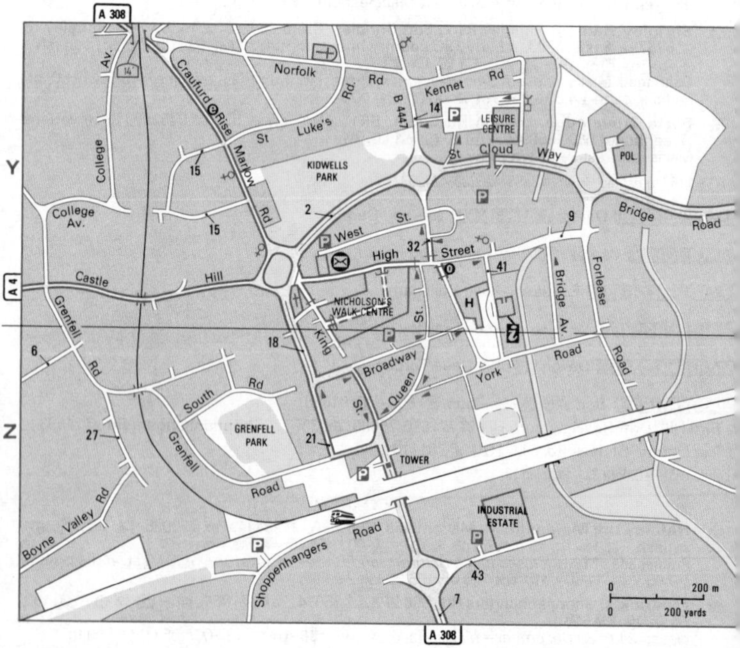

Thames Riviera, at the bridge, SL6 8DW, ☎ 74057, Fax 776586, ← – TV ☎ P – 50. AE VISA. V e
closed 26 to 30 December – **Jerome's: Meals** (light lunch Saturday) 14.50/17.50 **st.** and a la carte – **52 rm** 80.00/125.00 **st.**

Walton Cottage, Marlow Rd, SL6 7LT, ☎ 24394, Fax 773851 – TV ☎ P – 30. AE VISA. Y e
closed 23 December-4 January – **Meals** *(closed Friday to Sunday)* (dinner only) 15.95 **t.** 5.50 – **64 rm** 76.00/104.00 **t.**

Fredrick's (at Fredrick's H.), Shoppenhangers Rd, SL6 2PZ, ☎ 35934, Fax 771054, – P. AE VISA X c
closed Saturday lunch and 24 to 30 December – **Meals** 21.50/29.50 **t.** and a la carte 8.00.

Jasmine Garden, 29 High St., SL6 1JG, ☎ 20334 – AE VISA JCB Y o
Meals - Chinese - 12.50/25.00 **st.** and a la carte.

at Littlewick Green W : 3 1/4 m. by A 4 – V – ✉ Maidenhead – ☎ 01628 :

Crystals, Bath Rd, SL6 3RQ, on A 4 ☎ 822085, Fax 829211 – TV ☎ P – 30. AE VISA JCB.
Meals 13.95 **t.** and a la carte 4.00 – 5.00 – **19 rm** 70.00/85.00 **t.** – SB.

ATS Denmark St., Cordwallis Est. ☎ 20161

MAIDEN NEWTON Dorset 403 404 M 31 **The West Country G.** – pop. 937 – ✉ Dorchester – ☎ 01300.

Envir. : Cerne Abbas★, NE : 5½m..

London 143 – Bournemouth 35 – Bristol 55 – Taunton 34 – Weymouth 16.

Le Petit Canard, Dorchester Rd, DT2 0BE, ☎ 320536 – VISA
closed Sunday, Monday and 1 week early January – **Meals** (booking essential) (dinner only) 23.00 **t.** 5.50.

We suggest:

For a successful tour, that you prepare it in advance.

Michelin maps and guides will give you a great deal of useful information on route planning, places of interest, accommodation, prices etc.

MAIDSTONE Kent 404 V 30 **Great Britain G.** – pop. 136 209 – ☎ 01622.

Envir. : Leeds Castle★ *AC*, SE : 4½m. by A 20 and B 2163.

Tudor Park, Ashford Rd, Bearsted ☎ 734334.

The Gatehouse, The Old Palace Gardens, Mill St., ME15 6YE ☎ 673581/602169.

London 36 – Brighton 64 – Cambridge 84 – Colchester 72 – Croydon 36 – Dover 45 – Southend-on-Sea 49.

Stakis Maidstone, Bearsted Rd, ME14 5AA, NE : 1 ½ m. by A 249 ☎ 734322, Fax 734600, – rm rest TV ☎ P – 90. AE VISA JCB.
Meals 9.50/19.50 **st.** and dinner a la carte 9.95 – 8.75 – **136 rm** 85.00/97.00 **st.**, 3 suites – SB.

Grangemoor, 4-8 St. Michael's Rd, ME16 8BS, off Tonbridge Rd ☎ 677623, Fax 678246, – TV ☎ P – 100. AE VISA
Meals 12.00/16.00 **t.** and a la carte 3.80 – **47 rm** 38.00/52.00 **t.**

Travel Inn, London Rd, ME16 0HG, NW : 1 m. on A 20 ☎ 752515, Fax 672469 – rm TV P. AE VISA
Meals (grill rest.) – 4.95 – **40 rm** 34.50 **t.**

Rock House without rest., 102 Tonbridge Rd, ME16 8SL, ☎ 751616, Fax 756119 – TV P. AE VISA.
closed 24 December-1 January – **11 rm** 35.00/46.00 **st.**

at Bearsted E : 3 m. by A 249 on A 20 – ✉ Maidstone – ☎ 01622 :

Tudor Park H. Country Club Resort (Country Club), Ashford Rd, ME14 4NQ, E : 1 m. on A 20 ☎ 734334, Fax 735360, ←, park, – rm TV ☎ P – 300. AE VISA
Meals (carving lunch)/dinner 18.00 **t.** and a la carte 6.25 – 9.50 – **117 rm** 80.00 **st.** – SB.

Soufflé, The Green, ME14 4DN, off Yeoman Lane ☎ 737065, Fax 737065 – P. AE VISA
closed Monday – **Meals** 14.50/18.50 **t.** and a la carte 4.95.

at Boughton Monchelsea S : 4½ m. by A 229 on B 2163 – ✉ Maidstone – ☎ 01622 :

Tanyard, Wierton Hill, ME17 4JT, S : 1½ m. by Park Lane ☎ 744705, Fax 741998, ←, « 14C tannery standing in orchards », – rest TV ☎ P. AE VISA.
closed Christmas and first 2 weeks January – **Meals** *(closed lunch Saturday to Tuesday)* (lunch booking essential) 20.00/25.00 **t.** 5.00 – **6 rm** 60.00/125.00 **t.**

at Wateringbury SW : 4½ m. on A 26 – ✉ Maidstone – ☎ 01622 :

Wateringbury, Tonbridge Rd, ME18 5NS, ☎ 812632, Fax 812720, – rm TV ☎ P – 75. AE VISA
Meals a la carte 9.25/17.70 **st.** – **40 rm** 59.50/75.00 **st.** – SB.

at Larkfield W : 3 ¼ m. on A 20 – ✉ Maidstone – ☎ 01732 :

Larkfield Priory (Forte), 812 London Rd, ME20 6HJ, ☎ 846858, Fax 846786 – ⇔ TV ☎ P – 80. AE VISA JCB
Meals (bar lunch Monday to Saturday)/dinner a la carte 23.45/30.00 **st.** 6.10 – ☕ 8.50 **52 rm** 59.50 **st.** – SB.

ATS 165 Upper Stone St. ☎ 758738/758664

MALDON Essex 404 W 28 – pop. 10 781 – ☎ 01621.

Forrester Park, Beckingham Rd, Great Totham ☎ 891406 – 9, 9 Bunsay Downs, Littl Baddow Rd, Woodham Walter ☎ (01245) 412648/412369.

Coach Lane, CM9 7UH ☎ 856503.

London 42 – Chelmsford 9 – Colchester 17.

Five Lakes H. Golf & Country Club, Colchester Rd, Tolleshunt Knights, CM9 8HX NE : 8 ¼ m. by B 1026 ☎ 868888, Fax 869696, 18, park, indoor, squash – rest TV ☎ P – 450. AE VISA
Meals 13.25/15.25 **t.** and a la carte – **Camelot : Meals** (Wednesday to Saturday dinner an Sunday lunch) 25.00 **t.** and a la carte – ☕ 7.95 – **110 rm** 85.00/115.00 **st.**, 4 suites – SB.

Blue Boar (Forte), Silver St., CM9 4QE, ☎ 852681, Fax 856202 – ⇔ TV ☎ P – 30. AE VISA JCB.
Meals 12.95/25.00 **t.** and dinner a la carte – ☕ 8.50 – **29 rm** 65.00/75.00 **t.** – SB.

Chigborough Lodge, Chigborough Rd, Heybridge, CM9 4RE, NE : 2½ m. by A 414 of B 1026 ☎ 853590 – P. VISA
closed Sunday dinner, Monday, Tuesday, 2 weeks summer and 2 weeks winter – **Meal** (booking essential) a la carte 13.00/19.75 **st.**

ATS 143-147 High St. ☎ 856541

Le Guide change, changez de guide Michelin tous les ans.

MALMESBURY Wilts. 403 404 N 29 **The West Country G.** – pop. 5 853 – ☎ 01666.

See : Town★ – Market Cross★★ – Abbey★.

Town Hall, Market Lane, SN16 9BZ ☎ 823748.

London 108 – Bristol 28 – Gloucester 24 – Swindon 19.

Whatley Manor, Easton Grey, SN16 0RB, W : 2 ½ m. on B 4040 ☎ 822888 Fax 826120, ≤, « Part 18C manor house », heated, park, – TV ☎ P – 40. AE VISA
Meals 14.50/28.50 **t.** 6.25 – **29 rm** ☕ 76.00/112.00 **t.** – SB.

Old Bell, Abbey Row, SN16 0AG, ☎ 822344, Fax 825145, « Part 13C former abbot hostel », – TV ☎ P – 25. AE VISA JCB
Meals (light lunch)/dinner 24.00 **st.** – **32 rm** ☕ 60.00/115.00 **st.** – SB.

Knoll House, Swindon Rd, SN16 9LU, ☎ 823114, Fax 823897, – TV ☎ P. VISA
Meals 15.00/22.50 **st.** and a la carte 4.50 – **23 rm** ☕ 55.00/85.00 **st.** – SB.

at Crudwell N : 4 m. on A 429 – ✉ Malmesbury – ☎ 01666 :

Crudwell Court, SN16 9EP, ☎ 577194, Fax 577853, « 17C former vicarage, gardens » heated – ⇔ rest TV ☎ P. AE VISA
Meals 12.50/25.95 **t.** – **15 rm** ☕ 50.00/114.00 **t.** – SB.

Mayfield House, SN16 9EW, ☎ 577409, Fax 577977, – TV ☎ P – 30. AE VISA
Meals (bar lunch Monday to Saturday)/dinner 17.95 **t.** 3.75 – **20 rm** ☕ 40.00/58.00 **t.** – SB

MALPAS Ches. 402 403 L 24 – pop. 3 684 – ☎ 01948.

London 177 – Birmingham 60 – Chester 15 – Shrewsbury 26 – Stoke-on-Trent 30.

Market House, Church St., SY14 8NU, ☎ 860400, – VISA
closed Sunday dinner, Monday to Wednesday, 26 to 29 December and 1 to 4 January – **Meals** (booking essential) (dinner only and Sunday lunch)/dinner 11.75 **t.** and a la carte 5.75.

at Tilston NW : 3 m. on Tilston Rd – ✉ Malpas – ☎ 01829 :

Tilston Lodge, SY14 7DR, ☎ 250223, Fax 250223, « Rare breed farm animals », – ⇔ TV P.
Meals (by arrangement) 19.00 **s.** – **3 rm** ☕ 35.00/58.00 **s.**

MALTBY S. Yorks. 402 403 404 P 23 – see Rotherham.

MALTON N. Yorks. 402 R 21 **Great Britain G.** – pop. 4 294 – ☎ 01653.

Envir. : Castle Howard★★ (Park★★★) *AC*, W : 6 m..

18, 9 (2x) Malton & Norton, Welham Park, Welham Rd, Norton ☎ 692959.

58 Market Place, YO17 OLW ☎ 600048.

London 229 – Kingston-upon-Hull 36 – Scarborough 24 – York 17.

Green Man, 15 Market St., YO17 0LY, ☎ 600370, Fax 696006 – TV ☎ P – 80. AE VISA.
Meals (grill rest.) 10.00/15.50 **t.** and a la carte 7.50 – **23 rm** 55.00/110.00 **t.**, 1 suite – SB.

Greenacres Country, Amotherby, YO17 0TG, W : 2 ½ m. on B 1257 ☎ 693623, Fax 693623, – TV P. VISA.
closed mid November-February – **Meals** *(closed Sunday)* (residents only) (dinner only) 12.25 **st.** 3.50 – **9 rm** 27.25/54.50 **st.** – SB.

at Wharram-Le-Street SE : 6 m. on B 1248 – ✉ Malton – ☎ 01944 :

Red House, YO17 9TL, ☎ 768455, – TV P
closed 1 week Christmas – **Meals** (by arrangement) 13.00 **s.** 3.00 – **3 rm** 22.00/44.00 **s.** – SB.

ATS 27 Commercial St., Norton ☎ 692567/693525

MALVERN Heref. and Worcs. 403 404 N 27 – see Great Malvern.

MALVERN WELLS Heref. and Worcs. 403 404 N 27 – see Great Malvern.

MANCHESTER Gtr. Manchester 402 403 404 N 23 **Great Britain G.** – pop. 404 861 – ☎ 0161.
See : City★ - Castefield Heritage Park★ CZ – Town Hall★ CZ – City Art Gallery★ CZ **M2** – Cathedral★ (Stalls and Canopies★) CY.
Heaton Park, Prestwick ☎ 798 0295, ABV – Houldsworth Park, Houldsworth St., Reddish, Stockport ☎ 442 9611 – Chorlton-cum-Hardy, Barlow Hall, Barlow Hall Rd ☎ 881 3139 – William Wroe, Pennybridge Lane, Flixton ☎ 748 8680.
Manchester International Airport : ☎ 489 3000, S : 10 m. by A 5103 – AX – and M 56 – Terminal : Coach service from Victoria Station.
Town Hall, Lloyd St., M60 2LA ☎ 234 3157/8 – Manchester Airport, International Arrivals Hall, Terminal 1, M90 3NY ☎ 436 334.
London 202 – Birmingham 86 – Glasgow 221 – Leeds 43 – Liverpool 35 – Nottingham 72.

Plans on following pages

Victoria and Albert, Water St., M3 4JQ, ☎ 832 1188, Fax 834 2484, « Converted 19C warehouse, television themed interior », – rm rest TV ☎ P – 250. AE VISA. AX **u**
Cafe Maigret : Meals 14.95 **st.** and a la carte - (see also ***Sherlock Holmes*** below) – 11.95 – **128 rm** 132.00 **st.**, 4 suites – SB.

Holiday Inn Crowne Plaza Midland, Peter St., M60 2DS, ☎ 236 3333, Fax 932 4101, squash – rm TV ☎ P – 600. AE VISA JCB. CZ **x**
French rest. : Meals *(closed Sunday)* (dinner only) 32.50 **t.** and a la carte – **Trafford Room : Meals** (carving rest.) 17.95 **st.** – **Wyvern : Meals** *(closed Sunday)* a la carte 12.40/23.40 **t.** – 10.95 – **296 rm** 120.00 **t.**, 7 suites – SB.

Ramada, Blackfriars St., Deansgate, M3 2EQ, ☎ 835 2555, Telex 669699, Fax 835 3077 – rm rest TV ☎ P – 400. AE VISA JCB. CY **v**
Meals 12.50/18.50 **st.** and dinner a la carte 5.75 – 10.50 – **196 rm** 115.00 **st.**, 5 suites.

Copthorne Manchester, Clippers Quay, Salford Quays, M5 2XP, ☎ 873 7321, Telex 669090, Fax 873 7318, – rm rest TV ☎ P – 150. AE VISA. AX **n**
Meals 15.50/18.50 **st.** and a la carte 8.85 – 11.25 – **166 rm** 107.00/117.00 **st.**

Portland Thistle, 3-5 Portland St., Piccadilly Gdns, M1 6DP, ☎ 228 3400, Fax 228 6347, – rm rest TV ☎ P – 270. AE VISA JCB CZ **a**
Meals *(closed Sunday dinner and Bank Holidays)* 16.45/18.45 **st.** and a la carte 5.50 – 9.85 – **204 rm** 102.00/124.00, 1 suite.

Castlefield, Liverpool Rd, M3 4JR, ☎ 832 7073, Fax 839 0326, – rest TV ☎ P – 65 AX **v**
48 rm.

Comfort Friendly Inn, Birch St., Hyde Rd, West Gorton, M12 5NT, SE : 2½ m. by A 57 ☎ 220 8700, Fax 220 8848 – rm TV ☎ P – 100. AE VISA. BX **a**
Meals 9.75 **st.** and a la carte 3.50 – **90 rm** 36.50/52.00 **st.** – SB.

XXX **Sherlock Holmes** (at Victoria and Albert H.), Water St., M3 4JQ, ☎ 832 1188, Fax 832 2484 – P. AE VISA AX **u**
Meals *(closed Sunday)* 19.00/35.00 **st.** and a la carte.

XX **Brasserie St Pierre,** 57-63 Princess St., M2 4EQ, ☎ 228 0231, Fax 228 0231 – AE VISA CZ **s**
closed Saturday lunch, Monday dinner, Sunday, 24 December-2 January and Bank Holidays – **Meals** 12.95 **t.** and a la carte 6.95.

XX **Royal Orchid,** 36 Charlotte St., M1 4FD, ☎ 236 5183, Fax 236 8830. AE VISA CZ **o**
closed Monday and Saturday lunch and Sunday – **Meals** - Thai - 9.50/15.00 **t.** and a la carte.

XX **Isola Bella,** Dolefield, Crown Sq., M3 3EN, ☎ 831 7099, Fax 839 1561 – . AE VISA CZ **e**
closed Bank Holidays – **Meals** - Italian - a la carte 15.30/24.50 **st.** 5.50.

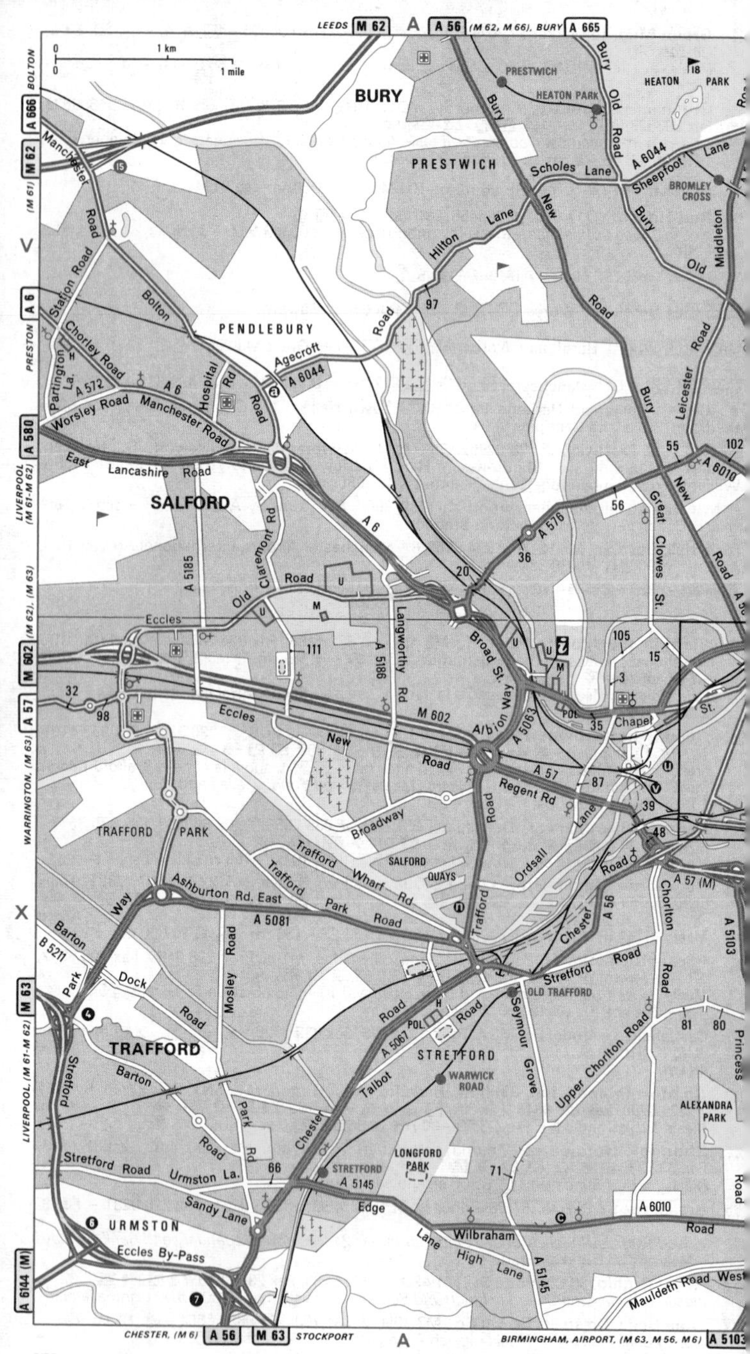
LEEDS M 62
A
A 56 (M 62, M 66), BURY A 665
BOLTON A 666
M 62 (M 61)
PRESTON A 6
LIVERPOOL (M 61-M 62) A 580
(M 62), (M 63) M 602
WARRINGTON, (M 63) A 57
LIVERPOOL, (M 61-M 62) M 63
A 6144 (M)
CHESTER, (M 6) A 56
M 63 STOCKPORT
BIRMINGHAM, AIRPORT, (M 63, M 56, M 6) A 5103
V
X
1 km
1 mile
BURY
PRESTWICH
HEATON PARK
HEATON PARK
BROMLEY CROSS
PENDLEBURY
SALFORD
SALFORD QUAYS
TRAFFORD PARK
TRAFFORD
STRETFORD
OLD TRAFFORD
WARWICK ROAD
LONGFORD PARK
ALEXANDRA PARK
URMSTON
Scholes Lane
Hilton Lane
Agecroft Road
Bury New Road
Bury Old Road
Sheepfoot Lane
Middleton Road
Leicester Road
Great Clowes St.
Manchester Road
Station Road
Bolton Road
Chorley Road
Partington La.
Worsley Road
Hospital Rd
East Lancashire Road
Claremont Rd
Old Road
Eccles Old Road
Langworthy Rd
Broad St.
Albion Way
Eccles New Road
Regent Rd
Ordsall Lane
Chapel St.
Broadway
Trafford Wharf Rd
Trafford Park Road
Trafford Road
Ashburton Rd. East
Trafford Way
Barton Dock Road
Mosley Road
Chester Road
Chorlton Road
Stretford Road
Seymour Grove
Upper Chorlton Road
Princess Road
Talbot Road
Barton Road
Park Rd
Stretford Road
Urmston La.
Sandy Lane
Edge Lane
Wilbraham Road
High Lane
Eccles By-Pass
Mauldeth Road West
A 6044
A 572
A 6
A 5185
A 5186
A 576
A 6010
A 5063
A 57
A 56
A 57 (M)
A 5103
A 5081
B 5211
A 5067
A 5145
M 602

MANCHESTER

BUILT UP AREA

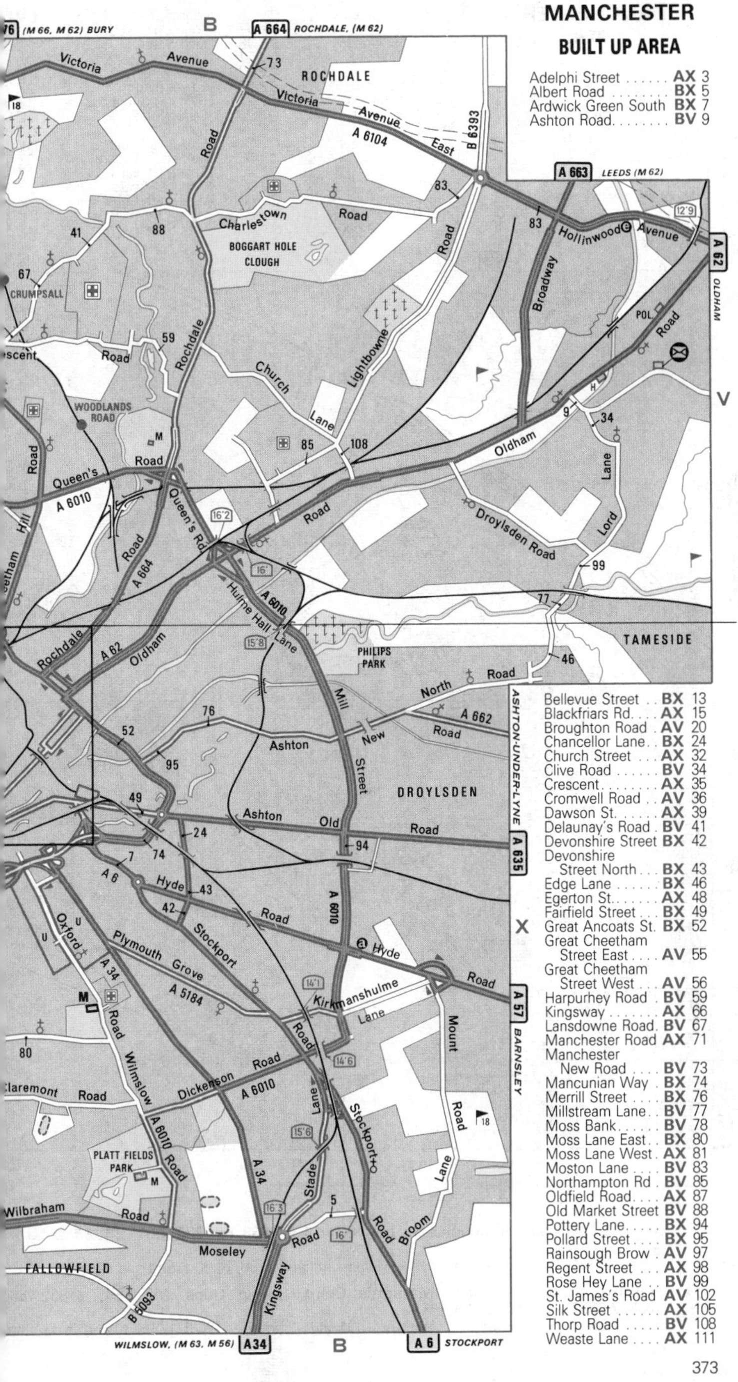

Street	Grid	No.
Adelphi Street	AX	3
Albert Road	BX	5
Ardwick Green South	BX	7
Ashton Road	BV	9
Bellevue Street	BX	13
Blackfriars Rd.	AX	15
Broughton Road	AV	20
Chancellor Lane	BX	24
Church Street	AX	32
Clive Road	BV	34
Crescent	AX	35
Cromwell Road	AV	36
Dawson St.	AX	39
Delaunay's Road	BV	41
Devonshire Street	BX	42
Devonshire Street North	BX	43
Edge Lane	BX	46
Egerton St.	AX	48
Fairfield Street	BX	49
Great Ancoats St.	BX	52
Great Cheetham Street East	AV	55
Great Cheetham Street West	AV	56
Harpurhey Road	BV	59
Kingsway	AX	66
Lansdowne Road	BV	67
Manchester Road	AX	71
Manchester New Road	BV	73
Mancunian Way	BX	74
Merrill Street	BX	76
Millstream Lane	BV	77
Moss Bank	BV	78
Moss Lane East	BX	80
Moss Lane West	AX	81
Moston Lane	BV	83
Northampton Rd	BV	85
Oldfield Road	AX	87
Old Market Street	BV	88
Pottery Lane	BX	94
Pollard Street	BX	95
Rainsough Brow	AV	97
Regent Street	AX	98
Rose Hey Lane	BV	99
St. James's Road	AV	102
Silk Street	AX	105
Thorp Road	BV	108
Weaste Lane	AX	111

MANCHESTER
CENTRE

XX **Giulio's Terrazza,** 14 Nicholas St., M1 4EJ, ℘ 236 4033, Fax 228 6501 – ▤. AE VISA JCB CZ
closed Sunday and Bank Holidays – **Meals** - Italian - 8.50/14.90 **t.** and a la carte 🍷 5.80.

XX **Gaylord,** Amethyst House, Marriott's Court, Spring Gdns, M2 1EA, ℘ 832 486 Fax 832 6037 – ▤. AE VISA CZ
closed 25 December and 1 January – **Meals** - Indian - 12.75/17.95 **t.** and a la cart 🍷 5.45.

Yang Sing, 34 Princess St., M1 4JY, ℘ 236 2200, Fax 236 5934 – ▤. VISA CZ **n**
closed 25 December – **Meals** - Chinese (Canton) - (booking essential) 15.40/32.50 **t.** and a la carte.

Chiang Rai, 16 Princess St., M1 4NB, ℘ 237 9511 – VISA CZ **u**
closed Sunday lunch and Bank Holidays – **Meals** - Thai - 9.00/21.30 **t.** and a la carte.

Market, 104 High St., M4 1HQ, ℘ 834 3743 – VISA JCB CY **o**
closed Sunday to Tuesday, 1 week Easter, August and 1 week Christmas – **Meals** - Bistro - (dinner only) a la carte 14.65/23.05 **t.** 4.75.

Koreana, Kings House, 40a King St. West, M3 2WY, ℘ 832 4330, Fax 832 2293 – VISA JCB CZ **z**
closed lunch Bank Holiday Mondays, Sunday and 1 week Christmas-New Year – **Meals** - Korean - 19.50 **t.**

at Northenden S : 5 ¼ m. by A 5103 – AX – ✉ Manchester – ☎ 0161 :

Forte Posthouse, Palatine Rd, M22 4FH, ℘ 998 7090, Fax 946 0139 – rm – 150. VISA JCB.
Meals a la carte 14.35/22.15 **t.** 6.25 – 7.95 – **190 rm** 59.00 **t.** – SB.

at Didsbury S : 5 ½ m. by A 5103 – AX – on A 5145 – ✉ Manchester – ☎ 0161 :

Est, Est, Est !, 756 Wilmslow Rd, M20 0RN, ℘ 445 8209 – ▤. VISA
closed 25 December – **Meals** - Italian - 9.95/12.95 **t.** and a la carte 4.95.

at Manchester Airport S : 9 m. by A 5103 – AX – off M 56 – ✉ Manchester – ☎ 0161 :

Manchester Airport Hilton, Outwood Lane, Ringway, M22 5WP, ℘ 436 4404, Fax 436 1521, – rm ▤ – 250. VISA JCB.
Meals *(closed Saturday lunch)* 19.50/30.00 **st.** and a la carte 8.00 – **Portico : Meals** *(closed Sunday)* (dinner only) a la carte 28.000 **st.** 9.20 – 12.50 – **222 rm** 111.00/170.00 **st.**

Forte Crest, Ringway Rd, M90 3NS, ℘ 437 5811, Telex 668721, Fax 436 2340, – rm ▤ – 45. VISA.
Meals 16.00/26.00 **st.** and a la carte – 11.00 – **283 rm** 99.00/108.00 **st.**, 2 suites – SB.

Etrop Grange (Regal), Thorley Lane, M90 4EG, ℘ 499 0500, Fax 499 0790 – rm – 40. VISA JCB
Meals 16.50/33.50 **st.** 6.95 – 9.50 – **38 rm** 97.50/110.00 **st.**, 2 suites – SB.

Travel Inn, Finney Lane, Heald Green, SK8 2QH, E : 2 m. by B 5166 ℘ 499 1944, Fax 437 4910 – rm – 70. VISA.
Meals (grill rest.) – 4.95 – **61 rm** 34.50 **t.**

Moss Nook, Ringway Rd, Moss Nook, M22 5WD, ℘ 437 4778, Fax 498 8089 – . VISA
closed Saturday lunch, Sunday, Monday and 2 weeks Christmas – **Meals** 16.50/29.50 **t.** and a la carte 4.50.

at Chorlton-Cum-Hardy SW : 5 m. by A 5103 on A 6010 – ✉ Manchester – ☎ 0161 :

Sabre D'or without rest., 392 Wilbraham Rd, M21 0UH, ℘ 881 5055, Fax 881 1546 – AX **c**
17 rm 25.00/45.00 **st.**

Peking Palace, 285 Barlow Moor Rd, M21 2GH, S : 1 m. on A 5145 ℘ 881 2954 – ▤. VISA
closed Monday except Bank Holidays – **Meals** - Chinese (Peking) - (dinner only) a la carte approx. 16.00 **st.**

at Eccles W : 4 m. by M 602 – AX – ✉ Manchester – ☎ 0161 :

Highbury, 113 Monton Rd, M30 9HQ, NW : 1 ¼ m. by A 576 on B 5229 ℘ 787 8545, Fax 787 9023 – rest . VISA.
closed 24 December-2 January – **Meals** (by arrangement) (residents only) (dinner only) 14.00 **st.** – **11 rm** 41.00/49.00 **st.**

at Worsley W : 7 ¼ m. by M 602 – AV – and M 62 (eastbound) on A 572 – ✉ Manchester – ☎ 0161 :

Novotel Manchester West, Worsley Brow, M28 2YA, at junction 13 of M 62 ℘ 799 3535, Fax 703 8207, heated – rm ▤ rest – 220. VISA
Meals 12.95/18.85 **st.** and a la carte – 7.50 – **119 rm** 52.50.

Tung Fong, 2 Worsley Rd, M28 4NL, on A 572 ℘ 794 5331, Fax 727 9598 – ▤. VISA
closed lunch Saturday and Sunday – **Meals** - Chinese (Peking) - 20.50/27.50 **st.** and a la carte 5.00.

at Pendlebury NW : 4 m. by A 6 on A 666 – ✉ Manchester – ☎ 0161 :

Henry Boddington, 219 Bolton Rd, M27 8TG, ℘ 736 5143, Fax 737 2786 – AV **a**
Meals (grill rest.) – **31 rm.**

at Swinton NW : 4 m. by A 580 – AV – and A 572 on B 5231 – ✉ Manchester – ☎ 0161 :

New Ellesmere Lodge (Premier), East Lancs Rd, M27 8AA, SW : ½ m. on A 580 ℘ 728 2791, Fax 794 8222 – rm . VISA.
Meals (grill rest.) 7.00/13.55 **t.** 3.95 – 4.45 – **27 rm** 39.50 **t.** – SB.

ATS Chester St. ℘ 236 5505
TS 98 Wilmslow Rd, Rusholme ℘ 224 6296
TS Warren Rd, Trafford Park ℘ 872 7631
ATS 122 Higher Rd, Urmston ℘ 748 6990/5923
ATS 20/28 Waterloo Rd ℘ 832 7752

MANNINGTREE Essex 404 X 28 – pop. 709 – ✉ Colchester – ☎ 01206.
◆London 67 – Colchester 10 – ◆Ipswich 12.

X **Stour Bay Café,** 39-43 High St., CO11 1AH, ✆ 396687, Fax 395462 – AE VISA
closed lunch Tuesday to Thursday, Sunday, Monday, 2 weeks January, 2 weeks Septemb and Bank Holidays – **Meals** a la carte 12.45/22.00 **t.**

MARAZION Cornwall 403 D 33 The West Country G. – pop. 1 417 – ✉ Penzance – ☎ 01736.
Envir. : St. Michael's Mount★★ (≤★★) – Ludgvan★ (Church★) N : 2 m. by A 30 – Chysauster N : 2 m. by A 30 – Gulval★ (Church★) W : 2½ m.
Praa Sands, Germoe Cross Rd ✆ (01736) 763445.
◆London 318 – Penzance 3 – Truro 26.

Mount Haven, Turnpike Rd, TR17 0DQ, ✆ 710249, Fax 711658, ≤ St. Michael's Mou and Mount's Bay – rest TV ☎ P. AE VISA
closed 3 to 15 January and 20 to 28 December – **Meals** *(closed lunch October-April)* (b lunch)/dinner 18.50 **t.** and a la carte 4.25 – **17 rm** 36.00/72.00 **t.** – SB.

at St. Hilary E : 2½ m. by Turnpike Rd, on B 3280 – ✉ Penzance – ☎ 01736 :

Enny's, Trewhelln Lane, TR20 9BZ, ✆ 740262, Fax 740262, « 17C manor hous working farm », heated, park, – rm TV P. AE VISA
closed December – **Meals** (by arrangement) 17.50 **t.** – **5 rm** 35.00/55.00 – SB.

at Perranuthnoe SE : 1¾ m. by A 394 – ✉ Penzance – ☎ 01736 :

Ednovean House, TR20 9LZ, ✆ 711071, ≤ St. Michael's Mount and Mount's Bay, – rest P. AE VISA
Meals 10.00/14.00 **st.** 4.25 – **9 rm** 21.00/46.00 **st.**

MARCH Cambs. 402 404 U 26 – pop. 16 832 – ☎ 01345.
Frogs Abbey, Grange Rd ✆ 52364.
◆London 93 – ◆Cambridge 34 – ◆Norwich 63.

Olde Griffin, High St., PE15 9JS, ✆ 52517, Fax 50086 – TV ☎ P – 100. AE VISA.
Meals 9.50/12.50 **st.** and dinner a la carte – **20 rm** 38.50/67.50 **st.** – SB.

MARDEN Heref. and Worcs. – see Hereford.

MARKET BOSWORTH Leics. 402 403 404 P 26 – pop. 2 019 – ✉ Nuneaton – ☎ 01455.
◆London 109 – ◆Birmingham 30 – ◆Coventry 23 – ◆Leicester 22.

Softleys, Market Pl., CV13 0JS, ✆ 290464 – TV ☎. AE VISA.
Meals *(closed Monday lunch and Sunday to non-residents)* (in bar) 10.50/15.95 and a la carte 4.50 – **3 rm** 40.00/50.00 **t.**

MARKET DEEPING Lincs. 404 T 25 – ✉ Peterborough (Cambs.) – ☎ 01778.
◆London 94 – ◆Leicester 39 – Lincoln 43 – ◆Nottingham 54.

XX **Caudle House** with rm, 43 High St., PE6 8ED, ✆ 347595, Fax 348529, – TV ☎. VISA.
closed first 2 weeks August – **Meals** *(closed Sunday dinner and Monday)* (bookir essential) (dinner only and Sunday lunch) 14.75/24.50 **st.** – **2 rm** 32.00/45.00 **st.** – SB.

MARKET HARBOROUGH Leics. 404 R 26 – pop. 16 563 – ☎ 01858.
Great Oxendon Rd ✆ 463684.
Pen Lloyd Library, Adam and Eve St., LE16 7LT ✆ 468106.
◆London 88 – ◆Birmingham 47 – ◆Leicester 15 – Northampton 17.

Three Swans, 21 High St., LE16 7NJ, ✆ 466644, Fax 433101 – rm TV ☎ P 85. AE VISA.
Meals *(closed Sunday dinner)* 12.95/18.95 **t.** and a la carte 7.50 – **36 rm** 67.00/87.00 s – SB.

Angel, High St., LE16 7NL, ✆ 462702, Fax 410464 – TV ☎ P – 120. AE VIS
Meals 10.95/14.95 **st.** and a la carte 4.75 – **30 rm** 55.00/70.00 **st.**

at Glooston NE : 7½ m. by A 6 and B 6047 off Hallaton Rd – ✉ Market Harborough ☎ 01858 :

X **Old Barn Inn** with rm, LE16 7ST, ✆ 545215 – rm TV P. AE VISA
closed lunch Monday to Friday and Sunday dinner – **Meals** 17.50 **st.** (dinner) and a la car 4.75 – **3 rm** 37.50/49.50 **st.**

at Marston Trussell (Northants.) W : 3½ m. by A 427 – ✉ Market Harborough ☎ 01858 :

Sun Inn, Main St., LE16 9TY, ✆ 465531, Fax 433155 – TV ☎ P – 60. AE VISA
Meals 14.95 **t.** and a la carte 5.25 – **19 rm** 39.50/55.00 **t.**

ATS 47-49 Kettering Rd ✆ 464535

MARKET LAVINGTON Wilts. 403 404 O 29 – see Devizes.

MARKET RASEN Lincs. 402 404 T 23 pop. 4 199 – ☎ 01673.

London 156 – Boston 41 – Great Grimsby 19 – Lincoln 16.

- **Bleasby House,** Legsby, LN8 3QN, SE : 4¼ m. by B 1202 ☎ 842383, « Working farm », … **Meals** (by arrangement) 12.00 **st.** – **3 rm** 18.00/36.00 **st.**

MARKET WEIGHTON Humbs. 402 R-S 22 pop. 4 371 – ✉ York – ☎ 01430.

London 206 – ♦Kingston-upon-Hull 19 – York 20.

- **Londesborough Arms,** 44 High St., YO4 3AH, ☎ 872214, Fax 872214 – TV ☎ P – 150. AE VISA JCB. **Meals** 11.95/20.95 **st.** and a la carte 4.95 – **16 rm** 35.00/80.00 **st.** – SB.

MARKFIELD Leics. 402 403 404 Q 25 – pop. 4 657 – ☎ 01530.

London 113 – ♦Birmingham 45 – ♦Leicester 6 – ♦Nottingham 24.

- Field Head, Markfield Lane, LE67 9PS, on B 5327 ☎ 245454, Fax 243740 – rm TV ☎ P – 50 **28 rm.**
- **Granada Lodge** without rest., Little Shaw Lane, LE6 0PP, NW : 1 m. on A 50 ☎ 244237, Fax 244580, Reservations (Freephone) 0800 555300 – TV ☎ P. AE VISA. – **39 rm** 39.95 **st.**

MARKHAM MOOR Notts. – ✉ Retford – ☎ 01777.

London 143 – Lincoln 18 – ♦Nottingham 28 – ♦Sheffield 27.

- **Forte Travelodge,** DN22 0QU, A 1 northbound ☎ 838091, Reservations (Freephone) 0800 850950 – TV P. AE VISA. **Meals** (grill rest.) – **40 rm** 34.50 **t.**

MARKINGTON N. Yorks. 402 P 21 – see Harrogate.

MARKS TEY Essex 404 W 28 – see Colchester.

MARLBOROUGH Wilts. 403 404 O 29 The West Country G. – pop. 6 788 – ☎ 01672.

See : Town★.

Envir. : Savernake Forest★★ (Grand Avenue★★★) SE : 2 m. by A 4 – Whitehorse (<★) NW : 5 m. – West Kennett Long Barrow★, Silbury Hill★, W : 6 m. by A 4.

Exc. : Ridgeway Path★★ – Avebury★★ (The Stones★, Church★) W : 7 m. by A 4 – Littlecote★★ (arms and armour★, Roman mosaic floor★) AC, E : 10 m. by A 4 – Crofton Beam Engines★ AC, SE : 9 m. by A 346 – Wilton Windmill★ AC, SE : 10 m. by A 346 and A 338.

The Common ☎ 512147.

Car Park, George Lane, SN8 1EE ☎ 513989.

London 84 – ♦Bristol 47 – ♦Southampton 40 – Swindon 12.

- **Ivy House,** High St., SN8 1HJ, ☎ 515333, Fax 515338 – TV ☎ P – 50. AE VISA **Garden : Meals** 10.95/18.00 **t.** and a la carte 4.50 – **26 rm** 25.00/85.00 **t.** – SB.
- **Castle and Ball** (Forte Heritage), High St., SN8 1LZ, ☎ 515201, Fax 515895 – TV ☎ P – 45. AE VISA **Meals** 12.25/17.95 **t.** and a la carte 6.70 – 8.50 – **36 rm** 70.00/100.00 **st.** – SB.
- **Moran's,** 2-3 London Rd, SN8 1PQ, ☎ 512405, Fax 512405 – *closed Sunday to Tuesday, 1 to 4 January and 10 January-2 February* – **Meals** (booking essential) (dinner only) a la carte 17.15/25.70 **t.** 4.50.

at Ogbourne St. George NE : 3¾ m. by A 346 – ✉ Marlborough – ☎ 01672 :

- **Laurel Cottage** without rest., Southend, SN8 1SG, S : ½ m. on A 346 ☎ 841288, « 16C thatched cottage », – TV P. **4 rm** 26.00/50.00 **st.**

at Burbage SE : 5¾ m. by A 346 – ✉ Marlborough – ☎ 01672 :

- **Old Vicarage** without rest., Eastcourt, SN8 3AG, by Taskers Lane ☎ 810495, Fax 810663, – TV P. AE VISA. *closed Christmas and New Year* – **3 rm** 35.00/60.00 **s.**
- **Loaves and Fishes,** East Sands, SN8 3AN, S : 1 m. via Suthmere Drive ☎ 810211 – VISA *closed Sunday dinner and Monday* – **Meals** a la carte 17.45/23.00 **t.** 6.50.

ATS 120/121 London Rd ☎ 512274

MARLOW Bucks. 404 R 29 – pop. 17 310 – ☎ 01628.

C/o Court Garden, Leisure Complex, Pound Lane, SL7 2AE ☎ 483597 (summer only).

London 35 – Aylesbury 22 – ♦Oxford 29 – Reading 14.

- **Danesfield House**, Medmenham, SL7 2EY, SW : 2 ½ m. on A 4155 ☎ 891010, Fax 890408, « Italian Renaissance style mansion, < terraced gardens and River Thames », heated, park, – rest TV ☎ P – 80. AE VISA JCB. **Meals** 17.50/32.50 **t.** 8.55 – **86 rm** 125.00/195.00 **t.**, 1 suites – SB.

Compleat Angler (Forte Heritage), Marlow Bridge, Bisham Rd, SL7 1RG, ✆ 48444, Fax 486388, ≤ River Thames, « Riverside setting and grounds », – rm 120. AE VISA JCB
Valaisan : **Meals** 22.95/32.50 **t.** and a la carte 7.50 – 11.95 – **60 rm** 125.00/190.00 s, 2 suites – SB.

Country House without rest., Bisham Rd, SL7 1RP, ✆ 890606, Fax 890983, – AE VISA.
9 rm 66.00/82.00 **st.**

Holly Tree House without rest., Burford Close, Marlow Bottom, SL7 3NF, N : 2 m. A 4155 and Wycombe Rd, off Marlow Bottom ✆ 891110, Fax 481278, heated, – AE VISA
5 rm 54.50/67.50 **st.**

Villa D'este, 2 Chapel St., SL7 1DD, ✆ 472012 – AE VISA
closed Saturday lunch – **Meals** - Italian - 12.00 **t.** (lunch) and a la carte 16.50/23.00 **t.** 4.0

MARPLE Gtr. Manchester 402 403 404 N 23 – pop. 19 829 – 0161.
London 190 – Chesterfield 35 – Manchester 11.

Springfield, 99 Station Rd, SK6 6PA, ✆ 449 0721, – rm . AE VISA.
closed 2 weeks August – **Meals** *(closed Friday to Sunday)* (dinner only) 14.50 **st.** 7.50 –
7 rm 40.00/50.00 **st.**

MARSDEN W. Yorks. 402 404 O 23 – Huddersfield – 01484.
London 195 – Leeds 22 – Manchester 18 – Sheffield 30.

Hey Green Country House, Waters Rd, HD7 6NG, NW : 1 ¼ m. by Station Rd and Reddisher Rd ✆ 844235, Fax 847605, – . AE VISA JCB.
Meals 19.50/23.00 **t.** and a la carte 5.25 – **9 rm** 49.50/80.00 **t.**

MARSTON MORETAINE Beds. 404 S 27 – see Bedford.

MARSTON TRUSSELL Northants. 404 R 26 – see Market Harborough.

MARTINHOE Devon – see Lynton.

MARTOCK Somerset 403 L 31 The West Country G. – pop. 4 982 – 01935.
See : Village★ - All Saints★★.
Envir. : Montacute House★★ *AC*, SE : 4 m. – Muchelney★★ (Parish Church★★) NW : 4½ m. by B 3165.
Exc. : Martock – Barrington Court Garden★ *AC*, SW : 7½ m. by B 3165 and A 303.
London 148 – Taunton 19 – Yeovil 6.

Hollies, Bower Hinton, TA12 6LG, S : 1 m. on B 3165 ✆ 822232, Fax 822249, – 100. AE VISA
Meals (in bar) a la carte approx. 15.85 **t.** 4.00 – **30 rm** 52.50/80.00 **t.** – SB.

MARWELL ZOOLOGICAL PARK Hants. – see Winchester.

MARY TAVY Devon 403 H 32 – see Tavistock.

MASHAM N. Yorks. 402 P 21 – pop. 1 171 – Ripon – 01765.
London 231 – Leeds 38 – Middlesbrough 37 – York 32.

King's Head, Market Pl., HG4 4EF, ✆ 689295, Fax 689070 – – 35. AE VIS
Meals (bar lunch Monday to Saturday)/dinner a la carte 7.95/14.50 **t.** 4.05 – **10 r** 39.00/58.00 **t.**

Bank Villa, HG4 4DB, on A 6108 ✆ 689605, –
March-October – **Meals** 15.00 **st.** 3.75 – **7 rm** 26.00/36.00 **st.**

Floodlite, 7 Silver St., HG4 4DX, ✆ 689000 – AE VISA
closed Tuesday to Thursday lunch, Monday and 2 weeks January – **Meals** 10.50 (lunch) and a la carte 4.35.

MATLOCK Derbs. 402 403 404 P 24 Great Britain G. – pop. 10 465 – 01629.
Exc. : Hardwick Hall★★ *AC*, E : 12½ m. by A 615 and B 6014.
The Pavilion, DE4 3NR ✆ 55082.
London 153 – Derby 17 – Manchester 46 – Nottingham 24 – Sheffield 24.

Riber Hall, Riber, DE4 5JU, SE : 3 m. by A 615 ✆ 582795, Fax 580475, « Pa Elizabethan manor house », – rest . AE VISA JCB
Meals 11.00/20.00 **t.** and dinner a la carte 6.50 – 8.00 – **11 rm** 83.00/144.50 **t.** – SB.

New Bath (Forte Heritage), New Bath Rd, Matlock Bath, DE4 3PX, S : 1 ½ m. on A ✆ 583275, Fax 580268, heated, – – 130. AE VI JCB
Meals 9.95/18.95 **t.** and a la carte 5.85 – 8.75 – **55 rm** 65.00/85.00 **st.** – SB.

Temple, Matlock Bath, DE4 3PG, S : 1 ¾ m. by A 6 ✆ 583911, Fax 580851, ≤, rest . AE VISA.
Meals 11.00/20.00 **st.** and a la carte 4.80 – **14 rm** 41.00/56.00 **st.** – SB.

Hodgkinson's, 150 South Par., Matlock Bath, DE4 3NR, S : 1 ¼ m. on A 6 ✆ 58217 « Victoriana » – – **7 rm.**

at Tansley E : 1 ¾ m. on A 615 – ✉ Matlock – ☎ 01629 :

Lane End House, Green Lane, DE4 5FJ, off Church St. ☎ 583981, – ⊭ TV P. VISA
closed Christmas – **Meals** (by arrangement) (communal dining) 14.95 – **4 rm** ☐ 29.00/50.00 **s.** – SB.

at Dethick SE : 4 m. by A 615 – ✉ Matlock – ☎ 01629 :

Manor Farmhouse without rest., DE4 5GG, ☎ 534246, ←, , park – ⊭ TV P.
closed Christmas – **3 rm** ☐ 18.00/36.00 **st.**

MAWDESLEY Lancs. 402 L 23 pop. 1 750 – ✉ Ormskirk – ☎ 01704.

London 217 – ♦Liverpool 28 – ♦Manchester 28 – Preston 15.

Mawdesley, Hall Lane, L40 2QZ, N : ½ m. ☎ 822552, Fax 822096, , TV ☎ ♿ P – 50. AE VISA.
Meals (grill rest.) a la carte 12.75/19.20 **t.** 4.25 – **35 rm** ☐ 41.00/51.00 **t.** – SB.

MAWNAN SMITH Cornwall 403 E 33 – see Falmouth.

MAYFIELD E. Sussex 404 U 30 – pop. 3 515 – ☎ 01435.

London 46 – ♦Brighton 25 – Eastbourne 22 – Lewes 17 – Royal Tunbridge Wells 9.

Rose and Crown, Fletching St., TN20 6TE, ☎ 872200, Fax 873809 – TV P. VISA.
Meals a la carte 8.90/14.45 **t.** 4.50 – ☐ 6.95 – **4 rm** 38.00/48.00 **t.**

Middle House, High St., TN20 6AB, ☎ 872146, Fax 873423, – TV ☎ P. AE VISA JCB.
Meals *(closed dinner Sunday and Monday)* (bar lunch)/dinner a la carte 16.85/19.25 **t.** 4.75 – **7 rm** ☐ 45.00/75.00 **t.** – SB.

at Five Ashes SW : 2 ¾ m. on A 267 – ✉ Mayfield – ☎ 01825 :

Coles Hall, TN20 6JH, S : ¾ m. on A 267 ☎ 830274, ←, , park – TV P
Meals (by arrangement) 8.50 – **3 rm** ☐ 18.00/32.00 **st.**

MEADOW HEAD S. Yorks. – see Sheffield.

MEALSGATE Cumbria 402 K 19 – ✉ Carlisle – ☎ 0169 73.

London 315 – ♦Carlisle 16 – Keswick 17.

Boltongate Old Rectory , Boltongate, CA5 1DA, SE : 1 ½ m. by B 5299 on Ireby rd ☎ 71647, Fax 71798, ←, – P. VISA.
Meals (by arrangement) (communal dining) 21.00 **s.** – **3 rm** ☐ 28.00/74.00.

MEDWAY SERVICE AREA Kent – ✉ Gillingham – ☎ 01634.

London 39 – Canterbury 22 – Maidstone 11.

Pavilion Lodge without rest., ME8 8PW, on M 2 ☎ 377337, Fax 360848 – ⊭ TV ♿ P
58 rm 39.95 **t.**

MELBOURN Cambs. 404 U 27 – pop. 4 006 – ✉ Royston (Herts.) – ☎ 01763.

London 44 – ♦Cambridge 10.

Melbourn Bury , Royston Rd, SG8 6DE, SW : ¾ m. ☎ 261151, Fax 262375, ←, « Tastefully furnished country house of Tudor origin », , park – ⊭ rm TV P. AE VISA.
closed Easter and Christmas-New Year – **Meals** *(closed Sunday dinner)* (booking essential) (residents only) (communal dining) (dinner only) 16.00 **st.** 5.00 – **3 rm** ☐ 48.00/80.00 **st.**

Chiswick House without rest., 3 Chiswick End, SG8 6LZ, NW : 1 m. by Meldreth rd, off Whitecroft Rd ☎ 260242, – ⊭ P
6 rm ☐ 33.00/40.00 **st.**

XXX **Sheen Mill** with rm, Station Rd, SG8 6DX, ☎ 261393, Fax 261376, ←, « Restored 17C water mill », – TV ☎ P. AE VISA.
Meals *(closed Sunday dinner, 26 to 28 December and Bank Holidays)* 15.95/23.50 **t.** and a la carte 4.25 – **8 rm** ☐ 50.00/85.00 **t.**

XX **Pink Geranium,** 25 Station Rd, SG8 6DX, ☎ 260215, Fax 262110, – ⊭ P. AE VISA
closed Saturday lunch, Sunday dinner, Monday except December, 26 December and 1 January – **Meals** (a la carte only Saturday dinner) 15.95/29.95 **t.** and a la carte.

MELKSHAM Wilts. 403 404 N 29 **The West Country G.** – pop. 13 074 – ☎ 01225.

Envir. : Corsham Court** *AC*, NW : 4 ½ m. by A 365 and B 3353 – Lacock* (Lacock Abbey* *AC*, High Street*, St. Cyriac*, Fox Talbot Museum of Photography* *AC*) N : 3 ½ m. by A 350.

Church St., SN12 6LS ☎ 707424.

London 113 – ♦Bristol 25 – Salisbury 35 – Swindon 28.

Beechfield House, Beanacre, SN12 7PU, N : 1 m. on A 350 ☎ 703700, Fax 790118, ←, « Country house and gardens », heated, – ⊭ rest TV ☎ P – 50. AE VISA
Meals *(closed Saturday lunch)* 11.00/22.00 **st.** – **24 rm** ☐ 66.00/99.00 **st.** – SB.

Shurnhold House without rest., Shurnhold, SN12 8DG, NW : 1 m. on A 365 ℘ 79055 « Jacobean manor house, gardens » – ⇔ TV ☎ P. VISA. ✻
☐ 4.25 – **4 rm** 48.00/115.00 **st.**

Sandridge Park, Sandridge Hill, SN12 7QU, E : 2 m. on A 3102 ℘ 70689 Fax 702838, ←, « Early Victorian mansion », park – ⇔ rm TV P. VISA JCB. ✻
closed Christmas – **Meals** (booking essential) (residents only) (communal dining) (dinn only) 20.00 **st.** 4.00 – **4 rm** ☐ 40.00/80.00.

Toxique with rm, 187 Woodrow Rd, SN12 7AY, NE : 1 ¼ m. by A 3102 and Forest ℘ 702129, – ⇔ rest P. AE VISA JCB. ✻
Meals (booking essential) 14.00/28.00 **st.** 5.10 – **4 rm** ☐ (dinner included) 90.00/135.00

at Shaw NW : 1 ½ m. on A 365 – ✉ Melksham – ☎ 01225 :

Shaw Country, Bath Rd, SN12 8EF, on A 365 ℘ 702836, Fax 790275, – ⇔ rest TV P. AE VISA JCB
Meals 13.95 **t.** and a la carte 4.55 – **13 rm** ☐ 40.00/74.00 **t.** – SB.

MELTHAM W. Yorks. 402 404 O 23 – pop. 7 514 – ✉ Huddersfield – ☎ 01484.

Thick Hollins Hall ℘ 850227.

London 192 – Leeds 21 – Manchester 23 – Sheffield 26.

Durker Roods, Bishops Way, HD7 3AG, ℘ 851413, Fax 851843, – TV ☎ P – 8 AE VISA JCB
Meals *(closed Saturday lunch and Sunday dinner)* a la carte 9.00/13.50 **t.** 4.50 – **31 r** ☐ 35.00/40.00 **t.**

La guida cambia, cambiate la guida ogni anno.

MELTON MOWBRAY Leics. 402 404 R 25 – pop. 24 348 – ☎ 01664.

Waltham Rd, Thorpe Arnold ℘ 62118.

Melton Carnegie Museum, Thorpe End, LE13 1RB ℘ 480992.

London 113 – Leicester 15 – Northampton 45 – Nottingham 18.

Stapleford Park Country House, LE14 2EF, E : 5 m. by B 676 on Stapleford ℘ (01572) 787522, Fax 787651, ←, « Part 16C and 19C mansion in park », – ⇔ rest TV ☎ P – 300. AE VISA
Meals (light lunch Monday to Saturday)/dinner a la carte 27.00/32.50 **t.** – ☐ 10.00 – **41 r** 135.00/200.00 **t.**, 1 suite – SB.

Quorn Lodge, 46 Asfordby Rd, LE13 0HR, ℘ 66660, Fax 480660 – ⇔ rest TV ☎ P. AE VISA JCB. ✻
Meals *(closed Sunday dinner and Monday lunch)* 8.50/11.50 **st.** and a la carte 3.50 **11 rm** ☐ 42.50/52.50 **st.** – SB.

Harboro (Forte), Burton St., LE13 1AF, ℘ 60121, Fax 64296 – ⇔ rm TV P. AE JCB
Meals (grill rest.) a la carte 9.30/15.70 **st.** – ☐ 5.45 – **26 rm** 31.95/41.95 **st.** – SB.

at Old Dalby NW : 8½ m. by A 6006 on Old Dalby rd – ✉ Melton Mowbray – ☎ 01664

Home Farm without rest., 9 Church Lane, LE14 3LB, ℘ 822622, – ⇔ P. AE VISA ✻
closed Christmas – **5 rm** ☐ 25.00/40.00 **s.**

ATS Leicester Rd ℘ 62072

MEMBURY Devon – see Axminster.

MEMBURY SERVICE AREA Berks. 403 404 P 29 – ✉ Newbury – ☎ 01488.

Forte Travelodge, Membury, Lambourn Woodlands, RG16 7TU, M 4 betwee junctions 14 and 15 (westbound carriageway) ℘ 71881, Reservations (Freephone 0800 850950 – TV P. AE VISA
Meals (grill rest.) – **40 rm** 34.50 **t.**

MENDLESHAM GREEN Suffolk 404 W 27 – see Stowmarket.

MERE Wilts. 403 404 N 30 **The West Country G.** – pop. 2 257 – ☎ 01747.

Envir. : Stourhead★★★ *AC*, NW : 4 m. by B 3095 and B 3092.

Exc. : Longleat House★★★ *AC*, N : 9½ m. by A 303 and B 3092.

The Square, BA12 6JJ ℘ 861211.

London 113 – Exeter 65 – Salisbury 26 – Taunton 40.

Chetcombe House, Chetcombe Rd, BA12 6AZ, ℘ 860219, – ⇔ TV P. AE VISA
Meals (lunch by arrangement)/dinner 13.50/15.00 **s.** 3.50 – **5 rm** ☐ 29.00/50.00 **s.** – SB.

Chantry, Church St., BA12 6DS, ℘ 860264, Fax 860264, « 15C chantry priest house », heated, – ⇔ rm P. ✻
closed Christmas and New Year – **Meals** (by arrangement) 18.00 **st.** – **3 rm** ☐ 27.00 54.00 **st.**

MERIDEN W. Mids. 403 404 P 26 – see Coventry.

MEVAGISSEY Cornwall 403 F 33 The West Country G. – pop. 3 655 – ☎ 01726.
See : Town★★.
London 287 – Newquay 21 – ◆Plymouth 44 – Truro 20.

Mevagissey House ⑤, Vicarage Hill, PL26 6SZ, ✆ 842427, Fax 842427, ≤, ⛆ – ⛌ ▣ ⓟ. VISA. ✻
March-October – **Meals** (by arrangement) 14.00 **s.** 4.25 – **6 rm** ⊒ 22.00/50.00 – SB.

MEYSEY HAMPTON Glos. – ✉ Cirencester – ☎ 01285.
London 101 – ◆Bristol 44 – Gloucester 26 – ◆Oxford 29.

Masons Arms, High St., GL7 5JT, ✆ 850164, Fax 850164 – ▣ ⓟ. VISA. ✻
Meals *(closed Sunday dinner)* a la carte 8.90/13.15 **st.** 4.50 – **8 rm** ⊒ 28.00/46.00 **st.**

MICHAELWOOD SERVICE AREA Glos. 403 M 29 – ✉ Dursley – ☎ 01454.

Forte Travelodge, Lower Wick, GL11 6DD, M 5 (northbound carriageway) ✆ 261513, Reservations (Freephone) 0800 850950 – ▣ ♿ ⓟ. AE ⓘ VISA
Meals (grill rest.) – **40 rm** 34.50 **t.**

MICKLEOVER Derbs. 402 403 404 P 25 – see Derby.

MICKLETON Glos. 403 404 O 27 – see Chipping Campden.

MICKLE TRAFFORD Ches. – see Chester.

MIDDLECOMBE Somerset – see Minehead.

MIDDLEHAM N. Yorks. 402 O 21 – pop. 754 – ECD : Thursday – ☎ 01969.
London 233 – Kendal 45 – ◆Leeds 47 – York 45.

Miller's House, Market Pl., DL8 4NR, ✆ 622630, Fax 623570, ⛆ – ⛌ rest ▣ ☎ ⓟ. VISA. ✻
closed January – **Meals** (dinner only) 19.50 **t.** 3.10 – **7 rm** ⊒ 35.00/85.00 **t.** – SB.

Waterford House, 19 Kirkgate, DL8 4PG, ✆ 622090, Fax 624020, « Part 17C house, antiques », ⛆ – ⛌ rest ▣ ⓟ. VISA
Meals (lunch by arrangement)/dinner 15.50/25.00 **st.** and a la carte 5.00 – **5 rm** ⊒ 40.00/75.00 **st.**

at Carlton SW : 4½ m. on Coverdale Rd – ✉ Leyburn – ☎ 01969 :

Foresters Arms with rm, DL8 2BB, ✆ 640272, Fax 640272 – ▣ ⓟ. VISA
Meals *(closed Sunday dinner and Monday)* a la carte 13.95/29.00 **t.** – **3 rm** ⊒ 30.00/55.00 **st.**

at West Scrafton SW : 6 m. by Coverdale Rd – ✉ Leyburn – ☎ 01969 :

Coverdale Country ⑤, Swineside, DL8 4RX, ✆ 640601, ≤, ⛆ – ⛌ rest ▣ ⓟ. VISA. ✻
March-October – **Meals** 10.00 **t.** 4.60 – **5 rm** ⊒ 31.00/62.00 **t.** – SB.

MIDDLESBROUGH Cleveland 402 Q 20 – pop. 140 849 – ☎ 01642.
Middlesbrough Municipal, Ladgate Lane ✆ 315533 – 18 Brass Castle Lane, Marton ✆ 316430.
Teesside Airport : ✆ (01325) 332811, SW : 13 m. by A 66 - AZ - and A 19 on A 67.
51 Corporation Rd, TS1 1LT ✆ 243425/264330.
London 246 – ◆Kingston-upon-Hull 89 – ◆Leeds 66 – ◆Newcastle upon Tyne 41.

Plan on next page

Baltimore, 250 Marton Rd, TS4 2EZ, ✆ 224111, Fax 226156 – ▣ ☎ ⓟ – 25. AE ⓘ VISA BZ **e**
Meals *(closed lunch Saturday and Sunday)* 13.75 **st.** and a la carte **st.** 5.50 – **30 rm** ⊒ 72.50/84.50 **st.**, 1 suite.

Marton Way Toby, Marton Rd, TS4 3BS, ✆ 817651, Fax 829409 – ⛌ rm ▣ ☎ ⓟ – 85. AE ⓘ VISA BZ **a**
Meals a la carte 9.90/17.40 **t.** – **53 rm** ⊒ 38.00/48.00 **t.** – SB.

Grey House, 79 Cambridge Rd, TS5 5NL, ✆ 817485, Fax 817485, ⛆ – ▣ ☎ ⓟ. VISA AZ **n**
closed Christmas and New Year – **Meals** (by arrangement) 8.50 **s.** – **9 rm** ⊒ 35.00/49.00 **s.**

ATS Murdock Rd (off Sotherby Rd), Cargo Fleet ✆ 249245/6

MIDDLESBROUGH

Cleveland Centre . . . . **ABY**
Corporation Road. . . . . **BY** 8
Dundas Street. . . . . **ABY** 12
Grange Road. . . . . **ABY**
Hill Street Centre . . . . **AY**
Linthorpe Road . . . . **AY**
Newport Road . . . . **AY**

Albert Road . . . . **BY** 2
Ayresome Green Lane. . . . . **AZ** 3
Bridge Street West . . . . **AY** 4
Bright Street. . . . . **BY** 5
Clairville Road. . . . . **BZ** 6
Cleveland Street . . . . **BY** 7
Devonshire Road . . . . **AZ** 10
Eastbourne Road . . . . **AZ** 14
Ferry Road . . . . **BY** 15
Finsbury Street . . . . **AZ** 16
Gresham Road . . . . **AZ** 18
Hartington Road . . . . **AY** 19
Longford Street. . . . . **AZ** 22
Ormesby Road . . . . **BZ** 24
Princes Road . . . . **AZ** 26
St. Barnabas Road . . . . **AZ** 27
Saltersgill Avenue . . . . **BZ** 28
Sussex Street . . . . **AY**
Tees Bridge
Approach Road . . . . **AZ**
West Terrace . . . . **BZ**
Westbourne Grove . . . . **BZ**
Wilson Street . . . . **AY**
Woodlands Road. . . . . **BZ**
Zetland Street . . . . **ABY**

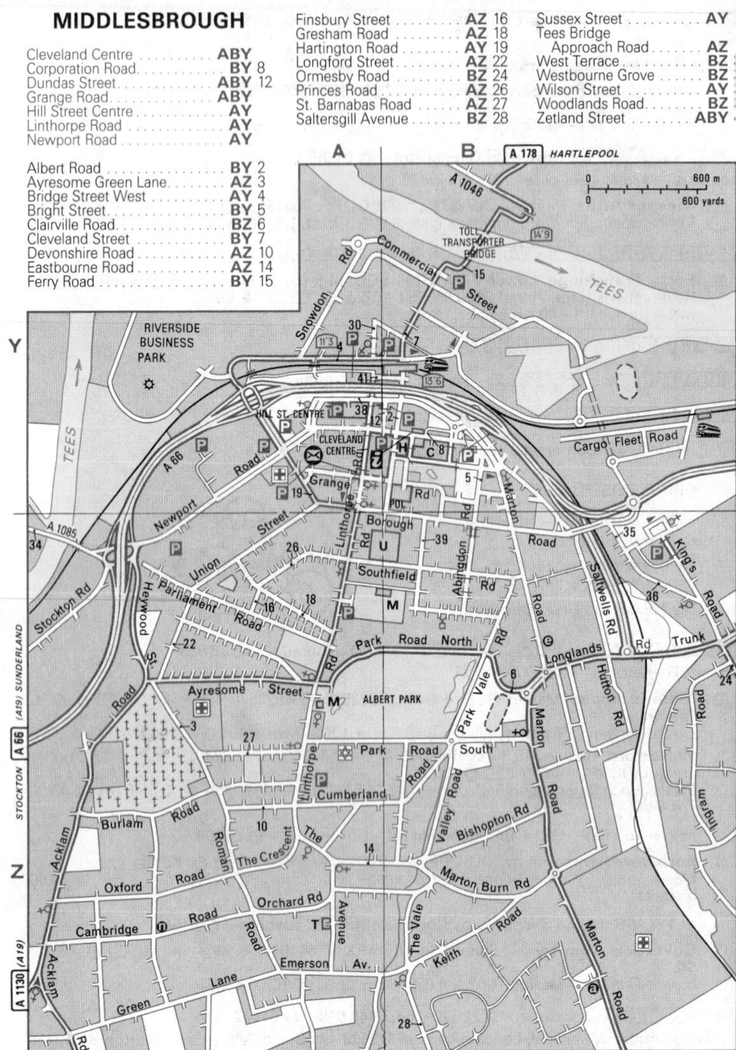

MIDDLETON N.Yorks. - see Pickering.

MIDDLETON-IN-TEESDALE Durham 401 402 N 20 – pop. 1 477 – ☎ 01833.

◆London 232 – ◆Carlisle 56 – ◆Leeds 78 – ◆Middlesbrough 35 – ◆Newcastle upon Tyne 49.

Teesdale, Market Sq., DL12 0QG, ✆ 640264, Fax 640651 – TV ☎ P. AE VISA
Meals (bar lunch Monday to Saturday)/dinner 17.95 **st.** and a la carte 5.20 – **10 r**
38.50/60.50 **st.** – SB.

MIDDLETON STONEY Oxon. 403 404 Q 28 – pop. 304 – ☎ 01869.

◆London 66 – Northampton 30 – ◆Oxford 12.

Jersey Arms, OX6 8SE, ✆ 343234, Fax 343565, – TV ☎ P. AE VISA JCB.
Meals *(closed Sunday dinner)* a la carte 17.10/25.45 **t.** 4.95 – **13 rm** 65.00/79.50
3 suites – SB.

MIDDLE WALLOP Hants. 403 404 P 30 – ✉ Stockbridge – ☎ 01264.

London 80 – Salisbury 11 – ♦Southampton 21.

Fifehead Manor, SO20 8EG, on A 343 ℘ 781565, Fax 781400, « Converted 16C manor house », – TV ☎ P. AE VISA
Meals 19.00/25.00 t. 5.80 – **15 rm** 40.00/105.00 **t.** – SB.

MIDHURST W. Sussex 404 R 31 – pop. 4 614 – ☎ 01730.

London 57 – ♦Brighton 38 – Chichester 12 – ♦Southampton 41.

Spread Eagle, South St., GU29 9NH, ℘ 816911, Fax 815668, « 15C hostelry, antique furnishings » – TV ☎ P – 50. AE VISA.
Meals 16.50/29.00 **t.** – 3.75 – **40 rm** 73.00/165.00 **t.**, 1 suite – SB.

Angel, North St., GU29 9DN, ℘ 812421, Fax 815928, « 16C coaching inn », – rm TV ☎ P – 60. AE VISA.
Brasserie : Meals 12.50/17.50 **t.** and a la carte 7.95 - (see also ***Cowdray Room*** below) – **21 rm** 75.00/155.00 **t.** – SB.

XXX **Cowdray Room** (at Angel H.), North St., GU29 9DN, ℘ 812421, Fax 815928, – P. AE VISA
Meals a la carte 20.50/31.00 **t.** 7.95.

X **Mida,** Wool Lane, GU29 9BY, ℘ 813284
closed Sunday, Monday, 1 week May and 1 week November – **Meals** (lunch by arrangement)/dinner a la carte 19.00/33.00 **t.**

X **Maxine's,** Red Lion St., GU29 9PB, ℘ 816271 – . VISA
closed Sunday dinner, Monday, Tuesday and 2 weeks January – **Meals** 13.95 **st.** and a la carte 5.25.

at Bepton SW : 2½ m. by A 286 on Bepton rd – ✉ Midhurst – ☎ 01730 :

Park House, South Bepton, GU29 0JB, ℘ 812880, Fax 815643, heated, – TV ☎ P. AE VISA
Meals (by arrangement) 10.50/18.50 **t.** 5.45 – **10 rm** 60.00/110.00 **t.**, 1 suite.

at Stedham W : 2 m. by A 272 – ✉ Midhurst – ☎ 01730 :

X **Nava Thai at Hamilton Arms,** School Lane, GU29 0NZ, ℘ 812555 – P. VISA
closed Monday and 27 to 29 December – **Meals** - Thai - 17.00 **t.** and a la carte 4.25.

at Trotton W : 3¼ m. on A 272 – ✉ Petersfield (Hants.) – ☎ 01730 :

Southdowns Country, GU31 5JN, S : 1 m. ℘ 821521, Fax 821790, – rm rest TV ☎ P – 100. AE VISA.
Meals 12.95/29.95 **t.** 5.50 – **20 rm** 66.00/109.00 **t.** – SB.

MIDSOMER NORTON Avon 403 M 30 – ✉ Bath – ☎ 01761.

London 129 – Bath 10 – ♦Bristol 15 – Wells 8.

Centurion, Charlton Lane, BA3 4BD, SE : 1 m. by B3355, Charlton Rd and Fosseway ℘ 417711, Fax 418357, , squash – TV ☎ P – 180. AE VISA.
closed 24 to 26 December – **Meals** 10.00/16.50 **t.** and a la carte – **44 rm** 60.00/80.00 **t.** – SB.

MILBORNE PORT Dorset 403 404 M 31 – see Sherborne.

MILFORD-ON-SEA Hants. 403 404 P 31 – pop. 4 434 – ✉ Lymington – ☎ 01590.

London 109 – Bournemouth 15 – ♦Southampton 24 – Winchester 37.

South Lawn, Lymington Rd, SO41 0RF, ℘ 643911, Fax 644820, – rest TV ☎ P. VISA.
closed 21 December-20 January – **Meals** (dinner only and Sunday lunch)/dinner 23.95 **t.** 6.80 – **24 rm** 47.50/95.00 **t.** – SB.

Westover Hall, Park Lane, SO41 0PT, ℘ 643044, Fax 644490, – TV ☎ P. AE VISA
restricted opening January-mid February – **Meals** 12.50/18.00 **st.** 6.90 – **14 rm** 40.00/100.00 **st.** – SB.

XX **Rocher's,** 69-71 High St., SO41 0QG, ℘ 642340 – AE VISA
closed Sunday dinner, Monday, Tuesday and 2 weeks June – **Meals** - French - (dinner only and Sunday lunch) 23.50 **t.**

MILTON DAMEREL Devon 403 H 31 – pop. 451 – ☎ 01409.

London 249 – Barnstaple 21.

Woodford Bridge, EX22 7LL, N : 1 m. on A 388 ℘ 261481, Fax 261585, , squash – TV ☎ P. AE VISA.
Meals (bar lunch Monday to Saturday)/dinner a la carte 11.30/23.80 **t.** 6.95 – **8 rm** 65.00 **t.**

Per spostarvi più rapidamente utilizzate le carte Michelin "Grandi Strade" :
n° 970 Europa, *n°* 976 Rep. Ceca/Slovacchia, *n°* 980 Grecia, *n°* 984 Germania,
n° 985 Scandinavia-Finlandia, *n°* 986 Gran Bretagna-Irlanda, *n°* 987 Germania-Austria-Benelux,
n° 988 Italia, *n°* 989 Francia, *n°* 990 Spagna-Portogallo, *n°* 991 Jugoslavia.

MILTON KEYNES Bucks. 404 R 27 – pop. 176 330 – 01908.

Abbey Hill, Monks Way, Two Mile Ash 563845 – Windmill Hill, Tattenhoe Lane Bletchley 378623 – , Wavendon Golf Centre, Lower End Rd, Wavendon 281811.

411 Secklow Gate East, The Food Hall, MK9 3NE 232525/231742.

London 56 – Birmingham 72 – Bedford 16 – Northampton 18 – Oxford 37.

Forte Crest, 500 Saxon Gate West, Milton Keynes Central, MK9 2HQ, 667722 Fax 674714, – rm – 150. AE VISA JCB
Meals 11.95/16.95 **st.** and a la carte – 10.85 – **148 rm** 95.00 **st.**, 2 suites – SB.

Hilton National Milton Keynes, Timbold Drive, Kents Hill, MK7 6HL, SE : 4 m. by A 4146 and A 421 off Brickhill St. (V10) 694433, Fax 695533, – rm rest – 300. AE VISA JCB
Meals 12.50/16.95 **st.** and dinner a la carte 6.25 – 10.25 – **137 rm** 95.00 **st.**, 1 suite – SB

Quality Friendly, Monks Way, Two Mile Ash, MK8 8LY, NW : 2 m. by A 509 and A 5 at junction with A 422 561666, Fax 568303, – rm – 120. AE VISA JCB
Meals (carving rest.) 9.95/13.50 **st.** 4.25 – **88 rm** 57.50/82.00 **st.** – SB.

Shenley Church Inn (Toby), Burchard Cres., Shenley Church End, MK5 6HQ, SW : 2 m by A 509 and Portway (H5) off Watling St. (V4) 505467, Fax 502308 – rm – 100. AE VISA
Meals (carving rest.) a la carte 10.80/17.40 **t.** 5.25 – **50 rm** 65.00/75.00 **st.**

Caldecotte Arms (Premier), Bletcham Way (H10), Caldecotte, MK7 8HP, SE : 5½ m. by A 509 and A 5, taking 2nd junction left signposted Milton Keynes (South and East) 366188, Fax 366603, « Windmill feature, lakeside setting » – . AE VISA
Meals (grill rest.) – 4.45 – **40 rm** 39.50 **t.** – SB.

Peartree Bridge Inn (Toby), Milton Keynes Marina, Waterside, Peartree Bridge, MK6 2DG, SE : 1¾ m. by A 509 off A 4146 691515, Fax 690274, « Marina setting beside the Grand Union Canal » – rm . AE VISA
Meals (grill rest.) a la carte 10.75/18.50 **st.** – **39 rm** 59.95/69.95 **st.**

Broughton, Broughton Village, MK10 9AA, E : 4 m. by A 509 off A 5130 667726 Fax 604844, – . AE VISA
accommodation closed 24 to 30 December – **Meals** (bar lunch Monday to Saturday) dinner 13.95 **t.** and a la carte 3.75 – **31 rm** 55.00/70.50 **t.**

Travel Inn, Secklow Gate West, Central Milton Keynes, MK9 3BZ, 663388 Fax 607481 – rm – 50. AE VISA
Meals (grill rest.) – 4.95 – **38 rm** 34.50 **t.**

Jaipur, Elder House, 502 Eldergate, Station Sq., MK9 1LR, 669796, Fax 694464 – AE VISA
Meals - Indian - (buffet lunch Sunday) 12.50/30.00 and a la carte 7.95.

at Hanslope NW : 9 m. by A 5 and A 508 on Hanslope rd – Milton Keynes – 01908

Hatton Court, Bullington End, MK19 7BQ, SE : 1½ m. on Wolverton rd 51004 Fax 510945, – rm – 50. AE VISA
Meals 12.95/18.95 **t.** and a la carte – 7.50 – **20 rm** 65.00/95.00 – SB.

ATS 38 Victoria Rd, Bletchley 640420

MILTON-UNDER-WYCHWOOD Oxon. – pop. 2 030 – 01993.

London 83 – Birmingham 52 – Gloucester 35 – Oxford 27.

Hillborough, The Green, OX7 6JH, 830501, Fax 832005 – . AE VISA
Meals 12.00/16.00 **t.** and a la carte 4.00 – **10 rm** 40.00/58.00 **t.** – SB.

MINCHINHAMPTON Glos. 403 404 N 28 pop. 5 173 – 01453.

London 115 – Bristol 26 – Gloucester 11 – Oxford 51.

Hunters Lodge without rest., Dr Brown's Rd, GL6 9BT, 883588, Fax 731449, « Cotswold stone house on Minchinhampton common », – .
closed Christmas – **3 rm** 25.00/44.00.

Markey's, The Old Ram, Market Sq., GL6 9BW, 882287 – . AE VISA
closed Sunday, Monday, by arrangement Tuesday, first 2 weeks January and last 2 weeks August – **Meals** 9.95 **t.** (lunch) and dinner a la carte 15.50/21.00 **t.**

MINEHEAD Somerset 403 J 30 **The West Country G.** – pop. 6 543 – 01643.

See : Town★ - Higher Town (Church Steps★, St. Michael's★) – West Somerset Railway★ *AC*

Envir. : Dunster★★ - Castle★★ *AC* (upper rooms ≤★) Water Mill★ *AC*, St. George's Church★ Dovecote★, SE : 2½ m. by A 39 – Selworthy★ (Church★, ≤★★) W : 4½ m. by A 39.

Exc. : Exmoor National Park★★ – Cleeve Abbey★★ *AC*, SE : 6½ m. by A 39.

The Warren, Warren Rd 702057.

17 Friday St., TA24 5UB 702624.

London 187 – Bristol 64 – Exeter 43 – Taunton 25.

Northfield ⑤, Northfield Rd, TA24 5PU, ☎ 705155, Fax 707715, ≤ bay, « Gardens », Fø, ⛱ – |♦| TV ☎ P – 🏃 60. AE ⓓ VISA
Meals 16.95 **st.** (dinner) and lunch a la carte 10.00/14.00 **st.** 4.50 – **26 rm** ☐ 52.00/94.00 – SB.

Benares ⑤, Northfield Rd, TA24 5PT, ☎ 704911, Fax 706373, ≤, « Gardens » – ⊬ rest TV ☎ P. AE ⓓ VISA
25 March-4 November – **Meals** (bar lunch)/dinner 18.00 **t.** 4.50 – **19 rm** ☐ 45.00/84.00 **t.** – SB.

Beacon Country House ⑤, Beacon Rd, TA24 5SD, ☎ 703476, ≤, ⛱, ⛁, park – TV ☎ P. VISA. ✗
Meals a la carte 21.70/23.75 **st.** 7.00 – **8 rm** ☐ 50.00/80.00 **t.** – SB.

Channel House ⑤, Church Path, TA24 5QG, off Northfield Rd ☎ 703229, ≤, ⛁ – TV ☎ P. ⓓ VISA JCB. ✗
mid March-late November and Christmas – **Meals** (dinner only) 18.00 **st.** and a la carte 4.50 – **8 rm** ☐ (dinner included) 76.00/112.00 **st.** – SB.

Wyndcott ⑤, Martlet Rd, TA24 5QE, ☎ 704522, ≤, ⛁ – TV ☎ P. AE VISA
Meals 9.95/16.95 **st.** – **11 rm** ☐ 43.95/97.90 **st.** – SB.

Beaconwood ⑤, Church Rd, North Hill, TA24 5SB, ☎ 702032, ≤ sea and Minehead, ⛱ heated, ⛁, ✗ – ⊬ rest TV ☎ P. VISA
March-November – **Meals** (bar lunch)/dinner 13.95 **st.** – **14 rm** ☐ 36.00/56.00 **st.** – SB.

Rectory House, Northfield Rd, TA24 5QH, ☎ 702611, ⛁ – ⊬ rest TV P. VISA
March-October – **Meals** (dinner only) 16.00 6.00 – **8 rm** ☐ 25.00/50.00.

at Middlecombe W : 1½ m. by A 39 – ✉ Minehead – ☎ 01643 :

Periton Park ⑤, TA24 8SW, ☎ 706885, Fax 706885, ≤, ⛁ – ⊬ TV ☎ P. AE VISA. ✗
Meals (dinner only) 20.00 **st.** 4.00 – **8 rm** ☐ (dinner included) 65.00/124.00 **st.** – SB.

ATS Bampton St. ☎ 704808/9

MINSTER Kent 404 Y 29 – see Ramsgate.

MINSTER LOVELL Oxon. 403 404 P 28 – pop. 1 613 – ✉ Witney – ☎ 01993.
London 72 – Gloucester 36 – ♦Oxford 16.

XX ✿ **Lovells at Windrush Farm** with rm, Windrush Farm, Old Minster Lovell, OX8 5RN, ☎ 779802, Fax 779802, ⛁ – ⊬ rest P. AE ⓓ VISA JCB
closed January – **Meals** *(closed Sunday dinner and Monday)* (booking essential) (lunch by arrangement Tuesday to Thursday and Saturday) 17.50/29.50 **t.** 9.00 – **3 rm** ☐ (dinner included) 90.00/160.00 **t.**
Spec. Red mullet with pesto mash, Fillet of beef with smoked bacon and potato rösti, Assiette of desserts.

MISTERTON Somerset 403 L 31 – see Crewkerne.

MOBBERLEY Ches. 402 403 404 N 24 – see Knutsford.

MONK FRYSTON N. Yorks. 402 Q 22 – pop. 722 – ✉ Lumby – ☎ 01977.
London 190 – ♦Kingston-upon-Hull 42 – ♦Leeds 13 – York 20.

Monk Fryston Hall, LS25 5DU, ☎ 682369, Fax 683544, « Italian garden », park – ⊬ rest TV ☎ P – 🏃 50. AE VISA
Meals 13.25/25.00 **t.** and a la carte 5.80 – **28 rm** ☐ 68.50/102.00 **t.** – SB.

MONKTON COMBE Avon – see Bath.

MONKTON FARLEIGH Wilts. 403 404 N 29 – see Bradford-on-Avon.

MONTACUTE Somerset 403 L 31 – see Yeovil.

MORCHARD BISHOP Devon 403 I 31 – pop. 978 – ✉ Crediton – ☎ 01363.
London 217 – Barnstaple 28 – Exeter 17 – Taunton 40.

Wigham ⑤, EX17 6RJ, NE : 1 m. on Eastington rd ☎ 877350, Fax 877350, ≤, « 16C longhouse, working farm », ⛱ heated – ⊬ TV P. AE VISA. ✗
Meals (communal dining) 18.50 **st.** 4.75 – **5 rm** ☐ (dinner included) 80.00/110.00 **st.** – SB.

MORCOTT SERVICE AREA Leics. – see Uppingham.

MORECAMBE Lancs. 402 L 21 – pop. 46 657 – ✆ 01524.

Bare ✆ 418050 – Heysham, Trumacar Park, Middleton Rd ✆ 851011.

Station Buildings, Central Promenade, LA4 4DB ✆ 582808/9.

♦London 248 – ♦Blackpool 29 – ♦Carlisle 66 – Lancaster 4.

Strathmore, Marine Rd, East Promenade, LA4 5AP, ✆ 421234, Fax 414242, ≤ – rest – 200. AE VISA.
Meals 11.15/30.00 **t.** and a la carte 4.95 – **51 rm** 59.00/78.00 **t.** – SB.

Prospect, 363 Marine Rd, East Promenade, LA4 5AQ, ✆ 417819, Fax 417819, ≤ – AE VISA
Easter-October – **Meals** (by arrangement) 7.00 **st.** – **14 rm** 17.50/35.00 **st.** – SB.

ATS Westgate ✆ 68075/62011

MORETON Mersey. 402 403 K 23 pop. 12 053 – ✆ 0151.

♦London 225 – Birkenhead 4 – ♦Liverpool 5.

Lee Ho, 308 Hoylake Rd, L46 6DE, W : ¼ m. on A 553 ✆ 677 6440 – AE VISA
closed Monday dinner, 25 and 26 December and Bank Holidays – **Meals** - Chinese - (dinn only) 24.00 **t.** and a la carte.

MORETONHAMPSTEAD Devon 403 I 32 **The West Country G.** – pop. 1 380 – ✉ Newton Abb – ✆ 01647 – **Envir.** : Dartmoor National Park★★ (Brent Tor ≤★★, Haytor Rocks ≤★).

Manor House Hotel ✆ 40355.

♦London 213 – Exeter 13 – ♦Plymouth 28.

Manor House ⛰, TQ13 8RE, SW : 2 m. on B 3212 ✆ 440355, Fax 440961, ≤, « Pa 19C », park, squash – 120. AE VISA
Meals 18.50 **st.** (dinner) and a la carte 4.80 – **89 rm** 72.50/120.00 **st.** – SB.

Wray Barton Manor without rest., TQ13 8SE, SE : 1 ½ m. on A 382 ✆ 44046 Fax 440628.
April-October – **6 rm** 17.50/47.00.

Moorcote without rest., TQ13 8LS, NW : ¼ m. on A 382 ✆ 440966.
16 March-14 October – **6 rm** 28.00/38.00.

Reverend Woodforde, 11a Cross St., TQ13 8NL, ✆ 440691 – VISA
April-December – **Meals** *(closed Sunday)* (dinner only) 20.00 **t.** 4.50.

MORETON-IN-MARSH Glos. 403 404 O 28 **Great Britain G.** – pop. 2 802 – ✆ 01608.

Envir. : Chastleton House★★, SE : 5 m. by A 44.

♦London 86 – ♦Birmingham 40 – Gloucester 31 – ♦Oxford 29.

Manor House, High St., GL56 0LJ, ✆ 650501, Fax 651481, « 16C manor hous gardens » – rest – 75. AE VISA.
Meals 9.50/19.50 **t.** and a la carte 6.50 – **38 rm** 59.50/95.00 **t.**, 1 suite – SB.

Redesdale Arms, High St., GL56 0AW, ✆ 650308, Fax 651843 – 80. VISA.
Meals (bar lunch Monday to Saturday)/dinner 14.00 **t.** and a la carte – 4.45 – **16 r** 39.50 **st.**, 1 suite – SB.

Treetops without rest., London Rd, GL56 0HE, ✆ 651036. VISA.
6 rm 30.00/40.00 **st.**

Townend Cottage and Coach House, High St., GL56 0AD, ✆ 650846 – rm
closed 24 to 28 December and February – **Meals** (by arrangement) 9.40 – **4 rm** 29.0 39.50.

Marsh Goose, High St., GL56 0AX, ✆ 652111, Fax 652403. AE VISA JCB
closed Sunday dinner and Monday – **Meals** 13.50/33.00 **t.** and lunch a la carte 4.50.

Annies, 3 Oxford St., GL56 0LA, ✆ 651981 – AE VISA
closed Sunday dinner and 15 January-9 February – **Meals** (dinner only and Sunday lunch dinner 20.00 **st.** and a la carte 5.25.

MORPETH Northd. 401 402 O 18 – pop. 14 394 – ✆ 01670.

The Common ✆ 519980 – The Chantry, Bridge St., NE61 1PJ ✆ 511323.

♦London 301 – ♦Edinburgh 93 – ♦Newcastle upon Tyne 15.

Linden Hall ⛰, Longhorsley, NE65 8XF, NW : 7 ½ m. by A 192 on A 697 ✆ 51661 Fax 788544, ≤, « Country house in extensive grounds », park, – rest – 300. AE VISA.
Meals 15.95/24.50 **st.** and a la carte – **49 rm** 97.50/195.00 **st.**, 1 suite – SB.

ATS Coopies Lane Ind. Est. ✆ 514627

MORSTON Norfolk – see Blakeney.

MORTEHOE Devon 403 H 30 – see Woolacombe.

MOTCOMBE Dorset 403 404 N 30 – see Shaftesbury.

MOULSFORD Oxon. 403 404 Q 29 The West Country G. – pop. 491 – ☎ 01491.

Exc. : Ridgeway Path★★.

♦London 58 – ♦Oxford 17 – Reading 13 – Swindon 37.

XXX **Beetle and Wedge** with rm, Ferry Lane, OX10 9JF, ℘ 651381, Fax 651376, <, « Thames-side setting », – TV ☎ P. AE VISA JCB.
The Dining Room: Meals *(closed Sunday dinner, Monday and 25 December)* (booking essential) 21.50/35.00 **t.** – **10 rm** 80.00/125.00 **t.** – SB.
X **Boathouse : Meals** *(closed 25 December)* (booking essential) a la carte 17.15/28.15 **t.**

MOULTON Northants. 404 R 27 – see Northampton.

MOULTON N. Yorks. 402 P 20 – pop. 197 – ✉ Richmond – ☎ 01325.

♦London 243 – ♦Leeds 53 – ♦Middlesbrough 25 – ♦Newcastle upon Tyne 43.

XX **Black Bull Inn,** DL10 6QJ, ℘ 377289, Fax 377422, « Brighton Belle Pullman coach » – P. AE VISA
closed Sunday and 24 to 27 December – **Meals** 13.75 **t.** (lunch) and a la carte 19.95/32.50 **t.**

MOUSEHOLE Cornwall 403 D 33 The West Country G. – ✉ Penzance – ☎ 01736.

See : Village★.

Envir. : Penwith★★ – Lamorna (The Merry Maidens and The Pipers Standing Stone★) SW : 3 m. by B 3315.

Exc. : Land's End★ (cliff scenery★★★) W : 9 m. by B 3315.

♦London 321 – Penzance 3 – Truro 29.

Lobster Pot, South Cliff, TR19 6QX, ℘ 731251, Fax 731140, < – rest TV ☎. VISA.
closed January and February – **Meals** (bar lunch Monday to Saturday)/dinner 15.95 **t.** and a la carte 5.85 – **25 rm** (dinner included) 45.50/63.00 **t.** – SB.

Carn Du, Raginnis Hill, TR19 6SS, ℘ 731233, < Mounts Bay, – rest TV P. AE VISA JCB.
Meals (booking essential for non-residents) (bar lunch)/dinner 14.95 **t.** 4.50 – **7 rm** 25.00/60.00 **t.** – SB.

MUCH BIRCH Heref. and Worcs. – see Hereford.

MUCH WENLOCK Shrops. 402 403 M26 Great Britain G. – pop. 3 232 – ☎ 01952.

See : Priory★ *AC*.

Envir. : Ironbridge Gorge Museum★★ *AC* (The Iron Bridge★★ - Coalport China Museum★★ - Blists Hill Open Air Museum★★ – Museum of the River and Visitor Centre★) NE : 4½ m. by A 4169 and B 4380.

The Museum, High St., TF13 6HR ℘ 727679 (summer only).

♦London 154 – ♦Birmingham 34 – Shrewsbury 12 – Worcester 37.

Bourton Manor, Bourton, TF13 6QE, SW : 2¾ m. on B 4378 ℘ (01746) 785531, Fax 785683, <, – TV ☎ P – 40. AE VISA JCB
Meals a la carte 16.00/20.50 **st.** – **8 rm** 45.00/110.00 **st.** – SB.

Wheatland Fox, High St., TF13 6AD, ℘ 727292 – TV ☎ P. AE VISA.
Meals *(closed dinner Sunday and Monday to non-residents)* a la carte 10.45/15.95 **st.** 4.25 – **5 rm** 37.50/55.00 **st.** – SB.

Old Barn without rest., 45 Sheinton St., TF13 6HU, ℘ 728191, – TV P.
closed December – **4 rm** 28.00/38.00.

MUDEFORD Dorset 403 404 O 31 – see Christchurch.

MULLION Cornwall 403 E 33 The West Country G. – pop. 2 646 – ✉ Helston – ☎ 01326.

See : Mullion Cove★★★ (Church★) – Lizard Peninsula★.

Envir. : Kynance Cove★★★, S : 5 m.

Exc. : Helston (Flora Day Furry Dance★★) (May) N : 7½ m. by A 3083 – Culdrose (Flambards Village Theme Park★) *AC*, N : 6 m. by A 3083 – Wendron (Poldark Mine★) N : 9½ m. by A 3083 and B 3297.

18 Cury, Helston ℘ 240276.

♦London 323 – Falmouth 21 – Penzance 21 – Truro 26.

Polurrian, TR12 7EN, SW : ½ m. ℘ 240421, Fax 240083, < Mounts Bay, heated, squash – rest TV ☎ P. AE VISA
Meals (bar lunch Monday to Saturday) 18.00 **t.** and a la carte 5.95 – **38 rm** (dinner included) 76.00/172.00 **t.**, 1 suite – SB.

MUNGRISDALE Cumbria 401 402 L 19 20 – pop. 330 – ✉ Penrith – ☎ 0176 87.

♦London 301 – ♦Carlisle 33 – Keswick 8.5 – Penrith 13.

Mill, CA11 0XR, ℘ 79659, – rest TV P
March-October – **Meals** (dinner only) 22.50 **t.** 4.15 – **7 rm** 35.00/70.00 **s.**

Mosedale House, Mosedale, CA11 0XQ, N : 1 m. by Mosedale rd ℘ 79371 – TV P
Meals 11.00 4.50 – **4 rm** 20.00/54.00 **st.**

NAILSWORTH Glos. 403 404 N 28 – pop. 5 242 – 01453.

♦London 120 – ♦Bristol 30 – Swindon 41.

Egypt Mill, GL6 0EA, 833449, Fax 836098, – TV ☎ P – 100. AE VISA.
Meals 9.80/14.75 **t.** and a la carte – **14 rm** 42.50/65.00 **st.** – SB.

Aaron Farm, Nympsfield Rd, GL6 0ET, W : ¾ m. by Spring Hill 833598, Fax 836737
rm TV P
Meals 10.00 **st.** – **3 rm** 25.00/36.00 **st.**

Waterman's, Old Market, GL6 0BX, 832808 – AE VISA
closed Sunday and Monday – **Meals** (dinner only) a la carte 16.20/24.65 **t.** 4.50.

William's Bistro, 3 Fountain St., GL6 0BL, 835507, Fax 835950 – VISA
closed Sunday, Monday, Christmas to New Year, Good Friday, Easter Saturday an[d] Tuesdays after Bank Holidays – **Meals** - Seafood - (dinner only) a la carte 17.00/26.00 **st.**

NANTWICH Ches. 402 403 404 M 24 – pop. 11 695 – 01270.

Church House, Church Walk, CW5 5RG 610983/610880.

♦London 176 – Chester 20 – ♦Liverpool 45 – ♦Stoke-on-Trent 17.

Rookery Hall , Worleston, CW5 6DQ, N : 2 ½ m. by A 51 on B 5074 61001[.]
Fax 626027, ≤, « Part 19C country house », , , park, – TV ☎ P – 9[.]
AE VISA.
Meals (booking essential) 16.50/35.00 **st.** – **42 rm** 98.50/150.00 **st.**, 3 suites – SB.

Oakland House without rest., 252 Newcastle Rd, Blakelow, Shavington, CW5 7E[.]
E : 2½ m. by A 51 on A 500 67134, – TV P. VISA.
6 rm 25.00/34.00 **s.**

Churche's Mansion, Hospital St., CW5 5RY, E : ¼ m. 625933, Fax 62783[.]
« Timbered Elizabethan house », – P. VISA
closed Sunday dinner, Monday and second week January – **Meals** 15.95/25.00 **t.**

at Burland W : 2½ m. on A 534 – ✉ Nantwich – 01270 :

Burland Farm without rest., Wrexham Rd, CW5 8ND, W : ¾ m. on A 534 52421[.]
Fax 524419, « Working farm », – TV P
closed Christmas and New Year – **3 rm** 25.00/50.00.

Great Britain and Ireland is now covered by an Atlas at a scale of 1 inch to 4.75 miles.

Three easy to use versions: Paperback, Spiralbound and Hardback.

NATIONAL EXHIBITION CENTRE W. Mids. 403 404 O 26 – see Birmingham.

NAWTON N. Yorks. – see Helmsley.

NAYLAND Suffolk 404 W 28 – 01206.

♦London 64 – Bury St.Edmunds 24 – ♦Cambridge 54 – Colchester 6 – ♦Ipswich 19.

Gladwins Farm , Harpers Hill, CO6 4NU, NW : ½ m. on A 134 262261, Fax 26300[.]
≤, , , park, – rm TV P. VISA
closed Christmas – **Meals** (by arrangement) 8.50 **st.** – **4 rm** 20.00/50.00 **st.**

Martha's Vineyard, 18 High St., CO6 4JF, 262888 – VISA
closed Sunday dinner, Monday to Wednesday, 2 weeks summer and 2 weeks winter
Meals (dinner only and Sunday lunch)/dinner 15.00/18.50 **t.** 5.50.

NEAR SAWREY Cumbria 402 L 20 – see Hawkshead.

NEEDHAM MARKET Suffolk 404 X 27 – pop. 4 377 – 01449.

♦London 77 – ♦Cambridge 47 – ♦Ipswich 8.5 – ♦Norwich 38.

Forte Travelodge without rest., Norwich Rd., IP6 8LP, Beacon Hill Service Are[a] at junction of A 14 with A 140 721640, Reservations (Freephone) 0800 850950 – TV [.]
P. AE VISA.
40 rm 34.50 **t.**

Pipps Ford, Norwich Rd roundabout, IP6 8LJ, SE : 1 ¾ m. by B 1078 at junction of A 1[.] with A 140 760208, Fax 760561, « Elizabethan farmhouse », , , , – P. [.]
closed mid December-mid January – **Meals** (by arrangement) (communal dining) 18.50
3.50 – **7 rm** 17.00/65.00 **t.**

NETHERTON Mersey. - see Liverpool.

NETHER WESTCOTE Oxon. – see Stow-on-the-Wold.

NETTLEBED Oxon. 404 R 29 pop. 699 – ✉ Henley-on-Thames – 01491.

♦London 44 – ♦Oxford 19 – Reading 9.

White Hart, High St., RG9 5DD, 641245, Fax 641423, « Part 15C inn », – rm [.]
☎ P – 40. VISA.
Meals a la carte 10.50/18.95 st. 4.00 – **6 rm** 49.50/79.50 **st.** – SB.

NETTLETON SHRUB Wilts. 403 404 N 29 – see Castle Combe.

EW ALRESFORD Hants. 403 404 Q 30 – pop. 5 041 – ✉ Alresford – ☎ 01962.
ondon 63 – ♦Portsmouth 40 – Reading 33 – ♦Southampton 20.

✗ **Hunters** with rm, 32 Broad St., S024 9AQ, ✆ 732468, Fax 732468, « Former coaching inn », – TV – 60. AE VISA.
closed 24 to 30 December – **Meals** *(closed Sunday)* 9.95/15.95 **t.** and dinner a la carte 4.50 – **3 rm** 37.50/47.50 **st.** – SB.

EWARK-ON-TRENT Notts. 402 404 R 24 **Great Britain G.** – pop. 24 749 – ☎ 01636.
e : St. Mary Magdalene★.
Kelwick, Coddington ✆ 626241.
The Gilstrap Centre, Castlegate, NG24 1BG ✆ 78962.
ondon 127 – Lincoln 16 – ♦Nottingham 20 – ♦Sheffield 42.

Grange, 73 London Rd, NG24 1RZ, S : ½ m. on Grantham rd (A 1) ✆ 703399, Fax 702328, – TV ☎ P. AE VISA.
closed 24 December-2 January – **Meals** (lunch by arrangement)/dinner 12.50 **t.** and a la carte 6.95 – **15 rm** 45.00/75.00 **t.** – SB.

✗ **Gannets Bistrot,** 35 Castlegate, NG24 1AZ, ✆ 610018 – . VISA JCB
closed Sunday and Monday – **Meals** a la carte 13.25/24.75 **st.** 5.25.

at North Muskham N : 4½ m. by A 46 and A 1 – ✉ Newark-on-Trent – ☎ 01636 :

Forte Travelodge, NG23 6HT, N : ½ m. on A 1 (southbound carriageway) ✆ 703635, Reservations (Freephone) 0800 850950 – TV & P. AE VISA.
Meals (grill rest.) – **30 rm** 34.50 **t.**

ATS 70 William St. ✆ 77531

EWBURGH Lancs. 402 L 23 – ☎ 01257.
ondon 217 – ♦Liverpool 26 – ♦Manchester 39 – Preston 20 – Southport 13.

Red Lion, Ash Brow, WN8 7NG, on A 5209 ✆ 462336, Fax 462827 – TV ☎ P. AE VISA.
Meals (bar meals)/dinner a la carte 7.25/13.80 **t.** 3.75 – 4.50 – **13 rm** 28.00/35.00 **t.**

EWBURY Berks. 403 404 Q 29 **The West Country G.** – pop. 136 700 – ☎ 01635.
c. : Littlecote★★ (arms and armour★, Roman mosaic floor★) *AC*, W : 10 m. by A 4.
Newbury and Crookham, Bury's Bank Road, Greenham Common ✆ 40035 – 18 Donnington lley, Old Oxford Rd ✆ 32488.
The Wharf, RG14 5AS ✆ 30267.
ondon 67 – ♦Bristol 66 – ♦Oxford 28 – Reading 17 – ♦Southampton 38.

Donnington Valley H. & Golf Course, Old Oxford Rd, Donnington, RG14 3AG, N : 1¾ m. by A 4 on B 4494 ✆ 551199, Fax 551123, 18, park – rest TV ☎ & P – 140. AE VISA
Gallery : Meals 15.00/17.50 **st.** and a la carte 5.95 – 7.50 – **58 rm** 87.50/122.50 **st.** – SB.

Foley Lodge, Stockcross, RG20 8JU, NW : 2 m. by A 4 on B 4000 ✆ 528770, Fax 528398, – rm TV ☎ P – 220. AE VISA
Meals a la carte 15.00/40.00 **t.** 5.95 – **68 rm** 95.00/130.00 **st.**, 1 suite – SB.

Jarvis Elcot Park, RG20 8NJ, W : 5 m. by A 4 ✆ (01488) 658100, Fax 658288, ←, , park, – rm rest TV ☎ & P – 110. AE VISA
Meals 15.00 **st.** and a la carte 6.00 – 8.25 – **75 rm** 90.00/110.00 **st.** – SB.

Hilton National, Pinchington Lane, RG14 7HL, S : 2 m. by A 34 ✆ 529000, Fax 529337, – rm rest TV ☎ & P – 200. AE VISA
Meals (bar lunch Saturday) 14.95/17.50 **st.** and dinner a la carte 5.95 – 10.25 – **109 rm** 87.00/105.00 **st.** – SB.

Stakis Newbury, Oxford Rd, RG20 8XY, N : 3¼ m. on A 34 ✆ 247010, Fax 247077, – rm rest TV ☎ & P – 30. AE VISA.
Meals (bar lunch Saturday and Bank Holidays) 9.75/15.95 **st.** and a la carte 8.00 – 8.50 – **109 rm** 83.00/93.00 **st.**, 2 suites – SB.

Blue Boar Inn, North Heath, RG20 8UE, N : 4¾ m. on B 4494 ✆ 248236, Fax 248506 – TV ☎ P. AE VISA.
Meals (in bar Sunday dinner) a la carte 14.95/22.40 – **15 rm** 45.00/57.00 **t.**

Limes, 368 London Rd, RG14 2QH, E : ½ m. on A 4 ✆ 33082, Fax 580023, – TV ☎ P. AE VISA JCB.
Meals (by arrangement) 12.00 **t.** 3.95 – **15 rm** 35.00/54.00.

at Woolton Hill SW : 4½ m. by A 34 off A 343 – ✉ Newbury – ☎ 01635 :

Hollington House , RG20 9XA, SW : ½ m. on East End rd ✆ 255100, Fax 255075, ←, « Edwardian country house, gardens », heated, park, – rm TV ☎ P – 45. AE VISA.
Meals 14.50/28.50 **t.** and a la carte – **19 rm** 90.00/350.00 **st.**, 1 suite – SB.

at Hamstead Marshall SW : 5½ m. by A 4 – ✉ Newbury – ☎ 01488 :

White Hart Inn, Kintbury Rd, RG20 0HW, ✆ 658201, Fax 657192, – TV ☎ P. AE VISA.
closed 25 and 26 December – **Meals** - Italian - *(closed Sunday)* a la carte 14.20/24.50 **t.** 5.25 – **6 rm** 40.00/65.00 **t.**

at Speen W : 1 ¾ m. on A 4 – ✉ Newbury – ☎ 01635 :

Hare & Hounds, Bath Rd, RG19 1QY, ✆ 521152, Fax 47708 – TV ☎ P
29 rm, 1 suite.

ATS 30 Queens Rd ✆ 42250

NEWBY BRIDGE Cumbria 402 L 21 **Great Britain G.** – ✉ Ulverston – ☎ 0153 95.

Envir. : Lake Windermere★★.

♦London 270 – Kendal 16 – Lancaster 27.

Lakeside, Lakeside, LA12 8AT, NE : 1 m. on Hawkshead rd ✆ 31207, Fax 31699, « Lakeside setting », – ◻ – TV ☎ P – 100. AE VISA
Meals (bar lunch)/dinner a la carte 16.00/25.00 **t.** 6.00 – **70 rm** 75.00/130.00 **t.**, 2 suite – SB.

Whitewater, The Lakeland Village, LA12 8PX, SW : 1½ m. by A 590 ✆ 31133, Fax 3188, squash – TV ☎ P – 70. AE VISA
Meals (bar lunch Monday to Saturday)/dinner a la carte 15.40/24.65 **st.** – **35 rm** 65.0 98.00 **st.** – SB.

Swan, LA12 8NB, ✆ 31681, Fax 31917, – TV ☎ P – 65. AE VIS
Meals (bar lunch Monday to Saturday)/dinner 24.00 **st.** and a la carte – **35 rm** 60.0 130.00 **st.**, 1 suite – SB.

at Cartmell Fell NE : 3¼ m. by A 590 off A 592 – ✉ Grange-over-Sands – ☎ 0153 95

Lightwood Farmhouse without rest., LA11 6NP, ✆ 31454, – TV P. VIS
closed Christmas – **8 rm** 30.00/50.00 **t.**

at Bowland Bridge NE : 4 ¼ m. by A 590 off A 592 – ✉ Grange-over-Sands ☎ 0153 95 :

Hare and Hounds, LA11 6NN, ✆ 68333, – TV ☎ P. VISA
Meals 8.95/12.00 **t.** and a la carte 4.50 – **16 rm** 35.00/66.00 **t.** – SB.

NEWBY WISKE N. Yorks. – see Northallerton.

NEWCASTLE AIRPORT Tyne and Wear 401 402 O 19 – see Newcastle upon Tyne.

NEWCASTLE-UNDER-LYME Staffs. 402 403 404 N 24 **Great Britain G.** – pop. 119 091 ☎ 01782.

Exc. : Wedgwood Visitor's Centre★ *AC*, SE : 6½ m. by A 34 Z.

18 Newcastle Municipal, Keele Rd ✆ 627596.

Ironmarket, ST5 1PB ✆ 711964.

♦London 161 – ♦Birmingham 46 – ♦Liverpool 56 – ♦Manchester 43.

Plan of Built up Area : see Stoke-on-Trent

NEWCASTLE-UNDER-LYME
CENTRE

High Street	YZ	
Roebuck Centre	YZ	
Albert Street	Y	
Barracks Road	YZ	
Blackfriars Road	Z	9
Brook Lane	Z	
Brunswick Street	Y	
Church Street	Y	20
Friarswood Road	Z	
George Street	Y	
Hassell Street	Y	
Higherland	Z	37
Iron Market	Y	38
King Street	Y	
Lancaster Road	Z	
Liverpool Road	Y	41
Lower Street	YZ	
Merrial Street	Y	47
Parkstone Avenue	Z	
Pool Dam	Z	
Queen Street	Y	
Ryecroft	Y	
Vessey Terrace	Z	73
Victoria Road	Z	

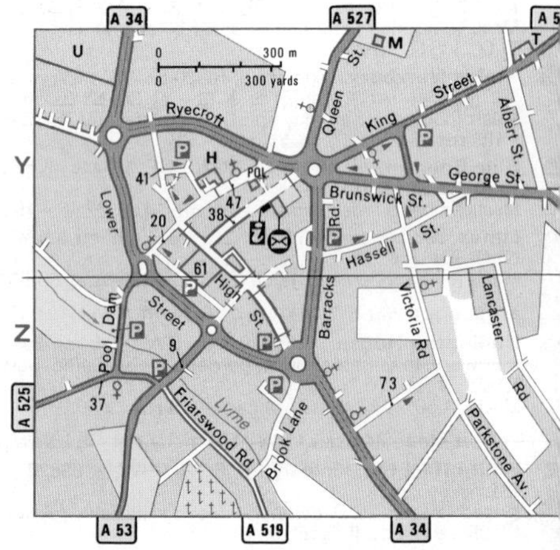

Forte Posthouse, Clayton Rd, Clayton, ST5 4DL, S : 2 m. on A 519 ☎ 717171, Fax 717138, Lø, ≘s, 🏊, ⛱ – ⇔ rm 📺 ☎ ℗ – 🎪 70. 🅂 AE ⓞ VISA JCB
Meals 11.00/18.50 **st.** and a la carte – ☐ 7.95 – **119 rm** 59.00 **st.** – SB.

Clayton Lodge (Jarvis), Clayton Rd, Clayton, ST5 4AF, S : 1 ¼ m. on A 519 ☎ 613093, Fax 711896 – ⇔ rm 📺 ☎ ℗ – 🎪 280. 🅂 AE ⓞ VISA
Hobsons : Meals 7.85/13.75 **st.** and a la carte 🍷 5.80 – ☐ 8.50 – **49 rm** 70.00/80.00 **st.** – SB.
on Stoke-on-Trent town plan V **e**

ATS Lower St. ☎ 622431

NEWCASTLE UPON TYNE Tyne and Wear 401 402 O 19 **Great Britain G.** – pop. 259 541 – ☎ 0191.

See : City★★ – Grey Street★ CZ – Quayside★ CZ : Composition★, All Saints Church★ (interior★) Castle Keep★ *AC* CZ – Laing Art Gallery and Museum★ *AC* CY **M1** – Museum of Antiquities★ CY **M2**.

Envir. : Hadrian's Wall★★, W : by A 69 AV.

Exc. : Beamish : North of England Open-Air Museum★★ *AC*, SW : 7 m. by A 692 and A 6076 AX Seaton Delaval Hall★ *AC*, NE : 11 m. by A 189 - BV - and A 190.

High Gosforth Park ☎ 236 2009 – Broadway East, Gosforth ☎ 285 6710, BV – City of Newcastle, Three Mile Bridge, Gosforth ☎ 285 1775, – Wallsend, Rheydt Av., Bigges Main ☎ 262 1973, NE : by A 1058 BV – Whickham, Hollinside Park ☎ 488 7309.

✈ Newcastle Airport : ☎ 286 0966, NW : 5 m. by A 696 AV – **Terminal** : Bus Assembly : Central Station Forecourt.

⛴ to Norway (Bergen, Haugesund and Stavanger) (Color Line) 2-3 weekly – to Denmark (Esbjerg) (Scandinavian Seaways) (summer only) (18 h) – to Sweden (Gothenburg) (Scandinavian Seaways) weekly (22 h) – to Germany (Hamburg) (Scandinavian Seaways) 1 daily (23 h 30 mn).

Central Library, Princess Sq., NE99 1DX ☎ 261 0691 – Main Concourse, Central Station, NE1 5DL ☎ 230 0030.

London 276 – ◆Edinburgh 105 – ◆Leeds 95.

Plans on following pages

Copthorne Newcastle, The Close, Quayside, NE1 3RT, ☎ 222 0333, Telex 53340, Fax 230 1111, ≤, Lø, ≘s, 🏊 – 🛗 ⇔ rm ▤ rest 📺 ☎ ♿ ℗ – 🎪 200. 🅂 AE ⓞ VISA JCB. ✻ CZ **z**
Meals 12.95/16.95 **st.** and dinner a la carte 🍷 5.75 – ☐ 10.95 – **156 rm** 112.00/125.00 **t.** – SB.

Vermont, Castle Garth (off St. Nicholas St. beside Castle Keep), NE1 1RQ, ☎ 233 1010, Fax 233 1234, ≤, Lø – 🛗 ⇔ rm ▤ rest 📺 ☎ ♿ ℗ – 🎪 200. 🅂 AE ⓞ VISA. ✻ CZ **s**
Brasserie : Meals 15.50 and a la carte 🍷 5.50 - (see also ***Blue Room*** below) – ☐ 9.50 – **95 rm** 105.00/125.00 **t.**, 6 suites – SB.

Forte Crest, New Bridge St., NE1 8BS, ☎ 232 6191, Fax 261 8529 – 🛗 ⇔ rm ▤ rest 📺 ☎ ♿ ℗ – 🎪 400. 🅂 AE ⓞ VISA JCB CY **n**
Meals 9.95/16.50 **st.** and a la carte 🍷 6.75 – ☐ 9.95 – **165 rm** 79.00 **st.**, 1 suite – SB.

County Thistle, Neville St., NE99 1AH, ☎ 232 2471, Fax 232 1285 – 🛗 ⇔ rm 📺 ☎ ℗ – 🎪 130. 🅂 AE ⓞ VISA JCB CZ **a**
Meals *(closed Saturday lunch)* 10.50/17.00 **st.** and dinner a la carte 🍷 5.95 – ☐ 9.25 – **115 rm** 77.00/97.00 **st.** – SB.

Surtees, 12-16 Dean St., NE1 1PG, ☎ 261 7771, Fax 230 1322 – 🛗 📺 ☎. 🅂 AE ⓞ VISA JCB. ✻ CZ **u**
Meals - Café-restaurant - (bar lunch Monday to Friday)/dinner a la carte approx. 13.70 **t.** – **27 rm** ☐ 57.50/69.50 **t.**

Novotel, Ponteland Rd, Kenton, NE3 3HZ, at junction of A 1 (M) with A 696 ☎ 214 0303, Fax 214 0633, Lø, ≘s, 🏊 – 🛗 ⇔ rm ▤ rest 📺 ☎ ♿ ℗ – 🎪 220. 🅂 AE ⓞ VISA AV **a**
Meals 12.95 **st.** and a la carte 🍷 5.25 – ☐ 7.50 – **126 rm** 52.50 **st.**

Bank Top Toby, Ponteland Rd., Kenton, NE3 3TY, at junction of A 1 (M) with A 696 ☎ 214 0877, Fax 214 0095 – ⇔ ▤ rest 📺 ☎ ♿ ℗ – 🎪 50. 🅂 AE ⓞ VISA. ✻ AV **a**
Meals 6.25/15.00 **t.** and a la carte 🍷 3.95 – **30 rm** ☐ 59.95/69.95 **t.** – SB.

Swallow, 1 Newgate Arcade, Newgate St., NE1 5SX, ☎ 232 5025, Fax 232 8428 – 🛗 ⇔ rm 📺 ☎ ℗ – 🎪 100. 🅂 AE ⓞ VISA CZ **o**
Meals 10.25/17.25 **st.** and a la carte 🍷 5.00 – **93 rm** ☐ 85.00/95.00 **st.** – SB.

Imperial Swallow, Jesmond Rd, NE2 1PR, ☎ 281 5511, Fax 281 8472, Lø, ≘s, 🏊 – 🛗 ⇔ rm 📺 ☎ ℗ – 🎪 120. 🅂 AE ⓞ VISA CY **c**
Meals 9.50/16.00 **st.** and dinner a la carte 🍷 6.00 – **121 rm** ☐ 70.00/95.00 **st.** – SB.

Waterside, 48-52 Sandhill, Quayside, NE1 3JF, ☎ 230 0111, Fax 230 1615 – 🛗 📺 ☎. 🅂 AE ⓞ VISA JCB. ✻ CZ **r**
Meals - Café-restaurant - *(closed lunch Sunday and Bank Holidays)* 7.95/25.00 **st.** and a la carte 🍷 3.70 – ☐ 5.50 – **20 rm** 48.00/75.00 **st.** – SB.

NEWCASTLE UPON TYNE

Adelaide Terrace . . . . AX 2
Atkinson Road . . . . AX 3
Bath Street . . . . BX 4
Bensham Road . . . . AX 6
Benton Bank . . . . BV 8
Buddle Street . . . . BV 13
Byker Bridge . . . . BV 15
Church Avenue . . . . AV 16
Church Road . . . . AV 18
Clayton Road . . . . BV 21
Coldwell Lane . . . . BX 22
Coldwell Street . . . . BX 24
Condercum Road . . . . AX 26
Fossway . . . . BV 31
Haddrick's Mill Road . . . . . BV 36
High Street West . . . . BV 37
Jesmond Dene Road . . . . . BV 39
Killingworth Road . . . . . . BV 42
Lobley Hill Road . . . . AX 45
Matthew Bank . . . . BV 49
Neptune Road . . . . BV 51
Red Hall Drive . . . . BV 61
Redheugh Bridge . . . . AX 62
Saltwell Road . . . . BX 69
Shipdon Road . . . . AX 71
Springfield Road . . . . AV 72
Station Road . . . . BX 73
Stephenson Road . . . . BV 74
Sunderland Road . . . . BX 76
Sutton Street . . . . BV 77
Swalwell Bank . . . . ABX 79
Waverdale Avenue . . . . . . BV 83
West Farm Avenue . . . . . . BV 87
Whickham Bank . . . . AX 88
Windy Nook Road . . . . BX 89

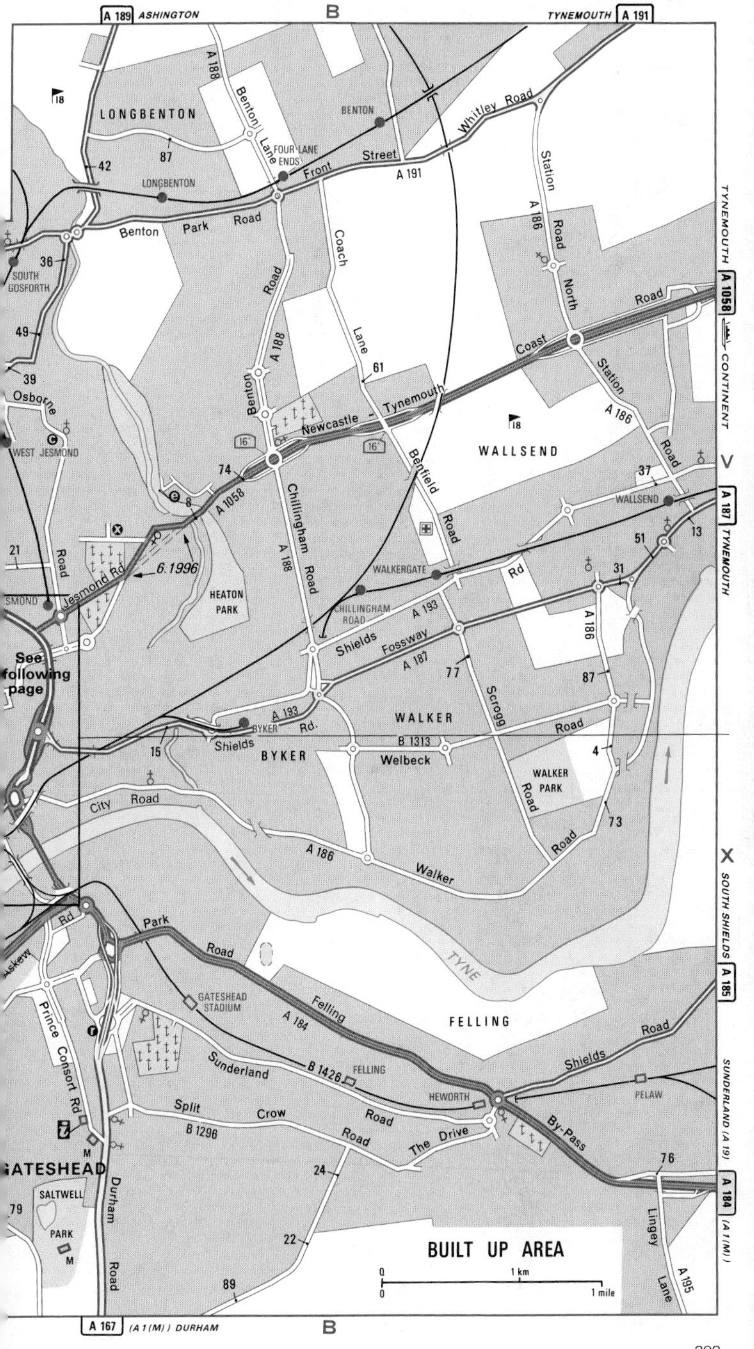
A 189 ASHINGTON
B
TYNEMOUTH A 191
LONGBENTON
BENTON
FOUR LANE ENDS
Front Street
Whitley Road
A 191
Benton Park Road
SOUTH GOSFORTH
Coach Lane
Station Road
North Road
A 186
Coast Road
TYNEMOUTH A 1058
CONTINENT
Newcastle - Tynemouth
WALLSEND
Benfield Road
Chillingham Road
A 188
Benton Road
Osborne
WEST JESMOND
Jesmond Rd
6.1996
HEATON PARK
A 1058
WALKERGATE
CHILLINGHAM ROAD
WALLSEND
A 187 TYNEMOUTH
V
See following page
Shields Rd.
A 193
Fossway
A 187
Scrogg Road
WALKER
BYKER
B 1313
Welbeck Road
WALKER PARK
City Road
A 186
Walker Road
X
SOUTH SHIELDS A 185
TYNE
Park Road
Felling
A 184
GATESHEAD STADIUM
FELLING
Askew Rd
Prince Consort Rd
Sunderland Road
B 1426
Split Crow Road
B 1296
HEWORTH
PELAW
Shields Road
SUNDERLAND (A 19)
By-Pass
The Drive
GATESHEAD
SALTWELL PARK
Durham Road
Lingey Lane
A 195
A 184 (A 1(M))
BUILT UP AREA
1 km
1 mile
A 167 (A 1(M)) DURHAM
B

NEWCASTLE UPON TYNE

Blackett Street . . . . **CY**
Eldon Square Shopping Centre . . . . . **CYZ**
Grey Street . . . . **CZ**
Newgate Street . . . . **CZ**
Pilgrim Street . . . . **CZ** 57

Bridge Street . . . . **CZ** 10
Broad Chare . . . . **CZ** 12
Collingwood Street . . . . **CZ** 25
Forth Street . . . . **CZ** 30
George Street . . . . **CZ** 32
Great North Road . . . . **CY** 33
Jesmond Road . . . . **CY** 40
John Dobson Street . . . . **CY** 41
Leazes Park Road . . . . **CY** 43
Low Friar Street . . . . **CZ** 46
Market Street . . . . **CZ** 47

Mosley Street . . . . **CZ** 50
Neville Street . . . . **CZ** 52
New Bridge St. West . . . . **CY** 53
Northumberland Street . . . . . . **CY** 56
Railway Street . . . . **CZ** 60
Rutherford Street . . . . **CZ** 63
St. Mary's Place . . . . **CY** 65
St. Nicholas Street . . . . **CZ** 66
Scotswood Road . . . . **CZ** 70
Thornton Street . . . . **CZ** 80
Wellington Street . . . . **CY** 84

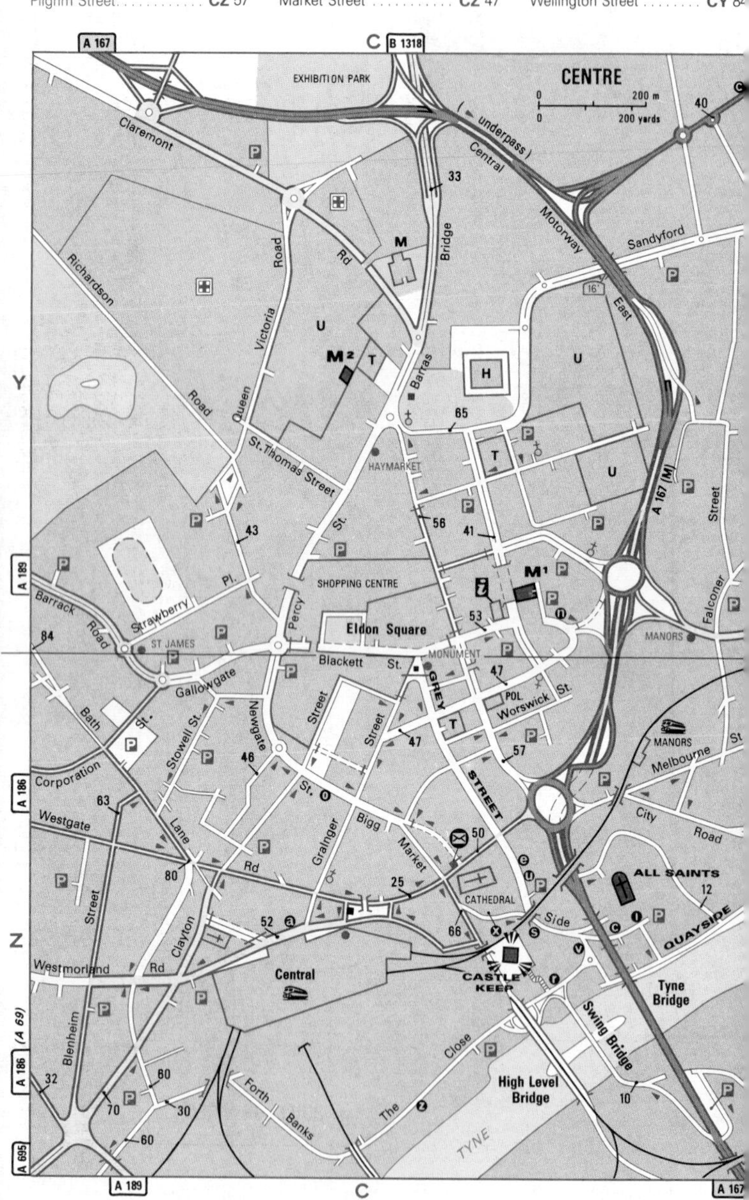

New Kent, 127 Osborne Rd, Jesmond, NE2 2TD, ✆ 281 1083, Fax 281 3369 – TV ☎ P. AE VISA. BV **c**
Meals (bar lunch)/dinner 12.50 **st.** and a la carte 5.05 – **32 rm** 60.00/75.00 **st.** – SB.

Forte Travelodge, Whitemare Pool, NE10 8YB, SE : 4 m. at junction of A 194 with A 184 ✆ 438 3333, Reservations (Freephone) 0800 850950 – TV P. AE VISA.
Meals (grill rest.) – **41 rm** 34.50 **t.**

Avenue, 2 Manor House Rd, NE2 2LU, at junction with Osborne Av. ✆ 281 1396 – TV ☎. VISA BV **x**
closed 23 December-14 January – **Meals** (by arrangement) – **10 rm** 22.00/42.00 **st.**

Blue Room (at Vermont H.), Castle Garth (off St. Nicholas St. beside Castle Keep), NE1 1RQ, ✆ 233 1010, Fax 233 1234 – P. AE VISA CZ **s**
Meals *(closed Sunday and Monday)* (dinner only) 27.50 **t.** and a la carte.

Fisherman's Lodge, Jesmond Dene, Jesmond, NE7 7BQ, ✆ 281 3281, Fax 281 6410 – P. AE VISA JCB BV **e**
closed Saturday lunch, Sunday and Bank Holidays – **Meals** 17.80/28.00 **st.** and a la carte 5.50.

21 Queen Street (Laybourne), 21 Queen St., Quayside, NE1 3UG, ✆ 222 0755, Fax 221 0761 – AE VISA CZ **c**
closed Saturday lunch, Sunday and Bank Holidays – **Meals** 15.00 **t.** (lunch) and a la carte 25.50/34.50 **t.** 6.00
Spec. Marinade of smoked salmon with a warm potato salad, Assiette of new season's lamb with roasted spring vegetables, Roasted turbot with onion confit, wild mushrooms and meat juices.

Vujon, 29 Queen St., Quayside, NE1 3UG, ✆ 221 0601, Fax 221 0602 – . AE VISA JCB CZ **i**
closed Sunday lunch and 25-26 December – **Meals** - Indian - 10.00/25.00 **st.** and a la carte 4.50.

The Blackgate, The Side, NE1 3JE, ✆ 261 7356 – AE VISA CZ **x**
closed Saturday lunch, Sunday, Monday dinner and Bank Holidays – **Meals** 13.20/17.15 **t.** and a la carte.

Leela's, 20 Dean St., NE1 1PG, ✆ 230 1261 – . AE VISA CZ **e**
closed Sunday, 1 to 15 January and Bank Holidays – **Meals** - South Indian - 9.95/16.95 **t.** and a la carte.

Courtney's, 5-7 The Side, NE1 3JE, ✆ 232 5537 – . AE VISA CZ **v**
closed Saturday lunch, Sunday, 2 weeks May, 1 week Christmas and Bank Holidays – **Meals** 15.00 **st.** (lunch) and dinner a la carte 17.95/25.00 **st.**

Barn Again Bistro, 21a Leazes Park Rd, NE1 4PF, ✆ 230 3338 – VISA CY **a**
closed Saturday lunch and Sunday – **Meals** 9.85 **t.** (lunch) and a la carte 11.65/20.25 **t.** 4.65.

at Gosforth N : 4 ¾ m. by B 1318 – AV – ✉ Tyneside – ✆ 0191 :

Swallow Gosforth Park, High Gosforth Park, NE3 5HN, on B 1318 ✆ 236 4111, Fax 236 8192, ≤, park, squash – rm rest TV ☎ P – 600. AE VISA JCB
Brandling : Meals 14.50/27.50 **t.** 8.00 – **Conservatory : Meals** 15.00 **st.** 8.00 – **173 rm** 83.00/120.00 **t.**, 5 suites – SB.

at Seaton Burn N : 8 m. by B 1318 – AV – ✉ Newcastle upon Tyne – ✆ 0191 :

Holiday Inn, Great North Rd, NE13 6BP, N : ¾ m. at junction with A 1 ✆ 201 9988, Fax 236 8091, – rm TV ☎ P – 400. AE VISA
Meals (carving lunch) 16.95 **st.** (dinner) and a la carte 15.35/25.90 **st.** – 9.95 – **149 rm** 98.50/108.50 **st.**, 1 suite – SB.

at Boldon E : 7 ¾ m. by A 184 – BX – ✆ 0191 :

Quality Friendly, Witney Way, Boldon Business Park, NE35 9PE, ✆ 519 1999, Fax 519 0655, – rm rest TV ☎ P – 200. AE VISA JCB.
Meals 8.25/13.50 **st.** and a la carte 4.25 – 7.75 – **82 rm** 57.50/82.00 **st.** – SB.

Forsters, 2 St. Bedes, Station Rd, East Boldon, NE36 OLE, ✆ 519 0929 – AE VISA
closed Sunday, Monday, 1 week June, 1 week August, Christmas, New Year and Bank Holidays – **Meals** (dinner only) 16.00 **t.** and a la carte 18.85/23.95 **t.** 4.00.

at Newcastle Airport NW : 6 ¾ m. by A 167 off A 696 – AV – ✉ Newcastle upon Tyne – ✆ 01661 :

Airport Moat House, Woolsington, NE13 8DJ, ✆ 401 9988, Telex 537121, Fax 860157 – rm rest TV ☎ P – 400. AE VISA.
Meals a la carte 14.15/26.00 **st.** 5.75 – 9.25 – **98 rm** 75.00/90.00 **st.**, 2 suites – SB.

at Ponteland NW : 8 ¼ m. by A 167 on A 696 – ✉ Newcastle upon Tyne – 01661 :

XX **Horton Grange** with rm, Seaton Burn, NE13 6BU, NE : 3½ m. by Morpeth rd 860686, Fax 860308, – rest . VISA JCB.
closed 25-26 December and 1 January – **Meals** *(closed Sunday to non-residents)* (booking essential) (dinner only) 32.00 **t.** 4.75 – **9 rm** 59.00/80.00 **st.** – SB.

X **Café 21,** 35 The Broadway, Darras Hall Estate, NE20 9PW, SW : 1 ½ m. by B 6323 and Callerton Lane 820357 – AE VISA
closed Sunday, Monday and Bank Holidays – **Meals** - Bistro - (bookings not accepted) 13.50 **t.** (lunch) and a la carte 16.00/22.00 **t.** 5.20.

ATS 80/90 Blenheim St. 232 3921/232 5031
ATS Newton Park Garage, Newton Rd, Heaton 281 2243
ATS White St, Walker 262 0811

NEWENT Glos. 403 404 M 28 pop. 5 373 – 01989.

◆London 109 – Gloucester 10 – Hereford 22 – Newport 44.

Orchard House, Aston Ingham Rd, Kilcot, GL18 1NP, SW : 2 ¼ m. by B 4221 on B 4222 720417, – . VISA.
Meals (communal dining) 15.50 **s.** 4.50 – **3 rm** 30.00/59.00 **s.**

NEWHAVEN E. Sussex 404 U 31 – pop. 10 210 – 01273.

to France (Dieppe) (Stena Line) 4 daily (4 h).

◆London 63 – ◆Brighton 9 – Eastbourne 14 – Lewes 7.

Hotels and restaurants see : Lewes NW : 7 m. by A 26.

NEWINGTON Kent 404 V/W 29 pop. 4 899 – 01795.

◆London 40 – Canterbury 20 – Maidstone 13.

Newington Manor, Callaways Lane, ME9 7LU, 842053, Fax 844273, – . AE VISA.
closed 26 to 31 December – **Meals** *(closed Saturday lunch, Sunday dinner and Bank Holiday Mondays)* 16.25 **st.** and a la carte 6.50 – 4.50 – **12 rm** 50.00/90.00 **st.** – SB.

NEWLYN Cornwall 403 D 33 – see Penzance.

NEWMARKET Suffolk 404 V 27 – pop. 16 498 – 01638.

18 Links, Cambridge Rd 662708.

63 The Rookery, CB8 8HT 667200.

◆London 64 – ◆Cambridge 13 – ◆Ipswich 40 – ◆Norwich 48.

Bedford Lodge, Bury Rd, CB8 7BX, NE : ½ m. on A 1304 663175, Fax 667391, , , , – – 200. AE VISA JCB.
Meals 15.95/16.95 **t.** and a la carte – **49 rm** 72.00/92.50 **t.**, 7 suites – SB.

Heath Court, Moulton Rd, CB8 8DY, 667171, Fax 666533 – rm – 80. AE VISA
Meals *(closed lunch Saturday and Bank Holidays)* a la carte 14.75/22.50 **st.** 6.10 – **44 rm** 60.00/95.00 **st.** – SB.

at Six Mile Bottom (Cambs.) SW : 6 m. on A 1304 – ✉ Newmarket – 01638 :

Swynford Paddocks, CB8 0UE, 570234, Fax 570283, <, , park, – rest – 25. AE VISA
closed 4 days Christmas-New Year – **Meals** 22.95 **t.** (dinner) and a la carte 15.25/24.95 **t.** 5.00 – **15 rm** 70.00/128.00 **t.** – SB.

ATS 2 Exeter Rd 662521

NEWMILLERDAM W. Yorks. – see Wakefield.

NEW MILTON Hants. 403 404 P 31 pop. 21 291 – 01425.

9, 18 Barton-on-Sea, Milford Rd 615308.

◆London 106 – Bournemouth 12 – ◆Southampton 21 – Winchester 34.

❀ **Chewton Glen**, Christchurch Rd, BH25 6QS, W : 2 m. by A 337 and Ringwood Rd on Chewton Farm Rd 275341, Fax 272310, <, , « Gardens », , , heated, , 9, park, indoor – rest – 120. AE VISA.
Marryat Room and Conservatory : Meals 26.00/42.00 **t.** and a la carte approx. 42.00 **t.** 8.00 – 14.50 – **40 rm** 194.25/262.50 **t.**, 14 suites – SB
Spec. Ravioli of langoustines with a nage of Noilly Prat flavoured scallops, Braised sea bass with shiitake mushrooms, ginger and lemon grass, Verbena crème brûlée.

NEW POLZEATH Cornwall 403 F 32 – ✉ Wadebridge – 01208.

◆London 283 – Newquay 27 – ◆Plymouth 49 – Truro 36.

Pentire Rocks, PL27 6US, 862213, Fax 862259, heated – rest . AE VISA JCB.
closed 4 January-4 February – **Meals** *(closed Sunday dinner)* 10.00/30.00 **t.** – **15 rm** 32.50/65.00 **t.** – SB.

EWPORT Essex 404 U 28 – pop. 2 178 – ✉ Saffron Walden – ☎ 01799.

ondon 38 – ◆Cambridge 21 – Colchester 41.

XX **Village House,** High St., CB11 3PF, ☎ 541560 – Ⓟ. VISA
closed Sunday, Monday and January – **Meals** (dinner only) a la carte 19.30/25.30 **t.** 5.25.

EWPORT Shrops. 402 403 404 M 25 **Great Britain G.** – pop. 25 028 – ☎ 01952.

xc. : Weston Park★★, SE : 6½ m. by A 41 and A 5.

London 150 – ◆Birmingham 33 – Shrewsbury 18 – ◆Stoke-on-Trent 21.

Royal Victoria, St. Mary's St., TF10 7AB, ☎ 820331, Fax 820209 – TV ☎ Ⓟ – 100. AE VISA JCB
Meals *(closed Sunday dinner)* (light lunch)/dinner 11.50 **t.** and a la carte – **24 rm** 35.00/49.50 **t.**

EWPORT PAGNELL Bucks. 404 R 27 – pop. 14 374 – ☎ 01908.

London 57 – Bedford 13 – Luton 21 – Northampton 15.

Coach House (Country Club), London Rd, Moulsoe, MK16 0JA, SE : 1½ m. by B 526 on A 509 ☎ 613688, Fax 617335, – rm TV ☎ Ⓟ – 180. AE VISA.
Meals (bar lunch Saturday and Bank Holiday Mondays) a la carte 11.40/22.40 **t.** 5.80 – 7.50 – **49 rm** 72.00/82.00 **t.** – SB.

Swan Revived, High St., MK16 8AR, ☎ 610565, Fax 210995 – TV ☎ Ⓟ – 70. AE VISA
Meals 14.25 **t.** and a la carte – **42 rm** 58.00/80.00 **t.** – SB.

EWQUAY Cornwall 403 E 32 **The West Country G.** – pop. 17 390 – ☎ 01637.

nvir. : Penhale Point and Kelsey Head★ (≤★★) SW : by A 3075 Y – Trerice★ *AC*, SE : 3½ m. by 392 - Y - and A 3058.

xc. : St. Agnes - St. Agnes Beacon (✻★★) SW : 12½ m. by A 3075 – Y – and B 3285.

Tower Rd ☎ 872091 Z – 9, 18 Treloy ☎ 878554.

Newquay Airport : ☎ 860551 Y.

Municipal Offices, Marcus Hill, TR7 1BD ☎ 871345.

London 291 – Exeter 83 – Penzance 34 – ◆Plymouth 48 – Truro 14.

Plan on next page

Bristol, Narrowcliff, TR7 2PQ, ☎ 875181, Fax 879347, ≤, – TV ☎ Ⓟ – 200. AE VISA JCB Z r
Meals 10.00/16.50 **t.** and a la carte 4.50 – **73 rm** 52.00/92.00 **t.**, 1 suite – SB.

Trebarwith, Trebarwith Cres., TR7 1BZ, ☎ 872288, Fax 875431, ≤ bay and coast, – rest TV ☎ Ⓟ. AE VISA JCB. Z a
March-October – **Meals** (bar lunch)/dinner 13.00 8.00 – **41 rm** (dinner included) 40.00/80.00 **st.** – SB.

Kilbirnie, Narrowcliff, TR7 2RS, ☎ 875155, Fax 850769, heated, – TV ☎ Ⓟ. VISA Z e
Meals (bar lunch)/dinner 15.50 **t.** – **66 rm** (dinner included) 40.00/80.00 **t.** – SB.

Esplanade, Esplanade Rd, Pentire, TR7 1PS, ☎ 873333, Fax 851413, ≤, – TV ☎ Ⓟ. AE VISA Y a
Meals (dinner only and Sunday lunch)/dinner 13.00 **st.** and a la carte 4.00 – **75 rm** (dinner included) 20.00/80.00 **st.** – SB.

Trenance Lodge, 83 Trenance Rd, TR7 2HW, ☎ 876702, Fax 872034, heated, – TV Ⓟ. VISA. Z u
Meals (dinner only) 17.50 **t.** and a la carte 4.00 – **5 rm** 25.00/50.00 – SB.

Whipsiderry, Trevelgue Rd, Porth, TR7 3LY, NE : 2 m. by A 392 off B 3276 ☎ 874777, Fax 874777, ≤, heated, – rest TV Ⓟ. AE VISA.
closed January, February and November – **Meals** (bar lunch)/dinner 18.95 **st.** and a la carte 4.95 – **23 rm** (dinner included) 29.00/80.00 **t.**

Windward, Alexandra Rd, Porth Bay, TR7 3NB, ☎ 873185 – rest TV Ⓟ. AE VISA. Y r
Meals (residents only) (bar lunch)/dinner 10.00 **st.** 3.95 – **14 rm** 26.00/48.00 **t.**

Water's Edge, Esplanade Rd, Pentire, TR7 1QA, ☎ 872048, ≤ Fistral Bay, – rest TV ☎ Ⓟ. VISA. Y u
Easter-September – **Meals** (residents only) (dinner only) 4.50 – **20 rm** (dinner included) 25.00/70.00 **t.** – SB.

Corisande Manor, Riverside Av., Pentire, TR7 1PL, ☎ 872042, ≤ Gannel Estuary, – rest TV Ⓟ. Y n
5 May-13 October – **Meals** (bar lunch)/dinner 12.50 **t.** 4.95 – **19 rm** (dinner included) 26.00/52.00 **t.** – SB.

Philema, Esplanade Rd, Pentire, TR7 1PY, ☎ 872571, Fax 873188, ≤, – TV ☎ Ⓟ. VISA JCB Y c
March-October – **Meals** (bar lunch)/dinner 13.50 **t.** 3.50 – **27 rm** 25.00/60.00 **t.** – SB.

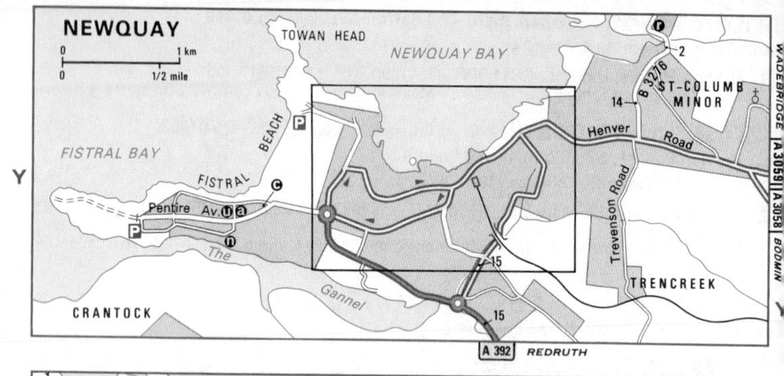

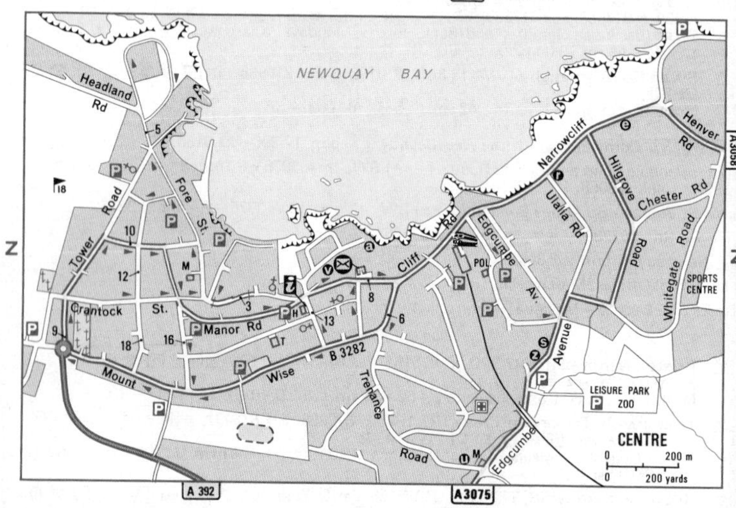

Bank Street . . . . Z 3	Beacon Road . . . . Z 5	Marcus Hill . . . . Z 13
East Street . . . . Z 8	Berry Road . . . . Z 6	Porth Way . . . . Y 14
Fore Street . . . . Z	Higher Tower Road . . . . Z 9	Trevemper Road . . . . Y 15
	Hope Terrace . . . . Z 10	St. Georges Road . . . . Z 16
Alexandra Road . . . . Y 2	Jubilee Street . . . . Z 12	St. John's Road . . . . Z 18

⌂ **Wheal Treasure,** 72 Edgcumbe Av., TR7 2NN, ✆ 874136 – ⊁ rest TV P. ✗ Z z
April-October – **Meals** (by arrangement) 7.00 **st.** 3.00 – **12 rm** (dinner included) 25.00/50.00 **st.** – SB.

⌂ **Copper Beech,** 70 Edgcumbe Av., TR7 2NN, ✆ 873376 – ⊁ rest TV P. ✗ Z s
Easter-October – **Meals** 11.00 **st.** – **15 rm** 17.50/45.00 **st.**

⌂ **Towan Beach,** 7 Trebarwith Cres., TR7 1DX, ✆ 872093 – ⊁ rest TV. VISA JCB. ✗
Meals (by arrangement) 8.50 **st.** 3.00 – **6 rm** 21.00/46.00 **st.** Z v

at Trerice SE : 4 ¾ m. by A 392 off A 3058 – Y – ✉ Newquay – ☎ 01872 :

⌂ **Trewerry Mill**, TR8 5HS, W : ½ m. ✆ 510345, – ⊁ P. ✗
Easter-October – **Meals** (by arrangement) 7.50 3.50 – **5 rm** 16.50/33.00.

at Crantock SW : 4 m. by A 3075 – Y – ✉ Newquay – ☎ 01637 :

Crantock Bay, West Pentire, TR8 5SE, W : ¾ m. ✆ 830229, Fax 831111, ≤ Crantock Bay, – ⊁ rest TV ☎ P. AE VISA JCB
restricted opening November-mid March – **Meals** (buffet lunch)/dinner 9.00/15.95 **t.** 4.50 – **34 rm** (dinner included) 43.00/86.00 **t.** – SB.

⌂ **Crantock Plains Farmhouse,** Cubert, TR8 5PH, SE : 1½ m. bearing right at the fork in the road ✆ 830253, – ⊁ P. ✗
closed Christmas – **Meals** (by arrangement) 8.50 **st.** 3.00 – **7 rm** 16.00/41.00 **st.**

EW ROMNEY Kent 404 W 31 – ☎ 01797.

ondon 71 – ♦Brighton 60 – Folkestone 17 – Maidstone 36.

Romney Bay House, Coast Rd, Littlestone, TN28 8QY, E : 1 ¼ m. off R 2071 ✆ 364747, Fax 367156, <, , – TV ☎ P. VISA.
closed Christmas – **Meals** (light lunch by arrangement) 20.00 **t.** (dinner) and lunch a la carte approx. 16.50 **t.** – **7 rm** 35.00/90.00 **t.** – SB.

EWTON POPPLEFORD Devon 403 K 31 – pop. 1 765 (inc. Harpford) – ✉ Ottery St. Mary – 01395.

ondon 208 – Exeter 10 – Sidmouth 4.

Coach House, Southerton, EX11 1SE, N : 1 m. by Venn Ottery Rd ✆ 568577, – TV ☎ P. VISA.
Meals *(closed Sunday lunch)* (booking essential) 7.50/14.00 **t.** and dinner a la carte 4.90 – **6 rm** 30.00/70.00 – SB.

EWTON SOLNEY Derbs. 402 403 404 P 25 – see Burton-upon-Trent (Staffs.).

ITON I.O.W. 403 404 Q 32 – see Wight (Isle of).

ORMAN CROSS Cambs. 404 T 26 – see Peterborough.

ORMANTON PARK Leics. – see Stamford.

ORTHALLERTON N. Yorks. 402 P 20 – pop. 9 628 – ☎ 01609.

The Applegarth Car Park, DL7 8LZ ✆ 776864.

.ondon 238 – ♦Leeds 48 – ♦Middlesbrough 24 – York 33.

Golden Lion (Forte), 114 High St., DL7 8PP, ✆ 777411, Fax 773250 – TV ☎ P – 150. AE VISA JCB
Meals (bar lunch Monday to Saturday)/dinner 16.95 **st.** and a la carte 5.80 – 8.50 – **21 rm** 55.00/65.00 **st.** – SB.

Windsor, 56 South Par., DL7 8SL, ✆ 774100 – TV.
Meals (by arrangement) 9.00 – **6 rm** 20.00/38.00 **st.**

Romanby Court, High St., DL7 8PG, ✆ 774918 – AE VISA JCB
closed Sunday and first 2 weeks August – **Meals** - Italian - 14.95 **t.** and a la carte 16.15/ 22.85 **t.** 4.95.

at Staddlebridge NE : 7½ m. by A 684 on A 19 at junction with A 172 – ✉ Northallerton – ☎ 01609 :

McCoys at the Tontine with rm, DL6 3JB, on southbound carriageway ✆ 882671, Fax 882660, « 1930's decor » – TV ☎ P. AE VISA
closed 25 and 26 December and 1 January – **Meals** (dinner only) a la carte 22.10/33.70 **t.** – **6 rm** 79.00/99.00 **t.**

Bistro : Meals a la carte 15.85/29.55 **t.** 6.00.

at Newby Wiske S : 2½ m. by A 167 – ✉ Northallerton – ☎ 01609 :

Solberge Hall, DL7 9ER, NW : 1 ¼ m. on Warlaby rd ✆ 779191, Fax 780472, <, , park – TV ☎ P – 100. AE VISA
Meals 6.95/21.95 **t.** and dinner a la carte – **24 rm** 70.00/80.00 **t.**, 1 suite – SB.

NORTHAMPTON Northants. 404 R 27 **Great Britain G.** – pop. 180 567 – ☎ 01604.

xc. : All Saints, Brixworth★, N : 7 m. on A 508 Y.

, Delapre, Eagle Drive, Nene Valley Way ✆ 764036/763957, Z – 18 Collingtree Park, Vindingbrook Lane ✆ 700000.

Visitor Centre, Mr Grant's House, 10 St. Giles Square, NN1 1DA ✆ 22677.

London 69 – ♦Cambridge 53 – ♦Coventry 34 – ♦Leicester 42 – Luton 35 – ♦Oxford 41.

Plan on next page

Swallow, Eagle Drive, NN4 7HW, SE : 2 m. by A 428 off A 45 ✆ 768700, Fax 769011, , , – rm rest TV ☎ P – 220. AE VISA JCB Z **a**
Spires : Meals 13.50/21.00 **st.** and a la carte 6.75 – **La Fontana : Meals** - Italian - *(closed Sunday)* 13.50/20.00 **st.** and a la carte 4.95 – **118 rm** 95.00/105.00 **st.**, 2 suites – SB.

Stakis Northampton, 100 Watering Lane, Collingtree, NN4 0XW, S : 3 m. on A 508 ✆ 700666, Fax 702850, , , , – rm rest TV ☎ P – 300. AE VISA.
Meals *(closed lunch Saturday and Bank Holidays)* (carving lunch) 13.75/18.95 **st.** and a la carte 8.00 – 9.75 – **136 rm** 97.00/107.00 **st.**, 3 suites – SB.

Northampton Moat House (Q.M.H.), Silver St., NN1 2TA, ✆ 739988, Fax 230614 – rm TV ☎ P – 600. AE VISA X **n**
Meals *(closed lunch Saturday)* 15.00/18.00 **st.** and a la carte 6.50 – 9.50 – **136 rm** 70.00 **st.**, 4 suites – SB.

Courtyard by Marriott, Bedford Rd, NN4 7YF, SE : 1 ½ m. on A 428 ✆ 22777, Fax 35454, – rm TV ☎ P – 30. AE VISA JCB Z **c**
Meals 13.95 **st.** and a la carte 5.55 – 8.25 – **104 rm** 66.00/86.00 **st.** – SB.

NORTHAMPTON

Street	Grid	No.
Abington Street	X	
Drapery	X	18
Gold Street	X	
Grosvenor Centre	X	
Weston Favell Centre	Y	

Street	Grid	No.
Abington Square	X	2
Bewick Road	Y	4
Billing Road	X	5
Bridge Street	X	6
Campbell Street	X	7
Castillian St.	X	8
Charnwood Avenue	Y	10
Church Lane	X	12
Cliftonville Rd.	Z	13
College Street	X	14
Derngate	X	15
Greyfriars	X	23
Guildhall Road	X	24
Hazelwood Rd.	X	25
Horse Shoe Street	X	28
Kettering Road	X	30
Kingsthorpe Grove	Y	34
Lower Mounts	X	35
Oaklands Drive	Y	38
Overstone Road	X	39
Park Avenue North	Y	40
Park Avenue South	Z	43
Rushmere Road	Z	44
St. Andrew's Road	Y	45
St. Edmund's Road	X	48
St. Edmund's St.	Z	49
St. James's Road	Z	50
St. John's Street	X	51
St. Leonard's Road	Z	52
St. Michael's Road	X	53
Sheep Street	X	54
Silver Street	X	55
Spencer Bridge Road	X, Z	57
Towcester Road	Z	58
Upper Mounts	X	59
Waveney Way	Y	60
West Bridge	X	62
Windrush Way	Y	63

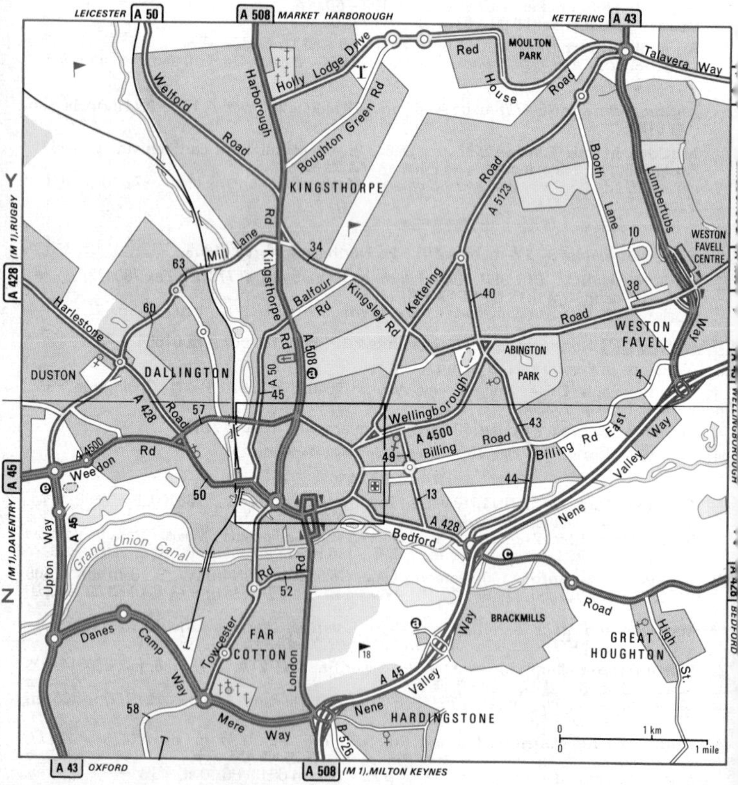

Midway Toby, London Rd, Wootton, NN4 0TG, S : 2 ½ m. on A 508 ☏ 769676, Fax 769523 – rest – 60. AE VISA
Meals (grill rest.) 13.00 **t.** (lunch) and a la carte 11.50/20.50 **t.** 3.95 – **31 rm** 59.95/69.95 **t.** – SB.

Lime Trees, 8 Langham Pl., Barrack Rd, NN2 6AA, ☏ 32188, Fax 233012 – rest . AE VISA. Y a
closed Sunday and 25 and 26 December – **Meals** (dinner only) 15.00 **t.** and a la carte – **25 rm** 46.00/60.00 **t.** – SB.

Travel Inn, Harpole Turn, Weedon Rd, NN7 4DD, W : 3 ¾ m. on A 45 ☏ 832340, Fax 831807 – rm – 60. AE VISA.
Meals (grill rest.) – 4.95 – **51 rm** 34.50 **t.**

Forte Travelodge, Upton Way (Ring Rd), NN5 6EG, SW : 1 ¾ m. by A 45 ☏ 758395, Reservations (Freephone) 0800 850950 – . AE VISA. Z e
Meals (grill rest.) – **40 rm** 34.50 **t.**

at Spratton N : 7 m. by A 508 off A 50 – Y – ✉ Northampton – ☎ 01604 :

Broomhill Country House , Holdenby Rd, NN6 8LD, SW : 1 m. on Holdenby rd ☏ 845959, Fax 845834, ≤, heated, , park, – . AE VISA.
closed 25 and 26 December – **Meals** *(closed Sunday dinner)* 13.25/20.40 **t.** and a la carte 5.90 – **13 rm** 60.00/70.00 **t.**

at Moulton NE : 4½ m. by A 43 – Y – ✉ Northampton – ☎ 01604 :

Poplars, 33 Cross St., NN3 7RZ, ☏ 643983, Fax 790233, – rm . AE VISA
closed 1 week Christmas – **Meals** (by arrangement) 12.50 **t.** 3.75 – **20 rm** 38.00/48.00 **t.** – SB.

ATS Kingsthorpe Rd ☏ 713303

NORTH BOVEY Devon 403 I 32 **The West Country G.** – pop. 254 – ✉ Newton Abbot – ☎ 01647.

Envir. : Dartmoor National Park★★ (Brent Tor ≤★★, Haytor Rocks ≤★).

London 214 – Exeter 13 – ♦Plymouth 31 – Torquay 21.

Blackaller House , TQ13 8QY, ☏ 440322, Fax 440322, ≤, – rest
closed January and February – **Meals** (by arrangement) 17.50 **t.** 4.35 – **5 rm** 27.00/66.00 **t.** – SB.

NORTHENDEN Gtr. Manchester 402 403 404 N 23 – see Manchester.

NORTH FERRIBY Humbs. 402 S 22 – see Kingston-upon-Hull.

NORTHFIELD W. Mids. 403 ㉒ 404 ⑳ – see Birmingham.

NORTHLEACH Glos. 403 404 O 28 **Great Britain G.** – pop. 1 654 – ☎ 01451.

See : Church of SS. Peter and Paul★ – Wool Merchants' Brasses★.

Cotswold Countryside Collection, GL54 3JH ☏ 860715 (summer only).

London 84 – ♦Birmingham 63 – Gloucester 21 – ♦Oxford 28 – Swindon 24.

XX Wickens, Market Pl., GL54 3EJ, ☏ 860421 – .

NORTH MUSKHAM Notts. 402 404 R 24 – see Newark-on-Trent.

NORTH NEWINGTON Oxon – see Banbury.

NORTH PERROT Somerset – see Crewkerne.

NORTH PETHERTON Somerset 403 K 30 – see Bridgwater.

NORTH STIFFORD Essex 404 ㊹ – ✉ Grays – ☎ 01708.

London 22 – Chelmsford 24 – Southend-on-Sea 20.

Stifford Moat House (Q.M.H), High Rd, RM16 5UE, at junction of A 13 with A 1012 ☏ 719988, Fax (01375) 390426, , – rm – 120. AE VISA.
Meals *(closed lunch Saturday and Bank Holidays)* 17.50/19.00 **t.** and a la carte 6.00 – 9.50 – **96 rm** 74.00/82.00 **st.** – SB.

NORTH STOKE Oxon. – see Wallingford.

NORTH WALSHAM Norfolk 403 404 Y 25 **Great Britain G.** – pop. 9 534 – ☎ 01692.

Exc. : Blicking Hall★★ *AC*, W : 8½ m. by B 1145, A 140 and B 1354.

London 125 – ♦Norwich 16.

Beechwood, 20 Cromer Rd, NR28 0HD, ☏ 403231, Fax 407284, – rest . AE VISA
Meals 6.20/12.00 **t.** and dinner a la carte 4.00 – **9 rm** 33.00/50.00 **t.** – SB.

Toll Barn without rest., NR28 0JB, S : 1½ m. on B 1150 ☏ 403063, Fax 406582, – . .
6 rm 44.00 **s.**

NORTH WALTHAM Hants. 403 404 Q 30 – pop. 727 – ✉ Basingstoke – ☎ 01256.
♦London 59 – Reading 24 – Southampton 24 – Swindon 52.

Wheatsheaf, RG25 2BB, S : ¾ m. on A 30 ✆ 398282, Fax 398253 – ⅹ rm TV ☎ P – 80. AE ⓓ VISA
Meals 9.50/16.95 **t.** and a la carte 5.25 – **28 rm** ☐ 57.50/69.00 **t.** – SB.

NORTON Shrops. – see Telford.

NORTON ST PHILIP Somerset 403 404 N 30 – see Bath (Avon).

NORWICH Norfolk 404 Y 26 **Great Britain G.** – pop. 120 895 – ☎ 01603.
See : City★★ - Cathedral★★ Y – Castle (Museum and Art Gallery★ *AC*) Z – Market Place★ Z.
Envir. : Sainsbury Centre for Visual Arts★ *AC*, W : 3 m. by B 1108 - X.
Exc. : Blicking Hall★★ *AC*, N : 11 m. by A 140 – V - and B 1354 – NE : The Broads★.
18 Royal Norwich, Drayton High Road, Hellesdon ✆ 425712, V – 18 Sprowston Park, Wroxham Rd ✆ 410657 – 18 Costessy Park, Costessey ✆ 746333 – 18 Bawburgh, Long Lane ✆ 746390.
✈ Norwich Airport : ✆ 411923, N : 3½ m. by A 140 V.
ℹ The Guildhall, Gaol Hill, NR2 1NF ✆ 666071.
♦London 109 – ♦Kingston-upon-Hull 148 – ♦Leicester 117 – ♦Nottingham 120.

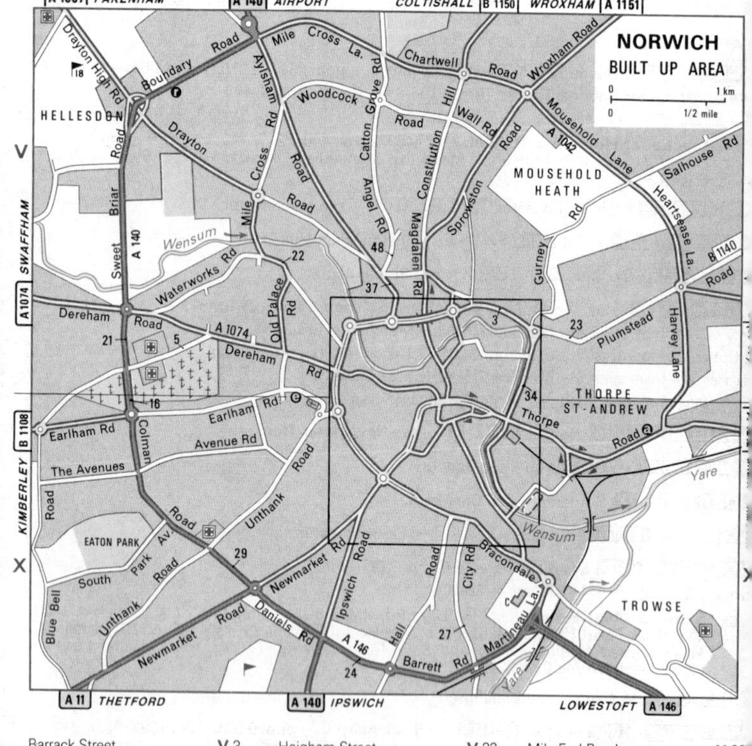

Sprowston Manor, Wroxham Rd, Sprowston, NR7 8RP, NE : 3 ¼ m. on A 1151 ✆ 410871, Fax 423911, ⅹ rest TV ☎ P – 120. AE ⓓ VISA
Meals 19.50/40.00 **t.** and a la carte 6.95 – ☐ 9.00 – **86 rm** 83.00/89.00 **t.**, 1 suite – SB.

NORWICH

astle Mall
Shopping Centre . . . . Z
m Hill . . . . Y
entleman's Walk . . . . Z 17
ndon Street . . . . YZ 26
. Andrew's Street . . . . Y 36
. Stephen's Street . . . . Z

Bank Plain . . . . Y 2
Bethel Street . . . . Z 4
Castle Meadow . . . . Z 6
Cattle Market Street . . . . Z 7
Chapel Field North . . . . Z 9
Charing Cross . . . . Y 10
Colegate . . . . Y 14
Exchange Street . . . . YZ 15
Grapes Hill . . . . Y 19
Market Avenue . . . . Z 28

Rampant Horse Street . . . . . . Z 32
Red Lion Street . . . . Z 33
St. George's Street . . . . Y 38
Thorn Lane . . . . Z 42
Timber Hill . . . . Z 43
Tombland . . . . Y 45
Upper King Street . . . . Y 46
Wensum Street . . . . Y 49
Westlegate . . . . Z 50
Whitefriars . . . . Y 51

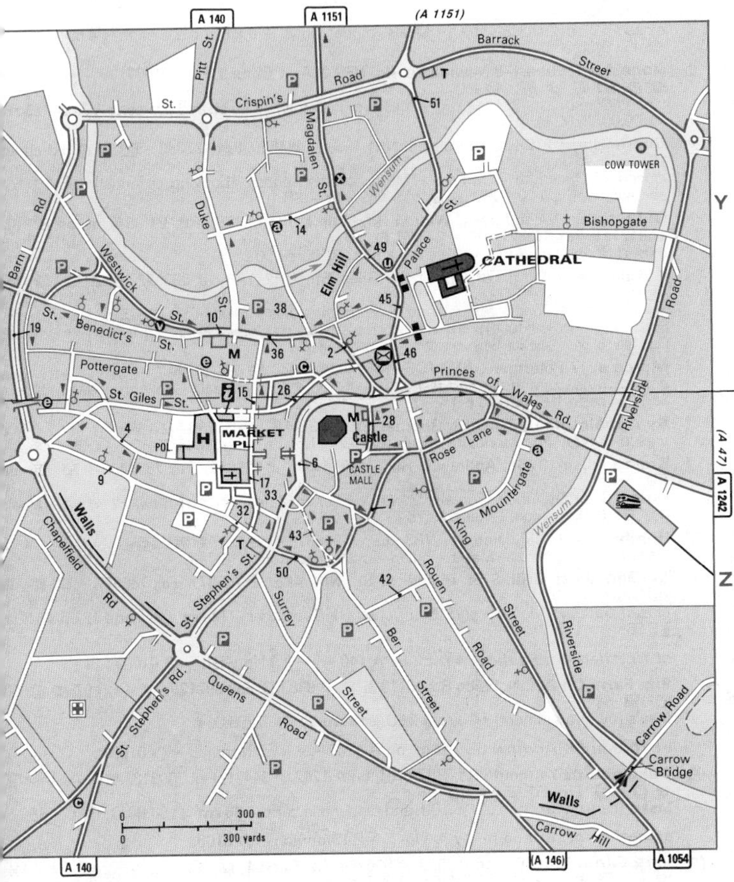

Nelson, Prince of Wales Rd, NR1 1DX, ℘ 760260, Fax 620008, <, Lδ, ≘s, ▣ – |‡| ⇔ rm ▤ rest TV ☎ & ℗ – 🏔 90. ⚿ AE ⓞ VISA. ⋙ Z **a**
Meals (bar lunch Saturday) 9.75/14.50 **st.** and a la carte 4.25 – **132 rm** ☐ 75.00/95.00 **st.** – SB.

Maid's Head (Q.M.H.), Tombland, NR3 1LB, ℘ 209955, Fax 613688 – |‡| ⇔ rm TV ☎ ℗ – 🏔 100. ⚿ AE ⓞ VISA JCB Y **u**
Meals 4.95/26.20 **t.** and a la carte – ☐ 10.75 – **80 rm** 69.00/89.00 **st.**, 1 suite – SB.

Stakis Norwich, Cromer Rd, NR6 6JA, N : 3 m. by A 140 ℘ 410544, Fax 789935, Lδ, ≘s, ▣ – |‡| ⇔ rm ▤ rest TV ☎ & ℗ – 🏔 450. ⚿ AE ⓞ VISA JCB
Meals 9.95/15.95 **st.** and a la carte 4.50 – ☐ 7.95 – **108 rm** 69.00/92.00 **st.** – SB.

Quality Friendly, 2 Barnard Rd, Bowthorpe, NR5 9JB, W : 3½ m. by A 1074 on A 47 ℘ 741161, Fax 741500, Lδ, ≘s, ▣ – ⇔ rm ▤ rest TV ☎ & ℗ – 🏔 180. ⚿ AE ⓞ VISA. ⋙
Meals (carving rest.) 9.90/13.50 **st.** and a la carte 4.50 – **80 rm** ☐ 57.50/88.00 **st.** – SB.

Forte Posthouse, Ipswich Rd, NR4 6EP, S : 2¼ m. on A 140 ☏ 456431, Fax 506400, – rm TV ☎ P – 65. AE VISA JCB
Meals a la carte 13.15/22.15 **st.** – 7.95 – **116 rm** 59.00 **st.** – SB.

Norwich, 121 Boundary Rd, NR3 2BA, on A 47 ☏ 787260, Fax 400466, – rm rest TV ☎ P – 300. AE VISA V
Meals *(closed lunch Saturday and dinner 25 and 26 December)* (carving lunch)/dinne 16.00 **st.** and a la carte 6.50 – **107 rm** 62.50/72.50 **st.** – SB.

Beeches, 4-6 Earlham Rd, NR2 3DB, ☏ 621167, Fax 620151, – TV ☎ P. AE VISA JCB. VX e
closed 22 to 29 December – **Meals** (dinner only) 12.00 **t.** and a la carte 4.50 – **27 rm** 45.00/58.00 **t.** – SB.

Annesley House, 6-8 Newmarket Rd, NR2 2LA, ☏ 624553, Fax 621577, – rest TV ☎ P. AE VISA. Z c
closed Christmas and New Year – **Meals** (dinner only) 15.95 **st.** and a la carte 3.95 – **23 rm** 55.00/75.00 **st.** – SB.

Cumberland, 212-216 Thorpe Rd, NR1 1TJ, ☏ 434550, Fax 433355 – TV ☎ P. AE VISA JCB. X a
closed 26 December-4 January – **Meals** *(closed Sunday)* (booking essential) 9.95/16.95 **t** and a la carte 4.00 – **25 rm** 34.90/59.90 **t.** – SB.

Old Rectory without rest., Watton Rd, Little Melton, NR9 3PB, W : 5½ m. on B 1108 ☏ 812121, Fax 812521, – TV P.
closed Christmas and New Year – **3 rm** 32.00/58.00 **st.**

XX ✿ **Adlard's** (Adlard), 79 Upper St. Giles St., NR2 1AB, ☏ 633522 – AE VISA JCB Z e
closed Monday lunch, Sunday and 1 week Christmas – **Meals** 16.50/35.00 **t.**
Spec. Foie gras and lentil terrine with sherry vinaigrette, Lunesdale duck with glazed apple chutney, gratin dauphinoise, Cassolette of prune and Earl Grey ice cream with hot spiced plums.

XX **Marco's,** 17 Pottergate, NR2 1DS, ☏ 624044 – AE VISA Y e
closed Sunday, Monday and last 2 weeks September – **Meals** - Italian - 14.00 **t.** (lunch) and a la carte 19.40/28.70 **t.** 4.50.

XX **By Appointment,** 27-29 St. Georges St., NR3 1AB, ☏ 630730 – VISA Y a
closed Sunday and Monday – **Meals** (dinner only) a la carte 20.65/25.40 **t.** 6.95.

XX **Brasted's,** 8-10 St. Andrew's Hill, NR2 1AD, ☏ 625949, Fax 766445 – AE VISA Y c
closed Saturday lunch, Sunday, 24 December to 2 January and Bank Holidays – **Meals** 15.00 **t.** (lunch) and a la carte 21.75/27.75 **t.** 7.00.

X **Bombay,** 9-11 Magdalen St., NR3 1LE, ☏ 666618 – AE VISA JCB Y x
closed 25 December – **Meals** - Indian - a la carte approx. 10.75 **t.**

X **St. Benedicts Grill,** 9 St. Benedicts St., NR2 4PE, ☏ 765377, Fax 765377 – AE VISA Y v
closed Sunday, Monday and 25 to lunch 31 December – **Meals** a la carte 12.85/18.20 **t.** 5.95.

at Horsham St. Faith N : 4½ m. by A 140 – V – ✉ Norwich – 01603 :

Elm Farm Chalet, Norwich Rd, NR10 3HH, ☏ 898366, Fax 897129, – TV ☎ P. AE VISA.
Meals (by arrangement) 14.00 **t.** 3.50 – **18 rm** 31.00/56.00 **t.**

at Thorpe St. Andrew E : 2½ m. on A 1242 – X – ✉ Norwich – 01603 :

Oaklands, 89 Yarmouth Rd, NR7 0HH, on A 1242 ☏ 34471, Fax 700318, – rest TV ☎ P – 110. AE VISA.
Meals (carving lunch) 6.95/15.50 **t.** and dinner a la carte – **38 rm** 54.00/68.00 **t.** – SB.

at Hethersett SW : 6 m. by A 11 – X – ✉ Norwich – 01603 :

Park Farm, NR9 3DL, on B 1172 ☏ 810264, Fax 812104, park, – rest TV ☎ P – 120. AE VISA.
Meals 10.75/15.50 **st.** and a la carte 5.95 – **38 rm** 60.00/115.00 **st.** – SB.

Forte Travelodge without rest., Thickthorn Service Area, NR13 9AU, at junction of A 11 with A 47 ☏ 57549, Reservations (Freephone) 0800 850950 – TV P. AE VISA
40 rm 34.50 **t.**

ATS Mason Rd, Mile Cross Lane ☏ 423471 ATS Aylsham Rd, Aylsham Way ☏ 426316

NOTTINGHAM Notts. 402 403 404 Q 25 **Great Britain G.** – pop. 270 222 – ✆ 0115.

See : Castle Museum★ (alabasters★) *AC*, CZ **M**.

Envir. : Wollaton Hall★ *AC*, W : 3 m. by A 609 AZ **M**.

Exc. : Newstead Abbey★ *AC*, N : 9 m. by A 611 - AY - and B 683.

18 Bulwell Forest, Hucknall Rd ✆ 977 0576, AY – 18 Wollaton Park ✆ 978 7574, AZ – 18 Mapperley, Central Av., Plains Rd ✆ 926 5611, BY – 18 Nottingham City, Lawton Drive, Bulwell ✆ 927 8021 – 18 Beeston Fields, Beeston ✆ 925 7062 – 18 Ruddington Grange, Wilford Rd, Ruddington ✆ 984 6141 BZ – 9, 9 Edwalton ✆ 923 4775, BZ - 9 (x 3) Cotgrave Place G & C.C., Stragglethorpe ✆ 933 3344/5500.

East Midlands Airport, Castle Donington : ✆ (01332) 852852 SW : 15 m. by A 453 AZ.

1-4 Smithy Row, NG1 2BY ✆ 947 0661 – at West Bridgford : County Hall, Loughborough Rd, NG2 7QP ✆ 977 3558.

♦London 135 – ♦Birmingham 50 – ♦Leeds 74 – ♦Manchester 72.

Plans on following pages

Royal Moat House International (Q.M.H.), Wollaton St., NG1 5RH, ✆ 936 9988, Fax 475667, squash – rm – 500. AE VISA. CY **e**
Avenue : Meals *(closed Saturday lunch and Sunday)* 8.95/15.25 **t.** 4.95 – **Marcellos : Meals** - Italian - *(closed Sunday lunch)* 9.95/14.50 **t.** 4.95 – 9.50 – **198 rm** 85.00/105.00 **st.**, 3 suites.

Forte Crest, St. James's St., NG1 6BN, ✆ 947 0131, Fax 948 4366 – rm – 600. AE VISA JCB CY **a**
Meals 12.50/14.95 **st.** and dinner a la carte 6.75 – 10.95 – **130 rm** 79.00/125.00 **st.** – SB.

Nottingham Gateway, Nuthall Rd, NG8 6AZ, NW : 3 ¼ m. on A 610 ✆ 979 4949, Fax 979 4744 – rm rest – 250. AE VISA.
Meals 10.00/20.00 **st.** and a la carte 4.50 – 6.50 – **106 rm** 55.00/65.00 **st.** – SB.

Rutland Square, St. James's St., NG1 6FJ, ✆ 941 1114, Fax 941 0014 – rm rest – 150. AE VISA. CZ **c**
Meals 7.50/20.00 **st.** and a la carte 6.50 – 7.75 – **103 rm** 58.00/65.00 **st.**, 1 suite – SB.

Strathdon Thistle, 44 Derby Rd, NG1 5FT, ✆ 941 8501, Fax 948 3725 – rm rest – 120. AE VISA CY **c**
Meals *(closed Saturday lunch)* 14.00/16.00 **st.** and a la carte 5.50 – 8.95 – **68 rm** 72.00/92.00 **st.** – SB.

Nottingham Moat House (Q.M.H.), 296 Mansfield Rd, NG5 2BT, ✆ 935 9988, Fax 969 1506 – rm – 180. AE VISA BY **u**
Meals 8.75/13.95 **t.** and a la carte 5.75 – 9.50 – **169 rm** 62.00/82.00 **st.**, 3 suites – SB.

Holiday Inn Garden Court, Castle Marina Park, off Castle Boulevard, NG7 1GX, ✆ 950 0600, Fax 950 0433 – rm rest – 40. AE VISA JCB
Meals *(closed lunch Saturday and Sunday)* 9.00/12.95 **st.** and dinner a la carte – 7.50 – **100 rm** 59.50/64.50 **st.** – SB. AZ **e**

Priory Toby, Derby Rd, Wollaton Vale, NG8 2NR, W : 3 m. on A 52 ✆ 922 1691, Fax 925 6224 – . AE VISA. AZ **s**
Meals 8.25 **st.** and a la carte – **31 rm** 62.00/73.00 **st.**

Quality George, George St., NG1 3BP, ✆ 947 5641, Fax 948 3292 – rm – 150. AE VISA JCB. DY **e**
Meals (buffet lunch)/dinner 13.50 **st.** and a la carte 5.00 – 7.75 – **70 rm** 54.50/70.00 **st.** – SB.

Stage, Gregory Boulevard, NG7 6LB, ✆ 960 3261, Fax 969 1040 – rm – 40. AE VISA JCB. AY **a**
Meals 7.95/11.95 **st.** and dinner a la carte 4.20 – **52 rm** 37.50/52.50 **st.** – SB.

Woodville, 340 Mansfield Rd, NG5 2EF, ✆ 960 6436, Fax 985 6846 – rest – 90. AE VISA. BY **c**
Meals *(closed lunch Saturday and Sunday and Bank Holidays)* 7.95/16.95 **st.** and dinner a la carte 4.75 – **45 rm** 45.00/60.00 **st.**

Greenwood Lodge, Third Av., Sherwood Rise, NG7 6JH, ✆ 962 1206, Fax 962 1206, – . VISA. AY **n**
Meals *(closed Sunday)* (residents only) (communal dining) (dinner only) a la carte 14.95/21.50 **s.** 4.50 – **5 rm** 25.00/45.00 **s.**

Lucieville St. James, 349 Derby Rd, NG7 2DZ, ✆ 978 7389, Fax 979 0346, – . AE VISA. AZ **c**
Meals (residents only) 12.50/25.00 **st.** and a la carte – 9.50 – **8 rm** 45.00/95.00 **st.** – SB.

Nuthall Lodge, 432 Nuthall Rd., NG8 5DQ, NW : 2 ¾ m. on A 610 ✆ 978 4080, Fax 979 0346 – . AE VISA AY **r**
Meals (residents only) (dinner only) 12.90 **t.** and a la carte – 7.50 – **7 rm** 35.00/45.00 **s.** – SB.

Claremont without rest., 2 Hamilton Rd, Sherwood Rise, NG5 1AU, ✆ 960 8587, Fax 960 8587, – . VISA JCB. BY **x**
closed 23 December-2 January – **14 rm** 25.00/35.00.

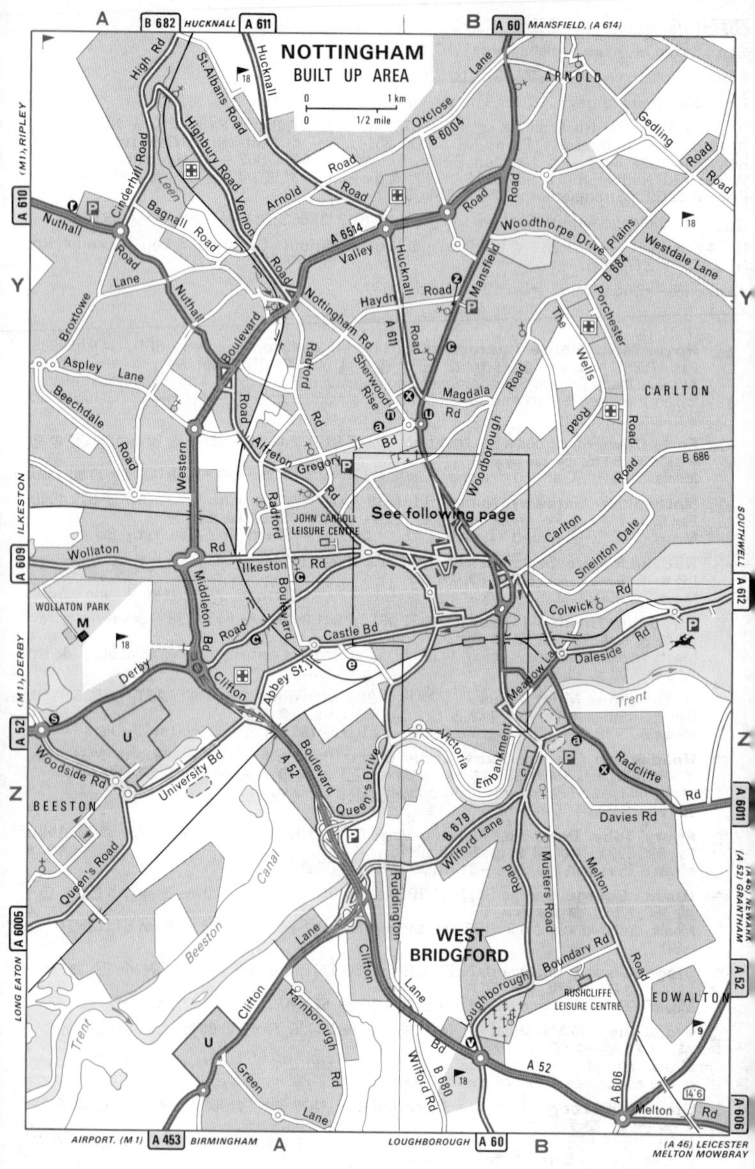

XX **Sonny's,** 3 Carlton St., NG1 1NL, ✆ 947 3041, Fax 950 7776 – AE VISA — DY **c**
closed 25 and 26 December and 1 January – **Meals** a la carte 16.70/22.75 **t.** 4.50.

XX **Saagar,** 473 Mansfield Rd, Sherwood, NG5 2DR, ✆ 962 2014 – AE VISA — BY **z**
closed 25 December – **Meals** - Indian - 7.00/11.00 **t.** and a la carte 5.25.

X **Ben Bowers,** 128 Derby Rd (basement), NG1 5FB, ✆ 941 3388 – AE VISA
closed Saturday lunch, Sunday, Monday and 25 to 27 December – **Meals** 7.90/13.95 **t.** 4.75. — CY **s**

X **Higoi,** 57 Lenton Boulevard, NG7 2FQ, ✆ 942 3379 – AE VISA JCB — AY **c**
Meals - Japanese - (dinner only and lunch Friday and Saturday) 8.90 **t.** (lunch) and a la carte 17.50/31.80 **t.**

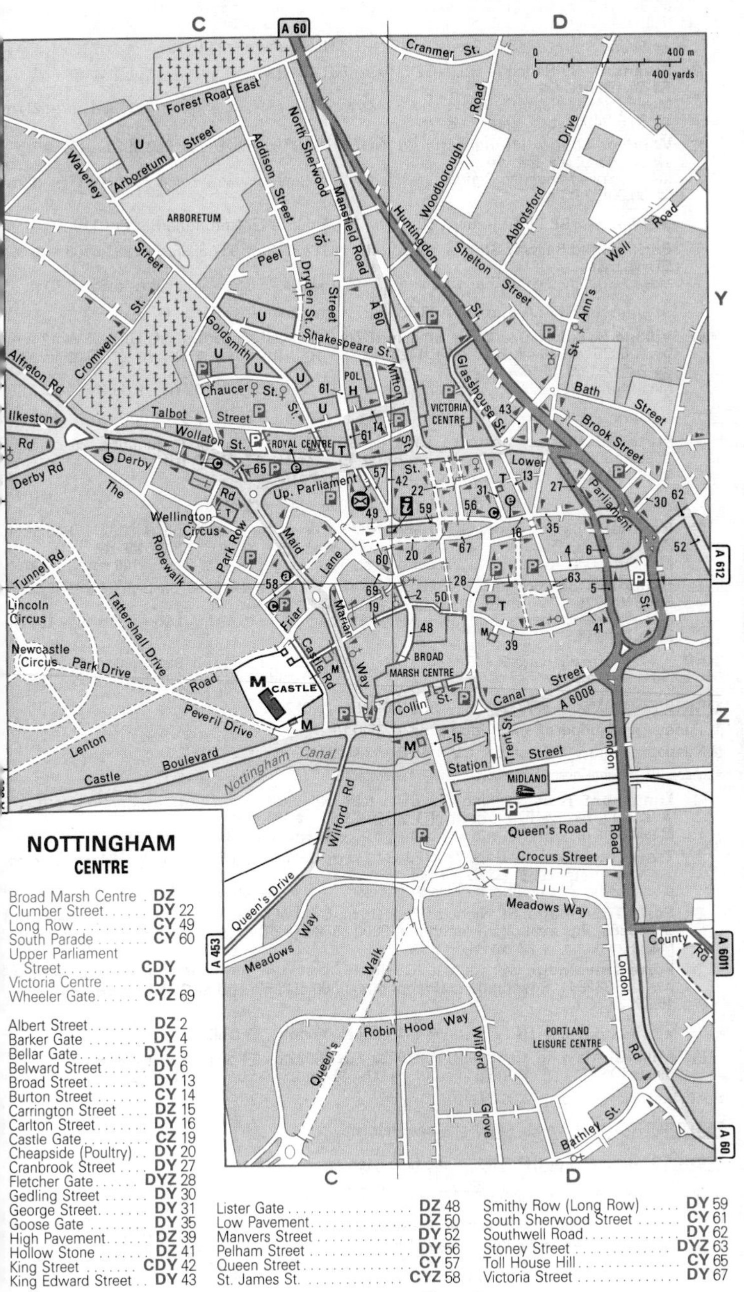

NOTTINGHAM
CENTRE

Broad Marsh Centre . . **DZ**
Clumber Street . . . . . . **DY** 22
Long Row . . . . **CY** 49
South Parade . . . . **CY** 60
Upper Parliament Street . . . . **CDY**
Victoria Centre . . . . . . **DY**
Wheeler Gate . . . . . . **CYZ** 69

Albert Street . . . . **DZ** 2
Barker Gate . . . . **DY** 4
Bellar Gate . . . . **DYZ** 5
Belward Street . . . . **DY** 6
Broad Street . . . . **DY** 13
Burton Street . . . . **CY** 14
Carrington Street . . . . **DZ** 15
Carlton Street . . . . **DY** 16
Castle Gate . . . . **CZ** 19
Cheapside (Poultry) . . **DY** 20
Cranbrook Street . . . . **DY** 27
Fletcher Gate . . . . . . **DYZ** 28
Gedling Street . . . . . . **DY** 30
George Street . . . . **DY** 31
Goose Gate . . . . **DY** 35
High Pavement . . . . . . **DZ** 39
Hollow Stone . . . . **DZ** 41
King Street . . . . **CDY** 42
King Edward Street . . **DY** 43

Lister Gate . . . . **DZ** 48
Low Pavement . . . . **DZ** 50
Manvers Street . . . . **DY** 52
Pelham Street . . . . **DY** 56
Queen Street . . . . **CY** 57
St. James St. . . . . **CYZ** 58

Smithy Row (Long Row) . . . . . **DY** 59
South Sherwood Street . . . . . . **CY** 61
Southwell Road . . . . **DY** 62
Stoney Street . . . . **DYZ** 63
Toll House Hill . . . . **CY** 65
Victoria Street . . . . **DY** 67

If you find you cannot take up a hotel booking you have made, please let the hotel know immediately.

at West Bridgford SE : 2 m. on A 52 – ✉ Nottingham – ☎ 0115 :

Swans, 84-90 Radcliffe Rd, NG2 5HH, ℘ 981 4042, Fax 945 5745 – 50. AE VISA. BZ **a**
Meals *(closed Saturday lunch and Sunday dinner)* 13.95 **st.** and a la carte 4.95 – **30 rm** 39.50/49.50 **t.**, 1 suite – SB.

Windsor Lodge, 116 Radcliffe Rd, NG2 5HG, ℘ 952 8528, Fax 952 0020 – 30. AE VISA. BZ **x**
Meals *(closed Friday to Sunday)* (residents only) (dinner only) 8.75/11.75 **st.** 3.50 – **48 rm** 36.00/52.00 **st.**

at Plumtree SE : 5 ¾ m. by A 60 – BZ – off A 606 – ✉ Nottingham – ☎ 0115 :

Perkins, Old Railway Station, Station Rd, NG12 5NA, ℘ 937 3695, Fax 937 6405 – . AE VISA
closed Sunday, Monday and Bank Holidays – **Meals** - Bistro - a la carte 14.80/18.10 **t.**

at Beeston SW : 4 ¼ m. on A 6005 – ✉ Nottingham – ☎ 0115 :

Village H. & Leisure Club, Brailsford Way, Cuilwell Meadows, NG9 6DL, SW : 2 ¾ m. by A 6005 ℘ 946 4422, Fax 946 4428, squash – rm – 220. AE VISA JCB
Meals (grill rest.) 8.95/21.00 **st.** and a la carte 4.50 – 7.95 – **92 rm** 79.00/99.00 **st.** – SB.

at Sandiacre (Derbs.) SW : 7½ m. by A 52 – AZ – on B 5010 – ✉ Nottingham – ☎ 0115 :

Forte Posthouse, Bostocks Lane, NG10 5NJ, SW : ¾ m. at junction 25 of M 1 ℘ 939 7800, Fax 949 0469 – rm – 50. AE VISA
Meals a la carte approx. 15.00 **t.** 5.50 – **91 rm** 56.00/69.50 **t.**

at Long Eaton (Derbs.) SW : 8 m. on A 6005 – AZ – ☎ 0115 :

Novotel, Bostock Lane, NG10 4EP, NW : 1 ¾ m. by A 6005 on B 6002 ℘ 946 5111, Fax 946 5900, heated, – rm – 200. AE VISA
Meals 10.00 **st.** (dinner) and a la carte 10.55/19.75 **st.** 8.75 – 7.50 – **105 rm** 42.50 **st.**

Sleep Inn, Bostock Lane, NG10 5NL, NW : 1 ¾ m. by A 6005 on B 6002 ℘ 946 0000, Fax 946 0726 – rm – 60. AE VISA.
closed 24 December-3 January – **Meals** a la carte 9.50/16.50 **t.** 4.95 – 5.45 – **101 rm** 29.95/39.95 **t.**

ATS 116 Highbury Rd, Bulwell ℘ 278824
ATS 66 Castle Boulevard ℘ 947 6678
ATS 126-132 Derby Rd, Stapleford ℘ 939 2986
ATS Oxford St., Long Eaton, Derbs. ℘ 973 2156

NUNEATON Warks. 403 404 P 26 – pop. 66 715 – ☎ 01203.

18 Purley Chase, Pipers Lane, Ridge Lane ℘ 393118.
Nuneaton Library, Church St., CV11 4DR ℘ 384027.
♦London 107 – ♦Birmingham 25 – ♦Coventry 10 – ♦Leicester 18.

Longshoot Toby, Watling St., CV11 6JH, NE : 2 ½ m. on A 47 at junction with A 5 ℘ 329711, Fax 344570 – rm . AE VISA.
Meals (grill rest.) 9.25 **t.** and a la carte 5.25 – **44 rm** 48.00/58.00 **t.** – SB.

Travel Inn, Coventry Rd, CY10 7PJ, S : 2½ m. by A 444 on B 4113 ℘ 343584, Fax 327156, – rm . AE VISA.
closed 24 to 26 December – **Meals** (grill rest.) – 4.95 – **48 rm** 34.50 **t.**

Forte Travelodge, St. Nicholas Park Drive, CV11 6EN, NE : 1½ m. by A 47 (Hinkley Rd) ℘ 353885, Reservations (Freephone) 0800 850950 – . AE VISA.
Meals (grill rest.) – **28 rm** 34.50 **t.**

Forte Travelodge without rest., CV10 7TF, S : 1 ½ m. on A 444 (southbound carriageway) ℘ 382541, Reservations (Freephone) 0800 850950 – . AE VISA.
40 rm 34.50 **t.**

at Sibson (Leics.) N : 7 m. on A 444 – ✉ Nuneaton – ☎ 01827 :

Millers', Main Rd, CV13 6LB, ℘ 880223, Fax 880223 – . AE VISA JCB
Meals 10.95/14.95 **st.** and a la carte 4.00 – **40 rm** 41.50/49.50 **st.** – SB.

ATS Weddington Rd ℘ 341130/341139

NUNNINGTON N. Yorks. 402 R 21 – see Helmsley.

OADBY Leics. 402 403 404 R 26 – see Leicester.

OAKHAM Leics. 402 404 R 25 – pop. 8 691 – ☎ 01572.
ℹ Oakham Library, Catmose St., LE15 6HW ℘ 724329.
♦London 103 – ♦Leicester 26 – Northampton 35 – ♦Nottingham 28.

Barnsdale Lodge, The Avenue, Rutland Water, LE15 8AH, E : 2 m. on A 606 ℘ 724678, Fax 724961, « Converted part 17C farmhouse » – rest TV ☎ P – 220. AE VISA JCB.
Meals 13.95/25.00 **t.** and a la carte 4.25 – **29 rm** 49.50/89.00 **t.** – SB.

Whipper-Inn, Market Pl., LE15 6DT, ℘ 756971, Fax 757759 – TV ☎ – 50. AE VISA
Meals 7.95/14.95 **t.** and a la carte – **24 rm** 57.00/84.00 **t.** – SB.

Boultons, 4 Catmose St., LE15 6HW, ℘ 722844, Fax 724473 – TV ☎ & P – 60. AE VISA
Meals 9.50/15.00 **st.** and a la carte 5.50 – **25 rm** 55.00/70.00 **st.** – SB.

at Hambleton E : 3 m. by A 606 – ✉ Oakham – ☎ 01572 :

❀ **Hambleton Hall** , LE15 8TH, ℘ 756991, Fax 724721, « Victorian country house, ≤ Rutland Water », heated, , park, – TV ☎ P. AE VISA
Meals 29.50/35.00 **st.** and a la carte 42.50/63.00 **st.** – 8.50 – **15 rm** 110.00/295.00 **st.** – SB
Spec. Fricassee of morels and asparagus with a light chicken mousse, Loin of local lamb with a tian of aubergines and red peppers, Caramelised lemon tart with slices of poached figs and honey ice cream.

OAKLEY Hants. 403 404 Q 30 – see Basingstoke.

OBORNE Dorset 403 404 M 31 – see Sherborne.

OCKHAM Surrey 404 S 30 – pop. 407 – ✉ Ripley – ☎ 01483.
♦London 27 – Guildford 9.

Hautboy , Ockham Lane, GU23 6NP, ℘ 225355, Fax 211176, – rest TV ☎ P. AE VISA.
closed 1 January – **Meals** 13.95/23.50 **t.** and a la carte – 7.95 – **5 rm** 78.00/125.00 **t.**

ODIHAM Hants. 404 R 30 – pop. 4 886 – ☎ 01256.
♦London 51 – Reading 16 – Winchester 25.

George, 100 High St., RG25 1LP, ℘ 702081, Fax 704213, « 15C inn » – rm TV ☎ P. AE VISA
Meals *(closed Saturday lunch and dinner Sunday)* 13.75 **t.** (lunch) and a la carte 18.75/33.45 **t.** 5.25 – **18 rm** 65.00/90.00 **t.**

OGBOURNE ST. GEORGE Wilts. 403 404 O 29 – see Marlborough.

OKEHAMPTON Devon 403 H 31 The West Country G. – pop. 4 641 – ☎ 01837.
Exc. : S : Dartmoor National Park★★ (Brent Tor ≤★★, Haytor Rocks ≤★) – Lydford★★ (Lydford Gorge★★) S : 8 m. by B 3260 and A 386.
18 Okehampton ℘ 52113.
ℹ 3 West St., EX20 1HQ ℘ 53020 (summer only).
♦London 226 – Exeter 25 – ♦Plymouth 30.

Forte Travelodge, Sourton Cross, EX20 4LY, SW : 4½ m. by B 3260 and A 30 on A 386 ℘ 52124, Reservations (Freephone) 0800 850950 – TV & P. AE VISA.
Meals (grill rest.) – **32 rm** 34.50 **t.**

at Sourton SW : 5 m. by B 3260 and A 30 on A 386 – ✉ Okehampton – ☎ 01837 :

Collaven Manor without rest., EX20 4HH, SW : ¾ m. on A 386 ℘ 861522, « 15C manor house, gardens » – TV P
Easter-October – **3 rm** 30.00/45.00 **t.**

ATS Crediton Rd ℘ 53277/52799

OLD Northants. pop. 290 – ☎ 01604.
♦London 77 – ♦Birmingham 58 – ♦Leicester 26 – Northampton 6.

Wold Farm , Harrington Rd, NN6 9RJ, ℘ 781258, , park – P.
Meals (by arrangement) (communal dining) 12.50 **st.** – **6 rm** 22.00/44.00 **st.**

OLD BROWNSOVER Warks. – see Rugby.

OLD BURGHCLERE Berks. 404 Q 29 – – ✉ Newbury – ☎ 01635.
♦London 77 – ♦Bristol 76 – Newbury 10 – Reading 27 – ♦Southampton 28.

XX **Dew Pond,** RG15 9LH, ℘ 278408, Fax 278408, ≤ – P. VISA
closed Sunday, Monday, first 2 weeks January and 2 weeks August – **Meals** (dinner only) 23.00/29.00 **st.** 6.00.

OLDBURY W. Mids. – see Birmingham.

OLD BYLAND N.Yorks. – see Helmsley.

OLD DALBY Leics. 402 404 R 25 – see Melton Mowbray.

OLDHAM Gtr. Manchester 402 404 N 23 – pop. 216 531 – ☎ 0161.

Crompton and Royton, High Barn, Royton ☎ 624 2154 – Lees New Rd ☎ 624 4986.

Central Library, 84 Union St., OL1 1DN ☎ 627 1024.

♦London 212 – ♦Leeds 36 – ♦Manchester 7 – ♦Sheffield 38.

Plan : see Manchester

- **Smokies Park,** Ashton Rd, Bardsley, OL8 3HX, S : 2 ¾ m. on A 627 ☎ 624 3405, Fax 627 5262, – – 150. AE VISA.
  Meals *(closed lunch Bank Holidays)* (dancing Friday and Saturday evenings) 13.50/25.00 **t.** and a la carte – **47 rm** 56.00/80.00 **t.** – SB.
- **Bower,** Hollinwood Av., Chadderton, OL9 8DE, SW : 3 ¼ m. by A 62 on A 6104 ☎ 682 7254, Fax 683 4605, – rm – 200 BV **e**
  63 rm.
- **Avant,** Windsor Rd, Manchester St., OL8 4AS, ☎ 627 5500, Fax 627 5896 – rm rest – 250. AE VISA.
  Meals *(closed Sunday lunch)* 8.50/15.50 **t.** and a la carte 6.75 – 8.50 – **101 rm** 60.00/70.00 **t.**, 2 suites – SB.
- **Periquito,** Manchester St., OL8 1UZ, ☎ 624 0555, Fax 627 2031, – rm – 320. AE VISA JCB.
  Meals (bar lunch Monday to Saturday)/dinner 14.00 **st.** and a la carte – 7.00 – **130 rm** 46.00 **st.** – SB.
- **Travel Inn,** The Broadway, Chadderton, OL9 8DW, SW : 3 ½ m. by A 62 on A 6104 ☎ 681 1373 – rm . AE VISA
  Meals (grill rest.) – 4.95 – **40 rm** 34.50 **t.**
- XX **White Hart Inn,** 51 Stockport Rd (1st floor), Lydgate, OL4 4JJ, E : 3 m. by A 669 ☎ 872566 – . VISA
  closed Sunday dinner and Monday – **Meals** (dinner only and Sunday lunch)/dinner 19.95/23.95 **t.**

ATS 169-171 Huddersfield Rd ☎ 633 1551   ATS 179-185 Hollins Rd ☎ 627 0180/665 1958

Si vous cherchez un hôtel tranquille,
consultez d'abord les cartes de l'introduction
ou repérez dans le texte les établissements indiqués avec le signe ou .

OLD SODBURY Avon 403 404 M 29 – ✉ Bristol – ☎ 01454.

Chipping Sodbury ☎ 312024.

♦London 110 – Bristol 14 – Gloucester 30 – Swindon 29.

- **Sodbury House,** BS17 6LU, on A 432 ☎ 312847, Fax 273105, – – 30. AE VISA JCB.
  closed 24 December-3 January – **Meals** *(closed Friday to Sunday)* (residents only) (dinner only) 12.50 **st.** 4.95 – **13 rm** 40.00/75.00 **st.**
- **Dornden** , 15 Church Lane, BS17 6NB, ☎ 313325, Fax 312263, <, –
  closed 3 weeks September-October and Christmas-New Year – **Meals** (by arrangement) 9.00 **t.** – **9 rm** 26.00/50.00 **t.**

OMBERSLEY Heref. and Worcs. 403 404 N 27 pop. 2 089 – ☎ 01905.

♦London 148 – ♦Birmingham 42 – Leominster 33.

- **Greenlands** without rest., Uphampton, WR9 0JP, NW : 1 ½ m. by A 449 taking second turning to Uphampton ☎ 620873, <, « 16C cottage », –
  3 rm 17.00/38.00 **st.**

ORMSKIRK Lancs. 402 L 23 – pop. 23 425 – ☎ 01695.

♦London 219 – ♦Liverpool 12 – Preston 18.

- **Beaufort,** High Lane, Burscough, L40 7SN, NE : 1 ¾ m. by B 5319 on A 59 ☎ 892655, Fax 895135 – – 40. AE VISA.
  Meals 7.50/12.95 **t.** and a la carte – **21 rm** 60.00/70.00 **t.** – SB.

OSWESTRY Shrops. 402 403 K 25 – pop. 33 508 – ☎ 01691.

Aston Park ☎ 610221 – Llanymynech, Pant ☎ 830542.

Mile End Services, SY11 4JA ☎ 662488 – The Heritage Centre, 2 Church Ter., SY11 2TE ☎ 662753.

♦London 182 – Chester 28 – Shrewsbury 18.

- **Wynnstay,** Church St., SY11 2SZ, ☎ 655261, Fax 670606, , , , – – 180. AE VISA
  Meals 12.50/25.00 **st.** and a la carte – 8.95 – **26 rm** 65.00/80.00 **t.**, 1 suite – SB.
- **Forte Travelodge,** Mile End Service Area, SY11 4JA, SE : 1 ¼ m. at junction of A 5 with A 483 ☎ 658178, Reservations (Freephone) 0800 850950 – . AE VISA.
  Meals (grill rest.) – **40 rm** 34.50 **t.**
- **Ashfield,** Llwyn-y-Maen, Trefonen Rd, SY10 9DD, SW : 1½ m. ☎ 655200, Fax 657367, <, – rest . AE VISA
  Meals (bar lunch)/dinner 18.50 **s.** and a la carte 4.00 – 5.00 – **10 rm** 34.00/40.00 **s.** – SB.

XX **Starlings Castle** with rm, Bron y Garth, SY10 7NU, NW : 7 ¼ m. by B 4579, via Selattyn ℘ 718464, Fax 718464, ← – TV P. VISA
Meals (dinner only and Sunday lunch)/dinner 18.50/22.50 **t.** 5.50 – 4.00 – **8 rm** 20.00/55.00 **t.**

X **Sebastian,** 45 Willow St., SY11 1AQ, ℘ 655444, Fax 653452 – VISA
closed Tuesday and Saturday lunch, Sunday, Monday, 25 and 26 December, 1 January and Bank Holiday Mondays – **Meals** 10.95/17.95 **t.** and dinner a la carte 4.50.

ATS Oswald Rd ℘ 653540/653256

OTLEY Suffolk 404 X 27 – pop. 1 381 – ✉ Ipswich – ☎ 01473.
♦London 83 – ♦Ipswich 7.5 – ♦Norwich 43.

Otley House, IP6 9NR, ℘ 890253, Fax 890009, ←, « Part 17C manor house », – TV P.
mid March-October – **Meals** *(closed Sunday)* (communal dining) (dinner only) 16.50/19.50 **st.** – **4 rm** 42.00/72.00 **st.**

Bowerfield House, Helmingham Rd, IP6 9NR, ℘ 890742, Fax 890059, « Converted 17C stable and barn », – rm TV P.
15 March-3 October – **Meals** (by arrangement) (communal dining) 16.50 **st.** – **3 rm** 34.00/46.00 **st.**

OTLEY W. Yorks. 402 O 22 – pop. 13 596 – ☎ 01943.
West Busk Lane ℘ 461015.
Council Offices, 8 Boroughgate, LS21 3AH ℘ 247 7707.
♦London 216 – Harrogate 14 – ♦Leeds 12 – York 28.

Chevin Lodge, Yorkgate, LS21 3NU, S : 2 m. by East Chevin Rd ℘ 467818, Fax 850335, « Pine log cabin village », park, – TV P – 120. VISA.
Meals 10.50/17.25 **st.** and a la carte 4.95 – **51 rm** 82.00/102.00 **st.** – SB.

OULTON Suffolk – see Lowestoft.

OUNDLE Northants. 404 S 26 – pop. 3 996 – ✉ Peterborough – ☎ 01832.
Benefield Rd ℘ 273267.
14 West St., PE8 4EF ℘ 274333.
♦London 89 – ♦Leicester 37 – Northampton 30.

Talbot (Forte Heritage), New St., PE8 4EA, ℘ 273621, Fax 274545, – TV P – 50. VISA JCB
Meals (bar lunch Monday to Saturday)/dinner 16.95 **st.** and a la carte 7.30 – 8.50 – **38 rm** 64.00/74.00 **st.**, 1 suite – SB.

at Fotheringhay N : 3 ¾ m. by A 427 off A 605 – ✉ Peterborough (Cambs.) – ☎ 01832 :

Castle Farm, PE8 5HZ, ℘ 226200, « Riverside garden » – rm TV P.
Meals (by arrangement) 10.00 **st.** – **6 rm** 30.00/48.00 **st.**

at Upper Benefield W : 5 m. on A 427 – ✉ Peterborough (Cambs.) – ☎ 01832 :

Wheatsheaf, PE8 5AN, ℘ 205254, Fax 205245, – TV P. VISA JCB
Meals a la carte 17.40/23.70 **t.** – **9 rm** 45.00/55.00 **t.** – SB.

OUTLANE W. Yorks. – see Huddersfield.

OVER PEOVER Ches. 402 403 404 M 24 – see Knutsford.

OWER Hants 403 404 P 31 – see Romsey.

OXFORD Oxon. 403 404 Q 28 **Great Britain G.** – pop. 110 103 – ☎ 01865.
See : City★★★ - Christ Church★★ (Hall★★ *AC*, Tom Quad★, Tom Tower★, Cathedral★ *AC* - Choir Roof★) BZ – Merton College★★ *AC* BZ - Magdalen College★★ BZ – Ashmolean Museum★★ BY **M2** – Bodleian Library★★ (Ceiling★★, Lierne Vaulting★) *AC* BZ **F** – St. John's College★ BY - The Queen's College★ BZ – Lincoln College★ BZ - Trinity College (Chapel★) BY – New College (Chapel★) *AC*, BZ – Radcliffe Camera★ BZ **A** – Sheldonian Theatre★ *AC*, BZ **G** – University Museum★ BY **M3** – Pitt Rivers Museum★ BY **M4**.
Envir. : Iffley Church★ AZ **A**.
Exc. : Woodstock : Blenheim Palace★★★ (The Grounds★★★) *AC*, NW : 8 m. by A 4144 and A 34 AY.
The Old School, Gloucester Green, OX1 2DA ℘ 726871.
♦London 59 – ♦Birmingham 63 – ♦Brighton 105 – ♦Bristol 73 – ♦Cardiff 107 – ♦Coventry 54 – ♦Southampton 64.

Plans on following pages

Randolph (Forte), Beaumont St., OX1 2LN, ℘ 247481, Fax 791678 – rm TV – 250. VISA JCB BY **n**
Spires : Meals 13.95/35.00 **t.** and dinner a la carte – 11.50 – **104 rm** 95.00/160.00 **st.**, 5 suites – SB.

Oxford Moat House (Q.M.H.), Wolvercote Roundabout, OX2 8AL, ℘ 489988, Fax 310259, squash – rm rest TV P – 150. VISA AY **e**
Meals (carving lunch) 10.50/16.50 6.00 – 9.50 – **155 rm** 98.00/130.00 **st.** – SB.

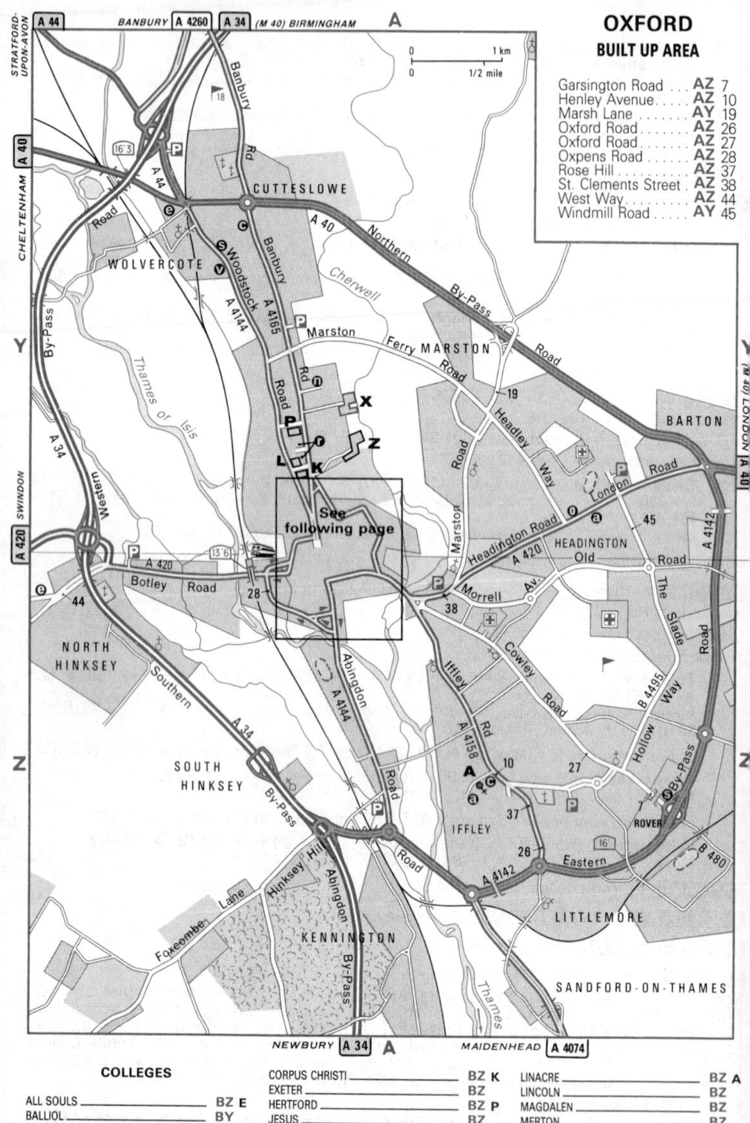

COLLEGES

ALL SOULS	BZ	E
BALLIOL	BY	
BRASENOSE	BZ	D
CHRIST CHURCH	BZ	
CORPUS CHRISTI	BZ	K
EXETER	BZ	
HERTFORD	BZ	P
JESUS	BZ	
KEBLE	BY	
LADY MARGARET HALL	AY	Z
LINACRE	BZ	A
LINCOLN	BZ	
MAGDALEN	BZ	
MERTON	BZ	
NEW	BZ	
NUFFIELD	BZ	B

Old Parsonage, 1 Banbury Rd, OX2 6NN, ☎ 310210, Fax 311262, « Part 17C house », – TV ☎ P. VISA. BY **e**
closed 24 to 26 December – **Meals** (room service and meals in bar only) a la carte 17.65/28.20 **t.** 6.25 – **30 rm** 110.00/190.00 **t.**

Eastgate (Forte Heritage), Merton St., OX1 4BE, ☎ 248244, Fax 791681 – rest TV ☎ P. VISA JCB BZ **c**
Meals a la carte 11.50/17.50 **st.** 6.85 – 8.50 – **43 rm** 92.00/110.00 **st.**

Linton Lodge (Hilton), Linton Rd, OX2 6UJ, ☎ 53461, Fax 310365, – TV ☎ P – 120. VISA AY **n**
Meals 12.95/16.50 **st.** and a la carte 6.50 – 10.25 – **70 rm** 90.00/120.00 **st.** – SB.

OXFORD

Broad Street	**BZ** 3
Clarendon Shopping Centre	**BZ**
Cornmarket Street	**BZ** 6
George Street	**BZ** 9
High Street	**BZ**
Queen Street	**BZ** 34
Westgate Shopping Centre	**BZ**
Blue Boar Street	**BY** 2
Castle Street	**BZ** 5
Hythe Bridge Street	**BZ** 12
Little Clarendon Street	**BY** 13
Logic Lane	**BZ** 14
Magdalen Street	**BYZ** 16
Magpie Lane	**BZ** 17
New Inn Hall Street	**BZ** 20
Norfolk Street	**BZ** 21
Old Greyfriars Street	**BZ** 23
Oriel Square	**BZ** 24
Park End Street	**BZ** 30
Pembroke Street	**BZ** 31
Queen's Lane	**BZ** 33
Radcliffe Square	**BZ** 35
St. Michael Street	**BZ** 40
Turl Street	**BZ** 41
Walton Crescent	**BY** 42
Worcester Street	**BZ** 47

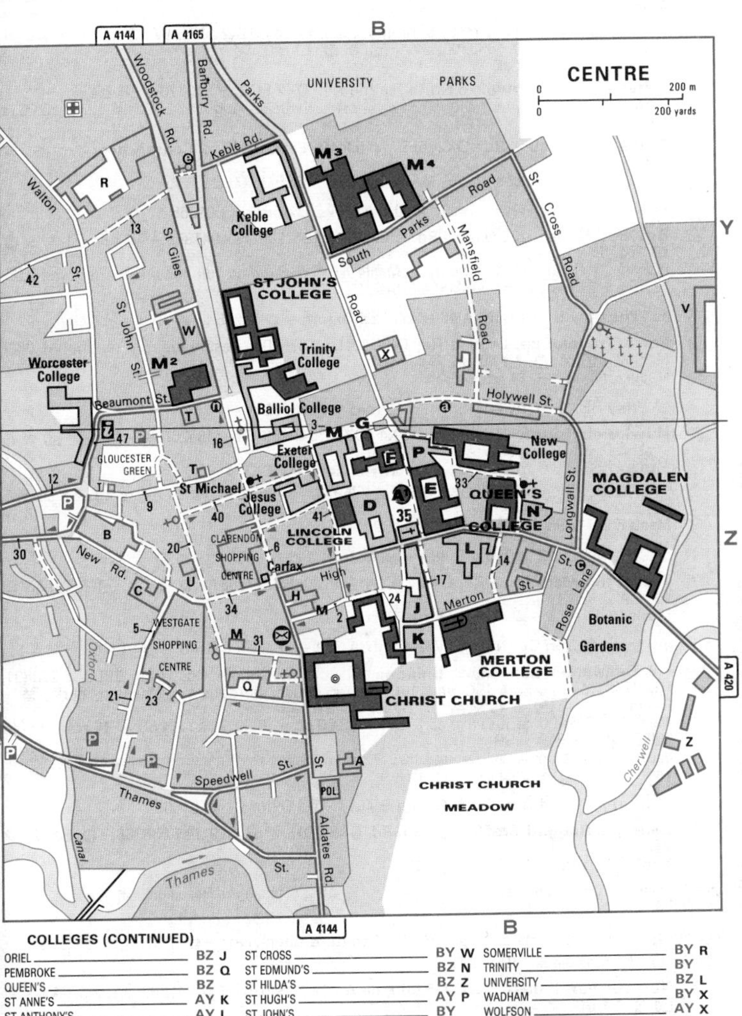

COLLEGES (CONTINUED)

ORIEL	**BZ J**
PEMBROKE	**BZ Q**
QUEEN'S	**BZ**
ST ANNE'S	**AY K**
ST ANTHONY'S	**AY L**
ST CATHERINE'S	**BY V**
ST CROSS	**BY W**
ST EDMUND'S	**BZ N**
ST HILDA'S	**BZ Z**
ST HUGH'S	**AY P**
ST JOHN'S	**BY**
ST PETER'S	**BZ U**
SOMERVILLE	**BY R**
TRINITY	**BY**
UNIVERSITY	**BZ L**
WADHAM	**BY X**
WOLFSON	**AY X**
WORCESTER	**BY**

Bath Place, 4-5 Bath Pl., OX1 3SU, ✆ 791812, Fax 791834, « 17C Flemish weavers cottages » – ⇔ rest ▤ rest TV ☎ P. AE VISA — BY **a**
Meals 14.00/25.50 **t.** and a la carte – ☕ 7.50 – **8 rm** 70.00/100.00 **t.**, 2 suites.

Cotswold House without rest., 363 Banbury Rd, OX2 7PL, ✆ 310558, Fax 310558, – ⇔ TV P. – *closed 23 December-2 January* – **7 rm** ☕ 37.00/55.00 **st.** — AY **c**

Chestnuts without rest., 45 Davenant Rd, OX2 8BU, ✆ 53375, Fax 53375 – ⇔ TV P. *closed 23 December-6 January* – **5 rm** ☕ 32.00/56.00 **s.** — AY **s**

Marlborough House without rest., 321 Woodstock Rd, OX2 7NY, ☎ 311321, Fax 515329 – TV ☎ P. VISA. AY **v**
closed 23 December-2 January – **12 rm** 55.00/65.00 **t.**

Mount Pleasant, 76 London Rd., Headington, OX3 9AJ, ☎ 62749, Fax 62749 – TV ☎ P. AE VISA JCB. AY **a**
Meals 15.25 **st.** and a la carte – **8 rm** 45.00/75.00 – SB.

Dial House without rest., 25 London Rd, Headington, OX3 7RE, ☎ 69944, – TV P AY **o**
8 rm 42.00/50.00.

Tilbury Lodge without rest., 5 Tilbury Lane, Botley, OX2 9NB, W : 2 m. by A 420 off B 4044 ☎ 862138, Fax 863700, – TV ☎ P. VISA. AZ **e**
9 rm 42.00/62.00 **st.**

Fifteen North Parade, 15 North Parade Av., OX2 6LX, ☎ 513773 – VISA AY **r**
closed Sunday dinner, Monday and last 2 weeks August – **Meals** 12.00/15.00 **t.** and a la carte.

Gee's, 61 Banbury Rd, OX2 6PE, ☎ 53540, Fax 310308, « Conservatory » – VISA AY **r**
closed 25 and 26 December – **Meals** a la carte 16.95/25.00 **t.** 6.95.

at Kidlington N : 4½ m. on A 4260 – AY – Oxford – 01865 :

Bowood House, 238 Oxford Rd, OX5 1EB, ☎ 842288, Fax 841858 – rest TV ☎ P. VISA.
closed 23 December-1 January – **Meals** *(closed Sunday)* (dinner only) a la carte 9.95/17.45 **t.** – **22 rm** 45.00/62.00 **t.** – SB.

at Wheatley E : 7 m. by A 40 – AY – Oxford – 01865 :

Forte Travelodge, London Rd, OX9 1JH, ☎ 875705, Reservations (Freephone) 0800 850950 – TV P. AE VISA.
Meals (grill rest.) – **24 rm** 34.50 **t.**

at Iffley SE : 2 m. by A 4158 – Oxford – 01865 :

Hawkwell House, Church Way, OX4 4DZ, ☎ 749988, Fax 748525, – rest TV ☎ P – 150. AE VISA. AZ **c**
Meals 12.50/20.00 **t.** and a la carte – **27 rm** 70.00/85.00 **t.** – SB.

The Tree, Church Way, OX4 4EY, ☎ 775974, Fax 747554, – TV ☎ P. AE VISA. AZ **a**
Meals 6.95/12.95 – **7 rm** 50.00/60.00 **t.**

at Cowley SE : 2½ m. by B 480 – Oxford – 01865 :

Travel Inn, Garsington Rd, OX4 2JZ, ☎ 779230, Fax 775887 – rm TV P. AE VISA AZ **s**
Meals (grill rest.) – 4.95 – **60 rm** 34.50 **t.**

at Great Milton SE : 12 m. by A 40 off A 329 – AY – Oxford – 01844 :

Le Manoir aux Quat' Saisons (Blanc), Church Rd, OX44 7PD, ☎ 278881, Fax 278847, « Part 15C and 16C manor house, gardens », heated, park, – rest rest TV ☎ P – 35. AE VISA JCB.
Meals 29.50/65.00 **st.** and a la carte 62.00/78.00 **st.** 16.00 – 14.50 – **16 rm** 175.00/325.00 **st.**, 3 suites – SB
Spec. Trois bouchées gourmandes aux parfums d'ailleurs, Courgette en fleur farcie au crabe et jus de truffes, Pêche de vigne pochée et figues farcies de glace au Porto.

at Cumnor W : 4¼ m. by A 420 on B 4017 – Oxford – 01865 :

Bear and Ragged Staff, Appleton Rd, OX2 9QH, ☎ 862329, Fax 865366 – P. AE VISA
Meals a la carte 19.85/29.85 **t.** 4.95.

ATS Pony Rd, Horspath Trading Est., Cowley ☎ 777188
ATS 2 Stephen Rd, Headington ☎ 61732

OXHILL Warks. 403 404 P 27 pop. 303 – Stratford-upon-Avon – 01926.
London 85 – Birmingham 32 – Oxford 25.

Nolands Farmhouse, CV35 0RJ, on A 422 ☎ 640309, Fax 641662, – rest TV P. VISA.
closed December – **Meals** *(closed Sunday and Monday)* (residents only) (dinner only) a la carte 9.50/16.00 **t.** 5.50 – **9 rm** 25.00/44.00 **st.**

En saison, *surtout dans les stations fréquentées, il est prudent de retenir à l'avance. Cependant, si vous ne pouvez pas occuper la chambre que vous avez retenue, prévenez immédiatement l'hôtelier.*

Si vous écrivez à un hôtel à l'étranger, joignez à votre lettre un coupon-réponse international (disponible dans les bureaux de poste).

PADSTOW Cornwall 403 F 32 **The West Country G.** – pop. 4 250 (inc. St. Merryn) – ☎ 01841.

See : Town★.

Envir. : Trevone (Cornwall Coast Path★★) W : 3 m. by B 3276 – Trevose Head★ (≤★★) W : 6 m. by B 3276.

Exc. : Bedruthan Steps★, SW : 7 m. by B 3276 – Pencarrow★, SE : 11 m. by A 389.

18, 9, 9 Trevose, Constantine Bay ☎ 520208.

Red Brick Building, North Quay, PL28 8AF ☎ 533449 (summer only).

London 288 – Exeter 78 – Plymouth 45 – Truro 23.

Metropole (Forte Heritage), Station Rd, PL28 8DB, ☎ 532486, Fax 532867, ≤ Camel Estuary, heated, – TV ☎ P – 50. AE VISA JCB
Meals (bar lunch Monday to Saturday)/dinner 18.95 **st.** a la carte 6.85 – 8.75 – **44 rm** 70.00/120.00 **st.** – SB.

Old Custom House Inn, South Quay, PL28 8ED, ☎ 532359, Fax 533372, ≤ Camel Estuary and harbour – rest TV ☎ P. AE VISA JCB
Meals (bar lunch)/dinner 16.00 **st.** and a la carte 4.95 – **26 rm** 64.00/84.00 **st.** – SB.

St. Petroc's House, 4 New St., PL28 8EA, ☎ 532700, Fax 533344 – TV ☎ P. VISA
30 November-27 December – **St. Petrocs Bistro : Meals** *(closed Monday)* 14.95 **t.** 6.00 – **8 rm** 25.00/77.00 **t.** – SB.

Dower House without rest., Fentonula Lane, PL28 8BA, ☎ 532317, Fax 532317 – TV P. VISA
April-December – **6 rm** 33.00/66.00 **st.**

Woodlands, Treator, PL28 8RU, W : 1 ¼ m. by A 389 on B 3276 ☎ 532426, – TV P.
March-5 November – **Meals** 10.00 **st.** 3.60 – **9 rm** (dinner included) 38.00/74.00 **t.** – SB.

Seafood with rm, Riverside, PL28 8BY, ☎ 532485, Fax 533344, ≤, « Attractively converted granary on quayside » – TV ☎ P. VISA
closed 17 December-2 February – **Meals** - Seafood - *(closed Sunday)* (booking essential) 21.50/29.30 **t.** and a la carte 32.95/48.35 **t.** 6.00 – **10 rm** 38.30/115.00 **t.** – SB.

at Little Petherick S : 3 m. on A 389 – ✉ Wadebridge – ☎ 01841 :

Molesworth Manor without rest., PL27 7QT, ☎ 540292, ≤, « Part 17C and 19C rectory », – P.
closed November – 1.75 – **10 rm** 19.00/50.00 **s.**

Old Mill Country House, PL27 7QT, ☎ 540388, « Part 16C corn mill », – rest P. AE VISA.
March-October – **Meals** 8.50 3.25 – **6 rm** 43.00/53.00.

at Constantine Bay SW : 4 m. by B 3276 – ✉ Padstow – ☎ 01841 :

Treglos, PL28 8JH, ☎ 520727, Fax 521163, ≤, – rest TV ☎ P. VISA.
14 March-2 November – **Meals** 11.50/21.00 **st.** 5.90 – **41 rm** 37.00/100.00 **st.**, 3 suites – SB.

at Treyarnon Bay SW : 4¾ m. by B 3276 – ✉ Padstow – ☎ 01841 :

Waterbeach, PL28 8JW, ☎ 520292, Fax 521102, ≤, – TV ☎ P. VISA.
April-October – **Meals** (bar lunch)/dinner 12.50 **t.** 3.50 – **16 rm** (dinner included) 32.00/88.00 **t.**, 5 suites.

PADWORTH Berks. 403 404 Q 29 pop. 545 – ✉ Reading – ☎ 01734.

London 58 – Basingstoke 12 – Reading 10.

Padworth Court (Country Club), Bath Rd, RG7 5HT, on A 4 ☎ 714411, Fax 714442 – TV ☎ P – 180. AE VISA.
Meals *(closed lunch Saturday and Bank Holidays)* a la carte 11.85/19.10 **st.** 4.65 – 7.50 – **50 rm** 72.00/90.00 **st.** – SB.

PAIGNTON Devon 403 J 32 **The West Country G.** – pop. 42 989 – ☎ 01803.

See : Torbay★ - Kirkham House★ *AC* Y **B**.

Envir. : Paignton Zoo★★ *AC*, SW : ½ m. by A 3022 AY (see Plan of Torbay).

The Esplanade, TQ4 6BN ☎ 558383.

London 226 – Exeter 26 – Plymouth 29.

Plan of Built up Area : see Torbay

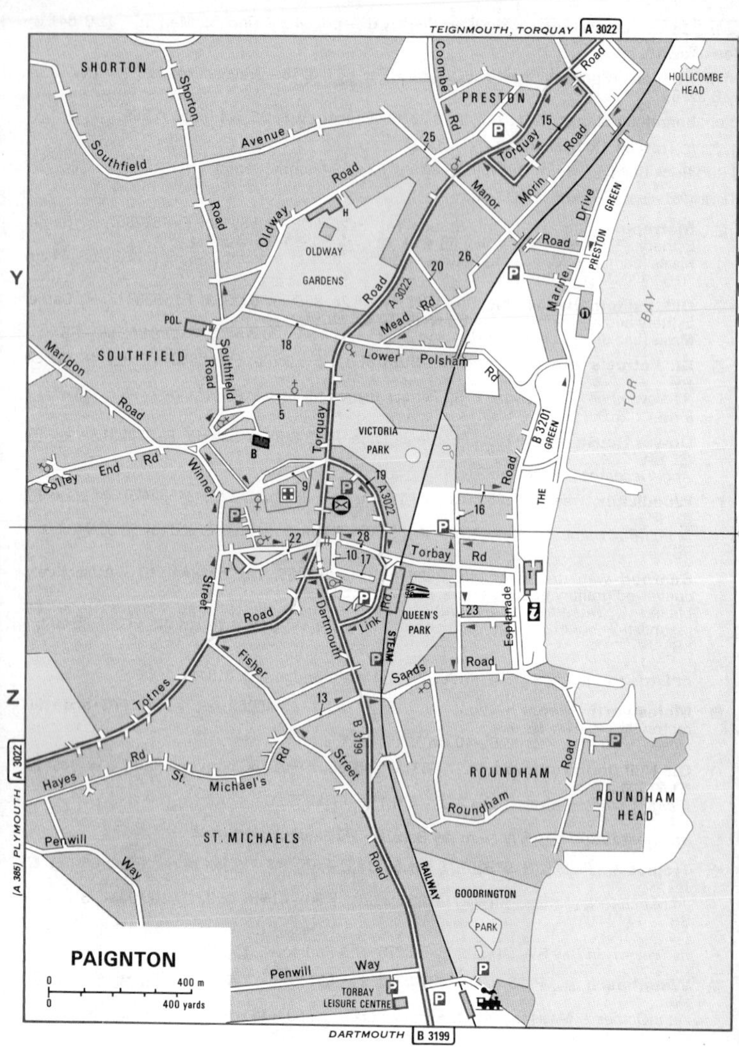

Hyde Road	**Y**	19
Torbay Road	**Z**	
Torquay Road	**Y**	
Victoria Street	**Z**	28
Cecil Road	**Y**	5
Church Street	**Y**	9
Commercial Road	**Z**	10
Elmsleigh Road	**Z**	13
Eugene Road	**Y**	15
Garfield Road	**Y**	16
Gerston Road	**Z**	17
Higher Polsham Road	**Y**	18
Kings Road	**Y**	20
Palace Avenue	**Z**	22
Queen's Road	**Z**	23
Upper Manor Road	**Y**	25
Upper Morin Road	**Y**	26

Redcliffe, 4 Marine Drive, TQ3 2NL, ☎ 526397, Fax 528030, ← Torbay, , , heated, , – rest ☎ – 40. AE VISA. Y n
Meals (bar lunch Monday to Saturday)/dinner 14.75 **t.** and a la carte 5.00 – **59 rm** 48.00/96.00 **t.** – SB.

ATS Orient Rd ☎ 556888/558975

Wenn Sie ein ruhiges Hotel suchen,
benutzen Sie zuerst die Karte in der Einleitung
oder wählen Sie im Text ein Hotel mit dem Zeichen oder .

PAINSWICK Glos. 403 404 N 28 **Great Britain G.** – pop. 4 142 – 01452.

See : Town★.

London 107 – ◆Bristol 35 – Cheltenham 10 – Gloucester 7.

Painswick , Kemps Lane, GL6 6YB, SE : ½ m. by Bisley St., St. Marys St. and Tibbiwell 812160, Fax 814059, « Part 18C Palladian house », – . AE VISA
Meals 14.75/28.50 **st.** and a la carte 5.25 – **20 rm** 63.00/130.00 **st.** – SB.

Country Elephant, New St., GL6 6XH, 813564, – VISA JCB
closed Monday, Tuesday and first 2 weeks January – **Meals** 15.00 **t.** (lunch) and a la carte 17.50/26.95 5.00.

PAKENHAM Suffolk 404 W 27 – see Bury St. Edmunds.

PARBOLD Lancs. 402 L 23 **Great Britain G.** – pop. 4 129 – ✉ Wigan – 01257.

Envir. : Rufford Old Hall★ (Great Hall★) *AC*, NW : 4 m. by B 5246.

London 212 – ◆Liverpool 25 – ◆Manchester 24 – Preston 19.

High Moor Inn, High Moor Lane, WN6 9QA, NE : 3 m. by B 5246 and Chorley Rd 252364, Fax 255120 – . AE VISA
Meals 11.00 **t.** (lunch) and a la carte 12.65/22.50 **t.**

PARKGATE Ches. 402 403 K 24 – pop. 3 789 – ✉ Wirral – 0151.

◆London 206 – Birkenhead 10 – Chester 11 – ◆Liverpool 12.

Parkgate, Boathouse Lane, L64 6RD, N : ½ m. on B 5135 336 5001, Fax 336 8504, – rm rest – 100. AE VISA
Meals (dancing Friday and Saturday night) 8.00/12.95 **t.** and a la carte – **27 rm** 49.50/69.00 **t.** – SB.

PARKHAM Devon 403 H 31 – 01237.

◆London 229 – Barnstaple 14 – Exeter 87 – ◆Plymouth 58.

Penhaven Country House , EX39 5PL, 451711, Fax 451878, , park – rest . AE VISA
Meals 9.50/13.95 **st.** and dinner a la carte 4.75 – **12 rm** (dinner included) 55.95/119.00 **st.** – SB.

Old Rectory , EX39 5PL, 451443, – rm . AE.
closed Christmas – **Meals** (by arrangement) (communal dining) 18.00 **s.** 4.00 – **3 rm** 50.00/78.00 **st.**

PATCHWAY Avon 403 404 M 29 – see Bristol.

PATELEY BRIDGE N. Yorks. 402 O 21 **Great Britain G.** pop. 2 504 – ✉ Harrogate – 01423.

Exc. : Fountains Abbey★★★ *AC* - Studley Royal★★ *AC* (≤★ from Anne Boleyn's Seat) - Fountains Hall (Façade★), NE : 8½ m. by B 6265.

14 High St., HG3 5AW 711147 (summer only).

◆London 225 – ◆Leeds 28 – ◆Middlesbrough 46 – York 32.

Grassfields Country House , Low Wath Rd, HG3 5HL, 711412, –
closed December-January – **Meals** (residents only) (dinner only) 12.00 **st.** 3.00 – **9 rm** 29.00/50.00 **st.** – SB.

at Low Laithe SE : 2¾ m. on B 6165 – ✉ Harrogate – 01423 :

Dusty Miller, Main Rd, Summer Bridge, HG3 4BU, 780837, Fax 780065 – . AE VISA
closed Sunday, Monday, 2 weeks August and 25 December to 1 January – **Meals** (dinner only) 24.00 **t.** and a la carte 16.70/34.80 **t.** 5.50.

at Wath-in-Nidderdale NW : 2¼ m. by Low Wath Rd – ✉ Harrogate – 01423 :

Sportsman's Arms with rm, HG3 5PP, 711306, Fax 712524, – rm . VISA.
closed 25 December – **Meals** (in bar Monday to Saturday lunch and Sunday dinner)/dinner 19.75 **st.** and a la carte 5.50 – **7 rm** 39.00/58.00 **st.** – SB.

at Ramsgill-in-Nidderdale NW : 5 m. by Low Wath Rd – ✉ Harrogate – 01423 :

Yorke Arms , HG3 5RL, 755243, Fax 755243 – rest . VISA.
Meals *(closed dinner 25 December)* (bar lunch Monday to Saturday)/dinner 19.50 **t.** and a la carte 4.50 – **13 rm** 40.00/100.00 **t.** – SB.

PATRICK BROMPTON N. Yorks. 402 P 21 – pop. 145 – ✉ Bedale – 01677.

◆London 228 – ◆Leeds 48 – ◆Newcastle upon Tyne 33 – York 41.

Elmfield House , Arrathorne, DL8 1NE, NW : 2 ¼ m. by A 684 on Richmond rd 450558, Fax 450557, , park – rest . VISA.
Meals (dinner only) 11.50 **st.** 4.50 – **9 rm** 29.50/44.00 **st.** – SB.

PAULERSPURY Northants. 403 404 R 27 – see Towcester.

PAYHEMBURY Devon – see Honiton.

PEASMARSH E. Sussex 404 W 31 – see Rye.

PEMBURY Kent 404 U 30 – see Royal Tunbridge Wells.

PENCRAIG Heref. and Worcs. – see Ross-on-Wye.

PENDLEBURY Gtr. Manchester 402 403 404 N 23 – see Manchester.

PENDOGGETT Cornwall 403 F 32 – ✉ Port Isaac – ☎ 01208.

♦London 264 – Newquay 22 – Truro 30.

Cornish Arms, PL30 3HH, on B 3314 ☎ 880263, Fax 880335, « Retaining 16C features » – TV ☎ P. AE VISA
Meals (bar lunch Monday to Saturday)/dinner 19.95 **t.** and a la carte 4.95 – **7 rm** 35.00/49.00 **t.** – SB.

PENKRIDGE Staffs. 402 403 404 N 25 pop. 8 565 – ✉ Stafford – ☎ 01785.

♦London 140 – ♦Birmingham 25 – Derby 41 – ♦Leicester 56 – Shrewsbury 27 – ♦Stoke-on-Trent 23.

Bridge House, Stone Cross, ST19 5AS, on A 449 ☎ 714426 – rm TV P
Meals *(closed Monday lunch and Sunday dinner)* 11.00/25.00 **st.** and a la carte 4.00 – **9 rm** 25.00/35.00 **st.**

PENRITH Cumbria 401 402 L 19 – pop. 13 330 – ECD : Wednesday – ☎ 01768.

18 Salked Rd ☎ 89191/65429.

Robinson's School, Middlegate, CA11 7PT ☎ 67466.

♦London 290 – ♦Carlisle 24 – Kendal 31 – Lancaster 48.

North Lakes, Ullswater Rd, CA11 8QT, S : 1 m. at junction 40 of M 6 ☎ 868111, Fax 868291, squash – rm TV ☎ P – 200. AE VISA
Meals *(closed Saturday lunch)* 11.50/18.00 **t.** and a la carte 6.95 – **84 rm** 89.00/128.00 **t.** – SB.

Forte Travelodge, Redhills, CA11 0DT, SW : 1 ½ m. by A 592 on A 66 ☎ 866958, Reservations (Freephone) 0800 850950 – TV P. AE VISA.
Meals (grill rest.) – **32 rm** 34.50 **t.**

Woodland House, Wordsworth St., CA11 7QY, ☎ 864177, Fax 890152 – TV P.
closed 2 weeks November – **Meals** (by arrangement) 9.50 **s.** 3.00 – **8 rm** 25.00/40.00 **s.**

ATS Gilwilly Ind. Est. ☎ 65656/7

PENSHURST Kent 404 U 30 **Great Britain G.** – pop. 1 509 – ☎ 01892.

Envir. : Hever Castle★ *AC*, W : 6 m. by B 2176 and B 2027.

♦London 38 – Maidstone 19 – Royal Tunbridge Wells 6.

Swale Cottage without rest., Old Swaylands Lane, TN11 8AH, SE : 1 m. by B 2176 off Poundsbridge Lane ☎ 870738, ≤, – TV P.
3 rm 38.00/58.00.

PENZANCE Cornwall 403 D 33 **The West Country G.** – pop. 20 284 – ☎ 01736.

See : Town★ - Outlook★★★ – Western Promenade (≤★★★) YZ – National Lighthouse Centre★ *AC* Y – Chapel St.★ Y – Maritime Museum★ *AC* Y **M1**.

Envir. : Penwith★★ – Trengwainton Garden★★ (≤★★) *AC*, NW : 2 m. by St. Clare Street Y – Sancreed - Church★★ (Celtic Crosses★★) W : 3½ m. by A 30 Z – St. Michael's Mount★★ (≤★★) E : 4 m. by B 3311 – Y - and A 30 – Lanyon Quoit★, NW : 3½ m. by St. Clare Street – Newlyn★ SW : 1½ m. by B 3315 Z – St. Madron (St. Maddern★) NW : 1½ m. by St. Clare Street Y.

Exc. : Morvah (≤★★) NW : 6 ½ m. by St. Clare Street Y – Zennor (Church★) NW : 6 m. by B 3311 Y – Prussia Cove★, E : 8 m. by B 3311 – Y – and A 394 – Land's End★ (cliff scenery★★★) SW : 10 m. by A 30 Z.

Access to the Isles of Scilly by helicopter ☎ 63871, Fax 64293.

to the Isles of Scilly (Hugh Town) (Isles of Scilly Steamship Co. Ltd) (summer only) (2 h 40 mn).

Station Rd, TR18 2NF ☎ 62207.

♦London 319 – Exeter 113 – ♦Plymouth 77 – Taunton 155.

Plan opposite

Abbey, Abbey St., TR18 4AR, ☎ 66906, Fax 51163, « Attractively furnished 17C house », – TV P. AE VISA Y u
closed 10 days at Christmas – **Meals** (booking essential) (dinner only) 22.50 **t.** – **6 rm** 65.50/140.00 **t.**, 1 suite – SB.

Beachfield, The Promenade, TR18 4NW, ☎ 62067, Fax 331100, ≤ – TV ☎. AE VISA Z a
Meals (bar lunch)/dinner 11.75 **st.** and a la carte 3.25 – **18 rm** 34.50/79.00 **st.** – SB.

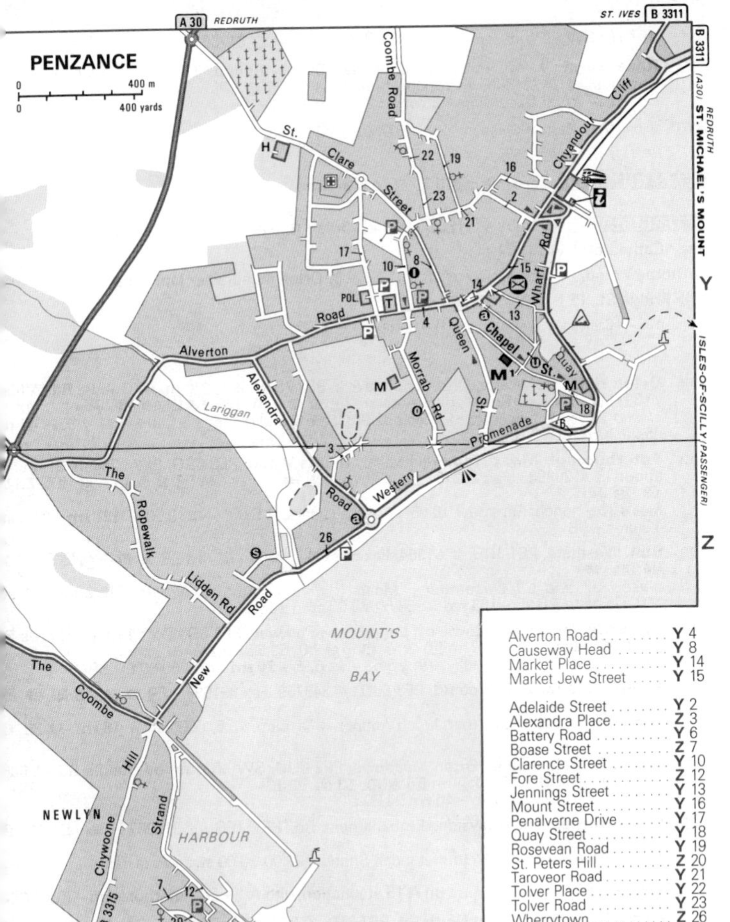

Tarbert, 11 Clarence St., TR18 2NU, ℘ 63758, Fax 331336 – TV ☎. AE VISA. Y **i**
closed 22 December-28 January – **Meals** (dinner only) 14.00 **st.** and a la carte 4.50 – **12 rm** 28.50/57.00 **st.** – SB.

Sea and Horses, 6 Alexandra Terr., TR18 4NX, ℘ 61961, Fax 330499 – rest TV ☎ P. AE VISA JCB. Z **s**
Meals (bar lunch)/dinner 14.00 **t.** 3.10 – **11 rm** 28.00/56.00 **t.** – SB.

Estoril, 46 Morrab Rd, TR18 4EX, ℘ 62468, Fax 67471 – TV ☎ P. VISA. Y **o**
closed January – **Meals** 12.00 **st.** 4.00 – **10 rm** 25.00/52.00 **st.** – SB.

Harris's, 46 New St., TR18 2LZ, ℘ 64408 – AE VISA Y **a**
closed Monday lunch, Sunday, 1 week February and 2 weeks November – **Meals** a la carte 18.50/29.95 **t.**

at ***Newlyn*** SW : 1 ½ m. on B 3315 – Z – ✉ Penzance – 01736 :

Higher Faugan , TR18 5NS, SW : ¾ m. on B 3315 ℘ 62076, Fax 51648, heated, , park, – TV ☎ P. AE VISA JCB
Meals (by arrangement November-February) (bar lunch)/dinner 17.00 **st.** 4.10 – **11 rm** 48.00/115.00 **st.** – SB.

at Drift SW : 2½ m. on A 30 – Z – ✉ Penzance – ☎ 01736 :

Rose Farm without rest., Chyanhal, Buryas Bridge, TR19 6AN, SW : ¾ m. c Chyanhal rd ☎ 731808, « Working farm », – TV P. closed 24 to 26 December – **3 rm** 22.50/38.00 **st.**

ATS Jelbert Way, Eastern Green Ind. Est ☎ 62768

ATS Units 25-26, Stable Hobba Ind. Est., Newlyn ☎ 69100

PERRANUTHNOE Cornwall 403 D 33 – see Marazion.

PETERBOROUGH Cambs. 402 404 T 26 **Great Britain G.** – pop. 153 166 – ☎ 01733.

See : Cathedral★★ *AC* Y.

Thorpe Wood, Nene Parkway ☎ 267701, BX – Orton Meadows, Ham Lane ☎ 237478, BX.

45 Bridge St., PE1 1HA ☎ 317336.

♦London 85 – ♦Cambridge 35 – ♦Leicester 41 – Lincoln 51.

Plans opposite

Orton Hall, The Village, Orton Longueville, PE2 7DN, SW : 2½ m. by Oundle Rd (A 605 ☎ 391111, Fax 231912, , park – rm TV ☎ P – 120. AE VISA JCB BX closed 26 to 30 December – **Meals** 12.95/16.95 **t.** and dinner a la carte – 7.95 – **49 rr** 55.00/105.00 **t.** – SB.

Peterborough Moat House (Q.M.H.), Thorpe Wood, PE3 6SG, SW : 2¼ m. at round about 33 ☎ 289988, Fax 262737, , , – rm rest TV ☎ P – 400. VISA JCB BX **Meals** (bar lunch Saturday) 15.95 **st.** and a la carte 5.50 – 9.50 – **121 rm** 72.00 st 4 suites – SB.

Bull, Westgate, PE1 1RB, ☎ 61364, Fax 557304 – rm rest TV ☎ P – 200. VISA Y *closed 27 and 28 December* – **Meals** (dancing Saturday evening) 13.50/28.00 **st** and a la carte 8.15 – **103 rm** 68.50/79.00 **st.**, 1 suite – SB.

Butterfly, Thorpe Meadows, off Longthorpe Parkway, PE3 6GA, W : 1 m. by Thorpe R ☎ 64240, Fax 65538 – rm TV ☎ P – 80. AE VISA BX **Meals** 12.25/24.00 **t.** and a la carte 5.50 – 6.95 – **70 rm** 57.50/80.00 **t.** – SB.

Thorpe Lodge, 83 Thorpe Rd, PE3 6JQ, ☎ 348759, Fax 891598 – TV ☎ P. AE VIS JCB. BX **Meals** *(closed Sunday)* (bar lunch)/dinner a la carte 7.25/12.30 **st.** – **18 rm** 36.00 48.00 **st.**

Travel Inn, Ham Lane, Orton Meadows, PE2 0UU, SW : 3½ m. by Oundle Rd (A 605 ☎ 235794, Fax 391055 – rm TV P. AE VISA BX **Meals** (grill rest.) – 4.95 – **40 rm** 34.50 **t.**

Grain Barge, The Quayside, Embankment Rd, PE1 1EG, ☎ 311967 – . AE VISA Z **Meals** - Chinese (Peking) - (buffet lunch Sunday) 20.00/30.00 **st.** and a la carte.

at Norman Cross S : 5¾ m. on A 15 at junction with A 1 – ✉ Peterborough – ☎ 01733

Forte Posthouse, Great North Rd, PE7 3TB, ☎ 240209, Fax 244455, , , – rm TV ☎ P – 50. AE VISA JCB BX **Meals** a la carte 13.35/24.20 **t.** 6.25 – 7.95 – **93 rm** 59.00 **t.** – SB.

at Alwalton SW : 5¾ m. on Oundle Rd (A 605) – ✉ Peterborough – ☎ 01733 :

Swallow, Peterborough Business Park, Lynch Wood, PE2 6GB, (opposite East o England Showground) ☎ 371111, Fax 236725, , , , – rm rest TV ☎ P – 275. AE VISA AX **Emperor** : **Meals 18.00/23.00 st.** and a la carte 5.50 – **Laurels** : **Meals** 14.00/16.75 **st** and a la carte 5.50 – **161 rm** 90.00/105.00 **st.**, 2 suites – SB.

Forte Travelodge, Great North Rd, PE7 3UR, A 1 (southbound carriageway) ☎ 231109 Reservations (Freephone) 0800 850950 – TV P. AE VISA. AX **Meals** (grill rest.) – **32 rm** 34.50 **t.**

at Wansford W : 8½ m. by A 47 – ✉ Peterborough – ☎ 01780 :

Haycock, PE8 6JA, ☎ 782223, Fax 783031, « Part 17C coaching inn », – TV ☎ P – 150. AE VISA AX **Meals** 18.95 **t.** (lunch) and a la carte 13.95/25.00 **t.** – **50 rm** 79.00/120.00 **st.**, 1 suite – SB.

Stoneacre without rest., Elton Rd, PE8 6JT, S : ½ m. on unmarked drive ☎ 783283 – TV P. AX **5 rm** 27.00/46.00 **st.**

ATS Wareley Rd (off George St.) ☎ 67112/3

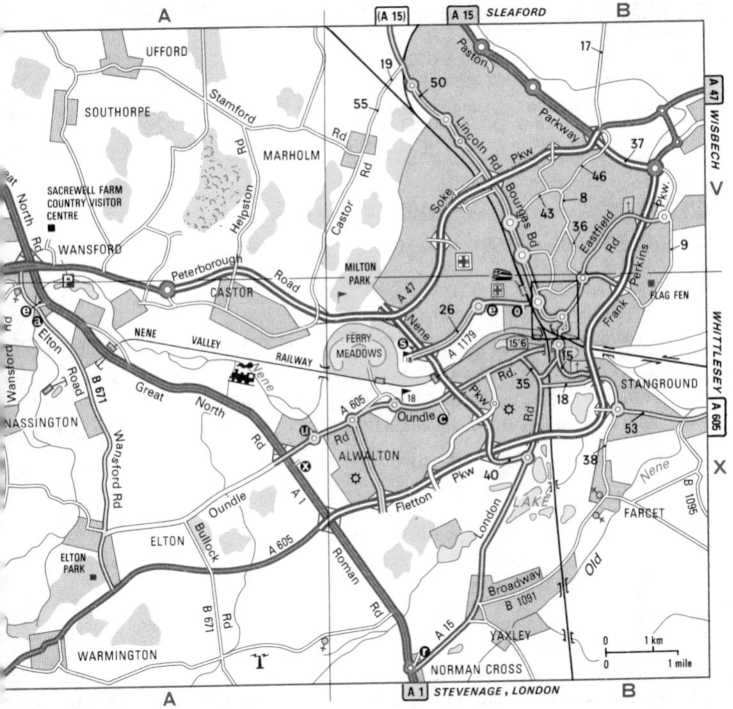

A B

(A 15) A 15 SLEAFORD

UFFORD · SOUTHORPE · Stamford Rd · MARHOLM · Helpston Rd · Castor Rd · SACREWELL FARM COUNTRY VISITOR CENTRE · WANSFORD · Peterborough Road · CASTOR · MILTON PARK · Paston Parkway · Lincoln Rd · Soke Pkw · Bourges Bd · Eastfield Rd · Frank Perkins Pkw. · FLAG FEN · A 47 WISBECH · WHITTLESEY · NENE VALLEY RAILWAY · FERRY MEADOWS · Nene · A 1179 · STANGROUND · A 605 · Elton Road · B 671 · Wansford Rd · Great North Rd · NASSINGTON · Oundle Rd · ALWALTON · Fletton Pkw · LAKE · FARCET · B 1095 · ELTON · ELTON PARK · Bullock Rd · Roman Rd · London Rd · Broadway B 1091 · Old Nene · YAXLEY · WARMINGTON · NORMAN CROSS · A 15 · A1 STEVENAGE, LONDON

V X

0 1 km · 0 1 mile

PETERBOROUGH

ridge Street	Z
hurch Street	YZ
ong Causeway	Y 25
ueensgate Shopping Centre	Y
ivergate Shopping Centre	Z
attle Market Road	Y 2
ty Road	Y 3
owgate	Y 5
ross Street	Z 6
ogsthorpe Road	BV 8
dgerley Drain Road	BV 9
mbankment Road	Z 12
xchange Street	Y 13
letton Avenue	BX 15
eneva Street	Y 16
untons Road	BV 17
igh Street	BX 18
urn Road	BV 19
ongthorpe Parkway	BX 26
larket Way	Y 28
lidgate	Y 29
lew Road	Y 34
lew Road	BX 35
ark Road	BV 36
aston Parkway	BV 37
eterborough Road	BX 38
horpres Way	BX 40
ivergate	Z 42
t Paul's Road	BV 43
horpe Road	Y 45
Velland Road	BV 46
Ventworth Street	Z 48
Verrington Parkway	BV 50
Vheelyard	Y 52
Vhittlesey Road	BX 53
Voodcroft Road	BV 55

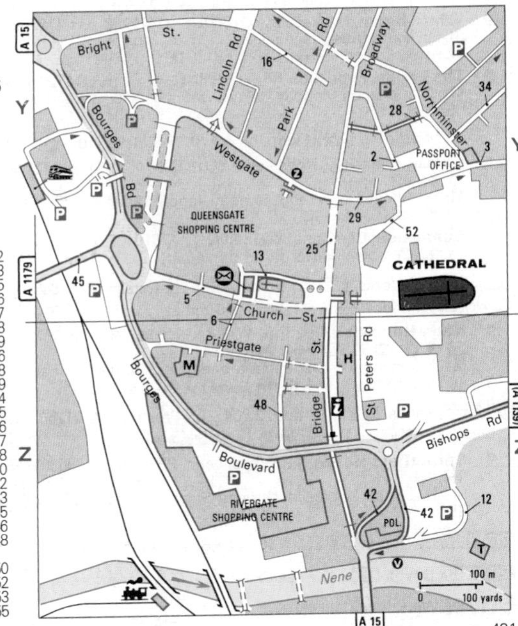

PETERSFIELD Hants. 404 R 30 – pop. 12 618 – ☎ 01730.

Heath Rd ℘ 263725.

County Library, 27 The Square, GU32 3HH ℘ 268829.

London 59 – Brighton 45 – Guildford 25 – Portsmouth 19 – Southampton 32 – Winchester 19.

Langrish House, Langrish, GU32 1RN, W : 3½ m. by A 272 ℘ 266941, Fax 260543, park – . AE VISA.
closed 24 December-2 January – **Meals** *(closed Sunday and Bank Holidays)* (bar lunch) 14.75 **st.** and a la carte 3.50 – **18 rm** 35.00/70.00 **t.** – SB.

ATS 15 & 31 Dragon St. ℘ 265151

PETERSTOW Heref. and Worcs. 403 404 M 28 – see Ross-on-Wye.

PETWORTH W. Sussex 404 S 31 **Great Britain G.** – pop. 3 866 – ☎ 01798.

See : Petworth House** *AC*.

9, 18 Osiers Farm ℘ (01903) 44097.

London 54 – Brighton 31 – Portsmouth 33.

Horseguards Inn with rm, Upperton Rd, Tillington, GU28 9AF, W : 1½ m. by A 272 ℘ 342332, – . VISA.
closed 25 December – **Meals** (booking essential) a la carte 15.50/23.75 t. – **3 rm** 58.00 st.

at Sutton S : 5 m. by A 283 – Pulborough – ☎ 01798 :

White Horse Inn, The Street, RH20 1PS, ℘ 869221, Fax 869291, – . AE VISA.
Meals a la carte 11.80/18.00 **t.** – **5 rm** 48.00/58.00 **st.** – SB.

En haute saison, et surtout dans les stations, il est prudent de retenir à l'avance.

PEVENSEY E. Sussex 404 V 31 pop. 2 833 – ☎ 01323.

London 74 – Brighton 25 – Folkestone 49.

Priory Court, BN24 5LG, ℘ 763150, – . VISA.
Meals a la carte 12.45/23.15 **st.** – **10 rm** 25.00/49.00 **st.** – SB.

PICKERING N. Yorks. 402 R 21 – pop. 6 269 – ☎ 01751.

Eastgate Car Park, YO18 7DP ℘ 473791.

London 237 – Middlesbrough 43 – Scarborough 19 – York 25.

Forest and Vale, Malton Rd, YO18 7DL, ℘ 472722, Fax 472972, – – 40. AE VISA
Meals 9.95/17.40 **t.** and a la carte 5.00 – **17 rm** 48.00/80.00 **t.** – SB.

White Swan, Market Pl., YO18 7AA, ℘ 472288, Fax 472288 – rm . AE VISA
St. Emilion : Meals (lunch by arrangement Monday to Saturday)/dinner 9.50/19.50 **t.** 4.20 – **12 rm** (dinner included) 65.00/100.00 **t.**, 1 suite – SB.

The Lodge, Middleton Rd, YO18 8NQ, W : ½ m. ℘ 472976, – . AE VISA.
Meals (bar lunch Monday to Friday)/dinner 19.50 **st.** and a la carte 4.25 – **9 rm** 29.00/58.00 **st.** – SB.

at Middleton NW : 1½ m. on A 170 – Pickering – ☎ 01751 :

Cottage Leas, Nova Lane, YO18 8PN, N : 1 m. ℘ 472129, Fax 474930, – . VISA
Meals (dinner only and Sunday lunch)/dinner 19.75 **t.** and a la carte 5.50 – **11 rm** 40.00/68.00 **t.** – SB.

Sunnyside, Carr Lane, YO18 8PD, ℘ 476104, Fax 476104, – rest . VISA
Easter-October – **Meals** (by arrangement) 12.00 – **3 rm** 24.00/38.00.

PICKHILL N. Yorks. 402 P 21 – pop. 412 – Thirsk – ☎ 01845.

London 229 – Leeds 41 – Middlesbrough 30 – York 34.

Nags Head Country Inn, YO7 4JG, ℘ 567391, Fax 567212, « Part 18C inn », – . AE VISA JCB.
Meals (lunch by arrangement Monday to Saturday) (in bar Sunday dinner)/dinner 18.50 **st.** and a la carte 4.25 – **15 rm** 34.00/48.00 **st.** – SB.

PILLING Lancs. 402 L 22 – pop. 2 204 – Preston – ☎ 01253.

London 243 – Blackpool 11 – Burnley 43 – Manchester 49.

Springfield House, Wheel Lane, PR3 6HL, ℘ 790301, Fax 790907, – . VISA.
Meals *(closed lunch Monday and Saturday)* 8.65/15.25 **t.** 4.35 – **7 rm** 30.00/55.00 **t.** – SB.

PIMPERNE Dorset 403 404 N 31 – see Blandford Forum.

PINHOE Devon 403 J 31 – see Exeter.

PITTON Wilts. – see Salisbury.

LUCKLEY Kent 404 W 30 – pop. 883 – ☎ 01233.

London 53 – Folkestone 25 – Maidstone 18.

⌂ **Elvey Farm** 🐎, TN27 0SU, W : 2 m. by Smarden rd and Marley Farm rd, off Mundy Bois rd ☎ 840442, Fax 840726, ⩽, « Converted oast house and barn », 🌳 – TV P. VISA JCB. ✻
Meals (by arrangement) 18.95 **t.** 3.95 – **8 rm** ☐ 35.50/59.50 **t.** – SB.

LUMTREE Notts. – see Nottingham.

LYMOUTH Devon 403 H 32 The West Country G. – pop. 243 373 – ☎ 01752.

ee : Town★★ - Smeaton's Tower (⩽★★) AC BZ **A** – Plymouth Dome★ AC BZ – Royal Citadel amparts⩽★★) AC BZ – Elizabethan House★ AC – City Museum and Art Gallery★ BZ **M**.

nvir. : – Saltram House★★ AC, E : 3½ m. BY **A** – Anthony House★ AC, W : 5 m. by A 374 – ount Edgcumbe (⩽★) AC, SW : 2 m. by passenger ferry from Stonehouse AZ.

xc. : NE : Dartmoor National Park★★ (Brent Tor ⩽★★, Haytor Rocks ⩽★) BY – Buckland obey★★ AC, N : 7 ½ m. by A 386 ABY – Yelverton Paperweight Centre★, N : 10 m. by 386 ABY.

Staddon Heights, Plymstock ☎ 402475 – 9 Elfordleigh Hotel G & C.C., Colebrook, Plympton 336428.

✈ Plymouth City (Roborough) Airport : ☎ 772752, N : 3½ m. by A 386 ABY.

⛴ to France (Roscoff) (Brittany Ferries) 1-2 daily (6 h) – to Spain (Santander) (Brittany erries) (23 h).

Island House, 9 The Barbican, PL1 2LS ☎ 264849.

London 242 – ◆Bristol 124 – ◆Southampton 161.

Plans on following pages

Copthorne Plymouth, Armada Centre, Armada Way, PL1 1AR, (via Western Approach southbound) ☎ 224161, Telex 45756, Fax 670688, Fō, ≘s, 🏊 – 🛗 ⇎ rm ▤ rest TV ☎ ♿ P – 🏛 70. AE ⓓ VISA JCB BZ **e**
Meals 16.95 **st.** and a la carte 6.25 – **Burlington : Meals** (dinner only and Sunday lunch) 16.95 **st.** and a la carte 6.25 – ☐ 9.50 – **135 rm** 79.00/120.00 **st.** – SB.

Plymouth Hoe Moat House (Q.M.H.), Armada Way, PL1 2HJ, ☎ 639988, Telex 45637, Fax 673816, ⩽ city and Plymouth Sound, Fō, ≘s, 🏊 – 🛗 ⇎ rm ▤ rest TV ☎ ♿ P – 🏛 400. AE ⓓ VISA. ✻ BZ **s**
Blue Riband : Meals (bar lunch Saturday) a la carte 11.50/19.75 **st.** 4.95 – ☐ 9.50 – **210 rm** 90.00/99.50 **st.**, 1 suite – SB.

Grand, Elliott St., The Hoe, PL1 2PT, ☎ 661195, Fax 600653, ⩽ – 🛗 TV ☎ P – 🏛 70. AE ⓓ VISA BZ **a**
Meals 8.50/18.50 **t.** and dinner a la carte 7.50 – **77 rm** ☐ 70.00/110.00 **st.** – SB.

Forte Posthouse, Cliff Rd, The Hoe, PL1 3DL, ☎ 662828, Fax 660974, ⩽ Plymouth Sound, 🏊 heated – 🛗 ⇎ rm TV ☎ P – 🏛 80. AE ⓓ VISA JCB AZ **v**
Meals a la carte 13.00/22.15 **st.** 5.95 – ☐ 7.95 – **106 rm** 56.00 **st.** – SB.

New Continental, Millbay Rd, PL1 3LD, ☎ 220782, Fax 227013, Fō, ≘s, 🏊 – 🛗 TV ☎ P – 🏛 400. AE VISA AZ **s**
Meals (bar lunch Saturday) 9.95/14.50 **st.** and a la carte – **99 rm** ☐ 65.00/120.00 **st.** – SB.

Novotel Plymouth, 270 Plymouth Rd., Marsh Mills Roundabout, PL6 8NH, ☎ 221422, Fax 221422 (ext. 126), 🏊 heated – 🛗 ⇎ rm ▤ rest TV ☎ ♿ P – 🏛 200. AE ⓓ VISA BY **i**
Meals a la carte 11.50/19.75 **st.** 4.95 – ☐ 7.50 – **100 rm** 49.50 **st.**

Campanile, Longbridge Rd, Marsh Mills, PL6 8LD, ☎ 601087, Fax 223213 – ⇎ rm TV ☎ ♿ P – 🏛 30. AE ⓓ VISA BY **a**
Meals 10.35 **st.** 4.95 – ☐ 4.95 – **51 rm** 36.50 **st.**

⌂ **Bowling Green** without rest., 9-10 Osborne Pl., Lockyer St., The Hoe, PL1 2PU, ☎ 667485, Fax 255150 – TV ☎. AE ⓓ VISA BZ **r**
closed 24 to 26 December – **12 rm** ☐ 28.00/46.00 **st.**

⌂ **Athenaeum Lodge** without rest., 4 Athenaeum St., The Hoe, PL1 2RH, ☎ 665005 – TV P. VISA. ✻ BZ **u**
9 rm ☐ 20.00/36.00 **st.**

⌂ **Cranbourne** without rest., 282 Citadel Rd, The Hoe, PL1 2PZ, ☎ 263858, Fax 263858 – TV. AE VISA BZ **r**
14 rm ☐ 15.00/35.00 **st.**

⌂ **Sea Breezes,** 28 Grand Par., West Hoe, PL1 3DJ, ☎ 667205 – TV. VISA JCB AZ **o**
Meals (by arrangement) 10.00 **s.** – **8 rm** ☐ 15.00/36.00 **s.**

⌂ **Berkeley's of St. James** without rest., 4 St. James Place East, The Hoe, PL1 3AS, ☎ 221654 – ⇎ TV. AE ⓓ. ✻ AZ **n**
5 rm ☐ 16.00/35.00 **t.**

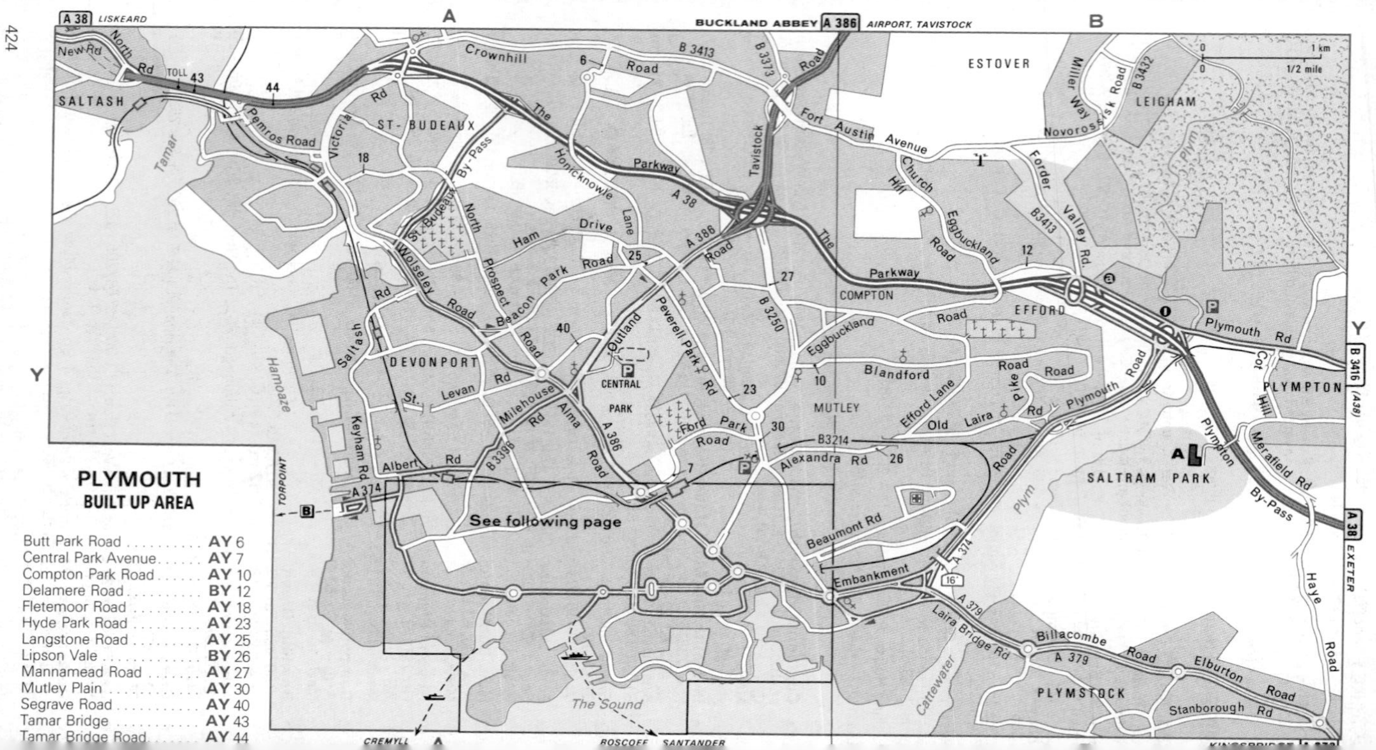

PLYMOUTH
BUILT UP AREA

Butt Park Road	AY	6
Central Park Avenue	AY	7
Compton Park Road	AY	10
Delamere Road	BY	12
Fletemoor Road	AY	18
Hyde Park Road	AY	23
Langstone Road	AY	25
Lipson Vale	BY	26
Mannamead Road	AY	27
Mutley Plain	AY	30
Segrave Road	AY	40
Tamar Bridge	AY	43
Tamar Bridge Road	AY	44

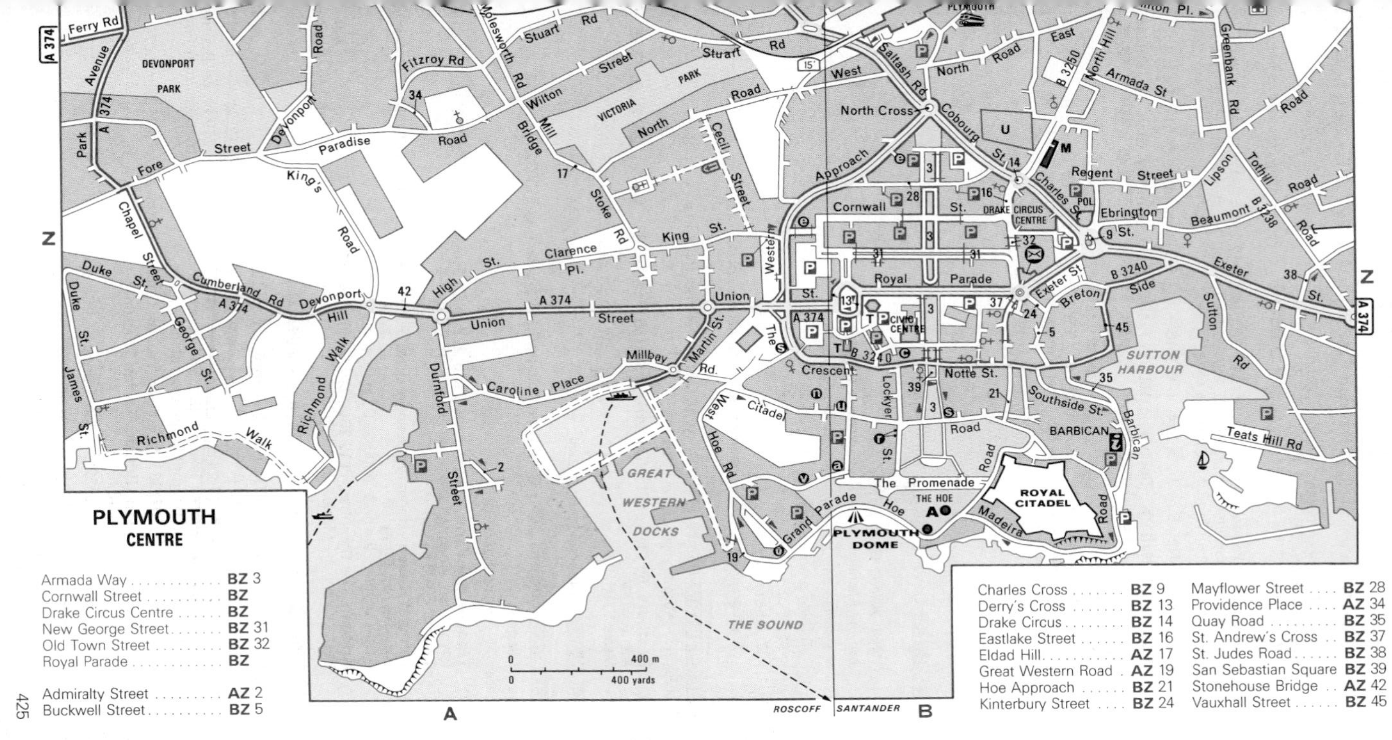

PLYMOUTH
CENTRE

Armada Way .... BZ 3
Cornwall Street .... BZ
Drake Circus Centre ...... BZ
New George Street .... BZ 31
Old Town Street .... BZ 32
Royal Parade .... BZ

Admiralty Street .... AZ 2
Buckwell Street .... BZ 5
Charles Cross .... BZ 9
Derry's Cross .... BZ 13
Drake Circus .... BZ 14
Eastlake Street ..... BZ 16
Eldad Hill .... AZ 17
Great Western Road . AZ 19
Hoe Approach ...... BZ 21
Kinterbury Street .... BZ 24
Mayflower Street .... BZ 28
Providence Place .... AZ 34
Quay Road .... BZ 35
St. Andrew's Cross .. BZ 37
St. Judes Road ..... BZ 38
San Sebastian Square BZ 39
Stonehouse Bridge .. AZ 42
Vauxhall Street ..... BZ 45

✕ ✲ **Chez Nous** (Marchal), 13 Frankfort Gate, PL1 1QA, ✆ 266793, Fax 266793 – VISA AZ
closed Sunday, Monday, 3 weeks February, 3 weeks September and Bank Holidays – **Meals** - French - 28.50 **t.** 10.50
Spec. Terrine de crabe et sa petite salade à l'orange, La bouillabaisse du Barbican, Glace tiramisu et ses fraises au vin rouge.

✕ **Bougie La Brasserie,** Princess St., PL1 2EX, ✆ 221177, Fax 221177 – AE VISA BZ
closed Saturday lunch, Sunday, 25 and 26 December, 1 January and Bank Holidays – **Meals** - French - 7.50/9.50 **t.** and a la carte.

at Plympton **NE : 5 m. by A 374 on B 3416 – BY – ✉ Plymouth – ☎ 01752 :**

Boringdon Hall, Boringdon Hill, PL7 4DP, N : 1 ½ m. by Glen Rd ✆ 344455, Fax 346578, « Part 16C manor », park, – rm TV ☎ P – 120. AE VISA
Meals 18.95 **st.** and a la carte 5.95 – **40 rm** 65.00/110.00 **st.** – SB.

Windwhistle Farm, Hemerdon, PL7 5BU, NE : 2 ½ m. by Glen Rd and B 3417 turning left beside telephone box after Miners Arms in Hemerdon ✆ 340600, – P.
Meals (by arrangement) (communal dining) 12.00 **s.** – **3 rm** 18.00/40.00 **s.**

ATS Teats Hill Rd, Coxside ✆ 266217/227964
ATS Miller Way, Novorossisk Rd, Estover ✆ 769123
ATS Strode Rd, Plympton ✆ 331001

PLYMPTON Devon 403 H 32 – see Plymouth.

When visiting Great Britain,
use the ***Michelin Green Guide*** **"Great Britain".**
- *Detailed descriptions of places of interest*
- *Touring programmes*
- *Maps and street plans*
- *The history of the country*
- *Photographs and drawings of monuments, beauty spots, houses...*

POCKLINGTON Humbs. 402 R 22 – pop. 6 878 – ✉ York (N. Yorks.) – ☎ 01759.
♦London 213 – ♦Kingston-upon-Hull 25 – York 13.

Feathers, 56 Market Pl., YO4 2AH, ✆ 303155, Fax 304382 – rest TV ☎ P. AE VISA JCB.
Meals 10.95/12.95 **st.** and a la carte 5.95 – **12 rm** 39.50/50.00 **st.** – SB.

PODIMORE Somerset – see Yeovil.

POLPERRO Cornwall 403 G 33 **The West Country G.** – ✉ Looe – ☎ 01503.
See : Village★.
♦London 271 – ♦Plymouth 28.

Trenderway Farm without rest., PL13 2LY, NE : 2 m. by A 387 ✆ 272214, ←, « 16C farmhouse, working farm », , park – TV P.
4 rm 60.00 **t.**, 1 suite.

Lanhael House without rest., Langreek Rd, PL13 2PW, ✆ 272428, Fax 273077, heated, – rest TV P.
April-October – **5 rm** 25.00/39.00 **st.**

✕ **Kitchen,** The Coombes, PL13 2RQ, ✆ 272780 – . VISA
Easter-October – **Meals** *(closed Sunday)* (dinner only) a la carte 15.50/20.50 **t.** 6.50.

PONTELAND Tyne and Wear 401 402 O 19 – see Newcastle upon Tyne.

POOLE Dorset 403 404 O 31 **The West Country G.** – pop. 133 050 – ☎ 01202.
See : Town★ - Museums★ *AC* (Waterfront **M1**, Scaplen's Court **M2**).
Envir. : Compton Acres★★, (English Garden ←★★★) *AC*, SE : 3 m. by B 3369 BX on Bournemouth town plan – Brownsea Island★ (Baden-Powell Stone ✲★★) *AC*, by boat from Poole Quay or Sandbanks BX on Bournemouth town plan.
18 Parkstone, Links Rd ✆ 707138 – 18 Bulbury Woods, Lytchett Matravers ✆ (01929) 459574.
to France (Cherbourg) (Brittany Ferries Truckline) 1-2 daily (4 h 15 mn) – to France (St. Malo) (Brittany Ferries) (8 h).
ℹ The Quay, BH15 1HE ✆ 673322 – Dolphin Shopping Centre.
♦London 116 – Bournemouth 4 – Dorchester 23 – Weymouth 28.

Plan opposite - Plan of Built up Area : see Bournemouth

POOLE

Dolphin Shopping Centre
Church Street 3
Emerson Road 4
Falkland Sq. 6
Fishermans Rd 7
Furnell Rd 8
Holes Bay Rd 10
Labrador Drive 12
Longfleet Rd 13
Market St. 14
New Orchard 16
New Street 17
Serpentine Rd 18
Thames St. 19
Towngate Bridge 21
Westons Lane 22

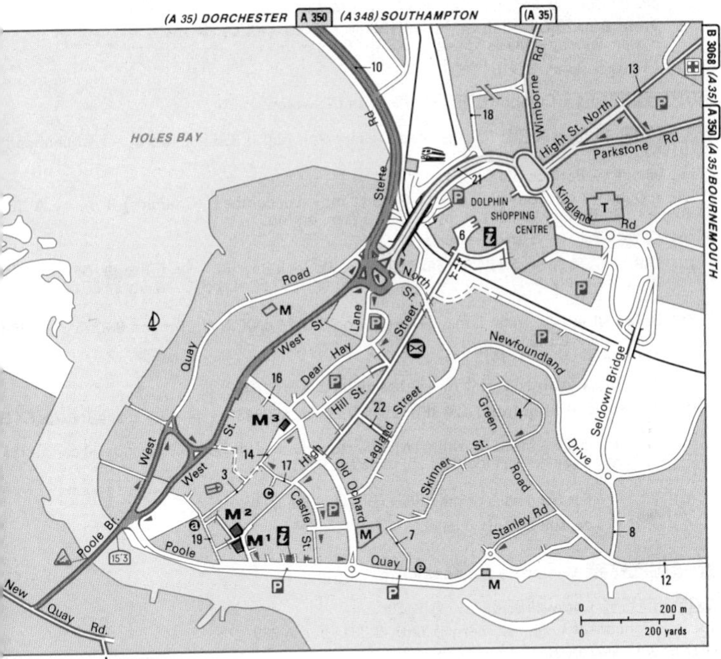

Haven, Banks Rd, Sandbanks, BH13 7QL, SE : 4 ¼ m. on B 3369 ℰ 707333, Fax 708796, ⩽ Ferry, Old Harry Rocks and Poole Bay, Lδ, ≘s, ⛱ heated, squash – |‡| TV ☎ P – 🔏 160. AE ① VISA. ✻ on Bournemouth town plan BX **c**
Meals 16.00/23.50 **t.** and a la carte 5.75 – (see also ***La Roche*** below) – **90 rm** ☐ 90.00/200.00 **st.**, 2 suites – SB.

Mansion House, 7-11 Thames St., BH15 1JN, off Poole Quay ℰ 685666, Fax 665709, « 18C town house » – ▤ rest TV ☎ P – 🔏 25. AE ① VISA JCB. ✻ **a**
Meals (in bar Saturday lunch and Sunday dinner) 17.00/21.50 **t.** 6.00 – **28 rm** ☐ 75.00/120.00 **st.** – SB.

Salterns, 38 Salterns Way, Lilliput, BH14 8JR, ℰ 707321, Fax 707488, ⩽, squash – ⇎ rm ▤ rest TV ☎ P – 🔏 80. AE ① VISA JCB on Bournemouth town plan BX **e**
Meals 15.50/25.00 4.00 – ☐ 9.50 – **20 rm** 66.00/86.00 **t.** – SB.

Quay Thistle ⛵, The Quay, BH15 1HD, ℰ 666800, Fax 684470 – |‡| ⇎ rm ▤ rest TV ☎ P – 🔏 30. AE ① VISA JCB. ✻ **e**
Meals 17.95/25.00 **t.** and a la carte 5.00 – ☐ 9.75 – **65 rm** 80.00/90.00 **t.** – SB.

Arndale Court, 62-66 Wimborne Rd, BH15 2BY, ℰ 683746, Fax 668838 – TV ☎ P – 🔏 30. AE ① VISA JCB on Bournemouth town plan ABX **r**
Meals *(closed Sunday dinner)* (dinner only and Sunday lunch)/dinner a la carte approx. 14.90 **st.** 3.95 – **32 rm** ☐ 48.00/59.50.

Sea Witch, 47 Haven Rd, Canford Cliffs, BH13 7LH, ℰ 707697, Fax 707494 – ⇎ TV ☎ P. VISA on Bournemouth town plan CX **u**
Meals *(closed lunch Tuesday and Sunday and Monday)* 7.45/14.95 **t.** and a la carte **t.** 3.75 – **10 rm** ☐ 37.50/60.00 **st.** – SB.

Inn in the Park, Pinewood Rd, Branksome Park, BH13 6JS, ℰ 761318 – TV P. VISA on Bournemouth town plan CX **a**
Meals *(closed dinner Sunday and Monday)* (bar lunch)/dinner 11.50 **t.** and a la carte – **5 rm** ☐ 32.50/45.00 **st.**

XX **La Roche** (at Haven H.), Banks Rd, Sandbanks, BH13 7QL, ℘ 707333, Fax 708796 – P. VISA
on Bournemouth town plan BX
closed Sunday – **Meals** (dinner only and Sunday lunch) a la carte 32.00/37.00 **t.** 5.75.

X **Isabel's,** 32 Station Rd, Lower Parkstone, BH14 8UD, ℘ 747885 – VISA
on Bournemouth town plan BX
closed Sunday and 26 to 28 December – **Meals** (dinner only) 19.00 **t.** and a la carte.

X **John B's,** 20 Old High St., BH15 1BP, ℘ 672440 – VISA
closed Sunday – **Meals** (dinner only) 19.50 **t.** 5.75.

ATS 1 Fernside Rd ℘ 733301/733326

POOLEY BRIDGE Cumbria 401 402 L 20 – see Ullswater.

PORLOCK Somerset 403 J 30 **The West Country G.** – pop. 1 395 (inc. Oare) – ✉ Minehead ☎ 01643.

See : Village★ - Porlock Hill (≤★★).

Envir. : Dunkery Beacon★★★ (≤★★★) S : 5 ½ m. – Luccombe★ (Church★) 3 m. by A 39 Culbone★ (St. Beuno) W : 3½ m. by B 3225, 1½ m. on foot.

◆London 190 – ◆Bristol 67 – Exeter 46 – Taunton 28.

Oaks, TA24 8ES, ℘ 862265, Fax 862265, ≤ Porlock Bay, – TV P. VISA
closed January and February – **Meals** (dinner only) 22.50 **st.** 5.75 – **9 rm** 50.00/80.00 **s** – SB.

Bales Mead without rest., West Porlock, TA24 8NX, NW : 1 m. on B 3225 ℘ 86256
≤, – TV P
3 rm 30.00/40.00 **st.**

at Porlock Weir NW : 1½ m. – ✉ Minehead – ☎ 01643 :

Anchor and Ship Inn, TA24 8PB, ℘ 862753, Fax 862843, ≤, – rest TV P. VISA
closed January – **Meals** (bar lunch Monday to Saturday)/dinner 18.95 **t.** and a la carte 6.7 – **20 rm** (dinner included) 72.75/135.50 **st.** – SB.

Prices	For full details of the prices quoted in the guide, consult the introduction.

PORTINSCALE Cumbria – see Keswick.

PORT ISAAC Cornwall 403 F 32 – ☎ 01208.

Exc. : – Pencarrow★, SE : 12 m. by B 3267, B 3314 and A 389.

◆London 266 – Newquay 24 – Tintagel 14 – Truro 32.

Port Gaverne, Port Gaverne, PL29 3SQ, S :½ m. ℘ 880244, Fax 880151, « Retaining 17 features » – rest TV P. VISA JCB
closed 7 January-17 February – **Meals** (bar lunch)/dinner a la carte 17.45/26.00 **t.** – **19 rm** 47.00/98.00 **t.** – SB.

Slipway, Harbour Front, PL29 3RH, ℘ 880264, Fax 880264, « Part 16C inn » – P. VISA JCB
closed 8 January-15 March – **Meals** (bar lunch)/dinner a la carte 17.00/24.50 **t.** 4.25 – **10 rm** 24.00/64.00 **t.** – SB.

Archer Farm, Trewetha, PL29 3RU, SE :½ m. by B 3267 ℘ 880522, ≤, – res TV P
April-October – **Meals** 15.00 3.75 – **5 rm** 22.50/28.00.

PORTLOE Cornwall 403 F 33 – ✉ Truro – ☎ 01872.

◆London 296 – St. Austell 15 – Truro 15.

Lugger, TR2 5RD, ℘ 501322, Fax 501691, ≤, – rest TV P. VISA JCB
9 February-17 November – **Meals** (bar lunch Monday to Saturday)/dinner 25.00 **st.** and a la carte 4.25 – **19 rm** (dinner included) 70.00/144.00 **t.** – SB.

PORTSCATHO Cornwall 403 F 33 **The West Country G.** – ✉ Truro – ☎ 01872.

Envir. : St. Just-in-Roseland Church★★, W : 4 m. by A 3078 – St. Anthony-in-Roseland (≤★★) S : 3½ m.

◆London 298 – ◆Plymouth 55 – Truro 16.

Roseland House, Rosevine, TR2 5EW, N : 2 m. by A 3078 ℘ 580644, Fax 580801, ≤ Gerrans Bay, – TV P. VISA.
Meals 10.50/18.00 **st.** 5.00 – **16 rm** (dinner included) 33.00/100.00 **st.** – SB.

Gerrans Bay, 12 Tregassick Rd, TR2 5ED, ℘ 580338, Fax 580250, ≤, – TV P. VISA JCB
April-October and Christmas – **Meals** (bar lunch Monday to Saturday)/dinner 21.00 **t.** 4.60 – **14 rm** (dinner included) 49.50/99.00 **t.** – SB.

ORTSMOUTH and SOUTHSEA Hants. 403 404 Q 31 **Great Britain G.** – pop. 174 697 – 01705.

ee : City★ – Naval Portsmouth BY : H.M.S. Victory★★★ *AC*, The Mary Rose★★, Royal Naval useum★★ *AC* – Old Portsmouth★ BYZ : The Point (≤★★) - St. Thomas Cathedral★ – Southsea astle★ *AC*) AZ – Royal Marines Museum, Eastney★ *AC*, AZ **M1**.

nvir. : Portchester Castle★ *AC*, NW : 5½ m. by A 3 and A 27 AY.

Great Salterns, Porthsmouth Golf Centre, Burrfields Rd ☏ 664549/699519 AY – 18 Crookhorn ne, Widley ☏ 372210/372299 – 18 Southwick Park, Pinsley Drive, Southwick ☏ 380131.

to France (Cherbourg) (P & O European Ferries Ltd) 2-3 daily (4 h 45 mn) day, (8 h 45 mn) ght – to France (Le Havre) (P & O European Ferries Ltd) 3 daily (5 h 45 mn) day, (7 h) night – France (Caen) (Brittany Ferries) 2-3 daily (6 h), (St. Malo) 1 daily (9 h) – to the Isle of Wight ishbourne) (Wightlink Ltd) frequent services daily (35 mn) – to Spain (Santander) (Brittany erries) (30 h) – to Spain (Bilbao) (P & O European Ferries Ltd) (30 h).

to the Isle of Wight (Ryde) (Wightlink Ltd) frequent services daily (15 mn) – from Southsea the Isle of Wight (Ryde) (Hovertravel Ltd) frequent services daily (10 mn).

The Hard, PO1 3QJ ☏ 826722 – Clarence Esplanade, PO5 3ST ☏ 832464 (summer only) – erminal Building, Portsmouth Ferryport ☏ 838635 102 Commercial Rd, PO1 1EJ ☏ 838382.

London 78 – ◆Brighton 48 – Salisbury 44 – ◆Southampton 21.

Plans on following pages

Hilton National, Eastern Rd, Farlington, PO6 1UN, NE : 5 m. on A 2030 ☏ 219111, Fax 210762, Fitness, Sauna, Pool, Garden – ⊭ rm TV ☎ ♿ P – 🏛 230. AE VISA — AY **c**
Meals (bar lunch Saturday) 15.95/17.95 **t.** and a la carte 6.00 – ☕ 10.25 – **118 rm** 75.00/115.00 **t.**

Innlodge, Burrfields Rd, PO3 5HH, ☏ 650510, Fax 693458, – ⊭ rm ▤ rest TV ☎ ♿ P – 🏛 120. AE VISA. — AY **u**
Meals a la carte 9.20/19.65 **t.** 5.25 – ☕ 6.50 – **73 rm** 42.00/55.00 **t.**

Forte Posthouse, Pembroke Rd, PO1 2TA, ☏ 827651, Fax 756715, Fitness, Sauna, Pool – lift ⊭ rm TV ☎ P – 🏛 220. AE VISA JCB — CZ **o**
Meals a la carte 13.40/20.95 **st.** – ☕ 7.95 – **163 rm** 59.00 **st.** – SB.

Hospitality Inn (Mount Charlotte), South Par., Southsea, PO4 0RN, ☏ 731281, Fax 817572, ≤ – lift ⊭ rm TV ☎ – 🏛 200. AE VISA JCB. — AZ **r**
Meals 14.50/16.50 **st.** and a la carte 4.50 – **113 rm** ☕ 69.00/79.00 **st.**, 2 suites – SB.

Green Farm Toby, Copnor Rd, Hilsea, PO3 5HS, ☏ 654645, Fax 654287 – ⊭ rm ▤ rest TV ☎ ♿ P – 🏛 35. AE VISA. — AY **e**
Meals (grill rest.) 7.90 **t.** (lunch) and a la carte 10.20/16.15 **t.** – **30 rm** ☕ 57.50/69.00 **t.** – SB.

Sallyport, High St., Old Portsmouth, PO1 2LU, ☏ 821860, Fax 821293 – TV ☎. AE VISA — BZ **a**
Meals 17.00 **st.** and a la carte 4.95 – **10 rm** ☕ 32.00/59.00 **st.** – SB.

Seacrest, 11-12 South Par., Southsea, PO5 2JB, ☏ 733192, Fax 832523, ≤ – lift ⊭ rest TV ☎ P. AE VISA — AZ **e**
Meals (residents only) (dinner only) 10.95 **t.** and a la carte 3.95 – **28 rm** ☕ 35.00/65.00 **t.** – SB.

Beaufort, 71 Festing Rd, Southsea, PO4 0NQ, ☏ 823707, Fax 870270 – ⊭ rest TV ☎ P. AE VISA. — AZ **n**
Meals (dinner only) 13.90 **st.** and a la carte 3.70 – **20 rm** ☕ 40.00/70.00 **st.** – SB.

Fortitude Cottage without rest., 51 Broad St., Old Portsmouth, PO1 2JD, ☏ 823748, Fax 823748 – ⊭ TV. VISA JCB. — BY **c**
closed 25 and 26 December – **3 rm** ☕ 25.00/44.00 **st.**

St. Margaret's, 3 Craneswater Gate, Southsea, PO4 0NZ, ☏ 820097, Fax 820097, – ⊭ rest TV. VISA. — AZ **i**
closed 23 December-3 January – **Meals** (by arrangement) 9.00 **st.** – **14 rm** ☕ 19.00/40.00 **st.** – SB.

Glencoe without rest., 64 Whitwell Rd, Southsea, PO4 0QS, ☏ 737413 – TV. VISA — AZ **u**
7 rm ☕ 16.50/35.00 **st.**

Cranbourne House without rest., 6 Herbert Rd, Southsea, PO4 0QA, ☏ 824981 – ⊭ TV — AZ **a**
3 rm.

Ashwood without rest., 10 St. David's Rd, Southsea, PO5 1QN, ☏ 816228, Fax 753955 – TV. — AZ **c**
7 rm ☕ 17.00/36.00.

XX **Bistro Montparnasse,** 103 Palmerston Rd, Southsea, PO5 3PS, ☏ 816754, Fax 816754 – AE VISA — CZ **a**
closed Sunday, Monday and Bank Holidays – **Meals** (dinner only) 12.50/20.00 **t.** and a la carte 17.50/24.60 **t.** 6.50.

at Cosham N : 4½ m. by A 3 and M 275 on A 27 – ✉ Portsmouth – ☏ 01705 :

Portsmouth Marriott, North Harbour, PO6 4SH, ☏ 383151, Fax 388701, Fitness, Sauna, Pool, squash – lift ⊭ rm ▤ TV ☎ ♿ P – 🏛 280. AE VISA JCB — AY **a**
Meals 15.95 **st.** and a la carte 5.25 – ☕ 10.25 – **169 rm** 75.00/90.00 **st.**, 1 suite.

ATS Sharps Close ☏ 665959

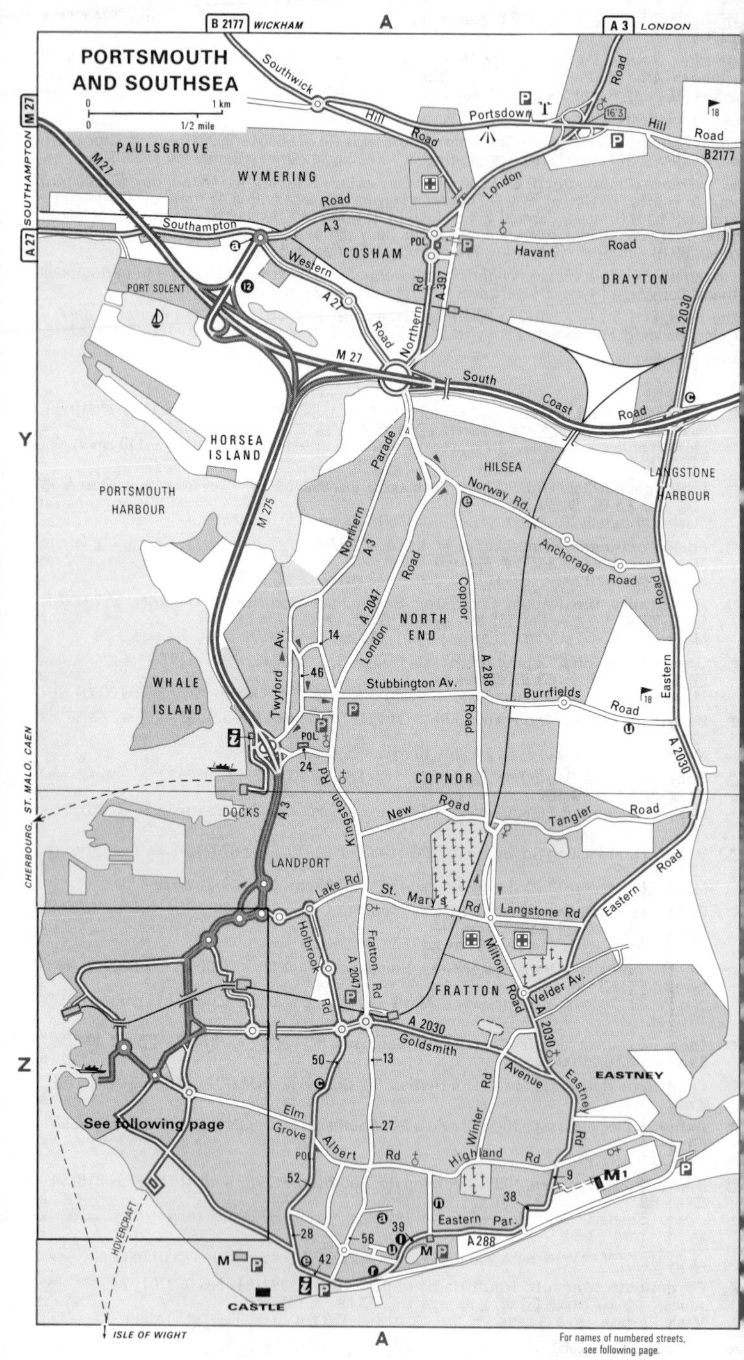

For names of numbered streets, see following page.

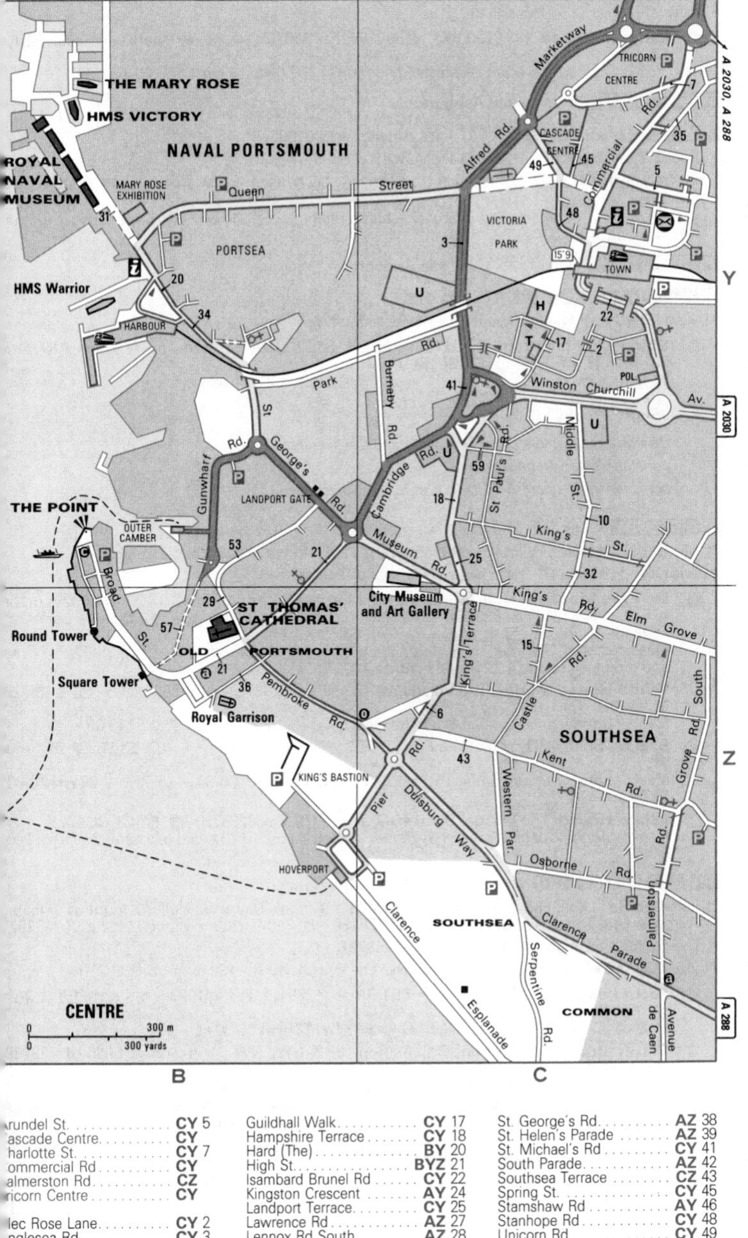

ɪrundel St. . . . . CY 5
ascade Centre. . . . . CY
harlotte St. . . . . CY 7
ommercial Rd . . . . CY
almerston Rd . . . . CZ
ricorn Centre . . . . CY

lec Rose Lane. . . . . CY 2
nglesea Rd . . . . CY 3
ellevue Terrace . . . . CZ 6
romwell Rd . . . . AZ 9
don St. . . . . CY 10
awcett Rd . . . . AZ 13
ladys Avenue . . . . AY 14
reat Southsea St. . . . . . . CZ 15

Guildhall Walk. . . . . CY 17
Hampshire Terrace . . . . . . CY 18
Hard (The) . . . . BY 20
High St. . . . . BYZ 21
Isambard Brunel Rd . . . . . CY 22
Kingston Crescent . . . . . . AY 24
Landport Terrace. . . . . CY 25
Lawrence Rd . . . . AZ 27
Lennox Rd South . . . . AZ 28
Lombard St. . . . . BYZ 29
Main Rd. . . . . BY 31
Norfolk St. . . . . CYZ 32
Ordnance Row . . . . BY 34
Paradise St. . . . . CY 35
Penny St. . . . . BZ 36

St. George's Rd. . . . . AZ 38
St. Helen's Parade . . . . . . AZ 39
St. Michael's Rd . . . . CY 41
South Parade. . . . . AZ 42
Southsea Terrace . . . . CZ 43
Spring St. . . . . CY 45
Stamshaw Rd . . . . AY 46
Stanhope Rd . . . . CY 48
Unicorn Rd . . . . CY 49
Victoria Rd North . . . . AZ 50
Victoria Rd South . . . . AZ 52
Warblington St. . . . . BY 53
Waverley Rd . . . . AZ 56
White Hart Rd. . . . . BYZ 57
Wiltshire St.. . . . . CY 59

POSTBRIDGE Devon 403 I 32 – ✉ Yelverton – ☎ 01822.
♦London 205 – Exeter 21 – ♦Plymouth 19.

- **Lydgate House** ⛰, PL20 6TJ, ☎ 880209, Fax 880202, ≤, 🎣, 🌳, park – ⇔ rest TV P. VISA
  closed 3 January-8 March – **Meals** (dinner only) 15.50 **st.** – **8 rm** ☐ 29.00/58.00 **t.**

POUNDSGATE Devon – see Ashburton.

POWBURN Northd 401 402 O 17 – ✉ Alnwick – ☎ 01665.
♦London 312 – ♦Edinburgh 73 – ♦Newcastle upon Tyne 36.

- **Breamish House** ⛰, NE66 4LL, ☎ 578266, Fax 578500, ≤, 🌳 – ⇔ rest TV ☎ P. VISA JCB
  closed 30 December-mid February – **Meals** (dinner only) 21.50 **t.** 6.25 – **11 rm** ☐ (dinner included) 74.00/146.00 **t.** – SB.

POWERSTOCK Dorset 403 L 31 – see Bridport.

POYNTON Ches. 402 403 N 23 – ☎ 01625.
♦London 193 – Chester 44 – ♦Manchester 12 – ♦Stoke-on-Trent 28.

- **Spinney** without rest., 59-61 Chester Rd, SK12 1HB, W : ¼ m. on A 5149 ☎ 871397, Fax 872143, 🌳 – TV P. AE VISA JCB
  12 rm ☐ 35.00/58.75 **s.**

"Short Breaks" (SB)

De nombreux hôtels proposent des conditions avantageuses
pour un séjour de deux nuits
comprenant la chambre, le dîner et le petit déjeuner.

PRESTBURY Ches. 402 403 404 N 24 – pop. 3 623 – ☎ 01625.
Mottram Hall Hotel, Wilmslow Rd, Mottram St. Andrews ☎ 828135.
♦London 184 – ♦Liverpool 43 – ♦Manchester 17 – ♦Stoke-on-Trent 25.

- **De Vere Mottram Hall,** Wilmslow Rd, Mottram St. Andrew, SK10 4QT, NW : 2¼ m. on A 538 ☎ 828135, Fax 829284, ≤, « Part 18C mansion », 🏋, ≘s, 🏊, 18, 🌳, park, 🎾, squash – 🛗 ⇔ rm TV ☎ ♿ P – 🏛 275. AE ⓓ VISA
  Meals *(closed Saturday lunch)* (dancing Friday and Saturday evening) 18.00/23.00 **st.** and dinner a la carte 7.00 – **129 rm** ☐ 110.00/145.00 **st.**, 3 suites – SB.
- **White House Manor,** The Village, SK10 4HP, ☎ 829376, Fax 828627, 🌳 – TV ☎ P. AE ⓓ VISA. ✻
  Meals - (room service or see ***White House*** below) – ☐ 8.50 – **8 rm** 65.00/110.00 **t.**
- **Bridge,** SK10 4DQ, ☎ 829326, Fax 827557, 🌳 – TV ☎ ♿ P – 🏛 100. AE ⓓ VISA JCB ✻
  Meals *(closed Sunday dinner)* 9.75/13.15 **t.** and a la carte 5.00 – ☐ 7.50 – **23 rm** 40.00/69.00 **st.** – SB.
- ✕✕ **White House,** The Village, SK10 4DG, ☎ 829376, Fax 828627 – P. AE ⓓ VISA
  closed Monday lunch and Sunday dinner – **Meals** 11.95/18.70 **t.** and a la carte 20.75/29.20 **t.** 5.50.

PRESTON Lancs. 402 L 22 – pop. 126 082 – ☎ 01772.
18 Fulwood Hall Lane, Fulwood ☎ 794234/700436 – 18 Ingol, Tanterton Hall Rd, Ingol ☎ 734556 – 18 Aston & Lea, Tudor Av., Blackpool Rd ☎ 726480 – 18 Penwortham, Blundell Lane ☎ 743207.
ℹ The Guildhall, Lancaster Rd, PR1 1HT ☎ 253731.
♦London 226 – ♦Blackpool 18 – Burnley 22 – ♦Liverpool 30 – ♦Manchester 34 – ♦Stoke-on-Trent 65.

- **Forte Posthouse,** The Ringway, PR1 3AU, ☎ 259411, Fax 201923 – 🛗 ⇔ rm TV ☎ P – 🏛 120. AE ⓓ VISA JCB
  Meals a la carte 15.90/21.95 **t.** 6.50 – ☐ 7.95 – **121 rm** 56.00 **st.** – SB.
- **Claremont,** 516 Blackpool Rd, Ashton, PR2 1HY, NW : 2 m. on A 5085 ☎ 729738, Fax 726274, 🌳 – TV ☎ P. AE ⓓ VISA. ✻
  Meals 10.95 **st.** and a la carte 3.70 – **14 rm** ☐ 37.50/51.00 **st.**
- **Tulketh,** 209 Tulketh Rd, off Blackpool Rd, Ashton, PR2 1ES, NW : 2 ¼ m. by A 6 off A 5085 ☎ 728096, Fax 723743 – ⇔ rest TV ☎ P. AE ⓓ VISA. ✻
  closed 23 December-2 January – **Meals** (residents only) (dinner only) a la carte 7.00/15.00 **st.** 4.20 – **12 rm** ☐ 36.50/49.50 **st.**
- ✕✕ **Heathcotes Brasserie,** 23 Winckley Sq., PR1 3JJ, ☎ 252732, Fax 203433 – AE VISA
  Meals (bookings not accepted) 10.50 **t.** (lunch) and a la carte 15.50/22.00 **t.**

at Broughton N : 3 m. on A 6 – ✉ Preston – ☎ 01772 :

- **Broughton Park H. Country Club Resort** (Country Club), 418 Garstang Rd, PR3 5JB, ☎ 864087, Fax 861728, 🏋, ≘s, 🏊, 🌳, squash – 🛗 ⇔ rm TV ☎ ♿ P – 🏛 200. AE ⓓ VISA. ✻
  Courtyard : Meals *(closed lunch Saturday and Bank Holidays except Christmas)* 13.25/19.95 **t.** and dinner a la carte 5.75 – ☐ 9.50 – **98 rm** 82.00/112.00 **t.** – SB.

at Samlesbury E : 2½ m. by A 59 – ✉ Preston – ☎ 01772 :

Swallow Trafalgar, Preston New Rd, PR5 0UL, E : 1 m. at junction of A 59 with A 677 ☎ 877351, Fax 877424, squash – rm rest – 250. AE VISA
Meals (closed Saturday lunch) 9.50/15.50 **st.** and a la carte – **78 rm** 85.00/110.00 **st.** – SB.

Tickled Trout, Preston New Rd, PR5 0UJ, W : 1 m. on A 59 ☎ 877671, Fax 877463, – rm – 100. AE VISA
Meals (buffet lunch) 10.50/19.00 **st.** and dinner a la carte 5.50 – 6.95 – **72 rm** 75.00/100.00 **st.** – SB.

at Bamber Bridge S : 5 m. by A 6 on B 6258 – ✉ Preston – ☎ 01772 :

Novotel, Reedfield Place, Walton Summit, PR5 6AB, SE : ¾ m. by A 6 at junction 29 of M 6 ☎ 313331, Telex 677164, Fax 627868, heated, – rm – 180. AE VISA
Meals a la carte 8.50/14.90 **st.** – 7.50 – **98 rm** 42.50 **st.**

Poachers, Lobstock Lane, PR5 6BJ, S : ½ m. on A 6 ☎ 324100, Fax 629525 – rm
Meals (grill rest.) – **40 rm.**

at Lea W : 3½ m. on A 583 – ✉ Preston – ☎ 01772 :

Travel Inn, Blackpool Rd, PR4 0XL, on A 583 ☎ 720476, Fax 729971 – rm . AE VISA.
Meals (grill rest.) – 4.95 – **38 rm** 34.50 **t.**

ATS 296-298 Aqueduct St, Ashton ☎ 257688

PRESTWICH Gtr. Manchester 402 403 404 N 23 – ✉ Manchester – ☎ 0161.
London 205 – Leeds 40 – Liverpool 30 – Manchester 5.

Village H & Leisure Club, George St., M25 8WS, S : 1 ¾ m. by A 56 ☎ 798 8905, Fax 773 5562, squash – – 120. AE VISA
Meals (grill rest.) (bar lunch)/dinner 13.00 **t.** and a la carte 5.25 – **39 rm** 62.50/73.00 **t.**

PRIDDY Somerset 403 L 30 – see Wells.

PUCKERIDGE Herts. 404 U 28 – see Ware.

PUCKRUP Glos. – see Tewkesbury.

PUDDINGTON Ches. 402 403 K 24 – see Chester.

PUDSEY W. Yorks. 402 P 22 – see Leeds.

PULBOROUGH W. Sussex 404 S 31 – pop. 4 309 – ☎ 01798.
8, 9 West Chiltington, Broadford Bridge Rd ☎ 813574.
London 49 – Brighton 25 – Guildford 25 – Portsmouth 35.

Chequers, Church Pl., RH20 1AD, NE : ¼ m. on A 29 ☎ 872486, Fax 872715, – . AE VISA
Meals (bar lunch Monday to Saturday)/dinner 20.50 **st.** and a la carte 3.50 – **11 rm** 49.50/85.00 **t.** – SB.

Stane Street Hollow, Codmore Hill, RH20 1BG, NE : 1 m. on A 29 ☎ 872819 – . VISA JCB
closed Sunday dinner, Monday, Tuesday, two weeks late May, 2 weeks late October and 24 December-5 January – **Meals** - Swiss - (booking essential) 13.50 **t.** (lunch) and a la carte 18.50/23.00 **t.** 6.00.

at West Chiltington E : 2 ¾ m. by A 283 on West Chiltington rd – ✉ Pulborough – ☎ 01798 :

New House Farm without rest., Broadford Bridge Rd, RH20 2LA, ☎ 812215, – .
closed Christmas – **3 rm** 25.00/50.00 **st.**

PURFLEET Essex 404 (44) – ☎ 01708.
London 16 – Hastings 56 – Maidstone 26 – Southend-on-Sea 24.

Travel Inn, High St., RM16 1QA, ☎ 865432, Fax 860852 – rm . AE VISA
Meals (grill rest.) – 4.95 – **30 rm** 34.50 **t.**

In this guide

a symbol or a character, printed in red or black, in **bold** or light type, does not have the same meaning.
Pay particular attention to the explanatory pages.

PURTON Wilts. 403 404 O 29 – pop. 3 926 – ✉ Swindon – ☎ 01793.

♦London 94 – ♦Bristol 41 – Gloucester 31 – ♦Oxford 38 – Swindon 5.

Pear Tree at Purton, Church End, SN5 9ED, S : ½ m. by Church St. on Lydiard Millicent rd ☎ 772100, Fax 772369, ←, « Conservatory restaurant », – TV ☎ P – 60. AE VISA JCB
Meals *(closed Saturday lunch)* 17.50/27.50 **st.** 7.00 – **16 rm** 75.00 **st.**, 2 suites.

QUORNDON Leics. – see Loughborough.

RAMSBOTTOM Gtr. Manchester 402 N 23 – pop. 13 743 – ☎ 01706.

♦London 223 – ♦Blackpool 39 – Burnley 12 – ♦Leeds 46 – ♦Manchester 13 – ♦Liverpool 39.

Old Mill, Springwood St., off Carr St., BL0 9DS, ☎ 822991, Fax 822291, – TV ☎ P. AE VISA JCB.
Meals 7.75/12.50 **t.** and a la carte 4.25 – **36 rm** 45.50/65.00 **t.** – SB.

Village, 18 Market Pl., BL0 9HT, ☎ 825070 – AE VISA
closed Sunday dinner, Monday and Tuesday – **Meals** 8.75/17.50 **t.** 4.50.

RAMSGATE Kent 404 Y 30 – pop. 37 895 – ☎ 01843.

to France (Dunkerque) (Sally Ferries) 5 daily (2 h 30 mn) – to Belgium (Ostend) (Sally Ferries) 6 daily (4 h).

19 Queen St., CT11 8HA ☎ 591086.

♦London 77 – ♦Dover 19 – Maidstone 45 – Margate 4.5.

Jarvis Marina Resort, Harbour Par., CT11 8LJ, ☎ 588276, Fax 586866, ←, – rm rest TV ☎ – 120. AE VISA.
Meals (bar lunch Monday to Saturday)/dinner a la carte 14.00/20.00 **t.** – **59 rm** 66.50/69.00 **t.** – SB.

San Clu, Victoria Par., East Cliff, CT11 8DT, ☎ 592345, Fax 580157, ← – TV ☎ P. AE VISA JCB
Meals (bar lunch Monday to Friday)/dinner 11.75 **st.** and a la carte – **32 rm** 50.00/130.00 **st.** – SB.

at Minster W : 5½ m. by A 253 on B 2048 – ✉ Ramsgate – ☎ 01843 :

Morton's Fork, 42 Station Rd, CT12 4BZ, ☎ 823000, Fax 821224 – rest TV ☎ P. AE VISA.
Meals *(closed Sunday dinner and Monday)* 13.95 **t.** and a la carte 5.60 – 6.50 – **3 rm** 35.00/46.00 **t.** – SB.

ATS 82-84 Bellevue Rd ☎ 595829

RAMSGILL-IN-NIDDERDALE N. Yorks. 402 O 21 – see Pateley Bridge.

RASKELF N. Yorks. – see Easingwold.

RAVENSTONEDALE Cumbria 402 M 20 – pop. 886 – ✉ Kirkby Stephen – ☎ 0153 96.

♦London 280 – ♦Carlisle 43 – Kendal 19 – Kirkby Stephen 5.

Black Swan, CA17 4NG, ☎ 23204, Fax 23604, – rest TV ☎ P. AE VISA JCB
Meals (lunch by arrangement Monday to Saturday) 9.95/22.00 **t.** and a la carte 4.50 – **15 rm** 45.00/70.00 **t.** – SB.

Fat Lamb, Crossbank, Fell End, CA17 4LL, SE : 2 m. by Sedbergh rd on A 683 ☎ 23242 ←, , park – P
Meals 11.50/18.00 **t.** and a la carte 3.50 – **12 rm** 32.00/56.00 **t.** – SB.

READING Berks. 403 404 Q 29 – pop. 128 877 – ☎ 01734.

18 Calcot Park, Calcot ☎ 427124.

Town Hall, Blagrave St., RG1 1QH ☎ 566226.

♦London 43 – ♦Brighton 79 – ♦Bristol 78 – Croydon 47 – Luton 62 – ♦Oxford 28 – ♦Portsmouth 67 – ♦Southampton 46

Plan opposite

Holiday Inn (Q.M.H.), Caversham Bridge, Richfield Av., RG1 8BD, ☎ 259988 Fax 391665, ←, « Thames-side setting », – rm rest TV ☎ P – 250. AE VISA. X
Meals 9.95/25.00 **t.** and a la carte 5.95 – 8.95 – **107 rm** 106.00 **st.**, 4 suites – SB.

Ramada, Oxford Rd, RG1 7RH, ☎ 586222, Fax 597842, – rm TV ☎ P – 220. AE VISA JCB. Z
Meals (buffet lunch Saturday) 15.00/30.00 **st.** 5.95 – 8.95 – **193 rm** 99.00 **st.**, 1 suite.

Forte Posthouse, 500 Basingstoke Rd, RG2 0SL, S : 2 ½ m. on A 33 ☎ 875485 Fax 311958, – rm TV ☎ P – 100. AE VISA JCB. X
Meals a la carte 11.65/22.15 **t.** – 8.95 – **138 rm** 69.00 **st.** – SB.

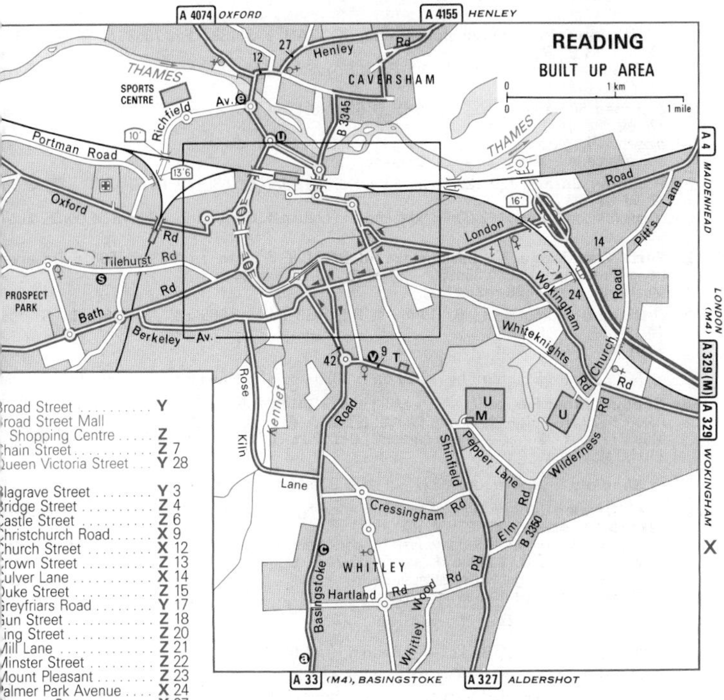

READING

BUILT UP AREA

road Street . . . . Y
road Street Mall
Shopping Centre . . . . . Z
hain Street . . . . Z 7
ueen Victoria Street . . . Y 28

lagrave Street . . . . Y 3
ridge Street . . . . Z 4
astle Street . . . . Z 6
hristchurch Road . . . . . . X 9
hurch Street . . . . X 12
rown Street . . . . Z 13
ulver Lane . . . . X 14
uke Street . . . . Z 15
reyfriars Road . . . . Y 17
un Street . . . . Z 18
ing Street . . . . Z 20
ill Lane . . . . Z 21
linster Street . . . . Z 22
lount Pleasant . . . . Z 23
almer Park Avenue . . . . . X 24
rospect Street . . . . X 27
t. Mary's Butts . . . . Z 29
tation Hill . . . . Y 30
tation Road . . . . Y 31

Tilehurst Road . . . . Z 33
Tudor Road . . . . Y 34
Valpy Street . . . . Y 37

Watlington Street . . . . Z 40
West Street . . . . Y 41
Whitley Street . . . . X 42

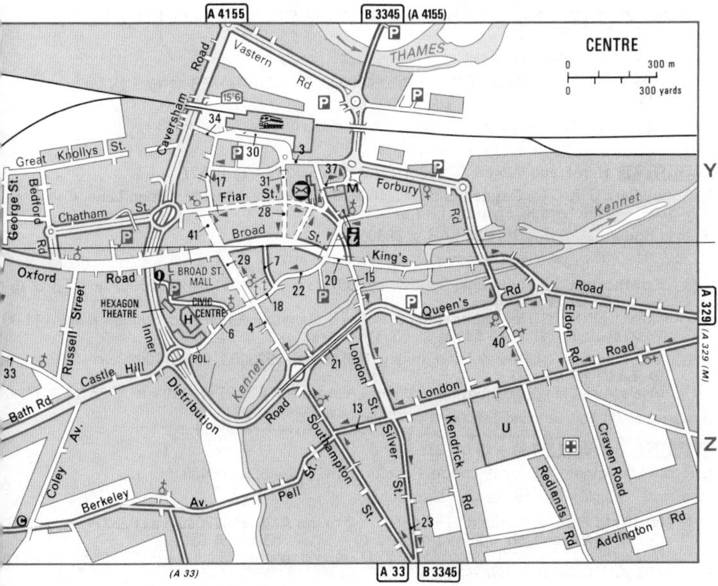

CENTRE

Hillingdon Prince, 39 Christchurch Rd, RG2 7AN, ✆ 311391, Fax 756357 – |‡| TV ☎ P – 100. AE VISA. X v
Meals *(closed Saturday lunch and Bank Holidays)* 12.95 **st.** and a la carte 4.95 – **36 rm** 50.00/75.00 **t.**

Upcross, 68 Berkeley Av., RG1 6HY, ✆ 590796, Fax 576517, – TV ☎ P – 45. AE VISA Z c
closed 27 December-2 January – **Meals** *(closed Saturday lunch)* 10.50/30.00 **st** and a la carte – **20 rm** 49.00/65.00 **st.** – SB.

Rainbow Corner, 132-138 Caversham Rd, RG1 8AY, ✆ 588140, Fax 586500 – TV ☎ P. AE VISA. X u
Meals *(closed Sunday)* 12.00/18.50 **t.** and a la carte 4.95 – 4.95 – **22 rm** 54.00/68.00 **t.** – SB.

Forte Travelodge, 387 Basingstoke Rd, RG2 0JE, S : 2 m. on A 33 ✆ 750618, Reservations (Freephone) 0800 850950 – TV P. AE VISA. X c
Meals (grill rest.) – **36 rm** 34.50 **t.**

Dittisham without rest., 63 Tilehurst Rd, RG3 2JL, ✆ 569483, – TV P. VISA X s
5 rm 19.50/45.00 **st.**

at Sindlesham SE : 5 m. by A 329 on B 3030 – X – ✉ Wokingham – ☎ 01734 :

Reading Moat House (Q.M.H.), Mill Lane, RG41 5DF, NW :½ m. by Mole Rd ✆ 499988, Fax 666530, – |‡| rm rest TV ☎ P – 80. AE VISA
Meals 17.50 **t.** (dinner) and a la carte 30.00/32.20 **t.** 7.00 – 10.00 – **95 rm** 100.00/110.00 **st.**, 1 suite.

at Shinfield S : 4 ¼ m. on A 327 – X – ✉ Reading – ☎ 01734 :

XXX ✿✿ **L'Ortolan** (Burton-Race), The Old Vicarage, Church Lane, RG2 9BY, ✆ 883783, Fax 885391, – P. AE VISA
closed Sunday dinner, Monday, last 2 weeks February and last 2 weeks August – **Meals** French - 28.00/37.00 **t.** and a la carte 52.50/74.50 **t.** 10.50
Spec. Millefeuille de rouget Niçoise en tapenade, Tournedos de chevreuil aux grains de cassis et purée Dubarry, Soufflé chaud aux abricots glace au lait d'amande.

ATS Basingstoke Rd ✆ 502225

READING SERVICE AREA Berks. – ✉ Reading – ☎ 01734.

Granada Lodge without rest., RG30 3UQ, M 4 eastbound between junctions 11 and 12 ✆ 566966, Fax 595444, Reservations (Freephone) 0800 555300 – TV ☎ P. AE VISA JCB.
40 rm 39.95 **st.**

REDCAR Cleveland 402 Q 20 – pop. 4 836 – ☎ 01642.

Wilton ✆ 465265 – Cleveland, Queen St. ✆ 483693 – Saltburn, Hob Hill, Saltburn-by-the-Sea ✆ (01287) 622812.

◆London 255 – ◆Middlesbrough 9 – Scarborough 43.

Park, 3-5 Granville Terr., TS10 3AR, ✆ 490888, Fax 486147 – TV ☎ P – 50
33 rm.

ATS Limerick Rd, Dormanstown ✆ 477100/477163 ATS 162 Lord St. ✆ 484013

REDDITCH Heref. and Worcs. 403 404 O 27 – pop. 73 372 – ☎ 01527.

Abbey Park G & C.C., Dagnell End Rd ✆ 63918 – Lower Grinsty, Green Lane, Callow Hill ✆ 543309 – Pitcheroak, Plymouth Rd ✆ 541054.

Civic Square, Alcester St., B98 8AH ✆ 60806.

◆London 111 – ◆Birmingham 15 – Cheltenham 33 – Stratford-upon-Avon 15.

Southcrest , Pool Bank, Southcrest, B97 4JS, ✆ 541511, Fax 402600, – TV ☎ P – 70. AE VISA JCB
closed 23 to 31 December – **Meals** *(closed Saturday lunch and Sunday dinner)* 11.00/13.00 **st.** and a la carte – **58 rm** 63.00/70.00 **st.**

Old Rectory , Ipsley Lane, Ipsley, B98 0AP, ✆ 523000, Fax 517003, – rest ☎ P. AE VISA.
Meals (residents only) (communal dining) (dinner only) 16.95 **st.** – **10 rm** 55.00/85.00 **st**

ATS Pipers Rd, Park Farm Ind. Est., Park Farm South ✆ 502002/502027

REDHILL Surrey 404 T 30 – ☎ 01737.

Redhill & Reigate, Clarence Lodge, Pendleton Rd ✆ 244626/244433.

◆London 22 – ◆Brighton 31 – Guildford 20 – Maidstone 34.

Nutfield Priory, Nutfield, RH1 4EN, E : 2 m. on A 25 ✆ 822066, Fax 823321, ≤, , , park, squash – |‡| rm TV ☎ P – 80. AE VISA
Meals *(closed Saturday lunch)* 15.00/22.00 **st.** and dinner a la carte 6.00 – 6.00 – **51 rm** 110.00/130.00 **st.**, 1 suite – SB.

Ashleigh House without rest., 39 Redstone Hill, RH1 4BG, on A 25 ✆ 764763, Fax 780308, heated, – TV P. VISA.
closed Christmas – **8 rm** 25.30/50.00 **st.**

at Salfords S : 2½ m. on A 23 – ✉ Redhill – ☎ 01737 :

Travel Inn, Brighton Rd, RH1 5BT, ✆ 767277, Fax 778099 – TV ☎ & P. AE VISA
Meals (grill rest.) – 4.95 – **42 rm** 34.50 **t.**

REDWORTH Durham – see Darlington.

REETH N. Yorks. 402 O 20 – pop. 939 – ✉ Richmond – ☎ 01748.
London 253 – ♦Leeds 53 – ♦Middlesbrough 36.

Burgoyne, On The Green, DL11 6SN, ✆ 884292, Fax 884292, ←, – TV ☎ P. VISA
closed 2 January-4 February – **Meals** (dinner only) 21.00 **t.** 5.95 – **9 rm** 50.00/80.00 **t.** – SB.

Arkleside, DL11 6SG, ✆ 884200, Fax 884619, ←, – TV P. VISA
closed January – **Meals** 14.50 **st.** – **9 rm** 28.50/75.00 **st.** – SB.

REIGATE Surrey 404 T 30 – pop. 52 007 – ☎ 01737.
London 26 – ♦Brighton 33 – Guildford 20 – Maidstone 38.

Bridge House, Reigate Hill, RH2 9RP, N : 1¼ m. on A 217 ✆ 246801, Fax 223756 – TV ☎ P – 50. AE VISA.
Meals *(closed Bank Holiday Mondays)* (dancing Wednesday to Saturday evenings) 16.00/25.00 **t.** and a la carte – 7.50 – **37 rm** 50.00/75.00 **t.**

Cranleigh, 41 West St., RH2 9BL, ✆ 223417, Fax 223734, heated, , – TV ☎ P. AE VISA JCB.
closed 24 to 31 December – **Meals** (by arrangement) (dinner only) 16.50 **t.** 4.50 – **9 rm** 42.00/75.00 **t.**

The Dining Room, 59a High St., RH2 9AE, ✆ 226650 – . AE VISA
closed Saturday lunch, Sunday, 1 week Easter, 1 week August and 2 weeks Christmas – **Meals** 13.95/30.00 **t.** and a la carte.

La Barbe, 71 Bell St., RH2 7AN, ✆ 241966, Fax 226387 – . AE VISA
closed Saturday lunch, Sunday and Bank Holidays – **Meals** - French - 16.45/23.95 **st.** 6.50.

RENDCOMB Glos. 403 404 O 28 – see Cirencester.

RETFORD Notts. – see East Retford.

REYDON Suffolk – see Southwold.

RICHMOND N. Yorks. 402 O 20 Great Britain G. – pop. 7 862 – ☎ 01748.
See : Castle★ *AC* – Georgian Theatre Royal and Museum★.
Bend Hagg ✆ 825319 – 18 Catterick Garrison, Leyburn Rd ✆ 833401.
Friary Gardens, Victoria Rd, DL10 4AJ ✆ 850252/825994.
London 243 – ♦Leeds 53 – ♦Middlesbrough 26 – ♦Newcastle upon Tyne 44.

King's Head, Market Pl., DL10 4HS, ✆ 850220, Fax 850635 – TV ☎ P – 150. AE VISA
Meals (bar lunch Monday to Saturday)/dinner 18.95 **st.** and a la carte 4.50 – **28 rm** 53.00/82.00 **st.** – SB.

West End, 45 Reeth Rd., DL10 4EX, W : ½ m. on A 6108 ✆ 824783, – TV P
closed Christmas-New Year – **Meals** 12.00 **st.** 4.30 **5 rm** 19.50/39.00 **st.**

Whashton Springs Farm , DL11 7JS, NW : 3½ m. on Ravensworth rd ✆ 822884, « Working farm », , park – TV ☎ P.
closed mid December-February – **Meals** (by arrangement) 12.50 **st.** 5.00 – **8 rm** 26.00/44.00 **st.**

at Kirby Hill NW : 4½ m. by Ravensworth rd – ✉ Richmond – ☎ 01748 :

Shoulder of Mutton Inn, DL11 7JH, ✆ 822772 – TV P.
Meals *(closed Monday lunch)* (in bar) a la carte 7.60/13.00 – **5 rm** 25.00/39.00 **st.**

ATS Reeth Rd ✆ 824182/3

RIDGEWAY Derbs. – see Sheffield (S. Yorks.).

RINGWOOD Hants. 403 404 O 31 – pop. 9 813 – ☎ 01425.
The Furlong, BH24 1AZ ✆ 470896 (summer only).
London 102 – Bournemouth 11 – Salisbury 17 – ♦Southampton 20.

Moortown Lodge, 244 Christchurch Rd, BH24 3AS, ✆ 471404, Fax 476052 – rest TV ☎ P. AE VISA.
closed 24 December-mid January – **Meals** *(closed Sunday to non-residents)* (dinner only) 14.95 **t.** 5.25 – **6 rm** 32.00/80.00 **t.** – SB.

at Avon S : 4 m. on B 3347 – ✉ Christchurch – ☎ 01425 :

Tyrrells Ford, BH23 7BH, ✆ 672646, Fax 672262, park – TV ☎ P – 25. AE VISA.
Meals 11.95/19.95 **t.** and dinner a la carte 5.00 – **16 rm** 55.00/100.00 **t.** – SB.

RIPLEY N. Yorks. 402 P 21 – pop. 193 – ✉ Harrogate – ☎ 01423.

◆London 213 – Bradford 21 – ◆Leeds 18 – ◆Newcastle upon Tyne 79.

Boar's Head, HG3 3AY, ✆ 771888, Fax 771509, « 18C coaching inn within estate village of Ripley Castle », – rm TV ☎ P. AE VISA
Meals 12.00 **t.** (lunch) and a la carte 23.50/31.00 **t.** – **25 rm** 75.00/105.00 **t.** – SB.

at Burnt Yates W : 2¾ m. on B 6165 – ✉ Harrogate – ☎ 01423 :

Bay Horse Inn, HG3 3EJ, on B 6165 ✆ 770230, – rm TV ☎ P. VISA.
Meals (bar lunch Monday to Saturday)/dinner 14.95 **t.** and a la carte 5.50 – **14 rm** 40.00/55.00 **t.** – SB.

RIPLEY Surrey 404 S 30 – pop. 1 697 – ☎ 01483.

◆London 28 – Guildford 6.

XXX **Michels',** 13 High St., GU23 6AQ, ✆ 224777, – AE VISA
closed Saturday lunch, Sunday dinner, Monday and 1 January – **Meals** 19.00/28.00 and a la carte 4.50.

RIPON N. Yorks. 402 P 21 **Great Britain G.** – pop. 13 806 – ☎ 01765.

See : Town★ - Cathedral★ (Saxon Crypt★★) *AC*.

Envir. : Fountains Abbey★★★ *AC* :- Studley Royal★★ *AC* (≤★ from Anne Boleyn's Seat) - Fountains Hall (Façade★), SW : 2½ m. by B 6265 – Newby Hall (Tapestries★) *AC*, SE : 3½ m. by B 6265.

Ripon City, Palace Rd ✆ 603640.

Minster Rd, HG4 1LT ✆ 604625 (summer only).

◆London 222 – ◆Leeds 26 – ◆Middlesbrough 35 – York 23.

Ripon Spa, Park St., HG4 2BU, E : ¼ m. on B 6265 ✆ 602172, Fax 690770, – TV ☎ P – 150. AE VISA JCB
Meals 9.95/16.50 **t.** and a la carte 9.95 – **40 rm** 60.00/90.00 **t.** – SB.

ATS Dallamires Lane ✆ 601579

ROADE Northants. – pop. 2 527 – ☎ 01604.

◆London 66 – ◆Coventry 36 – Northampton 5.5.

XX **Roadhouse,** 16 High St., NN7 2NW, ✆ 863372 – P. AE VISA
closed Saturday lunch, Sunday and Monday – **Meals** 15.00 **st.** (lunch) and dinner a la carte 18.00/23.50 **st.**

ROCHDALE Gtr. Manchester 402 N 23 – pop. 202 164 – ☎ 01706.

Edenfield Rd, Bagslate ✆ 46024 – Marland, Springfield Park ✆ 49801 – , Castle Hawk Heywood Rd ✆ 40841.

The Clock Tower, Town Hall, OL16 1AB ✆ 356592.

◆London 224 – ◆Blackpool 40 – Burnley 11 – ◆Leeds 45 – ◆Manchester 12 – ◆Liverpool 40.

Norton Grange, Manchester Rd, Castleton, OL11 2XZ, SW : 3 m. by A 58 on A 664 ✆ 30788, Fax 49313, – rm TV ☎ P – 100. AE VISA
Meals *(closed Saturday lunch)* 18.50 **t.** and a la carte – **49 rm** 82.50/92.50 **t.**, 1 suite – SB.

Castleton, Manchester Rd, Castleton, OL11 2XX, SW : 3 m. by A 58 on A 664 ✆ 357888, Fax 525757, – TV ☎ P. AE VISA.
Meals *(closed lunch Saturday and Bank Holidays)* 8.50/13.50 **t.** and a la carte 4.50 – **13 rm** 50.00/70.00 **t.**

XX **French Connection,** Edenfield Rd, Cheesden, Norden, OL12 7TY, W : 5 m. on A 680 ✆ 50167, ≤ – P. VISA
closed Monday and first 2 weeks August – **Meals** a la carte 20.25/28.30 **t.**

XX **After Eight,** 2 Edenfield Rd, OL11 5AA, W : 1 m. on A 680 ✆ 46432 – . AE VISA
closed Sunday dinner, Monday, first 2 weeks May, 26 December and 1 January – **Meals** (dinner only and Sunday lunch)/dinner 14.20/21.70 **st.** 4.40.

ATS Royds St. ✆ 32411/49935
ATS Castleton Moor, Nixon St. (ASDA) ✆ 57068

ROCHESTER Kent 404 V 29 Great Britain G. – pop. 23 971 – ✉ Chatham – ☎ 01634.

See : Castle★ *AC* – Cathedral★ *AC*.

Eastgate Cottage, High St., ME1 1EW ☎ 843666.

London 30 – ◆Dover 45 – Maidstone 8 – Margate 46.

Bridgewood Manor, Maidstone Rd, ME5 9AX, SE : 3 m. by A 2 on A 229 ☎ 201333, Fax 201330, 𝐿𝑎, ≘s, ⊠, ✂ – |‡| ⇔ rm ≡ rest TV ☎ ♿ P – 🏛 150. AE ① VISA
Meals 14.00/24.00 **t.** and a la carte 🍷 8.00 – **96 rm** ☐ 90.00/110.00 **t.**, 4 suites – SB.

Forte Posthouse, Maidstone Rd, ME5 9SF, SE : 2 ½ m. by A 2 on A 229 ☎ 687111, Fax 864876, 𝐿𝑎, ≘s, ⊠, 🌳 – |‡| ⇔ rm ≡ rest TV ☎ ♿ P – 🏛 110. AE ① VISA
Meals a la carte 12.65/23.20 **t.** – ☐ 7.95 – **105 rm** 59.00/69.00 **t.** – SB.

ROCHFORD Essex 404 W 29 – ☎ 01702.

London 46 – Chelmsford 19 – Colchester 39 – Southend-on-Sea 3.

Renouf, Bradley Way, SS4 1BU, ☎ 541334, Fax 549563, 🌳 – ≡ rest TV ☎ P – 🏛 30. AE ① VISA
closed 26 to 31 December – **Meals** *(closed Saturday lunch)* (residents only Sunday dinner) 15.50/35.00 **st.** and a la carte 🍷 5.00 – **23 rm** ☐ 57.50/88.00 **st.**

RODBOROUGH Glos. – see Stroud.

ROGATE W. Sussex 404 R 30 – pop. 1 785 – ✉ Petersfield (Hants.) – ☎ 01730.

London 63 – ◆Brighton 42 – Guildford 29 – ◆Portsmouth 23 – ◆Southampton 36.

Mizzards Farm 🐦 without rest., GU31 5HS, SW : 1 m. by Harting rd ☎ 821656, Fax 821655, ≤, « 17C farmhouse », ⛱ heated, 🌳, park – ⇔ TV P. ✻
closed Christmas – **3 rm** ☐ 36.00/55.00 **st.**

ROLLESTON-ON-DOVE Staffs. 402 403 404 P 25 – see Burton-upon-Trent.

ROMALDKIRK Durham 402 N 20 – see Barnard Castle.

ROMSEY Hants. 403 404 P 31 Great Britain G. – pop. 14 256 – ☎ 01794.

See : Abbey★ (interior★★).

Envir. : Broadlands★ *AC*, S : 1 m..

18 Dunwood Manor, Shootash Hill ☎ 340549 – 18 Nursling ☎ (01703) 732218 – 18 Wellow, Ryedown Lane, East Wellow ☎ 322872.

1 Latimer St., SO51 8DF ☎ 512987.

◆London 82 – Bournemouth 28 – Salisbury 16 – ◆Southampton 8 – Winchester 10.

White Horse (Forte Heritage), Market Pl., SO51 8ZJ, ☎ 512431, Fax 517485 – ⇔ TV ☎ P – 🏛 30. AE ① VISA
Meals (bar lunch Monday to Saturday)/dinner 17.95 **st.** and a la carte 🍷 7.05 – ☐ 8.50 – **33 rm** 65.00/85.00 – SB.

Spursholt House 🐦, Salisbury Rd, SO51 6DJ, W : 1 ¼ m. by A 31 on A 27 ☎ 512229, Fax 523142, « Part 17C mansion, gardens » – ⇔ rm TV P
Meals (by arrangement) 12.50 **st.** – **3 rm** ☐ 25.00/45.00 **st.**

XXX **Old Manor House,** 21 Palmerston St., SO51 8GF, ☎ 517353, « Timbered 16C house » – P. AE VISA
closed Sunday dinner, Monday and 24 December-8 January – **Meals** 13.50/17.50 **st.** and a la carte 22.50/29.90 **st.** 🍷 5.50.

at Ower SW : 3¼ m. on A 31 – ✉ Romsey – ☎ 01703 :

New Forest Heathlands, Romsey Rd, SO51 6ZJ, on A 31 ☎ 814333, Fax 812123, ≘s, 🌳 – ⇔ rest TV ☎ P – 🏛 200. AE ① VISA
closed 24 to 29 December – **Meals** 8.25/17.50 **t.** and dinner a la carte – **52 rm** ☐ 63.00/92.00 **st.** – SB.

ROSEDALE ABBEY N. Yorks. 402 R 20 Great Britain G. – pop. 332 (Rosedale) – ✉ Pickering – ☎ 01751.

Envir. : ≤★ on road to Hutton-le-Hole.

◆London 247 – ◆Middlesbrough 27 – Scarborough 25 – York 36.

Blacksmith's Arms, Hartoft End, YO18 8EN, SE : 2 ½ m. on Pickering rd ☎ 417331, Fax 417167, ≤, 🌳 – TV ☎ P. AE VISA
Meals 11.95/25.00 **t.** 🍷 4.95 – **14 rm** ☐ (dinner included) 65.00/110.00 **t.** – SB.

Milburn Arms, YO18 8RA, ☎ 417312, Fax 417312, 🌳 – TV ☎ P. ① VISA. ✻
Meals (bar lunch Monday to Saturday)/dinner a la carte 18.40/23.40 **t.** 🍷 3.95 – **11 rm** ☐ 44.50/74.00 **t.** – SB.

White Horse Farm, YO18 8SE, NW : ¼ m. by Thorgill rd ☎ 417239, Fax 417781, 🌳 – TV ☎ P. AE VISA
closed 24 and 25 December – **Meals** (bar lunch Monday to Saturday)/dinner 18.00 **t.** 🍷 5.45 – **15 rm** ☐ 44.00/68.00 **t.** – SB.

ROSSINGTON S. Yorks. 402 403 404 Q 23 – see Doncaster.

ROSS-ON-WYE Heref. and Worcs. 403 404 M 28 **Great Britain G.** – pop. 9 606 – ☎ 01989.
See : Market House★ – Yat Rock (≤★).
Envir. : SW : Wye Valley★ – Goodrich Castle★ *AC*, SW : 3½ m. by A 40.
ℹ Swan House, Eddie Cross St., HR9 7BZ ✆ 562768.
♦London 118 – Gloucester 15 – Hereford 15 – Newport 35.

Chase, Gloucester Rd, HR9 5LH, ✆ 763161, Fax 768330, – TV ☎ P – 250. AE ① VISA.
closed Christmas – **Meals** a la carte approx. 23.00 **st.** 4.50 – **39 rm** 65.00/80.00 **st.** – SB

Royal (Forte Heritage), Palace Pound, HR9 5HZ, ✆ 565105, Fax 768058, ≤, – TV ☎ P – 80. AE ① VISA JCB
Meals (bar lunch Monday to Saturday)/dinner 19.95 **t.** and a la carte 7.30 – 8.75 **40 rm** 65.00/95.00 **st.** – SB.

Edde Cross House without rest., Edde Cross St., HR9 7BZ, ✆ 565088, – TV.
booking essential, February-October – **3 rm** 30.00/46.00 **st.**

Sunnymount, Ryefield Rd, HR9 5LU, off Gloucester Rd ✆ 563880 – rest P. VISA.
closed 1 week at Christmas – **Meals** (by arrangement) 14.50 **st.** 5.25 – **6 rm** 28.00 50.00 **st.** – SB.

Pheasants, 52 Edde Cross St., HR9 7BZ, ✆ 565751 – AE ① VISA
closed Sunday, Monday, 25 December-2 January and 11 to 15 June – **Meals** (dinner only a la carte 22.05/28.75 **st.** 7.50.

at Yatton NE : 5¾ m. by A 449 – ✉ Ross-on-Wye – ☎ 01531 :

Rocks Place , HR9 7RD, ✆ 660218, Fax 660460, ≤, – rm TV ☎ P. VISA JCB
Meals *(closed Sunday dinner)* (lunch by arrangement Monday to Saturday)/dinner 14.95 5.00 – **7 rm** 35.00/65.00 **t.** – SB.

at Kerne Bridge S : 3¾ m. on B 4234 – ✉ Ross-on-Wye – ☎ 01600 :

Lumleys without rest., HR9 5QT, ✆ 890040, – ☎ P. VISA.
3 rm 25.00/42.00 **s.** – SB.

at Glewstone SW : 3¼ m. by A 40 – ✉ Ross-on-Wye – ☎ 01989 :

Glewstone Court , HR9 6AW, ✆ 770367, Fax 770282, ≤, « Part Georgian and Victorian country house », – TV ☎ P. AE VISA JCB
closed 25 to 27 December – **Meals** 11.95/24.75 **st.** 5.00 – **7 rm** 40.00/94.00 **st.** – SB.

at Pencraig SW : 3¾ m. on A 40 – ✉ Ross-on-Wye – ☎ 01989 :

Pencraig Court, HR9 6HR, ✆ 770306, Fax 770040, ≤, – TV ☎ P. AE ① VISA.
April-October – **Meals** (bar lunch)/dinner 13.50 **st.** and a la carte 3.75 – **11 rm** 45.00 60.00 **st.** – SB.

at Peterstow W : 2½ m. on A 49 – ✉ Ross-on-Wye – ☎ 01989 :

Pengethley Manor , HR9 6LL, NW : 1½ m. on A 49 ✆ 730211, Fax 730238, ≤ « Georgian country house », heated, , park – TV ☎ P – 50. AE ① VISA JCB
Meals 12.50/24.00 **t.** and a la carte 6.50 – **21 rm** 70.00/100.00 **t.**, 3 suites – SB.

Peterstow Country House , HR9 6LB, ✆ 562826, Fax 567264, ≤, « Converted Georgian rectory », , park – rest TV ☎ P – 30. AE ① VISA.
Meals 12.50/26.50 **st.** and a la carte 4.75 – **9 rm** 42.50/99.00 **st.** – SB.

ATS Ind. Est., Alton Rd ✆ 64638

ROSTHWAITE Cumbria 402 K 20 – see Keswick.

ROTHBURY Northd 401 402 O 18 **Great Britain G.** – pop. 1 805 – ✉ Morpeth – ☎ 01669.
See : Cragside House★ (interior★) *AC*.
ℹ National Park Information Centre, Church House, Church St., NE65 7UP ✆ 620887 (summer only).
♦London 311 – ♦Edinburgh 84 – ♦Newcastle upon Tyne 29.

Orchard, High St., NE65 7TL, ✆ 620684, – rest TV.
March-November – **Meals** 13.50 **t.** 3.50 – **6 rm** 32.50/70.00 **t.**

ROTHERHAM S. Yorks. 402 403 404 P 23 – pop. 251 637 – ☎ 01709.
18 Thrybergh Park ✆ 850466 – 18 Grange Park, Upper Wortley Rd, Kimberworth ✆ 559497 – 18 Phoenix, Pavilion Lane, Brinsworth ✆ 363788.
ℹ Central Library, Walker Pl., S65 1JH ✆ 823611.
♦London 166 – ♦Kingston-upon-Hull 61 – ♦Leeds 36 – ♦Sheffield 6.

Carlton Park (Q.M.H.), 102-104 Moorgate Rd, S60 2BG, ✆ 849955, Fax 368960, – rm rest TV ☎ P – 120. AE ① VISA
Meals (bar lunch Saturday) 8.95/16.95 **st.** and a la carte 6.50 – 9.20 – **77 rm** 68.00/74.00 **st.**, 3 suites – SB.

Swallow, West Bawtry Rd, S60 4NA, SE : 2¼ m. on A 630 ☎ 830630, Fax 830549, – rm – 300.
Meals 12.95/16.95 **st.** and a la carte 6.00 – **98 rm** 80.00/96.00 **st.**, 2 suites – SB.

Travel Inn, Bawtry Rd, S65 3JB, E : 2 m. by A 6021 on A 631 ☎ 543216, Fax 531546 – rm
Meals (grill rest.) – 4.95 – **37 rm** 34.50 **t.**

Campanile, Lowton Way, Hellaby Ind. Est., S66 8RY, E : 5 m. by A 6021 and A 631 off Denby Way ☎ 700255, Fax 545169 – rm
Meals a la carte 10.35/15.35 **t.** – 4.50 – **50 rm** 36.00 **t.**

at Bramley E : 4 m. by A 6021 off A 631 – ✉ Rotherham – ☎ 01709 :

Elton, Main St., S66 0SF, ☎ 545681, Fax 549100 – rm
Meals 11.50/19.50 **st.** and a la carte 5.50 – **29 rm** 52.00/78.00 **st.** – SB.

at Maltby E : 7 m. by A 6021 on A 631 – ✉ Rotherham – ☎ 01709 :

Hellaby Hall, Old Hellaby Lane, Hellaby, S66 8SN, W : 1 ¾ m. on A 631 ☎ 702701, Fax 700979, – rm – 140.
Meals (dancing Saturday evening) 11.95/18.50 **t.** and a la carte 5.50 – **51 rm** 78.00/98.00, 1 suite – SB.

ATS Eastwood Works, Fitzwilliam Rd ☎ 371556/372391

ROTHERWICK Hants – see Hook.

ROTHLEY Leics. 402 403 404 Q 25 – see Leicester.

ROTTINGDEAN E. Sussex 404 T 31 – pop. 8 949 – ✉ Brighton – ☎ 01273.

London 58 – ◆Brighton 4 – Lewes 9 – Newhaven 5.

Braemar without rest., Steyning Rd, BN2 7GA, ☎ 304263,
15 rm 15.00/30.00 **t.**

ROUGHAM GREEN Suffolk – see Bury St. Edmunds.

ROWDE Wilts. 403 404 N 29 – see Devizes

ROWNHAMS SERVICE AREA Hants. 403 404 P 31 – ✉ Southampton – ☎ 01703.

M 27 Services (westbound), SO1 8AW ☎ 730345.

Road Chef Lodge without rest., S016 8AP, M 27 between junctions 3 and 4 (southbound carriageway) ☎ 741144, Fax 740204, Reservations (Freephone) 0800 834719 –
closed Christmas-New Year – **39 rm** 37.50 **st.**

ROWSLEY Derbs. 402 403 404 P 24 **Great Britain G.** – pop. 451 – ✉ Matlock – ☎ 01629.

Envir. : Chatsworth★★★ (Park and Garden★★★) *AC*, N : by B 6012.

◆London 157 – Derby 23 – ◆Manchester 40 – ◆Nottingham 30.

Peacock (Jarvis), Bakewell Rd, DE4 2EB, ☎ 733518, Fax 732671, « 17C stone house, antiques », –
Meals 13.85/36.00 **t.** 8.50 – **14 rm** (dinner included) 85.00/140.50 **t.** – SB.

East Lodge, DE4 2EF, on A 6 ☎ 734474, Fax 733949, , park –
Meals 8.50/18.50 **t.** and a la carte 6.00 – **14 rm** 55.00/90.00 **t.** – SB.

ROWTON Ches. 402 403 L 24 – see Chester.

ROYAL LEAMINGTON SPA Warks. 403 404 P 27 – pop. 55 396 – ☎ 01926.

Leamington and County, Golf Lane, Whitnash ☎ 425961 on plan of Warwick.

Jephson Lodge, Jephson Gardens, The Parade, CV32 4AB ☎ 311470.

◆London 99 – ◆Birmingham 23 – ◆Coventry 9 – Warwick 3.

Plan on next page - Plan of Built up Area: See Warwick

Mallory Court, Harbury Lane, Bishop's Tachbrook, CV33 9QB, S : 2¼ m. by B 4087 (Tachbrook Rd) ☎ 330214, Fax 451714, <, « Country house in extensive gardens », , squash –
closed 2 to 11 January – **Meals** (booking essential) 24.50/32.00 **st.** – 11.75 – **10 rm** 120.00/375.00 **st.** – SB.

Regent, 77 Parade, CV32 4AX, ☎ 427231, Fax 450728 – rest – 100. V **a**
Meals 6.50/16.50 **st.** and a la carte 5.50 – **80 rm** 65.00/89.00 **st.** – SB.

Courtyard by Marriott, Olympus Av., Tachbrook Park, CV34 6RJ, SW : 1½ m. by A 452 ☎ 425522, Fax 881322, – rm rest – 50.
Meals *(closed lunch Saturday and Sunday)* 13.75 **t.** and a la carte 6.00 – **95 rm** 60.00/81.50 **st.** – SB. plan of Warwick Z **v**

Angel, 143 Regent St., CV32 4NZ, ☎ 881296 – – 30. U **c**
Meals *(closed Saturday lunch)* 8.95/12.50 **st.** and a la carte 3.00 – **48 rm** 49.50/59.00 **st.**

ROYAL LEAMINGTON SPA

Parade . . . . UV
Regent Street . . . . UV
Royal Priors Shopping Centre . . . U
Warwick Street . . . . U

Adelaïde Road V
Avenue Road . . . . V 2
Bath Street . . . . V 3
Beauchamp Avenue . . . . U
Beauchamp Hill . . . . U 4
Binswood Street . . . . U 6
Brandon Parade . . . . U 10
Church Hill . . . . UV 16
Clarendon Avenue . . . . U
Clarendon Place . . . . U 18
Dale Street . . . . UV
Hamilton Terrace . . . . V 21
High Street . . . . V 22
Holly Walk . . . . U
Kenilworth Road . . . . U
Leam Terrace V
Leicester Street . . . . U
Lillington Avenue . . . . U
Lillington Road . . . . U
Lower Avenue . . . . V 28
Newbold Terrace . . . . V 30
Northumberland Road . . . . U 33
Old Warwick Road V
Priory Terrace . . . . V 37
Radford Road V
Regent Grove . . . . UV 40
Rugby Road . . . . U
Russell Terrace V
Spencer Street . . . . V 44
Tachbrook Road . . . . V 47
Victoria Terrace . . . . V 49
Willes Road . . . . UV

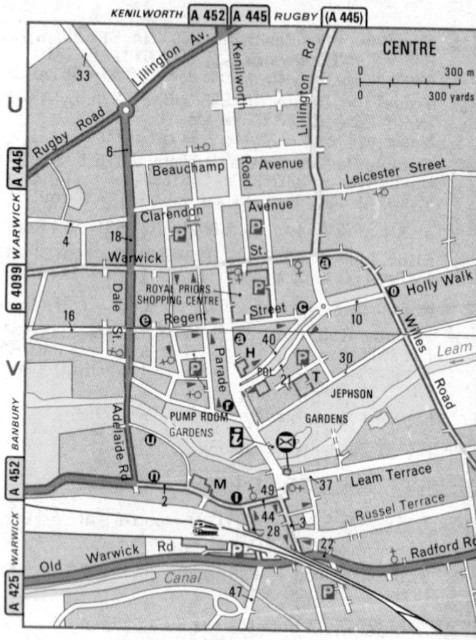

Manor House (Forte), Avenue Rd, CV31 3NJ, ℘ 423251, Fax 425933 – 100. VISA V
Meals (bar lunch Monday to Saturday)/dinner 16.95 **st.** and a la carte 6.50 – 8.50
53 rm 69.00/79.00 **st.** – SB.

Inchfield, 64 Upper Holly Walk, CV32 4JL, ℘ 883777, Fax 330467, – 40 AE VISA. U
Meals *(closed Saturday lunch and Sunday dinner)* 10.25/28.00 **t.** and a la carte 4.50
6.50 – **22 rm** 55.00/90.00 **t.** – SB.

Eaton Court, 1-7 St. Marks Rd, CV32 6DL, ℘ 885848, Fax 885848, – 100. AE VISA JCB. plan of Warwick Z
closed 24 December-2 January – **Meals** (lunch by arrangement)/dinner 13.95 **t.** and a la carte 4.00 – **36 rm** 45.00/75.00 **t.** – SB.

Lansdowne, 87 Clarendon St., CV32 4PF, ℘ 450505, Fax 421313 – rest AE VISA. U
closed 24 and 25 December – **Meals** (dinner only) 21.95 **t.** 4.85 – **15 rm** 49.95/59.90 **t.** – SB.

Adams, 22 Avenue Rd, CV31 3PQ, ℘ 450742, Fax 313110, – AE VISA V
Meals (lunch by arrangement)/dinner 20.00 **t.** and a la carte 4.75 – 7.50 – **12 rm** 45.00/52.00 **t.** – SB.

York House, 9 York Rd, CV31 3PR, ℘ 424671 – rm AE VISA. V
closed 24 to 31 December – **Meals** (by arrangement) 12.50 **t.** – **8 rm** 21.00/50.00 **t.** – SB

Coverdale House without rest., 8 Portland St., CV32 5HE, ℘ 330400, Fax 833388 – VISA U
7 rm 32.00/42.00 **st.**

Flowerdale House without rest., 58 Warwick New Rd, CV32 6AA, ℘ 426002 Fax 883699, – VISA. plan of Warwick Z
6 rm 25.00/42.00 **s.**

Les Plantagenets, 15 Dormer Pl., CV32 5AA, ℘ 451792, Fax 453171 – AE VISA
closed Saturday lunch, Sunday and Bank Holidays – **Meals** - French - 12.50/18.50 and a la carte. V

ATS 52-54 Morton St. ℘ 339643/4

***En saison,** surtout dans les stations fréquentées, il est prudent de retenir à l'avance. Cependant, si vous ne pouvez pas occuper la chambre que vous avez retenue, prévenez immédiatement l'hôtelier.*

Si vous écrivez à un hôtel à l'étranger, joignez à votre lettre un coupon-réponse international (disponible dans les bureaux de poste).

OYAL TUNBRIDGE WELLS Kent 404 U 30 Great Britain G. – pop. 60 272 – ☎ 01892.

ee : The Pantiles★ B **26** – Calverley Park★ B.

Langton Rd ✆ 523034 A.

The Old Fish Market, The Pantiles, TN2 5TN ✆ 515675.

.ondon 36 – ◆Brighton 33 – Folkestone 46 – Hastings 27 – Maidstone 18.

ROYAL TUNBRIDGE WELLS

alverley Road . . . . **B**
gh Street . . . . **B** 14
ount Pleasant Road . . . . **B** 25
ntiles (The) . . . . **B** 26
oyal Victoria Place Shopping Centre . . . . **B**

enhall Mill Road . . . . **A** 3

Bishop's Down . . . . **A** 4
Calverley Park Gardens . . . **B** 7
Crescent Road . . . . **B** 9
Fir Tree Road . . . . **A** 10
Grosvenor Road . . . . **B** 12
Hall's Hole Road . . . . **A** 13
High Rocks Lane . . . . **A** 16
Hungershall Park Road . . . **A** 17
Lansdowne Road . . . . **B** 18
Lower Green Road . . . . . . **A** 20

Major York's Road . . . . **A** 22
Mount Ephraim . . . . **A** 23
Mount Ephraim Road . . . . **B** 24
Prospect Road . . . . **A** 27
Rusthall Road . . . . **A** 28
St. John's Road . . . . **B** 29
Tea Garden Lane . . . . **A** 30
Vale Road . . . . **B** 33
Victoria Road . . . . **B** 34
Warwick Park . . . . **B** 35

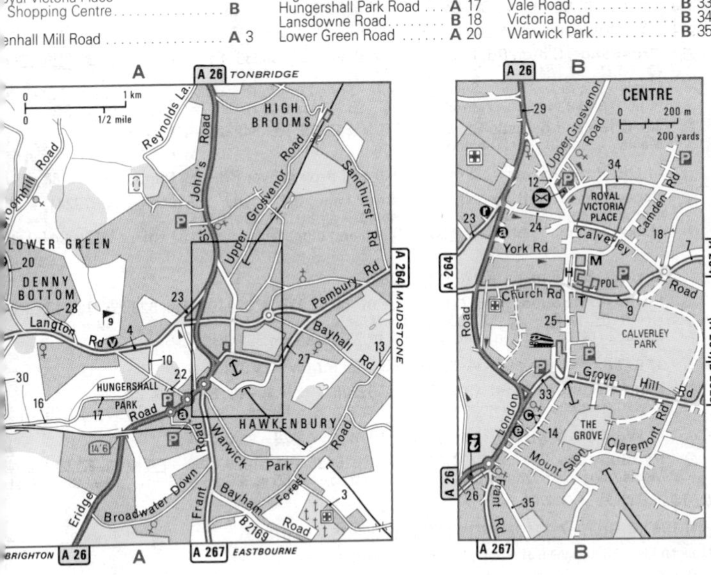

Spa, Mount Ephraim, TN4 8XJ, ✆ 520331, Fax 510575, ←, ⛳, ≘s, ▣, ⛲, park, 🎾 – ⇅ ✕ rm TV ☎ ♿ 🅿 – 🏛 250. 💳 AE ⓞ VISA. ✕ A **v**
Meals (bar lunch Saturday) a la carte 13.50/18.00 **t.** and a la carte 🍷 6.50 – ☕ 8.50 – **72 rm** 69.00/84.00 **st.**, 4 suites.

Russell, 80 London Rd, TN1 1DZ, ✆ 544833, Fax 515846 – ✕ rm TV ☎ 🅿. 💳 AE ⓞ VISA JCB. ✕ B **a**
Meals 13.95/17.95 **t.** and dinner a la carte 🍷 5.80 – **26 rm** ☕ 55.00/99.00 **t.** – SB.

Swan, The Pantiles, TN2 5TD, ✆ 541450, Fax 541465 – TV ☎ 🅿 – 🏛 55. 💳 AE ⓞ VISA JCB. ✕ A **a**
Meals (lunch by arrangement) 8.95/16.00 **t.** and a la carte – **17 rm** ☕ 45.00/80.00 **st.** – SB.

Cheevers, 56 High St., TN1 1XF, ✆ 545524, Fax 535956 – 💳 AE VISA B **c**
closed Sunday, Monday and 1 week Christmas – **Meals** 17.50/25.00 **t.** 🍷 4.65.

Chi, 26 London Rd, TN1 1DA, ✆ 513888, Fax 662489 – 💳 AE VISA B **e**
closed Sunday and 25-26 December – **Meals** - Chinese - 10.00/22.50 **t.** and a la carte.

Xian, 54 High St., TN1 1XF, ✆ 522930, Fax 540322 – 💳 AE VISA B **c**
closed lunch Sunday and Bank Holidays and 25 to 27 December – **Meals** - Chinese - 10.25/20.00 **t.** and a la carte 🍷 4.20.

at Pembury NW : 4 m. by A 264 off A 21 – A – ✉ Royal Tunbridge Wells – ☎ 01892 :

Jarvis Pembury, 8 Tonbridge Rd, TN2 4QL, ✆ 823567, Fax 823931, ≘s, ▣ – ✕ rm TV ☎ ♿ 🅿 – 🏛 200. 💳 AE ⓞ VISA
Meals *(closed Saturday lunch)* 9.95/17.95 **t.** and dinner a la carte – ☕ 9.50 – **74 rm** 79.00/89.00 **st.**, 5 suites – SB.

at Frant S : 2½ m. on A 267 – A – ✉ Royal Tunbridge Wells – ☎ 01892 :

Old Parsonage 🐦 without rest., Church Lane, TN3 9DX, ✆ 750773, Fax 750773, ←, « Georgian rectory », ⛲ – ✕ TV 🅿. 💳 VISA
3 rm ☕ 32.00/58.00 **st.**

at Rusthall W : 1 ¾ m. by A 264 – ✉ Royal Tunbridge Wells – ☎ 01892 :

Danehurst, 41 Lower Green Rd, TN4 8TW, ℘ 527739, Fax 514804, – TV P. VISA.
closed last 2 weeks August – **Meals** (by arrangement) 25.95 **s.** 3.95 – **5 rm** 32.5 65.00 **s.** – SB.

RUAN-HIGH-LANES Cornwall 403 F 33 – see Veryan.

RUCKHALL Heref. and Worcs. – see Hereford.

RUGBY Warks. 403 404 Q 26 – pop. 84 563 – ☎ 01788.
Whitefields Hotel Golf Complex, Coventry Rd, Thurlaston ℘ 521800.
The Library, St. Matthews St., CV21 3BZ ℘ 535348.
London 88 – Birmingham 33 – Leicester 21 – Northampton 20 – Warwick 17.

Grosvenor, Clifton Rd, CV21 3QQ, on B 5414 ℘ 535686, Fax 541297, – TV P. AE VISA JCB
Meals *(closed lunch Saturday and Sunday (June, July and August))* 9.95 (lunch) and a la carte 17.75/28.65 **st.** 7.95 – **20 rm** 67.50/77.50 **st.**, 1 suite – SB.

Mr Chan's, 3-5 Castle St., CV21 2TP, ℘ 542326, Fax 542326 – AE VISA
Meals - Chinese - 19.00 **t.** and a la carte.

at Old Brownsover N : 2 m. by A 426 and Brownsover Rd – ✉ Rugby – ☎ 01788 :

Brownsover Hall (Regal), Brownsover Lane, CV21 1HU, ℘ 546100, Fax 579241, « 19 Gothic style hall », – rm TV ☎ P – 80. AE VISA
Meals (bar lunch Saturday) 9.95/15.95 **st.** and dinner a la carte – **31 rm** 79.50/94.50 **st.** SB.

at Crick SE : 6 m. on A 428 – ☎ 01788 :

Forte Posthouse, NN6 7XR, W : ½ m. on A 428 ℘ 822101, Fax 823955, rm TV ☎ P – 200. AE VISA JCB
Meals 20.00 **st.** and a la carte 7.95 – 7.95 – **88 rm** 59.00 **st.** – SB.

at Kilsby SE : 6¼ m. by A 428 on A 5 – ✉ Rugby – ☎ 01788 :

Hunt House, Main Rd, CV23 8XR, ℘ 823282, – P. AE VISA JCB
closed Sunday, Monday and 26 to 30 December – **Meals** (dinner only) 21.50 **t.** 4.75.

at West Haddon (Northants.) SE : 10 m. on A 428 – ☎ 01788 :

Pytchley Inn, 23 High St., NN6 7AP, ℘ 510426, Fax 510209, – TV ☎ P. AE VISA.
Meals *(closed 25 December)* (grill rest.) approx. 11.55 **st.** 3.95 – **14 rm** 39.00/50.00 **st.**

ATS 73 Bath St. ℘ 574705

RUGELEY Staffs. 402 403 404 O 25 – pop. 22 975 – ☎ 01889.
London 134 – Birmingham 31 – Derby 29 – Stoke-on-Trent 22.

Forte Travelodge, Western Springs Rd, WS15 2AS, at junction of A 51 with A 46 ℘ 570096, Reservations (Freephone) 0800 850950 – TV P. AE VISA.
Meals (grill rest.) – **32 rm** 34.50 **t.**

ATS Mill Lane ℘ 582500

RUNCORN Ches. 402 403 L 23 – pop. 64 154 – ☎ 01928.
Clifton Rd ℘ 572093.
London 202 – Liverpool 14 – Manchester 29.

Forte Posthouse, Wood Lane, Beechwood, WA7 3HA, SE : ½ m. off junction 12 of M 5 ℘ 714000, Fax 714611, – rm TV ☎ P – 500. AE VISA JCB
Meals a la carte 17.45/23.35 **st.** – 7.95 – **135 rm** 59.00 **st.** – SB.

Campanile, Lowlands Rd, WA7 5TP, beside the railway station ℘ 581771, Fax 581730 rm TV ☎ P – 25. AE VISA JCB.
Meals 10.35 **st.** and a la carte – 4.50 – **53 rm** 36.50 **st.**

ATS Sandy Lane, Weston Point ℘ 567715/6

RUSHDEN Northants. 404 S 27 – pop. 23 592 – ☎ 01933.
London 74 – Cambridge 42 – Northampton 14 – Peterborough 25.

Forte Travelodge, NN10 9EP, on A 45 (eastbound carriageway) ℘ 57008, Reservation (Freephone) 0800 850950 – TV P. AE VISA.
Meals (grill rest.) – **40 rm** 34.50 **t.**

RUSHLAKE GREEN E. Sussex 404 U 31 – ✉ Heathfield – ☎ 01435.
London 54 – Brighton 26 – Eastbourne 13.

Stone House, TN21 9QJ, ℘ 830553, Fax 830726, « Part 14C, part Georgian countr house, antiques », , park – TV ☎ P.
closed 24 December-5 January – **Meals** (residents only) (dinner only) 26.50 **st.** 4.85 – **6 rm** 71.25/165.00 **st.**, 1 suite – SB.

RUSTHALL Kent – see Royal Tunbridge Wells.

RYE E. Sussex 404 W 31 Great Britain G. – pop. 4 207 – ECD : Tuesday – 01797.
See : Old Town★★ : Mermaid Street★, St. Mary's Church (<★).
The Heritage Centre, Strand Quay, TN31 7AY 226696.
London 61 – Brighton 49 – Folkestone 27 – Maidstone 33.

George (Forte Heritage), High St., TN31 7JP, 222114, Fax 224065 – – 60.
Meals (bar lunch Monday to Saturday)/dinner 18.95 **t.** 7.50 – 9.25 – **22 rm** 70.00/75.00 **st.** – SB.

Mermaid Inn, Mermaid St., TN31 7EU, 223065, Fax 225069, « 15C inn » –
Meals 11.50/21.00 **t.** and a la carte 6.50 – **28 rm** 59.00/120.00 **t.** – SB.

Jeake's House without rest., Mermaid St., TN31 7ET, 222828, Fax 222623 –
12 rm 23.50/82.00 **st.**

Green Hedges without rest., Rye Hill, TN31 7NH, N : ½ m. off A 268 on unmarked rd 222185, heated, –
closed Christmas and New Year – **3 rm** 40.00/58.00.

Old Vicarage without rest., 66 Church Sq., TN31 7HF, 222119, Fax 227466, –
closed Christmas – **6 rm** 36.00/59.00 **st.**

Flushing Inn, 4 Market St., TN31 7LA, 223292, « 15C inn with 16C mural » –
closed Monday dinner, Tuesday and first 2 weeks January – **Meals** - Seafood - 13.50/23.50 **t.** and a la carte 5.00.

Landgate Bistro, 5-6 Landgate, TN31 7LH, 222829 –
closed Sunday, Monday, 2 weeks June, 1 week October and 1 week Christmas – **Meals** (dinner only) 15.50 **st.** and a la carte 4.00.

at Rye Foreign NW : 2 m. on A 268 – 01797 :

Broomhill Lodge, TN31 7UN, on A 268 280421, Fax 280402, – rest
Meals 14.50/21.50 **st.** and a la carte 4.75 – **12 rm** 46.00/104.00 **t.** – SB.

at Peasmarsh NW : 4 m. on A 268 – Rye – 01797 :

Flackley Ash, London Rd, TN31 6YH, 230651, Telex 957210, Fax 230510, – – 100.
Meals 14.15/25.15 **st.** 5.00 – **30 rm** 69.00/98.00 **st.**, 2 suites – SB.

RYE FOREIGN E. Sussex – see Rye.

RYTON ON DUNSMORE W. Mids. 403 404 P 28 – see Coventry.

SAFFRON WALDEN Essex 404 U 27 Great Britain G. – pop. 14 019 – 01799.
See : Audley End★★ *AC*.
1 Market Pl., Market Sq., CB10 1HR 510444.
London 46 – Cambridge 15 – Chelmsford 25.

Saffron, 10-18 High St., CB10 1AY, 522676, Fax 513979 – – 70.
Conservatory : Meals *(closed Sunday dinner)* 14.25 **t.** and a la carte – **17 rm** 45.00/65.00 **t.** – SB.

Bridge End Orchard, 35 Bridge St., CB10 1BT, 522001, –
Meals (by arrangement) – **3 rm** 27.50/50.00 **st.**

at Littlebury Green W : 4½ m. by B 1383 – Saffron Walden – 01763 :

Elmdon Lee, CB11 4XB, 838237, Fax 838237, –
closed Christmas – **Meals** (by arrangement) (communal dining) (dinner only) 16.00/18.00 **s.** 4.00 – **4 rm** 27.50/55.00 **s.**

at Duddenhoe End W : 7½ m. by B 1052 and B 1383 off B 1039 – Saffron Walden – 01763 :

Duddenhoe End Farm without rest., CB11 4UU, 838258, , park –
3 rm 22.00/36.00.

at Elmdon W : 7½ m. by B 1052 and B 1383 off B 1039 – Saffron Walden – 01763 :

Elmdon Bury , CB11 4NF, 838220, Fax 838504, , , park, – rm
closed 23 December-6 January – **Meals** (by arrangement) (communal dining) (dinner only) (unlicensed) 12.00 **s.** – **3 rm** 26.00/44.00.

ATS Station Rd 521426

Se cercate un albergo tranquillo,
oltre a consultare le carte dell'introduzione,
rintracciate nell'elenco degli esercizi quelli con il simbolo o .

ST. AGNES Cornwall 403 E 33 **The West Country G.** – pop. 6 592 – ☎ 01872.

See : St. Agnes Beacon** (※**).

Envir. : Portreath*, SW : 5½ m..

Perranporth, Budnic Hill ☎ 572454.

London 302 – Newquay 12 – Penzance 26 – Truro 9.

Rose-in-Vale, Mithian, TR5 0QD, E : 2 m. by B 3285 ☎ 552202, Fax 552700, heated, – rest. *closed January and February* – **Meals** 8.95/17.95 **st.** and a la carte 4.25 – **19 rm** 42.50/105.00 **st.** – SB.

ST. ALBANS Herts. 404 T 28 **Great Britain G.** – pop. 126 202 – ☎ 01727.

See : City* - Cathedral* – Verulamium* (Museum* *AC*).

Envir. : Hatfield House** *AC*, E : 6 m. by A 1057.

Batchwood Hall, Batchwood Drive ☎ 833349 – Kinsbourne Green Lane, Redbourn ☎ 793493.

Town Hall, Market Pl., AL3 5DJ ☎ 864511.

London 27 – Cambridge 41 – Luton 10.

Sopwell House, Cottonmill Lane, AL1 2HQ, SE : 1½ m. by A 1081 and Mile House Lane ☎ 864477, Fax 844741, park – 300. **Bejerano's Brasserie : Meals** 16.00 **st.** (dinner) and lunch a la carte 14.00/18.00 **st.** - (see also ***Magnolia Conservatory*** below) – 9.50 – **90 rm** 105.00/125.00 **st.**, 2 suites – SB.

Noke Thistle, Watford Rd, AL2 3DS, SW : 2½ m. at junction of A 405 with B 4630 ☎ 854252, Fax 841906, – rm – 50. **Bertie's : Meals** *(bar lunch Saturday and Bank Holidays except Christmas)* 15.00/22.00 and a la carte **t.** 5.75 – 8.75 – **109 rm** 87.00/105.00 **t.**, 2 suites – SB.

St. Michael's Manor, Fishpool St., AL3 4RY, ☎ 864444, Fax 848909, « Part 16C, part William and Mary manor house, lake and gardens » – 35. **Meals** 13.00/24.00 **t.** and a la carte 7.95 – **24 rm** 78.00/140.00 **st.**

Pré, Redbourn Rd, AL3 6JZ, NW : 1¼ m. on A 5183 ☎ 855259, Fax 852239, – rest. **Meals** (grill rest.) a la carte 9.75/13.85 **t.** 5.15 – **11 rm** 45.00/55.00 **t.**

Nonna Rosa, 3 Manor Rd, AL1 3ST, ☎ 853613, Fax 853613, – **Meals** 18.00/20.00 **t.** and a la carte 3.60 – **10 rm** 36.00/47.50 **st.** – SB.

Ardmore House, 54 Lemsford Rd, AL1 3PR, ☎ 859313, Fax 859313, – rest. **Meals** (dinner only) 9.95 **st.** and a la carte – **26 rm** 45.00/57.50 **st.**

Black Lion Inn, 198 Fishpool St., AL3 4SB, ☎ 851786, Fax 859243 – **Meals** - Italian - *(closed Monday lunch and Sunday)* 12.00/25.00 **t.** and a la carte – **10 rm** 48.00/59.00 **st.**

XXX **Magnolia Conservatory** (at Sopwell House H.), Cottonmill Lane, AL1 2HQ, SE : 1½ m. by A 1081 and Mile House Lane ☎ 864477, Fax 844741 – *closed Saturday lunch, Sunday dinner and Bank Holidays* – **Meals** 16.95/23.50 **st.** and a la carte 6.00.

ATS Grimston Rd ☎ 835174 ATS Lyon Way, Hatfield Rd ☎ 852314

ST. AUSTELL Cornwall 403 F 32 **The West Country G.** – pop. 21 622 – ☎ 01726.

See : Holy Trinity Church*.

Envir. : St. Austell Bay** (Gribbin Head**) E : by A 390 and A 3082 – Carthew : Wheal Martyn Museum** *AC*, N : 2 m. by A 391 – Mevagissey**, S : 5 m. by B 3273 – Charlestown*, SE : 2 m. by A 390.

Exc. : Trewithen*** *AC*, NE : 7 m. by A 390 – Lanhydrock**, NE : 11 m. by A 390 and B 3269 – Polkerris*, E : 7 m. by A 390 and A 3082.

Carlyon Bay ☎ 814250.

London 281 – Newquay 16 – Plymouth 38 – Truro 14.

White Hart, Church St., PL25 4AT, ☎ 72100, Fax 74705 – 45. *closed 25 and 26 December* – **Meals** 6.95/12.00 **t.** 3.75 – **18 rm** 40.00/63.00 **t.** – SB.

Poltarrow Farm, St. Mewan, PL26 7DR, SW : 1¾ m. by A 390 on St. Mewan rd ☎ 67111, « Working farm », park – *closed Christmas* – **Meals** (by arrangement) – **5 rm** 25.00/40.00 **s.** – SB.

at Tregrehan E : 2½ m. by A 390 – ✉ St. Austell – ☎ 01726 :

Boscundle Manor, PL25 3RL, ☎ 813557, Fax 814997, « Tastefully converted 18C manor, gardens », heated, park – rest. *mid March-October* – **Meals** *(closed Sunday to non-residents)* (dinner only) 22.50 **st.** 5.00 – **8 rm** 65.00/110.00 **st.**, 2 suites – SB.

at Carlyon Bay E : 2½ m. by A 3601 – ✉ St. Austell – ☎ 01726 :

Carlyon Bay, PL25 3RD, ☎ 812304, Fax 814938, ≤ Carlyon Bay, « Extensive gardens », heated, – – 50. AE VISA
Meals 11.00/23.00 **t.** and a la carte – **73 rm** (dinner included) 83.00/202.00 **t.** – SB.

Wheal Lodge, 91 Sea Rd, PL25 3SH, ☎ 815543, Fax 815543, – . VISA
closed Christmas – **Meals** (residents only) 12.50 **st.** 3.95 – **6 rm** 39.00/80.00 **st.** – SB.

at Charlestown SE : 2 m. by A 390 – ✉ St. Austell – ☎ 01726 :

Pier House, PL25 3NJ, ☎ 67955, Fax 69246, ≤ – . VISA
Meals *(closed 25 December dinner)* a la carte 12.50/26.40 **t.** – **25 rm** 28.00/62.00 **t.**

Rashleigh Arms, PL25 3NJ, ☎ 73635, Fax 69246, – . VISA
Meals 7.50/10.20 **t.** and a la carte – **5 rm** 24.00/48.00 **t.**

T' Gallants without rest., 6 Charlestown Rd, PL25 3NJ, ☎ 70203, – . VISA
8 rm 25.00/36.00 **st.**

ATS Gover Rd ☎ 65685/6

ST. BLAZEY Cornwall 403 F 32 – pop. 8 837 – ☎ 01726.

London 276 – Newquay 21 – Plymouth 33 – Truro 19.

Nanscawen House without rest., Prideaux Rd, PL24 2SR, W : ¾ m. ☎ 814488, Fax 814488, ≤, heated, – . VISA JCB
closed 25-26 December – **3 rm** 58.00/78.00 **s.**

ST. HELENS Mersey. 402 403 L 23 – ☎ 01744.

Sherdley Park ☎ 813149 – London 207 – Liverpool 12 – Manchester 27.

Chalon Court, Chalon Way, Linkway West, WA10 1NG, ☎ 453444, Fax 454655, , – rm – 220. AE VISA
The Renaissance : Meals (dancing Friday and Saturday evening) 9.95/19.95 **st.** and a la carte 4.75 – 8.75 – **81 rm** 79.50 **st.**, 3 suites – SB.

Waterside, East Lancashire Rd, WA11 7LX, N : 1 ¾ m. at junction of A 580 with A 571 ☎ 23333, Fax 454231 – – 80. AE VISA
Meals (grill rest.) 7.00/12.00 **st.**and a la carte 5.10 – 4.95 – **43 rm** 39.00 **st.**

ATS Sutton Rd ☎ 613434

ATS Blackbrook Rd, Blackbrook ☎ 54175/6

ST. HILARY Cornwall – see Marazion.

ST. IVES Cambs. 404 T 27 – pop. 15 312 – ✉ Huntingdon – ☎ 01480.

London 75 – Cambridge 14 – Huntingdon 6.

Slepe Hall, Ramsey Rd, PE17 4RB, ☎ 463122, Fax 300706 – – 40. AE VISA
closed 25 to 29 December – **Meals** 13.95 **t.** and a la carte 3.95 – **15 rm** 52.00/62.00 **t.** – SB.

Dolphin, Bridge Foot, London Rd, PE17 4EP, ☎ 466966, Fax 495597 – – 150. AE VISA
closed 27-30 December – **Meals** 12.50/15.50 **st.** and a la carte 4.00 – **47 rm** 55.00/65.00 **st.**

Oliver's Lodge, Needingworth Rd, PE17 4JP, ☎ 463252, Fax 461150 – – 40. AE VISA JCB
Meals 14.50/17.50 **t.**and a la carte 4.25 – **15 rm** 52.00/65.00 **t.** – SB.

at Holywell E : 3 m. by A 1123 – ✉ Huntingdon – ☎ 01480 :.

Old Ferryboat Inn, PE17 3TG, ☎ 463227, Fax 494885, – – 40. VISA
accommodation closed 25 December – **Meals** a la carte 10.95/21.40 **t.** – **7 rm** 40.00/68.00 **t.**

ATS East St. ☎ 465572

ST. IVES Cornwall 403 D 33 **The West Country G.** – pop. 7 254 – ☎ 01736.

See : Town★★ - Barbara Hepworth Museum★★ *AC* Y **M1** – Tate Gallery ★★ - St. Nicholas Chapel (≤★★) Y – St. Ia★ Y **A** – **Envir.** : S : Penwith★★ Y – St. La★.

Exc. : St. Michael's Mount★★ (≤★★) S : 10 m. by B 3306 – Y - B 3311, B 3309 and A 30.

Tregenna Castle Hotel ☎ 795254 ext: 121 Y – West Cornwall, Lelant ☎ 753401.

The Guildhall, Street-an-Pol, TR26 2DS ☎ 796297 – London 319 – Penzance 10 – Truro 25.

Plan on next page

Porthminster, The Terrace, TR26 2BN, ☎ 795221, Fax 797043, ≤, , , heated, , – . AE VISA Y s
Meals (buffet lunch)/dinner 18.50 **st.** and a la carte – **46 rm** 53.00/122.00 **st.** – SB.

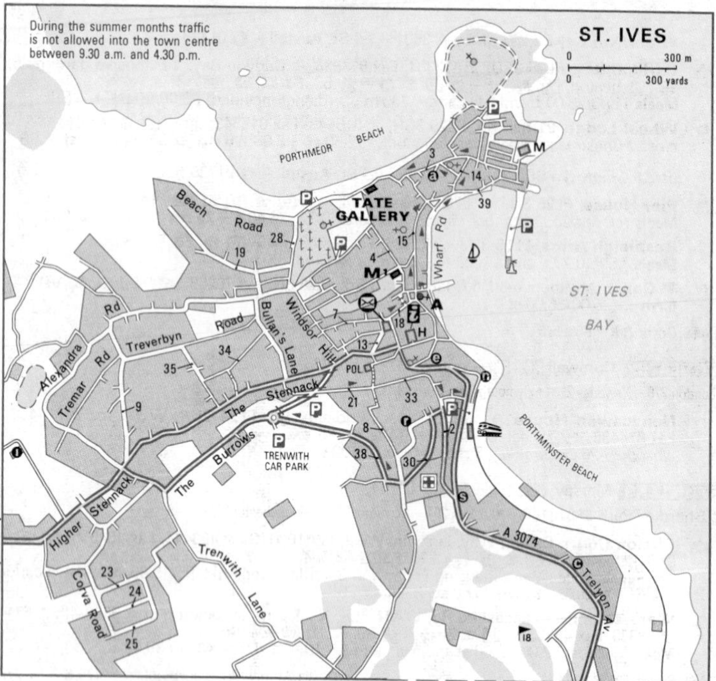

During the summer months traffic is not allowed into the town centre between 9.30 a.m. and 4.30 p.m.

ST. IVES

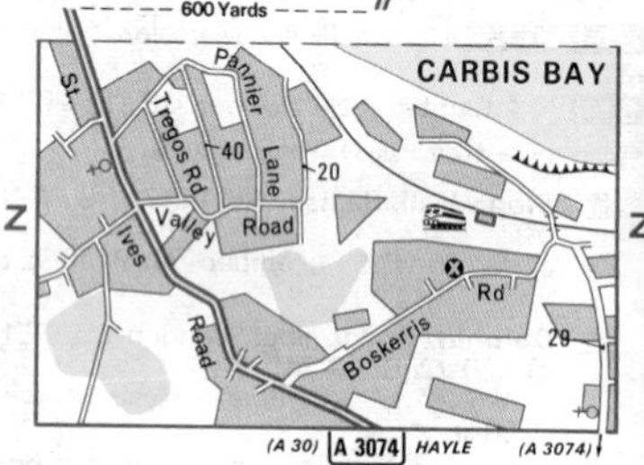

Countryman at Trink, Old Coach Rd, TR26 3JQ, S : 2½ m. by B 3306 and B 3311 on Hayle rd ☎ 797571, – rest TV P. AE VISA.
Meals (bar lunch)/dinner 16.00 **t.** and a la carte 4.75 – **6 rm** 35.00/50.00 **t.** – SB.

Pedn-Olva, The Warren, Porthminster Beach, TR26 2EA, ☎ 796222, Fax 797710, ≤ coast-line – TV ☎ P – **35 rm.** Y **n**

Skidden House, Skidden Hill, TR26 2DU, ☎ 796899, Fax 798619 – rest TV ☎ P. AE VISA JCB Y **e**
Meals *(restricted service November to March)* (bar lunch)/dinner 17.50 **st.** and a la carte 7.50 – **6 rm** 39.00/72.00 **st.** – SB.

Old Vicarage without rest., Parc-an-Creet, TR26 2ET, ☎ 796124, Fax 796124, – TV P. AE VISA JCB Y **i**
March-October – **8 rm** 21.00/46.00.

Blue Hayes, Trelyon Av., TR26 2AD, ☎ 797129, ≤, – rest TV P. VISA JCB.
mid March-mid October – **Meals** 15.00 – **9 rm** 32.50/69.00 **t.** – SB. Y **c**

Pondarosa, 10 Porthminster Terr., TR26 2DQ, ☎ 795875 – TV P. AE VISA JCB.
– **Meals** 8.00 **st.** 3.25 – **9 rm** 14.00/30.00 **st.** – SB. Y **r**

Pig'n'Fish, Norway Lane, TR26 1LZ, ☎ 794204 – VISA Y **a**
closed Sunday, Monday and November-February – **Meals** *(Mondays July and August only)* - Seafood - (dinner only) 17.50 **t.** and a la carte 20.00/24.00 **t.** 7.50.

at Carbis Bay S : 1 3/4 m. on A 3074 – ✉ St. Ives – ☎ 01736 :

Boskerris, Boskerris Rd, TR26 2NQ, ☎ 795295, Fax 798632, ≤, heated, – rest TV ☎ P. AE VISA Z x
Easter-October – **Meals** (bar lunch)/dinner 17.50 **st.** – **19 rm** 30.00/80.00 **st.** – SB.

T. JUST Cornwall 403 C 33 **The West Country G.** – pop. 4 424 – ☎ 01736.

ee : Church★.
nvir. : Penwith★★ – Sancreed - Church★★ (Celtic Crosses★★) SE : 3 m. by A 3071 – rengwainton Garden★★ (≤★★) *AC*, E : 4 1/2 m. by A 3071 – St. Buryan★★ (Church Tower★★) E : 5 1/2 m. by B 3306 and A 30 – Land's End★ (cliff scenery★★★) S : 5 1/2 m. by B 3306 and 30 – Cape Cornwall★ (≤★★) W : 1 1/2 m. – Geevor Tin Mine★ *AC*, N : 3 m. by B 3306 – Carn uny★, SE : 3 m. by A 3071 – Wayside Cross★ – Sennen Cove★ (≤★), S : 5 1/2 m. by B 3306 nd A 30.
xc. : – Porthcurno★, S : 9 1/2 m. by B 3306, A 30 and B 3315.
, Cape Cornwall G & C.C., ☎ 788611.
London 325 – Penzance 7.5 – Truro 35.

Boscean Country, TR19 7QP, NW : 1/2 m. by Boswedden Rd ☎ 788748, Fax 788748, ≤, – rest P. VISA.
April-October – **Meals** (dinner only)(residents only) 12.00 **t.** 3.50 – **12 rm** 24.00/40.00 **t.**

ST. JUST IN ROSELAND Cornwall – see St. Mawes.

ST. KEVERNE Cornwall 403 E 33 – ✉ Helston – ☎ 01326.
London 326 – Falmouth 17 – Penzance 24 – Truro 29.

Volnay, Porthoustock, TR12 6QW, NE : 1 m. ☎ 280183 – P
closed Sunday dinner, Monday, January and November – **Meals** (booking essential) (dinner only) a la carte 14.75/23.00 **st.** 4.25.

ST. LEONARDS E. Sussex 404 V 31 – see Hastings and St. Leonards.

ST. MARGARET'S AT CLIFFE Kent 404 Y 30 – see Dover.

ST. MARTINS Cornwall 403 ㉚ – see Scilly (Isles of).

ST. MARY'S Cornwall 403 ㉚ – see Scilly (Isles of).

ST. MAWES Cornwall 403 E 33 **The West Country G.** – ✉ Truro – ☎ 01326.
See : Town★ - Castle★ *AC* (≤★).
Envir. : St. Just in Roseland Church★★, N : 2 1/2 m. by A 3078.
London 299 – ◆Plymouth 56 – Truro 18.

Idle Rocks, 1 Tredenham Rd., TR2 5AN, ☎ 270771, Fax 270062, ≤ harbour and estuary – rest TV ☎. AE VISA
Meals 6.75/23.75 and lunch a la carte 4.95 – **24 rm** (dinner included) 61.00/122.00 **st.** – SB.

Rising Sun, The Square, TR2 5DJ, ☎ 270233 – TV ☎ P.
8 rm.

St. Mawes, The Seafront, TR2 5DW, ☎ 270266, ≤ – TV ☎. AE VISA JCB
mid February-mid November – **Meals** 11.00/16.00 **t.** 4.75 – **7 rm** (dinner included) 66.00/108.00 **st.** – SB.

at St. Just in Roseland N : 2 1/2 m. on A 3078 – ✉ Truro – ☎ 01326 :

Rose da Mar, TR2 5JB, N : 1/4 m. on B 3289 ☎ 270450, ≤, – P
March-October – **Meals** (booking essential) (dinner only) 13.75 **s.** – **8 rm** 25.00/62.00 **s.**

ST. MICHAELS-ON-WYRE Lancs. 402 L 22 – ☎ 01995.
◆London 235 – ◆Blackpool 24 – Burnley 35 – ◆Manchester 43.

Mallards, Garstang Rd, PR3 0TE, ☎ 679661 – P. VISA JCB
closed Sunday dinner, 1 week January and 2 weeks August – **Meals** (dinner only and Sunday lunch)/dinner 17.00 **t.** 6.00.

In this guide
a symbol or a character, printed in red or black, in **bold** or light type, does not have the same meaning.
Pay particular attention to the explanatory pages.

ST. NEOTS Cambs. 404 T 27 – pop. 25 110 – ☏ 01480.
See : Town★.
Envir. : Parish Church★★.
Abbotsley, Eynesbury Hardwicke ☏ 474000.
◆London 60 – Bedford 11 – ◆Cambridge 17 – Huntingdon 9.

Eaton Oak, Crosshall Rd, PE19 4AG, NW : 1 m. on B 1048 at junction with A 1 ☏ 219555
Fax 407520 – rest. AE VISA.
Meals (grill rest.) a la carte 10.40/16.50 **t.** 6.50 – **9 rm** 40.00/50.00 **t.**

at Wyboston (Beds.) SW : 2½ m. by B 1428 on A 1 – ✉ Bedford – ☏ 01480 :

Wyboston Lakes without rest., Great North Rd, MK44 3AL, N : ½ m. at junction of A 42
with A 1 ☏ 212625, Fax 223000, – rest – 120. AE VISA.
5.95 – **102 rm** 36.00/49.00 **st.** – SB.

ATS Brook St. ☏ 472920

*Die Gesamtkarte von **Großbritannien** und **Irland** ist die **Michelin-Karte** 986 im Maßstab 1:1 000 000.*

SALCOMBE Devon 403 I 33 **The West Country G.** – pop. 2 189 – ☏ 01548.
Envir. : Sharpitor (Overbecks Museum and garden) (≤★★) *AC*, S : 2 m. by South Sands Z.
Exc. : Prawle Point (≤★★★) E : 16 m. around coast by A 381 – Y - and A 379.
Council Hall, Market St., TQ8 8DE ☏ 842736/843927 (summer only).
◆London 243 – Exeter 43 – ◆Plymouth 27 – Torquay 28.

SALCOMBE

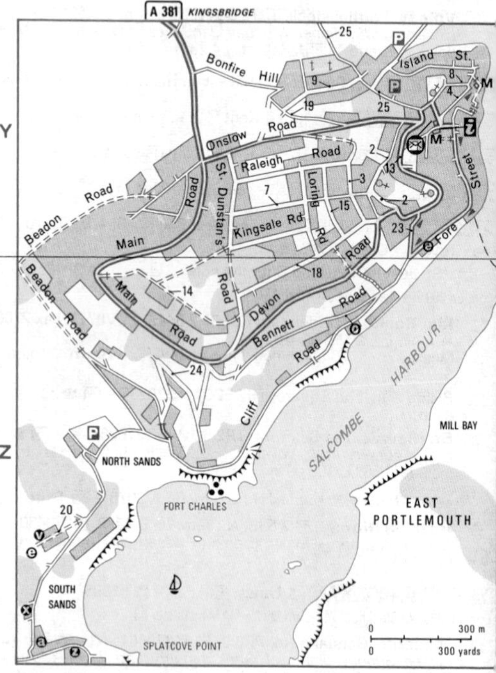

Town plans
roads most used by traffic and those on which guide listed hotels and restaurants stand are fully drawn; the beginning only of lesser roads is indicated.

Tides Reach, South Sands, TQ8 8LJ, ☏ 843466, Fax 843954, ≤ estuary, , squash – AE VISA Z
closed 22 December-15 February – **Meals** (bar lunch)/dinner 21.85 **st.** and a la carte 5.35 –
38 rm (dinner included) 82.00/162.00 **st.** – SB.

Marine, Cliff Rd, TQ8 8JH, ☏ 844444, Fax 843109, ≤ estuary, – rest AE VISA Y
Meals 22.00 **t.** and a la carte – **51 rm** (dinner included) 100.00/180.00 **t.** – SB.

South Sands, South Sands, TQ8 8LL, ℘ 843741, Fax 842112, ≤, heated, – TV ☎ P. VISA Z a
March-October – **Meals** (bar lunch)/dinner 18.75 **st.** and a la carte 4.65 – **30 rm** (dinner included) 46.00/110.00 **st.** – SB.

Bolt Head, South Sands, TQ8 8LL, ℘ 843751, Fax 843060, ≤ estuary, heated – TV ☎ P. AE VISA Z z
14 March-9 November – **Meals** (buffet lunch) 15.00/40.00 **t.** – **28 rm** (dinner included) 82.00/184.00 **st.** – SB.

Grafton Towers, Moult Rd, TQ8 8LG, ℘ 842882, ≤ estuary, – rest TV P. VISA Z v
April-September – **Meals** (dinner only) 16.00 and a la carte 4.75 – **13 rm** 31.00/65.00 **st.** – SB.

The Wood, De Courcy Rd, Moult Hill, TQ8 8LQ, by Moult Rd ℘ 842778, Fax 844277, ≤ estuary, – rest TV P. AE Z e
March-November – **Meals** (by arrangement) 16.00 **t.** – **5 rm** 28.00/76.00 **t.** – SB.

Bay View without rest., Bennett Rd, TQ8 8JJ, ℘ 842238, ≤ estuary – P. VISA. Z o
Easter-September – **3 rm** 50.00 **s.**

at Soar Mill Cove SW : 4 ¼ m. by A 381 via Malborough village – Y – ✉ Salcombe – ☎ 01548 :

Soar Mill Cove, TQ7 3DS, ℘ 561566, Fax 561223, ≤, heated, , , – rest TV ☎ P. VISA.
11 February-October – **Meals** (light lunch)/dinner 32.00 **t.** 6.50 – **16 rm** 100.00/154.00 **t.** – SB.

at Hope Cove W : 4 m. by A 381 via Malborough village – Y – ✉ Kingsbridge – ☎ 01548 :.

Lantern Lodge, TQ7 3HE, by Grand View Rd ℘ 561280, Fax 561736, ≤, , , – rest TV ☎ P. VISA JCB.
March-November – **Meals** (bar lunch)/dinner 14.50 **t.** – **14 rm** (dinner included) 40.30/110.20 **t.** – SB.

Port Light, Bolberry Down, TQ7 3DY, SE : 2 ¼ m. via Inner Hope ℘ 561384, ≤, – TV P. VISA
closed January and Monday February-April, November-December – **Meals** a la carte 10.25/17.75 **t.** 4.50 – **5 rm** (dinner included) 60.00 **t.** – SB.

SALE

Gtr. Manchester 402 403 404 N 23 – pop. 56 052 – ✉ Manchester – ☎ 0161.

Sale Lodge, Golf Rd ℘ 973 3404.

London 212 – Liverpool 36 – Manchester 6 – Sheffield 43.

Amblehurst, 44 Washway Rd, M33 1QZ, on A 56 ℘ 973 8800, Fax 905 1697, – rm TV ☎ P. AE VISA.
Meals *(closed Saturday lunch, Sunday dinner and Bank Holidays)* 11.95/13.95 **t.** and a la carte – **39 rm** 60.00/75.00 **t.**

Lennox Lea, Irlam Rd, M33 2BH, ℘ 973 1764, Fax 969 6059, – rest TV ☎ P. AE VISA
Meals *(closed Sunday and Bank Holidays)* (dinner only) 10.95 **t.** and a la carte 4.95 – **30 rm** 43.50/53.50 **t.**

Cornerstones, 230 Washway Rd, M33 4RA, ℘ 283 6909, Fax 283 6909, – TV ☎ P. VISA.
Meals *(closed Friday to Sunday)* (dinner only) 10.00/12.00 **s.** 4.50 – 3.00 – **9 rm** 21.50/40.00 **s.** – SB.

Summer Palace, 11-15 Tatton Rd, M33 1EB, ℘ 973 9980, Fax 976 2243 – . AE VISA – **Meals** - Chinese (Peking) - (dinner only) 10.00/40.00 **t.** and a la carte 4.50.

SALFORDS

Surrey 404 T 30 – see Redhill.

SALISBURY

Wilts. 403 404 O 30 The West Country G. – pop. 105 318 – ☎ 01722.

See : City★★ - Cathedral★★★ AC Z – Salisbury and South Wiltshire Museum★★ AC Z **M2** – Close★ Z : Mompesson House★ AC Z **A**, Museum of the Duke of Edinburgh's Royal Regiment★ AC Z **M1** – Sarum St. Thomas Church★ Y **B**.

Envir. : Wilton Village (Wilton House★★★ AC, Royal Wilton Carpet Factory★ AC) W : 3 m. by A 30 Y – Old Sarum★ AC, N : 2 m. by A 345 Y – Woodford (Heale House Garden★) AC, NW : 4½ m. by Stratford Rd Y.

Exc. : Stonehenge★★★ AC, NW : 10 m. by A 345 – Y - and A 303 – Wardour Castle★ AC, W : 15 m. by A 30 Y.

18, 9 Salisbury & South Wilts., Netherhampton ℘ 742645 – 18 High Post, Great Durnford ℘ 782231.

Fish Row, SP1 1EJ ℘ 334956.

London 91 – Bournemouth 28 – Bristol 53 – Southampton 23.

Plan on next page

Milford Hall, 206 Castle St., SP1 3TE, ℘ 417411, Fax 419444 – rest TV ☎ P – 70. AE VISA. Y a
Meals 9.95/25.30 **t.** and dinner a la carte 4.90 – **35 rm** 45.00/67.50 **t.** – SB.

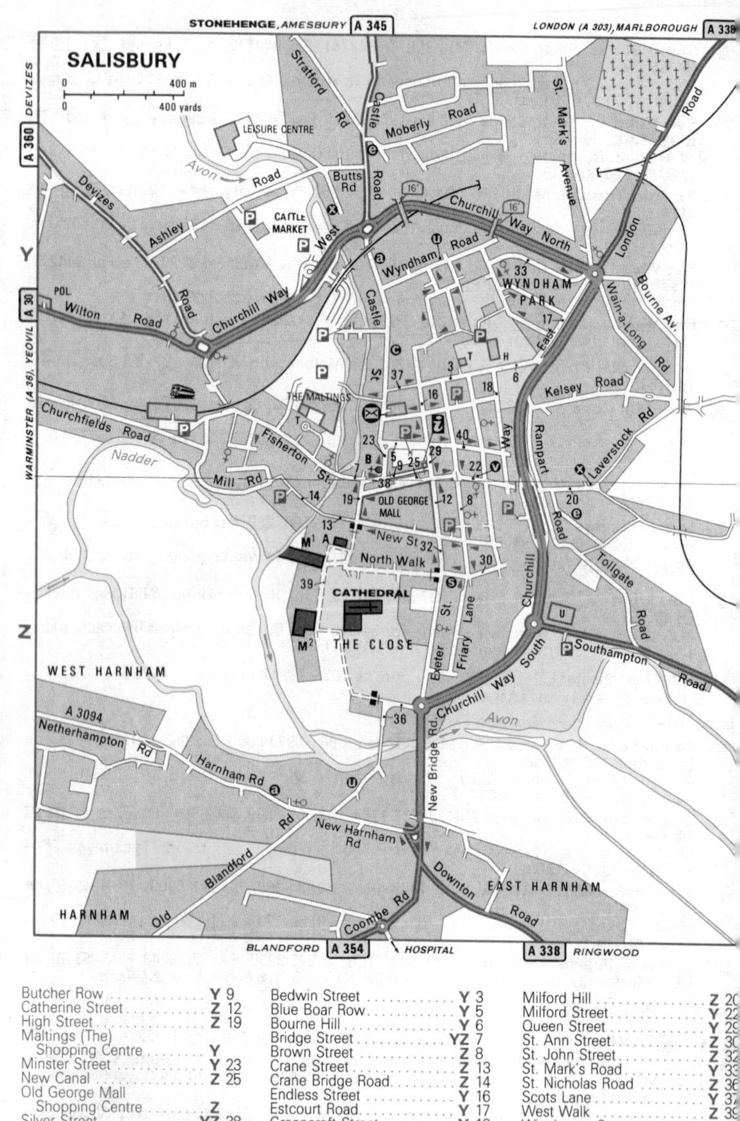

White Hart (Forte Heritage), 1 St. John's St., SP1 2SD, ☎ 327476, Fax 412761 – ⇔ TV ☎ P – 🏛 80. AE ① VISA Z
Meals *(closed Saturday lunch)* a la carte 17.00/25.60 **t.** 🍷 6.95 – ☐ 9.25 – **68 rm** 80.00/120.00 **t.** – SB.

Trafalgar, 33 Milford St., SP1 2AP, ☎ 338686, Fax 414496 – TV ☎ – 🏛 35. AE ① VISA Y
Meals (grill rest.) 9.95 **t.** and a la carte 🍷 4.20 – **18 rm** ☐ 45.00/60.00 **t.** – SB.

Byways House without rest., 31 Fowlers Rd, off Milford Hill, SP1 2QP, ☎ 328364 Fax 322146, – TV P. VISA Z
closed Christmas and New Year – **23 rm** ☐ 23.00/49.00 **st.**

Stratford Lodge, 4 Park Lane, SP1 3NP, N : off Castle Rd, 325177, Fax 412699, –
closed Christmas and New Year – **Meals** (by arrangement) 19.00 **t.** 5.00 – **9 rm** 34.50/54.00 **t.** – SB.

Cricket Field Cottage without rest., Wilton Rd, SP2 7NS, W : 1 ¼ m. on A 36 322595, –
5 rm 25.00/42.00 **st.** – SB.

Victoria Lodge, 61 Castle Rd, SP1 3RH, 320586, Fax 414507 – Y **e**
Meals (by arrangement) 8.50 **t.** – **13 rm** 27.50/40.00 **st.**

Glen Lyn without rest., 6 Bellamy Lane, Milford Hill, SP1 2SP, 327880 – YZ **x**
9 rm 20.00/40.00 **st.** – SB.

Malvern without rest., 31 Hulse Rd, SP1 3LU, 327995, – Y **x**
3 rm 30.00/36.00 **st.**

Wyndham Park Lodge without rest., 51 Wyndham Rd, SP1 3AB, 328851, Fax 328851 – Y **u**
4 rm 18.00/36.00 **s.**

Just Brahm's, 68 Castle St., SP1 3TS, 328402, Fax 328593 – VISA Y **c**
closed Sunday – **Meals** 7.95/9.95 **t.** and a la carte.

at Pitton E : 6 m. by A 30 – Y – Salisbury – 01722 :

Silver Plough, White Hill, SP5 1DZ, 712266 – AE VISA
Meals a la carte 13.95/19.95 **st.** 5.95.

at Whiteparish SE : 7 ½ m. by A 36 on A 27 – Salisbury – 01794 :

Newton Farmhouse, Southampton Rd, SP5 2QL, SE : 1 ½ m. on A 36 884416, , –
Meals (by arrangement) 13.50 – **8 rm** 25.00/40.00.

Brickworth Farmhouse without rest., Brickworth Lane, SP5 2QE, NW : 1 ½ m. off A 36 884663, Fax 884581, –
closed 23 December-2 January – **4 rm** 18.00/36.00 **s.**

at Downton S : 6 m. by A 338 – Z – on B 3080 – 01725 :

Warren without rest., 15 High St., SP5 3PG, 510263, –
closed 20 December-6 January – **6 rm** 30.00/42.00 **st.**

at Woodfalls S : 7 ¾ m. by A 338 – Z – on B 3080 – Salisbury – 01725 :

Woodfalls Inn, The Ridge, SP5 2LN, 513222, Fax 513220 – – 80. AE VISA
Meals 9.95/14.95 **t.** and a la carte 7.40 – **7 rm** 42.95/75.00 **t.**, 1 suite – SB.

at Harnham SW : 1 ½ m. by A 3094 – Salisbury – 01722 :

Rose and Crown (Q.M.H.), Harnham Rd, SP2 8JQ, 399955, Fax 339816, <, « Part 13C inn, riverside setting », – – 80. AE VISA Z **u**
Meals 8.00/30.00 **st.** and a la carte – 8.75 – **28 rm** 90.00/130.00 **st.** – SB.

Grasmere, 70 Harnham Rd, SP2 8JN, 338388, Fax 333710, <, – AE VISA Z **a**
Meals a la carte 13.50/25.50 **st.** 4.50 – **20 rm** 49.50/105.00 **st.** – SB.

at Broad Chalke SW : 8 m. by A 354 and Broad Chalke Valley Rd – Z – Salisbury – 01722 :

Queens Head, SP5 5EN, 780344 – VISA
Meals 10.00/25.00 **t.** and a la carte 6.00 – **4 rm** 30.00/45.00 **t.**

Stoke Farm , SP5 5EF, E : ¾ m. 780209, Fax 781041, « Working farm », , ,
– rm
March-October – **Meals** (by arrangement) 15.00 **st.** – **3 rm** 22.00/44.00 **st.**

at Teffont W : 10 ¼ m. by A 36 – Z – and A 30 on B 3089 – Salisbury – 01722 :

Howard's House with rm Teffont Evias, SP3 5RJ, on lane opposite Black Horse 716392, Fax 716820, <, « Part 17C former dower house », – rest AE VISA
Meals (dinner only and Sunday lunch)/dinner 25.00 **t.** 6.25 – **9 rm** 95.00/115.00 **t.** – SB.

at Little Langford NW : 8 m. by A 36 – Y – and Great Wishford rd – Salisbury – 01722 :.

Little Langford Farmhouse without rest., SP3 4NR, 790205, <, « Working farm », , park –
closed 24 December-1 January – **3 rm** 26.00/38.00 **st.**

ATS 155 Wilton Rd 336789 ATS 28 St. Edmund's Church St. 322390/322451

SALTASH Cornwall 403 H 32 The West Country G. – pop. 14 139 – ☎ 01752.
Envir. : Antony House★, S : 1 m. on A 38.
Exc. : St. Germans Church★, SW : 7 m. by A 38 and B 3249.
18, 18 St. Mellion ☎ (01579) 50101 – 18 China Fleet C.C. ☎ 848668.
♦London 246 – Exeter 38 – ♦Plymouth 5 – Truro 49.

Granada Lodge without rest., Callington Rd, Carkeel, PL12 6LF, NW : 1½ m. by A 388 c A 38 at Saltash Service Area ☎ 848408, Reservations (Freephone) 0800 555300 – ☎ & P. AE VISA.
31 rm 39.95 **st.**

ATS 99 St. Stephens Rd ☎ 848469

SALTFORD Avon 403 404 M 29 – see Bristol.

SAMLESBURY Lancs. 402 M 22 – see Preston.

SAMPFORD PEVERELL Devon 403 J 31 pop. 1 091 – ✉ Tiverton – ☎ 01884.
♦London 184 – Barnstaple 34 – Exeter 20 – Taunton 19.

Parkway House, EX16 7BJ, ☎ 820255, Fax 820780, – TV ☎ P – 130. AE VISA JCB.
Meals 10.50 **t.** and a la carte 3.85 – **10 rm** 35.00/45.00 **st.** – SB.

Old Cottage Inn, ✉ Uffculme, EX15 3ES, E : 1¾ m. by A 361 on A 38 ☎ 840328 – TV P AE VISA JCB.
closed 25 and 26 December – **Meals** (in bar) a la carte approx. 9.50 **t.** 4.00 – **10 rm** 33.50 **st.** – SB.

SAMPFORD PEVERELL SERVICE AREA Devon 403 J 31 – ✉ Tiverton – ☎ 01884.
♦London 184 – Barnstaple 34 – Exeter 20 – Taunton 19.

Forte Travelodge, EX16 7HD, M 5 junction 27 ☎ 821087, Reservations (Freephone 0800 850950 – TV & P. AE VISA.
Meals (grill rest.) – **40 rm** 34.50 **t.**

SANDBACH Ches. 402 403 404 M 24 – pop. 15 839 – ☎ 01270.
18 Malkins Bank ☎ 765931.
♦London 177 – ♦Liverpool 44 – ♦Manchester 28 – ♦Stoke-on-Trent 16.

Chimney House (Country Club), Congleton Rd, CW11 OST, E : 1 ½ m. on A 53 ☎ 764141, Fax 768916, – TV ☎ P – 120. AE VISA.
Meals 12.00/18.00 **t.** and a la carte – 7.50 – **48 rm** 65.00/110.00 **st.** – SB.

Old Hall, Newcastle Rd, CW11 OAL, ☎ 761221, Fax 762551, « 17C coaching inn », rest TV ☎ P. AE VISA JCB.
Meals *(closed Sunday dinner)* (dinner only and Sunday lunch)/dinner 12.00 **t.** and a la carte 5.75 – **14 rm** 62.50/75.00 **t.** – SB.

Saxon Cross, Holmes Chapel Rd, CW11 9SE, E : 1¼ m. by A 534 ☎ 763281, Fax 76872 – TV ☎ P – 50. AE VISA.
Meals *(closed Saturday lunch, Sunday dinner and Bank Holidays)* 8.60/15.00 **st.** and dinner a la carte 5.50 – **52 rm** 59.50/69.00 **st.** – SB.

SANDIACRE Derbs. 402 403 404 Q 25 – see Nottingham (Notts.).

SANDIWAY Ches. – ✉ Northwich – ☎ 01606.
♦London 191 – ♦Liverpool 34 – ♦Manchester 22 – ♦Stoke-on-Trent 26.

Nunsmere Hall, Tarporley Rd, CW8 2ES, SW : 1½ m. by A 556 on A 49 ☎ 889100 Fax 889055, ←, « Part Victorian house on wooded peninsula », park – TV ☎ P – 50. AE VISA JCB.
Meals 16.95/46.00 **st.** and dinner a la carte 7.25 – 13.50 – **31 rm** 95.00/135.00 **st.** 1 suite – SB.

SANDPLACE Cornwall – see Looe.

SANDRINGHAM Norfolk 402 404 V 25 Great Britain G. – pop. 430 – ✉ King's Lynn – ☎ 01485
See : Sandringham House★ *AC.*
♦London 111 – King's Lynn 8 – ♦Norwich 50.

Park House, PE35 6EH, ☎ 543000, Fax 540663, « Former Royal residence » Restricted to physically disabled and their companions, heated, park – rm TV ☎ & P. AE VISA.
closed 14 to 21 December – **Meals** (buffet lunch)/dinner 13.00 **st.** 5.00 – **16 rm** 40.00/128.00 **st.**

SANDWICH Kent 404 Y 30 Great Britain G. – pop. 4 729 – ☎ 01304.
See : Town★.
The Guildhall, Cattle Market, CT13 9AH ☎ 613565 (summer only).
♦London 72 – Canterbury 13 – ♦Dover 12 – Maidstone 41 – Margate 9.

Bell, The Quay, CT13 9EF, ☎ 613388, Fax 615308 – rm TV ☎ P – 120. AE VISA
Meals 9.95/21.50 **t.** and a la carte 5.00 – **29 rm** 70.00/120.00 **t.** – SB.

ANDY Beds. 404 T 27 – pop. 8 989 – ☎ 01767.
, 18 John O'Gaunt, Sutton Park, Biggleswade ☎ 260360.
ondon 49 – Bedford 8 – ◆Cambridge 24 – Peterborough 35.

Holiday Inn Garden Court, Girtford Bridge, London Rd, SG19 1DH, W : ¾ m. by B 1042 at junction of A 1 with A 603 ☎ 692220, Fax 680452 – rm TV ☎ P – 200. AE VISA JCB.
Meals *(closed Sunday)* (dinner only) 15.00 **st.** and a la carte – 6.50 – **56 rm** 45.00 **st.** – SB.

Highfield Farm without rest., Great North Rd, SG19 2AQ, N : 2 m. by B 1042 on A 1 (southbound carriageway) ☎ 682332, park – TV P
closed Christmas – **6 rm** 20.00/40.00 **s.**

ANDYPARK Devon 403 I 31 – see Chagford.

ARISBURY Hants. 403 404 Q 31 – pop. 5 805 – ✉ Southampton – ☎ 01489.
London 90 – ◆Portsmouth 16 – ◆Southampton 6.

Dormy House, 21 Barnes Lane, Sarisbury Green, SO31 7DA, S : 1 m. ☎ 572626 – rm TV ☎ P. AE VISA.
Meals (by arrangement) 9.95 **st.** 3.25 – **12 rm** 37.50/46.00 **st.**

Town plans : *the names of main shopping streets are indicated in red at the beginning of the list of streets.*

AUNTON Devon 403 H 30 – ✉ Braunton – ☎ 01271.
nvir. : Braunton★ – St. Brannock's Church★, E : 2½ m. on B 3231 – Braunton Burrows★, E : ½ n. on B 3231.
, 18 Saunton ☎ 812436.
London 230 – Barnstaple 8 – Exeter 48.

Preston House, EX33 1LG, ☎ 890472, Fax 890555, ≤ Saunton Sands, , heated, – TV ☎ P. AE VISA.
March-November – **Meals** (bar lunch)/dinner 15.00 **t.** 4.50 – **15 rm** 35.00/85.00 **t.** – SB.

SAWBRIDGEWORTH Herts. 404 U 28 – pop. 7 901 – ☎ 01279.
London 26 – ◆Cambridge 32 – Chelmsford 17.

The Manor of Groves , High Wych, CM21 0LA, SW : 1 ½ m. by A 1184 ☎ 600777, Fax 600374, ≤, , 18, , park, – TV ☎ P – 70. AE VISA.
Meals *(closed Saturday lunch)* 10.95/13.95 **t.** and a la carte 6.95 – **32 rm** 75.00/125.00 **st.** – SB.

SAWLEY Lancs. 402 M 22 – pop. 237 – ☎ 01765.
London 242 – ◆Blackpool 39 – ◆Leeds 44 – ◆Liverpool 54.

Spread Eagle, BB7 4NH, ☎ (01200) 441202, Fax 441973 – TV ☎ P. AE VISA
Meals 11.00/18.00 **t.** and a la carte 5.75 – **10 rm** 45.00/55.00 **st.** – SB.

SCALBY N. Yorks. 402 S 21 – see Scarborough.

SCARBOROUGH N. Yorks. 402 S 21 – pop. 38 809 – ☎ 01723.
18 Scarborough North Cliff, North Cliff Av., Burniston Rd ☎ 360786, NW : 2 m. by A 165 Y –
18 Scarborough South Cliff, Deepdale Av., off Filey Rd ☎ 360522, S : 1 m. by A 165 Z.
St. Nicholas Cliff, YO11 2EP ☎ 373333.
◆London 253 – ◆Kingston-upon-Hull 47 – ◆Leeds 67 – ◆Middlesbrough 52.

Plan on next page

Crown (Forte), 7-11 Esplanade, YO11 2AG, ☎ 373491, Fax 362271 – TV ☎ – 160. AE VISA JCB. Z i
Meals 9.95/16.95 **st.** and dinner a la carte 6.05 – 8.50 – **77 rm** 55.00/65.00 **t.**, 1 suite – SB.

Palm Court, St. Nicholas Cliff, YO11 2ES, ☎ 368161, Fax 371547, , – TV ☎ – 100. AE VISA. Z e
Meals 9.25/16.50 **t.** and dinner a la carte 5.70 – **46 rm** 37.00/78.00 **t.**, 1 suite – SB.

Bradley Court, 7-9 Filey Rd, YO11 2SE, ☎ 360476, Fax 376661 – TV ☎ P – 120. AE VISA Z r
Meals (bar lunch)/dinner 12.50 **t.** 7.50 – **40 rm** 39.50/79.00 **t.** – SB.

Pickwick Inn without rest., Huntriss Row, YO11 2ED, ☎ 375787, Fax 374284 – TV ☎. AE VISA. Z c
10 rm 22.50/35.00 **st.**

Old Mill, Mill St., YO11 1SW, by Victoria Rd ☎ 372735, Fax 372735, « Restored 18C windmill » – TV P. VISA Z u
Meals 12.00 **t.** 3.25 – **11 rm** (dinner included) 32.00/64.00 – SB.

Jade Garden, 121 Falsgrave Rd, YO12 5EG, ☎ 369099, Fax 363135 – AE VISA Z v
Meals - Chinese - (dinner only) 14.50 **t.** and a la carte.

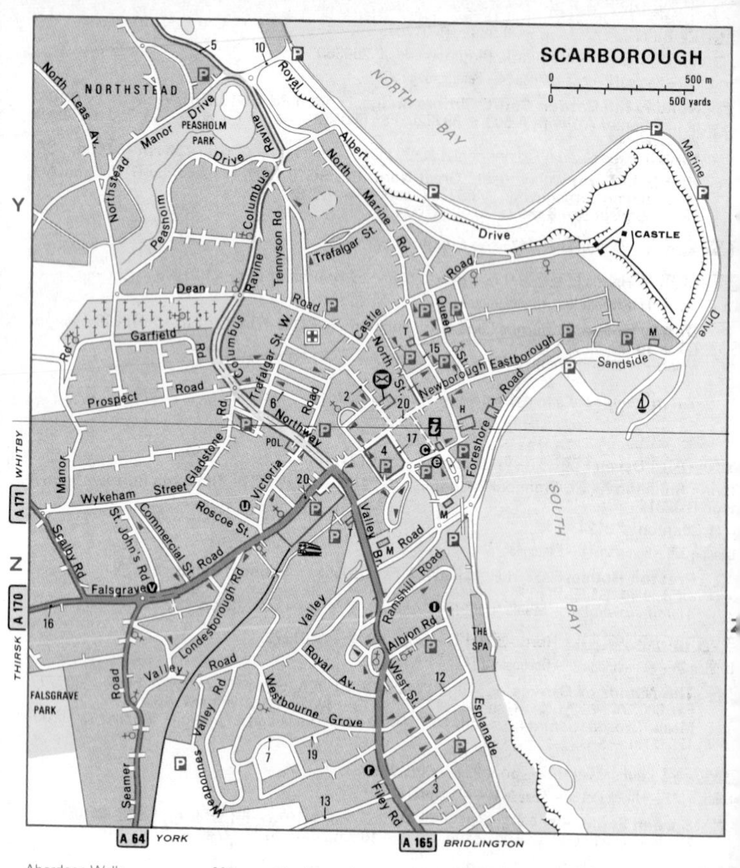

at Scalby NW : 3 m. by A 171 – Z – ✉ Scarborough – ☎ 01723 :

Wrea Head 🐎, YO13 0PB, by Barmoor Lane ☎ 378211, Fax 371780, ≤, « Victorian country house », park – TV ☎ P – 🏛 25. AE VISA
Meals 12.50/28.50 **t.** and dinner a la carte 🍷 7.50 – **20 rm** ☕ 57.50/115.00 **st.**, 1 suite – SB.

at Hackness NW : 7 m. by A 171 – Z – ✉ Scarborough – ☎ 01723 :

Hackness Grange 🐎, YO13 0JW, ☎ 882345, Fax 882391, « 18C country house », park, – rest TV ☎ P. AE VISA.
Meals 19.95/35.00 **st.** 🍷 6.95 – **27 rm** ☕ 67.50/135.00 **t.**, 1 suite.

SCILLY (Isles of) Cornwall 403 ㉚ **The West Country G.** – pop. 2 048.

See : Islands★ - The Archipelago (≤★★★).

Envir. : St. Agnes : Horsepoint★.

Helicopter service from St. Mary's and Tresco to Penzance : ☎ 0736 (Penzance) 63871.

✈ St. Mary's Airport : ☎ (01720) 422677, E : 1½m. from Hugh Town.

⛴ from Hugh Town to Penzance (Isles of Scilly Steamship Co. Ltd) (summer only) (2 h 40 mn).

ℹ Porthcressa Bank, St. Mary's, TR21 0JY ☎ 01720 (Scillonia) 422536.

Bryher The West Country G. – pop. 78 – ✉ Scillonia – ☎ 01720.

See : Watch Hill (<★) – Hell Bay★.

Hell Bay ⛰, TR23 0PR, ☎ 422947, Fax 423004, ⛱ – ⊭ rest ▣ ☎. ▣ VISA. ✻
April-September – **Meals** (bar lunch)/dinner 19.50 **st.** 5.00 –, **10 suites** ▭ 49.50/140.00 **st.** – SB.

Bank Cottage ⛰, TR23 0PR, ☎ 422612, Fax 422612, <, ⛱ – ⊭ rest. ✻
March-October – **5 rm** ▭ (dinner included) 35.00/76.00 **st.**

St. Martin's The West Country G. pop. 113 – ✉ St. Martin's – ☎ 01720.

See : Viewpoint★★.

St. Martin's ⛰, TR25 0QW, ☎ 422092, Fax 422298, < Tean Sound and islands, « Idyllic island setting », ▣, ⛱ – ⊭ rest ▣ ☎. ▣ AE ◑ VISA
March-October – **Tean : Meals** (bar lunch)/dinner 28.50 **st.** 9.50 – **22 rm** ▭ 40.00/170.00 **st.**, 2 suites – SB.

St. Mary's The West Country G. – pop. 1 607 – ✉ St. Mary's – ☎ 01720.

See : Garrison Walk★ (<★★) – Peninnis Head★.

⛳9 ☎ 422692.

Tregarthen's, Hugh Town, TR21 0PP, ☎ 422540, Fax 422089, < – ▣ ☎. ▣ AE ◑ VISA JCB. ✻
late March-late October – **Meals** (bar lunch) 20.00 **t.** 6.20 – **33 rm** ▭ (dinner included) 65.00/130.00 **t.** – SB.

Star Castle ⛰, TR21 0JA, ☎ 422317, Fax 422343, « Elizabethan fortress », ▣, ⛱, ✻ – ⊭ rest ▣ ☎ Ⓟ. ▣ ◑ VISA
mid March-mid October – **Meals** (bar lunch)/dinner 18.00 **t.** and a la carte – **28 rm** ▭ (dinner included) 49.00/130.00 **t.** – SB.

Atlantic, Hugh St., Hugh Town, TR21 0PL, ☎ 422417, Fax 423009, < St. Mary's Harbour – ⊭ rest ▣ ☎. ▣ VISA
mid February-mid November – **Meals** (dinner only) 22.00 **st.** and a la carte 7.00 – **24 rm** ▭ (dinner included) 61.50/131.00 **st.** – SB.

Carnwethers ⛰, Pelistry Bay, TR21 0NX, ☎ 422415, ≘s, ⛱ heated, ⛱ – ⊭ ▣
May-September – **Meals** 3.60 – **10 rm** ▭ (dinner included) 40.00/94.00 **st.**

Carn Warvel ⛰, Church Rd, Old Town, TR21 0NA, ☎ 422111, ⛱ – ⊭ rest ▣. ✻
March-November – **Meals** 10.50 **st.** 3.20 – **5 rm** ▭ (dinner included) 33.50/63.00 **st.**

Crebinick House, Church St., TR21 0JT, ☎ 422968 – ⊭. ✻
April-October – **Meals** (by arrangement) 8.50 **st.** 4.40 – **6 rm** ▭ (dinner included) 55.75/77.00 **st.**

Tresco The West Country G. – pop. 167 – ✉ New Grimsby – ☎ 01720.

See : Island★ - Abbey Gardens★ *AC* (Lighthouse Way <★★).

Island ⛰, Old Grimsby, TR24 0PU, ☎ 422883, Fax 423008, < St. Martin's and islands, « Idyllic island setting, sub-tropical gardens », ⛱ heated, park, ✻ – ⊭ rest ▣ ☎. ▣ AE VISA JCB. ✻
March-October – **Meals** (bar lunch)/dinner 20.00 **t.** and a la carte – **38 rm** ▭ (dinner included) 95.00/190.00 **t.**, 2 suites.

New Inn, TR24 0QQ, ☎ 422844, Fax 423200, <, ⛱ heated, ⛱ – ⊭ rest ▣ ☎. ▣ VISA JCB. ✻
Meals (bar lunch)/dinner 13.50/21.00 **t.** 7.45 – **12 rm** ▭ (dinner included) 48.00/130.00 **t.** – SB.

SCOLE Norfolk 404 X 26 – see Diss.

SCOTCH CORNER N. Yorks. 402 P 20 – ✉ Richmond – ☎ 01748.

ℹ Pavilion Service Area, A 1, DL10 6PQ ☎ 377677.

♦London 235 – ♦Carlisle 70 – ♦Middlesbrough 25 – Newcastle upon Tyne 43.

Pavilion Lodge without rest., Middleton Tyas Lane, D10 6PQ, ☎ (01325) 377719, Fax 377890 – ⊭ ▣ ♿ Ⓟ. ▣ AE ◑ VISA. ✻
50 rm 39.95 **t.**

Forte Travelodge, Skeeby, DL10 5EQ, S : 1 m. on A 1 (northbound carriageway) ☎ 823768, Reservations (Freephone) 0800 850950 – ▣ ♿ Ⓟ. ▣ AE VISA. ✻
Meals (grill rest.) – **40 rm** 34.50 **t.**

SCUNTHORPE Humbs. 402 S 23 – pop. 61 550 – ☎ 01724.

⛳18 Ashby Decoy, Burringham Rd ☎ 842913 – ⛳9 Kingsway ☎ 840945 – ⛳9, ⛳9 Grange Park, Butterwick Rd, Messingham ☎ 762945.

✈ Humberside Airport : ☎ (01652) 688456, E : 15 m. by A 18.

♦London 167 – ♦Leeds 54 – Lincoln 30 – ♦Sheffield 45.

Wortley House, Rowland Rd, DN16 1SU, ☎ 842223, Fax 280646 – ▣ ☎ Ⓟ – 🏛 250. ▣ AE ◑ VISA JCB
Meals 12.75/25.00 **st.** and a la carte 4.75 – **38 rm** ▭ 67.50 **st.** – SB.

at Broughton E : 7 m. by A 18 – ✉ Scunthorpe – ☎ 01652 :

Briggate Lodge Inn, Ermine St., DN20 0AQ, S : 1 m. ☎ 650770, Fax 650495, – ⇔ rm TV ☎ & P – 60. AE VISA JCB.
Meals 15.50/16.50 **st.** and a la carte 5.50 – **48 rm** 77.00/85.00 **st.**, 2 suites – SB.

ATS Grange Lane North ☎ 868191

SEACROFT W. Yorks. 402 ⑩ – see Leeds.

SEAFORD E. Sussex 404 U 31 – pop. 20 933 – ☎ 01323.

Southdown Rd ☎ 890139.

Station Approach, BN25 2AR ☎ 897426.

London 65 – Brighton 14 – Folkestone 64.

Quincy's, 42 High St., BN25 1PL, ☎ 895490 – AE VISA JCB
closed Sunday dinner and Monday – **Meals** (dinner only and Sunday lunch)/dinner 21.45 **t** 4.75.

at Westdean E : 3¼ m by A 259 – ☎ 01323 :

Old Parsonage without rest., BN25 4AL, ☎ 870432, ←, « 13C King John house », – ⇔ P.
closed Christmas and New Year – **3 rm** 35.00/65.00 **s.**

SEAHOUSES Northd 401 402 P 17 **Great Britain G.** – ☎ 01665.

Envir. : Farne Islands★ (by boat from harbour).

Beadnell Rd ☎ 720794.

Car Park, Seafield Rd, NE68 7SR ☎ 720884 (summer only).

London 328 – Edinburgh 80 – Newcastle upon Tyne 46.

Olde Ship, 9 Main St., NE68 7RD, ☎ 720200, Fax 721383, « Nautical memorabilia » – TV ☎ P. VISA JCB.
closed December and January – **Meals** (bar lunch)/dinner 12.50 **t.** 4.60 – **15 rm** (dinner included) 43.00/86.00 **t.** – SB.

Beach House, 12a St. Aidans, Seafront, NE68 7SR, ☎ 720337, Fax 720921, ←, – ⇔ rest TV ☎ & P. VISA
April-October – **Meals** (dinner only) 18.00 **t.** – **14 rm** 37.00/74.00 **t.** – SB.

SEALAND Clwyd 402 403 L 24 – see Chester.

SEATOLLER Cumbria – see Keswick.

SEATON BURN Tyne and Wear 402 P 18 – see Newcastle upon Tyne.

SEATON CAREW Cleveland 402 Q 20 – see Hartlepool.

SEAVIEW I.O.W. 403 404 Q 31 – see Wight (Isle of).

SEAVINGTON ST. MARY Somerset 403 L 31 **The West Country G.** – pop. 367 – ✉ Ilminster – ☎ 01460.

Envir. : Ilminster★ - St. Mary's★★, W : 2 m..

London 142 – Taunton 14 – Yeovil 11.

Pheasant, Water St., TA19 0QH, ☎ 240502, Fax 242388, – TV ☎ P. AE VISA.
Meals *(closed Sunday dinner)* (dinner only and Sunday lunch)/dinner a la carte 18.50/25.50 **t.** 4.75 – **8 rm** 50.00/80.00 **t.** – SB.

SEDGEMOOR SERVICE AREA Somerset – ☎ 01934.

Somerset Visitor Centre, M 5 South, BS26 2UF ☎ 750833.

Forte Travelodge, BS24 0JL, M 5 (northbound carriageway) between junctions 22 and 21 ☎ 750831, Fax 750450, Reservations (Freephone) 0800 850950 – TV & P. AE VISA.
Meals (grill rest.) – **40 rm** 34.50 **t.**

SEDLESCOMBE E. Sussex 404 V 31 – pop. 1 631 (inc. Whatlington) – ✉ Battle – ☎ 01424.

London 56 – Hastings 7 – Lewes 26 – Maidstone 27.

Brickwall, The Green, TN33 0QA, ☎ 870253, Fax 870785, heated, – TV ☎ P. AE VISA
Meals 11.50/17.50 **t.** 5.20 – **23 rm** (dinner included) 55.00/94.00 **t.** – SB.

SELBY N. Yorks. 402 Q 22 **Great Britain G.** – pop. 12 600 – 01757.
See : Abbey Church★.
Park St., YO8 0AA ✆ 703263.
London 202 – ◆Kingston-upon-Hull 36 – ◆Leeds 23 – York 14.

Londesborough Arms, Market Pl., YO8 0NS, ✆ 707355, Fax 701607 – 45.
Meals 9.95 **st.** and a la carte 4.15 – **26 rm** 45.00/55.00 **st.** – SB.

ATS Unit 1, Canal Rd (off Bawtry Rd) ✆ 703245/702147

SELLING Kent 404 W 30 – pop. 687 – ✉ Faversham – 01795.
London 56 – Canterbury 10 – ◆Dover 28 – Maidstone 25.

Parkfield House without rest., Hogben's Hill, ME13 9QU, NW : ½ m. ✆ (01227) 752898,
closed 24 to 26 December – **4 rm** 17.50/35.00 **s.**

SELSIDE Cumbria – see Kendal.

SEMINGTON Wilts. 403 404 N 29 – see Trowbridge.

SEMLEY Dorset 403 404 N 30 – see Shaftesbury.

SETTLE N. Yorks. 402 N 21 – pop. 2 730 – 01729.
Giggleswick ✆ 825288.
Town Hall, Cheapside, BD24 9EJ ✆ 825192.
◆London 238 – Bradford 34 – Kendal 30 – ◆Leeds 41.

Falcon Manor, Skipton Rd, BD24 9BD, ✆ 823814, Fax 822087, – rest
Meals (bar lunch Monday to Saturday)/dinner 19.50 **t.** and a la carte 4.35 – **19 rm** 55.00/110.00 **t.** – SB.

SEVENOAKS Kent 404 U 30 **Great Britain G.** – pop. 19 617 – 01732.
Envir. : Knole★★ *AC*, SE : ½ m. – Ightham Mote★ *AC*, E : 5 m. by A 25.
Woodlands , Tinkerpot Lane ✆ (01959) 523805 – Darenth Valley, Station Rd, Shoreham ✆ (01959) 522944.
Buckhurst Lane, TN13 1LQ ✆ 450305.
◆London 26 – Guildford 40 – Maidstone 17.

Royal Oak, Upper High St., TN13 1HY, ✆ 451109, Fax 740187, – rest rest – 35.
Meals *(closed Saturday lunch)* 8.95/13.95 **st.** and a la carte 7.95 – **37 rm** 60.00/80.00 **st.** – SB.

at Ivy Hatch E : 4¾ m. by A 25 on Coach Rd – ✉ Sevenoaks – 01732 :.

The Chantecler at The Plough, TN15 0NL, ✆ 810268, –
Meals 12.95 and a la carte.

SEVERN VIEW SERVICE AREA Avon – ✉ Bristol – 01454.

Pavilion Lodge without rest., BS12 3BJ, M 4 junction 21 ✆ 633313, Fax 633819 –
51 rm 39.95 **t.**

SHAFTESBURY Dorset 403 404 N 30 **The West Country G.** – pop. 6 203 – 01747.
See : Gold Hill★ (<★) – Local History Museum★ *AC*.
Envir. : Wardour Castle★ *AC*, NE : 5 m..
8 Bell St., SP7 8AE ✆ 853514.
◆London 115 – Bournemouth 31 – ◆Bristol 47 – Dorchester 29 – Salisbury 20.

Royal Chase, Royal Chase Roundabout, SP7 8DB, SE : at junction of A 30 with A 350 ✆ 853355, Fax 851969, – – 190.
Meals 13.50/18.50 **st.** and a la carte 7.00 – **34 rm** 55.00/97.40 **st.** – SB.

La Fleur de Lys, 25 Salisbury St., SP7 8EL, ✆ 853717 –
closed Monday lunch, Sunday dinner and 1 week January – **Meals** 19.45 **t.** (dinner) and a la carte 24.00/27.50 **t.**

Jesters, 4 Bell St., SP7 8AR, ✆ 854444 –
closed Sunday dinner, Monday and October – **Meals** a la carte 10.15/19.15 **t.** 4.75.

at Semley N : 3½ m. by A 350 – ✉ Shaftesbury – 01747 :

Benett Arms, SP7 9AS, ✆ 830221, Fax 830152 –
closed 25 and 26 December – **Meals** a la carte 12.80/20.85 **t.** 4.25 – **5 rm** 29.00/44.00 **t.** – SB.

at Compton Abbas S : 4 m. on A 350 – ✉ Shaftesbury – 01747 :

Old Forge without rest., Chapel Hill, SP7 0NQ, ✆ 811881, Fax 811881, « Blacksmiths forge museum »,
3 rm 25.00/45.00 **st.**

at Motcombe NW : 2½ m. by B 3081 – ✉ Shaftesbury – ☎ 01747 :

Coppleridge Inn ⛰, SP7 9HW, N : 1 m. on Mere rd ☎ 851980, Fax 851858, ⛱, park, ✂ – TV ☎ P. AE VISA
Meals a la carte 9.45/15.50 **t.** 4.00 – **10 rm** ☐ 40.00/70.00 **t.** – SB.

SHALDON Devon 403 J 32 – see Teignmouth.

SHANKLIN I.O.W. 403 404 Q 32 – see Wight (Isle of).

SHAW Wilts. 403 404 N 29 – see Melksham.

SHAWBURY Shrops. 402 403 404 M 25 – pop. 2 457 – ✉ Shrewsbury – ☎ 01939.
♦London 159 – ♦Birmingham 43 – Chester 39 – ♦Stoke-on-Trent 29 – Shrewsbury 7.

The Sett ⛰, Stanton-upon-Hine-Heath, SY4 4LR, NE : 2¼ m. by B 5063 ☎ 250391 « Working farm » – ⊁ P. VISA
closed Christmas and New Year – **Meals** 14.00 **st.** 3.00 – **3 rm** ☐ 22.00/40.00 **st.**

SHEDFIELD Hants. 403 404 Q 31 – pop. 3 558 – ✉ Southampton – ☎ 01329.
18, 9 Meon Valley Hotel, Sandy Lane, ☎ 833455, off A 334.
♦London 75 – ♦Portsmouth 13 – ♦Southampton 10.

Meon Valley H. Country Club Resort (Country Club), Sandy Lane, SO3 2HQ, off A 334 ☎ 833455, Fax 834411, ⛹, ♨, ⛆, 18, park, ✂, squash – ⊁ TV ☎ P – 🎪 100. AE VISA. ✗
Meals *(closed Saturday lunch)* 22.00/42.00 **t.** 4.50 – ☐ 9.00 – **83 rm** 75.00/105.00 **t.** – SB.

SHEEPWASH Devon 403 H 31 – see Hatherleigh.

SHEERNESS Kent 404 W 29 – pop. 11 653 – ☎ 01795.
♦London 52 – Canterbury 24 – Maidstone 20.

Hotels and Restaurants see : Maidstone SW : 20 m.

SHEFFIELD S. Yorks. 402 403 404 P 23 **Great Britain G.** – pop. 501 202 – ☎ 0114.
See : Cutlers' Hall★ CZ **A** – Cathedral Church of SS. Peter and Paul CZ **B** : Shrewsbury Chapel (Tomb★).
18 Tinsley Park, Darnall ☎ 256 0237 BY – 18 Beauchief Municipal, Abbey Lane ☎ 262 0648/262 0040 AZ – 18 Birley Wood, Birley Lane ☎ 264 7262, BZ – 18 Concord Park, Shiregreen Lane ☎ 257 0274/257 0053, BY – 18 Hillsborough, Worrall Rd ☎ 234 3608, AY – 18 Abbeydale, Twentywell Lane, Dore ☎ 236 0763, AZ – 18 Lees Hall, Hemsworth Rd, Norton ☎ 255 4402, AZ.
i Peace Gdns, S1 2HH ☎ 273 4671/2 – Railway Station, Sheaf St., S1 2BP ☎ 279 5901.
♦London 174 – ♦Leeds 36 – ♦Liverpool 80 – ♦Manchester 41 – ♦Nottingham 44.

Plans on following pages

Holiday Inn Sheffield, Victoria Station Rd, S4 7YE, ☎ 276 8822, Fax 272 4519 – ⊞ ⊁ rm TV ☎ P – 🎪 350. AE VISA JCB DY **a**
Meals *(closed Saturday lunch)* 12.95/15.95 **st.** and a la carte 4.95 – ☐ 9.95 – **100 rm** 77.00/109.00 **st.** – SB.

Charnwood, 10 Sharrow Lane, S11 8AA, ☎ 258 9411, Fax 255 5107 – ⊞ TV ☎ P – 🎪 80. AE VISA. ✗ CZ **u**
Brasserie Leo : Meals 12.00/25.00 **t.** and a la carte 4.75 – **Henfrey's : Meals** *(closed Sunday and Monday)* (dinner only) a la carte approx. 25.95 **t.** 4.50 – **22 rm** ☐ 75.00/90.00 **t.** – SB.

Swallow, Kenwood Rd, S7 1NQ, ☎ 258 3811, Fax 250 0138, ⛹, ♨, ⛆, ⛆, ⛱, park – ⊞ ⊁ rm TV ☎ P – 🎪 200. AE VISA AZ **r**
Meals 13.25/18.00 **st.** and a la carte 7.00 – **117 rm** ☐ 87.00/128.00 **st.** – SB.

Beauchief (Country Club), 161 Abbeydale Rd South, S7 2QW, SW : 3½ m. on A 621 ☎ 262 0500, Fax 235 0197, ⛹, ♨ – ⊁ rm TV ☎ ♿ P – 🎪 100. AE VISA. ✗
Meals 9.95/16.95 **t.** and a la carte 6.00 – ☐ 7.50 – **41 rm** 68.00 **st.** – SB.

Forte Posthouse, Manchester Rd, Hallam, S10 5DX, ☎ 267 0067, Fax 268 2620, ≤, ⛹, ♨, ⛆ – ⊞ ⊁ rm TV ☎ P – 🎪 300. AE VISA JCB AZ **a**
Meals 20.00 **st.** and a la carte 4.95 – ☐ 7.95 – **133 rm** 59.00 **st.**, 2 suites – SB.

Harley, 334 Glossop Rd, S10 2HW, ☎ 275 2288, Fax 272 2383 – ⊁ rm ▤ rest TV ☎ – 🎪 20. AE VISA. ✗ CZ **e**
Meals *(closed Saturday lunch and Sunday)* (dancing Friday and Saturday evenings) 9.75/36.50 **st.** and a la carte – ☐ 3.50 – **22 rm** 50.00/80.00 **t.**

Novotel, Arundel Gate, S1 2PR, ☎ 278 1781, Fax 278 7744, ⛆ – ⊞ ⊁ rm ▤ TV ☎ ♿ P – 🎪 170. AE VISA DZ **a**
Meals (bar lunch)/dinner 15.75 **st.** and a la carte 5.75 – ☐ 7.50 – **144 rm** 55.00/95.00 **st.**

Comfort Inn without rest., George St., S1 2PF, ☎ 273 9939, Fax 276 8332 – ⊞ ⊁ rm TV ☎. AE VISA JCB DZ **e**
closed 24 December-1 January – ☐ 5.95 – **50 rm** 39.95/44.95 **st.**

SHEFFIELD

BUILT UP AREA

See following page

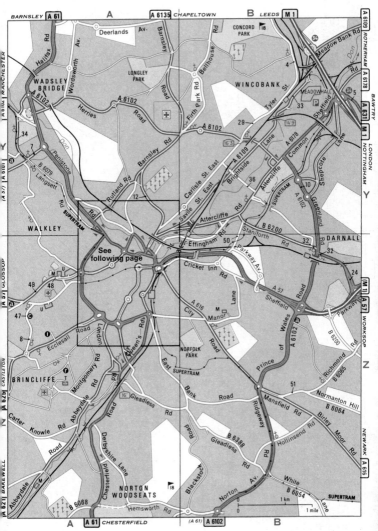

Forte Travelodge, 340 Prince of Wales Rd, S2 1FF, ℘ 253 0935, Fax 264 2731, Reservations (Freephone) 0800 850950 – rm TV ☎ & P – 80. AE VISA. BZ **a**
Meals (grill rest.) – **60 rm** 34.50 **t.**

Westbourne House without rest., 25 Westbourne Rd, S10 2QQ, ℘ 266 0109, Fax 266 7778, – TV P. AE VISA JCB AZ **c**
9 rm 43.00/60.00 **st.**

SHEFFIELD

CENTRE

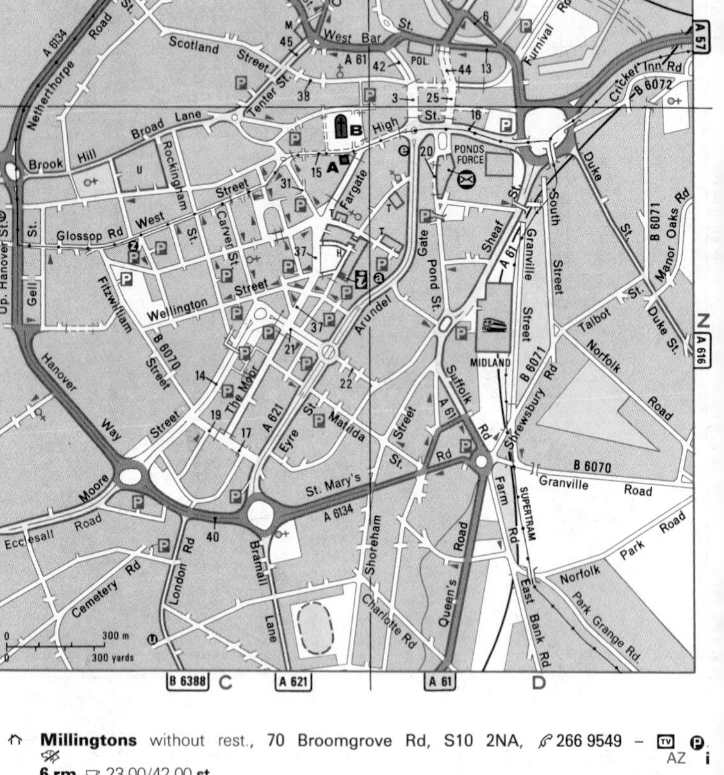

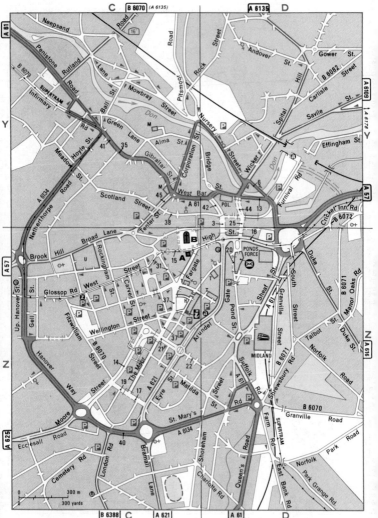

⌂ **Millingtons** without rest., 70 Broomgrove Rd, S10 2NA, ℘ 266 9549 – TV P. (no dogs) AZ **i**
6 rm ☕ 23.00/42.00 **st.**

⌂ **Coniston** without rest., 90 Beechwood Rd, Hillsborough, S6 4LQ, ℘ 233 9680 – TV P. (no dogs) AY **a**
closed Christmas and New Year – **4 rm** ☕ 15.00/30.00 **st.**

XX **Le Neptune,** 141 West St., S1 4EW, ☎ 279 6677, Fax 275 7868 – AE VISA CZ z
Meals - French - *(closed Saturday lunch and Sunday)* 10.00/17.95 **st.** and a la carte.

X **Rafters,** 220 Oakbrook Rd, Nether Green, S11 7ED, SW : 2½ m. by A 625 ☎ 230 4819. AE
closed Sunday, Tuesday and 28 August-10 September – **Meals** (dinner only) 16.95 **t.**

at Grenoside N : 4½ m. on A 61 – AY – ✉ Sheffield – ☎ 0114 :

Holme Lane Farm without rest., 38 Halifax Rd, S30 3PB, ☎ 246 8858, – TV ☎ P. VISA.
7 rm 26.00/45.00 **st.**

at Whitley N : 5 m. by A 6135 – AY – ✉ Sheffield – ☎ 0114 :

Whitley Hall, Elliot Lane, Grenoside, S30 3NR, off Whitley Lane ☎ 245 4444, Fax 245 5414, , park – TV ☎ P – 70. AE VISA
Meals *(closed Saturday lunch, 25 and 26 December, 1 January and Bank Holiday Mondays)* 13.00/22.00 **t.** and a la carte – **15 rm** 60.00/150.00 **t.**

at Chapeltown N : 6 m. on A 6135 – AY – ✉ Sheffield – ☎ 0114 :

Staindrop Lodge, Lane End, S30 4UH, NW : ½ m. on High Green rd ☎ 284 6727, Fax 284 6783 – TV ☎ P – 80. AE VISA.
Meals *(closed lunch Saturday and Monday, Sunday dinner and Bank Holidays)* 8.10/19.90 **t.** and a la carte 4.00 – **13 rm** 54.00/69.00 **t.** – SB.

XX **Greenhead House,** 84 Burncross Rd, S30 4SF, ☎ 246 9004 – P. VISA
closed Sunday to Tuesday, 2 weeks Easter, 2 weeks mid August and Christmas-New Year – **Meals** (booking essential) (dinner only) 27.75/30.75 **st.** 4.75.

at Ridgeway (Derbs.) SE : 6¾ m. by A 616 off B 6054 – BZ – ✉ Sheffield – ☎ 0114 :

XXX **Old Vicarage,** Ridgeway Moor, S12 3XW, on Marsh Lane rd ☎ 247 5814, Fax 247 7079, – P. AE VISA
closed Sunday dinner, Monday and 27 December-2 January – **Meals** (lunch booking essential) 35.00 **t.** 6.00.

at Meadow Head S : 5¼ m. on A 61 – AZ – ✉ Sheffield – ☎ 0114 :

Sheffield Moat House (Q.M.H.), Chesterfield Rd South, S8 8BW, ☎ 282 9988, Fax 237 8140, , – rm rest TV ☎ P – 500. AE VISA
Meals *(closed Saturday lunch)* 9.50/16.50 **st.** and a la carte – 9.50 – **89 rm** 79.00/92.00 **st.**, 5 suites – SB.

ATS 87/91 Clifton St., Attercliffe ☎ 244 9750/244 9759
ATS Herries Rd ☎ 234 3986/7

SHELLEY W. Yorks. 402 404 O 23 – ✉ Huddersfield – ☎ 01484.

London 193 – Leeds 22 – Manchester 30 – Sheffield 20.

Three Acres Inn, Roydhouse, HD8 8LR, NE : 1½ m. on Flockton rd ☎ 602606, Fax 608411 – rm TV ☎ P. AE VISA.
Meals *(closed Saturday lunch)* 12.95 (lunch) and dinner a la carte 16.15/24.15 5.95 – **19 rm** 47.50/57.50 **t.** – SB.

SHENINGTON Oxon. – see Banbury.

SHEPPERTON Surrey 404 S 29 – pop. 11 589 – ☎ 01932.

London 25.

Plan : see Greater London (South-West)

XX Edwinns, Church Sq., TW17 9JT, S : 1 m. ☎ 223543, Fax 253562

SHEPTON MALLET Somerset 403 404 M 30 The West Country G. – pop. 7 581 – ☎ 01749.

See : Town★ - SS. Peter and Paul's Church★.

Envir. : Evercreech (Church Tower★) SE : 4 m. by A 371 and B 3081 – Downside Abbey★ (Abbey Church★) N : 5½ m. by A 37 and A 367.

Exc. : Longleat House★★★ *AC*, E : 15 m. by A 361 and B 3092 – Wells★★ - Cathedral★★★, Vicars' Close★, Bishop's Palace★ *AC* (≤★★) W : 6 m. by A 371 – Wookey Hole★★ (Caves★ *AC*, Papermill★, Fairground Collection★) W : 6½ m. by B 371 – Glastonbury★★ - Abbey★★★ (Abbots Kitchen★) *AC*, St. John the Baptist★★, Somerset Rural Life Museum★ *AC* – Glastonbury Tor★ (≤★★★) SW : 9 m. by B 3136 and A 361 - Nunney★, E : 8½ m. by A 361.

18 Mendip, Gurney Slade ☎ 840570.

London 127 – Bristol 20 – Southampton 63 – Taunton 31.

Thatched Cottage Inn, 63-67 Charlton Rd, BA4 5QF, ☎ 342058, Fax 343265 rest TV ☎ P. AE VISA JCB.
Meals a la carte 10.50/16.85 **st.** – **8 rm** 44.50/67.50 **st.** – SB.

Shrubbery, Commercial Rd, BA4 5BV, ☎ 346671, Fax 346581, – TV ☎ P. VISA JCB
Meals (closed Sunday dinner to non-residents) 11.95/15.95 **t.** and a la carte 4.255 – **7 rm** 45.00/59.50 **t.** – SB.

XXX **Bowlish House** with rm, Wells Rd, BA4 5JD, W : ½ m. on A 371 ✆ 342022, Fax 342022 – TV P. VISA AE VISA
closed 1 week spring and 1 week autumn – **Meals** (booking essential) (dinner only) 22.50 **st** 4.50 – 3.50 – **3 rm** 48.00 **st.**

X **Blostin's,** 29 Waterloo Rd, BA4 5HH, ✆ 343648 – VISA JCB
closed Sunday, Monday, 2 weeks January and 2 weeks June – **Meals** (dinner only 14.95 **t.** and a la carte 5.95.

at Doulting E : 1½ m. on A 361 – ✉ Shepton Mallet – ☎ 01749 :

XXX **Brottens Lodge** with rm, BA4 4RB, S : 1 m. turning right at Abbey Barn Inn following sign for Evercreech ✆ 880352, Fax 880601, ←, – TV ☎ P. VISA
Meals *(closed Monday and Saturday lunch and Sunday)* 17.50/21.50 **st.** 4.25 – **3 rm** 45.00/75.00 **st.**

at Evercreech SE : 4 m. by A 371 on B 3081 – ✉ Shepton Mallet – ☎ 01749 :

Pecking Mill Inn, BA4 6PG, W : 1 m. on A 371 ✆ 830336, Fax 831316 – TV ☎ P. AE VISA.
closed 25 and 26 December – **Meals** *(closed Monday and Tuesday lunch)* a la carte 11.40/19.20 **st.** 4.25 – **6 rm** 33.00/45.00 **st.** – SB.

SHERBORNE Dorset 403 404 M 31 **The West Country G.** – pop. 7 606 – ☎ 01935.

See : Town★ - Abbey★★ – Castle★ *AC.*

Envir. : Sandford Orcas Manor House★ *AC,* NW : 4 m. by B 3148 – Purse Caundle Manor★ *AC,* NE : 5 m. by A 30.

Exc. : Cadbury Castle (←★★) N : 8 m. by A 30.

18 Clatcombe ✆ 812475.

3 Tilton Court, Digby Rd, DT9 3NL ✆ 815341.

♦London 128 – Bournemouth 39 – Dorchester 19 – Salisbury 36 – Taunton 31.

Eastbury, Long St., DT9 3BY, ✆ 813131, Fax 817296, – TV ☎ P – 60. AE VISA.
Meals 10.50/18.00 **t.** 6.50 – **14 rm** 55.00/95.00 **t.**

Antelope, Greenhill, DT9 4EP, ✆ 812077, Fax 816473 – TV ☎ & P – 80. AE VISA.
Meals 11.50 **t.** and a la carte 4.95 – **19 rm** 39.95/65.00 **st.** – SB.

Quinns, Marston Rd, DT9 4BL, ✆ 815008 – TV P
Meals (by arrangement) (communal dining) 14.50 **s.** – **3 rm** 21.00/54.00 **s.**

XX **Pheasants** with rm, 24 Greenhill, DT9 4EW, ✆ 815252, Fax 815252 – TV P. VISA.
closed 2 weeks mid January – **Meals** *(closed Sunday dinner and Monday to non-residents)* 12.75/22.00 **t.** and a la carte 4.25 – **5 rm** 37.50/65.00 **t.** – SB.

at Milborne Port – ✉ Sherborne – ☎ 01963 :

Old Vicarage , Sherborne Rd, DT9 5AT, NE : 1½ m. on A 30 ✆ 251117, Fax 251515, ←, – TV ☎ P. VISA
closed January – **Meals** *(closed Sunday dinner and Monday)* 10.50/25.00 **t.** and a la carte 6.50 – **7 rm** 30.00/80.00 **t.** – SB.

at Oborne NE : 2 m. by A 30 – ✉ Sherborne – ☎ 01935 :

XX **Grange** with rm, DT9 4LA, ✆ 813463, Fax 817464, ←, , – TV ☎ P. AE VISA.
closed 1 to 8 January and 19 August-5 September – **Meals** - Italian - *(closed Sunday dinner)* (dinner only and Sunday lunch)/dinner a la carte 15.30/24.00 **t.** 5.80 – **5 rm** 45.00/65.00 **t.** – SB.

at Hermitage S : 7½ m. by A 352 – ✉ Sherborne – ☎ 01963 :

Almshouse Farm without rest., DT9 6HA, ✆ 210296, ←, « Former monastery, working farm », – TV P.
closed Christmas and January – **3 rm** 25.00/40.00 **s.**

at Yetminster SW : 5½ m. by A 352 and Yetminster rd – ✉ Sherborne – ☎ 01935 :

Manor Farmhouse, DT9 6LF, ✆ 872247, « 17C farmhouse », – TV P. VISA.
Meals (by arrangement) 15.00 **t.** – **3 rm** 30.00/50.00 **st.**

SHERBOURNE Warks. – see Warwick.

SHERE Surrey 404 S 30 – see Guildford.

SHERIFF HUTTON N. Yorks. 402 Q 21 – pop. 2 299 – ✉ York – ☎ 01347.

♦London 313 – York 10.

Rangers House , The Park, YO6 1RH, S : 1 ¼ m. by Strensall rd ✆ 878397, Fax 878666, – P.
Meals 21.00 4.00 – **6 rm** 32.00/64.00 – SB.

SHERINGHAM Norfolk 404 X 25 – pop. 5 870 – ☎ 01263.
Sheringham ℘ 822038.
Station Approach, NR26 8RA ℘ 824329 (summer only).
♦London 128 – Cromer 4 – ♦Norwich 27.

Beacon without rest., 1 Nelson Rd, NR26 8BT, ℘ 822019, – P.
April-October – **6 rm** 22.00/44.00 **st.**

SHIFNAL Shrops. 402 403 404 M 25 – pop. 6 516 – ✉ Telford – ☎ 01952.
♦London 150 – ♦Birmingham 28 – Shrewsbury 16.

Park House, Park St., TF11 9BA, ℘ 460128, Fax 461658, , , – rm P – 180. AE VISA
Meals (bar lunch Saturday) 10.50/18.95 **st.** and a la carte 4.95 – 7.50 – **52 rm** 83.00/99.50 **st.**, 2 suites – SB.

SHINFIELD Berks. 404 R 29 – see Reading.

SHIPHAM Somerset 403 L 30 **The West Country G.** – pop. 1 094 – ✉ Winscombe – ☎ 01934.
Envir. : Cheddar Gorge★★ (Gorge★★, Caves★★, Jacobs's Ladder ※★) – Axbridge★★ – King John's Hunting Lodge★ – St. John the Baptist★, SW : 5 m. on A 38 – St. Andrew's Church★, S : 2½ m..
Mendip Spring, Honeyhall Lane, Congresbury, Avon ℘ 853337/852322.
♦London 135 – ♦Bristol 14 – Taunton 20.

Daneswood House, Cuck Hill, BS25 1RD, ℘ 843145, Fax 843824, ←, – P. AE VISA.
closed 25 December-5 January – **Meals** *(closed Sunday dinner to non-residents)* 18.95/25.95 **st.** 4.50 – **9 rm** 57.50/79.50 **st.**, 3 suites – SB.

Stadtpläne : *Die Auswahl der Straßen wurde unter Berücksichtigung des Verkehrs und der Zufahrt zu den erwähnten Häusern getroffen.*

Die weniger wichtigen Straßen wurden nur angedeutet.

SHIPLEY W. Yorks. 402 O 22 – pop. 29 753 – ☎ 01274.
Northcliffe, High Bank Lane ℘ 584085.
♦London 216 – Bradford 4 – ♦Leeds 12.

Hollings Hall (Country Club) , Hollins Hill, Baildon, BD17 7QW, NE : 2½ m. on A 6038 ℘ 530053, Fax 530187, , , park – rm P – 200. AE VISA.
Meals (bar lunch Saturday) 12.95/16.95 **st.** and a la carte 5.95 – 7.50 – **58 rm** 75.00 **st.**, 1 suite – SB.

Aagrah, 27 Westgate, BD18 3QX, ℘ 530880 – AE VISA
closed 25 December – **Meals** - Indian - (booking essential) (dinner only) a la carte 10.60/17.50 **t.** 4.00.

SHIPTON GORGE Dorset – see Bridport.

SHIPTON-UNDER-WYCHWOOD Oxon. 403 404 P 28 – pop. 1 154 – ☎ 01993.
♦London 81 – ♦Birmingham 50 – Gloucester 37 – ♦Oxford 25.

Lamb Inn, High St., OX7 6DQ, ℘ 830465, Fax 832025 – rest P. AE VISA.
Meals *(closed Monday)* (buffet lunch)/dinner 21.00 **t.** – **5 rm** 58.00/68.00 **t.**

SHIRLEY W. Mids. 403 404 O 26 – see Solihull.

SHOTTISHAM Suffolk 404 X 27 – see Woodbridge.

SHRAWLEY Heref. and Worcs. 403 404 N 27 – pop. 379 – ✉ Worcester – ☎ 01905.
♦London 152 – ♦Birmingham 45 – Leominster 33.

Lenchford, WR6 6TB, SE : ½ m. on B 4196 ℘ 620229, Fax 621125, ←, « Riverside setting », , – P – 80. AE VISA.
Meals (bar lunch Monday to Saturday) a la carte 13.95/19.15 **st.** – **15 rm** 39.50/55.50 **st.** – SB.

SHREWLEY Warks. 403 404 P 27 – see Warwick.

SHREWSBURY Shrops. 402 403 L 25 **Great Britain G.** – pop. 91 749 (inc. Atcham) – ☎ 01743.
See : Abbey★ D.
Exc. : Ironbridge Gorge Museum★★ *AC* (The Iron Bridge★★ - Coalport China Museum★★ - Blists Hill Open Air Museum★★ – Museum of the River and Visitor Centre★) SE : 12 m. by A 5 and B 4380.
Condover ℘ 872976 – Meole Brace ℘ 364050.
The Music Hall, The Square, SY1 1LH ℘ 350761.
♦London 164 – ♦Birmingham 48 – ♦Cardiff 10 – Chester 43 – Derby 67 – Gloucester 93 – ♦Manchester 68 – ♦Stoke-on-Trent 39 – ♦Swansea 124.

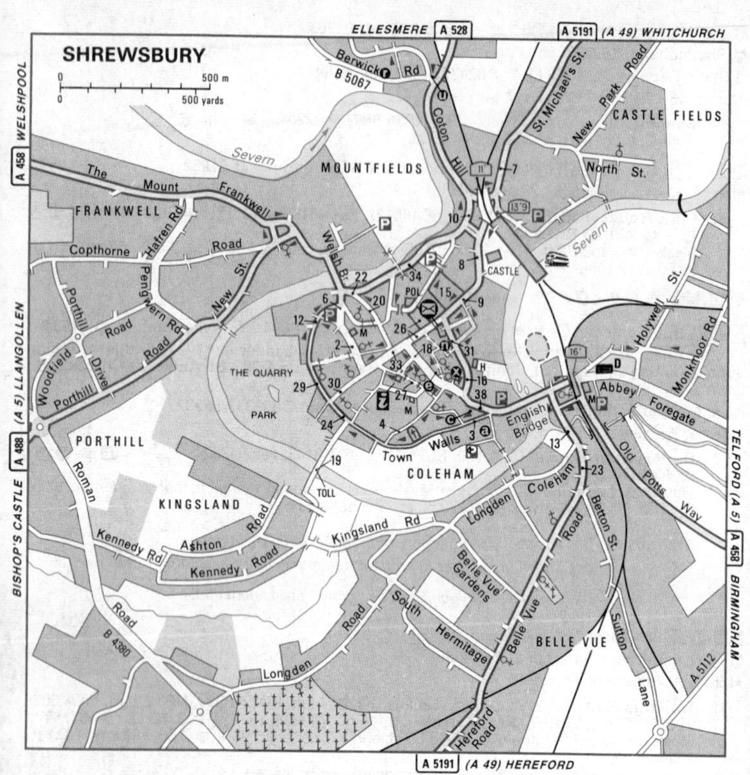

Darwin Centre 15
High Street 18
Pride Hill 26
Shoplatch 33

Barker Street 2
Beeches Lane 3
Belmont 4
Bridge Street 6

Castle Foregate 7
Castle Gates 8
Castle Street 9
Chester Street 10
Claremont Bank 12
Coleham Head 13
Dogpole 16
Kingsland Bridge 19
Mardol 20

Mardol Quay 22
Moreton Crescent 23
Murivance 24
Princess Street 27
St. Chad's Terrace 29
St. John's Hill 30
St. Mary's Street 31
Smithfield Road 34
Wyle Cop 38

Lion (Forte), Wyle Cop, SY1 1UY, ℘ 353107, Fax 352744 – ◫ ⊁ TV ☎ P – 200. AE ◑ VISA JCB
Meals 14.50/17.50 **st.** and a la carte 6.05 – ☕ 8.50 – **59 rm** 58.00/70.00 **st.** – SB. **c**

Prince Rupert (Q.M.H.), Butcher Row, SY1 1UQ, ℘ 499955, Fax 357306 – ◫ ▤ rest TV ☎ P – 70. AE ◑ VISA JCB
Meals 12.00/18.50 **t.** and a la carte 6.50 – ☕ 8.75 – **62 rm** 68.00 **t.**, 3 suites – SB. **n**

Pinewood House without rest., Shelton Park, The Mount, SY3 8BL, NW : 1 ½ m. on A 458 ℘ 364200, – TV P
4 rm ☕ 35.00/48.00.

Fieldside without rest., 38 London Rd, SY2 6NX, E : 1 ¼ m. by Abbey Foregate on A 5064 (via Shirehall) ℘ 353143, Fax 358645, – ⊁ TV ☎ P. AE ◑ VISA.
closed 3 weeks November – **6 rm** ☕ 28.00/42.00 **st.**

Cromwells, 11 Dogpole, SY1 1EN, ℘ 361440 – TV. AE VISA JCB
Meals a la carte 8.75/19.20 **t.** – **7 rm** ☕ 23.00/40.00 **t.** **x**

Sandford House without rest., St. Julians Friars, SY1 1XL, ℘ 343829, – TV. AE VISA
11 rm ☕ 31.00/43.50 **st.** **a**

Tudor House without rest., 2 Fish St., SY1 1UR, ℘ 351735, « 15C house » – TV.
3 rm ☕ 26.00/46.00 **st.** **e**

Sydney House, Coton Cres., off Coton Hill, SY1 2LJ, ☎ 354681, Fax 354681 – rest TV ☎ P. VISA. u
closed 24 December-1 January – **Meals** (by arrangement) 15.00 **st.** 4.00 – **7 rm** 35.00/65.00 **st.** – SB.

Roseville, 12 Berwick Rd, SY1 2LN, ☎ 236470 – P. r
closed 16 December-31 January – **Meals** (by arrangement) 14.00 **s.** – **3 rm** 22.00/44.00 **s.**

at Albrighton N : 3 m. on A 528 – ✉ Shrewsbury – ☎ 01939 :

Albrighton Hall, Ellesmere Rd, SY4 3AG, ☎ 291000, Fax 291123, park, squash – rm TV ☎ P – 260. AE VISA
Meals *(closed Saturday lunch)* 11.95/19.75 **t.** and a la carte 8.50 – 8.50 – **39 rm** 77.50/115.00 **t.** – SB.

Albright Hussey, Ellesmere Rd, SY4 3AF, ☎ 290571, Fax 291143, « 16C moated manor house », – TV ☎ P. AE VISA.
Meals 11.50/19.50 **t.** and a la carte – **5 rm** 57.50/135.00 **t.** – SB.

at Dorrington S : 7 m. on A 49 – ✉ Shrewsbury – ☎ 01743 :

Country Friends with rm, SY5 7JD, ☎ 718707, – P. AE VISA JCB.
closed 2 weeks mid July and 1 week October – **Meals** *(closed Sunday and Monday)* 24.85 **t.** 5.50 – **3 rm** (dinner included) 60.00/98.00 **t.**

at Hanwood SW : 4 m. on A 488 – ✉ Shrewsbury – ☎ 01743 :

White House, SY5 8LP, ☎ 860414, – rm P.
Meals (by arrangement) 16.00 **s.** 4.50 – **6 rm** 20.00/50.00 – SB.

Old School House without rest., SY5 8LJ, ☎ 860694, – TV P.
3 rm 16.50/31.00 **s.**

at Alberbury W : 7½ m. by A 458 – ✉ Shrewsbury – ☎ 01743 :

Rowton Castle, SY5 9EP, SW : ½ m. off A 458 ☎ 884044, Fax 884949, park – TV ☎ P – 110. AE VISA.
Meals 11.95/17.50 **t.** and a la carte – **19 rm** 50.00/65.00 **st.** – SB.

ATS Lancaster Rd, Harlescott ☎ 343954/232231

When visiting Great Britain,
use the *Michelin Green Guide* **"Great Britain".**
– *Detailed descriptions of places of interest*
– *Touring programmes*
– *Maps and street plans*
– *The history of the country*
– *Photographs and drawings of monuments, beauty spots, houses...*

SHURDINGTON Glos. 403 404 N 28 – see Cheltenham.

SIBSON Leics. – see Nuneaton (Warks.).

SIDFORD Devon 403 K 31 – see Sidmouth.

SIDMOUTH Devon 403 K 31 The West Country G. – pop. 12 982 – ☎ 01395.

Envir. : Bicton★ (Gardens★) *AC*, SW : 5 m..

18 Cotmaton Rd ☎ 513023.

Ham Lane, EX10 8XR ☎ 516441.

London 170 – Exeter 14 – Taunton 27 – Weymouth 45.

Belmont, The Esplanade, EX10 8RX, ☎ 512555, Group Telex 42551, Fax 579101, – TV ☎ P. AE VISA.
Meals (dancing Saturday evening) 11.50/22.50 **t.** and a la carte 5.50 – **51 rm** (dinner included) 84.00/232.00 **t.** – SB.

Riviera, The Esplanade, EX10 8AY, ☎ 515201, Fax 577775, – rest TV ☎ – 85. AE VISA
Meals 12.00/20.00 **t.** and a la carte 4.50 – **27 rm** 67.00/162.00 **t.** – SB.

Salcombe Hill House, Beatlands Rd, EX10 8JQ, ☎ 514697, Fax 578310, heated, – rest TV ☎ P. VISA JCB
closed January and February – **Meals** (bar lunch Monday to Saturday)/dinner 16.25 **t.** and a la carte – **30 rm** (dinner included) 53.00/132.00 **t.** – SB.

Fortfield, Station Rd, EX10 8NU, ☎ 512403, Fax 512403, – rest TV ☎ P. AE VISA
closed 2 weeks mid January – **Meals** (bar lunch)/dinner 16.00 **st.** – 5.50 – **57 rm** 34.50/69.00 **st.** – SB.

Littlecourt, Seafield Rd, EX10 8HF, ℘ 515279, heated, – rest. JCB
late March-late October and 5 days at Christmas – **Meals** (bar lunch)/dinner 14.00 **t.** 4.10 – **20 rm** (dinner included) 48.35/96.70 **t.** – SB.

Hunters Moon, Sid Rd, EX10 9AA, ℘ 513380, Fax 514270, – rest. VISA JCB
closed December-February – **Meals** (dinner only) 15.00 **st.** – **18 rm** 41.00/82.00 **st.**

Abbeydale, Manor Rd, EX10 8RP, ℘ 512060, – rest.
April-October – **Meals** (bar lunch Monday to Saturday and carving lunch Sunday)/dinner 13.00 **st.** 4.00 – **18 rm** (dinner included) 46.00/108.00 **st.** – SB.

Mount Pleasant, Salcombe Rd, EX10 8JA, ℘ 514694, –.
March-November – **Meals** (residents only) (dinner only) 15.00 **st.** 5.25 – **16 rm** (dinner included) 42.00/84.00 **st.** – SB.

Woodlands, Station Rd, Cotmaton Cross, EX10 8HG, ℘ 513120, – rest. VISA
Meals 5.45/10.50 **t.** 5.50 – **28 rm** 20.00/56.00 **t.** – SB.

Broad Oak without rest., Sid Rd, EX10 8QP, ℘ 513713, –.
March-November – **3 rm** 20.00/50.00.

Salcombe Cottage without rest., Hillside Rd, EX10 8JF, ℘ 516829, « 18C thatched cottage », –
4 rm 19.50/36.00 **st.**

at Sidford N : 2 m. – ✉ Sidmouth – ☎ 01395 :

Salty Monk, Church St., EX10 9QP, on A 3052 ℘ 513174, « Part 16C », – rest
7 rm.

ATS Vicarage Rd ℘ 512433

In alta stagione, e soprattutto nelle stazioni turistiche, è prudente prenotare con un certo anticipo.
Avvertite immediatamente l'albergatore se non potete più occupare la camera prenotata.

Se scrivete ad un albergo all'estero, allegate alla vostra lettera un tagliando-risposta internazionale (disponibile presso gli uffici postali).

SILCHESTER Hants. 403 404 Q 29 – pop. 1 428 – ✉ Reading (Berks.) – ☎ 01734.
London 62 – Basingstoke 8 – Reading 14 – Winchester 26.

Romans, Little London Rd, RG7 2PN, ℘ 700421, Fax 700691, heated, – 40. VISA
closed 24 December-3 January – **Meals** *(closed Saturday lunch)* 13.95 **t.** and a la carte 6.50 – **25 rm** 75.00/115.00 **t.** – SB.

SIMONSBATH Somerset 403 I 30 **The West Country G.** – ✉ Minehead – ☎ 01643.
Envir. : Exmoor National Park★★ – Exford (Church★) E : 5½ m. by B 3223 and B 3224.
London 200 – Exeter 40 – Minehead 19 – Taunton 38.

Simonsbath House, TA24 7SH, ℘ 831259, Fax 831557, ≤, « 17C country house », – rest. VISA.
closed December and January – **Meals** (dinner only) 22.00 **st.** 4.75 – **7 rm** 50.00/90.00 **t.** – SB.

SINDLESHAM Berks. – see Reading.

SINGLETON Lancs. 402 L 22 – see Blackpool.

SISSINGHURST Kent 404 V 30 – see Cranbrook.

SIX MILE BOTTOM Cambs. – see Newmarket (Suffolk).

SKELTON N. Yorks. 402 Q 22 – see York.

SKELWITH BRIDGE Cumbria 402 K 20 – see Ambleside.

SKIPTON N. Yorks. 402 N 22 **Great Britain G.** – pop. 13 583 – ☎ 01756.
See : Castle★ *AC*.
18 ℘ 795657.
9 Sheep St., BD23 1JH ℘ 792809.
London 217 – Kendal 45 – Leeds 26 – Preston 36 – York 43.

Randell's, Keighley Rd, BD23 2TA, S : 1 ¼ m. on A 629 ℘ 700100, Fax 700107, squash – rm 400.
Meals (bar lunch Monday to Saturday)/dinner 16.00 **st.** 5.45 – **76 rm** 84.50/99.50 **st.** – SB.

Unicorn, Devonshire Pl., Keighley Rd, BD23 2LP, ℘ 794146, Fax 793376 –
Meals (residents only) (dinner only) a la carte 9.70/13.50 **st.** 5.50 – **9 rm** 40.00/47.00 **st.** – SB.

Forte Travelodge, Gargrave Rd, BD23 1UD, W : 1 ¾ m. by Water St. at A 65/A 59 roundabout ℘ 798091, Reservations (Freephone) 0800 850950 –
Meals (grill rest.) – **32 rm** 34.50 **t.**

at Elslack W : 4½ m. by A 59 off A 56 – ✉ Skipton – 01282 :

Tempest Arms, BD23 3AY, ℘ 842450, Fax 843331 – 80.
Meals a la carte 13.50/16.30 **st.** 5.50 – **10 rm** 46.00/52.00 **st.** – SB.

ATS Carleton Rd Garage, Carleton Rd ℘ 795741/2

SLAIDBURN Lancs. 402 M 22 – pop. 302 – ✉ Clitheroe – 01200.

London 249 – Burnley 21 – Lancaster 19 – Leeds 48 – Preston 27.

Parrock Head, BB7 3AH, NW : 1 m. ℘ 446614, Fax 446313, ≤ Bowland Fells, – rest
Meals (bar lunch Monday to Saturday)/dinner 18.00 **t.** 5.50 – **9 rm** 40.00/70.00 **t.** – SB.

SLEAFORD Lincs. 402 404 S 25 – pop. 10 388 – 01529.

South Rauceby, Willoughby Rd ℘ 488273.

The Mill, Money's Yard, Carre St., NG35 7TW ℘ 414294.

London 119 – Leicester 45 – Lincoln 17 – Nottingham 39.

Lincolnshire Oak, East Rd, NG34 7EH, NE : ¾ m. on B 1517 ℘ 413807, Fax 413710, – 140.
Meals a la carte 13.85/17.65 **st.** – **14 rm** 47.00/65.00 **st.** – SB.

Forte Travelodge, NG34 8NP, NW : 1 m. on A 15 at junction with A 17 ℘ 414752, Reservation (Freephone) 0800 850950 –
Meals (grill rest.) – **40 rm** 34.50 **t.**

Tally Ho Inn, Aswarby, NG34 8SA, S : 4½ m. on A 15 ℘ 455205, ≤, –
closed 25 and 26 December – **Meals** (in bar Sunday dinner) a la carte 11.95/18.20 **t.** 3.50 – **6 rm** 30.00/45.00 **st.** – SB.

ATS 40 Albion Terr., off Boston Rd ℘ 302908

SLINFOLD W. Sussex – see Horsham.

SLOUGH Berks. 404 S 29 – pop. 101 066 – 01753.

London 29 – Oxford 39 – Reading 19.

Copthorne, Cippenham Lane, SL1 2YE, SW : 1 ¼ m. by A 4 on A 355 ℘ 516222, Telex 220250, Fax 516237, – rm – 200.
Reflections : Meals *(closed Sunday)* (dinner only) 19.50 **st.** and a la carte 7.50 – **Veranda : Meals** (dancing Saturday evening) a la carte 18.35/24.15 **st.** 7.50 – 10.50 – **217 rm** 120.00/130.00 **st.**, 2 suites.

Heathrow/Slough Marriott, Ditton Rd, Langley, SL3 8PT, SE : 2½ m. on A 4 ℘ 544244, Fax 540272, – rm – 300.
Meals (bar lunch Saturday) 15.50/22.00 **st.** and dinner a la carte 7.25 – 11.85 – **348 rm** 125.00 **st.**, 1 suite – SB.

Courtyard by Marriott, Church St., Chalvey, SL1 2NH, SW : 1 ¼ m. by A 4 on A 355 ℘ 551551, Fax 553333, – rm – 40.
Meals 14.25 **st.** and a la carte 5.95 – 8.25 – **148 rm** 77.00/85.00 **st.** – SB.

ATS 1A Furnival Av. ℘ 524214

SMITE Heref. and Worcs. – see Droitwich.

SOAR MILL COVE Devon – see Salcombe.

SOLIHULL W. Mids. 403 404 O 26 – pop. 199 859 – ☎ 0121.

Central Library, Homer Rd, B91 3RG ✆ 704 6130/704 6134.

♦London 109 – ♦Birmingham 7 – ♦Coventry 13 – Warwick 13.

Solihull Moat House (Q.M.H.), Homer Rd, B91 3QD, ✆ 623 9988, Fax 711 2696, – rm rest – 200. AE VISA JCB
Meals (light lunch Saturday) 16.75 **t.** (dinner) and a la carte 22.25/30.00 **t.** 5.70 – 9.50
115 rm 105.00/130.00 **st.** – SB.

St. John's Swallow, 651 Warwick Rd, B91 1AT, ✆ 711 3000, Fax 705 6629, – rm rest – 800. AE VISA JCB
Meals *(closed lunch Saturday and Bank Holidays)* (dancing Saturday evening) 13.50 19.50 **st.** and a la carte 7.00 – **176 rm** 95.00/110.00 **st.**, 1 suite – SB.

Jarvis International, The Square, B91 3RF, ✆ 711 2121, Fax 711 3374 – rm – 200. AE VISA
Meals 9.45/22.95 **st.** and a la carte 6.50 – 9.00 – **117 rm** 95.00/165.00 **st.**, 10 suites SB.

at Shirley W : 2½ m. by B 4025 – ✉ Solihull – ☎ 0121 :

Regency (Regal), Stratford Rd, B90 4EB, SE : 2 m. on A 34 ✆ 745 6119, Fax 733 3801, – rm rest – 150. AE VISA
Meals *(closed Saturday lunch)* 13.50/17.50 **st.** and a la carte 5.95 – **110 rm** 95.00 105.00 **st.**, 2 suites – SB.

Travel Inn, Stratford Rd, B90 4PT, SE : 2½ m. on A 34 ✆ 744 2942, Fax 733 7075 – rm . AE VISA.
Meals (grill rest.) – 4.95 – **51 rm** 34.50 **t.**

XX **Chez Julien,** 1036 Stratford Rd, Monkspath, B90 4EE, SE : 2½ m. on A 34 ✆ 744 7232 Fax 745 4775 – . AE VISA
closed Saturday lunch, Sunday and Bank Holidays – **Meals** - French - 11.80/23.00 **st** and a la carte 4.95.

SOMERTON Somerset 403 L 30 The West Country G. – pop. 4 489 – ☎ 01458.

See : Town★ - Market Place★ (cross★) – St. Michael's Church★.

Envir. : Long Sutton★ (Church★★) SW : 2½ m. by B 3165 – Huish Episcopi (St. Mary's Church Tower★★) SW : 4½ m. by B 3153 – Lytes Cary★, SE : 3½ m. by B 3151.

Exc. : Muchelney★★ (Parish Church★★) SW : 6½ m. by B 3153 and A 372 – High Ham (←★★, St Andrew's★) NW : 6½ m. by B 3153 – Midelney Manor★ *AC*, SW : 9 m. by B 3153 and A 378.

♦London 138 – ♦Bristol 32 – Taunton 17.

Lynch Country House without rest., 4 Behind Berry, TA11 7PD, ✆ 272316, Fax 272590 ←, « Attractively converted Regency house », park – . AE VISA.
5 rm 45.00/65.00 **t.**

ATS Bancombe Rd, Trading Est. ✆ 273467

SONNING-ON-THAMES Berks. 404 R 29 – pop. 1 354 – ☎ 01734.

♦London 48 – Reading 4.

Great House at Sonning, Thames St., RG4 6UT, ✆ 692277, Fax 441296, – – 80. AE VISA.
Meals a la carte 13.45/25.50 5.50 – 8.50 – **34 rm** 69.50/99.50 **st.**, 2 suites – SB.

XXX **French Horn** with rm, Thames St., RG4 6TN, ✆ 692204, Fax 442210, ← River Thames and gardens – . AE VISA.
closed Good Friday and 26 December – **Meals** (booking essential) 17.50/ 28.00 **st.** and a la carte 5.25 – **11 rm** 80.00/95.00 **st.**, 4 suites.

OURTON Devon 403 H 31 – see Okehampton.

SOUTHAMPTON Hants. 403 404 P 31 Great Britain G. – pop. 196 864 – 01703.

ee : Old Southampton AZ : Bargate★ **B** - Tudor House Museum★ **M1**.

, Southampton Municipal, Golf Course Rd, Bassett 768407, AY – Stoneham, Monks Wood Close, Bassett 768151, AY – Chilworth Golf Centre, Main Rd, Chilworth 740544, AY.

Southampton/Eastleigh Airport : 620021 N : 4 m. BY.

to France (Cherbourg) (Stena Line) 1-2 daily (5 h) – to the Isle of Wight (East and West Cowes) (Red Funnel Ferries) frequent services daily.

Above Bar, SO9 4XF 221106.

London 87 – ◆Bristol 79 – ◆Plymouth 161.

Plans on following pages

De Vere Grand Harbour, West Quay Rd, SO15 1AG, 633033, Fax 633066, – 450. AE VISA. AZ **a**
Meals 12.95/25.00 **st.** and a la carte 5.50 – **169 rm** 110.00/150.00 **st.**, 3 suites – SB.

Hilton National, Bracken Pl., Chilworth, SO16 3RB, 702700, Telex 47594, Fax 767233, – rm rest – 200. AE VISA AY **e**
Meals *(closed Saturday lunch)* 13.25/16.25 **t.** and a la carte 5.90 – 10.50 – **133 rm** 81.90/96.90 **st.**, 2 suites – SB.

Southampton Park, 12-13 Cumberland Pl., SO15 2WY, 343343, Fax 332538, – rm rest – 200. AE VISA AZ **u**
closed 24 to 27 December – **Meals** 15.95 **t.** – 7.50 – **72 rm** 52.50 **t.** – SB.

Novotel, 1 West Quay Rd, SO15 1RA, 330550, Fax 222158, <, – rm – 450. AE VISA AZ **x**
Meals 14.00 **st.** and a la carte 4.95 – 7.50 – **121 rm** 52.50 **st.** – SB.

County (Q.M.H.), 119 Highfield Lane, Portswood, SO17 1AQ, 359955, Fax 583910, – – 200. AE VISA BY **e**
Meals *(closed Saturday lunch)* 14.50/15.00 **st.** and a la carte 6.10 – 8.50 – **66 rm** 55.00/65.00 **st.** – SB.

Dolphin (Forte), 35 High St., SO9 2DS, 339955, Fax 333650 – – 75. AE VISA JCB AZ **i**
Meals (bar lunch Monday to Saturday)/dinner 15.95 **st.** and a la carte 6.70 – 8.50 – **71 rm** 50.00/60.00 **st.**, 2 suites – SB.

Forte Posthouse, Herbert Walker Av., SO1 0HJ, 330777, Fax 332510, <, – rm – 150. AE VISA JCB AZ **o**
Meals a la carte approx. 17.00 **t.** – 7.95 – **128 rm** 59.00 **t.** – SB.

Star, 26-27 High St., SO14 2NA, 339939, Fax 335291 – rm – 70. AE VISA AZ **z**
Meals (bar lunch Saturday) 8.00/12.00 **st.** and a la carte 4.00 – **45 rm** 39.50/46.50 **st.** – SB.

Rosida Garden, 25-27 Hill Lane, S015 5AB, 228501, Fax 635501, heated, – . AE VISA AZ **r**
closed 24 December-2 January – **Meals** (dinner only) a la carte 10.00 **t.** 3.00 – **27 rm** 40.00/60.00 **t.** – SB.

Travel Inn, Romsey Rd, Nursling, SO1 9XJ, NW : 4 m. on A 3057 732262 – rm . AE VISA. AY **a**
Meals (grill rest.) – 4.95 – **32 rm** 34.50 **t.**

Hunters Lodge, 25 Landguard Rd, SO1 5DL, 227919, Fax 230913 – rm . AE VISA. AZ **v**
closed 18 December-5 January – **Meals** (by arrangement) 10.00 **s.** 2.50 – **16 rm** 23.50/52.00 **st.**

XX **Kuti's Brasserie,** 37-39 Oxford St., SO1 1DP, 221585 – . AE VISA AZ **e**
closed 25 and 26 December – **Meals** - Indian - a la carte 11.75/20.90 **t.**

ATS West Quay Rd 333231 ATS 88-94 Portswood Rd 582727

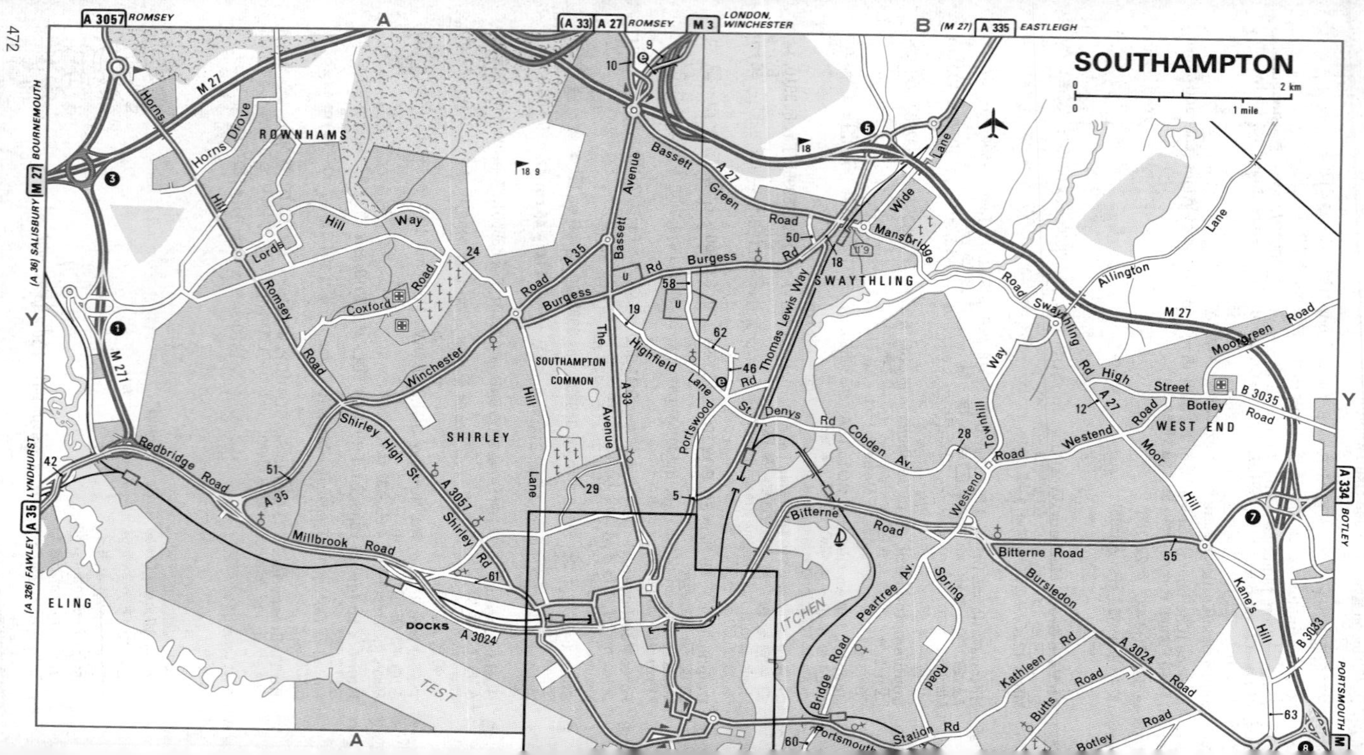
SOUTHAMPTON
0 1 mile
0 2 km
A 3057 ROMSEY
A
(A 33) A 27 ROMSEY
M 3 LONDON, WINCHESTER
B (M 27) A 335 EASTLEIGH
(A 36) SALISBURY M 27 BOURNEMOUTH
(A 326) FAWLEY A 35 LYNDHURST
A 334 BOTLEY
PORTSMOUTH M
Y
M 27
Horns Hill
Horns Drove
ROWNHAMS
Lords Hill Way
Romsey Road
Coxford Road
Winchester Road
M 271
Redbridge Road
A 35
Millbrook Road
Shirley High St.
A 3057
Shirley Rd
SHIRLEY
Hill Lane
SOUTHAMPTON COMMON
Burgess Road
Burgess Rd
Bassett Avenue
The Avenue
A 33
Bassett Green Road
A 27
Highfield Lane
Portswood Road
St. Denys Rd
Thomas Lewis Way
SWAYTHLING
Mansbridge
Wide Lane
Swaythling Road
Allington Lane
Moorgreen Road
High Street
Botley Road
B 3035
WEST END
Westend Road
Moor Hill
Townhill Way
Cobden Av.
Bitterne Road
Bursledon Road
A 3024
Kane's Hill
B 3033
Peartree Av.
Spring Road
Bridge Road
Kathleen Rd
Butts Road
Botley Road
Station Rd
Portsmouth
ITCHEN
DOCKS
A 3024
TEST
ELING

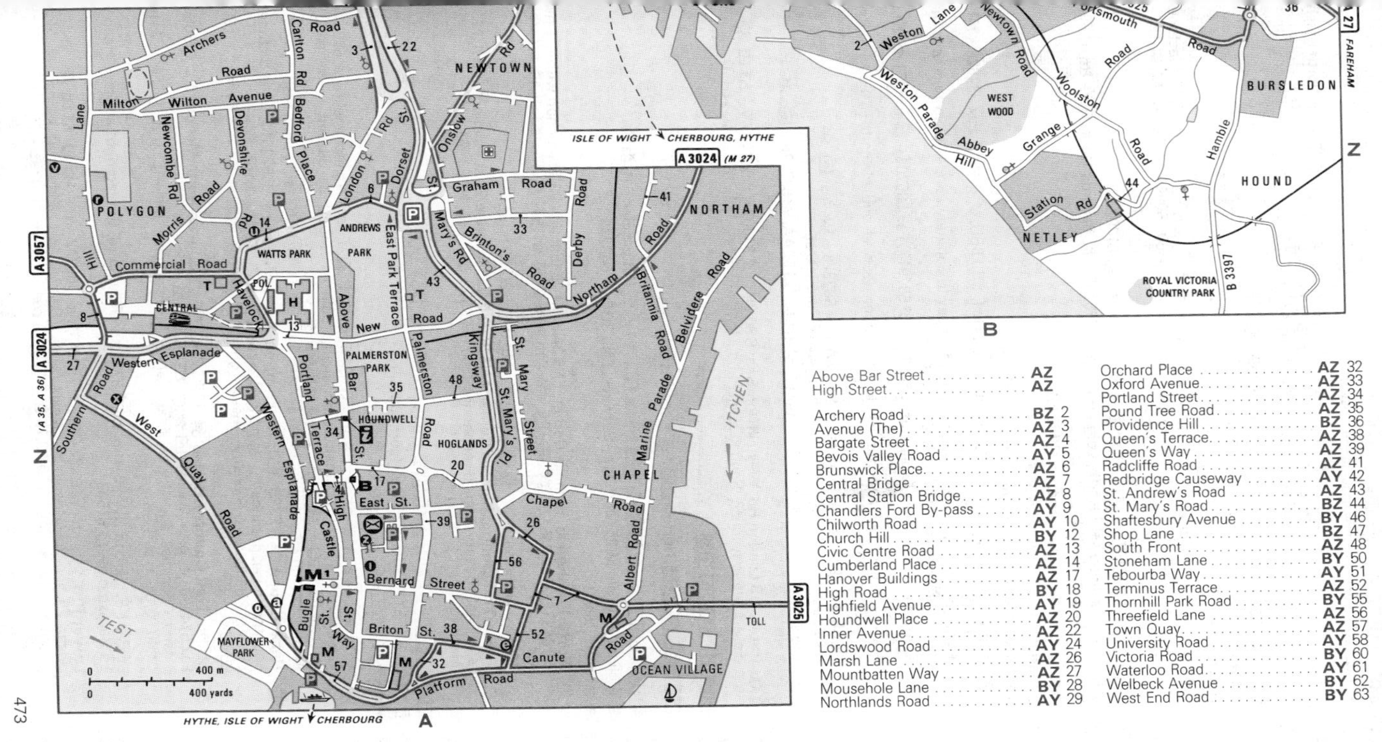

Above Bar Street	AZ	
High Street	AZ	
Archery Road	BZ	2
Avenue (The)	AZ	3
Bargate Street	AZ	4
Bevois Valley Road	AY	5
Brunswick Place	AZ	6
Central Bridge	AZ	7
Central Station Bridge	AZ	8
Chandlers Ford By-pass	AY	9
Chilworth Road	AY	10
Church Hill	BY	12
Civic Centre Road	AZ	13
Cumberland Place	AZ	14
Hanover Buildings	AZ	17
High Road	BY	18
Highfield Avenue	AY	19
Houndwell Place	AZ	20
Inner Avenue	AZ	22
Lordswood Road	AY	24
Marsh Lane	AZ	26
Mountbatten Way	AZ	27
Mousehole Lane	BY	28
Northlands Road	AY	29
Orchard Place	AZ	32
Oxford Avenue	AZ	33
Portland Street	AZ	34
Pound Tree Road	AZ	35
Providence Hill	BZ	36
Queen's Terrace	AZ	38
Queen's Way	AZ	39
Radcliffe Road	AZ	41
Redbridge Causeway	AY	42
St. Andrew's Road	AZ	43
St. Mary's Road	BZ	44
Shaftesbury Avenue	BY	46
Shop Lane	BZ	47
South Front	AZ	48
Stoneham Lane	BY	50
Tebourba Way	AY	51
Terminus Terrace	AZ	52
Thornhill Park Road	BY	55
Threefield Lane	AZ	56
Town Quay	AZ	57
University Road	AY	58
Victoria Road	BY	60
Waterloo Road	AY	61
Welbeck Avenue	BY	62
West End Road	BY	63

SOUTH BRENT Devon 403 I 32 – ✆ 01548.

♦London 227 – Exeter 29 – ♦Plymouth 16 – Torquay 16.

Brookdale House ⟡, North Huish, TQ10 9NR, SE : 4½ m. by B 3210 on North Huish ✆ 821661, Fax 821606, ⟡ – ⟡ rm ⟡ ⟡ ⟡. ⟡ AE VISA. ⟡
Meals a la carte 18.50/26.50 **st.** ⟡ 7.20 – **8 rm** ⟡ 55.00/90.00.

SOUTH CAVE Humbs. 402 S 22 – pop. 3 339 – ✆ 01430.

18 Cave Castle Hotel ✆ 421286/422245.

♦London 176 – ♦Kingston-upon-Hull 12 – ♦Leeds 40 – York 30.

Forte Travelodge, Beacon Service Area, HU15 1RZ, SW : 2½ m. on A 63 (eastbou carriageway) ✆ 424455, Reservations (Freephone) 0800 850950 – ⟡ ⟡ ⟡. ⟡ AE VISA.
Meals (grill rest.) – **40 rm** 34.50 **t.**

SOUTHEND-ON-SEA Essex 404 W 29 – pop. 158 517 – ✆ 01702.

18 Belfairs, Eastwood Rd North, Leigh-on-Sea ✆ 525345 – 18 Ballards Gore, Gore Rd, Cane don, Rochford ✆ 258917.

✈ Southend-on-Sea Airport : ✆ 340201, N : 2 m..

ℹ 19 High St., SS1 1JE ✆ 215120.

♦London 39 – ♦Cambridge 69 – Croydon 46 – ♦Dover 85.

Balmoral, 32-36 Valkyrie Rd, Westcliff-on-Sea, SS0 8BU, ✆ 342947, Fax 337828 – ⟡ ⟡. ⟡ AE VISA JCB. ⟡
Meals *(closed Sunday dinner)* (bar lunch Monday to Saturday)/dinner 12.95 **t.** and a la car ⟡ 4.00 – **28 rm** ⟡ 39.00/75.00 **st.**, 1 suite.

Camelia, 178 Eastern Esplanade, SS1 3AA, ✆ 587917, Fax 585704 – ⟡ rest ⟡ ⟡. ⟡ VISA JCB. ⟡
Meals (dinner only and Sunday lunch)/dinner 12.95 **st.** and a la carte ⟡ 4.50 – **16 r** ⟡ 42.50/70.00 **st.** – SB.

Pebbles, 190 Eastern Esplanade, SS1 3AA, ✆ 582329 – ⟡ rest ⟡. ⟡
Meals (by arrangement) 12.50 **st.** – **5 rm** ⟡ 25.00/40.00 **st.**

Moorings without rest., 172 Eastern Esplanade, SS1 3AA, ✆ 587575 – ⟡. ⟡
3 rm ⟡ 25.00/36.00 **s.**

XXX **Paris,** 719 London Rd, Westcliff-on-Sea, SS0 9ST, ✆ 344077, Fax 344077 – ⟡ AE VISA
closed Saturday lunch, Sunday dinner and Monday – **Meals** 14.50/23.95 **st.** ⟡ 6.00.

SOUTH KILVINGTON N. Yorks. – see Thirsk.

SOUTH LOPHAM Norfolk 404 X 26 – see Diss.

SOUTH MIMMS SERVICE AREA Herts. 404 T 28 – ✉ Potters Bar – ✆ 01707.

ℹ Welcome Break, M 25 Motorway Services, EN6 3QQ ✆ 643233.

♦London 21 – Luton 17.

Forte Posthouse, Bignells Corner, EN6 3NH, M 25 junction 23 at junction with A 1 (M ✆ 643311, Fax 646728, ⟡, ⟡, ⟡ – ⟡ rm ⟡ rest ⟡ ⟡ ⟡ – ⟡ 170. ⟡ AE ⟡ VISA JCB ⟡
Meals a la carte approx. 15.00 **t.** ⟡ 5.50 – **120 rm** 59.50/69.50 **st.**

Forte Travelodge, Bignells Corner, EN6 3QQ, M 25 junction 23 at junction with A 1 (M ✆ 665440, Reservations (Freephone) 0800 850950 – ⟡ ⟡ ⟡. ⟡ AE VISA. ⟡
Meals (grill rest.) – **52 rm** 34.50 **t.**

SOUTH MOLTON Devon 403 I 30 – pop. 4 066 – ✆ 01769.

ℹ 1 East St., EX36 3BU ✆ 574122 (summer only).

♦London 210 – Exeter 35 – Taunton 39.

Whitechapel Manor ⟡, EX36 3EG, E : 4 m. by B 3227 and Whitechapel rd ✆ 573377 Fax 573797, ⟡, « Elizabethan manor house built by Robert de Bassett », ⟡, park – ⟡ rest ⟡ ⟡ ⟡ – ⟡ 30. ⟡ AE ⟡ VISA JCB. ⟡
Meals (booking essential) 34.00 **st.** ⟡ 5.50 – **9 rm** ⟡ 70.00/170.00 **st.**, 1 suite – SB.

Park House ⟡, EX36 3ED, N : ½ m. on North Molton rd ✆ 572610, ⟡, « Victoria country house, gardens », ⟡, park – ⟡ rest ⟡ ⟡ ⟡. ⟡ AE ⟡ VISA. ⟡
closed 22 January-26 February – **Meals** (light lunch)/dinner 18.50 **st.** ⟡ 4.10 – **8 rm** ⟡ 49.00/ 88.00 **st.** – SB.

Marsh Hall Country House ⟡, EX36 3HQ, NE : 1½ m. on North Molton rd ✆ 572666 Fax 574230, ⟡, ⟡ – ⟡ rest ⟡ ⟡ ⟡. ⟡ AE ⟡ VISA. ⟡
closed Christmas and 3 weeks February – **Meals** (dinner only) 18.50 **st.** ⟡ 6.50 – **7 rm** ⟡ 40.00/84.00 **st.** – SB.

at East Buckland NW : 6¼ m. by B 3226 and Filleigh rd, turning right at Stags Head – ✉ Barnstaple – ✆ 01598 :

XX **Lower Pitt** ⟡ with rm, EX32 0TD, ✆ 760243, Fax 760243, ⟡ – ⟡ ⟡. ⟡ AE VISA. ⟡
closed 25 and 26 December – **Meals** *(closed Sunday and Monday)* (booking essential) (dinner only) a la carte 15.50/19.75 **st.** ⟡ 4.50 – **3 rm** ⟡ 55.00/110.00 **st.** – SB.

SOUTH NORMANTON Derbs. 402 403 404 Q 24 – pop. 8 034 – ☎ 01773.

London 130 – Derby 17 – ♦Nottingham 15 – ♦Sheffield 31.

Swallow, Carter Lane East, DE55 2EH, on A 38 ℘ 812000, Fax 580032, Fitness centre, Indoor pool, Sauna – No smoking rm ▤ rest TV ☎ ♿ P – 200. Cards: AE, Diners, VISA
Meals 12.50/19.95 **st.** and a la carte – **157 rm** ☕ 95.00/120.00 **st.** – SB.

SOUTHPORT Mersey. 402 K 23 – pop. 90 959 – ☎ 01704.

Southport Municipal, Park Road West ℘ 535286.

112 Lord St., PR8 1NY ℘ 533333.

London 221 – ♦Liverpool 20 – ♦Manchester 38 – Preston 19.

Scarisbrick, 239 Lord St., PR8 1NZ, ℘ 543000, Fax 533335 – Lift TV ☎ P – 180. Cards: AE, Diners, VISA. No dogs
Meals (dancing Saturday evening) 8.60/14.50 **t.** and a la carte 🍷 5.00 – **77 rm** ☕ 65.00/120.00 **st.** – SB.

Stutelea, Alexandra Rd, PR9 0NB, ℘ 544220, Fax 500232, Fitness centre, Indoor pool, Sauna, Garden – Lift TV ☎ P. Cards: AE, Diners, VISA. No dogs
Meals (bar lunch)/dinner a la carte 12.00/17.00 **t.** 🍷 4.90 – **24 rm** ☕ 45.00/90.00 **st.** – SB.

Cambridge House, 4 Cambridge Rd, PR9 9NG, NE : 1 m. on A 565 ℘ 538372, Fax 547183, Garden – No smoking TV ☎ P. Cards: AE, Diners, VISA. No dogs
Meals 11.95/16.95 **t.** and a la carte 🍷 5.00 – **18 rm** ☕ 33.00/59.00 **t.** – SB.

Radley, Promenade, PR8 1QU, ℘ 530310 – TV P
22 rm.

Ambassador, 13 Bath St., PR9 0DP, ℘ 543998, Fax 536269 – No smoking TV P. Cards: AE, VISA
closed Christmas and New Year – **Meals** 10.00 **st.** 🍷 3.50 – **9 rm** ☕ 29.00/46.00 **st.** – SB.

Gilton, 7 Leicester St., PR9 0ER, ℘ 530646, Fax 533791, Sauna, Garden – TV ☎ P. Cards: VISA. No dogs
Meals (by arrangement) 10.00 **st.** 🍷 3.15 – **13 rm** ☕ 25.00/40.00 **st.** – SB.

ATS 69 Shakespeare St. ℘ 534434

When looking for a quiet hotel
use the maps found in the introductory pages
or look for establishments with the sign (quiet) *or* (very quiet).

SOUTHSEA Hants. 403 404 Q 31 – see Portsmouth and Southsea.

SOUTH SHIELDS Tyne and Wear 401 402 P 19 – pop. 83 704 – ☎ 0191.

Cleadon Hills ℘ 456 0475 – Whitburn, Lizard Lane ℘ 529 2144.

Amphitheatre, Sea Rd, NE33 2LD ℘ 455 7411 (summer only) – Museum & Art Gallery, Ocean Rd, NE33 2HZ ℘ 454 6612.

London 284 – ♦Newcastle upon Tyne 9.5 – Sunderland 6.

Sea, Sea Rd, NE33 2LD, ℘ 427 0999, Fax 454 0500 – TV ☎ P. Cards: AE, Diners, VISA
Meals 6.95/9.95 **st.** and a la carte – **33 rm** ☕ 58.00/73.00 **t.** – SB.

ATS Western Approach ℘ 454 1060/4247

SOUTHWAITE SERVICE AREA Cumbria 401 402 L 19 – ✉ Carlisle – ☎ 0169 74.

M 6 Service Area, CA4 0NS ℘ 73445/73446.

London 300 – ♦Carlisle 14 – Lancaster 58 – Workington 48.

Granada Lodge without rest., CA4 0NT, M 6 between junctions 41 and 42 ℘ 73131, Fax 73669, Reservations (Freephone) 0800 555300 – No smoking TV ☎ ♿ P. Cards: AE, VISA. No dogs
– **39 rm** 39.95 **st.**

SOUTH WALSHAM Norfolk 404 Y 26 **Great Britain G.** – pop. 1 612 – ✉ Norwich – ☎ 01603.

Envir. : The Broads★.

London 120 – Great Yarmouth 11 – ♦Norwich 9.

South Walsham Hall H. & Country Club (quiet), South Walsham Rd, NR13 6DQ, ℘ 270378, Fax 270519, ≤, Outdoor pool heated, Tennis, Garden, park, Riding, squash – TV ☎ P. Cards: AE, Diners, VISA, JCB. No dogs
Meals 15.50/18.50 **t.** and a la carte 🍷 4.50 – **17 rm** ☕ 40.00/90.00 **st.** – SB.

SOUTHWELL Notts. 402 404 R 24 **Great Britain G.** – pop. 6 958 – ☎ 01636.

See : Minster★★ *AC*.

♦London 135 – Lincoln 24 – ♦Nottingham 14 – ♦Sheffield 34.

Saracen's Head (Forte Heritage), Market Pl., NG25 0HE, ℘ 812701, Fax 815408 – No smoking TV ☎ P – 100. Cards: AE, Diners, VISA
Meals 10.25/17.95 **st.** and a la carte 🍷 6.70 – ☕ 8.50 **27 rm** 60.00/85.00 **st.** – SB.

Old Forge without rest., 2 Burgage Lane, NG25 0ER, ℘ 812809, Garden – No smoking TV ☎ P. Cards: VISA
6 rm ☕ 32.00/48.00.

SOUTHWOLD Suffolk 404 Z 27 – pop. 5 951 – ☎ 01502.

The Common ☎ 723234.

Town Hall, Market Pl., IP18 6EF ☎ 724729 (summer only).

London 108 – Great Yarmouth 24 – Ipswich 35 – Norwich 34.

Swan, Market Pl., IP18 6EG, ☎ 722186, Fax 724800, – rest – 40. AE VISA.
Meals *(closed lunch Monday to Friday January-Easter)* 15.50/35.95 **t.** – **43 rm** 40.0 118.00 **t.**, 2 suites – SB.

Crown, 90 High St., IP18 6DP, ☎ 722275, Fax 727223 – – 40. AE JCB.
closed 1 week early January – **Meals** 15.50/19.95 **t.** – 4.50 – **12 rm** 40.00/69.00 **t.**

at Reydon NW : 1 m. by A 1095 on B 1126 – ✉ Southwold – ☎ 01502 :

Cricketers, Wangford Rd, IP18 6PZ, ☎ 723603, Fax 722194, – . VISA.
Meals (in bar) a la carte 10.70/13.10 **t.** 5.00 – **8 rm** 35.00/55.00 **t.** – SB.

SPALDING Lincs. 402 404 T 25 – pop. 19 561 – ☎ 01775.

Ayscoughfee Hall, Churchgate, PE11 2RA ☎ 725468/761161.

London 111 – Lincoln 40 – Leicester 56 – Norwich 65.

Queensgate, Westlode St., PE11 2AF, ☎ 711929, Fax 724205 – . AE VISA JC
Meals (in bar) 9.95/24.75 **st.** 3.95 – **11 rm** 40.00/49.00 **st.**

Bedford Court without rest., 10 London Rd, PE11 2TA, ☎ 722377, Fax 722377, –
4 rm 25.00/40.00.

ATS 10 Gosberton Rd ☎ 680251

SPEEN Berks. – see Newbury.

SPEEN Bucks. – ✉ Princes Risborough – ☎ 01494.

London 41 – Aylesbury 15 – Oxford 33 – Reading 25.

Old Plow (Restaurant), Flowers Bottom, HP27 0PZ, W : ½ m. by Chapel Hill an Highwood Bottom ☎ 488300, – . AE VISA
closed Sunday dinner, Monday, 24 December-3 January and 28 July-5 August
Meals 15.95/25.00 **t.** 5.50.

Bistro : Meals (booking essential) a la carte 15.00/28.00 **t.** 7.95.

SPORLE Norfolk – see Swaffham.

SPRATTON Northants. 404 R 27 – see Northampton.

STADDLEBRIDGE N. Yorks. – see Northallerton.

STAFFORD Staffs. 402 403 404 N 25 – pop. 117 788 – ☎ 01785.

Brocton Hall, Brocton ☎ 662627 – Stafford Castle, Newport Rd ☎ 223821.

The Ancient High House, Greengate St., ST16 2JA ☎ 40204.

London 142 – Birmingham 26 – Derby 32 – Shrewsbury 31 – Stoke-on-Trent 17.

De Vere Tillington Hall, Eccleshall Rd, ST16 1JJ, NW : 1½ m. on A 5013 ☎ 253531 Fax 259223, , , , – rm rest – 200. AE VISA
Meals *(closed Saturday lunch)* 9.00/14.75 **st.** and a la carte – **90 rm** 82.00/95.00 **st.** – SB

Garth (Regal), Moss Pit, ST17 9JR, S : 2 m. on A 449 ☎ 56124, Fax 55152, – rm rest – 120. AE VISA
Meals *(closed lunch Saturday and Bank Holidays)* 18.00/20.00 **t.** – **60 rm** 68.00/72.00 **st** – SB.

Vine, Salter St., ST16 2JU, ☎ 44112, Fax 46612 – . AE VISA.
Meals (in bar) a la carte 9.50/15.95 **t.** – **27 rm** 32.50/40.00 **t.**

ATS Kenworthy Rd, Astonfields Ind. Est. ☎ 223832/58118

STAINES Middx. 404 S 29 – pop. 51 167 – ☎ 01784.

London 26 – Reading 25.

Thames Lodge (Forte Heritage), Thames St., TW18 4SF, ☎ 464433, Fax 454858, – rest – 50. AE VISA JCB
Meals (bar lunch Monday to Saturday)/dinner a la carte 13.40/21.30 **t.** 6.70 – 8.50 – **44 rm** 85.00/95.00 **t.** – SB.

STAITHES N. Yorks. 402 R 20 – ✉ Saltburn (Cleveland) – ☎ 01947.

London 269 – Middlesbrough 22 – Scarborough 31.

Endeavour, 1 High St., TS13 5BH, ☎ 840825
closed Sunday except dinner July-September and mid January-mid March – **Meals** - Seafood - a la carte 16.85/23.15 **st.** 4.80.

STAMFORD Lincs. 402 404 S 26 Great Britain G. – pop. 13 566 – ☎ 01780.

See : Town★★ - St. Martin's Church★ – Lord Burghley's Hospital★ – Browne's Hospital★ *AC*.

Envir. : Burghley House★★ *AC*, SE : 1½ m. by B 1443.

Stamford Arts Centre, 27 St. Mary's St., PE9 2DL ℘ 55611.

♦London 92 – ♦Leicester 31 – Lincoln 50 – ♦Nottingham 45.

The George of Stamford, 71 St. Martin's, PE9 2LB, ℘ 55171, Fax 57070, « Part 16C coaching inn with walled monastic garden » – TV ☎ P – 50. AE VISA
Meals 19.50 **st.** (lunch) and a la carte 26.20/35.75 **st.** – **46 rm** 78.00/160.00 **st.**, 1 suite – SB.

Lady Anne's, 37-38 High St., St. Martin's Without, PE9 2LJ, ℘ 481184, Fax 65422, – rest TV ☎ P – 130. AE VISA JCB
closed 27 to 31 December – **Meals** 15.50 **t.** and a la carte 5.25 – **29 rm** 49.50/78.25 **t.** – SB.

Ram Jam Inn, Great North Rd, Stretton, LE15 7QX, NW : 8 m. by B 1081 on A 1 (northbound carriageway) ℘ 410776, Fax 410361, – TV ☎ P – 25. AE VISA.
closed 25 December – **Meals** a la carte 10.15/19.05 **t.** 6.25 – 5.00 – **7 rm** 41.00/51.00 **t.**

Garden House, 42 High St., St. Martin's, PE9 2LP, ℘ 63359, Fax 63339, – TV ☎ P. AE VISA
Meals 14.50 **st.** and a la carte – **20 rm** 49.75/79.50 **st.** – SB.

Raj of India, 2 All Saints St., PE9 2PA, ℘ 53556 – . AE VISA
Meals - Indian - a la carte 8.25/13.30 **t.** 4.80.

L'Incontro, The Old Barn Passage, St. Mary's St., PE9 2HG, ℘ 51675, « 16C barn » – AE VISA JCB
closed Monday lunch and Sunday – **Meals** - Italian - a la carte 12.50/18.75 **t.** 5.45.

at Empingham (Leics.) W : 5¾ m. on A 606 – ✉ Oakham – ☎ 01780 :

White Horse, 2 Main St., LE15 8PS, ℘ 460221, Fax 460521, – TV ☎ P – 60. AE VISA.
Meals (bar lunch)/dinner 15.95 **t.** and a la carte 4.50 – **14 rm** 32.00/60.00 – SB.

at Normanton Park (Leics.) W : 6½ m. by A 606 on Edith Weston Rd – ✉ Oakham – ☎ 01780 :

Normanton Park , South Shore, LE15 8RP, ℘ 720315, Fax 721086, <, , – rm TV ☎ P – 30. VISA
Meals a la carte 13.50/24.00 **t.** – **23 rm** 49.50/79.50 **t.** – SB.

STANDISH Gtr. Manchester 402 404 M 23 – pop. 12 196 – ✉ Wigan – ☎ 01257.

♦London 210 – ♦Liverpool 22 – ♦Manchester 21 – Preston 15.

Kilhey Court, Chorley Rd, WN1 2XN, E : 1¾ m. by B 5239 on A 5106 ℘ 472100, Fax 422401, , , , 18, , park – rm rest TV ☎ P – 180. AE VISA.
Laureate : Meals *(closed Saturday lunch)* 11.95/32.50 **t.** and a la carte – 8.50 – **61 rm** 75.00/120.00 **st.** – SB.

Wigan/Standish Moat House (Q.M.H.), Almond Brook Rd, WN6 0SR, W : 1 m. on A 5209 ℘ 499988, Fax 427327, , , – rm rest TV ☎ P – 150. AE VISA
Meals 8.50/12.50 **st.** and a la carte 4.95 – 7.50 – **113 rm** 65.00/95.00 **st.** – SB.

Ashfield House, Ashfield Park Drive, WN6 0EQ, SE : ¾ m. by A 49 ℘ 473500, Fax 400311, – TV ☎ P. AE VISA JCB.
Meals 11.95/19.95 **t.** and a la carte – **12 rm** 55.00/65.00 **t.**

Wrightington, Moss Lane, Wrightington (Lancs.), WN6 9PB, W : 1¾ m. by A 5209 ℘ 425803, Fax 425830, , , , squash – TV ☎ P – 150. AE VISA JCB
Meals *(closed Saturday lunch)* 9.95/15.95 **t.** 3.95 – **47 rm** 56.00/68.00 **t.** – SB.

The Beeches, School Lane, WN6 0TD, on A 5209 ℘ 426432, Fax 427503, – P.
Stable Brasserie.

ATS 23 Market St. ℘ 423146/423732

STANNERSBURN Northd. 401 402 M 18 – ✉ Hexham – ☎ 01434.

♦London 363 – ♦Carlisle 56 – ♦Newcastle upon Tyne 46.

Pheasant Inn , Falstone, NE48 1DD, ℘ 240382, Fax 240382 – TV P. VISA JCB.
closed 25 and 26 December – **Meals** (bar lunch Monday to Saturday)/dinner a la carte 11.00/16.40 **t.** 3.95 – **8 rm** 30.00/52.00 **t.** – SB.

STANSTEAD ABBOTS Herts. 404 U 28 – pop. 1 909 – ✉ Ware – ☎ 01279.

9 Briggens House Hotel, Briggens Park, Stanstead Rd ℘ 793742.

♦London 22 – ♦Cambridge 37 – Luton 32 – ♦Ipswich 66.

Briggens House (Q.M.H.), Stanstead Rd, SG12 8LD, E : 2 m. by A 414 ℘ 829955, Fax 793685, <, heated, 9, , park, – TV ☎ P – 100. AE VISA.
Meals 17.95/21.50 **st.** and a la carte 7.35 – 9.50 – **53 rm** 85.00/115.00 **st.**, 1 suite – SB.

STANSTED AIRPORT Essex 404 U 28 – ✉ Stansted Mountfitchet – ☎ 01279.

◆London 37 – ◆Cambridge 29 – Chelmsford 18 – Colchester 29.

Hilton National, Round Coppice Rd, CM24 8SE, ✆ 680800, Fax 680890, Iá, ≘s, ▣ – ▮ ⇹ rm ▤ ▣ ☎ ♿ ⓟ – 🏛 250. ▣ AE ⓓ VISA JCB
Meals 13.50/14.50 **st.** and a la carte 🍷 5.00 – ☕ 9.75 – **237 rm** 79.00/89.00 **st.** – SB.

Forte Travelodge without rest., Birchanger Service Area, Old Dunmow Rd, CN23 5QZ, at junction 8 of M 11 ✆ 656477, Reservations (Freephone) 0800 850950 – ⇹ ▣ ♿ ⓟ. ▣ AE ⓓ VISA
60 rm 34.50 **t.**

at Broxted NE : 3¾ m. by Broxted rd – ✉ Great Dunmow – ☎ 01279 :

Whitehall, Church End, CM6 2BZ, on B 1051 ✆ 850603, Fax 850385, ≤, « Part 12C and 15C manor house, walled garden », ⛱, 🎾 – ▣ ☎ ⓟ – 🏛 100. ▣ AE ⓓ VISA. ✻
Meals - (see below) – **25 rm** ☕ 79.00/155.00 **t.** – SB.

XXX **Whitehall** (at Whitehall H.), Church End, CM6 2BZ, on B 1051 ✆ 850603, Fax 850385 – ⓟ. ▣ AE ⓓ VISA
Meals 19.50/37.50 **t.** 🍷 7.50.

STANTON FITZWARREN Wilts. – see Swindon.

STANTON HARCOURT Oxon 403 404 P 28 – pop. 908 – ✉ Oxford – ☎ 01865.

◆London 71 – Gloucester 45 – ◆Oxford 13 – Swindon 27.

X **Harcourt Arms,** OX8 1RJ, ✆ 881931 – ⓟ. ▣ AE ⓓ VISA
closed 26 December – **Meals** 12.00 **t.** (dinner Monday to Friday) and a la carte 12.25/18.35 **t.** 🍷 5.50.

STANTON WICK Avon 403 404 M 29 – see Bristol.

STARBOTTON N. Yorks. – see Kettlewell.

STAVERTON Devon 403 I 32 – pop. 682 – ✉ Totnes – ☎ 01803.

◆London 220 – Exeter 20 – Torquay 33.

Kingston House 🐎, TQ9 6AR, NW : 1 m. on Kingston rd ✆ 762235, Fax 762444, ≤, « Georgian mansion, antiques and marquetry staircase », 🌳, park – ⇹ ☎ ⓟ. ▣ AE ⓓ VISA JCB. ✻
Meals (lunch by arrangement) 17.50/40.00 **st.** and a la carte – **3 rm** ☕ 60.00/105.00 **st.** – SB.

Sea Trout Inn, TQ9 6PA, ✆ 762274, Fax 762506, 🐟 – ▣ ☎ ⓟ. ▣ AE VISA
accommodation closed 24 to 26 December – **Meals** *(closed Sunday dinner)* (bar lunch Monday to Saturday)/dinner 18.50 **t.** and a la carte 🍷 4.65 – **10 rm** ☕ 39.50/60.00 **t.** – SB.

STEDHAM W. Sussex 404 R 31 – see Midhurst.

STEEPLE ASTON Oxon. 403 404 Q 28 – pop. 874 – ✉ Bicester – ☎ 01869.

◆London 69 – ◆Coventry 38 – ◆Oxford 10.

Hopcrofts Holt, OX6 3QQ, SW : 1¼ m. at junction of A 4260 with B 4030 ✆ 340259, Fax 340865, 🌳 – ⇹ rm ▣ ☎ ⓟ – 🏛 100. ▣ AE ⓓ VISA JCB
Meals *(closed Saturday lunch)* (carving lunch Sunday) 11.95/17.95 **t.** and a la carte 🍷 5.10 – **88 rm** ☕ 65.00/95.00 **t.** – SB.

STEVENAGE Herts. 404 T 28 **Great Britain G.** – pop. 75 147 – ☎ 01438.

Envir. : Knebworth House★ *AC*, S : 2½ m..

⛳18, ⛳9 Aston Lane ✆ 880424 – ⛳18, ⛳9 Chesfield Downs Golf Centre, Jack's Hill, Graveley ✆ (01462) 482929.

◆London 36 – Bedford 25 – ◆Cambridge 27.

Cromwell (Q.M.H.), High St., Old Town, SG1 3AZ, ✆ 779954, Fax 742169, 🌳 – ⇹ rm ▤ rest ▣ ☎ ⓟ – 🏛 200. ▣ AE ⓓ VISA. ✻
Meals 12.95/16.95 **t.** and a la carte – ☕ 8.75 – **56 rm** 85.00/95.00 **t.** – SB.

Hertfordpark (Q.M.H.), Danestrete, SG1 1EJ, ✆ 779955, Fax 741880 – ▮ ⇹ rm ▣ ☎ – 🏛 250. ▣ AE ⓓ VISA
Meals *(closed Saturday lunch)* 14.50/16.00 **st.** and a la carte – ☕ 9.50 – **98 rm** 59.50/62.50 **st.** – SB.

Novotel Stevenage, Knebworth Park, SG1 2AX, SW : 1½ m. by A 602 at junction with A 1 (M) ✆ 742299, Fax 723872, ⛱ heated – ▮ ⇹ rm ▤ rest ▣ ☎ ♿ ⓟ – 🏛 120. ▣ AE ⓓ VISA
Meals a la carte 11.65/20.85 **st.** 🍷 5.25 – ☕ 7.95 – **100 rm** 54.50 **st.**

Travel Inn, Corey's Mill Lane, SG1 4AA, NW : 2 m. on A 602 ✆ 351318, Fax 721609 – ▮ ⇹ rm ▣ ♿ ⓟ. ▣ AE ⓓ VISA. ✻
Meals (grill rest.) – ☕ 4.95 – **39 rm** 34.50 **t.**

at Broadwater S : 1 ¾ m. by A 602 on B 197 – ✉ Stevenage – ☎ 01438 :

Forte Posthouse, Old London Rd, SG2 8DS, ☎ 365444, Fax 741308, – rm TV ☎ P – 60. AE VISA JCB
Meals a la carte 14.35/23.50 **st.** – 7.95 – **54 rm** 56.00 **st.** – SB.

ATS 4-8 Norton Rd ☎ 313262

STEYNING W. Sussex 404 T 31 – pop. 5 629 – ☎ 01903.
◆London 52 – ◆Brighton 12 – Worthing 10.

Old Tollgate, The Street, Bramber, BN44 3WE, SW : 1 m. ☎ 879494, Fax 813399 – TV ☎ P. AE VISA.
Meals (carving rest.) 14.25/17.25 **t.** – 5.95 – **31 rm** 58.00/78.00 **t.** – SB.

Springwells without rest., 9 High St., BN44 3GG, ☎ 812446, Fax 879823, heated, – TV ☎ P. AE VISA.
closed Christmas and New Year – **11 rm** 34.00/70.00 **t.**

STILTON Cambs. 404 T 26 – pop. 3 765 – ✉ Peterborough – ☎ 01733.
◆London 76 – ◆Cambridge 30 – Northampton 43 – Peterborough 6.

Bell Inn, Great North Rd, PE7 3RA, ☎ 241066, Fax 245173, « Part 16C inn », – rm TV ☎ P – 100. AE VISA JCB.
closed 24 to 26 December – **Meals** 15.95/22.50 **t.** – **19 rm** 59.00/94.00 **t.**

Prices For full details of the prices quoted in the guide, consult the introduction.

STOCKBRIDGE Hants. 403 404 P 30 – pop. 570 – ☎ 01264.
◆London 75 – Salisbury 14 – Winchester 9.

Carbery, Salisbury Hill, SO20 6EZ, on A 30 ☎ 810771, Fax 811022, heated, – TV P.
closed 2 weeks Christmas – **Meals** (by arrangement) 11.50 **t.** – **11 rm** 23.00/49.00 **st.**

at Longstock N : 1 ½ m. by Longstock rd – ✉ Stockbridge – ☎ 01264 :

Peat Spade Inn, SO20 6DR, ☎ 810612, Fax 810612, – P. AE
closed Sunday dinner, 25-26 December, 2 weeks beginning February and 2 weeks end March – **Meals** 17.25 **t.** and a la carte 5.50.

STOCKPORT Gtr. Manchester 402 403 404 N 23 – pop. 284 395 – ☎ 0161.
Heaton Moor, Mauldeth Rd, Heaton Mersey ☎ 432 2134 - Romiley, Goosehouse Green ☎ 430 2392 – Ladythorn Rd, Bramhall ☎ 439 4057 – Hazel Grove ☎ 483 3217 – Offerton Rd, Offerton ☎ 427 2001.
Graylaw House, Chestergate, SK1 ING ☎ 474 3320/1.
◆London 201 – ◆Liverpool 42 – ◆Manchester 6 – ◆Sheffield 37 – ◆Stoke-on-Trent 34.

Old Rectory, Churchgate, SK1 1YG, E : ¼ m. by Wellington St. ☎ 429 0060, Fax 474 0076 – rm TV ☎ P. AE VISA.
Meals (grill rest.) 12.00 **st.** and a la carte – 4.95 – **30 rm** 45.00 **st.**

Saxon Holme, 230 Wellington Rd North, SK4 2QN, N : 1 m. on A 6 ☎ 432 2335, Fax 431 8076 – TV ☎ P. AE VISA
Meals (dinner only) 13.00 **st.** and a la carte 4.50 – **33 rm** 44.00/55.00 **st.** – SB.

Alma Lodge (Jarvis), 149 Buxton Rd, SK2 6EL, S : 1 ¼ m. on A 6 ☎ 483 4431, Fax 483 1983 – rm TV ☎ P – 200. AE VISA JCB
Meals *(closed Saturday lunch)* (carving rest.) 9.95/13.50 **st.** and a la carte 6.75 – 8.50 – **52 rm** 69.00/79.00 **st.** – SB.

Wycliffe, 74 Edgeley Rd, Edgeley, SK3 9NQ, E : 1 m. on B 5465 ☎ 477 5395, Fax 476 3219 – TV ☎ P. AE VISA.
Meals - Italian - *(closed Saturday lunch and Bank Holidays)* 8.00/15.50 **t.** and a la carte 4.75 – **20 rm** 39.00/50.00 **st.**

Travel Inn, Buxton Rd, SK2 6NB, S : 1 m. on A 6 ☎ 480 2968, Fax 477 8320 – rm TV P. AE VISA.
Meals (grill rest.) – 4.95 – **40 rm** 34.50 **t.**

ATS Hollingworth Rd, Bredbury ☎ 430 5221

STOCKTON-ON-TEES Cleveland 402 P 20 – pop. 173 912 – ☎ 01642.
Eaglescliffe, Yarm Rd ☎ 780098 – Knotty Hill Golf Centre, Sedgefield ☎ 620320 – Norton, Junction Rd ☎ 676385.
Teesside Airport : ☎ (01325) 332811, SW : 6 m. by A 1027, A 135 and A 67.
Theatre Yard, off High St., TS18 1AT ☎ 615080.
◆London 251 – ◆Leeds 61 – ◆Middlesbrough 4.

Swallow, 10 John Walker Sq., TS18 1AQ, ☎ 679721, Fax 601714, – rm rest TV ☎ P – 300. AE VISA JCB
Meals 13.00/18.00 **st.** and a la carte – **125 rm** 88.00/115.00 **st.** – SB.

at Eaglescliffe S : 3½ m. on A 135 – ✉ Stockton-on-Tees – ☎ 01642 :

Parkmore, 636 Yarm Rd, TS16 0DH, ℘ 786815, Fax 790485, – 140. AE VISA JCB
Meals 13.00/17.50 **st.** and a la carte ₫ 4.25 – **55 rm** 58.00/86.00 **st.** – SB.

ATS 18 Brunswick St. ℘ 675733 ATS 112 Norton Rd ℘ 604477

STOKE BRUERNE Northants. 404 R 27 – pop. 347 – ✉ Towcester – ☎ 01604.
London 69 – Coventry 33 – Northampton 9 – Oxford 33.

Bruerne's Lock, 5 Canalside, NN12 7SB, ℘ 863654, « Attractive canalside setting » – AE VISA
closed Saturday lunch, Sunday dinner, Monday, 1 week October and 26 December-4 January – **Meals** 16.00 **t.** (lunch) and dinner a la carte 22.15/28.70 **t.** ₫ 5.95.

STOKE BY NAYLAND Suffolk 404 W 28 – ☎ 01206.
London 70 – Bury St.Edmunds 24 – Cambridge 54 – Colchester 11 – Ipswich 14.

Angel Inn with rm, Polstead St., CO6 4SA, ℘ 263245, Fax 337324, « Part timbered 17C inn » – AE VISA.
closed 25 and 26 December – **Meals** a la carte 11.75/24.00 **t.** ₫ 3.70 – **6 rm** 45.00/59.00 **st.**

STOKE D'ABERNON Surrey 404 ㊷ – see Cobham.

STOKE FLEMING Devon 403 J 33 – see Dartmouth.

STOKE GABRIEL Devon 403 J 32 – see Totnes.

STOKE-ON-TERN Shrops. 402 403 404 M 25 – see Hodnet.

Es ist empfehlenswert, ***in der Hauptsaison*** *und vor allem in Urlaubsorten, Hotelzimmer im voraus zu bestellen.*
Benachrichtigen Sie sofort das Hotel, wenn Sie ein bestelltes Zimmer nicht belegen können.

Wenn Sie an ein Hotel im Ausland schreiben, fügen Sie Ihrem Brief einen internationalen Antwortschein bei (im Postamt erhältlich).

STOKE-ON-TRENT Staffs. 402 403 404 N 24 **Great Britain G.** – pop. 244 637 – ☎ 01782.
See : Museum and Art Gallery★ Y **M** – Gladstone Pottery Museum★ *AC* V.
Envir. : Wedgwood Visitor's Centre★ *AC*, S : 5½ m. by A 500 and A 34 V.
Exc. : Little Moreton Hall★★ *AC*, N : 8½ m. by A 500 on A 34 U.
Greenway Hall, Stockton Brook ℘ 503158, U – Parkhall, Hulme Rd, Weston Coyney ℘ 599584, V.
Potteries Shopping Centre, Quadrant Rd, Hanley, ST1 1RZ ℘ 284600.
London 162 – Birmingham 46 – Leicester 59 – Liverpool 58 – Manchester 41 – Sheffield 53.

Plans on following pages

Stoke-on-Trent Moat House (Q.M.H.), Etruria Hall, Festival Park, Etruria, ST1 5BQ, ℘ 609988, Fax 284500, – rm rest – 600. AE VISA. U **n**
Meals 12.50/34.00 **t.** and a la carte – 9.50 – **143 rm** 90.00/155.00 **st.**

Stakis Stoke-on-Trent, 66 Trinity St., Hanley, ST1 5NB, ℘ 202361, Fax 286464, – rm – 300. AE VISA. Y **c**
Chatterley's : Meals (carving lunch) (bar lunch Saturday) 11.00/14.50 **st.** ₫ 5.25 – 8.75 – **125 rm** 80.00/90.00 **st.** – SB.

at Basford NW : 1¾ m. by A 500 off A 53 – ✉ Stoke-on-Trent – ☎ 01782 :

Haydon House, 9 Haydon St., ST4 6JD, ℘ 711311, Fax 717470 – – 80. AE VISA U **a**
Clock : Meals *(closed Saturday lunch and Sunday)* 10.50/14.90 **st.** and a la carte – 6.00 – **24 rm** 52.50/62.50 **t.**, 6 suites.

at Talke NW : 4 m. on A 500 at junction with A 34 – ✉ Stoke-on-Trent – ☎ 01782 :

Forte Travelodge, Newcastle Rd, ST7 1UP, ℘ 777000, Fax 777162, Reservations (Freephone) 0800 850950 – AE VISA. U **e**
Meals (grill rest.) – **62 rm** 34.50 **t.**

ATS 25 Smithpool Rd, Fenton ℘ 47081 ATS 87/89 Waterloo Rd, Burslem ℘ 838493/836591

STOKE-ON-TRENT
NEWCASTLE-UNDER-LYME
BUILT UP AREA

lexandra Road . . . . U 3
edford Road . . . . U 4
rownhills Road . . . . U 12
hurch Lane . . . . U 19
Cobridge Road . . . . U 21
Davenport Street . . . . U 23
Elder Road . . . . U 24
Etruria Vale Road . . . . U 27
Grove Road . . . . V 30
Hanley Road . . . . U 31
Heron Street . . . . V 34
High Street . . . . U 35
Higherland . . . . V 37
Manor Street . . . . V 44
Mayne Street . . . . V 45
Moorland Road . . . . U 48
Park Hall Road . . . . V 54
Porthill Road . . . . U 59
Snow Hill . . . . U 63
Stoke Road . . . . U 68
Strand (The) . . . . V 69
Victoria Park Road . . . . U 75
Watlands View . . . . U 76
Williamson Street . . . . U 77

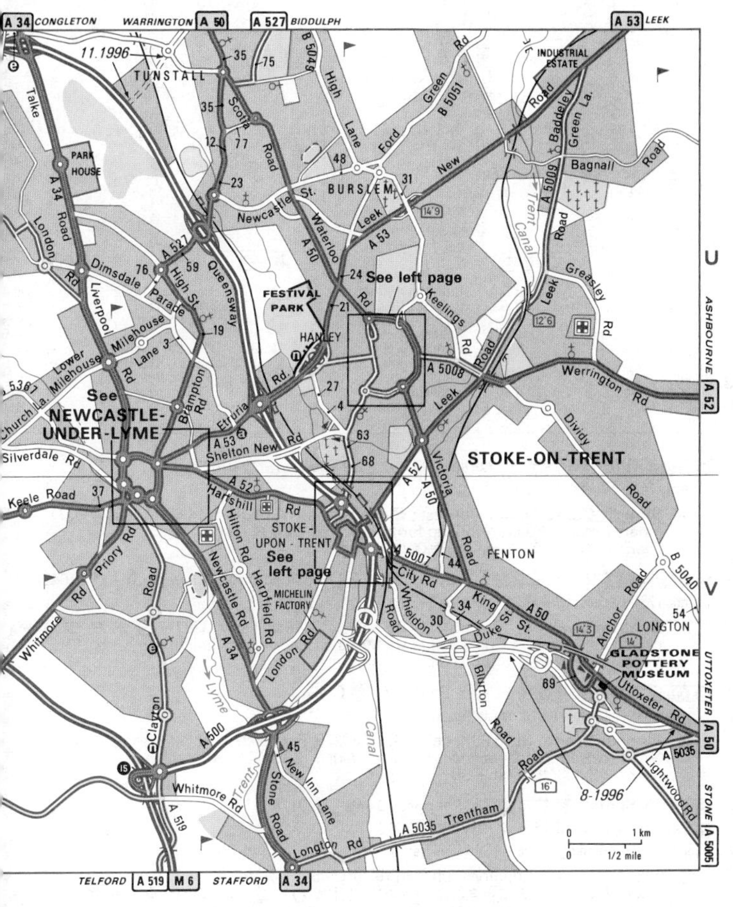

Die Videokassette

SCHLÖSSER AN DER LOIRE von Chambord bis Chinon

ergänzt den Grünen Michelin-Reiseführer Schlösser an der Loire. Thema des Films sind die Schlösser und die kultivierte Lebenskunst in der Touraine.

Sechs Versionen sind erhältlich :

0751 auf französisch SECAM
0752 auf französisch PAL
1752 auf englisch PAL
1753 auf englisch NTSC
2752 auf deutsch PAL
3752 auf italienisch PAL

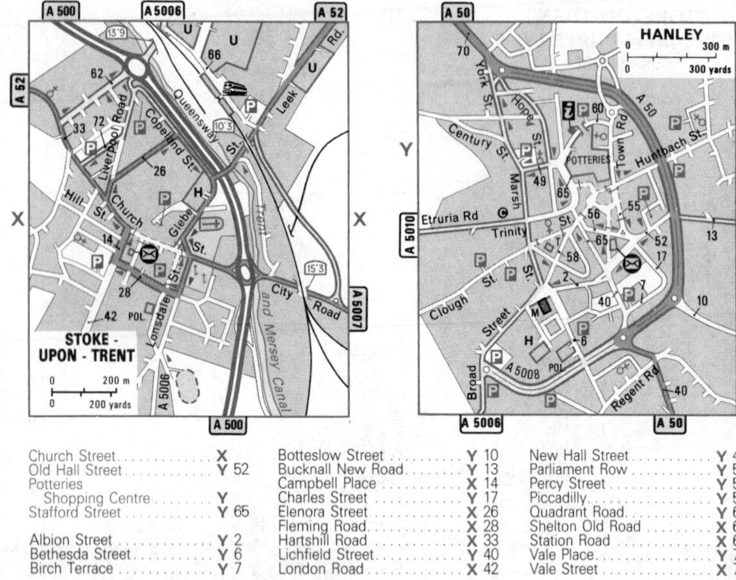

Church Street	X	Botteslow Street	Y 10	New Hall Street	Y 4
Old Hall Street	Y 52	Bucknall New Road	Y 13	Parliament Row	Y 5
Potteries Shopping Centre	Y	Campbell Place	X 14	Percy Street	Y 5
Stafford Street	Y 65	Charles Street	Y 17	Piccadilly	Y 5
		Elenora Street	X 26	Quadrant Road	Y 6
Albion Street	Y 2	Fleming Road	X 28	Shelton Old Road	X 6
Bethesda Street	Y 6	Hartshill Road	X 33	Station Road	X 6
Birch Terrace	Y 7	Lichfield Street	Y 40	Vale Place	Y 7
		London Road	X 42	Vale Street	X 7

STOKE ST. GREGORY Somerset 403 L 30 – ✉ Taunton – ☎ 01823.

♦London 147 – ♦Bristol 39 – Taunton 8.

Slough Court without rest., Slough Lane, TA3 6JQ, ℘ 490311, Fax 490311, « 14 moated manor house, working farm », ⛱, 🎾 – TV **P**. ✗
February-October – **3 rm** ☕ 30.00/48.00 **st.**

STOKESLEY N. Yorks. 402 Q 20 pop. 4 786 – ✉ Middlesbrough (Cleveland) – ☎ 01642.

♦London 239 – ♦Leeds 59 – ♦Middlesbrough 8 – York 52.

Chapter's with rm, 27 High St., TS9 5AD, ℘ 711888, Fax 713387 – TV ☎. AE VISA
closed 25 December and 1 January – **Meals** *(closed Sunday lunch)* a la carte 11.95/20.85 🍷 4.95 – **13 rm** ☕ 47.00/60.00 **t.**

STONE Glos. 403 404 M 29 – ✉ Berkeley – ☎ 01454.

♦London 130 – ♦Bristol 17 – Gloucester 18.

Elms at Stone, GL13 9JX, on A 38 ℘ 260279, Fax 260279, ⛱ – TV ☎ **P**. VISA
Meals *(closed Sunday dinner to non-residents)* 12.95/14.95 **st.** and lunch a la carte 🍷 4.95 **8 rm** ☕ 38.00/48.00 **st.** – SB.

STONE Staffs. 402 403 404 N 25 – pop. 12 645 – ☎ 01785.

⛳18 Barlaston, Meaford Rd ℘ (01782) 372795.

♦London 150 – ♦Birmingham 36 – ♦Stoke-on-Trent 9.

Stone House (Country Club), ST15 0BQ, S : 1 ¼ m. by A 520 on A 34 ℘ 81553
Fax 814764, 🏋, 🏊, 🏊, ⛱, 🎾 – ⇔ rm TV ☎ **P** – 🏫 150. AE VISA. ✗
Meals *(closed Saturday lunch and Bank Holidays)* a la carte 15.75/20.20 **t.** – ☕ 7.50 – **47 r**
65.00 **t.** – SB.

STON EASTON Somerset pop. 579 – ✉ Bath (Avon) – ☎ 01761.

London 131 – Bath 12 – Bristol 11 – Wells 7.

Ston Easton Park ⛰, BA3 4DF, ✆ 241631, Fax 241377, ≤, « Palladian country house », park, – rest TV ☎ P. VISA JCB.
Meals 26.00/38.50 **st.** and dinner a la carte 35.00/41.00 **st.** 7.50 – 12.00 – **19 rm** 115.00/320.00 **st.**, 2 suites – SB.

STONOR Oxon. 404 R 29 – see Henley-on-Thames.

STONY STRATFORD Bucks. 404 R 27 pop. 8 328 – ☎ 01908.

London 58 – Birmingham 68 – Northampton 14 – Oxford 32.

XX **Peking,** 117 High St., MK11 1AT, ✆ 563120, Fax 560084 – ▤. AE VISA
Meals - Chinese (Peking, Szechuan) - 8.50/25.00 **st.** and a la carte.

at Cosgrove (Northants.) N : 2½ m. by A 508 – ✉ Milton Keynes – ☎ 01908 :

Old Bakery, Main St., MK19 7JL, ✆ 262255, Fax 263620 – TV ☎ P. AE VISA.
closed 2 weeks at Christmas – **Meals** (residents only) (dinner only) a la carte 12.15/18.00 **st.** 4.50 – 6.50 – **8 rm** 36.00/43.50 **st.** – SB.

*Es ist empfehlenswert, **in der Hauptsaison** und vor allem in Urlaubsorten, Hotelzimmer im voraus zu bestellen. Benachrichtigen Sie sofort das Hotel, wenn Sie ein bestelltes Zimmer nicht belegen können.*

Wenn Sie an ein Hotel im Ausland schreiben, fügen Sie Ihrem Brief einen internationalen Antwortschein bei (im Postamt erhältlich).

STORRINGTON W. Sussex 404 S 31 – pop. 4 670 – ☎ 01903.

London 54 – Brighton 20 – Portsmouth 36.

Little Thakeham ⛰, Merrywood Lane, Thakeham, RH20 3HE, N : 1 ¾ m. by B 2139 ✆ 744416, Fax 745022, ≤, « Lutyens house with gardens in the style of Gertrude Jekyll », heated, – TV ☎ P. AE VISA JCB.
closed 2 weeks Christmas-New Year – **Meals** *(closed Monday lunch and Sunday dinner)* (lunch by arrangement)/dinner 32.50 **st.** 6.50 – **7 rm** 95.00/150.00 **st.**, 2 suites – SB.

XXX ✿ **Manley's** (Löderer), Manley's Hill, RH20 4BT, E : ¼ m. on A 283 ✆ 742331 – P. AE VISA
closed Sunday dinner, Monday and first week January – **Meals** 19.60/30.00 **t.** and dinner a la carte approx. 38.00 **t.** 6.90
Spec. Pan fried new season's lamb with grilled aubergines and jus reduction, Poached fillets of Dover sole with Riesling, shallots and langoustine, Lemon and orange soufflé cooked in honey and rum.

XX **Old Forge,** 6a Church St., RH20 4LA, ✆ 743402, Fax 742540 – AE VISA
closed lunch Tuesday and Saturday, Sunday dinner, Monday, 1 week late spring and 3 weeks October – **Meals** 12.00/22.00 **st.** and a la carte 20.00/27.00 **st.** 5.00.

STOURBRIDGE W. Mids. 403 404 N26 – pop. 55 624 – ☎ 01384.

London 147 – Birmingham 14 – Wolverhampton 10 – Worcester 21.

Plan : see Birmingham p. 2

Talbot (Regal), High St., DY8 1DW, ✆ 394350, Fax 371318 – TV ☎ P – 150. AE VISA AU **a**
Meals 9.50/19.50 **st.** and dinner a la carte – **25 rm** 45.75/55.50 **st.** – SB.

Limes, 260 Hagley Rd, Pedmore, DY9 0RW, SE : 1½ m. on A 491 ✆ (01562) 882689, – TV ☎ P AU **z**
10 rm.

at Hagley S : 2½ m. by A 491 – ✉ Stourbridge – ☎ 01562 :

Travel Inn, Birmingham Rd, DY9 9JS, NE : 1 ½ m. on A 456 (eastbound) ✆ 883120, Fax 884416 – rm TV & P. AE VISA. AU **r**
Meals (grill rest.) – 4.95 – **40 rm** 34.50 **t.**

at Kinver (Staffs.) W : 5 m. by A 458 – AU – ✉ Stourbridge – ☎ 01384 :

XX **Berkley's,** 5-6 High St., DY7 6HG, ✆ 873679 – AE VISA
closed Sunday, first 2 weeks February, 26 to 30 December and Bank Holiday Mondays – **Meals** (dinner only) a la carte 17.30/25.50 **t.** 4.25.

STOURPORT-ON-SEVERN Heref. and Worcs. 403 404 N 26 – pop. 18 739 – ☎ 01299.

London 137 – Birmingham 21 – Worcester 12.

County (Q.M.H.), 35 Hartlebury Rd, DY13 9LT, E : 1 ¼ m. on B 4193 ✆ 289955, Fax 878520, , , , , park, , squash – rm TV ☎ P – 350. AE VISA
Meals 13.50/16.50 **st.** and a la carte 5.25 – 8.50 – **66 rm** 62.00/72.00 **st.**, 2 suites – SB.

STOWMARKET Suffolk 404 W/X 27 – pop. 13 229 – ☎ 01449.

Wilkes Way, IP14 1DE ✆ 676800.

◆London 81 – ◆Cambridge 42 – ◆Ipswich 12 – ◆Norwich 38.

Gipping Heights, Creeting Rd, IP14 5BT, E : 1 m. by Station Rd East (B 1113) ✆ 675264 – TV P. VISA.
Meals *(closed 25 December)* (bar lunch)/dinner 11.50 **s.** 4.80 – **5 rm** 33.00/45.00 **s.** – SB.

Forte Travelodge, IP14 3PY, NW : 2 m. by A 1038 on A 14 (westbound) ✆ 615347 Reservations (Freephone) 0800 850950 – TV P. AE VISA
Meals (grill rest.) – **40 rm** 34.50 **t.**

at Mendlesham Green NE : 6 ¼ m. by B 1115, A 1120 and Mendlesham rd – ✉ Stowmarket – ☎ 01449 :

Cherry Tree Farm, Mendlesham Green, IP14 5RQ, ✆ 766376, « Part Elizabethan house », – P.
closed Christmas and January – **Meals** (by arrangement) (communal dining) 15.00 **st.** – **3 rm** 30.00/48.00 **st.**

STOW-ON-THE-WOLD Glos. 403 404 O 28 Great Britain G. – pop. 1 999 – ☎ 01451.

Exc. : Chastleton House★★, NE : 6½ m. by A 436 and A 44.

Hollis House, The Square, Gl54 1AF ✆ 831082.

◆London 86 – ◆Birmingham 44 – Gloucester 27 – ◆Oxford 30.

Wyck Hill House , GL54 1HY, S : 2¼ m. by A 429 on A 424 ✆ 831936, Fax 832243, « Part Victorian country house », , park – rest TV P – 50. AE VISA
Meals 13.50/29.50 **t.** and dinner a la carte – **29 rm** 78.00/108.00 **t.**, 1 suite – SB.

Grapevine, Sheep St., GL54 1AU, ✆ 830344, Fax 832278, « Mature grapevine in restaurant » – rest TV P – 25. AE VISA JCB.
closed 24 December-11 January – **Meals** (bar lunch Monday to Saturday)/dinner 16.00/23.00 **t.** – **23 rm** (dinner included) 74.00/154.00 **t.** – SB.

Fosse Manor, Fosse Way, GL54 1JX, S : 1¼ m. on A 429 ✆ 830354, Fax 832486, , – rest TV P – 40. AE VISA
closed 22 to 29 December – **Meals** 12.95/30.00 **t.** and a la carte 5.95 – **20 rm** 53.00/150.00 **t.** – SB.

Unicorn (Forte Heritage), Sheep St., GL54 1HQ, ✆ 830257, Fax 831090 – TV P. AE VISA JCB
Meals 11.95/16.95 **st.** and a la carte 7.20 – 8.50 – **20 rm** 70.00/85.00 **st.** – SB.

Stow Lodge, The Square, GL54 1AB, ✆ 830485, – TV P. AE.
closed Christmas and 3 January-early February – **Meals** (bar lunch)/dinner 15.00 **t.** and a la carte – **22 rm** 37.00/95.00 **t.** – SB.

Bretton House without rest., Fosseway, GL54 1JU, S : ½ m. on A 429 ✆ 830388, , – TV P
closed Christmas – **3 rm** 35.00/45.00.

Wyck Hill Lodge without rest., Wyck Hill, GL54 1HT, S : 2 m. by A 429 on A 424 ✆ 830141, , – TV P.
closed Christmas – **3 rm** 30.00/44.00 **st.**

Limes without rest., Evesham Rd, GL54 1EJ, ✆ 830034, – TV P
closed 24 December-2 January – **3 rm** 33.00/38.00.

Cross Keys Cottage without rest., Park St., GL54 1AQ, ✆ 831128 – TV.
3 rm 35.00/50.00.

at Broadwell NE : 1 ¾ m. by A 429 – ✉ Moreton-in-Marsh – ☎ 01451 :

College House, Chapel St., GL56 0TW, ✆ 832351, « 17C house », – TV P
closed Christmas – **Meals** (by arrangement) (communal dining) 16.50 **st.** – **3 rm** 48.00/58.00 **st.**

at Bledington SE : 4 m. by A 436 on B 4450 – ✉ Kingham – ☎ 01608 :

Kings Head, OX7 6HD, ✆ 658365, Fax 658902 – rm TV P. VISA.
closed 24 and 25 December – **Meals** (bar lunch)/dinner a la carte 11.45/17.15 **st.** 4.00 – **12 rm** 42.00/75.00 **st.** – SB.

at Nether Westcote SE : 4 ¾ m. by A 429 off A 424 – ✉ Kingham – ☎ 01993 :

Lavender Hill, OX7 6SD, ✆ 831872, – TV P
Meals (by arrangement) 15.00 **st.** – **3 rm** 34.00/48.00 **st.** – SB.

TRATFIELD TURGIS Hants. – pop. 94 – ✉ Basingstoke – ☎ 01256.

ondon 46 – Basingstoke 8 – Reading 11.

Wellington Arms, RG27 0AS, on A 33 ℘ 882214, Fax 882934, – TV ☎ P – 60. AE VISA
Meals *(closed Saturday lunch and Sunday dinner)* 17.95 **t.** and a la carte – **33 rm** 65.00/85.00 **t.**, 2 suites.

TRATFORD-UPON-AVON Warks. 403 404 P 27 **Great Britain G.** – pop. 105 586 – ☎ 01789.

ee : Town★ - Shakespeare's Birthplace★ *AC*, AB.

nvir. : Mary Arden's House★ *AC*, NW : 4 m. by A 3400 A.

xc. : Ragley Hall★ *AC*, W : 9 m. by A 422 A.

Tiddington Rd ℘ 297296, B – 18 Welcombe Hotel, Warwick Rd ℘ 299021, B – 18 Stratford aks, Bearley Rd, Snitterfield ℘ 731571, B.

Bridgefoot, CV37 6GW ℘ 293127.

ondon 96 – ◆Birmingham 23 – ◆Coventry 18 – ◆Oxford 40.

STRATFORD-UPON-AVON

idge Street ... B 8
enley Street ... A 29
gh Street ... A 31
heep Street ... AB 35
ood Street ... A 47

anbury Road ... B 2
enson Road ... B 3
ridge Foot ... B 6
hapel Lane ... A 13
hapel Street ... A 14
hurch Street ... A 16
opton Bridge ... B 18
ollege Lane ... A 19
y Street ... A 22
vesham Place ... A 24
reat William Street ... A 25
reenhill Street ... A 27
uild Street ... A 28
other Street ... A 32
cholars Lane ... A 33
ddington Road ... B 38
inity Street ... A 40
Varwick Road ... B 42
Vaterside ... B 43
Vindsor Street ... A 45

own plans : the names of ain shopping streets are dicated in red at the eginning of the list of streets.

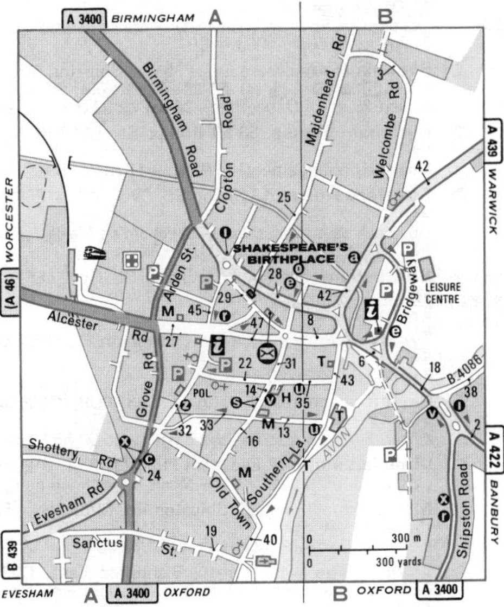

Welcombe H. & Golf Course, Warwick Rd, CV37 0NR, NE : 1½ m. on A 439 ℘ 295252, Telex 31347, Fax 414666, <, « 19C Jacobean style mansion in park », 18, – TV ☎ P – 80. AE VISA JCB.
Meals 18.50/29.50 **st.** 7.50 – **71 rm** 110.00/150.00 **st.**, 4 suites – SB.

Ettington Park, Alderminster, CV37 8BS, SE : 6 ¼ m. on A 3400 ℘ 450123, Fax 450472, <, « Victorian Gothic mansion », park, – TV ☎ P – 60. AE VISA JCB.
Meals 16.00/40.00 **t.** and dinner a la carte 8.00 – **43 rm** 115.00/175.00 **st.**, 5 suites – SB.

Stratford Moat House (Q.M.H.), Bridgefoot, CV37 6YR, ℘ 279988, Fax 298589, – rm TV ☎ P – 450. AE VISA JCB B **e**
Meals 10.95/20.25 **st.** 5.75 – 9.50 – **245 rm** 95.00/125.00 **st.**, 2 suites – SB.

Alveston Manor (Forte Heritage), Clopton Bridge, CV37 7HP, ℘ 204581, Fax 414095, « Part Elizabethan house », – rm TV ☎ P – 150. AE VISA JCB B **i**
Manor : Meals 21.50 **t.** and a la carte 8.50 – 9.75 – **105 rm** 80.00/95.00 **t.**, 1 suite – SB.

Shakespeare (Forte Heritage), Chapel St., CV37 6ER, ℘ 294771, Fax 415411, « 17C timbered inn » – rm TV ☎ P – 100. AE VISA A **v**
David Garrick : Meals 15.95/25.95 **t.** and a la carte – 10.00 – **62 rm** 95.00/125.00 **t.**, 1 suite – SB.

Arden Thistle, 44 Waterside, CV37 6BA, ☎ 294949, Fax 415874, – rm – 50. AE VISA JCB B u
Bards : **Meals** 10.50/21.00 **t.** and a la carte 6.30 – 8.50 – **63 rm** 70.00/130.00 **st.** – SB.

Windmill Park, Warwick Rd, CV37 0PY, NE : 3 m. on A 439 ☎ 731173, Fax 731131, park, – rm rest – 360. AE VISA
Meals 12.50/17.50 **st.** and a la carte – **103 rm** 87.50/105.00 **st.** – SB.

Grosvenor, 12-14 Warwick Rd, CV37 6YT, ☎ 269213, Fax 266087 – rest – 100. AE VISA JCB. B a
Meals (bar lunch Saturday) 12.50 **t.** and a la carte 5.95 – **59 rm** 65.00/98.00 **t.**, 1 suite – SB.

White Swan (Forte), Rother St., CV37 6NH, ☎ 297022, Fax 268773, « Part 16C inn » – – 40. AE VISA A
Meals (bar lunch Monday to Saturday)/dinner 17.95 **st.** and a la carte 5.95 – 8.50 – **37 rm** 75.00/90.00 **st.** – SB.

Forte Posthouse, Bridgefoot, CV37 7LT, ☎ 266761, Fax 414547, – rm – 150. AE VISA B v
Meals a la carte 15.85/22.40 **st.** 6.25 – 7.95 – **60 rm** 59.00 **st.** – SB.

Dukes, Payton St., CV37 6UA, ☎ 269300, Group Telex 31430, Fax 414700, – AE VISA JCB. AB c
closed Christmas and New Year – **Meals** *(closed Sunday)* a la carte 17.70/28.40 **t.** 4.95 – **22 rm** 52.50/120.00 **t.** – SB.

Sequoia House without rest., 51-53 Shipston Rd, CV37 7LN, ☎ 268852, Fax 414559, – – 40. AE VISA JCB. B
closed 20 to 28 December – **24 rm** 39.00/72.00 **st.**

Caterham House, 58-59 Rother St., CV37 6LT, ☎ 267309, Fax 414836 – . VISA A
Meals (by arrangement) 12.95 **st.** – **11 rm** 50.00/65.00 **st.**

Stratford House, 18 Sheep St., CV37 6EF, ☎ 268288, Fax 295580 – . AE VISA JCB. AB
closed 4 days Christmas – **Shepherd's : Meals** *(closed Sunday)* (dinner only) a la carte 14.75/21.70 **t.** – **11 rm** 60.00/88.00 **t.**

Stratheden without rest., 5 Chapel St., CV37 6EP, ☎ 297119, Fax 297119 – . VISA A
9 rm 35.00/60.00 **st.**

Twelfth Night without rest., Evesham Pl., CV37 6HT, ☎ 414595 – . VISA A
6 rm 28.00/56.00 **s.**

Payton without rest., 6 John St., CV37 6UB, ☎ 266442, Fax 266442 – . AE VISA JCB. A
closed 24 to 26 December – **5 rm** 40.00/56.00 **s.**

Virginia Lodge, 12 Evesham Pl., CV37 6HT, ☎ 292157, – . A
closed 23 to 26 December – **Meals** (by arrangement) – **8 rm** 19.00/46.00.

Melita without rest., 37 Shipston Rd, CV37 7LN, ☎ 292432, Fax 204867, – . AE VISA JCB B
closed Christmas – **12 rm** 40.00/68.00 **t.**

Victoria Spa without rest., Bishopton Lane, CV37 9QY, NW : 2 m. by A 3400 on Bishopton Lane turning left at roundabout with A 46 ☎ 267985, Fax 204728, – . VISA.
7 rm 45.00/50.00 **t.**

Carlton without rest., 22 Evesham Pl., CV37 6HT, ☎ 293548 – . A
6 rm 20.00/46.00 **st.**

Liaison, 1 Shakespeare St., CV3 6RN, ☎ 293400, Fax 297863 – AE VISA A
closed Saturday lunch, Sunday and first week January – **Meals** 14.95/21.50 **t.** and a la carte 7.50.

Hussain's, 6a Chapel St., CV37 6EP, ☎ 267506, Fax 415341 – . AE VISA A
closed 25 December – **Meals** - Indian - 6.95/10.95 **t.** and a la carte 3.50.

at Charlecote E : 4 ¾ m. by B 4086 on B 4088 – B – ✉ Stratford-upon-Avon – ☎ 01789

Charlecote Pheasant (Q.M.H.), CV35 9EW, ☎ 279954, Fax 470222, heated, – rm – 120. AE VISA
Meals 10.25/14.25 **st.** and a la carte 6.25 – 8.95 – **67 rm** 70.00/100.00 **st.** – SB.

at Wellesbourne E : 5 ¾ m. on B 4086 – B – ✉ Warwick – ☎ 01789 :

Chadley House, Loxley Rd, CV35 9JL, SW : 1 ¼ m. by A 429 ☎ 840994, Fax 84297 « Part Georgian farmhouse », – . VISA.
closed 25 and 26 December – **Meals** (lunch by arrangement) (light dinner Sunday residents only) 18.00/20.00 **t.** and dinner a la carte – **9 rm** 42.50/75.00 **t.** – SB.

Kings Head, Warwick Rd, CV35 9LX, ☎ 840206 –
9 rm.

at Long Marston SW : 7 m. by A 3400 – B – off B 4632 – ✉ Stratford-upon-Avon – ☎ 01789 :

Kings Lodge without rest., CV37 8RL, ℘ 720705, Fax 720705, – closed December and January – **3 rm** 20.00/50.00 **s.**

at Billesley W : 4½ m. by A 422 – A – off A 46 – ✉ Stratford-upon-Avon – ☎ 01789 :

Billesley Manor (Q.M.H.), B49 6NF, ℘ 279955, Fax 764145, ≤, « Part Elizabethan manor, topiary garden », park, – TV – 90. AE VISA. **Meals** 18.00/27.50 **t.** and a la carte – 8.75 – **39 rm** 99.00/170.00 **t.**, 2 suites – SB.

at Wilmcote NW : 3½ m. by A 3400 – A – ✉ Stratford-upon-Avon – ☎ 01789 :

Pear Tree Cottage without rest., 7 Church Rd, CV37 9UX, ℘ 205889, Fax 262862, « Part Elizabethan », – TV. *closed 18 December-1 January* – **7 rm** 28.00/44.00 **s.**

ATS Western Rd ℘ 205591

TRATTON Glos. 403 404 O 28 – see Cirencester.

TREATLEY Berks. 403 404 Q 29 Great Britain G. – pop. 986 – ✉ Goring – ☎ 01491.
nvir. : Basildon Park★ AC, SE : 2½ m. by A 329 – Mapledurham★ AC, E : 6 m. by A 329, B 471 id B 4526.
xc. : Ridgeway Path★★.
Goring & Streatley, Rectory Rd ℘ 872688.
ondon 56 – ♦Oxford 16 – Reading 11.

Swan Diplomat, High St., RG8 9HR, ℘ 873737, Fax 872554, « ≤ Thames-side setting », – TV – 100. AE VISA. **Meals** 19.25/35.00 **t.** and a la carte – 9.50 – **45 rm** 86.50/126.50 **t.**, 1 suite – SB.

TREET Somerset 403 L 30 The West Country G. – pop. 9 563 – ☎ 01458.
ee : The Shoe Museum★.
nvir. : Glastonbury★★ - Abbey★★★ (Abbots Kitchen★) AC, St. John the Baptist★★, Somerset ıral Life Museum★ AC, Glastonbury Tor★ (≤★★★) NE : 2 m. by A 39.
.ondon 138 – ♦Bristol 28 – Taunton 20.

Bear, 53 High St., BA16 0EF, ℘ 442021, Fax 840007, – TV – 80. VISA. **Meals** a la carte 7.85/18.70 **t.** – 6.95 – **17 rm** 48.00 **st.**, 1 suite.

TRETTON Ches. 402 403 404 M 23 – see Warrington.

TRETTON Staffs. 402 403 404 P 25 – see Burton-upon-Trent.

TROUD Glos. 403 404 N 28 – pop. 103 622 – ☎ 01453.
, 18 Minchinhampton ℘ 832642 (old course) 833866 (new course) – 18 Painswick ℘ 812180.
Subscription Rooms, George St., GL5 1AE ℘ 765768.
.ondon 113 – ♦Bristol 30 – Gloucester 9.

Stonehouse Court, Stonehouse, GL10 3RA, W : 3¼ m. on A 419 ℘ 825155, Fax 824611, – TV – 150. AE VISA. **Meals** 10.00/20.00 **st.** and a la carte – **35 rm** 55.00/90.00 **st.**, 1 suite – SB.

Old Nelson, Stratford Lodge, Stratford Rd, GL5 4AF, N : ½ m. by A 46 ℘ 765821, Fax 765964 – rm TV. AE VISA. **Meals** (grill rest.) a la carte approx. 12.95 **t.** 3.95 – 4.45 – **32 rm** 39.50 **st.** – SB.

Old Vicarage, 167 Slad Rd, GL5 1RD, ℘ 752315, Fax 752315, – TV. *closed January* – **Meals** (by arrangement) 15.00 **t.** 4.40 – **3 rm** 30.00/39.00 **s.** – SB.

at Brimscombe SE : 2¼ m. on A 419 – ✉ Stroud – ☎ 01453 :

Burleigh Court, Burleigh Lane, GL5 2PF, S : ½ m. by Burleigh rd via The Roundabouts ℘ 883804, Fax 886870, ≤, heated, – rest TV. VISA. **Meals** 16.50/27.00 **st.** 4.50 – **17 rm** 62.50/95.00 **st.** – SB.

at Rodborough S : ¾ m. by A 46 – ✉ Stroud – ☎ 01453 :

Bear of Rodborough (Forte Heritage), Rodborough Common, GL5 5DE, SE : 1½ m. on Minchinhampton rd ℘ 878522, Fax 872523, – TV – 70. AE VISA. **Meals** (bar lunch Monday to Saturday)/dinner 16.95 **st.** and a la carte 6.00 – 9.25 – **47 rm** 55.00/65.00 **st.** – SB.

at Amberley S : 3 m. by A 46 – ✉ Stroud – ☎ 01453 :

Amberley Inn, GL5 5AF, ℘ 872565, Fax 872738, – TV. AE VISA. **Meals** 12.00/15.95 **st.** and a la carte 4.25 – **14 rm** 55.00/80.00 **st.** – SB.

ATS Dudbridge Rd ℘ 758156/752191

STUCKTON Hants. – see Fordingbridge.

STUDLEY Warks. 403 404 O 27 – pop. 5 883 – ✉ Redditch – ☎ 01527.
◆London 109 – ◆Birmingham 15 – ◆ Coventry 33 – Gloucester 39.

XX **Pepper's,** 45 High St., B80 7HN, ☏ 853183 – ▤. AE VISA
closed lunch Saturday and Sunday and 25 to 26 December – **Meals** - Indian - a carte 8.35/16.00 **t.**

STURMINSTER NEWTON Dorset 403 404 N 31 **The West Country G.** – pop. 2 579 – ☎ 01258.
See : Mill★ *AC.*
◆London 123 – Bournemouth 30 – ◆Bristol 49 – Salisbury 28 – Taunton 41.

Stourcastle Lodge, Gough's Close, DT10 1BU, (off the Market Place) ☏ 47232 Fax 473381, – rest TV ☎ P. VISA.
Meals 15.00 **st.** – **5 rm** 27.00/68.00 **st.**

XXX **Plumber Manor** with rm, DT10 2AF, SW : 1 ¾ m. by A 357 on Hazelbury Bryan ☏ 472507, Fax 473370, ≤, « 18C manor house », park, – TV ☎ P. AE VIS
closed February – **Meals** (dinner only and Sunday lunch)/dinner 27.00 **st.** 5.00 – **16 r** 65.00/120.00 **st.**

GREEN TOURIST GUIDES

Picturesque scenery, buildings

Attractive routes

Touring programmes

Plans of towns and buildings.

SUDBURY Suffolk 404 W 27 **Great Britain G.** – pop. 11 291 – ☎ 01787.
See : Gainsborough's House★ *AC.*
Town Hall, Market Hill, CO10 6TL ☏ 881320 (summer only).
◆London 59 – ◆Cambridge 37 – Colchester 15 – ◆Ipswich 21.

Mill, Walnut Tree Lane, CO10 6BD, ☏ 375544, Fax 373027, ≤, « Converted 19C mill » ▤ rest TV ☎ P – 70. AE VISA
Meals a la carte 16.70/22.70 **t.** 4.95 – 7.50 – **56 rm** 50.00/78.00 **t.** – SB.

Hill Lodge, Newton Rd, CO10 6RG, on A 134 (Colchester rd) ☏ 377568, Fax 373636 rest TV P – 60. AE VISA JCB.
closed 1 week Christmas – **Meals** (by arrangement) (residents only) (dinner only) 8.00 **s.**
17 rm 23.00/38.00 **s.**

X **Mabey's Brasserie,** 47 Gainsborough St., CO10 7SS, ☏ 374298, Fax 374298 – ▤ AE VISA
closed Sunday and Monday – **Meals** a la carte 13.85/20.40 **t.** 5.25.

X **Red Onion Bistro,** 57 Ballingdon St., CO10 6DA, SW : ¾ m. on A 131 ☏ 376777 – P. VISA
closed Sunday and Bank Holidays – **Meals** 9.75 **t.** (dinner) and lunch a la carte 8.25/13.50 2.95.

at Belchamp Walter (Essex) W : 5 m. by A 131 and Belchamps rd – ✉ Sudbury ☎ 01787 :

St. Mary Hall, CO10 7BB, SW : 1 ½ m. on Great Yeldham rd ☏ 237202, « Part 15C part 16C house », heated, – rm P. VISA
Meals (by arrangement) (communal dining) 16.00 **st.** 4.00 – **3 rm** 28.00/60.00 **st.**

ATS Edgeworth Rd ☏ 374227

SUNDERLAND Tyne and Wear 401 402 P 19 – pop. 289 040 – ☎ 0191.
18 Whitburn, Lizard Lane ☏ 529 2144, A.
Unit 3, Crowtree Rd, SR1 3EL ☏ 565 0960/565 0990.
◆London 272 – ◆Leeds 92 – ◆Middlesbrough 29 – ◆Newcastle upon Tyne 12.

Plan opposite

Swallow Sunderland, Queens Par., Seaburn, SR6 8DB, ☏ 529 2041, Fax 529 4227, ≤ – rm ▤ TV ☎ P – 300. AE VISA. A
Meals 12.50/21.50 **st.** – **65 rm** 95.00/150.00 **st.** – SB.

Roker, Roker Terrace, Roker, SR6 0PH, ☏ 567 1786, Fax 510 0289, ≤ – TV ☎ P. VISA. A
Meals (grill rest.) a la carte 7.95/13.75 **st.** – 5.50 – **44 rm** 39.95 **st.** – SB.

Travel Inn, Wessington Way, SR5 3HR, NW : by A 1231, ☏ 548 9384, Fax 584 4148 rm TV P – 25. AE VISA.
Meals (grill rest.) – 4.95 – **40 rm** 34.50 **t.**

ATS Monkwearmouth Bridge ☏ 565 7694

SUNDERLAND

Fawcett Street	B	
High Street West	B	15
Holmeside	B	
John Street	B	16
The Bridges	B	

Albion Place	B	2
Barnes Park Road	A	3
Bedford Street	B	4
Borough Road	B	5
Bridge Street	B	6
Charlton Road	A	8
Chester Road	B	10
Crowtree Road	B	11
Derwent Street	B	12
Harbour View	A	14
Kayll Road	A	17
Livingstone Road	B	18
New Durham Road	B	19
Ormonde Street	A	21
Pallion Road	A	22
Park Lane	B	23
Queens Road	A	24
Roker Terrace	A	25
St. Luke's Terrace	A	26
St. Mary's Way	B	27
Shields Road	A	29
Southwick Road	B	30
Station Road	A	32
Trimdon Street	A	35
Vine Place	B	36
Wessington Way	A	38

Plans de villes :
Le nom des principales voies commerçantes est inscrit en rouge au début des légendes-rues.

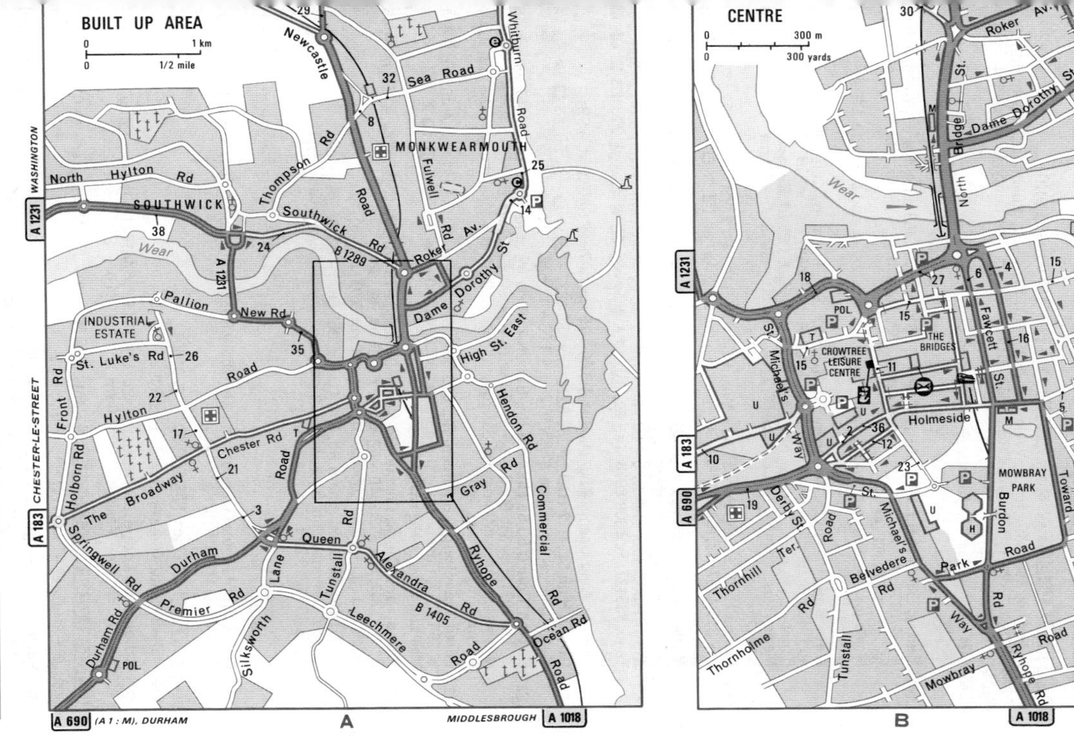

SUNNINGHILL Berks. 404 S 29 – see Ascot.

SUTTON W. Sussex – see Petworth.

SUTTON COLDFIELD W. Mids. 403 404 O 26 – pop. 106 001 – 0121.

Pype Hayes, Eachelhurst Rd, Walmley 351 1014, DT – 18 Boldmere, Monmouth Driv 354 3379, DT – 18 110 Thornhill Rd 353 2014 DT – 18, 18 The Belfry, Lichfield Rd, Wishaw (01675) 470301 DT.

London 124 – Birmingham 8 – Coventry 29 – Nottingham 47 – Stoke-on-Trent 40.

Plan : see Birmingham pp. 2 and 3

Belfry, Lichfield Rd, Wishaw, B76 9PR, E : 6½ m. by A 453 on A 446 (01675) 470301 Fax 470178, park, squash – rm rest – 300. VISA.
Meals *(closed Saturday and Sunday lunch)* 15.95/27.50 **st.** and a la carte 9.95 – **211 rm** 125.00/190.00 **st.**, 8 suites.

New Hall (Thistle), Walmley Rd, B76 1QX, SE : 1½ m. by Coleshill St., Coleshill Rd and Reddicap Hill on B 4148 378 2442, Fax 378 4637, « Part 13C moated manor house », park, – rest – 50. VISA JCB. DT
Meals *(closed Saturday lunch)* 18.50/37.00 **t.** 6.00 – 9.65. – **57 rm** 102.00/125.00 **st.** 5 suites – SB.

Penns Hall (Jarvis), Penns Lane, Walmley, B76 1LH, SE : 2¾ m. by A 5127 351 3111 Fax 313 1297, park, squash – rm – 400. VISA DT
Meals *(closed Saturday lunch)* 10.50/14.95 **st.** and a la carte 6.50 – 9.50 – **131 rm** 99.00/116.00 **st.**, 5 suites – SB.

Moor Hall, Moor Hall Drive, B75 6LN, NE : 2 m. by A 453 and Weeford Rd 308 3751 Telex 335127, Fax 308 8974, – rm – 200. VISA JCB. DT
Meals (carving lunch) 10.50/21.00 **st.** 6.00 – **75 rm** 78.00/140.00 **st.** – SB.

Royal, High St., B72 1UD, 355 8222, Fax 355 1837 – – 50. VISA.
Meals (grill rest.) a la carte 11.85/16.25 **t.** 4.65 – 5.50 – **22 rm** 43.95 **t.** DT

Sutton Court, 60-66 Lichfield Rd, B74 2NA, N : ½ m. at junction of A 5127 with A 45 355 6071, Fax 355 0083 – rm – 90. VISA JCB DT
Meals (bar lunch Monday to Saturday)/dinner 22.00 **t.** and a la carte 4.50 – 9.50 – **64 rm** 65.00/80.00 **st.** – SB.

Forte Travelodge, Boldmere Rd, B72 5UP, SW : 1¼ m. by A 5127 and A 453 on B 414 355 0017, Reservations (Freephone) 0800 850950 – rm VISA.
Meals (grill rest.) – **32 rm** 34.50 **t.** DT

Parson and Clerk, Chester Rd North, Streetly, B73 6SP, W : 3½ m. by A 453 on A 45 353 1747, Fax 352 1340 – VISA. CT
Meals a la carte 7.50/17.65 **st.** – 5.00 – **36 rm** 36.00 **t.**

La Truffe, 65 Birmingham Rd, B72 1QF, 355 5836 – VISA DT
closed Saturday lunch, Sunday, Monday, 2 weeks Easter and last week August – **Meals** 10.95/16.95 **t.** and a la carte 6.25.

at Curdworth SE : 6½ m. by A 5127, A 452 and A 38 on A 4097 – Sutton Coldfield – 01675 :

Old School House without rest., Kingsbury Rd, B76 9DR, on A 4097 470177 – **6 rm** 34.00/42.50 **t.**

SUTTON-ON-SEA Lincs. 402 404 U 24 – 01507.

London 151 – Boston 32 – Great Grimsby 30 – Lincoln 45.

Athelstone Lodge, 25 Trusthorpe Rd, LN12 2LR, 441521 – rest
March-October – **Meals** 10.00 **st.** – **6 rm** 17.00/34.00 – SB.

SUTTON SCOTNEY SERVICE AREA Hants. 403 404 P 30 – Winchester – 01962.

London 66 – Reading 32 – Salisbury 21 – Southampton 19.

Forte Travelodge, SO21 3JY, on A 34 761016 (northside), 760779 (southside), Reservations (Freephone) 0800 850950 – VISA.
Meals (grill rest.) – **71 rm** 34.50 **t.**

SWAFFHAM Norfolk 404 W 26 **Great Britain G.** – pop. 5 855 – 01760.

Exc. : Oxburgh Hall★★ *AC*, SW : 7½ m.

London 97 – Cambridge 46 – King's Lynn 16 – Norwich 27.

Strattons, Ash Close, PE37 7NH, off Market Sq. 723845, Fax 720458, « Part Queen Anne house », – VISA JCB
closed Christmas – **Meals** (booking essential for non-residents) (lunch residents only) 23.00 **st.** (dinner) 5.00 – **7 rm** 50.00/78.00 **st.**

George, Station St., PE37 7LJ, 721238, Fax 725333 – – 150. VISA
Meals 14.50 **t.** and a la carte 3.95 – **28 rm** 45.00/59.00 **t.** – SB.

at Sporle NE : 3 m. by A 47 – ✉ King's Lynn – ☎ 01760 :

Corfield House, PE32 2EA, on Necton rd ☎ 723636, – ⊁ TV P. VISA.
April-20 December – **Meals** 12.00 **st.** – **5 rm** 23.00/43.00 **st.**

ATS Unit 2a, Tower Meadow (off Station St.) ☎ 722543

SWANAGE Dorset 403 404 O 32 **The West Country G.** – pop. 9 037 – ☎ 01929.

See : Town★.

Envir. : St. Aldhelm's Head★★ (≤★★★) SW : 4 m. by B 3069 – Durlston Country Park (≤★★) : 1 m. – Studland (Old Harry Rocks★★, St. Nicholas Church★) N : 3 m. – Worth Matravers Anvil Point Lighthouse ≤★★) S : 2 m. – Great Globe★, S : 1¼ m.

Exc. : Corfe Castle★★ (≤★★) *AC*, NW : 6 m. by A 351.

Isle of Purbeck, Studland ☎ 44361.

The White House, Shore Rd, BH19 1LB ☎ 422885.

London 130 – Bournemouth 22 – Dorchester 26 – ◆Southampton 52.

Havenhurst, 3 Cranborne Rd, BH19 1EA, ☎ 424224 – ⊁ rest P.
Meals 15.00 **st.** and a la carte 3.50 – **17 rm** 25.00/50.00 **st.** – SB.

Crowthorne, 24 Cluny Cres., BH19 2BT, by Stafford Rd ☎ 422108 – ⊁ P. VISA.
March-October – **Meals** 10.00 – **8 rm** 20.00/44.00 – SB.

Cauldron Bistro, 5 High St., BH19 2LN, ☎ 422671 – AE VISA
closed Monday and Tuesday lunch except Bank Holidays in summer, Monday and Tuesday dinner in winter and first 3 weeks January – **Meals** - Seafood - a la carte 16.25/24.50 **t.** 6.25.

The Galley, 9 High St., BH19 2LN, ☎ 427299 – AE VISA JCB
closed January, February and 3 weeks mid November-first week December – **Meals** (dinner only) 16.50/21.00 **st.** 4.25.

Wenn Sie ein ruhiges Hotel suchen,
benutzen Sie zuerst die Karte in der Einleitung
oder wählen Sie im Text ein Hotel mit dem Zeichen ♨ *oder* ♨.

SWAVESEY SERVICE AREA Cambs. 404 U 27 – see Cambridge.

SWINDON Wilts. 403 404 O 29 **The West Country G.** – pop. 145 236 – ☎ 01793.

See : Great Western Railway Museum★ *AC* – Railway Village Museum★ *AC* Y **M**.

Envir. : Lydiard Park (St. Mary's★) W : 4 m. U.

Exc. : Ridgeway Path★★, S : 8½ m. by A 4361 – Whitehorse (≤★)E : 7½ m. by A 4312, A 420 and B 400 off B 4057.

Broome Manor, Pipers Way ☎ 532403 – Shrivenham Park, Penny Hooks ☎ 783853, Fax 782999 – Wootton Bassett ☎ 849999 – Wrag Barn, Shrivenham Rd, Highworth ☎ 861327.

37 Regent Street, SN1 IJL ☎ 530328/493007.

London 83 – Bournemouth 69 – ◆Bristol 40 – ◆Coventry 66 – ◆Oxford 29 – Reading 40 – ◆Southampton 65.

Plans on following pages

De Vere, Shaw Ridge Leisure Park, Whitehill Way, SN5 7DW, W : 2¾ m. by A 3102 and Tewkesbury Way (at Mannington junction) ☎ 878785, Fax 877822, – ⊁ rest TV ☎ & P – 400. AE VISA U **e**
Meals (bar lunch Saturday) (carving lunch) 14.25/18.95 **st.** and dinner a la carte 7.25 – **146 rm** 100.00/115.00 **st.**, 8 suites – SB.

Swindon Marriott, Pipers Way, SN3 1SH, SE : 1½ m. by Marlborough Road off B 4006 ☎ 512121, Fax 513114, squash – ⊁ rm TV ☎ & P – 250. AE VISA JCB. V **s**
Meals *(closed lunch Saturday, Sunday and Bank Holidays)* 14.00/17.00 **st.** and a la carte – 10.25 – **153 rm** 75.00/105.00 **st.** – SB.

Hilton National, Lydiard Fields, Great Western Way, SN5 8UZ, M 4, junction 16 ☎ 881777, Fax 881881, – ⊁ rm TV ☎ & P – 350. AE VISA V **a**
Meals (bar lunch Saturday) 14.75/17.75 **st.** and a la carte 5.50 – 10.50 – **150 rm** 85.00/135.00 **st.** – SB.

Forte Posthouse, Marlborough Rd, SN3 6AQ, ☎ 524601, Fax 512887, – ⊁ rm TV ☎ P – 70. AE VISA V **b**
Meals 20.00 **st.** and a la carte **t.** 6.75 – 7.95 – **98 rm** 59.00 **st.** – SB.

at Blunsdon N : 4½ m. on A 419 – U – ✉ Swindon – ☎ 01793 :

Blunsdon House, SN2 4AD, ☎ 721701, Fax 721056, park, squash – ⊁ rm TV ☎ & P – 300. AE VISA JCB. U **a**
Meals 10.75/11.75 **st.** and a la carte – **87 rm** 77.50/92.50 **st.**, 1 suite – SB.

SWINDON

Beechcroft Road . . . . **U** 4	Devises Road . . . . **V** 18	Rodbourne Road . . . . **U** 48
Bridge End Road . . . . **U** 6	Gipsy Lane . . . . **U** 25	Slade Drive . . . . **U** 51
Cheney Manor Road . . . . . . **U** 10	Hobley Drive . . . . **U** 28	Swindon Road . . . . **U** 57
Cirencester Way . . . . **U** 12	Kingsdown Road . . . . **U** 30	Vicarage Road . . . . **U** 61
	Newport Street . . . . **V** 36	Westcott Place . . . . **U** 64
	Oxford Road . . . . **U** 42	Whitworth Road . . . . **U** 66
	Park Lane . . . . **U** 43	Wootton Basset Road . . . . . . **U** 69

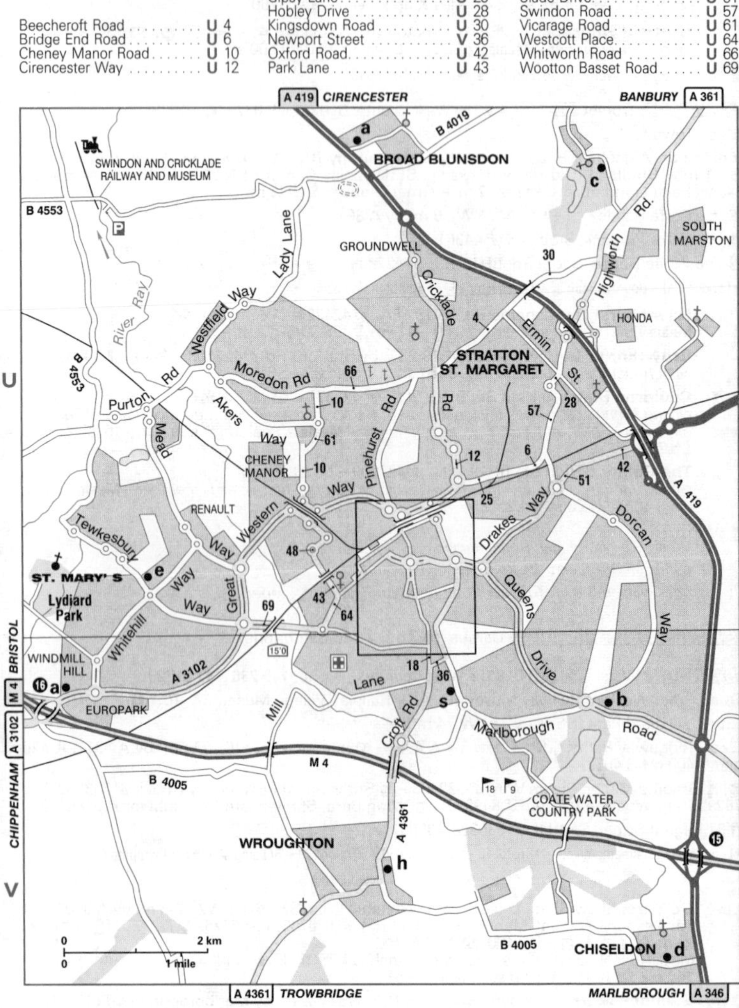

at Stanton Fitzwarren NE : 5 ¼ m. by A 4312 and A 419 off A 361 – ✉ Swindon – ☎ 01793 :

Stanton House, The Avenue, SN6 7SD, ℘ 861777, Fax 861857, ⇐, ☞, ✕ – 🛗 ▤ rest ☑ ☎ ♿ 🅟 – 🚣 110. 🆂 AE ⓓ VISA JCB. ✱ U **c**
Meals - Japanese - a la carte 16.50/25.00 **t.** 🍷 5.00 – **86 rm** ☐ 65.00/90.00 **t.**

at Wroughton S : 3 ¼ m. on A 4361 – V – ✉ Swindon – ☎ 01793 :

Moormead Country, Moormead Rd, SN4 9BY, ℘ 814744, Fax 814119 – ☑ ☎ ♿ 🅟 – 🚣 60. 🆂 AE ⓓ VISA V **h**
Meals 12.95/18.95 **st.** and a la carte – **34 rm** ☐ 60.00/100.00 **st.** – SB.

at Chiseldon S : 6 ¼ m. by A 4312, A 4259 and A 345 on B 4005 – V – ✉ Swindon – ☎ 01793 :

Chiseldon House 🐎, New Rd, SN4 0NE, ℘ 741010, Fax 741059, ⛱ heated, ☞ – ☑ ☎ 🅟. 🆂 AE ⓓ VISA. ✱ V **d**
Orangery : Meals *(closed Saturday lunch)* 14.95/22.95 **t.** 🍷 7.00 – **21 rm** ☐ 69.50/115.00 **t.** – SB.

SWINDON

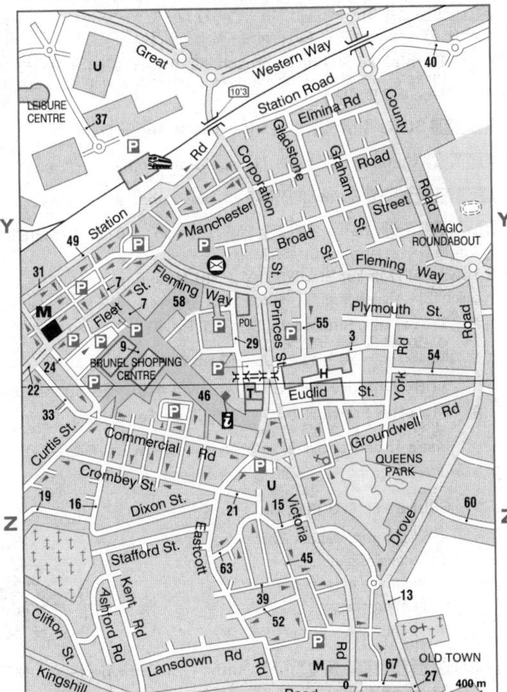

at Wootton Bassett W : 6 ¼ m. on A 3102 – ✉ Swindon – ☎ 01793 :

Marsh Farm, Coped Hall, SN4 8ER, N : 1 m. by A 3102 on Purton rd ☎ 848044, Fax 851528, – rest ▣ ☎ ⓟ – 110. AE VISA.
Meals *(closed Saturday lunch)* 15.50 **st.** and a la carte 5.50 – **30 rm** 52.00/85.00 **st.**

at Hook W : 6 ¼ m. by A 3102, B 4534 and Hook rd – ✉ Swindon – ☎ 01793 :

School House, Hook St., SN4 8EF, ☎ 851198, Fax 851025, – ▣ ☎ ⓟ. AE VISA.
Meals *(closed Sunday and Bank Holidays)* (dinner only) 18.95/23.00 **st.** 5.50 – **11 rm** 60.00/70.00 **st.**

ATS Cheney Manor Ind. Est. ☎ 521171 ATS 86 Beatrice St. ☎ 534867/431620

SWINTON Gtr.Manchester 402 403 404 N 23 – see Manchester.

SYMONDS YAT WEST Heref. and Worcs. 403 404 M 28 **Great Britain G.** – ✉ Ross-on-Wye – ☎ 01600.

See : Town★ – Yat Rock (≤★).

Envir. : S : Wye Valley★.

London 126 – Gloucester 23 – Hereford 17 – Newport 31.

Norton House, Whitchurch, HR9 6DJ, ☎ 890046, – ▣ ⓟ.
Meals (by arrangement) 15.00 **t.** – **3 rm** 27.50/44.00 **s.**

Cedars, Llangrove Rd, Whitchurch, HR9 6DQ, NW : ¾ m. ☎ 890351, – ▣.
Meals (by arrangement) 11.50 **t.** – **8 rm** 17.00/40.00 **t.** – SB.

Woodlea, HR9 6BL, ☎ 890206, Fax 890206, – rest ☎ ⓟ. VISA
Meals 16.45 **t.** 3.70 – **9 rm** 22.00/60.00 **t.** – SB.

TADCASTER N. Yorks. 402 Q 22 – ☎ 01937.

London 206 – Harrogate 16 – Leeds 14 – York 11.

Plough Inn, Headwell Lane, Saxton, LS24 9PX, S : 5 m. by A 162 ☎ 557242 – ⓟ. VISA
closed Sunday dinner and Monday – **Meals** a la carte 17.10/18.85 **t.**

TADWORTH Surrey 404 T 30 – ☎ 01737.
♦London 23 – ♦Brighton 36 – Guildford 22 – Maidstone 41.

XX **Gemini,** 28 Station Approach, KT20 5AH, ✆ 812179 – VISA
closed Saturday lunch, Sunday dinner, Monday, 2 weeks Christmas and 2 weeks June
Meals 13.50/22.50 **t.**

TALKE Staffs. 402 403 404 N 24 – see Stoke-on-Trent.

TALKIN Cumbria 401 402 L 19 – see Brampton.

TALLAND BAY Cornwall 403 G 32 – see Looe.

TAMWORTH Staffs. 402 403 404 O 26 – pop. 70 065 – ☎ 01827.
18 Eagle Drive, Amington ✆ 53850.
Town Hall, Market St., B79 7LY ✆ 59134 (summer only).
♦London 128 – ♦Birmingham 12 – ♦Coventry 29 – ♦Leicester 31 – ♦Stoke-on-Trent 37.

Travel Inn, Bitterscote, Bonehill Rd, B78 3HQ, on A 51 ✆ 54414, Fax 310420 – rm TV
& P. AE VISA.
Meals (grill rest.) – 4.95 – **40 rm** 34.50 **t.**

at Bodymoor Heath S : 6¾ m. by A 4091 – ✉ Sutton Coldfield – ☎ 01827 :

Marston Farm, B76 9JD, ✆ 872133, Fax 875043, park, – rest TV ☎ & P
50. AE VISA
Meals 15.75 **t.** and a la carte 5.50 – **37 rm** 75.00/90.00 **t.** – SB.

ATS Tame Valley Ind. Est., Watling St., Wilnecote ✆ 281983

GRÜNE REISEFÜHRER

Landschaften, Baudenkmäler
Sehenswürdigkeiten
Fremdenverkehrsstraßen
Tourenvorschläge
Stadtpläne und Übersichtskarten

TAMWORTH SERVICE AREA Staffs. – ✉ Tamworth – ☎ 01827.

Granada Lodge without rest., Green Lane, B77 6PS, A 5 / M 42 junction 10 ✆ 260120
Fax 260145, Reservations (Freephone) 0800 555300 – TV ☎ & P. AE VISA.
63 rm 39.95 **st.**

TANSLEY Derbs. – see Matlock.

TAPLOW Berks. 404 R 29 – ☎ 01628.
♦London 33 – Maidenhead 2 – Reading 12.

Cliveden , SL6 0JF, N : 2 m. by Berry Hill ✆ 668561, Fax 661837, « Mid-Victorian stately home, ≤ National Trust Gardens, parterre and River Thames », , , heated, , , park, , squash – rest TV ☎ P – 40. AE VISA JCB
Terrace : Meals 28.00/36.50 **st.** and a la carte 32.50/59.50 **st.** 11.00 – (see also **Waldo's** below) – 15.50 – **32 rm** 210.00/395.00 **st.**, 5 suites – SB.

XXXX ✿ **Waldo's** (at Cliveden H.), SL6 0JF, N : 2 m. by Berry Hill ✆ 668561, Fax 661837 –
P. AE VISA JCB
closed Sunday and Monday – **Meals** (dinner only) 45.00/60.00 **st.** 11.00
Spec. Cornish crab with lime, pimentos, scallops and a potato and chive salad, Fillet of beef with smoked foie gras girolles and artichokes poivrade, Hot apricot soufflé with a wild strawberry ice cream.

TARPORLEY Ches. 402 403 404 M 24 – pop. 2 308 – ☎ 01829.
18 Portal G & C.C., Cobblers Cross Lane ✆ 733933.
♦London 186 – Chester 11 – ♦Liverpool 36 – Shrewsbury 36.

Swan, 50 High St., CW6 0AG, ✆ 733838, Fax 732932 – TV ☎ P – 100. AE VISA.
Meals (lunch by arrangement) 17.00/19.00 **t.** and a la carte 4.50 – **13 rm** 45.00/70.00 **t**
– SB.

TARRANT MONKTON Dorset 403 404 N 31 – see Blandford Forum.

TATTENHALL Ches. 402 403 404 L 24 – pop. 3 263 – ☎ 01829.
♦London 200 – ♦Birmingham 71 – Chester 10 – ♦Manchester 38 – ♦Stoke-on-Trent 30.

Higher Huxley Hall , CH3 9BZ, N : 2¼ m. on Huxley rd ✆ 781484, Fax 781142, ≤
« Part 14C manor house, working farm », , – TV ☎ P. VISA JCB.
booking essential – **Meals** (communal dining) 20.00 **s.** 5.00 – **3 rm** 35.00/70.00 **s.**

Newton Hall without rest., CH3 9AY, N : 1 m. by Huxley Rd ✆ 770153, « Working farm », – TV P
closed 25 and 31 December – **3 rm** 25.00/40.00 **s.**

AUNTON Somerset 403 K 30 The West Country G. – pop. 41 545 – ☎ 01823.

ee : Town★ – St. Mary Magdalene★ – Somerset County Museum★ AC – St. James★ – ammett St.★ – The Crescent★ – Bath Alley★.

nvir. : Trull (Church★) S : 2½ m. by A 38.

xc. : Bishops Lydeard★ (Church★) NW : 6 m. – Wellington : Church★, Wellington Monument ★★) SW : 7½ m. by A 38 – Combe Florey★, NW : 8 m. – Gaulden Manor★ AC, NW : 10 m. by 358 and B 3227.

, 9 Taunton Vale, Creech Heathfield ℘ 412220 – 18 Vivary Park ℘ 289274 – 18 Taunton and ckeridge, Corfe ℘ 421240.

The Library, Corporation St., TA1 4AN ℘ 274785.

ondon 168 – Bournemouth 69 – ◆Bristol 50 – Exeter 37 – ◆Plymouth 78 – ◆Southampton 93 – Weymouth 50.

Castle, Castle Green, TA1 1NF, ℘ 272671, Fax 336066, « Part 12C castle with Norman garden » – 100. VISA.
Meals 17.90/35.00 **st.** 6.00 – **36 rm** 70.00/170.00 **st.** – SB
Spec. Potted pigeon and duck with spiced pears, Braised shoulder of lamb with thyme, garlic and vegetables, Baked egg custard with nutmeg ice cream.

Forte Posthouse, Deane Gate Av., TA1 2UA, E : 2½ m. by A 358 at junction with M 5 ℘ 332222, Fax 332266, – rm rest – 200. VISA JCB
Meals a la carte 13.95/22.45 **st.** 6.25 – 7.95 – **97 rm** 59.00 **st.** – SB.

Orchard House without rest., Fons George, Middleway, TA1 3JS, off Wilton St. ℘ 351783, Fax 351785, – . VISA JCB.
6 rm 35.00/55.00 **t.**

Travel Inn, 81 Bridgwater Rd, TA1 2DU, E : 1 ¾ m. by A 358 ℘ 321112, Fax 322054 – rm . VISA.
Meals (grill rest.) – 4.95 – **40 rm** 34.50 **t.**

Forde House without rest., 9 Upper High St., TA1 3PX, ℘ 279042, – .
closed Christmas and New Year – **5 rm** 26.00/48.00.

at Hatch Beauchamp SE : 6 m. by A358 – ✉ Taunton – ☎ 01823 :

Farthings, TA3 6SG, ℘ 480664, Fax 481118, « Georgian country house », – rest . VISA
Meals (lunch by arrangement) (light dinner Sunday residents only) 15.00/20.00 **t.** 4.50 – **8 rm** 55.00/85.00 **t.** – SB.

Frog Street Farm, Beercrocombe, TA3 6AF, SE : 1 ¼ m. by Beercrocombe Rd ℘ 480430, « 15C farmhouse, working farm », heated, – .
March-October – **Meals** (by arrangement) 15.00 **st.** – **3 rm** 25.00/54.00 **st.**

at Bishop's Hull W : 1 ¾ m. by A 38 – ✉ Taunton – ☎ 01823 :

Meryan House, Bishop's Hull Rd, TA1 5EG, ℘ 337445, Fax 322355, – . VISA.
Meals *(closed Sunday)* (dinner only) 18.00 **st.** – **12 rm** 40.00/60.00 **st.**

at West Bagborough NW : 10½ m. by A 358 – ✉ Taunton – ☎ 01323 :

Bashfords Farmhouse without rest., TA4 3EF, ℘ 432015, – .
3 rm 21.25/37.50.

) ATS 138 Bridgwater Rd, Bathpool ℘ 412826

TAUNTON DEANE SERVICE AREA Somerset 403 K 31 – ✉ Taunton – ☎ 01823.

Road Chef Lodge without rest., TA3 7PF, ℘ 332228, Fax 338131, Reservations (Freephone) 0800 834719 – . VISA.
closed Christmas and New Year – **39 rm** 37.50 **st.**

TAVISTOCK Devon 403 H 32 The West Country G. – pop. 10 222 – ☎ 01822.

Envir. : Morwellham★ AC, SW : 4½ m.

Exc. : E : Dartmoor National Park★★ (Brent Tor ≤★★, Haytor Rocks ≤★) – Buckland Abbey★★ AC, S : 7 m. by A 386 – Lydford★★ (Lydford Gorge★★) N : 8½ m. by A 386.

8 Down Rd ℘ 612049 – 18 Hurdwick, Tavistock Hamlets ℘ 612746.

Town Hall, Bedford Sq., PL19 0AE ℘ 612938 (summer only).

London 239 – Exeter 38 – ◆Plymouth 15.

Bedford (Forte), 1 Plymouth Rd, PL19 8BB, ℘ 613221, Fax 618034 – – 45. VISA JCB
Meals (bar lunch Monday to Saturday)/dinner 16.95 **st.** 5.50 – 8.50 – **30 rm** 57.50/67.50 **t.** – SB.

Neils, 27 King St., PL19 0DT, ℘ 615550 – . VISA
closed Sunday and Monday – **Meals** (dinner only) 17.00 **t.** and a la carte.

at Mary Tavy N : 3¾ m. on A 386 – ✉ Tavistock – ☎ 01822 :

Stannary with rm, PL19 9QB, ℘ 810897, Fax 810898, – . VISA.
closed Christmas – **Meals** - Vegetarian - *(closed Monday to Thursday except 14 February and 31 December)* (dinner only) 30.00 **st.** 5.00 – **3 rm** (dinner included) 70.00/120.00 **st.** – SB.

at Gulworthy W : 3 m. on A 390 – ✉ Tavistock – ☎ 01822 :

XX **Horn of Plenty** ⛶ with rm, PL19 8JD, ☎ 832528, Fax 832528, ≤ Tamar Valley and Bodmin Moor, – TV ☎ P. AE VISA
closed 25 and 26 December – **Meals** *(closed Monday lunch)* 14.50/28.50 **t.** 5.50 – 7.5 – **7 rm** 78.00/98.00 **t.** – SB.

ATS 2 Parkwood Rd ☎ 612545

TEESSIDE AIRPORT Durham 402 P 20 – see Darlington.

TEFFONT Wilts. – see Salisbury.

TEIGNMOUTH Devon 403 J 32 – pop. 13 403 – ☎ 01626.

The Den, Sea Front, TQ14 8BE ☎ 779769.

London 216 – Exeter 16 – Torquay 8.

Cliffden, Dawlish Rd, TQ14 8TE, ☎ 770052, Fax 770594, ≤, Restricted to the blind and their companions, – TV ☎ P. VISA
Meals (residents only) (bar lunch)/dinner a la carte 18.00 **st.** 3.50 – **21 rm** (dinner included) 38.00/76.00 **st.** – SB.

Thomas Luny House, Teign St., TQ14 8EG, ☎ 772976, « Georgian house built by Thomas Luny », – rest TV ☎ P.
closed January – **Meals** (residents only) (communal dining) (dinner only) 16.50 **s.** 6.50 – **4 rm** 30.00/60.00 **s.** – SB.

at Shaldon S : 1 m. on B 3199 – ✉ Teignmouth – ☎ 01626 :

Ness House, Marine Drive, TQ14 0HP, ☎ 873480, Fax 873486, ≤, – TV ☎ P. AE VISA.
Meals 15.00/22.50 **t.** and a la carte 5.25 – **12 rm** 40.00/95.00 **t.** – SB.

Glenside, Ringmore Rd, TQ14 0EP, W : ½ m. on B 3195 ☎ 872448, – rest TV P
Meals 13.00 3.25 – **10 rm** 24.00/48.00 **t.** – SB.

Si vous cherchez un hôtel tranquille,
consultez d'abord les cartes de l'introduction
ou repérez dans le texte les établissements indiqués avec le signe ⛶ ou ⛶.

TELFORD Shrops. 402 403 404 M 25 **Great Britain G.** – pop. 119 340 – ☎ 01952.

Envir. : Ironbridge Gorge Museum★★ *AC* (The Iron Bridge★★, Coalport China Museum★★, Blists Hill Open Air Museum★★, Museum of the River and Visitor Centre★) S : 5 m. by B 4373.

Exc. : Weston Park★★ *AC*, E : 7 m. by A 5.

18, 9 Telford Hotel G & C.C., Great Hay, Sutton Hill ☎ 585642 – 18 Wrekin, Wellington ☎ 244032 – 18, 9, 9, 9 The Shropshire, Muxton Grange, Muxton ☎ 677866.

The Telford Centre, Management Suite, TF3 4BX ☎ 291370.

London 152 – Birmingham 33 – Shrewsbury 12 – Stoke-on-Trent 29.

Holiday Inn, Telford International Centre, St. Quentin Gate, TF3 4EH, SE : ½ m. ☎ 292500, Fax 291949, squash – rm rest TV ☎ P – 250. AE VISA JCB.
Meals 15.95 **st.** and a la carte 6.50 – 9.95 – **100 rm** 89.00 **st.** – SB.

Telford Golf & Country Moat House (Q.M.H.), Great Hay, Sutton Hill, TF7 4DT, S : 4½ m. by A 442 ☎ 429977, Fax 586602, ≤, 9, 18, squash – rest TV ☎ P – 240. AE VISA
Meals 11.95/15.50 **st.** and a la carte 5.95 – **85 rm** 84.00/94.00 **st.**, 1 suite – SB.

Telford Moat House (Q.M.H.), Forgegate, Telford Centre, TF3 4NA, ☎ 429988, Fax 292012, – rm rest TV ☎ P – 400. AE VISA
closed 25 to 31 December – **Meals** a la carte 8.65/25.65 **t.** 6.95 – 8.95 – **143 rm** 82.00/92.00 **st.**, 4 suites – SB.

Madeley Court ⛶, Castlefields Way, Madeley, TF7 5DW, S : 4 ½ m. by A 442 and A 4169 on B 4373 ☎ 680068, Fax 684275, « Part 16C manor house », – TV ☎ P – 200. AE VISA.
Meals 18.00/30.00 **st.** and a la carte 7.50 – 7.95 – **47 rm** 79.50/98.00 **st.** – SB.

Forte Travelodge, Shawbirch Crossroads, Shawbirch, TF1 3QA, NW : 5½ m. by A 442 at junction with B 5063 ☎ 251244, Reservations (Freephone) 0800 850950 – TV P. AE VISA
Meals (grill rest.) – **40 rm** 34.50 **t.**

White House, Wellington Rd, Muxton, TF2 8NG, N : 4 ½ m. by A 442 off A 578 ☎ 604276, Fax 670336, – TV ☎ P. AE VISA JCB.
Meals *(closed Saturday lunch)* 8.95/12.50 **t.** and a la carte 3.50 – **30 rm** 49.50/67.50 **st.** – SB.

at Norton S : 7 m. on A 442 – ✉ Shifnal – ☎ 01952 :

Hundred House, Bridgnorth Rd, TF11 9EE, ☎ 730353, Fax 730355, « Tastefully decorated inn, antiques », – TV ☎ P. AE VISA JCB.
Meals 17.50 **t.** and a la carte 6.50 – **10 rm** 59.00/88.00 **t.** – SB.

at Wellington W : 6 m. by M 54 on B 5061 – ✉ Telford – ☎ 01952 :

Buckatree Hall 🔇, The Wrekin, Buckatree, TF6 5AL, SE : 2 3/4 m. by B 5061 ☎ 641821, Fax 247540, <, 🌳 – |‡| ⚡ rm 📺 ☎ 🅿 – 🪑 170. 💳 AE ⓓ VISA JCB
Meals 9.50/16.95 **t.** and a la carte – **59 rm** 75.00/89.50 **t.**, 2 suites – SB.

Charlton Arms (Premier), Church St., TF1 1DG, ☎ 251351, Fax 222077 – ⚡ rm 📺 ☎ 🅿 – 🪑 150. 💳 AE ⓓ VISA. ✂
Meals (grill rest) a la carte 8.50/16.00 **st.** 7.95 – 4.45 – **22 rm** 39.50 **st.**

ATS Queen St., Madeley ☎ 582820 — ATS Kensington Way, Oakengates ☎ 613810/612198

TEMPLE SOWERBY Cumbria 401 402 M 20 – pop. 329 – ✉ Penrith – ☎ 0176 83.

London 297 – ♦Carlisle 31 – Kendal 38.

Temple Sowerby House, CA10 1RZ, ☎ 61578, Fax 61958, « 17C farmhouse with Georgian additions », 🌳 – ⚡ rest 📺 ☎ 🅿. 💳 AE ⓓ VISA JCB
Meals (light lunch Monday to Saturday)/dinner 23.00 **st.** 5.00 – **12 rm** 55.00/75.00 **st.** – SB.

TENBURY WELLS Heref. and Worcs. 403 404 M 27 – ☎ 01584.

London 144 – ♦Birmingham 36 – Hereford 20 – Shrewsbury 37 – Worcester 28.

Cadmore Lodge 🔇, St. Michaels, WR15 8TQ, SW : 2 3/4 m. by A 4112 turning right opposite Cloisters College ☎ 810044, Fax 810044, <, 🏌9, 🎣, park, 🎾 – ⚡ rm 📺 ☎ 🅿 – 🪑 100. 💳 AE ⓓ VISA JCB. ✂
Meals 14.50 **t.** and a la carte – **8 rm** 34.50/57.50 **t.** – SB.

TENTERDEN Kent 404 W 30 – pop. 7 005 – ☎ 01580.

ℹ Town Hall, High St., TN30 6AN ☎ 763572 (summer only).

London 57 – Folkestone 26 – Hastings 21 – Maidstone 19.

Jarvis White Lion, 57 High St., TN30 6BD, ☎ 765077, Fax 764157 – ⚡ rm 📺 ☎ 🅿 – 🪑 50. 💳 AE ⓓ VISA
Meals 18.00 **t.** (dinner) and a la carte 10.10/16.75 **t.** – **15 rm** 55.00/85.00 **st.** – SB.

Little Silver Country, Ashford Rd, St. Michaels, TN30 6SP, N : 2 m. on A 28 ☎ (01233) 850321, Fax 850647, 🌳 – ⚡ 📺 ☎ 🅿 – 🪑 150. 💳 AE VISA. ✂
Meals (booking essential) (lunch residents only) 13.00/20.00 **t.** and a la carte 5.80 – **10 rm** 60.00/110.00 **t.** – SB.

Brattle House, Cranbrook Rd, TN30 6UL, W : 1 m. by A 28 ☎ 763565, <, 🌳 – ⚡ 🅿. ✂
closed 19 December-6 January – **Meals** (by arrangement) (communal dining) 16.50 **s.** – **3 rm** 40.00/56.00 **s.** – SB.

Collina House, 5 East Hill, TN30 6RL, ☎ 764852 – ⚡ rm 📺 🅿. 💳 AE VISA. ✂
Meals 30.00 **t.** 4.50 – **14 rm** 30.00/45.00 **st.** – SB.

TETBURY Glos. 403 404 N 29 **Great Britain G.** – pop. 5 065 – ☎ 01666.

Envir. : Westonbirt Arboretum★ *AC*, SW : 2½m. by A 433.

🏌9 Westonbirt ☎ (0166 88) 242.

ℹ The Old Court House, 63 Long St., GL8 8AA ☎ 503552 (summer only).

♦London 113 – ♦Bristol 27 – Gloucester 19 – Swindon 24.

The Close, 8 Long St., GL8 8AQ, ☎ 502272, Fax 504401, « 16C town house with walled garden » – ⚡ rest 📺 ☎ 🅿 – 🪑 30. 💳 ⓓ VISA. ✂
Meals 18.50/25.25 **t.** and a la carte – **15 rm** 85.00/160.00 **t.** – SB.

Snooty Fox, Market Pl., GL8 8DD, ☎ 502436, Fax 503479 – 📺 ☎. 💳 AE ⓓ VISA JCB. ✂
Meals 18.00 **t.** 5.75 – **12 rm** 60.00/110.00 **t.** – SB.

Number Sixty Five, 65 Long St., GL8 8AA, ☎ 503346 – 💳 AE VISA
closed Sunday dinner – **Meals** (dinner only and Sunday lunch)/dinner 18.25 **t.** and a la carte 5.00.

at Willesley SW : 4 m. on A 433 – ✉ Tetbury – ☎ 01666 :

Tavern House without rest., GL8 8QU, ☎ 880444, Fax 880254, « Part 17C former inn and staging post », 🌳 – ⚡ 📺 ☎ 🅿. 💳 VISA. ✂
4 rm 40.00/65.00.

at Calcot W : 3½ m. on A 4135 – ✉ Tetbury – ☎ 01666 :

Calcot Manor 🔇, GL8 8YJ, ☎ 890391, Fax 890394, « Converted Cotswold farm buildings », 🏊 heated, 🌳, 🎾 – ⚡ rest 📺 ☎ 🅿. 💳 AE ⓓ VISA. ✂
Meals 17.00/26.00 **st.** 6.00 – 5.00 – **20 rm** 75.00/125.00 **st.** – SB.

En saison, *surtout dans les stations fréquentées, il est prudent de retenir à l'avance. Cependant, si vous ne pouvez pas occuper la chambre que vous avez retenue, prévenez immédiatement l'hôtelier.*

Si vous écrivez à un hôtel à l'étranger, joignez à votre lettre un coupon-réponse international (disponible dans les bureaux de poste).

TEWKESBURY Glos. 403 404 N 28 Great Britain G. – pop. 9 546 – ☎ 01684.

See : Town★ – Abbey★★ (Nave★★, vault★).

Envir. : St. Mary's, Deerhurst★, SW : 4 m. by A 38 and B 4213.

Tewkesbury Park Hotel, Lincoln Green Lane ☎ 295405.

64 Barton St., GL20 5PX ☎ 295027.

♦London 108 – ♦Birmingham 39 – Gloucester 11.

Tewkesbury Park H. Country Club Resort (Country Club), Lincoln Green Lane, GL2 7DN, S : 1¼ m. by A 38 ☎ 295405, Fax 292386, ←, park, squash – 150.
Meals (bar lunch Saturday) 12.00/18.00 **t.** and dinner a la carte 6.00 – 9.00 – **78 rm** 75.00 **t.** – SB.

Bell, Church St., GL20 5SA, ☎ 293293, Fax 295938 – 40.
Meals (bar lunch Monday to Saturday)/dinner 17.95 **st.** and a la carte 4.50 – **25 rm** 59.50/95.00 **st.** – SB.

Jessop House, 65 Church St., GL20 5RZ, ☎ 292017, Fax 273076 –
closed 24 December-2 January – **Meals** *(closed Sunday)* (bar lunch)/dinner a la carte 14.50/22.90 **st.** 3.90 – **8 rm** 49.00/75.00 **st.** – SB.

Bistrot André, 78 Church St., GL20 5RX, ☎ 290357,
closed Sunday and February – **Meals** - French - (dinner only) a la carte 12.75/23.35 **st.**

at Puckrup N : 2½ m. on A 38 – ✉ Tewkesbury – ☎ 01684 :

Puckrup Hall, GL20 6EL, ☎ 296200, Fax 850788, ←, park – rm – 200.
Meals 18.50 **t.** (dinner) and a la carte 20.00/30.00 **t.** 6.00 – 6.00 – **82 rm** 75.50/105.00 **st.**, 2 suites – SB.

at Bredons Norton NE : 4¾ m. by B 4080 – ✉ Tewkesbury – ☎ 01684 :

Home Farm, GL20 7HA, NE : ¾ m. taking right turn at village hall ☎ 772322, « Working farm », park –
closed December – **Meals** (communal dining) 12.00 **s.** – **3 rm** 20.00/36.00 **s.**

at Kemerton NE : 5¼ m. by A 438 – ✉ Tewkesbury – ☎ 01386 :

Upper Court, GL20 7HY, take turning at stone cross in village ☎ 725351, Fax 725472, ←, « Georgian manor house, antique furnishings, gardens », heated, park –
closed Christmas and New Year – **Meals** *(closed Sunday and Monday)* (booking essential) (residents only) (communal dining) (dinner only) 25.00 **s.t.** 3.50 – **6 rm** 55.00/110.00 **st.**

at Corse Lawn SW : 6 m. by A 38 and A 438 on B 4211 – ✉ Gloucester – ☎ 01452 :

Corse Lawn House, GL19 4LZ, ☎ 780771, Fax 780840, « Queen Anne house », heated – 40.
Meals - (see *Corse Lawn House* below) – **17 rm** 70.00/90.00 **st.**, 2 suites – SB.

Corse Lawn House (at Corse Lawn House), GL19 4LZ, ☎ 780771, Fax 780840,
Meals 15.95/23.50 **st.** and a la carte 5.50.

ATS Oldbury Rd ☎ 292461

THAME Oxon. 404 R 28 The West Country G. – pop. 10 806 – ☎ 01844.

Exc. : Ridgeway Path★★.

Market House, North St., OX9 3HH ☎ 212834.

♦London 48 – Aylesbury 9 – ♦Oxford 13.

Spread Eagle, 16 Cornmarket, OX9 2BW, ☎ 213661, Fax 261380 – 250.
closed 29 and 30 December – **Meals** *(closed lunch Bank Holiday Mondays)* 17.45/19.95 **st.** and a la carte 4.75 – 7.95 – **31 rm** 76.00/100.00 **st.**, 2 suites – SB.

Thatchers, 29-30 Lower High St., OX9 2AA, ☎ 212146, Fax 217413 –
closed Sunday dinner – **Meals** a la carte 15.50/27.50 **t.** 8.50.

at Towersey E : 2 m. by A 4129 – ✉ Thame – ☎ 01844 :

Upper Green Farm without rest., Manor Rd, OX9 3QR, ☎ 212496, Fax 260399, « Part 15C and 16C thatched farmhouse, 18C barn »,
10 rm 32.00/50.00 **st.**

THATCHAM Berks. 403 404 Q 29 – pop. 20 226 – ✉ Newbury – ☎ 01635.

♦London 69 – ♦Bristol 68 – ♦Oxford 30 – Reading 15 – ♦Southampton 40.

Regency Park, Bowling Green Rd, RG18 3RP, NW : 1 ¾ m. by A 4 by Northfield Rd ☎ 871555, Fax 871571, rest – 110.
Meals 13.95/21.50 **st.** and a la carte 5.95 – 9.50 – **49 rm** 85.00/105.00 **st.**, 1 suite – SB.

THAXTED Essex 404 V 28 – pop. 2 681 – ☎ 01371.

London 44 – ♦Cambridge 24 – Colchester 31 – Chelmsford 20.

Four Seasons, Walden Rd, CM6 2RE, NW : ½ m. on B 184 ☎ 830129, Fax 830835 – ⇔ TV ☎ P. AE VISA JCB. ✻
Meals (residents only Sunday dinner and Bank Holidays) a la carte 17.50/24.75 **t.** 4.50 – **9 rm** ☐ 50.00/65.00 **t.** – SB.

Farmhouse Inn, Monk St., CM6 2NR, S : 1½ m. by B 184 ☎ 830864, Fax 831196 – TV ☎ P. AE VISA. ✻
Meals (bar lunch Monday to Saturday)/dinner a la carte 8.70/16.40 **t.** 3.75 – **11 rm** ☐ 32.50/42.50 **t.** – SB.

Folly House, Watling Lane, CM6 2QY, ☎ 830618, – ⇔ TV P. ✻
Meals (by arrangement) (communal dining) 15.00 – **3 rm** ☐ 35.00/50.00 **s.** – SB.

THELBRIDGE Devon 403 I 31 pop. 261 – ✉ Tiverton – ☎ 01884.

London 220 – Barnstaple 21 – Exeter 20 – Taunton 34.

Thelbridge Cross Inn, Thelbridge Cross, EX17 4SQ, on B 3042 ☎ 860316, Fax 860316, – ⇔ TV ☎ P. AE VISA. ✻
Meals a la carte approx. 8.95 **t.** – **8 rm** ☐ 35.00/70.00 **st.** – SB.

THETFORD Norfolk 404 W 26 – pop. 19 901 – ☎ 01842.

London 83 – ♦Cambridge 32 – ♦Ipswich 33 – King's Lynn 30 – ♦Norwich 29.

Bell (Forte Heritage), King St., IP24 2AZ, ☎ 754455, Fax 755552 – ⇔ TV ☎ P – 80. AE VISA JCB
Meals *(closed Saturday lunch)* 10.25/18.95 **t.** and a la carte 7.40 – ☐ 8.50 – **46 rm** 60.00/70.00 **st.**, 1 suite – SB.

ATS Canterbury Way ☎ 755529

THIRSK N. Yorks. 402 P 21 – pop. 4 162 – ☎ 01845.

Thornton-Le-Street ☎ 522170.

14 Kirkgate, YO7 1PQ ☎ 522755 (summer only).

♦London 227 – ♦Leeds 37 – ♦Middlesbrough 24 – York 24.

Sheppard's, Front St., Sowerby, YO7 1JF, S : ½ m. ☎ 523655, Fax 524720 – ⇔ rm TV ☎ P. VISA. ✻
closed first week January – **Meals** (in bar dinner Sunday and Monday and lunchtime) a la carte 15.70/23.35 **t.** 5.25 – **8 rm** ☐ 59.00/85.00 **st.**

Spital Hill , YO7 3AE, SE : 1¾ m. on A 19, entrance between 2 white posts ☎ 522273, , park – ⇔ ☎ P. AE VISA. ✻
Meals (by arrangement) (communal dinning) 18.50 3.25 – **3 rm** ☐ 37.00/63.00 **st.** – SB.

St. James House without rest., 36 The Green, YO7 1AQ, ☎ 524120 – ⇔ TV. ✻
mid March-mid November – **4 rm** ☐ 25.00/40.00.

Brook House without rest., Ingramgate, YO7 1DD, at far end of drive ☎ 522240, Fax 523133, – TV P. ✻
closed 2 weeks Christmas-New Year – **3 rm** ☐ 24.00/32.00 **s.**

at South Kilvington N : 1½ m. on A 61 – ✉ Thirsk – ☎ 01845 :

Thornborough House Farm, YO7 2NP, N : ¼ m., entrance between roundabout and A 19 junction ☎ 522103, Fax 522103, – ⇔ TV P. VISA
Meals (by arrangement) (communal dining) 9.00 **st.** – **3 rm** ☐ 17.00/34.00 **st.** – SB.

at Asenby SW : 5¼ m. by A 168 – ✉ Thirsk – ☎ 01845 :

Crab and Lobster, Dishforth Rd, YO7 3QL, ☎ 577286, Fax 577109, « Thatched inn, memorabilia », – P. AE VISA
closed Sunday dinner – **Meals** (booking essential) 13.95 **t.** (lunch) and a la carte 15.95/22.95 **t.** 4.50.

ATS Long St. ☎ 522982/522923

THORALBY N. Yorks. 402 N/O 21 – pop. 160 – ✉ Leyburn – ☎ 01969.

♦London 245 – Kendal 41 – ♦Leeds 64 – York 57.

Littleburn , DL8 3BE, W : ½ m. by unmarked lane taking left fork after ¼ m. ☎ 663621, ←, « 17C country house », – ⇔ P. ✻
Meals (by arrangement) (communal dining) 18.00 **s.** 3.45 – **3 rm** ☐ 30.00/60.00 **s.**

Low Green House, DL8 3SZ, SE : ¼ m. on unmarked lane ☎ 663623, – ⇔ TV P
Meals (by arrangement) 12.00 **s.** – **4 rm** ☐ 23.50/39.00 **s.**

THORNABY-ON-TEES Cleveland 402 Q 20 – pop. 12 108 – ✉ Middlesbrough – ☎ 01642.

Tees-Side, Acklam Rd ☎ 676249.

♦London 250 – ♦Leeds 62 – ♦Middlesbrough 3 – York 49.

Forte Posthouse, Low Lane, Stainton Village, TS17 9LW, SE : 3½ m. by A 1045 on A 1044 ☎ 591213, Fax 594989, , – ⇔ rm TV ☎ P – 100. AE VISA
Meals a la carte 13.00/20.00 **st.** 6.95 – ☐ 7.95 – **135 rm** 56.00 **st.** – SB.

THORNBURY Avon 403 404 M 29 – pop. 12 617 – ✉ Bristol – ☎ 01454.
♦London 128 – ♦Bristol 12 – Gloucester 23 – Swindon 43.

Thornbury Castle 🐌, Castle St., BS12 1HH, ✆ 281182, Fax 416188, « 16C castle gardens », park – ⊁ rest ▭ ☎ ⓟ. 🖾 AE ⓓ VISA. ⚘
closed 2 days January – **Meals** 18.50/31.00 **t.** – ☐ 8.95 – **16 rm** 75.00/200.00 **t.**, 1 suite.

THORNTHWAITE Cumbria 402 K 20 – see Keswick.

THORNTON CLEVELEYS Lancs. 402 L 22 – pop. 28 061 – ☎ 01253.
♦London 244 – ♦Blackpool 6 – Lancaster 20 – ♦Manchester 44.

XX **Victorian House** with rm, Trunnah Rd, Thornton, FY5 4HF, ✆ 860619, Fax 865350, « Victoriana », 🌳 – ▭ ☎ ⓟ. 🖾 AE VISA
Meals 10.00/21.00 **st.** and lunch a la carte 🍷 5.50 – ☐ 6.95 – **2 rm** 35.00/40.00 **st.**

THORPE Derbs. 402 403 404 O 24 Great Britain G. – pop. 201 – ✉ Ashbourne – ☎ 01335.
See : Dovedale★★ (Ilam Rock★).
♦London 151 – Derby 16 – ♦Sheffield 33 – ♦Stoke-on-Trent 26.

Peveril of the Peak (Forte Heritage) 🐌, DE6 2AW, ✆ 350333, Fax 350507, ≤, 🌳, 🎾 – ⊁ ▭ ☎ ⓟ – 🏛 50. 🖾 AE ⓓ VISA JCB
Meals 11.95/16.95 **st.** and a la carte 🍷 7.05 – ☐ 8.50 – **47 rm** 70.00/85.00 **st.** – SB.

THORPE MARKET Norfolk 404 X 25 – pop. 303 – ✉ North Walsham – ☎ 01263.
♦London 130 – ♦Norwich 21.

Green Farm, North Walsham Rd, NR11 8TH, ✆ 833602, Fax 833163 – ▭ ☎ ⓟ. 🖾 AE VISA
Meals (bar lunch)/dinner 18.50 **t.** and a la carte 🍷 4.95 – **9 rm** ☐ 52.50/75.00 **t.** – SB.

***En saison,** surtout dans les stations fréquentées, il est prudent de retenir à l'avance. Cependant, si vous ne pouvez pas occuper la chambre que vous avez retenue, prévenez immédiatement l'hôtelier.*

Si vous écrivez à un hôtel à l'étranger, joignez à votre lettre un coupon-réponse international (disponible dans les bureaux de poste).

THORPE ST. ANDREW Norfolk 404 Y 26 – see Norwich.

THRAPSTON SERVICE AREA Northants. 404 S 26 – ✉ Kettering – ☎ 01832.

Forte Travelodge, NN14 4UR, at junction of A 14 with A 605 and A 45 ✆ 735199, Reservations (Freephone) 0800 850950 – ▭ ♿ ⓟ. 🖾 AE VISA
Meals (grill rest.) – **40 rm** 34.50 **t.**

THREE BRIDGES W. Sussex – see Crawley.

THRELKELD Cumbria 402 K 20 – see Keswick.

THRUSSINGTON Leics. 402 403 404 Q 25 – see Leicester.

THURLESTONE Devon 403 I 33 – see Kingsbridge.

THURROCK SERVICE AREA Essex 404 V 29 – ✉ West Thurrock – ☎ 01708.
⛳18 Belhus Park, South Ockendon ✆ 854260.
ℹ Granada Motorway Service Area (M 25), RM16 3BG ✆ 863733.

Granada Lodge without rest., RM16 3BG, ✆ 891111, Fax 860971, Reservations (Freephone) 0800 555300 – 🛗 ⊁ ▭ ☎ ♿ ⓟ. 🖾 AE VISA. ⚘
– **44 rm** 39.95 **st.**

ATS Units 13/14, Eastern Av., Waterglade Ind. Park, West Thurrock, Grays ✆ 862237

TICEHURST E. Sussex 404 V 30 pop. 3 118 – ✉ Wadhurst – ☎ 01580.
⛳18 Dale Hill Hotel, Ticehurst ✆ 200112.
♦London 49 – Brighton 44 – Folkestone 38 – Hastings 15 – Maidstone 24.

Dale Hill Golf H., TN5 7DQ, NE : ½ m. on A 268 ✆ 200112, Fax 201249, Fō, ≘s, 🏊, ⛳18, park – 🛗 ▭ ☎ ♿ ⓟ – 🏛 30. 🖾 AE VISA. ⚘
Meals (bar lunch)/dinner 15.00 **t.** 🍷 5.10 – ☐ 3.00 – **31 rm** 45.00/70.00 **t.**, 1 suite.

TICKTON Humbs. – see Beverley.

TILSTON Ches. 402 403 L 24 – see Malpas.

TINTAGEL Cornwall 403 F 32 The West Country G. – pop. 1 721 – ☎ 01840.
See : Arthur's Castle (site★★★) *AC* – Tintagel Church★ – Old Post Office★ *AC*.
Envir. : Delabole Quarry★ *AC*, SE : 4½ m. by B 3263.
Exc. : Camelford★, SE : 6½ m. by B 3263 and B 3266.
♦London 264 – Exeter 63 – ♦Plymouth 49 – Truro 41.

Trebrea Lodge , Trenale, PL34 0HR, SE : 1 m. by Boscastle Rd (B 3263) and Trenale Lane on Trewarmett rd 770410, Fax 770092, <, « Part 18C manor house, 14C origins », VISA
closed 8 to 31 January – **Meals** (dinner only) 18.50 **t.** – **7 rm** 47.50/78.00 **t.** – SB.

Wootons Country, Fore St., PL34 0DD, 770170, Fax 778978 – VISA.
Meals (bar lunch)/dinner 15.50 **t.** and a la carte 3.25 – **11 rm** 25.00/55.00 **t.**

Bossiney House, Bossiney Rd, PL34 0AX, NE : ½ m. on B 3263 770240, Fax 770501, VISA
Easter-end October – **Meals** (bar lunch)/dinner 13.00 **st.** 3.75 – **19 rm** 31.00/52.00 **st.** – SB.

Polkerr, PL34 0BY, 770382,
closed 25 and 26 December – **Meals** (by arrangement) 7.50 **s.** – **7 rm** 17.00/40.00 **s.** – SB.

Old Borough House, Bossiney Rd, PL34 0AY, NE : ½ m. on B 3263 770475 – rest
Meals (by arrangement) 10.00 **s.** – **5 rm** 29.50/39.00 **s.**

Old Millfloor , Trebarwith, PL34 0HA, S : 1 ¾ m. by B 3263 770234, « Former flour mill », park –
April-October – **Meals** (by arrangement) 12.00 – **3 rm** 18.00/36.00.

TODDINGTON SERVICE AREA Beds. 404 S 28 – pop. 4 500 – Luton – 01525.

Granada Lodge without rest., LU5 6HR, M 1 junction 12 (southbound carriageway) 878424, Fax 878452, Reservations (Freephone) 0800 555300 – VISA.
43 rm 39.95 **st.**

TODWICK S. Yorks. – pop. 1 639 – Sheffield – 01909.

London 161 – Nottingham 35 – Sheffield 10.

Red Lion, Worksop Rd, S31 0DJ, on A 57 771654, Fax 773704 – rm – 50. VISA
Meals 8.95/12.95 **t.** and a la carte 4.95 – 6.00 – **30 rm** 39.95 **t.**

TONBRIDGE Kent 404 U 30 – pop. 101 763 (inc. Malling) – 01732.

Poult Wood, Higham Lane 364039.

Tonbridge Castle, Castle St., TN9 1BG 770929.

London 33 – Brighton 37 – Hastings 31 – Maidstone 14.

Rose and Crown (Forte), 125 High St., TN9 1DD, 357966, Fax 357194 – 100. AE VISA
Meals 8.95/18.95 **t.** and a la carte 6.90 – 8.50 – **48 rm** 55.00/65.00 **st.** – SB.

The Office, 163 High St., TN9 1BX, 353660 – AE VISA JCB
closed Sunday, 3 days Christmas and Bank Holidays – **Meals** a la carte 12.00/14.20 **t.**

at Golden Green NE : 4 m. by Three Elm Lane off A 26 – Tonbridge – 01732 :

Goldhill Mill without rest., Three Elm Lane, TN11 0BA, 851626, Fax 851881, « Part Tudor and Georgian water mill », park, – VISA.
closed 15 July-31 August – **3 rm** 60.00/75.00 **st.**

ATS 61/63 Pembury Rd 353800/352231

TORCROSS Devon 403 J 33 – see Kingsbridge.

TORQUAY Devon 403 J 32 The West Country G. – pop. 59 587 – 01803.

See : Torbay★ – Kent's Cavern★ *AC* CX **A**.

Envir. : Cockington★, W : 1 m. AX.

Petitor Rd, St. Marychurch 314591, B.

Vaughan Parade, TQ2 5JG 297428.

London 223 – Exeter 23 – Plymouth 32.

Plans on following pages

Imperial (Forte), Parkhill Rd, TQ1 2DG, 294301, Fax 298293, < Torbay, heated, squash – rm rest – 350. AE VISA JCB — CZ **a**
Regatta : Meals (dinner only and Sunday lunch)/dinner 32.00 **t.** and a la carte 9.50 – **Sundeck Brasserie : Meals** a la carte 13.75/24.25 **t.** 9.50 – 11.00 – **150 rm** 80.00/150.00 **st.**, 17 suites – SB.

Grand, Seafront, TQ2 6NT, 296677, Fax 213462, <, heated, – rest – 300. AE VISA — BZ **z**
Meals (dancing Saturday evening) 13.50/18.50 **st.** and a la carte – **100 rm** 75.00/125.00 **st.**, 11 suites – SB.

Palace, Babbacombe Rd, TQ1 3TG, 200200, Fax 299899, « Extensive gardens », heated, park, indoor, squash – rm – 350. AE VISA. — CX **u**
Meals 13.50/21.50 **t.** and a la carte 6.50 – **134 rm** 55.00/100.00 **t.**, 6 suites – SB.

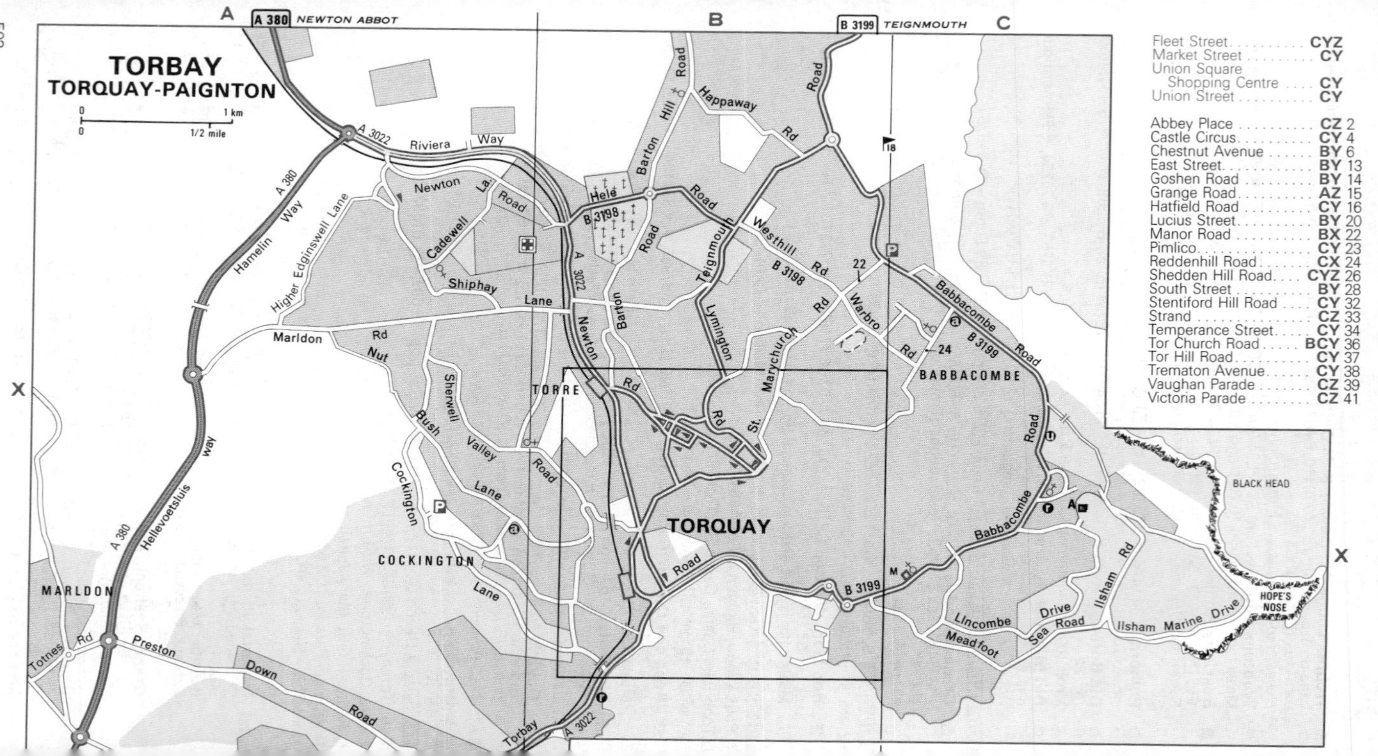
TORBAY
TORQUAY-PAIGNTON
0 1 km
0 1/2 mile
A
B
C
X
X
A 380 NEWTON ABBOT
B 3199 TEIGNMOUTH
Fleet Street CYZ
Market Street CY
Union Square Shopping Centre CY
Union Street CY
Abbey Place CZ 2
Castle Circus CY 4
Chestnut Avenue BY 6
East Street BY 13
Goshen Road BY 14
Grange Road AZ 15
Hatfield Road CY 16
Lucius Street BY 20
Manor Road BX 22
Pimlico CY 23
Reddenhill Road CX 24
Shedden Hill Road CYZ 26
South Street BY 28
Stentiford Hill Road CY 32
Strand CZ 33
Temperance Street CY 34
Tor Church Road BCY 36
Tor Hill Road CY 37
Trematon Avenue CY 38
Vaughan Parade CZ 39
Victoria Parade CZ 41
A 3022
Riviera Way
A 380
Hamelin Way
Hellevoetsluis way
Higher Edginswell Lane
Newton La.
Road
Cadewell
Shiphay
Lane
Marldon
Nut Rd
Sherwell Valley Road
Bush Lane
Cockington
COCKINGTON
Lane
TORRE
Newton Rd
Barton Road
Hele
B 3198
Barton Hill Road
Happaway Rd
Road
Teignmouth Road
Westhill Rd
B 3198
Lymington Rd
Marychurch Rd
St.
Warbro Rd
22
24
Babbacombe Road
B 3199
BABBACOMBE
Road
TORQUAY
Road
B 3199
Babbacombe
Lincombe
Meadfoot
Sea Road
Drive
Ilsham Rd
Ilsham Marine Drive
BLACK HEAD
HOPE'S NOSE
MARLDON
Totnes Rd
Preston
Down Road
Torbay
A 3022
18
M
A

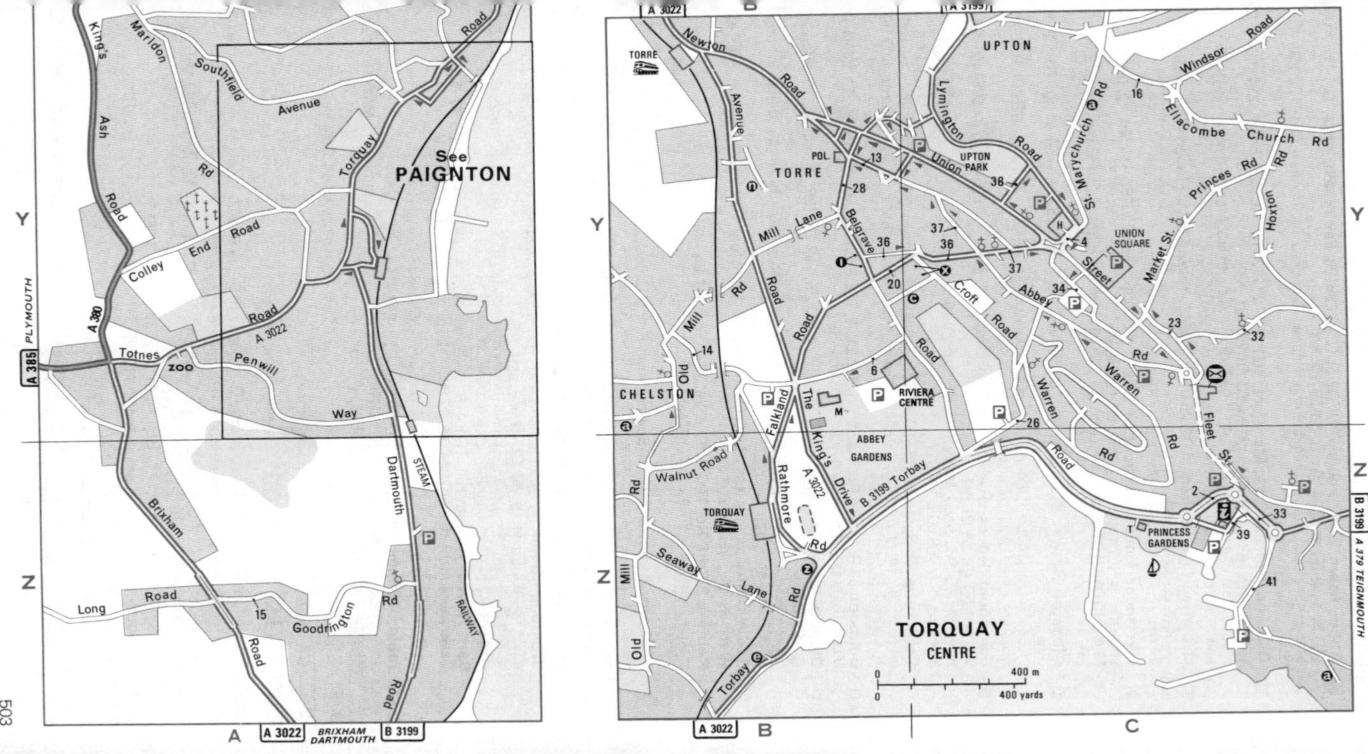
See
PAIGNTON
King's Ash Road
Marldon
Southfield
Avenue
Rd
Colley End Road
Torquay
Road
A 3022
Totnes
ZOO
Penwill
Way
A 380
A 385
PLYMOUTH
Dartmouth
STEAM
RAILWAY
Brixham
Road
Long Road
Goodrington Rd
15
A 3022
BRIXHAM
DARTMOUTH
B 3199
TORRE
UPTON
Newton Road
Avenue
Lymington Road
Union
UPTON PARK
TORRE
POL
Mill Lane
Belgrave
Road
Rd
Mill
Old
CHELSTON
Walnut Road
Seaway Lane
Falkland
The King's Drive
Rathmore Rd
TORQUAY
RIVIERA CENTRE
ABBEY GARDENS
A 3022
B 3199 Torbay
Torbay Rd
Croft Road
Abbey Road
Warren Rd
Warren Road
Fleet St.
St. Marychurch Rd
UNION SQUARE
Street
Market St.
Princes Rd
Hoxton Rd
Ellacombe Church Rd
Windsor Road
PRINCESS GARDENS
TORQUAY
CENTRE
400 m
400 yards
B 3199
A 379 TEIGNMOUTH

Abbey Lawn, Scarborough Rd, TQ2 5UQ, ℘ 299199, Fax 291460, ≤, heated, – ‖ 80. AE VISA JCB CY
Meals (bar lunch)/dinner 12.95 **t.** and a la carte – **56 rm** (dinner included) 41.00/98.00 **t.** – SB.

Osborne, Hesketh Cres., Meadfoot, TQ1 2LL, ℘ 213311, Fax 296788, ≤, heated, – 80. AE VISA CX
Meals (bar lunch) a la carte 11.25/13.45 **t.** – **Langtry's : Meals** (dinner only) 19.50 **st.** and a la carte 6.70 – **23 rm** (dinner included) 65.00/168.00 **st.** – SB.

Livermead Cliff, Seafront, TQ2 6RQ, ℘ 299666, Telex 42424, Fax 294496, ≤, heated, – 70 BX
64 rm.

Livermead House, Seafront, TQ2 6QJ, ℘ 294361, Fax 200758, ≤, heated, squash – 250. AE VISA BZ
Meals 10.00/20.00 **st.** and a la carte 4.25 – **64 rm** (dinner included) 60.00/122.00 **st.** – SB.

Albaston House, 27 St. Marychurch Rd, TQ1 3JF, ℘ 296758 – . VISA JCB CY
closed 5 December-5 January – **Meals** 10.00/15.00 **st.** 4.00 – **13 rm** 28.00/70.00 **st.** – SB.

Fairmount House, Herbert Rd, Chelston, TQ2 6RW, ℘ 605446, Fax 605446, – rest . AE VISA AX
early March-October – **Meals** *(closed Sunday dinner)* (bar lunch)/dinner 11.50 **t.** 4.95 – **8 rm** 29.00/58.00 **t.** – SB.

Cranborne, 58 Belgrave Rd, TQ2 5HY, ℘ 298046 – rest . VISA. BY
closed Christmas and New Year – **Meals** (by arrangement) 8.00 **st.** – **12 rm** 21.00/46.00 **st.** – SB.

Belmont, 66 Belgrave Rd, TQ2 5HY, ℘ 295028, Fax 295028 – rest . AE VISA BY
Meals 10.00 **st.** – **13 rm** 17.00/34.00 **st.** – SB.

Glenorleigh, 26 Cleveland Rd, TQ2 5BE, ℘ 292135, Fax 292135, heated, – rest . VISA. BY
February-September – **Meals** (by arrangement) 12.00 **st.** 3.50 – **16 rm** (dinner included) 35.00/70.00 **st.** – SB.

Cedar Court without rest., 3 St. Matthews Rd, Chelston, TQ2 6JA, ℘ 607851 – BY
10 rm 14.00/36.00 **st.**

Remy's, 3 Croft Rd, TQ2 5UF, ℘ 292359 – . VISA JCB CY
closed Sunday and Monday – **Meals** - French - (booking essential) (dinner only) 15.85 **t.** 5.00.

Mulberry Room with rm, 1 Scarborough Rd, TQ2 5UJ, ℘ 213639 – . CY
Meals *(closed Sunday dinner, Monday and Tuesday to non-residents)* 7.95 **st.** (lunch) and a la carte 10.00/14.50 **st.** 5.50 – **3 rm** 25.00/45.00 **st.** – SB.

Village Brasserie, 5 Ilsham Rd, Wellswood, TQ1 2JG, ℘ 290855 CX

at Maidencombe N : 3½ m. by B 3199 – BX – ✉ Torquay – 01803 :

Orestone Manor , Rockhouse Lane, TQ1 4SX, ℘ 328098, Fax 328336, ≤, heated, – rest . AE VISA JCB.
closed 2 January-4 February – **Meals** (bar lunch Monday to Saturday)/dinner 25.50 **st.** 5.00 – **18 rm** (dinner included) 65.00/160.00 **st.** – SB.

Barn Hayes , Brim Hill, TQ1 4TR, ℘ 327980, ≤, – rest . VISA
Meals (bar lunch)/dinner 13.00 **st.** 3.50 – **12 rm** 27.00/54.00 **st.** – SB.

at Babbacombe NE : 1½ m. – ✉ Torquay – 01803 :

Table, 135 Babbacombe Rd, TQ1 3SR, ℘ 324292 – . VISA CX
closed Sunday, Monday, 1 to 18 February and 1 to 18 September – **Meals** (booking essential) (dinner only) 28.00/32.50 **t.** 7.50.

ATS 20 Tor Church Rd ℘ 293985 ATS 100 Teignmouth Rd ℘ 329495

TORVER Cumbria 402 K 20 – see Coniston.

TOTLAND BAY I.O.W. 403 404 P 31 – see Wight (Isle of).

TOTNES Devon 403 I 32 **The West Country G.** – pop. 7 018 – 01803.

See : Town★ – St. Mary's★ – Butterwalk★ – Castle (≤★★★) *AC*.

Envir. : Paignton Zoo★★ *AC*, E : 4½ m. by A 385 and A 3022 – British Photographic Museum, Bowden House★ *AC*, S : 1 m. by A 381.

Exc. : Dartmouth★★ (Castle ≤★★★) SE : 12 m. by A 381 and A 3122.

18, 9 Dartmouth Golf & C.C., Blackawton ℘ 712686.

The Plains, TQ9 5EJ ℘ 863168.

London 224 – Exeter 24 – Plymouth 23 – Torquay 9.

Old Forge at Totnes without rest., Seymour Pl., TQ9 5AY, ℘ 862174, Fax 865385, « 14C working forge », – . VISA.
10 rm 32.00/64.00 **st.**

at Stoke Gabriel SE : 4 m. by A 385 – ✉ Totnes – ☎ 01803 :

Gabriel Court ⛯, TQ9 6SF, ℘ 782206, Fax 782333, heated, – TV ☎ P. AE VISA
Meals (dinner only and Sunday lunch)/dinner 23.00 **st.** 6.00 – **19 rm** 55.00/80.00 **st.**

at Ashprington S : 3½ m. by A 381 – ✉ Totnes – ☎ 01803 :

Waterman's Arms, Bow Bridge, TQ9 7EG, ℘ 732214, Fax 732214, « Part 15C inn », – TV ☎ P. VISA
Meals a la carte 9.75/15.75 **t.** 3.50 – **15 rm** 36.00/72.00 **t.** – SB.

at Tuckenhay S : 4¼ m. by A 381 – ✉ Totnes – ☎ 01803 :

Floyd's Inn (sometimes) with rm, Bow Creek, TQ9 7EQ, ℘ 732350, Fax 732651, ≤, « Riverside setting », – TV ☎ P. VISA
closed 25 and 26 December – **George's :** *(closed Sunday dinner and Monday)* a la carte 33.00/44.50 **t.** – 10.00 – **3 rm** 100.00/175.00 **t.**

The Canteen : Meals (in bar) a la carte 12.50/20.00 **t.**

at Dartington – ✉ Totnes – ☎ 01803 :

Cott Inn, TQ9 6HE, NW : 2 m. on A 385 ℘ 863777, Fax 866629, « 14C thatched inn », – TV ☎ P. AE VISA JCB
closed 25 December – **Meals** a la carte 13.00/19.25 **st.** 5.50 – **6 rm** 45.00/50.00 **st.** – SB.

ATS Babbage Rd ℘ 862086

TOTTENHILL Norfolk – see King's Lynn.

TOWCESTER Northants. 403 404 R 27 – pop. 7 006 – ☎ 01327.

18, 18, 9 West Park G. & C.C., Whittlebury, Towcester ℘ 858092 – 18 Farthingstone Hotel, Farthingstone ℘ 136291.

London 70 – Birmingham 50 – Northampton 9 – Oxford 36.

Saracens Head, 219 Watling St., NN12 7BX, ℘ 350414, Fax 359879 – TV ☎ P – 30. AE VISA.
Meals 15.95/19.95 **st.** 4.95 – **20 rm** 55.00/75.00 **st.**

Forte Travelodge, East Towcester bypass, NN12 6TQ, SW : ½ m. by Brackley rd on A 43 ℘ 359105, Reservations (Freephone) 0800 850950 – TV P. AE VISA.
Meals (grill rest.) – **33 rm** 34.50 **t.**

at Paulerspury SE : 3¼ m. by A 5 – ✉ Towcester – ☎ 01327 :

Vine House with rm, 100 High St., NN12 7NA, ℘ 811267, Fax 811309, – TV ☎ P. VISA.
closed 26 December-2 January – **Meals** *(closed Monday and Saturday lunch and Sunday)* a la carte 13.95/23.50 5.00 – **6 rm** 38.80/61.10 **t.**

TOWERSEY Oxon. 404 R 28 – see Thame.

TREGONY Cornwall 403 F 33 **The West Country G.** – pop. 729 – ✉ Truro – ☎ 01872.

Envir. : Trewithen★★★ *AC*, N : 2½ m.

London 291 – Newquay 18 – Plymouth 53 – Truro 10.

Tregony House, 15 Fore St., TR2 5RN, ℘ 530671, – P. VISA.
closed December and January – **Meals** (by arrangement) 11.00 **st.** – **6 rm** 19.25/44.50 **st.**

TREGREHAN Cornwall 403 F 32 – see St. Austell.

TRERICE Cornwall 403 E 32 – see Newquay.

TRESCO Cornwall 403 ㉚ – see Scilly (Isles of).

TREYARNON BAY Cornwall 403 E 32 – see Padstow.

TRING Herts. 404 S 28 – pop. 12 597 – ☎ 01442.

London 38 – Aylesbury 7 – Luton 14.

Pendley Manor, Cow Lane, HP23 5QY, E : 1½ m. by B 4635 off B 4251 ℘ 891891, Fax 890687, ≤, , park, – TV ☎ P – 200. AE VISA
Meals 16.00/30.00 **st.** and a la carte – **69 rm** 85.00/95.00 **t.**, 2 suites – SB.

Rose and Crown, High St., HP23 5AH, ℘ 824071, Fax 890735 – rm TV ☎ P – 80. AE VISA JCB.
Meals (bar lunch Saturday) 9.95/17.95 **t.** and a la carte 5.35 – **27 rm** 55.00/94.00 **t.** – SB.

Travel Inn, Tring Hill, HP23 4LD, W : 1½ m. on A 41 ℘ 824819, Fax 890787 – rm TV P. AE VISA.
closed 24 to 26 December – **Meals** (grill rest.) – 4.95 – **30 rm** 34.50 **t.**

TROTTON W. Sussex – see Midhurst.

TROUTBECK Cumbria 402 L 20 – see Windermere.

TROWBRIDGE Wilts. 403 404 N 30 The West Country G. – pop. 25 279 – ☎ 01225.

Envir. : Westwood Manor★, NW : 3 m. by A 363 – Farleigh Hungerford Castle★ (St. Leonard's Chapel★) *AC*, W : 4 m.

Exc. : Longleat House★★★ *AC*, SW : 12 m. by A 363, A 350 and A 362 - Bratton Castle (≤★★) SE : 7½ m. by A 363 and B 3098 – Steeple Ashton★ (The Green★) E : 6 m. – Edington (St. Mary St. Katherine and All Saints★) SE : 7½ m.

St. Stephen's Pl., BA14 8AH ☎ 777054.

London 115 – Bristol 27 – Southampton 55 – Swindon 32.

Old Manor ♨, Trowle, BA14 9BL, NW : 1 m. on A 363 ☎ 777393, Fax 765443, « Queen Anne house of 15C origin », – rm TV ☎ P. AE VISA JCB.
closed 4 days Christmas – **Meals** *(closed Sunday)* (residents only) (dinner only) 15.00 t. and a la carte 3.95 – **14 rm** 40.00/66.00 t.

Hilbury Court, Hilperton Rd, BA14 7JW, NE : ¼ m. on A 361 ☎ 752949, Fax 777990, – rest TV ☎ P. VISA.
closed 24 December-1 January – **Meals** *(closed Friday to Sunday and Bank Holidays)* (residents only) (bar lunch)/dinner 14.00 t. 3.90 – **13 rm** 32.00/52.00 t.

Brookfield House without rest., Vaggs Hill, Wingfield, BA14 9NA, SW : 4 m. by A 366 on B 3109 ☎ 830615, « Working farm », park – rm TV P.
3 rm 25.00/40.00 st.

at Semington NE : 3 m. by A 361 on A 350 – ✉ Trowbridge – ☎ 01380 :

Edwards Dining Room at Highfield House, BA14 6JN, on A 350 ☎ 870554 – P. AE VISA
closed Sunday dinner, Monday and Tuesday – **Meals** (dinner only and Sunday lunch)/dinner 16.50 t. 4.75.

ATS Canal Rd, Ladydown Trading Est. ☎ 753469

TRURO Cornwall 403 E 33 The West Country G. – pop. 16 522 – ☎ 01872.

See : Royal Cornwall Museum★ *AC*.

Envir. : Trelissick garden★★ (≤★★) *AC*, S : 4 m. by A 39 – Feock (Church★) S : 5 m. by A 39 and B 3289.

Exc. : Trewithen★★★, NE : 7½ m. by A 39 and A 390.

18 Treliske ☎ 72640.

Municipal Buildings, Boscawen St., TR1 2NE ☎ 74555.

London 295 – Exeter 87 – Penzance 26 – Plymouth 52.

Alverton Manor, Tregolls Rd, TR1 1XQ, ☎ 76633, Fax 222989, « Mid 19C manor house, former Bishop's residence and convent », – rest TV ☎ P – 200. AE VISA JCB.
Meals 12.95/18.50 **st.** and dinner a la carte 4.50 – **32 rm** 63.00/99.00 **st.**, 2 suites – SB.

Royal, Lemon St., TR1 2QB, ☎ 70345, Fax 42453 – rm TV ☎ P – 40. AE VISA.
Meals (grill rest.) a la carte 10.85/20.85 **st.** – **34 rm** 49.00/80.00 **st.** – SB.

Laniley House ♨ without rest., Newquay Rd, nr. Trispen, TR4 9AU, NE : 3½ m. by A 39 and A 3076 on Frogmore rd ☎ 75201, – TV P.
March-October – **3 rm** 25.00/36.00 **s.**

Blue Haze without rest., The Parade, Malpas Rd, TR1 1QE, ☎ 223553, Fax 223553, – TV P.
3 rm 21.00/38.00.

Conifers without rest., 36 Tregolls Rd, TR1 1LA, ☎ 79925 – TV P.
4 rm 17.50/35.00 **s.**

at Blackwater W : 7 m. by A 390 – ✉ Truro – ☎ 01872 :

Rock Cottage, TR4 8EU, ☎ 560252, Fax 560252 – TV P.
closed Christmas and New Year – **Meals** (by arrangement) 9.00 **s.** – **3 rm** 23.50/39.00 **s.**

✿ **Pennypots** (Viner), TR4 8EY, SW : ¾ m. ☎ (01209) 820347 – P. VISA
closed Sunday, Monday and 4 weeks winter – **Meals** (dinner only) a la carte 22.20/29.00 **t.**
Spec. Lobster ravioli with sea asparagus on an olive oil and basil dressing, Pan fried fillet of beef with a Madeira and wild mushroom sauce, Vanilla shortbread filled with raspberries and clotted cream.

ATS Tabernacle St. ☎ 74083 ATS Newham Rd ☎ 40353

TRUSHAM Devon pop. 152 – ✉ Newton Abbot – ☎ 01626.

London 208 – Exeter 16 – Plymouth 36.

Cridford Inn, TQ13 0NR, ☎ 853694, « 11C former hall house » – rest TV P. VISA.
closed 25 December – **Meals** *(closed Sunday dinner)* (booking essential) (bar lunch)/dinner a la carte 10.45/22.20 **t.** 5.75 – **4 rm** 37.50/55.00 **t.** – SB.

TUCKENHAY Devon – see Totnes.

TUNBRIDGE WELLS Kent 404 U 30 – see Royal Tunbridge Wells.

URNERS HILL W. Sussex 404 T 30 pop. 1 534 – ☎ 01342.
London 33 – Brighton 24 – Crawley 7.

Alexander House ⛛, East St., RH10 4QD, E : 1 m. on B 2110 ✆ 714914, Fax 717328, ←, « Part 17C country house in extensive parkland », ⛛, ⛛, ⛛, ⛛ – ⛛ ⛛ rest TV ☎ P. ⛛ AE ⛛ VISA. ⛛
Meals 16.75/24.95 **t.** and a la carte ⛛ 7.50 – ⛛ 12.50 – **9 rm** 95.00/125.00 **t.**, 6 suites – SB.

UTBURY Staffs. 402 403 404 O 25 **Great Britain G.** – pop. 3 249 – ✉ Burton-upon-Trent – ☎ 01283.
nvir. : Sudbury Hall★★ *AC*, NW : 5½ m. by A 50.
London 132 – Birmingham 33 – Derby 11 – Stoke-on-Trent 27.

Ye Olde Dog and Partridge, High St., DE13 9LS, ✆ 813030, Fax 813178, « Part 15C timbered inn », ⛛ – ⛛ rm TV ☎ P. ⛛ AE VISA. ⛛
closed 25 December – **Meals** (carving rest.) a la carte 11.00/14.45 **t.** ⛛ 5.20 – **17 rm** ⛛ 55.00/72.50 **t.**

Mill House without rest., Cornmill Lane, DE13 9HA, SE : ½ m. ✆ 813634, « Georgian house and watermill », ⛛ – ⛛ TV P. ⛛
closed 25 and 26 December – **3 rm** ⛛ 35.00/55.00 **st.**

TWO BRIDGES Devon 403 I 32 **The West Country G.** – ✉ Yelverton – ☎ 01822.
Envir. : Dartmoor National Park★★ (Brent Tor ←★★, Haytor Rocks ←★).
London 226 – Exeter 25 – Plymouth 17.

Prince Hall ⛛, PL20 6SA, E : 1 m. on B 3357 ✆ 890403, Fax 890676, ←, ⛛ – ⛛ rest TV ☎ P. ⛛ AE ⛛ VISA JCB
closed first 2 weeks January – **Meals** (dinner only) 19.50 **t.** ⛛ 4.50 – **8 rm** ⛛ (dinner included) 49.50/54.50 **t.** – SB.

***En saison**, surtout dans les stations fréquentées, il est prudent de retenir à l'avance. Cependant, si vous ne pouvez pas occuper la chambre que vous avez retenue, prévenez immédiatement l'hôtelier.*

Si vous écrivez à un hôtel à l'étranger, joignez à votre lettre un coupon-réponse international (disponible dans les bureaux de poste).

TWO MILLS Ches. – see Chester.

TYNEMOUTH Tyne and Wear 401 402 P 18 – pop. 8 921 – ☎ 0191.
London 290 – Newcastle upon Tyne 8 – Sunderland 7.

Hope House, 47 Percy Gdns, NE30 4HH, ✆ 257 1989, Fax 257 1989, ←, « Tastefully furnished Victorian house » – TV ⛛. ⛛ AE ⛛ VISA. ⛛
Meals (communal dining) (dinner only) 14.50 **s.** ⛛ 5.00 – **3 rm** ⛛ 35.00/55.00 **s.** – SB.

UCKFIELD E. Sussex 404 U 31 – pop. 12 087 – ☎ 01825.
London 45 – Brighton 17 – Eastbourne 20 – Maidstone 34.

Horsted Place ⛛, Little Horsted, TN22 5TS, S : 2½ m. by B 2102 and A 22 on A 26 ✆ 750581, Fax 750459, ←, « Victorian Gothic country house and gardens », ⛛, ⛛18, park, ⛛ – ⛛ ⛛ rest TV ☎ P – ⛛ 100. ⛛ AE ⛛ VISA. ⛛
Meals 14.95/30.00 **t.** and a la carte ⛛ 5.75 – ⛛ 3.50 – **15 rm** 100.00/180.00 **t.**, 5 suites – SB.

Hooke Hall, 250 High St., TN22 1EN, ✆ 761578, Fax 768025, « Queen Anne town house », ⛛ – TV ☎ P. ⛛ AE VISA. ⛛
closed 24 to 30 December – **La Scaletta : Meals** – Italian – *(closed Saturday lunch and Sunday)* 13.00 **t.** (lunch) and a la carte 18.70/24.00 **t.** ⛛ 5.00 – ⛛ 6.50 – **9 rm** 40.00/105.00 **st.**

UFFINGTON Oxon. 403 404 P 29 – ☎ 01367.
London 75 – Oxford 29 – Reading 32 – Swindon 17.

Craven, Fernham Rd, SN7 7RD, ✆ 820449, « Thatched 17C house », ⛛ – ⛛ rm P. ⛛ AE ⛛ VISA. ⛛
Meals (by arrangement) 15.50 **st.** ⛛ 3.25 – **5 rm** ⛛ 25.00/58.00 **t.**

ULLINGSWICK Heref. and Worcs. – pop. 237 – ✉ Hereford – ☎ 01432.
London 134 – Hereford 12 – Shrewsbury 52 – Worcester 19.

Steppes Country House ⛛, HR1 3JG, ✆ 820424, Fax 820042, « Converted farmhouse of 14C origins », ⛛ – ⛛ TV ☎ P. ⛛ AE VISA
closed December and January except Christmas and New Year – **Meals** (booking essential) (bar lunch)/dinner 24.00 **st.** ⛛ 4.95 – **6 rm** ⛛ 50.00/90.00 **st.** – SB.

ULLSWATER Cumbria 402 L 20 pop. 1 199 – ✉ Penrith – ☎ 0176 84.
ℹ Main Car Park, Glenridding, CA11 0PA ✆ 82414 (summer only).
London 296 – Carlisle 25 – Kendal 31 – Penrith 6.

at Howtown SW : 4 m. of Pooley Bridge – ✉ Penrith – ☎ 0176 84 :

Howtown ⛛, CA10 2ND, ✆ 86514, ←, ⛛ – P
April-October – **Meals** 8.75/12.00 **t.** – **13 rm** ⛛ 39.00/78.00 **t.**

at Pooley Bridge on B 5320 – ✉ Penrith – ☎ 0176 84 :

Sharrow Bay Country House, CA10 2LZ, S : 2 m. on Howtown rd ☎ 86301, Fax 86349, ≤ Ullswater and fells, « Lakeside setting, gardens, tasteful decor », – rest
closed late November-late February – **Meals** (booking essential) 31.75/41.75 **st.** – **24 rm** (dinner included) 95.00/320.00 **st.**, 4 suites
Spec. Duck foie gras served on a potato pancake with spinach and morel sauce, Grilled medallion of salmon on a leek purée with a Madeira and lemon sauce, Ginger and crème brûlée tart with rhubarb sauce.

at Watermillock on A 592 – ✉ Penrith – ☎ 0176 84 :

Leeming House (Forte Heritage), CA11 0JJ, on A 592 ☎ 86622, Fax 86443, ≤ « Lakeside country house and gardens », park – – 35. AE VISA JCB
Meals 28.50 **t.** (dinner) and a la carte 16.30/28.95 **t.** – 10.50 – **40 rm** 80.00/135.00 **t.** – SB.

Rampsbeck Country House, CA11 0LP, ☎ 86442, Fax 86688, ≤ Ullswater and fells, park – VISA
closed second week January-mid February – **Meals** 22.00/37.50 **t.** 5.00 – **19 rm** 50.00/120.00 **t.**, 1 suite – SB.

Old Church, CA11 0JN, ☎ 86204, Fax 86368, ≤ Ullswater and fells, « Lakeside setting », – rest
April-October – **Meals** *(closed Sunday)* (booking essential) (dinner only) a la carte 16.20/23.40 **st.** 6.50 – **10 rm** 59.00/119.00 **st.** – SB.

Knotts Mill Country Lodge, CA11 0JN, on A 592 ☎ 86472, Fax 86699, ≤, – rest
9 rm.

Die Preise Einzelheiten über die in diesem Führer angegebenen Preise finden Sie in der Einleitung.

ULVERSTON Cumbria 402 K 21 – pop. 11 866 – ☎ 01229.
18 Bardsea Park ☎ 582824.
Coronation Hall, County Sq., LA12 7LZ ☎ 587120.
London 278 – Kendal 25 – Lancaster 36.

Trinity House, 1 Princes St., LA12 7NB, off A 590 ☎ 587639, Fax 587639 – AE VISA JCB
Meals (dinner only) 13.95 **t.** and a la carte 5.00 – **6 rm** 41.00/60.00 **t.** – SB.

Church Walk House without rest., Church Walk, LA12 7EW, ☎ 582211 –
closed Christmas and New Year and restricted opening in winter – **3 rm** 22.00/40.00 **s.**

Bay Horse Inn with rm, Canal Foot, LA12 9EL, E : 2¼ m. by A 5087, Morecambe Rd and beyond Industrial area, on the coast ☎ 583972, Fax 580502, ≤ Morecambe bay – rest VISA
closed 2 January-2 February – **Meals** *(closed lunch Sunday and Monday)* (booking essential) 15.50 **t.** (lunch) and a la carte 18.95/24.20 **t.** – **7 rm** (dinner included) 80.00/150.00 **t.** – SB.

at Lowick Bridge N : 6¾ m. by A 590 and A 5092 on A 5084 – ✉ Ulverston – ☎ 01229 :

Bridgefield House with rm, LA12 8DA, SE : ½ m. by Nibthwaite rd ☎ 885239, Fax 885379, ≤, – rest VISA
Meals (booking essential) (dinner only) 22.50 **t.** – **5 rm** 35.00/70.00 **t.** – SB.

ATS The Gill ☎ 583442

UMBERLEIGH Devon 403 I 31 – ☎ 01769.
London 218 – Barnstaple 7 – Exeter 31 – Taunton 49.

Rising Sun, EX37 9DU, on A 377 ☎ 560447, Fax 560764, – VISA
Meals 7.95/14.95 **st.** and dinner a la carte 4.75 – **11 rm** 38.00/70.00 **st.** – SB.

UP HOLLAND Lancs. 402 M 23 – see Wigan.

UPLYME Devon 403 L 31 – see Lyme Regis.

UPPER BENEFIELD Northants. – see Oundle.

UPPER SLAUGHTER Glos. 403 404 O 28 – see Bourton-on-the-Water.

UPPINGHAM Leics. 404 R 26 – pop. 3 143 – ☎ 01572.
London 101 – Leicester 19 – Northampton 28 – Nottingham 35.

Rutland House without rest., 61 High St. East, LE15 9PY, ☎ 822497, Fax 822497, – VISA
4 rm 29.00/39.00 **st.**

Lake Isle with rm, 16 High St. East, LE15 9PZ, ☎ 822951, Fax 822951 – AE VISA
Meals *(closed Monday lunch and Sunday dinner to non-residents)* 11.00/25.50 **t.** 6.00 – **10 rm** 47.00/68.00 **t.**, 2 suites – SB.

at Morcott Service Area E : 4 ¼ m. by A 6003 on A 47 – ✉ Uppingham – ☎ 01572 :

Forte Travelodge, Glaston Rd, LE15 8SA, ✆ 87719, Reservations (Freephone) 0800 850950 – TV ♿ P. AE VISA. 🐕
Meals (grill rest.) – **40 rm** 34.50 **t.**

UPTON ST. LEONARDS Glos. – see Gloucester.

UPTON SNODSBURY Heref. and Worcs. 403 404 N 27 – see Worcester.

UPTON-UPON-SEVERN Heref. and Worcs. 403 404 N 27 – pop. 2 561 – ☎ 01684.
Pepperpot, Church St., WR8 0HT ✆ 594200 (summer only).
♦London 116 – Hereford 25 – Stratford-upon-Avon 29 – Worcester 11.

White Lion, High St., WR8 0HJ, ✆ 592551, Fax 592551 – TV ☎ P. AE ⓓ VISA
closed 25 and 26 December – **Meals** 15.25 **t.** and a la carte 🍷 4.95 – **10 rm** ☕ 54.50/74.50 **t.** – SB.

UTTOXETER Staffs. 402 403 404 O 25 **Great Britain G.** – pop. 11 707 – ☎ 01889.
Envir. : Sudbury Hall★★ *AC*, E : 5 m. by A 518 and A 50.
18 Wood Lane ✆ 565108.
♦London 145 – ♦Birmingham 33 – Derby 19 – Stafford 13 – ♦Stoke-on-Trent 16.

White Hart, Carter St., ST14 8EU, ✆ 562437, Fax 565099 – TV ☎ P – 50. AE ⓓ VISA. 🐕
Meals (grill rest.) 7.50 **t.** and a la carte 🍷 4.95 – ☕ 5.00 – **21 rm** 36.00/55.00 **t.**

Bank House, Church St., ST14 8AG, ✆ 566922, Fax 567565 – TV ☎ P – 30. AE ⓓ VISA
Meals 20.00 **t.** and a la carte 🍷 3.95 **15 rm** ☕ 37.50/69.50 **t.** – SB.

Forte Travelodge, Ashbourne Rd, ST14 5AA, at junction of A 50 with B 5030 ✆ 562043, Reservations (Freephone) 0800 850950 – TV ♿ P. AE VISA. 🐕
Meals (grill rest.) – **32 rm** 34.50 **t.**

at Doveridge (Derbs.) NE : 2½ m. by Derby rd on A 50 – ✉ Ashbourne – ☎ 01889 :

XX **Beeches Farmhouse** with rm, Waldley, DE6 5LR, NE : 2 m. by Marston Lane ✆ 590288, Fax 590288, « Working farm », – TV ☎ P. AE ⓓ VISA. 🐕
closed 23 to 30 December – **Meals** *(closed Sunday dinner)* (dinner only and Sunday lunch)/dinner a la carte 11.65/18.25 **st.** 🍷 3.75 – **10 rm** ☕ 38.50/46.00 **st.**

ATS Smithfield Rd ✆ 563848/565201

VENN OTTERY Devon 403 K 31 – ✉ Ottery St. Mary – ☎ 01404.
♦London 209 – Exeter 11 – Sidmouth 5.

Venn Ottery Barton, EX11 1RZ, ✆ 812733, – rest P. VISA
Meals 15.00 **t.** 🍷 4.00 – **16 rm** ☕ 23.00/50.00 **t.** – SB.

VENTNOR I.O.W. 403 404 Q 32 – see Wight (Isle of).

VERYAN Cornwall 403 F 33 **The West Country G.** – pop. 877 – ✉ Truro – ☎ 01872.
See : Village★.
♦London 291 – St. Austell 13 – Truro 13.

Nare, Carne Beach, TR2 5PF, SW : 1 ¼ m. ✆ 501279, Fax 501856, ≤ Carne Bay, heated, – TV ☎ P. VISA
closed 6 weeks January-February – **Meals** 13.00/27.00 **t.** and a la carte – **34 rm** ☕ 74.00/189.00 **t.**, 2 suites.

at Ruan High Lanes W : 1 ¼ m. on A 3078 – ✉ Truro – ☎ 01872 :

Hundred House, TR2 5JR, ✆ 501336, Fax 501151, – rest TV ☎ P. AE VISA
March-October – **Meals** (dinner only) 21.50 – **10 rm** ☕ (dinner included) 58.00/116.00 **t.** – SB.

Crugsillick Manor, TR2 5LJ, SE : ¾ m. by A 3078 on Veryan rd ✆ 501214, Fax 501214, « Queen Anne manor house of Elizabethan origins », – P. VISA. 🐕
Meals (by arrangement) (communal dining) 20.00 **st.** 🍷 6.00 – **3 rm** ☕ 35.00/88.00 **st.**

WADDESDON Bucks. 404 R 28 pop. 1 864 – ☎ 01296.
♦London 51 – Aylesbury 5 – Northampton 32 – ♦Oxford 31.

Five Arrows, High St., HP18 0JE, ✆ 651727, Fax 658596, – rm TV ☎ P. VISA. 🐕
Meals a la carte 13.35/25.15 **t.** – **6 rm** ☕ 55.00/70.00 **t.**

WADDINGTON Lancs. 402 M 22 – see Clitheroe.

Europe

If the name of the hotel
is not in bold type,
on arrival ask the hotelier his prices.

WADHURST E. Sussex 404 U 30 – pop. 4 499 – ☎ 01892.
♦London 44 – Hastings 21 – Maidstone 24 – Royal Tunbridge Wells 6.

Newbarn without rest., Wards Lane, TN5 6HP, E : 3 m. by B 2099 ℘ 782042, ≤ Bewl Water and countryside, – – P.
3 rm 20.00/44.00 **t.**

Kirkstone without rest., Mayfield Lane, TN5 6HX, ℘ 783204, – P
3 rm 18.00/36.00 **st.**

WAKEFIELD W. Yorks. 402 P 22 **Great Britain G.** – pop. 76 181 – ☎ 01924.
Envir. : Nostell Priory★ *AC*, SE : 4½ m. by A 638.
18 City of Wakefield, Lupset Park, Horbury Rd ℘ 367442 – 18 28 Woodthorpe Lane, Sandal ℘ 255104 – 9 Normanton, Snydale Rd ℘ 892943 – 9 Painthorpe House, Painthorpe Lane, Crigglestone ℘ 255083.
Town Hall, Wood St., WF1 2HQ ℘ 295000/295001.
♦London 188 – ♦Leeds 9 – ♦Manchester 38 – ♦Sheffield 23.

Cedar Court, Denby Dale Rd., Calder Grove, WF4 3QZ, SW : 3 m. on A 636 ℘ 276310, Telex 557647, Fax 280221 – rm TV P – 400. AE VISA
Meals *(closed Saturday lunch)* 8.50/19.95 **t.** and a la carte 5.95 – 8.50 – **144 rm** 75.00 **st.**, 5 suites – SB.

Swallow, Queen St., WF1 1JU, ℘ 372111, Fax 383648 – rm rest TV P – 200. AE VISA
Meals (light lunch)/dinner 17.00 **st.** and a la carte 7.00 – **63 rm** 78.00/114.00 **st.** – SB.

Forte Posthouse, Queen's Drive, Ossett, WF5 9BE, W : 2 ½ m. on A 638 ℘ 276388, Fax 276437 – rm rest TV P – 150. AE VISA
Meals 20.00 **st.** and a la carte – 7.95 – **99 rm** 59.00 **st.** – SB.

at Newmillerdam S : 3½ m. on A 61 – ✉ Wakefield – ☎ 01924 :

St. Pierre, Barnsley Rd, WF2 6QG, ℘ 255596, Fax 252746 – rm rest TV P – 40. AE VISA.
Meals 7.95/15.95 **t.** and a la carte 5.25 – 6.00 – **42 rm** 55.00 **t.**, 2 suites – SB.

ATS Bethel Pl., Thornes Lane ℘ 371638

WALBERSWICK Suffolk 404 Y 27 pop. 1 648 – ✉ Southwold – ☎ 01502.
♦London 97 – Great Yarmouth 28 – ♦Ipswich 32 – ♦Norwich 32.

Anchor, The Street, IP18 6UA, ℘ 722112, Fax 722283, – rest TV P. AE VISA JCB.
Meals (bar lunch Monday to Saturday)/dinner 17.50 **t.** and a la carte 4.00 – **13 rm** 50.00/80.00 **t.** – SB.

WALBERTON W. Sussex – see Arundel.

WALKINGTON Humbs. 402 S 22 – see Beverley.

WALLINGFORD Oxon. 403 404 Q 29 **The West Country G.** – pop. 6 616 – ☎ 01491.
Exc. : Ridgeway Path★★.
Town Hall, Market Place, OX10 0EG ℘ 826972.
♦London 54 – ♦Oxford 12 – Reading 16.

George (Mount Charlotte), 84 High St., OX10 0BS, ℘ 836665, Fax 825359 – rm TV P – 120. AE VISA JCB
Meals 10.50/28.00 **st.** and a la carte 5.50 – **39 rm** 62.00/72.00 **st.** – SB.

at North Stoke S : 2¾ m. by A 4130 and A 4074 on B 4009 – ✉ Wallingford – ☎ 01491 :

Springs , Wallingford Rd, OX10 6BE, ℘ 836687, Fax 836877, ≤, , heated, , park, – TV P – 50. AE VISA.
Meals 15.50/27.00 **st.** and a la carte – **34 rm** 90.00/155.00 **st.**, 2 suites – SB.

WALMERSLEY Gtr. Manchester – see Bury.

WALSALL W. Mids. 403 404 O 26 – pop. 259 488 – ☎ 01922.
18 Calderfields, Aldridge Rd ℘ 640540 CT.
♦London 126 – ♦Birmingham 9 – ♦Coventry 29 – Shrewsbury 36.

Plan of enlarged area : see Birmingham pp. 2 and 3

Quality Friendly, 20 Wolverhampton Rd West, Bentley, WS2 0BS, W : 2½ m. on A 454 ℘ 724444, Fax 723148, , , – rm TV P – 180. AE VISA JCB. BT **a**
Meals (carving rest.) 9.55/13.50 **st.** and a la carte 8.50 – 7.75 – **155 rm** 57.50/94.00 **st.** – SB.

Boundary (Forte), Birmingham Rd, WS5 3AB, SE : 1½ m. on A 34 ℘ 33555, Fax 612034, – rm rest TV P – 65. AE VISA JCB CT **e**
Meals (bar lunch Monday) 10.00/14.25 **st.** and a la carte – 7.95 – **94 rm** 57.50 **st.** – SB.

ATS Leamore Trading Est., Fryers Rd, Bloxwich ℘ 478631

WALSGRAVE ON SOWE W. Mids. – see Coventry.

WALTHAM ABBEY Essex 404 U 28 – pop. 11 207 – 01992.

London 15 – Cambridge 44 – Ipswich 66 – Luton 30 – Southend-on-Sea 35.

Swallow, Old Shire Lane, EN9 3LX, SE : 1½ m. on A 121 717170, Fax 711841, – rm rest – 220.
Meals 14.00/23.50 **st.** and a la carte 4.25 – **163 rm** 96.00/185.00 **st.** – SB.

ATS Unit 17, Lea Rd, Ind. Park 788050

WALTON-ON-THAMES Surrey 404 S 29 – 01932.

London 23 – Brighton 54 – Portsmouth 61 – Southampton 65.

Ashley Park, Ashley Park Rd, KT12 1JP, 220196, Fax 248721 – – 60.
Meals a la carte 12.75/20.50 **t.** – **29 rm** 65.00/80.00 **t.**

WANSFORD Cambs. 404 S 26 – see Peterborough.

WARE Herts. 404 T 28 – pop. 17 069 – 01920.

Whitehill, Dane End 438495.

London 24 – Cambridge 30 – Luton 22.

Hanbury Manor H. Country Club Resort (Country Club), Thundridge, SG12 0SD, N : 1 ¾ m. by A 1170 on A 10 487722, Fax 487692, ≤, « Jacobean style mansion in extensive grounds, walled garden », squash – rm rest – 140.
Conservatory : Meals 28.50 **st.**(dinner) and a la carte 27.50/32.00 **st.** 7.50 – **Vardon's : Meals** a la carte 19.00/28.75 **st.** 7.50 - (see also ***Zodiac Room*** below) – 12.50 – **91 rm** 143.00/299.00 **st.**, 5 suites – SB.

Ware County (Q.M.H.), Baldock St., SG12 9DR, N : ½ m. on A 1170 465011, Fax 468016 – rm rest – 200.
Meals *(closed Saturday lunch)* 9.95/13.95 **t.** 5.85 – 8.75 – **50 rm** 71.50/84.00 **t.** – SB.

XXXX **Zodiac Room** (at Hanbury Manor H.), Thundridge, SG12 0SD, N : 1 ¾ m. by A 1170 on A 10 487722, Fax 487692 – .
closed Sunday dinner – **Meals** (dinner only and Sunday lunch)/dinner 26.50/28.50 **st.** and a la carte 7.50.

at Puckeridge N : 5 ½ m. by A 1170 and A 10 at junction with A 120 – Ware – 01920 :

Vintage Court, Cambridge Rd, SG11 1SA, 822722, Fax 822877, – rm – 90.
closed 25 December-1 January – **Meals** 11.85/15.85 **t.** and a la carte – **24 rm** 65.45/73.40 **t.**

WAREHAM Dorset 403 404 N 31 The West Country G. – pop. 5 644 – 01929.

See : Town★ – St. Martin's★★.

Envir. : Blue Pool★ *AC*, S : 3½ m. by A 351 – Bovington★ (Bovington Camp Tank Museum★ *AC*, Woolbridge Manor★) W : 5 m. by A 352.

Exc. : Moreton Church★★, W : 9½ m. by A 352 – Corfe Castle★★ (≤★★) *AC*, SE : 6 m. by A 351 – Lulworth Cove★, SW : 10 m. by A 352 and B 3070.

Town Hall, East St., BH20 4NN 552740.

London 123 – Bournemouth 13 – Weymouth 19.

Priory, Church Green, BH20 4ND, 551666, Fax 554519, ≤, « Part 16C priory, riverside gardens », – rest .
Meals 12.95/28.50 **t.** and a la carte 7.00 – **17 rm** 70.00/195.00 **t.**, 2 suites – SB.

Springfield Country, Grange Rd, Stoborough, BH20 5AL, S : 1 m. by South St. and West Lane 552177, Fax 551862, heated, squash – – 75.
Meals (bar lunch)/dinner 15.00 **t.** and a la carte 5.00 – **32 rm** 75.00/126.00 **t.** – SB.

Kemps Country House, East Stoke, BH20 6AL, W : 2 ¾ m. on A 352 462563, Fax 405287, – rest – 70.
Meals *(closed Saturday lunch)* 9.95/18.95 **t.** and a la carte – **14 rm** 55.00/112.00 **t.** – SB.

Pleasant hotels and restaurants
are shown in the Guide by a red sign.

Please send us the names
of any where you have enjoyed your stay.

Your Michelin Guide will be even better.

XXXXX ... X

WAREN MILL Northd. – see Bamburgh.

WARMINSTER Wilts. 403 404 N 30 **The West Country G.** – pop. 16 267 – ☎ 01985.

Envir. : Longleat House★★★ *AC*, SW : 3 m – **Exc.** : Stonehenge★★★ *AC*, E : 18 m. by A 36 and A 303 – Bratton Castle (≤★★) NE : 6 m. by A 350 and B 3098.

☐ Central Car Park, BA12 9BT ☎ 218548.

◆London 111 – ◆Bristol 29 – Exeter 74 – ◆Southampton 47.

Bishopstrow House, BA12 9HH, SE : 1½ m. on B 3414 ☎ 212312, Fax 216769, ≤, heated, park, indoor – rest – 60.
Meals 12.50/36.00 **t.** and a la carte – **27 rm** 98.00/180.00 **t.**, 3 suites – SB.

Granada Lodge without rest., BA12 7RU, NW : 1¼ m. by B 3414 ☎ 219539, Fax 214380, Reservations (Freephone) 0800 555300 –
32 rm 39.95 **st.**

at Heytesbury SE : 3¾ m. by B 3414 – ✉ Warminster – ☎ 01985 :

Angel, High St., BA12 0ED, ☎ 840330, Fax 840931, « 17C inn »
closed 25 December – **Meals** (bar lunch Monday to Saturday)/dinner a la carte 12.50/21.50 **st.** 4.25 – **4 rm** 37.50/49.00 **st.**

at Crockerton S : 1¾ m. by A 350 – ✉ Warminster – ☎ 01985 :

Springfield House, BA12 8AU, on Potters Hill rd ☎ 213696, –
Meals (by arrangement) 15.00 **st.** – **3 rm** 29.00/48.00 **st.** – SB.

at Horningsham SW : 5 m. by A 362 – ✉ Warminster – ☎ 01985 :

Bath Arms, BA12 7LY, ☎ 844308, Fax 844150, –
Meals 9.50/25.00 **t.** and a la carte 4.00 – **7 rm** 35.00/52.00 **t.** – SB.

WARREN STREET Kent 404 W 30 – ✉ Maidstone – ☎ 01622.

◆London 51 – Folkestone 28 – Maidstone 12.

Harrow Inn, ME17 2ED, ☎ 858727, Fax 850026, –
closed 25 and 26 December – **Meals** a la carte 15.15/25.15 **t.** – **13 rm** 39.50/49.50 **t.** – SB.

WARRINGTON Ches. 402 403 404 M 23 – pop. 182 685 – ☎ 01925.

Hill Warren, Appleton ☎ 261620 – Walton Hall, Warrington Rd, Higher Walton ☎ 266775 – Kelvin Close, Birchwood ☎ 818819 – Leigh, Kenyon Hall, Culcheth ☎ 763130.

☐ 21 Rylands St., WA1 1EJ ☎ 442180/444400.

◆London 195 – Chester 20 – ◆Liverpool 18 – ◆Manchester 21 – Preston 28.

Village H. & Leisure Club, Centre Park, WA1 1QA, ☎ 240000, Fax 445240, , squash – rm – 200.
Meals *(closed Saturday lunch)* (grill rest.) 9.95/12.95 **st.** and a la carte 3.95 – **87 rm** 80.00/90.00 **st.** – SB.

Holiday Inn Garden Court, Woolston Grange Av., Woolston, WA1 4PX, E : 3¼ m. by A 57 at junction 21 of M 6 on B 5210 ☎ 838779, Fax 838859 – rm rest
Meals (dinner only) 20.00 **st.** and a la carte 7.95 – 8.45 – **98 rm** 61.00 **st.** – SB.

Travel Inn, Calver Rd, Winwick Quay Industrial Estate, WA2 8RN, N : 2¼ m. on A 49 ☎ 414417, Fax 414544 – rm
Meals (grill rest.) – 4.95 – **40 rm** 34.50 **t.**

at Stretton S : 3½ m. by A 49 on B 5356 – ✉ Warrington – ☎ 01925 :

Park Royal International, Stretton Rd, WA4 4NS, ☎ 730706, Fax 730740 – rest – 400.
Meals 9.45/16.45 **t.** and a la carte – 8.50 – **98 rm** 73.00/83.00 **t.**, 2 suites – SB.

ATS Grange Av., Latchford ☎ 632613

WARWICK Warks. 403 404 P 27 **Great Britain G.** – pop. 22 709 – ☎ 01926.

See : Town★ - Castle★★ *AC* Y – Leycester Hospital★ *AC* Y **B** – Collegiate Church of St. Mary★ (Tomb★) Y **A**.

Warwick Racecourse ☎ 494316 Y – ☐ The Court House, Jury St., CV34 4EW ☎ 492212.

◆London 96 – ◆Birmingham 20 – ◆Coventry 11 – ◆Oxford 43.

Plan opposite

Old Fourpenny Shop, 27-29 Crompton St., CV34 6HJ, ☎ 491360, Fax 411892 – Y **a**
Meals *(closed Monday dinner and Sunday to non-residents)* 8.50/14.00 **t.** and a la carte 4.50 – **11 rm** 35.00/65.00 **st.** – SB.

Park Cottage without rest., 113 West St., CV34 6AH, ☎ 410319, Fax 410319 – Y **e**
closed 24 to 26 December – **4 rm** 40.00/50.00 **st.**

WARWICK
ROYAL LEAMINGTON SPA

Les plans de villes sont disposés le Nord en haut.

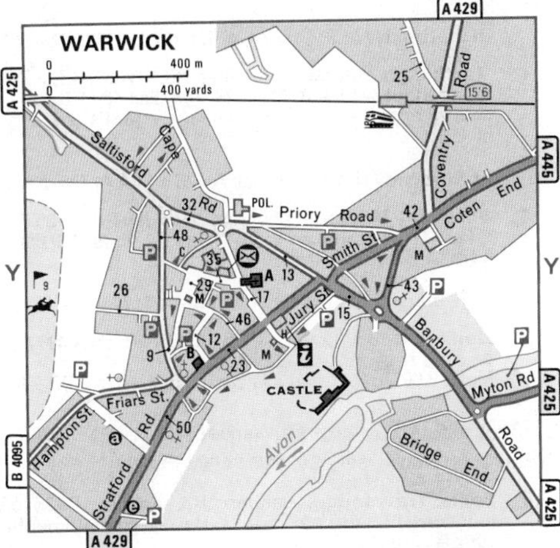

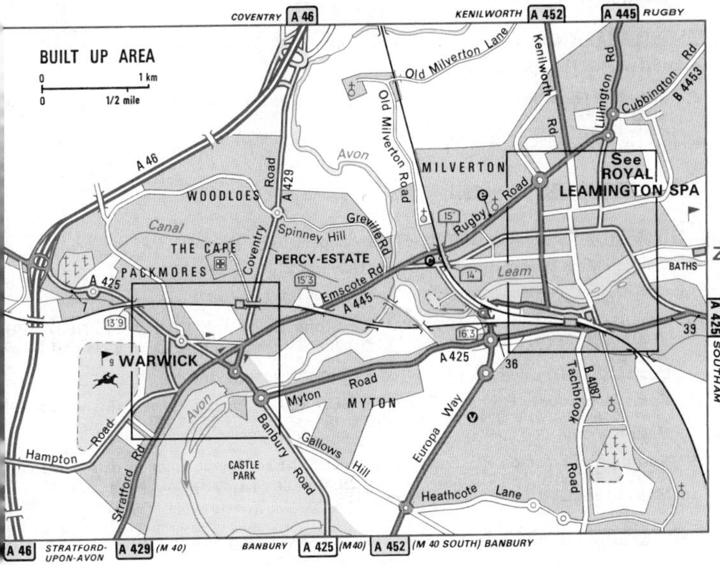

BUILT UP AREA
1 km
1/2 mile
COVENTRY A 46 — KENILWORTH A 452 — A 445 RUGBY
WOODLOES — THE CAPE — PACKMORES — PERCY-ESTATE — MILVERTON — MYTON — CASTLE PARK
See ROYAL LEAMINGTON SPA
A 46 STRATFORD-UPON-AVON — A 429 (M 40) — BANBURY A 425 (M40) — A 452 (M 40 SOUTH) BANBURY — A 425 SOUTHAM

at Barford S : 3½ m. on A 429 – Z – ✉ Warwick – ☎ 01926 :

Glebe House, Church St., CV35 8BS, on B 4462 ☎ 624218, Fax 624625, Fö, ≘s, ◻, 🛲 – |‡| ▤ rest ▣ ☎ **P** – 🔬 120. AE ⓓ VISA
Meals 10.00/15.50 **st.** and dinner a la carte ₰ 4.95 – **40 rm** ☐ 95.00/110.00 **st.**, 1 suite – SB.

at Longbridge SW : 2 m. on A 429 – Z – ✉ Warwick – ☎ 01926 :

Hilton National, Stratford Rd, CV34 6RE, at junction of A 429 with M 40 ☎ 499555, Fax 410020, Fö, ≘s, ◻ – |‡| ⇆ rm ▣ ☎ & **P** – 🔬 300. AE ⓓ VISA. ✻
Meals *(closed Saturday lunch)* (carving lunch) 14.75/19.50 **t.** and dinner a la carte ₰ 5.95 – ☐ 10.50 – **181 rm** 95.00/110.00 **t.** – SB.

at Sherbourne SW : 2¾ m. by A 429 – Z – ✉ Warwick – ☎ 01926 :

Old Rectory, Vicarage Lane, CV35 8AB, at junction with A 46 ☎ 624562, Fax 624562, 🛲 – ▣ **P**. VISA
Meals (residents only) (dinner only) a la carte 13.90/19.50 **st.** ₰ 2.90 – **14 rm** ☐ 33.00/56.00 **st.**

at Hatton NW : 3½ m. by A 425 on A 4177 – Z – ✉ Warwick – ☎ 01926 :

Northleigh House, Five Ways Rd, CV35 7HZ, NW : 2½ m. by A 4177, turning left at roundabout with A 4141 ✆ 484203, Fax 484006, – ⇔ TV P. VISA
closed mid December-31 January – **Meals** (by arrangement) 14.50 – **7 rm** 30.00/55.00 **st.**

at Shrewley NW : 4¾ m. by A 425 and A 4177 – Z – on B 4439 – ✉ Warwick – ☎ 01926

Shrewley House without rest., Hockley Rd, CV35 7AT, on B 4439 ✆ 842549, Fax 842216 « Part 17C farmhouse », – ⇔ TV ☎ P. VISA
4 rm 43.00/67.00 **st.**

at Honiley NW : 6¾ by A 425 on A 4177 – Z – ✉ Warwick – ☎ 01926 :

Honiley Court (Country Club), CV8 1NP, on A 4177 ✆ 484234, Fax 484474 – |‡| ⇔ rm TV ☎ ♿ P – 150. AE ① VISA
Meals 8.00/18.00 **t.** and a la carte 5.95 – 7.50 – **62 rm** 65.00 **t.** – SB.

WARWICK SERVICE AREA Warks. 404 P 27 – ☎ 01926.

The Court House, Jury St., CV34 4EW ✆ 492212.

Forte Travelodge, Banbury Rd, Ashorn, CV35 0AA, M 40 (northbound) between junctions 12 and 13 ✆ 651681, Reservations (Freephone) 0800 850950 – TV ♿ P. AE ① VISA
Meals (grill rest.) – **56 m** 34.50 **t.**

WASDALE HEAD Cumbria 402 K 20 – ✉ Gosforth – ☎ 0194 67.

◆London 324 – Kendal 72 – Workington 30.

Wasdale Head Inn, CA20 1EX, ✆ 26229, Fax 26334, < Wasdale Head, – ⇔ rest ☎ P. VISA
closed mid November-28 December – **Meals** (bar lunch)/dinner a la carte 12.50/19.20 **t.** 4.50 – **9 rm** 29.00/58.00 **t.**

WASHINGBOROUGH Lincs. 402 404 S 24 – see Lincoln.

WASHINGTON Tyne and Wear 401 402 P 19 – pop. 60 012 – ☎ 0191.

Washington Moat House, Stone Cellar Rd , Usworth ✆ 417 2626.

◆London 278 – Durham 13 – ◆Middlesbrough 32 – ◆Newcastle upon Tyne 7.

Washington Moat House (Q.M.H.), Stone Cellar Rd, District 12, NE37 1PH ✆ 402 9988, Fax 415 1166, squash – ⇔ rm TV ☎ P – 200. AE ① VISA.
Meals 8.25/30.00 **t.** and a la carte 6.00 – 10.00 – **105 rm** 70.00/95.00 **st.** – SB.

Forte Posthouse, Emerson, District 5, NE37 1LB, at junction of A 1 (M) with A 195 ✆ 416 2264, Fax 415 3371 – |‡| ⇔ rm TV ☎ P – 100. AE ① VISA JCB.
Meals a la carte 13.00/24.20 **t.** 6.95 – 7.95 – **138 rm** 59.00 **st.** – SB.

Campanile, Emerson Rd, Emerson, District 5, NE37 1LE, at junction of A 1(M) with A 195 ✆ 416 5010, Fax 416 5023 – ⇔ rm TV ☎ ♿ P – 25. AE ① VISA
Meals 10.35 **st.** 4.75 – 4.50 – **78 rm** 36.50 **st.**

WASHINGTON SERVICE AREA Tyne and Wear – ✉ Washington – ☎ 0191.

Granada Lodge without rest., DH3 2SJ, on A 1 (M) (southbound carriageway) ✆ 410 0076, Fax 410 0057, Reservations (Freephone) 0800 555300 – ⇔ TV ☎ ♿ P. AE VISA.
35 rm 39.95 **st.**

WATERHEAD Cumbria 402 L 20 – see Ambleside.

WATERHOUSES Staffs. 402 403 404 O 24 Great Britain G. – pop. 1 182 – ✉ Stoke-on-Trent – ☎ 01538.

Envir. : Dovedale★★ (Ilam Rock★) E : 6 m. by A 523.

London 115 – ◆Birmingham 63 – Derby 23 – ◆Manchester 39 – ◆Stoke-on-Trent 17.

XX ✿ **Old Beams** (Wallis) with rm, Leek Rd, ST10 3HW, ☎ 308254, Fax 308157, – rest TV ☎ P. AE VISA.
Meals *(closed Saturday lunch, Sunday dinner and Monday)* (booking essential) 12.00/36.00 **t.** 8.00 – ☕ 6.50 – **5 rm** 55.00/89.95 **t.**
Spec. Hot soufflé of scallops and lobster on a saffron olive oil dressing, Duet of lobster mousse and lobster meat with Dublin Bay prawn tortellinis, Boned young farmed rabbit with a light tarragon jus.

WATERINGBURY Kent 404 V 30 – see Maidstone.

WATERMILLOCK Cumbria 402 L 20 – see Ullswater.

WATER YEAT Cumbria – see Coniston.

WATFORD Herts. 404 S 29 – pop. 74 566 – ☎ 01923.

Bushey G & C.C., High St. ☎ (0181) 950 2283, BT – Bushey Hall, Bushey Hall Drive ☎ 222253, BT – Oxhey Park, Prestwick Rd, South Oxhey ☎ 248312, AT.

◆London 21 – Aylesbury 23.

Plan : see Greater London (North-West)

Hilton National, Elton Way, WD2 8HA, Watford bypass, E : 3½ m. on A 41 at junction with B 462 ☎ 235881, Fax 220836, – rm rest TV ☎ P – 375. AE VISA JCB. BT e
Meals *(closed Saturday lunch)* 12.50/19.50 **st.** – ☕ 10.50 – **194 rm** 94.00 **st.**, 1 suite – SB.

WATH-IN-NIDDERDALE N. Yorks. – see Pateley Bridge.

WEAVERHAM Ches. 402 403 404 M 24 – pop. 6 604 – ☎ 01606.

◆London 191 – Chester 15 – ◆Liverpool 28 – ◆Manchester 28.

Oaklands, Millington Lane, Gorstage, CW8 2SU, SW : 2 m. by A 49 ☎ 853249, Fax 852419, – TV ☎ P. AE VISA
Meals a la carte 12.20/22.55 **st.** 5.20 – **11 rm** ☕ 49.00/55.00 **st.** – SB.

Tall Trees Lodge without rest., Tarporley Rd, Lower Whitley, WA4 4EZ, N : 2¾ m. on A 49 at junction with A 533 ☎ (01928) 790824, Fax 791330 – TV ☎ P – 40. AE VISA
20 rm 34.50 **st.**

WEEDON BEC Northants. 403 404 Q 27 – pop. 2 363 – ✉ Northampton – ☎ 01327.

◆London 74 – ◆Coventry 18 – Northampton 8 – ◆Oxford 41.

Heyford Manor (Country Club), High St., Flore, NN7 4LP, E : 1½ m. on A 45 ☎ 349022, Fax 349017, – rm TV ☎ P – 80. AE VISA
Meals *(closed Saturday lunch)* 8.95 **t.** (lunch) and a la carte 11.65/19.40 **t.** – ☕ 7.50 – **53 rm** 59.00 **t.** – SB.

WELLAND Heref. and Worcs. 403 404 N 27 – see Great Malvern.

WELLESBOURNE Warks. 403 404 P 27 – pop. 5 230 – see Stratford-upon-Avon.

WELLINGBOROUGH Northants. 404 R 27 – pop. 41 602 – ☎ 01933.

Wellingborough Library, Pebble Lane, NN8 1AS ☎ 228101.

◆London 73 – ◆Cambridge 43 – ◆Leicester 34 – Northampton 10.

Hind (Q.M.H.), Sheep St., NN8 1BY, ☎ 222827, Fax 441921 – rest TV ☎ P – 80
34 rm.

at Finedon NE : 3½ m. by A 510 – ✉ Wellingborough – ☎ 01933 :

Tudor Gate, High St., NN9 5JN, ☎ 680408, Fax 680745 – TV ☎ P – 50. AE VISA JCB
Meals 11.50/15.95 **t.** and a la carte 4.50 – **27 rm** ☕ 60.00/75.00 **t.** – SB.

WELLINGTON Shrops. 402 403 404 M 25 – see Telford.

WELLINGTON Somerset 403 K 31 – ☎ 01823.

◆London 177 – Barnstaple 41 – Exeter 27 – Taunton 7.

Pinksmoor Millhouse, Pinksmoor, TA21 0HD, SW : 2¾ m. by A 38 ☎ 672361, Fax 672361, ←, « Working farm », – rm TV P.
closed Christmas and New Year – **Meals** (by arrangement) (communal dining) 11.50 **st.** – **3 rm** ☕ 21.00/37.00 **st.**

WELLINGTON HEATH Heref. and Worcs. 403 404 M 27 – see Ledbury.

WELLS Somerset 403 404 M 30 **The West Country G.** – pop. 9 763 – ☎ 01749.

See : City★★ – Cathedral★★★ – Vicars' Close★ – Bishop's Palace★ (≤★★) *AC*.

Envir. : Glastonbury★★ - Abbey★★★ (Abbots Kitchen★) *AC*, St. John the Baptist★★, Somerset Rural Life Museum★ *AC*, Glastonbury Tor★ (≤★★★) SW : 5½ m. by A 39 – Wookey Hole★ (Caves★ *AC*, Papermill★, Fairground Collection★) NW : 2 m.

Exc. : Cheddar Gorge★★ (Gorge★★, Caves★★, Jacob's Ladder ✻★) St. Andrew's Church★ NW : 7 m. by A 371 – Axbridge★★ (King John's Hunting Lodge★, St. John the Baptist Church★ NW : 8½ m. by A 371.

18 East Horrington Rd ✆ 672868.

ℹ Town Hall, Market Pl., BA5 2RB ✆ 672552.

♦London 132 – ♦Bristol 20 – ♦Southampton 68 – Taunton 28.

- **Swan**, 11 Sadler St., BA5 2RX, ✆ 678877, Fax 677647, squash – TV ☎ P – 150. VISA
  Meals 12.50/20.00 **t.** 4.95 – **38 rm** 65.00/86.00 **t.** – SB.
- **Beryl**, BA5 3JP, E : 1¼ m. by B 3139 off Hawkers Lane ✆ 678738, Fax 670508, « Victorian Gothic country house, antique furniture », heated, park – TV ☎ P. VISA
  closed 24 to 26 December – **Meals** (residents only) (communal dining) (booking essentia (dinner only) 18.00 **st.** 4.00 – **6 rm** 45.00/75.00 **st.**
- **White Hart**, Sadler St., BA5 2RR, ✆ 672056, Fax 672056 – TV ☎ P – 60. AE VISA
  Meals 12.95/14.95 **st.** and dinner a la carte 4.00 – **12 rm** 45.00/60.00 **st.** – SB.
- **Star**, 18 High St., BA5 2SQ, ✆ 670500, Fax 672654 – TV ☎. AE VISA
  Meals (in bar) 11.50 **t.** (dinner) and a la carte 9.15/19.15 **t.** – **12 rm** 50.00/60.00 **t.** – SB.
- **Infield House** without rest., 36 Portway, BA5 2BN, ✆ 670989, Fax 679093, – P. VISA
  closed January and December – **3 rm** 31.00/46.00 **st.**
- **Littlewell Farm**, Coxley, BA5 1QP, SW : 1½ m. on A 39 ✆ 677914, – TV P.
  Meals (by arrangement) (communal dining) 15.00 **st.** 5.50 – **5 rm** 22.00/42.00 **st.** – SB.

at Wookey Hole NW : 1¾ m. by A 371 – ✉ Wells – ☎ 01749 :

- **Glencot House**, Glencot Lane, BA5 1BH, ✆ 677160, Fax 670210, park – TV ☎ P – 30. AE VISA
  Meals *(closed Sunday and Monday to non-residents)* (dinner only) 22.50 **t.** 5.00 – **12 rm** 48.00/80.00 **t.** – SB.

at Priddy NW : 6¼ m. by A 39 – ✉ Wells – ☎ 01749 :

- **Highcroft** without rest., Wells Rd, BA5 3AU, SE : 1¼ m. ✆ 673446, ≤, park – P
  closed Christmas-New Year – **4 rm** 17.00/36.00.

WELLS-NEXT-THE-SEA Norfolk 404 W 25 **Great Britain G.** – pop. 2 400 – ☎ 01328.

Envir. : Holkham Hall★★ *AC*, W : 2 m. by A 149.

ℹ Staithe St., NR23 1AN ✆ 710885 (summer only).

♦London 117 – King's Lynn 31 – ♦Norwich 36.

- **Scarborough House**, Clubbs Lane, NR23 1DP, ✆ 710309 – TV P. AE VISA JCB
  closed 24 to 26 December – **Meals** (dinner only) 13.95 **t.** 3.95 – **14 rm** 29.00/58.00 **t.** – SB.
- **The Cobblers**, Standard Rd, NR23 1JU, ✆ 710155, – TV P.
  closed Christmas – **Meals** (by arrangement) 9.25 **st.** 2.50 – **8 rm** 18.50/37.00 **st.**
- **Moorings**, 6 Freeman St., NR23 1BA, ✆ 710949 –
  closed Thursday lunch, Tuesday, Wednesday, 2 weeks early June and 2 weeks early December – **Meals** - Seafood - (booking essential) a la carte approx. 18.50 **t.** 4.50.

WELWYN Herts. 404 T 28 – ☎ 01438.

♦London 31 – Bedford 31 – ♦Cambridge 31.

- **Tewin Bury Farm**, AL6 0JB, SE : 3½ m. by A 1000 on B 1000 ✆ 717793, Fax 840440, park – TV ☎ P – 50. AE VISA
  Meals *(closed Sunday dinner and Bank Holidays)* 8.25/18.50 **t.** 4.25 – **17 rm** 57.00/67.50 **st.**

WEM Shrops. 402 403 L 25 – ✉ Shrewsbury – ☎ 01939.

♦London 167 – ♦Birmingham 50 – Chester 32 – ♦Stoke-on-Trent 36 – Shrewsbury 8.

- **Soulton Hall**, SY4 5RS, E : 2 m. on B 5065 ✆ 232786, Fax 234097, « 16C manor house, working farm », park – TV ☎ P. VISA JCB
  Meals (by arrangement) 17.00 **st.** 4.65 – **6 rm** 29.50/58.50 **st.** – SB.

WENDLING Norfolk 404 W 25 - see East Dereham.

ENTBRIDGE W. Yorks. 402 404 Q 23 – ✉ Pontefract – ☎ 01977.
ndon 183 – ◆Leeds 19 – ◆Nottingham 55 – ◆Sheffield 28.

Wentbridge House, Old Great North Rd, WF8 3JJ, ✆ 620444, Fax 620148, – TV ☎ P – 120. AE VISA.
closed 25 December – **Meals** 15.00/21.00 **t.** and a la carte 6.25 – **16 rm** 70.00/100.00 **t.** – SB.

EOBLEY Heref. and Worcs. 403 L 27 – pop. 1 076 – ✉ Hereford – ☎ 01544.
ondon 145 – Brecon 30 – Hereford 12 – Leominster 9.

Red Lion, HR4 8SE, ✆ 318220, « 14C former inn » – rm TV P. VISA
Meals (residents only) (dinner only) 17.50 **st.** 4.50 – **5 rm** 42.50/59.50 **st.** – SB.

XX **Ye Olde Salutation Inn** with rm, Market Pitch, HR4 8SJ, ✆ 318443, Fax 318216 – TV P. AE VISA JCB.
Meals (bar meal Sunday dinner and Monday) a la carte 17.60/25.90 **t.** 4.75 – **4 rm** 33.00/60.00 **t.**

EST BAGBOROUGH Somerset 403 K 30 – see Taunton.

EST BEXINGTON Dorset – ✉ Dorchester – ☎ 01308.
ondon 150 – Bournemouth 43 – Bridport 6 – Weymouth 13.

Manor, Beach Rd, DT2 9DF, ✆ 897616, Fax 897035, <, – TV ☎ P. AE VISA.
Meals 13.00/21.00 **t.** – **13 rm** 49.00/84.00 **t.** – SB.

EST BRIDGFORD Notts. 403 404 Q 25 – see Nottingham.

I prezzi Per ogni chiarimento sui prezzi qui riportati, consultate le spiegazioni alle pagine dell'introduzione.

EST BROMWICH W. Mids. 403 404 O 26 – see Birmingham.

EST CHILTINGTON W. Sussex 404 S 31 see Pulborough.

EST COKER Somerset 403 404 M 31 – see Yeovil.

ESTDEAN E. Sussex – see Seaford.

EST DOWN Devon 403 H 30 – ☎ 01271.
London 221 – Exeter 52 – Taunton 59.

Long House, The Square, EX34 8NF, ✆ 863242, Fax 863242, – rest TV. VISA.
March-October – **Meals** 15.95 **st.** – **4 rm** 45.50/84.00 **st.** – SB.

ESTERHAM Kent 404 U 30 **Great Britain G.** – pop. 3 948 – ☎ 01959.
nvir. : Chartwell★ *AC*, S : 2 m. by B 2026.
London 24 – ◆Brighton 45 – Maidstone 22.

Kings Arms, Market Sq., TN16 1AN, ✆ 562990, Fax 561240 – TV ☎ P. AE VISA JCB
closed 25 to 31 December – **Meals** a la carte 17.50/25.25 **st.** 7.50 – 7.75 – **16 rm** 65.00/75.00 **st.** – SB.

ESTGATE Durham 401 402 N 19 – ✉ Weardale – ☎ 01388.
London 278 – ◆Carlisle 49 – ◆Middlesbrough 50 – ◆Newcastle upon Tyne 42.

Breckon Hill, DL13 1PD, E : ½ m. on A 689 ✆ 517228, <, – TV P.
March-November – **Meals** (communal dining) 12.50 **s.** 3.00 – **6 rm** 27.00/40.00 **s.** – SB.

EST HADDON Northants. 403 404 Q 26 – see Rugby.

ESTLETON Suffolk 404 Y 27 – pop. 1 317 – ✉ Saxmundham – ☎ 01728.
London 97 – ◆Cambridge 72 – ◆Ipswich 28 – ◆Norwich 31.

Crown, IP17 3AD, ✆ 648777, Fax 648239, – TV ☎ P. AE VISA.
Meals 17.50 **t.** (dinner) and a la carte – **19 rm** 52.50/95.00 **t.** – SB.

Pond House without rest., The Hill, IP17 3AN, ✆ 648773, – P.
3 rm 24.00/42.00 **st.**

WEST LULWORTH Dorset 403 404 N 32 **The West Country G.** – pop. 838 – ✉ Wareham – ☎ 01929.
See : Lulworth Cove★.
London 129 – Bournemouth 21 – Dorchester 17 – Weymouth 19.

Cromwell House, Main Rd, BH20 5RJ, ✆ 400253, Fax 400566, <, heated, – TV ☎ P. AE VISA
closed Christmas and New Year – **Meals** (dinner only) 12.00 **t.** and a la carte 4.50 – **14 rm** 24.50/59.00 – SB.

Gatton House without rest., Main Rd, BH20 5RU, ✆ 400252, Fax 400252, – rest TV P. VISA
March-October – **8 rm** 29.50/55.00 **st.**

WEST MALLING Kent 404 V 30 – pop. 2 479 – ☎ 01732.

♦London 27 – ♦Brighton 47 – Hastings 40 – Maidstone 6.

- **Heavers Farm** 🐎, Chapel St., Ryarsh, ME19 5JU, NW : 2 ½ m. by A 20 ☎ 84207 Fax 842074, – rest Ⓟ. closed Christmas and New Year – **Meals** (by arrangement) 15.00 **st.** – **3 rm** 20.0 36.00 **st.**

WEST MERSEA Essex 404 W 28 – pop. 6 602 – ✉ Colchester – ☎ 01206.

♦London 58 – Chelmsford 27 – Colchester 9.5.

- **Le Champenois, Blackwater H.** with rm, 20-22 Church Rd, CO5 8QH, ☎ 383338 – Ⓟ. VISA. *closed first 3 weeks January* – **Meals** *(closed Tuesday lunch and Sunday dinner)* a carte 17.80/25.60 **t.** 4.50 – **7 rm** 28.00/65.00 **t.** – SB.

WESTON-ON-THE-GREEN Oxon. 403 404 Q 28 – pop. 460 – ✉ Bletchington – ☎ 01869.

♦London 65 – ♦Birmingham 61 – Northampton 33 – ♦Oxford 8.

- **Weston Manor,** OX6 8QL, on B 430 ☎ 350621, Fax 350901, heated, park, squas – Ⓟ – 40. VISA JCB. **Meals** *(closed Saturday lunch and Bank Holidays)* 16.75/28.00 **st.** 6.50 – **35 rm** 90.0 110.00 **st.**, 1 suite – SB.

Pour voyager rapidement, utilisez les **cartes Michelin** *"Grandes Routes" :*
970 Europe, 976 République Tchèque-République Slovaque, 980 Grèce, 984 Allemagne, 985 Scandinavie-Finlande, 986 Grande-Bretagne-Irlande, 987 Allemagne-Autriche-Benelux, 988 Italie, 989 France, 990 Espagne-Portugal, 991 Yougoslavie.

WESTON-SUPER-MARE Avon 403 K 29 **The West Country G.** – pop. 64 935 – ☎ 01934.

See : Seafront (≤★★) BZ.

Exc. : Axbridge★★ (King John's Hunting Lodge★, St. John the Baptist Church★) SE : 9 m. b A 371 – BY – and A 38 – Cheddar Gorge★★ (Gorge★★, Caves★★, Jacob's Ladder ✳★) St. Andrew's Church★, SE : 10½ m. by A 371.

Worlebury, Monks Hill ☎ 623214, BY – Uphill Rd North ☎ 621360 AZ.

Beach Lawns, BS23 1AT ☎ 626838.

♦London 147 – ♦Bristol 24 – Taunton 32.

Plan opposite

- **Grand Atlantic** (Forte), Beach Rd, BS23 1BA, ☎ 626543, Fax 415048, ≤, – Ⓟ – 200. VISA BZ **Meals** (bar lunch Monday to Saturday)/dinner 16.95 **st.** and a la carte 5.55 – 8.50 **76 rm** 55.00/75.00 **st.** – SB.
- **Old Colonial,** 30 Knightstone Rd, BS23 2AW, ☎ 620739, Fax 642725, ≤ – Ⓟ. VISA. BZ **Meals** 12.95 **st.** and a la carte – **9 rm** 50.00/65.00 **st.** – SB.
- **Royal Pier,** 55-57 Birnbeck Rd, BS23 2EJ, ☎ 626644, Fax 624169, ≤ Weston Bay an Bristol Channel – Ⓟ – 70. VISA. AY **Meals** 8.25/14.95 **t.** and a la carte 5.95 – **36 rm** 45.00/75.00 **t.** – SB.
- **Commodore,** Beach Rd, Sand Bay, Kewstoke, BS22 9UZ, by Kewstoke rd (toll ☎ 415778, Fax 636483 – Ⓟ – 120. VISA. AY *closed Christmas* – **Meals** (bar lunch Monday to Saturday)/dinner a la carte 10.75/18.20 5.25 – **18 rm** 50.00/65.00 **t.** – SB.
- **Beachlands,** 17 Uphill Rd North, BS23 4NG, ☎ 621401, Fax 621966, – Ⓟ. VISA AZ *closed 24 December-1 January* – **Meals** (bar lunch Monday to Saturday) 14.75 **t.** 5.50 **17 rm** 34.50/79.00 **t.** – SB.
- **Queenswood,** Victoria Park, BS23 2HZ, off Upper Church Rd ☎ 416141, Fax 621759 rest rest . VISA JCB BZ **Meals** 8.50/15.50 **st.** 4.50 – **17 rm** 37.50/65.00 **st.** – SB.
- **Ormonde House** without rest., 19 Uphill Rd North, BS23 4NG, ☎ 412315, , , Ⓟ. VISA. AZ **6 rm** 22.50/35.00 **s.**
- **Braeside,** 2 Victoria Park, BS23 2HZ, off Upper Church Rd ☎ 626642, Fax 626642 rest BZ *closed October* – **Meals** (by arrangement) 8.50 **st.** – **9 rm** 22.50/45.00 **st.**
- **Duets,** 103 Upper Bristol Rd, BS22 8ND, ☎ 413428 – VISA BY *closed Sunday dinner, Monday, 1 week January, 1 week June and 1 week November* – **Meals** (lunch by arrangement) 15.50 **t.** and a la carte 5.50.

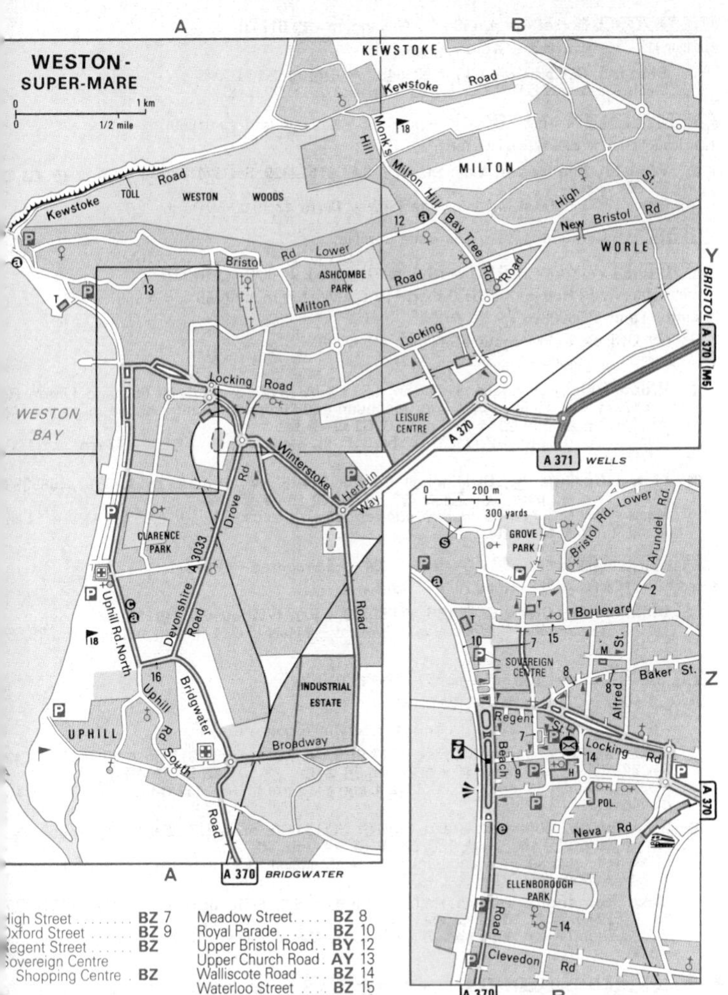

WEST PENNARD Somerset 403 M 30 – see Glastonbury.

WEST RUNTON Norfolk 404 X 25 – ✉ Cromer – ☎ 01263.

Links Country Park Hotel ☎ 838383.

London 135 – King's Lynn 42 – Norwich 24.

Links Country Park, Sandy Lane, NR27 9QH, ☎ 838383, Fax 838264, ≘, 🏊, 9, 🌳, 🎾 – |♦| ▤ rest 📺 ☎ 🅟 – 🔬 150. 🖾 AE VISA
Meals (bar lunch Monday to Saturday) 18.75 **t.** and a la carte 🍷 5.65 – **40 rm** ☕ 75.00/190.00 **t.** – SB.

Dormy House, Cromer Rd, NR27 9QA, on A 149 ☎ 837537, Fax 837537, 🌳 – |♦| ⇔ rest 📺 ☎ 🅟. 🖾 AE VISA. ❀
Meals (bar lunch Monday to Saturday)/dinner 15.50 **t.** and a la carte 🍷 4.20 – **14 rm** ☕ 52.00/98.00 **t.** – SB.

WEST SCRAFTON N. Yorks. – see Middleham.

WEST STOUR Dorset – pop. 159 – ✉ Gillingham – ☎ 01747.
♦London 119 – Bournemouth 35 – Salisbury 28 – Yeovil 15.

Ship Inn, SP8 5RP, on A 30 ✆ 838640, – . *Meals* a la carte 7.50/13.15 **t.** 3.95 – **6 rm** 28.00/42.00 **t.**

WEST WITTON N. Yorks. 402 O 21 – pop. 325 – ✉ Leyburn – ☎ 01969.
♦London 241 – Kendal 39 – ♦Leeds 60 – York 53.

Wensleydale Heifer, Main St., DL8 4LS, ✆ 622322, Fax 624183, – . VISA JCB
Meals 12.50/25.00 **st.** and a la carte 4.95 – **15 rm** 49.00/80.00 **st.** – SB.

WETHERAL Cumbria 401 402 L 19 – see Carlisle.

WETHERBY W. Yorks. 402 P 22 **Great Britain G.** – pop. 24 656 – ☎ 01937.
Envir. : Harewood House★★ (The Gallery★) *AC*, SW : 5½ m. by A 58 and A 659.
Linton Lane ✆ 580089.
Council Offices, 24 Westgate, LS22 6NL ✆ 582706.
♦London 208 – Harrogate 8 – ♦Leeds 13 – York 14.

Wood Hall , Trip Lane, Linton, LS22 4JA, SW : 3 m. by A 661 and Linton R ✆ 587271, Fax 584353, ←, « Part Jacobean and Georgian country house in park », – 140. AE VISA
Meals *(closed Saturday lunch)* 13.95/26.95 **st.** and a la carte 8.50 – **42 rm** 90.00/145.00 **st.** – SB.

Linton Springs , Sicklinghall Rd, LS22 4AF, W : 1 ¾ m. by A 661 ✆ 585353 Fax 587579, , park, – 30. AE VISA
Meals *(closed Sunday dinner to non-residents)* a la carte 13.40/18.90 **t.** 4.95 – **11 rm** 60.00/80.00 **t.**, 1 suite.

WETHERSFIELD Essex 404 V 28 – pop. 1 204 – ✉ Braintree – ☎ 01371.
♦London 52 – ♦Cambridge 31 – Chelmsford 19 – Colchester 22.

Dicken's, The Green, CM7 4BS, ✆ 850723, « Part 17C house » – . VISA
closed Sunday dinner, Monday and Tuesday – **Meals** 15.00 **t.** (lunch) and a la carte 18.55/23.40 **t.**

WEYBRIDGE Surrey 404 S 29 – pop. 7 919 – ☎ 01932.
♦London 23 – Crawley 27 – Guildford 17 – Reading 33.

Plan : see Greater London (South-West)

Oatlands Park, Oatlands Drive, KT13 9HB, NE : ¾ m. by A 317 on A 3050 ✆ 847242 Fax 842252, , , park, – rm – 300. AE VISA
Meals (bar lunch Saturday) 16.00/18.00 **t.** and a la carte 5.95 – **112 rm** 97.00/143.00 **st.** 4 suites – SB.

Ship Thistle, Monument Green, High St., KT13 8BQ, off A 317, ✆ 848364, Fax 857153 – rm rest – 150. AE VISA JCB.
Meals (bar lunch Saturday and Bank Holiday Mondays) 10.95/16.50 **t.** and dinner a la carte – 8.50 – **39 rm** 92.00/115.00 **t.** – SB.

Casa Romana, 2 Temple Hall, Monument Hill, KT13 8RH, on A 317, ✆ 843470 Fax 845221 – . AE VISA
closed Saturday lunch, 25 and 26 December – **Meals** - Italian - 14.95/16.95 **t.** and a la carte 5.00.

WEYMOUTH Dorset 403 404 M 32 **The West Country G.** – pop. 46 065 – ☎ 01305.
See : Town★ – Timewalk★ *AC* – Nothe Fort (←★) *AC* – Boat Trip★ (Weymouth Bay and Portland Harbour) *AC*.
Envir. : Chesil Beach★★ – Portland★ - Portland Bill (✻★★) S : 2½ m. by A 354.
Exc. : Maiden Castle★★ (←★) N : 6 ½ m. by A 354 – Abbotsbury★★ (Swannery★ *AC*, Sub-Tropical Gardens★ *AC*, St. Catherine's Chapel★) NW : 9 m. by B 3157.
Links Road ✆ 773981.
to Channel Islands : Guernsey (St. Peter Port) and Jersey (St. Helier) (Condor Ltd : hydrofoil) 2 daily.
The King's Statue, The Esplanade, DT4 7AN ✆ 765221/765223/785747.
♦London 142 – Bournemouth 35 – ♦Bristol 68 – Exeter 59 – Swindon 94.

Rex, 29 The Esplanade, DT4 8DN, ✆ 760400, Fax 760500 – . AE VISA
Meals (bar lunch)/dinner 10.00 **st.** and a la carte 4.60 – **31 rm** 46.00/82.00 **st.** – SB.

Streamside, 29 Preston Rd, Overcombe, DT3 6PX, NE : 2 m. on A 353 ✆ 833121 Fax 832043, – . AE VISA.
Meals 7.75/11.75 **t.** and dinner a la carte 3.75 – **15 rm** 46.00/68.00 **t.** – SB.

Bay Lodge, 27 Greenhill, DT4 7SW, ✆ 782419, Fax 782828 – . AE VISA.
closed November – **Meals** (dinner only) 14.75 **st.** and a la carte 3.75 – **12 rm** 25.00/67.00 **st.** – SB.

Chatsworth, 14 The Esplanade, DT4 8EB, ✆ 785012, Fax 766342 – ⇔ rest TV ☎. VISA.
Meals 12.00 **st.** 3.00 – **8 rm** 29.00/60.00 **st.** – SB.

Sou'West Lodge, Rodwell Rd, DT4 8QT, ✆ 783749 – ⇔ rest TV P
closed Christmas – **Meals** (by arrangement) 7.50 **st.** – **8 rm** 22.00/45.00 **st.** – SB.

Perry's, The Harbourside, 4 Trinity Rd, DT4 8TJ, ✆ 785799 – VISA
closed lunch Monday and Saturday, Sunday dinner October-March, 1 and 2 January, 26 and 27 December – **Meals** 12.50 **t.** (lunch) and a la carte 18.00/24.00 **t.** 5.75.

WHALLEY Lancs. 402 M 22 – pop. 3 195 – ✉ Blackburn – ☎ 01254.

Long Leese Barn, Clerkhill ✆ 822236.

London 233 – ♦Blackpool 32 – Burnley 12 – ♦Manchester 28 – Preston 15.

Foxfields, Whalley Rd, Billington, BB7 9HY, SW : 1 ¼ m. ✆ 822556, Fax 824613 – ⇔ rm TV ☎ & P – 150. AE VISA.
Meals - (see below) – **18 rm** 69.00/84.00 **st.**, **26 suites** 70.00/90.00 – SB.

Mytton Fold Farm, Whalley Rd, Langho, BB6 8AB, SW : 1 ½ m. ✆ 240662, Fax 248119, 18, – TV ☎ & P – 250. AE VISA.
closed 24 December-11 January – **Meals** (bar lunch Monday to Saturday)/dinner 13.95 **t.** and a la carte 5.15 – **27 rm** 46.00/69.00 **t.** – SB.

Foxfields (at Foxfields H.), Whalley Rd, Billington, BB7 9HY, SW : 1 ¼ m. ✆ 822556, Fax 824613 – P. AE VISA
Meals *(closed Saturday lunch)* 8.95/16.95 **st.** and a la carte 4.95.

Europe

Si le nom d'un hôtel figure en caractères maigres,
demandez à l'arrivée
les conditions à l'hôtelier.

WHAPLODE Lincs. 402 404 T 25 – pop. 1 929 – ✉ Spalding – ☎ 01406.

London 106 – Lincoln 45 – ♦Leicester 61 – ♦Norwich 60.

Guy Wells , Eastgate, PE12 6TZ, E : ½ m. by A 151 ✆ 422239, « Queen Anne house », – ⇔ P.
closed 25 and 26 December – **Meals** (by arrangement) 12.00 **st.** – **3 rm** 20.00/40.00 **st.**

WHARRAM-LE-STREET N. Yorks. – see Malton.

WHEATLEY Oxon. 403 404 Q 28 – see Oxford.

WHIMPLE Devon 403 J 31 – see Exeter.

WHITBY N. Yorks. 402 S 20 – pop. 13 640 – ☎ 01947.

18 Low Straggleton, Sandsend Rd ✆ 602768.

Langborne Rd, YO21 1YN ✆ 602674.

♦London 257 – ♦Middlesbrough 31 – Scarborough 21 – York 45.

Larpool Hall Country House , Larpool Lane, YO22 4ND, SE : 1 m. by A 171 ✆ 602737, Fax 602737, ≤, , park – ⇔ TV ☎ P. AE VISA.
Meals 9.50/24.95 **t.** and a la carte – **14 rm** 39.50/100.00 **t.** – SB.

at Dunsley W : 3 ¼ m. by A 171 – ✉ Whitby – ☎ 01947 :

Dunsley Hall , YO21 3TL, ✆ 893437, Fax 893505, ≤, , , , – TV ☎ P. VISA.
Meals (light lunch Monday to Saturday) 11.95/17.95 **st.** and dinner a la carte 4.95 – **7 rm** 49.50/79.00 **st.** – SB.

WHITEHAVEN Cumbria 402 J 20 pop. 9 358 – ☎ 01946.

9 St. Bees, Rhoda Grove, Rheda, Frizington ✆ 812105.

Market Hall, Market Pl., CA28 7JG ✆ 695678.

♦London 330 – ♦Carlisle 39 – Kendal 42.

Howgate, Howgate, CA28 6PL, NE : 1 m. by B 5345 on A 595 ✆ 66286, Fax 66286 – TV ☎ P. AE VISA.
closed 25 and 26 December and 1 January – **Meals** 14.75 **t.** and a la carte 5.00 – **20 rm** 45.00/60.00 **t.**

ATS Meadow Rd ✆ 692576

WHITEPARISH Wilts. 403 404 P 30 – see Salisbury.

WHITEWELL Lancs. 402 M 22 – pop. 5 617 – ✉ Clitheroe – ☎ 01200.

♦London 281 – Lancaster 31 – ♦Leeds 55 – ♦Manchester 41 – Preston 13.

Inn at Whitewell, Forest of Bowland, BB7 3AT, ✆ 448222, Fax 448298, ≤, « Antiques and memorabilia », , – TV ☎ P. AE VISA JCB
Meals (bar lunch)/dinner a la carte 15.00/19.40 **t.** 5.50 – **9 rm** 49.00/72.00 **t.**, 1 suite.

WHITLEY S. Yorks. – see Sheffield.

WHITLEY BAY Tyne and Wear 401 402 P 18 – ☎ 0191.
ℹ Park Rd, NE26 1EJ ✆ 252 4494.
♦London 295 – ♦Newcastle upon Tyne 10 – Sunderland 10.

Windsor, South Par., NE26 2RF, ✆ 251 8888, Fax 297 0272 – |♦| ▤ rest TV ☎ – 🏛 100. AE ⓓ VISA
Meals (bar lunch)/dinner 12.50 **st.** and a la carte 🍷 4.30 – **64 rm** ☐ 49.00/60.00 **st.** – SB.

Ambassador, South Par., NE26 2RQ, ✆ 253 1218, Fax 297 0089 – TV ☎ P – **27 rm.**

ATS John St., Cullercoats ✆ 253 3903

WHITNEY-ON-WYE Heref. and Worcs. 403 K 27 pop. 133 – ✉ Hereford – ☎ 01497.
♦London 150 – ♦Birmingham 56 – ♦Cardiff 73 – Hereford 17.

Rhydspence Inn, HR3 6EU, W : 1½ m. on A 438 ✆ 831262, « Part 14C inn », – TV P. AE VISA.
closed 25 December – **Meals** a la carte 17.45/25.45 **t.** 🍷 4.75 – **7 rm** ☐ 32.50/75.00 **t.** – SB.

WHITSTABLE Kent 404 X 29 – ✉ Whitstable – ☎ 01227.
♦London 68 – ♦Dover 24 – Maidstone 37 – Margate 12.

Whitstable Oyster Fishery Co., Royal Native Oyster Stores, The Horsebridge CT5 1BU, ✆ 276856, Fax 770666, ≤, « Converted warehouse ». AE ⓓ VISA JCB
closed Monday dinner, 25 and 26 December – **Meals** - Seafood - a la carte 16.85/24.90 **t.**

WHITTLE-LE-WOODS Lancs. 402 M 23 – see Chorley.

WICKFORD Essex 404 V 29 – ☎ 01268.
♦London 30 – Chelmsford 12 – Southend-on-Sea 10.

Chichester, Old London Rd, Rawreth, SS11 8UE, E : 2 ¾ m. by A 129 ✆ 560555 Fax 560580, – ▤ rest TV ☎ P – 🏛 100. AE ⓓ VISA.
Meals (bar lunch Saturday) 8.50/13.95 **t.** 🍷 4.90 – ☐ 6.50 – **35 rm** 53.50/56.50 **t.**

WICKHAM Hants. 403 404 Q 31 – pop. 2 941 – ☎ 01329.
♦London 74 – ♦Portsmouth 12 – ♦Southampton 11 – Winchester 16.

Old House, The Square, PO17 5JG, ✆ 833049, Fax 833672, « Queen Anne house », – TV ☎ P. AE ⓓ VISA.
closed 1 week Easter, 2 weeks August and 2 weeks Christmas – **Meals** *(closed lunch Monday and Saturday, Sunday and Bank Holidays)* 28.00 **st.** 🍷 7.25 – ☐ 10.00 – **12 rm** 65.00/85.00 **st.** – SB.

WIDEGATES Cornwall 403 G 32 – see Looe.

WIDNES Ches. 402 403 404 L 23 – pop. 57 162 – ☎ 0151.
⛳18 Highfield Rd ✆ 424 2440.
♦London 205 – ♦Liverpool 19 – ♦Manchester 27 – ♦Stoke-on-Trent 42.

Everglades Park, Derby Rd, WA8 0UJ, NE : 3 m. by A 568 on A 5080 ✆ 495 2040, Fax 424 6536 – ▤ rest TV ☎ P – 🏛 200. AE ⓓ VISA JCB.
Meals 12.95 **st.** (dinner) and a la carte 9.35/25.00 **st.** 🍷 4.75 – **32 rm** ☐ 55.00/67.00 **st.** – SB.

at Cronton NW : 2 m. by A 568 on A 5080 – ✉ Widnes – ☎ 0151 :

Hillcrest (Regal), Cronton Lane, WA8 9AR, ✆ 424 1616, Fax 495 1348 – |♦| TV ☎ P – 🏛 120. AE ⓓ VISA JCB
Meals (bar lunch Saturday) (carving lunch Sunday) 9.95/13.95 and dinner a la carte – **49 rm** ☐ 45.00/120.00 **t.** – SB.

ATS Tanhouse Lane ✆ 424 3011/2945

WIGAN Lancs. 402 M 23 – ☎ 01942.
♦London 203 – ♦Liverpool 18 – ♦Manchester 24 – Preston 18.

Wigan Oak, Riverway, WN1 3SS, access by Orchard St. ✆ 826888, Fax 825800 – |♦| ⇔ rm TV ☎ ♿ P – 🏛 170. AE ⓓ VISA.
Meals 8.95/14.95 **t.** and a la carte – ☐ 6.95 – **88 rm** 59.50/69.50 **st.** – SB.

at Up Holland W : 4¾ m. on A 577 – ✉ Wigan – ☎ 01695 :

Lancashire Manor, Prescott Rd, WN8 9PU, SW : 2¾ m. by A 577 and Stannanought Rd ✆ 720401, Fax 50953 – ⇔ rm TV ☎ ♿ P – 🏛 200. AE ⓓ VISA.
Meals *(closed lunch Saturday and Bank Holidays)* 16.50 **st.** and a la carte 🍷 5.50 – **55 rm** ☐ 57.00/85.00 **st.** – SB.

ATS 98 Warrington Rd, Newtown ✆ 42017/42442

VIGHT (Isle of) 403 404 PQ 31 32 Great Britain G. – pop. 124 577.

ee : Island★★.

nvir. : Osborne House, East Cowes★★ AC – Carisbrooke Castle, Newport★★ AC (Keep ≤★) – rading★ (Roman Villa★ AC, St. Mary's Church★, Nunwell House★ AC) – Shorwell : St. Peter's hurch★ (wall paintings★).

from East and West Cowes to Southampton (Red Funnel Ferries) frequent services daily from Yarmouth to Lymington (Wightlink Ltd) frequent services daily (30 mn) – from Fishbourne to Portsmouth (Wightlink Ltd) frequent services daily (35 mn).

from Ryde to Portsmouth (Hovertravel Ltd) frequent services daily (10 mn) – from Ryde to ortsmouth (Wightlink Ltd) frequent services daily (15 mn).

Alverstone – ✉ Isle of Wight – 01983.

Grange, PO36 0EZ, 403729, – rest. *closed December and January* – **Meals** 13.50 **st.** – **6 rm** 18.50/48.00 **st.**

Chale – pop. 717 – ✉ Isle of Wight – 01983.

Newport 9.

Clarendon H. and Wight Mouse Inn, Newport Rd, PO38 2HA, 730431, Fax 730431, ≤, – VISA
Meals 7.00/13.50 **st.** and a la carte 5.00 – **12 rm** 33.00/66.00 **st.**, 1 suite – SB.

Cowes – pop. 16 923 – ✉ Isle of Wight – 01983.

9 Osborne, East Cowes 295421.

The Arcade, Fountain Quay, PO31 7AR 291914.

Newport 4.

New Holmwood, Queens Rd, Egypt Point, PO31 8BW, 292508, Fax 295020, ≤, heated – – 150
23 rm, 2 suites.

Fountain, High St., PO31 7AW, 292397, Fax 299554 – . AE VISA
Meals a la carte 8.20/16.40 **t.** – **20 rm** 49.50/59.50 **t.** – SB.

Freshwater – pop. 5 073 – ✉ Isle of Wight – 01983.

Newport 13.

Yarlands Country House, Victoria Rd, PO40 9PP, 752574, – rest. *closed December and January* – **Meals** (dinner only) 12.00 **st.** 4.75 – **6 rm** 43.00/76.00 **st.**

Blenheim House without rest., Gate Lane, Freshwater Bay, PO40 9QD, S : 1 m. 752858, heated – .
June-August – **7 rm** 22.00/42.00 **st.**

Niton – ✉ Isle of Wight – 01983.

Windcliffe Manor, Sandrock Rd, Undercliff, PO38 2NG, 730215, Fax 730215, heated, – rest . AE VISA
Meals 9.50/16.95 **t.** and a la carte 4.80 – **14 rm** (dinner included) 44.00/92.00 **t.** – SB.

Pine Ridge, The Undercliff, PO38 2LY, 730802, Fax 731001, – rest . VISA
Meals 14.95 **t.** 3.95 – **9 rm** 20.00/60.00 – SB.

Seaview – ✉ Isle of Wight – 01983.

Seaview, High St., PO34 5EX, 612711, Fax 613729 – . AE VISA
Meals *(closed Sunday dinner except Bank Holidays)* a la carte 16.15/23.85 **t.** 3.95 – **16 rm** 40.00/92.00 **t.**, 1 suite – SB.

Shanklin – pop. 8 109 – ✉ Isle of Wight – 01983.

18 Fairway Lake, Sandown 403217.

67 High St., PO37 6JJ 862942.

Newport 9.

Brunswick, Queens Rd, PO37 6AN, 863245, , heated, , – rest . VISA
March-October and Christmas – **Meals** (bar lunch)/dinner 10.00 **st.** – **32 rm** 27.00/66.00 **st.**

Fern Bank, 6 Highfield Rd, PO37 6PP, 862790, Fax 864412, , , – rest . VISA
Meals (bar lunch Monday to Saturday)/dinner 11.50 **t.** and a la carte 4.00 – **22 rm** 36.75/95.50 **t.** – SB.

Bourne Hall Country, Luccombe Rd, PO37 6RR, 862820, Fax 865138, , heated, , , – . AE VISA.
closed December and January – **Meals** (bar lunch)/dinner 12.00 **t.** and a la carte 6.75 – **30 rm** (dinner included) 51.00/90.00 **t.** – SB.

Queensmead, 12 Queens Rd, PO37 6AN, ☎ 862342, heated, – rest TV P. AE VISA
March-October and Christmas – **Meals** (bar lunch)/dinner 10.00 **st.** and a la carte 3.95 – **30 rm** (dinner included) 42.00/84.00 **st.** – SB.

Luccombe Chine Country House, Luccombe Chine, PO37 6RH, S : 2 ¼ m. by A 3055 ☎ 862037, ←, – TV P. VISA.
closed December and January – **Meals** (dinner only) 13.50 **t.** 4.50 – **6 rm** 56.00/76.00 – SB.

Delphi Cliff, 7 St. Boniface Cliff Rd, PO37 6ET, ☎ 862179, Fax 862179, ←, – rest TV.
Easter-October – **Meals** (by arrangement) – **10 rm** (dinner included) 26.00/52.00 **st.** – SB

Cavendish House without rest., Eastmount Rd, PO37 6DN, ☎ 862460, Fax 862460 – ☎ P. VISA.
closed 2 weeks February and Christmas – **3 rm** 25.00/50.00 **s.**

Totland – pop. 2 316 – ✉ Isle of Wight – ☎ 01983.
Newport 13.

Sentry Mead, Madeira Rd, PO39 0BJ, ☎ 753212, Fax 753212, – rest TV P. VISA
Meals (bar lunch)/dinner 12.50 **t.** – **14 rm** 30.00/60.00 **t.**

Rockstone Cottage, Colwell Chine Rd, PO40 9NR, NE : ¾ m. by A 3054 ☎ 753723, – rest TV P
Meals (by arrangement) 10.00 3.25 – **5 rm** 22.00/44.00.

Littledene Lodge, Granville Rd, PO39 0AX, ☎ 752411 – rest P. VISA
March-October – **Meals** (by arrangement) 9.50 **st.** – **6 rm** 25.00/42.00 **st.** – SB.

Ventnor – pop. 7 956 – ✉ Isle of Wight – ☎ 01983.
Steephill Down Rd ☎ 853326.
34 High St., PO38 1RZ ☎ 853625 (summer only).
Newport 10.

Hillside, Mitchell Av., PO38 1DR, ☎ 852271, Fax 852271, ←, – rest TV P. AE VISA
Meals (by arrangement) 8.50 **st.** 3.50 – **11 rm** (dinner included) 30.00/60.00 **st.** – SB.

at Bonchurch – ✉ Isle of Wight – ☎ 01983 :

Winterbourne, PO38 1RQ, via Bonchurch Shute ☎ 852535, Fax 853056, « Country house ← gardens and sea », heated – rest TV ☎ P. AE VISA
April-October – **Meals** (bar lunch)/dinner 16.95 **t.** 6.80 – **12 rm** (dinner included) 48.00/144.00 **t.** – SB.

Highfield, 87 Leeson Rd, Upper Bonchurch, PO38 1PU, on A 3055 ☎ 852800, ←, – rest TV ☎ P. VISA.
March-October – **Meals** 7.50/16.00 **t.** and dinner a la carte – **12 rm** (dinner included) 33.00/74.00 – SB.

Lake, Shore Rd, PO38 1RF, ☎ 852613, Fax 852613, – rest TV P
March-October – **Meals** (dinner only) 9.50 **st.** 3.50 – **21 rm** (dinner included) 32.50/54.00 **st.** – SB.

Yarmouth – ✉ Isle of Wight – ☎ 01983.
Newport 10.

George, Quay St., PO41 0PE, ☎ 760331, Fax 760425 – TV ☎ – 40. AE VISA
George : Meals *(closed Monday)* (dinner only and Sunday lunch)/dinner 32.50 7.50 –
Brasserie : Meals a la carte 17.15/23.45 7.50 – **18 rm** 65.00/120.00 **st.** – SB.

WIGSTON FIELDS Leics. 402 403 404 Q 26 – see Leicester.

WILLERBY Humbs. 402 S 22 – see Kingston-upon-Hull.

WILLERSEY Heref. and Worcs. 403 404 O 27 – see Broadway.

WILLERSEY HILL Glos. 403 404 O 27 – see Broadway (Heref. and Worcs.).

WILLESLEY Glos. 403 404 N 29 – see Tetbury.

WILLITON Somerset 403 K 30 The West Country G. – pop. 2 410 – ✉ Taunton – ☎ 01984.
Envir. : Cleeve Abbey** AC, W : 2 m. by A 39 – London 177 – Minehead 8 – Taunton 16.

White House, 11 Long St., TA4 4QW, ✆ 632306 – rest
June-October – **Meals** (dinner only) 27.50 **t.** 7.75 – **12 rm** 32.00/84.00 **t.** – SB.

Fairfield House, 51 Long St., TA4 4QY, ✆ 632636 – VISA.
March-October – **Meals** (dinner only) 11.50 **st.** and a la carte 4.80 – **5 rm** 25.00/45.00 **t.** – SB.

Curdon Mill, Lower Vellow, TA4 4LS, SE : 2 ½ m. by A 358 on Stogumber rd ✆ 656522, Fax 656197, « Converted water mill on working farm », heated, park – VISA JCB.
Meals (by arrangement) 19.50 **t.** 3.90 – **6 rm** 35.00/60.00 **t.**

WILMCOTE Warks. 403 404 O 27 – see Stratford-upon-Avon.

WILMINGTON Devon 403 K 31 – see Honiton.

WILMINGTON East Sussex 404 U 31 – see Eastbourne.

WILMSLOW Ches. 402 403 404 N 24 – pop. 28 827 – ☎ 01625.
Great Warford, Mobberley ✆ (01565) 872148.
London 189 – Liverpool 38 – Manchester 12 – Stoke-on-Trent 27.

Stanneylands, Stanneylands Rd, SK9 4EY, N : 1 m. by A 34 ✆ 525225, Fax 537282, « Gardens » – rm rest – 100. AE VISA.
Meals *(closed dinner Sunday, 25 to 27 December and 1 January)* 13.75/27.50 **t.** and a la carte 5.75 – 10.45 – **32 rm** 86.90/95.70 **t.**

Wilmslow Moat House (Q.M.H.), Oversley Ford, Altrincham Rd, SK9 4LR, NW : 2 ¾ m. on A 538 ✆ 889988, Fax 531876, squash – rm – 300. AE VISA – **Meals** *(closed Saturday lunch)* 13.00/16.50 **st.** and a la carte 5.95 – 9.25 – **125 rm** 92.00/110.00 **st.** – SB.

at Handforth N : 3 m. on A 34 – ✉ Wilmslow – ☎ 01625 :

Pinewood Thistle, 180 Wilmslow Rd, SK9 3LG, S : 1 m. on A 34 ✆ 529211, Fax 536812, rm rest – 200. AE VISA
Meals 11.50/17.50 **st.** and a la carte 4.50 – 8.00 – **58 rm** 85.00/95.00 **st.** – SB.

Belfry, Stanley Rd, SK9 3LD, ✆ (0161) 437 0511, Fax 499 0597 – rm – 180. AE VISA JCB.
closed 26 December, 1 January, 5 and 8 April – **Meals** (dancing Friday evening) 14.00/21.50 **t.** and a la carte 6.80 – **78 rm** 77.00/88.00 **t.**, 2 suites.

WIMBORNE MINSTER Dorset 403 404 O 31 The West Country G. – pop. 15 274 – ☎ 01202 –
See : Town* – Priest's House Museum* AC.
Envir. : Kingston Lacy** AC, NW : 3 m. by B 3082.
29 High St., BH21 1HR ✆ 886116.
London 112 – Bournemouth 10 – Dorchester 23 – Salisbury 27 – Southampton 30.

Beechleas, 17 Poole Rd, BH21 1QA, ✆ 841684, Fax 849344, « Georgian townhouse » – AE VISA.
closed 24 December-21 January – **Meals** (dinner only) 19.75 **t.** – 8.50 – **9 rm** 53.00/83.00 **t.** – SB.

Stour Lodge, 21 Julians Rd, BH21 1EF, on A 31 (Dorchester rd) ✆ 888003, Fax 888003, –
closed 21 December-3 January – **Meals** (by arrangement) 10.00 3.50 – **3 rm** 25.00/45.00 **st.**

Les Bouviers, Oakley Hill, Merley, BH21 1RJ, S : 1 ¼ m. on A 349 ✆ 889555, Fax 889555 – AE VISA
Meals *(closed Saturday lunch)* 18.75/23.95 **t.** and a la carte.

at Horton N : 6 m. by B 3078 – ✉ Wimborne Minster – ☎ 01258 :

Northill House, BH21 7HL, NW : ½ m. ✆ 840407, – rest AE VISA.
– *closed 20 December-15 February* – **Meals** (bar lunch)/dinner 14.00 **st.** 4.70 – **9 rm** 38.00/67.00 **st.**

WINCHCOMBE Glos. 403 404 O 28 pop. 5 127 – ☎ 01242.
London 100 – Birmingham 43 – Gloucester 26 – Oxford 43.

White Lion, 37 North St., GL54 5PS, ✆ 603300, Fax 224609, « Part 15C inn », –
VISA.
Meals 10.00 **st.** and a la carte 6.95 – **6 rm** 32.50/67.50 **st.** – SB.

Isbourne Manor House without rest., Castle St., GL54 5JA, ✆ 602281, « Part Georgian and Elizabethan manor house », –
3 rm 35.00/50.00 **s.**

Sudeley Hill Farm without rest., GL54 5JB, E : 1 m. by Castle St. ✆ 602344, « Part 15C house, working farm », park –
closed Christmas – **3 rm** 28.00/42.00 **t.**

Wesley House with rm, High St., GL54 5LJ, ✆ 602366, Fax 602405, « Part 15C house » – rm AE VISA.
closed 14 January-10 February – **Meals** *(closed Sunday dinner except at Bank Holidays)* 14.00/23.00 **t.** and lunch a la carte 5.00 – **5 rm** 45.00/65.00 **t.** – SB.

WINCHELSEA E. Sussex 404 W 31 **Great Britain G.** – ☎ 01797.

See : Town★ – St. Thomas Church (effigies★).

◆London 64 – ◆Brighton 46 – Folkestone 30.

- **Strand House,** TN36 4JT, E : 1/4 m. on A 259 ✆ 226276, Fax 224806, « Part 14C and 15C house », – rest TV P. VISA
  Meals (by arrangement) 12.50 **st.** 4.00 – **10 rm** 32.00/45.00 **st.** – SB.

WINCHESTER Hants. 403 404 P 30 **Great Britain G.** – pop. 96 386 – ☎ 01962.

See : City★★ - Cathedral★★★ *AC* B – Winchester College★ *AC* B **B** – Castle Great Hall★ B **D** – God Begot House★ B **A.**

Envir. : St. Cross Hospital★★ *AC* A.

Guildhall, The Broadway, SO23 9LJ ✆ 840500/848180.

◆London 72 – ◆Bristol 76 – ◆Oxford 52 – ◆Southampton 12.

WINCHESTER

Street	Ref	Street	Ref	Street	Ref
High Street	B	Chilbolton Avenue	A 9	Park Road	A 26
Alresford Road	A 2	City Road	B 10	St. George's Street	B 32
Andover Road	B 3	Clifton Terrace	B 12	St. Paul's Hill	B 33
Bereweeke Road	A 5	East Hill	B 15	St. Peter's Street	B 34
Bridge Street	B 6	Eastgate Street	B 16	Southgate Street	B 35
Broadway (The)	B 8	Easton Lane	A 18	Stoney Lane	A 36
		Friarsgate	B 19	Stockbridge Road	B 37
		Kingsgate Road	A 22	Sussex Street	B 38
		Magdalen Hill	B 23	Union Street	B 39
		Middle Brook Street	B 24	Upper High Street	B 40

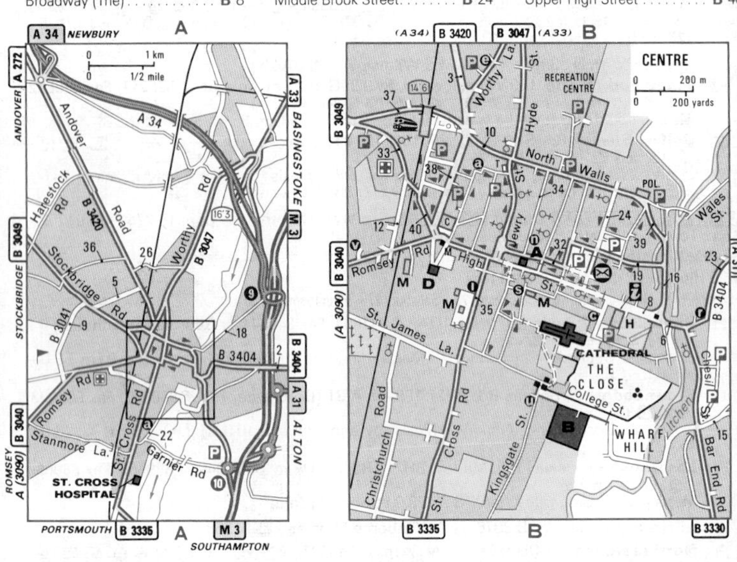

- **Lainston House** , Sparsholt, SO21 2LT, NW : 3 1/2 m. by A 272 ✆ 863588, Fax 776672 <, « 17C manor house », , park, – TV ☎ P – 80. AE VISA JCB
  Meals 18.50/35.00 **t.** and a la carte 7.00 – 10.00 – **37 rm** 95.00/225.00 **t.**, 1 suite – SB.
- **Forte Crest,** Paternoster Row, SO23 9LQ, ✆ 861611, Fax 841503, < – rm TV ☎ P – 100. AE VISA. B
  Meals 14.75/19.95 **t.** and a la carte 6.75 – 10.85 – **93 rm** 93.00 **st.**, 1 suite – SB.
- **Winchester Moat House** (Q.M.H.), Worthy Lane, SO23 7AB, ✆ 709988, Fax 840862 , – rm TV ☎ P – 200. AE VISA. B
  Meals 10.00/15.50 **st.** and a la carte 6.50 – 9.50 – **72 rm** 75.00/85.00 **st.** – SB.
- **Hotel du Vin,** 14 Southgate St., SO23 9EF, ✆ 841414, Fax 842458, « Georgian town house, wine memorabilia », – TV ☎ P – 40. AE VISA. B
  Meals - (see *Bistro* below) – 7.00 – **19 rm** 60.00/95.00 **t.**
- **Royal,** St. Peter St., SO23 8BS, ✆ 840840, Fax 841582, – rm TV ☎ P – 100. AE VISA JCB B
  Meals 17.50 **st.** (dinner) and a la carte 10.45/28.50 **st.** 5.75 – 8.95 – **75 rm** 75.00/105.00 **st.** – SB.

Wykeham Arms, 75 Kingsgate St., SO23 9PE, ℘ 853834, Fax 854411, « Traditional 18C inn, memorabilia », – TV ☎ P. VISA B u
closed 25 December – **Meals** *(closed Sunday)* (in bar) a la carte 10.90/18.85 **st.** 5.70 – **7 rm** 65.00/75.00 **st.**

East View without rest., 16 Clifton Hill, SO22 5BL, ℘ 862986, Fax 862986, ←, – TV P. VISA. B r
3 rm 35.00/45.00 **st.**

Florum House, 47 St. Cross Rd, SO23 9PS, ℘ 840427, Fax 840427, – rest TV P. VISA A a
Meals (by arrangement) 12.75 **st.** – **9 rm** 36.00/56.00 **st.** – SB.

Portland House without rest., 63 Tower St., SO23 8TA, ℘ 865195 – TV. B a
4 rm 38.00/48.00.

Nine The Square, 9 Great Minster St., The Square, SO23 9HA, ℘ 864004, Fax 879586 – AE VISA B s
closed Sunday, 1 to 8 January and Bank Holidays – **Meals** a la carte 18.45/26.70 **t.**

Bistro (at Hotel du Vin), 14 Southgate St., SO23 9EF, ℘ 841414, Fax 842458, – P B i
Meals a la carte 16.45/20.95 **t.** 6.00.

Old Chesil Rectory, Chesil St., SO23 8HV, ℘ 851555, « 15C » – VISA B v
closed Sunday, Monday, last week July, 2 weeks August and 1 week Christmas – **Meals** 20.00/25.00 **t.** and lunch a la carte 4.95.

at Marwell Zoological Park SE : 7 ¼ m. by A 33 – B – and B 3335 on B 2177 – ✉ Winchester – ☎ 01962 :

Marwell Safari Lodge, Thompsons Lane, SO21 1JY, ℘ 777681, Fax 777625, park – TV ☎ ♿ P – 180. AE VISA.
Meals (bar lunch)/dinner 20.00 **st.** and a la carte 8.75 – 7.50 – **68 rm** 65.00/75.00 **st.** – SB.

ATS 61 Bar End Rd ℘ 865021

WINDERMERE Cumbria 402 L 20 Great Britain G. – pop. 7 932 – ☎ 0153 94.

Envir. : Lake Windermere★★ – Brockhole National Park Centre★ *AC*, NW : 2 m. by A 591.

Cleabarrow ℘ 43123, E : 1½ m. by A 5074 - Z - on B 5284.

Victoria St., LA23 1AD ℘ 46499 at Bowness, Glebe Rd, LA23 3HJ ℘ 42895 (summer only).

London 274 – Blackpool 55 – Carlisle 46 – Kendal 10.

Plan on next page

Langdale Chase , LA23 1LW, NW : 3 m. on A 591 ℘ 32201, Fax 32604, ← Lake Windermere and mountains, « Lakeside setting », – rest TV ☎ P – 25. AE VISA
Meals 15.00/23.50 **t.** and dinner a la carte 10.90 – **31 rm** 47.00/115.50 **t.**, 1 suite – SB.

Holbeck Ghyll , Holbeck Lane, LA23 1LU, NW : 3¼ m. by A 591 ℘ 32375, Fax 34743, ← Lake Windermere and mountains, « Former hunting lodge », – rest TV ☎ P. AE VISA JCB
Meals (dinner only) 27.00 **t.** 6.25 – **13 rm** (dinner included) 80.00/180.00 **t.**, 1 suite – SB.

Miller Howe, Rayrigg Rd, LA23 1EY, ℘ 42536, Fax 45664, ← Lake Windermere and mountains, – rest rest TV ☎ P. AE VISA. Y s
early March-early December – **Meals** (booking essential) (dinner only) 28.00 **t.** 8.00 – **12 rm** (dinner included) 95.00/250.00 **t.** – SB.

Quarry Garth Country House, Troutbeck Bridge, LA23 1LF, NW : 2 m. on A 591 ℘ 88282, Fax 46584, park – rest TV ☎ P
10 rm.

Cedar Manor, Ambleside Rd, LA23 1AX, ℘ 43192, Fax 45970, – rest TV ☎ P. VISA Y i
Meals (dinner only) 20.50 **t.** 6.00 – **12 rm** (dinner included) 54.00/96.00 **t.** – SB.

Glenburn, New Rd, LA23 2EE, ℘ 42649, Fax 88998 – TV ☎ P. VISA JCB. Y u
Meals (dinner only) 15.50 **st.** 6.25 – **16 rm** 35.00/50.00 **st.** – SB.

Woodlands, New Rd, LA23 2EE, ℘ 43915 – TV P. AE VISA JCB. Y u
Meals (residents only) (dinner only) 13.50 **st.** 3.80 – **14 rm** 21.00/54.00 **st.**

Hawksmoor, Lake Rd, LA23 2EQ, ℘ 442110, – TV P. VISA JCB. Z s
closed 23 November-26 December – **Meals** (dinner only) (residents only) 10.75 **st.** 3.50 – **10 rm** 20.00/62.00 **st.** – SB.

Braemount House, Sunny Bank Rd, LA23 2EN, by Queens Drive ℘ 45967, Fax 45967 – TV ☎ P. VISA. Z u
Meals 17.50 **s.** 5.90 – **5 rm** 50.00/80.00 **s.** – SB.

Archway, 13 College Rd, LA23 1BU, ℘ 45613 – TV ☎. AE VISA. Y e
closed early December and late January – **Meals** (by arrangement) 11.50 **st.** – **4 rm** 40.00/52.00 **st.** – SB.

Beaumont without rest., Holly Rd, LA23 2AF, ℘ 47075, Fax 47075 – TV P. AE VISA. Y n
closed December and January – **10 rm** 35.00/56.00 **st.**

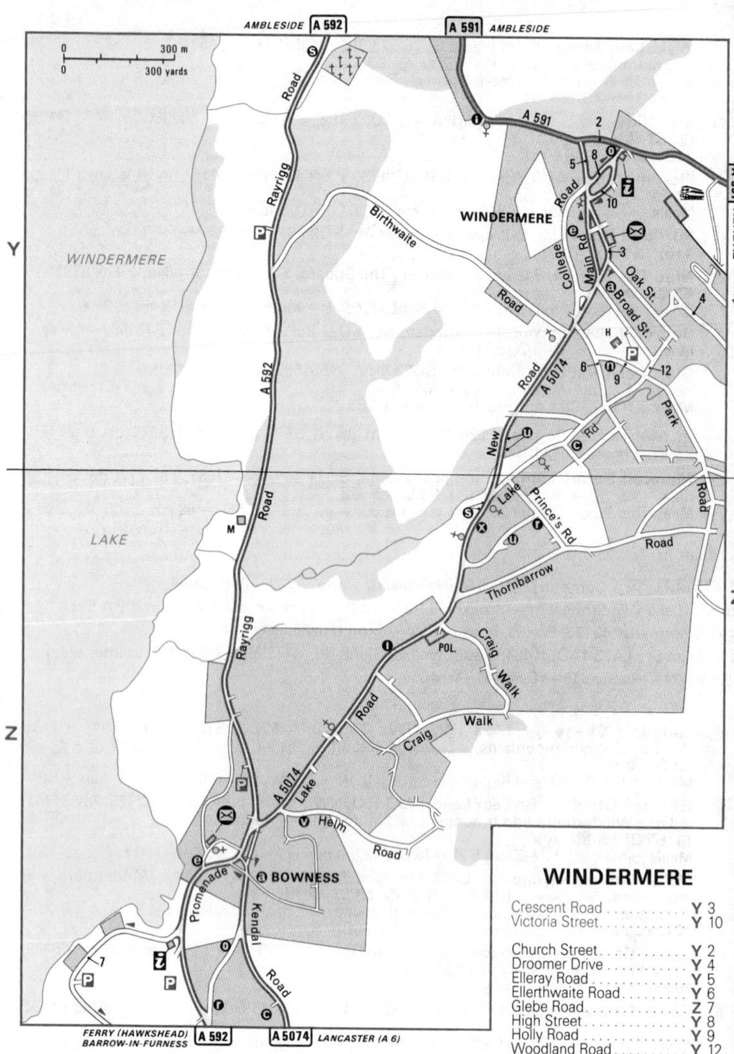

Fir Trees without rest., Lake Rd, LA23 2EQ, ℘ 42272, Fax 42272 – TV P. AE VISA – **7 rm** 31.00/52.00 **st.** Z

Glencree without rest., Lake Rd, LA23 2EQ, ℘ 45822 – TV P. VISA. *April-October* – **5 rm** 45.00/60.00. Z

Kirkwood without rest., Prince's Rd, LA23 2DD, ℘ 43907 – TV. VISA JCB **7 rm** 30.00/50.00 **st.** YZ

Oldfield House without rest., Oldfield Rd, LA23 2BY, ℘ 88445, Fax 43250 – TV P AE VISA JCB. *closed January* – **8 rm** 25.00/48.00 **st.** Y

Kay's Cottage without rest., 7 Broad St., LA23 2AB, ℘ 44146 – TV. VISA. *closed 24 to 26 December* – **4 rm** 27.00/35.00 **t.** Y

Roger's, 4 High St., LA23 1AF, ℘ 44954 – AE VISA Y
closed Sunday except at Bank Holidays, 1 week January and 1 week summer – **Meals** (lunch by arrangement)/dinner 16.00 **st.** and a la carte 5.50.

at Bowness-on-Windermere S : 1 m. – ✉ Windermere – ☎ 0153 94 :

Old England (Forte Heritage), LA23 3DF, ☎ 42444, Fax 43432, ≤ Lake Windermere and mountains, heated pool, garden – lift, non-smoking rooms, TV, ☎, parking – conference 90. Cards: AE, Diners, VISA, JCB. Z e
Meals (bar lunch Monday to Saturday)/dinner 19.75 **st.** and a la carte 7.55 – ☐ 8.95 – **76 rm** 65.00/130.00 **st.**, 2 suites – SB.

Linthwaite House (quiet), Crook Rd, LA23 3JA, S : ¾ m. by A 5074 on B 5284 ☎ 88600, Fax 88601, ≤ Lake Windermere and fells, « Extensive grounds and private lake », fishing – non-smoking rooms, TV, ☎, parking. Cards: AE, VISA, JCB.
Meals (light lunch Monday to Saturday)/dinner 29.50 **st.** 7.00 – **18 rm** ☐ 90.00/155.00 **st.** – SB.

Lindeth Fell (quiet), Lyth Valley Rd, LA23 3JP, S : 1 m. on A 5074 ☎ 43286, Fax 47455, ≤ Lake Windermere and mountains, « Country house atmosphere, gardens », fishing, park, tennis – non-smoking rest, TV, ☎, parking. Cards: VISA.
early March-mid November – **Meals** (light lunch)/dinner 20.00 **st.** 4.50 – **14 rm** ☐ (dinner included) 53.00/106.00 **st.**

Craig Manor, Lake Rd, LA23 2JF, ☎ 88877, Fax 88878, ≤ – non-smoking rest, TV, ☎, parking. Cards: AE, VISA. Z i
Meals (bar lunch Monday to Saturday)/dinner 16.50 and a la carte 5.75 – **16 rm** ☐ 49.00/104.00 **t.**

Burnside, Kendal Rd, LA23 3EP, ☎ 42211, Fax 43824, gym, sauna, indoor pool, garden, squash – lift, non-smoking rooms, TV, ☎, disabled access, parking – conference 100. Cards: AE, Diners, VISA. Z c
Meals (bar lunch Monday to Saturday)/dinner 18.00 **t.** and a la carte – **55 rm** ☐ (dinner included) 65.00/130.00 **t.**, 2 suites – SB.

Fayrer Garden House (quiet), Lyth Valley Rd, LA23 3JP, S : 1 m. on A 5074 ☎ 88195, Fax 45986, ≤, garden – non-smoking rest, TV, ☎, parking. Cards: AE, VISA.
Meals (dinner only) 22.50 **t.** and a la carte 4.25 – **14 rm** ☐ (dinner included) 65.00/130.00 **t.** – SB.

Burn How, Back Belsfield Rd, LA23 3HH, ☎ 46226, Fax 47000, sauna, garden – non-smoking rest, TV, ☎, parking. Cards: AE, Diners, VISA, JCB. Z r
closed January – **Meals** (bar lunch)/dinner 18.50 **st.** and a la carte 5.50 – **26 rm** ☐ 46.00/95.00 – SB.

Wild Boar, Crook Rd, LA23 3NF, SE : 4 m. by A 5074 on B 5284 ☎ 45225, Fax 42498, garden – non-smoking rooms, TV, ☎, parking – conference 40. Cards: AE, Diners, VISA.
Meals 8.95/19.95 **t.** and a la carte – **36 rm** ☐ 47.50/95.00 **st.** – SB.

Belsfield (Forte), Back Belsfield Rd, LA23 3EL, ☎ 42448, Fax 46397, ≤, sauna, indoor pool, garden, tennis – lift, non-smoking rooms, TV, ☎, disabled access, parking – conference 120. Cards: AE, Diners, VISA, JCB. Z o
Meals (bar lunch)/dinner 15.95 **st.** and a la carte 6.05 – **61 rm** ☐ 49.00/65.00 **st.**, 3 suites – SB.

Crag Brow Cottage, Helm Rd, LA23 3BU, ☎ 44080, Fax 46003, garden – non-smoking rest, TV, ☎, parking. Cards: VISA, JCB. Z v
Meals 9.95/19.95 **t.** and a la carte – **11 rm** ☐ (dinner included) 60.00/100.00 **t.** – SB.

Bordriggs Country House (quiet), Longtail Hill, LA23 3LD, S : 1 m. by A 592 on B 5284 ☎ 43567, Fax 46949, heated pool, garden – non-smoking rooms, TV, ☎, parking.
Meals (residents only) (dinner only) 14.00 **st.** 2.75 – **10 rm** ☐ 27.50/65.00 **st.** – SB.

White Foss (quiet) without rest., Longtail Hill, LA23 3JD, S : ¾ m. by A 592 on B 5284 ☎ 46593, ≤, garden – parking.
April-October – **3 rm** ☐ 40.00/46.00 **st.**

Laurel Cottage without rest., St. Martins Sq., LA23 3EF, ☎ 45594, Fax 45594 – TV, parking.
15 rm ☐ 23.00/52.00 **st.** Z a

Gilpin Lodge with rm, Crook Rd, LA23 3NE, SE : 2½ m. by A 5074 on B 5284 ☎ 88818, Fax 88058, ≤, garden, park – non-smoking rest, TV, ☎, parking. Cards: AE, Diners, VISA, JCB.
Meals 14.00/26.00 **st.** and lunch a la carte 5.65 – **9 rm** ☐ 65.00/140.00 **st.** – SB.

at Troutbeck N : 4 m. by A 592 – Y – ✉ Windermere – ☎ 0153 94 :

Mortal Man (quiet), LA23 1PL, ☎ 33193, Fax 31261, ≤ Garburn Hill and Troutbeck Valley, garden – non-smoking rest, TV, ☎, parking
mid February-mid November – **Meals** (dinner only and Sunday lunch)/dinner 20.00 **st.** 5.50 – **12 rm** ☐ (dinner included) 57.50/115.00 **st.** – SB.

This Guide is not a comprehensive list of all hotels and restaurants, nor even of all good hotels and restaurants in Great Britain and Ireland.

Since our aim is to be of service to all motorists, we must show establishments in all categories and so we have made a selection of some in each.

WINDSOR

North is at the top on all town plans.

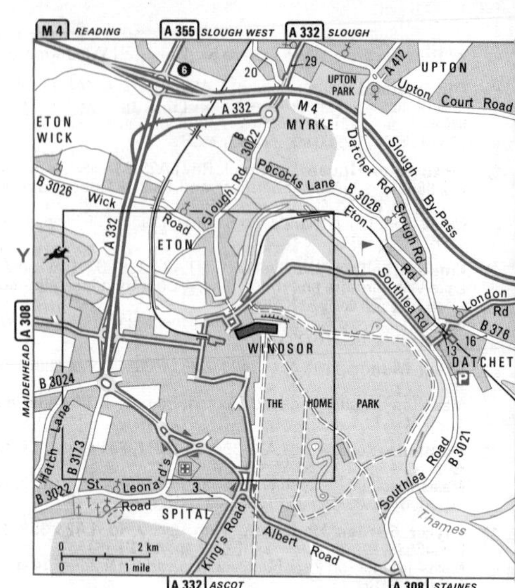

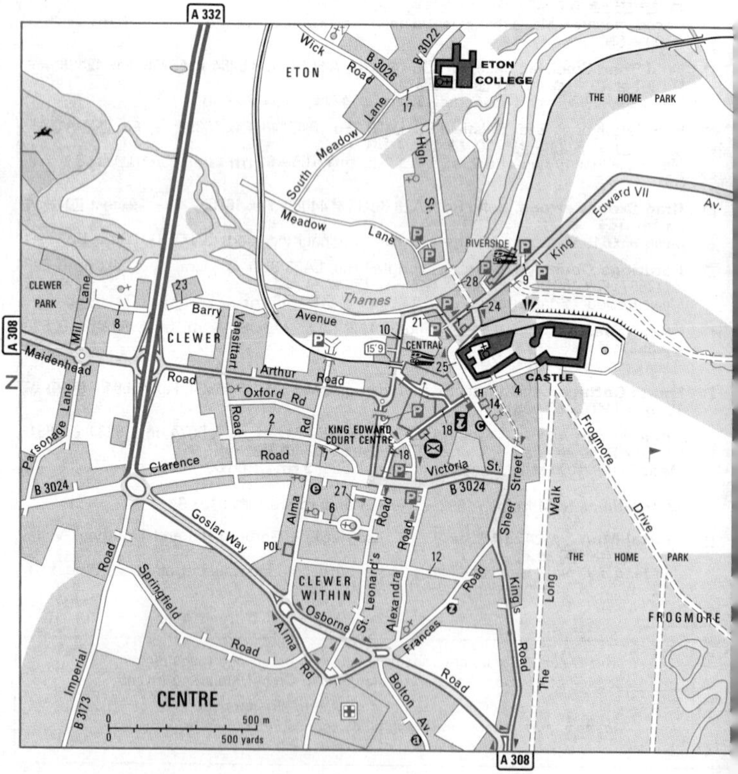

A 332
Wick Road
B 3026
B 3022
ETON
ETON COLLEGE
THE HOME PARK
Lane
High St.
South Meadow
Meadow Lane
King Edward VII Av.
RIVERSIDE
CLEWER PARK
Mill Lane
Thames
Barry Avenue
Vansittart Road
CLEWER
A 308
Maidenhead Road
Z
Arthur Road
Oxford Rd
CENTRAL
CASTLE
Frogmore Drive
Parsonage Lane
KING EDWARD COURT CENTRE
Victoria St.
Clarence Road
B 3024
Alma Road
Goslar Way
POL
Sheet Street
The Long Walk
THE HOME PARK
CLEWER WITHIN
St. Leonard's Road
Alexandra Road
Frances Road
King's Road
FROGMORE
Springfield Road
Osborne Rd
Alma Rd
Imperial Road
B 3173
CENTRE
Bolton Av.
0 500 m
0 500 yards
A 308

WINDSOR Berks. 404 S 29 Great Britain G. – pop. 30 136 (inc. Eton) – ☎ 01753.
See : Town★ – Castle★★★ : St. George's Chapel★★★ AC (stalls★★★), State Apartments★★ AC, North Terrace (≤★★) Z – Eton College★★ AC (College Chapel★★, Wall paintings★) Z.
Envir. : Windsor Park★ AC Y.
24 High St., SL4 1LH ☎ 852010.
London 28 – Reading 19 – Southampton 59.

Plan opposite

Oakley Court (Q.M.H.), Windsor Rd, Water Oakley, SL4 5UR, W : 3 m. on A 308 ☎ 609988, Telex 849958, Fax (01628) 37011, ≤, « Part Gothic mansion on banks of River Thames », park – TV ☎ P – 160. AE VISA JCB.
Oakleaf : Meals 22.00/32.00 **st.** and a la carte – **Boaters Brasserie : Meals** *(closed Sunday lunch)* a la carte 12.75/21.75 **st.** – 15.00 – **91 rm** 140.00/160.00 **st.**, 1 suite – SB.

Castle (Forte Heritage), High St., SL4 1LJ, ☎ 851011, Fax 830244 – TV ☎ P – 400. AE VISA Z **c**
Meals 12.50/26.50 **st.** and a la carte – 11.50 – **103 rm** 99.00/140.00 **st.**, 1 suite – SB.

Aurora Garden, 14 Bolton Av., SL4 3JF, ☎ 868686, Fax 831394, – TV ☎ P – 90. AE VISA Z **a**
Meals *(closed dinner 25 December)* 13.95/18.50 **t.** and dinner a la carte 5.50 – **14 rm** 65.00/85.00 **st.** – SB.

Dorset without rest., 4 Dorset Rd, SL4 3BA, ☎ 852669 – TV P. AE VISA Z **e**
5 rm 49.00/59.00 **st.**

Fairlight Lodge, 41 Frances Rd, SL4 3AQ, ☎ 861207, Fax 865963, – TV ☎ P. AE VISA Z **z**
Meals 7.00 **st.** 4.50 – **10 rm** 42.00/60.00 **st.**

WINEHAM W. Sussex 404 T 31 – see Henfield.

WINSCOMBE Avon 403 L 30 pop. 4 360 – ☎ 01934.
London 137 – Bristol 16 – Taunton 22.

Sidcot Arms (Premier), Bridgwater Rd, BS25 1NN, on A 38 ☎ 844145, Fax 844192 – rest TV ☎ P. AE VISA.
Meals 7.25 **t.** and a la carte – 4.45 – **31 rm** 39.50 **t.** – SB.

WINSFORD Somerset 403 J 30 The West Country G. pop. 270 – ✉ Minehead – ☎ 01643.
See : Village★.
Envir. : Exmoor National Park★★.
London 194 – Exeter 31 – Minehead 10 – Taunton 32.

Royal Oak Inn, Exmoor National Park, TA24 7JE, ☎ 851455, Fax 851009, « Attractive part 12C thatched inn », – TV ☎ P. AE VISA
Meals (bar lunch)/dinner 22.50 **t.** – **14 rm** 62.50/72.50 **t.** – SB.

Karslake House, Halse Lane, TA24 7JE, ☎ 851242, Fax 851242, – TV P
closed January and February – **Meals** 15.50 **st.** 4.60 – **7 rm** (dinner included) 55.00/90.00 **st.** – SB.

WINSLEY Wilts. 403 404 N 29 – see Bath (Avon).

WINSTER Derbs. 402 403 404 P 24 pop. 684 – ☎ 01629.
London 157 – Derby 21 – Manchester 46 – Nottingham 28 – Sheffield 28.

Dower House without rest., Main St., DE4 2DH, ☎ 650213, Fax 650894, « Elizabethan house », – TV P.
March-October – **3 rm** 23.00/55.00 **s.**

WINTERBOURNE Avon 403 404 M 29 – see Bristol.

WINTERINGHAM Humbs. 402 S 22 – pop. 4 714 – ✉ Scunthorpe – ☎ 01724.
London 176 – Kingston-upon-Hull 16 – Sheffield 67.

XXXX ✿ **Winteringham Fields** (Schwab) with rm, Silver St., DN15 9PF, ☎ 733096, Fax 733898, « Part 16C manor house », – TV ☎ P. AE VISA.
closed first week August and 2 weeks Chritmas – **Meals** *(closed lunch Saturday and Monday and Sunday)* 12.50/43.00 **st.** and a la carte 32.25/46.60 **st.** 6.00 – 7.00 – **6 rm** 65.00/95.00 **st.**, 1 suite
Spec. Charlotte of ox tongue with sautéed potatoes and warm spinach salad, Pan fried breast of free range marsh duckling with potato fondantes, Crystallline of apple with blackcurrant syrup and vanilla ice cream.

WISBECH Cambs. 404 U 25 pop. 18 583 – ☎ 01945.
London 103 – Cambridge 43 – Norwich 58.

White Lion, South Brink, PE13 1JD, ☎ 63060, Fax 63069 – rest TV ☎ P – 100. VISA.
Meals - Italian - a la carte 14.00/21.20 **t.** 5.25 – 4.95 – **12 rm** 39.90/59.85 **st.** – SB.

ATS North End ☎ 583214

WITCOMBE Glos. – see Gloucester.

WITHAM Essex 404 V 28 – pop. 26 872 – ☎ 01376.
♦London 42 – ♦Cambridge 46 – Chelmsford 9 – Colchester 13.

Jarvis Rivenhall, Rivenhall End, CM8 3BH, NE : 1½ m. by B 1389 on A 12 (southbound carriageway) ☎ 516969, Fax 513674, squash – rm – 150. AE VISA
Meals *(closed lunch Saturday and Bank Holidays)* 11.50/15.50 **t.** and a la carte – 8.50 – **55 rm** 59.00/69.00 **t.** – SB.

ATS Unit 15, Moss Rd Ind. Est. East ☎ 518360/515671

WITHERSLACK Cumbria 402 L 21 – see Grange-over-Sands.

WITHINGTON Glos. 403 404 O 28 – pop. 486 – ☎ 01242.
♦London 91 – Gloucester 15 – ♦Oxford 35 – Swindon 24.

Halewell, GL54 4BN, ☎ 890238, Fax 890332, « Part 15C monastery, country house atmosphere », heated, park – AE VISA.
Meals (booking essential) (residents only) (communal dining) (dinner only) 19.50 **st.** – **6 rm** 49.50/79.00 **st.**

WITHYPOOL Somerset 403 J 30 **The West Country G.** – pop. 196 – ✉ Minehead – ☎ 01643.
Envir. : Exmoor National Park★★ – Exford (Church★) NE : 4 m. by B 3223 and B 3224.
♦London 204 – Exeter 34 – Taunton 36.

Westerclose Country House, TA24 7QR, NW : ¼ m. ☎ 831302, Fax 831307, park – rest AE VISA
closed February – **Meals** *(closed lunch Monday)* (booking essential) 19.00/23.00 **t.** and a la carte 4.50 – **10 rm** 30.00/80.00 **t.** – SB.

Royal Oak Inn, TA24 7QP, ☎ 831506, Fax 831659, « Part 17C inn », – AE VISA
closed 25 and 26 December – **Meals** (bar lunch Monday to Saturday)/dinner 20.00 **t.** and a la carte 5.90 – **8 rm** 32.00/72.00 **t.** – SB.

During the season, particularly in resorts, it is wise to book in advance.

WITNEY Oxon 403 404 P 28 – pop. 19 041 – ☎ 01993.
Town Hall, Market Sq., OX8 6AG ☎ 775802.
♦London 69 – Gloucester 39 – ♦Oxford 13.

Witney Lodge, Ducklington Lane, OX8 7TJ, S : 1½ m. on A 415 ☎ 779777, Fax 703467, – rm – 160. AE VISA.
Meals 8.75/11.50 and a la carte 6.30 – 6.25 – **74 rm** 65.00/84.00 **st.** – SB.

at Hailey N : 1¼ m. on B 4022 – ✉ Witney – ☎ 01993 :

Bird in Hand, White Oak Green, OX8 5XP, N : 1 m. on B 4022 ☎ 868321, Fax 868702 – rm VISA
Meals 25.00 **st.** and a la carte 5.35 – 7.50 – **16 rm** 40.00 **t.** – SB.

at Barnard Gate E : 3¼ m. by B 4022 off A 40 – ✉ Eynsham – ☎ 01865 :

Boot Inn, OX8 6XA, ☎ 881231, Fax 881231 – VISA
closed 25 and 26 December – **Meals** a la carte 12.90/23.40 **st.** 4.50.

ATS Orchard Way, off Corn St. ☎ 704273

WITTERSHAM Kent 404 W 30 pop. 1 431 – ✉ Tenterden – ☎ 01797.
♦London 59 – ♦Brighton 54 – Folkestone 22 – Maidstone 28.

Wittersham Court, TN30 7EA, ☎ 270425, squash – rm
3 rm.

WIVELISCOMBE Somerset 403 K 30 **The West Country G.** – pop. 2 394 – ✉ Taunton – ☎ 01984.
Envir. : Gaulden Manor★ *AC*, NE : 3 m. by B 3188.
♦London 185 – Barnstaple 38 – Exeter 37 – Taunton 14.

Langley House, Langley Marsh, TA4 2UF, NW : ½ m. ☎ 623318, Fax 624573, – rest AE VISA
Meals (booking essential) (dinner only) 25.50/29.25 **st.** 5.25 – **8 rm** 68.50/115.00 **st.** – SB.

Jews Farm House, Huish Champflower, TA4 2HL, NW : 2½ m. turning right opposite postbox in wall onto rd marked as unsuitable for heavy vehicles; 2nd on left ☎ 624218, « 13C farmhouse », park – rm
closed December and January – **Meals** (by arrangement) (communal dining) 20.00 **s.** – **3 rm** 42.00/60.00 **s.**

Deepleigh without rest., Langley Marsh, TA4 2UU, NW : 1 m. on Whitefield rd ☎ 623379, « Converted 16C farmhouse », –
3 rm 19.50/39.00 **st.**

MICHELIN

Technology and fashion are driving our world forward at incredible speed and nowhere has change moved faster than in the motor industry.

Always one step ahead

Throughout these years of change, Michelin has always kept one step ahead, anticipating the demands of manufacturers and motorists and providing the tyres to carry their vehicles into the future.

This devotion to meeting change with improved performance has made Michelin the world's leading tyre company with products serving a multitude of roles in a myriad of countries.

Michelin is also the guiding light for thousands of travellers, charting changes in road networks and boundaries with a range of constantly updated maps and travel books.

Some things, however, never change. The company's commitment to improving quality and customer service remains the same as it has in the past.

And whatever lies ahead, travellers can be confident that Michelin will be there to get them to the end of their journey in safety and in comfort.

The Red Hotel and Restaurant Guide isn't the only Michelin publication designed to help you on your travels. Michelin offers a range of tourist literature, from maps to guides, which can be used together to give a complete picture of your destination.

Green Tourist Guides

As well as easy-to-follow driving itineraries, walking tours and maps, Green Guides list all the principal attractions with historical and cultural information. You'll end up knowing the area like a local.

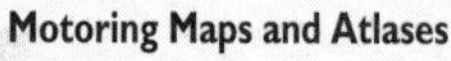

Finding your destination is easy with Michelin. Its maps and atlases are regularly updated to accommodate changing transport networks and give a wealth of other information that will prove invaluable on the road.

Michelin I-Spy

Even long car journeys are fun when children have I-Spy books with them. Each has literally hundreds of things to spot, with subjects ranging from Aircrafts to Zoos and from Dinosaurs to Dogs.

NEW departures for '96

Having brought you the best in travel publishing for nearly 100 years, Michelin is charting new territory with two totally new types of book.

I-Spy Guides

Anyone can be an instant expert with this exciting new series of mini-information books. Superbly written and illustrated, they offer a multitude of facts on two popular subjects - cars and birds - and are suitable for adults and children alike.

MICHELIN FRANCE

Landscape Architecture Tradition

This beautifully illustrated book is the perfect complement to Michelin Green Tourist Guides, capturing the memories of a trip to France in over 400 stunning photographs. Each picture is supported by narrative text to paint a vivid picture of the countryside, the buildings and the people in one of the most culturally and historically rich countries in the world.

The right choice

With so many makes, patterns and sizes, choosing car tyres has never been easy. So how can you be sure of selecting the right tyre, one that increases your driving enjoyment, fits your price range and meets the capabilities of your car? The answer is with Michelin. Michelin makes it simple to choose tyres by narrowing the choice to just three main ranges covering all types of driving.

Pilot

If you drive a high performance or luxury car, you need Michelin Pilots. SX for sports handling, CX for comfort and HX for demanding business use.

If you're concerned about economy, cut costs with low rolling resistance Michelin Energy tyres that save up to 5% on fuel but still give maximum grip and life.

new CLASSIC
MICHELIN

If you want real value for money, Michelin Classics offer the same mileage and grip as other Michelin tyres, but at a lower price.

For full details on the Michelin options available for your car, contact your nearest tyre dealer.

Built
TO WIN

Ever since 1891, when the Michelin brothers entered their new tyres in a Paris-Brest cycle race, Michelin has played a leading role in sport. This is thanks not only to innovations in technology, but to the expertise of its staff in providing competitors with the means to win. And in 1995, this commitment to victory again paid off.

In the British Touring Car Championship, Michelin gave John Cleland his grip on the driver's title while Renault secured the manufacturer's championship with their Michelin shod Laguna.

World-wide, the success story was the same with Michelin pushing to make it three in a row in the FIA World Supercup and grab its eighth consecutive victory in the World Rally Series. On two wheels, Michelin provided the winning edge for World Champions Carl Fogarty and Mick Doohan.

In fact, from the wide open spaces of North Africa in the Rally Raid World Cup to the mud and rock of the World Trials Championship, it was Michelin all the way. Expect to see more of the same in 1996.

ship
Pilot TEAM FORD
MICHELIN
Pilot
MICHELIN
It's got w
MICHELIN
L10 MWM
P&O

CLOCKING UP VICTORY AT LE MANS

Imagine covering 2,520 miles in a day, stopping only to refuel and pushing your car to the limit at speeds well over 200mph. Now imagine what it does to the tyres.

This day and nightmare of endurance is the Le Mans 24 hour Rally and in 1995, Michelin shared a unique victory with McLaren.

It was the 63rd event in the race's history and the first outing for the stunning British built **F1 GTR.** It was also one of the wettest Le Mans in living memory, so tyre choice was absolutely vital. But, as so often in the past, the Michelins were right on course, carrying McLaren to a staggering 298 laps of the 8.45 mile circuit.

In fact Michelin tyres were chosen by almost a third of the competitors, all eager to experience the benefits of the world's number one tyres. Because they knew that even in the worst conditions, you can always rely on Michelin.

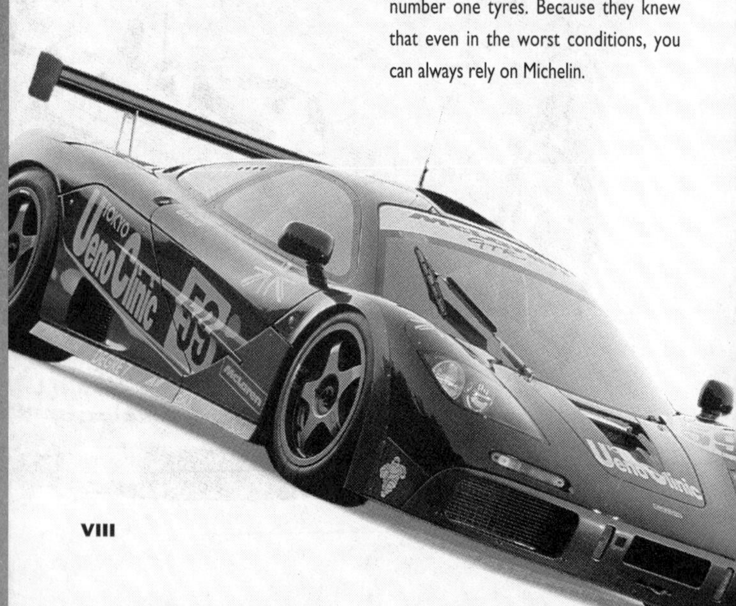

WIX Essex 404 X 28 – ✉ Manningtree – ☎ 01255.

♦London 70 – Colchester 10 – Harwich 7 – ♦Ipswich 16.

- **Dairy House Farm** without rest., Bradfield Rd, CO11 2SR, NW : 1 m. ☎ 870322, Fax 870186, ←, park – TV P.
3 rm 22.00/34.00.

WOBURN Beds. 404 S 28 **Great Britain G.** – pop. 1 534 – ✉ Milton Keynes – ☎ 01525.

See : Woburn Abbey★★.

♦London 49 – Bedford 13 – Luton 13 – Northampton 24.

- **Bedford Arms** (Mount Charlotte), 1 George St., MK17 9PX, ☎ 290441, Fax 290432 – rm TV ☎ P – 60. AE VISA.
Meals *(closed Saturday lunch)* 13.50/18.50 **st.** and a la carte 5.75 – 8.50 – **51 rm** 75.00/85.00 **st.**, 2 suites – SB.
- **Bell Inn**, 21 Bedford St., MK17 9QD, ☎ 290280, Fax 290017 – TV ☎ P. AE VISA.
closed 25 to 30 December – **Meals** - (see ***Bell Inn*** below) – **27 rm** 62.00/82.00 **st.** – SB.
- XXX **Paris House**, Woburn Park, MK17 9QP, SE : 2 ¼ m. on A 4012 ☎ 290692, Fax 290471, « Reconstructed timbered house in park », – P. AE VISA
closed Sunday dinner, Monday and February – **Meals** 25.00/42.00 **t.** 5.00.
- XX **Bell Inn** (at Bell Inn H.), 21 Bedford St., MK17 9QD, ☎ 290280, Fax 290017 – P. AE VISA
closed Saturday lunch, Sunday dinner and 25 to 30 December – **Meals** 15.95/18.95 **t.** 6.00.

WOKINGHAM Berks. 404 R 29 – pop. 29 424 – ☎ 01734 – Sandford Lane, Hurst ☎ 344355.

♦London 43 – Reading 7 – ♦Southampton 52.

- **Stakis Bracknell**, London Rd, RG40 1ST, E : 1½ m. on A 329 ☎ 772550, Fax 772526, , park, – rm rest TV ☎ P – 280. AE VISA.
Meals *(closed Saturday lunch)* (carving lunch) 14.95/19.75 **st.** and dinner a la carte 5.75 – 10.75 – **125 rm** 115.00/126.00 **st.**, 3 suites – SB.
- **Edward Court**, Wellington Rd, RG40 2AN, ☎ 775886, Fax 772018 – TV ☎ P. AE VISA.
Meals 12.95/15.95 **t.** and a la carte 4.50 – 7.50 – **25 rm** 55.00/70.00 **t.**

WOLVERHAMPTON W. Mids. 402 403 404 N 26 – pop. 242 190 – ☎ 01902.

18 Oxley Park, Stafford Rd, Bushbury ☎ 20506, A – 18 Wergs, Keepers Lane, Tettenhall ☎ 742225, A – 18 Perton Park, Wrottesley Park Rd ☎ 380103/380073, A.

18 Queen Sq., WV1 1TQ ☎ 312051.

London 132 – ♦Birmingham 15 – ♦Liverpool 89 – Shrewsbury 30.

Plans on following pages - Plan of Enlarged Area : see Birmingham pp. 2 and 3

- **Goldthorn**, 126 Penn Rd, WV3 0ER, ☎ 29216, Fax 710419, , – TV ☎ P – 140. AE VISA JCB — B c
Meals *(closed lunch Saturday and Bank Holidays)* 9.95/16.50 **st.** and a la carte 5.50 – **92 rm** 65.00/95.00 **st.** – SB.
- **Britannia**, Lichfield St., WV1 4DB, ☎ 29922, Fax 29923 – rm TV ☎ – 210. AE VISA — B e
Meals (bar lunch Monday to Saturday)/dinner 7.95 **st.** and a la carte – 6.50 – **116 rm** 42.00/90.00 **st.**, 1 suite – SB.
- **Mount** (Jarvis) , Mount Rd, Tettenhall Wood, WV6 8HL, W : 2 ½ m. by A 454 ☎ 752055, Fax 745263, – rm TV ☎ P – 160. AE VISA — A a
Meals *(closed Saturday lunch)* 10.50/17.75 **t.** and a la carte 6.00 – 8.50 – **55 rm** 69.00/85.00 **t.**, 1 suite – SB.
- **Novotel**, Union St., WV1 3JN, ☎ 871100, Fax 870054, heated – rm TV ☎ P – 200. AE VISA — B a
Meals (bar lunch)/dinner 12.00 **st.** and a la carte 5.95 – 7.50 – **132 rm** 49.50 **st.**
- Park Hall, Park Drive, Ednam Rd, WV4 5AJ, off Goldthorn Hill ☎ 331121, Fax 344760, – TV ☎ P – 400 — A e
56 rm, 1 suite.
- **Ely House**, 53 Tettenhall Rd, WV3 9NB, ☎ 311311, Fax 21098 – TV ☎ P. AE VISA. — B u
Meals (lunch by arrangement) 12.50/13.50 **t.** and a la carte 5.95 – **18 rm** 42.00/68.00 **t.**
- **Wheaton House** without rest., 285 Stafford Rd, Oxley, WV10 6DQ, N : 1½ m. on A 449 ☎ 28841 – TV P. — A c
4 rm 17.50/28.00.

ATS 35-39 Wednesfield Rd ☎ 455055 — ATS 2 Willenhall Rd ☎ 871417

WOLVERHAMPTON

Darlington Street . . . . B
Mander Centre. . . . . B
Victoria Street . . . . B 24
Wulfrun Centre . . . . B

Alfred Squire Road . . . . A 2
Birmingham New Road . . . . A 3
Bridgnorth Road . . . . A 6
Cleveland Street . . . . B 7
Garrick Street. . . . . B 8
High Street. . . . . A 9
Lichfield Road . . . . A 10

Lichfield Street. . . . . B
Market Street. . . . . B
Princess Street. . . . . B
Queen Square . . . . B
Railway Drive. . . . . B
Salop Street . . . . B
Thompson Avenue . . . . A

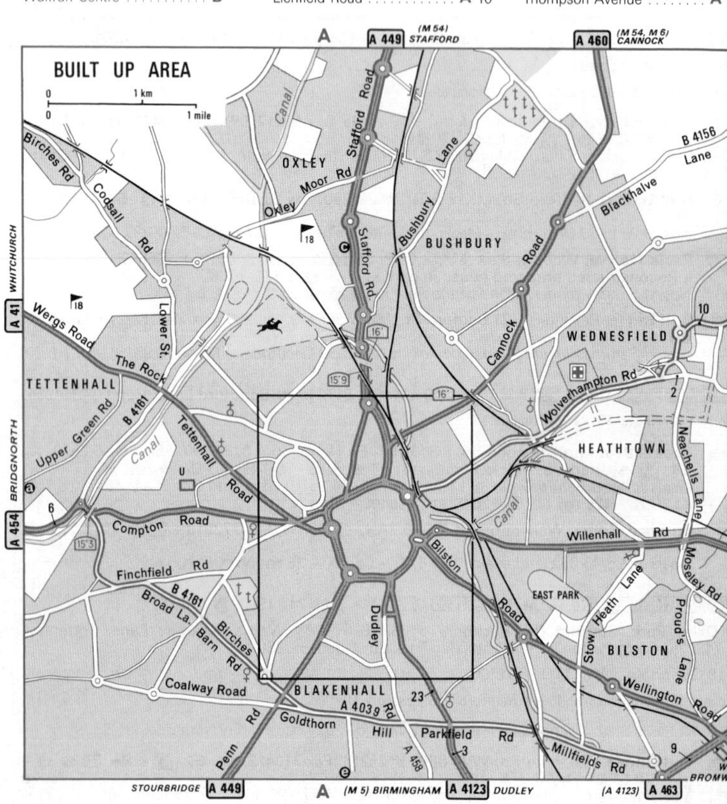

Benutzen Sie auf Ihren Reisen in **EUROPA :**

- die Michelin-Länderkarten
- die Michelin-Abschnittskarten
- die Roten Michelin-Führer (Hotels und Restaurants) :

Benelux, Deutschland, España Portugal, Europe, France, Great Britain and Ireland, Italia, Schweiz.

- die Grünen Michelin-Führer (Sehenswürdigkeiten und interessante Reisegebiete) :

Italien, Spanien

- die Grünen Regionalführer von **Frankreich** (Sehenswürdigkeiten und interessante Reisegebiete) :

Paris, Atlantikküste, Bretagne, Burgund Jura, Côte d'Azur (Französische Riviera), **Elsaß Vogesen Champagne, Korsika, Provence, Schlösser an der Loire**

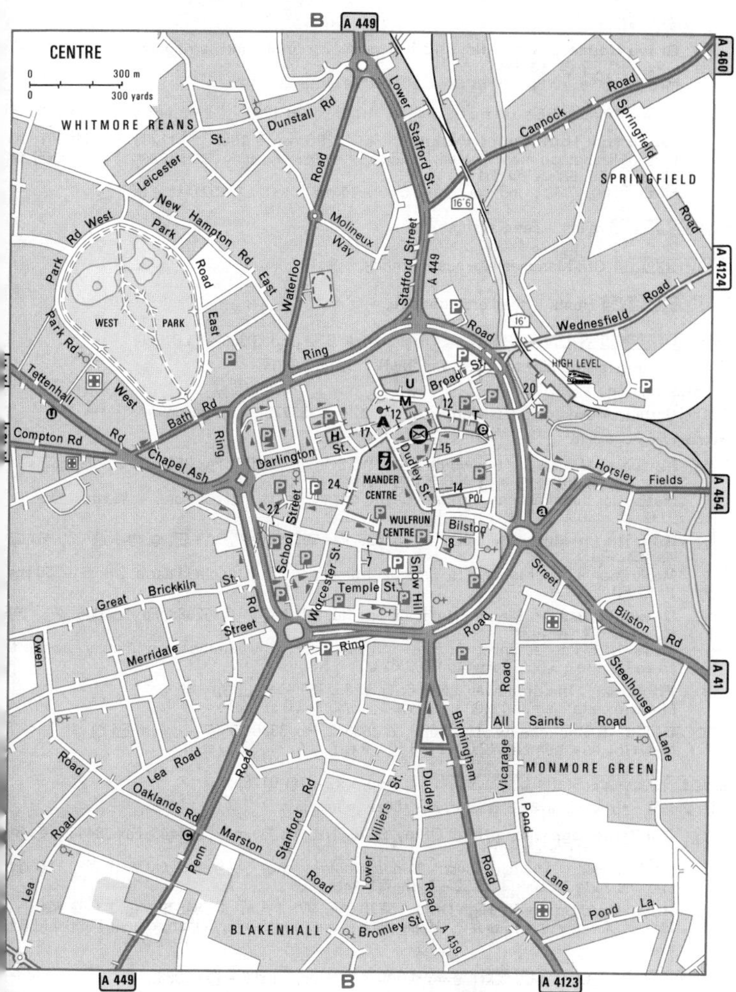

WOOBURN COMMON Bucks. – see Beaconsfield.

WOODBRIDGE Suffolk 404 X 27 – pop. 7 449 – ☎ 01394.

Cretingham, Grove Farm ☎ (01728) 685275 – Seckford Hall Rd, Seckford ☎ 388000.

London 81 – Great Yarmouth 45 – Ipswich 8 – Norwich 47.

- **Seckford Hall** ⚘, IP13 6NU, SW : 1 ¼ m. by A 12 ☎ 385678, Fax 380610, ≤, « Part Tudor country house », , , , , , park – rm rest – 100. AE VISA JCB
  closed 25 December – **Meals** 13.00 **st.** (lunch) and a la carte 23.65/33.45 **st.** 5.00 – **25 rm** 79.00/148.00 **st.**, 7 suites – SB.
- **Ufford Park,** Yarmouth Rd, Ufford, IP12 1QW, NE : 2 m. on B 1438 ☎ 383555, Fax 383582, ≤, , , , , park – – 150. AE VISA JCB.
  Meals *(closed Saturday lunch)* (carving rest.) 14.50/15.50 **st.** and a la carte – **37 rm** 70.00/90.00 **st.** – SB.
- Crown (Forte), Thoroughfare, IP12 1AD, ☎ 384242, Fax 387192 –
  20 rm.

Grove House, 39 Grove Rd, IP12 4LG, on A 12 (northbound carriageway) ℘ 382202, – rest.
Meals 14.50 **s.** 3.80 – **9 rm** 26.50/45.00 **s.** – SB.

at Shottisham SE : 5 ¾ m. by B 1438, A 1152 on B 1083 – ✉ Woodbridge – 01394 :

Wood Hall H. & Country Club, IP12 3EG, on B 1083 ℘ 411283, Fax 410007, ←, « Part Elizabethan manor house », heated, park, squash – rest – 150. AE VISA
Meals 15.00/17.50 **t.** and a la carte 5.00 – **14 rm** 60.00/145.00 **st.** – SB.

WOODFALLS Wilts. – see Salisbury.

WOODFORD Gtr. Manchester – see Bramhall.

WOODGREEN Hants. – see Fordingbridge.

WOODHALL SPA Lincs. 402 404 T 24 **Great Britain G.** – pop. 3 266 – 01526.

Envir. : Tattershall Castle★ *AC*, SE : 4 m. by B 1192 and A 153.

Woodhall Spa ℘ 352511.

The Cottage Museum, Iddlesleigh Rd, LN10 6SH ℘ 353775 (summer only).

◆London 138 – Lincoln 18.

Petwood House, Stixwould Rd, LN10 6QF, ℘ 352411, Fax 353473, ←, « Gardens », park – – 150. AE VISA
Meals (bar lunch Monday to Saturday)/dinner 15.00 **st.** and a la carte – **46 rm** 69.70/91.00 **st.** – SB.

Golf, The Broadway, LN10 6SG, ℘ 353535, Fax 353096, – – 150. AE VISA JCB
Meals (bar lunch Monday to Saturday)/dinner 14.95 **st.** and a la carte 4.95 – **50 rm** 57.50/85.00 **st.** – SB.

Dower House, Manor Estate, via Spa Rd, LN10 6PY, ℘ 352588, Fax 354045, – AE VISA JCB
Meals (booking essential Sunday dinner) (lunch by arrangement)/dinner 13.00 **t.** and a la carte 3.65 – **7 rm** 42.00/62.00 **t.** – SB.

Pitchaway, The Broadway, LN10 6SQ, ℘ 352969 – .
Meals (by arrangement) 6.00 **s.** – **7 rm** 16.00/36.00 **s.** – SB.

Oglee, 16 Stanhope Av., LN10 6SP, ℘ 353512, Fax 353512, – rm .
Meals (by arrangement) 12.00 **st.** 3.50 – **5 rm** 17.50/38.00 **st.**

WOODSEAVES Staffs. 402 403 404 N 25 pop. 1 974 – 01785.

◆London 155 – ◆Birmingham 38 – Shrewsbury 23 – ◆Stoke-on-Trent 15.

XX **Old Parsonage** with rm, High Offley, ST20 0NE, W : 1 ¼ m. ℘ 284446, Fax 284446, ←, – . AE VISA
Meals *(closed Monday lunch, Sunday dinner and Bank Holidays)* 15.00/19.50 **st.** and a la carte 5.95 – 5.00 – **4 rm** 40.00 **st.** – SB.

X **Royal Oak,** Grubb St., High Offley, ST20 0NE, W : 1 ¼ m. ℘ 284579 – . VISA
closed Monday and Tuesday – **Meals** (dinner only and Sunday lunch)/dinner 11.50/21.00 **t** 5.25.

WOODSTOCK Oxon. 403 404 P 28 **Great Britain G.** – pop. 2 898 – 01993.

See : Blenheim Palace★★★ (The Grounds★★★) *AC*.

Hensington Rd, OX20 1JQ ℘ 811038 (summer only).

◆London 65 – Gloucester 47 – ◆Oxford 8.

Bear (Forte Heritage), Park St., OX20 1SZ, ℘ 811511, Fax 813380, « Part 16C inn » – – 70. AE VISA
Meals 14.95/25.95 **st.** 7.50 – 8.95 – **41 rm** 95.00/115.00 **st.**, 3 suites – SB.

Feathers, Market St., OX20 1SX, ℘ 812291, Fax 813158, « Tastefully furnished 17C houses » – . AE VISA JCB
Meals 16.50 **t.** (lunch) and a la carte 26.75/38.00 **t.** 10.00 – 7.85 – **16 rm** 78.00/150.00 **t.** 1 suite – SB.

WOODY BAY Devon 403 I 30 – see Lynton.

WOOKEY HOLE Somerset 403 L 30 – see Wells.

When looking for a quiet hotel
use the maps found in the introductory pages
or look for establishments with the sign or .

WOOLACOMBE Devon 403 H 30 **The West Country G.** – ☎ 01271.

Envir. : Mortehoe★★ (St. Mary's Church★, Morte Point★, Vantage Point★) N : ½ m.

Red Barn Cafe Car Park, Barton Rd ☎ 870553 (summer only).

London 237 – Barnstaple 15 – Exeter 55.

Woolacombe Bay, South St., EX34 7BN, ☎ 870388, Fax 870613, ≤, Fь, ≘s, heated, , squash – |‡| TV ☎ P – 🏃 200. AE VISA. ✻
closed early January-mid February – **Meals** (dancing Tuesday evening) (light lunch Monday to Saturday)/dinner 18.00 **st.** and a la carte 5.50 – **64 rm** (dinner included) 53.00/156.00 **st.** – SB.

Little Beach, The Esplanade, EX34 7DJ, ☎ 870398, ≤ – TV ☎ P. VISA
March-October – **Meals** (dinner only) 14.50 **st.** 3.95 – **10 rm** 25.00/70.00 **st.** – SB.

at Mortehoe N : ½ m. – ✉ Woolacombe – ☎ 01271 :

Watersmeet, The Esplanade, EX34 7EB, ☎ 870333, Fax 870890, ≤ Morte Bay, heated, – rest TV ☎ P. AE VISA. ✻
closed December-mid February – **Meals** (bar lunch)/dinner 25.50 **st.** and a la carte 5.50 – **24 rm** (dinner included) 61.85/170.00 **st.** – SB.

Cleeve House, EX34 7ED, ☎ 870719, – TV P. VISA. ✻
April-October – **Meals** (dinner only and lunch June-September) 7.00/15.00 **st.** 3.50 – **6 rm** (dinner included) 43.50/75.00 **st.** – SB.

Sunnycliffe, Chapel Hill, EX34 7EB, ☎ 870597, Fax 870597, ≤ Morte Bay – TV P. ✻
February-October – **Meals** 15.00 **st.** – **8 rm** 30.00/60.00 **st.** – SB.

WOOLER Northd 401 402 N 17 pop. 1 975 – ☎ 01668.

London 321 – ◆Edinburgh 64 – ◆Newcastle upon Tyne 45.

Ryecroft, NE11 6AB, ☎ 281459, Fax 282214, – ☎ P. VISA
Meals (light lunch Monday to Saturday)/dinner 15.00 **st.** 4.75 – **9 rm** 22.50/45.00 **st.** – SB.

WOOLLEY EDGE SERVICE AREA W. Yorks. – ✉ Wakefield – ☎ 01924.

Granada Lodge without rest., WF4 4LQ, M 1 between junctions 38 and 39 ☎ 830569, Fax 830609, Reservations (Freephone) 0800 555300 – TV ☎ ♿ P. AE VISA. ✻
31 rm 39.95 **st.**

WOOLSTONE Glos. – see Cheltenham.

WOOLTON Mersey. 402 403 L 23 – see Liverpool.

WOOLTON HILL Berks. – see Newbury.

WOOTTON BASSETT Wilts. 403 404 O 29 – see Swindon.

WORCESTER Heref. and Worcs. 403 404 N 27 **Great Britain G.** – pop. 81 755 – ☎ 01905.

See : City★ – Cathedral★★ – Royal Worcester Porcelain Works★ (Dyson Perrins Museum★) M.

Exc. : The Elgar Trail★ – Perdiswell Municipal, Bilford Rd ☎ 754668.

The Guildhall, High St., WR1 2EY ☎ 726311/723471.

London 124 – ◆Birmingham 26 – ◆Bristol 61 – ◆Cardiff 74.

Plan on next page

Fownes, City Walls Rd, WR1 2AP, ☎ 613151, Fax 23742, « Converted glove factory » – |‡| TV ☎ ♿ P – 🏃 100. AE VISA **a**
Meals (bar lunch Saturday) 9.95/15.95 **st.** and dinner a la carte 7.00 – 8.50 – **58 rm** 80.00/95.00 **st.**, 3 suites – SB.

Giffard (Forte), High St., WR1 2QR, ☎ 726262, Fax 723458 – |‡| rm TV ☎ P – 🏃 140. AE VISA **r**
Meals (bar lunch Monday to Saturday)/dinner 14.95 **st.** and a la carte 5.80 – 7.95 – **100 rm** 52.50/62.50 **st.**, 3 suites – SB.

Diglis House, Severn St., WR1 2NF, ☎ 353518, Fax 767772, ≤, « Georgian house on banks of River Severn », – TV ☎ P. VISA. ✻ **o**
Meals 7.00/25.00 **t.** and a la carte – **11 rm** 52.00/120.00 **t.** – SB.

Number 40 without rest., 40 Britannia Sq., WR1 3DN, ☎ 611920, Fax 27152, « Regency townhouse » – TV. ✻ **n**
3 rm 40.00/60.00 **st.**

Heathside, 172 Droitwich Rd, Fernhill Heath, WR3 7UA, NE : 3 m. by A 449 on A 38 ☎ 458245, – TV ☎ P. VISA. ✻
Meals (by arrangement) 12.00 **t.** 3.50 – **9 rm** 18.00/45.00 **t.**

Brown's, 24 Quay St., WR1 2JJ, ☎ 26263, « Converted riverside corn mill » – AE VISA **c**
closed Saturday lunch, Sunday dinner, 1 week Christmas and Bank Holiday Mondays – **Meals** 16.00/30.00 **st.** 5.00.

Il Pescatore, 34 Sidbury, WR1 2HZ, ☎ 21444 – VISA **e**
closed Monday lunch and Sunday – **Meals** - Italian 11.50/18.50 **t.** and a la carte 5.25.

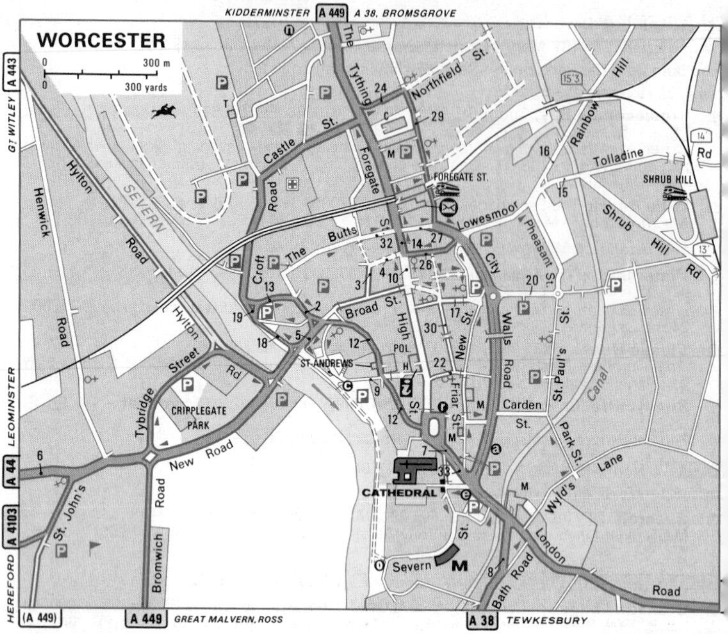

WORCESTER

at Upton Snodsbury E : 6 m. by A 44 on A 422 – ✉ Worcester – ☎ 01905 :

Upton House, WR7 4NR, on B 4082 (beside church) ✆ 381226, « Tastefully furnishe timbered house », – TV ☎ P.
closed Easter and Christmas – **Meals** (by arrangement) (communal dining) 23.50 **st.** – **3 r**
47.50/65.00 **st.**

ATS Little London, Barbourne ✆ 24009/28543

WORFIELD Shrops. – see Bridgnorth.

WORKINGTON Cumbria 402 J 20 – pop. 26 938 – ☎ 01900.

Branthwaite Rd ✆ 603460.

Central Car Park, Washington St., CA14 3AW ✆ 602923.

London 313 – Carlisle 33 – Keswick 20.

Washington Central, Washington St., CA14 3AW, ✆ 65772, Fax 68770, – rest TV ☎ P – 300. AE VISA.
Meals 12.95/17.25 **t.** and a la carte 4.50 – **40 rm** 49.50/69.50 **t.** – SB.

ATS Annie Pit Lane, Clay Flatts Trading Est. ✆ 602352

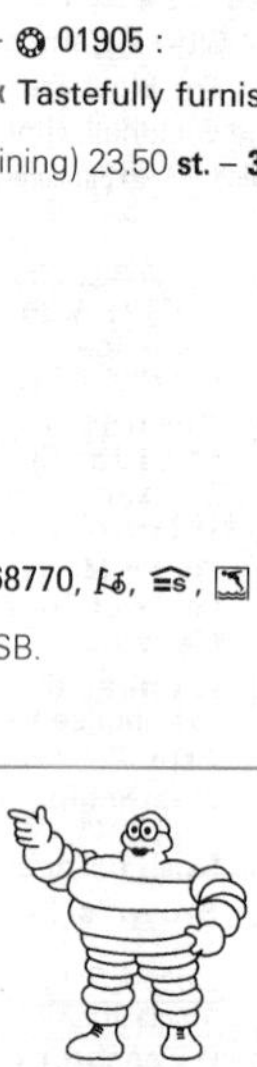

WORKSOP Notts. 402 403 404 C 24 – pop. 38 222 – ✆ 01909.

Kilton Forest, Blyth Rd ✆ 472488.

Worksop Library, Memorial Av., S80 2BP ✆ 501148.

London 163 – Derby 47 – Lincoln 28 – ◆Nottingham 30 – ◆Sheffield 19.

Clumber Park (Country Club), Clumber Park, S80 3PA, SE : 6½ m. by B 6040 and A 57 on A 614 ✆ (01623) 835333, Fax 835525, – TV ☎ P – 220. AE VISA.
Meals (bar lunch Saturday) a la carte 11.45/20.60 **t.** 5.80 – 7.50 – **47 rm** 59.00 **t.**, 1 suite – SB.

Forte Travelodge, Dukeries Mill, St. Annes Drive, S80 3QD, W : ½ m. by A 57 ✆ 501528, Reservation (Freephone) 0800 850950 – TV P. AE VISA.
Meals (grill rest.) – **40 rm** 34.50 **t.**

ATS 44-46 Carlton Rd ✆ 501818

WORMINGTON Glos. 403 404 O 27 – see Broadway (Heref and Worcs.).

WORSLEY Gtr. Manchester 402 403 404 MN 23 – see Manchester.

Town plans: *roads most used by traffic and those on which guide- listed hotels and restaurants stand are fully drawn; the beginning only of lesser roads is indicated.*

WORTHING W. Sussex 404 S 31 – pop. 96 157 – ✆ 01903.

Hill Barn, Hill Barn Lane ✆ 237301, BY – , Links Rd ✆ 260801 AY.

Shoreham Airport : ✆ (01273) 452304, E : 4 m. by A 27 BY.

Chapel Rd, BN11 1HL ✆ 210022 – Marine Parade ✆ 210022 (summer only).

◆London 59 – ◆Brighton 11 – ◆Southampton 50.

Plans on next page

Beach, Marine Par., BN11 3QJ, ✆ 234001, Fax 234567, ← – TV ☎ P – 80. AE VISA. AZ **e**
Meals 18.50 **t.** (dinner) and a la carte 19.45/23.70 4.25 – **77 rm** 51.00/86.50 **t.**, 3 suites – SB.

Chatsworth, Steyne, BN11 3DU, ✆ 236103, Fax 823726 – TV ☎ P – 150. AE VISA BZ **x**
Meals (carving lunch) 9.95/15.95 **t.** 4.50 – **107 rm** 49.90/90.00 **t.** – SB.

Windsor House, 14-20 Windsor Rd, BN11 2LX, ✆ 239655, Fax 210763, – rest TV ☎ P – 120. AE VISA. BY **i**
closed 26 to 30 December – **Meals** 10.50/18.00 **t.** and a la carte – **30 rm** 46.50/70.00 **st.** – SB.

Kingsway, 117-119 Marine Par., BN11 3QQ, ✆ 237542, Fax 204173 – TV ☎ P. AE VISA AZ **i**
Meals (carving rest.) 9.75/15.50 **t.** and a la carte 5.50 – **29 rm** 45.00/80.00 **t.** – SB.

Cavendish, 113-115 Marine Par., BN11 3QG, ✆ 236767, Fax 823840 – TV ☎ – 40. VISA JCB AZ **u**
Meals *(closed Sunday dinner)* 10.95/14.95 **t.** and a la carte 4.50 – **18 rm** 42.00/69.50 **t.** – SB.

Bonchurch House, 1 Winchester Rd, BN11 4DJ, ✆ 202492 – rest TV P. AZ **v**
Meals 11.00 **st.** – **6 rm** 19.00/40.00 **st.**

Beacons, 18 Shelley Rd, BN11 1TU, ✆ 230948, Fax 230948 – rest TV ☎ P. AE VISA JCB BZ **e**
closed Christmas – **Meals** 14.50 **t.** 3.00 – **6 rm** 27.00/46.00 **s.**

Upton Farm without rest., Upper Brighton Rd, Sompting Village, BN14 9JU, ✆ 233706, – TV P BY **a**
3 rm 20.00/35.00 **st.**

Trenchers, 118-120 Portland Rd, BN11 1QA, ✆ 820287 – VISA BZ **c**
closed Sunday dinner – **Meals** 10.00/19.50 **t.** and a la carte 5.00.

Paragon, 9-10 Brunswick Rd, BN11 3NG, ✆ 233367, Fax 233367 – AE VISA JCB AZ **c**
closed Sunday, Bank Holidays and 2 weeks Christmas – **Meals** 14.95/18.95 **st.** and a la carte 4.50.

Beijing, 1 Littlehampton Rd, BN13 1PY, ✆ 694508 – AY **a**
Meals - Chinese (Peking, Szechuan) rest.

Parsonage, 6-10 High St., Tarring, BN14 7NN, ✆ 820140, Fax 219386, , « 15C cottages » – AE VISA AY **c**
closed Sunday and Bank Holidays – **Meals** 9.95/15.95 **t.** and a la carte 3.75.

ATS 34 Thorn Rd ✆ 237640

WORTHING

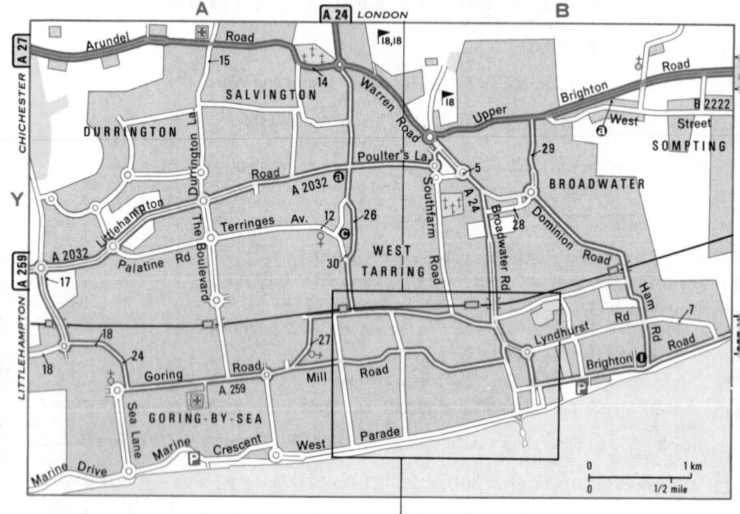

A
B
Y
A 24 LONDON
A 27
CHICHESTER
A 259
LITTLEHAMPTON
Arundel Road
SALVINGTON
DURRINGTON
Durrington La.
Warren Road
Upper Brighton Road
B 2222
West Street
SOMPTING
Poulter's La.
A 2032
BROADWATER
Littlehampton Road
The Boulevard
Terringes Av.
Southfarm Road
A 24
Broadwater Rd
Dominion Road
WEST TARRING
Palatine Rd
Ham Rd
Lyndhurst Rd
Brighton Road
Goring Road
A 259
Mill Road
GORING-BY-SEA
Sea Lane
Marine Crescent
West Parade
Marine Drive
0 1 km
0 1/2 mile

(A 2032)
A 24
A 259
WEST WORTHING
Becket Road
Pavilion Road
CENTRAL
Tarring Road
Teville Road
Newland Road
HOMEFIELD PARK
Upper High St.
Park Road
Heene Road
Shakespeare Road
VICTORIA PARK
Clifton Road
Victoria Road
Christchurch Rd
Chapel Road
North St.
Lyndhurst Rd
Grand Avenue
Downview Road
Rugby Road
Mill Road
AMELIA PARK
Richmond Road
Lansdowne Road
Manor Road
Heene Road
Gratwicke Road
Crescent Road
GUILDBOURNE CENTRE
MONTAGUE CENTRE
Shelley Road
South St.
Boundary Road
Rowlands Road
Montague St.
Bath Road
Marine Parade
West Parade
CENTRE
0 400 m
0 400 yards
Z
A
B

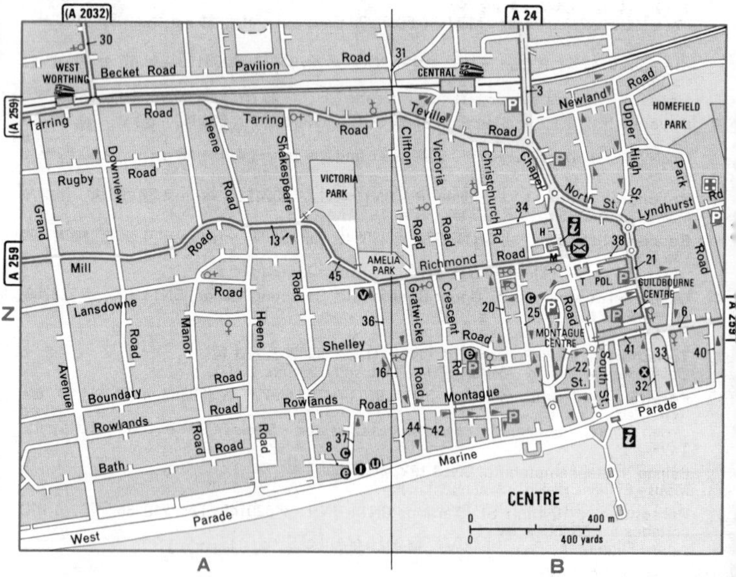

VRESSLE N. Yorks. 402 R 22 – ✉ Selby – ☎ 01757.
London 208 – ♦Kingston-upon-Hull 31 – ♦Leeds 31 – York 19.

- **Loftsome Bridge Coaching House,** YO8 7EN, S : ½ m. ☎ 630070, Fax 630070, – TV ☎ P. VISA.
  Meals *(closed Sunday dinner and Bank Holidays)* (dinner only and Sunday lunch)/ dinner 14.95 **st.** 3.50 – **15 rm** 35.00/50.00 **st.**

VROTHAM HEATH Kent 404 U 30 – pop. 1 767 – ✉ Sevenoaks – ☎ 01732.
London 35 – Maidstone 10.

- **Forte Posthouse,** London Rd, TN15 7RS, ☎ 883311, Fax 885850, – rm TV ☎ P – 60. AE VISA JCB
  Meals a la carte 14.00/24.00 **t.** – 7.95 – **106 rm** 59.00/69.00 **t.** – SB.
- **Travel Inn,** London Rd, TN15 7RX, ☎ 884214, Fax 780368 – rm TV P. AE VISA.
  Meals (grill rest.) – 4.95 – **40 rm** 34.50 **t.**

VROUGHTON Wilts. 403 404 O 29 – see Swindon.

VROXHAM Norfolk 404 Y 25 **Great Britain G.** – pop. 1 494 – ☎ 01603.
nvir. : The Broads★.
London 118 – Great Yarmouth 21 – ♦Norwich 7.

- **Garden Cottage** without rest., 96 Norwich Rd, NR12 8RY, ☎ 784376 – TV P. AE VISA.
  3 rm 25.00/42.50 **st.**
- **Staitheway House** without rest., Staitheway Rd, The Avenue, NR12 8TH, SW : ¾ m. by A 1151 ☎ 782148, Fax 782148, – TV P.
  3 rm 22.00/38.00.

"Short Breaks" (SB)

De nombreux hôtels proposent des conditions avantageuses
pour un séjour de deux nuits
comprenant la chambre, le dîner et le petit déjeuner.

VROXTON Oxon. 403 404 P 27 – see Banbury.

VYBOSTON Beds. – see St. Neots (Cambs.).

VYCH CROSS E. Sussex 404 U 30 – see Forest Row.

VYE Kent 404 W 30 pop. 1 954 – ✉ Ashford – ☎ 01233.
♦London 60 – Canterbury 10 – ♦Dover 28 – Hastings 34.

- XX **Wife of Bath** with rm, 4 Upper Bridge St., TN25 5AW, ☎ 812540, Fax 813630, – TV ☎ P. VISA.
  closed first 2 weeks September – **Meals** *(closed Sunday and Monday)* 12.50/22.95 **t.** and lunch a la carte 4.75 – **6 rm** 35.00/75.00 **t.**

VYLAM Northd. 401 402 O 19 – pop. 2 142 – ☎ 01661.
♦London 266 – ♦Carlisle 48 – ♦Newcastle upon Tyne 10.

- XX **Laburnum House,** NE41 8AJ, ☎ 852185 – AE VISA
  closed Sunday, 1-2 January and 26 December – **Meals** (dinner only) 15.50 **t.** and a la carte.

VYNDS POINT Heref. and Worcs. 403 404 M 27 – see Great Malvern.

YARCOMBE Devon 403 K 31 – ✉ Honiton – ☎ 01404.
♦London 180 – Exeter 25 – ♦Southampton 95 – Taunton 12.

- **Belfry,** EX14 9BD, on A 30 ☎ 861234, Fax 861579, – TV ☎ P. AE VISA
  closed last 2 weeks February and first 2 weeks November – **Meals** (dinner only)/ 13.95 **st.** and a la carte 4.95 – **6 rm** 42.00/64.00 **st.** – SB.

YARLINGTON Somerset – pop. 125 – ✉ Wincanton – ☎ 01963.
♦London 127 – ♦Bristol 32 – Taunton 30 – Yeovil 12.

- XX **Stags Head,** BA9 8DG, ☎ 440393 – P. VISA JCB
  closed Sunday dinner and Monday – **Meals** (dinner only and Sunday lunch)/dinner a la carte 19.25/22.55 **t.** 4.30.

YARM Cleveland 402 P 20 – pop. 8 929 – ☎ 01642.
♦London 242 – Middlesbrough 8.

- **Crathorne Hall**, Crathorne, TS15 0AR, S : 3½ m. by A 67 ☎ 700398, Fax 700814, « Converted Edwardian mansion », , park – rm TV ☎ P – 140. AE VISA
  Leven : Meals 14.50/22.75 **t.** and a la carte 6.00 – **37 rm** 99.00/125.00 **t.** – SB.

YARMOUTH I.O.W. 403 404 P 31 – see Wight (Isle of).

YATELEY Surrey 404 R 29 – pop. 15 663 – ✉ Camberley – ☎ 01252.
◆London 37 – Reading 12 – ◆Southampton 58.

Casa Dei Cesari, Handford Lane, Cricket Hill, GU17 7BA, ☎ 873275, Fax 870614, ... VISA. *closed 26 December* – **Meals** - Italian - 7.00/15.50 **st.** and a la carte 4.75 – **34 rm** 60.0 80.00 **t.**, 2 suites – SB.

YATTENDON Berks. 403 404 Q 29 pop. 288 – ✉ Newbury – ☎ 01635.
◆London 61 – ◆Oxford 23 – Reading 12.

Royal Oak (Regal), The Square, RG18 0UG, ☎ 201325, Fax 201926, ... VISA **Meals** *(closed Sunday dinner)* (booking essential) 15.50/25.00 **t.**

YATTON Heref. and Worcs. – see Ross-on-Wye.

YELVERTON Devon 403 H 32 The West Country G. – pop. 3 669 – ☎ 01822.
See : Yelverton Paperweight Centre★.
Envir. : Buckland Abbey★★ *AC*, SW : 2 m.
Exc. : E : Dartmoor National Park★★ (Brent Tor ≤★★, Haytor Rocks ≤★).
18 Golf Links Rd ☎ 853618.
◆London 234 – Exeter 33 – ◆Plymouth 9.

Moorland Links, PL20 6DA, S : 2 m. on A 386 ☎ 852245, Fax 855004, ≤, ... rm ... – 200. ... VISA **Meals** (bar lunch Saturday and Bank Holidays) 17.25/22.75 **st.** 5.50 – **44 rm** 61.9 89.95 **st.**, 1 suite – SB.

Harrabeer Country House, Harrowbeer Lane, PL20 6EA, ☎ 853302, ... VISA *closed Christmas and New Year* – **Meals** 12.50 **s.** 3.25 – **7 rm** 20.00/51.00 **s.** – SB.

Overcombe, Old Station Rd, Horrabridge, PL20 7RA, N : 1¼ m. on A 386 ☎ 853501, ... VISA **Meals** 12.60 **t.** 4.75 – **11 rm** 21.00/47.00 **t.** – SB.

Les prix	Pour toutes précisions sur les prix indiqués dans ce guide, reportez-vous à l'introduction.

YEOVIL Somerset 403 404 M 31 The West Country G. – pop. 28 317 – ☎ 01935.
See : St. John the Baptist★.
Envir. : Monacute House★★ *AC*, W : 4 m. on A 3088 – Fleet Air Arm Museum, Yeovilton★★ A NW : 5 m. by A 37 – Tintinhull House Garden★ *AC*, NW: 5½ m. – Ham Hill (≤★★) W : 5½ m. b A 3088 – Stoke sub-Hamdon (parish church★) W : 5¼ m. by A 3088.
Exc. : Muchelney★★ (Parish Church★★) NW : 14 m. by A 3088, A 303 and B 3165 – Lytes Cary N : 7½ m. by A 37, B 3151 and A 372 – Sandford Orcas Manor House★, NW : 8 m. by A 359 Cadbury Castle (≤★★) NE : 10½ m. by A 359 – East Lambrook Manor★ *AC*, W : 12 m. by A 30 and A 303.
18, 9 Sherborne Rd ☎ 75949.
Petter's House, Petter's Way, BA20 1SH ☎ 71279 – at Podimore, Somerset Visitor Centr Forte Services (A 303), BA22 8JG ☎ 841302 (summer only).
◆London 136 – Exeter 48 – ◆Southampton 72 – Taunton 26.

Manor (Forte), Hendford, BA20 1TG, ☎ 23116, Fax 706607 – ... – 60. ... VISA JCB **Meals** 9.95/18.95 **st.** and a la carte 5.80 – 8.50 – **41 rm** 65.00/90.00 **st.** – SB.

Yeovil Court, West Coker Rd., BA20 2NE, SW : 2 m. on A 30 ☎ 863746, Fax 863990 – ... – 50. ... VISA. **Meals** *(closed Saturday lunch and Sunday dinner)* a la carte 14.70/20.30 **st.** 5.25 – **17 r** 59.00/69.00 **st.**, 1 suite – SB.

at Podimore N : 9½ m. by A 37 off A 303 – ✉ Yeovil – ☎ 01935 :

Forte Travelodge, BA22 8JG, W : ½ m. ☎ 840074, Reservations (Freephone) 080 850950 – ... VISA. **Meals** (grill rest.) – **31 rm** 34.50 **t.**

at Barwick S : 2 m. by A 30 off A 37 – ✉ Yeovil – ☎ 01935 :

Little Barwick House with rm, BA22 9TD, ☎ 23902, Fax 20908, « Georgian dowe house », ... rest ... VISA *closed first 3 weeks January* – **Meals** *(closed Sunday to non-residents)* (booking essentia (dinner only) 24.90 **t.** 4.80 – **6 rm** 48.00/76.00 **t.** – SB.

at West Coker SW : 3½ m. on A 30 – ☎ 01935 :

Four Acres, High St., BA22 9AJ, ☎ 862555, Fax 863929, ... rest ... – 10 ... VISA. **Meals** 13.50 **st.** and a la carte – **24 rm** 66.00/82.00 **st.** – SB.

Skittles Inn, 1 Church St., BA22 9AH, ☎ 863986 – ... VISA *closed Sunday dinner and Bank Holidays* – **Meals** 15.00 **t.** and a la carte 6.00.

at Montacute W : 5½ m. on A 3088 – ✉ Martock – ☎ 01935 :

Kings Arms, Bishopston, TA15 6UU, ☎ 822513, Fax 826549, – TV ☎ P. AE VISA.
Meals *(closed Sunday dinner)* (buffet lunch) 10.50/16.50 **t.** and dinner a la carte 4.95 – **11 rm** 49.00/75.00 **t.** – SB.

XX **Milk House** with rm, The Borough Sq., TA15 6XB, ☎ 823823, – TV. VISA.
closed 22 December-2 January and 2 weeks summer – **Meals** *(closed Sunday and Tuesday)* (lunch by arrangement)/dinner 22.90 **st.** and a la carte 6.00 – **2 rm** 48.00/58.00 **st.** – SB.

ATS Penmill Trading Est., Lyde Rd ☎ 75580/71780

YETMINSTER Dorset 403 404 M 31 – see Sherborne.

YORK N. Yorks. 402 Q 22 **Great Britain G.** – pop. 98 745 – ☎ 01904.

See : City★★★ – Minster★★★ (Stained Glass★★★, Chapter House★★, Choir Screen★★) CDY – National Railway Museum★★★ CY – The Walls★★ CDXYZ – Castle Museum★ *AC* DZ **M2** – Jorvik Viking Centre★ *AC* DY **M1** – Fairfax House★ *AC* DY **A** – The Shambles★ DY **54**.

18 Lords Moor Lane, Strensall ☎ 491840, BY – 9 Heworth, Muncaster House, Muncastergate ☎ 424618 BY.

Exhibition Sq., YO1 2HB ☎ 62175 – York Railway Station, Outer Concourse, YO2 2AY ☎ 621756 – TIC Travel Office, 6 Rougier St., YO2 1JA ☎ 620557.

London 203 – Kingston-upon-Hull 38 – Leeds 26 – Middlesbrough 51 – Nottingham 88 – Sheffield 62.

Plans on next page

Middlethorpe Hall, Bishopthorpe Rd, YO2 1QB, S : 1 m. by A 19 ☎ 641241, Fax 620176, ≤, « William and Mary house, gardens », park – rest TV ☎ P – 60. AE VISA.
Meals 12.50/30.95 **st.** 5.95 – **Grill : Meals** *(May-September)* (dinner only Friday and Saturday and Sunday lunch) 25.95/30.95 **st.** 5.95 – 10.50 – **23 rm** 86.50/135.00 **st.**, 7 suites – SB.

Swallow, Tadcaster Rd, YO2 2QQ, ☎ 701000, Fax 702308, – rm TV ☎ P – 170. AE VISA AZ **a**
Meals 13.95/25.00 **st.** and a la carte 5.50 – **111 rm** 95.00/110.00 **st.**, 1 suite – SB.

York Viking Moat House (Q.M.H.), North St., YO1 1JF, ☎ 459988, Fax 641793, ≤, – rm rest TV ☎ P – 300. AE VISA JCB. CY **n**
Meals (carving lunch) 9.50/18.75 **st.** and a la carte 6.50 – 9.50 – **186 rm** 99.00/124.00 **st.**, 1 suite – SB.

Mount Royale, The Mount, YO2 2DA, ☎ 628856, Fax 611171, « Tasteful decor and furnishings », heated, – TV ☎ P. AE VISA JCB AZ **s**
Meals (dinner only) 26.50 **t.** – **20 rm** 75.00/90.00 **t.**, 1 suite – SB.

The Grange, Clifton, YO3 6AA, ☎ 644744, Fax 612453, « Regency town house » – TV ☎ P – 45. AE VISA CX **u**
Meals *(closed Saturday lunch)* 13.00/23.00 **st.** and a la carte 4.50 – **30 rm** 90.00/170.00 **st.** – SB.

Ambassador, 123-125 The Mount, YO2 2DA, ☎ 641316, Fax 640259, – rest TV ☎ P – 50. AE VISA. AZ **c**
Meals (dinner only) 18.00 **t.** and a la carte – **24 rm** 79.00/98.50 **t.** – SB.

York Pavilion, 45 Main St., Fulford, YO1 4PJ, S : 1 m. on A 19 ☎ 622099, Fax 626939, – rest TV ☎ P – 30. AE VISA JCB.
Meals 7.50/18.00 **t.** and a la carte 6.50 – **23 rm** 65.00/98.00 – SB.

Judges' Lodging, 9 Lendal, YO1 2AQ, ☎ 638733, Fax 679947 – TV ☎ P. AE VISA. CY **x**
Meals (bar lunch Monday to Saturday)/dinner 12.45 **t.** and a la carte – **12 rm** 67.50/120.00 **t.** – SB.

Novotel, Fishergate, YO1 4AD, ☎ 611660, Fax 610925, – rm rest TV ☎ P – 210. AE VISA DZ **o**
Meals 11.50/14.50 **st.** and a la carte 5.25 – 7.50 – **124 rm** 56.50/76.00 **st.** – SB.

Forte Posthouse, Tadcaster Rd, YO2 2QF, ☎ 707921, Telex 57798, Fax 702804, – rm TV ☎ P – 100. AE VISA AZ **r**
Meals a la carte approx. 15.00 **t.** 5.50 – **139 rm** 56.00/69.50 **st.**

Monkbar, St. Maurice's Rd, YO3 7JA, ☎ 638086, Fax 629195 – TV ☎ P – 70. AE VISA JCB. DX **a**
Meals 10.95/17.95 **st.** and a la carte 5.50 – **47 rm** 69.00/109.00 – SB.

4 South Parade, 4 South Par., YO2 2BA, ☎ 628229, Fax 628229, « Georgian town house » – TV ☎ P. CZ **n**
closed 24 to 27 December – **Meals** (by arrangement) 23.00 **st.** – **3 rm** 68.00/88.00 **st.**

Holmwood House without rest., 114 Holgate Rd, YO2 4BB, ☎ 626183, Fax 670899 – TV ☎ P. AE VISA AZ **x**
12 rm 45.00/65.00 **st.**

Arndale without rest., 290 Tadcaster Rd, YO2 2ET, ☎ 702424, – TV P. AZ **i**
closed Christmas and New Year – **10 rm** 45.00/59.00 **st.**

YORK

Street	Grid	No.
Blake Street	CY	5
Coney Street	CY	13
Davygate	CY	16
Lendal	CY	32
Parliament Street	DY	42
Shambles (The)	DY	54
Stonegate	CY	58
Bishopgate Street	CZ	3
Bishophill Senior	CZ	4
Campleshon Road	AZ	7
Church Street	DY	8
Clifford Street	DY	10
Colliergate	DY	12
Cromwell Road	CZ	15
Deangate	DY	18
Duncombe Place	CY	20
Fawcett Street	DZ	21
Fetter Lane	CY	22
Goodramgate	DY	25
High Ousegate	DY	26
High Petergate	CY	28
Knavesmire Road	AZ	29
Leeman Road	AY, CY	30
Lord Mayor's Walk	DX	33
Low Petergate	DY	35
Melrosegate	BY	36
Museum Street	CY	39
Pavement	DY	43
Peasholme Green	DY	45
Penley's Grove Street	DX	46
Queen Street	CZ	49
St. Helen's Road	AZ	50
St. Leonard's Place	CY	52
St. Maurice's Road	DXY	53
Station Road	CY	55
Stonebow (The)	DY	56
Tower Street	DZ	59
University Road	BZ	60

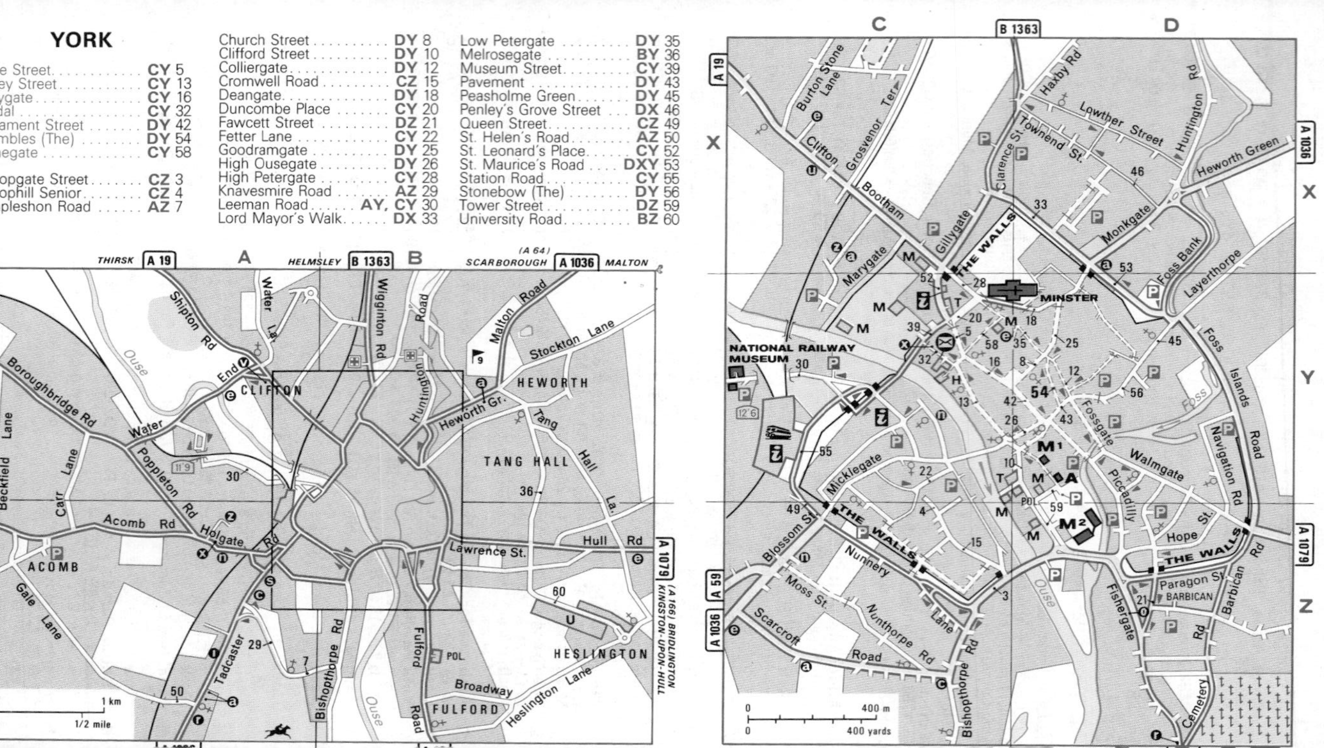

Curzon Lodge and Stable Cottages without rest., 23 Tadcaster Rd, YO2 2QG, ℘ 703157, – TV P. VISA. AZ **a**
closed Christmas and New Year – **10 rm** 39.00/60.00 **st.**

23 St. Mary's without rest., 23 St. Mary's, Bootham, YO3 7DD, ℘ 622738 – TV. CX **a**
closed Christmas and New Year – **9 rm** 28.00/60.00 **t.**

Kilima, 129 Holgate Rd, YO2 4DE, ℘ 625787, Fax 612083, – rest TV P. AE VISA. AZ **n**
Meals 10.50/17.95 **t.** and a la carte 4.75 – **15 rm** 47.25/86.50 **t.** – SB.

Grasmead House without rest., 1 Scarcroft Hill, YO2 1DF, ℘ 629996, Fax 629996 – TV. VISA JCB. – **6 rm** 45.00/58.00 **st.** CZ **a**

Heworth Court, 76-78 Heworth Green, YO3 7TQ, ℘ 425156, Fax 415290 – rest TV P. AE VISA. BY **a**
Meals 7.95/16.95 **t.** and a la carte – **25 rm** 42.00/76.00 **t.** – SB.

Clifton Bridge, Water End, YO3 6LL, ℘ 610510, Fax 640208 – rest TV P. AE VISA AY **e**
Meals (bar lunch)/dinner 10.00 **t.** and a la carte 4.95 – **14 rm** 40.00/64.00 **t.** – SB.

Cottage, 3 Clifton Green, YO3 6LH, ℘ 643711, Fax 611230 – TV P. AE VISA.
closed Christmas – **Meals** (dinner only) 11.50 **t.** and a la carte 4.95 – **18 rm** 30.00/60.00 **t.** – SB. AY **v**

Black Bull, Hull Rd, YO1 3LF, ℘ 411856, Fax 430667 – TV P. AE VISA.
Meals (bar lunch)/dinner a la carte 9.85/12.85 **st.** – 5.75 **40 rm** 38.50/44.00 **st.** BZ **e**

Priory, 126 Fulford Rd, YO1 4BE, ℘ 625280, Fax 625280, – TV P. AE VISA.
closed Christmas – **Meals** (dinner only) 15.00 **t.** and a la carte 4.95 – **20 rm** 30.00/50.00 **t.** – SB. DZ **r**

18 St. Paul's Square, 18 St. Paul's Sq., YO2 4BD, ℘ 629884, – . AZ **z**
closed Christmas and New Year – **Meals** (by arrangement) 18.50 **st.** – **3 rm** 37.50/60.00 **st.**

Ashbury without rest., 103 The Mount, YO2 2AX, ℘ 647339 – TV. CZ **e**
closed Christmas and New Year – **5 rm** 35.00/55.00 **st.**

Crook Lodge, 26 St. Mary's, Bootham, YO3 7DD, ℘ 655614 – rest TV P.
closed Christmas – **Meals** 10.50 **st.** 3.75 – **7 rm** 25.00/46.00 **st.** – SB. CX **z**

Hobbits without rest., 9 St. Peter's Grove, Clifton, YO3 6AQ, ℘ 624538, Fax 651765 – TV P. VISA. CX **e**
closed 23 to 30 December – **6 rm** 27.00/54.00 **s.**

XX **Melton's,** 7 Scarcroft Rd, YO2 1ND, ℘ 634341, Fax 629233 – . VISA CZ **c**
closed Monday lunch, Sunday dinner, 1 week late August and 24 December for 3 weeks – **Meals** (booking essential) 13.90/28.50 **st.** and a la carte 6.70.

X **19 Grape Lane,** 19 Grape Lane, YO1 2HU, ℘ 636366, Fax 702120 – VISA CY **e**
closed Sunday, Monday, last week January, first 2 weeks February, last 2 weeks September and 25 to 28 December – **Meals** - English - 12.50 **t.** (lunch) and a la carte 16.95/23.65 **t.**

at Kexby E : 6 ¾ m. on A 1079 – B – ✉ York – 01759 :

Kexby Bridge, Hull Rd, YO4 5LD, ℘ 388223, Fax 388822, – TV P – 100. VISA.
Meals 12.50/17.00 **t.** – **32 rm** 50.00/75.00 **t.** – SB.

at Escrick S : 5 ¾ m. on A 19 – B – ✉ York – 01904 :

Parsonage Country House, Main St., YO4 6LF, ℘ 728111, Fax 728151, – rest TV P – 160. AE VISA JCB.
Meals 11.50/18.50 **st.** and a la carte 5.25 – **13 rm** 75.00/95.00 **st.** – SB.

at Bilbrough SW : 5 ½ m. by A 1036 – AZ – off A 64 – ✉ York – 01937 :

Bilbrough Manor, YO2 3PH, ℘ 834002, Fax 834724, ←, « Tastefully decorated Victorian manor », , park – rest TV P. AE VISA.
closed 25 to 30 December – **Meals** 14.50/30.00 **t.** and a la carte 6.15 – **12 rm** 77.00/150.00 **t.** – SB.

Travel Inn, Bilbrough Top, Colton, YO2 3PP, S : ½ m. on A 64 (westbound carriageway) ℘ 835067, Fax 835934 – rm TV P – 40. AE VISA
Meals (grill rest.) – 4.95 – **60 rm** 34.50 **t.**

Forte Travelodge, Steeton, LS24 8EG, SW : ¾ m. on A 64 (eastbound carriageway) ℘ 531823, Reservations (Freephone) 0800 850950 – TV P. AE VISA
Meals (grill rest.) – **40 rm** 34.50 **t.**

at Long Marston W : 7 m. on B 1224 – AZ – ✉ York – 01904 :

Gill House Farm, Tockwith Rd, YO5 8PJ, N : ½ m. ℘ 738379, « Working farm », – TV P. VISA
Meals (by arrangement) 10.00 **st.** – **4 rm** 30.00/42.00 **st.**

at Skelton NW : 3 m. on A 19 – A – ✉ York – 01904 :

Fairfield Manor, Shipton Rd, YO3 6XW, ℘ 670222, Fax 670311, – rest TV P – 200 – **84 rm**, 6 suites.

ATS 2 James St. ℘ 412372/410375
ATS 36 Holgate Rd ℘ 654411
ATS 110 Layerthorpe ℘ 628479/625884

Wales

Place with at least

- a hotel or restaurant — ● Ruthin
- a pleasant hotel or restaurant — 🏨, ⌂, ✕
- a quiet, secluded hotel — 🐴
- a restaurant with ✿, ✿✿, ✿✿✿, Meals (M)
- See this town for establishments located in its vicinity — NEATH

Localité offrant au moins

- une ressource hôtelière — ● Ruthin
- un hôtel ou restaurant agréable — 🏨, ⌂, ✕
- un hôtel très tranquille, isolé — 🐴
- une bonne table à ✿, ✿✿, ✿✿✿, Meals (M)
- Localité groupant dans le texte les ressources de ses environs — NEATH

La località possiede come minimo

- una risorsa alberghiera — ● Ruthin
- Albergo o ristorante ameno — 🏨, ⌂, ✕
- un albergo molto tranquillo, isolato — 🐴
- un'ottima tavola con ✿, ✿✿, ✿✿✿, Meals (M)
- La località raggruppa nel suo testo le risorse dei dintorni — NEATH

Ort mit mindestens

- einem Hotel oder Restaurant — ● Ruthin
- ein angenehmes Hotel oder Restaurant — 🏨, ⌂, ✕
- einem sehr ruhigen und abgelegenen Hotel — 🐴
- einem Restaurant mit ✿, ✿✿, ✿✿✿, Meals (M)
- Ort mit Angaben über Hotels und Restaurants in der Umgebung — NEATH

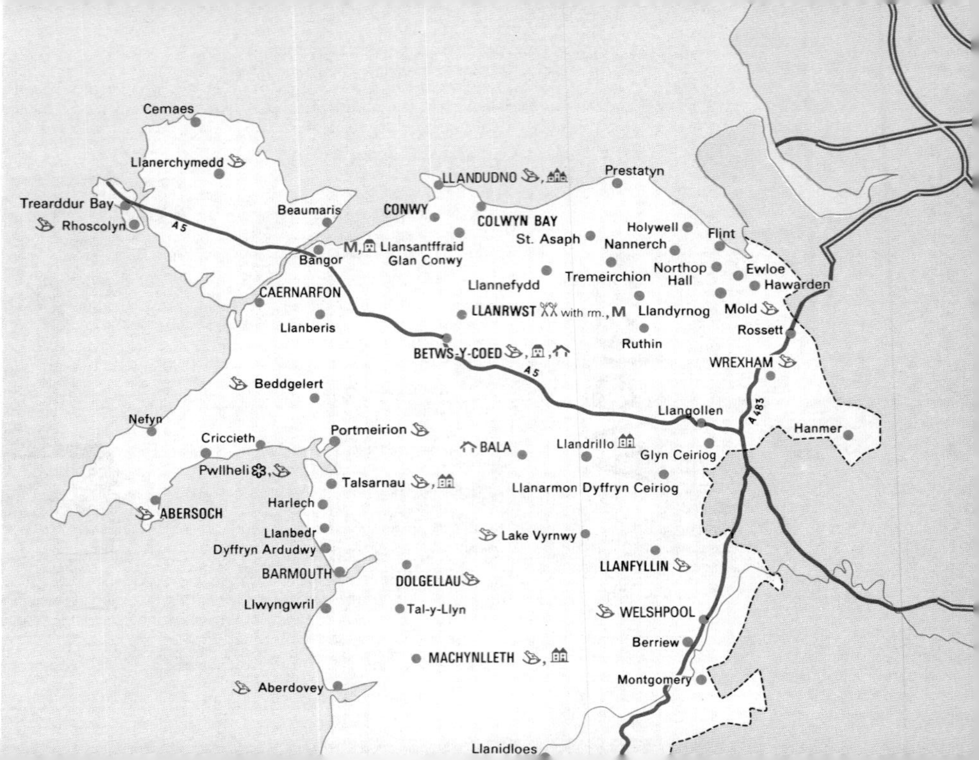

Cemaes
Llanerchymedd
Trearddur Bay
Rhoscolyn
A 5
Beaumaris
Bangor
M, Llansantffraid Glan Conwy
CONWY
LLANDUDNO
COLWYN BAY
Prestatyn
St. Asaph
Holywell
Flint
Nannerch
Northop Hall
Ewloe
Hawarden
Tremeirchion
Llannefydd
CAERNARFON
Llanberis
LLANRWST with rm., M
Llandyrnog
Mold
Rossett
Ruthin
BETWS-Y-COED
WREXHAM
A 483
Beddgelert
Llangollen
Hanmer
Nefyn
Criccieth
Portmeirion
BALA
Llandrillo
Glyn Ceiriog
Pwllheli
Talsarnau
Llanarmon Dyffryn Ceiriog
Harlech
ABERSOCH
Llanbedr
Dyffryn Ardudwy
Lake Vyrnwy
LLANFYLLIN
BARMOUTH
DOLGELLAU
Llwyngwril
Tal-y-Llyn
WELSHPOOL
Berriew
MACHYNLLETH
Aberdovey
Montgomery
Llanidloes

Llangurig
Cwmystwyth
Knighton
Rhayader
Presteigne
A 483
New Quay
LLANDRINDOD WELLS
ABERPORTH
Rhydlewis
Llanwrtyd Wells
CARDIGAN
Llangammarch Wells
Pumsaint
HAY-ON-WYE
Crug-y-bar
Cynghordy
Three Cocks
FISHGUARD
Newport
Boncath
Llyswen
Crymmych
Talgarth
Brechfa
Brecon
with rm.
Llangorse
ST. DAVIDS
Wolf's Castle
A 40
Llandeilo
Whitland
CRICKHOWELL
Haverfordwest
St. Clears
A 48
MONMOUTH
ABERGAVENNY
Cross Hands
Merthyr Tydfil
Raglan
Laugharne
Milford Haven
Saundersfoot
Swansea S.A.
Aberdare
PEMBROKE
TENBY
Pontypool
USK
Tintern
NEATH
Llantrisant
SWANSEA
Cwmbran
Chepstow
Porth
Port Talbot
Pontypridd
Magor S.A.
Sarn Park S.A.
M 4
NEWPORT
Miskin
Cardiff West S. A.
BRIDGEND
St. Brides-Super-Ely
PORTHCAWL
Cowbridge
CARDIFF
Llantwit Major
Barry

ABERDARE (Aberdâr) M. Glam. 403 J 28 pop. 13 484 – 01685.
London 178 – Cardiff 23 – Swansea 27.

Ty Newydd, Penderyn Rd, Hirwaun, CF44 9SX, NW : 5 m. on A 4059 ℘ 81343 Fax 813139, – TV ☎ P – 200. VISA.
Meals 9.30/14.00 **t.** and a la carte 3.50 – **28 rm** 45.15/64.15 **t.**, 1 suite – SB.

ATS Canal Rd, Cwmbach ℘ 873914/875491

ABERDOVEY (Aberdyfi) Gwynedd 403 H 26 – pop. 869 – 01654.
Aberdovey ℘ 767210.
London 230 – Dolgellau 25 – Shrewsbury 66.

Plas Penhelig Country House, LL35 0NA, E : 1 m. by A 493 ℘ 767676, Fax 76778 ≤, « Terraced gardens », park – TV ☎ P – 35. VISA JCB
11 March-December – **Meals** 14.50/21.00 **t.** 6.00 – **11 rm** 63.00/116.00 **t.** – SB.

Trefeddian, Tywyn Rd, LL35 0SB, W : 1 m. on A 493 ℘ 767213, Fax 767777, ≤ gol course and sea, , park, – rest TV ☎ P. VISA
2 March-2 January – **Meals** 8.75/15.75 **t.** – **46 rm** 50.00/124.00 **t.** – SB.

Penhelig Arms, LL35 0LT, ℘ 767215, Fax 767690, ≤, « Part 18C inn » – rm TV ☎ P VISA JCB
Meals (bar lunch Monday to Saturday)/dinner 18.75 **t.** – **10 rm** 39.00/78.00 **t.** – SB.

Harbour, LL35 0EB, ℘ 767250, Fax 767078, ≤ – TV. VISA
closed 25 and 26 December – **Meals** 15.00 **st.** (dinner) and a la carte 3.50 – **8 rm** 45.00 90.00 **st.**, 1 suite – SB.

Maybank, 4 Penhelig Rd, LL35 0PT, E : 1 m. on A 493 ℘ 767500, ≤ – TV P. VIS JCB.
closed 2 January-16 February and 8 November-23 December – **Meals** (booking essentia (dinner only) 22.45 **st.** 6.50 – **6 rm** 25.00/52.00 **st.** – SB.

Brodawel without rest., Tywyn Rd, LL35 0SA, W : 1¼ m. on A 493 ℘ 767347, ≤, – TV P.
May-September – **6 rm** 22.00/44.00 **st.**

ABERGAVENNY (Y-Fenni) Gwent 403 L 28 **Great Britain G.** – pop. 9 593 – 01873.
Exc. : Raglan Castle★ *AC*, SE : 9 m. by A 40.
Monmouthshire, Llanfoist ℘ 853171.
Swan Meadow, Monmouth Road, NP7 5HH ℘ 857588 (summer only).
London 163 – Gloucester 43 – Newport 19 – Swansea 49.

Llansantffraed Court (Mount Charlotte), Llanvihangel Gobion, NP7 9BA, SE : 6½ m. by A 40, B 4598 and Raglan rd ℘ 840678, Fax 840674, ≤, , park – rm TV ☎ P. VISA
Meals 12.95/17.95 **st.** and dinner a la carte 5.50 – **21 rm** 59.00/130.00 **st.** – SB.

Halidon House without rest., 63 Monmouth Rd, NP7 5HR, ℘ 857855, ≤, – P.
April-October – **5 rm** 15.00/35.00 **st.**

at Llanfihangel Crucorney N : 6½ m. by A 40 on A 465 – ✉ Abergavenny – 01873 :

Penyclawdd Court, NP7 7LB, S: ¼ m. by Pantygelli rd ℘ 890719, Fax 890848, ≤ « Tudor manor house », – rm TV P. VISA.
Meals (by arrangement) (communal dining) 20.00 **st.** – **3 rm** 45.00/60.00 **st.**

at Govilon W : 5¼ m. by A 465 on B 4246 – ✉ Abergavenny – 01873 :

Llanwenarth House, NP7 9SF, N : 1 m. on B 4246 ℘ 830289, Fax 832199, ≤, « 16C manor house », – rest TV P
closed mid January-February – **Meals** (by arrangement) (residents only) (communal dining (dinner only) 24.00 **st.** 5.80 – **5 rm** 56.00/76.00 **s.** – SB.

at Llanwenarth NW : 3 m. on A 40 – ✉ Abergavenny – 01873 :

Llanwenarth Arms, Brecon Rd, NP8 1EP, ℘ 810550, Fax 811880, ≤, – TV ☎ P. VISA.
Meals a la carte 12.95/20.00 **st.** – **18 rm** 39.00/59.00 **st.**

ATS 11 Monmouth Rd ℘ 854348/855829

ABERPORTH Dyfed 403 G 27 – pop. 2 147 – ✉ Cardigan – 01239.
London 249 – Carmarthen 29 – Fishguard 26.

Penrallt, SA43 2BS, SW : 1 m. by B 4333 ℘ 810227, Fax 811375, ≤, , , heated, , – TV ☎ P. VISA
closed 23 December-1 January – **Meals** (bar lunch)/dinner 16.00 **s.** and a la carte 4.95 – **17 rm** 48.00/95.00 **st.** – SB.

at Tresaith NE : 1¾ m. – ✉ Cardigan – 01239 :

Glandwr Manor, SA43 2JH, ℘ 810197, – P.
March-October – **Meals** *(closed Sunday to non residents)* (bar lunch)/dinner 12.00 **t.** and a la carte 3.70 – **7 rm** 27.00/56.00 **t.**

ABERSOCH Gwynedd 402 403 G 25 pop. 805 – ✉ Pwllheli – ☎ 01758.

Abersoch, Golf Rd ☎ 712622.

London 265 – Caernarfon 28 – Shrewsbury 101.

Abersoch Harbour, Lon Engan, LL53 7HR, ☎ 712406, ≤ – TV ☎ P. VISA JCB
Meals (bar lunch Monday to Saturday)/dinner 16.00 **t.** and a la carte 3.95 – **14 rm** 30.00/80.00 **t.** – SB.

Riverside, LL53 7HW, ☎ 712419, Fax 712671, – TV ☎ P. AE VISA.
March-mid November – **Meals** (bar lunch)/dinner 21.00 **t.** 5.25 – **12 rm** 30.00/80.00 **st.** – SB.

White House, LL53 7AG, ☎ 713427, Fax 713512, ≤, – TV ☎ P – 120. VISA
Meals (bar lunch residents only) 16.50 **t.** and a la carte 5.50 – **14 rm** 31.50/69.00 **t.** – SB.

Neigwl, Lon Sarn Bach, LL53 7DY, ☎ 712363, Fax 712363, ≤ Cardigan Bay – TV P. VISA.
Meals *(closed Sunday)* (dinner only) 20.00 **st.** – **9 rm** 36.00/60.00 **st.** – SB.

Tudor Court, Lon Sarn Bach, LL53 7EB, ☎ 713354, Fax 713354 – TV P. VISA
Meals 11.50/17.50 **t.** and a la carte 5.00 – **8 rm** 34.50/60.00 **t.** – SB.

at Bwlchtocyn S : 2 m. – ✉ Pwllheli – ☎ 01758 :

Porth Tocyn , LL53 7BU, ☎ 713303, Fax 713538, ≤ Cardigan Bay and mountains, heated, , – TV ☎ P. VISA
Easter-mid November – **Meals** (bar lunch Monday to Saturday)/dinner 25.50 **t.** 5.50 – 4.00 – **17 rm** 41.50/99.00 **t.** – SB.

Crowrach Isaf , LL53 7BY, ☎ 712860, ≤, , park – TV P.
Meals 12.50 **st.** – **3 rm** 17.00/40.00 **st.**

ABERYSTWYTH Dyfed 403 H 26 **Great Britain G.** – pop. 8 359 – ☎ 01970.

See : Town★ - ≤★ from the National Library of Wales.

Exc. : Devil's Bridge (Pontarfynach)★, E : 12 m. by A 4120 – Strata Florida★ *AC*, SE : 15 m. by B 4340.

Bryn-y-Mor ☎ 615104.

Terrace Rd, SY23 2AG ☎ 612125.

London 238 – Chester 98 – Fishguard 58 – Shrewsbury 74.

Belle Vue Royal, Marine Terrace, SY23 2BA, ☎ 617558, Fax 612190, ≤ – rm TV ☎ P – 40. AE VISA.
closed 24 to 26 December – **Meals** 11.50/20.00 **t.** 6.00 – **36 rm** 47.50/73.50 **t.** – SB.

Four Seasons, 50-54 Portland St., SY23 2DX, ☎ 612120, Fax 627458 – rest TV ☎ P. VISA.
Meals (bar lunch Monday to Saturday)/dinner 18.00 **t.** 4.50 – **14 rm** 46.00/68.00 **t.** – SB.

Groves, 44-46 North Par., SY23 2NF, ☎ 617623, Fax 627068 – TV ☎ P. AE VISA.
Meals 10.50/19.50 **st.** 5.45 – **9 rm** 42.00/60.00 **st.** – SB.

Sinclair, 43 Portland St., SY23 2DX, ☎ 615158, Fax 615158 – TV.
Meals 11.50 **st.** – **3 rm** 27.50/45.00 **st.**

at Chancery (Rhydgaled) S : 4 m. on A 487 – ✉ Aberystwyth – ☎ 01970 :

Conrah Country House , SY23 4DF, ☎ 617941, Fax 624546, ≤, « 18C country house », , , , park – rest TV ☎ P – 50. AE VISA JCB.
closed 1 week Christmas – **Meals** 15.75/25.50 **t.** and lunch a la carte 6.00 – **20 rm** 59.00/108.00 **t.** – SB.

ATS Glanyrafon Ind. Est., Llanbadarn ☎ 611166

ARTHOG Gwynedd 402 403 I 25 – see Dolgellau.

BALA Gwynedd 402 403 J 25 – pop. 1 922 – ☎ 01678.

Bala Lake Hotel ☎ 520344/520111.

Penllyn Road, LL23 7NH ☎ 521021 (Winter open Fri to Sun only).

London 216 – Chester 46 – Dolgellau 18 – Shrewsbury 52.

White Lion Royal, 61 High St., LL23 7AE, ☎ 520314 – TV ☎ P
26 rm.

Fron Feuno Hall , LL23 7YF, SW : 1 m. on A 494 ☎ 521115, Fax 521151, ≤ Bala Lake, , , park, – P.
April-October – **Meals** (by arrangement) (communal dining) 16.00 **st.** – **3 rm** 30.00/56.00 **st.**

Melin Meloch, LL23 7DP, E : 1 3/4 m. by A 494 on B 4401 ☎ 520101, « Part 13C converted water mill », – TV P.
closed January – **Meals** (by arrangement) (communal dining) 11.50 **st.** – **3 rm** 25.00/42.00 **st.**

Llidiardau Mawr without rest., Llidiardau, LL23 7SG, NW : 4 1/4 m. by A 4212 ☎ 520555, ≤, « 17C stone-built mill house », – P.
Easter-September – **3 rm** 20.00/40.00.

at Fron-Goch NW : 2 ¾ m. on A 4212 – ✉ Bala – ☎ 01678 :

Fferm Fron-Goch, LL23 7NT, ☎ 520483, Fax 520483, « 17C farmhouse, working farm », park – ⊭ TV P. ✻
Easter-October – **Meals** (by arrangement) 9.50 **s.** – **3 rm** ☐ 17.00/34.00 **s.**

BANGOR Gwynedd 402 403 H 24 – pop. 11 173 – ☎ 01248.

St. Deiniol, Pentryn ☎ 353098 – London 247 – Birkenhead 68 – Holyhead 23 – Shrewsbury 83.

Menai Court, Craig-y-Don Rd, LL57 2BG, ☎ 354200, Fax 354200, ≤, – ⊭ TV ☎ P – 60. VISA JCB
closed 26 December-8 January and 4 to 9 April – **Meals** *(closed lunch Saturday, Sunday and Bank Holidays)* (lunch by arrangement)/dinner 11.95/15.95 **t.** and dinner a la carte 6.20 – **13 rm** ☐ 48.00/71.50 **t.** – SB.

Travelodge, One Stop Services, Llandegai, LL57 4BG, SE : 2½ m. by A 5122, at junction of A 5 with A 55 ☎ 370345, Fax 370345 – ⊭ rm TV ♿ P. AE VISA. ✻
Meals (grill rest.) a la carte approx. 12.45 **t.** – ☐ 5.00 – **30 rm** 34.50 **t.**

BARMOUTH **(Abermaw)** Gwynedd 402 403 H 25 – pop. 2 386 – ☎ 01341.

The Old Library, Station Rd, LL42 1LU ☎ 280787 (summer only).

London 231 – Chester 74 – Dolgellau 10 – Shrewsbury 67.

Ty'r Graig Castle, Llanaber Rd, LL42 1YN, on A 496 ☎ 280470, Fax 281260, ≤, – ⊭ rest TV ☎ P. AE VISA JCB
Meals 9.95/15.50 **t.** and a la carte 5.50 – **12 rm** ☐ 38.00/71.00 **t.** – SB.

Cranbourne, 9 Marine Par., LL42 1NA, ☎ 280202 – ⊭ rest TV. VISA. ✻
closed Christmas – **Meals** 9.50 **st.** 2.50 – **10 rm** ☐ 15.50/50.00 **s.**

at Llanaber NW : 1½ m. on A 496 – ✉ Barmouth – ☎ 01341 :

Llwyndû Farmhouse ⑤, LL42 1RR, N : ¾ m. on A 496 ☎ 280144, Fax 281236, « Part 17C », – ⊭ TV P
closed 26 November-3 December – **Meals** (by arrangement) 22.00 **st.** 6.00 – **7 rm** ☐ 48.00/62.00 **st.** – SB.

BARRY **(Barri)** S. Glam. 403 K 29 – pop. 46 368 – ☎ 01446.

Brynhill, Port Rd, Colcot ☎ 735061 – RAF St. Athan ☎ 751043.

The Triangle, Paget Rd, Barry Island, CF62 5TG ☎ 747171 (summer only).

London 167 – Cardiff 10 – Swansea 39.

Egerton Grey Country House, CF62 3BZ, SW : 4½ m. by A 4226 and Porthkerry rd via Cardiff Airport ☎ 711666, Fax 711690, ≤, « Country house atmosphere », , park, – ⊭ rest TV ☎ P – 40. AE VISA JCB
Meals 12.50/25.50 **st.** 5.25 – **10 rm** ☐ 55.00/90.00 **st.** – SB.

Mount Sorrel, Porthkerry Rd, CF62 7XY, ☎ 740069, Fax 746600, ≘s, – TV ☎ P – 150. AE VISA
Meals (bar lunch)/dinner 15.50 **t.** – **43 rm** 55.00/90.00 **t.** – SB.

Aberthaw House, 28 Porthkerry Rd, CF62 7AX, ☎ 737314, Fax 732376 – TV ☎. VISA
Meals *(closed Sunday)* (dinner only) 25.00 **t.** and a la carte 3.95 – ☐ 3.50 – **10 rm** 32.50/52.50 **t.**

Cwm Ciddy Toby, Airport Rd, CF6 9BA, NW : 1½ m. by B 4266 ☎ 700075, Fax 700075 – TV ☎ P. AE VISA. ✻
closed 24-26 December – **Meals** (grill rest.) 15.50 **t.** and a la carte 4.95 – **14 rm** ☐ 49.00/59.00 **t.** – SB.

BEAUMARIS Gwynedd 402 403 H 24 Great Britain G. – pop. 2 050 – ☎ 01248.

See : Castle★★ *AC* – Envir. : Isle of Anglesey★★.

Exc. : Plas Newydd★★ *AC*, SW : 7 m. by A 545 and A 4080.

London 253 – Birkenhead 74 – Holyhead 25.

Ye Olde Bull's Head Inn, Castle St., LL58 8AP, ☎ 810329, Fax 811294 – ⊭ rm TV ☎ P AE VISA JCB. ✻
closed 25-26 December and 1 January – **Meals** - (see below) – **15 rm** ☐ 45.00/90.00 **t.** – SB.

Bishopsgate House, 54 Castle St., LL58 8BB, ☎ 810302, Fax 810166 – ⊭ rest TV ☎ P AE VISA JCB. ✻
closed January – **Meals** (bar lunch Monday to Saturday)/dinner 13.95 **t.** and a la carte 5.50 – **11 rm** ☐ 35.00/65.00 **t.** – SB.

Plas Cichle ⑤, LL58 8PS, NW : 2 ½ m. by B 5109 and Llanfaes Rd ☎ 810488, ≤ « Working farm », , park – ⊭ TV P. ✻
February-October – **Meals** 12.50 – **3 rm** ☐ 28.00/42.00 **st.**

XX **Ye Olde Bull's Head Inn** (at Ye Olde Bull's Head Inn H.), Castle St., LL58 8AP, ☎ 810329, Fax 811294 – P. AE VISA JCB
closed 25-26 December and 1 January – **Meals** (bar lunch Monday to Saturday)/dinner 19.95 **t.** and a la carte 6.50.

BEDDGELERT Gwynedd 402 403 H 24 Great Britain G. – pop. 535 – 01766.

Exc. : Snowdon★★★ (✻★★★ from summit) N : by marked footpaths or by Snowdon Mountain Railway from Llanberis.

♦London 249 – Caernarfon 13 – Chester 73.

- **Royal Goat,** LL55 4YE, ℘ 890224, Fax 890422, – . AE VISA
  Meals 11.00/14.00 **st.** and a la carte 5.50 – **28 rm** 42.00/68.00 **st.**, 2 suites – SB.
- **Sygun Fawr Country House**, LL55 4NE, NE : ¾ m. by A 498 ℘ 890258, ≤ mountains and valley, « Part 16C stone built house », , park – . VISA JCB
  closed January – **Meals** 17.00 **st.** 4.30 – **7 rm** 39.00/52.00 **st.** – SB.

BEREA Dyfed – see St. Davids.

BERRIEW (Aberriw) Powys 402 403 K 26 – pop. 1 305 – ✉ Welshpool – 01686.

♦London 190 – Chester 49 – Shrewsbury 26.

- **Lion,** SY21 8PQ, ℘ 640452, Fax 640604, « Part 17C inn » – . AE VISA JCB.
  Meals (booking essential) (bar lunch Monday to Saturday)/dinner a la carte 18.00 **t.** and a la carte 5.00 – **7 rm** 50.00/90.00 **t.** – SB.

Prices For full details of the prices quoted in the guide, consult the introduction.

BETWS-Y-COED Gwynedd 402 403 I 24 Great Britain G. – pop. 848 – 01690.

See : Town★.

Envir. : Swallow Falls★, NW : 2 m. by A 5.

Clubhouse ℘ 710556.

Royal Oak Stables, LL24 0AH ℘ 710426.

♦London 226 – Holyhead 44 – Shrewsbury 62.

- **Royal Oak,** Holyhead Rd, LL24 0AY, ℘ 710219, Fax 710603 – . AE VISA.
  Meals 9.00/20.00 **t.** and a la carte – **27 rm** 49.00/78.00 **t.** – SB.
- **Waterloo,** LL24 0AR, on A 5 ℘ 710411, Fax 710666, , , – . AE VISA JCB.
  closed 24 to 26 December – **Meals** (bar lunch Monday to Saturday)/dinner 17.50 **t.** and a la carte 4.50 – **39 rm** 49.50/79.00 **t.** – SB.
- **Tan-y-Foel Country House**, LL26 0RE, E : 4 m. by A 5 and A 470 on Nebo rd ℘ 710507, Fax 710681, ≤ Vale of Conwy and Snowdonia, « Part 16C manor house », , park – . AE VISA JCB.
  closed December, booking essential January – **Meals** (residents only) (dinner only) 26.00 **st.** 5.50 – **7 rm** 69.50/110.00 **st.** – SB.
- **Ty Gwyn,** London Rd, LL24 0SG, SE : ½ m. on A 5 ℘ 710383, Fax 710383, « 17C inn » – . VISA
  Meals 11.50/17.95 **t.** 4.50 – **13 rm** 19.00/80.00 **t.**
- **Park Hill,** Llanrwst Rd, LL24 0HD, NE : 1 m. by A 5 on A 470 ℘ 710540, Fax 710540, ≤ Vale of Conwy, , , – rest . AE VISA.
  Meals (dinner only) 14.50 **t.** 3.95 – **11 rm** 19.50/62.00 **t.** – SB.
- **Bryn Bella** without rest., Llanrwst Rd, LL24 0HD, ℘ 710627, ≤ Vale of Conwy – .
  4 rm 17.00/36.00 **st.**

at Penmachno SW : 4 ¾ m. by A 5 on B 4406 – ✉ Betws-y-Coed – 01690 :

- **Penmachno Hall**, LL24 0PU, ℘ 760207, – . VISA.
  closed 24 December-7 January – **Meals** (by arrangement) (communal dining) 16.50 **st.** 2.95 – **4 rm** 30.00/50.00 **st.**

BONCATH Dyfed 403 G 27 pop. 672 – 01239.

♦London 247 – Carmarthen 27 – Fishguard 17.

- **Pantyderi Mansion** without rest., SA37 0JB, W : 2 ¾ m. by B 4332 ℘ 841227, Fax 841670, ≤, « Working farm », heated, , , park – .
  February-November – **8 rm** 22.00/44.00 **t.**

BONTDDU Gwynedd 402 403 I 25 – see Dolgellau.

BRECHFA Dyfed 403 H 28 – ✉ Carmarthen – 01267.

♦London 223 – Carmarthen 11 – ♦Swansea 30.

- **Ty Mawr Country House** with rm, Abergorlech Rd, SA32 7RA, ℘ 202332, Fax 202437, « Part 15C and 16C house », – rm . AE VISA
  closed last 2 weeks January, last week November and 25-26 December – **Meals** *(closed Tuesday dinner to non-residents)* (lunch by arrangement) 12.50/22.00 **st.** 4.50 – **5 rm** 48.00/76.00 **st.** – SB.

BRECON (Aberhonddu) Powys 403 J 28 Great Britain G. – pop. 7 523 – 01874.
Exc. : Dan-yr-Ogof Caves** *AC*, SW : 18 m. by A 40 and A 4067.
18 Penoyre Park, Cradoc 623658 – 9 Newton Park, Llanfaes 622004.
Cattle Market Car Park, LD3 9DA 622485.
London 171 – Cardiff 40 – Carmarthen 31 – Gloucester 65.

Peterstone Court, Llanhamlach, LD3 7YB, SE : 3 ¼ m. on A 40 665387, Fax 665376, ←, « Georgian manor house », heated, – rm. AE VISA JCB
Meals 17.95/21.95 **st.** and a la carte 4.95 – **12 rm** 79.50/135.00 **st.** – SB.

ATS The Watton 624496/624163

BRIDGEND (Pen-y-Bont) Mid Glam. 403 J 29 – pop. 14 311 – 01656.
London 177 – Cardiff 20 – Swansea 23.

Heronston, Ewenny Rd, CF35 5AW, S : 2 m. on B 4265 668811, Fax 767391, heated, – – 120. AE VISA JCB
Meals (bar lunch Saturday) 14.95 **st.** and a la carte 5.75 – **76 rm** 65.00/80.00 **st.** – SB.

at Pencoed NE : 4½ m. by A 473 – Pencoed – 01656 :

Forte Travelodge, CF3 5HU, E : 1 ¼ m. by Felindre rd 864404, Reservations (Freephone) 0800 850950 – AE VISA
Meals (grill rest.) – **40 rm** 34.50 **t.**

at Coychurch (Llangrallo) E : 2¼ m. by A 473 – Bridgend – 01656 :

Coed-y-Mwstwr, CF35 6AF, N : 1 m. 860621, Fax 863122, ←, heated, park, – – 120. AE VISA
Meals 10.50/24.00 **t.** and a la carte 5.15 – **22 rm** 80.00/120.00 **t.**, 1 suites – SB.

at Southerndown SW : 5½ m. by A 4265 – Bridgend – 01656 :

Frolics, Beach Rd, CF32 0RP, 880127 – VISA
closed Sunday dinner, Monday and 25 to 29 December – **Meals** (dinner only and Sunday lunch)/dinner 15.50 **st.** and a la carte.

at Laleston W : 2 m. on A 473 – Bridgend – 01656 :

Great House with rm, High St., CF32 OHP, on A 473 657644, Fax 668892, – AE VISA.
Meals *(closed Saturday lunch, Sunday dinner and Bank Holiday Mondays)* 21.95 **t.** and a la carte 5.75 – **10 rm** 65.00/100.00 **t.** – SB.

ATS 122 Coity Rd 658775/6

BWLCHTOCYN Gwynedd 402 403 G 25 – see Abersoch.

CADOXTON W. Glam. 403 I 29 – see Neath.

CAERNARFON Gwynedd 402 403 H 24 Great Britain G. – pop. 9 695 – 01286.
See : Town*** – Castle*** *AC*.
18 Aberforeshore, Llanfaglan 673783/678359.
Oriel Pendeitsh, Castle St., LL55 2NA 672232.
London 249 – Birkenhead 76 – Chester 68 – Holyhead 30 – Shrewsbury 85.

Seiont Manor, Llanrug, LL55 2AQ, E : 3 m. on A 4086 673366, Fax 672840, park – – 100 – **28 rm.**

Pengwern, Saron, LL54 5UH, SW : 3 ¼ m. by A 487 on Llandwrog rd 831500, Fax 831500, « Working farm », park –
closed December and January – **Meals** (by arrangement) 13.50 **st.** – **3 rm** 25.00/50.00 **st.** – SB.

Isfryn, 11 Church St., LL55 1SW, 675628, Fax 675628 – rest
March-October – **Meals** (by arrangement) 15.50 **s.** – **6 rm** 17.50/40.00 **s.**

at Seion NE : 5½ m. by A 406 and B 4366 on Seion rd – Caernarfon – 01248 :

Ty'n Rhos Country House, Llanddeiniolen, LL55 3AE, SW : ¼ m. 670489, Fax 670079, ←, park – rest. AE VISA JCB.
closed 24 to 27 December – **Meals** (by arrangement) (residents only Sunday and Monday) (dinner only) 19.50 **t.** and a la carte 6.00 – **11 rm** 45.00/80.00 **st.** – SB.

ATS Bangor Rd 673110

Pleasant hotels and restaurants
are shown in the Guide by a red sign.
Please send us the names
of any where you have enjoyed your stay.
Your **Michelin Guide** will be even better.

CARDIFF (Caerdydd) S. Glam. 403 K 29 **Great Britain G.** – pop. 279 055 – ✪ 01222.

ee : City★ – Castle★ (interiors★) *AC* BZ – National Museum of Wales★ (Picture Collection★) *AC* BY – Llandaff Cathedral★ *AC* AV **B.**

nvir. : Welsh Folk Museum, St. Fagan's★★ *AC*, by St. Fagan's Rd AV – Castell Coch★ *AC*, W : 4½m. by A 470 AV.

xc. : Caerphilly Castle★★ *AC*, N : 7 m. by A 469 AV.

Dinas Powis, Old Highwalls ℘ 512727, AX.

Cardiff (Wales) Airport : ℘ (01446) 711111, SW : 8 m. by A 48 AX – **Terminal** : Central Bus Station.

Central Station, CF1 1QY ℘ 227281.

London 155 – ◆Birmingham 110 – ◆Bristol 46 – ◆Coventry 124.

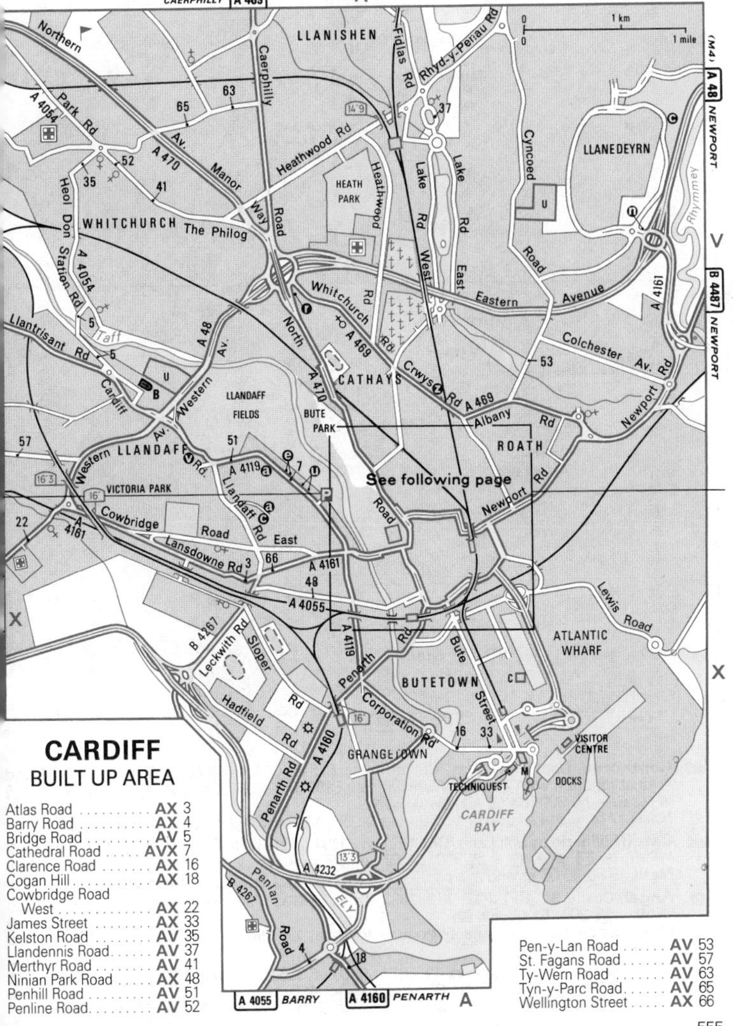

CARDIFF
BUILT UP AREA

Atlas Road . . . . AX 3
Barry Road . . . . AX 4
Bridge Road . . . . AV 5
Cathedral Road . . . . . AVX 7
Clarence Road . . . . AX 16
Cogan Hill . . . . AX 18
Cowbridge Road West . . . . AX 22
James Street . . . . AX 33
Kelston Road . . . . AV 35
Llandennis Road . . . . . AV 37
Merthyr Road . . . . AV 41
Ninian Park Road . . . . . AX 48
Penhill Road . . . . AV 51
Penline Road . . . . AV 52
Pen-y-Lan Road . . . . . . AV 53
St. Fagans Road . . . . . . AV 57
Ty-Wern Road . . . . AV 63
Tyn-y-Parc Road . . . . . . AV 65
Wellington Street . . . . . AX 66

CARDIFF

Copthorne, Copthorne Way, Culverhouse Cross, CF5 6XJ, W : 4 ¾ m. by A 4161 and A 48 at junction with A 4232 ✆ 599100, Fax 599080, Ⓛ, ≘s, ☒, ≈ – |♦| ⊬ rm ▤ rest ▣ ☎ ♿ Ⓟ – 🕴 300. ▣ AE ⊕ VISA JCB. ✻
Meals 17.00 **t.** and a la carte 🍷 5.50 – ☐ 9.95 – **134 rm** 95.00/115.00 **t.**, 1 suite – SB.

Cardiff Marriott, Mill Lane, CF1 1EZ, ✆ 399944, Fax 395578, ≤, Ⓛ, ≘s, ☒, squash – |♦| ⊬ rm ▤ ▣ ☎ ♿ Ⓟ – 🕴 300. ▣ AE ⊕ VISA JCB. ✻ BZ s
Meals 15.50/25.00 **st.** and a la carte – **178 rm** 82.00/92.00 **st.**, 4 suites – SB.

Angel, Castle St., CF1 2QZ, ✆ 232633, Telex 498132, Fax 396212, Ⓛ, ≘s – |♦| ⊬ rm ▣ ☎ Ⓟ – 🕴 300. ▣ AE ⊕ VISA BZ a
Meals (lunch by arrangement Monday to Saturday)/dinner 18.00 **st.** – ☐ 9.25 – **89 rm** 78.00/92.00 **st.**, 2 suites – SB.

Park (Mount Charlotte), Park Pl., CF1 3UD, ✆ 383471, Telex 497195, Fax 399309 – |♦| ⊬ rm ▣ ☎ Ⓟ – 🕴 300. ▣ AE ⊕ VISA JCB. ✻ BZ c
Meals 12.25/17.50 **st.** and a la carte 🍷 4.95 – ☐ 9.25 – **115 rm** 88.00/98.00 **st.**, 4 suites – SB.

Cardiff International, Mary Ann St., CF1 2EQ, ℘ 341441, Telex 498005, Fax 223742 – rm rest – 40. BZ **u**
Meals 10.95/14.95 **t.** and a la carte 4.25 – 8.95 – **140 rm** 85.00/100.00 **t.**, 3 suites – SB.

Cardiff Moat House (Q.M.H.), Circle Way East, Llanedeyrn, CF3 7XF, NE : 3 m. by A 48 ℘ 589988, Fax 549092, – rm rest – 300. AV **n**
Meals *(closed Saturday lunch)* 12.50/14.50 **st.** and a la carte – 9.50 – **130 rm** 75.00 **st.**, 2 suites – SB.

Forte Posthouse, Castle St., CF1 2XB, ℘ 388681, Fax 371495 – rm – 150. BZ **i**
Meals 7.95 **st.** and a la carte – 7.95 – **153 rm** 69.00 **st.**, 1 suite – SB.

Friendly, Merthyr Rd, CF4 7LD, NW : 5 m. by A 470 at junction with M 4 ℘ 529988, Fax 529977, – rm rest – 180.
Meals (carving rest.) 13.50 **st.** (dinner) and a la carte 4.50 – **95 rm** 57.50/94.00 **st.** – SB.

Churchills, Cardiff Rd, CF5 2AD, ℘ 562372, Fax 568347 – rest – 110. AV **v**
Meals 8.50/30.00 **st.** and a la carte 3.75 – 6.90 – **28 rm** 60.00/70.00 **st.**, 7 suites – SB.

Forte Posthouse, Pentwyn Rd, CF2 7XA, NE : 4 m. by A 48 ℘ 731212, Fax 549147, – rm rest – 120.
Meals a la carte 17.90/25.85 **st.** 6.25 – 7.95 – **142 rm** 59.00 **st.** – SB.

Cardiff Bay, Schooner Way, Atlantic Wharf, CF1 5RT, ℘ 465888, Fax 481491, – rest – 300. BZ **r**
Meals *(closed lunch Saturday)* 10.00/15.00 **st.** and a la carte 4.50 – 8.50 – **65 rm** 68.00/110.00 **st.**

Forte Travelodge, Circle Way East, Llanedeyrn, CF3 7ND, on Coed-y-Gores rd ℘ 549564, Reservations (Freephone) 0800 850950 – . AV **c**
Meals (grill rest.) – **32 rm** 34.50 **t.**

Townhouse without rest., 70 Cathedral Rd, CF1 9LL, ℘ 239399, Fax 223214 – . AV **u**
8 rm 39.50/49.50 **st.**

Briars without rest., 126-128 Cathedral Rd, CF1 9LQ, ℘ 340881, Fax 230122 – . AV **e**
10 rm 22.00/38.00 **st.** – SB.

Ferrier's, 130-132 Cathedral Rd, CF1 9LQ, ℘ 383413, Fax 383413 – . AV **e**
closed 1 week Christmas – **Meals** a la carte 8.45 **t.** – **26 rm** 20.00/48.00 **t.**

Annedd Lon without rest., 3 Dyfrig St., off Cathedral Rd, CF1 9LR, ℘ 223349 – . AV **u**
4 rm 18.00/38.00 **s.**

Georgian without rest., 179 Cathedral Rd, CF1 9PL, ℘ 232594, Fax 232594 – . AV **a**
8 rm 25.00/40.00 **st.**

XXXX **De Courcey's,** Tyla Morris Av., Pentyrch, CF4 8QN, NW : 6 m. by A 4119 on Pentyrch rd ℘ 892232, Fax 891949 – .
closed Sunday dinner, Monday and 24 to 30 December – **Meals** (dinner only and Sunday lunch) 18.50 **t.** and a la carte 5.00.

XX Indian Ocean, 290 North Rd, Gabalfa, CF4 3BN, ℘ 621349 – AV **r**
Meals -Indian rest.

X **Le Cassoulet,** 5 Romilly Cres., Canton, CF1 9NP, ℘ 221905, Fax 221905. AX **c**
closed Saturday lunch, Sunday, Monday, August and 2 weeks Christmas – **Meals** - French - 20.00/26.00 **t.** and a la carte 4.75.

X **Quayle's,** 6-8 Romilly Cres., Canton, CF1 9NR, ℘ 341264 – AX **a**
closed Sunday dinner, Tuesday, 26 December, 1 January and Bank Holidays – **Meals** - Bistro - 11.95 **t.** and a la carte 16.40/23.35 **t.** 4.75.

X **Blas-ar-Gymru (A Taste of Wales),** 48 Crwys Rd, CF2 4NN, ℘ 382132, Fax 565062 – . AV **z**
closed Saturday lunch, Sunday, lunch 2 weeks January and Bank Holiday Mondays – **Meals** 18.95 **t.** and lunch a la carte 4.50.

X **Thai House,** 23 High St., CF1 2BZ, ℘ 387404, Fax 640810 – BZ **o**
closed Sunday – **Meals** - Thai - 10.00 **t.** (dinner) and a la carte 12.20/26.75.

X **Armless Dragon,** 97 Wyeverne Rd, Cathays, CF2 4BG, ℘ 382357 –
closed Saturday lunch, Sunday, Monday, 25-26 December and 1 January – **Meals** 9.90 **t.** (lunch) and a la carte 14.70/17.70 **t.** 3.95. BY **n**

at Thornhill N : 5 ¼ m. by A 470 on A 469 – AV – ✉ Cardiff – ☎ 01222 :

New House Country 🐑, Caerphilly Rd, CF4 5UA, on A 469 ☎ 520280, Fax 520324, ≤ , park – TV ☎ P – 🏛 220. AE VISA. ✻
Meals 11.95/14.95 **t.** and a la carte 🍷 4.95 – ☕ 5.95 – **20 rm** ☕ 58.00/80.00 **st.** – SB.

Manor Parc, Thornhill Rd, CF4 5UA, on A 469 ☎ 693723, Fax 614624, , ✂ – TV ☎ P AE VISA. ✻
closed 24 to 26 December – **Meals** *(closed Sunday dinner)* 14.95/25.00 **t.** and a la carte 🍷 7.00 – **12 rm** ☕ 67.50/110.00 **st.** – SB.

at Castleton (Cas-Bach) (Gwent) NE : 7 m. on A 48 – AV – ✉ Cardiff – ☎ 01633 :

Travel Inn, Newport Rd, CF3 8UQ, ☎ 680070, Fax 681143 – ✕ rm TV ♿ P. AE VISA. ✻
Meals (grill rest.) – ☕ 4.95 – **47 rm** 34.50 **t.**

ATS Hadfield Rd ☎ 228251/226336

CARDIFF WEST SERVICE AREA S. Glam. – ✉ Pontycwn – ☎ 01222.
Central Station, CF1 1QY ☎ 227281.

Pavilion Lodge without rest., CF7 8SA, M 4 junction 33 ☎ 892255, Fax 892497 – ✕ TV ♿ P – 🏛 30. AE VISA JCB
50 rm 39.95 **t.**

CARDIGAN (Aberteifi) Dyfed 403 G 27 – pop. 4 409 – ☎ 01239.
Gwbert-on-Sea ☎ 612035.
Theatr Mwldan, Bath House Rd, SA43 2JY ☎ 613230.
♦London 250 – Carmarthen 30 – Fishguard 19.

Penbontbren Farm 🐑, Glynarthen, SA44 6PE, NE : 9 ½ m. by A 487 ☎ 810248 Fax 811129, park – TV ☎ ♿ P – 🏛 30. AE VISA JCB. ✻
closed 23 to 28 December – **Meals** (dinner only) a la carte 15.00 **st.** 🍷 4.20 – **10 rm** ☕ 35.00/68.00 **st.** – SB.

at Cilgerran S : 3 m. by A 478 and Cilgerran rd – ✉ Cardigan – ☎ 01239 :

Allt-y-Rheini Mansion 🐑, SA43 2TJ, S : ½ m. on Crymmych rd ☎ 612286, ≤, – TV P. VISA. ✻
Meals a la carte 12.85/15.85 **t.** 🍷 3.75 – **5 rm** ☕ 31.00/54.00 **t.**

at St. Dogmaels W : 1 m. by A 487 on B 4568 – ✉ Cardigan – ☎ 01239 :

Berwyn 🐑 without rest., Cardigan Rd, SA43 3HS, ☎ 613555, ≤, – TV P. ✻
3 rm ☕ 20.00/38.00 **st.**

at Gwbert on Sea NW : 3 m. on B 4548 – ✉ Cardigan – ☎ 01239 :

Gwbert, SA43 1PP, on B 4548 ☎ 612638, Fax 621474, ≤ Cardigan Bay – TV ☎ P. VISA. ✻
Meals (bar lunch Monday to Saturday)/dinner 14.50 **t.** (dinner) and a la carte 🍷 5.50 – **16 rm** ☕ 34.50/113.00 **t.** – SB.

ATS 4 Bath House Rd ☎ 612917

CASTLETON (Cas-Bach) Gwent 403 K 29 – see Cardiff (South Glam.).

CEMAES Gwynedd 402 403 G 23 **Great Britain G.** – ☎ 01407.
Envir. : Isle of Anglesey★★.
♦London 272 – Bangor 25 – Caernarfon 32 – Holyhead 16.

Hafod Country House, LL67 ODS, S : ½ m. on Llanfechell rd ☎ 710500, ≤, – ✕ TV P. ✻
March-October – **Meals** (by arrangement) 12.00 **st.** – **3 rm** ☕ 30.00/39.00 **st.** – SB.

CHANCERY (Rhydgaled) Dyfed 403 H 26 – see Aberystwyth.

CHEPSTOW Gwent 403 404 M 29 **Great Britain G.** – pop. 9 461 – ☎ 01291.
See : Castle★ *AC.*
Envir. : Wye Valley★ (Eagle's Nest Viewpoint, Windcliff★).
18, 18 St. Pierre, St. Pierre Park ☎ 625261.
Castle Car Park, Bridge St., NP6 5EY ☎ 623772 (summer only).
♦London 131 – ♦Bristol 17 – ♦Cardiff 28 – Gloucester 34.

St. Pierre H. Country Club Resort (Country Club), NP6 6YA, SW : 3 ½ m. on A 48 ☎ 625261, Fax 629975, Lб, ≘s, ⛆, 18, park, ✂, squash – ✕ TV ☎ P – 🏛 220. AE VISA JCB. ✻
Meals 15.00/21.00 **st.** and a la carte – ☕ 9.00 – **134 rm** 109.00 **st.**, 9 suites – SB.

George (Forte), Moor St., NP6 5DB, ☎ 625363, Fax 627418 – ✕ TV ☎ P – 🏛 30. AE VISA JCB
Meals (buffet lunch Monday to Saturday)/dinner 15.95 **st.** and a la carte 🍷 6.95 – ☕ 8.50 – **14 rm** 67.50/92.50 **st.** – SB.

Beaufort, Beaufort Sq., NP6 5EP, ✆ 622497, Fax 627389 – TV ☎ P – 30. AE VISA.
Meals 10.95/18.50 **t.** and a la carte 3.50 – 4.95 – **18 rm** 36.00/47.00 **st.** – SB.

Castle View, 16 Bridge St., NP6 5EZ, ✆ 620349, Fax 627397, – rest TV ☎. AE VISA
closed January – **Meals** *(Sunday dinner residents only)* (bar lunch Monday to Saturday)/ dinner 18.95 **st.** and a la carte – 5.45 – **13 rm** 35.00/56.50 **t.** – SB.

CILGERRAN Dyfed 403 G 27 – see Cardigan.

COLWYN BAY (Bae Colwyn) Clwyd 402 403 I 24 Great Britain G. – pop. 9 471 – 01492.
Envir. : Bodnant Garden★★ *AC*, SW : 6 m. by A 55 and A 470.
Abergele and Pensarn, Tan-y-Goppa Rd, Abergele ✆ (01745) 824034 – Old Colwyn, Woodland Av. ✆ 515581.
40 Station Rd, LL29 8BU LL28 8LD ✆ 530478 – The Promenade, Rhos-on-sea, LL28 4EP ✆ 548778 (summer only).
London 237 – Birkenhead 50 – Chester 42 – Holyhead 41.

Norfolk House, 39 Princes Drive, LL29 8PF, ✆ 531757, Fax 533781, – TV ☎ P – 35. AE VISA JCB
closed 24 December-9 January – **Meals** (bar lunch)/dinner 17.75 **t.** and a la carte 4.60 – **23 rm** 39.50/56.00 **t.** – SB.

Hopeside, 63-67 Princes Drive, West End, LL29 8PW, ✆ 533244, Fax 532850 – rm TV ☎ P – 50. AE VISA
Meals 10.00/20.00 **t.** and a la carte 3.50 – **17 rm** 35.00/50.00 **t.**

Café Niçoise, 124 Abergele Rd, LL29 7PS, ✆ 531555 – AE VISA JCB
closed lunch Monday-Tuesday, Sunday, 1 week January and 1 week June – **Meals** 13.95 **t.** and a la carte 4.95.

at Rhos-on-Sea (Llandrillo-yn-Rhos) NW : 1 m. – ✉ Colwyn Bay – 01492 :

Ashmount, College Av., LL28 4NT, ✆ 544582, Fax 545479 – TV ☎ P. AE VISA JCB
Meals (bar lunch)/dinner 16.45 **st.** and a la carte 3.95 – **17 rm** 35.50/61.00 **st.** – SB.

Great Britain and Ireland are covered entirely
at a scale of 16 miles to 1 inch by our «Main roads» map 986.

CONWY Gwynedd 402 403 I 24 Great Britain G. – pop. 3 627 – 01492.
See : Town★ – Castle★★ *AC* – Town Walls★★ – Plas Mawr★★ *AC*.
Envir. : Sychnant Pass (<★★) – Bodnant Garden★★ *AC*, S : 6 m. by A 55 and A 470.
Morfa ✆ 593400 – Penmaenmawr, Conway Old Rd ✆ 623330.
Conwy Castle Visitor Centre, LL32 8LD ✆ 592248.
London 241 – Caernarfon 22 – Chester 46 – Holyhead 37.

Castle (Forte), High St., LL32 8DB, ✆ 592324, Fax 583351 – TV ☎ P – 30
29 rm.

Berthlwyd Hall, Llechwedd, LL32 8DQ, SW : 2¼ m. by B 5106 and Sychnant rd, off Hendre rd ✆ 592409, Fax 572290, <, heated, – TV ☎ P. AE VISA.
Meals 14.50/19.50 **st.** and a la carte – 4.00 – **9 rm** 49.00/77.00 **st.** – SB.

at Roewen S : 3 m. by B 5106 – ✉ Conwy – 01492 :

Tir-y-Coed Country House, LL32 8TP, ✆ 650219, <, – rest TV P. AE.
March-October – **Meals** 11.50 **t.** 4.75 – **7 rm** 27.50/50.50 **t.** – SB.

at Tal-y-Bont S : 5¾ m. on B 5106 – ✉ Conwy – 01492 :

Lodge, LL32 8YX, ✆ 660766, Fax 660534 – rm TV ☎ P – 30. AE VISA
closed January – **Meals** *(closed Monday lunch except Bank Holidays and Tuesday lunch following Bank Holidays)* (booking essential Sunday and Monday in winter) 8.25/ 20.00 **st.** and dinner a la carte 4.95 – **10 rm** 39.50/60.00 **st.** – SB.

COWBRIDGE S. Glam. 403 J 29 – pop. 6 167 – 01656.
London 167 – Cardiff 12 – Swansea 30.

Stembridge Farmhouse without rest., Llandow, CF7 7NT, SW : 3½ m. ✆ 890389, <, – TV P.
closed December-January – **3 rm** 25.00/60.00 **st.**

COYCHURCH (Llangrallo) M. Glam. 403 J 29 – see Bridgend.

CRICCIETH Gwynedd 402 403 H 25 – pop. 1 720 – 01766.
Ednyfed Hill ✆ 522154.
London 249 – Caernarfon 17 – Shrewsbury 85.

Mynydd Ednyfed Country House, Caernarfon Rd, LL52 0PH, NW : ¾ m. on B 4411 ✆ 523269, <, , – TV ☎ P. AE VISA
closed 24 to 30 December – **Meals** (dinner only) 15.00 **t.** and a la carte 4.00 – **9 rm** 34.00/59.50 **t.** – SB.

CRICKHOWELL Powys 403 K 28 – pop. 2 166 – ☎ 01873.

♦London 169 – Abergavenny 6 – Brecon 14 – Newport 25.

- **Gliffaes Country House** ⛰, NP8 1RH, W : 3 ¾ m. by A 40 ☎ (01874) 73037 Fax 730463, ≤, « Country house and gardens on the banks of the River Usk », 🎣, pa 🎾 – TV ☎ P. AE VISA JCB. ✻
  closed 5 January-24 February – **Meals** (bar lunch Monday to Saturday)/dinner 19.95 and a la carte – **22 rm** 35.00/104.00 **st.** – SB.
- **Bear,** High St., NP8 1BW, ☎ 810408, Fax 811696 – TV ☎ P. AE VISA JCB
  Meals (bar meal Sunday dinner)/a la carte 15.00/22.50 **t.** 3.95 – **28 rm** 42.00/70.00 **t.**

at Llangenny E : 3 m. by A 40 via Glangrwyney – ✉ Crickhowell – ☎ 01873 :

- **Gellirhydd Farm** ⛰, NP8 1HF, N : 1 ½ m. taking unmarked road before brid ☎ 810466, ≤, 🎣, park – P. VISA. ✻
  closed 23 December-2 January – **Meals** (by arrangement) (communal dining) 10.00 – **3** 18.00/40.00 – SB.

at Llangattock SW : 1 ¼ m. by A 4077 and Llangynidr rd – ✉ Crickhowell – ☎ 01873

- **Ty Croeso** ⛰, The Dardy, NP8 1PU, ☎ 810573, Fax 810573, ≤, – TV ☎ P. AE V JCB
  closed 2 weeks January – **Meals** (dinner only and Sunday lunch) (bar lunch Ma September) 14.95 **t.** and a la carte 3.50 – **8 rm** 30.00/65.00 **t.** – SB.

CROSSGATES Powys 403 J 27 – see Llandrindod Wells.

CROSS HANDS Dyfed 403 H 28 – pop. 9 520 – ☎ 01269.

♦London 208 – Fishguard 63 – ♦Swansea 19.

- **Forte Travelodge,** SA14 6NW, on A 48 ☎ 845700, Reservations (Freephone) 08 850950 – TV & P. AE VISA. ✻
  Meals (grill rest.) – **32 rm** 34.50 **t.**

CRUG-Y-BAR Dyfed 403 I 27 – ✉ Llanwrda – ☎ 01558.

♦London 213 – Carmarthen 26 – ♦Swansea 36.

- **Glanrannell Park** ⛰, SA19 8SA, SW : ½ m. by B 4302 ☎ 685230, Fax 685784, ≤, 🎣, park – rest P. VISA JCB
  April-October – **Meals** *(closed Sunday lunch to non- residents)* (light lunch)/dinner 20.00 3.50 – **8 rm** 36.00/62.00 **t.** – SB.

CRYMMYCH Dyfed 403 G 28 – ✉ Whitland – ☎ 01994.

♦London 245 – Carmarthen 25 – Fishguard 19.

- Preseli Country House ⛰, SA34 0YP, S : 4 m. by A 478, on lane opposite disused quar ☎ 419425, Fax 419425, ≤, park – TV P
  7 rm.

CWMBRAN Gwent 403 K 29 – pop. 46 021 – ☎ 01633.

♦London 149 – ♦Bristol 35 – ♦Cardiff 17 – Newport 5.

- **Parkway,** Cwmbran Drive, NP44 3UW, S : 1 m. by A 4051 ☎ 871199, Telex 49788 Fax 869160, – rm TV ☎ & P – 500. AE VISA
  closed 24 December-2 January – **Meals** *(closed Saturday lunch and lunch July August)* 12.95 **t.** and dinner a la carte – 8.95 – **69 rm** 73.00/82.50 **t.**, 1 suite – SB.

ATS Station Rd ☎ 484964

CWMYSTWYTH Dyfed 403 I 26 – ✉ Aberystwyth – ☎ 01974.

♦London 231 – Aberystwyth 15 – Shrewsbury 73.

- Hafod Lodge ⛰ without rest., SY23 4AD, ☎ 282247, ≤, – P
  3 rm.

CYNGHORDY Dyfed 403 I 27 – ✉ Llandovery – ☎ 015505.

♦London 210 – Carmarthen 31 – ♦Swansea 41.

- **Llanerchindda Farm** ⛰, SA20 0NB, N : 2 ½ m. by Station rd and under viadu ☎ 750274, Fax 750300, ≤, « Working farm », – rest TV P
  Meals (residents only) 9.00 **st.** 2.75 – **7 rm** 21.00/42.00 **st.**

DEGANWY Gwynedd 402 403 I 24 – see Llandudno.

DOLGELLAU Gwynedd 402 403 I 25 – pop. 2 621 – ☎ 01341.

Pencefn Rd ☎ 422603.

Ty Meirion, Eldon Sq., LL40 1PU ☎ 422888.

♦London 221 – Birkenhead 72 – Chester 64 – Shrewsbury 57.

Penmaenuchaf Hall, Penmaenpool, LL40 1YB, W : 1 ¾ m. on A 493 422129, Fax 422129, ≤, « Country house atmosphere », park – rest TV P – 50. AE VISA JCB.
Meals 13.95/23.00 **t.** and a la carte 6.10 – **14 rm** 50.00/150.00 **t.** – SB.

Dolserau Hall, LL40 2AG, NE : 2 ¾ m. by A 494 422522, Fax 422400, ≤, – rest TV P. VISA
Meals (dinner only) 18.50 **t.** – **14 rm** (dinner included) 57.00/108.00 **t.** – SB.

George III, Penmaenpool, LL40 1YD, W : 2 m. by A 493 422525, Fax 423565, ≤ Mawddach estuary and mountains, – rest TV P. VISA JCB.
Meals 11.95 **t.** (lunch) and dinner a la carte 16.65/24.80 **t.** 4.40 – **12 rm** 37.50/88.00 **t.** – SB.

at Ganllwyd N : 5½ m. on A 470 – Dolgellau – 01341 :

Dolmelynllyn Hall, LL40 2HP, 440273, Fax 440273, ≤, park – TV P. AE VISA.
March-November – **Meals** (light lunch by arrangement)/dinner 22.50 **st.** 6.75 – **10 rm** 47.50/110.00 **st.** – SB.

at Llanfachreth NE : 3 ¾ m. – Dolgellau – 01341 :

Ty Isaf Farmhouse, LL40 2EA, 423261, ≤, « 17C longhouse », – P
Meals (communal dining) 12.00 **st.** – **3 rm** 24.00/48.00 **st.**

at Arthog SW : 7 m. on A 493 – Dolgellau – 01341 :

Cyfannedd Uchaf, LL39 1LX, S : 4½ m. by A 493 Cregennan Lakes rd, taking right turn at T. junction at end of road (gated roads) 250526, ≤ Barmouth, Mawddach estuary and mountains, park – P.
April-September – **Meals** 5.50 **st.** – **3 rm** 16.00/34.00 **st.**

at Bontddu W : 5 m. on A 496 (Barmouth Rd) – Dolgellau – 01341 :

Bontddu Hall Country House, LL40 2UF, 430661, Fax 430284, ≤ Mawddach estuary and mountains, « Victorian mansion in extensive gardens », park – rest TV P. AE VISA JCB
April-October – **Garden : Meals** 12.75/23.50 **t.** and a la carte – **17 rm** 52.50/90.00 **t.**, 3 suites – SB.

Borthwnog Hall, LL40 2TT, E : 1 m. on A 496 430271, Fax 430682, ≤ Mawddach estuary and mountains, « Part Regency house, art gallery », park – rest TV P. VISA.
closed 24 to 26 December – **Meals** (booking essential) (dinner only) 16.25 **t.** and a la carte 4.75 – **3 rm** 60.00/96.00 **t.** – SB.

DRENEWYDD YN NOTAIS **(Nottage)** M. Glam. – see Porthcawl.

DYFFRYN ARDUDWY Gwynedd 402 403 H 25 – pop. 1 452 (inc. Tal-y-bont) – 01341.
London 237 – Dolgellau 16 – Caernarfon 44.

Ael-Y-Bryn, LL44 2BE, on A 496 242701, Fax 242682, ≤, – TV P. VISA
Meals 12.40 **st.** (dinner) and a la carte approx. 12.40 **st.** 3.95 – **10 rm** 25.00/50.00 **st.** – SB.

Ystumgwern Hall Farm without rest., LL44 2DD, NW : 1 m. by A 496 247249, Fax 247171, « Working farm », park – TV P.
5 suites 20.00/40.00.

EGLWYSFACH Dyfed 403 I 26 – see Machynlleth (Powys).

EWLOE Clwyd pop. 3 263 – 01244.
Autolodge Site, Gateway Services, A 55 Expressway westbound, Northophall, CH7 6HE 541597.
London 200 – Chester 8.5 – Shrewsbury 48.

St David's Park, St. David's Park, CH5 3YB, on B 5125 at junction with A 494 520800, Fax 520930, – rm rest TV P – 270. AE VISA JCB
Fountains : Meals 11.95/17.50 **t.** 6.50 and a la carte – 8.95 – **121 rm** 85.00/95.00 **st.** – SB.

ATS Holywell Rd (Nr. Queensferry) 520380

FISHGUARD **(Abergwaun)** Dyfed 403 F 28 – pop. 5 061 (inc. Goodwick) – 01348.
to Republic of Ireland (Rosslare) (Stena Line) 2 daily (3 h 30 mn).
4 Hamilton St., SA65 9HL 873484.
London 265 – Cardiff 114 – Gloucester 176 – Holyhead 169 – Shrewsbury 136 – Swansea 76.

Manor House, 11 Main St., SA65 9HG, 873260, – TV. VISA
closed 23 to 28 December – **Meals** (dinner only) 18.00 **st.** 5.50 – **6 rm** 24.00/48.00 **st.**

Plas Glyn-Y-Mel without rest., Lower Town, SA65 9LY, 872296, ≤, park – TV P
5 rm 37.00/70.00 **t.**

XX **Three Main Street** with rm., Main St., SA65 9HG, ℘ 874275 – ⋟. ⋟
closed February – **Meals** *(closed Monday in winter and Sunday)* (light lunch)/dinner a la carte 15.75/21.45 **t.** – **3 rm** ⊒ 30.00/50.00 **t.** – SB.

at Pontfaen SE : 5½ m. by B 4313 – ✆ 01239 :

Tregynon Country Farmhouse ⋟, Gwaun Valley, SA65 9TU, E : 6¼ m. ℘ 820531 Fax 820808, ⋟, park – ⋟ TV ☎ P – 🔺 25. ⋟ VISA JCB. ⋟
Meals (booking essential) (dinner only) 15.50 **t.** – **8 rm** ⊒ 46.00/67.00 **t.** – SB.

at Letterston S : 5 m. by A 40 – ✆ 01348 :

Heathfield Mansion ⋟, SA62 5EG, NW : 1½ m. by B 4331 ℘ 840263 – ⋟ P
April-October – **Meals** (by arrangement) 8.00 **st.** ⋟ 3.00 – **4 rm** ⊒ 25.00/36.00 **st.** – SB.

at Welsh Hook SW : 7½ m. by A 40 – ✉ Haverfordwest – ✆ 01348 :

XX **Stone Hall** ⋟ with rm, SA62 5NS, ℘ 840212, Fax 840815, « Part 14C manor house with 17C extension », ⋟ – TV P. ⋟ AE ⋟ VISA. ⋟
closed 2 weeks January-February – **Meals** (dinner only) 17.00 **t.** and a la carte ⋟ 5.25 – **5 rm** ⊒ 46.00/65.00 **t.** – SB.

at Goodwick (Wdig) NW : 1½ m. – ✉ Fishguard – ✆ 01348 :

Ivybridge, Drim Mill, Dyffryn, SA64 0FT, E : ¾ m. by A 487 ℘ 872623, Fax 875366, park TV P. ⋟ VISA JCB
closed Christmas – **Meals** 12.95 **st.** ⋟ 4.75 – **6 rm** ⊒ 21.50/43.00 **st.** – SB.

ATS Scleddau ℘ 873522

FLINT **(Fflint)** Clwyd 402 403 K 24 pop. 12 564 – ✆ 01352.
♦London 226 – Chester 12 – Shrewsbury 58.

Green's Lodge, Northop Rd, Flint Mountain, CH6 5QG, S : 1½ m. on A 5119 ℘ 763127 Fax 763126, ⋟9 – TV ☎ P
21 rm.

ATS 31 Chester Rd ℘ 733401/734368

FRON-GOCH Gwynedd 402 403 J 25 – see Bala.

GANLLWYD Gwynedd 402 403 I 25 – see Dolgellau.

GLYN CEIRIOG Clwyd 402 403 K 25 – ✉ Llangollen – ✆ 0169 172.
♦London 194 – Shrewsbury 30 – Wrexham 17.

Golden Pheasant ⋟, Llwynmawr, LL20 7BB, SE : 1¾ m. by B 4500 ℘ 718281, Fax 718479, ≤, ⋟ – TV ☎ P. ⋟ AE ⋟ VISA
Meals 10.95/17.95 **st.** ⋟ 6.95 – **18 rm** ⊒ (dinner included) 45.00/110.00 **st.** – SB.

GOODWICK (Wdig) Dyfed 403 F 27 – see Fishguard.

GOVILON Gwent – see Abergavenny.

GUILSFIELD Powys 402 403 K 26 – see Welshpool.

GWBERT ON SEA Dyfed 403 F 27 – see Cardigan.

HANMER Clwyd 402 403 L 25 – pop. 565 – ✉ Whitchurch – ✆ 01948.
♦London 237 – Chester 26 – Shrewsbury 27 – ♦Stoke-on-Trent 28.

Hanmer Arms, SY13 3DE, ℘ 830532, Fax 830740, ⋟ – TV ☎ P – 🔺 40. ⋟ AE ⋟ VISA ⋟
Meals a la carte 8.10/17.50 **st.** ⋟ 4.30 – **18 rm** ⊒ 38.00/52.00 **st.**, 6 suites – SB.

HARLECH Gwynedd 402 403 H 25 **Great Britain G.** – pop. 1 880 – ✆ 01766.
See : Castle** *AC*.
⋟18 Royal St. David's ℘ 780203.
Gwyddfor House, High St., LL46 2YA ℘ 780658 (summer only).
♦London 241 – Chester 72 – Dolgellau 21.

Gwrach Ynys, LL47 6TS, N : 2¼ m. on A 496 ℘ 780742, Fax 781199, ⋟ – ⋟ rest TV ☎ P
closed Christmas and 1 January – **Meals** (by arrangement) 10.00 **st.** – **7 rm** ⊒ 20.00/40.00 **st.**

XX **Castle Cottage** with rm, Pen Llech, LL46 2YL, off B 4573 ℘ 780479 – ⋟ rest. ⋟ AE VISA. ⋟
closed 3 weeks February – **Meals** (booking essential) (dinner only and Sunday lunch)/dinner 18.50 **t.** ⋟ 4.95 – **6 rm** ⊒ 24.00/52.00 **t.** – SB.

HAVERFORDWEST **(Hwlffordd)** Dyfed 403 F 28 – pop. 11 099 – ✆ 01437.
⋟18 Arnolds Down ℘ 763565.
2 Old Bridge, SA61 2EZ ℘ 763110.
♦London 250 – Fishguard 15 – ♦Swansea 57.

Mariners, Mariners Sq., SA61 2DU, ✆ 763353, Fax 764258 – TV ☎ P – 35. AE VISA.
closed 25 to 27 December, 1 and 2 January – **Meals** (bar lunch)/dinner 12.00 **t.** and a la carte 5.00 – **30 rm** 46.50/70.00 **t.** – SB.

Wilton House, 6 Quay St., SA61 1BG, ✆ 760033, Fax 760297 – TV. AE VISA.
Meals (by arrangement) approx. 11.50 **st.** 3.25 – **8 rm** 29.00/47.00 **st.** – SB.

ATS Back Lane, Prendergast ✆ 763756/7

HAWARDEN (Penarlâg) Clwyd 402 403 K 24 pop. 11 812 – 01244.

London 218 – Chester 8 – Shrewsbury 50.

Swiss Restaurant Imfeld, 68 The Highway, CH5 3DH, ✆ 534523 – VISA
closed Monday – **Meals** (dinner only) 21.00 **t.** and a la carte 5.50.

ATS Holywell Rd, Ewloe, Deeside ✆ 520380

HAY-ON-WYE Powys 403 K 27 – pop. 1 407 – 01497.

Rhosgoch, Builth Wells ✆ 851251.

London 154 – Brecon 16 – Hereford 21 – Newport 62.

Swan, Church St., HR3 5DQ, ✆ 821188, Fax 821424, – rest TV ☎ P – 160. AE VISA JCB
Meals (bar lunch Monday to Saturday)/dinner 22.50 **t.** and a la carte 4.95 – **18 rm** 50.00/80.00 **st.** – SB.

Old Black Lion, Lion St., HR3 5AD, ✆ 820841, « Part 13C and 17C inn » – rest TV ☎ P. AE VISA.
Meals a la carte 16.45/20.70 **st.** 5.25 – **10 rm** 20.95/46.00 **st.** – SB.

York House, Hardwick Rd, Cusop, HR3 5QX, E : ½ m. on B 4348 ✆ 820705, – TV P. AE VISA
Meals (by arrangememt) 12.00 **st.** – **5 rm** 26.50/44.00 **st.**

at Llanigon SW : 2½ m. by B 4350 – ✉ Hay-on-Wye – 01497 :

Old Post Office without rest., HR3 5QA, ✆ 820008, « 17C house » – P
closed January – **3 rm** 20.00/40.00.

HOLYHEAD (Caergybi) Gwynedd 402 403 G 24 – pop. 11 796 – 01407.

to Republic of Ireland (Dun Laoghaire) (Stena Line) 2-4 daily (3 h 30 mn) – to Republic of Ireland (Dublin) (B & I Line) 2 daily (3 h 30 mn).

London 269 – Birkenhead 94 – Cardiff 215 – Chester 88 – Shrewsbury 105 – Swansea 190.

***Hotel see : Rhoscolyn** S : 5½ m.*

HOLYWELL (Treffynnon) Clwyd 402 403 K 24 – pop. 6 084 – 01745.

Holywell, Brynford ✆ 710040.

London 217 – Chester 19 – Liverpool 34.

Kinsale Hall, Llanerchymor, CH8 9DX, N : 3½ m. by B 5121 off A 548 ✆ 560001, Fax 561298, 18, park – rest TV ☎ P – 350. AE VISA.
Meals 14.00/18.00 **t.** and a la carte 5.50 – **27 rm** 70.00/90.00 **st.**, 2 suites.

Stamford Gate, Halkyn Rd, CH8 7SJ, ✆ (01352) 712942, Fax 713309 – TV ☎ P. VISA.
Meals (dancing Friday and Saturday) 9.50/14.75 **st.** and a la carte 4.00 – **12 rm** 38.00/45.00 **st.**

Forte Travelodge, Halkyn, CH8 8RF, SE : 3½ m. on A 55 (westbound carriageway) ✆ (01352) 780952, Reservations (Freephone) 0800 850950 – TV P. AE VISA.
Meals (grill rest.) – **31 rm** 34.50 **t.**

HOWEY Powys – see Llandrindod Wells.

KNIGHTON (Trefyclawdd) Powys 403 K 26 – pop. 2 851 – 01547.

Little Ffrydd Wood ✆ 528646.

The Offa's Dyke Centre, West St., LD7 1EW ✆ 528753.

London 162 – Birmingham 59 – Hereford 31 – Shrewsbury 35.

Milebrook House, Ludlow Rd, Milebrook, LD7 1LT, E : 2 m. on A 4113 ✆ 528632, Fax 520509, – rest TV P. AE VISA JCB.
Meals *(closed Monday lunch)* 10.75/19.50 **t.** and dinner a la carte 5.60 – **6 rm** 44.80/64.00 **t.** – SB.

LAKE VYRNWY Powys 402 403 J 25 – ✉ Llanwddyn – 01691.

Unit 2, Vyrnwy Craft Workshops, SY10 0LY ✆ 870346.

London 204 – Chester 52 – Llanfyllin 10 – Shrewsbury 40.

Lake Vyrnwy, SY10 0LY, ✆ 870692, Fax 870259, Lake Vyrnwy, « Victorian sporting estate », park, – TV ☎ P – 80. AE VISA JCB
Meals (lunch booking essential) 12.95/22.50 **st.** – **34 rm** 60.50/127.50 **t.**, 1 suite – SB.

LALESTON M. Glam. 403 J 29 – see Bridgend.

LAMPHEY Dyfed – see Pembroke.

LANGSTONE Gwent 403 L 29 – see Newport.

LAUGHARNE Dyfed 403 G 28 – pop. 1 272 – 01994.

♦London 233 – Carmarthen 13 – Fishguard 41.

Halldown without rest., SA33 4QS, N : 1½ m. on A 4066 ℘ 427452, – P
closed 25 and 26 December – **5 rm** 17.00/30.00 **st.**

LETTERSTON Dyfed 403 F 28 – see Fishguard.

LLANABER Gwynedd 402 403 H 25 – see Barmouth.

LLANARMON DYFFRYN CEIRIOG Clwyd 402 403 K 25 – – ✉ Llangollen – 0169 176.

♦London 196 – Chester 33 – Shrewsbury 32.

West Arms, LL20 7LD, ℘ 600665, Fax 600622, , – P – 30. AE VISA JCB
closed January – **Meals** (bar lunch Monday to Saturday)/dinner 23.50 **st.** and a la cart 5.45 – **11 rm** (dinner included) 75.00/140.00 **t.**, 1 suite – SB.

LLANBEDR Gwynedd 402 403 H 25 – pop. 1 101 – 01341.

♦London 262 – Holyhead 54 – Shrewsbury 100.

Pensarn Hall , LL45 2HS, N : ¾ m. on A 496 ℘ 241236, , – rest TV P. VISA
closed Christmas and New Year – **Meals** (dinner only) 11.50 **st.** 3.00 – **7 rm** 26.50 46.00 **st.** – SB.

Victoria Inn, LL45 2LD, ℘ 241213, – rest TV P. VISA
Meals 6.50/14.50 **st.** and dinner a la carte 3.95 – **5 rm** 26.00/48.50 **st.**

LLANBERIS Gwynedd 403 H 24 **Great Britain G.** – pop. 1 986 – 01286.

Envir. : Snowdon★★★ (✻★★★ from summit) SE : by Snowdon Mountain Railway or by marked footpaths.

41 High St., LL55 ℘ 870765 (summer only).

♦London 243 – Caernarfon 7 – Chester 65 – Shrewsbury 78.

Y Bistro, 43-45 High St., LL55 4EU, ℘ 871278 – . VISA JCB
closed Sunday except at Bank Holidays and Mondays in winter – **Meals** (booking essential) (dinner only) 25.00 **t.** 4.50.

LLANDEGLA Clwyd 402 403 K 24 – see Wrexham.

LLANDEGLEY Powys – see Llandrindod Wells.

LLANDEILO Dyfed 403 I 28 – pop. 850 – 01558.

18 Glynhir, Glynhir Rd, Llandybie, Ammanford ℘ (01269) 850472.

♦London 218 – Brecon 34 – Carmarthen 15 – ♦Swansea 25.

Plough Inn with rm, Rhosmaen, SA19 6NP, N : 1 m. on A 40 ℘ 823431, Fax 823969, – TV – P – 45. AE VISA JCB.
closed 25 December – **Meals** *(closed Sunday dinner to non-residents)* a la carte 14.75 22.00 **st.** 5.00 – 4.50 – **12 rm** 45.00/65.00 **st.**

ATS Towy Terr., Ffairfach ℘ 822567

LLANDRILLO Clwyd 402 403 J 25 – pop. 1 048 – ✉ Corwen – 01490.

♦London 210 – Chester 40 – Dolgellau 26 – Shrewsbury 46.

Tyddyn Llan Country House , LL21 0ST, ℘ 440264, Fax 440414, « Part Georgian country house », , – rest P. AE VISA JCB
Meals 10.75/25.00 8.00 – **10 rm** 56.50/97.00 **t.** – SB.

LLANDRINDOD WELLS Powys 403 J 27 **Great Britain G.** – pop. 4 943 – 01597.

Exc. : Elan Valley★★, NW : 12 m. by A 4081, A 470 and B 4518.

18 Llandrindod Wells ℘ 822010/823873.

Old Town Hall, Memorial Gardens, LD1 5DL ℘ 822600.

♦London 204 – Brecon 29 – Carmarthen 60 – Shrewsbury 58.

Metropole, Temple St., LD1 5DY, ℘ 823700, Fax 824828, , , – TV P – 250. AE VISA
Meals 9.75/16.95 **t.** 4.75 – **120 rm** 61.00/81.00 **t.**, 2 suites – SB.

Charis without rest., Pentrosfa, LD1 5AL, S : ¾ m. by A 470 ℘ 824732 – TV P
closed 23 December-2 January – **4 rm** 18.00/32.00.

Dillraj, Emporium Building, Temple St., LD1 5DL, ℘ 823843 – AE VISA JCB
Meals - Indian - 5.25/9.95 **t.** and a la carte.

at Crossgates NE : 3 ½ m. at junction of A 483 with A 54 – ✉ Llandrindod Wells ☎ 01597 :

Guidfa House, LD1 6RF, ☎ 851241, Fax 851875, ⚘ – ⟡ TV Ⓟ. VISA. ✽
Meals 12.50 **st.** 3.50 – **7 rm** ☕ 21.00/44.00 **st.** – SB.

at Llandegley E : 7 m. by A 483 on A 44 – ✉ Llandrindod Wells – ☎ 01597 :

Ffaldau Country House, LD1 5UD, ☎ 851421, ⚘ – ⟡ Ⓟ. VISA. ✽
Meals (booking essential) (residents only) (dinner only) 16.50 5.00 – **4 rm** ☕ 28.00/45.00.

at Howey S : 1 ½ m. by A 483 – ✉ Llandrindod Wells – ☎ 01597 :

Three Wells Farm ⛰, LD1 5PB, NE : ½ m. ☎ 824427, Fax 822484, ≤, « Working farm », ⚘, – ⟡ rest TV ☎ Ⓟ
closed Christmas – **Meals** 10.50 **t.** 3.00 – **10 rm** ☕ 18.00/38.00 **t.**, 4 suites – SB.

Corven Hall ⛰, LD1 5RE, S : ½ m. by A 483 on Hundred House rd ☎ 823368, ⚘ – ⟡ rest TV Ⓟ. ✽
February-October – **Meals** 10.00 **st.** 3.00 – **10 rm** ☕ 22.50/37.00 **st.** – SB.

Holly Farm ⛰, LD1 5PP, W : ½ m. ☎ 822402, « Working farm », ⚘ – ⟡ rest Ⓟ. ✽
April-October – **Meals** 8.00 **t.** – **3 rm** ☕ 20.00/36.00 **t.** – SB.

LANDUDNO Gwynedd 402 403 I 24 **Great Britain G.** – pop. 18 647 – ☎ 01492.

xc. : Bodnant Garden★★ *AC*, S : 7 m. by A 470.

Rhos-on-Sea, Penrhyn Bay ☎ 549641, A – 18 72 Bryniau Rd, West Shore ☎ 875325 A – Hospital Rd ☎ 876450 B.

1-2 Chapel St., LL30 2YU ☎ 876413.

London 243 – Birkenhead 55 – Chester 47 – Holyhead 43.

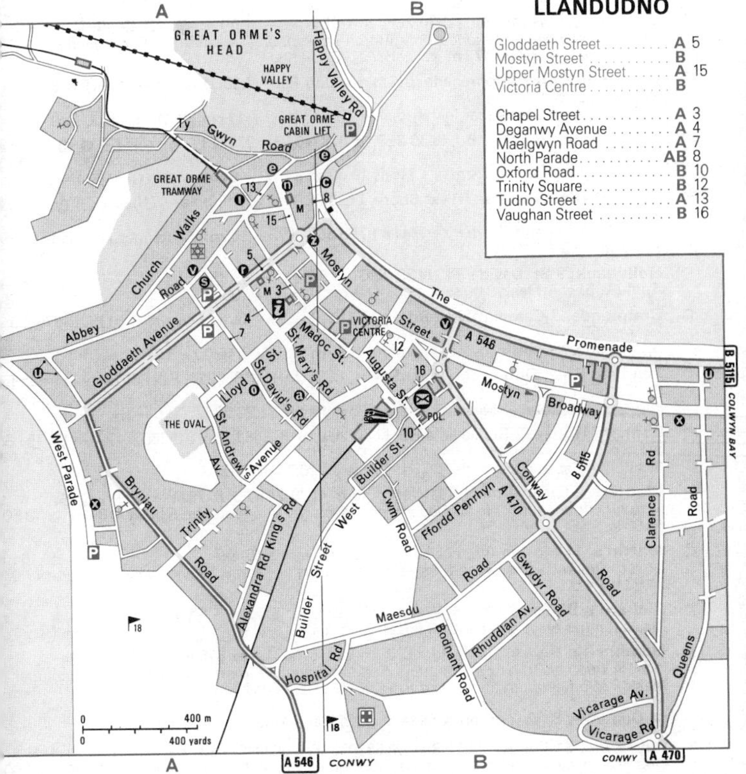

Bodysgallen Hall, LL30 1RS, SE : 2 m. on A 470 ℘ 584466, Fax 582519, ≤ garde and mountains, « Part 17C and 18C hall with terraced gardens », park,
– 50.
closed 2 to 16 January – **Meals** (booking essential) 13.50/36.00 **st.** 5.80 – 9.95 – **18** 85.00/165.00 **st.**, 16 suites – SB.

Imperial, The Promenade, LL30 1AP, ℘ 877466, Fax 878043, –
150. B
Meals 10.95/19.50 **st.** and a la carte – **97 rm** 60.00/90.00, 3 suites – SB.

Empire, 73 Church Walks, LL30 2HE, ℘ 860555, Fax 860791, « Collection of Russell Fl prints », heated, – rest – 40. A
closed 15 to 27 December – **Meals** (bar lunch Monday to Friday)/dinner 21.50 and a la carte 5.75 – **43 rm** 55.00/95.00 **st.**, 7 suites – SB.

Empire (No 72), 72 Church Walks, LL30 2HE, ℘ 860555, Fax 860791, « Victoriana »
closed 15 to 27 December – **8 rm** 65.00/100.00 **st.** – SB.

St. Tudno, North Parade, LL30 2LP, ℘ 874411, Fax 860407, ≤, – rest rest
A
Meals 15.50/27.50 **st.** 5.95 – **21 rm** 69.00/138.00 **st.** – SB.

Dunoon, Gloddaeth St., LL30 2DW, ℘ 860787, Fax 860031, –
mid March-October – **Meals** 8.00/15.60 **st.** – **55 rm** 36.00/72.00 **st.** – SB. A

Bedford, Promenade, Craig-y-Don, LL30 1BN, E : 1 m. on B 5115 ℘ 876647, Fax 8601
Gigolos : Meals - Italian - a la carte 14.00/19.65 **st.** 4.35 – **27 rm** 25.00/46.00 **st.** – S

Bryn Derwen, 34 Abbey Rd, LL30 2EE, ℘ 876804, Fax 876804, –
A
March-October – **Meals** (dinner only) 10.50 **t.** 4.00 – **9 rm** 38.50/77.00 **t.**

Wilton, 14 South Par., LL30 2LN, ℘ 876086, Fax 876086 – AB
closed December and January – **Meals** (dinner only) 8.00 **st.** 3.95 – **14 rm** 24.0 48.00 **t.** – SB.

Belle Vue, 26 North Par., LL30 2LP, ℘ 879547, ≤ – B
April-October and weekends only March-November – **Meals** (bar lunch)/dinner 10.00 and a la carte 5.00 – **17 rm** 22.50/55.00 **t.** – SB.

Bromwell Court, Promenade, 6 Craig-y-Don Par., LL30 1BG, ℘ 878416, Fax 874142 rest
B
April-October – **Meals** (bar lunch)/dinner 10.00 4.50 – **11 rm** 19.50/39.00 – SB.

Epperstone, 15 Abbey Rd, LL30 2EE, ℘ 878746, Fax 871223 – rest
A
March-October and Christmas – **Meals** 10.00 **st.** 6.50 – **8 rm** 24.00/50.00 **t.** – SB.

Sunnymede, West Par., West Shore, LL30 2BD, ℘ 877130, Fax 871824 –
A
closed January and February – **Meals** 10.95 **st.** 3.75 – **18 rm** (dinner included) 35.9 73.00 **st.** – SB.

Hollybank, 9 St. David's Pl., LL30 2UG, ℘ 878521 – A
April-October – **Meals** 8.00 **st.** 4.00 – **7 rm** 24.00/40.00 **st.**

Craiglands, 7 Carmen Sylva Rd, LL30 1LZ, E : 1 m. by A 546 off B 5115 ℘ 875090 rest
April-October – **Meals** (by arrangement) – **6 rm** 38.00/45.00 – SB.

Tan Lan, Great Orme's Rd, West Shore, LL30 2AR, ℘ 860221, Fax 860221 – rest
A
late March-October – **Meals** 12.50 **t.** 4.25 – **18 rm** 22.50/50.00 **t.** – SB.

Banham House, 2 St. David's Rd, LL30 2UL, ℘ 875680, Fax 875680 – rm
A
Meals 10.45 **st.** and a la carte 4.35 – **6 rm** 26.00/46.00 **st.**

Clontarf, 2 Great Orme's Rd, West Shore, LL30 2AR, ℘ 877621 – rm A
March-October and 24 to 28 December – **Meals** (by arrangement) 8.50 **st.** – **9 rm** 18.50 42.00 **s.** – SB.

Martin's, 11 Mostyn Av., LL30 1YS, ℘ 870070 – B
closed Sunday, Monday and first 2 weeks January – **Meals** (dinner only) a la carte 17.00 24.50 **t.** 4.50.

Richard's Bistro, 7 Church Walks, LL30 2HD, ℘ 877924 – A
Meals (dinner only) a la carte 13.85/21.85 **st.** 4.00.

Number 1's Bistro, 1 Old Rd, LL30 2HA, ℘ 875424, Fax 875424 –
closed lunch Sunday and Monday, Sunday dinner in winter and 25 to 28 December
Meals 13.95 **t.** (dinner) and a la carte 13.00/18.75 **t.** 5.95. A

at Deganwy S : 2 ¾ m. on A 546 – A – ✉ Llandudno – 01492 :

Paysanne, Station Rd, LL31 9EJ, ℘ 582079, Fax 583848 –
closed Sunday and Monday – **Meals** (booking essential) (dinner only) 13.00/18.50 **t.** 5.00

LANDYRNOG Clwyd 402 403 J/K 24 – ✉ Denbigh – ☎ 01824.
London 212 – Birkenhead 29 – Chester 21 – Shrewsbury 53.

Berllan Bach ≫, Fford Las, LL16 4LR, SE : 1¼ m. by Police Station rd on Llangynhafel rd ☎ 790732, ⚘ – TV P
Meals 12.50 **s.** – **3 rm** ☐ 25.00/38.00 **s.** – SB.

LLANERCHYMEDD Gwynedd 402 403 G 24 **Great Britain G.** – ☎ 01248.
Envir. : Isle of Anglesey★★.
London 262 – Bangor 18 – Caernarfon 23 – Holyhead 15.

Llwydiarth Fawr ≫, LL71 8DF, N : ¾ m. on B 5111 ☎ 470321, ≤, « Georgian farmhouse », ⚘, ⚘, park – ⇔ TV P. VISA. ⚘
closed Christmas – **Meals** (by arrangement) 13.50 **st.** – **3 rm** ☐ 25.00/50.00 **st.**, 2 suites – SB.

Tre'r Ddôl ≫, LL71 7AR, SW : 3½ m. by B 5112 ☎ 470278, ≤, « 17C farmhouse », ⚘, park – ⇔ rm TV P. ⚘
closed Christmas – **Meals** 12.00 **st.** – **4 rm** ☐ 25.00/40.00 **st.**

Drws-Y-Coed ≫, LL71 8AD, E : 1½ m. by B 5111 on Benllech rd ☎ 470473, ≤, ⚘, park – ⇔ TV P. ⚘
closed Christmas – **Meals** (by arrangement) 12.00 **s.** – **3 rm** ☐ 22.00/40.00 – SB.

LLANFACHRETH Gwynedd 402 403 I 25 – see Dolgellau.

LLANFIHANGEL Powys 402 403 J 25 – see Llanfyllin.

LLANFIHANGEL CRUCORNEY Gwent 403 L 28 – see Abergavenny.

LLANFYLLIN Powys 402 403 K 25 – pop. 1 267 – ☎ 01691.
London 188 – Chester 42 – Shrewsbury 24 – Welshpool 11.

Bodfach Hall Country House ≫, SY22 5HS, NW : ¼ m. on A 490 ☎ 648272, Fax 648272, ≤, ⚘, park – TV ☎ P. AE VISA
March-October – **Meals** *(closed Sunday dinner to non-residents)* (bar lunch Monday to Saturday)/dinner 16.50 **t.** – **9 rm** ☐ 33.50/70.00 **t.** – SB.

Seeds, 5 Penybryn Cottages, High St., SY22 5AP, ☎ 648604, « 16C cottages », ⚘ – ⇔. VISA
closed Monday except Bank Holidays September-May – **Meals** (Sunday dinner booking essential) 15.95 **t.** (dinner) and lunch a la carte 11.85/15.50 **t.** 5.75.

at Llanfihangel SW : 5 m. by A 490 and B 4393 on B 4382 – ✉ Llanfyllin – ☎ 01691 :

Cyfie Farm ≫, SY22 5JE, S : 1½ m. by B 4382 ☎ 648451, Fax 648451, ≤ Meifod valley, « Restored 17C longhouse, working farm », ⚘, park – TV P. ⚘
Meals (communal dining) 10.50 – **1 rm** ☐ 20.50/37.00, **3 suites** 49.00/50.00 – SB.

LLANGAMMARCH WELLS Powys 403 J 27 – ☎ 01591.
London 200 – Brecon 17 – Builth Wells 8.

Lake Country House ≫, LD4 4BS, E : ¾ m. ☎ 620202, Fax 620457, ≤, « Country house in extensive grounds », ⚘, ⚘, park, ⚘ – ⇔ TV ☎ P. AE VISA JCB
Meals 15.50/26.50 **st.** 5.95 – **7 rm** ☐ 75.00/120.00 **st.**, 11 suites 140.00/150.00 **st.** – SB.

LLANGATTOCK Powys 403 K 28 – see Crickhowell.

LLANGENNY Powys 403 K 28 – see Crickhowell.

LLANGOLLEN Clwyd 402 403 K 25 **Great Britain G.** – pop. 3 267 – ☎ 01978.
See : Plas Newydd★ *AC*.
Exc. : Chirk Castle★ *AC*, SE : 7½ m. by A 5.
18 Vale of Llangollen, Holyhead Rd ☎ 860613.
Town Hall, Castle St., LL20 5PD ☎ 860828.
London 194 – Chester 23 – Holyhead 76 – Shrewsbury 30.

Bryn Howel, LL20 7UW, E : 2¾ m. on A 539 ☎ 860331, Fax 860119, ≤, ⚘, ⚘, ⚘ – TV ☎ P – 300. AE VISA JCB. ⚘
closed 25 and 26 December – **Cedar Tree : Meals** a la carte 16.00/26.25 **t.** 7.50 – **35 rm** ☐ 73.00/96.00 **t.**, 1 suite – SB.

Royal (Forte), Bridge St., LL20 8PG, ☎ 860202, Fax 861824, ≤ – ⇔ TV ☎ P – 60. AE VISA JCB
Meals (bar lunch Monday to Saturday)/dinner 15.95 **st.** 6.55 – ☐ 8.50 – **33 rm** 55.00/65.00 **t.** – SB.

Gales Wine Bar, 18 Bridge St., LL20 8PF, ☎ 860089, Fax 861313 – ⇔ rm TV ☎ P. AE VISA JCB. ⚘
closed 24 December-2 January – **Meals** *(closed Sunday)* (in bar) a la carte 5.45/11.15 **t.** 3.90 – **12 rm** ☐ 34.00/46.50 **t.**, 2 suites.

LLANGORSE Powys 403 K 28 – ✉ Brecon – ☎ 01874.
London 177 – Abergavenny 15 – Brecon 5 – Newport 33.

Red Lion, LD3 7TY, ☎ 684238, Fax 658595 – TV P. ⚘
Meals *(closed Bank Holidays)* (bar lunch Monday to Saturday)/dinner 11.00 **st.** and a la carte – **10 rm** ☐ 25.00/40.00 – SB.

LLANGURIG Powys 403 J 26 – pop. 680 – ✉ Llanidloes – ☎ 0155 15.
♦London 188 – Aberystwyth 25 – Carmarthen 75 – Shrewsbury 53.

Old Vicarage without rest., SY18 6RN, ☎ 440280, Fax 440280 – ⊭ TV P
April-October – **4 rm** ☐ 28.00/40.00 **st.**

LLANGYBI Gwent – see Usk.

LLANIDLOES Powys 403 J 26 – ☎ 01686.
♦London 183 – Aberystwyth 30 – Carmarthen 80 – Shrewsbury 48.

Glyngynwydd without rest., Cwmbelan, SY18 6QQ, S : 2½ m. by B 4518 on A 4
☎ 413854, Fax 412012, « 17C farmhouse », – ⊭ P.
3 rm ☐ 18.50/36.00 **st.**

LLANIGON Powys 403 K 27 – see Hay-on-Wye.

LLANNEFYDD Clwyd 402 403 J 24 – pop. 567 – ✉ Denbigh – ☎ 01745.
♦London 225 – Chester 37 – Shrewsbury 63.

Hawk and Buckle Inn, LL16 5ED, ☎ 540249, Fax 540316, ← – ⊭ rm TV ☎ P. AE VISA
JCB.
closed 25 December – **Meals** *(closed Sunday and Monday) (restricted opening October-April)* (bar lunch Tuesday to Saturday and Sunday dinner)/dinner 18.00 and a la carte 5.
10 rm ☐ 38.00/50.00 **t.** – SB.

LLANRHIDIAN W. Glam. – see Swansea.

En haute saison, et surtout dans les stations, il est prudent de retenir à l'avance.

LLANRWST Gwynedd 402 403 I 24 – pop. 3 012 – ☎ 01492.
♦London 230 – Holyhead 50 – Shrewsbury 66.

Priory, Maenan, LL26 0UL, N : 2½ m. on A 470 ☎ 660247, Fax 660734, – TV ☎
AE VISA
Meals (lunch booking essential)/dinner 10.00 **st.** (dinner) and a la carte 13.00/22.45 **s**
5.00 – **12 rm** ☐ 39.00/49.00 – SB.

Bron Eirian, Town Hill, LL26 0NF, ☎ 641741, ←, – ⊭ TV P
Meals (communal dining) 14.00 **st.** – **3 rm** ☐ 26.00/40.00 **st.** – SB.

Cae'r Berllan with rm, LL26 0PP, S : 1 m. on A 470 ☎ 640027, « 16C manor house »
– ⊭ TV P. VISA.
mid March-October – **Meals** *(closed Sunday to Tuesday to non-residents)* (booking essential) (dinner only) 13.00 **t.** and a la carte 13.25/19.50 **t.** 4.00 – **2 rm** ☐ 60.00 **t.** – SB.

at Trefriw NW : 2 m. on B 5106 – ✉ Llanrwst – ☎ 01492 :

Hafod House, LL27 0RQ, ☎ 640029, Fax 641351, – ⊭ rest TV ☎ P. AE VISA
JCB.
Meals *(closed Sunday to Tuesday)* (dinner only and lunch Sunday and Bank Holidays)
18.95 **t.** 4.45 – **7 rm** ☐ 24.50/49.00 **t.** – SB.

Chandler's Brasserie, LL27 0JH, ☎ 640991 – ⊭ P. VISA
closed Sunday, Monday, Tuesday and Wednesday November-Easter, 2 weeks late January-early February, 2 weeks October and Christmas-New Year – **Meals** (dinner only) a la carte 14.65/20.75.

LLANSANFFRAID GLAN CONWY Gwynedd 402 403 I24 Great Britain G. – pop. 2 194
✉ Aberconwy – ☎ 01492.
Envir. : Bodnant Garden★★ *AC*, S : 2½ m. by A 470.
♦London 241 – Colwyn Bay 4 – Holyhead 42.

Old Rectory, LL28 5LF, on A 470 ☎ 580611, Fax 584555, ← Conwy estuary,
« Georgian country house with antique furnishings », – ⊭ TV ☎ P. AE VISA
JCB.
closed 20 December-1 February – **Meals** (dinner only) 27.50 **st.** 6.90 – **6 rm** ☐ 62.00/
114.00 **st.** – SB.

LLANTRISANT Gwent 403 L 28 – pop. 9 136 (inc. Pontyclun) – ✉ Usk – ☎ 01291.
♦London 148 – ♦Bristol 34 – Gloucester 43 – Newport 8.

Greyhound Inn, NP5 1LE, NE : ½ m. on Usk rd ☎ 672505, Fax 673255, – TV ☎ & P
VISA.
accommodation closed 24 and 25 December – **Meals** *(closed Sunday dinner)* a la carte 11.40/18.00 **t.** 4.50 – **10 rm** ☐ 48.00/58.00 **t.** – SB.

LLANTWIT MAJOR S. Glam. 403 J 29 – pop. 9 836 – ☎ 01446.
♦London 175 – ♦Cardiff 18 – ♦Swansea 33.

West House, West St., CF61 1SP, ☎ 792406, Fax 796147, – TV ☎ P. AE VISA JCB
Meals *(closed Monday and Bank Holidays)* 7.50/14.50 **t.** and a la carte 3.95 – **21 rm**
☐ 48.00/68.00 **t.** – SB.

LLANWENARTH Gwent – see Abergavenny.

LLANWRTYD WELLS Powys 403 J 27 – pop. 649 – ☎ 01591.

London 214 – Brecon 32 – Carmarthen 39.

Lasswade Country House, Station Rd, LD5 4RW, ℘ 610515, Fax 610611, ≤, – TV ☎ P. VISA
Meals (dinner only and Sunday lunch)/dinner 16.95 **t.** 4.95 – **8 rm** 32.50/55.00 **t.** – SB.

LLWYNGWRIL Gwynedd 402 403 H 25 – ✉ Dolgellau – ☎ 01341.

London 226 – Aberystwyth 44 – Birkenhead 80 – Chester 72 – Shrewsbury 67.

Pentre Bach, LL37 2JU, ℘ 250294, Fax 250885, ≤, – TV P. VISA.
closed November, 24 to 26 and 31 December – **Meals** (by arrangement) 17.70 – **3 rm** 19.00/48.00.

LLYSWEN Powys 403 K 27 – ✉ Brecon – ☎ 01874.

London 188 – Brecon 8 – ◆Cardiff 48 – Worcester 53.

Llangoed Hall, LD3 0YP, NW : 1 ¼ m. on A 470 ℘ 754525, Fax 754545, ≤, « Edwardian mansion by Sir Clough Williams-Ellis of 17C origins », – rest TV ☎ P – 50. AE VISA JCB.
Meals 16.00/29.50 **t.** and a la carte 28.00/36.50 **t.** 8.50 – **20 rm** 95.00/195.00 **t.**, 3 suites – SB
Spec. Venison sausage with celeriac and foie gras sauce, Suprême of salmon with a champagne butter sauce, Mango mousse with a brioche of cherries.

Griffin Inn, LD3 0UR, on A 470 ℘ 754241, Fax 754592, « Part 15C inn », – rest ☎ P. AE VISA JCB
Meals (residents only Sunday dinner) a la carte 13.75/19.95 **t.** 5.50 – **8 rm** 28.50/50.00 **t.** – SB.

MACHYNLLETH Powys 402 403 I 26 – pop. 1 110 – ☎ 01654.

Ffordd Drenewydd ℘ 702000.

Canolfan Owain Glyndwr, SY20 8EE ℘ 702401.

London 220 – Shrewsbury 56 – Welshpool 37.

Plas Dolguog, SY20 8UJ, E : 1 ½ m. by A 489 ℘ 702244, Fax 702530, ≤, « 17C country house », , park – TV ☎ P. VISA.
closed first two weeks February – **Meals** (dinner only and Sunday lunch)/dinner 15.00 **t.** 4.50 **9 rm** 27.50/56.00 **t.** – SB.

Bacheiddon Farm without rest., Aberhosan, SY20 8SG, SE : 5 ¼ m. on Dylife rd, via Forge ℘ 702229, « Working farm » – P.
May-September – **3 rm** 40.00.

at Eglwysfach (Dyfed) SW : 6 m. on A 487 – ✉ Machynlleth (Powys) – ☎ 01654 :

Ynyshir Hall, SY20 8TA, ℘ 781209, Fax 781366, ≤, « Georgian country house, gardens », park – TV ☎ P. AE VISA JCB.
Meals (booking essential) 17.50/29.00 **st.** – **6 rm** 75.00/120.00 **st.**, 2 suites – SB.

MAGOR SERVICE AREA Gwent 403 L 29 – ✉ Newport – ☎ 01633.

Granada Service West, Junction 23, M 4, NP6 3YL ℘ 881122.

Granada Lodge without rest., NP6 3YL, M 4 junction 23 ℘ 880111, Fax 881896, Reservations (Freephone) 0800 555300 – TV ☎ P. AE VISA.
– **43 rm** 39.95 **st.**

MERTHYR TYDFIL M. Glam. 403 J 28 – pop. 59 317 – ☎ 01685.

Morlais Castle, Pant, Dowlais ℘ 722822 – Cilsanws Mountain, Cefn Coed ℘ 723308.

14a Glebeland St., CF47 8AU ℘ 379884.

London 179 – ◆Cardiff 25 – Gloucester 59 – ◆Swansea 33.

Tregenna, Park Terr., CF47 8RF, ℘ 723627, Fax 721951 – TV ☎ P. AE VISA
Meals a la carte 9.20/16.45 **t.** 6.00 – **24 rm** 40.00/55.00 **st.** – SB.

MILFORD HAVEN (Aberdaugleddau) Dyfed 403 E 28 – pop. 13 649 – ☎ 01646.

Hubbertson ℘ 692368.

94 Charles St., SA73 2HL ℘ 690866 (summer only).

London 258 – Carmarthen 39 – Fishguard 23.

Lord Nelson, Hamilton Terr., SA73 3AL, ℘ 695341, Fax 694026, – TV ☎ P. AE VISA.
Meals (bar lunch)/dinner a la carte 12.35/18.05 **st.** 3.95 – **29 rm** 42.00/65.00 **st.**, 1 suite.

MISKIN M. Glam. – ✉ Cardiff – ☎ 01443.

London 169 – ◆Cardiff 22 – ◆Swansea 31.

Miskin Manor, CF7 8ND, E : 1 ¾ m. by A 4119 (Groes Faen rd) ℘ 224204, Fax 237606, ≤, , park, squash – TV ☎ P – 200. AE VISA.
closed 25 to 29 December – **Meals** 17.95 **st.** and a la carte – **31 rm** 80.00/125.00 **st.**, 1 suite – SB.

MOLD **(Yr Wyddgrug)** Clwyd 402 403 K 24 – pop. 9 168 – ☎ 01352.

Pantmywyn ✆ 740318/741513 – Old Padeswood, Station Rd ✆ (01244) 547401 – Padeswood & Buckley, The Caia, Station Lane, Padeswood ✆ (01244) 550537 – Caerwys ✆ 720692.

Library, Museum and Art Gallery, CH7 1AP ✆ 759331.

London 211 – Chester 12 – Liverpool 29 – Shrewsbury 45.

Soughton Hall, CH7 6AB, N : 2½ m. by A 5119 ✆ 840811, Fax 840382, ≤, « Early 18 ... Italianate mansion », – rest. **Meals** *(closed Sunday lunch)* a la carte 18.95/34.95 **st.** 6.00 – **12 rm** 70.00/119.00 ... SB.

Tower without rest., Nercwys, CH7 4ED, S : 1 m. by B 5444 and Nercwys ... ✆ 700220, « 15C fortified house », park. **3 rm** 40.00/60.00 **st.**

ATS Wrexham Rd ✆ 753682

MONMOUTH **(Trefynwy)** Gwent 403 L 28 **Great Britain G.** – pop. 8 204 – ☎ 01600.

Envir. : S : Wye Valley★.

Exc. : Raglan Castle★ *AC*, SW : 8 m. by A 40.

The Rolls of Monmouth, The Hendre ✆ 715353 – Leasebrook Lane ✆ 712212.

Shire Hall, Agincourt Sq., NP5 3DY ✆ 713899.

London 147 – Gloucester 26 – Newport 24 – Swansea 64.

Riverside, Cinderhill St., NP5 3EY, ✆ 715577 – 150. **Meals** (bar lunch Monday to Saturday) 12.00/25.00 **t.** and a la carte 4.00 – **17 rm** 49.00/69.00 **t.** – SB.

at Whitebrook SE : 8½ m. by A 466 – ✉ Monmouth – ☎ 01600 :

Crown at Whitebrook with rm, NP5 4TX, ✆ 860254, Fax 860607. *closed 2 weeks January and 2 weeks July* – **Meals** *(closed Monday lunch and Sunday dinner to non-residents)* 15.50/25.50 **st.** and lunch a la carte – **12 rm** (dinner included) 70.00/120.00 **st.** – SB.

ATS Wonastow Rd, Wonastow Ind. Est. ✆ 716832

MONTGOMERY **(Trefaldwyn)** Powys 403 K 26 **Great Britain G.** – pop. 1 059 – ☎ 01686.

See : Castle★.

London 194 – Birmingham 71 – Chester 53 – Shrewsbury 30.

Dragon, Town Square, SY15 6AA, ✆ 668359, Fax 668359, – rm. **Meals** 16.50 **t.** and a la carte 4.05 – **14 rm** 42.00/69.00 **t.** – SB.

Little Brompton Farm without rest., SY15 6HY, SE : 2 m. on B 4385 ✆ 66837... « Working farm », park. **3 rm** 40.00 **s.**

MOYLGROVE Dyfed 403 F 27 – see Newport.

MUMBLES (The) W. Glam. 403 I 29 – see Swansea.

NANNERCH Clwyd 402 403 K 24 – pop. 513 – ✉ Mold – ☎ 01352.

London 218 – Chester 19 – Liverpool 36 – Shrewsbury 52.

Old Mill, Melin-y-Wern, Denbigh Rd, CH7 5RH, NW : ¾ m. on A 451 ✆ 74154... Fax 740254, « Converted 19C corn mill and stables ». **Meals** (residents only) (dinner only) 19.50 **st.** 3.00 – **6 rm** 38.00/57.00 **st.** – SB.

NEATH **(Castell-Ned)** W. Glam. 403 I 29 pop. 19 528 – ☎ 01639.

Swansea Bay, Jersey Marine ✆ (01792) 814153/812198.

London 188 – Cardiff 40 – Swansea 8.

Castle, The Parade, SA11 1RB, ✆ 641119, Fax 641624, – rm, 120. **Meals** a la carte 8.25/17.50 **t.** 4.00 – **28 rm** 49.50/59.50 **t.** – SB.

at Cadoxton NW : 1½ m. by A 474 – ✉ Neath – ☎ 01639 :

Cwmbach Cottages, Cwmbach Rd, SA10 8AH, ✆ 639825, ≤, – rm. **Meals** (by arrangement) 14.00 **st.** – **5 rm** 22.00/40.00 **st.** – SB.

EFYN Gwynedd 402 403 G 25 – pop. 2 548 – ☏ 01758.

Nefyn & District, Morfa Nefyn ☎ 720218.

ondon 265 – Caernarfon 20.

Caeau Capel ≫, Rhodfar Mor, LL53 6EB, ☎ 720240, ☞ – TV P. VISA
Easter-October – **Meals** (bar lunch)/dinner 12.50 **t.** 4.45 – **18 rm** ☐ 23.65/46.00 **t.** – SB.

IEWPORT Dyfed 403 F 27 – pop. 1 162 – ☏ 01239.

Newport ☎ 820244.

London 258 – Fishguard 7.

Llysmeddyg, East St., SA42 0SY, on A 487 ☎ 820008, ☞ – ⇆ P. ✻
closed Christmas – **Meals** (by arrangement) 13.00 **st.** 4.50 – **4 rm** ☐ 18.50/37.00 **st.** – SB.

Grove Park, Pen-y-bont, SA42 0LT, on Moylegrove rd ☎ 820122 – ⇆ TV. ✻
closed 20 December-2 January – **Meals** 14.00 **st.** 3.65 – **4 rm** ☐ 40.00 **st.** – SB.

Cnapan with rm, East St., SA42 0SY, on A 487 ☎ 820575, Fax 820878, ☞ – ⇆ rest TV P. VISA. ✻
closed February and 25-26 December – **Meals** *(closed Tuesday Easter-October)* (booking essential) (light lunch Monday to Saturday) a la carte 8.70/17.50 **t.** 5.25 – **5 rm** ☐ 29.00/48.00 **t.**

at Moylgrove NE : 6 m. – ✉ Cardigan – ☏ 01239 86 :

Old Vicarage ≫, SA43 3BN, S : 1/4 m. on Glanrhyd rd ☎ 881231, ☞ – ⇆. ✻
March-November – **Meals** 12.50 **st.** 3.45 – **3 rm** ☐ 22.50/45.00 **st.**

NEWPORT (Casnewydd-Ar-Wysg) Gwent 403 L 29 **Great Britain G.** – pop. 133 318 – ☏ 01633.

nvir. : Caerleon (Fortress Baths★, Roman Amphitheatre★ *AC*) NE : 3½ m. on B 4596.

Tredegar Park, Bassaleg Rd ☎ 895219 – 9 Caerleon, Broadway ☎ 420342 – 18 Parc, Church ane, Coedkenew ☎ 680933.

Museum and Art Gallery, John Frost Sq., NP9 1HZ ☎ 842962.

London 145 – ◆Bristol 31 – ◆Cardiff 12 – Gloucester 48.

Celtic Manor H. & Country Club, Coldra Woods, NP6 2YA, E : 3 m. on A 48 ☎ 413000, Fax 412910, Fб, ⌂s, ☐, 18, park – |‡| ⇆ rm ▤ TV ☎ P – 🏛 300. AE ⓓ VISA. ✻
Meals a la carte 14.65/30.65 **st.** 7.00 - (see also ***Hedley's*** below) – ☐ 9.45 – **73 rm** 89.00/99.00 **st.** – SB.

Hilton National, The Coldra, NP6 2YG, E : 3 m. on A 48 ☎ 412777, Fax 413087, Fб, ⌂s, ☐ – ⇆ rm TV ☎ P – 🏛 350. AE ⓓ VISA
Meals *(closed Saturday lunch)* (carving rest.) (buffet lunch)/dinner 8.95/15.75 **st.** and dinner a la carte 7.95 – ☐ 9.25 – **119 rm** 80.00 **st.**

Westgate, Commercial St., NP9 1TT, ☎ 244444, Fax 246616 – |‡| TV ☎ & – 🏛 150. AE ⓓ VISA
Meals (dinner only) 13.95 **st.** – **69 rm** ☐ 57.50/78.00 **st.** – SB.

Kings, High St., NP9 1QU, ☎ 842020, Fax 244667 – |‡| TV ☎ P – 🏛 200. AE ⓓ VISA JCB. ✻
closed 24 to 30 December – **Meals** *(closed lunch Saturday and Sunday)* 9.95 **st.** (lunch) and dinner a la carte 9.95/15.00 **st.** 4.50 – ☐ 7.00 – **47 rm** 42.00/52.00 **st.** – SB.

Newport Lodge, 147 Bryn Bevan, Brynglas Rd, NP9 5QN, N : 3/4 m. by A 4042 ☎ 821818, Fax 856360 – TV ☎ P. AE VISA
Meals *(closed Sunday dinner)* (bar lunch)/dinner 12.50 **st.** and a la carte 4.50 – **27 rm** ☐ 52.00/67.00 **st.** – SB.

Kepe Lodge without rest., 46a Caerau Rd, NP9 4HH, ☎ 262351, ☞ – TV P. ✻
closed 1 week Christmas – **8 rm** ☐ 19.00/34.00 **t.**

Hedley's (at Celtic Manor H. & Country Club), Coldra Woods, NP6 2YA, E : 3 m. on A 48 ☎ 413000, Fax 412910 – P. AE ⓓ VISA
Meals *(closed Saturday lunch and Sunday)* 15.95/23.00 **st.** and a la carte 7.50.

at Langstone E : 4½ m. on A 48 – ✉ Newport – ☏ 01633 :

Stakis Newport, Chepstow Rd, NP6 2LX, ☎ 413737, Fax 413713, Fб, ⌂s, ☐, ☞ – ⇆ rm ▤ rest TV ☎ & P – 🏛 80. AE ⓓ VISA JCB. ✻
Meals *(closed Saturday lunch)* 10.50/17.25 **st.** and dinner a la carte 5.25 – ☐ 8.75 – **131 rm** 85.00/115.00 **st.**, 10 suites – SB.

at Redwick SE : 9½ m. by M4 off B 4245 – ✉ Magor – ☏ 01633 :

Brick House ≫, NP6 3DX, ☎ 880230, Fax 880230 – ⇆ TV P. ✻
Meals (by arrangement) 10.00 **st.** – **7 rm** ☐ 25.00/40.00 **st.**

ATS 101 Corporation Rd ☎ 216115/216117

NEW QUAY (Ceinewydd) Dyfed 403 G 27 – pop. 915 – ☏ 01545.

Church St., SA45 9NZ ☎ 560865 (summer only).

◆London 234 – Aberystwyth 24 – Carmarthen 31 – Fishguard 39.

Park Hall ≫, Cwmtydu, SA44 6LG, SW : 2 3/4 m. by A 486 and Llangrannog rd ☎ 560306, Fax 560306, ≤, ☞ – TV P
Meals (by arrangement) 19.50 **st.** 4.00 – **5 rm** ☐ 29.00/58.00 **st.** – SB.

NORTHOP HALL Clwyd 402 403 K 24 – pop. 4 155 (Northop) – ☎ 01244.
♦London 220 – Chester 9 – Shrewsbury 52.

All Seasons Lodge, Gateway Services, A 55 (westbound carriageway), CH7 6H, ☎ 550011, Fax 550763 – ⇔ rm TV ☎ ♿ P – 40. AE VISA. ✻
closed 25 and 26 December – **Meals** *(closed Sunday lunch)* 12.50 **st.** and a la carte 4 – ☐ 6.50 – **38 rm** 34.50/59.00 **st.** – SB.

Forte Travelodge, CH7 6HB, A 55 (eastbound carriageway) ☎ 816473, Reservatic (Freephone) 0800 850950 – TV ♿ P. AE VISA. ✻
Meals (grill rest.) – **40 rm** 34.50 **t.**

NOTTAGE (Drenewydd Yn Notais) M. Glam. 403 I 29 – see Porthcawl.

PANT MAWR Powys 403 I 26 – ✉ Llangurig – ☎ 0155 15.
♦London 219 – Aberystwyth 21 – Shrewsbury 55.

Glansevern Arms, SY18 6SY, on A 44 ☎ 440240, ← – TV P
closed 20 to 31 December – **Meals** *(closed Sunday dinner)* (booking essential) (dinner o and Sunday lunch)/dinner 17.75 **t.** 4.60 – **7 rm** ☐ 35.00/65.00 **t.** – SB.

PEMBROKE (Penfro) Dyfed 403 F 28 Great Britain G. – pop. 15 881 – ☎ 01646.
See : Castle★★ *AC*.
Defensible Barracks, Pembroke Dock ☎ 683817.
to Republic of Ireland (Rosslare) (B & I Line) 1-2 daily (4 h 15 mn).
Pembroke Visitor Centre, Commons Road, SA71 4EA ☎ 622388.
♦London 252 – Carmarthen 32 – Fishguard 26.

Underdown Country House ≫, Grove Hill, SA71 5PR, ☎ 622900, Fax 6212 « Antiques and gardens » – TV ☎ P. AE VISA. ✻
closed 22 to 27 December and 29 December-3 January – **Meals** (booking essential) (dinr only) a la carte 17.70/25.00 **t.** – **6 rm** ☐ 35.00/55.00 **t.** – SB.

at Lamphey E : 1 ¾ m. on A 4139 – ✉ Pembroke – ☎ 01646 :

Court ≫, SA71 5NT, ☎ 672273, Fax 672480, ≘s, park – TV ☎ P – 80. AE VISA JCB. ✻
Meals (light lunch)/dinner 15.95 **st.** and a la carte 4.95 – ☐ 7.50 – **30 rm** 56.00/120.00 s 7 suites – SB.

Bethwaite's Lamphey Hall, SA71 5NR, ☎ 672394, Fax 672369, – TV ☎ P. AE VISA. ✻
Meals 8.95/14.50 **t.** and dinner a la carte 4.50 – **10 rm** ☐ 35.00/50.00 **t.** – SB.

at Pembroke Dock NW : 2 m. on A 4139 – ✉ ☎ 01646 :

Cleddau Bridge, Essex Rd, SA72 6UT, NE : 1 m. by A 4139 on A 477 (at Toll Bridg ☎ 685961, Fax 685746, heated – TV ☎ P – 175. AE VISA
Meals 9.95/13.95 **t.** and a la carte 3.75 – **22 rm** ☐ 55.00/59.50 **t.**, 2 suites – SB.

ATS Well Hill Garage, Well Hill ☎ 683217/683836

PENALLY (Penalun) Dyfed 403 F 29 – see Tenby.

PENCOED M. Glam. 403 J 29 – see Bridgend.

PENMACHNO Gwynedd 402 403 I 24 – see Betws-y-Coed.

PONTFAEN Dyfed – see Fishguard.

PONTYPOOL (Pontypwl) Gwent 403 K 28 – ☎ 01495.
♦London 154 – Gloucester 54 – Newport 13 – ♦Swansea 59.

Pentwyn Farm ≫, Little Mill, NP4 0HQ, NE : 4 ½ m. by A 472 and A 4042 on A 47 ☎ 785249, Fax 785249, « 16C longhouse », heated, – P. ✻
closed Christmas and New Year – **Meals** (by arrangement) (communal dining) 11.00 **st.**
4 rm ☐ 20.00/38.00 **st.** – SB.

PONTYPRIDD M. Glam. 403 K 29 – ☎ 01443.
♦London 164 – ♦Cardiff 9 – ♦Swansea 40.

Llechwen Hall, Llanfabon, CF37 4HP, NE : 4 ¼ m. by A 4223 off A 4054 ☎ 74205 Fax 742189, – TV ☎ P – 80. AE VISA
Meals 10.95/17.95 **st.** – **11 rm** ☐ 48.50/95.00 **t.** – SB.

ATS Nile St., off Broadway ☎ 403796

PORTH M. Glam. 403 J 29 pop. 6 225 – ✉ Pontypridd – ☎ 01443.
♦London 168 – ♦Cardiff 13 – ♦Swansea 45.

Heritage Park, Coed Cae Rd, Trehafod, CF37 2NP, on A 4058 ☎ 687057, Fax 687060 rest TV ☎ ♿ P – 200. AE VISA
Meals a la carte 12.00/16.50 **st.** – ☐ 5.95 – **50 rm** 42.95/58.95 – SB.

Pour visiter une ville ou une région : utilisez les Guides Verts Michelin.

PORTHCAWL M. Glam. 403 I 29 – pop. 16 099 – ☎ 01656.
ℹ The Old Police Station, John St., CF36 3DT ✆ 786639.
♦London 183 – ♦Cardiff 28 – ♦Swansea 18.

Atlantic, West Drive, CF36 3LT, ✆ 785011, Fax 771877, ← – lift TV ☎ P. VISA JCB
Meals (bar lunch and Sunday dinner)/dinner 12.50 **t.** and a la carte 4.75 – **18 rm** 49.50/72.00 **t.** – SB.

at Nottage N : 1 m. by A 4229 – ✉ Porthcawl – ☎ 01656 :

Rose and Crown, Heol-y-Capel, CF36 3ST, N : 1 m. by A 4229 ✆ 784850, Fax 772345 – TV ☎ P. AE VISA.
Meals (carving rest.) a la carte approx. 10.00 **t.** 4.65 – **8 rm** 40.45/45.95 **t.**

PORTHGAIN Dyfed 403 E 28 – see St. Davids.

PORTMEIRION Gwynedd 402 403 H 25 Great Britain G. – ☎ 01766.
See : Village ★ *AC.*
♦London 245 – Caernarfon 23 – Colwyn Bay 40 – Dolgellau 24.

Portmeirion , LL48 6ET, ✆ 770228, Fax 771331, ← village and estuary, « Private Italianate village, antiques », heated, , park, – rest TV ☎ P – 100. AE VISA JCB.
closed 7 January-2 February – **Meals** *(closed Monday lunch)* 13.50/25.00 **t.** 5.00 – 8.50 – **26 rm** 70.00/115.00 **t.**, 8 suites – SB.

PORT TALBOT W. Glam. 403 I 29 – pop. 51 023 – ☎ 01639.
♦London 193 – ♦Cardiff 35 – ♦Swansea 11.

Travel Inn, Baglan Rd, SA12 8ES, M 4 Junction 42 ✆ 813017, Fax 823096 – rm TV P. AE VISA.
Meals (grill rest.) – 4.95 – **40 rm** 34.50 **t.**

ATS Afan Way ✆ 883895/885747

Les prix Pour toutes précisions sur les prix indiqués dans ce guide, reportez-vous à l'introduction.

PRESTATYN Clwyd 402 403 J 23 – ☎ 01745.
♦London 230 – Bangor 35 – Birkenhead 43 – Chester 35 – Holyhead 56.

Traeth Ganol, 41 Beach Rd West, LL19 7LL, ✆ 853594, Fax 886687 – TV P. VISA.
Meals *(closed Sunday dinner, Monday and Tuesday to non-residents)* 10.00/12.00 **t.** and a la carte 4.70 – **9 rm** 30.00/45.00 **t.** – SB.

PRESTEIGNE Powys 403 K 27 – pop. 2 141 – ☎ 01544.
ℹ The Old Market Hall, Broad St., LD8 2AW ✆ 260193 (summer only).
♦London 159 – Llandrindod Wells 20 – Shrewsbury 39.

Radnorshire Arms (Forte), High St., LD8 2BE, ✆ 267406, Fax 260418, – TV ☎ P 25. AE VISA
Meals 10.95/15.95 **t.** 5.55 – 8.50 – **16 rm** 65.00/75.00 **t.** – SB.

PUMSAINT Dyfed 403 I 27 – ☎ 01558.
♦London 208 – Carmarthen 28 – ♦Swansea 38.

Seguendo di Stagioni, Harford, SA19 8DT, NW : 2 m. on A 482 ✆ 650671, Fax 650671 – P
closed Sunday dinner, Monday and Tuesday – **Meals** - Italian - (dinner only and Sunday lunch) 14.95/22.95 **t.** and a la carte 4.95.

PWLLHELI Gwynedd 402 403 G 25 – pop. 3 974 – ☎ 01758.
18 Golf road ✆ 701644.
ℹ Min-y-Don, Station Rd, LL53 6HE ✆ 613000 (summer only).
♦London 261 – Aberystwyth 73 – Caernarfon 21.

XXX ✿ **Plas Bodegroes** (Chown) with rm, LL53 5TH, NW : 1 ¾ m. on A 497 ✆ 612363, Fax 701247, « Georgian country house », , park – TV ☎ P. AE VISA
closed Monday except Bank Holidays and November-February – **Meals** (booking essential) (dinner only) 30.00 **t.** 6.00 – **8 rm** (dinner included) 75.00/180.00 **t.** – SB
Spec. Lobster and smoked haddock fishcake with tartare sauce, Lamb kebab with garlic cream, Cinnamon biscuit.

RAGLAN Gwent 403 L 28 pop. 1 857 – ✉ Abergavenny – ☎ 01873.
♦London 154 – Gloucester 34 – Newport 18 – ♦Swansea 58.

X **Clytha Arms** with rm, NP7 9BW, W : 3 m. on Clytha rd (old Abergavenny Rd) ✆ 840206, Fax 840206 – TV P. VISA.
Meals *(closed Sunday dinner and Monday except Monday lunch in summer)* a la carte 13.85/21.75 **t.** 3.75 – **3 rm** 40.00/65.00 **t.**

REDWICK Gwent 403 L 29 – see Newport.

RHAYADER (Rhaeadr) Powys 403 J 27 Great Britain G. – pop. 1 626 – 01597.
Envir. : Elan Valley★★, SW : by B 4518.
The Leisure Centre, North St., LD6 5BU 810591.
♦London 180 – Brecon 34 – Hereford 46 – Shrewsbury 60.

Elan, West St., LD6 5AF, 810373 –
11 rm.

RHOSCOLYN Gwynedd 402 403 G 24 Great Britain G. – pop. 539 – Holyhead – 01407.
Envir. : Isle of Anglesey★★.
♦London 269 – Bangor 25 – Caernarfon 30 – Holyhead 5.5.

Old Rectory, LL65 2DQ, 860214, ≤, – VISA
closed 21 December-3 January – **Meals** (communal dining) 15.00 **st.** – **5 rm** 30.00/51.00 **st.** – SB.

RHOS-ON-SEA (Llandrillo-Yn-Rhos) Clwyd 402 403 I 24 – see Colwyn Bay.

RHYDLEWIS Dyfed 403 G 27 – Llandysul – 01239.
♦London 235 – Carmarthen 26 – Fishguard 38.

Broniwan, SA44 5PF, NE : ¼ m. by Plump rd, taking first turn right onto unmarked road 851261, « Working farm », , park –
Meals (by arrangement) 10.00 **s.** – **3 rm** 17.00/34.00 **st.** – SB.

ROEWEN Gwynedd – see Conwy.

ROSSETT (Yr Orsedd) Clwyd 402 403 L 24 – pop. 2 936 – 01244.
♦London 203 – Chester 8 – Shrewsbury 39.

Llyndir Hall, Llyndir Lane, LL12 0AY, N : ¾ m. by B 5445 571648, Fax 571258 « Part Strawberry Gothic country house », – rm – 150. AE VISA JCB.
Meals (bar lunch Saturday) 14.50/24.95 **t.** and a la carte 6.25 – 7.95 – **37 rm** 74.00/110.00 **t.**, 1 suite – SB.

Rossett Hall, Chester Rd, LL12 0DE, 571000, Fax 571505, – rm – 120. AE VISA JCB.
Meals *(closed Saturday lunch)* 11.00/22.00 **t.** 5.95 – 7.00 – **29 rm** 65.00/80.00 **st.** 1 suite – SB.

RUTHIN (Rhuthun) Clwyd 402 403 K 24 – pop. 5 029 – 01824.
Ruthin-Pwllglas 702296.
Ruthin Craft Centre, Park Rd, LL15 1BB 703992.
♦London 210 – Birkenhead 31 – Chester 23 – Shrewsbury 46.

Ruthin Castle, Corwen Rd, LL15 2NU, 702664, Fax 705978, « Reconstructed Victorian and part medieval castle », , park – – 140. AE VISA JCB.
Meals 6.25/16.50 **t.** and a la carte – **58 rm** 65.00/85.00 **t.** – SB.

Ye Olde Anchor Inn, Rhos St., LL15 1DX, 702813, Fax 703050 – rest . VISA
Meals 10.00/18.00 **st.** and a la carte 6.50 – **10 rm** 27.50/50.00 **st.** – SB.

Eyarth Station, Llanfair Dyffryn Clwyd, LL15 2EE, S : 1¾ m. by A 525 off Pwllglas rd 703643, Fax 707464, ≤, heated, – rm . VISA
Meals 14.00 **s.** 4.00 – **6 rm** 44.00 **st.** – SB.

ST. ASAPH (Llanelwy) Clwyd 402 403 J 24 Great Britain G. – pop. 3 399 – 01745.
See : Cathedral★.
Envir. : Rhuddlan Castle★★, N : 2½ m. by A 525 and A 547 – Denbigh Castle★, S : 6 m. by A 525 and A 543.
♦London 225 – Chester 29 – Shrewsbury 59.

Oriel House, Upper Denbigh Rd, LL17 0LW, S : ¾ m. on A 525 582716, Fax 585208 – – 250. AE VISA JCB
Meals 10.00/15.95 **t.** and a la carte – **19 rm** 36.00/66.00 **t.** – SB.

Plas Elwy, The Roe, LL17 0LT, N : ½ m. at junction of A 525 with A 55 582263 Fax 583864 – . AE VISA JCB.
closed 26 to 30 December – **Meals** *(closed Sunday dinner to non-residents)* (lunch by arrangement Monday to Saturday) 7.50/8.00 **t.** and a la carte 4.75 – **13 rm** 40.00/68.00 **t.**

ST.BRIDES-SUPER-ELY S. Glam. – 01446.
♦London 155 – ♦Bristol 51 – ♦Cardiff 9 – Newport 22.

Sant-Y-Nyll without rest., CF5 6EZ, 760209, Fax 760209, ≤, , park – . AE
6 rm 25.00/45.00 **st.**

ST. CLEARS (Sancler) Dyfed 403 G 28 – pop. 3 014 – ☎ 01994.

London 229 – Carmarthen 9 – Fishguard 37.

Forge Motel, SA33 4NA, E : 1 m. on A 40 ☎ 230300, Fax 230300, ≘s, 🏊, 🌳 – TV ☎ P. VISA
closed 25 and 26 December – **Meals** (grill rest.) a la carte 5.95/18.25 **t.** 4.00 – **18 rm** 36.00/55.00.

ST. DAVIDS (Tyddewi) Dyfed 403 E 28 Great Britain G. – pop. 1 959 – ✉ Haverfordwest – ☎ 01437.

See : Town★ – Cathedral★★ – Bishops Palace★ *AC*.

St. Davids City, Whitesands Bay ☎ 721751.

London 266 – Carmarthen 46 – Fishguard 16.

Old Cross, Cross Sq., SA62 6SP, ☎ 720387, Fax 720394, 🌳 – ⇔ rm TV ☎ P. VISA JCB
March-October – **Meals** (bar lunch)/dinner 16.00 **t.** and a la carte – **16 rm** 39.50/69.00 **t.** – SB.

Ramsey House, Lower Moor, SA62 6RP, SW : ½ m. on Porth Cleis Rd. ☎ 720321, 🌳 – ⇔
Meals 12.50 **st.** 4.45 – **7 rm** (dinner included) 63.00/76.00 **st.** – SB.

Morgan's Brasserie, 20 Nun St., SA62 6NT, ☎ 720508 – VISA
closed January and February – **Meals** *(closed Sunday except July and August and Monday and Wednesday November-December)* (dinner only) a la carte 17.70/21.15 **t.**

at Berea NE : 4½ m. by A 487, B 4583 and Llanrian rd – ✉ St. Davids – ☎ 01348 :

Cwmwdig Water 🐎, SA62 6DW, NE : ½ m. ☎ 831434, ≤, 🌳 – ⇔ P. VISA JCB
closed November and Christmas – **Meals** (by arrangement) 14.00 **t.** 4.40 – **12 rm** (dinner included) 34.00/68.00 **t.**

at Porthgain NE : 7¾ m. by A 487 via Llanrian – ✉ Haverfordwest – ☎ 01348 :

Harbour Lights, SA62 5BN, ☎ 831549 – VISA
closed Sunday, Monday, December and January – **Meals** (booking essential) 19.50 **t.** (dinner) and lunch a la carte 13.50/17.50 **t.** 5.75.

ST.DOGMAELS Dyfed 403 G 27 – see Cardigan.

SARN PARK SERVICE AREA M. Glam. – ✉ Bridgend – ☎ 01656.

M 4, Junction 36, CF32 9SY ☎ 654906.

London 174 – Cardiff 17 – Swansea 20.

Forte Travelodge, CF32 9RW, M 4 junction 36 ☎ 659218, Reservations (Freephone) 0800 850950 – TV ♿ P. AE VISA
Meals (grill rest.) – **40 rm** 34.50 **t.**

SAUNDERSFOOT Dyfed 403 F 28 – pop. 2 666 – ☎ 01834.

London 245 – Carmarthen 25 – Fishguard 34 – Tenby 3.

St. Brides, St. Brides Hill, SA69 9NH, ☎ 812304, Fax 813303, ≤, 🏊 heated – ⇔ rm ▤ rest TV ☎ P – 🏛 100. AE ⓓ VISA
closed 1 to 13 January – **Meals** 11.50/22.00 **st.** and a la carte 6.00 – **43 rm** 56.00/92.00 **st.**, 2 suites – SB.

Vine Farm, The Ridgeway, SA69 9LA, ☎ 813543, 🌳 – TV P
April-October – **Meals** (by arrangement) 10.50 **st.** – **5 rm** 20.00/43.00 **st.** – SB.

SEION Gwynedd 402 403 H 24 see Caernarfon.

SOUTHERNDOWN M. Glam. 403 J 29 see Bridgend.

SWANSEA (Abertawe) W. Glam. 403 I 29 Great Britain G. – pop. 181 906 – ☎ 01792.

See : Maritime Quarter★ B – Maritime and Industrial Museum★ B **M.**

Envir. : Gower Peninsula★ : – Cefn Bryn (✻★★) – Rhossili (≤★★★) W : by A 4067 A.

Morriston, 160 Clasemont Rd ☎ 771079, A – Clyne, 120 Owls Lodge Lane, Mayals ☎ 401989, A – Langland Bay ☎ 366023 – A – Fairwood Park, Blackhills Lane, Upper Killay ☎ 203648 – A – Inco, Clydach ☎ 844216, A.

to Republic of Ireland (Cork) (Swansea Cork Ferries) (10 h).

P O Box 59, Singleton St., SA1 3QG ☎ 468321.

London 191 – Birmingham 136 – Bristol 82 – Cardiff 40 – Liverpool 187 – Stoke-on-Trent 175.

Plans on next page

Swansea Marriott, Maritime Quarter, SA1 3SS, ☎ 642020, Fax 650345, ≤, Fø, ≘s, 🏊 – |‡| ⇔ rm ▤ TV ☎ ♿ P – 🏛 250. AE ⓓ VISA JCB B e
Meals 10.95/15.95 **st.** and a la carte – 10.25 – **117 rm** 76.00 **st.** – SB.

Forte Crest, 39 The Kingsway, SA1 5LS, ☎ 651074, Fax 456044, Fø, ≘s, 🏊 – |‡| ⇔ rm TV ☎ P – 🏛 250. AE ⓓ VISA JCB B a
Meals a la carte 12.00/22.85 **st.** 6.95 – 7.95 – **97 rm** 69.00 **t.**, 2 suites – SB.

SWANSEA

Zum besseren Verständnis der Stadtpläne lesen Sie bitte die Zeichenerklärung in der Einleitung.

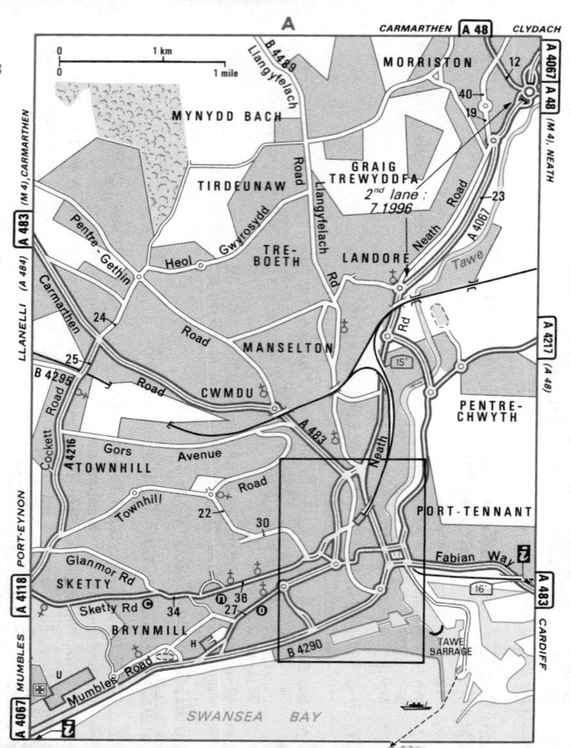

Fforest, Pontardulais Rd, Fforestfach, SA5 4BA, NW : 3 ½ m. on A 483 ☏ 588711, Fax 586219, – rm TV ☎ P – 200. AE VISA.
Meals 15.00 **t.** and a la carte 5.00 – **34 rm** 55.00/64.50 **t.** – SB.

Beaumont, 72-73 Walter Rd, SA1 4QA, ☏ 643956, Fax 643044 – TV ☎ P. AE VISA A n
Meals *(closed Sunday dinner)* (lunch by arrangement) 14.75/19.75 **t.** and a la carte 8.50 – **17 rm** 47.50/80.00 **t.** – SB.

Windsor Lodge, Mount Pleasant, SA1 6EG, ☏ 642158, Fax 648996 – TV ☎ P. AE VISA JCB B r
closed 25 and 26 December – **Meals** (lunch by arrangement) (bar meals Sunday) 10.00/25.00 **t.** 4.95 – **18 rm** 45.00/56.00 **t.** – SB.

Alexander, 3 Sketty Rd, Uplands, SA2 0EU, ☏ 470045, Fax 476012 – rest TV ☎. AE VISA. A c
closed Christmas – **Meals** (by arrangement) – **6 rm** 30.00/42.00 **st.**

Annie's, 56 St. Helen's Rd, SA1 4BE, ☏ 655603 – VISA A o
closed Monday except summer and Sunday – **Meals** (booking essential) (dinner only) 18.80 **st.** 4.45.

at Swansea Enterprise Park NE : 4 m. by A 4067 – A – off A 48 – ✉ Swansea – ☎ 01792 :

Hilton National, Phoenix Way, SA7 9EG, ☏ 310330, Fax 797535, – rm rest TV ☎ P – 180. AE VISA
Meals *(closed Saturday lunch)* 8.75/14.50 **st.** and a la carte 6.50 – 9.50 – **118 rm** 60.00/75.00 **st.**, 2 suites – SB.

at The Mumbles SW : 7 ¾ m. by A 4067 – ✉ Swansea – ☎ 01792 :

Norton House, 17 Norton Rd, SA3 5TQ, ☏ 404891, Fax 403210, – TV ☎ P. AE VISA.
Meals (bar lunch)/dinner 23.50 **t.** 4.95 – **15 rm** 55.00/80.00 **t.** – SB.

Osborne (Jarvis), Rotherslade Rd, Langland Bay, SA3 4QL, W : ¾ m. ☏ 366274, Fax 363100, ← – TV ☎ P – 50. AE VISA
Meals (bar lunch Monday to Saturday)/dinner 14.95 **st.** and a la carte 6.75 – **32 rm** 65.00/95.00 **st.** – SB.

Hillcrest, 1 Higher Lane, SA3 4NS, W : ¾ m. on Langland rd ☏ 363700, Fax 363768 – TV ☎ P. AE VISA.
closed 21 December-10 January – **Meals** *(closed Sunday dinner)* (dinner only and Sunday lunch) 17.50 **t.** – **7 rm** 50.00/70.00 **t.** – SB.

Wittemberg, 2 Rotherslade Rd, Langland, SA3 4QN, W : ¾ m. ☏ 369696, Fax 366995 – TV P. AE VISA.
closed January – **Meals** 10.00 **st.** 2.60 – **11 rm** 32.00/52.00 **st.** – SB.

at Llanrhidian W : 10 ½ m. by A 4118 – A – and B 4271 on B 4295 – ✉ Reynoldston – ☎ 01792 :

Fairyhill, Reynoldston, SA3 1BS, W : 2 ½ m. by B 4295 (Llangennith rd) ☏ 390139, Fax 391358, , park – TV ☎ P – 35. AE VISA JCB
Meals *(closed Sunday dinner September-Easter)* 13.95/24.50 **st.** 7.00 – **8 rm** 65.00/120.00 **st.** – SB.

ATS 139 Neath Rd, Hafod ☏ 456379

SWANSEA SERVICE AREA W. Glam. 403 I 28 – ☎ 01792.

P O Box 59, Singleton St., SA1 3QG ☏ 468321.

Pavilion Lodge without rest., Penllergaer, SA4 1GT, M 4 junction 47 ☏ 894894, Fax 898806 – TV P. AE VISA JCB
50 rm 39.95 **t.**

TALGARTH Powys 403 K 28 – pop. 1 818 – ☎ 01874.

London 182 – Brecon 10 – Hereford 29 – Swansea 53.

Olde Masons Arms, Hay Rd, LD3 0BB, ☏ 711688 – TV P. VISA
Meals (bar lunch)/dinner 10.50 **t.** and a la carte – **6 rm** 27.50/49.00 **t.** – SB.

TALSARNAU Gwynedd 402 403 H 25 – pop. 647 – ✉ Harlech – ☎ 01766.

London 236 – Caernafon 33 – Chester 67 – Dolgellau 25.

Maes-y-Neuadd, LL47 6YA, S : 1 ½ m. by A 496 off B 4573 ☏ 780200, Fax 780211, ←, « Part 14C country house », , park – rest TV ☎ P – 25. AE VISA JCB
Meals 12.75/23.00 **t.** – **15 rm** (dinner included) 75.00/199.00 **t.**, 1 suite – SB.

TAL-Y-BONT Gwynedd 402 403 I 24 – see Conwy.

TAL-Y-LLYN Gwynedd 402 403 I 25 – ✉ Tywyn – ☎ 01654.

♦London 224 – Dolgellau 9 – Shrewsbury 60.

Tynycornel, LL36 9AJ, on B 4405 ✆ 782282, Fax 782679, ← Tal-y-Llyn lake a[nd] mountains, ⌂, heated, ⌂, ⌂ – ⌂ rest TV ☎ P. ⌂ AE ⌂ VISA JCB
Meals (bar lunch Monday to Saturday)/dinner 18.00 **t.** 5.80 – **15 rm** ⌂ (dinner include[d]) 62.50/125.00 **t.**, 1 suite.

TENBY (Dinbych-Y-Pysgod) Dyfed 403 F 28 Great Britain G. – pop. 4 809 – ☎ 01834.

See : Town★ – Harbour and Seafront★★.

Envir. : Caldey Island★, S : by boat.

18 The Burrows ✆ 842787/842978.

The Croft, SA70 8AP ✆ 842402.

♦London 247 – Carmarthen 27 – Fishguard 36.

Waterwynch House ⌂, Narberth Rd, SA70 8TJ, N : 1 ¾ m. on A 478 ✆ 8424[6] Fax 845076, ←, ⌂, park – ⌂ rest TV ☎ P. ⌂ VISA
April-October – **Meals** *(closed Sunday dinner)* (dinner only and Sunday lunch) dinner 15.00 **t.** – **14 rm** ⌂ 38.00/76.00 **t.**, 3 suites.

Atlantic, Esplanade, SA70 7DU, ✆ 842881, Fax 842881 (ext. 256), ⌂, ⌂ – ⌂ TV ☎ P. ⌂ AE VISA. ⌂
closed 18 December-1 January – **Meals** (bar lunch)/dinner 16.00 **t.** 4.95 – **40 rm** ⌂ 35.0[0]/100.00 **t.** – SB.

Fourcroft, North Beach, SA70 8AP, ✆ 842886, Fax 842888, ←, ⌂, heated, ⌂ – ⌂ ☎ – ⌂ 80. ⌂ VISA JCB
Meals (bar lunch)/dinner 15.00 **st.** and a la carte 4.50 – **46 rm** ⌂ 45.00/83.00 **st.** – SB.

Broadmead, Heywood Lane, SA70 8DA, NW : ¾ m. ✆ 842641, Fax 845757, ⌂ – TV P. ⌂ VISA JCB. ⌂
closed January, February and November – **Meals** (bar lunch)/dinner 16.00 **t.** and a la ca[rte] 3.95 – **20 rm** ⌂ 20.00/52.00 **t.** – SB.

Buckingham, Esplanade, SA70 7DU, ✆ 842622, ← – ⌂ rm TV. ⌂ VISA
Easter-mid October – **Meals** 9.50 **st.** 6.00 – **8 rm** ⌂ 22.00/39.00 **st.** – SB.

Myrtle House, St. Marys St., SA70 7HW, ✆ 842508, Fax 842508 – ⌂ TV. ⌂ VISA JCB
Easter-October – **Meals** 10.00 – **8 rm** ⌂ 26.00/48.00.

at Penally (Penalun) SW : 2 m. by A 4139 – ✉ Tenby – ☎ 01834 :

Penally Abbey ⌂, SA70 7PY, ✆ 843033, Fax 844714, ←, ⌂ – TV ☎ P. ⌂ AE VISA JC[B] ⌂
Meals (dinner only) 23.50 **st.** 5.40 – **12 rm** ⌂ 64.00/104.00 **st.** – SB.

THORNHILL S. Glam. 403 K 29 – see Cardiff.

THREE COCKS (Aberllynfi) Powys 403 K 27 – ✉ Brecon – ☎ 01497.

♦London 184 – Brecon 11 – Hereford 25 – ♦Swansea 55.

Three Cocks with rm, LD3 0SL, on A 438 ✆ 847215, Fax 847215, « Part 15C inn », ⌂ P. ⌂ VISA. ⌂
closed December-10 February – **Meals** *(closed Sunday lunch and Tuesday)* 25.00/35.00 and a la carte 4.00 – **7 rm** ⌂ 45.00/62.00 **st.** – SB.

TINTERN (Tyndyrn) Gwent 403 404 L 28 Great Britain G. – pop. 749 – ✉ Chepstow – ☎ 0129[1]

See : Abbey★★ *AC*.

Envir. : Wye Valley★.

♦London 137 – ♦Bristol 23 – Gloucester 40 – Newport 22.

Jarvis Beaufort, NP6 6SF, on A 466 ✆ 689777, Fax 689727, ⌂ – TV ☎ P – ⌂ 50. ⌂ ⌂ VISA JCB
Meals (bar lunch Monday to Saturday)/dinner 17.95 **t.** and a la carte 7.00 – **24 r[m]** ⌂ (dinner included) 69.00/99.00 **t.** – SB.

Royal George, NP6 6SF, on A 466 ✆ 689205, Fax 689448, ⌂ – TV ☎ P. ⌂ AE ⌂ V[ISA] JCB
Meals (bar lunch)/dinner 17.50 **t.** and a la carte 4.50 – **19 rm** ⌂ 40.00/75.00 **t.** – SB.

Parva Farmhouse with rm, NP6 6SQ, on A 466 ✆ 689411, Fax 689557 – TV ☎ P. ⌂ VISA JCB
Meals (dinner only) 16.50 **st.** and a la carte 5.80 – **9 rm** ⌂ 42.00/62.00 **st.** – SB.

Dieser Führer ist kein vollständiges Hotel- und Restaurantverzeichnis.
Um den Ansprüchen aller Touristen gerecht zu werden,
haben wir uns auf eine Auswahl in jeder Kategorie beschränkt.

TREARDDUR BAY Gwynedd 402 403 G 24 – ✉ Holyhead – ☎ 01407.
♦London 269 – Bangor 25 – Caernarfon 29 – Holyhead 3.

Trearddur Bay, LL65 2UN, ✆ 860301, Fax 861181, ▢, ⛬ – TV ☎ P – 🏛 120. AE VISA JCB
Meals (bar lunch Monday)/dinner 26.00 **st.** – **30 rm** ▭ 70.00/126.00 **st.** – SB.

TREFRIW Gwynedd 402 403 I 24 – see Llanrwst.

TREMEIRCHION Clwyd 402 403 J 24 – ✉ St. Asaph – ☎ 01745.
♦London 225 – Chester 29 – Shrewsbury 59.

Bach-Y-Graig, LL17 0UH, SW : 2 m. by B 5429 and Heol Y Brenin off Dinbych rd ✆ 730627, « 16C brick built house, working farm », ⛬, park – TV P.
closed Christmas and New Year – **Meals** (by arrangement) (communal dining) 10.50 **s.** – **3 rm** ▭ 25.00/40.00 **s.** – SB.

TRESAITH Dyfed – see Aberporth.

USK (Brynbuga) Gwent 403 L 28 **Great Britain G.** – pop. 2 187 – ☎ 01291.
Exc. : Raglan Castle★ *AC*, NE : 7 m. by A 472, A 449 and A 40.
18 Alice Springs, Bettws Newydd ✆ (01873) 880772.
♦London 144 – ♦Bristol 30 – Gloucester 39 – Newport 10.

Glen-yr-Afon House, Pontypool Rd, NP5 1SY, ✆ 672302, Fax 672597, ⛬ – TV ☎ ♿ P – 🏛 120. AE VISA
Meals 17.00/25.00 **t.** and a la carte – **26 rm** ▭ 55.30/67.00 **t.** – SB.

at Llangybi S : 2½ m. on Llangybi rd – ✉ Usk – ☎ 01633 :

Cwrt Bleddyn, NP5 1PG, S : 1 m. ✆ 450521, Fax 450220, ▢, ⛬, park, squash – rm TV ☎ P – 🏛 200. AE VISA
Meals 14.95/24.50 **t.** – **32 rm** ▭ 82.50/105.00 **t.**, 4 suites – SB.

WELSH HOOK Dyfed – see Fishguard.

WELSHPOOL (Trallwng) Powys 402 403 K 26 **Great Britain G.** – pop. 5 900 – ☎ 01938.
Envir. : Powis Castle★★, S : 1 m. by A 483.
18 Golfa Hill ✆ 83249.
Flash Centre, Salop Rd, SY21 7DH ✆ 552043.
♦London 182 – ♦Birmingham 64 – Chester 45 – Shrewsbury 19.

Royal Oak, The Cross, SY21 7DG, ✆ 552217, Fax 552217 – TV ☎ P – 🏛 150. AE VISA JCB
Meals 7.95/14.95 **t.** and a la carte 4.50 – **25 rm** ▭ 40.00/75.00 **t.** – SB.

Moat Farm, SY21 8SE, S : 2¼ m. on A 483 ✆ 553179, « Working farm », ⛬, park – rest TV P.
April-October – **Meals** (by arrangement) (communal dining) 11.00 **st.** – **3 rm** ▭ 25.00/36.00 **st.** – SB.

at Guilsfield N : 3 m. by A 490 on B 4392 – ✉ Welshpool – ☎ 01938 :

Lower Trelydan, SY21 9PH, S : ¾ m. by B 4392 on unmarked rd ✆ 553105, Fax 553105, « 16C farmhouse, working farm », ⛬, park – P.
Meals (by arrangement) 12.00 **st.** 3.50 – **3 rm** ▭ 25.00/38.00 **st.**

WHITEBROOK Gwent – see Monmouth.

WHITLAND (Hendy-Gwyn) Dyfed 403 G 28 – pop. 1 518 – ☎ 01994.
♦London 235 – Carmarthen 15 – Haverfordwest 17.

Cilpost Farm, SA34 0RP, N : 1 ¼ m. by North Rd ✆ 240280, ≤, « Working dairy farm », ▢, ⛬ – P.
April-September – **Meals** 15.00 **t.** 3.00 – **7 rm** ▭ (dinner included) 29.00/68.00.

ATS Emporium Garage, Market St. ✆ 240587

WOLF'S CASTLE (Cas-Blaidd) Dyfed 403 F 28 pop. 616 – ✉ Haverfordwest – ☎ 01437.
♦London 258 – Fishguard 7 – Haverfordwest 8.

Wolfscastle Country, SA62 5LZ, on A 40 ✆ 741225, Fax 741383, ⛬, squash – rest TV ☎ P. AE VISA JCB
closed 24 to 26 December – **Meals** (lunch by arrangement Monday to Saturday)/dinner a la carte 14.05/21.15 **t.** 4.50 – **20 rm** ▭ 38.00/70.00 **t.** – SB.

WREXHAM (Wrecsam) Clwyd 402 403 L 24 **Great Britain G.** – pop. 40 614 – ☎ 01978.

See : St. Giles Church★.

Envir. : Erddig★ *AC*, SW : 2 m.

Holt Rd ☏ 261033 – , Chirk G & C.C. ☏ (0169) 1774407.

Lambpit St., LL11 1AY ☏ 292015.

◆London 192 – Chester 12 – Shrewsbury 28.

Llwyn Onn Hall , Cefn Rd, LL13 0NY, 2½ m. by A 534 ☏ 261225, Fax 363233, ←, rm – 25. AE VISA JCB.
Meals 15.00/20.00 **st.** and a la carte 4.00 – **13 rm** 54.00/110.00 **st.** – SB.

Cross Lanes, Marchwiel, LL13 0TF, SE : 3½ m. on A 525 ☏ 780555, Fax 780568, , park – – 100. AE VISA.
closed 25 and 26 December – **Meals** (bar lunch Saturday) 10.50/18.90 **t.** and a la car 5.25 – 4.50 – **15 rm** 54.00/78.00 **st.** – SB.

Forte Travelodge, Croes-Foel roundabout, Rhostyllen, LL14 4EJ, SW : 2½ m. on A 48 (Wrexham bypass) ☏ 365705, Reservations (Freephone) 0800 850950 – VISA.
Meals (grill rest.) – **32 rm** 34.50 **t.**

Travel Inn, Chester Rd, LL12 8PW, NE : 2½ m. by A 483 on B 5445 ☏ 853214 – AE VISA.
Meals (grill rest.) – 4.95 – **38 rm** 34.50 **t.**

at Llandegla W : 10 m. by A 525 – ✉ Wrexham – ☎ 01978 :

Bodidris Hall ,, LL11 3AL, NE : 1½ m. by A 5104 ☏ 790434, Fax 790335, « Part 15 manor », , , park – rest – 40. AE VISA.
Meals (lunch by arrangement) 10.50/25.00 **st.** and a la carte 6.50 – **12 rm** 80.00 125.00 **st.** – SB.

ATS Dolydd Rd, Croesnewydd ☏ 352301/352928

Scotland

Place with at least	
a hotel or restaurant	● Tongue
a pleasant hotel or restaurant	🏨, ⌂, ✗
a quiet, secluded hotel	🐎
a restaurant with	✿, ✿✿, ✿✿✿, **Meals (M)**
See this town for establishments located in its vicinity	ABERDEEN

La località possiede come minimo	
una risorsa alberghiera	● Tongue
Albergo o ristorante ameno	🏨, ⌂, ✗
un albergo molto tranquillo, isolato	🐎
un'ottima tavola con ✿, ✿✿, ✿✿✿,	**Meals (M)**
La località raggruppa nel suo testo le risorse dei dintorni	ABERDEEN

Localité offrant au moins	
une ressource hôtelière	● Tongue
un hôtel ou restaurant agréable	🏨, ⌂, ✗
un hôtel très tranquille, isolé	🐎
une bonne table à	✿, ✿✿, ✿✿✿, **Meals (M)**
Localité groupant dans le texte les ressources de ses environs	ABERDEEN

Ort mit mindestens	
einem Hotel oder Restaurant	● Tongue
ein angenehmes Hotel oder Restaurant	🏨, ⌂, ✗
einem sehr ruhigen und abgelegenen Hotel	🐎
einem Restaurant mit ✿, ✿✿, ✿✿✿,	**Meals (M)**
Ort mit Angaben über Hotels und Restaurants in der Umgebung	ABERDEEN

Galson
Kinlochbervie
Rhiconich
Scourie
Breasclete
Stornoway
ISLE OF LEWIS
Drumbeg
Kylesku
Lochinver
Ardvourlie
Tarbert
Achiltibuie
Ullapool
Scarista
ISLE OF HARRIS
Aultbea
Dundonnell
Poolewe
Gairloch
Flodigarry
Lochmaddy
NORTH UIST
Culnaknock
Talladale
Locheport
Uig
Grimsay
Torridon
Shieldaig
Strathconon
Liniclate
BENBECULA
Skeabost
M, Dunvegan
Portree
Lochcarron
SOUTH UIST
ISLE OF SKYE
Erbusaig
Plockton
Cannich
Kyle of Lochalsh
Dornie
Daliburgh
Lochboisdale
Broadford
Breakish
Glenelg
Pollachar
Ord
Isleornsay
Ardvasar
Invergarry
Castlebay
ISLE OF BARRA
Arisaig

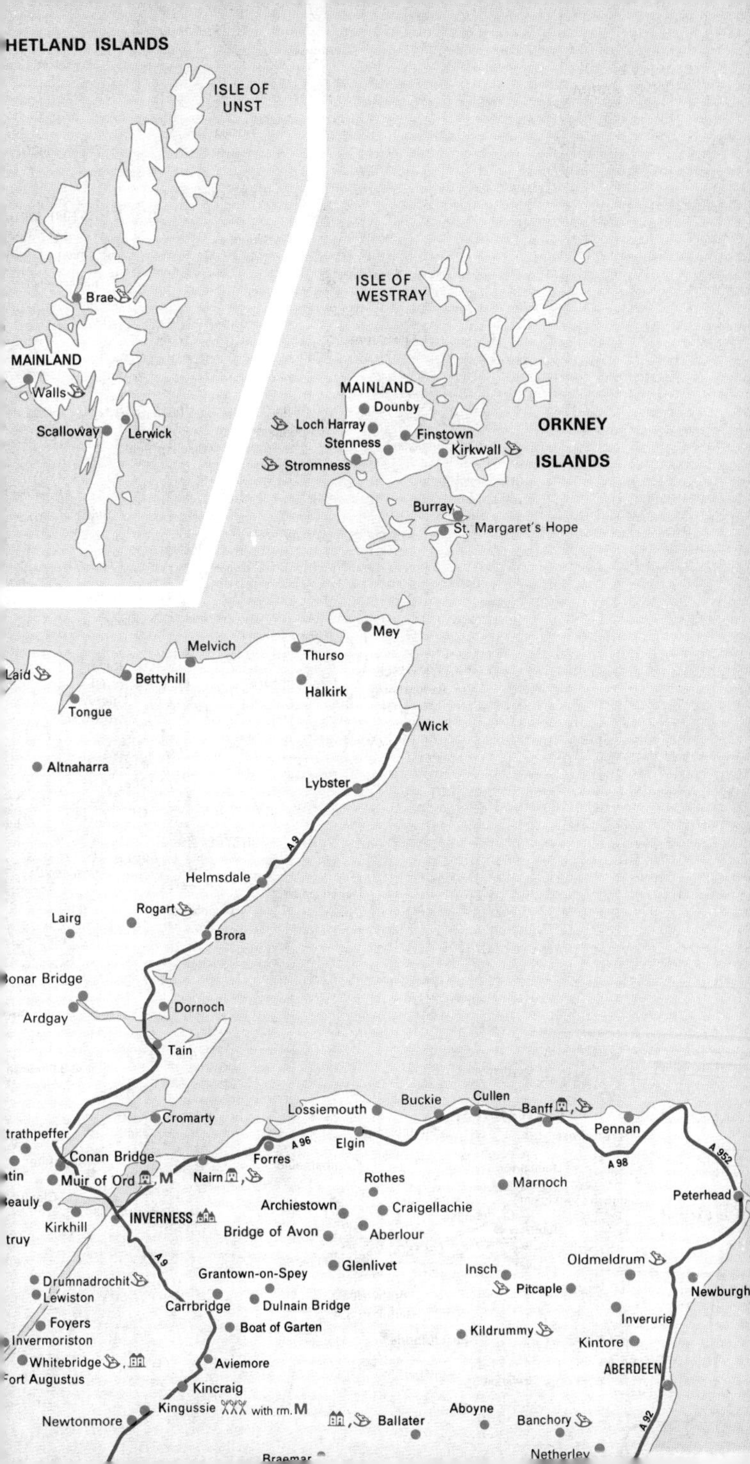
HETLAND ISLANDS
ISLE OF UNST
Brae
MAINLAND
Walls
Scalloway
Lerwick
ISLE OF WESTRAY
MAINLAND
Dounby
Loch Harray
Stenness
Finstown
Kirkwall
ORKNEY ISLANDS
Stromness
Burray
St. Margaret's Hope
Mey
Melvich
Thurso
Laid
Bettyhill
Halkirk
Tongue
Wick
Altnaharra
Lybster
A9
Helmsdale
Rogart
Lairg
Brora
Bonar Bridge
Ardgay
Dornoch
Tain
Buckie
Cullen
Lossiemouth
Banff
Cromarty
Pennan
trathpeffer
Elgin
A 96
A 98
A 952
Conan Bridge
Forres
Muir of Ord
M
Nairn
Rothes
Marnoch
Peterhead
eauly
Archiestown
Craigellachie
Kirkhill
INVERNESS
Bridge of Avon
Aberlour
truy
A9
Glenlivet
Oldmeldrum
Drumnadrochit
Grantown-on-Spey
Insch
Pitcaple
Newburgh
Lewiston
Carrbridge
Dulnain Bridge
Foyers
Inverurie
Boat of Garten
Invermoriston
Kildrummy
Kintore
Whitebridge
Aviemore
ABERDEEN
Fort Augustus
Kincraig
Kingussie
with rm. M
Aboyne
Newtonmore
Ballater
Banchory
A 92
Netherley
Braemar

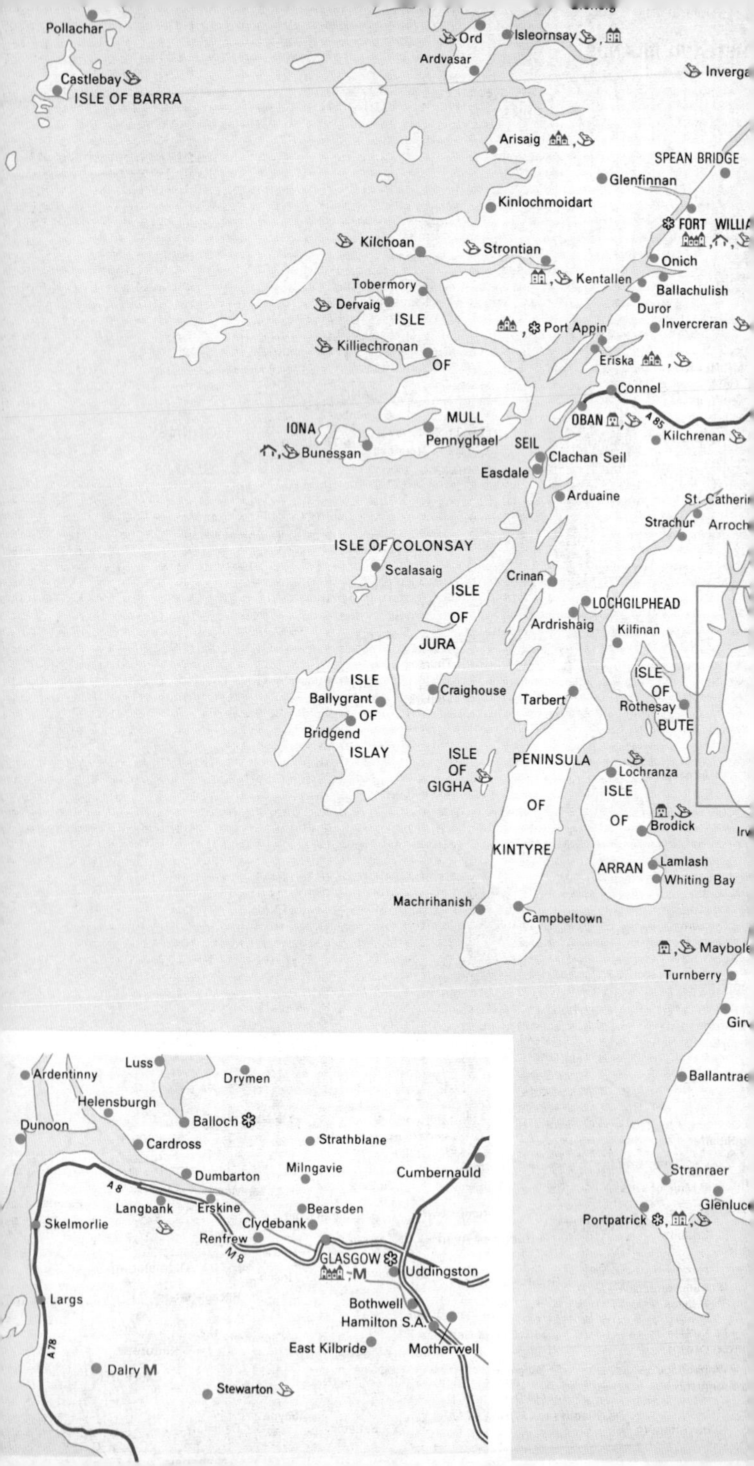

Pollachar
Ord
Isleornsay
Ardvasar
Inverga
Castlebay
ISLE OF BARRA
Arisaig
SPEAN BRIDGE
Glenfinnan
Kinlochmoidart
FORT WILLIA
Kilchoan
Strontian
Onich
Kentallen
Ballachulish
Tobermory
Dervaig
ISLE
Duror
Port Appin
Invercreran
Killiechronan
OF
Eriska
Connel
MULL
IONA
OBAN
A 85
Kilchrenan
Pennyghael
SEIL
Bunessan
Clachan Seil
Easdale
Arduaine
St. Catherin
Strachur
Arroch
ISLE OF COLONSAY
Scalasaig
Crinan
ISLE
OF
LOCHGILPHEAD
Ardrishaig
Kilfinan
JURA
ISLE
ISLE
OF
Craighouse
Tarbert
Ballygrant
Rothesay
OF
BUTE
Bridgend
ISLAY
ISLE
OF
GIGHA
PENINSULA
Lochranza
ISLE
OF
OF
Brodick
Irv
KINTYRE
Lamlash
ARRAN
Whiting Bay
Machrihanish
Campbeltown
Maybole
Turnberry
Girv
Ballantrae
Stranraer
Glenluce
Portpatrick
Luss
Ardentinny
Drymen
Helensburgh
Dunoon
Balloch
Cardross
Strathblane
Milngavie
Cumbernauld
Dumbarton
A 8
Langbank
Erskine
Bearsden
Skelmorlie
Clydebank
Renfrew
M 8
GLASGOW
M
Uddingston
Largs
Bothwell
Hamilton S.A.
East Kilbride
Motherwell
A 78
Dalry M
Stewarton

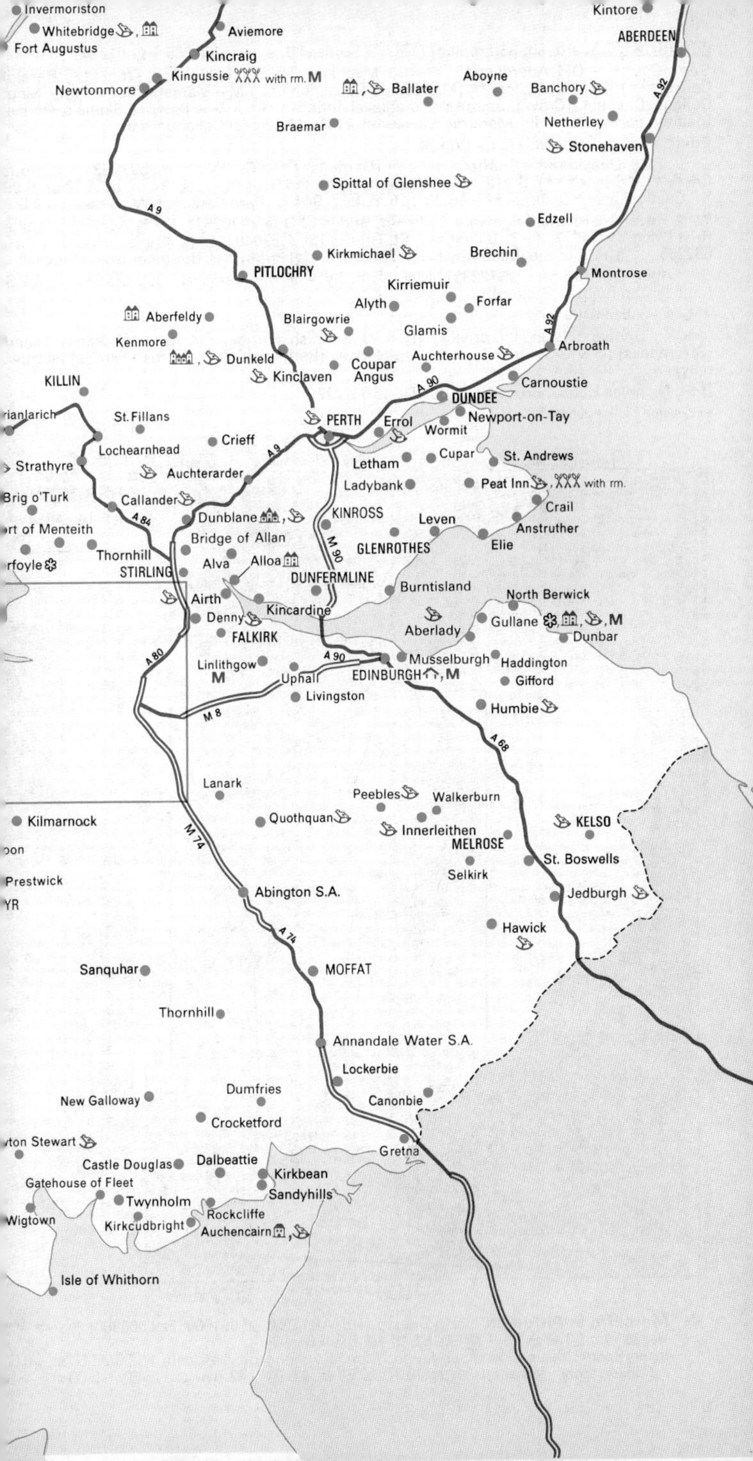
Invermoriston
Whitebridge
Fort Augustus
Aviemore
Kincraig
Kingussie with rm. M
Newtonmore
Kintore
ABERDEEN
A 92
Aboyne
Ballater
Banchory
Netherley
Braemar
Stonehaven
Spittal of Glenshee
A 9
Edzell
Kirkmichael
Brechin
PITLOCHRY
Montrose
Kirriemuir
Alyth
Forfar
Aberfeldy
Blairgowrie
Glamis
Kenmore
Arbroath
Dunkeld
Auchterhouse
Coupar Angus
Kinclaven
Carnoustie
KILLIN
A 90
DUNDEE
Crianlarich
St. Fillans
PERTH
Errol
Newport-on-Tay
Wormit
Lochearnhead
Crieff
Cupar
St. Andrews
Strathyre
Letham
Auchterarder
Ladybank
Peat Inn with rm.
Brig o'Turk
Callander
Crail
KINROSS
A 84
Dunblane
Leven
Anstruther
Port of Menteith
Bridge of Allan
M 90
GLENROTHES
Elie
Thornhill
Alva
Alloa
Aberfoyle
STIRLING
DUNFERMLINE
Burntisland
North Berwick
Airth
Kincardine
Gullane M
Denny
Aberlady
Dunbar
FALKIRK
A 80
A 90
Musselburgh
Haddington
Linlithgow
M
Uphall
EDINBURGH M
Gifford
Livingston
M 8
Humbie
A 68
Lanark
Peebles
Walkerburn
Kilmarnock
Quothquan
Innerleithen
KELSO
MELROSE
M 74
St. Boswells
Selkirk
Prestwick
AYR
Abington S.A.
Jedburgh
A 74
Hawick
Sanquhar
MOFFAT
Thornhill
Annandale Water S.A.
Lockerbie
Dumfries
New Galloway
Canonbie
Crocketford
Newton Stewart
Gretna
Castle Douglas
Dalbeattie
Kirkbean
Gatehouse of Fleet
Sandyhills
Twynholm
Rockcliffe
Wigtown
Kirkcudbright
Auchencairn
Isle of Whithorn

ABERDEEN Aberdeen. (Grampian) **401** N 12 **Scotland G.** – pop. 204 885 – 01224.

See : City★★ – Old Aberdeen★★ X – St. Machar's Cathedral★★ (West Front★★★, Herald Ceiling★★★) X **A** – Art Gallery★★ (Macdonald Collection★★) Y **M** – Mercat Cross★★ Y **B** – King College Chapel★ (Crown Spire★★★, medieval fittings★★★) X **D** – Provost Skene's House (painted ceilings★★) Y **E** – Maritime Museum★ Z **M1** – Marischal College★ Y **U**.

Envir. : Brig o' Balgownie★, by Don St. X.

Exc. : SW : Deeside★★ – Crathes Castle★★ (Gardens★★★) *AC*, SW : 16 m. by A 93 X – Dunottar Castle★★ *AC* (site★★★), S : 18 m. by A 92 X – Pitmedden Garden★★, N : 14 m. by A 92 on B 99 X – Castle Fraser★ (exterior★★) *AC*, W : 16 m, by A 944 X – Fyvie Castle★, NW : 6 m. on A 947.

18, 18 Royal Aberdeen, Balgownie, Links Rd, Bridge of Don ☎ 702571, X – 18 Auchmill, Provost Rust Drive ☎ 714577, X – 18 Balnagask, St. Fitticks Rd ☎ 876407 X – 18 King's Links, Golf Rd ☎ 632269 X – 18 Portlethen, Badentoy Rd ☎ 781090, X – 18, 9 Murcar, Bridge of Don ☎ 704345,

Aberdeen Airport : ☎ 722331, NW : 7 m. by A 96 X – **Terminal** : Bus Station, Guild S (adjacent to Railway Station).

☎ 0345 090700.

to Shetland Islands (Lerwick) (P & O Scottish Ferries) (14 h) – to Orkney Island (Stromness) (P & O Scottish Ferries) – to Norway (Bergen) (P & O Scottish Ferries) (summer only).

St. Nicholas House, Broad St., AB9 1DE ☎ 632727.

◆Edinburgh 130 – ◆Dundee 67.

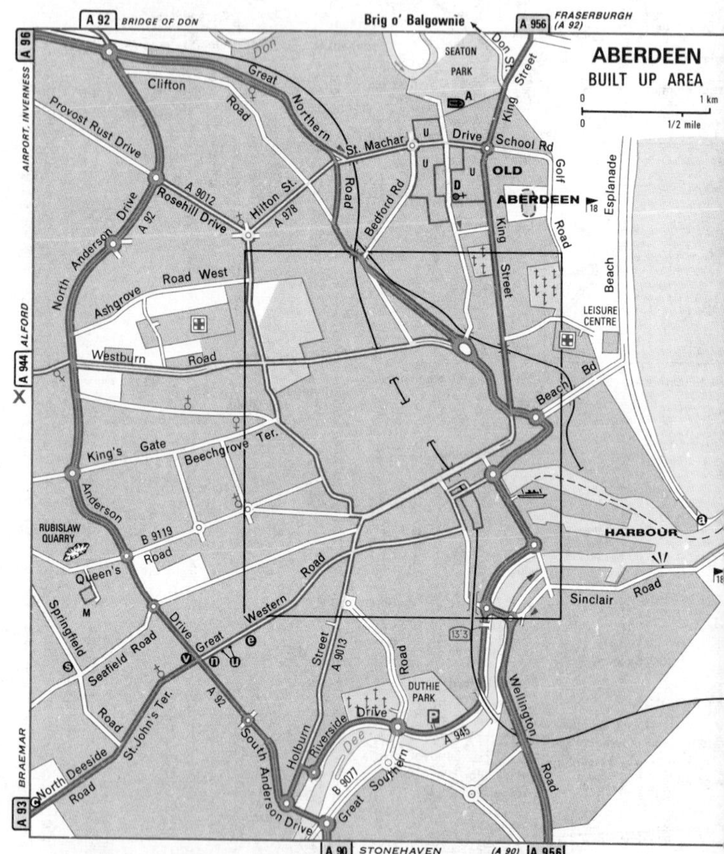

Marcliffe at Pitfodels, North Deeside Rd, AB1 9YA, ☎ 861000, Fax 868860, – rest – 90. VISA JCB X
Invery Room : Meals *(closed Sunday and Monday)* (dinner only) a la carte 26.50/35.50 **st.** 6.50 – **Conservatory : Meals** a la carte 15.70/23.50 **st.** 6.50 – **42 rm** 115.00/175.00 **st.** – SB

ABERDEEN

on Accord Centre . . . . Y
eorge Street. . . . . Y
. Nicholas Centre . . . . Y 29
. Nicholas Street . . . . YZ 30
inity Centre . . . . Z
nion Street . . . . Z

oad Street. . . . . Y 6
astle Street. . . . . Y 7

College Street. . . . . Z 9
Craigie Loanings . . . . Y 12
Denburn Road. . . . . YZ 14
East North Street. . . . . Y 16
Great Southern Road. . . . . . . Z 18
Guild Street . . . . Z 19
Justice Street. . . . . Y 21
Millburn Street. . . . . Z 23
Rosemount Terrace . . . . Y 25
Rosemount Viaduct . . . . Y 26
St. Andrew Street . . . . Y 28
School Hill . . . . YZ 32

South Esplanade West . . . . . Z 33
South Mount Street. . . . . Y 34
Springbank Terrace . . . . Z 35
Spring Garden . . . . Y 36
Trinity Quay . . . . Z 37
Union Terrace. . . . . Z 39
Upperkirkgate. . . . . Y 40
Victoria Street. . . . . Z 42
Waverley Place. . . . . Z 43
Wellington Place . . . . Z 45
Wellington Road. . . . . Z 47
Woolmanhill. . . . . Y 48

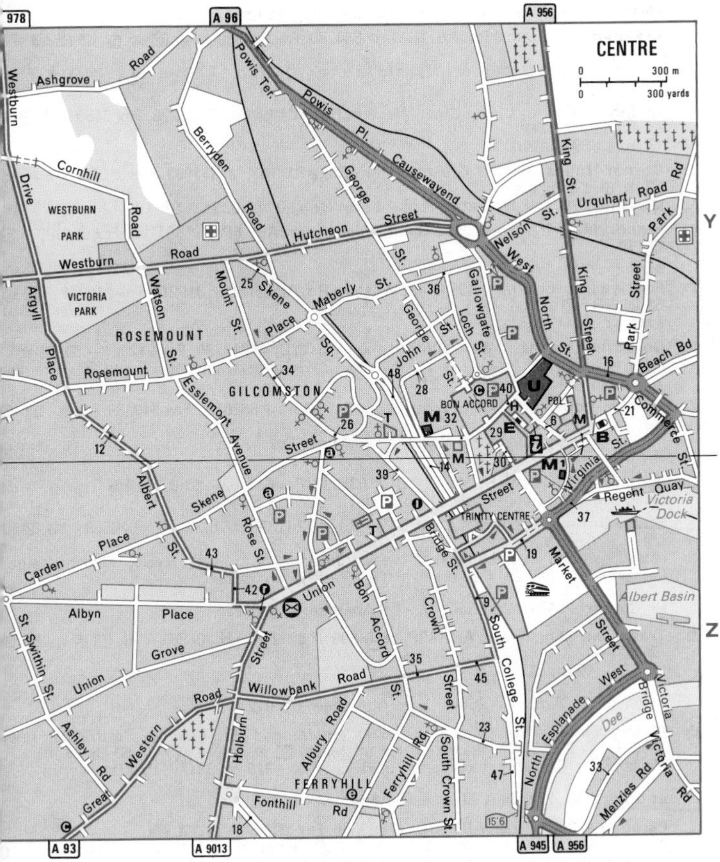

CENTRE
0 300 m
0 300 yards
A 96
A 956
978
A 93
A 9013
A 945
A 956
Y
Z
Ashgrove Road
Westburn Drive
Cornhill
WESTBURN PARK
Westburn Road
VICTORIA PARK
Argyll Place
ROSEMOUNT
Rosemount
GILCOMSTON
Berryden Road
Powis Ter.
Powis Pl.
Causewayend
George St.
Hutcheon Street
Watson St.
Mount St.
Skene Place
Maberly St.
Esslemont Avenue
Skene Street
Albert St.
Carden Place
Rose St.
Albyn Place
Union Grove
Union Street
Holburn Street
Great Western Road
Ashley Rd
St Swithin St.
Willowbank Road
Albury Road
FERRYHILL
Fonthill Rd
Ferryhill Rd
South Crown St.
Crown Street
Bon Accord St.
Bridge St.
South College St.
North Esplanade West
Market Street
TRINITY CENTRE
BON ACCORD
Gallowgate
Loch St.
John St.
West North St.
Nelson St.
King St.
King Street
Urquhart Road
Park Street
Park Rd
Beach Bd
Commerce St.
Virginia St.
Regent Quay
Victoria Dock
Albert Basin
Dee
Victoria Bridge
Victoria Rd
Menzies Rd

Caledonian Thistle, 10-14 Union Terr., AB9 1HE, ☎ 640233, Fax 641627 – 🛗 ⇔ rm 📺 ☎ 🅟 – 🏛 35. AE ⓓ VISA Z i
Meals 10.75/25.50 **st.** and a la carte 🍷 6.95 – ☕ 10.25 – **78 rm** 103.00/135.00 **st.**, 2 suites – SB.

Stakis Aberdeen, 161 Springfield Rd, AB9 2QH, ☎ 313377, Fax 312028, 🏋, ≘s, 🏊, ⛱, 🎾 – 🛗 ⇔ rm 📺 ☎ 🅟 – 🏛 900. AE ⓓ VISA JCB. ✻ X s
Meals *(closed Saturday lunch)* 10.00/14.00 **st.** and dinner a la carte – ☕ 9.50 – **109 rm** 99.00/109.00 **st.**, 1 suite – SB.

Ardoe House 🐎, South Deeside Rd, Blairs, AB1 5YP, SW : 5 m. on B 9077 ☎ 867355, Fax 861283, ≤, « Part 19C baronial mansion », ⛱, park – 🛗 ⇔ 📺 ☎ 🅟 – 🏛 120. AE ⓓ VISA
Meals *(closed Saturday lunch)* 26.75 **t.** (dinner) and a la carte 🍷 6.00 – ☕ 10.50 – **69 rm** 82.00/124.00 **t.**, 2 suites – SB.

Copthorne, 122 Huntly St., AB1 1SU, ☎ 630404, Fax 640573 – 🛗 ⇔ rm 📺 ☎ – 🏛 220. AE ⓓ VISA JCB. ✻ Z a
Meals *(closed lunch Saturday and Sunday)* 15.25 **t.** and a la carte – ☕ 10.25 – **89 rm** 107.00/132.00 **t.** – SB.

Quality, Bridge of Don, AB23 8BL, N : 3 m. on A 92 ✆ 706707, Fax 823923 – rm
Meals 18.00/25.00 **st.** and a la carte – 9.25 – **123 rm** 75.00/125.00 **st.** – SB.

Amatola (Jarvis), 448 Great Western Rd, AB1 6NP, ✆ 318724, Fax 312716 – rm – 400. X
Meals (bar lunch Monday to Saturday)/dinner 12.95 **st.** and a la carte – 8.75 – **53 rm** 79.00/99.00 **st.** – SB.

Malacca, 349 Great Western Rd, AB1 6NW, ✆ 588901, Fax 571621 – X
Meals - Seafood - a la carte 16.60/36.50 **t.** 7.50 – **21 rm** 65.00/75.00 **t.**

Craiglynn, 36 Fonthill Rd, AB1 2UJ, ✆ 584050, Fax 584050 – Z
closed 25 and 26 December – **Meals** (dinner only)/14.95 **st.** 4.50 – **9 rm** 34.00/62.50 **st.** – SB.

Cedars without rest., 339 Great Western Rd, AB1 6NW, ✆ 583225, Fax 585050 – X
13 rm 38.00/52.00 **st.**

Corner House, 385-387 Great Western Rd, AB1 6NY, ✆ 313063, Fax 313063 – rest X
Meals 13.00 **st.** and a la carte 3.75 – **17 rm** 42.00/56.00 **st.** – SB.

Manorville without rest., 252 Great Western Rd, AB1 6PJ, ✆ 594190, Fax 594190 – Z
3 rm 25.00/40.00 **t.**

Fourways without rest., 435 Great Western Rd, AB1 6NJ, ✆ 310218, Fax 310218 – X
7 rm 25.00/40.00 **s.**

Courtyard on the Lane, 1 Alford Lane, AB1 1YD, ✆ 213795, Fax 212961 –
closed Sunday, Monday, 1 and 2 January, 2 weeks mid July and 25 and 26 December – **Meals** a la carte 16.20/24.25 **t.** 6.00. Z

Rendez-vous, 210-212 George St., AB1 1BS, ✆ 633610, Fax 649389 – Y
closed Sunday lunch – **Meals** - Chinese (Peking) and Thai - 9.50 **t.** (lunch) and a la carte 13.00/16.90 **t.**

Nargile, 77-79 Skene St., AB1 1QD, ✆ 636093, Fax 636202 – Y
Meals - Turkish - (dinner only) 18.75 **st.** and a la carte 5.40.

Silver Darling, Pocra Quay, North Pier Rd, AB2 1DQ, ✆ 576229, Fax 626558 – X
closed Saturday lunch, Sunday, 2 weeks Christmas-New Year – **Meals** - French Seafood - (booking essential) 23.00 **t.** (lunch) and a la carte 24.95/30.50 **t.**

at Murcar N : 4½ m. on A 92 – X – ✉ Aberdeen – ☎ 01224 :

Travel Inn without rest., AB2 8BP, on B 999 ✆ 821217, Fax 706869 –
4.95 – **40 rm** 34.50 **t.**

at Altens S : 3 m. on A 956 – X – ✉ Aberdeen – ☎ 01224 :

Altens Skean Dhu (Mount Charlotte), Souterhead Rd, AB1 4LF, ✆ 877000, Telex 739631, Fax 896964, heated – rm rest – 400.
Meals 13.75/16.50 **st.** and a la carte 5.95 – 9.50 – **220 rm** 83.00/115.00 **st.**, 1 suite – SB.

at Cults SW : 4 m. on A 93 – X – ✉ Aberdeen – ☎ 01224 :

Faraday's, 2 Kirk Brae, AB1 9SQ, ✆ 869666, Fax 869666 –
closed Monday lunch, Sunday and 26 December-12 January – **Meals** (booking essential) 19.95 **t.** (dinner) and lunch a la carte approx. 10.80 **t.** 4.60.

at Maryculter SW : 8 m. on B 9077 – X – ✉ Aberdeen – ☎ 01224 :

Maryculter House, South Deeside Rd, AB1 0BB, ✆ 732124, Fax 733510, « Part 13C house on River Dee », – rm – 30.
Meals (bar lunch)/dinner 27.50 **t.** 6.50 – 9.50 – **23 rm** 105.00/125.00 **t.** – SB.

at Bucksburn NW : 4 m. by A 96 – X – on A 947 – ✉ Aberdeen – ☎ 01224 :

Holiday Inn Crown Plaza Aberdeen, Oldmeldrum Rd, AB2 9LN, ✆ 713911, Fax 714020, – rm – 180.
Meals 10.95/17.50 **st.** and a la carte – 10.95 – **144 rm** 105.00/130.00 **t.** – SB.

at Dyce NW : 5½ m. by A 96 – X – on A 947 – ✉ Aberdeen – ☎ 01224 :

Aberdeen Marriott, Riverview Drive, Farburn, AB2 0AZ, ✆ 770011, Fax 722347, – rm – 400.
Meals a la carte 20.00/28.00 **st.** – 10.75 – **153 rm** 99.00 **st.**, 1 suite – SB.

at Aberdeen Airport NW : 6 m. by A 96 – X – ✉ Aberdeen – ☎ 01224 :

Airport Skean Dhu Aberdeen (Mount Charlotte), Argyll Rd, AB2 0DU, ℘ 725252, Telex 739239, Fax 723745, heated – rm TV ☎ & P – 550. AE VISA JCB
Meals 12.25/18.50 **st.** and a la carte 5.95 – 9.25 – **148 rm** 83.00/150.00 **st.**

Speedbird Inn, Argyll Rd, AB2 0AF, ℘ 772884, Fax 772560 – rm TV ☎ & P. AE VISA
Meals *(closed lunch Saturday and Sunday)* a la carte 9.50/14.40 **st.** 3.95 – 3.95 – **100 rm** 42.50 **t.**

ATS Beach Boulevard ℘ 592727 ATS 214 Hardgate ℘ 589461

ABERFELDY Perth. (Tayside) 401 I 14 **Scotland G.** – pop. 4 083 – ☎ 01887.
See : Town★.
Envir. : St. Mary's Church (painted ceiling★) NE : 2 m. by A 827.
Exc. : Loch Tay★★, SW : 6 m. by A 827 – Ben Lawers★★, SW : 16 m. by A 827 – Blair Castle★★ AC, N : 20½ m. by A 827 and A 9.
Taybridge Rd ℘ 820535.
The Square, PH15 2DD ℘ 820276.
Edinburgh 76 – ♦Glasgow 73 – ♦Oban 77 – Perth 32.

Farleyer House , PH15 2JE, W : 2 m. on B 846 ℘ 820332, Fax 829430, ←, , park – rm TV ☎ P. AE VISA.
closed 2 weeks early January – **Menzies : Meals** (booking essential) (dinner only) 32.00/40.00 **t.** 4.50 – **Bistro : Meals** a la carte 17.60/24.95 **t.** 4.50 – **11 rm** 85.00/190.00 **t.** – SB.

Guinach House , Urlar Rd, PH15 2ET, off Crieff Rd ℘ 820251, Fax 829607, ←, – rest TV P. VISA
closed Christmas – **Meals** (dinner only) 22.50 **st.** – **7 rm** 37.50/75.00 **st.**

Benutzen Sie für weite Fahrten in Europa die **Michelin-Länderkarten** *:*
970 Europa, 976 Tschechische Republik-Slowakische Republik, 980 Griechenland,
984 Deutschland, 985 Skandinavien-Finnland, 986 Großbritannien-Irland,
987 Deutschland-Österreich-Benelux, 988 Italien, 989 Frankreich, 990 Spanien-Portugal,
991 Jugoslawien.

ABERFOYLE Stirling (Central) 401 G 15 **Scotland G.** – pop. 936 – ✉ Stirling – ☎ 01877.
Envir. : The Trossachs★★★ (Loch Katherine★★) N : 5 m. by A 821 – Hilltop Viewpoint★★★ (★★★) N : 2½ m. by A 821 – Inchmahone Priory (double effigy★) *AC*, E : 4 m. by A 81.
Exc. : Ben Lomond★★, W : 16 m. by B 829.
Braeval ℘ 382493.
Main St., ℘ 72352 (summer only).
Edinburgh 56 – ♦Glasgow 27.

XX ✿ **Braeval** (Nairn), FK8 3UY, E : 1 m. by A 821 on A 81 ℘ 382711, Fax 382400 – P. VISA
closed Sunday dinner, Monday, 1 to 4 January, 1 week mid March, 1 week June and 10 days October – **Meals** (booking essential) (dinner only and Sunday lunch) 28.95 **t.**
Spec. Crab soufflé with mint hollandaise, Roast breast of guinea fowl with roast vegetables and sauce tapenade, Poached pears with vanilla cream pastry and champagne syrup.

ABERLADY E. Lothian. (Lothian) 401 L 15 – pop. 1 033 – ☎ 01875.
Edinburgh 16 – Haddington 5 – North Berwick 7.5.

Green Craigs , EH32 0PY, SW : ¾ m. on A 198 ℘ 870301, Fax 870440, ←, – TV ☎ P. AE VISA.
closed 1 January – **Meals** 25.00 **t.** and a la carte 5.50 – **6 rm** 60.00/120.00 **t.** – SB.

Kilspindie House, Main St., EH32 0RE, ℘ 870682, Fax 870504 – TV ☎ P. VISA
Meals (dinner only) 13.00 **t.** and a la carte 5.30 – **26 rm** 39.00/66.00 – SB.

ABERLOUR Banff. (Grampian) 401 K 11 pop. 1 780 – ☎ 01340 Carron.
Edinburgh 192 – ♦Aberdeen 60 – Elgin 15 – ♦Inverness 55.

Dowans, AB38 9LS, SW : ¾ m. by A 95 ℘ 871488, Fax 871038, – TV ☎ P. VISA
closed January and February – **Meals** (bar lunch)/dinner 18.50 **t.** 4.50 – **17 rm** 39.00/70.00 **t.** – SB.

ABINGTON SERVICE AREA Lanark. (Strathclyde) – ✉ Biggar – ☎ 0186 42.
Edinburgh 43 – Dumfries 37 – ♦Glasgow 38.

Forte Travelodge, ML12 6RG, at junction of A 74 with M 74 ℘ 782, Reservations (Freephone) 0800 850950 – TV & P. AE VISA.
Meals (grill rest.) – **56 rm** 34.50 **t.**

ABOYNE Aberdeen. (Grampian) 401 L 12 **Scotland G.** – pop. 3 793 (inc. Cromar) – ☎ 0133 9
Exc. : Craigievar Castle★ *AC*, NE : 12 m. by B 9094, B 9119 and A 980.
Formanston Park ✆ 86328.
Ballater Road Car Park ✆ 86060 (summer only).
◆Edinburgh 131 – ◆Aberdeen 30 – ◆Dundee 68.

Birse Lodge, Charleston Rd, AB34 5EL, ✆ 86253, – . VISA
Meals 28.00 **t.** (dinner) and a la carte 10.00/22.00 **t.** 4.50 – **12 rm** 25.00/70.00 **st.** – SB

Hazlehurst Lodge, Ballater Rd, AB34 5HY, ✆ 86921, Fax 86660, « Contempora interior », – . AE VISA.
closed December-January – **Meals** (by arrangement) 22.00 **t.** 7.00 – **3 rm** 30.00/70.0 – SB.

ACHILTIBUIE Ross and Cromarty. (Highland) 401 D 9 – ☎ 01854.
◆Edinburgh 243 – ◆Inverness 84 – Ullapool 25.

Summer Isles, IV26 2YG, ✆ 622282, Fax 622251, « Picturesque setting ≤ Summ Isles », – rest
3 April-6 October – **Meals** (booking essential) (light seafood lunch) 33.00 **st.** (dinn and lunch a la carte 17.00 **st.** – **11rm** 45.00/97.00 **st.**, 1 suite.

AIRTH Stirling. (Central) 401 I 15 – pop. 1 519 – ✉ Falkirk – ☎ 01324.
◆Edinburgh 30 – Dunfermline 14 – Falkirk 7 – Stirling 8.

Airth Castle, FK2 8JF, ✆ 831411, Fax 831419, ≤, « Part 13C and 17C castle a stables in extensive grounds », , , , , park, – – 380.
VISA.
Meals 9.25/22.50 **t.** and a la carte 5.50 – **75 rm** 90.00/140.00 **st.** – SB.

Prices	For full details of the prices quoted in the guide, consult the introduction.

ALLOA Stirling. (Central) 401 I 15 **Scotland G.** – pop. 26 691 – ☎ 01259.
Exc. : Culross★★★ (Village★★★, Palace★★ *AC*, Study★ *AC*) SE : 7 m. by A 907, A 977 and B 90 – Castle Campbell★ (site★★★, ≤★) *AC*, NE : 8 m. by A 908 and A 91 – Stirling★★, W : 8 m. A 907.
◆Edinburgh 33 – ◆Dundee 48 – ◆Glasgow 35.

Gean House, Gean Park, Tullibody Rd, FK10 2HS, NW : 1 m. on B 9096 ✆ 21927 Fax 213827, ≤, – rest – 60. AE VISA.
Meals 11.50/29.00 **t.** and a la carte – **7 rm** 80.00/140.00 **t.** – SB.

ATS Union St. ✆ 724253

ALLOWAY Ayr. (Strathclyde) 401 402 G 17 – see Ayr.

ALTENS Aberdeen. (Grampian) – see Aberdeen.

ALTNAHARRA Sutherland. (Highland) 401 G 9 **Scotland G.** – ✉ Lairg – ☎ 01549.
Exc. : Ben Loyal★★, N : 10 m. by A 836 – Ben Hope★ (≤★★★) NW : 14 m.
◆Edinburgh 239 – ◆Inverness 83 – Thurso 61.

Altnaharra, IV27 4UE, ✆ 411222, Fax 411222, ≤, , – rest . VISA.
March-September – **Meals** (bar lunch)/dinner 19.00 **st.** 5.50 – **16 rm** 49.50/59.00 **st.**

ALVA Stirling.(Central) 401 I 15 pop. 7 475 – ☎ 01259.
◆Edinburgh 36 – ◆Dundee 46 – ◆Glasgow 35.

Farriers with rm, Woodland Park, Alva Stables, FK12 5HU, ✆ 762702, Fax 769782 –
. AE VISA.
Meals a la carte 12.65/21.35 **st.** 4.50 – **6 rm** 39.00/49.50 **st.**

ALYTH Perth. (Tayside) 401 J 14 – pop. 4 650 – ☎ 01828.
Pitcrocknie ✆ 632268.
◆Edinburgh 63 – ◆Aberdeen 69 – ◆Dundee 16 – Perth 21.

Lands of Loyal, Loyal Rd, PH11 8JQ, N : ½ m. by B 952 ✆ 633151, Fax 633313, ≤, – rest . AE VISA
Meals 21.75 **t.** (dinner) and a la carte 11.50/23.95 5.95 – **14 rm** 45.00/70.00 **t.** – SB.

Drumnacree House, St. Ninians Rd, PH11 8AP, ✆ 632194, Fax 632194, –
VISA
April-19 December – **Meals** *(closed Sunday and Monday to non-residents)* (bookin essential) (dinner only) 23.00 **t.** 6.00 – **6 rm** 35.00/65.00 **t.**

ANNANDALE WATER SERVICE AREA Dumfries (Dumfries and Galloway) – ✉ Lockerbie ☎ 01576.

Annandale Water Lodge, Johnstonebridge, DG11 1HD, junction 16 A 74 (M ✆ 470870, Fax 470644 – rm . AE VISA
Meals (grill rest.) a la carte approx. 9.00 **st.** – 5.25 – **42 rm** 34.50 **st.**

ANSTRUTHER Fife. (Fife) 401 L 15 Scotland G. – pop. 1 307 – ☎ 01333.
See : Scottish Fisheries Museum★★ *AC*.
Envir. : The East Neuk★★ – Crail★★ (Old Centre★★, Upper Crail★) NE : 4 m. by A 917.
Exc. : Kellie Castle★ *AC*, NW : 7 m. by B 9171, B 942 and A 917.
Marsfield Shore Rd ℘ 310956.
Scottish Fisheries Museum ℘ 311073 (summer only).
Edinburgh 46 – ♦Dundee 23 – Dunfermline 34.

- **Spindrift,** Pittenweem Rd, KY10 3DT, ℘ 310573, Fax 310573 – TV ☎ P. VISA.
  closed mid November-early December – **Meals** 16.00 **st.** 4.80 – **8 rm** 40.00/60.00 **st.** – SB.
- **Cellar,** 24 East Green, KY10 3AA, ℘ 310378, Fax 312544 – AE VISA
  closed Sunday, Monday except dinner in summer, 1 week January, 1 week November and Christmas – **Meals** - Seafood - 28.50 **t.** (dinner) and lunch a la carte 12.95/19.25.

ARBROATH Angus. (Tayside) 401 M 14 Scotland G. – pop. 24 002 (inc. St. Vigeans) – ☎ 01241.
See : Town★ – Abbey★ *AC*.
Envir. : St. Vigeans★, N : 1½m. by A 92.
Arbroath, Elliot ℘ 872069.
Market Pl., DD11 1HR ℘ 872609.
♦Edinburgh 72 – ♦Aberdeen 51 – ♦Dundee 16.

- **But 'n' Ben,** Auchmithie, DD11 5SQ, NE : 3 m. by A 92 ℘ 877223, « Converted fishermens cottages » – . VISA
  closed Tuesday – **Meals** (light lunch) a la carte 8.40/17.80 **t.** 5.95.

ARCHIESTOWN Moray. (Grampian) 401 K 11 – ✉ Aberlour (Banff) – ☎ 01340.
♦Edinburgh 194 – ♦Aberdeen 62 – ♦Inverness 49.

- **Archiestown,** AB38 7QX, ℘ 810218, Fax 810239, – rest TV ☎ P. AE VISA
  mid February-mid October – **Meals** - (see below) – **8 rm** 32.50/80.00 **t.**
- **Archiestown** (at Archiestown H.), AB38 7QX, ℘ 810218, Fax 810239 – P. AE VISA
  mid February-mid October – **Meals** (bar lunch)/dinner 25.00 **t.** 5.00.

ARDENTINNY Argyll. (Strathclyde) 401 F 15 – ✉ Dunoon – ☎ 01369.
♦Edinburgh 107 – Dunoon 13 – ♦Glasgow 64 – ♦Oban 71.

- **Ardentinny**, PA23 8TR, ℘ 810209, Fax 810345, ← Loch Long, « Lochside setting », – rest TV ☎ P. AE VISA
  21 March-October – **Meals** (bar lunch)/dinner 24.00 **st.** and a la carte 6.00 – **11 rm** 43.00/86.00 – SB.

ARDEONAIG Perth. (Central) 401 H 14 – see Killin.

ARDGAY Sutherland. (Highland) 401 G10 – ☎ 01863.
♦Edinburgh 205 – ♦Inverness 49 – Wick 77.

- Ardgay House, IV24 3DH, ℘ 766345, – TV P
  6 rm.

ARDRISHAIG Argyll. (Strathclyde) 401 D 15 – pop. 1 315 – ✉ Lochgilpead – ☎ 01546.
♦Edinburgh 132 – ♦Glasgow 86 – ♦Oban 40.

- **Allt-na-Craig,** Tarbert Rd, PA30 8EP, on A 83 ℘ 603245, ←, – P
  closed Christmas and New Year – **Meals** (by arrangement) 15.00 **s.** 4.00 – **6 rm** 28.00/60.00 **s.** – SB.
- **Fascadale House** without rest., PA30 8EP, on A 83 ℘ 603845, ←, – P.
  March-October – **3 rm** 20.00/44.00 **st.**

ARDUAINE Argyll. (Strathclyde) 401 D 15 Scotland G. – ✉ Oban – ☎ 01852.
Exc. : Loch Awe★★, E : 12 m. by A 816 and B 840.
♦Edinburgh 142 – ♦Oban 20.

- **Loch Melfort**, PA34 4XG, ℘ 200233, Fax 200214, ← Sound of Jura, , park – rest TV ☎ P. AE VISA.
  closed 5 January-20 February – **Meals** (bar lunch)/dinner 30.00 **t.** 6.95 – **27 rm** 59.00/95.00 **t.** – SB.

ARDVASAR Inverness. (Highland) 401 C 12 – see Skye (Isle of).

ARDVOURLIE Western Isles (Outer Hebrides) 401 Z 10 – see Lewis and Harris (Isle of).

ARISAIG Inverness. (Highland) 401 C 13 **Scotland G.** – ☎ 01687.

See : Village★.

Envir. : Silver Sands of Morar★, N : 5½ m. by A 830.

Traigh ✆ 450645.

♦Edinburgh 172 – ♦Inverness 102 – ♦Oban 88.

Arisaig House ⛰, Beasdale, PH39 4NR, SE : 3 ¼ m. on A 830 ✆ 450622, Fax 45062 ⩽ Loch nan Uamh and Roshven, « Gardens », park – rest. AE VISA.
3 April-1 November – **Meals** (booking essential) (light lunch)/dinner 36.75 **t.** 9.00 – 7.5 **12 rm** 70.00/221.00 **t.**, 2 suites.

Arisaig, PH39 4NH, ✆ 450210, Fax 450310, ⩽ – rest. VISA
Meals (bar lunch)/dinner a la carte 16.50/29.90 **t.** – **15 rm** 22.00/57.00 **st.** – SB.

Old Library Lodge with rm, High St., PH39 4NH, ✆ 450651, Fax 450219, ⩽ Loch na Ceall and Inner Hebridean Isles – . AE VISA.
April-October – **Meals** *(closed Tuesday lunch)* 21.00 **t.** and lunch a la carte – **6 rm** 45.0 62.00 **st.**

ARRAN (Isle of) Bute. (Strathclyde) 401 402 DE 16 17 **Scotland G.** – pop. 4 474.

See : Island★★ - Brodick Castle★★ *AC.*

from Brodick to Ardrossan (Caledonian MacBrayne Ltd) 4-5 daily (55 mn) – fron Lochranza to Kintyre Peninsula (Claonaig) (Caledonian MacBrayne Ltd) frequent service daily (30 mn).

– The Pier, Lochranza ✆ (01770) 830320 (summer only).

Brodick – pop. 822 – ✉ Brodick – ☎ 01770.

Brodick ✆ 302349 – Machrie Bay ✆ 850261.

The Pier TA27 8AU ✆ 302140/302401.

Auchrannie Country House, KA27 8BZ, ✆ 302234, Fax 302812, – rest. AE VISA.
Meals 22.00 **t.** (dinner) and a la carte 7.45/16.35 **t.** – **26 rm** 50.00/100.00 **st.**, 2 suite SB.

Kilmichael Country House ⛰, Glen Cloy, KA27 8BY, 1 m. by Shore Rd, taking lef turn opposite Golf Club ✆ 302219, – . VISA
closed Christmas – **Meals** *(closed Wednesday to non residents)* (dinner only) 27.50 **st** **5 rm** 55.00/110.00 **st.**, 1 suite.

Arran, Shore Rd, KA27 8AJ, ✆ 302265, Fax 302093, ⩽, – rest
16 rm.

Dunvegan House, Shore Rd, KA27 8AJ, ✆ 302811, ⩽, – rm.
Meals 12.50 **st.** 4.50 – **10 rm** 18.50/52.00 **st.**

Glen Cloy Farmhouse ⛰, KA27 8DA, ✆ 302351, – rest
March-7 November – **Meals** 15.00 **s.** – **5 rm** 22.00/50.00 – SB.

Lamlash – pop. 900 – ✉ Brodick – ☎ 01770.

Lamlash ✆ 200296.

Glenisle, Shore Rd, KA27 8LS, ✆ 600559, Fax 600966, ⩽, – . VISA
closed 4 January-11 February – **Meals** (bar lunch)/dinner 13.00 4.25 – **13 rm** (dinne included) 44.00/88.00 **t.**

Lilybank, Shore Rd, KA27 8LS, ✆ 600230, ⩽, –
closed January and February – **Meals** 20.00 **t.** – **6 rm** 20.00/55.00 **t.** – SB.

Carraig Mhor, Shore Rd, KA27 8LS, ✆ 600453, Fax 600453 – . VISA
closed Sunday except Bank Holiday weekends and mid January-mid February – **Meals** (dinner only) 18.50 **t.**

Lochranza – ✉ Lochranza – ☎ 01770.

Lochranza ✆ 830273.

The Pier ✆ 830320 (summer only).

Apple Lodge, KA27 8HJ, ✆ 830229, Fax 830229, – .
minimum stay 2 nights – **Meals** (communal dining) 15.50 **st.** – **3 rm** 45.00/55.00 **s.** 1 suite – SB.

Butt Lodge ⛰, KA27 8JF, SE : ½ m. by Brodick Rd ✆ 830240, ⩽, – . VISA.
Meals 12.50 **s.** – **5 rm** 31.00/52.00 **s.** – SB.

Whiting Bay – ✉ Whiting Bay – ☎ 01770.

Whiting Bay ✆ 700487.

Royal, Shore Rd, KA27 8PZ, ✆ 700286, Fax 700286, ⩽, – rest
March-October – **Meals** 12.00 **st.** – **6 rm** 24.00/48.00 **st.**

ARROCHAR Dunbarton (Strathclyde) 401 F 15 **Scotland G.** – pop. 833 – ☎ 0130 12.
Envir. : E : Ben Lomond★★.
Exc. : S : Loch Lomond★★.
Edinburgh 83 – ◆Glasgow 35 – ◆Oban 57.

Succoth Farmhouse ⛰ without rest., G83 7AL, N : ¾ m. on Succoth rd ☎ 702591, Fax 702591, 🌳 – ⊁ Ⓟ. ⊁
April-October – **3 rm** ☕ 15.00/30.00.

AUCHENCAIRN Kirkcudbright. (Dumfries and Galloway) 401 402 I 19 – ✉ Castle Douglas – ☎ 01556.
Edinburgh 98 – ◆Dumfries 21 – Stranraer 62.

Collin House ⛰, DG7 1QN, N : 1 m. by A 711 ☎ 640292, Fax 640276, « Part 18C country house, ⩽ Auchencairn Bay and Cumbrian Mountains », 🌳, park – ⊁ rest TV ☎ Ⓟ. VISA. ⊁
closed January-early March – **Meals** (dinner only) 28.00 **t.** – **6 rm** ☕ 57.00/88.00 **st.** – SB.

AUCHTERARDER Perth. (Tayside) 401 I 15 **Scotland G.** – pop. 3 910 – ☎ 01764.
Envir. : Tullibardine Chapel★, NW : 2 m.
Ochil Rd ☎ 662804 – Rollo Park, Dunning ☎ 684747.
90 High St. PH3 1BJ ☎ 663450.
Edinburgh 55 – ◆Glasgow 45 – Perth 14.

Gleneagles, PH3 1NF, SW : 2 m. by A 824 on A 823 ☎ 662231, Telex 76105, Fax 662134, ⩽, « Championship golf courses and extensive leisure facilities », 🏋, ≘s, 🏊, 9, 18, 🎣, 🌳, park, 🎾, squash – 🛗 ⊁ rm ▤ rest TV ☎ ♿ Ⓟ – 🪑 360. AE ⓓ VISA JCB
Strathearn : Meals (dinner only and Sunday lunch) 41.00 **t.** and a la carte – **Dormy Grill : Meals** *(closed Monday and Tuesday October-Easter)* (grill rest.) (dinner only) a la carte 18.75/24.75 **t.** 🍷 9.00 – **216 rm** ☕ 130.00/325.00 **st.**, 18 suites – SB.

Auchterarder House ⛰, PH3 1DZ, N : 1 ½ m. on B 8062 ☎ 663646, Fax 662939, ⩽, « Scottish Jacobean house », 🌳, park – ⊁ rest TV ☎ Ⓟ. AE ⓓ VISA
Meals (booking essential) 15.00/37.50 **t.** 🍷 7.00 – **13 rm** ☕ 90.00/195.00 **t.**, 2 suites – SB.

Duchally House ⛰, PH3 1PN, S : 4 m. by A 824 off A 823 ☎ 663071, Fax 662464, ⩽, 🌳, park – TV ☎ Ⓟ – 🪑 50. AE ⓓ VISA
Meals (lunch by arrangement) 10.50/24.50 **st.** and a la carte 🍷 4.75 – **13 rm** ☕ 65.00/90.00 **st.** – SB.

Collearn House, PH3 1DF, ☎ 663553, Fax 662376, 🌳 – ⊁ rm TV ☎ Ⓟ – 🪑 60. AE VISA. ⊁
Meals 15.00/24.00 **t.** and a la carte 🍷 4.75 – **8 rm** ☕ 60.00/100.00 **t.** – SB.

AUCHTERHOUSE Angus. (Tayside) 401 K 14 pop. 794 – ✉ Dundee – ☎ 01382.
Edinburgh 69 – ◆Dundee 7 – Perth 24.

XXX **Old Mansion House** ⛰ with rm, DD3 0QN, ☎ 320366, Fax 320400, ⩽, « Part 15C and 17C country house », 🏊 heated, 🌳, park, 🎾, squash – ⊁ rest TV ☎ Ⓟ. AE ⓓ VISA. ⊁
closed 24 December-5 January – **Meals** 15.95 **t.** (lunch) and a la carte 21.50/27.20 **t.** 🍷 4.95 – **6 rm** ☕ 80.00/125.00 **t.**

AULTBEA Ross and Cromarty. (Highland) 401 D 10 **Scotland G.** – ☎ 01445.
Envir. : Inverewe Gardens★★★ *AC*, S : 5½ m. by A 832.
Exc. : Loch Maree★★★, S : 10 m. by A 832.
◆Edinburgh 234 – ◆Inverness 79 – Kyle of Lochalsh 80.

Aultbea, IV22 2HX, ☎ 731201, Fax 731214, ⩽, 🌳 – TV ☎ Ⓟ. AE VISA
Meals (bar lunch)/dinner 21.50 **t.** and a la carte 🍷 3.95 – **8 rm** ☕ 35.50/79.00 – SB.

Cartmel, Birchburn Rd, IV22 2HZ, ☎ 731375, 🌳 – ⊁ Ⓟ
closed November-December – **Meals** 10.00 – **4 rm** ☕ 16.00/38.00.

AVIEMORE Inverness. (Highland) 401 I 12 **Scotland G.** – pop. 2 214 – Winter sports – ☎ 01479.
See : Town★.
Exc. : The Cairngorms★★ (⩽★★★) – ✳★★★ from Cairn Gorm, SE : 11 m. by B 970 – Landmark Visitor Centre (The Highlander★) *AC*, N : 7 m. by A 9 – Highland Wildlife Park★ *AC*, SW : 7 m. by A 9.
Grampian Rd, TH22 1PP ☎ 810363.
◆Edinburgh 129 – ◆Inverness 29 – Perth 85.

Stakis Four Seasons, Aviemore Centre, PH22 1PF, ☎ 810681, Fax 810534, ⩽ Cairngorms, 🏋, ≘s, 🏊 – 🛗 ⊁ rm TV ☎ Ⓟ – 🪑 110. AE ⓓ VISA JCB
Meals (dancing Saturday evening) 12.50/30.00 **t.** and a la carte 🍷 6.50 – **88 rm** ☕ (dinner included) 65.00/130.00 **st.** – SB.

Cairngorm, 77 Grampian Rd, PH22 1PE, ☎ 810233, Fax 810791 – ⊁ rest TV ☎ Ⓟ – 🪑 70. AE ⓓ VISA. ⊁
closed 25 and 26 December – **Meals** (bar lunch)/dinner 14.95 **t.** 🍷 5.45 – **32 rm** ☕ 44.00/64.00 **t.**

Corrour House, Inverdruie, PH22 1QH, SE : 1 m. on B 970 ☎ 810220, Fax 811500, – rest 📺 ☎ 🅟. AE VISA
February-October – **Meals** (dinner only) 18.00 **t.** 4.00 – **8 rm** 35.00/66.00 **t.** – SB.

Lynwilg House, Lynwilg, PH22 1PZ, S : 2 m. by B 9152 on A 9 ☎ 811685, Fax 811685, – 📺 🅟. VISA
closed November-27 December – **Meals** (by arrangement) 15.00 – **4 rm** 28.00/60.00.

AYR Ayr. (Strathclyde) 401 402 G 17 **Scotland G.** – pop. 47 872 – ☎ 01292.
Envir. : Alloway★ (Burns Cottage and Museum★ *AC*) S : 3 m. by B 7024 BZ.
Exc. : Culzean Castle★ *AC* (setting★★★, Oval Staircase★★) SW : 13 m. by A 719 BZ.
18 Belleisle, Bellisle Park, Doonfoot Rd ☎ 441258, BZ – 18 Dalmilling, Westwood Av. ☎ 263893, BZ – 9 Doon Valley, Hillside, Patna ☎ 531607, BZ.
Burns House, Burns Statue Square, KA7 1UD ☎ 284196.
◆Edinburgh 81 – ◆Glasgow 35.

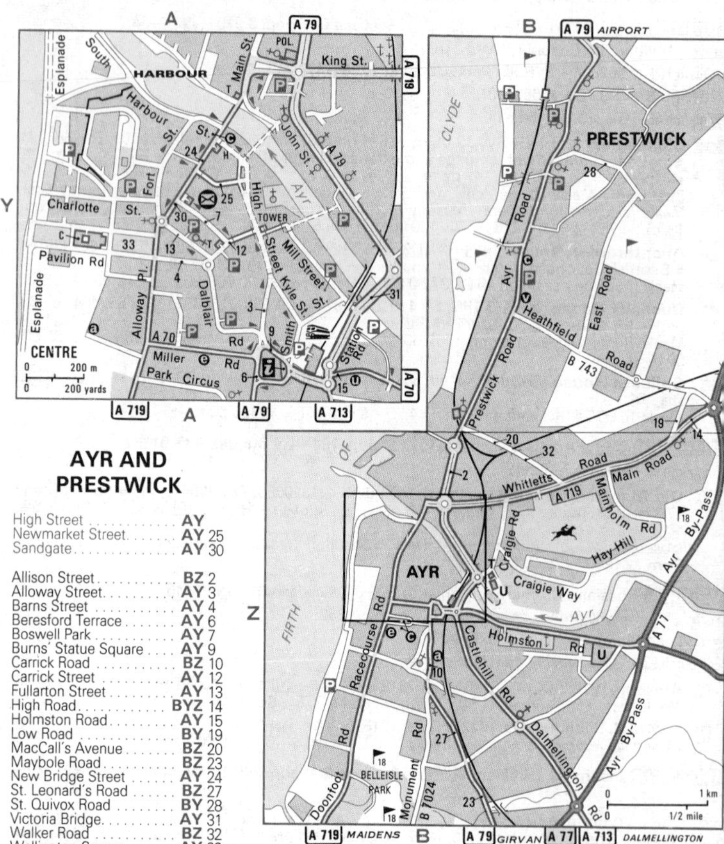

AYR AND PRESTWICK

High Street	AY
Newmarket Street	AY 25
Sandgate	AY 30
Allison Street	BZ 2
Alloway Street	AY 3
Barns Street	AY 4
Beresford Terrace	AY 6
Boswell Park	AY 7
Burns' Statue Square	AY 9
Carrick Road	BZ 10
Carrick Street	AY 12
Fullarton Street	AY 13
High Road	BYZ 14
Holmston Road	AY 15
Low Road	BY 19
MacCall's Avenue	BZ 20
Maybole Road	BZ 23
New Bridge Street	AY 24
St. Leonard's Road	BZ 27
St. Quivox Road	BY 28
Victoria Bridge	AY 31
Walker Road	BZ 32
Wellington Square	AY 33

Fairfield House, 12 Fairfield Rd, KA7 2AR, ☎ 267461, Fax 261456, – 📺 ☎ 🅟. AE VISA. AY a
Meals 11.20/19.95 **st.** and a la carte 6.25 – **33 rm** 75.00/149.00 **st.** – SB.

Kylestrome, 11 Miller Rd, KA7 2AX, ☎ 262474, Fax 260863 – 📺 ☎ 🅟 – 25. AE VISA. AY e
closed 1 January and 26 December – **Meals** 9.95/16.50 **st.** and a la carte 4.95 – **12 rm** 50.00/80.00 **t.** – SB.

Pickwick, 19 Racecourse Rd, KA7 2TD, ☎ 260111, Fax 285348 – 📺 ☎ 🅟. AE VISA. BZ e
Meals 8.95/15.95 **t.** and a la carte – **15 rm** 46.00/72.00 **t.** – SB.

Langley Bank without rest., 39 Carrick Rd, KA7 2RD, ☎ 264246, Fax 282628 – TV ☎ P. VISA. BZ a
6 rm 30.00/45.00 **s.**

Glenmore, 35 Bellevue Cres., KA7 2DP, ☎ 269830 – TV. BZ c
Meals (by arrangement) 10.00 **st.** – **5 rm** 20.00/45.00.

Crescent without rest., 26 Bellevue Cres., KA7 2DR, ☎ 287329, Fax 286779 – TV. BZ c
closed December – **4 rm** 30.00/48.00 **st.**

Coila without rest., 10 Holmston Rd, KA7 3BB, ☎ 262642 – TV P. VISA AY u
4 rm 36.00/45.00 **st.**

Fouters, 2a Academy St., KA7 1HS, ☎ 261391 – AE VISA AY c
closed Sunday lunch, Monday, 24 to 27 December, 31 December and 1 to 4 January – **Meals** a la carte 15.55/23.40 **t.** 4.95.

at ***Alloway*** S : 3 m. on B 7024 – BZ – ✉ Ayr – ☎ 01292 :

Northpark House, 2 Alloway, KA7 4NL, ☎ 442336, Fax 445572 – TV ☎ P. AE VISA.
Meals 15.00/24.80 **t.** and dinner a la carte 5.95 – **5 rm** 57.50/85.00 **t.** – SB.

Burns Monument, KA7 4PQ, ☎ 442466, Fax 443174, ←, – TV ☎
9 rm.

BALLACHULISH Argyll. (Highland) 401 E 13 **Scotland G.** – ☎ 01855.

Exc. : Glen Coe★★, E : 6 m. by A 82.

PA39 4JR ☎ 811296 (summer only).

◆Edinburgh 117 – ◆Inverness 80 – Kyle of Lochalsh 90 – ◆Oban 38.

Ballachulish, PA39 4JY, W : 2¼ m. by A 82 on A 828 ☎ 811606, Fax 821463, ←, – TV ☎ P. VISA
Meals (bar lunch)/dinner 11.00/25.00 **st.** and a la carte 6.00 – **52 rm** (dinner included) 77.50/134.00 **st.**, 2 suites – SB.

Isles of Glencoe, PA39 4HL, ☎ 811602, Fax 811770, ← Loch Leven and the Pap of Glencoe, – TV ☎ & P. VISA
closed January-mid February – **Meals** 11.00/19.50 **st.** and a la carte 6.00 – **39 rm** (dinner included) 76.00/131.00 **st.** – SB.

Ballachulish House, PA39 4JX, W : 2½ m. by A 82 on A 828 ☎ 811266, Fax 811498, ←, – P. VISA.
closed Christmas and New Year – **Meals** 23.50 **st.** 5.00 – **6 rm** 50.00/76.00 **st.**

Lyn Leven, White St., PA39 4JP, ☎ 811392, Fax 811600, ←, – rest TV P. VISA
closed Christmas – **Meals** (by arrangement) 9.00 **st.** 3.80 – **8 rm** 25.00/40.00 **t.**

BALLANTRAE Ayr. (Strathclyde) 401 402 E 18 pop. 672 – ✉ Girvan – ☎ 01465.

◆Edinburgh 115 – ◆Ayr 33 – Stranraer 18.

Balkissock Lodge, KA26 0LP, E : 4 m. by A 77 (south) taking first turn left after bridge ☎ 831537, Fax 831537, – TV P. VISA.
restricted opening November-January – **Meals** 14.75 – **3 rm** 26.50/53.00 **st.** – SB.

BALLATER Aberdeen. (Grampian) 401 K 12 – pop. 1 362 – ECD : Thursday – ☎ 0133 97.

Victoria Rd ☎ 55567.

Station Sq. ☎ 55306 (summer only).

◆Edinburgh 111 – ◆Aberdeen 41 – ◆Inverness 70 – Perth 67.

Craigendarroch H. & Country Club, Braemar Rd, AB35 5XA, on A 93 ☎ 55858, Fax 55447, ← Dee Valley and Grampians, , squash – TV ☎ P 110. AE VISA.
closed 1 week January – **Meals** 10.95 **t.** (dinner) and a la carte 11.15/21.15 **t.** 5.25 - (see also ***Oaks*** below) – **38 rm** 85.00/135.00 **st.**, 6 suites – SB.

Tullich Lodge, AB35 5SB, E : 1½ m. on A 93 ☎ 55406, Fax 55397, ← Dee Valley and Grampians, « Country house atmosphere », – ☎ P. AE VISA
April-October – **Meals** (booking essential) (bar lunch)/dinner 25.00 **st.** 6.00 – **10 rm** (dinner included) 100.00/200.00 **st.** – SB.

Darroch Learg, Braemar Rd, AB35 5UX, ☎ 55443, Fax 55252, ← Dee Valley and Grampians, – TV ☎ P. AE VISA
closed January – **Meals** (light lunch Monday to Saturday)/dinner 23.75 **st.** – **19 rm** 40.00/100.00 **st.** – SB.

Balgonie Country House, Braemar Pl., AB35 5RQ, W : 1 m. by A 93 ☎ 55482, Fax 55482, ←, – rest TV ☎ P. AE VISA
closed mid January-mid February – **Meals** (lunch by arrangement Monday to Saturday) 28.50 **t.** – **9 rm** 55.00/95.00 **t.** – SB.

Glen Lui, 14 Invercauld Rd, AB35 5RP, ☎ 55402, Fax 55545, ←, – TV ☎ P. AE VISA
closed February – **Meals** 16.00/20.00 **st.** and a la carte – **17 rm** 33.00/66.00 **st.**, 2 suites – SB.

Auld Kirk, Braemar Rd, AB35 5RQ, ℘ 55762, Fax 55707, « Former 19C church » – TV ☎ P. VISA
Meals 16.95 **st.** (dinner) and a la carte 10.00/15.50 **st.** 3.80 – **6 rm** 25.00/44.00 **st.** – SB.

Moorside House without rest., 26 Braemar Rd, AB35 5RL, ℘ 55492, – TV P. VISA.
April-October – **9 rm** 25.00/38.00 **st.**

Oaklands without rest., 30 Braemar Rd, AB35 5RL, ℘ 55013, – TV P.
May-October – **3 rm** 32.00/44.00 **s.**

XXX **Oaks** (at Craigendarroch H. & Country Club), Braemar Rd, AB35 5XA, on A 93 ℘ 55858, Fax 55447 – P. AE VISA
closed 1 week January – **Meals** (dinner only and Sunday lunch)/dinner 25.00 **st.** and a la carte 6.50.

X **Green Inn** with rm, 9 Victoria Rd, AB35 5QQ, ℘ 55701, Fax 55701 – TV. VISA
closed 4 days at Christmas and last week November-first week December – **Meals** *(closed Sunday dinner October-March)* (dinner only and Sunday lunch in summer) 10.50 **t.** (lunch) and dinner a la carte 19.50/25.75 **t.** – **3 rm** (dinner included) 60.00/89.00 **t.** SB.

BALLOCH Dunbarton (Strathclyde) 401 G 15 Scotland G. – ✉ Alexandria – 01389.

Envir. : N : Loch Lomond★★.

Balloch Rd, JH3 8LQ ℘ 753533 (summer only).

◆Edinburgh 72 – ◆Glasgow 20 – Stirling 30.

Cameron House H. & Country Estate , Loch Lomond, G83 8QZ, NW : 1½ m. by A 811 on A 82 ℘ 755565, Fax 759522, ≤ Loch Lomond, « Lochside setting », , , , 9, , , park, , squash – rest TV ☎ P – 300. AE VISA.
Brasserie : **Meals** a la carte 12.25/24.40 **t.** – (see also ***Georgian Room*** below) – **63 rm** 125.00/160.00 **st.**, 5 suites – SB.

XXX ✿ **Georgian Room** (at Cameron House H. & Country Estate), Loch Lomond, G83 8QZ, ℘ 755565, Fax 759522, ≤ Loch Lomond, « Lochside setting », – P. AE VISA
closed lunch Saturday and Sunday – **Meals** (booking essential) 14.95/35.00 **t.** and a la carte 35.40/41.75 **t.**
Spec. Layers of tomato, peppers and aubergine with a langoustine fricassee, Loin of lamb gently roasted with rosemary and served on Anna potatoes, Warm chocolate, almond apple and pistachio tart with Madeira sabayon.

BALLYGRANT Argyll. (Strathclyde) 401 B 16 – see Islay (Isle of).

BANAVIE Inverness. (Highland) 401 E 13 – see Fort William.

BANCHORY Kincardine. (Grampian) 401 M 12 Scotland G. – pop. 6 230 – 01330.

Envir. : Crathes Castle★★ (Gardens★★★) *AC*, E : 3 m. by A 93.

Exc. : Dunnottar Castle★★ (site★★★) *AC*, SW : 15½ m. by A 93 and A 957 – Aberdeen★★, NE : 17 m. by A 93.

18 Kinneskie ℘ 822365 – 9 Torphins ℘ (013398) 82115.

Bridge St. AB31 3SX ℘ 822000.

◆Edinburgh 118 – ◆Aberdeen 17 – ◆Dundee 55 – ◆Inverness 94.

Raemoir House , AB31 4ED, N : 2½ m. on A 980 ℘ 824884, Fax 822171, ≤, « 18C mansion with 16C Ha-House », , , , park, – rest TV ☎ P – 50. AE VISA.
Meals (bar lunch Monday to Saturday)/dinner 25.00 **t.** and a la carte 6.50 – **19 rm** 52.50/125.00 **t.**, 4 suites – SB.

Banchory Lodge , Dee St., AB31 3HS, ℘ 822625, Fax 825019, ≤, « Part 18C house on River Dee », , , – TV ☎ P. AE VISA
Meals 15.00/25.50 **st.** 4.95 – **22 rm** 75.00/125.00 **st.** – SB.

Tor-na-Coille, Inchmarlo Rd, AB31 4AB, ℘ 822242, Fax 824012, , squash – TV ☎ P – 90. AE VISA
closed 25 to 27 December – **Meals** 11.15/23.50 **t.** and dinner a la carte 9.80 – **23 rm** 56.50/70.50 **t.** – SB.

BANFF Banff. (Grampian) 401 M 10 Scotland G. – pop. 4 402 – 01261.

See : Town★ – Duff House★ (baroque exterior★) *AC* – Mercat Cross★.

18 Royal Tarlair, Buchan St., Macduff ℘ 832548/832897 – 18 Duff House Royal, The Barnyards ℘ 812062.

Collie Lodge, AB45 1AU ℘ 812419 (summer only).

◆Edinburgh 177 – ◆Aberdeen 47 – Fraserburgh 26 – ◆Inverness 74.

Eden House , AB45 3NT, S : 5 m. by A 98 and A 947 on Scattertie Dunlugas rd ℘ 821282, ≤, « Part 18C former shooting lodge overlooking River Deveron Valley », , , park, – P.
closed Christmas and New Year – **Meals** (booking essential) (communal dining) (dinner only) (unlicensed) 20.00/25.00 **st.** – **5 rm** 34.00/68.00 **st.**

ATS Carmelite St. ℘ 812234

BARRA (Isle of) Inverness (Western Isles) 401 X 12/13 pop. 1 316 – ✉ Castlebay – ☎ 01871.

Castlebay – ☎ 01871.

Isle of Barra ⛰, Tangusdale Beach, PA80 5XW, NW : 2 m. on A 888 ☎ 810383, Fax 810385, ≤ Tangusdale Beach – ⇔ rest TV P. VISA
mid March-mid October – **Meals** (bar lunch)/dinner 16.50 **t.** 4.00 – **30 rm** 32.50/76.00 **t.** – SB.

Castlebay ⛰, HS9 5XD, ☎ 810223, Fax 810455, ≤, – TV ☎. VISA
Meals (bar lunch)/dinner 15.00 **st.** 4.50 – **12 rm** 30.00/60.00 **st.** – SB.

Tigh na Mara without rest., HS9 5XD, ☎ 810304 – ⇔ TV.
closed Christmas-New Year – **5 rm** 18.00/36.00 **s.**

BEARSDEN Dunbarton. (Strathclyde) 401 G 16 – pop. 40 612 (inc. Milngavie) – ✉ Glasgow – ☎ 0141.

◆Edinburgh 51 – ◆Glasgow 5.

La Bavarde, 19 New Kirk Rd, G61 9JS, ☎ 942 2202 – AE VISA
closed Sunday, Monday and 5 to 13 July – **Meals** 6.75 **t.** (lunch) and dinner a la carte 8.30/19.65 **st.** 4.50.

BEATTOCK Dumfries (Dumfries and Galloway) 401 402 J 18 – see Moffat.

BEAULY Inverness. (Highland) 401 G 11 – pop. 1 154 – ☎ 01463.

◆Edinburgh 169 – ◆Inverness 13 – ◆Wick 125.

Lovat Arms, High St., IV4 7BS, ☎ 782313, Fax 782862 – ⇔ TV ☎ P. VISA
Meals (bar lunch)/dinner 25.00 **t.** 4.20 – **22 rm** 39.00/94.00 **t.** – SB.

Priory, The Square, IV4 7BX, ☎ 782309, Fax 782531 – TV ☎. AE VISA
Meals 12.50/27.50 **t.** and a la carte 3.50 – **23 rm** 43.50/74.50 **t.** – SB.

Chrialdon, Station Rd, IV4 7EH, ☎ 782336, – ⇔ rest TV P. VISA
March-November – **Meals** 19.50 **st.** 8.50 – **8 rm** 29.00/52.00 **st.**

BENBECULA Inverness. (Western Isles) 401 X 11 – see Uist (Isles of).

BETTYHILL Sutherland. (Highland) 401 H 8 – ✉ Thurso (Caithness) – ☎ 01641.

◆Edinburgh 262 – ◆Inverness 93 – Thurso 31.

Tigh Na Sgoil ⛰, Kirtomy, KW14 7TB, NE : 3 ¼ m. by A 836 on Kirtomy rd ☎ 521455, Fax 521457, – TV ☎ P.
Meals (communal dining) 11.00 **st.** 2.50 – **5 rm** 26.50/53.00 **st.**

BLAIRGOWRIE Perth. (Tayside) 401 J 14 **Scotland G.** – pop. 5 208 – ☎ 01250.

Exc. : Scone Palace★★ *AC*, S : 12 m. by A 93.

26 Wellmeadow, PH10 6AS ☎ 872960/873701.

◆Edinburgh 60 – ◆Dundee 19 – Perth 16.

Kinloch House ⛰, PH10 6SG, W : 3 m. on A 923 ☎ 884237, Fax 884333, ≤, « Country house atmosphere », , park – ⇔ rest TV ☎ P. AE VISA
closed 16 to 29 December – **Meals** 15.50/28.90 **st.** and lunch a la carte 5.40 – **21 rm** (dinner included) 79.00/165.00 **st.**

Altamount House ⛰, Coupar Angus Rd, PH10 6JN, on A 923 ☎ 873512, Fax 876200, – ⇔ rest TV ☎ P. AE VISA
closed 4 January-13 February – **Meals** *(closed Sunday dinner and Monday during winter)* (bar lunch Monday to Saturday)/dinner 19.50 **t.** 4.75 – **7 rm** 39.50/75.00 **t.** – SB.

Rosemount Golf, Golf Course Rd, PH10 6LJ, SE : 1 ¾ m. by A 923 ☎ 872604, Fax 874496, – TV ☎ P – 50. VISA
Meals 11.00/18.00 **st.** and a la carte 4.75 – **12 rm** 37.00/54.00 **st.** – SB.

Laurels, PH10 6LH, SW : 1 ¼ m. on A 93 ☎ 874920, – ⇔ TV P. AE VISA
closed December-mid January – **Meals** (by arrangement) 10.00 3.50 – **6 rm** 18.00/36.00.

BLAIRLOGIE Stirling. (Central) – see Stirling.

BOAT OF GARTEN Inverness. (Highland) 401 I 12 – ☎ 01479.

Boat of Garten ☎ 831282.

◆Edinburgh 133 – ◆Inverness 28 – ◆Perth 89.

The Boat, PH24 3BH, ☎ 831258, Fax 831414, – ⇔ rest TV ☎ P. AE VISA
closed 10 November-21 December – **Meals** (bar lunch)/dinner 20.00 **t.** 6.75 – **32 rm** 39.00/78.00 **t.** – SB.

Heathbank House, Spey Av., PH24 3BD, ☎ 831234, – ⇔ P.
closed November-25 December – **Meals** 18.00 **s.** 5.00 – **7 rm** 25.00/70.00 **s.**

BONAR BRIDGE Sutherland. (Highland) 401 G 10 – pop. 840 – ✉ Ardgay – ☎ 01863.
♦Edinburgh 206 – ♦Inverness 50 – ♦Wick 76.

Kyle House, Dornoch Rd, IV24 3EB, ☎ 766360, – rest P. *closed December and January* – **Meals** (by arrangement) 10.00 **s.** – **6 rm** 16.00/38.00 **s.**

BOTHWELL Lanark. (Strathclyde) 401 402 H 16 **Scotland G.** pop. 11 997 – ✉ Glasgow ☎ 01698.
See : Castle★ *AC.*
Envir. : Blantyre (David Livingstone Museum★) *AC*, W : 2 m. by A 724.
♦Edinburgh 39 – ♦Glasgow 8.5.

Silvertrees, 27-29 Silverwells Cres., G71 8DP, ☎ 852311, Fax 852311 ext : 200, – P – 120. AE VISA
Meals *(closed Sunday dinner)* 11.00/14.50 **t.** and a la carte 5.90 – **24 rm** 55.00/80.00 **t** 2 suites.

BRAE Shetland. (Shetland Islands) 401 P 2 – see Shetland Islands (Mainland).

BRAEMAR Aberdeen. (Grampian) 401 J 12 **Scotland G.** – ☎ 0133 97.
Envir. : Lin O'Dee★, W : 5 m.
Cluniebank Rd ☎ 41618.
The Mews, Mar Rd ☎ 41600 (summer only).
♦Edinburgh 85 – ♦Aberdeen 58 – ♦Dundee 51 – Perth 51.

Invercauld Arms Thistle, Invercauld rd, AB35 5YR, ☎ 41605, Fax 41428 – P – 60 – **68 rm.**

Braemar Lodge, Glenshee Rd, AB35 5YQ, ☎ 41627, Fax 41627, – P. VISA *closed November and December* – **Meals** (dinner only) 19.50 **st.** 6.00 – **5 rm** 35.00/70.00 **st.** – SB.

BREAKISH Inverness (Highland) 401 C 12 – see Skye (Isle of).

BREASCLETE Western Isles (Outer Hebrides) 401 Z 9 – see Lewis and Harris (Isle of).

Per spostarvi più rapidamente utilizzate le carte Michelin *"Grandi Strade"* :
n° 970 Europa, n° 976 Rep. Ceca/Slovacchia, n° 980 Grecia, n° 984 Germania,
n° 985 Scandinavia-Finlandia, n° 986 Gran Bretagna-Irlanda, n° 987 Germania-Austria-Benelux
n° 988 Italia, n° 989 Francia, n° 990 Spagna-Portogallo, n° 991 Jugoslavia.

BRIDGEND Argyll. (Strathclyde) 401 B 16 – see Islay (Isle of).

BRIDGE OF ALLAN Stirling. (Central) 401 I 15 – ☎ 01786.
♦Edinburgh 40 – ♦Glasgow 32 – Perth 30.

Old Manor, 129 Henderson St., FK9 4RQ, ☎ 832169, Fax 833990 – P. AE VISA
Meals a la carte 11.85/21.40 **t.** – **7 rm** 28.35/80.00 **t.**

BRIDGE OF AVON Banff. (Highland) 401 J 11 – ✉ Ballindalloch – ☎ 01807.
♦Edinburgh 157 – ♦Inverness 50.

Delnashaugh Inn, AB37 9AS, on A 95 ☎ 500255, Fax 500389, ≤ – P. VISA. *closed 5 November-3 March* – **Meals** (bar lunch)/dinner 22.50 **t.** – **9 rm** 55.00/130.00 **t.**

BRIG O'TURK Perth. (Central) 401 G 15 **Scotland G.** – ✉ Callander – ☎ 01877.
Envir. : The Trossachs★★★ (Loch Katherine★★) W : 2 m. by A 821 – Hilltop Viewpoint★★★ (✻★★★) SW : 3½m. by A 821.
♦Edinburgh 58 – ♦Glasgow 36 – Perth 47.

Dundarroch Country House without rest., Trossachs, FK17 8HT, ☎ 376200, Fax 376202, ≤, , , park – P. VISA.
April-October – **3 rm** 46.75/67.50 **t.**

BROADFORD Inverness (Highland) 401 C 12 – see Skye (Isle of).

BRODICK Bute. (Strathclyde) 401 402 E 17 – see Arran (Isle of).

BRORA Sutherland. (Highland) 401 I 9 – pop. 1 687 – ☎ 01408.
Golf Rd ☎ 621417.
♦Edinburgh 234 – ♦Inverness 78 – ♦Wick 49.

Royal Marine , Golf Rd, KW9 6QS, ☎ 621252, Fax 621181, , , , – P. AE VISA
accommodation closed 25 December – **Meals** a la carte 17.00/20.00 **t.** 5.00 – **11 rm** 50.00/90.00 **t.** – SB.

Links , Golf Rd, KW9 6QS, ☎ 621225, Fax 621383, ≤, , – P. AE VISA
April-October – **Meals** a la carte 16.00/20.00 **t.** 5.00 – **21 rm** 50.00/90.00 **t.**, 1 suite – SB.

Lynwood ⓢ, Golf Rd, KW9 6QS, ☎ 621226, Fax 621226, – rm TV P. VISA
closed January and February – **Meals** 12.00 **st.** – **4 rm** 22.00/40.00 **st.** – SB.

Tigh Fada ⓢ without rest., Golf Rd, KW9 6QS, ☎ 621332, Fax 621332, ←, – P.
closed Christmas and New Year – **3 rm** 16.50/39.00.

ROUGHTY FERRY Angus. (Tayside) 401 L 14 – see Dundee.

UCKIE Banff. (Grampian) 401 L 10 – pop. 8 324 – 01542.
Buckpool, Barhill Rd ☎ 832236 – 18 Strathlene ☎ 831798.
Cluny Sq. ☎ 834853 (summer only).
Edinburgh 195 – ◆Aberdeen 66 – ◆Inverness 56.

XX **Old Monastery,** Drybridge, AB56 2JB, SE : 3½ m. by A 942 on Deskford rd ☎ 832660, ←, « Former chapel overlooking Spey Bay » – P. AE VISA
closed Sunday, Monday, 2 weeks November and 3 weeks January – **Meals** a la carte 12.25/18.50 **t.** 6.00.

UCKSBURN Aberdeen. (Grampian) 401 N 12 – see Aberdeen.

UNESSAN Argyll. (Strathclyde) 401 B 15 – see Mull (Isle of).

URNTISLAND Fife. (Fife) 401 K 15 – pop. 5 951 – 01592.
nvir. : Aberdour★ – Aberdour Castle★ *AC*, W : 3 m. by A 921.
Burntisland Golf House Club, Dodhead ☎ 873247 – 18 Kinghorn Municipal, McDuff Cres. ☎ 890345.
4 Kirkgate, KY3 9BB ☎ 872667.
Edinburgh 20 – Dunfermline 10 – Kirkcaldy 6.

Kingswood, Kinghorn Rd, KY3 9LL, ☎ 872329, Fax 873123 – TV ☎ P – 100. AE VISA
Meals (bar lunch)/dinner 14.50 **t.** and a la carte 3.65 – **9 rm** 48.00/70.00 **t.** – SB.

URRAY Orkney. (Orkney Islands) 401 L 7 – see Orkney Islands.

USBY Lanark. (Strathclyde) 401 402 H 16 – see Glasgow.

UTE (Isle of) Bute. (Strathclyde) 401 402 E 16 – pop. 7 354.
from Rothesay to Wemyss Bay (Caledonian MacBrayne Ltd) frequent services daily 30 mn) – from Rhubodach to Colintraive (Caledonian MacBrayne Ltd) frequent services daily 5 mn).

Rothesay – ✉ Rothesay – 01700.
18 Canada Hill ☎ 502244.

Alamein House, 28 Battery Pl., Promenade, PA20 9DU, ☎ 502395, ← – rest TV P
closed 2 weeks October-November and Christmas-New Year – **Meals** 9.50 **st.** – **7 rm** 19.50/47.00 **s.** – SB.

CAIRNBAAN Argyll. (Strathclyde) 401 D 15 – see Lochgilphead.

CALLANDER Perth. (Central) 401 H 15 **Scotland G.** – pop. 3 268 – 01877.
See : Town★.
Exc. : The Trossachs★★★ (Loch Katrine★★) – Hilltop Viewpoint★★★ (✻★★★) W : 10 m. by A 821.
18 Aveland Rd ☎ 330090.
Rob Roy & Trossachs Visitor Centre, Ancaster Sq., PA28 6EF ☎ 330342.
◆Edinburgh 52 – ◆Glasgow 43 – ◆Oban 71 – Perth 41.

Roman Camp ⓢ, Main St., FK17 8BG, ☎ 330003, Fax 331533, ←, « Part 17C hunting lodge in extensive gardens », park – rest TV ☎ & P. AE VISA
Meals 19.00/34.00 **t.** and a la carte 6.00 – **11 rm** 60.00/135.00 **t.**, 3 suites – SB.

Arran Lodge, Leny Rd, FK17 8AJ, ☎ 330976, – TV P.
closed December and January – **Meals** (unlicensed) (residents only) (dinner only) 23.00 – **4 rm** 40.00/66.00 **s.** – SB.

Invertrossachs Country House ⓢ, Invertrossachs, FK17 8HG, SW : 5½ m. by A 81 and Invertrossachs rd taking no through road after 1 ¾ m. ☎ 331126, Fax 331229, ←, « Edwardian hunting lodge in extensive grounds », – rest TV ☎ P. AE VISA
closed 18 December-8 January – **Meals** (unlicensed) (by arrangement) (dinner only) 17.95 **st.** – **3 rm** 45.00/145.00 **st.**

Lubnaig, Leny Feus, FK17 8AS, ☎ 330376, Fax 330376, – rest TV P. VISA.
Easter-mid October – **Meals** (residents only) (dinner only) 18.00 **t.** 6.50 – **10 rm** 40.00/60.00 **t.** – SB.

Dalgair, Main St., FK17 8BQ, ☎ 330283, Fax 331114 – TV ☎ P. AE VISA
Meals (bar lunch)/dinner 10.00 **st.** and a la carte 5.00 – **8 rm** 26.00/52.00 **st.** – SB.

- **Priory** ⛰, Bracklinn Rd, FK17 8EH, ☏ 330001, Fax 330001, – ⊭ TV P. ✻ *closed 2 weeks February and 2 weeks November* – **Meals** 12.00 **st.** – **8 rm** ☕ 26.50/53.00 **s** – SB.
- **Brook Linn** ⛰, Leny Feus, FK17 8AU, ☏ 330103, Fax 330103, ≤, – ⊭ TV P *mid March-November* – **Meals** 12.00 **st.** 🍷 4.00 – **7 rm** ☕ 20.00/48.00 **st.** – SB.
- **East Mains House** without rest., Bridgend, FK17 8AG, ☏ 330535, – ⊭ TV P *April-October* – **5 rm** ☕ 18.00/38.00 **s.**
- **Highland House,** 8 South Church St., FK17 8BN, ☏ 330269 – ⊭ TV. AE VISA *March-November* – **Meals** 15.75 **st.** 🍷 3.95 – **9 rm** ☕ 23.50/47.00 **st.** – SB.

CAMPBELTOWN Argyll. (Strathclyde) 401 D 17 – see Kintyre (Peninsula).

CANNICH Inverness. (Highland) 401 F 11 – ✉ Beauly – ☎ 01456.

◆Edinburgh 184 – ◆Inverness 28 – Kyle of Lochalsh 54.

- **Mullardoch House** ⛰, IV4 7LX, W : 8½ m. ☏ 415460, Fax 415460, ≤ Loch Sealbanac and Affric Hills, « Converted shooting lodge », – TV P. AE VISA **Meals** (bar lunch)/dinner 19.00 **t.** 🍷 6.00 – **6 rm** ☕ 39.50/79.00 **t.** – SB.

CANONBIE Dumfries. (Dumfries and Galloway) 401 402 L 18 pop. 1 144 – ☎ 0138 73.

◆Edinburgh 80 – ◆Carlisle 15 – ◆Dumfries 34.

- XX **Riverside Inn** with rm, DG14 0UX, ☏ 71295 – ⊭ rest TV P. VISA. ✻ *closed 25 and 26 December, 1-2 January, 2 weeks February and 2 weeks November* **Meals** *(closed Sunday)* (booking essential) (bar lunch)/dinner 23.00 **t.** 🍷 4.00 – **6 rm** ☕ 55.00/72.00 **t.** – SB.

CARDROSS Dunbarton. (Strathclyde) 401 G 16 – ☎ 01389.

◆Edinburgh 63 – ◆Glasgow 17 – Helensburgh 5.

- **Kirkton House** ⛰, Darleith Rd, G82 5EZ, ☏ 841951, Fax 841868, ≤, – TV ☎ P. AE VISA *closed 20 December-15 January* – **Meals** 17.50 **st.** 🍷 3.50 – **6 rm** ☕ 37.50/59.00 **st.** – SB.

CARNOUSTIE Angus. (Tayside) 401 L 14 – pop. 12 337 – ☎ 01241.

18, 18 Monifieth Golf Links, Princes St., Monifieth ☏ (01382) 532767 – 18 Panmure, Barr ☏ 853120.

ℹ The Library, High St., DD7 6AN ☏ 852258 (summer only).

◆Edinburgh 68 – ◆Aberdeen 59 – ◆Dundee 12.

- XX **11 Park Avenue,** 11 Park Av., DD7 7JA, ☏ 853336, Fax 853336 – AE VISA *closed Sunday, and Monday* – **Meals** 25.00 **t.** (dinner) and a la carte 11.85/22.20 🍷 5.50.

CARRBRIDGE Inverness. (Highland) 401 I 12 – ☎ 01479.

9 Carrbridge ☏ 841623.

ℹ Main St. ☏ 841630 (summer only).

◆Edinburgh 135 – ◆Aberdeen 92 – ◆Inverness 23.

- **Feith Mho'r Country House** ⛰, Station Rd, PH23 3AP, W : 1¼ m. ☏ 841621, ≤, – ⊭ rest TV P *closed 10 November-27 December* – **Meals** 12.00 – **6 rm** ☕ 23.00/46.00.

CASTLEBAY Inverness (Western Isles) 401 X 12/13 – see Barra (Isle of).

CASTLE DOUGLAS Kirkcudbright. (Dumfries and Galloway) 401 402 I 19 **Scotland G.** – pop. 4 187 – ☎ 01556.

Envir. : Threave Garden★★ *AC*, SW : 2½ m. by A 75 – Threave Castle★ *AC*, W : 1 m.

9 Abercromby Rd ☏ 502801/502099.

ℹ Markethill Car Park ☏ 502611 (summer only).

◆Edinburgh 98 – ◆Ayr 49 – ◆Dumfries 18 – Stranraer 57.

- **Longacre Manor** ⛰, Ernespie Rd, DG7 1LE, NE : ¾ m. on A 745 ☏ 503576, – TV ☎ P. VISA **Meals** 15.00 **st.** 🍷 3.85 – **4 rm** ☕ 32.00/70.00 **st.**

ATS Station Yard ☏ 503121/2

CLACHAN SEIL Argyll. (Strathclyde) 401 D 15 – see Seil (Isle of).

CLEISH Fife. (Tayside) 401 J 15 – see Kinross.

CLYDEBANK Dunbarton. (Strathclyde) 401 G 16 strict, Hardgate ☏ (01389) 73289 – pop. 45 717 – ☎ 0141.

18 Clydebank Municipal, Overtoun Rd, Dalmuir ☏ 952 8698 – 18 Clydebank.

◆Edinburgh 52 – ◆Glasgow 6.

- **Patio,** 1 South Av., Clydebank Business Park, G81 2RW, ☏ 951 1133, Fax 952 3713 – ⊭ rm ▤ rest TV ☎ ♿ P – 150. AE VISA *closed 25 to 28 December and 1 to 3 January* – **Meals** *(closed lunch Saturday and Sunday)* 8.95/15.95 **st.** and a la carte 🍷 6.75 – ☕ 9.75 – **78 rm** 58.50/68.50 **st.**, 2 suites – SB.

COLONSAY (Isle of) Argyll. (Strathclyde) 401 B 15 – pop. 106 (inc. Oronsay) – ☎ 0195 12.

Isle of Colonsay ℘ 316.

– from Scalasaig to Oban via Port Askaig and Kennacraig (Caledonian MacBrayne Ltd) (2 h 15 mn).

Scalasaig – ✉ Colonsay – ☎ 01951.

Isle of Colonsay, PA61 7YP, ℘ 200316, Fax 200353, ←, – rest TV P. AE VISA JCB
closed 12 January-28 February and 5 November-27 December – **Meals** (bar lunch)/ dinner 21.75 **st.** 4.60 – **11 rm** (dinner included) 65.00/130.00 **st.** – SB.

CONAN BRIDGE Inverness 401 G 11 – ☎ 01349.

◆Edinburgh 168 – ◆Inverness 12.

Kinkell House, Easter Kinkell, IV7 8HY, E : 3 m. by B 9163 and A 835 on B 9169 ℘ 861270, Fax 861270, ←, – TV P. VISA
closed January and February – **Meals** *(closed Saturday lunch)* (booking essential) a la carte 9.75/17.95 **st.** 4.50 – **3 rm** 48.50/67.00 **st.** – SB.

CONNEL Argyll. (Strathclyde) 401 D 14 – ✉ Oban – ☎ 01631.

◆Edinburgh 118 – ◆Glasgow 88 – ◆Inverness 113 – ◆Oban 5.

Ards House, PA37 1PT, ℘ 710255, ←, – P. VISA.
closed December and January – **Meals** 16.50 **t.** 4.75 – **6 rm** 37.00/54.00 **t.** – SB.

Ronebhal, PA37 1PJ, ℘ 710310, ←, – TV P. VISA.
mid March-mid October – **Meals** a la carte approx. 15.00 – **6 rm** 19.50/60.00.

CONTIN Ross and Cromarty 401 G 11 pop. 1 194 – ✉ Strathpeffer – ☎ 01997.

◆Edinburgh 175 – ◆Inverness 19.

Coul House, IV14 9EY, ℘ 421487, Fax 421945, ←, – TV ☎ P. AE VISA JCB
Meals (lunch by arrangement)/dinner 25.50 **t.** and a la carte 7.70 – **21 rm** 46.00/94.00 **t.** – SB.

Achilty, IV14 9EG, NW : ¾ m. on A 835 ℘ 421355, Fax 421355 – TV P. VISA.
Meals (bar lunch Monday to Saturday)/dinner a la carte 9.20/19.45 **st.** – **12 rm** 19.50/ 55.00 – SB.

COUPAR ANGUS Perth. (Tayside) 401 K 14 pop. 3 844 – ✉ Blairgowrie – ☎ 01828.

◆Edinburgh 63 – ◆Dundee 14 – Perth 13.

Moorfield House, Myreiggs Rd, PH13 9HS, NW : 2 ½ m. by A 923 ℘ 627303, Fax 627339, – TV ☎ P – 120. AE VISA.
Meals (lunch by arrangement)/dinner 21.50 **t.** 5.25 – **12 rm** 35.00/96.00 **t.**

CRAIGELLACHIE Banff. (Grampian) 401 K 11 **Scotland G.** – ☎ 01340.

Envir. : Glenfiddich Distillery★, SE : 5 m. by A 941.

◆Edinburgh 190 – ◆Aberdeen 58 – ◆Inverness 53.

Craigellachie, Victoria St., AB38 9SR, ℘ 881204, Fax 881253, – rest TV ☎ P. AE VISA
Meals 14.50/28.00 **st.** and a la carte – **30 rm** 60.00/125.00 **t.** – SB.

CRAIGHOUSE Argyll. (Strathclyde) 401 C 16 – see Jura (Isle of).

CRAIL Fife. (Fife) 401 M 15 **Scotland G.** – pop. 1 537 – ☎ 01333.

See : Town★★ – Old Centre★★ – Upper Crail★.

Envir. : Scottish Fisheries Museum★★, NE : 4 m. by A 917 – The East Neuk★★, SW : 4 m. by A 917 – Kellie Castle★ *AC*, NE : 5½m. by B 9171 and A 917.

Crail Golfing Society, Balcomie Clubhouse ℘ 450278.

Museum & Heritage Centre, 62-64 Marketgate, KY10 3TC ℘ 450869 (summer only).

◆Edinburgh 50 – ◆Dundee 23 – Dunfermline 38.

Caiplie, 53 High St., KY10 3RA, ℘ 450564 rest
March-October – **Meals** 13.00 3.70 – **7 rm** 17.50/35.00.

CRIANLARICH Perth. (Central) 401 G 14 – ☎ 01838.

◆Edinburgh 82 – ◆Glasgow 52 – Perth 53.

Allt-Chaorain House, FK20 8RU, NW : 1 m. on A 82 ℘ 300283, Fax 300238, ←, – TV ☎ P. VISA
21 March-31 October – **Meals** (residents only) (communal dining) (dinner only) 18.00 **t.** – **8 rm** 46.00/72.00 **t.** – SB.

I prezzi Per ogni chiarimento sui prezzi qui riportati, consultate le spiegazioni alle pagine dell'introduzione.

CRIEFF Perth. (Tayside) 401 I 14 **Scotland G.** – pop. 6 096 – ☎ 01764.

See : Town★.

Envir. : Drummond Castle Gardens★ *AC*, S : 2 m. by A 822 – Comrie (Scottish Tartans Museum★) W : 6 m. by A 85.

Exc. : Scone Palace★★ *AC*, E : 16 m. by A 85 and A 93.

18, 9 Perth Rd ℘ 652909 – 9 Muthill, Peak Rd ℘ 681523.

Town Hall, High St., PH7 3HU ℘ 652578.

◆Edinburgh 60 – ◆Glasgow 50 – ◆Oban 76 – Perth 18.

Murraypark, Connaught Terr., PH7 3DJ, ℘ 653731, Fax 655311, – rest TV ☎ P – 25. AE VISA
Meals (bar lunch)/dinner 25.00 **t.** and a la carte 6.00 – **19 rm** 49.00/72.00 **t.**, 1 suite – SB.

Leven House, Comrie Rd, PH7 4BA, on A 85 ℘ 652529, ← – rest TV P
March-October – **Meals** 14.00 **st.** 3.90 – **10 rm** 20.00/40.00 **st.** – SB.

CRINAN Argyll. (Strathclyde) 401 D 15 **Scotland G.** – ✉ Lochgilphead – ☎ 01546.

See : Hamlet★.

Exc. : Kilmory Knap (Macmillan's Cross★) SW : 14 m.

◆Edinburgh 137 – ◆Glasgow 91 – ◆Oban 36.

Crinan, PA31 8SR, ℘ 830261, Fax 830292, « ← commanding setting overlooking Loch Crinan and Sound of Jura », – rest TV ☎ P. AE VISA
Meals 20.00/27.50 **t.** 5.50 – (see also ***Lock 16*** below) – **20 rm** 90.00/200.00 **t.**

Lock 16 (at Crinan H.), PA31 8SR, ℘ 830261, Fax 830292, « ← commanding setting overlooking Loch Crinan and Sound of Jura » – rest P. VISA
closed Sunday, Monday and October-Easter – **Meals** - Seafood - (booking essential) (dinner only) 40.00 **t.** 7.50.

Great Britain and ***Ireland*** *is now covered*
by an ***Atlas*** *at a scale of 1 inch to 4.75 miles.*

Three easy to use versions: Paperback, Spiralbound and Hardback.

CROCKETFORD Dumfries. (Dumfries and Galloway) 401 402 I 18 – ✉ Dumfries – ☎ 01556.

◆Edinburgh 73 – ◆Ayr 51 – Dumfries 10.

Galloway Arms, DG2 8RA, ℘ 690248 – rest TV P. AE VISA
Meals 13.00/21.00 **t.** and a la carte 4.80 – **13 rm** 37.50/60.00 **t.** – SB.

CROMARTY Ross and Cromarty. (Highland) 401 H 10 **Scotland G.** – pop. 865 – ☎ 01381.

Exc. : Fortrose (Cathedral Church setting★) SW : 10 m. by A 832.

18 Fortrose & Rosemarkie, Ness Road East ℘ 620529.

◆Edinburgh 182 – ◆Inverness 26 – ◆Wick 126.

Royal, Marine Terr., IV11 8YN, ℘ 600217, ← – TV P. AE VISA
Meals a la carte 11.00/16.00 **t.** 6.00 – **10 rm** 32.00/55.00 **t.** – SB.

CROSSFORD Fife. (Fife) 401 J 15 – see Dunfermline.

CULLEN Banff. (Grampian) 401 L 10 **Scotland G.** – pop. 1 522 – ☎ 01542.

See : Cullen Auld Kirk★ (Sacrament house★, panels★).

Envir. : Deskford Church (Sacrament house★) S : 4 m. by A 98 and B 9018 – Portsoy★, E : 5½m. by A 98.

18 The Links ℘ 840685.

20 Seafield St., AB56 2FH ℘ 840757 (summer only).

◆Edinburgh 189 – ◆Aberdeen 59 – Banff 12 – ◆Inverness 61.

Bayview, Seafield St., AB56 2SU, ℘ 841031, ← – TV ☎
6 rm.

CULLODEN Inverness. (Highland) 401 H 11 – see Inverness.

CULNAKNOCK Inverness. (Highland) 401 B 11 – see Skye (Isle of).

CULTS Aberdeen. (Grampian) 401 N 12 – see Aberdeen.

CUMBERNAULD Lanark. (Strathclyde) 401 I 16 – pop. 62 412 – ☎ 01236.

◆Edinburgh 40 – ◆Glasgow 11 – Stirling 13.

Westerwood, St. Andrews Drive, G68 0EW, N : 2 m. by A 8011 ℘ 457171, Fax 738478, 18, – rm TV ☎ P – 150. AE VISA
Meals (bar lunch Saturday) 9.95 **st.** (lunch) and a la carte 11.15/23.20 **st.** 4.95 **41 rm** 82.50/55.00 **st.** – SB.

Travel Inn, 4 South Muirhead Rd, G67 1AX, off A 8011 ℘ 725339, Fax 736380 – rm TV P. AE VISA.
Meals (grill rest.) – 4.95 – **37 rm** 34.50 **t.**

UPAR Fife. (Fife) 401 K 15 – pop. 8 174 – ☎ 01334.

The Granary, Coal Rd, PY15 5YQ ✆ 52874.

dinburgh 45 – ◆Dundee 15 – Perth 23.

✗ **Ostler's Close,** Bonnygate, KY15 4BU, ✆ 655574 – VISA
closed Sunday and Monday – **Meals** a la carte 13.90/27.00 **t.**

ATS St. Catherine St. ✆ 654003

ALBEATTIE Kirkcudbright. (Dumfries and Galloway) 401 402 I 19 **Scotland G.** – pop. 4 421 – 01556.

nvir. : Kippford★, S : 5 m. by A 710.

Dalbeattie ✆ 611421.

Town Hall, DJ5 ✆ 610117 (summer only).

Edinburgh 94 – ◆Ayr 56 – ◆Dumfries 14 – Stranraer 62.

Auchenskeoch Lodge, DG5 4PG, SE : 5 m. on B 793 ✆ (01387) 780277, Fax 780277, park – rest. VISA
April-December – **Meals** (by arrangement) 18.00 **st.** 6.50 – **3 rm** 35.00/55.00 **st.** – SB.

Briardale House, 17 Haugh Rd, DG5 4AR, ✆ 611468 –
closed November and December – **Meals** (by arrangement) 11.00 **s.** – **3 rm** 38.00 **s.** – SB.

DALCROSS Inverness. (Highland) – see Inverness.

DALIBURGH Inverness. (Western Isles) 401 X 12 – see Uist (Isles of).

DALRY Ayr (Strathclyde) 401 402 F 16 – ☎ 01294.

Edinburgh 70 – ◆Ayr 21 – ◆Glasgow 25.

✗✗ **Braidwoods,** Drumastle Mill Cottage, KA2 44LN, SW : 1½ m. by A 737 on Saltcoats rd ✆ 833544 – VISA
closed Tuesday lunch, Sunday dinner, Monday, 3 weeks January and 1 week October-November – **Meals** 12.50/27.00 **t.** 7.25.

DENNY Stirling. (Central) 401 I 15 **Scotland G.** – pop. 11 061 – ☎ 01324.

xc. : Stirling★★, N : 8 m. by A 872.

◆Edinburgh 34 – ◆Glasgow 25 – Stirling 7.

Topps Farm, Fintry Rd, FK6 5JF, W : 4 m. on B 818 ✆ 822471, Fax 823099, ← – VISA.
Meals (by arrangement) 18.00 **t.** – **8 rm** 32.00/42.00 **t.** – SB.

DERVAIG Argyll. (Strathclyde) 401 B 14 – see Mull (Isle of).

DORNIE Ross and Cromarty. (Highland) 401 D 12 – ✉ Kyle of Lochalsh – ☎ 01599 555 (3 fig.) and 01599 (6 fig.).

◆Edinburgh 212 – ◆Inverness 74 – Kyle of Lochalsh 8.

Dornie, IV40 8DT, ✆ 205, Fax 429 – VISA
Meals 18.00 **t.** and a la carte – **12 rm** 22.50/66.00 **t.**

Conchra House, Ardelve, IV40 8DZ, ✆ 555233, Fax 554433, ← Loch Long, « Part Georgian country house », – VISA.
Meals 18.00 **st.** – **6 rm** 34.00/64.00 **st.** – SB.

DORNOCH Sutherland. (Highland) 401 H 10 **Scotland G.** – pop. 2 042 – ☎ 01862.

See : Town★.

18, 18 Royal Dornoch, Golf Rd ✆ 810219.

The Square, IV25 35D ✆ 810400.

◆Edinburgh 219 – ◆Inverness 63 – ◆Wick 65.

Highfield without rest., Evelix Rd, IV25 3HR, ✆ 810909, Fax 810909, ←, –
3 rm 28.00/44.00 **s.**

Fourpenny Cottage, IV25 3QF, N : 3 m. by Embo rd on Golspie rd ✆ 810727, Fax 810727, ←, –
closed 18 December-15 February – **Meals** 15.00 **5 rm** 35.00/60.00 – SB.

DOUNBY Orkney. (Orkney Islands) 401 K 6 – see Orkney Islands (Mainland).

DRUMBEG Sutherland. (Highland) 401 E 9 – ✉ Lairg – ☎ 01571.

◆Edinburgh 262 – ◆Inverness 105 – Ullapool 48.

Drumbeg House (Taigh Druimbeag), IV27 4NW, ✆ 833209, –
March-October – **Meals** (communal dining) 15.00 – **3 rm** (dinner included) 45.00/70.00 **st.**

DRUMNADROCHIT Inverness. (Highland) 401 G 11 Scotland G. – pop. 852 – ✉ Milton ☎ 01456.

Envir. : Loch Ness★★ – Loch Ness Monster Exhibition★ *AC.*

♦Edinburgh 172 – ♦Inverness 16 – Kyle of Lochalsh 66.

Polmaily House 🐎, IV3 6XT, W : 2 m. on A 831 ☎ 450343, Fax 450813, « Country hous atmosphere », 🏊 heated, 🌳, park, 🎾 – 🚭 TV ☎ P. VISA
closed first 2 weeks December and last 3 weeks January – **Meals** 14.00/17.50 and a la carte 🍷 7.00 – **10 rm** 45.00/105.00 **t.** – SB.

DRYMEN Stirling. (Central) 401 G 15 Scotland G. – pop. 1 565 – ☎ 01360.

Envir. : Loch Lomond★★, W : 3 m..

ℹ Drymen Library, The Square, J63 0BL ☎ 60068 (summer only).

♦Edinburgh 64 – ♦Glasgow 18 – Stirling 22.

Buchanan Arms, Main St., G63 0BQ, ☎ 660588, Fax 660943, Ⅎ₆, ≘s, 🏊, 🌳, squash 🚭 TV ☎ P – 🎤 150. VISA JCB
Meals 9.75/18.50 **st.** and a la carte 🍷 4.95 – **51 rm** 78.00/114.00 **st.** – SB.

DULNAIN BRIDGE Inverness. (Highland) 401 J 12 – ✉ Grantown-on-Spey (Moray Highlanc – ☎ 01479.

♦Edinburgh 140 – ♦Inverness 31 – Perth 96.

Muckrach Lodge, PH26 3LY, W :½ m. on A 938 ☎ 851257, Fax 851325, ⩽, 🌳 – TV ☎ P – 🎤 40. AE VISA. ✗
Meals (bar lunch Monday to Saturday)/dinner 22.50 **t.** and a la carte 🍷 5.00 – **12 rm** 41.00/82.00 **st.** – SB.

Auchendean Lodge, PH26 3LU, S : 1 m. on A 95 ☎ 851347, Fax 851347, ⩽ Spey Valle and Cairngorms, 🌳 – 🚭 rest TV P. AE VISA
closed January-early February – **Meals** (dinner only) 23.50 **st.** 🍷 3.50 – **8 rm** 24.00/70.00 **st.** – SB.

"Short Breaks" (SB)

Molti alberghi propongono delle condizioni vantaggiose
per un soggiorno di due notti
comprendente la camera, la cena e la prima colazione.

DUMBARTON Dunbarton. (Strathclyde) 401 G 16 Scotland G. – pop. 77 173 – ☎ 01389.

See : Dumbarton Castle (site★) *AC.*

Envir. : Loch Lomond★★, N : 5½ m. by A 82.

⛳18 Vale of Leven, Northfield Rd, Bonhill ☎ 752351.

ℹ Milton, by Dumbarton A 82 (northbound) ☎ 42306 (summer only).

♦Edinburgh 64 – ♦Glasgow 12 – Greenock 17.

Forte Travelodge, Milton, G82 2TY, E : 3 m. by A 814 on A 82 ☎ 65202, Reservations (Freephone) 0800 850950 – TV ♿ P. AE VISA. ✗
Meals (grill rest.) – **32 rm** 34.50 **t.**

DUMFRIES Dumfries. (Dumfries and Galloway) 401 402 J 18 Scotland G. – pop. 21 164 – ☎ 01387.

See : Town★ – Midsteeple★ A **A.**

Envir. : Lincluden College (Tomb★) *AC*, N : 1½ m. by College St. A.

Exc. : Drumlanrig Castle★★ (cabinets★) *AC*, NW : 16½ m. by A 76 A – Shambellie House Museum of Costume (Costume Collection★) S : 7¼ m. by A 710 A – Sweetheart Abbey★ *AC*, S : 8 m. by A 710 A – Caerlaverock Castle★ (Renaissance façade★★) *AC*, SE : 9 m. by B 725 B – Glenkiln (Sculptures★) W : 9 m. by A 780 – A – and A 75 – Ruthwell Cross★, SE : 12 m. by A 780 – B – A 75 and B 724.

⛳18 Dumfries & Galloway, Laurieston Av., Maxwelltown ☎ 253582 A – ⛳9 Crichton Royal, Bankend Rd ☎ 41122, B.

ℹ Whitesands, DG1 4TH ☎ 253862, B.

♦Edinburgh 80 – ♦Ayr 59 – ♦Carlisle 34 – ♦Glasgow 79 – ♦Manchester 155 – ♦Newcastle upon Tyne 91.

Plan opposite

Cairndale, English St., DG1 2DF, ☎ 254111, Fax 250555, Ⅎ₆, ≘s, 🏊 – 🛗 🚭 rm TV ☎ P – 🎤 40. AE VISA. ✗ B a
Meals (carving lunch) 9.50/20.00 **st.** and a la carte 🍷 5.00 – **76 rm** 75.00/105.00 **st.** – SB.

Station, 49 Lovers Walk, DG1 1LT, ☎ 254316, Fax 250388 – 🛗 TV ☎ P – 🎤 70. AE VISA B e
Meals (bar lunch)/dinner 16.50 **st.** and a la carte 🍷 4.25 – **32 rm** 65.00/80.00 **st.** – SB.

Orchard House without rest., 298 Annan Rd, DG1 3JE, E : 1½ m. on A 780 (Carlisle rd) ☎ 255099, 🌳 – 🚭 TV ♿ P
3 rm 25.00/37.00.

ATS Glasgow St. ☎ 63837/8

DUMFRIES

High Street . . . . **A** 18
Loreburn Centre . . . . **A** 20

Aldermanhill Road . . . . **B** 2
Bank Street . . . . **A** 3
Buccleuch Street . . . . **A** 4
Cardoness Street . . . . **B** 5
Cassalands . . . . **A** 6
Castle Street . . . . **A** 7
Castle Douglas Road . . . . . . **A** 8
Catherine Street . . . . **B** 9
Corberry Avenue . . . . **A** 10
Cornwall Mount Rd . . . . **B** 12
Friars Vennel . . . . **A** 13
Galloway Street . . . . **A** 14
Glebe Street . . . . **B** 15
Great King Street . . . . **A** 16
Hermitage Drive . . . . **A** 17
Loreburn Street . . . . **A** 21
Nith Street . . . . **AB** 22
Queen Street . . . . **B** 23
Queensberry Street . . . . **A** 24
Rae Street . . . . **B** 26
St. Mary's Street . . . . **B** 27
St. Michael Street . . . . **B** 28
St. Michael's Bridge Road . . . . **A** 30
Shakespeare Street . . . . **B** 31
Union Street . . . . **A** 32
Whitesands . . . . **A** 34

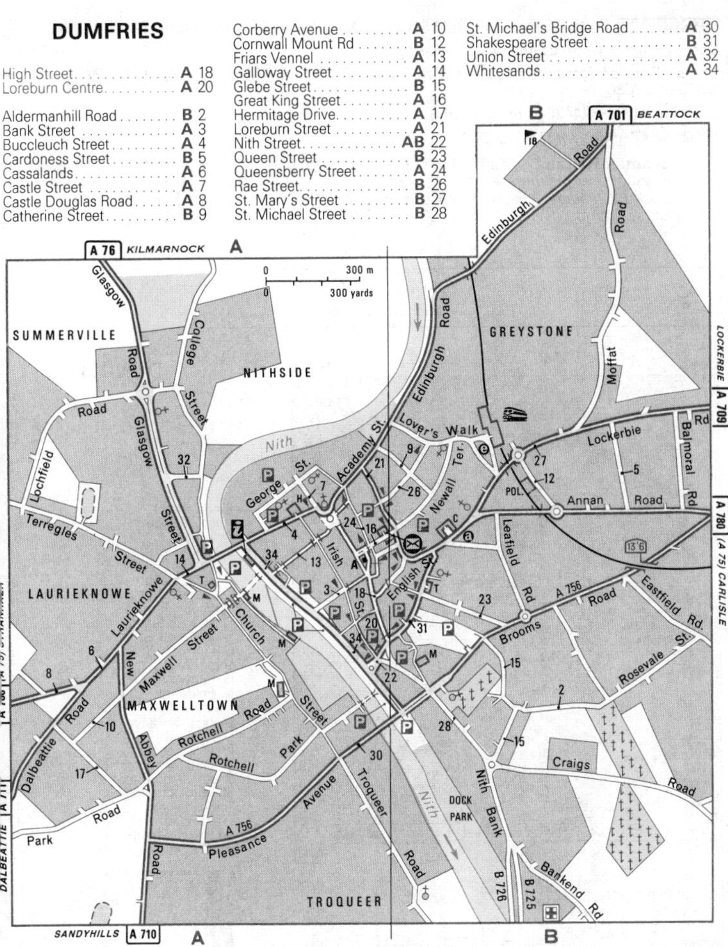

EUROPE on a single sheet
Michelin map no 970.

DUNAIN PARK Inverness. (Highland) – see Inverness.

DUNBAR E. Lothian. (Lothian) 401 M 15 **Scotland G.** – pop. 5 812 – ☎ 01368.

See : Tolbooth★ – John Muir's Birthplace★.

Exc. : Tantallon Castle★★ (clifftop site★★★) *AC*, NW : 10 m. by A 1087, A 1 and A 198 – Preston Mill★, W : 6 m. by A 1087, A 1 and B 1407 – Tyninghame★, NW : 6 m. by A 1 and A 198 – Museum of Flight★, W : 7 m. by A 1087, A 1 and B 1377.

18 East Links ☎ 862317 – 18 Winterfield, St. Margarets, North Rd ☎ 862280.

143 High St., EH42 1ES ☎ 863353.

◆Edinburgh 28 – ◆Newcastle upon Tyne 90.

Courtyard, Woodbush Brae, EH42 1HB, ☎ 864169 – TV P. AE VISA
Meals a la carte 12.45/18.65 **st.** 5.10 – **6 rm** 24.50/47.00 **st.** – SB.

St. Laurence without rest., North Rd, EH42 1AU, ☎ 862527, –
3 rm 17.50/35.00.

Marine, 7 Marine Rd, EH42 1AR, ☎ 863315, ←
April-September – **Meals** 10.00 **st.** – **9 rm** 16.00/32.00 **st.**

DUNBLANE Perth. (Central) 401 I 15 **Scotland G.** – pop. 8 007 (inc. Lecropt) – ☎ 01786.

See : Town★ – Cathedral★ (west front★★).

Envir. : Doune★ (castle★ *AC*) W : 4½ m. by A 820 – Doune Motor Museum★ *AC*, W : 5½ m. by A 820 and A 84.

ℹ Stirling Rd ✆ 824428 (summer only).

◆Edinburgh 42 – ◆Glasgow 33 – Perth 29.

Cromlix House 🐦, Kinbuck, FK15 9JT, N : 3½ m. on B 8033 ✆ 822125, Fax 825450, ⩽, « Antique furnishings », 🐟, 🎣, park, 🎾 – ⇄ rest 📺 ☎ 🅿 – 🏛 30. 🅂 AE ⓞ VISA. 🚫
closed 2 January-9 February – **Meals** (booking essential) (lunch by arrangement Monday to Friday October-May)/dinner 36.50 **t.** 🍷 6.00 – **6 rm** ☕ 105.00/180.00 **t.**, **8 suites** 200.00 **t.** – SB.

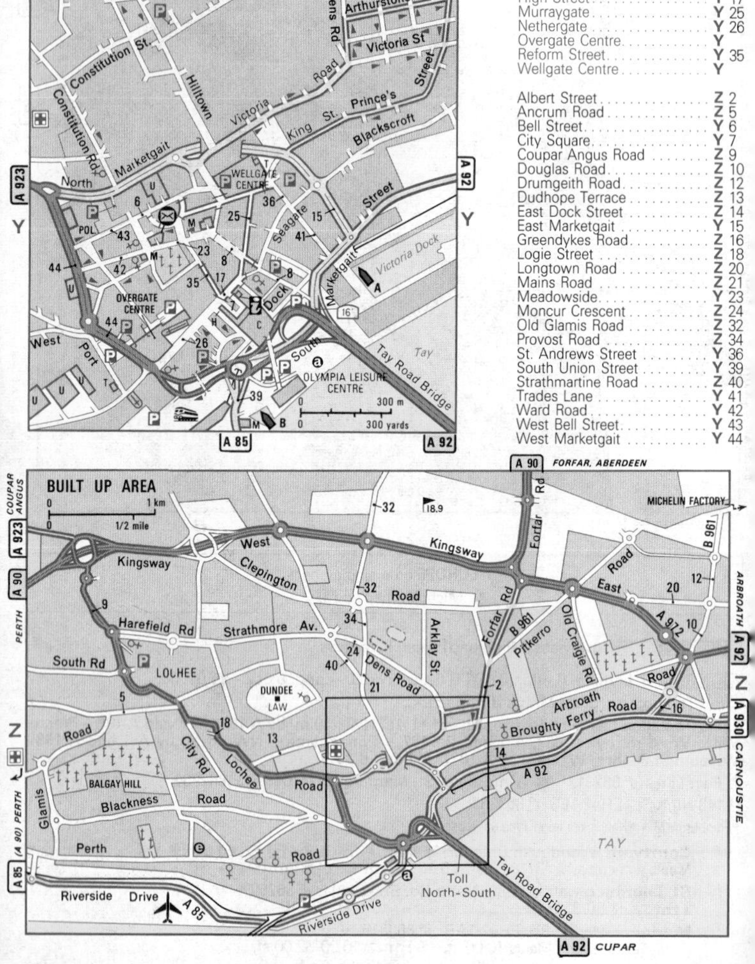

DUNDEE

Street	Grid	No.
Commercial Street	Y	8
High Street	Y	17
Murraygate	Y	25
Nethergate	Y	26
Overgate Centre	Y	
Reform Street	Y	35
Wellgate Centre	Y	
Albert Street	Z	2
Ancrum Road	Z	5
Bell Street	Y	6
City Square	Y	7
Coupar Angus Road	Z	9
Douglas Road	Z	10
Drumgeith Road	Z	12
Dudhope Terrace	Z	13
East Dock Street	Z	14
East Marketgait	Y	15
Greendykes Road	Z	16
Logie Street	Z	18
Longtown Road	Z	20
Mains Road	Z	21
Meadowside	Y	23
Moncur Crescent	Z	24
Old Glamis Road	Z	32
Provost Road	Z	34
St. Andrews Street	Y	36
South Union Street	Y	39
Strathmartine Road	Z	40
Trades Lane	Y	41
Ward Road	Y	42
West Bell Street	Y	43
West Marketgait	Y	44

DUNDEE Angus. (Tayside) 401 L 14 **Scotland G.** – pop. 165 873 – ☎ 01382.

See : The Frigate Unicorn★ *AC* Y **A** – RRS Discovery★ *AC* Y **B**.

8, 9 (2x) Caird Park, Mains Loan, Caird Park ✆ 453606 – 18 Camperdown Park ✆ 623398.

✈ Dundee Airport : ✆ 643242, SW : 1½ m. Z.

ℹ 4 City Sq., DD1 3BA ✆ 434664.

♦Edinburgh 63 – ♦Aberdeen 67 – ♦Glasgow 83.

Plan opposite

Stakis Dundee, Earl Grey Pl., DD1 4DE, ✆ 229271, Fax 200072, ←, Fö, ≘s, ☒ – |‡| ⊁ rm ▤ rest TV ☎ ♿ P – 🔥 400. AE ⓪ VISA JCB. ✻ Y **a**
Meals (carving rest.) 11.45/18.00 **st.** and dinner a la carte ₫ 6.80 – ☑ 9.50 – **104 rm** 88.00/115.00 **st.**, 2 suites – SB.

Swallow, Kingsway West (Dundee Ring Rd), DD2 5JT, W : 4¾ m. at junction of A 85 with A 90 ✆ 641122, Fax 568340, Fö, ≘s, ☒, ⁂ – ⊁ ▤ rest TV ☎ ♿ P – 🔥 80. AE ⓪ VISA
Meals 10.00/18.50 **st.** and a la carte – **107 rm** ☑ 87.50/130.00 **st.**, 1 suite – SB.

Shaftesbury, 1 Hyndford St., DD2 1HQ, ✆ 669216, Fax 641598 – ⊁ rest TV ☎. AE ⓪ VISA Z **e**
Meals (lunch by arrangement) (Sunday dinner residents only)/dinner 15.00 **t.** and a la carte ₫ 4.95 – **12 rm** ☑ 38.50/68.00 **st.** – SB.

Travel Inn, Discovery Quay, Riverside Drive, ✆ 203240, Fax 203237, ← – TV ♿. AE ⓪ VISA. ✻ Z **a**
Meals (grill rest.) – ☑ 4.95 – **40 rm** 34.50 **t.**

Travel Inn, Kingsway West, Invergowrie, DD2 5JU, NW : on A 90 ✆ 561115, Fax 568431 – ⊁ rm TV ♿ P. AE ⓪ VISA. ✻
Meals (grill rest.) – ☑ 4.95 – **40 rm** 34.50 **t.**

Invermark without rest., 23 Monifieth Rd, DD5 2RN, E : by A 930 ✆ 739430, Fax 739430, ⁂ – ⊁ TV P. VISA. ✻
4 rm ☑ 25.00/40.00.

at Broughty Ferry E : 4½ m. by A 930 – Z – (Dundee Rd) – ✉ Dundee – ☎ 01382 :

Tayview without rest., 71-73 Vincent St., DD5 2EZ, ✆ 779438 – ⊁. VISA. ✻
11 rm ☑ 40.00/65.00 **t.**

Beach House, 22 Esplanade, DD5 2EN, ✆ 776614, Fax 480241 – ⊁ rest TV ☎. VISA. ✻
Meals 11.00 ₫ 4.50 – **5 rm** ☑ 38.00/50.00.

ATS 332 Clepington Rd ✆ 858327

DUNDONNELL Ross and Cromarty. (Highland) 401 E 10 **Scotland G.** – ✉ Garve – ☎ 01854.

Envir. : Loch Broom★★, N : 4½ m. via A'lt na h-Airbhe.

Exc. : Falls of Measach★★, SE : 10 m. by A 832 – Corrieshalloch Gorge★, SE : 11½ m. by A 832 and A 835.

♦Edinburgh 215 – ♦ Inverness 59.

Dundonnell, IV23 2QR, ✆ 633204, Fax 633366, ← Dundonnell Valley – ⊁ rest TV ☎ P 🔥 60. AE VISA
April-mid November except Christmas-New Year – **Meals** (bar lunch)/dinner 22.75 **t.** and a la carte ₫ 4.50 – **30 rm** ☑ 47.00/90.00 **t.** – SB.

DUNFERMLINE Fife. (Fife) 401 J 15 **Scotland G.** – pop. 29 436 – ☎ 01383.

See : Town★ – Abbey★ (Abbey Church★★) *AC*.

Envir. : Forth Bridges★★, S : 5 m. by A 823 and B 980.

Exc. : Culross★★★ (Village★★★, Palace★★ *AC*, Study★ *AC*) W : 7 m. by A 994 and B 9037.

18 Canmore, Venturefair ✆ 724969 – 18 Pitreavie, Queensferry Rd ✆ 722591 – 9 Saline, Kinneddar Hill ✆ 852591.

ℹ 13-15 Maygate, KY12 7NE ✆ 720999 (summer only).

♦Edinburgh 16 – ♦Dundee 48 – Motherwell 39.

King Malcolm Thistle, Queensferry Rd, KY11 5DS, S : 1 m. on A 823 ✆ 722611, Fax 730865 – ⊁ rm ▤ rest TV ☎ P – 🔥 150. AE ⓪ VISA JCB
Meals *(closed lunch Saturday and Sunday)* 14.95 **st.** and a la carte ₫ 4.60 – ☑ 8.95 – **48 rm** 65.00/85.00 **st.** – SB.

at Crossford SW : 1¾ m. on A 994 – ✉ Dunfermline – ☎ 01383 :

Keavil House ♨, Main St., KY12 8QW, ✆ 736258, Fax 621600, Fö, ≘s, ☒, ⁂ – TV ☎ ♿ P – 🔥 150. AE ⓪ VISA
Meals 12.50/19.50 **t.** and dinner a la carte ₫ 5.00 – **30 rm** ☑ 55.00/100.00 **t.** – SB.

ATS 14 Dickson St., Elgin St. Est. ✆ 722802

Plans de ville : *Les rues sont sélectionnées en fonction de leur importance pour la circulation et le repérage des établissements cités.*

Les rues secondaires ne sont qu'amorcées.

DUNKELD Perth. (Tayside) 401 J 14 Scotland G. pop. 4 069 – ☎ 01350.

See : Village★ – Cathedral Street★.

Dunkeld & Birnam, Fungarth ☎ 727524.

The Cross, PH8 0AN ☎ 727688 (summer only).

◆Edinburgh 58 – ◆Aberdeen 88 – ◆Inverness 98 – Perth 14.

Kinnaird ⛯, Dalguise, PH8 0LB, NW : 6 ¾ m. by A 9 on B 898 ☎ (01796) 482440 Fax 482289, ← Tay valley and hills, « Sporting estate, antique furnishings », park – rest. closed Monday to Wednesday January-March – **Meals** 24.00/39.50 **t.** 8.00 – **8 rm** 190.00/240.00 **t.**, 1 suite.

Stakis Dunkeld ⛯, PH8 0HX, ☎ 727771, Fax 728924, ←, « Tayside setting », park – rm – 85. **Meals** (light lunch)/dinner 26.00 **t.** and a la carte 6.00 – 9.75 – **83 rm** 92.00 **st.**, 3 suites – SB.

Bheinne Mhor, Perth Rd, Birnam, PH8 0DH, S : ¾ m. by A 923 ☎ 727779, – . closed mid December-mid January – **Meals** (by arrangement) 13.00 – **3 rm** 29.00/40.00 **st.**

DUNOON Argyll. (Strathclyde) 401 F 16 – pop. 13 781 (inc. Kilmun) – ☎ 01369.

Innellan, Knockamillie Rd ☎ 3546.

from Dunoon Pier to Gourock Railway Pier (Caledonian MacBrayne Ltd) frequent services daily (20 mn) – from Hunters Quay to McInroy's Point, Gourock (Western Ferries (Clyde) Ltd) frequent services daily (20 mn).

7 Alexandra Par., PA23 8AB ☎ 3785.

◆Edinburgh 73 – ◆Glasgow 27 – ◆Oban 77.

Enmore, Marine Par., Kirn, PA23 8HH, N : 1 ¼ m. on A 815 ☎ 702230, Fax 702148, ← Firth of Clyde, squash – rest. closed 2 weeks Christmas – **Meals** 10.00/28.00 **st.** and a la carte 5.90 – **10 rm** 39.00/140.00 **st.** – SB.

Anchorage, Shore Rd, Ardanadam, PA23 8QG, N : 3 m. on A 815 ☎ 705108, Fax 705108 ←, – . **Meals** 22.00 **st.** (dinner) and a la carte 6.75/20.00 **st.** 4.00 – **5 rm** 42.00/51.00 **st.** – SB.

ATS 247 Argyll St. ☎ 2853

DUNVEGAN Inverness. (Highland) 401 A 11 – see Skye (Isle of).

DUROR Argyll. (Strathclyde) 401 E 14 – ✉ Appin – ☎ 01631.

◆Edinburgh 125 – Fort William 19 – ◆Oban 31.

Stewart ⛯, Glen Duror, PA38 4BW, ☎ 740268, Fax 740328, ←, – rest. *April-mid October* – **Meals** (bar lunch Monday to Saturday)/dinner 25.00 **t.** and a la carte 6.00 – **19 rm** 43.50/87.00 **t.** – SB.

DYCE Aberdeen. (Grampian) 401 N 12 – see Aberdeen.

EASDALE Argyll. (Strathclyde) 401 D 15 – see Seil (Isle of).

EAST KILBRIDE Lanark. (Strathclyde) 401 402 H 16 – pop. 73 378 – ☎ 0135 52 (5 fig.) and 01355 (6 fig.).

Torrance House, Strathaven Rd ☎ 48638.

◆Edinburgh 46 – ◆Ayr 35 – ◆Glasgow 10.

Stakis East Kilbride, Stewartfield Way, G74 5LA, NW : 2 ¼ m. on A 726 ☎ 36300, Fax 33552, squash – rm rest – 150. **Point Grill : Meals** 14.50/16.50 **st.** and a la carte - (see also ***Simpsons*** below) – 8.95 – **73 rm** 89.00/99.00 **st.**, 1 suite – SB.

Bruce Swallow, 34 Cornwall St., G74 1AF, ☎ 29771, Fax 42216 – rm – 250. **Meals** (bar lunch)/dinner 25.00 **st.** and a la carte 6.50 – **78 rm** 75.00/90.00 **st.** – SB.

Stuart, 1 Cornwall Way, G74 1JR, ☎ 21161, Fax 64410 – – 200. **Meals** 15.00/20.00 **t.** and a la carte – **38 rm** 57.00/90.00 **t.**, 1 suite.

Crutherland ⛯, Strathaven Rd, G75 0QZ, SE : 2 m. on A 726 ☎ 37633, Fax 37633, park – – 40 **18 rm**, 1 suite.

Travel Inn, Brunel Way, The Murray, G75 0JY, ☎ 22809, Fax 30517 – rm. **Meals** (grill rest.) – 4.95 – **40 rm** 34.50 **t.**

XXX **Simpsons** (at Stakis East Kilbride H.), Stewartfield Way, G74 5LA, NW : 2¼ m. on A 726 ☎ 36300, Fax 33552 – . *closed Sunday* – **Meals** (booking essential) (dinner only) 21.50 **st.**

EDINBURGH Midlothian. (Lothian) 401 K 16 **Scotland G.** – pop. 418 914 – ☎ 0131.

See : City★★★ – Edinburgh International Festival★★★ (August) – National Gallery of Scotland★★ DY **M4** – Royal Botanic Garden★★★ AV – The Castle★★ *AC* DYZ : Site★★★ – Palace Block (Honours of Scotland★★★) – St. Margaret's Chapel (※★★★) – Great Hall (Hammerbeam Roof★★) – ≤★★ from Argyle and Mill's Mount DZ – Abbey and Palace of Holyroodhouse★★ *AC* (Plasterwork Ceilings★★★, ※★★ from Arthur's Seat) BV – Royal Mile★★ : St. Giles' Cathedral★★ (Crown Spire★★★) EYZ – Gladstone's Land★ *AC* EYZ **A** – Canongate Talbooth★ EY **B** – New Town★★ (Charlotte Square★★★ CY **14** – Royal Museum of Scotland (Antiquities)★★ EZ **M2** – The Georgian House★ *AC* CY **D** – National Portrait Gallery★ EY **M3** – Dundas House★ EY **E**) – Scottish National Gallery of Modern Art★ AV **M1** – Victoria Street★ EZ **84** – Scott Monument★ (≤★) *AC* EY **F** – Craigmillar Castle★ *AC* BX – Calton Hill (※★★★ *AC* from Nelson's Monument) EY.

Envir. : Edinburgh Zoo★★ *AC* AV – Hill End Ski Centre (※★★) *AC*, S : 5½ m. by A 702 BX – The Royal Observatory (West Tower ≤★) *AC* BX – Ingleston, Scottish Agricultural Museum★, W : 6½ m. by A 8 AV.

Exc. : Rosslyn Chapel★★ *AC* (Apprentice Pillar★★★) S : 7½ m. by A 701 – BX – and B 7006 – Forth Bridges★★, NW : 9½ m. by A 90 AV – Hopetoun House★★ *AC*, NW : 11½ m. by A 90 – AV – and
A 904 – Dalmeny★ – Dalmeny House★ *AC*, St. Cuthbert's Church★ (Norman South Doorway★★) NW : 7 m. by A 90 AV – Crichton Castle (Italianate courtyard range★) *AC*, SE : 10 m. by A 7 – X – and B 6372.

18, 18 Braid Hills, Braid Hills Rd ☎ 447 6666, BX – 18 Craigmillar Park, 1 Observatory Rd ☎ 667 2837, BX – 18 Carrick Knowe, Glendevon Park ☎ 337 1096 AX – 18 Duddingston Road West ☎ 661 1005, BV – 18 Silverknowes, Parkway ☎ 336 3843, AV – 18 Liberton, 297 Gilmerton Rd ☎ 664 8580, BX – 9 Portobello, Stanley St. ☎ 669 4361, BV – 18 (2x) Dalmahoy Hotel C.C., Kirknewton ☎ 333 4105/1845, AX.

✈ Edinburgh Airport : ☎ 333 1000, W : 6 m. by A 8 AV – **Terminal :** Waverley Bridge.

☎ 0345 090700.

ℹ Edinburgh & Scotland Information Centre, 3 Princes St., EH2 2QP ☎ 557 1700 – Edinburgh Airport, Tourist Information Desk ☎ 333 2167.

◆Glasgow 46 – ◆Newcastle upon Tyne 105.

Plans on following pages

Caledonian (Q.M.H.), Princes St., EH1 2AB, ☎ 459 9988, Fax 225 6632 – ▮ ⇔ rm ▤ rest TV ☎ ♿ P – 🏛 300. AE ⓓ VISA. ✻ CY **n**
Carriages : Meals 20.60/29.40 **st.** and a la carte 🍷 7.20 - (see also ***Pompadour*** below) – ☐ 14.50 – **223 rm** 135.50/299.00 **st.**, 11 suites – SB.

Balmoral (Forte), Princes St., EH2 2EQ, ☎ 556 2414, Telex 727282, Fax 557 8740, Lδ, ≘s, ☐ – ▮ ⇔ rm ▤ rest TV ☎ ♿ – 🏛 380. AE ⓓ VISA JCB. ✻ EY **n**
Bridges : Meals 19.95/29.50 **st.** 🍷 7.50 - (see also ***Grill*** below) – ☐ 14.50 – **168 rm** 120.00/170.00 **st.**, 21 suites – SB.

Sheraton Grand, 1 Festival Sq., EH3 9SR, ☎ 229 9131, Fax 229 6254, Lδ, ≘s, ☐ – ▮ ⇔ rm ▤ TV ☎ ♿ P – 🏛 500. AE ⓓ VISA JCB. ✻ CDZ **v**
Grill : Meals *(closed Saturday lunch and Sunday)* 19.95/27.50 **t.** and a la carte 🍷 9.00 – **Terrace : Meals** 18.00 **t.** and a la carte 🍷 7.00 – ☐ 14.00 – **255 rm** 140.00/205.00 **st.**, 6 suites.

George Inter-Continental, 19-21 George St., EH2 2PB, ☎ 225 1251, Fax 226 5644 – ▮ ⇔ rm TV ☎ P – 🏛 200. AE ⓓ VISA JCB. ✻ DY **z**
Meals 12.95/16.95 **st.** and a la carte 🍷 6.00 – **193 rm** ☐ 90.00/165.00 **t.**, 2 suites – SB.

Dalmahoy H. Country Club Resort (Country Club) ⛰, Kirknewton, EH27 8EB, SW : 7 m. on A 71 ☎ 333 1845, Fax 333 1433, ≤, Lδ, ≘s, ☐, 18, ⛳, park, ✻, squash – ▮ ⇔ ▤ rest TV ☎ ♿ P – 🏛 190. AE ⓓ VISA. ✻
Meals *(closed Saturday lunch)* 14.50/23.50 **t.** and dinner a la carte – ☐ 9.50 – **150 rm** 109.00 **t.**, 1 suite – SB.

Howard, 32-36 Gt. King St., EH3 6QH, ☎ 557 3500, Fax 557 6515, « Georgian town houses » – ▮ ⇔ rest TV ☎ P – 🏛 40. AE ⓓ VISA DY **s**
closed 24 December-2 January – **Meals** (dinner only) a la carte 18.55/27.30 **st.** 🍷 6.95 – **16 rm** ☐ 110.00/225.00 **st.** – SB.

Swallow Royal Scot, 111 Glasgow Rd, EH12 8NF, W : 4½ m. on A 8 ☎ 334 9191, Fax 316 4507, Lδ, ≘s, ☐ – ▮ ⇔ rm ▤ rest TV ☎ P – 🏛 300. AE ⓓ VISA
Meals 15.50/21.00 **st.** and a la carte 🍷 6.50 – **255 rm** ☐ 105.00/135.00 **st.**, 4 suites – SB.

Hilton National, 69 Belford Rd, EH4 3DG, ☎ 332 2545, Telex 727979, Fax 332 3805 – ▮ ⇔ rm TV ☎ ♿ P – 🏛 130. AE ⓓ VISA JCB CY **i**
Meals (bar lunch Saturday and Sunday) 13.00/17.50 **st.** and dinner a la carte 🍷 7.00 – ☐ 11.00 – **144 rm** 90.00/250.00 **st.**

Edinburgh Capital (Q.M.H.), Clermiston Rd, EH12 6UG, ☎ 535 9988, Fax 334 9712, Lδ, ≘s, ☐ – ▮ ⇔ rm TV ☎ ♿ P – 🏛 300. AE ⓓ VISA AV **n**
Meals 16.75 **st.** (dinner) and a la carte 9.00/21.00 **st.** – ☐ 10.50 – **111 rm** 90.00/120.00 **st.** – SB.

Mount Royal (Jarvis), 53 Princes St., EH2 2DZ, ☎ 225 7161, Fax 220 4671, ≤ – ▮ TV ☎ – 🏛 50. AE ⓓ VISA. ✻ DY **a**
Meals 8.95/14.95 **st.** and dinner a la carte – ☐ 8.75 – **156 rm** 95.00/135.00 **st.** – SB.

EDINBURGH
FIRTH
CRAMOND
BLACKHALL
MURRAYFIELD
EDINBURGH ZOO
SIGHTHILL
JUNIPER
GREEN
ROYAL BOTANIC GARDENS
Queensferry Road
Glasgow Road
Corstorphine Road
Gorgie Road
Slateford Road
Calder Road
Lanark Road
Colinton Road
Comiston Rd
Union Canal
Water of Leith
FORTH-ROAD-BRIDGE
GLASGOW (M8) (M9) STIRLING
KILMARNOCK
AIRPORT
LANARK

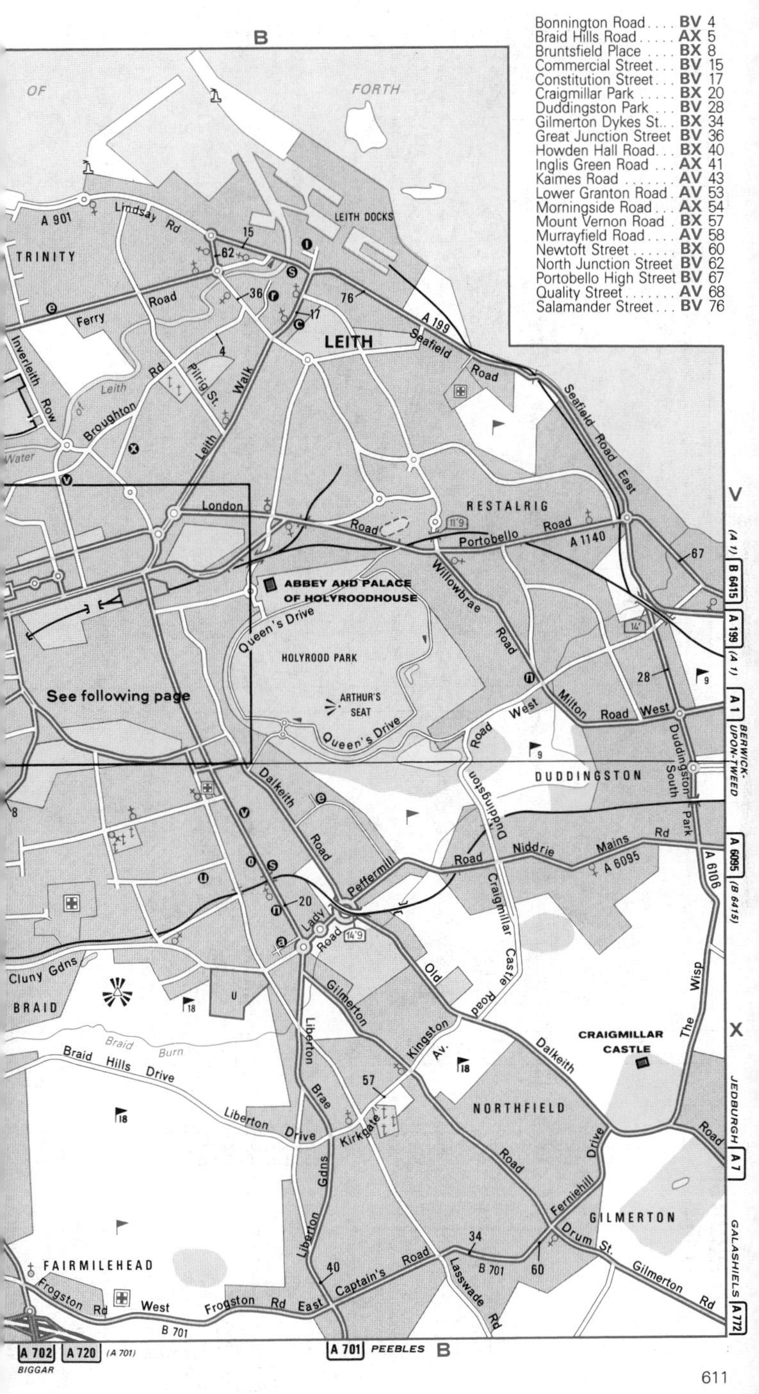

Bonnington Road	BV	4
Braid Hills Road	AX	5
Bruntsfield Place	BX	8
Commercial Street	BV	15
Constitution Street	BV	17
Craigmillar Park	BX	20
Duddingston Park	BV	28
Gilmerton Dykes St.	BX	34
Great Junction Street	BV	36
Howden Hall Road	BX	40
Inglis Green Road	AX	41
Kaimes Road	AV	43
Lower Granton Road	AV	53
Morningside Road	AX	54
Mount Vernon Road	BX	57
Murrayfield Road	AV	58
Newtoft Street	BX	60
North Junction Street	BV	62
Portobello High Street	BV	67
Quality Street	AV	68
Salamander Street	BV	76

EDINBURGH
CENTRE

Street	Grid	No.
Castle Street	DY	
Frederick Street	DY	
George Street	DY	
Hanover Street	DY	
High Street	EYZ	37
Lawnmarket	EYZ	46
Princes Street	DY	
St. James Centre	EY	
Waverley Market	EY	
Bernard Terrace	EZ	3
Bread Street	DZ	6
Bristo Place	EZ	7
Candlemaker Row	EZ	9
Castlehill	DZ	10
Chambers Street	EZ	12
Chapel Street	EZ	13
Charlotte Square	CY	14
Deanhaugh Street	CY	23
Douglas Gardens	CY	25
Drummond Street	EZ	27
Forrest Road	EZ	31
Gardner's Crescent	CZ	32
George IV Bridge	EZ	33
Grassmarket	DZ	35
Home Street	DZ	38
Hope Street	CY	39
Johnston Terrace	DZ	42
King's Bridge	DZ	44
King's Stables Road	DZ	45
Leith Street	EY	47
Leven Street	DZ	48
Lothian Street	EZ	51
Mound (The)	DY	55
North Bridge	EY	61
North St. Andrew Street	EY	66
Raeburn Place	CY	69
Randolph Crescent	CY	71
St. Andrew Square	EY	73
St. Mary's Street	EY	75
Shandwick Place	CYZ	77
South Charlotte Street	DY	78
South St. David Street	DEY	79
Spittal Street	DZ	83
Victoria Street	EZ	84
Waterloo Place	EY	87
Waverley Bridge	EY	89
West Maitland Street	CZ	92

Royal Terrace, 18 Royal Terrace, EH7 5AQ, ✆ 557 3222, Fax 557 5334, Fitness, sauna, pool, garden – lift TV ☎ – conference 80. Cards AE VISA JCB. ✱ EY i
Meals *(closed lunch Saturday and Sunday)* a la carte 14.95/27.00 **t.** – ☕ 9.50 – **92 rm** 105.00/145.00 **st.**, 1 suite.

Forte Posthouse Edinburgh, Corstorphine Rd, EH12 6UA, ✆ 334 0390, Fax 334 9237 – lift ⊬ rm TV ☎ P – conference 120. Cards AE VISA JCB. ✱ AV o
Meals a la carte 13.00/24.20 **st.** 6.95 – ☕ 7.95 – **204 rm** 69.00 **st.** – SB.

King James Thistle, 107 Leith St., EH1 3SW, ✆ 556 0111, Fax 557 5333 – lift ⊬ rm ▤ TV ☎ – conference 250. Cards AE VISA JCB. ✱ EY u
Meals 12.50/19.50 **t.** and a la carte 6.10 – ☕ 9.95 – **142 rm** 110.00/135.00 **st.**, 5 suites – SB.

Stakis Edinburgh Grosvenor, Grosvenor St., EH12 5EF, ✆ 226 6001, Fax 220 2387 – lift TV ☎ ♿ – conference 300. Cards AE VISA JCB CZ a
Meals *(closed lunch Saturday and Sunday)* 10.95/16.95 and a la carte 6.75 – ☕ 8.50 – **135 rm** 95.00/105.00 **st.**, 1 suite – SB.

Channings, South Learmonth Gdns, EH4 1EZ, ✆ 315 2226, Fax 332 9631 – lift ⊬ rest TV ☎. Cards AE VISA. ✱ CY e
closed 25 to 27 December – **Meals** (light lunch Saturday) 9.95/19.50 **st.** and dinner a la carte – **48 rm** ☕ 92.00/132.00 **st.** – SB.

Malmaison, 1 Tower Pl., Leith, EH6 7DB, ✆ 555 6868, Fax 555 6999, « Contemporary interior » – lift TV ☎ ♿ P – conference 30. Cards AE VISA BV i
Meals - Brasserie - a la carte 14.50/19.95 **t.** 8.50 – ☕ 10.00 – **19 rm** 75.00/85.00 **t.**, 6 suites.

Ellersly Country House (Jarvis), 4 Ellersly Rd, EH12 6HZ, ✆ 337 6888, Fax 313 2543, garden – lift ⊬ rm TV ☎ P – conference 70. Cards AE VISA AV v
Meals *(closed Saturday lunch)* 14.95 **t.** and a la carte 6.50 – ☕ 8.50 – **57 rm** 99.00/125.00 **t.** – SB.

Holiday Inn Garden Court, 107 Queensferry Rd, EH4 3HL, ✆ 332 2442, Fax 332 3408, ≤, Fitness – lift ⊬ rm ▤ rest TV ☎ ♿ P – conference 60. Cards AE VISA JCB AV x
Meals (bar lunch Monday to Saturday)/dinner 14.50 **st.** and a la carte 7.95 – ☕ 8.95 – **119 rm** 79.50/89.50 **st.** – SB.

Thrums, 14-15 Minto St., EH9 1RQ, ✆ 667 5545, Fax 667 8707, garden – TV ☎ P. Cards VISA. ✱ BX v
closed Christmas – **Meals** 12.00 **t.** (dinner) and a la carte 8.85/16.15 **t.** 6.00 – **14 rm** ☕ 37.00/68.00 **t.** – SB.

Lodge, 6 Hampton Terr., West Coates, EH12 5JD, ✆ 337 3682, Fax 313 1700 – ⊬ TV ☎ P. Cards VISA. ✱ AV u
closed 10 to 26 December – **Meals** *(closed Sunday)* (dinner only) 12.50/15.50 **t.** 4.95 – **12 rm** ☕ 40.00/80.00 **st.**

Travel Inn, 228 Willowbrae Rd, EH8 7NG, ✆ 661 3396, Fax 652 2789 – ⊬ rm TV ♿ P. Cards AE VISA. ✱ BV n
Meals (grill rest.) – ☕ 4.95 – **40 rm** 34.50 **t.**

Forte Travelodge, 48 Dreghorn Link, City Bypass, EH13 9QR, ✆ 441 4296, Reservations (Freephone) 0800 850950 – TV ♿ P. Cards AE VISA. ✱ AX a
Meals (grill rest.) – **40 rm** 34.50 **t.**

17 Abercromby Place without rest., 17 Abercromby Pl., EH3 6LB, ✆ 557 8036, Fax 558 3453, « Georgian town house » – ⊬ TV ☎ garage P. Cards VISA. ✱ DY r
closed Christmas – **6 rm** ☕ 35.00/70.00.

Drummond House without rest., 17 Drummond Pl., EH3 6PL, ✆ 557 9189, Fax 557 9189, « Georgian town house » – ⊬. Cards VISA. ✱ DY e
3 rm ☕ 65.00/90.00 **st.**

Sibbet House without rest., 26 Northumberland St., EH3 6LS, ✆ 556 1078, Fax 557 9445, « Georgian town house » – ⊬ TV ☎. Cards VISA. ✱ DY x
3 rm ☕ 55.00/70.00 **s.**

27 Heriot Row, 27 Heriot Row, EH3 6EN, ✆ 225 9474, Fax 220 1699, « Georgian town house », garden – ⊬ TV ☎. Cards VISA. ✱ DY v
Meals (by arrangement) (communal dining) 25.00/30.00 **st.** – **3 rm** ☕ 45.00/70.00 **st.**

Stuart House without rest., 12 East Claremont St., EH7 4JP, ✆ 557 9030, Fax 557 0563 – ⊬ TV ☎. Cards AE VISA. ✱ BV x
7 rm ☕ 33.00/75.00 **t.**

Dorstan, 7 Priestfield Rd, EH16 5HJ, ✆ 667 6721, Fax 668 4644 – ⊬ rest TV ☎ P. Cards VISA. ✱ BX e
closed Christmas – **Meals** (by arrangement) 15.00 **t.** – **14 rm** ☕ 29.00/75.00 **t.**

International without rest., 37 Mayfield Gdns, EH9 2BX, ✆ 667 2511, Fax 667 1109 – TV. ✱ BX s
8 rm ☕ 23.00/64.00 **s.**

Greenside, 9 Royal Terr., EH7 5AB, ✆ 557 0022, Fax 557 0022, garden – TV. Cards AE VISA. ✱ EY a
Meals 18.00 **t.** 5.90 – **14 rm** ☕ 40.00/70.00 **t.**

Teviotdale, 53 Grange Loan, EH9 2ER, ✆ 667 4376, Fax 667 4376 – ⊬ TV ☎. Cards AE VISA. ✱ BX u
closed 14 to 28 December and 4 January-7 February – **Meals** (by arrangement) 14.50 – **7 rm** ☕ 42.00/64.00 **t.**

Kew without rest., 1 Kew Terr., Murrayfield, EH12 5JE, ☎ 313 0700, Fax 313 0747 – TV. P. VISA AV
6 rm 30.00/65.00 **st.**

Ravensdown without rest., 248 Ferry Rd, EH5 3AN, ☎ 552 5438 – TV. BV
7 rm 38.00/40.00.

Parklands without rest., 20 Mayfield Gdns, EH9 2BZ, ☎ 667 7184 TV. BX
6 rm 30.00/52.00.

Galloway without rest., 22 Dean Park Cres., EH4 1PH, ☎ 332 3672 – TV CY
10 rm 28.00/50.00 **t.**

Glenisla, 12 Lygon Rd, EH16 5QB, ☎ 667 4877, Fax 667 4098 – VISA. BX
Meals 10.00 **t.** 4.00 – **8 rm** 23.00/52.00 **t.**

St. Margaret's without rest., 18 Craigmillar Park, EH16 5PS, ☎ 667 2202, Fax 667 2202 TV P. VISA. BX
closed January and February – **8 rm** 25.00/50.00 **st.**

XXXX **Pompadour** (at Caledonian H.), Princes St., EH1 2AB, ☎ 459 9988, Fax 225 6632 – P. AE VISA CY
closed lunch Saturday and Sunday – **Meals** 23.50/42.00 **st.** and dinner a la carte 7.60.

XXXX **Grill** (at Balmoral H.), 1 Princes St., EH2 2EQ, ☎ 556 2414, Telex 727282, Fax 557 3747 AE VISA JCB EY
closed lunch Saturday and Sunday – **Meals** 21.50/35.00 **st.** and a la carte 7.00.

XX **Vintners Room,** The Vaults, 87 Giles St., Leith, EH6 6BZ, ☎ 554 6767, Fax 467 7130 – AE VISA BV
closed Sunday and 2 weeks Christmas-New Year – **Meals** a la carte 11.50/24.75 **t.** 5.00

XX **Martins,** 70 Rose St., North Lane, EH2 3DX, ☎ 225 3106 – . AE VISA DY
closed Saturday lunch, Sunday, Monday, 1 week May-June, 1 week September-Octob and 23 December-22 January – **Meals** (booking essential) 15.00 **t.** (lunc and a la carte 24.50/30.55 **t.** 5.00.

XX **L'Auberge,** 56 St. Mary's St., EH1 1SX, ☎ 556 5888, Fax 556 2588 – . AE VI JCB EYZ
closed 25-26 December and 1 to 3 January – **Meals** - French - 16.50/24.50 **t.** and a la car 6.00.

XX **Raffaelli,** 10-11 Randolph Pl., EH3 7TA, ☎ 225 6060, Fax 225 8830 – AE VISA CY
closed Saturday lunch, Sunday and Bank Holidays – **Meals** - Italian - a la carte 13.95/22.90 4.90.

XX **Lancer's Brasserie,** 5 Hamilton Pl., Stockbridge, EH3 5BA, ☎ 332 3444 – VISA CY
Meals - North Indian - 8.95 **t.** (lunch) and a la carte 10.45/15.35 **t.**

XX **Indian Cavalry Club,** 3 Atholl Pl., EH3 8HP, ☎ 228 3282, Fax 225 1911 – AE VISA CZ
Meals - Indian - 6.95/16.95 **t.** and a la carte.

XX **Merchants,** 17 Merchant St.,, EH1 2QD, off Candlemaker Row, (under bridge ☎ 225 4009, Fax 557 9318 – AE VISA JCB EZ
closed Sunday – **Meals** (booking essential) 8.95/12.50 **t.** and a la carte 5.00.

XX **Denzler's 121,** 121 Constitution St., EH6 7AE, ☎ 554 3268, Fax 467 7239 – AE VIS JCB BV
closed Saturday lunch, Sunday, Monday, 25 and 26 December, 1 and 2 January and las 2 weeks July – **Meals** 7.75/17.50 **st.** and a la carte 5.35.

X **Atrium,** 10 Cambridge St., EH1 2ED, ☎ 228 8882, Fax 459 1060 – . AE VISA DZ
closed Saturday lunch, Sunday and 1 week Christmas – **Meals** a la carte 20.50/27.50 6.50.

X **Silvio's,** 54 The Shore, Leith, EH6 6RA, ☎ 553 3557, Fax 553 3557 – . AE VISA BV
closed Sunday, 25 and 26 December, 1 and 2 January – **Meals** - Italian - a la carte 14.60 19.20 **t.** 4.50.

X **Le Marche Noir,** 2-4 Eyre Pl., EH3 5EP, ☎ 558 1608, Fax 556 0798 – AE VISA BV
Meals (booking essential) 12.50/19.50 **t.**

at Edinburgh International Airport W : 7½ m. by A 8 – AV – ✉ Edinburgh – ☎ 0131

Stakis Edinburgh Airport, EH28 8LL, ☎ 519 4400, Fax 519 4422 – rm rest TV ☎ P – 220. AE VISA
Meals 5.95/25.00 **st.** and a la carte 6.50 – 8.50 – **134 rm** 89.00/99.00 **st.** – SB.

at Ingliston W : 7¾ m. on A 8 – AV – ✉ Edinburgh – ☎ 0131 :

Norton House, EH28 8LX, on A 8 ☎ 333 1275, Fax 333 5305, <, , park – rm TV ☎ P – 250. AE VISA
Meals *(closed Saturday lunch)* 15.50/22.50 **t.** and a la carte – **46 rm** 104.00/155.00 **st.** 1 suite – SB.

ATS 167 Bonnington Rd, Leith ☎ 554 6617 ATS 6 Gylemuir Rd, Corstorphine ☎ 334 6174

EDINBURGH INTERNATIONAL AIRPORT Midlothian (Lothian) 401 J 16 – see Edinburgh.

EDZELL Angus. (Tayside) 401 M 13 Scotland G. – pop. 830 – 01356.
Envir. : Castle★ AC (The Pleasance★★★) W : 2 m.
Exc. : Glen Esk★, NW : 7 m.
Trinity, Brechin 622383.
Edinburgh 94 – ◆Aberdeen 36 – ◆Dundee 31.

Glenesk, High St., DD9 7TF, 648319, Fax 647333, – – 100.
Meals 11.50/15.50 **t.** and a la carte – **25 rm** 48.00/80.00 **t.** – SB.

ELGIN Moray. (Grampian) 401 K 11 Scotland G. – pop. 11 855 – 01343.
See : Town★ – Cathedral★ (Chapter house★★)AC.
Exc. : Glenfiddich Distillery★, SE : 10 m. by A 941.
Moray, Stotfield Rd, Lossiemouth 812018 – Hardhillock, Birnie Rd 542338 – Hopeman, Moray 830578.
17 High St., IV30 1EJ 542666.
Edinburgh 198 – ◆Aberdeen 68 – Fraserburgh 61 – ◆Inverness 39.

Mansion House, The Haugh, IV30 1AW, via Haugh Rd and Murdocks Wynd 548811, Fax 547916, – rest – 200.
Meals 12.50/35.00 **t.** and a la carte – **23 rm** 75.00/140.00 **t.** – SB.

Mansefield House, 2 Mayne Rd, IV30 1NY, 540883, Fax 552491 – .
Meals 11.00 **t.** (lunch) and a la carte 18.50/22.25 **t.** 4.95 – **16 rm** 55.00/80.00 **t.** – SB.

Lodge, 20 Duff Av., IV30 1QS, 549981, – .
Meals (by arrangement) 13.50 **s.** – **8 rm** 22.00/42.00.

ATS Moycroft 546333

Prices For full details of the prices quoted in the guide, consult the introduction.

ELIE Fife. (Fife) 401 L 15 – pop. 903 – 01333.
◆Edinburgh 41 – ◆Dundee 29 – Dunfermline 29.

Bouquet Garni, 51 High St., KY9 1BZ, 330374, Fax 330374 –
closed Sunday, second and third week January and third week November – **Meals** 17.00/25.90 **t.** and a la carte.

ERBUSAIG Ross and Cromarty (Highland) 401 C 12 – Kyle of Lochalsh – 01599.
◆Edinburgh 206 – ◆Dundee 184 – ◆Inverness 84 – ◆Oban 127.

Old Schoolhouse with rm, IV40 8BB, 534369, Fax 534369, – .
April-October – **Meals** (booking essential) (dinner only) a la carte 17.00/24.00 **t.** 4.25 – **2 rm** 30.00/50.00 **t.**

ERISKA (Isle of) Argyll. (Strathclyde) 401 D 14 – Oban – 01631.

Isle of Eriska, PA37 1SD, 720371, Fax 720531, Lismore and mountains, « Country house atmosphere », park, – .
closed January – **Meals** (dinner only) 35.00 **st.** 4.00 – **17 rm** 140.00/305.00 **t.**

ERROL Perth. (Tayside) 401 K 14 pop. 1 772 – 01821.
◆Edinburgh 54 – ◆Dundee 14 – Perth 10.

Waterybutts Lodge, Grange, PH2 7SZ, NE : 2¼ m. by B 958 642894, Fax 642894, « Sporting lodge », – .
Meals (residents only) (communal dining) (dinner only) 15.00 **t.** 3.00 – **8 rm** 32.50/55.00 **t.**

ERSKINE Renfrew. (Strathclyde) 401 402 G 16 – 0141.
◆Edinburgh 55 – ◆Glasgow 9.

Forte Posthouse, Erskine Bridge, PA8 6AN, on A 726 812 0123, Fax 812 7642, – rm – 600.
Meals a la carte 12.00/22.85 **st.** – 7.95 – **166 rm** 59.00 **st.** – SB.

FALKIRK Stirling. (Central) 401 I 16 – pop. 42 353 – 01324.
Polmonthill, Grangemouth 711500 – Polmont, Manuel Rigg, Maddiston 711277.
2-4 Glebe St., SK1 1HU 620244.
◆Edinburgh 26 – Dunfermline 18 – ◆Glasgow 25 – Motherwell 27 – Perth 43.

Grange Manor, Glensburgh Rd, FK3 8XJ, NE : 2 m. by A 904 on A 905 474836, Fax 665861 – – 120.
Meals *(closed Sunday)* 11.50/17.50 **t.** and a la carte 4.45 – **7 rm** 54.00/79.00 **t.** – SB.

Stakis Falkirk, Camelon Rd, Arnothill, FK1 5RY, 628331, Fax 611593 – rm – 300.
Meals (bar lunch Saturday) 9.40/16.50 **st.** and a la carte – 8.50 – **55 rm** 72.00/82.00 **st.** – SB.

at Polmont SE : 3 m. on A 803 – ✉ Polmont – ☎ 01324 :

🏨 **Inchyra Grange,** Grange Rd, FK2 0YB, Kirk entry via Boness Rd ☎ 711911, Fax 71613 Fá, ≘s, ⊠ – 🛗 ⇔ rm TV ☎ P – 🎪 200. VISA
Meals (closed Saturday lunch) 9.95/19.25 **st.** and a la carte – ☕ 8.50 – **73 rm** 77.5(134.00 **st.** – SB.

ATS Burnbank Rd ☎ 622958

FINSTOWN Orkney. (Orkney Islands) 401 K 6 – see Orkney Islands.

FIONNPHORT Argyll. (Strathclyde) 401 A 15 – Shipping Services : see Mull (Isle of).

FLODIGARRY Inverness. (Highland) - see Skye (Isle of).

FORFAR Angus. (Tayside) 401 L 14 – pop. 14 159 – ☎ 01307.
18 Cunninghill, Arbroath Rd ☎ 462120.
ℹ The Library, West High St. ☎ 467876 (summer only).
♦Edinburgh 75 – ♦Aberdeen 55 – ♦Dundee 12 – Perth 31.

🏨 **Chapelbank House,** 69 East High St., DD8 2EP, ☎ 463151, Fax 461922 – ⇔ TV ☎ P VISA. ✗
Meals *(closed Sunday dinner and Monday)* 16.50 **t.** (dinner) and a la carte 10.00/20.45 🍷 3.95 – **4 rm** ☕ 48.00/70.00 **t.**

ATS Queenswell Rd ☎ 464501

When visiting Scotland,
use the ***Michelin Green Guide*** **"Scotland".**
– *Detailed descriptions of places of interest*
– *Touring programmes*
– *Maps and street plans*
– *The history of the country*
– *Photographs and drawings of monuments, beauty spots, houses...*

FORRES Moray. (Grampian) 401 J 11 **Scotland G.** – pop. 5 559 – ☎ 01309.
See : Town.
Envir. : Sueno's Stone★★, N : ½ m. by A 940 on A 96 – Brodie Castle★ *AC*, W : 3 m. by A 96.
Exc. : The Road The Isles★★, N : 1 m. by A 940 on A 96 – Elgin★ (Cathedral★, Chapter House★★ *AC*), E : 10¼ m. by A 96.
18 Muiryshade ☎ 672949.
ℹ 116 High St., IV6 0NP ☎ 672938 (summer only).
♦Edinburgh 165 – ♦Aberdeen 80 – ♦Inverness 27.

🏨 **Knockomie** 🐦, Grantown Rd, IV36 0SG, S : 1½ m. on A 940 ☎ 673146, Fax 673290, 🌳 park – TV ☎ ♿ P – 🎪 50. VISA
Meals 20.00/24.00 **t.** and a la carte 🍷 6.00 – **13 rm** ☕ 55.00/125.00 **t.**, 1 suite – SB.

🏨 **Ramnee,** Victoria Rd, IV36 0BN, ☎ 672410, Fax 673392, 🌳 – TV ☎ P – 🎪 100. VISA
closed 25 December and 1 to 3 January – **Meals** 10.00/21.00 **st.** and dinner a la carte 🍷 4.75 – **20 rm** ☕ 50.00/95.00 **st.** – SB.

FORT AUGUSTUS Inverness. (Highland) 401 F 12 **Scotland G.** – pop. 902 (inc. Glenmoriston) – ☎ 01320.
Exc. : Loch Ness★★ – The Great Glen★.
9 Markethill ☎ 366460.
ℹ Car Park ☎ 366367 (summer only).
♦Edinburgh 166 – Fort William 32 – ♦Inverness 36 – Kyle of Lochalsh 57.

🏨 **Lovat Arms,** PH32 4DU, ☎ 366206, Fax 366677, 🌳 – TV ☎ P. VISA
closed 24 and 25 December – **Meals** (bar lunch)/dinner 21.50 **st.** and a la carte 🍷 4.75 – **21 rm** ☕ 26.50/67.00 **st.**

🏨 **Inchnacardoch Lodge,** PH32 4BL, NE : ¾ m. on A 82 ☎ 366258, <, 🐟, 🌳 – ⇔ rest TV ☎ P. VISA. ✗
March-October – **Meals** (dinner only) 16.00 **t.** – **12 rm** ☕ 25.00/70.00 **t.**

🏨 **Brae,** PH32 4DG, ☎ 366289, Fax 366702, 🌳 – ⇔ TV P. VISA
March-October – **Meals** (dinner only) 25.00 **st.** 🍷 6.00 – **8 rm** ☕ (dinner included) 40.00/98.00 **st.** – SB.

🏠 **Sonas** without rest., PH32 4DH, on A 82 ☎ 366291, 🌳 – P
3 rm ☕ 22.00/34.00.

FORT WILLIAM Inverness. (Highland) 401 E 13 Scotland G. – pop. 10 391 – ☎ 01397.

See : Town★.

Exc. : Road to the Isles★★★ ≤★★ (Glenfinnan★ ≤★, Arisaig★, Silver Sands of Morar★, Mallaig★, Ardnamurchan Peninsula★★, Ardnamurchan Point ≤★★) NW : 46 m. by A 830 – SE : Ben Nevis★ (Ben Nevis★★ ≤★★ *AC*).

North Rd ☎ 704464.

☎ 0345 090700.

Cameron Centre, Cameron Sq., PH33 6AJ ☎ 703781.

Edinburgh 133 – ♦Glasgow 104 – ♦Inverness 68 – ♦Oban 50.

❀ **Inverlochy Castle** ⑤, Torlundy, PH33 6SN, NE : 3 m. on A 82 ☎ 702177, Fax 702953, ≤ loch and mountains, « Victorian castle in extensive park », ↘, ⚘, ✂ – ⊬ rest TV ☎ P. AE VISA. ✗
March-November – **Meals** (booking essential) 24.00/42.50 **st.** – **16 rm** ▭ 150.00/276.00 **st.**, 1 suite
Spec. Puff pastry pillow of asparagus topped with pan fried foie gras, Pan fried medallions of venison with a lemon and parsley coating, Raspberry crème brûlée.

Factor's House, Torlundy, PH33 6SN, NE : 3½ m. on A 82 ☎ 705767, Fax 701421, ⚘, ✂ – ⊬ rest TV ☎ P. AE VISA. ✗
closed 5 January-1 March – **Meals** *(closed Sunday and Monday)* (booking essential) (dinner only) a la carte 14.50/29.75 **t.** – **5 rm** ▭ 65.00/150.00 **st.**

Distillery House without rest., Nevis Bridge, North Rd, PH33 6LH, ☎ 700103, Fax 706277 – TV P. VISA
7 rm ▭ 25.00/60.00 **st.**

Grange without rest., Grange Rd, PH33 6JF, by Ashburn Lane ☎ 705516, ≤, ⚘ – ⊬ TV P. VISA. ✗
March-mid November – **3 rm** ▭ 64.00 **s.**

Crolinnhe without rest., Grange Rd, PH33 6JF, by Ashburn Lane ☎ 702709, ≤, ⚘ – ⊬ TV P. ✗
April-November – **5 rm** ▭ 52.00/66.00 **st.**

Ashburn House without rest., Achintore Rd, PH33 6RQ, S : ½ m. on A 82 ☎ 706000, Fax 706000, ⚘ – ⊬ TV P. VISA. ✗
February-October – **7 rm** ▭ 30.00/65.00.

Cabana House without rest., Union Rd, PH33 6RB, ☎ 705991, ⚘ – ⊬ TV P. ✗
closed February and November – **3 rm** ▭ 35.00/43.00 **s.**

at Banavie N : 3 m. by A 82 and A 830 on B 8004 – ✉ Fort William – ☎ 01397 :

Moorings, PH33 7LY, ☎ 772797, Fax 772441, ≤, ⚘ – ⊬ rest TV ☎ P. AE ⓓ VISA. ✗
closed 25 and 26 December – **Jacobean : Meals** (lunch by arrangement)/dinner 25.00 **t.** and a la carte 🍷 6.00 – **24 rm** ▭ 35.00/80.00 **t.** – SB.

FOYERS Inverness (Highland) 401 G 12 – ✉ Loch Ness – ☎ 01456.

Edinburgh 175 – ♦Inverness 19 – Kyle of Lochalsh 63 – ♦Oban 96.

Craigdarroch ⑤, IV1 2XU, N : ¼ m. on B 852 ☎ 486400, Fax 486444, ≤, park – ⊬ TV ☎ ♿ P. VISA
Meals a la carte 14.00/21.50 **st.** 🍷 6.50 – **15 rm** ▭ 60.00/100.00 **st.** – SB.

Foyers Bay House, Lower Foyers, IV1 2YB, W : 1 ¼ m. by B 852 on Lower Foyers rd ☎ 486624, Fax 486337, ≤, ⚘ – TV ☎ P. AE VISA. ✗
Meals *(dinner only)* 14.50 **t.** and a la carte – **3 rm** ▭ 62.00 **t.** – SB.

GAIRLOCH Ross and Cromarty. (Highland) 401 C 10 Scotland G. pop. 2 194 – ☎ 01445.

Envir. : Loch Maree★★★, E : 5½ m. by A 832.

Exc. : Inverewe Gardens★★★ *AC*, NE : 8 m. by A 832 – Wester Ross★★★ – S : from Gairloch to Kyle of Lochalsh★★★ (vista★★, ≤★★★) – N : from Gairloch to Ullapool★★ (≤★★★).

Gairloch ☎ 712407.

Auchtercairn ☎ 712130.

Edinburgh 228 – ♦Inverness 72 – Kyle of Lochalsh 68.

Creag Mor, Charleston, IV21 2AH, ☎ 712068, Fax 712044, ≤, ⚘ – TV ☎ P. VISA
March-mid November – **Meals** (bar lunch)/dinner 24.00 **st.** and a la carte 🍷 4.00 – **18 rm** ▭ 40.00/80.00 **st.**, 1 suite – SB.

Little Lodge ⑤, North Erradale, IV21 2DS, NW : 5½ m. on B 8021 ☎ 771237, ≤ Torridon Mountains and Skye, ⚘ – ⊬ P. ✗
April-October – **Meals** 17.00 – **3 rm** ▭ (dinner included) 55.00/88.00 – SB.

Birchwood without rest., IV21 2AH, ☎ 712011, ≤ – ⊬ P
April-October – **6 rm** ▭ 33.00/46.00.

GALSON Western Isles (Outer Hebrides) 401 A 8 – see Lewis and Harris (Isle of).

GATEHOUSE OF FLEET Kirkcudbright. (Dumfries and Galloway) 401 402 H 19 – pop. 919 – ☎ 01557.

Gatehouse of Fleet ☎ 814734.

Car Park, DJ7 2AE ☎ 814212 (summer only).

♦Edinburgh 113 – ♦Dumfries 33 – Stranraer 42.

Cally Palace ⑤, DG7 2DL, E : ½ m. on B 727 ☎ 814341, Fax 814522, ≤, ≘s, ◻, 18, park, – |‡| ✕ rest ▭ ☎ ⓟ. ◻ VISA. ✕
closed 3 January-1 March – **Meals** 11.00/21.00 **t.** and a la carte 7.20 – **50 rm** ◻ 62.00/135.00 **t.**, 6 suites – SB.

GATTONSIDE Roxburgh. (Borders) – see Melrose.

GIFFNOCK Renfrew. (Strathclyde) 401 ㊶ – see Glasgow.

GIFFORD E. Lothian. (Lothian) 401 L 16 **Scotland G.** – pop. 688 – ✉ Haddington – ☎ 01620.

See : Village★.

Exc. : Northern foothills of the Lammermuir Hills★★, S : 10½ m. by B 6355 and B 6368.

Edinburgh Rd ☎ 810591.

♦Edinburgh 20 – Hawick 50.

Tweeddale Arms, High St., EH41 4QU, ☎ 810240, Fax 810488 – ▭ ☎. ◻ AE VISA
Meals 12.95/19.50 **t.** 4.00 – **17 rm** ◻ 42.75/65.00 **t.** – SB.

GIGHA (Isle of) Argyll. (Strathclyde) 401 C 16 – ☎ 01583.

♦Edinburgh 168.

Gigha ⑤, PA41 7AA, ☎ 505254, Fax 505244, ≤ Sound of Gigha and Kintyre Peninsula, – ⓟ. ◻ VISA
March-October – **Meals** (bar lunch)/dinner 20.00 **t.** 4.50 – **13 rm** ◻ 54.50/98.00 **t.** – SB.

GIRVAN Ayr (Strathclyde) 401 402 F 18 pop. 7 719 – ☎ 01465.

18 Brunston Castle, Dailly ☎ 81471 – 18 Golf Course Rd ☎ 714272/714346.

♦Edinburgh 100 – ♦Ayr 20 – ♦Glasgow 56 – Stranraer 31.

Glendrissaig without rest., Newton Stewart Rd., KA26 0HJ, S : 1¾ m. by A 77 on A 714 ☎ 714631, ≤, – ✕ ⓟ. ✕
April-October – **3 rm** ◻ 23.00/50.00 **st.**

GLAMIS Angus. (Tayside) 401 K 14 **Scotland G.** pop. 648 – ✉ Forfar – ☎ 01307.

See : Village★ - Castle★★ *AC* – Angus Folk Museum★ *AC*.

Exc. : Meigle Museum★★ (early Christian Monuments★★) *AC*, SW : 7 m. by A 94.

♦Edinburgh 60 – ♦Dundee 11 – Perth 25.

Castleton House with rm, Eassie, DD8 1SJ, W : 3¾ m. on A 94 ☎ 840340, Fax 84050– ✕ rest ▭ ☎ ⓟ. ◻ AE VISA. ✕
Meals 11.75/22.50 **t.** and a la carte – **6 rm** ◻ 60.00/90.00 **t.** – SB.

LASGOW Lanark. (Strathclyde) 401 402 H 16 **Scotland G.** – pop. 662 853 – ☎ 0141.

ee : City★★★ – Cathedral★★★ (≤★) DZ – The Burrell Collection★★★ AX **M1** – Hunterian Art allery★★ (Whistler Collection★★★ – Mackintosh Wing★★★) *AC* CY **M4** – Museum of Trans- ort★★ (Scottish Built Cars★★★, The Clyde Room of Ship Models★★★) AV **M3** – Art Gallery and useum Kelvingrove★★ CY – Pollok House★ (The Paintings★★) AX **D** – Tolbooth Steeple★ DZ **A** Hunterian Museum (Coin and Medal Collection★) CY **M1** – City Chambers★ DZ **C** – Glasgow chool of Art★ *AC*, CY **B** – Necropolis (≤★ of Cathedral) DYZ.

xc. : The Trossachs★★★, N : 31 m. by A 879 – BV – A 81 and A 821 – Loch Lomond★★, NW : m. by A 82 AV.

Littlehill, Auchinairn Rd ☎ 772 1916, BV – 18 Deaconsbank, Rouken Glen Park, Stewarton Rd, astwood ☎ 638 7044 AX – 18 Linn Park, Simshill Rd ☎ 637 5871, BX – 18 Lethamhill, umbernauld Rd ☎ 770 6220, BV – 9 Alexandra Park, Dennistown ☎ 556 3991 BV – 9 King's ark, 150a Croftpark Av., Croftfoot ☎ 634 4745, BX – 9 Knightswood, Lincoln Av. ☎ 959 2131 V – 9 Ruchill, Brassey St. ☎ 946 7676 BV.

ccess to Oban by helicopter.

✈ Glasgow Airport : ☎ 887 1111, W : 8 m. by M 8 AV – **Terminal** : Coach service from Glasgow entral and Queen Street main line Railway Stations and from Anderston Cross and Buchanan us Stations.

✈ see also Prestwick.

☎ 0345 090700.

35 St. Vincent Pl., G1 2ER ☎ 204 4400 – Glasgow Airport, Tourist Information Desk, Paisley ☎ 848 4440.

Edinburgh 46 – ◆Manchester 221.

Plans on following pages

Glasgow Hilton, 1 William St., G3 8HT, ☎ 204 5555, Fax 204 5004, ≤, Fā, ≘s, ⊠ – |$| ⇔ rm ≡ TV ☎ ♿ P – 🏛 1000. AE ⓓ VISA JCB. ✂ CZ **s**
Minsky's : Meals 16.50/28.00 **t.** and a la carte 7.00 - (see also ***Camerons*** below) – ☕ 12.50 – **315 rm** 120.00/145.00 **st.**, 4 suites.

Glasgow Moat House (Q.M.H.), Congress Rd, G3 8QT, ☎ 306 9988, Fax 221 2022, ≤, Fā, ≘s, ⊠ – |$| ⇔ rm ≡ TV ☎ ♿ P – 🏛 800. AE ⓓ VISA. ✂ CZ **r**
Mariners : Meals 14.50/47.00 **t.** and dinner a la carte 7.50 – **Pointhouse : Meals** 15.95/18.95 **t.** and a la carte 7.50 – ☕ 10.95 – **267 rm** 112.00 **st.**, 16 suites – SB.

Glasgow Marriott, 500 Argyle St., Anderston, G3 8RR, ☎ 226 5577, Fax 221 7676, Fā, ≘s, ⊠, squash – |$| ⇔ rm ≡ TV ☎ ♿ P – 🏛 720. AE ⓓ VISA CZ **a**
Meals 12.95/15.95 **st.** and a la carte 7.00 – ☕ 10.25 – **293 rm** 84.00 **st.**, 5 suites – SB.

Forte Crest, Bothwell St., G2 7EN, ☎ 248 2656, Telex 77440, Fax 221 8986, ≤ – |$| ⇔ rm ≡ TV ☎ P – 🏛 800. AE ⓓ VISA CZ **z**
Meals 14.95 **st.** and a la carte – ☕ 10.95 – **248 rm** 99.00 **st.**, 3 suites – SB.

✿ **One Devonshire Gardens,** 1 Devonshire Gdns, G12 OUX, ☎ 339 2001, Fax 337 1663, « Opulent interior design » – TV ☎ – 🏛 50. AE ⓓ VISA AV **a**
Meals *(closed Saturday lunch)* 25.00/40.00 **t.** 8.00 – ☕ 13.50 – **25 rm** 135.00/160.00 **t.**, 2 suites
Spec. Seared scallops with Thai sauce, Tournedos of Scottish beef fillet on a confit of shallots and sweet garlic, Creamed cold baked rice pudding with Armagnac soaked prunes.

Glasgow Thistle (Mount Charlotte), 36 Cambridge St., G2 3HN, ☎ 332 3311, Telex 777334, Fax 332 4050 – |$| ⇔ rm TV ☎ ♿ P – 🏛 1500. AE ⓓ VISA JCB DY **z**
Meals (carving rest.) 12.00/25.00 **st.** and a la carte 6.00 – ☕ 11.50 – **304 rm** 90.00/140.00 **st.**, 3 suites – SB.

Devonshire, 5 Devonshire Gdns, G12 0UX, ☎ 339 7878, Fax 339 3980 – TV ☎ – 🏛 50. AE ⓓ VISA. ✂ AV **a**
Meals *(closed Saturday lunch and Sunday)* 15.00/35.00 **st.** and a la carte 7.95 – ☕ 10.75 – **14 rm** 105.00/175.00 **st.** – SB.

Copthorne Glasgow, George Sq., G2 1DS, ☎ 332 6711, Telex 778147, Fax 332 4264 – |$| ⇔ rm TV ☎ – 🏛 100. AE ⓓ VISA DZ **n**
Meals 12.95/15.95 **t.** and a la carte 5.25 – ☕ 9.25 – **136 rm** 96.50/109.00 **st.**, 4 suites.

Malmaison, 278 West George St., G2 4LL, ☎ 221 6400, Fax 221 6411, « Contemporary interior » – TV ☎. AE ⓓ VISA. ✂ CY **c**
Meals - Brasserie - a la carte 15.95/19.90 **st.** – ☕ 10.00 – **17 rm** 80.00 **st.**, 4 suites.

Swallow Glasgow, 517 Paisley Rd West, G51 1RW, ☎ 427 3146, Fax 427 4059, Fā, ≘s, ⊠ – |$| ≡ rest TV ☎ P – 🏛 350. AE ⓓ VISA AX **a**
Meals *(closed Saturday lunch)* (carving lunch) 12.00/16.75 **st.** and dinner a la carte – **117 rm** ☕ 85.00/130.00 **st.** – SB.

Tinto Firs Thistle, 470 Kilmarnock Rd, G43 2BB, ☎ 637 2353, Fax 633 1340 – TV ☎ P – 🏛 50. AE ⓓ VISA JCB AX **c**
Meals (bar lunch Monday and Saturday) 12.95/19.95 **t.** and a la carte 5.50 – **25 rm** ☕ 75.00/95.00 **st.**, 2 suites – SB.

GLASGOW
BUILT UP AREA

For Street Index see Glasgow p. 6

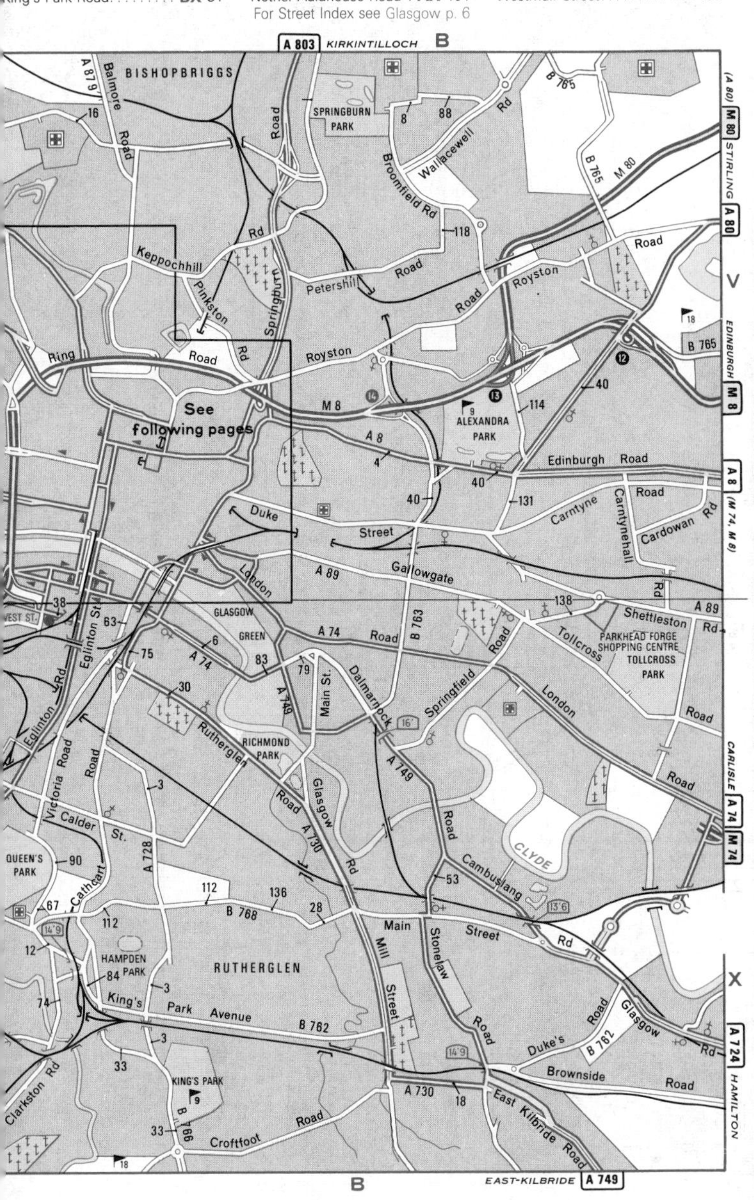

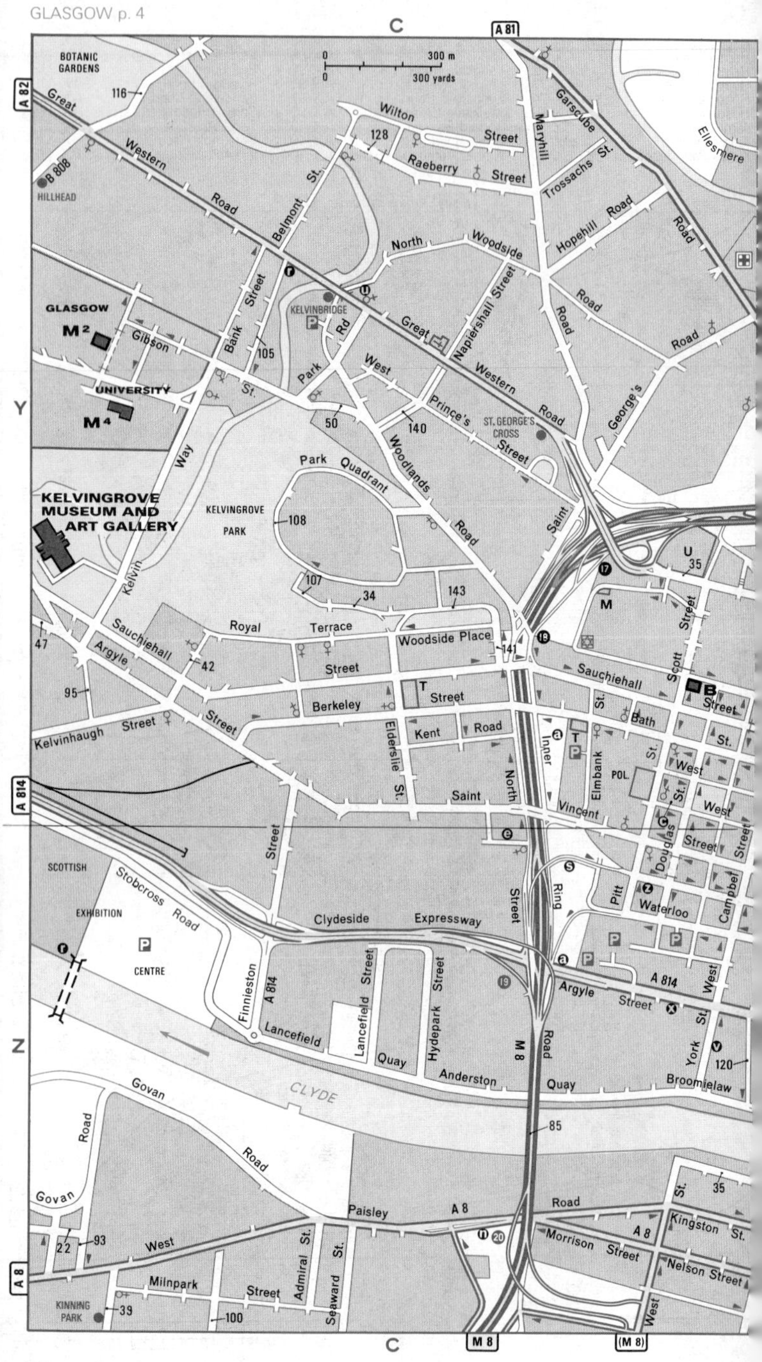
C
A 81
A 82
BOTANIC GARDENS
0 300 m
0 300 yards
116
Great Western Road
B 808
HILLHEAD
Wilton Street
128
Raeberry Street
Garscube Road
Maryhill Road
Trossachs St.
Ellesmere
Hopehill Road
Belmont St.
North Woodside Road
Napiershall Street
GLASGOW
M²
Gibson St.
Bank Street
105
KELVINBRIDGE
Park Rd
Great Western Road
St. George's Road
UNIVERSITY
M⁴
Y
West Prince's Street
50
140
ST. GEORGE'S CROSS
Kelvin Way
Park Quadrant
Woodlands Road
Saint
KELVINGROVE MUSEUM AND ART GALLERY
KELVINGROVE PARK
108
U
35
107
34
143
M
Royal Terrace
Woodside Place
141
Scott Street
47
Sauchiehall Street
42
Argyle Street
95
Berkeley Street
T
Sauchiehall St.
B
Bath St.
Kelvinhaugh Street
Elderslie St.
Kent Road
Inner Ring Road
T
Elmbank St.
West St.
A 814
POL.
North Street
Saint Vincent Street
West Street
Douglas St.
SCOTTISH EXHIBITION CENTRE
Stobcross Road
Pitt
Waterloo
Campbell
Clydeside Expressway
Finnieston
A 814
Lancefield Street
Hydepark Street
A 814
Argyle Street
West St.
York St.
Z
Lancefield Quay
Anderston Quay
M 8
Broomielaw
120
Govan Road
CLYDE
85
Road
St.
35
Govan
Paisley Road
A 8
Kingston St.
A 8
Morrison Street
22
93
West
Nelson Street
A 8
Milnpark Street
Admiral St.
Seaward St.
West
KINNING PARK
39
100
C
M 8
(M 8)

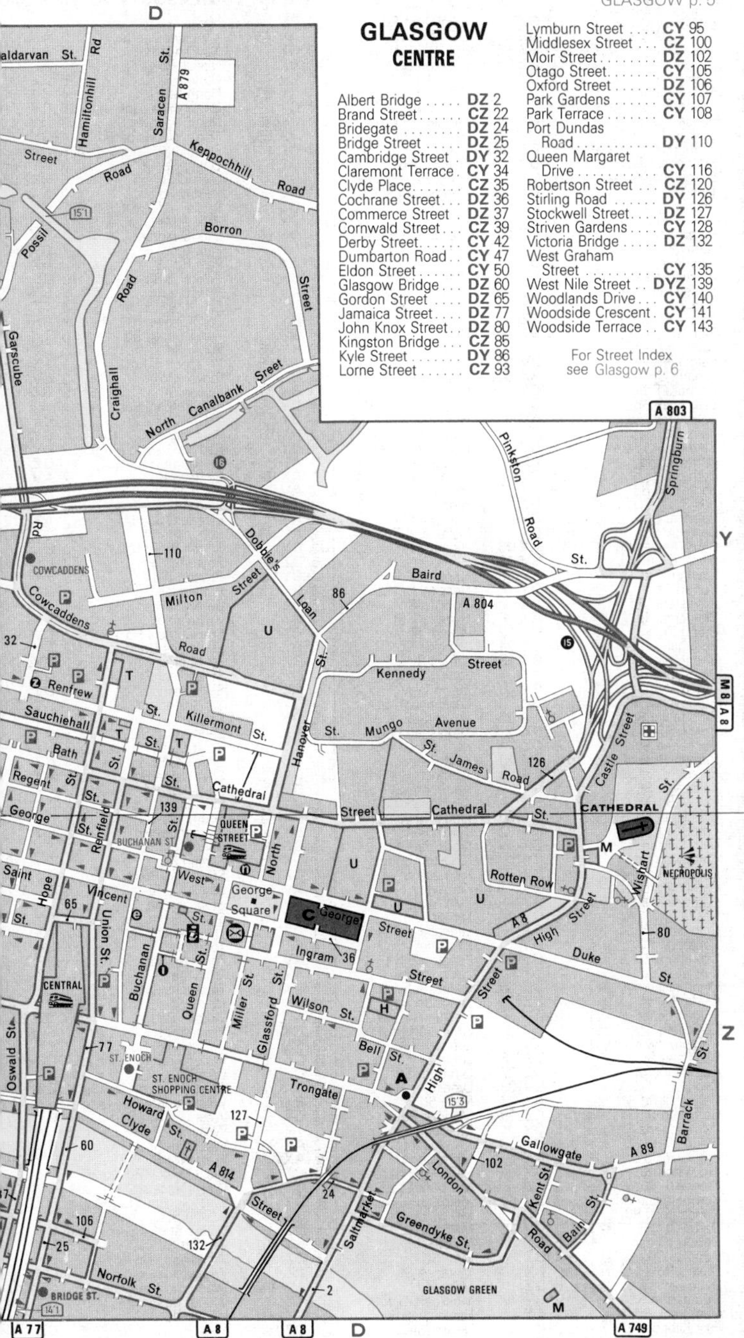
GLASGOW
CENTRE
Albert Bridge ..... DZ 2
Brand Street ...... CZ 22
Bridgegate .... DZ 24
Bridge Street ..... DZ 25
Cambridge Street . DY 32
Claremont Terrace . CY 34
Clyde Place .... CZ 35
Cochrane Street ... DZ 36
Commerce Street . DZ 37
Cornwald Street ... CZ 39
Derby Street ...... CY 42
Dumbarton Road .. CY 47
Eldon Street ...... CY 50
Glasgow Bridge ... DZ 60
Gordon Street ..... DZ 65
Jamaica Street .... DZ 77
John Knox Street .. DZ 80
Kingston Bridge ... CZ 85
Kyle Street .... DY 86
Lorne Street ...... CZ 93
Lymburn Street .... CY 95
Middlesex Street ... CZ 100
Moir Street .... DZ 102
Otago Street .... CY 105
Oxford Street ...... DZ 106
Park Gardens ...... CY 107
Park Terrace .... CY 108
Port Dundas Road .... DY 110
Queen Margaret Drive .... CY 116
Robertson Street ... CZ 120
Stirling Road ...... DY 126
Stockwell Street .... DZ 127
Striven Gardens .... CY 128
Victoria Bridge ..... DZ 132
West Graham Street .... CY 135
West Nile Street .. DYZ 139
Woodlands Drive ... CY 140
Woodside Crescent . CY 141
Woodside Terrace .. CY 143
For Street Index see Glasgow p. 6
D
Y
Z
A 803
A 804
A 879
M 8
A 8
A 77
A 749
A 89
A 814
Keppochhill Road
Borron Street
Possil Road
Saracen St.
Hamiltonhill Rd
Craighall Road
Garscube Rd
North Canalbank Street
Pinkston Road
Springburn
Baird St.
Dobbie's Loan
Milton Street
Cowcaddens Road
COWCADDENS
Kennedy Street
St. Mungo Avenue
St. James Road
Castle Street
CATHEDRAL
NECROPOLIS
Renfrew St.
Sauchiehall St.
Killermont St.
Bath St.
Regent St.
George St.
Cathedral Street
Hanover St.
North St.
QUEEN STREET
BUCHANAN ST.
West George St.
George Square
Saint Vincent St.
Hope St.
Union St.
Buchanan St.
Queen St.
Ingram Street
Miller St.
Glassford St.
Wilson St.
Bell St.
Rotten Row
High Street
Duke Street
Wishart St.
CENTRAL
ST. ENOCH
ST. ENOCH SHOPPING CENTRE
Trongate
Howard St.
Clyde Street
Saltmarket
London Road
Gallowgate
Kent St.
Bain St.
Barrack St.
Greendyke St.
GLASGOW GREEN
Oswald St.
Norfolk St.
BRIDGE ST.

STREET INDEX TO GLASGOW TOWN PLAN

Argyle St. p. 4 **CZ**
Buchanan St. p. 5 **DZ**
Gordon St. p. 5 **DZ** 65
Jamaica St. p. 5 **DZ** 77
Oswald St. p. 5 **DZ**
Parkhead Forge
Shopping Centre p. 3 **BX**
Renfield St. p. 5 **DZ**
St. Enoch
Shopping Centre **DZ**
St. Vincent St. p. 5 **DZ**
Sauchiehall St. p. 5 **DY**
Trongate p. 5 **DZ**
Union St. p. 5 **DZ**

Albert Bridge p. 5 **DZ** 2
Admiral St. p. 4 **CZ**
Aikenhead Rd p. 3 **BX** 3
Alexandra Par. p. 3 **BV** 4
Anderston Quay p. 4 **CZ**
Anniesland Rd p. 2 **AV**
Argyle St. p. 4 **CZ**
Bain St. p. 5 **DZ**
Baird St. p. 5 **DY**
Balgrayhill p. 3 **BV** 5
Ballater St. p. 3 **BX** 6
Balmore Rd p. 3 **BV**
Balornock Rd p. 3 **BV** 8
Balshagray Av. p. 2 **AV** 9
Bank St. p. 4 **CY**
Barrack St. p. 5 **DZ**
Barrhead Rd p. 2 **AX**
Bath St. p. 4 **CY**
Battlefield Rd p. 3 **BX** 12
Bell St. p. 5 **DZ**
Belmont St. p. 4 **CY**
Berkeley St. p. 4 **CY**
Berryknowes Rd p. 2 **AX** 15
Bilsland Drive p. 3 **BV** 16
Blairbeth Rd p. 3 **BX** 18
Borron St. p. 5 **DY**
Boydstone Rd p. 2 **AX**
Braidcraft Rd p. 2 **AX** 20
Brand St. p. 4 **CZ** 22
Bridegate p. 5 **DZ** 24
Bridge St. p. 5 **DZ** 25
Brockburn Rd p. 2 **AX**
Broomfield Rd p. 3 **BV**
Broomielaw p. 4 **CZ**
Broomloan Rd p. 2 **AV** 26
Brownside Rd p. 3 **BX**
Buchanan St. p. 5 **DZ**
Burnhill Chapel St. p. 3 **BX** 28
Byres Rd p. 2 **AV** 29
Caldarvan St. p. 5 **DY**
Calder St. p. 3 **BX**
Caledonia Rd p. 3 **BX** 30
Cambridge St. p. 5 **DY** 32
Cambuslang Rd p. 3 **BX**
Cardowan Rd p. 3 **BV**
Carmunnock Rd p. 3 **BX** 33
Carntyne Rd p. 3 **BV**
Carntynehall Rd p. 3 **BV**
Castle St. p. 5 **DY**
Cathcart Rd p. 3 **BX**
Cathedral St. p. 5 **DY**
Claremont Ter. p. 4 **CY** 34
Clarkston Rd p. 3 **BX**
Clyde Place p. 4 **CZ** 35
Clyde St. p. 5 **DZ**
Clyde Tunnel p. 2 **AV**
Clydeside
Expressway p. 2 **AV**
Cochrane St. p. 5 **DZ** 36
Commerce St. p. 5 **DZ** 37
Cook St. p. 3 **BV** 38
Corkerhill Rd p. 2 **AX**
Cornwald St. p. 4 **CZ** 39
Cowcaddens St. p. 5 **DY**
Craighall Rd p. 5 **DY**
Croftfoot Rd p. 3 **BX**
Crookston Rd p. 2 **AX**
Crow Rd p. 2 **AV**
Cumbernauld Rd p. 3 **BV** 40
Dalmarnock Rd p. 3 **BX**
Derby St. p. 4 **CY** 42
Dobbie's Loan p. 5 **DY**
Douglas St. p. 4 **CZ**
Duke's Rd p. 3 **BX**
Duke St. p. 5 **DZ**
Dumbarton Rd p. 4 **CY** 47
Dumbreck Rd p. 2 **AX**
East Kilbride Rd p. 3 **BX**
Edinburgh Rd p. 3 **BV**
Edmiston Drive p. 2 **AV** 48
Eglinton Rd p. 3 **BX**
Eglinton St. p. 3 **BX**
Elderslie St. p. 4 **CY**
Eldon St. p. 4 **CY** 50
Elmbank St. p. 4 **CY**
Farmeloan Rd p. 3 **BX** 53
Fenwick Rd p. 2 **AX** 55
Finnieston St. p. 4 **CZ**
Gallowgate p. 5 **DZ**
Garscube Rd p. 5 **DY**
George Square p. 5 **DZ**
George St. p. 5 **DZ**
Gibson St. p. 4 **CY**
Glasgow Bridge p. 5 **DZ** 60
Glasgow Rd
(PAISLEY) p. 2 **AX** 62
Glasgow Rd
(RENFREW) p. 2 **AV**
Glasgow Rd
(RUTHERGLEN) p. 3 **BX**
Glassford St. p. 5 **DZ**
Gorbals St. p. 3 **BX** 63
Gordon St. p. 5 **DZ** 65
Govan Rd p. 4 **CZ**
Grange Rd p. 3 **BX** 67
Great Western Rd p. 4 **CY**
Greendyke St. p. 5 **DZ**
Haggs Rd p. 2 **AX** 68
Hamiltonhill Rd p. 5 **DY**
Hardgate Rd p. 2 **AV**
Harriet St. p. 2 **AX** 70
Helen St. p. 2 **AV** 72
High St. p. 5 **DZ**
Hillington Rd p. 2 **AV**
Holmfauld Rd p. 2 **AV** 73
Holmlea Rd p. 3 **BX** 74
Hope St. p. 5 **DZ**
Hopehill Rd p. 4 **CY**
Hospital St. p. 3 **BX** 75
Howard St. p. 5 **DZ**
Hydepark St. p. 4 **CZ**
Ingram St. p. 5 **DZ**
Jamaica St. p. 5 **DZ** 77
James St. p. 3 **BX** 79
John Knox St. p. 5 **DZ** 80
Kelvin Way p. 4 **CY**
Kelvinhaugh St. p. 4 **CY**
Kennedy St. p. 5 **DY**
Kennishead Rd p. 2 **AX**
Kent Rd p. 4 **CY**
Kent St. p. 5 **DZ**
Keppoch Hill Rd p. 5 **DY**
Killermont St. p. 5 **DY**
Kilmarnock Rd p. 2 **AX**
King's Drive p. 3 **BX** 83
King's Park Av. p. 3 **BX**
Kings Park Rd p. 3 **BX** 84
Kingston Bridge p. 4 **CZ** 85
Kingston St. p. 4 **CZ**
Kingsway p. 2 **AV**
Kyle St. p. 5 **DY** 86
Lamont Rd p. 3 **BV** 88
Lancefield Quay p. 4 **CZ**
Lancefield St. p. 4 **CZ**
Langlands Rd p. 2 **AV**
Langside Av. p. 2 **AX** 89
Langside Drive p. 2 **AX**
Langside Rd p. 3 **BX** 90
Lincoln Av. p. 2 **AV** 91
Linthaugh Rd p. 2 **AX**
London Rd p. 3 **BX**
Lorne St. p. 4 **CZ** 93
Lymburn St. p. 4 **CY** 95
Lyoncross Rd p. 2 **AX** 97
Main St. p. 3 **BX**
Maryhill Rd p. 4 **CY**
Meiklerig
Crescent p. 2 **AX** 98
Merrylee Rd p. 2 **AX**
Middlesex St. p. 4 **CZ** 100
Milnpark St. p. 4 **CZ**
Milton St. p. 5 **DY**
Mill St. p. 3 **BX**
Miller St. p. 5 **DZ**
Minard Rd p. 2 **AX** 101
Moir St. p. 5 **DZ** 102
Morrison St. p. 4 **CZ**
Moss Rd p. 2 **AV** 103
Mosspark Blvd. p. 2 **AX**
Napiershall St. p. 4 **CY**
Nelson St. p. 4 **CZ**
Nether
Auldhouse Rd p. 2 **AX** 104
Newlands Rd p. 2 **AX**
Nitshill Rd p. 2 **AX**
Norfolk St. p. 5 **DZ**
North St. p. 4 **CY**
North Canalbank St. p. 5 **DY**
North Hanover St. p. 5 **DY**
North Woodside Rd p. 4 **CY**
Oswald St. p. 5 **DZ**
Otago St. p. 4 **CY** 105
Oxford St. p. 5 **DZ** 106
Paisley Rd p. 2 **AV**
Paisley Rd West p. 2 **AX**
Park Gdns p. 4 **CY** 107
Park Quadrant p. 4 **CY**
Park Ter p. 4 **CY** 108
Peat Rd p. 2 **AX**
Petershill Rd p. 3 **BV**
Pinkston Rd p. 5 **DY**
Pitt St. p. 4 **CZ**
Pollokshaws Rd p. 2 **AX**
Port Dundas Rd p. 5 **DY** 110
Possil Rd p. 5 **DY**
Prospecthill Rd p. 3 **BX** 112
Provan Rd p. 3 **BV** 114
Queen St. p. 5 **DZ**
Queen Margaret
Drive p. 4 **CY** 116
Raeberry St. p. 4 **CY**
Red Rd p. 3 **BV** 118
Renfield St. p. 5 **DZ**
Renfrew Rd p. 2 **AV**
Renfrew St. p. 5 **DY**
Ring Rd p. 3 **BV**
Riverford Road p. 2 **AX** 119
Robertson St. p. 4 **CZ** 120
Rotten Row p. 5 **DZ**
Royal Ter p. 4 **CY**
Royston Rd p. 3 **BV**
Rutherglen Rd p. 3 **BX**
St. Andrew's
Drive p. 2 **AX**
St. George's Rd p. 4 **CY**
St. James Rd p. 5 **DY**
St. Mungo Av. p. 5 **DY**
St. Vincent St p. 5 **DZ**
Saltmarket p. 5 **DZ**
Sandwood Rd p. 2 **AV** 123
Saracen St. p. 5 **DY**
Sauchiehall St. p. 5 **DY**
Scott St. p. 4 **CY**
Seaward St. p. 4 **CZ**
Shettleston Rd p. 3 **BX**
Shieldhall Rd p. 2 **AV**
Shields Rd p. 2 **AX** 124
Southbrae Drive p. 2 **AV**
Springburn Rd p. 3 **BV**
Springfield Rd p. 3 **BX**
Stirling Rd p. 5 **DY** 126
Stobcross Road p. 4 **CZ**
Stockwell St. p. 5 **DZ** 127
Stonelaw Rd p. 3 **BX**
Striven Gdns p. 4 **CY** 128
Thornliebank Rd p. 2 **AX**
Todd St. p. 3 **BV** 131
Tollcross Rd p. 3 **BX**
Trongate p. 5 **DZ**
Trossachs St. p. 4 **CY**
Union St. p. 5 **DZ**
Victoria Bridge p. 5 **DZ** 132
Victoria Rd p. 3 **BX**
Wallacewell Rd p. 3 **BV**
Waterloo St. p. 4 **CZ**
West St. p. 4 **CZ**
West Campbell St. p. 4 **CZ**
West George St. p. 5 **DZ**
West Graham St. p. 4 **CY** 135
Westmuir Place p. 3 **BX** 136
Westmuir St. p. 3 **BX** 138
West Nile St. p. 5 **DYZ** 139
West Paisley Rd p. 4 **CZ**
West Prince's St. p. 4 **CY**
West Regent St. p. 5 **DY**
Wilson St. p. 5 **DZ**
Wilton St. p. 4 **CY**
Wishart St. p. 5 **DZ**
Woodlands Drive p. 4 **CY** 140
Woodlands Rd p. 4 **CY**
Woodside Crescent p. 4 **CY** 141
Woodside Place p. 4 **CY**
Woodside Ter p. 4 **CY** 143
York St. p. 4 **CZ**

Carrick (Forte), 377 Argyle St., G2 8LL, ☏ 248 2355, Fax 221 1014 – rm – 80. CZ x
Meals 9.50/21.00 **st.** and dinner a la carte 3.75 – 8.95 – **121 rm** 62.00 **st.** – SB.

Charing Cross Tower, Elmbank Gdns, G2 4PP, pedestrianised area off Bath St. ☏ 221 1000, Fax 248 1000, ≤ – rm. CY a
Meals (bar lunch)/dinner 8.95 **st.** – 4.90 – **276 rm** 38.50 **st.**

Terrace House, 14 Belhaven Terr., G12 0TG, (off Great Western Rd) ☏ 337 3377, Fax 337 3377 – rest. AV x
Meals (dinner only) a la carte 15.20/22.65 **t.** 3.95 – **15 rm** 52.00/68.00 **t.** – SB.

Town House, 4 Hughenden Terr., G12 9XR, ☏ 357 0862, Fax 339 9605 – rest. AV a
Meals (dinner only) a la carte 15.50/20.45 **st.** 5.25 – **10 rm** 52.00/62.00 **st.**

Manor Park, 28 Balshagray Drive, G11 7DD, ☏ 339 2143, Fax 339 5842 –. AV u
Meals *(closed Sunday)* 10.00/16.50 **t.** and a la carte – **7 rm** 38.00/76.00 **t.** – SB.

Albion, 405-407 North Woodside Rd, G20 6NN, ☏ 339 8620, Fax 334 8159 – **16 rm.** CY u

Drumlin without rest., 4 Kelvin Drive, G20 8QG, ☏ 945 4877, Fax 945 5152 –. AV r
– **7 rm** 45.00/70.00.

Granada Lodge, 251 Paisley Rd, G5 8RA, ☏ 420 3882, Fax 420 3884, Reservations (Freephone) 0800 555300 – rm. CZ n
Meals (Harry Ramsden's) – **43 rm** 39.95 **st.**

Kirklee without rest., 11 Kensington Gate, G12 9LG, ☏ 334 5555, Fax 339 3828 –. AV c
9 rm 45.00/59.00 **st.**

Camerons (at Glasgow Hilton H.), 1 William St., G3 8HT, ☏ 204 5511, Fax 204 5004 –. CZ s
Meals *(closed Saturday lunch and Sunday)* 20.50/29.50 **t.** and a la carte 7.00.

Buttery, 652 Argyle St., G3 8UF, ☏ 221 8188, Fax 204 4639 –. CZ e
closed Saturday lunch, Sunday 1 January and 25 December – **Meals** 14.85 **st.** (lunch) and a la carte 21.35/31.00 **t.**

Yes, 22 West Nile St., G1 2PW, ☏ 221 8044, Fax 248 9159 –. DZ e
closed Sunday and Bank Holidays – **Meals** 11.95/24.95 **st.** and a la carte 10.50.

Rogano, 11 Exchange Pl., G1 3AN, ☏ 248 4055, Fax 248 2608, « Art Deco » –. DZ i
closed 1-3 January and 25-26 December – **Meals** - Seafood - 16.50 **t.** (lunch) and a la carte 25.40/31.75.

Ho Wong, 82 York St., G2 3LE, ☏ 221 3550, Fax 248 5330 –. CZ v
Meals - Chinese (Peking) 7.50/15.00 **t.** and a la carte 5.95.

Ubiquitous Chip, 12 Ashton Lane, off Byres Rd, G12 8SJ, ☏ 334 5007, Fax 337 1302 –. AV e
closed 1 January and 25 and 31 December – **Meals** a la carte 21.80/30.80 **t.**

La Parmigiana, 447 Great Western Rd, Kelvinbridge, G12 8HH, ☏ 334 0686 –. CY r
closed Sunday, 1-2 January and Bank Holidays – **Meals** - Italian - a la carte 14.60/25.15 **t.** 5.35.

at Stepps NE : 5½ m. by M 8 on A 80 – BV – ✉ Glasgow – ☏ 0141 :

Garfield House, Cumbernauld Rd, G33 6HW, ☏ 779 2111, Fax 779 2111 – – 120.
Meals 16.75 **t.** (dinner) and a la carte11.45/21.95 **t.** 6.05 – **46 rm** 64.00/95.00 **st.**

at Giffnock (Renfrew.) (Strathclyde) S : 5¼ m. by A 77 – AX – ✉ Glasgow – ☏ 0141 :

MacDonald Thistle, Eastwood Toll, G46 6RA, at junction of A 77 with A 726 ☏ 638 2225, Fax 638 6231, – – 160.
Meals (bar lunch Saturday and Bank Holidays) 9.50/20.50 **t.** and a la carte 5.10 – **52 rm** 72.00/87.00 **t.**, 4 suites.

Turban Tandoori, 2 Station Rd, G46 6JF, ☏ 638 0069 –
Meals - Indian - (dinner only) 13.00 **st.** and a la carte 6.50.

at Busby S : 7¼ m. by A 77 – AX – on A 726 – ✉ Glasgow – ☏ 0141 :

Busby, 1 Field Rd, Clarkston, G76 8RX, ☏ 644 2661, Fax 644 4417 – rm – 150.
Meals 8.75/19.00 **st.** and a la carte 7.75 – **32 rm** 59.50/79.50 **st.** – SB.

at Glasgow Airport W : 8 m. by M 8 – AV – ✉ Paisley – ☏ 0141 :

Travel Inn, Whitecart Rd, PA3 2TH, M8 junc. 28 ☏ 842 1563, Fax 842 1570 – rm – 30.
Meals (grill rest.) – 4.95 – **81 rm** 34.50 **t.**

ATS 192 Finnieston St. ☏ 248 6761
ATS Rutherglen Ind. Est., Glasgow Rd, Rutherglen ☏ 647 9341
ATS 1 Sawmillfield St., off Garscube Rd ☏ 332 1945

GLASGOW AIRPORT Lanark. (Strathclyde) 401 402 G 16 – see Glasgow.

GLENCARSE Perth. (Tayside) 401 K 14 -see Perth.

GLENELG Ross and Cromarty (Highland) 401 D 12 – 01599.
♦Edinburgh 229 – ♦Inverness 75 – Kyle of Lochalsh 25.

Glenelg Inn, IV40 8JR, 522273, Fax 522373, ← Glenelg Bay, – P
Easter-October – **Meals** 15.00/19.00 **st.** – **6 rm** 43.00/116.00 **st.**

GLENFINNAN Inverness. (Highland) 401 D 13 – ✉ Fort William – 01397.
♦Edinburgh 150 – ♦Inverness 85 – ♦Oban 66.

Prince's House, PH37 4LT, W : ¾ m. on A 830 722246, Fax 722307, ← – rest TV P. AE VISA
March-November – **Meals** (in bar) a la carte 15.95/25.95 **t.** – **9 rm** 44.00/82.00 **t.** – SB.

GLENLIVET Banff. (Grampian) 401 J 11 pop. 3 559 – ✉ Ballindalloch – 01807.
♦Edinburgh 180 – ♦Aberdeen 59 – Elgin 27 – ♦Inverness 49.

Minmore House, AB37 9DB, S : ¾ m. on Glenlivet Distillery rd 590378 Fax 590472, ←, – rest P. VISA
May-October – **Meals** (dinner only) 23.50 **st.** 4.50 – **10 rm** (dinner included) 60.00 120.00 **st.** – SB.

GLENLUCE Wigtown. 401 F 19 – ✉ Newton Stewart – 01581.
Wigtownshire County, Mains of Park, Newton Stewart 300420.
♦Edinburgh 126 – ♦Ayr 62 – Dumfries 65 – Stranraer 9.

Kelvin House, 53 Main St., DG8 0PP, 300303, Fax 300303 – TV. VISA.
Meals 8.50 **st.** and a la carte 4.25 – **5 rm** 26.00/53.00 **st.** – SB.

GLENROTHES Fife. (Fife) 401 K 15 **Scotland G.** – pop. 38 650 – 01592.
Envir. : Falkland★ (Village★, Palace of Falkland★ *AC*, Gardens★ *AC*) N : 5 ½ m. by A 92 and A 912.
Thornton, Station Rd 771111 – Golf Course Rd 754561/758686 – Balbirnie Park Markinch 752006 – Auchterderran, Woodend Rd, Cardenden 721579 – Leslie, Balsilli Laws 620040.
Rothes Halls, Rothes Sq., Kingddom Centre, 610784.
♦Edinburgh 33 – ♦Dundee 25 – Stirling 36.

Balbirnie House, Markinch, KY7 6NE, NE : 1 ¾ m. by A 911 and A 92 on B 913 610066, Fax 610529, « Part 18C mansion », park – rest TV P – 150. AE VISA.
Meals 27.50/45.00 **t.** (dinner) and lunch a la carte12.25/21.25 **t.** 6.25 – **28 rm** 90.00 180.00 **t.**, 2 suites – SB.

at Leslie W : 3 m. by A 911 – ✉ Leslie – 01592 :

Rescobie, 6 Valley Drive, KY6 3BQ, 742143, Fax 620231, – TV P. AE VISA
closed 25 to 27 December – **Meals** 16.00 **st.** (dinner) and a la carte 8.40/23.45 **st.** 5.20 – **10 rm** 48.00/70.00 **st.** – SB.

GRANTOWN-ON-SPEY Moray. (Highland) 401 J 12 – pop. 2 391 – 01479.
Abernethy, Nethy Bridge 821305.
High St., PH26 3EH 872773 (summer only).
♦Edinburgh 143 – ♦Inverness 34 – Perth 99.

Ravenscourt House, Seafield Av., PH26 3JG, 872286, Fax 873260 – rest TV P. VISA.
closed January – **Meals** *(closed Sunday dinner to non-residents)* (light lunch Tuesday to Saturday)/dinner 25.00 **t.** and a la carte 4.00 – **6 rm** 35.00/80.00 **st.** – SB.

Culdearn House, Woodlands Terr., PH26 3JU, 872106, Fax 873641, – TV P. AE VISA.
March-October – **Meals** (residents only) (dinner only) 3.95 – **9 rm** (dinner included) 49.50/99.00 **st.** – SB.

Ardconnel, Woodlands Terr., PH26 3JU, 872104, Fax 872104, – TV P. VISA
Easter-October – **Meals** 16.50 **st.** 6.00 – **6 rm** 30.00/60.00 **st.**

Ardlarig, Woodlands Terr., PH26 3JU, 873245, – rest TV P
closed 22 to 29 December – **Meals** 10.50 **st.** 5.95 – **7 rm** 18.50/37.00 **st.** – SB.

GRETNA Dumfries. (Dumfries and Galloway) 401 402 K 19 – pop. 2 678 – 01461.
The Old Blacksmith's Shop 337834 (summer only).
♦Edinburgh 91 – ♦Carlisle 10 – ♦Dumfries 24.

Garden House, Sarkfoot Rd, DG16 5EP, on B 7076 337621, Fax 337692, TV P – 150. AE VISA JCB.
Meals 15.95 **st.** and a la carte 4.00 – **21 rm** 39.00/90.00 **st.** – SB.

Gretna Chase, DG16 5JB, S : 1/4 m. on B 7076 ✆ 337517, Fax 337766, « Gardens » – TV ☎ P. AE VISA. ✻
Meals *(closed Sunday)* (bar lunch)/dinner a la carte 14.95 **t.** 4.50 – **8 rm** 38.00/80.00 **t.**

Forte Travelodge, DG16 5HQ, ✆ 337566, Fax 337752, Reservations (Freephone) 0800 850950 – TV & P. AE VISA. ✻
Meals (grill rest.) – **64 rm** 34.50 **t.**

GRIMSAY Western Isles (Outer Hebrides) 401 Y 11 – see Uist (Isles of).

GULLANE E. Lothian. (Lothian) 401 L 15 **Scotland G.** – pop. 2 229 – ✆ 01620.

Envir. : Dirleton★ (Castle★) NE : 2 m. by A 198.

18, 18, 18 Gullane ✆ 843115.

◆Edinburgh 19 – North Berwick 5.

Greywalls ⛺, Duncur Rd, Muirfield, EH31 2EG, ✆ 842144, Fax 842241, ≤ gardens and golf course, « Lutyens house, gardens by Gertrude Jekyll », ✻ – ⊁ rest TV ☎ P. AE VISA
April-October – **Meals** 20.00/33.00 **t.** and lunch a la carte 6.00 – **22 rm** 95.00/170.00 **t.** – SB.

✿ **La Potinière** (Hilary Brown), Main St., EH31 2AA, ✆ 843214 ⊁
closed lunch Friday and Saturday, dinner Sunday to Thursday, Wednesday, 25-26 December, 1-2 January, 1 week March, 1 week June and 1 week October – **Meals** (booking essential) 21.00/30.00 **t.** 5.00
Spec. Fried salmon fillet on spicy lentils with a morel sauce, Lamb fillet on a bed of spinach with a broad bean and tarragon sauce, Warm soft centred chocolate pudding.

HADDINGTON E. Lothian. (Lothian) 401 L 16 **Scotland G.** – pop. 7 342 – ✆ 01620.

See : Town★ - High Street★.

Envir. : Lennoxlove★ *AC*, S : 1 m..

Exc. : Tantallon Castle★★ (clifftop site★★★) *AC*, NE : 12 m. by A 1 and A 198 – Northern foothills of the Lammermuir Hills★★, S : 14 m. by A 6137 and B 6368 – Stenton★, E : 7 m..

18 Amisfield Park ✆ 823627.

◆Edinburgh 17 – Hawick 53 – ◆Newcastle upon Tyne 101.

Maitlandfield House, 24 Sidegate, EH41 4BZ, ✆ 826513, Fax 826713, ⛬ – TV ☎ P – 200. AE VISA
Meals 22.50 **st.** (dinner) and a la carte 6.60/15.85 **st.** 6.50 – **22 rm** 50.00/85.00 **st.** – SB.

Brown's with rm, 1 West Rd, EH41 3RD, ✆ 822254, Fax 822254, ⛬ – ⊁ rest TV ☎ P. AE VISA. ✻
Meals (booking essential) (dinner only and Sunday lunch)/dinner 17.50/26.50 **t.** – **5 rm** 55.00/78.00 **st.**

HALKIRK Caithness. (Highland) 401 J 8 pop. 1 913 – ✆ 01847.

◆Edinburgh 285 – Thurso 8 – ◆Wick 17.

Bannochmore Farm ⛺, (The Bungalow) Harpsdale, KW12 6UN, S : 3 1/4 m. ✆ 841216, « Working farm », park – ⊁ P. ✻
Meals (communal dining) 9.50 – **3 rm** 16.00/32.00 **t.**

HAMILTON SERVICE AREA Lanark. (Strathclyde) – ✆ 01698.

9 Larkhall, Burnhead Rd ✆ 881113 – 9 Strathclyde Park, Mote Hill ✆ 266155.

Road Chef Services, M 74 northbound, ML3 6JW ✆ 285590.

◆Edinburgh 38 – ◆Glasgow 12.

Road Chef Lodge without rest., ML3 6JW, M 74 between junctions 6 and 5 (northbound carriageway) ✆ 891904, Fax 891682, Reservations (Freephone) 0800 834719 – ⊁ TV ☎ & P – 25. AE VISA. ✻
closed Christmas and New Year – **36 rm** 39.95 **st.**

HARRIS (Isle of) Inverness. (Outer Hebrides) (Western Isles) 401 Z 10 – see Lewis and Harris (Isle of).

HAWICK Roxburgh. (Borders) 401 402 L 17 **Scotland G.** – pop. 16 127 – ✆ 01450.

Exc. : Jedburgh Abbey★★ *AC*, SW : 12 1/2 m. by A 698 – Waterloo Monument (✻★★) NE : 12 m. by A 698, A 68 and B 6400 – Hermitage Castle★, S : 16 m. by B 6399.

18 Hawick, Vertish Hill ✆ 372293 – 18 Minto, Denholm ✆ 870220.

Common Haugh, TD9 7AR ✆ 372547 (summer only).

◆Edinburgh 51 – ◆Ayr 122 – ◆Carlisle 44 – ◆Dumfries 63 – Motherwell 76 – ◆Newcastle upon Tyne 62.

Kirklands, West Stewart Pl., TD9 8BH, ℘ 372263, Fax 370404, – TV ☎ P. VISA.
closed 25-26 December and 1-2 January – **Meals** (bar lunch)/dinner 12.50 **t.** and a la carte 4.25 – **12 rm** 48.50/75.00 **t.** – SB.

Rubislaw, Newhouses, TD9 8PR, N : 3 m. by A 7 ℘ 377693, ← Rubers law and Cheviot hills, – TV P. VISA.
closed Christmas and New Year – **Meals** 20.00 **st.** 6.00 – **3 rm** 36.00/60.00 **st.**

ATS Victoria Rd ℘ 373369

HEITON Roxburgh. (Borders) – see Kelso.

HELENSBURGH Dunbarton. (Strathclyde) 401 F 15 **Scotland G.** – pop. 12 972 – 01436.
See : Hill House★ *AC.*
Envir. : Loch Lomond★★, NE : 4½ m. by B 832.
Exc. : The Clyde Estuary★.
to Gourock via Kilcreggan (Caledonian MacBrayne Ltd) 2-10 daily (except Sunday).
The Clock Tower, J84 7NY ℘ 672642 (summer only).
♦Edinburgh 68 – ♦Glasgow 22.

Commodore Toby, 112-117 West Clyde St., G84 8ES, ℘ 676924, Fax 676233, ← – TV ☎ P – 200. VISA.
Meals (grill rest.) 6.95/8.25 **st.** and a la carte 3.95 – **44 rm** 65.00/82.00 **st.**, 1 suite – SB.

HELMSDALE Sutherland. (Highland) 401 J 9 – 01431.
Coupar Park ℘ (04312) 640 (late March-Sept).
♦Edinburgh 227 – ♦Inverness 71 – Thurso 45 – ♦Wick 37.

Navidale House, KW5 6JS, N : ½ m. on A 9 ℘ 821258, Fax 821531, ←, – TV P. VISA.
closed mid November-mid January – **Meals** (bar lunch Monday to Saturday)/dinner 21.00 **t** 5.00 – **14 rm** (dinner included) 56.00/115.00 **t.** – SB.

HUMBIE E. Lothian (Lothian) 401 L 16 pop. 376 – 01875.
♦Edinburgh 19 – Hawick 44 – ♦Newcastle upon Tyne 92.

Johnstounburn House (Thistle), EH36 5PL, S : 1 m. on B 6368 ℘ 833696, Fax 833626, ←, « Part 17C country house in extensive gardens », park – TV ☎ P – 30. VISA JCB
Meals 16.00/27.50 **t.** – **20 rm** 99.00/160.00 **t.** – SB.

INGLISTON Midlothian. (Lothian) 401 K 16 – see Edinburgh.

INNERLEITHEN Peebles. 401 402 K 17 – 01896.
♦Edinburgh 30 – Galashiels 12 – Peebles 6.

The Ley, EH44 6NL, N : 2¼ m. on B 709 ℘ 830240, Fax 830240, , park – P.
mid February - mid October – **Meals** (by arrangement)(residents only)(dinner only) 19.50 **s** 4.25 – **3 rm** 44.00/74.00 **s.**

INSCH Aberdeen (Grampian) 401 M 11 **Scotland G.** – pop. 1 541 – 01464.
Exc. : Huntly Castle (elaborate Heraldic carvings★★★) *AC*, NW : 14½ m. by B 9002 and A 97.
Golf Terr. ℘ 820363.
♦Edinburgh 55 – ♦Aberdeen 25.

Leslie Castle, Leslie, AB52 6NX, SW : 3¾ m. by B 992 ℘ 820869, Fax 821076, « 17C fortified baronial house » – TV ☎ P. VISA.
closed 1-14 November – **Meals** (lunch by arrangement)/dinner 30.00 **st.** 5.00 – **4 rm** 93.00/136.00 **st.** – SB.

INVERCRERAN Argyll. (Strathclyde) 401 E 14 – ✉ Appin – 01631.
♦Edinburgh 142 – Fort William 29 – ♦Oban 19.

Invercreran Country House, Glen Creran, PA38 4BJ, ℘ 730414, Fax 730532 ← Glen Creran and mountains, , park – rest TV ☎ P. VISA.
March-November – **Meals** 28.00 **st.** (dinner) and lunch a la carte 16.00/24.00 **st.** 7.00 – **9 rm** 62.00/140.00 **st.** – SB.

INVERGARRY Inverness (Highland) 401 F 12 – ✉ Inverness – 01809.
♦Edinburgh 159 – Fort William 25 – ♦Inverness 43 – Kyle of Lochalsh 50.

Glengarry Castle, PH35 4HW, on A 82 ℘ 501254, Fax 501207, ←, , , park, – rest TV ☎ P. VISA
early April to late October – **Meals** 10.00/21.00 **st.** – **26 rm** 43.50/90.00 **st.** – SB.

Ardochy Lodge, Glengarry, PH35 4HR, W : 7 ½ m. by A 87 on Tomdoun rd ℘ 511232, ←, , , park – rest P. VISA
Meals (dinner only) 10.00 3.75 – **8 rm** (dinner included) 55.50/74.00 **st.** – SB.

Invergarry, PH35 4HG, ℘ 501206, Fax 501236, – rest TV ☎ P. VISA
closed 24-26 December – **Meals** (dinner only) 15.00 **st.** and a la carte 4.50 – **10 rm** 37.00/64.00 **st.** – SB.

ꞮVERMORISTON Inverness. (Highland) 401 G 12 **Scotland G.** – ✆ 01320.

ꞮVir. : Loch Ness★★.

dinburgh 168 – ◆Inverness 29 – Kyle of Lochalsh 56.

🏠 **Glenmoriston Arms,** IV3 6YA, ✆ 351206, Fax 351206, – TV ☎ P. VISA
Meals (bar lunch)/dinner 18.50 **t.** and a la carte 5.25 – **8 rm** 45.00/66.00 **t.** – SB.

ꞮVERNESS Inverness. (Highland) 401 H 11 **Scotland G.** – pop. 62 186 – ✆ 01463.

ɜe : Town★ – Museum and Art Gallery★ **M.**

ːc. : Loch Ness★★, SW : by A 82 – Clava Cairns★, E : 9 m. by Culcabock Rd, B 9006 and B 851
Cawdor Castle★ *AC*, NE : 14 m. by A 96 and B 9090.

Culcabock Rd ✆ 239882 – 18 Torvean, Glenurquhart Rd ✆ 711434.

Dalcross Airport : ✆ 232471, NE : 8 m. by A 96.

✆ 0345 090700.

Castle Wynd, IN2 3BJ ✆ 234353.

.dinburgh 156 – ◆Aberdeen 107 – ◆Dundee 134.

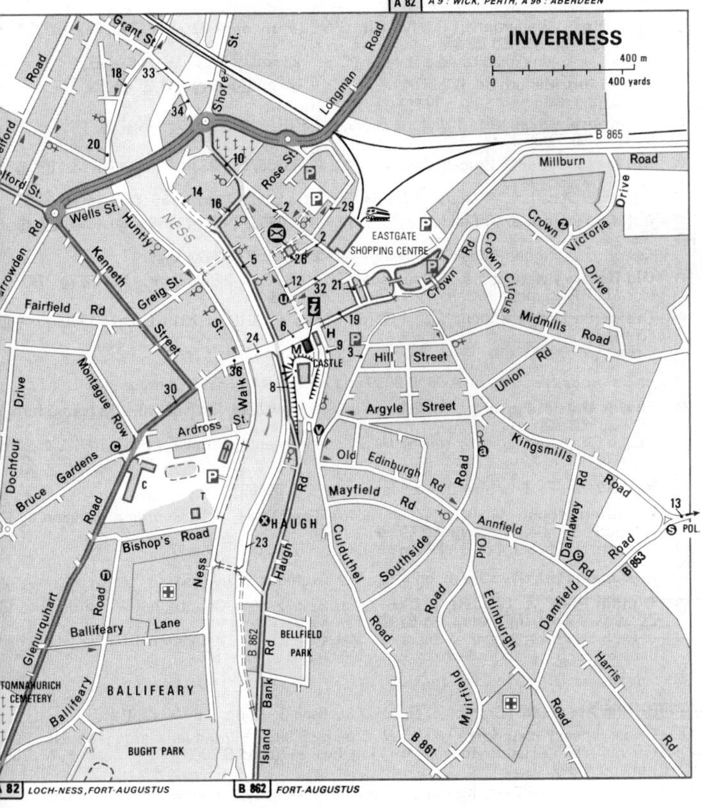

ːademy Street 2
ɪidge Street 6
ɪurch Street 12
ɪstgate
Shopping Centre
gh Street 19
ɪion Street 32
ɪdconnel Street 3

Bank Street 5
Castle Road 8
Castle Street 9
Chapel Street 10
Culcabock Road 13
Douglas Row 14
Friars Lane 16
Gilbert Street 18
Huntly Place 20

Inglis Street 21
Ness Bank 23
Ness Bridge 24
Queensgate 26
Strothers Lane 29
Tomnahurich Street 30
Waterloo Bridge 33
Waterloo Place 34
Young Street 36

Kingsmills (Swallow), Culcabock Rd, IV2 3LP, ☎ 237166, Fax 225208, – 60. VISA
Meals 13.50/21.50 **st.** and a la carte – **83 rm** 100.00/135.00 **st.**, 1 suite – SB.

Inverness Thistle, Millburn Rd, IV2 3TR, E : 1 m. on B 865 ☎ 239666, Fax 711145 – rm – 230. VISA JCB
Meals (bar lunch Saturday) (carving lunch) 10.00/25.00 **t.** and dinner a la carte – 8.95 – **117 rm** 75.00/105.00 **t.**, 1 suite – SB.

Caledonian (Jarvis), 33 Church St., IV1 1DX, ☎ 235181, Fax 711206, – – 300. VISA
Meals (bar lunch Monday to Saturday)/dinner 16.95 **st.** and a la carte – 8.50 – **103 r** 85.00/109.00 **st.**, 3 suites – SB.

Craigmonie, 9 Annfield Rd, IV2 3HX, ☎ 231649, Fax 233720, – – 140. VISA JCB.
Meals 12.00/24.00 **t.** and a la carte 5.50 – 8.50 – **32 rm** 55.00/80.00 **t.**, 3 suites – S

Glenmoriston, 20 Ness Bank, IV2 4SF, ☎ 223777, Fax 712378 – – 30. VISA.
Meals (dinner only) 22.00 **t.** and a la carte 5.95 – **19 rm** 55.00/80.00 **t.** – SB.

Glendruidh House, Old Edinburgh Rd South, IV1 2AA, SE : 2 m. ☎ 22649 Fax 710745, – VISA JCB.
Meals 12.00/19.50 **t.** 4.50 – **7 rm** 50.00/79.00 **t.** – SB.

Loch Ness, Glenurquhart Rd, IV3 6JL, SW : 1½ m. on A 82 ☎ 231248, Fax 239327, – 100. VISA
Meals (bar lunch) 20.50 **t.** and a la carte 5.50 – **22 rm** 52.50/95.00 **t.** – SB.

Travel Inn, Milburn Rd, IV2 3QX, ☎ 712010 – rm VISA
Meals (grill rest.) – 4.95 – **40 rm** 34.50 **t.**

Braemore without rest., 1 Victoria Drive, IV2 3QB, ☎ 243318, –
3 rm 35.00/55.00 **st.**

Moyness House, 6 Bruce Gdns, IV3 5EN, ☎ 233836, Fax 233836, – rest VISA.
closed 23 December-3 January – **Meals** 18.00 **st.** 5.00 – **7 rm** 29.00/58.00 **st.** – SB.

Ballifeary House, 10 Ballifeary Rd, IV3 5PJ, ☎ 235572, Fax 717583, – VISA.
Easter-mid October – **Meals** 16.00 **st.** 4.20 – **8 rm** 33.00/66.00 **st.**

Old Rectory without rest., 9 Southside Rd, IV2 3BG, ☎ 220969, –
closed 22 December-10 January – **4 rm** 24.00/36.00.

Craigside Lodge without rest., 4 Gordon Terr., IV2 3HD, ☎ 231576, Fax 713409, – VISA
6 rm 20.00/36.00 **t.**

at Dalcross NE : 9 m. by A 96, B 9039 and Ardersier rd – ✉ Inverness – 01667 :

Easter Dalziel Farm, IV1 2JL, on B 9039 ☎ 462213, Fax 462213, « Working farm – VISA
closed Christmas and New Year **Meals** (by arrangement) (communal dining) 11.00 **s.** – **3 r** 24.00/34.00 **s.**

at Culloden E : 3 m. by A 96 – ✉ Inverness – 01463 :

Culloden House, IV1 2NZ, ☎ 790461, Fax 792181, «, « Georgian mansion », park, – VISA JCB.
Meals 16.50/35.00 **t.** 6.10 – **22 rm** 125.00/175.00 **t.**, 1 suite.

at Dunain Park SW : 2½ m. on A 82 – ✉ Inverness – 01463 :

Dunain Park, IV3 6JN, ☎ 230512, Fax 224532, «, « Country house, gardens », park – rest VISA JCB
closed 3 weeks January-February – **Meals** (lunch by arrangement)/dinner a la car approx. 24.85 **t.** 6.50 – **8 rm** 55.00/150.00 **t.**, 6 suites – SB.

ATS Carsegate Rd North, The Carse ☎ 236167

INVERURIE Aberdeen. (Grampian) 401 M 12 **Scotland G.** – pop. 8 647 – 01467.

Exc. : Castle Fraser★ (exterior★★) *AC*, SW : 6 m. by B 993 – Pitmedden Gardens★★, NE : 10 r by B 9170 and A 920 – Haddo House★, N : 14 m. by B 9170 and B 9005 – Fyvie Castle★, N : 13 r by B 9170 and A 947.

18 Blackhall Rd ☎ 620207 – 18 Kintore ☎ 632631 – 18 Kemnay, Monymusk Rd ☎ 642225.

Town Hall, Market Pl., AB51 9SN ☎ 620600 (summer only).

♦Edinburgh 147 – ♦Aberdeen 17 – ♦Inverness 90.

Thainstone House H. & Country Club, AB51 9NT, S : 2 m. by B 993 on A ☎ 621643, Fax 625084, park – rest – 300. VISA.
Simpson's : Meals 12.50/29.50 **t.** 7.00 – **47 rm** 54.00/112.00 **t.**, 1 suite – SB.

Strathburn, Burghmuir Drive, AB51 4GY, NW : 1¼ by A 96 ☎ 624422, Fax 625133, – 30. VISA.
Meals 12.75/22.75 **st.** and dinner a la carte 5.25 – **25 rm** 60.00/90.00 **st.** – SB.

VINE Ayr. (Strathclyde) 401 402 F 17 **Scotland G.** – pop. 23 275 – ☎ 01294.

vir. : Kilmarnock (Dean Castle, arms and armour★, musical instruments★) *AC*, E : 5½ m. by 71 and B 7038.

Western Gailes, Gailes ✆ 311649 – 18 Irvine Ravenspark, Kidsneuk Lane ✆ 271293 – Bogside ✆ 78139.

dinburgh 75 – Ayr 14 – ◆Glasgow 29.

Hospitality Inn (Mount Charlotte), 46 Annick Rd, KA11 4LD, SE : 1 m. on B 7081 ✆ 274272, Telex 777097, Fax 277287, « Exotic indoor garden with ⛆ », 9 – ⇔ rm TV ☎ ♿ P – 🏛 300. AE VISA
Meals (carving lunch) 5.25/20.00 **t.** and dinner a la carte 5.10 – ☐ 8.75 – **126 rm** 75.00/100.00 **st.** – SB.

ATS 9 Kyle Rd, Ind. Est. ✆ 278727

LAY (Isle of) Argyll. (Strathclyde) 401 B 16 – pop. 3 840.

Machrie Hotel, Port Ellen ✆ (01496) 2310.

Port Ellen Airport : ✆ (01496) 302361/302022.

from Port Askaig to Isle of Jura (Feolin) (Western Ferries (Argyll) Ltd) (5 mn) – from Port en and Port Askaig to Kintyre Peninsula (Kennacraig) (Caledonian MacBrayne Ltd) 1-3 daily – m Port Askaig to Oban via Isle of Colonsay (Scalasaig) (Caledonian MacBrayne Ltd) h 30 mn).

at Bowmore, The Square ✆ (01496) 810254.

Ballygrant – ✉ Ballygrant – ☎ 01496.

Ballygrant Inn, PA45 7QR, ✆ 840277, Fax 840277, 🌳 – ⇔ P. VISA. ✻
Meals 12.95/18.00 **st.** – **3 rm** ☐ 23.50/50.00 **st.** – SB.

Bridgend – ✉ Bowmore – ☎ 01496.

Bridgend, PA44 7PJ, ✆ 810212, Fax 810673, 🌳 – TV ☎ P
Meals 15.00/20.00 **t.** 5.00 – **10 rm** ☐ 40.00/80.00 **t.**

GREEN TOURIST GUIDES

Picturesque scenery, buildings

Attractive routes

Touring programmes

Plans of towns and buildings.

SLE of WHITHORN Wigtown. (Dumfries and Galloway) 401 402 G 19 **Scotland G.** – op. 1 448 – ✉ Newton Stewart – ☎ 01988.

nvir. : Priory Museum (Early Christian Crosses★★) NW : 3 m. by A 750.

dinburgh 152 – ◆Ayr 72 – ◆Dumfries 72 – Stranraer 34.

Steam Packet, Harbour Row, DG8 8LL, ✆ 500334, ← – TV ☎. VISA
closed 25 December – **Meals** 13.50/13.50 **t.** (dinner) and a la carte6.50/16.50 **t.** 4.40 – **5 rm** ☐ 22.50/45.00 **t.**

SLEORNSAY Inverness. (Highland) 401 C 12 – see Skye (Isle of).

EDBURGH Roxburgh. (Borders) 401 402 M 17 **Scotland G.** – pop. 4 768 – ☎ 01835.

ee : Town★ - Abbey★★ *AC* – Mary Queen of Scots House Visitor Centre★ *AC* – The anongate Bridge★.

nvir. : Waterloo Monument (✳★★) N : 4 m. by A 68 and B 6400.

Jedburgh, Dunion Rd ✆ 863587.

Murray's Green, TD8 6BE ✆ 863435/863688.

Edinburgh 48 – ◆Carlisle 54 – ◆Newcastle upon Tyne 57.

Glenfriars, The Friars, TD8 6BN, ✆ 862000, Fax 862000, 🌳 – TV P. AE VISA
closed Christmas-New Year – **Meals** 17.00 4.25 – **6 rm** ☐ 35.00/64.00 – SB.

Hundalee House without rest., TD8 6PA, S : 1½ m. by A 68 ✆ 863011, Fax 863011, ←, 🌳, park – TV P. ✻
April-October – **5 rm** ☐ 25.00/40.00 **s.**

Spinney without rest., Langlee, TD8 6PB, S : 2 m. on A 68 ✆ 863525, Fax 863525, 🌳 – ⇔ P. ✻
March-November – **3 rm** ☐ 32.00/42.00 **st.**

OHN O'GROATS Caithness. (Highland) 401 K 8 – Shipping Services : see Orkney Islands.

URA (Isle of) Argyll. (Strathclyde) 401 C 15 – pop. 196.

from Feolin to Isle of Islay (Port Askaig) (Western Ferries (Argyll) Ltd) (5 mn).

Craighouse – ✉ Jura – ☎ 01496.

Jura, PA60 7XU, ✆ 820243, Fax 820249, ← Small Isles Bay, 🌳, 🌳 – P. AE VISA
closed 2 weeks Christmas and New Year – **Meals** (bar lunch)/dinner 15.75 **st.** 5.15 – **16 rm** ☐ 28.00/70.00 **st.**, 1 suite.

KELSO Roxburgh. (Borders) 401 402 M 17 **Scotland G.** – pop. 6 167 – ☎ 01573.

See : Town★ – Market Square★★ – ≤★ from Kelso Bridge.

Envir. : Floors Castle★ *AC*, NW : 1½ m. by A 6089.

Exc. : Mellerstain★★ (Ceilings★★★, Library★★★) *AC*, NW : 6 m. by A 6089 – Waterloo Monument (✻★★) SW : 7 m. by A 698 and B 6400 – Jedburgh Abbey★★ *AC*, SW : 8½ m. by A 698 – Dryburgh Abbey★★ *AC* (setting★★★), SW : 10½ m. by A 6089, B 6397 and B 6404 – Scott's View★★, W : 11 m. by A 6089, B 6397, B 6404 and B 6356 – Smailholm Tower★ (✻★★) NW : 6 m. by A 6089 and B 6397 – Lady Kirk (Kirk o'Steil★) NE : 16 m. by A 698, A 697, A 6112 and B 6437.

18 Berrymoss Racecourse Rd ☎ 223009.

Town House, The Square, PD5 7HC ☎ 223464 (summer only).

♦Edinburgh 44 – Hawick 21 – ♦Newcastle upon Tyne 68.

Ednam House, Bridge St., TD5 7HT, ☎ 224168, Fax 226319, ≤, « 18C house », – ☎ P – 150. VISA
closed Christmas amd New Year – **Meals** (bar lunch Monday to Saturday)/dinner 18.00 st. 7.50 – **32 rm** 48.00/93.00 **st.** – SB.

at Heiton SW : 3 m. by A 698 – ✉ Kelso – ☎ 01573 :

Sunlaws House , TD5 8JZ, ☎ 450331, Fax 450611, ≤, « Victorian country house », , park, – rest TV ☎ P. AE VISA
Meals 12.50/40.00 **st.** 9.50 – **22 rm** 95.00/175.00 **t.** – SB.

ATS The Butts ☎ 224997/8

KENMORE Perth. (Tayside) 401 I 14 **Scotland G.** pop. 596 – ☎ 01887.

See : Village★.

Envir. : Loch Tay★★.

Exc. : Ben Lawers★★, SW : 8 m. by A 827.

18 Taymouth Castle ☎ 830228 – 9 Mains of Taymouth ☎ 830226.

♦Edinburgh 82 – ♦Dundee 60 – ♦Oban 71 – Perth 38.

Kenmore, PH15 2NU, ☎ 830205, Fax 830262, , , 18, , , – rest TV P. AE VISA
Meals 20.00/25.00 **t.** and a la carte 4.50 – **38 rm** (dinner included) 48.50/125.00 **t.** – SB.

The Guide is updated annually so renew your Guide every year.

KENTALLEN Argyll. (Highland) 401 E 14 – ✉ Appin – ☎ 01631.

♦Edinburgh 123 – Fort William 17 – ♦Oban 33.

Ardsheal House , PA38 4BX, SW : ¾ m. by A 828 ☎ 740227, Fax 740342, ≤, « Country house atmosphere », , park, – rest ☎ P. AE VISA
Meals 18.00/32.50 **t.** 5.50 – **13 rm** (dinner included) 85.00/180.00 **t.** – SB.

KILCHOAN Argyll. (Highland) 401 B 13 – ✉ Acharacle – ☎ 01972.

♦Edinburgh 163 – ♦Inverness 120 – ♦Oban 84.

Meall Mo Chridhe , PH36 4LH, ☎ 510238, Fax 510238, ≤ Sound of Mull, , park, P
April-October – **Meals** (booking essential) (communal dining) (dinner only) (unlicensed) 26.95 **st.** – **3 rm** (dinner included) 79.00/138.00 **st.** – SB.

KILCHRENAN Argyll. (Strathclyde) 401 E 14 **Scotland G.** – ✉ Taynuilt – ☎ 01866.

Envir. : Loch Awe★★, E : 1¼ m.

♦Edinburgh 117 – ♦Glasgow 87 – ♦Oban 18.

Ardanaiseig , PA35 1HE, NE : 4 m. ☎ 833333, Fax 833222, ≤ gardens and Loch Awe, « Country house in extensive informal gardens beside Loch Awe », , park, – rest TV ☎ P. AE VISA
Easter- 2 October – **Meals** 15.00/33.50 **t.** and dinner a la carte 6.00 – **13 rm** 78.00/160.00 **t.**, 1 suite – SB.

Taychreggan , PA35 1HQ, SE : 1¼ m. ☎ 833211, Fax 833244, ≤ Loch Awe and mountains, « Lochside setting », , , park – rest ☎ P. AE VISA
Meals 30.00 **t.** (dinner) and lunch a la carte 28.00/30.00 4.00 – **20 rm** (dinner included) 80.00/160.00 **t.** – SB.

KILDRUMMY Aberdeen. (Grampian) 401 L 12 **Scotland G.** – ✉ Alford – ☎ 0197 55.

See : Castle★ *AC*.

Exc. : Huntly Castle (Heraldic carvings★★★) N : 15 m. by A 97 – Craigievar Castle★, SE : 13 m. by A 97, A 944 and A 980.

♦Edinburgh 137 – ♦Aberdeen 35.

Kildrummy Castle , AB33 8RA, S : 1¼ m. on A 97 ☎ 71288, Fax 71345, ≤ gardens and Kildrummy castle, « 19C mansion in extensive park », – rest TV ☎ P. VISA JCB
closed January – **Meals** 16.50/28.00 **st.** and a la carte 4.75 – **16 rm** 70.00/120.00 **st.** – SB.

KILFINAN Argyll. (Strathclyde) 401 E 16 pop. 906 – ✉ Tighnabruaich – ☎ 01700.

Edinburgh 124 – ◆Glasgow 78 – ◆Oban 78.

Kilfinan ⑤, PA21 2EP, ℘ 821201, Fax 821205, – rest TV ☎ P. AE VISA.
closed February – **Meals** 27.00 **st.** (dinner) and lunch a la carte 12.00/20.00 **st.** 5.00 – **11 rm** ☐ 48.00/72.00 **st.** – SB.

KILLIECHRONAN Argyll. (Strathclyde) 401 C 14 – see Mull (Isle of).

KILLIECRANKIE Perth. (Tayside) 401 I 13 – see Pitlochry.

KILLIN Perth. (Central) 401 H 14 Scotland G. – pop. 1 108 – ☎ 01567.

Exc. : Loch Tay★★, Ben Lawers★★, NE : 8 m. by A 827 – Loch Earn★★, SE : 7 m. by A 827 and A 85.

Killin ℘ 820312.

Bredalbane Folklore Centre, Falls of Dochart ℘ 820254 (summer only).

Edinburgh 72 – ◆Dundee 65 – Perth 43 – ◆Oban 54.

Dall Lodge Country House, Main St., FK21 8TN, ℘ 820217, Fax 820726, – rest TV ☎ & P. VISA
Meals 12.50/28.00 **st.** and a la carte **t.** 7.85 – **10 rm** ☐ 32.50/65.00 **st.** – SB.

Morenish Lodge Highland House ⑤, FK21 8TX, NE : 2 ½ m. on A 827 ℘ 820258, Fax 820258, ≤ Loch Tay and hills, – P. VISA.
Easter-October – **Meals** (dinner only) 15.00 **t.** 4.40 – **13 rm** ☐ (dinner included) 40.00/80.00 **t.** – SB.

Breadalbane House without rest., Main St., FK21 8UT, ℘ 820386, Fax 820386 – TV P. VISA.
5 rm ☐ 28.00/38.00 – SB.

at Ardeonaig NE : 6 ¾ m. – ✉ Killin – ☎ 01567 :

Ardeonaig ⑤, South Lochtayside, FK21 8SU, ℘ 820400, Fax 820282, ≤, – rest P
restricted opening November to March – **Meals** 23.50 **t.** (dinner) and lunch a la carte 13.55/20.85 **t.** – **15 rm** ☐ 62.50/125.00 **t.**

For the quickest route use the Michelin Main Road Maps :
970 Europe, 976 Czech Republic-Slovak Republic, 980 Greece, 984 Germany,
985 Scandinavia-Finland, 986 Great Britain and Ireland, 987 Germany-Austria-Benelux,
988 Italy, 989 France, 990 Spain-Portugal and 991 Yugoslavia.

KILMARNOCK Ayr. (Strathclyde) 401 402 G 17 – ☎ 01563.

◆Edinburgh 64 – ◆Ayr 13 – ◆Glasgow 25.

Forte Travelodge without rest., Kilmarnock bypass, Bellfield Interchange, KA1 5LQ, at junction of A 71 with A 76 and A 77 ℘ 73810, Reservations (Freephone) 0800 850950 – TV & P. AE VISA
40 rm 34.50 **t.**

KILMORE Argyll. (Strathclyde) 401 D 14 – see Oban.

KILNINVER Argyll. (Strathclyde) 401 D 14 – see Oban.

KINCARDINE Fife (Central) 401 I 15 Scotland G. pop. 1 089 – ☎ 01259.

Envir. : Culross★★★ (Village★★★, Palace★★ *AC*, Study★ *AC*) E : 4 m. by B 9037.

Tulliallan ℘ 730396.

◆Edinburgh 30 – Dunfermline 9 – ◆Glasgow 25 – Stirling 12.

Unicorn Inn, 15 Excise St., FK10 4LN, ℘ 730704 – AE VISA
closed Sunday lunch, Monday, 1-2 January, 2 weeks July and 25-26 December – **Meals** a la carte 15.70/21.95 **t.** 5.25.

KINCLAVEN Perth. (Tayside) 401 J 14 pop. 394 – ✉ Stanley – ☎ 01250.

◆Edinburgh 56 – Perth 12.

Ballathie House ⑤, PH1 4QN, ℘ 883268, Fax 883396, ≤, « Country house in extensive grounds on banks of River Tay », , park – rest TV ☎ & P. AE VISA JCB
Meals (bar lunch 17 October to Easter) 13.95/27.50 **t.** 5.00 – **26 rm** ☐ (dinner included) 97.50/210.00 **t.**, 1 suite – SB.

KINCRAIG Inverness. (Highland) 401 I 12 Scotland G. – ✉ Kingussie – ☎ 01540.

See : Highland Wildlife Park★ *AC*.

Exc. : The Cairngorms★★ (≤★★★) – ✻★★★ from Cairn Gorm, E : 14 m. by A 9 and B 970.

◆Edinburgh 119 – ◆Inverness 37 – Perth 75.

Ossian, The Brae, PH21 1QD, ℘ 651242, Fax 651633, ≤, – rest TV ☎ P. VISA
closed December and January except Christmas-New Year – **Meals** (bar lunch)/dinner a la carte 16.50/21.75 **t.** 5.00 – **9 rm** ☐ 28.00/56.00 **t.**

KINGUSSIE Inverness. (Highland) 401 H 12 **Scotland G.** – pop. 1 298 – 01540.

Envir. : Highland Wildlife Park★ *AC*, NE : 4 m. by A 9.

Exc. : Aviemore★, NE : 11 m. by A 9 – The Cairngorms★★ (≤★★★) – ✻★★★ from Cairn Gorr NE : 18 m. by B 970.

18 Gynack Rd 661374.

King St., PH21 1HP 661297 (summer only).

♦Edinburgh 117 – ♦Inverness 41 – Perth 73.

Scot House, Newtonmore Rd, PH21 1HE, 661351, Fax 661111 – rest TV P. VISA
closed January – **Meals** *(closed 25 December)* 20.00/25.00 **t.** and dinner a la carte 5.90 **9 rm** (dinner included) 50.00/95.00 **t.** – SB.

Columba House, Manse Rd, PH21 1JF, 661402, – TV P. VISA
Meals 15.00 **t.** (dinner) and lunch a la carte 5.50/8.95 **t.** 4.50 – **7 rm** 25.00/44.00 **t.** – S

Homewood Lodge, Newtonmore Rd, PH21 1HD, 661507, ≤, – P.
Meals (by arrangement) 10.50 **st.** – **4 rm** 19.50/39.00 **st.** – SB.

Avondale, Newtonmore Rd, PH21 1HF, 661731, Fax 661731, – TV P
Meals (by arrangement) 8.50 – **7 rm** 27.50/43.00.

St. Helens without rest., Ardbroilach Rd, PH21 1JX, 661430 – P.
3 rm 36.00/40.00 **s.**

XXX **The Cross** with rm, Tweed Mill Brae, Ardbroilach Rd, PH21 1TC, 66116 Fax 661080 – P. VISA.
closed 8 January-28 February and 1 -26 December – **Meals** *(closed Tuesday)* (bookin essential)(dinner only) 35.00 **st.** 5.00 – **9 rm** (dinner included) 105.00/170.00 **st.** – SB.

KINLOCHBERVIE Sutherland. (Highland) 401 E 8 **Scotland G.** – Lairg – 01971.

Exc. : Cape Wrath★★★ (≤★★) *AC*, N : 28½ m. (including ferry crossing) by B 801 and A 838.

♦Edinburgh 276 – Thurso 93 – Ullapool 61.

Kinlochbervie , IV27 4RP, 521275, Fax 521438, ≤ Loch Inchard and sea – re TV P. AE VISA
April-October – **Meals** (booking essential)(bar lunch)/dinner 27.50 **t.** 4.50 – **14 rn** 52.00/84.00 **t.** – SB.

KINLOCHMOIDART Inverness. (Highland) 401 C 13 – Lochailort – 01967.

♦Edinburgh 153 – ♦Inverness 110 – ♦Oban 74.

X **Kinacarra,** PH38 4ND, 431238, ≤ – P
Easter-October – **Meals** *(closed Monday)* (booking essential) (light lunch) a la carte 9.4C 20.25 **t.** 5.60.

KINROSS Kinross. (Tayside) 401 J 15 – pop. 5 047 – 01577.

18, 18 Green Hotel, 2 The Muirs 863407 – 9 Milnathort, South St. 864069 – 9 Bishopshire Kinnesswood (01592) 780203.

Kinross Service Area (junction 6, M 90) KY13 7BA 863680.

♦Edinburgh 28 – Dunfermline 13 – Perth 18 – Stirling 25.

Windlestrae, KY13 7AS, 863217, Fax 864733, , , , – rm TV P 250. AE VISA.
Meals 12.95/35.00 **st.** and a la carte 4.95 – **43 rm** 75.00/110.00 **st.**, 2 suites – SB.

Green, 2 The Muirs, KY13 7AS, 863467, Fax 863180, , , 18, , , , squash TV P – 140. AE VISA
Meals (bar lunch)/dinner 25.00 **st.** and a la carte 5.25 – **47 rm** 68.00/125.00 **t.** – SB.

Granada Lodge without rest., Kincardine Rd, KY13 7NQ, W : 1 m. by A 922 on A 97 864646, Fax 864108, Reservations (Freephone) 0800 555300 – TV P. VISA.
35 rm 39.95 **st.**

Lomond Country Inn, Kinnesswood, KY13 7HN, E : 4 ½ m. by A 922 on A 91 (01592) 840253, Fax 840693, ≤ – TV P. AE VISA.
Meals 9.50 **t.** and a la carte 4.00 – **11 rm** 35.00/55.00 **t.** – SB.

X **Croftbank House,** Station Rd, KY13 7TG, 863819 – P. VISA
closed Monday, 1 January and 25 December – **Meals** 13.50/24.00 **t.** and dinner a la cart 4.75.

at Cleish SW : 4½ m. by B 996 off B 9097 – Kinross – 01577 :

Nivingston House , KY13 7LS, 850216, Fax 850238, ≤, , park – TV P. VISA
Meals 15.50/25.00 **st.** and a la carte – **17 rm** 75.00/130.00 **st.** – SB.

KINTORE Aberdeen. (Grampian) 401 M 12 – 01467.

♦Edinburgh 136 – ♦Aberdeen 14 – ♦Inverness 91.

Torryburn, AB51 0XP, 632269, Fax 632271, , – rest TV P – 60. VISA
closed 1 January – **Meals** (bar lunch Monday to Saturday)/dinner 25.00 **st.** and a la carte 4.80 – **9 rm** 37.50/52.00 **st.**

KINTYRE (Peninsula) Argyll. (Strathclyde) 401 D 16 **Scotland G.**
See : Carradale★ – Saddell (Collection of grave slabs★).
, Campbeltown, Machrihanish ✆ (01586) 810213.
at Campbeltown (Machrihanish Airport) : ✆ (01586) 553021.
from Claonaig to Isle of Arran (Lochranza) (Caledonian MacBrayne Ltd) (summer only) frequent services daily (30 mn) – from Kennacraig to Isle of Islay (Port Ellen and Port Askaig) (Caledonian MacBrayne Ltd).

Campbeltown – ✉ Campbeltown – 01586.
MacKinnon House, The Pier, PA28 6EF ✆ 552056.
♦Edinburgh 176.

Seafield, Kilkerran Rd, PA28 6JL, ✆ 554385, Fax 552741 – TV ☎ P. VISA.
Meals 15.00/25.00 **t.** and a la carte 6.50 – **9 rm** 38.00/60.00 **t.** – SB.

Balegreggan Country House, Balegreggan Rd, PA28 6NN, NE : 1 m. by A 83 ✆ 552062, Fax 552062, ≤, – TV P. VISA.
Meals 22.50 **st.** 4.00 – **4 rm** 40.00/70.00 **st.**

Rosemount without rest, Low Askomil, PA28 6EN, ✆ 553552, ≤, – TV P
3 rm 21.00/38.00 **s.**

Machrihanish – pop. 5 722 – ✉ Campbeltown – 01586.
♦Edinburgh 182 – ♦Oban 95.

Ardell House without rest., PA28 6PT, ✆ 810235, ≤, – TV P
March-October – **11 rm** 22.00/50.00 **s.**

Tarbert – ✉ Tarbert – 01880.
Kilberry Rd, Tarbert ✆ 820565.
Harbour St. ✆ 820429 (summer only).

Columba, East Pier Rd, PA29 6UF, E : ¾ m. ✆ 820808, Fax 820808, ≤, – rest TV P. VISA
closed 25 December – **Meals** (bar lunch Monday to Saturday)/dinner 17.50 **t.** 4.95 – **10 rm** (dinner included) 42.95/91.90 **t.** – SB.

ATS Burnside St., Campbeltown ✆ 554404

Le Guide change, changez de **guide Michelin** *tous les ans.*

KIRKBEAN Dumfries (Dumfries and Galloway) 401 402 J 19 – ✉ Dumfries – 01387.
♦Edinburgh 89 – Carlisle 41 – ♦Dumfries 12.

Cavens Country House, DG2 8AA, ✆ 880234, Fax 880234, , park – rest TV P. VISA
Meals (by arrangement) 16.50 **st.** 4.00 – **6 rm** 35.00/56.00 **st.** – SB.

KIRKCUDBRIGHT Kirkcudbright. (Dumfries and Galloway) 401 402 H 19 **Scotland G.** – pop. 4 188 – 01557.
See : Town★.
Envir. : Dundrennan Abbey★ *AC*, SE : 5 m. by A 711.
Stirling Cres. ✆ 330314.
Harbour Sq., DJ6 4HY ✆ 330494 (summer only).
♦Edinburgh 108 – ♦Dumfries 28 – Stranraer 50.

Selkirk Arms, Old High St., DG6 4JG, ✆ 330402, Fax 331639, – TV ☎ P. AE VISA
Meals (bar lunch)/dinner 25.00 **st.** and a la carte 4.00 – **16 rm** 47.00/75.00 **st.** – SB.

Gladstone House without rest., 48 High St., DG6 4JX, ✆ 331734, Fax 331734, – TV. VISA.
3 rm 32.00/58.00 **s.**

KIRKHILL Inverness (Highland) 401 G 11 pop. 1 072 – ✉ Inverness – 01463.
♦Edinburgh 164 – ♦Inverness 8 – ♦Wick 130.

Inchberry House, Lentran, IV3 6RJ, E : 2 ½ m. by B 9164 off A 862 ✆ 831342, Fax 831342, ≤, – P
April-December – **Meals** (dinner only) 14.50 **s.** 4.50 – **6 rm** 36.00/42.00 **s.**

KIRKMICHAEL Perth. (Tayside) 401 J 13 **Scotland G.** pop. 542 – ✉ Blairgowrie – 01250.
Envir. : Glenshee (★★).
♦Edinburgh 74 – Perth 30 – Pitlochry 12.

Log Cabin, PH10 7NB, W : 1 m. ✆ 881288, Fax 881402, ≤, « Scandinavian pine chalet », – & P. AE VISA
closed 25 and 26 December – **Meals** 18.95 **t.** (dinner) and lunch a la carte 8.55/12.70 **t.** – **13 rm** (dinner included) 42.50/85.00 **t.** – SB.

KIRKWALL Orkney. (Orkney Islands) 401 L 7 – see Orkney Islands (Mainland).

KIRRIEMUIR Angus. (Tayside) 401 K 13 pop. 6 347 – ☎ 01575.
♦Edinburgh 65 – ♦Aberdeen 50 – ♦Dundee 16 – Perth 30.

- **Purgavie Farm,** Lintrathen, DD8 5HZ, W : 6 ¾ m. on B 951 ☎ 560213, Fax 560213, ≤ – ⊬ TV P
  Meals (communal dining) 9.50 – **3 rm** ☐ 16.00/36.00.

KYLE OF LOCHALSH Ross and Cromarty. (Highland) 401 C 12 **Scotland G.** – pop. 862 ☎ 01599.
Exc. : N : from Kyle of Lochalsh to Gairloch★★★ (Vista★★, ≤★★★) – Eilean Donan Castle★ AC (Site★★) E : 8 m. by A 87.
⛴ to Mallaig (Caledonian MacBrayne Ltd) (summer only) (5 mn).
ℹ Car Park, YV40 8DA ☎ 434276.
♦Edinburgh 204 – ♦Dundee 182 – ♦Inverness 82 – ♦Oban 125.

- **Lochalsh,** Ferry Rd, IV40 8AF, ☎ 534202, Fax 534881, ≤ Skye ferry and hills – |‡| ⊬ rm TV ☎ P. AE VISA
  Meals 13.50/28.00 **t.** and a la carte 🍷 6.95 – **36 rm** ☐ 65.00/85.00 **t.**, 2 suites – SB.

KYLESKU Sutherland. (Highland) – ☎ 01971.
♦Edinburgh 256 – ♦Inverness 100 – Ullapool 34.

- **Kylesku** ⛰, IV27 4HW, ☎ 502231, Fax 502313, ≤ Loch Glencoul and mountains, ⊬ rest TV. VISA
  February-October – **Meals** 12.50/18.50 **t.** and a la carte 🍷 4.50 – **7 rm** ☐ 22.50/60.00 **t.**
- **Newton Lodge** ⛰, IV27 4HW, S : 2 m. on A 894 ☎ 502070, ≤ Loch Glencoul and mountains – ⊬ TV P. VISA
  April-October – **Meals** (residents only) (dinner only) 12.00 **t.** 🍷 5.20 – **7 rm** ☐ 49.00 **t.**

LADYBANK Fife (Fife) 401 K 15 – pop. 1 373 – ☎ 01337.
Envir. : Falkland★ – Palace of Falkland★ – Gardens★ – Village★, S : ½ m. by A 914 on A 912.
♦Edinburgh 38 – ♦Dundee 20 – Stirling 40.

- **Redlands Country Lodge** ⛰ without rest., KY15 7SH, E : 1 m. on B 938 ☎ 831091, Fax 831091, – TV P.
  closed February – **4 rm** ☐ 28.00/46.00.

LAID Sutherland. (Highland) 401 F 8 – ✉ Lairg – ☎ 01971.
⛳9 Balnakeil, Durness ☎ 511364.
♦Edinburgh 242 – Thurso 59 – Ullapool 95.

- **Port-na-Con House** ⛰, by Altnaharra, IV27 4UN, ☎ 511367, Fax 511367, ≤ Loch Eribol, ⊬. VISA
  mid March-mid October – **Meals** 10.00 **st.** and a la carte 🍷 4.00 – **4 rm** ☐ 23.50/39.00 **st.**

LAIRG Sutherland. (Highland) 401 G9 – pop. 857 – ☎ 01549.
♦Edinburgh 218 – ♦Inverness 61 – ♦Wick 72.

- **Sutherland Arms,** IV27 4AT, ☎ 402291, Fax 402261, ≤, – TV ☎ P. AE VISA
  Meals (bar lunch Monday to Saturday)/dinner 18.00 **st.** and a la carte – **25 rm** ☐ (dinner included) 60.00/110.00 **st.** – SB.
- **Park House,** IV27 4AU, ☎ 402208, Fax 402208, ≤, – TV P
  Meals 11.00 – **3 rm** ☐ 31.00/42.00 – SB.

LAMLASH Bute. (Strathclyde) 401 E 17 – see Arran (Isle of).

LANARK Lanark. (Strathclyde) 401 402 I 16 – pop. 11 682 – ☎ 01555.
ℹ Horsemarket, Ladyacre Rd, ML11 7LQ ☎ 661661.
♦Edinburgh 34 – ♦Carlisle 78 – ♦ Glasgow 28.

- XX **Ristorante La Vigna,** 40 Wellgate, ML11 9DT, ☎ 664320, Fax 661400 – AE VISA
  closed Sunday lunch – **Meals** - Italian - (booking essential) a la carte 17.00/26.70 **t.** 🍷 4.95.

LANGBANK Renfrew. (Strathclyde) 401 G 16 – ☎ 01475.
♦Edinburgh 63 – ♦Glasgow 17 – Greenock 7.

- **Gleddoch House** ⛰, PA14 6YE, SE : 1 m. by B 789 ☎ 540711, Fax 540201, ≤ Clyde and countryside, ⛳18, , park, squash – ⊬ rm TV ☎ P – 🎤 80. AE VISA
  Meals 18.50/40.00 **t.** and a la carte 🍷 5.75 – **39 rm** ☐ 95.00/175.00 **t.** – SB.

LARGS Ayr. (Strathclyde) 401 402 F 16 **Scotland G.** – pop. 11 297 – ☎ 01475.
See : Largs Old Kirk★ *AC*.
⛳18 Irvine Rd ☎ 674681.
⛴ to Great Cumbrae Island (Cumbrae Slip) (Caledonian MacBrayne Ltd) frequent services daily (10 mn).
ℹ Promenade, KA30 8BG ☎ 673765.
♦Edinburgh 76 – ♦Ayr 32 – ♦Glasgow 30.

Brisbane House, 14 Greenock Rd, Esplanade, KA30 8NF, ℘ 687200, Fax 676295, ← – TV ☎ P – 50. VISA.
Meals 19.75 **t.** (dinner) and a la carte 9.25/30.20 **t.** 4.90 – **23 rm** 50.00/80.00 **t.** – SB.

Glen Eldon, 2 Barr Cres., KA30 8PX, ℘ 673381, Fax 673381 – rest TV ☎ P. AE VISA.
April-November – **Meals** (dinner only) 14.00 **st.** – **9 rm** 34.00/54.00 **st.** – SB.

ERWICK Shetland. (Shetland Islands) 401 Q 3 – see Shetland Islands (Mainland).

ETHAM Fife. (Fife) 401 K 15 – ✉ Cupar – 01337.
dinburgh 42 – Dundee 14 – Perth 28.

Fernie Castle, KY7 7RU, NE : ½ m. on A 914 ℘ 810381, Fax 810422, « Part 14C castle », park – TV ☎ P – 120. AE VISA.
Meals (bar lunch Monday to Friday)/dinner 19.50 **st.** and a la carte 5.95 – **15 rm** 49.00/100.00 **t.** – SB.

ESLIE Fife. (Fife) 401 K 15 – see Glenrothes.

EVEN Fife. (Fife) 401 K 15 – 01333.
dinburgh 33 – Dundee 33 – Stirling 42.

Old Manor, Leven Rd, Lundin Links, KY8 6AJ, E : 2 m. on A 915 ℘ 320368, Fax 320911, ←, – rest TV ☎ P. AE VISA
Meals 12.50/24.50 **st.** and a la carte 5.25 – **20 rm** 65.00/125.00 **st.** – SB.

EWIS and HARRIS (Isle of) Western Isles (Outer Hebrides) 401 A 9 **Scotland G.**
ee : Callanish Standing Stones★★ – Carloway Broch★ – St. Clement's Church, Rodel omb★).
from Stornoway to Ullapool (Caledonian MacBrayne Ltd) (3 h 30 mn) – from Kyles calpay to the Isle of Scalpay (Caledonian MacBrayne Ltd) 6-12 daily (except Sunday 1 daily) 0 mn) – from Tarbert to Isle of Skye (Uig) (Caledonian MacBrayne Ltd) 1-3 weekly h 45 mn) – from Tarbert to Isle of Uist (Lochmaddy) (Caledonian MacBrayne Ltd) 1-2 weekly from Tarbert to Portavadie (Caledonian MacBrayne Ltd) (summer only) 8-11 daily (30 mn).

LEWIS

Breasclete – 01851.

Eschol, 21 Breasclete, HS2 9ED, ℘ 621357, ←, – TV P.
March-October – **Meals** 16.00 – **4 rm** (dinner included) 39.00/100.00 – SB.

Galson – 01851.

Galson Farm, South Galson, PA86 0SH, ℘ 850492, ←, , park – P. VISA
Meals (communal dining) (by arrangement) 18.00 3.95 – **3 rm** 24.00/48.00 – SB.

Stornoway – 01851.
Lady Lever Park ℘ 702240.
26 Cornwell St., PA7 2DD ℘ 702088.

Cabarfeidh, Manor Park, HS1 2EU, N :½ m. on A 859 ℘ 702604, Fax 705572 – rest TV ☎ P – 300. AE VISA
Meals (bar lunch)/dinner 18.50 **st.** and a la carte 5.50 – **46 rm** 65.00/88.00 **st.** – SB.

County, 12-14 Francis St., HS1 2XB, ℘ 703250, Fax 706008 – TV ☎. VISA
Meals a la carte 8.50/17.70 **t.** 4.25 – **18 rm** 41.50/66.00 **t.**

Hebron without rest., 14 Maclean Terr., PA87 2QZ, NW : 1 m. by A 859 and McDonald Rd ℘ 702890 – TV.
3 rm 15.00/36.00 **s.**

HARRIS

Ardvourlie – 01859.

Ardvourlie Castle, HS3 3AB, ℘ 502307, ← Loch Seaforth and mountains, « 19C former hunting lodge on shore of Loch Seaforth », – rest P.
April-October – **Meals** (dinner only) 25.00 **st.** – **4 rm** (dinner included) 75.00/140.00 **st.**

Scarista – pop. 2 363 – 01859.

Scarista House, HS3 3HX, from Tarbert, SW : 15 m. on A 859 ℘ 550238, Fax 550277, ← Scarista beach and mountains, – ☎ P.
mid May-mid September – **Meals** (booking essential) (dinner only) 26.00 **st.** 6.00 – **8 rm** 61.00/100.00 **st.**

Tarbert – pop. 795 – ✉ Harris – 01859.

Harris, HS3 3DL, ℘ 502154, Fax 502281, – P. VISA
Meals 10.00/15.75 **t.** and lunch a la carte 4.95 – **24 rm** 29.90/64.40 **t.** – SB.

Leachin House, HS3 3AH, 502157, Loch Tarbert, – .
closed 15 December-15 January – **Meals** (communal dining) 20.00 **st.** – **3 rm** 35.0
70.00 **st.**

Allan Cottage, HS3 3DJ, 502146 –
April-September – **Meals** 16.00 **s. 3 rm** (dinner included) 41.00/82.00 **s.**

Two Waters, Lickisto, HS3 3EL, S : 10 m. by A 859 on C 79 530246, , ,
rest
May-September – **Meals** 13.00 **t.** – **4 rm** (dinner included) 50.00/86.00 **t.**

LEWISTON Inverness. (Highland) 401 G 12 **Scotland G.** – 01456.
Envir. : Loch Ness★★.
♦Edinburgh 173 – ♦Inverness 17.

Glen Rowan, West Lewiston, IV3 6UW, 450235, – .
closed 24 to 26 December – **Meals** 15.00 **st.** – **3 rm** 34.00/36.00 **st.**

LINICLATE Inverness (Western Isles) 401 XY 11 /12 – see Uist (Isles of).

LINLITHGOW W. Lothian. (Lothian) 401 J 16 **Scotland G.** – pop. 13 689 – 01506.
See : Town★★ – Palace★★ *AC* : Courtyard (fountain★★), Great Hall (Hooded Fireplace★★
Gateway★ – Old Town★ – St. Michaels★.
Envir. : Cairnpapple Hill★ *AC*, SW : 5 m. by A 706 – House of the Binns (plasterwork ceilings★
AC, NE : 4½ m. by A 803 and A 904.
Exc. : Hopetoun House★★ *AC*, E : 7 m. by A 706 and A 904 – Abercorn Parish Churc
(Hopetoun Loft★★) NE : 7 m. by A 803 and A 904.
Braehead 842585 – West Lothian, Airngath Hill 826030.
Burgh Halls, The Cross, EH49 7EJ 844600.
♦Edinburgh 19 – Falkirk 9 – ♦Glasgow 35.

Earl O' Moray Inn, Bonsyde, EH49 7NU, NE : 1¾ m. by A 803 842229, Fax 846233,
– – 30. VISA.
Meals a la carte 12.45/27.65 **t.** 4.95 – **8 rm** 70.00/100.00 **t.** – SB.

XXX **Champany Inn,** Champany, EH49 7LU, NE : 2 m. on A 803 at junction with A 90
834532, Fax 834302, « Converted horse mill », – . VISA JCB
closed Saturday lunch, Sunday, 25-26 December and 1-2 January – **Meals** (Beef Special-
ties) 13.75/35.00 **t.** and a la carte 26.50/39.40 **t.** 6.25.

LIVINGSTON Midlothian. (Lothian) 401 J 16 – pop. 22 357 – 01506.
Bathgate, Edinburgh Rd 652232 – Deer Park C.C., Knightsbridge 438843.
♦Edinburgh 16 – Falkirk 23 – ♦Glasgow 32.

Hilton National, Almondview, Almondvale, EH54 6QB, 431222, Fax 434666,
– rm – 100. VISA JCB.
Meals 12.50/17.95 **st.** and a la carte 7.25 – 9.75 – **120 rm** 75.00/120.00 **st.**

LOCHBOISDALE Western Isles (Outer Hebrides) 401 Y 12 – see Uist (Isles of).

LOCHCARRON Ross and Cromarty (Highland) 401 D 11 **Scotland G.** pop. 870 – 01520.
Envir. : Loch Earn★★.
Main St., 722357 (summer only).
♦Edinburgh 221 – ♦Inverness 65 – Kyle of Lochalsh 23.

Lochcarron, IV54 8YS, 722226, Fax 722612, Loch Carron – . VISA
Meals 15.50 **t.** (dinner) and a la carte 8.90/24.40 **t.** 4.95 – **10 rm** 36.50/80.00 **t.** – SB.

Rockvilla, IV54 8YB, 722379, Loch Carron – rest . VISA.
closed 25 December and 1 January – **Meals** 8.50/19.50 **st.** 4.95 – **4 rm** 50.00/60.00 **st.**

LOCHEARNHEAD Perth. (Central) 401 H 14 – 01567.
♦Edinburgh 65 – ♦Glasgow 56 – ♦Oban 57 – Perth 36.

Mansewood Country House, FK19 8NS, S : ½ m. on A 84 830213, –
VISA.
Meals (dinner only) 20.00 **t.** 3.25 – **6 rm** 29.00/40.00 **t.** – SB.

LOCHEPORT Western Isles (Outer Hebrides) 401 Y 11 – see Uist (Isles of).

LOCHGILPHEAD Argyll. (Strathclyde) 401 D 15 **Scotland G.** – pop. 2 421 – 01546.
Envir. : Loch Fyne★★, E : 3½ m. by A 83.
Blarbuie Rd 602340.
Lochnell St., PA31 8JN 602344 (summer only).
♦Edinburgh 130 – ♦Glasgow 84 – ♦Oban 38.

Empire Travellers Lodge without rest., Union St., PA31 8JS, 602381 – .
VISA.
closed 24 December-2 January – **9 rm** 18.00/36.00 **st.**

at Cairnbaan NW : 2 ¼ m. by A 816 on B 841 – ✉ Lochgilphead – ☎ 01546 :

Cairnbaan, PA31 8SJ, ☎ 603668, Fax 606045 – TV ☎ P. AE VISA.
closed first 2 weeks February – **Meals** (bar lunch)/dinner 19.50 **st.** and a la carte 5.00 – **11 rm** 50.00/90.00 **st.**

LOCH HARRAY Orkney. (Orkney Islands) 401 K 6 – see Orkney Islands (Mainland).

LOCHINVER Sutherland. (Highland) 401 E 9 **Scotland G.** – ✉ Lairg – ☎ 01571.

See : Village★.

Exc. : Loch Assynt★★, E : 6 m. by A 837.

Main St., ID27 4LF ☎ 844330 (summer only).

Edinburgh 251 – ♦Inverness 95 – ♦Wick 105.

Inver Lodge, IV27 4LU, ☎ 844496, Fax 844395, ≤ Loch Inver Bay, Suilven and Canisp mountains, park – rest TV ☎ P. AE VISA JCB
closed 1 January-3 April and 16 October-31 December – **Meals** (bar lunch Monday to Saturday) (buffet dinner Sunday)/dinner 27.00 **st.** and a la carte 5.00 – **20 rm** 75.00/130.00 **st.** – SB.

Albannach, Baddidarroch, IV27 4LP, W : 1 m. by Baddidarroch rd ☎ 844407, Fax 844407, ≤ Loch Inver Bay and Suilven, – P. VISA.
booking essential – **Meals** *(closed Monday lunch)* (light lunch) 25.00 **t.** (dinner) and lunch a la carte 10.00/15.00 5.50 – **4 rm** (dinner included) 50.00/96.00 **t.**

Veyatie without rest., 66 Baddidarroch, IV27 4LP, W : 1 ¼ m. by Baddidarroch rd ☎ 844424, ≤ Loch Inver Bay, Suilven and Canisp mountains, – P
April-October – **3 rm** 23.00/46.00 **t.**

Davar without rest., IV27 4LJ, W : ½ m. on Baddidarroch rd ☎ 844501, ≤ Loch Inver Bay and Suilven – TV P.
May-October – **3 rm** 26.00/40.00.

Lochinver Larder - Riverside Bistro, Main St., IV27 4JY, ☎ 844356, ≤ Loch Inver – . VISA
April-October – **Meals** (dinner only) a la carte 12.50/22.00 **t.**

LOCHMADDY Western Isles (Outer Hebrides) 401 Y 11 – see Uist (Isles of).

LOCHRANZA Bute. (Strathclyde) 401 402 E 16 – see Arran (Isle of).

LOCKERBIE Dumfries. (Dumfries and Galloway) 401 402 J 18 – pop. 2 301 – ☎ 01576.

Corrie Rd ☎ 203363 – Lochmaben, Castlehill Gate ☎ (01387) 810552.

Edinburgh 74 – ♦Carlisle 27 – ♦Dumfries 13 – ♦Glasgow 73.

Dryfesdale, DG11 2SF, NW : 1 m. by B 7068 ☎ 202427, Fax 204187, ≤, – TV ☎ & P.
AE VISA
Meals 11.00/17.00 **st.** and a la carte – **15 rm** 48.00/79.00 **st.** – SB.

LOSSIEMOUTH Moray. (Grampian) 401 K 10 – ☎ 01343.

Station Park, Pitgaveny St. ☎ 814804 (May-Sept).

Edinburgh 181 – ♦Aberdeen 70 – Fraserburgh 66 – ♦Inverness 44.

Stotfield, Stotfield Rd, IV31 6QS, ☎ 812011, Fax 814820, ≤, – TV ☎ P. AE VISA.
Meals 10.00/19.50 **t.** and dinner a la carte 5.50 – **45 rm** 38.00/75.00 **t.**

LUSS Dunbarton. (Strathclyde) 401 G 15 **Scotland G.** pop. 402 – ☎ 01436.

See : Village★.

Envir. : E : Loch Lomond★★.

♦Edinburgh 89 – ♦Glasgow 26 – Oban 65.

Lodge on Loch Lomond, G83 8NT, ☎ 860201, Fax 860203, ≤ Loch Lomond, – TV ☎ P. AE VISA
Meals a la carte 12.05/17.65 **t.** – 7.50 – **10 rm** 60.00 **t.** – SB.

LYBSTER Caithness. (Highland) 401 K 9 – ☎ 01593.

♦Edinburgh 251 – ♦Inverness 94 – Thurso 28 – ♦Wick 14.

Portland Arms, KW3 6BS, on A 9 ☎ 721208, Fax 721446 – TV ☎ P – 200. AE VISA
Meals 10.95/16.95 **st.** and a la carte 4.50 – **19 rm** 38.50/65.00 **st.** – SB.

MACHRIHANISH Argyll. (Strathclyde) 401 C 17 – see Kintyre (Peninsula).

MARNOCH Aberdeen. (Grampian) 401 L 11 **Scotland G.** pop. 1 706 – ✉ Huntly – ☎ 01466.
Exc. : Huntly Castle (elaborate Heraldic Carvings★★★) *AC*, SW : 10½ m. by B 9117, B 9118 a B 9022.
♦Edinburgh 170 – ♦Aberdeen 40 – Fraserburgh 39 – ♦Inverness 77.

Old Manse of Marnoch, AB54 5RS, on B 9117 ☎ 780873, Fax 780873, – re
TV P. VISA
Meals 25.00 6.00 – **5 rm** 60.00/90.00 – SB.

MARYCULTER Aberdeen. (Grampian) 401 N 12 – see Aberdeen.

MAYBOLE Ayr. (Strathclyde) 401 402 F 17 **Scotland G.** pop. 8 749 – ☎ 01655.
Envir. : Culzean Castle★ *AC* (setting★★★, Oval Staircase★★) W : 5 m. by B 7023 and A 719.

Ladyburn, KA19 7SG, S : 5 ½ m. by B 7023 off B 741 (Girvan rd) ☎ 74058 Fax 740580, ←, , park – TV ☎ P. AE VISA.
April-October – **Meals** *(closed Sunday dinner and Monday to non-residents)* (booki essential) (lunch by arrangement)/dinner 12.50/30.00 **t.** 6.00 – **8 rm** 90.00/140.00 **t** SB.

MELROSE Roxburgh. (Borders) 401 402 L 17 **Scotland G.** – pop. 2 414 – ☎ 01896.
See : Town★ - Abbey★★ (decorative sculptures★★★) *AC*.
Envir. : Eildon Hills (★★★) – Scott's View★★ – Abbotsford★★ *AC*, W : 4½ m. by A 6091 a B 6360 – Dryburgh Abbey★★ *AC* (setting★★★) SE : 4 m. by A 6091.
Exc. : Bowhill★★ *AC*, SW : 11½m. by A 6091, A 7 and A 708 – Thirlestane Castle (plasterwo ceilings★★) *AC*, NE : 21 m. by A 6091 and A 68 – 9 Melrose, Dingleton ☎ 822855.
Priorwood Gardens ☎ 822555 (summer only).
♦Edinburgh 38 – Hawick 19 – ♦Newcastle upon Tyne 70.

Burts, Market Sq., TD6 9PN, ☎ 822285, Fax 822870, – rest TV ☎ P. AE VISA
Meals 13.75/25.00 **t.** and dinner a la carte 4.95 – **21 rm** 45.00/78.00 **t.** – SB.

Bon Accord, Market Sq., TD6 9PQ, ☎ 822645, Fax 823474 – rest TV ☎. AE VIS
closed 25 December – **Meals** 20.00 **t.** (dinner) and a la carte 10.45/20.95 **t.** 4.95 – **9 r** 40.00/70.00 **t.** – SB.

Dunfermline House without rest., Buccleuch St., TD6 9LB, ☎ 822148, Fax 822148 –
TV.
5 rm 21.00/42.00 **s.**

at Gattonside NW : 2¼ m. by A 6091 on B 6360 – ✉ Melrose – ☎ 01896 :

Hoebridge Inn, TD6 9LZ, ☎ 823082 – P. VISA
closed Monday, 25 December, 1 January, 2 weeks April and 1 week October – **Mea** (dinner only) a la carte 13.95/19.65 **t.** 4.50.

MELVICH Sutherland. (Highland) 401 I 8 – ✉ Thurso. (Caithness) – ☎ 01641.
♦Edinburgh 267 – ♦Inverness 110 – Thurso 18 – ♦Wick 40.

Sheiling, KW14 7YJ, on A 836 ☎ 531256, Fax 531356, ←, – P
April-mid October – **Meals** (communal dining) 13.00 **st.** – **3 rm** 30.00/46.00 **st.**

MEY Caithness. (Highland) 401 K 8 – ☎ 01847.
♦Edinburgh 302 – ♦Inverness 144 – Thurso 13 – ♦Wick 21.

Castle Arms, KW14 8XH, ☎ 851244, Fax 851244 – TV ☎ & P. AE VISA
Meals (bar lunch)/dinner 15.50 **st.** and a la carte 4.95 – **8 rm** 35.00/52.00 **t.** – SB.

MILNGAVIE Lanark. (Strathclyde) 401 H 16 – pop. 12 592 – ✉ Glasgow – ☎ 0141.
♦Edinburgh 53 – ♦Glasgow 7.

Black Bull Thistle, 1-5 Main St., G62 6BH, ☎ 956 2291, Fax 956 1896 – TV ☎ P
100. AE VISA
Meals *(closed lunch Saturday and Bank Holiday Mondays)* 17.95 **t.** (dinner) and a la carte 21.20/28.75 **t.** – 8.95 – **27 rm** 65.00/88.00 **t.** – SB.

MOFFAT Dumfries. (Dumfries and Galloway) 401 402 J 17 **Scotland G.** – pop. 2 647 ☎ 01683.
Exc. : Grey Mare's Tail★★, NE : 9 m. by A 708.
18 Coatshill ☎ 220020.
Churchgate, DJ10 9EG ☎ 220620 (summer only).
♦Edinburgh 61 – ♦Dumfries 22 – ♦Carlisle 43 – ♦Glasgow 60.

Moffat House, High St., DG10 9HL, ☎ 220039, Fax 221288, – rest TV ☎ P. A
VISA
Meals (bar lunch)/dinner 19.50 **t.** 5.75 – **20 rm** 54.00/80.00 **t.** – SB.

Beechwood Country House ⊗, Harthope Pl., by Academy Rd, DG10 9RS, ☎ 220210, Fax 220889, ≤, 🌳 – ⇎ rest TV ☎ P. AE VISA
closed 2 January-15 February – **Meals** *(closed lunch Monday to Wednesday)* 13.50/21.00 **t.** 4.50 – **7 rm** ☐ (dinner included) 64.00/106.00 **t.** – SB.

Buccleuch Arms, High St., DG10 9ET, ☎ 220003, Fax 221291, 🌳 – TV ☎. AE VISA
Meals a la carte 11.45/21.75 **t.** 4.50 – **11 rm** ☐ 39.00/45.00 **t.** – SB.

Fernhill without rest., Grange Rd, DG10 9HT, ☎ 220077, 🌳 – ⇎ TV.
April-September – **3 rm** ☐ 20.00/33.00 **s.**

Alba House without rest., 20 Beechgrove, DG10 9RS, ☎ 220418, 🌳 – TV.
May-September – **3 rm** ☐ 30.00/37.00 **st.**

Hartfell House, Hartfell Cres., DG10 9AL, by Well St. and Old Well Rd ☎ 220153, 🌳 – ⇎ rest P
March-November – **Meals** (by arrangement) 11.50 **st.** 3.95 – **9 rm** ☐ 23.50/43.00 **st.**

Well View ⊗ with rm, Ballplay Rd, DG10 9JU, E : 3/4 m. by Selkirk Rd (A 708) ☎ 220184, Fax 220088, ≤, 🌳 – ⇎ TV P. AE VISA
Meals *(closed Saturday lunch)* 12.00/27.00 **t.** 4.50 – **5 rm** ☐ 44.00/78.00 **t.**, 1 suite – SB.

at Beattock SW : 2 1/4 m. by A 701 – ✉ Moffat – ☎ 01683 :

Auchen Castle ⊗, DG10 9SH, N : 2 m. by A 74 ☎ 300407, Fax 300667, ≤, 🐟, 🌳, park – TV ☎ P – 🎤 45. AE VISA
closed 3 weeks Christmas-New Year – **Meals** (bar lunch)/dinner a la carte 15.00/20.00 **st.** 4.70 – **25 rm** ☐ 47.50/86.00 **st.** – SB.

Broomlands Farm without rest., DG10 9PQ, S : 1/2 m. by A 74 ☎ 300320, Fax 300320, « Working farm », 🌳 – ⇎ TV P
April-October – **3 rm** ☐ 20.00/36.00.

MONTROSE Angus. (Tayside) 401 M 13 Scotland G. – pop. 8 473 – ☎ 01674.

Exc. : Edzell Castle★ (The Pleasance★★★) *AC*, NW : 17 m. by A 935 and B 966 – Cairn O'Mount Road★ (≤★★) N : 17 m. by B 966 and B 974 – Brechin (Round Tower★) W : 7 m. by A 935 – Aberlemno (Aberlemno Stones★, Pictish sculptured stones★) W : 13 m. by A 935 and B 9134.

18, 18 Traill Drive ☎ 672932.

The Library, High St., ☎ 672000 (summer only).

Edinburgh 92 – Aberdeen 39 – Dundee 29.

Park, 61 John St., DD10 8RJ, ☎ 673415, Fax 677091, 🌳 – TV ☎ P – 🎤 180. AE VISA
Meals 8.50/14.50 **t.** and a la carte 5.20 – **59 rm** ☐ 65.00/85.00 **t.** – SB.

Oaklands without rest., 10 Rossie Island Rd, DD10 9NN, on A 92 ☎ 672018, Fax 672018 – TV P. VISA – **7 rm** ☐ 18.50/33.00 **s.**

During the season, particularly in resorts, it is wise to book in advance.

MOTHERWELL Lanark. (Strathclyde) 401 I 16 – ☎ 01698.

Library, Hamilton Rd, ML1 3DZ ☎ 267676.

Edinburgh 38 – Glasgow 12.

Travel Inn without rest., Glasgow Rd, Newhouse, ML1 5SY, NE : 4 1/4 m. by A 723 and A 73 on A 775 ☎ 860277, Fax 861353 – ⇎ TV ♿ P – 🎤 100. AE VISA.
☐ 4.95 – **40 rm** 34.50 **t.**

MUIR OF ORD Ross and Cromarty. (Highland) 401 G 11 – pop. 2 033 – ☎ 01463.

18 Great North Rd ☎ 870825.

Edinburgh 173 – Inverness 10 – Wick 121.

Dower House ⊗, Highfield, IV6 7XN, N : 1 m. on A 862 ☎ 870090, Fax 870090, « Part 17C house », 🌳 – ⇎ TV ☎ P. VISA
Meals (lunch by arrangement)/dinner 30.00 **st.** 6.50 – **4 rm** ☐ 50.00/120.00 **st.**, 2 suites – SB.

MULL (Isle of) Argyll. (Strathclyde) 401 BC 14/15 Scotland G. – pop. 2 838.

See : Island★ - Calgary Bay★★ – Torosay Castle *AC* (Gardens★ ≤★).

Envir. : Isle of Iona★ (Madean's Cross★, St. Oran's Chapel★, St. Martin's High Cross★, Infirmary Museum★ *AC*).

9 Craignure, Scallastle ☎ (01680) 812370.

from Craignure to Oban (Caledonian MacBrayne Ltd) (40 mn) – from Fishnish to Lochaline (Caledonian MacBrayne Ltd) frequent services daily (15 mn) – from Tobermory to Isle of Coll (Arinagour) (Caledonian MacBrayne Ltd) 3 weekly (1 h 20 mn) – from Tobermory to Isle of Tiree (Scarinish) (Caledonian MacBrayne Ltd) 3 weekly (2 h 30 mn) – from Tobermory to Kilchoan (Caledonian MacBrayne Ltd) 5-11 daily (summer only) (35 mn) – from Tobermory to Oban (Caledonian MacBrayne Ltd) 3 weekly (2 h).

from Fionnphort to Isle of Iona (Caledonian MacBrayne Ltd) frequent services daily in summer (5 mn).

Main St., Tobermory ☎ 01688 (Tobermory) 302182.

Bunessan – ✉ Fionnphort – ☎ 01681.

Ardfenaig House ♨, PA67 6DX, W : 3 m. by A 849 ✆ 700210, Fax 700210, ≤, ⚘, par
⊬ ℗. 🅽 VISA. ✗
April-October – **Meals** (dinner only) 25.00 **st.** 4.50 – **7 rm** ⊏ (dinner included) 70.0C
170.00 **st.** – SB.

Dervaig – ✉ Tobermory – ☎ 01688.

Druimard Country House ♨, PA75 6QW, on Salen rd ✆ 400345, Fax 400345, ≤, ⚘
⊬ rest TV ☎ ℗. 🅽 VISA
April-October – **Meals** *(closed Sunday to non-residents)* (dinner only) 20.00 **t.** – **5 rn**
⊏ (dinner included) ⊏ 66.00/123.00 **t.**, 1 suite – SB.

Druimnacroish Country House ♨, PA75 6QW, S : 2 m. by B 8073 and Salen r
✆ 400274, Fax 400311, ≤ Bellart Glen, ⚘ – ⊬ rest TV ☎ ℗. 🅽 AE ⓓ VISA
May-October – **Meals** (dinner only) 20.00 **st.** – **6 rm** ⊏ 62.00/124.00 **st.**

Killiechronan – ☎ 01680.

Killiechronan House ♨, PA72 6JU, on B 8073 ✆ 300403, Fax 300463, ≤, ⚓, ⚘, park
☎ ℗. 🅽 AE VISA
March-October – **Meals** (booking essential to non-residents) (dinner only) 20.90 **t.** – **6 rn**
⊏ 60.00/104.00 **t.** – SB.

Pennyghael – ☎ 01681.

Pennyghael, PA70 6HB, ✆ 704288, Fax 704205, ≤, ⚘ – TV ☎ ℗. 🅽 VISA
Easter-mid October – **Meals** (booking essential to non-residents) (in bar) (dinner only
21.00 **t.** 5.50 – **6 rm** ⊏ (dinner included) 60.00/100.00 **st.**

Tobermory – pop. 2 708 – ☎ 01688.

⛳9 Tobermory ✆ 302020.

Western Isles, PA75 6PR, ✆ 302012, Fax 302297, ≤ Tobermory harbour and Calve
Island – ⊬ rest TV ☎ ℗. 🅽 AE VISA
closed 3 to 21 January and 18 to 28 December – **Meals** (bar lunch)/dinner 25.00 **t.** – **Spices**
Meals (dinner only) a la carte approx. 20.00 **t.** – **24 rm** ⊏ 42.50/140.00 **t.**, 1 suite – SB.

Ulva House, Strongarbh, PA75 6PR, ✆ 302044, ≤ Tobermory harbour and Calve Island,
⚘ – ⊬ ℗
April-October – **Meals** 15.95 **t.** 4.90 – **6 rm** ⊏ 34.95/65.00 **t.**

MURCAR Aberdeen. (Grampian) **401** N 12 – see Aberdeen.

MUSSELBURGH E. Lothian. (Lothian) **401** K 16 – pop. 18 425 – ☎ 0131.

⛳18 Monktonhall ✆ 665 2005 – ⛳18 Royal Musselburgh, Prestongrange House, Prestonpans ✆ (01875) 810276 – ⛳9 Musselburgh Old Course, Silver Ring Clubhouse, Millhill ✆ 665 6981.

ℹ Brunton Hall, EH21 6AF ✆ 665 6597 (summer only).

◆Edinburgh 6 – Berwick 54 – ◆Glasgow 53.

Granada Lodge without rest., Old Craighall, EH21 8RE, S : 1½ m. by B 6415 at junction
with A 1 ✆ 653 6070, Fax 653 6106, Reservations (Freephone) 0800 555300 – ⊬ TV ☎ ♿
℗. 🅽 AE VISA. ✗
44 rm 39.95 **st.**

NAIRN Nairn. (Highland) **401** I 11 **Scotland G.** – pop. 3 367 – ☎ 01667.

Envir. : Forres (Sueno's Stone★★) E : 11 m. by A 96 and B 9011 – Cawdor Castle★ *AC*, S : 5½m. by B 9090 – Brodie Castle★ *AC*, E : 6 m. by A 96.

Exc. : Fort George★, W : 7 m. by A 96, B 9092 and B 9006.

⛳18, ⛳9 Seabank Rd ✆ 452103 – ⛳18 Nairn Dunbar, Lochloy Rd ✆ 452741.

ℹ 62 King St. ✆ 452753 (summer only).

◆Edinburgh 172 – ◆Aberdeen 91 – ◆Inverness 16.

Golf View, 63 Seabank Rd, IV12 4HD, ✆ 452301, Fax 455267, ≤, Fø, ≘s, ⛱ heated, ⛱,
⚘, ✗ – 🛗 ⊬ rest TV ☎ ℗ – 🏛 100. 🅽 AE ⓓ VISA
Meals 12.70/21.50 **t.** and a la carte – **45 rm** ⊏ 57.00/120.00 **t.**, 3 suites – SB.

Clifton House ♨, Viewfield St., IV12 4HW, ✆ 453119, Fax 452836, ≤, « Antiques », ⚘
– ℗. 🅽 AE ⓓ VISA
closed December and January – **Meals** (booking essential) 12.50/25.00 **st.** and a la carte
4.00 – **12 rm** ⊏ 45.00/96.00 **st.** – SB.

Claymore House, 45 Seabank Rd, IV12 4EY, ✆ 453731, Fax 455290, ⚘ – ⊬ rest TV ☎
♿ ℗. 🅽 AE VISA JCB
Meals 15.00/25.00 **st.** and a la carte 4.00 – **16 rm** ⊏ 37.50/75.00 **st.** – SB.

Lochloy House ⚘, Lochloy Rd, Lochloy, IV12 5LE, NE : 2½ m. ✆ 455355, Fax 454809, ≤ Moray Firth, « Country house atmosphere », ⚘, ⚘, park, ⚘ – ⚘ ⚘ rest ☎ P. ⚘ VISA. ⚘
April-October (booking essential) – **Meals** (lunch by arrangement)/dinner 23.50 **st.** and a la carte 19.00/27.00 **st.** 6.00 – **8 rm** ⚘ 80.00/130.00 **st.**

Links, 1 Seafield St., IV12 4HN, ✆ 453321, Fax 456092, ⚘ – ⚘ rest TV ☎ P. ⚘ AE VISA
Meals *(closed Sunday and Monday in winter)* (dinner only) 15.00 **st.** – **10 rm** ⚘ 32.50/75.00 **st.** – SB.

Ramleh, 2 Academy St., IV12 4RJ, ✆ 453551, Fax 456577 – ⚘ rest TV P. ⚘ AE ⚘ VISA. ⚘
Fingal's : Meals 7.00/18.00 **t.** and a la carte 4.35 – **10 rm** ⚘ 20.00/55.00 **t.** – SB.

Longhouse, 8 Harbour St., IV12 4NU, ✆ 455532 – ⚘ AE VISA
closed Monday, 2 weeks January, 1 week October and 25 and 26 December – **Meals** (booking essential in winter) (dinner only) a la carte 13.75/23.00 **t.** 5.50.

NETHERLEY Kincardine. (Grampian) 401 N 12 **Scotland G.** – ✉ Stonehaven – ☎ 01569.
Envir. : Muchalls Castle (plasterwork ceilings★★) *AC*, SE : 5 m. by B 979 – Deeside★★, N : 2 m. by B 979 – Aberdeen★★, NE : 3 m. by B 979 and B 9077.
Exc. : Aberdeen★★, NE : 12 m. by – Dunnottar Castle★★ (site★★★) *AC*, S : 7 m. by B 979 – Crathes Castle★★ (Gardens★★★) *AC*, NW : 13 m. by B 979, B 9077 and A 93.
♦Edinburgh 117 – ♦Aberdeen 12 – ♦Dundee 54.

Lairhillock, AB3 2QS, NE : 1½ m. by B 979 on Portlethan rd ✆ 730001, Fax 731175 – P. ⚘ AE ⚘ VISA
Meals (bar lunch Monday to Saturday)/dinner 25.50 **t.** and a la carte 6.50.

NEWBURGH Aberdeen. (Grampian) 401 N 12 **Scotland G.** – ☎ 01358.
Exc. : Pitmedden Gardens★★ *AC*, W : 6½ m. by B 9000 – Haddo House★ *AC*, NW : 14 m. by B 900, A 92 and B 9005.
⚑18 McDonald, Ellon ✆ 720576 – ⚑9 Newburgh-on-Ythan, Ellon ✆ 789438.
♦Edinburgh 144 – ♦Aberdeen 14 – Fraserburgh 33.

Udny Arms, Main St., AB41 0BL, ✆ 789444, Fax 789012, ⚘ – TV ☎ P – ⚘ 45. ⚘ AE ⚘ VISA
Meals - (see below) – ⚘ 8.50 – **24 rm** 49.50/59.00 **t.** – SB.

Udny Arms (at Udny Arms H.), Main St., AB41 0BL, ✆ 789444, Fax 789012 – P. ⚘ AE ⚘ VISA
Meals 7.95/12.95 **t.** and a la carte 6.95.

NEW GALLOWAY Kirkcudbright. (Dumfries and Galloway) 401 402 H 18 **Scotland G.** – ☎ 01644 – Envir. : Galloway Forest Park★, Queen's Way★ (Newton Stuart to New Galloway) SW : 19 m. by A 712.
⚑9 New Galloway ✆ 737.
♦Edinburgh 88 – ♦Ayr 36 – Dumfries 25.

Leamington, High St., DG7 3RN, ✆ 420327 – ⚘ rest TV P. ⚘ VISA. ⚘
closed November – **Meals** (by arrangement) 11.50 **t.** 3.50 – **9 rm** ⚘ 14.00/40.00 **t.**

NEWPORT-ON-TAY Fife. (Fife) 401 L 14 – ☎ 01382.
♦Edinburgh 55 – ♦Dundee 4 – Perth 23 – St. Andrews 11.

Forgan House ⚘, DD6 8RB, SE : 2½ m. by B 995 and A 92 on Tayport rd ✆ 542760, Fax 542760, ⚘ – ⚘ TV P. ⚘ VISA. ⚘
Meals (by arrangement) (communal dining) 17.50 **s.** 5.00 – **4 rm** ⚘ 35.00/60.00 **s.**

NEW SCONE Perth. (Tayside) 401 J 14 – see Perth.

NEWTONMORE Inverness. (Highland) 401 H 12 – pop. 1 044 – ☎ 01540.
⚑18 Newtonmore ✆ 673328.
♦Edinburgh 113 – ♦Inverness 43 – Perth 69.

Pines ⚘, Station Rd, PH20 1AR, ✆ 673271, ≤, ⚘ – ⚘ P. ⚘
May-October – **Meals** 10.00 **s.** – **6 rm** ⚘ (dinner included) 34.00/68.00 **s.** – SB.

NEWTON STEWART Wigtown. (Dumfries and Galloway) 401 402 G 19 **Scotland G.** – pop. 2 543 – ☎ 01671 – Envir. : Galloway Forest Park★, Queen's Way★ (Newton Stewart to New Galloway) N : 19 m. by A 712.
⚑18, Kirroughtree Av., Minnigaff ✆ 402172.
🅸 Dashwood Sq., DG8 6DQ ✆ 402431 (summer only).
♦Edinburgh 131 – ♦Dumfries 51 – ♦Glasgow 87 – Stranraer 24.

Kirroughtree ⚘, DG8 6AN, NE : 1½ m. by A 75 on A 712 ✆ 402141, Fax 402425, ≤ woodland and Wigtown Bay, « 18C mansion in landscaped gardens », park, ⚘ – ⚘ rest TV ☎ P. ⚘ VISA. ⚘
closed 3 January-16 February – **Meals** 12.00/27.50 **st.** and lunch a la carte 6.00 – **15 rm** ⚘ (dinner included) 71.00/140.00 **st.**, 2 suites – SB.

Creebridge House ⑤, Minnigaff, DG8 6NP, ☎ 402121, Fax 403258, ⛱ – ⊭ rest TV ☎ ℗. Ⓢ AE VISA
Meals (bar lunch Monday to Saturday)/dinner 20.00 **t.** and a la carte ⧫ 4.50 – **20 rm** ☐ 45.00/75.00 **t.** – SB.

Crown, 101 Queen St., DG8 6JW, ☎ 402727, Fax 402727 – TV ☎ ℗. Ⓢ VISA. ⚘
Meals (bar lunch)/dinner 20.00 **t.** and a la carte ⧫ 4.00 – **11 rm** ☐ 29.50/50.00 **st.** – SB.

Rowallan House ⑤ without rest., Corsbie Rd, DG8 6JB, ☎ 402520, ⛱ – TV ℗. ⚘
April-October – **5 rm** ☐ 22.00/44.00.

NORTH BERWICK E. Lothian. (Lothian) 401 L 15 Scotland G. – pop. 5 871 – ☎ 01620.

Envir. : North Berwick Law (✳★★★) S : 1 m. - Tantallon Castle★★ (clifftop site★★★) *AC*, E 3½ m. by A 198 – Dirleton★ (Castle★ *AC*) SW : 2½ m. by A 198.

Exc. : Museum of Flight★, S : 6 m. by B 1347 – Preston Mill★, S : 8½ m. by A 198 and B 1047 - Tyninghame★, S : 7 m. by A 198 – Coastal road from North Berwick to Portseton★, SW : 13 m by A 198 and B 1348.

18 North Berwick, West Links, Beach Rd ☎ 892135 – 18 Glen, East Links ☎ 892221.

ℹ Quality St., EH39 4HJ ☎ 892197.

♦Edinburgh 24 – ♦Newcastle upon Tyne 102.

Marine (Forte Heritage), 18 Cromwell Rd, EH39 4LZ, ☎ 892406, Fax 894480, ≤ golf course and Firth of Forth, ≘s, ⛆ heated, ⛱, ⚘ – |‡| ⊭ TV ☎ ℗ – 🏛 250. Ⓢ AE ⓓ VISA JCB
Meals 8.95/29.95 **st.** and dinner a la carte ⧫ 6.50 – ☐ 10.95 – **74 rm** 70.00/100.00 **st.** 5 suites – SB.

Point Garry, 20 West Bay Rd, EH39 4AW, ☎ 892380, Fax 892848, ≤ – TV ☎ ℗. Ⓢ VISA
April-October – **Meals** 10.50/15.95 **t.** and dinner a la carte – **15 rm** ☐ 40.00/100.00 **t.** – SB.

Craigview without rest., 5 Beach Rd, EH39 4AB, ☎ 892257 – ⊭ TV. ⚘
2 rm ☐ 20.00/40.00 **st.**, 1 suite.

OBAN Argyll. (Strathclyde) 401 D 14 Scotland G. – pop. 8 203 – ☎ 01631.

Exc. : Loch Awe★★, SE : 17 m. by A 85 – Bonawe Furnace★, E : 12 m. by A 85 – Cruachan Power Station★ *AC*, E : 16 m. by A 85 – Sea Life Centre★ *AC*, N : 14 m. by A 828.

18 Glencruitten Rd ☎ 62868/64115.

Access to Glasgow by helicopter.

⛴ to Isle of Mull (Craignure) (Caledonian MacBrayne Ltd) (40 mn) – to Isle of Barra (Castlebay) via South Uist (Lochboisdale) (Caledonian MacBrayne Ltd) (summer only) – to Isle of Tiree (Scarinish) via Isle of Mull (Tobermory) and Isle of Coll (Arinagour) (Caledonian MacBrayne Ltd) 3 weekly (4 h 15 mn) – to Isle of Islay (Port Askaig) and Kintyre Peninsula (Kennacraig) (Caledonian MacBrayne Ltd) (summer only) – to Isle of Lismore (Achnacroish) (Caledonian MacBrayne Ltd) 2-4 daily (50 mn) – to Isle of Colonsay (Scalasaig) (Caledonian MacBrayne Ltd) (2 h 15 mn).

ℹ Boswell House, Argyll Sq., PA34 4AR ☎ 63122.

♦Edinburgh 123 – ♦Dundee 116 – ♦Glasgow 93 – ♦Inverness 118.

Manor House, Gallanach Rd, PA34 4LS, ☎ 562087, Fax 563053, ≤, ⛱ – ⊭ rest TV ☎ ℗. Ⓢ AE VISA
closed January – **Meals** (lunch by arrangement)/dinner 22.90 **t.** and a la carte ⧫ 4.90 – **11 rm** ☐ (dinner included) 80.00/140.00 **t.** – SB.

Barriemore, Corran Esplanade, PA34 5AQ, ☎ 566356, ≤ – ⊭ TV ℗. Ⓢ VISA
closed February and December – **Meals** *(closed Monday)* (dinner only) 18.50 **st.** ⧫ 4.95 – **13 rm** ☐ 54.00 **st.**

Kilchrenan House without rest., Corran Esplanade, PA34 5AQ, ☎ 562663, Fax 562663, ≤ – TV ☎ ℗. Ⓢ VISA. ⚘
Easter-October – **10 rm** ☐ 23.00/60.00 **t.**

at Kilmore S : 4 m. on A 816 – ✉ Oban – ☎ 01631 :

Glenfeochan House ⑤, PA34 4QR, S : ½ m. on A 816 ☎ 770273, Fax 770624, ≤, « Victorian country house in extensive gardens », ⛱, park – ⊭ TV ℗. Ⓢ AE VISA. ⚘
May-October – **Meals** (residents only) (communal dining) (dinner only) 30.00 **st.** ⧫ 6.95 – **3 rm** ☐ 100.50/134.00 **t.**

at Kilninver SW : 8 m. by A 816 on B 844 – ✉ Oban – ☎ 01852 :

Knipoch, PA34 4QT, NE : 1½ m. on A 816 ☎ 316251, Fax 316249, ≤, ⛱ – ⊭ rest TV ☎ ℗. Ⓢ AE ⓓ VISA. ⚘
mid February-mid November – **Meals** (lunch by arrangement)/dinner 29.50 **t.** ⧫ 6.20 – **17 rm** ☐ 65.00/130.00 **t.**

OLDMELDRUM Aberdeen. (Grampian) 401 N 11 – ☎ 01651.

♦Edinburgh 140 – ♦Aberdeen 17 – ♦Inverness 87.

Meldrum House ⑤, AB51 0AE, N : 1½ m. on A 947 ☎ 872294, Fax 872464, ≤, « Part 13C baronial house », ⛱, park – ⊭ rest TV ☎ ℗. Ⓢ VISA
Meals 11.50/26.50 **t.** ⧫ 6.00 – **9 rm** ☐ 80.00/120.00 **t.** – SB.

ONICH Inverness. (Highland) 401 E 13 – ECD : Saturday except summer – ✉ Fort William – ☎ 01855.

Edinburgh 123 – ◆Glasgow 93 – ◆Inverness 79 – ◆Oban 39.

The Lodge on the Loch, Creag Dhu, PH33 6RY, on A 82 ✆ 821237, Fax 821463, ⩽ Loch Linnhe and mountains, – rest TV ☎ ♿ P. VISA
closed January – **Meals** 11.00/27.00 **st.** and lunch a la carte 6.00 – **20 rm** (dinner included) 75.00/150.00 **st.** – SB.

Onich, PH33 6RY, on A 82 ✆ 821214, Fax 821484, ⩽ Loch Linnhe and mountains, « Lochside setting », – rest TV ☎ P. AE VISA JCB
Meals (bar lunch)/dinner 15.00 **st.** 4.50 – **27 rm** 31.00/76.00 **st.** – SB.

Allt-Nan-Ros, PH33 6RY, on A 82 ✆ 821210, Fax 821462, ⩽ Loch Linnhe and mountains, – rest TV ☎ P. AE VISA
Meals 19.50 **st.** (dinner) and lunch a la carte 10.50/14.50 – **20 rm** (dinner included) 69.50/155.00 **st.** – SB.

Cuilcheanna House, PH33 6SD, ✆ 821226, ⩽, – P. VISA
April-October – **Meals** 14.50 **st.** 4.00 – **6 rm** 33.00/46.00 **st.**

ORD Inverness (Highland) 401 C 12 – see Skye (Isle of).

ORKNEY ISLANDS Orkney. (Orkney Islands) 401 KL 6/7 Scotland G. – pop. 19 612.

See : Islands★★.

Envir. : Old Man of Hoy★★★ – Maes Howe★★ *AC* – Skara Brae★★ *AC* – Corrigal Farm Museum★ *AC* – Brough of Birsay★ *AC* – Birsay (⩽★) – Ring of Brodgar★ – Stromness★ (Pier Arts Centre, collection of abstract art★) – Unston Cairn★.

✈ see Kirkwall.

⛴ service between Isle of Hoy (Longhope), Isle of Hoy (Lyness), Isle of Flotta and Houton (Orkney Islands Shipping Co. Ltd) frequent services daily (except Sundays) – from Stromness to Scrabster (P & O Scottish Ferries) (1 h 45 mn) – from Stromness to Shetland Islands (Lerwick) via Aberdeen (P & O Scottish Ferries) – from Kirkwall to Westray, Stronsay via Eday and Sanday (Orkney Islands Shipping Co. Ltd) 2 daily – from Tingwall via Eglisay, Wyre and Rousay (Orkney Islands Shipping Co. Ltd) 5 daily – from Kirkwall to Shapinsay (Orkney Islands Shipping Co. Ltd) (25 mn) – from Stromness to Graemsay, Houton and Isle of Hoy (Lyness) (Orkney Islands Shipping Co. Ltd) 1 weekly – from Kirkwall to North Ronaldsay (Orkney Islands Shipping Co. Ltd) 1 weekly (2 h 30 mn).

⛴ from Burwick (South Ronaldsay) to John O'Groats (John O'Groats Ferries) (summer only) 4 daily (45 mn).

Burray – ☎ 01856.

Ankersted, KW17 2SS, E : ½ m. on A 961 ✆ 731217, ⩽ – TV P. VISA.
Meals (by arrangement) 11.00 **st.** – **4 rm** 16.00/32.00 **st.**

Dounby – ☎ 01856.

Smithfield, KW17 2HT, ✆ 771215, Fax 771494 – rest TV P. VISA.
April-October – **Meals** 10.00/15.00 **st.** and a la carte 3.70 – **7 rm** 25.00/50.00 **st.**

Finstown – ☎ 01856.

Atlantis Lodges, KW17 2EH, ✆ 761581, Fax 875361, ⩽ – TV ☎ P. VISA.
Meals (by arrangement) (dinner only) 30.00 5.00 – **1 rm** 23.00/46.00 **st.**, **13 suites** 36.00/45.00 **st.** – SB.

Kirkwall Scotland G. – pop. 5 952 – ☎ 01856.

See : Kirkwall★★ – St. Magnus Cathedral★★ – Earl's Palace★ *AC* – Tankerness House Museum★ *AC*.

Exc. : Western Mainland★★ – Italian Chapel★ *AC*.

18 Grainbank ✆ 872457.

✈ Kirkwall Airport : ✆ 872421, S : 3½ m.

6 Broad St., Kirkwall, KW15 1NX ✆ 872856.

Ayre, Ayre Rd, KW15 1QX, ✆ 873001, Fax 876289 – TV ☎ P – 150. AE VISA
Meals 18.00 **t.** (dinner) and a la carte 15.80/29.00 **t.** 4.00 – **33 rm** 52.00/84.00 **t.** – SB.

Foveran, St. Ola, KW15 1SF, SW : 3 m. on A 964 ✆ 872389, Fax 876430, ⩽, « Overlooking Scapa Flow », – rest TV ☎ P. VISA.
closed January – **Meals** *(closed Sunday to non-residents)* (dinner only) 25.00 **t.** and a la carte 4.50 – **8 rm** 45.00/70.00 **st.**

Albert, Mounthoolie Lane, KW15 1JZ, pedestrian area off Junction Rd ✆ 876000, Fax 875397 – TV ☎. AE VISA
closed 25 December and 1 January – **Meals** (bar lunch)/dinner 15.00 **st.** and a la carte – **19 rm** 48.00/75.00 **st.** – SB.

Queens, Shore St., KW15 1LG, ✆ 872200, Fax 873871 – TV ☎. VISA.
Meals (in bar) a la carte 7.40/17.55 **t.** – **9 rm** 26.00/40.00 **t.**

St. Ola without rest., Harbour St., KW15 1LE, ✆ 875090, Fax 875090 – TV ☎. VISA.
6 rm 28.00/40.00 **t.**

West End, Main St., KW15 1BU, ✆ 872368, Fax 876181 – TV ☎ P. VISA
Meals (bar lunch)/dinner 14.00 **st.** and a la carte 4.85 – **16 rm** 33.00/54.00 **st.**

Polrudden, Peerie Sea Loan, KW15 1UH, W : ¾ m. by Pickaquoy Rd ✆ 87476
Fax 874761 – rest TV P
Meals (by arrangement) 10.50 **s.** – **7 rm** 27.00/44.00 **st.**

Brekk-Ness, Muddisdale Rd, KW15 1RS, W : 1 m. by Pickaquoy Rd ✆ 87431
Fax 874317 – rest TV P
Meals (by arrangement) 11.00 **t.** – **11 rm** 28.00/46.00 **t.**

ATS Junction Rd, Kirkwall ✆ 872361/872158

Loch Harray – 01856.

Merkister, KW17 2LF, off A 986 ✆ 771366, Fax 771515, ←, – TV ☎ P.
VISA
April-October – **Meals** (bar lunch Monday to Saturday)/dinner 18.75 **t.** and a la carte 5.00
14 rm 33.00/72.00 **t.** – SB.

St. Margaret's Hope – 01856.

Murray Arms, Back Rd, KW17 2SP, ✆ 831205 – P.
Meals (residents only on Monday) (in bar) 8.00/13.20 **st.** and a la carte – **5 rm** 20.00
40.00 **st.**

Anchorage, Back Rd, KW17 2SP, ✆ 831456 – TV
Meals 18.00 – **4 rm** 17.00/34.00 **st.**

Creel with rm, Front Rd, KW17 2SL, ✆ 831311, ← – rm TV P. VISA.
closed Sunday to Thursday November-April and January – **Meals** (lunch by arrangement)
dinner 17.50/23.50 **st.** 5.75 – **3 rm** 27.00/50.00 **t.**

Stenness – 01856.

Standing Stones, KW16 3JX, on A 965 ✆ 850449, Fax 851262, – rm TV ☎ P
VISA.
Meals (booking essential) (bar lunch)/dinner 19.50 **st.** and a la carte – **17 rm** 37.50
90.00 **st.** – SB.

Stromness – 01856.

Stenigar, Ness Rd, KW16 3DW, S : ½ m. ✆ 850438, ←, – TV P.
May-October – **Meals** (by arrangement) (communal dining) 15.00 – **4 rm** 25.00/44.00 **st**

Thira, Innertown, KW16 3JP, W : 1½ m. by Back Rd, Outertown rd, then first right
onto unmarked road and left turn after ½ m. ✆ 851181, ← Hoy Island and Sound, –
TV P
closed December – **Meals** (by arrangement) 8.00 – **4 rm** 22.00/44.00 **st.**

PEAT INN Fife. (Fife) 401 L 15 – Cupar – 01334.
Edinburgh 45 – Dundee 21 – Perth 28.

The Peat Inn with rm, KY15 5LH, ✆ 840206, Fax 840530, – rest TV ☎ & P.
AE VISA
Meals *(closed Sunday, Monday, 25 December and 1 January)* (booking essential) 18.50/
28.00 **st.** and dinner a la carte 27.50/32.50 **st.** 9.00 – **1 rm** 95.00 **st.**, **7 suites** 135.00/
145.00 **st.**.

PEEBLES Peebles. (Borders) 401 402 K 17 **Scotland G.** – pop. 7 065 – 01721.
Exc. : Traquair House★★ *AC*, SE : 7 m. by B 7062 – Rosslyn Chapel★★ *AC*, N : 16½ m. by A 703, A 6094, B 7026 and B 7003 – The Tweed Valley★★, SE : 11 m. by A 72.
18 Kirkland St. ✆ 720197.
High St., EH45 8AG ✆ 720138 (summer only).
Edinburgh 24 – Hawick 31 – Glasgow 53.

Peebles Hydro, Innerleithen Rd, EH45 8LX, ✆ 720602, Fax 722999, ←, , , , ,
park, , squash – TV ☎ P – 450. AE VISA.
Meals 15.00/21.00 **st.** 6.50 – **135 rm** (dinner included) 65.00/122.50 **st.**, 2 suites – SB.

Cringletie House, EH45 8PL, N : 3 m. on A 703 ✆ 730233, Fax 730244, ←, « Victorian country house in extensive grounds », , park, – rest TV ☎ P. AE VISA
closed 2 January-7 March – **Meals** 24.50 **t.** (dinner) and lunch a la carte 11.25/12.75 **t.** –
13 rm 52.50/104.00 **s.** – SB.

Park, Innerleithen Rd, EH45 8BA, ✆ 720451, Fax 723510, – TV ☎ P. AE VISA
Meals (bar lunch)/dinner a la carte 10.70/16.20 **t.** 6.50 – **24 rm** (dinner included)
63.50/125.00 **t.** – SB.

PENNAN Aberdeen. (Grampian) 401 N 10 – – New Aberdour – 01346.
Edinburgh 181 – Aberdeen 51 – Fraserburgh 12 – Inverness 85.

Pennan Inn, 17-19 Main St., AB43 4JB, ✆ 561201, Fax 561437 – TV. AE VISA.
Meals *(closed Sunday and Monday)* (bar lunch)/dinner a la carte 8.75/26.00 **st.** 3.75 –
5.00 – **6 rm** 35.00/50.00 **st.**

ENNYGHAEL Argyll (Strathclyde) – see Mull (Isle of).

ERTH Perth. (Tayside) 401 J 14 **Scotland G.** – pop. 123 495 – ☎ 01738.

ee : City★ – Black Watch Regimental Museum★ Y **M1** – Georgian Terraces★ Y – Museum and rt Gallery★ Y **M2.**

nvir. : Scone Palace★★ *AC*, N : 2 m. by A 93 Y – Branklyn Garden★ *AC*, SE : 1 m. by A 85 Z – innoull Hill (≤★) SE : 1¼ m. by A 85 Z – Huntingtower Castle★ *AC*, NW : 3 m. by A 85 Y – Elcho astle★ *AC*, SE : 4 m. by A 912 – Z – and Rhynd rd.

xc. : Abernethy (11C Round Tower★), SE : 8 m. by A 912 – Z – and A 913.

Craigie Hill, Cherrybank ☎ 624377 Z – 18 King James VI, Moncreiffe Island ☎ 625170/632460 – 18 Murrayshall, New Scone ☎ 651171 Y – 18 North Inch, c/o Perth & Kinross District Council, High St. ☎ 336481 Y.

45 High St., PH1 5TJ ☎ 638353 – Caithness Glass Car Park, A 9 Western City by pass ☎ 638481 (summer only).

Edinburgh 44 – ◆Aberdeen 86 – ◆Dundee 22 – Dunfermline 29 – ◆Glasgow 64 – ◆Inverness 112 – ◆Oban 94.

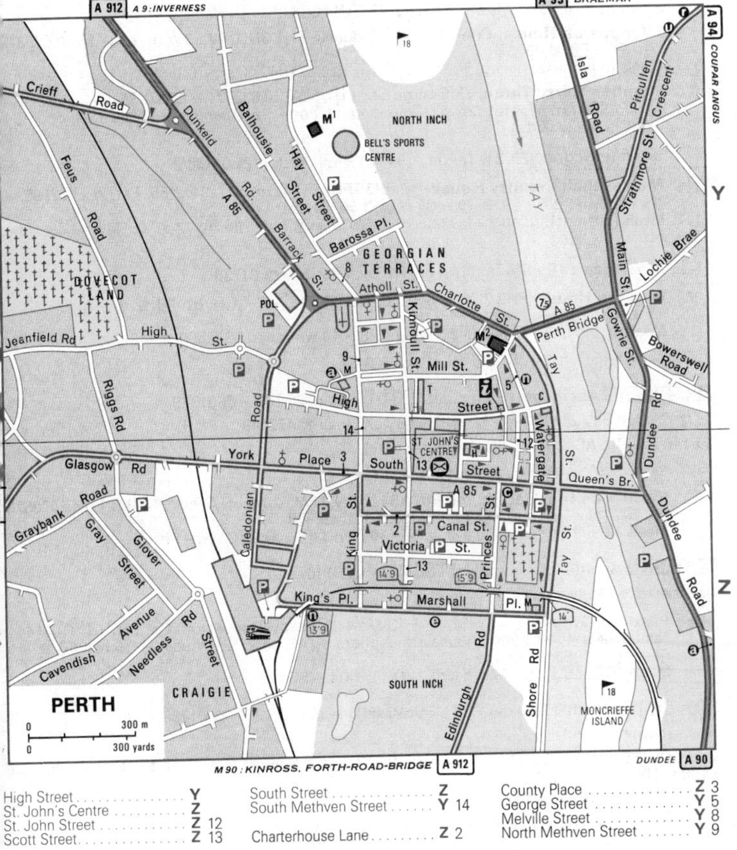

High Street	Y		South Street	Z		County Place	Z 3
St. John's Centre	Z		South Methven Street	Y 14		George Street	Y 5
St. John Street	Z 12					Melville Street	Y 8
Scott Street	Z 13		Charterhouse Lane	Z 2		North Methven Street	Y 9

Dupplin Castle ⛰, SW : 6¼ m. by A 93 on A 9 ☎ 623224, Fax 444140, ≤, « Country house atmosphere, gardens », park – ⇋ rm ☎ **P**. VISA JCB. ✱
Meals (residents only) (booking essential) (communal dining) (dinner only) 33.00 **t.** – **4 rm** ☐ 60.00/90.00 **t.**

Hunting Tower ⛰, Crieff Rd, PH1 3JT, W : 3½ m. by A 85, ☎ 583771, Fax 583777, TV ☎ **P** – 180. AE VISA
Meals 11.95/19.75 **t.** and a la carte 6.50 – **15 rm** ☐ 68.00/85.00 **t.**, 10 suites – SB.

Parklands, St. Leonard's Bank, PH2 8EB, ☎ 622451, Fax 622046, – rest TV ☎ P. AE VISA Z
closed 23 December-8 January – **Meals** 15.50/24.95 **t.** and a la carte – **14 rm** 70.00/120.00 **t.** – SB.

Stakis Perth, West Mill St., PH1 5QP, ☎ 628281, Fax 643423 – rm TV ☎ P – 150. AE VISA Y
Meals 16.50 **st.** and a la carte – 8.50 – **76 rm** 67.00/97.00 **st.** – SB.

Sunbank House, 50 Dundee Rd, PH2 7BA, ☎ 624882, Fax 442515, – TV ☎ P. VISA. Z
closed January – **Meals** (dinner only) 18.95 **t.** 5.75 – **9 rm** 38.00/64.00 **t.** – SB.

Lochiel House without rest., Pitcullen Cres., PH2 7HT, ☎ 633183 – TV P. Y
3 rm 19.00/38.00 **s.**

Pitcullen without rest., 17 Pitcullen Cres., PH2 7HT, ☎ 626506, Fax 628265 – TV P. VISA. Y
6 rm 18.00/40.00 **st.**

Park Lane without rest., 17 Marshall Pl., PH2 8AG, ☎ 637218, Fax 643519 – TV P. VISA. Z
February-early December – **6 rm** 22.00/44.00 **s.**

Ellengowan House, Crieff Rd, Almondbank, PH1 3NG, W : 3½ m. on A 85 ☎ 583372, – TV ☎ P.
Meals (communal dining) 10.50 **st.** – **3 rm** 23.00/40.00 **st.** – SB.

Number Thirty Three, 33 George St., PH1 5LA, ☎ 633771 – AE VISA Y
closed Sunday, Monday, 25 and 26 December and 9 to 30 January – **Meals** - Seafood - a la carte 11.60/23.00 **t.** 6.50.

at New Scone NE : 2½ m. on A 94 – Y – ✉ Perth – ☎ 01738 :

Murrayshall Country House , PH2 7PH, E : 1½ m. by A 94 ☎ 551171, Fax 552595, ←, 18, , park, – TV ☎ P – 60. AE VISA.
Meals (bar lunch)/dinner a la carte 16.50/20.90 **st.** 8.50 – **16 rm** 70.00/140.00, 3 suites – SB.

at Glencarse E : 6¼ m. on A 85 – Y – ✉ Perth – ☎ 01738 :

Newton House, PH2 7LX, ☎ 860250, Fax 860717, – rest TV ☎ P – 30. AE VISA
Meals 10.50/19.50 **st.** and a la carte 6.75 – **10 rm** 60.00/90.00 **st.** – SB.

ATS Inveralmond Ind. Est., Ruthvenfield Rd ☎ 629481

PETERHEAD Aberdeen. (Grampian) 401 O 11 – pop. 20 789 – ☎ 01779.

18, 9 Cruden Bay ☎ 812285 – 18, 9 Craigewan Links ☎ 472149.

54 Broad St., AB42 ☎ 471904 (summer only).

Edinburgh 165 – Aberdeen 35 – Fraserburgh 18.

Waterside Inn, Fraserburgh Rd, AB42 7BN, NW : 2 m. on A 952 ☎ 471121, Fax 470670, – rm TV ☎ P – 50. AE VISA
Meals 18.95 **t.** (dinner) and a la carte – **109 rm** 69.00/99.00 **st.** – SB.

PITCAPLE Aberdeen. (Grampian) 401 M 12 – ☎ 01467.

Edinburgh 51 – Aberdeen 21.

Pittodrie House , AB51 5HS, SW : 1 ¾ m. by Chapel off Garioch rd ☎ 681444, Fax 681648, ←, « Country house atmosphere », , park, , squash – rest TV ☎ P – 120. AE VISA
Meals 16.00/27.50 **t.** – **27 rm** 92.00/115.00 **t.** – SB.

PITLOCHRY Perth. (Tayside) 401 I 13 **Scotland G.** – pop. 3 126 – ☎ 01796.

See : Town★.

Exc. : Blair Castle★★ *AC*, NW : 7 m. by A 9 – Queen's View★★, W : 7 m. by B 8019 – Falls of Bruar★, NW : 11 m. by A 9.

18 Golf Course Rd ☎ 472792.

22 Atholl Rd, PH16 5BX ☎ 472215/472751.

Edinburgh 71 – Inverness 85 – Perth 27.

Pine Trees , Strathview Terr., PH16 5QR, ☎ 472121, Fax 472460, ←, , park – TV ☎ P. VISA.
Meals 15.50/23.00 **t.** – **20 rm** 51.00/94.00 **t.**

Green Park, Clunie Bridge Rd, PH16 5JY, ☎ 473248, Fax 473520, ←, – rest TV ☎ P. VISA.
28 March-27 October – **Meals** (bar lunch)/dinner 19.50 **t.** and a la carte 4.95 – **37 rm** 48.00/96.00 **t.** – SB.

Dunfallandy House ⑧, Logierait Rd, Dunfallandy, PH16 5NA, S : 1 ¼ m. by Bridge Rd ☎ 472648, Fax 472017, ≤, – TV P. VISA.
February-October – **Meals** (bar lunch)/dinner 16.50 **st.** 3.95 – **8 rm** 25.00/64.00 **st.** – SB.

Knockendarroch House, 2 Higher Oakfield, PH16 5HT, ☎ 473473, Fax 474068, ≤, – TV P. AE VISA
April-October – **Meals** (residents only) (dinner only) 15.00 **st.** 4.00 – **12 rm** (dinner included) 90.00/100.00 **t.** – SB.

Westlands of Pitlochry, 160 Atholl Rd, PH16 5AR, ☎ 472266, Fax 473994, – TV ☎ P. VISA
Meals (bar lunch)/dinner 18.50 **st.** 4.45 – **15 rm** 33.00/76.00 **st.** – SB.

Claymore, 162 Atholl Rd, PH16 5AR, ☎ 472888, Fax 474037, – TV ☎ P. VISA
closed January – **Meals** (bar lunch)/dinner 16.00 4.75 – **12 rm** 34.00/68.00 **st.** – SB.

Acarsaid, 8 Atholl Rd, PH16 5BX, ☎ 472389, Fax 473952 – rest TV ☎ P. VISA.
10 March-4 December – **Meals** (light lunch)/dinner 17.00 **st.** 4.00 – **18 rm** 27.50/65.00 **st.** – SB.

Balrobin, Higher Oakfield, PH16 5HT, ☎ 472901, Fax 474200, ≤, – rest TV P. VISA
March-October and New Year – **Meals** (residents only) (dinner only) 14.50 **t.** 5.00 – **15 rm** 25.00/59.00 **t.** – SB.

Birchwood, 2 East Moulin Rd, PH16 5DW, ☎ 472477, Fax 473951, – rest TV ☎ P. VISA.
March-November – **Meals** 15.00/18.00 **t.** and a la carte 5.25 – **17 rm** 28.00/70.00 **t.** – SB.

Torrdarach, Golf Course Rd, PH16 5AU, ☎ 472136, – TV P.
Easter-mid October – **Meals** (by arrangement) 15.00 **st.** – **7 rm** 25.00/50.00 **st.** – SB.

Dundarave, Strathview Terr., PH16 5AT, ☎ 473109, ≤, – rest TV P
March-November – **Meals** 13.95 **st.** – **7 rm** 28.00/56.00 **st.**

XX **East Haugh House** with rm, East Haugh, PH16 5JS, SE : 2 m. by A 924 ☎ 473121, Fax 472473, – rest TV ☎ P. VISA
closed 25 and 26 December – **Meals** (bar lunch)/dinner 23.95 **t.** 5.50 – **8 rm** 49.00/64.00 **t.** – SB.

at Killiecrankie NW : 4 m. by A 924 and B 8019 on B 8079 – ✉ Pitlochry – ☎ 01796 :

Killiecrankie, PH16 5LG, ☎ 473220, Fax 472451, ≤, – rest TV ☎ P. VISA
closed January, February and early March – **Meals** (bar lunch)/dinner 27.50 **t.** 5.50 – **9 rm** (dinner included) 76.00/152.00 **t.**, 1 suite – SB.

PLOCKTON Ross and Cromarty. (Highland) 401 D 11 Scotland G. – ☎ 01599.

See : Village★.

◆Edinburgh 210 – ◆Inverness 88.

Haven, 3 Innes St., IV52 8TW, ☎ 544223, Fax 544467, ≤, – rest TV ☎ P. VISA.
closed 20 December-1 February – **Meals** (lunch by arrangement) 8.50/22.00 **t.** 4.95 – **13 rm** (dinner included) 54.00/108.00 **t.** – SB.

Plockton, Harbour St., IV52 8TN, ☎ 544274, Fax 544274, ≤ Loch Carron, – TV. VISA
Meals (in bar) a la carte 8.95/18.75 **t.** 4.75 – **7 rm** 27.50/50.00 **t.**

POLLOCHAR Western Isles (Outer Hebrides) – see Uist (Isles of).

POLMONT Stirling. (Central) 401 402 I 16 – see Falkirk.

POOLEWE Ross and Cromarty. (Highland) 401 D 10 – ☎ 01445.

Envir. : Inverwe Gardens★★★, N : 1 m. on B 8057.

◆Edinburgh 234 – ◆Inverness 78 – Kyle of Lochalsh 74.

Pool House, IV22 2LE, ☎ 781272, Fax 781403, ≤ Loch Ewe – TV P. VISA.
closed January and February – **Meals** (bar lunch)/dinner 21.50 **st.** 7.50 – **12 rm** 36.00/80.00 **st.** – SB.

PORT APPIN Argyll. (Strathclyde) 401 D 14 – ✉ Appin – ☎ 01631.

◆Edinburgh 136 – Ballachulish 20 – ◆Oban 24.

⊛ **Airds** (Allen) ⑧, PA38 4DF, ☎ 730236, Fax 730535, ≤ Loch Linnhe and hills of Kingairloch, « Former ferry inn », – rest TV ☎ P. AE VISA.
Meals (light lunch)/dinner 35.00 **t.** – **12 rm** 95.00/195.00 **t.** – SB
Spec. Crab tart with salad and tomato coulis, Monkfish with lobster mousse, squat lobsters and a basil butter sauce, Roast fillet of lamb with spices, roast garlic and an aubergine fritatta.

PORT OF MENTEITH Perth. (Central) 401 H15 – ☎ 01877.

◆Edinburgh 53 – ◆Glasgow 30 – Stirling 17.

Lake ⑧, FK8 3RA, ☎ 385258, Fax 385671, ≤, « Lakeside setting » – rest TV ☎ P. AE VISA
Meals 15.95/21.90 **t.** and dinner a la carte 4.00 – **12 rm** (dinner included) 79.00/153.00 **t.** – SB.

PORTPATRICK Wigtown. (Dumfries and Galloway) 401 402 E 19 – pop. 842 – ✉ Stranraer – ☎ 01776.

18, 9 Portpatrick Dunskey, Golf Course Rd ℘ 810273.

◆Edinburgh 141 – ◆Ayr 60 – ◆Dumfries 80 – Stranraer 9.

- ✿ **Knockinaam Lodge** ⛰, DG9 9AD, SE : 5 m. by A 77 off B 7042 ℘ 81047 Fax 810435, ←, « Country house in picturesque coastal setting », ⛰, ⛰, park – ⛔ re TV ☎ P. ⛰ AE ⓘ VISA
  Meals (booking essential) (light lunch) 25.00/35.00 **t.** 🍷 8.00 – **10 rm** ☐ 80.00/160.00 **t.**
  Spec. Marinated scallops in a potato parcel with homemade courgette chutney, Roasted quail stuffed with a mousse chicken, sweetbreads and apricots, Layered mixed chocolate terrine with a caramelised orange sauce.
- **Fernhill,** Heugh Rd, DG9 8TD, ℘ 810220, Fax 810596, ←, ⛰ – TV ☎ ♿ P. ⛰ AE VISA
  closed 25 and 26 December – **Meals** 8.50/19.50 **t.** and a la carte 🍷 4.35 – **20 rm** ☐ 55.0 99.00 **t.** – SB.
- Crown, DG9 8SX, ℘ 810261, Fax 810551, ← – ⛔ rest TV ☎
  12 rm.
- **Blinkbonnie,** School Brae, DG9 8LG, ℘ 810282, ←, ⛰ – ⛔ TV P. ⛔
  closed December – **Meals** (by arrangement) 10.50 **st.** – **5 rm** ☐ 20.00/35.00 **st.** – SB.

PORTREE Inverness. (Highland) 401 B 11 – see Skye (Isle of).

PRESTWICK Ayr. (Strathclyde) 401 402 G 17 – pop. 13 705 – ☎ 01292.

✈ Prestwick Airport : ℘ 79822 – BY – **Terminal** : Buchanan Bus Station.

✈ see also Glasgow.

ℹ Prestwick Airport, KA9 2PL ℘ 79822 (summer only) – BY.

◆Edinburgh 78 – ◆Ayr 2 – ◆Glasgow 32.

Plan of Built up Area : see Ayr

- **Carlton Toby,** 187 Ayr Rd, KA9 1TP, ℘ 476811, Fax 474845 – TV ☎ P. ⛰ AE ⓘ VISA ⛔ BY
  Meals (bar lunch Thursday) 6.00/15.00 **st.** and a la carte 🍷 4.95 – **37 rm** ☐ 49.50/85.00 **st.** – SB.
- **Travel Inn,** Kilmarnock Rd, Monkton, KA9 2RJ, NE : 3 m. by A 79 at junction of A 77 with A 78 ℘ 678262, Fax 678248 – ⛔ rm TV ♿ P. ⛰ AE ⓘ VISA. ⛔
  Meals (grill rest.) – ☐ 4.95 – **40 rm** 34.50 **t.**
- **Kincraig,** 39 Ayr Rd, KA9 1SY, ℘ 479480 – TV P. ⛔ BY
  Meals (by arrangement) 7.00 – **6 rm** ☐ 22.00/38.00 **st.**

QUOTHQUAN Lanark. (Strathclyde) 401 J 27 **Scotland G.** – ✉ Biggar – ☎ 01899.

Envir. : Biggar★ (Gladstone Court Museum★ *AC* – Greenhill Covenanting Museum★ *AC*) SE 4½ m. by B 7016.

◆Edinburgh 32 – ◆Dumfries 50 – ◆Glasgow 36.

- **Shieldhill** ⛰, ML12 6NA, NE : ¾ m. ℘ 220035, Fax 221092, ←, « Victorian country house, 12C origins », ⛰ – ⛔ TV ☎ P – 🏛 25. ⛰ AE ⓘ VISA. ⛔
  Meals 10.00/31.00 **st.** and lunch a la carte – **11 rm** ☐ 68.00/152.00 **st.** – SB.

RENFREW Renfrew. (Strathclyde) 401 G 16 **Scotland G.** – pop. 24 116 – ☎ 0141.

Envir. : Paisley Museum and Art Gallery (Paisley Shawl Section★) SW : 2¾ m. by A 741.

◆Edinburgh 53 – ◆Glasgow 7.

- **Glynhill,** 169 Paisley Rd, PA4 8XB, ℘ 886 5555, Fax 885 2838, ⛰, ⛰, ⛰ – ⛔ rm TV ☎ P – 🏛 450. ⛰ AE ⓘ VISA JCB. ⛔
  Meals 9.75/29.00 **st.** and a la carte 🍷 4.75 – **125 rm** ☐ 72.00/164.00 – SB.

RHICONICH Sutherland. (Highland) 401 F 8 – ✉ Lairg – ☎ 01971.

◆Edinburgh 249 – Thurso 87 – Ullapool 57.

- **Rhiconich,** IV27 4RN, ℘ 521224, Fax 521732, ← Loch Inchard, ⛰, park – ⛔ rest TV ☎ P. ⛰ VISA
  Meals (bar lunch)/dinner a la carte 9.10/15.20 **st.** 🍷 3.95 – **7 rm** ☐ 29.50/60.00 **st.**

ROCKCLIFFE Kirkcudbright. (Dumfries and Galloway) 401 402 I 19 – ✉ Dalbeattie – ☎ 01556.

◆Edinburgh 100 – ◆Dumfries 20 – Stranraer 69.

- **Millbrae,** DG5 4QG, ℘ 630217 – ⛔ rest TV P
  Meals 9.00 – **5 rm** ☐ 24.00/34.00 **st.**
- **Torbay Farmhouse** ⛰, DG5 4QE, E : ¼ m. ℘ 630403, Fax 630403, ←, ⛰ – ⛔ P
  22 March-late October – **Meals** (by arrangement) 10.00 **st.** – **3 rm** ☐ 26.00/48.00 **st.** – SB.

OGART Sutherland. (Highland) 401 H 9 pop. 419 – ☎ 01408.
Edinburgh 229 – ◆Inverness 73 – ◆Wick 63.

Sciberscross Lodge 🐎, Strath Brora, IV28 3YQ, N : 7 m. by Balnacoil rd ☎ 641246, Fax 641465, ≤ Brora valley and hills, 🎣, 🌳 – **P**. VISA
February-October – **Meals** (communal dining) (dinner only) 45.00 **t.** – **4 rm** (dinner included) 85.00/170.00 **t.**

Rovie Farm 🐎, IV28 3TZ, W : ¾ m. by A 839 ☎ 641209, Fax 641209, ≤, « Working farm », 🌳, park – **P**.
Easter-November 12.00 **st.** – **6 rm** (dinner included) 30.00/60.00.

ROTHES Moray. (Grampian) 401 K 11 **Scotland G.** – pop. 1 520 – ☎ 01340.
Exc. : Glenfiddich Distillery★, SE : 7 m. by A 941.
Dufftown ☎ 820325.
Edinburgh 192 – ◆Aberdeen 62 – Fraserburgh 58 – ◆Inverness 49.

Rothes Glen 🐎, AB38 7AH, N : 3 m. on A 941 ☎ 831254, Fax 831566, ≤, « Country house atmosphere », 🌳, park – TV ☎ **P**. AE VISA
April-October – **Meals** 12.50/23.75 **st.** and a la carte 5.00 – **16 rm** 65.00/90.00 **t.** – SB.

ROTHESAY Bute. (Strathclyde) 401 402 E 16 – see Bute (Isle of).

ROYBRIDGE Inverness. (Highland) 401 F 13 – see Spean Bridge.

ST. ANDREWS Fife. (Fife) 401 L 14 **Scotland G.** – pop. 11 136 – ☎ 01334.
See : City★★ – Cathedral★ (✻★★) *AC* – West Port★.
Exc. : The East Neuk★★, SE : 9 m. by A 917 and B 9131 – Crail★★ (Old Centre★★, Upper Crail★) SE : 9 m. by A 917 – Kellie Castle★ *AC*, S : 9 m. by B 9131 and B 9171 – Ceres★, SW : 9 m. by B 939 - E : Inland Fife★.
18 (x5), 9 Eden, Jubilee, New, Old, Strathtyrum and Balgove Courses ☎ 475757 – 9 St. Michael's, Leuchars ☎ 839365.
78 South St. ☎ 472021.
◆Edinburgh 51 – ◆Dundee 14 – Stirling 51.

St. Andrews Old Course, Old Station Rd, KY16 9SP, ☎ 474371, Telex 76280, Fax 477668, ≤ golf courses and sea, 🏋, ≘, 🏊 – 🛗 ⇔ rm ▤ rest TV ☎ ♿ **P** – 🏛 300. AE VISA JCB
Conservatory : Meals 14.00 **t.** 7.25 – **Grill : Meals** (closed lunch in summer) 15.00/34.50 **t.** 7.25 – **108 rm** 170.00/290.00 **st.**, 17 suites – SB.

Rusacks (Forte Heritage), 16 Pilmour Links, KY16 9JQ, ☎ 474321, Fax 477896, ≤, ≘ – 🛗 ⇔ rest TV ☎ **P** – 🏛 100. AE VISA JCB
Meals 9.50/38.00 **st.** and dinner a la carte 8.40 – 9.50 – **48 rm** 80.00/160.00 **st.**, 2 suites – SB.

Rufflets, Strathkinness Low Rd, KY16 9TX, W : 1½ m. on B 939 ☎ 472594, Fax 478703, ≤, « Country house, gardens » – ⇔ TV ☎ **P** – 🏛 30. AE VISA.
Meals (bar lunch in winter) 16.00/26.00 **st.** and a la carte 7.00 – **25 rm** 69.00/158.00 – SB.

St. Andrews Golf, 40 The Scores, KY16 9AS, ☎ 472611, Fax 472188, ≤ – 🛗 ⇔ rest TV ☎ **P** – 🏛 200. AE VISA
Meals 9.95/25.00 **t.** and a la carte 6.50 – **23 rm** 74.00/122.00 **t.** – SB.

The Scores, 76 The Scores, KY16 9BB, ☎ 472451, Fax 473947, ≤, 🌳 – 🛗 ⇔ rest TV ☎ **P** – 🏛 180. AE VISA JCB.
closed 22 to 26 December – **Meals** (bar lunch)/dinner 22.50 **st.** 6.00 – **30 rm** 76.00/150.00 **st.** – SB.

Aslar House without rest., 120 North St., KY16 9AF, ☎ 473460, Fax 473460, 🌳 – TV. VISA.
5 rm 25.00/52.00 **s.**

ST. BOSWELLS Roxburgh. (Borders) 401 402 L 17 **Scotland G.** – pop. 2 092 – ☎ 01835.
Envir. : Dryburgh Abbey★★ *AC* (setting★★★) NW : 4 m. by B 6404 and B 6356.
Exc. : Bowhill★★ *AC*, SW : 11½ m. by A 699 and A 708.
9 St. Boswells ☎ 823858/823527.
◆Edinburgh 39 – ◆Glasgow 79 – Hawick 17 – ◆Newcastle upon Tyne 66.

Dryburgh Abbey 🐎, TD6 0RQ, N : 3½ m. by B 6404 on B 6356 ☎ 822261, Fax 823945, ≤, 🏊, 🎣, 🌳 – 🛗 ⇔ rest TV ☎ **P** – 🏛 120. VISA JCB
Meals 6.50/21.50 **t.** 5.50 – **24 rm** 55.00/150.00 **t.**, 2 suites – SB.

ST. CATHERINES Argyll. (Strathclyde) 401 E 15 **Scotland G.** – ✉ Cairndow – ☎ 01499.
Envir. : Loch Fyne★★.
Exc. : Inveraray★★ : Castle★★ (interior★★★) *AC*, NW : 12 m. by A 815 and A 83 – Auchindrain★, NW : 18 m. by A 815 and A 83.
◆Edinburgh 99 – ◆Glasgow 53 – ◆Oban 53.

Thistle House without rest., PA25 8AZ, on A 815 ☎ 302209, ≤, 🌳 – **P**. VISA
April-October – **5 rm** 25.00/42.00.

ST. FILLANS Perth. (Tayside) 401 H 14 – ☎ 01764.
♦Edinburgh 67 – ♦Glasgow 57 – ♦Oban 64 – Perth 30.

Four Seasons, PH6 2NF, ☎ 685333, Fax 685333, ≤ Loch Earn and mountains – rest TV ☎ P. AE VISA
closed January and February – **Meals** 13.95/24.50 **t.** and a la carte 4.75 – **12 rm** 42.0
86.00 **t.**

Achray House, PH6 2NF, ☎ 685231, Fax 685320, ≤ Loch Earn and mountains, –
☎ P. AE VISA.
March-October – **Meals** (bar lunch Monday to Saturday)/dinner 15.00/21.30 **t.** and a la ca
9 rm 38.00/65.00 **t.**

ST. MARGARET'S HOPE Orkney. (Orkney Islands) 401 K 6 – see Orkney Islands.

SANDYHILLS Kirkcudbright. (Dumfries and Galloway) 401 402 I 19 – ✉ Dalbeattie
☎ 01387.
♦Edinburgh 99 – ♦Ayr 62 – ♦Dumfries 19 – Stranraer 68.

Cairngill House, DG5 4NZ, ☎ 780681, ≤, – TV P.
Meals (bar lunch)/dinner 10.00 **st.** and a la carte 3.00 – **7 rm** 28.00/50.00 **st.** – SB.

SANQUHAR Dumfries (Dumfries and Galloway) 401 402 I 17 pop. 2 680 – ☎ 01659.
Blackaddie Rd ☎ 50577.
Tolbooth, High St. ☎ 50185 (summer only).
♦Edinburgh 58 – Dumfries 27 – ♦Glasgow 24.

Blackaddie House, Blackaddie Rd, DG4 6JJ, N : ¼ m. by A 76 ☎ 50270, Fax 5027
« Riverside setting », – TV P. VISA.
Meals a la carte 11.05/19.85 **t.** 4.95 – **10 rm** 32.00/54.00 **t.** – SB.

Great Britain and Ireland is now covered
by an Atlas at a scale of 1 inch to 4.75 miles.

Three easy to use versions: Paperback, Spiralbound and Hardback.

SCALASAIG Argyll. (Strathclyde) 401 B 15 – see Colonsay (Isle of).

SCALLOWAY Shetland. (Shetland Islands) 401 Q 3 – see Shetland Islands (Mainland).

SCARISTA Inverness. (Outer Hebrides) (Western Isles) 401 Y 10 – see Lewis and Harri
(Isle of).

SCOURIE Sutherland. (Highland) 401 E 8 Scotland G. – ✉ Lairg – ☎ 01971.
Exc. : Cape Wrath★★★ (≤★★) AC, N : 31 m. (including ferry crossing) by A 894 and A 838 –
Loch Assynt★★, S : 17 m. by A 894.
♦Edinburgh 263 – ♦Inverness 107.

Eddrachilles, Badcall Bay, IV27 4TH, S : 2½ m. on A 894 ☎ 502080, Fax 502477
≤ Badcall Bay and islands, , park – TV ☎ P. VISA.
March-October – **Meals** (bar lunch)/dinner 10.90 **t.** and a la carte 3.30 – **11 rm** 47.00
74.00 **t.** – SB.

Scourie, IV27 4SX, ☎ 502396, Fax 502423, ≤, – ☎ P. AE VISA
April-13 October – **Meals** (bar lunch)/dinner 15.50 **t.** 4.50 – **20 rm** 43.00/76.00 **t.** – SB.

SEIL (Isle of) Argyll. (Strathclyde) 401 D 15 – ✉ Oban – ☎ 01852.

Clachan Seil – ✉ Oban – ☎ 01852.

Willowburn, PA34 4TJ, ☎ 300276, ≤, – rest TV P. VISA.
April-October – **Meals** (bar lunch)/dinner 18.00 **t.** and a la carte 5.00 – **6 rm** (dinner
included) 48.00/96.00 – SB.

Easdale – ✉ Oban – ☎ 01852.

Inshaig Park, PA34 4RF, ☎ 300256, ≤ Inner Hebridean Islands, – rest TV P
Easter-mid October – **Meals** (bar lunch)/dinner 16.00 **st.** and a la carte – **6 rm** 44.00/
45.00 **st.**

SELKIRK Selkirk. (Borders) 401 402 L 17 Scotland G. – pop. 6 469 – ☎ 01750.
Envir. : Bowhill★★ AC, W : 3½ m. by A 708 – Abbotsbury★★ AC, NE : 5½ m. by A 7 and B 6360.
Exc. : Melrose Abbey★★ (decorative sculptures★★★) AC, NE : 8½ m. by A 7 and A 6091 – Eildon
Hills (★★★) NE : 7½ m. by A 699 and B 6359 – The Tweed Valley★★, NW : 7½ m. by A 707 and
A 72.

The Hill ☎ 20621.
Halliwell's House, TD7 4BL ☎ 20054 (summer only).
♦Edinburgh 40 – ♦Glasgow 73 – Hawick 11 – ♦Newcastle upon Tyne 73.

Philipburn House, TD7 5LS, W : 1 m. at junction of A 707 with A 708 ☎ 20747,
Fax 21690, heated, – TV ☎ P – 30. AE VISA.
Meals 7.50/25.00 **t.** and a la carte – **16 rm** 62.00/104.00 **t.** – SB.

SHETLAND ISLANDS Shetland. (Shetland Islands) 401 PQ 3 Scotland G. – pop. 22 522.

See : Islands★ - Up Helly Aa★★ (last Tuesday in January) – Jarlshof★★ *AC*.

Tingwall Airport : ✆ (01595) 84306, NW : 6½ m. of Lerwick by A 971.

Unst Airport : at Baltasound ✆ (0195 781) 404.

from Lerwick to Aberdeen via Orkney Islands (Stromness) (P & O Scottish Ferries) – from Lerwick to Republic of Ireland (Skerries) (Shetland Islands Council) booking essential 2 weekly (2 h 30 mn) – from Lerwick (Mainland) to Bressay (Shetland Islands Council) frequent services daily (5 mn) – from Laxo (Mainland) to Isle of Whalsay (Symbister) (Shetland Islands Council) frequent services daily (30 mn) – from Toft (Mainland) to Isle of Yell (Ulsta) (Shetland Islands Council) frequent services daily (20 mn) – from Isle of Yell (Gutcher) to Isle of Unst (Belmont) via Isle of Fetlar (Oddsta) (Shetland Islands Council) (booking essential) – from Fair Isle to Sumburgh (Gruntness) (Shetland Islands Council) 1-2 weekly.

MAINLAND

Brae – 01806.

Busta House, ZE2 9QN, SW : 1½ m. ✆ 522506, Fax 522588, ≤, « Part 16C and 18C country house », – rest TV ☎ P. AE VISA
closed 21 December-4 January – **Meals** (bar lunch)/dinner 22.50 **t.** 4.50 – **20 rm** 63.00/110.00 **t.** – SB.

Lerwick Scotland G. – pop. 7 590 – 01595.

Envir. : Gulber Wick (≤★) S : 2 m. by A 970.

Exc. : Mousa Broch★★★ *AC* (Mousa Island) S : 14 m. – Lerwick to Jarlshof★, S : 22 m. by A 970 – Shetland Croft House Museum★ *AC*, SW : 6 m. by A 970 and A 9073.

18 Lerwick ✆ 695369.

Market Cross, Lerwick, ZE1 0LU ✆ 3434.

Shetland, Holmsgarth Rd, ZE1 0PW, ✆ 695515, Fax 695828, ≤ – TV ☎ P – 250. AE VISA.
Meals (bar lunch)/dinner 26.50 **st.** and a la carte 3.95 – **62 rm** 74.00/85.50 **st.**, 1 suite – SB.

Kveldsro House, Greenfield Pl., ZE1 0AQ, ✆ 692195, Fax 696595 – rest TV ☎ P – 35. AE VISA.
closed 24 December-4 January – **Meals** (bar lunch)/dinner 18.50 **st.** 9.75 – **17 rm** 88.50/105.00 **st.** – SB.

Lerwick, 15 South Rd, ZE1 0RB, ✆ 692166, Fax 694419, ≤, – TV ☎ P. AE VISA
Meals 11.50/26.50 **st.** and a la carte 3.95 – **34 rm** 64.00/76.95 **st.**, 1 suite – SB.

Breiview, 43 Kantersted Rd, ZE1 0RJ, SW : 1 m. by A 970 ✆ 695956 – TV P.
Meals 8.00 **st.** – **5 rm** 25.00/40.00 **st.**

ATS 3 Gremista Ind. Est., Lerwick ✆ 3857

Scalloway – 01595.

Hildasay, Upper Scalloway, ZE1 0UP, NE : ½ m. by A 970 taking unmarked road on left after school ✆ 880822 – TV P
Meals (by arrangement) 8.50 – **3 rm** 21.00/38.00 **s.** – SB.

Broch House without rest., Upper Scalloway, ZE1 0UP, NE : ½ m. by A 970 taking unmarked road on left after school ✆ 880767, Fax 880731 – TV P. VISA.
3 rm 19.00/34.00 **s.**

Walls – 01595.

Burrastow House, ZE2 9PD, SW : 2½ m. ✆ 809307, Fax 809213, ≤, « Part 18C house overlooking Vaila Sound », , park – P. VISA
closed January-mid March – **Meals** *(closed dinner Sunday and Monday to non-residents)* (lunch by arrangement)/dinner 28.50 **t.** – **5 rm** (dinner included) 76.00/142.00 **t.** – SB.

SHIELDAIG Ross and Cromarty. (Highland) 401 D 11 Scotland G. – Strathcarron – 01520.

Exc. : Wester Ross★★★.

◆Edinburgh 226 – ◆Inverness 70 – Kyle of Lochalsh 36.

Tigh-An Eilean, IV54 8XN, ✆ 755251, Fax 755321, ≤ Shieldaig Islands and Loch, « Attractively furnished inn », – rest. AE VISA.
April-October – **Meals** (bar lunch)/dinner 20.50 **t.** 4.25 – **11 rm** (dinner included) 62.00/132.00 **t.**

SKEABOST Inverness. (Highland) 401 B 11 – see Skye (Isle of).

SKELMORLIE Ayr. (Strathclyde) 401 F 16 Scotland G. – pop. 1 736 – 01475.

Exc. : Greenock (≤★★) NE : 8½ m. by A 78 off A 770.

9 Skelmorlie ✆ 520152.

◆Edinburgh 78 – ◆Ayr 39 – ◆Glasgow 32.

Redcliffe House, 25 Shore Rd, PA17 5EH, on A 78 ✆ 521036, Fax 521894, ≤, – TV ☎ P. AE VISA.
Meals 20.00/25.00 **t.** and a la carte 4.50 – **10 rm** 47.50/90.00 **st.** – SB.

SKYE (Isle of) Inverness. (Highland) 401 B 11 /12 **Scotland G.** – pop. 8 868.

See : Island★★ – The Cuillins★★★ – Skye of Island's Life Museum★ *AC*.

Envir. : N : Trotternish Peninsula★★ – W : Duirinish Peninsula★ – Portree★.

from Armadale to Mallaig via Isles of Eigg, Muck, Rhum and Canna (Caledonian MacBrayne Ltd) 3-6 daily (except Sunday) (30 mn) – from Uig to Isle of Harris (Tarbert) (Caledonian MacBrayne Ltd) 1-3 daily (1 h 45 mn) – from Uig to North Uist (Lochmaddy) via Isle of Harris (Tarbert) (Caledonian MacBrayne Ltd) 1-2 daily – from Sconser to Isle of Raasay (Caledonian MacBrayne Ltd) 5 daily (except Sunday) (15 mn).

Ardvasar – 01471.

Ardvasar, IV45 8RS, 844223, – . VISA.
closed November and 21 December-7 January – **Meals** 12.00/25.00 **t.** and a la carte 7.00 – **10 rm** 35.00/65.00 **t.**

Breakish – 01471.

Seagull, IV42 8PY, 822001 – . VISA
Easter-early October – **Meals** (dinner only and lunch Saturday and Sunday) a la carte 11.25/22.70 **st.**

Broadford – 01471.

Dunollie, IV49 9AE, 822253, Fax 822060 – rest . VISA.
Early March-October – **Meals** (bar lunch)/dinner 12.00 **st.** and a la carte 4.50 – **87 rm** 30.00/70.00 **st.** – SB.

Ptarmigan without rest., Harrapool, IV49 9AQ, E : ¾ m. on A 850 822744, Fax 822745, Broadford Bay and islands, « Waterside setting », – . AE VISA
closed 2 weeks winter – **3 rm** 40.00/50.00 **st.**

Earsary without rest., Harrapool, IV49 9AQ, E : ¾ m. on A 850 822697, , , park – .
3 rm 20.00/40.00 **st.**

Westside without rest., Elgol Rd, IV49 9AB, on A 881 822320, – .
3 rm 17.00/36.00 **s.**

Culnaknock – Portree – 01470.

Glenview Inn, IV51 9JH, 562248, Fax 562211, – . VISA
closed 7 January-mid March – **Meals** a la carte 10.00/18.00 **t.** 4.20 – **4 rm** 30.00/60.00 **t.**

Dunvegan – 01470.

Harlosh House , IV55 8ZG, SE : 6 m. by A 863 521367, Fax 521367, Loch Bracadale and Islands – . VISA.
Easter-mid October – **Meals** - Seafood - (dinner only) 24.50 **t.** – **6 rm** 65.00/90.00 **t.**

Dunorin House , Herebost, IV55 8GZ, SE : 2½ m. by A 863 on Roag rd 521488, Fax 521488, , – . VISA.
April-mid November – **Meals** (dinner only) a la carte 18.00/23.00 **st.** 4.00 – **10 rm** 33.00/70.00 **st.** – SB.

Three Chimneys, Colbost, IV55 8ZT, NW : 5¾ m. by A 863 on B 884 511258 – . VISA
closed Sunday and November-March – **Meals** (booking essential) 27.50 **t** (dinner) and lunch a la carte 10.75/24.75 **t.** 6.25.

Flodigarry – Staffin – 01470.

Flodigarry Country House , IV51 9HZ, 552203, Fax 552301, Staffin Island and coastline, – . VISA
Meals (bar lunch Monday to Saturday)/dinner 30.00 **st.** 4.50 – **23 rm** 38.00/104.00 **st.** – SB.

Isleornsay – Sleat – 01471.

Kinloch Lodge , IV43 8QY, N : 3½ m. by A 851 833333, Fax 833277, Loch Na Dal, « 17C former shooting lodge », , , park – . VISA
March-November – **Meals** (dinner only) 35.00 **t.** 4.00 – **10 rm** 90.00/180.00 **t.**

Eilean Iarmain , Camus Cross, IV43 8QR, 833332, Fax 833275, , « 19C inn », – . AE VISA.
Meals 16.50/26.00 **t.** 5.25 – **12 rm** 60.00/85.00 **t.** – SB.

Ord – Sleat – 01471.

Fiordhem , IV43 8RN, 855226, Loch Eishort and Cuillin mountains, « Idyllic setting on shores of Loch Eishort », – .
April-October – **3 rm** (dinner included) 35.00/70.00.

Portree – pop. 2 126 – ☎ 01478.

ℹ Meall House, Portree, IV51 9BZ ✆ 612137.

Cullin Hills ⑤, IV51 9LU, NE : ¾ m. by A 855 ✆ 612003, Fax 613092, ≤, 🌳, park – ⇌ rest 📺 ☎ 🅿 – 🧑‍🏫 40. 🅂 AE VISA
Meals (bar lunch Monday to Saturday)/dinner 21.50 **t.** 🍷 5.95 – **25 rm** ☐ 45.00/100.00 **t.** – SB.

Bosville, Bosville Terr., IV51 9DG, ✆ 612846, Fax 613434, ≤ – ⇌ 📺 ☎ 🅿. 🅂 AE VISA
Meals *(closed Sunday to non-residents)* 9.95/18.00 **st.** and a la carte 🍷 6.00 – **11 rm** ☐ 45.00/80.00 **st.**, 3 suites – SB.

Rosedale, Beaumont Cres., IV51 9DB, ✆ 613131, Fax 612531, ≤ harbour, 🌳 – ⇌ rest 📺 ☎ 🅿. 🅂 VISA
12 May-September – **Meals** (dinner only) 23.00 **t.** 🍷 5.75 – **23 rm** ☐ 35.00/80.00 **t.**

Kings Haven without rest., 11 Bosville Terr., IV51 9DG, ✆ 612290 – 📺. 🅂 VISA. ✗
closed Christmas – **6 rm** ☐ 56.00 **t.**

Burnside without rest., 5 Budmhor, IV51 9DJ, NE : ½ m. by A 855 ✆ 612669, 🌳 – 📺 🅿
April-October – **3 rm** ☐ 18.00/36.00 **st.**

Skeabost – ✉ Skeabost Bridge – ☎ 01470.

⛳9 Skeabost ✆ 532202

Skeabost House ⑤, IV51 9NP, ✆ 532202, Fax 532454, ≤ Loch Snizort Beag, ⛳9, 🎣, 🌳, park – ⇌ rest 📺 ☎ 🅿. 🅂 VISA
April-October – **Meals** (buffet lunch)/dinner 28.00 and a la carte 🍷 6.00 – **26 rm** ☐ 48.00/110.00 **t.** – SB.

Uig – ☎ 01470.

Ferry Inn, IV51 9XP, ✆ 542242 – ⇌ rm 📺 🅿. 🅂 VISA
Meals a la carte 11.00/23.00 **t.** 🍷 4.50 – **6 rm** ☐ 30.00/58.00 **t.** – SB.

Woodbine, Kilmuir Rd, IV51 9XP, ✆ 542243 – 📺 🅿
Meals 10.50 **st.** – **4 rm** ☐ 24.00/37.00 **st.**

Prices For full details of the prices quoted in the guide, consult the introduction.

SPEAN BRIDGE Inverness. (Highland) 401 F 13 – ☎ 01397.
♦Edinburgh 143 – Fort William 10 – ♦Glasgow 94 – ♦Inverness 58 – ♦Oban 60.

Corriegour Lodge, Loch Lochy, PH34 4EB, N : 8¾ m. on A 82 ✆ 712685, Fax 712696, ≤, 🌳 – ⇌ rest 📺 🅿. 🅂 AE VISA. ✗
March-November – **Meals** (dinner only) 19.50 **t.** 🍷 5.00 – **8 rm** ☐ 30.00/80.00 **t.** – SB.

Old Pines ⑤, PH34 4EG, NW : 1½ m. by A 82 on B 8004 ✆ 712324, Fax 712433, ≤, park – ⇌ ♿ 🅿. 🅂 VISA. ✗
closed 2 weeks November – **Meals** (booking essential) 22.50 **st.** – **8 rm** ☐ (dinner included) 50.00/100.00 **st.** – SB.

✗✗ **Old Station,** Station Rd, PH34 4EP, ✆ 712535 – ⇌ 🅿. 🅂 VISA
closed January and Sunday to Wednesday November-March – **Meals** (booking essential) (dinner only) a la carte 14.40/22.00 **t.** 🍷 5.50.

at Roybridge E : 3 m. on A 86 – ☎ 01397 :

Glenspean Lodge ⑤, PH31 4AW, E : 2 m. on A 86 ✆ 712223, Fax 712660, ≤, 🌳 – ⇌ rest 📺 ☎ 🅿. 🅂 AE ⓓ VISA
Meals (bar lunch Monday to Saturday)/dinner 20.50 **t.** and a la carte 🍷 3.20 – **17 rm** ☐ 52.00/100.00 **t.** – SB.

SPITTAL OF GLENSHEE Perth. (Tayside) 401 J 13 **Scotland G.** – ✉ Blairgowrie – ☎ 01250.
Envir. : Glenshee (✳★★) (chairlift *AC*).
♦Edinburgh 69 – ♦Aberdeen 74 – ♦Dundee 35.

Dalmunzie House ⑤, PH10 7QG, ✆ 885224, Fax 885225, ≤, ⛳9, 🎣, 🌳, park, 🎾 – 🛗 🅿. 🅂 VISA
closed November and December – **Meals** (bar lunch)/dinner 20.00 **t.** – **17 rm** ☐ 54.00/88.00 **t.** – SB.

STENNESS Orkney. (Orkney Islands) 401 K 7 – see Orkney Islands.

STEPPS Lanark. (Strathclyde) 401 H 16 – see Glasgow.

STEWARTON Ayr. (Strathclyde) 401 402 G 16 **Scotland G.** – pop. 7 091 – ☎ 01560.
Envir. : Kilmarnock (Dean Castle, arms and armour★, musical instruments★ *AC*) S : 5½ m. by A 735 and B 7038.
♦Edinburgh 68 – ♦Ayr 21 – ♦Glasgow 22.

✗✗✗ **Chapeltoun House** ⑤ with rm, KA3 3ED, SW : 2½ m. by A 735 off B 769 ✆ 482696, Fax 485100, « Country house in extensive grounds », 🎣, 🌳, park – ⇌ rest 📺 ☎ 🅿. 🅂 AE VISA. ✗
closed first week January – **Meals** 15.90/26.40 **t.** – **8 rm** ☐ 69.00/139.00 **t.** – SB.

STIRLING Stirling. (Central) **401** I 15 **Scotland G.** – pop. 30 515 – ✆ 01786.

See : Town★★ – Castle★★ *AC* (Site★★★, external elevations★★★, Stirling Heads★★, Argyll and Sutherland Highlanders Regimental Museum★) B – Argyll's Lodging★ (Renaissance decoration★) B **A** – Church of the Holy Rude★ B **B**.

Envir. : Wallace Monument (✻★★) NE : 2½ m. by A 9 – A – and B 998.

Exc. : Dunblane★ (Cathedral★★, West Front★★), N : 6½ m. by A 9 A.

🅸 41 Dumbarton Rd, FK8 2LQ ℘ 475019 – Royal Stirling Visitor Centre, The Esplanade ℘ 479901 – Motorway Service Area, M 9/M 80, junction 9 ℘ 814111 (summer only).

♦Edinburgh 37 – Dunfermline 23 – Falkirk 14 – ♦Glasgow 28 – Greenock 52 – Motherwell 30 – ♦Oban 87 – Perth 35.

STIRLING

Street	Square	No.
Dumbarton Road	B	10
Leisure Centre	B	
Murray Place	B	15
Port Street	B	
Thistle Centre	B	
Upper Craigs	B	29
Barnton Street	B	2
Borestone Crescent	A	3
Causewayhead Road	A, B	4
Corn Exchange Road	B	5
Cornton Road	A	7
Coxithill Road	A	8
Drummond Place	B	9
Goosecroft Road	B	12
King Street	B	13
Newhouse	A	16
Park Place	A	18
Queen Street	B	20
Randolph Terrace	A	22
St. John Street	B	23
St. Mary's Wynd	B	24
Seaforth Place	B	25
Shirra's Brae Road	A	26
Spittal Street	B	27
Union Street	B	28
Weaver Row	A	31

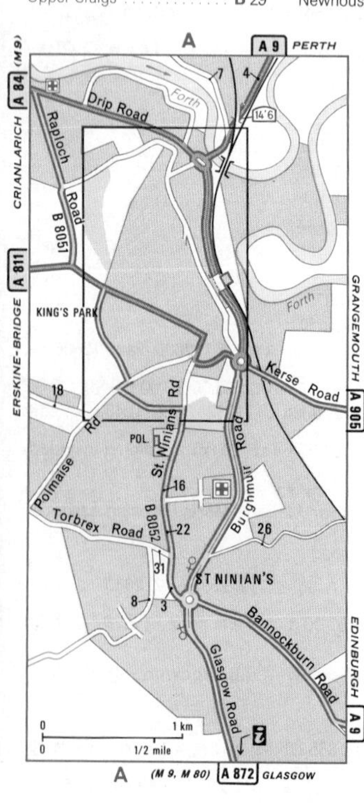

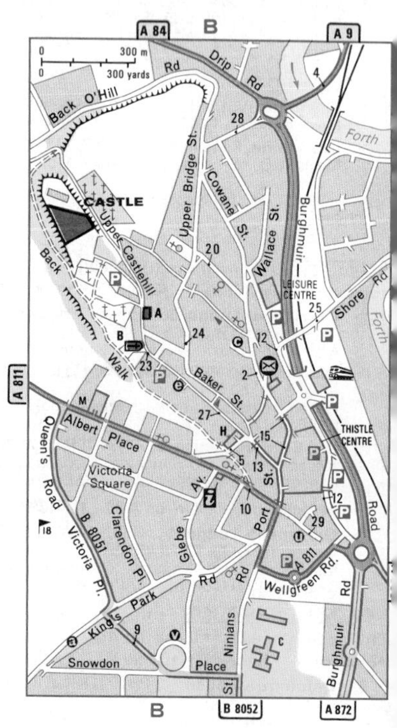

Stirling Highland, Spittal St., FK8 1DU, ℘ 475444, Fax 462929, squash – rm TV ☎ ♿ P – 150. AE VISA B **e**
Scholars : Meals *(closed Sunday dinner)* 21.50 **st.** – **Rizzios : Meals** - Italian - *(closed Saturday lunch)* a la carte 10.45/22.40 **st.** 5.95 – **72 rm** 88.00/114.00 **st.**, 4 suites – SB.

Park Lodge, 32 Park Terr., FK8 2JS, ℘ 474862, Fax 449748, « Tastefully decorated Georgian house, antiques », – TV ☎ P – 40. VISA B **a**
Meals (booking essential Sunday dinner in winter) 12.00/17.00 **st.** and a la carte **t.** 4.50 – **10 rm** 50.00/75.00 **st.** – SB.

Granada Lodge without rest., Pirnhall roundabout, Snabhead, FK7 8EU, S : 3 m. by A 872 ℘ 813614, Fax 815900, Reservations (Freephone) 0800 555300 – TV ☎ ♿ P. AE VISA.
37 rm 39.95 **st.**

Number 10, Gladstone Pl., FK8 2NN, ☎ 472681, – TV. B **v**
Meals (by arrangement) 6.00 **st.** – **3 rm** 20.00/36.00 **st.**

West Plean House without rest., FK7 8HA, S : 3½ m. on A 872 (Denny rd) ☎ 812208, « Working farm », , park – P.
closed 1 December-15 January – **3 rm** 25.00/44.00 **st.**

Fairfield, 14 Princes St., FK8 1HQ, ☎ 472685 – TV. B **c**
Meals (by arrangement) 7.50 **st.** – **6 rm** 20.00/40.00 **st.** – SB.

Regent, 30 Upper Craigs, FK8 2DG, ☎ 472513 – . AE VISA B **u**
Meals - Chinese (Canton, Peking) - 5.60/27.00 **t.** and a la carte 5.90.

at Blairlogie NE : 4½ m. by A 9 on A 91 – A – ✉ Stirling – 01259 :

Blairlogie House, FK9 5QE, ☎ 761441, Fax 761441, , park – TV ☎ P. VISA
closed 24 December-4 January – **Meals** *(closed Sunday)* 16.50 **t.** (dinner) and lunch a la carte approx. 10.00 3.90 – **7 rm** 49.00/68.00 **t.** – SB.

ATS 45 Drip Rd ☎ 450770

STONEHAVEN Kincardine. (Grampian) 401 N 13 – 01569.

◆ Edinburgh 114 – ◆ Aberdeen 16 – ◆ Dundee 51.

Muchalls Castle , AB3 2RS, N : 5 m. by B 979 and A 90 on Netherley rd ☎ 731170, Fax 731480, « Early 17C laird's house, plasterwork ceilings », – rm P.
closed January and February – **Meals** (booking essential) (residents only) (communal dining) (dinner only) 25.00 **st.** – **8 rm** 75.00/120.00 **st.**

ATS 64-72 Barclay St. ☎ 762077

STORNOWAY Ross and Cromarty. (Outer Hebrides) (Western Isles) 401 A 9 – see Lewis and Harris (Isle of).

STRACHUR Argyll. (Strathclyde) 401 E 15 **Scotland G.** pop. 628 – ✉ Cairndow – 01369.

Exc. : Inveraray★★ : Castle★★ (interior★★★) *AC*, NW : 17 m. by A 185 and A 83 – Loch Fyne★★.

◆Edinburgh 104 – ◆Glasgow 58 – ◆Oban 58.

Creggans Inn, PA27 8BX, on A 815 ☎ 860279, Fax 860637, ← Loch Fyne, , – rest TV ☎ P. AE VISA
Meals (bar lunch Monday to Saturday)/dinner 18.90 **t.** and a la carte – **20 rm** 40.00/70.00 **t.** – SB.

STRANRAER Wigtown. (Dumfries and Galloway) 401 402 E 19 **Scotland G.** – pop. 11 348 – 01776.

Exc. : Logan Botanic Garden★ *AC*, S : 11 m. by A 77, A 716 and B 7065.

18 Creachmore, Leswalt ☎ 870245.

to Northern Ireland (Belfast) (Stena Line) frequent services daily (2 h 20 mn) – to Northern Ireland (Belfast) (Hoverspeed Ltd) 4-5 daily (1 h 30 mn).

1 Bridge St., DG9 7JA ☎ 702595 (summer only).

◆Edinburgh 132 – ◆Ayr 51 – ◆Dumfries 75.

North West Castle, Portrodie, DG9 8EH, ☎ 704413, Fax 702646, , – TV ☎ P – 100. VISA
Meals 19.75 **t.** (dinner) and a la carte 14.50/22.00 **st.** 8.00 – **67 rm** 52.00/70.00 **st.**, 4 suites – SB.

Kildrochet House , DG9 9BB, S : 3¼ m. by A 77 on A 716 ☎ 820216, « Former 18C dower house », – P. VISA
Meals (by arrangement) 14.00 **s.** – **3 rm** 26.00/46.00 **s.**

ATS Commerce Rd, Ind. Est. ☎ 702131

STRATHBLANE Stirling. (Central) 401 H 16 – pop. 2 355 – ✉ Glasgow – ☎ 01360.

♦Edinburgh 52 – ♦Glasgow 11 – Stirling 26.

Kirkhouse Inn, G63 9AA, ✆ 770621, Fax 770896 – TV ☎ P – 🏛 30. AE VISA
Meals 12.95/15.00 **t.** and dinner a la carte – **15 rm** 45.00/65.00 **t.** – SB.

STRATHCONON Ross and Cromarty. (Highland) 401 F 11 **Scotland G.** – ✉ Muir of Ord ☎ 01997.

Exc. : Wester Ross★★★.

♦Edinburgh 184 – ♦Inverness 28.

East Lodge, IV6 7QQ, W : 11 m. from Marybank off A 832 ✆ 477222, Fax 477243, ≤, – TV ☎ P. VISA.
Meals (dinner only) 25.00 **st.** – **10 rm** 45.00/100.00 **st.** – SB.

STRATHPEFFER Ross and Cromarty. (Highland) 401 G 11 – pop. 966 – ☎ 01997.

18 Strathpeffer Spa ✆ 421219.

The Square, IV14 9DW ✆ 421415 (summer only).

♦Edinburgh 174 – ♦Inverness 18.

Holly Lodge, Golf Course Rd, IV14 9AR, ✆ 421254, , – TV P. VISA
Meals 14.50 **st.** (dinner) and lunch a la carte 8.50/10.00 **st.** 4.00 – **8 rm** 27.50/55.00 **st.**

Craigvar without rest., The Square, IV14 9DL, ✆ 421622, – TV ☎ P. VISA.
Easter-October – **3 rm** 26.00/44.00 **st.**

STRATHYRE Perth. (Central) 401 H 15 **Scotland G.** – ✉ Callander – ☎ 01877.

Exc. : The Trossachs★★★ (Loch Katherine★★) SW : 14 m. by A 84 and A 821 – Hilltop viewpoint★★★ (✳★★★) SW : 16½ m. by A 84 and A 821.

♦Edinburgh 62 – ♦Glasgow 53 – Perth 42.

Creagan House with rm, FK18 8ND, on A 84 ✆ 384638, Fax 384319, ≤ – P. AE VISA
closed February and 1 week October – **Meals** (booking essential) (dinner only and Sunday lunch)/dinner 21.00 **t.** 6.50 – **5 rm** 42.50/65.00 **t.** – SB.

STROMNESS Orkney. (Orkney Islands) 401 K 7 – see Orkney Islands.

STRONTIAN Argyll. (Highland) 401 D 13 – ☎ 01967.

Village Square, PH36 ✆ 402131 (summer only).

♦Edinburgh 139 – Fort William 23 – ♦Oban 66.

Kilcamb Lodge, PH36 4HY, ✆ 402257, Fax 402041, ≤, « Lochside setting », , park – TV P. VISA.
26 March-6 November – **Meals** (light lunch)/dinner 25.00 **t.** – **10 rm** (dinner included) 79.50/159.00 **t.**

STRUY Inverness (Highland) 401 F 11 – ✉ Beauly – ☎ 01465.

♦Edinburgh 191 – ♦Inverness 21 – Kyle of Lochalsh 61.

Cnoc, IV4 7JU, ✆ 761264, Fax 761207, ≤, – rest P. VISA.
Meals 7.50/11.50 **st.** and dinner a la carte 5.10 – **7 rm** 20.00/56.00 **st.** – SB.

TAIN Ross and Cromarty. (Highland) 401 H 10 – pop. 4 540 – ☎ 01862.

18 Tain ✆ 892314.

♦Edinburgh 191 – ♦Inverness 35 – ♦Wick 91.

Morangie House, Morangie Rd, IV19 1PY, ✆ 892281, Fax 892872 – rm TV ☎ P. AE VISA.
Meals 9.00/23.00 **t.** and a la carte 4.60 – **26 rm** 45.00/75.00 **t.** – SB.

Mansefield House, Scotsburn Rd, IV19 1PR, ✆ 892052, Fax 892260, – TV ☎ P – 30. AE VISA
Meals (bar lunch)/dinner a la carte 11.45/18.80 **t.** 4.65 – **17 rm** 45.00/85.00 **t.**

Golf View House without rest., 13 Knockbreck Rd, IV19 1BN, ✆ 892856, Fax 892856, ≤, – TV P.
closed 15 December-31 January – **5 rm** 20.00/38.00 **s.**

TALLADALE Ross and Cromarty (Highland) 401 D 10 **Scotland G.** – ✉ Achnasheen – ☎ 01445.

Envir. : Loch Maree★★★ – Victoria Falls★, N : 2 m. by A 832.

Exc. : Wester Ross★★★.

♦Edinburgh 218 – ♦Inverness 62 – Kyle of Lochalsh 58.

Old Mill Highland Lodge, IV22 2HL, ✆ 760271, – P.
Meals 16.50 – **5 rm** (dinner included) 48.50/97.00 – SB.

TARBERT Argyll. (Strathclyde) 401 D 16 – see Kintyre (Peninsula).

TARBERT Inverness. (Outer Hebrides) (Western Isles) 401 Z 10 – see Lewis and Harris (Isle of).

THORNHILL Dumfries. (Dumfries and Galloway) 401 402 I 18 **Scotland G.** – pop. 1 633 – ☎ 01848.

Envir. : Drumlanrig Castle★★ (cabinets★) *AC*, NW : 2½ m. by A 76.

♦Edinburgh 64 – ♦Ayr 44 – ♦Dumfries 15 – ♦Glasgow 63.

- **Trigony House,** Closeburn, DG3 5EZ, S : 1½ m. on A 76 ☎ 331211, – rest TV ☎ P. VISA.
  closed 25 December – **Meals** (bar lunch)/dinner 17.50 **t.** 4.80 – **8 rm** 36.00/70.00 **t.** – SB.

THORNHILL Stirling. (Central) 401 H 15 – pop. 550 – ✉ Stirling – ☎ 01786.

♦Edinburgh 46 – ♦Glasgow 36.

- **Corshill Cottage**, FK8 3QD, E : 1 m. on A 873 ☎ 850270, – P
  May-September – **Meals** (by arrangement) 13.00 – **3 rm** 25.00/40.00 **st.**

THURSO Caithness. (Highland) 401 J 8 **Scotland G.** – pop. 8 488 – ☎ 01847.

Exc. : Strathy Point★ (≤★★★) W : 22 m. by A 836.

18 Newlands of Geise ☎ 63807.

from Scrabster to Stromness (Orkney Islands) (P & O Scottish Ferries) (1 h 45 mn).

Riverside, KW14 8BU ☎ 62371 (summer only).

♦Edinburgh 289 – ♦Inverness 133 – ♦Wick 21.

- **Forss House**, Bridge of Forss, KW14 7XY, W : 5½ m. on A 836 ☎ 861201, Fax 861301, ≤, , park – rest TV ☎ P. AE VISA.
  Meals (bar lunch)/dinner 18.50 **st.** 4.30 – **10 rm** 45.00/80.00 **st.** – SB.
- **Murray House** without rest., 1 Campbell St., KW14 7HD, ☎ 895759 – TV P.
  closed 23 December-3 January – **4 rm** 16.00/40.00.

"Short Breaks" (SB)

De nombreux hôtels proposent des conditions avantageuses
pour un séjour de deux nuits
comprenant la chambre, le dîner et le petit déjeuner.

TOBERMORY Argyll. (Strathclyde) 401 B 14 – see Mull (Isle of).

TONGUE Sutherland. (Highland) 401 G 8 **Scotland G.** pop. 552 – ✉ Lairg – ☎ 01847.

Exc. : Cape Wrath★★★ (≤★★) W : 44 m. (including ferry crossing) by A 838 – Ben Loyal★★, S : 8 m. by A 836 – Ben Hope★ (≤★★★) SW : 15 m. by A 838 – Strathy Point★ (≤★★★) E : 22 m. by A 836 – Torrisdale Bay★ (≤★★) NE : 8 m. by A 836.

♦Edinburgh 257 – ♦Inverness 101 – Thurso 43.

- **Ben Loyal,** Main St., IV27 4XE, ☎ 611216, Fax 611212, ≤ Ben Loyal and Kyle of Tongue – rest TV P. VISA
  closed January and February – **Meals** (bar lunch)/dinner 18.50 **t.** and a la carte 6.95 – **12 rm** 38.00/70.00 **t.** – SB.

TORRIDON Ross and Cromarty (Highland) 401 D 11 – ✉ Achnasheen – ☎ 01445.

♦Edinburgh 234 – ♦Inverness 62 – Kyle of Lochalsh 44.

- **Loch Torridon**, IV22 2EY, S : 1½ m. on A 896 ☎ 791242, Fax 791296, ≤ Upper Loch Torridon and mountains, , , park – TV ☎ P. AE VISA.
  restricted service January and February – **Meals** (bar lunch)/dinner 35.00 **st.** 6.75 – **19 rm** 70.00/180.00 **st.**, 1 suite – SB.

TROON Ayr. (Strathclyde) 401 402 G 17 – pop. 15 116 – ☎ 01292.

18 (3x) Troon Municipal, Harling Drive ☎ 312464.

Municipal Buildings, South Beach ☎ 317696 (summer only).

♦Edinburgh 77 – ♦Ayr 7 – ♦Glasgow 31.

- **Marine Highland,** 8 Crosbie Rd, KA10 6HE, ☎ 314444, Fax 316922, ≤, , , , squash – TV ☎ P – 200. AE VISA
  Meals 10.95/24.95 **t.** and a la carte – **66 rm** 92.00/146.00 **t.**, 6 suites – SB.
- **Lochgreen House**, Monktonhill Rd, Southwood, KA10 7EN, SE : 2 m. on B 749 ☎ 313343, Fax 318661, , park, – rest TV ☎ P. AE VISA.
  Meals 16.95/26.00 **st.** 7.50 – **14 rm** 95.00/120.00 **st.**, 1 suite – SB.

Piersland House, 15 Craigend Rd, KA10 6HD, ✆ 314747, Fax 315613, – TV ☎ P – 100. VISA
Meals 11.95/18.95 **st.** and a la carte 5.60 – **19 rm** 75.00/97.50 **st.**, 4 suites – SB.

Ardneil, 51 St. Meddans St., KA10 6NU, ✆ 311611, Fax 318111 – TV P. VISA
Meals 8.50/15.00 **st.** and a la carte 4.50 – **9 rm** 25.00/50.00 **st.**

Highgrove House with rm, Old Loans Rd, Loans, KA10 7HL, E : 2 ½ m. by A 759 ✆ 312511, Fax 318228, ←, – TV ☎ P. VISA.
Meals 14.95/22.50 **t.** and a la carte 6.95 – **9 rm** 58.00/80.00 **st.** – SB.

TURNBERRY Ayr. (Strathclyde) 401 402 F 18 **Scotland G.** – ✉ Girvan – 01655.
Envir. : Culzean Castle★ *AC* (setting★★★, Oval Staircase★★) NE : 5 m. by A 719.
◆Edinburgh 97 – ◆Ayr 15 – ◆Glasgow 51 – Stranraer 36.

Turnberry H. & Golf Courses, KA26 9LT, on A 719 ✆ 331000, Telex 777779, Fax 331706, « Edwardian country house, ← golf courses, bay and Ailsa Craig », , , , 18, , , squash – TV ☎ P – 150. VISA JCB.
Turnberry : Meals (dinner only and Sunday lunch) a la carte 39.50/48.50 **t.** 9.50 –
Bay at Turnberry : Meals *(closed dinner November-March)* a la carte 20.50/28.25 **t.** 9.50 –
122 rm 205.00/260.00 **t.**, 10 suites – SB.

TWYNHOLM Kirkcudbright. (Dumfries and Galloway) 402 H 19 pop. 1 068 – 01557.
◆Edinburgh 107 – ◆Ayr 54 – ◆Dumfries 27 – Stranraer 48.

Fresh Fields, Arden Rd, DG6 4PB, SW : ¾ m. by Burn Brae ✆ 860221, Fax 860221, – P.
March-October – 4.25 **5 rm** (dinner included) 40.00/80.00 **st.**

UDDINGSTON Lanark. (Strathclyde) 401 402 H 16 – pop. 5 367 – ✉ Glasgow – 01698.
18 Coatbridge, Townhead Rd ✆ (01236) 28975.
◆Edinburgh 41 – ◆Glasgow 10.

Redstones, 8-10 Glasgow Rd, G71 7AS, ✆ 813774, Fax 815319 – TV ☎ P. VISA.
closed 1 and 2 January – **Meals** (in bar lunchtime and Sunday dinner)/dinner 15.50 **t.** and a la carte 4.95 – **18 rm** 52.00/74.50 **t.**

Il Buongustaio, 84 Main St., G71 7LR, ✆ 816000 – VISA
closed Sunday dinner and Tuesday – **Meals** - Italian - 5.95 **t.** (lunch) and a la carte 13.95/46.85 **t.** 5.50.

UIG Inverness. (Highland) 401 B 11 and 12 – see Skye (Isles of).

Your recommendation is self-evident if you always walk into a hotel Guide in hand.

UIST (Isles of) Western Isles (Outer Hebrides) 401 XY 11 /12 – pop. 3 510.
see Liniclate.
from Lochboisdale to Isle of Barra (Castlebay) and Oban (Caledonian MacBrayne Ltd) (summer only) – from Lochmaddy to Isle of Skye (Uig) (Caledonian MacBrayne Ltd) – from Lochmaddy to Isle of Harris (Tarbert) (Caledonian MacBrayne Ltd) (1 h 45 mn).

NORTH UIST

Grimsay – 01870.

Glendale, 7 Kallin, HS6 5HY, ✆ 602029, ← – P
Meals 10.00 – **3 rm** 18.00/30.00 **st.**

Locheport – 01876.

Langass Lodge, HS6 5HA, NW : 4½ m. by B 894 off A 867 ✆ 580285, Fax 580285, ←, – P. VISA
closed 1 January-1 April – **Meals** *(closed Sunday lunch)* 12.00/20.00 **st.** and a la carte 3.90 – **6 rm** 32.00/64.00 **st.**

Lochmaddy – 01876.

Lochmaddy, HS6 5AA, ✆ 500331, Fax 500210 – TV ☎ P. VISA
Meals (bar lunch)/dinner a la carte 16.00/24.00 **t.** 4.00 – **15 rm** 38.50/72.00 **t.**

BENBECULA

Liniclate – 01870.

Benbecula Airport : ✆ 602051.

Dark Island, HS7 5PJ, ✆ 603030, Fax 602347 – TV ☎ P. VISA
Meals 9.75/17.50 **st.** and a la carte 4.00 – **42 rm** 55.00/90.00 **st.** – SB.

SOUTH UIST

Daliburgh – ✉ Lochboisdale – ☎ 01878.

Askernish ☎ 700541.

Borrodale, HS8 5SS, ☎ 700444, Fax 700611, – TV P. VISA
Meals 8.00/16.50 **t.** and a la carte 5.40 – **13 rm** 36.00/70.00 **t.** – SB.

Lochboisdale – ☎ 01878.

Brae Lea, Lasgair, HS8 5TH, NW : 1 m. by A 865 ☎ 700497, – P
Meals 12.00 – **4 rm** 22.00/45.00 – SB.

Pollachar – ☎ 01878.

Polochar Inn, HS8 5TT, ☎ 700215, Fax 700768, ≤ Sound of Barra – TV ☎ P. VISA.
Meals a la carte 11.95/33.70 **t.** – **11 rm** 30.00/65.00 **t.** – SB.

LLAPOOL Ross and Cromarty. (Highland) 401 E 10 **Scotland G.** – pop. 1 231 – ☎ 01854.
ee : Town★.
nvir. : Loch Broom★★.
xc. : Falls of Measach★★, S : 11 m. by A 835 and A 832 - Corrieshalloch Gorge★, SE : 10 m. by 835 – Northwards to Lochinver★★, Morefield (≤★★ of Ullapool), ≤★ Loch Broom – S : from llapool to Gairloch★★ (≤★★★).
to Isle of Lewis (Stornoway) (Caledonian MacBrayne Ltd) (3 h 30 mn).
West Shore St., IV26 2UR ☎ 612135 (summer only).
Edinburgh 215 – ♦Inverness 59.

✿✿ **Altnaharrie Inn** (Gunn Eriksen), IV26 2SS, SW : ½ m. by private ferry ☎ 633230, ≤ Loch Broom and Ullapool, « Idyllic setting on banks of Loch Broom », – AE VISA.
Easter-early November – **Meals** (booking essential) (dinner only) 55.00/65.00 **st.** 5.70 – **8 rm** (dinner included) 195.00/340.00 **st.**
Spec. Fillet of Sika deer with a mushroom and grape ravioli and two sauces, Wild salmon with asparagus, capers and ginger in a champagne aspic, Clear 'soup' of lobster with lemon grass, herbs and a small pastry.

Ardvreck without rest., Morefield Brae, IV26 2TH, NW : 2 m. by A 835 ☎ 612028, Fax 612028, ≤ Loch Broom and mountains, – TV P.
10 rm 23.00/46.00 **t.**

Sheiling without rest., Garve Rd, IV26 2SX, ☎ 612947, ≤ Loch Broom, – P.
closed Christmas and New Year – **7 rm** 25.00/42.00 **st.**

Dromnan without rest., Garve Rd, IV26 2SX, ☎ 612333, Fax 612333, ≤, – TV P.
7 rm 40.00 **t.**

JPHALL W. Lothian. (Lothian) 401 J 16 pop. 14 600 – ☎ 01506.
Uphall, Houston Mains ☎ 856404.
♦Edinburgh 13 – ♦Glasgow 32.

Houstoun House, EH52 6JS, ☎ 853831, Fax 854220, « Gardens », park – TV ☎ P. AE VISA
Meals *(closed Saturday lunch)* 15.95/28.00 **st.** and a la carte 6.00 – 9.00 – **30 rm** 92.00/120.00 **st.** – SB.

WALKERBURN Peebles. (Borders) 401 402 K 17 **Scotland G.** – pop. 1 038 (inc. Traquair) – ☎ 01896.
Envir. : The Tweed Valley★★ – Traquair House★★, W : 4 m. by A 72 and B 709.
Exc. : Abbotsbury★★ *AC*, W : 10½ m. by A 72, A 6091 and B 6360.
Innerleithen, Leithen Water, Leithen Rd ☎ 830951.
♦Edinburgh 32 – Galashiels 10 – Peebles 8.

Tweed Valley, Galashiels Rd, EH43 6AA, ☎ 870636, Fax 870639, ≤, – rest TV ☎ P. AE VISA
closed 25 and 26 December – **Meals** (in bar) 16.00/24.00 **t.** and a la carte 6.75 – **16 rm** 43.00/86.00 **t.** – SB.

WALLS Shetland. (Shetland Islands) 401 PQ 3 – see Shetland Islands (Mainland).

WHITEBRIDGE Inverness. (Highland) 401 G 12 – ☎ 01456.
♦Edinburgh 171 – ♦Inverness 23 – Kyle of Lochalsh 67 – ♦Oban 92.

Knockie Lodge, IV1 2UP, SW : 3 ½ m. by B 862 ☎ 486276, Fax 486389, ≤ Loch Nanlann and mountains, « Tastefully converted hunting lodge », park – rest ☎ P. AE VISA.
May-October – **Meals** (residents only) (dinner only) 26.00 **st.** 4.00 – **10 rm** 50.00/150.00 **t.**

WHITING BAY Bute. (Strathclyde) 401 402 E 17 – see Arran (Isle of).

WICK Caithness. (Highland) 401 K 8 **Scotland G.** – pop. 9 713 – ☎ 01955.

Exc. : Duncansby Head★ (Stacks of Duncansby★★) N : 14 m. by A 9 – Grey Cairns of Camster (Long Cairn★★) S : 17 m. by A 9 – The Hill O'Many Stanes★, S : 10 m. by A 9.

Reiss ☎ 602726.

Wick Airport : ☎ 602215, N : 1 m.

Whitechapel Rd, KW1 4EA ☎ 602596.

♦Edinburgh 282 – ♦Inverness 126.

Clachan without rest., South Rd, KW1 5NH, on A 9 ☎ 605384, – TV.
3 rm 25.00/40.00 **st.**

WIGTOWN Wigtown. (Dumfries and Galloway) 401 G 19 **Scotland G.** – pop. 1 344 ✉ Newton Stewart – ☎ 01988.

Exc. : Whithorn Museum (early Christian crosses★★) S : 10 m. by A 746.

Wigtown & Bladnoch, Lightlands Terr. ☎ 403354.

♦Edinburgh 137 – ♦Ayr 61 – ♦Dumfries 61 – Stranraer 26.

Corsemalzie House, DG8 9RL, SW : 6 ½ m. by A 714 on B 7005 ☎ 86025
Fax 860213, , park – rest TV ☎ P. AE VISA
closed February and 25-26 December – **Meals** 19.50 **t.** (dinner) and a la carte 10.05/17.90
4.50 – **14 rm** 56.00/90.00 **t.** – SB.

WORMIT Fife. (Fife) 401 L 14 – ✉ Newport-on-Tay – ☎ 01382.

Scotscraig, Golf Rd, Tayport ☎ 552515.

♦Edinburgh 53 – ♦Dundee 6 – St. Andrews 12.

Sandford, DD6 8RG, S : 2 m. at junction of A 914 with B 946 ☎ 541802, Fax 542136,
, – TV ☎ P – 60. AE VISA
Meals a la carte approx. 23.40 8.50 – **16 rm** 80.00/95.00 – SB.

Northern Ireland

Place with at least

a hotel or restaurant ● Londonderry

a pleasant hotel or restaurant 🏨, ⌂, ✗

a quiet, secluded hotel 🐎

a restaurant with ✿, ✿✿, ✿✿✿, **Meals (M)**

See this town for establishments located in its vicinity **BELFAST**

Localité offrant au moins

une ressource hôtelière ● Londonderry

un hôtel ou restaurant agréable 🏨, ⌂, ✗

un hôtel très tranquille, isolé 🐎

une bonne table à ✿, ✿✿, ✿✿✿, **Meals (M)**

Localité groupant dans le texte les ressources de ses environs **BELFAST**

La località possiede come minimo

una risorsa alberghiera ● Londonder

Albergo o ristorante ameno 🏨, ⌂,

un albergo molto tranquillo, isolato

un'ottima tavola con ✿, ✿✿, ✿✿✿, **Meals (N**

La località raggruppa nel suo testo le risorse dei dintorni **BELFA**

Ort mit mindestens

einem Hotel oder Restaurant ● Londonder

ein angenehmes Hotel oder Restaurant 🏨, ⌂,

einem sehr ruhigen und abgelegenen Hotel

einem Restaurant mit ✿, ✿✿, ✿✿✿, **Meals (N**

Ort mit Angaben über Hotels und Restauran in der Umgebung **BELFAS**

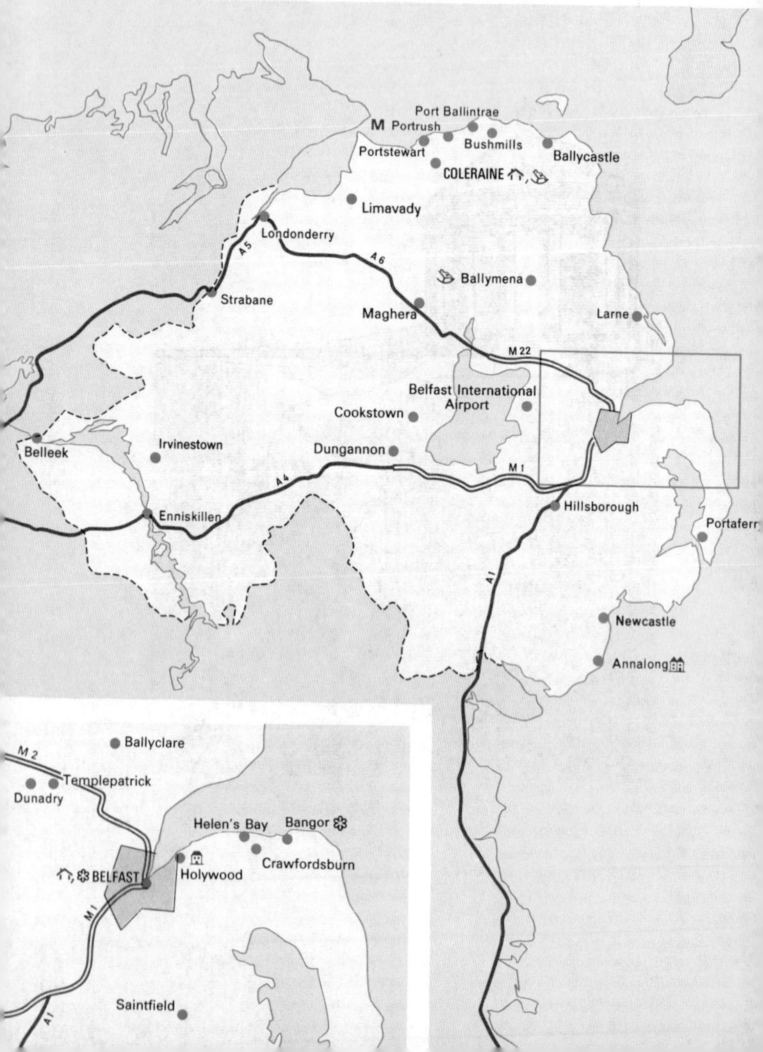

NNALONG (Áth na Long) Down 405 O 5 Ireland G. – pop. 1 937 – ☎ 0139 67.

xc. : W : Mourne Mountains★★ :– Bryansford, Tollymore Forest Park★★ AC, Annalong Marine ırk and Cornmill★ AC – Silent Valley Reservoir★ (≤★) – Spelga Pass and Dam★ – Drumena ashel and Souterrain★ – Kilbroney Forest Park (viewpoint★).

3elfast 37 – ♦Dundalk 36.

Glassdrumman Lodge, 85 Mill Rd, BT34 4RH, ☎ 68451, Fax 67041, ≤ Irish Sea and Mourne mountains, park – TV ☎ P. AE VISA.
Meals (communal dining) (dinner only) (booking essential) 27.50/35.00 **t.** and a la carte 5.00 – 12.50 – **8 rm** 85.00/110.00 **t.**, 2 suites – SB.

ALLYCASTLE (Baile an Chaistil) Antrim 405 N 2 – ☎ 01265 7.

Cushendall Rd ☎ 62536.

7 Mary St. BT54 6QH ☎ 62024.

Belfast 55 – Ballymena 27 – Coleraine 22.

Marine, North St., BT64 6BN, ☎ 62222, Fax 69507, ≤ Fair Head and Rathlin Island, – TV ☎ P – 150. AE VISA.
Meals 12.50/13.50 **st.** and dinner a la carte 4.10 – **31 rm** 45.00/65.00 **st.** – SB.

BALLYCLARE (Bealach Cláir) Antrim 405 N/O 3 – ☎ 01232.

25 Springvale Rd ☎ (019603) 42352/24542.

Belfast 10 – Ballymena 14 – Larne 10.

Ginger Tree, 29 Ballyrobert Rd, BT39 9RY, S : 3¼ m. by A 57 on B 56 ☎ 848176 – P. AE VISA JCB
closed Saturday lunch, Sunday, 12-13 July and 24 to 27 December – **Meals** - Japanese - 10.75/24.00 **t.** and a la carte 5.00.

BALLYMENA (An Baile Meánach) Antrim 405 N 3 Ireland G. – pop. 28 717 – ☎ 01266.

xc. : Antrim Glens★★★ :– Murlough Bay★★★ (Fair Head ≤★★★) Glengariff Forest Park★★ AC Waterfall★★) Glengariff★, Glendun★, Rathlin Island★ – Antrim (Shane's Castle Railway★ AC, Round Tower★) S : 9½ m. by A 26.

128 Raceview Rd ☎ 861207/861487.

Ardeevin, Council Offices, 80 Galgorm Rd, BT42 1AB ☎ 44111 – Morrows Shop, 17 Bridge St., BT42 1AB ☎ 653663 (summer only).

♦Belfast 28 – ♦Dundalk 78 – Larne 21 – ♦Londonderry 51 – ♦Omagh 53.

Galgorm Manor, BT42 1EA, W : 3 ¾ m. by A 42 on Cullybackey rd ☎ 881001, Fax 880080, ≤, « Part 19C country house on banks of River Main », park – rest TV ☎ P – 400. AE VISA JCB.
Meals 9.95/18.95 **st.** and dinner a la carte – **23 rm** 79.00/105.00 **st.** – SB.

Country House, 20 Doagh Rd, BT42 3LZ, SE : 6 m. by A 36 on B 59 ☎ 891663, Fax 891477, – TV ☎ P – 150. AE VISA
Meals *(closed Saturday lunch)* 10.95/14.95 **st.** and dinner a la carte 4.10 – **40 rm** 70.00/100.00 **st.** – SB.

ATS Antrim Rd ☎ 652888

BANGOR (Beannchar) Down 405 O/P 4 – ☎ 01247.

34 Quay St. BT20 5ED ☎ 270069.

♦Belfast 14 – Newtownards 5.

Marine Court, 18-20 Quay St., BT20 5ED, ☎ 451100, Fax 451200, – TV ☎ – 300. AE VISA.
closed 25 December – **Meals** (bar lunch Monday to Saturday) 15.00 **t.** (dinner) and a la carte 9.50/17.50 **t.** 4.00 – **51 rm** 75.00/95.00 **t.** – SB.

Clandeboye Lodge, Crawfordsburn Rd, Clandeboye, BT19 1UR, SW : 3 m. by A 2 and B 170 following signs for Blackwood Golf Centre ☎ 852500, Fax 852772, 18 – rm TV ☎ P – 300. AE VISA
closed 24 to 27 December – **Meals** (bar lunch)/dinner 17.00 **st.** and a la carte 5.60 – 6.25 – **43 rm** 75.00 – SB.

O'Hara's Royal, 26 Quay St., BT20 5ED, ☎ 271866, Fax 467810 – TV ☎ – 60. AE VISA.
closed 25 December – **Meals** 14.50 **t.** (dinner) and a la carte 15.95/22.75 **t.** 3.60 – **34 rm** 61.50/74.50 **t.**

Shelleven, 61 Princetown Rd, BT20 3TA, ☎ 271777, Fax 271777 – TV P. VISA.
Meals (by arrangement) 12.50 **st.** – **12 rm** 25.00/50.00 **st.**

✿ **Shanks**, The Blackwood, Crawfordsburn Rd, Clandeboye, BT19 1GB, SW : 3¼ m. by A 2 and B 170 following signs for Blackwood Golf Centre ☎ 853313, Fax 853785 – 18 P. AE VISA
closed Sunday and Monday – **Meals** (dinner only) 24.95 **t.**
Spec. Smoked chilli and basil risotto with roast prawns, Clandeboye estate venison, shallot confit, potato rösti and thyme aïoli, Pear and amaretti trifle.

ATS 161 Clandeboye Rd ☎ 271736

BELFAST (Béal Feirste) Antrim 405 O 4 Ireland G. – pop. 279 237 – ☎ 01232.

See : City★ - Ulster Museum★★ (Spanish Armada Treasure★★, Shrine of St. Patrick's Hand★) AZ **M1** – City Hall★ BZ – Donegall Square★ BZ **20** – Botanic Gardens (Palm House★) AZ – St Anne's Cathedral★ BY – Crown Liquor Saloon★ BZ – Sinclair Seamen's Church★ BY – St Malachy's Church★ BZ.

Envir. : Belfast Zoological Gardens★★ *AC*, N : 5 m. by A 6 AY.

Exc. : Carrickfergus (Castle★★ *AC*, St. Nicholas' Church★) NE : 9 ½ m. by A 2 – Talnotry Cottage Bird Garden, Crumlin★ *AC*, W : 13½ m. by A 52.

18 Balmoral, 518 Lisburn Rd ☎ 381514, AZ – 18 Belvoir Park, Newtonbreda ☎ 491693 AZ – 18 Fortwilliam, Downview Av. ☎ 370770, AY – 18 The Knock, Summerfield, Dundonald ☎ 482249, AZ – 18 Shandon Park, 73 Shandon Park ☎ 793730, AZ – 9 Cliftonville, Westland Rd ☎ 744158/746595, AY – 9 Ormeau, 50 Park Rd ☎ 641069, AZ.

Belfast International Airport : ☎ (01849) 422888, W : 15 ½ m. by A 52 AY – Belfast City Airport : ☎ 457745 – **Terminal** : Coach service (Ulsterbus Ltd.) from Great Victoria Street Station (40 mn).

to Isle of Man (Douglas) (Isle of Man Steam Packet Co. Ltd) (summer only) (4 h 30 mn) – to Stranraer (Stena Line) frequent services daily (2 h 20 mn), (SeaCat Scotland) (1 h 30 mn) – to Liverpool (Norse Irish Ferries Ltd) (11 h).

St. Annes Court, 59 North St., BT1 1NB ☎ 246609 – Belfast International Airport, BT29 4AB ☎ 422888 – Belfast City Airport, Sydenham By-pass, BT3 9JH ☎ 457745.

◆Dublin 103 – ◆Londonderry 70.

Plans on following pages

Europa, Great Victoria St., BT2 7AP, ☎ 327000, Fax 327800 – rm rest TV ☎ – 1000. AE VISA. – closed 25 December – **Gallery : Meals** *(closed Saturday lunch and Sunday dinner)* 13.95/21.50 **t.** and a la carte 5.00 – **Brasserie : Meals** a la carte 10.00/18.00 **t.** 5.00 – **179 rm** 94.00/130.00 **st.**, 5 suites – SB. BZ

Stormont, 587 Upper Newtownards Rd, BT4 3LP, E : 4½ m. by A 2 on A 20 ☎ 658621, Fax 480240 – rm rest TV ☎ – 400. AE VISA. *closed 25 December* – **McMaster's : Meals** *(closed Saturday lunch and Sunday dinner)* 16.50/22.50 **t.** and a la carte – **Brasserie : Meals** *(closed Sunday lunch)* a la carte approx. 14.00 **t.** – 9.00 – **109 rm** 89.00/160.00 **t.**

Dukes, 65 University St., BT7 1HL, ☎ 236666, Fax 237177, – rm rest TV ☎ – 130. AE VISA. **Meals** 8.50/15.00 **t.** – 6.50 – **21 rm** 75.00/85.00 **st.** – SB. AZ a

Stranmillis Lodge without rest., 14 Chlorine Gdns., BT9 5DJ, ☎ 682009, Fax 682009 – TV ☎. VISA. **6 rm** 40.00/60.00 **st.** AZ x

Ash Rowan, 12 Windsor Av., BT9 6EE, ☎ 661758, Fax 663227, – TV ☎. VISA. *closed 23 December-2 January* – **Meals** (by arrangement) 20.00 **st.** – **4 rm** 46.00/68.00 **st.** AZ c

Malone without rest., 79 Malone Rd, BT9 6SH, ☎ 669565 – TV. *closed Christmas and New Year* – **8 rm** 32.00/47.00 **st.** AZ n

✿ **Roscoff** (Rankin), 7 Lesley House, Shaftesbury Sq., BT2 7DB, ☎ 331532, Fax 312093, « Art Deco influenced interior » – . AE VISA *closed Sunday, Easter Monday, 12-13 July and 25-26 December* – **Meals** 15.50/23.50 **t.** Spec. Gratin of lobster with black spaghetti, courgettes and tarragon, Confit of duck with sweetbreads, asparagus and a garlic cream, Gingered crème brûlée with plum compote. AZ r

Nick's Warehouse, 37-39 Hill St. (1st Floor), BT1 2LB, ☎ 439690, Fax 230514 – . AE VISA *closed Saturday lunch, Monday dinner, Sunday, Easter Monday and Tuesday, 12-13 July and 25 to 27 December* – **Meals** 17.95 **t.** (dinner) and lunch a la carte 13.45/20.95 **t.** 4.00. BY a

La Belle Epoque, 61-63 Dublin Rd, BT2 7HE, ☎ 323244, Fax 323244 – AE VISA *closed Saturday lunch, Sunday, 11-12 July and 25-26 December* – **Meals** 10.75/30.00 **t.** and a la carte. AZ o

Strand, 12 Stranmillis Rd, BT9 5AA, ☎ 682266, Fax 663189 – AE VISA **Meals** a la carte 11.65/15.65 **st.** AZ e

La Bohème, 103 Great Victoria St., BT2 7AG, ☎ 240666, Fax 240040 *closed Sunday, 11-12 July and 25-26 December* – **Meals** - French Bistro - (dinner only) 18.95 **st.** and a la carte 4.95. AZ v

Saints and Scholars, 3 University St., BT7 1FY, ☎ 325137, Fax 323240 – AE VISA *closed Saturday lunch, 12 July and 25 December* – **Meals** a la carte 10.45/19.20 **t.** 5.05. AZ s

Manor House, 43-47 Donegall Pass, BT7 1DQ, ☎ 238755, Fax 238755 – . VISA *closed 12-13 July and 25-26 December* – **Meals** - Chinese (Canton) - 5.50/20.00 **t.** and a la carte 4.20. AZ u

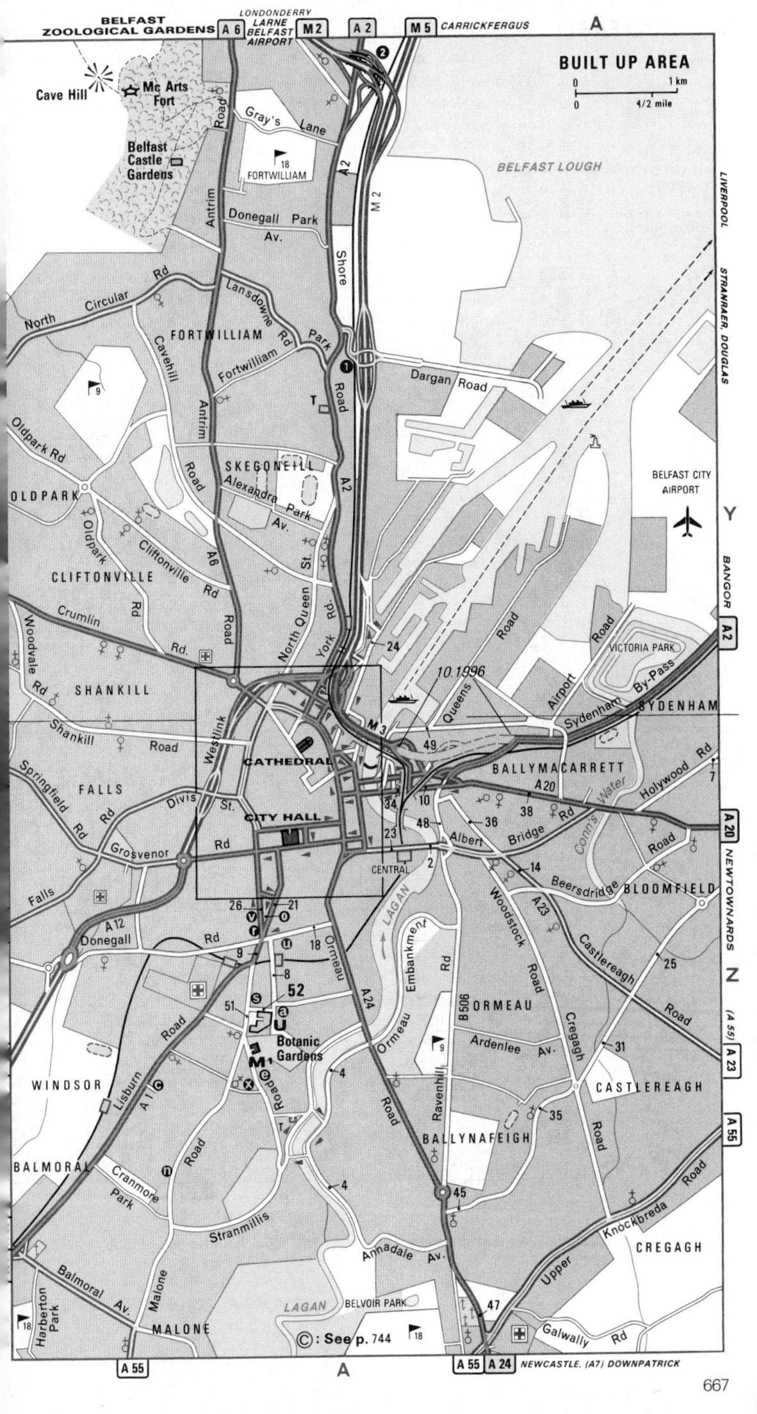
BUILT UP AREA
0
1 km
0
1/2 mile
BELFAST ZOOLOGICAL GARDENS
A 6
LONDONDERRY LARNE BELFAST AIRPORT
M 2
A 2
M 5
CARRICKFERGUS
A
Cave Hill
Mc Arts Fort
Belfast Castle Gardens
Gray's Lane
FORTWILLIAM
BELFAST LOUGH
LIVERPOOL
STRANRAER, DOUGLAS
Antrim Road
Donegall Park Av.
Shore Road
North Circular Rd
Lansdowne Rd
FORTWILLIAM
Park
Fortwilliam
Cavehill
Dargan Road
Oldpark Rd
SKEGONEILL
Alexandra Park Av.
OLDPARK
BELFAST CITY AIRPORT
Y
BANGOR
Oldpark Rd
Cliftonville Rd
CLIFTONVILLE
A6
North Queen St.
York Rd.
Crumlin Rd.
Woodvale Rd
SHANKILL
VICTORIA PARK
Airport Road
Queens Road
10.1996
Sydenham By-Pass
SYDENHAM
A2
Shankill Road
Westlink
M 3
CATHEDRAL
BALLYMACARRETT
Holywood Rd
Springfield Rd
FALLS
Divis St.
CITY HALL
A20
Connswater
A 20
Falls Rd
Grosvenor Rd
Albert Bridge Rd
CENTRAL
Beersbridge
BLOOMFIELD
NEWTOWNARDS
LAGAN
Donegall Rd
A 12
Ormeau
Embankment
Woodstock Road
A23
Castlereagh Road
52
Ormeau Rd
ORMEAU
B 506
Z
Botanic Gardens
Ardenlee Av.
Cregagh
(A 55)
A 23
WINDSOR
Lisburn Road
A 1
Road
Ormeau Road
Ravenhill
CASTLEREAGH
BALLYNAFEIGH
Road
A 55
BALMORAL
Cranmore Park
Stranmillis
Knockbreda Road
Annadale Av.
CREGAGH
Upper
Balmoral Av.
Malone
LAGAN
BELVOIR PARK
Harberton Park
MALONE
© : See p. 744
Galwally Rd
A 55
A
A 55
A 24
NEWCASTLE, (A7) DOWNPATRICK

BELFAST

Castlecourt Shopping Centre .... BYZ
Castle Place .... BZ
Donegal Place .... BZ
Royal Avenue .... BYZ

Albert Bridge .... AZ 2
Albert Square .... BY 3
Annadale Embankment .... AZ 4
Ann Street .... BZ 5
Belmont Road .... AZ 7
Botanic Avenue .... AZ 8
Bradbury Place .... AZ 9
Bridge End .... AZ 10
Bridge Street .... BZ 12
Castlereagh Street .... AZ 14
Clifton Street .... BY 15
Corporation Square .... BY 16
Donegall Pass .... AZ 18
Donegall Quay .... BYZ 19
Donegall Square .... BZ 20
Dublin Road .... AZ 21
East Bridge Street .... AZ 23
Garmoyle Street .... AY 24
Grand Parade .... AZ 25
Great Victoria Street .... BZ 26
High Street .... BYZ 28
Howard Street .... BZ 29
Ladas Drive .... AZ 31
Lagan Bridge .... BY 32
Middlepath St. .... AZ 34
Mount Merrion Avenue .... AZ 35
Mountpottinger Road .... AZ 36
Newtownards Road .... AZ 38
Queen Elizabeth Bridge .... BZ 40
Queen's Bridge .... BZ 41
Queen's Square .... BY 42
Rosemary Street .... BZ 44
Rosetta Park .... AZ 45
Saintfield Road .... AZ 47
Short Strand .... AZ 48
Sydenham Road .... AZ 49
University Road .... AZ 51
University Square .... AZ 52
Waring Street .... BY 54
Wellington Place .... BZ 55

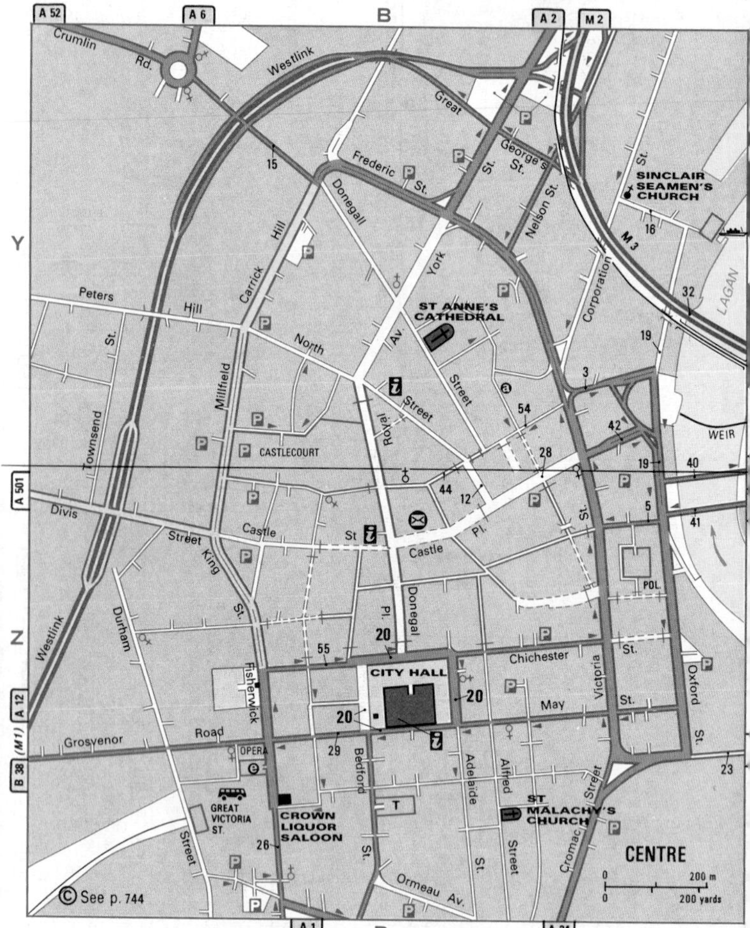

© See p. 744

In Northern Ireland traffic and parking are controlled in the town centres. No vehicle may be left unattended in a Control Zone.

The names of main shopping streets are indicated in red at the beginning of the list of streets.

at Dundonald E : 5½ m. on A 20 – AZ – ✉ Belfast – ☎ 01247 :

Cottage without rest., 377 Comber Rd, BT16 0XB, SE : 1 ¾ m. on Comber Rd (A 22) ✆ 878189, – ⚑. ✗
3 rm ☕ 18.00/34.00.

at Dunmurry SW : 5½ m. on A 1 – AZ – ✉ Belfast – ☎ 01232 :

Forte Posthouse, 300 Kingsway, BT17 9ES, ✆ 612101, Telex 74281, Fax 626546, , park – ⚑ rm ▤ rest TV ☎ ⓟ – 400. AE ⓓ VISA
Meals *(closed Saturday lunch)* a la carte 15.85/21.65 **t.** 6.95 – ☕ 7.95 – **82 rm** 75.00 **st.** – SB.

ATS 4 Duncrue St. ✆ 749531 ATS 37 Boucher Rd ✆ 663623

BELFAST INTERNATIONAL AIRPORT **(Aerphort Béal Feirste)** Antrim 405 N 4 – ✉ Aldergrove – ☎ 01849.

✈ Belfast International Airport : ✆ 422888.

♦Belfast 15 – Ballymena 20 – Larne 23.

Aldergrove Airport H., Aldergrove, BT29 4AB, ✆ 422033, Fax 423500, – ⚑ rm ▤ TV ☎ ⓟ – 230. AE ⓓ VISA. ✗
Meals 8.25/14.75 **t.** and dinner a la carte 5.95 – ☕ 7.50 – **108 rm** 67.00 **st.**

BELLEEK **(Béal Leice)** Fermanagh 405 H 4 – ☎ 0136 56.

♦Belfast 117 – ♦Londonderry 56.

Moohan's Fiddlestone without rest., Main St., BT93 3FY, ✆ 58008
5 rm.

BUSHMILLS **(Muileann na Buaise)** Antrim 405 M 2 **Ireland G.** – pop. 1 348 – ✉ Bushmills – ☎ 0126 57.

Exc. : Causeway Coast★★ : Giant's Causeway★★★ (Hamilton's Seat ≤★★), Carrick-a-rede Rope Bridge★★★, Dunluce Castle★★ *AC*, Gortmore Viewpoint★★ – Magilligan Strand★★, Downhill★ (Mussenden Temple★).

⛳9 Bushfoot, Portballintrae ✆ 31317.

♦Belfast 57 – Ballycastle 12 – Coleraine 10.

Bushmills Inn, 25 Main St., BT57 8QA, ✆ 32339, Fax 32048, « Part 18C inn » – TV ☎ ⓟ – 100. VISA
Meals 14.00 **t.** (dinner) and a la carte 11.00/18.80 **t.** 5.95 – **11 rm** ☕ 52.00/85.00 **st.** – SB.

CASTLEROCK **(Carraig Ceasail)** Londonderry – see Coleraine.

COLERAINE **(Cîil Raithin)** Londonderry 405 L 2 **Ireland G.** – pop. 20 721 – ☎ 01265.

Exc. : Antrim Glens★★★ :– Murlough Bay★★★ (Fair Head ≤★★★), Glenariff Forest Park★★ *AC* (Waterfall★★) – Glenariff★, Glendun★, Rathlin Island★ – Causeway Coast★★ : Giant's Causeway★★★ (Hamilton's Seat ≤★★) – Carrick-a-rede Rope Bridge★★★ – Dunluce Castle★★ *AC* – Gortmore Viewpoint★★ – Magilligan Strand★★ – Downhill★ (Mussenden Temple★).

⛳18, ⛳9 Castlerock, Circular Rd ✆ 848314 – ⛳9 Brown Trout, 209 Agivey Rd ✆ 868209.

ℹ Railway Rd, BT52 1PE ✆ 44723.

♦Belfast 53 – Ballymena 25 – ♦Londonderry 31 – ♦Omagh 65.

Bushtown House, 283 Drumcroone Rd, BT51 3QT, S : 2 ½ m. on A 29 ✆ 58367, Fax 320909, – ⚑ rm TV ☎ ⓟ – 250. AE VISA. ✗
Meals 10.50/17.50 **st.** and dinner a la carte 3.75 – **20 rm** ☕ 43.00/85.00 **st.** – SB.

Greenhill House , 24 Greenhill Rd, Aghadowey, BT51 4EU, S : 9 m. by A 29 on B 66 ✆ 868241, – ⚑ rest TV ⓟ. VISA. ✗
March-October – **Meals** (by arrangement) 15.00 – **6 rm** ☕ 27.00/44.00 – SB.

Camus House without rest., 27 Curragh Rd, BT51 3RY, SE : 3¾ m. on A 54 ✆ 42982, , park – ⚑ TV ⓟ. ✗
3 rm ☕ 25.00/40.00 **st.**

at Castlerock NW : 6 m. by A 2 on B 119 – ✉ Castlerock – ☎ 01265 :

Maritima House without rest., 43 Main St., BT51 4RA, ✆ 848388, ≤, – ⓟ. ✗
3 rm ☕ 21.00/38.00.

ATS Loguestown Ind. Est., Bushmills Rd ✆ 42329

COOKSTOWN **(An Chorr Chráochach)** Tyrone 405 L 4 – ☎ 01648 7.

⛳18 Killymoon, 200 Killymoon Rd ✆ 63762/62254.

ℹ 48 Molesworth St. BT80 8TA ✆ 66727.

♦Belfast 45 – Ballymena 27 – ♦Londonderry 49.

Tullylagan Country House , 40B Tullylagan Rd, Sandholes, BT80 8UP, S : 4 m. by A 29 ✆ 65100, Fax 61715, , park – TV ☎ ⓟ. VISA. ✗
closed 24 and 25 December – **Meals** *(closed Saturday lunch)* 9.95/15.95 **st.** and dinner a la carte 5.50 – **15 rm** ☕ 45.00/80.00 **st.** – SB.

CRAWFORDSBURN (Sruth Chráfard) Down 405 O 4 Ireland G. – pop. 572 – ☎ 01247.

Envir. : Heritage Centre, Bangor★, E : 3 m. by B 20.

Exc. : – Priory (Cross Slabs★) – Mount Stewart★★★ *AC*, SE : 12 m. by A 2, A 21 and A 20 – Scrabo Tower (≤ ★★★), SW : 8 m. – Ballycopeland Windmill★ *AC*, E : 13 m. by A 2, A 21 and B 172 – Strangford Lough★ (Castle Espie Centre★ *AC* - Nendrum Monastery★) – Grey Abbey★ *AC*, SE : 14 m. by A 2, A 21 and A 20.

♦Belfast 10 – Bangor 3.

Old Inn, 15 Main St., BT19 1JH, ✆ 853255, Fax 852775, – TV ☎ P – 25. AE VISA.
Meals *(closed Sunday dinner)* 18.00 **t.** (dinner) and a la carte 19.45/24.85 **t.** 4.50 – **33 rm** 70.00/135.00 **st.** – SB.

DUNADRY (Dîn Eadradh) Antrim 405 N 3 Ireland G. – ☎ 01849.

Envir. : Antrim (Round tower★, Shane's Castle Railway★ *AC*) NW : 4 m. by A 6.

Exc. : Crumlin : Talnotry Cottage Bird Garden★ *AC*, SW : 10½ m. by A 5, A 26 and A 52.

♦Belfast 15 – Larne 18 – ♦Londonderry 56.

Dunadry, 2 Islandreagh Drive, BT41 2HA, ✆ 432474, Fax 433389, – rm TV ☎ P – 300. AE VISA.
closed 24 to 26 December – **Meals** (buffet lunch Saturday) 12.50/17.50 **st.** and a la carte 5.00 – **67 rm** 90.00/112.00 **st.** – SB.

DUNDONALD (Dîn DÉnaill) Antrim 405 O 4 – see Belfast.

DUNGANNON (Dîn Geanainn) Tyrone 405 L 4 – ☎ 01868.

♦Belfast 42 – Ballymena 37 – Dundalk 47 – ♦Londonderry 60.

Cohannon Inn & Auto Lodge, 212 Ballynakelly Rd, BT71 6HJ, E : 6¼ m. by A 29 and M 1 on A 45 ✆ 724488, Fax 724488, – TV P – 30. AE VISA.
Meals a la carte 8.05/15.05 **st.** 3.95 – 3.95 – **22 rm** 31.95 **st.**

ATS 51 Oaks Rd ✆ 723772

DUNMURRY (Dún Muirígh) Antrim 405 N 4 – see Belfast.

ENNISKILLEN (Inis Ceithleann) Fermanagh 405 J 4 Ireland G. – pop. 11 436 – ☎ 01365.

Envir. : Castle Coole★★★ *AC*, SE : 1 m..

Exc. : NW : Lough Erne★★ : Cliffs of Magho Viewpoint★★★ *AC* – Devenish Island★ *AC* – Castle Archdale Country Park★ – White Island★ – Janus Figure★ – Tully Castle★ *AC* – Florence Court★★ *AC*, SW : 8 m. by A 4 and A 32 – Marble Arch Caves and Forest Nature Reserve★★ *AC*, SW : 10 m. by A 4 and A 32.

18 Castlecoole ✆ 325250.

Fermanagh Tourist Information Centre, Wellington Rd, BT74 7EF ✆ 323110.

♦Belfast 87 – ♦Londonderry 59.

Killyhevlin, Dublin Rd, BT74 4AU, SE : 1¾ m. on A 4 ✆ 323481, Fax 324726, ≤, park – TV ☎ P – 500. AE VISA.
Meals (carving lunch Sunday) 15.00/17.50 **st.** and a la carte 6.00 – **43 rm** 55.00/80.00 **st.**, 1 suite – SB.

Manor House Country, Killadeas, BT94 1NY, N : 7 ½ m. by A 32 on B 82 ✆ (01365 6) 21561, Fax 21545, – rm TV ☎ P – 300. AE VISA.
Meals 9.90/18.50 **t.** and a la carte 4.50 – **46 rm** 40.00/100.00 **t.** – SB.

HELEN'S BAY (Cuan Héilin) Down 405 O 3 – ☎ 01247.

♦Belfast 10 – Newtownards 9.

Deanes on the Square, 7 Station Sq., BT19 1TN, ✆ 852841, « Converted 19C railway station » – AE VISA
closed Sunday dinner, Monday, 1 week January and 1 week July – **Meals** (dinner only and Sunday lunch) 23.75 **t.**

HILLSBOROUGH (Cromghlinn) Down 405 N 4 Ireland G. – ☎ 01846.

See : Town★ – Fort★.

Exc. : – The Argory★, W : 25 m. by A 1 and M 1.

♦Belfast 13.

White Gables, 14 Dromore Rd, BT26 6HS, SW : ½ m. ✆ 682755, Fax 689532 – rm rest TV ☎ P – 120. AE VISA.
closed 25 December – **Meals** *(closed Saturday lunch and Sunday)* 15.75/21.00 **t.** and dinner a la carte 4.95 – 8.75 – **31 rm** 71.50/115.00 **t.**

Hillside, 21 Main St., BT26 6AE, ✆ 682765, Fax 682557 – AE VISA
closed Sunday – **Meals** (dinner only) 16.00 **t.** and a la carte 5.15.

HOLYWOOD **(Ard Mhic Nasca)** Down 405 O 4 **Ireland G.** – pop. 9 252 – ☎ 01232.

Envir. : Cultra : Ulster Folk and Transport Museum★★ *AC*, NE : 1 m. by A 2.

♦Belfast 5 – Bangor 6.

- **Culloden,** 142 Bangor Rd, BT18 0EX, E : 1½ m. on A 2 ☎ 425223, Fax 426777, ←, park, – rm – 500. VISA.
  Mitre : Meals *(closed Saturday lunch)* 15.00/18.50 **t.** and a la carte 7.00 – **Cultra Inn : Meals** – (grill rest.) a la carte 9.95/17.95 **t.** 7.00 – 9.00 – **83 rm** 104.00/135.00 **st.**, 6 suites SB.
- **Rayanne House,** 60 Demesne Rd, BT18 9EX, by High St. and Downshire Rd ☎ 425859, Fax 425859, ←, – rest. VISA.
  Meals *(closed Sunday)* (booking essential) (dinner only) (unlicensed) a la carte 19.50/24.30 **t.** – **6 rm** 49.00/70.00 **st.** – SB.
- **Sullivans,** Unit 5, Sullivan Pl., BT18 9JF, ☎ 421000, Fax 421000 – VISA
  closed Sunday and Bank Holidays – **Meals** (restricted lunch) (unlicensed) 8.50/15.95 **t.** and a la carte.

IRVINESTOWN **(Baile an Irbhinigh)** Fermanagh 405 J 4 **Ireland G.** – pop. 1 906 – ☎ 0136 56.

Exc. : NW : Lough Erne★★ : Cliffs of Magho Viewpoint★★★ *AC* – Devenish Island★ *AC* – Castle Archdale Country Park★ – White Island★ – Janus Figure★ – Tully Castle★ *AC*.

♦Belfast 78 – ♦Dublin 132 – Donegal 27.

- **Mahon's,** 2-10 Mill St., BT94 1GS, ☎ 21656, Fax 28344 – – 300. VISA.
  Meals 8.75/14.95 **st.** and a la carte 4.95 – **18 rm** 29.50/57.50 – SB.

LARNE **(Latharna)** Antrim 405 O 3 **Ireland G.** – pop. 17 575 – ☎ 01574.

Envir. : Glenoe Waterfall★, S : 5 m. by A 2 and B 99 – SE : Island Magee (Ballylumford Dolmen★).

Exc. : NW : Antrim Glens★★★ – Murlough Bay★★★ (Fair Head ← ★★★), Glenariff Forest Park★★ *AC* (Waterfall★★), Glenariff★, Glendun★, Rathlin Island★.

Cairndhu, 192 Coast Rd, Ballygally ☎ 583248.

– to Cairnryan (P & O European Ferries Ltd) 4-6 daily (2 h 15 mn).

Sir Thomas Dixon Buildings, Victoria Rd, BT40 1RU ☎ 272313 – Carnfunnock County Park, Coast Road ☎ 270541 Narrow Guage Rd, BT40 1XB ☎ 260088.

♦Belfast 23 – Ballymena 20.

- Magheramorne House, 59 Shore Rd, Magheramorne, BT40 3HW, S : 3½ m. on A 2 ☎ 279444, Fax 260138, ←, park – – 200
  22 rm.
- **Derrin House** without rest., 2 Prince's Gdns, BT40 1RQ, off Glenarm Rd (A 2) ☎ 273269, Fax 273269 – VISA
  closed 25 and 26 December – **7 rm** 20.00/36.00 **s.**

ATS Narrow Gauge Rd ☎ 274491

LIMAVADY **(Léim an Mhadaidh)** Derry 405 L 2 – ☎ 0150 47.

♦Belfast 62 – Ballymena 39 – Coleraine 13 – ♦Londonderry 17 – ♦Omagh 50.

- **Radisson Roe Park H. & Golf Resort,** Roe Park, BT49 9LB, W : ½ m. on A 2 ☎ 22212, Fax 22313, park – – 440. VISA.
  Meals (bar lunch)/dinner a la carte 23.00/27.00 **st.** – **63 rm** 70.00/110.00 **st.**, 1 suite – SB.

LONDONDERRY **(Doire)** Londonderry 405 K 2-3 **Ireland G.** – pop. 72 334 – ☎ 01504.

See : Town★ – City Walls and Gates★★ – Guildhall★ – St. Columb's Cathedral★ *AC* – Long Tower Church★ – Tower Museum★.

Envir. : Grianan of Aileach★★ (← ★) (Republic of Ireland) NW : 5 m. by A 2 and N 13.

Exc. : SE : by A 6 – Sperrin Mountains★ : Ulster-American Folk Park★★ – Glenshane Pass★★ (★★) – Sawel Mountain Drive★ (←★★) – Roe Valley Country Park★ – Ness Wood Country Park★ – Sperrin Heritage Centre★ *AC* – Beaghmore Stone Circles★ – Ulster History Park★ – Oak Lough Scenic Road★ – Eglinton★ – Gortin Glen Forest Park★ *AC*.

City of Derry, 49 Victoria Rd ☎ 311610/46369.

Eglinton Airport : ☎ 810784, E : 6 m. by A 2.

8 Bishop St., BT48 6PW ☎ 267284.

♦Belfast 70 – ♦Dublin 146.

- **Everglades,** Prehen Rd, BT47 2PA, S : 1½ m. by A 5 ☎ 46722, Fax 49200 – – 300. VISA.
  closed 25 December – **Meals** *(closed Saturday lunch)* 9.95/17.95 **t.** and dinner a la carte – **51 rm** 62.00/80.00 **t.**, 1 suite – SB.

Beech Hill House 🅂, 32 Ardmore Rd, BT47 3QP, SE : 3 ½ m. by A 6 ℘ 49279, Fax 45366, ⚟, 🌳, park, ✂ – ⚞ rest ▢ ☎ Ⓟ – 🎕 100. ▣ ▣ VISA. ⚘
closed 24 and 25 December – **Meals** 14.95/19.95 **t.** and a la carte 🍷 6.95 – **17 rm** ☐ 62.50/90.00 **t.** – SB.

Waterfoot H. & Country Club, 14 Clooney Rd, Caw Roundabout, BT47 1TB, NE : 3 ¾ m. at junction of A 39 with A 5 and A 2 ℘ 45500, Fax 311006, 🏋, ⚟, ▢ – ▢ ☎ ♿ Ⓟ – 🎕 100. ▣ ▣ ◐ VISA. ⚘
closed 25 and 26 December – **Meals** (grill rest.) a la carte 10.70/19.25 **st.** 🍷 4.70 – ☐ 5.00 – **48 rm** 52.50/65.00 **st.** – SB.

White Horse, 68 Clooney Rd, BT47 3PA, NE : 6 ½ m. on A 2 (Coleraine rd) ℘ 860606, Fax 860371 – ▢ ☎ Ⓟ – 🎕 350. ▣ ▣ ◐ VISA. ⚘
Meals (grill rest.) a la carte 11.30/19.50 **t.** – ☐ 5.25 – **43 rm** 42.50 **st.** – SB.

MAGHERA (Machaire Rátha) Londonderry 405 L 3 – ⊛ 01648.

♦Belfast 40 – Ballymena 19 – Coleraine 21 – ♦Londonderry 32.

Ardtara Country House 🅂, 8 Gorteade Rd, Upperlands, BT46 5SA, N : 3¼ m. by A 29 off B 75 ℘ 44490, Fax 45080, ≤, « 19C country house », 🌳, ✂ – ▢ ☎ Ⓟ. ▣ ▣ VISA. ⚘
closed 25 and 26 December – **Meals** *(closed Sunday dinner)* (booking essential) 12.50/25.00 **t.** and dinner a la carte 🍷 6.00 – **8 rm** ☐ 60.00/100.00 **t.** – SB.

NEWCASTLE (An Caisleán Nua) Down 405 O 5 Ireland G. – pop. 7 214 – ⊛ 01396 7.

Envir. : Castlewellan Forest Park★★ *AC*, NW : 4 m. by A 50 – Dundrum Castle★ *AC*, NE : 4 m. by A 2.

Exc. : SW : Mourne Mountains★★ : Bryansford, Tollymore Forest Park★★ *AC* – Annalong Marine Park and Cornmill★ *AC* – Silent Valley Reservoir★ (≤★) – Spelga Pass and Dam★ – Drumena Cashel and Souterrain★ – Kilbroney Forest Park (viewpoint★) – Loughinisland Churches★, NE : 10 m. by A 2 and A 24.

ℹ The Newcastle Centre, 10-14 Central Promenade, BT30 6LZ ℘ 22222.

♦Belfast 30 – ♦Londonderry 101.

Burrendale H. & Country Club, 51 Castlewellan Rd, BT33 0JY, N : 1 m. on A 50 ℘ 22599, Fax 22328, 🏋, ⚟, ▢, 🌳 – ⇅ ▢ ☎ ♿ Ⓟ – 🎕 150. ▣ ▣ ◐ VISA JCB. ⚘
Meals 16.00 **st.** (dinner) and a la carte 10.15/17.40 **st.** 🍷 4.00 – **51 rm** ☐ 55.00/90.00 **st.** – SB.

Briars Country House 🅂, 39 Middle Tollymore Rd, BT33 0JJ, N : 1½ m. by Bryansford Rd (B 180) and Tollymore Rd ℘ 24347, Fax 24347, ≤, 🌳 – ⚞ rm ▢ ☎ ♿ Ⓟ. ▣ VISA. ⚘
Meals (unlicensed) 12.00/22.00 **st.** – **9 rm** ☐ 35.00/50.00 **st.** – SB.

PORTAFERRY (Port an Pheire) Down 405 P 4 Ireland G. – pop. 2 324 – ⊛ 0124 77.

See : Aquarium★.

Envir. : Castle Ward★★ *AC*, SW : 4 m. by boat and A 25.

Exc. : SE : Lecale Peninsula★★ – Struell Wells★, Quoile Pondage★, Ardglass★, Strangford★, Audley's Castle★.

ℹ Shore St., Nr Strangford Ferry Departure Point (summer only).

♦ Belfast 29 – Bangor 24.

Portaferry, 10 The Strand, BT22 1PE, ℘ 28231, Fax 28999, ≤, « 18C, loughside setting » – ▢ ☎. ▣ ▣ ◐ VISA. ⚘
closed 24 and 25 December – **Meals** 13.50/20.00 **t.** and a la carte 🍷 5.00 – **13 rm** ☐ 49.50/89.00 **t.** – SB.

PORT BALLINTRAE (Port Bhaile an Trá) Antrim 405 M 2 Ireland G. – pop. 756 – ✉ Bushmills – ⊛ 0126 57.

Exc. : Causeway Coast★★ : Giant's Causeway★★★ (Hamilton's Seat ≤★★) – Carrick-a-rede Rope Bridge★★★ – Dunluce Castle★★ *AC* – Gortmore Viewpoint★★ – Magilligan Strand★★ – Downhill★ (Mussenden Temple★).

♦Belfast 68 – Coleraine 15.

Bayview, 2 Bayhead Rd, BT57 8RT, ℘ 31453, Fax 32360, ≤, ⚟, ▢ – ▢ ☎ Ⓟ – 🎕 100. ▣ VISA. ⚘
Meals 8.75/15.00 **t.** and dinner a la carte – **16 rm** ☐ 35.00/70.00 – SB.

PORTRUSH (Port Rois) Antrim 405 L 2 Ireland G. – pop. 5 703 – ⊛ 01265.

Exc. : Causeway Coast★★ : Giant's Causeway★★★ (Hamilton's Seat ≤★★) – Carrick-a-rede Rope Bridge★★★ – Dunluce Castle★★ *AC* – Gortmore Viewpoint★★ – Magilligan Strand★★ – Downhill★ (Mussenden Temple★).

18, 18, 9 Royal Portrush, Dunluce Rd ℘ 822311.

ℹ Dunluce Centre, Sandhill Dr., BT56 8BT ℘ 823333 (summer only).

♦Belfast 58 – Coleraine 4 – ♦Londonderry 35.

Magherabuoy House, 41 Magheraboy Rd, BT56 8NX, SW : 1 m. by A 29 ℘ 823507, Fax 824687, ≤, ≘s, – rest ☎ – 300. AE VISA. Meals (bar lunch)/dinner 15.00 **st.** 4.00 – **38 rm** 50.00/80.00 **st.** – SB.

O'Neill's Causeway Coast, 36 Ballyreagh Rd, BT56 8LR, NW : 1 ¼ m. on A 2 (Portstewart rd) ℘ 822435, Fax 824495, ≤ – ☎ – 500. AE VISA. Meals (bar lunch)/dinner 16.00 **st.** 5.70 – **21 rm** 55.00/75.00 **st.** – SB.

Glencroft, 95 Coleraine Rd, BT56 8HN, ℘ 822902, – . *closed 2 weeks Christmas* – **Meals** (by arrangement) 12.50 – **5 rm** 20.00/34.00 **st.** – SB.

Ramore, The Harbour, BT56 8BN, ℘ 824313, ≤ – . VISA *closed Sunday and Monday* – **Meals** (booking essential) (dinner only) a la carte 13.05/24.85 **t.** 5.75.

PORTSTEWART (Port Stíobhaird) Londonderry 405 L 2 **Ireland G.** – pop. 6 459 – 01265.

Exc. : Causeway Coast★★ : Giant's Causeway★★★ (Hamilton's Seat ≤★★) – Carrick-a-rede Rope Bridge★★★ – Dunluce Castle★★ *AC* – Gortmore Viewpoint★★ – Magilligan Strand★★ – Downhill★ (Mussenden Temple★).

Town Hall, The Crescent, BT55 7AB ℘ 832286 (summer only).

♦Belfast 67 – Coleraine 6.

Edgewater, 88 Strand Rd, BT55 7LZ, ℘ 833314, Fax 832224, ≤, ≘s – ☎ – 100. AE VISA. **Meals** 11.00/35.00 **st.** and dinner a la carte 4.95 – **30 rm** 44.50/72.00 **st.** – SB.

SAINTFIELD (Tamhnaigh Naomh) Down 405 O 4 pop. 2 780 – 01238.

♦Belfast 11 – Downpatrick 11.

The Barn, 120 Monlough Rd, BT24 7EU, NW : 1 ¾ m. by A 7 ℘ 510396, – . VISA *closed Sunday to Tuesday* – **Meals** (dinner only) 22.50 **t.** 5.00.

STRABANE (An Srath Bán) Tyrone 405 J 3 **Ireland G.** – pop. 11 981 – 01504.

Exc. : Sperrin Mountains★ : Ulster-American Folk Park★★ – Glenshane Pass★★ (★★) – Sawel Mountain Drive★ (≤★★) – Roe Valley Country Park★ – Ness Wood Country Park★ – Sperrin Heritage Centre★ *AC* – E : Beaghmore Stone Circles★ – Ulster History Park★ – Oak Lough Scenic Road★ – Eglinton★ – Gortin Glen Forest Park★ *AC*.

18 Ballycolman ℘ 382271/382007.

Abercorn Square, BT82 8DY ℘ 883735 (summer only) – Council Offices, 47 Derry Rd ℘ 382204.

♦Belfast 87 – Donegal 34 – ♦Dundalk 98 – ♦Londonderry 14.

Fir Trees, Melmount Rd, BT82 9JT, S : 1 ¼ m. on A 5 ℘ 382382, Fax 383116 – ☎ . AE VISA. **Meals** 10.50/12.95 **st.** and a la carte – **26 rm** 33.00/50.00 **st.** – SB.

TEMPLEPATRICK (Teampall Phádraig) Antrim 405 N 3 – pop. 1 414 – ✉ Ballyclave – 0184 94.

♦Belfast 12 – Ballymena 16 – ♦Dundalk 65 – Larne 16.

Templeton, 882 Antrim Rd, BT39 0AH, ℘ 432984, Fax 433406, – ☎ – 300. AE VISA JCB. *closed 25 and 26 December* – **Templeton : Meals** (dinner only and Sunday lunch)/dinner 16.95 5.95 – **Upton Grill : Meals** (grill rest.) a la carte 7.70/16.90 **st.** 5.95 – **20 rm** 85.00/100.00 **st.** – SB.

Channel Islands

Place with at least
a hotel or restaurant ● Catel
a pleasant hotel or restaurant 🏨, ⌂, ✕
a quiet, secluded hotel 🐎
a restaurant with ✿, ✿✿, ✿✿✿, **Meals (M)**

Localité offrant au moins
une ressource hôtelière ● Catel
un hôtel ou restaurant agréable 🏨, ⌂, ✕
un hôtel très tranquille, isolé 🐎
une bonne table à ✿, ✿✿, ✿✿✿, **Meals (M)**

La località possiede come minimo
una risorsa alberghiera ● Catel
Albergo o ristorante ameno 🏨, ⌂, ✕
un albergo molto tranquillo, isolato 🐎
un'ottima tavola con ✿, ✿✿, ✿✿✿, **Meals (M)**

Ort mit mindestens
einem Hotel oder Restaurant ● Catel
ein angenehmes Hotel oder Restaurant 🏨, ⌂, ✕
einem sehr ruhigen und abgelegenen Hotel 🐎
einem Restaurant mit ✿, ✿✿, ✿✿✿, **Meals (M)**

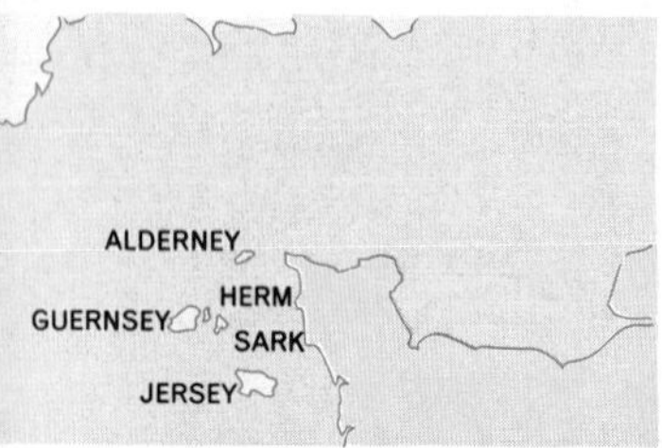

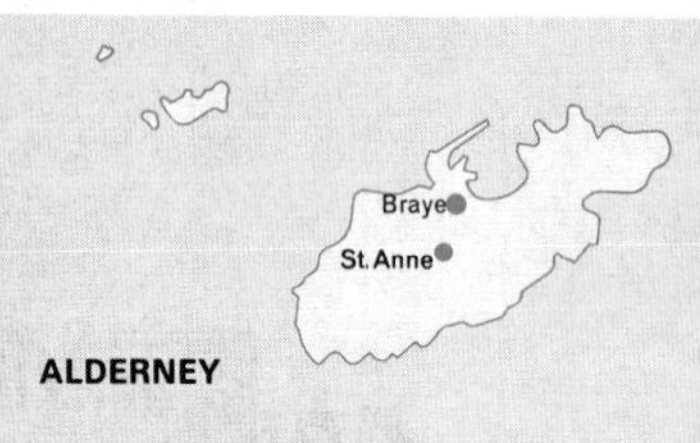

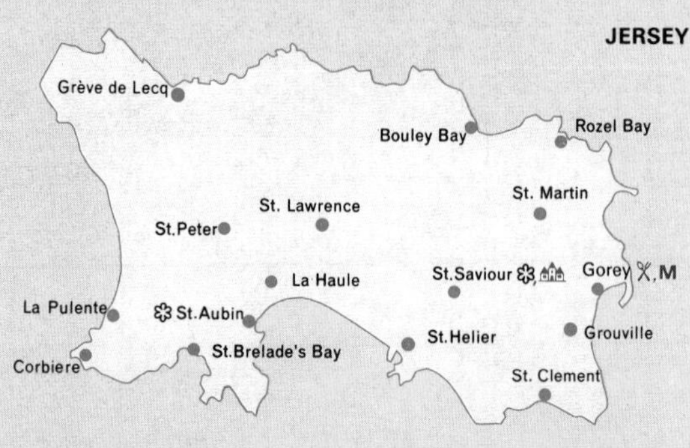

ALDERNEY 403 Q 33 and 230 ⑨ The West Country G. – pop. 2 297 – ☎ 01481.

See : Braye Bay★ – Mannez Garenne (<★ from Quesnard Lighthouse) – Telegraph Bay★ – Vallee des Trois Vaux★ – Clonque Bay★.

✈ ℘ 822551 - Booking Office : Aurigny Air Services ℘ 822889,.

⛴ to Guernsey (St. Peter Port) (Condor Ltd) (45 mn) – to Jersey (St. Helier) (Condor Ltd) (1 h 50 mn) – to France (St. Malo) (Condor Ltd) (4 h 20 mn).

ℹ States Office, Queen Elizabeth II St. JY9 3AA ℘ 822994/823737.

St. Anne – ☎ 01481.

⛳9 Route des Carrières ℘ 822835.

Chez André, Victoria St., ℘ 822777, Fax 822962 – ⇔ TV ☎. AE VISA
Meals (dinner only and Sunday lunch October-May) 14.50 **s.** and a la carte 4.00 – **11 rm** 31.50/70.00 **s.** – SB.

Inchalla, Le Val, GY9 3UL, ℘ 823220, Fax 824045, ≤, – ⇔ rest TV ☎ P. AE VISA.
closed 2 weeks Christmas – **Meals** *(closed Sunday dinner)* (dinner only and Sunday lunch)/dinner 13.75 and a la carte 3.50 – **9 rm** 39.50/79.00 – SB.

Rose and Crown, Le Huret, ℘ 823414, Fax 823615, – TV ☎. AE VISA JCB.
Meals (in bar) a la carte 7.50/15.45 **s.** 2.35 – **6 rm** 37.00/74.00 **s.**

Belle Vue, The Butes, ℘ 822844, Fax 823601 – ⇔ rest TV ☎. VISA JCB.
closed 24 to 26 December – **Meals** 8.50/12.50 **s.** and a la carte 4.75 – **27 rm** 37.50/75.00 **s.** – SB.

Maison de la Paix without rest., Petit Val, GY9 3DF, NW: ¾ m. by Les Mouriaux ℘ 823369, Fax 823369, < Platte Saline – ⇔ TV P.
closed Christmas and New Year – **3 rm** 34.00/48.00 **s.** – SB.

Chez Nous without rest., Les Venelles, GY9 3TW, ℘ 823633, Fax 823732 – ⇔ TV ☎. AE.
closed February – **3 rm** 26.00/44.00 **s.**

Georgian House, Victoria St., GY9 3UF, ℘ 822471, Fax 822471 – AE VISA
Meals *(closed Tuesday dinner)* 8.75/12.50 and a la carte 3.65.

Braye – ☎ 01481.

First and Last, ℘ 823162, < harbour – AE VISA JCB
25 March-31 October – **Meals** (closed Sunday dinner and Monday except Bank Holidays) (dinner only) a la carte 14.95/24.40 3.95.

GUERNSEY 403 OP 33 and 230 ⑨ ⑩ The West Country G. – pop. 58 867 – ☎ 01481.

See : Island★ – Pezeries Point★★ – Icart Point★★ – Côbo Bay★★ – St. Martins Point★★ – St. Apolline's Chapel★ – Vale Castle★ – Fort Doyle★ – La Gran'mere du Chimquiere★ – Moulin Huet Bay★ – Rocquaine Bay★ – Jerbourg Point★.

✈ Service Air ℘ 37682, Aurigny Air ℘ 37426, Midland Airport Services ℘ 37785.

⛴ to France (St. Malo) via Jersey (St. Helier) (Emeraude Lines) summer only – from St. Peter Port to Jersey (St. Helier) (Condor Ltd) 3 daily – from St. Peter Port to Weymouth (Condor Ltd) 3 daily – from St. Peter Port to Herm (Herm Seaway) (25 mn).

⛴ from St. Peter Port to France (Portbail and Carteret) (Service Maritime Carteret) (summer only) (1 h 5 mn) – from St. Peter Port to France (St. Malo and St. Quay Portrieux) via Jersey (St. Helier) (Emeraude Lines) (summer only) – from St. Peter Port to Weymouth (Condor Ltd : hydrofoil) 2 daily – from St. Peter Port to Sark (Isle of Sark Shipping Co. Ltd) (summer only) (40 mn) – from St. Peter Port to Alderney (Condor Ltd) (45 mn) – from St. Peter Port to Jersey (Channiland) (summer only) (50 mn).

ℹ Visitor Information Centre, North Plantation ℘ 723552 – The Airport, La Villiaze, Forest ℘ 37267.

Catel/Castel – ☎ 01481.

Belvoir Farm, Rue de la Hougue, GY5 7DY, ℘ 56004, Fax 56349, heated, – ⇔ rest TV P.
May-September – **Meals** (by arrangement) 9.00 **st.** 3.00 – **14 rm** (dinner included) 35.00/68.00 **s.** – SB.

Fermain Bay – ✉ St. Peter Port – ☎ 01481.

La Favorita, Fermain Lane, GY4 6SD, ℘ 35666, Fax 35413, <, ≤, – ⇔ rest TV ☎ P. AE VISA.
closed 20 December-1 January – **Meals** 16.50 **s.** (dinner) a la carte approx. 11.75 **s.** 4.75 – **36 rm** 46.00/87.00 **s.** – SB.

Le Chalet, GY4 6SD, ℘ 35716, Fax 35718 – TV ☎ P. AE VISA.
26 April-19 October – **Meals** (bar lunch Monday to Saturday)/dinner 15.50 and a la carte 3.50 – **44 rm** 40.00/100.00 – SB.

Forest – ☎ 01481.

Tudor Lodge Deer Farm without rest., Forest Rd, GY8 0AG, ✆ 37849, Fax 35662, park – TV ☎ P. VISA. ⋈
closed December-mid January – **5 rm** ⊏ 25.00/55.00.

Mon Plaisir without rest., Rue des Landes, GY8 0DY, ✆ 64498, Fax 63493, – TV P
closed 2 weeks December-January – **4 rm** ⊏ 25.00/42.00.

Pembroke Bay – ✉ Vale – ☎ 01481.

St. Peter Port 5.

Pembroke Bay ⊗, GY3 5BY, ✆ 47573, Fax 48838, heated, – TV ☎ P. VISA JCB.
closed 3 January-15 February – **Meals** 13.90 **s.** (dinner) and a la carte 14.65/28.25 **s.** 4.50
Ludwig's : Meals - Bavarian - *(closed Monday except July-August)* (dinner only) a la carte 12.70/18.65 **s.** 4.50 – **12 rm** ⊏ 45.00/77.00 **s.** – SB.

St. Martin – pop. 6 082 – ☎ 01481.

St. Peter Port 2.

Green Acres ⊗, Les Hubits, GY4 6LS, ✆ 35711, Fax 35978, heated, – rest rest TV ☎ P – 40. AE VISA.
Meals (bar lunch)/dinner 14.00 and a la carte 4.00 – **48 rm** ⊏ 38.00/76.00 – SB.

Idlerocks ⊗, Jerbourg Point, GY4 6BJ, ✆ 37711, Fax 35592, ≤ sea and neighbouring Channel Islands, heated, – rm TV ☎ P. AE VISA JCB
Meals (bar lunch Monday to Saturday)/dinner 16.00 **s.** 5.00 – **28 rm** ⊏ (dinner included) 50.00/178.00 – SB.

Saints Bay ⊗, Icart, GY4 6JG, ✆ 38888, Fax 35558, heated, – TV ☎ P. VISA.
April-October – **Meals** 12.50 and a la carte **s.** – **34 rm** ⊏ (dinner included) 55.00/96.00.

Bella Luce, La Fosse, Moulin Huet, GY4 6EB, ✆ 38764, Fax 39561, heated, –
TV ☎ P. AE VISA
Meals (bar lunch)/dinner 14.00 **s.** and a la carte 4.00 – **31 rm** ⊏ 45.50/88.00 – SB.

St. Margarets Lodge, Forest Rd., GY4 6UE, ✆ 35757, Fax 37594, heated, –
rest TV ☎ P – 80. AE VISA.
Meals 9.50/14.50 and a la carte 3.50 **46 rm** ⊏ 26.00/81.00 **s.**, 1 suite – SB.

Bon Port ⊗, Moulin Huet Bay, GY4 6EW, ✆ 39249, Fax 39596, ≤ Moulin Huet Bay and Jerbourg Point, – rest TV ☎ P. VISA JCB.
Meals 20.00/40.00 **s.** and a la carte **s.** – **15 rm** ⊏ 57.20/98.00 **s.**, 4 suites.

La Cloche ⊗, Les Traudes, GY4 6LR, ✆ 35421, Fax 38258, heated, – TV ☎ P
VISA.
May-October – **Meals** (residents only) (dinner only) 11.95 3.25 – **10 rm** ⊏ (dinner included) 31.50/82.00.

La Barbarie ⊗, Saints Bay, GY4 6ES, ✆ 35217, Fax 35208, heated, – TV ☎ P.
VISA.
Meals (bar lunch Monday to Saturday)/dinner 17.50 and a la carte 3.75 – **22 rm** ⊏ 43.50/87.00, 1 suite – SB.

Farnborough without rest., Les Damonettes Lane, GY1 1ZN, off Les Hubits ✆ 37756 Fax 34082, – TV P. VISA.
April-September – **11 rm** ⊏ 30.00/46.00 **st.**

La Michele ⊗, Les Hubits, GY4 6NB, ✆ 38065, Fax 39492, heated, – rest TV
☎ P. AE VISA.
April-October – **Meals** (residents only) (dinner only) 8.00 **s.** 3.50 – **13 rm** ⊏ (dinner included) 42.00/74.00 – SB.

Ambassador, Route De Sausmarez, GY4 6SQ, ✆ 38356, Fax 39280, – rest TV ☎
P. AE VISA.
14 April-October – **Meals** 10.50 4.95 – **19 rm** ⊏ (dinner included) 35.00/70.00 – SB.

St. Peter in the Wood pop. 2 242 – ✉ St. Peters – ☎ 01481.

St. Peter Port 6.

Café Du Moulin, Rue du Quanteraine, GY7 9DP, ✆ 65944, Fax 66468 – VISA
closed Sunday dinner and Monday – **Meals** 10.95/17.95 and a la carte 5.00.

St. Peter Port The West Country G. – pop. 16 648 – ☎ 01481.

See : Town★★ – St. Peter's Church★ Z – Hauteville House (Victor Hugo's House)★ *AC* Z – Castle Cornet★ (≤★) *AC* Z.

Envir. : Saumarez Park★, W : 2 m. by road to Catel Z – Little Chapel★, SW : 2 1/4 m. by Mount Durand road Z.

18 St. Pierre Park ✆ 727039, Z.

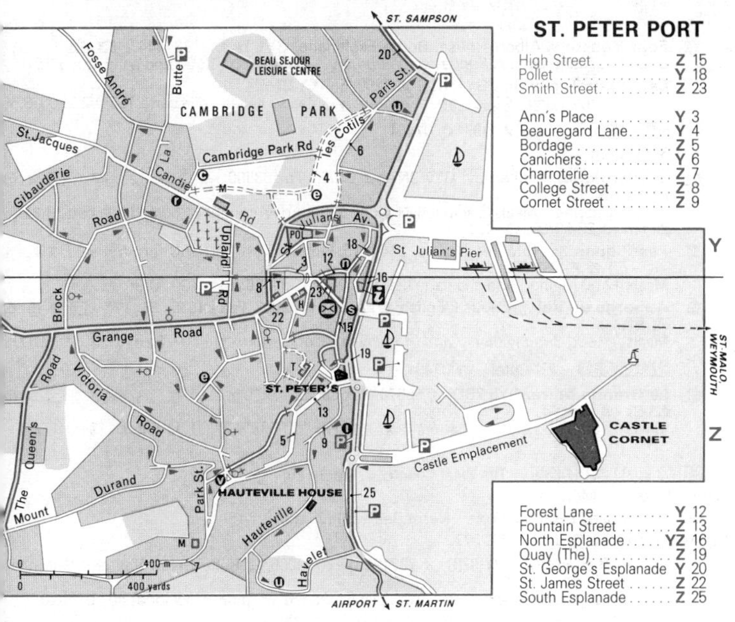

St. Pierre Park, Rohais, GY1 1FD, W : by Grange Rd., ℘ 728282, Telex 4191662, Fax 712041, ≤, park, – rm – 200. AE VISA JCB.
Café Renoir : Meals 11.95/17.95 **s.** and a la carte 6.50 (see also ***Victor Hugo*** below) – **132 rm** 105.00/145.00 **s.**, 3 suites.

Duke of Richmond, Cambridge Park, GY1 1UY, ℘ 726221, Fax 728945, heated – rest – 100. AE VISA Y **c**
Meals 9.50/15.00 **s.** and a la carte 4.50 – **74 rm** 45.00/85.00 **st.**, 1 suite – SB.

De Havelet, Havelet, GY1 1BA, ℘ 722199, Fax 714057, – . AE VISA Z **u**
Wellington Boot : Meals *(closed Sunday dinner)* (dinner only and Sunday lunch) 14.50 and a la carte 3.50 – **Havelet Grill : Meals** *(closed Monday dinner)* 14.50 and a la carte 3.25 – **34 rm** 53.50/104.00 – SB.

Moore's Central, Le Pollet, GY1 1WH, ℘ 724452, Fax 714037 – . AE VISA. Y **n**
Meals 17.50 **s.** (dinner) and a la carte15.00/30.50 2.50 – **48 rm** 31.00/130.00 – SB.

Midhurst House, Candie Rd, GY1 1UP, ℘ 724391, Fax 729451, – . VISA. Y **r**
Easter-mid October – **Meals** (residents only) (dinner only) 11.00 – **8 rm** 32.00/60.00 – SB.

Kenwood House without rest., Allez St., GY1 1NG, ℘ 726146, Fax 725632 – . VISA. Z **e**
closed 20 December-5 January – **6 rm** 15.00/44.00 **s.**

Marine without rest., Well Rd, GY1 1WS, ℘ 724978 – VISA JCB. Y **u**
11 rm 24.50/46.00 **s.**

XXXX **Victor Hugo** (at St. Pierre Park H.), Rohais, GY1 1FD, W : by Grange Rd., ℘ 728282, Telex 4191662, Fax 712041 – . AE VISA JCB
closed Saturday lunch and Sunday dinner – **Meals** - Seafood - 10.95/19.95 **s.** and a la carte 6.95. Z **i**

XX **La Frégate** with rm, Les Cotils, GY1 1UT, ℘ 724624, Fax 720443, ≤ town and harbour, – . AE VISA. Y **e**
Meals 12.50/18.00 **s.** and a la carte 4.50 – **13 rm** 55.00/95.00 **s.**

XX **The Absolute End,** Longstore, GY1 2BG, N : ¾ m. by St. George's Esplanade ℘ 723822, Fax 729129 – AE VISA
closed Sunday and January – **Meals** - Seafood - 11.00 **s.** (lunch)and a la carte 11.50/20.50 **s.** 4.00.

XX **Le Nautique,** Quay Steps, GY1 2LE, ℘ 721714, Fax 721786, ≤ – AE VISA JCB Z **s**
closed Sunday and first 2 weeks January – **Meals** a la carte 17.00/22.50 4.80.

XX **Four Seasons,** Albert House, South Esplanade, GY1 1AJ, ℘ 727444 – VISA Z i
closed Tuesday dinner, Sunday and February – **Meals** 10.00/13.50 and a la carte 4.50.

XX **La Piazza,** Trinity Sq., GY1 1LX, ℘ 725085 – AE VISA Z v
closed Sunday and 24 December-24 January – **Meals** - Italian - a la carte 16.20/27.00 3.50.

St. Saviour – pop. 2 419 – 01481.

St. Peter Port 4.

L'Atlantique, Perelle Bay, GY7 9NA, ℘ 64056, Fax 63800, ←, heated, – TV P. AE VISA.
March-October – **Meals** (bar lunch Monday to Saturday)/dinner 14.50 and a la carte 3.95 – **23 rm** 28.50/80.00 – SB.

Les Piques , Rue des Piques, ℘ 64515, Fax 65857, « Part 15C farmhouse », , , – TV P. VISA.
Meals 12.50 (dinner) and a la carte12.00/19.00 3.75 – **25 rm** 30.00/96.00.

Auberge du Val , Sous L'Eglise, GY7 9FX, ℘ 63862, Fax 64835, , – TV P. AE VISA.
Meals *(closed Sunday dinner and Monday)* a la carte approx. 14.00 – **8 rm** 30.00/60.00 **s.**

Vazon Bay – Catel – 01481.

La Grande Mare, GY5 7BD, ℘ 56576, Fax 56532, ←, heated, 18, , – TV P. AE VISA.
Meals 12.50/19.50 and a la carte 6.50 – **11 rm** 95.00/177.00, **13 suites** 113.00/177.00 – SB.

HERM 403 P 33 and 230 ⑩ **The West Country G.** – pop. 45 – 01481.

See : Le Grand Monceau★.

to Guernsey (St. Peter Port) (Herm Seaway) (25 mn).

Administrative Office, ℘ 722377.

White House , GY1 3HR, ℘ 722159, Fax 710066, ← Belle Greve Bay and Guernsey, heated, , park, – rest. VISA.
April-September – **Meals** 11.95/19.95 3.95 – **38 rm** (dinner included) 46.00/110.00.

The Guide is updated annually so renew your Guide every year.

JERSEY 403 OP 33 and 230 ⑪ **The West Country G.** – pop. 84 082 – 01534.

See : Island★★ – Jersey Zoo★★ *AC* – St. Catherine's Bay★ (←★★) – Grosnez Point★ – Devil's Hole★ – St. Matthews Church, Millbrook (glasswork★) – La Hougue Bie (Neolithic tomb★ *AC*, Chapels★, German Occupation Museum★ *AC*) – St. Catherine's Bay★ (←★★) – Noirmont Point★.

States of Jersey Airport : ℘ 492000.

to France (St. Malo) (Emeraude Lines) – from St. Helier to Weymouth via Guernsey (St. Peter Port) 3 daily.

from St. Helier to France (St. Quay Portrieux (Emeraude Lines), Granville and St. Malo (Emeraude Lines and Channiland)) (summer only) – from Gorey to France (Portbail and Carteret) (Emeraude Lines) (summer only) (30 mn) – from St. Helier to Alderney (Condor Ltd) (1 h 55 mn) – from St. Helier to Sark (Emeraude Lines) (summer only) – from St. Helier to Guernsey (St. Peter Port) (Emeraude Lines) (summer only) – from St. Helier to Weymouth via Guernsey (St. Peter Port) (Condor Ltd) – from St. Helier to Guernsey (St. Peter Port) (50 mn), to Sark (45 mn) (Channiland) (summer only).

Liberation Square, St. Helier, JE1 1BB ℘ 500700.

Bouley Bay – Trinity – 01534.

St. Helier 5.

Water's Edge, JE3 5AS, ℘ 862777, Fax 863645, ← Bouley Bay, , heated, – rest TV P. AE VISA JCB.
April-October – **Meals** 13.50/17.50 and a la carte 6.00 – **44 rm** 47.00/109.00, 7 suites – SB.

Corbiere – St. Brelade – 01534.

St. Helier 8.

XXX **Sea Crest** with rm, Petit Port, JE3 8HH, ℘ 46353, Fax 47316, ←, , – rest TV P. AE VISA.
closed mid January-mid February – **Meals** *(closed Sunday dinner November-March and Monday)* 11.50/19.00 and a la carte 6.00 – **7 rm** 59.50/95.00.

Gorey **The West Country G.** – St. Martin – 01534.

See : Mont Orgueil Castle★ (←★★) *AC* – Jersey Pottery★.

St. Helier 4.

Old Court House, Gorey Village, JE3 9FS, ℘ 854444, Fax 853587, , heated, – TV P. AE VISA
April-mid October – **Meals** (bar lunch)/dinner 13.00 **s.** and a la carte 3.00 – **58 rm** (dinner included) 35.00/108.00 **s.**

Moorings, Gorey Pier, JE3 6EW, 853633, Fax 857618 – rest. Meals 10.50/35.00 **s.** and la carte 2.90 – **16 rm** 32.00/94.00 **s.** – SB.

Maison Gorey, Gorey Village, JE3 9EP, 857775, Fax 857779 – rest.
May-September – **Meals** (bar lunch)/dinner 8.00 4.00 – **30 rm** 45.00/70.00.

Trafalgar Bay, Gorey Village, JE3 9ES, 856643, Fax 856922, heated, –.
May-September – **Meals** (bar lunch)/dinner 10.00 – **27 rm** (dinner included) 30.50/98.00 **s.**

Jersey Pottery (Garden Restaurant), Gorey Village, JE3 9EP, 851119, Fax 856403, « Working pottery », –.
closed Saturday January-April, Sunday and 10 days at Christmas – **Meals** - Seafood - (lunch only) a la carte 16.75/24.00 6.00.

Village Bistro, Gorey Village, JE3 9EP, 853429, Fax 853429.
closed Monday except Bank Holidays, 2 weeks February and 2 weeks November – **Meals** (dinner booking essential) 9.50 (lunch) and a la carte 18.50/23.90 3.00.

Grève De Lecq – St. Ouen – 01534.

Des Pierres, JE3 2DT, on B 65 481858, Fax 485273 –.
Meals (dinner only) 8.00 **s.** 2.95 – **16 rm** (dinner included) 37.00/76.00 **s.** – SB.

Grouville – 01534.

Lavender Villa, Rue a Don, JE3 9DX, on A 3 854937, Fax 856147, – rest.
24 March-2 November – **Meals** (dinner only) 7.00 3.00 – **21 rm** (dinner included) 34.00/68.00 **s.**

Mon Desir House without rest., La Rue Des Prés, JE3 9DJ, 854718, Fax 857798, –.
closed December-mid February – **13 rm** 16.00/48.00 **s.**

La Haule – St. Brelade – 01534.

La Place, Route du Coin, JE3 8BF, by B 25 on B 43 44261, Fax 45164, heated – 35.
Knights : Meals 10.50/19.00 and a la carte 6.00 – **39 rm** 82.00/126.00 – SB.

Au Caprice, JE3 8BA, on A 1 22083, Fax 26199 –.
April-October – **Meals** (by arrangement) 6.00 – **13 rm** 17.00/51.00.

La Pulente – St. Brelade – 01534.

Les Mielles, The Mount, Val de la Mare, St. Ouens 81947/82787.

St. Helier 7.

Atlantic, La Moye, JE3 8HE, 44101, Fax 44102, heated, – 60.
closed January and February – **Meals** 15.00/21.50 **s.** and dinner a la carte – **49 rm** 105.00/225.00 **s.**, 1 suite – SB.

Rozel Bay – St. Martin – 01534.

St. Helier 6.

Chateau La Chaire, Rozel Valley, JE3 6AJ, 863354, Fax 865137, –.
Meals - (see below) – **13 rm** 95.00/145.00 **s.**, 1 suite – SB.

Le Couperon de Rozel, JE3 5BN, 865522, Fax 865332, heated –.
25 April-5 October – **Meals** 12.95/17.95 **s.** and a la carte 4.00 – **35 rm** (dinner included) 51.50/115.00 **s.**

Chateau La Chaire (at Chateau La Chaire H.), Rozel Valley, JE3 6AJ, 863354, Fax 865137 –.
Meals 10.25/22.50 and a la carte 4.50.

St. Aubin – 01534.

St. Helier 4.

Somerville, Mont du Boulevard, JE3 8AD, S : 3/4 m. via harbour 41226, Fax 46621, St. Aubin's Bay, heated, –.
8 April-October – **Meals** (dancing 3 evenings a week) (bar lunch Monday to Saturday)/dinner 15.00 **s.** and a la carte 3.50 – **59 rm** 30.00/110.00.

La Tour, High St., JE3 8BR, 43770, Fax 47143, St. Aubin's Fort and Bay – rest.
April-November – **Meals** (dinner only) 10.50 and a la carte 3.75 – **25 rm** 34.00/68.00, 1 suite.

Mont de La Roque, Mont de La Roque, JE3 8BQ, ✆ 42942, Fax 47841, ≤ – TV ☎ P. VISA. ✱
closed January and February – **Meals** *(closed Monday)* 9.95/16.50 and a la carte 3.10 – **24 rm** 40.00/80.00 – SB.

Panorama without rest., High St., JE3 8BR, ✆ 42429, Fax 45940, ≤ St. Aubin's Fort and Bay, – TV. AE VISA. ✱
Easter-October – **17 rm** 40.00/70.00.

Bon Viveur, The Bulwarks, JE3 8AB, ✆ 41049, Fax 47540, ≤ – TV. AE VISA JCB. ✱
March-October – **Meals** 10.00 and a la carte 3.00 – **19 rm** 23.00/50.00.

Sabots d'or, High St., JE3 8BR, ✆ 43732 – TV. AE VISA
Meals (by arrangement) – **12 rm** (dinner included) 26.00/56.00 **s.**

St. Magloire, Rue de Crocquet, JE3 8BZ, ✆ 41302, Fax 44148 – rest TV. AE VISA. ✱
mid March-October – **Meals** (by arrangement) 6.00 2.75 – **12 rm** 16.00/48.00 **s.** – SB.

XXX ✿ **Broome's** (Broome), The Bulwarks, JE3 8AB, ✆ 42760, Fax 42760, – P. AE VISA JCB
closed Sunday and January – **Meals** 12.50/28.00 and a la carte 22.95/28.45 8.00
Spec. Roast sea scallops, jade sauce, Lambs sweetbreads tempura with a blood orange and saffron jus, Rhubarb and custard sandwich.

X **Old Court House Inn** with rm, St. Aubin's Harbour, JE3 8AB, ✆ 46433, Fax 45103, ≤, – TV ☎. AE VISA. ✱
closed Tuesday dinner and Wednesday October-March – **Meals** 15.50 and a la carte 3.50 – **8 rm** 40.00/80.00, 1 suite.

St. Brelade's Bay The West Country G. – pop. 9 331 – ✉ St. Brelade – 01534.

See : Fishermen's Chapel (frescoes★).

St. Helier 6.

L'Horizon, JE3 8EF, ✆ 43101, Fax 46269, ≤ St. Brelade's Bay, – TV ☎ P – 150. AE VISA. ✱
Crystal Room : Meals (dinner only) 14.00/23.75 5.75 - (see also ***Star Grill*** below) – **104 rm** 120.00/210.00 **s.**, 3 suites – SB.

St. Brelade's Bay, JE3 8EP, ✆ 46141, Fax 47278, ≤ St. Brelade's Bay, heated, – TV ☎ P. AE VISA. ✱
late April-early October – **Meals** 12.00/18.00 and a la carte – **80 rm** (dinner included) 90.00/180.00, 1 suite.

Golden Sands, La Route de la Baie, JE3 8EF, ✆ 41241, Fax 499366, ≤ – TV ☎. VISA ✱
April- 2 January – **Meals** (residents only)(dinner only) 11.50 and a la carte – **62 rm** 35.00/120.00.

Chateau Valeuse, Rue de la Valeuse, JE3 8EE, ✆ 46281, Fax 47110, heated, – TV ☎ P. VISA. ✱
April-21 October – **Meals** *(closed Sunday dinner to non-residents)* 9.50/15.00 and dinner a la carte 4.00 – **34 rm** (dinner included) 45.00/108.00 **s.**

Three Bay View without rest., La route de Noirmont, JE3 8AJ, on B 57 ✆ 42028 – P. ✱
7 rm 16.00/32.00.

XXX **Star Grill** (at L'Horizon H.), JE3 8EF, ✆ 43101, Fax 46269 – P. AE VISA
Meals 13.50 (lunch) and a la carte 23.45/37.20 5.75.

St. Clement – pop. 7 393 – 01534.

St. Clements ✆ 21938.

St. Helier 2.

Playa D'Or, Greve d'Azette, JE2 6SA, W : 2 m. on A 4 ✆ 22861, Fax 69668 – TV P AE VISA. ✱
closed December and January – **Meals** (by arrangement) 7.50 3.50 – **15 rm** 27.50/55.00 **s.**

Rocque-Berg View without rest., Rue de Samares, JE2 6LS, ✆ 852642, Fax 851694, heated – TV P. VISA. ✱
April-30 October – **9 rm** 30.00/40.00 **s.**

St. Helier The West Country G. – pop. 28 123 – 01534.

See : Jersey Museum★ *AC* Z – Elizabeth Castle (≤★) *AC* Z – Fort Regent (≤★ *AC*) Z.

Envir. : St. Peter's Valley (Living Legend★ *AC*) NW : 4 m. by A 1, A11 St. Peter's Valley rd and C 112.

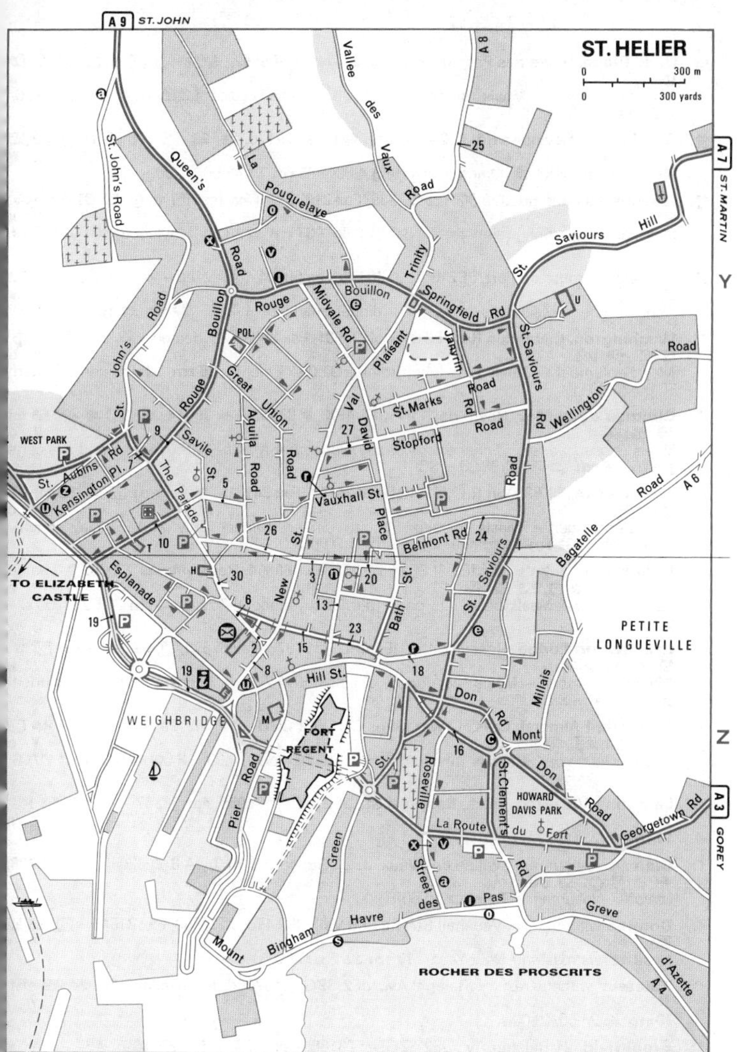

De Vere Grand, Esplanade, JE4 8WD, ☏ 22301, Fax 37815, ≤, Fь, ≘s, ☐ – |♦| ▤ rest TV ☎ ♿ P – 🏛 180. ☐ AE ⓘ VISA Y **u**
Meals (dinner only) 19.50 ꕃ 5.00 – (see also ***Victoria's*** below) – **110 rm** ☐ 85.00/160.00 **s.**, 5 suites – SB.

Pomme d'Or, Liberation Sq., JE2 3NR, ☏ 880110, Telex 4192309, Fax 37781 – |♦| ⨯ rm ▤ rest TV ☎ – 🏛 180. ☐ AE ⓘ VISA ⨯ Z **u**
Harbour Room : Meals (carving rest.) 8.00/15.50 ꕃ 3.55 (see also ***La Petite Pomme*** below) – **145 rm** ☐ 67.50/105.00 **s.**, 2 suites – SB.

De la Plage, Havre des Pas, JE2 4UQ, ☎ 23474, Fax 68642, ←, Ⅰ – |‡| TV ☎ P. AE VISA JCB. ✻ Z
May-13 October – **Meals** (dinner only) 20.00 **s.** and a la carte 3.55 – **78 rm** 35.00/112.00 **s.**

Apollo, 9 St. Saviour's Rd, JE2 4LA, ☎ 25441, Fax 22120, Ⅰ, ≘s, – |‡| TV ☎ P. VISA. ✻ Z
Meals (dinner only) 11.00 and a la carte 4.00 – **85 rm** 43.50/87.00 – SB.

Queens, Queens Rd, JE2 3GR, ☎ 22239, Fax 21930 – |‡| ⇔ rest TV ☎ P. AE VISA JCB ✻ Y
Meals (residents only) (dinner only) 8.00 3.50 – **37 rm** (dinner included) 40.00/96.00 s – SB.

Laurels, La route du Fort, JE2 4PA, ☎ 36444, Fax 59904, heated – ⇔ rest TV ☎ P. AE VISA. ✻ Z
April-October – **Meals** (residents only) (dinner only) 9.50 4.00 – **37 rm** 50.00/80.00.

Washington, Clarendon Rd, JE2 3YS, ☎ 37981, Fax 89899, heated – ⇔ rest TV ☎ P AE VISA Y
May-September – **Meals** (bar lunch)/dinner 9.50 **s.** 4.60 – **36 rm** (dinner included) 50.00/80.00.

Chateau de la Mer, Havre des Pas, JE2 4PX, ☎ 33366, Fax 36544, ← – TV ☎ P. VISA JCB Z
Meals *(closed Sunday dinner and Monday November-March)* 11.50/14.50 **s.** and a la carte 3.75 – **4 rm** 45.00/88.00 – SB.

Mornington, 60-68 Don Rd, JE2 4QD, ☎ 24452, Fax 34131 – |‡| ⇔ rest TV ☎. AE VISA. ✻ Z
April-September – **Meals** *(closed Sunday dinner)* (dinner only and Sunday lunch)/dinner 9.00 – **31 rm** (dinner included) 41.00/68.00 – SB.

Uplands, St. John's Rd, JE2 3LE, ☎ 873006, Fax 68804, Reservations 73006, heated ⇔ rest TV ☎ P. AE VISA. ✻ Y
April-October – **Meals** (residents only) (bar lunch)/dinner 8.75 **s.** – **43 rm** 33.00/66.00 **s.** – SB.

Greenwood Lodge, Roseville St., JE2 4PL, ☎ 67073, Fax 67876, heated – ⇔ TV ☎ AE VISA JCB Z
March-November – **Meals** (bar lunch)/dinner 7.50 2.95 – **32 rm** (dinner included) 35.00/62.00 – SB.

Almorah, 1 Almorah Cres., Lower Kings Cliff, JE2 3GU, ☎ 21648, Fax 68600, – ⇔ TV ☎ P. VISA. ✻ Y
closed December – **Meals** (residents only) (dinner only) 9.00 3.00 – **14 rm** 29.00/38.00 **s.** – SB.

La Bonne Vie without rest., Roseville St., JE2 4PL, ☎ 35955, Fax 33357 – ⇔ TV. VISA ✻ Z
10 rm 23.00/51.00.

Glen without rest., Vallee des Vaux, JE2 3GB, N : 1¼ m. by A 8 ☎ 32062, Fax 880738 – TV P. VISA. ✻
March-7 November – **7 rm** 25.50/51.00.

Domino without rest., Vauxhall St. (Rue du Val), JE2 4TJ, ☎ 30360, Fax 31546 – TV. AE VISA. ✻ Y
closed Christmas and New Year – **13 rm** 25.00/50.00.

Kaieteur without rest., 4 Ralegh Av., JE2 3ZG, ☎ 37004, Fax 67423 – TV. AE VISA ✻ Y
10 rm 24.50/49.00 **s.**

Brookfield, 24 Raleigh Av., JE2 3ZG, ☎ 23168, Fax 21543 – TV. VISA. ✻ Y
closed December and January – **Meals** (by arrangement) – **20 rm** (dinner included) 28.00/71.00.

De L'Etang, 33 Havre des Pas, JE2 4UL, ☎ 21996, Fax 37829, ← – TV. VISA. ✻
closed 20 December-20 January and 21 October-10 November – 3.50 – **13 rm** (dinner included) 29.50/52.50 – SB. Z

XXX **Victoria's** (at Grand H.), Peirson Rd, JE4 8WD, ☎ 872255, Fax 37815 – ▤ P. AE VISA Y
closed Sunday dinner – **Meals** (live music and dancing) 14.95/23.50 and a la carte 5.00.

XXX **La Petite Pomme** (at Pomme d'Or H.), Conway St., JE2 3NR, ☎ 66608 – ▤. AE VISA Z
closed lunch Saturday and Bank Holidays and Sunday – **Meals** 13.50/15.50 **s.** and a la carte **s.** 3.55.

XX **La Capannina,** 65-67 Halkett Pl., JE2 4WG, ☎ 34602, Fax 877628 – AE VISA Z
closed Sunday – **Meals** - Italian - 17.00 (dinner) and a la carte 11.20/22.90 4.90.

XX **Langtry's,** La Motte St., JE2 4SZ, ☎ 32668. AE VISA Z
closed Saturday lunch and Sunday – **Meals** 10.00/16.50 **s.** and a la carte 4.00.

St. Lawrence – pop. 4 561 – 01534.

St. Helier 3.

Elmdale Farm, Ville Emphrie, JE3 1EA, 34779, Fax 601115, heated, – . VISA.
Meals *(closed Mondays except Bank Holidays)* 6.50/17.00 and a la carte 3.50 – **13 rm** 25.00/50.00.

Villa d'Oro without rest., La Grande Route de St. Laurent, JE3 1NJ, on A 10 862262, Fax 863012 – . AE VISA.
closed November and 20 December-20 January – **12 rm** 15.00/40.00 **s.**

St. Martin – pop. 3 258 – 01534.

St. Helier 4.

Le Relais de St. Martin, JE3 6EA, 853271, Fax 855241, – rest . VISA.
Meals (by arrangement) 8.75 3.00 – **11 rm** 25.00/50.00.

La Franchise Farm without rest., JE3 6HU, NW : ¾ m. by B 30 on C 110 862224, – .
April-September – **7 rm** 19.00/48.00.

St. Peter – pop. 84 082 – 01534.

St. Helier 5.

Mermaid, Airport Rd, JE3 7BN, on B 36 41255, Fax 45826, heated, – – 80. AE VISA.
Meals 9.50/12.00 **s.** and a la carte 4.50 – **68 rm** 53.25/104.00 – SB.

Greenhill's Country, Coin Varin, Mont de l'Ecole, JE3 7EL, on C 112 481042, Fax 485322, heated – . AE VISA JCB.
Meals 12.50/17.00 **s.** and a la carte – **19 rm** 59.00/118.00 **s.** – SB.

St. Saviour – pop. 12 747 – 01534.

St. Helier 1.

Longueville Manor, Longueville Rd, JE2 7SA, on A 3 25501, Fax 31613, « Former manor house with Jacobean panelling », heated, park, – rest rest . AE VISA
Meals 17.00/30.00 **s.** and dinner a la carte 31.75/37.75 **s.** 10.00 – **30 rm** 180.00/230.00 **s.**, 2 suites – SB
Spec. Gateau of Jersey crab on a warm potato salad with marinated vegetables, Ragout of scallops and lobster with dumplings and a basil flavoured nage, Grilled Jersey sea bass on an aubergine terrine, tomato and olive sauce.

Champ Colin without rest., Rue du Champ Colin, Houge Bie, JE2 7UN, 851877, Fax 854902, – . AE VISA JCB.
3 rm 36.00/44.00.

SARK 403 P 33 and 230 ⑩ **The West Country G.** – pop. 560 – 01481.

See : Island★★ – La Coupee★★★ – Port du Moulin★★ – Creux Harbour★ – La Seigneurie★ *AC* – Pilcher Monument★ – Hog's Back★.

to France (St. Malo) via Jersey (St. Helier) (Emeraude Lines) (summer only) – to Guernsey (St. Peter Port) (Isle of Sark Shipping Co. Ltd) (summer only) (40 mn) – to Jersey (St. Helier) (Channiland) (45 mn).

832345.

Dixcart, GY9 0SD, 832015, Fax 832164, park – AE VISA JCB
Meals (booking essential in winter) 7.50/15.00 and a la carte 3.00 – **15 rm** 30.00/70.00 – SB.

Petit Champ, GY9 0SF, 832046, Fax 832469, coast, Herm, Jetou and Guernsey, « Country house atmosphere », heated, – rest. AE VISA.
Easter-early October – **Meals** 16.75 **s.** (dinner) and a la carte 9.00/23.95 **s.** 3.60 – **16 rm** (dinner included) 47.00/98.00 **s.**

Stocks, GY9 0SD, 832001, Fax 832130, . AE VISA JCB.
April-September – **Meals** 9.00/20.00 and a la carte 5.00 – **24 rm** (dinner included) 40.00/110.00 – SB.

Les Quatre Vents, GY9 0SE, off Harbour Hill 832247, Fax 832332, – rm .
closed December-2 January – **Meals** (by arrangement) 15.00 **s.** – **4 rm** 22.00/44.00.

La Sablonnerie with rm, Little Sark, GY9 0SD, 832061, Fax 832408, – AE VISA.
Easter-mid October – **Meals** 18.50/25.00 and a la carte 4.80 – **21 rm** (dinner included) 49.50/119.00, 1 suite.

Founiais, Harbour Hill, GY9 0SB, 832626, Fax 832642 – VISA
March-October – **Meals** a la carte 12.90/18.65 3.25.

Isle of Man

Place with at least

a hotel or restaurant	● Douglas
a pleasant hotel or restaurant	🏨, 🏠, ✕
a quiet, secluded hotel	🐴
a restaurant with	✿, ✿✿, ✿✿✿, **Meals** (M)

Localité offrant au moins

une ressource hôtelière	● Douglas
un hôtel ou restaurant agréable	🏨, 🏠, ✕
un hôtel très tranquille, isolé	🐴
une bonne table à	✿, ✿✿, ✿✿✿, **Meals** (M)

La località possiede come minimo

una risorsa alberghiera	● Douglas
Albergo o ristorante ameno	🏨, 🏠, ✕
un albergo molto tranquillo, isolato	🐴
un'ottima tavola con	✿, ✿✿, ✿✿✿, **Meals** (M)

Ort mit mindestens

einem Hotel oder Restaurant	● Douglas
ein angenehmes Hotel oder Restaurant	🏨, 🏠, ✕
einem sehr ruhigen und abgelegenen Hotel	🐴
einem Restaurant mit	✿, ✿✿, ✿✿✿, **Meals** (M)

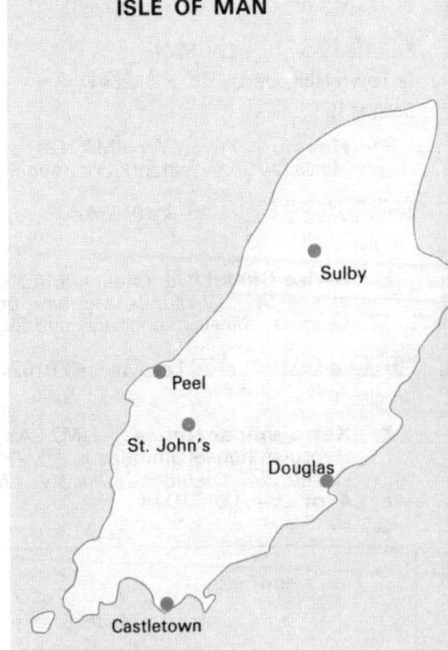

CASTLETOWN 402 G 21 **Great Britain G.** – pop. 3 152 – ☎ 01624.

Exc. : Cregneash Folk Museum★ *AC*, W : 6½ m. by A 5 and A 31.

Douglas 10.

- **Castletown Golf Links**, Derbyhaven, IM9 1UA, E : 2 m. ☎ 822201, Fax 824633, ≤ Irish Sea and golf links, ≘s, ⊠, 18, park – TV ☎ & P – 180. AE VISA
  Meals (bar lunch Monday to Saturday)/dinner 18.50 **st.** 5.50 – **58 rm** ☐ 50.00/80.00 **st.** – SB.

- **Chablis Cellar**, 21 Bank St., IM9 1AT, ☎ 823527 – VISA
  closed Sunday dinner and Monday – **Meals** 18.50/38.00 **t.** and a la carte 6.50.

DOUGLAS 402 G 21 **Great Britain G.** – pop. 22 214 – ☎ 01624.

Exc. : Snaefell★ (✻★★★) N : 8 m. by A 2 and mountain tramcar from Laxey – Laxey Wheel★★ NE : 8 m. by A 2.

18 Douglas Municipal, Pulrose Park ☎ 661558 – 18 King Edward Bay, Groudle Rd, Onchan ☎ 620430/673821.

Ronaldsway Airport : ☎ 823311, SW : 7 m. – **Terminal** : Coach service from Lord St.

to Belfast (Isle of Man Steam Packet Co. Ltd) (summer only) (4 h 30 mn) – to Republic of Ireland (Dublin) (Isle of Man Steam Packet Co. Ltd) (4 h 30 mn) – to Fleetwood (Isle of Man Steam Packet Co. Ltd) (summer only) (3 h 20 mn) – to Heysham (Isle of Man Steam Packet Co Ltd) (3 h 45 mn) – to Liverpool (Isle of Man Steam Packet Co. Ltd) (4 h).

Sea Terminal ☎ 686766.

- **Mount Murray H. & Country Club**, Santon, IM4 2HT, SW : 4¾ m. by A 5 ☎ 661111, Fax 611116, ≘s, ⊠, 18, park, squash – ⊫ rm TV ☎ & P – 300. AE VISA
  Meals *(closed Sunday lunch)* a la carte 10.50/16.00 **st.** – **Murray's : Meals** *(closed Saturday lunch, Sunday dinner and Monday)* 12.50/25.00 **t.** and dinner a la carte – **90 rm** ☐ 72.50/140.00 **st.** – SB.

- **Empress**, Central Promenade, IM2 4RA, ☎ 661155, Fax 673554, ≘s, ⊠ – ≡ rest TV ☎ – 150. AE VISA JCB
  Meals 7.50/12.50 **t.** and a la carte 5.75 – ☐ 7.50 – **99 rm** 59.00/65.00 **t.**, 3 suites – SB.

- **Sefton**, Harris Promenade, IM1 2RW, ☎ 626011, Fax 676004, ≤, ≘s, ⊠ – TV ☎ & P – 80. AE VISA JCB
  Meals 8.00/15.00 **st.** and dinner a la carte 6.00 – **77 rm** ☐ 47.50/67.50 **st.**, 2 suites.

- **Castle Mona**, Central Promenade, IM2 4LY, ☎ 624540, Fax 675360 – TV ☎ P – 120. AE VISA
  Meals 11.95 **st.** and a la carte – ☐ 5.95 – **66 rm** 46.50 **st.**, 1 suite – SB.

- **Admirals House**, 12 Loch Promenade, IM1 2LX, ☎ 629551, Fax 675021 – TV ☎. AE VISA
  Boncompte : Meals *(closed Saturday lunch and Sunday)* 11.00/16.50 **t.** and a la carte 4.75 – **12 rm** ☐ 50.00/110.00 **t.**

ATS Mount Vernon, Peel Rd ☎ 622661 ATS 5-7 South Quay ☎ 676532

PEEL 402 F 21 – ☎ 01624.

Town Hall, Derby Rd ☎ 842341.

Douglas 11.

- **Haven**, 10 Peveril Av., IM5 1QB, ☎ 842585, Fax 842585 – TV. VISA
  Meals (by arrangement) (communal dining) 10.50 **st.** – **3 rm** ☐ 23.00/34.00 **st.** – SB.

ST. JOHNS 402 G 21 – ☎ 01624.

Douglas 10.

- **Swiss Chalet**, Glen Helen, IM4 3NP, N : 2 m. on A 3 ☎ 801657 – P
  closed Sunday dinner, Monday, last week January-first week February and last week October – **Meals** (dinner only and Sunday lunch)/dinner 11.95 **t.** and a la carte.

SULBY 402 G 21 – ✉ Lezayre – ☎ 01624.

Douglas 16.

- **Kerrowmoar House**, IM7 2AX, E : ½ m. on Ramsey rd ☎ 897543, Fax 897927, « Part Georgian house, antiques », ⊠, park, – TV ☎ P.
  closed 23 December-2 January – **Meals** (by arrangement) (communal dining) 15.00 **s.** – **4 rm** ☐ 45.00/70.00 **s.**

Don't confuse:

Comfort of hotels	: ... , ,
Comfort of restaurants	: XXXXX X
Quality of the cuisine	: ✿✿✿, ✿✿, ✿, **Meals**

Republic of Ireland

Prices quoted in this section of the guide are in Irish pounds (punt)

Dans cette partie du guide, les prix sont indiqués en monnaie irlandaise « Punt »

In questa parte della guida, i prezzi sono indicati in livres irlandesi « Punt »

In diesem Teil des Führers sind die Preise in irländischer Währung « Punt » angegeben

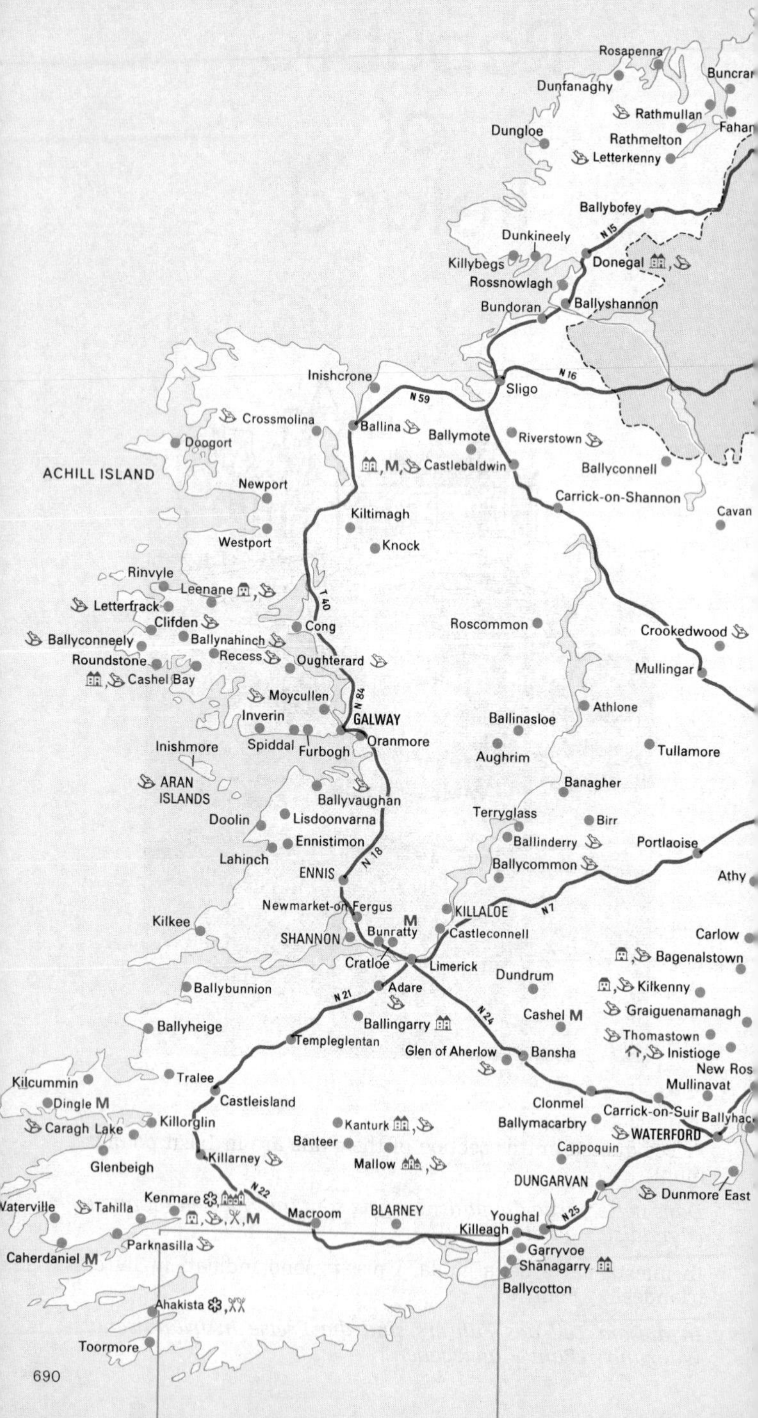
Rosapenna
Buncrana
Dunfanaghy
Rathmullan
Fahan
Dungloe
Rathmelton
Letterkenny
Ballybofey
N 15
Dunkineely
Killybegs
Donegal
Rossnowlagh
Bundoran
Ballyshannon
Inishcrone
N 16
Sligo
N 59
Crossmolina
Ballina
Ballymote
Riverstown
Doogort
M, Castlebaldwin
Ballyconnell
ACHILL ISLAND
Newport
Carrick-on-Shannon
Cavan
Kiltimagh
Westport
Knock
Rinvyle
Leenane
T 40
Letterfrack
Clifden
Cong
Roscommon
Crookedwood
Ballyconneely
Ballynahinch
Recess
Roundstone
Oughterard
Mullingar
Cashel Bay
Moycullen
N 84
Athlone
Inverin
GALWAY
Ballinasloe
Spiddal
Furbogh
Oranmore
Inishmore
Tullamore
Aughrim
ARAN ISLANDS
Banagher
Ballyvaughan
Terryglass
Doolin
Lisdoonvarna
Birr
Ennistimon
Ballinderry
Portlaoise
Lahinch
N 18
Ballycommon
ENNIS
Athy
Newmarket-on-Fergus
KILLALOE
N 7
Kilkee
M
SHANNON
Bunratty
Castleconnell
Carlow
Cratloe
Bagenalstown
Limerick
Dundrum
Adare
Kilkenny
Ballybunnion
N 21
Graiguenamanagh
N 24
Cashel M
Ballingarry
Ballyheige
Thomastown
Templeglentan
Glen of Aherlow
Bansha
Inistioge
New Ros
Kilcummin
Tralee
Mullinavat
Castleisland
Clonmel
Dingle M
Carrick-on-Suir
Ballyhac
Killorglin
Ballymacarbry
Caragh Lake
Kanturk
WATERFORD
Banteer
Cappoquin
Glenbeigh
Killarney
Mallow
DUNGARVAN
N 22
Dunmore East
Kenmare
Vaterville
Tahilla
M
BLARNEY
Youghal
Macroom
N 25
Killeagh
Parknasilla
Garryvoe
Caherdaniel M
Shanagarry
Ballycotton
Ahakista
Toormore

Place with at least
a hotel or restaurant ● Adare
a pleasant hotel or restaurant
a quiet, secluded hotel
a restaurant with ✿, ✿✿, ✿✿✿, Meals (M)
See this town for establishments located in its vicinity DUBLIN
Localité offrant au moins
une ressource hôtelière ● Adare
un hôtel ou restaurant agréable
un hôtel très tranquille, isolé
une bonne table à ✿, ✿✿, ✿✿✿, Meals (M)
Localité groupant dans le texte les ressources de ses environs DUBLIN
La località possiede come minimo
una risorsa alberghiera ● Adare
Albergo o ristorante ameno
un albergo molto tranquillo, isolato
un'ottima tavola con ✿, ✿✿, ✿✿✿, Meals (M)
La località raggruppa nel suo testo le risorse dei dintorni DUBLIN
Ort mit mindestens
einem Hotel oder Restaurant ● Adare
ein angenehmes Hotel oder Restaurant
einem sehr ruhigen und abgelegenen Hotel
einem Restaurant mit ✿, ✿✿, ✿✿✿, Meals (M)
Ort mit Angaben über Hotels und Restaurants in der Umgebung DUBLIN
M 22
M 1
Monaghan
astleblayney
Omeath
Carlingford
A 1
Carrickmacross
Dundalk
Virginia
N 1
DROGHEDA
Trim
Skerries
Dunshaughlin
Newbridge
Dunlavin
Glendalough
Laragh
Castledermot
WICKLOW
Aughrim
Redcross
Avoca
N 11
GOREY M
Courtown Harbour
Ferns
Enniscorthy
N 25
Wexford
Rosslare
ROSSLARE HARBOUR
Swords
Malahide
Portmarnock
Maynooth
M 4
Howth
DUBLIN ✿✿, ✿, M
Straffan
N 7
Dun Laoghaire
Kill
Killiney
Blessington
Bray
N 11
Greystones
Delgany
N 71
Cork M
Midleton
Glengarriff
Monkstown
Cobh
Ballylickey
Innishannon
Carrigaline
Dunmanway
Bandon
KINSALE
Durrus
Clonakilty
Ballinadee
Skull
Skibbereen
N 71
Glandore
XXX, M
Butlerstown
Baltimore

ACHILL ISLAND (Acaill) Mayo 405 B 5/6 Ireland G..

See : Island★.

Achill Sound ℘ 45384 (1 July-31 August).

Doogort (Dumha Goirt) – ✉ Achill Island – ☎ 098.

Keel ℘ 43202.

Gray's, ℘ 43244, – rest
Meals (by arrangement) 15.00 **t.** – **17 rm** 20.00/40.00 **t.**

ADARE (Áth Dara) Limerick 405 F 10 Ireland G. – pop. 899 – ☎ 061.

See : Town★ – Adare Friary★.

Exc. : Rathkeale (Castle Matrix★ AC) W : 7½ m. by N 21 – Newcastle West★, W : 16 m. by N 2 – Glin Castle★ AC, W : 29 m. by N 21, R 518 and N 69.

℘ 396255 (1 June-30 October).

♦Dublin 131 – ♦Killarney 59 – ♦Limerick 10.

Adare Manor, ℘ 396566, Fax 396124, ≤, « 19C Gothic mansion in extensiv parkland », – 180.
Meals 15.00/32.00 **t.** and a la carte – 10.50 – **63 rm** 200.00/300.00 **st.**, 1 suite – SB.

Dunraven Arms, Main St., ℘ 396633, Fax 396541, « Attractively furnished, antiques » – 150.
Meals - (see ***Maigue*** below) – 9.50 – **66 rm** 69.00/99.00 **t.** – SB.

Woodlands House, Knockanes, SE : 2 m. by N 21 on Croom rd ℘ 396118, Fax 39607 – 350.
closed 24 and 25 December – **Meals** (bar lunch Monday to Saturday)/dinner 16.75 s and a la carte 7.50 – **57 rm** 45.00/76.00 **st.** – SB.

Foxhollow without rest., Knockanes, SE : 2 ¼ m. by N 21 on Croom rd ℘ 39677 Fax 396779, – rm
3 rm 20.00/37.00 **st.**

Adare Lodge without rest., Kildimo Rd, ℘ 396629 –
6 rm 20.00/34.00 **st.**

Carrabawn House without rest., Killarney Rd, SW : ½ m. on N 21 ℘ 396067, –
7 rm 30.00/45.00.

Abbey Villa without rest., Kildimo Rd, ℘ 396113, Fax 396969 –
closed 20 December-2 January – **6 rm** 17.00/34.00 **st.**

Village House without rest., Main St., ℘ 396554, Fax 396903 –
March-October – **5 rm** 16.00/34.00 **st.**

Sandfield House without rest., Castleroberts, SE : 3 ¼ m. by N 21 on Croom r ℘ 396119, –
February-October – **4 rm** 21.00/34.00.

Maigue (at Dunraven Arms H.), Main St., ℘ 396633, Fax 396541, –
Meals (dinner only and Sunday lunch) 12.50/25.00 **st.** and a la carte 4.75.

AHAKISTA (Áth an Chiste) Cork 405 D 13 – ✉ Bantry – ☎ 027.

♦Dublin 217 – ♦Cork 63 – ♦Killarney 59.

✪ **Shiro** (Kei Pilz), ℘ 67030, Fax 67206, ≤ Dumnanus Bay, –
closed January – **Meals** - Japanese - (booking essential) (dinner only) 35.00 **st.** 10.00
Spec. Zensai: Azuke-Bachi, Suimono, Saka-Mushi.

ARAN ISLANDS (Oileáin Árann) Galway 405 CD 8 Ireland G..

See : Islands★ – Inishmore (Dun Aenghus★★★).

Access by boat or aeroplane from Galway city or by boat from Kilkieran, Rossaneel or Fisherstreet (Clare).

and by aeroplane from Inverin.

℘ 099 (Inishmore) 61263 (30 May-15 September).

Inishmore – ✉ Aran Islands – ☎ 099.

Ard Einne, Killeany, ℘ 61126, Fax 61388, ≤ Killeany Bay
March-October – **Meals** (by arrangement) 12.00 **st.** – **11 rm** 28.00/32.00 **st.** – SB.

ATHLONE (Baile Átha Luain) Westmeath 405 I 7 Ireland G. – pop. 8 170 – ☎ 0902.

Exc. : Clonmacnois★★★ (Grave Slabs★, Cross of the Scriptures★) S : 13 m. by N 6 and N 62 – N : Lough Ree (Ballykeeran Viewpoint★★, Glassan★) – Clonfinlough Stone★, S : 11½ m. by N 6 and N 62.

Hodson Bay ℘ 92073/92235.

Tourist Office, The Castle ℘ 92856 (May-mid October).

♦Dublin 75 – ♦Galway 57 – ♦Limerick 75 – Roscommon 20 – ♦Tullamore 24.

Hodson Bay, NW : 4¾ m. by N 61 ℘ 92444, Fax 92688, ≤, – 500.
Meals 9.50/21.00 **t.** and dinner a la carte 6.00 – **95 rm** 55.00/110.00, 2 suites – SB.

Shelmalier House, Retreat Rd, Cartrontroy, E : 2½ m. by Dublin rd ✆ 72245, Fax 73190, – TV ☎ P. VISA.
closed 24 to 26 December – **Meals** (by arrangement) 15.00 **st.** 4.95 – **7 rm** 18.00/30.00 **st.** – SB.

Cornloft, Tuam Rd, NW : 3½ m. by Roscommon rd on R 362 ✆ 94753 – P. AE VISA
closed Sunday dinner, Monday, 1-8 January, 1-8 April and 24-28 December – **Meals** 12.50/27.00 **st.** and a la carte 5.50.

ATHY (Baile Átha Á) Kildare 405 L 9 pop. 5 204 – ☎ 0507.
Dublin 40 – Kilkenny 29 – Wexford 59.

Tonlegee House with rm, SW : 2¼ m. by N 78 ✆ 31473, Fax 31473 – TV ☎ P. AE VISA.
Meals *(closed Sunday to non-residents)* (dinner only) 20.00 **st.** 5.50 – **9 rm** 45.00/80.00 **st.** – SB.

AUGHRIM (Eachroim) Galway 405 H 8 – ✉ Ballinasloe – ☎ 0905.
✆ 73939 (2 April-9 October).
Dublin 90 – Galway 43 – Limerick 60 – Tullamore 45.

Aughrim Schoolhouse,, on N 6 ✆ 73936 – P. AE VISA
closed Sunday dinner, Monday, Good Friday, 24 and 25 December and 1 January – **Meals** (dinner only and Sunday lunch) 18.50 **t.** and a la carte.

AUGHRIM (Eachroim) Wicklow 405 N 9 pop. 713 – ☎ 0402.
✆ 73939 (2 April-9 October).
Dublin 46 – Waterford 77 – Wexford 60.

Lawless's, ✆ 36146, Fax 36384, – TV ☎ P. AE VISA.
closed 24-26 December – **Meals** (bar lunch Monday to Saturday)/dinner 17.75 **t.** and a la carte 5.45 – **10 rm** 35.00/62.00 **t.** – SB.

We suggest:

For a successful tour, that you prepare it in advance.
Michelin maps and *guides will give you a great deal of useful information on route planning, places of interest, accommodation, prices etc.*

AVOCA (Abhóca) Wicklow 405 N 9 – pop. 494 – ☎ 0402.
Dublin 47 – Waterford 72 – Wexford 55.

Woodenbridge, Vale of Avoca, SW : 2 ¼ m. on R 752 ✆ 35146, Fax 35573, – TV ☎ P. AE VISA.
Meals 9.95/18.95 **st.** 6.25 – **12 rm** 35.00/60.00 **st.** – SB.

Keppel's Farmhouse, Ballanagh, S : 2 m. by unmarked rd ✆ 35168, ≤, « Working farm », , park – .
April-mid October – **Meals** (by arrangement) 13.00 **st.** – **5 rm** 25.00/34.00 **st.** – SB.

BAGENALSTOWN (Muine Bheag) Carlow 405 L 9 – ☎ 0503.
Dublin 63 – Carlow 10 – Kilkenny 13 – Wexford 37.

Kilgraney Country House,, S : 3 ¾ m. by R 705 ✆ 75283, Fax 75283, ≤, « Late Georgian house with collection of Philippine and other Eastern furnishings and artefacts », – P. VISA.
March-November – **Meals** *(closed Monday to Thursday, except June-August)* (booking essential) (communal dining)(dinner only) 22.00 **t.** 5.00 – **5 rm** 25.00/70.00 **t.** – SB.

BALLINA (Béal an Átha) Mayo 405 E 5 **Ireland G.** – pop. 6 563 – ☎ 096.
Envir. : Rosserk Abbey★, N : 4 m. by R 314.
Exc. : Moyne Abbey★, N : 7 m. by R 314 – Downpatrick Head★, N : 20 m. by R 314.
9 Mosgrove, Shanaghy ✆ 21050.
✆ 70848 (3 May-30 September).
Dublin 150 – Galway 73 – Roscommon 64 – Sligo 37.

Mount Falcon Castle, Foxford Rd, S : 4 m. on N 57 ✆ 70811, Fax 71517, ≤, « Country house atmosphere », , park, – ☎ P. AE VISA.
closed February, March and 1 week Christmas – **Meals** (by arrangement) (communal dining) (dinner only) 20.00 **t.** – **10 rm** 49.00/98.00 **t.**

Brigown without rest., Quay Rd, NE : 1 ¾ m. by N 59 ✆ 22609, – TV P
4 rm 16.00/32.00.

BALLINADEE (Baile na Daibhche) Cork 405 G 12 – ✉ Bandon – ☎ 021.
Dublin 174 – Cork 20.

Glebe Country House, ✆ 778294, Fax 778456, « Georgian rectory », – ☎ P. VISA
Meals *(closed Sunday)* (by arrangement) (communal dining)(unlicensed) 15.00/20.00 **st.** – **3 rm** 30.00/50.00 **st.** – SB.

BALLINASLOE (Béal Átha na Sluaighe) Galway 405 H 8 Ireland G. – pop. 5 793 – 0905.
Exc. : Turoe Stone, Bullaun★, SW : 18 m. by R 348 and R 350.
18 Ballinasloe 42126 – 9 Mountbellew 79259.
Main Street 42131 (1 July-31 August).
◆Dublin 91 – ◆Galway 41 – ◆Limerick 66 – Roscommon 36 – ◆Tullamore 34.

Haydens, Dunlo St., 42347, Fax 42895, – rest – 250.
closed 24 to 26 December – **Meals** *(closed Sunday dinner)* 10.00/19.00 **t.** and dinner a la carte 4.75 – 5.95 – **48 rm** 31.00/54.00 **t.** – SB.

BALLINCLASHET Cork 405 G 12 – see Kinsale.

BALLINDERRY (Baile an Doire) Tipperary 405 H 8 Ireland G. – Nenagh – 067.
Exc. : Portumna★ (castle★) N : 9½ m. by R 493 and N 65.
◆Dublin 111 – ◆Galway 53 – ◆Limerick 41.

Gurthalougha House, W : 1¾ m. 22080, Fax 22154, «, « Country house on banks of Lough Derg », park, –
March-October and weekends November-January – **Meals** (dinner only) 15.00 **t.** 5.50 – **7 rm** 30.00/72.00 **t.** – SB.

BALLINGARRY (Baile an GharraÁ) Limerick 405 F 10 – 069.
◆Dublin 141 – ◆Killarney 56 – ◆Limerick 18.

Mustard Seed at Echo Lodge, 68508, « Victorian house, former convent », – – 30.
early March-mid January – **Meals** *(closed Sunday lunch)* (communal dining Sunday dinner residents only) 22.00/29.00 **t.** 6.75 – **11 rm** 70.00/125.00 **st.**, 1 suite.

When looking for a quiet hotel
use the maps found in the introductory pages
or look for establishments with the sign or .

BALLYBOFEY (Bealach Féich) Donegal 405 I 3 – pop. 2 972 – 074.
18 Ballybofey & Stranorlar 31093.
◆Dublin 148 – ◆Londonderry 30 – ◆Sligo 58.

Kee's, Main St., Stranorlar, NE : ½ m. on N 15 31018, Fax 31917, , , –
Meals 9.50/18.50 **t.** and dinner a la carte – **36 rm** 39.50/77.00 **st.** – SB.

BALLYBUNNION (Baile an Bhuinneánaigh) Kerry 405 D 10 Ireland G. – pop. 1 346 – 068.
Exc. : Carrigafoyle Castle★, NE : 13 m. by R 551 – Glin Castle★ *AC*, E : 19 m. by R 551 and N 69
18, 18 Ballybunnion, Sandhill Rd 27146.
◆Dublin 176 – ◆Limerick 56 – Tralee 26.

Marine Links, Sandhill Rd, 27139, Fax 27666, –
9 March-October – **Meals** (bar lunch Monday to Saturday)/dinner 17.75 **t.** and a la carte 6.95 – **12 rm** 45.00/72.00 **t.** – SB.

Teach de Broc without rest., Link Rd, S : 1½ m. by Golf Club rd on Ballyduff rd 27581, Fax 27919, – .
6 rm 25.00/50.00 **t.**

BALLYCOMMON (Baile Uí Chomáin) Tipperary 405 H 9 – Nenagh – 067.
◆Dublin 28 – ◆Galway 66 – ◆Limerick 28.

St. David's Country House, NE : 5 m. by R 495 24145, Fax 24388, «, « Loughside setting », , , park – .
closed 15 January-15 March – **Meals** (booking essential) (dinner only and Sunday lunch) 26.00 **st.** 8.00 – **9 rm** 70.00/150.00 **st.** – SB.

BALLYCONNEELY (Baile Conaola) Galway 405 B 7 – Clifden – 095.
◆Dublin 189 – ◆Galway 54.

Erriseask House, 23553, Fax 23639, « Mannin Bay and mountains, park – .
April-October – **Meals** - (see below) – **12 rm** 40.00/85.00 **t.** – SB.

Erriseask House (at Erriseask House H.), 23553, Fax 23639 – .
April-October – **Meals** *(closed Thursday lunch)* (booking essential) 14.50/32.50 **t.** and a la carte 6.00.

BALLYCONNELL (Béal Atha Conaill) Cavan 405 J 5 – pop. 465 – 049.
◆Dublin 89 – Drogheda 76 – Enniskillen 23.

Slieve Russell,, SE : 1¾ m. on R 200 26444, Fax 26474, «, , , , 18, , park, , squash – rest – 800.
Meals (carvery lunch Monday to Saturday) 13.00/26.00 **st.** and dinner a la carte 9.75 – **145 rm** 70.00/160.00 **st.** – SB.

BALLYCOTTON (Baile Choitán) Cork 405 H 12 – ☎ 021.

♦Dublin 165 – ♦Cork 27 – ♦Waterford 66.

Bayview, ☎ 646746, Fax 646824, ≤ Ballycotton Bay, harbour and island, – – 40. AE VISA.
5 April-31 December – **Meals** 12.00/25.00 **st.** and dinner a la carte 8.50 – **33 rm** 50.00/80.00 **st.**, 2 suites – SB.

XX **Spanish Point** with rm, ☎ 646177, Fax 646179, ≤ Ballycotton Bay – . AE VISA
Meals *(closed 8 January-10 March)* (dinner only except July and August) 18.00 **t.** and a la carte 6.00 – **5 rm** 22.00/76.00 **st.**

BALLYEDMUND Wexford – see Gorey.

BALLYHACK (Baile Hac) Wexford 405 L 11 – pop. 221 – ✉ New Ross – ☎ 051.

♦Dublin 105 – ♦Waterford 8.5.

X **Neptune**, Ballyhack Harbour, ☎ 389284, Fax 389284 – AE VISA
April-October – **Meals** - Seafood - *(closed Sunday and Monday April-July and September)* (lunch by arrangement)/dinner a la carte 13.50/25.40 **t.**

BALLYHEIGE (Baile Uí Thaidhg) Kerry 405 C 10 pop. 656 – ☎ 066.

♦Dublin 186 – ♦Limerick 73 – Tralee 11.

White Sands, ☎ 33102, Fax 33357 – . AE VISA JCB
April-October – **Meals** (bar lunch Monday to Saturday)/dinner a la carte 13.75/20.00 **st.** – **75 rm** 39.00/70.00 **st.** – SB.

BALLYLICKEY (Béal Átha Leice) Cork 405 D 12 Ireland G. – ✉ Bantry – ☎ 027.

Envir. : Bantry Bay★ – Bantry House★ *AC*, S : 3 m. by R 584.

Exc. : Glengarriff★ (Garinish Island★★, access by boat) NW : 8 m. by N 71 – Healy Pass★★ (≤★★) W : 23 m. by N 71, R 572 and R 574 – Slieve Miskish Mountains (≤★★) W : 29 m. by N 71 and R 572 – Lauragh (Derreen Gardens★ *AC*) NW : 27½ m. by N 71, R 572 and R 574 – Allihies (copper mines★) W : 41½ m. by N 71, R 572 and R 575 – Garnish Island (≤★) W : 44 m. by N 71 and R 572.

9 Bantry Park, Donemark ☎ 50579.

♦Dublin 216 – ♦Cork 55 – ♦Killarney 45.

Ballylickey Manor House, ☎ 50071, Fax 50124, ≤, « Extensive gardens », heated, , park – . AE VISA.
mid March-early November – **Meals** *(closed Wednesday lunch)* 12.00/30.00 **t.** and a la carte 9.00 – **6 rm** 90.00 **t.**, 5 suites – SB.

Sea View House, ☎ 50462, Fax 51555, ≤, – . AE VISA
15 March-15 November – **Meals** (bar lunch Monday to Saturday)/dinner 22.50 **t.** 6.00 – **17 rm** 40.00/100.00 **st.** – SB.

Reendesert, ☎ 50153, Fax 50597 – – 100. AE VISA.
March-October – **Meals** (bar lunch Monday to Saturday)/dinner 16.00 **st.** and a la carte 4.50 – **18 rm** 31.50/59.00 **st.** – SB.

XX **Larchwood House** with rm, Pearsons Bridge, NE : 1¾ m. by R 584 ☎ 66181, ≤, – . AE VISA.
closed Sunday and 22 to 28 December – **Meals** (dinner only) 30.00 **t.** 6.00 – **4 rm** 22.00/44.00 **t.**

BALLYMACARBRY (Baile Mhac Cairbre) Waterford 405 I 11 Ireland G. – pop. 381 – ✉ Clonmel ☎ 052.

Exc. : W : Nier Valley Scenic Route★★.

♦Dublin 118 – ♦Cork 49 – Waterford 39.

Hanora's Cottage, Nire Valley, E : 4 m. by Nire Drive rd and Nire Valley Lakes rd ☎ 36134, Fax 36540, – . VISA.
closed Christmas – **Meals** (by arrangement) 17.50 **t.** 5.50 – **8 rm** 32.50/55.00 **t.** – SB.

BALLYMOTE (Baile an Mhóta) Sligo 405 G 5 – ✉ Sligo – ☎ 071.

♦Dublin 124 – Longford 48 – ♦Sligo 15.

Mill House without rest., Keenaghan, ☎ 83449, , – .
closed 20 December-7 January – **5 rm** 14.00/32.00.

BALLYNACOURTY Waterford 405 J 11 – see Dungarvan.

BALLYNAHINCH (Baile na hInse) Galway 405 C 7 – ✉ Recess – ☎ 095.

♦Dublin 140 – ♦Galway 41 – Westport 49.

Ballynahinch Castle, Ballinafad, ☎ 31006, Fax 31085, ≤ Owenmore river and woods, , , park, – . AE VISA.
closed February – **Meals** (bar lunch)/dinner 23.50/30.00 **t.**and a la carte 7.50 – **28 rm** 75.90/132.00 **st.** – SB.

BALLYSHANNON (Béal Atha Seanaion) Donegal 405 M 4 Ireland G. – pop. 2 426 – ☎ 072.
Envir. : Rossnowlagh Strand★★, N : 6 m. by R 231.
♦Dublin 157 – Donegal 13 – ♦Sligo 27.

Dorrian's Imperial, Main St., ☎ 51147, Fax 51001, – TV ☎ P – 30. VISA. *closed 23 to 31 December* – **Meals** 10.00 **t.** (lunch) and a la carte 11.50/18.85 **t.** 5.50 – **26 rm** 35.00/78.00 **st.** – SB.

BALLYVAUGHAN (Baile Uí Bheacháin) Clare 405 E 8 Ireland G. – pop. 181 – ☎ 065.
Envir. : The Burren★★ (Cliffs of Moher★★★, Scenic Routes★★, Aillwee Cave★ *AC* (Waterfall★) Corcomroe Abbey★, Kilfenora Crosses★).
♦Dublin 149 – Ennis 34 – ♦Galway 29.

Gregans Castle, SW : 3 ¾ m. on N 67 ☎ 77005, Fax 77111, ≤ countryside and Galway Bay, park – ☎ P. VISA JCB. *April-October* – **Meals** (bar lunch)/dinner 27.00 **t.** and a la carte 6.00 – **18 rm** 76.00/99.00 **t.**, 4 suites.

Hyland's, ☎ 77037, Fax 77131 – TV ☎ P. AE VISA. *closed 5 January-5 February and 18 to 27 December* – **Meals** (bar lunch)/dinner 25.00 **st.** 5.00 – **18 rm** 40.45/69.30 **st.** – SB.

Rusheen Lodge without rest., SW : ¾ m. on N 67 ☎ 77092, Fax 77152, – TV ☎ P. AE VISA. *March-October* – **8 rm** 30.00/40.00 **st.**

BALTIMORE (Dún na Séad) Cork 405 D 13 – ☎ 028.
♦Dublin 214 – ♦Cork 59 – ♦Killarney 77.

Baltimore Harbour, ☎ 20361, Fax 20466, – TV ☎ & P – 130. VISA. *Easter-November and Christmas* – **Meals** (bar lunch Monday to Saturday) 16.00 **t.** – **30 rm** 48.00/70.00 **t.** – SB.

Great Britain and Ireland is now covered by an Atlas at a scale of 1 inch to 4.75 miles.

Three easy to use versions: Paperback, Spiralbound and Hardback.

BANAGHER (Beannchar) Offaly 405 I 8 Ireland G. – pop. 1 428 – ☎ 0509.
Envir. : Clonfert Cathedral★ (West doorway★★).
♦Dublin 83 – ♦Galway 54 – ♦Limerick 56 – ♦Tullamore 24.

Brosna Lodge, Main St., ☎ 51350, Fax 51521, – TV ☎ P. VISA *closed 24 December-1 February* – **Meals** (bar lunch Monday to Saturday)/dinner 16.95 **st.** and a la carte 6.00 – **14 rm** 28.00/52.00 **st.** – SB.

Old Forge without rest., West End, ☎ 51504 – P. *closed Christmas* – **4 rm** 18.00/32.00 **t.**

BANDON (Droichead na Bandan) Cork 405 F 12 – ☎ 023.
♦Dublin 174 – ♦Cork 19.

Munster Arms, Oliver Plunkett St., ☎ 41562, Fax 41562 – rm TV ☎ – 25. AE VISA. *closed 25 December* – **Meals** 10.95/18.00 **st.** and a la carte – **34 rm** 30.00/60.00 **st.** – SB.

St. Anne's without rest., Clonakilty Rd, SW : ¾ m. on N 71 ☎ 44239, – P. AE VISA. **5 rm** 19.00/30.00 **st.**

BANSHA (An Bháinseach) Co. Tipperary 405 H 10 – ☎ 062.
♦Dublin 103 – ♦Cork 55 – ♦Limerick 30 – ♦Waterford 48.

Bansha House, ☎ 54194, Fax 54215, , park – P. VISA. *closed 20 December-1 January* – **Meals** 13.00 **t.** 7.00 – **8 rm** 25.00/40.00 **t.** – SB.

BANTEER (Bántár) Cork 405 F 11 – ☎ 029.
♦Dublin 158 – ♦Cork 30 – ♦Killarney 29 – ♦Limerick 48.

Clonmeen Lodge, E : 2 m. on Mallow rd ☎ 56238, Fax 56294, , park – P. VISA. **Meals** (booking essential) a la carte 15.00/20.00 **s.** 5.75 – **6 rm** 35.00/60.00 **st.**

BAREFIELD (Gort Lomán) Clare 405 F 9 – see Ennis.

BIRR (Biorra) Offaly 405 I 8 Ireland G. – pop. 3 280 – ☎ 0509.
See : Town★ – Birr Castle Demesne★★ *AC* (Telescope★).
Exc. : Roscrea★ (Damer House★ *AC*) S : 12 m. by N 62 – Slieve Bloom Mountains★, E : 13 m. by R 440.
18 The Glenns ☎ 20082.
☎ 20110 (16 May-11 September).
Athlone 28 – ♦Dublin 87 – Kilkenny 49 – ♦Limerick 49.

Dooly's, Emmet Sq., ✆ 20032, Fax 21332 – TV ☎ – 🏛 250. AE VISA. ✗
closed 24 to 26 December – **Meals** 9.00/18.00 **st.** and dinner a la carte 4.80 – **18 rm** 35.00/65.00 **st.** – SB.

County Arms, Railway Rd, ✆ 20791, Fax 21234, squash – TV ☎ P – 🏛 300. AE VISA JCB. ✗
Meals 9.00/20.00 **t.** and a la carte 6.50 – **18 rm** 42.00/80.00 **t.** – SB.

BLARNEY (An Bhlarna) Cork 405 G 12 **Ireland G.** – pop. 2 043 – ✉ Cork – ☎ 021.

See : Blarney Castle★★ *AC* – Blarney House★ *AC*.

♦Dublin 167 – ♦Cork 6.

Blarney Park, ✆ 385281, Fax 381506, ✗ – TV ☎ & P – 🏛 300. AE VISA. ✗
Meals (lunch by arrangement Monday to Saturday) 10.50/15.50 **st.** and dinner a la carte 5.50 – **76 rm** 56.00/104.00 – SB.

Killarney House without rest., Station Rd, NE : 1 m. ✆ 381841, – TV P. ✗
4 rm 22.00/32.00.

at Tower W : 2 m. on R 617 – ✉ Cork – ☎ 021 :

Ashlee Lodge without rest., ✆ 385346, – P. ✗
April-October – **5 rm** 20.00/32.00 **st.**

BLESSINGTON (Baile Coimán) Wicklow 405 M 8 – ☎ 045.

♦Dublin 19 – Kilkenny 56 – Wexford 70.

Tulfarris House, S : 6 m. by N 81 ✆ 864574, Fax 864423, ≤, park, ✗ – TV ☎ P. AE VISA JCB. ✗
closed 23 to 30 December – **Meals** (bar lunch Monday to Saturday)/dinner 21.00 **t.** 6.00 – **21 rm** 75.50/107.00 **st.**, 17 suites 88.00/107.00 **st.** – SB.

BRAY (Bré) Wicklow 405 N 8 **Ireland G.** – pop. 25 096 – ☎ 01.

Envir. : Powerscourt★★ (Waterfall★★★ *AC*) W : 4 m. - Killruddery House and Gardens★ *AC*, S : 2 m. by R 761.

18 Woodbrook, Dublin Rd ✆ 282 4799 – 18 Old Conna, Ferndale Rd ✆ 282 6055.

♦Dublin 13 – Wicklow 20.

Tree of Idleness, Seafront, ✆ 286 3498 – AE VISA
closed Monday, 2 weeks August-September and 1 week Christmas – **Meals** - Greek-Cypriot - (dinner only) 15.50 **t.** and a la carte 7.00.

BUNCRANA (Bun Cranncha) Donegal 405 J 2 – ☎ 077.

Exc. : – Malin Head★★★ (≤★★★) NE : 31½ m. by R 238 and R 242 – Inishowen Peninsula★★ – Carndonagh High Cross★, NE : 18½ m. by R 238 – Gap of Mamore★, NW : 8 m. – Lag Sand Dunes★, NE : 24½ m. by R 238 and R 242.

♦Dublin 160 – ♦Londonderry 15 – ♦Sligo 99.

Lake of Shadows, Grianan Park, ✆ 61005, Fax 62131 – TV ☎ P. AE VISA. ✗
closed 24 and 25 December – **Meals** 13.60 **st.** and a la carte 4.50 – **23 rm** 25.00/48.00 **st.** – SB.

BUNDORAN (Bun Dobhráin) Donegal 405 H 4 – ☎ 072.

Main St. ✆ 41350 (June-September).

♦Dublin 161 – Donegal 17 – ♦Sligo 23.

Great Northern, N : ¼ m. ✆ 41204, Fax 41114, ≤, 18, ✗ – TV ☎ & P. AE VISA
closed 3 January-14 February – **Meals** 9.50/23.00 **st.** and lunch a la carte 6.00 – **94 rm** 50.00/160.00 **st.** – SB.

Holyrood, ✆ 41232, Fax 41100, 18, ✗ – TV ☎ & P. AE VISA. ✗
Meals (bar lunch Monday to Saturday)/dinner 15.00 **t.** and lunch a la carte 10.00 – **85 rm** 48.00/70.00 **st.** – SB.

Allingham Arms, ✆ 41075, Fax 41171 – TV ☎ & P. AE VISA. ✗
Meals 8.00/17.00 **st.** and dinner a la carte – **88 rm** 42.50/65.00 **st.** – SB.

Bay View without rest., Main St., ✆ 41296, Fax 41147, ≤ – TV ☎. VISA. ✗
19 rm 24.00/34.00 **st.**

Le Chateaubrianne, W : 1 m. on N 5 ✆ 42160, Fax 42160 – P. VISA
closed Monday September-June and 3 weeks November – **Meals** (dinner only and Sunday lunch)/dinner 16.00/20.00 **t.** 7.00.

BUNRATTY (Bun Raite) Clare 405 F 9 **Ireland G.** – ☎ 061.

See : Castle and Folk Park★★ *AC* – Town★★.

♦Dublin 129 – Ennis 15 – ♦Limerick 8.

Fitzpatrick Bunratty Shamrock, ✆ 361177, Telex 72114, Fax 471252, – rest TV ☎ P – 🏛 200. AE VISA. ✗
closed 24 and 25 December – **Meals** 10.50/20.00 **t.** and dinner a la carte 6.50 – 8.00 – **115 rm** 79.00/120.00 **t.** – SB.

Bunratty Lodge without rest., N : 1½ m. ℘ 369402, – TV P.
March-October – **6 rm** 25.00/34.00 **st.**

Shannon View without rest., NW : 1 m. on N 18 ℘ 364056, Fax 364056, – P.
March-November – **4 rm** 16.50/33.00 **t.**

MacCloskey's, Bunratty House Mews, ℘ 364082, « Cellars of Georgian house » – P. VISA – *closed January* – **Meals** (dinner only) 26.00 **t.** 8.00.

BUTLERSTOWN (Baile an Bhuitléaraigh) Cork 405 F 13 **Ireland G.** – Bandon – 023.

Envir. : Courtmacsherry★, N : 3 m..

◆Dublin 193 – ◆Cork 32.

Dunworley Cottage, Dunworley, S : 2 m. ℘ 40314, Fax 40314 – P. AE VISA
closed Monday, Tuesday and November-mid March except Christmas – **Meals** (lunch by arrangement) a la carte 14.50/27.50 **st.**

CAHERDANIEL (Cathair Dónall) Kerry 405 B 12 – Killarney – 066.

◆Dublin 238 – ◆Killarney 48.

Derrynane Bay House, W : ½ m. on N 70 ℘ 75404, Fax 75404, ← – rm TV P. VISA.
closed 17 February-9 March – **Meals** 12.00 **s.** 5.00 **6 rm** 20.00/36.00 **s.** – SB.

Loaves and Fishes, ℘ 75273 – AE VISA
Easter-September – **Meals** *(closed Tuesday except June-September and Monday)* (dinner only) a la carte 18.35/24.85 5.50.

CAPPOQUIN (Ceapach Choinn) Waterford 405 I 11 **Ireland G.** – pop. 829 – 058.

Envir. : Lismore★ (Lismore Castle Gardens★ *AC*, St. Carthage's Cathedral★), W : 4 m. by N 72 – Mount Melleray Abbey★, N : 4 m. by R 669.

Exc. : The Gap★ (←★) NW : 9 m. by R 669.

◆Dublin 136 – ◆Cork 31 – ◆Waterford 40.

Richmond House with rm, SE : ½ m. on N 72 ℘ 54278, Fax 54988, « Georgian house », – TV P. VISA.
closed 23 December-1 February – **Meals** *(closed Sunday and Monday to non-residents)* (dinner only) 24.00 **t.** 6.00 – **10 rm** 28.00/64.00 **st.**

CARAGH LAKE (Loch Cárthaí) Kerry 405 C 11 **Ireland G.** – 066.

See : Lough Caragh★.

Exc. : Iveragh Peninsula★★★ (Ring of Kerry★★).

18 Dooks, Glenbeigh ℘ 68205/68200.

◆Dublin 212 – ◆Killarney 22 – Tralee 25.

Ard-Na-Sidhe , ℘ 69105, Fax 69282, ←, « Country house furnished with antiques, lakeside setting », , , park – rest P. AE VISA.
May-September – **Meals** (dinner only) 26.00 **st.** 8.50 – **20 rm** 68.00/132.00 **st.**

Caragh Lodge , ℘ 69115, Fax 69316, ←, « Country house atmosphere, lakeside setting », , , , – P. AE VISA.
7 April-12 October – **Meals** (dinner only) 24.00 **t.** 6.00 – **10 rm** 60.00/95.00 **t.**

CARLINGFORD (Cairlinn) Louth 405 N 5 **Ireland G.** – pop. 850 – 042.

See : Town★.

Exc. : Windy Gap★, NW : 8 m. by R 173.

◆Dublin 66 – ◆Dundalk 13.

McKevitt's Village, Market Sq., ℘ 73116, Fax 73144, – TV . AE VISA.
Meals 8.50/17.50 **st.** and a la carte 5.00 – **13 rm** 28.00/56.00 **t.** – SB.

Carlingford House without rest., ℘ 73118, – TV P.
March-November – **5 rm** 20.00/35.00.

CARLOW (Ceatharlach) Carlow 405 L 9 – 0503.

◆Dublin 50 – Kilkenny 23 – Wexford 47.

Barrowville Town House without rest., Kilkenny Rd, ℘ 43324, Fax 41953, – TV P. VISA.
7 rm 20.00/40.00 **st.**

Goleen without rest., Milford, SW : 5¼ m. on N 9 ℘ 46132, Fax 46132, – TV P. AE VISA. – *April-November* – **6 rm** 17.00/36.00 **s.**

CARRICKMACROSS (Carraig Mhachaire Rois) Monaghan 405 L 6 **Ireland G.** – pop. 1 678 – 042.

Envir. : Dún a' Rá Forest Park★, SW : 5 m. by R 179 – St. Mochta's House★, E : 7 m. by R 178.

18 Nuremore ℘ 61438.

◆Dublin 57 – Dundalk 14.

Nuremore ,, S : 1 m. on N 2 ℘ 61438, Fax 61853, ←, , , , 18, , , park, , squash – rest TV P – 200. AE VISA.
Meals 13.50/25.50 **st.** and a la carte 8.00 – **69 rm** 75.00/130.00 **st.** – SB.

CARRICK-ON-SHANNON (Cora Droma Rúisc) Leitrim 405 H 6 pop. 1 858 – ☎ 078.

See : Town★.

Exc. : Lough Rynn Demesne★.

♦Dublin 97 – Ballina 50 – ♦Galway 74 – Roscommon 26 – ♦Sligo 34.

Hollywell without rest., Liberty Hill, ☎ 21124, Fax 21124, ≤, « Part 18C country house », – P. VISA.
closed 22 to 31 December – **4 rm** 30.00/55.00 **st.**

CARRICK-ON-SUIR (Carraig na Siûire) Tipperary 405 J 10 – pop. 5 143 – ☎ 051.

Garravone ☎ 40047.

♦Dublin 95 – ♦Cork 68 – ♦Limerick 62 – ♦Waterford 16.

Carraig, Main St., ☎ 641455, Fax 641604 – rest TV ☎ P – 250. AE VISA.
closed Good Friday and Christmas Day – **Meals** 7.10/14.95 **st.** and dinner a la carte – **14 rm** 33.00/55.00 **st.** – SB.

CARRIGALINE (Carraig Uí Leighin) Cork 405 G 12 – ☎ 021.

♦Dublin 163 – ♦Cork 9.

Glenwood House without rest., Ballinrea Rd, N : 3/4 m. by R 611 (Cork rd) ☎ 373878, Fax 373878, – TV ☎ P. VISA.
closed 1 week Christmas – **8 rm** 30.00/50.00 **st.**

CASHEL (Caiseal) Tipperary 405 I 10 **Ireland G.** – pop. 2 473 – ☎ 062.

See : Town★★★ – Rock of Cashel★★★ *AC* – Cormac's Chapel★★ – Round Tower★ – Museum★ – Cashel Palace Gardens★ – Cathedrals★ – GPA Bolton Library★ *AC* – Hore Abbey★ – Dominican Friary★. Envir. : Holy Cross Abbey★★, N : 9 m. by R 660 – Athassel Abbey★, W : 5 m. by N 74.

Bolton Library ☎ 61333 (1 April-1 October).

♦Dublin 101 – ♦Cork 60 – Kilkenny 34 – ♦Limerick 36 – ♦Waterford 44.

Ros Guill House without rest., NE : 3/4 m. on R 691 ☎ 61507, – P. VISA.
May-October – **5 rm** 25.00/35.00 **st.**

Chez Hans, Rockside, ☎ 61177, « Converted 19C church » – P. VISA
closed Sunday, Monday, 24 to 26 December and 3 weeks January – **Meals** (dinner only) a la carte 23.20/27.50 **t.** 6.00.

Spearman, 97 Main Street, ☎ 61143 – AE VISA
closed Sunday dinner and Monday October-May and 24 to 26 December – **Meals** a la carte 14.95/20.95 **t.** 4.95.

CASHEL BAY (Cuan an Chaisil) Galway 405 C 7 **Ireland G.** – ☎ 095.

See : Town★.

♦Dublin 173 – Galway 41.

Cashel House, ☎ 31001, Fax 31077, ≤, « Country house atmosphere, gardens », park, – TV ☎ P. AE VISA
closed 10 January-10 February – **Meals** (bar lunch)/dinner 29.00 **t.** and a la carte 21.85/26.85 **t.** 7.50 – **32 rm** 49.00/172.00 **t.** – SB.

Zetland House, ☎ 31111, Fax 31117, ≤ Cashel Bay, « Country house, gardens », – ☎ P. AE VISA.
6 April-October – **Meals** 27.50 **t.** dinner and lunch a la carte 23.50/33.00 **t.** 6.50 – **20 rm** 75.00/140.00 **t.** – SB.

Glynsk House, SW : 5 3/4 m. on R 340 ☎ 32279, Fax 32342, ≤ – TV ☎ P. VISA.
Meals 8.50/15.00 **t.** and a la carte 6.00 – **12 rm** 32.00/50.00 **t.** – SB.

CASTLEBALDWIN (Béal Átha na gCarraigíní) Sligo 405 G 5 **Ireland G.** – ✉ Boyle (Roscommon) – ☎ 071.

Envir. : Carrowkeel Megalithic Cemetery (≤★★), S : 3 m..

Exc. : Arigna Scenic Drive★★, N : 2 m. by N 4 – Lough Key Forest Park★★ *AC*, SE : 10 m. by N 4 – View★★, N : 9 m. by N 4 on R 280 – Mountain Drive★, N : 6 m. on N 4 – Boyle Abbey★ *AC*, SE : 8 m. by N 4.

♦Dublin 118 – Longford 42 – ♦Sligo 15.

Cromleach Lodge, Ballindoon, SE : 3½ m. ☎ 65155, Fax 65455, ≤ Lough Arrow and Carrowkeel Cairns, , park – TV ☎ P. AE VISA.
February-October – **Meals** (dinner only) 29.50 **t.** 6.50 – **10 rm** 50.00/130.00 **t.** – SB.

CASTLEBLAYNEY (Baile na Lorgan) Monaghan 405 L 5 – pop. 2 029 – ☎ 042.

Muckno Park ☎ 40197.

♦Dublin 68 – ♦Belfast 58 – ♦Drogheda 39 – ♦Dundalk 17 – ♦Londonderry 80.

Glencarn, Monaghan Rd, ☎ 46666, Fax 46521, , – rest TV ☎ P. AE VISA.
Meals (bar lunch)/dinner 15.50 **t.** and a la carte – **27 rm** 33.00/60.00 **t.** – SB.

CASTLECONNELL (Caisleán Uí Chonaill) Limerick 405 G 9 Ireland G. – pop. 1 391 – ✉ Limerick – ☎ 061.

See : Town★.

◆Dublin 111 – ◆Limerick 9.

Castle Oaks House ⛰, ☎ 377666, Fax 377717, ≤, ₺, ≘s, ☒, ☜, ☞, park, ✗ – ▣ ☎ ⓟ – 🏛 200. ▣ AE ⓓ VISA. ✻
closed 25 to 27 December – **Meals** (bar lunch Monday to Saturday)/dinner 16.95 **st.** and a la carte 🍷 4.75 – **11 rm** ☐ 54.00/100.00 **t.** – SB.

CASTLEDERMOT (Díseart Diarmada) Kildare 405 L 9 Ireland G. – pop. 741 – ☎ 0503.

Exc. : Carlow Cathedral (Marble Monument★) NE : 7 m. by N 9.

◆Dublin 44 – Kilkenny 30 – Wexford 54.

Kilkea Castle ⛰, Kilkea, NW : 3 ¾ m. on R 418 ☎ 45156, Fax 45187, ≤, « Part 12C castle », ₺, ≘s, ☒, 18, ☜, ☞, park, ✗ – |‡| ▣ ☎ ⓟ – 🏛 200. ▣ AE ⓓ VISA. ✻
closed 24 to 28 December – **Meals** 15.50/26.00 **t.** and a la carte 🍷 6.00 – ☐ 11.00 – **31 rm** 115.00/140.00 **t.**, 7 suites – SB.

CASTLEISLAND (Oileán Ciarraá) Kerry 405 D 11 – ☎ 066.

◆Dublin 170 – ◆Cork 59 – ◆Killarney 16 – ◆Limerick 52 – Tralee 12.

River Island, Lower Main St., ☎ 42555, Fax 42544 – |‡| ▣ ☎. ▣ AE VISA. ✻
Meals (bar lunch Monday to Saturday)/dinner 13.50 **t.** and a la carte 🍷 5.95 – **50 rm** ☐ 30.00/60.00 **t.** – SB.

CAVAN (An Cabhán) Cavan 405 J 6 Ireland G. – pop. 3 332 – ☎ 049.

Envir. : Killykeen Forest Park★, W : 6 m. by R 198.

ℹ Farnham St. ☎ 31942 (June-September).

◆Dublin 71 – Drogheda 58 – Enniskillen 40.

Kilmore, Dublin Rd, E : 2 m. on N 3 ☎ 32288, Fax 32458 – ▣ ☎ ♿ ⓟ – 🏛 550
39 rm.

CHEEKPOINT (Pointe na Ságe) Waterford 405 K/L 11 – see Waterford.

CLIFDEN (An Clochán) Galway 405 B 7 – pop. 808 – ☎ 095.

Exc. : Connemara★★★, NE : by N 59 – Sky Road★★★, NE : by N 59 – Connemara National Park★, NE : 1 m by N 59.

ℹ Market Street ☎ 21163 (3 May-30 September).

◆Dublin 181 – Ballina 77 – ◆Galway 49.

Rock Glen Manor House ⛰, S : 1 ¼ m. by R 341 ☎ 21035, Fax 21737, ☞, ✗ – ▣ ☎ ⓟ. ▣ AE ⓓ VISA JCB. ✻
16 March-October – **Meals** (bar lunch)/dinner 23.00 **t.** and a la carte 🍷 6.00 – **29 rm** ☐ 53.00/114.00 **t.** – SB.

Ardagh ⛰, Ballyconneely rd, S : 1 ¾ m. on R 341 ☎ 21384, Fax 21314, ≤ Ardbear Bay, ☜ – ▣ ☎ ⓟ. ▣ AE ⓓ VISA JCB. ✻
April-October – **Meals** (bar lunch)/dinner 24.50 and a la carte 🍷 7.00 – **21 rm** ☐ 60.00/91.00 **s.** – SB.

Mal Dua without rest., Galway Rd, E : ½ m. on N 59 ☎ 21171, Fax 21739 – ⊁ ▣ ☎ ⓟ. ▣ AE VISA. ✻
closed December – **9 rm** ☐ 21.00/50.00 **st.**

Sunnybank House without rest., Sunny Bank, Church Hill, ☎ 21437, Fax 21976, ≘s, ☒ heated, ☞, ✗ – ▣ ☎ ⓟ. ▣ AE VISA. ✻
March-10 November – **10 rm** ☐ 35.00/50.00 **st.**

Failte ⛰ without rest., S : 1 ¼ m. by R 341 ☎ 21159, ≤ – ⓟ. ▣ AE VISA. ✻
April-September – **5 rm** ☐ 13.50/30.00 **st.**

Quay House, Beach Rd, ☎ 21369, Fax 21369, ≤. ▣ VISA
April-October – **Meals** (light lunch)/dinner a la carte 15.50/20.50 **t.** 🍷 7.00.

CLONAKILTY (Cloich na Coillte) Cork 405 F 13 Ireland G. pop. 2 576 – ☎ 023.

See : West Cork Regional Museum★ *AC*.

Envir. : Timoleague★ (Franciscan Friary★) E : 5 m. by R 600.

◆Dublin 193 – ◆Cork 32.

Árd na Gréine Farm House ⛰, Ballinascarthy, NW : 5 ¾ m. by N 71 ☎ 39104, Fax 39397, ☞ – ▣ ⓟ. AE VISA
Meals 10.00 **st.** – **6 rm** ☐ 20.00/34.00 **st.** – SB.

CLONEA STRAND Waterford – see Dungarvan.

CLONMEL (Cluain Meala) Tipperary 405 I 10 – pop. 14 531 – ☎ 052.

18 Lyreanearla, Mountain Rd ☎ 21138.

ℹ Community Office, Town Centre ☎ 22960.

◆Dublin 108 – ◆Cork 59 – Kilkenny 31 – ◆Limerick 48 – ◆Waterford 29.

Minella ⛰, Coleville Rd, ℘ 22388, Fax 24381, ≤, park – TV ☎ P – 600. AE ◑ VISA
Meals 12.00/25.00 **t.** and a la carte 6.50 – **67 rm** ☐ 65.00/120.00 **st.**, 3 suites – SB.

Clonmel Arms, Sarsfield St., ℘ 21233, Fax 21526 – TV ☎ – 450. AE ◑ VISA.
Meals 8.00/17.00 **t.** and a la carte 5.00 – ☐ 6.50 – **31 rm** 60.00/75.00 **t.** – SB.

COBH (An Cóbh) Cork 405 H 12 pop. 6 227 – 021.
◆Dublin 173 – ◆Cork 13 – ◆Waterford 71.

Tearmann ⛰, Ballynoe, N : 2½ m. by R 624 ℘ 813182, Fax 814011, – P.
April-October – **Meals** (by arrangement) 11.00 **st.** – **3 rm** ☐ 21.00/32.00 **st.**

CONG (Conga) Mayo 405 E 7 **Ireland G.** – pop. 183 – 092.
See : Town★ – **Envir.** : Lough Corrib★★.
Exc. : Ross Abbey★★ (Tower ≤★) – Joyce Country★★ (Lough Nafooey★★) W : by R 345.
◆Dublin 160 – Ballina 49 – ◆Galway 28.

Ashford Castle ⛰, ℘ 46003, Fax 46260, ≤, « Part 13C and 18C castle, in extensive formal gardens on shores of Lough Corrib », 9, park, – TV ☎ P – 110. AE ◑ VISA.
George V Room : Meals *(closed Christmas and New Year)* 16.50/34.50 **t.** and a la carte – (see also **Connaught Room** below) – ☐ 12.50 – **77 rm** 202.00/292.00 **st.**, 6 suites – SB.

XXXX **Connaught Room** (at Ashford Castle H.), ℘ 46003, Fax 46260, ≤ gardens, Lough Corrib and islands – P. AE ◑ VISA
April-October – **Meals** (booking essential) (dinner only) a la carte 35.00/70.00 8.50.

CORK (Corcaigh) Cork 405 G 12 **Ireland G.** – pop. 174 400 – 021.
See : City★★ – Shandon Bells★★ EY, St. Fin Barre's Cathedral★★ *AC* Z, Cork Public Museum★★ X **M** – Grand Parade★ Z , South Mall★ Z , St. Patrick Street★ Z , Crawford Art Gallery★ Y – Christ the King Church★ X **D** , Elizabethan Fort★ Z , Cork Lough★ X.
Envir. : Dunkathel House★ *AC*, E : 5¾ m. by N 8 and N 25 X.
Exc. : Fota Island★★ (Fota House★★) E : 8 m. by N 8 and N 25 X – Cobh★ (St. Colman's Cathedral★, Lusitania Memorial★) SE : 15 m. by N 8, N 25 and R 624 X.
18 Douglas ℘ 891086, X – 18 Mahon, Cloverhill, Blackrock ℘ 362480 X – 18 Monkstown, Parkgarriffe ℘ 841376, X – 18 Harbour Point, Clash, Little Island ℘ 353094, X.
Cork Airport : ℘ 313131, S : 4 m. by L 42 X – **Terminal** : Bus Station, Parnell Pl..
to France (Cherbourg and Le Harve) (Irish Ferries) 1 weekly (summer only), (Roscoff and St. Malo) (Brittany Ferries) 3 weekly (summer only) – to Swansea (Swansea Cork Ferries) (10 h) – Cork City, Grand Parade ℘ 273251.
◆Dublin 154.

CORK
BUILT UP AREA

Baker's Road . . . . . . X 4
Commons Road . . . . . . X 12
Curragh Road . . . . . . X 14
Dublin Street . . . . . . X 16
Gardiner's Hill . . . . . . X 20
Great William O'Brien Street . . . . . . X 22
Horgan Quay . . . . . . X 23
Lower Mayfield Road . . . . . . X 31
Thomas Davis Street . . . . . . X 49
Victoria Cross Rd . . . . . . X 50
Watercourse Road . . . . . . X 52
Western Road . . . . . . X 53
Wilton Road . . . . . . X 55

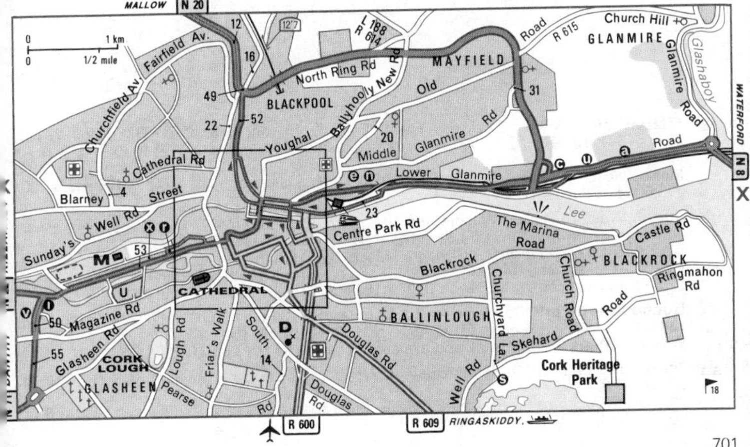

CORK

Merchant's Quay Shopping Centre .... Y
Oliver Plunkett Street .... Z
St. Patrick's Street .... Z

Camden Place .... Y 5
Coburg Street .... Y 10
Corn Market Street .... Y 13
Dominick Street .... Y 15
Eason's Hill .... Y 17
Emmet Place .... Y 18
Gerald Griffin St. .... Y 21
Infirmary Road .... Z 24
John Redmond Street .... Y 26
Lancaster Quay .... Z 28
Langford Row .... Z 29
Lower Glanmire Road .... Y 30
Merchant's Quay .... Y 32
Newsom's Quay .... Y 34
North Mall .... Y 35
O'Connell's Square .... Y 3
Parnell Place .... Z 3
Pembroke Street .... Z 3
Proby's Quay .... Z 4
Roman Street .... Y 4
St Patrick's Quay .... Y 4
Southern Road .... Z 4
South Link .... Z 4
South Main Street .... Z 4
Summer Hill .... Y 4
Wolfe Tone Street .... Y 5

Fitzpatrick's Silver Springs, Tivoli, E : 2 ½ m. on N 8 ☎ 507533, Telex 76111, Fax 507641, Fö, ≘s, ☐, ⛳9, ☐, park, ☐, squash – |☐| ☐ rm ☐ rest ☐TV ☎ Ⓟ – ☐ 800. ☐ AE ① VISA. ☐ X c
Meals *(closed Sunday dinner)* 10.50/20.50 **t.** and a la carte – ☐ 8.00 – **106 rm** 79.00/115.00 **st.**, 3 suites – SB.

Jurys, Western Rd, by Washington St., ☎ 276622, Fax 274477, Fö, ≘s, ☐ heated, ☐, squash – |☐| ☐ rm ☐ rest ☐TV ☎ ♿ Ⓟ – ☐ 500. ☐ AE ① VISA. ☐ Z v
closed 25 to 27 December – **Glandore : Meals** 16.00 **t.** (dinner) and a la carte 12.45/24.05 **t.** ☐ 5.85 – **Fastnet : Meals** *(closed Sunday and Monday)* (dinner only) 16.95/22.00 **t.** and a la carte ☐ 5.85 – ☐ 9.75 – **184 rm** 100.00/119.00 **t.**, 1 suite – SB.

Rochestown Park, Rochestown Rd, Douglas, SE : 3 m. by R 609 ☎ 892233, Fax 892178, Fö, ≘s, ☐, ☐ – |☐| ☐ rm ☐TV ☎ Ⓟ – ☐ 150. ☐ AE ① VISA. ☐
Windsor : Meals 12.00/20.00 **t.** and a la carte ☐ 5.50 – **63 rm** ☐ 57.00/85.00 **t.** – SB.

Morrisons Island, Morrisons Quay, ☎ 275858, Fax 275833 – |☐| ☐ rm ☐ rest ☐TV ☎ Ⓟ. ☐ AE ① VISA. ☐ Z a
closed 25 December – **Riverbank : Meals** 13.00 **t.** and a la carte ☐ 7.50 – ☐ 8.00 – **8 rm** 80.00/110.00 **t.**, **32 suites** 110.00 **t.** – SB.

Arbutus Lodge, Middle Glanmire Rd, Montenotte, ✆ 501237, Fax 502893, – rest – 100. VISA. X e
closed 24 to 28 December – **Meals** - (see ***Arbutus Lodge*** below) – **16 rm** 45.00/115.00 **st.**, 4 suites – SB.

Country Club, Middle Glanmire Rd, Montenotte, ✆ 502922, Fax 502082, – – 300. VISA X n
closed 24 to 26 December – **Meals** (bar lunch)/dinner 20.00 **st.** and dinner a la carte – **60 rm** 39.50/52.00 **st.** – SB.

Imperial, South Mall, ✆ 274040, Telex 75126, Fax 274040 – – 500. VISA Z n
closed 25 to 30 December – **Meals** 13.00/20.00 **st.** and dinner a la carte 8.00 – **100 rm** 50.00/150.00 **t.** – SB.

Jurys Cork Inn, Anderson's Quay, ✆ 276444, Fax 276144 – rm – 40. VISA. Y c
closed 24 to 27 December – **Meals** (bar lunch)/dinner 14.00 **t.** 5.25 – 6.00 – **133 rm** 49.00 **st.**

Victoria Lodge without rest., Victoria Cross, ✆ 542233, Fax 542572, – . VISA X v
closed 24 to 30 December – **40 rm** 28.00/44.00 **st.**

Lotamore House without rest., Tivoli, E : 3¼ m. on N 8 ✆ 822344, Fax 822219, – . VISA X a
closed 24 to 26 December – **20 rm** 28.00/50.00 **st.**

Forte Travelodge, Blackash, S : 2¼ m. by R 600 ✆ 310722, Reservations (Freephone) 0800 850950 (UK) - 1800 709709 (Republic of Ireland) – . VISA
Meals (grill rest.) – **40 rm** 34.50 **t.**

Garnish House without rest., Western Rd, ✆ 275111, Fax 273872 – . VISA. X r
14 rm 35.00/60.00 **st.**

Seven North Mall without rest., 7 North Mall, ✆ 397191, Fax 300811 – . VISA. Y a
closed 9 December-15 January – **5 rm** 40.00/60.00 **st.**

Killarney House without rest., Western Rd, ✆ 270290, Fax 271010 – . VISA. X x
18 rm 30.00/55.00 **t.**

Acorn House without rest., 14 St. Patrick's Hill, ✆ 502474 – . VISA. Y e
closed 22 December-10 January – **9 rm** 25.00/45.00 **st.**

Cliffords, 18 Dyke Par., ✆ 275333 – VISA JCB Z e
closed Saturday lunch, Sunday, Monday, last 2 weeks August and 1 week Christmas – **Meals** 11.50/25.50 **st.** 8.90.

Flemings with rm, Silver Grange House, Tivoli, E : 2¾ on N 8 ✆ 821621, Fax 821800, – . VISA JCB. X u
closed 24 to 27 December – **Meals** 12.50/22.00 **t.** and a la carte 6.50 – **4 rm** 39.00/65.00 **t.** – SB.

Arbutus Lodge (at Arbutus Lodge H.), Middle Glanmire Rd, Montenotte, ✆ 501237, Fax 502893, – . VISA X e
closed Sunday to non-residents and 24 to 28 December – **Meals** 14.50/22.50 **st.** and a la carte 6.80.

Lovett's (Restaurant), Churchyard Lane, off Well Rd, Douglas, ✆ 294909 – . VISA X s
closed Saturday lunch, Sunday, Bank Holidays and 24 to 30 December – **Meals** 14.50/24.00 **t.** and dinner a la carte 6.00.

Wylam, Victoria Cross, ✆ 341063, Fax 272146 – . VISA JCB X i
closed 24 and 25 December – **Meals** - Chinese - (dinner only) 16.50 **t.** and a la carte 6.50.

Michael's Bistro, 4 Mardyke St., ✆ 276887 – VISA Z e
closed Monday lunch, Sunday, 1 week Christmas and last 2 weeks August – **Meals** a la carte 13.20/20.50 **st.** 6.50.

Jacques, 9 Phoenix St., ✆ 277387, Fax 270634 – . VISA Z c
closed Saturday lunch, Sunday, 24 to 28 December and Bank Holidays – **Meals** a la carte 9.40/21.30 **t.**

COURTOWN HARBOUR (Cuan Bhaile na Cúirte) Wexford 405 N 10 – pop. 343 – ✉ Gorey – 055.

◆Dublin 62 – ◆Waterford 59 – Wexford 42.

Courtown, ✆ 25108, Fax 25304, – . VISA.
16 March-4 November – **Meals** 10.25/19.50 **t.** and dinner a la carte – **21 rm** 30.00/80.00 **t.** – SB.

CRATLOE (An Chreatalach) Clare 405 F 9 pop. 510 – ✉ Bunratty – ☎ 061.
◆Dublin 127 – Ennis 17 – ◆Limerick 7.

Bunratty View, ☎ 357352, Fax 357491, ←, 🌳 – ⊁ TV ☎ P. AE VISA. ✻
Meals (by arrangement) – **6 rm** ☐ 22.00/36.00 **s.**

CROOKEDWOOD (Tigh Munna) Westmeath 405 K 7 – ✉ Mullingar – ☎ 044.
◆Dublin 55 – ◆Drogheda 30 – Mullingar 6.

Crookedwood House ⛰, E : 1 ½ m. on Delvin rd ☎ 72165, Fax 72166, ←, « 18C rectory », 🌳 – TV ☎ P. AE ⓓ VISA. ✻
Meals - (see below) – **8 rm** ☐ 40.00/70.00 **t.** – SB.

XX **Crookedwood House** (at Crookedwood House H.), E : 1 ½ m. on Delvin rd ☎ 72165, Fax 72166, « 18C rectory », 🌳 – P. AE ⓓ VISA
closed Sunday dinner and Monday – **Meals** (dinner only and Sunday lunch)/dinner 19.50 and a la carte 6.00.

CROSSMOLINA (Crois Mhaoilíona) Mayo 405 E 5 **Ireland G.** – pop. 1 202 – ☎ 096.
Envir. : Errew Abbey★, SE : 6 m. by R 315.
Exc. : Broad Haven★, NW : 27 m. by N 59 and R 313.
◆Dublin 157 – ◆Ballina 6.5.

Enniscoe House ⛰, Castlehill, S : 2 m. on R 315 ☎ 31112, Fax 31773, ←, « Georgian country house, antiques », 🎣, park – P. AE VISA. ✻
closed February-March and 14 October-30 December – **Meals** (dinner only) 23.00 **st.** 7.00 – **6 rm** ☐ 50.00/104.00 **st.** – SB.

GREEN TOURIST GUIDES

Picturesque scenery, buildings

Attractive routes

Touring programmes

Plans of towns and buildings.

DELGANY (Deilgne) Wicklow 405 N 8 – pop. 6 682 (inc. Greystones) – ✉ Bray – ☎ 01.
⛳18 Delganny ☎ 287 4645/287 4536.
◆Dublin 19.

Glenview ⛰, Glen of the Downs, NW : 2 m. by L 164 on N 11 ☎ 287 3399, Fax 287 7511, ←, Fб, ≘s, 🏊, 🌳, park – 🛗 ⊁ rm TV ☎ ♿ P – 🏛 250. AE ⓓ VISA. ✻
Meals 15.00/24.00 **st.** and dinner a la carte 5.50 – **43 rm** ☐ 59.00/150.00 **st.** – SB.

DINGLE (An Daingean) Kerry 405 B 11 **Ireland G.** – pop. 1 272 – ☎ 066.
See : Town★ – Pier★, St. Mary's Church★.
Envir. : Gallarus Oratory★★★, NW : 5 m. by R 559 – NE : Connor Pass★★ – Kilmalkedar★, NW : 5½ m. by R 559.
Exc. : Mount Eagle (Beehive Huts★★) W : 9 m. by R 559 – Slea Head★★, W : 10½ m. by R 559 – Stradbally Strand★★, NE : 10½ m. via Connor Pass – Ballyferriter Heritage Centre★ *AC*, NW : 8 m. by R 559 – Mount Brandon★, N : 12½ m. by R 559 via Kilmalkedar – Blasket Islands★, W : 13 m. by R 559 and ferry from Dunquin.
ℹ Main St. ☎ 51188 (April-October).
◆Dublin 216 – ◆Killarney 51 – ◆Limerick 95.

Dingle Skellig, SE : ½ m. by T 68 ☎ 51144, Fax 51501, ←, ≘s, 🏊, 🌳, 🎾 – 🛗 TV ☎ P. AE ⓓ VISA. ✻
mid March-mid November – **Meals** 10.50/20.95 **t.** and dinner a la carte – **99 rm** ☐ 65.00/110.00 **t.**, 1 suite.

Milltown House ⛰, W : ¾ m. by Slea Head Drive ☎ 51372, Fax 51095, ←, 🌳 – TV ☎ ♿ P. VISA. ✻
closed 1 January-15 March – **Meals** *(closed Monday)* (dinner by arrangement) 15.00 **st.** 7.00 – **10 rm** ☐ 40.00/50.00 **st.**

Greenmount House without rest., Gortonora, by John St. ☎ 51414, Fax 51974, ← – ⊁ TV ☎ P. VISA. ✻
12 rm ☐ 30.00/50.00 **st.**

Doyle's Townhouse, 5 John St., ☎ 51174, Fax 51816 – TV ☎. ⓓ VISA
mid March-mid November – **Meals** - (see *Doyle's Seafood Bar* below) – **8 rm** ☐ 42.00/65.00 **t.**

Cleevaun without rest., Lady's Cross, Milltown, W : 1 ¼ m. on R 559 ☎ 51108, Fax 51108, ←, 🌳 – TV ☎ P. VISA. ✻
mid February-mid November – **9 rm** ☐ 35.00/43.00.

Captains House without rest., The Mall, ☎ 51531, Fax 51079, 🌳 – ⊁ rest TV ☎. AE VISA. ✻
closed 7 January-16 March – **8 rm** ☐ 25.00/40.00 **st.**

↑ **Bambury's** without rest., Mail Rd, E : on T 68 ✆ 51244, Fax 51786, ← – TV ☎ P. VISA. ✻
12 rm ☐ 34.00/44.00 **st.**

↑ **Alpine House** without rest., Mail Rd, E : on T 68 ✆ 51250, Fax 51966, – TV ☎ P. VISA. ✻
13 rm ☐ 16.50/37.00 **st.**

XX **Beginish** with rm, Green St., ✆ 51588, Fax 51591, – AE VISA
mid March-mid November – **Meals** - Seafood - *(closed Monday)* (light lunch)/dinner a la carte 17.00/24.00 **t.** 5.50, 3 suites ☐ 40.00/60.00 **t.**

X **Waterside,** ✆ 51458 – VISA
closed Tuesday and January-March – **Meals** a la carte 13.00/26.00 **st.** 5.00.

X **Doyle's Seafood Bar,** 4 John St., ✆ 51174, Fax 51816 – VISA. ✻
mid March-mid November – **Meals** *(closed Sunday)* (dinner only) 14.00 **t.** and a la carte 17.95/25.20 7.20.

DONEGAL (Dún na nGall) Donegal 405 H 4 Ireland G. – pop. 2 193 – 073.

See : Donegal Castle★ *AC*.

Exc. : Cliffs of Bunglass★★★, W : 30 m. by N 56 and R 263 – Glencolumbkille Folk Village★★ *AC*, W : 33 m. by N 56 and R 263 – Trabane Strand★★, W : 36 m. by N 56 and R 263 – Glenmalin Court Cairn★, W : 37 m. by N 56 and R 263 at Malin Beg.

Donegal Airport ✆ (075) 48232.

The Quay ✆ 21148 (April-October).

◆Dublin 164 – ◆Londonderry 48 – ◆Sligo 40.

St. Ernan's House, St. Ernan's Island, SW : 2 ¼ m. by N 15 ✆ 21065, Fax 22098, « Wooded island setting ← Donegal Bay », park – rest TV ☎ P. VISA. ✻
4 April-October – **Meals** (dinner only) 27.00 **st.** 6.00 – **12 rm** ☐ 120.00/144.00 **t.** – SB.

Harvey's Point Country, NE : 4½ m. by T 27 (Killibegs rd) ✆ 22208, Fax 22352, ←, « Loughside setting », park, – TV ☎ P – 50. AE VISA
April-October and restricted opening November-March – **Meals** - (see below) – **20 rm** ☐ 60.50/99.00 **st.** – SB.

↑ **Island View House** without rest., Ballyshannon rd, SW : ¾ m. ✆ 22411, ←, – TV P. ✻
4 rm ☐ 24.00/32.00.

XX **Harvey's Point Country** (at Harvey's Point Country H.), NE : 4½ m. by T 27 (Killibegs rd) ✆ 22208, Fax 22352, ←, « Loughside setting », – P. AE VISA
April-October and restricted opening November-March – **Meals** 10.45/25.00 **t.** and a la carte 7.50.

DOOLIN (Dúlainm) Clare 405 D 8 – 065.

◆Dublin 171 – ◆Galway 43 – ◆Limerick 50.

Aran View House, NE : ½ m. ✆ 74061, Fax 74540, ←, « Working farm », park rm TV ☎ P. AE VISA. ✻
March-October – **Meals** (bar lunch Monday to Saturday and Bank Holidays)/dinner 16.00 **t.** and a la carte 4.95 – **19 rm** ☐ 35.00/60.00 **t.** – SB.

↑ **Doonmacfelim House** without rest., ✆ 74503, Fax 74421, – ☎ P. VISA. ✻
8 rm ☐ 22.00/32.00 **t.**

DROGHEDA (Droichead Átha) Louth 405 M 6 pop. 23 848 – 041.

Envir. : Monasterboice★★, N : 6½ m. by N 1 – Boyne Valley★★, on N 51 – Termonfeckin (Tower House★) NE : 5 m. by R 166.

Exc. : – Newgrange★★, W : 3 m. by N 51 on N 2 – Old Mellifont★.

◆Dublin 29 – ◆Dundalk 22.

Boyne Valley, SE : 1 ¼ m. on N 1 ✆ 37737, Fax 39188, , , park, rm TV ☎ P – 350. AE VISA. ✻
Meals 9.50/22.50 **st.** and dinner a la carte 4.80 – **37 rm** ☐ 33.00/80.00 **st.** – SB.

↑ **Tullyesker House** without rest., Tullyesker, Monasterboice, N : 3½ m. by N 1 ✆ 30430, – TV P. ✻
closed 22 to 29 December – **5 rm** ☐ 36.00/44.00 **st.**

at Termonfeckin NE : 5 m. on R 166 – ✉ Drogheda – 041 :

XX **Triple House,** on R 166 ✆ 22616, Fax 22616, – P. VISA
closed Monday except June-August – **Meals** (dinner only and Sunday lunch) 15.00 **st.** and a la carte 5.00.

Bitte beachten Sie die Geschwindigkeitsbeschränkungen in Großbritannien
– 60 mph (= 96 km/h) außerhalb geschlossener Ortschaften
– 70 mph (= 112 km/h) auf Straßen mit getrennten Fahrbahnen und Autobahnen.

DUBLIN (Baile Átha Cliath) Dublin 405 N 7 Ireland G. – pop. 859 976 – ☎ 01.

See : City★★★ – Trinity College★★★ (Library★★★ *AC*) JY – Chester Beatty Library★★★ FV – Phoenix Park★★★ AS – Dublin Castle★★ HY – Christ Church Cathedral★★ HY – St. Patrick' Cathedral★★ HZ – Marsh's Library★★ HZ – National Museum★★ (Treasury★★), KZ – Nationa Gallery★★ KZ – Merrion Square★★ KZ – Rotunda Hospital Chapel★★ JX – Kilmainham Hosp tal★★ AT – Kilmainham Gaol Museum★★ AT **M6** – National Botanic Gardens★★ BS – No 29★ KZ – Liffey Bridge★ JY – Taylors' Hall★ HY – City Hall★ HY – St. Audoen's Gate★ HY **B** – S Stephen's Green★ JZ – Grafton Street★ JYZ – Powerscourt Centre★ JY – Civic Museum★ JY **M** – Bank of Ireland★ JY – O'Connell Street★ (Anna Livia Fountain★) JX – St. Michan's Church HY **E** – Hush Lane Municipal Gallery of Modern Art★ JX **M4** – Pro-Cathedral★ JX – Garden c Remembrance★ JX – Custom House★ KX – Bluecoat School★ BS **F** – Guinness Museum★ BT **M** – Marino Casino★ CS – Zoological Gardens★ AS – Newman House★ *AC* JZ.

Exc. : Powerscourt★★ (Waterfall★★★ *AC*), S : 14 m. by N 11 and R 117 EV – Russboroug House★★★, SW : 22 m. by N 81 BT – Rathfarnham Castle★, S : 3 m. by N 81 and R 115 BT.

18 Elm Park G. & S.C., Nutley House, Donnybrook ☎ 269 3438/269 3014, GV – 18 Milltown, Lower Churchtown Rd ☎ 977060/976090, EV – 18 Royal Dublin, North Bull Island, Dollymount ☎ 833 6346, CS – 18 Forrest Little, Cloghran ☎ 840 1183/840 1763, BS – 18 Lucan, Celbridge Rd, Lucan ☎ 628 0246, AS – 18 Edmondstown, Rathfarnham ☎ 493 2461, BT.

✈ Dublin Airport : ☎ 8444900, N : 5½ m. by N 1 BS – **Terminal** : Busaras (Central Bus Station) Store St..

⛴ to Holyhead (B & I Line) 2 daily (3 h 30 mn) – to the Isle of Man (Douglas) (Isle of Man Steam Packet Co. Ltd) (4 h 30 mn).

ℹ 14 Upper O'Connell St. ☎ 284 4768 – Arrivals Hall, Dublin Airport ☎ 284 4768.

Baggot Street Bridge ☎ 284 4768.

♦Belfast 103 – ♦Cork 154 – ♦Londonderry 146.

Conrad Dublin, Earlsfort Terr., D2, ☎ 676 5555, Telex 91872, Fax 676 5424 – |♦| ⇔ rm ▤ TV ☎ ♿ P – 300. AE ① VISA JCB. ✗ JZ **w**
Alexandra : Meals *(closed Saturday lunch, Sunday and Bank Holidays)* 18.50/27.50 **t.** and a la carte 6.50 – **Plurabelle Brasserie : Meals** 14.50/15.50 **t.** and a la carte 6.50 – ☕ 11.50 – **182 rm** 165.00/190.00 **t.**, 9 suites.

Berkeley Court, Lansdowne Rd, Ballsbridge, D4, ☎ 660 1711, Fax 661 7238 – |♦| ⇔ rm ▤ rest TV ☎ ♿ 🚗 P – 440. AE ① VISA. ✗ FU **c**
Berkeley Room : Meals 14.75/26.00 **t.** and a la carte 5.60 – **Conservatory Grill : Meals** 9.75/15.00 **t.** and a la carte 5.60 – ☕ 9.95 – **181 rm** 155.00/175.00 **st.**, 5 suites.

Shelbourne (Forte), 27 St. Stephen's Green, D2, ☎ 676 6471, Fax 661 6006 – |♦| ⇔ rm TV ☎ 🚗 – 400. AE ① VISA JZ **s**
Meals 15.50/26.00 and a la carte 5.65 – ☕ 11.50 – **155 rm** 130.00/172.00, 9 suites – SB.

Westbury, Grafton St., D2, ☎ 679 1122, Telex 91091, Fax 679 7078 – |♦| ⇔ rm ▤ rest TV ☎ 🚗 – 150. AE ① VISA JCB. ✗ JY **b**
Meals 16.50/24.00 **t.** and a la carte 5.60 – ☕ 10.00 – **195 rm** 155.00/175.00 **t.**, 8 suites.

Jurys H. & Towers, Pembroke Rd, Ballsbridge, D4, ☎ 660 5000, Telex 93723, Fax 660 5540, heated – |♦| ⇔ rm ▤ rest TV ☎ ♿ P – 850. AE ① VISA. ✗ FU **p**
Kish : Meals - Seafood - (dinner only) 25.00 **t.** and a la carte 6.00 – **Embassy Garden : Meals** 12.50/21.00 **t.** and a la carte 6.00 – ☕ 9.75 – **378 rm** 121.00/180.00 **t.**, 6 suites – SB.

Burlington, Upper Leeson St., D4, ☎ 660 5222, Telex 93815, Fax 660 3172 – |♦| ⇔ rm ▤ rest TV ☎ ♿ P – 1000. AE ① VISA JCB. ✗ EU **e**
Meals 14.50/17.50 **t.** and a la carte 5.50 – ☕ 9.35 – **448 rm** 115.00/135.00 **t.**, 4 suites.

Gresham, O'Connell St., D1, ☎ 874 6881, Telex 32473, Fax 878 7175 – |♦| ▤ rest TV ☎ ♿ 🚗 – 250. AE ① VISA. ✗ JX **k**
Meals 12.50/24.20 **st.** and a la carte 7.90 – ☕ 11.00 – **194 rm** 80.00/160.00 **t.**, 6 suites.

DUBLIN
BUILT UP AREA

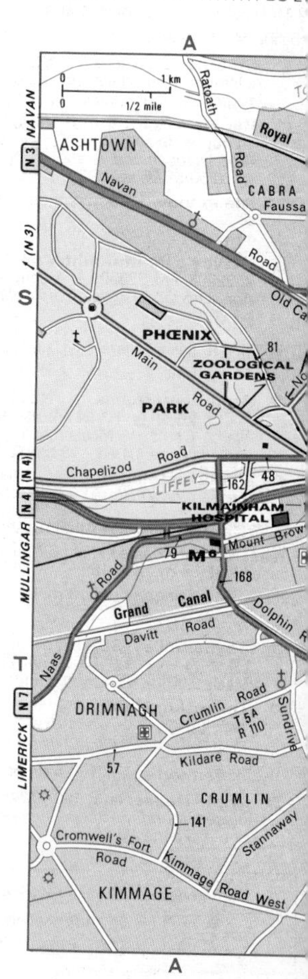

Hibernian, Eastmoreland Pl., Ballsbridge, D4, ✆ 668 7666, Fax 660 2655 – TV ☎ ♿ P. AE VISA. EU **x**
closed 24 to 29 December – **Patrick Kavanagh Room : Meals** *(closed Saturday lunch)* 13.95/29.95 **t.** and dinner a la carte 5.95 – **29 rm** 90.00/157.00 **st.** – SB.

Doyle Montrose, Stillorgan Rd, D4, SE : 4 m. by N 11 ✆ 269 3311, Fax 269 1164 – rest TV ☎ ♿ P – 80. AE VISA JCB. GV **y**
Meals 9.35/16.50 **t.** and a la carte 5.80 – 7.40 – **179 rm** 83.00/143.00 **t.**

Mespil, Mespil Rd, D4, ✆ 667 1222, Fax 667 1244 – rm rest TV ☎ ♿ P – 40. AE VISA. EU **u**
closed 24 to 26 December – **Meals** (bar lunch)/dinner 17.95 **t.** and a la carte 5.25 – 6.50 – **153 rm** 65.00/80.00 **t.** – SB.

Canal Road	**BT**	30
Clanbrassil Street	**BT**	40
Conyngham Road	**AS**	48
Denmark Street	**BS**	52
Donnybrook Road	**CT**	54
Dorset Street	**BS**	55
Drimnagh Road	**AT**	57
Eglinton Road	**CT**	63
Grand Parade	**BT**	72
Inchicore Road	**AT**	79
Infirmary Road	**AS**	81
James' Street	**BT**	84
Leeson Street Upper	**BT**	94
Macken Street	**BST**	99
Morehampton Road	**BT**	108
Mount Street Upper	**BT**	112
Palmerston Park	**BT**	123
Phibsborough Road	**BS**	132
Rathmines Road Upper	**BT**	135
Ringsend Road	**CT**	139
St Agnes Road	**AT**	141
St Alphonsus Road	**BS**	144
St John's Road West	**AS**	147
Sandford Road	**BT**	151
Shelbourne Road	**CT**	157
Shrewsbury Road	**CT**	159
South Circular Road	**AS**	162
Suir Road	**AT**	168
Terenure Road East	**BT**	172
Thomas Street West	**BT**	174
Victoria Quay	**BS**	178
Western Way	**BS**	184
Wolfe Tone Quay	**BS**	195

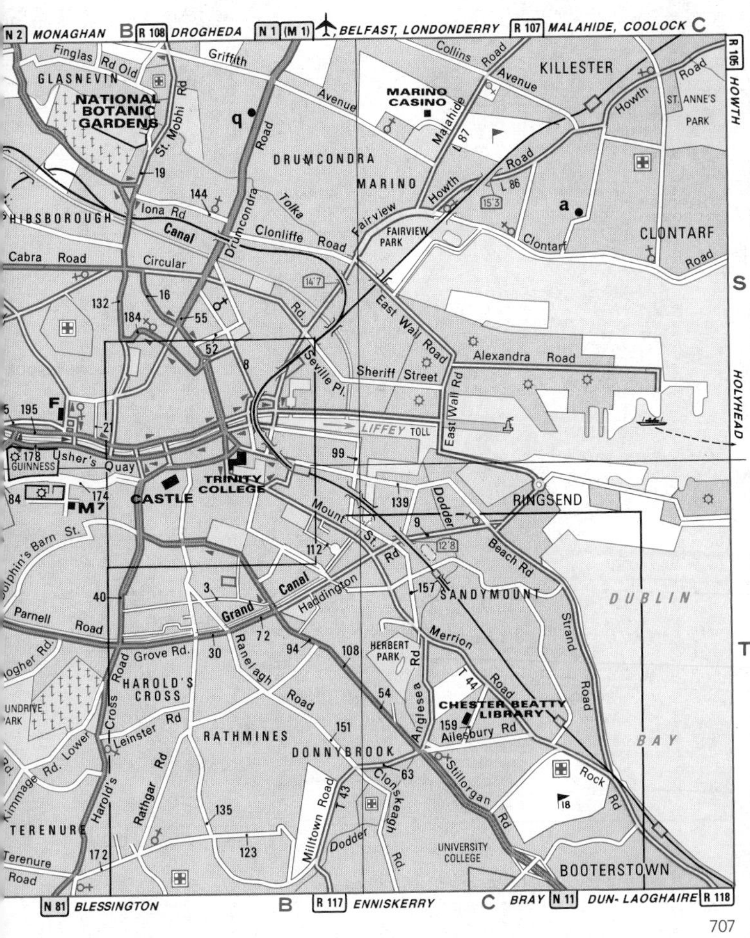

DUBLIN
SOUTH EAST BUILT UP AREA

Street	Grid	No.
Ailesbury Road	**FV**	4
Baggot Street Upper	**EU**	7
Beech Hill Avenue	**FV**	10
Beechwood Road	**EV**	12
Belgrave Road	**DV**	13
Bloomfield Avenue	**DU**	18
Brighton Road	**DV**	22
Camder Street	**DU**	28
Castlewood Avenue	**DV**	31
Charlemont Street	**DU**	34
Charlotte Street	**DU**	36
Chelmsford Road	**EV**	37
Church Avenue	**FU**	39
Clyde Road	**EFU**	43
Eastmoreland Place	**EU**	61
Elgin Road	**EFU**	64
Harrington Street	**DU**	73
Herbert Place	**EU**	76
Irishtown Road	**FU**	82
Lansdowne Road	**FU**	90
Lea Road	**GU**	91
Leeson Street Lower	**EU**	93
Leinster Road West	**DV**	96
Londonbridge Road	**FU**	97
Maxwell Road	**DV**	102

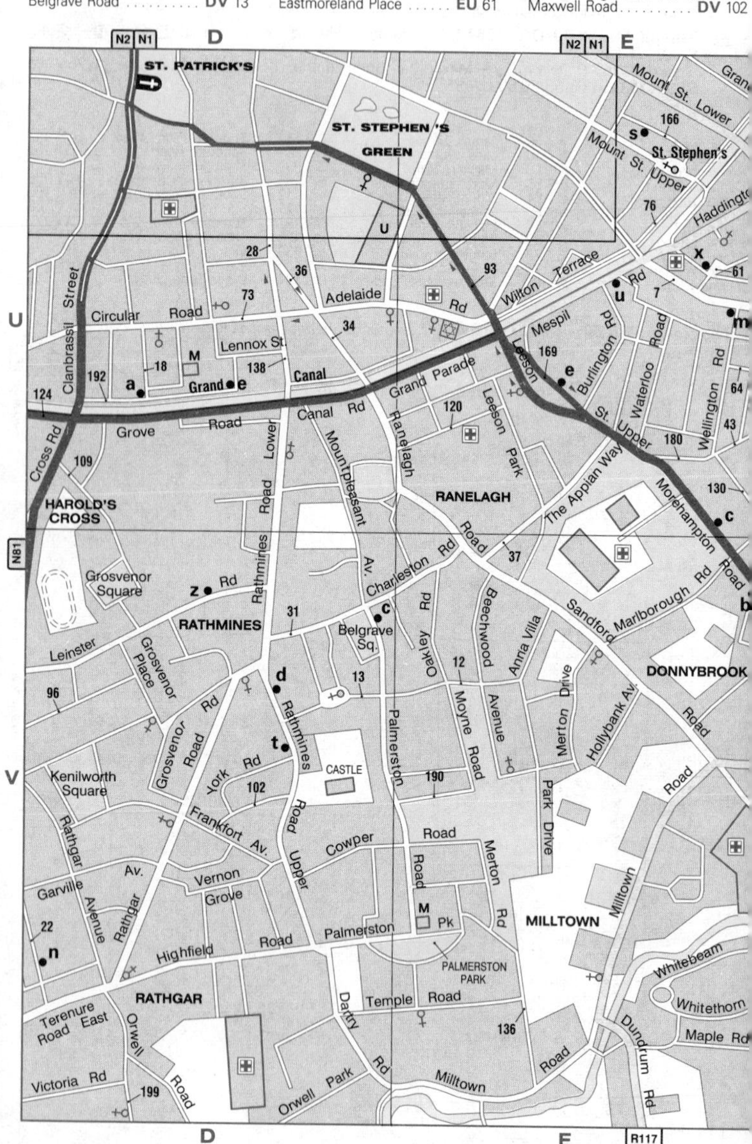

If you find you cannot take up a hotel booking you have made, please let the hotel know immediately.

lerlyn Park . . . . GV 105
ount Drummond Av. . . DU 109
ewbridge Avenue . . . . . . FU 115
ewgrove Avenue . . . . . . GU 117
orthbrook Road . . . . EU 120
utgrove Park . . . . FV 121
arnell Road . . . . DU 124
embroke Park . . . . EU 130
aglan Road . . . . FU 133

Richmond Avenue South . EV 136
Richmond Street South . . DU 138
St Alban's Park . . . . GV 142
St John's Road East . . . . . GV 145
Seafort Avenue . . . . GU 153
Sean Moore Road . . . . . . GU 154
Serpentine Avenue . . . . . . FU 156
Simmonscourt Road . . . . . FU 160
South Lotts Road . . . . FU 163

Stephen's Lane . . . . EU 166
Sussex Road . . . . EU 169
Trimbleston Avenue . . . . . GV 175
Victoria Avenue . . . . FV 177
Wellington Place . . . . EU 180
Windsor Road . . . . EV 190
Windsor Terrace . . . . DU 192
Wynnsward Drive . . . . FV 198
Zion Road . . . . DV 199

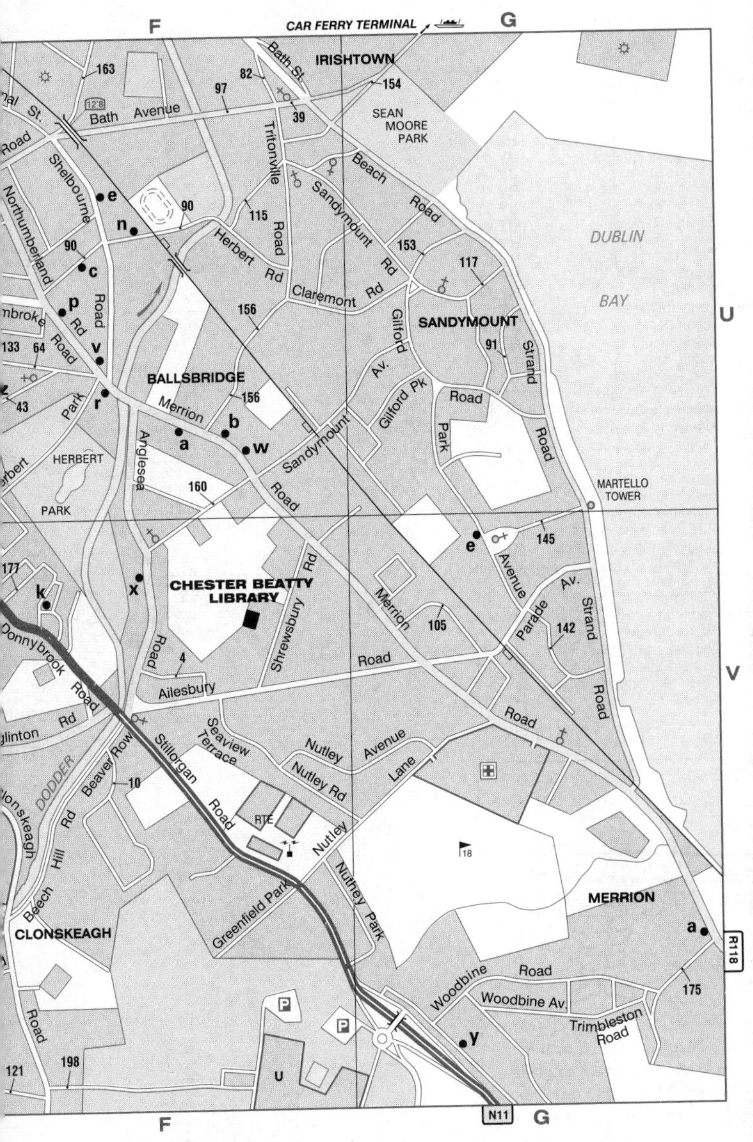

Prévenez immédiatement l'hôtelier si vous ne pouvez pas occuper la chambre que vous avez retenue.

DUBLIN CENTRE

Street	Grid	No.
Anne Street South	**JYZ**	6
Dawson Street	**JYZ**	
Duke Street	**JY**	58
Grafton Street	**JYZ**	
Henry Street	**JX**	
Ilac Centre	**HJX**	
Irish Life Mall Centre	**JKX**	
O'Connell Street	**JX**	

Street	Grid	No.
Brunswick Street North	**HX**	24
Buckingham Street	**KX**	25
Bull Alley	**HZ**	27
Chancery Street	**HY**	33
Clanbrassil Street	**HZ**	40
College Green	**JY**	45
College Street	**JY**	46
Cornmarket	**HY**	49
D'Olier Street	**JY**	51
Earlsfort Terrace	**JZ**	60
Essex Quay	**HY**	66
Fishamble Street	**HY**	67
George's Quay	**KY**	69
Golden Lane	**HZ**	70
Henrietta Street	**HX**	75
High Street	**HY**	78
Kevin Street Upper	**HZ**	85
Kildare Street	**JKZ**	87
King Street South	**JZ**	88
Marlborough Street	**JX**	100
Merchants Quay	**HY**	103
Montague Street	**JZ**	106
Mount Street Upper	**KZ**	112
Nicholas Street	**HY**	118
Parnell Square East	**JX**	126
Parnell Square North	**JX**	127
Parnell Square West	**HJX**	129
St Mary's Abbey Street	**HY**	148
St Patrick Close	**HZ**	150
Stephen Street	**HJY**	165
Tara Street	**KY**	171
Wellington Quay	**HJY**	181
Werburgh Street	**HY**	183
Westland Row	**KY**	186
Westmoreland Street	**JY**	187
Wexford Street	**HZ**	189
Winetavern Street	**HY**	193
Wood Quay	**HY**	196

Town plans: roads most used by traffic and those on which guide-listed hotels and restaurants stand are fully drawn; the beginning only of lesser roads is indicated.

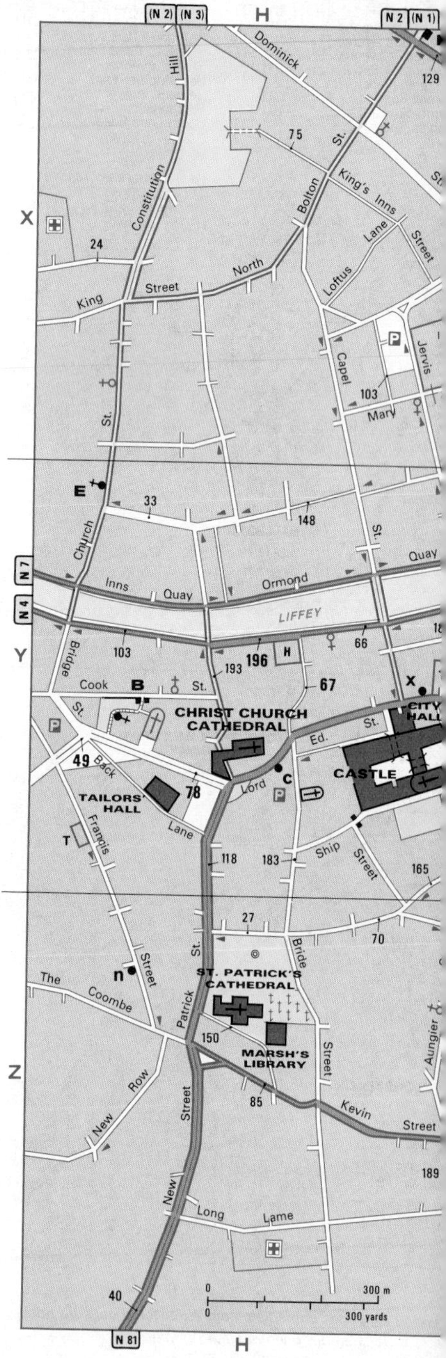

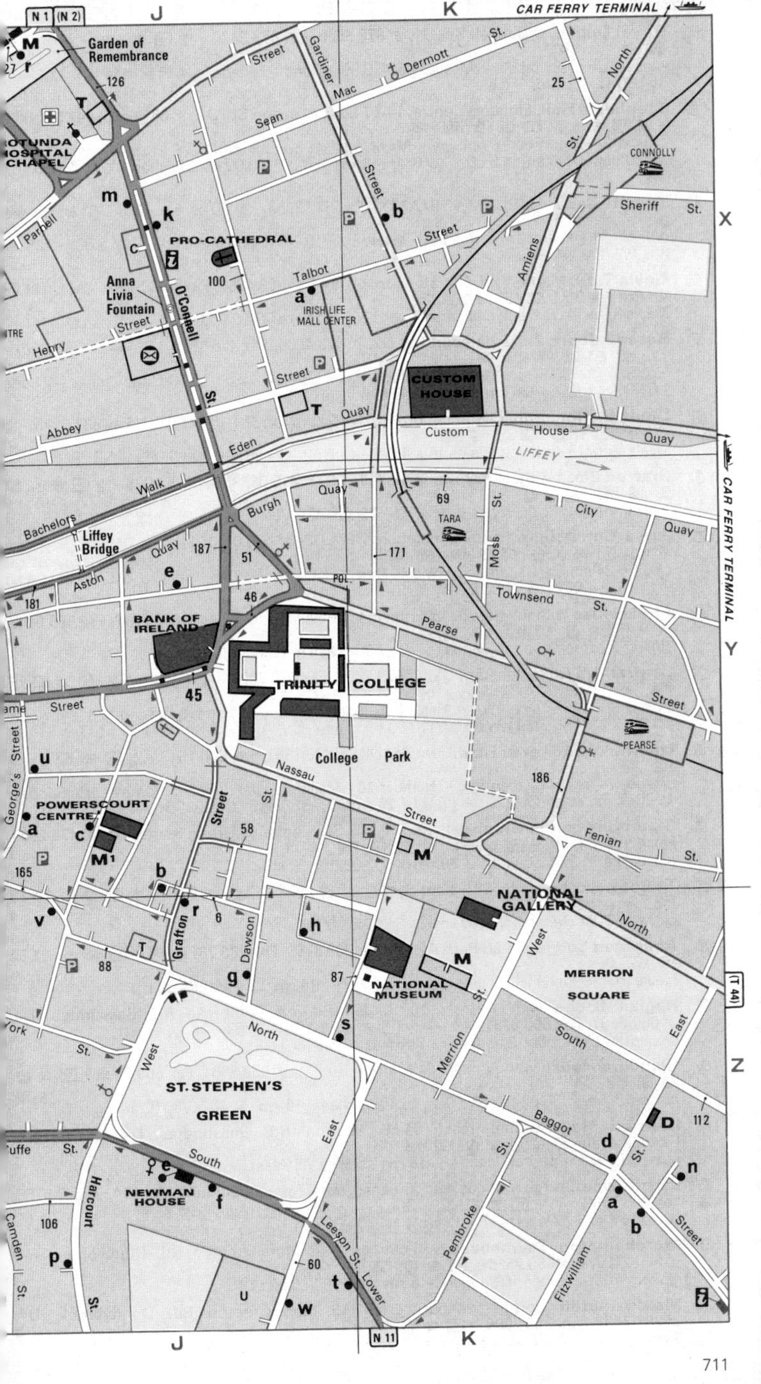

CAR FERRY TERMINAL
Garden of Remembrance
ROTUNDA HOSPITAL CHAPEL
PRO-CATHEDRAL
Anna Livia Fountain
IRISH LIFE MALL CENTER
CUSTOM HOUSE
CONNOLLY
Sheriff St.
Amiens
Talbot Street
Sean Mac Dermott St.
Gardiner Street
North St.
O'Connell St.
Henry Street
Abbey Street
Eden Quay
Custom House Quay
LIFFEY
Bachelors Walk
Liffey Bridge
Burgh Quay
Aston Quay
City Quay
TARA
Moss St.
Townsend St.
Pearse Street
BANK OF IRELAND
TRINITY COLLEGE
College Park
PEARSE
Nassau Street
Fenian St.
POWERSCOURT CENTRE
George's Street
Grafton Street
Dawson St.
NATIONAL GALLERY
NATIONAL MUSEUM
MERRION SQUARE
Merrion St.
York St.
ST. STEPHEN'S GREEN
Baggot Street
Pembroke St.
Fitzwilliam St.
Leeson St. Lower
NEWMAN HOUSE
Harcourt St.
Camden St.
Cuffe St.

Royal Dublin, O'Connell St., D1, ✆ 873 3666, Fax 873 3120 – |‡| TV ☎ – 220. AE VISA. JX r
closed 25 December – **Meals** 11.50/18.95 **st.** and a la carte 4.75 – **114 rm** 83.00/104.00 **st.**, 3 suites – SB.

Stephen's Hall, Earlsfort Centre, 14-17 Lower Leeson St., D2, ✆ 661 0585, Fax 661 060 – |‡| TV ☎ . AE VISA. JZ
closed 24 December-4 January – **Meals** *(closed Sunday and Bank Holidays)* 9.50/15.00 and dinner a la carte 5.00 – 8.00 – **3 rm** 100.00/140.00 **st.**, **34 suites** 140.00/200.00 **t.** – SB.

Temple Bar, Fleet St., D2, ✆ 677 3333, Fax 677 3088 – |‡| TV ☎ – 30. AE VISA. JY
closed 23 December-4 January – **Meals** 8.25/18.00 **st.** and a la carte – 6.00 – **108 rm** 85.00/110.00 **st.** – SB.

Doyle Tara, Merrion Rd, D4, SE : 4 m. on T 44 ✆ 269 4666, Fax 269 1027 – |‡| rest TV ☎ P – 300. AE VISA. GV
Meals 8.90/14.00 **t.** and a la carte – 6.50 – **113 rm** 76.00/99.00 **t.**

Russell Court, 21-25 Harcourt St., D2, ✆ 478 4066, Fax 478 1576 – |‡| rm TV ☎ P – 150. AE VISA. JZ
closed 24 to 29 December – **Meals** (bar meals Sunday) 12.50/16.00 **t.** and dinner a la carte 6.50 – 6.50 – **36 rm** 60.00/90.00 **t.**, 6 suites – SB.

Doyle Skylon, Upper Drumcondra Rd, N : 2½ m. on N 1 ✆ 837 9121, Fax 837 2778 – |‡| rest TV ☎ P. AE VISA. BS c
Meals 9.50/13.25 **t.** and a la carte 4.60 – 6.50 – **92 rm** 76.00/99.00 **t.** – SB.

Grafton Plaza without rest., Johnsons Pl., D2, ✆ 475 0888, Fax 475 0908 – |‡| TV ☎ . AE VISA. JZ v
closed 24 to 26 December – 7.50 – **75 rm** 70.00/95.00 **st.**

Jurys Christchurch Inn, Christchurch Pl., D8, ✆ 475 0111, Fax 475 0488 – |‡| rm rest TV ☎ P. AE VISA. HY c
closed 24 to 26 December – **Meals** (bar lunch)/dinner 13.50 **st.** and a la carte 4.95 – 6.00 – **182 rm** 51.00 **st.**

Ariel House without rest., 52 Lansdowne Rd, Ballsbridge, D4, ✆ 668 5512, Fax 668 5845, – TV ☎ P. VISA. FU n
closed 24 December-14 January – 7.50 – **28 rm** 60.00/140.00 **t.**

Central, 1-5 Exchequer St., D2, ✆ 679 7302, Fax 679 7303 – |‡| TV ☎ – 80. AE VISA. JY u
closed 24 to 27 December – **Meals** (bar lunch Monday to Friday) a la carte 13.90/17.65 **t.** 5.95 – 7.50 – **69 rm** 60.00/110.00 **t.**, 1 suite.

Longfield's, 10 Lower Fitzwilliam St., D2, ✆ 676 1367, Fax 676 1542 – |‡| TV ☎. AE VISA. KZ d
closed 24 to 27 December – **Number 10 : Meals** *(closed lunch Saturday and Sunday)* 14.20/31.50 **st.** and a la carte 6.00 – **26 rm** 79.50/115.00 **st.** – SB.

Stauntons on the Green without rest., 83 St. Stephen's Green South, D2, ✆ 478 2300, Fax 478 2263, – TV ☎ . AE VISA. JZ f
closed 24 to 27 December – **30 rm** 50.00/105.00 **st.**

Talbot without rest., 95-98 Talbot St., D1, ✆ 874 9202, Fax 874 9672 – |‡| TV ☎ P. AE VISA. JX a
closed 23-27 December – **40 rm** 35.00/55.00 **st.**

Aberdeen Lodge, 53-55 Park Av., D4, ✆ 283 8155, Fax 283 7877, – TV ☎ P. AE VISA. GV e
Meals (dinner only) 21.00 and a la carte 7.00 – **16 rm** 45.00/90.00 **t.**

Raglan Lodge without rest., 10 Raglan Rd, off Pembroke Rd, Ballsbridge, D4, ✆ 660 6697, Fax 660 6781, – TV ☎ P. AE VISA. FU z
closed 22 December-2 January – **7 rm** 45.00/100.00 **st.**

Glenogra House without rest., 64 Merrion Rd, D4, ✆ 668 3661, Fax 668 3698 – TV ☎ P. AE VISA. FU w
closed 2 weeks February and 1 week Christmas – **10 rm** 40.00/80.00 **st.**

Merrion Hall without rest., 54-56 Merrion Rd, Ballsbridge, D4, ✆ 668 1426, Fax 668 4280, – TV ☎ P. VISA. FU b
closed 20 December-3 January – **15 rm** 40.00/90.00 **st.**

Lansdowne Lodge without rest., 6 Lansdowne Terr., Shelbourne Rd, D4, ✆ 660 5755, Fax 660 5662, – TV ☎ P. VISA FU e
closed 24 to 27 December – **12 rm** 49.00/66.00 **t.**

Morehampton Townhouse without rest., 46 Morehampton Rd, Donnybrook, D4, ✆ 660 2106, Fax 660 2566 – TV ☎ P. VISA. EU c
closed 15 December-10 January – **6 rm** 45.00/60.00 **st.**

Morehampton Lodge without rest., 113 Morehampton Rd, Donnybrook, D4, ✆ 283 7499, Fax 283 7595 – TV ☎ P. VISA EV b
5 rm 50.00/70.00 **st.**

Belgrave Guest House without rest., 8-10 Belgrave Sq., Rathmines, D6, ℘ 496 3760, Fax 497 9243, – TV ☎ P. VISA. DV **c**
closed 22 December-1 January – **24 rm** 32.50/55.00 **st.**

Uppercross House, 26-30 Upper Rathmines Rd, Rathmines, D6, ℘ 4975486, Fax 4975361 – TV ☎. AE VISA DV **d**
Meals (dinner only) 9.95 **st.** and a la carte 5.50 – **14 rm** 37.50/60.00 **st.**

Anglesea Town House without rest., 63 Anglesea Rd, Ballsbridge, D4, ℘ 668 3877, Fax 668 3461 – TV ☎. AE VISA. FV **x**
closed 20 December-4 January – **7 rm** 45.00/90.00 **t.**

Clara House without rest., 23 Leinster Rd, Rathmines, D6, ℘ 497 5904, Fax 497 5904 – TV ☎ P. VISA DV **z**
13 rm 35.00/58.00 **st.**

Grafton House without rest., 26-27 South Great Georges St., D2, ℘ 679 2041, Fax 677 9715 – TV ☎. VISA. JY **a**
closed Christmas – **11 rm** 40.00/70.00 **st.**

Glenveagh Town House without rest., 31 Northumberland Rd, Ballsbridge, D4, ℘ 668 4612, Fax 668 4559 – TV ☎. VISA. FU **u**
closed 22 to 28 December – **11 rm** 50.00/70.00 **st.**

St. Aiden's without rest., 32 Brighton Rd, Rathgar, D6, ℘ 4906178, Fax 4920234 – TV ☎ P. VISA. DV **n**
closed 23 to 26 December – **8 rm** 30.00/66.00 **st.**

Glen without rest., 84 Lower Gardiner St., D1, ℘ 855 1374 – TV ☎ P. VISA. KX **b**
12 rm 30.00/48.00 **t.**

XXX ✿✿ **Patrick Guilbaud,** 46 James' Pl., James' St., off Lower Baggot St., D2, ℘ 676 4192, Fax 661 0052 – ▤. AE VISA KZ **n**
closed Sunday, Monday, 1 to 10 January and Bank Holidays – **Meals** - French - 18.50/30.00 **t.** and a la carte 32.00/38.00 **t.** 8.00
Spec. Cassolette of Dublin Bay prawns with lemon butter, Crubeens (pigs trotters) served with a mushroom pudding, Croustade aux pommes.

XXX ✿ **The Commons,** Newman House, 85-86 St. Stephen's Green, D2, ℘ 475 2597, Fax 478 0551, « Contemporary collection of James Joyce inspired Irish Art » – AE VISA JZ **e**
closed Saturday lunch, Sunday, 2 weeks Christmas and Bank Holidays – **Meals** 18.00/30.00 **t.** and a la carte 30.50/43.50 **t.** 7.00
Spec. Pan fried slices of duck foie gras with grilled Clonakilty black pudding, Grilled turbot fillet, pea and smoked bacon confit, beluga caviar sauce, Braised loin of lamb with parsley dumplings, fennel, thyme and Parmesan.

XXX **Ernie's,** Mulberry Gdns, off Morehampton Rd, Donnybrook, D4, ℘ 269 3300, Fax 269 3260, « Contemporary Irish Art collection » – ▤. AE VISA FV **k**
closed Saturday lunch, Sunday, Monday and 1 week Christmas – **Meals** 10.00/25.00 **t.** and dinner a la carte 24.00/33.50 **t.** 7.50.

XXX **Viking at Clontarf Castle,** Castle Av., Clontarf, D3, NE : 3 ½ m. ℘ 833 2271, Fax 833 4549 – ▤ P. AE VISA CS **a**
closed Sunday, Monday, Good Friday and 24 to 26 December – **Meals** (dinner only) 14.50 **t.** and a la carte 5.50.

XXX **Le Coq Hardi,** 35 Pembroke Rd, D4, ℘ 668 9070, Fax 668 9887 – P. AE VISA JCB EU **m**
closed Saturday lunch, Sunday, 2 weeks August, 2 weeks Christmas and Bank Holidays – **Meals** 18.00/30.00 **t.** and a la carte 8.00.

XX **Chapter One,** The Dublin Writers Museum, 18-19 Parnell Sq., D1, ℘ 873 2266, Fax 873 2330 – ▤ P. AE VISA JX **r**
closed Saturday lunch, Monday dinner, Sunday, 25 to 26 December and Bank Holidays – **Meals** 12.50/22.50 **t.** and dinner a la carte 18.25/23.75 **t.** 6.00.

XX ✿ **Thornton's** (Thornton), 1 Portobello Rd, D8, ℘ 454 9067, Fax 454 9067 – ▤. AE VISA DU **e**
closed Sunday and Monday – **Meals** (booking essential) (dinner only) 28.50 **t.** and a la carte 26.50/32.45 **t.** 6.75
Spec. Marinated wild Atlantic salmon with cucumber jelly, Sautéed loin of lamb with courgette clafoutis and thyme jus, Nougat pyramid with glazed fruit and orange sauce.

XX **Locks,** 1 Windsor Terr., Portobello, ℘ 4543391, Fax 4538352 – AE VISA DU **a**
closed Saturday lunch, Sunday, last week July-first week August and 1 week Christmas – **Meals** 13.95/22.00 **t.** and a la carte 5.95.

XX **Polo One,** 5-6 Molesworth Pl., off Molesworth St., D2, ℘ 662 2233, Fax 678 9593. AE VISA JZ **h**
closed Sunday – **Meals** 10.00/17.50 **t.** and a la carte 5.50.

XX **Zen,** 89 Upper Rathmines Rd, D6, ℘ 4979428 – ▤. AE VISA DV **t**
closed lunch Monday, Tuesday, Wednesday, Saturday and 25 to 26 December – **Meals** - Chinese (Szechuan) - 8.00/18.00 **st.** and a la carte 5.00.

XX **Les Frères Jacques,** 74 Dame St., D2, ℘ 679 4555, Fax 679 4725 – AE VISA HY
closed Saturday lunch, Sunday, 25-30 December and Bank Holidays – **Meals** - French - 13.00/20.00 **t.** and dinner a la carte 5.50.

XX **L'Ecrivain,** 109 Lower Baggot St., D2, ℘ 661 1919, Fax 661 0617, – ▤. AE VISA KZ
closed Saturday lunch, Sunday, 25 to 27 December and Bank Holidays – **Meals** (booking essential) 11.00/25.00 **t.** and dinner a la carte 6.50.

XX **La Stampa,** 35 Dawson St., D2, ℘ 677 8611, Fax 677 3336 – AE VISA JZ
closed lunch Saturday and Sunday, Good Friday and 25 December – **Meals** 10.50 **t** (lunch) and dinner a la carte 17.40/27.40 **t.** 6.00.

XX **Peacock Alley,** 112 Lower Baggot St., ℘ 662 0760, Fax 662 0776 – AE VISA
closed Saturday lunch, Sunday, 23 December to lunch 31 December and Bank Holidays – **Meals** (booking essential) 15.95/35.00 **t.** KZ

XX **Old Dublin,** 90-91 Francis St., D8, ℘ 4542028, Fax 4541406 – AE VISA HZ
closed Saturday lunch, Sunday and Bank Holidays – **Meals** - Russian-Scandinavian - 12.50/19.50 **t.** and dinner a la carte 5.95.

XX **Chandni,** 174 Pembroke Rd, Ballsbridge, D4, ℘ 668 1458 – ▤. AE VISA FU
closed Sunday lunch – **Meals** - Indian - 7.95/39.95 **st.** and dinner a la carte.

XX **Fitzers Café,** RDS, Merrion Rd, Ballsbridge, D4, ℘ 667 1301, Fax 667 1299 – P. AE VISA FU
closed 25-26 December, 1 January and Good Friday – **Meals** (booking essential) 10.50/35.95 **t.** and a la carte 6.95.

X **Dobbin's,** 15 Stephen's Lane, off Lower Mount St., D2, ℘ 676 4679, Fax 661 3331 – ▤ P. AE VISA EU
closed Saturday lunch, Monday dinner, Sunday and Bank Holidays – **Meals** - Bistro - 14.50/23.00 **st.** and a la carte 6.25.

X **Roly's Bistro,** 7 Ballsbridge Terr., Ballsbridge, D4, ℘ 668 2611, Fax 660 8535 – ▤. AE VISA FU
closed Good Friday and 25 to 26 December – **Meals** 9.50 **t.** (lunch) and dinner a la carte 14.40/20.95 **t.** 4.50.

X **Cooke's Café,** 14 South William St., D2, ℘ 679 0536, Fax 679 0546 – ▤. AE VISA JY
closed 25 to 26 December, 1 January and Bank Holidays – **Meals** 13.75 **t.** and a la carte.

X **Chili Club,** 1 Anne's Lane, South Anne St., D2, ℘ 677 3721, Fax 493 8284 – AE VISA JZ
closed lunch Saturday and Bank Holidays and Sunday – **Meals** - Thai - (booking essential) 9.95/125.00 **t.** and a la carte 5.75.

at Foxrock SE : 7½ m. by N 11 – ✉ Dublin – ☎ 01 :

X **Bistro One,** 3 Brighton Rd., D18, ℘ 289 7711 – VISA
closed Sunday, Monday, first 2 weeks August and 24 to 26 December – **Meals** (booking essential) (dinner only) a la carte 12.00/18.75 **t.** 4.95.

DUNDALK (Dun Dealgan) Louth 405 M 5/6 pop. 25 843 – ☎ 042.

♦Dublin 51 – Drogheda 22.

Carrickdale, Carrickcarnon, N : 8 m. on N 1 ℘ 71397, Fax 71740, – TV ☎ P. AE VISA.
closed 25 December – **Meals** 10.00/20.00 **st.** and dinner a la carte 5.00 – **47 rm** 35.00/70.00 **st.** – SB.

DUNDRUM (Dún Droma) Tipperary 405 H 10 pop. 247 – ✉ Cashel – ☎ 062.

♦Dublin 104 – ♦Cork 66 – ♦Limerick 33.

Dundrum House, SE : ¾ m. on R 505 ℘ 71116, Fax 71366, 18, park, – TV ☎ P – 150. AE VISA.
Meals (bar lunch Monday to Saturday)/dinner 26.00 **t.** and a la carte 5.50 – **54 rm** 48.00/88.00 – SB.

DUNFANAGHY (Dún Fionnachaidh) Donegal 405 I 2 Ireland G. – pop. 280 – ✉ Letterkenny – ☎ 074.

Envir. : Horn Head Scenic Route★, N : 2½ m.

Exc. : Doe Castle★, SE : 7 m. by N 56 – The Rosses★, SW : 25 m. by N 56 and R 259.

♦Dublin 172 – Donegal 54 – ♦Londonderry 43.

Arnold's, Main St., ℘ 36208, Fax 36352, ←, – TV ☎ P. AE VISA.
16 March-9 November – **Meals** 9.50/22.00 **t.** and a la carte 5.50 – **34 rm** 37.00/74.00 **t.** – SB.

Carrig Rua, Main St., ℘ 36133, Fax 36277, ← – TV ☎ P. AE VISA.
18 March-October – **Meals** (carving lunch)/dinner 18.00 **t.** and a la carte 4.50 – **22 rm** 28.00/70.00 **t.** – SB.

DUNGARVAN (**Dún Garbháin**) Waterford 405 J 11 pop. 6 920 – ☎ 058.

Dublin 118 – ◆Cork 44 – Waterford 30.

🏨 **Lawlors,** Meagher St., ✆ 41122, Fax 41000 – 🛗 ▤ rest 📺 ☎ – 🎤 250. AE VISA. ✻
closed 25 December – 8.75/16.50 **st.** and a la carte – **89 rm** ☐ 34.00/62.00 **t.** – SB.

at Clonea Strand E : 3¾ m. by Clonea Strand rd – ✉ Dungarvan – ☎ 058 :

🏨 Clonea Strand, ✆ 42416, Fax 42880, ←, 🏋, ≋, 🏊, ⛳9 – 🛗 📺 ☎ 🅟 – 🎤 200 – **58 rm.**

at Ballynacourty SE : 3¼ m. by R 675 – ✉ Dungarvan – ☎ 058 :

🏨 Gold Coast Golf, ✆ 42249, Fax 43378, ←, ⛳9, 🎾 – 🛗 📺 ☎ 🅟 – 🎤 100 – **37 rm.**

DUNGLOE (**An Clochán Liath**) Donegal 405 G 3 – ☎ 075.

Dublin 173 – ◆Londonderry 51 – ◆Sligo 76.

🏨 **Ostan na Rosann,** ✆ 21088, Fax 21365, ←, ≋, 🏊 – 📺 ☎ 🅟. AE VISA. ✻
Easter-October – **Meals** (bar lunch)/dinner 17.00 **st.** and a la carte 🍷 4.95 – **48 rm** ☐ 50.00/77.00 **st.** – SB.

DUNKINEELY (**Dún Cionnaola**) Donegal 405 G 4 – ☎ 073.

Dublin 157 – ◆Londonderry 56 – ◆Sligo 50.

✗✗ **Castle Murray** with rm, St. Johns Point, SW : 1 ¼ m. by N 56 and St. Johns Point rd turning left at T junction ✆ 37022, Fax 37330, ← – 📺 ☎ 🅟. VISA
closed 3 weeks January-February, Monday and Tuesday November-Easter – **Meals** - French - (dinner only and Sunday lunch)/dinner 16.00/23.00 **st.** and a la carte – **10 rm** ☐ 26.00/52.00 **st.**

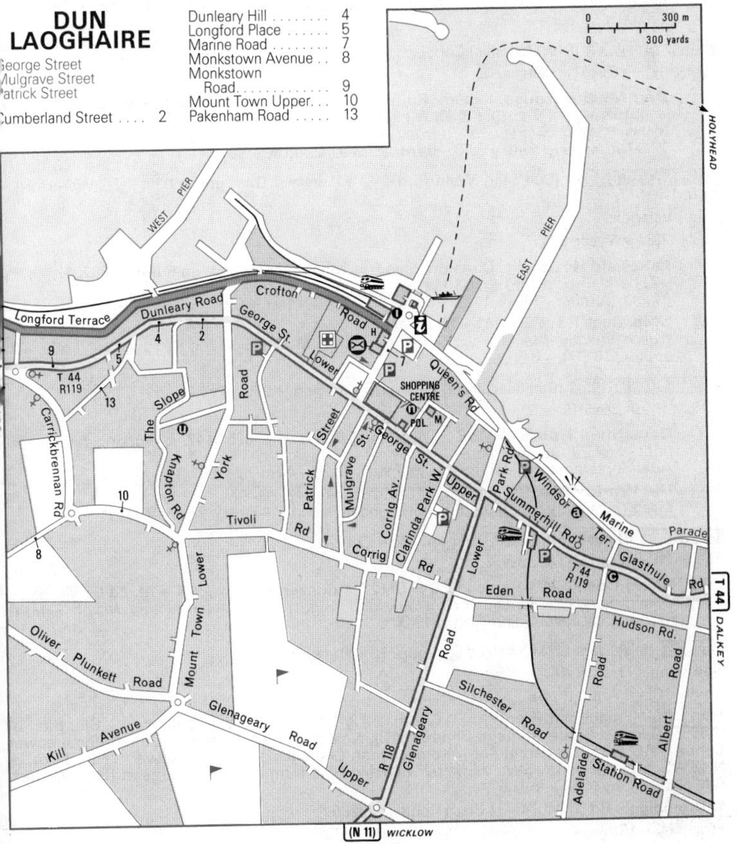

DUN LAOGHAIRE (Dún Laoghaire) Dublin 405 N 8 – pop. 55 540 – ☎ 01.
Envir. : – ≤★★ of Killiney Bay from coast road south of Sorrento Point.
⛴ to Holyhead (Stena Line) 2-4 daily (3 h 30 mn) – ℹ St. Michaels Wharf ☎ 2844768.
♦Dublin 9.

Plan on preceding page

- **Royal Marine,** Marine Rd, ☎ 280 1911, Fax 280 1089, ≤, – rest 500. **Meals** *(closed Saturday lunch)* 9.50/17.95 **st.** and a la carte 5.50 – 7.95 – **104 rm** 80.00/115.00 **t.** – SB.
- **Chestnut Lodge** without rest., 2 Vesey Pl., Monkstown, ☎ 280 7860, Fax 280 1466 « Regency house, antiques », – . **5 rm** 35.00/55.00 **t.**
- **Sandycove House,** Marine Parade, Sandycove, ☎ 284 1600, Fax 284 1600 – . **Meals** (dinner only) a la carte 16.85/21.85 **st.** – **10 rm** 30.00/43.00 **st.**
- XXX **Na Mara,** 1 Harbour Rd, ☎ 280 6767, Fax 284 4649 – *closed Sunday, 1 week Christmas and Bank Holidays* – **Meals** - Seafood - 11.00/23.00 and a la carte 6.00.
- XX **Morels Bistro,** 1st floor (above Eagle House), 18 Glasthule Rd, ☎ 230 0210, Fax 230 0466 – *closed Monday* – **Meals** (dinner only and Sunday lunch) a la carte 18.70/24.50 **st.** 6.60.

DUNLAVIN (Dún Luáin) Wicklow 405 L 8 – pop. 720 – ☎ 045.
♦Dublin 31 – ♦Kilkenny 44 – Wexford 61.

- **Rathsallagh House** , SW : 2 m. on Grangecon Rd ☎ 403112, Fax 53343, ≤, « 18C converted stables, walled garden », , , , park, – – 50. *closed 23 to 27 December* – **Meals** (dinner only) 29.00/35.00 **st.** 7.00 – **16 rm** 70.00/170.00 **st.**, 1 suite – SB.

DUNMANWAY (Dún Mánmhaí) Cork 405 E 12 – pop. 1 404 – ☎ 023.
♦Dublin 191 – ♦Cork 37 – ♦Killarney 49.

- **Dún Mhuire House,** Kilbarry Rd, W : ½ m. by R 586 taking first right at fork junction ☎ 45162, – . **Meals** *(closed Sunday to Tuesday September-May)* (booking essential) (dinner only) 12.00 **st.** and a la carte 5.00 – **6 rm** 26.00/40.00 **st.** – SB.

DUNMORE EAST (Dún Mór) Waterford 405 L 11 **Ireland G.** – pop. 1 038 – ✉ Waterford – ☎ 051.
See : Village★.
♦Dublin 108 – ♦Waterford 12.

- **Lakefield House** , Dunmore East Rd, Rosduff, NW : 5 m. on R 684 ☎ 382582, ≤, , park – rest . *March-October* – **Meals** 14.00 – **5 rm** 21.00/32.00 **st.** – SB.
- X **Ship,** Dock Rd, ☎ 383141 – *closed Sunday, Monday and November-April* – **Meals** - Seafood - (dinner only) a la carte approx. 16.95 **t.** 6.50.

DUNSHAUGHLIN (Dún Seachlainn) Meath 405 M 7 pop. 1 275 – ☎ 01.
♦Dublin 17 – Drogheda 19.

- **Gaulstown House** , NE : 1½ m. by Ratoath rd ☎ 825 9147, « Working farm », , park – . *April-September* – **Meals** (by arrangement) 13.00 – **4 rm** 22.00/34.00 – SB.
- **Old Workhouse,** Ballinlough, ☎ 8259251, – . **Meals** (by arrangement) (communal dining) 15.00 **st.** – **4 rm** 25.00/44.00 **st.**

DURRUS (Dúras) Cork 405 D 13 – pop. 188 – ☎ 027.
♦Dublin 210 – ♦Cork 56 – ♦Killarney 53.

- XX **Blairs Cove,** SW : 1 m. on L 56 ☎ 61127, « Converted barn », – . *closed Sunday, Monday except July and August and November-mid March* – **Meals** (booking essential) (dinner only) 19.00 **t.**

ENNIS (Inis) Clare 405 F 9 **Ireland G.** – pop. 13 730 – ☎ 065.
See : Ennis Friary★ *AC*.
Envir. : Clare Abbey★, SE : 1 m. by R 469.
Exc. : Quin Franciscan Friary★, SE : 6½ m. by R 469 – Knappogue Castle★ *AC*, SE : 8 m. by R 469 – Carrofin (Clare Heritage Centre★ *AC*), N : 8½ m. by N 85 and R 476 – Craggaunowen Centre★ *AC*, SE : 11 m. by R 469 – Kilmacduagh Churches and Round Tower★, NE : 11 m. by N 18 – Scattery Island★, SW : 27 m. by N 68 and boat from Kilrush – Bridge of Ross, Kilkee★, SW : 35½ m. by N 68 and N 67.
Drumbiggle Rd ☎ 24074 – ℹ Clare Road ☎ 28366.
♦Dublin 142 – ♦Galway 42 – ♦Limerick 22 – Roscommon 92 – ♦Tullamore 93.

Auburn Lodge, Galway Rd, N : 1½ m. on N 18 ☎ 21247, Fax 21202, ⁂, ⁂ – TV ☎ P. AE VISA. ⁂
Meals 9.50/17.00 **st.** and dinner a la carte – **99 rm** 48.00/90.00 **st.** – SB.

Cill Eoin House without rest., Killadysert Cross, Clare Rd, SE : 1½ m. at junction of N 18 with R 473 ☎ 41668, Fax 20224, ⁂, ⁂ – ⁂ TV ☎ P. AE VISA. ⁂
closed 1 to 7 January – **14 rm** 20.00/32.00 **t.**

Magowna House ⁂, Inch, Kilmaley, SW : 5 m. by R 474 (Kilmaley rd) ☎ 39009, Fax 39258, ≤, ⁂ – ☎ P. AE VISA. ⁂
closed 24 to 26 December – **Meals** 15.95 **st.** 5.00 – **5 rm** 23.00/36.00 **st.** – SB.

at Barefield NE : 3½ m. on N 18 – ✉ Ennis – ☎ 065 :

Carraig Mhuire, Bearnafunshin, NE : 1 ¾ m. on N 18 ☎ 27106, Fax 27375, ⁂ – P. ⁂
Meals 11.00 **s.** – **4 rm** 16.00/32.00 **st.** – SB.

ENNISCORTHY (Inis Córthaidh) Wexford 405 M 10 pop. 4 127 – ☎ 053.

♦Dublin 76 – Kilkenny 46 – Waterford 34 – Wexford 15.

Ballinkeel House ⁂, Ballymurn, SE : 6½ m. by unmarked rd on Curracloe rd ☎ 38105, Fax 38468, ≤, « 19C country house, antiques », ⁂, park, ⁂ – ⁂ rm P. VISA JCB. ⁂
closed 13 November-28 February – **Meals** (booking essential) (communal dining) (dinner only) 18.00 **st.** – **5 rm** 43.00/70.00 **st.**

ENNISTIMON (Inis Díomáin) Clare 405 E 9 – ☎ 065.

♦Dublin 158 – ♦Galway 52 – ♦Limerick 39.

Grovemount House without rest., Lahinch Rd, W : ½ m. on N 67 ☎ 71431, Fax 71823, ⁂ – ☎ P. VISA. ⁂
Easter-September – **8 rm** 25.00/40.00 **st.**

FAHAN (Fathain) Donegal 405 J 2 Ireland G. – pop. 309 – ✉ Inishowen – ☎ 077.

Exc. : Inishowen Peninsula★★ : (Dun Ree Fort★ *AC*), N : 11 m. by R 238.

North West, Lisfannon ☎ 61027.

♦Dublin 156 – ♦Londonderry 11 – ♦Sligo 95.

XX **St. John's,** ☎ 60289, « Loughside setting », ⁂ – ⁂ P. AE VISA JCB
closed Monday, Good Friday and 25 and 26 December – **Meals** (dinner only) 20.00 **t.** 5.95.

FERNS (Fearna) Wexford 405 M 10 pop. 859 – ✉ Enniscorthy – ☎ 054.

Exc. : – Mount Leinster★, NW : 17 m..

♦Dublin 69 – Kilkenny 53 – Waterford 41 – Wexford 22.

Clone House ⁂, S : 2 m. by Boolavogue rd off Monageer rd ☎ 66113, Fax 66113, « Working farm », ⁂, ⁂, park – ⁂ TV P. ⁂
March-October – **Meals** (by arrangement) (communal dining) 14.00 **st.** – **4 rm** 23.00/36.00.

FOXROCK (Carraig an tSionnaigh) Dublin 405 N 7 – see Dublin.

FURBOGH/FURBO (Na Forbacha) Galway 405 E 8 – ☎ 091.

♦Dublin 42 – ♦Galway 7.

Connemara Coast, ☎ 592108, Fax 592065, ≤, ⁂, ⁂, ⁂, ⁂, ⁂ – ⁂ rm TV ☎ P – 500. AE VISA. ⁂
Meals (bar lunch)/dinner 22.00 **st.** and a la carte 6.75 – **111 rm** 50.00/135.00 **st.**, 1 suite – SB.

GALWAY (Gaillimh) Galway 405 E 8 Ireland G. – pop. 50 855 – ☎ 091.

See : City★★ – Lynch's Castle★ BY – St. Nicholas' Church★ BY – Roman Catholic Cathedral★ AY – Eyre Square : Bank of Ireland Building (Mace★) BY **D.**

Envir. : NW : Lough Corrib★★.

Exc. : W : by boat, Aran Islands (Inishmore – Dun Aenghus★★★) BZ – Thoor Ballylee★★, SE : 21 m. by N 6 and N 18 BY – Athenry★, E : 14 m. by N 6 and R 348 BY – Dunguaire Castle, Kinvarra★ *AC*, S : 16 m. by N 6, N 18 and N 67 BY – Knockmoy Abbey★, NE : 19 m. by N 17 and N 63 BY – Coole Park (Autograph Tree★), SE : 21 m. by N 6 and N 18 BY – St. Mary's Cathedral, Tuam★, NE : 21 m. by N 17 BY – Loughrea (St. Brendan's Cathedral★) SE : 22 m. by N 6 BY.

Galway, Blackrock, Salthill ☎ 22169/27622.

Carnmore Airport : ☎ 752874, NE : 4 m..

Victoria Pl., Eyre Sq. ☎ 63081.

♦Dublin 135 – ♦Limerick 64 – ♦Sligo 90.

GALWAY

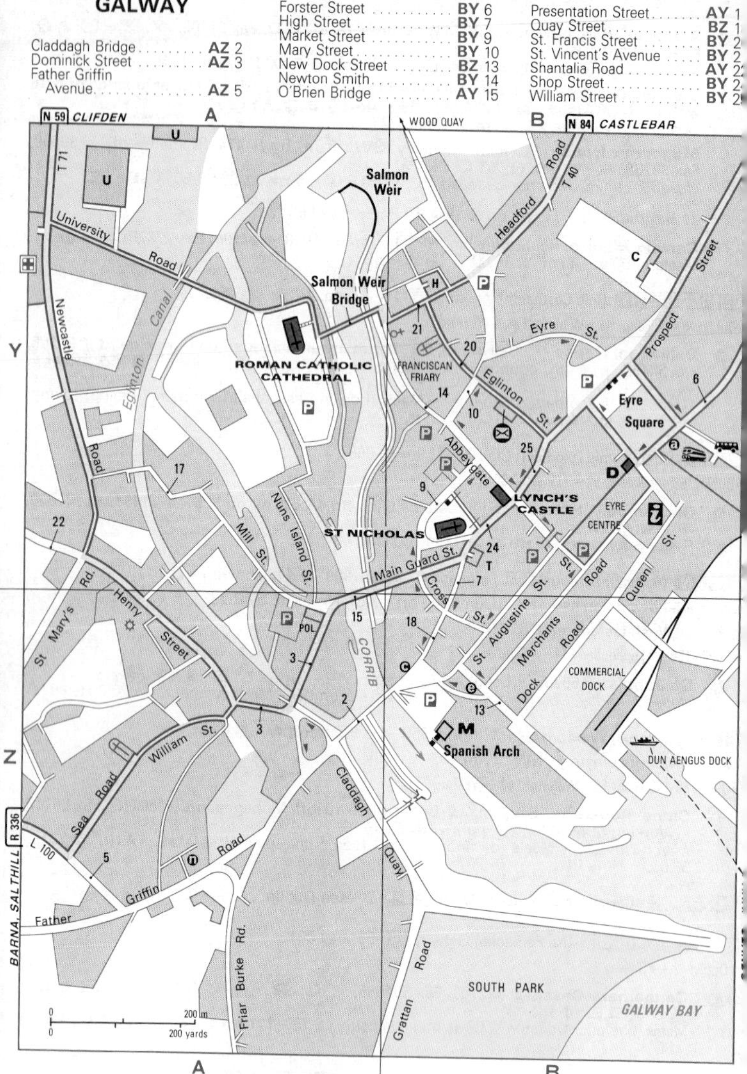

Glenlo Abbey, Bushypark, NW : 3¼ m. on N 59 ☎ 526666, Fax 527800, « Restored part 18C house and church », 9, park – lift rest TV ☎ & P – 100. AE VISA. **Ffrench Room : Meals** (booking essential) (bar lunch Monday to Saturday)/dinner 26.00 **st.** 8.50 – 10.00 – **42 rm** 100.00/150.00 **st.**, 3 suites – SB.

Great Southern, Eyre Sq., ☎ 64041, Fax 66704, – lift rm TV ☎ P – 450 **115 rm**, 1 suite. BY **a**

Corrib Great Southern, Dublin Rd, E : 1¾ m. on N 6 ☎ 755281, Fax 751390, – lift rm rest TV ☎ & P – 850. AE VISA. **Meals** *(closed Saturday lunch)* 11.00/18.00 **t.** and dinner a la carte 7.00 – 7.00 – **176 rm** 67.50/104.00 **t.**, 4 suites – SB.

Ardilaun House, Taylor's Hill, W : 1½ m. on R 336 ☎ 521433, Fax 521546, – lift rm TV ☎ P – 450. AE VISA JCB – *closed 18 to 22 December* – **Meals** (bar lunch Saturday) 10.00/25.00 **t.** and a la carte 6.50 – **89 rm** 60.00/95.00 **t.**, 1 suite – SB.

Jurys Galway Inn, Quay St., 66444, Fax 68415, – rm – 40. BZ c
closed 24 December-3 January – **Meals** (bar lunch)/dinner 14.00 **t.** and a la carte 5.25 – 6.00 – **128 rm** 55.00 **st.**

Brennan's Yard, Lower Merchants Rd, 68166, Fax 68262 – . BZ e
Meals (booking essential) (bar lunch)/dinner 10.00/20.00 **t.** and a la carte – **24 rm** 70.00/100.00 **t.** – SB.

Galway Ryan, Dublin Rd, E : 1¼ m. on N 6 753181, Telex 50149, Fax 753187, , , – rest – 60.
closed 24 and 25 December – **Meals** (bar lunch)/dinner 17.00 **st.** and a la carte 5.50 – 8.00 – **96 rm** 85.00/120.00 **t.** – SB.

Adare House without rest., 9 Father Griffin Pl., Lower Salthill, 582638, Fax 583963 – . AZ n
closed 24 to 27 December – **11 rm** 37.00 **t.**

Casey's Westwood, Newcastle, NW : 1¾ m. on N 59 21442, Fax 21400, – .
closed Good Friday and 24 to 26 December – **Meals** 10.95/25.00 **st.** and a la carte 5.50.

at Salthill SW : 2 m. – AZ – Salthill – 091 :

Jameson's, Upper Salthill, 28666, Fax 28626 – – 50.
Meals *(closed Sunday dinner)* 6.00/16.00 **st.** and a la carte 10.00 **20 rm** 38.00/70.00 **st.**

Tysons Rockbarton Park, 5-7 Rockbarton Park, 522286, Fax 527692 – .
closed 24 to 30 December – **Meals** *(closed Sunday)* (dinner only) 17.00 **st.** and a la carte 5.00 – **11 rm** 30.00/60.00 **st.** – SB.

Devondell without rest., 47 Devon Park, Lower Salthill, off Lower Salthill Rd 523617 – .
closed 20 to 30 December – **4 rm** 17.00/34.00.

GARRYVOE (Garraí Uí Bhuaigh) Cork 405 H 12 – Castlemartyr – 021.

Dublin 161 – Cork 23 – Waterford 62.

Garryvoe, 646718, Fax 646824, , , – – 300.
closed 25 December – **Meals** 10.00/20.00 **st.** and dinner a la carte 8.50 – **20 rm** 35.00/60.00 **st.** – SB.

GLANDORE (Cuan Dor) Cork 405 E 13 – 028.

Dublin 196 – Cork 44 – Killarney 75.

Rectory, 33072, Fax 33600, – .
closed 4 days Christmas – **Meals** *(weekends only November-March)* (dinner only) 25.00 **t.** and a la carte 22.00/25.50 **t.** 7.00.

GLENBEIGH (Gleann Beithe) Kerry 405 C 11 – 066.

Dublin 197 – Killarney 21 – Tralee 24.

Foxtrot without rest., Mountain Stage, SW : 3 m. on N 70 68417, Fax 68552, – .
March-October – **4 rm** 20.00/32.00 **st.**

GLENDALOUGH (Gleann dá Loch) Wicklow 405 M 8 – 0404.

Dublin 28 – Kilkenny 68 – Wexford 63.

Glendalough, 45135, Fax 45142, – – 150.
closed January – **Meals** 8.00/19.00 **t.** and a la carte 5.00 – **43 rm** 45.00/70.00 **t.** – SB.

GLENGARRIFF (An Gleann Garbh) Cork 405 D 12 – 027.

63084 (July-August).

Dublin 213 – Cork 60 – Killarney 37.

Cois Coille without rest., 63202, , – .
April-October – **6 rm** 21.00/34.00 **st.**

GLEN OF AHERLOW (Gleann Eatharlaí) Tipperary 405 H 10 Ireland G. – Tipperary – 062.

See : Glen of Aherlow★.

Exc. : Caher Castle★★ *AC* – Town Square★ – St. Paul's Church★ – Swiss Cottage★ *AC*, SE : 7 m. by N 24 and R 670 – Clonmel★ (County Museum★, St. Mary's Church★, Riverside★, Quay★), NE : 16 m. by N 24 – Kilmallock★★ :- Abbey★, Collegiate Church★, Blossom's Gate★, Town Walls★, King's Castle★ – W : 27½ m. by R 664 and R 515.

Dublin 118 – Cahir 6 – Tipperary 9.

Aherlow House , 56153, Fax 56212, Galty Mountains, park – .
Meals 9.95/18.50 **st.** 5.00 – 7.50 – **30 rm** 33.00/120.00 **st.** – SB.

GOREY (Guaire) Wexford 405 N 9 Ireland G. – pop. 2 198 – 055.

Exc. : Ferns★, SW : 11 m. by N 11.

Courtown, Kiltennel 25166/25432.

Town Centre 21248 (July and August).

♦Dublin 58 – Waterford 55 – Wexford 38.

Marlfield House, Courtown Rd, E : 1 m. 21124, Fax 21572, ≤, « Regency house, conservatory », park, – . *closed 15 December-25 January* – **Meals** 18.50/32.00 **t.** and lunch a la carte 15.00/28.00 **t.** 7.00 – **18 rm** 87.50/144.00 **t.**, 1 suite.

at Ballyedmund S : 10½ m. on R 741 – Gorey – 054 :

Eugenes, on R 741 89288 – . *closed Tuesday, 1-8 March, 1-14 September, Christmas and Good Friday* – **Meals** (lunch by arrangement) 9.50/14.95 **t.** 7.55.

GRAIGUENAMANAGH (Gráig na Manach) Kilkenny 405 L 10 – 0503.

♦Dublin 77 – Kilkenny 20 – ♦Waterford 25 – Wexford 34.

Stablecroft, Mooneen, N : 2 m. by R 705 off R 703 24714, ≤, – rm . **Meals** (communal dining) 14.00 **s.** – **3 rm** 13.50/34.00 **st.**

GREYSTONES (Na Clocha Liatha) Wicklow 405 N 8 pop. 9 649 – 01.

♦Dublin 22.

Hungry Monk, Southview Church Rd, 287 5759, Fax 872 2809 – . *closed Monday and 25-26 December* – **Meals** (dinner only and Sunday lunch)/dinner 22.95 **t.** and a la carte 6.75.

HOWTH (Binn Éadair) Dublin 405 N 7 Ireland G. – Dublin – 01.

See : Town★ – The Summit★.

Deer Park Hotel, Howth Castle 832 2624.

♦Dublin 10.

Marine, Sutton Cross, W : 1½ m. 839 0000, Fax 839 0442, ≤, – 200. *closed 24 to 26 December* – **Meals** 12.50/21.00 **t.** and dinner a la carte 6.60 – **26 rm** 52.00/96.00 **st.** – SB.

Howth Lodge, W : 1 m. 832 1010, Fax 832 2268, ≤, – – 200. *closed 23 to 27 December* – **Meals** *(closed Sunday dinner)* (bar lunch Monday to Saturday)/dinner 22.00 **t.** and a la carte 5.50 – **46 rm** 55.00/100.00 **st.** – SB.

Deer Park,, W : ¾ m. 832 2624, Fax 839 2405, ≤, park – rest – 100. *closed 25 and 26 December* – **Meals** (bar lunch Monday to Saturday)/dinner 17.00 **t.** and a la carte 5.00 – **49 rm** 47.00/82.00 **st.** – SB.

King Sitric, Harbour Rd, East Pier, 832 5235, Fax 839 2442 – . *closed Sunday, 10 days January, 10 days Easter and Bank Holidays* – **Meals** - Seafood - (light lunch Monday to Saturday May-September) (dinner only October-April)/dinner 24.00 **t.** and a la carte 6.00.

INISHCRONE (Inis Crabhann) Sligo 405 E 5 – 096.

♦Dublin 160 – Ballina 8 – ♦Galway 79 – ♦Sligo 34.

Ceol na Mara, Main St., 36351, Fax 36351, ≤ – . *February-October* – **Meals** (by arrangement) 14.00 **st.** 4.00 – **9 rm** 20.00/34.00 **st.** – SB.

INISHMORE (Inis Mór) Galway 405 CD 8 – see Aran Islands.

INISTIOGE (Inis Tíog) Kilkenny 405 K 10 – 056.

♦Dublin 82 – Kilkenny 16 – ♦Waterford 19 – Wexford 33.

Berryhill, SE : ¾ m. by R 700 58434, Fax 58434, ≤, « Working farm », park – . *closed March and Christmas* – **Meals** (by arrangement) (communal dining) 25.00 **s.** 5.25 – **3 rm** 36.00/70.00 **s.**

Rathsnagadan House, SE : 4½ m. by R 700 (051) 23641, ≤, park – rm . *closed December-January* – **Meals** (by arrangement) 16.00 **st.** 5.00 – **3 rm** 25.00/40.00 **st.**

Motte, Plass Newid, NW : ¼ m. on R 700 58655 – . *closed Sunday, Monday and 1 week Christmas* – **Meals** (dinner only) 18.90 **t.** 5.40.

NNISHANNON **(Inis Eonáin)** Cork 405 G 12 – pop. 319 – 021.

Dublin 169 – Cork 15.

Innishannon House, S : ¾ m. on R 605 775121, Fax 775609, ←, « Riverside setting », park – TV ☎ P. AE VISA
closed January-February – **Meals** 12.00/26.00 **t.** and a la carte 6.50 – **14 rm** 65.00/150.00 **st.** – SB.

NVERIN **(Indreabhán)** Galway 405 D8 – 091.

Dublin 149 – Galway 17.

Tigh Chualáin without rest., Kilroe East, on R 336 83609 – TV ☎ P.
April-October – **9 rm** 20.00/30.00.

KANTURK **(Ceann Toirc)** Cork 405 F 11 **Ireland G.** – pop. 1 777 – 029.

See : Town★ - Castle★.

Fairy Hill 50534.

Dublin 161 – Cork 33 – Killarney 31 – Limerick 44.

Assolas Country House, E : 3 ¼ m. by R 576 off R 580 50015, Fax 50795, ←, « Part 17C and 18C country house, gardens, riverside setting », park, – ☎ P. VISA JCB.
April-October – **Meals** (booking essential) (dinner only) 28.00 **st.** 7.50 – **9 rm** 72.00/154.00 **st.** – SB.

Duhallow Lodge, S : 3¼ m. by R 579 on N 72 56042, Fax 56152 – rm TV ☎ P – 250. VISA.
Meals (bar lunch Monday to Saturday)/dinner 12.00/24.00 **t.** 5.50 – **22 rm** 40.00/70.00 **st.** – SB.

For the quickest route use the Michelin Main Road Maps :
970 Europe, 976 Czech Republic-Slovak Republic, 980 Greece, 984 Germany, 985 Scandinavia-Finland, 986 Great Britain and Ireland, 987 Germany-Austria-Benelux, 988 Italy, 989 France, 990 Spain-Portugal and 991 Yugoslavia.

KENMARE **(Neidín)** Kerry 405 D 12 **Ireland G.** – pop. 1 366 – 064.

See : Site★.

Exc. : Iveragh Peninsula★★★ (Ring of Kerry★★) – Healy Pass★★ (←★★), SW : 19 m. by R 571 and R 574 – Mountain Road to Glengarriff (←★★) S : by N 71 - Slieve Miskish Mountains (←★★), SW : 30 m. by R 571 - Gougane Barra Forest Park★★, SE : 10 m. – Lauragh (Derreen Gardens★ AC), SW : 14½ m. by R 571 – Allihies (Copper Mines★), SW : 35½ m. by R 571 and R 575 – Garnish Island (←★), SW : 42½ m. by R 571, R 575 and R 572.

Kenmare 41291.

Heritage Centre, The Square 41233 (April-October).

Dublin 210 – Cork 58 – Killarney 20.

Park, 41200, Fax 41402, ← Kenmare Bay and hills, « Antiques, paintings », park, – TV ☎ P – 35. AE VISA.
6 April-5 November and 24 December-2 January – **Meals** (dinner only) 28.50/38.00 **t.** and a la carte 34.65/46.00 8.00 – **47 rm** 104.00/214.00 **t.**, 2 suites – SB
Spec. Carpaccio of prawns with caviar and lime crème fraîche, Pan fried fillet of turbot on a spicy cucumber salad, Hot ravioli of hazelnut and chocolate, orange ice cream, Cointreau sauce.

Sheen Falls Lodge, SE : 1¼ m. by N 71 41600, Fax 41386, « Wooded setting on banks of Sheen River and Kenmare Bay, ← Sheen Falls », park, – TV ☎ P – 120. AE VISA JCB.
closed 2 January-5 February – **La Cascade : Meals** (bar lunch Monday to Saturday)/dinner 38.50 **st.** 10.50 – 13.50 – **32 rm** 180.00/235.00 **st.**, 8 suites
Spec. Lasagne of langoustine with green asparagus tips scented with coriander, Noisettes of lamb topped with ratatouille on a purée of smoked aubergine, Brûlée of sweet rice with a compote of cherries.

Dromquinna Manor, Blackwater Bridge P.O., W : 3 m. by N 71 on N 70 41657, Fax 41791, ←, « Situated on the banks of Kenmare river », park, – TV ☎ P. AE VISA.
Meals 12.50/25.00 **t.** and a la carte 5.90 – **28 rm** 29.50/100.00 **st.**, 1 suites – SB.

Sallyport House without rest., S : ¼ m. on N 71 42066, Fax 41752, ←, « Antique furniture », – TV ☎ P.
April-October – **4 rm** 30.00/60.00 **st.**

Shelburne without rest., Killowen Rd, E : ½ m. on R 569 (Cork Rd) 41013, Fax 42135, « Stylishly decorated 18C house », – TV ☎ P. VISA.
June-September – **Meals** - (see ***Packie's*** below) – **5 rm** 40.00/60.00 **t.**

Dunkerron, Sneem Rd, W : 2½ m. on N 70 41102, Fax 41102, park – ☎ P. VISA.
April-October – **Meals** (booking essential) (lunch by arrangement) 12.00/19.00 and a la carte 6.00 – **10 rm** 32.00/56.00 **st.**

Foleys, Henry St., 41361, Fax 41799 – TV. VISA.
Meals (bar lunch)/dinner 13.95 **st.** and a la carte 5.75 – **10 rm** 30.00/44.00 **st.** – SB.

Mylestone House without rest., Killowen Rd, E : ¼ m. ✆ 41753, – P. VISA.
March-mid November – **5 rm** ☐ 25.00/34.00 **st.**

Ceann Mara, E : 1 m. on Kilgarvan rd ✆ 41220, ≤ Kenmare Bay and hills, – P.
May-September – **Meals** (by arrangement) 15.00 – **4 rm** ☐ 23.00/34.00 **st.**

Ard Na Mara without rest., Pier Rd, ✆ 41399, Fax 41399, ≤ Kenmare Bay and hills, P.
4 rm ☐ 20.00/29.00 **t.**

d'Arcys with rm, Main St., ✆ 41589, Fax 41589 – VISA
closed Monday except Bank Holidays, last 2 weeks January and 24 to 27 December – **Meal** (dinner only) 15.00/20.00 **t.** and a la carte 16.00/24.50 **t.** 6.00 – **5 rm** ☐ 20.00/32.00 **st.**

Lime Tree, Shelbourne St., ✆ 41225, Fax 41402, « Characterful former schoolhouse » P. VISA
April-October – **Meals** (dinner only) a la carte 14.40/22.45 **t.** 6.50.

Packies, Henry St., ✆ 41508 – VISA
closed Sunday and mid November-March – **Meals** (dinner only) a la carte 14.50/22.30 5.00.

An Leath Phingin, 35 Main St., ✆ 41559 – VISA
Meals *(closed lunch Sunday and Monday and November)* 12.50 **t.** (dinner and a la carte 12.50/20.50 **t.** 5.00.

KILCUMMIN (Cill Chuimán) Kerry 405 B 11 – ✆ 066.

♦Dublin 203 – ♦Killarney 34 – ♦Limerick 85 – Tralee 21.

Strand View House without rest., ✆ 38131, ≤ – P.
closed November and December – **4 rm** ☐ 25.00/33.00.

The Guide is updated annually so renew your Guide every year.

KILKEE (Cill Chaoi) Clare 405 D 9 pop. 1 315 – ✆ 065.

♦Dublin 177 – ♦Galway 77 – ♦Limerick 58.

Halpin's, Erin St., ✆ 56032, Fax 56317 – TV ☎. AE VISA.
15 March-31 October – **Meals** (bar lunch Monday to Saturday)/dinner 17.00 **t.** and a la carte 7.00 – **12 rm** ☐ 30.00/75.00 **t.** – SB.

KILKENNY (Cill Chainnigh) Kilkenny 405 K 10 Ireland G. – pop. 8 515 – ✆ 056.

See : Town★★ – St. Canice's Cathedral★★ – Kilkenny Castle and Grounds★★ *AC* – Cityscope★ *AC* – Black Abbey★.

Exc. : Dunmore Cave★ *AC*, N : 7 m. by N 77 and N 78 – Kells Priory★, S : 9 m. by R 697.

18 Glendine ✆ 22125/65400.

Rose Inn St. ✆ 51500.

♦Dublin 71 – ♦Cork 86 – ♦Killarney 115 – ♦Limerick 69 – ♦Tullamore 52 – ♦Waterford 29.

Kilkenny, College Rd, SW : ¾ m. at junction with N 76 ✆ 62000, Fax 65984, , , , – TV ☎ P – 400. AE VISA.
Meals 9.50/22.50 **st.** and a la carte 4.95 – **79 rm** ☐ 57.50/110.00 **st.**, 1 suite – SB.

Newpark, Castlecomer Rd, N : 1 m. on N 77 ✆ 22122, Fax 61111, , , , , park – rest TV ☎ P – 600. AE VISA.
Meals 11.50/22.00 **t.** and dinner a la carte – ☐ 7.00 – **84 rm** 47.00/77.00 **t.** – SB.

Blanchville House, Dunbell, Maddoxtown, SE : 7 ½ m. by N 10 (eastbound) ✆ 27197, Fax 27636, ≤, « Georgian country house », , park – P. VISA.
March-October – **Meals** *(closed Sunday)* (by arrangement) (residents only) (communal dining) (dinner only) (unlicensed) 20.00 **st.** – **6 rm** ☐ 30.00/60.00 **st.** – SB.

Butler House without rest., 15-16 Patrick St., ✆ 65707, Fax 65626, – TV ☎ P – 70. AE VISA.
closed 24 to 29 December – **11 rm** ☐ 49.50/79.00 **t.**, 2 suites.

Shillogher House without rest., Callan Rd, SW : 1 m. on N 76 ✆ 63249, – TV ☎ P. VISA.
5 rm ☐ 30.00/35.00.

Lacken House with rm, Dublin Rd, E : ¾ m. on N 10 ✆ 61085, Fax 62435, – rest TV ☎ P. AE VISA JCB.
Meals *(closed Sunday and Monday)* (dinner only) 23.00 **t.** and a la carte 6.00 – **8 rm** ☐ 25.00/72.00 **t.** – SB.

Ristorante Rinuccini, 1 The Parade, ✆ 61575, Fax 51288
closed Sunday dinner October-May except Bank Holiday weekends – **Meals** - Italian - a la carte 8.55/24.15 **t.** 5.95.

KILL (An Chill) Kildare 405 M 8 pop. 1 518 – ✆ 045.

♦Dublin 15 – Carlow 36.

Ambassador, on N 7 ✆ 877064, Fax 877515 – TV ☎ P – 220. AE VISA.
Meals (carving lunch Monday to Saturday) 8.50/18.50 **t.** and dinner a la carte 5.50 – **36 rm** ☐ 45.00/80.00 **st.** – SB.

KILLALOE (Cill Dalua) Clare 405 G 9 Ireland G. – pop. 956 – 061.

See : Town★ – St. Flannan's Cathedral★.

Envir. : Graves of the Leinstermen★, N : 4½ m. by R 494.

Exc. : Nenagh★ (Heritage Centre★★ *AC*, Castle★), NE : 12 m. by R 496 and N 7 – Holy Island★ *AC*, N : 8 m. by R 463 and boat from Tuamgraney.

Lock House, 376866 (1 June-11 September).

Dublin 109 – Ennis 32 – Limerick 13 – Tullamore 58.

- **Lakeside,** 376122, Fax 376431, ←, ... – 300. AE VISA
  closed 23 to 25 December – **Meals** 9.50/22.00 **st.** and a la carte 5.50 – **45 rm** (dinner included) 55.00/100.00 **st.** – SB.

at Ogonnelloe N : 6¼ m. on R 463 – Ogonnelloe – 061 :

- **Lantern House**, 923034, Fax 923139, ←, ... AE VISA
  mid February-October – **Meals** (by arrangement) 16.00 **t.** 4.55 – **6 rm** 20.00/40.00.

KILLARNEY (Cill Airne) Kerry 405 D 11 Ireland G. – pop. 7 275 – 064.

See : Town★★ – Knockreer Demesne★ – St. Mary's Cathedral★.

Envir. : Killarney National Park★★★ – Muckross House★★ *AC*, S : 3½ m. by N 71 – Torc Waterfall★★, S : 5 m. by N 71 – Gap of Dunloe★★, SW : 6 m. by R 582 – Muckross Abbey★, S : 3½ m. by N 71.

Exc. : Iveragh Peninsula★★★ (Ring of Kerry★★) – Ladies View★★, SW : 12 m. by N 71 – Moll's Gap★, SW : 15½ m. by N 71.

18, 18 Mahoney's Point 31034.

Kerry (Farranfore) Airport : 066 (Farranfore) 64644, N : 9½ m. by N 22.

Town Hall 31633.

Dublin 189 – Cork 54 – Limerick 69 – Waterford 112.

- **Europe**, Fossa, W : 3½ m. on R 562 31900, Fax 32118, ← lake and mountains, ..., park, ... – 500. AE VISA
  April-October – **Meals** (light lunch)/dinner 26.00 **st.** and a la carte 25.10/29.50 **st.** 8.50 – **199 rm** 96.00/134.00 **st.**, 6 suites – SB.
- **Killarney Park,** Kenmare Pl., 35555, Fax 35266, ... – rest ... – 70. AE VISA
  closed 24 to 26 December – **Park : Meals** 9.00/25.00 **st.** and a la carte 8.50 – **66 rm** 100.00/150.00 **st.** – SB.
- **Aghadoe Heights**, NW : 3½ m. by N 22 31766, Fax 31345, ← countryside, lake and Macgillycuddy's Reeks, ... – 100. AE VISA
  Meals - (see ***Fredrick's at the Heights*** below) – **57 rm** 110.00/155.00 **st.**, 3 suites – SB.
- **Great Southern,** East Avenue Rd, 31262, Fax 31642, ..., park, ... – 900. AE VISA
  closed 5 January-20 February – **Meals** (bar lunch) – **Dining Room : Meals** (dinner only) 17.00 **t.** 6.00 – 7.50 – **176 rm** 56.50/113.00 **t.**, 3 suites – SB.
- **Dunloe Castle**, Beaufort, W : 6 m. by R 562 44111, Fax 44583, ← Gap of Dunloe, countryside and mountains, ..., park, ... rm ... – 900. AE VISA JCB
  April-October – **Meals** 10.00/25.00 **st.** and dinner a la carte 8.50 – **119 rm** 62.00/125.00 **st.**, 1 suite – SB.
- **Muckross Park,** S : 2¾ m. on N 71 31938, Fax 31965, ... – 40. AE VISA
  closed January and February – **Meals** (bar lunch)/dinner 22.95 **st.** and a la carte – **25 rm** 80.00/120.00 **st.**, 2 suites – SB.
- **Randles Court,** Muckross Rd, 35333, Fax 35206 – ... AE VISA
  closed January and February – **Meals** (bar lunch Monday to Saturday)/dinner 10.00/20.00 **st.** 6.00 – **37 rm** 55.00/110.00 **st.** – SB.
- **Cahernane**, Muckross Rd, S : 1 m. on N 71 31895, Fax 34340, ←, ... AE VISA JCB
  April-October – **Meals** (bar lunch)/dinner 26.50 **st.** and a la carte 7.00 – **48 rm** 85.00/150.00 **st.** – SB.
- **Ross,** Kenmare Pl., 31855, Fax 31139, ... rest rest ... AE VISA
  March-November – **Meals** (bar lunch Monday to Saturday) 17.00 **st.** and a la carte 7.50 – **32 rm** 61.00/86.00 **st.** – SB.
- **Royal,** College St., 31853, Fax 34001 – ... VISA
  closed 1 week Christmas – **Meals** (bar lunch Monday to Saturday)/dinner 20.00 **t.** and a la carte 6.95 – **49 rm** 45.00/110.00 **t.** – SB.

Torc Great Southern, Park Rd, ☎ 31611, Fax 31824, ≘s, ▣, ⛶, % – TV ☎ P. AE ⊙ VISA. ✻
8 April-October – **Meals** (bar lunch) 16.00 **t.** 10.00 – **94 rm** ☐ 58.00/88.00 – SB.

Foley's Townhouse, 23 High St., ☎ 31217, Fax 34683 – ▤ rest TV ☎ P. AE VISA. ✻
5 April-October – **Meals** *(closed 23-26 December)* (bar lunch)/dinner 20.00 **st.** and a la carte 7.50 – **12 rm** ☐ 38.00/70.00 **t.** – SB.

Killeen House, Aghadoe, W : 4 m. by R 562 ☎ 31711, Fax 31811, ⛶ – TV ☎ P. AE ⊙ VISA
March-10 November – **Meals** (bar lunch)/dinner 21.50 **st.** 5.50 – **15 rm** ☐ 39.60/78.20 st.

Kathleens Country House without rest., Tralee Rd, N : 2 m. on N 22 ☎ 32810, Fax 32340, ←, ⛶ – ⋟ TV ☎ P. AE VISA. ✻
17 March-13 November – **17 rm** ☐ 60.00/70.00.

Fuchsia House without rest., Muckross Rd, S : ¾ m. on N 71 ☎ 33743, Fax 36588, ⛶ – ⋟ TV ☎ P. AE VISA. ✻
closed December – **10 rm** ☐ 38.00/48.00 **st.**

Victoria House without rest., Muckross Rd, S : 1 ¼ m. on N 71 ☎ 35430, Fax 35439 – TV ☎ P. AE VISA. ✻
15 rm ☐ 28.00/40.00 **st.**

Beaufield House without rest., Cork Rd, E : 1 m. ☎ 34440, Fax 34663, ⛶ – TV ☎ P. AE VISA. ✻
closed 20 to 30 December – **14 rm** ☐ 25.00/38.00 **st.**

Lime Court without rest., Muckross Rd, S : ¾ m. on N 71 ☎ 34547, Fax 34121 – TV ☎ P AE VISA. ✻
12 rm ☐ 25.00/50.00 **st.**

Gleann Fia ⚘ without rest., Deerpark, N : 1 ½ m. by N 22 bypass ☎ 35035, Fax 35000, « Riverside setting », ⛶ – ⋟ TV ☎ P. AE VISA. ✻
15 March-October – **10 rm** ☐ 25.00/40.00 **st.**

Naughton's Villa without rest., Muckross Rd, ☎ 36025 – TV ☎ P. ✻
April-October – **5 rm** ☐ 25.00/40.00 **st.**

Sika Lodge without rest., Ballydowney, W : 1 m. on R 562 ☎ 36304, Fax 36746 – TV ☎ P. ✻
– **6 rm** ☐ 25.00/36.00 **st.**

Avondale House without rest., Tralee Rd, N : 3 m. on N 22 ☎ 35579, ←, ⛶ – TV P. ✻
March-10 November – **5 rm** ☐ 20.00/30.00 **st.**

Lake Lodge without rest., Muckross Rd, S : ¾ m. on N 71 ☎ 33333, Fax 35109 – TV ☎ P. AE VISA. ✻
13 rm ☐ 18.00/38.00 **st.**

XXX **Fredrick's at the Heights** (at Aghadoe Heights H.), NW : 3 ½ m. by N 22 ☎ 31766, Fax 31345, ← Countryside, lake and Macgillycuddy's Reeks – ▤ P. AE ⊙ VISA
Meals (booking essential) (buffet lunch Sunday) 17.50/29.50 **st.** and a la carte 6.95.

XX **Gaby's,** 27 High St., ☎ 32519, Fax 32747 – AE ⊙ VISA
closed lunch Sunday, Monday and November-Easter, 1 week Christmas and February – **Meals** - Seafood - a la carte 18.00/37.70 **t.** 6.10.

XX **West End House,** Lower New St., ☎ 32271, Fax 35979 – AE VISA
closed Monday and November – **Meals** (light lunch Tuesday to Saturday) 16.50 **t.** (dinner) and a la carte.

X **Strawberry Tree,** 24 Plunkett St., ☎ 32688, Fax 32689 – AE ⊙ VISA
closed Sunday, January and February – **Meals** (dinner only) a la carte 21.25/26.45 **t.** 6.50.

KILLEAGH (Cill Ia) Cork 405 H 12 – ☎ 024.

♦Dublin 151 – ♦Cork 23 – ♦Waterford 53.

Ballymakeigh House ⚘, N : 1 m. ☎ 95184, Fax 95370, « Working farm », ⛶, park, % – P. ✻
10 February-October – **Meals** (by arrangement) 20.00 **st.** 8.00 – **5 rm** ☐ 28.00/44.00 **st.** – SB.

KILLINEY (Cill Iníon Léinín) Dublin 405 N 8 – ☎ 01.

Killiney ☎ 851983.

♦Dublin 8 – Bray 4.

Fitzpatrick Castle, ☎ 284 0700, Telex 30353, Fax 285 0207, ←, Fō, ≘s, ▣, ⛶, %, squash – |‡| ⋟ rm TV ☎ P – 🔺 400. AE ⊙ VISA JCB. ✻
Truffles : Meals 12.50/20.50 **t.** and dinner a la carte – **Castle Grill : Meals** (dinner only and Sunday lunch) a la carte approx. 16.95 – ☐ 8.00 – **84 rm** 79.00/124.00 **t.**, 6 suites – SB.

Court, Killiney Bay, ☎ 285 1622, Fax 285 2085, ←, ⛶ – |‡| ⋟ rm ▤ rest TV ☎ P – 🔺 250. AE ⊙ VISA. ✻
Meals 11.50/20.95 **t.** and a la carte 5.50 – **86 rm** ☐ 70.00/90.00 **st.** – SB.

Europe

If the name of the hotel is not in bold type, on arrival ask the hotelier his prices.

KILLORGLIN (Cill Orglan) Kerry 405 C 11 pop. 1 229 – 066.

Dublin 207 – ♦Killarney 12 – Tralee 16.

Bianconi, Annadale Rd, 61146, Fax 61950, – TV ☎. AE VISA
closed 23 to 28 December – **Meals** (bar meals lunch and Sunday dinner) 25.00 **t.** and a la carte 5.95 – **15 rm** 27.00/50.00 **t.** – SB.

Westfield House, Glenbeigh Rd, W : 3/4 m. by N 70 61909, Fax 61996, – rm TV ☎ P. VISA
Meals (by arrangement) 12.50 **st.** – **10 rm** 22.00/35.00 **st.** – SB.

Grove Lodge without rest., Killarney Rd, E : 1/2 m. on R 562 61157, Fax 61157, « Riverside setting », – TV ☎ P. VISA
closed 1 to 28 December – **5 rm** 25.00/36.00 **st.**

KILLYBEGS (Na Cealla Beaga) Donegal 405 G 4 – 073.

Exc. : – Glengesh Pass★★★, SW : 15 m. by N 56 and R 263 – Gweebarra Estuary★, NE : 19 m. by R 262 and R 252.

♦Dublin 181 – Donegal 17 – ♦Londonderry 64 – ♦Sligo 57.

Bay View, Main St., 31950, Fax 31856, <, – rest TV ☎ &. AE VISA
Meals (bar lunch Monday to Saturday)/dinner 17.00 **t.** and a la carte 4.80 – **36 rm** 45.00/75.00 **st.**, 2 suites – SB.

KILTIMAGH (Coillte Mach) Mayo 405 EF 6 pop. 652 – 094.

♦Dublin 138 – ♦Galway 52 – Westport 26.

Cill Aodain, 81761, Fax 81838 – TV ☎. VISA.
Meals (carving lunch Monday to Saturday)/dinner 18.00 **st.** and a la carte 4.75 – **15 rm** 30.00/62.00 **st.** – SB.

KINSALE (Cionn Eitigh) Cork 405 G 12 **Ireland G.** – pop. 1 759 – 021.

See : Town★★ – St. Multose Church★ – Kinsale Regional Museum★ *AC*.

Envir. : Summercove★ (<★) E : 1 1/2 m. – Charles Fort★ *AC*, E : 1 3/4 m..

Pier Rd 774417 (March-November).

♦Dublin 178 – ♦Cork 17.

Acton's (Forte), Pier Rd, 772135, Fax 772231, <, – TV ☎ P – 300. AE VISA
Meals (bar lunch Monday to Saturday)/dinner 18.50 **st.** and a la carte 6.00 – **56 rm** 75.00/110.00 **st.** – SB.

Blue Haven, 3 Pearse St., 772209, Fax 774268 – TV ☎. AE VISA.
closed 9 to 25 January – **Meals** - Seafood - (bar lunch)/dinner a la carte 18.25/29.25 **t.** 6.00 – **18 rm** 65.00/120.00 **st.** – SB.

Old Bank House without rest., 11 Pearse St., 774075, Fax 774296 – TV ☎. AE VISA.
closed 23 to 26 December – **9 rm** 50.00/110.00 **st.**

Moorings without rest., Scilly, 772376, Fax 772675, < Kinsale harbour – TV ☎ P. VISA.
8 rm 35.00/90.00.

Scilly House Inn without rest., Scilly, 772413, Fax 774629, <, – ☎ P. AE VISA.
8 April-October – **6 rm** 65.00/80.00 **st.**, 1 suite.

Quayside House without rest., Pier Rd, 772188, Fax 772664 – TV ☎. VISA.
6 rm 35.00/50.00 **st.**

Kilcaw Guesthouse without rest., E : 1 m. on R 600 774155 – TV ☎ P. VISA
7 rm 25.00/50.00 **t.**

Murphys Farm House without rest., NE : 1 1/2 m. by R 600 772229, – P.
March-October – **3 rm** 22.00/39.00 **st.**

Chez Jean Marc, Lower O'Connell St., 774625, Fax 774680 – AE VISA
closed Sunday and Monday in winter and February – **Meals** (dinner only) 18.00 **t.** and a la carte.

Max's, Main St., 772243 – VISA
March-October – **Meals** 12.00 **t.** and a la carte.

at Ballinclashet E : 5 m. by R 600 – ✉ Kinsale – 021 :

Oystercatcher, 770822, Fax 770822 – P. AE VISA
Easter-mid November – **Meals** *(closed Monday)* (dinner only) 26.95 **t.** 7.75.

KNOCK (An Cnoc) Mayo 405 F 6 **Ireland G.** – pop. 440 – 094.

See : Basilica of our Lady, Queen of Ireland★.

Knock (Connaught) Airport : 67222, NE : 9 m. by N 17.

Knock Airport 67247 (June-September).

♦Dublin 132 – Galway 46 – Wesport 32.

Hotel and Restaurant see : Cong SW : 36 m. by N 17, R 331, R 334 and R 345.

LAHINCH (An Leacht) Clare 405 D 9 Ireland G. – pop. 550 – ☎ 065.

Envir. : Cliffs of Moher★★★.

Lahinch ℘ 81003 – Spanish Point, Miltown Malbay ℘ 84198.

♦Dublin 162 – ♦Galway 49 – ♦Limerick 41.

Aberdeen Arms, ℘ 81100, Fax 81228, ≘s, ✂ – ▤ rest TV ☎ P – 🏛 200. AE ◑ VISA ✻
Meals 10.45/18.00 **st.** and a la carte 4.50 – **55 rm** 45.00/86.00 **st.** – SB.

Atlantic, Main St., ℘ 81049, Fax 81029 – TV ☎ P. VISA. ✻
Meals (bar lunch Monday to Saturday)/dinner 20.00 **st.** 6.00 – **14 rm** 37.50/55.00 **st.** – SB.

LARAGH (Láithreach) Wicklow 405 N 8 pop. 248 – ✉ Wicklow – ☎ 0404.

♦Dublin 26 – Kilkenny 70 – Wexford 61.

Laragh Trekking Centre ⑤, Glendalough East, NW : 1½ m. on Sallygap rd ℘ 45282, Fax 45204, ≤, ⌒, 🌳 – ⇔ TV ☎ P. VISA
Meals (by arrangement) 14.50 – **6 rm** 25.00/37.00 **st.** – SB.

LEENANE (An Líonán) Galway 405 C 7 Ireland G. – ✉ Clifden – ☎ 095.

See : Killary Harbour★.

Envir. : Joyce Country★★ – Aasleagh Falls★, NE : 2½ m..

Exc. : Lough Nafooey★★, SE : 8½ m. by R 336 – Doo Lough Pass★, NW : 9 m. by N 59 and R 335

♦Dublin 173 – Ballina 56 – ♦Galway 41.

Delphi Lodge ⑤, NW : 8 ¼ m. by N 59 on Louisburgh rd ℘ 42211, Fax 42296, ≤ « Georgian sporting lodge, loughside setting », ⌒, park – ☎ P – 🏛 30. VISA. ✻
February-September – **Meals** (residents only) (communal dining) (dinner only) 25.00 **t.** – **11 rm** 55.00/100.00 **t.**

Portfinn Lodge, ℘ 42265, Fax 42315, ≤ – ☎ P. VISA
April-October – **Meals** (by arrangement) 22.50 **t.** 7.50 – **8 rm** 27.00/38.00 **t.**

LETTERFRACK (Leitir Fraic) Galway 405 C 7 – ☎ 0195.

♦Dublin 189 – Ballina 69 – ♦Galway 57.

Rosleague Manor ⑤, W : 1½ m. on N 59 ℘ 41101, Fax 41168, ≤ Ballynakill harbour and Tully mountain, ≘s, 🌳, park, ✂ – ⇔ rest ☎ P. AE VISA
Easter-October – **Meals** (bar lunch)/dinner 25.00 **t.** and a la carte 17.00/22.95 **t.** 8.00 – **20 rm** 65.00/120.00 **t.** – SB.

LETTERKENNY (Leitir Ceanainn) Donegal 405 I 3 Ireland G. – pop. 7 166 – ☎ 074.

Exc. : Glenveagh National Park★★ (Gardens★★), NW : 12 m. by R 250, R 251 and R 254 – Grianan of Aileach★★ (≤★) NE : 17½ m. by N 13 – Church Hill (Colmcille Heritage Centre★ *AC*, Glebe House and Gallery★ *AC*) NW : 10 m. by R 250.

Barnhill ℘ 21150 – Dunfanaghy ℘ 36335.

♦Dublin 150 – ♦Londonderry 21 – ♦Sligo 72.

Castlegrove House ⑤, Ramelton Rd, NE : 4 ½ m. by N 13 off R 245 ℘ 51118, Fax 51384, ≤, « Late 17C country house », ⌒, 🌳, park – ⇔ ☎ P. AE ◑ VISA. ✻
closed 23 to 27 December and 9 to 30 January – **Meals** *(closed Sunday and Monday October-April)* (dinner only) 25.00 **t.** and a la carte 6.00 – **8 rm** 45.00/160.00 **t.** – SB.

Gleneany, Port Rd, ℘ 26088, Fax 26090 – ▤ rest TV ☎ P. VISA. ✻
Meals 8.50/15.50 **t.** and a la carte **22 rm** 28.00/48.00.

LIMERICK (Luimneach) Limerick 405 G 9 Ireland G. – pop. 52 083 – ☎ 061.

See : City★★ - St Mary's Cathedral★★ Y – Limerick Museum★★ Z – King John's Castle★ *AC* Y – John Square★ Z **20** – St. John's Cathdral★ Z.

Envir. : Hunt Museum, Limerick University★ *AC*, E : 2 m. by N 7 Y – Cratloe Wood (≤★) NW : 5 m. by N 18 Z.

Exc. : Lough Gur Interpretive Centre★ *AC*, S : 11 m. by R 512 and R 514 Z – Clare Glens★, E : 13 m. by N 7 and R 503 Y – Monasteranenagh Abbey★, S : 13 m. by N 20 Z.

✈ Shannon Airport : ℘ 061 (Shannon) 471444, W : 16 m. by N 18 Z – **Terminal** : Limerick Railway Station.

ℹ Arthur's Quay ℘ 317522 Y.

♦Dublin 120 – ♦Cork 58.

Plan opposite

Castletroy Park, Dublin Rd, E : 2¼ m. on N 7 ℘ 335566, Fax 331117, ⚒, ≘s, ▣, 🌳 – |‡| ⇔ rm TV ☎ ♿ P – 🏛 450. AE ◑ VISA JCB. ✻
closed 25 to 30 December – **McLaughlin's : Meals** *(closed Saturday lunch and Sunday dinner)* 14.50/26.00 **t.** and dinner a la carte 7.50 – **105 rm** 93.00/119.00 **st.**, 2 suites – SB.

Limerick Inn, Ennis Rd, NW : 4 m. on N 18 ℘ 326666, Fax 326281, ⚒, ≘s, ▣, 🌳, ✂ – |‡| ▤ rest TV ☎ ♿ P – 🏛 600. AE ◑ VISA. ✻
Meals 11.95/23.00 **st.** and dinner a la carte 5.00 – 7.50 – **149 rm** 90.00/110.00 **st.**, 4 suites – SB.

LIMERICK

rthur Quay
Shopping Centre . . . . Y
'Connell Street . . . . Z
atrick Street . . . . YZ 32
oches Street . . . . Z
arfield Street . . . . Y 39
/illiam Street . . . . Z

rthur Quay . . . . Y 2
aal's Bridge . . . . Y 4
ank Place . . . . Y 5
arrington Street . . . . Z 6

Bridge Street . . . . Y 7
Broad Street . . . . Y 8
Castle Street . . . . Y 10
Cathedral Place . . . . Z 12
Charlotte's Quay . . . . Y 13
The Crescent . . . . Z 14
Cruises Street . . . . Z 15
Gerald Griffen St. . . . . Z 16
Grattan Street . . . . Y 17
High Street . . . . Z 18
Honan's Quay . . . . Y 19
John Square . . . . Z 20
Lock Quay . . . . Y 21
Lower Cecil Street . . . . Z 22
Lower Mallow St. . . . . Z 23

Mathew Bridge . . . . Y 24
Mount Kenneth . . . . Z 26
Newtown Mahon . . . . Z 28
North Circular Rd. . . . . Z 29
O'Dwyer Bridge . . . . Y 30
Penniwell Road . . . . Z 33
Rutland Street . . . . Y 34
St Alphonsus St. . . . . Z 35
St Gerard St. . . . . Z 36
St Lelia Street . . . . YZ 37
Sexton Street North . . . . . . Y 40
Shannon Street . . . . Z 42
South Circular Rd. . . . . Z 43
Thomond Bridge . . . . Y 45
Wickham Street . . . . Z 47

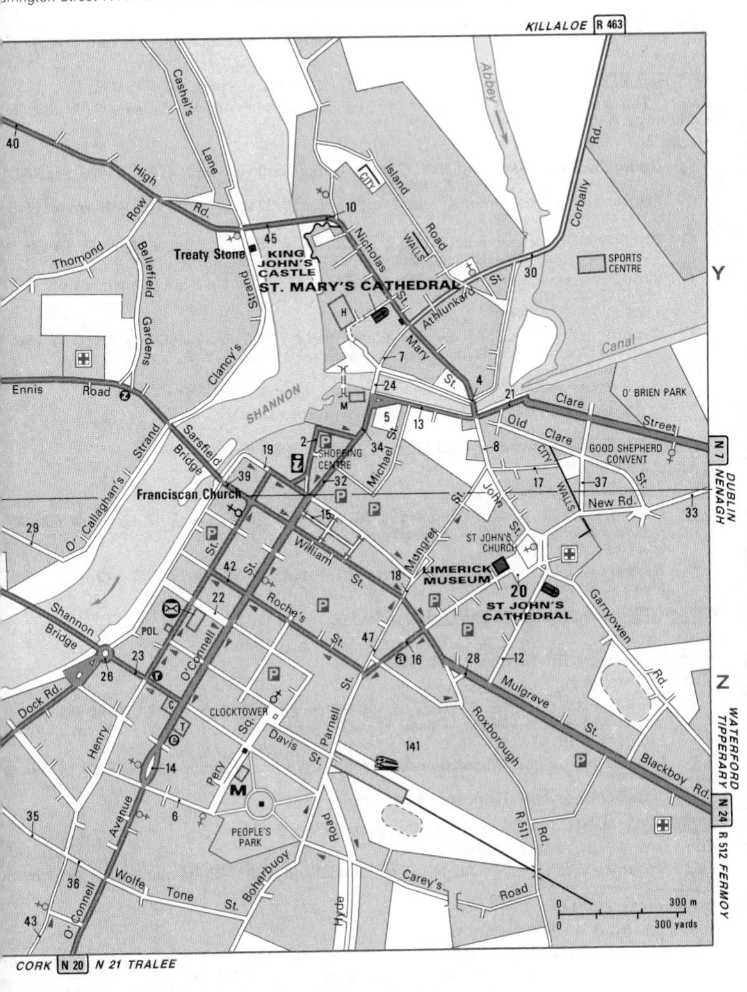

Jurys, Ennis Rd, ☎ 327777, Telex 70766, Fax 326400, ⛶, ≘s, 🏊, 🌳, 🎾 – ▤ rest 📺 ☎ Y z
Ⓟ – 🚻 200. AE ① VISA.
closed 24 to 27 December – **Copper Room : Meals** (dinner only and Sunday lunch)/dinner 21.00 **t.** and a la carte 🍷 6.05 – ☕ 8.00 – **93 rm** 80.00/125.00 **t.**, 1 suite – SB.

Limerick Ryan, Ennis Rd, NW : 1 ¼ m. on N 18 ☎ 453922, Fax 326333, 🌳 – 🛗 ⚡ rm ▤ rest 📺 ☎ ♿ Ⓟ – 🚻 120. AE ① VISA.
Meals 9.50/21.00 **t.** and a la carte 🍷 5.95 – ☕ 9.00 – **179 rm** 70.00/100.00 **t.**, 2 suites – SB.

Clifton House without rest., Ennis Rd, NW : 1¼ m. on N 18 ℘ 451166, Fax 451224, TV ☎ P. VISA.
closed 22 December-4 January – **16 rm** 25.00/36.00.

Clonmacken House without rest., Clonmacken Rd, off Ennis Rd, NW : 2 m. by N 1 ℘ 327007, Fax 327007, – TV ☎ P. VISA.
closed 21 December-7 January – **10 rm** 25.00/38.00 **st.**

De La Fontaine, 12 Upper Gerald Griffin St., ℘ 414461 – AE VISA JCB Z
closed Sunday – **Meals** - French - (dinner only and Friday lunch) 15.00 **t.** and a la carte.

Quenelle's, Upper Henry St., ℘ 411111, Fax 400111 – AE VISA Z
closed Sunday, Monday, 1 week March and 1 week December – **Meals** (dinner onl 21.50 **t.**

Silver Plate, 74 O'Connell St., ℘ 316311 – AE VISA JCB Z
closed Sunday, Monday and 24 to 26 December – **Meals** (dinner only) a la carte 15.00/18.5 5.00.

LISDOONVARNA (Lios Dúin Bhearna) Clare 405 E 8 Ireland G. – pop. 842 – 065.

Envir. : The Burren★★ (Cliffs of Moher★★★, Scenic Routes★★, Aillwee Cave★ *AC* (Waterfall★ Corcomroe Abbey★, Kilfenora Crosses★).

♦Dublin 167 – ♦Galway 39 – ♦Limerick 47.

Ballinalacken Castle , NW : 3 m. by N 67 (Doolin rd) on R 477 ℘ 74025, Fax 7402 ≤, park – rest TV ☎ P. VISA.
mid April-4 October – **Meals** (light lunch)/dinner 14.00 **st.** and a la carte – **13 rm** 35.0 60.00 **st.**

Sheedy's Spa View, Sulphir Hill, ℘ 74026, Fax 74555, – ☎ P. AE VISA.
4 April-7 October – **Meals** - (see ***Orchid*** below) – **11 rm** 35.00/54.00 **t.**

Woodhaven without rest., Doolin Coast Rd, W : 1 m. by N 67 (Doolin rd) off R 47 ℘ 74017, – P.
4 rm 21.00/32.00.

Orchid (at Sheedy's Spa View H.), Sulphir Hill, ℘ 74026, Fax 74555 – P. AE VISA
4 April-7 October – **Meals** (dinner only) a la carte 19.50/30.10 **t.** 9.50.

Great Britain and *Ireland* are covered entirely
at a scale of 16 miles to 1 inch by our *«Main roads» map* 986.

MACROOM (Maigh Chromtha) Cork 405 F 12 – pop. 2 303 – 026.

Lackaduve ℘ 41072.

♦Dublin 186 – ♦Cork 25 – ♦Killarney 30.

Castle, Main St., ℘ 41074, Fax 41505, squash – TV ☎ P – 60. AE VISA.
closed 24 to 28 December – **Meals** 8.00/12.50 **t.** and a la carte 7.00 – **26 rm** 25.0 55.00 **t.** – SB.

Bower , Gortanaddan, Kilnamartyra, W : 8 m. by N 22 ℘ 40192, – P
Meals 11.00 **st.** – **5 rm** 14.00/31.00 **st.**

MALAHIDE (Mullach Íde) Dublin 405 N 7 Ireland G. – pop. 12 088 – 01.

See : Castle★.

18, 9 Beechwood, The Grange ℘ 846 1611.

♦Dublin 9 – Drogheda 24.

Grand, ℘ 845 0000, Fax 845 0987, ≤ – rm TV ☎ P – 750. AE VISA.
closed 25 and 26 December – **Meals** 11.00/20.00 **t.** and a la carte 5.50 – **100 rm** 75.00 140.00 **st.** – SB.

Liscara without rest, Malahide Rd, Kinsealy, S : 3 m. on Dublin rd ℘ 848 3751 – P
closed December and January – **6 rm** 25.00/32.00.

MALLOW (Mala) Cork 405 F 11 Ireland G. – pop. 6 238 – 022.

See : Town★ – St. James' Church★.

Exc. : Doneraile Wildlife Park★ *AC*, NE : 6 m. by N 20 and R 581 – Buttevant Friary★, N : 7 m. b N 20.

18 Balleyellis ℘ 21145.

♦Dublin 149 – ♦Cork 21 – ♦Killarney 40 – ♦Limerick 41.

Longueville House , W : 3½ m. by N 72 ℘ 47156, Fax 47459, ≤, « Georgian mansio in extensive grounds », – TV ☎ P – 25. AE VISA.
closed 18 December-March – **Presidents : Meals** (booking essential) (bar lunch Monday t Saturday)/dinner 27.00/38.00 **t.** and a la carte 8.00 – **20 rm** 58.00/144.00 **t.**

Springfort Hall , N : 4¾ m. by N 20 on R 581 ℘ 21278, Fax 21557, , park – TV ☎ P. AE VISA.
closed 24 December-2 January – **Meals** *(closed Sunday)* (dinner only) a la carte 19.50 26.00 **st.** 6.00 – **24 rm** 40.00/90.00 **st.** – SB.

Central, Main St., ℘ 21527, Fax 21527 – TV ☎ P – 350. AE VISA.
closed 25 December – **Meals** a la carte 7.20/19.85 **st.** 4.95 – **20 rm** 21.00/60.00 **st.** – SB

AYNOOTH (Maigh Nuad) Kildare 405 M 7 – pop. 6 027 – ☏ 01.

vir. : Castletown House★★ *AC*, SE : 4 m. by R 405.

blin 15.

Moyglare Manor ⑤, Moyglare, N : 2 m. ☎ 628 6351, Fax 628 5405, ←, « Georgian country house, antique furnishings », park – ☎ P – 35. AE VISA. *closed 24 to 29 December* – **Meals** (*closed Saturday lunch to non-residents*) 15.00/25.00 **t.** and dinner a la carte 7.95 – **17 rm** 85.00/130.00 **t.**

Moyglare Glebe ⑤, Moyglare, N : 1 ¾ m. ☎ 629 0689, Fax 628 5405, ← heated, – TV ☎ P. AE VISA. **Meals** (booking essential) (residents only) (dinner only) 25.00 **t.** 7.95 – **7 rm** 65.00/90.00 **t.**

IDLETON (Mainistir na Corann) Cork 405 H 12 pop. 2 990 – ☏ 021.

East Cork, Gortacue ☎ 631687.

Jameson Heritage Centre ☎ 613702 (April-September).

ublin 161 – ◆Cork 12 – ◆Waterford 61.

Midleton Park, Old Cork Rd, ☎ 631767, Fax 631605, – rest TV ☎ & P – 400. AE VISA *closed 25 December* – **Meals** 10.95/17.50 **st.** and a la carte 4.95 – **39 rm** 45.00/75.00 **st.**, 1 suite – SB.

Bailick Cottage without rest., S : ½ m. by Broderick St. ☎ 631244, – P. **6 rm** 23.50/50.00.

IONAGHAN (Muineachán) Monaghan 405 L 5 – ☏ 047.

ublin 83 – ◆Belfast 43 – Drogheda 54 – ◆Dundalk 22 – ◆Londonderry 75.

Hillgrove, Old Armagh Rd, SE : ¾ m. by N 2 ☎ 81288, Fax 84951 – rest TV ☎ & P – 800. AE VISA. **Meals** (carving lunch)/dinner 17.50 **st.** and a la carte 5.00 – **44 rm** 45.00/90.00 **st.** – SB.

Four Seasons, Coolshannagh, N : 1 m. on N 2 ☎ 81888, Fax 83131, , , – TV ☎ P. AE VISA. **Meals** (carving lunch) 9.00/25.00 **t.** and dinner a la carte 5.20 – **40 rm** 34.00/80.00 **t.** – SB.

IONKSTOWN (Baile na Mhanaigh) Cork 405 G/H 12 – ☏ 021.

Dublin 163 – ◆Cork 9.

Raffeen Lodge without rest., SW : 2 m. by R 610 ☎ 371632, Fax 371632 – TV P. *March-October* – **6 rm** 20.00/30.00 **st.**

IOYCULLEN (Maigh Cuilinn) Galway 405 E 7 – pop. 545 – ☏ 091.

Dublin 139 – ◆Galway 7.

Knockferry Lodge ⑤, Knockferry (on Lough Corrib), NE : 6 ½ m. by Knockferry rd ☎ 80122, Fax 80328, ←, , – rest P. AE VISA. *April-30 October* – **Meals** (dinner only) 15.50 **st.** – **10 rm** 25.00/42.00 **st.** – SB.

Moycullen House ⑤, SW : 1 m. on Spiddle rd ☎ 85566, Fax 85566, – rm P. AE VISA. *March-October* – **Meals** (communal dining) (by arrangement) – **5 rm** 37.50/60.00 **st.**

Drimcong House, NW : 1 m. on N 59 ☎ 85115, « 17C estate house », – P. AE VISA *closed Sunday, Monday and Christmas-March* – **Meals** (booking essential) (dinner only) 16.95/21.00 **t.** and a la carte 22.50/30.50 **t.** 5.00.

MULLINAVAT (Muileann an Bhata) Kilkenny 405 K 10 pop. 283 – ☏ 051.

Dublin 88 – Kilkenny 21 – Waterford 8.

Rising Sun, Main St., ☎ 898173, Fax 898173 – TV ☎ P. VISA *closed 23 to 28 December* – **Meals** (bar lunch Monday to Friday)/dinner 10.00 **t.** and a la carte 4.50 – **10 rm** 24.00/40.00 **t.** – SB.

MULLINGAR (An Muileann gCearr) Westmeath 405 JK 7 **Ireland G.** – pop. 8 003 – ☏ 044.

nvir. : Belvedere House and Gardens★ *AC*, S : 3½ m. by N 52.

xc. : Multyfarnhan Franciscan Friary★, N : 8 m. by N 4 – Tullynally Castle★ *AC*, N : 13 m. by N 4 nd R 394 – Fore Abbey★, NE : 17 m. by R 394.

Belvedere ☎ 48366/48629.

Dublin Road ☎ 48650.

◆Dublin 49 – ◆Drogheda 36.

Greville Arms, Pearse St., ☎ 48563, Fax 48052 – rest TV ☎ P – 100. AE VISA. **Meals** 8.50/18.00 **st.** and a la carte 6.50 – **40 rm** 35.00/85.00 **st.** – SB.

Hilltop Country House without rest., Rathconnell, NE : 2 ½ m. by R 52 ☎ 48958, Fax 48013, – P. *March-October* – **5 rm** 21.00/34.00 **st.** – SB.

NEWBRIDGE (An Droichead Nua) Kildare 405 L 8 Ireland G. – pop. 11 778 – ☎ 045.

See : Town★.

Envir. : Tully★★★ (Japanese Gardens★★★ AC, Irish National Stud★★ AC) SW : 6 m. by N 7 – Kildare★ (Cathedral★★) SW : 5½ m. by N 7.

Curragh ℘ 41238/41714.

Main Street, ℘ 33835 (July-August).

◆Dublin 28 – Kilkenny 57 – ◆Tullamore 36.

Keadeen, Ballymany, SW : 1 m. ℘ 431666, Fax 434402, – – 350. VISA.
Meals 10.00/40.00 **t.** and dinner a la carte 6.00 – **32 rm** 60.00/150.00 **st.**, 1 suite – SB

NEWMARKET-ON-FERGUS (Cora Chaitlín) Clare 405 F 7 – pop. 1 583 – ☎ 061.

◆Dublin 136 – Ennis 8 – ◆Limerick 15.

Dromoland Castle , NW : 1½ m. on N 18 ℘ 368144, Fax 363355, ≤, « Converted castle », , park, – – 450. VISA.
Meals 16.50/34.00 **t.** and a la carte 8.00 – 12.50 – **67 rm** 202.00 **st.**, 6 suites.

Clare Inn, NW : 2 m. on N 18 ℘ 368161, Fax 368622, , , , , – 400. VISA.
Meals (bar lunch Monday to Saturday)/dinner 20.00 **st.** 5.50 – 7.00 – **121 rm** 50.00/85.00 **st.** – SB.

Carrygerry House , SW : 8 m. by N 18 ℘ 472339, Fax 472123, , park – rm VISA.
closed 4 days Christmas – **Meals** *(closed Sunday)* (bar lunch)/dinner 21.50 **t.** and a la carte 5.00 – **12 rm** 47.50/85.00 **t.** – SB.

En saison, *surtout dans les stations fréquentées, il est prudent de retenir à l'avance. Cependant, si vous ne pouvez pas occuper la chambre que vous avez retenue, prévenez immédiatement l'hôtelier.*

Si vous écrivez à un hôtel à l'étranger, joignez à votre lettre un coupon-réponse international (disponible dans les bureaux de poste).

NEWPORT (Baile Uí Fhiacháin) Mayo 405 D 6 Ireland G. – pop. 512 – ☎ 098.

Envir. : Burrishoole Abbey★, NW : 2 m. by N 59 – Furnace Lough★, NW : 3 m. by N 59.

◆Dublin 164 – Ballina 37 – ◆Galway 60.

Newport House , ℘ 41222, Fax 41613, « Country house atmosphere, antiques », , park – rest VISA.
19 March-2 October – **Meals** (dinner only) 29.00 **st.** 8.00 – **18 rm** 66.00/132.00 **st.**

NEW ROSS (Ros Mhic Thriúin) Wexford 405 L 10 Ireland G. – pop. 5 018 – ✉ Newbawn – ☎ 051.

See : St. Mary's Church★.

Exc. : Kennedy Arboretum, Campile★ AC, S : 7½ m. by R 733 – Dunbrody Abbey★, S : 8 m. by R 733 – Inistiage★, NW : 10 m. by N 25 and R 700 – Graiguenamanagh★ (Duiske Abbey★) N : 11 m. by N 25 and R705.

Tinneranny ℘ 21433.

Town Centre ℘ 21857 (mid June-August).

◆Dublin 88 – Kilkenny 27 – ◆Waterford 15 – Wexford 23.

Cedar Lodge, Carrigbyrne, E : 8 m. on N 25 ℘ 28386, Fax 28222, – VISA.
closed 23 December-1 February – **Meals** (lunch booking essential)/dinner 22.00 **st.** 8.95 – **28 rm** 55.00/85.00 **st.** – SB.

Riversdale House without rest., Lower William St., ℘ 22515, – .
February-October – **4 rm** 22.00/32.00 **st.**

OGONNELLOE (Tuath Ó gConaíle) Clare 405 G 9 – see Killaloe.

OMEATH (Ó Méith) Louth 405 N 5 pop. 249 – ☎ 042.

◆Dublin 63 – ◆Dundalk 10.

Omeath Park , NW : ½ m. on B 79 ℘ 75116, Fax 75116, ≤, , park – VISA.
closed 24 to 26 December – **Meals** (bar lunch Monday to Saturday)/dinner 20.00 **st.** and a la carte 5.00 – **13 rm** 35.00/80.00 **st.** – SB.

Granvue House, ℘ 75109, Fax 75415, ≤ – VISA.
closed 21 to 30 December – **Meals** (bar lunch Monday to Saturday)/dinner 12.00 6.00 – **9 rm** 25.00/44.00 **t.** – SB.

ORANMORE (Órán Mór) Galway 405 F 8 – ☎ 091.

◆Dublin 131 – ◆Galway 7.

Mooring's, Main St., ℘ 790462, Fax 790462 – – 30. VISA.
Meals (dinner only) 18.00 **t.** and a la carte 5.25 – **6 rm** 35.00/60.00 **st.**

UGHTERARD (Uachtar Ard) Galway 405 E 7 Ireland G. – pop. 711 – ☎ 091.
ee : Town★.
nvir. : Lough Corrib★★ (Shore road – NW – ≤★★) – Aughnanure Castle★ *AC*, SE : 2 m. by
59.
Gortreevagh ℘ 82131.
Main street ℘ 82808.
ublin 149 – ◆Galway 17.

Connemara Gateway, SE : ¾ m. on N 59 ℘ 82328, Fax 82332, ≦s, ⊡, ⊼, ⚔ – ▤ rest
⊡ ☎ ⓟ. ⊡ AE ⓞ VISA. ✻
closed December and January except 3 days at New Year – **Meals** (bar lunch)/dinner 13.50 **t.** and a la carte ⸢ 5.95 – **61 rm** ⊒ 45.00/105.00 **st.**, 1 suite – SB.

Currarevagh House ⊛, NW : 4 m. ℘ 82312, Fax 82731, ≤, « Country house atmosphere », ⊸, ⊼, park, ⚔ – ⊬ rest ⓟ. ✻
April-October – **Meals** (booking essential) (dinner only) 19.50 **t.** ⸢ 4.90 – **15 rm** ⊒ 44.00/88.00 **t.** – SB.

Ross Lake House ⊛, Rosscahill, SE : 4½ m. by N 59 ℘ 80109, Fax 80184, ⊼, ⚔ – ☎
ⓟ. ⊡ AE ⓞ VISA. ✻
closed November-17 March – **Meals** (dinner only) 19.00 **t.** ⸢ 5.50 – **13 rm** ⊒ 40.00/80.00 **t.** – SB.

Boat Inn, ℘ 82196, Fax 82694 – ⊡ ☎. ⊡ AE ⓞ VISA
Meals *(restricted opening November-February)* a la carte 8.20/13.50 **st.** ⸢ 4.50 – **11 rm** ⊒ 24.00/46.00 **st.** – SB.

Cnoc na Curra ⊛ without rest., Pier Rd, ℘ 82225, ≤, ⊸, ⊼ – ⊬ ☏ ⓟ. ✻
15 May-September – **4 rm** ⊒ 20.00/40.00 **st.**

"Short Breaks" (SB)

De nombreux hôtels proposent des conditions avantageuses
pour un séjour de deux nuits
comprenant la chambre, le dîner et le petit déjeuner.

ARKNASILLA (Páirc na Saileach) Kerry 405 C 12 Ireland G. – ☎ 064.
nvir. : Sneem★, NW : 2½ m. by N 70.
xc. : Iveragh Peninsula★★★ (Ring of Kerry★★) – Staigue Fort★, W : 13 m. by N 70.
Dublin 224 – ◆Cork 72 – ◆Killarney 34.

Great Southern ⊛, ℘ 45122, Fax 45323, ≤ Kenmare River, bay and mountains, ≦s, ⊡, ⛳9, ⊸, ⊼, park, ⚔ – ⊡ ⊡ ☎ ♿ ⓟ – 🔬 80. ⊡ AE ⓞ VISA. ✻
closed 2 January-10 March – **Meals** (bar lunch)/dinner 25.00 **st.** and a la carte ⸢ 8.00 – **83 rm** ⊒ 103.00/170.00 **st.**, 1 suite – SB.

PORTLAOISE (Port Laoise) Laois 405 K 8 Ireland G. – pop. 8 360 – ☎ 0502.
nvir. : Rock of Dunamase★ (≤★), E : 4 m. by N 80 – Emo Court★ *AC*, NE : 7 m. by N 7.
xc. : Stradbally★, E : 6½ m. by N 80 – Timahoe Round Tower★, SE : 8 m. by R 426.
The Heath ℘ 46533.
James Fintan Lawlor Av. ℘ 21178 (May-December).
Dublin 54 – Kilkenny 31 – ◆Limerick 67.

Killeshin, Dublin Rd, E : 1 m. on N 7 ℘ 21663, Fax 21976 – ⊬ rm ⊡ ☎ ⓟ. ⊡ AE ⓞ VISA. ✻
closed 24 to 27 December – **Meals** 8.15/17.90 **t.** and a la carte ⸢ 5.00 – **44 rm** ⊒ 29.70/55.00 – SB.

Aspen without rest., Dunamase, E : 4½ m. by N 80 ℘ 25405, Fax 25442, ≤, ⊼ – ⊬ ⓟ. ✻
April-October – **4 rm** ⊒ 20.00/34.00 **st.**

PORTMARNOCK (Port Mearnóg) Dublin 405 N 7 – pop. 9 173 – ☎ 01.
Dublin 5 – Drogheda 28.

Portmarnock H. & Country Club, ℘ 846 0611, Fax 846 2442, ≤, ⛳18, ⊼ – ⊡ ☎ ⓟ – 🔬 750. ⊡ AE ⓞ VISA. ✻
Meals (dinner only and Sunday lunch)/dinner 16.75 **t.** and a la carte ⸢ 5.00 – **18 rm** ⊒ 62.50/135.00 **st.** – SB.

RATHMELTON (Ráth Mealtain) Donegal 405 J 2 – ☎ 074.
Dublin 154 – Donegal 37 – ◆Londonderry 27 – ◆Sligo 76.

Ardeen ⊛ without rest., ℘ 51243, ⊼, ⚔ – ⓟ. AE
Easter-October – **4 rm** ⊒ 19.00/35.00 **t.**

RATHMULLAN (Ráth Maoláin) Donegal 405 J 2 Ireland G. – pop. 536 – ✉ Letterkenny – ☎ 074.
Exc. : Knockalla Viewpoint★★, N : 8 m. by R 247 – Rathmelton★, SW : 7 m. by R 247.
Otway, Saltpans ℘ 58319.
Dublin 165 – ◆Londonderry 36 – ◆Sligo 87.

Rathmullan House ⑤, N : ½ m. on R 247 ℘ 58188, Fax 58200, ≤ Lough Swilly and hi « Part 19C country house, gardens », ⇌, ⊡, ↘, park, ✗ – ⇹ rest TV ☎ P. AE VISA. ✗
April-October – **Meals** (bar lunch Monday to Saturday)/dinner 22.50 **t.** 5.50 – **21 r** ⊒ 37.50/120.00 **t.** – SB.

Fort Royal ⑤, N : 1 m. by R 247 ℘ 58100, Fax 58103, ≤ Lough Swilly and hills, ⛱, pa ✗, squash – ⇹ rest TV ☎ P. AE ⓘ VISA
April-October – **Meals** (bar lunch Monday to Saturday)/dinner 18.00 **st.** 7.00 – **15 r** ⊒ 60.00/100.00 **st.** – SB.

RATHNEW (Ráth Naoi) Wicklow 405 N 8 – see Wicklow.

RECESS (Sraith Salach) Galway 405 C 7 – ☎ 095.
Exc. : Lough Nafooey★★, NE : by N 59 on R 345 – Lough Corrib★★, SE : by R 336 on N 59.
♦Dublin 173 – Ballina 72 – ♦Galway 36.

Lough Inagh Lodge ⑤, NW : 4 ¾ m. by N 59 on R 344 ℘ 34706, Fax 34708, ≤ Lou Inagh and The Twelve Bens, ↘ – TV ☎ P. AE ⓘ VISA JCB
April-October – **Meals** (bar lunch)/dinner 23.00 **t.** and a la carte 7.00 – **12 rm** ⊒ 69.0 120.00 **t.** – SB.

REDCROSS (Chrois Dhearg, An) Wicklow 405 N 9 – ✉ Wicklow – ☎ 0404.
♦Dublin 39 – Kilkenny 66 – Wexford 47.

Saraville, ℘ 41745 – P. ✗
17 March-September – **Meals** (by arrangement) (communal dining) 12.00 – **4 rm** ⊒ 19.0 32.00.

*Le Guide change, changez de **guide Michelin** tous les ans.*

RINVYLE/RENVYLE (Rinn Mhaoile) Galway 405 C 7 – ☎ 095.
♦Dublin 193 – Ballina 73 – ♦Galway 61.

Renvyle House ⑤, ℘ 43511, Fax 43515, ≤ Atlantic Ocean, ⛱ heated, 9, ↘, ⛱, par ✗ – TV ☎ P. AE ⓘ VISA JCB. ✗
closed 3 January-1 March – **Meals** (light lunch Monday to Saturday)/dinner 22.00 **t.** 8.00 **64 rm** ⊒ 58.00/116.00 **t.**, 1 suite – SB.

RIVERSTOWN (Baile idir Dhá Abhainn) Sligo 405 G 5 – pop. 274 – ☎ 071.
♦Dublin 123 – ♦Sligo 13.

Coopershill ⑤, ℘ 65108, Fax 65466, ≤, « Georgian country house », ↘, ⛱, park, ✗ ⇹ ☎ P. AE ⓘ VISA JCB. ✗
15 March-October – **Meals** (residents only) (dinner only) 22.00 **st.** 5.00 – **7 rm** ⊒ 57.5 95.00 **st.**

ROSAPENNA (Rosapenna) Donegal 405 I 2 **Ireland G.** – ☎ 074.
Envir. : N : Rosguill Peninsula Atlantic Drive★.
18 Downings ℘ 55301.
♦Dublin 216 – Donegal 52 – ♦Londonderry 47.

Rosapenna Golf, Downings, ℘ 55301, Fax 55128, ≤, 18, ✗ – TV ☎ P. AE ⓘ VISA
March-October – **Meals** (light lunch)/dinner 22.00 **t.** and a la carte 5.00 – **45 rm** ⊒ 55.0 115.00 **t.**

ROSCOMMON (Ros Comáin) Roscommon 405 H 7 **Ireland G.** – pop. 1 314 – ☎ 0903.
See : Castle★.
Exc. : Castlestrange Stone★, SW : 7 m. by N 63 and R 362 – Famine Museum★, Strokestow Park House★ *AC*, N : 12 m. by N 61 and R 368 – Castlerea : Clonalis House★ *AC*, NW : 19 m. b N 60.
9 Moate Park ℘ 26382.
℘ 26342 (20 June-4 September).
♦Dublin 94 – ♦Galway 57 – Limerick 94.

Abbey ⑤, on N 63 ℘ 26240, Fax 26021, ⛱ – TV ☎ ♿ P – 200. AE ⓘ VISA. ✗
Meals 10.00/25.00 **st.** and dinner a la carte 6.00 – **25 rm** ⊒ 45.00/100.00 **st.** – SB.

ROSSLARE (Ros Láir) Wexford 405 M 11 – pop. 847 – ☎ 053.
18, 9 Rosslare Strand ℘ 32113.
Rosslare Terminal ℘ 33622.
♦Dublin 104 – ♦Waterford 50 – Wexford 12.

Kelly's Resort, Strand Rd, ℘ 32114, Fax 32222, ≤, ⛱, ⇌, ⊡, ⛱, ✗, squash – rest TV ☎ ♿ P. AE VISA. ✗
closed 3 December-1 March – **Meals** 12.65/24.50 **st.** 5.50 – **99 rm** ⊒ 47.00/94.00 – SB.

Cedars, Strand Rd, ℘ 32124, Fax 32243, ⇌, ⛱ – ⇹ rm rest TV ☎ P. VISA. ✗
April-December – **Meals** 12.50/18.00 **st.** and a la carte 4.95 – **34 rm** ⊒ 42.00/80.00 **st.** – SB.

ROSSLARE HARBOUR (Calafort Ros Láir) Wexford 405 N 11 Ireland G. – pop. 968 – ☎ 053.
Envir. : Lady's Island★, SW : 6 m. by N 25 and R 736 – Tacumshane Windmill★, SW : 6 m. by N 25 and R 736.
– to Fishguard (Stena Line) 2 daily (3 h 30 mn) – to Pembroke (B & I Line) 1-2 daily (4 h 15 mn).
Kilrane ☎ 33232 (May-mid September).
Dublin 105 – ♦Waterford 51 – Wexford 13.

Great Southern, ☎ 33233, Fax 33543, – 150. VISA.
7 April-October – **Meals** (bar lunch)/dinner 17.00 **t.** and a la carte 7.00 – 7.00 – **99 rm** 49.00/70.00 **t.** – SB.

Rosslare, ☎ 33110, Fax 33386, « Nautical memorabilia », squash – . AE VISA
Meals 10.50/18.00 **st.** and a la carte 4.95 – **25 rm** 25.00/78.00 **t.** – SB.

Tuskar House, St. Martins Rd, ☎ 33363, Fax 33363, – . AE VISA.
Meals *(closed 25 December)* 7.50/15.95 **t.** and a la carte 4.95 – **30 rm** 35.00/60.00 **t.** – SB.

Devereux, Wexford Rd, ☎ 33216, Fax 33301, – . AE VISA JCB.
closed 24 and 25 December – **Meals** (bar lunch Monday to Saturday)/dinner a la carte 9.95/19.20 4.95 – **16 rm** 35.00/52.00 – SB.

at Tagoat W : 2½ m. on N 25 – ✉ Rosslare – ☎ 053 :

Churchtown House , N : ½ m. on Rosslare rd ☎ 32555, Fax 32555, – rm . VISA.
15 March-15 November – **Meals** (booking essential) (residents only) (unlicensed) 14.00 **st.** – **11 rm** 25.00/70.00.

"Short Breaks" (SB)

Zahlreiche Hotels bieten Vorzugspreise bei einem Aufenthalt von zwei Nächten.
Diese Preise umfassen Zimmer, Abendessen und Frühstück.

ROSSNOWLAGH (Ros Neamhlach) Donegal 405 H 4 – ☎ 072.
♦Dublin 153 – Donegal 14 – ♦Sligo 31.

Sand House , ☎ 51777, Fax 52100, bay, beach and mountains, – . AE VISA.
Easter-mid October – **Meals** (bar lunch Monday to Friday)/dinner 16.00 **t.** and a la carte 6.50 – **45 rm** 45.00/95.00 **t.** – SB.

ROUNDSTONE (Cloch na Rón) Galway 405 C 7 pop. 281 – ☎ 095.
♦Dublin 193 – ♦Galway 47.

Eldon's, ☎ 35933, Fax 35921, – . AE VISA.
14 March-10 November and New Year – **Meals** 18.00 **t.** (dinner) and a la carte 17.95/20.45 4.95 – **13 rm** 29.50/54.00 **st.** – SB.

SALTHILL (Bóthar na Trá) Galway 405 E 8 – see Galway.

SHANAGARRY (An Seangharraí) Cork 405 H 12 Ireland G. – pop. 242 – ✉ Midleton – ☎ 021.
Envir. : Ballycotton★, SE : 2½ m. by R 629 – Cloyne Cathedral★, NW : 4 m. by R 629.
Exc. : Rostellan Wood★, W : 9 m. by R 629 and R 631 on R 630.
♦Dublin 163 – ♦Cork 25 – ♦Waterford 64.

Ballymaloe House , NW : 1 ¾ m. on L 35 ☎ 652531, Fax 652021, « Part 16C, part Georgian country house », heated, park, – rest . AE VISA.
closed 24 to 26 December – **Meals** (buffet Sunday) 18.00/32.00 **st.** 8.00 – **32 rm** 80.00/130.00 **st.**

SHANNON (Sionainn) Clare 405 F 9 – pop. 7 920 – ☎ 061.
18 Shannon ,Airport ☎ 471020.
Shannon Airport : ☎ 471444.
Shannon Airport ☎ 471664.
♦Dublin 136 – Ennis 16 – ♦Limerick 15.

Oak Wood Arms, on N 19 ☎ 361500, Fax 361414 – rm – 200. AE VISA.
closed 24 and 25 December – **Meals** (carving lunch)/dinner 18.00 **t.** and a la carte 5.95 – **43 rm** 65.00/96.00 **st.**, 2 suites – SB.

at Shannon Airport SW : 2½ m. on N 19 – ✉ Shannon – ☎ 061 :

Great Southern, ☎ 471122, Telex 72078, Fax 471982 – rm rest – 200. AE VISA.
Meals (carving lunch)/dinner 14.00 **st.** and a la carte 6.00 – 7.00 – **113 rm** 66.00/92.00 **st.**, 2 suites – SB.

SKERRIES (Na Sceirí) Dublin 405 N 7 – pop. 7 032 – ☎ 01.

Skerries ☎ 849 1204.

Community Office ☎ 849 0888.

♦Dublin 19 – Drogheda 15.

XX **Red Bank,** 7 Church St., ☎ 849 1005, Fax 849 1598 – AE VISA
closed Monday – **Meals** - Seafood - 13.75/22.00 **t.** and dinner a la carte 5.75.

SKIBBEREEN (An Sciobairán) Cork 405 E 13 – ☎ 028.

♦Dublin 205 – ♦Cork 51 – ♦Killarney 64.

Liss Ard Lake Lodge, SE : 2¾ m. by R 596 on Tragumna rd ☎ 22365, Fax 22839, ≤
« Minimalistic interior, themed feature gardens », park, – TV
– 25. AE VISA.
closed 17 January-12 February – **Meals** (restricted menu Tuesday, residents only) (bookin
essential) (dinner only) 24.00 **st.** and a la carte 14.00 – **10 rm** 75.00/240.00 **st.** – SB.

SKULL/SCHULL (An Scoil) Cork 405 D 13 – pop. 579 – ☎ 028.

♦Dublin 226 – ♦Cork 65 – ♦Killarney 64.

Corthna Lodge Country House without rest., W : ¾ m. by R 592 ☎ 28517
Fax 28517, ≤, – . – *April-October* – **6 rm** 25.00/40.00 **st.**

XX **Restaurant in Blue,** W : 2½ m. on R 592 ☎ 28305 – . AE VISA
closed January and February – **Meals** (booking essential) (dinner only and Sunda
lunch) 21.00 **t.** and a la carte 7.00.

SLIEVEROE (Sliabh Rua) Waterford – see Waterford.

SLIGO (Sligeach) Sligo 405 G 5 **Ireland G.** – pop. 17 302 – ☎ 071.

See : Town★★ – Abbey★ – **Envir.** : SE : Lough Gill★★ – Carrowmore Megalithic Cemetery★ *AC*
SW : 3 m. – Knocknarea★ (≤★★★) SW : 6 m. by R 292.

Exc. : Parke's Castle★★ *AC*, E : 9 m. by R 286 – Glencar Waterfall★, NE : 9 m. by N 16
Creevelea Abbey, Dromahair★, SE : 11½ m. by N 4 and R 287 – Creevykeel Court Cairn★, N
16 m. by N 15.

Rosses Point ☎ 77134/77186.

Sligo Airport, Strandhill : ☎ 68280.

Temple St. ☎ 61201.

♦Dublin 133 – ♦Belfast 126 – ♦Dundalk 106 – ♦Londonderry 86.

Sligo Park, Pearse Rd, S : 1 m. on N 4 ☎ 60291, Fax 69556, – TV
– 100. AE VISA.
Meals (bar lunch Saturday) 8.50/17.95 **st.** and dinner a la carte 4.65 – **89 rm** 55.00
89.00 **st.** – SB.

Benwiskin Lodge without rest., Shannon Eighter, N : 2 m. by N 15 ☎ 41088, – TV
. VISA.
closed 24 to 31 December – **5 rm** 16.00/32.00 **st.**

Tree Tops without rest., Cleveragh Rd, S : ¼ m. by Dublin rd ☎ 60160, Fax 62301,
TV . VISA.
closed 15 December-15 January – **5 rm** 21.00/32.00 **st.**

SPIDDAL (An Spidéal) Galway 405 E 8 – ☎ 091.

♦Dublin 143 – ♦Galway 11.

Bridge House, Main St., ☎ 83118, – TV . AE VISA.
closed 20 December-14 February – **Meals** 10.00/20.00 **st.** and a la carte 4.95 – **14 rm**
35.00/70.00 **st.** – SB.

Ardmor Country House without rest., W : ½ m. on R 336 ☎ 83145, Fax 83596, ≤,
. VISA.
8 rm 22.00/32.00.

STRAFFAN (Teach Srafáin) Kildare 405 M 8 – pop. 341 – ☎ 01.

Naas, Kerdiffstown ☎ (0145) 97509.

♦Dublin 15 – Mullingar 47.

Kildare H. & Country Club, ☎ 627 3333, Fax 627 3312, ≤, « Part early 19C countr
house on banks of the River Liffey », , park, indoor, squash –
TV – 70. AE VISA.
Byerley Turk : Meals 22.00/39.00 and a la carte 46.50/60.50 8.00 – **Legends** (in K Club)
Meals a la carte 16.35/27.35 **t.** 7.00 – 13.00 – **38 rm** 190.00/290.00 **t.**, 7 suites – SB.

Barberstown Castle, N : ½ m. ☎ 628 8157, Fax 627 7027, « Part Elizabethan, par
Victorian house with 13C castle keep », – TV . AE VISA.
closed 24 to 26 December – **Meals** (dinner only and Sunday lunch)/dinner 25.0
and a la carte 6.50 – **10 rm** 65.00/110.00 **t.** – SB.

Barberstown House without rest., N : ½ m. on R 403 ☎ 627 4007, « Georgian house »
– TV . VISA.
closed 21 December-4 January – **5 rm** 30.00/45.00 **st.**

SWORDS (Sord) Dublin 405 N 7 – pop. 17 705 – ☎ 01.

Balcarrick, Corballis, Donabate ☎ 843 6228.

Dublin 8 – Drogheda 22.

Forte Travelodge, Miltons Field, S : ½ m. on N 1 ☎ 840 9233, Reservations (Freephone) 0800 850950 (UK), 1800 709709 (Republic of Ireland) – TV & P. AE VISA.
Meals (grill rest.) – **40 rm** 34.50 **t.**

TAGOAT (Teach Gót) Wexford 405 M 11 – see Rosslare Harbour.

TAHILLA (Tathuile) Kerry 405 C 12 Ireland G. – ☎ 064.

Exc. : Iveragh Peninsula*** (Ring of Kerry**).

Dublin 222 – Cork 70 – Killarney 32.

Tahilla Cove, ☎ 45204, Fax 45104, ≤ Tahilla Cove and mountains, « Waterside setting », park – TV ☎ P. AE VISA
Easter-mid October – **Meals** (bar lunch)/dinner 16.50 **t.** – **9 rm** 43.00/66.00 **st.** – SB.

TEMPLEGLENTAN (Teampall an Ghleanntáin) Limerick 405 E 10 Ireland G. – ☎ 069.

Exc. : Newcastle West*, NE : 4½ m. by N 21.

Newcastle West, Ardagh ☎ 76500.

Dublin 154 – Killarney 36 – Limerick 33.

Devon, on N 21 ☎ 84122, Fax 84122 – TV ☎ P – 60. AE VISA.
closed 24 and 25 December – **Meals** 8.50/13.50 **st.** and dinner a la carte 5.25 – **37 rm** 35.00/80.00 **st.** – SB.

TERMONFECKIN Louth 405 N 6 – see Drogheda.

TERRYGLASS (Tír Dhá Ghlas) Tipperary 405 H 8 – ✉ Nenagh – ☎ 067.

Dublin 114 – Galway 51 – Limerick 43.

Riverrun House, ☎ 22125, Fax 22187, – ☎ P. AE VISA
Meals (by arrangement) – **6 rm** 27.50/45.00 **st.**

THOMASTOWN (Baile Mhic Andáin) Kilkenny 405 K 10 Ireland G. pop. 1 487 – ✉ Kilkenny – ☎ 056.

See : Ladywell Water Garden* *AC.*

Envir. : Jerpoint Abbey**, SW : 1½ m. by N9.

18 Mount Juliet ☎ 24725.

Dublin 77 – Kilkenny 11 – Waterford 30 – Wexford 38.

Mount Juliet, NW : 1½ m. ☎ 24455, Fax 24522, « 18C manor and sporting estate, ≤ River Nore and park », 18, – TV ☎ P – 40. AE VISA.
closed 2 to 17 January – **Meals** (dinner only) 33.00 **t.** – **30 rm** 135.00/195.00 **t.**, 2 suites.

Hunters Yard at Mount Juliet, NW : 1½ m. ☎ 24725, Fax 24522, « Converted 18C stables », 18, park, – TV ☎ P – 40. AE VISA.
closed 2 to 17 January – **Meals** a la carte 21.00/28.00 **t.** – **13 rm** 125.00 **t.**, 8 suites.

TOORMORE (An Tuar Mór) Cork 405 D 13 – ✉ Goleen – ☎ 028.

Dublin 221 – Cork 68 – Killarney 65.

Fortview House, Gurtyowen, NE : 1½ m. on Durrus rd (R 591) ☎ 35324 – rest P.
March-October – **Meals** (by arrangement) 12.00 **st.** – **5 rm** 17.00/36.00 **st.** – SB.

TOWER Cork 405 G 12 – see Blarney.

TRALEE (Trá Lí) Kerry 405 C 11 Ireland G. – pop. 17 225 – ☎ 066.

Envir. : Blennerville Windmill** *AC,* SW : 2 m. by N 86 – Ardfert Cathedral*, NW : 5½ m. by R 551.

Exc. : Banna Strand**, NW : 8 m. by R 551 – Crag Cave** *AC,* W : 13 m. by N 21 – Rattoo Round Tower*, N : 12 m. by R 556.

Ashe Memorial Hall, Denny St. ☎ 21288.

Dublin 185 – Killarney 20 – Limerick 64.

Grand, Denny St., ☎ 21499, Fax 22877 – rm rest TV ☎ – 250. AE VISA.
Meals 9.00/15.00 **t.** and a la carte 5.00 – **44 rm** 30.00/60.00 **t.** – SB.

Ballyseede Castle, SE : 3¼ m. by N 22 ☎ 25799, Fax 25287, park – TV ☎ P. VISA.
Meals *(closed dinner November-February)* (bar lunch October-April)/dinner 15.00 **t.** and a la carte 6.25 – **14 rm** 50.00/110.00 **t.** – SB.

Barnakyle without rest., NW : 1½ m. on R 551 ☎ 25048, Fax 25048, – P. closed 20 to 31 December – **4 rm** 22.00/32.00 **st.**

Kilteely House, Ballyard, S : 1 m. via Princes St. ☎ 23376, Fax 25766, – res P. VISA. closed 20 to 31 December – **Meals** (by arrangement) 15.00 **st.** – **11 rm** 25.00/50.00 **st.** – SB.

Knockanish House without rest., The Spa, W : 3 m. by R 551 on R 558 ☎ 36268, – P. 18 March-31 October – **6 rm** 20.00/34.00 **st.**

TRIM (Baile Átha Troim) Meath 405 L 7 pop. 1 784 – 046.

See : Trim Castle★★ – Town★.

Envir. : Bective Abbey★, NE : 4 m. by R 161.

◆Dublin 27 – Drogheda 26 – Tullamore 43.

Crannmór without rest., Dunderry Rd, N : 1¼ m. ☎ 31635, – P. VISA. April-September – **4 rm** 21.00/32.00 **st.**

TULLAMORE (Tulach Mhór) Offaly 405 J 8 pop. 8 622 – 0506.

◆Dublin 65 – Kilkenny 52 – ◆Limerick 80.

Sea Dew House without rest., Clonminch Rd, SE : ¼ m. on N 80 ☎ 52054, Fax 52054, – P. VISA. closed 22 December-2 January – **10 rm** 30.00/50.00 **st.**

Pine Lodge, Screggan, SW : 4½ m. by N 52 on Mountbolus rd ☎ 51927, Fax 51927, – P. closed 15 December-15 February – **Meals** (by arrangement) 17.50 **st.** – **4 rm** 27.00/44.00 – SB.

La guida cambia, cambiate la guida ogni anno.

VIRGINIA (Achadh an Iúir) Cavan 405 K 6 pop. 720 – 049.

◆Dublin 51 – Drogheda 39 – Enniskillen 60.

Sharkey's, ☎ 47561, Fax 47761, – P. VISA. **Meals** (bar lunch Monday to Saturday)/dinner 18.00 **t.** and a la carte 4.50 – **10 rm** 32.00/62.00 **t.** – SB.

WATERFORD (Port Láirge) Waterford 405 K 11 **Ireland G.** – pop. 40 328 – 051.

See : Town★ – City Walls★ – City Hall and Theatre Royal★.

Envir. : Waterford Crystal★, SW : 1½ m. by N 25.

Exc. : Tramore★, S : 9 m. by R 675 – Duncannon★, E : 12 m. by R 683, ferry from Passage East and R 374 (south) – Dunmore East★, SE : 12 m. by R 684 – Tintern Abbey★, E : 13 m. by R 683, ferry from Passage East, R 733 and R 734 (south).

18 Newrath ☎ 74182.

Waterford Airport, Killowen : ☎ 75589.

41 The Quay ☎ 75788.

◆Dublin 96 – ◆Cork 73 – ◆Limerick 77.

Waterford Castle, The Island, Ballinakill, E : 2½ m. by R 683, Ballinakill Rd and private ferry ☎ 78203, Fax 79316, ≤, « Part 15C and 19C castle, river island setting », 18, park, – P. AE VISA. **Meals** (bar lunch November-April) 16.00/33.00 **st.** 6.75 – 10.00 – **14 rm** 150.00/200.00 **t.**, 5 suites – SB.

Granville, Meagher Quay, ☎ 55111, Fax 70307 – rm rest – 180. AE VISA JCB. closed 25 and 26 December – **Meals** 9.95/17.00 **st.** and a la carte 5.15 – **Bells** : **Meals** *(closed Sunday)* (dinner only) a la carte 18.00/20.25 **st.** 5.40 – **74 rm** 48.50/93.00 **st.** – SB.

Jurys, Ferrybank, ☎ 832111, Fax 832863, ≤ City, park, – rm P – 700. AE VISA. closed 24 to 28 December – **Meals** 11.00/13.00 **t.** and a la carte 6.25 – 7.95 – **97 rm** 71.00/93.00 **t.**, 1 suite – SB.

Bridge, The Quay, ☎ 77222, Fax 77229 – – 250. AE VISA. closed 24 to 26 December – **Meals** (bar lunch)/dinner 15.50 **st.** and a la carte 5.95 – **80 rm** 35.00/65.00 **st.** – SB.

Dooley's, The Quay, ☎ 73531, Fax 70262 – rm . AE VISA JCB. closed 25 to 27 December – **Meals** 10.50/15.50 **t.** and a la carte 6.00 – **34 rm** 38.00/70.00 **st.** – SB.

Coach House, Butlerstown Castle, Butlerstown, SW : 5¼ m. by N 25 ☎ 384656, Fax 384751, ≤, – P. closed 22 December-10 January – **Meals** *(closed Sunday and Monday)* (booking essential) (dinner only) 18.95 **st.** 5.50 – **7 rm** 31.00/50.00 **st.** – SB.

Foxmount Farm ⛰, SE : 4 ½ m. by R 683, off Cheekpoint rd ✆ 74308, Fax 54906, ≤, « Working farm », park, – P.
9 March-3 November – **Meals** (by arrangement) 15.00 – **6 rm** 27.00/40.00 – SB.

Dwyer's, 8 Mary St., ✆ 77478 – VISA
closed Sunday, first 2 weeks July and 1 week Christmas – **Meals** (dinner only) 14.00 **t.** and a la carte 6.00.

Prendiville's, Cork Rd, SW : ¾ m. on N 25 ✆ 78851, Fax 74062 – P. VISA
closed Saturday lunch, Sunday and 23 to 30 December – **Meals** 9.50/15.50 **t.** and dinner a la carte 6.25.

at Slieveroe NE : 2 ¼ m. by N 25 – ✉ Waterford – ☎ 051 :

Diamond Hill without rest., ✆ 832855, Fax 32254, – P. VISA.
10 rm 35.00 **st.**

at Cheekpoint E : 7 m. by R 683 – ✉ Waterford – ☎ 051 :

Three Rivers ⛰ without rest., ✆ 382520, Fax 382542, ≤ – P. VISA.
14 rm 28.00/56.00 **st.**

WATERVILLE (An Coireán) Kerry 405 B 12 **Ireland G.** – pop. 463 – ☎ 066.

Exc. : Iveragh Peninsula★★★ (Ring of Kerry★★) – Skellig Islands★★, W : 8 m. by N 70 , R 567 and ferry from Ballinskelligs – Derrynane National Historic Park★★ *AC*, S : 9 m. by N70 – Leacanabuaile Fort (≤★★), N : 13 m. by N 70 – Cahergall Fort★, N : 12 m. by N 70.

Ring of Kerry ✆ 74102/74545.

♦Dublin 238 – ♦Killarney 48.

Butler Arms, ✆ 74144, Fax 74520, ≤, – TV P. VISA.
16 April-19 October – **Meals** (bar lunch)/dinner 18.00 **t.** and a la carte 5.50 – **30 rm** 75.00/110.00 **t.** – SB.

Waterville House and Golf Links without rest., ✆ 74244, Fax 74567, ≤, heated, – TV P. VISA.
16 April-October – **6 rm** 50.00/100.00 **t.**, 4 suites.

Golf Links View without rest., Murreigh, N : 1 m. on N 70 ✆ 74623, Fax 74623 – TV P. VISA.
March-October – **4 rm** 19.50/32.00 **t.**

Klondyke House without rest., N : ½ m. on N 70 ✆ 74119, Fax 74666, ≤ – P. VISA.
6 rm 19.00/28.00 **st.**

WESTPORT (Cathair na Mart) Mayo 405 D 6 **Ireland G.** – pop. 3 688 – ☎ 098.

See : Town★★ (Centre★) – Westport House★★ *AC*.

Exc. : SW : Murrisk Peninsula★★ – Silver Strand★★, SW : 21 m. by R 335 – Ballintubber Abbey★, SE : 13 m. by R 330 – Croagh Patrick★, W : 6 m. by R 335 – Bunlahinch Clapper Bridge★, W : 16 m. by R 335.

Carowholly ✆ 25113/27070.

The Mall ✆ 25711.

♦Dublin 163 – ♦Galway 50 – ♦Sligo 65.

Westport Woods, Louisburgh Rd, W : ½ m. ✆ 25811, Fax 26212, – TV P. VISA.
closed January – **Meals** (dinner only and Sunday lunch)/dinner 15.00 **st.** and a la carte 4.95 – **57 rm** 61.00/88.00 **st.** – SB.

Wilmaur ⛰ without rest., Rosbeg, W : 2 m. by R 335 ✆ 25784, Fax 26224, ≤, – P.
Easter-September – **5 rm** 25.00/33.00 **st.**

WEXFORD (Loch Garman) Wexford 405 M 10 **Ireland G.** – pop. 15 393 – ECD : Thursday – ☎ 053.

See : Town★ – Main Street★ – Franciscan Friary★.

Envir. : Irish Agricultural Museum, Johnstown Castle★★ *AC*, SW : 4 ½ m. – Irish National Heritage Park, Ferrycarrig★ *AC*, NW : 2½ m. by N 11 – Curracloe★, NE : 5 m. by R 741 and R 743.

Exc. : Tacumshane Windmill★, S : 11 m. by N 25 – Lady's Island★, S : 11 m. by N 25 – Kilmore Quay★, SW : 15 m. by N 25 and R 739 (Saltee Islands★ - access by boat) – Enniscorthy Castle★ (County Museum★ *AC*) N : 15 m. by N 11.

Mulgannon ✆ 42238.

Crescent Quay ✆ 23111 (1 March-4 November).

♦Dublin 88 – Kilkenny 49 – ♦Waterford 38.

Ferrycarrig ⛰, Ferrycarrig Bridge, NW : 2¾ m. on N 11 ✆ 20999, Fax 20982, ≤, – TV P – 400. VISA.
Meals (bar lunch)/dinner 19.50 **st.** and a la carte 5.00 – **38 rm** 50.00/80.00 **st.**, 1 suite – SB.

Talbot, Trinity St., ℘ 22566, Fax 23377, squash – TV. AE VISA.
Meals 7.50/16.50 **t.** and a la carte 5.50 – **99 rm** 42.00/74.00 **t.** – SB.

Whitford House, New Line Rd, W : 2¼ m. on R 733 ℘ 43444, Fax 46399, – rest TV. VISA.
closed 23 December-14 January – **Meals** (bar lunch)/dinner 19.50 **t.** 7.00 – **23 rm** 26.50/59.00 **t.** – SB.

White's, George St., ℘ 22311, Fax 45000, – TV – 200. AE VISA JCB.
Meals 10.00/20.00 **st.** and a la carte 5.90 – **81 rm** 41.00/82.00 **st.**, 1 suite – SB.

Newbay Country House, W : 4 m. by N 25 and Clonard rd ℘ 42779, Fax 46318, park – VISA.
closed 1 December-10 January – **Meals** *(closed Sunday and Monday)* (by arrangement) (residents only) (communal dining) (dinner only) 25.00 **st.** 6.00 – **6 rm** 43.00/70.00 **st.**

Slaney Manor, Ferrycarrig, NW : 4 m. by N 11 on Killurin rd ℘ 45751, Fax 46510, park TV. VISA
closed December and January – **Meals** (by arrangement) (residents only) 8.00/18.00 **st.** 4.50 – **12 rm** 37.00/60.00 **st.** – SB.

Ardruadh without rest., Spawell Rd, ℘ 23194, « Gothic style Victorian house », – TV. AE VISA.
closed 1 week Christmas – **5 rm** 20.00/34.00.

Gateway, Rosslare Rd, Drinagh, S : 2½ m. ℘ 43295, Fax 45827, squash – TV. AE VISA.
closed Good Friday and 25 December – **Meals** (bar lunch Monday to Saturday)/dinner 15.00 **st.** and a la carte 4.50 – **11 rm** 28.00/48.00 **st.** – SB.

Rathaspeck Manor, Rathaspeck, SW : 4 m. by R 733 off N 25 ℘ 42661, « Georgian country house », – TV.
May-October – **Meals** (by arrangement) (residents only) (dinner only) 14.00 – **7 rm** 24.00/40.00 **s.**

Clonard House, Clonard Great, SW : 2½ m. by R 733 ℘ 43141, Fax 43141, « Georgian country house, working farm », park – TV. VISA.
Easter-mid November – **Meals** (by arrangement) 13.00 **st.** – **9 rm** 22.00/36.00 **st.**

McMenamin's Townhouse without rest., 3 Auburn Terr., Redmond Rd, ℘ 46442, Fax 46442, « Victorian town house » – TV. VISA.
closed 20 to 30 December – **5 rm** 22.50/40.00 **st.**

Killiane Castle, Drinagh, S : 3½ m. by Rosslare Rd ℘ 58885, Fax 58885, « Working farm », park, – VISA
March-November – **Meals** (by arrangement) 14.00 – **8 rm** 24.00/36.00 **st.**

"Un atlante della Gran Bretagna e dell' Irlanda è disponibile in tre versioni : rilegato, in brossura e a spirale."

WICKLOW (Cill Mhantáin) Wicklow 405 N 9 **Ireland G.** – pop. 5 847 – 0404.

Envir. : Mount Usher Gardens, Ashford★ *AC*, NW : 4 m. by R 750 and N 11 – Devil's Glen★, NW : 8 m. by R 750 and N 11.

Exc. : Glendalough★★★ : – Lower Lake★★★, Upper Lake★★, Cathedral★★, Round Tower★, St. Kevin's Church★, St. Kieran's Church★, St. Kevin's Cross★, St. Saviour's Priory★ – W : 14 m. by R 750, N 11, R 763, R 755 and R 756 – Wicklow Mountains★★ :– Avondale Forest Park★★ *AC*, Wicklow Gap★★, Sally Gap★★, Meeting of the Waters★, Glenmacnass Waterfall★, Glenmalur★ – Loughs Tay and Dan★.

Blainroe ℘ 68168.

Fitzwilliam St. ℘ 69117.

♦Dublin 33 – ♦Waterford 84 – Wexford 67.

Grand, ℘ 67337, Fax 69607, – rm rest TV – 240. VISA.
Meals 10.00/18.00 **t.** and dinner a la carte 6.00 – **32 rm** 39.00/68.25 **st.** – SB.

Old Rectory, NW : ¼ m. on R 750 ℘ 67048, Fax 69181, – rest TV. AE VISA.
29 March-27 October – **Meals** (booking essential) (dinner only) 27.00 **st.** and a la carte 8.00 – **5 rm** 69.00/92.00 **st.** – SB.

Lissadell House, Ashtown Lane, S : 1½ m. by R 751 ℘ 67458, –
March-October – **Meals** (by arrangement) 14.00 **st.** – **4 rm** 21.00/32.00 **st.**

at Rathnew NW : 2 m. on R 750 – Wicklow – 0404 :

Tinakilly House, on R 750 ℘ 69274, Fax 67806, « Part Victorian country house », – TV – 60. AE VISA JCB.
Meals 18.50/30.00 **st.** 7.00 – **26 rm** 93.00/160.00 **st.**, 3 suites – SB.

Hunter's, Newrath Bridge, N : ¾ m. by N 11 on R 761 ℘ 40106, Fax 40338, « Converted 18C inn, gardens » – rest. AE VISA.
closed 24 to 26 December – **Meals** 16.00/22.50 **t.** 4.90 – **16 rm** 45.00/90.00 **t.**

YOUGHAL (Eochaill) Cork 405 I 12 Ireland G. – pop. 5 532 – ☎ 024.

See : Town★ – St. Mary's Collegiate Church★★ – Town Walls★★ – Clock Gate★ – The Red House★.

Exc. : Helvick Head★★ (≤★★), NE : 22 m. by N 25 and R 674 – Ringville (≤★★), NE : 20 m. by N 25 and R 674 – Dungarvan★ (King John's Castle★) NE : 19 m. by N 25 – Ardmore★ – Round Tower★ – Church★ (arcade★), N : 10 m. by N 25 and R 673 – Whiting Bay★, SE : 12 m. by N 25, R 673 and the coast road.

18 Knockaverry ℘ 92787.

Heritage Centre ℘ 92390 (June-mid September).

◆Dublin 146 – ◆Cork 30 – ◆Waterford 47.

Aherne's, 163 North Main St., ℘ 92424, Fax 93633 – TV ☎ ♿ P. AE VISA. ✻
closed 24 to 29 December – **Meals** - (see ***Aherne's Seafood Bar*** below) – **10 rm** ☕ 60.00/100.00 **st.**

Devonshire Arms, Pearse Sq., ℘ 92827, Fax 92900 – TV ☎ P. AE VISA
closed 25 to 28 December – **Meals** (lunch by arrangement) 9.00/19.00 **st.** and a la carte – **10 rm** ☕ 30.00/60.00 – SB.

XX **Aherne's Seafood Bar** (at Aherne's H.), 163 North Main St., ℘ 92424, Fax 93633 – P. AE VISA. ✻
closed 24 to 29 December – **Meals** 13.50/23.00 **t.** and a la carte 🍷 7.00.

Major hotel groups
Principales chaînes hôtelières
Principali catene alberghiere
Die wichtigsten Hotelketten

COPTHORNE HOTELS	COPTHORNE	*0800 414741 (Freephone)*
COUNTRY CLUB HOTEL GROUP (Country Club Resorts/Hotels)	COUNTRY CLUB	*01582 562256*
DE VERE HOTELS PLC	DE VERE	*01925 265050*
RADISSON EDWARDIAN HOTELS	RADISSON EDWARDIAN	*0800 191991 (Freephone)*
FORTE HOTELS	FORTE	*(0345) 404040 or 0800 404040 (Freephone)*
TRAVELODGES		*0800 850950 (Freephone)*
FRIENDLY HOTELS	FRIENDLY	*0800 591910 (Freephone)*
GRANADA HOTELS & LODGES	GRANADA	*0800 555300 (Freephone)*
HILTON HOTELS	HILTON	*0990 445866*
HOLIDAY INN WORLDWIDE	HOLIDAY INN	*0800 897121 (Freephone)*
HYATT HOTELS	HYATT	*0171 5808197*
INTERCONTINENTAL HOTELS LTD	INTER-CON	*0181 8472277 or calls from outside London 0345 581444*
JARVIS HOTELS	JARVIS	*(0345) 581811*
MARRIOTT HOTELS	MARRIOTT	*0800 221222 (Freephone)*
MOUNT CHARLOTTE/THISTLE HOTELS	MT. CHARLOTTE THISTLE	*0800 181716 (Freephone) 0113 2439111*
NOVOTEL	NOVOTEL	*0171 7241000*
PREMIER LODGES & INNS	PREMIER	*0800 118833 (Freephone)*
QUEENS MOAT HOUSES PLC	Q.M.H.	*0500 213214 (Freephone) or 01708 766677*
RAMADA INTERNATIONAL	RAMADA	*0800 181737 (Freephone)*
SHERATON HOTELS	SHERATON	*0800 353535 (Freephone)*
STAKIS HOTELS	STAKIS	*0800 262626 (Freephone)*
SWALLOW HOTELS LTD	SWALLOW	*0191 4194666*
TRAVEL INNS	TRAVEL INN	*01582 414341*

Note : *abbreviations used in the Guide and central reservation telephone numbers*

Important : *abréviations utilisées dans nos textes et centraux téléphoniques de réservation*

Importante : *abbreviazoni utilizzate nei nostri testi e centrali telefoniche di prenotazione*

Wichrig : *im Führer benutzte Abkürzungen der Hotelketten und ihre Zentrale für telefonische Reservierung*

Distances

All distances in this edition are quoted in miles. The distance is given from each town to other nearby towns and to the capital of each region as grouped in the guide. Towns appearing in the charts are preceded by a diamond ♦ text.

To avoid excessive repetition some distances have only been quoted once – you may therefore have to look under both town headings.

The distances in miles quoted are not necessarily the shortest but have been based on the roads which afford the best driving conditions and are therefore the most practical.

Distances en miles

Pour chaque région traitée, vous trouverez au texte de chacune des localités sa distance par rapport à la capitale et aux villes environnantes. Lorsque ces villes sont celles des tableaux, leur nom est précédé d'un losange noir ♦.

La distance d'une localité à une autre n'est pas toujours répétée aux deux villes intéressées : voyez au texte de l'une ou de l'autre.

Ces distances ne sont pas nécessairement comptées par la route la plus courte mais par la plus pratique, c'est-à-dire celle offrant les meilleures conditions de roulage.

Dublin - Sligo : **136 Miles**

	Belfast	Cork	Dublin	Dundalk	Galway	Killarney	Limerick	Londonderry	Omagh	Sligo	Tullamore
Cork	260										
Dublin	106	154									
Dundalk	54	207	53								
Galway	196	122	138	155							
Killarney	286	54	181	233	133						
Limerick	225	57	119	172	65	68					
Londonderry	72	287	144	102	174	298	230				
Omagh	68	268	111	70	156	254	213	33			
Sligo	125	202	136	107	89	213	145	85	68		
Tullamore	142	126	67	84	82	139	72	158	127	95	
Waterford	204	71	99	151	135	112	78	245	212	177	82

Distanze in miglia

Per ciascuna delle regioni trattate, troverete nel testo di ogni località la sua distanza dalla capitale e dalle città circostanti. Quando queste città sono comprese nelle tabelle, il loro nome è preceduto da una losanga ♦.

Le distanza da una località all'altra non è sempre ripetuta nelle due città interessate : vedere nel testo dell'una o dell'altra.

Le distanze non sono necessariamente calcolate seguendo il percorso più breve, ma vengono stabilite secondo l'itinerario più pratico, che offre cioè le migliori condizioni di viaggio.

Entfernungsangaben in meilen

Die Entfernungen der einzelnen Orte zur Landeshauptstadt und zu den nächstgrößeren Städten in der Umgebung sind im allgemeinen Ortstext angegeben. Die Namen der Städte in der Umgebung, die auf der Tabelle zu finden sind, sind durch eine Raute ♦ gekennzeichnet.

Die Entfernung zweier Städte voneinander können Sie aus den Angaben im Ortstext der einen oder der anderen Stadt ersehen.

Die Entfernungsangaben gelten nicht immer für den kürzesten, sondern für den günstigsten Weg.

Distances between major towns
Distances entre principales villes
Distanze tra le principali città
Entfernungen zwischen den grösseren Städten

Edinburgh - Southampton 431 Miles

	Aberdeen	Ayr	Birmingham	Blackpool	Brighton	Bristol	Cambridge	Cardiff	Carlisle	Coventry	Dover	Dumfries	Dundee	Edinburgh	Glasgow	Inverness	Ipswich	Kingston-upon-Hull	Leeds	Leicester	Liverpool	London	Manchester	Middlesbrough	Newcastle	Norwich	Nottingham	Oban	Oxford	Plymouth	Portsmouth	Sheffield	Southampton	Stoke-on-Trent	Swansea
Ayr	184																																		
Birmingham	433	291																																	
Blackpool	325	184	133																																
Brighton	600	459	166	301																															
Bristol	513	372	87	214	159																														
Cambridge	468	353	99	226	120	171																													
Cardiff	537	396	111	238	192	44	205																												
Carlisle	231	90	203	96	371	284	265	308																											
Coventry	450	308	22	150	155	97	79	126	220																										
Dover	585	487	201	329	106	198	120	232	398	180																									
Dumfries	210	57	235	127	402	315	296	339	33	252	430																								
Dundee	70	111	364	256	531	444	399	468	162	381	516	141																							
Edinburgh	125	76	297	190	465	378	341	402	96	314	459	74	56																						
Glasgow	150	35	299	192	467	380	361	404	98	316	494	77	77	46																					
Inverness	105	205	457	350	625	538	500	562	256	474	618	234	127	158	171																				
Ipswich	522	407	153	281	126	207	55	240	319	133	127	350	453	396	415	555																			
Kingston-upon-Hull	362	247	145	145	263	234	146	258	159	144	263	191	293	236	255	395	174																		
Leeds	326	211	122	90	265	212	152	236	123	122	270	154	257	200	219	359	206	61																	
Leicester	424	307	44	149	168	130	71	154	219	24	186	250	355	297	315	456	125	103	103																
Liverpool	358	217	103	59	271	184	196	172	129	120	298	160	289	223	225	383	250	132	77	118															
London	549	408	115	250	55	123	57	157	320	101	75	351	480	400	416	574	79	200	205	108	220														
Manchester	354	213	90	55	258	171	166	195	125	107	285	156	285	218	221	378	220	99	44	100	36	207													
Middlesbrough	275	189	181	129	324	270	205	294	102	180	323	132	206	149	197	308	260	89	64	161	140	264	107												
Newcastle	231	147	210	138	353	299	234	323	60	209	352	90	162	105	155	264	288	129	93	190	169	292	136	42											
Norwich	493	378	165	246	169	234	67	267	290	145	169	321	424	367	386	526	45	156	178	120	227	115	191	231	260										
Nottingham	396	281	53	128	196	143	89	167	193	53	215	224	327	270	289	429	143	98	75	30	104	136	73	134	162	124									
Oban	180	125	389	282	557	470	450	494	188	406	584	166	118	124	92	117	505	345	309	405	315	506	310	271	226	476	379								
Oxford	502	361	68	203	106	75	83	108	273	57	146	304	433	366	369	526	136	197	174	77	172	55	160	233	262	149	105	459							
Plymouth	632	491	206	333	212	119	276	156	403	215	289	434	563	497	499	657	312	353	330	249	302	228	290	389	418	339	262	589	197						
Portsmouth	585	443	151	285	48	95	139	137	355	140	142	387	516	449	451	609	163	279	257	159	255	80	242	315	344	205	188	541	85	173					
Sheffield	362	255	86	97	229	176	125	200	167	86	247	198	293	236	263	395	179	70	35	67	78	169	43	99	128	150	39	352	138	295	221				
Southampton	567	425	132	267	61	75	136	117	337	121	143	369	498	431	433	591	172	261	238	141	237	88	224	297	326	198	170	523	67	151	21	203			
Stoke-on-Trent	388	247	47	89	215	128	140	152	159	64	242	190	319	253	255	413	195	129	91	60	58	164	46	155	183	207	53	345	117	247	199	55	181		
Swansea	531	390	146	232	227	79	240	41	302	161	267	333	462	395	398	555	275	293	271	189	186	192	230	329	358	302	202	488	143	191	172	235	152	187	
Wick	212	313	565	457	732	645	608	669	363	582	726	342	235	265	279	109	662	503	466	564	490	681	486	416	371	634	536	226	634	764	717	502	699	520	663

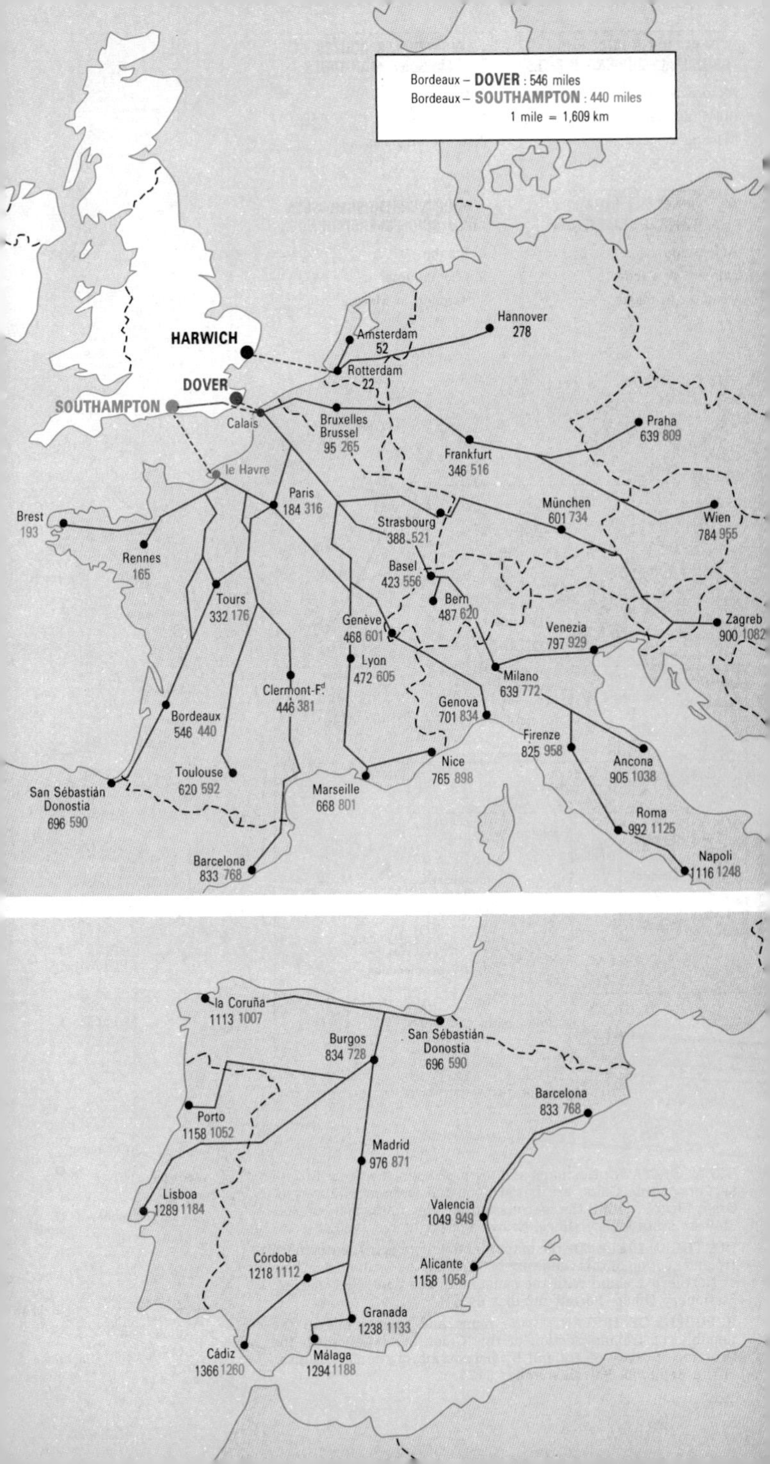

Bordeaux – DOVER : 546 miles
Bordeaux – SOUTHAMPTON : 440 miles
1 mile = 1,609 km
HARWICH
DOVER
SOUTHAMPTON
Hannover 278
Amsterdam 52
Rotterdam 22
Calais
Bruxelles Brussel 95 265
Frankfurt 346 516
Praha 639 809
le Havre
Paris 184 316
Strasbourg 388 521
München 601 734
Wien 784 955
Brest 193
Rennes 165
Basel 423 556
Bern 487 620
Tours 332 176
Genève 468 601
Venezia 797 929
Zagreb 900 1082
Lyon 472 605
Milano 639 772
Clermont-Fd 446 381
Genova 701 834
Bordeaux 546 440
Firenze 825 958
Nice 765 898
Ancona 905 1038
Toulouse 620 592
Marseille 668 801
San Sébastián Donostia 696 590
Roma 992 1125
Napoli 1116 1248
Barcelona 833 768
la Coruña 1113 1007
Burgos 834 728
San Sébastián Donostia 696 590
Barcelona 833 768
Porto 1158 1052
Madrid 976 871
Lisboa 1289 1184
Valencia 1049 949
Alicante 1158 1058
Córdoba 1218 1112
Granada 1238 1133
Cádiz 1366 1260
Málaga 1294 1188

MAJOR ROADS AND PRINCIPAL SHIPPING ROUTES	
Motorway	
Road number	A 4.T 35. N 2
Mileage	20

PRINCIPALES ROUTES ET LIAISONS MARITIMES	
Autoroute	
N° de route	A 4.T 35. N 2
Distance en miles	20

PRINCIPALI STRADE E ITINERARI MARITTIMI	
Autostrada	
Numero di strada	A 4.T 35. N 2
Distanza in miglia	20

HAUPTVERKEHRSSTRASSEN UND SCHIFFSVERBINDUNGEN	
Autobahn	
Straßennummer	A 4.T 35. N 2
Entfernung in Meilen	20

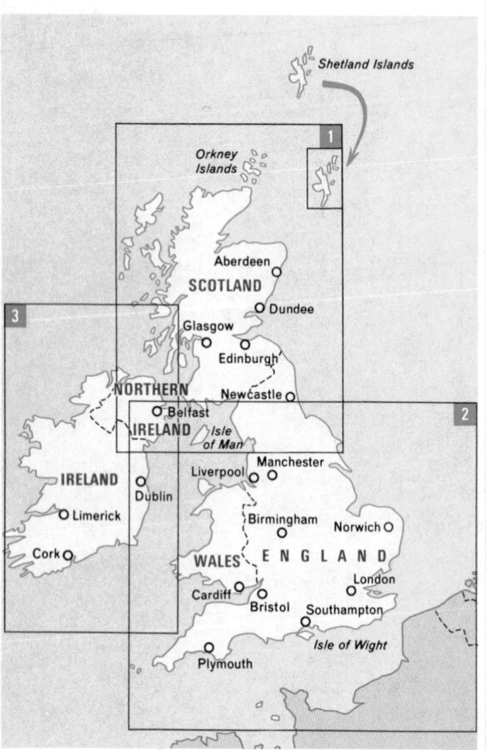

GREAT BRITAIN : the maps and town plans in the Great Britain Section of this Guide are based upon the Ordnance Survey of Great Britain with the permission of the Controller of Her Majesty's Stationery Office, Crown Copyright reserved.

NORTHERN IRELAND : the maps and town plans in the Northern Ireland Section of this Guide are based upon the Ordnance Survey of Northern Ireland with the sanction of the Controller of H.M. Stationery Office, Permit number 845.

REPUBLIC OF IRELAND : the maps and town plans in the Republic of Ireland Section of this Guide are based upon the Ordnance Survey of Ireland by permission of the Government of the Republic, Permit number 6124.

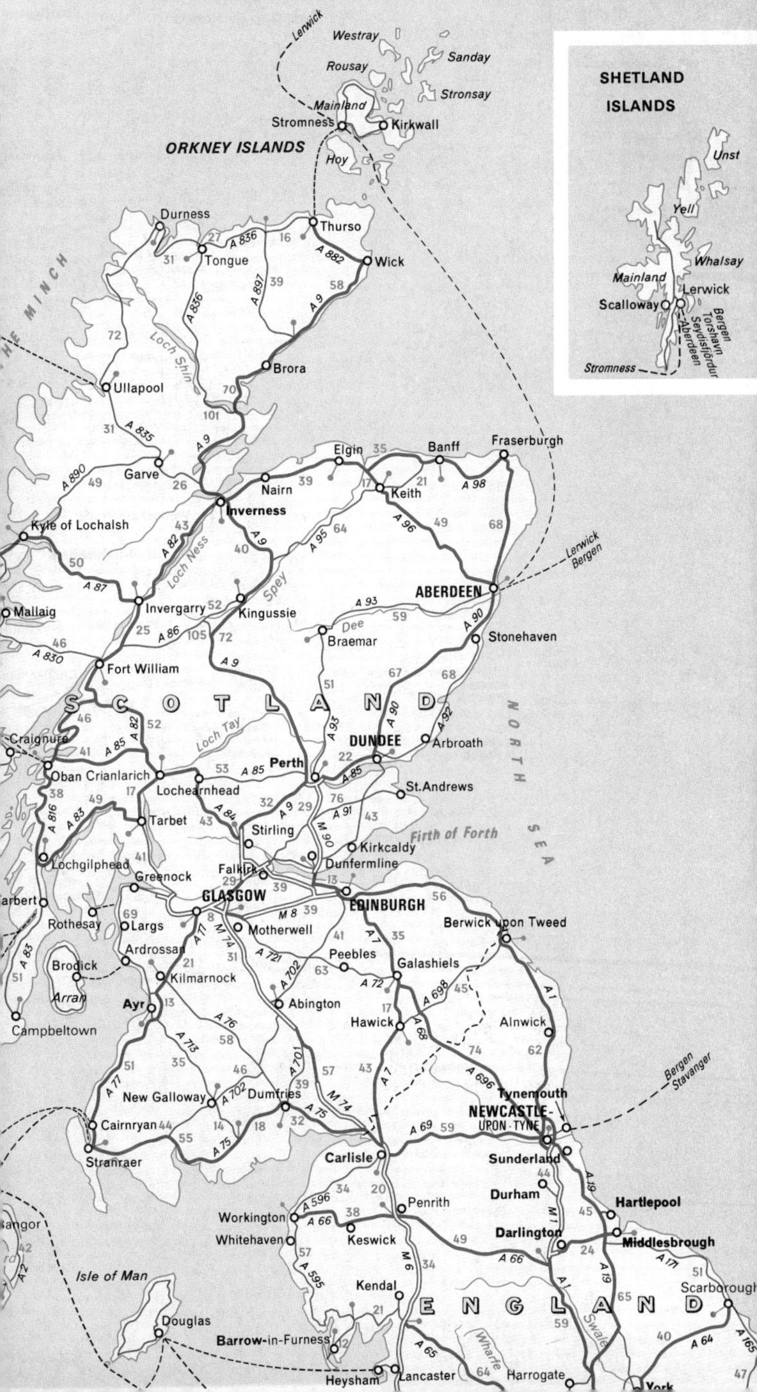

SHETLAND ISLANDS
ORKNEY ISLANDS
SCOTLAND
ENGLAND
NORTH SEA
Firth of Forth
Isle of Man
GLASGOW
EDINBURGH
ABERDEEN
DUNDEE
NEWCASTLE-UPON-TYNE
Inverness
Perth
Stirling
Fort William
Oban
Ayr
Dumfries
Carlisle
Kirkwall
Stromness
Lerwick
Thurso
Wick
Ullapool
Kyle of Lochalsh
Mallaig
Stranraer
Cairnryan
Douglas
Berwick upon Tweed
Sunderland
Durham
Darlington
Middlesbrough
Hartlepool
Scarborough
Kendal
Penrith
Keswick
Lancaster
Heysham
Harrogate

NORTHERN IRELAND
Larne
Lough Neagh
Belfast
Bangor
Strangford Lough
Armagh
Banbridge
Newcastle
Dundalk / Dun Dealgan
Drogheda / Droichead Átha
Boyne
Kells
DUBLIN / BAILE ÁTHA CLIATH
Naas
Dun Laoghaire
Bray
Wicklow
Arklow
Enniscorthy
Wexford
Rosslare
IRISH SEA
Isle of Man
Douglas
Stranraer
ST GEORGE'S CHANNEL
le Havre
Cherbourg
Roscoff
Holyhead / Caergybi
Bangor
Caernarfon
Colwyn Bay / Bae Colwyn
Mold / Yr Wyddgrug
Wrexham / Wrecsam
Dolgellau
Welshpool / Y Trallwng
Aberystwyth
Llangurig
Llandrindod Wells
WALES
Fishguard / Abergwaun
Carmarthen / Caerfyrddin
Brecon / Aberhonddu
Merthyr Tydfil
Milford Haven / Aberdaugleddau
Pembroke Dock / Doc Penfro
Swansea / Abertawe
Newport / Casnewydd
CARDIFF / CAERDYDD
Bristol Channel
Carlisle
Workington
Whitehaven
Penrith
Keswick
Kendal
Barrow-in-Furness
Heysham
Lancaster
Sunderland
Durham
Darlington
ENGL
Wharfe
Harrogate
LEEDS
BLACKPOOL
Preston
Blackburn
Bradford
Burnley
Halifax
Southport
Wigan
Bolton
Oldham
LIVERPOOL
Birkenhead
MANCHESTER
Stockport
Warrington
Chester
Macclesfield
Matlock
STOKE-ON-TRENT
Shrewsbury
Wolverhampton
Walsall
Dudley
BIRMINGHAM
Ludlow
Severn
Warwick
Worcester
Stratford-upon-Avon
Wye
Hereford
Ross
Gloucester
Cheltenham
THAMES
Swindon
BRISTOL
Bath
Wells
Ilfracombe
Minehead
Barnstaple
Bridgwater
Taunton
Salisbury
Avon
Yeovil
Bude
EXETER
Honiton
Dorchester
BOURNEMOUTH
Exmouth
Weymouth
Newquay
Bodmin
PLYMOUTH
Torquay Torbay
Truro
Penzance
Falmouth
Isles of Scilly
Santander
Roscoff
St.Malo
ENGLISH
Rosslare
Alderney
Cherbourg
Guernsey
Sark
St.Peter-Port
Jersey
St.Hélier

Hartlepool
Middlesbrough
Scarborough
AND
NORTH SEA
York
KINGSTON UPON HULL
Wakefield
Scunthorpe
Immingham
Rotterdam
Zeebrugge
Great Grimsby
Doncaster
Rotherham
SHEFFIELD
Lincoln
Skegness
Boston
Cromer
NOTTINGHAM
King's Lynn
NORWICH
Wisbech
LEICESTER
Stamford
Great Yarmouth
Peterborough
Lowestoft
Coventry
Ely
Rugby
Bury St.Edmunds
CAMBRIDGE
Zeebrugge
Northampton
Bedford
Ipswich
Esbjerg
Göteborg
Hoek van Holland
Hamburg
Felixstowe
Stevenage
Colchester
Harwich
Luton
Aylesbury
Harlow
Chelmsford
OXFORD
LONDON
Tilbury
Southend-on-Sea
Thames
Reading
Margate
Zeebrugge
Newbury
Windsor
Sheerness
Ramsgate
OOSTENDE
BRUGGE
Basingstoke
Canterbury
Deal
Guildford
Maidstone
Dunkerque
BELGIË
BELGIQUE
Crawley
Royal-Tunbridge Wells
Dover
Winchester
Folkestone
Channel Tunnel
Calais
SOUTHAMPTON
BRIGHTON
Chichester
Hastings
St-Omer
Worthing
Eastbourne
Boulogne
PORTSMOUTH
Newhaven
LILLE
Newport
Isle of Wight
St-Malo
Arras
Cambrai
Abbeville
CHANNEL
Dieppe
AMIENS
Somme
St-Quentin
Rosslare
FRANCE
Beauvais
Compiègne
LE HAVRE
ROUEN
Lisieux
Senlis
CAEN
Seine

3

Colonsay
Jura
Port Askaig
Islay
Port Ellen
ATLANTIC
OCEAN
NORTH CHANNEL
Letterkenny
Londonderry
Coleraine
Waterfoot
Ballymena
Larne
Donegal
Strabane
Omagh
NORTHERN
IRELAND
Lough Neagh
BELFAST
Strangford Lough
Ballygawley
Enniskillen
Sligo/
Sligeach
Armagh
Banbridge
Newcastle
Monaghan
Ballina
L. Allen
Boyle
Cavan
Dundalk/
Dun Dealgan
Westport
Castlebar
L. Mask
Longford
Kells
Roscommon
Drogheda/
Droichead Átha
Clifden
L. Corrib
Boyne
L. Ree
Mullingar
Galway/
Gaillimh
Athlone
DUBLIN/
BAILE ÁTHA CLIATH
Ballinasloe
Tullamore
Dun Laoghaire
Bray
Lisdoonvarna
IRELAND
Naas
River Shannon
Ennis/
Inis
Roscrea
Wicklow
Kilkee
Thurles
Suir
Carlow
Arklow
LIMERICK/
LUIMNEACH
Kilkenny/
Cill Chainnigh
Cashel/
Caiseal
Barrow
Enniscorthy
Tralee
Dingle
Caher
Carrick on Suir
Wexford
Killarney/
Cill Airne
Fermoy
R. Blackwater
Lismore
Waterford/
Port Lairge
Rosslare
ST GEORGE'S CHANNEL
CORK/
CORCAIGH
Cobh
Youghal
Glengarriff
Bantry
Milford H
Aberdaugled
le Havre
Cherbourg
Roscoff
CELTIC SEA

European dialling codes
Indicatifs téléphoniques européens
Indicativi telefonici dei paesi europei
Telefon-Vorwahlnummern europäischer Länder

	from/de dal/von		to/en in/nach	from/de dal/von	to/en en/mach
AND	Andorra	1944	Great Britain	0033628	Andorra
A	Austria	0044	»	0043	Austria
B	Belgium	0044	»	0032	Belgium
BG	Bulgaria	0044	»	00359	Bulgaria
CZ	Czech Republic	0044	»	0042	Czech Republic
DK	Denmark	00944	»	0045	Denmark
FIN	Finland	99044	»	00358	Finland
F	France	1944	»	0033	France
D	Germany	0044	»	0049	Germany
GR	Greece	0044	»	0030	Greece
H	Hungary	0044	»	0036	Hungary
I	Italy	0044	»	0039	Italy
FL	Liechtenstein	0044	»	004175	Liechtenstein
L	Luxembourg	0044	»	00352	Luxembourg
M	Malta	0044	»	00356	Malta
MC	Monaco	1944	»	003393	Monaco
NL	Netherlands	0944	»	0031	Netherlands
N	Norway	09544	»	0047	Norway
PL	Poland	0044	»	0048	Poland
P	Portugal	0044	»	00351	Portugal
IRL	Rep. of Ireland	0044	»	00353	Rep. of Ireland
RO	Romania	–	»	0040	Romania
SK	Slovakia	0044	»	0042	Slovakia
E	Spain	0744	»	0034	Spain
S	Sweden	00944	»	0046	Sweden
CH	Switzerland	0044	»	0041	Switzerland

	from/de dal/von		to/en in/nach	from/de dal/von	to/en en/nach
AND	Andorra	19353	Rep. of Ireland	0033628	Andorra
A	Austria	00353	»	0043	Austria
B	Belgium	00353	»	0032	Belgium
BG	Bulgaria	00353	»	00359	Bulgaria
CZ	Czech Republic	00353	»	0042	Czech Republic
DK	Denmark	009353	»	0045	Denmark
FIN	Finland	990353	»	00358	Finland
F	France	19353	»	0033	France
D	Germany	00353	»	0049	Germany
GB	Great Britain	00353	»	0044	Great Britain
GR	Greece	00353	»	0030	Greece
H	Hungary	00353	»	0036	Hungary
I	Italy	00353	»	0039	Italy
FL	Liechtenstein	00353	»	004175	Liechtenstein
L	Luxembourg	00353	»	00352	Luxembourg
M	Malta	00353	»	00356	Malta
MC	Monaco	19353	»	0033	Monaco
NL	Netherlands	09353	»	0031	Netherlands
N	Norway	095353	»	0047	Norway
PL	Poland	00353	»	0048	Poland
P	Portugal	00353	»	00351	Portugal
RO	Romania	–	»	0040	Romania
SK	Slovakia	00353	»	0042	Slovakia
E	Spain	07353	»	0034	Spain
S	Sweden	009353	»	0046	Sweden
CH	Switzerland	00353	»	0041	Switzerland

Illustrations : Rodolphe Corbel p. 284 et 328.

Manufacture française des pneumatiques Michelin
Société en commandite par actions au capital de 2 000 000 000 de francs
Place des Carmes-Déchaux – 63 Clermont-Ferrand (France)
R.C.S. Clermont-Fd B 855 200 507

Michelin et Cie, Propriétaires-Éditeurs 1996
Dépôt légal Janvier 96 – ISBN 2-06-006569-0

Printed in E.C. 12-95-50

Photocomposition : APS, Tours – Impression : MAURY Imprimeur S.A., Malesherbes
Reliure : N.R.I., Auxerre